THE OXFORD DICTIONARY OF THE

Classical World

THE OXFORD
DICTIONARY OF THE
Classical
World

EDITED BY JOHN ROBERTS

OXFORD

UNIVERSITY PRESS

OXFORD
UNIVERSITY PRESS

Great Clarendon Street, Oxford OX2 6DP

Oxford University Press is a department of the University of Oxford.
If furthers the University's objective of excellence in research, scholarship,
and education by publishing worldwide in

Oxford New York

Auckland Cape Town Dar es Salaam Hong Kong Karachi
Kuala Lumpur Madrid Melbourne Mexico City Nairobi
New Delhi Shanghai Taipei Toronto

With offices in

Argentina Austria Brazil Chile Czech Republic France Greece
Guatemala Hungary Italy Japan Poland Portugal Singapore
South Korea Switzerland Thailand Turkey Ukraine Vietnam

Oxford is a registered trade mark of Oxford University Press
in the UK and in certain other countries

Published in the United States
by Oxford University Press Inc., New York

© Oxford University Press 2005

British Library Cataloguing in Publication Data

Data available

Library of Congress Cataloging in Publication Data

Data available

Typeset by SPI Publisher Services, Pondicherry, India
Printed in Great Britain on acid-free paper by Biddles Ltd

ISBN 0-19-280145-7
ISBN 978-0-19-280145-6

1 3 5 7 9 10 8 6 4 2

Contents

Preface

The third edition of *The Oxford Classical Dictionary* (*OCD3*) is, as claimed by its editors, indisputably the most 'authoritative one-volume guide to all aspects' of the classical world. 'All aspects' is no exaggeration. In the second half of the 20th century there had been an explosion of scholarship in classical studies, widening the geographical and cultural parameters of the subject. The near east and the history of the Jews were no longer largely ignored, and women were no longer virtually invisible. *OCD3* gave an influential voice to these innovations. It is fair to claim therefore that as a result of the publication of *OCD3* in 1996, the 'classical world' that we now perceive is larger and much more interesting than before.

The Oxford Dictionary of the Classical World (*ODCW*) is an abridgement of *OCD3*. Containing just over a third of its content, it aims to bring the essence of its parent *Dictionary* to students, teachers, and the general reader in an accessible, portable, and affordable format. To reduce what its editors recognized as *OCD*'s 'terrible size' (1.6 million words) it would be necessary to use certain parameters to aid the editing process. Rough chronological limits were set: for Greek history the main emphasis falls on the Archaic and Classical periods, and a lighter emphasis on the Hellenistic period; for Roman history, the emphasis falls on the later republic, starting with the First Punic War, and on the earlier empire, ending with the death of Marcus Aurelius, creating a timeframe spanning 776 BC–AD 180 (see Chronology). For reasons of space, too, minor mythical figures like Narcissus have been omitted if they do not figure in the major myths of the ancient world.

Geographically, Greece and Italy are the core areas. The book contains five maps, which, between them, show all the places, countries, provinces, and islands mentioned in the text. Great care has been taken to make the book user friendly, thus many entries have been simplified, all bibliographies removed, technical terms explained, Greek transliterated. Two new appendices add to the usefulness of this book: an essay on money and its value in the classical world, and a two-way gazetteer of ancient and modern place names. The book also contains a chronology of events in Greece and the East, and in Rome and the West, and a list of major classical authors, from Homer and Hesiod to Plutarch.

Thematic entries, drawing upon innovative scholarship, explore such topics as animals, attitudes to; barbarian; bilingualism; constellations and named stars; death, attitudes to; democracy, Athenian; economic theory, Greek; Etruscan language; freedom in the ancient world; gladiators; imperialism; medicine; myth and mythology; *polis*; sin; slavery; and women. *ODCW*'s 2,500 entries demonstrate the continuing relevance of Graeco-Roman civilization. This pre-Christian culture is very like ours in many ways, very different in others.

I am deeply indebted to *ODCW*'s two consultants for all their help: Jane Gardner, Emeritus Professor of Ancient History at the University of Reading, advised on Roman politics and Roman law; Robin Osborne, Professor of Ancient History at King's College, Cambridge, gave guidance on Greek history, politics, and culture. They answered my unending queries promptly and in all necessary detail. They are not responsible for blemishes in *ODCW*; they are responsible for countless improvements.

Dr Liv Yarrow rendered an invaluable service to the *Dictionary*. She readily agreed to take on a Herculean labour, reducing by far the largest entry, Rome (History), 11,590 words, to a little more than 4,000. This she did while preserving the glow of the narrative, an achievement for which I shall always be grateful.

Two distinguished scholars have contributed original articles to *ODCW*: Dr Catherine Osborne on Atomism, and Andy Meadows of the Department of Coins and Medals at the British Museum, on Money and its Value in the Classical World. I thank them both most warmly.

The idea of a two-way gazetteer was prompted by a letter from Professor Daniel Hughes, formerly a mathematician resident in Siena, who complained about one defect in *OCD3*, which in almost every other respect was 'proving a great joy'.

Pam Coote has watched over the enterprise from the start to what is at the time of writing the beginning of the end. It was reassuring to know that in moments of perplexity her experience and wisdom were there to guide. When others were restive, she was patient. Patience is commonly counted a minor virtue; I have come to think it should be raised to the rank of cardinal. I hope that the finished product will make it all seem worthwhile. An experienced copy-editor, Tom Chandler, energetically expunged blemishes.

'Editor, Reference' hardly does justice to the unfailing support of Rebecca Collins and Judith Wilson, for which I am most grateful. My wife has, over many years, helped me in many ways in my every literary endeavour, including this one—*sine qua non*.

I dedicate this book to Andrew and Anna, no strangers to classical woods and pastures.

J.R.

Bladon
August 2004

Abbreviations

abbrev.	abbreviated	lb.	pound(s)
acc. to	according to	lit.	literally
b.	born	lt.	litre(s)
bk.	book	m.	metre(s)
c.	*circa*, about	masc.	masculine
cent.	century	mi.	mile(s)
ch.	chapter	ml.	millilitre(s)
cm.	centimetre(s)	Mt.	Mount
col.	column	NE	north-east(ern)
cp.	compare	neut.	neuter
d.	died	nr.	near
dr.	drachma(e)	NT	New Testament
esp.	especially	NW	north-west(ern)
fem.	feminine	OP	Old Persian
f., ff.	and following	opp.	opposed to
fl.	flourished	OT	Old Testament
fr.	fragment	*OT*	Sophocles' *Oedipus Tyrannus*
ft.	foot/feet	oz.	ounce(s)
g.	gram(s)	p.a.	*per annum*, annually
gal.	gallon(s)	para.	paragraph
Gk.	Greek	pl.	plural
ha.	hectare(s)	ps.-	pseudo-
i.a.	*inter alia*, among other	pt.	part
	things	sing.	singular
IE	Indo-European	SE	south-east(ern)
in.	inch(es)	sq.	square
kg.	kilogram(s)	SW	south-west(ern)
km.	kilometre(s)	suff.	suffect
Lat.	Latin		

Major Authors, from Homer and Hesiod to Plutarch

This list of 56 famous writers gives some idea of the diversity of the authors' areas of activity. A striking feature of the Classical World is that so many of these early writers still speak to us powerfully. They come the closest to us.

Aeschines Athenian orator and rival of Demosthenes in the courts.
Aeschylus Tragic poet. Six of his tragedies (possibly seven) survive, including the *Oresteia* trilogy.
Alcaeus Lyric poet of Mytilene on Lesbos.
Alcman Lyric poet, active in Sparta.
Apollonius Rhodius Poet of the epic *Argonautica*.
Aristophanes Greatest poet of Attic Old Comedy.
Aristotle Polymath. Extant works fall into three categories: Logic and Metaphysics (first, i.e. fundamental, philosophy); Nature, Life (esp. zoology), Mind; Ethics, Politics, Art.
Augustus *Res Gestae* (*RG*; 'Achievements').
Caesar *Gallic War*; *Civil War*. See IULIUS CAESAR (1), GAIUS.
Catullus 'Neoteric': innovative Roman poet.
Cicero Greatest Roman orator. In addition to his speeches, his prose works fall into three groups: works on Rhetoric, Letters, works on Philosophy. See TULLIUS CICERO, MARCUS.
Demosthenes Greatest Athenian orator. Many public speeches survive, and some private (lawcourt speeches). He lived and died for liberty.
Diogenes Laertius *Lives of the Philosophers*.
Dionysius of Halicarnassus *Roman Antiquities*, a learned history of early Rome, praising Roman virtues.
Euripides Tragic poet. By chance, more than twice as many of his plays survive than those of either Aeschylus or Sophocles (18). Plays include *Medea*, *Hippolytus*, *Trojan Women*.
Gellius, Aulus Roman miscellanist, author of *Attic Nights*.
Herodotus of Halicarnassus *Histories*, mainly about the Persian Wars, but also about very many other things.
Hesiod of Ascra *c.*700 BC. Hexameter poet of *Theogony* (origin and genealogy of the gods), and *Works* (agricultural) *and Days*.
Homer Poet of the *Iliad* and probably the *Odyssey*. If Homer slightly preceded Hesiod, and the *Iliad* preceded the *Odyssey*, then the work commonly accounted the greatest in Greek literature was also the earliest.
Horace Rome's first lyric poet, modelled himself on the Greek lyric poet Alcaeus in his *Carmina*, 'Odes'. He wrote also *Satires* and *Epistles*.
Isocrates Athenian rhetor and writer of rhetorical texts. He set up a higher education school for discussing 'general and practical matters'.
Juvenal Roman satirist. The city of Rome is his scene, but he was not a sociologist.

Livy History of Rome from its Foundation, in 142 books, of which about one-third survive. A patriotic, but not chauvinistic, writer.

Lucan Roman poet, author of the epic *Civil War* (49–48 BC; 'Pharsalia'). He tells a tale of horror and criminality leading to the destruction of the republic.

Lucian of Samosata Versatile belletrist, excelled in comic prose dialogue.

Lucretius Roman Epicurean poet, author of *De Rerum Natura*, 'On the Nature of Things'. In six books of hexameter verse, he presents the case for Epicureanism.

Lysias As a foreigner resident in Athens (metic), wrote skilful, elegant speeches for others to deliver in court.

Martial Roman poet, born in Spain; author of more than 1,500 epigrams, short poems, ending with a punch line. The scene is the city of Rome.

Nepos The earliest extant biographer in Latin.

Ovid Roman poet. By AD 8 he was the leading poet of Rome, but in that same year Augustus banished him to Tomis on the western shore of the Black Sea. His *Metamorphoses*, 'miraculous transformations', has had great influence on Western art and literature.

Persius Roman poet, author of six 'satires', preaching Stoic morality.

Pindar Greek lyric poet, author of songs composed in celebration of victories in the four panhellenic festivals.

Plato Greek philosopher, author of some two dozen dialogues, founder of the Academy. Firm believer in the objectivity of values. For good reason, his *Republic* is his most famous book.

Plautus Roman writer of comedy. His 21 plays are the earliest Latin works to have survived.

Pliny the Elder Roman polymath. *Natural History*.

Pliny the Younger Roman letter-writer.

Plutarch Greek moral philosopher and biographer. In addition to 78 miscellaneous works, 50 Lives survive, including 23 pairs, of his *Parallel Lives* of Greeks and Romans. His aim was to exemplify individual virtue (or vice) in the careers of great men.

Polybius Greek historian of Rome's rise to imperial power.

Propertius Roman elegiac poet. His military service is love.

Quintilian Roman teacher of rhetoric. *Education of the Orator*.

Sallust Roman historian. *Catalinarian War, Jugurthan War*.

Seneca the Elder Born in Spain, educated in Rome. Lifelong student of rhetoric.

Seneca the Younger Son of the Elder. Moral philosopher (Stoic by conviction, and tragic poet. Six plays survive, drawn from, not tied to, Athenian originals esp. Euripides).

Sophocles Tragic poet. Seven plays survive. Three of them concern two descendants of Labdacus King of Thebes—Oedipus and his daughter Antigone.

Statius Roman poet, author of the epic *Thebaid*, which recounts the war between the sons of Oedipus for the kingship of Thebes.

Suetonius Roman biographer. After *On Famous Men*: teachers of language and literature, and of rhetoric, poets, orators, historians, philosophers, came *Caesars*: twelve imperial biographies from Caesar to Domitian.

Tacitus Historian of the early Roman empire. The text of both *Histories* and *Annals* is incomplete, but quite enough survives to establish that Tacitus is a great historian.

Terence Roman writer of comedy, who died young. All his six plays survive.

Theocritus Poet from Syracuse, creator of the bucolic (cowherd song) or pastoral genre. A Greek word meaning 'vignettes' was given at an unknown date as a generic title for all the 30 poems. Its transliteration into 'idylls', suggesting pleasant rural scenes, does not prepare the reader for the sophistication ahead.

Theognis Elegiac poet of Megara. In the manuscript tradition a corpus of some 1,400 lines are attributed to him, but the lines are the work of many hands. The collection is our best source for the cultured man's ideas about life, friendship, fate, death, and other matters, between the late 7th and early 5th cent.

Theophrastus Of Eresos in Lesbos, associate of Aristotle, and successor to him as head of the Lyceum. Like him a polymath. The father of botany, the only area in which most of his work survives intact. Also intact is his *Characters*, sketches of 30 more or less undesirable types of personality.

Thucydides Of Athens, historian of the Peloponnesian War. The most interesting thing about the War is that it was recorded by Thucydides.

Tibullus Roman elegiac poet. Like Propertius, his military service is love.

Varro Polymath. Extant in entirety *On Farming*; partially *On the Latin Language*.

Virgil Rome's greatest poet: *Eclogues* (originally *Bucolics*, cowherd songs), *Georgics*, the epic *Aeneid*. Of twelve books three are the most memorable. 2. Aeneas tells Dido the story of the fall of Troy. 4. Aeneas and Dido become lovers; Mercury is sent to remind him of his mission, and his departure leads Dido to take her own life. 6. Advised by his dead father in a dream, he consults the Sibyl of Cumae. She takes him to the Underworld, where he receives a vision of the future of Rome.

Xenophon Of Athens (to begin with). A prolific prose author. His works fall into four groups. 1. Long (quasi-) historical narratives, including *Anabasis* ('March Up-country', account of his saving 10,000 Greek mercenaries). 2. Socratic texts, including (Xenophon's) *Recollections of Socrates*. 3. Three technical treatises. 4. Four monographs, including *Constitution of the Spartans*. The exiled Xenophon was settled by the Spartans near Olympia.

Notes to the Reader

Aphabetical Arrangement
Entries appear in letter-by-letter alphabetical order up to the first punctuation (if any) in the headword.

Personal Names
If the names of two or more different persons are spelt in exactly the same way, the names are differentiated by number, and (1) indicates the earliest bearer of the name. Thus Zeno (1) invented paradoxes in the 5th cent. BC, and Zeno (2) invented Stoicism *c*.300 BC. Mythical characters are listed before historical.

Romans of the republican and imperial periods are listed by their second name—their *nomen*, i.e. family name—rather than by their *cognomen*, i.e. third or other additional name (see NAMES, PERSONAL, ROMAN). For example, the famous man we call Julius Caesar had three names: Gaius Iulius Caesar. (J was not a letter of the Roman alphabet.) The first is the *praenomen*, the second the *nomen* (indicating family or *gens*), and the third the *cognomen*; and he appears under the headword **Iulius**. However, there are two persons called Gaius Iulius Caesar in the *Dictionary*. Thus we have **Iulius Caesar** (1), **Gaius** and **Iulius Caesar** (2), **Gaius**. The famous man happens to be the earlier of the two; so he is (1). Under **Caesar** the reader will find a cross-reference: **Caesar** See IULIUS CAESAR (1), GAIUS. Within a *gens* like that of the Cornelii, the sequence is alphabetical, starting with the feminine, Cornelia.

A slight departure from these principles is to list mainly literary figures (so not Julius Caesar or Cicero), and emperors, in the form in which they are most usually known. So readers will find some literary figures under the *cognomen*, such as **Catullus, Gaius Valerius,** rather than under Valerius. Emperors are listed by the component of the (often long) name which is most familiar, such as **Nero (Claudius Caesar)** rather than Claudius Caesar, Nero. Nicknames (Caligula, Caracalla) are cross-referenced.

Pronunciation
Greek and Latin poetry was still being written to be heard long after the invention of Greek alphabetic writing *c*.740 BC. Guidance on pronunciation of Latin and transliterated Greek words is mostly restricted to indicating by macron (e.g. ē) and breve (e.g. ĕ) which vowels were long and, if necessary, which were short, unless the accepted English pronunciation (esp. of the last syllable) differs. Setting aside last syllables, unmarked vowels are likely to have been short. If a macron or breve appears somewhere above a headword, it will not reappear above that word, should it recur in the text. If a transliterated Greek or Latin word appears more than once within the text of an entry, it will carry macron or breve on its first appearance only. In Greek, *ai, au, eu, oi, ou* are diphthongs ('Zeus' rhymes with 'juice'), as are *ae, oe* in Latin. The possibility of a diphthong may be ruled out by use of a macron over the first vowel (Alphēus) or a breve over the second (Alcinoŭs). Occasionally a stress accent (′) is used (Hippódamus). Most Greek proper names have been Latinized; so, Alpheus,

not Alpheios. Three *praenomina* deserve macrons: Gāius, Lūcius, Mānius (see NAMES, PERSONAL, ROMAN). Latin *c* and *g* were hard, as in *coat* and *goat*.

Cross-Referencing

An asterisk (*) in front of a word in the text signals a cross-reference to a related entry. Cross-referencing by this method normally occurs only once in an entry, and normally on the first appearance of that word. Sometimes the asterisked word may differ from the signalled headword by as much as a syllable, but only if there is no near-by headword that might confuse. The other method of cross-referencing is 'see' or 'see also', followed by a headword in SMALL CAPITALS.

Literary Titles

Partly for the sake of brevity, literary titles are mostly shorn of the definite article (*Antigone*, not *The Antigone*). Likewise with many Greek place names: so, Piraeus, not the Piraeus; Peloponnese, not the Peloponnese.

Architectural Terms

Technical terms in architecture are explained not only in ARCHITECTURE, but also in ORDERS and TEMPLE, and some account of pottery shapes/uses will be found in both POTTERY, GREEK and SYMPOSIUM. See also AGONES; AMPHORAE, GREEK; PANATHENAEA.

Academy, public *gymnasium at Athens, sacred to the hero Academus, NW of the Dipylon gate. It gave its name to the school founded there by *Plato in the early 4th cent. and maintained by an unbroken line of successors until the 1st cent. BC. The school's private property was never there, but, at least during the 4th cent., at Plato's nearby house.

The Early Academy is the phase of doctrinal Platonism under Plato himself (d. 347) and his successors *Speusippus, Xenocratēs, *Polemon, and Cratēs.

The 'New Academy' is the phase, from c.269 to the early or mid-1st cent. BC, in which the school, initially under *Arcesilaus, interpreted true Platonism as scepticism. Dialectical criticism of doctrines, usually Stoic, was orchestrated to demonstrate the impossibility of knowledge, resulting in *epochē*, suspension of judgement. *Carneades, its most influential head, was a systematic critic of all doctrines.

Accius, Lūcius (170–c.86 BC), Roman tragic poet and literary scholar. Although of conservative political views, he believed that literary talent demanded in its context more respect than nobility of birth. He had a touchy sense of his own importance, always avenging insults. Contemporaries were amused by the outsize statues of himself he had placed in the temple of the Muses.

Over 40 tragic titles are transmitted. Many of them concerned the Trojan cycle of legends. A lengthy *hexameter poem, the *Annals*, found Greek origins for Roman religious festivals. The *Didascalica* ran to at least nine books and included *i.a.* the history of both the Athenian and the Roman theatre. Accius wrote here in a mixture of prose and diverse poetical metres.

The grandeur of Accius' tragic style caused some contemporaries to laugh. *Cicero, however, who was proud to have known him personally, admired his plays almost as highly as he did those of *Pacuvius and cited extensive passages in his dialogues. *Columella and *Seneca the Younger continued to read him.

acclamation Vocal expressions of approval and good wishes in ritual form were an important part of Roman life, both private (e.g. at weddings) and public (for actors and the presiding magistrate at public performances, and above all at a *triumph). The title of *imperator* was based on the soldiers' acclamation. A magistrate leaving for his province was escorted by crowds shouting ritual acclamations, and his return was received in a corresponding way. (See PROVINCIA, 2.) Under the empire, these rituals were magnified, but confined to the emperor and approved members of his family. They were also ritually greeted at public appearances, esp. at games and on their birthdays. By the late republic, rhythmical shouting at games, sometimes organized, expressed approval or disapproval of politicians. Cicero takes it seriously, as expressions of public opinion (which counted only in the city of Rome), and *Clodius Pulcher organized such shouting at *contiones to simulate public opinion. Under the empire, such acclamations, esp. at games, became the only expression of public opinion, and they could rarely be suppressed. They were normally combined with ritual greetings of the emperor to express approval or disapproval of prominent persons and demand rewards or punishments for them. Ritualized acclamations spread to recitations (see RECITATIO) and *declamations, and claques could be collected and even paid for this. Nero formed a large claque for his performances, importing the Alexandrian tradition of musical accompaniment to their chants.

In the senate ritual shouts of greeting and approval for the emperor appear very early. They were used to attract the emperor's notice by demanding punishment of 'traitors' (see MAIESTAS), and at the death of a hated emperor would demand (probably with more spontaneity) his *damnatio memoriae* and punishment for his creatures. On Trajan's accession the acclamations welcoming him were first recorded on published documents, and that practice spread. By this time acclamations also greeted (e.g.) the announcement of the names of designated consuls.

accountability, accounts See EUTHYNA.

Achaea Region in NE *Peloponnese, beside the Corinthian Gulf. Historically a federation of small territories.

Achaean Confederacy, federal organization developed by the twelve Achaean cities united in cult of Zeus. First mentioned in 453 BC as Athenian allies, Achaea's independence was guaranteed in 446 (*Thirty Years Peace). In the Peloponnesian War neutrality proved impossible, and Achaea fell into Sparta's sphere of influence. Common citizenship existed by 389. In the 2nd cent. the confederacy expanded to absorb all *Peloponnese.

Achaemenid art The official sculpture of the Persian empire was made in a style which owed much to Mesopotamian forerunners, and like them tended to the glorification of the ruler. The Median, Persian, Babylonian, Sardian, Egyptian, and Ionian artisans who worked on the great palace complexes subordinated any indigenous traits to an international style devised to articulate the ideology of Achaemenid kings.

Only a few sculptured reliefs are preserved from Pasargadae, the city of *Cyrus (1). *Darius I is shown triumphant over a prostrate usurper in the *Bisitun relief, while Ahuramazda hovers above. A colossal statue of Darius in Egyptian granite found at *Susa presents problems: was it originally made for an Egyptian setting, or was it commissioned for Darius' Susan palace? The tombs of Darius and his successors at *Naqš-i Rustam show a royal personage on a platform borne by personifications of the lands of the empire. The façades of the *apadana at Persepolis showed the king granting an audience to an official, ranks of tribute-bearers and courtiers, and lions attacking bulls. The theme of royal victory occurs in reliefs representing struggles between royal heroes and mythical beasts, motifs which are often repeated on seal-stones.

Achaemenids The term, as used by Herodotus, refers to one of the three clans of the Pasargadae tribe to which the Persian kings belonged; its eponymous ancestor was supposedly Achaemenēs. The statement corresponds in part to *Darius I's account at *Bisitun, where he links himself explicitly to Achaemenes: 'For this reason we are called Achaemenids. From long ago we have been noble. From long ago we have been kings.' But this is the official version promulgated by Darius after his seizure of power. This also led him to erect inscriptions in *Cyrus' (1) name at Pasargadae (NE of *Persepolis) describing the founder of the empire as an Achaemenid: they served to hide the fact that Darius himself had no genealogical claim to the throne in 522 BC. Throughout Persian history, the term 'Achaemenid' had two quite distinct meanings: (1) the extensive circle of clan members, part of the Pasargadae tribe; (2) politically and dynastically, it describes only the fictional line of ancestors created by Darius and his descendants. When speaking of the Achaemenid dynasty and empire, the term is used in the second sense. Darius I's descendants (the royal line), down to, and including, *Darius III, effectively retained exclusive access to the kingship, and no 'outsider' was ever able to seize royal power. See PERSIA.

Achaia, official name for the Roman province of *Greece, commemorating Rome's defeat of the *Achaean Confederacy in 146 BC.

Acharnae, the largest Attic *deme. It lay in the NW corner of the Attic plain, near the pass from the Thriasian plain along which *Archidamus II and the Spartans marched in 431 BC. Although famous as charcoal-burners in Aristophanes, the Acharnians lived primarily by growing corn and cultivating vines and olives. They were also famously brave and had, appropriately, a sanctuary to *Ares: the temple was moved to the Athenian Agora in the Roman period.

Achātēs, in myth, faithful lieutenant of *Aeneas in the *Aeneid*.

Achelōūs, the longest Greek river, rising in central Epirus and debouching into the NW corner of the Corinthian Gulf. Its lower reaches were affected by heavy alluviation and constituted the much disputed frontier between Acarnania and Aetolia. Acheloüs was personified early as a water- and *river-god (the son of *Oceanus and Tēthys), from whom all seas, rivers and springs derived.

Achillēs, son of *Peleus and *Thetis; greatest Greek hero in the Trojan War; central character of *Homer's *Iliad*. He is king of Phthia, or 'Hellas and Phthia', in southern Thessaly, and his people are the Myrmidons. The size of his kingdom, and of his contingent in the Trojan expedition (50 ships), is not outstanding. But martial prowess is the measure of excellence for a Homeric hero, and Achilles' status as 'best of the Achaeans' is unquestioned. We are reminded of his absolute supremacy throughout the poem, even during those long stretches for which he is absent from the battlefield.

His *character is complex. In many ways he carries the savage ethical code of the Homeric hero to its ultimate and terrifying conclusion. When *Agamemnon steals his concubine Briseis, his anger at the insult to his personal honour is natural and approved by gods and men; but he carries this anger beyond any normal limit when he refuses an offer of immense compensation. Again, when he finally re-enters the war after the death of his friend Patroclus, his ruthless massacre of Trojans, culminating in the killing of *Hector, expresses a 'heroic' desire for revenge; but this too is taken beyond normal bounds by his contemptuous maltreatment of Hector's corpse.

But what makes Achilles remarkable is the way in which his extreme expression of the 'heroic code' is combined with a unique degree of insight and self-knowledge. Unlike Hector, Achilles knows well that he is soon to die. In his speech at *Iliad* 9. 308–429 he calls the entire code into question, saying that he would rather live quietly at home than pursue glory in the Trojan War; but it is his 'heroic' rage against Agamemnon that has brought him to this point. In his encounter with Lycaon, his sense of common mortality (the fact that Patroclus has died and Achilles himself will die) is a reason, not for sparing his suppliant, but for killing him in cold blood. Finally at *Iliad* 24, when *Priam begs him to release Hector's body, it is human feeling, as well as the gods' command, that makes him yield; but even then he accepts a ransom, and his anger still threatens to break out afresh.

Later writers seldom treated the subject-matter of the *Iliad* (though *Aeschylus did so, portraying Achilles and Patroclus as lovers). But they did provide many further details of Achilles' career, often derived from cyclic epics (see EPIC CYCLE) such as the *Cypria* and *Aethiopis*. As a boy he was brought up by the wise *Centaur Chiron on Mt. Pelion. Later his mother Thetis, knowing that he would be killed if he joined the expedition to Troy, hid him at the court of King Lycomedes on Scyros, disguised as a girl. There he fell in love with the king's daughter Dēidamīa, who bore him a son, Neoptolemus. *Odysseus discovered his identity by trickery, and he joined the Greek army at Aulis, where he was involved in the story of *Iphigenia. On the way to Troy he wounded Telephus. His exploits at Troy included the ambush and killing of Priam's son *Troilus, a story linked with that of his love for Priam's daughter Polyxena. After the events of the *Iliad* he killed two allies of the Trojans: the *Amazon queen Penthesilea, with whom also he is said to have fallen in love, and the Ethiopian king *Memnon. Finally he was himself killed by *Paris and *Apollo (as predicted at *Iliad* 22. 358–60). The fight over his body, and his funeral, are described in a dubious passage of the *Odyssey*. His famous arms were then given to Odysseus. After the fall of Troy his ghost demanded the sacrifice of Polyxena. Several of these episodes, including the ambush of Troilus and the killing of Penthesilea, were popular with vase-painters.

A late addition is the motif of Achilles' heel: Thetis sought to make the infant Achilles *invulnerable by dipping him in the *Styx, but omitted to dip the heel by which she held him, and it was there that he received his death-wound.

Acragas (Lat. Agrigentum) was founded *c*.580 BC by the Geloans in central southern Sicily. One of the largest and richest Greek cities, it occupied a large bowl of land, rising to a lofty acropolis on the north side. Its early acquisition of power was owed to Phalaris, the first important Sicilian *tyrant. In 480 *Theron was the ally of *Gelon in his victory at *Himera. After expelling Theron's son, Acragas had a limited democratic government, in which *Empedocles, its most famous citizen, took part. Acragantine 6th- and 5th-cent. prosperity is attested by a remarkable series of temples, the remains of which are among the most impressive of any Greek city, and by its extensive, wealthy necropoleis.

acropolis See ATHENS, TOPOGRAPHY.

acrotēria Decorative sculpture above the corners of a pediment.

acta means 'things done' and has two specialized, overlapping senses in Roman history; one is a gazette, the other is official acts, esp. of an emperor.

The *Acta diurna* was a gazette, whose publication dates from before 59 BC; from the late republic onwards it recorded not only official events and ceremonies, but lawsuits and public speeches, and was read both at Rome and in the provinces. The *Acta senātūs* constituted the official record of proceedings in the senate, first published in 59. Under the Principate a senator was selected by the emperor to be responsible for the record. The proceedings were available to senators, but *Augustus forbade their wider publication. Tacitus used, or depended on, authorities who used both the *Acta senatus* and the *Acta diurna*.

The definition of *acta* meaning enactments was not easy. The term was eventually held to cover the '*constitutions of emperors'. Under the republic magistrates took an oath, on entering office, to respect the laws of the state. The first recorded use of an oath to observe *acta* was that taken by all the magistrates to observe the *acta* of *Caesar in 45 BC. When his *acta* were ratified by the senate after his murder, the looseness of the term gave scope for confusion and corruption. Oaths were taken to observe the *acta* of Augustus in 29 and in 24 BC. In order to equate the emperor's enactments with other sources of law, magistrates, emperors included, took the oath to observe the *acta* of previous emperors, except those whose *acta*, directly after their death, were explicitly rescinded or at least excluded from the oath, though the wise enactments of even bad emperors might survive their death. However, the relation of the *acta* of the living emperor to those of his predecessors raised problems. At first moderate emperors, such as *Tiberius and *Claudius, sought to restrict the oath to the *acta* of Divus Augustus, excluding their own *acta*, but with the increase of autocracy, the oath came to include the *acta* of reigning emperors.

Actium, a flat sandy promontory at the entrance to the Ambracian Gulf, forming part of the territory of Anactorium, as well as the NW extremity of Acarnania. A cult of Apollo was located here as early as the 6th cent. BC. A temple stood on a low hill near the tip of the promontory, where games were celebrated in honour of the god as late as the end of the 3rd cent. In 31 BC the cape was the site of Marcus *Antonius' camp, and gave its name to the naval battle, fought just outside the gulf, in which he was defeated by *Octavian. A few years later, when Octavian founded Nicopolis ('victory city') on the opposite side of the strait, he took care to enlarge Apollo's sanctuary at Actium by rebuilding the old temple and adding a monumental naval trophy.

actors See COMEDY (GREEK); COMEDY, LATIN; DIONYSUS, ARTISTS OF; THEATRE STAGING, GREEK; TRAGEDY, GREEK and LATIN.

Acts of the Apostles The second of two volumes, which continues the story of the rise and spread of *Christianity begun in the gospel of Luke. Its narrative starts with Jesus' ascension in Jerusalem and ends with *Paul preaching in Rome, where he had been taken after his appeal to the emperor. The focus of the material on the earliest Jerusalem church around Peter and, later in the book, on the Christian career of Paul shows the concern of the author to relate the Jewish and Gentile missions and to demonstrate their basic unity. Only occasional glimpses are offered of the conflict in early Christianity which is evident in the Pauline corpus. Acts has for a long time been a cause of controversy between those who maintain the substantial authenticity of its historical account (while allowing for its apologetic interests) and those who see the document as a work of skilful narrative propaganda, whose historical value is negligible. Knowledge of contemporary Graeco-Roman institutions should not mask the difficulties in accepting the historicity of Acts, a particular problem being the reconciliation of the accounts of Paul's career in Acts, Galatians 1–2, and the Corinthian correspondence. The references to Paul's theology indicate a markedly different set of ideas from what we find in the letters to the Romans and Galatians. For this and other reasons Acts has proved to be disappointing to the historian of Christian origins as a source for early Christian history. The history of the Jerusalem church after the start of the Pauline mission is touched on only in so far as it helps the author explain Paul's career as apostle to the Gentiles. Whereas Luke's gospel portrays Jesus as a Palestinian prophet with a controversial, indeed subversive, message for Jewish society, there is little in Acts (apart from the idealized accounts of the common life of the Jerusalem church) of that radicalism. The antagonism to *Jews and the sympathetic account of Roman officials evident in the gospel of Luke is continued in Acts. Jews in Acts are regarded as responsible for the harassment of nascent Christianity, though there are occasional glimpses of more openness to Judaism elsewhere in the book than the concluding verses would indicate.

Various suggestions have been made with regard to its (and the related gospel of Luke's) purpose. They have included an apologia for

Christianity to the Roman state, an explanation for the delay of the Second Coming by stressing the role of the church in the divine purpose, an essay in anti-Jewish polemic, and a defence of Paul when his case was heard in Rome. Like his contemporary *Josephus, the author of Acts seeks to demonstrate that divine providence is at work.

adlection A man acquired the right of speaking in the Roman *senate on election as *quaestor; he became a full member when his name was placed on the senatorial roll. *Caesar, *dictator or overseer of public morals, and the *triumvirs adlected men directly into the senate. This unpopular proceeding was avoided by emperors until *Claudius, *censor in AD 47–48.

Admētus See ALCESTIS.

Adōnis Name given by the Greeks to a divine personage whom they thought to be eastern in origin, but whose eastern prototypes are very different from the picture which became established in Greece. Adonis aroused the love of *Aphrodite, who hid him in a chest and entrusted him to *Persephone, but she, captivated in her turn, refused to give him back. Then *Zeus decreed that the young man should spend four months of the year in the Underworld (see HADES) and four months with Aphrodite—whom Adonis chose also for the final four months, left to his own decision. He was born from a myrrh tree, and dying young in a hunting accident, was changed into an anemone, a flower without scent. A festival for the young god, known as Adonia, is attested only at Athens, Alexandria, and Byblos. In 5th cent. BC Athens, women sowed seed at midsummer in broken pots and placed them on the roof-tops, so that germination was rapidly followed by withering. In this lively, noisy celebration, which has been brought into opposition with the *Thesmophoria, mourning is secondary; at Byblos, the ritual involves the whole population, expressing at two different times mourning and laments, and resurrection and joy, but there is no trace of the 'gardens of Adonis'. The festival at Alexandria, like that of Athens, presents a picture of a women's ritual including mourning, but above all rejoicing centred on the couple, Aphrodite and Adonis.

adoption

Greek Greeks counted on their heirs for support in old *age, and for continuation of their families (*oikoi*; see HOUSEHOLD, *Greek*) and tendance of their tombs after death. But high mortality ensured that many had no surviving children. Adoption was a common recourse, probably encouraged by the great variation in fertility characteristic of populations with unreliable means of contraception. The fullest accounts can be provided for *Gortyn and *Athens in the Classical period.

The *polis* was not concerned to maintain separate *oikoi* through adoption, though individuals certainly were; adoption was essentially a private matter, regulated by the *phratries and *demes into which adopted children were introduced, in which the archon took no initiative.

Roman *Adoptiō* is a legal act by which a Roman citizen enters another family and comes under the *patria potestas* of its chief. Only a *paterfamilias* could adopt. When the adopted person, male or female, was previously in the paternal power of another, the act was *adoptio*; when a male who was not in paternal power but himself the head of a family, it was *adrogātiō*. Women could not be adrogated. Both acts involved a reduction of legal status. *Adrogatio* fused two families, for with the adoptee all under his power and his property pass into the family of the adopter. Adoption of adult men was a convenient recourse for childless aristocrats and for emperors in need of successors.

Adriatic Sea See IONIAN SEA.

adultery

Greek At Athens, a law (attributed to *Draco or *Solon) allowed a man who killed another he found in the sexual act with his wife, mother, sister, daughter, or concubine held for the purpose of bearing free children, to plead justifiable homicide; such adulterers might also be held for ransom. It is probable that there was also a *graphe* against adulterers, possible that those caught in the act were delivered to the *Eleven for summary execution or trial. Adulterous wives had to be divorced, and were excluded from public sacrifices. As for unmarried women, Solon supposedly permitted a *kȳrios* ('controller', male representative at law) to sell a daughter or sister into slavery if he discovered she was not a virgin. No instances are known, however, and indeed some husbands probably preferred to respond (or not) to adultery without recourse to the law, so avoiding public dishonour. Many states are said to have allowed adulterers to be killed with impunity. But the law code of *Gortyn envisages adulterers paying ransoms, varying with the status of the parties and the setting of the acts, and pecuniary penalties are stipulated in some marriage contracts from Hellenistic Egypt. Punishments in other (mostly later) communities stress public humiliation. Laws at both Athens and Gortyn provided protection against entrapment and false accusations. There was allegedly no Lycurgan law against adultery at Sparta, a tradition informed by the custom by which Spartans could share their wives with fellow citizens for procreative purposes. (See MARRIAGE LAW, Greek.)

Roman Roman tradition ascribed to fathers and husbands great severity in punishing illicit sexual behaviour by daughters or wives. Such misconduct was stuprum in married or unmarried women, an offence against chastity (pudīcitia); adulterium described sexual intercourse between a married woman and a man other than her husband. Until the legislation of Augustus, regulation was chiefly in the hands of the family: adultery probably always justified divorce; a family council might advise the paterfamilias (husband or father in whose power the woman was (see PATRIA POTESTAS)) on this and other sanctions, possibly including execution. The immediate killing of adulterers/ adulteresses taken in the act was defensible (morally and in court) but probably not legally prescribed. Other physical violence against the adulterer is a literary commonplace. Adultery in the late republic, like the seduction or rape of an unmarried woman, entitled the father or husband to sue the man for damages (for *iniuria, insult) and not only to divorce the wife but to retain part of her dowry. Magistrates occasionally proceeded against adulterers/adulteresses.

*Augustus, in the Julian law on repression of adulteries, passed apparently shortly after the marriage law of 18 BC, made illicit sexual intercourse (extramarital intercourse by and with a respectable free woman) a crime, to be tried by a special court under a praetor (in practice, often the senate). The law detailed restricted circumstances in which homicide by father or husband was justifiable. The normal judicial penalty for adulterers was *relegatio (banishment) to different islands, and partial confiscation of property and dowry (one half). The husband with clear evidence had to divorce or be liable to a charge of procuring; penalties similar. On divorce, husband or father might bring an accusation within 60 days, or anyone within the next four months.

A woman might not be accused while married. (See MARRIAGE LAW, Roman.)

advocacy as a profession. A party to a Roman trial might entrust the presentation of his case to an advocate (advocātus, *patronus). These men, who appear as a class in the late republic under the influence of Greek rhetoric, and of whom *Cicero and *Pliny the Younger are prominent representatives, were orators rather than *lawyers. They would necessarily have, or acquire, some knowledge of law (Cicero knew a lot), but their reputations were founded on their skill in forensic rhetoric. They and the jurists regarded each other as distinct classes, with different (and in the eyes of the other class inferior) functions, though occasionally an advocate might become a jurist. Advocates were forbidden to accept any reward for their services, but this rule was evidently often ignored.

Aeacus, ancestral hero of *Aegina, whose eponymous nymph bore him to *Zeus; to give him company, Zeus turned the island's ant population into humans. As a primeval figure, he was naturally close to the gods, and he retained their favour; acc. to Pindar, he helped *Apollo and *Poseidon build the walls of *Laomedon's Troy and even settled disputes among the gods themselves. Famous for his justice and piety in life, he became a judge in the Underworld. He was the founder of the warrior clan of the Aeacidae: his sons *Peleus and *Telamon, exiled for the murder of their brother, fathered *Achilles and Ajax (see AIAS (1)) respectively.

aediles, Roman magistrates. The aediles originated as two subordinates of the tribunes of the plebs whose sacrosanctity they shared. Their central function was to supervise the temples (aedes) and cults of the plebs, those of *Ceres and *Diana on the *Aventine, but they also acted as the executives of the tribunes. With the addition in 367 BC of two curule aediles (see MAGISTRACY, ROMAN) elected from the patricians, the aedileship became a magistracy of the whole people, but the subsequent functions of both sets of aediles can be chiefly explained as patronage of the urban plebs. After the admission of plebeians, the curule magistracy was held alternately by each order. Aediles were elected annually. Curules ranked below praetors, plebeians at first below tribunes but eventually with the curules. The office was not essential in the *cursus honorum. The main duties of all aediles were the *cura urbis, cura annōnae, and cura lūdōrum. Cura urbis meant care for the fabric of the city and what went on in it, including the streets of Rome, public order in cult practices, the water supply, and the market. In addition they acted as protectors of the plebs against the usurpation of public land, extortionate money-lending, rape, and insults to the plebs, prosecuting offenders for a financial penalty before their assembly. Out of the cura urbis developed the cura annonae, the maintenance and distribution of the corn supply. (See FOOD SUPPLY, Roman.) This duty passed under Augustus to the corn *prefect and other officials. An important aspect of the urban administration was the public games (*ludi). Here the growth of wealth and political rivalry in the later republic encouraged the aediles to spend an increasing amount of their own money to gain electoral advantage. The Ludi Romani and Megalenses fell to the curules, the Ludi Ceriales and Plebeii to the plebeians. Augustus, however, transferred the games to the praetors. Under Caesar's dictatorship and the Principate the aediles lost most of their quasi-police functions, but retained their concern for the market and related issues, such as the operation of sumptuary laws. The curule aediles acquired formal jurisdiction over cases relating to sales.

Aegae, in northern Pieria, overlooking the coastal plain of Macedonia. Founded by the first of the Temenid kings and thereafter the site of their tombs, it has been made famous by M. Andronikos, who excavated a pre-Temenid cemetery of tumuli and then, in 1977, three royal tombs of the 4th cent. BC. Two were intact. The frescos, the offerings in gold, silver, ivory, and bronze, and the weapons were of the highest artistic quality.

Aegeus, Athenian hero, father of *Theseus. When king of Athens, he consulted the *Delphic oracle about his childlessness, but failing to understand the reply (a figurative injunction to abstain from sex until his return home) fathered Theseus on Aethra, daughter of Pittheus, king of Troezen. Later he married *Medea, who attempted to poison Theseus on his arrival in Athens, and was therefore driven out by him. When Theseus returned from Crete, he or his steersman forgot to raise the agreed sign on the ship, and Aegeus, thinking his son was dead, threw himself off the Acropolis or into the sea (in this version called 'Aegean',

after him). Aegeus was one of the tribal *eponymoi (see PHYLAI). But his popularity in the 5th cent. was largely due to his position as father of Theseus.

Aegina, island in Saronic Gulf. Early in the first millennium BC it was settled by Greeks from *Epidaurus. Aeginetans participated at *Naucratis. The scale of Aegina's trade is indicated by its population of c.40,000 on territory which could support only 4,000 from its own agricultural resources. Like other prosperous places, Aegina had a tyrant, Pheidon. It struck *coins early.

In the 6th cent. BC Aegina and Athens came to blows, a naval war which simmered on during the Persian War period (when however Aegina fought well on the Greek side), and ended only with Aegina's forcible incorporation (paying a steep 30 talents annual tribute) into the *Athenian empire in 458/7. This was a watershed in 5th-cent. Greek history, given that Aegina was Dorian. In 431 Athens evicted the Aeginetans from Aegina, alleging that they were 'chiefly responsible for the war', a reference to Aeginetan complaints at Sparta that their *autonomy under 'the treaty'—the *Thirty Years Peace of 446—had been infringed. Athenian *cleruchs were installed. This is the effective end of independent Aeginetan history, though *Lysander restored the island to the Aeginetans in 405.

aegis, divine attribute, represented as a large all-round bib with scales, fringed with snakes' heads and normally decorated with the gorgoneion (see GORGON). In Homer *Zeus' epithet 'aegis-holding', and the story that the aegis was given to him by *Hephaestus suggests a primary association with Zeus, who lends it to *Apollo. It is unclear whether Athena's aegis is also borrowed. In post-Homeric times the aegis is most closely associated with *Athena, who is commonly shown wearing it over her dress. In the Iliad the aegis is ageless and immortal, with a hundred tassels, and it is decorated with (a representation of) the Gorgon's face. Its shaking by Zeus or Apollo brings victory to the side the god supports and fear to its enemies. It protects from attack; not even Zeus' thunderbolt can break it.

Aegisthus, in myth the son of Thyestēs who survives to avenge the deaths of his brothers at the hands of *Atreus. In Aeschylus he is only a baby when Atreus kills the other boys, and perhaps for this reason survives. A version makes him the incestuous offspring of Thyestes and his daughter after the murder of the elder sons; an oracle had advised that a son thus born would avenge their deaths. When he grew up, he learnt the truth and avenged the murder of his brothers by killing Atreus and later, with *Clytemnestra, *Agamemnon. All this is post-Homeric: in the *Iliad* there is harmony between the brothers Atreus and Thyestes, and in the *Odyssey* Aegisthus is a baron with an estate near the domains of Agamemnon, and no reason is given for Agamemnon's murder except Aegisthus' relationship with Clytemnestra, whom he had seduced despite a warning from the gods. In all versions Aegisthus rules the kingdom securely for some years after Agamemnon's death, until he in his turn is killed in revenge by Agamemnon's son, *Orestes. The death of Aegisthus is a favourite subject in Archaic and Classical art.

Aelian (AD 165/70–230/5), acc. to the *Suda*, a freedman born in *Praeneste, learned his Greek from a sophist and was an admirer of *Herodes Atticus. After a brief career as a declaimer he turned to writing. His *Indictment of the Effeminate* (a posthumous attack on the emperor Elagabalus), *On Providence* and *On Divine Manifestations* are lost; fragments of the last show them to have been collections of stories designed to reveal the operations of divine forethought and justice. *On the Nature of Animals* (extant) similarly claims to be illustrating the reality of divine providence in the animal kingdom, though its examples of extraordinary characteristics go far beyond his self-imposed programme. Extraordinary facts about animals also occur in the *Miscellany*, though there the emphasis falls on (generally 'improving') anecdotes from human life and history. The *Rustic Letters* is a co-ordinated set of 20 vignettes of life in the Attic countryside of 5th- and 4th-cent. BC literature (in the manner of *Alciphron). Aelian writes throughout with an extreme, mannered simplicity, and was much admired in later antiquity for the purity of his Attic diction. He was widely read and drawn on by Christian writers.

Aelius Aristides See ARISTIDES, PUBLIUS AELIUS.

Aelius Sēiānus, Lūcius (Sejanus), of Volsinii, d. AD 31. Sejanus' father was an *equestrian, Seius Strabo. Sejanus, who had attended Augustus' grandson Gaius *Iulius Caesar (2) in the east,

was made Strabo's colleague as *praetorian *prefect by *Tiberius in AD 14, and soon, on his father's appointment as prefect of Egypt, became sole commander; by 23 he had concentrated the guard in barracks near the porta Viminalis. After the death of Tiberius' son Drusus *Iulius Caesar in 23 (murder was later imputed) his influence was paramount; a succession of prosecutions eliminated opponents (chiefly adherents of *Vipsania Agrippina (2)). Tiberius allegedly refused to allow a marriage with Drusus' widow Livia Iulia (25), but retired from Rome in 26, further increasing Sejanus' influence (he allegedly encouraged the move); honours and oaths were offered to him as to Tiberius. In 29 Agrippina and her eldest son Nero Iulius Caesar were deported; her second, Drusus Iulius Caesar, was imprisoned in 30. That year Sejanus was elected consul for 31 with Tiberius amid engineered demonstrations; proconsular *imperium* followed, and he hoped for tribunician power. In October, however, Tiberius, allegedly warned by his sister-in-law *Antonia (2), sent a letter to the senate which ended by denouncing him (certainly for plotting against *Germanicus' youngest son, *Gaius (1) 'Caligula'). Sejanus was arrested, the guard having been transferred to *Sutorius Macro, tried in the senate, and executed; the punishment of Livia Iulia and of adherents, real or alleged, followed; even his youngest children were killed. Tiberius acted quickly and in fear of the outcome. Sejanus has been suspected of planning a coup against him; more probably he intended a gradual accession to partnership, involving Livia Iulia's son Iulius Caesar Nero 'Gemellus'.

Aemilius Lepidus (1), **Marcus,** joined Sulla and enriched himself in the *proscriptions. Elected consul 78 BC, with *Pompey's support and against Sulla's wishes, with Lutatius Catulus as colleague, he agitated against Sulla's settlement and after Sulla's death prepared to attack it. As proconsul he held *Gaul (Cisalpine) through his *legate Iunius Brutus, collected forces in Transalpine Gaul and made contact with *Sertorius in Spain. Marching on Rome, he was defeated by Catulus and fled to Sardinia, where he was again defeated and died. The first to realize the strategic importance of a unified province of Gaul, he lacked the military ability to profit by his insight. *Caesar, though sympathetic, refused to join him but remembered his example.

Aemilius Lepidus (2), **Marcus,** younger son of *Aemilius Lepidus (1). As praetor 49 BC, he supported *Caesar, then governed Nearer Spain (48–47), intervening in the dissensions in Further Spain and returning to triumph. He was consul (46) and Caesar's *magister equitum* (46–44). On Caesar's death he gave armed support to Marcus *Antonius (Mark Antony), who in return contrived his appointment as *pontifex maximus* in Caesar's place. He then left to govern the provinces assigned him by Caesar, Gallia Narbonensis and Nearer Spain. When Antony retreated into Gaul, Lepidus assured Cicero of his loyalty to the republic but in May 43 joined forces with Antony and was declared a public enemy by the senate. At Bononia in October he planned the Triumvirate with Antony and *Octavian, accepting Further Spain with his existing provinces as his share of the empire; and demanding (or conceding) the proscription of his brother *Aemilius Paullus (2). After triumphing again 'from Spain' he held a second consulship (42) and took charge of Rome and Italy during the campaign of *Philippi. After their victory his colleagues deprived him of his provinces, on the rumour of collusion between him and Sextus *Pompeius, but nothing serious was proved; and after helping Octavian ineffectively in the war against *Antonius (Pietas), he was allowed by Octavian to govern Africa, where he had sixteen legions and was acclaimed *imperator*. Kept out of the discussions at Tarentum over the renewal of the Triumvirate (37) and ignored in the arrangements, he asserted himself when summoned by Octavian to aid in the war against Sextus Pompeius. He tried to take over Sicily, but Octavian won over his army, ousted him from the Triumvirate and banished him to Circeii, though he later contemptuously allowed him to enter Rome. He kept his title of *pontifex maximus* until his death in 13 or 12, when Augustus took it over. Superior to his two partners in social rank and inherited connections, he lacked their ability to gather support and their total dedication to the pursuit of power.

Aemilius Papiniānus (Papinian), a leading lawyer of the Severan age and a close associate of the emperor *Septimius Severus. In AD 205 he became *praetorian *prefect, but on the death of Septimius in 211 was dismissed by Caracalla (see AURELIUS ANTONINUS). After the murder of Caracalla's brother and joint emperor Septimius Geta in 212, he was prosecuted by the praetorians and, without protest from Caracalla,

put to death, an event which entered into legend as the martyrdom of a just man.

Papinian is best known for 37 books of 'Problems', and 19 of 'Ordered Opinions', not confined to his own practice but drawing on a wide range of sources. His efforts to explore the ethical basis of legal rules goes along with a more crabbed style than is usual with Roman lawyers, but when properly understood his reasoning is as impressive as his technical mastery. Papinian was long regarded as the greatest Roman lawyer.

Aemilius Paullus (1), **Lūcius,** became an *augur in 192 BC and governed Further Spain as praetor in 191, with command extended to 190 and 189. A defeat in 190 was retrieved by a victory in the following year. Later in 189 he went to Asia as one of the ten commissioners who administered the settlement after the defeat of the *Seleucid Antiochus III. He did not reach the consulship until 182, when he operated in *Liguria; his command was extended to 181 when he eventually forced the Ligurian Ingauni to surrender. In 171 he was one of the patrons chosen by the peoples of Spain to represent their complaints against Roman governors. He was elected to a second consulship for 168, and ended the Third Macedonian War by his victory at *Pydna. His triumph was marred by the death of his two young sons; his two elder sons had been adopted and became Quintus Fabius Maximus Aemilianus and Publius *Cornelius Scipio Aemilianus. He was elected censor in 164 and died in 160, by no means a rich man; of the booty (see MANUBIAE) from the war against Perseus king of Macedon he had kept for himself nothing but Perseus' library. Paullus had a keen interest in Greek culture, giving his sons a Greek as well as a traditional Roman education, and undertaking an archaeological tour of Greece after the war with Perseus (see EDUCATION, GREEK and ROMAN; TOURISM). That did not prevent him from willingly carrying out the senate's order to sack Epirus, and from sanctioning other acts of brutality by Roman troops. See also PORCIUS CATO (1).

Aemilius Paullus (2), **Lūcius,** Elder son of *Aemilius Lepidus (1) and brother of *Aemilius Lepidus (2), the triumvir, accused *Catiline of violence in 63 BC. In 56, as curule *aedile, he began to rebuild the Basilica Aemilia. He was praetor 53 and consul 50. Previously a consistent *optimate, he was now bought by *Caesar for 1,500 talents, which he needed for the basilica, gave him at least passive support in 50, and remained neutral during the ensuing Civil War.

Aemilius Scaurus, Marcus, of patrician, but recently impoverished and undistinguished family, acc. to Cicero had to work his way up like a *novus homo*. He amassed wealth (not always reputably), gained the support of the Caecilii Metelli, and became consul (with a Metellus) 115 BC, defeating *Rutilius Rufus. As consul he triumphed over *Ligurian tribesmen and was made *princeps senatus* by the censors (one a Metellus) although probably not the senior patrician. Increasingly powerful in the senate, he married *Caecilia Metella and became the leader of the Metellan family group, then at the height of its glory. Censor 109, he built the first Roman canals in the Po (Padus) valley for navigation and for drainage. About 105, he received a *cura annonae*, superseding the quaestor *Appuleius Saturninus. In 100 he moved the *senatus consultum ultimum* against Saturninus and his supporters. After Rutilius' conviction (92) he avoided prosecution and became one of the chief advisers of *Livius Drusus. He was dead by late 89, when Metella married *Sulla. Throughout his life he was involved in numerous trials, not always successful in prosecution, but never convicted. He was the last great *princeps senatus*: 'his nod all but ruled the world'. He wrote an autobiography, perhaps the first. (See BIOGRAPHY, ROMAN.) Cicero's admiration for him has coloured much of our tradition.

Aenēas, character in literature and myth, son of *Anchises and *Aphrodite. In the *Iliad* he is a prominent Trojan leader, belonging to the younger branch of the royal house, and has important duels with *Diomedes and *Achilles, from both of which he is rescued by divine intervention. His piety (see PIETAS) towards the gods is stressed, and *Poseidon prophesies that he and his children will rule over the Trojans.

This future beyond the *Iliad* is reflected in the version in the lost *Sack of Troy* (see EPIC CYCLE) that Aeneas and his family left Troy before its fall to retreat to Mt. Ida, which led later to accusations of his treachery. The departure of Aeneas from Troy is widely recorded, and the image of Aeneas' pious carrying of his father Anchises on his shoulders in the retreat is common in Greek vases of the 6th cent. BC found in Etruria.

A visit to Carthage, possibly involving a meeting with *Dido, is certainly part Aeneas' itinerary by the time of *Naevius' *Punic War*, where it

is seen as an ancestral cause of the enmity between Rome and *Carthage. As Rome confronted a Greek-speaking Mediterranean world in the 3rd cent., it found it useful to claim as its founder Aeneas, famous through his appearance in Homer but also an enemy of the Greeks; a particular stimulus was the invasion of Italy by *Pyrrhus of Epirus, who claimed descent from Achilles and saw Rome as a second Troy. So, Roman poets, historians, and antiquarians stressed the Trojan origins of Rome; considerations of chronology eventually led to the view that Aeneas founded not Rome but a preceding city, Lavinium, and that Rome's eponymous founder *Romulus was his distant descendant.

*Virgil's version of the Aeneas-legend in the *Aeneid* aims at literary coherence rather than antiquarian accuracy. Aeneas' wanderings, apart from the stay at Carthage, are compressed into a single book; his war in Latium is the subject of the second half of the poem, and he appears there and at other times to have links with *Augustus, who claimed him as ancestor. The Virgilian Aeneas' central traits of *pietas* and valour continue his Homeric character, but he is also a projection of the ideal patriotic Roman, subordinating personal goals to national interest. And yet he never loses his human vulnerability; he is in despair in his first appearance in the poem, he is deeply affected by love for Dido, and the poem ends not with his triumphant apotheosis, anticipated earlier, but with his killing of Turnus in a moment of passion.

Aenēas Tacticus, the earliest(-surviving) and most historically interesting of the ancient military writers. Of several treatises only his *Siegecraft* is extant, internally datable to the mid-4th cent. BC. Concerned more with defence against than prosecution of siege-warfare, it offers unique insights into the stresses of life in small communities with warfare and revolution constantly threatening. See SIEGECRAFT, GREEK.

Aenesidēmus of Cnossus, Sceptical philosopher, revived Pyrrhonism (see PYRRHON) in the 1st cent. BC.

Aeolis, the territory of the northernmost group of Greek immigrants to the west coast of Asia Minor, covering the coastal strip from the entrance of the Hellespont to the mouth of the Hermus—a linguistic and ethnological unit. The Aeolians, deriving from *Boeotia and *Thessaly, planted their first settlements in *Lesbos c.1000 BC, and thence expanded northwards to

Urban life in North Africa was of pre-Roman origin, both Punic and (under Punic influence) Numidian. In spite of the destruction of Carthage, a number of towns of Phoenician or Carthaginian origin survived on the coast, such as Hadrumetum and *Lepcis Magna. Under Roman control, urbanization increased greatly, and refounded Carthage became the largest city in the western empire after Rome (see URBANISM, Roman). Over 600 communities ranked as separate *civitates* (see CIVITAS), of which many in due course obtained the rank of *municipium or colony. The area of densest urbanization was around Carthage and the Bagrada valley. Some were established on the sites of early legionary fortresses; Lambaesis grew out of the settlement outside the final fortress chosen for legion III Augusta; others were settled as colonies for retired legionaries. Roman *equestrians of African origin are known from the mid-1st cent. AD, soon followed by senators. During the 2nd cent. African senators (including *Cornelius Fronto) formed the largest western provincial group. The influence of Africans reached its height under *Septimius Severus, who was born at Lepcis Magna.

The wealth of Africa, largely agricultural, was proverbial throughout the Roman period. Corn was the most important product, and with Egypt Africa replaced Sicily as Italy's major supplier during the empire (see FOOD SUPPLY, Roman). Esp. from the 2nd cent. *olive-growing and the production of oil for export became an increasingly important part of the African economy. Large estates in the hands of a few men were commonplace, the largest landowner being the emperor, but there were plenty of medium-sized estates as well, most of them owned not by Italians but by prosperous members of the Romano-African urban élite, whose wealth was conspicuously displayed in the public monuments they paid for in their home towns. Other exports from Africa included fish-pickle, esp. from Proconsularis (see FISHING), and wild animals destined for *amphitheatres in Italy and elsewhere, including lions, leopards, and *elephants, the capture of which is featured on a number of African *mosaics. The arts flourished, with several vigorous local schools of sculptors working in both limestone and marble, while mosaic workshops, in response to the demand for elaborate polychrome figured mosaics in both private houses and public buildings such as baths, adopted from the second quarter of the 2nd cent. onwards an original and creative approach to mosaic design, which by the

4th cent. had left its influence on mosaic floors in Italy and several other provinces as well.

Africānus See CORNELIUS SCIPIO AFRICANUS.

afterlife See ART, FUNERARY; DEATH, ATTITUDES TO; ELYSIUM; HADES; ISLANDS OF THE BLEST; ORPHIC LITERATURE; TARTARUS; TRANSMIGRATION.

Agamemnon, in myth, son of *Atreus, brother of *Menelaus, and husband of *Clytemnestra; king of *Mycenae, or *Argos, and, in Homer, commander-in-chief of the Greek expedition against Troy, taking with him 100 ships, the largest single contingent. He had a son, *Orestes, and three daughters, Chrysothemis, Laodice, Iphianassa; *Iphigenia, whom Homer does not mention, seems to be a later substitution for Iphianassa, as does Electra for Laodice.

Homer depicts Agamemnon as a man of personal valour, but lacking resolution and easily discouraged. His quarrel with *Achilles, who withdrew in anger and hurt pride from battle when Agamemnon took away his concubine Briseis, supplies the mainspring of the *Iliad*'s action, with Achilles' refusal to fight leading to tragedy. The *Odyssey* tells how, on Agamemnon's return home, *Aegisthus, Clytemnestra's lover, treacherously set on him and his men at a banquet and killed them all, Clytemnestra also killing his Trojan captive *Cassandra, daughter of *Priam. Eight years later Orestes came from Athens and avenged his father's murder. This whole story became a favourite among later authors, who retold it with various elaborations and changes. Aeschylus makes Clytemnestra a powerful and awe-inspiring woman who, quite alone, kills Agamemnon after she has pinioned him in a robe while he is unarmed in his bath.

The *Cypria* (see EPIC CYCLE) is the earliest evidence of the sacrifice of Agamemnon's daughter Iphigenia. Agamemnon caught a stag, then boasted that he was a better huntsman than *Artemis, whereupon the offended goddess held the Greek fleet wind-bound at Aulis. *Calchas told them to appease her by sacrificing Iphigenia, whom they sent for on the pretext of marriage to Achilles. Here the guilt for the killing seems to be laid on the Greeks in general; moreover Iphigenia was snatched away and made immortal by Artemis, who left a deer on the altar in her place (as in Euripides' *Iphigenia among the Taurians*). But again matters are very different in Aeschylus, where Iphigenia is a

Tenedos, and along the mainland coast to the east and south. Most of their cities derived their livelihood from agriculture. The religious centre of the settlements in the south was the temple of *Apollo at Gryneum. The chief city was *Cyme. The north Aeolian settlements occupied the coastal part of *Troas.

aerārium, derived from *aes, means 'treasury'. The main *aerarium* of Rome was the *aerarium Saturni*, so called from the temple below the Capitol, in which it was placed. Here were kept state documents, both financial and non-financial, and the state treasure. The *Tabularium was built near it in 78 BC. The *aerarium* was controlled by two urban *quaestors under the supervision of the senate. Caesar in 49 BC seized the reserve for his own use.

The *aerarium mīlitărĕ*, situated on the Capitol, was founded by Augustus in AD 6 to provide for the pensioning of discharged soldiers. Augustus provided for it a capital sum of 170 million sesterces from his own funds and an income from the 1 per cent tax on sales by auction and the 5 per cent tax on inheritances. It was administered by three ex-praetors.

aes, bronze, also more loosely copper or brass, hence money, coinage, pay, period for which pay is due, campaign. In the late 140s BC, the Roman state changed from reckoning in asses (coins originally weighing about a pound) to reckoning in sesterces = $\frac{1}{4}$ *denarius* = 4 asses.

Aeschinēs (1) (*c*.397–*c*.322 BC), Athenian orator whose exchanges with *Demosthenes (2) in the courts in 343 and 330 provide much of the evidence for the relations of Athens and Macedon in the 340s and the 330s. His origins were obscure enough to allow Demosthenes' invention full play. After hoplite service of some distinction in the 360s and early 350s, and a period as an actor, he embarked on a public career as a supporter of *Eubulus. In 347/6 both Aeschines and Demosthenes were members of the council (*boule*), and their disagreements led to sixteen years of enmity.

Aeschines was a member of the embassy sent to negotiate with Philip after the battle of *Chaeronea (338), but from then on he withdrew from politics only to re-emerge on two occasions when circumstances seemed favourable for an attack on Demosthenes. The first was in early 336 when Ctesiphon proposed that Demosthenes should be crowned in the theatre at the *Dionysia for the excellence of his services to the

city: earlier Demosthenes had been similarly honoured without protest, but, at a time when Demosthenes' gloomy predictions after Chaeronea seemed mocked by the opening of the Macedonian invasion of Persia, Aeschines indicted the decree under the *graphe paranomon*. However, the murder of Philip made the future too uncertain for Aeschines to be confident of success, and he abandoned the indictment for the moment. In 330 after the defeat of Persia at *Gaugamela, Athens was in almost complete isolation with no prospect of liberation from Macedon, and Aeschines thought the moment suitable for him to proceed with his prosecution of Ctesiphon. In his *Against Ctesiphon*, he reviewed the career of Demosthenes, somewhat selectively, and sought to show that Demosthenes was unworthy of the crown. In *On the Crown* Demosthenes replied with all the devastating effect that his great rhetorical gifts could command, and Aeschines failed to secure the necessary fifth of the jury's votes to save him from a fine and the limitation of the right to prosecute. He chose to retire from Athens to Rhodes, where he taught rhetoric.

The supremacy of Demosthenes as an orator has to a large extent beguiled posterity into the opinion that he alone fully appreciated the menace of Macedon and correctly diagnosed the causes of Philip's success, and Aeschines has been represented as an opportunist with little judgement and less principle. In fact, there was no obvious way of saving Athens and Greece, and it is probable that Aeschines no less than Demosthenes sought to maintain his city's power and independence.

Speeches The only genuine speeches of Aeschines known to the critics of the Roman period were the three that we have. Aeschines was a man of dignified presence and fine voice, who deprecated the use of extravagant gestures by an orator. Proud of his education, he displays it by frequent quotation of poetry. In the use of historical argument he cannot compare with Demosthenes, but in a battle of wits he more than holds his own. Ancient critics ranked him lower than he deserves; the fact is that he was not aiming at literary perfection; his object was to produce a powerful effect on his audiences, and he was justified by the result.

Aeschinēs (2) **Socraticus** (4th cent. BC), of the *deme of Sphettus in Attica, a devoted follower of *Socrates, was present at his trial and death. He wrote speeches for the lawcourts and taught oratory, but fell into poverty and took refuge at the court in *Syracuse, returning to Athens after the expulsion of *Dionysius (2) II in 356. Best known as the author of Socratic dialogues which resemble *Xenophon's more than *Plato's, Aeschines was apparently not an original thinker, and his Socrates expounds common ethical views. The dialogues were esteemed for their style and their faithfulness to Socrates' character and conversational manner.

Aeschylus, Athenian tragic poet (?525/4–456/5 BC). He fought in the battle of *Marathon. His first tragic production was in 499, his first victory in 484. He gained thirteen victories altogether. His epitaph makes no reference to his art, only to his prowess displayed at Marathon; this estimate of what was most important in Aeschylus' life—to have been a loyal and courageous citizen of a free Athens—will reflect his own death-bed wishes or those of his family.

Works Aeschylus' total output is variously stated at between 70 and 90 plays. Seven plays have survived, of which *Prometheus Bound* is of disputed authenticity. Many of Aeschylus' productions were connected 'tetralogies', comprising three tragedies presenting successive episodes of a single story (a 'trilogy') followed by a satyr-play based on part of the same or a related myth. This seems to have been common practice in his day. See SATYRIC DRAMA.

Technique Aeschylus was the most innovative and imaginative of Greek dramatists. His extant plays, though covering a period of only fifteen years, show a great and evolving variety in structure and presentation.

The three earliest extent plays (*Persians, Seven against Thebes*, and *Suppliants*) are designed for a theatre without a *skēnē* (stage building; see THE-ATRE STAGING, GREEK) but containing a mound or elevation (tomb of Darius, Theban acropolis, Argive sanctuary, the two latter with cult-images on them). There are two actors only; the main interactions are less between character and character than between character and chorus (often expressed in dialogue between singing chorus and speaking actor). There is a wide variety of structural patterns, some of them probably unique experiments, but all built round the basic framework of a series of episodes framed by entries and exits and separated by choral songs. The pace of the action is usually slow.

By 458 (the year of the *Oresteia* trilogy: *Agamemnon, Libation-bearers, Eumenides*) the dramatist had available to him a *skene* and probably an *ekkyklēma* and *mēchanē* also (see THEATRE STAGING, GREEK), as well as a third actor. Aeschylus makes imaginative, and once again very varied, use of the new opportunities. After composing the first half of *Agamemnon* entirely in his old style (with no actor–actor dialogue), he centres the play on a verbal trial of strength between *Agamemnon and *Clytemnestra, meanwhile keeping *Cassandra long silent and then making her narrate Agamemnon's death prophetically before it happens. The house and its entrance are firmly controlled throughout by the 'watch-dog' Clytemnestra. In the second half of *Libation-bearers* the action increasingly accelerates as the climax approaches, and then abruptly slows as Clytemnestra for a time staves off her doom with brilliant verbal fencing. In *Eumenides* a series of short scenes, full of surprises and changes of location, and including a trial-scene with some virtuoso four-sided dialogue, leads to a conclusion mainly in the old mode for one actor and chorus (with a second chorus at the very end).

Aeschylus' plots tend to be characterized, not by abrupt changes of direction (*peripeteiai*), but by a build-up of tension and expectation towards a climax anticipated by the audience if not by the characters. He was quite capable of contriving *peripeteiai* when he wished, as witness *Seven against Thebes*, where the whole action pivots on Eteocles' discovery that he has unwittingly brought about a combat between himself and his brother and thus fulfilled his father's curse; the trilogy form, however, encourages sharp changes of direction and mood between plays rather than within them.

The central interest in Aeschylean drama is in situation and event rather than in character. Even important figures in a play (like *Orestes) can be almost without distinctive character traits: if their situation gives them effectively no choice how to act, their personal qualities are irrelevant and are ignored. On the other hand, characters who make (or have previously made) decisions vitally affecting the action, when alternative choices were possible, are portrayed as far as is necessary for illuminating these decisions: Eteocles is usually calm and rational but can be carried away by strong emotions, Agamemnon is one who values prestige above all. The character most fully drawn is Clytemnestra, because the plot requires her to be a unique individual, 'a woman with a man's mind'.

For similar reasons, Aeschylean choruses nearly always have a strong and distinctive personality. Their words are often of the utmost importance in drawing attention to the deeper principles underlying events (even when they do not themselves fully understand these principles or their implications) and, together with their music and dance, in establishing the mood and theme of a whole play. The women of *Seven*, dominated almost throughout by fear, contrast sharply with the Danaids, utterly determined in their rejection of marriage and coercing King Pelasgus by a cool threat of suicide; the Argive elders of *Agamemnon*, enunciators of profound moral principles yet unable to understand how these principles doom Agamemnon to death, share a trilogy with the *Erinyes, hellish bloodsuckers yet also divine embodiments of these same principles. Aeschylus' choruses often have a substantial influence on the action; the Danaids and the Erinyes are virtually the protagonists of their plays, the women's panic in *Seven* causes Eteocles' promise to fight in person, while in *Libation-bearers* it is the chorus who ensure that Aegisthus is delivered unguarded into Orestes' hands. Sometimes a chorus will surprise the audience near the end of a play (as when the Argive elders defy Aegisthus); it is a distinctly Aeschylean touch in *Prometheus Bound* when the hitherto submissive Oceanids resolve to stay with Prometheus despite Hermes' warning of impending destruction.

Aeschylus' lyric language is smooth and flexible, and usually more easily understood than that of *Pindar or Sophocles, provided the listener was attuned to a vocabulary that tended towards the archaic and the Homeric. In iambic dialogue (see METRE, GREEK, 4(a)), where he had fewer models to follow, he sometimes seems stiff compared with Sophocles or Euripides, though he can also create an impression of everyday speech through informal grammar and phraseology. He excels at devising patterns of language and imagery, elaborating them down to minute detail, and sustaining them all through a play or a trilogy.

Aeschylus is consistently bold in exploiting the visual aspects of drama. The contrast between the sumptuous dress of Atossa at her first, carriage-borne entry and the return of Xerxes alone and in rags; the chaotic entry of the chorus in *Seven*; the African-looking, exotically dressed Danaids and their confrontation with brutal Egyptian soldiers; the purple cloth over which Agamemnon walks to his death, and the display of his corpse in the bath-tub with Cassandra beside him and Clytemnestra 'standing where I struck' (a scene virtually repeated in *Libation-bearers* with a different killer and different victims); the Erinyes presented anthropomorphically on stage (probably for the first time), yet tracking Orestes like hounds by the scent of blood; the procession that ends the *Oresteia*, modelled on that at the Great *Panathenaea—these are far from exhausting the memorable visual images in only six or seven plays, quite apart from numerous careful touches of detail (e.g. at the end of *Agamemnon* where Aegisthus, that 'woman' of a man, alone of those on stage has neither weapon nor staff in his right hand).

Thought Aeschylus is well aware of, and vividly presents, the terrible suffering, often hard to justify in human terms, of which life is full; nevertheless he also believes in the ultimate justice of the gods. In his surviving work (leaving aside *Prometheus*), all human suffering is clearly traceable, directly or indirectly, to an origin in some evil or foolish action—Xerxes' ill-advised decision to attempt the conquest of Greece; Laius' defiance of an oracular warning to remain childless; the attempt by the sons of Aegyptus to force the Danaids to be their wives; the adultery of Thyestes with Atreus' wife; the abduction of Helen by Paris. The consequences of these actions, however, while always bringing disaster to the agents, never end with them, but spread to involve their descendants and ultimately a whole community; some of these indirect victims have incurred more or less guilt on their own account, but many are completely innocent. In some of Aeschylus' dramas, like *Persians* or the Theban trilogy, the action descends steadily towards a nadir of misery at the end (*Seven against Thebes*). In the *Oresteia*, however, it proves possible to draw a line under the record of suffering and reach a settlement that promises a better future; each time a key element in the final stages is the substitution of persuasion for violence, as when in the *Oresteia* a chain of retaliatory murders is ended by the judicial trial of Orestes, and the spirits of violent revenge, the Erinyes, are persuaded to accept an honoured dwelling in Athens.

In dramas of the darker type described above, the gods are stern and implacable, and mortals often find themselves helpless prisoners of their own or others' past decisions; though they may still have considerable freedom to choose how to face their fate (compare the clear-sighted courage of Pelasgus or Cassandra with Xerxes or Agamemnon). Elsewhere, a different concept of divinity may appear. In the *Oresteia* ethical advance on earth, as the virtuous Electra and an Orestes with no base motive succeed the myopic Agamemnon and the monstrous Clytemnestra, is presently answered by ethical advance on Olympus as the amoral gods of *Agamemnon* and *Libation-bearers* turn in *Eumenides* into responsible and even loving protectors of deserving mortals.

Aeschylus is intensely interested in the shared life of the *polis*, and all his surviving genuine works have strong political aspects. He seems to be a firm supporter of democracy (a word whose elements first appear together in his phrase 'the sovereign hand of the people'), and of Athens' wars of the early 450s, while recognizing the overriding importance of avoiding civil conflict by conciliating rival interests. To later generations, who from time to time continued to see his plays, Aeschylus, who may have come of age in the year of *Cleisthenes' (2) reforms and whose death coincided with the peak of Athenian power, was (as in Aristophanes' *Frogs*) the poet of Athens' greatness, of the generation of Marathon, where he had lived what to him was the supreme day of his life. See also TRAGEDY, GREEK.

Aesculāpius The miraculous transfer of *Asclepius god of healing from *Epidaurus to Rome and the origin of the healing-cult on Tiber island in 291 BC were important moments in the Roman story of their religion; the summoning of a prestigious god from Greece, in accordance with the Sibylline Books (see SIBYL), to remedy a Roman crisis (*plague), represented a stage in the domestication of external religion and acted as a model for the closely related tale of the summoning of the Magna Mater in 204. (See CYBELE.) In fact the cult was spreading widely. By the imperial period, in Italy and the provinces, a Roman cult is hard to disentangle from the very popular and varied combinations of healing deities blending local cults with a broadly Asclepian tradition.

Aesop, as legendary a figure as Homer. What we call *fables, are first alluded to by *Hesiod and *Archilochus, but by the 5th cent. BC fables in prose are regularly attributed to Aesop. Herodotus places him in the 6th cent. as the slave of a Samian later murdered by Delphians. The first known collection of Aesopic fables was made by *Demetrius of Phaleron.

Afrānius Burrus, Sextus, *equestrian *procurator of *Livia Drusilla, *Tiberius, and *Claudius, came from Narbonensis (see GAUL (TRANSALPINE)). As favourite of *Iulia Agrippina, he was appointed sole praetorian *prefect by Claudius in AD 51 and retained his post under *Nero. He was Nero's adviser for many years, and, with *Seneca the Younger, was responsible for the first period of Nero's government. In 59 he managed Nero's relations with the public after the murder of his mother. He opposed Nero's divorce from *Claudia Octavia, which took place only after his death in 62. That he was poisoned is asserted by Suetonius and Cassius Dio, but regarded by Tacitus as unproven.

Africa, Roman The *Punic Wars made Rome heir to the Carthaginian empire. In 146 BC she left most territory in the hands of *Masinissa's descendants, but formed a new province (Africa) in the most fertile part. It was governed by a praetor from *Utica. Except for Utica and six other towns of Phoenician origin which had supported Rome in the Punic Wars, most of the land became *ager publicus*. Although the attempt by Gaius *Sempronius Gracchus to found a colony (see COLONIZATION, ROMAN) at Carthage failed, Roman and Italian traders and farmers settled in the province in large numbers, and many of *Marius' veterans settled west of the boundary line. After the battle of Thapsus in 46 *Caesar added to the existing province the Numidian territory of Juba I. Caesar's intention to colonize Carthage afresh was carried out by *Augustus.

Under him, the united province, now called Africa Prōconsulāris, extended from the edge of Cyrenaica to western Algeria. At least eleven colonies were founded in Proconsularis, in addition to the thirteen colonies settled on the coast of Mauretania. Africa Proconsularis was governed from Carthage by a proconsul, who (unusually for the governor of a province not controlled by the emperor) also commanded *legion III Augusta. Under *Gaius (1) command of the legion was handed over to an imperial *legate, who became responsible for the government of Numidia and the frontier districts. The provincialization of North Africa was completed by Claudius with the creation of two provinces in *Mauretania. Resistance to Roman rule on the fringes of the Sahara and in the mountainous regions was only sporadic, and for over three centuries the whole area from Cyrenaica to the Atlantic was protected by a single legion and auxiliaries.

Urban life in North Africa was of pre-Roman origin, both Punic and (under Punic influence) Numidian. In spite of the destruction of Carthage, a number of towns of Phoenician or Carthaginian origin survived on the coast, such as Hadrumetum and *Lepcis Magna. Under Roman control, urbanization increased greatly, and refounded Carthage became the largest city in the western empire after Rome (see URBANISM, *Roman*). Over 600 communities ranked as separate *civitates* (see CIVITAS), of which many in due course obtained the rank of *municipium or colony. The area of densest urbanization was around Carthage and the Bagrada valley. Some were established on the sites of early legionary fortresses; Lambaesis grew out of the settlement outside the final fortress chosen for legion III Augusta; others were settled as colonies for retired legionaries. Roman *equestrians of African origin are known from the mid-1st cent. AD, soon followed by senators. During the 2nd cent. African senators (including *Cornelius Fronto) formed the largest western provincial group. The influence of Africans reached its height under *Septimius Severus, who was born at Lepcis Magna.

The wealth of Africa, largely agricultural, was proverbial throughout the Roman period. Corn was the most important product, and with Egypt Africa replaced Sicily as Italy's major supplier during the empire (see FOOD SUPPLY, *Roman*). Esp. from the 2nd cent. *olive-growing and the production of oil for export became an increasingly important part of the African economy. Large estates in the hands of a few men were commonplace, the largest landowner being the emperor, but there were plenty of medium-sized estates as well, most of them owned not by Italians but by prosperous members of the Romano-African urban élite, whose wealth was conspicuously displayed in the public monuments they paid for in their home towns. Other exports from Africa included fish-pickle, esp. from Proconsularis (see FISHING), and wild animals destined for *amphitheatres in Italy and elsewhere, including lions, leopards, and *elephants, the capture of which is featured on a number of African *mosaics. The arts flourished, with several vigorous local schools of sculptors working in both limestone and marble, while mosaic workshops, in response to the demand for elaborate polychrome figured mosaics in both private houses and public buildings such as baths, adopted from the second quarter of the 2nd cent. onwards an original and creative approach to mosaic design, which by the

4th cent. had left its influence on mosaic floors in Italy and several other provinces as well.

Africānus See CORNELIUS SCIPIO AFRICANUS.

afterlife See ART, FUNERARY; DEATH, ATTITUDES TO; ELYSIUM; HADES; ISLANDS OF THE BLEST; ORPHIC LITERATURE; TARTARUS; TRANSMIGRATION.

Agamemnon, in myth, son of *Atreus, brother of *Menelaus, and husband of *Clytemnestra; king of *Mycenae, or *Argos, and, in Homer, commander-in-chief of the Greek expedition against Troy, taking with him 100 ships, the largest single contingent. He had a son, *Orestes, and three daughters, Chrysothemis, Laodice, Iphianassa, *Iphigenia, whom Homer does not mention, seems to be a later substitution for Iphianassa, as does Electra for Laodice.

Homer depicts Agamemnon as a man of personal valour, but lacking resolution and easily discouraged. His quarrel with *Achilles, who withdrew in anger and hurt pride from battle when Agamemnon took away his concubine Briseis, supplies the mainspring of the *Iliad*'s action, with Achilles' refusal to fight leading to tragedy. The *Odyssey* tells how, on Agamemnon's return home, *Aegisthus, Clytemnestra's lover, treacherously set on him and his men at a banquet and killed them all, Clytemnestra also killing his Trojan captive *Cassandra, daughter of *Priam. Eight years later Orestes came from Athens and avenged his father's murder. This whole story became a favourite among later authors, who retold it with various elaborations and changes. Aeschylus makes Clytemnestra a powerful and awe-inspiring woman who, quite alone, kills Agamemnon after she has pinioned him in a robe while he is unarmed in his bath.

The *Cypria* (see EPIC CYCLE) is the earliest evidence of the sacrifice of Agamemnon's daughter Iphigenia. Agamemnon caught a stag, then boasted that he was a better huntsman than *Artemis, whereupon the offended goddess held the Greek fleet wind-bound at Aulis. *Calchas told them to appease her by sacrificing Iphigenia, whom they sent for on the pretext of marriage to Achilles. Here the guilt for the killing seems to be laid on the Greeks in general; moreover Iphigenia was snatched away and made immortal by Artemis, who left a deer on the altar in her place (as in Euripides' *Iphigenia among the Taurians*). But again matters are very different in Aeschylus, where Iphigenia is a child, dead, and Agamemnon himself her killer, for which Clytemnestra never forgave him.

Agatharchus, painter, of Samos. He was the first to make a *skēnē* (stage building; see THEATRE STAGING, GREEK), for Aeschylus (probably for a revival at the time of the *Peloponnesian War), and wrote a book on '*skēnē*-painting', which inspired *Anaxagoras and *Democritus to write on perspective. He was the first painter to use perspective on a large scale (isolated instances occur on vases from the mid-6th cent. BC), probably in architectural backgrounds for plays. His quick work is contrasted with *Zeuxis' slowness. He was apparently compelled by *Alcibiades (*c.*430?) to paint his house (with perspective scenes?). The story suggests that private houses were usually unpainted. See PAINTING, GREEK.

Agathon of Athens was the most celebrated tragic poet after the three great masters. (See TRAGEDY, GREEK.) He won his first victory in 416 BC, and the occasion of *Plato's *Symposium* is a party at his house in celebration of that victory. Plato emphasizes his youth in *Symposium* and portrays him as a boy in *Protagoras*, of which the dramatic date is *c.*430; so he must have been born after 450. In *Protagoras* he is seen in the company of the *Prodicus, and he appears to have been influenced in style by *Gorgias. In 411 he heard and approved *Antiphon's speech in his own defence—this suggests anti-democratic sentiments—and in the same year he was caricatured in Aristophanes' *Thesmophoriazusae*. The play ridicules him for effeminacy and passive *homosexual tastes, and Plato, portraying him as the long-term boyfriend of one Pausanias, partly confirms the charge. Before 405 he left Athens (like *Euripides) for the court of *Archelaus of Macedon, and he died there.

*Aristotle says that he wrote a tragedy in which all the characters were invented, not taken from legend; that he wrote a tragedy which failed because he tried to include too much material, as if writing an epic; and that he was the first to write choral odes that were mere interludes, unconnected with the plot. All these developments can be seen as exaggerations of tendencies found in the later work of Euripides.

age The division of life into age-groups was prominent in antiquity, though there was disagreement over their precise identification. *Pythagorean philosophers identified four, whereas Hippocratic writers (see HIPPOCRATES) acknowledged seven ages of man, each seven years in length. Since adult society was primarily organized on a two-generational principle, a threefold division probably served most practical purposes, namely boy, young man, old man. There were minimum age qualifications for administrative and executive posts. So an Athenian councillor had to be 30 years old, as, probably, did a Spartan *ephor. Similarly, the Roman *cursus honorum or ladder of office prescribed minimum ages for all magistracies. Belief in sacred *numbers, notably seven and three, meant that certain ages were believed fraught with danger. *Augustus is said to have expressed considerable relief 'at having survived my climacteric, the sixty-third year'.

It is estimated that in Rome 'more than a quarter of all live-born Roman babies died within their first year of life'. About one-third of the children who survived infancy were dead by the age of 10. Upper-class females in their early teens tended to marry males who were at least ten years older. In Rome, however, the legal age for marriage was 12 and 14 for females and males respectively (see MARRIAGE LAW). Life expectancy was appreciably lower for *women at all social levels, largely because of the debilitating and often lethal effects of *childbirth. Probably less than one per cent of the population attained the age of 80 and anyone who did so was judged remarkable. Despite the brevity of most human life, threescore years and ten constituted the proper quota of years. Old age is commonly described as hateful in classical literature, and many lives would have been characterized by increasing incapacitation and loss of mobility from the beginning of the third decade onwards. Many Greeks and Romans would have had only an approximate notion of their exact age in years, as the expression *P(lus) M(inus)* 'more or less', which is often found on Roman tombstones, indicates. See POPULATION.

ager pūblicus, public land, comprised lands acquired by Rome by conquest from her enemies or confiscation from rebellious allies. By tradition there was, as early as the 5th cent. BC, dispute between patricians and plebeians over whether such lands should be retained in public ownership but open to exploitation on lease by rich possessors (not owners) or distributed in private ownership amongst the poorer classes. In practice much of this land seems to have been assigned to the use of Roman and, after 338, Latin colonies (see IUS LATII). The Licinio-Sextian laws of 367 BC purported to limit the amount of public land possessed by any one citizen to 500 *iugera* or 140 ha. (350 acres).

Public land continued to be acquired during subsequent centuries; the conquest of Cisalpine *Gaul added large areas of land which were either distributed amongst colonies or offered to citizens as smallholdings on permanent lease. Elsewhere, esp. in southern Italy, large tracts remained in the hands of the state and were regularly leased out by the *censors to rich citizens in return for large rents. There is evidence that in these distributions the legal limits were ignored and the collection of dues was lax.

The agrarian reforms associated with the Gracchi aimed at redistributing much of these large properties as smallholdings. In 133 BC (see SEMPRONIUS GRACCHUS (2), TIBERIUS) a commission was established to identify those lands possessed over the legal limits. Much land was regained by the state as a result and redistributed. A similar scheme was revived by Gaius *Sempronius Gracchus in 123, but the new distribution eventually ceased, following his violent death in 122; the whole exercise threatened the economic position of rich landowners.

In 111 BC an agrarian law was passed which in effect privatized all the Gracchan smallholdings, abolishing the rent which had been previously imposed and turning the lessees into owners. There remained some public lands in Italy which continued to be leased by the censors, but subsequently acquired lands, for example those seized by *Cornelius Sulla from the cities which opposed him, were usually distributed to veterans immediately. *Caesar in 59 gave much of the surviving censorial lands to *Pompey's soldiers. Thereafter the only significant public land in Italy, other than inalienable property such as parks in Rome and roads, comprised the property of individual municipalities and common open pasture.

The gradual disappearance of public lands in Italy was in contrast to the position in the provinces. All provincial land was, in legal theory, owned either by the people of Rome or the emperor. In practice nearly all was effectively in the hands of permanent possessors, and the theory affected only the remedies by which they might seek to protect their property. Truly publicly owned property was limited to lands seized from conquered communities and the like, but there was a tendency to redistribute these, for example to colonies, rather than retain them in public keeping, so that, as in Italy, such land as remained public was in the hands of municipalities (see MUNICIPIUM).

Agēsilāus II (*c*.445–359 BC), Spartan king of Eurypontid line. Son of *Archidamus II by his second wife, he was not expected to succeed his older half-brother *Agis II and so went through the prescribed educational curriculum (*agoge*) like any other Spartan boy. In 400 he unexpectedly secured the succession, with the aid of his former lover *Lysander, ahead of Agis' son Leotychidas, whose parentage was suspect (rumour had it that his true father was the exiled *Alcibiades).

The first king to be sent on campaign in Asia, where his declared aim was to liberate the Greeks from Persian suzerainty, Agesilaus achieved some success against the Persian viceroys *Pharnabazus and *Tissaphernes in 396–395 before his enforced recall to face a coalition of Sparta's Greek enemies in central and southern Greece. The battle of Coronea (394) was a Pyrrhic victory, and, despite some minor successes of his, the coalition was defeated not on land by Agesilaus but at sea by the Spartan admiral *Antalcidas with a Persian-financed fleet. Agesilaus, however, threw himself wholeheartedly behind the Peace of Antalcidas, or *King's Peace (386), which he interpreted to suit what he took to be Sparta's best interests. Pro-Spartan oligarchs were brought to power in *Mantinea, Phlius, and *Olynthus, but the most flagrant violation of the autonomy clause of the peace was the occupation of *Thebes (382). Partly by condoning that breach, Agesilaus provoked a further anti-Spartan coalition supported by Persia. Despite some success of Agesilaus in Boeotia, the Thebans and their *Boeotian federation eventually proved too strong for an enfeebled Spartan alliance at *Leuctra in 371. The Theban ascendancy of 371 to 362, presided over by *Epaminondas and Pelopidas, and the consequent liberation of *Messenia from Sparta, are directly attributable to Agesilaus' unremitting hostility to Thebes. Agesilaus nevertheless did not lose face or influence at home, and continued to direct Spartan counsels in the years of his city's humiliation. He organized the defence of the city against Epaminondas' coalition, and sought to augment the state's revenues by foreign service as a mercenary. He died in Cyrenaica on the return journey from Egypt, aged *c*.84.

Though born lame in one leg, and displaying a streak of romanticism, Agesilaus was typically Spartan in his qualities and limitations. He was an efficient soldier, but a better tactician than strategist, who failed to understand the importance of siegecraft and *sea power. At home, no Spartan king ever exploited better than he the resources of charisma and patronage available to a blue-blooded *Heraclid king. But the narrowness of his personal loyalties and political sympathies dissipated those moral assets by which alone Sparta might have maintained her Greek hegemony, in the face of a sharply dwindling citizen population and the constant hostility of the *helots at home and Sparta's Greek and non-Greek enemies beyond her borders.

Agis II, Spartan king of the Eurypontid house (the first to be given a name belonging naturally to the Agiads) from *c*.427 to 400 BC; he was son of *Archidamus II. He achieved widespread prominence in 418, as nominal victor of the battle of *Mantinea, a success that both stilled powerful domestic criticism of his leadership and restored Sparta's authority in the Peloponnese and outside. In 413, perhaps glad to escape scandal on his own doorstep, he was appointed general commanding the Peloponnesian forces in central Greece, and permanently occupied a fortified base within Athens' borders at Decelea. The centre of the *Peloponnesian War, however, shifted to Asia, and Agis' role in the eventual reduction of Athens by siege in 404 was subsidiary to that of *Lysander. His death (400) occasioned the succession dispute that brought *Agesilaus to the throne.

agōgē, the Spartan public upbringing. The Classical *agoge*, supervised by the *paidonomos* ('boy-herdsman'), embraced males aged 7–29. Only the immediate heirs to the kingships were exempt. There were three stages, the *paidēs*, *paidiskoi*, and *hēbōntēs*, probably representing ages 7–17, 18–19, and 20–29. The *paides* were trained in austerity, obedience, and mock battles by older youths within companies, subdivided into herds of age-mates with their own internal leadership. At age 12 they entered an institutionalized pederastic relationship with a young adult (see HOMOSEXUALITY). The *paidiskoi* were army reservists and (probably a select group) participants in the *krypteia*. The *hebontes* joined the *syssitia* and army, could marry, but remained in barrack life, competing for places among the 300 *hippeis*, the kings' bodyguard. Separating boys from their families, the *agoge* inculcated conformity and the priority of collective interests, but also promoted the emergence of future élites. Girls, also, were educated in the interests of the state, to be the mothers of future warriors; so the emphasis fell on physical training and athletics, but music and *dancing were not neglected.

agōnĕs 1. The term *agōn* and its derivatives can denote the informal and extempore rivalries that permeated Greek life in the general fight for survival and, success esp. philosophical, legal, and public debates; action between opposing sides in war; medical disputes. A corollary of the agonistic drive was the prominence as a motive for action of love of honour (*philotīmia*), which could turn into over-ambition and jealous rivalry, and, in its worst form, lead to *stasis* (strife) and political upheaval.

2. Gatherings of people, usually for formal contests in honour of a god or local hero.

Before the 8th cent. BC *agones* seem to have been small-scale events, centring round a shrine or sanctuary. But the *agon* at *Olympia came to acquire a special status: traditionally founded in 776 BC, by the end of the 8th cent. it was, because of the wide range of *athletic contests it offered and its lack of political ties, attracting increasing numbers of foreigners (esp. from among the athletic Spartans) and was organized as a panhellenic *agon* (see OLYMPIC GAMES; PANHELLENISM). With interstate relationships assuming increased importance during the 7th cent., local *agones* were reorganized at other places too. The *Pythian Games became panhellenic in 582; its range of athletics events followed the Olympic model, but it preserved its identity and associations with *Apollo through its emphasis on musical competitions. With the reorganization of the *Isthmian (*c*.581) and *Nemean Games (*c*.573), a group of four panhellenic *agones* came to form an athletics circuit. At Athens the Great *Panathenaea (founded 566) was also panhellenic, but for athletes never achieved the status of the other four. Despite this development, local *agones* with athletic contests continued to flourish: *Pindar's victory odes mention more than 20 local games, and a 5th-cent. Laconian inscription records 72 victories won by a father and son at eight *agones* in Peloponnese.

Contests were often in athletics, but music, poetry, and equestrian events were also popular. *Hesiod won a poetry-singing competition in *Chalcis; the Pythian Games included three types of musical contest and a painting competition. In Athens tragedies, comedies, and *dithyrambs were performed in competitions at the City *Dionysia, and at the Panathenaea *rhapsodes competed in Homer-reciting contests. *Horse- and chariot-races were mainly entered by rich men who paid charioteers or jockeys to ride on their behalf, and hoped for political prestige from good performances. The chariot-race was often long (about 14 km. (nearly 9 mi.) at the Olympic Games) and dangerous. Beauty contests, and drinking contests (see ANTHESTERIA) are also recorded.

At the four major panhellenic *agones*, victors were honoured with a *wreath: olive at Olympia, laurel at the Pythian Games, varieties of *selīnon* (parsley or celery) at the Isthmus and Nemea. On returning home the victor might receive more substantial rewards: free meals, the privilege of a front seat when spectating at *agones*, and gifts. Athens was esp. generous to victors, and at the Great Panathenaea in the 4th cent. BC money, gold crowns, bulls, and large numbers of amphorae containing olive oil were awarded as prizes (100 amphorae, *c*.4,000 lit. (880 gal.), for a victor in the men's *stadion* race, a very valuable prize).

agora, Gk. term for an area where people gather together, esp. for the political functions of the *polis*, normally sited centrally in cities, or at least central to the street lines where the actual centre may be occupied by other features (such as the Acropolis at Athens); the area was sacred. In unplanned cities its shape depends on the nature of the available site, irregular at Athens, on low-lying ground bordered by rising land to west (Kolonos Agoraios) and south (the slopes of the Acropolis). In planned cities the required number of blocks in the regular grid plan are allocated, giving a strictly rectangular shape. See URBANISM, Greek and Roman.

Architecturally, the agora need be no more than the space defined by marker stones rather than buildings, as, originally, at Athens. When spectacular buildings develop for the various functions of the agora, they are placed along the boundary, which they help to define, rather than in the agora space. These include lawcourts, offices, and meeting-places for officials (and the formal dining which was part of their office). These may be integrated with extended porticoes—*stoas—and it is these that come to dominate the architecture of the agora, often with long lines of rooms behind them, though sometimes as colonnades pure and simple. Such colonnades, extended along the boundaries, define the agora more obviously than marker stones and are normal in the developed (and esp. the planned) agoras of the 4th cent. BC and the Hellenistic period.

In unplanned agoras, streets normally run through the open area; thus the 'Panathenaic Way' enters the Athenian agora at its NW corner, and leaves at the SE. As the buildings on the borders develop, the agora tends more and more to be closed off, streets being diverted to pass outside the surrounding stoas, with perhaps one main street being allowed through (though by Roman times this may have to pass through formal, and closable, gateways).

The central area of the agora was the locality for special monuments and dedications, statue groups such as the Tyrannicides (see ARISTOGITON) at Athens, the line of *exedrae* at Priene. So long as the space was needed for crowds (all those voting in an *ostracism* at Athens, as an extreme example) it had to remain open; it was only with the restricted political life of Greek cities in the Roman period that it might include large buildings such as the *odeum of Agrippa at Athens. See ATHENS, TOPOGRAPHY.

agrarian laws and policy Allocation of land by the community is attested in the Greek world at the times of new city foundations (see COLONIZATION, GREEK), and when land was annexed (*cleruchies). There is also some evidence for legislation restricting the disposal of allotments by sale or inheritance, in order to maintain the original land-units, which sustained the households. On the other hand, there developed strong resistance to the notion of redividing the city's territory so as to change the proportions of private landholdings: a promise not to propose anything of the kind was included in the oath of the Athenian jurors. See also SPARTA.

At Rome agrarian legislation played a large part in the history of the republic and the struggles between the aristocracy and the *plebs. Legislation arose originally from annexation of land after Roman military expansion. It thus concerned land which was the public territory of the Roman people (see AGER PUBLICUS), not land belonging to private individuals (private land remained free from interference by the community except where it could be shown that a public right existed over it, such as access to a water supply). One type of law established new cities (colonies) with their associated land, a second assigned new allotments in a wide tract of territory, such as those in the *ager Gallicus* in Picenum, a third restricted the exploitation at will of unassigned public land by reference to area occupied or number of beasts grazed. The first known law of the last type, the *lex Licinia* of 367 BC, was probably a response to the opportunities created by the acquisition of all the land of Veii. During the middle republic, when Italy and Cisalpine *Gaul were gradually subjected to Roman power, land demands were satisfied by new allocations. However, in the late 2nd cent. BC, with a rising number of landless and a shortage of new land available for distribution in the peninsula, the Gracchi passed laws which sought to recover what was still technically public land from rich men who were exploiting it illegally to excess, and to redistribute it to the poor. This was regarded by rich landholders as a subversive move. Nevertheless the Gracchan programme (see SEMPRONIUS GRACCHUS (2), TIBERIUS and SEMPRONIUS GRACCHUS, GAIUS) was largely completed, and such redistribution seems to have remained part of agrarian policy until the death of *Livius Drusus (tribune of the *plebs* 91), though settlements were also made in territory acquired by conquest abroad. The *Social War followed by *Sulla's *proscriptions led to big changes in landholding in Italy, which favoured the larger landholders against the peasants. Some attempt was made to return to Gracchan policies in the late republic, but the chief means of public acquisition of land in Italy now had to be purchase from private individuals. The proscriptions by the triumvirs (see TRIUMVIRI) after Caesar's murder made land available for distribution to their soldiers, but *Augustus returned to purchase in order to secure land for his *veterans after Actium.

Agricola See IULIUS AGRICOLA.

agricultural writers Agricultural manuals, written by practising landowners, flourished at Rome from *Porcius Cato (1) (*c.*160 BC) to Palladius (*c.*mid-5th cent. AD), enjoying higher status than other technical literature. Greece had produced notable works (*Varro knew more than 50), but written mostly from a philosophical or scientific viewpoint; and an influential (lost) Punic work by Mago had been translated into both Greek and Latin. Agriculture, as gradually defined and systematized, embraced, in Varro's work (*c.*37 BC), arable cultivation, livestock, *arboriculture, market gardens, luxury foods, slave management, and *villa construction. A century later, *Columella doubted whether one man could know it all, and, from the early empire onwards, specialized works appeared. While Varro criticized *Theophrastus for excessive theory, modern scholars have doubted the practicality of the Roman writers. Recent rural archaeology has given grounds for greater confidence. The villa excavated at Settefinestre has substantiated in remarkable detail the recommendations of Varro and Columella, as has the discovery of a large vineyard at *Pompeii. But the agricultural writers describe not just one ideal type of estate. Crop by crop they discuss various methods of cultivation, according to species, soil, topography, and custom—a regional diversity confirmed by archaeological survey. See also AGRICULTURE, ROMAN.

agriculture, Greek Life in historical Greece was sustained by barley and wheat, sown mostly in the autumn as field crops dependent on rainfall between autumn and spring. Cultivation with a simple wooden plough (ard), sometimes tipped with iron, to break up the surface of the soil for receiving seeds in autumn, is treated as normal by ancient sources, but it is uncertain whether smallholders could produce enough to feed a pair of plough-oxen in addition to their own households. For them hand cultivation by spade and hoe must have been common.

The practice of leaving half the land in uncultivated fallow is also regarded as normal by our sources, while repeated ploughing of the fallow was desirable. But again, smallholders may have been forced to risk long-term depletion of the soil by resting much less than half their land each year. Some leguminous field crops (broad beans and various lentils (pulses)) were known in Mycenaean times and in *Homer. By the 4th cent. BC they were recommended as partial alternatives to fallow (either as crops in their own right or as green manure to be ploughed under); it is not clear how early or how widely they were employed in rotation with wheat and barley. The moisture and soil requirements of wheat made it an often unreliable crop in the Greek *climate. Barley, somewhat less nutritious and much less esteemed, was probably grown more widely. (See CEREALS.) Frequent local crop failures required supplementation through trade with less affected neighbours or over longer distances. While it is unlikely that overseas settlements of the 8th and 7th cents. BC had as a prime goal assistance to the grain supply of the mother cities, once established in *Magna Graecia and *Sicily or, later, on the north Black (*Euxine) Sea coast and its approaches, the existence of surpluses in the new settlements at times of shortage in the old lessened the chances of famine and set in motion rhythms of trade with far-reaching consequences. How early the larger Greek towns came to depend on imported grain is disputed. Some have seen Athenian colonies on the *Hellespont in the later 6th cent. as established on the route of the city's corn supply, but for Athens explicit evidence comes only in the late

5th cent. Meanwhile by *c*.470 Teos included interference with the city's grain supply among the targets of public curses.

Other crops, chiefly olives, grapes, and the vegetables and fruits grown in irrigated gardens, supplemented the largely cereal diet. *Olive oil and *wine also permitted *trade, not least for the acquisition of grain in times of shortage. Greeks rarely settled at elevations or latitudes too cold for the olive. Since the trees matured slowly (in ten to fifteen years), they were planted for long-term benefits and not always in large numbers. Olive cultivation was not demanding once young trees had been established and no longer needed *irrigation, but harvesting and, with only primitive *technology, oil production required much labour. By contrast, vines grew fast and demanded much hard work from the start.

For the Greeks improvement of agricultural property meant, after the creation of suitable plots of land, investment in trees and vines (see ARBORICULTURE) together with the necessary equipment, including store-rooms and containers for storing and shipping oil and wine. However, interplanting of cereals, pulses, vines, and trees in a single plot, or polyculture using separate plots, were probably always more common than specialization in a single crop.

Animal husbandry on a small scale (ploughoxen and mules, donkeys as pack animals, some sheep, goats, and pigs) probably had a place on all but the smallest properties. Larger herds were moved to mountain pastures in the summer (see PASTORALISM; TRANSHUMANCE). The value of manuring was appreciated, and organic wastes were collected conscientiously from settlements and applied esp. to trees and vines. But the amount available in the absence of lush pastures and large numbers of cattle close to the farms limited its effect.

Nowhere in mainland Greece did the geography and the nature of the agriculture favour large, unitary estates farmed by a large labour force, though properties increased in size in Hellenistic and esp. Roman times. The rich usually owned several parcels of land, whose environmental diversity may have been advantageous. Poorer farmers were more limited. The particular agricultural regimes in use varied with local social and economic conditions as well as with geography. *Thessaly's extensive good grain land was long controlled by a small upper class and farmed by a large population of serfs, as were *Laconia and *Messenia, less suited

to grains but probably slow to develop crops for trading. The islands of *Chios and Corcyra had rich estates concentrating on vines and olives and cultivated by unusually large numbers of slaves (see SLAVERY).

*Attica up to the *Peloponnesian War was also known for its fine country houses, a measure of rural prosperity. Its relatively large landless (or inadequately landed) population were not primarily farm labourers, and significant use of slave labour by the top three property classes is indicated. But for all except the rich, hired or slave labour only supplemented that of the landowner and his family.

The range of possibilities open to the Greek farmer for increasing production was restricted, and most required additional labour. Intensity and efficiency of agricultural production were neither uniform nor static, nor independent of social and economic factors, even if the ideal of self-sufficiency was prevalent. The agricultural information in *Xenophon's *Oeconomicus*, informative for us, was no doubt banal. But beginning in the 4th cent. an extensive technical literature developed.

agriculture, Roman By modern standards Roman agriculture was technically simple, average yields were low, transport was difficult and costly, and storage was inefficient. This limited urbanization (and hence 'industrialization') and obliged the bulk of the population to live and work on the land. Nevertheless, in the late republic and earlier *Principate agriculture and urbanization (see URBANISM, *Roman*) developed together to levels probably not again matched until the late 18th cent. Roman agriculture broadly fits the pattern which is commonly seen as characteristic of the Mediterranean region: based on the triad of *cereals, vines (see WINE) and *olives, at the mercy of a semi-arid *climate with low and unreliable rainfall, and dominated by small farms practising a polyculture aimed principally at self-sufficiency and safety. But two factors—the geophysical diversity of Italy (let alone of Rome's provinces), and the effects of political and social developments—led to important variations between areas and across time in the practice of agriculture. Recent decades have seen an enormous growth in archaeological research—surface survey of rural areas, excavations of farmsteads, study of the ancient environment—which is taking our understanding of Roman agriculture far beyond what could be discovered from the evidence of the literary sources.

In Archaic Rome the land seems to have been controlled by the élite, and most Romans were dependant labourers. The concept of private ownership of land had probably developed by the late 6th cent. BC, and by the later 4th cent. Rome had become a state of citizen-small-holders. The political aim behind this development was the creation of a large conscript army of smallholders who could afford to arm themselves (the *assidui*); as this army defeated Rome's Italian neighbours, the Roman state annexed tracts of their territories, which were often distributed in small plots to create more *assidui*, although some was left as nominally 'public' land (*ager publicus*) and appears to have been dominated by the élite, who now used enslaved enemies as their main agricultural workforce. This cycle of conquest, annexation, and settlement continued, almost without interruption, into the early second century BC, and settlement schemes, albeit thereafter using confiscated land, continued into the early Principate. The face of Italy was changed: forests were cleared and drainage schemes undertaken, as in southern Etruria and in the Po (*Padus) valley; the territories of the ubiquitous Roman colonies were divided into small farms of similar size by rectangular grids of ditches, banks, and roads (*centuriation), which are often still traceable today; these examples and the obligation on most of Rome's Italian allies to supply infantry on the Roman model encouraged the wider diffusion of this pattern of peasant smallholding.

Rome's massive overseas expansion in the 2nd and 1st cent. BC speeded agricultural developments which had already begun in the 3rd cent. The large and long-serving armies of conquest required huge supplies of corn, wine, wool, and leather, the Celtic aristocracy under and beyond Roman rule enthusiastically adopted wine-drinking as a mark of status, and the city of Rome swelled as the capital of an empire and the centre for conspicuous consumption and display by its ever richer leaders. The boom in demand for agricultural produce, and the continuous supply of cheap slave labour, encouraged the élite to expand their landholdings and to invest in market-oriented production. A significant differentiation between larger and smaller farms emerges in the archaeological record, and also regional patterns of types of agriculture. While in southern Italy relatively extensive forms of agriculture, i.e. cereal cultivation using chain-gangs of slaves and large-scale stockbreeding with seasonal movement between upland summer pastures and

winter stations in the coastal plains (*transhumance), were probably predominant, central west Italy (the semicircle around Rome and her main ports) was dominated by the so-called '*villa system', i.e. intensive production on medium-sized estates (around 25 to 75 ha.; 60 to 185 acres) of wine, olive oil, and other cash crops, including wheat (see CEREALS), vegetables, fruit (see FOOD AND DRINK), and also small game and poultry, with a permanent nucleus of skilled slave labour topped up at seasonal peaks with casual labour hired from the free rural poor. These forms of agriculture flourished into the 2nd cent. AD with some reorientation: consumption by the frontier-based armies of the Principate and the Celtic aristocracy was increasingly met by the development of local Roman-influenced agricultural production, but the growth of Rome and general urbanization of Italy in the Augustan period greatly increased domestic demand in Italy. Roman estate owners showed much interest in technical and technological improvements, such as experimentation with and selection of particular plant varieties and breeds of animal, the development of more efficient presses and of viticultural techniques in general, concern with the productive deployment and control of labour, and, arguably, a generally 'economically rational' attitude to exploitation of their landholdings (see TECHNOLOGY). A technical literature of estate management emerged, drawing on Carthaginian and Hellenistic predecessors, which is represented to us principally by the manuals of *Porcius Cato (1), *Varro, and *Columella (see also AGRICULTURAL WRITERS).

The development of this estate agriculture put pressure on the peasant smallholders, although military needs led to some dramatic and bitterly opposed attempts to revive an independent peasantry in central Italy, notably the Gracchan programme (see SEMPRONIUS GRACCHUS (2), TIBERIUS and SEMPRONIUS GRACCHUS, GAIUS) of the later 2nd cent. and the settlement schemes for veterans in the 1st cent. BC. The decline of the peasantry can be exaggerated: excavated small farms show that some peasants too produced for and profited from the same markets as the large estates, and in hillier areas and the Po valley the peasantry remained strong. But as the Roman army became mercenary and then, under Augustus, professional and more cosmopolitan, the political will to maintain an independent peasantry in Italy gradually evaporated, and it seems that peasants increasingly became tenants rather than owners of small farms. See LATIFUNDIA; PEASANTS.

Agrippa See VIPSANIUS AGRIPPA.

Agrippa I–II, Herodian kings. See IULIUS AGRIPPA (1–2).

Agrippa Postumus See IULIUS CAESAR, AGRIPPA.

Agrippīna See IULIA AGRIPPINA ('Agrippina the Younger'); VIPSANIA AGRIPPINA (1); VIPSANIA AGRIPPINA (2) ('Agrippina the Elder').

Aias (Lat. *Aiax*). (1) Son of *Telamon, king of *Salamis. He brought twelve ships from Salamis to Troy. In the *Iliad* he is enormous, head and shoulders above the rest, and the greatest Greek warrior after *Achilles. His stock epithet is 'bulwark of the Achaeans', and his characteristic weapon a huge shield of seven-fold ox-hide. He clearly has the better of *Hector in a duel, after which the heroes exchange gifts, Aias giving Hector a sword-belt in return for a sword; and he is at his memorable best when with unshakeable courage he defends the Greek wall and then the ships. He is also a member of the Embassy to Achilles, when he gives a brief but effective appeal to Achilles on friendship's grounds. At *Patroclus' funeral games he draws a wrestling match with *Odysseus, strength against cunning.

The *Aethiopis* (see EPIC CYCLE) told how after Achilles' death Aias carried his body off the field of battle while Odysseus held back the Trojans. The *Little Iliad* told how the arms of Achilles were then adjudged to Odysseus instead of Aias, who went mad with anger, killed the herds of the Greeks, believing them to be the Greek leaders, and then killed himself. *Sophocles dramatizes these later events in his *Ajax*, but at the end of the play Aias is taken to an honourable burial, in marked contrast to his treatment in the *Little Iliad* where he is denied the customary burial honours. In the *Odyssey*, when Odysseus is in Hades, he meets the shade of Aias who, in anger at his loss of Achilles' arms, refuses to speak and stalks away in magnificent *silence.

Scenes from Aias' life popular in art, some from the 7th cent. BC, are combats with Hector and others, dicing with Achilles, lifting Achilles' body, the argument and voting about Achilles' arms, and (an especial favourite) his suicide.

Aias (2) Son of Oïleus, the Locrian chieftain. In Homer Aias leads the Locrian contingent to Troy with 40 ships. He is 'much lesser' than Telamonian Aias (hence often called the Lesser Aias), quick-footed, and often paired with his great namesake as a brave fighter. He can, however, be an unpleasant character, on occasion grossly rude, hated by *Athena, and finally drowned by *Poseidon for blasphemy against the gods while scrambling ashore after shipwreck. In the *Sack of Troy* he dragged *Cassandra away from the statue of Athena to rape her, and in so doing loosened the statue from its plinth. This is a favourite scene in Archaic and Classical art.

Aidōs 'Shame'. See NEMESIS; HUBRIS; SUICIDE.

Ajax See AIAS (1) and (2).

ālae ('wings') In the republic *alae sociōrum* were two bodies of Roman allies, including cavalry and infantry, each equivalent in size to a *legion, which fought on the wings of the battleline. After the *Social War the Romans increasingly recruited cavalry from native peoples, and *Caesar used Gallic and German cavalry units to great effect, usually placing them under their own commanders. During the Civil War some native contingents were used by the military dynasts under the command of Roman officers or veteran soldiers. In *Augustus' reorganization of the army, many non-Roman infantry and cavalry units were incorporated into the formal structure of the army as *auxilia*. Alae (now used exclusively of cavalry) normally consisted of about 480–500 men divided into sixteen troops. Alae were commanded by *equestrian *prefects, who in the three posts often held by equestrian officers ranked above the prefects of auxiliary infantry cohorts and military tribunes. Cavalrymen of the *alae* probably received 1,050 sesterces a year under Augustus, equivalent to the pay of a legionary cavalryman and more than that of a legionary infantryman (see STIPENDIUM). Alae were originally enlisted from ethnic groups, and although this racial character was later diluted by wider recruiting including the admission of some citizens, they often retained their regional titles (e.g. 'first *ala* of Spanish'); a few bore personal names indicating the officer who had first raised or commanded them (e.g. '*ala Agrippiana*'); many were named after an emperor as a mark of honour or because he had recruited them; and some titles indicated methods of fighting.

Albānus mons, the Alban hills and more specifically their dominating peak, 21km. (13 mi.) SE of Rome. Until *c*.1150 BC the Albanus mons was an active volcano; the volcano, however, has been inactive in historical times. On the summit stood the Latin federal sanctuary of Jupiter Latiaris, where Roman consuls celebrated the *feriae Latinae* (see LATINS). Here at least five Roman generals celebrated *ovations after being refused regular *triumphs in Rome.

album An *album* was a whitened board or tablet on which information could be published in writing. Such tablets were widely used in Roman public life, e.g. to publicize the *praetors' edicts. *Album* was also the standard term for a published list or register. The *album senātōrium* was the official list of members of the *senate which was posted outside the senate-house from the time of *Augustus. See also ANNALES MAXIMI.

Alcaeus, Greek *lyric poet, of *Mytilene on Lesbos. Probably b. *c*.625–620 BC, since he was old enough to participate in the struggle against Athens for *Sigeum, in which *Pittacus distinguished himself. Lesbian politics at this period were violent and confused. After the death of the tyrant Myrsilus, the people elected Pittacus 'tyrant' for ten years. Alcaeus' poetry is full of attacks on and abuse of Pittacus, for perjury and faithlessness, low birth (probably false), drunkenness, unbridled ambition, and physical defects (see INVECTIVE). Popular opinion was with Pittacus, as in general is that of posterity.

Alcaeus' poetry was divided by the Alexandrians into at least ten books. It was composed for a solo singer in a variety of lyric metres in two- or four-line stanzas, including the alcaic stanza, named after him. His range is rivalled only by *Archilochus in the Archaic period. He dealt with politics, war, wine, love, hymns to the gods, moralizing, and myth. There is much variety in the treatment of each theme. Politics may be dealt with through personal abuse or the grandeur of myth and ritual or both; the invitation to drink may be supported by myth or the imperatives of the weather. He is open to a range of influences. In his use of lyric for abuse he blurs the difference between lyric and iambus. His hymns are influenced by the rhapsodic tradition (see RHAPSODES). He has a vivid descriptive power and an impressive vigour, esp. in his arresting openings. He was popular at Attic *symposia and a favourite with *Horace.

Alcestis, in myth, daughter of *Pelias, wife of Admētus king of Pherae, who is prepared to die in his place. Pelias promised Alcestis to whoever could yoke a lion and boar to a chariot. Admetus

was assisted in this feat by his lover Apollo, who had been punished by serfdom to Admetus for killing the *Cyclopes or the Pythian snake. But at his marriage Admetus forgets to sacrifice to *Artemis and finds the bridal chamber full of snakes, an omen of imminent death. On *Apollo's advice he appeases Artemis and even obtains from the Fates the concession that someone may die in his place. In the event, only Alcestis will, but Korē (*Persephone) sends her back from death or (in tragedy) *Heracles rescues her by wrestling with Death (Thanatos).

Alcestis' self-sacrifice belongs with a sequence of *folk-tale functions: (*a*) a young man faces early death; (*b*) he can be saved only if another will die for him; (*c*) only his wife will; (*d*) the lord of life and death grants life to this wife. Alcestis is mentioned in the *Iliad* for her beauty and offspring but then the tradition is silent till *Phrynichus' play *Alcestis*. The myth is best known from Euripides' *Alcestis* (438 BC).

Alcibiadēs (451/0–404/3 BC), son of Cleinias, Athenian general and politician, killed at *Coronea. Brought up in the household of his guardian *Pericles, he became the pupil and intimate friend of *Socrates. A flamboyant aristocrat, he competed in politics with the new-style *demagogues, and his ambitious imperialism drew Athens into a coalition with *Argos and other enemies of *Sparta. This policy, half-heartedly supported by the Athenians, was largely discredited by the Spartan victory at *Mantinea (418). Though Alcibiades temporarily allied with *Nicias to avoid *ostracism, the two were normally adversaries and rivals, and when Alcibiades sponsored the plan for a major Sicilian expedition, Nicias unsuccessfully opposed it. Both were appointed, together with Lamachus, to command this expedition (415). After the mutilation of the *herms, Alcibiades had been accused of involvement in other religious scandals, and soon after the fleet had reached Sicily he was recalled for trial. He escaped, however, to Sparta, where he encouraged the Spartans to send a general to Syracuse, and to establish a permanent Spartan post at Decelea in Attica (which was eventually done in 413).

In 412 he was involved in Sparta's decision to concentrate on the Aegean rather than the Hellespont, but he soon lost the confidence of the Spartans and fled to the Persian satrap *Tissaphernes. He tried to secure his return to Athens by obtaining the support of Persia and bringing about an oligarchic revolution, but the negotiations with Persia were unsuccessful. The

Athenian fleet at *Samos appointed him general, and for several years he skilfully directed operations in the Hellespont, winning a brilliant victory at Cyzicus in 410. On returning to Athens in 407 he was cleared of the religious charges hanging over him and was appointed to an extraordinary command; but when a subordinate was defeated by *Lysander at Notium (406) he withdrew to Thrace, and his approach to the Athenians before Aegospotami was rebuffed (405). He took refuge with the satrap *Pharnabazus, who had him murdered at the request of Lysander.

Alcibiades was a competent military leader and a master of intrigue, but his personal ambition and the excesses of his private life aroused the distrust of the Athenians, and he was not given the chance to show whether his ambitious policies, carried out under his leadership, could bring about success.

Alcmaeon (1), the son of *Amphiaraus and Eriphȳlē, who killed his mother in revenge for his father's death. Bribed by Polynīcēs (see ETEOCLES) with the necklace of Harmonia (see CADMUS), Eriphyle gave judgement in favour of Adrastus against her husband when adjudicating between them on whether Amphiaraus should join the expedition of the *Seven against Thebes despite his prophetic knowledge that all the participants except Adrastus would die. Amphiaraus ordered Alcmaeon to avenge his death with hers. After killing her Alcmaeon went mad and wandered about pursued by the *Erinyes.

Alcmaeon (2) of Croton (5th cent. BC) wrote a philosophical book dedicated to a group of *Pythagoreans, and known to *Aristotle and *Theophrastus. It mostly concerned the nature of man. Alcmaeon explained the human condition by the interplay of opposites, e.g. health as 'equal rights' of hot and cold, wet and dry, etc., disease as 'monarchy' of one of them. He held that 'passages' linked the sense-organs to the brain, which, followed by *Plato, he took to be the seat of understanding.

Alcmaeonids, a noble Athenian family prominent in politics. Its first eminent member was Megaclēs, who as archon (see ARCHONTES), perhaps in 632/1 BC, involved it in a hereditary *curse (see CYLON). This led to an immediate expulsion of the family. Its fortunes were to be haunted by this curse. Sixth-century members of the family, now back in Athens, had close links with *Croesus, *Pisistratus (see MEGACLES), and *Delphi (the family helped rebuild the temple). *Cleisthenes (2) served as archon under *Hippias (1) before turning democratic reformer.

In 490 (see PERSIAN WARS) they were suspected of collusion with the Persian invaders, and this may explain the almost total eclipse in our evidence of the male line after 480. *Pericles, son of Xanthippus and the Alcmaeonid Agariste, could ignore the Spartan invocation of the curse in 432/1, and *Alcibiades, despite his Alcmaeonid mother, escaped it altogether.

Alcman, Greek lyric poet, active in the mid- to late 7th cent. BC in *Sparta. The *Suda credits him with six books of lyric songs. Those songs, mostly choral, included maiden-songs. We also hear of hymns and wedding-songs. The most important surviving works are fragments of two maiden-songs found on papyri. Both poems share a richness of sensuous imagery and a pronounced homoerotic tenor. There is an evident taste for puns, and a proliferation of proper names, many of significance only to the original audience. Alongside this parochiality we find a taste for the exotic. Together the two songs show a gaiety and humour not usually associated with Sparta. Alcman's descriptive power is shown in an account of the sleep of nature.

Alcmēnē, mother of *Heracles. Her father was Electryon, king of *Mycenae, who was accidentally killed by her husband Amphitryon, heir to the throne of Tiryns; she followed Amphitryon into exile in *Thebes, but refused to sleep with him until he had avenged the death of her brothers on the Teleboans. *Zeus came to her in Amphitryon's shape a little before the latter's return, and she gave birth to twins—Heracles by Zeus, Iphiclēs by Amphitryon. *Hera in jealousy delayed the birth, thus ensuring that *Eurystheus was born before Heracles and so became king of *Argos. After the death of Heracles, Alcmene with the rest of his family was persecuted by Eurystheus, and in *Euripides' Heraclids took refuge with them in Athens, insisting on Eurystheus' death after his defeat in battle. At her own death she was taken to the *Islands of the Blest to marry Rhadamanthys.

alcoholism

Greece The ancient Greeks were well aware of self-destructive drinking, though they did not recognize addiction. *Homer, *Plato, *Aristotle, and *Plutarch, amongst others, did recognize the pernicious effects of *wine. Some groups, e.g. the Macedonians, drank with heroic intensity. Distinguished topers included *Cleomenes I, *Alcibiades, *Philip II of Macedon, *Alexander (2) the Great, and *Dionysius (2) II. In classical antiquity, however, allegations of intemperance often serve as vehicles for character assassination (see INVECTIVE); thus, each case must be considered on its merits.

Rome The ancient Romans were as interested in the harmful effects of excessive drinking and chronic intoxication as their Greek counterparts. The descriptions of the psychological and physical effects of chronic intoxication given by *Seneca the Younger and *Pliny the Elder presage modern observations. Mark Antony (Marcus *Antonius), *Iulia (2) (daughter of Augustus), and the emperors *Tiberius, *Claudius, *Vitellius, and *Commodus are among the prominent Romans accused of heavy drinking.

The alcoholic beverage of choice for both Greeks and Romans was *wine, customarily diluted with water, though the Macedonians were reputed to drink their wine unmixed.

Alexander (1) **I,** 'the Philhellene', king of Macedon c.498–454 BC. Subject to Persia from 492, he used his influence to extend his territory eastwards to the mines of Mt. Dysoron, which provided the silver for his coinage; and in 480/79 he was active in the campaigns of *Xerxes and *Mardonius. The tradition in Herodotus that he was responsible for the murder of Persian envoys (c.512) and maintained secret relations with the Hellenic leaders in 480 is propaganda to preserve his position and to broadcast his overtly philhellene policies. Acknowledged even before 480 as *proxenos and benefactor of the Athenians, he was recognized (in 476?) at Olympia as Hellenic ruler of a barbarian people; and he fostered the myth that his ancestors were Temenids from *Argos. The propaganda no doubt helped him preserve his independence against Athenian expansion in the wake of Xerxes' invasion.

Alexander (2) **III** ('the Great') of Macedon (356–323 BC), son of *Philip II and *Olympias. As crown prince he was taught by *Aristotle; he was his father's deputy in Macedon (340) and fought with distinction at the battle of *Chaeronea (338). Philip's last marriage created a serious rift, but a formal reconciliation had been effected by the time of his death (autumn 336), and Alexander was proclaimed king against a background of dynastic intrigue, in which his rivals were eliminated. A show of

force in southern Greece saw him acknowledged Philip's successor as leader of the *Corinthian League; and in 335, when the Thebans took advantage of his absence campaigning on the Danube and rebelled, he destroyed the city and enslaved the survivors. The exemplary punishment enabled him to leave the Greek world under the supervision of *Antipater with little fear of revolt, while he turned to the war of revenge against Persia.

2. In early 334 Alexander led his grand army across the Hellespont. In all some 43,000 foot and 5,500 horse (including the expeditionary force under *Parmenion), it was the most formidable array ever to leave Greek soil. The Macedonians were its indispensable nucleus. The infantry phalanx, c.15,000 strong and armed with the fearsome 6-m. (19$\frac{1}{2}$-ft.) pike (sarisa), comprised a guard corps (hypaspists) and six regionally levied battalions; and the cavalry, originally 1,800 strong, was also divided into regional squadrons. In pitched battle the *phalanx, in massed formation, was practically unbreakable on level ground, and Alexander was able to generate a cavalry charge from the flank which had decisive momentum. The hypaspists, usually supplemented by javelin-men and archers, were deployed in rapid-moving columns along with the cavalry, and were an irresistible combination in mountain warfare. These units were far superior to any they encountered, and, supplemented by a large reserve of secondary troops (Thracians, Illyrians, and the hoplites of the Corinthian League), they gave Alexander an overwhelming military advantage.

3. Alexander's superiority was immediately asserted at the Granicus (334), where a composite satrapal army was outmanœuvred and its large mercenary phalanx exterminated. That allowed him to march directly to occupy *Sardis, *Ephesus, and *Miletus. The most serious threat came from a superior Persian fleet, which sustained the stubborn defence of *Halicarnassus, and Alexander took the risk of demobilizing his own fleet and abandoning the coast. He moved east via Lycia, Pamphylia, and Phrygia (where he 'cut' the Gordian knot, fulfilling a presage of empire), and largely ignored a major Persian counter-offensive in the Aegean, which—fortunately for him—the Great King (*Darius III) crippled by withdrawing a large segment of the fleet to swell his royal army (summer 333). Alexander made Cilicia his base for the critical campaign and lured the vast Persian army into the narrow coastal plain south of Issus, where its numbers

were ineffective. He disrupted the front line with his standard cavalry charge from the right and gradually forced the entire Persian army into panic retreat. This overwhelming victory (c. Nov. 333) gave him control of the near east as far as the Euphrates. There was some resistance, notably at *Tyre and *Gaza, which he crushed, preferring protracted and costly sieges (seven months at Tyre) to diplomacy and negotiation. All challenges were met directly, whatever the human cost.

4. After a winter (332/1) in Egypt, which was surrendered peacefully, he invaded Mesopotamia and won his crowning victory at Gaugamela (1 October 331). Darius' forces were outmanoeuvred again, on chosen ground and unrestricted plain; Alexander sacrificed his left wing, leaving it to be enveloped while he extended the enemy line to the right, created a gap and drove inwards at the head of his cavalry. Again a general rout ensued, and Mesopotamia in turn lay open to him. *Babylon and *Susa fell without resistance, and he forced the Persian Gates against determined opposition to occupy the heartland of Persis (winter 331/0). At *Persepolis he acquired the accumulated financial reserves of the Persian empire and burnt its great palace during (it would seem) an orgiastic *symposium, later representing it as the final act of the war of revenge. That in effect came during the summer of 330 when Darius fled from his last refuge at Ecbatana, to be murdered by his closest entourage (led by Bessus, *satrap of Bactria). Alexander honoured his rival's body and closed the war by discharging his Hellenic troops *en masse*.

5. A new challenge arose when Bessus, who had withdrawn to his satrapy, proclaimed himself King of Kings under the regnal name Artaxerxes V. He appointed counter-satraps in central Asia and fomented revolt. Alexander left his satraps to cope with the insurgency, while he moved in a great swathe through Areia, Drangiana, and Arachosia (eastern Iran and western Afghanistan) and crossed the Hindu Kush to invade Bactria (spring 329). Bessus was soon gone, arrested in his turn by his nobles and surrendered to Alexander for exemplary punishment. Shortly afterwards, when Alexander reached the NE limit of the empire, a new uprising began in Sogdiana, rapidly spreading south to Bactria. One of Alexander's (non-Macedonian) columns was ambushed by the insurgents' nomad auxiliaries west of Marakanda (Samarkand), a military and moral reverse which impressed the need for slow,

systematic pacification. The conquest of the area fortress by fortress witnessed deliberate massacre, enslavement, and transplantation of recalcitrant populations, and, when the revolt ended (spring 327), the NE satrapies were left exhausted under a large garrison of mercenaries and a network of new city foundations, in which a Hellenic military élite was supported by a native agrarian work-force—the invariable model for the dozens of Alexandrias he founded in the eastern empire. It was in this same spring that he married for the first time—Roxanē, the beautiful daughter of a Bactrian noble, and a former prisoner.

6. From Bactria Alexander moved into *India at the invitation of the local dynasts of the Kabul valley and Punjab. He was willing enough to reaffirm the traditional Achaemenid claims to the Indus lands. Resistance was treated as rebellion, and his progress was marked by massacre and destruction, as in Sogdiana. Even the remote rock-fortress of Aornus was reduced by siege at the cost of prodigious hardship, to demonstrate that there was no escape from his dominion. The spring of 326 saw him at Taxila, east of the Indus, poised for a campaign against Porus, who held the Jhelum (*Hydaspes) against him. After a series of diversionary manoeuvres he crossed the river under cover of a spring thunder-storm and defeated Porus, whose war *elephants could not compensate for his cavalry inferiority. The victory was commemorated in two city foundations (Bucephala and Nicaea), and a remarkable issue of silver decadrachms depicts Alexander (crowned by Victory) in combat with Porus and his elephant. Alexander continued eastwards, crossing the rivers of the Punjab in the face of an increasing monsoonal deluge, until his troops' patience was exhausted. They refused to cross the Hyphasis (Beas) and invade the Ganges basin, and Alexander reluctantly acceded. A river fleet (commissioned in the summer) was ready at the Hydaspes by November 325, and the army proceeded by land and water to the southern Ocean. The journey was marked by a vicious campaign against the Malli, unprovoked except for their failure to offer submission, and Alexander's impetuousness cost him a debilitating chest wound. Further south the kingdoms of Sambus and Musicanus were visited with fire and slaughter when their allegiance wavered, and, as he approached his base in the Indus delta, the natives fled in terror (July 325).

7. Alexander now returned to the west, deputing *Nearchus to take his fleet across the

southern coastline while he led the main army through the Gedrosian desert, in emulation—so Nearchus claimed—of *Cyrus (1). The horrors of heat and famine which ensued were considerable, but perhaps exaggerated in the sources, which attest no great loss of life among the Macedonian army. Reunited with the fleet in Carmania (c. Dec. 325), he returned to Persepolis and Susa (March 324), where some 80 of his staff joined him in taking wives from the Persian nobility. For the next year there was a lull in campaigning, but there were grandiose preparations in the Levant, where he commissioned a war fleet allegedly 1,000 strong, some of which was conveyed to Babylon in summer of 323. The first stage of conquest was certainly the *Persian Gulf and Arabian littoral, which Alexander intended to conquer and colonize, but the sources refer to projects of conquest in the western Mediterranean aimed at Carthage and southern Italy—and plans are even alleged of a circumnavigation of Africa. The reality is perhaps beyond verification, but it is likely enough that Alexander conceived no practical limit to his empire.

8. Alexander's monarchy was absolute. From the outset he regarded Asia Minor as liberated territory only in so far as he displaced the Persians, and he announced the fact of possession by imposing his own satraps upon the erstwhile Persian provinces. By 332 he regarded himself as the proper ruler of the Persian empire, and after Gaugamela he was acclaimed king of Asia. From 330 his status was displayed in his court dress, which combined the traditional Macedonian hat and cloak with the Persian diadem, tunic, and girdle. He used Persian court ceremonial and promoted Persian nobles, but there is no evidence of a formal 'policy of fusion' with Persians and Macedonians assimilated into a single ruling class. The Macedonians were entrenched in a position of superiority. The Susa marriages would indeed give rise to a mixed offspring (as would the liaisons of his soldiers with native women), but in both cases the ultimate aim was probably to counter the regional and family loyalties which had been the curse of both Persian and Macedonian monarchs. At another level he had cut across the traditional regional basis of his army and introduced Iranians even to the élite Companion cavalry (see HETAIROI). There was to be a single loyalty—to the crown.

9. Alexander naturally experienced opposition in various forms. His Macedonian troops proved increasingly reluctant to be enticed into further conquest. He gave way once, at the Hy-

phasis, but at Opis (324) he confronted their contumacious demands for repatriation with summary executions and a devastating threat to man his army exclusively from Persians. He had deliberately made his Macedonians dispensable and demonstrated the fact. The same ruthlessness marked his reaction to opposition at court. He isolated and struck down *Parmenion because of his resistance to imperial expansion, and the adolescent pages, who seriously threatened his life for reasons which are obscure, were tortured and stoned to death. Insubordination was as intolerable as conspiracy. Alexander's return to the west in 325/4 witnessed a spate of executions of satraps who had exceeded their authority or arrogated power. Misgovernment as such was a secondary consideration. Relations with the Greek world became increasingly strained. At first the machinery of the Corinthian League was effective; and the challenge by Agis III of Sparta had limited support and was quickly crushed. But Alexander undermined the provisions of the league by his Exiles' Decree (324), which threatened Athens' possession of *Samos and gave almost every city the problem of repatriating long-term exiles. The last year of his reign was punctuated by tense and heated diplomacy, and his death precipitated general war in southern Greece.

10. Given Alexander's uncompromising claims to sovereignty, it can be readily understood how he came to conceive himself divine. A Heraclid by lineage, he believed himself the descendant of *Heracles, *Perseus, and (ultimately) *Zeus, and by 331 he had begun to represent himself as the direct son of Zeus, with dual paternity comparable to that of Heracles. He was reinforced in his belief by his pilgrimage (in 331) to the oracle of *Ammon (recognized as a manifestation of Zeus at Siwa), and thereafter styled himself son of Zeus Ammon. But divine sonship was not divinity, and by 327, after conquest had followed conquest, Alexander was encouraged (esp. in the liberated atmosphere of the symposium) to believe that his achievements deserved apotheosis at least as much as Heracles'. *Proskynēsis*, the prostration of inferior to superior, was *de rigueur* at the Persian court, but Alexander attempted to extend it to Macedonians and Greeks, for whom the gesture was an act of worship. The experiment failed, thanks to the resistance of his court historian Callisthenes, but the concept remained, and there is a tradition that he wrote to the cities of Greece in 324, suggesting that it would be appropriate for divine honours to be voted him

along with a *hero-cult for *Hephaestion. Cults were certainly established, mainly in Asia Minor, and persisted long after his death.

11. Portraits of Alexander tend to follow the model created by his favourite sculptor, Lysippus, who perpetuated the leftward inclination of his neck and the hair thrown back from a central parting. His profile, first illustrated on the 'Alexander sarcophagus' (311), appears repeatedly on coins, most strikingly on the commemorative tetradrachms of *Lysimachus. His personality is far more elusive, thanks to the tendency in antiquity to cite him as an example of good or evil and the propensity of moderns to endue him with the qualities they would admire in themselves. His reputation for invincibility, which he studiously fostered, has been a source of fascination (notably for *Pompey, *Trajan, and Napoleon), mostly for ill. The process began when he died (10 June 323) after a ten-day illness (which contemporaries ascribed to poison), and the marshals who sought to emulate him rapidly dismembered his empire.

Alexandria was founded by *Alexander (2) the Great in 331 BC when he took *Egypt from the Persians. It was developed principally by the first two Ptolemies, who made it the capital of their kingdom and the main Mediterranean port of Egypt (see PTOLEMY (1)). It was founded as a theoretically autonomous city (*polis) of the traditional Greek type, modelled in several respects on Athens: it had an exclusive hereditary citizenship organized by *demes, probably with an assembly (*ekklesia), council (*boule), and annually elected magistrates, it had its own territory, restricted to citizen-owners and exempt from direct royal taxation, its own coinage, and its own laws. Its founding citizens were recruited from all over the Greek world; there were also numerous non-citizen residents of Egyptian and other ethnic origin, including a large Jewish community which acquired special privileges though not full citizenship. Alexandria soon became one of the largest and grandest cities of the Mediterranean world, famed for the monumental magnificence of its two main intersecting streets, its palace-quarter with the tomb of Alexander and the *Museum and *Library, *gymnasium, and Pharus, the *lighthouse at the entrance to its two capacious artificial harbours. As a royal capital Alexandria could not be a normal *polis*: its coinage and, probably, its laws were used throughout Egypt; in the course of the dynastic struggles of the later Ptolemies, in which its citizens naturally took a prominent part, Alexandria was, it seems, punished with the loss of its assembly and council, and its magistrates became more like royal officials. These struggles also ignited the notorious antagonism between the 'Greek' citizen-body and the Jewish community, which continued to flare up in the Roman period (see JEWS).

When Egypt came under Roman rule, the citizens of Alexandria retained most of their surviving privileges; they were also used extensively in the new administration of the province, and only they, in Egypt, could acquire Roman *citizenship. Despite several appeals to the Julio-Claudian emperors, Alexandria regained a council only in AD 200/1 when *Septimius Severus granted councils to all the major cities of Egypt; this development, and the universal grant of Roman citizenship in 212, undermined Alexandria's political primacy in Egypt, but not her Mediterranean-wide economic and cultural importance. With over 500,000 inhabitants, Alexandria was the second city of the Roman empire; it was also the main port of the eastern Mediterranean for state and private shipping, straddling the luxury trade between India and Rome. Fine public and private buildings continued to be erected, and the arts and crafts and intellectual pursuits flourished.

alliance (Greek) An agreement between states to fight together against a common enemy. Such alliances might be made either for a limited period or for all time. In a full offensive and defensive alliance it was commonly stated that the participating states were to 'have the same friends and enemies': that formulation might be used when the alliance was on an equal basis, but it could be adapted to circumstances in which one participant was inferior to the other, as in 404 BC when *Athens undertook both to have the same friends and enemies as *Sparta and to follow Sparta's lead.

The *Peloponnesian League, built up by Sparta in the second half of the 6th cent. BC, was the first instance of a league of allies united for purposes of foreign policy. Such leagues tended to be formed with a dominant state as leader, influential through possession of executive power even if not formally privileged in decision-making, and with a council which played a part in decision-making and enabled representatives of the member states to express opinions and vote. Other examples were the *Delian League, the Second Athenian Confederacy, and the *Corinthian League organized by *Philip

II of Macedon. In the Delian League Athens came to interfere in various ways with the *autonomy of the members; and to win support for her Second Confederacy, she gave undertakings that such interference would not be repeated.

alliance (Roman) See AMICITIA; FOEDUS; SOCII.

alphabet, Greek In early Greece various forms of alphabet were current, but they all derived from a *Phoenician (Semitic) source, which must have reached the Aegean in the earlier 8th cent. (before our earliest Greek examples of *c.*740). The alphabet was taken in the order of the Semitic model:

	Greek names	English equivalents
A	Alpha	a
B	Bēta	b
Γ	Gamma	g
Δ	Delta	d
E	Epsīlon	ĕ
F	Vau	w
I	Zēta	sd
H	Ēta	ē
Θ	Thēta	th
I	Iōta	i
K	Kappa	k
Λ	Lambda	l
M	Mū	m
N	Nū	n
Ξ	Xī	ks
O	Omikron	ŏ
Π	Pī	p
M	San	
ϙ	Qoppa	
P	Rhō	rh
Σ	Sigma	s
T	Tau	t
Υ	Upsīlon	u
Φ	Phī	ph
X	Khī	kh
Ψ	Psī	ps
Ω	Ōmega	ō

Not all states used all letters, but all probably retained them in the original order. The most striking feature in the Greek adaptation of the Phoenician model is that by altering (consciously or unconsciously) the original significance of *AEIO* and adding *Υ* Greek, unlike Phoenician, achieved an independent representation of vowel-sounds. *ΥΦΧΨΩ* are all Greek additions. *Υ* appears to be a variant of *F*. *Ω*, an

Ionic invention, is also a doublet, formed by breaking the O. Received Semitic shapes were generally 'tidied up' in Greece—with verticals and horizontals conditioning the appearance of individual letters; hence a number of 'indeterminate' Semitic shapes yielded different Greek versions. The three double-consonant letters *ΦΧΨ* all appear early.

Most colonies used the script of their *metropolis*. One variety of the eastern alphabets, namely the East Ionic, eventually became predominant. It was officially adopted by Athens in the archonship of Euclīdēs (403–402 BC). Its acceptance by the whole Greek world was complete by about 370. Many changes in letter shape were also introduced, largely in the late 4th and 3rd cents., from writing in ink, so-called 'cursives'; they present rounded, simplified forms, c from *Σ*, *ε* from *E*, *ω* from *Ω*, and the like.

altars Indispensable adjunct of *sacrifice in ancient religion.

Greek The chief type was the raised *bōmos*, on which a wood fire was lit for the cremation of the victim's thigh-bones and spit-roasting of the entrails; *hero-cults by contrast commonly employed the *eschara*, a low altar, onto which the victim's blood was made to flow; the domestic altar was for bloodless offerings (natural produce, cakes, etc.). In Greek *sanctuaries monumental open-air *bōmoi*, usually of dressed stone (the ash altar of Zeus at *Olympia was unusual), are well attested archaeologically from the 6th cent. BC onwards; they were typically rectangular and sometimes approached by a flight of steps. Independent altars on a spectacular scale are a feature of the Hellenistic age—e.g. the so-called Great Altar of *Pergamum (early 2nd cent. BC), incorporating a sculptured frieze *c.*120 m. (130 yds.) long; the tradition was continued in the Roman east with the so-called Great Antonine Altar of *Ephesus (begun *c.* AD 166). In Greek myth and real life altars were traditionally places of refuge, the suppliants protected by the deity to whom the altar belonged.

Roman The Latin terms *altāria* (pl.) and *āra* derive from roots denoting 'burning' (of sacrificial offerings). Normally of stone, of varying size, from small *cippī* (stone markers) to large structures (as the *Ara Pacis), most often rectangular (occasionally round), and decorated with reliefs, they were dedicated to a particular deity, and stood either separately or in front of temples (inside only for incense and bloodless offerings).

Alyattēs, fourth *Lydian king (c.610–560 BC), of the house of *Gyges and father of *Croesus, finally drove back the Cimmerians, extended Lydian control to the Halys, and made war on Cyaxarēs the Mede (585), during which occurred a solar eclipse (supposedly foretold by *Thales). Peace was concluded with the marriage of Alyattes' daughter to Astyages. He continued Lydian campaigns against *Ionia, captured Smyrna, but failed against Clazomenae and *Miletus. Lydia prospered, electrum *coinage was used for the first time, and there was increasing interaction with the Greeks. Alyattes built two temples to Athena near Miletus and sent offerings to *Delphi; he has been seen as the founder of the Lydian empire. His vast burial mound, praised by Herodotus and Strabo, is now excavated.

Amazons, mythical race of female warriors. The name was popularly understood as 'breast-less' (*maza*, 'breast') and the story told that they 'pinched out' or 'cauterized' the right breast so as not to impede their javelin-throwing. No real etymology is known.

Amazons exist in order to be fought, and ultimately defeated, by men in an Amazonomachy ('Amazon-battle'). In the *Iliad* we hear of *Bellerophon killing them in Lycia, and of their defeat at the river Sangarios in Phrygia. In *Aethiopis* (see EPIC CYCLE) their Thracian queen, Penthesilea 'daughter of *Ares', arrives to help the Trojans, but *Achilles kills her (and *Thersites for alleging Achilles loved her). *Heracles' ninth labour was to fetch the belt of the Amazon queen, Hippolytē, resulting in another Amazonomachy. *Theseus joined Heracles and as a result had to defeat an Amazon invasion of *Attica, a story told in a late 6th-cent. BC *Theseid*. Amazon tombs are frequent in central Greece, presumably because of local Amazonomachy myths. Appropriately for a group inverting normal Greek rules, Amazons live at the edge of the world. Their usual homeland is next to a river Thermodon in a city in remote Pontic Asia Minor. Real Amazons would need men for procreation. *Diodorus (2) Siculus' Amazons at the Thermodon cripple their male children, but his second set, in Libya, have house-husbands to whom they return (like Greek males) after their period of military service. It is part of the mythologizing of *Alexander (2) the Great that stories were quick to surface that he had met Amazons and threatened or pleasured their queen.

Women warriors and hunters are quite frequent in myth and *folk-tale and inversely reflect the actual distribution of roles between the sexes. Amazonomachies and genre studies of Amazons are represented copiously in art from the late 7th cent. on, propelled by their special importance at Athens.

amber, a fossil resin, has a wide natural distribution in nothern Europe: so far as is known, the amber from the classical Mediterranean was Baltic. Amber was common in Archaic Greece, but not after c.550 BC; *Thales was the first to note its power of attraction. The main centre of amber carving under the Roman empire was Aquileia: amber was by then a fashionable luxury and played an important part in imperial trade with the free Germans.

ambitus, 'going round', is related to *ambitiō*, the pursuit of public office, but always, unlike *ambitio*, denotes reprehensible activity which has been declared illegal.

Specifically it refers to obtaining electoral support (see ELECTIONS AND VOTING, *Roman*) through gifts, favours, or the promise of these. In 181 BC a law instituted a system of trials, which was developed in the late republic by further laws about *ambitus* and related matters—the use of bribery agents, associations, and expenditure on public dinners. These laws seem to have been a response to fiercer competition for office. However, Roman tradition did not discourage the cultivation of voters through material benefits. What established politicians disliked was the stealing of votes by new men (see NOVUS HOMO) who outbid former patrons and the damage this caused to traditional claims of *patronage. In the late republic the distortion of politics by massive expenditure became scandalous in spite of the new legislation. Under the Principate, in so far as genuine competition for office persisted, *ambitus* remained an issue both in Rome and, perhaps more importantly, in the municipalities (see MUNICIPIUM) throughout the empire. The fact that penalties do not seem to have been very severe suggests toleration of traditional behaviour. See also CORRUPTION.

ambrosia (lit. 'immortality') and **nectar** are the food and drink of eternal life—usually in that order. They are thus properly reserved for the gods, as traditional stories emphasize: see *Odyssey* 5 on *Odysseus' meals with Calypso. *Heracles was formally served with a draught of immortal spirit by Athena on his assumption into Olympus, but the dying *Tydeus was refused the same favour at the last moment when the goddess found him devouring his enemy's brain. One version of *Tantalus' crime claims that, having tasted divine food himself, he tried to smuggle some away for others who were not so privileged. Those who ingest such rarefied substances naturally have not blood but a special fluid called *ichor* coursing through their veins. As the ultimate preservative, ambrosia may also be administered by goddesses to their favourites by external application: it is used by *Thetis to keep Patroclus' corpse fresh and by Athena to sustain the fasting *Achilles, and as a face cream to beautify *Penelope.

amīcitia, friendship in Roman political terminology. The relationship might be between Rome and either another state or an individual (see CLIENT KINGS), or between individuals. Although *amicitia* involved no treaty or formal legal obligations, the term was often associated with alliance (*societās*) and might describe strong ties and indeed dependency. In Roman political and social life the friends of an eminent man acted as his advisers in public and personal matters and might form a group of devoted political adherents (though the word suggests equality of status, such men might well be subordinates). Ideally *amicitia* involved genuine trust and affection; in practice it might be only an alliance to pursue common interests. Such friendships often conflicted. Nevertheless, their making and breaking were formal. Under the Principate the friends of the emperor formed, with his kinsmen and freedmen, his court (see AMICUS AUGUSTI). Loss of this friendship was close to condemnation as a criminal. See also CLIENS.

amīcus Augustī Political leaders of the 1st cent. BC made friendship a technical term of Roman political life. The emperors adopted the term *amicus* to identify, essentially as courtiers under the nascent monarchic system, favoured members of the *equestrian and senatorial orders, and as an increasingly formal label for the inner circle who made up their advisory *consilium.

Ammiānus Marcellīnus (*c.* AD 330–395), the last great Latin historian of the Roman empire, was born at Antioch. Assigned by *Constantius II to the personal staff of the general Ursicinus, Ammianus saw service in northern Italy, Gaul, and Germany (the early campaigns of *Julian), Illyricum and Mesopotamia. It was here, in the siege and capture by the Persians of Amida in 359, that the first phase of Ammianus' military career came to an end. He escaped from the city, but Ursicinus was dismissed from office. Ammianus later participated in the disastrous Persian campaign of Julian (363). Afterwards he travelled before coming to Rome in the mid-380s. It was here that he completed his history. The work is composed in 31 books, of which the first thirteen, covering the period from Nerva to 353, seem to have been lost by the early 6th cent. The earlier of the lost books were apparently not very full or original, but the scale of the narrative enlarged as Ammianus approached his own day. The surviving books describe in great detail the events and personalities of Ammianus' active lifetime through a period of just 25 years. The culmination of the work is the Gothic invasions of 376–8 and the battle of Adrianople (378) at which the emperor Valens was killed.

In the earlier books, narrating his service under Ursicinus, Ammianus' own experiences form a major element, and events are largely seen through the often biased eyes of his patron; with their vivid narrative of sometimes very detailed events and the subjectivity of their judgements, these books have seemed to readers to resemble personal memoir rather than formal history. Despite his own participation—which was at a less privileged level than his experiences with Ursicinus—his narrative of the Persian campaign of Julian is less personally involved, relying sometimes on written sources, and the books on Valentinian and Valens are less detailed, and despite moments of intense involvement, not focused on the author's own experiences. The centrepiece of the history was the government, first in Gaul as Caesar and then in the east as sole Augustus, of Julian. Ammianus deeply admired Julian, esp. for his military and administrative abilities. He was openly critical of other aspects of Julian's regime, not least his religious policies.

Himself a *pagan of a more traditional cast, Ammianus disliked Julian's intolerance, and was hostile to the emperor's devotion to sacrifice, and of his submission to the influence of philosophers who, in the end with disastrous results, indulged Julian's interest in Neoplatonic techniques of *divination. He is scathing about the ostentation of the bishops of Rome, criticizes those of *Alexandria for their ambition, and ironically refers to the failure of Christianity to live up to its 'pure and simple' professions.

Ammianus' elaborate, individual, and often very intense style is notable for its strong pictorial sense and for its ability to portray character, in which it displays the influence of physiognomical writing and exploits often very vivid comparisons of human character with that of wild beasts. It contains many passages, esp. of military narrative, in which individuals are shown at close quarters and in situations of personal stress and great danger. It is influenced too by the language of *satire, as when Ammianus denounces the behaviour of the nobility and common people of Rome, or the behaviour of lawyers. The subject-matter is wide, and the history contains many geographical and ethnographical digressions (describing the non-Roman as well as the Roman worlds), as well as scientific and antiquarian excursuses, in which the author's Greek culture is acknowledged, sometimes with quotations of Greek words in which Ammianus refers to Greek as his 'own' first language. For the contemporary period, Ammianus' narrative was based on personal knowledge and the accounts of eyewitnesses. The most persuasive literary influence is that of *Cicero, whose writings are constantly referred and alluded to. See HISTORIOGRAPHY, ROMAN.

Ammōn, *Hellenized name of Amun, the great god of Egyptian *Thebes and chief divinity of the developed Egyptian pantheon; thus naturally identified with *Zeus. Greek interest, probably mediated through *Cyrene (on whose coins his head is shown from the early 5th cent. with the typical ram's horns) centred on the oracular cult at the oasis of Siwa, in the Libyan desert; Herodotus assumes its fame, and Plutarch claims consultations by several prominent 5th-cent. Greeks including *Cimon, *Lysander, *Alcibiades, and *Nicias. In the 4th cent., in line with the growth of foreign cults, his worship is attested at Athens (where one of the two sacred triremes was renamed 'Ammonias' in his honour) and elsewhere in the Greek homeland; but it was above all *Alexander (2) the Great's visit in 331, after his victory at Issus, which caught the ancient imagination—even if the story of Zeus Ammon's acknowledgment of his own paternity of the young king, and so of Alexander's divinity, is a later elaboration.

amnesty To propose or demand the recall of *exiles was common throughout the Greek world, and attempts by such exiles to recover confiscated property often provoked further strife. Far less common was an amnesty in the formal sense of an act of state. The most famous ancient 'amnesty' was not a legislative act but part of an agreement at Athens in 403 BC between opponents and former supporters of the *Thirty Tyrants; the (incomplete) text at *Athenaion politeia 39 prohibits mnēsikakein ('remembering wrongs', sc. in a lawcourt) against all except specified oligarchic officials. Narrative sources present this agreement as the successful achievement of democratic magnanimity, though it was evidently imposed by the Spartan king *Pausanias (2).

Amphiarāus, seer descended from *Melampus, resident at *Argos, whence he joined the expedition of the *Seven against Thebes. In one tradition, he died with all the other champions save Adrastus. Since he knew that the expedition was doomed, Amphiaraus was unwilling to go, but—as pre-arranged with Adrastus—he was obliged to obey the judgement of his wife Eriphȳlē (sister of Adrastus), who had been bribed by Polynīcēs with the necklace of Harmonia (see CADMUS).

There is another version, that Amphiaraus was not killed at Thebes, but, while fleeing from the city, was swallowed up live, chariot and all, in a cleft made by *Zeus' thunderbolt. At some time between the development of the story of the Seven, and the first reference to his survival, Amphiaraus was associated with an underground oracular deity. His major *sanctuary was near Orōpus, in disputed territory between Attica and *Boeotia. It became popular during the *Peloponnesian War, when the Athenians invested Amphiaraus with healing powers on the model of *Asclepius. Consultation was by incubation: the consultants/patients bedded down on a ram-skin on the ground, and were visited by Amphiaraus as they slept. The sanctuary, which has been excavated, was popular in the 4th cent. under the Athenians, under the Hellenistic Boeotian Confederacy, and under the Romans, thanks to the impetus given by *Sulla, who granted it tax-free status.

amphictiony (from amphiktionēs, 'dwellers around') is the name given to Greek leagues connected with *sanctuaries and the maintenance of their cults. Most were concentrated near the sanctuary, but the amphictiony of Anthela and *Delphi came to include representatives from much of Greece. They could punish those who offended against the sanctuary, and the Delphic amphictiony could even declare a *Sacred War against an offending state.

Amphidromia See CHILDBIRTH; CHILDREN; NAMES, PERSONAL, GREEK.

Amphipolis, on the east bank of the Strȳmōn, which surrounds the city on three sides (hence its name), 5 km. (3 mi.) from its seaport Eïon; it was originally the site of a Thracian town, Ennea Hodoi ('nine ways'; see THRACE). After two unsuccessful attempts, it was colonized by the Athenians, with other Greeks, under Hagnon, in 437/6 BC. It owed its importance partly to its strategic position on the coastal route between northern Greece and the Hellespont, and partly to its commercial wealth as the terminal of trade down the Strymon valley, a depot for the minerals of Pangaeus and a centre for ship-timber. In 424 Amphipolis surrendered to *Brasidas. It remained independent until 357, when it was captured by *Philip II who gave it a favoured status in the Macedonian kingdom. *Alexander (2) the Great made it the chief mint in his domains. Under the Romans as an important station on the *via Egnatia it was declared a '*free city'.

amphitheatres The earliest surviving permanent amphitheatres are found in *Campania, the well-preserved example at *Pompeii, being the only closely datable example (c.80 BC). At Rome, although gladiatorial games were held in the *forum Romanum from an early date with spectators accommodated in temporary wooden stands, the first permanent building was erected by *Statilius Taurus in the *Campus Martius in 29 BC. Nero built a much larger wooden structure there, destroyed by the fire of AD 64. Rome finally gained a permanent, monumental amphitheatre with the *Colosseum. Amphitheatres are common in the west provinces from the late republic but are rarer in the east, where from the 2nd cent. AD onwards many *theatres were adapted for this purpose. The use of gladiatorial techniques for training the Roman army led to small amphitheatres also becoming a normal adjunct of military *camps, the earliest surviving examples being Augustan. The earliest masonry arenas such as Pompeii and *Emerita Augusta (8 BC) had retaining walls to support earth mounds; self-contained monumental masonry structures (e.g. Arelate), combining radial and annular vaulted passages to solve problems of access and circulation for large numbers of spectators, mainly appear under the inspiration of the Colosseum. The amphitheatre should be distinguished from the *ludus* (see LUDI) or gladiators' training-school, generally having much less seating and a proportionately larger arena. See GLADIATORS; VENATIONES.

Amphitryon See ALCMENE.

amphorae, Greek The amphora is one of the most versatile and long-lived pot shapes. A two-handled jar (*amphi-phoreus*, 'carried on both sides'), it can vary enormously in size, detail of shape, and manner of decoration. Plain or part-decorated jars were used widely for storage and transport; we see them often in vase scenes, and literary and epigraphic texts fill out the picture. The average capacity of Classical and Hellenistic jars is 20–25 lt. (4½–5½ gal.). Early transport amphorae (late 8th cent., esp. Attic and Corinthian) probably contained *olive oil; later, *wine becomes the major commodity; jars supplement, then supplant skins.

amphorae, Roman Amphorae, ceramic coarseware jars used for transporting a range of goods, provide the most abundant and meaningful archaeological data on the nature, range, and scale of Roman inter-regional trade in commodities such as *olive oil, *wine, marine products and fish-pickle (see FISHING), preserved fruits, etc. Amphorae were most heavily used in long-distance transport, esp. maritime or riverine, and are thus a good guide to regional economic activity. (Monte Testaccio is an artificial hill covering c.22,000 sq. m. (26,300 sq. yd.) in the Emporium district of Rome near the *Tiber, and composed entirely of broken amphorae, mostly oil amphorae from *Baetica.) The contents were clearly intended to be recognizable from the distinctive outward appearance of the most common amphora types, though painted inscriptions were sometimes added to the jar. The epigraphic evidence associated with amphorae, adds further to their value in studies of the economy. Most amphorae share a number of features: a narrow mouth, two opposed handles, thickish walls for strength, a tapering base (often a spike, though some amphorae had flat bottoms) to facilitate pouring and stacking in ships. Size and weight were important; amphorae were designed to be portable by one or at most two men.

amulets were magically potent objects worn for protection against witchcraft, illness, the evil eye, accidents, robbery, etc., also to enhance love, wealth, power, or victory. Houses, walls, and towns could be protected in the same way. Any kind of material might be employed: stones and metals as well as (parts of) animals and plants, since to every sort of material could be attributed an inherent 'magical' virtue (see

MAGIC); also parts of human bodies (esp. of people who had suffered a violent death: *gladiators, executed criminals, victims of *shipwreck etc.) were used as amulets. Their efficacy might be enhanced by engraved figures, e.g. deities or symbols, esp. on stones and gems in rings. Powerful names taken from exotic (esp. Egyptian and Hebrew) myth and cult were popular.

Belief in amulets remained active in Greece and Italy in all classes of the population throughout antiquity and into modern times.

Anacreon (b. c.575–570 BC) Greek *lyric poet, native of Teos. Little is known of his life. He probably joined in the foundation of Abdera by the Teans fleeing before the threat of the Persian general Harpagus in 545. He joined the court of *Polycrates (1), tyrant of *Samos. After the murder of Polycrates by the satrap Oroetes he joined the *Pisistratid court at Athens.

The range of what survives is narrow. Wine and love (both homosexual and heterosexual) figure prominently. His control of form produces an appearance of effortlessness. Many poems have an epigrammatic quality. Words are positioned with great effect. Striking images for love abound. Delicacy, wit, paradox, irony, and self-mockery are prominent. He also produced biting abuse in the iambic tradition (see IAMBIC POETRY, GREEK). His wit inspired a corpus of frivolous imitations in and after the Hellenistic period, the *Anacreontea*.

analogy and **anomaly** were two themes in the investigation of the Greek and Latin languages in the classical era. They turned on the question, to what extent can regularity (*analogia*, analogy) be recognized in rules and classes (e.g. *scrībō:scrībens* (I write, writing); *legō:legens* (I read, reading); *equus* (one horse), *equī* (more than one)) and how far must exceptions (*anomalia*, anomaly) be accepted (e.g. *bonus, melior, optimus* (good, better, best); *Zeūs, Zēnos* (Zeuls, of Zeus); *Athēnai*, formally pl., the city of Athens). In part this related to the contemporary discussion on the natural or the conventional origin of language.

The topic arose in the Greek world in Hellenistic times, and was part of the context in which grammatical science itself developed. The *Stoics favoured anomaly, and the Alexandrian scholars argued for analogy in the establishing of correct texts in the Homeric poems and in the teaching of Greek. Only on the evidence of analogies could the apparent disorderliness of language be brought into order. In an early statement on the objectives of grammar (c.100

BC) the 'working out of analogies' was given an explicit place.

In the Roman world *Caesar wrote a (lost) treatise on analogy, but our most extensive and detailed treatment of the subject comes from *Varro's *On the Latin Language*. In it both approaches to language are set out in separate sections as a formal debate. His series of corresponding case forms led later Latin grammarians to establish the five declensions by the end of antiquity.

Anatolia The Greek-derived (from *anatolē*, 'sunrise') equivalent of Roman *Asia Minor and modern Turkey, between the Aegean and the Euphrates.

Anaxagoras (probably 500–428 BC), of Clazomenae (see PANIONIUM); the first philosopher known to have settled in Athens. The evidence for his biography is confused and confusing. He may have arrived in Athens in 456/5 and philosophized there for c.20 years, until his prosecution on a charge of impiety. He resettled in Lampsacus in northern *Troas, perhaps with the aid of *Pericles. There he died and was buried with high honours. His name was associated with the fall of a large meteorite at Aegospotami in *Thrace (c.467); his explanations of other physical phenomena are reflected in Aeschylus' *Suppliants* (c.463) and *Eumenides* (458).

*Simplicius preserves extensive fragments of Anaxagoras' one book, which began with the words: 'All things were together'. The longest and most eloquent surviving passage explains how our differentiated cosmos was created from the original *mélange* by the action of mind, an entirely discrete principle, unmixed with any other substance but capable of ordering and controlling them. Anaxagoras' most striking and paradoxical claim is the thesis that, despite the consequent separation of dense from rare, hot from cold, etc., 'as things were in the beginning, so now they are all together': 'in everything—except mind—a portion of everything'. Ancient commentators supplied examples: what we call black contains a predominance of portions of black, but portions of white also, for how else could water turn into snow? Similarly sperm contains flesh, hair, and indeed everything else, for hair cannot come from not-hair, flesh from not-flesh, etc.

If analysis or division were thoroughgoing, would it not be possible to reach particles of pure flesh or pure black? This idea is explicitly rejected by Anaxagoras: 'the small is unlimited', and as complex as the large. The ultimate constituents of the world never exist as discrete physical entities, only as stuffs or powers of which—hence the designation 'portions'—such entities consist. When Anaxagoras talks of an infinity of 'seeds' both in the beginning and now in our world, we should probably think not of particles but of the potentiality of latent portions to become manifest.

To Anaxagoras is attributed the maxim: 'The appearances are a glimpse of what is not apparent'. Infinite variety in phenomena reflects infinite variety in seeds; things as we perceive them are very like things as they really are. This position is far removed from Parmenidean metaphysics and epistemology. (See PARMENIDES.) Yet engagement with *Eleatic ideas is evidently responsible for some key features of Anaxagoras' thought, e.g. the doctrine of the fundamental homogeneity of reality, his 'all together' echoing Parmenides' own words, and the explicit rejection of the concepts of birth and death in favour of mixture and dissolution. Modern scholars have been fascinated by the subtlety with which these ontological principles are applied in Anaxagoras' system. By contrast his cosmology is perceived as a mere reworking of *Anaximenes, even if the claim that the sun is a huge incandescent stone shocked contemporary opinion. More original is Anaxagoras' theory of mind, as both Plato and Aristotle recognize, while lamenting its failure to offer teleological explanations of natural processes.

Anaximander, of *Miletus (d. soon after 547 BC), said to be an associate or disciple of *Thales, was the first Greek to write a prose treatise 'On the Nature of Things'. He thus initiated the tradition of Greek natural philosophy by elaborating a system of the heavens, including an account of the origins of human life, and by leaving his speculation behind in written form. He was the first to make a *map of the inhabited world.

Anaximander's view of the cosmos is remarkable for its imagination and for its systematic appeal to rational principles and natural processes as a basis for explanation. The origin of things is the *apeiron*, the limitless or infinite, which apparently surrounds the generated world and 'steers' or governs the world process. Symmetry probably dictates that the world-order will perish into the source from which it has arisen, as symmetry is explicitly said to explain why the earth is stable in the centre of things, equally balanced in every direction.

The world process begins when the opposites are 'separated out' to generate the hot and the cold, the dry and the wet. By a process that is both biological and mechanical, earth, sea, and sky take shape, and huge wheels of enclosed fire are formed to produce the phenomena of sun, moon, and stars. The size of the wheels was specified, corresponding perhaps to the arithmetical series 9, 18, 27. The earth is a flat disc, three times as broad as it is deep. Mechanical explanations in terms of the opposites are offered for meteorological phenomena (wind, rain, lightning, and thunder) and for the origin of animal life. The first human beings were generated from a sort of embryo floating in the sea.

The *apeiron* is ageless, deathless, and eternal; unlike the anthropomorphic gods, it is also ungenerated. The cosmos, on the other hand, is a world-order of coming-to-be and perishing according to a fixed law of nature, described in the one quotation from Anaximander's book (perhaps the earliest preserved sentence of European prose): out of those things from which beings are generated, into these again does their perishing take place 'according to what is needful and right; for they pay the penalty and make atonement to one another for their wrongdoing, according to the ordinance of time'.

Anaximenēs, of *Miletus (traditional fl. 546–525 BC) followed in the footsteps of *Anaximander in composing a treatise in Ionian prose in which he developed a world system on the basis of an infinite or unlimited principle, which he identified as *aēr*. His system differed from that of his predecessor in several respects. Instead of suspending the earth in the centre of the universe by cosmic symmetry, he supported it from below by cosmic air. And instead of leaving the infinite starting-point for world formation indeterminate in nature, he specified it as elemental air, which he probably conceived as a kind of vital world-breath that dominates the world order as our own breath-soul rules over us. World formation he attributed to the condensation and rarefaction of the air. Air becomes fire by rarefaction; by motion it becomes wind; by condensation it becomes water and, by more condensation, earth and stones. Milesian cosmology as reformulated by Anaximenes became standard for Ionian natural philosophy in the 5th cent.

'ancestral constitution' See PATRIOS POLITEIA.

Anchīsēs, character in literature and myth, father of *Aeneas, and member of the Trojan royal house (see DARDANUS). He does not appear in person in *Homer's *Iliad*, but the *Homeric *Hymn to Aphrodite* recounts his union with that goddess on the slopes of Mt. Ida. He was warned by *Aphrodite not to reveal her identity as the mother of the resulting child, *Aeneas, but disobeyed; as punishment, he was lamed by a thunderbolt or blinded. Most versions of the Aeneas-legend tell how Anchises was carried on his son's back from Troy; some say that he went with Aeneas to Carthage and Italy, but in the *Aeneid* he dies in Sicily before reaching either place. Anchises' character in *Aeneid* bks. 2–3 is that of a frail and wise counsellor and priest-like religious authority; mutual affection between him and Aeneas is evident, esp. when Aeneas descends to the Underworld to see his dead father, who offers both a philosophical revelation and a pageant of the future of Rome.

Andocidēs (*c.*440–*c.*390 BC), a member of an aristocratic family, whose grandfather had been one of the ten Athenian envoys who negotiated the *Thirty Years Peace of 446. In 415, shortly before the *Sicilian Expedition was due to depart, the Athenians were dismayed to discover that in the night the statues of *Hermes around the city (see HERMS) had been mutilated: Hermes being the god of travellers, this act was presumably intended to affect the progress of the expedition, but it was also taken as a sign that the democracy itself was in danger. In the subsequent accusations the young Andocides and his associates in a club, which was probably suspected of oligarchic tendencies (see HETAIR-EIAI), were named as having shared both in the mutilations and in the profanation of the Eleusinian mysteries (see DEMETER; ELEUSIS), and were arrested. Andocides, to secure immunity and, as he claimed, to save his father, confessed to a share in the mutilations and gave an account of the whole affair, which, though it may have been far from the truth, was readily accepted by the Athenians. This secured his release, but shortly afterwards, when the decree of Isotimides, aimed esp. at him, forbade those who had confessed to an act of impiety to enter temples or the *Agora, Andocides preferred to leave the city and began to trade as a merchant, in which role he developed connections all over the Aegean and in Sicily and Italy. In 411, seeking to restore himself to favour at Athens, he provided oars at cost price to the fleet in Samos, and shortly afterwards returned to Athens to plead for the removal of the limitation on his rights. Unfortunately for him, the revolution of the *Four Hundred had just installed in power the very class of citizens whom his confession had affected, and he was imprisoned and maltreated. Released, perhaps at the fall of the Four Hundred, he resumed trading. At some time after the restoration of the democracy in 410, he returned to the city to renew his plea, but was again unsuccessful. Returning finally under the *amnesty of 403, he resumed full participation in public life, and in 400 (or 399) successfully defended himself in *On the Mysteries* against an attempt to have him treated as still subject to the decree of Isotimides: the sixth speech of the *Lysian corpus, *Against Andocides*, was delivered by one of his accusers. In 392/391 he was one of the Athenian envoys sent to Sparta to discuss the making of peace, and on his return in the debate in the assembly he delivered *On Peace* urging acceptance of the proffered terms, which were in fact very similar to those of the *King's Peace of 387/6. The Athenians, however, rejected the peace, and Andocides and the other envoys were prosecuted. Andocides anticipated condemnation by retiring into exile, and we hear no more of him.

Andromachē, daughter of the king of Thebe in *Troas, and wife of *Hector. Her father and seven brothers were killed by *Achilles. After the fall of Troy her son Astyanax was killed by the Greeks, and she herself became *Neoptolemus' slave and concubine. She bore him three sons. Acc. to Euripides' *Andromache*, she was threatened with death by Neoptolemus' wife Hermione during the visit to Delphi in which he was killed, but was protected by *Peleus, Neoptolemus' aged grandfather.

Andromeda, in myth, daughter of Cepheus, king of *Ethiopia, and his wife Cassiepeia. Cassiepeia boasted that she was more beautiful than the *Nereids; they complained to *Poseidon, who flooded the land and sent a sea-monster to ravage it. On consulting *Ammon, Cepheus learned that the only cure was to offer up Andromeda to the monster, and so she was fastened to a rock on the sea-shore. At this point *Perseus came by on his way from taking the head of the *Gorgon Medusa. He fell in love with Andromeda, and got her and her father's consent to his marrying her if he could kill the monster. This he did; but Cepheus' brother Phineus, who had been betrothed to Andromeda, plotted against him. Perseus showed him and his followers the head of Medusa, turning them all to stone. He and Andromeda stayed for a time with Cepheus, and left their eldest son, Perses, with him; from Perses the Persian kings were descended. They then went on to Seriphus, then to *Argos and Tiryns. Andromeda, Perseus, Cepheus, Cassiepeia, and the monster were all turned into *constellations bearing their names (the monster is Cetus).

Androtion (c.410–340 BC) was a rich Athenian politician and atthidographer (see ATTHIS). His long political career involved service to Athens in many capacities. For some reason he ended his life in exile in *Megara, where he wrote his *Atthis*. This eight-book work was more concerned with contemporary events than earlier *Atthidēs*; the last five books covered the period 404–c.340. We have 68 fragments. They show the chauvinism of a local historian, moderated by a scholarly concern for accuracy.

angels (angeloi), 'messengers'. *Hermes was the messenger of Zeus. *Iris was ascribed the same function; for *Plato the two are the divine *angeloi*. By the 3rd cent. AD, angels played a large part in Judaism and *Christianity, and they became important too for paganism as intermediaries (along with lesser gods and demons) of the true God, not just in *Gnosticism and *Neoplatonism but also in 'mainstream' belief: thus an oracle from *Claros inscribed at *Oenoanda (c. AD 200?) represents even Apollo as an angelic 'small part' of God.

animals, attitudes to This was the subject of a huge debate among philosophers. Already in the 6th and 5th cents. BC *Pythagoras and *Empedocles had attacked the killing or maltreatment of animals, partly on the grounds that *transmigration made us literally akin to them. But vegetarianism was made difficult by the interconnections between religious sacrifice and meat-eating. Justice was treated as a gift of God to benefit humans, not animals, both by *Hesiod and in the myth ascribed to *Protagoras in *Plato's *Protagoras*.

The decisive step was taken by *Aristotle, who denied reason and belief to animals. Compensatingly, he allowed them a rich perceptual life, which he carefully disentangled from reliance on reason or belief. In ethics, he surprisingly combined the view that animals can be praised and blamed for their voluntary acts with the view that we owe them no justice, because we have nothing in common, and can conduct a just war against them. Aristotle's successor *Theophrastus, disagreed. We are, in an extended sense, akin even in reasonings, and killing harmless animals is unjust.

The Epicureans and Stoics (see EPICURUS; STOICISM) sided with Aristotle in denying reason to animals, and hence justice. Only *Plutarch was to ask 'why not kindness, if not justice?' The Epicurean rationale is that justice is owed only where there is a contract, hence only among rational agents. The Stoics denied that animals, as non-rational, could be treated as belonging (oikeiōsis: lit. a welcoming into the household)— and that despite the prevalence of *pets. Hence justice could not be extended to them. Unlike Aristotle, they denied animals memory, emotion, foresight, intention, and voluntary acts.

From then on, the philosophical debate turned on animal rationality. Animal pain and terror were seldom cited before *Porphyry. Pythagoras and *Apuleius exploited them only in the case of humans transformed into animals. Outside philosophy, attitudes were sometimes broader. The Athenians punished a man for flaying a ram alive. When *Pompey staged a slaughter of *elephants, the public was more concerned for the terrified elephants, the Stoic *Seneca the Younger for the loss of human life. The philosophers' praise of animals is sometimes only to downgrade humans (*Cynics) or glorify the Creator (*Augustine), while vegetarianism was often based merely on *ascetic or medical grounds.

The chief defenders of animals, in response to the Stoics, were the Neopythagoreans and certain Platonists. By far the most important work is Porphyry's *On Abstinence from Animal Food*. Of its four books, the first records the case against animals, but forbids meat on ascetic grounds; the second rejects animal sacrifice; the third claims rationality and justice for animals; the fourth is an anthropology of vegetarian nations. But Porphyry's probable pupil *Iamblichus felt it necessary to reinstate sacrifice. To defend this, he reinterpreted the belief of Pythagoras and that of Plato in transmigration of human souls into animals, the first belief as excluding sacrificial animals the second as metaphorical. He denied a rational soul to animals. The western Christian tradition was fatefully influenced by Augustine, who ignored the pro-animal side of this debate and backed the Stoic ground for killing animals. See also ANIMALS, KNOWLEDGE OF; ANIMALS IN CULT; HUNTING; PETS; SACRIFICE, GREEK and ROMAN; SEMONIDES; and particular animals (CAMELS; DOGS; ELEPHANTS; HORSES).

animals, knowledge of 1. Greek and Roman writing and thinking about animals was as often ethical as what we might call scientific in character. The archaeological record provides ample evidence that animals were closely observed by artists, and further evidence for the ancient study of animals comes from early medical observations about the role of animals and animal products in human regimen.

In the Homeric epics, animals exemplify many types of human qualities. Lions are brave, deer are prone to flight, bees swarm like crowds of people, dogs tread the treacherous path between loyalty and servility. (The story of Odysseus' dog, who died of joy on recognizing the scent of his long-lost master, was regarded by the later medical Empiricists as a miracle of *diagnosis.) Many similar examples can be found in the early Greek lyric poets. In the late 7th cent. BC, *Semonides of Amorgos wrote a poem comparing animals with different types of women; the only good woman is like a bee, the best of a terrible collection. Specific qualities retain their associations with specific animals. *Herodotus' story of *Arion's rescue from pirates by a dolphin stands at the head of a long line of similar tales about these intelligent and compassionate creatures. Much later, *Plutarch marvelled at the society of ants in their anthills, and in a series of treatises considered the problems of whether animals have souls and the capacity for reason, and feeling. (See preceding article.) The ethical, metaphorical, use of animals to explain the organization of human society reaches its fullest expression in the anecdotal zoology of *Aelian, in the Aesopic collection of *fables, and ultimately in the medieval bestiaries.

2. The earliest surviving systematic studies of the physical nature of animals are those of Aristotle—many would insist that no one in antiquity after Aristotle rivalled the breadth and depth of his interests. The biological treatises account for well over one-fifth of the surviving Aristotelian corpus, and lists of Aristotle's works suggest that there is much more that has not survived. In spite of the amount of material, there is disagreement even about the aims of Aristotle's zoological investigations. He was probably the first to devise a detailed zoological taxonomy, and this formed an important part of his general study of the *physics of the sublunary sphere.

In his famous exhortation to the study of animals, Aristotle speaks of the low status enjoyed by the enterprise—some philosophers, he says, considered the subject matter trivial if not disagreeable—but he maintains that the study of even the meanest of creatures is worthwhile if only because the means to discover their beauty, form, and purpose are close at hand. Modern disagreement about the nature of Aristotle's zoological enterprise is due in part to the difficulty of arranging the relevant treatises in a clear chronological sequence. Aristotle himself would have us approach his work on animals as an example of his scientific method in action.

In the treatises which make up the so-called *Organon* (esp. the *Posterior Analytics*), Aristotle set out the goals of scientific inquiry. He stressed the importance of firm, logically tested scientific knowledge, and elaborated the deductive apparatus for its achievement. In practice, Aristotle's method meant that he could begin an investigation into animals, for example, by collecting the relevant material—observations, information from others, along with the results of a preliminary assessment of these data, all of which go to make up what he calls the 'phenomena', together with the opinions of earlier authorities. Not all the phenomena are the result of *autopsy—Aristotle himself acknowledges debts to all kinds of people, and *Pliny the Elder noted that with the help of *Alexander (2) the Great, Aristotle was able to order thousands of fowlers, fishermen, beekeepers, hunters, and herdsmen to inform him about every creature they encountered.

The results of the first step in Aristotle's zoological investigation are set out in 'Researches into Animals'. The range covered is extraordinary—the lives, breeding habits, and structure of some 540 different genera. Such a huge amount of raw material needed to be arranged in some provisional way; listing the 'differences' between animals, Aristotle arranged his evidence in his 'Researches' under preliminary headings. He drew a broad distinction, for example, between bloodless and blooded creatures. Bloodless animals (of which he enumerates 120 altogether) are of four main types. Blooded animals include man, viviparous quadrupeds and cetacea, oviparous quadrupeds and animals without feet, birds, and fish.

In 'On the Parts of Animals' problems of division are addressed in detail, as are other theoretical questions about the relative importance of the various causal factors which all need to be understood if an animal's existence is to be properly explained. In general, Aristotle advocates investigating the attributes common to a group of animals, then explaining their existence ultimately in terms of their purpose (the Final Cause). He also includes accounts of the matter from which they come (the Material Cause), the process which led to their generation (the Efficient Cause), and their shape (the Formal Cause). The parts of animals are divided into those whose division yields a part which can be called by the same name as the whole—flesh, hair, bone, blood, marrow, milk, cartilage, etc.—and those whose division yields something with a different name—hands for instance, whose parts cannot be called 'hands', faces, skeletal structures, the internal organs, and so on. These are the 'non-uniform' parts. Concentrating attention exclusively on these characteristics as a prelude to explanation is not enough, and Aristotle criticizes certain of his predecessors for privileging the matter of an animal, and the material aspects of its generation, over its *raison d'être*. Aristotelian explanation in zoology is dominated by questions of purpose and function. Aristotle argued that the good of a particular animal, or part of an animal, is explicable in terms of that animal's contribution to its own survival, or the survival of its species. This does not lead to inflexibility; some things may be necessarily so without any obvious purpose—the colour of one's eyes, the existence of breasts in men, and so on—but Aristotelian teleological explanation can deal even with them as instances of natural necessity. Problems related to the origins and means of animal locomotion are investigated in 'On the Movement of Animals' and 'On the Progression of Animals'. But how does the soul move the body? What is the ultimate source of movement? Aristotle elaborates his ideas about the 'unmoved mover' in many different contexts, but the specific problems raised here lead into the investigation presented in 'On the Soul'.

animals in cult Numerous features of Greek religion attest links between animals and gods, usually between one animal or group of animals and one divinity. Thus *Athena is associated with various *birds (in Athens esp. the owl); *Dionysus is called 'bull' in an Elean hymn and seen as a bull by Pentheus in Euripides' *Bacchae*. There are traces, too, of a closer identification, in which gods (and/or their worshippers) appear in animal or part-animal form. Arcadia was in historical times the special home of theriomorphic deities; here we find a myth of *Poseidon's rape of *Demeter in equine form along with *Pausanias' (3) reference to a horse-headed statue of Demeter. But rituals involving the imitation of animals are found in other parts of the Greek world, a well-known example being the *arkteia* of *Brauron, where little girls played the part of bears in a ceremony for *Artemis.

By far the most important religious role of real animals in both Greece and Rome was that of *sacrificial victim. Animals for sacrifice were normally domesticated; sheep, goats, pigs, and cattle were the commonest species used, and it is likely that throughout antiquity most of the meat consumed from these animals would have been sacrificial meat. Deviant sacrifices, as of horses, fish, and also of wild animals more normally killed in hunting, are rare. The actions of some animals (esp. birds) were often seen as supplying omens, and prophecy from the entrails of sacrificial victims was also practised, in Greece, but more esp. by the Etruscans and thence the Romans (see DIVINATION). See also ANIMALS, ATTITUDES TO.

ankhisteia, a kinship group, extending to second cousins, or perhaps only to first cousins once removed. In Athenian law the nearest relatives within this group had the right to inherit property (see INHERITANCE, *Greek*); if a group member was killed, it was their duty to prosecute the killer. Relatives on the father's side took precedence over those on the mother's.

annālēs maximī, a chronicle kept by the *pontifex maximus*. Under the republic the *pontifex maximus* used to keep an annual record, and to publish a version of it outside the *Regia on a whitened board, which was probably repainted every year. The chronicle contained the names of magistrates, and apparently registered all kinds of public events. Although *Porcius Cato (1) was irritated by its frequent references to food shortages and eclipses, it was an important source for the earliest Roman historians, who also adopted its plain style and perhaps also its chronicle form. The *annales maximi* continued to be compiled until the time of the *Gracchi.

Annia Galeria Faustīna, younger daughter of *Antoninus Pius, was betrothed at *Hadrian's wish to the future Lucius *Verus in AD 138; this was set aside by Antoninus after Hadrian's death in favour of his wife's nephew Marcus *Aurelius. The marriage took place in 145. Her first child, Domitia Faustina, was born in 147, and she at once became Augusta. She bore Marcus at least a dozen children, six of whom survived her, five daughters and a son, *Commodus. The latter was alleged to be illegitimate; Faustina's loyalty as well as her marital fidelity were subject to question, not least in reports that she encouraged the rebellion of Avidius Cassius. But Marcus, who gave her the title 'mother of the camp' in 174, ignored these rumours and had her deified on her death in 175.

Annius Milō, Titus, of a prominent family of Lanuvium, as tribune 57 BC worked for Cicero's recall from exile and, with Sestius, organized armed gangs to oppose those led by *Clodius Pulcher, which had long prevented it. Fighting between Clodius and Milo in the city continued for several years, since—short of the *senatus consultum ultimum*, impossible to pass—there was no legitimate way of using public force to suppress it. Both Milo and Clodius ascended through the official career (see CURSUS HONORUM), at times unsuccessfully prosecuting each other for *vis*, until Milo's men met and defeated Clodius' near Bovillae in January 52. Clodius, wounded in the fighting, was killed on Milo's orders, chiefly to clear the way for Milo's candidacy for the consulship of 52, elections for which had been prevented by Clodius with *Pompey's support. After continued rioting Pompey was made sole consul and passed legislation including a strict law on *vis*, under which Milo was prosecuted. Cicero, intimidated by Pompey's soldiers guarding the court, broke down and was unable to deliver an effective speech for the defence. Milo was convicted and went into *exile at *Massalia. *Caesar, in part out of loyalty to Clodius' memory, refused to recall him along with other political exiles, and in 48, while Caesar was away in the east, Milo joined *Caelius Rufus in an attempt to raise rebellion among the poor in Italy and was killed.

annōna See FOOD SUPPLY, *Roman*.

Antalcidas, Spartan statesman. He first appears as Sparta's representative at the Graeco-Persian conference at *Sardis in 392 BC. He negotiated a Sparto-Persian alliance with *Artaxerxes (2) II in 388 and, as admiral, blockaded the Hellespont with Persian naval assistance, forcing the Athenians and their allies to agree to the *King's Peace (or Peace of Antalcidas) in 387/6. Its terms abandoned the Greek cities of Asia to Persia and established peace (probably the first officially named 'Common Peace') in mainland Greece and the Aegean based upon the principle of *autonomy, although the practical effect was the establishment of Spartan hegemony.

Antēnor, Athenian sculptor, active *c*.530–500 BC. Acc. to *Pausanias (3), he made the first bronze group of the tyrannicides Harmodius and *Aristogiton for the Athenian *agora; *Pliny the Elder dates it to 510. *Xerxes took it to Persia in 480, but the Athenians soon asked *Critius to replace it. *Alexander (2) the Great, *Seleucus I, or Antiochus I returned it, and thereafter it stood beside Critius' group. Antenor's only extant work is the monumental *korē* (see SCULPTURE, GREEK) dedicated by the potter Nearchus.

Anthestēria, a festival of *Dionysus, which despite its name (suggesting *anthos*, flower) was associated esp. with the new wine. It was celebrated in most Ionian communities, but almost all details are known from Athens. It was celebrated in the correspondingly named month Anthesterion, roughly late February. On the evening of the first day, 'Jar-opening' (Pithoigia), *pithoi* of the previous autumn's vintage were taken to the sanctuary of Dionysus in the Marshes, opened, offered to the god, and sampled. On the following day, drinking-parties of an abnormal type were held: participants sat at separate tables and competed, in silence, at draining a *chous* or five-litre (nine-pint) measure (whence the day's name Choes); slaves too had a share. Miniature *choes* were also given as toys to children, and 'first Choes' was a landmark. The third day was called Chytroi, 'Pots', from pots of seed and vegetable bran that were offered, it seems, to the dead. It was almost certainly during the Anthesteria that the wife of the *basileus* (see ARCHONTES) was somehow 'given as a bride' to Dionysus (whose image may have been escorted to her on a 'ship-chariot', a rite known from vases). A series of vases which show a mask of Dionysus on a pillar, in front of which women draw wine from mixing-bowls while others dance, may evoke a part of the same ceremony. The main problem posed by the festival is to see how its different elements relate to one another.

anthology The first artistically arranged anthology of *epigrams seems to be the *Garland* of *Meleager (2), *c*.100 BC. Our fullest source of information for both contents and arrangement is the so-called *Palatine Anthology* (*Anth. Pal.*), which preserves (*a*) Meleager's own preface, listing every poet included; and (*b*) in *Anth. Pal.* 5–7, 9, and 12 a series of more or less unbroken blocks of epigrams by poets named in the preface.

Philippus of Thessalonica compiled under *Nero another *Garland*, arranged by alphabetical order of the first word of each poem and thematic arrangement inside the letter groups. The literary quality of the second *Garland* is generally lower, less love and more rhetoric. Under (probably) Hadrian Straton produced his own collection of pederastic epigrams, and *c*.567/8 Agathias a *Cycle* of epigrams by his contemporaries, arranged like Meleager's *Garland*.

Around AD 900 a Byzantine schoolteacher called Constantine Cephalas put together a massive collection based on all these earlier collections, and much other material from a variety of sources, in particular a large number of inscriptional epigrams collected from various parts of Greece and Asia Minor. Around 940 a scholar known as J produced in *Anth. Pal.* an amplified redaction of Cephalas (some 3,700 epigrams in all). To this MS and its *scholia we owe almost our entire knowledge of Greek epigram from Meleager to Agathias.

The contents of *Anth. Pal.* are conventionally described as follows. 1, Christian epigrams; 2, an *ekphrasis* of statues in a bath in Constantinople; 3, epigrams from a temple; 4, prefaces of Meleager, Philippus, and Agathias; 5, amatory epigrams; 6, dedicatory epigrams; 7, epitaphs; 8, epitaphs by Gregory of Nazianzus; 9, declamatory epigrams; 10, hortatory eipgrams; 11, convivial and satirical epigrams; 12, pederastic epigrams; 13, poems in various metres; 14, oracles, riddles, and problems; 15, a miscellaneous appendix. Blocks from Meleager, Philippus, and Agathias alternate with sections compiled and arranged by Cephalas himself.

Finally in 1301 Maximus Planudes produced a much reduced anthology (*Anth. Plan.*) based on an abridged Cephalas. *Anth. Pal.* was unknown during most of the Renaissance (lurking in London and Louvain), not brought to the attention of scholars till 1606 and not finally published till the 19th cent. Till then *Anth. Plan.* was *the* Greek Anthology.

The Greek Anthology is one of the great books of European literature, a garden containing the flowers and weeds of fifteen hundred years of Greek verse, from doggerel to the purest poetry.

anthropology The Greeks and Romans developed a range of ideas about their own identity and the identity of others; about the nature of human societies, their history, and organization. Greeks designated non-Greek speakers '*barbarian'—after the Greek verb for 'babble'—and language remained an important index of racial and cultural difference. (*Herodotus introduced many Greeks to foreigners and

their customs for the first time; a foreign tongue might be likened to the twittering of birds.) Language served equally to differentiate Greek-speaking groups—the various Greek dialects (see GREEK LANGUAGE, 3) had their own distinctive written as well as spoken forms. Poets, philosophers, doctors, and others tried to define what it is to be human (an *anthrōpos*). One may mention the use of animal similes and metaphors in the Homeric epics (see HOMER) as aids to understanding human behaviour, *Semonides' misogynistic poem attributing various animal characteristics to different kinds of woman (see ANIMALS, KNOWLEDGE OF), *Hesiod's *Works and Days*, where man is distinguished from brute beasts through his possession of justice, and medical works concerned with issues such as the physiological difference between male and female, and the validity of using the study of animal physiology and anatomy to illuminate the human body (see MEDICINE). Many medical theories were formulated against a background of the assumed inferiority of the female sex. The natural world of *Aristotle has man, as opposed both to woman and mankind, firmly placed in the centre.

Moreover, there was widespread and sustained interest throughout Graeco-Roman antiquity in explaining the evolution of human —not just Greek—language, culture, and behaviour. The variety of ancient models of human history fall into two broad lines of argument. One line is represented most clearly by the Homeric and Hesiodic poems, and argues nostalgically that human society declined from an ancient '*golden age' through other ages of increasing metallic baseness to the present. This model is common in poetry (both Greek and Latin) from *Pindar to *Juvenal and beyond. The other line of argument has it that civilization gradually progressed through the discovery of technological, political, and linguistic benefits. A fragment of *Xenophanes illustrates this position: 'The Gods did not show everything to mortals from the beginning, but through investigation mortals have discovered over time what is better'. On this view, man has some control over his progress.

Behind this apparently straightforward dichotomous summary there lies much that is not straightforward. For a start, there was no single, orthodox 'Myth of the Golden Age' in which life for mankind becomes progressively worse with time. Baser metallic ages, even in Hesiod, still have their good points, and Hesiod's golden age is apparently devoid of normal humans altogether—only godlike creatures remote and free from toil and grief. And *Cornelius Celsus held that in the distant past medicine was necessary only for the treatment of wounds and other injuries because men lived virtuous and moderate lives. Yet the development of medicine, he suggests, has gone a long way towards counteracting the effects of the decline in moral standards.

Generalization is difficult. Certain philosophical models which allow that human society is capable of improvement often insist that this improvement is dependent on men embracing the appropriate philosophical way of life. (This is as true of *Epicureans like Lucretius as it is of Plato.) Moreover, even those who saw social institutions and the arts as constantly progressing had no place for progress on the part of nature herself—say, by suggesting that animal species too might be in a state of constant development. On the contrary, philosophers and natural scientists from *Anaximander to Aristotle and beyond seem to have held that the successful adaptation of animals to their environment was simply the result of one-off changes in their form.

antidosis ('exchange') in Athens was a legal procedure concerned with *liturgies. Liturgies were supposed to be performed by the richest men. If a man appointed to perform one claimed that another man, who had not been appointed and was not exempt, was richer than himself, he could challenge him either, if he admitted being richer, to perform the liturgy or, if he claimed to be poorer, to exchange the whole of his property for that of the challenger, who would then perform it. If the challenged man failed to fulfil either alternative, the case went to trial by a jury, who decided which man should perform the liturgy; this was probably the most usual upshot, though actual exchanges of property did sometimes take place.

Antigonē daughter of *Oedipus and Iocasta, sister of *Eteocles, Polynīcēs, and Ismēnē.

*Sophocles' (1) *Antigone* deals with events after the Theban War, in which Eteocles and Polynices killed one another (see SEVEN AGAINST THEBES). Antigone's uncle *Creon (1), the new king of Thebes, has issued an edict forbidding anyone to bury the body of the traitor Polynices. Antigone, though urged not to by Ismene, insists on defying the edict. She is arrested and brought before Creon, and proudly defends her action. He decrees that she should be imprisoned in a tomb and left to die, although she is engaged to his son Haemon. Creon is left unmoved by Haemon's arguments against such punishment, but is finally made to change his mind by the prophet *Tiresias, who reveals that the gods are angry at the exposure of Polynices and the burial of Antigone. He buries Polynices but arrives at Antigone's tomb too late: she has hanged herself, and Haemon, who has broken into the tomb, kills himself in front of his father. Creon's wife Eurydice also kills herself, leaving Creon a broken man.

Antigone's role in the play has been the subject of endless dispute, with some critics claiming that she is wholly in the right, others that she and Creon are equally right and equally wrong. Most would now agree that she is no saint (she is harsh and unfair to Ismene, and her defiance of male authority would have shocked an Athenian audience), but still find her admirable. While her story is unlikely to be pure invention by Sophocles, her earlier history is uncertain. Sophocles portrayed Antigone again in *Oedipus at Colonus*, where she accompanies her blind father in his exile.

Antigonus I (c.382–301 BC), 'the One-eyed', Macedonian noble, was prominent under *Philip II and governed Greater Phrygia for *Alexander (2) the Great (334–323). Victorious over Persian refugees from Issus (332), he remained unchallenged in his satrapy until he fell foul of the regent *Perdiccas, whom he denounced to *Antipater in Macedon (322), unleashing war. Within half-a-dozen years, he had gained control of territory from the Hindu Kush to the Aegean, but his success brought immediate war with erstwhile allies: *Cassander, *Lysimachus and *Ptolemy (1) (315). The 'Peace of the Dynasts' (summer 311) briefly ratified the status quo. Antigonus now directed his attention to the Greek world, broadcasting his liking for freedom and autonomy, and ultimately reactivated the *Corinthian League as a weapon against Cassander (303/2). Athens welcomed him and his son, Demetrius (Poliorcētēs), with open arms and exaggerated honours (307), and in the following year the two had themselves proclaimed kings. But the achievements belied the propaganda. The invasion of Egypt (306) was abortive, as was Demetrius' year-long siege of *Rhodes (305/4). Finally the coalition of 315 was reforged. At Ipsus (in *Phrygia) the combined Antigonid forces were defeated decisively and Antigonus died in battle. His ambitions had been too patent, his resources inadequate to contain the reaction they provoked.

Antipater (?397–319 BC), Macedonian statesman. Trusted lieutenant of *Philip II, he twice represented the king at Athens, and governed Macedon during the Danubian campaign of *Alexander (2) the Great (335). From 334 he acted as viceroy in Europe. Later his relations with Alexander were soured, and in 324 *Craterus was sent to replace him in Macedon. Alexander's death (323) resolved the tension but unleashed the *Lamian War, in which a formidable Hellenic coalition, headed by the Athenians and Aetolians, came close to victory. The arrival of Craterus and his veterans redressed the balance, and the critical victory at Crannon (August 322) allowed Antipater to impose the settlement which brought oligarchy and a Macedonian garrison to Athens.

Antiphon (*c.*480–411 BC), of the *deme of Rhamnus, the first Attic orator whose works were preserved. From a prominent family, he participated in the intellectual movement inspired by the *sophists, taking a particular interest in law and rhetoric; he reportedly taught *Thucydides (2). Many scholars are now inclined to identify him with Antiphon 'the Sophist', fragments of whose work *Truth* are concerned with the nature of justice and the relationship between *nomos* ('law, convention') and *physis* ('nature').

Thucydides praises Antiphon highly for ability (*aretē*), intelligence, and power of expression, adding that he stayed in the background himself but made his reputation giving advice to others. He credits Antiphon with planning the oligarchic coup that overturned the democratic constitution of Athens for a few months in 411 BC (see FOUR HUNDRED). When democracy was restored, most leaders of the coup fled, but Antiphon and Archeptolemus remained to stand trial for treason; both were convicted and executed. Antiphon's speech in his own defence, a small papyrus fragment of which survives, was the finest speech Thucydides knew. When congratulated by *Agathon on its brilliance, Antiphon replied that he would rather have satisfied one man of good taste than any number of common people.

Antiphon was apparently the first to compose speeches for other litigants and thus the first to write them down. His clients included well-known political figures and foreign allies of Athens. We have six complete works: three courtroom speeches and three *Tetralogies*. All concern homicide cases, though the fragmentary speeches treat many other issues. The courtroom speeches and the datable fragments come from the last two decades of Antiphon's life (430–411). In *Against the Stepmother* a young man accuses his stepmother of having employed a servant-woman to poison his father. He may have brought the case from a sense of duty, for he offers little evidence. In *The Murder of Herodes* a Mytilenean is accused of murdering Herodes during a sea voyage: Herodes went ashore one stormy night and never returned. He defends his innocence by appeal both to facts and to probabilities, and accuses his opponent of trumping up the charge for political reasons and personal gain. In *On the Chorus Boy* a *chorēgos* (see CHOREGIA) is accused of the accidental death of a boy who was given a drug to improve his voice. The *choregos* argues that he was not even present at the time and that the prosecution is politically motivated.

The *Tetralogies* are Antiphon's earliest works. Their authenticity is disputed, but their arguments concerning probability, causation, and similar issues fit the period and Antiphon's interests. Using the sophistic method of opposed arguments (see PROTAGORAS) and displaying a self-conscious virtuosity, the *Tetralogies* illustrate methods of argument that could be applied to a wide variety of cases. Each consists of four speeches for hypothetical cases, two on each side. In the *First Tetralogy* a man is murdered and circumstantial evidence points to the accused, who argues that others are more likely to be the killers. In the *Second Tetralogy* a boy is accidentally killed by a javelin; the defence argues that the boy himself, not the thrower, is guilty of unintentional homicide because he was the cause of his own death. In the *Third Tetralogy* a man dies after a fight and the accused argues that the victim is to blame because he started it.

Antiphon stands at the beginning of the tradition of literary Attic prose. He is an innovator and experimenter; he is fond of antithesis (in both word and thought), and poetic vocabulary. Compared with successors like *Lysias, Antiphon lacks grace of expression, clarity of organization, and the vivid presentation of character, but the force and variety of his arguments may account for his success.

Antisthenēs (mid-5th–mid-4th cent. BC), associate of *Socrates, one of those named by *Plato as having been present at his final conversation. A professional teacher, he continued the sophistic tradition by writing voluminously on many subjects, and in a variety of genres, including

Socratic dialogues, declamations, and *diatribes against various people, including Plato.

He followed Socrates in holding that virtue is sufficient for happiness, 'requiring nothing more than Socratic strength'. So he stressed the austerity of the Socratic lifestyle and was vehemently hostile to pleasures except those of a hard and simple life. This emphasis on the self-sufficiency and detachment of the virtuous agent was taken up by the Stoics (see STOICISM) and (with special emphasis on physical austerity) the Cynics; later writers treat Antisthenes as the founder of the Cynic tradition. See CYNICS. Following *Xenophanes and others, he was critical of conventional religion, maintaining that while in common belief there are many gods, in reality there is only one.

Antistius Labeō, Marcus, was a leading Roman lawyer in the time of *Augustus. His father, also a lawyer, was killed fighting for the republican cause. As a member of a commission to reconstitute the senate in 18 BC he showed his independent spirit. Out of sympathy with the new order, his political career stopped at the praetorship: the consulship belatedly offered him by Augustus he refused. *Tacitus contrasts his attachment to republican principle with the obsequiousness of his contemporary Ateius Capito. He acquired expertise not only in law but also in dialectics, language, literature, and grammar, which he brought to bear on legal problems. Author of many innovations, he divided his time equally between teaching in Rome and writing in the country, and wrote in all some 400 books. He drew a line under republican jurisprudence, which was henceforth cited largely through him.

Antōnia (1), elder daughter of Marcus *Antonius (Mark Antony) and *Octavia, b. 39 BC, was the wife of Domitius Ahenobarbus. Their children were Gnaeus, consul AD 32 (father of *Nero), Domitia and Domitia Lepida (mother of *Valeria Messallina).

Antōnia (2), younger daughter of Marcus *Antonius (Mark Antony) and *Octavia, b. 36 BC, married Nero *Claudius Drusus; their children were *Germanicus, Livilla (Livia Iulia), and *Claudius. After Drusus' death in 9 BC she refused to marry again, and after *Livia Drusilla's death brought up her grandchildren *Gaius (1) (the future emperor Caligula) and *Iulia Drusilla. Gaius, on his accession, conferred numerous honours upon her, including the name 'Au

gusta' (see AUGUSTUS, AUGUSTA, AS TITLES), but soon found her criticisms irksome and, it was said, drove her to suicide (37). Claudius rehabilitated her memory.

Antonine emperors and period See ANTONINUS PIUS; AURELIUS, M.; COMMODUS; ROME, HISTORY 2.2.

Antōnīnus Pius, Roman emperor AD 138–161, b. 86, son of Aurēlius Fulvus (consul 89). His mother was daughter of Arrius Antoninus (consul 69 and 97), whose name he bore. He married Annia Galeria Faustina, and became consul in 120. Apart from the traditional magistracies, his only posts were those of consular legate in Italy (an innovation of Hadrian), in his case in Etruria and Umbria, where he owned land, and proconsul of Asia (135/6).

His links with the Annii Veri, combined with his wealth, popularity, and character, led *Hadrian to choose him as adoptive son and successor on the death of Aelius Caesar. Given *imperium and the tribūnicia potestās (see TRIBUNI PLEBIS) in February 138, he became Imperator Titus Aelius Aurelius Antoninus Caesar and at Hadrian's wish adopted both the young son of Lucius Aelius (the future Lucius *Verus) and his nephew by marriage Annius Verus (Marcus *Aurelius). His accession at Hadrian's death, July 138, was warmly welcomed by the senate, which overcame its reluctance to deify Hadrian at Antoninus' insistence and named him Pius in acknowledgement of his loyalty. His wife Faustina was named Augusta (see AUGUSTUS, AUGUSTA, AS TITLES) and his only surviving child, also *Annia Galeria Faustina, was betrothed to Marcus Aurelius Caesar, his nephew and elder adoptive son. Pius became consul for a second term and *Pater Patriae in 139, consul for a third term in 140 with Marcus Aurelius as colleague, and held one further consulship, in 145, again with Marcus Aurelius, whose marriage to the younger Faustina took place the same year. On the birth of a child to this couple in late 147, Marcus Aurelius received tribunicia potestas, and Faustina (whose mother had died in 140) became Augusta. The dynastic succession thus clearly established—but, despite Hadrian's intention, the younger adoptive son received neither any powers nor the name Caesar— Antoninus' longevity and steady hand made 'Antonine' a byword for peace and prosperity. This impression is largely influenced by Aelius *Aristides' To Rome, delivered in 143 or 144, by the portrayal of the tranquil life of the imperial family, entirely confined to Italy, in *Fronto's Letters*, by the impressive tribute to Antoninus in Marcus Aurelius' *Meditations*, and by the uniformly favourable attitude of the scanty historical sources.

Hadrian's policies were rapidly changed in some areas: the consular legates for Italy, unpopular with the senate, were abolished, and southern Scotland reconquered by the governor, Hadrian's Wall being replaced by the '*wall of Antoninus*' between Forth and Clyde. This campaign, for which Antoninus took the acclamation 'Imperator' for the second time in late 142, was the only major war, but Moorish incursions in North Africa were dealt with by sending reinforcements to Mauretania in the 140s, minor campaigns kept the peace in Dacia, a show of force at the beginning of the reign deterred a Parthian invasion, and in the late 150s a minor extension of territory in Upper Germany was marked by the construction of a new 'outer' *limes*. Direction of military policy (and much else) was doubtless left to the praetorian *prefect Gavius Maximus, who held office for almost the entire reign. The senatorial *cursus honorum*—and other parts of the imperial system—settled down in a stable pattern, contributing to the emperor's popularity with the upper order. Two conspiracies against him are mentioned. A highlight of the reign was the celebration of Rome's 900th anniversary in 148, when Antoninus' otherwise thrifty financial policy was relaxed (by a temporary debasement of the silver coinage). He cut down on excess expenditure, although relieving cities affected by natural disasters, and left a surplus of 675 million *denarii* at his death. In spite of his conservatism and sceptical attitude towards Greek culture, Greeks advanced to the highest positions in his reign (*Claudius Atticus Herodes, consul 143, being the best-known case); other provincials also rose, not least from Africa, helped by the prominence of Fronto, a native of Cirta. The long, peaceful reign allowed the empire a breathing-space after Trajan's wars and Hadrian's restless travels. Antoninus' last watchword for the guard, 'equanimity', sums up his policy well; but he was angry with 'foreign kings' in his last hours, and clouds were looming. He died near Rome in March 161 and was deified 'by universal consent'.

Antōnius, Marcus, 'Mark Antony', Roman statesman and general b. in 83 (or, less likely, 86) BC. His youth was allegedly dissipated. He distinguished himself as cavalry commander under *Gabinius in Palestine and Egypt (57–54), then joined *Caesar in Gaul, where, apart from an interval in Rome, he remained till the end of 50; in 51 he was *quaestor. As tribune (see TRIBUNI PLEBIS) in 49 he defended Caesar's interests in the senate, fled to his camp when the 'last decree' was passed (see SENATUS CONSULTUM ULTIMUM), took part in the fighting in Italy, and was left in charge of Italy during Caesar's Spanish campaign. In 48 he served in Greece and commanded Caesar's left wing at Pharsalus. Caesar then sent him to impose order on Italy as his *magister equitum* (till late in 47), but he was only partly successful, and he held no further post till 44 when he was Caesar's consular colleague. On 15 February 44 he played a prominent role in the incident of the *Lupercalia, offering a diadem, which Caesar refused.

After the Ides of March he at first played a delicate game, combining conciliation of the Liberators with intermittent displays of his popular and military support. He acquired and exercised a strong personal dominance, but this was soon threatened by the emergence of *Octavian, and the two locked in competition for the Caesarian leadership. Octavian deftly acquired support and allies, and by early 43 Antony faced an armed coalition consisting of Iunius Brutus Albinus, whom he was blockading in Mutina, the consuls *Hirtius and Vibius Pansa, both moderate Caesarians, and Octavian, backed by the senate's authority and Cicero's eloquence. In April he was compelled to retreat into Gallia Narbonensis (See GAUL (TRANSALPINE)). He was, however, joined there by the governors of the western provinces, *Aemilius Lepidus (1), *Asinius Pollio, and *Munatius Plancus, and later reconciled with Octavian.

By the *lex Titia* (Nov. 43) Antony, Lepidus, and Octavian were appointed *'triumvirs for putting the state in order' for five years. The *proscription of their enemies (esp. the rich) was followed in 42 by the defeat of *Cassius and *Brutus at Philippi, which established Antony's reputation as a general. By agreement with Octavian he now undertook the reorganization of the eastern half of the empire; he also received Gaul, strategically vital if there were to be any renewal of fighting in the west. In 41 he met *Cleopatra VII at Tarsus and spent the following winter with her in Egypt. Their twins Alexander Helios and Cleopatra Selene were born in 40. The defeat of his brother *Antonius (Pietas) in Perusia compelled him to return to Italy early in 40, despite the Parthian invasion of Syria; but a new agreement was reached, the Pact of

*Brundisium, whereby Antony surrendered Gaul, which Octavian had already occupied, and married Octavian's sister *Octavia. The division of the empire into east and west was becoming more clear-cut. At Misenum in 39 the triumvirs extended their agreement to Sextus *Pompeius, after which Antony returned with Octavia to the east. By 38 his lieutenant Ventidius had expelled the Parthians from Syria. In 37, new differences between Antony and Octavian were settled at Tarentum, and the Triumvirate was renewed for another five years; but this time he left Octavia behind when he set out for the east, and renewed his association with Cleopatra more firmly. Their third child Ptolemy Philadelphus was born in 36.

This liaison had political attractions. Egypt was one of several important kingdoms which Antony strengthened and expanded; nor did he grant all that Cleopatra wished, for he refused to take territory from *Herod (1) of Judaea, another able and valued supporter. The allegiance of the east was courted by religious propaganda. By 39 he had already presented himself as *Dionysus in Athens, and he and Cleopatra could now be presented as *Osiris and *Isis, linked in a sacred marriage for the prosperity of Asia. But in 36 Antony's Parthian expedition ended in a disastrous reverse, while the defeat of Sextus *Pompeius and the elimination of Lepidus correspondingly strengthened Octavian. It took time for Antony to accept that a decisive clash with Octavian was inevitable. At first he continued to concentrate on the east, planning a further invasion of Parthia and annexing Armenia in 34: this was marked in *Alexandria by a ceremony (hostile sources regarded it as a sacrilegious version of a Roman *triumph) after which Cleopatra and her children—including Caesarion, whom Antony provocatively declared to be Caesar's acknowledged son—were paraded in national and regal costumes of various countries, just as if they might inherit them dynastically. The propaganda exchanges with Octavian intensified in 33. Early in 32 Octavian intimidated many of Antony's supporters, including the consuls, into leaving Rome. Antony divorced Octavia; then Octavian outrageously seized and published Antony's will, in which he allegedly left bequests to his children by Cleopatra and requested burial in Alexandria. Octavian proceeded to extract the annulment of Antony's remaining powers and a declaration of war against Cleopatra: Antony would now seem a traitor if he sided with the national enemy.

The spring and summer of 31 saw protracted military engagements in western Greece. Antony's initial numerical superiority was whittled away by *Agrippa's skilful naval attacks. During the summer Antony was deserted by most of his most influential Roman supporters, including Plancus: they had allegedly been alienated by Cleopatra's presence. In September 31 Cleopatra and Antony managed to break the blockade at *Actium and escape southwards, but the campaign was decisively lost, and their supporters defected to Octavian in the following months. Antony killed himself as Octavian entered Alexandria (August 30).

Much of *Plutarch's portrayal of Antony carries some conviction—the great general, with unusual powers of leadership and personal charm, destroyed by his own weaknesses. But it is easy to underestimate his political judgement. True, Octavian won the war of propaganda in Italy, but till a late stage Antony continued to have strong support from the east and from influential Romans (many old republicans preferred him to Octavian). He looked the likely winner until the Actium campaign itself, and it is arguable that military rather than political considerations sealed his downfall. His administrative arrangements in the east were clear-sighted, and most were continued by Augustus.

Antony was married to his cousin Antonia, whom he divorced in 47; in 47 or 46, to *Fulvia; in 40, to Octavia. By Antonia he had a daughter; by Fulvia two sons; by Octavia two daughters, *Antonia (1) the Elder and *Antonia (2) the Younger, through whom he was the ancestor of the emperors *Gaius (1), *Claudius, and *Nero. His 'marriage' to Cleopatra would not have been seen as such by Italian observers.

Antōnius Pallas, Marcus, freedman of *Antonia (2) the Younger and financial secretary of her son *Claudius. His wealth, success, and arrogant temper made him unpopular. Devoted to *Iulia Agrippina and alleged to be her lover, he successfully promoted her candidature in the competition to marry Claudius after the execution of Messallina; he also hastened Claudius' adoption of her son *Nero. The senate voted him *ornamenta praetoria and a sum of money: he refused the money and received public commemoration for virtue and frugality. After the accession of Nero, Pallas, like Agrippina, was gradually and firmly thrust aside from power. Compelled to resign his office, he stipulated that no questions should be asked, that his accounts be regarded as balanced. Finally, he was put to death by Nero, because of his wealth, it is said (AD 62).

Antōnius (Pietās), Lūcius, Younger brother of Marcus *Antonius (Mark Antony), was quaestor in Asia 50 BC and in charge of the province for part of 49. As tribune 44, he carried a law allowing Caesar to appoint half the magistrates except for consuls; after Caesar's death he allowed Octavian to address a *contio and later was made chairman of a commission to distribute public land (see AGER PUBLICUS) to *veterans and the poor. For his work on this (later annulled by the senate) he was made patron of the 35 tribes (see TRIBUS) and of the ex-military tribunes; he also (we do not know why) became patron of the *equestrians and of the *bankers and was honoured with statues in the Forum. He served as a *legate under his brother Antony in the war of Mutina, which successfully resisted Antony in 43, and, as consul 41, worked in Antony's interest against Octavian, trying to impress Antony's partisans by assuming the *cognomen '*Pietas'. When he championed Italian cities against Octavian's veterans, Octavian, after securing the neutrality of Antony's commanders, attacked him. He was besieged in Perusia and forced to surrender (40). Octavian pardoned him and sent him to a command in Spain, where he died.

Anytus, a rich Athenian and democratic leader, best known as a prosecutor of *Socrates (399 BC). General in 409, he failed to prevent the loss of *Pylos; at his trial he reportedly bribed the entire jury. After 403 he was a respected, moderate leader of the restored democracy. *Plato (*Meno* 91) introduces him as a passionate enemy of the *sophists. His prosecution of Socrates for impiety was probably motivated less by religious concerns than by anger at Socrates' disdain of democratic politicians.

apadana, 'the public part of a royal palace'. Attested only at *Susa, the word is usually applied to the large multi-columned halls in the palaces at Susa and *Persepolis.

Apatūria, an *Ionian festival. Acc. to Herodotus, Ionians are all those who 'derive from Athens and celebrate the festival Apaturia. All Ionians celebrate it except Ephesians and Colophonians.' Almost all details are known from Athens. It is unique among Greek festivals in its special association with a particular social grouping, the *phratry: the phratries celebrated

it, in the autumn month Pyanopsion, at their separate centres throughout Attica, and its main function was to enrol new phratry members (who by this registration acquired a title to *citizenship). It lasted three days, called (1) Dorpia, from the 'dinner' the *phratores* held together on assembling in the evening; (2) Anarrhysis, from the 'drawing back' of the necks of the victims sacrificed to *Zeus Phratrios and *Athena Phratria that day; (3) Koureōtis, the day of admission-sacrifices brought by the relatives of prospective new members: if the *phratores* ate of the animal, the candidate was thereby acknowledged. Three types of admission-sacrifice are known, the occasions of which appear to have been: 'lesser', a preliminary offering made during early childhood; 'hair-cutting', on entry to the *ephebate; 'marriage offering', brought by newly-married *phratores* on behalf of their wives.

Apellai was a monthly festival of *Apollo held at Sparta and elsewhere. On this day the stated meetings of the Spartan assembly (see EKKLESIA) were held. The assembly comprised all Spartiate male citizens in good standing. With the concurrence of the *gerousia* (council of elders), and under the presidency of an *ephor, it had the right to vote on laws, decide on peace or war and the conclusion of treaties, elect ephors and other officials and members of the *gerousia*, appoint military commanders and emancipate *helots—all normally by shouting, not the counting of individual votes.

Apellēs, painter, of Colophon, later of Ephesus. He is mentioned more often, and generally considered better, than any other painter. *Pliny the Elder dates him 332 BC (from the portrait of *Alexander (2) the Great). He was taught by Pamphilus at Sicyon. He painted portraits of *Philip II, Alexander (who allowed no other artist to paint him), and their circle, and a self-portrait (probably the first). He died in *Cos while copying his 'Aphrodite', probably early in the 3rd cent.

About 30 works are recorded. He showed Alexander mounted and with a thunderbolt; also with the *Dioscuri and Victory; and in triumph with War personified as a bound captive. Thus he fully reflected the eastern aspects of Alexander's rule in a Greek medium. His 'Aphrodite Anadyomene' (rising from the sea wringing out her hair) was in Cos, later in Rome. 'Sacrifice', also in Cos, was described by *Herodas. The tone of his pictures was due to a secret varnish. He wrote a book on painting: he claimed to know when to take his hand from a picture, and that his works had charm, *charis*. His 'Nude Hero' was said to challenge nature herself; horses neighed only at Apelles' horses. See PAINTING, GREEK.

Aphrodisias, was a *Carian city, probably established in the 2nd cent. BC as the political centre of communities honouring a mother-goddess, called *Aphrodite perhaps from the 3rd cent. and later identified with Roman *Venus. That identification encouraged a special relationship with Rome and with the family of *Caesar; so Aphrodisias resisted *Mithradates VI in 88 and the Liberators after Caesar's death, earning privileges which Rome conferred in 39. The wall-circuit, *c*.3.5 km. (2.2 mi.) long and containing many inscribed blocks reused, a stadium, and columns have always been visible; excavation has now uncovered civic buildings and much sculpture—see next entry. Numerous inscriptions, including an 'archive' of official communications from Rome inscribed on a wall in the theatre, throw important light on Roman history, late antiquity, ancient entertainments, and the Jewish Diaspora.

Aphrodisias, school of The existence of an Aphrodisian sculptural school was first proposed in 1943, on the basis of numerous statues in Roman and other museums signed by sculptors bearing the ethnic 'Aphrodisieus'. Excavations at *Aphrodisias have confirmed a rich sculptural tradition beginning in the 1st cent. BC and lasting into the 5th cent. AD. Large-scale production was facilitated by the existence of quarries of fine white *marble 2 km. (just over a mile) away. Portraits, architectural marbles (both narrative and decorative), *sarcophagi, copies and small-scale versions of classical originals constitute the school's main output.

Aphrodītē Born from the severed genitals of *Uranus acc. to *Hesiod, or in the *Homeric version daughter of *Zeus and Diōnē, Aphrodite is the representative among the gods of an ambivalent female nature combining seductive charm, the need to procreate, and a capacity for deception, elements all found in the person of the first woman, *Pandora. There is no agreement on her historical origins; the Greeks themselves thought of her as coming from the east, and in literature she is often called Cypris, 'the Cyprian'. (See CYPRUS.) The double tradition of her birth shows how the Greeks felt Aphrodite to be at the same time Greek and foreign, but

also, on the level of myth, that they perceived her as a powerful goddess whom it would be prudent to place under the authority of Zeus.

Aphrodite's cults extend very widely over the Greek world. *Cyprus is the home of her most famous cults, at Paphos and Amathus. There, probably in the Archaic period, the name Aphrodite became attached to an indigenous goddess who was also subject to numerous oriental influences. In Greece itself, one or more cults of Aphrodite are known in every region. She was worshipped above all as presiding over sexuality and reproduction—necessary for the continuity of the community. Thus in many cities girls about to be married sacrificed to Aphrodite so that their first sexual experience might be propitious. This is the particular sphere of Aphrodite, compared with other goddesses involved in marriage like *Hera and *Demeter. The close bond which the Greeks felt to exist between human fertility and the fruitfulness of the land lies behind Aphrodite's connections with vegetation and the earth in general. In Athens, Aphrodite 'in gardens', was worshipped together with Athena at the *Arrephoria, a rite concerned with fertility and with the sexuality of the *arrephoroi* as future wives of citizens. This Aphrodite was also worshipped by prostitutes. Epithets such as *Hetaira ('courtesan') and Pornē ('prostitute') show her as protectress of this profession, whose essential stock-in-trade was seduction. Corinth was esp. well known for the beauty and luxurious living of its prostitutes, who certainly revered the local Aphrodite.

If Aphrodite was worshipped primarily by women, men also took part in her cult, notably in connection with her role as patron of seafaring. Aphrodite is also concerned with magistrates in their official capacity, being the deity of concord and civic harmony. The title Pandemos, which is hers conspicuously in Athens, indicates her protection of the whole citizen body. The title Urania, 'heavenly', occurs often in cult and refers to the power of the goddess who presides over every type of union. It is with this epithet that the name Aphrodite is used as the Greek designation of foreign goddesses, a process found already in *Herodotus. The title also expresses one of Aphrodite's ambiguities, making her simultaneously 'daughter of Uranus' and 'the goddess who has come from elsewhere'. Acc. to *Pausanias (3), there were several statues showing an armed Aphrodite, esp. at Sparta. Considering the special characteristics of the upbringing of Spartiate girls, it is not too surprising that the goddess of femaleness should be given male attire. Her association with *Ares, prominent in the literary tradition, has more to do with a wish to bring opposites together than with any similarity of function.

From *Sappho to *Lucretius, literature celebrates the power of love and the dominion of Aphrodite. Ares, *Adonis, *Hermes, and *Dionysus are all at various times given as her lovers, as is the mortal *Anchises.

Apicius See COOKERY.

apoikia, 'a settlement far from home, a colony', and hence a Greek community regarded as distinct from the kind of trading-post conventionally known as an *emporion. In effect, an apoikia may be defined as a *polis established abroad by a polis (or *metropolis: 'mother city') at home: the official processes required the appointment of a leader/founder. The development of the polis at home in Greece coincided chronologically with the colonizing movement that was in progress between c.734 and 580 BC. Given the continuing importance of trade to the main colonizing cities, it follows that the distinction between apoikia and emporion—the settlement type characteristic of the pre-colonial phase—is in some cases more apparent than real. Certain apoikiai could well have been considered in effect as emporia first and poleis second; and the sheer size and population-density of at least one early emporion, *Pithecusae, seemingly established on a typically pre-colonial ad hoc basis, soon brought about a degree of social organization that might reasonably be expected of a 'true' apoikia. See FOUNDERS OF CITIES; COLONIZATION, GREEK.

Apollo, Greek god, son of *Zeus and *Leto, brother of *Artemis, for many 'the most Greek of Greek gods'. His *epithet Phoibos means 'radiant'. Among his numerous and diverse functions healing and *purification, prophecy, care for young citizens, for poetry, and music are prominent. In iconography, he is always young, beardless, and of harmonious beauty, the ideal *ephebe and young athlete; his weapon is the bow, and his tree the laurel.

In *Homer and *Hesiod, his myth and cult are fully developed, and his main centres, *Delos and *Delphi, are well known, though none goes back to the bronze age: Apollo's cult must have been introduced and brought to panhellenic importance during the Dark Age. Epic poetry, where Apollo is prominent, had its decisive share in this development. The key document

is the Homeric *Hymn to Apollo; it consists of two aetiological parts, a Delian part which tells the story of Apollo's birth and a Delphic part about the foundation of the oracular shrine in Delphi.

Apollo has a widespread role as the divinity responsible for the introduction of young initiated adults into society: he receives the first cut hair at the end of *initiation, and his cult has to do with military and athletic training and with the citizen-right of the sons. His cult on Delos, where Leto gave birth, became the religious focus of Archaic Ionia at least from the late 8th cent. onwards. While a Delian temple of Artemis existed in the 8th cent., a temple of Apollo was built only in the mid-6th cent.; his cult centred around the altar of horns.

Apollo's interest in music and poetry could derive from the same source, music and poetry having a major educational role in Greece (see EDUCATION, GREEK). Apollo's instrument is the lyre, whose well-ordered music is opposed to the ecstatic rhythms of pipe and drums which belong to *Dionysus and *Cybele; acc. to the Homeric Hymn to Hermes, he received it from *Hermes, its inventor. He is, together with the *Muses, protector of epic singers and citharaplayers; later, he is 'Leader of the Muses' in Pindar and on Archaic images. When philosophy takes over a similar educational function, he is associated with philosophy, and an anecdote makes him the real father of *Plato.

His own song, the paean, is sung and danced by the young Achaeans after the sacrifice to Apollo when bringing back *Chryseis to her father: even if not necessarily a healing-song in this passage, it was understood as such later and so was transferred to Asclepius as well. Ionian Apollo the Healer had cult in most Black (*Euxine) Sea cities, and as Medicus Apollo was taken over by the Romans during a *plague in the 5th cent. Only the rise of *Asclepius in the 5th and 4th cents. eclipsed this function. In Iliad 1 he is responsible both for sending and for averting the plague. The image of a god sending plague by shooting arrows points to the near east where Reshep 'of the arrow' is the plague-god in bronze age Ugarit in north Syria and on Cyprus; details of iconography point to a transfer from Cyprus to Spartan Amyclae.

Disease is the result of impurity, healing is purification—in myth, this theme later crystallized around *Orestes, whom Delphic Apollo cleansed of the murder of his mother, and of the concomitant madness. *Oracular Apollo is often connected with purification and plague. But this is only a small part of the much wider oracular function which Apollo had not only in his shrines at Delphi and the Boeotian Ptoion on the Greek mainland, and at Branchidae (see DID-YMA), *Claros, and Gryneum in Asia Minor, but also in his relationship with the *Sibyl(s) and other seers like Bacis or *Cassandra; while the Sibyls are usually priestesses of Apollo, Cassandra refused Apollo as a lover. Apollonian prophecy was usually ecstatic: the Delphic Pythia was possessed by the god, as were the Sibyls, Cassandra, and Bacis; and the *thespiōdos* of Claros attained ecstasy through drinking water. Apollo's wisdom is beyond human rationality.

In Archaic and Classical Greece, Delphi was the central oracular shrine. Though his cult had grown out of purely local worship in the 8th cent., myth saw its foundation as a primordial event, expressing it in the theme of dragon-slaying. Like the island of Delos, marginal Delphi achieved international political importance in Archaic Greece through being marginal. But from his role as a political adviser, Apollo acquired no further political functions—and only a slightly moralistic character.

In Italy, Apollo's arrival in Rome during a plague in 433 BC was due to a recommendation of the Sibylline Books: to avert the plague, a temple of Apollo Medicus was vowed and built just outside the *pomerium*. Mainly in response to Mark Antony's adoption of Dionysus (see ANTO-NIUS, MARCUS), *Augustus made Apollo his special god. In 31, he *vowed a second temple to Apollo in Rome after the battle of *Actium, where, from his nearby sanctuary, the god was said to have helped against Mark Antony and Cleopatra; the temple was built and dedicated in 28, close to the house of Augustus on the *Palatine, with a magnificent adjoining library. See DIVINATION; ORACLES.

Apollodōrus (1) (c.394–after 343 BC), the elder son of the Athenian banker *Pasion, was a minor politician and assiduous litigant. He is the speaker of seven speeches, wrongly attributed to *Demosthenes (2), which provide much information about him and his family. He repeatedly quarrelled with his step-father *Phormion (2) over money, and in c.349 made an unsuccessful attempt to prosecute him for embezzlement. In the late 340s he prosecuted Neaera, the wife of a political opponent, for illegal usurpation of Athenian *citizenship (see Demosthenes 59). She was a former courtesan, and the speech is a rich source of information about the Athenian *demi-monde* (see HETAIRAI).

Apollodōrus (2), of Athens (c.180–after 120 BC), the last of a series of intellectual giants in *Alexandria.

His *Chronicle* was based on the researches of *Eratosthenes, although it extended coverage beyond the death of *Alexander (2) the Great to Apollodorus' time. Written in comic trimeters which made it easy to memorize, it covered successive periods of history, philosophical schools, and the life and work of individuals from the fall of Troy (1184) to 146/5; later it was continued to 119 or 110/9 BC. Apollodorus often synchronized events and used archon lists for dating. *On the Gods* was a rationalistic account of Greek religion, much used by later writers, including *Philodemus.

Apollodorus' authority gave rise to imitations, including the extant *Library*, a study of Greek heroic myth, which presents an uncritical summary of traditional mythology (1st or 2nd cent. AD). See TIME-RECKONING; MYTHOGRAPHERS.

Apollodōrus (3), of *Damascus, building-expert (*architektōn*), to whom are attributed the *forum Traiani and baths of *Trajan (he may therefore be responsible for *Trajan's Column) and Trajan's bridge over the upper Danube. He is said to have disagreed with *Hadrian, having mocked his innovative architectural interest in 'pumpkins'—the complex vaulted structures that were to be so characteristic of the imperial villa at *Tibur—and to have been banished and later killed for criticizing the emperor's temple of Venus and Rome.

Apollōnius (1) **Rhodius,** a major literary figure of 3rd-cent. *Alexandria, royal tutor, head of the Library, and poet of the *Argonautica*, the only extant Greek *hexameter *epic written between *Homer and the Roman imperial period.

Works

Argonautica Hexameter epic on the *Argonautic legend in four long books. It was very important at Rome, where it was translated, is a major influence on *Catullus 64 and *Virgil's *Aeneid*, and, with the *Aeneid*, forms the basis of *Valerius Flaccus' *Argonautica*.

Books 1–2 deal with the outward voyage, to recover the Golden Fleece, from Iolcus in Thessaly to the Colchian city of Aia at the eastern edge of the Black (*Euxine) Sea, which is ruled over by Aiētēs, the cruel son of *Helios. The major events of this voyage are a stay at Lemnos, where the local women, who have murdered the entire male population, seize the chance for procreation, and *Jason (1) sleeps with Queen

*Hypsipylē; the loss of *Heracles from the expedition; a boxing-match between Amycus, king of the Bebrycians, and Polydeuces (see DIOSCURI); meeting with the blind prophet Phineus, whom the Argonauts save from the depredations of the Harpies ('snatchers', winged female personifications of stormy weather) and who, in return, tells them of the voyage ahead; passage through the Clashing Rocks (Symplēgadēs) which guard the entrance to the Black Sea; meeting on the island of Ares with the sons of Phrixus, who had fled Greece on the golden-fleeced ram. In bk. 3 Jason asks Aietes to grant him the fleece; this the king agrees to do on the condition that Jason ploughs an enormous field with fire-breathing bulls, sows it with dragon's teeth, and slays the armed warriors who rise up from the ground. Jason succeeds in this, because, at the instigation of Jason's protector Hera, the king's daughter, *Medea, falls in love with the hero and supplies him with a magic salve to protect him and give him superhuman strength. In bk. 4 Medea flees to join the Argonauts and secures the Fleece for them from the grove where it is guarded by a sleepless dragon. The Argonauts flee via a great river which is pictured as flowing from the Black Sea to the Adriatic; at the Adriatic mouth, Jason and Medea lure her brother, Apsyrtus, who commands the pursuing Colchians, to his death, a crime for which Zeus decides that they must be purified by Medea's aunt *Circe, who lives on the west coast of Italy. They reach Circe via rivers (the Po (*Padus) and the Rhône) imagined to link NE Italy with the western Mediterranean. From there they sail to Drepanē (Corfu), Homer's Scheria, where Jason and Medea are married, and are then driven to the wastes of Libya where they are again saved by divine intervention. They finally return home via Crete, where Medea uses her magic powers to destroy the bronze giant Talos who guards the island.

The central poetic technique of Apollonius is the creative reworking of *Homer. While the Hellenistic poet takes pains to avoid the repetitiveness characteristic of Archaic epic, Homer is the main influence on every aspect of the poem, from the details of language to large-scale *narrative patterns, material culture, and technology (e.g. sailing), which is broadly 'Homeric'. This is most obvious in set scenes such as the Catalogue of Argonauts, corresponding to Homer's Catalogue of Ships, the meeting of *Hera, *Athena, and *Aphrodite on *Olympus at the start of bk. 3, which has many forerunners in Homer, the scenes in the palace of Aietes, corresponding to the scenes of the *Odyssey* on

Scheria, and the voyage in the western Mediterranean, corresponding to *Odysseus' adventures on his way home. These scenes function by contrast: the Homeric 'model' is the base-text by which what is importantly different in the later poem is highlighted. Individual characters too owe much to Homeric predecessors, while also being markedly different from them: e.g. Jason/*Odysseus, Medea/Nausicaa and Circe. After Homer, the two most important literary influences are Pindar's account of the Argonauts and Euripides' *Medea*; the events of the tragedy are foreshadowed in a number of places in the epic—perhaps most strikingly in the murder of Apsyrtus, who goes to his death 'like a tender child'—and the epic shows that the events of the tragedy were 'inevitable', given the earlier history of Jason and Medea.

The *Argonautica* is a brilliant and disturbing achievement, a poem shot through with intelligence and deep irony.

Apollōnius (2), mathematician (fl. 200 BC). Born at Pergē in Pamphylia, he composed the first version, in eight books, of his *Conics* in *Alexandria 'somewhat too hurriedly'. Of the revised version of *Conics* the first four books survive in Greek and the next three in Arabic translation; the eighth is lost. Apollonius states that the first four books form an elementary introduction, while the remainder are particular extensions. He claims no originality for the content of *Conics* 1–4, but says quite correctly that he expounds the fundamental properties 'more fully and generally' than his predecessors.

Apollonius did for conics what Euclid had done for elementary geometry: both his terminology and his methods became canonical and eliminated the work of his predecessors. Like Euclid, too, his exposition follows the logical rather than the original sequence of working. Investigation of the latter has revealed how 'algebraic' his methods are. His silence on some features of conics is not due to ignorance, but to the elementary nature of the treatise; the specialized investigations of bks. 5–7 cover only a selection of possible topics, but bk. 5 in particular reveals Apollonius as an original mathematical genius.

Apollōnius (3) (3rd cent. BC) served *Ptolemy (1) II as chief minister in Egypt and is best known as holder of a large crown-gift estate in the *Fayūm. It formed the centre of a series of agricultural experiments (in arboriculture, viticulture, crops, and livestock) and was managed by Zenon of Caunus, who came to the Fayūm in

256 and stayed on in the area after leaving Apollonius' service. The collection of Zenon's papyri is the largest from the period. It illustrates these and Apollonius' other interests: textile-manufacturing at *Memphis, his contacts in *Alexandria, and commercial dealings, including slave-trading, in the Levant (see SLAVERY).

Apollōnius (4), **of Tyana** (in Cappodocia), a Neopythagorean holy man, whose true history and persona are elusive. Acc. to the only full account, the highly untrustworthy 'biography' of *Philostratus, he was born at the beginning of the 1st cent. AD and survived into the reign of *Nerva. He led the life of an *ascetic wandering teacher, visited distant lands (including India), advised cities (e.g. Sparta), had life-threatening encounters with Nero and Domitian, of whose murder he became clairvoyantly aware in mid-lecture, and on his own death underwent heavenly assumption. He was the object of posthumous cult attracting the patronage of the Severan emperors; pagan apologists compared him favourably to Jesus.

appāritōrēs, salaried officials who attended Roman magistrates and priests. They constituted one of the few resources of executive agency and administrative expertise available to magistrates, and gained power which they often abused. Appointed by the patronage of the magistrates, they served for more than their patron's year of office. These officials held the highest public appointment open to non-senators under the republic, and constituted an order, entry to which provided a reflection of social promotion for *freedmen and people from outside Rome; during the empire the social standing of the grander *apparitores* was little lower than the *equestrian order. Their standing was reflected in a complex organization into corporations according to function, which seems to have been reordered in the early empire, when new grades serving the emperor as magistrate were created. The *scribae* (broadly 'clerks', though serving also as accountants and cashiers) were the highest in prestige (*Horace was at least briefly *scriba* to the quaestors who ran the treasury, see AERARIUM), followed by the *lictors* who carried the insignia of *imperium*, the *fasces*, and acted as a bodyguard, the *viatores* or general errand-runners, and the *praecōnēs* or public criers.

Appendix Vergiliana, a collection of Latin poems of varied provenance and genre traditionally ascribed to *Virgil.

Appian, Greek historian. Born in *Alexandria at the end of the 1st cent. AD, he experienced the Jewish rising of AD 116/17, became a Roman citizen, moved to Rome as an *advocate and eventually gained, through the influence of his friend *Cornelius Fronto, the rank of a *procurator under *Antoninus Pius, which enabled him to devote his time to writing a Roman History. After the preface and bk. 1 on Rome in the period of the kings, the work is arranged ethnographically, dealing with the individual peoples as Rome conquered them: bk. 2, Italians; 3, Samnites; 4, Celts; 5, Sicilians; 6, Iberians; 7, *Hannibal; 8, Carthaginians (Libyans and Nomads); 9, Macedonians and Illyrians; 10, Greeks and Ionians; 11, Syrians (Seleucids) and Parthians; and 12, *Mithradates VI.; 13–17 treat the Civil Wars; 18–21, the wars in Egypt; 22, the century up to *Trajan; 23, Trajan's campaigns against Dacians, Jews, and Pontic peoples; and 24, Arabians. A survey of Rome's military and financial system was apparently not yet written when Appian died in the 160s. The preface, bks. 6–9, and 11–17 survive complete, apart from 8b on the Nomads and 9a on the Macedonians (of which only fragments exist) as well as 11b on the Parthians (11b was perhaps unfinished at Appian's death); 1–5 are fragmentary, 10 and 18–24 lost.

In order to accommodate a millennium of Roman history in a single work, Appian greatly, but not always successfully, reduced the material he chose from a variety of Greek and Latin authors, among them *Hieronymus of Cardia, *Polybius, and Roman annalists like *Asinius Pollio, *Caesar, and *Augustus. Since some of his valuable sources, esp. on the Civil Wars, are otherwise lost, his work gains historical importance for us, even though it does not simply reproduce these sources. Recent research has stressed Appian's own conscious contribution not only in choosing, reducing, and arranging the material, but also in the independent composition of speeches, in the introduction of episodes from the rhetorical repertoire, and in detailed interference with the sources in view of his avowed aims: a proud citizen of Alexandria, Appian makes events in Egypt the climax of his work; a convinced monarchist, he explains, not always correctly, Roman republican institutions to his Greek audience; a stout conservative, he regards a lack of popular concord, as witnessed in the Civil Wars, as cataclysmic; unusually interested in administration and finance, he preserves more social and economic information than most historiographers; above all, an ardent admirer of Rome, Appian explains her success through reference to the Romans' good counsel, endurance, patience, moderation, and, esp., overall virtue.

Appuleius Sāturnīnus, Lūcius, of praetorian family and a good popular orator, as quaestor at *Ostia was superseded in his *cura annonae by *Aemilius Scaurus and turned against the ruling oligarchy. As tribune 103 he sought the favour of *Marius by passing a law assigning land to his African veterans. Probably in that year, he passed a corn law against violent opposition by *optimate tribunes and a law setting up a permanent tribunal of inquiry (*quaestio) on *maiestas, directed (if in 103) against unpopular *nobiles. He and Servilius Glaucia continued turbulent action in 102 and 101. Caecilius Metellus Numidicus tried, as censor, to expel them from the senate, but was prevented by his colleague. Tribune again in 100, he again co-operated with Marius by proposing to settle the veterans of his German war in Transalpine Gaul and to give Marius a limited (and probably traditional) right to enfranchise non-Roman colonists. An oath of obedience, to be taken by all magistrates and senators, was attached to the law. Marius found an evasive formula allowing senators to swear it without disgrace, but Metellus refused and went into exile. Marius and Saturninus were later suspected of conspiring to bring this about. With the help of Glaucia, now praetor and supported by the *equestrians because of his extortion law, Saturninus also proposed colonies and land assignments for Roman and Italian veterans of other armies that had fought in Thrace and Sicily and of *proletarii. Re-elected tribune for 99, he hoped to have Glaucia as consul, but Marius, now suspicious of their ambitions, rejected Glaucia's candidacy as illegal. After having a hostile candidate murdered in the electoral assembly, Saturninus, by massive use of force in the *concilium plebis, tried to pass a law allowing Glaucia's candidacy. In the resulting riot, the senate, on the motion of the *princeps senatus Aemilius Scaurus, passed the *senatus consultum ultimum—its first use against a tribune in office—and Marius organized an attack on the agitators. On receiving an official promise of safety, they surrendered to him and were imprisoned in the senate-house, but were murdered by a mob without receiving any protection from Marius (probably autumn 100). This embittered their surviving adherents against Marius. Saturninus' colonies were not founded, but his land assignments seem to have been recognized.

Apuleius, writer and orator, b. *c.* AD 125 of prosperous parents at Madaurus in Africa Proconsularis, and educated in Carthage, Athens, and Rome; at Athens he gained enough philosophy to be called *philosophus Platōnicus* by himself and others. He claims to have travelled widely as a young man, and was on his way to *Alexandria when he arrived at Oea, probably in the winter of AD 156. The story from that point is told by Apuleius himself in his *Apology*, no doubt in the most favourable version possible; at Oea he met an ex-pupil from Athens, who persuaded him to stay there for a year and eventually to marry his mother Pudentilla in order to protect her fortune for the family. Later, Apuleius was accused by other relatives of Pudentilla of having induced her to marry him by magical means; the case was heard at Sabratha, near Oea, in late 158 or early 159. We can infer from the publication of the *Apology* (see below) that he was acquitted. Apuleius was active as a public speaker and philosophical lecturer in Carthage in the 160s, and he seems to have been made priest of the imperial cult for his province; nothing is known of him after 170.

Works (1) The *Apology*, Apuleius' speech of defence against charges of *magic (see above) is a rhetorical *tour de force*. In rebutting the charges Apuleius digresses hugely in order to show a vast range of learning, and presents himself as a committed intellectual and philosopher. The title recalls *Plato's *Apology*, the argumentation Cicero at his most colourful.

(2) The *Metamorphoses*, sometimes called the *Golden Ass*, is the only Latin *novel which survives whole. On an epic scale (eleven books) and full of narratological cleverness, erotic, humorous, and sensational by turns, it is a fascinating work. The story is that of the young man Lucius, who through his curiosity to discover the secrets of witchcraft is metamorphosed into an ass and undergoes a variety of picaresque adventures before being retransformed through the agency of *Isis. This plot is punctuated by a number of inserted tales, which have in fact a close thematic relation to the main narrative; the most substantial and best known of them is that of Cupid and Psyche ('Soul' in Greek, see PSYCHE), which parallels the main story of Lucius by presenting a character (Psyche) whose disastrous curiosity causes troublesome adventures before her rescue through divine agency. The last book provides a much discussed and controversial double twist: after his rescue by Isis, Lucius' low-life adventures are

interpreted in a new religious and providential light, and the identity of the narrator seems to switch from Lucius to Apuleius himself, a final metamorphosis. The novel's literary influences are various, including much Greek and Latin poetry; the main ass-tale is partly paralleled by the *Ass* dubiously ascribed to *Lucian, and the two may well have a common source. Many of the stories may derive from the tradition of bawdy Milesian Tales, and that of Cupid and Psyche, with its element of Platonic allegory, may owe at least something to a Greek source.

(3) The *Flōrida* ('colourful passages') are a short collection, derived from a longer one, of choice excerpts from Apuleius' showy *declamations given at Carthage in the 160s, containing passages of narrative, description, and anecdote, which show considerable talent.

(4) *On the God of Socrates* is a declamation on the *daimonion* of *Socrates, probably based on a Greek original, showing Apuleius' Platonic interests as well as his oratorical skills.

The style of Apuleius is admired by many; it is the apex of '*Asianism' in Latin, full of poetic and archaic words and apparent coinages, rhyming cola, and coloured with colloquialism and Graecisms; it is best seen in the great set pieces of the *Metamorphoses*. His literary personality is strongly projected in all his works, and in the range they cover: proud of his abilities as a speaker and writer, possessed of certitude and a vast if indiscriminate learning, he is best seen as a Latin sophist, matching in the Roman west the extravert and self-promoting characters who were his contemporaries in the Greek *Second Sophistic. Some of his later fame is initially owed to St *Augustine, his fellow-African, who was aware of Apuleius' prestige in his home province and was careful to attack him, but the *Metamorphoses* have been deservedly popular from the early Renaissance on.

Aquae Sulis The hot springs (hence mod. Bath) were developed from the Neronian period and attained great elaboration, rivalling the largest Gallic establishments. The hot spring was enclosed in a polygonal reservoir in the SE corner of a colonnaded precinct within which stood the temple with its altar in front. The temple of Sulis *Minerva carried the famous *Gorgon pediment. South of the precinct the spring connected with the principal suite of baths. The defences (constructed in the late 2nd cent.) enclosed other less well-known structures within their 9.3 ha. (23 acres). There was an extensive extramural settlement. Many inscrip-

tions record visitors from Britain and abroad, whilst excavation of the sacred spring has produced 130 curse-tablets (see CURSES), the most important such archive for Romano-Celtic religion yet published.

aqueducts In a Mediterranean climate, correcting the accidents of rainfall distribution through the management of water-sources transforms *agriculture by extending the growing-season through the dry summer by means of *irrigation, allows agglomerations of population beyond the resources of local springs or wells, eases waterlogging through drainage in the wetter zones, and protects against floods caused by violent winter rainfall.

Hydraulic engineering was therefore both useful and prestigious. It was quickly adopted by the nascent cities of the Greek world and their leaders: ground-level aqueducts bringing water from extramural springs into Greek cities were at least as old as the 6th cent. BC: notable late-Archaic examples are at Athens, using clay piping (see ATHENS, TOPOGRAPHY), and on *Samos, where the water was channelled by rock-hewn tunnel through the acropolis. A more elaborate system was constructed in the 2nd cent. BC by *Eumenes II at *Pergamum. It may have helped inspire the first important aqueduct at Rome, the aqua Marcia of 144 BC. It was the first to use *arches on a large scale. The city was, however, already served by two water-leats, for the most part in underground tunnels, called aqua Appia (312) and aqua Anio Vetus (272).

A copious supply of clean water was needed for a steadily increasing population. Most aqueducts, moreover (more or less legally), provided some water for irrigation in the market-garden belts in and around city walls. But the growing popularity of water-intensive services such as *baths and fountains (see NYMPHAEUM) also promoted the development of the aqueduct system, while there was considerable kudos to be gained by such spectacular reworkings of the dispositions of nature. By the imperial period, aqueducts became a widespread status symbol, and the great bridges (like the Pont du Gard on the Nîmes aqueduct) owe something to the need for visibility and show.

Imperial benefaction created the most ambitious projects. As a sign of Rome's status as world-capital and to supply their elaborate waterworks, Agrippa and Augustus added three aqueducts to its stock, and established an administrative infrastructure for maintaining the system (see CURA(TIO)). Aquae Iuliae or Augustae became standard in the repertoire of what favoured cities in Italy might receive. The Claudian aqueducts at Rome, aqua Claudia and Anio Novus, were also on the most ambitious scale, with very long sections on arches to maintain the head of water necessary for access all across the city of Rome. Further additions to the network were made under Trajan and Caracalla (for his baths): we know less about the period after the work of *Iulius Frontinus, our outstandingly detailed description of Rome's aqueducts in c. AD 100. Dues were payable for private use of water, but no attempt was made in any city to cover the cost of the system, which always remained a public benefaction. See WATER.

Arabs, ancient tribes and peoples who lived in, and around the modern Arabian peninsula. *Herodotus was acquainted with the Arabs of southern Palestine and the Sinai, and mentions the Arabs of the *incense region. For classical authors the defining features of the Arabs (in the Bible as well) are *nomadism, pastoralism, and the *camel-based caravan trade.

Aramaic, a Semitic language, was used in the near east from early in the 1st millennium BC and through the Roman period. Originating in upper Mesopotamia, it was used widely by the Assyrian and Persian administrations. After the fall of the Persian empire Aramaic continued to be used in the *Hellenizing cities of Palmyra, Petra, etc., as well as in the *Parthian east. There are many Greek–Aramaic bilingual inscriptions.

Āra Pācis, a monumental altar erected in the northern *Campus Martius near the via Lata, one of the major products of Augustan public art. It was voted in 13 BC by the senate, as *Augustus records in his *Res Gestae, to commemorate his safe return from Gaul and Spain; and finished in 9. The altar proper was surrounded by a walled precinct with entrances to east and west, and decorated with sculptured reliefs on two tiers. Internally there were festoons slung from ox-heads above and fluting below; externally the lower frieze was filled with complex acanthus scrolls, above which on the east and west were mythical panels, on the north and south a religious procession showing the imperial family, *lictors, priests, magistrates, and representations of the Roman people. Smaller reliefs on the inner altar, showing *Vestals, priests, sacrificial animals,

etc., continue the procession on the outer walls. The event represented by this procession is disputed.

In 1937–8 the site was thoroughly explored and the monument reconstructed, with most of its surviving sculptures, between the Mausoleum of Augustus and the Tiber. See SCULPTURE, ROMAN.

Arātus, Greek poet, c.315 to before 240 BC. Born in Cilicia, he studied at Athens, where he imbibed *Stoicism from *Zeno (2) and was introduced to Antigonus Gonatas, king of Macedon, who invited him to the court at Pella. There he celebrated the king's marriage, and composed a *Hymn to *Pan* glorifying Antigonus' victory over the Celts (277).

Aratus' best-known work, and the only one extant, is a poem entitled *Phaenomena* ('Celestial Phenomena'), undertaken at the suggestion of Antigonus. The first and longest part of this is a versification of a prose treatise by *Eudoxus which gave a detailed description of the make-up and relative positions of the *constellations. After a proem to *Zeus, Aratus describes the poles and the north constellations, the south constellations, enumerates the principal circles of the celestial sphere, and lists the simultaneous risings and settings of many combinations of the constellations, supposedly for telling the time at night. The second part of the poem deals with weather signs. Although it has a separate title and is derived from a different source, it is an integral part of the poem. After enumerating the days of the lunar month, and mentioning the seasons and *Meton's 19-year calendaric cycle, Aratus gives weather prognostications, not only from the celestial bodies, but also from terrestrial phenomena and animal behaviour. The poem is enlivened by mythical allusions and picturesque digressions, longest being descriptions of the *golden age and of storms at sea. The author's Stoicism is apparent esp. in the proem, where 'Zeus' is the Stoic all-informing deity.

Phaenomena achieved immediate fame and lasting popularity beyond the circle of learned poets: it became the most widely read poem, after the *Iliad* and *Odyssey*, in the ancient world, and was one of the very few Greek poems translated into Arabic. Latin translations were made by *Cicero, and *Germanicus. It was read more for its literary charm than its astronomical content, but some commentaries criticized the many grave astronomical errors which it contains.

arboriculture, tree cultivation. In the first millennium BC there was a remarkable expansion of fruit-tree cultivation around the Mediterranean. The productivity of *agriculture was increased because trees were often intercropped with cereals and legumes, increasing total yields per unit area. These developments laid the economic foundations for the prosperity of Greek and Roman civilization and made diets more diverse and more nutritious. The most important of the trees in question were the *olive, vine (see WINE), fig, apple, pear, plum, pistachio, walnut, chestnut, carob, date-palm, peach, almond, pomegranate, sweet and sour cherry-trees. The cultivation of many of these species of trees depended on the spread of the technique of grafting. The Roman *agricultural writers tell us about arboriculture. Trees were also important for *timber. It was needed for shipbuilding, houses, firewood and many other purposes. *Theophrastus describes the uses of different types of timber in his *Research on Plants*. The demand for timber sometimes resulted in deforestation.

'Arcadia' See PASTORAL POETRY, GREEK and LATIN; VIRGIL (section on '*Eclogues*').

Arcesilāus or **Arcesilas,** of Pitane in Aeolis, 316/5–242/1 BC, head of the *Academy from c.269. He introduced scepticism (see SCEPTICS) into Plato's school, thereby founding the 'New Academy'. He seems to have appealed to the examples of *Socrates and Plato. Like Socrates, Arcesilaus would examine or argue against a given thesis and make no assertions of his own. His professed attitude of withholding assent was adopted to avoid error and rashness of judgement.

Arcesilaus' most influential and famous argument was directed against the Stoic theory of knowledge (see STOICISM). He argued that given the definition of the Stoic criterion of truth, the so-called cognitive impression, one could show that nothing could be grasped or apprehended, since it was impossible to find an impression of such a kind that it could not be false. For any true and clear impression one could describe a situation in which an otherwise indistinguishable impression would be false. Since the Stoics held that the wise man would never assent to a false impression, it followed that the Stoic sage must withhold judgement on all matters. To the Stoic objection that suspension of judgement would make action, and hence life, impossible, Arcesilaus replied that it was possible to act

without assenting to anything, and that in the absence of certain knowledge a wise man could be guided by 'what is reasonable'.

The thesis that 'nothing can be grasped' has been described as a doctrine of the sceptical Academy, but this is a mistake: Arcesilaus and his successors down to *Carneades insisted that they did not know or assert that nothing could be known, any more than they knew or asserted any other philosophical thesis.

arch, triumphal See TRIUMPHAL ARCH.

archaeology, classical, the study of the material culture of ancient Greece and Rome. *Epigraphy, the study of inscriptions on permanent materials, is today seen as a branch of historical rather than of archaeological enquiry; while numismatics, the study of *coins, has become a largely independent discipline.

The collection of works of art, a prerogative of wealth rather than of learning, helped to confer on the subject in its early years a social prestige at least as prominent as its intellectual. Such excavation as took place before the mid-19th cent. was usually explicitly directed towards the recovery of works of art, with the textual evidence serving as a guide or, where it was not directly applicable, as an arbiter. Once the volume of available finds reached a certain critical mass, a further motive came into play: that of providing models for the better training of artists and architects.

Textual evidence, collectors' preference, and the frequency of recovery combined to make *sculpture pre-eminent among the visual arts. Only in the opening years of the 19th cent., with the transport of the *Parthenon, *Bassae, and *Aegina sculptures to London and to Munich, did even the learned world begin to glimpse the full scope of classical sculpture. From then on, leadership in this field passed to Germany.

With classical *painting, the natural starting-point was the rich series of murals excavated at *Herculaneum, *Pompeii, and other sites from the Vesuvian destruction of AD 79, in the years from 1739 on. Some reflection of lost Greek masterpieces was recognized in these, but in this case there was no salvation to come from the later recovery of the originals. Instead, attention was diverted to Greek painted vases which (though not yet recognized as Greek) had begun to appear in numbers in Italian graves in the 1720s (see POTTERY, GREEK). Then, later in the same century, the foundations were laid for a branch of classical archaeology which, for the first time, owed almost nothing to the surviving textual evidence. Interest was at first directed to the interpretation of the figured scenes on the vases. Late in the 19th cent., there was a shift to the increasingly detailed study of classification, chronology, and, above all, attribution of the works to individual artists. This phase, with which the name of Beazley (1885-1970) is inseparably associated, lasted for three generations and absorbed the energies of some of the most distinguished figures in the history of the discipline. With Beazley's death, the unique authority of his attributions was no longer available and there was a marked reversion to the study of the content of the scenes (see IMAGERY). Meanwhile Roman wall-painting and *mosaic came to be increasingly treated as manifestations of Roman culture in its own right, rather than as reflections of lost Greek work. The interaction of such art with its architectural setting has become a particular object of research.

The modern history of fieldwork in the Greek world—that is, its redirection towards the goal of recovery of the entire range of the preserved material culture—began with the adoption of a more systematic strategy in the excavation of Pompeii from 1860 on, and received its greatest single stimulus from the discoveries of Schliemann at *Troy, *Mycenae, and Tiryns in the 1870s and 1880s. The revelation that the soil could still hold secrets on the scale of whole civilizations—those of the bronze age Aegean—whose existence had not previously been suspected, acted as a spur to many other large-scale projects. In Greece, these have primarily been directed at the great *sanctuaries, with the German expedition to *Olympia (1875-) giving a notable lead, followed by the Greek excavations on the Athenian Acropolis (1882- ; see ATHENS, TOPOGRAPHY), and the French missions to *Delphi (1892-) and *Delos (1904-). Large areas of major settlement-sites have also been excavated, notably by the Americans at *Corinth (1896-), *Olynthus (1928-38), and the *Agora of Athens (1931-). In Italy the greatest single focus of interest has naturally been Rome itself, where the discoveries cover almost every aspect of ancient urban life and span many centuries. By far the most extensive field of activity, however, involving intensive work in at least 30 modern countries, has been the archaeology of the Roman empire.

The most prominent recent innovation in fieldwork has been the introduction of intensive surface survey. This technique involves the systematic searching of a tract of landscape, without discrimination in favour of 'likely' locations, to find traces of the pattern of past settlement and activity. It is directed at the acquisition of regional knowledge, esp. for the rural sector. Scientific techniques—for determining the provenance of manufactured objects, for the fuller classification of organic matter, for detection of buried features, and esp. for dating—have been used increasingly. In the last-named field, the most striking progress has been made by dendrochronology, which, by building up a sequence from a series of trees extending backwards in time, makes it possible to offer absolute dates for tree-rings in structural timbers and other large wooden objects.

Archelāus, king of Macedon (413-399 BC). He gained the throne by murder and was eventually assassinated by two male lovers. His reign is notable for co-operation with Athens (supply of shipbuilding materials), increasing security (fortress- and road-building; improvement of infantry and cavalry; matrimonial alliances), increasing wealth (resumption of silver coinage), transfer of major residence to Pella (strategically important; became the largest Macedonian city), and a 'Hellenizing' policy (theatre festival at Dium; patronage of *Zeuxis, *Timotheus, *Agathon, and *Euripides).

archers (Greek and Hellenistic) In *Homer's *Iliad* the bow is used by only one or two heroes on either side, and there is some suggestion that archers were despised. *Pandarus' bow was clearly composite, since horn was used in its construction. Horn was also used in the construction of *Odysseus' bow, and he apparently strings it sitting down, for such a bow was easier to string if one end could be anchored under a leg.

In historical times, archery continued to flourish in *Crete, and Cretan archers often figure as *mercenaries down to Roman times. But bowmen rarely appear among the troops of other Greek states. Athens also had some presumably native archers at the battle of *Plataea, and by 432 both mounted and foot-archers; four regularly served on Athenian *triremes.

Despite the respect accorded to Persian archers, they evidently had little effect on *hoplites. At the battle of *Marathon the Greek charge at the double was probably intended to leave the Persian archers as little time to shoot as possible, but at Plataea, although the Spartans and their comrades allegedly endured their fire for some time, casualties were slight. This probably explains why Greek states hardly bothered to raise organized forces of archers.

The rise of *Macedon ushered in an era when all arms were integrated into more complex forces, and archers played a more important role, *Alexander (2) the Great, using both Cretan and Macedonian archers. But even in Hellenistic warfare, archers were never battle-winners. Only, perhaps, at Carrhae in 53 BC, when *Crassus was overwhelmed by the *Parthians, was a large-scale battle won by archery fire, and this was in exceptional circumstances.

The extreme range of the ancient bow has been estimated to be between 300 and 250 m. (328 and 273 yds.), but its effective range was probably only up to 150–200 m. (164–219 yds.). Thus, at the double, advancing infantry would have been under fire for only about two minutes, allowing archers perhaps between 20 and 30 volleys.

arches In Greek architecture openings are normally covered by horizontal lintels or beams. The first description of arched construction using voussoirs locked into place by a keystone is attributed to *Democritus by *Seneca the Younger. The earliest attested vaults in Greek architecture are those of the Macedonian tombs, from the mid-4th cent. BC onwards. Arched gateways occur (but rarely) thereafter, esp. in the Hellenistic period.

Arches (and vaults) have been attributed to the *Etruscans, though again early dates are unprovable, and a borrowing from 4th-cent. and Hellenistic Greece seems more likely. Apart from the free-standing *triumphal arch (and the architecturally similar arched gateways in city walls) the most significant Roman use of the arch is in *aqueducts and in continuous arcading, combined with engaged half-columns supporting an overall entablature, first attested in the *Tabularium at Rome, and later used as the normal system for external walls of *amphitheatres and theatre auditoria.

Archidāmus, 'leader of the *dāmos' (*demos), was the name of several Eurypontid kings of Sparta, of whom the most notable was Archidamus II, who married an aunt and reigned for over 40 years (?469–427 BC). He first distinguished himself by his resolute response to the *earthquake of 464, which had prompted a massive revolt of the *helots aided by communities of the *perioikoi in Messenia. But even his seniority

could not dissuade the Spartan assembly from voting for war with Athens in 432, and he led the allied forces in invasions of Attica on three occasions (431, 430, 428); in 429 he started the siege of *Plataea. Twice married, he was allegedly fined on the first occasion for marrying a too short wife (the mother of *Agis II); his second marriage produced *Agesilaus II.

Archilochus, Greek iambic (see below) and elegiac poet, from *Paros. He mentioned *Gyges, who died c.652 BC, and a total solar eclipse which was almost certainly that of 6 April 648; a memorial to his friend Glaucus in late 7th-cent. lettering, has been found on Thasos, where Archilochus spent part of his life. His poetry was concerned with his personal affairs and with contemporary public events— politics, shipwrecks, war, etc. Its tone varied widely, from grave to gay, from pleasantly bantering to bitter. Archilochus was famous throughout antiquity for the stinging wit with which he lashed his enemies and sometimes his friends, and for what appeared to be carefree admissions of such outrageous conduct, as fleeing from battle and abandoning his shield, or compromising young ladies. He repeatedly attacked one Lycambes, who had apparently betrothed his daughter Neobulē to Archilochus but later revoked the agreement. The vengeful poet then produced a series of poems in which he recounted in explicit detail the sexual experiences that he and others had enjoyed with both Neobule and her sister. This (so the legend goes) induced Lycambes and his daughters to hang themselves for shame. We have several fragments from sexual narratives. However, in the 'Cologne Epode' discovered in 1974 Neobule is represented as available for Archilochus, but he dismisses her as overblown and promiscuous, while gently seducing the younger sister. The whole business has to be considered against the background of the Ionian *iambos* (see IAMBIC POETRY, GREEK) and its conventions of bawdy narrative and abuse of individuals.

Archimēdēs, mathematician and inventor (c.287–c.212/11 BC). Born at *Syracuse, son of an astronomer, and killed at the sack of the city by the Romans under *Claudius Marcellus (1), he was on intimate terms with its king *Hieron (2) II. He visited Egypt, but lived most of his life at Syracuse, corresponding with *Conon (2), *Eratosthenes, and others. Popular history knew him as the inventor of marvellous machines used against the Romans at the siege of

Syracuse, and of devices such as the screw for raising water; for his boast 'give me a place to stand and I will move the earth'; for his determination of the proportions of gold and silver in a wreath made for Hieron ('*Eureka*! I've got it!'); for his construction of two 'sphaerae' (a planetarium and a star globe) which were taken to Rome; and for his tomb, which by his wish depicted a cylinder circumscribing a sphere, with the ratio 3:2 which he discovered between them.

His extant works, with the principal features of each, are, in Greek: (1) *On the Sphere and Cylinder*, two books: formulae for the surface-area and volume of a sphere and any segment of it. (2) *Measurement of the Circle*: by inscribing and circumscribing regular polygons of 96 sides, upper and lower limits of $3\frac{1}{7}$ and $3\frac{10}{71}$ are found to the value of π; Archimedes incidentally gives a rational approximation to the square root of 3 and of several large numbers. (3) *On Conoids and Spheroids*: determination of the volumes of segments of solids formed by the revolution of a conic about its axis. (4) *On Spirals*: properties of tangents to the 'Archimedean' spiral and determination of its area. (5) *Equilibriums of Planes* or *Centres of Gravity of Planes*, two books: the theory of the lever is propounded and the centres of gravity of various rectilinear plane figures and of segments of conics are established. (6) *Quadrature of the Parabola*: the area of a parabola is determined first by 'mechanical' (see below) and then by geometrical means. (7) *The Sand-reckoner*: description of a system for expressing enormously large numbers in words (in effect a notation in which 100,000,000 is used as a base as we use 10). Archimedes employs it to express the number of grains of sand which, on certain assumptions, the universe is calculated to contain. It is the only surviving work of Archimedes touching on astronomy, and is our best source for the heliocentric system of *Aristarchus (1). (8) *Method of Mechanical Theorems*: description of the method invented by Archimedes for finding by 'mechanical' means the areas and volumes of the parabola, sphere, etc. (9) *On Floating Bodies*: deals with the positions which segments of a solid of revolution can assume when floating in a fluid; for this Archimedes invented a science of *hydrostatics. The Greek text of the latter two works was discovered in 1906.

The most notable characteristic of Archimedes' mathematical work is its freedom from the trammels of traditional Greek mathematics. It is true that in the *proofs* of those theorems for which the integral calculus is now used (e.g. those determining the surface-area and volume of a sphere or the area of a parabola) he uses the standard Greek method of bypassing infinitesimals (invented by *Eudoxus (1) and employed in Euclid bk. 10). But the *Method* (no. 8 above) reveals that for the *discovery* of these theorems he used a technique which consists of dividing two figures into infinitely thin strips, weighing these strips against each other, and then summing them to get the ratio of the two whole figures. This is analogous to the practice of the developers of the integral calculus in the 17th cent., but unlike them Archimedes recognized its lack of rigour, and used it only as a heuristic procedure. The same freedom of thought appears in arithmetic in the *Sand-reckoner*, which shows an understanding of the nature of a numerical system immeasurably superior to anything else from antiquity. It is this breadth and freedom of vision, rather than the amazing ingenuity which Archimedes displays in the solution of particular problems, which justifies calling him the greatest mathematician of antiquity. His work in hydrostatics (see (9) above) was epoch-making (although the effect in antiquity was negligible). The same is true of statics, though here he probably had predecessors.

architects The names of architects are preserved in literary sources as well as inscriptions. Theodorus, architect of the temple of Asclepius at *Epidaurus, is paid at only double the level of the ordinary craftsmen, suggesting a similar status, but this may be misleading, representing expenses rather than a living wage. *Vitruvius records treatises written by architects, such as Chersiphon and Metagenes, who built the Archaic temple of Artemis at Ephesus, *Ictinus and Carpion on the Parthenon, and the *Carian architect whose writings profoundly influenced him, Hermogenes; this suggests comparability with other educated men (as indeed, his 'On Architecture' requires). Roman architects are mostly anonymous; an exception is *Apollodorus (3).

From the inscriptions, in particular, their role is extensive. In Classical Greece they have to prepare the design (probably not detailed, scale plans, but possibly including full-size examples to be copied) and to draw up specifications to be submitted to the appropriate commissioning bodies (in Athens, ultimately, the assembly), as well as calculating the quantities of material to be ordered, including stone, and the exact dimensions of blocks to be delivered from the *quarries. Though details are lacking from the Roman period, it is clear that the more important architects would have to be masters of design, which included the complex calculations needed for planning the structure of major concrete buildings such as the *Pantheon.

During construction, they would have to supervise the laying out of buildings, calculating the exact positioning of different elements (such as the columns in temples) on the spot. Important Greek buildings sometimes reveal layout marks to facilitate this. They also supervised day by day; the architect named on inscriptions for the work of any year may not be the original designer, esp. if construction was protracted over many years. See ARCHITECTURE; ARTISANS AND CRAFTSMEN.

architecture

Greek The forms of Greek architecture evolved essentially in the 7th and 6th cents. BC. After the collapse of *Mycenaean civilization, construction methods relapsed into the simplest forms of mud-brick and timber, mostly in small hut structures, the main exception being the great 10th-cent. apsidal building at *Lefkandi.

The development of the Archaic period centred on *temples, which in size and expense always constituted the most important building type in the Greek world. Some of the earliest examples such as the little temple of c.750 BC at Perachora retained the apsidal form, while one at *Eretria was curvilinear. This soon gives way to the rectangular cella, in major buildings entered by a porch at one end, balanced by a similar but false porch at the back (western Greek temples omit this in favour of an adytum, an internal room at the back of the cella) and surrounded by a colonnade. Such temples of the first part of the 7th cent. as that to Poseidon at Isthmia, and to *Hera in the Argive and Samian Heraia were, like Lefkandi, 'hundred-footers', with steps and wall-footings of cut stone, but with wooden columns. They anticipated the forms of the Classical *orders of architecture.

Construction in stone, employing the Doric or Ionic orders, developed in the late 7th cent., when the Greeks began to have direct experience of Egypt, learning the methods of quarrying and working stone. The architectural form of temples built early in the 6th cent., the temples of *Artemis at *Corcyra (Doric), and the House of the Naxians on *Delos—probably a temple of Apollo—(Ionic), shows that the arrangements and details of the orders were established by then, and in the case of Doric, they clearly imitate forms evolved from the earlier wooden structures. Thereafter architecture as applied to temples is a matter of refinement and improvement, rather than radical development and change. Ionic architects (esp. in the *Cyclades) were using *marble in the early 6th cent. Limestone remained the normal material in Peloponnese, even for major temples such as that of *Zeus at *Olympia (c.470), and in the temples of Sicily and Italy, but the opening of the quarries of *Pentelicon in the late 6th cent. led to the splendid series of Athenian marble temples of the 5th century.

Refinement concentrated on detail: the balance of proportions in all parts of the structure, in the precise form of column, capital, entablature, and above all the decorative mouldings. Colour was also used, now generally lost from temples and other normal buildings but well preserved on the façades and interiors of the built Macedonian vaulted tombs of the 4th cent. and later (such as the royal tombs at Vergina; see AEGAE). Here the façades, which imitate temple and related architectural forms, have their painted decoration perfectly preserved because they were buried immediately after the decoration was added. The colours are harsh, positive blues and reds, with some patterning in contrasting yellow and gold. Refinement of architectural form involves the use of subtle curves rather than straight lines for the profiles of the columns: these evolve from the cruder curvature of early Doric, perhaps itself derived from the naturalistic curvature of Egyptian plant-form columns, and curvature of the temple base carried up to the entablature may be intended to correct optical illusion, as also the slight inward inclination of columns. Ionic buildings always used slender columns; Doric, very massive at first, becomes more slender— though the continued refinement into the Hellenistic period suggests that the 5th-cent. marble forms of Periclean Athens were not recognized as ideal, and 'Ictinus' interest in the mathematical relationship of various parts, particularly the ratio $2^2:3^2$, demonstrated in the *Parthenon, is not generally imitated.

The procedures of design employed by *architects are uncertain. Scale plans are known in Egypt, but their use in Greece was probably restricted by lack of drawing material and the limitations of the Greek numerical system, esp. for fractions. Procedures were more likely based on experience and tradition, details of layout being worked out *in situ*. 'Examples', probably full-scale, of detailed elements would be supplied to the *quarries and craftsmen as necessary. Structural systems were simple, based on the principle of post and beam, and dimensions were restricted by the size of available timber beams, generally not more than 12 m. (39 ft.). In temple architecture there is no complexity of plan, apart from the quite exceptional *Erechtheum at Athens.

Other building forms evolve more slowly, and are always influenced by concepts employed in temples. Usually they are less lavish, and economy in construction is an important factor. Colonnades, which had developed largely as a decorative or prestige factor, could be employed extensively in more utilitarian structures, either as free-standing buildings (stoas) or extended round courtyards, both providing scope for adding rooms behind the resulting portico, which could be put to a variety of purposes (see STOA). As a result, a new principle of architectural design emerges. Temples were essentially free-standing buildings, viewed from the surrounding space. Buildings based on the courtyard principle, which by the 6th cent. had been adapted as the normal arrangement for Greek *houses, were intended to be seen from within, from the space they surrounded. These developments are seen in more progressive places, such as Athens in the 5th cent. BC, esp. in the buildings surrounding the Agora. Theatre structures were still relatively undeveloped (see THEATRE STAGING, GREEK), and the theatre at Athens did not attain architectural form until the construction of the stone-seated auditorium in the second half of the 4th cent. Buildings might now be more complex in plan, though simple rectangles, or rectangular courtyards, were still preferred, with single roof levels. Curvilinear forms are rare, restricted to a few circular buildings (such as the *tholos, and the curvilinear auditorium of theatres). Some complex plans exist, such as the *Propylaea to the Athenian acropolis (436–432 BC), or the near contemporary Erechtheum, but even here the architect is constrained to think in terms of the juxtaposition of rectangular blocks, though using different roof levels, rather than a fully integrated overall design.

The Hellenistic period sees the widest application of Greek architectural forms, with developed arrangements, based on courtyard principles, for exercise grounds and planned agoras. Much structure remained in mud-brick and timber, but there was now more application of stone construction, with columns, to buildings other than temples. Here the simpler Doric order was generally preferred to Ionic.

Roman Roman architecture represents the fusion of traditional Greek elements, notably the trabeated *orders, with an innovative approach to structural problems resulting in the extensive exploitation of the *arch and vault, and the evolution of a new building material, concrete. While the orders remained synonymous with the Greek-inspired architecture of temples and colonnades, it was the structural experiments which facilitated the creation of new building types in response to the different political, social, and economic conditions of Rome's expanding empire.

The importance of the orders reflects the early pre-eminence of temple architecture in central Italy, where the Tuscan order evolved probably under the inspiration of Archaic Greek Doric. By the 2nd cent. BC distinctive Italian forms of Ionic and Corinthian were also in widespread use. A purely decorative use of the orders, incorporating many features later to be associated with the Italian 'baroque', was esp. common in the 2nd and 3rd cents. AD, gaining impetus from the increasing availability of various precious marbles. Monumental columnar façades, two to three storeys high, decorated theatre stages throughout the empire, and the device was also employed in the eastern empire and at Rome for public fountains (see NYMPHAEUM), *libraries, and large bath-buildings. Colonnaded streets also became popular.

New building types evolved in the 3rd and 2nd cents. BC, some, such as the *amphitheatre, purely Roman, while *baths and theatres showed more influence from Hellenistic Sicily and *Magna Graecia. Sophisticated timberwork allowed for the roofing of large spans in the *basilica, covered theatre (*odeum), and atrium house (see HOUSES, ITALIAN), while the adoption of barrel-vaulting for terracing structures such as villa platforms and monumental sanctuaries (e.g. sanctuary of Fortuna at *Praeneste) provided the basic structural system later used in utilitarian buildings such as the Porticus Aemilia and in free-standing theatres and amphitheatres. The high status of the orders in Roman architectural thought led to their being applied as decorous adjuncts to arched façades by the late republic (e.g. the Forum façade of the *Tabularium), a motif which found full expression in the theatre of Marcellus and the *Colosseum.

The decisive developments in Roman concrete architecture in the early imperial period also took place in the context of domestic or non-traditional building types, such as Nero's *Domus Aurea, *Domitian's palace on the Palatine, and Hadrian's villa at *Tibur as well as the great imperial baths, which in turn influenced the later Basilica of Maxentius; the *Pantheon, as a temple, is exceptional. The flexibility and structural properties of the new material were used to create an architecture in which the dominant factor was not the solid masonry but the space which it enclosed. Instead of the structural rationality and sculptural quality of Classical Greek architecture, this was an architecture of illusion and suggestion, in which subtly curvilinear forms based on complex geometries in plan and elevation, splendidly lit and clothed in light-reflecting material such as marble veneer and coloured-glass mosaic, contrived to negate the solidity of the structures themselves. Here too the columnar orders often formed an integral part of the visual effect, e.g. in the *frigidaria* (see BATHS) of the imperial bath-buildings, although their structural role was generally negligible. Treatment of exteriors remained simple and traditional, often decorated in either veneer or stucco imitation of ashlar, although in the later empire the curves of the vaults were often allowed free expression outside as well as inside. It was this exploitation of interior space which found its fulfilment in the architecture of Byzantium and remains the most important Roman contribution to all later architectural thought. See BRICK-STAMPS; BRIDGES; BUILDING MATERIALS; MARBLE; TRIUMPHAL ARCH.

archives

Greek In Archaic Greece, documentation was minimal, laws being the most important public documents; lists of officials and agonistic victors (see AGONES) were evidently recorded (and later published), but the public inscriptions themselves were probably the 'stone archives' (see RECORDS AND RECORD-KEEPING). Temples were safe deposits from early on (e.g. *Heraclitus deposited in a temple a copy of his own book), and might contain public inscriptions: hence they often came to house the archives of the city. Documents were also kept separately by the officials concerned, or in their offices, e.g. the Athenian cavalry archive, and the records of the *poletai; there was little centralization. Athens acquired a central archive, the Mētrōon, in the late 5th cent. BC; manned by slaves, housed official documents of the *boule

and assembly (*ekklesia), i.e. mainly decrees, some foreign letters, and treaties with other cities; the laws were probably not kept there until the late 4th cent., nor were private documents like *Epicurus' will. Even after the creation of the Metroon, public inscriptions were regarded as authoritative texts.

Roman Rome's early records were rudimentary: lists of magistrates (*fasti), copies of treaties, and priestly records, which were not systematically arranged till the late 4th cent. (see ANNALES MAXIMI). The main archive was the *aerarium, in the temple of Saturn, established in the early republic and supervised by urban *quaestors. It contained copies of laws and *senatus consulta, which were not valid until properly deposited; also *acta senatus (later), public contracts, records of official oaths, lists of public debtors, and Marcus *Aurelius' new register of Roman births. It is unclear how strictly the archives were separated from the *aerarium*'s financial functions; the closely associated monumental complex nearby on the slopes of the Capitol contained a *tabularium. Romans continue to speak of records going into the *aerarium*. Access was not always straightforward (see RECORDS AND RECORD-KEEPING). Another archive was used by the *plebs in the temple of Ceres on the *Aventine (holding *plebiscita and *senatus consulta*). Inscriptions, like the bronze tablets of laws visible on the Capitol, formed a public source of reference. Under the empire, the focus is increasingly on the emperor's archival records.

archontēs ('rulers'), the general Greek term for all holders of office in a state. But the word was often used as the title of a particular office, originally at least the highest office of the state. *Archontes* are found in most states of central Greece, including *Athens, and in states dependent on or influenced by Athens.

In Athens by the 6th cent. BC there were nine annually appointed archons. The powers of the original hereditary king (*basileus*) came to be shared among three officials: the *basileus*, who retained the religious duties; the *archōn*, who became the civilian head of state; and the *polemarchos* ('war-leader'), who commanded the army. Six *thesmothetai* ('statute-setters'), judicial officials, were added to the original three; and in the 5th or 4th cent. membership was raised to ten with the addition of the secretary to the thesmothetai, so that one could be appointed from each of *Cleisthenes' (2) ten tribes (*phylai*).

Whether direct election was retained throughout the 6th cent. is disputed; from 487/6 the method used was allotment from an elected short list; and at a later date allotment replaced election for the first stage. See SORTITION. By the early 5th cent. the two highest property classes (*pentakosiomedimnoi* and **hippeis* (3)) were eligible for appointment, and in 457/6 eligibility was extended to the third class, the **zeugitai*. Almost certainly, a man could be a member of the board of archons only once in his life; after his year of office he became a member of the council of the **Areopagus* for the rest of his life.

By the 6th cent. the archons and in particular the one entitled *archon* were the most important officials of the Athenian state. **Solon* was *archon* when he was commissioned to reform the state in 594/3, and it is a sign of continuing trouble afterwards that there were years when no *archon* was appointed and that an *archon* called Damasias refused to retire at the end of his year. **Hippias* (1) was *archon* in the first available year (526/5) after the death of his father **Pisistratus*. However, the creation by Cleisthenes of ten **strategoi* ('generals'), appointed annually by election and eligible for re-election, began a process by which in the 5th cent. the generals became the most important Athenian officials, while the archons became routine officials.

In the later 5th and 4th cent. the archons' duties were mainly religious and judicial: earlier they had given verdicts on their own account, but now they conducted the preliminary enquiry and presided in the jury-court which decided the verdict. The *archon* was responsible for a number of religious festivals, and for lawsuits concerning family matters. The *basileus* was responsible for the largest number of religious matters, and for homicide suits. The *polemarchos* was responsible for some festivals, including the games in honour of the war-dead, and for lawsuits involving non-citizens. The *thesmothetai* were responsible for the system of jury-courts as a whole, and for most 'public' lawsuits (in which any citizen might prosecute). In the elaborate organization of the court system developed in the 4th cent. all ten members of the board were involved in the selection of the jurors who were to serve each day, each supervising the procedure in his own tribe.

By the end of the 5th cent. it had become standard practice to identify each year by its *archon*, and so he is sometimes referred to as the eponymous *archon*, but that expression is not found in Greek texts until the Roman period. (In other articles the transliterated Greek '*archōn*' is anglicized as 'archon'.)

Archytas (fl. *c.*400–350 BC), Pythagorean philosopher and mathematician from **Tarentum*. He was elected general seven times and sent a ship to rescue **Plato* from **Dionysius* (2) II of Syracuse in 361. He figures prominently in several Platonic letters whose authenticity is controversial, but he is never mentioned in the dialogues. Fragments 1–3 are probably authentic. He argued that study of sciences such as astronomy, geometry, arithmetic, and music (harmonics) was crucial to the understanding of reality, and his reference to them as 'sisters' may have influenced Plato. In fragment 3 he praises 'correct calculation' as the source of political harmony. He was most famous as the founder of **mechanics* and for solutions to specific mathematical problems such as the doubling of the cube.

Areopagus, the 'Hill of Ares' at **Athens*, NW of the Acropolis, and the ancient council associated with it. There are no substantial remains on the hill; the council's meeting-place may have been on a terrace on the NE side rather than on the summit. Probably the council was called simply *boulē* ('council') at first, and was named after the hill when a second council from which it had to be distinguished was created, probably by **Solon*.

In early Athens the membership of the council will have been aristocratic. By the time of Solon, if not earlier, it came to comprise all ex-archons (see ARCHONTES), who entered it at the end of their year of office and remained members for the rest of their lives. The annual entry of nine new members in middle life maintained a strength of *c.*150. Changes in recruitment depended on changes in the recruitment of the archons: based on wealth rather than family from the time of Solon; including the **zeugitai*, the third property class, from 457/6 BC; and no longer attracting the men with the highest political ambitions from the first half of the 5th cent., when the archonships became routine offices.

It is likely that the council began as a body advising first the king and later the archons; and it certainly had acquired some jurisdiction, in homicide cases *i.a.*, before the time of Solon. Descriptions of it as guardian of the state or of the laws gave expression to its powerful position in early Athens, and may have been exploited as a basis for exercising new powers not formally conferred on it. Solon gave it or confirmed for it the right to try *eisangeliai*, charges of major offences against the state, but his creation of a new council to prepare business for the assembly began the decline in the powers of the Areopagus.

There may have been no further formal change in its powers until the reform of *Ephialtes (2) in 462/1. By this time the archons were appointed by lot from an elected short list, to an office which was overshadowed by the generalship (see STRATEGOI); so a powerful Areopagus was coming to seem an anachronism; and practice in participating in *Cleisthenes' (2) political machinery was giving the Athenian citizens the taste for controlling their own destiny. That Athens was dominated by the Areopagus after the *Persian Wars may be an invention of later writers to explain why reform of the Areopagus was necessary, but if the Areopagus had been exercising its judicial powers to the advantage of *Cimon, that may have provoked Cimon's opponents to attack it.

Ephialtes is said to have taken away the judicial powers which gave the Areopagus its guardianship of the state: they probably included the trial of *eisangeliai*, and procedures which enabled it to control the magistrates, such as *doki-masia*, the vetting before they entered office, and *euthynai*, the examination of their conduct when they left office. The Areopagus retained the right to try cases of homicide, wounding, and arson (and the *ephetai*, 'referees', who tried some categories of homicide cases were probably members of the Areopagus), and also some religious cases. The reform was contentious—Cimon was *ostracized, Ephialtes was murdered—but it held.

Arēs, the Greek war-god as embodiment of the ambivalent (destructive but often useful) forces of war, in contrast to *Athena who represents the intelligent and orderly use of war to defend the *polis*. In *Homer's *Iliad*, his image is mostly negative: he is brazen, ferocious, 'a glutton for war', his cry sounds like that of 'nine or ten thousand men', Zeus hates him, he fights on the Trojan side, his attendants are Deimos 'Fear' and Phobos 'Panic', and he is often opposed to Athena. On the other hand, a brave warrior is 'a shoot from Ares', and the Danai (see HELLENES) are his followers. As with the ecstatic *Dionysus, the myth of his Thracian origin illustrates his position outside the ordered, 'Greek' world of the *polis* and has no historical value.

Myth makes Ares the son of *Zeus and *Hera, thus inscribing him in Zeus' world-order, and the lover of *Aphrodite, whose eroticism is at least as liable to subvert the *polis* order. Offspring of Ares and Aphrodite are Deimos and Phobos, *Eros, and Theban Harmonia (see CADMUS). Among other children of Ares, unruly and disruptive figures abound.

In Rome, Ares was identified with *Mars; the Augustan temple of Ares in the Athenian Agora (perhaps the transferred 4th-cent. temple of Acharnae) meant Mars as the ancestor of Rome; Greek Ares would have been unthinkable in an agora.

Arginūsae, small islands between *Lesbos and the mainland, scene of a battle between the Athenian and Spartan fleets in 406 BC. Sparta's 120 triremes were probably in a single line abeam, Athens' 150 in a double line abeam. *Xenophon says the Athenians, on this occasion having the inferior fleet, adopted this formation in order to prevent the enemy breaking through their line in the manœuvre known as *diekplous*, and then swinging round to attack from the stern. The result was a victory for the Athenians, but it was marred by the failure to pick up survivors from their crippled ships, when a storm arose.

Argonauts, one of the earliest and most important Greek sagas, set in the generation before the Trojan War and involving heroes esp. associated with *Thessaly, central Greece, and *Peloponnese. King *Pelias of Iolcus sought to rid himself of the threat to his kingship posed by the legitimate heir, *Jason (1), by sending the young man off to recover the fleece of a ram upon which Phrixus (see HELLĒ) had fled to the fabulous kingdom of the sun, Aia, ruled by King Aiētēs. At least as early as the *Epic Cycle Aia was identified with the kingdom of Colchis at the east end of the Black (*Euxine) Sea. With Athena's help Jason had a marvellous ship, the *Argo*, built. The greatest heroes of the age gathered to join him on the voyage. Lists differ widely, but among the most prominent Argonauts in many versions were *Heracles, who in some versions did not complete the voyage, *Orpheus, the *Dioscuri, the steersman Tiphys, Lynceus who could see even beneath the earth, *Telamon, *Peleus, the sons of the north wind *Boreas, and *Theseus. The supernatural powers of many of the Argonauts differentiate the story markedly from the Homeric epics. The main protecting goddess for the voyage was *Hera, who wished to punish

Pelias for neglecting to honour her. For the main events of the outward voyage, see APOLLONIUS (1) RHODIUS. In Aia, Jason requests the fleece from Aietes, but the king sets him tasks to accomplish: he must plough with fire-breathing bulls, sow dragon's teeth, and kill the armed warriors which spring up from the ground (cp. *Cadmus). Jason succeeds with the help of Aietes' daughter *Medea, who supplies him with protecting potions and helps him take the fleece from the grove where it is guarded by a dragon.

Important events of the return voyage include the killing of Medea's young brother Apsyrtus, adventures in Libya during which the Argonauts carry their ship through the desert—they were intimately connected with the foundation legends of *Cyrene—and the encounter with the bronze giant Talos who protected Crete.

The saga is of a common folkloric quest type, but also clearly expresses, and was used by Greek writers to reflect, the confrontation between what was Greek and what 'other' and hence the very qualities which represented 'Greekness'. Ancient scholars themselves saw the story as a reflection of the age of colonization and expansion or, more banally, the search for gold.

Argos, a city in the southern Argive plain 5 km. (3 mi.) from the sea. In the Dorian invasion Argos fell to Temenus, the eldest of the *Heraclids. Early in the 7th cent. BC perhaps, a strong king, Pheidon, defeated the Spartans, presided in person over the Olympic Games, and made Argos the first power in Greece. Though *Herodotus attributed to him the giving of weights and measures to Peloponnese, he cannot have been responsible for the introduction of silver coinage, now generally agreed not to have happened until the 6th cent. In the 6th cent., Argive power receded in the face of the growth of Sparta. Henceforth Argos maintained a suspicious neutrality, fighting once a generation with Sparta. Her heaviest defeat was c.494, when *Cleomenes I was barely repelled from the walls by the women of Argos, rallied by the poetess Telesilla. In 480–479 the Argives observed a benevolent neutrality towards Persia. Shortly afterwards they set up a form of democracy. They were repeatedly allied with Athens against Sparta, but remained ineffective.

The territory of Argos in Classical times included *Mycenae, Tiryns, Nauplia, and other strongholds in the Argive plain. The great Argive goddess was *Hera, worshipped at the Heraion 10 km. (6 mi.) NE of Argos. Argive sculptors of the early Classical period were pre-eminent; the greatest was *Polyclitus.

Ariadnē, in myth, daughter of *Minos and Pāsiphaē. In Cnossus *Daedalus built her a dancing-floor. She fell in love with *Theseus and gave him a thread of wool to escape from the *Labyrinth after killing the Minotaur. Theseus fled with Ariadne but abandoned her on *Naxos either by choice or because the gods commanded him. *Dionysus found and married her there. In another version, Ariadne was already married to Dionysus when she followed Theseus and was killed by Artemis on Dia (Naxos). Originally Ariadne was a Minoan goddess of nature whose invocatory name ('Very Holy') suggests that she was expected to appear to her worshippers in *epiphany. Her myth centres on marriage and death, combining the sorrowful and happy aspects of the annual decay and renewal of vegetation.

Ariadne's desertion by Theseus on Naxos/Dia, her rescue by, and marriage to, Dionysus are popular themes in literature esp., and in vase-painting from the early 5th cent. BC through all periods of Greek and Roman art. Other parts of the myth occurred in the painter's repertoire in the 7th cent. She appears assisting Theseus against the Minotaur; and on the François vase she is shown facing Theseus, who leads the dance of Athenian youths and maidens whom he has rescued from the Minotaur. In *Polygnotus' 'Underworld' in the club-house of the *Cnidians at *Delphi, Ariadne appeared sitting on a rock gazing at her sister Phaedra (see HIPPOLYTUS).

Arianism See ARIUS.

Arīon, a *citharode from Methymna in Lesbos, spent most of his life at the court of the Corinthian tyrant *Periander, who ruled from 625 to 585 BC. He was said to have been thrown overboard while returning from a profitable visit to Italy and Sicily, but to have returned to *Corinth after being taken by a dolphin to Taenarum. He seems to have transformed the *dithyramb from an improvised processional song into a formal stationary one.

Aristagoras, deputy tyrant of *Miletus c.505–496 BC in *Histiaeus' absence, and influential rebel with too many causes. Trying to extend Miletus' Aegean power, he promoted a joint Ionian–Phoenician expedition of 100 ships against *Naxos in 500. Failing in the four-month siege, facing large military debts, and

perhaps contemplating an independent east Aegean empire, he arrested and deposed fellow
autocrats before demobilization (and thereby
curried favour with ordinary Greeks along the
coast), seized the Persians' Ionian fleet, abdicated Histiaeus' *de iure* tyrannical powers at
Miletus, and promoted revolt against *Persia
from the Black (*Euxine) Sea to *Cyprus. Control
of land and sea was quickly achieved. Seeking
allies and cash, Aristagoras sailed to Europe
(499/8). Spartans declined, Athenians and Eretrians (see ERETRIA) briefly enlisted, but, faced
with Phoenician sea-power and Persian access
by land, the *Ionian Revolt faltered. Although
Aristagoras superficially united Ionian communities during the six-year revolt, his authority
over Miletus and allied forces remained anomalous. As financial support diminished and allies bickered, he secured refuge and resources in
strategically important Myrcinus, Histiaeus'
base of operations (497/6). While expanding
power and revenues there, he was ambushed
and killed by *Thracians.

Herodotus calls Aristagoras the originator of
the Ionian Revolt. Despite impressive early successes, he later proved an easy scapegoat for
self-justifying survivors, victims of Persian retribution, and Athenian and Spartan self-glorifica-
tion. Later events confirmed his belief in the
possibility of Anatolian Greek independence,
but his revenues, diplomatic skills, and strategic
planning proved inadequate. History vilifies
losers and tyrants.

Aristarchus (1), of Samos, astronomer, is
dated by his observation of the summer solstice
in 280 BC. He put forward the heliocentric (see
GEOCENTRICITY) hypothesis, that 'the fixed stars
and sun remain unmoved, and that the earth
revolves about the sun on the circumference of
a circle, the sun lying in the middle of the orbit'
(Archimedes, *Sand-reckoner*); he also assumed
that the earth rotates about its own axis. His
only extant treatise, *On the Sizes and Distances of
the Sun and Moon*, is, however, on the geocentric
basis.

Aristarchus (2), of Samothrace (*c.*216–144 BC),
sat at the feet of Aristophanes of Byzantium at
*Alexandria. He became head of the Alexandrian
*Library *c.*153. On the accession of Ptolemy VIII
(145) he left Alexandria for *Cyprus, where he
died. With him real scholarship began, and his
work covered the wide range of grammatical,
etymological, orthographical, literary, and textual criticism. He wrote critical recensions of

poetic texts, commentaries on poets and also
Herodotus, and critical treatises on particular
matters relating to the *Iliad* and *Odyssey*. The
school which he founded at Alexandria and
which lasted into the Roman imperial period
had many distinguished pupils, e.g. *Apollodorus (2) and Dionysius Thrax.

Aristīdēs early 5th-cent. BC Athenian politician, probably archon (see ARCHONTES) in 489/
8, less probably general in 490 at the battle of
*Marathon. Famously just, he is often repre-
sented as an upright and 'aristocratic' foil to
duplicitous and 'democratic' *Themistocles; but
the contrast is unsound. *Ostracism befell him
in 483/2. Surviving *ostraka* accuse him of *Medism and spurning suppliants. He returned from
exile under an act of recall, and at the battle of
*Salamis in 480 led a hoplite engagement on the
island of Psyttaleia. He commanded at *Plataea
and after the Persian Wars helped Themistocles
fool the Spartans over the building of Athens'
city walls. He assessed the initial tribute of
*Delian League members. He died *c.*467.

Aristīdēs, Publius Aelius (AD 117–after
181), sophist (see SECOND SOPHISTIC) and man
of letters. Born in Mysia, he studied in Athens
and *Pergamum. Aged 26, he suffered the first of
a long series of illnesses, which ended his hopes
of a great public career and drove him to spend
much of his time as a patient at the Asclepieum
(see ASCLEPIUS) of Pergamum. The rest of his life
was passed mainly in Asia Minor, where he
made his home in Smyrna, and when not ill
occupied himself in writing and lecturing.

His many-sided literary output (built on an
intimate knowledge of the Classical literary
heritage) made him a giant in his own day and,
through its subsequent popularity, a 'pivotal
figure in the transmission of Hellenism'. It includes addresses delivered on public and private
occasions, declamations on historical themes,
polemical essays, prose hymns to various gods,
and six books of *Sacred Teachings*. Among the
public addresses, *To Rome* paints an impressive
picture of the Roman achievement, as seen by
an admiring provincial, while the *Panathenaic
Oration* provides a potted history of Classical
Athens. The historical declamations show an
equal facility with Classical oratorical style and
with the fine details of 5th and 4th cent. BC
history. Of the polemical works, the most interesting are *On Rhetoric* and *In Defence of the Four*,
which answer *Plato's attack on rhetoric and
politicians in *Gorgias*. The prose hymns were an

influential model for later writers. The *Sacred Teachings* are in a class apart. A record of revelations made to Aristides in *dreams by Asclepius, and of his obedience to the god's instructions, they supply both evidence for the practices associated with temple medicine (see MEDICINE, 2) and the fullest first-hand report of personal religious experiences that survives from any pagan writer.

aristocracy ('rule of the best'). The term is applied by modern scholars to the regimes of early Greece in which states were ruled by the noble families which had emerged from the Dark Age with the most landed property and political power, but the word *aristokratia* is not found before the 5th cent. BC, perhaps coined in response to *democracy. Thereafter it was the preferred term of those wishing to give a favourable picture of *oligarchy. In the threefold classification of monarchy (*kingship), oligarchy, and democracy, aristocracy is the good form of oligarchy. See NOBILES, NOBILITAS; OPTIMATES.

Aristogīton, Athenian tyrannicide. He and Harmodius, both of the family of Gephyraei, provoked, acc. to *Thucydides (2), by amorous rivalry, plotted along with others to kill *Hippias (1) at the Panathenaic festival of 514 BC (see PANATHENAEA) and end the tyranny. The plot miscarried, only *Hipparchus (1) was killed, and the tyrannicides were executed.

After the expulsion of Hippias in 510 by Sparta, the tyrannicides were elevated as heroes. Bronze statues of them by *Antenor were erected, probably quite early; carried off by *Xerxes in 480, they were replaced in 477/6 by a second group by *Critius and Nēsiōtēs; the epigram inscribed on the base was composed by *Simonides. Their tomb was placed in the *Ceramicus; the *polemarchos sacrificed annually to them, and their descendants received free meals in the *prytaneion. Certain *scolia were sung claiming that they brought Athens *isonomia. It was a popular belief, rebutted by Thucydides, that Hipparchus was the tyrant at the time. Other conflicting claims clustered round the role of the tyrannicides, but the view that 5th-cent. popular tradition literally thought they, rather than Sparta, ended the tyranny, is undermined by Thucydides and comedy. It is likely that all parties concerned concurred in honouring them from early on as a convenient, simple, and patriotic symbol for the defeat of tyranny. Later, they were seen as having ended the tyranny.

Aristophanēs, the greatest poet of Old Attic Comedy (see COMEDY (GREEK), OLD). Since he considered himself too young in 427 BC to produce ('direct' might be nearer the mark) a play himself (Callistratus produced his first three plays), he may have been born as late as 450. He died in or shortly before 386. Eleven of his plays survive; we have in addition 32 titles and nearly 1,000 fragments and citations. The surviving plays, and the datable lost plays (°) are:

427: °*Banqueters.* It contained an argument between a profligate son and his father and also between the profligate and a virtuous young man.

426: °*Babylonians.* Dionysus was a character in the play, and by its 'attacks on the magistrates' it provoked a prosecution—apparently unsuccessful—by *Cleon.

425 (first prize): *Acharnians* ('*Ach.*'); the 'hero' makes, and enjoys to the full, a private peace-treaty.

424 (first prize): *Knights* ('*Kn.*'), produced by Aristophanes himself; Cleon is savagely handled and worsted in the guise of a favourite slave of *Demos, and a sausage-seller replaces him as favourite.

423 (bottom prize): *Clouds* ('*Cl.*'), ridiculing *Socrates as a corrupt teacher of rhetoric. We have only the revised version of the play, dating from the period 418–416; the revision was not completed and was never performed.

422 (second prize): *Wasps*, ridiculing the enthusiasm of old men for jury-service.

421 (second prize): *Peace*, celebrating the conclusion of peace with Sparta.

414: °*Amphiaraus.*

414 (second prize): *Birds*, a fantasy in which an ingenious Athenian persuades the birds to build a city in the clouds and compels the gods to accept humiliating terms.

411: *Lysistrata* ('*Lys.*'), in which the citizens' wives in all the Greek states compel their menfolk, by a 'sex strike', to make peace; and *Thesmophoriazusae* ('*Thesm.*') in which the women at the *Thesmophoria plan to obliterate *Euripides, and an elderly kinsman of his takes part in their debate, disguised as a woman.

408: the first °*Plutus.*

405 (first prize): *Frogs*, in which *Dionysus descends to Hades to bring back Euripides, finds that he has to be the judge in a contest between *Aeschylus and Euripides, for the throne of poetry in *Hades, and ends by bringing back Aeschylus.

392: *Ecclesiazusae* ('*Eccl.*'), in which the women take over the running of the city and introduce community of property.

388: the second *Plutus* ('*Plut.*'), in which the god of wealth is cured of his blindness, and the remarkable social consequences of his new discrimination are exemplified.

In the first period, down to 421, Aristophanes followed a constant procedure in constructing his plays, esp. in the relation of the *parodos* (entry of the chorus) and the *parabasis* (address by the chorus to the audience) to the rest of the play. From *Birds* onwards we see significant changes in this procedure, culminating, in *Eccl.* and *Plut.*, in the introduction of choral songs irrelevant to the action of the play, and in *Plut.* the chorus seems, for the first time, an impediment to the unfolding of the plot (see COMEDY (GREEK), MIDDLE). At the same time *Eccl.* and *Plut.* show a great reduction of strictly topical reference. The evidence suggests that Aristophanes was a leader, not a follower, in the changes undergone by comedy in the early 4th cent. Aristophanes' language is colourful and imaginative, and he composes lyric poetry in every vein, humorous, solemn, or delicate. He has a keen eye and ear for the absurd and the pompous; his favoured weapons are parody, satire, and exaggeration to the point of fantasy, and his favourite targets are men prominent in politics, contemporary poets, musicians, scientists, and philosophers, and manifestations of cultural change in general. His sympathetic characters want to be left alone to enjoy traditional pleasures in traditional ways, but they are also ingenious, violent, and tenaciously self-seeking in getting what they want. Having been born into a radical democracy Aristophanes nowhere advocates oligarchic reaction, least of all in 411, when this reaction was an imminent reality. His venomous attack on Cleon in *Kn.* is explained by Cleon's earlier attack on him (see above), and his treatment of other politicians does not differ significantly from the way in which 'we' satirize 'them' nowadays. No class, age-group, or profession is wholly exempt from Aristophanes' satire, nor is the citizen-body as a whole, and if we interpret his plays as moral or social lessons, we never find the lesson free of qualifications and complications. Aristophanes' didactic influence does not seem to have been significant. In *Ap.* Plato blames him for helping to create mistrust of Socrates. On the other hand, *Ach.* and *Lys.* do not seem to have disposed the Athenians to negotiate for peace, and Cleon was elected to a generalship shortly after the first prize had been awarded to *Kn.*

See also COMEDY (GREEK), OLD and MIDDLE; LITERARY CRITICISM IN ANTIQUITY, paras. 2, 3.

Aristotle (384–322 BC), b. in Stagira, son of Nicomachus, a member of the medical guild of the Asclepiads (see ASCLEPIUS) and court physician to Amyntas II of Macedon. Aristotle may have spent part of his childhood at the court in Pella. Aged 17 he travelled to Athens and entered *Plato's *Academy, remaining until Plato's death in 348/7. Plato's philosophical influence is evident in all of Aristotle's work. Even when he is critical, he expresses deep respect for Plato's genius. At Plato's death Aristotle left Athens, probably because of political difficulties connected with his Macedonian ties. Accepting an invitation from Hermias, tyrant of Assos and Atarneus in *Troas and a former fellow student in the Academy, he went to Assos, where he stayed until Hermias' fall and death in 345, marrying his adopted daughter Pythias. While at Assos, and afterwards at *Mytilene, he did the biological research on which his later scientific writings are based. (The treatises often refer to place-names and species of that area.) His observations, esp. in marine biology, were unprecedented in their detail and accuracy. (See ANIMALS, KNOWLEDGE OF, 2.)

Invited by *Philip II of Macedon to Pella in 342, he became tutor to Philip's son *Alexander (2) the Great. In 335 he returned to Athens. Like Plato before him, he established a school in a *gymnasium. His choice was the Lyceum to the east of the city. (The school later took its name from its covered walk or *peripatos*.) He delivered some popular lectures, but most of his time was spent in writing or lecturing to a smaller group of serious students, including some, such as *Theophrastus and Eudemus, who achieved distinction. He amassed a large library, and encouraged his students to undertake research projects, esp. in natural science and political history (where he projected a collection of historical and comparative descriptions of 158 constitutions).

Pythias died early in this period; they had one daughter. For the rest of his life Aristotle lived with a slave-woman named Herpyllis, by whom he had a son, Nicomachus. Although in his will Aristotle praises Herpyllis' loyalty and kindness, he freed her from legal slavery only then. On the death of Alexander in 323, an outbreak of anti-Macedonian feeling forced Aristotle to leave Athens once again. Alluding to the death of *Socrates, he said that he was leaving to prevent the Athenians from 'sin[ning] twice against philosophy'. He retired to *Chalcis, where he died in 322.

Aristotle left his papers to Theophrastus, his successor as head of the Lyceum. *Strabo reports that Theophrastus left them to one Neleus of Scepsis (in Troas), whose heirs hid them in a cellar, where they remained until a rich collector, Apellicon, purchased them and brought them to Athens early in the first century BC. But some of Aristotle's major works were used by his successors in the Lyceum, as well as by *Epicurus and numerous *Alexandrian intellectuals. At this stage the works were not edited in anything like the form in which we know them. A list of Aristotle's works, probably dating from the 3rd cent. BC, appears to cover most of the major extant texts under some description, as well as a number of works now lost. Among the lost works are dialogues, some of which were still well known in *Cicero's Rome. Cicero describes their style as 'a golden river'.

When *Sulla captured Athens (86), Apellicon's collection was brought to Rome, where it was edited around 30 BC, by Andronicus of Rhodes, whose edition is the basis for all later editions. Andronicus grouped books into works, arranged them in a logical sequence, and left copious notes about his views on authenticity. We possess most of the works he considered genuine and important, in manuscripts produced between the 9th and 16th cents. The transmission during the intervening period is represented by several papyrus fragments, plus the extensive papyri from which the (dubious) *Athenaion Politeia has been edited.

The extant works may be grouped under three headings: (*a*) Logic and Metaphysics (*Categories*, *On Exposition*, *Prior Analytics*, *Posterior Analytics*, *Topics*, *Sophistical Refutations*, *Metaphysics*); (*b*) Nature, Life, and Mind (*Physics*, etc.; zoological works; psychological works, etc.); (*c*) Ethics, Politics, Art (*Eudemian Ethics*, *Nicomachean Ethics* (*Nic. Eth.*); *Politics*; *Rhetoric*; *Poetics*).

Of the works surviving only in fragments, the most important and substantial is *On the Forms*, a critical discussion of Plato's theories.

Many questions have been raised about the status of the 'Aristotelian corpus'. The most plausible view is that the extant treatises are written lectures. The exact wording of most of the material is Aristotle's. We cannot rely on the order of books within a treatise as Aristotelian, or even the grouping of distinct books into a single treatise. All titles and many introductory and concluding sentences are likely to be the work of later editors. Throughout we are faced with textual problems, some of which require the transposition of substantial passages for their solution. Some sections, furthermore, may have been left poorly organized by Aristotle

himself, and are best regarded as assorted notes that were never worked into a finished discussion. The most serious philosophical problems raised by the state of the corpus come from its duplications.

Aristotle was the first Greek philosopher to attempt a general account of validity in inference. *Prior Analytics* is thus a towering achievement; though displaced in the Hellenistic period by Stoic propositional logic, it became the dominant account of formal logic from the early Middle Ages until the early 20th cent. *Topics* and *Sophistical Refutations* show Aristotle's keen interest in methods of *dialectical argumentation and in the analysis of common fallacies and paradoxes.

In *Posterior Analytics* Aristotle sets out the conditions under which scientific demonstration will convey genuine understanding. Conclusions must be deducible, ultimately, from first principles that are true, basic, necessary, and explanatory of the other conclusions of the science. The scientist has understanding when he is able to show how the more basic principles of his science explain the less basic. *Posterior Analytics* argues that understanding is based on the experience of many particulars, and requires insight into the explanatory role of first principles.

In *Metaphysics* 4, Aristotle undertakes the defence of two esp. basic logical principles: the Principle of Non-Contradiction and the Principle of the Excluded Middle. Non-Contradiction, which is called 'the most basic starting-point of all', is established not by a proof from other principles, but by an 'elenctic demonstration', i.e. one that establishes that the opponent who challenges this law must rely on it if he is to think and speak at all. For to say anything definite he must rule something out—at the least, the contradictory of what he sets forth.

Throughout his work Aristotle is intensely concerned with experience, including the record of experience contained in what people say. It is common for an inquiry, in science as well as in ethics, to begin by 'setting down the *phainomena*, the 'appearances', which usually include perceptual observation and the record of reputable belief. Aristotle clearly believes that scientific inquiry involves examining common conceptions as well as looking at the world; indeed the two often interpenetrate. Aristotle is also very careful to survey the views of the reputable thinkers who have approached a problem. As he states at the start of his inquiry into number in *Metaphysics* 13, he can hope in this way to avoid making the same mistakes, and can perhaps hope to progress a little beyond what the tradition has already accomplished. Although we may find fault with his treatment of one or another previous thinker, he was the first Greek thinker to make engagement with the books of others a central part of his method.

'Metaphysics' is not an Aristotelian term (it refers to the placing of that work 'after *Physics*' in ancient editions), but Aristotle's study of the most general characteristics of things gives later metaphysics its agenda. Aristotle holds that the central question about that which is (*to on*), for both his predecessors and himself, has been a question about *ousia*, usually translated 'substance'. Since *ousia* is a verbal noun formed from the participle *on*, this is not a perspicuous statement. But from Aristotle's procedures we can get a better idea of his problem. Two questions appear to drive the search for substance: a question about *change*, and a question about *identity*. Since a central part of our experience of nature is that of change—the cycle of the seasons, changes in living bodies—an account of nature needs to find a coherent way to speak about process. Aristotle holds that this, in turn, requires the ability to single out some entities as (relatively) stable 'subjects' or 'substrates' of change, things to which the change happens. At the same time, discourse about the world also requires asking and answering the question 'What is it?' about items in our experience. This means being able to say what it is about an individual that makes it the very thing it is, and to separate that aspect from more superficial attributes that might cease to be present while the individual remained the same. This question, Aristotle holds, leads us to search for (what we now call) the thing's 'essence' (here we borrow a Ciceronian rendering of Aristotle's odd yet homely term, *to ti ēn einai*, 'the what it was to be'). The two questions might seem to point in opposite directions: the first in the direction of matter as the basic substance, since that persists while animals and people are born and die; the second in the direction of the universal, since 'human being' or 'tree' seem promising accounts of the 'what is it' of particulars. But it is Aristotle's view that in reality the two must be held closely together and will ultimately converge on a single account of the basic substances. For any adequate theory of change must single out as its substrates items that are not only relatively enduring, but also definite and distinct; and any account of the essence of a particular should enable us to say

what changes it can undergo while still remaining one and the same. Aristotle pursues the two prongs of his question through several treatises, with results that appear to undergo development and are always difficult to interpret. In *Metaphysics* 12, Aristotle articulates his idea of god as an eternally active and unaffected substance, whose activity is thinking and who inspires movement in the heavenly spheres by becoming an object of their love.

Metaphysics describes the development of philosophy as a search for explanations of natural events that inspire wonder. In *Physics* Aristotle describes the types of explanation a natural philosopher should be prepared to give. He begins from the question 'Why?' (*dia ti*)—asked either about a thing or a state of affairs; he suggests that there are four basic ways in which we can answer such a 'why' question. First, we may cite the materials of which a thing is composed. This answer is inadequate on its own, since we need to be able to pick out the thing as a structure of a certain sort before we can enumerate its constituents. Second, we may mention a thing's form or characteristic organization. Third, we may mention some agent or event that made the event or thing come about—this sort of answer is called by Aristotle 'the origin of change', and by the tradition 'the efficient cause'. Finally, we may mention 'the end' or 'that for the sake of which' a thing is. Aristotle often insists that we should explain processes or subsystems of creatures by showing how they contribute to the overall functioning of the creature. The characteristic organization of a species is in that sense an 'end' towards which processes should be seen as contributing. *Physics* also contains valuable discussions of place, time, and the nature of change. On **Psyche* is a general study of life and the living. After criticizing materialist and Platonist accounts of *psyche*, he defends the view that *psyche* is the substance of a living thing; he argues that this substance will be not its material constituents but its species-form.

Aristotle's ethical treatises search for an adequate account of *eudaimonia*, 'human flourishing'. *Eudaimonia* is the 'target' of human choice, and that it involves being active. Reflection, Aristotle holds, will show common candidates such as pleasure and honour to be inadequate accounts of what *eudaimonia* is; it must be understood as 'activity of soul in accordance with complete excellence'. This complex end has many constituent elements; Aristotle investigates a long list of excellences of character (such as courage, moderation, generosity, justice), which are, in general, stable dispositions to choose activities and to react in ways that are neither excessive nor deficient in each area of choice; this 'mean' standard is given by looking to the choices of the 'person of practical wisdom', i.e. to paradigms of human excellence. Excellence of character requires and is required by practical wisdom, an excellence of the intellect.

Aristotle stresses that practical wisdom requires a grasp of many particulars, which must be derived through experience. Like medicine and navigation, good judgement (in law as well as in ethics) requires a grasp of rules laid down in advance, but also the ability to adjust one's thinking to the complex requirements of the current situation. His account of 'equity' in public judgement is continuous with reflections on that theme in the *Attic orators; it has had enormous influence in the history of western law. Closely connected with Aristotle's accounts of practical wisdom are his reflections on voluntary action and excusing factors, and on choice.

Friendship (see LOVE AND FRIENDSHIP), Aristotle holds, is one of the most important elements in a good human life. Even if one were free of need and doing well in all other respects, one would still view life as not worth living without friends. Aristotle seems to hold that any genuine friendship requires mutual awareness and mutual activity seeking to benefit the other for the other's own sake. Friendships, however, come in different types, according to the characteristics of the parties that are the ground or basis for the friendship. There are friendships of pleasure, of utility, and of character, the last being both the most stable and the richest.

In two separate discussions Aristotle argues that pleasure is not equivalent to the good. (His accounts of pleasure differ, and may not be compatible.) In the final book of *Nicomachean Ethics* he then goes on to praise the life that is devoted to contemplating the eternal. He appears to praise this activity not just as one among the other constituents of *eudaimonia*, but as something of supreme value, to which maximal attention should be given.

The investigation of human flourishing is a part of the science of politics, since legislators need to know about human ends in order to design schemes that promote these ends. But *political theory requires, in addition, a critical and empirical study of different constitutions, and an attempt, on that basis, to consider what the best form of government would be. In the process, Aristotle makes Greek philosophy's most distinguished contribution to *economic theory.

In *Rhetoric*, Aristotle argues, against Platonic strictures, that rhetoric can be a systematic science. Defining rhetoric as 'the capability of recognizing in each case the possible means of persuasion', he argues for its autonomy and offers a comprehensive discussion of persuasion through speech. The work includes many discussions of broader interest, including a survey of ordinary beliefs about many ethical topics, and an analysis of the major emotions (see RHETORIC, GREEK).

Aristotle's *Poetics* should be read in close connection with his ethical writings, which insist, against Plato, that good people can sometimes fall short of *eudaimonia* through disasters not of their own making. Tragic action, Aristotle holds, inspires two emotions in its audience: *pity* (a painful emotion felt at the undeserved and serious suffering of another person), and *fear* (a painful emotion felt at the thought of serious disasters impending). We pity the tragic hero as someone undeserving of his misfortune, and fear for him, seeing him as someone similar to ourselves. (Plato's *Republic* had argued that both of these emotions are pernicious: literature that inspires them should be removed.) In this way, poetry proves more philosophical than historical narration, since it presents universals, things 'such as might happen' in a human life. Like other forms of representation (*mimēsis*), it gives rise to the pleasure of learning and recognition. The tragic hero's reversal (*peripeteia*) inspires pity if it is due not to wickedness of character but rather to some *hamartia*, by which Aristotle seems to mean some error in action, sometimes blameworthy and sometimes not. Scholars will never agree on the proper interpretation of the *katharsis* through pity and fear that is the result of watching tragic action. The central concepts of this work remain disputed.

Aristotle's achievements have been fundamental to much of the later history of western philosophy. His undisputed greatness has produced at times an attitude of deference that he might well have deplored. On the other hand, few if any philosophers have so productively stimulated the inquiries of other distinguished philosophers; few philosophers of the remote past, if any, are so conspicuously alive in the range of questions they provoke and in the resourcefulness of the arguments they offer.

See ANIMALS, KNOWLEDGE OF; BOTANY; EXPERIMENT; METEOROLOGY; MUSIC; PERIPATETIC SCHOOL; PHYSICS.

Aristoxenus, of *Tarentum (b. *c.*370 BC), best known for musical writings but also a philosopher, biographer, and historian. He was trained in *music, possibly to professional standards. Later he studied with the Pythagorean (see PYTHAGORAS) Xenophilus, pupil of *Philolaus, before joining *Aristotle's Lyceum. Here his success made him expect to inherit the headship; and when Aristotle bequeathed it to *Theophrastus instead, his remarks about Aristotle (acc. to the *Suda) were memorably rude. The waspishness of criticisms levelled at others in his writings makes this believable; but his intellectual orientation is unmistakably Aristotelian, and his one surviving reference to Aristotle is also the one unqualified compliment paid to anyone in that work. Most influential were his writings on harmonics, of which three incomplete books survive. Aristoxenus saw himself as pioneering a wholly new and scientific approach to harmonics. Pythagoreans had conceived pitches as quantities, and studied their mathematical relations. Earlier empiricists had sought merely to tabulate various forms of attunement and scale. Aristoxenus takes his subject, melody or attunement, to be a 'nature' existing solely in the audible domain; and he holds that the science must therefore represent it as it appears to the ear, not through a physicist's conception of sounds as movements of the air, since sounds are not heard in that guise, and specifically harmonic or musical properties attach only to what is heard. The main task of harmonics is to identify the components of audible melody, to abstract the principles governing their relations, and to demonstrate that aesthetic distinctions between melodic and unmelodic sequences and structures are determined by these principles. Harmonics is to be a science of the sort analysed in Aristotle's *Posterior Analytics*.

His biographies included Lives of at least four philosophers, Pythagoras, *Archytas, *Socrates, and *Plato. Fragments of the latter two are scurrilous and vituperative; but his work on Pythagoras probably underlies much of the later tradition.

Arius (*c.* AD 260–336) was the most important of early Christian heretics. He became a leading presbyter at *Alexandria. In 318 or 320/1 he began propagating subordinationist views about Christ's person. Controversy flared up, and he was condemned at the council of Nicaea (325). His characteristic teaching was that the Son or Word was a creature, created before time

and superior to other creatures, but like them changeable and distinct in essence from the Father.

armies, Greek and Hellenistic Apart from what little archaeology can tell us, our earliest evidence comes from *Homer, but it is uncertain how far the poems can be taken as depicting real warfare. To some extent, what happens on Homeric battlefields is dictated by the nature of the poetry. However, all troops are implied to be of the same type, and there is no cavalry. The constant use of the throwing-spear implies a normally loose formation.

By *Tyrtaeus' time, the fundamental distinction between 'heavy' infantry fighting hand-to-hand and 'light', missile-armed infantry, has appeared, at any rate in *Sparta, but the chariot has disappeared, and there is still no cavalry. What organization there is, is based on the three *Dorian *phylai. Archaeological evidence confirms that by the mid-7th cent. BC *hoplites had appeared, and thereafter, for some three centuries, they dominated the battlefield, though some states (e.g. *Macedon and *Thessaly) relied more on cavalry and the *Boeotians also had fine cavalry (see HIPPEIS, 2) in addition to hoplites. Some of the less urbanized areas (e.g. Aetolia) also still tended to make more use of light, missile-armed troops, and all states probably had them. Most armies seem to have been recruited locally. After the reforms of *Cleisthenes (2), Athenian hoplites were divided into ten units (*taxeis*) based on the ten *phylai*, and the cavalry was similarly divided into two groups of five units.

Most Greek troops were essentially militia. Cavalry and hoplites were drawn from the better off, since they mostly provided their own equipment. Possibly for this reason, there appears to have been little or no training at least until the 4th cent., and very little organization. The smallest unit in the Athenian army, for example, seems to have been a *lochos*, probably consisting of several hundred men.

The exception was Sparta. Not only were Spartan soldiers trained from boyhood (see AGOGE) and liable for service from 20 to 60, but their army was highly organized, giving it an ability to manœuvre that other armies lacked. The Spartan ideal was clearly an army of citizen-hoplites (*homoioi*, 'peers', see SPARTA, 2), but by 425 it appears that they made up only *c.*40 per cent, and there were fewer still by the time of *Leuctra. It is usually assumed that the numbers were made up by *perioikoi, but it is possible that

Spartans who had lost their full citizenship continued to serve in the army, and that the *perioikoi* were always separately brigaded.

The defeat of the Spartan army at Leuctra ushered in a short period of Theban dominance, and saw the beginnings of a new form of warfare, in which the traditional hoplite *phalanx was combined with cavalry and other arms. These changes culminated in the army of *Alexander (2) the Great. Macedon had long had good cavalry, known as *hetairoi (i.e. 'companions' of the king), but it was possibly Philip who first raised and organized the '*pezetairoi*' or 'foot companions', who, with the '*hypaspistai*' (lit. 'shield-bearers'), constituted the heavy infantry. By Alexander's time the *pezetairoi* were divided into *taxeis* of 1,500 men, subdivided down to files of sixteen men; the hypaspists into *chiliarchai* of 1,000 men.

But what marked Alexander's army out from its predecessors was the number of different types of unit all interacting with each other—*pezetairoi* and hypaspists, light infantry armed with missiles, heavy and light cavalry. Alexander's conquests owed as much to his soldiers' ability to cope with any situation, as to his own strategic and tactical skills.

Under his successors there was a tendency for the cavalry to decline, with a corresponding increase in the importance of the phalanx. The latter's unwieldiness was sometimes compensated for by interspersing more mobile infantry units among the heavy infantry, notably by *Pyrrhus in his Italian campaigns. But, in the end, the Macedonian-type army proved no match for the Roman *legions, and manpower problems, esp. in Macedonia itself, meant that its kings could not afford to lose even a single battle, whereas the Romans could survive even the most appalling defeats.

armies, Roman Traditionally, Servius Tullius (see REX) made the first attempt to channel the resources of the Roman state into military organization by dividing the citizens into wealth groups, so that the weapons they could afford determined their military role, with the richest serving as cavalry. Below these groups were the *capite censi* ('assessed by a head-count')—men with no property, who were excluded from the army. Military service, therefore, although integral to the duties of citizenship, was also a privilege. This organization of the citizens probably emerged gradually and not through the act of an individual. By *c.*400 BC a small allowance had been introduced for each soldier to help pay his

expenses on active service. The body of infantry was called the *legiō* ('levying', *legion) and by 311 had been divided into four legions; they were supported by contingents of Rome's Italian allies (*socii) and subjects, grouped in formations comparable in size to the legions and commanded by Roman officers. Archers and other specialist fighters were supplied by *mercenaries.

The *Punic Wars stretched Roman manpower resources to the limit. The system of recruitment had been designed for a small city-state fighting short annual campaigns in Italy. Rome now waged long wars, sometimes overseas, and after the defeat of *Carthage in 201, began to acquire provinces that needed a permanent military presence. So, there was a reduction in the property qualification for military service. The annual levy selected citizens of military age (17–46), who were expected to serve for up to six consecutive campaigns but be available for enlistment for up to sixteen years, or ten years in the case of a cavalryman. The army was commanded by the chief magistrates, the consuls.

Throughout the 2nd cent. there was increasing discontent with the levy as Rome faced a series of foreign wars, and the property qualification was further reduced. Then in 107 the consul *Marius extended this practice by accepting volunteers from the propertyless and had them equipped at the state's expense for the war in Africa (see JUGURTHA). Undoubtedly conscription along the normal lines still continued, but many volunteers probably chose to serve for sixteen years, and this contributed to the development of a professional, long-term army. The consequences of the *Social War (91–87) were also far-reaching, since Rome's defeated Italian allies were absorbed into the citizen body, significantly increasing the reservoir of manpower. Non-Italians now provided auxiliary forces of cavalry (see AUXILIA). But the state had no policy of granting appropriate discharge payments to its troops. Generals, often holding long-term commands, used their reputation, and promises of generous benefits, to recruit men with whom they then built up a personal rapport. Increasingly soldiers owed their allegiance to their commander rather than to the Roman state, and became instruments of violent political change. The precedent set by *Sulla in 88 of seizing power by military might was not to be expunged, and the republic succumbed to the rival mercenary armies of military dynasts.

*Augustus united these disunited legions in loyalty to his person and created a fully professional, standing army. This was not revolutionary in itself, but his detailed provision for the troops' service conditions and emoluments (see AERARIUM; STIPENDIUM; VETERANS), the incorporation of the non-citizen *auxilia* into the formal military structure, the establishment of a personal bodyguard (*praetorians), the permanent policing of Rome (see COHORTES URBANAE), and the apportionment of legions and *auxilia* as permanent garrisons of individual provinces, shaped Roman military thinking until the 3rd cent. AD and made military organization an integral part of imperial policy. The most striking development in the command of the Roman army was that from the end of the 1st cent. AD onwards, the emperor, who in his nomenclature and public portrayal bore the attributes of a Roman general, took personal charge of all major campaigns.

arms and armour

Greek In the Homeric poems the champions begin by throwing spears at each other, and when these are gone, they proceed to close combat with swords. The standing type of the Archaic and Classical soldier was the *hoplite, ultimately derived from the soldier of the transition from bronze to iron age. The trend now was towards heavier armour and fighting based on weight of manpower. Shields were made of bronze and leather, and spears and swords of iron. In addition hoplites wore breastplates, greaves, and helmets as defensive armour. The spear as used by hoplites and cavalry (see HIPPEIS, 2) had become a pike for thrusting, not throwing, and was usually some 2 m. (c.7 ft.) in length. Only light-armed troops and some light cavalry used instead the throwing-spear. Along with the use of the spear as a pike, the sword (at least of the Athenian hoplite) had developed a short, straight-edged blade; it could be used only for very close fighting.

The 4th cent. saw the evolution of a more flexible type of equipment than the hoplite's. Experiments were first made with the *peltast, but the final change was the establishment of the Macedonian type as employed in the *phalanx. The spear was increased still more in length to a maximum of just over 5 m. (17 ft.), and the shield reduced to a small target. The different ranks of the phalanx used different lengths of spear. The equipment for light-armed infantry and light- and heavy-armed cavalry was also specialized at this period. At all periods, soldiers competed over the excellence of their armour, some of which might be highly decorated. See WAR, ART OF, GREEK.

Roman Artistic representations, military treatises, other literary and subliterary references, and archaeological artefacts are the main sources of information. Pre-imperial artefacts are sparse and come mainly from siege sites. Imperial finds are plentiful, associated mainly with ordered dismantlement-deposits in frontier installations. Roman military equipment represented a constantly evolving and adapting *mélange* of cultural traits.

In the regal and early republican periods the Roman infantry was equipped on the Greek *hoplite model. A long thrusting-spear (*hasta*) was the chief offensive weapon, and the defensive armour varied with individual wealth, the richest men having cuirasses, round shields, greaves, and helmets of Greek or Italic form.

By the mid-2nd cent. BC, however, the heavy javelin (*pīlum*) replaced the *hasta* in the first two legionary lines (*hastātī* and *principēs*; see LEGION). A short sword was used for close fighting. Men of all three lines carried a long, curving, oval shield. Helmets were of Celtic type. A bronze plate was worn by the poorer soldiers, and a coat of mail by the richest. The legionary light infantry had a small round shield, light javelins, sword, and helmet. The legionary cavalry wore a helmet and cuirass, and carried a round shield and spear. During the last century of the republic (if not before) the *pīlum* became universal for legionary infantry, a change associated perhaps with cohort organization (see COHORS), relaxing property qualifications, and increased state supply of equipment.

In the first two centuries AD new forms of helmets developed from Celtic models. The legionary shield continued to be large and curving. Scale, mail, and articulated-plate cuirasses were current. The last consisted of steel plates articulated on leather strips, and developed from the first half of the 1st cent. AD into the 3rd. Spears and light javelins were carried by some legionaries instead of *pila*, and all continued with the short sword. Auxiliary infantry and cavalry (see AUXILIA) were also armoured in mail or scale (not plate), but large flat shields of varying shapes were carried. Infantry used short swords, cavalry the long Celtic *spatha*. Most carried spears and/or javelins, while specialist units carried composite bows or lances (cavalry).

In all periods the *mercenaries, allies, native levies, etc., valued for their specialized fighting skills, used their own ethnic military equipment.

Equipment was manufactured in cities and was largely a matter of individual acquisition and ownership before the 1st cent. BC. Thereafter, the state organized production, manufacture, and supply (individual ownership continued in the Principate), based principally on legionary workshops and craftsmen. Army expansion necessitated the establishment of additional, city-based, state arms factories from c. AD 300 onwards.

Arrephoria Athenian festival, at which a rite was performed by the *arrēphoroi*, two or four girls between the ages of 7 and 11, chosen by the *basileus* (see ARCHONTES) to serve *Athena Polias. They lived on the *Acropolis, they played a ritual game of ball, and they participated in the weaving of the *peplos* (see DRESS) offered to Athena at the *Panathenaea. They helped the priestess of Athena Polias. At the Chalkeia they and the priestess set up the loom for the *peplos*. They are probably represented with the priestess in the central scene on the *Parthenon frieze. At the rite marking the end of their service, at night, they put on their heads covered baskets given them by the priestess who knew no more than the girls what they contained, and through an underground passage they descended to the precinct of *Aphrodite in the Gardens, where they left what they were carrying and took and brought to the Acropolis something else covered up. After this they were replaced by others.

Arria the Elder, the wife of Caecina Paetus, celebrated for her courage and self-control. Thus when her husband was condemned by *Claudius for his part in a conspiracy (AD 42), she stabbed herself and, handing him the dagger, said, 'It doesn't hurt, Paetus'.

Arrian, c. AD 86–160. Born in *Nicomedia, he held local office and pursued studies with *Epictetus, whose lectures he later published. In Greece between 108 and 112 he attracted the friendship of *Hadrian, who later *adlected him to senatorial rank and after his consulate employed him for six years (131–7) as *legate of Cappadocia. Later he retired to Athens, where he held the archonship (145/6).

One of the most distinguished writers of his day, Arrian represented himself as a second *Xenophon and adopted a style which fused elements of Xenophon into a composite, artificial (yet outstandingly lucid) diction based on the great masters, *Herodotus and *Thucydides (2). *On Hunting* is an explicit revision of

Xenophon's monograph in the light of the revolution in *hunting brought by the Celtic greyhound; and Xenophon's influence is demonstrable in the short essays he wrote in Cappadocia: *Voyage Round the Black Sea*, *Essay on Tactics*, and, most remarkable, *Order of Battle against the Alans*, which expounds his tactics to repel the incursion of the Alans (135).

Celebrated as a philosopher in his lifetime, Arrian is today mainly known as a historian. His most famous work deals with the age of *Alexander (2) the Great. The period after Alexander's death (323–319 BC) was covered expansively in the ten books of *Affairs after Alexander* (significant fragments of which survive). The only extant history is the so-called 'Anabasis of Alexander', a history of Alexander in seven books from his accession to his death. A short companion piece, the *Indikē*, provides a digest of Indian memorabilia, based explicitly upon *Megasthenes, *Eratosthenes, and *Nearchus, and recounts Nearchus' voyage from southern India to Susa. Arrian's work is conceived as a literary tribute to Alexander's achievements, to do for him what *Homer had done for *Achilles, and the tone is eulogistic, mitigating standard criticisms and culminating in a panegyric of extraordinary intensity. The sources Arrian selected were *Ptolemy (1) I and Aristobulus, contemporaries and actors in the events and appropriately favourable to Alexander; and the narrative is worked up from material they provided, supplemented by *logoi* ('stories'), mostly from late rhetorical sources and chosen for their colour. Arrian's priority was excellence of style, not factual accuracy. So his account is rich in detail and eminently readable, but is marred by demonstrable errors and misunderstandings.

Arsacids, the Iranian royal dynasty with its original centre in *Parthia, ruling c.250 BC–AD 224; named after the tribal chieftain Arsacēs, who had invaded the former Seleucid satrapy of Parthia from the north and killed its ruler. Arsaces' kingly successors later claimed descent from, and the political heritage of, the *Achaemenids. They drove the *Seleucids from Iran and Mesopotamia and from 92 BC on were neighbours and rivals of Rome on the Euphrates–Armenian border.

art, ancient attitudes to

Artists and their Work The Greeks regularly equated art with craft, *technē*, which *Aristotle defined as the 'trained ability of making something under the guidance of rational thought'.

Until the late Hellenistic period, there is no evidence that sculpture and painting were viewed as fundamentally different from shoemaking or any other profession which yields a product.

From an aristocratic point of view artists were regarded as social inferiors because they were obliged to do physical work for others, and such a life was held to degrade their bodies and minds. Although this aristocratic prejudice is documented throughout antiquity, not everyone adhered to it. Artists like *Phidias, *Polyclitus, *Parrhasius, and *Zeuxis were clearly respected in their own time, and the quality and value of their work was recognized. Respect for the art of painting seems to have grown during the Classical period.

The modest position of artists in most Greek social and philosophical thought did not prevent some of them from becoming respected and even rich. Phidias was part of *Pericles' inner circle; *Polygnotus, whom Plutarch describes as 'not just one of the common workmen', served as Cimon's artistic impresario; the family of *Praxiteles belonged to the upper level of Athenian society in the 4th cent., and one of Praxiteles' sons, the sculptor Cephisodotus, undertook *trierarchies for the city; and in the Hellenistic period a number of sculptors are recorded as having held magistracies and been the recipients of honours in various Greek cities. The reputation and influence of artists was further enhanced by the *patronage of Hellenistic monarchs. *Alexander (2) the Great gave special status to Lysippus and *Apelles; and the early Ptolemies (see PTOLEMY (1)) invited prominent artists to their court.

In the late Hellenistic period a new theory of artistic creativity was developed in which certain artists, esp. Phidias, were recognized as inspired visionaries whose insight and creative ability surpassed that of ordinary people and made them sages of a sort.

Evolving Uses of Art, Greek There was a significant distinction in the Greek world between public and private art. The major arts of sculpture and painting fall primarily, if not exclusively, into the category of public art, which had two subdivisions: works with a religious purpose, such as cult-images, temple sculptures, and *votives; and works with a political or cultural commemorative function, such as portraits of civic leaders, personifications of political ideas, paintings of famous battles, and victory monuments connected with public competitions (see AGONES). For funerary sculpture, see next two entries.

Small-scale works of art which had a primarily decorative purpose, such as paintings on *pottery, engravings on gems, and jewellery, belong to the category of private art. Some *terracotta statuettes may fall into this class, although most of them were probably votive. In the 4th cent. figural *mosaic pavements became an increasingly common decorative element in private houses, and Plutarch's story of *Alcibiades' efforts to compel the painter *Agatharchus to decorate his house suggests that mural paintings could also be part of domestic decoration, at least in aristocratic circles.

Over time there were two major shifts of emphasis within these categories. First, beginning in the 5th cent. the line between religious and commemorative-political art became blurred as traditional subjects were adapted to convey political meanings (e.g. the Amazonomachy, the Gigantomachy; see AMAZONS; GIANTS). The sculptures of the *Parthenon and the great altar and other Attalid dedications at *Pergamum are notable examples of this trend. Second, as the idea of acquiring works of art for private delectation developed among Hellenistic monarchs, the major arts of sculpture and painting gradually also became part of the world of private art.

Evolving Uses of Art, Roman Art in Rome had the same functions as it had in Greece, but private patronage of artists played a much wider role in the Roman world, and the commemorative aspect of public art tended to have a different emphasis.

The formation of private art collections was a distinctive phenomenon of the later Roman republic and was apparently first stimulated by the vast quantities of Greek art taken as *booty by the Romans in the 3rd and 2nd cents. Captured sculptures and paintings were first used to adorn *triumphal processions and later to decorate villas and houses of the triumphators. In time, possessing an art collection became a badge of cultural sophistication, and the drive to acquire collections spread beyond the world of victorious generals. When the supply of looted works of art dried up, the demand created by collectors was met by Greek artists who migrated to Rome, and some of them could command huge prices for their work. By the 1st cent. BC a lively 'art world' had taken shape, populated not only by artists and collectors but also by dealers and even forgers. One significant outcome of this development was the creation of Europe's first public art galleries, in which extensive private collections could be exhibited.

The Romans were more interested than the Greeks in using the arts to record the details of specific historical events. Public buildings often bore inscriptions celebrating the largess and achievements of the prominent citizens who had built them, and both paintings and relief sculptures documented military campaigns and important public ceremonies. See ARA PACIS; TRAJAN'S COLUMN.

A fusion of this deep-seated historical self-consciousness with the growing importance of private patronage in late republican Rome resulted in an expansion of the scope of ancient *portraiture. The Greeks had produced portraits only of prominent public figures (e.g. military men and civic leaders). By the early empire, however, Roman portraits came to be commissioned not only by rulers and aristocrats but also by citizens of quite humble status, such as freedmen.

See ART, FUNERARY, GREEK and ROMAN; ARTISANS AND CRAFTSMEN; EKPHRASIS; IMAGERY; PAINTING, GREEK and ROMAN; SCULPTURE, GREEK and ROMAN.

art, funerary, Greek

Archaic period (c.700–c.480). The period's chief innovations were the funerary statue and carved gravestone. *Kouroi* (standing, usually nude, youths) marked graves on Thera by c.630. Funerary *korai* (standing, draped, young women) appear shortly after 600, as do painted and sculpted gravestones. At Athens, these *stelai* soon became lavish, until banned by sumptuary legislation, apparently c.490. Athletes, warriors, hunters, and elders are common subjects. The less rich or less pretentious continued to favour earth mounds, though built tombs of stone or brick appeared c.600.

Classical Period (c.480–c.330). At Athens, the legislation mentioned above decreed that no tomb could be made by more than ten men in three days. So, until c.430 Attic funerary art is restricted to white-ground *lēkythoi*: small, clay oil-flasks usually painted with domestic or mourning scenes in applied colour. Some show scenes at the tomb itself, complete with *lekythoi* standing on the stepped bases of the simple stone slabs that now served as grave-markers.

Around 430, for reasons perhaps relating either to the outbreak of the *Peloponnesian War (431) or the plague (430), grave-*stelai* began to reappear in Athens. They soon developed a standard repertoire of subjects: athlete, warrior,

mistress and maid, father and son, married couple, family group, funeral banquet, and so on. Though most are in the form of small shrines in high relief, low-relief slab-*stelai* furnished a cheap alternative; stone *lekythoi* were also popular, and unmarried women received a marble *loutrophoros* (vase used in nuptial bath). Dead and living are often linked by a handshake, and the mood is usually sombre. During the 4th cent., the *stelai* became larger and more elaborate, until *Demetrius (1) of Phaleron banned them in 317.

In Asia Minor, Greek architects and sculptors built sumptuous tombs for local rulers. In Lycia, the most elaborate is the 'Nereid Monument' from Xanthus, now in the British Museum. Constructed c.380, it consisted of a square podium embellished with battle-reliefs and surmounted by a small Ionic temple; Nereids stood between the columns. The Carian ruler *Mausolus used many elements of this design for his *Mausoleum at Halicarnassus. Begun c.365, this most grandiose of all sculpted tombs was widely imitated.

Hellenistic period (c.330–c.30). *Alexander (2) the Great's sumptuous hearse set a new standard in funerary magnificence. His own mausoleum at *Alexandria has disappeared, but other royal tombs have survived. In Macedonia, kings and aristocrats were buried in vaulted chambers painted with a wide variety of subjects: hunts, Amazonomachies, Centauromachies (see CENTAURS), *Hades and *Persephone, chariot-races and so on. The most famous of these, Tomb II at Vergina (see AEGAE), was probably constructed for King Philip Arrhidaeus and Eurydice (d. 317/6). Sculpted monuments include the 'Alexander Sarcophagus' from Sidon.

art, funerary, Roman

Early republican tombs at Rome have none of the decorative features of contemporary Etruscan funerary art (see ETRUSCANS), but by the mid to late republic some aristocratic tombs show a desire for elaboration (e.g. the façade of the tomb of the Scipio family, painted and decorated with statues in niches). From the last years of the republic onwards funerary art ceased to be the prerogative of the rich: even *freedmen and slaves decorated their tombs and bought funerary monuments. Several media were used to decorate the tomb outside and inside, and to provide memorials for the dead. The exterior might have decorations in relief (stone or terracotta) alluding to the deceased's offices or profession (e.g. *fasces and curule chair for a magistrate, or a scene of everyday business). Portraits of the deceased were also popular, esp. with freedmen in the late republic and early empire. Inside the tomb there were sculpted free-standing monuments, including the containers for the remains of the deceased—ash-chests in the early empire and, increasingly from *c*. AD 100 onwards, *sarcophagi. The interior of the tomb itself might be decorated with stucco, *painting, and *mosaic. In the *catacombs painting was the dominant form of decoration, but here biblical stories and Christian symbols replaced the pagan ones in use elsewhere. Mosaic was used primarily for the floors of tombs, but also appears on ceilings and walls.

The iconographic repertoire of Roman funerary art is rich. Motifs might refer directly to the deceased: *portraiture, whether full-length or in bust form, was popular throughout the imperial period, and portraits are found both on the façades of tombs and on a variety of monuments such as sarcophagi, where they can appear both in relief on the chest and as a reclining figure on the lid. The deceased might also be represented engaged in an everyday activity, on their deathbed, or in heroized and idealized form, with the attributes of a deity or hero, and women might be represented with the beauty and attributes of *Venus. Battle and hunt scenes, designed to show the deceased's manliness, were widely used on sarcophagi. Mythical scenes were popular, and a wide selection of episodes from Greek myth was used in all contexts. Motifs from the natural world abound. There were many other motifs, such as cupids, seasons, sphinxes, and griffins, which could be combined in different ways. Some of these designs alluded allegorically to beliefs in and hopes for an after-life. The *mystery cults, with their promise of salvation, gained in popularity, and Bacchic themes (see DIONYSUS) and *Hercules (paradigm of a mortal attaining immortality) appeared more often.

Much of the private, non-state art of Rome was funerary, and the production of sarcophagi became a major industry (see MARBLE; QUARRIES), with partially carved chests travelling considerable distances. Usually standardized motifs were taken from pattern books, personalization being achieved by the addition of an inscription or portrait. Nevertheless, commemoration of the dead, as lavish as could be afforded, was a major concern for most Romans of the imperial period. See CEMETERIES; DEAD, DISPOSAL OF; DEATH, ATTITUDES TO; IMAGERY; SCULPTURE, ROMAN.

Artaxerxes (1) **I** (465–424 BC), a son of *Xerxes, who came to power in the obscure situation following his father's murder. The Egyptian Revolt, helped by Athens, ended with the reimposition of *Achaemenid control (454); fighting in Asia Minor seems to have finished with a serious Persian set-back—but the historicity of the Peace of Callias (449/8; see CALLIAS, PEACE OF) remains debated.

Artaxerxes (2) **II** (405/4–359/8 BC), eldest son of *Darius II, Arsu/Arses succeeded his father smoothly. His reign is usually seen as initiating a period of accelerated decline. This vision, based on an uncritical reading of polemical, 4th-cent. Greek sources, misrepresents the longest reign in *Achaemenid history. The extensive building-works and the development of cults of *Mithra and Anahita show the continued vitality of politico-religious ideology.

Artemidōrus (mid/late 2nd cent. AD), of *Ephesus but called himself 'of Daldis' after his mother's native city in Lydia, whose chief deity *Apollo instigated his work on predictive *dreams. His *Onirocritica*, the product of travels to collect dreams and their outcomes and of study of the numerous earlier works on the subject, is the only extant ancient dream-book. It is of interest both for its categories of dream interpretation and for its religious and social assumptions.

Artemis Daughter of *Zeus and *Leto, *Apollo's elder twin sister, a major Olympian deity, a virgin and a huntress, who presided over crucial aspects of life. She presided over women's transitions (see RITES OF PASSAGE), esp. their transformation from virgin (*parthenos*) to (fully acculturated and fully 'tamed') woman (*gynē*), and over *childbirth and child-rearing. She was also concerned with male activities, often (as at Sparta, see below) with their rites of transition to adulthood, also *hunting and certain aspects of war. Like all deities, she had different cults in the different parts of the Greek world, but the above-mentioned concerns are part of her panhellenic persona and recur commonly in local cults; the same is even more strongly the case with her firm association with the wild and her persona as protector of young animals as well as of hunting.

In the Classical period Artemis is usually represented with a bow and arrow, and she is often associated with a deer. One of her epithets is Elaphēbolos (the 'Shooter of Deer'), after which was named the month Elaphebolion. Sometimes, esp. in the Archaic period, she was represented as Mistress of the Animals, usually winged, flanked by animals.

In *Homer, Artemis was, like Apollo, on the side of the Trojans. She was a death-bringing deity, for she sent sudden death to women, as Apollo did to men. Apollo and Artemis together killed the children of Niobē, who had boasted about the large number of children she had in comparison to Leto's two. She or Apollo, or both, killed *Gaia's son Tityus who had tried to rape Leto. Some of the more important myths assigning her the role of punishing deity are that of Actaeon (whom she transformed into a stag and had torn apart by his own hounds), that of her companion Callisto (for having lost her chastity to Zeus), and her demand that *Iphigenia be sacrificed.

In Attica her most important cults are those of Artemis Brauronia, Munichia, and Agrotera. As Brauronia and Munichia she was above all concerned with female transitions, esp. that from *parthenos* to *gynē*. At her sanctuaries at *Brauron and Munichia little girls between the ages of 5 and 10 served Artemis as *arktoi* (bears), a premenarche ritual that turned girl-children into marriageable *parthenoi*. Artemis Brauronia was a women's goddess, and she included a strong child-rearing function. Artemis Munichia was also a *kourotrophos*, and she was also concerned with *epheboi*; at her festival, the Munichia, ephebes sailed from Zea to the harbour of Munichia in 'the sacred ships', and held races at sea. Then they processed for Artemis and sacrificed, celebrations said to be in commemoration of and thanksgiving for the battle of *Salamis.

Artemis Agrotera had some involvement with war. The Spartans sacrificed a goat to her before battle, while the Athenians, we are told, before the battle of *Marathon vowed to sacrifice to Artemis Agrotera as many goats as enemies killed. In the event they could not find enough goats; so they vowed to sacrifice 500 a year, which they did, on her festival day, which thus involved a strong element of thanksgiving for Marathon. This festival included a procession to the temple in which the ephebes took part. The sanctuary of Artemis Agrotera was suburban, at Agrae.

Artemisia, early 5th-cent. BC ruler, under Persian suzerainty, over *Halicarnassus and *Cos. In the *Persian Wars Artemisia accompanied Xerxes' expedition with five ships. Acc. to the Halicarnassian *Herodotus, she was a 'warner'

figure, who unsuccessfully urged Xerxes not to fight at Salamis, but fought bravely and escaped by sinking a ship in her way. Xerxes remarked 'my men have become women and my women men'. Afterwards she urged him to retreat and transported part of his family to *Ephesus.

Artemisium, battle of (480 BC). Pevki bay near Artemisium on the NE coast of *Euboea was probably the base of the Greek fleet during the three days of fighting which coincided with the battle of *Thermopylae. With fewer and slower ships, the Greeks nevertheless took the initiative for two days, though careful to fight towards evening so that they could break off if necessary. But on the third day, perhaps to coincide with the final assault on Thermopylae, the Persian fleet came out at midday, and although still technically the victors, the Greeks had so many ships damaged that they were already considering withdrawal when the news of what had happened at Thermopylae reached them. Though indecisive, Artemisium, as *Pindar said, was where the Greeks 'laid the shining foundation of freedom'. See PERSIAN WARS.

artillery Evidence for Greek and Roman artillery comes from the surviving technical treatises, incidental historical and subliterary references, and, most importantly, finds of both machine-fittings and projectiles. The latter at present date from the 2nd cent. BC to the 4th cent. AD.

In 399 BC artificers of *Dionysius (1) I apparently invented the first artillery piece. The *gastraphetēs* shot arrows only, and somewhat resembled an early medieval crossbow. Propulsive force was supplied by a composite bow, which, being too powerful for a man to draw by hand, was bent by means of a slide and stock. Later *gastraphetai*, some of which were stone-throwers, used a winch and had a stand.

Torsion catapults appeared *c.*340, possibly invented by *Philip II's engineers. Stock, winch, and base remained much the same, but two springs, bundles of rope made from animal sinew, horsehair, or human hair, and held at high tension in a metal-plated wooden frame, now provided propulsive power. Torsion machines improved continuously in efficiency through the Roman period. From *c.*270 a technical literature of calibrating formulae and standard dimensions developed (see CTESIBIUS). The torsion *katapeltēs oxybelēs* shot bolts only, the *lithobolos* hurled stone-shot (*weights of ten *minae* to three talents). Both types had a maximum effective range of well over 300 m. (330 yds.).

Each imperial Roman legion had artillery specialists and workshops to design, manufacture, repair, and deploy its *c.*70 *catapultae* and *ballistae*. The small but powerful engines illustrated on *Trajan's Column and described by Heron, with all-metal frames, were probably developed in the 1st cent. AD. They continued in use into the late Roman period. By the 4th cent. AD the one-armed, stone-throwing *onager* was also developed.

Artillery figured most prominently in sieges, esp. those associated with Rome's eastern wars, and its use spread to the *Sasanids through Roman contacts. Whilst *Alexander (2) the Great used artillery in the field, lack of mobility restricted it before the Roman period. Long range made artillery a valuable naval weapon. See FORTIFICATIONS; SIEGECRAFT, GREEK and ROMAN; WAR, ART OF, GREEK and ROMAN.

artisans and craftsmen (see ART, ANCIENT ATTITUDES TO; CLUBS, GREEK and ROMAN; INDUSTRY; MARKETS). In Greece the prejudices of the (largely landowning) citizen-élites against the activities of 'mechanics' (*banausoi*), often slaves, *freedmen, or *metics, subjected artisans to formal handicaps in the oligarchic *polis, including limitation of political rights, restriction of their freedom of movement, and exclusion from the *gymnasium. In the Athenian *democracy their social standing was higher, despite the condescension of Athenian 'intellectuals'. Craftsmen themselves could be proud of their products, if the 'signatures' on painted *pottery are really those of their makers, as too of their occupations, to judge from the Athenian artisans who stated them in their dedications, including a 'washerwoman', the last a reminder of the considerable involvement of women in the humbler crafts, esp. *textile production. Although entrepreneurs could prosper through artisanal activity, craftsmen as a group were largely powerless, since the citizen body, beyond taxing sales and charging rents for market- and workshop-space, had no interest in promoting industry as such.

The larger scale of the Roman economy gives greater visibility to the entrepreneurial artisan in Roman society, such as the contract-baker Vergilius Eurysaces, whose grandiose tomb in Rome still stands, although there is little clear evidence for manufacturing enterprises of more than local significance (but see AMPHORAE (ROMAN)) and—apart from the exceptional case of brick production (see BRICKSTAMPS)—the Roman élite cannot easily be linked with manufacture. On the other hand, upper-class disdain for the crafts hardly encouraged the open admission of such links, which certainly accounted for some of the wealth of successful Roman *freedmen.

Ascanius, in literature and myth, son of *Aeneas. He appears in the Aeneas-legend by the 5th cent. BC, at first as one of several sons of Aeneas. The *gens Iūlia* claimed him as eponymous founder with an alternative name of 'Iūlus'. In the *Aeneid* he is a projection of typical and sometimes ideal Roman youth, but still too young to play a major part; other versions tell of his later career as king of Lavinium and founder of Alba Longa, the city from which Rome was founded.

asceticism The Greek word *askēsis* implies disciplined and productive effort. At first mainly physical in sense—alluding to the skill of the craftsman and the vigour of the athlete—it quickly acquired a moral sense also, clear in *Xenophon. He contrasted the ascetic with the self-willed amateur, stressing submission to a tradition of instruction, and he made a connection with self-mastery, overlaying with that positive moral note the more general notion of *labour. The ascetic improved upon nature, remaining in that sense a craftsman.

Asceticism was associated thereafter with philosophical rather than religious practice. Philosophers rejected ritual as a guarantee of liberation or virtue. Their moderation was distinct from the self-denial of priests, initiates, and devotees, even when that involved *fasting or sexual restraint.

Linked thus with philosophy, asceticism adopted forms dictated by different schools. With Platonism ascendant, its general aim veered naturally towards truth and knowledge understood in increasingly exalted and visionary senses. Followers of *Pythagoras, believing a divine element was imprisoned in the body, recommended release through *silence as an aid to contemplation, with fasting an added option (perhaps more symbolic than effective). Some Cynics may have furthered the ascetic cause, esp. when, like *Crates, they advocated simplicity and detachment. The *Stoics armed themselves against what they called 'passion' and relinquished some goods to safeguard others: sound judgement mattered more than willpower. No less, in their way, the disciples of

*Epicurus chose some goods over others in pursuit of true happiness and should be allowed the title of 'ascetic' in a strict sense. Finally, Neopythagoreanism from the 1st cent. BC on prompted more severe criticism of cult as a moral tool and emphasized the inner quality of true piety—an emphasis that would mirror if not reinforce the suspicion of some Christian ascetics about the usefulness of sacramental religion. By the time of *Philostratus and *Iamblichus, those different elements had begun to conflate—a process confirmed within *Neoplatonism.

Not surprisingly, therefore, asceticism made its appearance in a Christian context precisely when Christians opened themselves fully, during the 2nd cent., to the classical philosophical tradition. The chief exemplars are *Clement and *Origen of Alexandria.

Asclēpius, hero and god of healing.

In *Homer's *Iliad*, he is a hero, the 'blameless physician', taught by the *Centaur Chiron; his two sons, the physicians Machaon and Podalirius, lead a contingent from Tricca in *Thessaly. Later he was said to be the son of *Apollo and Coronis. Coronis had become Apollo's beloved, but then married a mortal; when a raven denounced the girl to the god, he killed her, but snatched the unborn baby from the pyre, and entrusted him to Chiron. When grown up, Asclepius became a great healer who even raised men from the dead, which provoked *Zeus into killing him with his thunderbolt. Angered, Apollo retaliated by killing the *Cyclopes who had made the thunderbolt; in order to punish him, Zeus sent him into servitude with Admetus, king of Pherae (see ALCESTIS). Unlike ordinary heroes, Asclepius must have been very early emancipated from the attachment to a local grave; this allowed him to develop a god-like stature, though he stayed attached to his father Apollo.

Expansion of Asclepius must have begun in late Archaic times; both *Cos and *Epidaurus became famous during the 5th cent. Cos was the home of a school of physicians who called themselves the descendants of Asclepius or Asclepiads. When, in 366/5, the city of Cos was rebuilt, Asclepius received a *sanctuary in a grove of Apollo; the famous oath, sworn to Apollo, Asclepius, (his daughters) Hygieia and Panacea, 'and all gods and goddesses', belongs to the same period. Asclepius must have arrived at Epidaurus c.500, and it became the centre for later expansion. Asclepius came to *Sicyon in the 5th cent., brought on a mule cart and in the form of his snake. Similarly, the god sent his snake to Athens where he arrived in 420/19, coming by sea to his sanctuary in *Piraeus (the snake stayed with *Sophocles until his new sanctuary was ready); not long after, he was transferred by cart, together with Hygieia, to his sanctuary on the west slope of the Acropolis, above the theatre of Dionysus. To cure a plague in 293, the *Sibylline books caused the Romans to fetch the god's snake by ship from Epidaurus to Rome, where the snake chose *Tiber island as its home.

The success of Asclepius was due to his appeal to individuals in a world where their concerns became more and more removed from *polis* religion and even from the healer Apollo, whose appeal was still discernible in his expansion to Rome in 433 and in his popularity in the Black (*Euxine) Sea towns: with the one exception of Asclepius' transfer to Rome, it was individuals who were responsible for the expansion. The hero, 'best of the physicians', son of Apollo but still enough of a human to try to cancel death, the fundamental borderline between man and god in Greek thinking, was more easily accessible than Apollo, who could proclaim lofty indifference towards man and his destiny; even as a god, Asclepius was never so distant (see the very personal attachment of Aelius *Aristides in the 2nd cent. AD to Asclepius).

Most Asclepiea share certain features. The children of Asclepius, his sons Machaon and Podalirius and his daughter Hygieia, have cult in most, as has Apollo, whom official inscriptions from Epidaurus always name before Asclepius. Most sanctuaries contain a sacred snake. A central feature of the cult is *incubation, the receiving of dreams in which the god prescribes the healing; such dreams are preserved in the *Sacred Teachings* of Aelius Aristides and in the accounts of more or less miraculous healings inscribed in Epidaurus, Pergamum, and Rome. Often, actual medical therapy followed the dream: Asclepiea developed into sacred hospitals and nursing-homes, but, owing to their wide appeal, also constituted meeting-places for local intellectuals and places of philosophical instruction. Most Asclepiea were situated outside the town, sometimes on the seashore or in a lone valley, or at least in a marginal position in town. They share such sites with oracular shrines; both constituted places where man could meet the divine directly (in his sanctuary, Asclepius 'reveals himself in person to man').

In iconography, Asclepius generally appears as a mature, bearded man, similar to Zeus, but with a milder expression. His most constant attributes are the staff and the snake, often coiled about the staff. Generally, the god is standing; in the chryselephantine statue from Epidaurus (see coins), the god is seated, the staff in his left hand, his right extended above the head of a serpent.

Asia, Roman province *Attalus III of *Pergamum bequeathed his kingdom to the Romans. After his death in 133 BC it was constituted as *provincia Asia*. Originally it consisted of Mysia, *Troas, *Aeolis, *Lydia, Ionia (see IONIANS), the islands along the coast, much of *Caria, and at least a land corridor through *Pisidia to Pamphylia. Under the empire Asia was bounded in the north by *Bithynia, in the south by Lycia, and in the east by *Galatia.

Asia was rich in natural resources and in the products of agriculture and industry. Woollen fabrics were a speciality of the interior. Trade routes ran from the interior along the valleys of the Hermus and the Maeander rivers to the harbours of the Aegean. Roman republican governors and capitalists exploited the new province with predatory rapacity and aroused widespread hatred, which was exploited by *Mithradates VI when he stirred up much of Asia to revolt between 88 and 85 BC. Allegedly 80,000 Italians were murdered in a single day at his instigation. After defeating Mithradates *Sulla reorganized the province in 85/4 BC. and revised the administrative pattern in eleven assize-districts. Asia continued to suffer from heavy taxation and arbitrary exactions through the civil wars of the late republic. The province picked the losing side in the wars between Mithradates and Rome, between *Pompey and *Caesar, between the tyrannicides and Antony (Marcus *Antonius), and between Antony and *Octavian. Neither victors nor losers in these wars hesitated to milk its rich resources. The principate of Augustus brought relief and was welcomed with genuine hope and enthusiasm, which is reflected above all in the organization of *ruler-cult throughout the province.

Asia was now governed by a proconsul (see PRO CONSULE), who normally served for one year, assisted by three *legates and a quaestor. He traditionally landed at *Ephesus, the headquarters of the republican *publicani and later of the imperial *procurators, but spent much of his time visiting the assize centres (*conventus) of the province according to a fixed rotation, where he heard cases and conducted other judicial business. Ephesus eclipsed Pergamum, although these cities and Smyrna remained locked in rivalry for the rank of leading city.

Under the Principate new cities were created in the interior regions of Mysia, Lydia, and Phrygia; the province thus comprised a conglomeration of self-governing cities, on which the Roman system of provincial government depended. The cities were responsible for local administration, for their own finances and building, for law and order on their territories, and for tax collection. The province was represented as a unity by the council of Asia, a general assembly of representatives from all the cities and other communities, which met annually in one of the five provincial cities (Ephesus, Smyrna, Pergamum, *Sardis, and Cyzicus) and organized the provincial imperial cult. Progress towards provincial unity, however, was always hampered by inter-city rivalry, esp. among the communities of the western coast and the Maeander valley.

In the first two centuries AD the cities of Asia enjoyed great prosperity, attested by splendid ruins and handsome monuments, and reflected e.g. in the panegyric speeches of Aelius *Aristides. The wealth of inscriptions, locally minted coins, and material remains makes Asia one of the best documented of all Roman provinces. The cities had changed from autonomous states into administrative centres, but countless inscriptions attest the eagerness of members of the city aristocracies for public service, their generosity in providing civic amenities (doubtless at the expense of the rural populations which they exploited), and the entry of many families into the senatorial and *equestrian orders. The glittering and extravagant society of the coastal cities, with their rich *rhetors and sophists, contrasts with the traditional, rural-based society of the interior. Urbanization brought Graeco-Roman culture up-country, but the basic Anatolian character of the population of regions such as Lydia and Phrygia persisted and was esp. conspicuous in their religious cults. The strict, self-disciplined morality of pagan belief in the hinterland of the province provided fertile ground where Jewish and early Christian groups flourished. Much of the interior had apparently converted to Christianity before the beginning of the 4th cent.

Asia Minor The term 'Asia Minor' denotes the westernmost part of the Asian continent, equivalent to modern Turkey between the

Aegean and the Euphrates. The west and south coastal fringes were part of the Mediterranean world; the heartland of Asia Minor lay in the hilly but fertile uplands of Phrygia, the steppic central plateau, and the rugged and harsh country of Cappadocia. These areas were framed by the Pontic ranges, which rise steeply from the Black Sea in the north, and the long range of the Taurus, which snakes through southern Asia Minor from Lycia to the Euphrates and separates Asia Minor from Syria. In the Graeco-Roman period the region's history is illuminated by an almost limitless flood of information, which makes it possible to identify the separate languages, cultures, and religious traditions of its various regions, and also to document the influence of external powers and cultures, above all of Persia, Greece, and Rome. Asia Minor was one of the economic powerhouses of the Persian empire. Much of the population of eastern Asia Minor had strong Iranian connections, and Persian settlements were also widespread in the west after the mid-6th cent. BC. Greek influence—*Hellenism—was naturally strongest in the coastal areas, where Greeks had established settlements between c.1100 and 600 BC. The cultural process, however, was not one-way, and the Greeks of Caria and Pamphylia were also much influenced by pre-existing cultures. During the 4th cent. Hellenization spread to the indigenous inhabitants of Pisidia and Lycia in the SW; most of the interior, however, was barely touched before the 1st cent. BC. Roman rule made the strongest impact. In the time of Hadrian Asia Minor was divided into six provinces: Asia, Pontus and Bithynia, Galatia, Lycia and Pamphylia, Cilicia, and Cappadocia. The creation of an all-embracing road network, the universal *ruler-cult, the founding of cities to act as administrative centres, a permanent military presence, and the creation of far-reaching systems of *taxation forged a new society in Asia Minor, which was as much Roman as it was *Anatolian.

Asianism and Atticism The Greek orators of *Asia Minor during the Hellenistic period developed a new style of oratory, marked by wordplay, emotional effect, bombast, and rhythm. An inevitable reaction is seen clearly in the work of the Augustan critics *Dionysius (3) of Halicarnassus and Caecilius of Caleacte, in favour of the stylistic norms of 5th-cent. Attic oratory (see ATTIC ORATORS). The confrontation of styles is best known from its Latin repercussions. *Cicero, with his Greek educational background and florid manner, was criticized as an 'Asian' by what he represents in *Brutus* and *Orator* as a minority of extremists who even thought the style of *Thucydides (2) appropriate in a Roman court. The tendencies of *Silver Age Latin might be thought to suggest an 'Asian' victory in the west; in the east, the admirers of Attic prose were able to suppress the productions of their rivals (see RHETORIC; SECOND SOPHISTIC).

Asinius Pollio, Gāius (76 BC–AD 4), supported *Caesar, as praetor in 45, commanding in Spain in 44, and then joined Antony (Marcus *Antonius); in Cisalpine Gaul in 41 he saved *Virgil's property from confiscation. Consul in 40, he celebrated a triumph over the Parthini of Illyria in 39; from the booty he built the first public *library in Rome. Then, with full honours, he retired from politics to devote himself to literature, arranging the first public recitations. In youth an associate of *Catullus, he later enjoyed the friendship of *Horace and Virgil. His own work included poetry, tragedy, and oratory in Atticist style (see ASIANISM AND ATTICISM), but he was above all a historian. His *Histories* treated the period from 60 BC to the battle of Philippi in 42; analytical, critical, and serious, they were used by *Plutarch and *Appian. A sharp critic, he corrected Cicero and Caesar, Sallust for archaism, and Livy for provincialism; and he maintained his republican independence even against Augustus.

Aspasia, Milesian-born partner of *Pericles from c.445 BC when he divorced his wife. She is said to have taught rhetoric, and to have had discussions with *Socrates. She was the target of attacks and jokes in comedy because of her supposed influence over Pericles: Aristophanes' *Acharnians* blames her for the *Peloponnesian War. Her (later legitimated) son by Pericles, also a Pericles, was one of the generals put to death after *Arginusae. See also EPITAPHIOS.

assembly See EKKLESIA.

assizes See CONVENTUS (2).

associations See CLUBS.

assonance, Latin Assonance, the recurrence of sounds in proximity, is a common feature of language, observable in all periods of Latin. Three kinds may be mentioned.

Alliteration The repetition of initial sounds appears in formulaic language of all levels in (*a*) idioms and proverbs; (*b*) prayers; (*c*) legal formulae.

Homoeoteleuton The repetition of final sounds is an almost inevitable consequence of Latin inflexion, e.g. 'excitatus senatus, inflammatus populus Romanus'. Its effectiveness in fixing formulaic language is seen in idiomatic and religious language.

Rhyme Latin inflexion also facilitates occasional rhyme, which reinforces syntactic or metrical boundaries. Over one-fifth of elegiac pentameters (see METRE, GREEK, 4(b) Dactylic) display internal rhyme, between the two halves of a line, almost always involving an adjective and noun in agreement.

astrology, the art of converting astronomical data (i.e. the positions of the celestial bodies) into predictions of outcomes in human affairs. Astrology developed in the Hellenistic age, an import from Babylon (see BABYLONIA), which equally furnished many of its astronomical parameters. *Alexandria was its major centre. By the 1st cent. BC, it had emerged as a sophisticated technical art, commanding widespread credence and respect. So it remained until the late empire, when its incompatibility with *Christianity led to its formal suppression (though not extinction).

There are several branches of astrology, of which the most important is genethlialogy, the art of foretelling an individual's life from the positions of the stars (i.e. sun, moon, planets, and fixed stars) at birth or conception; see CONSTELLATIONS. The basic astronomical data for calculating a 'nativity' (i.e. a horoscope) are (*a*) the positions of the seven known planets (including sun and moon) relative to one another (their 'aspects') and to the twelve signs of the zodiac, and (*b*) the position of the circle of the zodiac (and thus of the planets moving round it) relative to a second circle of twelve 'places' (mod. 'houses') whose cardinal points ('centres') are the rising- and setting-points on the horizon and the zenith and nadir.

astronomy The use of the heliacal rising and setting of prominent stars or star-groups to mark points in the year is found in the earliest literature of the Greeks (*Homer and *Hesiod), and no doubt goes back to prehistoric times. This 'traditional' Greek astronomy continued (with some refinements borrowed from 'scientific' astronomy) to the end of antiquity. It was embodied in the 'astronomical calendars' which

began with *Meton and Euctemon in the 5th cent. BC and of which several examples are preserved in manuscript and on stone. These mark important points of the year (including solstices and equinoxes), and use the risings and settings of stars as a basis for weather predictions (the latter already in Hesiod).

2. Scientific astronomy in Greece hardly predates the 5th cent. BC. The cosmological speculations of the earlier Presocratics are irrelevant, and the scientific feats attributed to some of them (e.g. *Thales' prediction of an eclipse) by later writers are unworthy of belief. However, some of the basic concepts necessary to later astronomy were enunciated in the course of the 5th cent. *Parmenides mentioned the sphericity of the earth and stated that the moon receives its light from the sun. *Empedocles went beyond this to infer the cause of solar eclipses, as did *Anaxagoras. Yet how unfamiliar this was even to an educated man of the late 5th cent. is shown by the remark of *Thucydides (2) that solar eclipses *seem* to occur only at new moon. *Democritus, according to Seneca the Younger, said that he *suspected* that there were several planets but gave neither number nor names. Significant for the future development of Greek astronomy is the transmission of elements from *Babylonia (which had a tradition of observational astronomy going back to the 8th cent.): the twelve signs of the zodiac appear in Greece perhaps as early as the late 6th cent. certainly the nineteen-year luni-solar cycle of Meton was derived from Babylon; but this, like Meton's solstice observations, is still directed towards the goals of 'traditional' astronomy.

3. The 4th cent. saw the introduction of the most characteristic Greek contribution to astronomical theory, the idea that the apparently irregular motions of the heavenly bodies should be explained by geometrical models based on uniform circular motion. The first system embodying this idea was constructed by Plato's contemporary *Eudoxus. He was also the first to establish axiomatic rigour in geometry: this success may have led to the notion of extending the explanatory power of geometry to other fields, including the heavens. Eudoxus' system of 'homocentric spheres', centred on the fixed, spherical earth, and rotating with uniform motions about different poles, combined simplicity with mathematical ingenuity, and was able, in principle, to account for the retrogradations of the planets and the latitudinal deviations of all bodies, including the moon. The observational elements involved were few. Yet even these

represent a considerable advance over the ignorance prevalent 50 years earlier: Eudoxus is the first Greek who is *known* to have recognized all five planets. Here again we may suspect Babylonian influence in the observational data, esp. since there are Mesopotamian elements also in the description of the *constellations which Eudoxus published. For all its mathematical elegance, Eudoxus' system exhibited serious discrepancies from easily observable facts. In particular no homocentric system could account for the obvious variations in size and brightness of e.g. the moon and Venus. Nevertheless his pupil Callippus modified Eudoxus' model to eliminate some of the grosser discrepancies, and this revised model has come down to us because *Aristotle accepted it, transforming what had probably been for Eudoxus a purely geometrical scheme into a physical mechanism with contiguous solid spheres. Scientific astronomy in the 4th cent. remained at this purely theoretical level: practical astronomy was concerned with traditional topics, the calendar, and the risings and settings of stars. The earliest extant astronomical works, those of Autolycus and *Euclid, are little more than a treatment of the latter in terms of elementary geometry.

4. At an unknown date, probably not long after Callippus, the epicyclic and eccentric hypotheses for planetary motion were proposed. These provided a remedy for the most glaring defect of the homocentric system, by producing variation in the distance of a heavenly body, while at the same time giving a simple representation of the 'anomalies' (variations in speed and direction) of the bodies; they became the standard models used in Greek theoretical astronomy. No doubt the complete geometric equivalence of epicyclic and eccentric forms, which was assumed in the planetary theory of *Apollonius (2), was discovered soon after these models were proposed. Perhaps it was in examining the transformation of one to the other that *Aristarchus (1) of Samos (*c*.280) came to see that one can transpose the geocentric universe to a heliocentric one, and so put forward his famous hypothesis (see GEOCENTRICITY). This, like the earlier suggestion of *Heraclides (1) Ponticus that the earth rotates on its axis, appears never to have been taken seriously by practising astronomers, although the grounds for rejecting it were 'physical' rather than astronomical. There was more observation, of solstices by Aristarchus and *Archimedes, of the declinations of fixed stars by Aristyllus and Timocharis, and of the moon (including eclipses) by Timocharis.

But theoretical astronomy remained at the stage of explaining the phenomena by means of geometrical models and deriving the mathematical consequences. This is evident in Apollonius' use of the epicyclic/eccentric hypothesis to determine stationary points on planets' orbits, and also in the single astronomical work surviving from this time, Aristarchus' treatise on the distances of the sun and moon: this is a mathematical exercise showing how the limits for those distances can be derived from certain numerical assumptions (about the inaccuracy of which the author appears unconcerned, although it must have been obvious). The topic of the distances of the heavenly bodies was much discussed, by Archimedes and Apollonius amongst others, but no one before Hipparchus devised a reliable method of computing even the moon's distance.

5. Astronomy was transformed by *Hipparchus (2) between *c*.145 and 125 BC. His great innovation was the idea of using the geometrical models, which his predecessors had developed to *explain* the phenomena, in order to *predict* or calculate them for a given time. He did not himself fully succeed in this (we are told that he renounced any attempt at constructing a theory of the planets), but he contributed several essential elements, including the development of *trigonometry, ingenious methods for the application of observational data to geometrical models, and the compilation of observations, not only of his own and other Greeks, but esp. from the massive Babylonian archives (to which he seems to have had privileged access). Although sporadic Mesopotamian influences appear in Greek astronomy from at least the time of Meton, it is apparently Hipparchus who was the main conduit to the Greek world of Babylonian astronomy, including not only observations, but also astronomical constants (e.g. very accurate lunar periods), the sexagesimal place-value notation for expressing fractions, and methods of calculation. The latter were sophisticated arithmetical procedures for predicting celestial phenomena, and now that the original *cuneiform documents have been analysed, it seems likely that it was the Babylonian success in applying mathematical methods to astronomical prediction which inspired Hipparchus to attempt the same within the Greek theoretical framework. He got as far as constructing a viable epicyclic model for the moon, and made many other individual advances, including the discovery of the precession of the equinoxes, to which he was perhaps led by noticing the discrepancy

between the year-length which he had derived from observations of equinoxes (the tropical year) and that used by the Babylonians (which was in fact a sidereal year). He also recorded a large number of star positions to be marked on his star-globe.

6. The history of astronomy in the 300 years between Hipparchus and *Ptolemy (2) is obscure, because the unchallenged position of the *Almagest* in later antiquity resulted in the loss of all earlier works on similar topics. In his magisterial *Almagest* (c. AD 150) Ptolemy ignores (apart from an occasional contemptuous aside), the work of his immediate predecessors, singling out Hipparchus as the sole peer worthy of his imitation and criticism. Starting from first principles, and rigidly excluding arithmetical methods, he constructed an edifice of models for sun, moon, planets, and fixed stars based on a combination of epicycles and eccentrics employing uniform circular motions, the numerical parameters of which he determined by rigorous geometrical methods from carefully selected observations. These were supplemented by tables allowing the computation of all celestial positions and phenomena pertinent to ancient astronomy, to a suitable accuracy. The result is a work of remarkable power and consistency, which dominated astronomy for 1,300 years.

7. Ptolemy himself regarded his work as provisional, but it was treated as definitive by his ancient successors, who confined themselves to explicating the *Almagest*, although there were serious defects in it even by ancient standards, notably in the solar theory, producing errors which increased with the lapse of time. That these were completely unnoticed in later antiquity is an indication both of the lack of independent observation and of the state of the science after Ptolemy. However, important corrections to the solar theory and other individual details of Ptolemaic astronomy were made after it experienced a revival through its transmission to the Islamic world (the *Almagest* was translated into Arabic c. AD 800), but even there the edifice as a whole remained undisturbed. Ancient astronomy did not begin to become obsolete until Copernicus.

8. The astronomy of the Greeks covered only a part of what is now denoted by the term. It can be considered the most successful of the ancient applied sciences, if one accepts the ancient view that its task is confined to describing and predicting observed motions by means of a consistent mathematical model. Physical astronomy, however, remained at a very low level (like physics in general). But it is not entirely ignored even in the *Almagest*, and in his *Planetary Hypotheses* Ptolemy attempted to fit the kinematical models of the *Almagest* into a unified physical system. This was based on Aristotelian notions, including the crucial thesis that nature is not wasteful. In it Ptolemy describes a universe in which each planetary 'shell' is contiguous with that of the bodies immediately above and below it. This system enabled him to compute the absolute dimensions and distances of all parts of the universe out to the sphere of the fixed stars, which he found to be less than 20,000 earth-radii from the central earth (less than the distance from the earth to the sun by modern computation). This vision of a small and completely determined universe became the canonical view in the Middle Ages, in both east and west. It was a strong argument against consideration of the heliocentric hypothesis, which entailed a vastly larger universe in which the fixed stars were at enormous distances.

Atalanta, a mythical heroine. She was exposed at birth and nursed by a bear before being brought up by hunters. When she reached maturity, she chose to remain a virgin and to spend her time hunting as a companion of *Artemis. She killed the Centaurs who had tried to rape her, she took part in the hunt of the Calydonian boar, where *Meleager (1) fell in love with her, and at the funeral games for *Pelias she defeated *Peleus in wrestling. Later, when her father wished to give her in marriage, she promised to marry the man who could defeat her in a foot-race. After several young men were defeated and put to death, Hippomenēs, or Mēlanion, was victorious in the test, having dropped some golden apples (see HESPERIDES) on the track, which Atalanta stopped to pick up. During a hunt, the couple made love in a sanctuary of *Zeus (or *Cybele) and as punishment for their impiety they were changed into lions.

Ātē, mental aberration, infatuation causing irrational behaviour which leads to disaster. A hero's *ate* is brought about through psychic intervention by a divine agency, usually *Zeus, but can also be physically inflicted. *Homer's *Agamemnon blames Zeus, *Fate, and the *Erinyes for the delusion that made him take *Briseis and lead the Achaeans to the brink of defeat. Ate is personified as the daughter of Zeus whom he expelled from Olympus to bring harm to men. A similarly pessimistic notion of divine punishment for guilt underlies Homer's Parable of the Prayers. In this early allegory swift-footed Ate outruns the slow Prayers and forces men into error and punishment.

Atellāna (sc. *fabula*), in origin a native Italian farce. It was a masked drama, largely improvised, with stock characters. It became a literary form for a short time in the period of *Sulla. *Atellanae* continued to be performed at least until the time of *Juvenal. They seem to have been primarily low-life comedies, often in coarse language, set in a small Italian town and giving a humorous portrait of rustic and provincial life; the familiar characters were shown in a variety of situations. See COMEDY, LATIN.

Ath. pol. See ATHENAION POLITEIA.

Athamas, mythical king of *Orchomenus, husband of Ino and father of Phrixus, *Helle, Melicertes, and Learchus. The first two were the children of Nephelē ('Cloud'), Athamas' first wife; their stepmother Ino concocted a bogus oracle demanding their deaths in sacrifice in order to restore the fertility of the land, but they were borne away on a golden-fleeced ram (see HELLE). Later, Ino and Athamas brought up the child *Dionysus, in revenge for which *Hera drove them mad. Athamas killed their son Learchus, and Ino ran from him carrying Melicertes and jumped into the sea, where mother and son were transformed into deities.

Athanasius (*c.* AD 295–373), outstanding theologian and Church leader, who as a deacon played an influential part at the council of Nicaea (325). Appointed bishop of *Alexandria in 328, he vigorously championed the Nicene doctrine of the consubstantiality of Father and Son against Arianism (see ARIUS), being five times deposed and exiled. Two of his exiles he spent in the west, to which he introduced monasticism. In the last decades of his life he developed the doctrine of the divinity and personality of the Holy Spirit, and did much to promote understanding between the different anti-Arian groups in the Church. His surviving writings include apologetic, dogmatic, and ascetic treatises, historical essays, and letters.

atheism The Greek for atheism is 'not to recognize the gods' or 'deny that the gods exist' or, later, 'to remove the gods'. The Greek word *atheos* can be applied to atheism (e.g. in Plato's *Apology*), but in the earliest instances it means

'impious, vicious' or 'hated, abandoned by the gods', and these senses persist along with the other. Christians and pagans were to swap charges of atheism, by which they meant 'impious views about the divine'.

The gods of popular polytheism were rejected or drastically reinterpreted by all philosophers from the 6th cent. BC onwards, but most preserved a divine principle of some kind (as in different ways *Plato, *Aristotle, and *Stoicism were to do). Radical atheism is hard to detect, and was never an influential intellectual position in the ancient world. *Anaxagoras and *Thucydides (2) have been suspected of it, because of their silences; a character in the satyrplay *Sisyphus* famously argues that gods are an invention of a 'wise lawgiver' to deter secret crime; on the other hand, *Democritus, whose system is compatible with atheism, appears to speak of gods in some fragments, and *Prodicus did not necessarily reject the divine in every form merely because he offered a rationalizing account of the origin of human belief in the gods of myth. Much the most important testimony to the reality of atheism is Plato's in *Laws* 10, where he speaks of contemporary thinkers who hold that the world is governed by nature or chance, not god, that morality is man-made and the best life is that according to nature. Who Plato had in mind is disputed; he goes on to say that such radical atheism was already on the wane.

A second view combated by Plato in *Laws* 10 is that the gods exist, but are indifferent to the doings of mankind. Such 'practical atheism' had doubtless always existed, and became the declared position of Epicurus (who however urged that the gods should still be honoured); philosophical opponents asserted that only fear of public opinion had restrained Epicurus from 'abolishing the gods' altogether. For agnosticism see PROTAGORAS.

Athēna In *Iliad* 5 *Homer describes how Athena took off the finely wrought robe 'which she herself had made and worked at with her own hands' and 'armed herself for grievous war'. This incident encapsulates the paradoxical nature of a goddess who is as skilled in the making of clothes as she is fearless in battle; who thus unites in her person the characteristic excellences of both sexes. At the greater *Panathenaea in Athens, she was presented with a robe, the work of maidens' hands (see ARREPHORIA), which traditionally portrayed the battle of the gods and *Giants in which she was the outstanding warrior on the side of the gods.

Her patronage of crafts is expressed in cults such as that of Athena Erganē, Athena the Craftswoman or Maker; it extends beyond the 'works' of women to carpentry, metalworking, and technology of every kind, so that at Athens she shared a temple and a festival with *Hephaestus and can be seen on vases seated (in armour!) in a pottery. Her love of battle is evident, as we saw, in myth, and also in such cults as that of Athena Victory (*Nike); she is regularly portrayed armed, one leg purposefully advanced, wearing her terror-inducing *aegis.

She is also closely associated with the masculine world in her mythological role as a helper of male heroes, most memorably seen in her presence beside Heracles on several of the metopes of the temple of *Zeus at *Olympia. Indeed her intervention in battle often takes the form of 'standing beside' a favourite. Her virginity is a bridge between the two sides of her nature. Weaving is a characteristic activity of ordinary young girls, but a perpetual virgin, who is not subject to the distinctively feminine experience of *childbirth, is a masculine woman, a potential warrior.

The warlike Athena is scarcely separable from Athena Polias, the goddess of the Acropolis (see ATHENS, TOPOGRAPHY) and protectress of cities. 'City-protecting' was more commonly performed by goddesses than gods; and the other great protectress was the other great warrior-goddess of the *Iliad*, Athena's close associate *Hera. Athena exercised this function in many cities besides Athens, including Sparta and (in the *Iliad*) Troy. Athens was unique only in the degree of prominence that it assigned her in this role.

Athena is unique among Greek gods in bearing a connection with a city imprinted in her very name. The precise linguistic relation between place and goddess is hard to define: the form of her name in early Attic inscriptions is the adjectival 'Athenaia', which suggests that she may in origin be 'the Athenian' something, the Athenian Pallas for instance. But this account still leaves the shorter name-form 'Athena' unexplained. Athenians themselves, stressed the goddess's association with their city. She was foster-mother of the early king *Erechtheus/*Erichthonius, and had competed, successfully, with Poseidon for possession of Attica. In panhellenic mythology, however, she shows no special interest in Athens or in Athenian heroes. The association with Athens does not appear to affect her fundamental character.

Her most important myth is that of her birth from the head of Zeus. It stresses her unique closeness to Zeus, a vital quality in a city-protecting goddess, and at the same time the gap that divides her, a child without a mother, from the maternal side of femininity. In the oldest version Zeus became pregnant with Athena after swallowing Metis; she was thus also a kind of reincarnation of *mētis*, 'cunning intelligence'.

It has been suggested that Athena's characteristic mode of action, a mode that unifies her apparently diverse functions while differentiating them from those of other gods with which they might appear to overlap, is the application of *mētis*. Her *mētis* appears obviously in her association with crafts and in her love for wily *Odysseus. In warfare she would express rational force, in contrast to the mindless violence of *Ares.

Athenaeus (fl. *c.* AD 200), of *Naucratis. His only extant work, *Deipnosophists* ('Doctors at Dinner'), was probably completed soon after the death of Commodus in 192. It belongs to the learned variety of the symposium form (see SYMPOSIUM LITERATURE). It is now in fifteen books; there is also an *Epitome, which covers existing gaps. At the dinner, which extends over several days, philosophy, literature, law, medicine, and other interests are represented by a large number of guests, who in some cases bear historical names (most notably *Galen); a Cynic philosopher is introduced as a foil. The Roman host, Larensis, probably the author's patron, is attested epigraphically. The sympotic framework, if not devoid of occasional humour, is subordinate in interest to the collections of excerpts which are introduced into it. They relate to all the materials and accompaniments of convivial occasions; they are drawn from a vast number of authors, esp. of the Middle and New *Comedy, whose works are now lost; they are valuable both as literature and as illustrating earlier Greek manners. Athenaeus cites some 1,250 authors, gives the titles of more than 1,000 plays, and quotes more than 10,000 lines of verse.

Athēnaiōn polīteia ('Athenian Constitution', Aristotelian). *Aristotle is credited with works on the constitutions of 158 states: a papyrus containing all but the opening few pages of the *Athenian Constitution* was acquired by the British Museum, and was published in 1891. The first two-thirds (chs. 1–41) give a history of the constitution to the restoration of the democracy after the regime of the Thirty (see THIRTY TYRANTS). This part derives from a mixture of sources, and is of uneven merit, but at its best it contains valuable information which does not survive in any other text. The remaining third (42–69) gives a factual account of the working of the constitution in the author's time, and appears to be based on the laws of Athens and the author's own observation.

There has been much argument as to the authorship of the work: it was regularly attributed in antiquity to Aristotle, and was written when he was in Athens; there are some striking agreements between the *Athenaion Politeia* and Aristotle's *Politics* (e.g. that *Solon should not be blamed for the extreme *democracy which was built on his foundations), but also some striking disagreements (e.g. on Solon's provisions for the appointment of the *archontes); except in a few passages the style differs from that of the Aristotelian corpus, but this is a different kind of work from those in the main corpus. Some scholars believe that Aristotle himself wrote the *Athenaion Politeia*; but Aristotle can hardly himself have written all the works attributed to him, and he was neither an Athenian nor an admirer of the Athenian democracy; so the work is more probably to be attributed to a pupil. Its value to historians is considerable, whether Aristotle was the author or not.

Athenian Constitution, Aristotelian See ATHENAION POLITEIA.

Athenian empire See DELIAN LEAGUE.

Athens, history Tradition held that *Theseus was responsible for the *synoecism, or political unification of the Athenian (Attic) state. The synoecism is now generally put *c.*900 BC after a tumultuous period in which refugees from Attica settled in Ionia (see IONIANS) from *c.*1050 BC onwards. Athenian imperial propaganda later exaggerated the organized character of this process, turning it into a movement of *colonization which would justify the *metropolis making hegemonial demands of the 'daughter-cities'. Another later propaganda item was the myth of 'autochthony' (Attica had 'always had the same inhabitants'). This was false, but useful for scoring off the *Dorian 'newcomers' See AUTOCHTHONS.

The Attic countryside was settled from the centre in the 8th cent. by 'internal colonization': Athens was not among the first genuinely colonizing states. The early Attic state was aristocratic and politically hardly distinctive. There was nothing even embryonically democratic

about the annual *archontes who were the chief officers of state.

Attica's long coastline is one of the features which made it exceptional. Others were an imposing city acropolis, with its own water-supply; a mountain-system which formed a first line of defence for Athens itself; and valuable resources in the silver-bearing *Laurium region of east Attica.

In 632 'the Athenians', a collective noun now first used for a political agent, resisted *Cylon's attempt at a *tyranny; there is no reason to link this rejection of revolution with *Draco's law-code in the 620s. Athens' first overseas settlement at *Sigeum in *c.*610 may be an indicator of economic restlessness of the kind which produced *Solon. His economic and political reforms in the 590s created an Attica of small-holders; enhanced Athenians' sense that they were a political élite; and widened eligibility for political office. But proper democracy was still in the future, and Solon could not save Athens from the tyranny, later in the 6th cent., of *Pisistratus and sons. The tyranny was not oppressive until shortly before the end (510), and did more for Athens' later military and naval prominence than 5th-cent. historians allowed.

It was *Cleisthenes (2) in 508 who, after a short phase of aristocratic struggle, established the democracy which provoked Persia by helping the *Ionian Revolt and then defeated Persia at *Marathon and ten years later at *Salamis. Full democracy did not arrive until the 460s and the reforms associated with *Ephialtes and *Pericles. Meanwhile Athens had in 478/7 become an imperial city: see DELIAN LEAGUE. Against a background of increasing tension with Sparta, the displaced leader of Greece, the Athenians now exploited their Persian War achievement. Military successes against Persia culminated in the battle of the Eurymedon in the early 460s, and more subject-allies were brought under Athenian control. The Athenian empire survived the First *Peloponnesian War of *c.*461–446, though the *Thirty Years Peace of 446 ended Athens' ten-year control of *Boeotia. But increasing Athenian expansionism in the early 430s alarmed Sparta, and the outbreak in 431 of the 27-year *Peloponnesian War ended the *Pentekontaetia* or 50-year period from the Persian Wars.

In the Archidamian War (431–421), the Spartans failed in their programme of 'liberating' Greece from the tyrant city, Athens. Nor did Athens' catastrophic Sicilian Expedition of 415–413 or the oligarchic regime of the *Four

Hundred (411), or even the definite commitment of rich Persia to the Spartan side (407) end the war, which included Athenian successes like Cynossema (411), Cyzicus (410), and *Arginusae (406) before the final defeat at Aegospotami in 405. Athens became a subject-ally of Sparta and a second, Spartan-sponsored oligarchy took power in 404, the *Thirty Tyrants.

But by a recovery even more remarkable than that of 413, Athens climbed back to independent and even semi-imperial status in the early 4th cent. Fifth-century Athens had been an imperial, Hellenistic Athens was a university, city; 4th-cent. Athens was something in between. Democracy was restored in 403 and the constitution was mildly reformed, though not in a way which can be associated with any named reformer. From now on the democracy was more efficient but noticeably less radical. In foreign affairs, Athens soon dared to confront the Spartans as one of the coalition which fought the *Corinthian War of 395–386 and, remarkably, included Sparta's recent backer, Persia. The battle of Cnidus of 394 was a naval victory over Sparta, won by a Persian-sponsored fleet but with an Athenian commander, Conon. The *King's Peace of 386 (see GREECE, HISTORY) ended this first phase of Athenian recovery. But Spartan aggressions and unpopularity enabled Athens to launch a *Second Athenian Confederacy in 378.

Initially the confederacy was successful and welcome: its members included Thebes, now a rising power. Athens defeated Sparta twice in the mid-370s. But Thebes' defeat of Sparta at *Leuctra in 371 led to a *rapprochement* between Athens and Sparta in the 360s. Meanwhile Athenian attempts to turn their empire into something more like its 5th-cent. predecessor, esp. attempts to recover *Amphipolis and the *cleruchy put in on *Samos in 366, were unpopular. Major island allies rebelled in 357–355. Because of distractions like this and the Third *Sacred War, not to mention sheer shortsightedness, it was not until 351 that Athens and *Demosthenes (2) realized the threat posed by *Philip II of Macedon. A brief war (early 340s) ended with the Peace of *Philocrates (346); Athens now acknowledged the loss of Amphipolis. The end, militarily, to Athenian great-power status came in 338 at *Chaeronea, though this did not signal either the death of the *polis generally or of Athens in particular.

The Athens of *Eubulus and *Lycurgus pursued, in the 330s and 320s, ostensibly backward-looking policies of retrenchment which actually anticipate Athens' Hellenistic role as cultural centre. Athens did not openly resist *Alexander (2) the Great, but when at the end of his life he restored Samos to the Samians, Athens embarked on and was defeated in the *Lamian War of 323–322, after which democracy was suppressed. Under *Cassander, Athens was ruled tyrannically by *Demetrius (1) of Phaleron (318–307), a period of peace but imposed cultural austerity. He was expelled by the rapturously welcomed Antigonid Macedonian Demetrius Poliorcētēs.

Athens, topography

Acropolis The central fortress and principal sanctuary of *Athena, patron goddess of the city. In the later 13th cent. BC the steep hill was enclosed by a massive wall. Within, there are Mycenaean terraces. The first monumental temples and sculptural dedications date to the 6th cent. Two large Doric temples of limestone with marble trim were built, along with a half-dozen small temples or treasuries. Later quarrying has obliterated the foundations of all but one of the colonnaded temples (c.510) which stood on the north side of the hill, just south of the later Erechtheum. A marble temple, the Older Parthenon, was under construction on the southern half of the hill in 480 when the Persians took and sacked the city. The debris from this devastation was buried on the Acropolis, and no major construction took place for about a generation. In the 450s a monumental bronze statue of Athena Promachus was set up to celebrate victory over the Persians, and in the second half of the 5th cent. four major buildings were constructed. First came the *Parthenon (447–432); the *Propylaea (437–432), gateway to the Acropolis, occupied the western approaches to the citadel. Soon after, an old shrine of Athena Nike (Victory) was refurbished and a small temple of the Ionic order was built just outside the Propylaea. Finally, the *Erechtheum was constructed during the last quarter of the 5th cent. Only a few buildings were added to Acropolis in later times: a sanctuary of Brauronian *Artemis (see BRAURON) and the Chalkothēkē, where bronzes were stored. A tall pier built just outside the Propylaea in the 2nd cent. BC first carried statues of *Eumenes II and Attalus II, kings of *Pergamum and benefactors of Athens, later replaced by one of Agrippa. The Roman presence in Greece is reflected on the Acropolis by the construction after 27 BC of a small round temple dedicated to Rome and

Augustus and built in an Ionic order closely copying the Erechtheum.

Environs of the Acropolis Numerous sanctuaries clustered around the base of the Acropolis. The sanctuaries of 'the nymph' (7th cent. BC), *Asclepius (420 BC), and *Dionysus (c.500 BC) lay on the south slope. The theatre of Dionysus was built of limestone and marble in the 330s BC and renovated several times in the Roman period. To the west lay a stoa built by Eumenes II and beyond that the local millionaire *Claudius Atticus Herodes built a huge *odeum in memory of his wife (c. AD 160). The ground east of the theatre was taken up by the odeum of Pericles (c.443 BC), a replica of the tent of Xerxes, captured by the Greeks at *Plataea. A broad street lined with tripods set up by victorious *chorēgoi* (see CHOREGIA) in the choral contests led from the theatre around the east end and north side of the Acropolis. The small Corinthian Lysicrates monument (335 BC) is the best-preserved surviving tripod base. In this eastern area were to be found several other cults (Aglaurus, *Dioscuri, *Theseus), as well as the Prytaneion, hearth of the city (all unexcavated). The north side of the Acropolis sheltered cults of *Aphrodite and *Eros, *Pan, *Apollo, and *Demeter and *Persephone (Eleusinium). The *Areopagus, a low hill NW of the Acropolis, was the seat in early times of a council and lawcourt as well as a shrine of the Eumenides (see ERINYES). St *Paul addressed the court of the Areopagus, though by the 1st cent. AD the council almost certainly met in the lower city and not on the hill.

Agora The civic centre of Athens, lay NW of the Acropolis on ground sloping down to the Eridanus stream. Traversed by the Panathenaic Way, the Agora was a large open square reserved for a wide variety of public functions, lined on all four sides by the principal administrative buildings of the city. First laid out in the 6th cent. BC, it remained a focal point for Athenian commerce, politics, and culture for centuries, surviving the Persian sack and the Sullan siege of 86 BC (see CORNELIUS SULLA FELIX). Here in the Classical period were to be found the *bouleutērion* (council-house), the *Tholos (dining-hall for the *prytaneis*), the Metrōon (*archives), mint, lawcourts, and magistrates' offices (Royal Stoa, and South Stoa I), along with sanctuaries (Hephaisteion, Altar of the Twelve Gods, Stoa of Zeus Eleutherius, Apollo Patroüs), fountain-houses, and stoas (*Stoa Poecile, Stoa of the Herms). More large stoas (Attalus II, Middle Stoa, South Stoa II) were added in the 2nd cent. BC. To the

2nd cent. perhaps should be dated the elaborate octagonal marble water-clock known today as the Tower of the Winds, built some 200 m. (220 yds.) east of the Agora. This eastern area was later occupied by the market of Caesar and Augustus, which supplanted many of the commercial functions of the old Agora. In the 2nd cent. AD a huge peristyle court with library was built by Hadrian just north of the Roman market. Roman additions to the Agora also reflect Athenian prominence in cultural and educational affairs: an odeum given by *Agrippa (c.15 BC) and a library dedicated by Pantaenus (c. AD 100). Pnyx, the meeting-place of the Athenian assembly (*ekklesia*), was built on a hill, 400m. (c.440 yds.) SW of the Agora. Originally laid out in either c.500 or 462/1 BC, and remodelled at the end of the 5th cent., the final phase was built in c.340 BC. This third phase consists of a rock-cut speaker's platform (*bēma*) and a massive curved retaining wall for the auditorium. By the Hellenistic period most meetings took place in the theatre of Dionysus. North of the Pnyx the ridge was given over to the worship of the *Nymphs, while the south end of the ridge was the site first of a Macedonian garrison fort in Hellenistic times and then the mausoleum of Iulius Antiochus Epiphanes Philopappus (d. AD 114/16).

SE Athens In this quarter of town were to be found the oldest cults of the city: Dionysus in 'the Marshes', Olympian Zeus, Gē (Earth), and Pythian Apollo. Best preserved is the colossal *Olympieum. It was approached through an arch bearing inscriptions delimiting the old town of Theseus from the new Athens built by *Hadrian. Nearby, to the north, a *gymnasium with a sanctuary of Apollo Lyceus gave its name to *Aristotle's school, the Lyceum. Other shrines and the old Enneakrounos fountain-house lay further out, along the banks of the Ilissus river. Across the river lay the Panathenaic stadium, built by *Lycurgus, rebuilt in marble by Claudius Atticus Herodes, and restored in 1896.

Fortifications An Archaic city wall was replaced in 479 BC, immediately after the Persian sack, by a new expanded circuit, hastily constructed at the behest of Themistocles. Its length of $6\frac{1}{2}$ km. (4 mi.) was pierced by at least fifteen gates, the principal one being the *Dipylon, to the NW. Moats and outer walls were added in the 4th cent. in response to threats from Macedonia, and a large extension was added to the east in Roman times. Communication between Athens and the harbours of *Piraeus was assured by means of three *Long Walls.

Cemeteries Burials were made outside the city walls, all around the circuit. The principal cemetery, known as the *Ceramicus, lay along the two major roads leading NW from the city. It was used as a burial ground from *c.*1100 BC until the 6th cent. AD, and excavations have recovered hundreds of graves, along with sculpted and inscribed grave-markers. In this same area lay the National Cemetery for the war-dead as well as other notables. Further on lay the *Academy.

athletics

Greek At the core of Greek athletics was an individual's struggle to gain victory over an opponent; hence it included not only (as 'athletics' implies nowadays) track and field events but also *boxing, *wrestling, and equestrian events (see HORSE- AND CHARIOT-RACES), and excluded team competitions and performances aimed at setting records ('athletics' derives from the root *athl-*, denoting struggle, competition for a prize, and misery). Athletics was a popular activity; valuable contemporary evidence for it is provided by vase-paintings and the victory odes of *Pindar and *Bacchylides.

The first substantial description of Greek practice comes from *Homer's account of the funeral games for Patroclus in *Iliad* 23. Eight events are mentioned there (*chariot-racing, boxing, wrestling, running, *javelin*, an event similar to fencing, throwing the weight, and archery); the five in italics regularly formed the central part of all later games.

From the middle of the 5th cent. the four major venues for athletics competitions were the *Olympic, *Pythian, *Nemean, and *Isthmian Games. The running-races were the *stadion* (a length of the stadium, 192 m. (210 yds.) at Olympia), *diaulos* (there and back), and *dolichos* (twelve laps at Olympia). There was no marathon, although acc. to Herodotus *Phidippides, who ran from Athens to Sparta, trained as an ultra-distance runner for the purpose of delivering messages. A race in armour, derived from military training, was introduced into athletics programmes at the end of the 6th cent., and there was a *pentathlon consisting of long-jump, *stadion*, discus, javelin, and wrestling. At the Olympic and Pythian Games there were separate events for men and boys, while at the Nemean and Isthmian Games there was also an intermediate category for youths (*ageneioi*, lit. 'beardless').

Training took place in the *gymnasium, or *xystos* (covered colonnade); for the running events, esp. the *dolichos*, long training-runs must have been done outside the confines of these buildings. The need for athletes to have a suitable diet (see DIETETICS) was widely recognized. Sometimes an athlete's father would act as his coach; often, past victors became coaches. Before the Olympic games, the wise precaution was taken of making competitors swear by Zeus that for the previous ten months they had trained properly. When training or competing, athletes covered their bodies with olive oil to keep off the dust and were generally naked, though there is some disputed evidence pointing to the use of loincloths. Male sexual interest in young athletes, admired for their physique, was commonplace (see HOMOSEXUALITY).

Women competed at Olympia in separate games, the Heraea in honour of *Hera; there was just one event, a shortened *stadion*-race. During the men's athletics, married women were forbidden to watch, but virgin girls were permitted, a custom perhaps derived from a conception of the games as an occasion for girls to meet future husbands.

It is hard to evaluate athletics performances, because running-races were not timed, and distances in field events not measured; a sign that standards may have been low is the fact that *Pausanias (3) records many examples of men who had been able to win in several different types of event.

Roman At Rome colourful *circus spectacles (esp. chariot-racing) and ball games were the most popular sporting activities. But Augustus promoted traditional athletics, staging athletic competitions in the Campus Martius and exhibition-running in the Circus; he himself was keen on watching boxing. Ultra-distance running was also practised: 'Some men can do 160 [Roman] miles in the Circus' (Pliny, *Natural History*). Interest in athletics was maintained by the establishing of Greek-style games at Rome and elsewhere. In (?)4 BC *Tiberius won the chariot-race at the Olympic Games; from then on, Romans (mostly either provincials with Roman citizenship, or those with sufficient authority to bend the rules, as Nero did in AD 67) won at Olympia with increasing regularity. See AGONES.

atīmia, in a Greek state, the loss of some or all rights. It originally amounted to outlawry, total loss of rights *vis-à-vis* the community that the man made *atīmos* had wronged; later it came usually to denote loss of civic rights (including the right to go to law to protect one's personal rights). In Athens *atimia* could be temporary (men in debt to the state lost their rights until the debt was discharged), and it could be limited to specific disabilities.

Atlantis, i.e. '(the island of) *Atlas', 'the island lying in the Atlantic'; the oldest surviving wonderland in Greek philosophy. *Plato is the earliest and chief source for the story, said to have been told to *Solon by Egyptian priests, of a huge and rich island of this name outside the Pillars of Heracles which once ruled 'Libya...as far as Egypt' and 'Europe as far as Tyrrhenia [= Etruria]' until, in an expedition to conquer the rest, its rulers were defeated by the Athenians, the island shortly after sinking overnight beneath the Atlantic after 'violent earthquakes and floods' (*Timaeus*).

Atlas, probably 'much-enduring', the *Titan son of Iapetus and brother of *Prometheus. In the *Odyssey* he is the 'malign' father of Calypso, 'who knows the depths of the whole sea, and holds the tall pillars which keep earth and heaven apart'. In *Hesiod he lives at the edge of the world beside the *Hesperides and holds up the heaven. The 'rationalizing' identification of the Titan with the *Atlas mountains is first found in *Herodotus. Atlas was the father of various *constellations. From an early date he was associated with Heraclean legends. Sent to fetch the golden apples of the Hesperides, *Heracles—on the advice of Prometheus—asked Atlas to get them while he held up the sky; Atlas refused to take back the sky but Heracles tricked him into doing so.

Atlas in art Atlas is depicted in art from the mid-6th cent. BC, usually with Heracles in the Garden of the Hesperides, notably on the early Classical metope from *Olympia. In Hellenistic and Roman art he supports the globe with great effort. *Pausanias (3) notes him on the chest of *Cypselus and the throne of Amyclae.

atomism The term 'atomism' is used of theories that posit the existence of small indivisible particles as the ultimate components of matter. The Greek term *atomon*, used by some ancient philosophers to describe these ultimate components, means 'indivisible'. The theories in ancient philosophy that fall under the general term 'atomism' share certain features: all posit an infinite number of these microscopic particle-type entities (atoms) as the physical occupants of the universe; these atoms are in motion through empty space, and the space itself has neither boundaries nor distinct places within it; atoms come in different varieties, which are differentiated in shape and have certain fundamental features such as solidity, resistance, texture, and possibly weight. The atom's intrinsic features never change, but when the atoms gather together, their intrinsic or primary qualities account for other secondary effects belonging to larger bodies, including the appearance of colour, flavour and scent (what we might call secondary qualities). These derivative effects can change as the arrangement of the atoms changes.

Leucippus and *Democritus in the early period, and *Epicurus and his followers in the Hellenistic period (including the work of the Roman poet *Lucretius), are the primary candidates for the description 'atomists'. In none of them was the atomic hypothesis either prompted or defended by experimental investigations into physics, since all were prompted by theoretical questions, including metaphysical puzzles about the nature of reality, whether things really change, and how we can know; some were also prompted by puzzles in mathematics and logic.

Because these puzzles arise from difficulties raised by other philosophers, the atomic theories need to be placed in their context. Leucippus and Democritus can be treated as a group, since it is hard to disentangle the record of what each separately might have contributed to what has come to be seen as a joint enterprise. Chronologically they occupy a position at the very end of what we call Presocratic philosophy (Democritus' working life actually coincides with that of Socrates, but his philosophical responses are mostly to his immediate predecessors, and so he is regarded as Presocratic in outlook). In metaphysics their chief concern is to counter the arguments against plurality and change that had been put forward by *Parmenides, and then re-affirmed by other thinkers, including *Zeno of Elea and Melissus. Some, at least, of Zeno's notorious paradoxes seem to be designed to show that division into parts is logically impossible, whether that division is supposed to end up with finite numbers of discrete component parts or an unending succession of finer divisions and subdivisions. The early atomists respond by proposing finite discrete component parts, themselves solid matter and uncuttable, but separated by portions of empty space or nothingness.

This latter proposal, asserting the existence of 'nothing' or 'what is not'—and that this 'nothing' occupied space between things—was the most controversial. Such apparent nonsense flies in the face of Parmenides' foundational claims (to the effect that only what *is* something can be included in the contents of the logically possible world). On the contrary, the atomists boldly claim, the world contains what is something and what is nothing, and parts of space, between the things that are something, is occupied by what is nothing. This means that bodies can be distinguished by being detached from each other, so that there can be more than one thing in reality even if all bodies are made of the same kind of stuff.

The suggestion that there is empty space also solves another puzzle, namely Melissus' claim that motion is impossible because things would need empty space to move about in: by positing the void, the atomists make space for the movement of atoms within it, and thereby explain changes in the macroscopic appearance of things. Since arrangements and collections of atoms account for the perceivable appearance, while atoms themselves are too small to see, it is only the appearance of things that changes. There is no change in what is there underneath: atoms themselves never change their shape or their instrinsic features. In this way the atomists deny that anything real has ceased to exist, since the impressions created by conglomerations of things are mere appearances, not genuine parts of reality. This kind of escape route from problems of change, and the consequent distinction between the primary and secondary qualities of things, motivates the sceptical attitude to the senses that is prominent in Democritus' work.

In the Hellenistic period, Epicurean philosophy advocates atomism along similar lines. Developments can be identified in the conception of the void (arguably now envisaged as pure extension, which may be occupied or unoccupied, as opposed to being a place occupied by 'nothing') and in the idea that atoms themselves contain 'minimal parts': that is, even though an atom is small, it has some size, and we can think of it having an edge and a middle, a left side and a right side; these parts not only cannot be physically cut apart, but they also have finite size: here too there is a limit to how far we can subdivide the magnitude in our mind, and the result must be a finite number of parts of finite size. These and other features of the Epicurean version of atomism were prompted by work on time, space and infinite tasks by *Aristotle and *Diodorus (1) Cronus.

Epicurus also invokes the atomic theory in a range of other areas besides physics and

metaphysics strictly understood: perception, thought, dreams and other psychological phenomena, religious belief, freedom of the will and causation in general are all to be accounted for with reference to a generally materialistic vision, in which the possibilities are defined by what can be supposed to happen to minute bodies falling randomly through an infinite universe of empty space. The most accessible systematic exploration of this vision is provided (with missionary zeal) by Lucretius in *De rerum natura*.

Atreus, in myth, son of *Pelops and Hippodamia and brother of Thyestēs. In *Homer there is harmony between the brothers, but from late epic on they had shared an implacable feud. Atreus married Āeropē, but she committed adultery with Thyestes and secretly gave him the golden lamb which carried with it claim to the kingship. *Zeus, however, expressed disapproval by reversing the course of the sun. Atreus banished Thyestes; but later, when he learnt of Aerope's adultery, he pretended a reconciliation with his brother and at a feast served up to him the flesh of the latter's own sons. At the end of the meal Atreus showed his brother the heads and hands of his sons, then once more banished him. By Aerope Atreus was father of *Agamemnon and *Menelaus. Atreus was finally killed by *Aegisthus, Thyestes' only surviving son.

Atthis was the title eventually given to the genre of Greek *historiography that narrated the local history of *Attica. The genre was probably created by *Hellanicus in the late 5th cent. It was most popular in the 4th cent. when *Atthides* were written by Cleidemus, *Androtion, and Phanodemus. *Philochorus, the last and most respected atthidographer, wrote in the 3rd.

In structure the *Atthis* was a chronicle, based upon a hypothetical list of kings (for the legendary period) and, after 683/2 BC, on the archons (see ARCHONTES). In the case of the latter the entries began with the archon's name, followed by his patronymic or demotic (see NAMES, PERSONAL, GREEK), and then the formula, 'in the time of this man such and such happened'. Within an entry, material was also arranged chronologically, but the structure was not conducive to showing relationship between events or cause and effect. The subject-matter of an *Atthis* was typical of a local history, covering such diverse material as the origins of religious *festivals and cults, etymology of place-names, geography, ethnography, and the creation of financial and political institutions. In short, the *Atthis* was a blend of mythical fantasy and accurate historical detail, the latter esp. as the account came closer to the historian's own day. The style was 'monotonous and hard for the reader to stomach'. The tone was patriotic, though more chauvinistic in some than others.

Attic From or relating to *Attica or *Athens; see also ASIANISM AND ATTICISM.

Attica, the territory of *Athens, a triangular promontory some 2,400 sq. km. (930 sq. mi.) in area divided from the rest of the Greek mainland by the mountain range of Parnes. Attic topography is varied, with fertile upland valleys, waterlogged lowland valley-bottoms, more or less barren mountain slopes and productive coastal and inland plains. Almost all the peninsula falls below the 400 mm. (16 in.) isohyet, making agriculture a precarious occupation. The rugged hills of southern Attica were a source of silver and lead, exploited from the bronze age (*Laurium), and the mountain ranges of Hymettus and Pentelicon were a source of fine *marble, used from the 6th cent.

Athens is the only place in Dark Age Attica where continuity of occupation can be clearly shown, and some archaeologists see the Archaic and Classical settlement pattern in Attica as resulting from 'internal colonization' from Athens. Archaic Attica is notable for outstanding dedications and burials, marking an élite rooted in the countryside; this is consistent with the traditions about the Solonian crisis (see SOLON) and about the locally based factional struggles which led to the tyranny of *Pisistratus. Local factions are absent from the Classical historical record, presumably as a result of *Cleisthenes' (2) reforms, which institutionalized a voice for some 139 local communities (*demes) on his new council of 500 (see BOULE). The continued vigorous life of these demes testifies to the extent to which Athenian lives remained rooted in the countryside.

Continued expenditure in the countryside is marked by 5th-cent. building at all the major rural *sanctuaries (*Eleusis, *Sunium, Rhamnus, *Brauron). Extension of *agriculture into marginal areas, along with the apparent agricultural base of most élite wealth, suggests that even when Athens could afford to become reliant on imported foodstuffs, there was no exodus from the land. In the Hellenistic period evidence for rural occupation declines; by Roman times much of Attica is in the hands of only a few landowners.

Some forts were constructed along Attica's northern border in the 5th cent., and forts on the coast were added during the latter stages of the *Peloponnesian War, but only in the 4th cent. was a system of forts constructed, and garrison duty became part of military training.

Attic cults and myths Most Greek states honoured most Greek gods; the differences between them are of emphasis and degree. As characteristic Athenian emphases one might mention: the extraordinary prominence of *Athena, unusual even for a city-protecting goddess; the international standing of the mysteries of *Demeter and Kore (*Persephone) at *Eleusis; the rich development of *deme religion, and the related abundance of *hero-cults; the honours acquired in the second half of the 5th cent. by *Hephaestus, usually a minor figure; the modest role of *Hera.

Acc. to one 5th-cent. observer (see OLD OLIGARCH), Athens had more *festivals than any other Greek state; only a small selection can be mentioned here. The great show-pieces, which attracted foreign visitors, were the *Panathenaea, the City *Dionysia (when tragedies and comedies were performed), and the Eleusinian *mysteries. Further major landmarks of the domestic year, each lasting several days, were the *Thesmophoria (Demeter and Kore), the most important women's festival; *Anthesteria, the new-wine festival; *Apaturia, the phratry festival. The other 'literary festivals' (*Lenaea, Rural Dionysia, Dionysia in *Piraeus, *Thargelia) were also very popular. Other traditional festivals that were widely or universally celebrated (sometimes impinging on domestic life, through the custom of preparing special food) or that affected many families from time to time were the Diasia (*Zeus Meilichios), Cronia (see CRONUS), Pyanopsia (*Apollo), and several initiatory festivals of *Artemis, chief among them the *Brauronia.

The most important Attic myths concerned: the conflict of Athena and *Poseidon for possession of Attica; the birth from earth of the first two kings *Cecrops and *Erechtheus/*Erichthonius, which founded symbolically the Athenians' claim to be 'autochthonous'; the adventures of the daughters of these two kings; the arrival in Attica of *Dionysus and, esp., Demeter (the latter event being the origin of the Eleusinian mysteries); the mission of Triptolemus, who distributed wheat worldwide, and above all the varied career of *Theseus. A distinctive canon of four Athenian achievements was shaped in the special context of the Funeral Speech (see EPITAPHIOS) for the war-dead: the war of Erechtheus against *Eumolpus of Eleusis and his Thracian allies; the war of Theseus against the invading *Amazons; succour in the cause of right given by the Athenians to the *Heraclids and to the mothers of the *Seven against Thebes. In contrast to these public and patriotic myths is the rich cycle attaching to the misfortunes of *Cephalus and Procris.

Attic Orators By the 2nd cent. AD there was a list of ten Athenian orators (*Lysias, *Isaeus, *Hyperīdēs, *Isocratēs, *Dīnarchus, *Aeschinēs (1), *Antiphōn, *Lycurgus, *Andocidēs, *Dēmosthenēs (2) whose classic status was recognized. Paradoxically, Lysias, Isaeus, and Dinarchus, being metics, could not *deliver* speeches to Athenian juries or to the assembly, and Isocrates never addressed a large audience; so this entry would be better entitled 'Speech-writers active in Athens', which is what all ten did, and we have only their surviving scripts by which judge their rhetorical powers. See CANON.

Atticus See POMPONIUS ATTICUS.

augurs, official Roman diviners. They formed one of the four great colleges of priests (see COLLEGIUM), instituted (so the tradition) in the regal period; originally made up of three (patrician) members, the complement was increased to nine in 300 BC when plebeians were admitted (five plebeians, four patricians), to fifteen by *Sulla, and sixteen by *Caesar. New members were admitted (for life) through co-optation; from 103 through popular election by the assembly of seventeen tribes (see TRIBUS) from the candidates nominated by two college members. As a college the augurs were a body of experts whose duty was to uphold the augural doctrine which governed the observation and application of the auspices (see AUSPICIUM) in Roman public life. They passed decrees either on their own initiative or more often responding to questions posed by the senate or the magistrates (*responsa*). These replies often dealt with cases of ritual fault which would nullify the auspices or with the removal of *religio*, a ritual obstacle to an action. The senate was free either to accept or to reject the advice. Individual augurs were both experts and priests. They could give *responsa* (to be distinguished from those of the college); in their capacity as priests they

celebrated various rites, and also (when asked) performed inaugurations of priests and temples. They could assist the magistrates in taking the auspices and, in particular, an augur had the right of making a binding announcement of adverse unsolicited omens (see PORTENTS), esp. at the popular assemblies.

Augusta Trēverōrum *civitas*-capital of the Treveri, developed from a settlement around a fort established under Augustus to guard a crossing of the Moselle. In the early empire it became the seat of the imperial *procurator of Belgica and the Germanies (see GAUL (TRANSALPINE); GERMANIA), and eventually also that of the governor of Belgica. It soon gained colonial status. Later, the advantages of its position brought it even more success. The colony covered well over 280 ha. (690 acres). Impressive remains include a bridge, an amphitheatre, bath-buildings, the 'porta Nigra' gateway, the cathedral, and an imperial audience hall. Its environs are rich in remains.

Augustālēs, members of a religious and social institution common in the cities of the western Roman empire. There are numerous variations on the title, which taken together appear in some 2,500 inscriptions. Nearly all *Augustales* were *freedmen, as well as Trimalchio (see PETRONIUS ARBITER) and his friends, the only *Augustales* depicted in literature. They often acted as benefactors (see EUERGETISM), funding public entertainments and building-projects as well as paying entry fees. In return, they enjoyed the prestige of their office, which functioned almost as a magistracy. *Augustales* were entitled to honorific insignia and were often selected by the town councillors. As their title indicates, their formal responsibilities may have centred on the imperial cult (see RULER-CULT), in the context of which they probably arranged sacrifices and games. They usually performed these duties for a year, after which they retained membership in an order, sometimes organized like a *collegium*, whose members held a rank just below that of the local council. The institution thus provided rich freedmen, who were legally barred from holding civic magistracies, with opportunities for public display and prestige.

Augustine, St (AD 354–430), b. at Thagaste, son of Patricius, a modest town councillor of pagan beliefs, and a dominant Catholic mother, Monica. Educated at Thagaste, Madauros, and

Carthage, he taught rhetoric at Thagaste, Carthage, and Rome and (384–6) as public orator at Mediolanum (mod. Milan), then the capital of the emperor Valentinian II. Patronized at Rome by Symmachus, the pagan orator, he hoped, by an advantageous marriage (to which he sacrificed his concubine, the mother of a son) to join the 'aristocracy of letters' typical of his age. At 19, however, he had read the *Hortensius* of *Cicero. This early 'conversion to philosophy' was the prototype of successive conversions: to Manichaeism, a *Gnostic sect promising Wisdom, and, in 386, to a Christianized *Neoplatonism patronized by Ambrose, bishop of Mediolanum. Catholicism, for Augustine, was the 'Divine Philosophy', a Wisdom guaranteed by authority but explored by reason: 'Seek and ye shall find', the only scriptural citation in his first work, characterizes his life as a thinker.

Though the only Latin philosopher to fail to master Greek, Augustine transformed Latin *Christianity by his Neoplatonism: his last recorded words echo *Plotinus. Stimulated by abrupt changes—he was forcibly ordained priest of Hippo in 391, becoming bishop in 395—and by frequent controversies, Augustine developed his ideas with an independence that disquieted even his admirers. He has left his distinctive mark on most aspects of Christianity.

Augustine's major works are landmarks in the abandonment of Classical ideals. His early optimism was soon overshadowed by a radical doctrine of grace. This change was canonized in an autobiographical masterpiece, the *Confessions* (*c*.397–400), a vivid if highly selective source for his life to 388 and, equally, a mirror of his changed outlook. *Christian Doctrine* sketched a literary culture subordinated to the Bible. *The Trinity* provided a more radically philosophical statement of the doctrine of the Trinity than any Greek Father. *The City of God* (413 to 426) presented a definitive juxtaposition of Christianity with literary paganism and Neoplatonism, esp. with *Porphyry. After 412, he combated in Pelagianism views which, 'like the philosophers of the pagans', had promised men fulfilment by their unaided efforts. In his *Retractations* (427) Augustine criticized his superabundant output of 93 works in the light of a Catholic orthodoxy to which he believed he had progressively conformed—less consistently, perhaps, than he realized.

Letters and verbatim sermons richly document Augustine's complex life as a bishop; the centre of a group of sophisticated ascetics (see ASCETICISM), the 'slave' of a simple congrega-

tion, he was, above all, a man dedicated to the authority of the Catholic Church. This authority had enabled his restless intellect to work creatively: he would uphold it, in Africa, by every means, from writing a popular song to elaborating the only explicit justification in the early Church of a policy of religious persecution.

Augustus (63 BC–AD 14), the first Roman emperor, who presided over the inception of much of the framework of the imperial system of the first three centuries AD. The longevity of his system, and its association with a literary milieu that came to be regarded as the *golden age of Latin literature, make him uniquely important in Roman history, but no narrative history of his lifetime survives except for the account of *Cassius Dio (manuscripts defective from 6 BC), and the rest of the evidence is deeply imbued with partisan spirit. An estimation of his personal contribution is hard to achieve.

Son of a *novus homo* (Gaius Octavius, praetor 61, d. 59) from Velitrae in the Alban hills, Octavius was typical of the junior senators in the third quarter of the 1st cent. BC, perceiving that the way to success lay through the support of the great dynasts. In this he had a head start: his mother Atia was the daughter of *Caesar's sister, which made him one of the closest young male relatives of the dictator, a connection emphasized when in 51 he gave the funeral oration for his maternal grandmother. In 47 he was made *pontifex*; with Caesar in Spain in 45, he was enrolled as a patrician, and when the dictator drew up his will (September 45) he adopted the 17-year-old Octavius and made him his heir. The young man spent the winter in study at Apollonia in Illyria, but reacted with decision and alacrity when Caesar was murdered and the will read. Over the next months he consolidated his position as the leader of the friends of Caesar, commemorating his adoptive father, and wooing his *veterans; a course of action which brought him into conflict with Antony (Marcus *Antonius). It brought him also the support of the cause that prevailed over Antony at Mutina (April 43), after which he seized the consulship by force. At Bononia the differences between him, Antony, and *Aemilius Lepidus (2) were resolved and the *Triumvirate established. The next years were marked by the crushing of *Antonius (Pietas) and *Fulvia at Perusia, with singular violence, the settling of veterans on confiscated land, and the *proscriptions, in which he was as ruthless as the others. He married *Scribonia as a gesture to Sextus *Pompeius, and she bore his only child *Iulia (2) (in 39 he divorced her to marry *Livia Drusilla); to seal the political dispositions made at *Brundisium in October 40, Antony married his sister *Octavia. All the politicians of the time made use of *imperium, one of the few surviving constitutional principles of any potency, and Caesar's heir now took the first name Imperator.

Over the 30s, events combined with astute responses enabled Imp. Caesar to represent himself as defender of an Italian order. His principal local rival for this position, Sex. Pompeius (finally defeated at Naulochus in 36), he represented as a pirate-leader. He took advantage of his control of the ancient centre of *imperium* and retained the favour of the disaffected and volatile *populus* who still in theory granted it. After a half-hearted attempt to attain some military reputation against a foreign enemy (the *Illyrians) he turned to representing Antony in *Alexandria as alien, immoral, and treacherous. In 32 a formal oath expressed the mass loyalty of Italy to his cause. The advantages of this policy were not wholly symbolic. Italy offered material resources, manpower, and the land with which to reward its loyalty. Imp. Caesar and his close supporters of these years and afterwards (esp. *Vipsanius Agrippa, *Statilius Taurus, and *Maecenas) were victorious against Antony, whose pro-Egyptian policy and reverse at Parthian hands in Armenia (36) had lost him much of his eastern support. The battle of *Actium (31) was the turning-point; the capture of Alexandria in the next year ended the war and led to the incorporation of Egypt in the *imperium*. Victory in the east, the vindication of his political promises in Italy, and the booty of the Ptolemies gave him an unassailable position, soon expressed in terms of divinity.

From his consulship of 31 (he held it every year down to 23) there began a down-playing of the irregularity of the triumviral system, which culminated in a formal *restitutio* of the *res publica*, a restoration in the sense of repair or revival. He returned to Rome in mid-29, triumphed, beautified the city by the dedication of important temples, and signalled an end to war by the closing of the temple of *Janus. Agrippa was his colleague in the consulship for 28 and 27: at the beginning of 27 he made the formal gesture of reinstating the magistrates, senate (reduced in numbers through a purge of undesirable elements), and people in their old constitutional role. In return he received a major grant of proconsular *imperium*, and many honours, including the name 'Augustus' (see AUGUSTUS, AUGUSTA,

AS TITLES), and departed to carry out the military duties of his new command.

Before 7 BC Augustus spent a great deal of time in the provinces (only in 23, 18, 17, and 12 did he spend the whole year in Rome, and he was absent for the whole of 26/5, 21/0, and 15/14). The Civil Wars had shown that power at Rome was to be won in the provinces, and with ever greater numbers of Roman citizens outside Italy, Augustus had to form an empire-wide system. The creation of a huge proconsular *provincia* on the model of the commands of Pompey and the triumvirs, which gave Augustus *imperium* over most of Rome's soldiers, was the core of this, and the most important part of the 'settlement' of 28/7. Delegation was essential in so unwieldy an entity, and, like his predecessors, Augustus appointed senatorial *legates and *equestrian prefects to serve his *imperium*. If these men ran units which were analogous to the *provinciae* of the proconsuls who continued to be sent to the parts of the Roman dominion that lay outside Augustus' command, that is not to say that the settlement envisaged two types of province. Such an innovation would have been far less subtle than the skill with which the legal flexibility of the assignment of proconsular commands and the convenient precedents of the previous generation were adapted to Augustus' purpose.

There were difficulties, since holders of *imperium* had been accustomed to a greater independence than Augustus could afford to allow them. Already in 30 the claim of Licinius Crassus to the *spolia opima* had tested the limits of self-determination; this bid for an antique honour was, characteristically, thwarted by a display of greater erudition from Augustus. Egypt's temptations proved too much for even the equestrian prefect *Cornelius Gallus (26). In 23, again following the precedent of *Pompey, the proconsular *imperium* was clearly labelled *maius* (superior), which also clarified the position of the other holders under Augustus of wide-ranging commands, such as Agrippa and *Iulius Caesar (2).

The maintenance of the loyalty of the soldiers finally depended on Augustus' capacity to pay them. That in turn depended on the organization of revenues so that they would regularly accrue to him directly. A simple fiscal logic transformed the empire: previously, the maintaining of cash flows to the centre, where they might be squandered by one's enemies, was of little interest to provincial governors. Now, the efficiency of the exaction system was the only guarantee of the survival of the new order. The whole world was enrolled, and noticed it (Luke 2: 1). Taxation was reformed and new provinces made so that their tribute might swell Augustus' takings. The enthusiastic imposition of such burdens caused rebellion and disaster, esp. in Germany. A military treasury on the Capitol announced the theoretical centrality of the fiscal arrangements to the whole *imperium* from AD 6 (see AERARIUM).

The incorporations of this period doubled the size of the provincial empire: NW Spain and the provinces of the Alps and the Alpine foreland. A fair show of military activity was a sensible ingredient in Augustan political strategy and provided the glory which maintained the standing of the ruling cadre. Some of this took the form of expeditions which brought in no additional taxation: like Augustus' own trip to the Danube (35–33 BC), Aelius Gallus' Arabian campaign (25–24), and the wars in southern Egypt of Cornelius Gallus (29) and Petronius (25). The main point of such trips was the glamour of the geography and ethnography, celebrated in poetry and on Agrippa's *map, which spread the belief that Augustus' Rome ruled the whole inhabited world. This impression was reinforced by Augustus' generally successful use (continued in the east from Antony's careful practise) of the traditional diplomatic relations with local magnates, kings, or communities, in places outside the direct *imperium* of a Roman governor. Ritual courtesies on both sides could suggest that the empire included India or *Britain, and had a practical role in settling outstanding issues with *Parthia in 20 in a negotiation which Augustus made a great deal of. When a serious military threat appeared, in the shape of the Pannonian Revolt, 'the worst war since those against Carthage', or the German war that followed the massacre of *Quinctilius Varus and his three legions, the system nearly collapsed.

For all his absences, Rome itself was at the heart of Augustus' vision. City-foundations in the provinces, and benefactions to existing *coloniae* (*see* COLONIZATION, ROMAN) and *municipia*, encouraged the imitation of the metropolis and the recognition of that constituency of Italians spread across the Mediterranean world that had played such a vital part in the Civil Wars. He could not avoid a real concern for the urban populace of Rome itself, who caused major disturbances of the traditional kind at intervals throughout his ascendancy. In 23, the choice of *tribunicia potestas* (see TRIBUNI PLEBIS) as the 'indication of the highest station', and the way in which Augustus counted the years of his 'reign'

thereafter, signalled also his descent from the *populārēs* (see OPTIMATES) of the late republic, many of whose policies he continued (albeit sometimes with a show of reluctance): he made provision against famine, fire, and flood, and reorganized the districts of the city (spreading his own cult in the process). The popular assembly duly ratified his legislation, and was represented *en masse* in displays of loyalty at important moments.

*Varro had taught Romans to be proudly aware of their traditions, and Augustus was eager to advance the process. The ancient messages of cult and civic ritual offered many opportunities, which he was making use of already in the 30s. After Actium the serious development of the cult of Palatine Apollo as a parallel to Capitoline Jupiter, and the restoration of dozens of Rome's ancient sanctuaries; after 12 (when he finally became *pontifex maximus* on the death of Lepidus) the formation of the House of the *Pater Patriae in 2 BC, and the inauguration of a replacement forum (see FORUM AUGUSTUM), to which many state ceremonies were removed; the creation of a 'suburb more beautiful than the city' on the *Campus Martius, for the enjoyment of the populace: the reduplication of Rome's glories cleverly allowed him to be a new founder without damaging the old system, and to surpass all past builders and benefactors without departing from or belittling their precedent. He thus underlined his relationship with the Roman past in a Roman history that culminated in his ascendancy.

His management of *lex* (statute law) was equally historic: giving his name to far more laws than any legislator before him, and announcing his control of the legislative assembly in the process, he became the city-founding lawgiver of the new Rome. The control of religion was the interpretative vehicle of much of this, and learning, interpretation, and doctrine, of law or ritual precedent, history or geography, were the indispensable servants of all these projects. Hence the cultural and literary acme that later generations of Romans perceived at this epoch. These processes came together in the years 19–17 BC, when he had made the last modifications to his position in the *res publica*, settled the eastern and western provinces, and acquired his first grandson (*Iulius Caesar (2), the child of *Iulia (2) and Agrippa). Now came the ethical and social laws, and in 17 the great celebration of the longevity that the Fates had given to Rome by making her populace virtuous and therefore fecund, in the *Secular Games.

His concern for the institutions of state allowed him to insert himself into the annals of Roman history as a continuator or reformer rather than as an intruder or revolutionary, while the flexibility of the institutions gave him a wonderful repertoire of gambits both for shaping opportunities for political success for his supporters and for social promotion, of which the most important form was the identification of a successor to his office. The very happy accident of his long life allowed readjustment of many of his innovations in a process of trial and error, a refining process which explains the success and long survival of many of them: the city *prefect, the public *postal service, the *vigiles, and so on.

The arrangement of a successor proved the most difficult task. The calculation of auctōritās in which he excelled, and which his very name evoked, entailed that no merely dynastic principle could be guaranteed; it would belittle his own carefully constructed reputation for real ability to have a successor who owed everything, as he had done, to a name. At the same time he had been unable (and had perhaps not wanted) to avoid accumulating honours for his family, and using for that very consolidation of auctoritas the image of a Father and the model of the state as a super-household, one conducted like his own and under his benign but omnicompetent tutelage. There was in the end a dissonance between the role of those who had to be permitted to acquire the necessary auctoritas to maintain the image of effective governance, esp. through largely contrived campaigns, and the need to rely on his own blood-line to keep alive the charisma of his own divine associations. Agrippa was a compliant assistant in the public sphere, and Livia in the private; but *Tiberius and *Drusus, Livia's children by her first marriage, were not good at playing second fiddle, and Iulia, his daughter and only child, on whom the whole dynastic construction relied, nearly wrecked the enterprise by probably calculated sexual misbehaviour. This called into question the credentials of the model family, the legitimacy of her offspring, and the feasibility of using ethics as a constitutional strategy, while potentially irradiating her partners (who included Antony's son Iullus *Antonius) with her share of the ancestral charisma.

What saved Augustus was the fact that he had (since he did not have the option of destroying them wholesale) re-created the Roman aristocracy and given them a new role in his social system. As an antidote to the Civil Wars; social mobility was to be curbed; freedmen were discouraged from promotion, the plebs was indulged but controlled; the two upper classes were encouraged to procreate, and each had its precise place in the religious system, at the theatre, and in government. As an ornament to the whole thing, and to camouflage the prerogatives that he ascribed to his own family, survivors of the great lines of the historic Roman past were encouraged to live up to their ancestors' images, and given a part to play in a system whose regulation, through his censorial function, it was Augustus' job to manage. Hence—and the power derived also from his fatherly pretensions—the ethical content of much of his legislation, which did the nobility the credit of thinking them worthy of the past while giving their arbiter a useful way of coercing them if they failed to live up to it. The seeds of the disastrous use of the laws on *adultery and *maiestas over the next generations were therefore sowed by Augustus, who was not himself faced by coherent opposition.

Later authors dated the establishment of the imperial monarchy to 31 or 27 BC. In many ways, as Augustus probably saw, and Tacitus appreciated, the new arrangements, many times modified, and threatened by diverse instability, could not be regarded as established until someone had succeeded to them, and then shown himself willing to continue their essentials. See also ROME, HISTORY, 2.1

Augustus, Augusta, as titles Republican usage was religious ('venerable'). On 16 January 27 BC *Octavian received the title from the senate, and he intended *Tiberius also to take it. Tiberius did not formally accept, but it was used in official documents and taken by all later emperors. Denied to other male members of the dynasty, it became the imperial title par excellence, and so was transmitted to military units and cities. The title 'Augusta' was conferred on the emperor's wife (*Livia Drusilla, in Augustus' will, the first), exceptionally on other relatives (*Antonia (2)).

aulos, pipe or double pipe; see MUSIC, 2.2(a).

Aurelian (Lūcius Domitius Aurēliānus) (c. AD 215–275), a man of humble origin from the Danubian region, achieved high military rank under the emperor Gallienus, but helped organize the plot that destroyed him. Appointed by Claudius II to the chief command of the cavalry, he served with distinction against the

Goths. Though Aurelian was the obvious successor to Claudius, he did not immediately declare himself on the latter's death. However, it was not long before he was proclaimed emperor by his troops and disposed of his rival (270).

Barbarian invasions first claimed his attention. He defeated the Vandals in Pannonia and then repulsed a dangerous incursion into Italy by the Alamanni and Iuthungi, pursuing the latter over the Danube. On his return to Rome, he surrounded the city with walls to protect it against further barbarian attacks (*wall of Aurelian). With characteristic ruthlessness, he also disposed of early political opponents to his rule.

He next dealt with Palmyra. *Zenobia, ruling for her young son, Septimius Vaballathus, had recently exploited Roman civil war to occupy Egypt and Asia Minor up to Bithynia (autumn 270). Coins and papyri show that she was now calling Vaballathus Imperator, but not Augustus, and was projecting him as the—albeit junior—colleague of Aurelian. Aurelian tolerated the compromise for only as long as he had to; early in 272 he marched east. Defeated at Antioch, Zenobia withdrew south, and proclaimed Vaballathus Augustus (spring 272). Aurelian pursued the rebels to Emesa, broke their main strength, and forced them to take refuge in Palmyra, which he then besieged. In summer 272, Zenobia was captured on her way to seek aid from Persia, and Palmyra surrendered.

Marching back westward, Aurelian defeated the Carpi on the Danube, but was recalled by a further revolt in Palmyra. He quickly crushed the uprising, and then proceeded to Egypt to suppress violent disturbances. He now turned west and ended the Gallic empire at Châlons, defeating Tetricus (early 274). Tetricus and Zenobia headed the captives from all Aurelian's victories in a magnificent triumph. Early in 275 Aurelian set out against Persia, but was murdered near *Byzantium, in a household plot.

Aurelian's energy and military talents restored the unity of the empire after a decade of division; and he was not just a successful general. Towards the end of his reign (274) he had the courage to abandon the old province of *Dacia—by now reduced to the Transylvanian highlands—and relocate its garrison, civilian administrators, and those of the rest of the population able and willing to join the evacuation, south of the Danube. He sought to reform the silver coinage, much damaged by 40 years of continual debasement. And, with the help of the booty won from Palmyra, he attempted to establish the worship of *Sol Invictus—with himself as this deity's chosen vicegerent—at the centre of Roman state religion (see ELAGABALUS, DEUS SOL INVICTUS; SOL). Thus in many ways he pioneered the work of Diocletian and Constantine I; yet he lacked the originality to bring the period of crisis to its conclusion. His murder was followed by a further ten years of uncertainty.

Aurēlius, Marcus (AD 121–180), emperor 161–180. He was named Marcus Annius Verus. His homonymous grandfather, an influential relative of *Hadrian, brought him up after his father's early death. His mother inherited a fortune. From early childhood Marcus was a favourite of Hadrian. When Hadrian died, Marcus was betrothed to *Antoninus Pius' daughter, his own cousin *Annia Galeria Faustina. Elected consul in 140 and 145, he married Faustina in the latter year; his first child was born on 30 November 147; the next day he received *tribunicia potestas* (see TRIBUNI PLEBIS) and *imperium, and Faustina became Augusta (see AUGUSTUS, AUGUSTA, AS TITLES). Marcus had been educated by many famous teachers, including *Fronto; many of their letters survive. His tranquil family life is vividly portrayed in his correspondence and recalled with affection in his *Meditations*. In 161 Marcus succeeded Antoninus, and at once requested the senate to confer the rank of co-emperor on his adoptive brother Lucius, as Hadrian had intended. Lucius took Marcus' name *Verus, while Marcus assumed that of Antoninus. There were thus two Augusti for the first time, equal rulers, except that only Marcus was *pontifex maximus* and he had greater *auctōritās*. The coinage proclaimed the harmony of the Augusti. Faustina now gave birth to twin sons, their names honouring Antoninus and Lucius (Lucius Aurelius *Commodus). But Antoninus' death had unleashed trouble on the frontiers: in Britain; Upper Germany; along the Danube; and, most seriously, in the east. The *Parthians seized Armenia and invaded Syria. It was decided that an expeditionary force was needed, to be led by Verus, with an experienced staff. Verus left Italy in 162 and was based at Antioch on Orontes until 166, but was merely a figurehead. After the expulsion of the Parthians from Armenia by Statius Priscus (163), he took the title 'Armeniacus' (accepted by Marcus in 164), crowning a new king. Other generals, notably Avidius Cassius, defeated the Parthians in Mesopotamia. Verus became Parthicus Maximus, Marcus soon following suit. In 166 further success led to the title 'Mēdicus'. But plague had broken out in the eastern army; the threat in the north was becoming acute—the despatch of three legions to the east had weakened the Rhine–Danube *limes. Verus was obliged to make peace, celebrating a joint triumph with Marcus. Each became *Pater Patriae, and Marcus' surviving sons, Commodus and Annius Verus, each became Caesar.

Marcus planned a new campaign to relieve the Danube frontier. Two new legions were raised in 165; V Macedonica was moved to *Dacia on its return from the east. But the *plague, reaching Rome in 166, delayed the expedition until spring 168; meanwhile Pannonia and Dacia were both invaded. The emperors went to the Danube in 168 and reinforced the frontier, stationing the new legions in western Pannonia. They wintered at Aquileia, where the plague broke out; the *praetorian *prefect was a victim, and *Galen, the imperial physician, refused to stay. At Verus' insistence, he and Marcus also left in January 169, but Verus died of a stroke. Marcus deified him and obliged his widow Lucilla to marry the Syrian *novus homo Claudius Pompeianus, who had distinguished himself in Pannonia. In spite of further bereavement—his younger son died—he pressed on with preparations, auctioning imperial treasures to raise funds, and returned north, in autumn 169.

Apparently planning to annex territory beyond the Danube, he launched an offensive in spring 170, but suffered a severe defeat. The Marcomanni and Quadi of Bohemia and Slovakia invaded, outflanked Marcus and swept over the Julian Alps. It was the worst such crisis since the German invasions at the end of the 2nd cent. BC. Desperate measures, led by Pompeianus and Helvius Pertinax, cleared Italy, Noricum, and Pannonia. The Marcomanni were defeated as they tried to recross the Danube with their booty. But the Balkans and Greece were invaded by the Costoboci, requiring further emergency measures, and Spain was ravaged by the Moors, dealt with by Marcus' friend Aufidius Victorinus. Marcus, based at Carnuntum, first used diplomacy to detach some tribes from the 'barbarian conspiracy'; some peoples were settled within the empire. The offensive, resumed in 172, is depicted at the start of the Aurelian column in Rome. In spite of the death of the praetorian prefect, the Marcomanni were defeated: victory was claimed, with the title 'Germānicus'. In a battle against the Quadi Roman troops were saved by a 'rain miracle', shown on the column, later claimed to have been achieved by the prayers of Christian legionaries; Marcus gave the credit to the Egyptian Hermes 'Āerius'. In 173 he pacified the Quadi, moving to Sirmium in 174 to take on the *Sarmatian Iazyges of the Hungarian plain. After some successes, he was obliged to make an armistice when Avidius Cassius, who had had special powers in the east, was proclaimed emperor. The revolt collapsed after three months, but Marcus, now Sarmaticus, toured the east, taking Faustina, who died in late 175 and was deified, and Commodus. He went through Asia and Syria to Egypt, returning via Athens to Rome. Here he held a triumph and raised Commodus to Augustus. In summer 178, renewed warfare in the north took him there again. He remained, evidently planning to annex Marcomannia and Sarmatia, until his death (March 180).

Marcus has been universally admired, as a philosopher-ruler, to the present day, criticized only for leaving his unworthy son as successor. This no doubt seemed the best way to ensure stability, and he left Commodus experienced advisers, including his numerous sons-in-law. Despite Marcus' lack of military experience he had taken personal command against the first wave of the great *Volkerwanderung* that ultimately destroyed the empire, setting an example that inspired his contemporaries in the view of *Ammianus.

Works

Meditations Marcus is most famous for a work his subjects never saw, the intimate notebook in which he recorded (in Greek) his own reflections on human life and the ways of the gods, perhaps before retiring at night. The title *Meditations* is modern: 'to himself' found in our manuscripts may not go back to the author, but is surely accurate. The closest analogies for the thought are with *Epictetus, but Marcus is less interested in sustained exposition. The style, often eloquent and poetic, can also be compressed, obscure, and grammatically awkward. All of this is understandable if he was writing memoranda for his eyes alone.

Although divided by moderns into twelve 'books', the work seems not to have a clear structure. Brief epigrams are juxtaposed with quotations (usually of moral tags, occasionally of longer passages) and with more developed arguments on divine providence, the brevity of human life, the necessity for moral effort, and tolerance of his fellow human beings. These *pensées* are nearly all generalized: we do not learn Marcus' thoughts about his family, members of the court, or strategy. We do, however, get some idea of his personality and pre-occupations.

The first book of the *Meditations* is more coherent than the others. Here Marcus goes through a list of his closer relatives and several teachers, recording what he owes to each. This list culminates in two long passages on what he owes to his predecessor *Antoninus Pius, and to the gods. Though often allusive and obscure, they give us unique access to the mind of an ancient ruler, and the whole book is a precious personal document.

In the rest of the work, though technical discussion of Stoic doctrine is avoided, certain recurrent themes stand out: the need to avoid distractions and concentrate on making the correct moral choice; the obligation of individuals to work for the common good (e.g. 'What does not benefit the hive does not benefit the bee'); the unity of mankind in a world-city; insistence on the providence of the gods, often combined with rejection of the Epicurean alternative that all is random movement of atoms. Duty and social responsibility are strongly emphasized; Marcus was keenly aware of the temptations of power. Thoughts of providence lead him to contemplate the vastness of time and space, and the guiding pattern that acc. to the Stoics gives order to the universe. There is also a more melancholy note, of resignation and pessimism. Marcus is fascinated by life's transience and the way in which all great men, even philosophers and emperors, pass on and are forgotten. His most lasting achievement is a work which has inspired readers as different as Sir Thomas Browne, Matthew Arnold, and Cecil Rhodes.

Aurēlius Antonīnus, Marcus (AD 188–217), nicknamed **Caracalla**, emperor AD 198–217. Elder son of *Septimius Severus; renamed after Marcus Aurelius and made Caesar in 195. Augustus in 198, he was consul for the first time with his father in 202 and for the second time with his brother Septimius Geta in 205, when he had his hated father-in-law killed. Consul for the third time in 208, again with Geta, whom he also hated, he accompanied his father to *Britain, sharing command against the Caledonians. When Severus died (211), he and Geta abandoned Scotland, making the *wall of Hadrian the frontier again, and returned to Rome. Caracalla had Geta killed, and a drastic purge followed. To conciliate the soldiers, he raised their pay, creating financial problems. One solution was the 'Antonine *constitution'; he simultaneously doubled the inheritance tax paid only by citizens, which funded the *aerarium militare*. In 215 a new coin was struck, evidently tariffed at two *denarii*, but weighing only 1.5: this was to lead to inflation.

In 213 he fought the Alamanni (the first time they are mentioned), and became Germanicus Maximus. In 214 he attacked the Danubian Carpi and reorganized *Pannonia, each province now having two legions (Britain was split into two provinces at this time; Nearer Spain was also subdivided). Obsessed by *Alexander (2) the Great, he raised a Macedonian phalanx and went east in his footsteps, through Asia Minor and Syria to *Alexandria, where large numbers who had mocked him were killed. When his offer to marry a Parthian princess was rejected, he attacked Media. While preparing a further campaign he was murdered near Carrhae (April 217).

aurum corōnārium ('gold for crowns') Gold *crowns were offered to rulers and conquerors in the ancient near east and in the Hellenistic world. Similar offerings were made from the early 2nd cent. BC to Roman generals and rapidly came to be exacted by them. A law of *Caesar (59 BC) enacted that it should not be demanded until a *triumph had been formally decreed. Under the empire, gold for crowns went to the emperor alone and was exacted with increasing frequency, not only for triumphs (*Res Gestae* 21) but on imperial accessions, anniversaries, adoptions, and so forth, and then became an irregular form of taxation on communities.

auspicium, literally 'bird-watching', but the term was applied to various types of *divination. There were five types of auspical sign: from the sky (thunder and lightning), from birds (their number, position, flight, cries, and feeding), from sacred chickens (kept hungry in a cage; if food fell from their beaks when they were eating, this was an excellent sign), from quadrupeds (e.g. a wolf eating grass), and from unusual, threatening occurrences. They were either unsolicited or solicited. Through the auspices the gods only expressed their approval or disapproval of an action either contemplated or in progress. They were valid for one day only, and pertained solely to the timing of an action, not to its substance. Auguries were the auspices that pertained not only to timing but also to substance. At inaugurations of priests and temples the deity gave approval not only for the day of the ceremony but also for the person or the place to be inaugurated. The auguries had no time limit, and to remove their effects a special ceremony was necessary. The auguries could be conducted only by the *augurs; any person could use the auspices, hence the division into private and public auspices. The latter were administered by the magistrates. All public acts were performed after a consultation of solicited auspices, e.g. elections, census, military operations.

autarky (Gk. *autarkeia*) The ideal of (economic) self-sufficiency.

autobiography See BIOGRAPHY, GREEK and ROMAN.

autochthons in myth, are figures born lit. from the earth, with no human parents. While the idea of 'mother' Earth is influential here, autochthony is not normally presented as the origin of humanity in general (the story of *Deucalion and Pyrrha comes closest to this) but rather serves to make a statement about a particular group of people. True autochthons (as opposed to the merely earthborn) remain in the land where they were born. Thus the autochthonous ancestor, like the founder-figure, expresses and forms the group's sense of its identity, making an implicit claim to superiority over non-autochthonous groups. The Spartoi (see CADMUS), the autochthonous 'sown men' of *Thebes, may at one time have represented a special class in the city, while the autochthon *Erichthonius expressed the claim of all Athenians to be the original inhabitants of *Attica.

autonomy In internal affairs it obtains when a community is responsible for its own laws; in this sense it is opposed to *tyranny and means self-determination, whereas *freedom (*eleutheria*) means absence of external constraint. But 'autonomy' is also regularly used in the context of interstate relations, where it indicates a limited independence permitted by a stronger power to a weaker, that is, external constraints are relevant to autonomy too. *Aegina's complaint about infringed autonomy was an issue at the beginning of the *Peloponnesian War. See FREE CITIES.

autopsy, a Greek-derived word for personal inspection—e.g. by historians, geographers, or doctors.

auxilia In the 1st cent. BC Rome often employed men recruited outside Italy as cavalry or light infantry, or in specialist roles, and during the Civil Wars Gallic and German cavalry and the forces of local kings, esp. in Asia Minor

and Syria, were important. Some of these were temporary formations serving under their own leaders near their homeland in accordance with their treaty obligations to Rome, and this practice continued. But *Augustus formally incorporated many ethnic auxiliary units into the army; they comprised non-citizens from the less developed provinces, and often took their title from a district or tribe ('of British'), or a city ('of the people of Antioch'), or from their armament ('of archers'), sometimes with the addition of an imperial name (e.g. *Flāvia*). Later, men were recruited to supplement existing units, first from areas with plentiful manpower, esp. Belgica (see GAUL (TRANSALPINE)), Pannonia, and *Thrace, and then locally from areas close to the camps of the *auxilia* units, or from adjacent provinces. So, the ethnic character of the *auxilia* was gradually diluted. In the 1st cent. AD, although many *auxilia* were volunteers, most were probably conscripted.

It is hard to calculate the total number of *auxilia*. By the Flavian period they probably numbered about 180,000, rising to over 220,000 in the mid-2nd cent. The *auxilia* consisted of infantry cohorts and cavalry wings (*alae*), and part-mounted cohorts containing cavalry and infantry (see COHORS). Regular auxiliary regiments were commanded by Roman officers of *equestrian rank, either tribunes or prefects, and the most senior was the prefect of an *ala*.

Auxiliary infantrymen were probably paid at five-sixths the rate of a legionary, receiving 750 sesterces a year under Augustus, with proportionally higher rates for cavalrymen (see STIPENDIUM). Service-time was eventually established at 25 years, and by the early 2nd cent. all *auxilia* were receiving citizenship on discharge for themselves and their children.

Gradually more citizens began to enlist in auxiliary units, and the distinction between auxiliaries and legionaries became blurred as the former took a growing part in fighting and in maintaining provincial garrisons.

Aventine, the southernmost hill of Rome, overlooking the Tiber. Temples here included those dedicated to *Diana and to Juno Regina. Until AD 49 the hill lay outside the *pomerium*. The temple of *Ceres, Liber (see LIBER PATER), and Libera was headquarters of the plebeian *aediles; the hill itself was *ager publicus* given to the *plebs* for settlement in 456, and it remained a cosmopolitan centre of popular politics under the late republic. Gaius *Sempronius Gracchus, perhaps imitating the second *secession, was besieged here in 121. Under the empire, however, it became principally a centre of élite housing. To the SW lay the Emporium and Monte Testaccio, a huge mound of broken *amphorae.

Babrius composed not later than the 2nd cent. AD 'Fables of *Aesop in Iambics', being metrical versions of *fables. 144 fables survive. The literary and artistic claims made in his two extant proems are such as to suggest that, despite the apparent artlessness of his style, he wrote for the delectation of an educated public rather than for the schoolroom.

Babylon The ruins of the city extend over several mounds in the vicinity of mod. Hillah (c.80 km. (50 mi.) south of Baghdad); the most important are Babil, Kasr, Merkes, Homera. Babylon became politically important under Hammurabi (1792–1750 BC); but its time of greatest splendour was as capital of the Neo-Babylonian empire (605–539 BC). Most of its famous buildings date from this period. Babylon was an important centre for the *Achaemenid and *Seleucid rulers, who supported its cults (in which they sometimes participated personally) and continued to use and maintain its palace.

The city area inside the double fortifications (described by *Herodotus) was c.400 ha. (990 acres). Eight gates pierced the walls; the summer palace (Babil) and New Year Festival temple lay outside them to the north. The ancient course of the *Euphrates, crossed by a stone-built bridge, divided the city in half; the citadel with palace (Kasr) lay on the east bank on the north edge of the city. Next to the palace lay the Ishtar gate, decorated with brilliantly coloured glazed-brick reliefs; from here southwards ran the similarly decorated processional way to the ziggurat (the temple-tower of Etemenanki) and central sanctuary of Bel-Marduk. East of Etemenanki, lay the dwelling quarters, Merkes and Homera.

Babylonia, country stretching from mod. Baghdad to the Arab-Persian Gulf, drained by the *Euphrates and Tigris rivers. From the 15th cent. BC Babylonia formed a territorial state with *Babylon as its capital. It was subject to Assyria

from the late 8th cent. until the Babylonian general Nabopolassar fought back the Assyrians and, with Median help, destroyed Assyria's empire (626–609). Nabopolassar founded the Neo-Babylonian empire, stretching from Palestine to the Iranian frontier, ruled from Babylon. The most famous Neo-Babylonian king was his son, Nebuchadnezzar II (604–562), who rebuilt Babylonia's cities extensively and sacked *Jerusalem (587). The last Neo-Babylonian ruler, Nabonidus (555–539), was defeated by *Cyrus (1) the Great of Persia. *Alexander (2) the Great conquered Babylonia in 331, detaching its northern region (Mesopotamia). *Seleucus I and *Antigonus I disputed, and fought for, control of Babylonia (316–309) and it became a core-region of the Seleucid empire.

Babylonia was perceived by Greeks and Romans as the source of astronomical and astrological lore. They associated this activity with 'Chaldaeans'—the name of a number of tribal groups in Babylonia. There is no evidence that Babylonians ever linked any particular learning with these tribes. *Astronomy and *mathematics were an important and highly developed part of Babylonian scholarship; most of the latest preserved *cuneiform texts are of this scientific nature. See ASTROLOGY; ASTRONOMY, 5; MATHEMATICS.

Bacchānālia usually translates the Greek *mysteries (*orgia*), with special reference to the worship suppressed by the Roman authorities in 186 BC. We have an account of the suppression in Livy and an inscribed version of the senatorial decree against the cult, in the form in which it was circulated to the allied states of Italy. These sources can be supplemented by references in *Plautus' plays and now by archaeological evidence to show that the Bacchic cult, perhaps of south Italian Greek origin, was widespread in Italy, decades before the senate chose to act against it. The form of the Italian cult seems to differ from other Hellenistic examples in admitting men as well as women to the mysteries and in increasing the frequency of meetings.

The surviving decree concentrates on the structure of Bacchic cells—their oaths of loyalty, their organization and funding, their membership, their property. This suggests that it was the power of cell-leaders over worshippers, cutting across traditional patterns of family and authority, that disturbed the senate, rather than alleged criminal actions or orgiastic rites; but any allegation would have helped to discredit a powerful and well-embedded cult; Livy's vivid account has valuable elements, and in substance shows knowledge of the decree itself; but its highly literary elaboration shows the influence of the senate's propaganda against the cult. The senate's persecution succeeded at least in removing the cult from prominence, though artistic evidence shows its long-sustained influence. Later Italian evidence shows a domesticated, family version of the cult, well subordinated to élite authority.

See DIONYSUS.

Bacchiads, aristocrats of *Corinth, claimed *Heraclid descent from King Bacchis. After suppressing the kingship c.750 BC they ruled, 200 in number, until *Cypselus overthrew them c.657. Corinth's western interests were established under them; they founded *Syracuse and *Corcyra, and were allies of *Chalcis in the Lelantine War (see GREECE (HISTORY), *Archaic period*). They married only among themselves (see ENDOGAMY), and were more exclusive than most Greek *aristocracies; that was the main reason for their fall.

Bacchus See DIONYSUS.

Bacchylidēs (c.520–450 BC), Greek lyric poet, nephew of *Simonides. Although he was well known in Hellenistic and Roman times, only a handful of lines had survived in quotations when a papyrus containing his book of victory odes almost complete and the first half of his book of *dithyrambs was found in Egypt in 1896. His patrons, apart from *Hieron (1) I of Syracuse, included athletes from Ceos, *Aegina, Phlius, Metapontum, and *Thessaly. Several of his dithyrambs were composed for competitions at Athens, one for Sparta. Stylistically, his dithyrambs are like ballads, using lively narrative, often allusive and selective, as well as direct speech. They exploit the pathetic potential of the myths, as do those victory odes which contain a mythical narrative as their centrepiece.

Baetica, the heart of the province originally (197 BC) called Further Spain, comprising a range of sophisticated and urbanized peoples formerly controlled by *Carthage. As Roman territory increased, an administrative division, beginning south of *Carthago Nova, between Nearer and Further Spain was formed. In 27 BC the old settled province east and south of the Anas was assigned to the senate as Hispania Baetica. It was divided for judicial purposes into four *conventūs centred at Gades, Corduba (the capital), Astigi, and Hispalis. Moreover, Caesar and Augustus created many colonies in this heavily urbanized province, while their grants of municipal status (see MUNICIPIUM) to native communities were greatly extended by Vespasian. Baetica was one of the richest provinces in the Roman west, exporting metals (see GOLD), *olive oil, and fish-pickle (see FISHING; FOOD AND DRINK) to Rome and the northern frontiers.

Balbus, Cornēlius See CORNELIUS BALBUS (1) and (2).

banishment See EXILE.

banks Banking in the Greek world appears to have evolved out of professional money-changing: a response to the multiplicity of state coinages (*trapezĩtēs* or 'banker' refers to the *trapeza* or changer's table). Changers, and presumably bankers, existed all over the Classical and Hellenistic Greek worlds, but our knowledge is concentrated in Athens, where, from the 4th cent. BC, the names are known of some twenty bankers. The most successful Athenian bankers were rich. *Pasion, beginning as a bankers' slave, gained his freedom, took over control of his former masters' bank, and eventually became a citizen. His own banking slave, *Phormion (2), followed an almost identical path from rags to riches.

In the Roman west, the basic problem is distinguishing between rich men of affairs who might offer financial services, including credit (e.g. *Pomponius Atticus) and professional dealers in money. Whereas the former might be rich through ownership of land, the latter were generally of lower status, made most of their living through financial transactions, and might be organized into *collēgia* (see CLUBS, ROMAN).

barbarian While we associate Classical culture primarily with emphasis on *citizenship (membership of a *polis), Classical Greek literature also assigns considerable importance to defining a common Greek identity and creating the figure of the 'barbarian' in contrast (see ANTROPOLOGY). That contrast was not important in Archaic literature. The factors that brought it to the fore were (a) the imposition of Persian control over western Asia Minor from the mid-6th cent. BC and the successful armed resistance to Persia by 31 Greek cities in 480/79 BC (see PERSIAN WARS); (b) justification of Athenian hegemony over the *Delian League on the grounds that Greeks should unite to continue resistance against Persia; and (c) the appearance of considerable numbers of non-Greek slaves at Athens, after the economic exploitation of the indigenous poor had been curtailed by *Solon's *seisachtheia* (alleviation of *debt).

With *Aeschylus' Persians (472 BC), a consistent image of the barbarian appears in Athenian literature and art. Apart from a lack of competence in Greek, the barbarian's defining feature is an absence of the moral responsibility required to exercise political freedom: the two are connected, since both imply a lack of *logos*, the ability to reason and speak (sc. Greek) characteristic of the adult male citizen. Barbarians are marked by a lack of control regarding sex, food, and cruelty. In *Homer, the breaking of such taboos had been associated with superhuman heroes; in Classical thought, they were 'barbarous' (the myth of Tereus, thought originally to have been a *Megarian hero, includes rape, tearing out a tongue, a mother's murder of her own child, and cannibalism: so, Tereus had to be reclassified as a *Thracian king. Absence of political freedom entails rule by tyrants, and often women, and the use of underhand weaponry like bows and poison; the absence of moral self-control entails the wearing of wasteful and 'effeminate' clothing, drinking wine neat, and enjoying emotional ('Lydian' or 'Ionian') music. Somatic differences might be used by writers (or vase-painters) to reinforce the image of the barbarian, but it did not matter whether he was black African or Thracian (see RACE).

The Greek/barbarian polarity continued to be a major element in Greek literature throughout antiquity; it compensated for the military and political powerlessness of Greek cities in the Hellenistic and Roman periods. Along with other elements of Greek culture, it became part of the ideological baggage of Latin literature. Its importance in practical terms is less clear: 'barbarians' were excluded from the *Olympic Games and other religious ceremonies, e.g. at *Eleusis. Roman rhetoric could represent opponents, both non-Roman and Roman, as either 'barbarians' or 'barbarous' (representations of *Cleopatra VII or *Boudicca), though such language masked much more real distinctions (principally that between the Roman citizen and the non-citizen), and Roman moral discourse symbolized disapproval in different terms (e.g. Etruscan luxury). While some Greek intellectuals stretched the polarity to its limits (e.g. Aristotle's Politics on barbarians being slaves 'by nature'), others questioned the usefulness of the concept. The polarity might be associated with a more universal distinction between 'us' at the centre of the world and 'them' at the periphery: the barbarians who inhabited the 'edge' of the world might be savages without laws, settled homes, or agriculture (see NOMADS), but alternatively they might have created an earthly paradise (the Hyperboreans, the 'Kingdom of the Sun' in the Indian Ocean (see EUHEMERUS)). Like kings, women, children, old people, or slaves, some barbarians might be closer to the divine world than the adult male citizen (Celtic *Druids, Persian magi, Indian gymnosophists).

In the Hellenistic period, the distinction between Greek and barbarian came to be seen as insignificant even by some of those imbued by the literary culture (*Stoicism); its irrelevance was explicitly expressed by Christians (Col. 3: 11). Nevertheless the prejudice against 'barbarians' remained latent in the literary tradition.

basileus, basileia See KINGSHIP; for the *basileus* (an official) at Athens see ARCHONTES; LAW AND PROCEDURE, ATHENIAN.

basilica, the name applied to a wide range of Roman building forms, esp. to the large, multipurpose public halls which regularly accompanied the *forum in the western half of the Roman world, and corresponded roughly in function to the Greek and Hellenistic *stoa. The earliest known was built in Rome by *Porcius Cato (1) in 184 BC. The name came, by extension, to be used for any large covered hall in domestic, commercial, military, or religious use.

The first basilicas may have been the administrative halls of the Hellenistic kings. A typical basilica is rectangular, open either along one side or at one end, with the roof in two sections, the central part being raised over a clerestory supported on an internal colonnade. An apsidal niche at one end contained the platform or *tribūnal* for magistrates. Basilicas can be free-standing, or placed along one side of the enclosed fora. The roofs of basilicas are supported by timber beam construction. This, and the large number of columns required to support them, are a required feature of basilical architecture.

Basilicas of traditional type continued to be built in the 3rd cent. AD (the Severan basilica at *Lepcis Magna). Since they were designed to hold large numbers of people, they responded to the needs of Christian worship following the official recognition of *Christianity, and the early *churches at Rome and elsewhere are essentially basilicas with the apisidal *tribunal*, using the columns and timber form of construction.

Bassae, in SW Arcadia, the site of one of the best-preserved Greek temples. It was dedicated to *Apollo the Helper (*Epikourios*). It dates to the latter part of the 5th cent. BC with an interruption due to Spartan occupation of the area during the *Peloponnesian War. The greater part of the temple is in the local limestone, with carved decoration applied in marble. The orientation, followed also by its predecessor, was towards the north instead of the east, and the early sunlight, instead of entering through the main doorway, was admitted to the adytum through an opening in the eastern side-wall. Ten engaged Ionic columns decorated the side walls of the cella internally, with a single central Corinthian column—one of the earliest of its kind, and one of the most beautiful (see ORDERS)—between the cella and the adytum. The sculptured frieze is now in the British Museum. Apollo with the epithet *Epikourios* may be regarded as the protector of Arcadians serving as *mercenaries.

baths, one of the most characteristic and widely distributed types of Roman building, had their origins in the Greek world where public baths were common from at least the 4th cent. BC. Surviving 3rd-cent. Greek baths centre on a series of hip-baths arranged around the walls of one or more rooms, often circular, with niches above the tubs, and were furnished with hot water which was poured over the seated bather. Baths of this type are found in southern Italy and Sicily, where, together with local traditions of therapeutic baths at volcanic springs, they were instrumental in the development of the purely Roman type. These replaced the individual tubs with communal pools, and often incorporated the dry sweating-rooms and exercise grounds of the Greek *gymnasium in the same establishment. The basic features of these early Roman baths were a changing-room (*apodytērium*), an unheated *frigidārium* with a cold-water basin, an indirectly heated warm room (*tepidārium*) sometimes containing a tepid pool, and a strongly heated room (*caldārium*) containing a hot plunge pool and a separate water-basin on a stand. The evolution of under-floor heating (the hypocaust) and wall-heating systems after c.100 BC, replacing the less efficient braziers, and the introduction of window-glass in the 1st cent. AD permitted the development of an elaborately graded system often with the incorporation of several wet and dry sweating-rooms. With increasingly assured water supply to towns (see AQUEDUCTS), large cold and even heated swimming-pools also became common adjuncts.

Public baths, often located near the *forum, were a normal part of Roman towns in Italy by the 1st cent. BC. The baths (*thermae*) in the Campus Martius donated to the Roman people by *Agrippa c.20 BC set new standards of luxury and architectural elaboration, and heralded a new civic role for the baths in the towns of the empire. In Rome they were followed by the baths of *Nero, *Titus, and *Trajan, the latter being the first of the truly monumental complexes set in a vast enclosure containing gardens, lecture-halls, libraries, and other cultural facilities, reflecting the influence of the Hellenistic gymnasium. The symmetrical plan of the bathing-block centred on a triple cross-vaulted *frigidarium* was influential both in Rome (baths of *Caracalla and *Diocletian) and in the provinces. The influence of the 'imperial' type can be seen in the increased size and elaboration of many baths in the provinces from the late 1st cent. onwards, along with an increase in the amount of space devoted to non-bathing functions.

Bathing occupied a central position in the social life of the day; by the 2nd cent., any sizeable community, civil or military, had at least one set of public baths, while private baths were common in *villas and in rich town houses. Larger towns often had one or more substantial buildings, which were show-pieces for the community as well as a number of smaller, privately owned *balnea* to serve everyday needs. See HOUSES, ITALIAN; WATER.

Baucis and her husband Philēmon were elderly peasants who entertained *Zeus and *Hermes with the resources of their meagre larder when the gods paid an incognito visit to *Phrygia; for their piety they were spared from the flood which drowned their inhospitable neighbours. They lived out the rest of their lives as priests of the temple into which their humble shack was transformed, and were themselves finally transfigured into an oak and a linden-tree springing from the same trunk. The tale, which has genuine roots in ancient Anatolian tree-cult (see TREES, SACRED), has its first and canonical telling in Ovid, *Metamorphoses* 8.

beards See COSMETICS; PORTRAITURE, ROMAN.

Behistun See BISITUN.

Bellerophon In *Homer's account he is son of Glaucus and grandson of *Sisyphus, and a native of Ephyre (generally identified with *Corinth). Proetus, king of Tiryns, had a wife Anteia (Stheneboea in later versions) who fell in love with Bellerophon and tried to seduce him. When he rejected her advances, she falsely accused him of trying to rape her. So Proetus sent him to Iobatēs, king of Lycia and Anteia's father, with a sealed letter containing instructions to kill the bearer. Iobates set Bellerophon tasks likely to bring about his death, sending him to kill the Chimaera (a composite monster), and to fight the Solymi and the *Amazons. When Bellerophon returned triumphant from all these tasks, and survived an ambush laid for him by Iobates, the king married him to his daughter and gave him half his kingdom. In versions after Homer, Bellerophon accomplished his tasks with the help of the winged horse *Pegasus, which *Athena helped him to catch. Acc. to *Euripides, he also used Pegasus to take vengeance on Stheneboea, and offended the gods by trying to fly on him to Olympus. In Homer, although there is no direct mention of Pegasus, Bellerophon became 'hated by all the gods', which presumably was caused by the attempt to reach Olympus. Bellerophon on Pegasus attacking the Chimaera is found in art from before the mid-7th cent. BC.

Bendis, a Thracian goddess. Greek artists represented her as a booted huntress, like Artemis. Her cult was introduced to Athens in two stages: by 430/29 BC she shared a small treasury under the control of the Treasurers of the Other Gods; and a decree of (probably) 413/12 assigned her a priestess and founded the great festival in *Piraeus known from the opening of *Plato's *Republic*, at which twin processions, of native Thracians and of Athenians, were followed by a torch-race on horseback and an 'all-night celebration' The immediate motivation for the introduction of the goddess's cult is unknown; at bottom, the Athenians' interest in Bendis must be a product of their preoccupation with Thrace, which goes back to the 6th cent. See RELIGION, THRACIAN; THRACE.

beneficiāriī were junior officers in the Roman army below the rank of *centurion. They were appointed through the favour (*beneficium*) of their commander, and the title existed at least from the time of *Caesar. In the imperial period a *beneficiarius* ranked among the *principālēs*, who received pay at one-and-a-half times or twice normal legionary rates (see STIPENDIUM), and performed administrative duties. Normally a man was promoted *beneficiarius* after serving as an *immūnis* (a soldier on basic pay who performed a specialist function for which he received exemption from routine duties), and then holding one or more posts in the century (see CENTURIA)—officer in charge of the watch, standard-bearer, or orderly. The rank of each *beneficiarius* depended on the status of the official to whose office he was attached (these included senior military officers, procurators, provincial governors, the city *prefect, the *praetorian prefects), and he could often expect promotion to the centurionate.

betrothal

Greek *Engyē* was a contract between two men, the groom and the bride's father (or other 'controller', male representative at law), which established that a union was a fully valid marriage. In Classical Athens, this contract was oral, more or less formulaic, aimed at assuring the legitimacy of children, and accompanied by an agreement concerning dowry; the bride herself did not need to be present, or even of an age to understand the proceedings, and the celebration of the marriage and cohabitation might be long delayed or in the end not take place. Marriages at Sparta too might involve betrothal; Another marriage custom was mock abduction.

Roman *Sponsalia* in the republic consisted of reciprocal promises, and breach-of-promise actions (in the form of actions for damages) existed. The tendency of classical Roman law was to remove constraint, and the term *sponsalia* came near to an informal agreement to marry, voidable at will (except that the intending husband was required to return such dowry as had been given to him and the intending bride was expected to return the much more usual gift from her intending husband). The betrothal was solemnized with a kiss, and the intending husband put an iron *ring on the third finger of his partner's left hand; it was the occasion for a party (also called *sponsalia*).

See also MARRIAGE LAW, *Greek* and *Roman*.

bilingualism Widespread bilingualism at some level was characteristic of the ancient world. Latin and esp. Greek were the languages of culture and education (in the Roman empire, Latin was the language of law and army), as well as power, so that while many other languages coexisted alongside Latin and Greek, neither Greeks nor Romans ever had to impose their language on others.

Greek unwillingness to learn other languages was linked to their assurance of cultural superiority. *Herodotus learned no other languages (and suffered at interpreters' hands, Greek thinkers categorize languages as Greek or *barbarian. Yet this monolingualism may be more characteristic of the literary élite and of high culture. Other Greeks—mercenaries in Egypt, those in Persian service, traders and colonizers—must have acquired other languages and often married non-Greek women. The *orientalizing period of Greek culture is hard to envisage with merely monolingual Greeks. Late 5th-cent. Athens has a mixture of customs and languages 'from all the Greeks and barbarians' (*Old Oligarch). However, by the Classical period, the bilinguals in a Greek city would be mainly foreigners, traders, and slaves, i.e. outsiders.

The picture becomes more complex with *Alexander (2) the Great's conquests of large non-Greek-speaking areas. In the *Seleucid empire, there is a mixture of Greek and *Aramaic in the administration. In Ptolemaic Egypt, Greek became the language of administration; the extent to which Egyptians learnt Greek and became bilingual, however, or Greeks integrated at all into Egyptian society, is difficult to gauge. There is evidence for individuals with double names, one Egyptian, one Greek, and for scribes fluent in both demotic and Greek. So the weight of administrative documents in Greek may hide greater Egyptian participation. Individual bilingualism, esp. among prominent and ambitious Egyptian officials, must have been widespread.

The Roman empire was bilingual at the official, and multilingual at the individual and non-official, level. With the increasing Hellenization of Rome itself (see HELLENISM), educated Romans were expected to be bilingual in Latin and Greek, esp. from the 1st cent. BC, at least for cultural purposes. *Quintilian advised that children start learning Greek before Latin. Greek was widely used in diplomacy: Licinius Crassus,

proconsul of Asia in 131 BC, who spoke five Greek dialects, was exceptional. *Tiberius tried, too late, to discourage Greek in the senate, a rare case of Latin chauvinism. Most Roman emperors were fluent in Greek: Marcus *Aurelius, despairing of Latin, wrote his *Meditations* in Greek.

The Romans made little attempt to impose Latin on the empire. The language of administration in the west was certainly Latin, and ambitious provincials simply had to acquire it. In the Greek-speaking east, administration was mostly conducted in Greek, and *edicts, imperial *constitutions, and letters sent by Rome to Greek cities were usually translated into Greek first (and inscribed in Greek). Greek-speakers were unenthusiastic about learning Latin, and Roman colonies in the east were linguistically quickly absorbed. However, the extent of bilingual inscriptions implies there was no strict single language policy. Decisions of the Roman courts were probably always given in Latin, and Latin was necessary in law for certain documents for Roman citizens.

biography, Greek Biography in antiquity was not a rigidly defined genre. *Bios*, 'life', or *bioi*, 'lives', spanned a range of types of writing. So the boundaries with neighbouring genres—the encomium, the biographical novel on the model of *Xenophon's *Cyropaedia*, the historical monograph on the deeds of a great man like Alexander (2) the Great—are blurred.

The impulse to celebrate the individual finds early expression in the *dirge and the funeral speech (see EPITAPHIOS); composing a literary work around an individual's experiences is as old as the *Odyssey* (see HOMER). In the 5th cent. biographical interest was pursued in various ways. *Ion of Chios gossiped about contemporary figures in his 'Visits', while Stesimbrotus of Thasos wrote colourfully on *Themistocles, *Thucydides (1) son of Melesias, and *Pericles. *Thucydides (2) included selective sketches of several figures, notably *Pausanias (1) and Themistocles. In the 4th cent. appeared two influential encomia, *Isocrates' *Evagoras* (Evagoras was king of Cypriot Salamis), enumerating its subject's qualities in a loosely chronological framework, and Xenophon's *Agesilaus*, giving first a focused narrative of achievements, then a catalogue of virtues. Xenophon's 'Socratic Memoirs' (*Memorābilia*), along with the Platonic corpus, developed the personality of *Socrates.

*Aristotle gave biography a new impetus. Under his influence interest in ethical and cultural history encouraged the writing of more generalized *bioi*. *Dicaearchus and Clearchus treated different lifestyles; *Theophrastus' *Characters* are clearly related. *Aristoxenus wrote Lives of philosophers, in which an interest in lifestyle combined with malicious stories about *Socrates' irascibility and *Plato's plagiarism. This anecdotal style heralds a distinctive kind of biography of cultural figures. Chamaeleon's Lives of various poets were notable for their wild inferences of biographical data from an author's work, and his model was followed. The tendency to collect Lives in series became a standard mode of presenting intellectual history, and the 'succession' of teachers and pupils was a helpful way of explaining influences.

Rather than clear-cut political Lives, we have works with biographical affinities. The impact of *Alexander (2) the Great was important. Early monographs centred on the king's person; the fragmentation of the Hellenistic world into dynasties encouraged monographs on other kings. The biographical novel on the model of *Cyropaedia* also revived, with its typical emphasis on a king's upbringing. Onesicritus' *How Alexander Was Brought Up* belongs here, and so later does *Nicolaus of Damascus' *On Augustus' Life and Education*.

The Christian Gospels have points of contact with the Greek tradition, with their charismatic hero and their anecdotal narrative texture. A different moral earnestness is found in Plutarch's *Parallel Lives*. Their scale, ambition, and historical sobriety are hard to parallel in earlier tradition; so is the depth of characterization. The comparison of a Greek and a Roman hero draws attention to nuances of personality.

*Philostratus' *Life of Apollonius* (see APOLLONIUS (4)) veers towards hagiography: readers would probably not have taken it as literal truth. The first book of Marcus *Aurelius provides an exploratory form of intellectual autobiography. *Galen is similar but less perceptive. *Diogenes (4) Laertius exemplifies the abridging and synthesizing of the materials of literary biography.

See also CHARACTER.

biography, Roman Roman biography did not wholly derive from its Greek equivalent: their own political and family customs led Romans to value the recording of the deeds of their great men. We hear of dirges at funerals, and of funeral laudations (see LAUDATIO FUNEBRIS). Such laudations were preserved and kept among the family records, together with the portrait masks (*imagines*) of distinguished

ancestors: Cicero complains about the inaccuracies of these laudations. Sepulchral inscriptions became very elaborate, often giving details of private as well as public matters (see 'LAUDATIO TURIAE'). The flavour of such formal memorials is as recurrent in Roman biography as that of encomium in the Greek counterpart.

The competitive quest for glory also stimulated writers to self-justification and self-defence. The award of a triumph might depend on the bulletins sent home by generals. More elaborate apologetic or propagandist autobiography found a natural home in Rome. *Caesar's *Commentaries* presented an esp. nuanced form of self-projection; *Cicero too wrote about his own career and achievement both in Latin and Greek. Under the Principate, it was esp. members of the imperial family who wrote political memoirs: *Augustus, *Tiberius, *Iulia Agrippina, *Hadrian, *Septimius Severus.

Justification was not limited to autobiography. Gaius *Sempronius Gracchus' two books *To Pomponius* presented a picture of his brother Tiberius *Sempronius Gracchus (2) which similarly contributed to contemporary debate. In a letter to Lucceius Cicero seems to assume that a historical monograph will naturally centre on a single person and his achievements, and playfully pleads for a liberal attitude to the truth.

The political heat of the late republic produced further writings designed to praise and defend, or sometimes attack, not only political actions but private character or philosophy. The influence of forensic rhetoric, so often describing the life of client or opponent, is here strong. The death of *Porcius Cato (2) inspired works by Cicero and *Brutus, which were answered first by *Hirtius, then by Caesar in his *Anticato*. Such works represent the beginnings of a considerable literature, a blend of martyrology and ideological propaganda, which came to cluster around the Stoic opponents of the 1st-cent. Principate (see STOICISM). Tacitus' *Agricola* explores political life under a tyrant, though it praises restrained collaboration rather than ostentatious martyrdom; its use of one man's life to sketch a political ambience is deft.

*Jerome named *Varro, *Nepos, and *Suetonius in a canon of biographers. Varro may be named for his *On Poets* or for his *Portraits*, or even for his *Life of the Roman People*, a Roman imitation of *Dicaearchus. Suetonius' *Caesars* reduces the element of historical narrative, providing instead a learned survey of an emperor's character and behaviour under a series of headings. The style of the *Caesars* proved congenial as spectators increasingly saw Roman history in terms of the ruling personality, and biography supplanted historiography as the dominant mode of record.

There is little intimacy in Roman biography. Much Latin poetry is self-revealing and self-analytical, but the most ambitious formal autobiography and biography is centred on public figures, and exploration of inner life is felt inappropriate. Cicero does tell us something of his education and development, analysing his debt to various teachers; but there are no Latin pieces of self-exploration comparable with Marcus *Aurelius' *Meditations* until we reach St *Augustine.

biology See ANATOMY AND PHYSIOLOGY; ANIMALS, KNOWLEDGE OF; BOTANY; GYNAECOLOGY; PHARMACOLOGY.

birds, sacred Though the Greeks and Romans did not consider any bird actually divine, many birds, like other animals, were closely associated with the gods, and all birds could bring messages from the gods by omens (see AUSPICIUM; PORTENTS). *Divination from the activities of birds (often eagles or other birds of prey) is well attested in *Homer and in tragedy. In Rome, watching birds was one of the chief forms of divination (see AUGURS). Not only was the behaviour of wild birds watched for signs, but on military expeditions chickens were kept for the purpose.

Numerous divine associations developed in Greece. The eagle as the bird of *Zeus was almost universal. *Athena takes the form of several different birds in Homer; her connection with owls seems to be post-Homeric and is esp. linked with Athens. *Apollo was associated with the falcon and the swan, *Hera with the peacock; this last pairing must be of recent date, since the peacock was still a novelty to Greeks in the 5th cent. BC. None of these birds was considered inviolate by virtue of association with a god. In fact, the association was occasionally sacrificial: doves, which along with sparrows were *Aphrodite's sacred bird, were often sacrificed to her. Most of these traditions were taken over when the Roman gods were identified with Greek counterparts; there were also some native Italian associations of birds with gods, such as that of the woodpecker with *Mars.

birthday Among the Greeks the birthdays of several major Olympian deities (e.g. of *Artemis on the sixth, *Apollo on the seventh, and *Poseidon on the eighth) were in early times assigned to days of the month and were treated as sacred. Throughout Greek history these 'monthly' birthdays continued to be recognized and were often the focal points of the deities' annual festivals. For humans the day of birth itself was marked by congratulatory visits and presents from relatives and friends, but in the Archaic and Classical periods there seems to have been no recurring monthly or annual celebrations of the day. Birthdays of humans first attained significance for the Greeks when they began to assimilate rulers and outstanding individuals to gods (see RULER-CULT). *Plato shared Apollo's birthday, and after his death his followers gave him special veneration each year, probably on his birthday. In his will *Epicurus endowed an annual banquet for his followers on his birthday. The birthdays and accession days of the Ptolemies (see PTOLEMY (1)), *Seleucids, and Attalids were publicly fêted during their lifetimes throughout their kingdoms, both monthly and annually.

The Romans, unlike the Greeks, marked only anniversaries and from earliest times annually celebrated their own birthdays and those of family members, friends, and patrons with gifts, offerings, prayers, vows, and banquets. Roman poets developed a specific type of poem for the occasion. The rituals of the Roman birthday formed part of the cult of the *genius* of a man or the *iuno* of a woman. Under the empire the people celebrated annually, as an important part of imperial cult, the birthdays of past and present emperors and members of the imperial family.

Bisitun, a cliff 30 km. ($18\frac{1}{2}$ mi.) east of Kermanshah, with a relief and a long trilingual inscription (Elamite, Babylonian, Old *Persian) by *Darius I. The three versions differ in details. Cols. 1–4 report on his victories over the usurper Gaumata and other rebel kings in his first regnal year. The inscription was carved in stages; the OP version was added last. Copies were sent out and parts have been found at *Elephantine (*Aramaic) and *Babylon. Bisitun is the only narrative OP text. Col. 5, on Darius' second and third years, is similar to the ahistoric style of the later OP inscriptions.

Bithynia, a territory in NW Asia Minor. Although much of the land is mountainous and covered with forest, the river Sangarius with its tributaries and the valleys that run back from the Propontis form fertile plains and provide easy communications. It was one of the richest regions of *Asia Minor, possessing fine marble quarries and good harbours, and crossed by the main roads to the Anatolian plateau and to Pontus.

In 75/4 King Nicomedes IV bequeathed Bithynia to Rome. In organizing the province of Pontus and Bithynia in 63 *Pompey divided the land between eleven cities for convenience in maintaining order and collecting taxes. Despite heavy exploitation by the *publicani in the 1st cent. BC, which led to much land being transferred to Italian owners, the region became very prosperous under the Roman empire. Pontus and Bithynia was at first governed by proconsuls, but the importance of the highways to the eastern frontiers and to Syria and of the maritime connections in the Black (*Euxine) Sea led imperial *procurators to assume greater responsibilities than usual under the Julio-Claudian emperors; and special imperial *legates replaced proconsuls under *Trajan and *Hadrian. The conditions of city life in Bithynia in the early 2nd cent. AD are unusually well documented, with the correspondence of Pliny the Younger and *Trajan c. AD 110 and the speeches of Dio Cocceianus revealing peculation by magistrates, unwise and extravagant building, and bitter rivalries between the cities. Foremost rivals were Nicomedia, the chief city, and Nicaea.

Bocchus I, king of *Mauretania and father-in-law or son-in-law of *Jugurtha. His offer of alliance, early in the Jugurthine War, was rejected by Rome. He later joined Jugurtha, receiving western *Numidia as his price. With Jugurtha, he twice nearly defeated *Marius, but was finally induced by *Sulla to surrender Jugurtha. He became a 'friend of the Roman People' and retained part of Numidia. The surrender of Jugurtha to Sulla, with whom Bocchus maintained a close connection, was depicted on Sulla's signet ring, to Marius' irritation, and in a controversial group of statues dedicated by Bocchus on the Capitol in 91 BC.

Boeotia and Boeotian Confederacy
Boeotia was a region in central Greece, bounded in the north by *Phocis and Opuntian Locris. The east faces the Euboean Gulf, and Mts. Parnes and Cithaeron form the southern boundary with Attica. On the west Mt. *Helicon and some lower heights separate a narrow coastline from the interior. Lake Copais divided the region into a smaller northern part, the major city of which was *Orchomenus, and a larger southern part

dominated by *Thebes. Geography and the fertility of the soil encouraged the growth of many prosperous and populous cities and villages.

Boeotia enters history with *Hesiod of Ascra, whose *Works and Days* indicates an agricultural society of smallholdings. In his time several *basileis* (see KINGSHIP) in *Thespiae possessed the judicial power to settle inheritances. Other large cities exercised power over their smaller neighbours. The result was the development of well-defined political units that formed the basis of an early federal government. The union of these cities in a broader political system was aided by their common culture, ethnicity, language, and religion. By the last quarter of the 6th cent. BC some of these cities formed the Boeotian Confederacy, doubtless under the hegemony of Thebes (see FEDERAL STATES). The Boeotians, as a people, not as a confederacy, were early members of the Delphic *Amphictiony.

From the outset of the Persian Wars until the *Pax Romana*, Boeotia was the 'dancing-floor of war' in Greece. Boeotian reaction to the Persian invasion was mixed. Plataea, Thespiae, and some elements in Thebes originally favoured the Greeks, but after the battle of *Thermopylae only Plataea remained loyal to the Greek cause. The Persian defeat entailed the devastation of Boeotia. A truncated confederacy may have survived, but the region was politically unimportant. In 457 BC Boeotia allied itself with Sparta, which resulted in the battles of Tanagra and Oenophyta, the latter a major Boeotian defeat. Afterwards, Athens held control of Boeotia until the battle of *Coronea in 447. Thereafter, Boeotia rebuilt its confederacy, and remodelled its federal government along the lines described by the *Hellenica Oxyrhynchia* (see OXYRHYNCHUS).

Boeotia supported Sparta in the *Peloponnesian War. It defeated Athens at the battle of *Delion in 424, and contributed substantially to its eventual defeat. After the peace treaty of 404 relations between Boeotia and Sparta cooled. See EPAMINONDAS.

Boēthius (c. AD 480–c.524). The Ostrogothic king of Italy Theoderic appointed this leading nobleman consul (510). He resisted official oppression, was implicated in a senatorial conspiracy, imprisoned, and executed. His *Consolations of Philosophy* is a prison dialogue with Philosophy, a *Menippean mixture of prose and verse. It justifies providence on a Stoic and Neoplatonic basis (see STOICISM; NEOPLATONISM), without overt *Christianity; its reconciliation of free will and divine prescience is philosophically notable; it shows high literary genius, and an astounding memory for classical texts under trying conditions. (King Alfred, Chaucer, and Elizabeth I were to translate it.) Boethius' Greek scholarship was rare in Italy; he planned introductions and translations for the mathematical and logical disciplines, and translations of all *Plato and *Aristotle. The project was not completed, and much is lost or fragmentary.

Bona Dea (the Good Goddess—title, not a name), an Italian goddess, worshipped esp. in Rome and Latium. In Rome, she had an annual nocturnal ceremony held at the house of a chief magistrate, from which men were rigorously excluded (See CLODIUS PULCHER); it was led by the women of the magistrate's family with the help of the *Vestals. It was a state ritual, performed in secret, for the welfare of the Roman people.

books, Greek and Roman Books existed in *Egypt long before they came into use in Greece. Systems of writing had been invented and developed for administrative purposes in both Egypt and Mesopotamia by c.3000 BC. While the Sumerians and Babylonians used clay tablets for their *cuneiform scripts, the Egyptians used papyrus (see PALAEOGRAPHY; PAPYROLOGY, GREEK).

The papyrus plant grew mainly in the Nile delta. It was used for many purposes: to make ropes, sandals, baskets, boats, and—most importantly—writing material. Papyrus remained the dominant writing material throughout classical antiquity. A papyrus roll (on average 6–8 m. (20–26 ft.) long) would take a book of *Thucydides (2), or a play of c.1,500 lines, or two to three books of *Homer. The text is arranged in columns; the number of lines per column varies between 25 and 45.

Although writing may have been employed early on in the composition of Greek poetry (and the complex structure of both Iliad and Odyssey is hardly conceivable without it), the performance of poetry continued to be oral throughout the Archaic and Classical periods. Much of early epic poetry is reflected in both lyric poetry and black-figure vase-painting, Corinthian and Attic, and it seems doubtful whether this can be accounted for by oral transmission (by itinerant *rhapsodes and choirs) alone. So it is reasonable to assume that book-rolls played a part in the transmission of Greek poetry in the 7th and 6th cents., if only as aides-mémoire to the performers. In the 6th cent., the tyrants *Poly-

crates (1) of Samos and *Pisistratus of Athens are said to have been admired for their collections of books. Pisistratus is credited with a revision of the texts of Homer which until then had been 'confused'; he is also said to have inserted lines about *Salamis and *Theseus into the texts. There clearly was, in the later 6th cent., an authoritative text of Homer which served as a basis for rhapsodic recitals at the *Panathenaea.

From c.500 onwards, book-rolls (evidently of papyrus) appear on Attic vases; as far as the writing can be identified, they all contain poetry. The Duris cup in Berlin of c.485 BC illustrates the use of book-rolls in schools, and Aristophanes' Clouds. describes the 'ancient education', i.e. in the schools of c.500, where the children were made to memorize epic poetry and to sing it in the traditional mode. In Aristophanes' Frogs (405) *Dionysus says he read *Euripides' Andromeda on board ship. The earliest references to booksellers are in *Eupolis and in *Plato (Apology 26d), where *Socrates says that a copy of *Anaxagoras could be bought 'from the orchestra' (in the Agora of Athens?) for one drachma 'at most'. *Xenophon (Anabasis) refers to 'many written books' being exported on ships from Athens to the Black (*Euxine) Sea, and in Memorakília *Socrates asks Euthydemus whether he wants to become a *rhapsode, having bought the complete works of Homer.

The intellectual revolution of the *sophists and the interest in dithyrambs and tragedy raised demand for books in Athens, where book production and the book trade flourished in the 4th cent. It made the vast collecting activities of *Aristotle and his pupils possible and led to the formation of *libraries, notably that of Aristotle himself.

The oldest surviving specimens of literary papyrus rolls date from the second half of the 4th cent. The *Timotheus papyrus (Persians), written in long lines in large, clumsy letters, may antedate *Alexander (2) the Great's conquest of Egypt. The carbonized papyrus roll found at Derveni, near *Thessalonica, a commentary on an *Orphic cosmogony, is written in small letters in a careful, skilled hand, which makes the columns look almost like inscriptions exactly aligned vertically. Given the regularity and elegance of Attic writing on vases, the Derveni papyrus has a stronger claim to being a typical representative of a 4th-cent. book. From the beginning of the Ptolemaic period through to the 8th cent. AD, an uninterrupted series of book-rolls and, later, codices chiefly from Egypt illustrates the development of Greek books and their scripts.

The *Museum and the Library at *Alexandria, became the most important centre of scholarship for centuries to come. The work of the Alexandrian scholars led to a standardization in the formats of Greek books and in the layout of the texts.

The most important innovation in the shape of the book was Roman in origin. The codex was created when the wooden panels of writing-tablets fastened together with thongs were replaced by parchment. At first used as notebooks, parchment codices had come into use for classical literature by the 1st cent. AD, while the normal form of the book was, in the Latin west as in the Greek east, the papyrus roll. What eventually established the codex was its adoption by the Christians; nearly all biblical and NT texts from the early 2nd cent. onwards are in codex form.

booty 'It is a law established for all time among all men that when a city is taken in war, the persons and the property of its inhabitants belong to the captors' (Xenophon, *Cyropaedia*). 'Booty' referred not just to movable and inanimate objects (e.g. precious metals), but could include animals and livestock, human beings, and even whole cities and territory. War was one of the major suppliers of the slave trade (see SLAVERY). It was rare after *Homer for wars to be fought solely and openly for acquisitive purposes. But it was always assumed that success in war would lead to appropriation by the victor of the property and persons of the vanquished, and sometimes of territory as well. Hence the largest sudden transfers of wealth in the ancient world were the result of successful warfare: e.g. *Sparta's conquest of *Messenia and the Messenians in the late 8th cent. BC, the *Persian Wars and the *Delian League down to *c.*450. *Alexander (2) the Great's conquest of the Persian empire and the wars of the Successors (see DIADOCHI), who all regarded their conquests as 'spear-won territory', and the numerous wars of the expanding Roman republic. On a smaller scale raiding between neighbouring states was endemic, as were *piracy at sea and *brigandage on land, except when a stronger power was able to impose peace in its sphere of influence (Athens in the 5th cent., Rhodes in the Hellenistic period, Rome under the empire). Throughout antiquity, it was also assumed that armies would sustain themselves from the territory in which they operated. For a Roman commander's right to dispose of booty, see MANUBIAE.

Borĕas, the north Wind, which brings to the Greeks an icy blast from *Thrace; 'King of the Winds' for Pindar, and the most strongly personified of the wind-gods. This vivid characterization is owed to the story of his seizing of the Athenian princess Oreithyia, daughter of *Erechtheus, from the banks of the Ilissus (Plato, *Phaedrus*); from the marriage he fathered the flying heroes Calaïs and Zētēs. The legend dates from the early 5th cent. BC, when a crop of vase-paintings showing the god as a rough and hirsute winged figure attest the sudden popularity of the kidnap story. Herodotus provides a possible explanation: the northerly gale which wrecked the Persian fleet before *Artemisium is supposed to have been summoned up by Athenians praying to 'their son-in-law' for aid, and they are said to have founded a cult by the Ilissus in gratitude.

Bosporus (1), **Thracian,** a strait 27 km. (17 mi.) long connecting the Black (*Euxine) Sea with the sea of Marmara. Together with the Hellespont the Bosporus separated Asia from Europe and provided a marine passage between the Black Sea and the eastern Mediterranean. Despite a strong current that runs from the Black Sea towards the Aegean, the Bosporus was navigable in antiquity, and was not a barrier to the armies that occasionally crossed it from one continent to the other. The Scythian rivers that flowed into the Black Sea provided food for the spawning mackerel and tuna that migrated through the Bosporus into the sea of Marmara. Phoenicians and Greeks exploited these rich fishing areas (see FISHING), and the Greeks developed extensive trade between native towns and their own coastal colonies along the Black Sea.

Bosporus (2), **Cimmerian,** the straits connecting the Black (*Euxine) Sea and the sea of Azov (Maeotis). The straits were the centre of a kingdom, which was known, accordingly, as the Bosporan kingdom or simply the Bosporus. Its main cities were Panticapaeum on the western shore (the Crimea) and Phanagoreia on the eastern shore.

Upon the death of *Mithradates VI, *Pompey had his treacherous son, Pharnaces II, recognized as king of the Bosporus, but he was defeated by *Caesar in 47 at the battle of Zela, the occasion of his famous claim, 'I came, I saw, I conquered'.

botany From earliest times, Greeks and Romans had expert familiarity with plants and their growth cycles; agriculture dominates, alongside command of medicinal herbs, including production of oils and perfumes. Exact nomenclatures were quite irrelevant; everyone 'knew' plants and flowers carpeting fields and mountain valleys in season; flower metaphors are common in *Homer and the lyric poets. There is nothing esoteric about early botanical lore; locals understood their plants—from various wheats (see CEREALS) and vegetables to the widespread poisons (hemlocks, mandrake, the opium poppy, etc.)—and they spoke of parts (roots, seeds, flowers, stems, leaves) *as* plants providing particulars: food, medicines, poisons, oils, beverages (wine, beer).

*Aristotle incorporated plants into his scheme of living things, endowing them with three faculties of the *soul: nutrition, growth, reproduction, but not motion or perception. *Theophrastus provides the best Greek account of botany in *Inquiry into Plants* and *Causes of Plants.* An acute observer of plants, Theophrastus distinguished long before modern botany between dicotyledons and monocotyledons, based on precise morphology; he is not ignorant of plant sexes, but chooses to tabulate by forms, flower to fruit, showing that he understood the essential relation of flowering to fruiting; anticipating *Dioscorides, Theophrastus notes geography to account for differences in shapes and properties of plants when used as medicines—and very good are his descriptions of plants and their parts, their cultivation as crops or as pot-herbs—and he often quotes from the ubiquitous root-cutters the special uses of plants, from medicines to quasi-magical potions and aphrodisiacs; bk. 9 of his *Inquiry* is a priceless document in its own right, the earliest extant herbal manual in Greek. See AGRICULTURAL WRITERS; ARBORICULTURE; OLIVE; PHARMACOLOGY; TIMBER; WINE.

bottomry See MARITIME LOANS.

Boudicca (name uncertain, but 'Boadicea' has neither authority nor meaning), wife of Prasutagus, who was established as client king of the *Iceni by the Romans. On his death (AD 60/1) he had left the emperor co-heir with his daughters, but imperial agents had Boudicca flogged and her daughters raped. Under Boudicca the Iceni, assisted by the *Trinovantes, rose in rebellion while the governor, *Suetonius Paulinus, was occupied in the west. *Camulodunum, *Londinium, and Verulamium were successively sacked. Venturing a battle, however, with Paulinus' main force, Boudicca's troops were easily routed, and she herself took poison.

boulē, in Greek states, a council; often the council which had day-to-day responsibility for the state's affairs. Its membership and powers varied with the complexion of the regime: in the Homeric world it was a meeting of nobles called to advise the king; in an oligarchic state eligibility might be restricted, membership might be for a long term, and the council might be powerful and the citizens' assembly weak (cp. the *gerousia,* council of elders, in *Sparta); in a democratic state eligibility would be broader, a limited term of office would ensure that more of the citizens served at some time, and the council would be the servant rather than the master of the assembly. The council would be involved in *decision-making, administration and jurisdiction. Most states had a council of this kind. In the cities of *Boeotia in the Classical period one-quarter of the citizens with full rights served at a time as the council.

In Athens the original council, the body which advised first the kings and later the archons, and came to be composed of ex-*archontes,* was the council of the *Areopagus. *Solon in 594/3 BC has been credited with the creation of a second council to perform the function of *probouleusis,* prior consideration of the assembly's business: a council of 400, 100 from each of the four tribes. Some have doubted its existence, but the evidence is as good as we could expect for a 6th-cent. institution.

In 508/7 BC *Cleisthenes (2) replaced this with a council of 500, 50 from each of the ten new tribes (*phylai), and within each tribe appointed from the *demes in proportion to their size. Membership was open to all but the lowest of the four property classes (i.e. to *pentakosiomedimnoi,* *hippeis, *zeugitai, but not *thetes); by the second half of the 5th cent. appointment was by lot for a year; and by the 4th cent. service was limited to two years in a man's life. The council met every day except holidays and impure days; by the late 5th cent. members were paid, but service made heavy demands on a conscientious member's time, and the richer citizens seem to have served in more than due proportion.

By the 450s BC the 50 members from one tribe served as the *prytaneis ('presidents') for one-tenth of the year, in an order determined by lot. They acted as a standing committee of the whole council; one of their number served as *epistatēs* ('chairman') for a single day, and he and the *prytaneis* from one *trittys* ('third') remained on duty for the whole twenty-four hours. They also convened the council and assembly; from the 450s to the early 4th cent. the *prytaneis* presided; from the early 4th cent. this duty was transferred to a new board of *proedroi*.

The function of Solon's council, inherited by Cleisthenes, was prior consideration of the assembly's business. In Athens the principle was interpreted so as to minimize the restriction imposed on the assembly: the assembly could not reach a decision on any subject until it had been considered by the council and placed on the assembly's agenda; but, although the council's *probouleuma* ('prior resolution') could incorporate a specific proposal, it did not have to do so, and in the assembly any citizen could propose a motion or an amendment; if a new topic emerged during the assembly's debate, the assembly could commission the council to produce a *probouleuma* for a later meeting. Only a member of the council could propose a *probouleuma*: a non-member who wanted to raise an item of business would commonly make a formal approach to the council through the *prytaneis*, or else arrange informally for a member to raise his business in the council.

This council probably began to acquire administrative and judicial powers with the reform of the Areopagus by *Ephialtes in 462/1 BC. It became the general overseer of Athens' administrative machinery, supervising the work of the many boards appointed for specific duties and itself providing the members for several of them. Its responsibilities included the state's finances and the sacred treasuries, warships (*triremes) and naval equipment in general, the cavalry and their horses (see HIPPEIS, 2), prizes for the *Panathenaea, public buildings, and the invalids who were given a maintenance grant by the state.

In Greek states the administration was weak, and it was believed that administrative bodies needed to be strengthened with judicial powers. In Athens many of the council's judicial powers were concerned with officials and with the official duties of private citizens: it was involved in the *dokimasia* (vetting before entry into office) of the *archontes* and the following year's councillors; it provided the interim *logistai* ('accountants') who checked officials' financial accounts each prytany, and it could try charges against officials; and it provided the *euthynoi* ('straighteners', see EUTHYNA) who received accusations of non-financial offences against officials when they left office (but the annual *logistai* who checked officials' final accounts were not members of the council). It was also involved in the procedure of *eisangelia* ('impeachment') for the trials of major offences against the state.

The council was the keystone of the democratic constitution, preparing business for the assembly and providing a focus between the assembly's meetings, and holding together the fragmented administration of the state. It was prevented from dominating by the fact that its members were appointed for a limited term and not from a limited class: the council could not easily acquire an interest different from that of the state as a whole.

See also EKKLESIA.

boxing In Greek and Roman boxing there was no classification of competitors by weight and so the advantage was generally with the heavier man. The Greeks bound leather thongs round their wrists and knuckles, to protect them rather than to increase the severity of the blow. For training they used softer padded gloves. The face was always the principal target.

The Romans used the *caestus*, a glove weighted with pieces of iron and having metal spikes placed round the knuckles, and boxing was often more of a gladiatorial show than an athletic sport. See AGONES; ATHLETICS; GLADIATORS; PANKRATION.

Brasidas (d. 422 BC), Spartan commander. Following distinguished action as a trierarch at *Pylos in 425, he was sent to northern Greece in 424 with a small force of *helots and mercenaries. After saving *Megara *en route*, he rapidly gained several important cities, including *Amphipolis and Torone, ignoring the armistice of 423 by supporting the revolts of *Scione and Mendē. Although unable to protect all his successes adequately, he permanently injured Athens' interests in the region. In 422 he defeated an Athenian army under *Cleon at Amphipolis, but was himself mortally wounded. Brasidas served as a prototype for Sparta's later conduct of foreign campaigns through semi-independent Spartiate military governors (harmosts) commanding non-Spartiate troops, and his success encouraged her future use of helots freed for military service.

Brauron, site of a *sanctuary of *Artemis on the east coast of *Attica. In the sanctuary itself there is a temple built in the 6th cent. and an architecturally innovative Pī-shaped *stoa with dining-rooms built in the later part of the 5th cent. Cult activity at Brauron was esp.

associated with the *arkteia*, a ritual, known also at the sanctuary of Artemis Munichia in *Piraeus, in which young girls between the ages of 5 and 10 'became' bears. The aetiological myth for the *arkteia* related that this service was required of all Athenian girls before marriage because of an incident in which a bear belonging to the sanctuary had been killed after becoming savage with a young girl. Modern scholars suggest that the ritual was a *rite of passage which marked the physical maturation of pubescent girls and prepared them for taming by marriage by stressing their wildness. The sanctuary included a cave sacred to *Iphigenia, and dedications were also made in celebration of successful *childbirth. The Brauronia was a quadrennial festival involving a procession from Athens out to Brauron.

bread See FOOD AND DRINK.

bribery, Greek Much of the Greek vocabulary for bribery is noticeably neutral ('persuade by gifts/money', 'receiving gifts'), although pejorative terms like 'gift-swallowing' are found in *Hesiod. In Attic tragedy, we hear of accusations of bribery against e.g. seers like Tiresias; Thucydides' *Pericles affirms that he has *not* taken bribes; clearly the normal expectation was that politicians did. Accusations of bribery are frequent in the 4th-cent. orator (see INVECTIVE), partly because it was necessary to prove bribery in order to make a treason accusation (*eisangelia) stick. See also CORRUPTION.

bribery, Roman See AMBITUS; CORRUPTION.

brickstamps, Roman Stamped bricks began to be used in Rome during the 1st cent. BC. Except for the brickstamps of military units throughout the Roman empire, these inscriptions became historically and archaeologically important documents only after the fire of Rome in AD 64, when there was an unprecedented demand for fired bricks as a great rebuilding programme was instituted. For more than a century the building activity in the city made large-scale production of bricks profitable. The raw materials were available close at hand, esp. in the lower Tiber valley on estates largely owned by members of distinguished Roman families, often of senatorial rank. From the mid-1st cent. AD the content of the stamps becomes more exact and more complex, indicating where the bricks were produced, and eventually including the names of the owner, the foreman, and the workers employed there.

In AD 110 the names of the consuls appear in a brickstamp for the first time.

bridges Timber bridges must have been built from an early period, and stone bridges constructed on the pillar-and-lintel principle are known from the 5th cent. BC. The bridge over the sacred stream at *Brauron has five parallel rows of orthostats (upright stone slabs) spanned by lintels. In the Hellenistic period bridges up to 300 m. (980 ft.) long were built, e.g. in northern Greece and in Asia Minor. There is a splendid example near *Cnidus. Piers of masonry, carefully built on the rocky bed, were so shaped as to create an efficient slipstream, and they carried a removable roadway of planking. It is uncertain whether any surviving example of a stone bridge with true arches dates from before the Roman period. The wooden bridge is associated with the very existence of Rome, but the stone bridge is a late development, the earliest dated example being the pons Aemilius of 179 BC, followed by *pons Mulvius in 109. Typical of the state of affairs outside Rome is the statement of Augustus (*Res Gestae* 20.5): 'I repaired the *via Flaminia...and all the bridges on it except the Mulvian and Minucian.' Nearly all monumental bridges belong to the imperial age. In Italy the most complete are those of Augustus at Ariminum and of Hadrian at Rome, the most imposing those of Augustus at Narnia and at Asculum Picenum. But they are far outclassed in length by the Augustan bridge at *Emerita, and in height by the famous bridge which several Spanish communities combined to erect over the Tagus gorge at Alcantara. The tradition of wooden bridge-building, however, continued in the hands of military engineers. *Caesar's description of his temporary wooden bridge on the Rhine is famous. *Vegetius describes pontoon bridges of boats, anticipated by the bridge of boats *Xerxes had thrown across the *Hellespont, while many bridges of timber more durably constructed than these must have carried even the most important trunk roads. Bridges spanning powerful rivers, however, were usually built with stone piers and wooden superstructure, as the Flavian Rhine bridge at Mogontiacum or *Trajan's Danube bridge (see DANUVIUS). British examples are the Thames bridge at *Londinium, the Tyne bridges at Corbridge and Pons Aelius, where stone piers of the same kind are known to have been used.

brigandage (Lat. *latrōcinium*), the unlawful use of personal violence to maraud by land, was not condemned wholesale by the Classical Greeks. A left-over from pre-state times, it remained a respectable occupation among some communities. Brigandage was esp. prevalent in uplands, over which even the ancient empires exercised only nominal control, and where pastoral mobility (see NOMADS; TRANSHUMANCE) facilitated illegal behaviour. With the Roman state's claim to the monopoly of force, *latrocinium* came to include feuding and raiding. The urban populations saw brigandage as an all-pervasive threat beyond the city gates (this was true even in Italy at the height of empire). In its attempts to control bandits (never permanently successful, not least because they often had the support of élite landowners), the Roman state relied on the army, more usually on the uncoordinated efforts of local police and vigilantes, backed up by the most brutal forms of exemplary punishment of culprits. See PIRACY.

Britain, Roman, the province of Britannia. The islands were known to the Mediterranean world from the 3rd cent. BC. After 120, as trading contacts between Transalpine Gaul and areas to the north intensified, Britain began to receive goods such as wine *amphorae, and Gallo-Belgic coinage was introduced. Close political contacts with northern Gaul provided the pretext for *Caesar's expeditions in 55 and 54 BC. His campaigns did not aim at conquest, although he did impose tribute on *Cassivellaunus before withdrawing. Contacts with the Continent intensified with the *Romanization of Gaul from *Augustus onwards, and Rome maintained an interest in British affairs.

Annexation had apparently been contemplated by Augustus and *Gaius (1) and was achieved by *Claudius in AD 43. The army of four legions, with *auxilia, quickly overran the territory of the Catuvellauni, with a set-piece battle at Camulodunum. The army then moved west and north, so that by the time of the *Boudiccan revolt (60/1) the lowlands south of the Trent and much of Wales were held. Romanization was advancing, and towns were well established at *Londinium, Verulamium, and *Camulodunum. The revolt was crushed, but territorial expansion slowed for perhaps a decade. A succession of able Flavian governors enlarged the province by completing the conquest of Wales and pushing into Scotland. The last of these, *Iulius Agricola (c.77/8–83/4), advanced far into Scotland and defeated the Caledonians in a great battle at mons Graupius. After his withdrawal the rest of Scotland remained uncon-

quered, and there began a gradual retreat, eventually to the Tyne–Solway line (by the period of *Trajan). The Stanegate road which marked this line became a *de facto* frontier until the construction of the *wall of Hadrian from *c.* AD 122. Although *Scotland was again occupied first in the period *c.*139–164, when the *wall of Antoninus was the frontier, and then during *Septimius Severus' campaigns of 208–211, it was never incorporated, and Hadrian's Wall remained the effective permanent frontier of the province.

Britain was an imperial province which contained a substantial military garrison throughout the Principate. In the 2nd cent. the army comprised three legions—II Augusta at Isca 2, XX Valeria Victrix at Deva, and VI Victrix at *Eburacum—and perhaps 75 auxiliary units. These were predominantly based in the north and Wales and brought wealth to these regions, which nevertheless remained less Romanized than areas to the south and east.

Local government was based on the Gallic cantonal system, with sixteen *civitates* (see CIVITAS) known. In addition there were four *coloniae* (see COLONIZATION, ROMAN) at Camulodunum (founded 49), Lindum (90–96), Glevum (96–98), and Eburacum (early 3rd cent.), together with Londinium which, although the provincial capital, is of uncertain status. The *civitates* were large, and some 70 lesser urban centres served the countryside away from the principal towns. None of the towns was well provided with public buildings. Most of those known are of later 1st- or 2nd-cent. date. During the 2nd and 3rd cents. most towns were provided with defences. In the 4th cent. the principal towns became more residential than productive centres. Although important as defended locations, none of them survived with urban characteristics for long into the 5th cent.

Agriculture remained the mainstay of the province with perhaps 90 per cent of the late Roman population of *c.*3.6 million living rurally. Most of these people continued to inhabit traditional farmsteads with only about one in 100 sites becoming a *villa. Villa-building began soon after the conquest and continued steadily through the 2nd and 3rd cents. with a peak in both numbers and opulence during the 4th cent. *Mosaics were common by the 4th cent., and there is abundant evidence for the existence of a rich, rurally based aristocracy in southern Britain.

Other economic activities known from archaeology show growth to a peak of prosperity during the 4th cent. Metal extraction (of *gold, *silver, and *lead) began very soon after the conquest but did not become dominant. Local craft-based production was widespread, its success attested by the abundant collections of objects found on most settlements. In the early empire there was heavy dependence on other provinces for the supply of consumer goods, imported initially through the military supply networks. Later, local production grew to sustain the bulk of the province's needs, and substantial factories for items like *pottery developed, esp. in rural locations in the south and east.

Art and culture in Britain developed as a hybrid of Celtic and classical features. The religions of the Mediterranean spread to Britain with the army and administrators, but the Celtic gods were worshipped across most of the province (see RELIGION, CELTIC). However, they took on new forms, with the increased use of Romano-Celtic styles of temple architecture and the adoption of Latin epigraphy on altars and dedications. Particular gods are associated with certain regions and *civitates*. Many soldiers also adopted Celtic gods whom they identified with gods of the Roman pantheon (see SYNCRETISM). Christianity is found throughout the province in the 4th cent. In art new materials (esp. stone sculpture and mosaic) supplanted the metalwork used in the iron age styles. Latin was widely adopted, although writing was most used on military and urban sites (see VINDOLANDA TABLETS).

During the later empire Britain enjoyed more peace than other provinces. Problems with raiders from across the North Sea may have led to the piecemeal construction of the Saxon Shore forts in the south-east from the mid-3rd cent. onwards. These and other coastal installations in the north and in Wales hint at increasing military threats, although the continued use of the traditional style of garrisons on Hadrian's Wall, combined with the general absence of the late Roman field army, implies that there were few serious military problems. There is little else to suggest any serious military threats until early in the 5th cent. By then the depleted British garrison could not cope, and the more pressing threats to Rome herself prevented aid from being sent. Britain, left to defend herself, gradually fell to the Saxons.

Britannicus See CLAUDIUS CAESAR BRITANNICUS.

bronze The ancients used the words *khalkos*, *aes*, indiscriminately for copper and for the harder and more fusible bronze, an alloy of copper and *tin. Until the introduction of *iron, bronze was the sole metal for utilitarian purposes, and it continued in general use to the end of antiquity for sculpture, many domestic objects, and, after the 5th cent. BC, for small-denomination coins. The principal sources of supply were, for Greece, *Chalcis and *Cyprus, and for Italy, Bruttium, Etruria (see ETRUSCANS), and Elba, while under Roman rule *Spain produced largely.

The technical processes employed were: hammering into plates which were riveted together, used in the making of utensils, and, during the Archaic period, of statues; and casting with wax, either solid (usually in the case of statuettes or the handles, rims, and feet of vessels) or hollow over a core of clay or plaster to produce large-scale sculpture. Relief decoration was produced in repoussé work; incised ornament is also common, esp. on mirrors. Tin and copper solders were used in addition to riveting for joins. The dull patina of bronzes in museums is the result of time; ancient bronzes were kept bright to resemble gold.

Brundisium a Messapian city on the Adriatic coast, and an important harbour. In 244 BC, a Latin colony (see IUS LATII) was founded there, and the *via Appia was extended from Tarentum to Brundisium. Thereafter, it was the principal route from Italy to Greece and the east. It was strategically vital during the Punic Wars and the conquest of the east, and was exempted from *portoria by *Sulla. It was captured by *Caesar (49), to cut off *Pompey's retreat. It was the location for the Pact of Brundisium, agreed by the *triumvirs (40).

Brutus See IUNIUS BRUTUS.

bucolic See PASTORAL POETRY, GREEK and LATIN.

building materials

Greek In its developed stages Greek *architecture was based on the use of finely dressed stone masonry, mainly limestone. Where available, white *marble was used for the finest structures. Transport costs would influence the choice of stone: local stone would often be used as an economy. In major buildings the dressed blocks were regularly fastened with clamps and dowels of wood or metal, but without mortar; and although exceptionally almost entire buildings might be of marble, including ceilings of quite large span (e.g. the *Propylaea at Athens), considerations of cost often meant that the less conspicuous parts were built in local limestone. See QUARRIES. Inferior materials were regularly surfaced with fine marble stucco to resemble masonry. In Hellenistic buildings all but the best materials were plastered on the interior often to receive painted decoration (see PAINTING, GREEK). In simpler buildings, walls were still built of mud-brick. Tiles were usually *terracotta, occasionally marble. *Bronze was used for many decorative purposes and facings (e.g. the temple of Athena Chalkioikos at Sparta). Waterproof cement was regularly used for hydraulic works and for floors which required frequent washing.

Roman Roman building practice was everywhere based on locally available materials. The only building materials widely transported in the empire were *marble and *timber for roofing. In Rome itself the plentiful local supplies of soft, easily dressed, volcanic tufa were used from the 6th cent. BC onwards and remained in use at all periods as a general-purpose building material (see QUARRIES). From the 2nd cent. BC travertine was quarried near *Tibur. This was a fine building stone, used esp. in the later republic until the large-scale use of marble was developed under Augustus. For much domestic architecture the use of timber-framed unfired brick (see BRICKSTAMPS) was widespread in Rome before the fire of AD 64. The major Roman contribution to architectural development was the exploitation and perfection of *opus caementicium*, Roman concrete. This comprised a hydraulic mortar laid in alternate courses with aggregate. It derived its unique strength from the use of the local volcanic deposits. In Rome from the 2nd cent. BC onwards it was increasingly employed in monumental building, at first faced with small irregularly shaped stones and later with small squared stones set diagonally. Building in concrete was flexible and cheap and allowed the construction of vaulted chambers on a large scale. The aggregate was often skilfully graded by weight, the supreme example being the dome of the *Pantheon; from the time of Hadrian the vaulting-load might be further lightened by the incorporation of large jars. In Rome and central Italy concrete from the 1st cent. AD was faced with fired brick. From the 1st cent. BC Roman *architecture made extensive use of white and coloured marble for columns, veneer, and paving (see CARRARA). Roof tiles were made of *terra-

cotta or stone. Waterproof mortars and *lead and terracotta piping were regularly employed for hydraulic installations (see BATHS).

bureaucracy, Greek Because the Greek world was composed of separate, small states, and because those states entrusted their administration as far as possible to individual citizens or boards of citizens, often appointed for a single year, rather than to professional administrators, bureaucracy in the Greek world is not a large subject. However, administrative machinery had to be kept in motion, documents had to be drafted, and *records had to be kept and retrieved; and, even in the amateur culture of the Greek city-states, there were some opportunities for specialization in this kind of work.

Athens, as usual, is the state about which we are best informed. Inventories were compiled, and often inscribed, of the contents of temple treasuries and of dockyards; there were contracts for tax-collection, mine leases, and the like; there were records of decrees and of law-court verdicts. Some public slaves were used for keeping records and producing them when required, and for assisting in the elaborate procedures of the jury-courts; one inscription orders a named slave to record what is stored in the arsenal and the public secretaries to verify the record. At a higher level Athens had a number of citizen secretaries and under-secretaries, and with the passage of time there was a tendency for secretarial posts to become less like magistracies, in which any public-spirited citizen might take his turn, and more like specialist posts which would be held by men with appropriate interests and skills. They were subject to the general rule that a man could hold a particular post for only one year, but several posts of this kind existed, and it was possible for a man to hold several of them over a period.

See also ARCHIVES.

Burrus See AFRANIUS BURRUS.

Byzantium, city on the European side of the southern end of the *Bosporus (1), between the Golden Horn and the *Propontis. The Greek city occupied only the eastern tip of the promontory, in the area now covered by the Byzantine and Ottoman palaces of Constantinople/Istanbul. The evidence of cults and institutions confirms the claim of the Megarians (see MEGARA) to be the main founders (c.660 BC). Except during the *Ionian Revolt the city was under Persian control from *Darius I's Scythian expedition until 478. In the Athenian empire (see DELIAN LEAGUE) it paid fifteen talents' tribute or more, deriving its wealth from tuna fishing and from tolls levied on passing ships. The city also had an extensive territory not only in European *Thrace but also in *Bithynia and Mysia in Asia. It revolted from Athens in 440–439 and 411–408. Although under Spartan control after the battle of Aegospotami (405), alliance coins show that it joined the anti-Spartan sea league formed after the battle of *Cnidus in 394. It became a formal ally of Athens when resisting *Philip II of Macedon in the siege of 340–339. *Hecate is supposed to have helped the besieged on this occasion, and her symbols, the crescent and star (later adopted as the emblem of the Turkish state), appear on the city coinage. Constantine I refounded Byzantium as New Rome, *Constantinople, AD 330, extending its bounds to new city walls and adorning it with magnificent new buildings.

Cadmus, legendary Phoenician founder of *Thebes, whose origins are still disputed: Phoenicia, Egypt, Mycenaean Greece, Archaic Greece, have all been proposed. In *Homer, he appears indirectly, as father of *Ino-Leucothea, and through the names Cadmeii, Cadmeiones given to the inhabitants of Thebes.

The generally accepted story is that Cadmus was sent by his father Agenor to find his sister *Europa, who had been abducted (by *Zeus, as it turned out). He failed in his search (Europa ended up in Crete, while Cadmus went to the Greek mainland), but was ordered by Delphi (see DELPHIC ORACLE) to be guided by a cow and establish a city where the animal lay down. Thus he founded Thebes, having killed a dragon, and peopled the place with men sprung from the dragon's teeth (Spartoi).

Cadmus married Harmonia, daughter of *Ares and *Aphrodite. He gave her a robe and a necklace made by Hephaestus (see AMPHIARAUS). They had four daughters: *Ino, *Semele, Autonoë and Agave (see PENTHEUS).

Cadmus was said to have brought writing to Greece (see ALPHABET, GREEK). In their old age he and Harmonia went off to Illyria and finally were turned into snakes. His dynasty ended with Thersander, son of *Polynices.

Caelius mons, the most SE of the *seven hills of Rome, lay south of the *Esquiline. Crossed by the *wall of Servius, it was densely populated in the republic; after a devastating fire in AD 27 it was largely occupied by the houses and gardens of the rich. The chief buildings on the hill included the temple of Divus *Claudius, begun by his widow *Iulia Agrippina, which was largely destroyed by her son *Nero to build a monumental *nymphaeum as part of his *Domus Aurea, but restored by *Vespasian; Nero's Macellum Magnum (AD 59), a new food-market; and barracks for several of the military units stationed in Rome, including *vigiles, and the mounted bodyguard of the emperor.

Caesar See IULIUS CAESAR (1), GAIUS.

Caesarea in Palestine, under its original name of Strato's Tower, was attached to the province of Syria by Pompey in 63, and given to *Herod (1) by Octavian in 30. Between c.22 and 10 BC, Herod rebuilt the city on a lavish scale, renaming it after the emperor, and constructing a huge artificial harbour. Tensions over the control of the constitution between the large Jewish minority and the Graeco-Syrian majority led to riots, and delegations were sent to Nero. His decision against the Jews was followed by attacks on the synagogue, and then the elimination of the Jewish population of 20,000, allegedly in a single day, provoked the First Jewish Revolt against Rome in AD 66. The city was the administrative capital of Judaea under the procurators and again after 70. *Vespasian made it a Roman colony. In the 3rd and 4th cents., it was a cosmopolitan cultural centre, home to well-known *rabbis, to the great Christian library of *Origen, and, after him, to *Eusebius.

Calchas, in Homer's *Iliad* a diviner who accompanied the Greek army to Troy. He reveals the reason for the plague on the camp and foretells the length of the war. After *Homer he is introduced into several episodes, such as the sacrifice of *Iphigenia, the building of the Wooden Horse, and generally the actions by which it was fated that Troy should be captured. An oracle had foretold that Calchas would die when he met a diviner better than himself, and this occurred when he met Mopsus, grandson of *Tiresias.

calendar, Greek There was no single Greek calendar. Almost every Greek community had a calendar of its own, differing from others in the names of the months and the date of the New Year. All were, at least originally, lunar. The months were named after festivals held or deities specially honoured in them. Dios and Artemisios, Macedonian months, were named after

*Zeus and *Artemis; Anthesterion at Athens from the festival *Anthesteria. Such month names are found in *Hesiod.

The Athenian calendar is best known. The year began, in theory, with the appearance of the first new moon after the summer solstice, and the months were Hekatombaion, Metageitnion, Boedromion, Pyanopsion, Maimakterion, Posideon, Gamelion, Anthesterion, Elaphebolion, Mounichion, Thargelion, and Skirophorion. All were named after festivals held in the month, some very obscure to us and probably to 5th- and 4th-cent. Athenians. Each month was in length 29 or 30 days; an ordinary year was 354 $\pm$ 1, a leap year 384 $\pm$ 1 days. A leap year was created by inserting a 'second' or 'later' month. The Athenians appear not to have followed any regular scheme, such as the 'Metonic Cycle' (see METON) used by the *Seleucids, in determining leap years.

calendar, Roman March remained the first month of the year until 153 BC. From then the official year of the consuls and most other Roman magistrates began on 1 January. March, May, Quintilis (July), and October had 31 days each (Nones on 7th, Ides on 15th), February 28, and the rest 29 (Ides on 13th): total 355.

To intercalate, February was shortened to 23 or 24 days and followed by an intercalary month of 27 days. This intercalating was so clumsily done that by the time of *Caesar the civic year was about three months ahead of the solar. In his capacity as *pontifex maximus, and advised by the astronomer Sōsigenēs, he intercalated sufficient days to bring the year 46 BC to a total of 445 days, which was thus 'the last year of the muddled reckoning'. From the next year onwards the Egyptian solar calendar (see TIME-RECKONING) was adapted to Roman use.

Caligula, Roman emperor. See GAIUS (1).

Callias (1), son of Hipponicus, of one of the richest families in 5th-cent. Athens; the family was also religiously important as one of the *genos Kērȳkēs, which supplied some of the priests for the mysteries at *Eleusis, esp. the dadouchos ('torchbearer'); Callias himself was dadouchos. He married Elpinīcē, sister of *Cimon. He distinguished himself at the battle of *Marathon. His colossal wealth may derive from early exploitation of the *Laurium silver-mines. He supposedly negotiated the *Callias Peace of c.450 BC with Persia and was one of the negotiators of the *Thirty Years Peace with Sparta in 446. He was father of Hipponicus, a

general in the *Archidamian War, and grandfather of *Callias (2). He was probably *proxenos of Sparta, because Xenophon makes his grandson say he inherited the role.

Callias (2) (c.450–370 BC), Athenian aristocrat, grandson of Callias (1), notorious for his wealth and extravagance. He was dadouchos of the Eleusinian mysteries (see CALLIAS (1)). He was ridiculed by comic poets, and attacked by *Andocides, whom he accused of sacrilege. More sympathetic pictures of his house and life are given by *Xenophon (Symposium) and *Plato (Protagoras). He was a general 391/0 in the *Corinthian War, and took part in a famous victory over Spartan *hoplites.

Callias, Peace of, a mid-5th-cent. treaty between Athens and Persia. Its historicity is disputed, chiefly because *Thucydides (2) does not mention it explicitly, though some passages in his History are probably indirect evidence. The date of the Peace is disputed; some evidence points to 449 but other items suggest the 460s, and this may mean that the 449 agreement was a renewal. Certainly direct Athenian–Persian hostilities ceased in mid-century.

Callicratēs Athenian *architect of the 5th cent. BC, responsible for work at the *Nike sanctuary and the central long wall to *Piraeus (see ATHENS, TOPOGRAPHY). He was associated with *Ictinus (see PARTHENON).

Callimachus (1), Athenian *polemarchos and (though this is controversial) commander-in-chief in the campaign of *Marathon, 490. He accepted *Miltiades' plan to meet the Persians in the field. His part in the actual battle, in the last stage of which he was killed, has been obliterated by the personality and achievements of Miltiades, but his share in the victory was fully recognized in the wall-paintings on the *Stoa Poecile, where he was portrayed among the Athenian gods and heroes.

Callimachus (2), of *Cyrene, Greek poet and scholar. He flourished under *Ptolemy (1) II (285–246 BC) and continued into the reign of Ptolemy III. He was credited with more than 800 books, but, apart from six hymns and some 60 epigrams, only fragments survive.

Works

1. Aetia ('Origins'), in four books: a miscellany of *elegiac pieces. The common subject is the origins in myth or history of Greek cults, festivals, cities, and the like. In the

'prologue' the poet answers the critics who complain that he does not compose a 'continuous poem' on the deeds of kings or heroes: poetry should be judged by art, not quantity; Apollo recommended the slender Muse, the untrodden paths; better be the cicada than the braying mule. Like *Hesiod, he had met the *Muses, in a dream, and they related the *Aetia* to him.

2. *Iambi*: thirteen poems, written in iambic metres (see METRE, GREEK, 4(a)). In the first, the 6th-cent. poet Hipponax speaks, returned from the dead; in the last, the poet names Hipponax as the exemplar of the genre. Personal *invective, and the *fable, play their part, as in the traditional *iambus* (see IAMBIC POETRY, GREEK). But these poems range much wider. The framing poems continue literary polemic.

3. *Hecalē*, a hexameter narrative (see METRE, GREEK, 4(b)) of something over 1,000 lines. *Theseus leaves Athens secretly to face the bull of *Marathon; a storm breaks; he takes shelter in the cottage of the aged Hecale; he leaves at dawn and subdues the bull; he returns to Hecale, finds her dead, and founds the *deme Hecale and the sanctuary of Zeus Hekaleios in her memory. This heroic (but not Homeric) material was deviously elaborated, with Hecale rather than Theseus at the centre. The scene of rustic hospitality became famous.

4. The *Hymns* reanimate the traditional (Homeric) form (see HYMNS), but with no view to performance. The hymns to *Zeus, *Artemis, and *Delos elaborate the god's birth and virtues with quizzical learning and virtuoso invention. Those to Apollo, *Athena, and *Demeter are framed as dramas, in which the narrator-celebrant draws the hearer into an imagined ritual.

5. The *Epigrams* (a selection preserved in *Meleager' (2) anthology) cover the full range of literary, erotic, dedicatory, and sepulchral themes.

6. Callimachus wrote many and various prose works. He was among the founders of lexicography and paradoxography (the collection of marvels). The *Pinakes* ('Tables of Those who have Distinguished themselves in Every Form of Culture and of What they Wrote') presented, in 120 books, a bibliography of Greek literature and a catalogue of the Alexandrian *Library, arranged by subject ('rhetoric', 'laws', 'miscellaneous prose'); they included some biographical notes, and cited the first line of each work, and the number of lines.

Callimachus often states his preferences in poetry and among poets. He defends shorter (and discontinuous) poems, the small drop from the pure spring; diversity of genre; 'a big book equals a big evil'. This 'new' aesthetic (which might seem less novel if we had the poetry of the 4th cent.) quotes the example of past poets. Callimachus invokes Hesiod, and condemns the *Epic Cycle; Homer is all-present, but formal emulation and verbal pastiche are rigorously avoided. Of contemporaries, Callimachus commends *Aratus.

From *Alexandria Callimachus looks to Greece, and the Greek past; he has a scholar's systematic knowledge of the Greek literary inheritance, an exile's feeling for the old country and its links (through *aitia*) with the contemporary world. His work often reaches out to the Archaic world, crossing the centuries of drama and prose—to Hesiod, Hipponax, Pindar. But this past is transmuted. Verbal borrowing is rare; genres are shifted or mixed, myth transformed by mannerism, words and motifs juxtaposed in postmodern incongruities. Callimachus' poems are (by epic standards) short; various in style, metre, and genre. To Roman poets he became the exemplar of sophistication.

Calpurnia (1), daughter of *Calpurnius Piso Caesoninus, married *Caesar in 59 BC, cementing an alliance between her husband and father. Though Caesar considered divorcing her to marry *Pompey's daughter in 53, her affection for him was great, and she attempted to keep him from the senate on the Ides of March. After the murder she handed his papers and 4,000 talents to Marcus *Antonius (Mark Antony).

Calpurnia (2), third wife of *Pliny the Younger, whom she accompanied to *Bithynia. She was granddaughter of Calpurnius Fabatus, to whom Pliny excused her miscarriage on grounds of her youth and inexperience. His affectionate letters to her established the theme of conjugal love in Latin literature.

Calpurnius Bibulus, Marcus, *Caesar's colleague in the curule *aedileship and the *praetorship and finally, after a bribery fund had been set up for him by the *nobiles*, in the consulship of 59 BC. After being forcibly prevented from vetoing Caesar's agrarian law, he attempted to invalidate all legislation of that year by remaining at his house and announcing that he was 'watching the heavens' for unfavourable omens (see PORTENTS)—a device of doubtful legality. In the 50s he consistently supported the *optimates* and was chosen to propose Pompey's sole consulship in 52. In 51–49 he governed

Syria, where one of his officers won a minor success, for which he was awarded a triumph, largely through the efforts of his father-in-law *Porcius Cato (2). Assigned a naval command with a large fleet in 49, he was unable to prevent Caesar's crossing to Epirus and died in 48. He had three sons by a first wife. He later married *Porcia, daughter of Cato, and had one son by her, who wrote a brief *biography of Marcus *Iunius Brutus, Porcia's second husband.

Calpurnius Pīsō, Gāius, the figurehead of the great conspiracy against *Nero in AD 65, had been exiled by *Gaius (1), who compelled his wife to leave her husband in favour of himself and then accused the pair of adultery. Under *Claudius, Piso became suffect consul, but he showed no real ambition. He lived in magnificent style and was one of the most popular figures in Rome, with his charming manners and oratorical gifts, which he put at the service of rich and poor alike. Already in 62 he was suspect to Nero's advisers, but in the actual conspiracy he proved a futile leader, and after its betrayal thought only of suicide.

Calpurnius Pīsō, Gnaeus (consul 7 BC) was appointed governor of Syria in AD 17, for the avowed purpose of lending counsel and assistance to *Germanicus when he journeyed to the east. His previous experience had lain in other lands: proconsul of Africa and *legate of Hispania *Tarraconensis. After reciprocal bickering and open quarrel, Germanicus broke off his *amicitia with Piso. Germanicus' death (19) was attributed by his friends to magical devices or poisoning by Piso and his forceful wife, Monātia Plancina. Returning to Rome, Piso was prosecuted in the senate (20), but took his own life before the trial was over, protesting his innocence and his loyalty to Tiberius. The text of a *senatus consultum about Piso's trial and disgrace, including an account of his activities in Syria, was found in Spain in the 1980s.

Calpurnius Pīsō Caesōnīnus, Lūcius, rapidly rose to the consulship, which he held in 58 BC (with *Gabinius) after marrying his daughter to *Caesar (consul 59). He refused to support *Cicero against *Clodius Pulcher, and as a reward was given the province of Macedonia by a law of Clodius. His administration there (57–55) was attacked by Cicero in two speeches. He was censor (50) and remained neutral in the Civil War, which he did his best to prevent. After Caesar's death he again tried to prevent civil

war (against Marcus *Antonius), but died soon after.

An Epicurean and friend of *Philodemus, he was open to attack as a voluptuary (see INVEC-TIVE); but he was no worse than many of his contemporaries, and his political influence was pacific. He is generally regarded as the owner of a villa in *Herculaneum where Epicurean papyri, including work by Philodemus, were discovered.

Cambȳsēs, eldest son of *Cyrus (1); acceded on the death of his father (530 BC). He completed his father's grand plan by conquering Egypt, where he was successful in promoting a policy of collaboration with the local élites. The Egyptian documents contradict the information collected later by *Herodotus on this point. *Babylonia is a good example of how Cambyses placed the great sanctuaries under tight control. The news of the revolt of his brother, Smerdis, forced Cambyses to leave Egypt in haste in 522; he died in Syria.

camels, long domesticated in Arabia and neighbouring lands, were unfamiliar in *Anatolia in 546 BC when *Cyrus's (1) baggage-camels terrified the Lydian horses. In the Hellenistic and Roman periods camels were widely used in Asia and North Africa.

Campānia, region of west central Italy bounded by the river Liris, the Apennines and the Sorrentine peninsula, in prosperity, political importance, and social organization closely tied to the region of Rome in the late republic and early empire (Augustus' First Region included both, and the name came to refer to the neighbourhood of Rome, the *Campagna*). The well-watered and mineral-rich plains and foothills e.g. *ager Campānus, ager Falernus* and the numerous harbours and beach-heads combined to give it a wider Italian and Mediterranean significance. Early seaborne contacts were followed by the establishment of a sequence of *apoíkiai, *Pithecusae on Ischia, and *Cumae on the mainland opposite, with its daughter-settlements Dicaearchia (later *Puteoli) and Neapolis. Etruscan cultural influence shaped the principal cities of the interior, Nola and *Capua.

camps When *Polybius described the construction of a military camp c.143 BC, he was referring to a well-established practice. Archaeological and aerial surveys have revealed about 400 marching-camps in *Britain, mostly square or oblong protected by a ditch and rampart of turves surmounted by a palisade, and with at least four gates. Some were practice camps (to teach soldiers building techniques); others were large enough to accommodate an army. At *Masada several siege camps with their internal stone walls have survived.

However, archaeological evidence rarely illuminates the internal layout of temporary camps. Acc. to Polybius, when a consular army of two legions and an equal number of allies encamped, the general's tent (*praetorium) was located in a central position, with an open space (*forum*) on one side, and the quaestor's tent on the other. In front of these were the tribunes' tents. The main street (*via principālis*), ran parallel to the *praetorium*, being intersected at right angles by other streets along which were encamped the legions and allies. The most important of these streets was the *via praetōria*, which formed a T-junction opposite the *praetorium*. Each of the two main roads of the camp led to fortified gates.

Campus Martius comprised most of the Tiber flood-plain bounded by the Pincian, Quirinal, and Capitoline hills. Taking its name from an altar to Mars, it was originally pasture outside the *pomerium, and therefore used for army musters and exercises and for the *comitia centuriata; here too armies gathered before processing in *triumph through the city. As a result, the Campus and the Circus Flaminius (221 BC), a monumentalized open space just to the south, through which the procession passed, were during the republic increasingly filled with temples, porticoes, and other monuments set up to commemorate (and thank the gods for) military victories, at the same time impressing the assembled electorate. The theatre of *Pompey (52) with huge portico, foreshadows the immense buildings of the Augustan *virī triumphālēs*, including *Statilius Taurus' amphitheatre (29), *Caesar's Saepta Iulia, completed by *Agrippa (26), who also built the *Pantheon, and baths with water-gardens; and the theatres of *Claudius Marcellus (2) and *Cornelius Balbus (2) of 13. Dominating the north of the Campus were Augustus' mausoleum (28), the Solarium (10), and the *Ara Pacis (9 BC). Imperial buildings gradually filled the remaining space in the Campus, which changed from being political and military in character to an area primarily concerned with imperial commemoration and entertainment. *Nero built baths (AD 62–64) and *Domitian the Divorum (dedicated to *Vespasian and *Titus), a stadium (now Piazza Navona), and odeum.

*Antoninus Pius honoured *Hadrian with a temple (145), and is himself commemorated by the Column of Antoninus, with famous panels on its base; the Column of Marcus Aurelius is decorated with spiral reliefs of the Marcomannic wars. Eventually, the whole area was included within the *wall of Aurelian.

Camulodunum (mod. Colchester) Substantial earthworks surrounded an iron age *oppidum* of the Augustan period. This was the capital and mint of Cunobel(l)inus. Captured in *Claudius' campaign of AD 43, a fortress of *legion XX Valeria was constructed beside it, and in 49 a colony was founded on the site of the fortress. This became the first provincial capital, with the temple of Divus Claudius and a theatre with an adjacent forum. This unwalled town was sacked by *Boudicca in 60/1 and later rebuilt to cover an area of *c*.43 ha. (106 acres). Its defences were a clay bank to which, it appears, a stone wall was added in the early 2nd cent.

canabae, civil settlements which developed close to legionary bases. They attracted *veterans, traders, and local women, with whom soldiers often formed liaisons; their sons, if they enlisted, gave their origin as 'in the camp'. *Canabae* were administered by a legionary *legate, although Roman citizens in them could act as *de facto* magistrates.

canals *Darius I completed the canal begun by Necho (see SAÏTES) to connect the Pelusiac branch of the Nile above (south of) Bubastis to the Red Sea. Ptolemy II built a longer canal, from the still undivided Nile near Heliopolis, which exploited the earlier workings of Necho and Darius. This canal, later improved by Trajan and Hadrian, enabled *Alexandria, which was linked to the Nile by its Canobic branch, to become the principal centre for seaborne trade between the east and the Mediterranean. See also *AEMILIUS SCAURUS; IRRIGATION.

candidātus, a candidate for a Roman magistracy. Officially named *petitor* (his rivals were therefore styled *competitōrēs*), he was called *candidatus* because he wore a whitened toga when greeting electors in the forum. A slave (*nōmenclātor*) reminded him of the names of the electors, and he had a crowd of partisans from the *plebs including his own freedmen and other clients, whose numbers were taken as an index of his likely success. In the late republic these activities often began a full year before the election, but the traditional period of canvass was over the last three market-days; this brought the candidate's name to the notice of the presiding magistrate. Originally candidacies, even of those absent, might be accepted on election day, but such concessions were limited by laws of the late republic. Under the Principate names might be given to the presiding consul or to the emperor who would pass the names on, if he had no objection (*nōminātiō*). By the end of *Augustus' reign, however, some senior magistrates were 'Caesar's candidates', who were elected without the need to canvass or the risk of rejection. See ELECTIONS AND VOTING.

Cannae, Apulian town on the right bank of the river Aufidus, where *Hannibal defeated the Romans in 216 BC. The battle was probably fought downstream from the town and on the same side of the river, with the Carthaginian left and Roman right resting on its bank. The Romans probably outnumbered Hannibal in infantry (80,000 : 40,000?), though 15,000 may have been left to guard their camps, but had fewer cavalry (6,000 : 10,000). Hannibal threw his centre infantry forward, keeping back his Africans on both wings, and when the Roman infantry drove in his centre, they were outflanked by the Africans. Meanwhile, Hannibal's left-wing cavalry, having driven off the Roman cavalry, rode round to help his right-wing cavalry defeat the Roman allied cavalry, and then repeatedly charged the Roman rear. Virtually surrounded, the Roman army perhaps suffered higher casualties in a single day's fighting than any other western army before or since. The army had been led by *Aemilius Paullus (1) and Terentius Varro. *Livy disparages Varro, but the decision to face *Hannibal in open battle again had been taken by the whole senate, and after the disaster he received a vote of thanks from senate and people.

canon In Classical Greek the word *kanōn* (lit. 'rod') was used to mean 'rule' or 'standard'; hence its use as the title of a manual on proportions by *Polyclitus and as the name of a statue illustrating his principles. The word was later applied by Christian writers to what became the approved selection of books of the Bible, but it was not used in pagan antiquity in the sense of a list of chosen 'best authors'. The idea of compiling lists of the best writers in a particular genre, such as the Nine Lyric Poets, was attributed by Roman writers to Alexandrian scholars, esp. *Aristarchus (2) and Aristophanes of Byzantium. This makes sense in so far as

much of the scholarship of the time was devoted to the rescue, classification, and interpretation of earlier literature, and the Alexandrians could use the books in their Library, with *Callimachus' (2) *Pinakes* as the major work of reference, to tell them which authors had stood the test of time. But they must also have been familiar with the much earlier lists of the type 'the Nine *Muses' or 'the *Seven Sages', and it is possible that (e.g.) the Nine Lyric Poets already formed a recognizable group.

The Alexandrians themselves seem to have used the term 'those included' for the select authors; in Latin the favoured term was *classicī*. The 'included' authors had a much better chance of survival than those not listed, partly because their works (or some of them) attracted scholarly commentary and were thus more easily studied, and more likely to be available for recopying, by successive generations. Papyrus discoveries have tended to confirm the influence of the Alexandrian lists.

The choice of certain numbers, esp. three and multiples of three, gives a misleading sense of authority and fixity to lists which were in fact subject to variation. Even the famous three great tragedians, familiar without further identification as early as the 4th cent. BC, could appear in a list with *Ion of Chios and Achaeus as well as on their own, and the Ten *Attic Orators are not always the same Ten (or ten at all). Even the biblical canon, with its strong theological implications, has not always been defined in exactly the same terms, despite belief in its divine authority and unalterability.

Capitol, Capitōlium, or **mons Capitōlinus,** the smallest of the hills of Rome: an isolated mass with two peaks, conventionally known as Capitolium proper and Arx ('citadel'). It is the site of the great temple begun by the Tarquins (see REX) and dedicated to *Jupiter Optimus Maximus, *Juno, and *Minerva. It was successfully defended against the Gauls in 386 BC. Here the consuls sacrificed at the beginning of the year and provincial governors took vows before going to their provinces; a sacrifice here was the culmination of the triumphal procession (see TRIUMPH). The original platform of the temple still exists; but the original temple was burnt in 83 BC. The new temple of *Lutatius Catulus (69 BC), was renovated and repaired by Augustus; it was burnt down during the course of fighting on the hill in AD 69, while *Vespasian's temple perished in the fire of 80. The last rebuilding was undertaken by *Domitian. Two other temples on the capitol were those of Fīdēs (good faith personified) and Ops (plenty personified). On the northern summit of the hill, the Arx, lay the temple of Juno Monēta (344 BC), and the Tarpeian Rock, which overlooked the *forum Romanum. The east face of the hill was occupied by a massive building usually identified as the *Tabularium and the approach-road from the Forum.

Both hill and temple of Jupiter were reproduced in many cities of Italy and (esp. western) provinces; *Jerusalem, as refounded by *Hadrian, was styled *Aelia Capitolina*.

Capua By *c*.600 BC, Capua was an *Etruscan city and head of a league of twelve cities. The surrounding area was known as the *ager Campanus* (see CAMPANIA). After 474, when the Etruscans were defeated by a combined force of Syracusans and Cumaeans (see SYRACUSE; CUMAE), Etruscan power in Campania began to wane. Oscan expansion, which had hitherto taken the form of gradual peaceful settlement, became more rapid and aggressive, and in *c*.425 Capua was conquered, along with *Cumae (421), Paestum (410), and most of inland Campania. Under Oscan rule, Capua became one of the most powerful cities in Italy. It became Oscanized, and was proverbial in later authors for wealth and arrogance. Initial contacts with Rome developed *c*.343. Capua is central to the problem of the First Samnite War, which resulted in Roman control of northern Campania. There was little Capuan involvement in the Second and Third Samnite Wars. It remained loyal to Rome, although there were pro-Roman and anti-Roman factions in most Campanian cities. The construction of the *via Appia between Rome and Capua in 312 emphasized the growing links between Rome and Campania. In 216, however, the anti-Roman faction at Capua gained power, and the city defected to Carthage, remaining an important ally of *Hannibal until its recapture in 211. The leaders of the revolt were executed and Capua deprived of both its territory and its political rights; it was now directly governed by a Roman praetor. A colony was founded there in 83, and it regained its civic rights in 58. Part of the fertile *ager Campanus* was used for colonies, but most of it was rented out by the censors at considerable profit. Exempt from the Gracchan land reforms (see SEMPRONIUS GRACCHUS (2) TIBERIUS), it was distributed to 20,000 colonists by Caesar. Imperial Capua was a prosperous city, as reflected in many public buildings and inscriptions.

Caracalla See AURELIUS ANTONINUS.

Carātacus, son of *Cunobel(l)inus. He took part in the resistance in *Britain to the Roman invasion of AD 43. He escaped over the Severn to the Silures, where he renewed hostilities against *Ostorius Scapula, by whom, however, he was defeated somewhere in the hills of the Welsh border. He fled to *Cartimandua, who surrendered him to the Romans (51). Tacitus puts into his mouth a rhetorical speech delivered in Rome to *Claudius, who spared his life.

Carbo See PAPIRIUS CARBO.

careers

Greek In Greek-speaking areas no *cursus honorum* on the Roman republican model emerged. Though *Thucydides (2) credited the Spartan army with a clear hierarchical command structure, promotions and careers within it were by appointment and co-optation rather than by election. Hence they were as much a matter of belonging to a notable lineage, or of influence with kings or ephors, as of merit. At Athens a simple hierarchy of military command in both infantry and cavalry is attested. Re-election to the generalship (see STRATEGOI) was common, but repeated re-election (see NICIAS; PERICLES) was not. In contrast, careers in civilian office-holding in Classical Athens were effectively precluded by the short-term tenure and non-repeatability of office, by collegiality, and above all by selection by lot (see SORTITION). A young politician had to use the assembly (*ekklesia) rather than office-holding, and tended to begin by lawcourt advocacy or by serving a senior politician as his 'friend' or 'flatterer' before establishing his own position and his own clique of followers.

Roman Ancient society was not so ordered as to provide a course of professional employment which afforded opportunity for advancement. The Latin phrase normally translated as 'career' is the Ciceronian *cursus honorum*, which refers to the series of elective magistracies: those of *quaestor, held at 30 from *Sulla's legislation onwards, but five years younger under the Principate; of *aedile; of *praetor, held at 39 under the late republic, but by some at 30 under the Principate; and of *consul, held at 42 after Sulla, by patricians at 33 under the Principate, and by new men (see NOVUS HOMO) at 38 or later. Election to these posts depended on birth and achievement, military and civil. Success might be achieved in preliminary offices civil or military (as one of the *vigintisexviri or *tribuni militum) and in the magistracy that preceded, and also in positions held at Rome, in Italy, or the provinces, under the republic often involving command of troops, that normally followed the praetorship and consulship (pro-praetorships, -consulships, allocated by seniority and the lot, see PRO CONSULE, PRO PRAETORE); or that were devised under the Principate to get previously neglected work done (e.g. supervision of roads in Italy; see CURA(TIO)). After AD 14 elections were effectively conducted in the senate and a man's success depended on the judgement of his peers or on his ability to strike bargains with his rivals' supporters; but a law of *Augustus (see IUS LIBERORUM) provided speedier advancement for men married with children, while the opinion of the emperor, known or surmised, was of great and increasing weight, hence too the favour of his advisers. Some posts, notably legionary commands and governorships of regions that were part of his 'province' (e.g. *Syria, *Gaul (Transalpine) outside Narbonensis), were in his direct gift, though the senate ratified such appointments (both types of officer were '*legates of Augustus'.

The word 'career' is often applied to the posts offered by the emperor to men of *equestrian or lower status, whether in official positions (e.g. praetorian *prefect or *procurators of Augustus in his provinces, supervising tax collecting) or as his private agents (also procurators) managing his private estates. But although such posts mostly had their distinctive standing, and were normally preceded by up to three military posts, and although (because of this) recognizable patterns of advancement developed, appointments were again ad hoc, *ad hominem*, intermittent, and accepted on a basis of mutual goodwill, with character rather than professionalism the overt criterion. Imperial freedmen and even slaves who held subordinate positions in the organizations enjoyed lower standing, but their continuous service over long periods of time justifies the application of the term 'career' to their activities (see FREEDMEN; SLAVERY).

In the army below the rank of tribune it is legitimate to speak of a career, since the minimum period of service outside the *praetorian guard was 20 years. Men often record their advance through minor posts of privilege to (e.g.) one of the 60 centurionates of a legion, or upwards through legionary centurionates (see CENTURIO). Elsewhere the word is inappropriate.

Caria, mountainous region in SW Asia Minor south of the *Maeander, with Greek cities (*Cnidus and *Halicarnassus) occupying the salient peninsulas and mixed communities on the shores of the gulfs. Until the 4th cent. BC the pastoral Carians lived mainly in hilltop villages grouped under native dynasties (some of which paid tribute to the Athenian empire in the 5th cent.), the principal seat being Mylasa. See also MAUSOLUS.

carmen, 'something chanted', a formulaic or structured utterance, not necessarily in verse. In early Latin the word was used esp. for religious utterances such as spells and charms: the laws of the *Twelve Tables contained provisions against anyone who chanted a *malum carmen*, 'evil spell' *Carmen* became the standard Latin term for song, and hence poem (sometimes esp. lyric).

Carnea, the main festival of the *Dorians, honouring *Apollo Carneius. At *Sparta it took place in late summer and lasted nine days. It was above all a choral and musical festival of *panhellenic importance.

Carnĕădēs of *Cyrene (214/13–129/8 BC), the most important representative of the sceptical *Academy. He studied philosophy in the Academy, but also took lessons in Stoic *dialectic from Diogenes of Babylon. Carneades became scholarch some time before 155, when he was sent by Athens on an embassy to Rome together with Diogenes and the Peripatetic Critolaus. Carneades was famous for his dialectical and rhetorical skills. He attracted many students, and his lectures drew large audiences. He left no writings, but his arguments were recorded.

Carneades used the method of arguing for and against any given view to criticize all dogmatic philosophies. He also continued the debate between the Academy and the Stoa, whose doctrines had been defended against earlier sceptical objections by *Chrysippus. In the dispute about the criterion of truth, he expanded the argument about the impossibility of distinguishing between cognitive and non-cognitive impressions. Most influential became his reply to the standard objection that sceptical withholding of assent makes life impossible. He confronted the Stoics with a dilemma: if there is no cognitive impression, then either the wise man will hold opinions—an alternative abhorred by the Stoics—or else he will suspend judgement on everything. In the latter case, he will still be able to act, since it is possible to follow impressions without full assent, and the wise man may make reasonable decisions if he is guided by impressions that are plausible or convincing and checked for consistency with other relevant impressions. Carneades' account of the plausible was introduced to refute the Stoic claim that life is impossible without cognitive impressions. (See SCEPTICS; STOICISM.)

Carneades' criticisms of the belief in gods (see ATHEISM) and *divination were much used by Cicero and *Sextus Empiricus. In ethics, he is credited with a classification of all possible views about the highest good, invented no doubt in order to argue that none of these options can be conclusively defended. Again his main target was *Stoicism. On the occasion of the famous embassy to Rome, he gave speeches for and against justice on two consecutive days. Carneades' performance was so impressive that *Porcius Cato (1) demanded a speedy departure of the Athenian delegation in order to protect Roman youths from the subversive influence of the philosophers.

Carrara, white *marble *quarries in NW Italy. Perhaps first exploited on a small scale by the *Etruscans, they were further developed after the foundation of the colony of Luna in 177 BC, which acted as a port. Large-scale quarrying began in the 1st cent. BC. Mamurra, *Caesar's *praefectus fabrum* ('ADC'), was the first to veneer the walls of his house with Carrara, and may have opened up the quarries for Caesar's building programme, ending the use of Attic white marbles from Peutelicon. The reconstruction of the *Regia (37 BC) is often regarded as the earliest example of large-scale use of Carrara, and the industry (for buildings, sculpture, and *sarcophagi) reached its peak under Trajan, before giving way to the employment of marbles from the eastern Mediterranean.

Carthage a *Phoenician colony and later a major Roman city on the coast of NE Tunisia.

Acc. to tradition, Carthage was founded from *Tyre in 814/13 BC, but no archaeological evidence has yet been found earlier than the second half of the 8th cent. The site provided anchorage and supplies for ships trading in the western Mediterranean for *gold, *silver, and *tin, and soon outstripped other Phoenician colonies because of its position, its fertile hinterland, and its better harbour.

Trade was more important to Carthage throughout its history than perhaps to any other ancient state. Initially most of it was conducted by barter with tribes in Africa and Spain, where metals were obtained in return for wine, cloth, and pottery; but early contact with the Greek world is shown by the presence of Attic *amphorae in the earliest levels at Carthage. Voyages of exploration were undertaken along the Atlantic coast of North Africa and Spain. Carthage controlled much of the trade in the western Mediterranean, settling its own trading-posts in addition to those founded by the Phoenicians, so that Carthaginian influence extended from Tripolitania to Morocco, as well as to western Sicily, Sardinia, and southern Spain.

Carthage was ruled at first by a governor, responsible to the king of Tyre. By the 6th cent. the constitution had become oligarchic, headed by at first one 'judge', later two, called *suffetes* in Latin; they were elected annually on a basis of birth and wealth. Military commands were held by separately elected generals. There was a powerful 'senate' of several hundred life-members. The powers of the citizens were limited. A body of 104 judges scrutinized the actions of generals and other officials. Largely through this body the ruling class was successful in preventing the rise of *tyranny either through generals manipulating the mercenary armies or officials encouraging popular discontent. Military service was not obligatory on Carthaginians; instead mercenaries were hired from various west Mediterranean peoples.

In the 5th cent., owing to setbacks in Sicily, Carthage occupied much of the hinterland of north and central Tunisia, and agriculture flourished. The native Numidian population in the areas to the west of Carthage adopted urbanism and other elements of Punic culture and religion from the late 3rd cent. onwards, and esp. under enlightened rulers such as *Masinissa, so that considerable parts of North Africa outside formal Carthaginian control were already Punicized before the arrival of Rome.

The chief external policy of Carthage was to control the sea routes to the west. From c.600 it was clear that rival claims must lead to war between *Etruscans, Carthaginians, and Greeks. The westward thrust of *Phocaea and *Massilia was crushed by the Etruscan and Carthaginian fleets (c.535). The western end of *Sicily remained in Carthaginian hands down to the 3rd cent. For three centuries Carthaginians and Greeks fought intermittently for Sicilian territory.

With Rome Carthage concluded treaties in 508 and 348, in which she jealously guarded her monopoly of maritime trade while refraining from interference in Italy. When *Pyrrhus attacked (280), her fleet helped Rome to victory. But sixteen years later Sicilian politics brought the two states into open conflict. Carthaginian intervention on the side of the *Mamertines at Messina in 264 precipitated the first of the *Punic Wars, which ended in the destruction of Carthage (146). Rome decreed that neither house nor crop should rise again. But Carthaginian blood survived, and the awesome pantheon still persisted: worship of Baal-Hammon, Tanit, and Melqart was too deep-rooted in many parts of North Africa to die with the destruction of Carthage, and it was to continue until the rise of *Christianity.

Carthage was content to copy and adapt artistic styles imported from Egypt and Greece. She manufactured and exported carpets, rugs, *purple dyes, jewellery, pottery, lamps, tapestry, timber, and hides. Her agricultural skill, which made excellent use of the fertile Tunisian plains, profited her Roman conquerors: Mago's 32 books on scientific farming were translated into Latin; see AGRICULTURAL WRITERS.

The site of Carthage was too attractive to remain unoccupied for long. The attempt of Gaius *Sempronius Gracchus to establish the colony of Junonia on suburban land failed, but the city was colonized by Augustus in fulfilment of Caesar's intentions, and became the capital of Africa Proconsularis (see AFRICA, ROMAN). By the 2nd cent. AD Carthage had become a city second only to Rome in the western Mediterranean. A few urban troops and a cohort of *legion III Augusta sufficed to keep order. But through his control of the vital African corn-trade, the proconsul was a potential danger to the emperor.

Carthage became an outstanding educational centre, esp. famous for orators and lawyers. In the 3rd cent. the genius of *Tertullian and the devotion of Cyprian made her a focus of Latin Christianity. Her bishop held himself the equal of the bishop of Rome.

Carthago Nova, a town in Nearer Spain. It lay on a peninsula within one of the best harbours of the Mediterranean. Originally named Mastia, it was refounded as New Carthage in 228 BC as a base for the Carthaginian conquest of Spain. It was captured by *Scipio Africanus in 209, made a colony, probably by 42 BC. Excavations have revealed the amphitheatre, theatre, streets, private houses, and the late Roman walls. It was famous for its *silver-mines (which brought the Roman treasury a daily revenue of

2,500 drachmas in the mid-2nd cent. BC), and its fish-pickle (see FISHING).

Cartimandua, queen of the Brigantes, the most populous tribe in Britain, whose treaty-relationship with *Claudius protected the early northern borders of Roman *Britain. In AD 51, true to her obligation, she handed over the fugitive *Caratacus, but was weakened by the resulting breach with her husband, the patriot Venutius, and twice required the help of Roman troops in the period 52–57. Later, planning to deprive him of support, she divorced Venutius and married his squire Vellocatus; but with the Roman world otherwise engaged in 68–69, Venutius seized his chance and drove her out. The result was the conquest of Brigantia under *Vespasian and its incorporation into the province.

caryatids, column-shafts carved in the form of draped women. Apparently named after Caryae in *Laconia, where virgins danced to *Artemis Caryatis. Of near-eastern derivation, they appear in Greece c.550 BC, and are popular on late Archaic treasuries at *Delphi; the most famous are those of the Athenian *Erechtheum. The Erechtheum accounts, however, simply call them *korai*; in this case, perhaps, they were civic versions of the private *korē* dedications of the past (see ART, FUNERARY, GREEK (*Archaic period*)). Copies of the Erechtheum caryatids embellished the *forum Augustum, the *Pantheon, and Hadrian's villa at *Tibur.

Cassander (d. 297 BC), son of *Antipater, represented his father at Babylon (323), where *Alexander (2) the Great treated him with naked hostility. In the struggles of the Successors he first impinges at Triparadeisus (late 321), where he was appointed chiliarch (cavalry commander and grand vizier). Chiliarch he remained at Antipater's death (autumn 319), subordinate to the regent Polyperchon; but he defected to *Antigonus I and with Antigonus' support established bases in *Piraeus and *Peloponnese (318/17). An inconclusive invasion of Macedon was followed by a wholly successful one, which overthrew *Olympias. From 316 he was master of Macedon and promoted the memory of *Philip II over that of Alexander. He ceremonially refounded *Thebes (316). A leading figure in the coalition war against Antigonus (315–311), he secured recognition of his position as general in Europe in the 'Peace of the Dynasts' (311) and later had himself proclaimed 'King of the Macedonians', later his official title. His death left Macedon temporarily stable, but soon to be convulsed by the quarrels of his heirs.

Cassandra, in myth, daughter of *Priam and *Hecuba. In *Homer she is mentioned as being the most beautiful of Priam's daughters, and she is the first to see her father bringing home the body of *Hector. The *Sack of Troy* (see EPIC CYCLE) adds that during the sack she took refuge at the statue of Athena, but *Aias (2) the Locrian dragged her away to rape her, and in so doing loosened the statue from its plinth. Perhaps Homer knew of this episode, for in the *Odyssey* he says that Aias was 'hated by Athena'; but he makes no direct mention of it. Nor does he mention Cassandra's prophetic powers for which in later tradition she was famous. The *Cypria* first mentions her prophecies. Aeschylus' *Agamemnon* tells how Apollo gave her the power of prophecy in order to win her sexual favours, which she promised to him. But she broke her word; so he turned the blessing into a curse by causing her always to be disbelieved. She commonly appears, in tragedy and elsewhere, as forewarning of terrible events, like the evil fate which *Paris would bring on Troy or the disasters which the Wooden Horse would cause, but having her warnings unheeded. After the sack of Troy, Cassandra was given to *Agamemnon as his concubine, and on his return home *Clytemnestra killed them both. There is a memorable scene in Aeschylus' *Agamemnon* where Cassandra sings of the horrors which have already polluted the house of *Atreus and foretells her own death and that of Agamemnon. A favourite scene in Archaic and Classical art is that of Cassandra clutching the image of Athena while Aias seizes her.

Cassius (tyrannicide). See CASSIUS LONGINUS.

Cassius Dio (*c.* AD 164–after 229), Greek senator and author of an 80-book history of Rome from the foundation of the city to AD 229. Dio came from a prominent family of Nicaea in *Bithynia. He was praetor in 194 and suffect consul *c.*204. From 218 to 228 he was successively *curator of *Pergamum and Smyrna, proconsul of *Africa, and *legate first of Dalmatia and then of Upper Pannonia. In 229 he held the ordinary consulship with Severus Alexander as colleague and then retired to Bithynia. Dio lived through turbulent times: he and his fellow senators quailed before tyrannical emperors and lamented the rise of men they regarded as upstarts, and in Pannonia

he grappled with the problem of military indiscipline. These experiences are vividly evoked in his account of his own epoch and helped to shape his view of earlier periods.

Dio tells us that, after a short work on the dreams and portents presaging the accession of *Septimius Severus, he went on to write first a history of the wars following the death of *Commodus and then the *Roman History*, and that for this work he spent ten years collecting material for events up to the death of Severus (211) and a further twelve years writing them up. Dio's words suggest that he began work *c.*202. His plan was to continue recording events after Severus' death as long as possible, but absence from Italy prevented him giving more than a cursory account of the reign of Severus Alexander and he ended the history with his own retirement.

The *Roman History* is only partly extant. The portion dealing with the period 69 BC to AD 46 survives in various manuscripts, with substantial lacunae after 6 BC. For the rest we depend on excerpts and *epitomes. Like its author, the work is an amalgam of Greek and Roman elements. It is written in Attic Greek, with much antithetical rhetoric and frequent verbal borrowings from the classical authors, esp. *Thucydides (2). The debt to Thucydides is more than merely stylistic: like him, Dio is constantly alert to discrepancies between appearances and reality. In its structure, however, the history revives the Roman tradition of an annalistic record of civil and military affairs arranged by the consular year. Dio shows flexibility in his handling of the annalistic framework: there are many digressions, usually brief; external events of several years are sometimes combined in a single narrative cluster; introductory and concluding sections frame the annalistic narratives of emperors' reigns.

For his own times Dio could draw on his own experience or oral evidence, but for earlier periods he was almost entirely dependent on literary sources, chiefly earlier histories. Attempts to identify individual sources are usually futile. Dio must have read widely in the first ten years, and in the ensuing twelve years of writing up he probably worked mainly from his notes without going back to the originals. Such a method of composition may account for some of the history's distinctive character. It is often thin and slapdash; errors and distortions are quite common, and there are some surprising omissions. However, Dio does show much independence, both in shaping his material and in interpretation: he freely makes causal links between events and attributes motivations to his characters, and many of these explanations must be his own contribution rather than drawn from a source.

One notable feature of the work is the prominence of the supernatural: Dio believed that divine direction played an important part in his own and others' lives, and he devoted much space to *portents. Another is the speeches, which are free inventions and sometimes on a very ample scale. Many of them are commonly dismissed as mere rhetorical set-pieces, but they generally have a dramatic function, often heavily ironic. In *Maecenas' speech of advice to *Augustus Dio combines an analysis of the problems facing Augustus and of the imperial system as it evolved under the emperors with a sketch of how he himself would have liked to see the empire governed.

The *Roman History* is dominated by the change from the republic to the monarchy of the emperors, repeatedly endorsed by Dio on the grounds that only monarchy could provide Rome with stable government. The late republic and the triumviral years (see TRIUMVIRI) are accorded much more space than other periods. Dio anachronistically treats the conflicts of the late republic as struggles between rival contenders for supreme power. His account of the settlement of 27 BC perceptively explores the ways in which it shaped the imperial system under which he still lived. Dio's treatment of individual emperors' reigns reflects the values and interests of the senator: his overriding concern is with the respects in which emperors measured up to or fell short of senators' expectations.

Cassius Longīnus, Gāius, the tyrannicide, was quaestor 54 BC and proquaestor under *Licinius Crassus in 53. He escaped from Carrhae, collected the remnants of the army, and organized the defence of Syria, staying on as proquaestor till 51; in 52 he crushed an insurrection in Judaea and in 51 repelled a Parthian invasion. As tribune 49 he supported *Pompey and was appointed by him to a naval command; in 48 he operated in Sicilian waters but on the news of *Pharsalus abandoned the war and obtained Caesar's pardon. Peregrine *praetor 44, he played a leading part in the conspiracy against *Caesar. Soon after the deed he was forced by popular hostility to leave Rome, and was assigned by the senate in June the task of importing corn from Sicily, and later the unim-

portant province of *Cyrene. After quarrelling with Marcus *Antonius (Mark Antony) he sailed instead for Asia and from there to Syria, where, early in 43, the governors of Bithynia and Syria put their armies at his disposal. Caecilius Bassus, whom they had been besieging, followed suit; a force on its way from Egypt to Cornelius Dolabella was intercepted and made to join him; and after the capture of (Syrian) Laodicea he took over Dolabella's army too. The senate had given him, with *Brutus, command over all the eastern provinces; but in the autumn they were outlawed for the murder of Caesar under the law of Quintus *Pedius. After raising more troops and money, Cassius crossed with Brutus to Thrace in summer 42 and encountered Antony and *Octavian at *Philippi. In the first battle his camp was captured and, probably under the impression that the day was altogether lost, he killed himself.

More perceptive and practical than Brutus, Cassius seems nevertheless to have been less respected and less influential. He was a man of violent temper and sarcastic tongue, a strict disciplinarian, and ruthless in his exactions. The charge of covetousness may have been well founded; but there is no convincing evidence that he was influenced by petty motives in the conspiracy against Caesar.

Cassius Longīnus Ravilla, Lūcius, as tribune in 137 BC passed a law extending voting by ballot to trials before the assembly, except for treason. He was consul 127 and censor 125. Renowned for severity as a *iudex (called 'scopulus reōrum', the rock on which the guilty foundered), he gained fame by formulating the question 'Cui bonō?' ('Who profited?') as a principle of criminal investigation. In 113, when three *Vestals had been accused of unchastity and two acquitted by the *pontifex maximus, he was appointed a special investigator and condemned them and some men involved.

Cassivellaunus, king presumably of the *Catuvellauni, appointed supreme commander of the SE Britons on the occasion of *Caesar's second invasion (54 BC). After an initial defeat in Kent, he endeavoured to avoid battle and hamper his enemies' foraging strategy with guerrilla tactics which much embarrassed Caesar, who managed, however, to capture his capital. A peace was arranged through Caesar's agent Commius, by which Cassivellaunus agreed to pay a tribute and allow the independence of the *Trinovantes. Following his submission,

Caesar withdrew to Gaul. Subsequently the Catuvellauni expanded to become the dominant tribe in SE *Britain.

Castor and Pollux The temple of the *Dioscuri at Rome, in the Forum, was attributed to the deities' miraculous intervention in 484 BC in the battle of Lake Regillus (against the *Latins) in response to the vow of the dictator Postumius (they brought the news of the victory to Rome in person). Recent excavation has shown that the first temple is indeed of about this date, and that it was little smaller than the rebuildings of 117 and of Tiberius (dedicated AD 6), lavish though the last was. So this was one of the first monumental structures in the Forum, and long the most imposing—testimony to the importance of the cavalry in the early Roman state. The temple on its high podium was a vantage-point in the Forum, and played an big part in the turbulent popular politics of the end of the republic.

catacombs, a term derived from the Greek name of a locality near the church of St Sebastian on the *via Appia, about 5 km. (3 mi.) south of Rome. The name was in use in the 4th and 5th cents. AD for the Christian cemetery associated with St Sebastian's in the form *ad catacumbās* or *catacumbae*. This famous cemetery was a series of narrow underground galleries and tomb-chambers cut in the rock. Their walls are lined with tiers of coffin-like recesses for inhumation, holding one to four bodies apiece and sealed with a stone slab or tiles. The affinity to the *columbarium* is evident, but the type itself seems to have been derived from Jewish catacombs, where Jews, like Christians, remained a household of the faithful, united in death as in life. Catacombs were not confined to Rome. All are associated with soft rocks, where tunnelling was easy.

The catacombs at Rome, however, are much the most extensive, stretching for at least 550 km. (340 mi.). Their distribution (some 50 are attested), along the main roads outside the city, is explained by their later growth out of, and side by side with, pagan cemeteries lying beyond the city boundaries in conformity with the law (see DEAD, DISPOSAL OF). The Domitilla catacomb, on the via Ardeatina, developed from the underground chamber tomb of the Flavii. The official organization by the Church of public catacombs, mainly for the poor of Rome's Christian community, began c.200, when the then pope directed St Callixtus to provide the cemet-

ery which is represented by the oldest part of the catacomb beside the via Appia that bears St Callixtus' name today.

In the tomb-chambers of the catacombs are altar-tombs and arched recesses for the bodies of popes and martyrs. Walls and ceilings received paintings (see PAINTING, ROMAN) which represent the first development of Christian art and are executed in the same technique and style as contemporary pagan work. Their subjects are biblical (scenes from the OT far outnumbering those from the NT) or symbolic (the Good Shepherd, Christ-*Orpheus, Christ as lawgiver, eucharistic and celestial banquets, etc.). A remarkable and probably private catacomb, dating from the 4th cent. and discovered on the via Latina, has paintings which include a medical class and six episodes from the *Hercules-cycle (see HERACLES), as well as biblical scenes more elaborate and showing a much wider range of content than those in the official public catacombs. Furniture in the catacombs included carved *sarcophagi, lamps, pottery, and painted-glass medallions.

The presence of these large cemeteries is explained partly by the size of the Christian community in Rome and partly by the long periods of toleration. About a century after the official recognition of the Church, the catacombs fell into disuse and became centres of *pilgrimage.

catapults See ARTILLERY; SIEGECRAFT, GREEK.

Catiline See SERGIUS CATILINA.

Cato (the Censor) See PORCIUS CATO (1).

Cato (of Utica) See PORCIUS CATO (2).

Catullus, Gāius Valerius, Roman poet, came from a distinguished family of Verona but spent most of his life in Rome. He was probably born in 84 BC or a little earlier, and probably died in 54 BC. Since he was sent to Rome as a young man, his family were probably thinking of a political career, but he seems to have lacked political ambitions. His only known public activity was service on the staff of the propraetor *Memmius, governor of Bithynia in 57/6 BC. The political events of the turbulent decade he passed in Rome are little mentioned in his work. On one occasion his politically active friend Licinius Calvus involved him in a literary campaign against the triumvirs, esp. *Caesar (with his minion, Mamurra), but this outburst of ill-humour did not last, and when Caesar magnanimously offered him his hand in reconciliation, he did not refuse it.

Catullus was at the centre of the radical social change that marked the end of the republic. He lived in the circles of the *jeunesse dorée* who had turned away from the ideals of early Rome and embraced Hellenistic culture. This environment affected not only Catullus' outlook and views but also his language, which acquired a facility previously unknown in Roman literature. He was surrounded by a group of young poets, the so-called 'neoterics', who shared the same rejection of traditional norms and the same search for new forms and content, and, as in their lifestyle, Hellenistic culture provided the most important model (see HELLENISTIC POETRY AT ROME). In these same aristocratic circles Catullus met the married woman whom he called 'Lesbia'. He depicts her as self-assured, beautiful, and cultured, and regards her becoming his lover as the peak of felicity. But when he realizes that she has been false to him with a succession of partners, his happiness turns to despair. The ups and downs of this affair provide Catullus with the central theme of his poetry. His love poetry is quite different from the light-hearted frivolity of Hellenistic literature, as presented in the epigrams of the Greek *Anthology*; he sought in love not sexual transport but a deep human union which would last a whole lifetime. Apuleius tells us that behind the name Lesbia was a Clodia, and this seems to offer a secure historical context, since we know of a Clodia with similar characteristics living in Rome at this time, the sister of *Clodius Pulcher and wife to the consul of 60, Caecilius Metellus Celer. Cicero gives a picture of her in his speech on behalf of Caelius Rufus which for all its bias must have had some basis in fact. Even if the identification cannot be proved, Cicero's picture of the historical *Clodia is instructive for the social background to Catullus' poetry.

Catullus died young, and left behind only a slim corpus of work amounting to 116 poems of extremely varied length and form. The book is primarily ordered on metrical grounds. Sixty short poems in lyric or iambic (see METRE, GREEK) metres are followed by poems 61–68, which are long poems in a variety of metres: the remainder of the book consists of *epigrams.

The three major groupings of poems within the corpus differ considerably in their approach. The short poems (1–60) contain much that one might term 'social poetry' from a thematic point of view, though they also include expressions of stronger emotions. These poems are not artless

productions of a moment's reflection: Catullus models himself in them on the elegance and facility of the shorter Hellenistic forms. The group of longer poems in more elevated style begins with two wedding poems: poem 63 describes the fate of a young man who has become a devotee of *Cybele, the '*epyllion' 64 contrasts happy and unhappy love in the stories of *Peleus and *Ariadne, and 65–68 are a series of elegiac poems on various themes (see ELEGIAC POETRY, LATIN). Poem 66 (with the introductory poem 65) contains a translation of the *Lock of Berenice* which concludes *Callimachus' (2) *Aetia*; 68 is often seen as a precursor of the love elegies of *Propertius and *Tibullus. The epigrams (69–116) differ radically from the other poems. Even when they deal with the painful circumstances of the poet's own life, they are never simply representations of a momentary emotion, but rather reflective analyses of a situation or the poet's own experience.

Catuvellauni, the most powerful south British tribe. *Cassivellaunus probably ruled it; later kings were Tasciovānus and his son Cunobel(l)īnus. under whom *Camulodunum became a major *oppidum* and centre for Roman imports. After AD 43 a *civitas* was created with its capital at Verulamium. The region was mainly agricultural with a cluster of villas around Verulamium.

cavalry See AUXILIA; EQUITES; HIPPEIS, 2.

caves, sacred The Greeks associated caves with the primitive, the uncanny, and hence the sacred. In myth they witness divine births (Zeus on Mt. Dicte), are home to monsters (the *Cyclopes), and conceal illicit sex (see SELENE). Remote and wild, real caves attracted the cult of *Pan and the *Nymphs, for whom several dozen cave-sanctuaries are known, or, as openings to the Underworld, oracles of the dead. In Italy the most celebrated holy cave was the Lupercal on the Palatine (see LUPERCALIA). Of imported cults, the most closely associated with caves was Mithraism (see MITHRAS), whose rites were celebrated in real or make-believe caves because the cave was considered an 'image of the universe'.

Cecrops, a mythical king of Athens. Athenians regarded him as their archetypal ancestral figure. No parents are recorded for him, and probably he was thought of as autochthonous (see AUTOCHTHONS). He was described as 'double-natured', with reference to his form as half-man, half-snake—the normal style of his depiction on red-figure vases, where he is a popular figure in many Athenian scenes. Cecrops was the father of Aglaurus, Pandrosus, and Herse, and of one son who died young. His deeds mark him out as a civilizing figure, the one who established monogamous marriage, writing, funeral rites, and other customs perceived as important to contemporary, 'normal', society. The foundation of many religious cults was also ascribed to him.

Celsus, medical author, see CORNELIUS CELSUS.

Celsus, author of a comprehensive polemic against *Christianity, The True Doctrine,* written probably between 175 and 181. The work is primarily known through *Origen's Against Celsus,* which preserves most of it through direct quotation. Celsus wrote from the perspective of a Middle Platonic philosopher, though in one section of his work he also appears to have adopted the criticism levelled against Christianity by a Jew. *The True Doctrine* is important evidence for knowledge of Christian doctrine among Gentiles, as well as for the difficulty outsiders had in determining the difference between 'orthodox' Christians and *Gnostic fringe groups. The importance of Celsus' book is suggested by the fact that Origen's massive refutation was written in the 240s.

Celts, a name applied by ancient writers to a population group occupying lands mainly north of the Mediterranean region from Galicia in the west to Galatia in the east. (Its application to the Irish, the Scots, and the Welsh is modern.) Their unity is recognizable by common speech and common artistic traditions. (1) Dialects of Celtic are still spoken (Ireland, Scotland, Wales, Brittany), or are attested by inscriptions, quotations, and place-names in this area. (2) The artistic unity is most apparent in the La Tène style (called from the Swiss type-site) which appears *c.*500 BC. It is a distinctive art of swinging, swelling lines, at its best alive and yet reposeful.

La Tène culture was so strong that it gave Celtic warriors the power to break through the defences of the classical world and reach the Mediterranean. In 386 they sacked Rome (see BRENNUS); and while in 279 one band raided *Delphi, in 278 another crossed the Hellespont and eventually settled the territory called Galatia, where Celtic was still spoken in the 5th cent. AD. It was a developed Celtic La Tène society that *Caesar confronted and described in Gaul in the mid-1st cent. BC, and indeed the

migration of the Helvetii may be interpreted as the last great ancient Celtic population-movement. But by then the tide was running against the Celts. The ancients knew them as fierce fighters and superb horsemen, and noticed the savagery of their religious rites conducted by the priesthood, the *Druids, who derived their doctrine from Britain. Yet the Celts' political sense was weak, and they were crushed between the migratory Germans and the power of Rome, to be ejected by the former and conquered outright by the latter.

cemeteries A formal cemetery, a space reserved for the disposal of the *dead, was an important element of the ancient city. Burial within the settlement had been common in many parts of the Mediterranean world in the early iron age, but after the 8th cent. BC it was rare. Cemeteries lined the roads leading away from cities. They usually consisted of numerous small grave-plots, which were rarely used for more than two or three generations, although some cemeteries, such as the *Ceramicus at Athens, remained in use for *c.*1,500 years.

censors, a pair of senior Roman magistrates, elected by the centuriate assembly (see CENTURIA) to hold office for eighteen months. Although they lacked *imperium and the right to an escort of *lictors, the censors possessed considerable authority and influence owing to the range of their responsibilities. The censorship was established in 443 BC as a civil magistracy with the primary function of making up and maintaining the official list of Roman citizens, previously the task of the consuls (see CENSUS). The censors were initially exclusively patrician. A law of 339 required that at least one of the censors be a plebeian, but not until 131 were both censors plebeian. The office came to be regarded as the highest position in the *cursus honorum and to be held as a rule only by ex-consuls. Censors were normally elected every four (later five) years, but practice varied greatly. After *Sulla, by whom the powers of the censors were for a time greatly reduced, election was irregular, and no censors were elected after 22 BC. Thereafter the emperors themselves assumed responsibility for censorial functions or delegated them to lesser officials.

The powers of the censors extended well beyond the conduct of the census itself. At the most general level they exercised a supervision of the morals of the community. When the lists of citizens were drawn up, the censors, if they agreed and stated the reason, might place a mark of censure (*nota*) against the name of a man whose conduct, public or private, they found reprehensible. The effect of this was to remove the man in question from his tribe (*tribus*). The censors also revised the membership of the senate. Here the censorial *nota* meant exclusion from the senate. Initial admission to the senate was dependent upon the censors down to the time of Sulla, by whose legislation election to the quaestorship automatically brought membership of the senate.

The censors were the officials responsible for the leasing of revenue-producing public property (land, forests, mines, etc.), and it was they who made the contracts with the *publicani* for the collection of the revenue arising therefrom (*vectigal*), as for the collection of the harbour-taxes (*portoria*) within Roman territory. The contract for the collection of the taxes of an entire province could also be sold to *publicani* by the censors at Rome, as was most notably the case with the province of Asia (from 123 or 122 BC). In addition, the censors were usually responsible for the letting of contracts for public works (roads, buildings, etc.); the amount available for these was determined by the senate. As Rome's dominion grew, so did the financial operations of the censors, giving rise both to potentially great fortunes for the *publicani* and to tension between the censors and senate on one side and the *publicani* and equestrian order on the other.

censorship See INTOLERANCE, INTELLECTUAL AND RELIGIOUS.

census, a national register prepared at Rome, on the basis of which were determined voting rights and liability for military service and taxation. The census was held from 443 BC by the *censors. One was normally held every four (later five) years. Men were required to state their full name, age, name of their father or *patrōnus*, domicile, occupation, and the amount of their property. The names of women and children were not included in the census, but fathers gave details about families. On the basis of the information received the censors registered citizens in tribes, *tribus (by domicile, except in the case of *freedmen who were, for most of the republic, registered in one or more of the four urban tribes), and centuries (see CENTURIA) (by property and age). Those whose property did not qualify them for enrolment in one of the five classes were registered in a single century of *capite censi* ('counted by head'; see

PROLETARII). The taking of a census was concluded with a religious ceremony of purification, the *lustrum* (*lustration). At the end of the republic the census was taken irregularly. It was held three times by *Augustus. The last known census in Italy was held by *Vespasian and *Titus: taxation, conscription, and voting had ceased to be Italian concerns. Not until the reign of Augustus were provincial censuses conducted by the central government.

Centaurs a tribe of 'beasts', human above and horse below; a wild and dangerous counterpart of the more skittish *satyrs, who are constructed of the same components but conceived of as amusing rather than threatening creatures. In both cases it is the very closeness of the horse to humanity that points up the need to remember that a firm line between nature and culture must be drawn. *Pirithous king of the Lapiths, a *Thessalian clan, paid for his failure to absorb this lesson when he invited the Centaurs to his wedding-feast; the party broke up in violence once the guests had tasted *wine, that quintessential product of human culture, and made a drunken assault on the bride. 'Ever since then', says Antinoüs in the *Odyssey*, 'there has been conflict between Centaurs and men.' Their uncontrolled lust, violence, and greed for alcohol (see ALCOHOLISM) challenge the hard-won and ever fragile rules of civilization, which are symbolically reasserted by the victory of *Heracles (whose wife Deianira the Centaur Nessus had tried to rape) over the savage horde. Centaurs belong to the forested mountains of Arcadia and northern Greece, the fringes of human society; so it is natural that in the 'Centauromachies' so popular in Archaic art they fight with uprooted trees and boulders against armed and disciplined Greek heroes.

Their double-natured ambivalence is further emphasized in traditions which single out two of their number, Chiron and Pholus, as wise and civilized exceptions to the rule. Pholus, it is true, eats his steak raw like an animal when entertaining Heracles, but his self-control is shown by his ability to hold his liquor—a specially aged vintage donated by Dionysus—until the other members of his tribe scent the bouquet of the wine, go berserk, and have to be shot down by Heracles. Chiron is a more complex character, blurring the human–animal boundary still further: vase-painters often make the point by giving him human rather than equine front legs and draping him in decorous robes. His bestial side is demonstrated by the way he feeds the baby *Achilles, deserted by his mother *Thetis, on the still-warm blood of the hares which in art he habitually carries over his shoulder as a portable game-larder (hence, in turn, the savagery of the hero); but he is also a source of wisdom on natural medicine, and is recorded as an educator of *Jason (1) and *Asclepius as well as Achilles.

By the 5th cent. BC, Centaurs (like *Amazons) come to symbolize all those forces which opposed Greek male cultural and political dominance; on the *Parthenon metopes, with their heroically nude boxers and wrestlers, the triumph over Persia is a clear subtext. (See PERSIAN-WARS TRADITION.) Of later literary treatments, *Ovid's account of the Lapith wedding (*Metamorphoses*. 12) is not to be missed.

centuria, lit. a group of 100, was the smallest unit of the Roman legion; 60 centuries made up a legion. It was also the name given to the constituent units of the centuriate assembly (*comitia centuriāta*). The bulk of the assembly was made up of eighteen centuries of horsemen (*equitēs*), and 170 of foot-soldiers (*peditēs*). The *pedites* were divided into five *classēs* according to their *census. There were in addition five centuries of non-combatants, of which four (of carpenters and musicians) were attached to one or other of the *classes*, and one (the *capite censī* ('counted by head') or *proletarii*), made up of those whose property fell below the minimum required for the fifth *classis*, were ranked separately below all the rest. The voting order of the assembly was fixed: first the *equestrian centuries, then the *classes*, then the *capite censi*.

centuriation, a system of marking out the land in squares or rectangles, by means of boundaries, normally before distribution in a colonial foundation. The centuriation systems which remain visible today are mostly those in relatively homogeneous terrain, esp. where the *līmitēs* (sing. *līmes*) between lots were also ditches which served for drainage. *Limites* might otherwise be anything from a drystone wall to a row of markers.

centurions were the principal professional officers in the Roman army. In the post-Marian army each of the ten cohorts (see COHORS; MARIUS) had six centuries, except in the case of the first cohort. Between these centuries there was little difference in status apart from seniority. The first cohort had, probably from early in the empire, only five centuries and was double the size of the others. Its centurions were *prīmus*

pīlus (see PRIMIPILUS), *princeps*, *hastātus*, *princeps posterior*, and *hastātus posterior*. Within this group strict seniority was observed, with the post of *primus pīlus* as the final honour.

During the republic centurions were selected from the ranks; under the Principate, most centurions continued to be promoted legionaries, but some were men who had transferred from an *equestrian career, or ex-praetorians. They were attracted by high pay, and good prospects on retirement. Centurions are found also in the *auxilia* and the *praetorians.

Cephalus, a famous mythical hunter known to the *Epic Cycle. His cult is known only in Attica. He married Procris daughter of *Erechtheus, but was abducted by *Eos, by whom he had a son. On returning to his wife, he disguised himself in order to test her fidelity, but found it wanting. Procris fled in shame to *Crete, but on her return she tried the same trick, with the same result. Cephalus accidentally killed her when she was spying on him as he went hunting, and was brought to trial at the *Areopagus by her father. Exiled from Attica, he took part with his inescapable hound in the hunt of the Teumessian fox, and finally went to Cephallēnia.

Ceramīcus, Kerameikos, large and (in ancient authors) loosely defined district of NW Athens based on the potters' (*kerameis*) quarter. Within the Themistoclean wall it embraced the area from the *Dipylon gate up to and including the Agora, for which it could be a virtual synonym, although Classical authors used it above all of the famous extramural cemetery (including the National Cemetery, see EPITAPHIOS) lining the routes which fanned out from the Sacred and Dipylon gates. Excavations provide detailed information about Athenian mortuary practices over 1,500 years. Many fine funerary monuments, both ceramic and sculpted, are now displayed in the Athens archaeological museum (see ART, FUNERARY, GREEK). The *deme Kerameis lay in this area. See ATHENS, TOPOGRAPHY; CEMETERIES.

Cerberus monstrous hound that guards the entrance to the Underworld, often called 'the dog of *Hades'. Hesiod makes him a child of Echidna and Typhon, 'brass-voiced and fifty-headed'; three heads are more normal in literary descriptions and in art, while Attic vase-painters usually make do with two. A shaggy mane runs down his back, and he may sprout writhing snakes. Despite his impressive appearance, however, he failed to keep out *Orpheus, who lulled him to sleep with music; while *Heracles (with Athena's help) even managed to chain him up and drag him away to the upper world, where he terrified *Eurystheus with the captive beast. The scene was already depicted in Archaic art on the so-called 'Throne of Amyclae'; a water-pot in the Louvre handles the theme with exuberance.

cereals, the most important component of the diet (see FOOD AND DRINK). The Greeks and Romans cultivated wheat, barley, oats, rye, and millet. The botanical works of *Theophrastus, the Roman *agricultural writers, and medical writers provide much information on cereals. These sources may be supplemented with the evidence of palaeobotanical remains of cereals found on archaeological sites.

By the end of antiquity wheat was the most important cereal. Innovations such as the spread of the rotary grain-mill, from the 4th cent. BC onwards, and the use of finer sieves to separate grain from chaff, made it possible to produce purer flour, although it was still coarse by modern standards. Wheat came to be preferred to the other cereals because it contains a higher proportion of gluten (which raises loaves during baking) than other cereals. This development led to the gradual displacement of the original Greek and Latin words for wheat by the words for corn in general (*sītos* and *frūmentum*).

Barley was also very important. It was often made into a kind of cake. Barley needs less water than wheat and is better adapted to semi-arid environments. Its significance declined because it produces inferior bread. Barley was eaten by slaves and the poor. In Attica it was probably more important than wheat as late as the 4th cent. BC. The *helots paid a rent in barley to the Spartans.

See also FOOD SUPPLY.

Cerēs, an ancient Italo-Roman goddess of growth, commonly identified in antiquity with *Demeter. In cult she is found associated with *Tellus. The occurrence of her Cerialia on the calendars and the existence of a *flamen Cerialis* testify to the antiquity of Ceres' cult at Rome. Her most famous cult, that on the *Aventine (introduced 493 BC), is largely under Greek influence. She is there worshipped with *Liber Pater and Libera. The temple became a centre of plebeian activities (see PLEBS) and was supervised by the plebeian *aediles.

Cestius Epulō, Gaius, a senator, who built himself the conspicuous pyramid-tomb beside the via Ostiensis in Rome. The tomb, with its grandiose Egyptian aspirations, and an inscription recording the execution of Cestius' will (*Agrippa was an heir), shows the pride and wealth of a *novus homo* in the Augustan system.

Chaerephon (5th cent. BC), Athenian, of the *deme of Sphettus, a friend and enthusiastic admirer of *Socrates. With other democrats he was banished by the *Thirty Tyrants and returned with *Thrasybulus (2) in 403, but died before Socrates' trial in 399. He is best known for reporting the *Delphic oracle's opinion that no one was wiser than Socrates (in Plato's *Apology*, 21). The story is probably true, being related by both *Plato and *Xenophon, but Chaerephon's motivation and the statement's meaning remain uncertain. In Aristophanes' *Clouds* he is joint proprietor with Socrates of the Thinkery (or just a pupil).

Chaeronea, battles of The town of Chaeronea commands the route south down the Cephissus valley. In 338 BC *Philip II of Macedon won a crushing victory over an alliance of southern Greek states, led by Athens and *Thebes, effectively putting an end to the era of the independent *polis. It is not certain how the victory was won. The stone lion east of the modern village clearly commemorates the battle, but its precise significance is unknown: it may mark the resting-place of the Theban élite 'Sacred Band'—254 skeletons were found nearby. In 86 *Sulla won a victory here over the army of *Mithradates VI of Pontus.

Chalcidicē, a big peninsula projecting from Macedonia and ending in three promontories, was inhabited originally by the Sithonians. Their name survived in 'Sithonia', the central promontory between the western 'Pallene' and the eastern 'Acte'. The first Greek colonists from *Chalcis in the 8th cent. BC dispossessed the Sithonians and founded c.30 settlements, perhaps giving the name 'Chalcidice' to the entire peninsula. *Eretria and Andros also founded colonies.

Followers perforce of *Xerxes, the cities joined the *Delian League and became subjects of Athens. Revolting in 432/1 they established a common capital at *Olynthus, thus inaugurating the 'Chalcidic Confederacy'. (See FEDERAL STATES.) The member cities shared a common citizenship and common laws; the confederacy struck a magnificent silver coinage.

Chalcis, the chief city of *Euboea throughout antiquity, controlling the narrowest part of the Euripus channel and (after 411 BC) a bridge to the mainland. In the 8th cent. Chalcis, with its neighbour *Eretria, planted colonies in *Italy and *Sicily. In the later 8th cent. it disputed with Eretria possession of the Lelantine plain, which lay between them (see GREECE (HISTORY); LEFKANDI). In the 7th cent. colonies were sent to the north Aegean. A centre of trade and manufacture, Chalcis was famous for its metalwork. In 506 it was compelled to cede part of its plain to Athenian cleruchs (see CLERUCHY). The city made common cause, however, with Athens during the invasion of *Xerxes. It led a revolt of Euboea against Athens (446) but was defeated and became a tributary ally until 411.

Chaos 'First of all Chaos came into being', says *Hesiod; it did not exist from everlasting. What it was like he does not say; the name means 'gaping void'.

character, *Aristotle was not alone in being interested in analysing ethically good and bad character, i.e. virtue and vice. The typical approach consists of the tabulation of virtues and vices, conceived both as modes of human behaviour and as psychological structures. In the Aristotelian model, human beings are taken to be adapted by nature (*phŷsis*) to develop relatively stable patterns of emotion and desire ('dispositions') which, in conjunction with value-laden beliefs and reasoning, form the basis for the choice-based actions and speeches in which people display their *ēthos* ('character', understood as 'ethical quality'). The social contexts of family, friendship-bond, city-state (and, for some, philosophical school) provide the framework for the development, as well as the definition, of these qualities. Other ancient philosophers emphasize an idea found also in Aristotle (Nicomachean Ethics) that only the virtuous have real stability and cohesion of character and that the non-virtuous are dominated by 'unreasonable' and fluctuating desires or 'passions'.

Absent from ancient thought is the interest in unique individuality and the subjective viewpoint which figures in modern western thinking about character. What is prominent, however, in ancient literature from Homer's *Iliad* onwards is the sympathetic presentation of abnormal and problematic psychological states and ethical stances. See also BIOGRAPHY.

chariots See HORSE- AND CHARIOT-RACES; TRANSPORT.

Charitĕs, 'Graces', goddesses personifying grace, charm, and beauty. *Hesiod, names them Aglaea (Radiance), Euphrosynē (Joy), and Thalīa (Flowering). He calls them daughters of *Zeus. They are closely associated with *Aphrodite in Homer, and later. In Hesiod, they and the Horae deck *Pandora. They enjoy poetry, singing, and dance and perform at the wedding of *Peleus and *Thetis. They make roses grow, have myrtles and roses as attributes, and the flowers of spring belong to them.

The Charites have no independent mythology, associating with gods of fertility, esp. Aphrodite, whose birth they attend. Often they are shown standing, processing, or dancing. *Pausanias (3) details cults and depictions of the Charites, particularly at *Orchomenus. The Charites were originally draped, later naked. The familiar group of three naked women is Hellenistic in origin, and became standard in many Roman copies in several media.

charities See EUERGETISM; FOOD SUPPLY.

Charon, mythological ferryman, who takes the shades across a river (usually Acheron) or a lake into *Hades proper. His first known visual representations occur *c.*500 BC on two black-figure vases; a few decades later he became popular on Attic white-ground *lēkythoi*. *Polygnotus painted him in his *Underworld* in the club-house of the Cnidians at *Delphi. It was said that Charon, out of fear, ferried Heracles, who had gone to fetch *Cerberus, into Hades, and was punished for this dereliction with a year in fetters.

chastity

Before Christianity Chastity (i.e. lifelong virginity) was not recommended in Greek *medicine before *Soranus. In pagan religion, certain goddesses chose to remain virgins (e.g. *Athena/*Minerva, *Hestia/*Vesta, *Artemis/*Diana) and some priestesses—not necessarily those serving virgin goddesses—remained lifelong virgins while others could hold the position only until the age of marriage.

In contrast to the Hippocratics (see HIPPOCRATES), who believed that a girl must be 'opened up' for the sake of her health, Soranus recommended perpetual virginity as positively healthful for both men and women. He argued that desire harms the body, and loss of seed is damaging to health, while pregnancy and *childbirth exhaust the body. However, Soranus does concede that intercourse is necessary for the survival of the human race. In contrast to Christian writers of the early Roman empire (see below), Soranus recommends virginity neither for spiritual health nor as part of rejecting the world, but to make life easier.

Christian Celibacy and *asceticism are endemic to *Christianity and are typical of the distinctive outlook on life which runs throughout much of early Christian literature. The lifestyle of John the Baptist and the canonical gospels' portrayal of the seeming celibacy of Jesus and his *eschatological message set the pattern for later Christian practice. The background to this form of religious observance is to be found in the ascetical practices of certain forms of sectarian Judaism. The level of purity demanded by the Qumran sect (see DEAD SEA SCROLLS) reflects the regulations with regard to sexual activity in Leviticus and the requirements laid upon men involved in a holy war in Deuteronomy. Elsewhere there is evidence that asceticism was a central part of the mystical and apocalyptic tradition of Judaism (e.g. Daniel 10; see RELIGION, JEWISH). The centrality of eschatological beliefs for Christianity meant that from the first much Christian practice demanded a significant distance from the values and culture of the day. The hope for the coming of a new age of perfection in which members of the Church could already participate placed rigorous demands on those who would join. Some evidence suggests that baptized men and women thought that they had to live like angels (cp. Luke 20: 35), putting aside all those constraints of present bodily existence which were incompatible with their eschatological state. *Paul's approach in 1 Corinthians 7 in dealing with the rigorist lifestyle of the Corinthian ascetics is typical of the compromise that evolved, in which there is a grudging acceptance of marriage and an exaltation of celibacy. The emerging monastic movement, therefore, drew on a long history of ascetical practice.

Chersonese, Thracian, a long, narrow peninsula forming the European side of the *Hellespont (Dardanelles). Running in an east–west direction, it connects the sea of Marmara with the Aegean. It was noted for its fertility and for its strategic location as a crossing between Europe and Asia. Several Greek cities lay along the protected southern (Hellespontine) shore, leaving no doubt about their ability to control sea traffic through the straits. It was settled by Aeolian and Ionian Greeks in the 8th and 7th cents. BC. Private Athenian interest began in the late 7th cent., with settlers involved in both local agriculture and trade and in the growing Greek commerce with the Black (*Euxine) Sea. By the 5th cent. the Athenian state took an official interest in protecting the corn trade, and a number of Chersonese cities became tributary states in the Athenian empire (see DELIAN LEAGUE). In the 4th cent. a wall was built across the narrow neck of the peninsula as a defence against Thracian incursions. *Philip II of Macedon ruled the area, and, after passing through the hands of *Alexander (2) the Great's successors, the Chersonese became a part of *Pergamum's domain (189). Thence it passed into Roman hands (133) as *ager publicus, and was converted into an imperial estate under *Augustus. See MILTIADES.

childbirth was generally the concern of women, either family and neighbours or experienced *midwives, who were sometimes ranked as doctors, but male doctors expected to be called in for difficult cases. Several treatises in the Hippocratic corpus (see HIPPOCRATES) include some discussion of childbirth. Dissection by Herophilus, in the 3rd cent. BC, revealed that the uterus is muscular, and Galen argues that it has the power to retain or expel the foetus. The most detailed account of labour and delivery is in the 1st-cent. AD handbook written by *Soranus for midwives, the *Gynaecology*.

In Greek tradition, childbirth ritually polluted those present because blood was shed, and delivery on sacred ground was therefore forbidden (see POLLUTION). Olympian goddesses are not represented as giving birth. The deities most often invoked in labour were *Artemis Eileithyia or *Hera in Greece, *Juno Lūcīna in Rome. There are allusions to rituals in which the father lifts the child from the earth or carries it round the hearth (*amphidromia*; see CHILDREN), but these would not always be practicable, and it was the name-day celebration, some ten days after the birth, which publicly acknowledged the child as a family member. See MOTHERHOOD; POLLUTION.

children In Greece the decision whether to raise a child rested with the father except in *Sparta where 'elders of the tribes' were required to pronounce upon its fitness to live. In Rome a law attributed to Romulus allegedly required all parents to 'bring up all their male offspring and the first-born of the girls'. The exposure of infants is often commented upon in both Greek and Latin authors, but this does not help us to determine how frequent it was in practice. Categories at high risk, however, include girls, those with a *deformity, illegitimate offspring, and slave offspring. Being less 'popular' than boys, many girls may have been undernourished. Whether this led to a marked imbalance among the sexes is unknown. From the time of *Trajan onwards some families in Roman cities were given financial aid called *alimenta* to help defray the cost of raising their children.

A boy, like a slave, was a marginal figure, but unlike a slave his marginality was only temporary. Girls, however, even upon attaining adulthood, always remained under the control of a male (see MARRIAGE LAW, *Greek*). In Athens a ceremony called the *amphidromia*, held probably on the fifth day after birth, signalled a child's entry into the family. Soon afterwards boys were registered in hereditary associations known as *phratries. Boys and girls until aged about 6 spent most of their time in the women's quarters. In *Sparta at this age boys left home and entered the public educational system called the *agoge*, which was designed to produce a well-disciplined army. A variety of *rites of passage for males signalled the end of childhood in the Greek world. The Roman equivalent to the *amphidromia* was the *lustratio*, 'purification', which took place on the eighth or ninth day. There was no subsequent ceremony of incorporation for Roman children. Childhood ended for boys around 16 with the putting on of the plain white adult toga in place of the *toga praetexta* with purple border.

In light of the probably high level of infant mortality there has been much speculation about the intensity of parental affect in antiquity. The keen desire for children that we observe both in literature and in the popularity of *adoption admittedly reflects in part the pragmatic acknowledgement that many parents in their old age were dependent upon offspring for support. A child's duty to its parents extended in the case of the Greeks to the legal requirement to maintain its parents in old age. No such ruling existed in the Roman world before the 2nd cent. AD.

Corporal punishment was often administered to children. The Roman *paterfamiliās* or household head had the right of life and death over his offspring (see PATRIA POTESTAS), though it was little exercised in the late republic and empire,

apart from cases of abandonment at birth and *adultery. The nurse and *paedagōgus* (lit. child-leader), both slaves, were important figures in a child's upbringing. Since the age gap between fathers and children was about 30 years, many children would have come under the supervision of a guardian (see GUARDIANSHIP). The Greeks and Romans believed that intelligence was a function of age and hence tended to regard the child as intellectually inferior. Largely because of their ritual purity children played a significant role in religion, singing in choirs and even serving as priests. Esp. important was the child whose parents were both still alive and so had not been polluted by contact with the dead.

Our perception of childhood in antiquity is largely based on what unrepresentative adults such as *Plato and *Aristotle have chosen to record. The concept of play, for instance, receives prominent attention in the *Laws* of Plato, who sees it as fulfilling a major role in the moulding of personality. Toys, commonly found in graves or depicted in vase-paintings, provide the most evocative picture of childhood. Representations of children in Greek art begin in the late-5th cent. BC and in Roman art at the beginning of the imperial era. Roman children are often mentioned in funerary inscriptions and lawcodes. See AGE; CHILDBIRTH; EDUCATION; MOTHERHOOD.

Chilon, Spartan *ephor (*c.*556 BC), whose wit and wisdom gained him place among the '*Seven Sages' of Greece. Related by marriage to kings of both houses, he was said to have been the first to 'yoke the ephors alongside the kings', a possible reference to the monthly renewed compact between Spartan kings and ephors. After his death he was worshipped at *Sparta as a hero (see HERO-CULT).

Chios, an *Ionian *polis* on the large Aegean island of the same name, some 7 km. (4$\frac{1}{2}$ mi.) from Asia Minor. *Thucydides (2) calls it the greatest *polis* of Ionia and its citizens among the richest Greeks. The plain beside the large eastern bay has always supported the main settlement. Literary figures included *Homer (supposedly), *Ion, and *Theopompus.

Reputedly colonized from *Euboea in the 9th cent. BC (also the date of the earliest Greek burials), in Archaic times Chios was often at loggerheads with Erythrae on the Asiatic mainland (where Chians had land) and with *Samos. The inscribed 'constitution' of *c.*575–550 refers to a 'council of the people' and to the duties of officials. Archaeology suggests that early trade concentrated on the Black (*Euxine) Sea, Egypt, and the west. The only major colony was at Maroneia, though Chians helped found the Hellenion at *Naucratis, where their pottery has been identified. They built an ostentatious altar at Delphi (late Archaic).

The Chians established a *modus vivendi* with *Croesus and *Cyrus (1), but later came under a Persian-backed tyrant. They played a leading part in the *Ionian Revolt, manning 100 ships at Lade. On the basis of that figure the free population is put at between 60,000 and 120,000; slaves were numerous from an early date. Settlement was dispersed: there are many Classical to Roman farmsteads.

The Chians encouraged Athens to set up the *Delian League, in which they were leading ship-contributors. Loyal to Athens during the Samian revolt and *Sicilian Expedition, they revolted in 412. *Lysander installed a harmost (Spartan military governor); after the Spartan withdrawal Chios was to become the first member of the *Second Athenian Confederacy.

Chiron See CENTAURS.

chorēgia At Athens the *choregia* was a *liturgy or public service performed by a rich citizen for the *polis*. A *chorēgos* (lit. 'leader of a chorus') was responsible for the recruitment, training, maintenance, and costuming of *choreutai* (members of a chorus) for competitive performance at a festival.

The *choregia* was central to the organization and funding of the dramatic *festivals in Athens and its demes. The actors were appointed and remunerated separately by the *polis*, but the chorus involved the main part of the expense in these productions. In the City *Dionysia choruses were required for each kind of performance: five for comedy (with 24 *choreutai* in each), three for tragedy and satyr-play (see SATYRIC DRAMA) (12 or 15 *choreutai*) and ten each for the two categories of *dithyramb, men's and boys' (50 *choreutai*). The competition at these festivals was as much between rival *choregoi* and their choruses as between poets, and the efforts of a *choregos* could crucially affect the success of a dramatic entry.

The history of the *choregia* roughly corresponds with the period of Athenian *democracy. *Choregoi* for dithyramb at the City Dionysia were chosen by the ten *phylai* ('tribes') and the *chorēgos* represented his tribe in the competition. *Choregoi* for tragedy and, until the mid-4th cent., for comedy at the City Dionysia were appointed by the archon, for the *Lenaea by the *basileus* (see ARCHONTES), from the richest Athenians liable for the duty. Thereafter comic *choregoi* were chosen by the tribes. *Choregoi* were chosen several months in advance of the next festival; this allowed for a long period of training and perhaps also for the possibility that a *chorēgos* might claim exemption or undertake an *antidosis. No one could be required to perform a major liturgy such as a *choregia* in two consecutive years, though rich men eager to secure the goodwill of their fellow citizens might volunteer to serve beyond what was officially required. In his speech *Against Meidias* *Demosthenes (2) presents himself as having saved the honour of his tribe by volunteering as its dithyrambic *choregos* after it had failed to appoint one for two years running. *Choregoi* belonged to the highest socio-economic tier, roughly one per cent of the citizen population. The sums spent on *choregiai* show that the duty could elicit vast expenditure. One extremely enthusiastic *choregos* catalogues a list which represents an outlay of nearly two and a half talents. This includes a dithyrambic *choregia* at the Little *Panathenaea for 300 drachmae, and a tragic *choregia* for 3,000 dr. The latter figure is roughly ten times what a skilled worker might have earned annually. This was probably for the City Dionysia, whose prestige encouraged lavish outlay, and where the tragic *choregia* covered the costs for a group of three tragedies and a satyr-play. In the same passage a comic *choregia* is said to have had 1,600 dr. spent on it, 'including the dedication of the equipment'. A *choregia* for dithyramb at the City Dionysia, with its 50 *choreutai*, was likely to be a costly undertaking. The system was also widely adopted for festivals in the Attic *demes (esp. the Rural Dionysia), though on a much smaller scale of expenditure.

Once chosen, the first duty of the *choregos* was to recruit the members of his chorus. Participation in choruses was confined to citizens, although it seems that *metics were allowed to participate as *choreutai* and *choregoi* at the smaller and less prestigious Lenaea. For dithyramb, *choreutai* were drawn from the *choregos'* own tribe; for tragedy and comedy they were probably selected from the citizen body as a whole; *choreutai* known for their skill must have been esp. sought after. A *choregos* had some legal powers to facilitate recruitment, at least in the case of a boys' chorus, where parents may have been reluctant to hand over their son to the charge of the *choregos*. In the 4th cent. the *choregos* for such a chorus was required to be over 40 years of age. The *choregos* provided a place for the training of the chorus, and sometimes an expert trainer, who might be the poet himself. The *choregos* was also responsible for the maintenance of his *choreutai* and for the provision of the masks and costumes of the chorus. In comedy *choregoi* are sometimes reviled for their meanness. However, costumes afforded an opportunity for ostentatious display by the *choregos*: Demosthenes provided his 50 *choreutai* with gold crowns and robes. Dramatic *choregoi* may also have been called on to furnish 'extras' and a secondary chorus when needed. Such arrangements were doubtless made in close consultation with the poets to whom the *choregoi* chosen for a festival were assigned by lot. In dithyramb, where the musical accompaniment was esp. important, the *choregoi* may have drawn lots for the choice of piper.

A victorious *choregos* in dithyramb received a bronze tripod from the *polis* which he frequently erected, often as part of a more elaborate monument, in a public place such as the street called 'Tripods' or near the theatre. It is not clear whether victorious *choregoi* in drama received any prize beyond an ivy crown, but the spirit of competition and the desire for honour (*see* PHILOTIMIA) were so strong among *choregoi* that the glory of a victory was its own reward. Winners in drama often erected a commemorative inscription and may have commissioned to mark the occasion vases of the kind that survive with images related to theatrical productions. These could also serve as commemorations of the victory-celebration which a victorious *choregos* was expected to give his 'team'. The *choregia* was at once a legal obligation on the rich and an opportunity for its performers to acquire a high public profile. Rich men would cite their glorious *choregiai* and other liturgies in public speeches with the explicit expectation of being shown political or forensic favour in return. On the other hand, some of the rich saw the system as a means of popular extortion. The *Old Oligarch complains that the *demos* (people) has spoilt musical activities, and demands to be paid for its performances, an indication that *choregoi* may have been expected to remunerate their *choreutai* with direct cash payment and not simply maintenance. Yet service as *choregos* could also be a way of garnering glory at the expense of one's fellows in a fiercely competitive arena before a large civic audience. The stories of the *choregiai* of *Alcibiades indicate a desire for self-display and recognition that shows itself in behaviour of an aristocratic and anti-democratic nature—such

as the wearing of *purple robes and the physical assault of a fellow competitor.

Throughout the 4th cent., social and economic strains put pressure on the system. Doubts were raised about the value of the enormous expenditure on *choregiai* in view of the competing needs of military funding and in the absence of imperial revenue. In *c.*310 *Demetrius (1) of Phaleron abolished the system of competitive *choregiai*.

Christianity Christianity began as a Jewish (see RELIGION, JEWISH) sect and changed its relationship with the Jewish community at a time when both groups were affected by later *Hellenism. The first followers of Jesus lived under the Roman empire, which regarded Jews as singular. The senate had recognized in *Herod (1) the Great (confirmed as king of Judaea in 40 BC) a useful ally against opponents of Roman expansion. The Jews, monotheists, for whom race and religion ware closely linked, survived in the Roman context only because exceptions were made: suspending in this instance a characteristic readiness to absorb the religion of an alien people, Rome allowed the Jews a controlled political independence in several territories (although Judaea itself, after Herod's death, passed under direct administration).

Many Jews lived willingly with resulting contradictions. Now the encroachment of Rome gave new edge to revulsion from the Gentile world, and the frequent brutality of the conquerors strengthened the hand of those more dubious about the benefits of alliance.

Jesus lived, therefore, in a divided Palestine. The rule of Rome and the fortunes of her Jewish allies seemed secure; but the cruelty of Herod had kept alive strong forces of resistance and revolt. One must ask where Jesus stood on issues of religious and political loyalty, although his native Galilee was subject to a *tetrarch rather than a Roman governor during his lifetime.

It is likely that Jesus reflected several tendencies in the Judaism of his day. Followers saw him variously as a holy man, wonder-worker, and prophet. He emphasized the imminent ending of the visible world and the judgement of God upon it. He promoted also a sense of liberty, to be enjoyed by those willing to repudiate family and career, and he taught that sins might be forgiven. That, and the number of his followers in the volatile atmosphere of *Jerusalem at pilgrimage time, was enough to set him at odds with the Jewish high-priestly establishment, wedded to the social order required by Rome.

Those who had not known Jesus well, if at all, were less simple and less dramatic in their interpretations. The NT reveals how they broadened the religious context within which he was seen as significant, in pagan as well as Jewish terms. They also postponed the consummation he had seemed to herald. Partly as a consequence, they felt it proper to debate the value and authority of the Roman dispensation and the contrasting force of Jewish tradition. They also passed judgement on the Temple. In spite of strident voices defending the unique and separate quality of their life, some elements of the religious practice of the Jews invited comparison with *pagan-ism: blood *sacrifice, priesthood, ritual purity.

At a time, therefore, when Jews were divided over the nature of their privilege and separation, one group among them began actively to seek recruits among the Gentiles (see PAUL, ST). Distance from other Jews was not achieved simply. The destruction of the Temple in AD 70, occurring in the midst of the earliest Christian readjustment, was built into the Church's founding documents. The Jewish revolts of 115–117 and 132–135, however, attracted little Christian comment. The Church's distinctiveness, by then, was more obvious. Christian texts with a strong Jewish flavour gave way to more deliberate competition for both respectability and a claim on the past. The apologist *Justin Martyr (d. c.165), while defending his new religion against the Roman élite, asserted also against Jews Gentile claims to the heritage of Israel.

*Origen established in the next generation a new style of dialogue with Jews, all in pursuit of his own biblical research. The Jews in Palestine had by that time acquired new confidence, after the disasters of 66–73 and 132–135. Their rabbinic leaders had completed the publication of the Mishnah (a collection of legal opinions that became the foundation document of rabbinic Judaism); and, under the leadership of a Patriarch, a disciplined community had been established, contrasting markedly with enduring elements of Hellenistic Jewry elsewhere. Origen's purpose was to demonstrate in Christianity the fulfilment of OT prophecy.

The full sense of a seamless inclusion of the OT within the Christian tradition came with *Eusebius of Caesarea (c.260–c.340). His History of the Church contributed much to a sense of continuity between the orthodox Christians of Constantine's reign and the faith and practice of the Apostolic age; his Preparation of the Gospel and Demonstration of the Gospel are no less significant for their Christian appropriation of the Hebrew past.

Christianity presented itself from an early stage as a universal religion. It did not merely invite adherence but demanded it: all men and women were thought able to achieve their destiny only within its embrace. One possible response to so aggressive an invitation was resentment; and here we touch upon the 'persecution' of Christianity by the Roman state. Legal proceedings against the Church were intermittent and often moderate; violent demonstrations outside the law were unusual. The heroism revered in the Acts of the Martyrs seems to have been invited as often as it was imposed. Nevertheless, we find occasional confrontation. The famous attack by *Nero on Christians in Rome in 64 had no lasting significance. More generally significant in political terms may have been the situation described in *Pliny the Younger's letters of 112; but *Trajan's insistence on the observance of legal procedure and the avoidance of harassment says as much as his governor's distaste. Christians in that period may have attracted suspicion partly through a presumed association with rebellious Jews. As the political hopes of the Jews began to fade, Christians were exposed as possible enemies of the state in their own right. It was then that famous martyrs such as Justin made their names. It was not, however, until the middle of the 3rd cent. that forceful opposition was sanctioned by central authority but the growing strength of the Church made it less susceptible to intolerance.

Throughout the earlier period, several paradoxes had been laid bare, connected with the universal vision of the Church, the analogous breadth of Rome's claims to government, and its desire to tolerate nevertheless a variety of religious beliefs and practices. State and Church faced similar problems: how should one balance universalist demands and individual variety? The state's solution was to demand, in the interest of unity, a minimum but inescapable conformity in religious practice, and to display, when it came to controlling belief, a prudent reticence. The devotee of an alien cult should not oppose, at least, the gods of Rome. The difference between loyalty to the empire and enthusiasm for local deities was more easily made clear with the growth of the imperial (*ruler-) cult (which called for the simplest obeisance) and the extension of citizenship by the Antonine *Constitution of 212. Christians resolutely branded that policy a subterfuge, demanding particular rights for what they thought of in their case as absolute values.

chronology   See CALENDARS; CLOCKS; ECLIPSES; TIME-RECKONING.

Chrȳsēis, in *Homer's *Iliad* the daughter of Chrȳsēs, priest of *Apollo at Chrȳsē in *Troas, who has been captured and awarded to *Agamemnon. On Agamemnon's refusal to let Chryses ransom her, Apollo sends a plague on the Greek camp. *Calchas explains the situation and Chryseis is returned, but Agamemnon takes Achilles' concubine Brīsēis for himself, thus causing *Achilles' anger.

Chrȳsippus, of Soli (c.280–207 BC), succeeded *Cleanthes as head of the Stoa in 232 (see STO-ICISM). He came to Athens c.260 and studied in the sceptical *Academy, learning the importance of argument for and against given positions. He studied under Cleanthes and adopted the Stoic position, defending it voluminously. He is said to have told Cleanthes that he needed only to know the positions, and would provide the proofs himself. Another saying has it that 'if there had been no Chrysippus, there would have been no Stoa'; his extensive writings (we have a partial list in *Diogenes (4) Laertius) argued for all aspects of Stoicism so competently that his position became Stoic orthodoxy, eclipsing earlier Stoics other than *Zeno (2), whose views Chrysippus took pains to preserve and explain. Through him Stoicism became a well-argued position, with extensive resources for debate on many fronts. He esp. developed Stoic logic.

churches (early Christian)   The first Christians met in the private houses of the faithful. Gradually, as local Christian communities became more numerous and richer, they might acquire their own church-houses, using them specifically as places of worship and for other religious activities, such as the granting of charity and the instruction of converts. Externally these buildings looked just like other private houses, though internally they might be adapted for their new function, e.g. by combining rooms to create a large enough space for worship. Before the conversion of Constantine I, and his conquest of the empire between 312 and 324, some Christian communities may already have commissioned halls specifically for worship, and certainly small shrines, such as the 2nd-cent. *aedicula* over the supposed tomb of St Peter in Rome (see VATICAN), were already being built over the bodies of martyrs.

However, the accession of an emperor with Christian sympathies and the granting of secur-ity, wealth, and privileged status to the Church transformed church-building. Large buildings were constructed inside towns, to serve as halls of worship for the rapidly expanding Christian community, and outside, to glorify the shrines of martyrs and to serve as the focus for Christian burial-grounds. In Rome itself massive investment by Constantine rapidly gave the city one huge intramural church (St John Lateran) and a string of martyr-churches outside the walls including St Peter's.

The Christians wished their buildings to look different from pagan shrines, and their principal need was for large halls that could contain many people worshipping together, unlike pagan *temples, with a focal point for rituals involving few people at a time. The principal influence on early Christian architecture was, therefore, the *basilica. Christian basilicas varied greatly in detail, but all shared the aim of containing many people at one time, with an architectural, decorative, and liturgical focus on one end of the building, where the clergy officiated at the altar (which in many cases was sited over the body of a saint).

Probably because more happened inside churches than inside temples, decoration tended to be mainly internal. Many late antique churches, like S. Vitale in *Ravenna, are plain structural shells on the outside, but inside are lavishly decorated with marble fittings, veneer, and floor- and wall-mosaics; and would once also have been filled with gold and silver plate and fittings, and with drapes of precious fabrics.

Cicero   See TULLIUS CICERO (1), MARCUS.

Cimon   (Gk. *Kimōn*), rich and noble 5th-cent. BC Athenian, son of *Miltiades and the daughter of the Thracian king Olorus; Cimon and *Thucydides (2), son of an Olorus, were thus related. His sister Elpinícē married *Callias (1); an *ostrakon* (see OSTRACISM) alleges *incest between them ('let Cimon take his sister Elpinice and get out'). He married an *Alcmaeonid. His sons were: Lacedaemonius, Oulios, Thettalus, pro-grammatic names (he was *proxenos* for Sparta and Thessaly). On Miltiades' death in 489 he paid his 50-talent fine. He joined an embassy to Sparta in 479 and thereafter was often *strategos*. In 478 he helped *Aristides bring the maritime Greeks into the Delian League and commanded most of its operations 476–463. He drove *Pausanias (1) out of *Byzantium; captured Eion-on-Strymon from the Persians (?476/5); and conquered Scȳros, expelling the Dolopians (pirates), installing a *cleruchy, and bringing back the 'bones of *Theseus' to Athens. Cimon's greatest achievement was the *Eurymedon victory over Persia, c.466; this brought places as far east as Phaselis into the league. Next he subdued Thracian *Chersonese and reduced revolted *Thasos in 465–463, but was prosecuted on his *euthyna by *Pericles for allegedly accepting bribes from *Alexander (1) I of Macedon; he was acquitted. He next persuaded Athens to send him (462) with a large hoplite force to help Sparta against the *helots, now in revolt. But the Athenians were sent humiliatingly home on suspicion of 'revolutionary tendencies', and Cimon's *ostracism followed (461). The exact connection between this and *Ephialtes' reforms is obscure, but Cimon was no hoplite conservative. True, he spent lavishly on entertainments and public works, as part of rivalry with radical leaders like *Themistocles, Ephialtes, and *Pericles. Again, after his ostracism his pro-Spartan policy was abandoned. But despite personal ties and sympathies with Sparta he was no enemy of the democracy or the empire: Eurymedon was as much the achievement of the naval *thetes as of hoplites; hoplites and thetes admittedly competed for military glory in the post-Persian War period, but both were excluded from top office until 458; so that opposition is unreal; Sparta at least saw Cimon and his hoplites as revolutionaries, i.e. compromised by the reforms hatching back home; and Cimon approved the Ionian propaganda of the empire, expanded it as much as Pericles, and like him forcibly opposed secession from it.

In 457 Cimon tried to help fight for Athens against Sparta at Tanagra but was rebuffed and not yet recalled from ostracism. When he did return at the end of the 450s, he arranged a five-year truce with Sparta and fought Persia on Cyprus, where he died.

Cinna See CORNELIUS CINNA.

Circē, powerful sorceress of mythology, daughter of *Helios. *Homer places her island of Aeaea at the extreme east of the world, but as early as *Hesiod she is associated also with the west and often placed at Monte Circeo on the coast of *Latium. In the Odyssey, Circe transforms a group of *Odysseus' men into pigs (though they retain human intelligence); Odysseus rescues them by resisting the goddess's magic, thanks to the power of the plant 'mōly' which *Hermes gives him. Odysseus and his men stay with her for a year, after which she dispatches them to the Underworld to consult *Tiresias. On their return she gives them more detailed instructions on how to confront the perils of the homeward journey. In the Telegony (see EPIC CYCLE), her son by Odysseus, Telegonus, accidentally killed his father when raiding Ithaca, and she herself married *Telemachus. Moralists often interpreted Circe as a symbol of luxury and wantonness, the pursuit of which turns men into beasts.

circus, the Roman arena for chariot-racing. The most important at Rome was the Circus Maximus (c.650 × 125 m.: c.711 × 137 yds.), in the valley between the Palatine and Aventine, traditionally founded in the regal period and progressively adorned during the republic. The distinctive form with parallel sides and one semi-circular end fitted with tiered seating, and with twelve starting-gates at the open end, was created under *Caesar and preserved in the monumental rebuilding by *Trajan. The area was divided into two tracks by a long central barrier, marked at the ends with conical turning-posts and decorated with Augustus' obelisk and other monuments, including the movable eggs and dolphins which marked the ends of the seven laps in each race. Four, six, eight or twelve teams of horses competed under different colours, red and white at first, then also green and blue. Other circuses at Rome included the Circus Flaminius in the *Campus Martius, formalized c.220 BC but without permanent seating, and the Vatican Circus of *Gaius (1) and *Nero, the site of Christian martyrdoms, close to the later St Peter's basilica. Best preserved is the Circus of Maxentius outside the city on the via Appia, dedicated in AD 309. Circuses are found elsewhere in Italy and in many parts of the empire. See HORSE- AND CHARIOT-RACES.

Cisalpine Gaul See GAUL (CISALPINE).

citharode, a singer to his own lyre-playing. See MUSIC, 3.

cities See POLIS; URBANISM.

citizenship, Greek Greek citizenship stemmed from the fusion of two elements, (a) the notion of the individual state as a 'thing' with boundaries, a history, and a power of decision, and (b) the notion of its inhabitants participating in its life as joint proprietors. The first element was a product of the various processes of state formation which eroded personal chieftainship by centralizing power and exercising it through a growing number of offices or magistracies with limited length of tenure: at first denoted by an extended use of the word *polis, it later engendered the more abstract term *polīteia*, 'polity', 'constitution', or 'commonwealth'. The second element developed from the informal but ineradicable roles which *epic already portrays as being played in communal life by the *demos (the territory or settlement and its inhabitants) and the *lāos* (the people in roles—esp. military— and relationships): reflected in various ways in early texts, it was formalized in the word *polītēs* (citizen) and in the assembly (*ekklesia*) as an institution. The fusion of the two elements was expressed in the fundamental phrase 'to have a share in the polity'. It implied that all citizens shared in public responsibilities (deciding, fighting, judging, administering, etc.) and in public privileges (access to land, distributions, or power) as if they were shareholders in a company.

Political pressures and political theory crystallized round the questions 'Should shares be equal?' and 'Who should be a citizen?'. Aspirations towards equality, opposed by *oligarchs, were expressed by terms such as *homoioi* ('peers', full Spartiates), *isēgoria* ('freedom to speak in assembly'), and *isonomia* ('equality of political rights'), by the diffusion of power among the citizenry, and by the notion of 'ruling and being ruled by turns' which shaped *Aristotle's functional definition of citizenship. So, the boundary between citizen and non-citizen needed explicit definition. Some formulations admitted all free residents, as *Cleisthenes' (2) reform in Athens probably did. Others required descent from a real or imagined founder or group, and therefore emphasized legitimacy of birth. Others envisaged 'those best able to serve (the city) financially and physically', or (as in Sparta) disfranchised those unable to contribute fully to the common table. Such formulations tended to equate citizenship with four abilities—to fight, to vote (in assembly and lawcourt), to hold office, to own land—and thereby to make citizen bodies into closed, privileged, all-male corporations, outside which lay various inferior or adjunct statuses such as *perioikoi* ('dwellers-round'), *metoikoi* (*metics), and *apeleutheroi* (*freedmen). For female citizenship in Athens, see STATUS, LEGAL AND SOCIAL, *Greek*.

citizenship, Roman In both the Greek and the Roman world in the Archaic period, it seems that communities were open to the arrival of people from elsewhere, at all social levels. Detailed rules for citizenship were developed in both civilizations, as the city evolved, in the 7th to 5th or 6th to 5th cents. BC. In the case of Rome, Roman citizenship clearly developed in dialogue with the citizenships of other Latin communities. It involved the observance of the Roman civil law; and the struggles of the plebeians gradually brought protection for citizens from magisterial *imperium.

At all events, Roman citizenship came to possess two features which distinguished it from *polis* citizenship and which later surprised Greek observers: the automatic incorporation of freed slaves of Romans into the Roman citizen body; and the ease with which whole communities of outsiders could be admitted as citizens. By the time that Rome faced the invasion of *Hannibal in 218, she had a long history of giving citizenship to Italian communities, either with the vote or without the vote (*sine suffrāgio*). (The latter communities were usually later granted the vote.) Apart from Roman communities of these two types and allies, *socii, Italy also contained numerous Latin communities, whose members shared a number of rights with Romans and whose citizenships were interchangeable with that of Rome, and vice versa, if the person concerned changed domicile. One of the rights shared with Romans was *conubium*. A child born to two Romans was a Roman; but so was a child born to a Roman father and a mother from a people possessing *conubium*. (See IUS LATII; LATINS; MUNICIPIUM.)

All citizens, after the abolition of the ban on *conubium* between patricians and plebeians, had *conubium*; they were also liable to *tributum and military service. If they had the vote, they were also eligible to stand for magistracies.

In the course of the 2nd cent., grants of citizenship dried up, except for a few communities *sine suffragio* granted the vote; and Rome sought also to restrict the access of Latins to Roman citizenship. Attempts were made to respond to the desire of Latins and Italians alike for citizenship, by *Fulvius Flaccus in 125, by Gaius *Sempronius Gracchus in 122, and by *Livius Drusus in 91. The failure of Flaccus provoked the revolt of Fregellae; and when the last attempt failed, most of the allies went to war with Rome to achieve their end, the so-called *Social War; and in order to ensure the loyalty of the rest, as also of the Latins, who had for the most part remained loyal, Rome granted them citizenship by the *lex Iulia* of 90. Citizenship was in fact also extended to former rebels. By the time of *Sulla, Italy south of the Po (*Padus) and former Latin colonies north of the Po were

Roman; actual registration in the Roman *census, however, remained very incomplete.

The last generation of the Roman republic and the Civil War which followed witnessed demands for citizenship in those areas of Italy which still did not have it—demands which were satisfied by *Caesar—and the increasing spread of citizenship overseas as a reward for service of one kind or another. In the established imperial system, Roman citizens enjoyed in theory and often in practice protection against the *imperium* of a provincial governor, and a relatively favourable tax status.

Roman citizenship continued to spread, for three main reasons. (1) Communities were granted Latin status and their magistrates automatically acquired Roman citizenship, a right which was probably created after the Social War for new Latin communities north of the Po. (2) Citizenship was granted to auxiliaries (see AUXILIA) and their families on discharge. (3) Legionaries were supposed to be recruited among citizens only, but were clearly also recruited among provincials and deemed to be citizens. Their families on their discharge—between *Augustus and *Septimius Severus serving soldiers could not marry—if their wives were of citizen status, helped to spread Roman citizenship. (4) In the east, from *Pompey on, citizenship was conferred on individuals, typically members of the provincial city-élites.

Citizenship was finally granted to virtually all the free population of the empire by *Caracalla, in the so-called Antonine *constitution. But by this time, the right to vote had long disappeared; provincial Romans had lost their exemption from taxation; and many of the most important personal privileges of citizenship had been restricted to the élite, the *honestiores, as opposed to the humiliores. And thereafter the essential distinction was between slave and free, and, within those who were free, between honestiores and humiliores.

Civil Wars, Roman See ROME, HISTORY.

cīvitās, 'citizenship, citizen community' (for the first, see CITIZENSHIP, ROMAN), term of Roman administrative law referring, like Greek *polis, to any free-standing community, and specifically, in the imperial period, to the lowest grade of autonomous member-community of the provincial empire. In areas of the empire newly under Roman rule (as often in Gaul, Britain, Spain, and Africa in the early empire) such a civitas formed from a local ethnic unit,

had a citizenry, council and magistrates, and a set of procedural rules adaptable to local custom. In many cases there was also encouragement to form a city to provide a physical setting for the new institutions. The next step might be the grant of full municipal status (see MUNICIPIUM). Meanwhile, the civitas could be relied on to carry out the *census and collect taxes, and its officials became the connection with representatives of the Roman state such as governors or procurators.

Claros, *oracle and grove of *Apollo belonging to the city of Colophon. The oracle appears to have been founded by the 8th cent. BC. The *sanctuary was discovered 1907, and excavation turned up the oracular chamber under the temple and numerous inscriptions relating to its operation. From these inscriptions and literary texts, we know that there were 'sacred nights' upon which the consultations would take place, when there would be a procession of consultants to the temple of Apollo with sacrifices and singing of hymns. Consultants would then hand over questions to the priests, who would descend into the innermost sanctuary to a place outside the room in which the divine spring flowed. Within this room the thespiōdos ('oracular singer'), a man, would drink from the spring and utter his responses to the questions of each consultant. These would then be written down in verse by the 'prophet' and delivered to the consultants. Claros was a major oracular site from roughly the 3rd cent. BC to the mid-3rd cent. AD.

classicism The modern use of 'classicism' to refer either to the art and literature of a period held to represent a peak of quality, or to the conscious imitation of works of such a period, derives from *Cornelius Fronto's use of classicus (lit. 'belonging to the highest class of citizens') to denote those ancient writers whose linguistic practice is authoritative for imitators. The possibility of designating a period as 'classical', and of the consequent appearance of 'classicizing' movements, arises with the Hellenistic consciousness of the present as set off from, but heir to, a great past tradition, and with the self-conscious development of a theory of imitation (see IMITATIO). A full-blown classicizing movement emerges in 1st-cent. BC Rome, fostered by Greek writers like *Dionysius (3) of Halicarnassus who champion *Thucydides (2) as a model for historians and argue for the superiority of 'Attic' over 'Asianic' rhetorical models (see

ASIANISM AND ATTICISM); in the visual arts there is a parallel movement to imitate Greek models of the 5th and 4th cents. BC. In modern scholarship 'Classical' has been used as a period term (often with evaluative overtones), opposed to 'Archaic', 'Hellenistic', 'baroque', etc., to refer esp. to the art and literature of 5th- and 4th-century BC Athens and of late republican and Augustan Rome.

classis A *classis* ('class') was a group of Roman citizens who could meet a certain minimum wealth qualification. Servius Tullius (see REX) is supposed to have divided property owners into five *classēs* for military purposes. The first three classes were equipped as heavy infantry, the last two as light-armed skirmishers. This system, together with the monetary values given in our sources to the levels of wealth required for membership of the various classes, cannot be earlier than *c.*400 BC.

In early times, then, the term *classis* signified Rome's armed forces; a vestige of this survived in the later use of *classis (nāvālis)* to mean 'navy'. The cognate term *classicus* ('belonging to the first rank') gives us the modern word 'classical' (see CLASSICISM).

The later republican division into five classes was instituted for fiscal purposes, as a means of taxing citizens on a sliding scale according to their wealth (see TRIBUTUM), and as the basis for distributing citizens into voting units in the *comitia centuriata*. By that time the army was recruited indiscriminately from all those who could meet the minimum property qualification for membership of the fifth class, a qualification that seems to have been reduced at various stages during the 2nd cent. BC until the time of *Marius.

Claudia Octavia, daughter of *Claudius and *Valeria Messallina, b. by AD 40. She was betrothed in 49 to *Iulia Agrippina's son Domitius Ahenobarbus (*Nero), whom she married in 53. Nero, who disliked and neglected her, divorced her in 62 for sterility in order to marry *Poppaea Sabina, and sent her to live in Campania under military surveillance. When a rumour that she had been reinstated provoked demonstrations of popular approval, he contrived fresh charges, banished her to Pandateria, and soon had her put to death. For the *praetexta* on her fate, see OCTAVIA.

Claudius (Tiberius Claudius Nero Germānicus), (10 BC–AD 54), Roman emperor,

was born at *Lugdunum, the youngest child of Nero *Claudius Drusus the Elder and of *Antonia (2). Hampered by a limp, trembling, and a speech defect, and by continual illnesses, he received no public distinction from Augustus beyond the augurate, and was twice refused a magistracy by Tiberius. Claudius retained *equestrian status until on 1 July 37 he became suffect consul with his young nephew, the emperor *Gaius (1); for the rest of the reign he received little but insults. After the assassination of Gaius he was discovered in the palace by a soldier, taken to the *praetorian barracks, and proclaimed emperor while the senate was still discussing the possibility of restoring the republic. Senators did not easily forgive him for the way he came to power, but he had the support of the army. Claudius stressed his bond with guard and legions and, making up for previous inexperience, briefly took a personal part in the invasion of *Britain (43). The capture of *Camulodunum occasioned an impressive pageant, and Claudius made a leisurely progress back to Rome for his triumph (44). (Britain was never to be fully conquered, and in the long run its garrison of three legions was a strategic waste.) By the end of his principate he had received 27 *acclamations as *imperator.* He was also consul four more times, and revived the office of censor, which he held with Lucius *Vitellius in 47–48.

Although he reverted from the absolutism of Gaius (whose acts, however, were not annulled wholesale), and stressed civility to the senate, the precariousness of his position made him liable to take sudden and violent action against threats real, imagined by himself, or thought up by advisers; offenders who were given a trial were often heard by few advisers in private. His early career and mistrust of the senate led him to rely on the advice of freedmen, esp. *Narcissus and *Antonius Pallas, whose influence and wealth were hated; but his dependence on his third and fourth wives *Valeria Messallina and *Iulia Agrippina was due as much to their political importance as to uxoriousness. Messallina was the mother of his only surviving son *Britannicus, b. 41 (Claudius' earlier wives left him with only a daughter). She was hard to dislodge for that reason, but fell in 48, in what looks like a struggle between freedmen on the one hand and senators and equestrians on the other. Agrippina, daughter of Claudius' popular brother *Germanicus, was a figure in her own right, and esp. desirable after the loss of face entailed by Messallina's fall. The son she brought with her was older than Britannicus, and in 50 he was adopted by Claudius as a partner for his own son to assure their joint accession to power; in 53 Nero married Claudius' daughter *Claudia Octavia. But while Nero's career was accelerated, with a grant of proconsular power outside Rome coming in 51, Britannicus was pushed aside. Claudius' death in 54 conveniently made it impossible for him to give his natural son the *toga of manhood, but the story that he was poisoned by Agrippina has been questioned.

In youth Claudius wrote historical works. He was steeped in religion and tradition, but his celebration of the *Secular Games (47), and extension of the *pomerium had the political purpose of reassuring the Roman people about the stability and success of his regime. Claudius was attentive to the welfare of the urban populace. Building the harbour north of *Ostia intended to secure the corn supply, as was his offer of privileges to those who invested in building corn ships.

Claudius' interest in government, from which he had been excluded, inclined him to intervene whenever he found anything amiss, and he berated senators who failed to take an active part in debate. He was esp. interested in jurisdiction, and was indefatigable, if emotional and inconsistent, in dispensing justice. Legislation had clear aims: to discourage sedition; to protect inheritance within the clan and the rights of individual property owners; more 'liberal' measures increased the rights of slaves, women, and minors. Arguments for his legislation invoked traditional *mōrēs* and the upholding of status, but in his senatorial speech advocating the admission of Gauls to the senate, Claudius' preoccupation with the place of innovation in Roman life shows him coming to terms with changes in economy and society.

Claudius was noted for generosity with the citizenship, though his advisers also sold it without his knowledge. (See CITIZENSHIP, ROMAN.) A few widespread grants of Latin rights (see IUS LATII), along with his favourable response to the request of long-enfranchised Gallic chieftains for permission to stand for senatorial office (resented by existing senators), made him seem more generous than he was: proven merit was his own criterion for grants. His grant of additional jurisdiction to provincial *procurators, and the introduction of that title for equestrian governors of provinces, previously called 'prefects', relieved him of the job of hearing appeals and stressed the dependence of the governors upon their emperor.

Claudius added other provinces to the empire besides Britain, although that left few resources for an active policy against the Germans: the two Mauretanias, Lycia (43), and *Thrace (46); and he resumed overseas colonization. His dealings with Judaea and the *Parthians, however, were inept. In Judaea the procurators who replaced the deceased King Agrippa I in 44 proved unsatisfactory, and by 54 Claudius' eastern governors had allowed the Parthians to gain control of Greater Armenia, a serious blow to Roman prestige.

Claudius was deified on death, enhancing his adoptive son's prestige, but in Nero's early years the failings of the regime (influence of women and freedmen, corruption, trials held in private, the bypassing of the senate, favour to provincials), were excoriated: *Seneca the Younger's *Apocolocyntōsis* reveals the tone. Under *Vespasian a more balanced view prevailed and Claudius' temple was completed, but *Tacitus is merciless. His accession and survival, preserving the imperial peace, and his recognition of social changes were his main domestic achievements.

Claudius Atticus Hērōdēs, Tiberius, 'Herodes Atticus' (*c.* AD 101–177), Athenian sophist and benefactor of Greek cities, consul 143; friend of Marcus *Aurelius, whom he taught (along with *Verus). A controversial public figure, he quarrelled with *Fronto and the Quintilii brothers, governors of *Achaia, and was accused of 'tyranny' by Athenian enemies (174) before Marcus Aurelius, whose efforts to reconcile the two parties emerge from a long Athenian inscription; his gifts of buildings, esp. at Athens (see ATHENS, TOPOGRAPHY), were not always appreciated by fellow Greeks (see OLYMPIA). His declaiming style was straightforward, elegant, and restrained, and it influenced a wide circle of pupils. His works included lectures and diaries. *Philostratus made him the centrepiece of his *Lives of the Sophists*. See SECOND SOPHISTIC.

Claudius Caecus, Appius, censor 312 before holding other high office; consul 307 and 296, praetor 295: in the latter two years he fought in Etruria (see ETRUSCANS), *Campania, and *Samnium. In 280, now old and blind, he successfully opposed peace with *Pyrrhus (2) after the Roman defeat at Heraclea.

Claudius was the first live personality in Roman history. As censor, he commissioned the building of the *via Appia from Rome to *Capua and the first *aqueduct (aqua Appia). In drawing up the list of the senate he left out men regarded as superior to those included, even enrolling the sons of freedmen. He distributed the lower classes through all the rural tribes, thus increasing their influence in the tribal assembly; the move was reversed by the censors of 304 (see CENSOR; CENSUS).

Claudius Cogidubnus, Tiberius, *client king of the British Atrebates *c.* AD 43–75. *Tacitus notes his loyalty, rewarded by rule over additional *civitates*. An inscription from Chichester dedicating a temple to *Neptune and *Minerva records his title *Rex magnus Brit(anniae)*, 'Great King of Brit(ain)'. There are many signs of his successful philo-Roman policy. The Fishbourne villa may have been built for his old age. The *cīvitās Rēg(ī)nōrum* (see REG(I)NI) derives its name from his kingdom. See ROMANIZATION, *In the west*.

Claudius Drūsus, Nero, 38–9 BC, second son of Tiberius *Claudius Nero and *Livia Drusilla, younger brother of *Tiberius, later emperor. After Tiberius Nero's death in 33 he was brought up by Octavian. In 19 he was permitted to stand for magistracies five years before the legal ages, and in 18 was quaestor. In 15 with Tiberius he subdued the Raeti and Vindelici, and established the later via Claudia Augusta over the Alps into Italy. In 13, left in charge of the Three Gauls, he organized a census and on 1 August 12 founded an altar to Rome and Augustus at *Lugdunum. Augustus entrusted the conquest of Germany to him, while Tiberius subdued the Balkans (12–9). In 12, after routing two tribes that had raided Gaul, he sailed along a canal dug for the purpose, through the lakes into the sea, and won over the Frisii, who later helped him away when his ships were stranded. He began the year 11 in Rome as urban praetor, then marched as far as the Weser, leaving forts behind him. After celebrating an *ovatio and receiving *ornamenta triumphalia he attacked the Chatti in 10 as proconsul, and returned to Rome with Augustus and Tiberius. In 9 as consul he fought his way to the Elbe; but died in camp after falling from his horse. Tiberius reached him before his death.

Drusus' conquests were extensive and well garrisoned. The senate bestowed on him and his descendants the surname 'Germānicus'; but the achievements in Germany were largely swept away with *Quinctilius Varus in AD 9. He was popular, and his views considered 'republican'; Tiberius disclosed to Augustus a letter expressing them. He was buried in Augustus'

own mausoleum. An unknown poet wrote his mother the *Consōlātio ad Liviam*. His wife *Antonia (2) bore him *Germanicus—who, emulating his father, in AD 15–16 tried to recover Roman territory in Germany—*Livia Iulia, and *Claudius.

Claudius Marcellus (1), Marcus, one of Rome's most outstanding commanders, served in the First *Punic War, and thereafter became an *augur, curule aedile, and praetor. As consul in 222 BC he campaigned successfully against the Insubrian Gauls, and winning the *spolia opīma by killing the Gallic chief in single combat; with his colleague he captured Mediolanum; he celebrated a triumph. Marcellus played an important part in the war against *Hannibal; he supported the fundamental Fabian strategy (see FABIUS MAXIMUS VERRUCOSUS), but showed more initiative than Fabius in his willingness to engage Hannibal when a favourable opportunity arose. He held a second praetorship in 216, resisting Hannibal's attack on Nola. He was elected *suffect consul in 215, but abdicated when the augurs declared that his election had been faulty. Since he was replaced by Fabius and became consul the following year, he may have accepted his removal from office on the assurance of Fabius' support for 214. In both 215, when he received proconsular command, and in 214 he continued to resist Hannibal's attempts to take Nola, and in the latter year he and Fabius captured Casilinum. In the autumn of 214 he was appointed to command in Sicily, and in 213 began the siege of *Syracuse, which he captured in 212. Marcellus' treatment of the city was harsh, and he indulged his taste for Greek culture by carrying off to Rome many works of art (see BOOTY). After mopping-up operations against Carthaginian forces, he returned to Rome and celebrated an *ovatio. As consul in 210 and proconsul in 209 he was eager to bring Hannibal to a pitched battle; when he succeeded, he was defeated. In 208, consul yet again, he and his colleague were aiming to recapture Locri Epizephyrii, but were ambushed; Marcellus was killed immediately and Crispīnus fatally wounded.

Claudius Marcellus (2), Marcus, son of Claudius Marcellus and of *Octavia, sister of *Augustus, was born in 42 BC. In 25 he and *Tiberius served in Spain under Augustus, whose preference for Marcellus was shown by Marcellus' marriage in the same year to *Iulia (2); and in 24 a more rapid anticipation of the normal *cursus honorum* was decreed for Marcellus than for Tiberius. In 23, as *aedile, Marcellus gave esp. magnificent games. He began to be thought of as a rival to *Agrippa for the position of heir to the monarchy, and his ambition gave cause for concern, but he died late in 23. He was buried in Augustus' own mausoleum; Octavia named a library after him and Augustus a theatre. His death was lamented by Virgil and Propertius.

Claudius Nero, Tiberius was quaestor 48 and commanded *Caesar's fleet in the Alexandrian War (48–47). In 46 he was entrusted with the settlement of veterans in Narbonese Gaul (see GAUL (TRANSALPINE)). In 44, however, he proposed that Caesar's murderers should be rewarded. Praetor 41, he supported *Antonius (Pietas) against *Octavian, and took part in the defence of Perusia. Early in 40 he escaped, tried in vain to incite a slave-rising in *Campania, and joined Sextus *Pompeius in Sicily with his wife *Livia Drusilla and infant son *Tiberius, the future emperor. Later, disagreeing with Sextus, he joined Antony in Greece, and returned to Rome after the Pact of Mīsēnum (39). In January 38 Octavian persuaded him to divorce Livia so that he might marry her himself. His second son Nero *Claudius Drusus was born three months after the marriage.

clāvus angustus, lātus The *angustus clavus* was a narrow, the *latus clavus* a broad, purple upright stripe (possibly two stripes) stitched to or woven into the Roman tunic (see DRESS). The former indicated equestrian, the latter senatorial rank. Under the emperors the *latus clavus* was worn before admission to the senate, on the assumption of the *toga virilis, by sons of senators as a right. The *latus clavus* could also be granted by emperors to men of non-senatorial origin; the award of the *latus clavus* gave such men the right to stand for senatorial office. Military tribunes (*tribuni militum) in the legions were distinguished as *tribuni angusticlavii* or *tribuni laticlavii* according to whether they were pursuing an equestrian or senatorial career.

Cleanthēs of Assos (331–232 BC), student of *Zeno (2) and his successor as head of the Stoa (see STOICISM). His religious spirit is distinctive; after the writings of *Chrysippus had established a Stoic orthodoxy, this came to seem less central. We have a long fragment of his *Hymn to Zeus*, which allegorizes the active principle of Stoic physics and displays a distinctive use of *Heraclitean ideas. He was interested in the detail of Stoic physics, and wrote on the nature of the cosmos, stressing the role of *fire. His version of ethics uncompromisingly stressed the distinctive value of virtue and downplayed the importance of factors like pleasure. He denied the usefulness of moral rules unless based on an understanding of basic principles.

Cleisthenēs (1), of *Sicyon, the greatest tyrant of the family of Orthagoras, which ruled for the record period of a century (probably *c.*665–565 BC). His reign (*c.*600–570) was allegedly marked by a movement against the Argive *Dorian ascendancy (see ARGOS): the three traditional Dorian tribes (*phylai) were given derogatory names while the non-Dorian was called *Archelāoi* ('Rulers'); the competition between *rhapsodes was suppressed because Homer celebrated the deeds of the Argives, an Argive hero was replaced by a Theban, and a new festival of *Dionysus was established. His daughter Agaristē (mother of the Athenian *Cleisthenes (2)) married the *Alcmaeonid *Megacles after a year-long house party for her suitors. In the First *Sacred War Cleisthenes was prominent on the winning side: he destroyed the offending city, and won the chariot-race in the first *Pythian Games.

Cleisthenēs (2), Athenian politician, of the *Alcmaeonid family, son of *Megacles and Agaristē, daughter of *Cleisthenes (1) of *Sicyon. He was archon (see ARCHONTES) under the tyrant *Hippias (1) in 525/4 BC, but later in Hippias' reign the Alcmaeonids went into exile and put pressure on Sparta through the *Delphic oracle to intervene in Athens and overthrow the tyranny. In the power vacuum which followed, Cleisthenes and Isagoras were rivals for supremacy; Isagoras obtained the archonship for 508/7; but Cleisthenes appealed for popular support with a programme of reform. Isagoras appealed to King *Cleomenes I of Sparta, who came to Athens with a small force, invoked the hereditary curse of the Alcmaeonids, and forced Cleisthenes and others to withdraw; but he met with strong popular resistance and was forced to withdraw in turn, taking Isagoras with him. Cleisthenes returned, and his reforms were enacted and put into effect.

Cleisthenes' main achievement was a new organization of the citizen body. The four *Ionian tribes (*phylai) and other older units were deprived of political significance. For the future each citizen was to be a member of one of 139 local units called *demes (*dēmoi*, see DEMOS), and the demes were grouped to form 30 new *trittyes* ('thirds') and 10 new *phylai*; citizenship and the political and military organization of Attica were to be based on these units (e.g. *Solon's council, *boule, of 400 became a council of 500, with 50 members from each tribe and individual demes acting as constituencies). The main purpose of the reform was probably to undermine the old channels of influence (and perhaps to give the Alcmaeonids an advantageous position in the new system); its main appeal to the ordinary citizens was perhaps the provision of political machinery at local level; and working this machinery educated the citizens towards democracy. (See DEMOCRACY, ATHENIAN.) The institution of *ostracism is almost certainly to be attributed to Cleisthenes.

In the 5th cent. Cleisthenes came to be regarded as the founder of the democracy, but in the political disputes at the end of the century the democrats looked further back, to Solon or even to *Theseus.

Cleitarchus, historian of *Alexander (2) the Great. His work achieved great popularity. Its date was probably early (c.310 BC) and derived from first-hand information. Cleitarchus was the source of the so-called 'vulgate tradition' (the numerous passages of *Diodorus (2) Siculus, *Curtius Rufus, and Justin, which transmit the same information). This common tradition supplements and sometimes corrects the court-based account of *Arrian, notably in the vivid reports of the sieges of *Halicarnassus and *Tyre, and the detailed narrative of operations in central Asia. There was a propensity for scenes of slaughter and suffering, perhaps exaggerated but revealing more sensitivity to the human cost of conquest than Arrian's somewhat sanitized account.

Cleitus 'the Black' (d. 328 BC), Macedonian noble and brother of the wet-nurse of *Alexander (2) the Great, commanded the royal Squadron of Companions (see HETAIROI) and saved Alexander's life at the *Granicus. In 330 he was raised to the command of the entire Macedonian cavalry alongside the royal favourite, *Hephaestion. Alienated by the absolutist trends at court, he lost control at a *symposium, criticizing the king's divine aspirations and the fashionable denigration of *Philip II, and was struck down by Alexander in a paroxysm of drunken fury. The murder became a standard example of royal excess in rhetoric and popular philosophy (see ALCOHOLISM).

Clement of Alexandria was born c. AD 150, probably at Athens and of pagan parents. He was converted to *Christianity and after extensive travels to seek instruction from Christian teachers received lessons from Pantaenus, whose catechetical school in *Alexandria was then an unofficial institution giving tuition to converts. Clement affects a wide acquaintance with Greek literature, since his writings abound in quotations from *Homer, *Hesiod, the dramatists, and the Platonic and Stoic philosophers. His *Protrepticus* (see below) is a copious source of information about the Greek *mysteries, though his wish to represent them as a perversion of Scriptural teachings must have led to misrepresentation. After ordination he succeeded Pantaenus as head of the school some time before 200, and held the office till 202, when, on the eve of the persecution under *Septimius Severus, he fled Alexandria. Clement died between 211 and 216.

His *Protrepticus* or 'Hortatory Address to the Greeks' (c.190) is designed to prove the superiority of Christianity to pagan cults and way of life. His *Paedagogus* or 'Tutor' (c.190–192) is an exposition of the moral teaching of Christ, not only in general, but also with application to such details as eating, drinking, dress, and use of money.

Cleobis and **Bitōn,** the two Argive brothers (see ARGOS) mentioned by *Solon to *Croesus, in *Herodotus' story, as among the happiest of mortals. Their mother, presumably a priestess of *Hera, found that her oxen had not been brought in time for a festival, and they drew her cart the 45 stades (c.8 km.: 5 mi.) to the temple. She prayed to the goddess to grant them the greatest boon possible for mortals, and Hera caused them to die while they slept in the temple. The Argives honoured them with statues at *Delphi.

Cleomenēs I, Agiad king of Sparta (reigned c.520–490 BC), son of Anaxandridas II by a second, bigamous union. His long, activist reign was one of the half-dozen most influential on record. He pursued an adventurous and at times unscrupulous foreign policy aimed at crushing *Argos and extending Sparta's influence both inside and outside the Peloponnese. It was during his reign, but not entirely according to his design, that the *Peloponnesian League came formally into existence. He embroiled *Thebes with Athens and frustrated Thebes' plans for a united *Boeotian federation by referring Plataea to Athens for alliance (probably in 519). He intervened twice successfully in Athenian affairs, overthrowing the tyranny of *Hippias (1) in 510 and expelling *Cleisthenes (2) in favour of Isagoras in 508. But his attempt to restore Isagoras by a concerted expedition of Sparta's Peloponnesian and central Greek allies in c.506 was frustrated by the opposition of the Corinthians and of his Eurypontid fellow king *Demaratus. In 494 Cleomenes defeated Argos at Sepeia near Tiryns and unscrupulously exploited his victory by burning several thousand Argive survivors to death in a sacred grove, for which impiety he was tried at Sparta and acquitted.

But he disliked overseas commitments, refusing to interfere in the affairs of *Samos (c.515), or to support the *Ionian Revolt (499); and he showed no certain awareness of the Persian danger before 491 when his attempt to punish *Aegina for *Medism was thwarted by Demaratus. He thereupon bribed the *Delphic oracle to declare Demaratus illegitimate and had him deposed, but the intrigue came to light and he fled Sparta, possibly to stir up revolt among the Arcadians. Recalled to Sparta, he met a violent end, perhaps at his own hands.

Clĕōn, Athenian politician, b. c.470 BC, the son of a rich tanner. He was perhaps involved in the attacks on *Pericles through his intellectual friends in the 430s, and in the opposition to Pericles' strategy of refusing battle against the invaders in 431. In 427 he proposed the decree (overturned the next day) to execute all the men of *Mytilene after the suppression of its revolt. In 426 he attacked the *Babylonians* of *Aristophanes as a slander on the state. In 425, after the Athenians had worsted the *Spartans at *Pylos, he frustrated their peace proposals and later accused the generals in charge of the siege of Sphaktēria of incompetence. When *Nicias offered to resign the command to him, he was obliged to take it. In co-operation with *Demosthenes (1), the general on the spot, he rapidly obtained the Spartans' surrender. In the same year he doubtless approved the measure increasing the tribute paid by the allied states; and he was responsible for increasing the jurors' pay from two to three obols. In 423 he proposed the decree for the destruction of *Scione and the execution of all its citizens. In 422, as general, he led an expedition to the Thraceward area, and recovered Torōnē, but he was defeated by *Brasidas and killed in a battle outside *Amphipolis.

We have a vivid picture of Cleon in *Thucydides (2) and Aristophanes, both of whom had reasons for disliking him. He was an effective, if vulgar, speaker, and seems to have been given to extravagant promises and extravagant accusations against opponents. He was a politician of a new kind, who was not from the old aristocracy, and whose predominance depended on persuasive speeches in the assembly and lawcourts rather than on regular office-holding; when he did serve as general, the undisputed facts include both successes and failures. See also DEMAGOGUES, DEMAGOGY.

Cleopatra VII (69–30 BC), the last and best known of the Ptolemies, was daughter of Ptolemy XII (Aulētēs, 'Piper'). On the latter's death in 51 she became queen, alone at first and later with her younger brothers, first Ptolemy XIII (who opposed Caesar) and then (47–45) with Ptolemy XIV. A joint reign with Ptolemy XV Caesar (Caesarion, reputedly Caesar's son) is recorded from 45 BC. She died by her own hand (and the bite of a royal asp) soon after Octavian (see AUGUSTUS) took Alexandria on 3 August 30.

Best known for her successful relations first with Caesar (Gaius *Iulius Caesar (1)), who besieged and captured Alexandria in 48–47, and later with Antony (Marcus *Antonius), following a colourful encounter at Tarsus in 41, she managed to increase her kingdom territorially in return for financial support. Internally Cleopatra was strong, using her position as pharaoh to gain backing from the people. An expert linguist, she was reportedly the first Ptolemy to have known Egyptian, and acc. to *Plutarch it was her conversation rather than her looks that explained her success.

The legend of Cleopatra has proved more powerful than her historical record. Her exploitation of Egyptian royal symbolism with its eastern tradition of luxury was used against her by her opponents; for Roman poets she was 'monster' and 'wicked woman'. Her visit to Rome in 46–44 achieved little but embarrassment for Caesar. Following his murder, her attempts to aid the Caesarians in 42 were thwarted by *Cassius, and by contrary winds. The summons to Tarsus by Antony followed. Her liaison with Antony formed the focus of Octavian's propaganda, based on fear of Egyptian wealth. Yet the skilful manipulation of power by this queen preserved Egypt from the direct rule of Rome longer than might otherwise have been the case. See ACTIUM; OCTAVIA.

Clĕōphon, Athenian politician, d. 404 BC. He is represented as a lyre-maker, and his mother was alleged to be Thracian (see THRACE). He was already a public figure at the time of the ostracism of *Hyperbolus, and was the most prominent *demagogue, in the manner of *Cleon, after the democratic restoration in 410. He introduced a payment of two obols a day, possibly to citizens not otherwise receiving public funds. He attacked both *Critias and *Alcibiades, and was opposed to peace with *Sparta both after Athens' victory at *Cyzicus in 410 and after her defeat at Aegospotami in 405 (see ATHENS, HISTORY). His elimination on a charge of treason paved the way for the peace settlement negotiated by *Theramenes.

cleruchy, a special sort of Greek colony (see COLONIZATION, GREEK) in which the settlers kept their original citizenship and did not form a completely independent community. In Classical Greek history the term is confined to certain Athenian settlements founded on conquered territory (Greek and non-Greek) from the end of the 6th cent. BC, esp. during the period of the *Delian League. It is often hard to decide whether a settlement of the 5th cent. is a cleruchy, as ancient authors do not always distinguish cleruchies from other colonies (see APOIKIA), and because it seems that colonists did not forfeit their Athenian citizenship any more than did cleruchs.

The numbers in a cleruchy varied from 4,000 (Chalcis) to 250 (Andros). Settlers each received an allotment which maintained them as *zeugitai*. The cleruchs probably resided in the cleruchies (rather than living in Athens as *rentiers*), and the cleruchies may sometimes have served the purpose of garrisons in addition to providing land for the poor. As Athenian citizens, cleruchs were liable for military service, paid war-tax (*eisphora*), and took part in religious activity at Athens.

cliens In Rome a client was a free man who entrusted himself to another and received protection in return. Clientship was a hereditary social status consecrated by usage and recognized, though not defined or enforced, by the law. The rules of the law were however binding in the special case of the freedman, who was *ipso facto* a client of his former owner (see FREEDMEN). Ordinary clients supported their patron (*patrōnus*) in political and private life, and demonstrated their loyalty and respect by going to his house to greet him each morning (*salūtātiō*), and attending him when he went out. The size of a man's clientele, and the wealth and status

of his individual clients, were a visible testimony to his prestige and social standing (and therefore to his political influence). In exchange clients received favours and benefits of various kinds, including daily subsistence in the form of food or money and assistance in the courts.

This reciprocal exchange of goods and services between persons of unequal social standing is only one facet of a much wider phenomenon in Roman society, in which power and status at all levels depended on personal connections and the trading of benefits and favours. At the level of the élite, Roman grandees dispensed huge sums of money to favoured protégés, and obtained administrative and military appointments for them through personal contacts with high-ranking public officials, above all from the emperor himself. In Rome political power and social prestige certainly depended on the manipulation of personal connections and the exchange of favours and benefits between individuals of unequal standing. On the other hand, in literary sources the parties to exchanges of benefits tend to refer to each other as friends (see AMICITIA), rather than as clients, which implied social inferiority. To be labelled '*cliens*' was hateful. In *Martial '*cliens*' effectively means parasite.

In the provinces Roman individuals and families built up large *clientēlae*: whole communities could become clients, and obtained access to the centre of power through the mediation of individual patrons.

client kings The term 'client kings' denotes a range of monarchs and quasi-monarchs of non-Roman peoples who enjoyed a relationship with Rome that was essentially harmonious but unequal. These were rulers under the patronage of the Roman state, but the less abrasive language of friendship (see AMICITIA) was the norm. The Roman state called such kings 'king and ally and friend', in a formal recognition by the senate. Grand ceremony seems often to have accompanied such recognitions, under republic and Principate alike.

From the 3rd cent. BC at the latest Rome developed such relationships with a view to consolidating or expanding her empire in Italy and beyond. *Hieron (2) II of Syracuse is often regarded as the first client king (c.263 BC), but he doubtless had predecessors. And Rome continued to build and maintain relationships with client kings throughout her history. Many kingdoms did indeed become provincial territory over the centuries, usually when Rome felt the need to step in to control local unrest: e.g. where kings failed to manage their succession, where a dynasty ended, or where local conditions had changed. See PROVINCIA, PROVINCE.

Client kingdoms were usually located at the margins of Roman control, whether on the edge of the empire or in an area which Rome would find difficult and expensive to administer directly. At the frontier, client kingdoms were important reservoirs of manpower, resources, and local knowledge. Rome expected client kings to meet her demands whenever she saw fit to make them, but client kings were not required to pay regular taxes. In return, client kings expected Rome to ensure their positions locally. The nearest Roman legions forestalled the movements of client kings' enemies, both internal and external, by their very presence. Where necessary, Roman forces came to the aid of client kings, who might ultimately take refuge on Roman territory. On occasion, Rome might prefer to come to an arrangement with the enemies of her client kings, but it was the unspoken promise of Roman support that kept client kings loyal to Rome (or loyal enough). One expression of that expectation was the occasional bequest by client kings of their kingdoms to Rome where no other acceptable successor was available to them (e.g. Attalus III of *Pergamum).

Client kings, like cities and others, exercised their relationship with Rome through more personal relations with leading individuals and families at Rome. Under the Principate such personal bonds continued to proliferate, but the emperor and his family now became the most attractive source of patronage for client kings, so that they became pre-eminent in royal relations as in all else. Augustus seems deliberately to have made kings more a part of the Roman empire, following a trend set esp. by *Caesar and Antony (Marcus *Antonius). Most client kings now held Roman citizenship: by AD 100 they had begun to enter the senate. They regularly sent their sons to grow up in Rome, preferably with the imperial family. *Augustus is said to have encouraged marriages among client royalty. In their kingdoms, client kings named their cities after the emperor or members of his family: they also celebrated the imperial (*ruler-) cult, and a few kings were priests of that cult. The ruling emperor was depicted on royal coinage. Coercion was not required: the relationship between client king and Rome, however unequal, was based upon mutual advantage.

climate The Mediterranean climate is characterized by cool, wet winters and hot, dry summers. There is a high degree of interannual climatic variability, which makes farming (see AGRICULTURE) risky and sometimes causes *famines. Only exceptional years stood a chance of being recorded. The rain, predominantly in winter, is usually adequate for dry-farming of cereals, and for evergreen trees resistant to the summer drought. However, it is not sufficient for dense forests. Westerly winds bring most of the rain, so that areas in the rain shadow on the eastern side of Greece, e.g. *Attica, are much drier than regions in western Greece. Rainfall often takes the form of short, intense showers. It runs off the land and does not help plants. There are statistical correlations between cereal yields, total annual precipitation and the monthly distribution of rainfall during the year. The winters generally remain warm enough for plants like the olive-tree, with a low degree of frost tolerance, while the summers are hot enough to support subtropical vegetation.

Cloāca Maxima, originally a stream draining NE Rome from the Argiletum to the Tiber through the *forum Rōmānum and Velabrum. The main sewer is largely due to *Agrippa's overhaul in 33 BC with later repairs and extensions. See SANITATION.

clocks The usual instrument for telling time in antiquity was the sundial. This employed the shadow of a pointer cast on a surface marked with lines indicating the seasonal hours (one seasonal hour was $\frac{1}{12}$ of the length of daylight at a given place: hours of constant length were used only by astronomers). The sundial was not commonly used until the 3rd cent BC, when the mathematical theory necessary for correctly drawing the hour-lines had been developed. Before then the popular way to tell time was a crude shadow-table, using the measured length of a man's own shadow.

At night the ancients used the water-clock, which measured time by the flow of water from a vessel. A primitive form was in use in Athenian courts of the 5th cent. BC, but accuracy was not achieved until Ctesibius (3rd cent.) invented a device to ensure a uniform flow. See TIME-RECKONING.

Clōdia, second of the three sisters of *Clodius Pulcher, b. *c*.95 BC, had married her first cousin Caecilius Metellus Celer by 62. Her bitter enemy

*Cicero (but gossip said she had once offered him marriage) paints a vivid picture of her in his *Letters* from 60 BC onwards, and above all in his speech on behalf of *Caelius Rufus. Her affair with *Catullus—the identification with Lesbia is widely admitted—began before the death of Metellus in 59, which Clodia was said to have caused by poison: by the end of that year Caelius was her lover. After the Caelius case her political importance ceases.

Clōdius Pulcher, Publius, youngest of six children of Claudius Pulcher, b. *c.*92 BC. In 68 he incited the troops of his brother-in-law *Licinius Lucullus to mutiny in Armenia. On his return to Rome he had been apparently friendly with *Cicero, but in May 61 Cicero gave damaging evidence against him when he was on trial for trespassing on the *Bona Dea festival disguised as a woman the previous December. However, Clodius was narrowly acquitted by a jury said to have been heavily bribed. Next year he sought transference into a plebeian *gens* (see PLEBS): this was at first resisted, but in March 59 *Caesar as *pontifex maximus* presided over the *comitia curiata* (see CURIA (1)) at which the adoption was ratified. There were suggestions of later disagreements with Caesar and *Pompey, but in the event he was elected tribune for 58. His measures included free corn for the *plebs*, restoration of *collēgia* (see CLUBS, ROMAN), grant of new provinces to the consuls, a bill exiling those who had condemned Roman citizens to death without popular sanction, a bill confirming the exile of Cicero (who departed in late March), and the despatch of *Porcius Cato (2) to *Cyprus. Clodius then turned against Pompey, threatening his life, and suggesting that Caesar's acts of 59 were invalid because of *Calpurnius Bibulus' religious obstruction. These attacks on Pompey were continued in 57, esp. over the question of Cicero's recall, and in the early part of Clodius' aedileship in 56; but after the meeting of Caesar and Pompey at Luca his attitude changed, and by agitation and violence he helped to bring about the joint consulship of Pompey and *Crassus in 55. He continued to control large sections of the urban *plebs*. He stood for the praetorship of 52, but owing to rioting the elections had not been held when he was murdered by *Annius Milo. His clients among the *plebs* burned the senate-house as his pyre.

Clodius, who like two of his sisters used the 'popular' spelling of his name, probably saw the tribunate as a vital step in his political career: revenge on Cicero need not have been his main aim in seeking transfer to the *plebs*, nor Caesar's aim in granting it. The one consistent motif is his courting of the urban *plebs* and the promotion of its interests.

Clōdius Thrasea Paetus, Publius (suffect consul AD 56), *Stoic, renowned for his uprightness and belief in senatorial freedom. He composed a biography of *Porcius Cato (2). He at first co-operated with *Nero but, after trying to stem senatorial servility, he showed opposition by abstention. Condemned under Nero in 66, he took his own life in the presence of his son-in-law *Helvidius Priscus and the Cynic philosopher Demetrius but dissuaded his wife Arria from taking hers, as he had once tried to dissuade her mother, *Arria the Elder.

closure, the sense of finality or conclusiveness at the end of a work or some part of it. In addition to the basic fulfilment of expectations raised by particular texts, some ancient genres show marked closural conventions; examples include the choral coda of Euripidean tragedy, the *plaudite* of Roman comedy (see COMEDY, LATIN), and the rhetorical peroration. *Aristotle tells us in his *Poetics* that a plot must have an ending, which follows from something but from which nothing follows, and that different endings suit different genres. The most telling ancient comment on the significance of endings as the opportunity for 'retrospective patterning' is to be found in *Solon's advice, recorded by Herodotus, to call no one happy until he is dead.

clothing See DRESS.

clubs, Greek Greek clubs, sacred and secular, are attested as early as the time of *Solon, one of whose laws gave legal validity to their regulations, unless they were contrary to the laws of the state; and we hear of political clubs (*hetaireiai*) in Athens in the 5th cent. BC. In the Classical period the societies known to us are mostly religious, carrying on the cult of some hero or god not yet recognized by the state, such as the votaries of *Asclepius, and Dexion, the heroized *Sophocles. In Hellenistic times, clubs become much more frequent and varied, and though many of them have religious names and exercise primarily religious functions, their social and economic aspects become increasingly prominent and some of them are purely secular. They are found throughout the Graeco-Roman world, but are esp. common in such cosmopolitan trade-centres as *Piraeus, *Delos, and

*Rhodes, in *Egypt, and in the flourishing cities of *Asia Minor, and they appear to have played a valuable role in uniting in a common religious and social activity different elements of the population—men and women, slaves and free, citizens and aliens, Greeks and '*barbarians'. On the titles and aims of these guilds, their cults and festivals, their social and economic aspects, their membership and officials, their organization and finance, much light has been thrown by inscriptions. See ERANOS.

clubs, Roman The Latin words corresponding most closely to the English 'club' are *collēgium and sodālitas (see SODALES). The former was the official title of the four great priestly colleges, *pontifices, *septemviri epulones, *quindecimviri sacris faciundis, and *augurs, and the word had religious associations even when the object of the club was not primarily worship. Few, if any, collegia were completely secular. All ancient societies from the family upwards had a religious basis. Collegia are associated with trades and professions (merchants, scribes, musicians, workers in wood and metal) and also with districts (see VICUS) of the city of Rome.

Few collegia existed before the Second Punic War. There were no legal restrictions on association down to the last century of the republic, though the action taken by the senate against the Bacchānālēs (see BACCHANALIA) in 186 BC shows that the government might intervene against an objectionable association. Membership of many clubs came to be dominated by freedmen, and slaves also were admitted to plebeian clubs. In the Ciceronian age the collegia became involved in elections and other political action; many were suppressed in 64 and again by *Caesar, after a temporary revival by *Clodius Pulcher. Augustus created new associations in the city districts, associated with the cult of the emperor's *numen or genius. On the other hand he also enacted that every club must be sanctioned by the senate or emperor. This permission is sometimes recorded on club inscriptions, and undoubtedly was freely given, though the policy of different emperors varied (*Trajan forbade the formation of clubs in Bithynia) and suspicion of clubs as a seed-bed of subversion remained. An extant *senatus consultum shows that general permission was given for burial clubs, provided that the members met only once a month for the payment of contributions. In practice these clubs engaged in social activities and dined together on certain occasions, e.g. the birthdays of benefactors.

Although many collegia were composed of men practising the same craft or trade, there is no evidence that their object was to maintain or improve their economic conditions. In most cases they were probably in name burial clubs, while their real purpose was to foster friendliness and social life among their members. Many clubs of *iuvenes existed mainly for sport, and associations were formed among *veterans. Several lists of members survive. They are headed by the names of the patrōnī, rich men, sometimes of senatorial rank, who often had made gifts to the clubs. The members bore titles recalling those borne by municipal officials. In these clubs the humbler population found some compensation for their exclusion from municipal honours. The fact that at the distributions of money or food a larger share was given to the officials or even to the patroni implies that the object of the clubs was not primarily philanthropic, though they no doubt fostered goodwill and generosity among their members.

Clytemnestra (Clytaem(n)estra; the shorter form is better attested); daughter of *Tyndareos and *Leda; sister of *Helen and the *Dioscuri; wife of *Agamemnon; mother of a son, *Orestes, and of three daughters, named by *Homer Chrysothemis, Laodice, and Iphianassa, although *Iphigenia, whom Homer does not mention, seems to be a later substitution for Iphianassa, as does Electra for Laodice. During Agamemnon's absence at Troy she took his cousin *Aegisthus as a lover, and on Agamemnon's return home after the ten-year war they murdered him, along with his Trojan captive, *Cassandra. Years later Orestes avenged his father's murder by killing both Clytemnestra and Aegisthus.

Her legend was a favourite one from Homer on, and given a variety of treatments. Homer makes her a good but weak woman led astray by an unscrupulous Aegisthus, and 'hateful' or 'accursed' only in retrospect. Agamemnon is killed by Aegisthus, while Clytemnestra kills Cassandra. Here there is no direct mention of her own murder by Orestes, although it is implied. *Stesichorus blames *Aphrodite, who made Tyndareos' daughters unfaithful because he had neglected her. But it is *Aeschylus' Clytemnestra, in his Oresteia of 458 BC, who dominates the extant literature which incorporates this legend. Before Aeschylus, Aegisthus and Clytemnestra were, as far as we can tell, joint partners-in-crime in Agamemnon's murder, with Aegisthus taking the dominant role. In Agamemnon, Clytemnestra has long nursed grief and rage because of her husband's sacrifice of Iphigenia at Aulis, then on his return home kills him entirely on her own, and with a fierce joy, after netting him in a robe while he is unarmed in his bath. Here she is an immensely powerful figure, a woman with the heart of a man, while Aegisthus' role has dwindled, and he becomes a blustering weakling who appears on stage only at the end of the play. *Sophocles and *Euripides in their *Electras* still make her the more prominent figure, but tend to increase the relative importance of Aegisthus again; in Sophocles she is depicted as a truly evil woman, but Euripides treats her more sympathetically, making her somewhat sorry for all that has happened. When the time comes for her death at Orestes' hands, in Aeschylus she tries to resist him and threatens him with the *Erinyes, whom her ghost afterwards stirs up against him; in the two other tragedians she simply pleads for her life.

Cnidus, a *Dorian city, founded perhaps *c.*900 BC, and claiming descent from Sparta, was situated on a long peninsula, in the gulf of *Cos, and was a member of the Dorian Hexapolis. Originally set on the SE coast of the peninsula, the Cnidians later moved to a magnificent strategic and commercial site at the cape. The fortifications and two protected harbours may still be seen. Failing in the attempt to convert their peninsula into an island, the Cnidians yielded to the Persians (after 546). After the Persian Wars they joined the *Delian League, but warmly espoused the Spartan cause after 413. Cnidus again came under Persian rule by the *King's Peace (386). Subjected to Ptolemaic control (see PTOLEMY (1)) in the 3rd cent. and perhaps Rhodian in the early 2nd, Cnidus was a *free city under Roman rule from 129 BC. Notable citizens were *Ctesias, *Eudoxus, and Sostratus (architect of the *Pharus of Alexandria). Cnidus was famous for its medical school, its wines, and the Aphrodite of *Praxiteles.

cōdex originally denotes leaves of wood, papyrus, or (esp.) parchment bound together in the form of a modern book as opposed to a roll. (See BOOKS, GREEK AND ROMAN.) Christian Scriptures took this convenient form, which made it easier to find the passage one wanted.

coercitiō, the right, held by every magistrate with *imperium*, of compelling reluctant citizens to obey his orders and decrees, by inflicting punishment. Against this compulsion, which magistrates exercised not as judges but as holders of executive authority, *provocatio* might be employed or an appeal to the tribunes. Moreover, the *provocatio* laws made it an offence to inflict capital punishment in face of appeal and banned the flogging of citizens, except in certain contexts, esp. those of military service, the games, and the stage. Hence, where citizens were concerned, *coercitio* would usually take the form of imprisonment (see PRISON), fine, exaction of pledges, or *relegation from Rome.

Cogidubnus See CLAUDIUS COGIDUBNUS.

cognōmen See NAMES, PERSONAL, ROMAN.

cohors (pl. *cohortēs*) In the early Roman republic the infantry provided by the allies were organized in separate *cohortes* of varying strength, each under a Roman or native *prefect. In the legions the cohort was first used as a tactical unit by *Cornelius Scipio Africanus in Spain, but for over a century it was employed alongside the manipular organization (see MANIPULUS) before the latter was superseded in the field. The cohort was made up of three maniples, or six centuries. There were ten *cohortes* in a legion.

From the time of *Cornelius Scipio Aemilianus, the general's personal bodyguard was known as the *cohors praetōria*. By the middle of the 1st cent. BC, the term was used also to describe the group of personal friends and acquaintances which accompanied a provincial governor. This entourage was the origin of the emperor's 'cohort of friends'; the military *cohortes praetoriae* were formalized in the *praetorian guard.

In the imperial *auxilia* infantry were organized in cohorts, nominally 500 strong under prefects. In Rome, the urban troops and the *vigiles also were organized in cohorts under tribunes.

cohortēs urbānae ('city cohorts'), the police force of Rome, established by *Augustus under the command of the city *prefect. A permanent police force in Rome was an innovation, and the first prefect *Valerius Messalla Corvinus resigned, declaring that he did not understand how to exercise his powers. Originally there were three cohorts, each commanded by a tribune and six centurions, numbered X–XII in continuation of the sequence in the *praetorian guard; under the Flavians there were four cohorts in Rome. Single 'city' cohorts (so named because they were originally withdrawn from Rome) are found at *Puteoli, *Ostia, and *Carthage, presumably protecting the shipment of corn to Rome, and at *Lugdunum, where there was an important mint. Each cohort contained 500 men. They were recruited from Italians, served for 20 years, were paid half the rate of praetorians. Normally the soldiers of the city cohorts would, like the praetorians, provide additional protection for the emperor.

coinage, Greek

Definitions Coinage to the Greeks was one of the forms of *money available to measure value, store wealth, or facilitate exchange. Coins were made from precious metal such as *gold or *silver, or from a copper alloy; they were of regulated weight and had a design (type) stamped on one side or both. Lumps of bullion too could be weighed to a standard and stamped with a design, but the stamp on a coin indicated that the issuing authority, normally a state or its representative(s), would accept it as the legal equivalent of some value previously expressed in terms of other objects, including metal by weight. Merchants and others therefore were expected to accept it in payment.

In the Archaic and Classical periods many of the Greek communities established around the Mediterranean and Black (*Euxine) Seas produced coins, and they often influenced their neighbours to do the same: Persians (see PERSIA) in western *Anatolia, Carthaginians (see CARTHAGE) in North Africa and Sicily, *Etruscans in Italy, *Celts in western Europe. The coins of these peoples, although they usually bear images and inscriptions appropriate to their traditions, were in general inspired by Greek models. After 334 the conquest of the Persian empire by *Alexander (2) the Great inaugurated a massive extension of the area covered by coinage, esp. in the Successor kingdoms (see DIADOCHI), Syria, Egypt and so on. In effect the term 'Greek coinage' includes most of the non-Roman coinage of the ancient world issued between the Straits of Gibraltar and NW India.

Beginnings Coinage began in western Anatolia, at the point of contact between Greek cities on the Aegean coast and the Lydian kingdom in the interior. The first coins were of electrum, an alloy of gold and silver occurring naturally in the river Pactolus, which flowed into the Hermus to the west of *Sardis. A date of c.600 BC or a little later for their introduction fits their appearance in a miscellaneous deposit of jewellery and figurines discovered in the foundations of the temple of Artemis at *Ephesus, and also the subsequent development of coinage in Anatolia

and the wider Aegean world. The first coins of electrum were followed in *Lydia by coins of pure gold and silver, with the type of confronting foreparts of a lion and of a bull. Such coins have traditionally been attributed to the Lydian king *Croesus (c.560–546), but hoard evidence suggests that most, if not all, are later than his reign and were part of the coinage issued in the area by the Persians.

Purpose Given the nature of the earliest coins—esp. their standardized weights and the lion's head that features on many of them—it is a plausible hypothesis that they were issued to make a large number of uniform and high-value payments in an easily portable and durable form, and that the authority or person making the payment, perhaps to *mercenaries, was the king of Lydia. For the original recipients coins were simply another form of movable wealth, but many pieces might thereafter be exchanged for goods or services and so pass into general circulation as money.

Coin Types The type of a Greek coin is a mark of its origin, whether a community or an individual. The earliest coins, found in the temple of Artemis at Ephesus, had types only on the obverse and their variety makes it difficult to assign them to a specific minting authority. The commonest type, a lion's head, has been attributed to the kingdom of Lydia; others, such as a seal's head or a recumbent lion, may belong to Phocaea and Miletus respectively. The significance of the earliest types was not usually reinforced by any letter or inscription. A coin type originated as the personal seal or badge of the authority responsible for its issue. By the end of the 6th cent. Initial letter or letters of an ethnic might be introduced (as a *koppa* on coins of Corinth or *Athe* on those of Athens), and in course of time the tendency was to lengthen the inscription. When written out in full, it was often in the genitive case, signifying [a coin] of whoever the issuing authority was.

After an initial period of variation the types of individual cities settled down and changed little: familiarity encouraged acceptability. Most coin types are connected with religion in the widest sense. Sometimes a divinity is represented directly, in other cases indirectly, through an animal or an attribute. Even some of the types illustrating a local product belong in this category: for example an ear of barley can symbolize Demeter, goddess of corn. Many types refer to local legends or religious traditions, for example those connected with the foundation of a city.

The Spread of Coinage (*Archaic and Classical*) In the second half of the 6th cent. the coin-producing cities of Anatolia turned from electrum to silver. Coinage in gold became a rarity, although from the early 5th cent. the Persians issued gold darics with the same type as their silver *sigloi*, a crowned figure representing the king of Persia. ('Darics' were so named by the Greeks after the Persian king *Darius I; *siglos* is a Greek form of the Semitic 'shekel'.) These coins were issued for use in those parts of the Persian empire in closest contact with the Greeks, and the institution of coinage did not initially travel far east of its birthplace.

To the west and north the story was different. By *c.*550 coinage had crossed the Aegean to communities close to the isthmus of Corinth—Aegina, Corinth, and Athens—and not much later had taken root among the Greek cities and the tribes of the Thraco-Macedonian area (see THRACE; MACEDONIA). The rich metal resources of the latter gave rise to coinage in a remarkable range of denominations, including the heaviest of all Greek silver coins, the double octadrachm. Such coins travelled far, esp. to the east, and may have been made for export. The first Athenian coins share some of the characteristics of the early coins of Anatolia, notably their changing types, their lack of any indication of origin, and the use of electrum as well as silver for some issues. In the later part of the 6th cent. these issues were replaced by the famous 'owls', with obverse helmeted head of Athena, reverse owl, and the abbreviated name of the city. These coins too travelled a long way, another example of the export in the form of coin of silver mined in the territory of the issuing state.

From the Aegean area coinage spread rapidly to the western Greeks settled around the coasts of southern Italy and Sicily, France, and Spain. The coins of the western Greeks attained the highest standards of artistic excellence and esp. in the late 5th and early 4th cents. the careers of many of the artists can be traced from their signatures on dies.

Hellenistic In the 4th cent. the Greek world of independent city-states began to give way to the ambitions of individuals and the growing power of Rome. In the east the exploitation by *Philip II of Macedon of the mines of Pangaeus after 356 left a rich legacy of coinage in gold and silver, which was adapted and expanded by *Alexander (2) the Great to cover the whole near east. He adopted the Attic weight-standard for both his gold and silver coinage, and struck coins with the same designs at more than one mint. After Alexander's death in 323, the currency system he had introduced remained remarkably stable.

coinage, Roman The progressive extension of Roman hegemony over central Italy brought booty in the form of *gold, *silver, and *bronze; the means to create a coinage on the Greek model were at hand. The stimulus was probably provided by Roman involvement with the Greek cities of *Campania, after the building of the *via Appia in the late 4th cent. BC; Rome now struck a coinage of silver pieces worth two (probably) drachmas, with the legend ROMANO, otherwise indistinguishable from the Greek coinages of the south. There was nearly a generation before the next issue, probably contemporary with the Pyrrhic War. (See PYRRHUS.) From this point, there is a virtually unbroken sequence of Roman coinage to the end of the Roman empire in the west.

A silver coinage with a token coinage in bronze and a heavy cast bronze coinage went on side by side down to the outbreak of the Second *Punic War in 218. It is probably in this period that Roman coinage penetrated the territories of the peoples of the central Apennines for the first time; and it is likely that, just as military needs may explain much of the production of Roman coinage in this period, so it was returning soldiers who carried it to Samnite and other communities.

The enormous strain of the war against *Hannibal led to the debasement of the silver coinage. The first coinage system of Rome collapsed, and *c.*211 a new system was introduced; it included a new silver coin, the *dēnārius*, which remained the main Roman silver coin until the 3rd cent. AD. The issue was financed initially by unprecedented state levies on private property, thereafter by booty as the war went better for Rome. The end of the war saw the virtual cessation of minting by other Italian communities; and most coinage other than Roman disappeared rapidly from circulation in Italy.

Despite the creation of the *denarius*, bronze remained the most important element in the Roman monetary system for some years; a belief similar to those held by *Porcius Cato (1) even led to the virtual suppression for a decade of the silver coinage, a symbol of increasing wealth and of declining public morality. But the consequences of Rome's conquest of the world could not be suppressed for ever; the booty in silver *i.a.* which flowed into Rome from 194 onwards and the mines in *Macedonia which Rome controlled from 167 found expression in a vastly increased issue of silver coinage from 157. It became normal for Rome to coin in a year as much as a Greek city might coin in a century. In the years after 157, the coinage came accurately to reflect the position of Rome as ruler of the world by omitting the ethnic: no identification was needed.

The period after the Second Punic War saw the beginning of the process whereby Roman coinage came to be the coinage of the whole Mediterranean world. The *denarius* rapidly became the silver coin of Sicily, flanked both by Roman bronze and by bronze city issues. In Spain, the Romans permitted or encouraged the creation of silver and bronze coinages modelled on the denarius coinage, probably in the 150s. As more and more of the Mediterranean world came under direct Roman rule and became involved in the civil wars that brought the republic to an end, so the use of Roman monetary units and Roman coins spread, to Africa, Greece and the east, and Gaul. Only Egypt, incorporated in 30, remained monetarily isolated from the rest of the Roman world.

The military insurrection of Sulla in 84 had seen the production of a gold as well as a silver coinage, the availability of the metal combining with an urgent need for coinage to pay his soldiers; the precedent of Sulla was followed by *Caesar: the vast quantities of gold derived as booty from Gaul and Britain were converted in 46 by *Hirtius into the largest gold issue produced by Rome before the reign of *Nero; by 44 the distribution of gold coins, or *aurei*, to the troops was a normal occurrence. Caesar's rival *Pompey had become from the exploitation of the eastern provinces the richest man of his time; in outdoing him in wealth as well as in prestige, Caesar in effect superseded the state as a minting authority.

The civil wars which followed the death of Caesar saw the production of coinage in a variety of metals by most of the rival contenders; unity of minting authority and uniformity of product returned when the last survivor of the civil wars finally suppressed the institutions of the free state and established an autocracy. The coinage of Caesar Octavianus (see AUGUSTUS) became the coinage of Rome.

Meanwhile, the types displayed by the Roman republican coinage had also come to mirror accurately the escalating internal conflict of the nobility. By 211, the production of coinage was in the hands of moneyers (see TRIUMVIRI), young men at the beginning of a political career. The possibilities offered by the coinage for self-advertisement gradually became apparent during the 2nd cent. BC, and by the last third of the century the issue produced by a moneyer was as far as its types were concerned effectively a private concern; a moneyer might recall his town of origin, the deeds of his ancestors, eventually the contemporary achievements of a powerful patron; with Caesar, the coinage began to display his portrait, an overtly monarchical symbol; even *Brutus, the self-styled Liberator, portrayed on his last issue two of the daggers which had murdered Caesar on one side and his own portrait on the other. In striking contrast to Marcus *Antonius (Mark Antony), the future Augustus gradually suppressed on his coinage any reference to his lieutenants; and the coinage with which he paid the troops who defeated Antony and *Cleopatra at Actium was already a coinage which displayed only the portrait and attributes of a single leader.

The mainstream coinage of the Roman empire consisted of *aurei* and *denarii*, at a ratio of 1 : 25, and base metal fractions. (The *sesterce* was worth a quarter of a *denarius*.) Although at all periods much, even most, was struck at Rome, this was not necessarily so: it is likely that between Augustus and the changes under *Nero most of the precious metal coinage was struck in Gaul. But the shift of minting back from Gaul to Rome began a process of concentration of minting which lasted till the Severans (see ROME, HISTORY). Thereafter, the evolution of the empire saw more and more of the mainstream coinage being produced in the provinces. And the base metal coinage of the east consisted for a long time of a range of provincial bronze coinages. The kaleidoscopic variety of the coinage of the empire was completed by hundreds of city coinages, in the west till *Claudius, in the east till the 3rd cent. AD. All these coinages, however, were probably based on, or compatible with, Roman monetary units. It is less clear how far the empire formed a single circulation area: the most probable view is that even mainstream coinage, once it had reached an area, tended to stay there; but the compartmentalization of circulation became more marked with the shift from a monetary to a natural economy in the third century AD.

The monetary system of the Roman empire always operated on very narrow margins. It is possible to calculate that in normal times perhaps 80 per cent of the imperial budget was covered by tax revenues, the rest by the topping up of what came in with coins minted from newly mined metal. Prudent emperors managed; the less prudent did not. See FINANCE, ROMAN.

collēgium (1) Magisterial or priestly: a board of officials. (2) Private: any private association of fixed membership and constitution (see CLUBS, ROMAN).

The principle of collegiality was a standard feature of republican magistracies at Rome. Arbitrary power was avoided by ensuring that every magistracy should be filled by at least two officials, and in any case by an even number. They were to possess equal and co-ordinate authority, but subject to mutual control. Thus a decision taken by one consul was legal only if it did not incur the veto (*intercessio*) of the other. This principle led to alternation in the exercise of power by the consuls each month. Under the Principate emperors might take as a colleague in their tribunician power (see TRIBUNI PLEBIS) their intended successors, who in many cases were co-emperors.

The name *collegium* was also applied to the two great priesthoods of the *pontifices* and the *augurs* and to the *quindecimviri sacris faciundis*, who had charge of the Sibylline oracles (see SIBYL). The lesser priesthoods were known as *sodalitates* (see SODALES).

Colōnia Agrippīnensis, command-centre of the Rhine frontier (see RHENUS), and one of the most important cities of the western Roman empire. In 38 BC *Agrippa transferred the Ubii to the left bank of the Rhine. Around 9 their capital, *Oppidum Ubiōrum*, was chosen to accommodate an altar for the imperial (*ruler-) cult, and was therefore renamed *Āra Ubiorum*. This probably signifies the Roman intention to make the city the capital of a new province of Germany. About the same time two legions were stationed close by. However, the defeat of *Quinctilius Varus returned the frontier to the Rhine, and the legions were later transferred. The city was henceforth capital of Lower Germany. In 50 *Claudius founded a veteran colony (*Colonia Claudia Ara Agrippinensium*) in honour of *Iulia Agrippina his wife. A naval base, headquarters of the Rhine fleet, was established a little upstream. The colonists and the Ubii merged rapidly. The colony enjoyed great prosperity. Its fine glassware was widely exported. A large mercantile port developed between the colony and the river.

colonization, Greek 'Colonization', in the language of a former imperial power, is a somewhat misleading term for the process of major Greek expansion that took place between c.734 and 580 BC. In fact, the process itself was not so much 'Greek' as directed in different ways and for different reasons by a number of independent city-states (see POLIS). This at least emerges with relative clarity from both the historical and the archaeological evidence.

There is little doubt about the areas first colonized and of the identity of the chief colonizing cities: *Chalcis, *Eretria, *Corinth, *Megara, *Miletus, and *Phocaea. Of these, the *Euboean cities (Chalcis, Eretria) must rank as pioneers. Eretrian *Corcyra was the first Greek colony in the Adriatic, which suggests that it was intended mainly as a way-station on the route to the west; and the primarily Chalcidian foundation of *Cumae on the bay of Naples is the most northerly as well as the earliest (before 725) Greek colony on the mainland of southern Italy—known to later historians as *Magna Graecia. Cumae was a natural extension of the precolonial Euboean venture at the *emporion of *Pithecusae, itself a result of earlier commercial experience—not least in a Levant (*Al Mina) that had been aware of western resources (*Sardinia) since the bronze age. Chalcidians extended their reach to eastern Sicily with the foundation of *Naxos (2) in 734, soon followed by Leontini and Catana; on the straits of Messina (see MESSANA), they were joined by Cumaeans at Zancle, and control of the vital passage was completed at Rhegium c.720. Nearer home, the *Chalcidicē peninsula takes its name from the early and extensive Euboean presence on the northern shores of the Aegean. The Euboean domination of this area, motivated by land hunger rather than commerce, was not broken until c.600, when Corinth established *Potidaea to trade with *Macedonia. By then, Corinthians (and Corinthian pottery) had long enjoyed a substantial western presence, built on precolonial experience that had extended to expatriate ceramic production at Pithecusae. In 733, Corinth evicted the Eretrians from Corcyra and founded *Syracuse, which had the best harbour in east Sicily and for long conditioned the history of nearby Megara Hyblaea, founded by Corinth's near neighbour at home, Megara—which elsewhere gained control by c.660 of the approaches to the Black (*Euxine) Sea with Chalcedon and the superior site of *Byzantium.

Early Euboean and Corinthian achievements in the west concentrated the attention of others, both on the west itself and on other areas as yet unopened. Of the former, the Achaeans were responsible from c.720 for Sybaris, Croton, Metapontum, and Poseidonia (i.e. Paestum). In the last decades of the 8th cent., *Sparta founded its only colony by taking possession of the finest port in south Italy, *Tarentum; Rhodians and Cretans (see RHODES; CRETE) combined to establish *Gela on the south coast of Sicily in 688. By now, daughter-foundations were a standard feature of the western scene: two of them, Selinus and *Acragas, representing extensions into west Sicily by Megara Hyblaea and Gela respectively, boast temples that are no less magnificent than those of Greece itself.

At the other end of the Greek world, the literary evidence is less reliable, and excavation has been less extensive: but it is claimed that Miletus founded numerous cities along the Anatolian coast to Trapezus, north from the *Bosporus (1) to the Danube, and in the Crimea. In a different direction, Thera founded *Cyrene in North Africa c.630. And from c.600, Phocaeans safeguarded their far western trade by founding colonies on the Mediterranean coast on either side of the Rhône delta: *Massalia, Nicaea, and Antipolis, and the aptly named Emporion in northern Spain. (See EMPORION.)

By 580 all the most obvious areas in the then available world had been occupied to at least some extent by Greeks. The factors that influenced any given colonizing city, or indeed the foundation of any given colony, were various: it is not possible to compile a generally applicable assessment of the interlocking claims of overpopulation and land hunger at home, opportunities for commercial advancement abroad, 'internal' (Greek vs. Greek) rivalry, and reaction to external pressure. No less various were the relations between colony and mother city, and the effects of Greek colonization on the indigenous inhabitants of the regions colonized. Many different natural resources were doubtless targeted for exploitation, and markets were accordingly made: but the cultural 'Hellenization of the *barbarians' (see HELLENISM) was at no time consciously planned, nor did all the 'barbarians' share an unswerving predilection for the Greek point of view.

See also APOIKIA; CLERUCHY; FOUNDERS OF CITIES; METROPOLIS.

colonization, Hellenistic *Plutarch, in his eulogy of *Alexander (2) the Great, made the foundation of cities the linchpin of the achievement of Alexander, who wished to spread Greek civilization throughout his realm, and it is true that Alexander's conquest opened the countries of the near east to Greek immigration. The Greeks, however, could envisage only life in cities with Greek-style houses, streets, public buildings, civic institutions, and a rural territory where the colonists could hold plots of land (klēroi; see CLERUCHY). Begun by Alexander, usually as military colonies rather than cities proper (*Alexandria in Egypt is an exception), this policy was followed by his successors (see DIADOCHI) and developed further by the *Seleucids. All their foundations received a Greek and/or Macedonian population. However, the Graeco-Macedonian dominance in the new cities implies neither an enforced Hellenization of the local peoples nor their marginalization. (See HELLENISM.)

colonization, Roman The earliest colonies of Roman citizens were small groups of 300 families at *Ostia, Antium (338 BC), and Tarracina (329). Others were added as the Roman territory expanded, through reluctance to maintain a permanent fleet. In 218 there were twelve such maritime colonies. Colonists retained Roman citizenship because the early colonies were within Roman territory, and were too small to form an independent state. Citizen colonies are distinct from Latin, which, though largely manned by Romans, were autonomous states established outside Roman territory and with acknowledged strategic aims (see IUS LATII; LATINS). Maritime colonies seem normally to have been exempt from legionary service, though the exemption was revocable, and colonists were bound not to absent themselves by night from their colonies in time of war.

About 177 the system of citizen colonies was reorganized. They were assimilated to Latin colonies, and the use of the latter abandoned. Henceforth citizen colonies were large—2,000–5,000 men—and were employed for the same purpose as Latin colonies formerly. Not all the original Roman colonies remained small and static. *Puteoli (194), though exceptional because of its position, was showing administrative complexity and magisterial jurisdiction in a public building contract of 105. The first deployment of large Roman colonies was in Cisalpina (see GAUL (CISALPINE)), where the strategic and cultural situation was different from that of 4th-cent. Latium. Generous allotments of land were given to the new colonies and their internal organization was changed also. They remained citizen colonies but received extensive powers of local government for their annual magistrates and council. Not many of the new-style colonies were founded till the *Gracchan age, when a further change took place in their employment. Henceforth they were founded for social and political as much as for strategic reasons, either as emigration schemes for the landless or to provide for veteran soldiers. They could cause friction with the original inhabitants and give rise to unrest, notably the revolts of 78 and 63 BC.

The first foundation outside Italy was the Gracchan Junonia at *Carthage (122). Its charter was revoked, but the colonists retained their allotments. In 118 *Narbo was successful. In 103 and 100, *Appuleius Saturninus and *Marius proposed large-scale colonization in certain provinces, and effected a few settlements in Africa, Corsica, and Provence. But extensive colonization outside Italy became regular only under *Caesar and *Octavian, when, reflecting the changed locus of political power, colonies began to adopt the names of their founders and benefactors as titles of honour (so *Colonia Claudia Ara Agrippinensium*, AD 50; see COLONIA AGRIPPINENSIS). Some colonists were still being drawn from the civilian population, notably at the refounding of Carthage and *Corinth (*c.* 44). Augustus, discharging his *veterans and avoiding Italy after 27, established numerous colonies not only in Narbonensis (see GAUL (TRANSALPINE)), the Spanish provinces, *Africa, and Mauretania, but also in the east. There had already been Caesarian foundations in Asia Minor. After *Philippi, Octavian gave veterans Italian land, but the Perusine war showed that if not sent home (*Res Gestae* 16) they would have to be settled elsewhere, and the numbers of Antonian troops to be discharged indicated the east. (See ANTONIUS, MARCUS.) Augustan colonies were thickly scattered, mainly on the seaboard of Greece and NW Asia Minor. In Pisidia (25 BC) and at Berytus (*c.*15 BC) they provided a military presence when legions could not be afforded. In the east an existing *polis* could survive colonization; colonization may be seen as part of a movement in populations that included the individual settlement of Italian businessmen, soldiers, and others, as well as the creation of hybrids like Nicopolis: colonization was sometimes unofficial in both east and west. In the later republic, casual immigrants established the assembly of Roman citizens (see CONVENTUS (1)) in native communities, thus forming the basis of a future *municipium.

Eastern colonies used the standard constitution of *duovir* and *decuriones; where there was a genuine settlement, the use of Latin for official purposes was persistent, and the eastern colonies were a fruitful source of senators and *equestrians, for their size; but the overall picture, in language, constitution, religion, and architecture, is of a rich mix. To possess a *capitōlium* (see CAPITOL) was important, and some colonies were miniature Romes. If colonies sent to places where native communities already existed provided the latter with the model of how Romans and Italians lived, and brought some means of following it, that was incidental (see ROMANIZATION). None the less the original communities would often eventually receive citizenship and coalesce with the colony.

Eastern colonization continued under *Claudius and *Vespasian but increasingly became a means of enhancing the status of existing cities (even though the concomitant privileges did not include exemption from tribute) rather than of finding homes for veterans or of constructing military outposts. *Colonia Aelia Capitolina* (*Jerusalem, AD 135) was a special punitive case. Claudius also began the regular colonization of the Balkan provinces and the northern frontier, which continued till *Hadrian. Thenceforth no new colonies were founded. Instead, the title 'colony' with colonial rights became a privilege increasingly sought by *municipia* as the highest grade of civic dignity. The process began when Claudius conferred the title on the capital cities of certain Gallic communities, but only became considerable in the 2nd cent. (see IUS ITALICUM).

colōnus (*a*) A member of a *colōnia* (see COLONIZATION, ROMAN); (*b*) a tenant farmer.

Colophōn See PANIONIUM.

Colosseum, the medieval name of the Flavian *amphitheatre, near the colossus of Nero, on the site of the lake in the *gardens of the *Domus Aurea. Begun by Vespasian, it was continued by Titus, and dedicated in June AD 80. Domitian was probably responsible for only the complex substructures of the arena. The building measures 188 × 156 m. (205 × 170 yds.) along the axes, and is 52 m. (170 ft.) high. The travertine façade has three storeys of superimposed arcades framed by half columns of the Doric, Ionic, and Corinthian orders, surmounted by a masonry attic decorated with Corinthian pilasters on a low podium; there are windows in the podium and in the spaces between the pilasters, alternating with bronze shields. There were also mast-corbels for the awning, worked by sailors. The seating, supported by concrete vaults, was in three tiers, with standing room above it. The arena was cut off by a fence and a high platform carrying marble chairs for guilds and officials, including boxes for the emperor and magistrates on the short axis. The arena was floored in timber, covering cages for beasts, mechanical lifts, and drains. Audiences, estimated at 50,000, were marshalled outside the building in an area bordered by bollards, and held tickets corresponding to the 76 numbered arcades, whence an elaborate system of staircases serviced all parts of the auditorium.

colours, sacred Three colours are esp. important for sacral purposes in antiquity; they are white, black, and red, the last being understood in the widest sense, to include *purple, crimson, even violet.

White is in general a festal colour, associated with things of good omen, such as sacrifices to the celestial gods (white victims are regular for this purpose in both Greece and Rome). See e.g. Homer's *Iliad* 3. 103, where a white lamb is brought for sacrifice to *Helios; as the Sun is bright and male, a white male lamb is brought for him, while Earth, being dark and female, gets a black ewe-lamb. It is the colour of the clothing (see DRESS) generally worn on happy occasions. In Rome, white horses drew the chariot of a *triumphātor*.

Black on the contrary is associated with the *chthonian gods and mourning, and with the dead. These facts explain why 'white' and 'black' respectively mean 'lucky' and 'unlucky' when used of a day, etc. (See RACE.) The natural association of white with light and black with darkness is explanation enough, but note also that white garments are conspicuously clean, black ones suggest the unwashed condition of a mourner; see DEAD, DISPOSAL OF.

Red might suggest blood, and therefore death and the Underworld, but also blood as the source or container of life, and also the ruddy colour of healthy flesh and various organs of the body. Perhaps because red, or purple (stress falling on sheen), is the colour of light, red is on occasion protective, e.g. the *praetexta* (see TOGA) of Roman magistrates and children. But it is also associated with the burning heat of summer.

columbārium (1), a Roman dovecot. These were sometimes small and fixed in gables, sometimes very large tower-like structures, fitted with nesting-niches in rows, perches, and running water.

(2) *Columbarium* is also a type of tomb, popular in early imperial Rome, so called because of its similarity to a dovecot. Often totally or partially subterranean, such tombs had niches arranged in rows in the walls with pots sunk into them to contain the ashes of the dead. These provided comparatively cheap but decent burial for the poorer classes: the occupants of each niche could be identified by an inscription, and might be commemorated by more expensive memorials (such as a portrait bust or marble ash-chest). The largest columbaria could hold the remains of thousands and were built to accommodate the slaves and freedmen of the Julio-Claudian imperial households. Smaller *columbaria* appear to have been built by speculators or burial clubs (see CLUBS, ROMAN). See also ART, FUNERARY, ROMAN.

Columella, Lūcius Iūnius Moderātus fl. AD 50, b. Gades, author of the most systematic extant Roman agricultural manual (written *c.* AD 60–65) in twelve books. Book 1: introduction, layout of villa, organization of slave workforce; 2: arable cultivation; 3–5: viticulture (mainly) and other arboriculture; 6, 7: animal husbandry; 8, 9: specialized breeding of poultry, fish and game, and bees; 10: horticulture (in *hexameter verse); 11: duties of *vīlicus* (slave estate-manager), calendar of farm work and horticulture; 12: duties of *vīlica* (female partner of *vilicus*), wine and oil processing and food conservation. Columella defends the intensive slave-staffed villa— characterized by capital investment, close supervision by the owner, and the integration of arable and animal husbandry—against influential contrary views on agricultural management. His calculation of the profits of viticulture has aroused lively modern debate. Columella treats vines at greater length than cereals, but that reflects the complexity of viticulture not the supposed demise of Italian arable cultivation. He owned several estates near Rome but had firsthand knowledge of agriculture elsewhere in Italy and in the provinces. Continually aware of the effects of various climatic conditions, soils, and land formations, he does not describe just one ideal estate. The serious nature of his work is further illustrated by the ample bibliography of Greek, Punic, and Roman authors, while his practical experience ensured a critical use of all sources. Columella's stylish prose, citations of Virgil, and book of verse were designed to give his work greater credibility among contemporary literary landowners, e.g. *Seneca the Younger and his brother Gallio (see ANNAEUS NOVATUS); they do not undermine its practical worth. See AGRICULTURAL WRITERS; AGRICULTURE, ROMAN; VILLA.

comedy (Greek), Old 'Old Comedy' is best defined as the comedies produced at Athens during the 5th cent. BC. An early form of comedy was composed in *Sicily by Epicharmus, the connection of which with Attic comedy is hypothetical. In Athens itself no transition from Old to Middle Comedy occurred precisely in 400, but the two extant plays of *Aristophanes which belong to the 4th cent. differ in character from his earlier work, esp. in the role of the chorus (see para. 2 below). The provision of comedies at the City *Dionysia each year was made the responsibility of the relevant magistrate in 488/7 or 487/6 BC. Comedies were first included in the *Lenaea shortly before 440. Before and after the *Peloponnesian War five comedies were performed at each festival; there is evidence that the number was reduced to three during the war, but the question is controversial. In the 4th cent. comedies were performed also at the Rural *Dionysia, and it is likely, given the existence of early theatres in several Attic *demes, that such performances were widespread before the end of the 5th cent. No complete plays of any poet of the Old Comedy except *Aristophanes survive, and he belongs to the last stage of the genre, but we have many citations from the work of his elders (notably *Cratinus) and contemporaries (notably *Eupolis). Some of these support generalizations about Old Comedy based on Aristophanes, but where support is absent or doubtful, one must remember Aristophanes' date and not assume that the structural features common to his earliest plays constitute, as a whole, a formula of great antiquity.

2. The chorus, which had 24 members, was of primary importance in Old Comedy, and many plays (e.g. *Babylonians*, *Banqueters*, *Acharnians*) take their names from their choruses. In Aristophanes the chorus addresses the audience in the *parabasis*, which has a central position in the play, and again at a later stage. In parts of the *parabasis* the chorus maintains its dramatic role (as Acharnians, knights, clouds, jurors, etc.), while in others it speaks directly for the poet; in the former case dramatic illusion is partly broken, in the latter case wholly. The entry of the chorus is sometimes a moment of violence and excitement; it may be (as in *Acharnians* and *Wasps*) hostile to the 'hero' of the play, and it has to be won over; thereafter it is on his side, applauding and reinforcing what he says and does.

3. The plots of Old Comedy are usually fantastic. In their indifference to the passage of time, the ease with which a change of scene may be assumed without any complete break in the action (places which in reality would be far apart can be treated as adjacent), and the frequency of their references to the audience, the theatre, and the occasion of performance, they resemble a complex of related charades or variety 'turns'. The context of the plot is the contemporary situation. In this situation, a character takes some action which may violate the laws of nature (e.g. in Aristophanes' *Peace* Trygaeus flies to the home of the gods on a giant beetle in order to release the goddess Peace from imprisonment and bring her back to earth) or may show a complete disregard for practical objections (e.g. in *Acharnians* Dikaiopolis makes a private peace treaty with his country's enemies and enjoys the benefits of peace). Events in Old Comedy are sometimes a translation of metaphorical or symbolic language into dramatic terms, sometimes the realization of common fantasies; they involve supernatural beings of all kinds. The comic possibilities of the hero's realization of his fantasy are often exploited by showing, in a succession of short episodes, the consequences of this realization for various professions and types. The end of the play is festive in character (Aristophanes' *Clouds* is a striking exception), a kind of formal recognition of the hero's triumph, but the logical relation between the ending and the preceding events may be (as in Aristophanes' *Wasps*) very loose, as if to drown the question 'But what happened *then*?' in the noise of song and dance and to remind us that we are gathered together in the theatre to amuse ourselves and Dionysus by a cheerful show.

4. Men prominent in contemporary society are vilified, ridiculed, and parodied in Old Comedy. Sometimes they are major characters, either under their own names (e.g. '*Socrates' in *Clouds* and '*Euripides' in *Thesmaphoriazusae*) or under a very thin disguise (e.g. the 'Paphlagonian slave' in *Knights*, who is *Cleon). Many plays, e.g. *Hyperbolus* and *Cleophon*, actually bore real men's names as their titles (see HYPERBOLUS; CLEOPHON). The spirit in which this treatment was taken by its victims and by the audience raises a difficult question in the study of Old

Comedy. A man would hardly become a comic poet unless he had the sense of humour and the natural scepticism which combine to make a satirist, and prominent politicians are always fair game for satire. Equally, artistic or intellectual change is a more obvious and rewarding target for ridicule than traditional practices and beliefs. There is nothing in the comic poets' work to suggest that as a class they positively encouraged an oligarchic revolution, and their own art was characterized by elaborate and continuous innovation. There is some evidence for attempts to restrict the ridiculing of individuals by legislation; the evidence for their scope and effect is scanty.

5. Mythology and theology are treated with extreme irreverence in Old Comedy; some plays were burlesque versions of myths, and gods (esp. Dionysus) were made to appear (e.g. in Aristophanes' *Frogs* and Cratinus' *Dionysalexandros*) foolish, cowardly, and dishonest. Yet the reality of the gods' power and the validity of the community's worship of them are consistently assumed and on occasion affirmed, while words and actions of ill-omen for the community are avoided. It is probable that comic irreverence is the elevation to a high artistic level (Demodocus' tale of *Ares and *Aphrodite in *Odyssey* 8 may be compared) of a type of irreverence which permeates the folklore of polytheistic cultures. The essential spirit of Old Comedy is the ordinary man's protest—using his inalienable weapons, humour and fantasy—against all who are in some way stronger or better than he: gods, politicians, generals, artists, and intellectuals.

6. The actors wore grotesque masks, and their costume included artificial exaggeration (e.g. of belly and *phallus) for comic effect; the phallus may have been invariable for male roles until the 4th cent. No limit seems to have been set, in speech or action, to the humorous exploitation of sex (normal and unorthodox) and excretion, and the vocabulary used in these types of humour eschews the euphemism characteristic of prose literature.

7. Most of the extant comedies of Aristophanes require for their performance four actors and, on occasion, supernumeraries.

See also: ARISTOPHANES.

comedy (Greek), Middle The term 'Middle Comedy' was coined by a Hellenistic scholar to cover plays produced in the years between Old and New Comedy (*c*.404–*c*.321 BC). This was a time of experiment and transition; different types of comedy seem to have predominated at

different periods; probably no single kind of play deserves to be styled 'Middle Comedy' to the exclusion of all others.

The defeat of Athens in 404 vitally affected the comic stage; the loss of imperial power and political energy was reflected in comedy by a choice of material less intrinsically Athenian and more cosmopolitan. In form at least the changes began early. *Aristophanes' *Ecclesiazusae* ('Assembly-women': probably 393 BC) and *Plutus* ('Wealth': 388), now generally acknowledged to be early examples of Middle Comedy, reveal the atrophy of the comic chorus.

The presentation of contemporary types, manners, and pursuits was a characteristic of Middle Comedy. This interest in the details of ordinary life may well have been associated with the development of one particular type of play, which dealt with a series of more or less plausible everyday experiences, such as love affairs and confidence tricks, and featured a group of stock characters ultimately (though with the distortions of caricature) drawn from life. This was the type of play that later prevailed in New Comedy. Virtually all its stock figures (e.g. cooks, *parasites, pimps, soldiers, courtesans (see HETAIRAI), angry or avaricious old men, young men in love) can be identified in the fragments and titles of Middle Comedy. Although several of these characters can be traced back, at least embryonically, to Old Comedy (thus the braggart soldier has a prototype in the *Lamachus of Aristophanes' *Acharnians*; *Eupolis named one play *Flatterers*, after its chorus), it is clear that the middle of the 4th cent. had the greatest influence on their typology. That was the time when, e.g., the cook began to receive his typical attributes of braggadocio and garrulousness, and the *parasite to be called regularly by this name in place of the older term 'flatterer'.

comedy (Greek), New, comedy written from the last quarter of the 4th cent. BC onwards, but generally regarded as ending its creative heyday in the mid-3rd cent., composed mainly but not exclusively for first performance at Athens. *Philemon, *Menander, and Diphilus are commonly seen as the leading playwrights of the period, and above all Menander, who, though not the most successful in his own lifetime, was soon recognized as the outstanding practitioner of this type of drama. Although Athenian citizenship and marriage-laws are integral to many of the plays, the presentation of characters, situations, and relationships is true to such universal elements of human experience that the plays could be enjoyed then as now by audiences far removed from Athens. Political references are rare and subordinate to the portrayal of the private and family life of fictional individuals; there are social tensions (between rich and poor, town and country, citizens and non-citizens, free and slave, men and women, parents and children), but they are not specific to one time or place. Love or infatuation (always heterosexual) plays a part and is regularly shown triumphing over obstacles in a variety of contexts. But this is not the only ingredient; Menander excelled at the sympathetic portrayal of many kinds of personal relationship and of the problems that arise from ignorance, misunderstanding, and prejudice. These generate scenes that the audience can perceive as comic because of their own superior knowledge, enjoying the irony of the situation; but Menander often plays games with his audience's expectations as well.

The playwrights' skill lay partly in their ability to give fresh treatment to familiar material. Comedy had become simpler and tamer by the end of the 4th cent.: there was little metrical variety (and the chorus was reduced to performing interludes that marked the act-breaks in a standard five-act structure) and very little obscenity (the costume of male characters no longer included a phallus), and the exuberant fantasies of Old Comedy were not found. But there were boastful stock characters, stock situations (such as the rediscovery of long-lost children), and familiar comic routines (such as the door-knocking scene which is central to the presentation of the main character in the third act of Menander's *Dyscolus* and can be traced back to Aristophanes' *Acharnians*).

comedy, Latin This term has come to be synonymous with *fabula* *palliata, since the *palliatae* of *Plautus and *Terence are the only complete Latin comedies to have survived from antiquity. But there were other types of comedy in Latin (see ATELLANA; FABULA; MIME; TOGATA), and there was clearly some overlap of subject-matter, titles, and style between the various types. The *palliata*; at first happy to allow the inclusion of Roman elements in its Greek setting (as in the plays of Plautus), came to favour greater consistency and thereby perhaps encouraged the development of a separate type of comedy with an Italian setting. Plautus and Terence continued to be performed, and new *palliatae* to be written, at least until the time of Horace, and *togatae* too were occasionally re-

vived; but the comic stage came to be dominated by the coarser *Atellana* (still performed in Juvenal's day) and above all (for several centuries) the mime. It is generally assumed that all actors were male, except in mimes. They certainly wore masks in *Atellana*, almost certainly in *palliata*, and perhaps also in *togata*, but not in mimes.

comitia In Rome the *Comitium was the place of assembly. *Comitia* is a pl. word meaning an assembly of the Roman people summoned in groups by a magistrate possessing the formal right to convene them. He had to convene them on a proper 'comitial' day, after the *auspices had been taken. When only a part of the people was summoned, the assembly was strictly a *concilium*. When the whole people was summoned, but not by groups, the assembly was a *contio. In the *comitia* the majority in each group determined the vote of the group. The *comitia* voted only on proposals put to them by magistrates, and they could not amend them.

The three types of *comitia* were the *comitia cūriāta*, the *comitia centuriāta*, and the *comitia tribūta*, the constituent voting groups being, respectively, *curiae* (see CURIA (1)), *centuriae, and *tribus. Resolutions of the *comitia* (and possibly of the *concilium plebis*) were subject to formal ratification by the patrician senators before they could become laws.

Comitia curiata This was the earliest form of Roman assembly, and its functions were progressively taken over by the *comitia centuriata*, although it continued throughout the republic to confirm the appointment of magistrates, and witnessed the appointment of priests, adoptions, and wills, probably under the chairmanship of the *pontifex maximus. In *Cicero's time the 30 *curiae* were represented in the *comitia* by 30 *lictors.

Comitia centuriata This was a wealth-based assembly. Its functions were to enact laws, to elect senior magistrates (consuls, praetors, censors), to declare war and peace, and to inflict the death penalty on Roman citizens who had exercised their right of appeal (see PROVOCATIO), or at least on those who were arraigned on political charges. An interval (*trinundinum) was observed after the notification of a meeting, during which preliminary discussions (*contiones*) of the proposals were held. In the judicial *comitia* a preliminary investigation before a *contio* had to be held, lasting for three days; after a *trinundinum* the vote was taken. The *comitia centuriata* met outside the *pomerium, usually in the *Campus Martius, and in military order. This reflects the military origins of the comitia centuriata.

The voting centuries in the comitia centuriata numbered 193 in all, and were divided among the five property classes in such a way that the higher census classes, which were numerically the smallest, contained the largest number of centuries; at the bottom the proletarians (*proletarii), who fell below the minimum property qualification for membership of the fifth class, were enrolled in a single century and were effectively disfranchised. Each class was also divided equally between centuries of seniors (men aged 46 and over) and juniors (men aged between 17 and 45), although the latter were far more numerous than the former. The result was that the rich could outvote the poor, and the old could outvote the young. A reform of the system in the 3rd cent. went only a little way towards redressing the balance, and the assembly retained an inbuilt conservative bias to the end of the republic.

Comitia plēbis tributa The assembly of the *plebs was strictly a concilium, but after plebiscites acquired the force of law it too was generally called comitia. The voting units in the plebeian assembly were the territorial tribes. The assembly elected plebeian tribunes and aediles, enacted plebiscites and held trials for non-capital offences; its procedures were quicker and less cumbersome than in the comitia centuriata.

The comitia populi tributa were founded in imitation of the plebeian assembly, at an uncertain date. The procedure was the same, but the comitia populi were convened by consuls or praetors, and patricians were admitted. The comitia elected quaestors, curule aediles, and military tribunes, enacted laws, and held minor trials.

From the 3rd cent. BC the pontifex maximus was elected by a special assembly of seventeen tribes chosen by lot. In 104 this system was extended to the other pontifices, the *augurs and the *quindecimviri sacris faciundis.

The Roman comitia were far from democratic. The centuriate assembly was blatantly weighted in favour of the propertied classes, while the tribal assembly, though ostensibly more democratic, in fact discriminated against both the urban plebs, who were confined to four of the 35 tribes, and the rural population, who lived too far from Rome to attend in person. The enfranchisement of Italy after the *Social War aggravated these problems. Attempts at reform were half-hearted and either abortive or too late,

and in the 1st cent. BC the assemblies ceased to be an effective means of expressing popular will. The election of magistrates was transferred to the senate by *Tiberius; only the declaration of the result was still performed before the people. The judicial and legislative functions of the comitia also lapsed in the early empire.

See also DEMOCRACY (NON-ATHENIAN).

Comitium, the chief place of political assembly in republican Rome occupying an area north of the *forum Romanum at the foot of the Capitoline. It is associated with seven levels of paving from the late 7th to the mid-1st cent. BC, after which it ceased to exist as a recognizable monument owing to Caesar's reorganization of the area.

commendātiō Under the Roman republic distinguished politicians influenced the elections of magistrates by open canvassing on behalf of friends. This practice was continued by emperors, and, when done in absence, by letter or by posting a list of recommended candidates, was known as commendatio. This method became normal when the emperor was infirm, or absent. Such candidātī Caesaris were normally sure of success; that made Tiberius careful to limit their numbers and delicate in his handling of the consulship. However, *Vespasian, in order to give his candidates a better chance, had them voted on separately. Any pretence that imperial influence was not decisive disappeared by the end of the 1st cent.

commentāriī, 'memoranda', were often private or businesslike, e.g. accounts, notebooks for speeches, legal notes, or teaching materials. Their public use developed in the priestly colleges (e.g. *pontifices), and with magistrates (*consuls, *censors, *aediles) and provincial governors. They apparently recorded decisions and other material relevant for future consultation: this could amount to a manual of protocol. Under the empire the 'imperial memoranda' provided an archive of official constitutions, rescripts, etc: entering a decision in the commentarii conferred its legal authority.

In the late republic a more literary usage developed, 'memoir' rather than 'memoranda'. Various records, handbooks, and other learned works were so described, but esp. autobiographies: thus perhaps the work of *Sulla, more certainly *Cicero's accounts of his consulship and above all *Caesar's commentarii. Such works favoured a plain style, ostensibly concentrating on content rather than the more obvious forms of rhetoric: they might purport to provide raw material for others to work up, but that pretence was sometimes thin.

Commentāriolum petitiōnis An essay in epistolary form, *c.*5,000 words, on the technique of electioneering, purporting to be addressed by Quintus *Tullius Cicero to his brother Marcus *Tullius Cicero (1) on the occasion of the latter's consular candidature in 64 BC. Its authenticity has been repeatedly impugned; the arguments against it are conclusive. The level of contemporary reference implies, at all events, much familiarity with the history of the period. The only plausible later context for the production of such a document would be that of a rhetorical exercise (see DECLAMATION). The content is divided into three sections: first, the means necessary to overcome the disadvantage of being a *novus homo*; second, methods of building up support, (*a*) through personal connections and (*b*) through canvassing the popular vote, the latter regarded as less important; third, a short section on how to prevent or counteract bribery. See ELECTIONS AND VOTING, ROMAN.

Commodus, Lūcius Aurēlius, sole emperor AD 180–192, one of twin sons born to Marcus *Aurelius and *Annia Galeria Faustina in 161, the first emperor 'born in the purple' (i.e. after his father's accession). Given the title Caesar in 166, he was summoned to his father's side after the usurpation of Avidius Cassius in 175, received *imperium* and *tribunicia potestas* at the end of 176, and was consul in 177, now Augustus and co-ruler. He left Rome with Marcus for the second Marcomannic War. On his father's death in March 180 he became sole emperor, taking the names Marcus Aurelius Commodus Antoninus, rapidly made peace, and abandoned the newly annexed territories, holding a triumph in October 180.

Major wars were avoided during the reign, the exception being in Britain, where, following a breach of the northern frontier, victories were won for which Commodus assumed the title 'Britannicus' in 184. Commodus at first retained his father's ministers, e.g. the praetorian *prefect Taruttienus Paternus, but after an assassination attempt in 182, in which the emperor's sister Annia Aurelia Galeria Lucilla was implicated, Paternus was dismissed and soon killed along with many others. The praetorian prefect Tigidius Perennis effectively ran the government from 182 to 185, when he was lynched by mutinous troops. Aurelius Cleander, the freedman chamberlain, was the next favourite to hold power, even becoming praetorian prefect. After his fall in 190, following riots in Rome, power was shared by the emperor's favourite concubine Marcia, the chamberlain Eclectus, and (from 191) the practorian prefect Aemilius Laetus. Commodus, by now obsessively devoted to performing as a *gladiator, appeared to be deranged. Proclaiming a new *golden age, he shook off his allegiance to his father's memory, calling himself Lucius Aelius Aurelius Commodus, as well as eight other names: each month was given one of these names; Rome itself became the *Colōnia Commodiāna*. Numerous senators had been executed; others feared the same fate, and Laetus, probably with the connivance of Helvius Pertinax, had Commodus strangled in the last night of 192. Though of humble origin, Pertinax was a most distinguished soldier, and that same night an enraptured senate declared him emperor. The memory of Commodus was at once condemned (see DAMNATIO MEMORIAE), but was restored by *Septimius Severus in 195.

commūnēs locī, 'commonplaces', were 'arguments that can be transferred to many cases'. They were practised at school among the *progymnasmata*, and theorists laid down headings; declaimers made them part of their stock-in-trade. The types are well illustrated in the pages of *Seneca the Elder. The danger of commonplaces was that they might be dragged in regardless of strict relevance. See TOPOS.

Companions See HETAIROI.

Concordia The cult of personified harmonious agreement (Gk. *homonoia*) within the body politic at Rome is indicative of its absence. The first temple overlooking the *Forum from the lower slopes of the Capitoline was linked to the troubles associated with the Licinio-Sextian legislation of 367 BC (see CONSUL); a major rebuilding by *Opimius in 121 commemorated the suppression of Gaius *Sempronius Gracchus and his followers, and the grandest rebuilding by *Tiberius (vowed 7 BC, dedicated as Concordia Augusta, AD 10) was intended to celebrate a really elusive solidarity within *Augustus' household. Some of the lavish marble architecture of the last temple survives.

confederacies See FEDERAL STATES.

Conōn (1), Athenian general. First attested at Naupactus (414 BC), he was re-elected *strategos* on *Alcibiades' restoration (407/6) and after Notium reorganized the fleet. Blockaded in Mytilēnē, he survived the witch-hunt after the resultant battle of *Arginusae (406). When *Lysander pounced at Aegospotami (405) he escaped, re-emerging from self-imposed exile as a Persian fleet-commander (397). Despite financial problems (he protested personally to *Artaxerxes (2) II) operations flourished, culminating in Sparta's defeat at *Cnidus (394), and he returned home (393), bringing money for fortifications and mercenaries.

Conōn (2), of *Samos (first half of 3rd cent. BC), mathematician and astronomer. After observing star-risings and weather phenomena in Italy and Sicily, he became famous by his identification (c.245 BC) of a group of stars near the *constellation Leo as the 'asterization' of the lock of hair dedicated by Queen Berenīcē of Egypt to the victory of her husband Ptolemy III. This flattery was celebrated by *Callimachus (2) in a poem imitated by *Catullus (66). In mathematics he wrote on intersecting conics and was a correspondent of *Archimedes, who respected him and regretted his early death.

consilium principis ('advisers to the *princeps'*). A Roman magistrate was always free to summon advisers in deliberation or on the bench. The fluctuating body of advisers summoned to the Roman emperors retained this semi-official character, though the gathering of friends (see AMICUS AUGUSTI) was increasingly strengthened by judicial and administrative personnel (the praetorian *prefect was regularly a member), and its meetings must be distinguished from consultation of individuals.

consolation The practice of offering words of comfort to those afflicted by grief is reflected in the earliest Greek poetry. Later, under the twin influences of rhetoric and philosophy, a specialized consolatory literature began to develop, initiating a tradition which persisted throughout Graeco-Roman antiquity. This literature took a number of forms. Philosophers wrote treatises on death and the alleviation of grief. Letters of consolation were written to comfort those who had suffered bereavement or some other loss-experience, such as exile or illness; they might be highly personal, or possess the more detached character of an essay. Funeral speeches (see LAUDATIO FUNEBRIS) often contained a substantial consolatory element. Poets sometimes wrote verse consolations. Greek cities voted prose-decrees of consolation for the kin of deceased worthies.

Consolation proper is regularly associated with the expression of sympathy (in itself a form of consolation), and with exhortation; eulogy of the deceased is also a frequent ingredient. Arguments typically employed include the following: all are born mortal; death brings release from the miseries of life; time heals all griefs; future ills should be prepared for; the deceased was only 'lent'—be grateful for having possessed him. Normally grief is regarded as natural and legitimate, though not to be indulged in.

The best surviving examples of pagan material are probably Servius *Sulpicius Rufus' letter to *Cicero on the occasion of the death of his daughter Tullia, and *Seneca the Younger's *To Marcia*. In *Boethius' *Consolations of Philosophy*, Philosophy herself consoles the author for his misfortunes. Christian writers make full use of pagan *topoi* (see TOPOS), but firm belief in a blissful afterlife and the wealth of relevant material available in Scripture ensured that consolation acquired a different character in Christian hands. See also CRANTOR.

Constantine I, 'the Great' (c. AD 272/3–337), b. in the Balkan province of Moesia, was son of Constantius I and Helena. When Constantius, now senior Augustus, died at *Eburacum (306), his troops proclaimed Constantine Augustus. Only after 20 years of struggle did Constantine emerge as sole Augustus.

In November 324 Constantine founded *Constantinople on the site of *Byzantium. The need for an imperial headquarters near the eastern and Danubian frontiers had been seen by *Diocletian. The city's dedication with both pagan rites and Christian ceremonies took place in May 330. From the beginning it was 'New Rome', though lower in rank. Many traditional features of Rome (not temples and cults) were in time reproduced. To speak of the foundation of a capital is misleading; yet a permanent imperial residence in the east did in the end emphasize division between the empire's Greek and Latin parts.

In a reunited empire Constantine was able to complete Diocletian's reforms and introduce innovations. The separation of civil and military commands was completed. A substantial field army was created under new commanders responsible directly to the emperor: its soldiers had higher pay and privileges than the frontier troops. Constantine radically reorganized the government. He tried vainly to stop *corruption in the steadily growing bureaucracy. He gave senatorial rank freely, and reopened many civilian posts to senators, who began to recover some of their lost political influence. From his reign survive the first laws to prevent tenant farmers and other productive workers from leaving their homes and work. His open-handedness harmed the economy: taxation (mostly in kind) rose inexorably despite the confiscation of the vast temple treasures. He established a gold coinage, but the other coinage continued to depreciate.

Resident now in the more Christianized east, his promotion of the new religion became clearer. He openly rejected *paganism, though without persecuting pagans, favoured Christians as officials, and welcomed bishops at court, but his actions in Church matters were his own. He now confronted another dispute which was rending Christianity, the theological questions about the nature of Christ raised by *Arius. To secure unity Constantine summoned the council which met at Nicaea in 325 (later ranked as the First Ecumenical Council), and proposed the formula which all had to accept. Dissidents were bludgeoned into agreement; but *Athanasius' view that his opponents had put an unorthodox interpretation on the formula was seen by Constantine as vexatious interference with attempts to secure unity. Even if his success in this aspect was superficial, he nevertheless brought *Christianity from a persecuted minority sect to near-supremacy in the religious life of the empire.

He spent the generally peaceful last dozen years of his reign in the east or on the Danube, though he visited Italy and Rome, and campaigned on the Rhine. Victory over the Goths was followed by a campaign against the *Sarmatians, many thousands of whom were then admitted within the empire as potential recruits. In 336 he fought north of the Danube, even recovering part of *Dacia. The empire's prestige seemed fully restored; a Persian war loomed but did not break out until after his death. Baptized when death approached (such postponement was common at the time), he died near Nicomedia in Bithynia (May 337).

Constantinople (*Constantinopolis*). Constantinople was founded by *Constantine I on the site of *Byzantium in AD 324. The city was styled 'New Rome' from the start, but it is not likely that Constantine had any thought of superseding Rome. He was simply building his own tetrarchic capital: the New Rome motif took on new significance after Alaric's sack of Rome (410) and the disappearance of the western empire.

Though not such an obvious site as has been claimed (being vulnerable from its hinterland and deficient in drinking-water), the new foundation grew rapidly in size and importance, though it did not become a regular imperial residence till the end of the century. By 373 an elaborate system of *aqueducts had been installed to provide enough water for the growing population. The Constantinian walls were demolished in 413, and the present walls built about $1\frac{1}{2}$ km. (1 mi.) further west. The area of the city was thus doubled. Like Rome, the city was divided into fourteen regions, though not till 413, with one of the regions across the Golden Horn and one outside the walls. As at Rome, there was also a free issue of corn (probably necessary to support the expansion).

Several pagan temples were left untouched, but Constantine at once built a number of churches, notably the Holy Apostles, where he and many of his successors were buried. He also rebuilt the hippodrome and adorned the streets and squares with statues brought from all over the empire (as *Jerome put it, 'Constantinople is dedicated by denuding every other city'). The bishop of Constantinople soon acquired great prestige, and in 381 the council of Constantinople declared that 'he should have the primacy of honour after the bishop of Rome because it was the New Rome'.

In 425 a number of professorial chairs were established: five and three in Greek and Latin *rhetoric, ten in Greek and Latin *grammar, one in philosophy, and two in law. But it was a long time before Constantinople managed to attract scholars of the first rank. The city prospered because it housed the imperial court and the government of the east. It was also the seat of the supreme courts of appeal with all their lawyers, and of the patriarchate with its numerous clergy, and thronged with petitioners and litigants, ecclesiastical, civil, and military.

constellations and named stars From the earliest times the Greeks, like many other peoples, named certain prominent stars and groups of stars. Homer speaks of the Pleiades, the Hyades, Orion, Boötes, the Bear ('also called the Wain'), and the 'Dog of Orion' (i.e. Sirius). Hesiod mentions all of these, and uses their heliacal risings and settings to mark the seasons and times for agricultural operations (e.g. the rising of the Pleiades for harvesting, and their setting for ploughing). This traditional 'agricultural calendar' was elaborated and codified in the later 'astronomical calendars' of *Meton, Euctemon and their successors (see ASTRONOMY). The above are the only stars and star-groups known to have been named in Archaic times, and the division of the *whole* visible sky into constellations seems not to precede *Eudoxus. However, the twelve signs of the zodiac (see below) were introduced from *Mesopotamia long before then.

2. Eudoxus (*c*.360 BC) extended and codified the previously unorganized material into a description of the heavens, in which he divided the whole of that region of the sky visible from Greece into named constellations, which (with some minor changes and additions at later periods) became canonical. In doing so he subsumed some previously named star-groups (such as the Pleiades and Hyades) into larger constellations. Although the original has not survived, we have a good idea of the content of his work from its adaptation in the *Phaenomena* of *Aratus and the commentary of *Hipparchus (2). The constellations were conceived not merely as star-groups but as the outlines of actual figures in the heavens, on which the individual stars are located (e.g. 'the star on the right foot of the Great Bear (Ursa Major) is the same as the one on the tip of the left horn of the Bull (Taurus)'. Although the idea is found in much older Babylonian texts, the wording of Eudoxus implies the existence of a star-globe on which the figures representing the constellations were actually drawn and the most prominent stars too located. Representations of such globes survive from antiquity, and *Ptolemy (2) gives detailed instructions for constructing one.

3. Like other peoples of antiquity, the Greeks identified some star-groups with mythological beings. Thus Hesiod calls the Pleiades 'daughters of Atlas'. This kind of identification was, at least in the system of Eudoxus, embedded in the very name of some constellations: the whole *Perseus myth is reflected in the names of the constellations Perseus, *Andromeda, Cetus (the sea-monster), Cassiopeia, and Cepheus. But it was only in Hellenistic times that systematic attempts were made to connect all constellations with traditional mythology. Aratus already has numerous mythological excursuses and allusions, but the most influential work of this kind was the *Catasterisms* (star-myths) of *Eratosthenes. A later epitome of this survives. Although we possess only a small part of the extensive ancient literature on astral mythology, even this is enough to show that there was no 'standard' version, but that different myths were often attached to the same constellation. The sign Gemini, which gets its name from the Babylonian MAŠ-MAŠ ('twins'), was identified not only with the famous divine twins Castor and Pollux (see DIOSCURI), but also with the Theban heroic twins Amphion and Zethus.

4. Connected with the mythology, but only partly determined by it, is the iconography of the constellations. This too was far from uniform, even among the professional astronomers. But there are certain traditional and unchanging characteristics, e.g. Taurus is always represented as only the forepart of a bull: it is probable that this is a relic of the Mesopotamian iconography of the constellation, as is certain for the representations of the zodiacal signs Capricorn (as a 'goat-fish') and Scorpius.

5. Of the 48 canonical constellations, the constellations of the belt known as 'the zodiac' are as follows:

(1) Ariēs (the Ram).

(2) Taurus (the Bull). The name and iconography are of Mesopotamian origin. The constellation includes the old Greek star-groups of the Hyades (Piglets) and Pleiades (meaning unknown).

(3) Gemini (the Twins); see para. 3 above.

(4) Cancer (the Crab). The name goes back to Babylon.

(5) Leo (the Lion). The name goes back to Mesopotamia. The star-group 'Coma Berenices' was given a separate name by *Conon (2).

(6) Virgo (the Maiden), represented with wings.

(7, 8) Libra and Scorpius. In Mesopotamia these were represented together as a huge scorpion, of which the first sign was the claws and the second the body and tail. In Greek sources too the first sign is often called 'the Claws', and so represented. But the name 'the Scales' (of a balance) and the corresponding representation is also found. The second sign is accordingly either a whole or partial scorpion.

(9) Sagittarius (the Archer), represented as a *Centaur with a bow, an iconography derived from Mesopotamia.

(10) Capricorn (the Goathorn); the representation as a mixture of goat and fish goes back to Mesopotamia.

(11) Aquarius (the Water-carrier).

(12) Piscēs (the Fishes). The constellation is called 'Fish' (singular) in Mesopotamia; the

representation as two fishes joined by a line is probably a Greek innovation.

constitution, Antonine is the name given to the edict of Caracalla (*Aurelius Antoninus), probably of AD 212, which made all free men and women in the empire Roman citizens. Acc. to *Cassius Dio, the emperor's motive was to increase the numbers liable to taxes imposed on citizens such as inheritance tax. A surviving papyrus points to religious motives. In any event the concept of universal citizenship fitted the egalitarian outlook which the Severan dynasty (193–235), rooted in Africa and Syria, shared with such contemporaries as *Galen and *Ulpian. The new citizens took Roman names and became subject to Roman law. In the long run the effect of the Antonine constitution was profound, since it promoted in both east and west a uniform legal system and a consciousness of being Roman that lasted until the fall of the empire, and sometimes beyond it.

Constitution of the Athenians attributed to *Aristotle: see ATHENAION POLITEIA; attributed to *Xenophon: see OLD OLIGARCH.

constitutions, the generic name for legislative enactments by Roman emperors: *edicts, decrees (judicial decisions), rescripts (written answers to officials or petitioners).

consul, the title of the chief annual civil and military magistrates of Rome during the republic. Two consuls were elected annually for most, if not all, of the republic by the centuriate assembly (see COMITIA) at a meeting called for the purpose, normally by a consul, exceptionally by a *dictator, or *interrex.

As the highest office of state the consulship figured in the 'struggle of the orders' between *patricians and plebeians (see PLEBS). Plebeian consuls were few in the 5th cent., and it was not until 367 BC that a Licinian plebiscite required the election of at least one plebeian consul and not until 342 that this became regular in fact. The first entirely plebeian college held office in 172.

The consul's power, or *imperium*, was effectively that of the king, limited by the period of office and the presence of a colleague with the same *imperium*. The importance of the principle of collegiality here is reflected in the fact that if a consul died or resigned, his colleague was bound to hold an election to fill his place for the remainder of the year (as *suffect consul). Over time, some functions were removed from the consuls. The conduct of the *census was taken over by the *censors from 443, and civil jurisdiction passed effectively to the praetor from 366. In the city consuls could exercise *coercitio, a general power of enforcing order and exacting obedience to their commands, but the extent of their power within the city was subject from the earliest times to *provocatio. The power of the consul in the field was virtually unrestricted, as symbolized by the addition of the axe to the *fasces when the consul left the city on campaign. The consuls could and usually did act together, e.g. in calling the senate or an assembly, and use of the veto (*intercessio) against one another was rare. When division of labour in the city was indicated, this might be arranged by agreement or by lot, or by use of the custom whereby each assumed duties (and the *fasces) for a month at a time. When both consuls were on campaign together, the normal practice was for each to assume overall command for a day at a time.

Under the empire consuls continued, but in an appropriately attenuated way. With *Augustus consular *imperium* came to be part of the emperor's arsenal and to be held by the emperor independently of the office of consul itself. With the suppression of the centuriate assembly and popular election, the emperors either recommended the candidates (see COMMENDATIO) or held the office themselves. The position continued to confer honour, as shown by the increasing use of pairs of suffect consuls during the same year after the initial brief tenure of the *consulēs ordinārii*, who gave their name to the year as the republican consuls had done. The republican age limits (fixed by a law of *Sulla's dictatorship: in the late republic no one under 42 could be elected) were often disregarded as imperial relatives and protégés were signalled by the bestowal upon them of the consulship.

contio (*conventio*, a coming together) was a public meeting at Rome from which no legal enactment actually emerged, even though it might form part of a longer formal procedure, such as a trial before the people. Hence it did not have to be held in an area hallowed by the taking of the auspices (see AUSPICIUM). It could be convened by a magistrate or a priest. Apart from trials, it was used for preliminary discussion of legislation or simply as a means of providing a politician with a political platform to pronounce on matters of the moment. A magistrate could call away a meeting summoned by an inferior, and a tribune could veto (see INTERCESSIO) the making of a speech at any meeting. The right of addressing the audience depended on the discretion of the convener. He addressed the gathering from a platform, to which he might summon speakers of sufficient importance, while others spoke from ground level. These meetings generally took place in or near the Forum, but could be held outside the *pomerium so that a pro-magistrate might attend without losing his *imperium. See COMITIA.

contubernium meant a 'dwelling together', as of soldiers or animals, but referred esp. to a quasi-marital union between slave and slave or slave and free. Since a slave lacked juristic personality, a *contubernium* was not a marriage but a factual situation, at the pleasure of the slaveowner, creating no legal consequences. Children were the property of the mother's owner; no slave-woman could be guilty of adultery; manumission of one or both parents need not extend to their issue. Sepulchral inscriptions indicate that *contubernia* were highly valued. But how widespread *de facto* slave 'families' were and which social contexts best favoured them cannot be known. Slave-owners always retained the right to separate slave family members, and commonly did so, to judge from records of slave sales and bequests.

conventus, 'assembly', is technically used (1) for associations of Italians abroad; (2) for provincial assizes.

(1) By the early 2nd cent. BC Italians (esp. in the east) united for religious and other purposes under elected *magistri*. In the late republic these associations often gained a position of great political importance locally; the governor would rely on them for service on juries and on his council and for advice on local conditions. In the Caesarian and Augustan period such an association often formed the nucleus for the foundation of a new colony or *municipium. In the long term with the spread of *Romanization, esp. in the west, these associations disappeared.

(2) In most provinces, by the late republic, assizes (where the provincial governor held court) were held in fixed centres. Under the Principate the status of assize centres became a much sought after privilege, comparable to that of being a centre for the imperial (*ruler-) cult, which was in the gift of the emperor. In the province of Asia, which had at least 300 urban communities, there were fourteen assize centres in the 2nd cent. AD. The annual assize-tour of the provincial governor constituted the practical framework within which he exercised all his routine administrative and jurisdictional duties.

conversion The term implies rejection of one way of life for another, generally better, after brief and intense insight into the shortcomings of self or the demands of circumstance. Ancient religious cult did not require such radical or sudden shifts. Devotees could embrace one allegiance without renouncing others. The characteristic word for conversion in the NT, *metanoia* (change of heart or mind), was used also by Classical philosophers. Acc. to the Stoic Hierocles, 'conversion is the beginning of philosophy'.

There was among the Romans a contrasting admiration for *constantia*, 'steadfastness', whereby those deserving moral approbation were as likely to maintain the gifts and inclinations of their breeding as to renounce their past in favour of novel commitments.

convīvium The Roman *convivium* was modelled on the Etruscan version of the Greek *symposium. These Italian feasts differed from their Greek prototypes in four important respects: citizen women were present; equality was replaced by a hierarchy of honour; the emphasis was on eating and the *cēna* (see MEALS), rather than on the later drinking session; the entertainment was often given by one man for his inferior friends and clients (see CLIENS). The Roman *convivium* was therefore embedded in social and family structures, rather than largely independent of them; the difference is captured by the remark of *Porcius Cato (1) that the Romans were right to emphasize the aspect of 'living together' by calling a group of reclining friends a *convivium* rather than a *symposium*.

The differences between Greek and Roman customs produced some tensions. The presence of respectable women is archaeologically attested in Etruria (see ETRUSCANS) and early Rome, and was already denounced by *Theopompus; it led to a series of attempts by Roman antiquarians to explain that originally Roman women had been prohibited from drinking wine or reclining. Later moralists were obsessed with the consequent dangers of *adultery, which became a specifically Roman vice. Inequality and the tendency to excessive display of wealth gave rise to an emphasis on the need for moderate behaviour, and satires on ostentation. The activities of the *parasite and pretensions towards Greek-style literary sophistication in private banquets were ridiculed, and contrasted with the public feasts given by politicians and emperors. The result was a complex convivial culture, whose literature was descriptive and moralizing, rather than designed for actual performance at the *convivium*, and was much concerned with differences between Greek and Roman customs.

Roman religion involved special forms of the feast. In 399 BC the *lectisternium* was introduced, a ritual in which images of the gods were arranged as banqueters on couches, and for which the *septemviri epulones* seem to have had responsibility. Other *collegia* such as the *arval brethren dined together according to complex rituals. The Saturnalia (see SATURNUS) was a traditional carnivalesque feast of reversal.

The Roman *dining-room was based on the *triclinium* arrangement of couches, traditionally with three couches and nine participants. This produced a space for entertainment facing the diners, rather than enclosed by them, and encouraged displays that were more lavish than in Greece, but did not involve participation.

cookery The religious importance of *sacrifice gave cooking a powerfully expressive role in ancient society: the order of the exposing of meat to different sources of heat, esp. boiling and roasting, mattered ritually. The public meat-cook (*mageiros*) was a man; other food preparation was among the private, household tasks of a woman (see HOUSEWORK). Food could be prepared at the hearth of the city and consumed as a public activity, like the meals in the Athenian *prytaneion*; it was normally a household matter. But the staples of domestic diet (see MEALS), esp. grains (of which there was a wide variety, see CEREALS), could also be cooked in special forms as offerings.

Cereals could be boiled (like pulses) or made into coarse or fine flours, which could also be boiled; the heat necessary for bread-making makes provision of communal ovens desirable outside very large households. The spread of bakeries is a part of a gradual and partial displacement of cookery from the household, reaching its acme in the Roman tavern, with its cheap wine and cooked food a sign of the advantages available to urban populations (see INNS, RESTAURANTS). Even in urban settings much cooking was still done in the household on a brazier. The kitchens of *Pompeii and *Herculaneum have told us much about practical technique.

The standard pattern of meals remained the combination of nutritious staples with tasty condiments. Quality in food reflected the excellence of these, and became—by 5th-cent. BC Athens if no earlier—an ingredient in social stratification. Raw materials were carefully calibrated: their places of origin acquired precise reputations. The preparation of speciality vegetables or meats through careful tending was part of the process. The combination of condiments, often exotic—e.g. as sauces based on fish products (see FISHING), *wine and its derivatives, *olive oil, or the cooking juices of fish or meat—was also a matter for ingenuity and skill, and this was the base of the claim of the ancient connoisseur to knowledge of an art.

Corbulō See DOMITIUS CORBULO.

Corcyra, northernmost of the western Greek islands, located in the *Ionian Sea just off the western coast of Epirus. Verdant and remote, Corcyra was identified with *Homer's Scheria. During the 8th cent. (traditionally in 734 BC), *Corinth established a colony on the island's east side, and expelled a group of *Eretrians in the process. Their city, named Corcyra, commanded three harbours, and prospered as a staging-point for voyages from Greece to the northern *Adriatic, Italy, and the western Mediterranean. Although Corcyra contributed to the general settlement of colonies in the region by Corinth (at Epidamnus and Apollonia, it was a co-founder), relations between colony and mother city were not always cordial. Corcyra fought the Corinthians in a sea battle c.660 and may have contributed to the fall of the *Bacchiad clan. A generation later, *Periander temporarily reasserted Corinthian control over the colony, but after his death, Corcyra regained its independence. Thereafter, the colony offended Corinth in various ways—by not participating in the *Persian War, by opposing the spread of Corinthian influence in the Ionian Sea, and by staying aloof from Greek politics in general. Circumstances surrounding a civil war at Epidamnus eventually drew it into a war with Corinth and forced it to ally with Athens for protection. An Athenian fleet was sent to Corcyra in 433, and again in 427 and 425 when Corinthian fleets attempted to co-operate with disaffected elements on the island. These years saw Corcyra convulsed by a savage civil war, during which the democrats massacred hundreds of their oligarchic opponents. In 410, Corcyra's democrats shook off their Athenian connection for a generation.

Corinth

Greek and Hellenistic The city lies near the isthmus which joins central Greece to *Peloponnese. Copious springs make the site extremely attractive, and it commands both the Isthmus and a rich coastal plain. Acrocorinth, the citadel, is too high to be a normal acropolis; the city lay by the springs at its northern foot. Development was continuous from the late 10th cent. BC. Corinthians exploited their unrivalled position for western voyages early. Pottery reached *Delphi by the early 8th cent., and soon after Ithaca and inland Epirus. Further west, it is found in the earliest levels at *Pithecusae; and when other colonies were established, they became the core of a market for Corinthian painted pottery (see POTTERY, GREEK) which covered the whole Greek world until the mid-6th cent., when it gave way to Attic except at home. Corinthian agriculture was always important, but the economy was remarkably diverse already in the 7th cent.: trade was extensive, and *Herodotus observed that Corinthians despised craftsmen less than did other Greeks. Corinth played a large part in developing the Doric order (see ORDERS): it evolved in temples built at Corinth and Isthmia, and many in NW Greece on which Corinthians worked.

The aristocratic *Bacchiads ruled until *Cypselus overthrew them c.657 BC; he passed the tyranny to his son *Periander, and the last tyrant fell c.585. An unusually narrow *oligarchy followed: the council of 80, with eight *probouloi*, was the main organ of government. Corinth became a *Spartan ally probably soon after 550, perhaps to secure protection against *Argos; they failed to overthrow *Polycrates (1) of Samos in a joint expedition c.525. During the reign of *Cleomenes, Corinth became alarmed at the growth of Spartan power and successfully led opposition among the allies to Spartan interventions in Athens. Corinth was inscribed with Athens and Sparta on the second coil of the Serpent Column at Delphi for its part in the defence of Greece against *Xerxes (see PERSIAN WARS). Corinthian aggression against *Megara led to the First *Peloponnesian War when the victim appealed to Athens for help; Corinth was extremely active and suffered heavily early in the war, but was satisfied with the balance established by the Thirty Years Peace, and took a leading role in preventing intervention against Athens when *Samos revolted in 440. Since 480, the Corinthians had exploited fears of *Corcyra to win influence in NW waters; when they thought their interests there were threatened by the Athenian alliance with Corcyra (433), they agitated energetically for war. Their success in procuring the *Peloponnesian War was matched by failure during it: their performance as Sparta's main naval ally was disastrous. The Corinthians voted against the Peace of *Nicias because it required them to accept their war losses; their attempts to renew hostilities against Athens succeeded only in embarrassing Sparta. When Athens attacked *Syracuse, Corinth enjoyed unaccustomed success in defence of its colony, helped partly by technical improvements which reinforced the prows of its *triremes. In 404 Sparta's refusal to destroy Athens began a rapid deterioration in relations, and within a decade Corinth joined Argos, *Boeotia, and Athens to fight Sparta in the *Corinthian War, so called because much of the action was in Corinthian territory—which suffered extensively. Corinth fought against *Philip II at *Chaeronea. The *Corinthian League was established at a meeting held in the city, but its central location had another consequence: Acrocorinth became the seat of a Macedonian garrison. After the Second Macedonian War, a Macedonian garrison gave place to a Roman successor, which *Quinctius Flamininus ostentatiously withdrew to demonstrate the reality of Greek 'freedom'; *Mummius destroyed Corinth in 146 to intimidate Greece into proper use of it.

See also DIOLKOS.

Roman Corinth was refounded (44 BC) as a Caesarian colony (see IULIUS CAESAR (1), GAIUS). The original colonists were mainly Roman freedmen, swelled by an influx of Roman businessmen (see NEGOTIATORES). By the late 1st cent. AD the colony was a flourishing centre of commerce, administration (see ACHAIA), the imperial cult, and entertainment. At first a self-conscious enclave of *Rōmānitās*, it became progressively Hellenized (see HELLENISM); under *Hadrian Greek replaced Latin as the language of official inscriptions. From the time of St *Paul it was the centre of early *Christianity in Greece.

Corinthian League, modern name for organization of Greek states created by *Philip II of Macedon after *Chaeronea: the details were agreed at Corinth. It provided (despite various Macedonian garrisons) for the *autonomy of all signatories and required collective action against states which contravened its terms. New features reflected Philip's intention to use it as the basis for his relations with the Greek states. Signatories swore not to overthrow the kingdom of Philip and his descendants; there was a meeting to take decisions, and a leader: Philip himself. The military obligations of members were determined by size.

Corinthian War, 395 to 386 BC, fought against Sparta by a combination of Athens, *Thebes, *Corinth, Persia, and others. The surface cause was trouble between *Locris and *Phocis, in which Thebes and Sparta intervened; the deeper cause was general fear of Spartan expansionism. The war was fought at sea (where the battle of Cnidus, 394, was a decisive blow to Sparta) and on land round Corinth, hence the name. It was ended by the *King's Peace.

Coriolānus See MARCIUS CORIOLANUS.

corn See CEREALS.

Cornēlia, second daughter of *Cornelius Scipio Africanus, married Tiberius *Sempronius Gracchus (1). Of her twelve children only three reached adulthood: Sempronia, who married *Cornelius Scipio Aemilianus, and the two famous tribunes Tiberius *Sempronius Gracchus (2) and Gaius *Sempronius Gracchus. After her husband's death she did not remarry, devoting herself chiefly to the education of her children. Traditions about her attitude to the tribunes' political activities vary, but she made Gaius abandon his attack on *Octavius. After Tiberius' death she retired to a villa at Misenum (where she heard of Gaius' death) and devoted herself to cultural pursuits and correspondence and conversation with distinguished men.

Cornēlius Balbus (1), **Lūcius,** b. in Gades (NW of Gibraltor), and distinguished as 'Balbus maior'. He acquired Roman citizenship at *Pompey's instance in 72 BC. He moved to Rome, where his political sense and the wealth derived from his adoption (c.59) by Theophanes of Mytilene gave him enormous influence. Part architect of the coalition of 60, he gradually shifted his allegiance from Pompey to *Caesar, serving the latter as ADC in 62 and 59, and later managing his interests in Rome. In 56 he was prosecuted for illegal usurpation of the citizenship, and was successfully defended by *Cicero in an extant speech. In the Civil War he was outwardly neutral. Actually he favoured Caesar,

and after Pharsalus became, with Oppius, Caesar's chief agent in public affairs. In 44 he supported *Octavian, though cautiously, and in 40 became Rome's first foreign-born consul. He had wide literary interests over which he constantly corresponded with Cicero. He bequeathed 25 *dēnāriī* to every citizen of Rome.

Cornēlius Balbus (2), **Lūcius,** nephew of Lucius *Cornelius Balbus (1) and distinguished as 'Balbus minor' in Cicero's letters, received the Roman *citizenship with his uncle. In 49 and 48 BC he undertook diplomatic missions for *Caesar; in 43 he was proquaestor in Further Spain under *Asinius Pollio, who complained of his tyrannical conduct at Gades and of his absconding with the pay-chest. *Augustus made him a *pontifex and gave him consular *ornamenta. Proconsul of Africa (21–20?), he defeated the Garamantes and other peoples and triumphed, a unique distinction for one not born a Roman. (See TRIUMPH.) He built a new town and docks at Gades and a theatre at Rome, which he dedicated in 13.

Cornēlius Celsus, Aulus, lived in the reign of *Tiberius (AD 14–37), and wrote an encyclopaedia on the arts/sciences (*artēs*), including books on agriculture, military science, and rhetoric. Only the medical books survive. The eight books of his *On Medicine* include a historical introduction to Greek medicine and a discussion of origins of *dietetics and medical theory (bk. 1, with proem), *pathology and therapeutics (bk. 2), special treatments (bks. 3–4), drug-lore (bks. 5–6, see PHARMACOLOGY), surgery (bk. 7), and skeletal anatomy (bk. 8). The proem to book 1 is one of the most important ancient sources for the history of Greek medicine, covering the period from the Homeric epics to Celsus' own day. See BOTANY; MEDICINE.

Cornēlius Cinna, Lūcius, of patrician family, fought successfully in the *Social War and, against the opposition of *Sulla, became consul 87 BC. Trying to rescind Sulla's legislation as passed by force, he was driven out of Rome by his colleague Octavius and illegally deposed. Collecting Italians and legionaries, he was joined by *Papirius Carbo and *Sertorius, and by *Marius, whom he summoned back to Italy. They marched on Rome and captured it late in 87. He punished those who had acted illegally, but tried (not very successfully) to stop indiscriminate violence on Marius' orders. Consul 86 with Marius and, after Marius' death, with Valerius Flaccus, he sent Flaccus to fight against *Mithradates VI, while he restored ordered government in Italy. He gained the co-operation of the *equestrians and the people by financial reforms, and that of eminent consulars by moderation and return to 'ancestral custom', although he could not repair the economic disruption of Italy due to the Social War and the Civil War. Following Marius' precedent, he held the consulship again in 85 and 84 with Carbo, owing to the emergency caused by the Mithradatic War and the threatening behaviour of Sulla, with whom he continued to negotiate. Embarking on a campaign in Liburnia early in 84, probably to train an army for a possible conflict with Sulla's veterans, he was killed in a mutiny. Sulla now rebelled and the government disintegrated. Our uniformly hostile accounts of him derive from supporters of Sulla.

Cornēlius Frontō, Marcus (c. AD 95–c.166), orator, *suffect consul 142; b. in Cirta; completed his education in Rome; a leading advocate under *Hadrian, he was appointed tutor by *Antoninus Pius to Marcus *Aurelius and his adoptive brother Lucius *Verus, remaining on intimate terms with them until his death, probably from the *plague of 166/7.

Though famous for his oratory ('not the second but the other glory of Roman eloquence', an allusion to *Cicero), Fronto is known today through his correspondence, chiefly with Marcus. The letters expound and illustrate his stylistic theories: the orator must seek out the most expressive word in Early Latin texts, preferring the unusual to the commonplace, provided it is not obscure or jarring; he must dispose his words in the best order and cultivate rhetorical figures, the *sententia, and the image-like description. Among Fronto's favourite authors are *Porcius Cato (1), *Plautus, *Ennius, and *Sallust; Cicero, though unsurpassed as a letter-writer, is criticized as an orator for taking insufficient pains to find 'unexpected and surprising words'. *Virgil is ignored, *Lucan and *Seneca the Younger damned.

The letters also illustrate Fronto's distaste for *Stoicism, his distress at its hold on Marcus, his constant ill-health, his family joys and sorrows, and the difficulties of life at court. He complains that Romans have no capacity for affection, nor even a name for it; Marcus, silent on Fronto's rhetorical tuition, acknowledges that he has learnt from him the hypocrisy of courts and the coldness of Roman patricians. Their own correspondence is marked by extreme displays of affection.

Fronto was more remarkable for mastery of language and warmth of heart than for keenness of intellect or strength of purpose; but our few fragments of his speeches tend to justify his ancient fame.

Cornēlius Gallus, Gāius appears in Rome in 43 BC as a mutual acquaintance of *Asinius Pollio and *Cicero. In 41 he had some sort of supervision of the confiscations of land, which involved *Virgil's family farm. In 30 he took an active military part in *Octavian's Egyptian campaign after *Actium and laid out a Forum Iulium in or near *Alexandria; this he recorded in an inscription, erased after his downfall, on an obelisk that is now in front of St Peter's in Rome. Octavian made him the first prefect of the new province of *Egypt. He suppressed a rebellion in the Thebaid, marched south beyond the first cataract, negotiated the reception of the king of *Ethiopia into Roman protection, and established a buffer-zone with a puppet king. He celebrated these achievements in a boastful trilingual inscription at Philae dated 15 April 29 and in inscriptions on the Pyramids, and set up statues of himself all over Egypt. He was apparently recalled, and, because of the insolence to which his pride had encouraged him, was banned from the house and provinces of Augustus. He was then indicted in the senate, and driven to kill himself (27/6 BC).

He wrote four books of love-elegies, addressed to Cythēris, a freedwoman actress who had been the mistress of Antony (Marcus *Antonius) 49–45 BC, under the pseudonym Lycōris. As well as one already-known pentameter, nine lines have been recovered from a papyrus. These lines confirm the position of Gallus as creator of the new genre of love-elegy and his influence, long suspected, on *Propertius; the appearance of the word domina also confirms the view that it was Gallus who, developing *Catullus, created the basic situation for Augustan elegists of the inamorata's dominance over the enslaved and helpless lover. See ELEGIAC POETRY, LATIN.

Cornēlius Scīpiō Aemiliānus Africānus (Numantīnus), Publius, b. 185/4 BC as second son of *Aemilius Paullus (2), adopted as a child by Cornelius Scipio, son of *Cornelius Scipio Africanus. In 168 he fought under Paullus at *Pydna. Back in Rome, he met *Polybius, who became his friend and his mentor in preparing him for a public career. In 151, though asked by the Macedonians, as Paullus' son, to settle their problems, he instead volunteered for arduous service as a military tribune under *Licinius Lucullus in Spain, thus persuading others to volunteer. In the fighting he won the *corona mūrālis* (see CROWNS AND WREATHS). When sent to request *elephants from *Masinissa, he renewed Africanus' patronal relations with him and vainly tried to mediate peace between him and *Carthage after a battle he had witnessed. In 149 and 148 he served as a military tribune in Africa (see PUNIC WARS) and again distinguished himself both in the fighting, where he won the *corona graminea*, and in diplomacy, persuading a Carthaginian commander to defect. After Masinissa's death he divided the kingdom among his three legitimate sons according to the king's request. Coming to Rome to stand for an *aedileship for 147, he was elected *consul, contrary to the rules for the *cursus honorum*, by a well-organized popular demand that forced the senate to suspend the rules. He was assigned Africa by special legislation and, after restoring discipline and closing off the enemy's harbour, he overcame long and desperate resistance and early in 146 captured Carthage after days of street-fighting. After letting his soldiers collect the *booty, he destroyed the city and sold the inhabitants into slavery. Anyone who should resettle the site was solemnly cursed. With the help of the usual senate commission he organized the province of Africa and after giving magnificent games returned to celebrate a splendid triumph, earning the name 'Africanus' to which his adoptive descent entitled him. He distributed some captured works of art among cities in Sicily and Italy.

In 140–39 he headed an embassy to the kings and cities of the east, with *Panaetius as his companion. After his return he presumably guided senate policy in those areas, esp. towards *Pergamum, the *Seleucids, and the *Jews. In 142 he was censor with *Mummius, who mitigated some of his severity. They restored the pons Aemilius (see BRIDGES) and adorned the *Capitol.

In 136 he secured the rejection of the peace in Spain negotiated by his cousin and brother-in-law Tiberius *Sempronius Gracchus (2). This deeply offended Gracchus, even though Scipio saved him from personal disgrace. In 135, again by special dispensation and without campaigning for the office, he was elected consul 134 and sent to *Numantia, with an army consisting chiefly of his own clients (see CLIENS) because of the shortage of military manpower. He

starved Numantia into surrender in just over a year, destroyed it, and sold the survivors into slavery, returning in 132 to celebrate a second triumph and acquire the (unofficial) name 'Numantinus'. By approving of Gracchus' murder he incurred great unpopularity. It was increased when, in 129, defending the interests of Italian clients holding public land, he was responsible for a senate decree that paralysed the agrarian commission by transferring its judiciary powers to the consuls, usually hostile or absent. When, soon after, he was found dead, various prominent persons, including his wife (Gracchus' sister) and *Cornelia (Gracchus' mother), were suspected of responsibility, though the funeral laudation written by his friend *Laelius specified natural death.

His personal morality and civil and military courage made him a friend of *Porcius Cato (1). But he was a patron of poets and philosophers, with a genuine interest in literature (he was himself an able orator) and in Greek philosophy, as transmitted by Polybius, which he combined with a traditional aristocratic Roman outlook. He believed in the 'balanced constitution', with the people entitled to choose their leaders. But he foresaw the ultimate fall of the republic, which could be delayed by stopping signs of decay, esp. the decline in aristocratic morality, and the danger of the democratic element, under the tribunes, leading the state into anarchy and tyranny. Utterly ruthless towards Rome's enemies, he believed in loyal patronage (both for Rome and for himself) over client-friends, whether monarchs like Masinissa or Italian allies. In his *Republic*, Cicero depicts him as the ideal Roman statesman.

Cornēlius Scīpiō Africānus, Publius, b. 236 BC, is said to have saved his father's life at the battle of the Ticinus in 218 and, as military tribune, to have rallied the survivors of the battle of *Cannae. He was curule *aedile 213, and in 210 was appointed by the people to the command in Spain, the first person to have received consular *imperium* without having previously been *consul or *praetor. In 209 he captured *Carthago Nova, the main Carthaginian supply base in Spain, by sending a wading party across the lagoon, which, he had discovered, normally ebbed in the evening. In 208, he defeated Hasdrubal Barca at Baecula. When Hasdrubal escaped towards the Pyrenees and the route to Italy, he decided not to pursue him. In 206 he defeated Mago and Hasdrubal at Ilipa. Thereafter only mopping-up operations remained in Spain; a mutiny in his army was quelled, and the ringleaders executed. Scipio crossed to Africa to solicit the support of Syphax, and met *Masinissa in western Spain.

Elected consul for 205, Scipio wanted to carry the war to Africa. Opposition in the senate was led by *Fabius Maximus Verrucosus, but he was assigned Sicily with permission to invade Africa if he saw fit. Denied the right to levy new troops, he crossed to Sicily accompanied only by volunteers, returning to south Italy to recapture Locri Epizephyrii. In 204 he landed in Africa, began the siege of *Utica, and wintered on a nearby headland. Hasdrubal and Syphax encamped a few miles south. In the course of feigned peace negotiations Scipio discovered the details of their camps, which were made of wood or reeds, and in the spring of 203 a night attack led to their destruction by fire and the death of large numbers of Carthaginian troops. Later Scipio defeated Hasdrubal and Syphax at the battle of the Great Plains, *c.*120 km. (75 mi.) west of Carthage. He now occupied Tunis but was forced to use his transport ships to block a Carthaginian attack on his fleet at Utica, losing 60 transports. During an armistice, peace terms were agreed, and accepted at Rome, but in the spring of 202 an attack by Carthage on Roman ships, and then on envoys sent by Scipio to protest, led to the resumption of hostilities. Hannibal had now returned to Carthage, and after further abortive peace negotiations Scipio defeated him at the battle of *Zama; peace was concluded on Rome's terms. Scipio received the *cognōmen* 'Africanus' and returned to Rome to celebrate a triumph.

Scipio now enjoyed great prestige at Rome. The capture of Carthago Nova, when Scipio is said to have told his troops that Neptune had appeared to him in a dream and promised him help, led to the belief that he was divinely inspired. The Iberians had saluted him as a king, but there is no evidence that he ever envisaged playing other than a traditional role in Roman politics. His success, however, meant that he had many enemies among the nobility, some alarmed by the stories circulating about him, others merely jealous of his success. He was elected *censor in 199, but his tenure of the office was unremarkable: he became *princeps senatus*, a position confirmed by the following two pairs of censors. Consul for the second time in 194, he wanted to succeed *Quinctius Flamininus in Greece, believing that a continued military presence was necessary as security against the *Seleucid Antiochus III, but the senate voted that the army should be withdrawn. As an ambassador to Africa in 193 he failed to settle a dispute between Carthage and Masinissa. In 190 he volunteered to go to Asia as a *legate under his brother Cornelius Scipio Asiāgenēs. He rejected the bribe which Antiochus offered him in order to secure a favourable peace; shortly before the battle of *Magnesia Antiochus returned his captive son. He took no part in the battle itself because of illness, but was chosen to present the Roman peace terms after Antiochus' defeat. At Rome there now began a series of conflicts between the Scipio brothers (and their allies) and their opponents, among whom *Porcius Cato (1) was prominent, culminating in the much debated 'trials of the Scipios'. The accusations involved the embezzlement of public funds. It is probable that Publius was attacked in the senate in 187, and Lucius put on trial, and that Publius was accused in 184, but avoided trial by retiring into voluntary exile on the Campanian coast, where he died the following year.

Cornēlius Scīpīo Nāsīca Serāpiō, Publius,

In 133 he vigorously opposed his cousin Tiberius *Sempronius Gracchus (2). When Gracchus mobilized a mob to seek re-election as tribune, he was accused of aiming at tyranny, but the consul saw no reason to take action. Scipio, calling on those who wanted to keep the republic safe to follow him, led a charge by senators and their clients (see CLIENS) against Gracchus, in which the latter was killed. The deed was ever after applauded by *optimates* and execrated by *populares*. Sent to Asia as head of a mission in connection with the annexation of the province, but in part to remove him from popular fury, he died at *Pergamum.

Cornēlius Sulla, Faustus,

son of *Cornelius Sulla Felix and of Caecilia Metella. His *praenōmen* and that of his twin sister, Fausta, were given to symbolize their father's good fortune. As his father's heir he was repeatedly threatened with prosecution. Serving as military tribune under Pompey, he was the first to scale the walls of the Temple in Jerusalem. On his return, he gave magnificent games in his father's memory (60 BC), was made *augur, and in 56 issued coins chiefly celebrating his father and Pompey. He was quaestor 54 and supported his half-brother *Aemilius Scaurus and, in 52, his brother-in-law *Annius Milo in their trials. He was put in charge of the restoration of the senate-house destroyed after *Clodius Pulcher's death. In the Civil War he joined *Pompey, fled to Africa after Pharsalus, and after Thapsus was captured and killed.

Cornēlius Sulla Fēlix, Lūcius, b. c.138 BC of an old patrician family, after a dissolute youth inherited a fortune from his stepmother, which enabled him to enter the aristocratic *career. Chosen by *Marius as his *quaestor (107) he distinguished himself in the Numidian War, finally securing the surrender of *Jugurtha by *Bocchus I through diplomacy and thus ending the war. He again served under Marius against the Germans in 104 and 103, then joined the army of Lutatius Catulus and enabled him to join in the final victory. Omitting the *aedileship, he failed to become *praetor for 98, but succeeded through lavish bribery in becoming urban praetor 97. He was assigned Cilicia as proconsul, then instructed to instal Ariobarzanes in Cappadocia. He accomplished this largely with local levies and displayed Roman power to the eastern kingdoms, including (for the first time) *Parthia. A Chaldaean's prophecy that he would attain greatness and die at the height of good fortune influenced him for the rest of his life. He stayed in Cilicia for several years. In 91 the senate, promoting him against Marius, granted Bocchus permission to dedicate on the Capitol a group showing the surrender of Jugurtha. Marius' reaction almost led to fighting, but the *Social War supervened.

In the war Sulla distinguished himself on the southern front and in 89, promoted esp. by the Metelli, gained the consulship of 88 with Pompeius Rufus, whose son married Sulla's daughter. Sulla himself married Caecilia Metella, widow of *Aemilius Scaurus, and was now one of the leading men in the state.

Given the command against *Mithradates VI by the senate, he was deprived of it by the tribune Publius *Sulpicius Rufus, who transferred it to Marius in order to gain Marius' aid for his political plans. Sulla pretended to acquiesce, but finding support among his troops, who hoped for rich booty in Asia, he marched on Rome and took the unprepared city by force. His officers, except for his quaestor (his relative *Licinius Lucullus) deserted him, and his methods shocked even his supporters. He had Sulpicius killed in office and his allies hunted down (Marius escaped to Africa), then passed several laws by armed force. General opposition compelled him to send his army away and allow the election of his enemy *Cornelius Cinna as consul 87, over his own candidate. Leaving Rome and ignoring a summons to stand trial,

he embarked for Greece, where Braetius Sura, a *legate of the commander in Macedonia, had already driven the enemy back to the sea. Sulla's hope of safety lay in winning the war: he ordered Sura to return to Macedonia and took charge of the fighting.

Outlawed, but not molested, under Cinna, he agreed (it seems) to refrain from attacking Valerius Flaccus, who had been given the command against Mithradates. He himself twice defeated Mithradates' general Archelaus and sacked *Piraeus and (in part) *Athens. After Lucullus had saved Mithradates from Flavius Fimbria, who had taken over Flaccus' army, Sulla made peace with the king at Dardanus (85), granting him his territory, recognition as an ally, and impunity for his adherents in return for surrender of his conquests and support for Sulla with money and supplies. He then dealt with Fimbria, reconciled his own army (disgruntled at the peace with the enemy of Rome) by quartering it on the cities of Asia, which he bled of their wealth, and on hearing of Cinna's death abandoned negotiations with the government and openly rebelled (84). Invading Italy, he was soon joined by most aristocrats—esp. Caecilius Metellus Pius, *Licinius Crassus, and *Pompey—and within a year had defeated all the loyalist forces. Finding the Italians hostile, he swore not to diminish their rights of citizenship, but massacred those who continued resistance (esp. the Samnites) and imposed severe penalties and confiscations on whole communities. After securing Rome through his victory at the Colline gate, he was appointed dictator under a law of the *interrex, another Valerius Flaccus, whom he made his magister equitum, and was voted immunity for all his actions, past and future. He continued and legalized his massacres by publishing *proscription lists.

During 81 he enacted a legislative programme designed to put power firmly in the hands of the senate, whose numbers (traditionally 300, but now much reduced) he raised to 600 by adlecting *equestrians supporting him. He now (1) curbed the tribunate by requiring the senate's approval for tribunician bills, limiting the veto (*intercessio) and debarring ex-tribunes from other magistracies, thus making the office unattractive to ambitious men; (2) returned the *quaestiones to the enlarged senate; (3) increased the number of praetors to eight and that of quaestors to 20, chiefly to ensure that tenure of provinces was not (in general) prolonged beyond one year; (4) laid down a stricter *cursus honorum, making the quaestorship as well as the praetorship compulsory before the consulship could be reached at a minimum age of 42; (5) made quaestors automatically members of the senate, thus abolishing the censors' right of selection, and did away with the powerful post of *princeps senatus*; (6) subjected holders of *imperium* outside Italy to stricter control by the senate. His veterans were settled on confiscated land (esp. in *Campania and Etruria, see ETRUSCANS) as guarantors of his order. Then, believing in the old prophecy that he now had not long to live, he gradually divested himself of power and restored constitutional government, becoming consul (with Metellus Pius) in 80 and returning to private status in 79. He retired with Valeria, his fifth wife, to Campania, where he died of a chronic disease in 78. His funeral was impressively staged to display the power of his veterans, esp. in view of the agitation of the consul *Aemilius Lepidus (1). In fact, his constitutional settlement, weakened by concessions during the 70s, was overthrown in 70 by his old adherents *Pompey and *Crassus; but his administrative reforms survived the end of the republic and beyond.

Despite his mystical belief in his luck, despite his arrogance and ruthlessness, Sulla never aimed at permanent tyranny: he did not even put his portrait on his coins. He wished his settlement to succeed, and he thought it out carefully, to eliminate the 'two-headedness' (thus *Varro) that Gaius *Sempronius Gracchus had introduced into the republic and to restore a strengthened senate to unchallenged power. His arrangements were consistent, practical, and neither visionary nor reactionary. Yet he had no appreciation of deep-seated problems: he made no attempt to remove the threat of client armies, such as had supported his own rebellion, by putting the senate in charge of providing for veterans, and he seems actually to have abolished the provision of corn to the poor at a controlled price. His own example not only set a precedent for the use of client armies against the republic, but helped to destroy the morale of those on whom resistance to an imitator would depend. After sparing the only powerful enemy of Rome for his personal advantage, he had prepared the ground for that enemy's resurgence by ruining the cities of Asia; he had weeded out those most loyal to the republic in Rome and Italy and rewarded and promoted those who, for whatever reason, had joined in his rebellion. A sense of duty and public service could not be expected of those now making up the senate who had welcomed the opportunities

for power and enrichment provided by a rebel; and a generation later it became clear that Italy, having suffered for its loyalty to the republic, was unwilling to defend Sulla's beneficiaries and their corrupt successors against Caesar when he followed Sulla's example.

That example did instil a horror of civil war that lasted for a generation: his beneficiaries praised his rebellion that had brought them to power, but shuddered at his cruelty after victory. Yet that memory was bound to fade. His career and the effects of his victory made another civil war almost inevitable, and a politic *clēmentia* now made a successful rebel unobjectionable to the majority.

corn supply See FOOD SUPPLY.

corruption Charges of corruption (fraud, *bribery, *ambitus, double-dealing, peculation, or the sale of offices) should be viewed against the norms of the society in which the accusation is made. Most of the surviving classical evidence comes from works whose primary purpose is denigration. Accusations of corruption were part of a rhetoric of execration intended to damn an opponent in as many memorable ways as possible. These claims should be accorded the same degree of credibility as *invective concerning dubious ancestry, sexual perversion, or *deformity.

The insults traded between *Demosthenes (2) and *Aeschines (1) were an accepted part of their rivalry and their advocacy of competing political programmes. In his speech against *Verres *Cicero included accusations of extortion, bribery, and taxation fraud. These were aspects of a long, lurid, and highly rhetorical description of Verres' vices—indispensable elements in any properly constructed character assassination. Provincial governorships were in fact widely regarded as a legitimate source of income (Cicero himself did well while governor of Cilicia), and very few cases of maladministration were ever successfully prosecuted in the Roman courts.

Some wrongdoers were caught and punished. In AD 38, the citizens of *Alexandria secured the conviction of Avillius Flaccus, a former prefect of Egypt, on charges of extortion. He was exiled and later executed on the orders of Caligula (see GAIUS (1)). In the early 3rd cent. AD, the emperor Severus Alexander discovered an official receiving money for his (apparently illusory) influence at court; a practice known colloquially as selling smoke. In a blunt example of imperial wit,

Severus ordered a fire of wet logs to be made. The offender was asphyxiated. These incidents represent isolated reactions. They are attempts to police esp. blatant or excessive abuses or to eliminate rivals, rather than evidence of any widespread condemnation of these practices themselves. No doubt most played safe, following the maxim of *Septimius Severus and *Caracalla that governors should be careful to take 'neither everything, nor every time, nor from everyone'.

Coruncānius, Tiberius, from Tusculum, consul 280 BC, dictator (for elections) 246, died 243. As consul he celebrated a triumph over the Etruscan cities of Volsinii and Vulci and was active with his colleague against *Pyrrhus. *Pontifex* from an unknown date, he became (between 255 and 252) the first plebeian *pontifex maximus*. As an early jurist, he was the first to admit members of the public to his consultations, thereby rendering jurisprudence a profession instead of a mystery (see LAWYERS, ROMAN).

Cos, a fertile island in the SE Aegean, on the north–south trading route along the coast of Anatolia and onwards to Cyprus, Syria, and Egypt. The island was colonized, in the Dark Age, by *Dorians. It was a member of the Dorian hexapolis (with Camirus, *Cnidus, *Halicarnassus, Ialysus, Lindus).

In the late Archaic period the island was subject initially to Persia and to the Lygdamid (see ARTEMISIA) dynasty of Halicarnassus, and then to Athens. In 366, the Coans, previously organized in separate cities, united to form one city-state (see SYNOECISM), founding a new city on the NE coast, which was fortified and where a good, artificial *harbour was built. The island fell under the control of *Mausolus and probably remained Hecatomnid until 'liberated' by *Alexander (2) the Great's admiral in 332.

For most of the 3rd cent. Cos was independent, an ally, of the Ptolemies (see PTOLEMY (1)), enjoying a democratic constitution, and trading, political, and cultural links with *Alexandria; the poets *Philitas, *Theocritus, and *Herodas exemplify the literary ties. The rich corpus of Coan inscriptions indicates the continuing vitality and importance of 'traditional' Greek cults through the Hellenistic period. The corpus attests too the continuing activity of Coan doctors, deriving from the local 'school of medicine' founded by *Hippocrates in the 5th cent., whose services Greek states asked for, and gained, usually in times of famine, war or revolution.

There are rich archaeological remains on Cos, from e.g. the excavations of the Asclepium (see ASCLEPIUS), outside the city, to those of the agora, the port quarter, a gymnasium, and the Hellenistic temple and altar of *Dionysus.

cosmetics Most of the aids to beauty known today were to be found in ancient times on a woman's dressing-table; and in both Greece and Rome men paid great attention to cleanliness, applying *olive oil after exercise and bathing (see BATHS), and scraping the limbs with strigils: dandies went further and would remove the hair from every part of their body with tweezers, pitch-plaster, and depilatories.

Many specimens have been found of ancient cosmetic implements. Mirrors were usually made of polished copper alloy. Combs were of the tooth-comb pattern, with one coarse and one fine row of teeth. Razors, made of bronze, were of various shapes, the handle often beautifully engraved. Safety-pins and brooches had many forms elaborately inlaid with enamel and metal.

Cosmetics and perfumes were freely used. Athenian women attached importance to white cheeks, as a marker of status; they applied white lead, and also used an orchid-based rouge. Roman women also had a great variety of salves, unguents, and hair-dyes kept in a toilet box with separate compartments for powders, paints, and toothpastes. Several recipes for these commodities are given by *Ovid in his mock-didactic poem 'Cosmetics for the Female Face'.

Greek women usually wore their hair arranged simply in braids and drawn into a knot behind; and the same style was often adopted in Rome. But under the empire a fashion arose of raising a structure of hair on the top of the head, either in a wig or painfully arranged by a lady's maid. Blondes were fashionable in Rome, and brunettes could either dye their hair or use the false hair which was freely imported from Germany.

Men in early Greece and Rome wore beards and allowed the hair of the head to grow long. From the 5th cent. BC the Greeks cut the hair of their heads short, and from the time of *Alexander (2) the Great they shaved their chins. The Romans followed suit in the 3rd cent. BC, but from the time of Hadrian they again wore beards. See DRESS; PORTRAITURE, GREEK and ROMAN.

council See BOUL.

courtesans See HETAIRAI.

craftsmen See ARTISANS AND CRAFTSMEN; INDUSTRY.

Crantor of Soli in Cilicia (c.335–275 BC), philosopher of the Early *Academy, and the first Platonic commentator. His commentary on Plato's *Timaeus* sided with those who denied a literal creation of the world. His ethical writings were much admired. One passage described a contest between the various Goods, with Virtue the eventual winner. His *On Grief* (Cicero's model for his own *Consolation*) opposed the *Cynic-inspired ideal of eradicating this emotion (see CONSOLATION). See also ATLANTIS.

Crassus See LICINIUS CRASSUS.

Craterus (d. 321 BC), marshal of *Alexander (2) the Great. First attested in charge of a Macedonian infantry battalion, he commanded the left of the phalanx at Issus and *Gaugamela. After the removal of *Philotas and *Parmenion, in which he played an unsavoury role, he assumed Parmenion's mantle and commanded numerous independent detachments during the campaigns in Sogdiana and India. At Opis (324) he was appointed viceroy in Europe in *Antipater's stead and commissioned to repatriate 10,000 Macedonian veterans. Alexander's death found him in Cilicia, and he could not participate in the Babylon settlement. In 322 he moved to Europe, where his forces were instrumental in winning the *Lamian War. A staunch defender of Macedonian tradition, he was intensely popular with the Macedonian rank and file, who cherished his memory.

Cratēs, of *Thebes (c.368/365–288/285 BC), *Cynic philosopher and poet. Having gone to Athens as a young man, he became a follower of *Diogenes (2) and gave his wealth to the poor. How far he maintained Diogenes' philosophy is disputed. He claimed to be 'a citizen of Diogenes', espousing a similar cosmopolitanism; notoriously enacted Diogenes' prescriptions regarding free and public sex in his relations with Hipparchia, with whom he shared a Cynic way of life; and often expressed ethical sentiments as extreme and intolerant as Diogenes'. But he did not insist on the complete renunciation of wealth or that everybody should become a Cynic, and he conceded a certain legitimacy to existing occupations; and the deployment of his considerable charm and kindliness in proclaiming his message, comforting the afflicted, and reconciling enemies, won him a reputation for humanity which endured throughout antiquity. Granted their obvious differences in personality and missionary approach, Crates seems himself to have followed Diogenes rigorously, while (sometimes) allowing greater latitude to others. This partial moral relativism makes him the link between 'hard' and 'soft' Cynicism; he is also, through *Zeno (2) (his most famous follower), the link between Cynicism and *Stoicism.

Cratīnus was regarded, with *Aristophanes and *Eupolis, as one of the greatest poets of Old Attic Comedy (see COMEDY (GREEK), OLD). He won the first prize six times at the City *Dionysia and three times at the *Lenaea. We have 27 titles and over 500 citations. His *Dionysalexandros* attacked *Pericles for 'bringing the war upon Athens', and must belong to 430 or 429. The *hypothesis of *Dionysalexandros* is largely preserved in a papyrus; in this play *Dionysus—as the title suggests—was represented as carrying *Helen off to Troy; there was a chorus of *satyrs. Cratinus' language and style were inventive, concentrated, and allusive, and Aristophanes was much influenced by him.

Cratylus, a younger contemporary of *Socrates. He pressed the doctrine of *Heraclitus to an extreme point, denying to things even the slightest fixity of nature. Acc. to *Aristotle he was *Plato's first master in philosophy, and Plato drew the conclusion that since fixity does not exist in the sensible world, there must be a non-sensible world to account for the possibility of knowledge.

credit, the temporary transfer of property rights over money or goods, was central to the functioning of ancient society. Almost all credit operations would have been informal transactions between relatives, neighbours, and friends, marked by the absence of interest, security, or written agreement. These day-to-day transactions, with their basis in *reciprocity, created and strengthened bonds between individuals. Hence the hostility felt by *Plato towards formal credit agreements, implying as they did a lack of trust. In Athens the range of possible sources of credit extended beyond family and friends to include professional money-lenders, bankers, and usurers (providing short-term high-interest loans). In these latter cases, relationships between the parties would be more impersonal, justifying interest and formal precautions. From the Roman world, detailed testimony from the republic focuses on credit transactions between members of the élite, juggling their resources with an eye towards political advantage. *Cicero writes of the obligation to take over the debts of an *amīcus* (see AMICITIA). Those thrown back on formal sources of credit could turn to a range of specialist lenders. See BANKS.

Cremūtius Cordus, Aulus, Roman historian, writing under *Augustus and *Tiberius, treated the period from the Civil Wars to at least 18 BC. Refusing to glorify Augustus, he celebrated *Cicero, *Brutus, and *Cassius, 'the last Roman'. Prosecuted at the instigation of *Sejanus, he killed himself (AD 25). His work was burnt, but copies, preserved by his daughter, were published in abridged form under *Gaius (1).

Creon (1), of *Thebes, brother of Iocasta. (See OEDIPUS.) He offered her and the kingdom to anyone who would rid Thebes of the *Sphinx. After Oedipus' fall and again after the death of *Eteocles, he became king or regent of Thebes. During the attack by the *Seven against Thebes, he lost his son Menoeceus. Another son, Haemon, was either killed by the Sphinx or took his own life after the suicide of *Antigone, his betrothed, or on a later occasion. Creon was almost as unfortunate in his daughters, whom he gave in marriage to *Heracles and Iphicles. The former, Megara, was killed by Heracles in a fit of madness. Creon was killed by *Theseus in a battle over the burial of the Seven.

Creon (2), a king of *Corinth whom *Medea killed by magic and fled, leaving her children behind to be killed by the Corinthians. *Euripides has her kill Creon's daughter (*Jason's betrothed) with a poisoned costume and murder her own sons.

Although the name 'Creon' means simply the 'lord' or 'ruler', and is used to fill in gaps in genealogies, it is a measure of the skill of *Sophocles and *Euripides that they make these two figures into credible, if not lovable, human beings.

Cresilas, sculptor from Cydonia in Crete, active c.440–410 BC. His statues of *Pericles and of Dieitrephes shot through with arrows stood on the Acropolis; their signed bases survive. Acc. to *Pliny the Elder, his *Amazon for *Ephesus was placed third after those of *Polyclitus and *Phidias. Copies of Pericles' head survive.

Crete In historical times the island was mainly *Dorian. Cretans prided themselves that *Zeus was born on Crete. Of Homer's 'Crete of the hundred cities' over 100 names survive, but there seem to have been in the Classical and Hellenistic periods only about 40 city-states. The island's position on the sea-routes to and from *Cyprus, the Levant, and *Egypt secured it an important place in the development of Archaic Greek art: important innovations were attributed to the mythical Cretan *Daedalus. It had a reputation as the home of mercenary slingers and *archers, and of lawgivers (see GORTYN; LAW IN GREECE). Aristocratic society persisted in the island, and the constitutions (though without kings) resembled that of *Sparta, which was said to have been derived from Crete, and impressed *Plato and *Aristotle. In the Classical period the island lay outside the mainstream of Greek history. See also LANDSCAPES (ANCIENT GREEK).

Critias (c.460–403 BC), one of the *Thirty Tyrants at Athens. Born of a rich old family to which *Plato also belonged, he, like his close friend *Alcibiades, was an associate of Socrates. He is often included with the *sophists, and surviving fragments of his tragedies and other works evince an interest in current intellectual issues.

Critias was implicated in the mutilation of the *herms (415) but was released on the evidence of *Andocides. He played little or no part in the oligarchic coup in 411. In perhaps 408 he proposed the recall of Alcibiades. The latter's second exile in 406 was probably linked to Critias' own exile; he went to *Thessaly. He was an admirer of *Spartan ways, about which he wrote several works, and upon the Spartan defeat of Athens in 404 he returned from exile to become one of the Thirty Tyrants. In *Xenophon's narrative he appears as the leader of the extremists, violent and unscrupulous, who proposes the execution of his colleague *Theramenes; but the account in *Athēnaiōn politeia does not mention him. He was killed fighting against *Thrasybulus (2) in spring 403. His reputation did not recover after his death; but Plato honoured his memory in several dialogues.

Critius, Athenian (?) sculptor, active c.490–460 BC. Author, with Nēsiōtēs, of six dedications on the Acropolis, all bronzes. The two were famed for their bronze Tyrannicides (Harmodius and *Aristogiton), commissioned in 477/6 to replace those by *Antenor, stolen by *Xerxes in 480.

Copies of them survive; they are often considered to represent the 'official birthday' of the early Classical or Severe style in Greek sculpture. Attributions include the 'Critius Boy' from the Acropolis.

Critolāus, of Phaselis, head of the *Peripatetic school, was probably an old man when he took part, with *Carneades (see ACADEMY) and Diogenes the Stoic (see STOICISM), in the philosophers' delegation to Rome in 155 BC. His headship of the school marks a renewal of its scientific and philosophical activities. He defended the Aristotelian doctrine of the eternity of the world against the Stoic periodic conflagration.

Croesus, last king of *Lydia (c.560–546 BC), son of *Alyattes. He completed the subjugation of the Greek cities on the Anatolian coast. His later relations with the Greeks were not unfriendly though tribute was imposed; he contributed to the rebuilding of the Artemisium at *Ephesus and made offerings to Greek shrines, esp. *Delphi; anecdotes attest his friendliness to Greek visitors and his wealth. The rise of *Persia led Croesus to seek support in Greece and Egypt, but *Cyrus (1) anticipated him: Sardis was captured and Croesus overthrown. By crossing the river Halys (into Persian territory) he was said to have destroyed a great empire. His subsequent fate soon became the theme of legend: he is cast or casts himself on a pyre, but is miraculously saved by *Apollo and translated to the land of the Hyperboreans or becomes the friend and counsellor of Cyrus.

Cronus, the youngest of the *Titans, sons of *Uranus (Heaven) and *Gaia (Earth). His mythology is marked by paradoxes. Acc. to one myth, he castrated his father at the instigation of his mother. From his marriage with his sister Rhea the race of the (Olympian) gods was born: *Hestia, *Demeter, *Hera, *Hades, *Poseidon, and *Zeus. Fearing to be overcome by one of his children he swallowed them on birth, save only the last, Zeus, saved by Rhea, who wrapped a stone in swaddling-clothes which Cronus swallowed instead. The infant Zeus was hidden in *Crete, where he was protected by the Cūrētēs (young, divine, male warriors). Later, by the contrivance of Gaia, Cronus vomited up all his children and was overcome by them after a desperate struggle. He was incarcerated in Tartarus. Later authors give roughly the same story, differing mainly on his place of exile, clearly under the influence of the second group of Cronus myths.

In these Cronus is pictured as king of the *golden age, a utopian wonderland. He maintains this role in the hereafter at the borders of the earth, as the ruler of the *Islands of the Blest. Later he becomes the model for the Italic god *Saturnus, civilizer of Latium and Italy.

The stark contradiction between the extreme cruelty manifested in the first version and the utopian blessings in the second has fostered conjectures concerning different origins. While Cronus as king of the golden age was supposed to have been an authentic Greek (or at least *Indo-European) contribution, the cruel tyrant was assumed to have been derived from another culture. Indeed, similar myths of swallowing fathers can be found all over the world, but none as close as the Hurrian–Hittite myth of Kumarbi. In his *Theogony* Hesiod must have (indirectly) borrowed the theme from this near-eastern myth.

Cronus is predominantly a mythical god: rites, cults, and cult-places are scarce. His festival, the Cronia, celebrated in Athens and a few other places after the harvest, is a carnivalesque feast of exultation and abundance: masters and slaves feast together. One source even reports that masters served their servants during the festival. However, other (legendary) cult practices involve human sacrifices, while foreign gods associated with human sacrifice, like Bel, are consistently identified with Cronus.

crowns and wreaths

Greek These were worn by Greeks for various ceremonial purposes: by priests when *sacrificing, by members of dramatic choruses, orators and symposiasts (see SYMPOSIUM). They served as prizes at games and as awards of merit. Originally made from the branches of trees and plants, each having a specific connotation (e.g. olive/*Olympic victory, funerals; vine and ivy/*Dionysus; rose/*Aphrodite, symposium), crowns began to be made in gold and occasionally silver. Less solid examples were made for funerary use, and some are preserved in the archaeological record. Gold crowns occur often in the epigraphic sources relating to Athens and *Delos. The crown-making stage was often bypassed, and the recipient simply pocketed the money.

Roman Crowns and wreaths were awarded by the Romans as decorations for valour, and in the republic the nature of the achievement dictated the type of award, the most distinguished being the *corōna grāminea*, a crown of grass granted to a man who raised a siege. *Pliny the Elder lists only eight recipients, ending with *Augustus. The *c. cīvica*, made of oak leaves, was granted to anyone who had saved a comrade's life in battle. The *c. nāvālis* (also *classica* or *rostrāta*—decorated with a ship's prow) was reserved for distinguished conduct in naval battles. A *c. mūrālis* was awarded to the first man to scale a town or camp wall under assault. A gold crown (*c. aurea*) rewarded general acts of gallantry, as did a miniature spear, standard, necklaces, bracelets, and metal discs which could be attached to body armour. Commanders celebrating a *triumph wore a crown of laurel, those with an *ovatio, a crown of myrtle. In the late republic rank rather than merit became the overriding factor in the type of award. This was developed in the imperial period, and although the *c. civica* was open to all soldiers, most military decorations were granted on a fixed scale according to rank.

crucifixion was a form of punishment apparently borrowed by the Romans from elsewhere, probably *Carthage. As a Roman penalty it is first certainly attested in the *Punic Wars. It was normally confined to slaves or non-citizens and later in the empire to humbler citizens; it was not applied to soldiers, except in the case of desertion. *Constantine I abolished the penalty. Normal practice was to begin with flagellation of the condemned, who was then compelled to carry a cross-beam to the place of execution, where a stake had been firmly fixed in the ground. He was stripped and fastened to the cross-beam with nails and cords, and the beam was drawn up by ropes until his feet were clear of the ground. Some support for the body was provided by a ledge which projected from the upright, but a footrest is rarely attested, though the feet were sometimes tied or nailed. Death probably occurred through exhaustion: it could be hastened by breaking the legs. After removal of the body the cross was usually destroyed. See also PUNISHMENT.

Ctēsias (late 5th cent. BC) of *Cnidus, Greek doctor at the court of *Artaxerxes (2) II, who wrote a history of *Persia in 23 books, consisting mostly of romantic stories, based on either oral traditions or court gossip, and now preserved only in fragments. Ctesias' claim that he consulted the royal records is not corroborated by the information he gives. Both in antiquity and modern times his work has been found unreli-

able, albeit entertaining. He also wrote the first separate work on India.

Ctēsibius, inventor (fl. 270 BC), was the son of a barber in *Alexandria, and employed by *Ptolemy (1) II. He was the first to make devices employing 'pneumatics', i.e. the action of air under pressure. His work on the subject is lost, but descriptions of some of his inventions are preserved by Philon, *Vitruvius, and Heron. These include the pump with plunger and valve, the water-organ, the first accurate water-*clock and a war-catapult. No great theoretician, Ctesibius was a mechanical genius, some of whose inventions were of permanent value. Many of the basic ideas in the works of Philon and Heron on mechanical devices probably derive from him.

culture-bringers, mythical figures who are credited with the invention of important cultural achievements. Around the 6th cent. BC the Greeks started to ascribe a number of inventions to gods and heroes. So *Athena Polias planted the first *olive tree, and as Ergane she invented weaving (see TEXTILE PRODUCTION); *Demeter taught sowing and grinding corn; *Dionysus was connected with viticulture (see WINE), and *Apollo thought up the *calendar. Of the heroes, Argive Phorōneus invented fire, and the Telchīnes of Rhodes metal-working; panhellenic *Heracles founded the *Olympic Games. In Athens, *Prometheus became important; to him it owed architecture, meteorology, astronomy, numbers, writing, domestication and harnessing of animals, sailing, medicine, *divination, mining—in short all *technai* (practical skills; Aeschylus, *Prometheus Bound* 506).

The *sophists became much interested in the origin of culture, witness *Protagoras' lost *On the Original State of Man.* *Prodicus considered Demeter and Dionysus to have been deified because of their inventions. His views were an instant success, and he was followed by *Euhemerus, whose Zeus takes a great interest in 'inventors who had discovered new things that promised to be useful for the lives of men'.

Cūmae (Gk. Cȳmē), *Euboean colony, founded c.740 BC opposite *Pithecusae. It was the earliest colony on the Italian mainland, and dominated coastal *Campania from 700, in turn founding Neapolis, Dicaearchia (see PUTEOLI), and Zancle (see MESSANA). In 421, it fell to the Oscans. Although substantially Oscanized, Greek culture was not eradicated. During the Archaic period, it had enjoyed cordial relations with Rome, but they soured after the Oscan conquest. It became a *cīvitās sine suffrāgiō* (see CITIZENSHIP, ROMAN) in 338, and remained loyal to Rome in the *Punic Wars. In 180 it adopted Latin as its official language, and probably obtained full citizenship soon after. The developing port of *Puteoli eclipsed Cumae economically, but it remained important. Many of the Roman élite had villas there, and the harbour and acropolis were sumptuously rebuilt by Augustus, who also granted Cumae colonial status. The Cumaean *Sibyl and cult of *Apollo were important in Augustan ideology (as can be seen in Virgil's *Aeneid*, bk. 6), and Cumae was popular among Roman aristocrats because of its Greek culture.

Cunaxa, a small town on the *Euphrates near Baghdad, where *Cyrus (2), younger son of *Darius II of Persia, was defeated and killed by his elder brother, *Artaxerxes (2) II, in 401 BC. The battle is chiefly interesting for the ease with which Cyrus' Greek *mercenaries, commanded on his right by the Spartan Clearchus, defeated Artaxerxes' left, with the loss of only one man. *Xenophon, who was serving among the Greeks, has left us a vivid description of their charge at the double, shouting their war-cry, and some clashing their spears on their shields to frighten the enemy horses. Even after Cyrus himself had been killed and the rest of his army had fled, the Greeks still managed to rout the remainder of Artaxerxes' army, in a second attack. It was after this battle, and the subsequent treacherous capture of their commanders (see TISSAPHERNES), that the Greeks began the long march home which is the main subject of Xenophon's *Anabasis*.

cuneiform is wedge-shaped writing by impressing the triangular cross-section of a reed upon clay. The script uses more than 500 signs to write syllables, logograms, determinatives, etc., each sign having various values. It was gradually replaced by alphabetic scripts.

cūra(tiō), cūrātor Among many more general meanings, these words refer to a specific duty inhering in a regular office; thus *Cicero defines the *aediles as *cūrātōrēs* of the city (i.e. its buildings, *sanitation, *policing, etc.), the *annona*, and the games (see LUDI). As Roman commitments expanded, some tasks came to surpass the powers of annual magistrates. In 145 BC the urban praetor Marcius Rex was retained in office in order to complete an *aque-

duct. This was later avoided by the conferment of special *curae*, in principle detached from office, for time-consuming tasks. In particular, the far-flung network of *roads in Italy, or its constituent parts, often received *curatores* after 100; thus *Caesar gained popularity by lavish spending as *curator* of the *via Appia *c.*67. Other *curae* were conferred as required. In 78 the consul Lutatius Catulus was made *curator* for restoring the Capitol, a task that dragged on for years. About 105 the *princeps senatus* *Aemilius Scaurus superseded the quaestor at Ostia *Appuleius Saturninus in the latter's regular charge of imports of corn. In 57, *Pompey, in a major innovation, received a *cura annonae* with *imperium* *pro consule* for five years. *Augustus assumed a *curatio annonae* based on this precedent at a time of famine. (He already had the *imperium*.) Occasional *curationēs* continue under the empire when required, e.g. the consular *curatores* for the restoration of *Campania appointed by *Titus after the eruption of *Vesuvius. However, under Augustus many routine functions of magistrates came to be entrusted to boards of experienced (consular or praetorian) *curatores*. In 22, he established praetorian *curatores* for distributing corn, in 20 for the roads, in 11 for the city's water supply. The senate decree creating that office shows the regulations establishing the powers and duties of such boards. *Curatores* for public buildings and for monitoring and regulating the *Tiber followed in Augustus' lifetime, and several more such boards later. The system was at once imitated in Roman colonies and municipalities and for a long time ensured the smooth functioning of urban life.

cūria (1) was the most ancient division of the Roman people. The *curiae* were 30 in number. Some bore local names, others personal ones. Membership of the *curiae* was determined by birth, but as they also seem to have been local groupings, each with its own meeting-place, it is probable that originally they comprised the families resident in particular localities. Each *curia* was headed by an official called the *cūriō*, aged at least 50 and elected for life. One of these leaders was chosen as head of all the *curiae*, the *curio maximus*. The post was held by patricians until 209 BC, when a plebeian was elected for the first time. See COMITIA.

Cūria (2), the senate-house of Rome. The original building on the north side of the *Comitium in the forum Romanum was orientated by cardinal points. It was restored by Sulla after 81

BC, damaged following the funeral of *Clodius Pulcher in 52 and rebuilt by Faustus *Cornelius Sulla. Caesar began a new building, on a slightly different site and orientation in 44 as part of his forum, which was inaugurated by *Augustus in 29. Restored by *Domitian in AD 94, it was rebuilt by *Diocletian after the fire of 283, following the Caesarian plan. The sumptuous oblong hall of brick-faced concrete decorated externally with imitation stucco ashlar, has a central door facing a magistrates' dais and lateral marble benches.

curses A curse expresses a wish that evil may befall a person or persons. Several different types can be distinguished, according to setting, motive, and condition. The most direct curses are maledictions lacking any explicit religious, moral, or legal legitimation. This category is exemplarily represented by the so-called curse tablets, thin lead sheets inscribed with maledictions intended to influence the actions or welfare of persons. If a motive is mentioned, it is generally inspired by feelings of envy and competition, esp. in the circus and the (amphi)-theatre, litigation, love, and commerce. Nearly all these texts are anonymous and lack argumentation or references to deserved punishment of the cursed person(s). If gods are invoked, they belong to the sphere of death, the Underworld, and witchcraft. In later times the magical names of exotic demons and gods abound. Spirits of the dead are also invoked, since the tablets were often buried in graves of the untimely dead. The tablets might be rolled up and transfixed with a needle, and sometimes 'voodoo dolls' were added. These tablets first appear in the 6th cent. BC often with simple formulas ('I bind the names of . . . ') and develop into elaborate texts in the imperial age. More than 1,500 have been recovered.

Included in the well-known collections of curse tablets, yet a distinct genre, are prayers for justice or 'vindictive prayers'. They differ from the binding curses in that the name of the author is often mentioned, the action is justified by a reference to some injustice done by the cursed person (theft, slander), the gods invoked are great gods (e.g. *Helios), and they are begged to punish the culprit and rectify the injustice. This variant becomes popular only in the Hellenistic and Roman periods and is found all over the Roman empire, but esp. in *Britain.

Both these types of curse are concerned with past and present occurrences. Another type refers to future events. Conditional curses damn the unknown persons who dare to infringe certain laws, prescriptions, treaties. They are prevalent in the public domain and are expressed by the community through its representatives (magistrates, priests). A special subdivison in this category is the conditional self-curse as contained in oath formulae. Here the person who offends against the oath brings upon himself the curse he has himself pronounced and the wrath of the gods. Similar imprecations, both public and private, are common in funerary inscriptions against those who violate graves.

cursus honōrum Down to the 3rd cent. BC there were perhaps few rules concerning the *cursus honorum* (career path) other than a requisite period of military service before seeking the political offices open to one's order, and some restrictions on iteration. The senatorial establishment in the early 2nd cent. continued to support a loosely regulated *cursus*, surely because it facilitated use of private influence in elections. However, in or soon after 197, when the number of *praetors was set at six, a new law stipulated that all *consuls be ex-praetors. Henceforth, the basic progression was *quaestor–praetor–consul. If the tribunate of the *plebs* and the aedileship were held, the former usually and the latter always followed the quaestorship; the censorship traditionally went to ex-consuls (see AEDILES; CENSOR; TRIBUNI PLEBIS). The *cursus* acquired further rigidity from the *lex Villia annalis* of 180 (see VILLIUS (ANNALIS)), which set minimum ages for each of the curule magistracies (see MAGISTRACY, ROMAN). *Cornelius Sulla Felix added an age requirement for the quaestorship, which he made compulsory. In the early Principate the pattern was extended. The vigintivirate (see VIGINTISEXVIRI) became a prerequisite for the quaestorship; between these two offices it was customary (though not mandatory) to serve as military tribune. All except patricians were obliged to hold either the tribunate of the *plebs* or the aedileship before reaching the praetorship. Career patterns beyond the praetorship were less structured, though promotions to provincial governorships and the new non-magisterial posts (see CURA(-TIO)) show certain regularities. Established patterns of advancement eventually developed for equestrian careers, esp. for the senior prefectures, but with greater variations than in the senatorial *cursus*. See CAREERS, ROMAN.

Cybelē, the great mother-goddess of Anatolia, associated in myth, and later at least in cult, with her youthful lover Attis. Pessinus was her chief sanctuary, and the cult appears at an early date in *Lydia. The queen or mistress of her people, Cybele was responsible for their well-being in all respects; primarily a goddess of fertility, she also cures (and sends) disease, gives oracles, and, as her mural crown indicates, protects her people in war. The goddess of mountains, she is also mistress of wild nature, symbolized by her attendant lions. Ecstatic states inducing prophetic rapture and insensibility to pain were characteristic of her worship.

By the 5th century BC Cybele was known in Greece and was early associated with *Demeter. It is likely that the cult was largely Hellenized. (See HELLENISM.) Cybele was officially brought to Rome in 205–204, but under the republic, save for the public games (see LUDI), the Megalensia, which were celebrated by the *aediles and the old patrician families, and processions of the priests of Cybele with the participation of the *quindecimviri sacris faciundis, she was confined to her Palatine temple and served only by oriental priests. Thanks to its official status and early naturalization in Rome and *Ostia, the cult spread rapidly through the provinces, esp. in Gaul and Africa. Its agrarian character made it more popular with the fixed populations than with the soldiery, and it was esp. favoured by women.

See also EUNUCHS; METRAGYRTES.

Cycladēs, an archipelago in the south Aegean, comprising some 30 habitable islands, ranging in size from a few square kilometres to over 400 sq. km. (155 sq. mi.), and many small islands deserted through most of history. They offer a favourable route across the Aegean: land is always in sight and refuge close at hand.

The Cyclades are mountainous and lack extensive arable land, but are rich in minerals. Their *marble, esp. from *Paros and *Naxos, is among the finest. An extreme Mediterranean climate with low annual rainfall and strong winds prevails. Barley and vines fare best.

Ancient geographers defined the Cyclades as the islands encircling *Delos. From c.1000 BC they were settled by *Ionians with Delos as their cult centre. The southern Cyclades were colonized from c.900 BC by *Dorians from Peloponnese. From the 8th until the 5th cent. the Ionian Cyclades flourished as independent states governed by rich aristocracies. From c.550 external interference increased, from mainland Greece and Asia Minor. During the *Persian Wars many submitted and contributed ships to the Persian fleet, the western string remaining loyal to the Greek allies. Afterwards the Ionian Cyclades joined the *Delian League; the Dorian islands remained independent until the Peloponnesian War. Many again joined the *Second Athenian Confederacy after 377.

Cyclōpēs are one-eyed giants. In *Homer they are savage and pastoral, and live in a distant country without government or laws. *Odysseus visits them in his wanderings and enters the cave of one of them, Polyphēmus, who imprisons him and his men and eats two of them raw, morning and evening, until they escape by blinding him while he is in a drunken sleep, and getting out among the sheep and goats when he opens the cave in the morning. Polyphemus is the son of *Poseidon, and the god, in answer to his prayer for vengeance, opposes the homecoming of Odysseus in every possible way, bringing to pass the *curse that he may return alone and find trouble when he arrives. The blinding is a popular theme of early vase-painting. Elsewhere we find an amorous Polyphemus, who lives in *Sicily and somewhat ludicrously woos the nymph Galatea, who prefers Acis.

But in *Hesiod the Cyclopes are three, Brontes, Steropes, and Arges (Thunderer, Lightener, Bright). They are divine craftsmen who make *Zeus his thunderbolt in gratitude for their release from imprisonment by their father *Uranus (Heaven; their mother is Earth). They often appear as *Hephaestus' workmen, and often again are credited with making ancient fortifications, as those of Tiryns.

Cylon, an Athenian nobleman; winner at *Olympia, perhaps in 640 BC. He married the daughter of Theagenēs, tyrant of *Megara, and with his help and a few friends seized the Acropolis at Athens, with a view to a tyranny, in an Olympic year (632?, see OLYMPIC GAMES). The masses, however, did not follow him, and he was besieged. He himself escaped; his friends surrendered and, though suppliants at an *altar, were killed. Hence arose the *curse, which attached to those said to be responsible, esp. to Megaclēs the archon (see ARCHONTES) and his family, the *Alcmaeonids.

Cȳmē, the most powerful of the Aeolian cities (see AEOLIS) on the seaboard of *Asia Minor, occupying a naturally strong harbour site. It was dominated successively by the Persians, the Athenians (to whose empire it belonged; see DELIAN LEAGUE), the *Seleucids, the Attalids of

*Pergamum, and the Romans. *Hesiod's father came from Cyme to *Boeotia, and its most distinguished citizen was the historian *Ephorus.

Cynics ('the dog-like'), term used of *Diogenes (2) 'the dog' (so called for his shamelessness) and his followers. Cynicism was never a formal philosophical school but rather a way of life grounded in an extreme primitivist interpretation of the principle 'live according to nature'. Diogenes having discovered the true way of life, there was little diversity or development within Cynicism, though 'hard' Cynics (rigorous exponents of the original prescription, found at all periods) can be distinguished from 'soft' Cynics (who compromised varyingly with existing social and political institutions), practical Cynicism from literary Cynicism (Cynicism as written or written about), and Cynics (in some sense) from those influenced by Cynicism.

'Hard' Cynicism was best expounded by Diogenes and (to some extent) *Crates. From 320 to 220 BC 'soft' Cynicism was represented by e.g. Onesicritus, who portrayed *Alexander (2) the Great as a Cynic philosopher-king. Practical Cynicism declined in the 2nd and 1st cents. BC but revived in the early empire. Greek cities swarmed with Cynics. Cynicism produced remarkable individuals, including Dio Chrysostom (Dio Cocceianus). The Roman authorities inevitably clashed with 'hard' Cynics (qua anarchists). Later, Cynic and Christian ascetics were sometimes confused, sometimes distinguished.

Cynicism greatly influenced Greek and Roman philosophy, rulership ideology, literature, and (later) religion. Crates' follower *Zeno (2) founded *Stoicism, a development of Cynicism with a proper theoretical grounding: Stoic ethics are essentially Cynic ethics, Stoic cosmopolitanism a development of Cynic; Diogenes' *Republic* influenced Zeno's and *Chrysippus'. The legitimacy of Cynicism was debated within Stoicism, reactions ranging from nearly total acceptance (Ariston) to partial acceptance (Zeno, Chrysippus), to rejection (*Panaetius), to bowdlerizing and idealizing redefinition (*Epictetus). The very extremeness of Cynic positions on material possessions, individual ethics, and politics provided the definition of other philosophies' positions: apart from the Stoics, the Epicureans (see EPICURUS), though greatly influenced by Cynic ethics, polemicized against Cynicism. Diogenes and Crates are generally celebrated in popular philosophy. Cynic ethics influenced Christian *asceticism.

To maximize their audience the Cynics (despite avowed rejection of literature) wrote more voluminously and variously than any ancient philosophical school. The Cynic *diatribe, anecdotal tradition, satiric spirit, and serio-comic discourse had enormous and varied philosophical and literary influence (e.g. on the diatribes of *Seneca the Younger and *Plutarch; philosophical biography and the gospels; Roman satire; the epistles of Horace, St Paul, and Seneca; Lucian).

Cyprus, third largest Mediterranean island. Though mountainous, its central plain is fertile. Rainfall is uncertain, drought endemic, and fertility dramatically responsive to irrigation capacity. Copper ore has been exploited since prehistory. Timber resources played a major role in the region's naval history.

The iron age settlement-pattern was based on a nexus of city-kingdoms—Salamis, Citium, Amathus, Paphos, Soli, etc.—which largely lasted throughout antiquity. Citium was for long a *Phoenician city (Phoenician influence was very strong elsewhere in the island). The kings ruled as autocrats. From the late 8th cent., if no earlier, Cyprus was sucked into eastern Mediterranean politics; its kings acknowledged at least the nominal suzerainty of a succession of great powers. While the 7th cent. seems to have been largely a period of independence, the island was dominated by *Egypt in the earlier 6th cent. In 545 came voluntary submission to Persia; there was Cypriot help for the Persians in the conquest of *Babylon and, in 525, their attack on Egypt. When *Darius I reorganized the empire, Cyprus found itself in the fifth satrapy with *Phoenicia and *Syria-Palestine; tribute was imposed. The cities (except Amathus) joined the *Ionian Revolt, egged on, it seems, by dissidents who gained control in Salamis, where crucial land and sea battles were fought. Though the Ionian fleet was victorious, ashore the Cypriots were defeated, and their leader killed. The cities were reduced by the Persians, Soli holding out the longest. The Cypriots had an uncomfortable time in the subsequent long struggle between Greece and Persia; their ships fought poorly on the Persian side in 480–479. The island was constantly campaigned over during Athenian efforts under *Cimon to deny it to the Persians, but Cimon's death during the 449/8 campaign raised the siege and, temporarily, pro-Persian rulers became everywhere dominant; but the king of Salamis, Evagoras I (c.411–374) was conspicuously pro-Greek, in fact as well as theory. Later, the kings intervened decisively on behalf of *Alexander (2) the Great at the siege of *Tyre in 331, where their ships were badly mauled.

Cypselus, tyrant of *Corinth, traditionally (and probably in fact) c.657–627 BC. He overthrew the *aristocracy of the *Bacchiads, and established the earliest tyrant dynasty (see TYRANNY), and one of the longest lasting. The Bacchiads treated him as one of them, though his father was not; that enabled him to exploit discontent with their exclusive control. He drew active support only from rich Corinthians, but his popularity is reflected in Aristotle's view that he became tyrant 'through demagogy' (see DEMAGOGUES): he had no bodyguard i.e. (perhaps) did not *need* one. His most important achievement was to remove the Bacchiads: we hear little of his actions in power. He founded colonies in NW Greece with his bastard sons as founders and tyrants, and established a long-lasting Corinthian interest there: the most important was Ambracia.

Cypselus, chest of, a chest of cedar-wood decorated with figures in ivory, gold, and wood, exhibited at *Olympia in the temple of Hera. It is said to have been the one in which the infant *Cypselus was hidden, and afterwards to have been dedicated by either Cypselus or his son *Periander. Nothing of this famous chest survives, but *Pausanias' (3) long description of the decorations suggests that they were in the style of contemporary painted pottery, i.e. that of the 7th to 6th cent. BC.

Cyrenaics, a school of philosophers, influential in the later 4th and early 3rd cent. BC. Its main tenets were that sense-impressions are the only things which are knowable, and that the sensory pleasure of the present moment is the supreme good. The claim of pleasure to be the supreme good was supported by the argument that all living things pursue pleasure and shun pain. The predominance of the pleasure of the moment was supported by the sceptical epistemology implied by the claim that only sense-impressions are knowable; since both past and future lie beyond the scope of present impressions, the wise agent will live only in and for the present. These doctrines may have had some influence on Epicureanism (see EPICURUS), partly by way of reaction.

Cyrēnē, the major Greek colony in Africa (see COLONIZATION, GREEK), was founded from Thera c.630 BC, and reinforced by later groups of colonists, who were, before the Hellenistic period, mainly *Dorian. It gave its name to the surrounding territory, apparently claiming authority (sometimes resisted) as *metropolis* of all Greek settlements there.

For the foundation, the account in *Herodotus is supplemented by an inscription purporting to give the substance of the Theraean decree which organized the colonial expedition; after two initial failures, a site was found, with Libyan help, c.12 km. ($7\frac{1}{2}$ mi.) from the sea, in a fertile area with a freshwater spring and normally good rainfall, but shading into pre-desert southwards; other Greek settlements followed swiftly. Communications with these and exploitation of the country required Libyan co-operation, which was withdrawn on arrival of a new wave of colonists in the 6th cent. Libyan/Egyptian opposition was defeated c.570, and Greek expansion continued, with more dependent settlements and the cities of Barca and Euhesperides. Within city territories Libyans presumably provided dependent labour; outside them they were free, and, apparently, peaceable; Herodotus notes their Hellenization (see HELLENISM), as well as their cultural influence on Greeks. There was intermarriage and, by the Hellenistic period, marked racial mixture. Cyrene's own territory became unusually large for a *polis*, with organized villages reminiscent of Attic *demes; its cereals, vines, olives, and grazing were notable, and the grazing extended into the pre-desert, which was also the source of silphium, Cyrene's characteristic export and emblem (see PHARMACOLOGY); like silphium-collection, animal husbandry must often have been in the hands of Libyans. The horses were esp. famous, horse-drawn chariots became a feature of Cyrene's armies, and chariot-racing, with teams victorious in Greek Games, a predilection of the rich (see HORSE- AND CHARIOT-RACES). The resultant wealth financed buildings, sculptures, painting, and a tradition of learning and literature. The great names (e.g. *Carneades, *Callimachus (2), *Eratosthenes) cluster in the Hellenistic period.

The *founder (Aristoteles Battus) and his heirs ruled as kings. The dynasty survived civic unrest and revolution as well as family infighting, submitted to *Persia in 525, but recovered independence in the 5th cent.; it was finally overthrown c.440. See PTOLEMY (1).

Cyrēnē, edicts of, five edicts of *Augustus preserved in a Greek inscription from *Cyrene. The first four belong to 7–6 BC and apply to the public (i.e. senetorial) province of *Crete and Cyrene alone; the fifth, which introduces a *senatus consultum*, dates from 4 BC and applies to the whole empire. The documents prove that Augustus received an *imperium maius* (see IMPERIUM) over the public provinces and demonstrate his ably balanced treatment of provincials.

Cyrus (1) the Great son of Cambyses I, became *c.*557 BC king of the small kingdom of Anshan in *Persia, at that time subject to the Median king. From 550 he fought extensive campaigns in which he conquered Media (550/549), *Sardis and *Lydia (546), *Babylonia, and the neo-Babylonian empire (539). At some point he conquered central Asia. He was thus the first Persian king to bring together territories into an imperial framework, to whose organization he contributed substantially. In general, the Greek (esp. Xenophon's *Cyropaedia*), Babylonian ('Cyrus cylinder'), and Judaean sources (Ezra) present him as a conqueror welcomed by the local inhabitants. This apologetic tendency reflects both the expectations nourished by certain groups (e.g. the Jews, who received permission to return to Jerusalem) and a policy continued by his successors: i.e. forging collaborative links with the local élites. This willingness to accommodate local conditions went hand-in-hand with tight control, as shown by the fact that land was confiscated to benefit the crown and Persian nobility. The royal administration also maintained a close watch over the fiscal obligations of the Babylonian sanctuaries. His achievement as founder of the empire was symbolized by the building of a royal residence in Persia, Pasargadae, where also his tomb was built. He was buried there by his son, *Cambyses II, after his death in 530 following a campaign in central Asia.

Cyrus (2) the Younger, second son of *Darius II and Parysatis. In 408 BC, because of dissension between the satraps *Pharnabazus and *Tissaphernes he was given an overarching command in Asia Minor to enable him to mount an effective fight against Athenian positions. When his ally *Lysander defeated Athens (405/4), he was actually at the Persian court for the coronation of his elder brother, who took the regnal name *Artaxerxes (2) II. Supported by his mother, he returned to Sardis, where he began preparations for a coup. He mounted his attack with an army of regular contingents from Asia Minor, reinforced by Greek mercenaries, in the spring of 401, thus taking full advantage of the problems faced by the Persians in Egypt, which was slipping from their control at the time. He led his army to Babylonia; a battle was fought at *Cunaxa, in which Cyrus lost his life. The reasons for his defeat were primarily political. Contrary to assertions in apologetic literature (esp. Xenophon's *Anabasis*), he failed to gain the adherence of the Persian nobility and the empire's élites, who remained largely loyal to Artaxerxes II.

Cythēra, an island off Cape Malea (Peloponnese) with *murex* in abundance (see PURPLE). Perhaps *c.*550 BC Sparta seized it from *Argos, installing a garrison and governor; its inhabitants became *perioikoi*. An obvious strategic threat to Sparta, 'better sunk beneath the sea' said *Chilon, it was captured by *Nicias and held for Athens from 424 to 421. In myth it was the birthplace of *Aphrodite, who had a sanctuary there.

Dacia lay in the loop of the lower Danube (see DANUVIUS), consisting mainly of the plateau of Transylvania. The Dacians were an agricultural people, but under the influence of Celtic invaders (see CELTS) in the 4th cent. BC they absorbed Celtic culture and developed the gold, silver, and iron mines of the Carpathians. From *c*.300 BC they traded with the Greeks, by way of the Danube; from the 2nd cent. they also had dealings with the Greek cities of Illyria (see ILLYRIANS) and Epirus via Roman traders seeking slaves. Their chief import was wine.

Under Augustus the Dacians caused few problems, but their military power grew under *Decebalus, who defeated Roman armies in AD 85 and 86. After a Roman victory *Domitian made peace, recognizing Decebalus as a client ruler (see CLIENT KINGS). *Trajan conquered Dacia in the First and Second Dacian Wars (101/2, 105/6). Decebalus' stronghold Sarmizegethusa was taken and destroyed. These campaigns are depicted on the spiral frieze of *Trajan's Column.

Daedalus, a legendary artist, craftsman, and inventor. *Homer calls artful works *daidala* and associates them with *Hephaestus. Homer locates Daedalus himself in *Crete (a precociously *orientalizing culture), ascribing to him the dancing-ground of *Ariadne at *Cnossus. Later sources add the Minotaur's *labyrinth, a statue of *Aphrodite, Ariadne's thread, and the bull that captivated Pāsiphaē—enraging her husband, *Minos, who imprisoned Daedalus.

His escape with his son Icarus on wings of feathers and wax may appear in Greece *c*.560 BC, on a vase from Athens. Icarus flew too close to the sun and the wax melted, but Daedalus crossed safely to *Sicily, where he was protected by King Cocalus, whose daughters boiled the pursuing Minos alive in a steam bath. There Daedalus was credited with numerous marvels, including a fortress near *Acragas, the platform for Aphrodite's temple on Mt. Eryx, and his own

steam bath at Selinus on sicily's SW coast. Greek encounters with *Phoenicians already in Sicily perhaps inspired these tales. 5th-cent. Attic dramatists wrote satyr-plays and comedies about his adventures, and *Aeschylus turned him into a maker of 'living' statues. Next he was credited with the invention of the walking pose for *kouroi*, whose Egyptian connections were soon noticed. By *c*.500, the Athenians had begun to claim him for themselves. A chameleon-like figure mutating with changing political and cultural circumstance, he gained a new lease of life in Rome, where his Sicilian flight caught *Ovid's imagination (*Metamorphoses* 8), and was popular in Roman painting.

daimōn Etymologically *daimōn* means 'divider' or 'allotter'; from *Homer onwards it is used mainly in the sense of performer of more or less unexpected, and intrusive, events in human life. In early authors, gods, even Olympians, could be referred to as *daimōnĕs*. Rather than referring to personal anthropomorphic aspects, however, *daimōn* appears to correspond to supernatural power in its unpredictable, anonymous, and often frightful manifestations. So, the adjective *daimonios* means 'strange', 'incomprehensible', 'uncanny'. Hence *daimōn* soon acquired connotations of Fate. Hesiod introduced a new meaning: the deceased of the *golden age were to him 'wealth-giving *daimones*' functioning as guardians or protectors. This resulted in the meaning 'personal protecting spirits', who accompany each human's life and bring either luck or harm. A lucky, fortunate person was *eudaimōn* ('with a good *daimon*': already in Hesiod), an unlucky one was *kakodaimōn* ('with a bad *daimon*': from the 5th cent. BC). Centuries later, Christian theologians, concentrating on their negative aspects, saw in *daimones* the true nature of the pagan gods: they were the embodiment and source of evil and *sin.

damnātiō memoriae After the deaths of persons deemed by the senate enemies of the state, measures to erase their memory might follow. Originally there was no set package but a repertoire: images might be destroyed (*Sejanus; *Valeria Messallina), and their display penalized (*Appuleius Saturninus), the name erased from inscriptions, and a man's *praenōmen* banned in his family. With emperors their acts were abolished. *Claudius prevented the senate from condemning *Gaius (1); but decrees were passed against *Domitian, *Commodus, and Elagabalus.

Damon pioneering Athenian musicologist, pupil of *Prodicus and teacher of *Pericles, admired by *Socrates and *Plato. He is said to have invented the 'relaxed Lydian' attunement. His views on *music's political significance, and on ethical effects of various rhythms (probably also of *harmoniai*, 'attunements') are reflected in Plato, *Republic* 3. Damon was ostracized in the 440s BC.

Danaŭs and **the Danaïds** Danaus was the son of Belus, the brother of Aegyptus, eponym of the Egyptians, and the brother-in-law of Phoenix, eponym of the Phoenicians. He himself is the eponym of the Danaans (Danaoi), a word used commonly by Homer and other poets to mean the Greeks.

He was the father of 50 daughters, the Danaids. They were betrothed to their cousins, the 50 sons of Aegyptus. In order to escape this marriage, they fled with their father to *Argos (whence their ancestor *Io had fled to Egypt) and were received as suppliants by its king, Pelasgus. Their reception and their pursuit by the sons of Aegyptus are the subject of the *Suppliants* of *Aeschylus. This is generally thought to have been the first play of a connected tetralogy of which the other plays were *Egyptians*, *Danaids*, and the satyric *Amymonē*. Pelasgus failed to protect the Danaids from the Egyptians, and Danaus ordered his daughters to kill their new husbands on their wedding night. All obeyed except one, Hypermestra, who spared her husband Lynceus (probably out of love), and became the ancestor of subsequent kings of Argos. Surviving accounts of this story include Horace, *Odes* 3. 11 (a famous evocation of Hypermestra's heroism), and Ovid, *Heroides* 14 (a letter from Hypermestra to Lynceus).

We do not know how Aeschylus resolved the issues, except that *Aphrodite had a role in *Danaids* and made a speech in favour of love.

*Pindar says that Danaus found new husbands for his daughters by offering them as prizes in a foot-race. A frequent motif in Latin literature is that of the Danaids' punishment in the Underworld, where they continually pour water into a leaking vessel.

dancing From earliest times, the dance played an important role in the lives of the Greeks, and was sometimes regarded by them as the invention of the gods. It was generally associated with music and song or poetry in the art called *mousikē*, and often made use of conventionalized *gestures. The dance had a place in religious festivals, in the *mysteries, in artistic competitions, in the education of the young, and even in military training, esp. in Sparta. People danced at weddings, at funerals, at the 'naming-days' of infants (see NAMES, PERSONAL, GREEK), at harvests, at victory celebrations, in after-dinner merrymaking, in joyous dance processions (*kōmoi*) through the streets, in animal mummery, and even in incantations. Performances by professional dancers were enjoyed, esp. at the *symposium; such dancers were almost all slaves or *hetairai*.

Greek dances included the *geranos* (a nocturnal serpentine dance); the pyrrhic and related dances by men and boys in armour; the *partheneion*, a song-dance performance by maidens; the *hyporchēma*, a lively combination of instrumental music, song, dance, and pantomime; and the uproarious *askōliasmos*, performed on greased wine-skins. In the worship of *Dionysus the wild *oreibasia*, or 'mountain-dancing' of frenzied women, by Classical times was toned down into a prepared performance by a group of trained devotees. In the Athenian theatre, the *tyrbasia* of the *dithyrambic choruses, the lewd *kordax* of comedy, the stately *emmeleia* of tragedy, and the rollicking *sikinnis* of the satyr-play were distinctive.

The Romans were much more restrained than the Greeks in their use of the dance. Some of them, including *Cicero, openly expressed contempt for dancers. There are records of a few ancient dances used in religious ceremonies—e.g. the leaping of the armed *Salii and the *fratres arvales* (arval brothers). *Etruscan and Greek dancers, from the 4th cent. BC on, exerted some influence, and the introduction of various *oriental cults brought noisy and ecstatic dances to Rome. Dancing by professionals, usually slaves, often furnished entertainment at dinner-parties (see CONVIVIUM). With the coming of the *pantomime, popular interest in the dance became great. See MASKS; MIME; MUSIC.

Dānuvius, ancient name for the Danube, originally denoted only the upper course down to the whirlpools and cataracts of the Iron Gates below Belgrade. This stretch remained unknown to the Greeks, long acquainted with the lower course down to the Black Sea as the *Ister, the sources of which long remained a matter of speculation. By the 1st cent. BC, when a Roman army first reached the river, the identity of the two had been realized, though many Roman poets preferred the Greek name. Under Augustus the province of Illyricum was extended to the Danube c.12 BC, which, except for advances into Germany and Dacia (2nd–3rd cents. AD), remained the northern limit of the empire for four centuries. Revered locally as a deity, the river was held in awe by the Romans. It was bridged in AD 105 by *Trajan, a construction of the architect *Apollodōrus (3) depicted on Trajan's Column. This followed repair of the towpath through the gorges in AD 100 and, in the following year, the excavation of a *canal to by-pass the barrier of the Iron Gates and permit navigation between the upper and lower courses.

Daphnis, a Sicilian herdsman, named from the laurel-tree (*daphnē*), he was the son, or favourite, of *Hermes and loved by a nymph who demanded his fidelity. When he was made drunk by a princess and slept with her, the nymph blinded him. Daphnis consoled himself by inventing pastoral music or perhaps was the first subject of the genre when other herdsmen sang of his misfortunes.

Daphnis and Chloē See LONGUS.

Dardanus, ancestor of the Trojan kings. In bk. 20 of *Homer's *Iliad* we have the genealogy *Zeus–Dardanus–Erichthonius–Tros, and thereafter

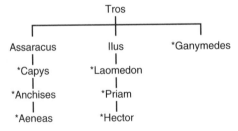

Tros

Assaracus — Ilus — *Ganymedes
| |
*Capys   *Laomedon
| |
*Anchises *Priam
| |
*Aeneas   *Hector

Acc. to Homer, Dardanus was Zeus' favourite of all his sons by mortal women.

Darīus I son of Hystaspēs, a Persian of noble lineage already known in the reigns of *Cyrus (1) and *Cambyses. He seized power after a bloody struggle against an individual said by him to have been the *magus Gaumata. The person he assassinated may in fact have been Bardiya (Gk. Smerdis), the brother of Cambyses (522 BC). He then had to quell numerous revolts by subject peoples and deal with the insubordinate Oroetes, satrap of *Sardis. His achievements were commemorated for posterity, in text and picture, on the rock of *Bisitun in Media. To mark what he presented as a refoundation of the empire, he created two new royal residences: Susa and *Persepolis. He also extended the empire in the east (Indus valley) and west (*Thrace). Soon after his crushing of the *Ionian Revolt (c.500–493), he put Datis in command of an army which conquered the Aegean islands, before meeting a setback at the battle of *Marathon (490). Until his death in 486, Darius worked to perfect the administration and tributary structure of the empire, as described by *Herodotus. His work is illustrated even better by the thousands of Elamite tablets found in the treasury and fortifications of Persepolis. See ACHAEMENIDS; PERSIAN WARS.

Darīus III acceded to the throne of Persia after the assassination of Artaxerxēs IV (336 BC). Since antiquity he has been judged negatively—a distortion of a complex reality. His dynastic legitimacy is well established; he prepared himself well for the confrontation with *Alexander (2) the Great; to the last he adhered to a coherent strategy in coping with an exceptional opponent. He died in 330 as a result of a plot, when his struggle against Alexander had plainly failed.

dead, disposal of Correct disposal of the dead was a crucial element in easing the *soul of the deceased into the next world. However, the forms of burial varied enormously. Great significance was attached to the choice of inhumation, cremation, or some other rite, but one can rarely see a direct correlation between specific methods and specific racial, social, or religious groups.

Greece After the destruction of the Mycenaean world c.1200 BC, regional variations returned in the Dark Age. There were, however, a few generally observed rules. Cremation with the ashes placed in a metal urn (usually bronze), in the Homeric style, tended to be associated with warrior burials throughout antiquity. Children were rarely cremated, and in most places infants were buried inside amphoras or storage pots. Starting in the 6th cent. there was a trend towards simpler burials, which may have been accompanied by sumptuary laws. Inhumation in pit-graves or tile graves was adopted for adults in most parts of Greece by the 6th or 5th cent.

Rich grave goods and elaborate tomb markers went out of fashion everywhere for most of the 5th cent., but returned c. 425. There was a great flowering of funerary sculpture at Athens in the 4th cent. Funerary spending rose still further after 300, and in the 3rd–1st cents. the massive 'Macedonian'-style vaulted tombs, often with painted interiors, are found all over Greece. The most spectacular of these are the late 4th-cent. royal tombs, possibly of *Philip II and his court, at Vergina in Macedonia (see AEGAE). Athens was an exception to this pattern. Cicero says that *Demetrius (1) of Phaleron banned lavish tombs, probably in 317, and indeed no monumental burials are known from Attica between then and the 1st cent. BC. In Roman times inhumation was the strict rule throughout the whole Greek east.

Rome Few burials are known from republican times, suggesting that rites were so simple as to leave few archaeological traces. By the 3rd cent. BC some of the rich were being cremated with their ashes placed in urns and buried in communal tombs. By the 1st cent., cremation was the norm, and acc. to *Cicero and *Pliny the Elder even the ultra-conservative Cornēliī gave up inhumation in 78 BC. At about the same time, Roman nobles began building elaborate tombs modelled on those of the Greek east, with monumental sculptures and elaborate stone architecture. The spiralling cost of élite tombs ended abruptly under Augustus, who built himself a vast mausoleum. Other nobles were careful to avoid being seen as trying to rival the splendour of the imperial household (but see CESTIUS EPULO). Simpler tombs, organized around modest *altars, came into fashion for the very rich, while the not-quite-so-rich and the growing number of funerary clubs (see CLUBS, ROMAN) adopted the *columbarium (2).

See further ART, FUNERARY, GREEK and ROMAN; CEMETERIES; DEATH, ATTITUDES TO.

Dead Sea Scrolls, documents made of leather and papyrus, and, in one case, of copper, found between 1947 and 1956 in caves near Qumran by the Dead Sea. The scrolls, written by Jews, are mostly in Hebrew and *Aramaic, but a small number are in Greek. Many are fragments of texts from the OT and from Jewish religious compositions otherwise preserved only through Christian manuscript traditions. The scrolls were written in the last centuries BC and 1st cent. AD.

Of particular significance in the study of Judaism in this period are the texts composed by sectarians, who are probably to be identified with Jews who used the nearby site at Qumran as a religious centre. These texts include community rules, hymns, liturgical texts, calendars, and works of biblical interpretation. Among this last group is found the *pesher* type of interpretation, characteristic of this sect and rarely found elsewhere in Jewish literature, in which the real meaning of scriptural passages is alleged to lie in hidden allusions to more recent events.

death, attitudes to

Greek The Greek attitude towards *Hades is best summed up by *Achilles, 'I'd rather be a day-labourer on earth working for a man of little property than lord of all the hosts of the dead' (Homer *Odyssey.* 11. 489–491). The Homeric dead are pathetic in their helplessness, inhabiting draughty, echoing halls, deprived of their wits, and flitting purposelessly about uttering batlike noises. Athenian lawcourt speeches urge the jury to render assistance to the dead as if they were unable to look after their own interests. The precise relationship between the living body and the *psyche* (spirit of the dead) is unclear, since the latter is referred to only in connection with the dead. The necessity of conducting burial rites and the insult to human dignity if they are omitted are often mentioned in literature. Except in philosophy and *Orphism, belief in a dual after-life is largely absent from Greek *eschatology. In Homer the Underworld judge *Minos merely settles lawsuits between the litigious dead. Only gross *sinners (e.g. *Tantalus, Tityus, and *Sisyphus) receive retributive punishment (in Tartarus, the deepest region of the underworld), while the favoured few end up in the Elysian Fields (see ELYSIUM). Fear of the after-life was therefore largely absent.

The deceased's journey to the next world was effected by elaborate ritual conducted by the relatives of the deceased, primarily women. The funeral, from which priests were debarred for fear of incurring *pollution, was a three-act drama, which comprised laying out the body (*prothesis*), the funeral cortège (*ekphora*), and the interment. Cremation and inhumation were often practised concurrently in the same community, with no apparent distinction in belief. From c.500 BC intramural burial was forbidden in Athens. No tomb-cult was practised in early times, but in Classical Athens women paid regular visits to the grave. Offerings included cakes and *libations mainly of pure water. The attention that the dead received from the living in this period was judged to be so important that it constituted a reason for adopting an heir. In the Archaic period a funeral provided a perfect showcase for the conspicuous display of aristocratic wealth and power and many communities passed legislation designed to limit its scope and magnificence.

Funerary ritual was substantially modified for those who died in their prime, the unburied dead, victims of murder, suicides, heroes, etc. Special sympathy was felt towards women who died at a marriageable age but unmarried. To underline their pathos, a stone marker in the form of a vase used in the nuptial bath was placed over the grave. Victims of murder were vengeful and malignant, as indicated by the grisly practice of cutting off their extremities. Most powerful were the heroic dead, who in *Plutarch's day still received blood sacrifice.

Geometric vases (see POTTERY, GREEK, 2) depict only the *prothesis* and *ekphora*, whereas Athenian white-ground oil flasks often depict tomb-cult. Hades is rarely represented in Greek art or in literature (*Odyssey* 11 and Aristophanes' *Frogs* are notable exceptions). The belief in Hades as the home of the undifferentiated dead predominated and never lost its hold over the popular imagination (it persisted as a theme in epitaphs).

Roman In the Roman tradition death is conceived of as a blemish striking the family of the deceased, with the risk of affecting all with whom it had contact: neighbours, magistrates, priests, and sacred places. So ritual established a strict separation between the space of the deceased and that of the living. Cypress branches announced the blemished house, and on days of sacrifice for the dead *sanctuaries were closed.

The time of death spanned above all the period when the deceased's corpse was exposed in his or her home, its transport to the *cemetery, and its burial. These operations were usually completed after eight days. After 40 days, the deceased was deemed to have joined a new category: those members of the community, the *dī mānes*, who lived outside towns on land set aside for this purpose and managed by the *pontifices*. The *di manes* were thought of as a collective divinity (Romans spoke of the *di manes* of

such-and-such a person), and received regular cult. The immortality which they enjoyed was conditional on the existence of descendants, or at least of a human presence (a proprietor of the land on which the tomb was located, or a funerary *collēgium*: see CLUBS, ROMAN), since it was the celebration of funerary cult, in the form of sacrifices, which ensured the deceased's survival. The unburied dead were called *lemurēs* and thought of as haunting inhabited areas and disturbing the living. Usually anonymous they none the less received cult at the Lemuria, supposedly to appease them.

Along with these forms of survival, conceived generally as menacing and undesirable, there existed a third belief about life after death—deification. Combining Roman tradition with Hellenistic practices and ideas deriving from Hellenistic philosophy, the deification of exceptional individuals was instituted at Rome after *Caesar's assassination. Thereafter elevation to the status of a god (*dīvus*) by a *senatus consultum* became the rule for emperors and some members of their families (see RULER-CULT).

See CONSOLATION; DEAD, DISPOSAL OF; EPIGRAM.

debt, the creation of obligations in cash or kind, existed at all levels of society throughout the ancient world: from loans of seed and implements between peasants to lending of small sums and household objects between city-dwellers, from borrowing to cope with unforeseen crises to substantial cash loans between the wealthy to support an élite lifestyle. Clear enough are the socio-political implications of widespread indebtedness, plausibly linked with the 'Solonian Crisis' (see SOLON) in Archaic Athens and the 'Struggle of the Orders' in early *Rome. In time of siege or revolution, the indebted could be a force to be reckoned with. Athens after Solon was exceptional in its successful prohibition of loans secured on the person; debt-bondage and other forms of debt-dependence were common throughout the rest of the Greek and Roman worlds. Frequent laws intended to regulate debt were rarely enforceable and generally had only limited effect. Forms of debt-bondage continued in Rome long after legislation which reputedly prohibited imprisonment for debt. Wider implications of indebtedness were also apparent at the upper end of society. Rich Athenians risked their status by raising loans on the security of property to fulfil *eisphora* (tax) and *liturgy obligations. In the late

Roman republic, indebtedness was intertwined with élite politics: the massive debts incurred by politicians in the pursuit of power could result in credit crises (49 BC, on the eve of the Civil War) and, in extreme cases, point the way to revolution (the conspiracy of *Catiline). A possible alternative was exploitation of the provincials: *Cicero, while governor in Cilicia, records with more dismay than surprise loans at usurious rates of interest by *Iunius Brutus to the city of Salamis on *Cyprus, and by *Pompey to the king of neighbouring Cappadocia.

decarchies were juntas, lit. 'ten-man rules', established under the aegis of *Lysander in parts of the former Athenian empire (see DELIAN LEAGUE) following Sparta's victory in the *Peloponnesian War. They were absolute dictatorships, sometimes supported by a garrison under a Spartan commander known as a harmost. They collected their city's share of the war-tax levied by Sparta and in other ways functioned as instruments of Sparta's short-lived Aegean empire.

Decebalus, king of *Dacia, a shrewd and resourceful commander, led several campaigns against Rome (AD 85–89). Although the Dacians were defeated in 88, *Domitian, faced with military rebellion in Germany and offensive moves by the Marcomanni and Quadi on the Danube, concluded a generous peace by which Decebalus was established as a king friendly to Rome (see CLIENT KINGS), was granted the assistance of Roman engineers, and received an annual subsidy. *Trajan, suspicious of Decabalus' power and eager for military glory, invaded Dacia (101/2) and after a tough campaign imposed a peace settlement which left Roman garrisons there. In 105 Trajan went to war again, apparently in response to Decebalus' infractions of the treaty. Sarmizegethusa, the capital, was captured, Decebalus killed himself, and the province of Dacia was created (106).

decision-making (Greek) A Greek state was the community of its citizens, and at least the most important decisions were made by an assembly of the citizens. *Democracies and *oligarchies differed not over that principle but over its application: how many of the free adult males were full citizens, entitled to participate in the assembly; which decisions were reserved for the assembly and which could be made by 'the authorities' (the magistrates and/or a council). The widespread principle of *probouleusis*, 'prior

consideration' by a council of business for the assembly, provided further scope for variation. In democratic Athens the council (see BOULE) had to approve items for the assembly's agenda, and could, but did not have to, propose a motion; but in the assembly any citizen could speak, and could propose a motion or an amendment to a motion already proposed. In more oligarchic states proposals might be allowed only from the magistrates and/or the council, and the right to address the assembly might be limited to magistrates and members of the council.

Larger organizations often entrusted decisions to a representative council. The Delphic *Amphictiony was a body of Greek peoples and had a council in which the peoples were represented: that was the main decision-making body, though there were sometimes meetings of an assembly. Federal Boeotia (see BOEOTIAN CONFEDERACY) in the late 5th and early 4th cents. BC had a council of 660 (60 from each of eleven electoral units), within which one-quarter played a probouleutic role.

declamation was the main means employed by *rhetors to train their pupils for public speaking. It was invented by the Greeks, who brought it to Rome and the Roman world generally. Its developed forms were known in Latin as the *controversia*, a speech in character on one side of a fictional law case, and the *suasoria*, a deliberative speech advising a course of action in a historical, pseudo-historical, or mythological situation; the first trained for the courts, the second for the political assembly or committee room.

The *sophists of the 5th cent. BC regarded it as their principal task to teach rhetoric. Surviving display speeches from this period, apparently intended as models for students, are clear forerunners of the *controversia*. *Antiphon's *Tetralogies*, arranged in speeches for and against, exemplify techniques of argument. *Gorgias' *Palamedes* displays a clear articulation that marks off parts of the speech and stages in the argument, and is plainly intended to train the student in systematic exposition. For *Philostratus, sketching the so-called *Second Sophistic, it was *Aeschines who, after his exile to Rhodes, introduced the use of stock characters, poor man and rich man, hero and tyrant. It must have been in the Hellenistic period that the characteristic form of the *controversia* evolved. The master would lay down a law, or laws, often imaginary, to govern the case, together with a *theme* detailing the supposed facts and stating the point at issue (e.g. 'A girl who has been raped may choose either marriage to her ravisher without a dowry or his death. On a single night a man raped two girls. One demands his death, the other marriage'). The case would be fictional, and names would be given only if it concerned historical circumstances. The speaker, whether pupil or rhetor, would take one side or the other, sometimes playing the part of an advocate, usually that of a character in the case. Thus training was given in all branches of rhetoric. Attention was paid to the articulation of the speech and to the forging of a persuasive argument; style would be inculcated by precept and example; memory was trained too, for speeches were not read out, and delivery (experience of an audience was given by the occasional introduction of parents and friends). Esp. important was the 'invention' (finding) of arguments. The *stasis* system, which owed much to Hermagoras (*c*.150 BC), enabled a speaker to establish the type of the case (e.g. 'conjecture', did X do Y?) and draw on a checklist of topics appropriate to that type (e.g. in the case of conjecture, motive and opportunity) with their associated arguments. The rhetor would teach the rhetorical system in abstract and exemplify it in his own model speeches.

These practices are presupposed by the earliest Latin rhetorical handbooks, *Cicero's On Invention* and the anonymous *Rhetoric for Herennius*, both based on Greek teaching. *Seneca the Elder probably gives a distorted picture: he is most interested in epigram and the clever slanting of a case, not in the technicalities of the *stasis* system or the elaboration of a complex argument. *Quintilian, though critical of the unreality of contemporary practice (as were *Petronius Arbiter and *Tacitus), never questions the basis of declamation, and his book is a handbook for the declaimer as well as for the orator.

decuriōnēs were the councillors who ran Roman local government in both colonies and municipalities (see MUNICIPIUM), Latin and Roman. They did so as members of the local council. They were recruited mainly from ex-magistrates and held office for life. The list of councillors was revised every five years. The qualifications included criteria of wealth, age, free birth, and reputation. The minimum age was 25. Members of influential families could however be made honorary members even if they lacked the standard qualifications. The number of councillors varied, but was often 100. They controlled the public life of the community, its administration, and finances, including the voting of honorary decrees and statues. They had charge of its external relations, including the sending of embassies and petitions to the emperor or provincial governor. The local popular assemblies did little apart from electing magistrates.

In time the class of *decuriones* became hereditary, membership descending in the male line; and nomination to office replaced popular election. *Decuriones* were privileged. Their toga had a purple stripe and, more important, they counted as *honestiores* and so were exempt from certain degrading punishments. Indeed their privileged position was essential to the running of the empire, since they were responsible for collecting imperial taxes in the local area and for performing a number of other public duties (*munera*; see MUNUS); and they were personally liable for default.

dēdicātiō Transfer of a thing from the human into the divine sphere was accomplished through the act of *dedicatio* and *consecrātiō*, the former indicating surrender of an object into divine ownership, the latter its transformation into a *rēs sacra* ('thing consecrated'). Dedications of temples, places, and altars were legally binding only if performed by competent authorities, such as the magistrates with *imperium*. At dedications of temples, the dedicant held a doorpost and pronounced (without interruption, hesitation, or stumbling) a formula dictated to him by a *pontifex*, with other *pontifices* often present. It contained a precise description of the object, the ground on which it stood, and the conditions of its use, with a written record as the title-deed.

dedications, literary (For non-literary dedications, see VOTIVES.)

Greek A literary dedication is a symbolic presentation of a work or collection to a dedicatee as a mark of affection or respect. It is usually embodied in a formal opening (or near-opening) address. In Pindar poetry is not the poet's gift but the 'gift of the Muses', and an opening address is reserved for divinities like the Muse herself. Dedication implies secularization.

Latin Honorific reference to a particular person in a work of prose or poetry, or in one part of a work, is common in Latin literature. This is connected with the important role played by the relationships of patronage (see PATRONAGE, LITERARY, LATIN) and friendship in the production and circulation of Latin literary texts. Dedication, by once and for all connecting the literary text with a particular person, is in itself a great compliment, and it is also usually accompanied by explicit expressions of praise. It is usually placed at or near the beginning of the work; in works in more than one book, a dedication to the same person is often repeated at the beginning of some (e.g. *Quintilian) or all (e.g. *Columella) of the books. Alternatively, the various books may be dedicated to different people: each of the three books of *Varro's *On Farming* is addressed to a different dedicatee, while in his *On the Latin Language* 2–4 are dedicated to Septimius, 5 onwards to *Cicero.

defamation See INIURIA.

deformity In antiquity far fewer congenitally deformed persons would have survived infancy than do so today, because Greeks and Romans would have had little compunction about withholding the necessities of life from those they deemed incapable of leading an independent life. (See INFANTICIDE.) In *Sparta the abandonment of deformed infants was a legal requirement. Likewise *Aristotle recommended that there should be a law 'to prevent the rearing of deformed children'. A law attributed to Romulus permitted the exposure of a monstrous infant on condition that five witnesses approved the decision. The Romans regarded the birth of a deformed child or animal as portentous in the extreme: *monstrum* (*'portent') is etymologically related to *monēre* ('to warn'). Prodigies were recorded year by year in the pontifical records. Acc. to Livy, 'the most abhorred portents of all' were hermaphrodites.

   Few individuals are known to have been congenitally deformed. One is *Agesilaus II, both diminutive and congenitally lame. It is unclear whether *Claudius was actually deformed or merely disabled. The deformed could expect to be stigmatized, like the hunchbacked *Thersites. The absence of physical blemish was a requirement for holding Greek or Roman priesthoods (see PRIESTS). *Plutarch says that the demand for freak slaves was so great in Rome that there even existed a 'monster market', and there are many references in the late republican and early imperial period to their popularity as household *pets. Hunchbacks, cripples, dwarfs and obese women were popular entertainers at drinking-parties, as numerous artistic representations indicate.

Book 4 of Aristotle's *Generation of Animals* provides an illuminating discussion of the classification and aetiology of congenital deformity. His most significant contribution to the subject was his insistence that deformities were an integral and necessary part of nature. See CHILDBIRTH.

Dēiphobus, in mythology, son of *Priam and *Hecuba, and one of the more powerful Trojan fighters. *Athena impersonated him so as to deceive *Hector and cause his death. After *Paris had been killed, Deiphobus married *Helen; he went with her to examine the Wooden Horse; and after the capture of Troy, *Menelaus and *Odysseus went first to his house, where the fighting was hardest. He was killed and mutilated by Menelaus after being, acc. to *Virgil, betrayed by Helen.

deisidaimonia Although originally the term had a laudatory sense ('scrupulousness in religious matters'), it is mainly pejorative and denotes an excessive pietism and preoccupation with religion, first and most explicitly in *Theophrastus' sixteenth *Character*. He defines *deisidaimonia* as 'cowardice vis-à-vis the divine' and gives the following characteristics: an obsessive fear of the gods, a penchant for adoration and cultic performance, superstitious awe of *portents both in daily life and in *dreams, and the concomitant inclination to ward off or prevent possible mishaps by magical or ritual acts, esp. through continuous *purifications.

Delian League, a modern name for the alliance formed 478/7 BC against the Persians. ('Athenian empire' might be a better title for this article). In 478 the Greeks, led by the Spartan *Pausanias (1), campaigned in *Cyprus and secured *Byzantium; but Pausanias abused his power and was recalled to Sparta. At the request of the allies, who pleaded Pausanias' behaviour and '*Ionian kinship', Athens accepted leadership. The Peloponnesians acquiesced, and a new alliance was formed with its headquarters on *Delos—a traditional Ionian festival centre but with an appeal to Dorian islanders also. Athens provided the commander of the allied forces and settled which cities were to provide ships and which money; the treasurers also, ten *hellēnotamiae*, were Athenians, and the Athenian *Aristides made the first assessment. But at the outset policy was determined at meetings on Delos at which every member, including Athens, had just one equal vote. The nucleus of the alliance was formed by the Ionian cities of the west coast of *Asia Minor, the *Hellespont, and the Propontis, and most of the Aegean islands. *Chios, *Samos, *Lesbos, and some other states with a naval tradition provided ships; the remainder brought annual tribute to the treasury at Delos. Members took permanently binding oaths of loyalty.

At first the anti-Persian objectives were vigorously pursued. Persian garrisons were driven out of *Thrace and *Chersonese; Greek control was extended along the west and south coast of Asia Minor; new members joined until there were nearly 200. The climax was *Cimon's victory at the mouth of the river Eurymedon (c. 466). Meanwhile Carystus in *Euboea was forced to join (c.472), *Naxos tried to secede and was forced back in (c.467), and in 465 Thasos revolted because of Athenian encroachment on Thasian mainland holdings. Thasos surrendered 462 and stiff terms were imposed, but nearby on the Strymon a large colony of Athenian allies was wiped out by the natives. If Cimon made a first peace of Callias (see CALLIAS, PEACE OF) after Eurymedon, it ended with his *ostracism, and fighting against Persia resumed in 460, when a strong Athenian force sailed to *Cyprus but was diverted to Egypt to support a Libyan prince in revolt from Persia. The Egyptian expedition ended in disaster for Athens in 454, and in that year the treasury was moved from Delos to Athens (?for security; but the date of the move is not absolutely certain). See TRIBUTE LISTS, ATHENIAN. But Athenian power spread in Greece and the Aegean: Dorian *Aegina was coerced in 458, and the First *Peloponnesian War gave Athens control over *Boeotia 457–446. At sea Cimon, back from ostracism, led a force to Cyprus, but this phase of resumed expansion ended with his death at the end of the 450s. Meanwhile Athens exploited the propaganda potential of *Apollo's sanctuaries at Delos and *Delphi; a struggle took place throughout the century between Athens and the Peloponnesians at this level as well as the military (see DELPHI).

The main Callias Peace of 450 (see CALLIAS, PEACE OF), if historical, restricted Persian movement west of Phaselis and outside the *Euxine, and Persia made other concessions. The removal of the original justification of the league led to restlessness among Athens' allies, but this was checked, and tribute-levying (perhaps discontinued for a year) was resumed. *Cleruchies and other repressive institutions were imposed. By now only Chios, Samos, and Lesbos contributed ships, the rest paid tribute perforce. Epigraphic evidence shows a shift to harsher

terminology, 'the allies' being replaced by 'the cities which the Athenians rule'.

Boeotia revolted in 447 or 446, Athens was defeated at *Coronea, and the crisis—revolts by *Megara and Euboea, and a Spartan invasion—was settled by the *Thirty Years Peace. In 440 Samos defied Athens, was besieged and subdued and forced to pay a large indemnity. Whether or not a technical democracy was now installed or an *oligarchy tolerated is uncertain; it was perhaps more important to Athens, here and elsewhere, that the governing group should be pro-Athenian (see DEMOCRACY, NON-ATHENIAN). Back at Athens, the popular courts (see DEMOCRACY, ATHENIAN, 2; LAW AND PROCEDURE, ATHENIAN) played a major part in the control of empire.

When the *Peloponnesian War began, this Athenian control was firm; Spartan hopes for large-scale revolt from Athens were disappointed, nor did the Spartans make best use of their opportunities, e.g. on Lesbos, which Athens crushed. In 425 the Athenians raised the tribute assessment to nearly 1,500 talents (the original assessment is said to have been 460 talents). In 416 when *Melos refused to join the alliance, Athens reduced the island, executed the men, and enslaved the women and children, a small atrocity but one long remembered against Athens. After the Sicilian disaster of 415–413 Chios, *Miletus, Thasos, Euboea, and other key places revolted, but even this wave of revolt was contained, partly because of Persian behaviour and Spartan limpness, partly because Athens had learned to avoid counterproductive reprisals.

The Athenian empire brought benefits to the poorer cities: *piracy was suppressed to the great advantage of trade, and the Athenian navy offered well-paid service, esp. attractive to the population of the *islands. Pride in Athenian imperial success and cultural achievement may not have been confined to Athens' own citizens, though these are not aspects on which our main source Thucydides dwells. He does not even bring out the extent to which the upper classes at Athens benefited from overseas territorial possessions in the empire, acquired in defiance of local rules. But such possessions help to explain why there was so little principled objection to the empire, and to the democracy which ran it, on the part of the Athenian élite. They also show that the literary picture of solidarity between the Athenian *demos* and the *demos* in the allied states is too simple. Thucydides, or rather one of his speakers, hints that the allies would prefer independence from either Athens or Sparta.

The allies did not in fact make much contribution to the defeat of Athens, and when Sparta took Athens' place, the cities soon had reason to regret the change. In less than 30 years they again united under Athenian leadership (see SECOND ATHENIAN CONFEDERACY). In 377 Athens repudiated cleruchies, garrisons, and overseas possessions; no wonder she had been unpopular in 431.

Dēlion, precinct and temple of *Apollo on the NE coast of *Boeotia, where the Boeotians defeated the Athenians in 424 BC. The Athenians, with 7,000 *hoplites and some cavalry, but no proper light troops, had fortified the precinct and were caught returning to Attica by a Boeotian army also of 7,000 hoplites, but with more than 10,000 light troops, 500 *peltasts, and some cavalry. The battle provides the first example of the Boeotian tactic of deploying hoplites in a deep *phalanx—here the Thebans (see THEBES) on the right were 25 deep, whereas the Athenians were only eight deep. The Thebans defeated the Athenian left, and although the Athenian right was at first successful, it fled in panic at the sudden appearance of Boeotian cavalry, sent round behind a hill to support their left. Athenian losses, at over 14 per cent, were perhaps the heaviest ever suffered by a hoplite army.

Dēlos, a small island between Myconos and Rheneia, regarded in antiquity as the centre of the *Cyclades. It is barren and almost waterless and was incapable of supporting its inhabitants. Delos, the only place to offer shelter to *Leto, was the birthplace of *Apollo and *Artemis, as recounted in the Homeric *Hymn to Apollo. This was the basis of its historical importance.

Delos was colonized by *Ionians c.950 BC, but the sanctuary's prominence originates in the 8th cent. It became the principal cult centre of the Ionians of the Cyclades, Asia Minor, Attica, and Euboea. *Naxos and *Paros were its most conspicuous patrons in the early Archaic period. In the later 6th cent. first *Pisistratus and then *Polycrates (1) of Samos asserted their authority. The Athenians purified (see PURIFICATION, GREEK) the island by removing burials within view of the sanctuary. Polycrates dedicated Rheneia to Apollo, providing the basis for the sanctuary's subsequent wealth. Delos emerged unscathed from the *Persian Wars and soon became the meeting-place and treasury of the

*Delian League. After their removal to Athens in 454 the Athenians assumed administration of the sanctuary but did not impose tribute. In 426 Athens carried out a second purification. Henceforth women about to give birth and the dying had to be removed to Rheneia. They also reorganized their quadrennial festival (the Delia), celebrated with particular splendour by *Nicias in 417. In 422 the Delians were expelled by Athens on a charge of impurity but were soon recalled. Its independence following liberation in 405 was short-lived, administration of the sanctuary reverting to Athens from 394.

Athenian domination lasted until 314. For the next century and a half Delos was independent and functioned as a normal city-state.

Independence ended in 166 BC when Rome handed control of Delos to Athens. Its inhabitants were expelled and replaced by Athenian *cleruchs. Delos was made a free port to the detriment of Rhodian commerce. In conjunction with its commercial growth in the later 2nd and early 1st cent. its population expanded enormously and it became increasingly cosmopolitan, merchants and bankers from Italy and the Hellenized east forming distinct communities (see NEGOTIATORES). Delos became the most important market for the slave trade (see SLAVERY). Although Athenians filled the civic posts, guilds and associations of the foreign communities and trading groups administered their own affairs. Sacked in 88 BC by Archelaus, *Mithradates VI's general, and again in 69 BC by pirates (see PIRACY), Delos never recovered its former greatness.

Delphi Delphi, one of the four great *panhellenic *sanctuaries, lies on the lower southern slopes of Parnassus, c.610 m. (2,000 ft.) above the gulf of *Corinth. The area was settled probably during the 10th cent. BC, and the first dedications (tripods and figurines) appear c.800. The first temple of *Apollo was built in the late 7th cent. The earliest archaeological links are with Corinth and Thessaly. The first *Pythian Games were held in either 591/0 or 586/5.

The sanctuary was enclosed by a wall. Inside it were the monuments dedicated by the states of Greece to commemorate victories and public events, together with c.20 'treasuries' (the oldest are those of Cypselid Corinth (see CYPSELUS; PERIANDER); *Sicyon, c.560; *Cnidus, c.550; and Siphnos, c.525), a small theatre, and the main temple of Apollo, to which the Sacred Way wound up from the road below. The *Persian Wars were architecturally celebrated with special panache, and heroes like *Miltiades were commemorated more assertively here than was possible in democratic Athens. The first temple was destroyed by fire in 548; debris, including many *votives (notably chryselephantine statuary), was buried under the Sacred Way. This destruction led to an architectural reorganization of the sanctuary. The great new temple was built in the late 6th cent. with help from the *Alcmaeonids, and was itself destroyed by earthquake in 373. A third temple was built by subscription.

Delphi was attacked by the Persians in 480 and by the Gauls in 279, but suffered little damage. Excavation began in 1880. Apart from revealing the main buildings of the enclosure and the remains of numerous monuments there have been notable finds of sculpture: the metopes of the Sicyonian and Athenian treasuries, the frieze of the Siphnian treasury, pedimental sculptures of the 'Alcmaeonid' temple, and the bronze Charioteer. Below the modern road and the Castalian Spring are public buildings (palaestra, etc.), the mid-7th-cent. temple of Athena Pronaea, the 4th-cent. *tholos, and the treasury of *Massalia (c.530).

The affairs of the sanctuary were administered by an ancient or ostensibly ancient international organization, the Delphic *Amphictiony. Influence at Delphi could be exercised in various ways and (mostly) via this amphictiony: by imposing fines for religious offences, by declaring and leading *sacred wars, and by participation in prestigious building projects. Thus from the age of Archaic *tyranny to the Roman period, Delphi (like other pan-hellenic sanctuaries but more so, because of its centrality and fame) was a focus for interstate competition as well as for contests between individuals. Control of *Thessaly was always desirable because Thessaly had a built-in preponderance of amphictionic votes. Delphi was also a *polis*, which issued decrees that survive on stone.

Delphic oracle *Oracle of *Apollo. Its origins are dated to the very end of the 9th cent. BC, and eventually it developed into the most important Greek oracle. It was consulted by *poleis* (see POLIS) as well as individuals, and played a guiding role in the formation of the Greek *poleis* and in *colonization; it gave guidance on *pollution, 'release from evils', and, above all, cult.

The earliest temple belongs to the second half of the 7th cent. The temple whose remains are visible was built in the 4th cent. The oracular consultation took place in the innermost sanc-

tuary (adytum), in which stood the *omphalos* marking the centre of the world as determined by Zeus, who released two eagles, one from the east and one from the west, which met at Delphi. Also in the adytum grew a laurel-tree (*daphnē*; see TREES, SACRED). The enquirer had to pay a consultation tax. At the altar outside the temple was offered the preliminary sacrifice before the consultation, which on regular consultation days was offered by the Delphic *polis* on behalf of all enquirers. On other days it was offered by the enquirer. If the preliminary ritual was successful, i.e. if the animal had reacted as it should when sprinkled with water, it was sacrificed, and the enquirer entered the temple, where he offered a second sacrifice, depositing either a whole victim or parts of one on an offering-table, at the entrance of the adytum. He then probably went with the *prophētai* (interpreters) and other cult personnel to a space from which he could not see the Pythia (see below) in the adytum. The Pythia, who had prepared herself by *purification at the Castalian spring, burnt laurel leaves and barley meal on the altar called *hestia* inside the temple; crowned with laurel, she sat on the tripod, became possessed (see POSSESSION, RELIGIOUS) by the god, and, shaking a laurel sprig, prophesied under divine inspiration—or in a self-induced trance. Her pronouncements were then somehow shaped by the *prophetai*. Exactly what form the Pythia's pronouncements took and what the *prophetai* did are matters of controversy. Perhaps she saw things which she put into words as best she could, and the *prophetai* interpreted them, shaping them into coherent, if ambiguous, responses; this was not an attempt to hedge their bets, but a result of the ambiguity inherent in the god's signs and the Greek perception that ambiguity is the idiom of prophecy, that there are limits to man's access to knowledge about the future: the god speaks ambiguously, and human fallibility intervenes and may misinterpret the messages.

The most important of the oracle's religious personnel (consisting of Delphians) were: the Pythia, an ordinary woman who served for life and remained chaste (see CHASTITY) throughout her service; the *prophetai*; the *hosioi*, who participated in the ritual of the consultation and shared tasks with the *prophetai*, and the priests of Apollo. The Pythia is not mentioned in the oldest 'document' informing us about the Delphic cult and oracle, the Homeric *Hymn to Apollo*, where the god gives oracular responses 'from the laurel-tree', an expression that corresponds closely to that ('from the oak-tree') used in the *Odyssey* for the prophecies at *Dodona, where the oak-tree spoke the will of *Zeus, which was interpreted by priests. A similar practice involving the laurel may have been practised at Delphi at an early period. Control of the oracle was in the hands of the Delphic *Amphictiony, run by the amphictionic council, whose duties included the conduct of the panhellenic *Pythian Games, the care of the finances of the sanctuary, and the upkeep of the temple. The amphictiony, we are told, fought a war against Crisa and defeated it; this is the First *Sacred War, the historicity of which has been doubted, but the traditional date for its end (c.590 BC) coincides with the beginning of a serious upgrading of the sanctuary, not the least of its manifestations being the building of several treasuries. The first Pythian Games were held to celebrate the amphictiony's victory. Other Sacred Wars followed, of which the fourth ended in 338 with the victory of *Philip II of Macedon at *Chaeronea. The oracle's influence had not diminished as a result of its suspect position in the *Persian Wars. Its influence continued, only its 'political' role inevitably diminished in the radically changed circumstances of the Hellenistic and Graeco-Roman world.

Dēmadēs (c.380–319 BC) Athenian statesman, influential in the two decades following the Greek defeat at *Chaeronea (338 BC). Taken prisoner in the battle, he was nevertheless chosen by *Philip II of *Macedon as an envoy and used by the Athenians to negotiate the so-called Peace of Demades. From then on he was regularly called on by the city to get it out of troubles caused by those who did not share his view that Macedon was too strong for the Greeks to revolt with a real chance of success. Having counselled against supporting *Thebes' revolt of 335, he was able to dissuade *Alexander (2) the Great from persisting in his demand for the surrender of *Demosthenes (2), *Hyperides, and other advocates of war. He seems to have sought the suspension of the Exiles' Decree in 324 by proposing a flattering decree that Alexander be voted a god (which earned him a ten-talent fine), but his greatest service was successfully to negotiate with *Antipater the end of the *Lamian War. In 319 he went on an embassy to Antipater to request the withdrawal of the garrison from Munichia, but *Cassander had him executed.

His policies of appeasement leagued him often with *Phocion. He deserved the statue that had been erected in the Agora. He began

life as a rower and received no formal training in rhetoric. He developed his great natural talent by speaking in the assembly. *Theophrastus opined that as an orator Demosthenes was worthy of the city, Demades too good for it.

demagogue, demagogy, 'leader(ship)' of the people', a phenomenon esp. associated with Classical Athens in the 5th cent. BC, though the 4th cent. had its (less extreme) demagogues too. Unlike their English counterparts, the Greek words were not initially or necessarily disparaging, i.e. the root meaning was 'leader' not 'misleader'. But 'demagogue' did become pejorative. The role of demagogues, a term which should be extended to include 'respectable' figures like *Pericles and *Nicias as well as more obvious ones like *Cleon and *Hyperbolus, was important in Athenian *democracy. (Plato's *Gorgias* makes Pericles flatter the people, contrast Thucydides 2. 65.) On the most favourable view, demagogues were the 'indispensable experts', esp. on financial matters, whose grasp of detail kept an essentially amateur system going. Certainly inscriptions, our main source of financial information about Classical Athens, help correct the hostile picture in Thucydides and *Aristophanes. In antiquity, *Theopompus and Idomeneus wrote on the Athenian demagogues.

Dēmarātus, Eurypontid king of Sparta (reigned c.515–491 BC). He twice obstructed his Agiad co-king *Cleomenes I. Dethroned on a false charge of illegitimacy manipulated through Delphi by Cleomenes, he *Medized by fleeing to *Darius I. He accompanied *Xerxes in 480, presumably in hopes of recovering his throne, but served in *Herodotus as a tragic warner of his city's die-hard resistance. Demaratus was rewarded for his services to Persia with four cities in *Troas.

demes, *dēmoi* local districts—villages, in effect—in Greece, and, by extension, the inhabitants or members thereof. The first of these twin meanings was always common, but of greater significance is the second, which at local level—*demos* as the word for an entire citizen body being another story—expresses the fact that a Classical or Hellenistic state's *demoi* sometimes served as its official, constitutional subdivisions, besides sustaining internally organized communal functions of their own. In post-Cleisthenic Athens (see CLEISTHENES (2)) 139 *demoi*, encompassing the city itself and the Attic countryside, became the building-blocks of Cleisthenes' three-tier civic structure. As natural units of settlement they varied in size, from hamlets to substantial towns like *Acharnae or *Eleusis, but equalizing mechanisms operated at the levels of *trittyes* and *phylai*, including proportional representation on the *boule of 500. Deme membership was hereditary in the male line, irrespective of any changes of residence, and served as guarantee of membership of the *polis itself. Registration of 18-year-olds as demesmen was thus the most far-reaching of the many functions supervised by the *dēmarchos*, the one official to be found in every deme. Besides the demarch, though, a deme assembly could devise and appoint whatever officials it liked, as one instance of the high degree of self-determination it enjoyed generally. To its own (resident) members their deme felt like a *polis* in miniature, and where possible it behaved as such, levying and spending income, organizing local cults and *festivals, and commemorating its decision-making on the inscriptions from which much of our evidence derives. Ambitious Athenians might occasionally see their deme as a stepping-stone to higher things, but *prosopographical evidence more strongly indicates the microcosm(s) and macrocosm as separate spheres, with life in the small pool remaining rewarding enough for many a big fish.

Dēmētēr, the Greek goddess of corn, identified in Italy with *Ceres. She controls all crops and vegetation, and so is the sustainer of life for men and animals. In early epic corn is called 'Demeter's grain', and in a Homeric simile 'blonde Demeter' herself winnows grain from chaff. Her daughter by Zeus, *Persephone, was called simply *Kŏrē*, 'the Girl', and the two were so closely linked that they were known as 'the Two Goddesses'. Because the life of plants between autumn and spring is one of hidden growth underground, Persephone was said to have been carried off by her uncle *Hades, lord of the Underworld, and compelled to spend the winter months with him as his wife, returning to the upper world with the flowers of spring. Thus as Kore she was a deity of youth and joy, the leader of the *Nymphs, with whom she looked after the growth of the young, but as Hades' wife she was also queen of the dead, governing the fate of souls, and thus an awesome and dread goddess.

As deities of *agriculture and growth, associated with a settled rhythm of life, Demeter and Kore were regarded as important influences in the development of civilization. Their title 'Thesmophoros' was traditionally interpreted as due to their role as givers of law and morality. The Greek religious calendar was closely linked to the farmer's year, and many of their festivals coincided with the seasonal activities of ploughing, sowing, reaping, threshing, and storing the harvest. One of the most important and widespread, the *Thesmophoria, normally took place in autumn, near to sowing-time, and included ceremonies intended to promote fertility. Like many festivals of Demeter, it was secret and restricted to women. Their secrecy seems to have been due primarily to the sense of awe and fear generated by contemplation of the powers of the earth and Underworld.

The most important festivals of Demeter and Kore were the ceremonies of initiation known as '*mysteries', the most famous of which were those of *Eleusis. By guaranteeing to initiates the favour of the goddesses, they offered above all the promise of a better fate after death, but they also promised prosperity in life, personified by *Plutus (Wealth), who was the child of Demeter.

Many legends told how, when Demeter was searching for her daughter after Hades had carried her off, she received information or hospitality from the inhabitants of different places in Greece, and in gratitude taught them how to practise agriculture and to celebrate her rituals. The chief claimants for this honour were Eleusis and *Sicily, her most important cult centres. The oldest and best-known version of the myth is the Homeric *Hymn to Demeter, an epic poem probably of the Archaic period. It tells how, after Kore was carried off, Demeter wandered the earth in search of her, disguised as an old woman, until she came to Eleusis where she was welcomed by the family of King Celeŭs. She became the nurse of his baby son Dēmophŏn, and tried to immortalize him by anointing him with *ambrosia and holding him in the fire at night to burn away his mortality. She was interrupted by Celeus' wife, and so prevented from making him immortal. Instead, she revealed her true identity, promised Demophon heroic honours after death, and ordered the Eleusinians to build her a temple and altar. She withdrew to her speedily built new temple and caused a universal famine, until Zeus was forced to order Hades to release her daughter. Hades, however, gave Persephone a pomegranate seed to eat, and because she had tasted food in the Underworld she was compelled to spend a third part of every year there, returning to earth in spring. Demeter then restored the fertility of the fields and taught the princes of Eleusis how to perform her mysteries, whose absolute secrecy is stressed. The poem closes with the promise of divine favour to the initiates both in life and after death. The Great Mysteries at Eleusis were celebrated in early autumn (Boedromion), and were preceded by the Lesser Mysteries at Agrae, just outside Athens, in spring.

The famine, in the *Homeric Hymn*, reflects another form of the belief that the death of vegetation has a divine cause. Persephone's absence and Demeter's anger and grief both combine to create sterility. The hymn assumes the existence of agriculture before the Rape, but the Athenians in the Classical period claimed that Demeter had given to *Triptolemus, one of the princes of Eleusis, the gifts of corn and the arts of agriculture, and that he then travelled the world teaching these to other nations (see CULTURE-BRINGERS).

Sicily was always regarded as esp. consecrated to the Two Goddesses, and in the Hellenistic and Roman periods versions of the myth of Kore which placed her Rape and Return here became popular. She was said to have been carried off from a meadow near Enna in the centre of the island, and to have disappeared underground at the site of a spring near *Syracuse, where an annual festival was held.

In art Demeter is shown both on her own and with Persephone, with related figures of cult such as Hades and Triptolemus, and in groups with the other Olympian deities. Esp. popular scenes are those of the Rape and Return of Persephone, and the Mission of Triptolemus. She carries a *sceptre, ears of corn and a poppy, or torches, and she and her daughter are often portrayed as closely linked and similar in iconography.

Dēmētrius of *Phaleron (b. *c*.350 BC), Athenian *Peripatetic philosopher (pupil of *Theophrastus) and statesman, began his political life in 325/4 and was probably elected *strategos* for many of the next few years. As a pro-Macedonian he escaped death in 318, and *Cassander made him absolute governor at Athens, where he held power for ten years. He passed comprehensive legislation: military and other service was limited, various forms of extravagance were curbed, measures were taken to regularize contracts and titles to property, and 'guardians of the laws' were set up. When Demetrius Poliorcētēs took Athens (307), Demetrius fled to *Boeotia, and was later librarian at *Alexandria (297).

Works Moral treatises, popular tales, declamations, histories, literary criticism, rhetoric, and collections of letters, *fables, and *proverbs. Though an outstanding orator, Demetrius produced a superficial amalgam of philosophy and rhetoric. He assisted his fellow Peripatetics, and under him Athens enjoyed relative peace.

Dēmocēdēs, of Croton in southern Italy (6th cent. BC), one of the most famous doctors (see MEDICINE) of his time, and origin of Croton's medical reputation, practised in *Aegina, *Athens, and then for *Polycrates (1) of Samos. After the murder of Polycrates *c.* 522, he won great repute at *Darius I's court, but the picturesque Herodotean story of his escape back to Croton, and marriage to the daughter of Milon the wrestler, looks like a folk-tale.

democracy, Athenian Athenian democracy from 508/7 to 322/1 BC is the best known example in history of a 'direct' democracy as opposed to a 'representative' or 'parliamentary' democracy.

1. Ideology In ancient Greece *dēmokratia* was a hotly debated form of constitution, often criticized by oligarchs and philosophers. Athenian democrats themselves, however, connected *dēmokratia* with the rule of law and, like modern democrats, they believed that democracy was inseparably bound up with the ideals of liberty and equality. *Demokratia* was what the word means: the rule (*kratos*) of the people (**dēmos*), and decisions of the assembly were introduced with the formula 'Resolved by the people'. When an Athenian democrat said *demos*, he meant the whole body of citizens, regardless of the fact that only a minority turned up to meetings of the assembly. Critics of democracy, on the other hand, esp. philosophers, tended to regard the *demos* as a class, i.e. the 'common people' or the 'city poor'.

The fundamental democratic ideal was liberty (see FREEDOM), which had two aspects: political liberty to participate in the democratic institutions, and private liberty to live as one pleased. The most important aspect of liberty was freedom of speech, which in the public sphere was every citizen's right to address his fellow citizens in the political assemblies, and in the private sphere was everyone's right to speak his mind. Critics of democracy, esp. philosophers, took democratic freedom to be a mistaken ideal that led to a deplorable pluralism and prevented people from understanding the true purpose of life.

The democrat concept of equality was not based on the view that all are equal (although philosophers wanted to impute this view to democrats). The equality advocated by democrats was that all should have an equal opportunity to participate in politics (*isonomia*), esp. an equal opportunity to speak in the political assemblies (*isēgoria*), and that all must be equal before the law. The concept of equality was purely political and did not spread to the social and economic aspects of life.

2. Institutions A description of the political system should focus on the 4th cent. BC, esp. on the age of *Demosthenes (2), where the sources are plentiful enough to allow a reconstruction of the organs of democracy.

Political rights were restricted to adult male Athenians. Women, foreigners, and slaves were excluded. An Athenian came of age at 18, when he became a member of his father's *deme and was enrolled in the deme's roster; but, as *epheboi*, most young Athenians were liable for military service for two years before, at the age of 20, they could be enrolled in the roster of citizens who had access to the assembly or *ekklesia*. And full political rights were obtained only at the age of 30.

The citizen population totalled some 30,000 adult males over 18, of whom some 20,000 were over 30 and thus in possession of full political rights. The population of Attica—citizens, foreigners, and slaves of both sexes and all ages—may have amounted to some 300,000 persons. (See POPULATION, GREEK.)

Any citizen over 20 had the right to speak and vote in the assembly. The people met 40 times a year, mostly on Pnyx; a meeting was normally attended by at least 6,000 citizens, the quorum required for (among other things) ratification of citizenship decrees, and a session might last only a couple of hours. The assembly was summoned by the 50 *prytaneis and chaired by the nine *proedroi*. The debate consisted of a number of speeches made by the politically active citizens, and all votes were taken by a show of hands, assessed by the *proedroi* without any exact count of the hands (see ELECTIONS AND VOTING). The Athenians distinguished between laws (general and permanent rules, called *nomoi*) and decrees (temporary and/or individual rules, called *psēphismata*); see LAW AND PROCEDURE, ATHENIAN, 1. The assembly was not allowed to pass laws but did, by decree, make decisions on foreign policy and on major issues of domestic policy. Furthermore, the people in assembly

were empowered (*a*) to elect the military and financial magistrates; (*b*) to initiate legislation by appointing a panel of legislators (*nomothetai*); and (*c*) to initiate a political trial (*eisangelia*) by referring the case to a jury-court (see below).

Citizens over 30 were eligible to participate in the annual sortition of a panel of 6,000 jurors, who for one year served both as legislators and as judges. When a law was to be enacted, the assembly decreed the appointment, for one day only, of a board of e.g. 1,000 legislators (*nomothetai*) selected by lot from the 6,000 jurors. Having listened to a debate, the *nomothetai* decided by a show of hands all amendments to *Solon's laws', i.e. the Solonian law code of 594/3 as revised and codified in 403/2. Boards of *nomothetai* were appointed only rarely.

Jurisdiction was much more time-consuming. The jury-courts (*dikastēria*; see LAW AND PROCEDURE, ATHENIAN, 2,4) met on roughly 200 days in a year. On a court day members of the panel of 6,000 jurors showed up in the morning in the *Agora, and a number of courts were appointed by sortition from among those present. These courts consisted of 201 or 401 jurors each in private actions and 501 or more in public actions. Each court was presided over by a magistrate, and in a session of some eight hours the jurors had to hear and decide either one public action or a number of private actions. The two most important types of political trial were (i) the public action against unconstitutional proposals (*graphe paranomon*), brought against proposers of decrees, and (ii) denunciation to the people in assembly (*eisangelia*), used most often against generals (*strategoi*) charged with treason or *corruption.

In addition to the decision-making organs of government (*ekklēsia, nomothetai, dikastēria*) Athens had about 1,200 magistrates, chosen from among citizens over 30 who presented themselves as candidates. About 100 were elected by the assembly, whereas the other 1,100 were selected by lot viz. 500 councillors and *c*.600 other magistrates, often organized in boards of ten with one representative from each tribe. The period of office was restricted to one year and a magistrate selected by lot could hold a particular office only once, whereas elected magistrates could be re-elected. Before entering office magistrates had to undergo vetting (*dokimasia*) before a jury-court and, on the expiration of their term of office, to render accounts (*euthynai*) before another jury-court.

The magistrates' principal tasks were to summon and preside over the *decision-making bodies, and to see to the execution of the decisions made. Apart from routine matters, the magistrates could not decide anything but only hold preliminary investigations. The council of 500 (*boule*) prepared business for the assembly and the *nomothetai*, the other magistrates for the jury-courts.

The *boulē* was composed of 50 men from each of the ten tribes (*phylai*), who for a tenth of the year (a prytany of 36 or 35 days) served as *prytaneis*, i.e. as executive committee of the council, which again served as executive committee of the assembly. Every day except holidays the council met in the council-house on the Agora to run the financial administration of Athens and to consider in advance every matter to be put before the people.

Of the other boards of magistrates the most important were the ten generals, who commanded the Athenian army and navy, the board for the Theoric Fund (see THEORIKA) who in the 350s under *Eubulus, supervised the financial administration, and the nine archons (see ARCHONTES), who in most public and private actions had to summon and preside over the jury-courts and supervised the major festivals, e.g. the *Panathenaea and the city *Dionysia.

In all matters the initiative was left to the individual citizen. At any time about 1,000 citizens must have been active as speakers and proposers of laws and decrees or as prosecutors (or assistant prosecutors) before a jury-court. But it was always a small group of about 20 citizens who more or less professionally initiated Athenian policy. They were called *rhētores* (speakers) or *politeuomenoi*, whereas the ordinary politically active citizen is referred to as an *idiōtēs* (amateur). There were no political parties, and the people did not just vote according to the crack of their leaders' whip. But by persuasion and charisma major political leaders sometimes succeeded in dominating the political assemblies for a longer period, as did *Pericles from 443 until his death in 429, and *Demosthenes (2) in the period 341–338.

Ordinary citizens were reimbursed for attending assemblies or serving as jurors or councillors. Very few magistrates were paid regularly, but many obtained perquisites instead. Speakers and proposers in the assemblies were unpaid, and those who attempted to make a profit out of politics were regarded as *sycophants and liable to punishment.

The council of the *Areopagus was a survival of the Archaic period and in the period 461–404 mainly a court for cases of homicide. In the 4th

cent., however, the activity of the Areopagus was again progressively enlarged in connection with attempts to revive the 'ancestral' or 'Solonian' democracy.

3. History In 510 the Pisistratid tyrants (see PISISTRATUS; HIPPIAS (1)) were expelled from Athens. There followed a power struggle between the returning aristocrats led by *Cleisthenes (2) and those who had stayed behind led by Isagoras. With the help of the common people Cleisthenes successfully opposed Isagoras and, reforming the Solonian institutions of 594, he introduced popular government, which was arising in several Greek city-states at the time. The term *dēmokratia* can be traced back to *c.470 and may go back to Cleisthenes. His major reforms was dividing Attica into 139 municipalities (*demes), which were distributed among ten tribes. Citizen rights were linked to membership of a deme, and a council of 500 was introduced, with 50 representatives from each of the ten tribes, and a fixed number of seats assigned to each of the demes according to its number of demesmen. Finally, to avoid a repeat of the power struggle of 510–507 Cleisthenes introduced *ostracism.

During the next century the new democracy was buttressed by other reforms: in 501 command of the army and navy was transferred from the *polemarch to a board of ten elected generals. In 487/6 the method of chosing the nine archons was changed from election to selection by lot from an elected short list. *Ephialtes' reforms of 462 deprived the Areopagus of its political powers, which were divided between the assembly, the council of 500, and the jury-courts. Shortly afterwards, on the initiative of Pericles, political pay was introduced for the jury-courts and the council, so that even poor citizens could exercise their political rights. Athenian citizenship became a much-coveted privilege, and in 451 Pericles passed a law confining *citizenship to the legitimate sons of an Athenian mother as well as father.

The defeats in the *Peloponnesian War resulted in a growing opposition to democracy, and twice the anti-democratic factions succeeded for some months in establishing an *oligarchy, in 411 a moderate oligarchy led by the council of *Four Hundred and in 404/3 a radical oligarchy under a junta which fully earned the name 'the *Thirty Tyrants'. In 403/2 democracy was restored in a modified form. Legislation (in 403) and all jurisdiction in political trials (in *c*.355) were transferred from the people in assembly to the panel of 6,000 jurors acting both as legislators and judges. In the 330s a kind of minister of finance was introduced. He was elected for a four-year period and could be re-elected, and for twelve consecutive years the administration of Athens was entrusted to *Lycurgus. These and other reforms were allegedly a return to the 'ancestral' or 'Solonian' democracy, but the gradual and moderate transformation of democratic institutions came to an abrupt end in 322/1 when the Macedonians after their victory in the *Lamian War abolished the democracy and had it replaced by a 'Solonian' oligarchy.

4. Tradition Between 322 BC and *c*. AD 1850
Athenian democracy was almost forgotten, and, if mentioned, the focus was on the mythical 'Solonian democracy' known from *Plutarch's *Life of Solon* and *Aristotle's *Politics*. It was not until *c*.1800, when history began to emerge as a scholarly discipline, that the Athenian democratic institutions were studied seriously and reconstructed from sources such as *Thucydides (2), Demosthenes, and inscriptions. And it was only from *c*.1850 that the new understanding of Classical Athenian democracy was connected, principally by George Grote, with a budding interest in democracy as a form of government, though now in the form of a 'representative' or 'parliamentary' democracy and no longer as an 'assembly' democracy in which power was exercised directly by the people.

democracy, non-Athenian and post-Classical Democracy was not an Athenian monopoly or even invention. (See DEMOCRACY, ATHENIAN.) The Archaic Spartan constitutional document preserved by *Plutarch explicitly says that 'the people shall have the power', but Sparta soon ossified. Sixth-cent. BC *Chios, as an inscription reveals, had a constitution with some popular features, though Classical Chios, like Classical Sparta, was no longer democratic. Classical Greek states other than Athens, such as *Argos, were or were perceived as democracies, but Athenian influence can usually be assumed (see DEMOCRACY, ATHENIAN). Thus assembly pay, a feature of the developed Athenian democracy (introduced only after the main *Peloponnesian War) is also attested at Hellenistic Iasus and *Rhodes, no doubt exported there originally from Athens. But imperial Athens, despite sweeping remarks in some ancient literary texts, was not doctrinaire about insisting on democracies in the subject states. It was more important to install or support favourably minded personnel. In any case, to impose 'democracy' on a tiny place like Erythrae in Ionia did not mean much, given the demographic facts: thus the mid 5th-cent. 'Erythrae decree' shows that the rules for the council established there by Athens were much less rigidly democratic than those at Athens itself.

*Polybius treated some aspects of the Roman constitution in the middle republic as if they were fully democratic, not without reason. *Porcius Cato (1), for instance, can plausibly be seen as an essentially popular politician. But there were always big differences from Classical Athens: at Rome, popular meetings (COMITIA; CONTIONES) could be summoned only by a magistrate; and at the end of the republic the enormous power of the military dynasts undermined even such democracy as there was. The prevalence of electoral bribery or *ambitus always, and esp. in the late republic when the stakes were higher, meant that elections expressed the popular will only approximately. (But in both republic and Principate there were other, cruder, outlets for popular feeling, such as demonstrations at the theatre or games; see ACCLAMATION). City assemblies tended to be dominated by the city population. Rome was not unique in this, but the size of Italy meant that the problem was esp. acute. The puzzle of apparently popular elections within an essentially oligarchic framework can be solved by seeing instances of genuinely contested elections as occasional submissions to popular will—an agreed form of arbitration. See also OPTIMATES; POLITICS, *At Rome*.

Dēmocritus, of Abdera, b. 460–457 BC, 40 years after *Anaxagoras acc. to his own statement quoted by *Diogenes (4) Laertius. He travelled widely, acc. to various later accounts, and lived to a great age. In time he became known as 'the laughing philosopher', probably because he held that 'cheerfulness' was a goal to be pursued in life. There is a story that he visited Athens— 'but no one knew me'; this may be a reflection of the undoubted fact that *Plato, although he must have known his work, never mentioned him by name.

Works   Diog. Laert. mentions 70 titles, classified as follows: Ethics, Physics, Unclassified, Mathematics, Music (which includes philological and literary criticism), Technical, and Notes. None of these works survives. Of his physical theories, on which his fame rests, only meagre quotations and summaries remain; most of the texts that have come down to us under his name are brief and undistinguished moral maxims.

From the time of *Aristotle, Democritus and Leucippus are jointly credited with the creation of the atomic theory of the universe (see ATOMISM); it is now impossible to distinguish the contribution of each. Aristotle's account of the origin of the theory rightly relates it to the Eleatic School. *Parmenides had argued that what is real is one and motionless, since empty space is not a real existent; motion is impossible without empty space, and plurality is impossible without something to separate the units. Division of what is real into units in contact, i.e. with no separating spaces, is ruled out because (a) infinite divisibility would mean there are no real units at all, and (b) finite divisibility is physically inexplicable. Against these arguments, says Aristotle, Leucippus proposed to rescue the sensible world of plurality and motion by asserting that empty space, 'the non-existent', may nevertheless serve to separate parts of what exists from each other. So the universe has two ingredients: Being, which satisfies the Eleatic criteria by being 'full', unchanging, and homogeneous, and Non-being or empty space. The pieces of real Being, since it is their characteristic to be absolutely indivisible units, are called 'atoms' (lit. 'uncuttables'). They are said to be solid, invisibly small, and undifferentiated in material; they differ from each other in shape and size only (perhaps also in weight), and the only change they undergo is in their relative and absolute position, through movement in space.

By their changes of position the atoms produce the compounds of the changing sensible world. Compounds differ in quality according to the shape and arrangement of the component atoms, their congruence or otherwise (i.e. their tendency to latch together because of their shape), and the amount of space between them. It is a matter of controversy whether the atoms have a natural downward motion due to weight (as later in Epicurean theory: see EPICURUS, *Doctrines*) or move randomly in the void until their motion is somehow directed by collisions with other atoms. In the course of time, groups of atoms form 'whirls' or vortices, which have the effect of sorting out the atoms by size and shape, like to like. Some of these are sorted in such a way as to produce distinct masses having the appearance of earth, water, air, and fire: thus worlds are formed—not one single world, as in most Greek cosmologies, but an indeterminate number scattered throughout the infinite void, each liable to perish through random atomic motions, as they were originally formed. Leucippus and Democritus produced an account of the evolution within worlds of progressively more complex stages of organization, including human cultures.

The *soul, which is the cause of life and sensation, is made of fine round atoms, and is a compound as perishable as the body. Perception takes place through the impact of *eidōla* (thin atomic films shed from the surfaces of sensible objects) upon the soul-atoms through the sense organs. Perceptible qualities are the product of the atoms of the sensible object and those of the perceiving soul. They therefore have a different mode of existence from atoms and void—'by convention' as opposed to 'in reality'. See ATOMISM.

Little is known about Democritus' mathematics, although mathematical writings appear in the lists of his works; he must have been a diligent biologist, for Aristotle quotes him often.

Many surviving fragments deal with ethics, but they are mostly short maxims, hard to fit together into a consistent and comprehensive doctrine. His positions, as reported, are close to those of Epicurus, but it is hard to know whether this is historically genuine. His ethical ideal seems to include the idea that the soul-atoms should be protected from violent upheavals; well-being which leads to 'cheerfulness' is a matter of moderation and wisdom. It is important not to let the fear of death spoil life, and to recognize the limits within which man is confined. Pleasure is in some sense the criterion of right action, but there must be moderation in choosing pleasures. In social ethics, Democritus was apparently prepared to link his view of contemporary society with his theory of the evolution of human communities; he saw that a system of law is necessary for the preservation of society.

Democritus has suffered intolerably from the triumph of his opponents, Plato, Aristotle, and the Stoics (see STOICISM). He defended the infinite universe, plural and perishable worlds, efficient, non-teleological causes, and the atomic theory of matter. The best brains preferred his opponents' arguments, and Epicurus and *Lucretius were his only influential followers until the post-Renaissance scientific revolution—by which time his books were lost.

dēmos See DEMES; DEMOCRACY, ATHENIAN. The Greek word means originally 'district, land', hence esp. (in *Attica and elsewhere) the villages or *demes (*demoi*, pl. of *demos*) which were the main units of country settlement. From 'the place where the people live' the word comes to mean 'the people', as in compounds like *dēmo-kratia*, 'people-power' or '*democracy'; *demos* sometimes means 'the sovereign people', sometimes 'the common people'.

Dēmosthenēs (1) (d. 413 BC), Athenian general. After an unsuccessful invasion of Aetolia in 426 he won two brilliant victories against a Peloponnesian and Ambraciot army invading Amphilochia. In 425 his occupation of *Pylos led to a most valuable success, the capture of a body of Spartan hoplites on the adjacent island of Sphacteria. He surprised Nisaea in 424, but failed to take *Megara, and in a triple attack on Boeotia, for which he was perhaps responsible, he was unable to land troops at Siphae, since the enemy was forewarned. He was not again entrusted with a major command until 413 when he was sent to reinforce *Nicias at *Syracuse. After failing to regain Epipolae by a night attack, he urged withdrawal from Syracuse, which was delayed until the Athenians had lost control of the sea and were driven to attempt escape by land. The rearguard, led by Demosthenes, surrendered on the sixth day, and he was later put to death.

Dēmosthenēs (2) (384–322 BC), the greatest Athenian orator. When Demosthenes was 7 years old, his father died, leaving the management of his estate to his brothers and a friend. The trustees mismanaged the business, and Demosthenes at the age of 18 found himself almost without resources. He claimed his patrimony from his guardians, who spent three years in attempts to compromise. In the mean time, he was studying rhetoric and legal procedure under *Isaeus and at 21 he brought a successful action against his guardians, but two more years elapsed before he received the remnants of the property. By now he was engaged in the profession of speech-writer, and the reputation gained in private cases led to his being employed as an assistant to prosecutors in public trials.

From 355/4 onwards he came more and more to devote himself to public business. In 353/2 he turned on *Eubulus in a speech which seems directed partly against the allocation of surpluses to the *theōrika—he sneers at the public works of Eubulus—and partly against the policy of abstaining from all but essential military enterprises.

In late 352 Philip's attack on the Odrysian (see THRACE) king Cersobleptes carried him very near the *Chersonese, and Demosthenes' eyes were opened. In 351 he delivered the *First Philippic* which pleaded for more vigorous prosecution of the war for *Amphipolis: his proposals were not accepted; deeper involvement in the long fruitless struggle may have seemed to endanger the power to defend the vital areas of *Thermopylae and Chersonese. In mid-349 *Olynthus was attacked by Philip and appealed to Athens for help: in the three *Olynthiacs*, delivered in quick succession, Demosthenes demanded the fullest support and, in the last, an end to the law assigning surpluses to the *theorika*; again he scathingly alluded to the works of Eubulus. One consequence of his opposition to Eubulus was that he became embroiled in an absurd wrangle with Midias, a prominent supporter of Eubulus, who had slapped his face at the *Dionysia of 348: the case was settled out of court and the speech *Against Midias* was never delivered.

In mid-348, before the fall of Olynthus, Demosthenes successfully defended *Philocrates when he was indicted under the *graphe paranomon for his proposal to negotiate with Philip, and in 347/6, when Demosthenes like *Aeschines (1) was a member of the *boule, the partnership continued, and Demosthenes played a leading part in securing acceptance of the Peace of Philocrates. On the two embassies to Macedon he cut a poor figure before Philip and got on badly with his fellow ambassadors, but the decisive moment came after the second embassy's return when, in the assembly, it was known that Philip had occupied the Gates of Thermopylae and that Phocis could not be saved. Demosthenes was shouted down and Aeschines made the speech to which Demosthenes constantly recurred. What Demosthenes wanted that day is not clear: if he did want the city to denounce the new Peace, to march out to support Phocis attacked by the Macedonians and *Thessalians from the north and the Thebans from the south, his judgement was seriously awry. From that day Demosthenes determined to undo the Peace, but for the moment contented himself with the attack on Aeschines from which he was forced to desist by the successful countercharge against his own associate, Timarchus.

The year 344 brought Demosthenes his opportunity to attack the Peace. Rumours reached Athens that Philip was preparing to intervene in the Peloponnese in support of *Argos and

Messene, and Demosthenes went on an embassy to those cities to warn them of the dangers of consorting with Philip: Philip protested, and offered to turn the Peace into a Common Peace (a peace-treaty applicable to all cities on the basis of *autonomy). In mid-343, after the success of *Hyperides' prosecution of Philocrates, Demosthenes judged the moment suitable to resume his attack on Aeschines; *On the False Embassy* sought to exploit the support of Eubulus' party for continuing the Peace and to suggest that Aeschines was really responsible for Philip's use of the peace negotiations to intervene in Phocis in 346. With the support of Eubulus and *Phocion, Aeschines was narrowly acquitted.

With the final collapse in early 342 of proposals to amend the Peace, Philip either began to intervene directly in Greece or was represented by Demosthenes as so doing, and amidst mounting hostility to Macedon Demosthenes went on an embassy to the Peloponnese to set about arranging an Hellenic alliance for the war he was determined to have. For the moment his efforts came to little, but in 341 in *On the Chersonese* and shortly after, in the *Third Philippic*, he argued that, since Philip's actions already amounted to war, it was absurd to heed the letter of the Peace. In 341/0 he formed an alliance with *Byzantium, and by autumn 340, when Philip finally declared war and seized the Athenian cornfleet, Demosthenes was in full charge of the war he had sought. In mid-339 he moved the suspension of the allocation of surpluses to the *theorika*, and with Thebes unlikely to side with Philip after having expelled the Macedonian garrison from the Gates, Demosthenes could expect not to have to face Philip in Greece. The sudden seizure of Elatea in Phocis threw Athens into horrified perplexity, but Demosthenes proposed and effected alliance with Thebes, which he later pretended always to have wanted, and Athens and Thebes fought side by side at *Chaeronea in autumn 338.

Demosthenes was present at the battle, and returned so quickly to organize the city's defences that Aeschines could accuse him of running away. He provided corn, repaired the walls, and was so much the man of the hour that he was chosen to deliver the Funeral Oration (see EPITAPHIOS) for 338. With Philip in Greece, the people looked to Demosthenes, and he successfully met the frequent attacks on him in the courts. In 337/6 he was theoric commissioner, and Ctesiphon proposed that he be *crowned at the Dionysia for his constant service to the city's

best interests: perhaps encouraged by the opening of the Macedonian attack on Persia, Aeschines indicted Ctesiphon, but with the changing events of the next few months he preferred for the moment to let the case lapse. Demosthenes, hoping that the death of Philip was the end of Macedonian domination in Greece, sought to foment troubles for his successor, but *Alexander (2) the Great quickly marched south and Demosthenes had to accept the new monarch. In 335 Demosthenes actively aided the Thebans in their revolt and narrowly escaped being surrendered to Alexander. From then on he seems to have looked to Persia to accomplish the liberation of Greece: such at any rate seems to be the meaning of the many charges of receiving money from the Persians. When Persia was crushed at *Gaugamela (331), Athens was left in disastrous isolation. Aeschines seized the opportunity to renew his attack on Demosthenes through Ctesiphon. The case was heard in mid-330, and Demosthenes defended his acts in *On the Crown*, which is his masterpiece. He declined to fall into the trap of discussing recent events and with supreme art interspersed his discussion of events long past with lofty assertions of principle. Fewer than one-fifth of the jury voted for Aeschines, and he retired to Rhodes. Demosthenes was left in triumph, and the city settled down to acceptance of Macedonian rule, until in 324 word reached Greece that at the coming Olympic Games Alexander's emissary Nicanor was to proclaim an edict ordering the restoration of exiles. Since this would affect Athens' *cleruchy on *Samos, an agitation began which was to end in the *Lamian War. Demosthenes led a deputation to protest. Later he engaged in the discussion at Athens about divine honours (see RULER-CULT) for Alexander, having also taken the lead in dealing with the sudden appearance of *Harpalus by proposing first that Harpalus be kept prisoner and his money stored on the Acropolis, and then that the *Areopagus investigate the losses. The Areopagus declared Demosthenes guilty of appropriating 20 talents, and he was found guilty and fined 50 talents, but, even if he did take the money, he may have intended to use it in service of the state. He went into exile, and lent his support to Hyperides in the creation of the alliance for the Lamian War. He was then recalled to Athens, but after the Macedonian victory at Crannon in 322 he left the city again, and was condemned to death by a decree of *Demades. Pursued by the agents of *Antipater, he killed himself in Calauria (322).

Modern opinions of Demosthenes' political importance have varied greatly. He has been lauded as a solitary champion of liberty and censured as the absurd opponent of progress. The high esteem in which the works of Demosthenes have been rightly held as works of art has tended to obscure the possibility that, while his devotion to liberty is one of its supreme monuments, his methods and his policies were not best suited to attain their end, and that those of his opponents, which we must largely infer from his attacks, were no less directed to maintaining the city's power and independence, and perhaps more apt.

Demosthenes has much to say about Philip's success being due to bribery, and he was convinced that his own opponents had been corrupted, but in his obsession with this dubitable view he seems blind to the real problem of his day, which was how Greece could be united to counter effectively the military power of the new national state—far greater than the power of any single city-state. There was much to be said against Demosthenes' determination to involve the full military resources of Athens in a war in the north, in particular that in such a war Athens stood to gain most and the other Greeks would not unite for that result. For the defence of Greece itself against invasion there was some hope of uniting the cities in a Common Peace, and this appears to have been the policy of Demosthenes' opponents. The situation of Greece was tragic, and Demosthenes was certainly of heroic stature.

Private lawcourt speeches The subjects of the private speeches include guardianship, inheritance, claims for payment, *maritime loans, mining rights, forgery, trespass, assault, etc. In his *Callicles* (which has flashes of humour, seldom found in Demosthenes) the plaintiff alleges that the defendant has flooded his land by blocking a watercourse; in *Conon*, a brilliant piece of writing, some dissolute young rowdies and their father are summoned for assault.

Demosthenes had many rivals in his lifetime; but later critics considered him the greatest of the orators. His claim to greatness rests on his singleness of purpose, his sincerity, and his lucid and convincing exposition of his argument. In many instances he produces a great effect by the use of a few ordinary words. In his most solemn moments his style is at its plainest and his language most moderate. A master of metaphor, he uses it sparingly, and hardly at all in his most impressive passages. His style varies infinitely according to circumstances.

Deucalion, in mythology, the Greek Noah, son of *Prometheus, married to Pyrrha. When *Zeus floods the earth in anger at the *sins of the age of bronze, Deucalion and Pyrrha, on the advice of Prometheus, build a chest and live there for nine days and nine nights. When they come to land, they repopulate the earth by casting over their shoulders stones from which people spring. Greek *genealogy begins with Deucalion's son Hellen ('Greek'), eponymous ancestor of the *Hellenes. Deucalion is held to have founded the temple of Olympian Zeus in Athens (see OLYMPIEUM), and there was an annual sacrifice commemorating the final ebbing away of the waters down the crevice there. The purpose of the flood is to create a new beginning for a new world-order.

Diadochi ('Successors'). This term was applied in a special sense to the more important of *Alexander (2) the Great's officers who ultimately partitioned his empire: *Antigonus I, *Antipater, *Cassander, *Lysimachus, *Ptolemy (1) I, *Seleucus I. The period of the Diadochi lasted from Alexander's death (323 BC) at least to the battle of Ipsus (301), which ended the efforts of Antigonus I to reassemble the whole empire under his own rule, and perhaps to the battle of Corupedium (281), which fixed the main political boundaries of the Hellenistic world for the next century.

diagnosis, lit. 'the means of distinguishing, or recognizing'. Much ancient medical literature is concerned with the way in which the doctor should discern the nature, history, and future course of the patient's *disease. Each case dealt with by the doctor involved the recognition of a number of signs which needed to be distinguished and ordered so that the correct treatment could be prescribed, and the progress of the disease anticipated. Prognosis is effectively a part of diagnosis, and many ancient diagnoses result not so much in naming the disease as in predicting its outcome. Effective prognosis not only increased the patient's confidence in the doctor, but could also encourage the doctor to avoid hopeless cases.

dialectic, the science of conducting a philosophical dialogue by exploring the consequences of premises asserted or conceded by an interlocutor. *Aristotle considered *Zeno (1) of Elea its founder, no doubt for his antinomies, which derived contradictory consequences from a disputed hypothesis. *Socrates' method of cross-examination, the *elenchos*, was a further landmark in the history of dialectic. But it was his pupil *Plato who formally developed the idea of a dialectical science, and who probably coined the term 'dialectic' itself. While Socrates' arguments had regularly taken the form of refutations, Plato presented dialectic as co-operative investigation based on agreed premises, in contrast to the essentially obstructive method of 'eristic'. In his middle and late periods Plato virtually equated dialectic with correct philosophical method, esp. for securing definitions. This for him normally means conceptual inquiry into the hierarchy of forms, and can involve the twin analytic methods of collection (into a genus) and division (into species). In the *Republic* dialectic is the supreme science, uniting the first principles of all individual disciplines under a single unhypothetical principle, the Good. Even here it is still viewed as taking the form of oral debate, and as including *elenchos* as one component.

Aristotle's *Topics*, whose origins lie largely in Plato's *Academy, is his handbook on dialectical method. For him dialectic, while still integral to investigative method and the proper route to knowledge of first principles, differs from scientific 'demonstration' because of the less secure status of its premises, operating as it does from *endoxa*, 'reputable' opinions held 'either by all or most people, or by the wise'. In so operating, dialectic applies Aristotle's standard method of proceeding from 'what appears' or from 'that which is better known to us'. Training in dialectic includes mastery of debating skills, of complex definitional theory, of rules of inference, and (as covered in his *On Sophistical Refutations*) of the analysis of fallacies.

The Dialectical school, influential in the later 4th and early 3rd cents. BC, was a Socratic movement which made dialectical virtuosity its focal concern, perhaps influenced by Socrates' description (in Plato's *Apology*) of dialectical activity as the greatest human good. In the Hellenistic period the *Stoics treated dialectic as a broad division of philosophy, embracing logic, grammar, definition and division, and the study of sophisms. The Stoic sage is said to be the only true dialectician, and to possess 'dialectical virtue'. The Epicureans rejected the whole of dialectic as superfluous. The Academics, as critics of all doctrinal stances, were leading practitioners of dialectic, yet also sought to undermine it by attacking its foundational axioms, such as the law of bivalence (statements are either true or false).

dialects, Greek See GREEK LANGUAGE.

dialogue As a special literary–philosophical form of writing, dialogue has its origin in *Socrates' philosophical activity; *Aristotle's description of written philosophical dialogues as 'Socratic *logoi*' reflects the association of the form with representations of Socratic conversations, often written by members of Socrates' circle (like *Plato), in which he himself is often the, or a, main speaker. A typical 'Socratic' conversation, or *dialogos*, will be one in which question-and-answer plays a leading role. As the genre develops in antiquity, this element declines in importance, being replaced by long speeches either exclusively by the main speaker with short interjections by others, or more often by different speakers. The beginnings of such developments are already visible in the Platonic corpus, although there they are partly the result of experimentation with the genre.

*Diogenes (4) Laertius says that some people claimed that *Zeno (1) of Elea was the first writer of dialogues; but it is Diogenes' view that it was Plato who closely defined the form, and that it was his dialogues which 'would justly win first prize for their beauty and invention'.

The writing of dialogues in Greek was revived by *Plutarch in the 1st and 2nd cents. AD, and a little later by *Lucian. *Plutarch's dialogues are modelled esp. on Plato's, but are lighter in content, while *Lucian's stance is more usually that of satirist than of philosopher; his range is greater even than Plato's, and shows the influence not only of Socratic conversations but, rather more obviously, of New *Comedy.

The first Roman known to have written in the manner of Plato and his successors, was Marcus Iunius Brutus (father of the tyrannicide), who composed three books on civil law, evidently in the form of a dialogue with his son. Cicero adopted the dialogue as the medium for most of his philosophical and rhetorical writing, employing Roman characters and settings. His first dialogues were explicitly modelled on Plato and contain a number of Platonic allusions.

Diana ('the bright one', originally a moon goddess), an Italian goddess anciently identified with *Artemis, from whom she took over the patronage of margins and savageness. One of her most famous shrines was on Mt. Tifata near *Capua; the name Tifata means 'holm-oak grove', which suits Diana's character as a goddess of the wilderness. Most famous of all was her ancient cult near Aricia (on the shore of the volcanic lake known as the Mirror of Diana, below the modern Nemi, i.e. *nemus*, 'grove'). Her temple stood in a grove. It was an old religious centre of the Latin League, and it is probable that the foundation of her temple on the *Aventine was an attempt to transfer the headquarters of this cult to Rome, along with the headship of the league. See further REX NEMORENSIS. That she was later largely a goddess of women is shown by the processions of women bearing torches (symbols of her name and original function) in her honour at Aricia.

diatribe, term (derived from Gk. word meaning 'spending' (of time)) given by modern scholars to works of Greek or Roman popular philosophy and generally implying the following: that they are direct transcriptions or literary developments of addresses given by *Cynic or *Stoic philosophers on the streets, before large audiences or (in the case of philosophers concerned with moral exhortation rather than systematic argument) to pupils; that they focus on a single theme; that their main aim is to attack vices (hence the modern usage); that they employ a vigorous, hectoring, colloquial (sometimes vulgar) style, with colourful, everyday imagery; that they sometimes have an anonymous interlocutor, thereby providing a dramatic illusion, a degree of argument and (usually) a butt. Such works are regarded as the pagan equivalent of the Christian sermon, which they are supposed to have influenced (from Paul onwards).

Dicaearchus, of *Messana, Greek polymath and prolific writer, pupil of *Aristotle and contemporary of *Theophrastus and *Aristoxenus: fl. *c.*320–300 BC. Fragments only survive of his works, but they show a remarkable range:

Literary and Cultural History (1) The *Life of Greece*, a pioneering history of culture in three books: it began with an idealized worldwide *golden age and went on to trace the evolution of contemporary Greek culture, pointing the contribution of Chaldaeans and Egyptians as well as Greeks. (2) *On Lives*, in several books, treating *Plato, *Pythagoras, and other philosophers. The title suggests a discussion of different lifestyles rather than straightforward biographies, and he presented his subjects as men of action as well as of reflection.

Philosophical (1) *On the Soul*, a dialogue on the corporeal nature and mortality of the *soul (one way in which he departed from Aristotelian teaching). (2) *On the Destruction of Man*, arguing that man is destroyed more by man than by natural disasters. (3) *On Prophecy*, accepting the possibility of the soul's prophetic power in dreams and in frenzy, but doubting its moral value and advisability. (4) *Descent into the *Trophonian Cave*, including immoralities of its priests.

Geographical *Tour of the World*, apparently including *maps. This established with some accuracy a main parallel of latitude from the straits of Gibraltar to the Himalayas and the assumed eastern Ocean. See GEOGRAPHY.

Dicaearchus' learning was as remarkable as his range and originality. He influenced many later writers. *Cicero admired him greatly, taking him as the model advocate of the 'practical' life and Theophrastus as that of the 'theoretical'.

dictator, an extraordinary supreme magistracy at Rome, used first in military, later in domestic crises.

As an emergency magistracy the dictatorship is found often in the annals of the republic down to the end of the 3rd cent. BC; it was not used during the 2nd cent. but reappeared in a more powerful form, when granted to *Sulla and then *Caesar. Normally dictators were simply nominated in public by a magistrate with *imperium (*consul, *praetor, or *interrex) after authorization by the senate—for Sulla and Caesar the authorization was provided by a law. The dictator's function was either to command the army or to perform a specific task, such as holding elections or dealing with a sedition. His 24 *lictors indicated a concentration of the powers of the consuls. The dictator immediately appointed a cavalry commander (*magister equitum) as his subordinate. Existing magistrates remained in office but were subordinate to him. Originally dictators resigned as soon as their task was completed, being permitted to remain in office for at most six months. They were therefore not appropriate for emergency overseas commands, and specially chosen proconsuls were used instead (see PRO CONSULE). In the middle and later republic the dictator's actions were in theory exempt neither from veto (see INTERCESSIO) by the tribunes nor from *provocatio. Nor was he himself free from prosecution after leaving office. Although after 202 no short-term dictators were appointed, it appears that this was contemplated in 54/3; in 52, on the senate's advice, *Pompey was created sole consul instead (senators apparently feared he might abuse dictatorial power). Both Sulla and Caesar, when they were appointed to this office in order to lend constitutional form to their *de facto* supremacy, were given the task 'putting the state in order'.

didactic poetry embraces a number of poetic works (usually in *hexameters) which aim to instruct the reader in a particular subject-matter, be it science, philosophy, hunting, farming, love, or some other art or craft. Didactic poems are normally addressed to a particular individual who is seen as the primary object of instruction and acts as a model for the reader. The text usually encourages the reader to identify with the addressee, though exceptions exist (e.g. Perses in *Hesiod's *Works and Days*).

didaskalia, lit. 'teaching', came to be used in Greece as the standard term for the production of a performance at a dramatic festival. *Dithyrambs, *tragedies, satyr-plays (see SATYRIC DRAMA), and *comedies were all performances that entailed the 'teaching' (*didaskein*) of choruses; *didaskalia* denoted both the training of the chorus and actors and the production itself, whether of a single play or of a group, and eventually was applied to a poet's entire output. The pl. *didaskaliai* was used of the official list of productions staged at a particular festival; this is the sense in which modern scholars use the word. The keeping of such records by the *archontes* in charge of the festivals is probably as old as the institution of *choregia.

The earliest example of dramatic records inscribed on stone dates from the 340s BC, which for each year's City *Dionysia gives the names of the archon, the winning tribe and *chorēgos* in the boys' and men's dithyrambic chorus, and the victorious *choregos* and poet in comedy and tragedy, with the name of the victorious leading actor added after the introduction of the contest for the best actor in 449. The beginning of this inscription is missing: the earliest year listed is 473/2, but the record probably went back to the late 6th cent.

*Aristotle probably composed his lost books *Victories at the Dionysia, Didaskaliai,* and *On Tragedies* at Athens in the period 334–322. He too must have drawn on the *archontes*' records, and his work must have been a source for the Alexandrian scholars who worked on drama and the festivals. Some traces of this research are evident in the *hypotheseis* to some of the surviving plays. The most important of the later inscriptions from Athens is a list, going back to the 5th cent., of tragedies and comedies at the City Dionysia and the *Lenaea, which gives the name of the archon, the poets in order of success, and the title of each play with the name of the leading actor who took part in it.

Dīdō, legendary queen of *Carthage, daughter of a king of Tyre called Belus by *Virgil. Acc. to *Timaeus, the earliest extant source for her story, her *Phoenician name was Elissa, and the name Dido ('wanderer') was given to her by the Libyans. Her husband was murdered by her brother Pygmalion, now king of Tyre, and Dido escaped with some followers to Libya (North Africa), where she founded Carthage. In the earlier tradition, in order to escape marriage with a Libyan king Dido built a pyre as though for an offering and leapt into the flames. The story of the encounter of *Aeneas and Dido (chronologically difficult given the traditional dating of Carthage's foundation four centuries after the destruction of Troy) probably appeared in *Naevius' epic 'The Punic War'. Acc. to *Varro, it was Dido's sister Anna who killed herself for love of Aeneas. In the classic version (*Aeneid* bks. 1 and 4) Aeneas lands on the coast of Carthage after a storm and is led by Venus to Dido's new city; Dido's infatuated love for the stranger is consummated in a cave during a storm while they are *hunting. Mercury (see MERCURIUS) descends to remind Aeneas of his mission to travel to Italy; as Aeneas departs obedient to the call of fate, Dido kills herself on top of a pyre that she has built. Her curse on the Trojans will eventually be fulfilled in the historical wars between Carthage and Rome. Many readers also detect a more recent historical allusion to the charms of *Cleopatra VII in the Virgilian Dido. She has enjoyed a vigorous after-life, in art, in literary reworkings, and in numerous operas. Her chastity has also been defended against Virgil by partisans including *Tertullian and Petrarch.

Didyma, oracular shrine of *Apollo (see ORACLES), located about 16 km. (10 mi.) south of *Miletus. In the Archaic period, it was administered by a priestly clan, the Branchidae, and rose to great prominence in the 6th cent. BC. Three prose oracular responses survive from this period, as does one dedication. In 494 the shrine was destroyed by *Darius I, and the Branchidae themselves were exiled to Sogdiana. The oracle was refounded in the time of *Alexander (2) the Great, and rapidly regained its standing. In the imperial period, it ranked with *Claros as one of the great oracular centres of Asia Minor.

Excavations have revealed a massive structure begun when the oracle was refounded. The total building measures 118 × 60 m. (129 × 66 yds.) at the platform. A double Ionic colonnade contains 108 columns and a further twelve in the forecourt. The west wall of the forecourt is pierced by an 8-m. (26-ft.)-wide entrance raised 1.5 m. (5 ft.) above the floor of the forecourt. The cella (roofed room) contains two Ionic columns to support the roof, and opens on the north and south sides to small rooms containing staircases, which may have led to a terrace at the level of the cella roof. The west end of the cella is pierced by three doors leading to a great staircase giving access to the adytum or innermost area (never roofed). Within the adytum there is a *naiskos* (chapel) surrounding the sacred spring. The priestess gave her oracles here.

Oracles could be given on only a limited number of days. The absolute maximum was once every four days, and the interval was probably far greater—possibly some months. The session itself began with a three-day *fast by the priestess, during which time she apparently resided in the adytum. On the appointed day, the priestess would take a ritual bath and enter the *naiskos*, while those who wished to put questions to her sacrificed outside and choruses sang hymns to the gods. Within the *naiskos*, the priestess sat on an axle suspended over the sacred spring and, when a question was put to her, she would dip her foot (or her dress) in the spring, but not drink from it, before giving her answer. These answers would probably have been in prose and would then have been turned into verse by the priests. The priests were appointed by the city of Miletus.

dietetics Many ancient medical authorities believed that therapeutic medicine had its origins in the gradual discovery of connections between health and the regulation of one's day-to-day life (*diaita*). A group of treatises in the Hippocratic corpus (see HIPPOCRATES) is concerned specifically with the study of the living-patterns of both sick and healthy. When *Cornelius Celsus wrote the preface to his *On Medicine*, dietetics had long been established as one of the three main branches of therapeutics, along with surgery and *pharmacology. Dietetics was originally thought to have developed in the context of the regulation of life for those training for the Games.

Hippocratic dietetic strategy involved the doctor with the healthy as much as the sick. Certain activities were known to be risky, and were thus to be discouraged—too much sex, drinking (see ALCOHOLISM), reading, inactivity, massage, and

so on. Doctors were encouraged to observe with great care all the factors, both internal and external, which might influence the body for good or ill.

dikastēria See DEMOCRACY, ATHENIAN; LAW AND PROCEDURE, ATHENIAN, 2.

Dikē (1), personification of Justice, daughter of *Zeus and *Themis, and one of the *Horae. She reports men's wrongdoing to Zeus, and sits beside him. In *Aratus and Roman poets she is the *constellation Virgo or Astraea, who left the earth when the bronze age began. In Archaic art she punishes Injustice, and later she is shown with a sword in Underworld scenes.

dikē (2) ('lawsuit'). See LAW AND PROCEDURE, ATHENIAN, 3.

Dīnarchus (*c*.360–*c*.290 BC), the last of the Ten *Attic Orators. Born at *Corinth, he went to Athens to study rhetoric under *Theophrastus and from 336/5 constantly and successfully practised the profession of speech-writer. As a *metic, he was barred from a political career, nor was he able himself to speak in court, but when after the *Lamian War the leading orators of the age, *Demosthenes (2) and *Hyperides, had met their deaths, Dinarchus was left in unchallenged and lucrative supremacy, and the period of rule by *Demetrius of Phaleron, his friend and patron, was his heyday. When Demetrius had to retire from Athens in 307/6, Dinarchus, suspect for his wealth and perhaps even more his friendship with 'those who dissolved the democracy', withdrew to *Chalcis. He marks the beginning of the decline in Attic oratory.

dining-rooms Reclining on couches while dining was introduced in Greece from the near east, probably *c*. 700 BC. Special rooms were built to accommodate the couches along the lengths of the wall, often on a slightly raised plinth. Floors are durable (cement or mosaic), presumably to allow for swabbing down. Each couch had a low table alongside. Such rooms were referred to by the number of couches they held. Eleven is a frequent number, the resulting dimensions (*c*.6.3 m. (21 ft.) square) thus giving a reasonable size for general conversation across the room. Dining-rooms in private houses are generally small, those for ritual feasting in *sanctuaries may be larger or very large halls for over 100 couches.

In later Hellenistic times the arrangement called *triclīnium* developed. Three large couches in a Pi (π) arrangement, each for three diners with head to centre, feet to the outside, making conversation easier. This system was adopted by the Romans. Each couch had its significance: the left couch was the lowest in rank where the family would dine, the host at the top (i.e. on the left); the guests would recline on the other two, the middle one (next to the host) being more honourable: the place on the right was the position of chief honour. See CONVIVIUM; MEALS; PALACES; SYMPOSIUM; THOLOS.

Dio (Cassius), historian. See CASSIUS DIO.

Diocletian originally named Dioclēs. Of obscure origins, b. in Dalmatia perhaps in the early 240s AD, he rose to command the bodyguard of the emperor Numerianus on the Persian campaign of 283/4. When Numerianus was killed by his *praetorian prefect Aper, the army proclaimed Diocles Augustus at *Nicomedia; he killed Aper. Before long Diocletian was sole emperor. Visiting Italy, he proclaimed his comrade-in-arms Maximian as Caesar. Maximian was soon made Augustus (286) and spent the next years defending Gaul. Diocletian spent most of his reign on the Danube (see DANUVIUS) or in the east.

In 293 Diocletian established the '*tetrarchy*'. To the two Augusti, now known as Iovius and Herculius respectively to emphasize their quasi-divine authority, were added Caesars, Constantius I and Galerius; they were adopted into the Jovian or Herculian houses by the marriage of Galerius to Diocletian's daughter Valeria and of Constantius to Maximian's (?step-)daughter. The arrangement would provide an imperial presence in different areas; it might deter usurpers; and the Caesars might become acceptable to the armies and live to succeed as Augusti. To raise the dignity of the imperial office Diocletian adopted an oriental court ceremonial and seclusion. Each tetrarch had his own staff, and was often on the move in his territory. In practice the empire was divided into two; Maximian and Constantius ruled the west, Diocletian and Galerius the east. After five years of sucessful fighting there was a lull in rebellions and wars; tetrarchic authority was secure.

Diocletian pursued systematically a long-established policy of dividing provinces into smaller units; by 314 there were about 100, twice the number of a century earlier (see PROVINCIA). The purpose was to ensure closer supervision, esp.

over law and finance, by governors and their numerous staffs; critics saw it as leading to never-ending condemnations and confiscations. In the later part of his reign, Diocletian began an important reform, separating military from civil power in frontier provinces. Senators remained excluded from military commands. His conception of defence was conservative; he made little or no effort to increase the size of the élite field army, which had been formed in the late 3rd cent. But a huge programme of building and reconstruction of defensive works was undertaken on all frontiers, and they were to be held by sheer force of numbers; the size of the Roman army was perhaps nearly doubled.

The army and the increase of administrative personnel were a heavy financial burden. Diocletian reformed the system of taxation to take inflation into account and to regularize exactions in kind. Most revenue and expenditure was now in kind. By the Currency Edict (301) Diocletian attempted to create a unified currency, doubling the value of at least some coins, but he could not establish confidence in this revaluation. Late in 301 he tried to halt inflation by the Price Edict. In great detail it fixed maximum prices and wages; despite savage penalties it became a dead letter, as goods disappeared from the market.

Many legal decisions show Diocletian's concern to maintain or resuscitate Roman law in the provinces. He was an enthusiast for what he understood of Roman tradition and discipline, to reinforce imperial unity. This policy forms the backdrop to the persecution of Christians, undertaken possibly on the insistence of Galerius. (See CHRISTIANITY.) Earlier attempts had been made to purge the court and the army, but the first persecuting edict was designed to prevent the Church from functioning, by requiring the burning of Scriptures and the demolition of churches, and the banning of meetings for worship; recusants were deprived of any rank, and thus made liable to torture and summary execution and prevented from taking action in court; imperial freedmen were re-enslaved. The later edicts were not promulgated outside the areas controlled by Diocletian and Galerius.

Late in 303 Diocletian visited Rome for the only time, to celebrate with Maximian the 20th anniversary of his accession. A collapse in health caused him to return to Nicomedia, where on 1 May 305 he abdicated (Maximian reluctantly did the same at Mediolanum), leaving Constantius and Galerius as Augusti. He attended Galerius' conference at Carnuntum (308) but refused to resume the purple and spent his last years at Salonae; remains of the palace he built survive. He died c.312. His wife Prisca and only child Valeria were exiled and then beheaded. Diocletian's genius was as an organizer; his measures did much to preserve the empire in the 4th cent., and many lasted much longer in the east. The tetrarchy as such broke down when Diocletian's personality was removed, but for most of the 4th cent. more than one emperor was the rule. His reforms were completed by *Constantine (1) I, who introduced further innovations, esp. in the army and in religion.

Diodōrus (1) **Cronus,** of Iasus (d. c.284 BC), master of *dialectic. His pupils included *Zeno (2), and his own five daughters. His work combined the dialectical traditions founded by *Zeno (1) of Elea and by *Socrates. He profoundly influenced Hellenistic philosophy. His 'master argument', which established his definition of 'possible' as 'what is or will be true', set the terms of the Hellenistic debate about modality. He gave his own account of a valid conditional, as one which neither was nor is able to have a true antecedent and a false consequent. He defended a theory of word-meaning as purely conventional, which he illustrated by changing a slave's name to 'However'. He also elaborated, and perhaps tried to solve, logical paradoxes like the Sorites and the Liar (see EUBULIDES).

Diodōrus (2) of Agyrium, Sicily (hence **Diodorus Siculus**), is the author of the 'Library', a universal history from mythological times to 60 BC. Only 15 of the original 40 books survive fully (bks. 1–5; 11–20); the others are preserved in fragments. Despite his claim to cover all known history, Diodorus concentrates on Greece and his homeland of Sicily, until the First *Punic War, when his sources for Rome become fuller. But even in its fragmentary state, the 'Library' is the most extensively preserved history by a Greek author from antiquity. For the period from the accession of *Philip II of Macedon (359) to the battle of Ipsus (301), it is fundamental; and it is the essential source for Classical Sicilian history and the Sicilian slave revolts of the 2nd cent. BC.

Diodorus probably visited *Egypt c.60–56, where he began researching his history. By 56, he may have settled in Rome, completing the 'Library' there c.30. He read Latin and had access to written materials in Rome, but, despite his admiration for *Caesar, there is no evidence that he personally knew Romans of prominence.

Books 1–6 include the geography and ethnography of the 'inhabited world' and its mythology and marvels before the Trojan War; bks. 1–3 cover the east, bks. 4–6 the west. Esp. significant are the description of Egypt in bk. 1; the discussion of India in bk. 2, drawn from *Megasthenes; and the highly fragmentary Euhemeran material in bk. 6 (see EUHEMERUS).

The fully preserved historical books cover 480–302 and are arranged annalistically, with Olympic, Athenian archon, and Roman consular years synchronized—often erroneously. The main source for most of the narrative of the Greek mainland is *Ephorus; *Hieronymus of Cardia is the prime authority for the outstanding narrative of the *Diadochi. For Sicily Diodorus uses *Timaeus extensively. Certain themes recur throughout the 'Library' independently of Diodorus' current source. Character assessments, with a strong insistence on personal and collective morality, and an emphasis on the civilizing power of individual benefactors suggest late Hellenistic influence and therefore Diodorus' own philosophy.

Diogenēs (1), of Apollonia (on the Black or *Euxine Sea), is generally reckoned the last of the Presocratic philosophers. The best evidence of his date is Aristophanes' *Clouds* (423 BC), where his views are parodied.

Diogenes' central argument defended an Anaximenean form of material monism (see ANAXIMENES). The first move established the truth of monism as such: interaction between bodies would be impossible if they were essentially different. Next came proofs reminiscent of Anaxagoras that there is much intelligence in the world, as witness its orderly structure and the life of men and other animals. From this Diogenes inferred his principal thesis: the basic body must be air, since air is what pervades and disposes all things and supports life and intelligence. Differentiation in air explains differences between species. The causal connection between air and life and intelligence was substantiated in a detailed account of the blood channels. Diogenes evidently applied his causal scheme systematically. Theophrastus has a long passage on the senses, and many physical phenomena were explained on the analogy of sweating and absorption of moisture (e.g. magnetism, the flooding of the *Nile).

Diogenēs (2) the *Cynic (c.412/403–c.324/321 BC). The distortions in the ancient traditions about Cynicism ('doggishness') multiply in the case of Diogenes, who provoked extremes of admiration, hostility, and invention. *Diogenes (4) Laertius preserves Diogenes' essential thought.

Accused with his father, moneyer at Sinope, of 'defacing the currency' (a phrase which was to yield a potent metaphor), Diogenes was exiled and spent the rest of his life in Athens and Corinth. He evolved a novel way of life from diverse, mainly Greek, elements: the belief that wisdom was a matter of action rather than thought; the principle (advanced by various *sophists, 5th-cent. primitivists, and *Antisthenes) of living in accordance with nature rather than law/convention; the tradition, perhaps sharpened by contemporary disillusionment with the *polis, of promulgating ideal societies or constitutions; a tradition of 'shamelessness'; Socratic rejection of all elements of philosophy except practical ethics; Socrates' pursuit of philosophy in the *agora rather than in a school; an anti-intellectual tradition; the tradition (variously represented by *Odysseus, *Heracles, the Spartans, and to some extent by Socrates) of physical toughness as a requirement of virtue; the image of the suffering hero and the wanderer (Odysseus, Heracles, various tragic figures); the tradition of mendicancy (represented both in literature and in life); the life of *asceticism and poverty (as represented by various wise men and holy men and labourers); the tradition of the wise or holy man who promises converts happiness or salvation; and various humorous traditions (the jester's practical and verbal humour; Old Comedy's outspokenness and crudity (see COMEDY (GREEK), OLD); Socrates' serio-comic wit).

Diogenes pursued a life as close as possible to the 'natural' life of primitive man, of animals, and of the gods. This entailed the minimum of material possessions (coarse cloak, staff for physical support and protection, purse for food) and of sustenance (obtained by living off the land and by begging); performance in public of all natural functions; training in physical endurance, and a wandering existence. Freedom, self-sufficiency, happiness, and virtue supposedly followed. It also entailed complete rejection of civilized life and of all forms of education and culture as inimical to the ideal life. Hence Diogenes' attacks on convention, marriage, family, politics, the city, all social, sexual, and racial distinctions, worldly reputation, wealth, power and authority, literature, music, and all forms of intellectual speculation. Such attacks are imposed by the Cynic's duty metaphorically to 'deface the currency'. Hence the modern implications of the word 'cynic' are misleading. Indeed, humane attitudes came easily to Diogenes (e.g. his advocacy of sexual freedom and equality stemmed naturally from rejection of the family).

Although proclaiming self-sufficiency, Diogenes tried to convert others by his own outrageous behaviour (which went beyond the requirements of the natural life), by direct exhortation employing all the resources of his formidable wit and rhetorical skills, and by various written works. He expounded his views in a *Republic*, and several tragedies. Such writings, which compromise the ideal of the practical demonstration of philosophical truth and the formal rejection of literature, did not imply real debate with conventional philosophers. Diogenes sparred verbally with *Plato but dismissed his philosophy as absurd; his own '*Republic*', while a serious statement of Cynic positions, parodied 'serious' philosophers' pretensions.

Diogenes' missionary activity entailed what his aggressiveness sometimes obscured: recognition of the common humanity of Cynics and non-Cynics. 'Philanthropy' (concern for one's fellow human beings) is integral to Cynicism and essential to Diogenes' celebrated concept of 'cosmopolitanism' (the belief that the universe is the ultimate unity, of which the material and animal worlds, human beings, and the gods are all intrinsic parts, with the Cynic representing the human condition at its best, at once human, animal, and divine).

Ancient and modern reactions to Diogenes range from appreciation of his wit to admiration for his integrity, denial of his philosophical significance, revulsion at his shamelessness, dislike of the threat he posed to conventional social and political values, and misguided attempts to make him respectable. Yet, whatever the detailed distortions in the Stoic history of philosophy, it was right to locate Diogenes within the great tradition, as even Plato half-conceded when he dubbed him a 'mad Socrates'.

See also CRATES.

Diogenēs (3), of *Oenoanda, author of a massive Greek inscription presenting basic doctrines of Epicureanism. The inscription was carved in a *stoa, probably in the 2nd cent. AD. The inscription occupied several courses of a wall c.80 m. (87 yds.) long. In the lowest inscribed course was a treatise on ethics dealing with pleasure, pain, fear, desire, dreams, necessity, and free will; beneath it was inscribed a selection of Epicurus' *Principal Doctrines* and other maxims. Immediately above was a treatise on *physics, the surviving sections of which include criticisms of rival schools and discussions of epistemology, the origins of civilization and language, astronomy, and theology. Above these main treatises were more maxims, letters of Epicurus, at least three letters written by Diogenes to Epicurean friends, and Diogenes' defence of old age.

Diogenes records that he was ailing and aged when he set up the inscription, and that he was moved by a desire to benefit his fellows at home and abroad as well as future generations. Although most of the inscription remains buried, the recovered fragments illuminate Epicurean theory and the activity of the school under the Roman empire. See EPICURUS.

Diogenēs (4) **Lāertius,** author of an extant compendium on the lives and doctrines of philosophers from *Thales to *Epicurus. He probably lived in the first half of the 3rd cent. AD. Nothing is known of his life.

After an introduction on some non-Greek 'thinkers' such as the magi (see MAGUS), and some of the early Greek sages, he divides the philosophers into two 'successions', an Ionian or eastern (bk. 1. 22 to bk. 7) and an Italian or western (bk. 8), and ends with important philosophers who did not found successions (bks. 9–10). This arrangement disperses the Presocratics in bks. 1, 2, 8, and 9. Bk. 10 is devoted entirely to Epicurus and preserves the texts of several of his works.

In 10. 138 Diogenes speaks of giving the finishing touch to his entire work; but the book is such a tissue of quotations industriously compiled, mostly from secondary sources, that it could have been expanded indefinitely. Diogenes usually drew his material on any one philosopher from more than one earlier compilation. Thus Diogenes' material often comes to us at several removes from the original. Fortunately, he usually names his sources, mentioning over 200 authors and over 300 works by name. As a rule he changes sources continually. Hence his reliability and value also change from passage to passage. For example, his account of Stoic doctrine is reliable and his long quotations from *Epicurus are invaluable when separated from the inserted marginalia that sometimes interrupt the sense. But some Lives, as *Heraclitus', are mere caricatures, and some summaries of doctrine are distorted.

See BIOGRAPHY, GREEK.

diolkos, stone trackway across the isthmus of *Corinth, for transporting ships and/or cargoes between the Saronic and Corinthian gulfs. Archaeology suggests a date under *Periander. Wheeled wagons (see TRANSPORT, WHEELED) ran in carved grooves; traffic probably moved in one direction at a time. *Triremes used it during the *Peloponnesian War, perhaps after modifications; it was probably constructed for merchant vessels.

Diomedēs son of *Tydeus; one of the chief Achaean warriors in the Trojan War and leader of a contingent of 80 ships from *Argos and Tiryns. In books 5 and 6 of the *Iliad* his great charge leads to the death of Pandarus, the removal of *Aeneas from looming defeat by his mother *Aphrodite, and the wounding of the goddess herself and of *Ares; later we are shown a more restrained side of his character as he declines to fight with his 'guest-friend' Glaucus (see FRIENDSHIP, RITUALIZED). Throughout the poem, but esp. in the second half, he offers shrewd and bold advice to the Greek war-council. In the funeral games for Patroclus he wins both the chariot-race and (against *Aias (1)) the spear-fight. He is esp. associated with *Odysseus in various actions, killing Dolon and *Rhesus in Bk. 10, and in the poems of the *Epic Cycle sharing in the murder of *Palamedes, bringing *Philoctetes back from Lemnos, and stealing the *Palladium, from the Trojan citadel.

Dionysia Many festivals of *Dionysus had special names, e.g. *Anthesteria, *Lenaea, etc. This article concerns those Attic festivals known as (a) the Rural Dionysia, and (b) the City or Great Dionysia. Festivals of Dionysus were widespread throughout the Greek world, but we know most about the *Attic ones, for which almost all surviving Greek drama was written.

(a) The Rural Dionysia were celebrated, on various days by the different *demes, in the month of Posideon (roughly December). They provided an opportunity for the locality to reproduce elements of the City Dionysia, and we hear of performances of *tragedy, *comedy, and *dithyramb. There survive various inscriptions concerning the proceedings. In Aristophanes' *Acharnians* Dicaeopolis goes home to celebrate the festival: he draws up a little sacrificial procession in which his daughter is *kanēphoros* ('basket-bearer'), two slaves carry the *phallus, Dicaeopolis himself sings an obscene song to Phales, and his wife watches from the roof. The song may be of the kind from which, acc. to Aristotle, *comedy originated.

(b) The City Dionysia belonged to Dionysus Eleuthereus, who was said to have been introduced into Athens from the village of Eleutherae, on the borders of Attica and *Boeotia. The festival is generally regarded as having been founded, or at least amplified, during the *tyranny of *Pisistratus. But in fact the archaeological, epigraphic, and literary evidence is so uncertain as to be no less consistent with a date for its foundation right at the end of the 6th cent., just after the establishment of *democracy, in which case the title 'Eleuthereus' would perhaps have been taken to connote political liberty.

The festival was celebrated at the end of March, when the city was again full of visitors after the winter. On 10 Elaphebolion, a splendid procession followed an unknown route to the sacred precinct (next to the theatre), where animals were sacrificed and bloodless offerings made. In the procession were carried phalli, loaves, bowls, etc., and the metics were dressed in red. The theatrical performances took place from the 11th to the 14th. Their precise arrangement is unknown, but normal practice in the Classical period was as follows. Three tragedians competed, each with three tragedies and a satyr-play (see SATYRIC DRAMA). There were five comic poets, each competing with a single play. And each of the ten tribes provided one dithyrambic chorus for the men's contest and one for the boys'. Before the performance of the tragedies the sons of citizens killed in battle were paraded in full armour in the theatre, and so was the tribute brought by Athens' allies. Various fragmentary inscriptions survive with the remains of lists of the annual performances (or victors). See also CHOREGIA; DIDASKALIA; PROAGON; TRAGEDY.

Dionysius (1) **I,** b. c.430 BC, son of a well-to-do *Syracusan; secretary to the generals (406), he distinguished himself in the *Acragas campaign against Carthage. By unscrupulous *demagogy he secured the dismissal of the generals and his own election as general plenipotentiary, obtained a bodyguard, occupied and fortified the citadel (Ortygia), and assumed control of the state. With a large allied army, he failed to raise the Carthaginian siege of Gela (405), but crushed a revolt of the aristocracy, and concluded the Peace of Himilco, which cost Syracuse her possessions. Besieged in Ortygia by the rebellious Syracusans (404–403), he came

to terms with them (less the exiled aristocracy), giving them, although disarmed, a measure of autonomy. After subjugating eastern Sicily with a mercenary army (402–399), he prepared for war with Carthage, fortifying Epipolae, amassing war-material, building a huge fleet, rearming the Syracusans, hiring mercenaries, and forming matrimonial alliances with Syracuse (Andromachē) and Locri Epizephyrii (Doris). He invaded the Carthaginian province (397) and stormed Motya, but (396) retired before Himilco to Syracuse; here he was besieged until 395, when, with some Corinthian and Spartan aid, he overthrew Himilco's plague-stricken forces. He restored his east Sicilian empire, attacked Rhegium and countered a new Carthaginian threat (395–392); but when the Syracusan army mutinied, he concluded a peace with Carthage (392) that recognized his suzerainty of east Sicily. He again attacked Rhegium (390) and starved it into surrender (387), allied himself with the Lucanians, crushed the forces of the Italiot League (of Greek cities) 389, and incorporated south Calabria in his empire. In 387 he helped Sparta to impose the *King's Peace on Greece. To improve his supply of silver, timber, horses, and mercenaries, he extended his power into the Adriatic, founding colonies. The chronology and details of his greatest war (383– probably 375), against the Italiots and allied Carthage, are unclear. After suffering a serious defeat by the Carthaginians in Sicily, he made a peace that established the Halycus as the common frontier. He sent expeditions to Greece, to assist Sparta against the *Boeotians; and Athens, hitherto hostile, voted him a *crown and (368) conferred her citizenship on him and his sons. He again invaded western Sicily (368) and besieged Lilybaeum, but his fleet was captured at Drepanum and he concluded an armistice. At the *Lenaea in Athens in 367 his play, The Ransom of Hector, won the prize, and a mutual defence treaty was negotiated, whose ratification was perhaps prevented by his death.

Dionysius was a born leader of men, in peace and war; orator and diplomat, planner and administrator, patron of religion, of his native city, of literature and the arts, a dramatist perhaps no worse than the generality in an age of decline— above all, the greatest soldier that, apart from the Macedonians, ancient Greece produced. He applied mind to warfare, introducing *artillery, Phoenician siege-technique, and the quinquereme. He could handle large *mercenary armies and small light-infantry detachments; he knew the importance of reconnaissance. If his subordinates had not constantly let him down, he might well have achieved his life's ambition, to drive the Carthaginians from Sicily. Dionysius represents the irruption onto the historical scene of the new individualism of his age. Portrayed by the anecdotal tradition, above all by the *Academy, as the archetypal tyrant—paranoid, oppressive, obsessed with power—he looms through the historical tradition rather as the first of the Romantic 'great men'; the precursor of *Alexander (2) the Great, *Hannibal, and Napoleon: obsessed not with power but with glory.

Dionysius (2) **II**, tyrant of *Syracuse (367–357 BC); b. *c*.396, eldest son of *Dionysius (1) I and Doris. Unwarlike and short-sighted, he was estranged from his father. Inheriting an empire 'secured with bonds of adamant', he ruled successfully for ten years. Encouraged by Dion, brother of his father's other wife, Andromachē, and *Plato himself, he conceived a passion for philosophy, which split his court between the 'reformers' and the 'old guard', led by *Philistus, and caused a rupture with Dion and eventually (360) with Plato. During his absence in Italy (357), Dion 'liberated' Syracuse and dissolved his empire. Dionysius was confined to the citadel (Ortygia), which, after the death of Philistus (356), he entrusted to his son, and withdrew to Locri Epizephyrii. In 346 he recovered Syracuse. The Locrians then revolted and massacred his family. Dionysius soon retired into private life in Corinth. He was neither an ineffectual ruler nor a despot; but the abandonment of his father's crusade against Carthage deprived the regime of its purpose and glamour, and it was weakened internally by division and by Dionysius' ill-advised attempt to reduce his soldiers' pay.

Dionysius (3), of *Halicarnassus, Greek critic and historian, lived and taught *rhetoric at Rome, arriving 'when *Augustus put an end to the civil war', and publishing the first part of his *Roman Antiquities* 22 years later. The 20 books of this great work go down to the outbreak of the First *Punic War; we have the first eleven (to 441 BC), with excerpts from the others. Dionysius used the legends of Rome's origins to demonstrate that it was really a Greek city, and his whole history is a learned panegyric of Roman virtues. It is also very rhetorical, abounding in long speeches. He doubtless thought of it as exemplifying his literary teaching, which was directed towards restoring Classical prose after

what he saw as the aberrations of the Hellenistic period. The treatises in which he developed this programme seem mostly to have been written before the *Antiquities*. Dionysius is an acute and sensitive stylistic critic; and he understood the importance of linking historical study (e.g. on questions of authenticity) with the purely rhetorical and aesthetic.

Dionysus is the twice-born son of *Zeus and *Semele. Snatched prematurely from the womb of his dying mother and carried to term by his father, he was born from the thigh of Zeus. Perceived as both man and animal, male and effeminate, young and old, he is the most versatile and elusive of all Greek gods. His myths and cults are often violent and bizarre, a challenge to the established social order. Always on the move, he is the most *epiphanic god, riding felines, sailing the sea, and even wearing wings. His commonest cult name was *Bakch(e)ios* or *Bakchos*, after which his ecstatic followers were called *bakchoi* and *bakchai*. Adopted by the Romans as *Bacchus*, he was identified with the Italian *Liber Pater.

He was first and foremost the god of *wine and intoxication. His other provinces include ritual madness or *ecstasy; the *mask, impersonation, and the fictional world of the theatre; and, paradoxically, the mysterious realm of the dead and the expectation of an after-life blessed with the joys of Dionysus. The common factor is his capacity to transcend existential boundaries. Both 'most terrible and most sweet to mortals' in Attic tragedy (Euripides, *Bacchae* 861), he was called 'Eater of Raw Flesh' as well as Meilichios ('who can, but needs to, be propitiated') in cult.

In Archaic epic, Dionysus is referred to as a 'joy for mortals' and 'he of many delights'. The source of all this pleasure is *wine, the god's ambivalent 'gift', which brings both 'joy and burden'. Dionysus 'invented' wine, just as *Demeter discovered *agriculture (see CULTURE-BRINGERS). By a common metonymy, the wine-god is also synonymous with his drink and is himself 'poured out' to the other gods as a ritual liquid. In vase-painting, Dionysus is never far from the wine. Surrounded by cavorting *satyrs and silens, *nymphs or *maenads, he presides over the vintage and the successive stages of wine-making on numerous black-figure vases. Holding in one hand a grapevine and in the other one of his favourite drinking-vessels, either a *cantharus* or a *rhyton*, he is often depicted receiving wine from a male or female cupbearer such as his son by *Ariadne, or pouring it on an altar as a *libation, or lying on a couch in typical sympotic posture (see SYMPOSIUM). Yet he is never shown in the act of consuming his own gift. His female followers, too, keep their distance from the wine, at least in maenadic iconography.

Wine festivals were celebrated in many parts of the Greek world. The oldest festival of Dionysus, the Ionian–Attic *Anthesteria, was held each spring. In Athens, the highlight consisted of the broaching of the new wine followed by a drinking-contest. On this occasion, as on others, citizen women were excluded from the ceremonial drinking of wine. In Attica, myths were told which connected the arrival of Dionysus and the invention of the wine with the murder of Icarius (taught by Dionysus how to make wine, with ill consequences). Here and elsewhere, Dionysiac myths emphasize the darker aspects of the god, and the perversion of his gifts.

Of Dionysus' four provinces, wine predominates. Drunkenness can cause violence and dementia (see ALCOHOLISM). Yet the ritual madness associated with Dionysus in myth and cult had nothing to do with alcohol or drugs. Seized by the god, initiates into Bacchic rites acted much like participants in other *possession cults. Their wild dancing and ecstatic behaviour were interpreted as 'madness' only by the uninitiated. As numerous cultic inscriptions show, worshippers did not employ the vocabulary of madness to describe their ritual ecstasy; rather, they used the technical but neutral language of *bakcheia* and *bakcheuein*. The practitioners of *bakcheia* were usually women. While men, too, could 'go mad' for Dionysus, they could not join the bands of maenadic women who went 'to the mountain' every other year in many Greek cities to celebrate their rites. Their notional leader was always the god himself, who appears in the Homeric version of the Lycurgus myth—the earliest reference to maenadic ritual—as Dionysus *mainomenos*, 'the raving god'. Ritual maenadism was never practised within the borders of Attica. Athenian maenads went to *Delphi to join the Delphic Thyiads on the slopes of Mt. Parnassus. Halfway between Athens and Delphi lies *Thebes, the home town of Dionysus and 'mother city (*metropolis) of the Bacchants', from where professional maenads were imported by other cities. In poetry and vase-painting, Dionysus and his mythical maenads tear apart live animals with their bare hands and eat them raw. But the divinely inflicted madness of myth was not a blueprint for actual rites.

Tragedy and comedy incorporate transgressive aspects of Dionysus, but they do so in opposite ways. While comedy re-enacts the periods of ritual licence associated with many Dionysiac festivals, tragedy dramatizes the negative, destructive traits of the god and his myths. *Aristotle connected the origins of tragedy and comedy with two types of Dionysiac performance—the *dithyramb and the phallic song respectively. Yet, in his own analysis of the tragic genre, he ignored Dionysus and indeed the central role of the gods in the drama. The actors' masks and choral song provide the plainest link between Attic drama and Dionysiac ritual. Tragic and comic choruses who refer to their own dancing always associate their choral performance with Dionysus, *Pan, or the maenads. Tragedy has much to do with Dionysus. The tragedians set individual characters, entire plays, and indeed the tragic genre as a whole in a distinct Dionysiac ambience (see COMEDY (GREEK); TRAGEDY, GREEK).

The god so closely associated with exuberant life is also connected with death. '*Hades and Dionysus are the same', acc. to *Heraclitus. On an Apulian funerary vase, Dionysus and Hades are shown in the Underworld each grasping the other's right hand, while figures from Dionysiac myth surround them. Acc. to one myth, Dionysus descends to the Underworld to rescue Semele from Hades; Aristophanes' comic parody (in *Frogs*) of the god's descent has Dionysus retrieve *Aeschylus. In many parts of the ancient world, tombs were decorated with Dionysiac figures and emblems like the maenad, the *cantharus*, and the ivy. (See also DEATH, ATTITUDES TO; ORPHIC LITERATURE; ORPHISM).

No other deity is more often represented in ancient art than Dionysus. Until about 430 BC, Dionysus is almost always shown as a mature, bearded, and ivy-wreathed adult wearing a long *chitōn* often draped with the skin of fawn or feline, and occasionally presenting a frontal face like his satyrs; later he usually appears youthful and beardless, effeminate, and partially or entirely nude. Major mythical subjects comprise the Return of *Hephaestus and the Gigantomachy (see GIANTS); Dionysus' birth and childhood; his punishments of two 'resisters' Lycurgus and *Pentheus, and the impious sailors whom he turns into dolphins; and his union with Ariadne.

The existence of Dionysus in the Mycenaean pantheon came as a complete surprise when it was revealed by Ventris in 1953. In classical antiquity Dionysus was considered a foreign god, whose original home was Thrace or Phrygia, and who did not arrive on the Greek scene until the 8th cent. BC. In 1933, W. F. Otto had stressed instead the Greek nature of Dionysus as the epiphanic god who comes and disappears.

Dionysus, artists of generic name for the powerful guilds into which itinerant Greek actors and musicians formed themselves from the 3rd cent. BC. Their formation reflects the demand for Attic-style drama from the 4th cent. in both Greece and the Hellenistic kingdoms, where they came under royal *patronage. They chiefly served to secure benefits for members, notably personal inviolability in their travels and exemption from military service and local taxes. See CLUBS, GREEK.

Dioscorides (1st cent. AD), of Cilician Anazarbus, wrote a five-book work on the drugs employed in medicine. He travelled extensively collecting information about the medicinal uses of herbs, minerals, and animal products. He visited the Greek mainland, Crete, Egypt, and Petra, but he mentions plants from much further afield. In the Preface he describes his travels as leading to a 'soldier-like life'.

Dioscorides' 'Materials of Medicine' lists c.700 plants and just over 1,000 drugs. His method was to observe plants in their native habitats and to research previous authorities on these subjects. Finally he related the written and oral data to his clinical observations of the effects the drugs had on and in the body. He also provided data on preparations, adulterations, and veterinary and household uses. Dioscorides boasted that his method of arrangement surpassed that of previous works. His scheme was first to arrange by categories, such as whole animals, animal parts and products, minerals, and plants—the last subdivided into roots, pot-herbs, fruits, trees, and shrubs. Within each category he arranged drugs according to their physiological effect on the body. This arrangement by drug affinities was not explained, and so many later copyists of his text rearranged his system according to the alphabet, thereby obscuring the genius of his contributions. Dioscorides' information aims at medical precision, and his account is relatively free of supernatural elements, reflecting keen, critical observation of how drugs act. His medical judgements were well regarded until the 16th cent. Manuscripts of the 'Materials of Medicine' in Greek, Latin, and Arabic are often beautifully illuminated and indicate that Dioscorides' original text was accompanied by illustrations. See BOTANY; PHARMACOLOGY.

Dioscūri, 'sons of Zeus', a regular title of Castor and Polydeuces (Pollux), who on the human plane are also sons of *Tyndareos. They are the brothers of *Helen, Tyndareos' daughter, in *Homer's *Iliad*, where they are treated as being dead; but in *Odyssey*. 11 they are 'alive' even though 'the corn-bearing earth holds them', and the author explains that they are honoured by *Zeus and live on alternate days, 'having honour equal to gods'. Here and in *Hesiod they are sons of Tyndareos and *Leda.

They were gods friendly to men, 'saviours', in a variety of spheres. Their characteristic mode of action is the *epiphany at a moment of crisis. Such interventions are regularly also an expression of their trustworthiness, their eagerness to help those who honour them or put their trust in them. *Simonides was denied his fee by the *Thessalian prince Scopas, on the grounds that his poem had paid more honour to the Dioscuri than to the mortal patron. A little later, two youths summoned Simonides outside during a banquet in Scopas' palace; the roof collapsed, killing all within. Above all they brought aid at sea, where their saving presence in storms was visible in the electric discharge known as St Elmo's fire.

Both in art and literature they are constantly associated with horses. Similarities have often been noted between the Dioscuri and the divine twins of other mythologies, esp. the Vedic Aśvins, who like them are closely associated with horses.

di penātes See PENATES, DI.

Diploma, a modern term describing a pair of small folding bronze tablets copied from the record of soldiers' privileges inscribed in Rome, and first issued by *Claudius to individual auxillaries and sailors.

Dipylon, the double gateway in Athens' city wall leading into the *Ceramicus and to the cemetery immediately outside the wall in that area. The gateway comprised a rectangular courtyard open on the land side, closed by two double doors on the city side; each corner was enlarged to form a tower; a fountain-house adjoined the gateway on the city side. The complex dates from immediately after the *Persian Wars, but was rebuilt in the 3rd cent. BC. The road from the *Agora to the *Academy passed through this gate. Some 75 m. (82 yds.) SW a similar smaller gateway protected the passage of the Sacred Way to *Eleusis. Between the two gates stood the Pompeion, the marshalling-place for the Panathenaic procession (see PANATHENAEA). From the 11th cent. BC onwards the area was the principal burial-ground of Athens. The best impression of the cemetery is given by *Pausanias (3), who observed here the tombs of the war-dead and individual monuments to Harmodius and *Aristogiton, *Cleisthenes (2), *Pericles, and other prominent politicians.

dirge, in Greek literature a song of lamentation sung antiphonally by a company of mourners and one or more soloists, either over the corpse, or on subsequent commemorative days. The earliest evidence for such dirges is Homeric. The form continued and was elaborated in the *kommos* of tragedy. In Latin literature the dirge (*nēnia*), containing lamentation and praise of a deceased person, wa sung to a pipe accompaniment, by a hired female mourner, whose assistants made responses, before the house of mourning, during the funeral procession, and beside the pyre.

disease, the main cause of death in antiquity, is a topic for which there are more sources than for most aspects of life in the ancient world, thanks mainly to the Hippocratic corpus (see HIPPOCRATES), and the numerous works of *Galen. Additional information may be obtained from the study of diseases found in human skeletal remains. Ancient medical literature concentrates on chronic and endemic diseases, rather than the major epidemic diseases.

Malaria and tuberculosis are the most prominent diseases in ancient literature. Malaria occurred in antiquity in three forms. All three produce fevers recurring every two or three days, which were easily noticed, if not understood, by ancient doctors. Malaria depends for its transmission on certain species of mosquito. The Pomptine Marshes, SE of Rome, was one area stricken with the disease, which the Romans personified as Febris. Tuberculosis mostly affected young adults. It was probably common in crowded urban centres.

Ancient authors say hardly anything about childhood diseases, but infantile viral diarrhoea and amoebic dysentery probably accounted for much of the high infant mortality observed in cemeteries. Chickenpox, diphtheria, mumps, and whooping cough are all described in connection with attacks on adults. The common cold certainly existed, as did some sexually transmitted diseases, such as genital herpes

and trachoma. Some cancers were well known. Galen says that breast cancer was common.

Some chronic malnutrition diseases were quite common, esp. in childhood. The Greeks and Romans also took an interest in diseases of animals and plants because of their importance in agriculture. See PLAGUE.

dissection See ANIMALS, KNOWLEDGE OF; VIVISECTION.

Dissoi logoi (lit. 'Double Arguments', i.e. 'Arguments For and Against'), a short sophistic work of unknown authorship, written some time after 400 BC. It consists mainly of arguments for and against various evaluative theses, with frequent appeals to relativity, and also discusses the teachability of virtue.

dithyramb, choral song in honour of *Dionysus. There are three phases in the history of the genre: (1) pre-literary dithyramb; (2) the institutionalization of dithyramb in the 6th cent. BC; and (3) the latest phase, which began in the mid-5th cent.

Already in phase (1) dithyramb was a cult song with Dionysiac content. It was sung by a group of singers under the leadership of an *exarchōn*. Phase (2) has its roots in the cultural and religious policies of the tyrants (see TYRANNY; PISISTRATUS) and the young Athenian democracy. *Herodotus says that *Arion in late 7th-cent. *Corinth was the first to compose a choral song, rehearse it with a choir, and produce it in performance, and that he gave the name 'dithyramb' to this new kind of choral song. Lāsus of Hermionē is connected with dithyramb at Athens: he organized (c.508) a dithyrambic contest in the first years of the democracy. Each of the ten Athenian tribes (see PHYLAI) entered the competition with one chorus of men and one of boys, each consisting of 50 singers. The financing of the enterprise (payment for the poet, the trainer of the chorus, and the pipe-player; and the outlay on costuming the chorus) was the responsibility of the *chorēgos* (see CHOREGIA). The winning *choregos* could put up a tripod with a dedicatory inscription in the Street of the Tripods. The dithyrambic contest was a competition between the tribes, not the poets. Dithyrambs were performed at the following Athenian festivals: the City *Dionysia, the *Thargelia, the (Lesser) *Panathenaea, the Prometheia, the Hephaestia. In the first part of the 5th cent. *Simonides (with 56 victories), *Pindar, and *Bacchylides were the dominant dithyrambic poets. Pindar's dithyrambs are recognizable as such by their Dionysiac character. The standard content of a Pindaric dithyramb included some mention of the occasion which had given rise to the song, and of the commissioning *polis*; praise of the poet; narration of a myth; and some treatment of Dionysiac theology. From the mid-5th cent. (phase 3), dithyramb became the playground of the musical avant-garde: they introduced astrophic form (i.e. their poems were not arranged according to strophe and antistrophe, see METRE, GREEK, 3), instrumental and vocal solos, and 'mimetic' music.

Our knowledge of dithyrambic poetry, esp. Pindar and Bacchylides, is based chiefly on papyrus finds (see PAPYROLOGY, GREEK). For phase (3) we are chiefly dependent on citations by *Athenaeus and on the criticisms of comic poets and *Plato.

divination

Greek Divination lies at the heart of Greek religion: *Sophocles represented a challenge to *oracles as a challenge to religion itself (*OT* 897–910), and *Xenophon in listing the benefits conferred on man by the gods regularly stresses guidance through 'sayings and *dreams and omens' (see PORTENTS) and sacrifices. His *Anabasis* presents the best panorama of the place of divination in a person's experience. Before joining *Cyrus' (2) expedition, which he realized might lead him into political difficulties, Xenophon had, on Socrates' advice, consulted the *Delphic oracle. At a moment of crisis, he received a dream from, as he thought, Zeus the King, containing both a threat and a promise: 'what it means to see such a dream one can judge from the consequences' (i.e. the rest of the *Anabasis*). During the campaign, the army regularly took omens from sacrifice, before marching off or joining battle (bad omens could cause a four-day delay), and Xenophon also records the consultative sacrifices that he performed whenever an important decision, personal or collective, had to be made. Through divinatory sacrifice Xenophon could, as it were, consult an oracle wherever he found himself, posing the question in exactly the form in which he might have put it to an oracle: 'is it more beneficial and advantageous to stay with King Seuthes or to depart?', for instance. He also mentions an omen from a sneeze.

Xenophon thus presents at least five ways in which the will of the gods was revealed (whether spontaneously or in response to a mortal inquiry): at fixed oracular shrines, through

dream-interpretation, observation of birds, sacrifice, and 'chance' omens such as a sneeze or an encounter or something said casually at a significant moment. Four forms are found in Homer, but not the very important technique of divination by sacrifice, which probably entered Greece from the near east in the early Archaic period. Also influential were the collections of verse oracles deployed by 'oracle-mongers'; they were commonly ascribed to mythical seers such as Bacis, *Musaeus, and the *Sibyl. Professional diviners included dream-interpreters and above all seers, *manteis*, who specialized in sacrificial divination but no doubt claimed a broader competence. *Isocrates mentions 'books on divination' bequeathed by a seer to a friend, who then took up the art and grew rich, and the literature on dream interpretation, of which *Artemidorus' *Onirocritica* is a late example, is said to go back to a work by Antiphon 'the sophist' (5th cent. BC). See PROPHECIES.

Professional seers were always exposed to ridicule and accusations of charlatanism, but societies which depend on seers also regularly deride them; attacks on individual seers must be distinguished from a more general scepticism. The philosophical debate on the subject is splendidly presented in *Cicero's *On Divination*. *Xenophanes, the *Epicureans, *Carneades and others denied the possibility of divination. Some Peripatetics defended 'inspired' prophecy such as the Pythia's (see DELPHIC ORACLE) or that through *dreams, while rejecting inductive divination from signs; most Stoics (notably Posidonius) vigorously defended both types, basing their justification upon the powers of gods, fate, and nature or the doctrine of 'sympathy' between the different parts of the world. See STOICISM.

Roman Divination stems from the belief that gods send meaningful messages. These messages were classified in a variety of intersecting ways: according to the character of signs through which the message was conveyed, and whether these signs were unsolicited or solicited; the time-frame to which a sign was taken to refer (future, present, past) and the content of the message itself (prediction, warning, prohibition, displeasure, approval); and, most importantly, whether the message pertained to the private or public sphere, the observation and interpretation of the latter category of signs forming part of Roman state religion.

The divine message was either intuitively conveyed or required interpretation. *Cicero adopts the division of divination (elaborated by the Stoics, see STOICISM) into two classes, artificial (external) and natural (internal). The latter relied upon divine inspiration, and was characteristic of prophets and dreamers. The former was based on art and knowledge. To this category belonged the observation of birds, celestial signs, entrails, unusual occurrences, also astrology and divination from lots. But inspired utterances (see SIBYL) and dreams also required interpretation.

The Roman state employed three groups of divinatory experts: the *augurs, the board of priests for the performance of sacred rites (see QUINDECIMVIRI SACRIS FACIUNDIS), who were in charge of the Sibylline books, and the *haruspicēs*. The first two were the official state priests; the *haruspices* were summoned from Etruria as needed (see RELIGION, ETRUSCAN). Their special province was the observation of the entrails of sacrificial victims, esp. the liver. Both augurs and *haruspices* observed and interpreted avian and celestial signs esp. thunder and lightning, but they treated them differently.

All signs were either solicited or unsolicited. The latter could function either as unsolicited auspices or as prodigies (see DEFORMITY; PORTENTS). The former referred solely to a specific undertaking, the prodigies on the other hand to the state of the republic. They were indications that the normal relationship with deity, the 'peace of the gods', was disturbed. Esp. potent were unusual occurrences. In the case of adverse auspices the action in question was to be abandoned; in the case of prodigies it was imperative to find out the cause of divine displeasure (this task often fell to the *haruspices*) and to perform ceremonies of appeasement.

The Roman state did not employ astrologers (occasionally they were banned from Rome) or dream-interpreters, but their services were sought by many, including emperors (see ASTROLOGY). Predictions were made also from involuntary motions, sneezing, and from lifeless objects, esp. from (inscribed) lots drawn from a receptacle. Poets too were so used, esp. *Virgil (*sortēs Vergiliānae*).

Popular divination was often scorned as charlatanry (by *Ennius, Cicero, and *Porcius Cato (1): a *haruspex* could not but laugh on meeting another *haruspex*), and the government was esp. suspicious of astrologers and inspired prophets. In the Christian empire all forms of divination were prohibited and persecuted, though never eradicated.

divorce See MARRIAGE LAW.

Dōdōna, the sanctuary of *Zeus Naïos in Epirus, and reputedly the oldest Greek oracle. The god's temple-sharer is Dione Naïa, and they are shown together on coins. Traditionally oracular responses emanated from the rustling leaves of the sacred oak or from doves sitting in the tree. *Odysseus claimed to have gone to Dodona in order to 'hear Zeus' will from the lofty oak'. Achilles prayed to the Pelasgian Zeus at Dodona, whose prophets, 'sleep on the ground with unwashed feet'. By the mid-5th cent. BC the oracle was operated by three priestesses, who later on were themselves called 'the Doves'. Their method of issuing responses in a trance was borrowed from *Apollo's oracle at *Delphi. The Dodonian oracle generally offered advice on private problems. The enquirer scratched his question on a lead tablet and was answered with a simple 'yes' or 'no'.

dogs were used by Greeks and Romans as watchdogs; to guard livestock; for hunting; and as *pets. *Odysseus, who, attacked by the dogs of the swineherd Eumaeus, sits immobile until rescued by the animals' master, is pointed out as an example to the modern traveller in Greece; later in the *Odyssey* the king's own hound Argos provides one of the most moving moments in the poem, when he greets his disguised master and dies. Among breeds mentioned by classical authors, the Laconian was esp. valued by *Xenophon for hunting. A small breed, like the Maltese terrier, appears on Attic vases.

dokimasia, the vetting of candidates for office at Athens, before the *thesmothetai* (except candidates for the *boule*, who were examined by the outgoing *boule*). Men already chosen, whether by lot or by vote, but primarily the former, were formally interrogated to ascertain whether they were eligible: e.g. whether they were 30 years old; whether (in the case of certain offices at certain periods, e.g. the archonship: see ARCHONTES) they belonged to a particular census-class; and whether they were not precluded from one office, because they had held it before, or were holding another, or through being under some form of *atimia.*

domains In the Homeric poems the *basileis* (see KINGSHIP) have special lots, or *temenē*, like those set aside for Glaucus and *Sarpedon in Lycia, the gardens of Alcinoüs, or the orchards of Laertes. These were tracts of fertile land, yielding fine produce useful for exchange. The title of others to the land they worked is not clear, but the idea of extensive private ownership of land was to spread, and become under the Roman law of property the dominant mode, and that which antiquity bequeathed to European culture.

Certain special types of property remained important throughout antiquity. The common land of early Greek *poleis* (see POLIS) was sometimes really common to the citizen body, and could, as in many new foundations, be assigned in shares equal by surface area, another step towards the regime of private property. The gods were also proprietors on a large scale, owning *temene* not unlike those of the Homeric heroes, administered for the running of the cult and *sanctuary. Under the Roman empire the legacy of these practices was the wide dispersal of civic holdings (Arpinum for instance, home town of *Marius and *Cicero, owned land in *Gaul (Cisalpine)) the revenues from which were vital to the survival of urban institutions. Italian temples and priesthoods like the *Vestals also owned estates. The Roman state had started with public land like any *polis*, but for whatever reason the Roman theory of *ager publicus* developed in a very special and important way, fuelled by the Struggle of the Orders; it was constantly controversial because of the growing size of revenues from it and its potential importance for the settlement of veterans or plebeians.

The royal lands of the Hellenistic kingdoms represent a quite different tradition, based on the theory of the total ownership of the land by the king. In *Egypt royal land was for the most part leased to small producers. The Roman emperors were the heirs of all these traditions. Forming huge portfolios of landed interests like their senatorial predecessors and contemporaries, they acquired a privileged share of the most productive assets, such as forests (see TIMBER), *quarries, or *mines. Even outside areas that had once experienced Hellenistic royal government, their land-holdings were increasingly run as distinctively imperial estates, with special rules and supervision.

Domitian (Titus Flāvius Domitiānus), younger son of *Vespasian, b. AD 51, remained in Rome during his father's campaign against *Vitellius. Surrounded on the Capitol with his uncle, he managed to escape and on Vitellius' death was proclaimed Caesar by the Flavian army, though the real power lay with *Licinius Mucianus until Vespasian's arrival. In 71 he participated in the triumph of Vespasian and *Titus, and between 70 and 80 held seven consulships. Although Domitian exercised no formal power,

he was clearly part of the dynastic plan, and he succeeded his brother smoothly in 81.

The literary sources, esp. *Tacitus and *Pliny the Younger, represent a senatorial tradition hostile to Domitian. This viewpoint illustrates the tension between aristocratic officials and autocrat. *Suetonius' account, though basically hostile, is better balanced and suggests that a more favourable view did exist, apart from the flattery of poets like *Statius and *Martial.

Domitian was conscientious in the performance of his duties, adopting a stance of moral rectitude, maintaining public decency at Games (see LUDI), and showing respect for religious ritual; three *Vestals were put to death for breaking their vows of chastity; later, Cornēlia, the chief Vestal, was buried alive. He promoted festivals and religious celebrations, showing particular devotion to *Jupiter and *Minerva, and performed the *Secular Games; many public buildings were erected, completed, or restored, including the *Capitol, the *Colosseum, and a great palace on the *Palatine. For the people there were frequent spectacles and banquets, though his cash grants were restrained. He raised military pay by a third, and bestowed by edict additional privileges on *veterans and their families; he remained popular with the army and *praetorians.

Domitian administered legal affairs diligently and tried to suppress corruption. Although authoritarian in his attitude to the provinces, Domitian tried to impress probity and fairness on his appointees; Pliny the Younger's letters to *Trajan show that Domitian's administrative decisions were generally endorsed. The role and influence of *equestrians in the administration increased in his reign, but as part of a continuing trend rather than deliberate policy. He probably left a surplus in the treasury; his confiscation of the property of his opponents was for political rather than financial reasons.

Domitian was the first reigning emperor since *Claudius in 43 to campaign in person, visiting the Rhine once, and the Danube three times. Iulius *Frontinus reports favourably on Domitian's personal control of strategy and tactics. In 82/3 he fought a successful war against the Chatti on the middle Rhine, brought the Taunus area under Roman control, and accepted a triumph and the name 'Germānicus'. But the military balance was shifting towards the Danube, and in 85 the *Dacians, under *Decebalus, invaded the Balkan province of Moesia killing its governor. Domitian came in person in 85 and 86; and after the defeat and death of the praetorian prefect, the governor of Upper Moesia won a victory at Tapae in 88. Since Domitian was facing trouble from the Marcomanni and Quadi in Pannonia, he made peace with Decebalus before launching a campaign against them (spring 89); at the end of 89 he celebrated another triumph. Then early in 92 a legion was destroyed in Pannonia by an incursion of the *Sarmatian Iazyges and the Suebi, which was eventually contained under Domitian's personal direction. There was also considerable military activity in Britain, where *Iulius Agricola continued the invasion of north Scotland; his recall in 84 after an unusually long governorship of seven years, probably reflects military needs elsewhere rather than imperial jealousy.

Domitian failed to find a working relationship with the *senate. He was sometimes tactless and did not conceal the reality of his autocracy, holding ten consulships as emperor, wearing triumphal dress in the senate, having 24 lictors, and becoming *censor perpetuus* in 85, symbolically in charge of the senate; his manner was arrogant, and he allegedly began an official letter: 'Our lord god orders that this be done'. There was a conspiracy in 87, and a rebellion in 89 by the governor of Upper Germany. He apparently had little support among his troops and was easily crushed, but Domitian thereafter forbade two legions to be quartered in one camp. He became more ruthless against presumed opponents, and factions in the aristocracy produced many senators willing to act as accusers. The executions of at least twelve exconsuls are recorded in the reign, mainly for dissent or alleged conspiracy, and not because they were *Stoics, although Domitian did expel philosophers. The emperor himself observed: 'no one believes an emperor's claim to have uncovered a conspiracy until he has been murdered'. The execution in 95 of *Flavius Clemens, his cousin, whose sons he had adopted as heirs, was a mistake, since it seemed that now no one was safe. A plot was formed by intimates of his entourage possibly including his wife, Domitia (see DOMITIUS CORBULO), and he was murdered on 18 September 96; his memory was condemned by the senate.

Domitius Corbulō, Gnaeus, through the six marriages of his mother Vistilia, was connected with many prominent families: one of his stepsisters married the emperor *Gaius (1). In AD 47 he was *legate of Lower Germany when he fought successfully against the Chauci, but was not allowed by *Claudius to go further. A strict disciplinarian, he made his troops dig a canal between the Meuse and Rhine. Proconsul of Asia under Claudius, he was soon after *Nero's accession made *legate of Cappadocia and *Galatia with the command against *Parthia in the war about the control of Armenia. This started in earnest only in 58, when Corbulo had reorganized the Roman army in the east. He captured Artaxata and Tigranocerta, installed Tigrānēs V as king of Armenia, and received the governorship of *Syria. But Tigranes was driven out of Armenia, the war was renewed in 62, and at Corbulo's request a separate general was sent to Armenia. After his defeat, Corbulo obtained in 63 a *maius* *imperium* and was again put in charge of Cappadocia–Galatia, as well as Syria. He restored Roman prestige, and concluded a durable agreement with Parthia: Tīridātēs, the Parthian nominee to the throne of Armenia, admitted a Roman protectorate. Corbulo probably did not abuse his popularity, but his son-in-law conspired. In October 66 Nero invited Corbulo to Greece and compelled him to take his own life. His daughter Domitia became wife of *Domitian in 70. It was the homage of the new dynasty to the name and influence of the greatest general of his time. The account of his achievements in Tacitus and *Cassius Dio derives from Corbulo's own memoirs.

Domitius Ulpiānus ('Ulpian'), came from *Tyre, where an inscription honouring him has been found. He followed an *equestrian career in Rome, drafting replies to petitions (see CONSTITUTIONS) for *Septimius Severus, to judge from their style, from AD 202 to 209, and at least from 205 onwards did so as secretary for petitions. On Severus' death at *Eburacum in 211 he sided with Caracalla, who in 212 by the *constitūtio Antōnīniana* (see CONSTITUTION, ANTONINE) extended Roman citizenship to all free inhabitants of the empire. Presumably in response to this extension, which suited his outlook, Ulpian was galvanized into activity in the following years (213–217), systematically composing more than 200 books in which he expounded Roman law for the benefit, among others, of the new citizenry, emphasized its rational and universal character and appealed to its basis in natural law. Probably under the emperor Elagabalus he became *prefect of the corn supply, in which capacity he is attested early in the reign of Severus Alexander, who in the same year made him *praetorian prefect and set him over the two existing prefects. The resulting clashes allowed the praetorian troops, with whom he lacked authority, to mutiny and murder him in 223.

Ulpian had an exalted idea of a lawyer's calling: lawyers were 'priests of justice' devoted to 'the true philosophy'. His fame was immediate and lasting, his works more widely used than those of any other lawyer. His clarity and forthright self-confidence make him an attractive writer, inspired by cosmopolitan tendencies, a search for consensus, and a regard for private rights. His work, both comprehensive and closely documented, foreshadows Justinian's *Digesta* (see JUSTINIAN'S CODIFICATION) which incorporated so much of it. For these reasons he has proved the most influential of Roman lawyers, having done more than anyone to present the law in a form in which it could be adapted to the very different needs of medieval and Renaissance Europe.

Domus Aurea (Golden House), *Nero's residence created after the fire of AD 64, and notorious for its novelties and extravagance. Nero was esp. castigated for turning a vast area of the centre of Rome into a regal park, with residential nuclei dispersed within landscaped *gardens extending from the *Palatine to the Oppian and Caelian hills around an artificial lake. The main entrance was from the Forum along the new *via Sacra through a colonnaded vestibule housing a colossal bronze statue of Nero. New palatial buildings were added to existing imperial properties on the Palatine and Esquiline, the best preserved of which is the Oppian wing incorporated into the substructures of the *baths of Trajan. The long colonnaded structure, developed on at least two levels with symmetrical five-sided courts either side of a remarkable domed octagonal hall, borrows much from Hellenistic palaces and Roman *villa architecture but uses vaulted concrete construction in an unprecedented fashion (see BUILDING MATERIALS).

donative, in the imperial period an irregular monetary payment to soldiers, perhaps originally associated with distributions of *booty. Donatives celebrated important events linked to the emperor—imperial birthdays, the defeat of conspiracies, military victories, and esp. accession to power. Augustus in his will had bequeathed 1,000 sesterces each to the *praetorians, 500 each to the urban soldiers (see COHORTES URBANAE), and 300 each to legionaries, sums which *Tiberius doubled in his own name. But in AD 41 *Claudius paid 15,000 sesterces per man to ensure the crucial support of the praetorians, confirming the importance of a substantial donative in the emperor's own name at his accession and linking the army more closely to his person. Claudius probably made a proportionate payment to other citizen troops, and thereafter a donative accompanied every accession. Donatives depended on circumstances and were not directly related to regular pay rates; the largest known donative, 25,000 sesterces (more than six times praetorian pay), was paid in 193 at the notorious 'auction' of the empire.

Dorians in historical times were the people who spoke Doric Greek (see DIALECTS, GREEK): in SE and NE Peloponnese (*Sparta, *Argos, *Corinth, *Megara), on islands in the south Aegean (*Melos, *Crete, *Rhodes, *Cos), and on the mainland facing Cos (*Cnidus, *Halicarnassus). Their main festival was the *Carnea. They were divided into three *phylae. Tension between Dorians and Lonians became acute in the 5th cent. For the myth of the arrival of the Dorians in Peloponnese, see HERACLIDS. Archaeology throws an uncertain light on the prehistoric truth about the Dorian invasion.

Draco, acc. to Athenian tradition, was a lawgiver who introduced new laws, probably 621/0 BC. This was the first time that Athenian laws were put in writing. Acc. to one account, he established a constitution based on the franchise of *hoplites, but elsewhere he is said only to have made laws against particular crimes. The penalties were very severe: when asked why he specified death as the penalty for most offences, he replied that small offences deserved death and he knew of no severer penalty for great ones; and *Demades later remarked that Draco wrote his laws in blood instead of ink. *Solon repealed all his laws except those dealing with homicide. Such was the tradition current in Athens in the 5th and 4th cents. BC. At that period no one doubted that the homicide laws then in force were due to Draco. Modern scholars have treated the tradition with varying degrees of scepticism. Some have even doubted whether Draco existed at all.

drainage, drain See CLOACA MAXIMA; SANITATION.

drama, Greek See COMEDY (GREEK); TRAGEDY, GREEK.

drama, Roman See COMEDY, LATIN; TRAGEDY, LATIN.

dreams Most ancients accepted that there were both significant and non-significant dreams (e.g. Homer's *Odyssey* 19: true dreams come from gates of horn, delusory dreams from gates of ivory). This basic division might itself be subdivided, most elaborately into a five-fold classification: non-predictive dreams, subdivided into those caused by the day's residues and distorted visions that come between sleeping and waking states; predictive dreams subdivided into: *oneiroi* that need symbolic interpretation, prophetic visions, and advice from a god. The last category is well attested epigraphically by *votives put up by people as the result of successful advice or instructions from a god received in a dream, and in the remarkable diary kept by Aelius *Aristides, which included numerous visions of *Asclepius and other gods. Dreams were indeed an important aspect of *diagnosis in *sanctuaries of Asclepius (see INCUBATION).

The idea that dreams could be significant, but might need professional interpreters, is found from Homer onwards. Dream-books were written from the 5th cent. BC onwards; the only surviving example from antiquity is that by *Artemidorus.

Philosophers and others discussed whether dreams had a divine origin. The Hippocratic author (see HIPPOCRATES) of *On the Sacred Disease* urged that dreams were caused merely by disturbances in the brain, and the author of *On Regimen* explained how to use dreams for medical diagnosis. *Plato argued that some dreams came from the gods and were reliable sources of knowledge, *Aristotle that physiological explanations applied, while *Epicurus and *Lucretius located dreams in a theory about the nature of sense perceptions. For *Cicero the possibility of prophetic dreams was an example of *divination that worked in practice, but which was impossible to justify theoretically.

dress In classical antiquity, items of clothing and jewellery were major personal possessions. The prominence of drapery, i.e. clothing, in Greek and Roman art reflects the importance of dress in daily life.

Most garments were made of *wool, though linen was used for some tunics and underclothing, and silk was worn by richer women; usually the fibre was left undyed, though women's clothes were more colourful than men's; the clothing of both sexes commonly had areas of decoration in wool dyed either with 'real purple' from whelks or in imitation of *purple; such decoration was generally very simple, consisting of woven bands and geometric motifs. Clothes were made of large pieces of cloth with simple outlines which had been woven to shape on traditional looms; though certain garments were characteristic of the Greeks and others of the Romans, there was no real difference between Greek and Roman clothes in techniques or materials; most classical garments belonged either to the category of mantles and cloaks that were 'thrown around', or to those items, including tunics, that were 'entered into', the former often served at night as blankets; all clothes were cleaned by washing and were stored folded-up in chests.

Draped mantles were the characteristic garment of freeborn citizens. The mantle worn by Greek men, and eventually by men and women throughout the eastern Mediterranean and by Roman women, was the *himation*, in Latin *pallium* or *palla*. This was a rectangle, which could be draped in various ways, but which was usually supported on the left arm, leaving the right arm free. The mantle worn by Roman men, the Etruscans, and, originally, Roman women too was the *toga, a semicircular piece of cloth which over time became extremely large. Cloaks were worn by men, either pinned on the right shoulder or joined at the front of the body. Pinned cloaks, used esp. by horsemen, could be rectangular or semicircular.

The traditional Greek woman's garment, the *peplos*, somewhere between a mantle and a tunic, was a roughly square piece of cloth worn with the top third or so folded over and pinned on both shoulders. By the 4th cent. BC the *peplos* had been largely replaced in the cities by the *himation* but was still worn in the country and by all women during cold weather.

Acc. to tradition, the *peplos*, *himation*, and toga had all at first been worn without a tunic. However, the tunic, *chitōn* or *tunica*, had an early history as an independent garment and by the 4th cent. the combination of draped mantle and tunic was the normal form of civilian dress for both men and women. Married Roman women wore the ankle-length *stola*, a mark of respectability.

Underclothes, like tunics, were probably worn more widely than ancient art or literature suggests. A tunic of linen was often worn under a tunic of wool and men probably mostly wore a triangular loincloth, as did women in menstruation. A number of cloth bands were also used as underclothes, notably the *strophion* or *mamillāre*, with which women bound their breasts.

Men's hats and foot wear might be made of felt. Leather was the usual material for shoes and sandals, but, except in the army, it was not used for clothing.

The simplicity and conservatism of classical dress was set off, in the case of women, by elaborate coiffures, jewellery, and make-up. For both men and women, hairstyles and footwear shapes changed more rapidly than those of clothing and so are a better guide when dating works of art. See COSMETICS; TEXTILE PRODUCTION.

Druids See RELIGION, CELTIC.

Drusus See CLAUDIUS DRUSUS, NERO (38–9 BC) and IULIUS CAESAR, DRUSUS (c.13 BC–AD 23), brother and son respectively of the emperor Tiberius.

Duīlius, Gaius, consul 260 BC, appointed to command in west *Sicily; took over command of Rome's first battle-fleet. Using a rotatable boarding-bridge, he defeated the Carthaginians under Hannibal (not the famous Hannibal) off Mylae. After returning to Italy (259), he celebrated Rome's first naval triumph, commemorated by the *columna rostrāta* (a column decorated with the beaks of captured ships in the Forum). From the *booty of Mylae, Duilius built a temple to *Janus in the forum Holitorium. He was censor in 258 and dictator to hold elections in 231.

dyeing was a well-established urban professional craft in the classical world and a branch of empirical chemistry, as the surviving Graeco-Roman dye recipe-books reveal. *Wool was dyed 'in the fleece' before spinning; flax (for linen) was dyed (if at all) as yarn, as was silk. Dyestuffs were drawn from many sources: plants, insects, and shellfish. Most plant dyes would not 'take' unless the textile fibres had been pretreated with a mordant like alum or iron. See TEXTILE PRODUCTION.

eagles See BIRDS, SACRED; SIGNA MILITARIA; STANDARDS, CULT OF.

Earth See GAIA, GE.

earthquakes The Mediterranean is a zone of intense earthquake activity. Notable earthquakes in antiquity include: *Sparta c.464 BC, where an age class perished; Helicē in *Achaea 373 BC, where the city was submerged under the sea; *Rhodes 227/6 BC, when the Colossus collapsed; *Pompeii AD 62, which suffered severe damage. Earthquakes were associated with *Poseidon in mythology: Poseidon the Homeric 'earth-shaker' was fervently worshipped also as 'earth-holder' and 'stabilizer', in Sparta and elsewhere. Herodotus was unusual in his seismological explanation of Thessalian geomorphology (see THESSALY). Ancient philosophers and 'scientists', however, often speculated about the causes of earthquakes.

Eburacum (also **Eboracum**) (York), on the Ouse in the Roman province of Britain. The legionary fortress lay on the east bank; founded during the campaigns of *Petillius Cerialis in AD 71–74, it was rebuilt by *Agricola c.79 and under Trajan, 107/8. Excavations within the fortress have been limited, although the headquarters-complex has been explored beneath York Minster. Eburacum was the seat of the northern command; *Septimius Severus and Constantius I died there whilst using it as a campaign base. The *canabae* (civil settlements) lay east of the Ouse; the mercantile settlement west of the river became a colony before 237. The city became the capital of Lower Britain under Severus, and had a bishopric before 314.

eclipses Solar and lunar eclipses rank with the most impressive celestial phenomena. They were widely considered ominous (see PORTENTS)—as the story of *Nicias' final defeat in Sicily shows—and some 250 reports of them occur in ancient sources. The Babylonian records of lunar eclipses to which *Ptolemy (2) had access apparently began in the 8th cent. BC. By the 5th cent., well-informed Greeks like *Thucydides (2) understood that solar eclipses can take place only at new, and lunar ones at full moon. Recorded eclipses in Greek and Roman literature provide the only absolute dates for historical events: the dated eclipses recorded by historians of the later Roman republic make it possible to trace the deviation of the months of the republican calendar from their proper positions.

ecology (Greek and Roman) *Empedocles devised the theory of the four *elements, leading to the idea of opposites and the theory of the four *humours, in which an imbalance of the humours causes *disease. Different climates cause different humours to prevail in different peoples, producing the theory of environmental determinism in *Hippocrates. The observed regularities in nature led to a belief in purpose in nature. *Herodotus thought that different types of animal had different rates of reproduction appropriate to their natures, an argument for purposeful creation. Other such arguments included the unity and harmony of the universe; the apparent design of human organs, e.g. the eye (*Socrates in Xenophon's *Memorakilia*); the regularities in astronomical phenomena, which led to *astrology and *Ptolemy' (2) theory of cosmic environmentalism in which the stars influence life on earth; and the idea that the creator acted like an artisan, a theory—very important for *Plato, *Cicero, and *Seneca the Younger—that was adopted by the early Christian Fathers and laid the foundations for natural theology in later ages. *Aristotle turned the concept of purpose in nature into an all-embracing teleology, but rejected Plato's artisan deity. Possibly Aristotle thought that nature advances unconsciously towards ends. *Theophrastus expressed doubts about teleology in biology, invented plant biogeography, and considered climatic change caused by human modification of the environment. The Epicureans (See EPI-CURUS) rejected design in nature. The *Stoics fused the aesthetic attitude towards nature, evident in Hellenistic *pastoral poetry, with utilitarian attitudes. The earth is both beautiful and useful.

economic theory (Greek) It is a common-place that the Greek philosophers had no eco-nomic theory. Three reasons are advanced for this absence: (1) the merely embryonic exist-ence of the relevant institutions, esp. the mar-ket; (2) aristocratic disdain for *trade and exchange; (3) the priority assigned to ethical concerns over technical considerations of ex-change and accumulation. While each of these claims contains some truth, the third assumes a modern conception of the autonomy of eco-nomics against which ancient theory may make a pertinent challenge.

*Plato's discussion of the market is sketchy. Economic analysis proper begins in *Aristotle's *Politics*. Fundamental to the entire discussion is the idea that material goods are tools of human functioning. Their proper use has a limit set by those requirements. Poverty placing people beneath this limit is a problem for public planning; accumulation above this limit is 'un-natural' and morally problematic. The accumu-lation of goods began as a way of ensuring the presence of needed resources. Because some of these had to be imported from a distance, barter arose; barter led, in turn, to the temporary ac-cumulation of surpluses useful for trade. Even-tually coined money was introduced to facilitate deferred exchanges. This, however, gave rise to the idea of accumulating a surplus without ref-erence to need or limit, as if wealth were an end in itself. Aristotle's analysis bears on recent criticisms of welfare and development econom-ics which appeal to notions of human function-ing in interpreting economic notions such as 'the standard of living' and 'the quality of life'. Elsewhere, Aristotle analyses the relationship between level of wealth and political behaviour, arguing that the essential difference between *democracy and *oligarchy lies in whether rule is by the poor or the rich; it happens that in every city the poor are many and the rich are few.

Hellenistic thought about money focuses on limiting the desire for possessions. Stoic tele-ology (see STOICISM) is the background for Adam Smith's conception of the 'invisible hand', which should not be understood apart from Stoic ideas of providence and justice. See ECONOMY, GREEK; WEALTH, ATTITUDES TO.

economy, Greek Even if there was 'an econ-omy' in ancient Greece, Greece itself was not a single entity, but a collection of more than 1,000 separate communities. One should there-fore speak of Greek economies rather than the Greek economy, and they may be divided into three groups. First, there is the 'Archaic' group, represented by *Sparta. At the opposite extreme is Athens, distinguished both by the size and number of its economic transactions, and by the sophistication of its economic institu-tions. In between fall the vast range of 'normal' Greek cities or communities, differentiated from the latter chiefly in the scale and, from the for-mer principally, in the nature of their economic arrangements.

Consider the last group first. Our 'economy' is derived from the Gk. *oikonomia*, but this meant originally and usually the management of a pri-vate household (*oikos*) rather than that of a 'na-tional' economy (see HOUSEHOLD, *Greek*). Each 'normal' Greek household (comprising a two-generation nuclear family, free dependants, slaves, animals, land, and other property) aimed to be as self-sufficient as possible, making allowance for the basic constants of the chan-ging domestic life-cycle, and the amount and nature of available land and labour. Household economy in Greece was overwhelmingly rural economy, the number of genuine cities or even genuinely urban residential centres being countable on the fingers of a single hand. See URBANISM, *Greek and Hellenistic*.

Most Greeks living in 'normal' communities were *peasants, farming a couple of hectares (say, 5 acres) planted to a mix of *cereals (mainly barley, some wheat) and drought-resistant crops (*olives, grapevines (see WINE), figs above all). Small stock animals, esp. sheep and goats (see PASTORALISM, GREEK), constituted a necessary complement to agriculture and herbiculture in the absence of artificial fertilizers. In coastal settlements there were always some specialist fishermen (see FISHING), but, apart from the Black (*Euxine) Sea, Greek waters were not fa-vourable to sizeable and predictable shoals of easily catchable fish. Fish remained a luxury food by comparison with the staple 'Mediterra-nean triad' (cereals, wine, olive oil) of the Greek peasant diet.

Self-sufficiency remained for most an ideal, so that economic exchange of various kinds was obligatory (see TRADE, GREEK). But such exchanges were typically conducted between individuals—neighbours or at any rate members of the same community—either directly and by barter in kind or through the use of some monetary medium in the local market. The economy of Athens was exceptional in the degree to which the survival of the community depended on the exchange through long-distance trade of a staple commodity, corn (see FOOD SUPPLY). Athens enjoyed a near-unique means of paying for such imports—the silver deposits in the *Laurium district of SE Attica. The mines were worked almost entirely by chattel-slave labour (see SLAVERY). Athens was also fortunate, and unusual, in that much of *Attica's soil and climate was esp. well suited to olive cultivation; the export of olive oil was officially encouraged from 600 BC.

These factors permitted the development during the 5th cent. of a genuinely urban sector of the Athenian citizen body, concentrated in what was almost a second city around *Piraeus. But most of those directly and exclusively engaged in Piraeus commerce, as in the other non-agricultural sectors of Athenian economy, were non-Athenian and often non-Greek foreigners, resident (*metics and slaves) and transient. Both absolutely and as a proportion of the total population (which itself was overgrown by 'normal' Greek standards) the foreign element was greater in Athens than in any other Greek community.

Sparta represented the opposite pole from Athens. So far from being encouraged as economically desirable or even necessary, foreigners—Greek as well as non-Greek—were periodically expelled from Sparta. The Spartans did regularly practise economic exchange, but within their territory, and with a politically subordinate free population known as *perioikoi, on whom they depended, not least, for supplies of iron. Agriculture and stockraising were left to, or rather forced upon, a subjugated local population of *helots, Greek in speech and culture but servile in status. By dint of exploiting the helots, the Spartans themselves contrived to do no economically productive work (except in the sense that war was itself a means of production). Some other Greek communities exploited workforces of a similar collective character and servile status, but none combined that exploitation with the Spartans' peculiar disdain of all non-military forms of economic activity. The Spartans were not unique in refusing to coin silver or bronze for economic or political purposes, but their retention of a non-convertible domestic 'currency' of iron spits symbolizes their economic eccentricity. See COINAGE, GREEK.

economy, Roman The economy of Rome, like all ancient Mediterranean economies, involved the interaction of the circumstances of local *agriculture with the available *labour supply in the context of opportunities for inter-regional redistribution in which the exchange of other commodities was involved. From the 7th cent. BC. Rome was privileged among other *Tiber valley communities as a centre for the movement of people and materials from peninsular Italy out into the world of Mediterranean contacts.

The exploitation of allotted public land (see AGER PUBLICUS) rapidly became linked with the formation of estate centres (see LATIFUNDIA) for the production of cash crops for mass-marketing, the *villas of the late republic, which were also central to the cultural life of the rich families that owned them. The cities grew as *markets and centres of processing, distribution, and consumption of the products of this agriculture, and as centres for the control and management of a labour force which included, partly as a result of the victories of the 2nd cent., numerous slaves (see SLAVERY). From the beginnings of the large-scale export of *wine from Italy in the mid-2nd cent. the network of economic exchanges involved entrepreneurs, Roman military forces in the field, dependent consumers inside and outside Roman territory, and the city of Rome itself in an increasingly complicated web, in which the non-agricultural resources of the growing imperial state, esp. metals (see MINES AND MINING), were an important ingredient. The production of olive oil in *Baetica, *Africa, and Tripolitania (western Libya) transformed these regions, with concomitant gain to their market centres and port outlets (see AMPHORAE, ROMAN). The economy of the empire included connections with networks of exchange reaching across northern Europe, and central Asia, and via the Red Sea with the Indian Ocean area, to which *Alexandria was central. Rome itself was a consumer on an enormous scale, and therefore powerfully influenced Mediterranean production and exchange. But the complexity of the network, the continued local interdependence of the regions of the empire, and the existence of very many smaller centres of consumption, and marketing, ensured that the economic life of the Roman world was not wholly directed towards Rome.

See ARTISANS AND CRAFTSMEN; COINAGE (ROMAN); INDUSTRY; TRADE, ROMAN.

ecstasy The Gk. term *ekstasis* may refer to any situation in which (part of) the mind or body is removed from its normal place or function. It is used for abnormal conditions of the mind such as madness, unconsciousness, or 'being beside one-self'. In the Hellenistic and later periods the notion is influenced by the Platonic concept of 'divine madness', a state of inspired possession distinct from lower forms of madness and as such providing insights into objective truth. *Ekstasis* now acquires the notion of a state of trance in which the soul, leaving the body, sees visions as Peter and *Paul in Acts. In later, esp. Neoplatonist theory, *ekstasis* is the central condition for escape from restraints of either a bodily or a rational-intellectual nature and thus becomes the gateway to union with God; see DIONYSUS.

edict High Roman magistrates (praetors, aediles, quaestors, censors, the governors of provinces) proclaimed by edicts the steps which they intended to take in the discharge of their office. Formally an edict was valid only for the term of office of the magistrate issuing it, but the new magistrate customarily took over his predecessor's edict, with only such deletions or additions as he thought desirable. The content of the edict therefore remained largely constant. The edict of the urban *praetor was esp. important for the development of the private law. His province was in form merely to apply the existing laws affecting Roman citizens, but in his edict he was able to promise new actions and other remedies and thus to create a mass of new rules. In the formulation of his edict and in its administration during his year of office, the praetor would rely on the advice of jurists (see LAWYERS, ROMAN). It was no doubt this indirect professional control which enabled the edict to play its vital formative function in the private law. Hadrian commissioned the jurist Salvius Iulianus to compose a revised version of the edict (c. AD 130), which was confirmed by a *senatus consultum. It thus acquired a permanent form (*ēdictum perpetuum*) and the praetors lost the power to change it.

education, Greek

1. **Early Period** Greek ideas of education (*paideia*) encompassed upbringing and cultural training in the widest sense, not merely schooling. The poets were regarded as the educators of society, esp. in the Archaic period, but also well into the Classical, when *Plato could attack *Homer's status as educator of Greece. Other educators were the laws and *festivals of the *polis, and later the institutions of *democracy and their procedures.

Before the 5th cent., there must have been training for any specialized skill; most of it was like an apprenticeship. There was a school of 120 boys at *Chios by 494. Attic vase-paintings show scenes of schooling. That schooling would be non-technical ('liberal'), and, would be primarily concerned with music (including poetry; see below, 3) and *athletics. This type of education, or at least its higher levels, was transformed by the *sophists and their successors into one involving the techniques of *rhetoric, which came to form the most typical part of higher education.

2. **Sparta** *Crete and Classical *Sparta practised a totalitarian and militaristic form of education controlled by the state; See AGOGE.

3. **Classical Athens**

Elementary education

Explicit evidence for schools (see above) is much later than the introduction of the *alphabet to Greece. *Ostracism at Athens may presuppose widespread basic *literacy by the time of *Cleisthenes (2).

There were three main elements to elementary education, normally taught in different establishments. The *paidotribēs* dealt with athletics and general fitness, mainly in the *palaestra. The *kitharistēs* taught music and the works of the lyric poets in the lyre school. The *grammatistēs* taught reading, writing, and arithmetic, as well as literature, which consisted of learning by heart the work of poets, esp. Homer, who were regarded as giving moral training. Thus after learning the alphabet, pupils would progress to learning the poets. Athletics and music (including poetry and *dance) were the fundamentals.

In a single day, the pupil might start with athletics, then proceed to the lyre school, and end with letters. But the system was private and fee-paying, far from rigid, and parents might not want their children to participate in all three. Girls, as we see from vase-painting, might be educated in all three elements, as well as dancing, though not normally in the same schools as boys or to the same extent. The teacher was normally a free man. Assistants might be slaves or free men. Boys were always accompanied to school by a *paidagōgos*, a slave who helped to bring up the child and maintain order at school. Discipline was strict: the symbol of the *paidotribes'* power to punish was the forked stick, of other teachers the cane. Pupils had to recite what they had learned, and the regular public competitions (See AGONES), whether literary, musical, or athletic, were an important arena for proving their skill.

The development of group schooling, in which the education previously reserved for the aristocracy spread to other citizens, may be related, at least in Athens, to the development of the *democracy. The balance between the physical and intellectual sides was disputed by some thinkers, and the military uses of physical education may have given that side ascendancy (See EPHEBOI). *Xenophanes and *Euripides scoffed at the athletic (and aristocratic) ideal, while *Pindar, perhaps Aristophanes, and *Xenophon supported it. Plato, *Isocrates, and Aristotle subordinated the physical side to the intellectual. Most Athenian schooling was undergone between the ages of *c*.7 and 14, and did not necessarily last all seven years. Between the ages of 14 and 18 upper-class boys seem to have run more or less wild.

Higher education

From the late 5th cent. it was possible to pursue more specialist education by joining one of the courses offered by the *sophists, or listening to their lectures and disputations. Or there were the specialized schools of rhetoric or philosophy or *medicine. The most famous were Isocrates' school of rhetoric, founded *c*.390, Plato's *Academy with its scientific, mathematical, and philosophical curriculum founded soon after, and *Aristotle's Lyceum, founded in 335.

The great educators and theorists

See SOPHISTS; HIPPIAS (2); SOCRATES; PLATO; ISOCRATES.

Teaching methods

Private tuition, individual tuition, and teaching in small groups are all attested, even for athletics. Learning by heart, with a view to recitation, was standard. Even Plato accepted the usefulness of games in elementary education (arithmetic). At a higher level, pedagogic techniques were most developed in rhetorical teaching. Students memorized commonplaces (See TOPOS), stock situations, and stock phrases, along with sample passages like *Gorgias' *Funeral Speech* (see EPITAPHIOS) as material for later improvisation (on which much store was set). Psychology, techniques of persuasion, and the art of arguing both sides of a case were also taught. In addition, the sophists, and esp. Isocrates, supplemented this

with further general knowledge (See RHETORIC, GREEK).

The sophists developed both the dialectical method and the lecture, which might take the form of the display speech or the full technical lecture, which even Plato often used, though he preferred *dialectic. The dialectic method involves question and answer, in which the respondent makes a real contribution to discussion (as opposed to the Socratic technique). This method was developed by Isocrates into a seminar technique of group discussion and criticism. The Socratic method proceeds by reducing the pupil to a state of *aporia* (or bafflement) and admission of complete ignorance (not to mention irritation), and then drawing out knowledge by a process of questioning, a process of intellectual 'midwifery'. It is well illustrated in the geometry lesson of Plato's *Meno*. Xenophon advocated the 'activity' method in his *Cyropaedia* where pupils learn justice by practising it in real-life group situations.

4. Hellenistic Education For the Hellenistic period, there is a wealth of inscriptions (see EPIGRAPHY, GREEK) which illuminate the public side of education, and rich *papyrological evidence for school activity (e.g. school exercises). The pattern of education established in Classical Athens was brought in the early years of the Hellenistic period to a definitive form, which endured with only slight changes to the end of the ancient world. Greater attention was paid to the education of the ordinary citizen.

Higher education

After secondary education there were several options. For really serious 'higher education' in the recognizably modern sense, there were the great centres of learning—Athens, *Pergamum, and *Rhodes for philosophy and rhetoric; *Cos, Pergamum, or Ephesus for medicine; *Alexandria for the whole range of higher studies (see MUSEUM).

See also EPHEBOL; LITERACY; ORALITY.

education, Roman

1. Early Italy and the Republic In the early period education was centred on the family and was probably based upon apprenticeship supervised by the father—in poorer homes an apprenticeship to agriculture or trade, in more aristocratic circles to military service and public life. The authority of the father, legalized as *patria potestas*, was absolute. The Roman mother had a more restricted, domestic role, but she was expected to set a strong moral example

(see MOTHERHOOD, *Roman*). Institutions like the religious calendars, the census, and the codification of the *Twelve Tables suggest that by the 5th cent. BC *literacy was becoming part of many men's everyday life, and by the end of the 4th cent. it would certainly have been hard for a Roman senator to do without reading and writing. It is not known how such elementary instruction was given, though it was often reckoned to be a parental responsibility.

2. **The Later Republic and the Empire** As Rome's contacts with the Greek-speaking world grew in the 3rd and 2nd cents., a pattern of education evolved which owed much to Greece (see EDUCATION, GREEK), but which omitted both *palaestra and *gymnasium and also the *kitharistēs* and his lyre school. Aristocratic Roman families often employed Greek-speaking tutors for their children (*Livius Andronicus and *Ennius were early examples) and these tutors—often slaves or freedmen—commonly taught both Greek and Latin; competence in both languages remained a feature of an upper-class education until the western and eastern empires parted company. This tradition of tutors in rich families continued alongside the growth of schools. A freedman, Spurius Carvilius, is credited with opening the first fee-paying school for elementary reading and writing in the second half of the 3rd cent., and thereafter the elementary teacher (*lūdī magister*) running a small school became a lowly, noisy, and familiar part of Roman life. The Greek custom of a family *paedagōgus* who took children to and from school and supervised their life and habits was also adopted; the custom burgeoned esp. after the Third Macedonian War when cheap, well-qualified Greek slaves became easily available. The second stage of education was in the hands of the *grammaticus, who taught language and poetry and who might be either a family's private tutor or a teacher with his own school. He could be a person of some learning and consequence. Teachers of *rhetoric (rhetors), the third stage of Greek and Roman education, first appear in the 2nd cent. at Rome, and, in the absence of Latin instructional material, taught Greek theory and practice. Latin materials corresponding to the Greek rhetorical manuals appeared in the 1st cent. and Plotius Gallus is said to have opened the first school for teaching rhetoric in Latin *c*.94 BC. Cicero's works on oratory were a major contribution to such teaching, and *Quintilian's, 'Education of the Orator' published *c*. AD 95 includes a picture of Roman rhet-

orical training at its best. From the middle of the 2nd cent. BC, when three visiting Greek philosophers made a deep impression with their lectures in Rome, philosophy could play a significant part in the education of some rich young Romans. Teachers were soon available in Italy, though the young were glad to travel and attend one of the four famous schools in *Athens or other centres where philosophers taught. From the 1st cent. AD there were law schools in Rome which founded an important tradition of legal education culminating in the great law school at Berytus in the eastern empire. Augustus attempted with some success to use Roman and Italian traditions to create a Roman counterpart to the Greek *ephēbeia* (see EPHEBOI); in this there was more than a hint of political education. Later emperors, local communities, and benefactors like *Pliny the Younger sometimes subsidized charitable and educational activity from personal interest, generosity, a sense of duty, or political expediency, but there was no national or regional provision for education.

3. **Levels and Subjects of Study** The three levels of Roman education represented by the *ludi magister*, the *grammaticus*, and the rhetor were never rigidly differentiated. Although formal education usually began when children were about 7 years old and transfers to the *grammaticus* and rhetor often happened at about the ages of 12 and 15 respectively, progress between the levels was often more a matter of achievement than age group; the roles of teachers sometimes overlapped considerably. All three levels followed a Greek pattern: the elementary teacher, for instance, taught reading by the familiar progression—letters, syllables, words—with much use of the gnomic example sentence (*sententia*). Writing and some basic mathematics were also his province. The *grammaticus* advanced the study of both language and poetry. As Roman grammarians like *Varro adapted Alexandrian grammatical theory to Latin, some systematic morphology was taught; syntax was rather diffusely approached via correctness of speech and the avoidance of solecism. In teaching poetry, attention was paid to expressive reading followed by the teacher's explanation and, where appropriate, analysis. Homer's preeminent place in Greek schools was originally taken by poets like Livius Andronicus (who supplied the *Odyssey* in *Saturnian verse translation), Naevius, and Ennius. Virgil supplanted most earlier poets (Terence becoming the Roman counterpart to *Menander). The teaching of

rhetoric followed the Greek model closely with a series of preliminary exercises (*progymnasmata*—sometimes taught by the *grammaticus*) leading on to the theory and practice of *declamation with the two major groupings of *suasoriae* (advice offered in historical or imaginary situations) and *controversiae* (courtroom cases). The five traditional parts of rhetoric were the basis of instruction: invention, arrangement, style, memory, and delivery (See RHETORIC, GREEK).

4. Schools and Teachers Elementary teachers seem usually to have worked in suitable spaces in public porticoes or squares, in hired accommodation off the street, or in their own rooms. The *grammaticus* and the rhetor probably commanded better but not institutional accommodation. Most schools were small, and though the monthly fees doubtless varied, such evidence as there is suggests that elementary teachers of some kind were affordable by most. Under the empire towns but not villages might be expected to have teachers and schools. Boys were in a majority, but some girls did attend too. The regular equipment for pupils consisted of waxed or whitened wooden writing-tablets, *stilus* or pen (though exercises were written on papyrus when it could be afforded). In the elementary school lessons began at dawn and discipline was strict and unashamedly physical.

The status of elementary teachers was low; many were ex-slaves and had only a small and hazardous income. The *grammaticus* was better respected, and *Suetonius' 'On grammatici' gives sketches of a poor but not ill-regarded profession. The rhetor could charge higher fees, and the most famous could become men of some consequence under the empire. The ratio of maximum fees payable to the *ludi magister*, the *grammaticus*, and the rhetor in *Diocletian's Price Edict was 1 : 4 : 5. The rhetor was at first an object of suspicion in Rome; in 161 Greek rhetors were expelled from the city, and Latin rhetors suffered the same fate in 92. However, from the time of *Caesar teachers were more favoured; now and then they received various immunities, exemptions, and privileges by imperial edict, though imperial patronage was largely reserved for the highest levels. *Vespasian endowed imperial chairs in Greek and Latin rhetoric at Rome, *Quintilian being the first holder of the Latin chair; Marcus *Aurelius endowed four chairs of philosophy and a chair of rhetoric at Athens. Emperors and politicians sought visibility and prestige in exchange for their generosity.

Egypt

Pre-Ptolemaic During the New Kingdom (Dynasties 18–20, c.1575–1087 BC) Egypt expanded into Asia. This great age of Egyptian militarism created in the 18th Dynasty an empire which stretched from the Euphrates to beyond the Fourth Cataract in Nubia, and the resources generated made possible remarkable achievements in the visual arts, esp. great temples such as those of Karnak and Luxor and the mortuary temples of west Thebes as well as the brilliantly decorated tombs in the Valleys of the Kings and Queens. The decline in Egypt's imperial position at the end of the dynasty was reversed by Seti I and Ramesses II in the early 19th Dynasty, but they never succeeded in recovering all the territory lost in Asia. The later New Kingdom is largely characterized by gradual decline. The Late Dynastic period (Dynasties 21–31, c.1087–332) is marked by long periods of foreign occupation by Libyans, Nubians, and Persians punctuated by short, if sometimes brilliant, periods of national resurgence (see SAITES). It terminates with the occupation by *Alexander (2) the Great in 332.

Ptolemaic In the period from the death of Alexander in 323 until the defeat of *Cleopatra VII with Antony (see ANTONIUS, MARCUS) at Actium in 31 BC the Egyptian throne was held by Macedonians, and from 304 by the one family, descended from Alexander's general Ptolemy son of Lagus. Externally the main problem remained the extent of the kingdom, while internally the nature of administrative control and relations with the native Egyptians formed the major concerns of this new resident dynasty of foreign pharaohs. Contemporary historical analysis is limited in period, much of it concentrating on the scandalous and sensational, and while numerous papyri and *ostraka*, preserved in the dry desert, join with inscriptions to make Egypt better documented than other Hellenistic kingdoms, they illustrate the details of administration and everyday life without its wider context.

Internally the Ptolemies used local expertise as they set up their royal administration based on the traditional divisions or nomes (see NOMOS (1)) of Egypt. Self-governing cities were few: *Alexandria, which served as capital from 312, *Naucratis, and Ptolemais, founded by Ptolemy I as a Greek city in the south. Through a hierarchical bureaucracy, taxation of rich agricultural land and of the population and their livestock was based on a thorough census and land-survey. Greek was gradually introduced as the language of the administration, and Greeks were privileged, both socially and in the tax-structure. The classification 'Greek' was now not an ethnic one, but rather one acquired, through employment and education. The wealth of the country (from its irrigation-agriculture and from taxes) was employed both for further development in the countryside (with agricultural initiatives and land-reclamation, esp. in the *Fayūm) and, in Alexandria, for royal patronage and display. The cultural life of the capital, with the *Museum and *Library strongly supported under the early Ptolemies, played an important role in the definition of contemporary Hellenism.

Like other Hellenistic monarchs, the Ptolemies depended for security on their army, and Ptolemaic troops were tied in loyalty to their new homes by land-grants in the countryside. In a soft approach to Egyptian ways, the Ptolemies early recognized the importance of native temples, granting privileges, and supporting native cults. The Ptolemies were both Egyptian pharaohs and Greek monarchs. General tolerance and even financial support for native temples characterize the religious policy of the regime. Two separate legal systems continued in use. The sister-marrying Ptolemaic dynasty is, from the late 3rd cent., consistently represented as in decline. From the mid-2nd cent. the shadow of Rome loomed large, yet Egypt was the last Hellenistic kingdom to fall under Roman sway.

Roman After two centuries of diplomatic contacts, Egypt was annexed as a province of the Roman people in 30 BC by Octavian (*Augustus) after his defeat of Antony and Cleopatra. Although the Romans adapted many individual elements of the centralized bureaucracy of the Ptolemaic kingdom, and although the emperor could be represented as a pharaoh, the institutions of the Ptolemaic monarchy were dismantled, and the administrative and social structure of Egypt underwent fundamental changes. The governor (prefect) and other major officials were Roman *equestrians appointed, like the administrators of other 'imperial' provinces, by the emperor for a few years. Egypt was garrisoned with three, later two, legions and a number of auxiliary units. For private business pre-existing Egyptian and Greek legal forms and traditions were generally respected, but under the umbrella of the principles and procedures of Roman law. A closed monetary system based on the Alexandrian silver tetradrachm was maintained, but the tetradrachm was made equivalent to the Roman *dēnārius*. The Egyptian temples and priesthood were allowed to keep most of their privileges, but in tacit return for the ubiquitous spread of the Roman imperial cult (see RULER-CULT). Local administration was gradually converted to a liturgical system, in which ownership of property brought an obligation to serve.

Egyptian deities the Graeco-Roman view of Egyptian religion is sharply fissured. Many writers of all periods, and probably most individuals, found in the Egyptians' worship of animals a polemical contrast to their own norms, just as, conversely, the Egyptians turned animal-worship into a symbol of national identity. The first Egyptian divinity to be recognized by the Greek world was the oracular *Ammon of the Siwa oasis; but *oracles have a special status. The only form of Late Egyptian religion to be assimilated into the Graeco-Roman world was to a degree untypical, centred on anthropomorphic deities—*Isis, Sarapis, and Harpocrates—and grounded in Egyptian vernacular enthusiasm quite as much as in temple ritual. The other gods which became known in the Graeco-Roman world, Anubis, Apis, Bubastis the cat-goddess, Horus, Osiris, etc., spread solely in their train.

eisangelia ('impeachment') in Athenian law was the name of distinct types of prosecution.

1. The accuser denounced someone to the *ekklesia or the *boule for treason. In the 4th cent. BC a law specified offences for which this procedure could be used: subversion of the *democracy, betrayal of Athenian forces or possessions to an enemy, and corrupt deception of the people by an orator (see BRIBERY, GREEK). In the 5th cent. it had been possible to use *eisangelia* for serious offences not specified in any law; the best known cases are the prosecutions for profanation of the *mysteries (see ELEUSIS) and mutilation of the *herms in 415. But in the 4th cent. this seems to have been no longer permitted, and prosecutors sometimes made tortuous efforts to bring various charges under one or other of the headings specified in the law. A case might be either referred to a jury or tried by the *ekklesia* itself, but after the middle of the 4th cent. no instances of trial by the *ekklesia* are known.

2. The accuser denounced an official to the *boule* for maladministration. The *boule* could impose a fine up to 500 drachmas. If it considered

a heavier penalty was required, it referred the case to a jury.

3. The accuser denounced a guardian (see GUARDIANSHIP, *Greece*) for maltreatment of an orphan, and prosecuted him before a jury.

A common feature was that in *eisangelia*, unlike other public actions, the prosecutor suffered no penalty if he obtained less than one-fifth of the jury's votes.

eisphora ('paying-in'), a general word for payments made for a common cause by a plurality of contributors; and in particular the name of a property tax known in a number of Greek states and in the Ptolemaic empire.

In Athens *eisphora* was an extraordinary tax which could be levied after a vote of immunity in the assembly, and *Thucydides (2) mentions a levy in 428/7, but we have no details about the 5th-cent. tax. In the 4th cent. *eisphora* was a proportional levy, imposed when the assembly chose and at a rate which the assembly chose, on all whose declared property exceeded a certain value; probably the class of *eisphora*-payers was larger than the class of *liturgy-performers; *metics were liable, on disadvantageous terms. The total assessment of all men or of all liable for *eisphora*, is said to have been 5,750 or 6,000 talents.

ekklēsia, the assembly of adult male citizens which had the ultimate *decision-making power in a Greek state. There was room for variation, according to the complexion of the regime, in the membership of the assembly (an *oligarchy might use a property qualification to exclude the poor), the frequency of its meetings, and the extent to which the business it could discuss and its freedom in discussing it were limited by the prerogatives of the magistrates and/or a council.

In the Homeric world (see HOMER) assemblies met occasionally, to deal with the business of the king or noble who summoned them. Active participation was limited to the leading men and the religious experts, while the ordinary men would shout their approval or remain ominously silent. In *Iliad* 2 the commoner *Thersites presumes to make a speech, but *Odysseus' rebuke to him meets with general applause.

In *Sparta the assembly of full citizens was guaranteed regular meetings and a final right of decision by the Great Rhetra attributed to Lycurgus (see APELLAI). The assembly appears more powerful, and the *gerousia* (council of elders) less powerful, in the narratives of

*Thucydides (2) and *Xenophon than in the Rhetra and in *Aristotle's *Politics*: ordinary members could not speak or make proposals, and the assembly was perhaps most powerful when the *gerousia* was divided. Voting was by acclamation.

At Athens, as elsewhere, the character of the assembly developed with progress towards *democracy. Probably the poorest citizens were never formally excluded, but at first were not expected to play an active part. Originally, the assembly perhaps decided only questions of peace and war, and formally elected the magistrates; it was probably involved in the special appointments of *Draco and *Solon; Solon's creation of a second council to prepare business for the assembly was probably coupled with regular meetings for the assembly, and his *eliaia* may have been a meeting of the assembly for judicial purposes. *Cleisthenes' (2) new organization of the citizen body had no direct effect on the assembly, but the high level of participation which his system required will have had an indirect effect. The assembly gained further powers from *Ephialtes' reform of the *Areopagus, including perhaps the right to try *eisangeliai*. By the second half of the 5th cent. all major and many minor decisions were taken by the assembly.

The regular meeting-place of the assembly was Pnyx. Eventually there were four regular meetings in each of the ten prytanies (see PRYTANEIS) of the year, and probably extraordinary meetings could be summoned in addition when necessary: the increase from one regular meeting per prytany may have been made in the second half of the 5th cent. Meetings were summoned by the *prytaneis* on behalf of the council. The requirement of a quorum of 6,000 for some categories of business suggests that an attendance of that size could be, but was not always, attained. In the 5th cent. citizens were not paid to attend the assembly, but payment for attending was introduced shortly after the democratic restoration of 403. Voting was by ballot when it was necessary to check that a quorum had been achieved, but otherwise by show of hands, when there was not a precise count but the presiding officers adjudged the majority.

Some items of business were prescribed by law for particular occasions in the year; every item on which the assembly was to make a decision had to be the subject of a *probouleuma* (prior resolution by the council), which could, but did not have to, incorporate a specific proposal, but in the assembly any citizen could speak and could propose a motion or an amendment. From the early 6th cent. to the late 5th laws could be enacted only by a decree of the assembly; the 4th cent. tried to distinguish between decrees (*psēphismata*), which were particular and/or ephemeral but included all decisions in foreign affairs, and laws (*nomoi*), which were general and permanent, and for which a more elaborate procedure was devised. Various precautions were taken against improper and overhasty decisions in the assembly, but they did not always prove effective in a crisis.

ekphrasis, an extended and detailed literary description of any object, real or imaginary. 'There are *ekphraseis* of faces and objects and places and ages and many other things' (*Hermogenes).

Elagabalus, deus Sōl invictus ('Invincible Sun-god Elagabalus'), oracular deity of Emesa on *Orontes, his sacred symbol a conical black stone. His cult was established in Rome from the later 2nd cent. AD. In 218 his hereditary priest at Emesa became emperor as Elagabalus and made the god the supreme official deity of the empire with precedence over Jupiter. This short-lived promotion (including translation of the sacred stone to the Palatine) was ended by the emperor's assassination, although the cult survived to enjoy the patronage of *Aurelian. See SOL INVICTUS.

Electa See ORESTES.

elections and voting

Greek In the Greek states voting was used in councils, assemblies, and lawcourts; appointments were made by election or by allotment (see SORTITION) or sometimes by a combination of the two. In Athens and elsewhere *psēphisma* (from *psēphos*, 'voting-stone') became the standard word for a decree of the council (*boule) or assembly (*ekklesia), and *cheirotonia* ('raising hands') was used for elections; but in *Athens voting was normally by show of hands (not precisely counted) in the council and assembly both for decrees and for elections, but by ballot in the lawcourts (See LAW AND PROCEDURE, ATHENIAN, 4). Ballots seem first to have been used when a count was necessary to check that a quorum had been achieved. The mechanics of ostracism will have alerted Athenians to the possibility of secret voting. In *Sparta voting by acclamation survived to the Classical period for elections and for decrees of the assembly.

Roman At Rome adult male citizens had the right to vote to elect the annual magistrates, to make laws, to declare war and peace, and, until the development of the public courts in the late republic, to try citizens on serious charges. But matters were never decided by a simple majority. Votes were always cast in assigned groups, so that a majority of individual votes decided the vote of each group, and a majority of groups decided the vote of the assembly as a whole. The three groupings of the *cūriae* (*curia (1)), centuries (*centuria), and tribes (*tribus) made up the different types of *comitia*.

In the two important *comitia* the procedures for voting were similar. Cicero noted that Romans considered matters and voted standing up, whereas the Greeks sat down. The vote was preceded by a *contio, a public meeting, to present the issues or the candidates involved. The presiding magistrate dissolved it by commanding the citizens to disperse into the areas roped off for each group. From their enclosures the groups of citizens proceeded, when called, across raised gangways, erected at the site of the assembly. Originally each voter was asked orally for his vote by one of the officials, who put a mark against the appropriate name or decision on his official tablet. From 139 to 107 BC a series of four laws introduced the secret ballot. Now the voter was handed a small boxwood tablet covered in wax on which he recorded his vote with a stylus. In most cases a single letter was sufficient: in legislation, V for assent (*utī rogās*, 'as you ask') and A for dissent (*antīquō*, 'status quo'); in judicial cases L for acquittal (*līberō*) and C for condemnation (*condemnō*); in elections the voter was expected to write the names for himself (*Porcius Cato (2) is said to have rejected many votes clearly written in the same hand). The completed tablet was then dropped into a voting-urn under the control of guardians, who forwarded it to the sorters. In the *comitia centuriāta* people voted successively, class by class, and the results were announced as they went along. In the *comitia tribūta* successive voting was used in legislative and judicial assemblies, but simultaneous voting probably in elections. This may explain why legislative assemblies regularly took place in a variety of places, some quite restricted, such as the *forum Romanum, *Capitol, and Circus Flaminius (see CIRCUS), while the large spaces of the *Campus Martius were needed for elections. It was here that Caesar planned a huge building, the Julian Enclosures (Saepta Iulia), to house the electoral process. The project was continued by *Aemilius

Lepidus (2) and completed in 26 BC under Augustus by *Vipsanius Agrippa.

The lot played a vital role in the electoral process. It was used to pick the tribe or the century which voted first and provided a lead for the other voters. The lot also determined the order of voting by the tribes or the order in which the votes were announced. This was important, because the first candidates to achieve a simple majority of the groups were declared elected up to the number of posts available, even though they might not have polled the largest number of votes if all the votes of all the groups had been counted.

The great lengths to which members of the élite went to win votes (see COMMENTARIOLUM PETITIONIS) shows that the voting assemblies represent a truly democratic element in republican Rome. (See DEMOCRACY, NON-ATHENIAN.) In typical Roman fashion the voting procedures, in a modified form, remained under the Principate, even when the substantive decision-making had passed to the emperor and the senate.

elegiac poetry, Greek This may be initially defined as poetry in elegiac couplets (see METRE, GREEK 3, 4). The term *elegeion* normally meaning 'elegiac couplet', is derived from *elegos*, a sung lament that must have been characteristically in this metre, but the metre was always used for many other purposes.

A stricter definition distinguishes between elegiac poetry (elegy) and *epigram (which was often in elegiac metre). Elegy, in the early period, was composed for oral delivery in a social setting, as a communication from the poet to others; an epigram was information written on an object (a tombstone, a dedication, etc.). The distinction was not always so clear after the 4th cent. BC, when the epigram came to be cultivated as a literary genre.

Archaic elegy is already established on both sides of the Aegean by c.650 BC when the first recorded elegists appear: *Archilochus, Callinus of Ephesus, and *Tyrtaeus. From then till the end of the 5th cent. BC elegy was a popular medium; some poets used no other.

Many pieces presuppose the *symposium as the setting in which they were designed to be heard. *Theognis expects that his elegies addressed to Cyrnus will often be sung by young men at banquets to the accompaniment of *auloi. There are other mentions of an aulete (*aulos*-player) accompanying the singing of elegy in the symposium, and an early 5th-cent. vase-painting shows a reclining symposiast with

words of an elegiac verse issuing from his mouth while an aulete plays. Certain elegists (Tyrtaeus, *Mimnermus) are said to have been auletes themselves.

A common use of elegy in the 7th cent. was in exhorting the poet's fellow citizens to fight bravely for their country. In other poems of Tyrtaeus and Solon the exhortation is political, presumably delivered to a social gathering from which participants might pass the message on to other gatherings. Solon, at least, also wrote elegies of a more personal, convivial character. Mimnermus was famous for elegies celebrating the pleasures of love and youth. He also used the versatile elegiac for his *Smyrneis*, a quasi-epic, complete with invocation of the Muses, on the Smyrnaeans' heroic repulse of the Lydians around the time of the poet's birth (see GYGES).

The largest surviving body of Archaic elegy is the collection of poems and excerpts, some 1,400 lines in all, transmitted under the name of Theognis. He is actually only one among many poets represented, ranging in date from the 7th to the early 5th cent. BC. Here we find a wide cross-section: political and moralizing verse, social comment, personal complaint, convivial pieces, witty banter, love poems to nameless boys. Other items are reflective or philosophic, and develop an argument on some ethical or practical question. This *dialectic element was a feature of elegy from the start, but became more prominent later, e.g. in *Xenophanes.

*Simonides used the medium to celebrate the great battles of 480/79 BC; his grandiose poem on Plataea recalls Mimnermus' *Smyrneis* (see PLATAEA, BATTLE OF). By the end of the 5th cent. the symposium was fast losing its songfulness, and elegy in the classical style was drying up.

elegiac poetry, Latin *Ennius introduced the elegiac couplet (see METRE, GREEK, 3, 4) into Latin. The careers of *Catullus and *Ovid bound the elegiac genre's most concentrated and distinctive period of Roman development. In particular, by early Augustan times elegy emerges as the medium for cycles of first-person ('subjective') poems describing the tribulations, mostly erotic, of a male poet who figuratively enslaves himself to a single (pseudonymous) mistress, distances himself from the duties associated with public life, and varies his urban *mise en scène* with escapist appeals to other worlds, mythological (*Propertius, Ovid) or rural (*Tibullus). 'Love-elegy', though the term is widely used by modern critics, was not for the Romans a formal poetic category. However, a canonical sequence of *Cornelius Gallus (as originator), Tibullus, Propertius, and Ovid is explicitly offered by Ovid; and *Quintilian's later adoption of this same canon to represent Latin elegy at large may well reflect the central role of Augustan 'love-elegy' in defining the genre.

Even in the heyday of 'love-elegy', the associations of the genre were never exclusively amatory. 'Verses unequally joined framed lamentation first, then votive epigram': Horace's interest in defining the genre in terms of its traditional origins finds some reflection in the practice of his own elegiac contemporaries. With its stress upon separation and loss, and its morbid flights of fancy (esp. in Propertius), Roman elegiac love may be implicated from the outset in funereal lament. As in Greek, the elegiac couplet is a multi-purpose metre, but its sphere of operation can often be defined negatively as 'not *epic'. The paired contrasts between public and private, martial and peaceful, hard and soft, weighty and slight which dominate the vocabulary of late republican and early imperial poetry are associated above all with an opposition between epic and elegy. Epic is constantly the term against which elegy defines itself—even in those long narrative elegies which come near to closing the gap between the two genres. Ovid's career as an elegist, from 'subjective' *Amores* to epistolary *Heroides*, didactic *Ars Amatoria*, aetiological *Fasti*, funereal *Tristia*, and vituperative *Ibis*, is the pre-eminent demonstration of the ability of a classical Roman genre to expand its range without losing its identity.

After Ovid the metre was used chiefly for epigrams and short occasional poems. The use of elegy for epigram reached a peak in the work of *Martial, whose couplets can excel Ovid's in wit and technical virtuosity.

Metre The disyllabic ending to the pentameter (see GREEK METRE, 4(b)) became the rule in Propertius' later poems and in Ovid. The strict Ovidian form of the couplet is ideally suited to pointed expression, conveyed through variation and antithesis: half-line responding to half-line, pentameter to hexameter, couplet to couplet. See HELLENISTIC POETRY AT ROME.

elements The Gk. *stoicheia* gradually became standard for 'elements'. Etymologically *stoicheion* means 'one of a series'. The term has important connotations in logic, mathematics, and discussions of scientific method as well as natural philosophy. *Aristotle defined an element as the primary constituent in something—be it object, speech, or a geometrical proof—which is indivisible into any other kind of thing. The elements of an object might be the four Empedoclean roots (see below), those of speech the letters which make up a word, or those of a geometrical proof the axioms and indemonstrables upon which the proof depends. The concept of elements is fundamental to the widely held Greek—not just Aristotelian—conceptions of science as axiomatic-deductive in character. Basic mathematical works are often called *Elements*; best-known examples include the *Elements* of *Euclid, and the *Elements of Harmonics* by *Aristoxenus.

Most of the first philosophers, Aristotle says, supposed that the only origins of all things were material. 'That out of which everything is made, that from which things first came, that into which they finally resolve, and that which persists even though modified by actions performed upon it—this they called an element, an origin of things which exist'. Aristotle reports that *Thales gave water this status, *Anaximenes air, *Anaximander 'the boundless', while *Empedocles named earth, air, fire, and water. It is far from clear that these early thinkers were really seeking to answer precisely the questions which *Aristotle attributes to them. In fact, it is likely that Empedocles' four 'roots' were the first clearly stated elemental substances into which everything in the world could be resolved. Empedocles' theory, in various forms, remained the dominant element theory for the rest of antiquity.

The early atomists Leucippus and *Democritus are credited with a different kind of theory, which sought to explain the qualitative variety in the physical world by appeals to the interaction of indivisible, impassive particles moving in a void (see ATOMISM). Plato, on the other hand, took on the four Empedoclean elements, but traced them further back to their origins in two types of elementary triangle. Throughout antiquity, there was a keen debate over the relative importance of the Empedoclean elements, and *fire's status was esp. problematic.

Among the Stoics (see STOICISM), *Zeno (2) and *Chrysippus defined the elements of the material world—earth, air, fire, and water—as substances out of which everything else is initially composed through alteration, and into which everything is dissolved, without suffering either of these fates themselves during the lifetime of a particular world.

Elephantinē, a nome-capital (see NOMOS (1)) in Upper *Egypt, on an island off Aswan below the first Nile cataract, occupied till the Arab period as a military post and custom-house on the frontier with Nubia. Jewish mercenaries formed a garrison here from the 26th Dynasty (see SAÏTES) onwards and established a temple of Yahweh. Their *papyri and *ostraka allow detailed insights into Persian administration in Egypt and the daily life of the community. Many Ptolemaic *ostraka* survive. There were temples (with nilometers).

elephants Although *ivory is mentioned in *Homer, Greeks first encountered war-elephants at *Gaugamela in 331 BC. The ivory probably came originally from Africa, but the first war-elephants were Indian. Although not used by *Alexander (2) the Great, war-elephants were used by his successors, esp. the *Seleucids and Ptolemies (see EGYPT, *Ptolemaic*).

When the Seleucids gained control of the Indian sources, the Ptolemies managed to capture and train African 'forest' elephants, then found in the hinterland of the Red Sea. Smaller than Indian elephants, they are not to be confused with East African 'bush' elephants, the latter being larger than the Indian and unknown to the ancients. The 'forest' elephant is now almost extinct. The main difference between the two types was that the Indian was large enough to carry a howdah containing one or more missile-armed soldiers in addition to the mahout, whereas the African carried a single mahout, and although he could carry javelins, the elephant itself was the main weapon. When the two types met at Raphia (217 BC), the Africans were defeated, but they were heavily outnumbered.

The Romans first encountered elephants when *Pyrrhus used Indians in his invasion of Italy. Both at Heraclea in 280 BC and at A(u)sculum Satrianum in 279, they had marked success, in the first routing the Roman cavalry—untrained horses will not face elephants—in the second actually breaching the Roman infantry line after it had been driven back by Pyrrhus' phalanx.

By this time the Carthaginians were also using African elephants, drawn from the forests of the Atlas region. They fought against the Romans in the First *Punic War, in Sicily and in the defeat of Atilius Regulus in Africa. *Hannibal, famously, took elephants across the Alps in 218. They helped win his first victory at the Trebia, but all save one died during the winter of 218/17. It carried Hannibal through the marshes of

the Arno in 217. But although Hannibal received more in 215, and used them in an attempt to break the siege of *Capua in 211, it was only at *Zama that he used them again in quantity, and there *Cornelius Scipio Africanus nullified their effectiveness by opening lanes through his ranks.

The Seleucids continued until their downfall to make use of elephants, but although the Romans also sometimes used them in war, they were mainly kept for the arena (see ANIMALS, ATTITUDES TO) or ceremonial. During the empire there was an imperial herd in *Latium. They were never used as pack-animals or for road-building.

Eleusis, the most famous *deme in Athens after *Piraeus, on a land-locked bay with a rich plain, merged with Athens sometime before the 7th cent. BC. Its hill and *sanctuary were enclosed by fortification walls in the late 6th century, and it became one of the three main fortresses for the defence of western *Attica. There was a theatre of *Dionysus there, and the sanctuary of *Demeter and Korē (See PERSEPHONE) was the site of many festivals of local or national importance, but the fame of Eleusis was due primarily to the annual festival of the *mysteries, which attracted initiates from the entire Greek-speaking world. Within the sanctuary of the Two Goddesses the earliest building that may be identified as a temple is Geometric (See POTTERY, GREEK, 2). Its replacement by increasingly larger buildings culminating in the square hall with rock-cut stands built under *Pericles, the largest public building of its time in Greece, bears witness to the ever increasing popularity of the cult. The unusual shape of this temple reflected its function as hall of initiation (usually called Anaktoron, sometimes Telesterion). Destroyed in AD 170, it was rebuilt under Marcus *Aurelius, who also brought to completion the splendid propylaea, a copy of the *Propylaea on the Athenian acropolis.

Eleven, Athenian officials, appointed by lot, who had charge of the prison and executions. They took into custody persons accused of serious theft or certain other crimes. If the thief was caught red-handed and admitted his guilt, they had him executed without trial; otherwise they presided over the court which tried him. (See LAW AND PROCEDURE, ATHENIAN.)

ēliaia, often but less correctly spelled *hēliaia,* was a meeting of Athenian citizens to try a legal case. It has generally been thought that, when *Solon introduced trials by the people in the early 6th cent. BC, the *eliaia* was simply the *ekklesia*, called by this different name when it was performing a judicial function. After the middle of the 5th cent., when a plurality of jury-courts certainly existed, the name *eliaia* was used either for all these courts collectively or for any one of them. It was also the name of a large court building, used for trials over which the *thesmothetai* presided.

Elis, the plain of NW *Peloponnese, famed for horse-breeding. In historical times it was occupied by a people related by race and language to the Aetolians, arriving from the north. The Eleans presided over the *Olympic Games. They were early and loyal allies of Sparta, until in 420 Sparta championed the independence of Lepreum, whereupon Elis joined Athens and *Argos; she was punished in 399 with the loss of Triphylia. The town of Elis on the Penēus was built c.471 BC, and replaced Olympia as a political centre. Considerable remains have been excavated, including the theatre.

Elysium (Elysian Fields or Plain), a paradise inhabited by the distinguished or (later) the good after their death. In the *Odyssey* it is the destination of Menelaus as husband of *Helen. It is situated at the ends of the earth and is the home of *Rhadamanthys; a gentle breeze always blows there, and humans can enjoy an easy life like that of the gods. Such a destiny is unique in Homer, and, as in the case of the clearly comparable *Islands of the Blest, Elysium tends to be reserved for the privileged few, although the base broadens with time. Its name may derive from Gk. *enēlysios* 'struck by lightning', death by lightning being regarded as a kind of apotheosis.

Ēmerita Augusta, a colony in SW Spain founded by Augustus in 25 BC for *veterans of *legions V and X. It was approached from the south by a 64-arch bridge. Many monuments partly survive, including an amphitheatre, circus, and temple: *Agrippa presented it with a great theatre. It also had colonial and provincial fora. Its aqueducts were fed from a large reservoir constructed near by. It was capital of Lusitania.

Empedoclēs (c.492–432 BC), a philosopher from *Acragas. Most details of his life are uncertain. There is no reason to doubt his aristocratic background, that he was involved in political life, or that he was active in both the religious and the philosophical spheres. Pythagoreanism was clearly a philosophical inspiration. Equally important was *Parmenides, whose thought shaped the basic ideas underlying Empedocles' philosophy.

Acc. to Diogenes Laertius, he was the author of two poems, *On Nature* and *Purifications*. Other authors refer to one poem or the other, not both. The relationship between these two poems is problematic, with no consensus about the distribution of the fragments. Hence the suspicion that *On Nature* and *Purifications* are alternative titles for a single work.

Empedocles is important for:

1. *His response to Parmenides*, who argued that no real thing could change or move and that the world was static. Empedocles accepted that *real* objects did not change; but against Parmenides he claimed that there could be several such things, his four 'roots' or *elements, which moved under the influence of Love and Strife. All six of Empedocles' realities were often personified as gods. The events of the world's history result from the interaction of these entities.

2. *Introducing the notion of repeated world cycles.* The influence of Love and Strife alternated; hence the history of the cosmos was cyclical. When Love is supreme, the world is a homogeneous whole; when Strife has conquered, the elements are completely separated.

3. *The claim that there are only four basic forms of perceptible matter*: earth, water, fire, and air. Empedocles thought that these forms of matter were unchangeable.

4. *The effluence theory.* A simple mechanism of pores and effluences was used to explain perception (effluences from sense-objects entering into the pores of sense organs), mixture, and many other natural processes. This notion had a major influence, esp. on *atomism.

5. *A theory of reincarnation and the transmigration of the soul.* Despite the claim that *transmigration occurs, there is no clear indication of whether the *daimonēs* (see DAIMON) which move from body to body survive for ever or only until the end of the current world cycle. His claim that even human thought is identifiable with the blood around the heart points to the physical nature of the transmigrating *daimon*.

emporion, 'a trading-post'. An *emporion* was an ad hoc community where a mixed and possibly shifting population of traders engaged in activities that would be well understood in the quarter of *Piraeus of the same name. Outside

Greece, a trading-post did not need to be established with the official acts deemed appropriate to the foundation of a true *apoikia: an *emporion* could be the result of nothing more solemn than market forces. Such was clearly the case at *Pithecusae, inhabited by Chalcidians, Eretrians, and some Levantines. This centre, however, supported a population of thousands rather than hundreds from the earliest 'pre-colonial' times so far attested archaeologically, with all that this required—and had received long before the end of the 8th cent. BC—in the way of just such organization as is commonly attributed to the *polis. At Pithecusae an *emporion* seems to have evolved into an overseas Euboean *polis*, i.e. an *apoikia*, whether officially recognized as such at home or not. The Pithecusan experience may have accelerated the development of the *polis*-concept for future use—at home no less than abroad. See TRADE, GREEK.

endogamy, marrying within (1) the citizen body or (2) the kin group. 1. Colonists and others on the margins of the Greek world often intermarried with native populations, and the Archaic élite regularly made marriage alliances with their peers in other Greek cities; prominent Athenian sons of such unions include *Themistocles and *Cimon. *Pericles' law (451/0) requiring Athenian citizens to have two citizen parents effectively precluded marriages with foreigners. Within communities, *Hesiod recommended taking a wife who lived nearby, and in Athens at least there was a tendency outside the élite to marry within the *deme (and so presumably the neighbourhood). At Rome, *conubium*, legal capacity to marry, ordinarily characterized citizens only, but cities and individuals could be granted this right as a mark of special status. Otherwise marriages were invalid. Yet they certainly occurred, esp. among soldiers debarred from marriage during service. Both Greeks and Romans tended to marry within the same social and economic class.

2. The *Bacchiads of *Corinth were reportedly endogamous, a tendency widespread in the Greek world, though generally less extreme. At both *Gortyn and *Athens the rules concerning the marriage of an heiress favoured kin, the father's brothers and their sons, and unions between uncles and nieces, first cousins, and other kin (esp. on the father's side) were regular at Athens. There is also evidence for endogamy in the royal houses of *Sparta. At Rome, however, marriages between uncle and niece were long illegal, and those between first cousins apparently less common than at Athens.

Ennius, Quintus (239–169 BC), Roman poet, an immigrant of upper-class Messapian origin brought to Rome in 204 by *Porcius Cato (1) and given the *citizenship in 184 by Fulvius Nobilior. Cato had found him serving in a Calabrian regiment of the Roman army in Sardinia. At Rome he made himself acceptable to noble clans. He lived in a modest house on the *Aventine and taught Greek and Latin grammar to the young men of the great families. He wrote plays for the public festivals down to the year of his death. He also wrote much non-dramatic verse. Fulvius Nobilior took him on his staff to Aetolia in 189. Biographers noted a fondness for alcohol (see ALCOHOLISM) and declared him to have died of gout.

In addition to numerous tragedies and a few comedies, he wrote a narrative poem in fifteen units on the history of the Roman people from the fall of Troy to the seizure of Ambracia and the triumphal return of the elder Nobilior. Its title, *Annals*, appropriated that of the record which the *pontifex maximus* kept of religiously significant events (see ANNALES MAXIMI). Instead of the ancient *Camenae*, Ennius invoked the *Muses, newly imported and given a home by Nobilior in a new temple on the *Campus Martius. He claimed to be a reincarnation of Homer and replaced *Saturnian verse with a Latin version of the dactylic *hexameter. Books 1–3 took Ennius' story down to the expulsion of the last king and the foundation of the republic; 4–6 dealt with the reduction of Etruria and Samnium and the seeing off of *Pyrrhus; 7–9 with the driving of the Carthaginians back to North Africa and the incorporation within the Roman state of the Greek cities of south Italy and Sicily; 10–12 with the campaigns of the first decade of the 2nd cent. on the Greek mainland and in Spain; 12–15 with the defeats inflicted on the Macedonian Philip V, the *Seleucid Antiochus III, and the Aetolian Confederacy. The poem emphasized the constant expansion of the Roman empire and the eclipse suffered by the Greek states which had sacked Troy and by their descendants. The gods of Olympus were made to support and assist the expansion. There was little on the other hand about the internal politics of the city of Rome. A number of Ennius' themes were foreign to the old Greek epic tradition. e.g. autobiography, literary polemic, grammatical erudition, and philosophical speculation. Ennius added a further three books to the *Annals* in the last years of his life.

Ennius wrote pieces on *Cornelius Scipio Africanus (d. 184). The notion that Scipio's soul might have been assumed into heaven went against conventional Roman doctrine on the after-life, as did the deification of Romulus. The *Epicharmus* presented an account of the gods and the physical operations of the universe. The poet dreamed he had been transported after death to a place of heavenly enlightenment.

The *Euhēmerus* presented a very different theological doctrine in a mock-simple prose modelled on the Greek of *Euhemerus and earlier theological writers. Acc. to this doctrine, the gods of Olympus were not supernatural powers still actively intervening in the affairs of men, but great generals, statesmen, and inventors of olden times commemorated after death in extraordinary ways. The relationship of such a view to what Ennius expounded elsewhere can only be guessed at. The remains of six books of *Satires* show a wide variety of metres. A frequent theme was the social life of Ennius himself and his upper-class Roman friends and their intellectual conversation.

Ennius stands out among Latin writers for the variety of his work. Some of his tragedies were still performed during the late republic. The *Annals* was carefully studied by *Cicero, *Lucretius, *Catullus, *Virgil, *Ovid, and *Lucan. Recitations were given during the time of *Hadrian. See TRAGEDY, LATIN.

Ēōs, the goddess of the dawn, daughter of the sun-god *Hyperion. In Homer her formulaic epithets are 'rosy-fingered' and 'saffron-robed', reflecting the pale shades of the dawn sky; and while the Sun himself has a four-horse chariot, Eos, to mark her subsidiary status, is content with a chariot and pair.

Her mythology centres on her role as a predatory lover: she carries off the handsome hunters *Cephalus or Orion as they stalk their own prey in the morning twilight, or seizes the Trojan prince Tithonus to be her heavenly gigolo. It is the latter whose bed she leaves when day breaks at the start of *Odyssey*. bk. 5, and by whom she became the mother of *Memnon, the eastern warrior-prince and Trojan ally. She begged immortality for Tithonus from *Zeus, but forgot to ask for eternal youth to go with it, so that he shrivelled away until nothing was left but a wizened, piping husk (hence the origin of the cicadas); she locked him into a room and threw away the key. The explanation of these stories,

in which a goddess's love is used as a metaphor for death, is to be found in the Greek practice of conducting funerals at night, with the *soul departing at daybreak.

In art she is usually winged, first appearing in the 6th cent. BC in scenes concerning the death of her son: she balances *Thetis in the *psychostasia* ('weighing') of the fates of *Achilles and Memnon or at the fight itself, or (on Duris' fine cup in the Louvre) she weeps over his corpse in a moving *pietà*. For the 5th cent. the favoured theme is the pursuit and abduction of Cephalus or Tithonus.

Epamīnondas (d. 362 BC), Theban general, victor at the battles of *Leuctra and *Mantinea. By 371 he was one of the Boeotarchs (Boeotian federal officials), and, as such, represented Thebes at the peace conference in Sparta, walking out when *Agesilaus II refused to allow him to take the oath on behalf of the Boeotians as a whole.

Although all seven Boeotarchs were at Leuctra, Epaminondas was clearly regarded as the architect of victory, and was re-elected for 370. Late in the year he went to the aid of the Arcadians (of central Peloponnese), and was largely responsible for the crucial decision to press on with the the invasion of the Spartan homeland—the first in historical times—and, above all, to free *Messenia. In the summer of 369 he led a second invasion of Peloponnese, which succeeded in further eroding Spartan influence, without quite matching previous triumphs. But his successes and, possibly, high-handed behaviour, aroused jealousy, and he was not re-elected Boeotarch for 368. Re-elected for 367, his third invasion of Peloponnese finally put an end to Sparta's 300-year-old *Peloponnesian League. The removal of the fear of Sparta, however, aroused old antagonisms, and by 362 Thebes found herself fighting many of her erstwhile allies in alliance with Sparta. At the battle of Mantinea, Epaminondas was killed in the moment of victory.

Though an innovative tactician, Epaminondas' strategic and political sense may be questioned. But his traditional nobility of character presumably reflects how he appeared to contemporaries, and he possibly lacked the ruthlessness necessary to impose Thebes' will on her quarrelsome allies, once they had ceased to fear Sparta. He may honestly have wanted to create an alliance of independent states in which Thebes would be no more than first among equals.

Epaphrodītus, *Nero's freedman and secretary, received military honours for helping him unmask the Pisonian conspiracy (see CAL-PURNIUS PISO, GAIUS) and accompanied him in his final flight. He was again secretary for petitions of *Domitian, by whom he was killed (AD 95), apparently because he had helped Nero to commit suicide. *Epictetus was his slave.

ephēboi originally meant boys who had reached the age of puberty, and was one of several terms for age classes; but in 4th-cent. BC Athens it came to have a special paramilitary sense, boys who in their nineteenth year had entered a two-year period of military training. In the first year they underwent, in barracks in Piraeus, training by *paidotribai* (physical trainers) and technical weaponry instructors, all under the general supervision of a *kosmētēs* and of ten *sōphronistai*, one from each of the tribes (*phylai). In the second year they served at the frontier posts of Attica as *peripoloi*.

Despite the military amateurism of which Thucydides (2) makes Pericles boast, it is unlikely that there was no system of training before the 4th cent., and traces of the later 'oath of the ephebes' have been detected in Thucydides and *Sophocles. And structuralist accounts of the ephebate bring out its function as a rite of passage; they point to the marginal character of service on the frontiers and to the civic exemptions and exclusions to which ephebes were subject, i.e. ephebes were made non-hoplites in preparation for being real *hoplites. But there is no hard evidence for a formal ephebic system before the mid-330s.

From the 3rd cent. BC the *ephēbeia*, based on the *gymnasium, was a universal feature of the *polis. The institution flourished for as long as the *polis*. It had become a civic instrument for relaying a basic and surprisingly uniform cultural Hellenism to the rising generation.

Ephesus, city at the mouth of the river Caÿster on the west coast of *Asia Minor, which rivalled and finally displaced *Miletus as the seaport of the Maeander valley. It was founded by *Ionians. It did little at sea before Hellenistic times, was oligarchic in temper, and open to indigenous influences. The city maintained itself against the Cimmerians and also *Lydia until its capture by *Croesus, who contributed to the construction of the great temple of Artemis. Under *Persia it shared the fortunes of the other coastal cities; it was a member of the *Delian League, but revolted c.412 BC and sided

with Sparta. The Archaic temple of Artemis, burnt down in 356, was rebuilt in the 4th cent., the Ephesians refusing *Alexander (2) the Great's offer to fund the cost. The city was replanned by *Lysimachus, and passed with *Attalus III's kingdom of *Pergamum to Rome in 133. An enthusiastic supporter of *Mithradates VI (88–85 BC), it was deprived by Sulla of its free status. Under the Principate it eclipsed Pergamum as the economic and administrative hub of provincial *Asia (See PORTORIA). Seat of Roman officialdom and one of the province's original *conventus* centres, it was also its chief centre for the (Roman) *ruler-cult. Acts 19 gives a vivid picture of the Artemisium's religious and economic importance for the Roman city.

ephetai were an Athenian jury, 51 in number. In the 5th cent. BC they seem to have been selected by lot from the members of the *Areopagus and to have been concerned with homicide cases only. Under the presidency of the *basileus* (see ARCHONTES) they tried almost all kinds of homicide not considered important enough for trial by the Areopagus itself.

Ephialtēs, Athenian politician, about whom little is known. In the late 460s he became the leading opponent of *Cimon. He resisted the sending of help to the *Spartans in 462 during the *helot revolt, on the ground that Sparta was Athens' rival for power. Supported by *Pericles, he took advantage of Cimon's absence, or less probably of the feeling of anger on his dismissal from Sparta, to pass measures taking from the *Areopagus its judicial powers of political importance. This aroused such strong feelings that Cimon was ostracized (see OSTRACISM), but later Ephialtes was assassinated.

ephors, probably 'overseers', civil magistrates attested in several Dorian states besides *Sparta. Here, the board of five were elected annually by the citizens (by an 'excessively childish' procedure, acc. to *Aristotle), and the senior ephor gave his name to the year. Combining executive, judicial, and disciplinary powers, and unconstrained by written laws, they dominated the everyday running of affairs, subject only to the requirement of majority agreement and the knowledge that their office was held for one year only and was unrepeatable. The eligibility of all Spartans for the office and their relationship with the kingship suggest that the ephors were created in some sense as popular, anti-aristocratic officials.

Each month they exchanged oaths with the kings, the king swearing to rule according to the city's established laws, the ephors swearing on behalf of the city to keep the king's position unshaken so long as he abided by his oath. The balance of obligation is clear. The ephors had a general control over the kings' conduct, could prosecute them before the Spartan supreme court (*gerousia* (council of elders) plus ephors), settle disputes between them, and enforce their appearance before their own board at the third summons. Two ephors accompanied the kings on campaign. Spartan political history was not, however, a straightforward contest between kings on the one hand and ephors on the other.

In administration they negotiated with representatives of other states, convened and presided over the assembly, supervised the state educational regime (See AGOGE), and gave orders for the mobilization and dispatch of the army. They could depose and prosecute other officials. In major political trials they both presided and executed the sentences. They dealt more summarily with the *perioikoi*, and most summarily of all with the *helots*, over whom they exercised an arbitrary power of life and death through the *krypteia*.

Ephorus, of *Cyme (c.405–330 BC), a historian whose lost work is important because *Diodorus (2) Siculus followed it extensively. The 30-book *History* avoided the mythological period, beginning with the Return of the *Heraclids and reaching the siege of Perinthus, in 340. His work was grand in scope and far longer than 5th-cent. histories. Acc. to *Polybius, he was the first universal historian, combining a focus on Greek history with events in the barbarian east. Ephorus provided each book with a separate proem. Individual books were apparently devoted to a particular area (southern and central Greece, Macedonia, Sicily, Persia), but within each book events were sometimes retold episodically, sometimes synchronically.

Ephorus drew on diverse sources, at times using good judgement (he preferred the *Oxyrhynchus historian to *Xenophon), at other times making unfortunate choices (he coloured *Thucydides' (2) account with material from 4th-cent. pamphleteers). Esp. interesting to Ephorus were migrations, the founding of cities, and family histories (see GENEALOGY).

The *History* was widely quoted in antiquity and was generally commended for its accuracy (except in military descriptions). In paraphrasing Ephorus, Diodorus supplies crucial information, esp. about 4th-cent. mainland history.

epic The purely metrical ancient definition of epic as verse in successive *hexameters includes such works as *Hesiod's *didactic poems and the philosophical poems of the Presocratics. In its narrower, and now usual, acceptance 'epic' refers to hexameter narrative poems on the deeds of gods, heroes, and men, a kind of poetry at the summit of the ancient hierarchy of *genres. The cultural authority of epic throughout antiquity is inseparable from the name of *Homer, generally held to be the earliest and greatest of Greek poets; the *Iliad* and the *Odyssey* establish norms for the presentation of the heroes and their relation with the gods, and for the omniscience of the inspired epic narrator. Acc. to Herodotus (2. 53), Homer and Hesiod established the names, functions, and forms of the Greek gods.

Epic in Rome begins with *Livius Andronicus' translation in *Saturnian verse of the *Odyssey* (3rd cent. BC). This was followed by *Naevius' historical epic in Saturnians, his *Punic War*. The commemorative and panegyrical functions of epic esp. appealed to the Romans; for a century and a half the classic Roman epic was *Ennius' *Annals*, the hexameter narrative of Roman history (finished before 169). Republican generals and statesmen had themselves commemorated in both Greek and Latin epics; *Cicero composed autobiographical epics on his own successes. *Virgil revolutionized the genre by combining the legendary and the historical strands of epic in the *Aeneid*, which immediately established itself as the central classic of Roman literature. Later Latin epics, both legendary (*Ovid's *Metamorphoses*, *Statius' *Thebaid*, *Valerius Flaccus' *Argonautica*) and historical (*Lucan's *Civil War*, *Silius Italicus' *Punica*), are composed through a continuous dialogue with the *Aeneid*.

Epic Cycle, a collection of early Greek epics, artificially arranged in a series so as to make a narrative extending from the beginning of the world to the end of the heroic age. Apart from the *Iliad* and *Odyssey* (See HOMER), we possess only meagre fragments of the poems involved, and our knowledge of what poems were involved is itself incomplete. We are best informed about those that dealt with the Trojan War and related events: there were six besides the *Iliad* and *Odyssey*, and summaries of their contents are preserved in some Homer manuscripts.

2. The poems were composed by various men, mainly or wholly in the 7th and 6th cents. BC. The Cycle is not mentioned as a whole before the 2nd cent. AD. But a Trojan Cycle, at least, seems to have been drawn up not later than the 4th cent. BC.

3. The Cyclic poems (this term by convention excludes the *Iliad* and *Odyssey*) were sometimes loosely attributed to Homer; but *Herodotus rejects this for the *Cypria* and queries it for the *Epigoni*, and later writers generally use the names of obscurer poets or the expression 'the author of (the *Cypria*, etc.)'. The poems seem to have been well known in the 5th and 4th cents., but little read later.

4. The poems known or presumed to have been included in the Cycle were as follows.

(1) In first place stood a theogony.

(2) *Titanomachia*.

(3) *Oedipodia*.

(4) *Thebais*. Highly esteemed by *Pausanias (3). See SEVEN AGAINST THEBES.

(5) *Epigoni*. Cited by Herodotus and parodied by *Aristophanes. See EPIGONI.

(6) *Cypria*. The poem dealt with the preliminaries of the Trojan War (wedding of Peleus and Thetis, judgement of Paris, rape of Helen) and all the earlier part of the war down to the point where the *Iliad* begins. The title seems to refer to the poem's place of origin.

(7) *Iliad*. There were alternative versions of the beginning and end which linked it with the adjacent poems.

(8) *Aethiopis*. The main events were the deaths of the *Amazon Penthesilea, *Thersites, *Memnon, and Achilles. The title refers to Memnon's Ethiopians.

(9) *Little Iliad*. The suicide of *Aias (1), the fetching of *Philoctetes and *Neoptolemus, the Wooden Horse, Sinon, the entry into Troy. The poem must have acquired the name *Ilias* independently of the *Iliad*, and then been called 'little' to distinguish it.

(10) *Sack of Troy*. The Trojan debate about the horse, *Laocoön, the sack of Troy, and departure of the Greeks. Aeneas left the city before the sack, not as in Virgil.

(11) *Homecomings*. The returns of various Greek heroes, ending with the murder of *Agamemnon, *Orestes' revenge, and *Menelaus' homecoming. The *Odyssey* alludes to these events—so much that it cannot have been intended to accompany the *Homecomings*—and its poet knew 'the Homecoming of the Achaeans', as a theme of song.

(12) *Odyssey*. Aristophanes of Byzantium and *Aristarchus (2) put the end of the poem at 23. 296, and so perhaps counted what followed as part of the *Telegony*.

(13) *Telegony*. An element of romantic fiction was conspicuous here (see ODYSSEUS).

Epictētus (mid-1st to 2nd cent. AD), Stoic philosopher from Hierapolis in Phrygia; in early life a slave of *Epaphroditus in Rome. Eventually freed by his master, he studied with Musonius Rufus. Epictetus taught in Rome until *Domitian banished the philosophers in 89. He set up a school at Nicopolis (see ACTIUM), where his reputation attracted many upper-class Romans. *Arrian published the oral teachings (*Discourses*) of Epictetus. Four books of these survive, along with a summary of key teachings known as the *Manual*. These writings and his personal reputation influenced Marcus *Aurelius; the *Manual* has been an inspirational book in both ancient and modern times.

Epictetus' teaching took two forms. He taught basic works of *Stoicism, esp. those of *Chrysippus, and shows considerable familiarity with technical matters. In the *Discourses*, however, he stresses the need to put philosophical sophistication to work in reforming moral character; learning is of little value for its own sake.

Epictetus' philosophy was largely consistent with earlier Stoicism, although its idiom differs markedly. A major doctrinal innovation was his commitment to the innate character of moral beliefs; for earlier Stoics, such ideas were natural but not innate. New also was the arrangement of his teaching: Epictetus divided it into three 'themes', concerning (1) the control of desires and passions, (2) actions, and (3) assent. Other leading ideas include: (*a*) a contrast between what is 'up to' the agent and what is not; beliefs, desires, plans, reactions, and interpretations of experience are up to us, while events which happen to us are not. This leads him to emphasize the *use* we make of our presentations in contrast to their mere reception. (*b*) An intense focus on the power of individual moral choice. (*c*) The Socratic claim that all men act according to what they believe to be good for them; hence, the proper response to moral error is an effort at education and not anger. (*d*) A powerful belief in divine providence. He interprets the rational, cosmic deity of Stoicism in a more personal sense with an emphasis on the need to harmonize one's will with that of the deity.

Epicūrus (b. *Samos, 341 BC; d. Athens, 270), moral and natural philosopher. His father and mother, Athenians, emigrated to the Athenian *cleruchy in Samos. He served as an *ephebe in Athens, when Xenocratēs was head of the *Academy and *Aristotle was in *Chalcis. He rejoined his family, who had settled on the Asian mainland at Colophon. At this time or earlier he learnt about the *atomist philosophy of *Democritus. At 32 he moved to *Mytilene, then to Lampsacus; at both places he set up a school and began to acquire pupils and loyal friends.

About 307/6 he bought a house in Athens, with a garden that became the eponymous headquarters of his school of philosophy. Apart from occasional visits to Asia Minor, he stayed in Athens until his death, when he left his garden and school to Hermarchus of Mytilene (his will survives).

The Epicurean School (The Garden). He and his followers lived together, secluding themselves from the affairs of the city and maintaining a modest and even austere life style, in accordance with the Master's teaching. They included slaves and women. Contemporary Epicureans mentioned in the literature were his most devoted companion, Metrodorus of Lampsacus, who died before Epicurus; Leontius and his wife Themista, also of Lampsacus; Hermarchus, his successor; and a slave called Mys.

The school was much libelled in antiquity and later, perhaps because of its determined privacy, and because of Epicurus' professed hedonism. The qualifications that brought this hedonism close to *asceticism were ignored, and members of rival schools accused the Epicureans of many kinds of profligacy. In Christian times, Epicureanism was anathema because it taught that man is mortal, that the cosmos is the result of accident, that there is no providential god, and that the criterion of the good life is pleasure.

Writings Diogenes Laertius reports that Epicurus wrote more than any other philosopher—about 300 rolls. Most of them are now lost. Fragments of his 37 books *On Nature* survive at *Herculaneum, and efforts to restore and interpret them, begun *c.*1800, are now proceeding with renewed vigour. The following three letters and two collections of maxims have been preserved intact: (1) Letter to Herodotus: a summary of his philosophy of nature; (2) Letter to Pythocles: a summary of astronomy and *meteorology; (3) Letter to Menoeceus: a summary of Epicurean morality; (4) *Kȳriai doxai*, or *Principal Doctrines*: 40 moral maxims.

Modern knowledge and appreciation of Epicurean philosophy depends heavily on the Latin epic poem of his later follower, *Lucretius' *De rerum natura* ('On the Nature of Things').

Doctrines The purpose of philosophy is practical: to secure a happy life. Hence moral philosophy is the most important branch, and physics and epistemology are subsidiary.

1. Epistemology

Epicurus held that sense perception is the origin of knowledge, and defended its reliability with a physical account of it. Physical objects, being made of atoms, give off from their surface thin films of atoms, called *eidōla*, which retain the shape and some other characteristics of their parent body and implant its appearance on the sense organs of the perceiver. This appearance is somehow transmitted to the soul-atoms which constitute the mind. The appearance itself is never false: falsehood occurs only in the opinion that the mind forms about it. If appearances conflict, a closer look or a sound argument or experience of the context may serve to 'counter-witness' all but one consistent set of opinions: in some cases (esp. in astronomy, where no closer look is possible) we must accept that all beliefs not counter-witnessed are somehow true.

Epicurus was apparently unable to articulate an explanation of concept-formation and theorizing by minds made of atoms and void. The extant texts show frequent use of analogical reasoning, from phenomena to theoretical entities.

2. Physics

Epicurus adopted the atomist theories (see ATOMISM) of Democritus, with some changes that can often be seen as attempts to answer Aristotle's criticisms.

The original atomist theory was a response to *Parmenides, *Zeno (1), and *Melissus. Arguments about Being and Not-being show that there must be permanent elements—atoms of matter. Arguments about divisibility show that there must be indivisibles—construed by Epicurus as inseparable parts of atoms. The observed fact of motion proves that there must be empty space in which atoms can move.

Change is explained as the rearrangement of unchangeable atoms. The universe is infinite, both in the number of atoms and in the extent of space. Our cosmos, bounded by the region of the heavenly bodies, came into being through random collisions of suitable atoms, and it will some day dissolve again into its component atoms. It is one of an indefinite number of cosmoi, past, present, and future.

Atoms move naturally downwards at constant and equal speed because of their weight, unless they collide with others. But they would never collide unless some of them sometimes swerved from the straight downward path. (This postulate, which also accounts for the self-motions of animals (see below), is not mentioned in any surviving text of Epicurus, but is set out at some length by Lucretius, mentioned by other classical writers, and generally agreed to have been advanced by Epicurus himself.)

Gods exist, atomic compounds like everything else, but take no thought for this cosmos or any other, living an ideal life of eternal, undisturbed happiness—the Epicurean ideal. It is good for men to respect and admire them, without expecting favours or punishments from them. Both creation, as in *Plato's Timaeus*, and the eternity of the cosmic order, as in Aristotle's world picture, are rejected: natural movements of atoms are enough to explain the origin and growth of everything in the world. A theory of the survival of the fittest explains the apparently purposeful structure of living things.

Epicurus was a thoroughgoing physicalist in his philosophy of mind. The *soul is composed of atoms, all extremely small but distinguished by shape into four kinds: fire, air, and breath (but all somehow different from their ordinary namesakes), and a fourth, unnamed kind. At death the component atoms are dispersed. The swerve of atoms somehow accounts for the possibility of actions performed by choice, by humans and some other animals: without the swerve, apparently, all actions would be as fully determined as the fall of a stone dropped from a height. How this works is a matter of continuing controversy.

3. Moral philosophy

'We say that pleasure is the beginning and end of living happily.' It is a datum of experience that pleasure is naturally and congenitally the object of human life. Since it is a fact, however, that some pleasures are temporary and partial, and involve pain as well, it is necessary to distinguish between pleasures, and to take only those which are not outweighed by pains. Pain is caused by unsatisfied desire; so one must recognize that those desires that are natural and necessary are easily satisfied; others are unnecessary. The limit of pleasure is the removal of pain; to seek always for more pleasure is simply to spoil one's present pleasure with the pain of unsatisfied desire. Pleasure is not so much the process of satisfying desires but rather the state of having desires satisfied.

Pleasure of the soul, consisting mainly of contemplation or expectation of bodily pleasure, is more valuable than bodily pleasure. The ideal is *ataraxia*, tranquillity. The study of philosophy is the best way to achieve the ideal. By teaching that the soul, made of atoms as the body is, dies with the body, it persuades us that after death there is no feeling: what happens after our death, like what happened before our birth, is 'nothing to us'. By teaching that the gods do not interfere and that the physical world is explained by natural causes, it frees us from the fear of the supernatural. By teaching that the competitive life is to be avoided, it removes the distress of envy and failure; by teaching one how to avoid intense emotional commitments, it frees us from the pain of emotional turmoil.

Epicurean moral philosophy thus finds room for most of the conventional Greek virtues of the soul; its main difficulty is to justify the virtues that are concerned with the well-being of other people—esp. justice. Those who are wise will avoid injustice, Epicurus argues, because one can never be certain of remaining undetected. But Epicurean morality was less selfish than such statements made it appear. The Epicurean communities were famous even among their enemies for the friendship which bound members to each other and to the founder. See also DIOGENES (3) OF OENOANDA.

Epidaurus, one of the small states of the Argolic Acte, on a peninsula of the Saronic Gulf. By the Classical period it was recognized as a *Dorian community. Its best-preserved monument is the theatre. The *sanctuary of Asclepius lies some 7 km. ($4\frac{1}{2}$ mi.) inland, towards *Argos, near a small sanctuary of Apollo Maleatas. The healing-cult of Apollo's son *Asclepius, elevated to divine status, seems to have been given impetus by the effects of the *plague at the time of the Peloponnesian War, developing considerably in the 4th cent. The temple was built *c*.370. Adjacent to it was the *abaton*, where the sick spent the night in hope of a healing visitation from the god (see INCUBATION).

Epigoni, sons of the '*Seven against Thebes': as with the latter, the names and number vary. The sons succeeded where their fathers had failed, drove the Cadmeans out of Thebes, and restored Thersander to the throne sought by his father Polynices. All the Epigoni but one survived.

epigram, Greek

Archaic An epigram was originally an inscription on an object or monument to say whose it is or who made it, who dedicated it to which god, or who is buried beneath it. The earliest known are in *hexameters, but by c.500 they were predominantly in what was to be the classic metre of epigram, the elegiac couplet (see METRE, GREEK, 3–4). The earliest consist largely of formulae plus the appropriate proper names in stereotyped epicizing phraseology.

Classical Epigrams written for monuments are normally anonymous; the earliest signed by the author date from c.350. The first poet credited with writing epigrams is *Simonides, though only one of the many ascribed to him can be accepted, the simple and dignified epitaph on the seer Megistias. Many others are attributed in Hellenistic and later times to famous poets. It is hard to believe *Euripides wrote the undistinguished couplet that *Plutarch read on a monument to the Athenians who died in Sicily, but there seems no reason to doubt *Aristotle's authorship of the epigram on a statue of his friend Hermias at Delphi.

See too ANTHOLOGY and individual epigrammatists, esp. MELEAGER (2).

epigram, Latin The use of metrical inscriptions in Latin is attested from the second half of the 3rd cent. BC. The two oldest epitaphs in the tomb of the Scipios are in *Saturnians, and limit themselves to a sober indication of the name, career, achievements, and civic virtues of the subject, in accordance with traditional Roman models for the praise of the great. More elaborate are the two Scipionic inscriptions in Saturnians, c.150, which lament figures whose early deaths prevented their attaining glory. There is little trace of Greek culture or style in these early epitaphs, but the Latin taste for such verbal effects as alliteration and antithesis is much in evidence.

*Ennius introduced into Latin not only the *hexameter but also the elegiac couplet (see METRE, GREEK, 3–4), the usual metre of Greek epigram. All the extant epigrams of Ennius preserve the norms of Roman honorific inscriptions. Two refer to the tomb of Scipio Africānus. The sober, monumental solemnity, the recall to communal values (Ennius celebrates his role as poet of Roman glory), and the usual verbal

effects of archaic Latin style recall the Scipionic inscriptions, but the metre, the density of expression (three of the epigrams consist of a single couplet), the motif of the dead man speaking in the first-person from his tomb and declining lament, the elevated conception of the poet's role, and the fact that he dedicates an epigram to himself as poet—all these are to be explained by Ennius' grafting of Hellenistic Greek culture onto the Roman tradition. Inscriptional verse, esp. epitaphs, continued to develop. There is clear evidence for a degree of professional composition, using a repertory of formulae and motifs dealing with the dead, their virtues, their survival through renown or the affection of their loved ones, and the loss felt at their departure.

From the end of the 2nd cent., the band of Greek intellectuals attached to the great Roman families began to include epigrammatists, whose poems served as a cultured accompaniment and ornament for the lives of their patrons. The epigram now became the ideal genre for the leisure hours of the refined upper-class amateur. This composition of everyday minor verse at Rome increased in the time of Caesar and Augustus. It was still practised by Greek epigrammatists living in Roman high society, and it was an important element in the work of *Catullus and the other 'new' poets, who wrote short poems to accompany gifts, to console or thank, invite or congratulate, to celebrate (seriously or humorously) the most diverse events of the society in which they lived, and to engage in polemic and invective on public or private matters. The Catullan or neoteric 'revolution' was the use of this genre and language to express an intensely personal emotional world and to affirm a system of values in which even the smallest day-to-day event, rather than being merely the subject of amateur versifying, became the occasion for poetry of the highest level. In this way, Catullus gave dignity to Roman minor verse, and became its classic practitioner. He never uses epigraphic forms: they are avoided even in the poems for the death of his brother (101) and the sparrow (3).

*Martial considers Catullus the canonical model of Latin epigram. His own epigrams reflect above all the varied and lively nature of the preceding Roman tradition: they offer homage and celebrate events public and private, accompany the events of everyday social life and turn them into elegant expressions of culture, offer space for moral reflection and for literary and personal polemic, and entertain with pungent wit, jokes, and pornography. He develops the satiric epigram and the epigram as a part of social relationships: i.e. precisely those aspects which seem to most 'epigrammatic'.

epigraphy, Greek, the study of inscriptions engraved on stone or metal in Greek letters. Interest in inscriptions is not a modern phenomenon; in antiquity people studied specific inscriptions. In the early 3rd cent. BC Craterus published a collection of Athenian decrees in at least nine books, with extensive commentary. With the Renaissance, interest in antiquities went hand in hand with admiration for the ancient literary inheritance. With Cyriac of Ancona there began a long series of travelling scholars, who in their notebooks produced beautiful descriptions and drawings of ancient sites and the inscriptions on them. Initially, inscriptions tended to be disregarded or even despised by the champions of the revered literary sources; but when the latter came under the attack of Cartesian rationalism and Pyrrhonian scepticism, epigraphical shares increased in value on the historical stock exchange: inscriptions were authentic and direct and could not be disqualified as forgeries or highly biased accounts. Since then, inscriptions have increasingly become part of the standard menu of scholars interested in any aspect of Greek civilization and society.

First find your inscriptions: excavations and research-motivated travel are the two main sources. Modern construction-work hitting on ancient substructures, the demolition of an old house, a peasant ploughing his land: these all can produce inscriptions which the modern traveller may (or may not) be lucky enough to find on his path. Some finds may reach the local museums; others find their way illegally to the European and American antiquities market; still more end up as building material in new peasant dwellings or are simply smashed. Systematic excavations of urban centres and temple complexes yield(ed) numerous texts: *Delphi, *Delos, the Athenian agora (see ATHENS, TOPOGRAPHY), *Olympia, Thasos, *Ephesus, Priene, *Claros are examples of sites which were highly productive. Once an inscription has been found, the next stage is that of cleaning and deciphering it. The human eye may be helped by a photo or a paper or latex squeeze. Inscriptions are engraved in uninterrupted lines of capitals; punctuation is virtually non-existent, though in Roman times dots are occasionally used to separate words, but never systematically. The Greeks began to write in the early Archaic period (8th cent. BC):

initially brief texts on ceramics and on stone, betraying the Semitic origin of the script. Where and when exactly the borrowing from the Semites took place remains disputable. It probably happened in a NW Semitic setting shortly after 800. The so-called *boustrophedon* style, in which lines, like ploughing oxen, move from right to left, from left to right, and so on until the end, is an adaptation of the Semitic habit of writing from right to left. In due course a general *koinē*-alphabet (see GREEK LANGUAGE; ALPHABET) came into existence, whose letter-forms slowly evolved between the Classical and the Roman imperial period. For decipherment a clear eye and knowledge of the Greek capital script as given in any grammar for beginners will suffice; for further judgement on the style of lettering and the ensuing date of the text, certain general principles have to be applied in combination with the most intricate technical expertise.

Inscriptions are often mutilated: either the format of the entire text is preserved but the wear and tear of time has obscured various letters or lines; or part of the stone is missing. In both cases the art of restoring illegible passages or half-preserved lines has to be applied. Restorations can be offered only on the basis of parallels. One must be able to recognize certain key terms or expressions which are characteristic of a specific category of texts (e.g. a dedication, an honorary decree for a specific category of people). After having collected a fair sample of unrestored parallel-texts one might be able to offer some suggestions. In other words, restoration of mutilated inscriptions enlarges our dossier of related texts; it does not enlarge our knowledge of ancient phenomena. Finally, the interpretation of the deciphered and, if possible, restored text must be attempted, i.e. the application of up-to-date knowledge of the larger context of our text. This presupposes a detailed knowledge of the main categories of inscriptions and their local varieties (epitaphs, epigrams, dedications, decrees, royal/imperial letters) and a decent command of what is already known from other sources about specific persons or topics recorded in our text.

Inscriptions were ubiquitous in ancient cities: in the *agora, in *sanctuaries and in *cemeteries. Lately there has been lively study of the relation between the omnipresence of inscribed stones (plus graffiti) and *literacy; in addition attention has been drawn to the symbolic value of inscriptions, often so long and occasionally put up so high on a wall that nobody actually could, or probably wanted to, read them. Studies of 'the epigraphic habit' and the reasons for both the growth and decline of inscribed stones under the empire will shed further light on the formation of the political culture and mentality of late antiquity.

Inscriptions function as a sort of '*archive' for the historian. They are not archival documents. In fact they are a selection of the papyrus documents stored in city archives. It is in the Hellenistic-Roman period that city archives became important: not only public documents but also private records were stored (and thereby ratified) in archives. Not all texts stored in archives were inscribed on stone; nor did all the inscribed ones survive the wear and tear of time. So, surviving inscriptions have undergone a double process of selection; through their mere number and the enormous variety in their subject-matter, for the ancient historian they are the equivalent of the more systematically preserved paper archives studied by the medievalist and the early modern historian.

epigraphy, Latin, the study of Latin texts inscribed on durable objects, usually of stone or bronze. It is concerned both with the form of the inscriptions and with their content, and so impinges on many other fields, e.g. art history, *palaeography, *linguistics, history, law, religion.

The epigraphist must first decipher all that can be read on the inscribed object, however badly damaged, and then, where possible, propose restorations of what is illegible or lost: processes for which modern techniques, such as computer-enhanced photographs and computerized indices of formulae, are currently supplementing long-standing aids, such as photographs taken in raking lights and squeezes (impressions made with absorbent paper or latex). The resulting text can then be interpreted as a historical document.

The texts may be formal documents such as laws, treaties, legal contracts, wills, or records of individuals and their activities, whether inscribed in their honour, at their commission, or, quite casually, by themselves (*graffiti*); epitaphs form the largest single group (see EPIGRAM, LATIN). The earliest show the *Latin language at a date well before any surviving literature, the later its development in everyday usage. They can give information on governmental policy and administration, on persons and events, and on many aspects of life and thought on which the literary sources are silent

or inadequate. The cumulative evidence even of trivial examples may be enlightening; and any text may prove more informative than it appears, if it is considered in its archaeological context.

epiphany occurs in both myth and cult when a god reveals his presence or manifests his power to a mortal or group of mortals, who 'see' or 'recognize' the god. Gods may appear in anthropomorphic form (as extraordinarily beautiful or larger than life; in the likeness of their cult statue; or disguised as ordinary mortals), as a disembodied voice, or as animals. Divine epiphanies take the form of waking or *dream visions; they may be accompanied by miracles or other displays of power, be protective or punitive; they may be sudden and spontaneous, or occur in response to a prayer. The concept is much older than the term. From Homer onwards, epiphany scenes constitute an essential element of epic narrative (Athena in *Iliad* 1, and *Odyssey*) and hymnic poetry (self-revelation of *Demeter, *Aphrodite, and *Dionysus in their respective *Homeric *Hymns*). Stage epiphanies are more frequent in tragedy than in extant comedy. From the 4th cent. onwards, epiphany emerges increasingly as a function of cult. Throughout the Hellenistic period, collections of divine epiphanies promoted faith and served religious propaganda in the cults of such gods as *Asclepius, *Apollo, Athena, as well as *Isis and Sarapis. In contrast to the importance of omens (see PORTENTS), epiphany is not a feature of Roman state religion. However, Roman poets and historians freely adapted Greek epiphanic conventions.

epitaphios (sc. *logos*), a funeral speech, delivered, according to Athenian custom, by a citizen chosen on grounds of intellect and distinction (Thucydides 2. 34, perhaps just a way of introducing *Pericles), at a public funeral of the war-dead of the previous campaigning season. This practice, said to have been unique to Athens and perhaps introduced 464 BC, was continued into Roman times, and the occasion was clearly solemn and important. But before *Hyperides the only certain names of speakers chosen are those of Pericles in 440 and 431, *Demosthenes (2) after the battle of *Chaeronea (338), and Archinus at some date in between.

The conventional form comprised: tribute to the virtues of the dead, sometimes with particular reference to their youth; summary of their country's glorious achievements in the past (esp. in the *Persian Wars (Marathon, Salamis), but see also ATTIC CULTS AND MYTHS, last para.); *consolation to relatives; and exhortation to the survivors to imitate their virtues. *Thucydides (2) purports to give in full the Funeral Speech delivered by Pericles at the end of the first year of the *Peloponnesian War, but this speech may have been idiosyncratic in its concentration on the Athens of the present and its silence on the after-life.

As a contrast to the impersonal austerity of Pericles we have the speech of Hyperides on *Leosthenes (a personal friend) and the other dead of the *Lamian War. We also have a florid fragment by *Gorgias; *Lysias, which may be genuinely Lysianic; and Demosthenes 60 (not genuinely Demosthenic). Finally, *Socrates in Plato's *Menexenus* recites a funeral speech implausibly said to have been composed by *Aspasia for delivery by Pericles. See also LAUDĀTIO FUNEBRIS.

epithalamium, a song (or speech) given 'at the bridal chamber (Gk. *thalamos*)'; a regular feature of marriages (see MARRIAGE CEREMONIES). Strictly speaking, it is distinct from the general 'wedding song', and from the 'hymenaeus', the processional song which accompanied the newly married couple to their house. In literature, however, the title 'epithalamium' predominates. The tradition is old. *Sappho's wedding songs were famous. Comedy and tragedy provide examples. Among Hellenistic poems *Theocritus 18 (Helen and Menelaus) stands out. But Latin poetry offers more: e.g. *Catullus 61, 62, and 64 (Peleus and Thetis).

epithets, divine

Greek It is necessary to distinguish between epithets or surnames appearing only as literary (esp. epic) ornaments and those known to have been used in cult. Thus we have no proof that *Athena was ever addressed in ritual as 'grey-eyed'; it is her stock epithet in *Homer, *Zeus' pet-name for her. It seems unlikely that *Ares was prayed to as 'ruinous to mortals'; he is so addressed by Athena, which is a very different thing, and it is his stock epithet. But there are many borderline cases, hard to decide. We have no instance of *Athena being called Pallas in cult, yet it is hard to suppose that so familiar a name was never used for her by worshippers; Zeus' stock epithet, 'cloud-gatherer', appears in the vocative in epic in many places where it is syntactically a nominative, strongly suggesting

that its form had become fixed by some ancient liturgical phrase, which, however, is lost to us. The immediate function of the epithet in epic is often to form with the proper name a convenient metrical unit. Now and then an epithet is used to avoid mentioning an ill-omened name; *Hades in Sophocles' *Oedipus at Colonus* is Zeus *chthonios* ('of the earth'), and in Aeschylus *Suppliants* he is even Zeus *allos* ('other', 'another').

The epithets which are known to have been used in cult may be grouped as follows. (1) Purely local, meaning that the deity in question is worshipped, or has a temple or altar, at such-and-such a place. Thus *Apollo *Delios* is simply Apollo who is worshipped in *Delos, and differs from the Pythian (see DELPHI), or any other similarly named Apollo, just as Our Lady of Lourdes does from Our Lady of Loreto. Such titles may tell us something of the history of the cult, if the title does not fit the immediate locality. (2) Titles indicating association with another god. (3) Most of the epithets, refer to the functions of the god or goddess. Thus, Zeus has many titles denoting his control of the weather and all that depends on it; he is Thunderer, God of the thunderbolt, Sender of rainstorms, Rainer, and as a natural consequence, Farmer; also God of favourable winds, and so forth. *Aphrodite has epithets denoting her power over the sexual life of mankind, as 'Delayer of old age'; her connection with love whether licit or illicit, e.g. 'Goddess of the whole people', in her Athenian worship as a deity of marriage; and on the other hand Hetaira (see HETAIRAI) and even Pornē (see PROSTITUTION, SECULAR). These last belong to subclass in which the characteristics of the worshipper are transferred to the deity; both signify the goddess who is worshipped by harlots.

Epithets referring to the higher (moral or civic) qualities of a deity are not uncommon: e.g. Apollo the Founder, or Athena of the *boulē*.

Roman Each deity had its name, but this name could be hidden or unknown (hence the formula in addresses 'whether god or goddess'). If it was known, and could be uttered (as the hidden name could not), it was often accompanied by epithets or surnames (*cognōmina*). They are either descriptions used informally or true names occurring in actual cult (attested in formulas, dedications, and names of temples). We can distinguish several classes of epithets and surnames: (1) Purely literary descriptions, e.g. of *Mars by *Virgil as harsh, wicked, untamed, savage, or powerful in arms. (2) Popular descriptions derived either from a special feature (often iconographic) of a deity, e.g. *Hercules, 'Wearing a *bulla*' (an *amulet worn by young boys), 'Youthful', 'Small', or from a story concerning a deity, e.g. *Minerva Capta, 'Captured', because she was transported to Rome after the capture of Falerii Veteres in 241 BC. (3) Geographical and local descriptions, e.g. *Bona Dea Subsaxana because she had her shrine *sub Saxo*, 'under the Rock' (of the Aventine) or *Diana Aventinensis. (4) Epithets referring to the civic standing of a deity: Jupiter Optimus Maximus, 'the Best (and) the Greatest, *Juno Regina, 'the Queen'. (5) Most numerous are epithets describing the function of a deity or its particular manifestation: *Apollo Medicus, 'Healer', Bona Dea Nutrix, 'Nurse', Jupiter Tonans, 'Thunderer', Stator, 'Stayer' (he stopped the advance of the enemy), Mars Ultor, 'Avenger' (he helped *Augustus avenge the murder of *Caesar), Venus Verticordia, 'Changer of Hearts' (she averted women's minds from lust to chastity). Deities for whom the most epithets are attested are Jupiter (over 100), Fortuna, Juno (over 40), Hercules, Mars, Venus (over 30), *Lares, *Mercurius (over 20).

epitome The Hellenistic age was the first to feel the growth of recorded literature as a burden; and the age which cast doubt on the propriety of a 'big book' also pioneered the abridgement of long works, esp. technical treatises. The practice became a common, even an obsessive, feature of post-Classical Greece. Convenient and informative compendia based on the writings of others were being produced at Rome by the end of the republic, esp. in history.

epōnymoi are those, usually gods or heroes, after whom something is named or thought to be named. Most often regions or cities are thought to be named after a hero, such as Arcas for Arcadia. Historical characters also gave their names to cities (Antioch, Alexandria). Divisions of the populace also had heroic eponyms. In Athens, the *eponymoi* (with no further qualification) were the ten heroes who gave their names to the ten Cleisthenic tribes created in 508/7 BC (see CLEISTHENES (2); PHYLAI). These heroes, who were said to have been picked by *Delphi from a list of 100 submitted, all had separate, presumably pre-existing cults, to which members of the new tribes gradually became in some measure attached; they had also, apparently, a collective cult in the Agora (see ATHENS, TOPOGRAPHY), where statues of the ten stood on a high base and tribal notices were posted.

A quite different case is the 'eponymous magistrate' who gives his name to his year of office, like the Athenian archon (see ARCHONTES).

epyllion is the term applied in modern times to 'miniature epic', a narrative poem of up to c.600 *hexameters, usually about an episode from the life of a mythological hero or heroine. This was a favourite form from *Theocritus and *Callimachus (2) until the 'new' poets contemporary with *Catullus. The topic is preferably unfamiliar, the love motif (often pathological love) becomes prominent in the later specimens, and often a second theme or a description of an object is enclosed within the main narrative; the style tends to be more subjective and emotional than in formal *epic, and the scale of the narrative is uneven, with some events elaborated (esp. emotional speeches) and others quickly passed over.

equestrians See following entry.

equitēs

Republic In the republic 1,800 cavalry (*equites*) had their horses supplied and maintained by the state (*equites equō pūblicō*), and in the centuriate assembly (see COMITIA) they formed eighteen *centuriae ('centuries'). They were enrolled by the *censors, after financial, physical, and moral scrutiny. At least from 304 BC, though rarely in the late republic, they paraded to the Capitol on 15 July. Men of aristocratic birth always had preference for enrolment.

About 400, men on their own horses (*equites equō prīvātō*) were added to the cavalry. They did not share the voting privilege, but were given at least some of the status marks, of the others. In the 3rd cent. Roman cavalry proved increasingly ineffective in war and by 200 was largely replaced by *auxilia. But *equites* retained their social eminence and became a corps from which officers and the staffs of governors and commanders were drawn. This new 'equestrian' service was within the reach of any rich and well-connected family, and the old exclusiveness was undermined. In 129 senators were excluded from the equestrian centuries. This marks the beginnings of the later equestrian order as a distinct body. Gaius *Sempronius Gracchus excluded senators from service on the *extortion court (see OPTIMATES). The qualification for service was wealth. Gracchus' prescription was followed in other *quaestiones; as a result, the composition of juries became, for a generation (106–70), an object of bitter contention between the senatorial and the equestrian orders, firmly establishing their distinctness.

*Pliny the Elder derives the equestrian order from the Gracchan jurors, and what evidence we have supports him. The rich *publicani* gradually became the dominant element on juries and within the order: Cicero could rhetorically identify them with it. By 50, the influx of Italians, to whose leading men the jury courts had been opened since 70, made a return to the old restriction politically impossible. The law allocating special rows of seats to equestrians probably confirmed the definition by wealth.

The new order was a disparate body. Round an aristocratic Roman core (men like *Pomponius Atticus) were grouped leading men from colonies and *municipia*, *publicani*, and even *negotiatores*—many of similar background, but some self-made men. Free birth and a landed interest were prerequisites for social recognition. Senators and equestrians in the late republic thus formed a plutocracy sharing both landed and business interests, in a range of proportions.

In social standing, equestrians were almost equal to senators, freely intermarrying even with patrician nobles and gaining entry to the senate (though not the consulship—see NOBILITAS) if they wanted it. But as a class they preferred the pursuit of money and pleasure to political responsibility, and they thus formed the non-political section of the upper class rather than (as in the empire) an intermediate class. Their history is an important part of that of the late republic, esp. in view of their control of the *quaestiones* during most of that time. Various *populares* (see OPTIMATES) tried to mould them into a political force opposed to the senate and the *nobiles*; but their social and economic interests, esp. after the enfranchisement of Italy, were too similar to permit this. *Sulla, after decimating them in the proscriptions, deprived them of leadership by adlecting the most prominent survivors to the senate, and of power by taking the courts from them. But strengthened by the influx of Italians and by increasing financial power, wooed by Pompey, and largely restored to the courts by the law of Aurelius Cotta, they rose to unprecedented influence in the 60s, when Cicero and the senate—aware of the basic community of interests of the two classes—tried to unite them behind the leading men of the state in a 'harmony of the orders'. Yet, though often united on a single issue (e.g. against threats to financial stability by demagogues or threats to freedom of profiteer-

ing by statesmen), sometimes even for a lengthy period, they were too disparate in composition and too non-political to form a stable grouping. Preventing necessary reform (esp. in the provinces), they remained a disruptive and irresponsible element with no programme or allegiance, until the Civil War substituted military for economic power. Caesar deprived them of the Asian tithe, but opened a new avenue for them by making prominent equestrians like Oppius and *Cornelius Balbus (1)—a splendid example of a non-traditional equestrian—his political and financial agents. The support of these men, as well as the precedent, proved important to Augustus.

Imperial period Under the emperors the equestrians constituted a second aristocratic order which ranked only below the senatorial order in status. Equestrians in the wider sense (see below) provided the officer corps of the Roman army and held a wide range of posts in the civil administration (see PROCURATOR) as it developed from its limited beginnings under Augustus.

The precise criteria for membership of the order remain disputed. On a wider definition, all Roman citizens of free birth who possessed the minimum census qualification of 400,000 sesterces automatically qualified as members of the order. Thus when *Pliny the Younger offered a friend from Comum a gift of 300,000 sesterces 'to make up the wealth required of an equestrian', he implies that this gift of itself would be sufficient to make his friend an equestrian. However, it may be that these were necessary but not sufficient criteria and that, in addition, some formal act of authorization, perhaps even the grant of the public horse (see below), by the emperor was necessary.

The equestrian order, widely defined, was much more numerous than the senatorial order and socially and politically (in the range of its public roles) more heterogeneous. Although the total number of equestrians at any time cannot be determined, already under Augustus they were numerous. *Strabo records that recent censuses had revealed 500 men of equestrian census in both Gades and Patavium. During the first two centuries the possession of equestrian rank spread widely through the provinces. This diffusion mirrored the extension of Roman *citizenship. From the beginning of the Principate *Baetica and Narbonensis are well represented; in the 1st cent. AD and after, Africa and the Greek east. Far fewer equestrians are attested in the Danubian provinces, Germany,

Gaul, and Britain. The order came to consist largely of the landed gentry of the municipalities of Italy and of the cities of the most urbanized provinces. Although these men were eligible to take up the military and civilian posts reserved for equestrians, most of them continued rather to play a local political role as senior magistrates or councillors, or as high priests of the imperial cult.

Within the order three specific subsets of unequal importance can be identified, namely the holders of the public horse, the jurors at Rome, and the military and civilian office-holders. The re-emergence of the category of *equites equo publico* under Augustus formed part of his traditionalist social policies. He restored the long disused parade of 15 July. This subset of equestrians formed a distinct corporation which might dedicate statues or play a role in the funeral of an emperor. The grant of this status was at the discretion of the emperor, who could also withdraw it. Augustus also established four boards of jurors, each of 1,000 men, who were of equestrian rank. Owing to the pressure for places Gaius (1) added a fifth board. Like the public horse the status of juror was solely in the gift of the emperor. Both statuses, as dignities conferred by the emperor, came to be honorific privileges which did not necessarily involve the performance of actual duties at Rome.

Under the Principate the most significant subset of equestrians consisted of those who served as equestrian officers in the army and as senior civil administrators. Each year there were *c*.360 posts available for senior officers of equestrian rank: prefectures of auxiliary (see AUXILIA) cohorts, military tribunates, and prefectures of auxiliary cavalry units. Some of these officers were not typical equestrian landed gentry but instead prominent soldiers who had attained the rank of senior centurion (*primipilus*) in a legion and thereby acquired equestrian status. Tenure of these officer-posts was normally the necessary precursor for advancement to the senior civil administrative posts, reserved for equestrians. In the provinces emperors appointed equestrians as procurators who had prime responsibility for fiscal administration; at Rome from the reign of Augustus key officials, such as the praetorian *prefect or the prefect of the corn supply, were always equestrians. From the late 1st cent. the posts of the palace officials, e.g., control of the imperial correspondence, were transferred from freedmen to equestrians. Senior equestrian administrators formed with senior senators the political élite of the empire.

They intermingled socially with senators; they married into senatorial families; like senators they could be summoned to serve on the emperor's *consilium*. Sons of leading equestrian officials were the prime source of recruitment of new senatorial families. On occasion, esp. under *Vespasian and Marcus *Aurelius, senior equestrians might be adlected (see ADLECTION) by the emperor into the senate.

eranos a Greek institution, involved *reciprocity: at first of food, and later of money. In *Homer, *eranos* refers to a meal for which each diner contributed a share; alternatively, the venue might be rotated. This earlier meaning was never lost; but, by the later 5th cent. BC, the concept had evolved to include a *credit system, common in Athens, whereby contributors lent small sums to help out a common acquaintance in need. The strong obligation to lend was matched by a reciprocal obligation to repay as soon as possible. The reciprocity inherent in *eranos* is reflected in metaphorical usage: to die in battle for the *polis* was to offer one's 'finest contribution', receiving in return 'immortal praise'. Readiness to contribute towards *eranos* loans could be cited in Athenian courts as an aspect of civic virtue; failure to repay as indicative of general degradation.

Eratosthenēs, of *Cyrene (*c*.285–194 BC), pupil of *Callimachus (2). After spending several years at Athens, he accepted the invitation of Ptolemy III Euergetes to become royal tutor and to succeed *Apollonius (1) Rhodius as head of the Alexandrian Library. He thus became a member of the Cyrenaean intelligentsia in Alexandria, of which the central figure was Callimachus. His versatility was renowned and criticized, and the eventual Alexandrian rating was 'B-class' (i.e. 'next after the best specialist in each subject'), and as a pentathlete or 'all-rounder'. Others, more kindly, called him 'a second *Plato'. In more than one field, however, and esp. in chronology and mathematical and descriptive *geography, of which, thanks to *Strabo, we know most, his work long retained much of its authority.

He was the first scholar so to describe himself (*philologos*). His was the first serious attempt to fix the dates of political and literary history. He investigated a wide range of mathematical problems and was accepted as an equal by *Archimedes, who dedicated his *Method of Mechanical Theories* to him. In his *On the Measurement of the Earth* he treated mathematical geography, calculating with a higher degree of accuracy than his predecessors the circumference of the earth. He was the first systematic geographer, and his *Geographica* dealt with mathematical, physical, and ethnographical geography.

Eratosthenes' chance utterances reveal him as a man of insight and conviction. In his *Geographica* he avers that both Greek and '*barbarian' (the Indians and the Arians, and also the Romans and the Carthaginians, 'with their wonderful political systems') should be judged by the criterion of morality and not of race.

See GEOGRAPHY; MAPS.

Erechthēum, the third outstanding building on the Athenian Acropolis, begun in 421 BC and finished, after a lapse, in 407; built of Pentelic marble, with friezes of black *Eleusis stone to take applied white marble relief sculpture. Exact details of its construction are known from a contemporary inscription. The main structure is divided into four compartments: the largest (east cella) has an Ionic portico; the west end is closed by a wall with engaged columns and corner piers. At this end is a unique and boldly projecting (though small) south feature—the 'porch of the maidens', with draped female figures (*caryatids) serving as supports—and, nearly opposite on the north side, a still more boldly projecting porch with Ionic columns standing on a lower level and having the tallest order of the whole composition.

The temple replaced to some extent the large 6th-cent. temple of *Athena whose foundations can be seen between it and the *Parthenon. We know from *Pausanias (3) that the Erechtheum housed a number of ancient cults (this may partly account for its complicated form) and many sacred spots and objects—the venerable image of Athena Polias, a golden lamp made by Callimachus, a salt well and the mark of *Poseidon's trident, an altar of Poseidon and *Erechtheus, and altars of Boutēs and *Hephaestus. Near the west end of the building were shrines of *Cecrops and his dutiful daughter Pandrosus, and the original sacred olive of Athena.

The Erechtheum was much admired in antiquity: the caryatids were copied for the *forum Augustum and Hadrian's villa at *Tibur.

Erechtheus, a cult figure worshipped on the Athenian Acropolis, formally identified with *Poseidon but often regarded as an early king of Athens. The Iliadic Catalogue knows an Erechtheus who was born from Earth (*Gaia), brought up by Athena and installed in her sanctuary, and who is worshipped with sacrifice of bulls and rams; this gives the kernel of his myth and cult.

Eretria, a city of *Euboea. It joined its neighbour *Chalcis in trade in Syria, and colonizing in Italy, Sicily, and the north Aegean. In the late 8th cent. they fought over the Lelantine plain. *Aristagoras of Miletus obtained its help for the *Ionian Revolt against Persia, and in the avenging expedition sent by Darius the city was besieged and burnt. Eretria was in the *Delian League, revolted in 446, but was recovered. In 411 it revolted again, with the rest of Euboea.

Erichthonius, an Athenian hero connected with the Acropolis and its cults. He may originally have been identical with *Erechtheus, the older attested name. He is distinguished from his near homonym by the emphasis placed on his birth and infancy. *Hephaestus tried to rape *Athena, but succeeded only in spilling his semen on her thigh; she wiped it off with a piece of wool, and dropped it on the ground, whereupon Earth conceived Erichthonius. After his birth she handed him over to Athena—an episode popular with red-figure vase-painters. Athena shut the child in a chest or basket and in turn entrusted him to the daughters of *Cecrops, two of whom with disastrous results disobeyed her order not to look inside.

Erīnўĕs, chthonian (lit. 'of the earth') powers of retribution for wrongs and blood-guilt esp. in the family. Individually or collectively they carry out the *curses of a mother or father. Outside the family, the Erinys blinds a man's reason; and, as *daimon beneath the earth, she protects a solemn oath. She also looks after beggars and generally ensures the natural order of things, like guarding the rights of an elder brother or silencing *Achilles' horse Xanthus, given a voice by *Hera. Heraclitus extends the Erinyes' control over the cosmos. Aeschylus calls them daughters of Night and brings them on stage repulsively dressed in black, with snakes for hair but wingless. Acc. to Hesiod's genealogy, which is closer to their divine chthonian origins, they spring from *Earth, made pregnant by *Uranus' blood. Their cult as Semnai ('August') in Athens and Eumenidēs ('Kindly') in *Sicyon reveal attempts at neutralizing the Erinyes' dark powers through euphemisms.

Eris, 'Strife', often personified as a goddess in poetry. She appears in several Homeric battle scenes. In his *Theogony* °Hesiod makes her the daughter of Night and mother of Toil, Pain, Battles, Bloodshed, Lies, Ruin, and the like. In *Works and Days*, however, he declares that there is not just one Eris but two, a bad Eris who fosters war and a good Eris who stimulates men to work through a spirit of competition. See PHILOTIMIA. Eris is given a mythical role by the *Cypria* (see EPIC CYCLE): she attended the wedding of °Peleus and °Thetis and there created rivalry between °Athena, °Hera, and °Aphrodite, which led to the Judgement of °Paris and thus to the Trojan War. Much later sources say that she was angry at not being invited to the wedding and created the rivalry by tossing the 'Apple of Discord' among the guests as a prize for the most beautiful.

Ĕrōs, god of love. Eros personified does not occur in Homer, but the Homeric passages in which the word *ĕrōs* is used give a clear idea of the original significance. It is the violent physical desire that drives Paris to Helen, Zeus to Hera, and shakes the limbs of the suitors of Penelope. A more refined conception of this Eros who affects mind and body appears in the Archaic lyric poets. Because his power brings peril, he is cunning, unmanageable, cruel; in °Anacreon he smites the lovestruck one with an axe or a whip. He comes suddenly like a wind. Eros is playful, but plays with frenzies and confusion. He symbolizes all attractions which provoke love. He is young and beautiful, he walks over flowers, and the roses are 'a plant of Eros' of which he makes his crown. He is sweet and warms the heart.

Eros is a constant companion of °Aphrodite, although he can appear with any god, whenever a love story is involved. °Hesiod seems to have transformed the Homeric conception of Eros. Although he describes Eros in terms almost identical with Homer as the god who 'loosens the limbs and damages the mind', he also makes him, together with °Earth and Tartarus, the oldest of all gods, all-powerful over gods and men. With Eros as a cosmic principle, °Parmenides found a place for him, perhaps as the power which reconciles opposites. This philosophic conception contributed to the Euripidean picture of omnipotent Eros, took abstruse mythological shape in Orphic cosmogonies (see ORPHIC LITERATURE; ORPHISM), and formed the background for Plato's discussions of Eros in *Symposium* and *Phaedrus*.

Hellenistic poets continue the more playful conception of Anacreon, the tricks Eros plays on mortals, the tribulations of those who try to resist him, and the punishments he receives for his misdeeds. His bow and arrows, first mentioned by Euripides, play a big part in these accounts. Often a plurality of Erotĕs is introduced because both love and the god who symbolized it could multiply.

Eros had some ancient cults and much individual worship. He was always the god of love directed towards male as well as female beauty. Hence his images in the gymnasia and his cult among the °Sacred Band in Thebes.

eschatology Doctrines about the last things—death, judgement, etc.

Esquiline The eastern plateau formed in Rome by the Oppian and Cispian hills, the *regiō Esquilīna* being the second of the republican Four Regions (See REGIO). It was included within the republican wall (°wall of Servius) and provided later sites for Nero's °Domus Aurea and the °baths of °Titus and °Trajan. Under Augustus the name was applied to Regio V, outside the republican wall, which contained °gardens belonging to rich aristocrats, notably the Gardens of °Maecenas; many of these later came into the possession of the emperors.

Eteoclēs, the older son of °Oedipus. After the blinding and retirement of their father, he and his brother Polynīcēs twice insulted him; so Oedipus cursed them. The two brothers agreed to reign in alternate years, Eteocles taking the first year, Polynices leaving °Thebes for °Argos. At the end of his year Eteocles refused to give up the throne; Polynices returned with his father-in-law Adrastus and the rest of the 'Seven'; in the ensuing battle, the two brothers met and killed each other (see SEVEN AGAINST THEBES).

Ethiopia was a name usually applied by the Greeks to any region in the far south. Early Greek interest in Ethiopia was largely concerned with the source of the °Nile. From Herodotus onwards 'Ethiopia' designated esp. the lands south of Egypt comprising the ancient Kush, Meroē, and Axumis. Ethiopians formed contingents in the Persian army during °Xerxes' invasion of Greece.

ethnics name the people of, for example, a certain city (Corinthians) or country (Egyptians).

ethnos The *ethnos* was a category of Greek state which existed alongside the °*polis*. *Ethnē* (pl.) are diverse, with no single form of constitution. In *ethne*, by contrast with *poleis* (which retained autonomy), individual communities surrendered some political powers (usually control of warfare and foreign relations) to a common assembly. By contrast with *poleis*, the role of urban centres in *ethne* varied greatly; settlement structures range from a high degree of urbanization and local autonomy (e.g. *Boeotia, which was tantamount to a collection of small *poleis*) to scattered villages with little urban development (e.g. Aetolia). Although the *ethnos* is sometimes equated with primitive tribalism, social and political developments from the 8th cent. BC onwards (e.g. in religion and *colonization) often bear comparison with evidence from *poleis*, and the *ethnos* was a long-lived phenomenon.

Etruscan discipline, Etruscan religion
See RELIGION, ETRUSCAN.

Etruscan language The Etruscan language is no longer obscure and mysterious, even if there are still large gaps in our knowledge of its grammar and lexicon and in our understanding of the texts—larger than is the case with other languages of comparable attestation. For access to Etruscan is made harder by its genealogical isolation. The only language that has so far been shown to be 'related' to Etruscan, i.e. to be descended from a common source, is the pre-Greek idiom of Lemnos, and the evidence even for this is limited to just a few texts. It may at best provide some support for the Lydian claim reported by *Herodotus that the Etruscans came from *Lydia.

Our sources for Etruscan are: (*a*) *c*.9,000 epigraphic texts, dated *c*.700–10 BC; (*b*) a linen book, two-thirds of which (*c*.1,500 words) is preserved in the binding of an Egyptian mummy; (*c*) 40–50 glosses, i.e. meanings given for Etruscan words in Latin or Greek texts; (*d*) a series of Etruscan loanwords in Latin and of Latin or Greek loanwords in Etruscan. The number and usefulness of the glosses is limited. The Etruscan–Latin bilingual inscriptions contain almost nothing but personal names. Beyond this, only an indirect approach to Etruscan is possible, consisting of three steps: (1) deducing the 'message' of the text from the archaeological context—possible only with context-bound texts such as captions to images, signatures, or epitaphs; (2) breaking down the 'message' into its parts, to be correlated with parts of the text—possible only with short texts, and made easier by comparing similar texts in better-known languages from the same cultural milieu; (3) checking the hypoth-

eses thus produced by applying the values to all instances of a word or form; by this means access may also be gained to parts of longer context-independent texts. Naturally this procedure does not provide an explanation of every detail.

The Etruscan script is an *alphabet, taken over (before 700) from a (west) Greek school-alphabet, and in its turn the source of the Latin script. It can therefore be read, i.e. we know roughly how the letters were pronounced. Etruscan is an agglutinating language. So in the noun, for instance, number and case are each marked by an individual affix: *clan* 'son', genitive *clen-s*, pl. *clen-ar*, gen. pl. *clen-ar-as*.

Etruscans, historically and artistically the most important of the indigenous peoples of pre-Roman Italy, and acc. to *Porcius Cato (1) the masters of nearly all of it—a claim confirmed by archaeology for the area between the Tridentine Alps and the gulf of Salerno.

The possessors of the indigenous culture between the Arno and the Tiber were iron age Etruscans, who gained much in the 9th and 8th cents. from the interest shown by the outside world in their mineral resources, and in the 7th were able to acquire and commission luxury goods and adornments of eastern Mediterranean (*orientalizing') types for the tombs of their 'princes'. Foremost among the early bearers of outside influences were the Euboean traders who had established themselves at *Pithecusae by the mid-8th cent.: their alphabet was modified to accommodate the pre-existing phonetic systems already characteristic of different Etruscan-speaking zones.

The continuity in settlement and in the basic culture of the 8th and 7th cents. at the main Etruscan centres was accompanied by major developments both in society and in artistic production. The *praenōmen–nōmen* combination, a clear sign of proto-urban organization, is attested epigraphically from the beginning of the 7th cent., as are recognizably local schools of fine painted pottery, soon joined by *bucchero* (Grey ware), bronze-work, and jewellery—categories in which the contributions of native Etruscan and expatriate Greek and Levantine specialists and entrepreneurs are inextricably linked. Oil and wine were also produced and exported on a large scale by the mid-6th cent. By then, too, the social class represented by the early orientalizing princely tombs had given way to a broader, *polis*-based, category of prosperous merchants and landowners. Their last resting-places take the form of single-family chamber-tombs, ranged along streets in well-planned cemeteries which have yielded a rich harvest of imported vases from all the best Attic black-figure and red-figure workshops. The chambers at *Tarquinii and a few other centres have preserved the largest extant complex of pre-Roman painting in the classical world: its naturalistic and often cheerful depiction of banquets, games, and hunting affords a welcome glimpse of the 'real' Etruscan character underneath the veneer of Hellenization (see HELLENISM) constituted by the mass of prestige goods imported (and made locally) not only for deposition in tombs but also to supply the *votive requirements of major sanctuaries.

The expansion of some Etruscan centres beyond the confines of Etruria proper began at an early stage with the foundation of the Tarquin dynasty at Rome (see REX). The presence of the Tarquins, who turned Rome into a city, doubtless facilitated control of the land route to *Campania, where *Capua became the chief Etruscan city. Felsina enjoyed a similar status in the Po valley from the late 6th cent., when growing Greek activity on land and at sea to the south made it imperative to cultivate new markets—not least with the mysterious Celtic communities north of the Alps. In the event, the *Celts added their own weight to the pressure on the Etruscans that was already building up from Rome (whence the Tarquins were expelled in 509), from the Greek south (where the battle of *Cumae was lost in 474) and from other quarters as well (the Carthaginians and the Italic peoples). Of these, the inexorable advance of Rome into Etruria and Umbria was by far the most serious threat to the survival of what was still an essentially cantonal phenomenon as distinct from a nation: city-states, loosely organized in a League of Twelve Peoples, capable of meeting in council and of denying federal assistance to Veii, threatened by Rome since the end of the 5th cent., for primarily religious reasons. *Livy's comment on this episode, to the effect that the Etruscans paid more attention than any other people to religious considerations, is one of the few positive statements about the Etruscans in the ancient sources: no Etruscan literature has survived, and Greek and Roman authors were far from objective observers of such matters as commercial rivalry (which they defined as piracy) and social customs (notably those concerning the position of women) that were not those of Greece or Rome. See ETRUSCAN LANGUAGE; RELIGION, ETRUSCAN.

etymology in the classical world was always closely connected with questions concerning the ultimate origin of language. Was the sound of a word merely a matter of convention, or was there some natural relationship between the sign and the thing signified (the theory of *physis*)? In general the latter view prevailed. The popular assumption that the study of a name could reveal 'the truth' about the thing accounts for the importance attached to etymology in ancient thought and literature. But their etymologies never attained any degree of accuracy.

Euboea, also called Long Island. The chief cities in antiquity were *Chalcis and *Eretria; in between was *Lefkandi, where remarkable 10th-cent. BC finds have revised notions of the Dark Age of Greece. Other cities were Histiaea, and marble-rich Carystus. In the 8th cent. Chalcis and Eretria were active mercantile centres, which led the islanders to involvement in an *emporion* at Al Mina in Syria by 800. They established colonies on the NW shores of the Aegean and in Italy and Sicily (see COLONIZATION, GREEK; PITHECUSAE) and fought over the Lelantine plain, which lay between them, in the 8th cent. In 506 Athens compelled Chalcis to surrender part of the plain and installed a *cleruchy. In 490 the Persian Datis attacked Euboea, capturing Eretria and Carystus. Euboean contingents fought Persia at *Salamis and *Plataea. Owing to Boeotian intrigues, Euboea revolted from Athens in 446, but was reconquered by *Pericles, who planted more cleruchies. The cities remained tributary allies of Athens in the *Delian League, and in the *Peloponnesian War, acc. to Thucydides, Euboea was 'more valuable to Athens than Attica itself'; it revolted in 411.

Eubūlidēs, of Miletus, mid-4th cent. BC, *dialectician. He was an outspoken critic of *Aristotle, a teacher of *Demosthenes (2), and the reputed author of several classic puzzles. Some of these—the Sorites ('How many grains make a heap?'), the Liar Paradox ('Is "I am lying" simultaneously true and false?'), and the Horned Argument ('Have you lost your horns?')—raise problems for the simple true/false dichotomy.

Eubūlus (c.405–c.335 BC), Athenian statesman of the period 355–342. In 355, after thirteen years' struggle to regain *Amphipolis and the *Chersonese and the brief but disastrous Social War, the imperialistic advocates of war were discredited and the state near bankruptcy. Eubulus as a theoric (see THEORIKA) commissioner gradually assumed control of Athens' finances, and raised public and private prosperity to a level probably not attained since the 5th cent. The most important guarantee of economic recovery was a law which made it hard for the assembly to draw on the routine revenues of the state for inessential military operations. Thus he was able to use the annual surpluses on a programme of public works. In the wider spheres of policy, he sought to concentrate Athens' military resources on the defence of the essential interests of Athens and of Greece, and to exclude *Philip II from Greek affairs by uniting the Greeks in a Common Peace, his chief associates being Midias, *Aeschines (1), and *Phocion. Like most Athenian politicians, he felt himself forced to accept the peace negotiated in 346 by *Philocrates and Demosthenes. After Philip used the peace to intervene in *Phocis, Demosthenes determined to renew the war, but Eubulus and his supporters sought to maintain and extend the peace. In 342 Demosthenes and the war-party were in control. No more is heard of Eubulus after *Chaeronea.

Euclid, mathematician (between 325 and 250 BC). His fame rests on the *Elements* which goes under his name. It is in thirteen books (bks. 1-6 on plane geometry, 7-9 on the theory of numbers, 10 on irrationals, 11-13 on solid geometry). The work as it stands is the classical textbook of elementary *mathematics. which remained the standard (in many languages and versions) for 2,000 years. It incorporates (and eliminated) many works on the *'elements' by earlier writers, notably *Eudoxus.

Eudoxus, of *Cnidus (*c*.390-*c*.340 BC), was an outstanding mathematician and did important work in *astronomy and geography; he was versatile in 'philosophy' in general. After starting to teach in Athens, he came to know Plato.

In geometry he invented the general theory of proportion, applicable to incommensurable as well as commensurable magnitudes, found in Euclid bk. 5. This greatly helped to assure the primacy of geometry in Greek *mathematics. He also developed the method of approach to the limit which became the standard way of avoiding infinitesimals in ancient mathematics, He was thus able to prove that cone and pyramid are one-third of the cylinder and prism respectively with the same base and height.

In astronomy he was the first Greek to construct a mathematical system to explain the apparent motions of the heavenly bodies: that of the 'homocentric spheres'. *Simplicius' account of this reveals both the high level of mathematics and the low level of observational astronomy of the time: Eudoxus combined uniform motions of concentric spheres about different axes with great ingenuity to produce a qualitatively correct representation of the retrogradations of some planets; but the underlying observational data are few and crude, and the discrepancies of the results with the actual phenomena often gross. Its adoption in a modified form by Aristotle was responsible for its resurrection in later ages. More practical (and very influential) was Eudoxus' description of the *constellations, with calendaric notices of risings and settings. The version entitled *Phainomena* (i.e. Celestial Phenomena) is known through its adaptation by *Aratus in his popular poem of the same name. His 'Circuit of the Earth' was a work of mathematical and descriptive geography.

euergetism, a neologism to describe the socio-political phenomenon of voluntary gift-giving to the ancient community. Embracing the beneficence of Hellenistic kings and Roman emperors, whose subjects saw such philanthropy as a cardinal virtue of rulers (see KINGSHIP), it has lately been studied in relation to the *polis, of which benefaction by wealthy citizens (including women) becomes a defining characteristic from the 3rd cent. BC until late antiquity, as is attested by thousands of honorific inscriptions memorializing donors; it is also a feature of republican Rome, where the liberality of senators in kind at least (public building, spectacle) resembles that of their humbler Greek contemporaries, and of the (Mediterranean) Roman city in general. In Greece the origins of euergetism go back to the aristocratic ideal of liberality found in Homer and echoed by *Aristotle, who gave feasting the city as an example of 'magnificence'. In Classical Athens beneficence in this tradition, while lingering into the 5th cent., was essentially inimical to the ideal equality of Athenian *democracy, which preferred instead to impose on rich citizens the duty of the *liturgy. Although 4th-cent. Athens conferred the title 'benefactor' on foreigners, only in the 3rd cent. does the type of the 'benefactor politician' emerge clearly in the Greek city. Aristotle saw munificence in office as a cynical device of rich oligarchs. Civic euergetism was a mixture of social display, patriotism, and political self-interest. It was not charity, since its main beneficiary was the citizen body.

Euhēmerus, of Messene, was perhaps active as late as 280 BC. He wrote a *novel of travel which was influential in the Hellenistic world. Euhemerus described an imaginary voyage to a group of *islands in the uncharted waters of the Indian Ocean and the way of life on its chief island, Panchaea. The central monument of the island, a golden column on which the deeds of *Uranus, *Cronus, and *Zeus were recorded, gave the novel its title 'Sacred Scripture'. From this monument Euhemerus learnt that Uranus, Cronus, and Zeus had been great kings in their day and that they were worshipped as gods by the grateful people. Earlier authors had written of imaginary utopias, but the utopia of Euhemerus was esp. relevant to the position of those Hellenistic rulers who claimed to serve their subjects and on that account to receive worship for their services (see RULER-CULT, GREEK). Euhemerism could be interpreted according to taste as supporting the traditional belief of Greek epic and lyric poetry which drew a clear line between gods and great men, which could sometimes be crossed with divine help; as advancing a justification for contemporary ruler-cults; or as a work of rationalizing *atheism.

The theory of god and man which was advanced by Euhemerus seems to have made little impression on the Greeks, but *Diodorus (2) Siculus, apparently taking the romance for fact, embodied it in his sixth book. In Latin it had more success after the publication of the *Euhemerus* of *Ennius. Christian writers liked to use it as evidence of the real nature of the Greek gods. Euhemerus' name survives in the modern term 'euhemeristic', applied to mythological interpretation which supposes certain gods (e.g. *Asclepius) to be originally heroes. See also CULTURE-BRINGERS; PRODICUS.

Eumenēs II (d. 158 BC), king of *Pergamum (197–158). The family solidarity of Eumenes, his mother, and his three brothers gave unusual inner strength to the dynasty. Eumenes, immediately threatened by the *Seleucid Antiochus III, was Rome's major ally in the war against him, culminating in the battle of *Magnesia (189), and he made the greatest gains from the ensuing Peace of Apamea (188), which divided Seleucid territory north of the Taurus (mountains in southern *Anatolia) between Pergamum and *Rhodes. Pergamum became immediately rich but also a guarantor of stability in the Roman interest, though Roman support did not mean peace. In the 170s Eumenes' building programme transformed Pergamum into a splendidly equipped capital city and produced the zenith of Pergamene plastic art (e.g. the Great Altar of Zeus); contacts with major Greek centres—*Athens, *Miletus, *Delphi, *Cos—were marked by massive gifts.

Eumenides See ERINYES.

Eumolpus, the 'fair singer', was the mythical ancestor of the Eleusinian clan (see GENOS) of the Eumolpidae. He appears first in the *Homeric *Hymn to Demeter* as one of the rulers of *Eleusis instructed by the goddess in the *mysteries. Acc. to the Eumolpidae, he was the son of *Poseidon and became the first *hierophantes. In art he holds a *sceptre, like the *hierophantes*, who with his melodious voice, saw himself as re-enacting the role of Eumolpus.

eunomia ('good order'). See POLIS; TYRTAEUS; SPARTA. In mythology, Eunomia is daughter of *Dike (1).

eunuchs

Religious In the Classical period, religious eunuchs are a feature of several Anatolian cults of goddesses. As a whole the institution created a class of pure servants of a god. Its significance derives from a double contrast, with the involuntary castration of boys for court use and the normal obligation to marry. The adult self-castrate expressed in his body both world-rejection and -superiority. Self-castration was a (decisive) step into a status 'between worlds', parallel to poverty, homelessness, self-laceration, ecstatic dancing. Cross-dressing (esp. earrings) and face-whitening advertised the anomalous state (see TRANSVESTISM, RITUAL).

Secular To the ancient Greeks eunuchs were despised figures who haunted the courts of oriental monarchs. The Persian king employed them prominently as guardians of his harem and loyal protectors of his throne, even exacting boys for castration as tribute from some subject peoples. The disgust expressed by Greek authors at the alien customs of Persia was tempered by an acknowledgement of the trustworthiness which the eunuchs displayed to their royal masters.

By the time of Augustus eunuchs had begun to enter the households of some leading Romans, notably *Maecenas and *Sejanus. Later the *praetorian *prefect of *Septimius Severus had 100 Roman citizens castrated to provide eunuch attendants for his daughter. The presence of eunuchs around prominent courtiers reflected the trend set by emperors themselves: *Claudius already had a favourite eunuch among his freedmen, while the licentious behaviour attributed to *Nero and others involved eunuchs as accomplices. Nero even placed a eunuch in command of a detachment of troops.

Euphrates, the more westerly of the Two Rivers of *Mesopotamia. Originating in the Armenian highlands, it flows SW to the Taurus, then SE. In the alluvial plain of Babylonia it was connected, in antiquity, to the Tigris by numerous navigation and irrigation *canals. In classical times it was crossed by a number of bridges, e.g. at Zeugma and *Babylon. The Parthian empire reached the permanent limit of its expansion westwards at the Euphrates in 53 BC. After the Romans in AD 66 had recognized the rule of an *Arsacid king over Armenia, they began the construction of a military *limes along the upper and middle course of the river; forts along its right bank guarded for more than 500 years the imperial frontier against first the Parthian, later the *Sasanid kings.

Eupolis was regarded as one of the greatest poets of the Old Comedy. His first play was produced in 429 BC; he won three victories at the *Lenaea and at least one at the City *Dionysia.

Flatterers (421) ridiculed *Callias (1), for cultivating the company of *sophists. *Maricas* (also 421) was an attack on *Hyperbolus, comparable with *Aristophanes' attack on *Cleon in *Knights*. In *Demes* great Athenians of the past were brought up from the Underworld to give advice to the present. In *Taxiarchs* the soft-living *Dionysus is subjected to hard military and naval training by *Phormion (1).

Euripidēs, Athenian tragic poet.

Career Euripides, b. probably in the 480s BC, first took part in the dramatic competitions of the City *Dionysia in 455, he died in *Macedonia 407/6, leaving, like *Sophocles later in the same year, plays still unperformed (*Iphigenia at Aulis* (*IA*), *Alcmaeon in Corinth, Bacchae*), with which he won a last, posthumous victory. In his lifetime he won only four victories at the Dionysia: he was thus far less successful in the competition than Aeschylus (13 victories) or Sophocles 18 victories).

Plays Euripides wrote c.90 plays. By chance we have nineteen, more than twice as many as we have of Aeschylus or Sophocles. They fall into two categories: the first, a group of ten plays which have been transmitted to us in our medieval manuscripts complete with *scholia. They represent the same kind of volume of 'selected plays' as we have for the other two playwrights. They are: *Alcestis, Medea, Hippolytus, Andromache, Hecuba, Trojan Women, Phoenician Women, Orestes, Bacchae*, and *Rhesus*. The last is probably not by Euripides; the plays are in their likely chronological order; *Bacchae* has lost its scholia and the end of the play is partly missing. The other nine plays are: *Helen, Electra, Heraclids, Heracles, Suppliant Women, IA, Iphigenia among the Taurians (IT), Ion, Cyclops*. They are in a rough (Greek) alphabetical order. There is little doubt that they represent the chance survival of one volume (perhaps two) of the 'complete plays' of Euripides, which circulated in alphabetical order: they therefore represent a random sample of Euripides' work. Nine of the surviving plays are dated: *Alcestis* (438), *Medea* (431), *Hippolytus* (428), *Trojan Women* (415); *Helen* (412); *Phoenician Women* (409); *Orestes* (probably 408); *Bacchae* and *IA* (between 408 and 406).

'Realism', Fragmentation, Formalism Ever since *Aristophanes' portrayal of Euripides, in *Frogs*, as an intellectual iconoclast who insisted on confronting the darker and more disturbing aspects of everyday reality (*Frogs* 959), and *Aristotle's quotation of an opaque remark attributed to Sophocles, to the effect that he (Sophocles) presented men 'as they ought to be', while Euripides presented them 'as they are', Euripides has tended to be read as a 'realist'. Moreover it has seemed obvious to many critics that a naturalistic treatment of human psychology, esp. female psychology, is another hallmark of Euripidean theatre. There certainly are strands of 'realism' in Euripides' writing: for example, *Medea's presentation of herself as mistrusted 'foreigner' and oppressed and exploited 'woman' and her subsequent slow, tortured progress to infanticide. But these are strands only in a fragmented whole.

If we read *Medea* attentively, we find that the Medea we have encountered in the passage already referred to exists, within the world of the play, alongside other Medeas: before the passage mentioned, she has been heard off-stage, giving incoherent voice only to pain, and articulate only in universal cursing and damnation, of herself and her own children as well as of her enemies; immediately after it, she is transformed into a subtle adversary who easily outwits her most powerful enemy. Later she becomes successively brilliant orator, pathetic victim, devious manipulator, exultant (and uncanny) avenger, tormented mother until her final metamorphosis (involving a stunning *coup de théâtre*) into the demonic figure who, in an aerial chariot drawn by snakes, closes the play with prophecies and taunts sent down from beyond his reach upon the husband who deserted and humiliated her.

Moreover, Euripidean 'realism' is conveyed to the reader/spectator through the medium of a marked, if equally fragmented, formalism. Euripides characteristically opens his plays with a markedly non-naturalistic 'prologue', in the form of a monologue, which acts like a separate overture. Almost as characteristically, he closes them with a detached tailpiece: the shape of the action is broken and brought to a halt by the intervention, sometimes (as in *Medea*) of a character from that action, now transformed, but more often a divinity. The divinity often apparently makes a highly theatrical apparition in mid-air, the so-called '*deus ex māchina*'. Confrontation between characters often takes the form of an exchange of symmetrical and brilliantly rhetorical speeches, transparently forensic in tone, a special kind of set piece which modern scholars have called an *agōn*.

Innovation and Recurrence In *Frogs* Aristophanes presents Euripides (comically) as a compulsive innovator and subverter of tradition. In his handling of the traditional stories which he (like the other 5th-cent. playwrights) took as the material out of which to make his plays, he clearly innovates. But innovation is not in itself an esp. Euripidean trait: Aeschylus (esp. in *Suppliant Women* and *Oresteia*) and Sophocles (esp. in *Philoctetes*) both gave themselves the freedom to reshape traditional stories in order to create new fictional worlds for the tragic theatre.

At least as characteristic of Euripides is the tendency to create theatre, almost obsessively, out of recurring dramatic situations which echo and resonate with each other. Very often these situations have women at their centre, women as victims and/or deadly avengers. Sometimes structural echoing (as between *Medea* and *Hippolytus*), situational parallels (as between *Electra* and *Orestes* or between *Hecuba* and *Trojan Women*), or emotional resonances (as between *Medea* and *Ion*) almost give the impression that the later play is a reworking of the earlier. Similarly *Bacchae* reverts to the theme of divine revenge through the subjugation and perversion of human will that he had treated in *Hippolytus*. But these are not 'revivals' under another name. Each reworking offers a different vision of the human condition.

Speech and Song: The Late Plays The late plays of Euripides (the plays that come after *Trojan Women* (415) and *Heracles*) have thrown up major problems of interpretation. The underlying assumption has been that in these plays ('escapist' or 'melodramatic', except for *Bacchae*) Euripides has turned away from the painful realities of tragic experience to offer his audiences less demanding, more 'entertaining' forms of theatre.

The late plays are also often seen as the moment in Athenian theatre history when the chorus goes into terminal decline: its songs become fewer.

Sung and spoken text together form the 'script' of the Attic tragic theatre from the earliest surviving play, Aeschylus' *Persians* of 472, to the last, Euripides' *Bacchae* and *IA* and Sophocles' *OC*, and in almost all the extant plays actors and chorus both sing and speak (it is generally assumed that the spoken lines marked 'Chorus' in our manuscripts were in fact spoken only by the chorus-leader). But song is the characteristic mode of choral utterance and speech that of actors. In the late plays of Euripides this distinction becomes much less clear as actors are increasingly given arias and duets to sing, and moments of great emotional intensity in these plays are marked by such songs. At the same time choral songs are becoming rarer, though the stanzas that form them are becoming longer.

Moreover, Euripides increasingly uses song not composed of the responding, metrically 'rhymed' stanzas that throughout the history of tragedy had characterized the song of both chorus and actors. The new music of *Timotheus and the writing that goes with it, composed of long sentences, free in syntax, that seem to float without ultimate closure (they are brilliantly *parodied by Aristophanes in *Frogs*), are clearly the medium for a different perception of human experience from that of the earlier plays. It is not that Euripides' perception is no longer 'tragic' (though a number of the late plays, such as *Ion*, *IT*, and *Helen*, do end with apparent 'happiness'); rather Euripides now seems to see human beings not just as articulately analytical in confronting suffering but simultaneously as living in a world of shifting, unstable, and often conflicting emotions. It is through song that such fleeting and unstable forms of consciousness are conveyed in the late plays.

Alongside this almost operatic use of song, Euripides also employs in the late plays other new formal devices. They include vastly extended passages of *stichomythia and the use of metres taken from much older forms of tragedy. The result is a series of plays whose emotional atmosphere is much more difficult to seize and characterize. Their themes still include human isolation and inexplicable suffering, failures of communication, the victimization of women, and the drive to revenge, even the terrors of madness, themes that have marked earlier Euripidean theatre but in a bewildering variety of new dramatic modes.

The last two plays that we have, *Bacchae* and *IA*, point up the paradoxical and disconcerting multiplicity of Euripides' theatrical imagination. *Bacchae* eschews almost all the formal innovations of the other late plays and offers a vision of human experience that combines a stark and shocking view of the power of divinity with a luxuriant but ambiguous emotionalism which veers from joyful calm to exultant savagery. *IA* takes us into another world. It makes much use of actor arias and duets; it deploys greatly extended passages of stichomythia. The choral songs are more numerous than in other late plays, and the first of them (the entry-song of the chorus) is very long. Above all it creates an emotionally charged but unstable world marked by botched deception and exciting disclosure, by an anti-hero, Agamemnon, who is tormented by indecision, and by a young Iphigenia, who combines a childlike innocence with heroic self-determination. The worlds of *IA* and of *Bacchae* barely touch and yet, in the theatre, they were juxtaposed, played one after the other before the same audience. They attest not merely the variety of Euripides' theatrical imagination but also the fact that his audiences were accustomed to experience tragedy not in the form of a single play but as a sequence of three separate tragic fictions, rounded off by anti-tragic burlesque.

Europa, in myth, is usually said to be the daughter of the Phoenician king Agenor. *Zeus saw her when she was playing with her companions on the seashore and was filled with desire for her. So he turned himself into, or sent, a beautiful bull, which approached her and enticed her by its mildness to climb on its back. At once it made off with her and plunged into the sea, then swam to *Crete. There Zeus made love to her, and she bore him two or three children, *Minos, Rhadamanthys, and, in post-Homeric accounts, *Sarpedon. She was then married to Asterius, king of Crete, who adopted her sons as his own. Zeus gave her three presents: the bronze man Tālōs to guard the island, a hound which always caught its quarry, and a javelin which always hit its mark. The last two passed afterwards to Minos, thence to Procris and so to her husband *Cephalus. Agenor, anxious about Europa, sent his sons *Cadmus, Phoenix, and Cilix to find her, and their mother went too. But when they failed to find Europa, they all chose to settle elsewhere, and Agenor never saw them again. The bull whose form Zeus had taken became the *constellation Taurus.

Eurōpē The name originally stood for central Greece. It was soon extended to the whole Greek mainland and by 500 BC to the entire land mass behind it. The boundary between the European continent and Asia was usually fixed at the river Don. *Homer's range of information hardly extended north of Greece or west of Sicily. The Mediterranean seaboard of Europe was chiefly opened up by the Greeks between c.750 and c.550 (see COLONIZATION, GREEK). The Atlantic coasts and 'Tin Islands' were discovered by the Phoenicians; *Pytheas circumnavigated Britain and followed the mainland coast at least to Heligoland. Thule remained a land of mystery. The Greeks penetrated by way of the Russian rivers as far as Kiev. North of the Balkans they located the mythical Hyperboreans. Greek pioneers ascended the Danube (see DANUVIUS) to the Iron Gates, and the Rhône perhaps to Lake Léman. But Herodotus had only a hazy notion of central Europe, and the Hellenistic Greeks knew little more.

The land exploration of Europe was chiefly accomplished by Roman armies. They completed the Carthaginian discovery of Spain; under Caesar they made Gaul known; under Augustus' generals, Licinius Crassus, *Tiberius, and Drusus (see CLAUDIUS DRUSUS, NERO), they opened up the Balkan lands, the Alpine massif, and the Danube basin. Tiberius and Drusus also overran western Germany to the Elbe.

The Europe–Asia polarity was important in Greek ideology; the two together were taken to represent the whole inhabited space (Africa/Libya being sometimes added as a third constituent). A Eurocentric chauvinism is evident in Roman thought: acc. to *Pliny the Elder, Europe is 'by far the finest of all lands'.

Eurystheus, in mythology, granted rule of the Argolid by *Zeus through *Hera's trickery. *Heracles was enslaved to him while he performed his twelve Labours, on the orders of the *Delphic oracle and as a punishment for killing his wife and children in a fit of madness. In art Eurystheus is depicted as a coward, hiding fearfully in a great jar when Heracles delivers e.g. the Erymanthian boar. Even after Heracles' death, Eurystheus persecuted his descendants, the *Heraclids.

Eusēbius, of Caesarea (c. AD 260–339), prolific writer, biblical scholar and apologist, founder of the Christian genres of Church history and chronicle, and the most important contemporary source for the reign of *Constantine I. His intellectual formation at *Caesarea owed much to the influence of Pamphilus (martyred 310), by whom he was apparently adopted, and to their joint use of the library of *Origen. From his election as bishop of Caesarea c.313 until his death in 339, Eusebius played a significant role in ecclesiastical politics in the eastern empire.

euthȳna, euthȳnai ('straightening'), the examination of accounts which every public official underwent on expiry of his office. At Athens the examination fell into two parts, the *logos* ('account'), concerned with his handling of public money and dealt with by a board of ten *logistai* ('accountants'), and the *euthynai* proper, an opportunity to raise any other objection to his conduct in office, dealt with by a board of ten *euthȳnoi* ('straighteners') appointed by the council (*boule). These officials could dismiss accusations or pass them on to the courts.

Euxine ('the hospitable'), the Greek name for the Black Sea, evidently a euphemism. From a Mediterranean perspective, it was cold, very deep, not very saline, and prone to storms. It carried extensive trade both between its shores and with the Mediterranean world. Most Greek settlements around the Black Sea were established during the 6th cent. BC and regarded themselves as Milesian foundations. The earliest extant treatment of the Black Sea is that of Herodotus, whose errors and misconceptions are such that it has been claimed that he never went there. See COLONIZATION, GREEK; MILETUS; TRADE.

evidence, attitudes to (Greek and Roman). There are various contexts in which Greeks and Romans sought to demonstrate things. Problems of knowledge were raised by philosophers at least as early as *Plato (this is one function of the theory of forms), even though theory of knowledge did not become an independent issue until the rise of scepticism (see PYRRHON). In history, however, the question esp. interested the founders of the genre. *Herodotus repeatedly identifies his informants, even when he explicitly rejects their accounts. *Thucydides (2) too uses oral testimony, but realizes the dangers of oral tradition (see ORALITY): this presumably is why he sticks to contemporary history, where he combines an explicit theory of cross-examination with a steadfast refusal to acknowledge his sources. One later Greek historian, *Polybius, pays at least lip-service to Thucydides' views on evidence, but the question did not apparently worry Roman writers: *Livy's Preface displays an explicit commitment to the truth, but he makes no use of primary sources; and even this commitment seems to be undermined by the half-heartedness with which *Cicero acknowledges the historian's duty not to lie.

The principal arena for evidence is the lawcourt. Witnesses in Classical Athens took precedence over documents (See LITERACY; ORALITY), but they could not be cross-examined (indeed, after c.380 BC their evidence was submitted in writing), and although they are cited over 400 times in the surviving speeches, they serve mainly to confirm the version of events given by the litigant as speaker. Only a free adult male could witness in an Athenian court: a woman could swear an evidentiary *oath, and a slave could be required to give evidence under torture, but in each case this required the consent of both litigants, and none of the 42 attested challenges to torture was ever carried through. Greek rhetorical theorists distinguish various categories of persuasive arguments. *Aristotle notably classifies laws as forms of evidence alongside witnesses, agreements, oaths, and torture, but this reflects a system where to cite the law is the litigant's privilege, not the judge's duty.

evidence, Roman Evidence, in the sense of the methods by which the facts at issue in a legal proceeding are established, was of little interest to the Roman *jurists. For them the proof of facts was the concern of the advocates (see ADVOCACY). This division between law and fact was embodied in the division between the proceedings before the magistrate and before the lay judge. Witnesses play a prominent part in Roman law, but there was no legal preference for their evidence, as opposed to proof by other means.

exchange See FINANCE; GIFT; MONEY; RECIPROCITY.

exedra, a recess with benches.

exile

Greek   Exile (*phygē*, lit. 'flight') is permanent or long-term removal from one's native place, usually as a punishment imposed by government or other superior power. In Greece it was from earliest times a standard consequence of homicide, and was as much a religious way of getting rid of a source of *pollution as a punishment.

In Classical Greece exile was a punishment for various offences, such as professional failure by a general or ambassador. Sometimes, however, the ambiguity of the word 'to flee'—'be exiled' or 'flee'—means we do not know if an individual was formally exiled or simply fled voluntarily to escape worse. In addition, we often hear of political exiles, as individuals or groups. Again, it is sometimes unclear whether such exiles were driven out by actual decree or because life was for whatever reason intolerable. Decrees of exile were sometimes reversed. As a result of *Alexander (2) the Great's 'Exiles' Decree', exiles returned to their origins. As beneficiaries of this general policy, Samians returned to *Samos in 322, 44 years after their expulsion by Athens, which therefore found itself with an influx of refugees of its own; the *Lamian War between Athens and Macedon was the result. The 5th-cent. Athenian institution of *ostracism was an unusual sort of exile in that it was for ten years only and involved no loss of property. *Argos and *Syracuse had or borrowed similar practices.

Roman   Exile, either undertaken voluntarily to escape a penalty (usually death), or imposed as a punishment, was common in the ancient world. In Rome it was originally voluntary. A person threatened by criminal proceedings for a capital offence could, even after the proceedings had begun, but before sentence, remove himself from Roman jurisdiction. This self-banishment was tolerated by the magistrates, provided that the person did not return from exile. In the late republic this *exsilium* was institutionalized as, in effect, a substitute for the death penalty. The magistrates were required to allow a condemned person time to escape before a capital sentence was executed. After his departure a decree denying water and fire excluded him from all legal protection and threatened him with death if he returned illicitly. This kind of exile was replaced under the Principate by a formal sentence of deportation or of the milder penalty of *relegation.

experiment   Greek and Roman scientists did not refer directly to the experimental method. However, in a variety of contexts they described testing procedures that were clearly deliberate investigations designed to throw light on problems or to support theories. Examples can be found in the Presocratic philosophers, the Hippocratic writers (see HIPPOCRATES), *Aristotle, Erasistratus, *Ptolemy (2), and *Galen.

We should distinguish first the areas where experimental investigation is possible from those where it is not. Direct experiments in astronomy are out of the question. This was also true, in antiquity, in relation to most problems in meteorology (thunder and lightning) and in geology (*earthquakes). In such cases ancient scientists often conjectured analogies with other more accessible phenomena that were directly investigable. Some of the experimental interventions described in the Hippocratic writers incorporate an element of analogy. The writer of *Diseases* 4 describes a system of intercommunicating vessels which can be filled or emptied by filling or emptying one of them. He uses this to explain the movements of the humours between the main sources in the body (stomach, heart, head, spleen, liver). What this shares with an experiment is the careful construction of an artificial set-up. Where it differs from experiment in the strict sense is that its relevance to the physiological problem discussed depends entirely on the strength of the analogy suggested (in this case a mere conjecture).

Sometimes, however, direct interventions are proposed. Examples can be given from *physics, harmonics, optics, physiology, and anatomy. Thus Aristotle states that he has proved by testing that sea water on evaporation becomes fresh: however, he then goes on to claim that the same is true of other flavoured liquids including wine—a typical risky extension of an experimental result.

Optics provides one of our fullest examples of a series of careful experiments, though the results have been adjusted to suit the general theory proposed. In his *Optics* Ptolemy describes his investigations of refraction between three pairs of media (from air to water, air to glass, and water to glass). He describes the apparatus used and records the results to within a half degree for angles of incidence at 10-degree intervals. However, the results all exactly confirm a general 'law'. Elsewhere he provides convincing experimental proof of the elementary laws of reflection, to establish, for instance, that the angle of incidence equals the angle of reflection.

Experiments in the strict sense were attempted also in the life sciences. Erasistratus described one in which a bird is kept in a vessel without food for a given period of time, after which he weighed the animal together with the visible excreta and compared this with the original weight. This he took to show that there are invisible effluvia from animals—again an over-interpretation of a correct result. Galen used experimental *vivisections on animals to investigate various problems. He showed the peristalsis of the stomach in one, and produced a detailed account of the courses of the nerves in systematic experiments on the spinal cords of pigs. In the latter case no general theory is at stake: what the experiments reveal is the precise connection between vital functions and particular nerves.

Ancient scientists thus showed considerable ingenuity in devising testing procedures. However, what this exemplifies is not so much the idea of a crucial experiment, an ideally neutral means of adjudicating between theories antecedently deemed to be of equal plausibility, as the appeal to tests specifically to support or to falsify a theory. In this way, experiments in antiquity are an extension, though an important one, of the use of evidence. See EVIDENCE, ANCIENT ATTITUDES TO.

extortion See REPETUNDAE.

Fabius Maximus Verrūcōsus, Quintus, as consul 233 BC celebrated a *triumph over the *Ligurians and unsuccessfully opposed the agrarian bill of *Flaminius. He was *censor 230, consul for the second time 228, and *dictator (probably) 221. Dictator again in 217, after the Roman defeat at Lake Trasimene, he began his famous policy of attrition, believing that Hannibal could not be defeated in a pitched battle; this earned him the name 'Cunctator' (the Delayer). He allowed Hannibal to ravage the plain of *Campania, but then blocked his exits; Hannibal, however, escaped by a stratagem. Opposition to Fabius' policy at Rome led to his *magister equitum, Minucius Rufus, receiving *imperium equal to his. When Minucius was enticed into a rash venture, Fabius rescued him. The traditional policy of fighting fixed battles was resumed in 216, but after the disaster at *Cannae there was no alternative to Fabius' policy. Helped by his position as the senior member of the college of *augurs, he became suffect consul for the third time for 215, operating in Campania. He was re-elected for 214, helped to recapture Casilinum and had a number of successes in *Samnium. Direct control of affairs now passed to other men, but Fabius reached his final consulship in 209, when he recaptured *Tarentum and was made *princeps senatus. In 205 he strongly opposed *Cornelius Scipio Africanus' plan to invade Africa. He was no doubt alarmed by Scipio's growing prestige, but genuinely believed that taking the war to Africa posed unnecessary dangers. Scipio brought the war to an end, but Fabius' cautious strategy had made victory possible. Fabius died in 203. He had been *pontifex since 216 as well as augur, a distinction unique until *Sulla and *Caesar.

Fabius Pictor, Quintus, the first Roman historian. He wrote in Greek. A member of the senate, he went on an embassy to *Delphi in 216 BC. His reasons for writing in Greek were both literary—the possibility of writing in Latin did not occur to him—and political, the need to defend Roman policy to the Greek world. Like other early historians of Rome, he appears to have dealt at length with the foundation legend and then passed rapidly to recent history.

fable, a short story in the popular tradition of Greece and other ancient cultures. Fables usually deal with a conflict in which animals speak and intervene, but the characters may also be plants, sundry objects, men, or gods, Fable normally deals with the triumph of the strong, but also portrays the cunning of the weak and their mockery of, or triumph over, the strong. Fables also stress the impossibility of changing nature; some give aetiological explanations. Usually there is a comic element; sometimes the 'situation' of a protagonist is depicted, from which the audience may draw analogies. The boundaries of fable overlap with those of myth, animal proverbs, anecdotes, tales, and clever sayings. Fable is normally fiction, but does at times use anecdotes about real characters. It reflects popular literature and may satirize the values and abuses of the dominant social classes.

Greek fable originated in Greece, but clearly absorbed foreign traditions, esp. Mesopotamian fable. In its turn, Greek fable influenced Indian fable. From the time of *Lucilius (1) Greek fable gave rise to numerous fables in Latin. In Greek literature fable appears as an example, used alongside myth and the historical or fictitious anecdote, from the time of *Hesiod ('The Hawk and the Nightingale'). Thereafter it is found above all in the writers of iambics (*Archilochus, *Semonides), and was used by elegists (*Theognis), lyric poets (*Simonides) and playwrights. It appears in prose in *Herodotus and is a favourite medium of the Socratic writers.

From the end of the 5th cent. BC, the authorship of fables was often attributed to *Aesop, whom a dubious tradition identifies as a Phrygian slave in Samos. From the Hellenistic era on, classical fable produced new versions, and new fables were constantly being created. The chief means of diffusion was the collection of fables, the first of which was compiled by *Demetrius of Phaleron *c.*300 BC. From this collection derived various others, some anonymous, others 'signed' by authors like *Phaedrus and *Babrius, who attempted to turn fable into a poetic genre.

fābula (besides meaning 'story', 'talk', '*fable') was the general Latin term for 'play' or 'drama'. The following types of Latin *fabulae* are mentioned: *fabula *Atellāna*; *palliāta*, sometimes used of all drama with a Greek setting, but normally restricted to comedy (*pallium* = Greek cloak); *plānipedia* (= *mime; *plānipēs*, 'flatfoot', was a term for a mime-actor); *praetexta(ta)*, serious drama on Roman historical subjects (the *toga praetexta* was worn by high magistrates).

family, Greek See HOUSEHOLD, GREEK.

family, Roman Biologically, an individual human being is related to parents, through them to ascendants, aunts, uncles, siblings, and cousins, and may, by sexual intercourse with someone of the other sex, in turn become a parent, linked by blood to descendants. Blood relations for Romans were *cognātī*, the strongest ties normally being with parents and children and the siblings with whom an individual grew up. Relationship established through the sexual tie of marriage was *adfinitās*; kin by marriage were *adfīnēs*. Law initially stressed blood relationship through males: *agnātī* (father's children other than oneself, father's siblings, father's brothers' children, a man's own children, etc.) inherited on intestacy. If she entered *manus* (marital power), a married woman came into the same agnate group as husband and children; if she did not, her legal ties and rights were with her natal family.

The group under the power of a *paterfamiliās* (see PATRIA POTESTAS), whether or not they lived in the same building, was sharply distinguished; there might be other living agnates outside this group. Agnatic forebears were present in family consciousness as recipients of ritual, as *imagines* (portrait–masks) in an aristocratic house, and as links between the living. For the Romans, *familia* could originally mean the patrimony; its more normal usages were to describe (1) those under the power of a *paterfamilias*, kin, or slaves, or (2) all the agnates who had been in such power, or (3) a lineage, like the Julian house, or (4) a group or household of slaves. A lineage in the broadest possible sense, a group allegedly descended from a common mythical ancestor, was *gens*; its members shared a middle name (*nōmen gentilicium*), e.g. Tullius/a, as members of an agnatic *familia* might share a last name (*cognōmen*), e.g. Cicero. *Domus*, besides meaning the building in which someone lived (home or residence: see HOUSES, ITALIAN), covers (1) the *household of free, slave, and freed persons and (2) a broader kinship group including cognates (e.g. the imperial 'family' or dynasty, *domus Caesarum*). Increasingly, descent in the female line came to be valued in sentiment, appraisal of status, and inheritance practices.

The nuclear family is described, in relation to its male head, as consisting of wife and children. Similarly a list of those closest to a particular individual would be drawn up to suit various contexts: Cicero for instance in writing to his brother Quintus at an emotional moment might stress his brother, his daughter, his own son, his wife, his nephew (his only surviving close kin), his wife. In relation to an individual, the kin or *affines* who count change with the phases of life and accidents of survival. The evidence of epitaphs illustrates close family ties as they existed at the time of commemoration: the person(s) who pay for a monument may do so out of love, duty as kin, or duty as beneficiary/ies. Where the commemorator is specified, we get a glimpse of how the family operated, as we do from juristic sources, e.g. on dowry or succession, or literary sources, which chiefly reflect the expectations and practice of the upper classes. Although ties with remoter relations by blood or marriage are acknowledged when they exist, emphasis is normally on the nuclear family.

famine The typical natural and man-made causes of famine were omnipresent: crop failure caused by the unreliable Mediterranean rainfall (see CLIMATE) or pests and diseases, destruction in war, state oppression or incompetence, poor arrangements for transport, storage, and distribution, and profiteering by the élite. Specific food-shortages of varying intensity and chronic malnutrition of the poor were common, but most of the population were subsistence farmers whose primary strategy of production was to minimize risk, and the political culture helped town-dwellers to press their leaders to resolve food crises before they became critical. The exaggerated references to 'famine' in the ancient sources echo the political rhetoric of an urban society where famine was a frequent threat but a rare experience. Local climatic variation meant that relief supplies were normally available within the region, given the political will to obtain them. Most famines were local, brief, and primarily man-made. See FOOD SUPPLY.

fascēs comprised bundles of rods, *c*.1.5 m. (5 ft.) long, and a single-headed axe; they were held together by red thongs and carried by *lictors. A miniature iron set from a late 7th-cent. tomb supports the later tradition of their Etruscan origin. They were the primary visible expression of magisterial authority and hence the focus of a complex symbolism of the magistrates' legitimacy and of their powers *vis-à-vis* citizens, subjects, and each other. They were regularly regarded (and in the republican period used) as instruments of execution, and the absence of the axe from the *fasces* of magistrates (other than *dictators and triumphing generals) within Rome symbolized citizen rights of appeal (**provocatio*) against capital *coercitio*. The alternation of precedence between the two *consuls was manifested in alternate 'tenure' of the *fasces*, and the number of a magistrate's *fasces* depended on his rank: consuls (and in the republic proconsuls) had twelve; dictators probably had 24, *praetors and *magistri equitum* (see MAGISTER EQUITUM) probably six. In the Principate, senatorial governors had the number appropriate to their previous magistracy, imperial *legates had five. In 19 BC Augustus was given the right to twelve *fasces* 'everywhere in perpetuity'; as *imperātōrēs* emperors always had their *fasces* laurelled.

fastī, the calendar of *diēs fasti*, *dies comitiālēs*, and *dies nefastī*, which indicated when a specific legal process organized by the urban *praetor and when assemblies might or might not take place; it received definitive publication in 304 BC. Vulgarly, *dies nefasti* came to be thought of as ill-omened days.

The word *fasti* also covers other listings: *fasti consulārēs* (of consuls, who gave their names to the year), *fasti triumphālēs* (of triumphs), and *fasti sacerdōtālēs* (of priests). Of *fasti consulares* we have the exemplar from Antium (84–55 BC) and the so-called *fasti Capitolīnī*, which were inscribed on an arch in the forum Romanum 18/17 BC. *Fasti triumphales* were also inscribed on the same arch, from Romulus down to the last 'republican' triumph, that of *Cornelius Balbus (2) in 19 BC. The *fasti consulares* and *triumphales* from *c*.300 BC appear consistently accurate, presumably using full regular records. See ANNALES MAXIMI.

fasting is the temporary abstinence from all food for ritual, ascetic, or medicinal purposes. Alien to Roman practice, it was rare in Greek cult, where feasting was more central than fasting. The Greeks, who used the meat of sacrificial animals, amongst other foodstuffs, as offerings to the gods and as meals for human worshippers (see SACRIFICE, GREEK), did not recognize extended periods of ritual fasting on the scale of Ramadan or Lent. In the few cults that made fasting a ritual requirement, its observance was always brief, lasting up to an entire day, and in exceptional circumstances up to three days.

Acc. to *Clement of Alexandria, those initiated into the Eleusinian *mysteries declared that they had performed the required rites preliminary to initiation by reciting the following 'password': 'I fasted, I drank the ritual drink (*kykeōn*), I took from the chest, and having worked [with the sacred implements] I removed [them] into the basket and from the basket into the chest.' In fact, the initiation proper was preceded by a whole day of fasting, which ended at nightfall with the drinking of the *kykeōn*. The initiates' fast, like their breaking of it, had a precedent in the fasting of *Demeter herself, who roamed the earth for nine days abstaining from *ambrosia and nectar, and even from bathing. Later, at Eleusis, 'wasting away with longing for her deep-bosomed daughter, she sat unsmiling, tasting neither food nor drink', until the jests of Iambe prompted her to laugh and to drink the *kykeōn*. Similarly, Achilles refused food after the death of Patroclus. In Greek culture, as in many others, self-neglect was an outward sign of extreme grief and mourning. Fasting was equally integral to another women's festival of Demeter, the *Thesmophoria. On its second day, called 'the Fast' by the Athenians, the participating women 'fasted like mullets', a fish known for its empty stomach. On this day, the 'gloomiest day' of the festival, the subversive women in Aristophanes' *Thesmophoriazusae* hold their assembly while keeping a strict fast. In addition to fasting, the celebrants at the Thesmophoria had to be sexually abstinent for several days. Fasting and sexual abstinence often went hand in hand as techniques designed to promote ritual purity (see PURIFICATION). More importantly, for the Greeks they signal a ritual departure from the social conventions of normal life.

See also ASCETICISM.

fate The common Greek words for fate mean 'share', 'portion'. One's share is appointed or falls to one at birth. The most important share is man's universal fate of death from which not even the gods can protect him. In *Homer's *Iliad* *Zeus considers saving his son *Sarpedon and favourite *Hector from imminent death, but *Hera and *Athena dissuade him from upsetting the natural order of things.

The workings of fate can appear irrational. At one moment the Pythia (see DELPHIC ORACLE) tells Lydian enquirers that 'no one, not even the god, can escape his appointed *moira*', at the next *Apollo postpones the sack of *Sardis for three years to help *Croesus. Nevertheless a governing principle of proper order attaches to the basic meaning of 'share' in *moira*, *aisa*, and their derivatives, even when they do not obviously refer to fate. They can describe a section of land, share of booty, or portions of meat. The developed notion of due order determined all shares, including that of fate and death, which fitted into a kind of prescribed order of the world.

The notion of a universal power of fate was less evident in Roman thought. Like the personified plural Fāta, the Parcae became goddesses of fate through assimilation with the three Moirai. See also STOICISM; TYCHE.

Favōrīnus (c. AD 85–155), sophist, philosopher, and man of letters. Born in Gallic Arelate, he learned Greek, and worked only in that language throughout his professional career. His speaking tours took him to Athens, Corinth, and Ionia, where he contracted a bitter feud with his fellow sophist Polemon. He was a friend of *Plutarch, and the teacher and associate of *Herodes Atticus, *Fronto, and Aulus *Gellius (who quotes and refers to him often). At Rome he moved in the circle of *Hadrian, was advanced to *equestrian rank, and held the office of a provincial high priest. He fell into disfavour, c.130. Under *Antoninus Pius he recovered his position. His extensive writings may be divided into three categories: (a) Miscellanies, esp. the *Memoirs* and the *Miscellaneous History*, of which the first was devoted to stories about philosophers. (b) Declamations. (c) Philosophical works, in which Favorinus presented himself as an adherent of the 'old' scepticism of the *Academy.

Fayūm, a natural depression in west-central Egypt, in whose centre is the remnant of Lake Moeris. Far more extensive in Herodotus' day, King Ptolemy II instigated its drainage. Many papyri and inscriptions survive from its towns and villages.

federal states are found in the Greek world from the late 6th cent. BC. The term is used of those organizations in which the separate city-states (see POLIS) of a geographical and ethnic region were combined to form a single entity at any rate for purposes of foreign policy, while for local purposes retaining their separate identity as city-states and their separate citizenship. Thus *Boeotia was a federal state in which the individual communities were still regarded as cities, whereas *Attica formed the city-state of Athens and the *demes did not have the degree of *autonomy appropriate to cities. Tribal states in the less urbanized parts of Greece (e.g. Aetolia) were like federal states in that the tribal organization comprised units with a considerable degree of local autonomy. There is no ancient Greek term which precisely denotes a federal state: the words most often used are *koinon* ('commonwealth') and *ethnos* ('nation').

The earliest evidence of a federal state is in (probably) 519 BC, when *Plataea resisted incorporation in a Boeotian federal state dominated by *Thebes and gained the protection of Athens; there are references to the Boeotarchs, the chief magistrates of the federation, in 480–479. The federation may have broken up after the Persian Wars, and for a time Boeotia was controlled by Athens, but it was revived after 446, and we have evidence for its basic mechanisms. The individual cities had similar constitutions, with one-quarter at a time of the full citizens who satisfied a property qualification acting as a probouleutic (see BOULE) council. The federation was based on electoral units, eleven after 427; the largest cities with their dependencies accounted for more than one unit, while the smallest were grouped together to form a unit; each unit provided one Boeotarch and 60 members of a council of 660, and within the council one-quarter at a time acted as the probouleutic body.

Felix, brother of *Antonius Pallas, was appointed *procurator of Judaea by *Claudius in AD 52, although an imperial *freedman. One of his three wives was a daughter of Antony (see ANTONIUS, MARCUS ASCUS) and *Cleopatra VII. He captured and crucified bandits, and massacred the followers of an Egyptian prophet. He was preached to by St *Paul, whom he kept in prison in *Caesarea for two years. The quarrel over control of Caesarea between Jews and 'Greeks' led to his recall by the emperor.

festivals

Greek Greek festivals were religious *rituals re-curring, usually every year, two years, or four years, at fixed times in the calendar. Unlike *sacrifices and other rituals performed for specific occasions (e.g. marriage) or in times of crisis, they were intended to maintain or renew the desired relationship with supernatural powers. In the Classical period it was believed that this relationship was maintained by rendering honour, at the appropriate time and in the appropriate manner, to the deity.

The festivals of Athens (see ATTIC CULTS) are best known, and their origins, like those of all Greek festivals, are multifarious, with some going back to pre-Greek neolithic times, some instituted to honour contemporary Hellenistic kings. Over the centuries new elements were added to old festivals (e.g. the *Panathenaea), and separate festivals on consecutive days may have coalesced into one (e.g. *Anthestēria). Many lasted one day only (e.g. *Thargēlia); some, like the City *Dionysia in Athens, lasted five or six days. Athens devoted at least 60 days a year to annual festivals.

The religious concerns of the Greeks were many, and the variety of the festivals and rituals reflects this. Rarely does a single festival address only one concern. It is possible to distinguish some major types of developed festivals. Agonistic (see AGONES) festivals, each eventually assigned to an Olympian deity, consisted initially of a *pompē* (procession), a *thysia* (sacrifice), an *agōn* (contest), and a banquet, in that order. The contests might be 'athletic' (human and equestrian races of various types, boxing, wrestling, etc.) or 'musical' (lyre- and pipe-playing, recitations, dancing, and drama), or both. The original *agon* at *Olympia was, acc. to myth, simply a 200-m. (*c*.220-yd.) foot-race. As contests were added, some were placed before the procession, and by the 5th cent. BC the programmes had become very large.

Periodic fertility rituals, many going back to the neolithic period, were often performed by women, often in secret. Some were genuine *mysteries (as at Eleusis). Those centred on agriculture naturally occurred at critical times in the farming cycle, e.g. at ploughing (Proērosia), at seeding (*Thesmophoria), and at harvest (Thargelia), with rituals appropriate to the deity and crop in question. Because concepts of human, animal, and crop fertility were intertwined, sympathetic *magic played a role. For this reason, and because of their secrecy and the combining of two or more festivals, the rituals of fertility festivals are esp. complex and opaque.

Through certain annual rituals, again of great antiquity, the Greeks initiated young people into adult society, in Athens esp. at the *Apaturia for young men and at the Brauronia (see BRAURON) for young women. The rituals differed significantly from city to city, but generally followed the pattern of separation, liminal experience, and reintegration characteristic of such *rites of passage.

A festival presumes a group, in the Greek context the smallest being a village (a deme in Athens), the usual the *polis*, a few confederations (see FEDERAL STATES), and the largest all the Greeks (see PANHELLENISM). By the Classical period the *polis* had absorbed many village festivals and now financed and administered them. Through festivals a *polis* like Athens might celebrate its own origins (the Synoecia, see SYNOECISM), its national identity and accomplishments (Panathenaea), or, in later times, its military victories. The festivals could be integrated into the legendary history of the city, as, at Athens, the Oschophoria were tied to Theseus' expedition to Crete. In all festivals the roles and often even dress of the participants maintained traditional divisions of citizen status, sex, age, and office; and thus a festival could provide cohesion to the group but simultaneously reassert traditional social orders. On the other hand, a few festivals, the Cronia (see CRONUS) in Athens and the Hybristica in *Argos provided a temporary reversal of the social order, with slaves acting as masters or women as men. Confederations of states with both tribal and geographical ties had cult centres with their own festivals, e.g. the Panionia (see PANIONIUM) for *Poseidon at Mycale.

Roman (feriae) The basic notion included not only the honouring of the gods, but also restrictions on public life: the courts were closed, some agricultural work was restricted, and in some cases holidays given to other workers. Festivals were of various kinds: some fixed by the regular calendar of the *fasti* (see CALENDAR, ROMAN); movable festivals were held annually on days appointed by priests or magistrates; special festivals were ordered, again by priests or magistrates, because of a specific event, a prodigy (see PORTENTS), a disaster, or a victory. A major element in many public festivals was the accompanying games (see LUDI).

fētiālēs, priests of the Latin states, concerned with the procedures and laws of declaring wars and making treaties. Our information comes from Rome, where they formed a college (*collegium*) of 20 members, who advised the senate on issues of peace and war, and had their own legal tradition. The institution presupposes that similar priests, with whom Roman *fetiales* interacted, existed in the other Latin states.

finance, Greek The collective deployment of resources by the community inevitably has socio-political implications (who pays? who benefits?). But public finance in Greek states rarely had economic aims beyond the broad balancing of incomings and outgoings. *Oikonomia* ('economics') as applied to state finance preserved autarkic (see AUTARKY) attitudes appropriate to its original meaning of 'household management'. Recurring expenditure (primarily on administration, cult, ambassadors, defence, maintenance of fortifications, gymnasia, and public buildings) would be met from a variety of revenues (rents and royalties from state property, including mines and quarries, court fees and fines, taxes on non-citizens, sales taxes, excise duties and customs dues). Collection of taxes was regularly farmed out by auction to private individuals. Extraordinary expenditure (typically arising from warfare or food shortage; occasionally, on public building) was met by ad hoc measures: property and poll taxes, public loans, creation of monopolies, contributions, or confiscations. Warfare itself was seen as potentially productive, and would occasionally prove so. Systems of Greek public finance may be assessed in so far as they conform to or deviate from these norms.

In Homeric society *reciprocity between aristocratic households prevailed. Resources were deployed by the giving of gift and counter-gift (see GIFT, GREECE): in return for their contributions to the élite, the people received protection. Arrangements in Archaic and even Classical *Sparta resembled Homeric organization in the near absence of any centralized system of finance. The mainstay of the regime was the agricultural produce appropriated from the *helots by individual Spartiates, who passed on a portion to their *syssition (public mess). Details are obscure (the *perioikoi may have made contributions in cash or kind), but the small scale of resources under central control helps to account for the poor showing of late 5th-cent. Sparta as a city. Much the same might be said of the rudimentary systems of finance operated by the

aristocracies dominating early Archaic *poleis*. Archaic tyrants provide a stark contrast: their characteristically heavy expenditure on public buildings and central, civic institutions gave the *polis* a new, urban emphasis. Necessary resources were raised by a combination of personal taxes and other, extraordinary measures: in Athens, a tax on agricultural produce. Also characteristic of Archaic tyranny was the effective merging of the tyrant's own resources with those of the state. The ending of *tyranny caused an immediate reaction against the tyrants' financial methods: taxes on the person became a symbol of oppression, restricted to non-citizens and those of low status.

Archaic Athens broadly conformed to this pattern; as late as the 480s, it was proposed that a windfall gain of 100 talents from the silver mines at *Laurium be parcelled out among the citizen body. Shortly after, Athenian finances were transformed by the acquisition of a tribute-paying empire (see DELIAN LEAGUE). Figures from the eve of the Peloponnesian War give a crude impression of scale: from a total annual revenue of *c*.1,000 talents some 600 talents derived from the empire. This made possible the maintenance of a massive navy, an extended programme of public building, provision of public pay, and the accumulation on the Acropolis of a strategic reserve of at least 6,000 talents. Against this, expenses of war were heavy: one talent in pay to keep one trireme at sea for one month. As the Peloponnesian War progressed, there was (in addition to an upward reassessment of the tribute in 425; see TRIBUTE LISTS, ATHENIAN) increasing reliance on payments of *eisphora*—an extraordinary property tax falling on the rich. By contrast, the Spartan system was poorly placed to generate the resources needed for extended warfare. Appeals for contributions from sympathetic individuals proved inadequate, and only massive subventions of Persian gold made possible the eventual Spartan victory. The importance of imperial revenues for Athens' *democracy became apparent in the 4th cent., when the range of public payments was actually extended to include assembly pay and payments from the theoric fund (see THEORIKA). Collective aspirations may be read into the explicit aim behind the proposals in *Xenophon's *Revenues*: maintenance of the citizen body at public expense. Attempts to revive the tribute-paying empire failed and heavier burdens therefore fell on the rich. The degree to which increasing demands disrupted and alienated the Athenian élite is disputed. There emerged in the course of the 4th cent. a group of financial experts (including *Eubulus and culminating in *Lycurgus), who held tailor-made offices and made the most of Athens' internal resources.

Characteristic of finance in Classical Athens was the *liturgy system, requiring the élite to perform public services (*trierarchy and *choregia). Liturgies were an integral part of the democratic system: in return for their services, liturgists might (or might not) receive popular consideration in politics and the courts. Aristotle recommends that oligarchies attach expensive duties to high public office, so excluding all but the rich. This privileging of wealth ties in with the broadly post-democratic practice of *euergetism, common in Hellenistic cities. The 'benefactor' earned enhanced status, and possibly material rewards, by making donations in cash or kind to the advantage of the citizen body.

finance, Roman 'Taxes are the sinews of the state.' So claimed both Cicero and *Domitius Ulpianus (Ulpian). Despite this recognition of the central importance of taxation, no systematic ancient treatment of Roman public finance survives. Extended financial documents are also rare. Many details about (e.g.) the allocation and collection of taxes or about the character of fiscal institutions remain obscure. Even so, the broad features of the history and development of Roman public finance through the republic and the Principate can be delineated with some confidence.

In the republic there were two major types of revenue namely the regular *vectigalia and the *tributum, an extraordinary (in principle) levy on the property of Roman citizens. The total size of this levy was decided by the senate and varied from year to year. The earliest detailed account of republican public finance survives in the sketch of the Roman constitution in bk. 6 of *Polybius, reflecting conditions in the mid-2nd cent. BC. The *aerarium, the central depository of the state for both cash and documents, was managed by two urban quaestors; but all decisions as to payments from it were made by the senate. On setting out on campaign a consul could draw funds on his own responsibility. But further payments, for the supplies, clothing, or pay of the army, had again to be authorized by the senate. The senate also made a quinquennial grant to the censors, on the basis of which they let out contracts for building and repairs of public buildings in Rome and the *municipia and

colonies of Italy and for the exploitation of public properties—rivers, harbours, gardens, *mines, and land. Ultimate control of the contracts, e.g. in altering the terms, again lay with the senate.

The most important development, not reflected in Polybius' account of the last two centuries of the republic, was the acquisition of a territorial empire overseas. At first resources were extracted from the conquered via *booty and war indemnities, in the medium term by the imposition of regular taxation (tribute) in cash or kind. Provincial governors (and their quaestors) were responsible for the supervision of the collection of tribute and for expenditure in their province. After 123 in Asia certainly (and perhaps elsewhere) the process of collection of tribute was contracted out to *publicani. Two prime consequences ensued from this development. First, the levying of tribute on Roman citizens in Italy was abandoned from 167 onwards. Secondly, the revenues of the state were greatly increased. On one estimate annual revenues in the early 2nd cent. were 12.5 to 15 million dēnārii. By the late 60s they had increased to 50 million; and acc. to a difficult passage of Plutarch, Pompey's great conquests in the 60s further increased revenues to either 85 or 135 million. The continuing access of new revenues both ensured that Rome's continuous wars were in the long term self-financing and allowed the creation of novel forms of public expenditure such as the distribution of subsidized, later free, corn to Roman citizens. (See FOOD SUPPLY.) Even so, public revenues remained modest in relation to the private wealth of the élite. The fortune of *Crassus alone amounted to 48 million denarii.

The establishment of imperial rule entailed far-reaching changes in public finance and the creation of an elaborate fiscal state. First, although the senate retained the function of making routine votes of funds, effective control over the state's finances came to lie with the emperor and his agents. Under Augustus we meet for the first time the publication of general accounts (ratiōnēs) of the public funds. At his death full details of the state's finances were in the hands of his personal slaves and freedmen. The public post of ā ratiōnibus ('financial secretary', first held by imperial freedmen, later by senior *equestrians) soon emerged. By the late 1st cent. AD this official was responsible for estimating the revenues and expenditure of the state. Secondly, direct taxation in the provinces, in the form of the poll tax and the land tax, was placed on a new footing through the introduction by *Augustus and *Agrippa of periodic provincial censuses (see CENSUS). These mapped out the human and physical resources of the provinces and formed the basis for the assessments of tribute for each city and its territory. Whenever a new province was annexed, a census was taken. Provincial governors and imperial procurators supervised the collection of tribute; the process of collection devolved on the individual civic authorities. Thirdly, Rome's revenues were vastly increased, although no secure figures survive. The annexation of new provinces (that of Egypt in 30 BC was esp. important) of itself increased revenues. A new array of indirect taxes was introduced. The most important were, probably, the 5 per cent tax on inheritances of AD 6 (hypothecated to the discharge payment for veterans) and the 4 per cent tax on the sale of slaves of AD 7 (hypothecated to the pay of the *vigiles). The first three centuries AD also saw the steady accretion of landed property (via legacies, gifts, and confiscations) in the hands of the emperor. The importance of revenue from such crown property was considerable, if unquantifiable, and is already manifest in Augustus' own account, in his *Res Gestae, of his expenditure on public needs. This formidable array of revenues (tribute in cash and kind, indirect taxes, revenues from crown property) enabled the imperial state to carry out, routinely, key political functions such as the distribution of the corn-dole at Rome, the upkeep of the imperial court, the construction and maintenance of an elaborate road network (see ROADS) across the empire, the payment of salaries to senatorial and equestrian officials (one million sesterces p.a. for a proconsul) and, above all, the funding of the vast standing armed forces of c.350,000 men. This fiscal system presupposed, in its mature form in the 2nd cent., a basic predictability of expenditure and revenue and the state's ability to exercise uncontested authority over the territory of the empire. However, potential problems in the form of sudden emergencies or increases in expenditure were already apparent in the later 2nd cent. The great northern wars under Marcus *Aurelius rapidly depleted the reserves of the treasury. In turn the major pay rises for the army of *Severus and *Caracalla were funded in part by significant debasements of the silver coinage. (See COINAGE, ROMAN.)

fire Acc. to Greek myth, *Prometheus stole fire from the gods for mortals with dire conse-quences. The name of the god *Hephaestus is often synonymous with fire. Fire figures prominently in the cosmologies of *Heraclitus, *Parmenides, the Pythagoreans (see PYTHAGORAS), and *Empedocles.

The status of fire as an *element presented problems throughout antiquity. *Theophrastus noted at the beginning of his treatise *On Fire* that 'of the simple substances fire has the most special powers'; much of the rest of the work is concerned with describing its various manifestations, and coming to terms with the problem of how such an element can exist only in the company of a material substrate, and how it can generate itself and be generated in such a variety of ways. Heat, flame, and light are different species of fire in many theories, including that of *Aristotle. Fire's dynamic properties, and its natural tendency to move upwards in space, figure in physiological and cognitive theories. In many biological theories, fire's special status is linked to breath, and life itself. In Stoic physics (see STOICISM), fire is the one element which remains constant even when one particular world-order comes to an end.

Fire was not easy to kindle, and the easiest way to ensure its availability was to keep a flame or glowing embers burning. If a fire went out, and could not be relit from a neighbour's hearth, it could be restarted by rubbing together two pieces of wood surrounded by tinder. The fire-drill consisted of a drill and a base made of hardwood. The drill was rotated with the aid of a bow-like contrivance. Fire could also be kindled from sparks struck from flint or pyrite, or with the help of a burning-glass. Burning-glasses are mentioned in Aristophanes' *Clouds*, but this method of fire-lighting seems to have been rare; *Archimedes may have known that fire could be kindled by suitably arranged mirrors, although the story that he set fire to the Roman fleet besieging Syracuse in this way must be apocryphal.

Fire is also normally essential to animal sacrifice, see SACRIFICE, GREEK.

first-fruits (Gk. *aparchai). The custom of offering firstlings to the gods from the produce of agriculture, hunting, or fishing was widespread in ancient Greece, ranging in scale from simple gifts in humble agrarian settings to organized donations made in the context of the Eleusinian *mysteries. One common form is known as *panspermia*, the bringing of a mixture of fruits at various festivals, sometimes cooked in a pot (at the *Thargelia and Pyanopsia

('Bean-boiling')). Firstlings of animal sacrifice are offered by the swineherd Eumaeus in *Odyssey* 14. At the mysteries *aparchai* of wheat and barley are requested of all Athenians, allies, and even other Greeks, to be delivered after the harvest, and were sold to provide sacrifices and a dedication. Acc. to the Greeks, first-fruits were brought in order to ensure fertility.

fiscus originally meant 'basket' or 'money-bag' and thence came to denote the private funds of an individual or, in an administrative context, the public funds held by a provincial governor. In the Principate it came to denote both the private funds of the emperor and the whole financial administration controlled by the emperor.

fishing Numbers of *Mediterranean fish vary from year to year: gluts occur, but dearth is so frequent that it is unwise to make fish protein more than a supplement to a subsistence diet. The nutritional usefulness is greatly increased by drying and salting. Even in times of glut, and assuming very favourable conditions for fishing, total yields cannot have made an important contribution to the protein needs of even small ancient populations, compared with *cereal or legume staples (see FOOD AND DRINK). They did, however, play a significant role in diversifying a diet based on those staples, which was important both nutritionally and culturally in the classic Mediterranean pairing of staple and 'relish'—Gk. *opson*. Salted or pickled fish was the *opson par excellence*, and widely available for use in small quantities.

To the producer, this demand gave the catch the economic status of a cash crop, and enabled the secondary purchase of more protein than could easily have been acquired through consuming the fish. On this base of widely disseminated eating of fish-pickle, the fisherman could rely on a more lucrative market in fresh fish, which could fetch high prices. This combination of ready availability of fish *opsa* with the opulent associations of fresh fish prized by the connoisseur underlies the great prominence of fish in the Athenian comic tradition. What had been characteristic of Athens became a feature of most towns in the Hellenistic and Roman periods; study of the *amphorae reveals the scale and complexity of the trade in *garum* (as the pickle came to be known), while the competitive consumption of the exquisites of high society provided a continuing stock of anecdote about colossal prices and singular specimens.

The fisherman became a type of opportunism and poverty.

Fishing in the open sea was chancy and hazardous, but essential for the most prized fish. Many local markets were supplied from the rocky shores. The fisheries of the once extensive wetland lagoons of the Mediterranean coasts were the easiest to develop artificially, because they were sheltered, shallow, and had controllable inlets and outlets, and systematic pisciculture grew from their management. Both archaeological and literary evidence shows the extent to which Roman pisciculture developed, and the elaboration of fishponds for both fresh and salt-water fish. Processing plants for making pickle were also built on a grand scale, from the early Hellenistic period in the Black (*Euxine) Sea area, and in the Roman period on the coasts of southern Spain and Mauretania. This economy depended on, and is an indicator of, a developed interdependence of markets in the Mediterranean. See MEALS; OPPIAN.

flāmines (sing. *flāmen*), Roman priests within the college of the *pontifices*. There were three major, twelve minor *flamines*, each of them assigned to the worship of a single deity, though this did not preclude their taking part in the worship of other deities. The three major ones were the *flamen Diālis, Martiālis*, and *Quirīnālis*—of *Jupiter, *Mars, and Quirīnus (a peaceful 'double' of Mars); acc. to the system of Dumézil, these three gods formed the most ancient and senior triad of Roman gods, representing the three *Indo-European functions of law, warfare, and production. Of the twelve deities served by a minor *flamen*, we know ten, including *Ceres, *Flora, and *Volcanus; but little is known of their priests' duties.

The three major *flamines* were always *patricians and chosen by the members of the pontifical college, never elected. The *Dialis* in historic times was bound by an elaborate system of ritual rules, marking the holiness of his person and protecting it from pollution. He and his wife (the *flaminica*) had perpetual religious obligations. By the later republic the other *flamines* could hold high office, even up to the consulship; successive *pontifices maximi* did, however, dispute the right of the *flamines* to abandon priestly duty, leave Rome, and so hold provincial commands, like other politician-priests. Since the flaminate was the only priesthood devoted to a specific deity, it was the natural model for the new priesthood devised first for Caesar and then for successive emperors after their deaths.

Specific rules and privileges were borrowed from old to new *flamines*, but not the full set of restrictions. See RULER-CULT.

Flāminīnus See QUINCTIUS FLAMININUS.

Flāminius, Gāius, was the only politician before the Gracchi to mount a serious challenge to the senatorial establishment on behalf of the *populares* (see OPTIMATES). A *novus homo, he was tribune of the *plebs* 232 BC, and, against opposition led by *Fabius Maximus Verrucosus, carried a law distributing the *ager Gallicus*—land confiscated from the Senones 50 years earlier—in individual lots to needy Roman citizens. *Polybius describes the law as the beginning of the perversion of the people, and claims that it caused the Gallic invasion of 225. Praetor in 227, Flaminius was the first annual governor of Sicily. As consul in 223 he led the first Roman army to cross the river Po (*Padus), and won a victory over the Insubres. Later sources say that prodigies (see PORTENTS) caused the senate to annul the results of the elections, and they sent a letter to the consuls ordering them to abdicate, but Flaminius refused to open it until after the battle. It is said that his triumph was voted by the people. Acc. to Plutarch, the consuls were eventually forced to abdicate. As censor in 220 he built the *via Flaminia and the *Circus Flaminius. He is said to have been the only senator to support the law of the tribune Quintus Claudius providing that no senator or son of a senator might own a ship capable of carrying more than 300 amphorae (218). He was elected consul for the second time for 217, is said to have neglected to take the *auspicia at Rome, to have entered office at Ariminum, and to have ignored unfavourable omens. He took up position at Arretium, but *Hannibal marched past him towards the heart of Etruria. Flaminius followed, and because of morning fog was caught in ambush at Lake Trasimene. He was killed and 15,000 men with him. The defeat was ascribed to his neglect of religious observances.

Flavian emperors and period See ROME, HISTORY, 2.2.

Flāvius Clēmens (consul AD 95), grandson of *Vespasian's brother Flavius Sabinus and husband of Flavia Domitilla (niece of *Domitian); an ineffectual person, he was put to death and his wife exiled soon after his consulship. They are said to have been guilty of impiety, i.e., by implication, of practising Judaism; later tradition alleges that they were Christians. Domitian intended two of the seven children of Clemens—Vespasian and Domitian as they were to be called—to succeed him; they are not heard of after 96. Acc. to Suetonius, Clemens' death hastened that of Domitian: want of an adult heir probably encouraged assassins.

Flōra, an Italian goddess of flowering or blossoming plants, mainly cereals. The antiquity of her cult in Rome is proved by the existence of a *flamen Florālis* (see FLAMINES). Flora had an old temple on the *Quirinal, but, shortly after the foundation of the Floralia in 240 BC, and on the advice of the Sibylline books, she was given a second temple in 238 close to the Circus Maximus. Her Games (*lūdī Florālēs*) were celebrated annually from 173. They included indecent farces (see MIME, *Roman*).

foedus means a treaty, solemnly enacted, which established friendship, peace and alliance between Rome and another state in perpetuity. A *foedus* was distinct from *indūtiae* ('truce'), which ended a state of war and lasted for an agreed number of years (up to a century). Treaties of alliance were either equal or unequal. An equal treaty enjoined each party to give military assistance to the other in the event of an attack. In an unequal treaty the second party was required to acknowledge and respect the *māiestās* (lit. 'greaterness') of the Roman people, and was effectively compelled to provide Rome with military forces on demand. Treaties were often negotiated by Roman military commanders, but they needed ratification at Rome by a vote of the *comitia centuriata*. The religious formalities, which included oaths and sacrifices, were supervised by the *fetiales. Treaties were engraved on bronze tablets.

folk-tales are popular stories transmitted orally. Polished and perfected over centuries by generations of peasant storytellers, they tap into deep strata of psychological and social wisdom, and are badly served by their relegation to the nursery, as 'fairy tales'. They typically engage with the problems faced by the powerless (poor, young, unregarded) male hero in his attempts to assert himself in a world of hostile forces, aided by animal or supernatural helpers; the goal and climax consists in maturity and marriage. Encouraging or consolatory templates for female behaviour make a natural complement. But the range is wide, and the invention fertile. Greek folk-tales are not easily distinguished from myth, legend, saga, popular history, biography, etc., and they reach us because they have been preserved in *literary* texts; so they have been contaminated by the requirements of *genre. All the same, the careers of *Perseus and *Bellerophon well exemplify the basic type. The Odyssean episode of the hero trapped in the giant's cave (see CYCLOPES; ODYSSEUS) finds parallels from Finland to Mongolia, and though some of these may be derived from the famous Homeric account, it cannot be true of *all* other versions; early oral diffusion of the powerfully attractive theme, from some undetermined source, seems probable. Herodotus too adapts many folk-tales to the purposes of his Histories, notably the pranks of the unnamed trickster-thief who pitted his wits against the Pharaoh Rhampsinitus. Even 5th-cent. drama draws up plots from the folk-tale reservoir (e.g. Euripides' *Alcestis*), and the same is true of Hellenistic poetry. There are grounds for supposing that some ancient Greek tales have managed to retain their core structure intact through constant retellings right down to modern times. In Latin, the classical example is the Cinderella-like story of Cupid and Psyche, recounted in a much elaborated version by Apuleius in *Metamosphoses* bks. 4–6.

food and drink The ancient diet was based on cereals, legumes, oil, and wine. *Cereals, esp. wheat and barley, were the staple food and the principal source of carbohydrates. They were eaten in many different ways, e.g. as bread and porridge. The rich could afford a more diversified diet and ate less cereal than the poor. *Athenaeus describes many types of bread and cakes. Probably only the rich could afford 'white' bread, but even the best bread available in antiquity was much coarser than modern bread.

Legumes (field beans, peas, chick-peas, lentils, lupins, etc.), a common find in archaeological excavations at *Pompeii, were an important part of the diet. They were incorporated into bread and complemented cereals because they are a rich source of protein.

The Greeks used the term *opson* for 'food eaten with bread or other cereal products'. Fish (see FISHING), which might be fresh, dried, or pickled, occupied a prominent place in *opson*, esp. at Athens. It was important as a source of protein and oils. Many species were known. However, fish are scarce in the Mediterranean because of the absence of large stretches of continental shelf. They probably did not make a major contribution to the diet.

*Olive oil was the main source of fats, which are necessary to make a cereal-based diet palatable. Fats, which have a very high calorific value, were also obtained from other sources, e.g. sesame oil. The use of butter was a mark of *barbarians; so was the drinking of beer and to some extent that of milk. Milk was generally used for making cheese. The main beverage was *wine, usually diluted and often artificially flavoured. It was drunk even by young children. *Honey was used for sweetening.

Meat was a luxury for most people. In Classical Athens it was generally eaten only at feasts accompanying religious *festivals. (See SACRIFICE.) Poultry, game, and eggs played a large part in Roman cookery, but there was little butcher's meat, apart from pork. Peasants generally kept pigs. Wild birds (partridges, quails, pheasants) were also eaten. The soldiers of the Roman army had a higher standard of living and a more varied diet than most inhabitants of the Roman empire.

For ordinary people vegetables (e.g. onion, garlic, turnip, radish, lettuce, artichoke, cabbage, leek, celery, cucumber) provided the most important addition to the basic diet. Among fruit, figs, grapes, apples, and pears played a leading part. Sauces, such as the Roman fish-pickle *garum* (see FISHING), and condiments and herbs were very popular. The Romans disliked the natural tastes of most cooked foods. See COOKERY; MEALS.

food supply

Greek For Greek city-states of the Archaic and Hellenistic periods the ethos of *autarky dominated the ideology of food supply. Few Greek cities ever outgrew the food production capacities of their territory, and the small number which did responded by intensifying production. This is well documented in the case of Athens. However, most Greek states operated in politically and environmentally unstable conditions. Weather (see CLIMATE) and warfare posed constant, but unpredictably timed, hazards. So, some shortfall in food supply could be expected perhaps as often as once in five years.

By 'food' (*sītos*) is meant *cereals. Though other crops were grown and important, corn was the preferred staple, esp. wheat and barley. Hence shortfalls in these crops proved the most troublesome. Corn was at the heart of the political discourse which evolved around the problem of food supply in most city-states.

Corn was grown not by cities but by individual households, on private land. So shortages had to be met with ad hoc measures on the part of government, city-states virtually never having either central corn production or storage facilities. General shortfalls in the cereal harvest enhanced class tensions, since rich landowners would have suffered less than small-scale cultivators. Shortfalls also provided opportunities for the rich to gain political capital and to manipulate grain supplies. From the 4th cent. BC onwards, benefactions of corn by rich men are regularly documented in inscriptions, and become part of the political strategies employed in élite competition for power (see EUERGETISM).

City-states could do little in the event of corn shortage. Generally states behaved as middlemen, aiming to encourage imports, or donations and subsidized sales by the rich. Incentives might be offered to private traders, but many were not citizens, and the profits they made were greatly resented.

It is sometimes hard to tell how 'genuine' food shortages were. Barley, which was considered inferior as food, was not imported. Wheat, the preferred cereal (and most of the time probably the prerogative of the rich) was the usual corn from overseas. It is hard to know how much of this imported wheat the poor ever ate. However, ensuring the supply of wheat itself became a political issue, as is shown by the careful diplomacy with which the Bosporan kingdom (a major supplier of wheat to Athens) was treated (See BOSPORUS (2)). See also AGRICULTURE, GREEK; FAMINE.

Roman The growth of Rome to a city of perhaps 250,000 inhabitants in the time of the *Gracchi and of up to one million under *Augustus, far outstripping the productive capacity of her hinterland, created an unprecedented demand for imported foodstuffs. The supplying of Rome was left mainly to private enterprise, and the main source was always Italy (including Sicily and Sardinia), but the political pressure on the Roman government to deal with actual or feared shortages led to some institutionalized public underpinning of the mechanisms of supply, which were enabled by exploitation of Rome's imperial revenues. In the early and middle republic individual magistrates competed either to win popular favour by securing extra supplies from subject or allied states where they had some personal influence, or to win noble approval by quashing popular complaints. Gaius *Sempronius Gracchus took the momentous step of establishing a regular public distribution of a set monthly ration of corn at a set price to adult male citizen residents, which *Clodius Pulcher made free in 58 BC. Other legislation alternately cut and increased the number of entitled recipients, called the *plebs frūmentāria*, until in 2 BC Augustus stabilized it at or below 200,000. Augustus also reorganized the system of storage and distribution under an imperial appointee of *equestrian status, the *prefect of the corn supply, who also had a more general remit to watch over food supplies. This public supply, drawing on the corn paid to the state as rent or tax in Sicily, Africa, and (from 30 BC) Egypt, helped the privileged minority who held tickets of entitlement, which could be inherited or sold. But the monthly ration did not meet a family's need for corn, and the tickets did not necessarily go to the poor. All residents will still have relied on the private market to some extent (or, if they had them, on produce from their farms), and most will have used it for most of their supplies. Shortages could and did occur, esp. in the supply of wheat (see CEREALS), which led emperors to make ad hoc interventions to hold down prices, or stimulating long-term improvements such as the successive new ports at *Ostia. Rich private individuals often gave free meals or tokens for food to their clients (see CLIENS), but this generosity was unreliable and also not esp. directed at the poor. At the end of the 2nd cent. AD *Septimius Severus added free *olive oil to the rations received by the *plebs frumentaria*, and in the 270s *Aurelian added free pork and cheap *wine, and the monthly wheat ration was replaced with a daily issue of bread. As Rome ceased to be the empire's capital in the 4th cent., the responsibility for maintaining supplies to the decreasing population fell first on the senatorial nobility and then on the Church. See FAMINE; GRANARIES.

fortifications

Greek Extensive town walls began to develop in the 6th and, esp., 5th cents. BC. They are usually of mud-brick on a stone footing. The Athenian walls at *Pylos were built with stone facings, with rubble and clay packing, an increasingly common form of construction, while the system of *Long Walls shows how large-scale fortifications were used for strategic ends. Fourth-century improvements in *siegecraft and the introduction of *artillery created increasing problems. Fortification designers steadily responded to the challenge. Experiments were made to improve the structure of the walls, dividing their lengths into compartments and using binding courses through the entire thickness of the wall. Techniques employed by the Phoenicians at *Tyre, blocks of outsize dimensions and mortared together with gypsum were not adapted in the Aegean area. The final defences of Syracuse, designed by *Archimedes, present the acme of Hellenistic fortification. Though the advantage was always with the attacker, defences sometimes included numerous sally-ports to facilitate active resistance.

Roman Early Roman fortifications derived from Etruscan and Greek antecedents, which were both a defence and a civic monument. For the early wall of Rome (6th cent. BC), see WALL OF SERVIUS. A free-standing stone wall of 4th-cent. date bounds the early fort at *Ostia. The fortifications of Roman republican colonies in Italy usually took advantage of naturally defensible sites, with walls in ashlar or polygonal masonry and powerful gateways. The Punic and Greek wars familiarized the Romans with the methods of and defences against Hellenistic siege warfare, and the Civil Wars of the late republic promoted more advanced defensive ideas at some Italian sites.

During the relative peace of the Principate urban fortifications were largely a matter of civic pride, requiring authorization from Rome. Augustan veteran colonies generally received defences of carefully laid walls, towers of various shapes, and monumental gateways. A few other important western towns acquired walls before AD 200 (e.g. *Augusta Treverorum), as did several in Africa. Britain had a tradition of 1st- and 2nd-cent. earthwork defences. Military defences (earth, timber, and turf to c. AD 100, stone thereafter) were more functional, but elaborate gateways suggest motives of display.

From the 3rd cent. AD the revival of Persia, barbarian invasions in Europe, and chronic civil war caused more general fortification. Late Roman defences, military and civilian, usually consisted of thick, high walls, regularly spaced projecting towers (sometimes for artillery), small gateways, and large ditches. In the west, Rome was provided with an elaborate new circuit of defences (see WALL OF AURELIAN) in the later 3rd cent.

forum, an open square or market-place in a Roman town. In contrast to the *forum Boarium

(cattle market) and forum Holitorium (vegetable market) at Rome, the *forum Romanum was also a place of public business, a role later shared with the imperial fora. Public fora of this kind, combining political, judicial, and commercial functions, formed the focal point of most Roman towns, esp. in the western empire. A typical forum, as at *Pompeii, was a long, rectangular open space flanked by a variety of public buildings, including variously temples, basilicas, speakers' platforms, senate-house, and other public offices, as well as *tabernae* (see INNS, RESTAURANTS), often in an informal arrangement with colonnades on two or more sides; the open space was adorned with honorific statues and other minor monuments. The imperial fora at Rome provided models for more monumental complexes, most common in the European provinces but also found in North Africa. These were symmetrical colonnaded squares, dominated by either a major temple (usually either a *capitōlium* (see CAPITOL, CAPITOLIUM) or dedicated to the imperial (*ruler-cult)) or a transverse *basilica across one short end, or both. See AGORA; MARKETS; URBANISM, *Roman*.

forum Augustum or **Augusti,** dedicated in 2 BC, the vast precinct of *Mars Ultor in Rome, vowed by Octavian at *Philippi. The octastyle marble Corinthian temple stood on a lofty podium at the northern end; the interior of the cella, flanked by columns, terminated in an apse housing colossal statues of Mars, *Venus, and Divus Julius. *Caesar's sword and many works of art were kept there. The temple was set against a high precinct wall which cut off the populous Subura. Broad flights of steps flanking the temple led from the Subura into the forum through *triumphal arches, dedicated to Drusus (see CLAUDIUS DRUSUS, NERO) and *Germanicus in AD 19. The forum area was flanked by Corinthian porticoes enriched with coloured marble, and crowned by a tall attic decorated with *caryatids copied from the *Erechtheum at Athens; behind these were large semicircular *exedrae. Statues of *Romulus and of *Aeneas adorned the *exedrae*, while others representing the Julian family and Roman state heroes decorated the porticoes; laudatory inscriptions from the bases of the statues survive. Here youths assumed the *toga virilis* (the symbol of manhood) and provincial governors ceremoniously departed or returned.

forum Boārium, the area of ancient Rome bounded by the *Capitol, *Palatine, and

*Aventine hills, near *Tiber island, named after the city's cattle market (See MARKETS). Its importance as a commercial and port area from an early date is reflected both by the 8th-cent. BC Greek pottery found here, and the presence of cults with Greek (and Phoenician) associations such as that of *Hercules at the Ara Maxima.

forum Caesaris or **Iūlium,** dedicated by *Caesar in 46 BC, on land bought eight years earlier for 60 million sesterces, and completed by Octavian (*Augustus). The forum had long colonnades on the east and west sides and a series of shops behind the west colonnade. The main entrance was at the south end, and by the SW corner lay the new Cūria Iūlia. (See CURIA.) The focal point of the forum was the octastyle temple of *Venus Genetrix, mythical foundress of the Julian *gens, which was completely rebuilt after a fire and rededicated in AD 113 by *Trajan.

forum Nervae or **Transitōrium** in Rome, built by *Domitian, was dedicated by *Nerva in AD 97. It converted the Argiletum, which approached the *forum Romanum between the *forum Augustum and the temple of Peace (see TEMPLUM PACIS), into a monumental avenue. At the east, against the south *exedra of the forum Augustum, stood a temple to *Minerva, Domitian's patron goddess; reliefs illustrating her cult and legends decorated the marble frieze and attic of the precinct wall, divided into shallow bays by detached marble columns. Traffic from the bustling Subura district entered through a curved monumental portico, south of the temple; at the western end was a monumental arch.

forum Rōmānum (Forum), the chief public square of Rome, surrounded by monumental buildings, occupied a swampy trough between the *Palatine, Velia, Quirinal, and *Capitol. The area was made suitable for building in the late 7th cent. BC by the canalizing of the *Cloaca Maxima, and the deposition of considerable quantities of fill. The *Regia and temple of *Vesta were traditionally associated with this period, while the earliest dated monuments are the temples of *Saturnus (497) and *Castor (484). The Forum became the centre of Roman religious, ceremonial, and commercial life, as well as the political activities which took place in the adjacent *Comitium; balconies were built (338) above the shops surrounding the forum, to allow for the viewing of the gladiatorial shows which took place there. Butchers and fishmon-

gers were, however, soon relegated to the *macellum* (see MARKETS) and *forum piscārium,* as more monumental buildings were constructed around the Forum. *Basilicas were introduced in 184 by *Porcius Cato (1); his work was soon imitated by the basilica Aemilia (179) on the north side of the square, and basilica Sempronia (170) on the south.

The growing population of Rome and the increasing importance of popular politics were reflected by the transfer from the Comitium to the Forum of the *comitia tributa* in 145; in 121 *Opimius restored the temple of *Concordia, following the death of Gaius *Sempronius Gracchus and his supporters, and built a new adjacent basilica. In the same year the first *triumphal arch was set up over the *via Sacra beside the Regia.

Much of the present setting is due to *Sulla, *Caesar, and *Augustus. Sulla rebuilt the *Curia (2) on a larger scale to accommodate the senate of 600 members, obliterating much of the Comitium in the process; Caesar planned a new basilica Iulia, to replace the old basilica Sempronia, which, like his Curia Iulia, was finished by Augustus. After Caesar's assassination a column was erected to mark the site of his pyre and later (29) replaced by the temple of Divus Iulius; this, and the adjacent Parthian arch of Augustus (19), had the effect of monumentalizing the eastern end of the Forum. New *Rostra in front of the temple of Divus Iulius faced the 'old' Rostra, rebuilt by Caesar and then Augustus. Many ancient monuments were restored.

Fewer changes were made to the topography of the Forum under the empire; the imperial fora, the Campus Martius, and the Palatine provided more scope for emperors keen to make their mark on the city. New temples were, however, dedicated to deified emperors and empresses, while Domitian set up an equestrian statue of himself in 91; and the arch of *Septimius Severus was built in 203. A fire in 283, however, provided an opportunity for a major reconstruction under *Diocletian.

forum Traiani or **Ulpium,** the greatest of the imperial fora in Rome, paid for by Dacian spoils, was built for *Trajan by *Apollodorus (3) and dedicated in AD 112. The colonnaded court lay between the *Capitol and Quirinal, impinging on the slopes of both by immense semicircular *exedrae.* A single portico closed the south, where its main entrance, adorned by a *triumphal arch in 117, faced the *forum Augustum; the lateral porticoes were double. The basilica Ulpia, with broad nave, double aisles, and two huge apsidal tribunals, occupied the forum's north side. Behind it lay Greek and Latin *libraries, flanking a colonnaded court framing *Trajan's Column. The inscription on the base states that its purpose was to show the depth of the cutting required for the forum: this refers to the scarping of the Quirinal, where an elaborate complex of shops on six levels, linked by streets and staircases and with an interesting market-hall, screens a terraced rock-face separated from the forum by a fire-wall and street. The libraries and column originally marked the end of the complex, but Hadrian added the temple of Deified Trajan beyond them.

founders of cities Founders were chiefly important before *Alexander (2) the Great in the case of colonies (see APOIKIA), founded under the leadership of an oikist, whose achievements often led to his posthumous worship as a hero (see HERO-CULT). In 5th-cent. BC Athens oikists were state officials who returned home after completing their task, as with Hagnon at *Amphipolis. Among Hellenistic founders of cities kings naturally loomed largest, although not all attended in person the founding rituals like Alexander.

fountains See NYMPHAEUM; WATER.

Four Hundred, the, a revolutionary *oligarchic council set up to rule Athens in 411 BC. The movement started in the fleet at *Samos in summer 412, when *Alcibiades offered to win Persian help for Athens if an oligarchy were established. *Pisander was sent to Athens to prepare the way, and secured an embassy to negotiate with Persia. Though the Persian negotiation failed and the oligarchs discarded Alcibiades, it was then too late to stop. In spring 411 the oligarchic clubs (*hetaireiai) murdered prominent democrats and intimidated the council (*boule) and assembly (*ekklesia). So far the published programme was 'moderate': abolition of civilian stipends (see DEMOCRACY, ATHENIAN, 3 for such political pay) and the restriction of the franchise to 5,000, those 'best able to serve the city physically and financially'. But after Pisander's return to Athens in May a meeting of the assembly, summoned to hear the proposals of a constitutional commission, was persuaded into electing five men who, indirectly, selected 400 to act as a council with full powers to govern. The supporters of the original 'moderate' programme were overwhelmed by the extremists

of the 400, who never summoned the 5,000, and who attempted unsuccessfully to negotiate with Sparta. But the democrats regained the upper hand in the fleet at Samos; and when the Peloponnesians attacked *Euboea, the squadron hastily sent by the 400 was defeated. *Theramenes, who had been one of the men behind the oligarchy, now came out for the moderates, the 400 were overthrown, and the 5,000 were instituted (September); but after the victory at *Cyzicus (410) full democracy was restored.

free cities formed a privileged category in Rome's system of provincial government. In the east the status ultimately derived from the blanket declaration of Greek freedom by *Quinctius Flamininus (196 BC); by the late republic a free city was one with a special agreement with Rome allowing it local autonomy and sometimes tax-immunity (*immunitas). With dependence implicit, the status was liable to Roman encroachment and sudden cancellation, although emperors respected its outward forms.

freedmen, freedwomen Emancipated slaves were more prominent in Roman society than in Greek city-states or Hellenistic kingdoms (see SLAVERY). Lat. *libertus/a* designates the ex-slave in relation to former owner (*patronus/a), *libertinus/a* in relation to the rest of society. In Greek communities, freed slaves usually merged with other free non-citizens. In Rome, the slave freed by a citizen was normally admitted to citizenship (see CITIZENSHIP, ROMAN). A slave might be released from the owner's control by a fictitious claim before a magistrate with executive power (*imperium) that he/she was free, by being ordered to present himself to the censors for registration as a citizen (public authority attested citizen status and made it impossible for the slave to be a slave), or by will (implementation of the owner's command was postponed until he/she died and depended on acceptance of the inheritance and public validation). A slave freed informally lacked citizenship and other rights, but was protected by the praetor, until Augustus introduced Latin rights, with the possibility (expanded by later emperors) of promotion to full citizenship. Augustus also regulated the previously untrammelled right to manumit.

In Greece, the ex-slave might be bound to perform services while the ex-owner lived; in Rome, continuing dependency took the form of part-time services, possible remunerated work, the obligation of dutifulness. Freedmen were usually registered in the four urban voting tribes (*tribus*), excluded from major public offices and military service, but given a role in local elective office and cult. Children born after their mother's manumission were freeborn and under no legal disabilities, though servile descent might be remembered (esp. by the upper classes) for several generations. Freed slaves document their activity in urban trades and crafts; the most prominent, rich, and envied were usually freed by the upper classes: literature emphasizes the exceptions—writers such as *Terence, the fictitious millionaire Trimalchio (see PETRONIUS ARBITER) or the bureau-chiefs of the early emperors such as *Narcissus and *Antonius Pallas. See NAMES, PERSONAL, ROMAN.

freedom in the ancient world The distinction free–unfree is attested in the earliest Greek and Roman texts (Linear B, Homer, *Twelve Tables). As 'chattel *slavery' became predominant, earlier status plurality was often replaced by a sharp contrast: slave–free. *Freedmen were enfranchised in Rome but not in Greece (See CITIZENSHIP, GREEK and ROMAN).

Freedom was first given *political* value by the Greeks, in a world of small *poleis* (see POLIS) which were not subject to imperial control, where power was not centralized, autocratic, or divinely sanctioned but broadly distributed, and communal well-being depended on many citizens, so that early forms of equality survived and gained importance over time. Loss of freedom was frequent, both for individuals (war, piracy, debt bondage), and communities (tyranny). Nevertheless, freedom was articulated politically only when *Lydian and esp. *Persian expansion to the Aegean for the first time subjected Greek *poleis* to foreign rule, often supporting local tyrants (see TYRANNY). This danger of double 'enslavement' and the confrontation with the autocratic Persian state made the Greeks aware of the free character of their societies. Earliest allusions to political freedom and the emergence of an abstract noun (*eleutheria*; from adj. *eleutheros*) date to the Persian Wars of 480/79 and their aftermath.

Vowing the continued defence of Greek liberty against Persia. Athens assumed leadership in the *Delian League (478), which was soon converted into a naval empire; allies became subjects who could hope only to preserve self-administration (AUTONOMY). Freedom quickly deteriorated into a political slogan. In the *Peloponnesian War, *Sparta proclaimed the liberation of Hellas from Athens as tyrant city,

though primarily protecting its own interests and soon turning oppressor itself.

Domestically, freedom initially meant 'absence of tyranny'. Constitutional development was dominated first by 'good order' (the *eunomia* of Sparta's traditional founder, Lycurgus), then by political equality (*isonomia*), which, in democracy, eventually included all citizens, thus approximating *isonomia* to *dēmokratia*. *Eleutheria* was claimed by democracy when democracy and oligarchy were perceived as mutually exclusive, partisan forms of rule, so that the *demos* could be free only by controlling power itself. Similarly, a new term for 'freedom of speech', i.e. 'frankness' (*parrhēsia*) supplemented 'equality of speech' (*isēgoria*). Rejecting the extension of full rights to all citizens, *oligarchs accepted as 'free citizens' only those rich enough to engage in 'liberal' (*eleutherios*) arts and occupations, and public service. When *eleutherios* was set against *eleutheros*, the concept of the 'free citizen' was divided ideologically.

In the 4th cent. Sparta, Athens, and *Thebes claimed to promote the liberty of those subjected by others. The liberty of the Greeks in Asia, sacrificed by Sparta in 412, was definitively yielded in the *King's Peace (386). The charter of the *Second Athenian Confederacy guaranteed the members' *eleutheria* and *autonomia*. The Messenian *helots were freed by Thebes after *Leuctra (371). To end continuous internecine warfare, *Isocrates called for a panhellenic crusade against Persia to liberate the Hellenes—a programme realized by *Alexander (2) the Great only after Greek liberty was crushed at *Chaeronea (338).

In the Hellenistic period, the kings, competing for political and material support, presented themselves as protectors of Hellenic civilization and liberty. Declarations of freedom for the Hellenes were thus an old tradition when *Quinctius Flamininus pronounced that European Greeks 'shall be free, exempt from tribute, and subject to their own laws'.

Philosophers had their own concerns. Fifth-cent. *sophists emphasized the strong individual's right to cast off enslavement by *nomos* ('law') and rule over the weaker in accordance with nature. Others contested the validity of traditional social distinctions; *Alcidamas declared slavery contrary to nature. Despite *Aristotle's elaborate defence (*Politics* bk. 1), this view was echoed by the Stoics and discussed thoroughly by Roman jurists (see LAWYERS, ROMAN).

One aspect of democratic *eleutheria* was 'to live as you please'. Plato caricatured such 'excessive' freedom in *Republic* bks. 8–9; Isocrates denounced it when advocating *patrios politeia*. Originating in popular morality, the notion of freedom from 'enslavement' (esp. to material goods and to passions) induced generations of thinkers (*Antisthenes, *Diogenes (2)) to stress self-control as the means to achieve inner freedom.

Loss of political freedom and the need for new orientations gave philosophy broad appeal as a means to achieve happiness (*eudaimonia*: see DAIMON). Despite fundamental differences, both Epicureans and Stoics believed in freedom as the goal and principle of life. (See EPICURUS; STOICISM.)

We cannot be certain about the process by which *libertas* was politicized in Rome. The late republican élite developed an aristocratic concept of *libertas*, supporting equality and opposing *regnum* ('kingship') and extraordinary power of individuals and factions. By contrast, the freedom of the people was not egalitarian and did not aim at political participation. It was primarily defensive, focusing on equality before the law and the protection of individual citizens from abuse of power by magistrates. *Libertas* rested on institutions; it was embodied by the *tribuni plebis* and their rights of *provocatio and auxilium* (personal protection) ('twin poles of the defence of liberty'). In late republican conflicts *libertas* was claimed by *populares* against oppression by *optimates* (thus connected with the secret ballot; see ELECTIONS AND VOTING, Roman) or a party of the few.

During the empire, power was concentrated in one man's hands. Although *libertas* remained a favoured slogan of imperial ideology, nevertheless, acc. to *Tacitus, *principātus ac libertas* were not reconciled before *Nerva. Even so, liberty was increasingly reduced to the elementary meaning of security and protection under the law.

While freedom lost political significance, *eleutheria/libertas* became an important element in Christian teaching, emphasized esp. by *Paul. Through God's gift and Christ's sacrifice his followers are liberated from sin, the finality of death, and the old law. Such freedom, however, involves subjection to the will of God: Christ's followers are God's 'slaves'. The freedom promised to Christians is available to all humans, including the lowly and slaves, but it is not of this world and does not militate against existing social dependencies and political or ethical obligations. So, Christians did not oppose slavery as an institution, but in accepting slaves into their community they anticipated the universal brotherhood of the free expected in another world.

friendship, Greek The principal terms customarily translated as 'friendship' have a semantic range wider than this translation suggests. *Philia* and *oikeiotēs* could both be used of *kinship ties, while *hetaireia* could also denote confraternities and political associations. The scarcity in the Greek world of institutions for the provision of vital services may partly explain this semantic difference. Friends provided 'services analogous to those provided by bankers, lawyers, hotel owners, insurers and others today'. Hence the great importance that the Greeks attached to their most intimate circles of friends. Friends, like kin, could be called upon in any emergency; they could be expected to display solidarity, lend general support, and procure co-operation. The obligations of friendship were less rigidly defined than those of kinship or ritualized *friendship. One's circle of friends, however, probably exerted an even more pervasive influence on one's behaviour and outlook than one's kin or ritualized friends. Friends were therefore supposed to be alike: a friend was ideally conceived of as one's 'other self'.

friendship, philosophical See LOVE AND FRIENDSHIP.

friendship, ritualized (or guest-friendship), a bond of trust, imitating kinship and reinforced by rituals, generating affection and obligations between individuals belonging to separate social units. In Greek sources this bond is called *xenia*; in Latin, *hospitium*. The individuals joined by the bond (usually men of roughly equal social status) are said to be each other's *xenos* or *hospes*. As the same terms designated guest–host relationships, *xenia* and *hospitium* have sometimes been interpreted as a form of hospitality. *Xenia, hospitium*, and hospitality do overlap to some extent, but the first two relationships display a series of additional features which assimilate them into the wider category called in social studies ritualized personal relationships, or pseudo-kinship. The analogy with kinship did not escape the notice of the ancients themselves.

A lexicographer defined *xenos* as 'a friend from abroad', and this definition holds good for Roman *hospes*: a ritualized friendship pair could consist of an Athenian and a Spartan, or a Roman and an Epirote, but very rarely consisted of two Athenians or two Romans. From its first appearance in *Homer onwards, ritualized friendship has been abundantly attested in both Greek and Latin sources from all periods and areas of classical antiquity.

One feature that ritualized friendship shared with kinship was the assumption of perpetuity: once the relationship had been established, the bond was believed to persist in latent form even if the partners did not interact with one another. This assumption had two practical consequences. First, the bond could be renewed or reactivated after years had elapsed, a variety of symbolic objects signalling that it once existed. Secondly, the bond did not expire with the death of the partners themselves, but outlived them, passing on in the male line to their descendants. The beginning of the relationship had to be marked with a ceremony, as did the reactivation of a relationship after many years. The rites of initiation into *xenia* and *hospitium* consisted of a diversity of symbolic elements enacted in sequence: a solemn declaration ('I make you my *xenos*', and 'I accept you'), an exchange of symbolic gifts (see GIFT, GREECE), a handshake, and finally feasting.

Ritualized friends were, by virtue of their prescribed duties, veritable co-parents. A *xenos* or *hospes* was supposed to show a measure of protective concern for his partner's son, to help him in any emergency, and to save his life. Acc. to *Euripides' Electra* and *Orestes*, *Orestes was brought up, following the murder of *Agamemnon, in the household of Agamemnon's *xenoi*. Neglect of co-parental duties was strongly disapproved of. Betrayal of ritualized friendship in general sometimes appears as a sin against the gods.

Ritualized friendship was an upper-class institution in both Greece and Rome. The people involved in it belonged to a small minority, renowned for their wealth and identified by lofty titles such as 'hero', 'tyrant', '*satrap', 'nobleman', 'consul', 'governor', 'emperor'. Throughout antiquity, such people lent each other powerful support, often at the expense of their inferiors, so often that ritualized friendship may be regarded as a tool for perpetuating class distinctions. The forms of mutual support practised included the exchange of valuable resources (e.g. money, troops, or corn), usually called 'gifts', and the performance of important services, usually called 'benefactions' (see EUERGETISM). The circulation of these goods and services created networks of ritualized friendship. The Greek and Roman worlds differed markedly in how these informal networks were integrated into their wider political systems.

In the Homeric world, *xenia* and the networks to which it gave rise were of paramount importance to the hero. The hero abroad found in a *xenos* an effective substitute for kinsmen, a protector, representative, and ally, supplying in case of need shelter, protection, men, and arms; the community was not sufficiently organized to interfere with this sort of cooperation. The relationship being largely personal, ritualized friendship was, together with marriage, the Homeric forerunner of political and military alliances. The emergence of the *polis* during the 8th and 7th cents. was accompanied by significant interactions between its nascent systems and this pre-existing network of personal alliances. Nor did the fully fledged *polis* lead to the abolition of this network: throughout the Classical period, dense webs of ritualized friendship still stretched beyond its bounds, at times facilitating, at times obstructing the conduct of foreign affairs. For the upper classes of the Classical period, these networks offered means of pursuing their own interests different from the civic system. The impact of *xenia* upon the Greek civic system is most evident in the creation by the *polis* of *proxenia*, a bond of trust, clearly modelled upon *xenia*, between a *polis* and a prominent individual outside it (see PROXENOS).

Under the republic, prominent Romans maintained extensive ties of *hospitium* with prominent non-Romans both elsewhere in Italy and overseas. In the law courts both *Cicero and *Caesar defended members of the aristocracy from various Italian communities. *Hospitium*, like *patronage, was instrumental in the *Romanization of local élites, in their upward social mobility, and in their integration into the Roman ruling class.

friendship, Roman See AMICITIA; FRIENDSHIP, RITUALIZED.

Frontīnus See IULIUS FRONTINUS.

Fronto See CORNELIUS FRONTO.

Fulvia, offspring of two noble families, became the best-known of late republican women active in politics and a prototype of empresses. Born in the late 70s BC, she married *Clodius Pulcher, supported his policies and called for vengeance after his murder. Briefly married to Scribonius Curio, she married Marcus *Antonius (Mark Antony) after Curio's death, took an active part in his management of politics after Caesar's death and later in the *proscriptions, greatly enriching herself. When Antony took charge of the east, she supported his cause in Italy, ultimately combining with his brother Antonius (Piets) in opposing Octavian. Besieged with him at Perusia (41), where her presence was exploited by hostile propaganda, she was allowed to join her husband after its fall, but was badly received by him and soon died. In later literature she became the type of the wicked matron, contrasted with the virtuous *Octavia, sister of Octavian.

funerals See DEAD, DISPOSAL OF; DEATH, ATTITUDES TO.

Furies See ERINYES.

furniture Table, chair, and couch are the central items of ancient furnishing. Their principal characteristic is portability, essential in the circumstances of ancient domestic life, with use of space, and even choice of house, at least among the élite, varying with season and occasion. The prevailing theory of habitation revolved round the current location of the principal persons of the family; their environment had to be speedily arranged for them, if not around them, with screens, curtains, and equipment for the current activity, be it eating, drinking, sleeping, writing—and portable furniture to support small utensils, *lamps, containers. Furniture was also a form of capital accumulation, deriving value from rare materials, ebony in Greek usage, citron (a North African tree) in Roman; or workmanship (fine figured representations, as on the chest of *Cypselus, were common). The very rich needed large quantities to equip communal dining: *Seneca the Younger had 500 citron-wood tables with *ivory legs. Oak and beech were used for cheaper furniture; cypress, cedar, and maple had a good reputation. Fine bronze, gold, silver, and enamel became widespread, as the finds of *Pompeii and *Herculaneum testify; luxury furniture of this kind was held to have reached Rome from Anatolia. Representations in Greek vase-painting and Roman wall-paintings attest a great variety of styles. See HOUSES, GREEK and ITALIAN.

G

Gabinius, Aulus, was military tribune under *Sulla and later his envoy to *Mithradates VI. As *tribune of the *plebs* 67 BC, he passed a law setting up a command with wide powers against the pirates, intended for *Pompey. He served under Pompey in the east and was made consul 58 by the three dynasts, with *Calpurnius Piso Caesoninus. The consuls supported *Clodius Pulcher against Cicero, and Gabinius ultimately received the rich province of Syria as his reward. There he alienated the *publicani* by largely taking over the tax collection for his own benefit. He restored as king of Egypt Ptolemy XII ('Piper') (who reportedly paid him 10,000 talents), left Roman legionaries to support him, and intervened in Judaea. Guilty of contravening several laws, and having made important enemies, he was prosecuted on his return and finally convicted of *extortion, even though his enemy Cicero had been forced by Pompey to defend him. He went into exile (54), was recalled by *Caesar and fought for him in Illyria.

Gaia, Gē, Earth, a primordial goddess. In Hesiod's *Theogony* the original entity was *Chaos, then came Gaia and other beings like *Eros. Gaia had many children from her son *Uranus, including the *Titans. In the Titanomachy she helps *Zeus by telling him what he needs to do to win. But after the defeat of the Titans she produces, from her union with Tartarus (also her son), the monster Typhon, who was a threat to the order of the Olympians, but was defeated by Zeus. The Olympians chose Zeus as their ruler on Gaia's advice. She is generally ambivalent: she can be deceitful and threatening, dangerous, and gives birth to creatures that pester gods and men. But she is also a positive nurturing figure. A popular episode in Attic art is the representation of the birth of *Erichthonius, where Gaia is shown as a woman emerging from the ground, handing the baby Erichthonius to Athena.

Gāius (1), the emperor, 'Caligula' (Gaius Iulius Caesar Germanicus, AD 12–41), son of *Germanicus and *Agrippina the Elder. In 14–16 he was on the Rhine with his parents and, dressed in miniature uniform, was nicknamed 'Caligula' ('Bootee') by the soldiers. He went with his parents to the east in 17 and, after Germanicus' death in 19, lived in Rome with his mother until her arrest in 29, then successively with *Livia Drusilla and *Antonia (2) until he joined *Tiberius on Capreae. The downfall of *Sejanus in 31 was to Gaius' advantage, and it was probably engineered by him and associates such as the *prefect of the watch (*vigiles*) *Macro, who also benefited. After the death of his brother Drusus Iulius Caesar in 33 Gaius was the only surviving son of Germanicus and, with Iulius Caesar Nero 'Gemellus'—*Claudius' claim not being considered—next in succession. He became *pontifex* in 31 and was quaestor two years later, but received no other training in public life. Tiberius made Gaius and Gemellus joint heirs to his property, but, supported by Macro, now *praetorian prefect, Gaius was proclaimed emperor (March 37), Tiberius' will being declared invalid by the senate, although his acts as a whole were not invalidated; Gaius made an appropriately perfunctory effort to have him deified.

Gaius' accession was greeted with widespread joy and relief, and his civility promised well. One symbolic gesture was the restoration of electoral choice to the popular assemblies, taken from them in 14 (it failed, and Gaius had to revert to Tiberian procedure). Gaius needed to enhance his authority and held the consulship four times; he became *Pater Patriae, a title refused by Tiberius, in September 37. In the early months of his rule he honoured the memory of his mother, father, and brothers and spoke abusively of Tiberius. Antonia, a restraining influence, died May 37. In October Gaius was seriously ill, and this may have brought the succession question into prominence: in

38, Gaius executed both Macro and his rival Gemellus. In 39 Gaius quarrelled with the senate, revised his attitude towards Tiberius' memory, announcing the return of slandering the emperor as a treasonable offence. The same year he married his fourth wife, who had already borne him a daughter, proving her fertility. The autumn and winter of 39–40 Gaius spent in Gaul and on the Rhine; a conspiracy was revealed whose leader, Cornelius Lentulus Gaetulicus, commander of the Upper Rhine army, was executed. This conspiracy may be connected with the simultaneous disgrace of his brother-in-law (and possible successor) Aemilius Lepidus and of Gaius' surviving sisters *Iulia Agrippina and Iulia Livilla. After his return to Rome (in *ovation, in August 40) Gaius was in constant danger of assassination, having no successor to avenge him, displayed increasing brutality, and was murdered in the palace in January 41. His wife and daughter were also murdered.

The government of Gaius was autocratic and capricious, and he accepted extravagant honours which came close to deification. He seems to have been engaged in discovering the limits of his power ('for me anything is licit'). He was a person of the highest descent, which helps to account for the unprecedented attention paid to his sisters, *Iulia Drusilla, whose death in 38 was followed by a public funeral and deification, Agrippina, and Livilla; he was brilliant and destructively witty; and he demanded exceptional homage and was savage if his superiority was not recognized. A gifted orator, who delivered Livia's *laudatio funebris* at the age of 17, he enjoyed writing rebuttals of successful speeches. By insisting on primacy in everything Gaius left even courtiers no role of their own. He had terrified the senators, humiliated officers of the praetorian guard (who carried out the assassination), and only the masses seem to have regretted his passing.

Gaius was a keen builder, interested in the state of Italy's roads and in Rome's water supply (he began the aqua Claudia (see AQUEDUCTS) and Anio Novus). He also completed the reconstruction of the theatre of Pompey and created a circus in the Vatican; other constructions were for his own pleasure, e.g. the bridge of boats from *Puteoli to Bauli (39), an ephemeral extravagance to outdo *Xerxes or overawe a Parthian hostage.

Gaius' high expenditures were economically advantageous, ending the sluggishness of Tiberius' regime. His achievements abroad, with the exception of his deployment of client rulers, were negative. He probably raised two new *legions for an invasion of Germany or Britain. However, his forays into Germany in the autumn of 39 may have been exercises intended to restore discipline after the fall of Gaetulicus and to commemorate the campaigns of Germanicus in 13–16; here the Chauci and Chatti were still causing trouble in 41. The conquest of Britain was only mooted, and was considered achieved when the son of Cunobelinus, king of the *Catuvellauni, came to render homage (Gaius could not afford to leave the centres of empire in 39–40). For the Jews under Gaius see below.

Gaius and the Jews Soon after his accession, Gaius conferred a kingship in Palestine upon his friend, the Herodian *Agrippa I. However, their understanding did not prevent discord between the inconsistent emperor and his Jewish subjects. A savage conflict between Jews and Greeks in *Alexandria stood unresolved when Gaius died. The prefect, Avillius Flaccus, seemingly abandoning any pretence at even-handedness when Gaius succeeded, had backed the Greek side in the long-standing dispute with the Jews over citizen rights. Agrippa I, visiting *en route* for his kingdom, was mocked by the Greek crowd and a pogrom thereby unleashed. It was on the emperor's birthday that Jews who had survived the assaults on their quarter were rounded up in the theatre and made to eat pork. While Gaius did have Flaccus arrested and replaced in late 38, he disdainfully ignored the delegations sent to Rome by both groups, leaving his successor to investigate and settle the matter.

Among the Jews of Palestine, Gaius' policy was heading for disaster when he died. A statue of the emperor was to be placed in the Jerusalem Temple and worshipped. Stalling by the governor of Syria, apparently sympathetic to Jewish pleas, delayed developments; and the intervention of Agrippa, whose long and perhaps genuine letter to Gaius is quoted by *Philon (2), is said to have caused the dropping of the plan.

Gāius (2), the famous 2nd-cent. AD law teacher, was lecturing in 160/1 and still alive in 178. Though a Roman citizen, he was known, and apparently chose to be known, by the single undistinctive name 'Gaius'. He is best known for his *Institutes* ('Teaching Course'), elementary lectures for students delivered in 160–161. A 5th-cent. manuscript of these lectures is probably genuine. It is marked by clarity of style, attention to history, concern for classification, and a critical attitude to legal rules, e.g. the lifelong tutelage of women. It employs a 'Socratic' method of teaching (see SOCRATES) which often leaves unanswered the problem raised.

Gāius Caesar See IULIUS CAESAR (2), GAIUS

Galba, the emperor (Servius Sulpicius Galba, 3 BC–AD 69), from an ancient patrician family, through the empress *Livia's favour moved in the highest social circles of the Julio-Claudian era. He was governor of Aquitania, consul (33), governor of Upper Germany (40–42), and proconsul of Africa (44–45); his standing was recognized by the award of triumphal insignia and three priesthoods. Governor of Hispania *Tarraconensis from 60, he was approached in 68 by *Iulius Vindex, who was instigating revolt against *Nero. Galba had his troops proclaim him as representative of the senate and people of Rome, and enrolled a new *legion in addition to the one in his province. Although Vindex was defeated, Nero's suicide and the support of Nymphidius Sabinus and his *praetorians encouraged Galba to march on Rome, accompanied by *Otho, governor of Lusitania. Once in power, Galba tried to recover Nero's extravagant largess, but the execution of several opponents, and the brutal killing of soldiers recruited by Nero from the fleet, cast a shadow. His avarice was notorious. He declined to pay the praetorians the *donative promised by Nymphidius, saying that it was his practice to levy his troops not to buy them. He compounded this mistake by failing to control his own supporters, and by sending his newly recruited legion to Pannonia. 'By universal consent he was capable of ruling—had he never ruled' (Tacitus *Histories*). When the legions of Upper Germany, who felt that they had been cheated of their reward for defeating Vindex, renounced their allegiance, Galba decided to adopt a successor. Otho, coveting this role for himself, fomented revolt among the praetorians, who murdered Galba January 69.

Galen, of *Pergamum (AD 129–?199/216) in a spectacular career rose from gladiator physician in Asia Minor to court physician in the Rome of Marcus *Aurelius. The son of a rich architect, he enjoyed an excellent education in rhetoric and philosophy in his native town before turning to medicine. After studying medicine further in Smyrna and *Alexandria, he began practising in Pergamum, 157, and went to Rome, 162.

Driven out by hostile competitors, or fear of the *plague, 166, he returned in 169, and remained in imperial service until his death. A prodigious polymath, he wrote on subjects as varied as grammar and gout, ethics and eczema, and was highly regarded in his lifetime as a philosopher as well as a doctor.

Although *Plato and *Hippocrates were his gods, and *Aristotle ranked only slightly below them, he was anxious to form his own independent judgements, and his assertive personality pervades all his actions and writings. His knowledge was equally great in theory and practice, and based in part on his own considerable library. Much of our information on earlier medicine derives from his reports alone, and his scholarly delineation of the historical Hippocrates and the writings associated with him formed the basis for subsequent interpretation down to the 20th cent.

He strove to encompass the whole of medicine, deriding those who were mere specialists or who rejected any engagement with theory. The best physician was, whether he knew it or not, also a philosopher, as well as a man good with his hands. Galen reports some spectacular surgical successes, like his removal of a suppurating breastbone, and he expected even moderate healers to be able to perform minor surgery. Although he rarely refrained from laying down the law on how to diagnose and treat patients, he equally stressed the inadequacy of general rules in an individual case. Although contemporaries credited him with almost miraculous skills in prognosis (which incorporated *diagnosis), esp. in what might be termed stress-related diseases, he replied that they were easily derived from Hippocratic first principles and that a sound diagnosis depended on close observation of every detail. His authoritative bedside manner would also have contributed to his success with patients.

Galen was esp. productive as anatomist and physiologist. Dissecting animals carefully and often, he collected and corrected the results of earlier generations by *experiment, better factual information, and logic. His physiological research was at times masterly, esp. in his series of experiments ligating or cutting the spinal cord. At others, his reliance largely on non-human anatomy, coupled with his belief that the basic structures of the human body had been described by Hippocrates, led him to 'see' things that were not there.

His *pathology, founded on the doctrines of the four *humours and of three organic systems, heart, brain, and liver, explained disease mainly as an imbalance, detectable esp. through qualitative changes in the body. His *pharmacology and *dietetics were largely codifications of earlier learning, enlivened by personal observations and occasional novel ideas, as with his (unfulfilled and later influential) attempt to classify drugs according to twelve grades of activity.

His philosophy was equally eclectic. His great effort to create a logic of scientific demonstration, surviving only in fragments, went beyond Aristotle and the *Stoics in both the range and precision of its arguments. In his psychology, he favoured a Platonic tripartite *soul over the Stoic unity, bringing the evidence of anatomy to support his case, in the same way as he used Aristotelian ideas on mixture to explain changes in the physical humours. His 'philosophical autobiography', *On My Own Opinions*, reveals the interactions between his medicine and his philosophy, as well as the limits he placed on certitude.

Galen's monotheistic views, his ardent belief in teleology, and his religious attitude—even anatomy was a veneration of God, and he was convinced of the personal protection of *Asclepius—foreshadow the Middle Ages. His dominant influence on later generations, comparable only to that of Aristotle, is based on his achievements as scientist, logician, and universal scholar, and on his own self-proclaimed insistence on establishing a medicine that was beyond all sectarianism. The dissension of earlier science could be conquered by an eclectic rationality based ultimately on notions in which all shared, and be turned into a stable system of Galenic medical and practical philosophy. See MEDICINE, 6.

Galerius, of peasant stock, was born in the AD 250s on the Danube. A herdsman, tough and uneducated, he rose high in the army and (perhaps) became *praetorian *prefect of *Diocletian, to whom his loyalty was unswerving. On the establishment of the *tetrarchy Diocletian proclaimed him Caesar (293); he divorced his wife and married Diocletian's daughter. Defending the frontier with Persia, he was severely defeated in 297, but raising reinforcements from the Balkans he attacked through Armenia, marched down the Tigris, and returned up the Euphrates, gaining total victory (298). The peace treaty was entirely favourable to Rome: substantial territory was annexed. Thereafter he moved to the Danube provinces. Various campaigns against the Marcomanni, Carpi, and *Sarmatians

followed; he settled many Sarmatians within the empire. His religious views coincided with those of Diocletian. He urged Diocletian to begin the persecution of *Christians at Nicomedia (303). On Diocletian's abdication, Galerius became Augustus (305); his subordination to *Constantius I meant little, as both Caesars were his men. Senior Augustus from Constantius' death (306), he reluctantly accepted *Constantine I as Caesar. Summoning Diocletian after a troubled period, he attempted a new settlement of the empire at Carnuntum (308), but Diocletian refused to resume the throne. Suffering from an agonizing illness, Galerius issued an edict ending the Christian persecution (311) but died very shortly afterwards.

Gallic Wars, the name given to the campaigns by which Gaius *Iulius Caesar (1) completed the Roman conquest of *Gaul (58–50 BC). The survival of Caesar's own account of this conquest (his *Commentaries*) makes us uniquely well informed about it. However, modern research has shown the dangers of unquestioning acceptance of Caesar's story: his attitudes to, dealings with, and description of Gauls and Germans were always determined by deep-rooted cultural prejudices and immediate political needs, and often by an expedient combination of the two. The Gallic conquest was probably unpremeditated; and is certainly incomprehensible if considered in isolation from the late republican power-struggle. Acc. to Caesar, appeals for his intervention on behalf of one Gallic tribe against another, or against German intruders, involved him in campaigns beyond the existing Roman province in southern Gaul, and drew him as far as the Rhine. At the end of 58 Caesar took up winter quarters in the NE, an act threatening permanent occupation of all Gaul. So, in 57 he had to meet preventive attacks by the peoples of northern Gaul; by his victories over them he brought northern France and Belgium under Roman control. In 56 Caesar had evidently resolved on the complete subjugation of Gaul, for in this year he forced the submission of the peoples of the Atlantic seaboard. It is uncertain whether the peoples of central Gaul at this time came to terms with him; but they were now ringed off within the Roman area of occupation, and Caesar at this stage considered the pacification of Gaul as complete.

In this belief Caesar spent the campaigning seasons of 55 and 54 in Germany and Britain. But sporadic revolts in northern Gaul kept him occupied throughout the winter of 54/3 and the following summer, and in 52 he was confronted by a formidable coalition of peoples in central Gaul under the leadership of *Vercingetorix. The decisive duel between Caesar and Vercingetorix, the most critical event in the Roman conquest of Gaul, culminated in the siege of Alesia. The reduction of Alesia by famine and the capture of Vercingetorix broke Gallic resistance, and the local rebellions which flared up here and there in 51 were easily dealt with. Caesar's principal subordinate throughout had been his *legate, Labienus, who in 49 deserted to *Pompey. For the results of the conquest, see GAUL (TRANSALPINE).

Gallus (poet) See CORNELIUS GALLUS.

Games (i.e. ritual contests) See AGONES; ATHLETICS; LUDI.

games A favourite game at Athens was draughts. The board was divided into 36 squares, and on them the oval pieces were moved. More popular still was the 'Wine-throw' (kottabos), esp. at the end of dinner (see SYMPOSIUM). The players, reclining on their left elbow, had to throw with their right hand the last drops of wine from their cups at a target. At Rome the two favourite games were 'Twelve Lines' and 'Robbers'. The first resembled our backgammon. The other, also played on a board, had pieces of different value, and the object was either to take or check your opponent's pieces.

gardens The main traditions go back to the gardens of the Fertile Crescent, including the Persian combination of preserve and pleasaunce known as paradeisos (see HUNTING). Early Greek intensive horticulture created places whose amenity, for abundance of shade or the presence of water, was esteemed (see DOMAINS), and this was the style of the Garden of *Epicurus. Trees were planted in *sanctuaries for their cultic significance (see TREES, SACRED) or for shade, and by extension, in public places such as the *agora. But a high aesthetic tradition dates only from the domestication of the paradeisos in the 4th cent. BC and esp. the Hellenistic and Roman periods.

This garden-art gave rise to the Roman name of formal gardening, ars topiāria (which went far beyond 'topiary', though this was one of its techniques). Use of slopes, views of different scenery, the deployment of sculptures, and the evocation of specific literary or traditional landscapes or stories were among the themes (as in Hadrian's villa at *Tibur); natural features such as springs, streams, hills, caves, and woods, were improved or created ex novo. In all this plants were important, but not central; specimen exotics evoked alien worlds (as birds and animals, which might also be ultimately destined for the table, did too) or pleased through scent, foliage contrast, or shade. Flowers were prized, but in Mediterranean conditions and before much improvement of the strain, were very limited in their season (hence the value of twice-blooming roses) and grown more for their use in garlands (see CROWNS AND WREATHS) than for their effect in a bed.

Remembering the days when a hortus was the lot of a citizen, the whimsical Roman élite labelled its suburban garden-palaces 'vegetable gardens', horti, and these often achieved remarkable levels of costly complexity. On a humbler scale, the features of ars topiaria were very widely disseminated across the Roman world. For our understanding, the town gardens of *Pompeii are esp. important, with the garden-paintings which complemented them.

Gaugaméla, village in Iraq, scene of *Alexander (2) the Great's decisive victory over *Darius III of Persia in 331 BC. The battle appears to have opened with a Persian attempt to outflank Alexander's right, which was defeated, while a charge of scythed chariots in the centre was also routed by Macedonian light troops. Then Alexander led his Companions (See HETAIROI), and the right and centre of his *phalanx, to attack a developing gap in the centre of the Persian line, whereupon Darius fled with Alexander in pursuit. The Macedonian left came under extreme pressure. However, this attack was eventually contained, and turned into a rout on news of the flight of the rest of the Persian army.

Gaul (Cisalpine) The northern region comprising the Po (*Padus) plain and its mountain fringes from the Apennines to the Alps was known to the Romans as Cisalpine Gaul. In the middle republic it was not considered part of Italy, which extended only to the foothills of the Apennines along a line roughly from Pisae to Ariminum. Beyond the Apennines lay Gaul, a land inhabited by Celtic peoples whom the Romans looked upon with fear and wonder. (See GAUL (TRANSALPINE).)

By the early 4th cent. the Gauls had displaced the Etruscans in the Po valley, and had begun to make raids across the Apennines into peninsular Italy (in one of which, c.386 BC, they sacked

Rome). Further Gallic invasions occurred sporadically throughout the 4th and 3rd cents., culminating in the great invasion of 225, which the Romans and their Italian allies defeated at Telamon on the Etruscan coast.

The Romans responded by invading Cisalpine Gaul, which they overran in a three-year campaign of conquest ending with the capture of Mediolanum in 222. Their efforts to consolidate the conquest were interrupted by *Hannibal's invasion, which prompted the Gauls to rebel. After defeating Hannibal, the Romans resumed their plan of conquest, which they completed in 191 with a victory over the Boii, the most powerful of the Cisalpine Gallic tribes. Colonies at Placentia and Cremona were refounded, and further colonies were settled at Bononia, 189, Parma, and Mutina. In 187 the via Aemilia was constructed from Ariminum to Placentia. As a result of this great programme of colonization (still evident in aerial photographs which show traces of *centuriation throughout the region), nearly all the land south of the Po was occupied by settlers from peninsular Italy, while the northern part of the plain remained largely in the hands of its Celtic inhabitants, who were henceforth known to the Romans as Transpadani.

After the *Social War Cisalpine Gaul was formally separated from Italy and became a province, with its southern border at the Rubicon; but all the colonial settlers who were not already Roman citizens were enfranchised. The rest of the free population, which effectively meant the Transpadani, were given *Latin rights, a decision that they greatly resented; the demand for full citizen rights became a hot political issue in the following decades, until the Transpadani were finally enfranchised by Caesar in 49. In 42 Cisalpine Gaul was fully integrated within Italy, and under Augustus was divided into four of the eleven administrative regions of Italy (VIII–XI).

In the centuries after 200 Cisalpine Gaul was rapidly and thoroughly Romanized, and few traces of Celtic language and culture remained by the time of the empire. An area of rich agricultural land, much of which was reclaimed by Roman drainage schemes in the lower Po valley, Cisalpine Gaul achieved great prosperity; by the time of *Strabo, who gives an eloquent description of it, it had become one of the most prosperous parts of Europe.

Gaul (Transalpine) comprised the area from the Pyrenees and the Mediterranean coast of France to the English Channel, and from the Atlantic to the Rhine and the western Alps. As a geopolitical entity, it emerged in the 1st cent. BC and lasted into the 5th cent. AD. Augustus divided Gaul into four provinces: Narbonensis, Lugdunensis, Aquitania, and Belgica.

Gaul was largely Celtic in culture (see CELTS), but it contained Germanic immigrants in the NE, and the south had been heavily influenced by Greek *colonization. 'Gaul' was not a natural unit, but a Roman artefact. In order to protect the route to Spain, Rome helped *Massalia against bordering tribes. The result was, in 121 BC, the formation of 'the Province' (*Provincia*), from the Mediterranean to Lake Geneva, with its capital at Narbo. In 58–50, Caesar seized the remainder of Gaul, justifying his conquest by playing on Roman memories of savage attacks over the Alps by Celts and Germans. Italy was now to be defended from the Rhine (*Rhenus).

Initially, indeed, the Romans treated the Gauls as *barbarians. They disparaged Gaul beyond the Province as *Gallia Comāta*—'Long-haired Gaul', and generally mismanaged the Province itself. However, Gaul was not far behind Rome. In the Celtic core, Caesar found nations (see CIVITAS) establishing urban centres which, though hardly classical cities, had significant socio-economic functions. Under the more prudent rule of the emperors, the Province, now Narbonensis, was seeded with military colonies, and became a land of city-states, comparable with Italy. In the other 'Three Gauls', colonies were few and the *civitates* were retained, but their leaders vied with each other in acquiring the conquerors' culture.

The *Romanization of northern Gaul is illustrated by the dominance of Latin, and the emergence of the Graeco-Roman city. The *civitates* were too large to be city-states, but they contained towns that could be designated as their administrative centres and developed, under local magnates, in accordance with classical criteria. Most were unwalled. On the land, Romanization took the form of *villas—at this time working farms as much as country seats.

The population of Gaul was large: c.10,000,000. Agriculture flourished. One of the great engines of its success was the Rhine army, which stimulated trade by purchasing supplies from the interior. Commerce was facilitated by an extensive road- and river-network. The metropolis of high imperial Gaul was *Lugdunum, at a main junction of these networks. There was little resistance to Roman rule. Localized revolts were easily suppressed; they probably accelerated the demise of the pre-Roman aristocracy. Few Gauls subsequently involved themselves in Roman imperial careers.

Gellius, Aulus, Roman miscellanist, b. between AD 125 and 128, author of *Attic Nights* in 20 books. All knowledge of Gellius comes from his work. Most of his life was spent in Rome. He knew *Cornelius Fronto; but the deepest impression was made on him by *Favorinus. He spent at least a year in Athens completing his education; he visited *Claudius Atticus Herodes in his summer retreat at Cephisia, attended the Pythian Games, and enjoyed the life of a student and a tourist. After his return he was appointed a judge to try private cases; but his interest in the law is essentially antiquarian.

Attic Nights is a collection of mainly short chapters, based on notes or excerpts he had made in reading, on a great variety of topics in philosophy, history, law, and esp. grammar in its ancient sense, including literary and textual criticism. Acc. to his preface, Gellius conceived the notion of giving literary form to his notes during the long winter's nights in Attica (whence the title), but completed the project (some 30 years later) as an instructive entertainment for his children. Variety and charm are imparted by the constant changes of topic, purportedly reproducing the chance order of Gellius' notes (a cliché of such works), and by the use of *dialogue and reminiscence as literary forms for conveying information; the dramatizations are generally fictitious, though in settings based on Gellius' own experience. The characters of Gellius' friends and teachers are finely drawn; the fictitious persons are less individual. Gellius is well read in Latin, less so in Greek; his judgement is sensible rather than incisive. He shares the age's preference for Early Latin and *Sallust over Augustan and *Silver Age writers, but admires *Virgil and will hear no ill of *Cicero.

Gelōn, son of Deinomenes, greatest of Sicilian tyrants before *Dionysius (1) I. On the death (c.491 BC) of Hippocrates, he seized the tyranny of Gela. He formed an alliance with *Theron of *Acragas, married his daughter Damarete, and with him fought the Phoenicians of western Sicily. He restored the exiled aristocracy of *Syracuse (485), but seized the city, which became the seat of his power; his brother *Hieron (1) I became ruler of Gela. He enlarged his empire by alliance and conquest. He transferred half the population of Gela to Syracuse. In these ways he built up the strongest single military power

in Hellas. The growth of his power, allied to Theron's, alarmed Anaxilas of Messana, Terillus of *Himera, and the Phoenicians; and from 483, Carthage prepared for war. Gelon was prevented from helping the metropolitan Greeks against *Xerxes by Hamilcar's arrival in NW Sicily. The victory of Himera (480) left Gelon, by alliances and the submission of his enemies, virtually the overlord of Sicily, and gave two generations of peace with Carthage. Gelon was now the accepted ruler of Syracuse. He enfranchised 10,000 mercenaries, and built temples at Himera and Syracuse, where his public works, and peace, gave great prosperity, and his reign was looked back on as a golden age. He died in 478/7, and was succeeded by Hieron.

genealogy, the enumeration of descent from an ancestor. Legendary pedigree was esp. important in Greece. Before fighting, *Homeric heroes boast of their ancestry, citing between two and eight generations of ancestors. Even aristocrats in Classical Athens (which put more stress on recent achievements) claimed descent from important local and Homeric heroes, and thence from the gods. Other groups, cities, colonies, or tribes, might trace descent from a single legendary figure (see FOUNDERS OF CITIES), and genealogies were sometimes akin to king-lists (e.g. *Sparta). Some of the first prose writers recorded (or worked out) genealogies, mostly legendary, as well as their chronological implications: *Hecataeus (c.500 BC) and *Hellanicus. Genealogies and their enumeration were popular, esp. in Sparta, as *Hippias (2) found. They reflect the enormous significance attributed by the Greeks to origins and the original ancestor in determining the character of future generations. Prestige, status, even moral character, might be derived from the original progenitor, preferably legendary, heroic, or divine. (Romans, more interested in their recent ancestors, adopted the Greek penchant for legendary ancestry only in the course of Hellenization (see HELLENISM) from the 2nd cent. BC.) Political and tribal affiliations might, similarly, be seen in genealogical terms. Given the value of the original ancestor, it is not surprising that the intervening links were sometimes vague or forgotten. Such is the moral or political importance of ancestry, that genealogy tends to reflect the current position or claims of a family, and thus it is usually the least reliable of historical traditions.

generals See; IMPERATOR; IMPERIUM; PRO CONSULE, PRO PRAETORE; STRATEGOI; and names of individual generals.

genos The word *genos* was widely and variously used in Greek of all periods to denote 'species', 'genus', 'sort', 'category', 'birth', 'kin', 'race', 'lineage', 'family', 'generation', 'posterity', etc. Probably from its use to denote '(noble) lineage', it came to be used in 4th-cent. BC Athenian orators and inscriptions in a quasi-precise sense to denote a set of families or individuals who identified themselves as a group by the use of a collective plural name. Some such names were geographical or occupational, but most were patronymic in form, implying the descent of their members from a fictive or real common male ancestor. About 60 such groups are known. Some 4th-cent. evidence suggests that a *genos* could be a constituent part of a *phratry, perhaps as its most prominent *oikos* ('house').

genre, a grouping of texts related within the system of literature by their sharing features of form and content. Ancient theoretical discussions of specific literary genres operate according to criteria which are one-sidedly formal (generally metrical), thematic (the characters' moral or social quality, the general subject-matter), or pragmatic (the situation of performance), but scarcely attempt to correlate or justify them. *Plato differentiates a number of existing poetic genres by their modes of presentation: mimetic (tragedy, comedy), narrational (dithyramb), or mixed (epic). But among the theoreticians it is only *Aristotle who provides a genuinely complex theory, combining considerations of form, content, the author's and audience's psychology, metre, language, performance, traditionality, and evolution. Yet his surviving *Poetics* focuses mostly upon a single genre and is often elliptical and tentative: it furnishes many of the elements of a useful theory but does not fully work them out.

gens ('lineage') derives from a Lat. root denoting procreation, and the *gens* was often conceived as comprising the free-born descendants of a common ancestor in the male line. That distant ancestor was often a fiction, and a real or supposed kinship link between those claiming membership of the same *gens* became increasingly difficult to demonstrate. Since all members of a *gens* bore the same *nomen* (normally ending in -*ius*), by the late republic alternative definitions based membership of a *gens* on tenure of the same *nomen*, not kinship. See NAMES, PERSONAL, ROMAN.

geocentricity The theory that the earth lies at the centre of the universe belongs to Greek scientific astronomy. The first man to whom the notion that the earth is spherical and lies at the centre of a spherical universe is credibly attributed is *Parmenides (early 5th cent.). By the time of *Eudoxus (*c.*360) the standard view was that the stationary spherical earth lies at the centre, around which rotates the outermost sphere of the fixed stars, once daily about the poles of the equator, carrying with it the intermediate spheres of the other heavenly bodies (also centred on the earth, but rotating in the other sense about different poles). That is the basis of *Aristotle's picture of the world, which dominated the cosmology of antiquity and the Middle Ages. Acc. to this, the sublunar region is composed of the four mutable *elements, earth, air, fire, and water, whose natural motion is in a straight line, i.e. 'down' towards the earth, or 'up' away from its centre. Everything above that region (including the visible heavenly bodies) is composed of an immutable 'fifth element' whose natural motion is circular. See ARISTARCHUS (1).

geography by the 5th cent. BC had three distinct strands: small-scale documentation of the actualities, as of particular sea routes; wider theories about the layout of land and sea on a global scale; and ideas about the place of the *oikoumenē* (inhabited world) in the order of the cosmos. Both of the more theoretical approaches are apparent in *Hecataeus and *Herodotus (who combined a geographical and ethnographical perspective): it is plausible to suggest an origin in 6th-cent. Ionia, in which new approaches to the physical nature of the universe, inspired in part by contacts with the Fertile Crescent and Egypt, combined with the active seafaring experience of states like Miletus and Samos. The invention of the map was attributed to *Anaximander.

Learned geography, coupled with *astronomy, came during the 4th cent. to an advanced understanding of the nature of the earth as a rotating sphere of a realistic size; and the theory of the latitudinal zones was refined. A mathematical geography emerged (limited in the end by the available instruments), advanced in the work of *Eratosthenes and *Hipparchus (2), which culminated in the 2nd cent. AD in the work of

*Ptolemy (2), the most detailed attempt made in antiquity to project the layout of the physical and human world on the surface of the globe. By 300 BC it was known to the informed that the *oikoumene* of which detailed information was available could occupy only a small portion of the northern hemisphere. It was also at this time that the idea of accumulating information systematically on the edges of received knowledge began. The work of the companions and followers of *Alexander (2) the Great, above all, established a link between formal geography and political dominion. It also offered, through the development of the ethnographic tradition, an analytical content for the genre which went beyond description and cataloguing.

Eratosthenes, whose contribution to geography as a separable discipline was enormous, set new standards of verification by rejecting the Homeric tradition and insisting on a clear distinction between fictitious wonder-descriptions and the recording of fact, established a blend of descriptive and mathematical geography as a new genre, made the mapping of the *oikoumenē* its centre, deployed a coherent system of co-ordinates of latitude and longitude in order to do so, and applied the benefits of Ptolemaic statecraft: e.g. his accurate estimate of the earth's circumference depended on the measurement of *Egypt in the interests of land management.

Geographical ordering became central to the formation of administrative units. Borrowing perhaps from the geographically defined satrapies of the *Achaemenid dominion, the Athenians had subdivided their empire into five units. Geographical organization of a sometimes complex kind was also a feature of the states of Alexander and his Successors (*Diadochi), and the usefulness of correct topographical information for coercion and exaction was established. Roman contributions were of a practical kind: the *commentarii* of commanders and governors; Gaius *Iulius Caesar (1) has a place of honour here, blending the claim to *autopsy with Herodotean ethnographical themes. Pomponius Mela, from *Baetica wrote a pioneering Latin geography at the time of *Claudius' invasion of Britain (AD 43–44). It was used by *Pliny the Elder.

Geometric (period) See POTTERY, GREEK, 2.

geometry See MATHEMATICS.

Germānia a name aplied by the Romans both to lands east of the Rhine (*Rhenus), occupied by the 'free' Germans, and to imperial provinces for the most part to the west of this river, carved out of *Gaul.

Germānicus See IULIUS CAESAR, GERMANICUS.

Germans (*Germāni*), after the *Celts the second major linguistic and cultural grouping encountered by the Graeco-Roman world in northern Europe. It was the Romans' failure, between 12 BC and AD 9 (when a German chieftain, Arminus, destroyed the three legions of *Quinctilius Varus near the *Teutoburgian forest), to absorb the Germanic peoples of the Elbe that compelled them to centre the defence of their western empire on the Rhine (*Rhenus) and upper Danube (*Danuvius).

Modern research has shown how much our two best informants about the Germanic peoples, *Caesar and *Tacitus, were influenced by their cultural prejudices and their literary strategies. (For example, Caesar's emphasis on the Rhine as a distinct boundary between Celts and Germans is now recognized as political, not ethnographic, in origin.)

Combining our best literary information about Germanic society (esp. Tacitus' *Germania*) with modern archaeological research produces a picture of a simple (by comparison with the Celtic) but developing iron age society, with permanent farms and villages. Agriculture was both arable and pastoral, and produced raw materials which could be traded for the finished goods of the Roman empire. Though there might be nominal kings, real political power was diffused among local clan chiefs: unlike the Celtic, the Germanic peoples produced no proto-urban settlements which might accommodate central administrations. They were effectively unified only in time of war, under a battle-leader—the final decision on whom, as with all matters of importance, was taken by the warriors in a tribal assembly. This absence of a clearly defined state-structure afforded the Germans a highly flexible response to Roman aggression, and protected them from conquest.

gestures convey attitude, intention, and status. Greeks and Romans moved trunk and limbs to precede, accompany, intensify, undercut, and replace words. Posture, orientation, separating social-distance (proximity in supplication), facial expression (frowns, arched brows), and paralinguistic cues (pauses, pitch-changes, silences, hissing) also express emotion and modulate speech. Social meaning is divulged through ritualized acts (saluting, drink-pledges) and informal behaviour (pursed lips, nodding, nail-biting). Behaviour may be intended (handclasp, embrace, kiss) or unintended (shriek, hiccough, horripilation, odour), sometimes even unconscious (sweat, lip-biting, eye-tics). The latter two categories of psychophysical reactions 'leak' hidden feelings. Some kinds of behaviour exhibit ethological constants (tears, grins, cowering, shrinking); others are culture-specific (Hellenic ethnogests: thigh-slapping, negative upward head-nod).

Giants, in myth a race of monstrous appearance and great strength. Acc. to *Hesiod, they were sons of *Gaia/Gē (Earth) from the blood of *Uranus which fell upon earth; he describes them as valiant warriors. *Homer considers them a savage race of men who perished with their king. The prevailing legend of the fight of the gods and the Giants was formulated in Archaic epics and was embroidered by many later writers. A substantial account is given by *Apollodorus (2). When the gods were attacked by the Giants, they learned that they could win only if they were assisted by a mortal. They called in *Heracles, who killed the giant Alcyoneus and many others with his arrows. *Zeus, who led the gods, smote with his thunderbolt Porphyrion who attempted to ravish *Hera; *Athena killed Pallas or Enceladus; *Poseidon crushed Polybotēs under the rock that became the island of Nisyros; *Apollo shot Ephialtēs; *Hermes slew Hippolytus; *Dionysus killed Eurytus and many other Giants besides who were caught in his vine; and Hephaestus aided the gods, throwing red-hot iron as missiles. The Giants were defeated and were believed to be buried under the volcanoes in various parts of Greece and Italy, e.g. Enceladus under Aetna.

The Gigantomachy was one of the most popular myths in Greece, and so the names of participants and the episodes of the battle vary from writer to writer and from representation to representation. Zeus, Heracles, Poseidon, and later Athena, are the usual protagonists. In its early stage the myth seems to represent a variation of the popular motif of the tribe that attempted to dethrone the gods; in a more advanced stage of culture the myth was interpreted as the fight of civilization against barbarism. In art the Giants are first shown as warriors or wild men, later as snake-legged monsters. The most famous sculptural renderings are found on the Archaic treasury of the Siphnians at *Delphi and on the Hellenistic altar of *Pergamum.

gift, Greece In the Homeric poems, gift-giving perhaps receives more attention than any other peaceful heroic activity. It has three outstanding features. First, gifts have an extremely wide range of functions. The word 'gift' (*dōron*) covered a diversity of actions and transactions (payment for services, rewards, prizes, bribes). Secondly, gifts are often very valuable; those referred to include cattle, armour, women, and even entire cities. Thirdly, gifts are often given within contexts such as *marriage, *funerals, friendship, and ritualized friendship (see FRIENDSHIP, GREEK and FRIENDSHIP, RITUALIZED), either to initiate or to perpetuate amiable relationships.

At all periods of Greek history, gift exchange differed sharply from such exchanges as trade, conducted outside the context of amiable relationships. In trade, the exchange was a short-term, self-liquidating transaction, generating neither binding relationships nor moral involvement. Within the context of amiable relationships, a gift was not merely meant to 'pay off' a past gift or service, but to render the recipient indebted, and thus set going a *reciprocity mechanism. Gifts served a multiplicity of purposes: they repaid past services, created new obligations, and acted as continual reminders of the validity of a bond. Gift-exchange differed from trade in that the exchange of goods was not the primary object of the transaction. Commodities of high use value (e.g. metal objects, *timber, and grain) circulated as gifts, and some of these commodities could not always be obtained by means of trade.

The *polis made a half-hearted attempt to curb the prevalence of gift-giving. By opening alternative channels of commodity supply, it presumably reduced the volume of vital resources circulating as gifts. Inside the *polis*-framework, the sort of gift-giving which could have hindered the impersonal functioning of political institutions (e.g. 'gifts' made to individual citizens in return for their votes) seems effectively to have been checked. Outside the *polis*, however, reality remained very much like the one reflected in the Homeric poems; élite members integrated into politically separated communities went on circulating substantial resources amongst themselves as gifts. The channels through which these resources moved coincided to a great extent with networks of ritualized *friendship.

This external involvement had important consequences both for the *polis*' social structure and for its political life: citizens involved in this sort of network could significantly improve their standing within the community by means of resources obtained from outside. In general, the community looked favourably upon donations made to it by such citizens. Receiving gifts from an outsider could also be seen as *bribery, however: the gift became a bribe if there was some suspicion that the countergift might involve trading with communal interests. See also CORRUPTION.

The expression 'Greek gifts' is an allusion to Virgil's *Aeneid* bk. 2, 'I fear the Greeks even when they bring gifts', said about the Trojan Horse.

gift, Rome See AMBITUS; EUERGETISM; FRIENDSHIP, RITUALIZED.

gladiators, combatants at games Gladiatorial combats, held at the funerals of dead warriors in Etruria (see ETRUSCANS), were introduced to Rome in 264 BC, when three pairs fought at the funeral games given in honour of Iunius Pera. Down to *Caesar's Games in 46 the justification (or pretext) was always the death of a male relative, but these were in part commemorative of Caesar's daughter *Iulia (1), in part not commemorative at all. These contests, like beast-fights (see VENATIONES), became an increasingly important route to popular favour for their promoter, forming a gripping, though normally brief (because highly expensive) item in games held in Rome and other towns (see AEDILES). However, 5,000 pairs fought in eight different games given by *Augustus (*Res Gestae* 22. 1) and the same number in a single series of games given by *Trajan to celebrate the conclusion of the Dacian War in AD 107. In Rome the original venue was the *forum Romanum. The first stone amphitheatre was built by *Statilius Taurus under Augustus, but it was only with the building of the Flavian amphitheatre (*Colosseum) that Rome had a specialized venue larger than those in quite small Italian towns (the amphitheatre in *Pompeii goes back to the early years of the Sullan colony). The *Seleucid Antiochus IV introduced these bloodiest of games to Antioch, *c.*170 BC, and later they spread to all parts of the Roman empire. Greek cities became wildly enthusiastic. Gladiators were of four types: the *murmillō*, with a fish for the crest on his helmet, and the Samnite, both heavily armed with oblong shield, visored helmet, and short sword; the *rētiārius*, lightly clad, fighting with net and trident; and the Thracian with round shield and curved scimitar.

Prisoners of war and condemned criminals were compelled to fight as gladiators. Those who fought professionally were either slaves, bought for the purpose, or free volunteers, who for a fee bound themselves to their owner by an oath which permitted him to kill or maim them (in practice a gladiator was too valuable an investment to be wasted outside the games, and the life of a defeated combatant was often spared by the audience's wish). They were trained in schools (see LŪDI (3)) under a *lanista* (who was sometimes a retired gladiator) and might be acquired as an investment, to be hired or sold to games-promoters. In the late republic they were often used as the core of a gang or armed entourage. Apparently even members of the senatorial and equestrian orders were attracted to a gladiatorial career, which derived a macabre glamour from courage, physical strength, and sexual potency. So there was legislation under Augustus and *Tiberius to prevent members of these orders becoming gladiators, which remained an infamous profession. Female gladiators were not unknown. After *Domitian gladiatorial games could be given at Rome only by emperors; outside Rome they required official sanction. Restrictions on games in the towns of the empire seem to be related more to the expenditure involved for the promoters than to any distaste. Opposition to such games centred on the shedding of blood for fun, but for *Cicero and *Pliny the Younger this did not apply if those fighting were condemned criminals. Gladiatorial combats were first prohibited in AD 325, when *Constantine I decided that they were too bloodthirsty a peacetime activity.

glass Glazed objects are common on Greek sites of the Archaic period, some of them Egyptian imports, others probably made locally. In the 6th cent. BC small vases made by the sandcore process became known in Greece; they have opaque blue, brown, or white bodies and a marbled effect was produced on their surface by means of a comb or spike. In the Hellenistic period mould-made bowls, mainly from Egypt, come into fashion.

The invention of glass-blowing in the 1st cent. BC (probably in Syria) wrought great changes in the glass industry, which, hitherto limited to expensive surrogates for luxury goods, now became capable of cheap mass-production, but even then the most highly valued glass was 'colourless and transparent, as closely as possible resembling rock crystal' (Pliny the Elder).

Window glass, made by a primitive process of rolling, was known at *Pompeii, and later became common; in the later empire also begins the use of glass for mirrors (see COSMETICS).

gnōmē, a maxim or aphorism: an important facet of Greek literary expression from the earliest period. Hesiod's *Works and Days* 694 is representative: 'keep the rules: proportion is best in all things.' The subject is usually human life or the terms of human existence, articulated as a succinct general truth or instruction. *Gnomai* are used: (*a*) in argument, to relate or distinguish particular and general: 'the Athenian war-dead will never be forgotten—heroes have the whole world for their tombstone' (Thucydides 2. 43); 'women (they say) live safe at home while men go to war . . . I would rather take up arms three times than give birth once' (Euripides *Medea* 248–251); (*b*) singly, as self-sufficient maxims, like the Delphic 'know thyself' and 'nothing in excess'. See PROVERBS.

Gnosticism is a generic term primarily used of theosophical groups which broke with the 2nd-cent. Christian Church; see CHRISTIANITY. A wider, more imprecise use of the term describes a syncretistic religiosity diffused in the near east, contemporaneous with and independent of Christianity. In recent years (esp. after the publication of the Coptic Gnostic texts discovered at Nag Hammadi in Upper Egypt in 1946), the diversity of beliefs in the various 'Gnostic' sects has been increasingly emphasized.

gods, Olympian See OLYMPIAN GODS, OLYMPIANS; RELIGION, GREEK; THEOS.

gold is rare in Greece, and the source of the rich treasures found in bronze age tombs (*Mycenae, etc.) is unknown. The island of Siphnos prospered in the 6th cent. BC by its gold production; later the mines were flooded. Mines on Thasos, opened by the *Phoenicians, were working in *Thucydides' (2) day, but have not been found. *Macedonia and *Thrace had a large auriferous area, where the mines of Mt. *Pangaeus were working before 500 BC. In Asia Minor, gold came from Mysia, Phrygia, and *Lydia; their wealth is attested by the stories of *Midas (1), *Croesus, and the river Pactolus. Electrum, a natural alloy of gold and silver, was panned in the rivers of Asia Minor, and was used for the earliest coins (see COINAGE, GREEK) and for jewellery. Colchis also furnished gold, Scythians brought supplies from central Asia, and *Carthage received gold from west Africa. Yet there was a scarcity of gold in

Greece until the conquests of *Alexander (2) the Great made available the hoards of Persia.

Early *Etruscan tombs show much gold furniture. At Rome the metal long remained rare; it probably first became common through war indemnities. Under the late republic and early empire the main source of supply (apart from *booty from the Hellenistic east) was Spain, where the NW and *Baetica yielded immense quantities. Gold was also mined in southern France and dredged from rivers in other parts of Gaul; there are also workings in south Wales. After the 1st cent. AD the western goldfields were largely superseded by those of the Balkans, Noricum, and *Dacia.

golden age, an imagined period in early human history when human beings lived a life of ease, far from toil and *sin. The most important text is *Hesiod, *Works and Days* 109–126, which talks of a 'golden *genos*', i.e. species or generation, as the first in a series: reference to a golden *age* occurs first in Latin. The golden age is associated esp. with *Cronus or *Saturnus and is marked by communal living and the spontaneous supply of food: its end comes with a series of inventions that lead to the modern condition of humanity (first plough, first ship, first walls, and first sword). Rationalist thinkers tended to reject the model in favour of 'hard' primitivism or a belief in progress, but the function of the myth was always to hold up a mirror to present malaises or to presage a future return to the idyll (as in Virgil's fourth *Eclogue*).

Golden Fleece See ARGONAUTS; JASON (1); MEDEA; PELIAS.

Golden House See DOMUS AUREA.

Gordium, capital of ancient Phrygia, situated where the river Sangarius is crossed by the main route westward from the Anatolian plateau to the sea (the Persian '*Royal Road'). Gordium became the main Phrygian centre in the 8th cent., at the end of which it reached its greatest prosperity under King *Midas (2). The site had massive fortifications and impressive palace buildings, and many richly furnished tumuli were built around it in the 8th to 6th cents., including one which has been identified as the tomb of Midas himself. Gordium was destroyed by the invading Cimmerians in the early 7th cent. but recovered, only to lose importance under Persian domination. It was visited by *Alexander (2) the Great (333), who cut the famous 'Gordian Knot'.

Gorgias of Leontini (c.485–c.380 BC), *sophist, important both as a thinker and as a stylist. His visit to Athens as an ambassador in 427 is traditionally seen as a landmark in the history of *rhetoric, introducing Sicilian techniques into the Athenian tradition of oratory. Certainly, his stylistic influence was enormous. The extant *Encomium of Helen* and *Defence of Palamedes*, as well as the fragment of his *Epitaphios, illustrate clearly the seductions of his antithetical manner, with its balancing clauses, rhymes, and assonances. There is a wonderful *parody of the style in Agathon's speech in *Plato's *Symposium*. At the same time, these speeches contain serious reflection on the power of words and on moral responsibility. We also possess summaries of a philosophical work. Apparently, Gorgias argued that 'nothing is', and even if something is, it cannot be known, or indicated by one person to another. How serious these sceptical arguments were has been much debated.

Gorgon/Medūsa, female monsters in Greek myth. Acc. to the canonical version of the myth *Perseus was ordered to fetch the head of Medusa, the mortal sister of Sthenno and Euryale; with their horrific gaze these Gorgons turned to stone anyone who looked at them. With the help of *Athena, *Hermes, and *nymphs, who had supplied him with winged sandals, *Hades' cap of invisibility, and a sickle, Perseus managed to behead Medusa in her sleep; from her head sprang the immortal winged horse *Pegasus. Although pursued by Medusa's sisters, Perseus escaped and, eventually, turned his enemy Polydectes to stone by means of Medusa's face.

*Hesiod knows the myth, which shows oriental influence. Gorgons were very popular—often with an apotropaic function, as on the west pediment of the temple of Artemis on *Corcyra—in Archaic art, which represented them as women with open mouth and dangerous teeth, but in the 5th cent. they lost their frightening appearance and became beautiful women.

See AEGIS; ORIENTALISM.

Gortyn, Gortyn law code Gortyn was a city in central *Crete. From the 7th cent. BC are known a temple to Athena on the acropolis, and one to *Apollo Pythios on the plain; an agora lies at the foot of the acropolis.

Of Gortyn's various early inscribed laws the most extensive is the Gortyn law code. It consists of various laws probably enacted since at least the 6th cent., and only slightly reorganized

when they were inscribed c.450. The inscription is built into an odeum restored in AD 100 on one side of the agora, but had probably always been displayed in this area. The laws deal with the family and family property, with slaves (see SLAVERY), surety, donations, mortgage, procedure in trials, and other items. Slaves had certain rights for their protection; they were also allowed to have their own property and even to marry free women. There was also a clear distinction, esp. in matters of hereditary right, between family and private property. There were detailed regulations on *adoption, and the property rights of heiresses and of the divorced wives of citizens. The modern distinction between criminal and family law does not apply, nor does the modern expectation that laws are egalitarian. For example, rape was not a criminal offence, but led to a fine, the level of which varied widely in accord with the status of the victim (whether male or female) and of the rapist. Witnesses, some on oath, and the oath of the party, served to establish a case; but the judge decided at his own discretion. The laws of Gortyn are probably the most important source for Archaic–Classical Greek law, and reveal a high level of juristic conceptions. See INHERITANCE, GREEK; LAW IN GREECE.

government/administration   **(Greek)**
Greek states involved their citizens, as far as possible, in carrying out decisions as well as in making decisions, and did little to develop a professional *bureaucracy. The need for regular administrators was reduced by such practices as tax-farming, the system of *liturgies, and reliance on individuals to prosecute offenders not only for private wrongs but also for wrongs against the state.

Democratic Athens, with its large number of citizens, its extensive overseas interests, and money with which to pay stipends, developed an esp. large number of administrative posts. The work of administration, where it could not be devolved, was divided into numerous separate, small jobs, and most of those were entrusted to boards of ten men, one from each tribe, appointed by lot for one year and not eligible for reappointment to the same board: it was assumed that the work required loyalty rather than ability. The council of 500, itself appointed by lot for a year, acted as overseer of the various boards. (See BOULE.) Thus when a partnership of citizens made a successful bid for the collection of a particular tax in a particular year, the contract would be made by the *poletai ('sellers') in the presence of the council. If they paid the money on time, they would pay it to the apodektai ('receivers') in the presence of the council, and if they defaulted, the council would use the praktores ('exactors') to pursue them. See generally DEMOCRACY, ATHENIAN.

Gracchi (the tribunes). See SEMPRONIUS GRACCHUS (2), TIBERIUS, and SEMPRONIUS GRACCHUS, GAIUS.

Graces See CHARITES.

grain supply See FOOD SUPPLY.

grammar, grammarians See LINGUISTICS, ANCIENT.

grammaticus is the Latin term denoting the professional teacher of language and literature, esp. poetry; 'grammarian' is a misleading translation. After their initial appearance at Rome (late 2nd–early 1st cent. BC) Latin grammaticī came to serve as instructors of upper-class boys with responsibility: for teaching correct Latinity via the grammatical handbook (ars), for giving line-by-line explication of poetic texts, and (often) for providing preliminary exercises in composition, before their pupils advanced to the *rhetor. Commonly slaves and freedmen in the earliest period, grammatici later more often belonged to the 'respectable' classes (*honestiores), like the children they taught. See EDUCATION, ROMAN; LINGUISTICS, ANCIENT.

granaries

Greek Large storerooms would have been required for the corn imported in quantities by Classical Athens, and would have been adjacent to the Great Harbour of *Piraeus, where the corn market (Alphitopolis Stoa) was built in the time of *Pericles.

Roman Purpose-built structures (horrea) for storing corn and other commodities developed in the late republic for the provisioning of Rome, and later at forts for military provisions. At Rome and *Ostia horrea were brick or masonry courtyard-structures surrounded by storerooms (sometimes on dwarf walls for ventilation). Military granaries were large sheds of timber or stone raised on posts or dwarf walls, the corn being kept in bins.

Grānīcus, river in NW Asia Minor, scene of *Alexander (2) the Great's first victory over the Persians (334 BC). Alexander began the battle on the right, launching an attack on the Persian cavalry lining the river-bank with the left squadron of Companions (see HETAIROI) and other cavalry between them and the phalanx to their left. The attack was driven back, but when the Persians pursued into the river-bed, Alexander led his remaining Companions obliquely to the left into their disordered ranks. After a short fight, the Persian cavalry fled, leaving their Greek mercenaries, stationed in the plain beyond the river, to be surrounded and annihilated.

graphē in Athenian law was a type of prosecution, the commonest public action. The name seems to imply that when this procedure was instituted its distinctive feature was that the charge was made in writing, whereas in other actions the charge was made orally. Any Athenian with full citizen rights who wished could prosecute; and since prosecution by anyone who wished was introduced by *Solon, it is probable that it was Solon who introduced graphe. By the 4th cent. BC charges in other actions also were put in writing, but the name graphe continued to be used for an ordinary public action (see LAW AND PROCEDURE, ATHENIAN, 3).

graphē paranomōn in Athens was a prosecution for the offence of proposing a decree or law which was contrary to an existing law in form or content. As soon as the accuser made a sworn statement that he intended to bring a graphe paranomon against the proposer, the proposal, whether already voted on or not, was suspended until the trial had been held. If the jury convicted the proposer, his proposal was annulled and he was punished, usually by a fine; if a man was convicted three times of this type of offence, he suffered disfranchisement.

The two earliest known cases were brought in 415 BC and thereabouts. *Ostracism was by then obsolescent, and in its place a graphe paranomon became a popular method of attacking prominent politicians. The most famous example is the prosecution of Ctesiphon by *Aeschines (1) for his proposal to confer a crown on *Demosthenes (2), the orator; the surviving speeches of Aeschines, Against Ctesiphon, and Demosthenes, On the Crown, were written for this trial.

grave-reliefs See ART, FUNERARY, GREEK.

Greece (geography) Greece is poor in minerals. Clay for pottery comes from particular local sources. Sometimes limestone has become crystalline under great pressure; hence the marbles of *Paros, *Naxos, Thasos, and of Pentelicon in Attica. Small deposits of iron ore are frequent, but tin and most of the copper for making bronze had to be imported. The silver-mines of *Laurium were essential to the economy of Athens.

Greece has a sharply seasonal Mediterranean *climate. The winter rainy season (typically October–May) is warm, seldom frosty, and the time of activity and growth. The dry season of summer is hot, rainless, relentlessly sunny, and is the dead season. The mountains intercept rain-bearing depressions, producing a disparity between the wet west of Greece and the dry east. The west coast of Asia Minor is again well watered in winter. Summer temperatures sometimes reach 40°C (104°F), esp. inland, but are tolerable because of north winds and dry air. Mountain areas, as in Arcadia in central *Peloponnese, are always difficult to live in because there are cold winters as well as dry summers: the growing season is very short, and frost-sensitive crops, esp. olives, cannot be grown. Traditional Greek *agriculture was based on cereals, olives, vines, and herding animals. It involved seasonal hard work, ploughing, sowing, picking olives, and tending vines; an unhurried harvest; and long periods of relative leisure.

It was seldom difficult to make *roads between the fertile basins. Seafaring called for great skill: the coasts are wild and terrible with cliff-bound promontories, and razor-edged reefs. There were few good harbours, and no tide to help in getting in or out. Sailors feared the sea in winter, and land travel was then difficult because of flooded fords. See LANDSCAPES (ANCIENT GREEK).

Greece (history)

Archaic, Classical, Hellenistic

Archaic period
(776–479). The conventional date for the beginning of the historical period of Greece is 776, the date of the first *Olympic Games on the reckoning of *Hippias (2). This may be about right for the event in question; but the early 8th cent. was innovatory in several other ways. Iron began to be worked with new sophistication; the alphabet was taken over from *Phoenicia; and colonies began to be sent out in a more organized way (see COLONIZATION, GREEK), esp. from *Euboea, which between 750 and 730 colonized *Cumae and *Pithecusae in the west and was involved in Al Mina in the east. The 8th cent. was also the age of *polis formation and

political *synoecism, perhaps themselves a result, in part, of the colonizing movement, but also of the rise of religious leagues or *amphictionies. The emergence of the *polis* was marked by the placing of *sanctuaries, often dedicated to *Hera, at the edge of *polis* territory. Some of these developments, not just writing, but perhaps even the idea of the self-determining community, may actually be Phoenician in inspiration. But whatever the truth about Semitic primacy, early Greek society soon acquired distinctive features and institutions, most of which continued to be important in classical times and later. Among these were athletics and religiously based athletic events like the Olympic Games; the *gymnasium, which provided training for both athletics and its elder brother, warfare; the *symposium, at which aristocratic values were inculcated; and *homosexuality, which was related to the three phenomena just mentioned. Some other characteristic features of Greek society are more easily paralleled elsewhere, e.g. ritualized *friendship; but institutionalized *proxeny, which developed out of it, was specifically Greek.

All this contributed to such shared Greek consciousness as there was (see ETHNICITY; NATIONALISM), but the chief way in which early Greek states interacted was through warfare, a paradoxical activity in that in Greece at most periods it was conducted according to shared custom (see WAR, RULES OF), but at the same time war is, obviously, an assertion of separateness. Equally the four great panhellenic ('all-Greek', see PANHELLENISM) sanctuaries, *Olympia, *Delphi, Isthmia (see ISTHMIAN GAMES), *Nemea, were a symbol of what Greeks had in common, but they were also a focus for interstate competition (see DELPHI), and constituting an alternative to war; indeed struggles for influence at sanctuaries sometimes developed into wars proper, see SACRED WARS. And sanctuaries were the repositories of tithes or tenth-parts of the *booty which was a reason for and result of warfare; this booty was often turned into dedications (see VOTIVES).

The first war which can be called in any sense general was the 8th-cent. Lelantine War fought by *Chalcis and *Eretria for control of the plain between them; but each side had allies from further away. Commercial and economic prosperity on the one hand, and individual ambition on the other, combined on *Thucydides' view to produce *tyranny. Colonization and trade were certainly connected, and the combination meant that Greece was exposed to luxuries on a new scale. But the chief modern explanation for tyranny is military. *Hoplite warfare involved a partial repudiation of individual aristocratic fighting methods, corresponding to that political repudiation of control by hereditary aristocracies which was the essence of tyranny. The first tyrannies, of Pheidon at Argos and *Cypselus at Corinth, are best put at mid-7th cent., when hoplites appear.

Two states which did not have tyrannies in this first phase are *Sparta and *Athens, indeed Sparta famously avoided tyranny until Hellenistic times. Sparta was remarkable in other ways also, e.g. by not sending out many colonies in the historical period (with the important exception of *Tarentum, Gk. Taras, in south Italy) but above all in having annexed its next-door neighbour *Messenia in the later 8th cent. The inhabitants were turned into *helots. Other neighbours of Sparta became *perioîkoi, a subordinate status to which some communities of *Laconia also belonged. Sparta later became a tight and repressive place, but Archaic Sparta guaranteed political power to the *dãmos* or people—meaning perhaps only the class of hoplite fighters—at an impressively early date (?7th cent.) when *democracy elsewhere was still in the future. But the political momentum at Sparta was lost, partly through the need to hold down Messenia and the helots; this in turn called for the strict *agoge*. Simple infantry strength enabled Sparta to coerce much of *Peloponnese by the later 6th cent., though propaganda also helped, the deliberate muting of Sparta's unpopular *Dorian aspect.

Athens also was unusual among Greek states, esp. in the size of its directly controlled territory, *Attica, its natural assets (esp. silver), and its physical suitability for a naval role (see ATHENS, *History*). Athens, like Sparta, avoided tyranny in the 7th cent., but unlike Sparta, Athens did experience an attempt at one at this time, the failed coup of *Cylon *c.*630. A generation later *Solon's reforms (594) both resembled and circumvented—for the moment—tyrannical, anti-aristocratic solutions imposed elsewhere. His creation of a new *boule* of 400 members was a big step towards democracy, as was the opening of high political office on criteria of wealth not birth; but even more crucial was abolition of the demeaning status of hectemorage (see HEKTE-MOROI). Indirect but important consequences of this abolition were the development of a self-conscious citizen élite (see CITIZENSHIP, GREEK) and the related rise of chattel *slavery. Solon also permitted appeal to the *eliaia* (see DEMOCRACY,

ATHENIAN; LAW AND PROCEDURE, ATHENIAN), and legislated in the social sphere; but some of the detailed traditions about his economic reforms are suspect because they imply the existence of *coinage, which in fact begins in the middle of the 6th cent., too late to be relevant to developments at the beginning of it.

Solon's reforms were critical for the longer-term development of Athens and indeed Greece, but in the short term they failed because Athens did after all succumb, for much of the second half of the 6th cent., to a tyranny, that of *Pisistratus and his sons *Hippias (1) and *Hipparchus (1). Under these rulers, Athenian naval power was built up, a vigorous foreign policy pursued, splendid buildings erected, and roads built. But the tyrants were driven out in 510, and *Cleisthenes (2) reformed the Athenian constitution in a democratic direction in 508/7.

Meanwhile Achaemenid *Persia had been expanding since *Cyrus (1) overthrew *Croesus in 546, and the new power had begun to encroach on the freedom of the east Greeks in Ionia (see IONIANS) and even islands like *Samos. The Athenians, like other mainland Greeks, were shielded from immediate danger by their distance from Ionia, but they were in the racial and religious senses Ionians too, and when in 499 the *Ionian Revolt broke out, Athens sent help to the rebels, who, however, were defeated at Lade (494).

How far this help provoked the *Persian Wars, by drawing *Darius I's vengeful attention to Athens, and how far they were simply an inevitable consequence of Persian dynamism, is not clear from the account of *Herodotus. A first expedition led by Datis and Artaphernes failed at *Marathon, in Attica (490); then at the battles of *Thermopylae, *Artemisium, *Salamis (all 480), and *Plataea (479) a far larger Persian invasion by *Xerxes was beaten back. The Greek successes of the Persian Wars were of enormous importance in conditioning Greek attitudes to themselves, to each other (see MEDISM; THEBES), and to the '*barbarian' (as Persians were now more aggressively defined), for centuries to come: see PERSIAN-WARS TRADITION. The victories were immediately commemorated by state dedications in the great sanctuaries (see DELPHI; OLYMPIA). Poetry by *Aeschylus and *Simonides, and the prose of Herodotus, signalled the Great Event in literature, as did buildings on the Athenian acropolis.

The pentēkontaëtia

(*c.*50-year period 479–431 BC). In the west (Italy and Sicily), the Greek states shared the culture of their *metropoleis in Greece itself (see esp. OLYMPIA), but there were differences. Here Greeks (like *Cyrene with its Berber neighbours) always had to live alongside non-Greeks (e.g. Messapians *Etruscans, *Carthaginians). At *Himera and *Cumae the western Greeks under their tyrants *Gelon and *Hieron (1) I defeated Carthage and the Etruscans in battles which contemporaries compared to the high points of the Persian Wars. But inter-Greek tensions were no less acute. Athenian and Peloponnesian interest in the west was always lively, partly for corn and partly for shipbuilding *timber from south Italy.

The great struggle of the 5th cent. was between the Athenians and the Peloponnesians led by Sparta. The germs of this are detectable even in the Persian Wars, and when the Athenians took over the leadership of Greece in 487 (see DELIAN LEAGUE), Sparta's response was mixed. But Sparta, despite having crushed for the moment her perennially ambitious rival *Argos in 494, had internal problems in the Peloponnese and, for several years from the mid-460s, difficulties with the helots to cope with. So stretched were the Spartans that they invited the Athenians in to help them against the helots, but the Athenian democracy moved on a step in just this period (see EPHIALTES) and the Athenians under *Cimon were dismissed from Sparta. Sparta's troubles enabled the Athenian empire to expand without check from the Greek side until the end of the 460s and the outbreak of the First *Peloponnesian War (460–446), when Sparta did, as often in its history, take some action to protect or further its interests (including religious) in central Greece. So far from curbing Athenian expansion, that war saw Athenian influence rise to its maximum extent: for over ten years after the battle of Tanagra Athens even controlled *Boeotia (457–446). It may be that the take-over was possible because Athens exploited *stasis inside the cities of Boeotia. Democratic Athens did not however insist on democracy in Boeotia, allegedly permitting oligarchies instead; nor is it certain that the *Boeotian Confederacy ceased to exist in the Athenian period, although Athens' departure in 446 may have led to a federal reorganization.

Despite preoccupations in Greece, Athens in this period continued the struggle against Persia which was the ostensible purpose of the Delian League; but after the Eurymedon victory of c.466 a preliminary peace may have been made, see CALLIAS, PEACE OF. A great Athenian expedition against Persia in Egypt in the 450s failed utterly, and in 450 the main Callias peace was made. Thereafter, until 413, Athens and Persia were in a state of uneasy peace.

The Peloponnesian War

The First Peloponnesian War ended with the *Thirty Years Peace of 446, and this instrument regulated Athenian–Spartan relations until the main *Peloponnesian War of 431–404. The Archidamian War (431–421), ended by the Peace of *Nicias, failed to achieve the Peloponnesian objective of 'liberating' Greece, i.e. breaking up the Athenian empire. Athenian exuberance climbed to its highest level in 415, when the *Sicilian Expedition was launched, to end in catastrophe two years later. Persia re-entered the picture in 413, an important moment because it introduced a long phase of Greek history, ending only with *Alexander (2) the Great, in which Persia's voice would often be decisive. As Athens and Sparta wore each other down, *Macedon grew in resources and self-confidence, esp. under the strong rule of *Archelaus; and *Thebes, another 4th-cent. heavyweight, profited from the war, notably by annexing *Plataea in 427. Small states tried to protect their territorial integrity by aligning with the strongest and closest power of the moment.

The Fourth Century

The end of the war in 404 coincided with another equally momentous event, the establishment in power of *Dionysius (1) I in Sicily, the prototype for many a 4th-cent. and Hellenistic strong man: tyranny, in fact, revives. Even in conservative Sparta there are traces of personality cult, detectable in *Lysander's victory monument at Delphi for the final victory at Aegospotami. And he got cult at *Samos. See RULER-CULT, *Greek.

Lysander's methods were harsh, and Spartan aggression in this period led, startlingly soon after the end of the Peloponnesian War, to the outbreak of the anti-Spartan *Corinthian War, ended by the *King's Peace (386). This curtailed Sparta's activities in Asia Minor (of which the most famous episode was the *Anabasis* or Persian expedition of *Xenophon and the Ten Thousand, in its initial phase a covertly Spartan operation to replace Artaxerxes II by his brother *Cyrus (2)). But the price of eliminating Sparta was surrender of the region to Persia, and a general Greek political retreat east of the Aegean. However, over the next 50 years cultural *Hellenism advanced, alongside Persian and indigenous culture, through activity by e.g. *Mausolus.

Much strengthened in Greece by the King's Peace, Sparta proceeded to fresh aggressions in northern and central Greece, always a tendency when domestic or other preoccupations permitted. Sparta's coercion of *Olynthus aroused no general protest, but the occupation of the acropolis of Thebes in 382 shocked and alarmed Greek opinion, and in 379 Thebes was liberated with Athenian help. Thebes and other places now joined a *Second Athenian Confederacy (378). But as Thebes' power itself grew, esp. after it had defeated Sparta at *Leuctra (371), Athens and Sparta found themselves driven together in the 360s when Thebes tried to usurp Athens' position at sea and (with more success) to weaken Sparta in Peloponnese by founding Arcadian Megalopolis and reconstituting *Messenia after centuries.

*Philip II of Macedon succeeded to a politically weak but economically strong Macedon in 359, which he rapidly strengthened further at the expense of all his neighbours, Greeks included. The story of Athens' diplomatic relations with him is intricate (see DEMOSTHENES (2)); features of the Peace of *Philocrates may indicate that he planned to invade Persia as early as 346, but he was obliged to defeat the Greeks at the battle of *Chaeronea in 338 before the expedition could start. In the event he was assassinated in 336. Alexander, his son, carried the project through (334–323) in a whirlwind campaign which took him to Egypt, Persia, Afghanistan, India, and the Persian Gulf. For the campaigns see ALEXANDER (2). The city-foundations of Alexander (see ALEXANDRIA) are the most important part of his legacy but hard to estimate in detail.

Hellenistic period

(323–31 BC). After Alexander had died aged 32, there was never much chance that the unity of his empire would be perpetuated by any one of his Successors—the name given to a whole clutch of his former marshals, controlling different areas but at overlapping times. (See DIADOCHI.) The 'satrapies' were distributed at Babylon in 323 and again at Triparadeisus in 320; another arrangement was reached in 311. The generation after Alexander's death is full of complex military and political history, recorded by *Hieronymus of Cardia, who described the Successors' attempts to acquire as much 'spear-won territory' as possible, while mouthing slogans about the 'freedom of the Greeks' (see FREEDOM IN THE ANCIENT WORLD); the closest any of them got to a dominant position was *Antigonus I (helped by his son Demetrius the Besieger).

Greek language

1. Introduction In the Classical period Greek was spoken in mainland Greece (including Peloponnese), in the islands of the Aegean (including Crete, Rhodes, and Cyprus), and in the Greek colonies in Asia, Africa, and Italy. It is the European (and Indo-European, abbrev. IE) language with the longest attested history; the first documents belong to the second half of the second millennium BC, and there is no real break between ancient Greek and the modern language of Greece. Most of the evidence from the 8th cent. BC until now is written in the Greek *alphabet, but at an early stage two syllabic scripts were also in use: Linear B in the second half of the second millennium rendered the Greek spoken by the Mycenaeans (see MYCENAEAN LANGUAGE), while a distantly related script was used for the local dialect of Cyprus.

2. Origins Greek is related to language groups such as Italic, Germanic, Indo-Iranian, Celtic, Slavic, Anatolian, Armenian, Albanian, etc., all of which descend from an unattested parent language (IE), which we partially reconstruct through comparison. IE speakers must have reached Greece from elsewhere, though the language may have acquired its main characteristics in Greece itself.

3. Dialects When we speak of Greek, we often mean Attic, i.e. the dialect of Athens. Yet from the Mycenaean period until the late Hellenistic period there was no standard Greek language, and all cities or regions had different forms of speech, which they transmitted to their colonies. These local 'dialects' had equal or similar status, and presumably most of them were mutually intelligible. Until the late 4th cent. BC (and often much later) they were used in normal oral intercourse and for written documents, laws, letters, etc. The contemporary inscriptions provide the best evidence for the differences. On the basis of shared features modern scholars classify the various forms of Greek into groups: Attic-Ionic, Arcado-Cyprian, Aeolic (which includes Boeotian, Thessalian, and Lesbian), Doric (which includes dialects like Laconian and Argolic, spoken in SE and NE Peloponnese), and NW Greek.

In spite of the absence of a standard language, from the 5th cent. at the latest—but probably much earlier—the Greeks thought of themselves as speaking a common language; for Herodotus 'Hellenism' was based on shared blood, language, customs, and religion. See HELLENISM,

HELLENIZATION. Greek was not identified with any of the dialects, but by the early 3rd cent. the Athenians were reproached for behaving as if Greek and Attic were the same thing. In the same period we begin to find that in local inscriptions the dialect is sometimes replaced by a form of language which is very close to Attic; it is the beginning of the so-called Attic-Ionic *Koinē* (common language), which eventually prevailed and provided Greece with a standard language. By the end of the 2nd cent. BC most local inscriptions were no longer in dialect; in contrast with the many dialects of the earlier colonies, the language brought to Asia and Africa by *Alexander (2) the Great and his Successors was a form of *koinē*.

4. Literary Greek Literary texts too were composed in different dialects, but the dialect was mostly determined by the literary *genre and its origin rather than by the author's origin. *Hesiod, who spoke Boeotian (an Aeolic dialect), composed *hexameters in the same mixed dialect (based on Ionic) as *Homer, while *Pindar, also a Boeotian, wrote choral poetry in a very different mixed dialect which included some Doric features. The iambic lines of Attic tragedy are written in a very literary Attic heavily influenced by Homer and by Ionic, but the choruses are written in Doric or rather in a literary form of Attic with superimposed Doric features.

grōmaticī, Roman land-surveyors. They were more commonly called *mensōrēs* or *agrimensores*, *gromatici* being a late term derived from the *grōma*, the most important of the surveyor's instruments. The primary objective of the land surveyor was to establish *līmitēs* (see LIMES), roadways or baulks intersecting at right angles and dividing the land into squares or rectangles (see CENTURIATION). He first plotted the two basic *limites*, and then more *limites* were established parallel to them.

Civilian surveyors were often *freedmen and constituted a professional group whose services were much in demand at the end of the republic and in the early Principate, when vast amounts of land were distributed to soldiers (see VETERANS). They established boundaries on private estates, assessed land for the census and land-tax, and most importantly measured and divided public land (*ager publicus) for the establishment of colonies; when they had taken the colonists to their allocations and completed a map of the settlement and a register of each holding, the founder signed the records, copies of which were kept in the colony and in Rome. Surveyors also advised in all kinds of land disputes. They were expected to master not only practical implementation, but also law and jurisdiction relating to land-holding.

guardianship

Greece The development of the law of guardianship in Greece and Rome was influenced by the change in the conception of guardianship itself, which began as a right of preserving and protecting the ward's property in the interest of the whole kin (as contingent heir of the ward), but became gradually a duty of the guardian in the interest of the ward. This explains the restrictions imposed upon the guardian with regard to his control over the child's property, and the increasing supervision of public authorities over his activity as guardian. The Greek guardian was either *epitropos* (lit. 'trustee', 'steward') of boys and girls until their majority—18 years in the case of boys (see DEMOCRACY, ATHENIAN, 2)—or *kȳrios* (lit. 'master', 'controller') of women. Guardians were appointed by the father's will; failing testamentary appointment the next relatives (brother or uncle), being the most likely successors, were entitled to claim the guardianship; in the absence of these an official (the archon in Athens) appointed the guardian. The guardian had to provide for the ward's education, attend to all his interests, and represent him in legal transactions: in general he was required to act on his behalf with the same solicitude as for a child of his own. The administration of property by the guardian, esp. of landed property, was submitted to the control of magistrates. Action for damages caused by the guardian might be brought against him by the ward within five years of the end of the guardianship. The principles of guardianship of women were analogous; but a woman could dispose freely of objects of lesser importance, without the help of her *kyrios*. See INHERITANCE.

Rome Roman law distinguished *tūtēla* and *cūra* as types of guardianship of persons not subject to father or husband (by *patria potestas* or *manus (see MARRIAGE LAW)). *Tutela* concerned children below the age of puberty (*impūberēs*, eventually boys under 14, girls under 12) and women, *cura* those above these ages but under 25 (minors), lunatics, and spendthrifts.

The original purpose of guardianship, conservation of property, is clear in the rule which gave *tutela* of an *impūbes* on the death of the *paterfamiliās* (see PATRIA POTESTAS) to the nearest male agnate (relation through males) as *tutor lēgitimus* (guardian indicated by statute), the person who would inherit if the ward died. But already in the *Twelve Tables the father could appoint someone else by will. Later, failing these, a magistrate would appoint one. *Tutela* of males ended with puberty, when the ward could beget an heir who would exclude the agnate from the inheritance. But a female's children did not fit this definition; so *tutela* of women was for life. In classical law it became attenuated because of changing attitudes to family. By *Cicero's day, many upper-class women could treat the guardian's authorization as a 'rubber-stamp', necessary but easily obtained.

Tutela's shift from privilege to burden appears in the evolution of the *tutor's* liability for misconduct. In early law he was liable only for fraudulent misappropriation, but in the later republic he could be required to account for his conduct according to the principles of good faith. Rules accrued, as did grounds which exempted from service as guardian one appointed by a will or by an official.

The *tutor's* concern was with property, not a child's custody or upbringing or a woman's personal life. He might administer it directly (but the ward might repudiate his acts when he came of age) or validate the ward's acts. A woman's *tutor* did not (in classical law) administer, but his authorization was needed for important transactions such as purchase of slaves or land, *manus*, and dowry (but not marriage itself).

guest-friendship See FRIENDSHIP, RITUALIZED.

Gȳgēs, king of *Lydia (c.680–645 BC), founded the Mermnad dynasty by murdering King Candaules and marrying his widow. The word 'tyrant' (see TYRANNY) first appears in Greek applied to Gyges. He started the exploitation of *gold from the Pactolus; attacked *Miletus and Smyrna, captured Colophon and sent sumptuous offerings to *Delphi. He gained Assyrian protection against the Cimmerians, but lost it later by helping Psammetichus I of Egypt. He was killed in a new Cimmerian invasion; his tomb was famous and has been identified in the royal tumulus cemetery at Bin Tepe.

gymnasiarch In Classical Athens gymnasiarchs were appointed annually from the ten tribes (*phylai*) to organize *torch-races; the post was a burdensome *liturgy. The gymnasiarch of the Hellenistic and Roman *polis* was general

supervisor of the civic *gymnasium (or gymnasia), responsible for its administration and the moral supervision (e.g. the policing of *homosexuality) of its youthful users (see EPHEBOI), for whom he was a fearsome authority-figure empowered to fine and flog. The heavy costs of physical training, mainly oil (see OLIVE) for *athletics and fuel for hot *baths, made the office a target for the *euergetism of rich citizens.

gymnasium In Greek cities, the gymnasium originated as a place of exercise for the citizens, specifically to fit the *epheboi for the rigours of service as *hoplites. At first no more than an open space, with a water supply, often sited in conjunction with a *sanctuary or shrine, as late as the 5th cent. BC gymnasia seem not to have needed architectural development, shade and shelter being provided rather by groves of trees. Descriptions of the Athenian gymnasia, the Lyceum, Cynosarges, and above all the Academy conform with this (see ATHENS, TOPOGRAPHY).

Frequented also by older citizens, and esp. from the connection with 4th-cent. philosophers, they became more intellectual centres. Though the element of exercise was never lost, the concept of education became more important. Some—esp. those at Athens—through the interests of the philosophical schools became in effect universities. More usually in the cities of the Hellenistic age they functioned as secondary schools. More specialized architecture was required, and the gymnasia became enclosed areas, their buildings arranged largely on the courtyard principle. The *Academy at Athens acquired such a courtyard, with shrine-building and fountain-house, but is badly preserved and not fully understood. Better-preserved examples are found in Anatolian cities. The lower gymnasium at Priene adjoins the stadium, which provides *athletic facilities. The gymnasium itself is wholly a school building, comprising a small courtyard with rooms opening off. One, its walls liberally inscribed by the pupils, is the classroom; another provides tubs and running cold water for washing. Gymnasia were generally provided by the city. As a centre of education, it became a focus for the maintenance of Greek identity in the face of non-Greek settlement and Roman political control.

See EDUCATION, GREEK; GYMNASIARCH; PALAESTRA.

gynaecology existed in the ancient world as a medical specialism, but its separate identity was not always permitted by wider medical theories. The significant question was this: do women have diseases peculiar to their sex, or are they subject to the same conditions as men, requiring a separate branch of medicine only to the extent that they have different organs to be affected? In other words, is gynaecology necessary?

Most of the surviving gynaecological treatises come from the Hippocratic corpus (see HIPPOCRATES) and probably date to the late 5th and early 4th cents. BC. These treatises include three volumes of *Gynaikeia*, usually translated as 'Diseases of Women'. These texts include long lists of remedies using plant and animal ingredients. The third volume concerns the treatment of barren women. A separate short treatise discusses the medical problems of unmarried girls at puberty, while others focus on the process of generation. Many of the case histories in *Epidemics* trace the progress of disease in women patients.

In keeping with a culture in which women could be seen to constitute a separate 'race', *Gynaikeia* criticizes those doctors who make the mistake of treating women with diseases as if they were men. For the Hippocratics of the *Gynaikeia*, women require a separate branch of medicine because they are seen as fundamentally different from men, not merely in their reproductive organs, but in the texture of their flesh, seen as 'wet' and 'spongey', like wool. Because of this texture, women are thought to absorb more fluid from their diet, menstruation being necessary to remove the surplus. There was, however, no uniformity on female difference.

The debate on the status of gynaecology continued. Alexandrian anatomy, associated esp. with *Herophilus, moved from fluids to organs, and women came to be seen more as reverse males than as a separate race. Whereas men's reproductive organs are outside, women were seen as having the same organs inside. Papyri show that Hippocratic prescriptions for women's diseases continued to be transmitted. *Soranus summarizes the position before his own time. See BOTANY; CHILDBIRTH; PHARMACOLOGY.

Hades, son of *Cronus and Rhea and husband of *Persephone, is 'Lord of the dead' and king of the Underworld, the 'house of Hades', where he rules supreme. After Homer, Hades is not only the god of the dead, but also the god of death, even death personified. 'Hades' refers normally to the god; in non-Attic literature, the word can also designate the Underworld. Cold, mouldering, and dingy, Hades is a 'mirthless place'. The proverbial 'road to Hades' is 'the same for all'. *Aeacus, son of *Zeus, 'keeps the keys to Hades'; the same is said of Pluton. The 'gates of Hades' are guarded by 'the terrible hound', *Cerberus, who wags his tail for the new arrivals, but devours those attempting to leave. Without burial, the dead cannot pass through Hades' gates. Once inside, they are shrouded in 'the darkness of pernicious Hades'.

Like the *Erinyes/Eumenides ('Angry/Kindly Ones') and *Demeter ('Earth-mother'), Hades lacked a proper name. He was referred to by descriptive circumlocutions as 'chthonian (lit. 'of the earth') Zeus', 'the chthonian god', 'king of those below', 'Zeus of the departed' and 'the other Zeus', 'the god below', or simply 'lord'. As the Lord of the dead, he was dark and sinister, a god to be feared and kept at a distance. Paradoxically, he was also believed to 'send up' good things for mortals from his wealth below.

The two opposite but complementary aspects of his divinity are reflected in a host of positive and negative epithets. Of the latter, Hades, 'the invisible one' acc. to ancient etymology, recalls the darkness of his realm. The 'wolf's cap of Hades', worn by *Athena in the *Iliad*, makes its wearers invisible. Other negative epithets are 'hateful', 'implacable and adamant', 'tearless' and 'malignant'. Epithets which euphemistically address his benign and hospitable aspects include 'Renowned', 'Good Counsellor', 'the Beautiful-haired One', 'Of Good Repute', 'Leader of the People', 'Lord over All', 'Receiver of Many', 'Host to Many' and Pluton ('Wealth'). During the 5th cent. BC 'Pluton' became Hades' most common name in myth as well as in cult.

Hades was not a recipient of cult. Like Thanatos ('death'), he was indifferent to prayer or offerings. Apart from the story of his abduction of Persephone, few myths attach to Hades. By giving her the forbidden food of the dead to eat—the pomegranate—he bound Demeter's daughter to return periodically to his realm. Their union was without issue; its infertility mirrors that of the Underworld. When the sons of Cronus divided the universe amongst themselves, Hades was allotted the world of the dead, Zeus obtained the sky, and Poseidon the sea. As ruler of the dead, Hades was always more ready to receive than to let go. Two kindred gods, Demeter and *Dionysus, as well as heroes like *Heracles, *Theseus, and *Orpheus, descended alive to Hades and returned to earth. Ordinary mortals went there to stay; Alcestis, Eurydīcē, and Protesilaus, the first Greek ashore at Troy, were among the few allowed to leave. Heracles wrestled with Thanatos and wounded Hades with an arrow.

Alcestis' death vision of Hades, who comes to get her, is dim but frightening (Euripides, *Alcestis* 259–262: 'Someone is leading me, leading me away—don't you see?—to the hall of the dead. He stares at me from under his dark-eyed brow. He has wings—it's Hades!'). In Greek art, Hades and Pluton—differentiating between the two is not always possible—are wingless human figures lacking any terrifying aspects. Zeus-like and bearded, Hades-Pluton is a majestic, elderly man holding a *sceptre, twig, cornucopia, pomegranate, or *cantharus*. Unlike Hades, Thanatos is represented with wings.

Hades was the universal destination of the dead until the second half of the 5th cent., when we first hear of the souls of some special dead ascending to the upper air (*aither*), while their bodies are said to be received by the earth (Athenian epitaph, *c*.432). The souls of the heroized daughters of *Erechtheus 'do not go to Hades', but reside in heaven. See DEATH, ATTITUDES TO, GREEK.

Hadrian (Publius Aelius Hadrianus), emperor AD 117–138. The Aelii of Italica in *Baetica were among the earliest provincial senators; his mother Domitia Paullina was from Gades. When his father died, Hadrian became the ward of *Trajan, his father's cousin, and of Acilius Attianus (85). Early devotion to Greek studies earned the nickname *Graeculus* ('little Greek'); a passion for hunting was apparent when he visited Italica (90). After the vigintivirate (see VIGINTISEX-VIRI, VIGINTIVIRI), he was tribune in *legion II Adiūtrix (95) and V Macedonica (96). Sent to congratulate Trajan on his adoption by *Nerva in 97, he remained in Upper Germany as tribune of XXII Prīmigenia, under his brother-in-law Iūlius Ursus Serviānus. In 100 he married Trajan's great-niece *Sabina Augusta, a match arranged by Trajan's wife Pompeia Plotina, a devoted supporter. He joined Trajan for the First *Dacian War; was tribune of the *plebs*; then legate of I Minervia in the Second Dacian War. He governed Lower Pannonia and was suffect consul (108). When Trajan's closest ally Licinius Sura died, Hadrian took over as imperial speech-writer. In 112 he was archon at Athens, where he was honoured with a statue. When the *Parthian expedition began (October 113), he joined Trajan's staff, becoming governor of Syria at latest in 117; and was designated to a second consulship for 118. His position was thus very strong when Trajan died on 8 August 117. The next day his adoption by Trajan was announced. It was rumoured that Plotina had staged an adoption after Trajan had died. Hadrian was disliked by his peers and had rivals, but the army recognized him; the senate had to follow suit. Plotina and the praetorian *prefect Attianus took Trajan's body to Rome, while Hadrian faced the crisis in the east. He abandoned the new provinces, dismissed Trajan's favourite Lusius Quietus from his command in Judaea (see JEWS). A rising in Mauretania, no doubt provoked by the dismissal of Quietus, a Moor, was suppressed by Hadrian's friend *Marcius Turbo. Britain was also disturbed; the governor of Lower Moesia was probably sent to Britain to restore control when Hadrian reached the Danube in spring 118. He evacuated the Transdanubian part of Lower Moesia annexed by Trajan. The governor of Dacia had died campaigning; Hadrian summoned Turbo to govern part of Dacia, with Lower Pannonia. Dacia was divided into three provinces. Turbo, an *equestrian, was given the same rank as the prefect of Egypt.

Meanwhile Attianus was active. Four ex-consuls, including Lusius Quietus, were executed for plotting treason. When Hadrian reached Rome (July 118), the senate was hostile. He claimed not to have ordered the executions but took steps to win popularity. First came a post-humous triumph for Trajan's Parthian 'victory'. Crown-gold (*aurum coronarium*) was remitted for Italy and reduced for the provinces; a new, more generous, largess was disbursed to the *plebs*; overdue tax was cancelled on a vast scale; bankrupt senators received a subsidy; lavish gladiatorial games were held.

Hadrian, consul again for 118, took as colleague Pedanius Fuscus, husband of his niece Fuscus was a likely heir. In 119 he was consul for the third and last time, and changed praetorian prefects. One new prefect was Septicius Clarus, to whom *Pliny the Younger had dedicated his Letters; *Suetonius Tranquillus, protégé of Pliny and Septicius' friend, became secretary for correspondence. The second prefect was Turbo: he was to take charge during Hadrian's absences, together with Annius Verus, a senator of Spanish origin, and kinsman of Hadrian. Verus, consul for the second time in 121 and city prefect, was rewarded by a third consulship in 126. On 21 April 121, the birthday of the city, Hadrian inaugurated a vast temple of *Venus and Rome in the Forum, designed by himself: one of many fields in which he dabbled and claimed expertise (see APOLLODORUS (3)). A poet, he boasted of his cithara-playing and singing, was expert in mathematics—and in military science. A favourite occupation was debating with sophists (see SECOND SOPHISTIC). *Favorinus yielded: 'who could contradict the Lord of Thirty Legions?' To the legions Hadrian now turned, leaving in 121 for the Rhineland. In Upper Germany and Raetia he erected a continuous palisade, Rome's first artificial *limes, symbolizing his policy of peace within fixed frontiers. Legions and *auxilia were mostly to remain in the same bases, local recruiting became prevalent. Hadrian set out to improve discipline and training—*Arrian was to dedicate his *Essay on Tactics* to Hadrian, registering the emperor's innovations. In 122 he crossed to Britain, taking his friend Platorius Nepos, promoted from Lower Germany to Britain, and VI Victrix. Sabina, Septicius, and Suetonius also went. An obscure imbroglio involving these three led to the men's dismissal. The main business was 'the wall to separate Romans and barbarians'. The *wall of Hadrian was far more elaborate than any other *limes*: the bridge at the E. end of the wall bore his name, Pons Aelius. From Britain he made for Spain, via southern Gaul, where he commemorated his horse in verse and Plotina with a basilica (she died early in 123). He wintered at Tarraco, calling a meeting of delegates from the peninsula: military service was on the agenda. Italica was not favoured with a visit, but he granted it the status of colony. Conscious perhaps of the coming 150th anniversary of 27 BC, Hadrian now shortened his names to Hadrianus Augustus: a claim to be a new founder of the empire.

News from the east determined his next move. His goal was the Euphrates, to confirm peace with Parthia. After an extensive tour of Asia Minor, he sailed (autumn 124) to Athens. There he was initiated in the Eleusinian *mysteries, visiting many other cities before his return to Rome, via Sicily, in summer 125. He stayed in Italy for three years, touring the Po valley for six months in 127; during this period he created, to the senate's displeasure, four 'provinces' in Italy, each with a consular governor. In 128 he accepted the title Pater Patriae; then began his last tour with a visit to Africa and Mauretania, creating another *limes*. Briefly at Rome in late summer, he crossed to Athens, where he wintered again, dedicated the *Olympieum and assumed the name 'Olympius'. After participating in the mysteries (spring 129), he went via Ephesus to Syria, wintering at Antioch, visiting Palmyra in spring 130, and going through Arabia and Judaea to Egypt. In Judaea he founded a *colonia* at Jerusalem, Aelia Capitolina, and banned circumcision: measures to Hellenize the Jews—a fatal provocation. Hadrian was accompanied not only by Sabina but by a young Bithynian, Antinoüs: his passion for the youth, embarrassing to many Romans, was a manifestation of his *Hellenism. After inspection of the tombs of *Pompey and *Alexander (2) the Great, debates in the Museum, and hunting in the desert, a voyage on the Nile ended in disaster: Antinoüs was drowned. Hadrian's extreme grief was assuaged only by declaring his beloved a god (duly worshipped all over the empire) and naming a new city on the Nile (perhaps already planned) Antinoöpolis. Hadrian went from Egypt to Lycia; by the winter of 131/2 he was back in Athens, to inaugurate the Olympieum and found the Panhellenion, an Athens-based loyalist organization of eastern cities.

In 132 the Jews rebelled under Bar Kokhba, rapidly gaining control of much territory. Hadrian was briefly in Judaea, summoning his foremost general from Britain to crush the revolt. It lasted until 135; by then Hadrian had been back in Rome for a year, worn out and ill, staying mostly at his *Tibur villa. In 136 he turned his mind to the succession. The aged Servianus and his grandson Pedanius Fuscus had aspirations; but Hadrian hated both and forced them to suicide. To universal surprise, he adopted one of the consuls of 136, as Lucius Aelius Caesar. But Aelius died suddenly on 1 January 138. Hadrian now chose Aurelius *Antoninus (Pius) and ensured the succession far ahead by causing him to adopt in turn his nephew Marcus (= Marcus *Aurelius) and Aelius' young son Lucius (= Lucius *Verus). Marcus, a favourite of Hadrian and grandson of Annius Verus, had been betrothed to Aelius' daughter. Hadrian died (10 July 138) with a quizzical verse address to his restless soul. He was buried in his new mausoleum (Castel Sant'Angelo) and deified by a reluctant senate. An intellectual and reformer (the Perpetual Edict and the extension of Latin rights were major measures (see EDICT; IUS LATII), by his provincial tours, amply commemorated on the coins, by his frontier policy, and promotion of Hellenism, he made a deep impact on the empire.

Hadrian's Wall See WALL OF HADRIAN.

Halicarnassus, Greek city of *Caria, founded c.900 BC. In classical times its culture was Ionian, but a high proportion of its citizens had Carian names. It was the capital of a minor dynasty which included *Artemisia. It joined the *Delian League and served as an Athenian naval station after the allies revolted in 412. *Mausolus, dynast and *satrap of the Persian province of Caria, made his capital at Halicarnassus c.370. Thereafter, with its great wall circuit, closed harbour, dockyard, public buildings, and the funerary temple of the dynasty (the *Mausoleum), Halicarnassus was one of the spectacular cities of the ancient world. It was captured by *Alexander (2) the Great after an arduous siege in 334.

Hamilcar Barca, father of *Hannibal, took over command of the Carthaginian fleet in 247 BC. After the Carthaginian defeat at the battle of the Aegātēs isles in 241 he negotiated the peace terms. When attempts to suppress the subsequent revolt of the mercenaries in the service of Carthage failed, he was appointed to replace his enemy Hanno as commander (240). A bitter struggle, with appalling atrocities on both sides, ended in 238 or 237, when Hamilcar and Hanno were eventually persuaded to co-operate. After the end of the mercenary war he was sent to

*Spain, taking his 9-year-old son Hannibal with him. Starting from Gades, he conquered south and SE Spain. In 231 Rome sent an embassy to investigate the situation; Hamilcar replied that the aim of his conquests was to secure money with which to pay the indemnity for the First Punic War. He died in 229. Although the story that he made Hannibal swear an oath never to be a friend of Rome is credible, it does not follow that Hamilcar was himself planning war with Rome. But after the loss of Sicily and Sardinia he wanted to add Spain's mineral wealth and manpower to Carthage's resources, thus enabling it to fight a new war effectively when it came.

Hannibal, Carthaginian general, b. 247 BC, the eldest son of *Hamilcar Barca. Hamilcar took him to Spain in 237, where he stayed during the commands of both his father and his brother-in-law Hasdrubal. In 221 he assumed the supreme command in Spain on the death of Hasdrubal and reverted to his father's policy of pushing north Regarding Rome's alliance with Saguntum as a threat to Carthage's position in Spain, he decided to defy her, and put pressure on Saguntum. He rejected a Roman protest, and after consulting Carthage began the siege of Saguntum in spring 219, knowing that war with Rome would result, and took the city eight months later.

Hannibal had decided, without waiting for a Roman declaration of war, to take the initiative by invading Italy; probably less with the object of destroying Rome than of detaching her allies (an expectation warranted by Carthage's experience in her wars with the Greeks) and so weakening her that she would give up Sicily, Sardinia, and Corsica, and undertake not to molest Carthage's North African and Spanish empire. He left his capital, *Carthago Nova, in May 218, with a professional army of 90,000 infantry and 12,000 cavalry (Iberians, Libyans, and Numidians) and *elephants, leaving his brother Hasdrubal to hold Spain; and subdued, regardless of cost, the area between the Ebro and the Pyrenees. He remained there until September, presumably in the expectation of meeting and destroying the army of the consul Cornelius Scipio before invading Italy. Then, with 50,000 infantry, 9,000 cavalry, and 37 elephants, he marched to the Rhône, avoided battle with Scipio (belatedly *en route* to Spain), and continued towards the Alps, which he crossed in about fifteen days, with great difficulty and enormous loss of life. The route he took remains uncertain.

He arrived in the area of Turin about the end of October, defeated Scipio (who had returned to Italy) in a cavalry skirmish at the Ticinus, and then, having been joined by many Gauls, won the first major battle of the war at the Trebia, west of Placentia, against the combined forces of Scipio and Sempronius Longus (end of December). In May 217 Hannibal crossed the Apennines (losing an eye in the passage of the Arno), ravaged Etruria, and with the help of early-morning fog, trapped the consul *Flaminius in an ambush at Lake Trasimene. Flaminius and 15,000 men were killed and 10,000 captured. Hannibal proceeded to Apulia, and thence to *Samnium and *Campania, while the dictator *Fabius Maximus Verrucosus embarked on his strategy of following Hannibal but avoiding a pitched battle. Hannibal returned to Apulia (eluding Fabius) for the winter. In 216 he inflicted a devastating defeat on both consuls, who commanded over-strength armies, at *Cannae; only 14,500 Romans and allies escaped death or captivity. After each battle he dismissed the Italian prisoners to their homes while holding the Romans.

Cannae led to the defection of south Italy, including *Capua, the second city in Italy, and part of Samnium; but central Italy and all the Latin colonies remained loyal to Rome, and with Roman commanders avoiding another pitched battle, Hannibal achieved little in the following three years (215–213), although he concluded an alliance with Philip V of Macedon (215), and helped to bring about the revolt of *Syracuse (214). He received no assistance from Spain, where Hasdrubal was on the defensive, and little from Carthage. He failed to gain control of a port, despite attacks on *Cumae, Neapolis, *Puteoli and *Tarentum; several towns were recaptured by Rome. In 212, however, he captured Tarentum by stealth, although the citadel remained in Roman control, and this was followed by the defection of three neighbouring Greek cities. In 211, in an attempt to relieve the siege of Capua (begun the previous year), Hannibal marched on Rome itself but failed to force the Romans to withdraw troops from Capua, and returned to the south; soon afterwards Capua fell, its fall being preceded by that of Syracuse. Hannibal was now being pressed ever further south, and he suffered a further blow in 209 when Fabius recaptured Tarentum. In 208, however, he caught both consuls in an ambush in Lucania; one, *Claudius Marcellus (1), was killed immediately, his colleague fatally wounded. In Spain, *Cornelius Scipio Africanus had captured Carthago Nova (209) and defeated Hasdrubal at Baecula (208). Hasdrubal slipped out of Spain, but in 207 his defeat and death on the Metaurus dashed Hannibal's hopes of receiving reinforcements. Hannibal was now confined to Bruttium, where he stayed until 203 when he was recalled to Africa to defend Carthage. After abortive peace negotiations with Scipio, he was decisively defeated at *Zama (202), and successfully urged his countrymen to make peace on Rome's terms.

Hannibal now involved himself in domestic affairs; as suffete (chief magistrate) in 196 he introduced constitutional reforms to weaken the power of the oligarchs, and reorganized the state's finances so that the war indemnity could be paid to Rome without levying additional taxes. His enemies reacted by alleging to Rome that Hannibal was intriguing with the Seleucid Antiochus III. When a Roman commission of enquiry arrived, Hannibal fled, ultimately reaching Antiochus (195). He urged Antiochus to go to war with Rome; he asked for a fleet and an army with which to stir Carthage to revolt, or, failing that, to land in Italy. He accompanied Antiochus to Greece in 192, and advised him to bring Philip V into the war and invade Italy. In 190, bringing a fleet from Syria to the Aegean, he was defeated by the Rhodians. The peace agreed between Rome and Antiochus provided for his surrender; he fled to Crete and then to Prusias I of *Bithynia, whom he supported in his war with *Eumenes II of Pergamum. In 183 or 182 *Quinctius Flamininus persuaded Prusias to surrender Hannibal, a fate which he forestalled by taking poison.

Hannibal was one of the greatest generals in history. He perfected the art of combining infantry and cavalry, he understood the importance of military intelligence and reconnaissance, and he commanded the unflagging loyalty of his troops. But he failed against Rome because all the assumptions upon which his strategy was based—that huge numbers of Gauls would follow him to Italy, that Carthage would recover the command of the sea and reinforce him from Africa, and that Hasdrubal would bring him reinforcements from Spain, and, above all, that Rome's confederation would break up following Rome's defeat in the field—proved false. Roman propaganda accused Hannibal of perfidy and cruelty; as far as the latter charge is concerned, although he could be chivalrous at times, his attitude to those who resisted him was uncompromising. But the record of Rome's treatment of defectors makes far grimmer reading.

Harmodius See ARISTOGITON.

Harpalus (d. 324 BC), Macedonian noble and boyhood friend of *Alexander (2) the Great, enjoyed high favour after Alexander's accession. He deserted the expedition shortly before the battle of Issus (333) but was reinstated in 331 and placed over the central treasuries of the empire. Based at *Babylon, he controlled the finances of the central satrapies and lived in regal style. On Alexander's return to the west he fled to mainland Greece, where his presence was disruptive. Admitted into Athens in summer 324, he was arrested and his moneys sequestered on the Acropolis. He escaped amidst accusations of bribery (which eventually ruined *Demosthenes (2) and *Demades) and took his mercenary army to Crete, where he was murdered.

healing gods *Disease has always been a crisis in the lives of both individuals and communities; to overcome such a crisis has been a major task of religion. Specific gods became patrons of human healers or were renowned for their ability to help individuals, some presiding over healing springs; a frequent strategy was to regard disease as the result of *pollution and then to try to cure it with cathartic rituals; see PURIFICATION.

In Greece, the main god responsible for healing was *Apollo, who in the *Iliad* sent the *plague and took it away again; behind this function, there lie ancient near-eastern conceptions. Apollo remained a healer throughout the Archaic and Classical periods; in Ionian cities (and their colonies), he often bore the epithet 'physician'; as Apollo Medicus, his cult was introduced to Rome in 433 BC. In the course of the 5th cent., Apollo's role as a healer was contested and slowly replaced by the much more personal and specialized hero *Asclepius, whom myth made Apollo's son and whose fame radiated chiefly from his Epidaurian sanctuary; in his main sanctuaries (*Epidaurus, *Cos, *Pergamum), Asclepius succeeded Apollo, who, however, still retained a presence in spite of the fame of his son. The ritual of Asclepius developed *incubation as a specific means to obtain healing in *dreams.

Rome followed the course set by Greece, introducing first Apollo Medicus, then, in 293 BC, Asclepius (Lat. *Aesculapius) from Epidaurus. Rome also venerated Febris, 'Fever' (i.e. malaria). Besides, and from time immemorial, Italy had a large number of local shrines, often of motherly goddesses who were supposed to heal; one of their main concerns, to judge from the many anatomic *votives, was with female fertility. Chiefly in Gaul and Britain, cults at healing springs were important (see RELIGION, CELTIC); their divinities kept their Celtic names or were identified with Roman gods, like Apollo or, in Roman Bath, Sulis Minerva; see AQUAE SULIS.

heating for cooking and warmth was primarily supplied in the classical world by charcoal stoves: hence the importance of charcoal-burning. In the Roman empire, heating was revolutionized by the introduction of the heated floor or hypocaust, at first only in public and private *baths, but later also in living areas.

Heaven See URANUS; ZEUS; and entries listed under AFTERLIFE.

Hēbē, a personification of the standard Greek word for 'adolescence, puberty' (hence too *epheboi). Hebe is normally a daughter of *Hera and *Zeus. She is often mentioned and depicted as cupbearer of the gods and as bride of *Heracles; this marriage is always viewed from the perspective of the groom, to whom it brought reconciliation with Hebe's mother Hera, a home on *Olympus, and eternal youth (i.e. godhead).

Hecataeus, of *Miletus, the most important of the early Ionian prose-writers (see LOGOGRAPHERS). For his date we depend on Herodotus' account of his role in the planning of the *Ionian Revolt; his prudent opposition suggests a senior figure.

Besides improving *Anaximander's map of the world, which he envisaged as a disc encircled by the river *Oceanus, he wrote a pioneering work of systematic *geography, 'Journey round the World', divided into two books, *Europe* and *Asia* (which included Africa). It described the places and peoples to be encountered on a clockwise coastal voyage round the Mediterranean and the Black (*Euxine) Sea, starting at the Straits of Gibraltar and finishing on the Atlantic coast of Morocco, with diversions to the islands of the Mediterranean and inland to Scythia, Persia, India, Egypt, and Nubia. It is uncertain how far his information rested on his own observations, as is the extent of Herodotus' debt to his work. We have over 300 fragments.

His *mythographic work, *Genealogies*, occupied at least four books (see GENEALOGY). Our fragments reveal a rationalizing approach to the legends of families claiming a divine origin (including, apparently, his own). He evidently believed that behind the fabulous elaborations of tradition lay historical facts distorted by exaggeration or by literal interpretation of metaphors. His opening proclaims his intellectual independence: 'Hecataeus of Miletus speaks thus. I write what seems to me to be true; for the Greeks have many tales which, as it appears to me, are absurd.'

Ancient critics regarded his style as clear but much less varied and attractive than that of Herodotus.

Hecatē was a popular and ubiquitous goddess from the time of *Hesiod until late antiquity. Unknown in *Homer and harmless in Hesiod, she emerges by the 5th cent. as a more sinister figure associated with magic and witchcraft, lunar lore and creatures of the night, dog sacrifices and illuminated cakes, as well as doorways and crossroads. In Hesiod's *Theogony*, she is praised as a powerful goddess who 'has a share' of earth, sea, and sky—but not the Underworld—and who gives protection to warriors, athletes, hunters, herdsmen, and fishermen.

Throughout her long history, Hecate received public as well as private cult, the latter often taking abnormal forms. She was worshipped in liminal places, and sacrifices to her were as anomalous as the goddess herself. In Athens altars and cult images of Hecate stood in front of private homes and esp. at forks in the road. Her favourite food offerings consisted of a scavenging fish tabooed in other cults—the red mullet—of sacrificial cakes decorated with lit miniature torches, and, most notoriously, of puppies. The illuminated cakes were offered at the time of the full moon.

Hecate's nocturnal apparitions, packs of barking hell-hounds, and hosts of ghost-like revenants, occupied a special place in the Greek religious imagination. She protected the crossroads as well as the graves by the roadside. Having become a permanent fixture of the Greek and Roman Underworld, she gives Virgil's *Sibyl, a priestess of Apollo and Hecate, a guided tour of Tartarus. Because of her association with the Underworld and the ghosts of the dead, Hecate looms large in ancient *magic. Sorceresses of all periods and every provenance invoke her name as one who makes powerful spells more potent.

Representations of Hecate in art fall into two broad categories—her images are either single-faced or three-faced. After *c.*430 BC, the goddess of the crossroads is often shown as a standing female figure with three faces or bodies, each corresponding to one of the crossing roads.

Hector, in myth, son of *Priam and *Hecuba, husband of *Andromache and father of Astyanax, and the greatest of the Trojan champions. In the *Iliad* he first appears leading the Trojans out to battle; he reproaches *Paris for avoiding *Menelaus, and arranges the truce and the single combat between the two. He takes a prominent part in the fighting of bks. 5 and 6, but in the latter goes back to the city to arrange for offerings to be made to the gods. He thus meets Andromache and Astyanax on the city walls in one of the best-known scenes of the *Iliad*, then returns with Paris to the battle. In bk. 7 he challenges any Greek hero to single combat, and is met by the greater *Aias (1), who has the better of the encounter; they part with an exchange of gifts. In bk. 8 he drives the Greeks back to their camp and bivouacs on the plain. In the long battle of bks. 11–17 he takes a prominent part, leading the main attack on the fortifications of the Greek camp, which nearly succeeds in burning the Greek ships. During the battle he is struck down with a stone thrown by Aias, but restored to strength by *Apollo at the command of Zeus. He kills Patroclus, and strips him of his arms despite the efforts of the Greeks. After the appearance of *Achilles at the trench, full of rage at Patroclus' death, Hector again bivouacs on the plain, against the advice of Polydamas. After the Trojan rout on the following day, he alone refuses to enter Troy, but stands his ground and waits for Achilles despite the entreaties of his parents. At Achilles' approach he flees, but after a long chase halts, deceived by Athena into thinking that *Deiphobus has come to his aid. In the subsequent fight he is killed, and with his dying words begs Achilles to return his body to Priam, then predicts Achilles' own death. But Achilles, still overcome with rage and hatred, drags Hector's body behind his chariot, though the gods keep it safe from harm. Finally, when Priam comes by night to the Greek camp to beg for the return of his son, Achilles' anger is eased and replaced by pity. The body is ransomed, an eleven-day truce is agreed, and the *Iliad* ends with Hector's funeral.

Hector is depicted in art from the 7th cent. on, setting out for battle, fighting Aias or some other hero, meeting his death at Achilles' hands, and his body being dragged and ransomed.

Hecuba (Gk. Hekabē), wife of *Priam. She was the mother of nineteen of Priam's 50 sons, including *Hector and *Paris. In *Homer she is a stately and pathetic figure, rarely coming into the foreground. In Euripides she is more prominent. The first half of his *Hecuba* deals with the sacrifice of her daughter Polyxena, the second with her revenge on the Thracian king Polymestor, who has murdered her youngest son Polydorus. Turning from victim to savage avenger she blinds Polymestor and kills his sons, and he makes a curious prophecy of her end. In *Trojan Women* she is again the central character, battered by a succession of woes. Incidents include her moral victory in a debate with *Helen and her allotment as a prize to *Odysseus.

hektēmoroi, 'sixth-parters', a class of peasants in Attica before *Solon. Exactly what they were and what Solon did for them is much disputed. They had to hand over to the rich one-sixth of the produce of the land they worked for them, on penalty of enslavement for themselves and their families, and this obligation was signalled by markers of wood or stone; Solon abolished the status and uprooted the markers, thus 'freeing the black earth' as he put it.

Helen, daughter of *Zeus and *Leda; wife of *Menelaus; the beautiful woman whose abduction by Paris was the cause of the Trojan War. Helen was also worshipped (at *Sparta and on *Rhodes) as a goddess associated with trees (see TREES, SACRED). She was, it seems, a goddess before she was a mortal heroine. In *Homer she is entirely human. As we see her in the *Iliad*, she is deeply conscious of the shame of her position at Troy, though it is unclear how far she is responsible for this. *Hector and *Priam treat her kindly; the Trojan elders marvel at her beauty; and she is in general a sympathetic character. In the *Odyssey*, after her return to Sparta, she is seen as a respectable wife and queen, though Menelaus' curious story of her role in the episode of the Trojan Horse presents a less complimentary picture.

Later writers supply further mythical details: how she was born from an egg (Zeus having visited Leda in the form of a swan); how she was abducted by Theseus but rescued by her brothers, Castor and Polydeuces (see DIOSCURI); how she was wooed by all the greatest heroes of Greece before her marriage to Menelaus. She now generally stands condemned for having willingly accompanied Paris to Troy. A story often illustrated on vases is that Menelaus, after the capture of Troy, intended to kill her, but dropped his sword on seeing her breasts.

*Stesichorus wrote a poem in which he held Helen to blame, but then, we are told, was punished with blindness for having slandered a goddess. His sight returned when he wrote a palinode saying that she never went to Troy at all: the gods lodged her in Egypt for the duration of the war and put a phantom Helen in her place. This version is then rationalized in *Herodotus.

The tragedians, esp. *Euripides, often condemn Helen for her adultery. An attempt at self-defence is refuted by *Hecuba in a debate in *Trojan Women*, and she is presented as vain and shallow in *Orestes*. In his *Helen*, however, Euripides follows the version of Stesichorus' palinode: Menelaus, returning from Troy with the phantom Helen, is astonished to find the real Helen in Egypt, and the pair then escape by trickery. *Gorgias composed a *Defence of Helen* as a light-hearted rhetorical exercise, and this is carried further in an encomium by *Isocrates.

hēliaea See ELIAIA.

Helicon, mountain in SW *Boeotia sacred to the *Muses. It overlooks Lake Copais to the NE and the Corinthian gulf to the SW. Its most famous feature is the Valley of the Muses, the site of Ascra, the unbeloved home of Hesiod. Thespiae celebrated a festival of the Muses, and the oldest tripod dedicated was reputedly that of Hesiod. Above the Grove of the Muses was Hippocrene, a fountain supposedly created when *Bellerophon's horse struck the ground with his hoof.

Hēlios, the sun. In early Greece Helios was always treated with reverence but received little cult. *Anaxagoras' announcement that the 'sun was a red-hot mass' caused outrage, and it was not uncommon to salute and even pray to the sun at its rising and setting, but *Aristophanes can treat the practice of sacrificing to sun and moon as one that distinguishes *barbarians from Greeks. Hence evidence for actual cults is scarce. The exception was *Rhodes, where Helios—subject of the 'colossus of Rhodes'—was the leading god and had an important festival; the myth explaining this prominence is told in *Pindar. In Homer he is invoked and receives an offering as witness to an oath, and his all-seeing, all-nurturing power is often stressed in poetry.

He is regularly conceived as a charioteer, who drives daily from east to west across the sky (a conception with both *IE and near-eastern parallels). His most important myth concerns his son Phaethon's unsuccessful attempt to guide the solar chariot. His journey back each night in a cup is already attested in *Mimnermus. The identification of the Sun with *Apollo was familiar in the 5th cent. BC, but did not become canonical until much later. It was not until the later Roman empire that Helios/*Sol grew into a figure of central importance in actual cult.

Hell See DEATH, ATTITUDES TO; HADES.

Hellanīcus of *Mytilene (*c*.480–395 BC) was an important mythographer, ethnographer, and chronicler. Though his background was in the tradition of Ionian research begun by *Hecataeus, he deserves to be ranked with *Herodotus and *Thucydides (2) in the effect he had on the development of Greek *historiography. He wrote extensively, but only some 200 fragments survive.

His five works of *mythography brought together the efforts of earlier mythographers to collate and integrate the disparate corpora of myths into a coherent and chronologically consistent narrative. The effect of this creative activity upon the whole classical tradition is incalculable.

His ethnographic works were even more extensive, ranging from areas of Greece to foreign countries (Egypt, Cyprus, Scythia, and Persia). They were, however, less influential, partly because they were largely unoriginal, partly because they were overshadowed by Herodotus.

His other area of interest was the Universal Chronicle. Hellanicus pioneered the use of victor lists (Carnean Games; see CARNEA) and of magistrates (priestesses of *Hera at *Argos) to establish a common chronology for Greek history (see TIME-RECKONING).

He combined all his talents late in life in Athens to create the first local history of *Attica (*Atthis*), based upon his ordering of the succession of mythical kings and the list of archons. His *Atthis* (called *Attikē Syngraphē* by Thucydides) covered in two books all Athenian history to the end of the *Peloponnesian War. Its tone was influenced by Athenian national propaganda. Thucydides criticized Hellanicus but used his *Priestesses*.

Hellē, daughter of *Athamas and sister of Phrixus, who, while escaping with her brother from their stepmother Ino (see CADMUS), fell into the sea from the flying ram with the Golden Fleece which was carrying them to Colchis; the sea was thereafter known as Helle's sea or *Hellespont.

Hellēnĕs, the name by which the Greeks called, and still call, themselves. Originally it and the territorial name 'Hellas' appear to have been confined to an area south of the river Spercheios, near *Thermopylae. In Homer the Greeks are called 'Achaeans', 'Argives', or 'Danai', but 'Panhellenes' (see PANHELLENISM) appear under *Aias (2), the Locrian hero, and 'Hellenes' under *Achilles, whose home was the Spercheios valley. Similarly, 'Hellas' is a district in Achilles' kingdom.

Hellenism, Hellenization, Greek culture and the diffusion of that culture, a process usually seen as active. The relation between the two modern words is controversial: should the longer word be avoided (see ORIENTALISM) because of its suggestion of cultural imperialism?

For non-Greeks to be 'Hellenized' (see HELLENES) was, most obviously, for them to learn to speak Greek, but in the 'Hellenistic' period (from the death of *Alexander (2) the Great in 323 BC to the victory of Octavian at *Actium in 31 BC) much more than the Greek language was diffused, to different degrees in different places, over the area that Alexander had conquered. Often the eventual outcome was not so much the diffusion of Greek culture as the fusion of practices Greek and non-Greek.

Hellenistic period See preceding entry and GREECE (HISTORY).

Hellenistic poetry at Rome The influence of Hellenistic Greek poetry on Roman poetry can hardly be overestimated. Latin poetry is from its beginnings based on scholarly appreciation of the literary production of the Greeks, and it was from the perspective of the literary and scholarly activity of the Hellenistic period that the Romans viewed Greek literature as a whole. The fragmentary nature of early Latin poetry means that the first stages of the *reception of Hellenistic poetry at Rome remain obscure. When, however, *Ennius in his *Annals* proclaims himself as a student of language proud of his stylistic superiority over his predecessors, and describes his poetic initiation, he has in mind *Callimachus' (2) *Aetia.*

For *Catullus and a few like-minded contemporaries (Cicero's 'new poets' or 'neoterics'), the ideal of Hellenistic elegance and style was represented by Callimachus. They cultivate a studied elegance in vocabulary, word order, metre, and narrative form with the aim of bringing Callima-

chean refinement to Latin poetry. *Epic and drama give way to polymetric experiments in lyric and iambic poetry, to *epigram and narrative elegy, and to the *epyllion. After the neoterics came the Augustans. *Virgil, *Horace, *Propertius, *Tibullus, and *Ovid all owe much to Hellenistic models and the Callimachean aesthetic. But there is more to Hellenistic poetry at Rome than Callimachus. *Philitas, *Theocritus, *Aratus, *Apollonius (1) Rhodius, and the epigrammatists collected in the *Garland* of *Meleager were all read and imitated.

hellēnotamiai ('treasurers of the Greeks'), were the chief financial officials of the *Delian League. Their office was in *Delos until 454/3 BC, in Athens after that; but from the first they were Athenians appointed by Athens (one from each tribe). They received the tribute from the allies, and from 453 paid the *aparchē* (*first-fruits) to the treasury of Athena (see TAMIAI); and they made payments on the instructions of the assembly, chiefly to generals for their campaigns but sometimes for other purposes (such as the Acropolis buildings).

Hellespont, the narrow strait dividing Europe from Asia at the final exit of the waters of the Black (*Euxine) Sea and Marmara into the Aegean—the modern Dardanelles. It was crossed by the Persian army under *Xerxes between Abydos and Sestos. It was again crossed by *Alexander (2) the Great. A strong current runs out from the Hellespont into the Aegean. Callipolis, Lampsacus, Sestos, and Abydos are on its shores, with the sites of Troy and Dardanus on the Asiatic side. All these cities derived much of their wealth from the fisheries (see FISHING), and from the passage of people and armies from Europe to Asia and vice versa. The name 'Hellespont' is connected with the legend of Phrixus and *Helle.

helots Some Greek states had servile populations that were not privately owned chattel slaves or *douloi* (see SLAVERY), but, because their status seemed superior in important respects, came to be categorized as 'between free men and (chattel) *douloi*'. Unlike the latter, they were not imported individually but enslaved collectively as a national group. Very little is known about any of them except the helots of *Sparta, and the evidence even for the helots is defective.

The name 'helots' is probably derived from a root meaning 'capture', and acc. to the usual view, first the Laconian and then the Messenian helots (see LACONIA; MESSENIA) were reduced to servitude by conquest between about the 10th and the 7th cents. BC; it was at any rate as a conquered people that the Spartans treated the helots in the historical period, actually declaring war on them annually by proclamation of the *ephors. Greek writers stressed Spartan brutality towards the helots, and the *krypteia system of helot control, which also served as a manhood *initiation ritual for would-be Spartiates, was indeed brutal. But not all helots wanted to eat their Spartan masters, even raw, as one disaffected Spartan agitator claimed; indeed, some of them established close working relationships with them, and it was these—mainly Laconians, presumably—who were employed on a large scale in the army and, esp. during and after the *Peloponnesian War, freed in substantial numbers. By contrast, the helots of Messenia seem to have nursed a permanent hostility born of 'national' cohesion, and the great helot revolts were largely if not wholly Messenian affairs. See NATIONALISM.

Actual figures for helots are lacking. Herodotus implies an unacceptably high 7:1 ratio, but Xenophon confirms that they outnumbered their masters by some way. Perhaps they even outnumbered the total free population of Laconia and Messenia, a balance unknown in communities with a chattel-slave population. Unlike such slaves, too, the helots reproduced themselves through family relations, albeit under threat of dissolution by murder, and were granted some property rights. But they were like slaves in being also themselves property—of the Spartan community rather than individual Spartan men and women. The Spartan assembly alone had the power to free them, which it exercised exceptionally—and duplicitously esp. to compensate for the dearth of citizen manpower that became ever more apparent from c.450 on. *Epaminondas freed the Messenians in 369.

Apart from their military obligations to the community as a whole, the main responsibility of the helots was to provide their individual Spartan masters and mistresses with a fixed quota of natural produce. From that contribution—or tribute—the Spartan citizen paid over to his mess (see SYSSITIA) the amount required to maintain his citizen standing. The helots thus 'enjoyed' the ambivalent position of being both the bedrock of the entire Spartan polity, and the enemy within.

Helvidius Priscus, son of a *primipilaris* (see PRIMIPILUS) from *Samnium, was tribune of the

plebs in AD 56, praetor in 70. In early youth he studied philosophy, and about 55 married (as his second wife) Fannia, daughter of *Clodius Thrasea Paetus, whose political doctrines he shared. Exiled after his father-in-law's condemnation in 66, he returned under *Galba, and though earlier a friend of *Vespasian, he took a critical attitude towards the Flavian regime from the start. Later his attacks on the emperor became vehement, and he was exiled by 75 and subsequently executed. Though he had clearly refrained from holding office in the later tyrannical phase of Nero's reign, his Stoic principles were compatible with acceptance of the Principate as a political system (see STOICISM). He did insist on senatorial independence and freedom of expression. His criticism of Vespasian's son or sons probably related to their conduct and not to the idea of hereditary succession in itself. Helvidius' son by his first marriage, a friend of *Tacitus and *Pliny the Younger, became consul under *Domitian but was executed c.93.

Helvius Cinna, Gāius, a friend of *Catullus, with whom he was probably in *Bithynia in 57/6 BC. Cinna was a 'learned poet', of the 'Alexandrian' school. His miniature epic *Zmyrna*, the work of nine years, was a masterpiece of the 'new' poetry and much admired. Its subject, the Cyprian legend of the incestuous love of Zmyrna (or Myrrha) for her father, gave opportunity for developing the Alexandrian interest in the psychology of passion, and its allusive learning was such that in Augustan times it already needed a commentary. He was tribune in 44 and was lynched at Caesar's funeral because he was mistaken for the anti-Caesarian Cornēlius Cinna. See HELLENISTIC POETRY AT ROME.

Hēphaestion (d. 324 BC), Macedonian noble. Perhaps the most intimate friend of *Alexander (2) the Great, he came to prominence after the death of *Philotas (330), when he shared command of the Companion cavalry with *Cleitus the Black. Later he held many independent commands, notably the commission to advance down the Kabul valley and bridge the Indus (327). One of the élite Bodyguard, he was further distinguished by his elevation to the chiliarchy, the principal ceremonial office at court, and at the mass marriage at Susa (324) his bride (like Alexander's) was a daughter of *Darius III. His sudden death at Ecbatana (autumn 324) plunged Alexander into a paroxysm of grief, and a colossally extravagant pyre was planned (but never executed) for his obsequies. His importance is measured by Alexander's affection. Nothing suggests that his abilities were outstanding.

Hēphaestus, Greek god of *fire, of black-smiths, and of *artisans.

In *Homer, Hephaestus owns fire and helps fight Scamander with it; in a formula, his name is used for fire. On the other hand, he is the divine master-artisan who fabricates *Achilles' shield and miraculous automata, self-moving tripods, golden maidservants, or watchdogs for Alcinous. In the divine society of Homer, he is an outsider: he works, even sweats; he is laughed at when he tries to replace Ganymedes; he is married to *Aphrodite but cuckolded; his feet are crippled (in Archaic iconography they are turned backwards): the outsider even lacks divine bodily perfection. His mother *Hera had conceived him without a male partner; seeing the crippled offspring, she cast him out of *Olympus, and he grew up with the sea goddesses Eurynome and *Thetis; or Zeus had thrown him out because he had sided with Hera, and he had landed on Lemnos. But he has strengths: his works evoke wonder; when serving the gods he intentionally provokes laughter; and he takes his cunning revenge on *Ares and Aphrodite and on Hera, and is brought back into Olympus. Thus, the Homeric picture preserves amid an aristocratic society the likeness of a cunning smith whose professional skills are highly admired and secretly feared. Such is the position smiths have in Archaic societies. Hephaestus' workshop was located beneath active volcanoes, esp. Aetna, and the *Cyclopes were assigned to him as his workmen.

In Athenian cult he is connected with Athena, the goddess of cunning intelligence. In his temple above the Agora ('Theseion'), which was built after 450 BC, there stood a group of Hephaestus and Athena Hephaestia, set up in 421/0 by Alcamenes. At the same time, the Hephaestia in honour of Hephaestus and Athena was reorganized as a festival celebrated every four years, with a splendid *torch-race and lavish sacrifices: the splendour of the festival reflects the position of artisans in the Athenian state. The same holds true for the Chalkeia, a festival dedicated to Athena and Hephaestus when the artisans processed through the town. The god was also important in the *Apaturia when the participants in their best robes and with torch in hand offered a hymn and a sacrifice to the god. Here and in the Hephaestia, the torch alludes to the theme of new fire. Athenian myth tells of Hephaestus' abortive attempt to rape *Athena; from his

spilled semen grew *Erichthonius, the ancestor of the autochthonous Athenians—the myth explains Hephaestus' role in the Apaturia and the theme of (new) beginnings. He was very early identified with Roman *Volcanus.

In Archaic iconography, Hephaestus appears esp. in the scene of his return to Olympus under the guidance of *Dionysus. He is also shown helping Zeus to give birth to Athena (east pediment of the *Parthenon) and in the assembly of the gods. The statue of a standing Hephaestus by Alcamenes with a discreet indication of his limp was famous.

Hēra, daughter of *Cronus and wife of *Zeus. Acc. to Homer, Hera's favourite cities were *Argos, *Sparta, and *Mycenae; several cults are attested at Sparta, and her most famous *sanctuary was on the hill dominating the Argive plain, where there was a temple perhaps from the 8th cent. BC. Sanctuaries with buildings at least as ancient are known at Perachora, Tiryns, and *Olympia. Of island sites, the best known is the sanctuary on *Samos, where the main building, rebuilt in the 6th cent., was mentioned by Herodotus, who comments on its magnificence (see POLYCRATES (1)). Thus the most ancient and important temples were those of Hera. Her cults also spread at an early date to the western colonies, where later she became identified with the Roman *Juno.

In the Classical period, Hera is distinguished from other goddesses by her double connection with royalty and marriage. Thus she is closely associated with Zeus, who made her 'last of all, his flourishing wife'. Her queenliness and noble beauty are abundantly stressed in her epithets and in artistic representations. She is described as 'golden-throned', and is often thus represented, sometimes seeming to surpass her husband in importance: at Olympia, an Archaic statue showed Zeus standing beside Hera enthroned, while in the Argive Heraion the famous chryselephantine statue by *Polyclitus represented the god in the form of a cuckoo perched on the *sceptre held by the goddess—in her other hand she held a pomegranate; and on her head-dress were figures of the *Charites and the *Horae.

Marriage is stressed constantly in Hera's myths and cults. *Motherhood, though part of Hera's personality, is little stressed in cult. Her children are *Ares, *Hebe, and Eileithyia, goddess of childbirth. She suckled *Heracles, a scene often shown on Etruscan mirrors, but her relationship with the hero, whose name could be taken to mean 'glory of Hera', is ambivalent. She acted as nurse to monsters born to *Gaia (Earth), the Lernaean Hydra and the Nemean lion; she was also the sole parent of the monster Typhon and also, acc. to Hesiod, *Hephaestus, whom she produced in anger, to defy her husband. But these episodes by their exceptional nature in fact illustrate Hera's close links with the marriage bond, which she herself protects and guarantees.

The marriage of Zeus and Hera is part of a complex symbolism including the natural world of plants and animals. This is shown by Hera's oldest sanctuaries, which are often situated in fertile plains away from urban settlements. The statue of Polyclitus mentioned above is relevant here. The sacred marriage described by Homer in *Iliad* 14, despite the alterations due to epic, still bears traces of this natural symbolism, and we also find mentioned the flourishing garden at the edge of the Ocean, which served as marriage-bed for the two deities. We can see a relationship between the goddess called Boōpis ('ox-eyed') and herds of cows, esp. in connection with a sacred marriage. Io, changed into a heifer by Zeus in bull form, was the priestess of Hera at Argos, where Hera's rule extended over the animal herds of the plain (see CLEOBIS AND BITON).

Hera was also worshipped as protector of cities and other social groups, esp. at Argos and Samos; *Alcaeus calls her 'mother of all', in a hymn of invocation where she appears between Zeus and Dionysus. In this context she is sometimes shown armed. At Argos the prize at the games held during the Heraia festival was a shield. Despite this protecting function, literary presentations, from the *Iliad* onwards, tend to stress the destructive and capricious side of her nature.

Hēraclēs, the greatest of Greek heroes. His name is that of a mortal, and has been interpreted as 'Glorious through *Hera'. In this case, the bearer is taken as being—or so his parents would hope—within the protection of the goddess. This is at odds with the predominant tradition (see below), wherein Heracles was harassed rather than protected by the goddess.

Heracles shared the characteristics of, on the one hand, a hero (both cultic and epic), on the other, a god. As a hero, he was mortal, and like many other heroes, born to a human mother and a god (*Alcmene and *Zeus). Legends of his epic feats arose early, and they were added to constantly throughout antiquity. These stories may have played a part in the transformation of Heracles from hero (i.e. a being of mortal origin, who, after death, exercised power over a limited geographical area, his influence residing in his mortal remains) to god (an immortal, whose power is not limited geographically). See HERO-CULT.

Outside the cycle of the Labours (see below), the chief events of Heracles' life were as follows: Hera pursued him with implacable enmity from before his birth, which she managed to delay until after that of *Eurystheus. She then sent serpents to *Thebes to attack Heracles in his cradle, but the infant strangled them. Later, she drove him mad and caused him to murder his Theban wife, Megara, and their children (there are different versions). In his youth, Heracles led the Thebans in their successful revolt against *Orchomenus. He also took part in an expedition against Troy (see LAOMEDON), accompanied the *Argonauts (but left the expedition to search for Hylas), founded the *Olympic Games, and ultimately died by burning on Mt. Oeta (death came as a relief from the poison given him unwittingly by his wife Deianira who had hoped to regain his love thereby: the dying *Centaur Nessus, from whom Heracles rescued his wife, had given her the poison as a love potion. She used it when Heracles brought Iolē home).

The Labours themselves (twelve is the canonical number, but there is little agreement on the full complement) support, by their geographical distribution, the contention that, however popular Heracles became in other parts of the ancient world, his origins lay in *Peloponnese, and more specifically in the Argolid. He was sent to perform them by Eurystheus, to whom he was bound in vassalage. Six belong to northern Peloponnese, and might be taken to represent either a gradual spread of Argive ambitions in that region, or, with equal likelihood, the growing popularity of Heracles over a steadily widening area. These tasks were to deal with (1) the Nemean lion (northern border of the Argolid; see NEMEA); (2) the Lernaean Hydra (SW Argolid); (3) the Erymanthian boar (NW Arcadia); (4) the hind of Ceryneia (*Achaea); (5) the Stymphalian birds (NE Arcadia); (6) the stables of Augeas (*Elis). The other Labours are situated at the ends of the habitable world or beyond: the Cretan bull to the south, the man-eating mares of the Thracian King Diomedes to the north, the quest for the belt of the *Amazon queen to the east, the search for the cattle of Geryon to the west, the apples of the *Hesperides at the edge of the world, and *Cerberus in the

Underworld. Many of the Labours are already depicted in Greek art of the Geometric (see POT-TERY, GREEK, 2) and early Archaic periods. Also early to appear are two feats outside the canon, encounters with Centaurs, and a fight with *Apollo for the Delphic tripod (see OMPHALE).

The iconography of Heracles was firmly established by the Archaic period, but even before then one can identify him from the subject-matter. The major identifying symbols were the lion-skin cape and hood (flayed from the Nemean lion), his club, and his bow and arrows.

Throughout his life and many adventures, Heracles was guided closely by *Athena, by whom he was introduced to *Olympus after his death. The apotheosis of Heracles was represented in literature and art by giving him—after his death—a wife in the person of *Hebe, i.e. 'youth', or rather the embodiment of the prime of life, for it is the permanent possession of this boon which most distinguishes gods from men. The story is attested by the 6th cent. In popular cult, Heracles was recognized and invoked as a god from at least late in the 6th cent. *Herodotus writes approvingly of those Hellenes who worship Heracles both as an immortal Olympian and as a hero.

The cult of Heracles spread at least partly through the absorption of local cult figures of similar nature. Individuals adopted Heracles as a more or less personal patron; at the communal level, he presided over ephebes (see EPHE-BOI) as their ideal in warfare and their patron in military training, whence his patronage of the *gymnasium (a role often shared with *Hermes), and over the young in general. He was primarily associated with the activities of men rather than women, which may explain the regulations barring women from his rites or even his sanctuaries.

The geographical distribution of his cults is as wide as that of his legends. Evidence from Tiryns and Argos is sparse. That he was established at Thebes by the Homeric period cannot be doubted, although the earliest contemporary evidence for cult occurs in the 5th cent. He was widely worshipped in Boeotia, and neighbouring *Attica. One of the earliest places to produce archaeological evidence for a cult of Heracles is the *sanctuary on Mt. Oeta. Another important early site is at Thasos, where evidence extends from soon after the foundation of the colony. The Thasian cult exemplifies several features of the worship of Heracles: first, his treatment as a god; second, his function as champion or protector of the community (esp. its urban centre;

see below); third, the tendency to syncretize (see SYNCRETISM) Heracles with other deities (with Melqart of *Tyre in the case of Thasos). The sanctuary at Thasos included not only a sacrificial area, but also a temple and extensive dining-facilities; descriptions of other Herakleia would lead us to expect the existence of athletic facilities as part of the complex. All this public devotion to bodily well-being would have helped to produce the impression of Heracles as a boisterous glutton.

Heracles was adopted by individuals or states as a symbol or protecting deity, to which numerous towns named after him bear eloquent testimony. Thebes used Heracles as its symbol from at least the second half of the 5th cent. In the preceding century *Pisistratus of Athens made Heracles his personal divine protector and legitimator of his actions. The Macedonian royal family ('Argeads' or 'Temenids') claimed lineal descent from Heracles for similar motives. Most notoriously, however, the *Dorian rulers of *Peloponnese sought to legitimate their claims to sovereignty by tracing their descent to Heracles through his sons, the *Heraclids, who, as the tale was told, 'returned' to the Peloponnese from the north to claim their inheritance.

Heraclids The myth of the return of the descendants of *Heracles to *Peloponnese functioned, above all, as a charter myth for the division of Peloponnese between different *Dorian states. *Tyrtaeus told how *Zeus had granted *Sparta to the Heraclids who left 'windy Erineos' in the Dorian heartland of northern Greece.

*Eurystheus, persecutor of Heracles, continued to persecute the exiled sons of Heracles after their father's death; the Athenians esp. gave them aid (see ATTIC CULTS AND MYTHS, last para.). After various adventures, the Heraclids enquired of Delphi (see DELPHIC ORACLE) when they could return, and were told to do so at the third harvest. Hyllus supposed this to mean the third year, but failed and was killed. A hundred years later his descendant Temenus again inquired, and got the same reply, which was now interpreted for him as meaning the third generation. The Dorians therefore tried again, in three companies, led by Temenus, Cresphontes, and the twin sons of Aristodemus, Eurysthenes and Procles. They entered by Elis. Conquering Peloponnese, they divided it into three parts, of which Cresphontes took *Messenia, Temenus *Argos, and the sons of Aristodemus *Lacedaemon, thus founding the dual kingship of *Sparta.

Hēraclītus (fl. c.500 BC), of Ephesus. Of aristo-cratic birth, he may have surrendered the (hon-orific) *kingship voluntarily to his brother. He is said to have compiled a book and deposited it in the temple of *Artemis. The surviving fragments are aphorisms, dense and cryptic. With implicit self-description, Heraclitus writes that the Del-phic god (see DELPHIC ORACLE) 'neither says nor conceals, but gives a sign'. The fragments form a cross-referring network rather than a linear ar-gument.

Heraclitus' central concept is that of *logos*, by which he apparently means at once his own discourse, connected discourse and thought in general, and the connected order in things that we apprehend. Most people, he holds, go through life like sleepers, experiencing the world with little understanding, each lost in a private vision. Waking up to the shared public order requires inquiry, sense-experience, and self-examination: 'I went in search of myself.'

The order we experience is a constant process of change; thus, stepping into the same river, we find different waters constantly flowing by us. Change, indeed, is necessary to the mainten-ance of cosmic order: 'the barley drink separates if it is not stirred.' Criticizing *Anaximander, who had contrasted the strife of the elements with their due order or *Dike*, Heraclitus insists that *Dike* is strife, and that nature is comparable to a taut bow, with tensions in opposite direc-tions. Developing his dynamic conception of periodic orderly change, he selects *fire as a basic element, by which all things are meas-ured, and whose measures are preserved over time. Stoic thinkers (see STOICISM) understood him to predict the periodic conflagration of the entire cosmos; they may have been right.

*Aristotle charged Heraclitus with denial of the Principle of Non-Contradiction because he asserts that certain opposites (the way up and the way down, day and night, etc.) are 'one'. Very likely, however, Heraclitus was charting the many ways in which opposites figure in our discourse. Sometimes one and the same thing will be seen to have opposite properties in relation to different observers; sometimes a thing will have opposite properties when viewed from different perspectives; sometimes one opposite cannot be understood or defined without reference to the other opposite. This excavation of the logical structure of language is part of inquiry into nature.

Heraclitus is the first Greek thinker to have a theory of *psyche* or '*soul' as it functions in the living person. He connects *psyche* with both *logos*

and fire, and appears to think of it as a dynamic connectedness that can be overwhelmed by a 'watery' condition, which spells death. He con-nects this idea with praise of temperate living and of those who pursue 'ever-flowing fame' rather than bestial satiety. He attacks the Dio-nysian cult (see DIONYSUS), and shows disdain for a central aspect of popular religion, saying 'corpses are more to be thrown away than dung'.

In politics he shows aristocratic sympathies, but insists on the importance of public law. All human laws, he insists, are nourished by one divine law—presumably speaking of the unitary divinity that he identifies with the changing order of nature.

heralds in *Homer were important aides of the kings, used for such tasks as maintaining order in meetings, making proclamations, and bearing messages. They were under the protec-tion of *Hermes, were inviolable, and carried a *sceptre or staff. In later Greece they assisted magistrates in assemblies and lawcourts and bore messages to other states. In this capacity they differed from ambassadors, who were not similarly inviolable but might be authorized not only to transmit formal messages but also to negotiate. Heralds could circulate freely even during wars, and so were sometimes sent to open negotiations by requesting permission to send ambassadors. The Roman public crier was a humbler attendant of magistrates. See APPARITORES.

Herculāneum Roman *municipium* on a spur of Vesuvius commanding the coast-road, 8 km. (5 mi.) from Neapolis.

Recent discoveries have made its municipal life seem vigorous, but restricted hinterland, limited communications, and a small harbour denied it much economic opportunity. The streets (whose plan is more regular than that of *Pompeii) show little sign of heavy traffic; shops and workshops are unobtrusive. As the centre of a resort-coast, however, renowned for its beauty and healthy climate, and close enough to Neapo-lis to be a luxury suburb, the town benefited from the wealth of local proprietors (including Roman senators). The grandest property, the Villa of the Papyri, NW of the town, on terraces overlooking the sea, was embellished with gardens, waterworks, and statues. The name de-rives from the papyrus scrolls found there. Though carbonized, they can be painstakingly unrolled: Epicurean in taste (see EPICURUS), they include many of the works of *Philodemus of Gadara. Many of the town houses were also expensively equipped. See HOUSES, ITALIAN.

The town was damaged by the *earthquake of AD 63 and obliterated by the eruption of 79. Deeply buried by ash which solidified, the remains (esp. organic material such as wood or papyrus) are better preserved, but much more difficult to excavate, than those of Pompeii. The first explorations, using tunnels, date from the early 18th cent.; some 5 ha. (12 acres) have since been completely uncovered (c.25 per cent of the urban core and inner suburbs). The houses appear more varied in plan than those of Pompeii; they preserve much evidence of the upper storey. Public buildings, mostly dating from the Julio-Claudian period, are less well attested. On the ancient coast are important baths, and recent work has uncovered the skeletal remains of many dozens of the inhabitants killed at the harbour while attempting to escape the eruption.

Herculēs, from *Hercles*, Italic pronunciation of the name *Heracles. His was perhaps the earliest foreign cult to be received in Rome, the Ara Maxima, which was his most ancient place of worship, being within the *pomerium of the *Palatine settlement. The probable intention was to put the commercial *forum Boarium, in which it stood, under the protection of a god better known than the local deities. His cult had become very popular with merchants, no doubt because of his supposed ability to avert evil (see HERACLES) and the long journeys involved in his Labours and other exploits. It was common to pay him a *tithe of the profits of an enterprise. In his worship at the Ara Maxima no other god was mentioned; women and dogs were excluded. The sacrificial meat had to be eaten or burnt daily: hence the popularity of the sanctuary.

Hermēs Myths about Hermes mostly concern his childhood, told in the *Homeric Hymn to Hermes* (last third of the 6th cent. BC; see HYMNS). He was the son of *Zeus and the *nymph Maia, b. on Mt. Cyllene in *Arcadia. On the day of his birth, he left his cradle, found a tortoise, from the shell of which he made a lyre, then went to Pieria where he stole 50 cows belonging to *Apollo, which he led backwards to a cave, where he sacrificed two and hid the others, before returning to Cyllene; finally he made up his quarrel with Apollo. Later, he invented the syrinx or pan-pipe. He has no recognized wife, but two sons, Eudorus and *Pan, are attributed to him. He is character-

ized by a great variety of functions. Above all, he is a messenger god, who carries out the orders of Zeus respectfully. In this capacity, he appears as a subordinate deity, e.g. giving the ultimatum of Zeus to *Prometheus, or acting as his go-between when he is enamoured of Ganymedes. He is generally well disposed, and negotiates the ransom of Hector with pleasantness and good humour. His titles stress his speed and beneficence. He is also the god who guides: he shows shepherds the way and leads teams of animals; he guides people, esp. travellers, for whom he marks out the route in the form of a pillar or herm (see below). He takes divine children to safety (thus he gives *Dionysus to the Nymphs of Nysa, as depicted in the famous statue attributed to *Praxiteles), and is generally a patron of children; he also helps heroes such as *Perseus, for whom he obtains the bronze sickle used by the hero to decapitate Medūsa (see GORGON), and Heracles. He leads *Hera, *Aphrodite, and *Athena to *Paris, the judge in their beauty contest. As god of movement, he is leader of the Nymphs and the *Charites. Finally, as the guide of *souls, he leads the dead to *Hades, summoning them to the journey beyond, taking them by the hand and accompanying them on to *Charon's boat.

Hermes is also a god of abundance, fertility and prosperity. He is the patron of herdsmen and of the fruitfulness of herds and flocks; he is himself a cowherd and shepherd. More generally, he is the god of every kind of prosperity. The herm, a quadrangular pillar topped with a head, with tenons on its sides and an erect phallus, was very popular from the end of the 6th cent. onwards, and not only recalls Hermes' powers of fertility but, as an apotropaic talisman, also guarantees the success of all sorts of undertakings. (See HERMS.) Hermes is also the god of trade.

Hermes is an ingenious god, expert in both technology and magic. From his birth onwards, he was skilled in trickery and deception, and in the *Homeric Hymn* he is 'prince of thieves'. Even in cult, he is attested as trickster and thief. But most often he uses his power in mischief, illusion, and mystery. He creates a lyre out of the shell of a tortoise. Like a magician he knows how to put the enemy camp to sleep and to call up the dead. As a corollary, this god of *mētis* (prudence, cunning) and of mediation, has no part in violence. He is the least warlike of the gods; he is dragged into the battle with the *Giants. He prefers persuasion to weapons, and appears often as patron of orators. Only in a late period, as Trismegistus ('thrice-greatest'), does he come to preside over mystical revelations, as the successor to the Egyptian god Thoth and god of the 'hermetic'. A final function of Hermes is that of god of athletes—one linked, no doubt, to the youthful appearance and charm which the god assumed for seduction. See ATHLETICS. In this role he is often associated, esp. in the *gymnasium, with *Heracles.

Hermes' main aspects are shown in his physical appearance and iconography. His attributes are: the herald's *sceptre or staff, which he almost always carries, the traveller's hat, with or without wings, and the winged sandals which evoke his speed. He is generally bearded in the earlier period, but an unbearded type develops from the 4th cent. onwards. He wears a pinned cloak (*chlamys*). Side by side with this very frequent representation of the god of herds and flocks, the god of music, the messenger and guide of the living and of the dead, we find the herm (see HERMS), whose identity as Hermes is sometimes stressed by a sceptre painted on the shaft. This form, attested in sculpture as well as on vases, was very popular and could symbolize most of the functions of the god.

The cult of Hermes is esp. widely diffused in Peloponnese, where Pausanias mentions numerous myths, rituals, cults, and herms. In Athens, Hermes had a very ancient cult, and in the form of the herm he was present everywhere in the city. Hermes was essentially kindly, one of the most familiar gods in the daily lives of the Greeks. See also MERCURIUS.

Hermocratēs, Syracusan statesman and general; see SYRACUSE. At the peace conference at Gela (424 BC) he alerted the Sicilian Greeks, and at Syracuse (418–416) his fellow citizens, to the threat posed to their liberty by Athens. He played a prominent part in the defeat of the Athenian expedition as adviser (415), general plenipotentiary (414), and as adviser to the Spartan commander Gylippus (413). Sent as admiral to Asia (412), he was exiled *in absentia* by the democracy, after the battle of Cyzicus (410). Provided with funds by *Pharnabazus, he returned to Sicily (409), and with a private army ravaged the Carthaginian province. Refused an amnesty in 408, he attempted to seize Syracuse with the aid of partisans inside the city (including *Dionysius (1) I) and was killed. He was praised as a patriot by *Thucydides (2).

Hermogenēs, of Tarsus (2nd cent. AD), *rhetor, wrote a comprehensive set of textbooks on rhetoric. We have two works which are certainly genuine: one on *staseis* (types of issue, see RHETORIC, GREEK), and one on *ideai* (types of style). The book on types of style deals with seven types, all to be seen as ingredients in the perfection of *Demosthenes (2), but identifiable, in various proportions, in other authors: they are clarity, grandeur, beauty, rapidity, character (qualities like simplicity, subtlety, and sweetness), sincerity, and forcefulness.

herms were marble or bronze four-cornered pillars surmounted by a bust. Male herms were given genitals. Herms originated in piles of stones (Gk. *hermata*) used as road- and boundary-markers, but early on developed into stylized images of *Hermes. As such they were viewed as protectors of houses and cities. The Athenians claimed credit for the developed sculptural form and herms were esp. common in Athens—at crossroads, in the countryside, in the Agora, at the entrance of the Acropolis, in *sanctuaries, and at private doorways. The mutilation of the herms in 415 BC led to the exile of *Alcibiades.

hero-cult Heroes were a class of beings worshipped by the Greeks, generally conceived as the powerful dead, and often as forming a class intermediate between gods and men. Not until the 8th cent. do hero-cults become widespread and normal. The cult paid to heroes cannot be sharply distinguished from that paid to gods.

While heroes' *sanctuaries tended to be smaller and less splendid than those of gods, often indeed occupying a small space within a divine sanctuary, a few heroes, such as *Hippolytus at Troezen, had sanctuary complexes as impressive as those of any god. Hero-shrines were often constructed around tombs, real or supposed, and the hero had a very close connection with that particular place. The exception to this is *Heracles, who is in any case as much god as hero.

Concepts of heroes were as variable as their cult, if not more so. There is some evidence that heroes as a class were viewed as at least potentially malign, to be placated with apotropaic ritual rather than worshipped in the normal sense, but this is true only rarely of individual heroes, who more often appear as patrons or saviours of their city, as helpers in sickness or personal danger, and generally as benefactors. The traditions of their lives, deaths, and actions after death, however, usually contain some element of singularity or paradox. Many cult heroes were identified with the characters of heroic *epic, but the newly dead might be given heroic honours, generally by oracular command, if they conformed to one of the heroic patterns, e.g. by instituting a divine cult or founding a city.

Herod (1) **the Great** (c.73–74 BC), son of the Idumaean Antipater, was through him made governor of Galilee in 47 BC and then, with his brother, designated tetrarch (see TETRARCHY) by Marcus *Antonius (Mark Antony). Herod escaped the Parthian invasion of 40, and, while the Parthian nominee occupied the throne, Herod was declared king of Judaea (see JEWS) by Antony and the senate. In 37 Herod took *Jerusalem, with the assistance of the governor of Syria. *Octavian, whom Herod supported at *Actium, confirmed his rule. The kingship and high priesthood were now again separate in Judaea, though the latter was in the king's gift: he promoted a new high-priestly class. The palace élite, of mixed ethnic affiliation, also grew. Herod was an able administrator and a skilful financier. He taxed the country heavily, but also developed its resources, to which end his artificial harbour at *Caesarea contributed. Spectacular building projects were a hallmark of his reign, including the rebuilding of Samaria as Sebaste, a string of fortress-palaces, most notably *Masada, and Herodium, also his burial place. *Jerusalem acquired an amphitheatre as well as a theatre, whose decorations aroused the suspicion of some Jews. But his greatest undertaking, the rebuilding of the Temple, was left entirely to priests, to preserve purity. There, offence was given by a golden eagle put over the gate at the very end of his reign, a time when tensions with the Pharisees, earlier his friends, were running high. Lavish donations outside Palestine established Herod as a benefactor on an empire-wide scale, as well as a flamboyant *philhellene; the *Olympic Games and the city of Athens were among the beneficiaries. Through his personal good offices, his visits to Rome, and the mediation of *Nicolaus of Damascus and of *Vipsanius Agrippa, Herod long retained Augustus' confidence. But, in 9 BC, an unauthorized war incurred imperial displeasure. Also increasingly unacceptable was his savagery towards the large family produced by his ten wives: intrigues led him to execute his favourite, Mariamme I, in 29, her two sons in 7, and his eldest son and expected heir a few days before his death. Serious disturbances then allowed Roman intervention, and the division of his kingdom between his remaining sons,

*Herod (2) Antipas, Archelaus, and Philip, was formalized.

Herod (2) **Antipas,** following the will left by his father *Herod (1), was appointed by Augustus *tetrarch of Galilee (where he rebuilt the city of Sepphoris and founded Tiberias) and of Peraea, a non-adjacent territory across the Jordan. Both John the Baptist and Jesus were active in Antipas' territory. John was imprisoned as a troublemaker in the fortress of Machaerus and then executed (perhaps at the instigation of Salome, daughter of his niece and second wife). Luke has *Pontius Pilatus trying unsuccessfully to transfer to Antipas, who happened to be in Jerusalem, the responsibility for trying Jesus.

Herod (so called in Acts of the Apostles) See IULIUS AGRIPPA (1–2), MARCUS.

Hērōdas, Greek composer of *iambic *mimes. Seven poems survive more or less complete. Herodas was probably active c. 250 BC. Poem 2 and probably 4 are set on *Cos; poem 1 is set outside Egypt but refers to the glories of *Alexandria, and poem 8 very likely refers to the literary squabbles of the Alexandrian Museum; *Pliny the Younger names Herodas in the same context as *Callimachus (2). Herodas, like Callimachus in his *Iambics*, claims *Hipponax as his model (poem 8), and his iambic mimes are written in a creative, literary approximation to the Ionic of Hipponax. In style and theme, however, Herodas is more indebted to comedy and the *mime tradition of Sophron.

Each poem, except 8, has more than one speaking 'part'; each poem assumes the presence of mute extras. It is disputed whether they were originally composed only to be read, to be performed by a single mime, or by a troupe. Their learned character suggests that Herodas envisaged the possibility of a reading audience.

The very diverse background of the poems shows them to be typical of their age—both modern and archaizing, learned and 'low'. They are 'realistic' in the sense that the characters and what they say have 'real life' analogues, but they depend upon an audience which knows how stylized is the view of life presented and can appreciate the productive clash between versification and language on one side and subject-matter on the other. See MIME, GREEK.

Herōdēs Atticus See CLAUDIUS ATTICUS HERODES.

Herodotus of *Halicarnassus (?484BC–420s), historian. Author of a very long historical narrative, the earliest we possess. It looks back to the fall of the *Lydian kingdom in western *Anatolia in 545 and forwards to events in the Archidamian War (431–421), but it has as its focus and *raison d'être* the 'war between Greeks and non-Greeks', which we call the *Persian Wars. We know very little about the life of its author.

2. Herodotus' narrative is built from smaller narratives. He ends his first sentence: 'What caused Greeks and non-Greeks to go to war?' Events, large and small, need explanations. After surveying traditions which traced the origin of the conflict to the reciprocal abduction of legendary princesses, Herodotus declares his own view that the story cannot reliably be taken back beyond the reign of the Lydian king *Croesus, who began the process of absorbing the Greek communities of the Aegean coast into his kingdom and whose fall brought Persian power into contact with these communities, which were promptly forced into submission. The first book explains how these events occurred, deals with the Persian conquest of the Median kingdom which embroiled Lydia and led to its annexation by Persia, and continues the expansionist reign of the Persian king *Cyrus (1) the Great to his death in battle in 530. Bk. 2 takes the form of a massive excursus on the geography, customs, and history of *Egypt, which was the next target of Persian expansionism, under Cyrus' son and successor, *Cambyses. (This excursus makes it clear that Herodotus was not just a political and military historian.) Bk. 3 continues the reign of Cambyses down to his death in 522, after a failed attempt to invade *Ethiopia; it goes on to describe the turmoil that followed and the eventual emergence of *Darius as the new king of Persia, and deals with his administrative settlement of the empire. Bk. 4 covers Darius' abortive attempt to subdue the *Scythian tribes who lived to the north and east of the Danube and across southern Russia, and deals also with Persian expansion along the north African coast. Bk. 5 traces further Persian expansion, into northern Greece and the southern Balkans, and narrates the unsuccessful attempt of the Aegean Greek communities to free themselves from Persian control (the so-called *Ionian Revolt): Herodotus signals, ominously, the fatal support that *Athens gave to that revolt. Bk. 6 begins the story that runs continuously to its end in bk. 9: the Persian determination to have revenge for Athenian interference in the affairs of its empire and the first seaborne

attack on mainland Greece, which was defeated at Marathon in 490. Bks. 7–9 embrace the huge expedition mounted in 480–479 by Darius' son and successor, *Xerxes, and the Greek response to that threat; the opening engagements, at sea off *Artemisium and on land at *Thermopylae; the climactic battles of *Salamis and *Plataea, which forced the Persian army and navy to withdraw to the north; and the carrying of the war back across the Aegean, ending in the battle of Mycale, on the Ionian coast opposite *Samos. At various points, episodes in the history of Greek communities not at first directly in contact with Persian power, such as *Sparta, Athens, *Corinth, and Samos, are interleaved, often at length, with the main narrative of Persian expansion as they explain how these communities became involved or failed for a time to be involved, until all are seamlessly joined together in bks. 7–9.

3. The stories from which Herodotus' narrative is built derive sometimes from distinguished individuals, sometimes from 'collective' informants ('the Corinthians say . . . '; 'we Spartans have a story . . . '). Occasionally his source may have been a document (e.g. his description of the satrapy system set up by Darius to administer the Persian empire). But the overwhelming mass of his material must derive from oral tradition, and that tradition will always have been local, even familial. Thus the overall conception of a narrative that would draw on these local traditions but would connect them so as to span more than 70 years and take in much of the known world was Herodotus' own, and it is his most brilliant and original achievement. Herodotus spoke only Greek, but he writes of interpreters in Egypt and at the Persian court, where also there were Greek officials in high places. He writes repeatedly of what was told to him in an astonishing range of places: where he could, he preferred to trust what he could see for himself (see AUTOPSY) and could enquire into (Herodotus' word for 'enquiry' is *historiē*, which brought the word 'history' into the languages of Europe). Where he could not, he listened (see ORALITY). He writes of enquiries made in the northern Aegean, in southern Italy, round the shores of the Black (*Euxine) Sea, in Egypt (where he travelled as far up the *Nile as *Elephantine), at *Dodona, and at *Cyrene; of things seen on the Dnieper in southern Russia; in *Babylon; at *Tyre of talking to *Carthaginians and to the inhabitants of *Delphi. He is familiar with the geography of Samos, of *Attica, and of the Nile delta. He takes for granted a detailed knowledge

of the topography of *Delos, of the Athenian Acropolis, and of Delphi. Everywhere he writes of what was said to him by 'the locals'. It is of the essence of Herodotus' method of historiē that he builds the process of enquiry into his narrative: he writes not only of his sources, their agreements and disagreements, but also of his own belief and disbelief at what he is told (he is, he writes, under an obligation to report what was said to him, but under no obligation to believe it: 7. 152. 3); sometimes too he records his inability to decide, or the impossibility of arriving at an answer to some question he is enquiring into (sometimes because it is beyond the reach of human memory; sometimes because it lies too far away, too far beyond the limits of his travels). Unlike *Thucydides (2), he does not present his account of the past as smoothly authoritative, the result of work not to be done again but as one man's struggle, not always successful, to discover and record what heroic men, non-Greek as well as Greek, have achieved, before those achievements are obliterated by time.

4. It is not merely Herodotus' travels that cover an astonishing range but also his understanding of the variety of human experience. He does not disguise the fact that the Greek-speaking world was the cultural as well as the geographical centre of his perceptions. But he writes, almost always open-mindedly, of the differences that distinguish Persians from Scythians, Babylonians, Indians, and Egyptians, as well as from Greeks. He is not very successful in grasping the 'ideologies' that made one religion different from another. That is hardly surprising: he records religious practice everywhere with precision, but he has nothing to teach him the 'meaning' of *ritual, as he has for Greek religion in the poems of *Homer and *Hesiod. He is sure that for all men, however much they know of other cultures, their own culture is superior. But when he is faced with something quite alien to his experience and to Greek experience generally, such as the culture of the Scythian nomads, who have no aspect of permanence to their lives (no statues, altars, or temples, except to *Ares; no agriculture, no buildings, no walls or settlements even), though he can admire their ability to escape Persian domination by never staying to confront the enemy, 'for the rest', he writes, 'I do not like them'. They offer him no point of resemblance and they do not fit. None the less, he describes their culture also dispassionately. For Herodotus it is important that things should fit: he is at home with symmetries.

5. Herodotus' vast narrative coheres because it is strung on two lines of connection which pass through time. The first is kinship; the second *reciprocity. Reciprocity is the demand that all men respond to what is done to them with like for like ('equals for equals', in Herodotus' own phrase): with good for good and with hurt for hurt. The demands of reciprocity are absolute, admit of no exceptions and, Herodotus believes, are common to all men. They also outlive time, since they are inherited. The principle of reciprocity is essential to Herodotus' writing: to answer the question 'why did this happen?' it is necessary to ask the further question: 'to what previous act was this act a response?' The chain of reciprocity may reach far back and encompass many people. Thus the search for a 'beginning' is common to all narrative and it is no surprise that, faced with the question 'why did Greeks and non-Greeks go to war ⟨in the 5th cent. BC⟩?', Herodotus finds an answer in events far distant in space and more than three generations in the past, with Croesus and his 'beginning of wrongful acts against Greeks'. It is the logic of reciprocity that explains not only the two Persian invasions of Greece but also, for example, the bitter hostility between Athens and *Aegina, which lasted from the mid-6th cent. until the Athenians expelled the Aeginetans from their island in 431. For the most part, the question 'why?' does not trouble Herodotus. Events that are too uncanny, shocking, or momentous for merely human explanation call into play the actions of divinity which are assumed also to be determined by the logic of reciprocity. He seems too to be at ease with the question of the 'meaning' of events. Both in his own person and also in the person of various 'warners' who appear in his narrative (men such as *Solon; the pharaoh Amasis; Xerxes' uncle Artabanus, and Croesus, after his downfall), the thread of events seems to be illuminated by general statements: 'human success stays nowhere in the same place', Herodotus; 'divinity is jealous and disruptive', 'man is the creature of chance', and 'in everything one must look to the end', 'Solon'; 'there is a cycle of human experience: as it revolves, it does not allow the same men always to succeed', 'Croesus'. These statements are what ancient Greeks called *gnomai and their function is closer to that of the *proverb than to any 'law' of historical process: they are not discountenanced by contradiction. Nor do references to 'what was going to be', to notions of a man's 'portion', or 'what is assigned' (see FATE) make Herodotus a historical determinist. Rather they

represent the storyteller's sense of the shape of his story. Closer perhaps to the heart of Herodotus' sense of things are 'wonder' (a very Herodotean word) at human achievement, the 'great and wonderful deeds of men' and the emotional undercurrent to events that so often gives his narrative a tragic colour: two compelling and haunting examples are the story of the deadly quarrel between *Periander, tyrant of Corinth, and his own son, and the astonishing moment at Abydos when Xerxes, engaged in reviewing his vast invasion force, bursts into tears on reflecting that in 100 years not one of these splendid warriors would be living. Artabanus replies that more painful still is the fact that in so short a life there was not one who would not, again and again, wish himself dead to escape the distress of living (see PESSIMISM, GREEK).

6. The singularity of Herodotus' methods and achievement has always made him problematic to his readers. He has been read with most enthusiasm and greatest understanding in periods of the rapid expansion of men's horizons, such as the period of *Alexander (2) the Great's eastern conquests and in the Age of Discovery. But two adverse responses constantly recur: the first that he is a mere storyteller, charming perhaps but not a serious historian (that view, without the acknowledgement of charm, goes back to Thucydides); the other view is that he is a liar. This view also has ancient supporters (esp. *Plutarch in his bizarre essay, On the Malice of Herodotus: Plutarch's beloved *Thebes does not emerge well from Herodotus' account of events). There are problems about believing everything that Herodotus says he saw or was told, but they are not so great as the problem of believing that Herodotus' narrative is essentially fiction.

Hēsiod, one of the oldest known Greek poets, often coupled or contrasted with *Homer as the other main representative of early epic. Which was the older of the two was much disputed from the 5th cent. BC on. Hesiod's absolute date is now agreed to be c.700 BC. Of his life he tells us something himself: that his father had given up a life of unprofitable sea-trading and moved from Aeolian *Cyme to Ascra in Boeotia; that he, as he tended sheep on Mt. *Helicon, had heard the *Muses calling him to sing of the gods; and that he once won a tripod for a song at a funeral contest at *Chalcis. For his dispute with Perses see below (2). Two extant poems have a good claim to be authentic.

Works

1. *Theogony* The main part of the poem, which is prefaced by a hymn to the Muses, deals with the origin and genealogies of the gods (including the divine world-masses Earth, Sea, Sky, etc.), and the events that led to the kingship of *Zeus: the castration of *Uranus by *Cronus and the overthrow of Cronus and the *Titans, the 'former gods', by the Olympians. This 'Succession Myth' has striking parallels in Akkadian and Hittite texts, and seems originally to have come from the near east. Hesiod's version shows some stylistic awkwardness and incongruity, but is not without power. Interlaced with it are the genealogies, which run smoother. The first powers born are *Chaos, Earth (see GAIA), and *Eros. From Chaos and Earth, in two separate lines, some 300 gods descend; they include personified abstracts, whose family relationships are clearly meaningful. There is a passage in praise of the un-Homeric goddess *Hecate, further myths, notably the aetiological tale of *Prometheus, and a detailed description of Tartarus, the deepest region of the Underworld. The poem ends with the marriages of Zeus and the other Olympians, and a list of goddesses who slept with mortal men. This last section is agreed to be post-Hesiodic.

2. *Works and Days* This poem, apparently composed after *Theogony*, would be more aptly entitled 'the Wisdom of Hesiod'. It gives advice for living a life of honest work. Hesiod inveighs against dishonesty and idleness by turns, using myths (Prometheus again, with the famous story of *Pandora; the five World Ages), parable, allegory, *proverbs, direct exhortation, and threats of divine anger. The sermon is ostensibly directed at a brother Perses, who has bribed the 'kings' and taken more than his share of his inheritance; but Perses' failings seem to change with the context, and it is impossible to reconstruct a single basic situation. Besides moral advice, Hesiod gives much practical instruction, esp. on agriculture (the year's 'Works'), seafaring, and social and religious conduct. There is a fine descriptive passage on the rigours of winter. The final section, sometimes regarded as a later addition, is the 'Days' (765–828), an almanac of days in the month that are favourable or unfavourable for different operations. The poem as a whole is a unique source for social conditions in early Archaic Greece.

It has always been the most read of Hesiodic poems. There was even a 'tradition' that it was Hesiod's only genuine work, but he names himself in *Theogony* 22, and links of style and thought between the two poems confirm identity of authorship. Both bear the marks of a distinct personality: a surly, conservative countryman, given to reflection, no lover of women or of life, who felt the gods' presence heavy about him.

Hesperidēs, the daughters of Night and Erebus, guarded a tree of golden apples given by *Earth to *Hera at her marriage. From the same tree came the apples thrown down by Hippomenēs (or Mēlanion) in his race against *Atalanta. The garden of the Hesperides was popularly located beyond the Atlas mountains at the western border of the Ocean. *Heracles succeeded in taking the apples after slaying Ladon, the dragon that also guarded the tree. The subject was popular in Greek art, esp. on painted pottery.

Hestia, the goddess of the hearth, closely related to *Vesta. Respect for and worship of the hearth are characteristic of the Greeks from earliest times. In the Mycenaean age the king's throne-room (*megaron*) was the architectural centre of the palace, and in the very centre of that room was a low, round hearth. After the fall of monarchies, the kings' hearths as political centres and sites for asylum and the entertainment of foreign visitors were succeeded by official state hearths housed in public buildings called *prytaneia*. There, at least in some cities, the fire was kept continuously burning. To unify Attica (see SYNOECISM) Theseus reputedly eliminated the various local *prytaneia* in favour of a single *prytaneion* in Athens. As a token of continuity a *metropolis* sent to a newly founded colony fire from its own hearth. Similarly, each family had its own hearth where small offerings were placed at meal times. Newborns, brides, and new slaves were initiated into the family by various rituals at or around the hearth. After the *Persian occupation of much of Greece in 480 BC, *Delphi ordered the Greek states to extinguish their fires, because they had been polluted by the Persians (see POLLUTION), and take new fire from the *prytaneion* at Delphi.

Although one of the twelve Olympians, Hestia has little mythology, unable as she was to leave the house. She is not mentioned by *Homer. *Hesiod and authors after him make her a daughter of *Cronus and Rhea. She 'liked not the works of *Aphrodite', rejected *Apollo and *Poseidon as suitors, and swore herself to lifelong virginity. So Zeus granted her 'to sit in the middle of the house, receiving the "fat" of offerings', to be honoured in all temples, and to be a goddess 'senior and respected among all men'. Even at sanctuaries and sacrifices of other gods Hestia regularly received a preliminary offering; in *prayers and *oaths she was usually named first. 'To begin from Hestia' became a proverb. Hestia's extremely close tie to one physical object, the hearth, is uncharacteristic of Greek gods and probably limited her development in both myth and cult.

hetairai ('companions', sing. *hetaira*) is an Attic euphemism for those women, slave, freed, or foreign, who were paid for sexual favours (see PROSTITUTION, SECULAR). There was a class and semantic distinction, but not a legal one, between the *hetaira* and the *pornē* ('buyable woman'), at least in later sources. A *porne*, even a lowly brothel slave, could gain her freedom, become an independent contractor, become the lover (*hetaira*) of some rich man or men, and thereby exert her own influence and herself become rich. Membership of the category *hetaira* implied beauty, education, and the ability to inspire ruinous infatuation in both foolish young men and those older and presumably wiser.

Greek literature about *hetairai* cannot yield concrete historical evidence for the realities of their lives, but instead constructs, from a male viewpoint, those women whose function it was to provide pleasure within a social ideology which defined women as wives, concubines, or prostitutes and allotted to each her separate place. Because the category 'prostitute' was the most fluid and the most exotic of the three, it was the most dangerous for men and the most productive of literary comment, ranging from the cynical to the romantic.

hetaireiai, associations of *hetairoi* ('comrades'). The *hetaireiai* best known to us are clubs in Athens, esp. of young, upper-class men, which combined a social function with a political: the furtherance of the ambitions of their leading members, and mutual assistance in the lawcourts and at elections. They are sometimes called *synōmosiai*, 'sworn groups', from the oaths of loyalty which might be required. The mutilation of the *herms in 415 BC was said to be the work of a *hetaireia* to which *Andocides belonged; and the informal political activity which led to the oligarchic regimes of the *Four Hundred in 411 and the *Thirty Tyrants in 404 was conducted in part through the *hetaireiai*. In reaction against that, the revised law code of the 4th cent. included provisions against subversive *hetaireiai*. See also CLUBS, GREEK.

hetairoi, the 'Companions' of early *Macedonian kings. Personal status at the Macedonian court was principally defined by relationship to the king; *hetairoi* were at first an élite because they were the king's friends, his retinue, who functioned equally as senior officers of state and militarily as the king's own cavalry, among them his Bodyguards. As the state grew and its royal structures became firmer, so the number of *hetairoi* also grew. Under *Philip II, after the major expansion and consolidation phase (c.340 BC), acc. to *Theopompus there were 800 of them, some from Macedonia, some from *Thessaly, some from further south in Greece, who participated in Philip's distribution of newly conquered lands. These men were, even now, personally selected by the king, but within them different circles of status developed—not all could be daily advisers, and those who were, the esp. close personal companions, formed an informal council of state. From Philip's time, adolescent sons of *hetairoi* were recruited to be royal pages.

Militarily *hetairoi* were cavalry—perhaps at first the only cavalry. As numbers of cavalry available grew, the *hetairoi* became an élite unit serving closely with the king, until *Alexander (2) the Great called all Macedonian cavalry 'Companion Cavalry'. The same development occurred with the heavy infantry, whom Alexander named *Pezetairoi* ('Infantry Companions').

heterosexuality and *homosexuality were not sharply opposed in the Graeco-Roman world. Discussions of sex could focus on either pleasure or procreation. Pleasures were categorized and valued on the distinction between active (penetrating an orifice with a penis) and passive. Heterosexual acts (not people) were distinguished from homosexual not as radically differing pleasures but primarily on the basis of social consequence: only the former produce children.

What was most important in heterosexual acts was the status of the woman and the man's degree of responsibility towards her and her offspring: wife, concubine, *hetaira, prostitute, slave. The purpose of wives was to produce legitimate children. Marriage was primarily a nexus of social and economic exchange (see MARRIAGE LAW). Love between husband and wife was not required. However, mutual re-spect, affection, and love could and did arise. Expressions of wives' love for husbands are common, less common the reverse. A strict double standard was enforced. Men had recourse to *hetairai* for love affairs and sophisticated entertainment, or to prostitutes for quick relief (see PROSTITUTION, SECULAR). Slaves, male or female, could routinely be used for sex. Concubinage offered a stable, legal (sometimes contractual) status to those for whom marriage was impossible or undesirable; see CONTUBERNIUM.

Control of wives' sexuality (virginity, *adultery) was important to assure the legitimacy of the children and so social stability. Athenian fathers could sell their corrupted unmarried daughters into slavery (no known cases). Tests (if ever applied) for virginity were mostly magical: the hymen was not fully recognized even by anatomists.

Adultery meant intercourse with a married woman: she was the object of adulteration. The offence was against her husband and a matter of 'self-help' justice until *Augustus' *lex Iūlia*. A man caught in the act (seduction or rape) with another's wife, mother, sister, daughter, or concubine, could be killed, sexually abused, or fined. Adulterous wives had to be divorced and were barred from public ceremonies. Roman law permitted fathers to kill adulterous daughters. Rape of a free male or female was subject to monetary fine; half for a slave.

Female orgasm is acknowledged but largely ignored by the (male) sources. At the same time women were thought to be sexually voracious. Roman (and to a lesser extent Greek) sources illustrate a marked scale of pleasure for the agent and humiliation for the object: vagina, anus, mouth. Anal intercourse, considered a Spartan proclivity, was also practised as a form of birth control. Receiving fellatio was esp. prized. Cunnilingus was most vile and degrading to the giver.

Reproduction was controlled through infant exposure (see INFANTICIDE), contraception, and abortion. Most forms of contraception were useless, but some barriers or mild spermatocides may have been intermittently successful. Surgical abortion was dangerous and avoided by doctors.

Vase-painting (c.575–450 BC) and other artistic (e.g. mirrors) and literary sources illustrate a wide variety of postures for intercourse. Sexual violence, group-sex, as well as occasional scenes of tenderness (kisses, caresses, eye-contact) are shown. Sex reappears in Hellenistic and Roman decorative arts, depicting primarily heterosexual intercourse of individual couples in domestic rather than symposiastic settings (see SYMPOSIUM).

Love as a theme in literature shows a marked periodicity. The personal celebrations of the lyric poets largely disappeared in the Classical period. Love re-emerged in New Comedy (see COMEDY (GREEK), NEW) and the *novel in a predominantly social, domestic, and hence heterosexual form. Hellenistic poetry focused on forbidden and pathological love. *Epigram worked conceits on pleasure and pain with both women and boys. Roman comedy transmitted some of this to poetry. *Catullus made romantic love in our sense central to his life and poetry. The theme of erotic passion was continued by the elegists, was parodied by *Ovid, and largely disappeared from the western tradition until its rediscovery in Courtly Love. See EROS; LOVE AND FRIENDSHIP; PORNOGRAPHY; SEXUALITY.

hexameter(s) See METRE, GREEK, 3; METRE, LATIN, 2(a).

Hieron (1) **I**, regent at Gela for his brother *Gelon (485–478 BC), and tyrant (see TYRANNY) of *Syracuse (478–466). He completed the subjugation of the Ionian cities of the east coast of Sicily, destroying Naxos and Catana. He refounded Catana, adding territory taken from the Sicels, renaming it Aetna. Hieron died in 466 at Aetna, and was buried there, being accorded, as founder, the heroic honours he craved. By nature suspicious and more despotic than Gelon, he envied the glamour and the heroic status of his brother, and sought to emulate his reputation by pursuing an energetic foreign policy and by his patronage both of the great Greek *festivals and their centres and of such poets as *Bacchylides, *Pindar, *Simonides, *Xenophanes, and *Aeschylus.

Hieron (2) **II**, tyrant (see TYRANNY), later king, of *Syracuse (c.271–216 BC). Between 275 and 271, Hieron was elected general, seized power as the result of a military coup, allied himself with the popular faction, and was perhaps elected general plenipotentiary. He attacked the *Mamertines, and after a severe defeat and further preparation, routed them on the Longanus river (west of *Messana) (265). He was then acclaimed king. Alarmed by the Mamertines' alliance with Rome, Hieron joined the Carthaginians (see CARTHAGE) in besieging Messana (264); but forced by the Romans to withdraw, and besieged in Syracuse, he came to terms (263), preserving much of his kingdom, but becoming in effect a subordinate of Rome. His loyalty to Rome in the First *Punic War earned him the revision of his treaty (248): it became a treaty as between equals (see FOEDUS), he received additions to his kingdom, and the indemnity still outstanding was remitted. Hieron maintained an efficient navy and policed the sea, enjoyed friendly relations with Carthage (after 241), *Rhodes, and *Egypt, improved (with the help of his friend *Archimedes) the defences of Syracuse, and enriched Syracuse and his kingdom by his building. He supplied Rome with grain, both before and during the Second *Punic War, and co-operated with her at sea and sent troops and money. He died shortly after *Cannae (216). 'Naturally regal and statesmanlike' (*Polybius), Hieron was realistic enough to jettison his early imperial aspirations in favour of loyalty to Rome and the prosperity and well-being of his people. His system of taxation, adopted by Rome after her annexation of Sicily (241)—the *lex Hieronica*—was regarded as both efficient and equitable.

Hieronymus, of Cardia, historian and statesman. His great history spanned the period from *Alexander (2) the Great's death (323) to at least the death of *Pyrrhus (272). The extant fragments only hint at its dimensions and content. Excellently informed, he supplied documentation such as the text of Alexander's Exiles' Decree, and carefully explained the motives of the various protagonists. The lively and lucid narrative was varied by pertinent digressions like the descriptions of Alexander's funeral car and the Indian practice of suttee.

hierophantēs, chief priest of the Eleusinian *mysteries, was chosen for life from the clan of the Eumolpidae. He was distinguished by a head-band, myrtle wreath, and a robe probably of purple, and like many priests he carried a *sceptre. Among Athenian priests he was the most revered. An impressive, melodious voice was an important requirement for appointment. Before the celebration he sent out *heralds to proclaim truce for the period of the mysteries. He opened the ceremonies with a proclamation that *barbarians (unlikely to know much Greek), murderers, and those defiled must keep away. In presenting the mysteries to the initiates he was assisted by the *dadouchos*, 'torchbearer'.

Hīmera, on the north coast of *Sicily, was founded *c.*649 BC by the Zanclaeans (see MESSANA). *Stesichorus was its most famous citizen. In the early 5th cent. it was controlled by a tyrant Terillus who, on his expulsion by *Theron of *Acragas, appealed to Carthage. The Carthaginian expedition was decisively defeated at Himera (480), where a fine Doric temple in the lower town celebrated the triumph of *Gelon and Theron. On the plateau above, a sanctuary with three temples has been excavated. Himera was razed by Carthage in 409 as an act of revenge.

Hipparchus (1), younger son of *Pisistratus of Athens (6th cent. BC). Closely associated with his elder brother *Hippias (1), he was known esp. as patron and lover of the arts. He invited *Anacreon and *Simonides to Athens, and set up *herms around *Attica with words of gnomic wisdom; see GNOME. He may have added Homeric recitals to the *Panathenaea (see RHAPSODES). It is unclear how much of the artistic momentum of Pisistratid Athens (esp. the temple of Olympian *Zeus) should be associated specifically with him. He was murdered by Harmodius and *Aristogīton in 514.

Hipparchus (2), astronomer, (fl. second half of 2nd cent. BC). His recorded observations range from 147 to 127. His only extant work, the *Commentary on the Phainomena of Eudoxus and Aratus*, contains criticisms of their descriptions and placings of the *constellations and stars (see ARATUS; EUDOXUS), and a list of simultaneous risings and settings. Valuable information on Hipparchus' own star co-ordinates has been extracted from it. Most of our knowledge of Hipparchus' other astronomical work comes from *Ptolemy's (2) *Almagest*.

Hipparchus transformed Greek *astronomy from a theoretical to a practical science, by applying to the geometrical models (notably the eccentric/epicyclic hypothesis) that had been developed by his predecessors numerical parameters derived from observations, thus making possible the prediction of celestial positions for any given time. In order to do this he also founded trigonometry, by computing the first trigonometric function, a chord table. He constructed viable theories for the sun and moon, and, using several ingenious methods for determining the lunar distance (which he was the first to estimate accurately), developed a theory of parallax. He was thus able to compute both lunar and solar eclipses. For the planets, however, he refused to construct a theory, contenting himself with compiling a list of observations from which he showed the insufficiency of previous planetary models. He is famous for his discovery of the precession of the equinoxes, which is connected both with his investigations of the length of the year and his observations of star-positions.

Hipparchus was a systematic and careful observer, who invented several instruments. He had a critical and original mind and a fertile mathematical invention. But he could not have achieved what he did without the aid of Babylonian astronomy, of which he displays a knowledge far deeper than any Greek before or after him, and the success of which in predicting phenomena he evidently wished to emulate. Not only did he have access to the wealth of Babylonian observational records (which he seems to have been instrumental in transmitting to the Greek world), but he also adopted many numerical parameters directly from Babylonian astronomy, and used a number of Babylonian arithmetical procedures, which were only later replaced (by *Ptolemy (2)) with strictly geometrical methods. Hipparchus' skill in combining the Babylonian and Greek traditions in astronomy was crucial to the successful propagation of the science in that form for over 1,000 years.

Hipparchus' geographical treatise was a polemic against the *Geography* of *Eratosthenes, criticizing descriptive and esp. mathematical details. He also wrote on *astrology, and his establishment of methods for computation of celestial positions undoubtedly contributed to the enormous expansion of that 'science' in the Graeco-Roman world soon after his time.

hippeis

1. Aristocracies In some Greek states the aristocracy was known as the 'hippeis'. Aristotle, while observing that only the rich possessed *horses, seems to have thought that this was the basis of their political power, since their states depended upon cavalry in war. But although there is some evidence for cavalry in early wars, it is doubtful whether many Greek states south of Boeotia had powerful forces of cavalry in early times. The term may rather reflect a time, real or imagined, when heroes rode to battle in chariots, as they do in *Homer, where *hippeis* means charioteers. Even when the war-chariot was abandoned, it may have continued in use among the rich for ceremonial

purposes—at funerals or in funeral games—and those who used it may have continued to be called 'charioteers'.

2. Cavalry Archaeological evidence shows that *horses were originally used in Greece to pull chariots, not for riding, and if the Homeric poems reflect real, contemporary warfare, this was still true in the 8th cent. BC. Even after men had started to ride horses, it is possible that in most places they originally simply rode them to the battlefield, and then dismounted to fight on foot, at least once *hoplites had become the dominant force. In any case, cavalry was never used on a large scale except in areas suited to the breeding of horses, such as *Macedonia, *Thessaly, and *Boeotia. Only the rich could afford horses, and in most areas any cavalry force was bound to be small. Thus the Athenians instituted a proper cavalry force only after the *Persian Wars, drawn from the second of *Solon's orders (see 3 below), and even by 431 it was only 1,000 strong. Sometimes it was very effective, but it was never a battle-winner. Similarly, the Spartans did not raise a proper cavalry force until 424, and then although the rich provided the horses, they did not themselves form the cavalry, and *Xenophon is strongly critical of its effectiveness. Thessalian cavalry, on the other hand, was famous from the time of the Lelantine War (see GREECE (HISTORY), *Archaic period*), and Theban cavalry performed excellently at the battles of *Plataea and *Leuctra. All these cavalry forces, however, were missile-armed and incapable of defeating infantry, unless the latter was caught in the wrong terrain or not properly formed.

Cavalry came into its own in the Macedonian army and in those of *Alexander (2) the Great's successors, and it was his 'Companions' (see HETAIROI) who gave Alexander victory in all three of his great battles. The key to the success of Macedonian cavalry was its use of a lance made of cornel wood, as opposed to javelins. This at last gave cavalry the capability of breaking enemy infantry, though it was still mostly used to exploit gaps already forming in infantry lines, as probably at the battle of *Chaeronea, and certainly at *Gaugamela.

3. Athenian Class At Athens *hippeis* may originally have been used of all the richest citizens, but in his constitution *Solon gave the name to the second of his four orders, comprising men whose land yielded between 300 and 500 *medimnoi* of corn or the equivalent in other produce. The archonship (see ARCHONTES) was open to members of this class by the beginning of the 5th cent. BC if not originally; in 457/6 eligibility was extended to the third order, the *zeugitai (the hoplites).

Hippias (1), tyrant (see TYRANNY) of Athens 527–510 BC, elder son and successor of *Pisistratus, in close association with his brother *Hipparchus (1). His rule was at first mild. Leading aristocrats held the archonship (see ARCHONTES), *Cleisthenes (2) in 525/4, *Miltiades in 524/3; Hipparchus patronized the arts. The famous Attic owl coinage probably begins in his reign (see COINAGE, GREEK), as does work on the temple of Olympian Zeus (*Olympieum), the largest in contemporary Greece; extensive work on the temple of Athena on the Acropolis (*c.*520); and the altar of the Twelve Gods in the Agora. His rule became harsher after Hipparchus' assassination. The *Alcmaeonids, based at Leipsydrion, in the foothills of Mt. Parnes, tried in vain to oust him; the Spartans under *Cleomenes I, spurred on by *Delphi and Cleisthenes, invaded Attica and finally succeeded. He and his family escaped to *Sigeum and later to *Darius I 's court. He was with the Persian forces at the battle of *Marathon.

Hippias (2), of *Elis, *sophist, a younger contemporary of *Protagoras. He acquired fame and wealth as a teacher and orator, claiming competence in arithmetic, geometry, astronomy, music (i.e. harmonics) grammar, poetry, and history, as well as in various handicrafts and in mnemonic techniques. His voluminous works included an elegy on the drowning of a chorus of boys from *Messenia, a collection of historical material, and a list of Olympic victors (see OLYMPIC GAMES).

Hippocratēs, of *Cos, probably a contemporary of Socrates (469–399 BC), was the most famous physician of antiquity and one of the least known. The important early corpus of medical writings bears his name (see MEDICINE, 4), but he cannot be confidently connected with any particular treatise, let alone with any specific doctrines. He remains for many a 'name without a work'; and even in antiquity the nature of his personal contributions to medicine were the subject of speculation.

A claim that he was acquainted with certain 5th-cent. *sophists is supported by *Cornelius Celsus, who says that the historical Hippocrates was the first to separate medicine from philosophy, and much more strongly by *Plato, who mentions Hippocrates several times. Plato suggests that he taught medicine for a fee and offers a cryptic glimpse into his medical thought, reporting that he claimed that one could not understand the nature of the body without understanding the nature of the whole. This difficult passage in *Phaedrus* attracted much comment in antiquity, and has continued to do so, since it represents the only early independent reference to Hippocrates' method.

See also DIETETICS.

Hippódamus, of *Miletus, b. *c.*500 BC, was the most famous Greek town-planner. Towards the middle of the 5th cent. he planned *Piraeus for the Athenians, and boundary stones found there are probably evidence of his work. The agora there was known as the Hippodamian. In 443 he went with the colony to *Thurii, and he may well have been responsible for its gridiron plan. Aristotle speaks of Hippodamus' foppish appearance and his political theories, and notes that he thought that the ideal size for a city was 10,000 (i.e. probably citizens). See URBANISM.

Hippolytus, son of *Theseus and an *Amazon, was devoted to the hunt and to the virgin *Artemis, ignoring *Aphrodite, who responded by afflicting Hippolytus' stepmother Phaedra, sister of *Ariadne, with a passion for him. When he rejected her, she accused Hippolytus to Theseus (just returned from consulting an oracle) of making advances to her, and hanged herself. *Poseidon, responding to the prayer of Theseus, sent a bull from the sea which caused the death of Hippolytus in a chariot crash as he left Troezen for exile.

The story was famous. It was dramatized in lost tragedies by *Sophocles and *Euripides, in both of which it seems that Phaedra is, as in the much later play by *Seneca the Younger, lustful and unscrupulous. In a second, surviving version by Euripides, on the other hand, Phaedra has a strong sense of modesty, which struggles with her passion, and it is the nurse rather than Phaedra herself who approaches Hippolytus. The myth was also handled by *Ovid in *Heroides* 4.

In cult also Hippolytus is associated with Aphrodite. At Athens she had a shrine 'by Hippolytus' on the Acropolis. At Troezen, the place of his death, he had a precinct containing a temple of Aphrodite and a hero-cult in which girls about to marry lamented for him and offered him their hair. Hippolytus embodies the persistence of virginal resistance to marriage, a resistance which the girls themselves must abandon.

Hirtius, Aulus (consul 43 BC), since *c.*54 an officer of *Caesar, who sent him as envoy to *Pompey in December 50. In the Civil Wars he served in Spain, and was at Antioch in spring 47; in 46 he was praetor and next year governed Transalpine *Gaul. After Caesar's murder he was consul designate, and Cicero induced him to take up arms against Antony (Marcus *Antonius) (43). With Octavian he raised Antony's siege of Mutina, but was killed in the victory, receiving with his colleague Pansa a public funeral. Hirtius added to Caesar's *Gallic War* an eighth book, and probably also wrote the *Alexandrian War*; his correspondence with Cicero, published in nine books, and the draft for Caesar's *Anticato* have not survived. A notorious epicure, Hirtius was also a fluent and reasonably painstaking writer.

Histiaeus, tyrant of *Miletus, loyal servant of Persia (*c.*515–493 BC), saved *Darius' I expedition beyond the Danube (see DANUVIUS), his unsuccessful atack on *Scythia, when fellow Greek autocrats pondered betraying their overlord (*c.*513). He protected Darius' interests in the western provinces of Anatolia, and gained Darius' gift of Myrcinus on the river Strymon, a hub for Ionian penetration and economic exploitation of the *Thracian–*Macedonian coastlands.

Suspected of potential rebellion or excessive power by Persian grandees, he was summoned to Susa, the winter capital, long detained, and honoured by Darius as his Aegean expert. Histiaeus overboldly promised (499) to regain the allegiance of Miletus and other Ionian cities that *Aristagoras, his appointed deputy, had led into rebellion. See IONIAN REVOLT. Like *Hecataeus, he appreciated Persian power and Hellenic inadequacies. Sent to pacify Ionia, after several Ionian repulses, he dared not return to Susa and so departed for his Thracian project. He later launched shipping-raids from *Byzantium and descents on *Chios, Thasos, and *Lesbos. As he foraged near Atarneus, Persian units captured and impaled him (493). Herodotus found only hostile Greek and Persian sources. He does acknowledge Histiaeus' steady services to Darius that led Harpagus and Artaphernes to execute him.

historiography, Greek *Homer is slippery ground for the historian. But his characters show awareness of the past, and they long to leave glory behind them; thus *Achilles sings of the famous deeds of men and *Helen weaves into a web the story of the sufferings she has herself brought about. The poet speaks of 'men who exist nowadays' by contrast with inhabitants of the world he describes. *Genealogies, of the sort that feature in Homeric battle-challenges, are essential to a historical perspective on human events, and they form the link between Homer and *Hecataeus, the first true Greek historian: he wrote on genealogy and mythology, as well as a description of the world known to him. His younger critic and improver was *Herodotus: the urge to correct and improve on a predecessor is one of the main dynamics of Greek historiography. But the prose of Hecataeus was not Herodotus' only stimulus: Herodotus' nine-book work may owe at least as much to poets who (unlike Homer) did treat historical events in verse: it is now known that *Simonides handled the Persian War in detail and compared it explicitly to the Trojan War.

Herodotus' repudiation of myth was less explicit and famous than that of *Thucydides (2), but equally or (because earlier) more important: Herodotus restricts himself to historical time and to information he can check. How far he did check that information has been controversial since antiquity, but the sceptical case has not been made out. On the contrary, Herodotus' work shows many authentic traces of the oral tradition (see ORALITY) on which its author drew.

Thucydides knew and reacted against Herodotus' work, and there are obvious differences, above all a more linear narrative which concerns itself more narrowly with war and politics, oligarchic and democratic, and hence with men; and less attention is paid to the influence of religion on Greek affairs. But there are similarities too; thus Homeric influence is detectable in detail not just on Herodotus but on Thucydides also, who has a rhetoric of his own and should not be crudely opposed to Herodotus as *literacy is opposed to *orality: Thucydides' famous preface declares his work to be *not so much* a prize composition (a word which hints at the displays of the *sophists) as a possession for ever. By including (i.e. inventing) speeches at all, both historians were copying Homer, and Thucydides' very difficult speeches resemble Homer's in that their style is different from the narrative.

Local historians studied the great states of mainland Greece, producing above all the *Atthides* or histories of Athens (see ATTHIS). The first Atthidographer was, however, not an Athenian, *Hellanicus of *Mytilene. But the great 4th- and 3rd-cent. Atthidographers, *Androtion and *Philochorus, were Athenians who used their literary works to express definite political viewpoints; theirs was not directionless antiquarianism.

The exiled Athenian *Xenophon is preoccupied in his *Hellenica* with *Peloponnese, but his perspective is too wide for this work to be called local history. He takes his chronological starting-point and some other obvious external features from Thucydides, but his religious values and his use of the illuminating digression are more reminiscent of Herodotus. His *Anabasis* is a snapshot of Persian Anatolia which reveals his gifts as a social historian and is a prime source for modern students of religion and warfare.

Thucydides never ceased to have influence even in the 4th cent. when to find him cited by name is rare, though another and more hardheaded continuator of Thucydides than Xenophon, the *Oxyrhynchus historian, does mention him. Thucydides' remarks on speeches were discussed by Callisthenes, whose *Hellenica* faintly transmits an important alternative tradition to that of Xenophon. 'Faintly', because Callisthenes resembles other big names of 4thcent. Greek historiography in that he survives only in fragments or quotations. The same is true of *Ephorus, whose universal history drew on Thucydides for the 5th cent., then on the Oxyrhynchus historian (late 5th and early 4th), then on Callisthenes. But Ephorus also comes down to us mediated by *Diodorus (3) Siculus. The sources of Diodorus' Persian material for the 4th cent. are disputed, even more so his Sicilian material.

Another Thucydidean continuator and partial imitator (he echoes the Thucydidean Funeral Speech) was *Theopompus, who wrote about *Philip II of Macedon in a way which may owe something to Thucydides' fascination with the individual *Alcibiades. But the great individual of the age was the new Achilles, *Alexander (2) the Great, whose 'Deeds' reported by Callisthenes, by *Cleitarchus, and by *Ptolemy (1) I and *Aristobulus (1), take us back to Homer—where this survey began.

historiography, Roman Presentation of the Roman past was firmly rooted in the Roman present. Historians proclaimed a desire to help and inspire contemporary readers in their public life, and the past was often moulded to provide antecedents for contemporary events or rephrased in contemporary terms, sometimes for tendentious reasons, sometimes just to make the story more excitingly familiar. Roman writers were also more often public men than their Greek counterparts (e.g. *Porcius Cato, *Sallust, *Asinius Pollio, *Tacitus), and their contemporary narrative told of events in which they had played a part: the result was an emphasis on this recent history, which usually comprised the bulk even of those works which covered Rome's history from its foundation (*ab urbe conditā*).

Still, historiography was not simply a masked version of the memoir. It aspired to tell the story of the Roman state, not just of an individual's experiences. At first this usually involved an outline of Rome's history from its beginnings, with special emphasis on the inspiring foundation stories. The result was an hourglass structure, with most space given to the beginnings and the present, and a sketchier account of the period in between: that is already visible in *Fabius Pictor, traditionally the earliest Roman historian, and survives in most of his *ab urbe condita* successors (including *Ennius, who did much to shape the Roman view of history). Another aspect, as *Cicero ruefully observed, was the evocation of traditional Roman annals. Writers may only rarely have consulted the *annales maximi* themselves, but the texture of such material—bare lists of omens, magistrates, triumphs, etc.—was still familiar. The annalistic structure, organizing material in a year-by-year fashion, also became regular.

Sallust's *War with Catiline* and *War with Jugurtha* abandoned annalistic form and developed the monograph, using these two episodes to illustrate themes of wider significance, esp. that of moral decline. The analysis is schematic, but is carried through with concentration and structural deftness; and Sallust moulded an appropriate style, concise, epigrammatic, rugged, and abrupt. Meanwhile *Caesar had written a different sort of monograph in his commentaries; their form (see COMMENTARII) leaves them outside the main stream. Asinius Pollio wrote of the Civil War (between Caesar and *Pompey) and its antecedents, beginning with 60 BC. His incisive and independent analysis influenced the later Greek versions of *Appian and *Plutarch.

Pollio was less influential in Rome itself, largely because *Livy's 142-book *ab urbe condita* came to dominate the field. A great Roman history had been written at last. Livy offered something new, with a more even treatment of past and present: the great bulk of his history was pre-contemporary, partly, as he explains in the preface, because decline was relatively recent,

and the best ethical examples were to be found in the earlier centuries. His moralizing is, however, more than Roman bias; it is also a form of explanation, isolating the strengths which carried Rome to its success, and might yet prove her salvation. The preface suggests that his contemporary books may have projected a less rosy view of Rome's morality, with degeneration explaining the less happy developments of the last century.

Livy's bulky eminence deterred rivals. History too changed, and the early Principate shows writers adjusting to a new world where the achievements of the Roman people, with the annual rhythm of changing magistracies, no longer captured the central themes of imperial reality. *Velleius Paterculus devoted increasingly much of his second book to three leading men—Caesar, *Augustus, and *Tiberius—and treated his material with rhetorical exuberance. His enthusiasm for the new world contrasted with *Cremutius Cordus' nostalgia for the old, and Cremutius paid with his life; *Seneca the Elder dealt more safely with the transition from republic to Principate.

Tacitus was in many ways highly traditional. He kept the annalistic form; he chose relatively recent events; he wrote of senate and generals, not just emperors and courts. Yet the old forms are at odds with their content, so often pointing the contrast with the republic. The annual rhythms are overridden by the impact of emperors and their changing characters; further themes cut across the years and reigns—the power of advisers and the great ladies of the court, the regrettable necessity of one-man rule in a world unfit to rule itself, the inert senators who exchange hypocrisies with their prince. Brilliant rhetorical sharpness and devastating analysis serve each other well. Livy, at least in his surviving books, was the historian of a romanticized past; Tacitus exposed dispiriting reality.

Tacitus defied imitation as much as did Livy. Imperial historiography was always in danger of collapsing into imperial biography; that had been clear since Velleius, and from the 2nd cent. AD biography dominated the field (see BIOGRAPHY, ROMAN). The classical historians stimulated *epitomes or at most rhetorical reformulation; they were not imitated until the last flowering of the genre with *Ammianus Marcellinus, who finally addressed a great theme, and was equal to the task.

Homer The ancient world attributed the two *epics, the *Iliad* and the *Odyssey*, the earliest and greatest works of Greek literature, to the poet Homer. Most scholars now see each epic as the work of one author. Whether both epics are the work of the same author is less certain. There is general agreement to date the poems between 750 and 650 BC, with the *Iliad* the earlier. *Chios and Smyrna have the strongest claims to have been Homer's birthplace.

2. The *Iliad* (i.e. the poem about Ilios or Troy) is the longer of the two by a third, consisting of over 15,600 lines, divided into 24 books. There is broad agreement that we have the poem virtually as it was composed, with the exception of bk. 10, where the evidence for later addition is strong. For the rest, an individual intelligence is shown by the theme of the anger of *Achilles, begun in the quarrel with *Agamemnon in 1, kept before us in the Embassy of 9, transferred from Agamemnon to *Hector in 18, and resolved in the consolation of *Priam, Hector's father, in 24; also by the tight time-scale of the epic, for, in place of a historical treatment of the Trojan War (see TROY), the *Iliad*, from bk. 2 to 22, records merely four days of fighting from the tenth year, separated by two days of truce. Even the beginning and end add only a few weeks to the total.

Thus the action is concentrated, but the composition subtly expands to include the whole war, with echoes from the beginning in bks. 2 to 4, and the final books repeatedly looking ahead to the death of Achilles and the fall of Troy. The centre is occupied by a single day of battle between 11 and 18, with the Trojans temporarily superior, Greek leaders wounded, their strongest and most mobile fighter (Achilles) disaffected, only Ajax (see AIAS (1)) and some warriors of the second rank holding the defence. The turning-point is in 16, when Patroclus, acting on a suggestion from *Nestor in 11, persuades Achilles to let him go to the rescue of their comrades, and thus starts the sequence that leads to his own death (16), Achilles' return (18), Hector's death (22), and the conclusion of the epic (24).

3. High among the qualities of the *Iliad* is a vast humanity, which justifies comparison with Shakespeare. The poet understands human behaviour and reactions. There are numerous well-differentiated portraits of leading figures, introduced on the Greek side in the first four books, whose successes in action reinforce their heroic status, and whose personal feelings and relationships are expressed in the frequent speeches. Figures of the second rank support the leaders; and a large number of minor characters, who appear only to be killed, add a sense of the pathos and waste of war, through background

details, esp. reference to families at home. The Trojans have their leaders too, but their efforts are essentially defensive, and the desperate situation of their city, and the threat to the women and children, contrast with the more straightforward heroics of the Greeks. Three women of Troy, *Hecuba, *Andromache, and *Helen, appear at key moments in bks. 6 and 24, the first two also in 22.

There is also what Pope called 'invention', a constant brilliance of imagination infusing the reports of action, speeches of the characters, and descriptions of the natural world. The language has a kind of perfection, due to a combination of phrases worn smooth by traditional use and the taste and judgement of the poet; and features which had been technical aids to the oral bard seem to have assumed the form of art in the *Iliad*—the use of formulae and repeated story patterns, ring-composition in the construction of speeches, the pictorial effects of extended similes.

4. The *Odyssey*, c.12,000 lines long, was probably composed in its present form in imitation of the already existing *Iliad*. Its 24 books show exact construction. Four books set the scene in *Ithaca ten years after the end of the war, and send Odysseus' son *Telemachus to two of the most distinguished survivors, *Nestor at *Pylos and *Menelaus at *Sparta, in search of news of his father. The next four show *Odysseus himself released after seven years from the island of Calypso and reaching the land of the Phaeacians, fertile Scheria, a half-way house between the fairy-tale world of his adventures and the real world of Ithaca which awaits him. There, in 9 to 12, he recounts his adventures to the Phaeacians. That completes the first half; the second is devoted to Odysseus' return home, the dangers he faces, and his eventual slaughter of the suitors of his wife *Penelope. In bk. 15, the two strands of the first half are brought together, when Telemachus returns from Sparta and joins his father.

For reasons difficult to guess, the quality of composition fades at the end, from 23. 296, which two Alexandrian scholars confusingly describe as the 'end' of the *Odyssey*. However, at least two parts of the 'continuation' (i.e. what follows 23. 296) are indispensable for the completion of the story—the recognition of Odysseus by his old father Laertes, and the avoidance of a blood feud with the relatives of the dead suitors.

5. The *Odyssey* is a romance, enjoyable at a more superficial level than the heroic/tragic

Iliad. We can take sides, for the good people are on one side, the bad on the other. Even the massacre of the suitors and the vengeance on the servants who had supported them are acceptable in a story of this kind. The poem depends very much more than the *Iliad* on a single character; and Odysseus has become a seminal figure in European literature, with eternal human qualities of resolution, intellectual curiosity, and love of home. Apart from bks. 9 to 12, the settings are domestic, Ithaca, Pylos, Sparta, and Scheria. So the gentler qualities of politeness, sensitivity, and tact come into play, as in the delicate interchanges between Odysseus and Nausicaa (the princess on Scheria) and her parents. On the other hand, the boorish behaviour of the suitors shows a break-down of the social order.

For many readers the adventures are the high point. The Lotus-eaters, the Cyclops (see CYCLOPES), king of the winds, cannibal giants, witch *Circe, *Sirens, Scylla, and Charybdis are part of the *folk-tale element in western consciousness. They are prefaced by a piratical attack on a people in *Thrace, and concluded on the island of the Sun, an episode which results in the elimination of Odysseus' surviving companions, leaving him to face the return home alone. In the middle, in bk. 11, comes the visit to the Underworld, where he sees figures from the past and receives a prophecy of the future.

The combination of precision of observation and descriptive imagination is on a par with the *Iliad*; examples are Odysseus in the Cyclops' cave, Odysseus in his own house among the suitors of his wife, the recognition by his old dog Argos. One gets the impression, however, more strongly with the *Odyssey* than the *Iliad*, that the tale has been told many times before, and some superficial inconsistencies may be the effect of variant versions (e.g. the abortive plans for the removal of the arms in 16).

6. The dactylic hexameter (see METRE, GREEK, 3) has a complex structure, with from twelve to seventeen syllables in the lines, and some precise metrical requirements. Milman Parry demonstrated that features of composition, notably pervasive repetition in the phraseology, derive from the practice of illiterate oral bards, who would learn the traditional phrases (formulae) in their years of apprenticeship; see ORALITY. This explains many aspects that worried analytical critics since the days of the Alexandrians; for repetition of a half-line, line, or sequence of lines had been taken by readers used to the practice of later poets as evidence of corruption in the text, and an adjective used inappropriately had seemed to be a fault, instead of the inevitable consequence of the use of formulae.

Of equal significance to the repetition of formulaic phrases in the composition of oral poetry is the repetitive, though flexible, use of what are called typical scenes, patterns in the story, sometimes described as 'themes'. These range from the four arming-scenes in the *Iliad*, scenes of arrival and departure, performance of sacrifices, descriptions of fighting, to the repeated abuse directed at Odysseus in the second half of the Odyssey. Such 'themes' performed a function parallel to the formulae, giving the experienced bard material for the construction of his songs in front of an audience.

It is now accepted that oral poetry theory has added to our understanding. Difference remains about whether Homer himself was an illiterate bard, or whether his position at the end of a long tradition shows a bard using the possibilities of literacy while still retaining the oral techniques. The ultimate problem of the survival of the two epics is inextricably bound up with this question. Three possibilities divide the field. Either the poet composed with the help of writing, the *alphabet having become available at just the right time; or the poems were recorded by scribes, the poet himself being illiterate; or they were memorized by a guild of public reciters (*rhapsodes) for anything up to 200 years (there being evidence for a written text in Athens in the 6th cent.).

7. The language in which the poems are composed contains a mixture of forms found in different areas of the Greek world. The historical implications of this mixture of dialects (see GREEK LANGUAGE, 3) are obscure. What is clear, however, is that the linguistic picture is consistent with that presented by oral theory. Some features are very ancient (often preserved in the formulaic phrases), some quite recent. An important conclusion is that late linguistic forms are not to be seen as post-Homeric interpolations, but more probably come from the language of the poet himself, while earlier ones had reached him through the tradition.

8. The assumed date of the Trojan war falls in the 13th cent. BC, towards the end of the *Mycenaean age; for the Mycenaean palaces on the mainland were destroyed from *c.*1200. There is thus a gap of half a millennium between the date of composition of the *Iliad* and the legendary past which is its setting. The 8th cent. is more important for the epics than the 13th: the epics reflect the society and political aspirations of

*c.*700 BC, but the history of the Mycenaean age and of the shadowy times (Dark Age) that lay between is naturally of great interest. Here archaeologist and historian combine. We have the discoveries of Schliemann at *Mycenae, and the excavations at Troy itself by Schliemann, Blegen, and Korfmann (1981–). Historical evidence from the 13th cent. has come to the surface. It is, however, unsafe to assume a close connection with Homer. For the passage of time, and a retrospective view of a heroic age, have moved the picture nearer to fiction than reality. Only fossilized memories of the Mycenaean age survive in his work. It must have been during the Dark Age that heroic poetry developed and spread, even if it originated in the Mycenaean age.

9. Hexameter poetry continued after Homer, with Hesiod and the *Homeric *Hymns, and the poems of the *Epic Cycle, which described the two legendary wars of the heroic age, those against Thebes and Troy. The Theban epics are lost, but for the Trojan we have summaries of the contents of six poems, which had been fitted round the *Iliad* and *Odyssey* to create a complete sequence from the marriage of *Peleus and *Thetis to the death of Odysseus. These cyclic epics were obviously later than the Homeric poems, and from a time when oral composition had ceased and public performance was by rhapsodes, not traditional bards. Their significance for us is that they represent the subject-matter of heroic poetry as it was before Homer; for the *Iliad* itself, being the individual creation of a poet of genius, was not typical. Thus the partially known later material can make some claim to priority over the earlier. Episodes in bks. 8 (rescue of Nestor), 17 (recovery of the body of Patroclus), 18 (mourning of Thetis), and 23 (funeral games) may echo situations connected with Achilles in the repertoire of the oral bards, which later appeared in the cyclic *Aethiopis*. If so, we get an insight into the creativity of the poet of the *Iliad*.

homicide See AREOPAGUS; LAW AND PROCEDURE, ATHENIAN and ROMAN (3).

homonoia, lit. 'oneness of mind', a political ideal first met in Greek writers of the later 5th cent. BC, signifying either (1) concord within the *polis and esp. the avoidance of *stasis or (2) the achievement of *panhellenic unity against the *barbarian (i.e. *Persia or *Macedon). See CONCORDIA.

homosexuality Greek and Roman men understood sex to be a matter of sexual penetration and phallic pleasure. The physical act of sex itself required, in their eyes, a polarization of the sexual partners into the categories of penetrator and penetrated as well as a corresponding polarization of sexual roles into 'active' and 'passive'. Those roles in turn were correlated with superordinate and subordinate social *status, with masculine and feminine styles, and (in the case of males, at least) with adulthood and adolescence. Phallic insertion was a sign of male precedence; it also expressed social domination and seniority. So Roman custom placed the sons of Roman citizens off limits to men. In Classical Athens, by contrast, free boys could be openly courted, but a set of elaborate protocols served to shield them from the shame associated with bodily penetration, thereby enabling them to gratify their male suitors without compromising their future status as adult men.

Pederasty Paiderastia is the Greek for the sexual pursuit of 'boys' by 'men' By 'boy', the ancients designated what we would call an adolescent rather than a child. Moreover, 'man' and 'boy' can refer in both Greek and Latin to the senior and junior partners in a pederastic relationship, or to those who play the respective sexual roles appropriate to each, regardless of their actual ages. Although some Athenian men may have entertained high-minded intentions towards the boys they courted, it would be hazardous to infer from their occasional efforts at self-promotion that Greek pederasty aimed chiefly at the education and moral improvement of boys instead of at adult sexual pleasure.

'Greek Love' Greek custom carefully differentiated the sexual roles assigned to men and to boys in their erotic relations with one another. Good-looking boys supposedly exerted a powerful sexual appeal that men, even when good-looking, did not. So, men were assumed to be motivated in their pursuit of boys by a passionate sexual desire (*erōs*) which the boys who were the targets of that desire did not conventionally share, whence the Greek habit of referring to the senior partner in a pederastic relationship as a *subject* of desire, or 'lover' (*erastēs*), and the junior partner as an *object* of desire, or 'beloved' (*erōmenos*). A boy who chose to 'gratify' the passion of his lover might be actuated by a variety of motives, including (at the baser end of the scale) material gain or social climbing and (at the higher end) affection, esteem, respect, and non-passionate love (*phília*), but—although a man might stimulate a boy sexually—neither sexual desire nor sexual pleasure represented an acceptable motive for a boy's compliance with the sexual demands of his lover. Even pederastic relationships characterized by mutual love and tenderness retained an irreducible element of emotional and erotic asymmetry, as is indicated by the consistent distinction which the Greeks drew in such contexts between the lover's *erōs* and the beloved's *philia*. By contrast, women were believed capable of returning their male lovers' sexual passion, and so could be spoken of as exhibiting *anterōs* ('counter-desire').

The asymmetries structuring pederastic relationships reflected the underlying division of sexual labour. Whereas a boy, lacking his lover's erotic motivation, was not expected to play what the Greeks considered an 'active' sexual role, a man was expected to do just that, either by thrusting his penis between the boy's thighs (which was considered the most respectful method, because it did not violate the boy's bodily integrity) or by inserting it into his anus. Respectable erotic relations between men and boys preserved the social fiction, to which some honourable lovers may have adhered in practice, that sexual penetration of the boy took place only between the legs (the so-called intercrural position), never in the anus or—what was even worse—in the mouth. It was not a question of what people actually did in bed (the boy was conventionally assumed to be anally receptive to his older lover) so much as how they behaved and talked when they were out of bed. Hence the story about Periander, tyrant of Ambracia, who asked his boy, 'Aren't you pregnant yet?': the boy, who had apparently raised no objection to being anally penetrated repeatedly, was sufficiently outraged by this question when it was put to him aloud—and doubtless in the presence of others—that he responded by killing the tyrant in order to recover his masculine honour.

The Greek insistence on distinguishing between the beloved's *philia* and the lover's *erōs* can be explained. Whatever a boy might do in bed, it was crucial that he not seem to be motivated by passionate sexual desire for his lover, because sexual desire for an adult man signified the desire to be penetrated, to be subordinate—to be like a woman, whose pleasure in sexual submissiveness disqualified her from assuming a position of social and political mastery. A boy who indicated that he derived any enjoyment from being anally receptive risked identifying himself as a *kinaidos*, a pathic, a catamite. The earliest attestation of female homoerotic desire

occurs in the work of a male author—namely, in the *partheneia* of *Alcman, who wrote choral odes to be performed by a cohort of unmarried girls in which individual maidens extol the beauty and allure of named favourites among their leaders and age-mates. Further expressions of homoerotic desire can be found a few decades later in the fragmentary poetry of *Sappho, who came from *Mytilene on the island of Lesbos.

Deviance and Toleration Ancient sources assume that most free adult males are at least capable of being sexually attracted by both good-looking boys and good-looking women; such attraction was deemed normal and natural. No specifically sexual stigma attached to the act of sexual penetration of a woman, boy, foreigner, or slave by a man, although certain kinds of sexual licence incurred disfavour: e.g. the corruption of free boys, and the *adulterous pursuit of citizen women. It would not have been unexpected to ask of a man who confessed to being in love whether his object was a boy or a woman (Aristophanes, *Frogs* 56). Songs of Harmodius and *Aristogīton, which celebrated the pederastic couple who supposedly freed Athens from tyranny, functioned in the democratic period as something like the Athenian national anthem. See EDUCATION; GYMNASIARCH; LOVE AND FRIENDSHIP; SEXUALITY.

honestiōrēs (lit. 'more honoured') The Romans made a broad distinction, which was at first social but acquired in the Principate and thereafter an increasing number of legal consequences, between an upper class usually termed *honestiores* and a lower class of *humiliōrēs* (lit. 'lowlier'). No legal definition of the two classes is found, and the allocation of an individual to one or the other was probably at the discretion of the court. The legal consequences were most marked in the criminal law, *honestiores* being subject to milder penalties than *humiliores* (rarely the death penalty, never death by crucifixion or by being thrown to wild beasts; *relegation to an island in place of forced labour in the mines, etc.).

honey, the chief sweetener known to the ancients, who understood apiculture and appreciated the different honey-producing qualities of flowers and localities. Thyme honey from Hymettus in Attica was famous, both for its pale colour and sweet flavour; Corsican, harsh and bitter; Pontic, poisonous and inducing madness. Honey was used in cooking, confectionery, and as a preservative. It was used in medicines, e.g. for coughs, ulcers, and intestinal parasites. It had an important role in religion, cult, and mythology. Its religious associations derive from the idea that it was a 'heavenly dew', which fell on to flowers from the upper air for bees to gather. Acc. to poets, it dripped from trees in the *golden age. It was used in *libations to the dead, in rites for *Persephone and *Hades, for *Hestia, and in the cult of *Mithras.

honour See PHILOTIMIA.

hoplites, Greek heavy infantry. Equipment included bronze helmet, corslet, originally of bronze, but later of leather or linen, and bronze greaves; sometimes extras such as arm-guards. Most important was a circular shield of wood or stiffened leather, faced with bronze, about 80 cm. (*c*.30 in.) in diameter, held by inserting the left arm through a central band, and gripping a cord or strap at the rim. Offensive weapons were a thrusting-spear, 2.5–3 m. (8–10 ft.) long, with iron point and butt, and short iron swords, sometimes straight, sometimes curved. The equipment was expensive and since hoplites were normally expected to provide their own, they had to be quite rich.

They deployed for battle shoulder to shoulder, usually eight or more deep, each man relying on his right neighbour's shield for the protection of his right side, since the shield-grip meant that half the shield projected to the left. At a signal the *phalanx advanced at the double or at a walk, and when within spear-thrust, the front ranks stabbed at their opponents, usually overarm. But with the rear ranks possibly literally pushing against the backs of those in front, sooner or later the opposing lines crashed together and the 'shoving' began. When one or other side gave way, pursuit was not carried far, since once ranks broke, hoplites became much more vulnerable. Though the hoplite phalanx was unwieldy, it was formidable when driving forward, as the Persians found at the battles of *Marathon and *Plataea. It could be defeated by other troops if attacked in flank or rear, or if caught in broken terrain.

Horace (Quintus Horātius Flaccus) (65–8 BC). Son of a *freedman with a modest landholding in Venusia. As a public auctioneer, his father earned enough to send him to Rome and then Athens for an education matching that of a typical upper-class Roman of the time. This ambitious education was intended to help Horace rise in society, and at first the plan met with success. While in Athens, Horace joined the army of *Brutus as a *tribunus militum, a post usually held by *equestrians. But these high hopes were brought to nothing by the fall of Brutus and the loss of the family's property. Horace counted himself lucky to be able to return to Italy, unlike many of his comrades-in-arms, and to obtain the position of scriba quaestorius (see APPARITORES). It was then that he wrote his first poems, which brought him into contact with *Virgil and *Varius Rufus. They recommended him to *Maecenas, then gathering around him a circle of writers; and when Maecenas accepted him into this circle in 38 BC and later gave him a *Sabine farm, his financial position was secure. His property put him in the higher reaches of the equestrian census, and he now had the leisure to devote himself to poetry. He was on friendly terms with many leading Romans. In his later years *Augustus also sought to be on close terms, as several letters written in a warm and candid tone attest. But Horace knew how to preserve his personal freedom. Augustus offered him an influential post on his personal staff, but Horace declined it, and he showed a similar independence towards Maecenas.

Works

Epodes The *Epodes* or *Iambi* form a slender book of 17 poems. The collection as a whole seems to have been published *c*.30 BC. Horace's formal model was *Archilochus, the founder of *iambus*. He thus introduced into Rome not only the metrical form of early Greek iambus, but also some of the matter. See IAMBIC POETRY, GREEK and LATIN. Horace's adoption of this early form did not represent a rejection of the Callimachean principle (see CALLIMACHUS (2)) that every detail of a poem should be artistically controlled and contribute to the total effect. The central theme of iambic poetry was traditionally *invective, and Horace may have taken up the genre in his affliction after the battle of *Philippi as a way of preserving his self-respect in hard times. But only some of the *Epodes* are invectives, and even in these the targets are either anonymous or obscure.

Satires Contemporaneously with the *Epodes*, Horace composed his two books of *hexameter *satires. He also calls them Sermōnēs, 'conversations'. Horace's model is *Lucilius (1), but he represents himself as determined to write with greater care and attention to form, and thus, again, as a follower of Callimachus. Another difference from Lucilius is that Horace's satires are less aggressive. While the pugnacious poet of the 2nd cent. took sides in the political struggles of his time, Horace chooses a purely private set of themes. In *Satires* 1. 4 and 2. 1 he represents personal abuse as a typical element in satire, but declares that he himself does not attack any contemporary public figures. When he names people as possessed of particular vices, the names clearly represent types rather than individual targets. The criticism of vice occurs less for its own sake than to suggest a correct way of life through an apprehension of error. In these passages Horace comes close to the doctrines and argument-forms of popular philosophy (so-called *diatribe). His style is 'to tell the truth through laughter' and not only to show others the way but also to work at improving himself and making himself more acceptable to his fellow human beings. The autobiographical aspect of many satires is another Lucilian element. Like Lucilius, he makes his own life a subject for his poetry.

Odes (Carmina) After the publication of the *Epodes* and *Satires*, Horace turned to lyric poetry. The earliest datable reference is in *Odes* 1. 37, which celebrates Augustus' defeat of *Cleopatra VII at *Actium. The first three books of the *Odes*, 88 poems in all, seem to have been published as a collection in 23 BC. The concluding poem looks back on the work as a completed unit, and does not envisage a sequel. After the composition, at Augustus' bidding, of the *Carmen saeculārĕ* in 17, however, a fourth book of fifteen poems was added, which also seems to have been inspired by Augustus.

Horace declares that his main literary model in the *Odes* was the early Greek *lyric poetry from *Lesbos, esp. that of *Alcaeus. He is indebted to this model for the metrical form of the *Odes*, but he also begins a series of poems with an almost literal translation of lines by Alcaeus (the so-called 'mottoes'), which serve as a springboard for his own developments. He also takes over motifs from other early lyric poets, such as *Sappho, *Anacreon, and *Pindar. His view of this early poetry, however, is that of a poet trained in the contemporary Hellenistic style: the *Odes* are full of the dense and sophisticated allusivity that reflected the complex literary world of Augustan Rome. He also takes over some themes from Hellenistic poetry, esp. from Greek epigram. See HELLENISTIC POETRY AT ROME.

Although the major themes of the *Odes* are the usual ones of ancient poetry, Horace's treatment of them is different. The hymns to the gods, for instance, are not meant for cult performance but meet the world of Greek divinity more with aesthetic pleasure than in an act of pious worship. His love poetry takes a different line from that of his contemporaries. While Catullus and the elegists (see ELEGIAC POETRY, LATIN) had tended to make a single beloved the focus of their life and poetry, Horace's poems are concerned with a variety of women (and boys; see HOMOSEXUALITY). Although passionate obsession is not entirely alien to the *Odes*, typically Horace tries to free himself from extreme emotion and move himself and his beloved towards a calm and cheerful enjoyment of the moment. The sympotic poetry (see SYMPOSIUM) diverges distinctively from that of Alcaeus. Horace does not set out to drown his sorrows, but to give himself and his friends at the drinking-party (see CONVIVIUM) a brief moment of freedom from care, in poems which, as earlier in the *Satires*, lead often to reflection on the right way to live. Friendship is an important theme throughout the *Odes*: they are hardly ever soliloquies, but poems addressed to a friend offering help and advice. The political themes begun in the *Epodes* are taken further. Although Horace declines to celebrate Augustus or Agrippa in the traditional Roman form of panegyric epic, from the time of the poem celebrating the defeat of Cleopatra on he offers explicit praise of the new ruler as one who had brought peace and through his policies maintained it. He also declares his support for the attempt by Augustus to restore 'ancient Roman' customs and morality. In the later *Ode* 3. 14, in the *Carmen saeculare*, and in the poems of bk. 4, the panegyric of the Augustan epoch comes even more to the fore, and it is celebrated as an epoch of peace, a second *golden age.

Horace's *Odes* differ in one essential respect from the norms of modern, esp. post-Romantic, lyric poetry. Modern lyric strives as far as possible for a unity of atmosphere within one poem, but this is found in Horace only in his shortest poems. More commonly within a single poem there are significant movements and changes in content, expression, and stylistic level. Poems written in high style with important content often conclude with a personal and apparently insignificant final turn.

Epistles book 1 After the publication of the *Odes*, Horace returned to hexameter poetry and the conversational style of his earlier *Sermones*, but this time in the form of letters addressed to a variety of recipients, which gave Horace a concrete starting-point and a unified speech-situation. In the programmatic *Epistle* 1. 1 Horace grounds his choice of the new form in his advancing old age: philosophical reflection and a concentration on questions of how to live now suit him better than the usual themes of lyric. The philosophical meditation that this declaration places at the centre of his work is an essential theme of the book, but not its only concern. Horace writes also more generally of the circumstances of his own life, and offers his friends various forms of counsel. Many elements recall the *Satires*, but the choice of the letter-form brings a more unified tone to the varied content. The last epistle (20) is an address to the book itself, portrayed as a young slave eager to be free of its master.

Epistles book 2, *Ars poetica* Poetry itself is the central theme of the two long poems in *Epistles* bk. 2 (2. 1. to Augustus and 2. 2 to Florus), and the *Ars poëtica*. In the letter to Augustus, Horace complains that the taste of the contemporary public turns more to the cheap theatrical effects of earlier Latin writers than the authors of his own generation. He accuses the older writers of being careless and deficient in taste. In his letter to his friend Florus Horace explains why he no longer writes poetry but has turned to philosophy, and offers a candid picture of the difficulties of a poet's life at Rome. The *Ars poetica* begins with the proposition that every poem must be a unified whole, and after a few lines on the necessary ordering of material turns to poetic language and the correspondingly appropriate style. In the final section the reader is offered general rules for the poet's craft. This varied subject-matter is given unity by the recurring insistence on such values as appropriateness, clarity, and artistic composition. Horace's teaching lies in the tradition of *Aristotle's school, the *Peripatetic. Horace's own contribution lies in his poetic transformation of that tradition through images and vignettes.

Hōrae, goddesses of the seasons. *Hesiod makes them daughters of *Zeus and of *Themis ('Divine Law') and names them *Eunomia ('Good Order'), *Dike ('Justice'), and Eirēnē ('Peace'). They guard the gates of *Olympus, and are regularly linked with the birth, upbringing, and marriages of gods and heroes; common associates are the Graces or *Charites, *Demeter 'bringer of the Seasons', and *Aphrodite. In a grand procession of *Ptolemy (1) II Philadelphus in the 3rd

cent. BC marched four Horae, each bearing her appropriate fruits. Such differentiated 'season Horae' were a favourite theme of Graeco-Roman art thenceforth.

horse- and chariot-races In the funeral games for Patroclus the chariot-race is the premier event (Homer *Iliad* 23). The heroes drive two-horse chariots normally used in battle over an improvised cross-country course, round a distant mark and home again. Similar funeral games for other heroes are recorded. But, despite the story of the race by which *Pelops won his bride, equestrian events were not the oldest in the historic Olympia festival (see OLYMPIC GAMES). *Pausanias (3) records the introduction of four-horse chariots in the 25th Olympiad (680 BC); of ridden horses in the 33rd; and of other equestrian events at irregular intervals thereafter. Regular hippodromes were now used. No material remains survive; but literary evidence shows that competitors raced to a marker *c.*550 m. (*c.*600 yds.) distant, round which they made a 180° left-hand turn before galloping back to round another marker. The number of laps varied (twelve for the four-horse chariots). Over 40 teams might take part, and the sport was dangerous, though elaborate arrangements (at least at Olympia) were made to ensure a fair start. Owners, not drivers or riders, received the glory. Equestrian events were supported by tyrants, and commemorated by poets.

At Rome, the chariots that drew vast crowds to the Circus Maximus (see CIRCUS) and its provincial equivalents were managed by factions, whose distinguishing colours—white, red, blue, and green—were thought by *Tertullian to represent the seasons. It is uncertain when the factions were formed. Blue and green eventually predominated. Horses (supplied by large stud-farms) and drivers became famous, many names being preserved in inscriptions, including leaden *curse-tablets. Races resembled the Greek ones but with no more than twelve entries. A raised barrier connected the turning-points. For emperors the races provided occasions for public display; for men-about-town opportunities to impress girlfriends.

horses The Homeric epics and Geometric art (see POTTERY, GREEK, 2) suggest that in Greece chariots. were used until the 8th cent. BC as transports for armoured men who fought on foot; thereafter Greek and Roman literature and art show the widespread use of ridden horses for warfare, racing, and hunting.

Well-to-do Romans, including women, also travelled on horseback. Mules were used to plough, and to pull carts; but both Greeks and Romans used horses mainly for riding and light draught, including under the empire not only chariot-racing but the *postal service and the pleasure-vehicles of courtesans. The unsuitability of ancient harness to equines has been exaggerated. The horse remained a 'status symbol' long after cavalry service ceased to be the privilege of the rich (see HIPPEIS); and the broken-down horse in the mill or carrying manure was pitied or despised as an example of fallen pride. Many different breeds are named in ancient literature, from the Nisaeans of Media to the smooth-gaited pacing horses of Spain. Breeding was generally unscientific, chosen stallions being admitted to herds of free-ranging mares. Descriptions of ancient veterinary practice are found in the Roman *agricultural writers. Of more general interest is *Xenophon's *On Horsemanship*. See HORSE- AND CHARIOT-RACES.

Hortensius, Quintus, a plebeian who was appointed *dictator to reconcile the orders after a debt crisis had provoked the final secession of the *plebs to the Janiculum c.287 BC. He carried a *lex Hortensia* by which plebiscites (see PLEBISCITUM) were to be binding on the whole people, and thus became indistinguishable from laws (see LEX). The measure gave the plebeian assembly the same unfettered legislative competence as the other assemblies (see COMITIA), and marked a decisive stage in the struggle of the orders.

Hortensius Hortalus, Quintus (b. 114 BC), was one of the foremost Roman orators. He served in the *Social War, became prominent during *Sulla's absence from Rome, joined him in time, and dominated the courts in 70, using a florid 'Asianic' style, and resorting to shameless bribery. Defeated by *Cicero in the *Verres case, despite his best efforts at legal trickery and intimidation, he was consul 69 and remained an eminent speaker and defender of the *optimates. He opposed *Pompey's special commands, but joined Cicero in several *causes célèbres*, with Cicero always speaking last. Like his friend *Licinius Lucullus, he gradually withdrew from politics into cultivated luxury. (Cicero puts him among the aristocrats solely concerned about their fishponds; see FISHING.) He died in 49. Cicero always distrusted him, but incurred a heavy moral obligation when Hortensius sponsored him for the augurate (see AUGURS). After Hortensius' death he amply repaid it in his rhetorical and philosophical works, esp. in *Brutus* and even more in *Hortensius*, where, with Cicero, he is the chief speaker.

Hostilius, Tullus, the sixth king of Rome (see REX).

household

Greek   The household (*oîkos*) was the fundamental social, political and economic unit of ancient Greece. At one level it was a co-resident group, many (though not all) of whose members were kin or affines (related by marriage). Patrilateral kinship was probably more common than matrilateral in household settings, since marriage was patrilocal, i.e. women tended to move into their husband's house and household on marriage. Though a nuclear family (parents and children) might form the household's core, there is much evidence for the regular appearance of stem families (nuclear family plus a grandparent) and various kinds of extended family, esp. incorporating unmarried female relatives (aunts, sisters, nieces, cousins, etc.). The senior man in the household usually took control of 'official' relations with the outside world and acted as the head of household (*kŷrios*). None the less, women never relinquished membership of the household into which they were born and might move back into it if the marriage were dissolved. Women, then, usually lived out their lives in two households, men in only one.

Households also included non-kin members, of lower, non-citizen status. Most notable were slaves, who belonged to the well-off households mentioned in the sources; see SLAVERY. But other dependants such as freedmen or freedwomen might also be present. Lodgers, might also have been considered household members during their sojourn. Households, esp. rich ones, must often have been quite large. Given the modesty of even rich Greek *houses (e.g. at 4th-cent. BC *Olynthus the size-range of houses was 150–300 m.²: 1,600–3,200 ft.²), living conditions must have been crowded by modern standards. See HOUSES, GREEK.

The concept of the household rose above its physical reality and covered not only people but property, land, and animals as well. At this level the households of the élite often expanded in scope beyond the co-resident unit to include other estates, farms, and businesses. The household formed the most significant structure of economic management in ancient Greece. (See ECONOMY, GREEK.) Transmission of property to the succeeding households of the next generation was via partible inheritance (see IN-HERITANCE, *Greek*). Because the household conceptually constituted the limits of trust and loyalty, businesses and long-term financial arrangements rarely expanded beyond it.

Roman 'Household' is the usual English translation of Latin *familia*, a term with several senses: the household property; the persons comprising a household (e.g. patron and freedman); a body of persons united by a common legal tie such as all kin subject to a living *paterfamilias*; a body of slaves; and all blood descendants of an original family founder. So, study of the Roman household can range from archaeological investigation of the structures in which Romans lived (see HOUSES, ITALIAN) to just household slaves. But it is now primarily associated with the field of family history, the principal constituents of which are the composition, organization and evolution of the family through its life-course. Understood ideally to comprise a married couple, their children, the house in which they lived, and their common property (which could include human property), the household in *Cicero's view was the foundation of society. The special case of Roman *Egypt apart, it is about the household at the social level Cicero represents that most is known.

The orientation of the household was strictly patriarchal, with its head wielding enormous power (*patria potestas*) over his dependants, including the power of life and death over his children and slaves. In reality the implicit harshness of the regime towards adult children who could not become legally independent and own property until their fathers died, was probably tempered by demographic factors that released many from its constricting effects as they reached their early and mature adult years. The role of the *māterfamiliās*, stereotypically conceived, was subordinate and, beyond reproduction in marriage, largely confined to matters of domestic management in a context where ideas of economic self-sufficiency were all-important (see MOTHERHOOD). It does not follow, however, that Roman wives and mothers were devoid of all social and economic power, as the example of Cicero's wife Terentia indicates. The ideal was propagated that marriage (see MARRIAGE LAW) was a union for life, but because of early spousal death and divorce both men and women might expect a succession of marriages through their adult lives. This often produced family and household reconstitution, with principals commonly finding themselves aligned in complex familial arrangements, involving both kin and non-kin members. So, the composition of the Roman household was far from simple, its membership constantly in flux, and, esp. because of the presence of servants (to whom the day-to-day care of children was often entrusted), not confined to immediate nuclear attachments.

houses, Greek Private houses of the Classical and Hellenistic periods were much the same throughout the Greek world. Most rooms opened onto one or more sides of a small, rectangular courtyard, reached via a short passage leading from the front door. Windows were few and small, and living areas were not visible from the street. An upper storey, reached by a ladder or, more rarely, a built stairway, was common, but is often hard to detect. Construction was in mud-brick on stone footings. Interior walls were plastered and often painted simply, mostly in red and white. Floors were of beaten earth. In most houses, on the ground floor, one or two rooms with heavier floors and provisions for bathing, heating water, and cooking can be identified, but cooking could take place on simple hearths or portable braziers in any room or in the courtyard. The concept of the hearth and its goddess, *Hestia, symbolized the identity and cohesion of the *household, but formal, fixed hearths were not common. Roofs were either pitched and covered with *terracotta tiles or flat, depending on regional climate and traditions.

Often a more elaborately decorated room with a distinctive floor-plan served to receive guests, all male (the *andrōn*, 'men's room'). The floor, in cement, was raised slightly around all four sides for the placing of dining-couches, usually five, seven, or eleven in number, which resulted in the room's doorway being off-centre (see DINING-ROOMS; SYMPOSIUM). The lower rectangle in the middle of the room was sometimes decorated with pebble *mosaics. The *andron* has been found in modest as well as large houses, in country as well as town, all over Greece.

Women's quarters are mentioned in literary sources but cannot be securely identified in the surviving architecture. Certain rooms or areas of the house were assigned primarily to women. The house as a whole may have been regarded as women's domain (see WOMEN), apart from the *andron* and wherever unmarried men, slave or free, slept. No distinct quarters for slaves are distinguishable architecturally, although female slaves might be separated by a locked door from the male.

The household was an economic as well as social unit. Much of the processing and storage of the products of the family's land took place in the house. Stone parts of oil-presses have been found in the houses of towns inhabited mostly by farmers. Wells, cisterns for rainwater, and pits for collecting waste for manure are found in courtyards; see WATER SUPPLY. If a craft was practised, that too took place in the house; separate workshops are rare. One room, opening onto the street, was sometimes separated to serve as a shop, not necessarily occupied by the residents of the house.

The private house was similarly designed in city, village, and countryside. In the last the courtyard might be larger to accommodate animals and equipment and commonly a tower of two or three storeys, round or square, and more heavily built than the rest, was entered from the courtyard. Such towers, often the only conspicuous remains of houses in the countryside, have been identified in towns as well. They appear to have been used primarily for the safe keeping of goods and persons, slave and free, esp. in more isolated locations.

The development of the Greek house is inseparable from that of the settlement. Houses were contiguous, sharing party-walls. The privacy of each adjacent unit and the concomitant independence of each *oîkos* were vital. When new settlements were established, streets were laid out orthogonally (see URBANISM); initially house plots were probably of uniform size, though in the course of time changes occurred. The modesty of the Classical houses of all classes is striking. Houses with two courtyards are first found in *Eretria in the 4th cent. BC and in Hellenistic towns. Courtyards may have a peristyle on four sides. The *palaces of monarchs and tyrants (see TYRANNY) were elaborations of the larger private houses.

houses, Italian By the 6th cent. BC the Roman élite was living along the *via Sacra, beside the Forum, in a series of sizeable, roughly equal house-plots, which shaped the topography of the area until the great fire of AD 64. The Roman aristocracy thus identified itself with a historic home in the city centre.

The 3rd–2nd-cent. BC houses of *Pompeii show a regular plan and a systematic division of urban space, but also a wide variety of size and levels of wealth, the House of the Faun being outstanding by the standards of anywhere

in the Mediterranean world. In these houses it is quite easy to identify the features which *Vitruvius, our principal literary source, regarded as canonical. The traditional houses of the centre of Rome seem also to have adhered to the basic pattern of atrium (see below) with rooms round it; where more space was available, this traditional arrangement could be combined with peristyles and gardens, offering scope for planned suites of rooms, and providing more flexible spaces for living, entertaining, politics, and the cultural activities which were integral to upper-class life. Luxury in domestic appointments was thought to have taken off dramatically in the 1st cent. BC.

The salient feature of this traditional plan was the atrium—a rectangular space open to the sky at the centre, columned in the more elaborate forms, with wide covered spaces on each of the four sides, one of which gave onto the outside world through a vestibule. Originally the site of the family hearth, whose smoke caused the blackening (*āter*) which gave the place its name, this was also the abode of the household deities, and housed the copies of the funerary masks which were the sign of the family's continuity and identity (see IMAGINES; LARES). The adjacent rooms were flexible in their use. A *trīclīnium* for convivial dining was an early and frequent adjunct, but *meals could be taken in various rooms, if available, according to season and weather (see CONVIVIUM; DINING-ROOMS).

*Augustus' house on the *Palatine, reached by passing along the street of venerable aristocratic addresses (the houses had been rebuilt many times) from the Forum, consisted of an amalgamation of several houses of the traditional sort, so that he could enjoy the advantages of considerable space while claiming moderation in his domestic circumstances. The building of very large complexes nearby under *Gaius (1) (e.g. the platform of the 'Domus Tiberiana', which supported a country villa in the heart of Rome) and *Nero, whose Golden House (*Domus Aurea) spread over a large section of the city centre, took a different line, but *Domitian's enormous palace, overpowering and monarchic though it was, is recognizably an ancient house on a hugely inflated scale (see PALACES).

For most inhabitants of the Roman city, however, this spacious life was impossible; it was normal to live in someone else's property, and in much less space. The rich had long accommodated slaves, dependants, and visitors around the principal spaces of their houses—on the street frontages, from which the principal rooms were averted, on upper floors, or even under the floors of the main premises, in warrens of small rooms. Parts of the house accessible from outside could be let profitably for accommodation or for trade. Purpose-built rental accommodation, in the form of whole blocks in the city or its environs, goes back to the middle republic. The demand for such premises grew so fast that those who could afford to build them saw a valuable source of rental income, and a style of architecture developed which had this type of dwelling-space in mind. By the imperial period, multi-storey tenement blocks, *insulae* ('islands'), housed almost all the population of Rome and other big cities. Not all this accommodation was poor; some was sited in attractive areas, some apartments were large enough, those on the lower floors were not inconvenient, and many people of some status could afford no better. The introduction of kiln-fired brick almost certainly made these developments safer and healthier than had been the case in the republic (see BUILDING MATERIALS, ROMAN). Estimates of the living conditions in the *insulae* we know best, those of *Ostia—where we cannot tell if we are looking at privileged or marginal housing—illustrate a more general difficulty in the study of the Roman house, that of understanding the density of occupation.

housework 'Women's work' meant weaving and the other tasks required in fabric-making: cleaning and carding wool, spinning and dyeing thread. *Xenophon, in his *Oeconomicus*, envisages a young wife whose only domestic training is in fabric-making: he suggests that she can train slaves to make fabric, supervise household supplies, equipment, and labour, and, for exercise, fold clothes and bedding and knead dough. *Columella says that the bailiff's wife on a Roman estate should supervise wool-working and preparation of meals, and should ensure that the kitchens, the shelters for animals, and esp. the sickroom are clean. But there is silence on the details of ordinary daily tasks.

hubris, intentionally dishonouring behaviour, was treated as a serious crime in Athens. The term was highly pejorative.

The best ancient discussion of *hubris* is found in *Aristotle's *Rhetoric*: his definition is that *hubris* is 'doing or saying things which bring shame on the victim, not in order to achieve anything other than what is done, but simply to get pleasure from it. For those who act in return for some

wrong do not commit *hubris*, they avenge themselves. The cause of pleasure for those committing *hubris* is that they think that by wronging others they prove themselves superior; that is why the young and the rich are hubristic, as they think themselves superior when they commit *hubris*'. This account, locating *hubris* within a framework of ideas concerned with the honour and shame of the individual, which took a central place in the value-systems of the ancient Greeks, fits neatly nearly all texts exploiting the notion, from *Homer till well after Aristotle's own time. While '*hubris*' primarily denotes gratuitous dishonouring by those who are, or think they are, superior, it can also denote the insolence of accepted 'inferiors', such as women, children, or slaves, who disobey or claim independence.

Hubris is usually the insulting use of violence: classic cases are Midias' punch on *Demosthenes' (2) face in the theatre (Demosthenes 21), and the assaults by Conon and sons on the speaker of Dem. 54, when the middle-aged Conon allegedly gloated over the body of their battered victim like a triumphant fighting-cock. Further common forms of hubristic acts are sexual assaults (*rape, seduction, or deviant practices), where emphasis is thereby placed on the dishonour inflicted on the victims or on the male householders responsible for them (see HOUSEHOLD, Greek). Since states too seek to protect their honour, *hubris* is commonly applied to invasions, imperialist 'enslavement', or military savagery, often when committed by '*barbarian' powers. Unchecked *hubris* was held to be characteristic of *tyrannies, or of *oligarchies or *democracies serving their own interests (depending on one's viewpoint), and to be a major cause of *stasis or civil war. In Athens, probably from *Solon's laws, a legal action for *hubris* existed, and its public significance was signalled by the possibility of the heaviest penalties, and by the fact that the action was (as a *graphe) open to any Athenian with full citizen rights, not restricted to the victim of the dishonour.

Hubris is not essentially a religious term; yet naturally enough the gods were often supposed to punish instances of it, either because they might feel themselves directly dishonoured, or, more often, because they were taken to uphold Greek moral and social values. Attic tragedy is not centrally concerned to display divine punishment of hubristic heroes; tragedy focuses rather on unjust or problematic suffering, whereas full-scale acts of *hubris* by the powerful tend to deprive them of the human sympathy necessary for tragic victims.

humiliōrēs See HONESTIORES; STATUS, LEGAL AND SOCIAL, *Roman.*

humours The corresponding Gk. and Lat. words strictly suggest some kind of fluid substance and are most commonly found in medical contexts. The explanation of disease—and even human behaviour—in terms of the interactions and relative proportions of fluids in the body is a very ancient one. There was, however, little agreement about which fluids counted as humours, and which were the most important. Many kinds of humoral theory were in circulation. Most influential were those which related the qualities of the humours to qualities which had been associated with the Empedoclean *elements, where earth, water, *fire, and air were sometimes analysed in terms of two pairs of opposites: hot and cold, wet and dry. This in turn enabled a correlation to be made with the four seasons. *Galen gives the four humours of the Hippocratic treatise *On the Nature of Man*—blood, phlegm, yellow bile, and black bile—a special status, which they continued to enjoy.

hunting Epic heroes (see HOMER) hunt to fill their bellies or to rid the land of dangerous beasts. The boar is the most formidable antagonist; venison is highly valued; mentions of lions are problematic. Hunters go on foot, armed with spear or bow. In Greek Classical literature the educational value of hunting is emphasized, but hunting is still for the pot and the methods described in *Xenophon's *On Hunting* are often unsporting. These include the use of snares and the beating of fawns so that their cries will draw their mothers within range. Hare-hunting receives special attention; the hunters, on foot, drive the hares into nets with the help of hounds. Hounds and nets are also used for boar-hunting; but the beast must ultimately be faced by men on foot armed with boar-spears. Opportunities for hunting on horseback are generally to be found in the east (e.g. in the 'paradises' or game-parks of the Persian *satraps). *Alexander (2) the Great's conquests enabled the Macedonian nobles to hunt on a gigantic scale and established the hunt as a paradigm of manly (esp. kingly) virtue, which is reflected in funerary art (notably the 'Tomb of *Philip II' at Vergina (see AEGAE), and the 'Alexander Sarcophagus'. The Roman conquerors took over the apparatus of the Macedonian kings, though enthusiasm for hunting was not universal—a 'slavish' occupation, acc. to

*Sallust. The distinction between amateur sportsmen and 'slavish' professionals (already found in *Plato and Xenophon) becomes marked in the Roman period. Professionals (including wildfowlers using nets and lime-twigs) hunt for the market, or to supply their masters. Sportsmen follow Greek methods; but often hunt on horseback. *Dido's hunt may be based on the actual practice of driving game from the hills to be ridden down on level ground. *Hadrian distinguished himself as a big-game hunter—lion, bear, and boar; but his friend *Arrian, whose *On Hunting* was professedly written to supplement Xenophon's work, coursed hares on horseback, taking more pleasure in the chase than in the kill. Country sports, including boar-, stag-, fox-, and hare-hunting, and the hunt breakfast, are depicted in the mosaic of the 'Little Hunt' at *Piazza Armerina. The slaughter of captured beasts in the *amphitheatre forms a separate subject; see VENATIONES.

hybris See HUBRIS.

Hydaspēs, river of the Punjab, where *Alexander (2) the Great defeated Porus in 326 BC. After continually stretching the enemy by marching and countermarching along the river, Alexander crossed it before dawn under cover of a thunderstorm, probably with only 6,000 foot and 5,000 horse. Porus sent forward an advance force of Indian cavalry and chariots, which was routed by Alexander's cavalry screen, and interspersed his infantry with *elephants, placing cavalry and chariots on the wings. But under attack by Alexander's cavalry, the Indian horse took refuge amongst the infantry, causing confusion, and uncovering its flanks and rear. In the centre the Macedonian infantry were able to open gaps in their line to accommodate elephants where necessary, and to use their pikes to drive others back on their own infantry, after dislodging their mahouts. Virtually surrounded, the Indian army was all but annihilated, and Porus himself captured.

hymns, Greek, 'Hymn' is a simple transliteration of a Greek word; but the relation of Greek to English hymns is not simple. *Hymnos* has at least three meanings: (1) a song of any kind; (2) any song in honour of a god; (3) a particular type of song in honour of a god. Use (1) is standard in Archaic poetry; (2) would perhaps have been judged normal by a Greek of the Classical period; (3) distinguishes the hymn from other forms of song in honour of gods, such as the *paean.

The only complete hymns that survive from before the year 400 BC are the *Homeric Hymns*, *hexameter compositions ranging from a handful of lines to several hundred. Typical features of hymns include: lists of the god's powers and interests and favourite places; accumulations of the god's *epithets; portrayals of the god engaged in characteristic activities; greetings, summonses, and *prayers to the god; and, most important of all, accounts of how the god was born and acquired his or her 'honours' and functions. For the hymn, the fundamental form of 'theology' is 'theogony'.

hymns, Roman See CARMEN.

Hypatia, woman learned in mathematics, astronomy, and philosophy (d. AD 415). Daughter of the mathematician Theon of *Alexandria, she revised the third book of his *Commentary on the Almagest*. Commentaries by her are lost. Influential in Alexandria as a teacher of Neoplatonist philosophy, she was torn to pieces by a mob of Christians.

Hyperbolus (d. 411 BC), 5th-cent. Athenian *demagogue during and after the Archidamian War (431–421; see PELOPONNESIAN WAR), esp. prominent after the death of *Cleon. He is sneered at in comedy for his doubtful paternity and foreign origin, but *ostraka* (see OSTRACISM WAR) show his father had a perfectly normal and reputable Greek name. In *c*.416 an ostracism was held by which Hyperbolus expected to secure the removal of *Alcibiades or *Nicias, but they secretly allied against him, and he was himself ostracized. He went to *Samos, where he was murdered by oligarchical revolutionaries. He is condemned by *Thucydides (2) in unusually strong terms; but, since he was the constant butt of comic poets, his influence must have been considerable. To some extent he can be rehabilitated by sensible-looking decrees which he proposed or amended.

Hyperīdēs (389–322 BC), Athenian statesman, rated by the ancients second only to *Demosthenes (2) amongst the Ten Orators (see ATTIC ORATORS). He studied rhetoric under *Isocrates and began his career by writing speeches for others. His political career opened with prosecutions of leading figures, the most notable being his successful prosecution of *Philocrates in 343 which heralded his future bitter opposition to Macedon (see PHILIP II), and after the battle of *Chaeronea he assumed a leading role. Immediately after the action, in which 1,000 Athenians had died and 2,000 were captured, he sought to provide replacements by making *metics citizens and freeing slaves; he was himself duly indicted for this unconstitutional measure, but it showed his determination to resist, as did his prosecution of *Demades and other collaborationists and his vigorous plea to the Athenians not to accede to *Alexander (2) the Great's demand in 335 for Demosthenes and others. In 324/3 he led the attack on Demosthenes and others who were accused of appropriating the money deposited by *Harpalus. Presumably he wanted it for the coming revolt against Macedon. Indeed Hyperides was the chief supporter of *Leosthenes and of Athenian action in the *Lamian War. Fittingly he was chosen to deliver the Funeral Oration (see EPITAPHIOS) of late 323, a speech of which much survives. With the collapse of Greek resistance, Hyperides had to flee. He was captured and put to death, *Antipater, in one version, first ordering the cutting out of the tongue which had so bitterly assailed him and Macedon, a not ignoble end for one of the heroes of Greek liberty.

Works In tone his speeches resembled those of *Lysias. He borrowed words and phrases from comedy, thus bringing his language into touch with the speech of everyday life. *'Longinus' *On the Sublime* notes his wit, his suavity and persuasiveness, his tact and good taste. He can be sarcastic and severe without becoming offensive; his reproof often takes the form of humorous banter. He speaks with respect of his adversaries and avoids scurrilous abuse.

hypothesis, literary (Greek). Prefixed to plays. Nearly all Athenian dramas have an introductory note giving an outline of the plot and often other information.

Hypsipylē Because the women of Lemnos neglected the rites of *Aphrodite, she made them stink, and their husbands left them to take concubines from *Thrace. They then murdered all the males on the island, except that Hypsipyle hid her father King Thoas, son of *Dionysus, and spirited him out of the country. She now governed Lemnos and received the *Argonauts when they came. The women mated with them, and Hypsipyle had two sons by *Jason (1).

iambic poetry, Greek 'Iambic' metre (see METRE, GREEK) got its name from *iambos*, a term associated with traditional jesting and ribaldries in certain festivals of *Demeter and *Dionysus. At *Eleusis the ribaldry was traced back to the mythical Iambē, who made the mourning Demeter laugh. In Ionia in the 7th and 6th cents. BC the *iambos* achieved literary status when *Archilochus and others published monologues and songs composed for *festivals and characterized by satirical denunciation of individuals or types, amusing narrations, and lubriciousness. The term 'iambic poetry' applies primarily to this material and to later literature inspired by it.

A recurrent feature in the Ionian texts is the first-person account of extravagant sexual adventures that the speaker claims to have had. He might adopt a character role such as a cook, a peasant farmer, or a burglar. The three principal iambographers of the Archaic period are Archilochus, *Semonides of Amorgos, and Hipponax of Ephesus.

iambic poetry, Latin See LUCILIUS (1); CATULLUS; HORACE.

Iamblichus (*c.* AD 245–*c.*325), *Neoplatonist philosopher, b. at Chalcis in Coele Syria, probably studied with *Porphyry; later he founded his own school in Syria. Extant writings include a compendium of Pythagorean philosophy (largely compiled from extracts derived from earlier writers). Bk. 1 is *On the Pythagorean Life*. Iamblichus incorporated in Neoplatonic philosophy what he took to be the 'theologies' of the ancients (Egyptians, Persians, Chaldaeans, Orphics (see ORPHISM), Pythagoreans), their demonology and their rites, esp. Chaldaean *theurgy.

Icarus See DAEDALUS.

Icenī, a British tribe in Norfolk and Suffolk; see BRITAIN. The tribe voluntarily made a treaty with *Claudius, but in AD 47 rebelled against forcible disarmament. *Prasutagus was established as *client king until his death in AD 60/1, when the attempted suppression of independence by Roman officials caused the rebellion of the tribe under his widow *Boudicca. After the harsh suppression of this outbreak (from which economic recovery was slow) a self-governing *civitas was created. Apart from its pottery industry, the *civitas* was agricultural, but with few villas. The area was none the less rich and has produced a series of silver and gold hoards (e.g. Mildenhall and Thetford).

iconography See IMAGERY.

Ictīnus was one of a number of fine *architects who worked at Athens in the time of *Pericles. In conjunction with *Callicrates he designed the *Parthenon and with a certain Carpion, otherwise unknown, as co-author, wrote a (lost) account of it. He was also one of a series of architects—Coroebus, Ictinus, Metagenes—who worked at *Eleusis on the great hall in which the performance of the *mysteries took place; the plan of the hall, with its rows of columns supporting the roof, was repeatedly modified.

From the design of the Parthenon it is clear that Ictinus was much interested in the ideal mathematical relationships between the different elements of temple architecture; his imposition of the ratio $2^2 : 3^2$ demonstrates an ability to go beyond the traditional evolutionary approach to proportions. No doubt his book explained his theorizing.

Īdomeneus, in mythology grandson of *Minos. He was one of the suitors of *Helen, and later led the Cretan contingent to Troy with 80 ships. He is a major figure in the *Iliad*, older than most of the other Greek leaders, but a great warrior, and one of the nine who volunteered to stand against *Hector in single combat. Running into a great storm on his journey home after the war, he vowed that if he returned safely he would sacrifice to *Poseidon the first living creature to meet him when he landed in *Crete. This turned out to be his own son. When he fulfilled, or tried to fulfil, the vow, a plague broke out, and to appease the gods he was forced to leave Crete for Italy.

Iliad See ACHILLES; HOMER.

Illyrians, the large group of related *Indo-European tribes that occupied in classical times the western side of the Balkan range from the head of the Adriatic (*Ionian) Sea to the hinterland of the gulf of Valona. The Romans called their territory Illyricum.

imagery The identification of scenes in sculpture, painting and the minor arts has long been a major activity of classical *archaeology, although it has traditionally been accorded less emphasis than the identification of artists' hands. In all the figurative arts conventional schemes were developed, sometimes under the influence of near-eastern iconography, for portraying particular mythical figures and episodes. Individual artists exploited conventional imagery not simply by replicating it, but by playing variations on a theme or by echoing the conventional scheme for one episode when portraying a different one. An extreme form of this is iconographic parody.

The origins of particular iconographic schemes, and the reasons why the popularity of scenes changes over time, are rarely clear. Ceramic vessels may owe some of their imagery to lost gold or silver *plate, and some vases can reasonably be held to take over the imagery of lost wall-paintings or of famous sculptures, such as the Tyrannicides group (see ARISTOGITON). Direct representation of scenes from comic drama is popular in 4th-cent. BC south Italian pottery. In the Greek world, public sculpture often carried broadly political meaning, using the otherness of more or less fantastic figures, *Centaurs or *Amazons, to define the behaviour of the good citizen.

Recent work on the non-mythical imagery on painted pottery has helped to uncover the ideology of the Greek city, stressing the way in which imagery can create ways of seeing as well as reflect them. Changes in the popularity of particular scenes or types of scene over time, at least when those changes extend over the work of several different painters, may indicate changing social concerns. The imagery on pots has a close relationship with the use to which those pots are put, and this can be seen esp. clearly with both vessels deposited in graves and vessels used at the *symposium, many of which are self-referential. One valuable source of information here lies in the way in which painters restrict scenes of certain types of activity to imaginary characters, such as *satyrs. But it is unsafe to assume that the attitudes displayed at the symposium were shared by society as a whole. The preservation of extensive areas of private housing at *Pompeii and *Herculaneum, enables us to see programmes of imagery with which some rich people surrounded themselves, and the care and originality with which they constructed visual narratives out of linked imagery.

Images were a major part of religious cult. Cult statues sometimes incorporated whole programmes of mythical imagery, as in the *Athena Parthenos; see PHIDIAS. In the Roman world religious imagery became increasingly complex, and more or less arcane symbolic programmes are associated with mystery cults. Christianity, with its use of types and antitypes drawn from pagan mythology as well as from both OT and NT, further enriched the interpretative range of familiar imagery. See ART, ANCIENT ATTITUDES TO; ART, FUNERARY; MYTH AND MYTHOLOGY; PAINTING; PISISTRATUS; POTTERY; SCULPTURE.

imāginēs, wax portrait-masks of Romans who had held the higher magistracies (see MAGISTRACY, ROMAN), were prominently displayed in the family mansion (see HOUSES, ITALIAN), with lines of descent and distinctions indicated. They were worn by actors impersonating the deceased in full ceremonial dress at public sacrifices and family funerals, at first only of male descendants, after c.100 BC gradually of female descendants as well (see IULIUS CAESAR (1), GAIUS). The right to this, and to having one's own *imagō* preserved, was forfeited by criminal conviction, by *proscription, and, under the empire, by *damnatio memoriae. The families 'known' (see NOBILES) to the public through these processions formed the *nobilitas*. By the early empire, and probably even in the late republic, the *imagines* of all qualified men to whom the deceased was related by birth or marriage seem to have been displayed at his funeral. The custom lasted into the late empire. These *imagines* played a part in the development of Roman *portraiture.

imitātio (Gk. *mimēsis*), the study and conspicuous deployment of features recognizably characteristic of a canonical author's style or content, so as to define one's own generic affiliation (see GENRE).

In rhetoric the term '*mimesis*' designates a later writer's relation of acknowledged dependence upon an earlier one. The *Muse is the daughter of memory: poets have always learned from other poets and are listeners or readers before they become singers or writers. But starting with the *sophists, the careful study and imitation of (usually written) models of discourse became an established educational technique. Throughout antiquity, a strong continuity in method and attitude linked school exercises on canonical texts (memorization, excerpting, paraphrase, translation, commentary, variation of theme or style, comparison) with a poetic practice which drew attention to its skilled use of models, 'not so as to filch but to borrow openly, in the hope of being recognized' (*Seneca the Elder, on Ovid).

immūnitās was the exemption of a community or an individual from obligations to the Roman state or of an individual from obligations to a local community. Cities acquired immunity from Roman taxation by *lex or *senatus consultum or imperial decree. See FREE CITIES. Immunity for life from Roman taxation could also be granted to individuals. Immunity from local *munera* (see MUNUS) might be granted either by Rome or by the community. Besides personal grants there was general exemption under the empire for such groups as shippers supplying corn to Rome, and local philosophers, *rhetors, and doctors.

imperātor, a generic title for Roman commanders, became a special title of honour. After a victory the general was acclaimed *imperator* by his soldiers (see ACCLAMATION). He assumed the title after his name until the end of his magistracy or until his triumph. The first certainly attested *imperator* is *Aemilius Paullus (2) in 189 BC. The title was assumed esp. by proconsuls (see PRO CONSULE) and gained new importance through *Sulla before he was appointed dictator. The increasing influence of the army in the late republic made *imperator* the symbol of military authority. Sulla occasionally stated (and *Pompey emphasized) that he was acclaimed *imperator* more than once. *Caesar first used the title permanently. *Agrippa in 38 BC refused a triumph for victories won under

*Octavian's superior command and established the rule that the *princeps* should assume the acclamations and the triumphs of his *legates. Henceforth, apparently, Octavian used *imperator* as *praenōmen* (*imperator Caesar*, not *Caesar imperator*). Thus the title came to denote the supreme power and was commonly used in this sense. But, officially, *Otho was the first to imitate Augustus, and only with *Vespasian did *Imperator* ('emperor') become a title by which the ruler was known. On the death of a *princeps*, or during a rebellion, the acclamation of a general as an *imperator* by an army indicated that he was the candidate of that body for the imperial dignity.

The use of the *praenomen* did not suppress the old usage of *imperator* after the name. After a victory the emperor registered the *salūtātiō imperātōria* after his name (e.g.: Imp. Caesar... Traianus... imp. VI).

imperialism

Greek and Hellenistic One Greek definition of *freedom included the ability of a state to exercise rule over others. The 5th-cent. BC Athenians justified their rule over other Greeks by appealing to the motives of fear, honour, and interest: 'it has always been the law that the weaker should be subject to the stronger.' *Thucydides (2) interpreted the early history of Greece as the gradual emergence of greater powers with superior resources. It was common for the major states to seek to dominate weaker ones, as Sparta and Athens on the mainland of Greece and in the Aegean (see PELOPONNESIAN LEAGUE; DELIAN LEAGUE). Smaller states did the same. But the fragmentation of the Greek world into hundreds of states, the consequent dispersal of resources, and the strong Greek attachment to independence and its symbols, all militated against the emergence of lasting empires in the Greek world, and even inhibited the formation of durable alliance systems except in special circumstances. The territorial empires of the near east, based on deliberate military conquest and the imposition of regular tribute on subjects, were long familiar to the Greeks (see LYDIA; PERSIA). But this eastern model did not transfer easily to Greek conditions. The future lay with military monarchies that could command greater resources and work on a scale that would eventually transcend the Greek world itself. *Dionysius (1) I of Syracuse, *Jason (2) of Pherae, and *Mausolus of Caria may variously be seen as precursors to *Philip II of Macedon. His transformation of Macedonian power provided the basis for *Alexander (2) the Great's conquest of the Persian empire and the subsequent emergence of the kingdoms of the Successors (or *Diadochi).

Roman The expansion of Roman power in Italy and esp. the creation of its Mediterranean and European empire from the 3rd cent. BC to the 1st cent. AD would nowadays count as a case of 'imperialism'.

Rome in the early and middle republican periods (5th to 2nd cents. BC) was a profoundly military society, as can be seen from e.g. the military nature of the political power of the city's magistrates (*imperium*), the need of any aspiring magistrate to have performed ten years of military service, and the religious and political importance attached to the *triumph. By the end of the war with *Pyrrhus in 272, Rome controlled the greater part of Italy south of the Po (see PADUS) by a network of relationships which had grown out of the fighting against the Aequi, *Volsci, and *Etruscans in the 5th and early 4th cents., the *Latins and the *Campanians in the mid-4th cent., and the *Samnites and other south Italians, of which the final stage was the Pyrrhic wars (see PYRRHUS). Some communities (mostly former Latin and Campanian allies) were incorporated into the Roman people (though geographically distinct from it, and often without full political rights), and the rest were classified as allies (*socii), either as part of a reconstituted 'Latin' alliance or with a separate treaty of their own. Of these, only the Roman communities were properly speaking part of the expanded city of Rome, while the allies were under an obligation to provide military assistance and (esp. in the case of the Latins) held certain rights from the Romans.

In the period of the two great wars against the Carthaginians (264–241 and 218–201; see PUNIC WARS), the Romans, backed by this military alliance, became involved in wars in *Sicily, Sardinia, Corsica, *Spain, *Greece, and North Africa (see AFRICA, ROMAN). From this grew the beginnings of the Roman empire outside Italy. Roman magistrates were assigned commands by the senate by the allocation of a *provincia or area of responsibility. Such *provinciae* were not essentially territorial, nor were they permanent; but in areas in which the Romans wished to exercise a long-term military control through the presence of armed forces it became necessary to allocate a *provincia* according to rules. Sometimes this seems to have occurred much later than the conflict that initially brought Roman soldiers to the area. Within this essentially military pattern, other elements of imperial control developed, esp. taxation of the local communities and jurisdiction exercised by Roman commanders over non-Romans.

In the first half of the 2nd cent. BC, and esp. in the context of the wars with the Hellenistic powers of the eastern Mediterranean, Roman imperialism took a different form. Roman armies were sent to Greece during the Macedonian wars and to Asia Minor to fight against the *Seleucid Antiochus III. Here long-term *provinciae* were not established when the fighting ended, and control of the regions was exercised in a more remote fashion, through treaties and diplomacy. For *Polybius however, this represented an extension of Roman control as real as that exercised directly in the western Mediterranean.

Further large-scale additions were made as a result of the organization of the east by *Pompey, after the defeat of *Mithradates VI (66–63), and of the campaigns of *Caesar in Gaul (58–50). The largest expansion, however, came under *Augustus, who not only completed the conquest of the Iberian peninsula but also added the new provinces of Raetia, Noricum, Pannonia, and Moesia along the line of the river Danube (see DANUVIUS). It appears that he was prevented from a further expansion into the part of Germany (see GERMANIA) between the Rhine and the Elbe only by the disastrous defeat of *Quinctilius Varus in AD 9. Thereafter, apart from *Claudius' conquest of southern Britain in 43, *Trajan alone (97–117) made further large-scale additions, of which only Dacia and Arabia survived the retrenchment of his successor, *Hadrian.

Although the mechanisms of Roman imperialism are fairly clear, Roman motivation has been the subject of much debate. Throughout the period of expansion, the political classes at Rome were determined that other states should do what Rome required of them, and, although it is rash to offer a single explanation of so complex a phenomenon as Roman imperialism, it seems that it was changes in the Roman understanding of what were the most effective means of achieving this control that shaped the way the empire grew.

imperium was the supreme power, involving command in war and the interpretation and execution of law (including the infliction of the death penalty), which belonged at Rome to the kings (see REX) and, after their expulsion, to *consuls, *praetors, *dictators, and masters of the horse (see MAGISTER EQUITUM). *Imperium* represents the supreme authority of the community in its dealings with the individual, and the magistrate in whom *imperium* is vested represents the community in all its dealings. *Imperium* may be seen as the power to give orders and to exact obedience to them. It was symbolized by the *fasces*, the bundle of rods borne by the *lictors, to which was added the axe when the magistrate left the precincts of the city. Later in the republic *imperium* was held also by proconsuls and propraetors (see PRO CONSULE, PRO PRAETORE), who were either ex-magistrates or private individuals upon whom a special command had been conferred, and by members of certain commissions (e.g. boards for the distribution of land). Its application was progressively restricted: first, when two consuls replaced the king, by the principle of collegiality and tenure of office limited to one year; the dictator, who had no colleague, held office for a maximum of six months. Secondly, magistrates were not allowed to execute citizens in Rome without trial because of the citizen's right of *provocatio* to the people. This right of appeal was extended, to citizens abroad. Thirdly, the *imperium* of promagistrates was generally restricted to the bounds of their *provincia*. *Imperium* needed ratification by a *lex curiata*, a convention which persisted at least to the end of the republic. To a promagistrate, *imperium* was granted for a year at a time, or until his commission was achieved. Grants of *imperium* for a specified term of several years occur only towards the end of the republic, the earliest being the grant of *imperium* to *Pompey for three years by the *lex Gabinia* of 67; this *imperium* was further distinguished by being *infinitum*, i.e. not subject to the usual territorial limits of a *provincia*.

Under the republic, in case of conflict, the *imperium* of a consul could probably override that of a praetor. As between consuls and proconsuls, each with twelve *fasces*, the consul could override the proconsul by virtue of the prestige (*auctoritas*) of his office. Conflict in the same area between proconsuls arose first in 67 between Pompey (pursuing pirates with proconsular *imperium*; see PIRACY) and the proconsul of Crete. So, in 57, the question of allowing Pompey, in virtue of his corn commission, *imperium* greater than that of other proconsuls was mooted, and *Brutus and *Cassius were granted *imperium maius* in the east by the senate in 43.

*Octavian held *imperium*, first *pro praetore* and later as consul in 43, as *triumvir from 42 to 33,

and as consul in 31–23 (and, from 27, as proconsul of a large number of provinces). When in 23 he resigned the consulship, his proconsular *imperium* was made *maius*, and it was provided that it could be exercised from within the city. *Imperium* was granted to him for ten-year periods in 27 and 8 BC and AD 3 and 13, and for five-year periods in 18 and 13 BC. It was voted to succeeding emperors at their accession by the senate.

Imperium maius was sometimes granted to others besides the emperor for the creation of a single military command, as to *Germanicus in the east in AD 17 and to *Corbulo in 63. It might also be conferred as a way of associating an individual with the *imperium* of the emperor and thereby signalling him as a suitable successor, as with *Tiberius.

As Rome's dominion came to extend overseas in the 3rd and 2nd cents. BC (see IMPERIALISM, ROMAN), it was conceived of as the power to issue orders and to exact obedience to them, i.e., as *imperium*. The first official expression of this is found in Greek. The treaty between Rome and Maroneia from the 160s BC refers to 'the Roman people and those under them', and this standard phrase appears in Latin in Rome's treaty with Callatis on the Black Sea as 'the Roman people and those under their *imperium*'. It was with reference to the principle and nature of supreme authority within the state that the authority of Rome itself over others was perceived and defined, and so it was to the *imperium Romānum* of the republic that the Roman empire succeeded.

impiety, official action against See INTOLERANCE, INTELLECTUAL AND RELIGIOUS.

incense is the name given to various aromatic gum-resins which, when heated, produce a fragrant odour. Often used interchangeably with 'frankincense', it was widely burnt as a religious offering in the ancient world, as an accompaniment to acts of divination, on the occasion of a burial, and as a gesture of homage. See below. Arabian frankincense was always the main variety in the ancient world, and given the amounts of frankincense consumed, it is natural that a lively trade should have developed in this commodity. In the earlier periods it was transported overland to Gaza, and thence on to the cities of the eastern Mediterranean. In the Roman era, maritime trade was more important.

Incense in religion Fragrance of burning wood, herbs, spices, and resins fulfilled ritual functions on three levels: first, to neutralize the smell of burning sacrificial flesh, hair, hoofs and horns, etc. (see SACRIFICE); secondly, to generate appropriate mood and ambience; thirdly, metaphorically, incense was an expression of the felt presence of the divine as well as the 'rising' to heaven of either prayers or souls of the dead. Myrrh and frankincense were most common in Greek religion, imported from south Arabia since the 8th cent. BC via Phoenicia (see PHOENICIANS) and *Cyprus and retaining their Semitic names. Granules of incense were thrown directly onto the altar or burnt separately in special braziers.

incest, sexual intercourse or marriage with close kin, was restricted throughout classical antiquity. However, the particular relations prohibited varied with place and time. Sexual relations involving parent and child were forbidden everywhere we have evidence; their occurrence in Greek myth generally evokes horror, yet the participants are sometimes marked as numinous by their transgression of the usual limits of human conduct (see HERO-CULT). Siblings of the same father could marry at *Athens, of the same mother at *Sparta. Even marriages between full siblings were recognized among the Greeks of Hellenistic and Roman *Egypt, an unusual practice, perhaps intended to preserve the ethnic identity of a small and isolated settler élite and the privileges to which it provided access.

incubation, *ritual sleep in a *sanctuary in order to obtain a dream, mostly for healing. Incubation is known from sanctuaries of *Asclepius, but also from other healing sanctuaries like the Amphiaraion at *Oropus. Such sanctuaries mostly had specific halls where patients slept during the night, with high walls to prevent prying. *Aristophanes in Plutus gives a detailed description of a night in the Asclēpiēum in *Piraeus, while the healing inscriptions from *Epidaurus, Rome, and *Pergamum although directly aimed at promoting the cult, allow some insights into the nature of the *dreams, as does the diary of Aelius *Aristides.
See HEALING GODS.

Indo-European and Indo-Europeans Languages such as Greek, Latin, and Sanskrit share regularities which indicate a close historical relationship (see LINGUISTICS). This grouping, termed Indo-European (IE) to indicate its geographical extent in historical times, includes some nine major living language-groups and also extinct ones known only through inscriptions. The earliest recorded examples belong to the second millennium BC, and include the bronze age form of Greek written in Linear B (e.g. at Cnossus, 14th cent. BC); but many unrecorded languages and language-groups of this family must once have existed, only some of which gave rise to successors which have left evidence in written or spoken form. The peoples who spoke any of this family of related languages may be termed—in a purely linguistic sense—Indo-Europeans.

industry Industry in the sense of hard *labour most Greeks and Romans knew all too well; total freedom from productive labour (scholē, ōtium) remained a governing ideal from one end of pagan antiquity to the other. But industry in the modern sense of large-scale manufacturing businesses they knew hardly at all, let alone as the standard form of manufacturing unit. That role was always filled by the individual workshop, and the largest Greek or Roman industrial labour force on record barely reached three figures. Nor did élite Greeks and Romans value labourers any more highly than labour as such; this was partly because manual labour, even when not actually performed by slaves (see SLAVERY), was nevertheless apt to attract the opprobrium of slavishness. As Herodotus put it, the Corinthians (see CORINTH) despised manual craftsmen the least, the *Spartans the most—but all élite Greeks despised them. On the other hand, they felt boundless admiration for skill (technē, ars), and some forms of ancient craftsmanship demanded that quality in the highest degree. See ART, ANCIENT ATTITUDES TO; ARTISANS AND CRAFTSMEN.

*Homer and *Hesiod mention a wide variety of craftsmen, some of the more expert and specialized being non-Greek. But only the metalworkers had their own workshops, and this accords with the flowering of bronze-working associated with the panhellenic sanctuaries of *Olympia, *Delphi, and *Delos. Their standards were eventually matched by the potters and (if they were separate) vase-painters, esp. those of *Athens, *Argos, and Corinth; the last could also boast at least one shipbuilder of distinction by 700. In the course of the 7th and 6th cents. workshops and studios proliferated, no longer tied principally to sanctuaries. Depictions of potters, leather-workers, and smiths occur on Attic black- and red-figure vases, themselves often products of the highest craft and finish. As is shown by workers' names, many of the craftsmen were non-Greek slaves.

The concomitant development of the Athenian empire and *Piraeus in the 5th cent. provided a further stimulus to craftsmanship, both quantitative and qualitative. The Athenian *trireme was a triumph of design and construction. No one, acc. to *Plutarch, would wish actually to be Phidias, but the products of *Phidias' extraordinary skill were universally admired. The anonymous labours of an army of stone-carvers have left us a legacy of finely dressed masonry and decorative sculptural detail carved in the hardest material (marble). Gem-cutters and die-engravers (see COINAGE, GREEK) like those who produced the decadrachms of *Syracuse were hardly less accomplished. At Athens craftsmanship interacted with high culture and politics. Plato's *Socrates was fond of analogies from craftsmanship, and the real Socrates was reputedly the son of a stonemason. The fathers of *Cleon, *Isocrates, and *Demosthenes (2) made their money through employing skilled slave craftsmen—tanners, *aulos-makers, and cutlers respectively. But the biggest 'industrialists' on record in Classical Athens were the *metic brothers Polemarchus and *Lysias, even if it is not certain that their 120 slaves all worked full time in the family shield-making business (esp. lucrative, thanks to the *Peloponnesian War). Some such skilled slaves were privileged to be set up in business on their own account by their masters. The craftsmen of Athens were sedentary, but itinerant Greek craftsmen operated as far afield as southern Russia and the Alps, working on the spot under commission from local rulers.

The Hellenistic period produced a growth of the Greek workshop system but also to some degree marked a return to the Mycenaean pattern of palace-centred industries. Textile and food production were affected. Several glass-producers of the 1st cent. BC seem to have had workshops in more than one town. *Glass-blowing was invented in the late 1st cent. BC. The Ptolemies (see PTOLEMY (1); EGYPT, *Ptolemaic*) 'nationalized' several Egyptian crafts: the production of papyrus scrolls, oil, perfumes, textiles (other than woollen), and beer became government monopolies. Craftsmen in these trades became government employees, who were controlled by tax-farmers and government officials, received salaries, and, in the production of oil, a share of the profits. A government production-schedule was issued annually, and the workers received their tools and raw materials from central stores. Large enterprises for fish-curing, metalworking, and brick-making were also properties of the Ptolemies.

In Rome of the kings (see REX), acc. to tradition, specialized crafts of metal- and leather-workers, potters, dyers, musicians, and *fabri* (all-purpose handymen) were organized in societies known as *collegia* (see CLUBS, ROMAN). In later republican times Roman craftsmanship developed on Greek lines. This was a period of enormous expansion of the Roman empire and intense specialization of all kinds of economic activity (see ECONOMY, ROMAN), and among the many imports to Rome and Italy from the Greek east were not only luxury finished goods but skilled Greek craftsmen, many of whom had been reduced to servitude by their slave-hungry imperial masters. As in Greece, an attempt was made to erect social barriers between the political élite and the sordid business of production and commerce, but even the Roman senate included some manufacturing entrepreneurs. The large and assured demand provided by Roman armies outside Italy was often a vital factor stimulating the production and distribution of consumable commodities. The politicization of the *collegia* at Rome was another late republican phenomenon, prompting official measures to dissolve or curb them.

Under the Principate craftsmanship of the Greek and Roman workshop type spread throughout the provinces of the empire. Remnants of administered economy persisted, esp. in mining districts, temples, and public domains; but even the Ptolemaic monopolies were broken up or changed into monopolistic concessions for small districts farmed out to independent craftsmen. The local markets of provincial districts were furnished with bricks, coarse pottery, cheap leather goods and metalwork, *terra sigillāta* (see POTTERY, ROMAN), cheap textiles, and so on by craftsmen working from public and private estates. There were, however, local exceptions to the general pattern both in scale and in management: an apparently huge private-enterprise development of olive-growing and *olive oil distribution in Cyrenaica (see CYRENE), traceable physically through the surviving containers (see AMPHORAE, ROMAN), and an imperially inspired development of stone *quarries in the mons Claudianus area of Egypt, are two conspicuous instances. See also TECHNOLOGY; TRADE; TRADERS.

infāmia as a legal term embraces a variable number of disabilities (the common one being an incapacity to act or appear for another at law) imposed in a variety of circumstances. It is at root social, involving loss of reputation or good name, but is given legal content by *lex, *senatus consultum, imperial *constitution, or by the praetor's *edict in specific situations, such as condemnation in ordinary criminal prosecutions, condemnation in civil actions for delict and in other civil actions in which the defendant was guilty of a breach of faith, or engaging in certain disreputable occupations.

infanticide, killing of infants ('putting outside' was probably a euphemism), a method of family limitation. The term as generally used by historians also covers exposure, because it is seldom possible to ascertain what actually happened in specific cases. Infanticide is often mentioned in myths and legends, e.g. *Oedipus, *Cyrus (1) the Great, *Romulus and Remus. Its frequency probably varied temporally and regionally. The Egyptians and the Jews were said to rear all their children, while the Carthaginians sacrificed children to Moloch (see CARTHAGE). *Soranus discussed reasons for not bringing up infants. Infants might have been exposed if they were deformed (see DEFORMITY), as in Sparta and Rome, or if they were the product of *rape or *incest. Poverty is another possible motive, although the poor often have more children than the rich. There is little evidence for selective female infanticide. The *Gortyn law code permitted infanticide in certain circumstances, while in *Thebes a law forbade infanticide but allowed poor parents to sell children. In *Ephesus too children could be sold in cases of extreme poverty. In Rome *patria potestas in principle allowed a father to execute his own children. The rise of *Christianity to become the official religion of the Roman empire caused considerable changes. The Christian Apostolic traditions rejected infanticide. A law of AD 374 treated infanticide as equivalent to *parricide.

inheritance

Greek In Athens, if a deceased man left legitimate sons, they shared the property equally (partible inheritance); if a son predeceased his father leaving sons of his own, those sons inherited their father's share. If the deceased man left a daughter but no son, the daughter's sons inherited. If she did not yet have a son, she was *epiklēros* (imprecisely translated 'heiress') and could be claimed in marriage by the nearest male relative, who took charge of the property until their son was old enough to take it over. If there were no legitimate children, relatives within the *ankhisteia* could claim. A man without sons could in effect choose an heir by adoption: the adoptee became legally the son of the adopter and so inherited the property, but could not oust an *epiklēros*; he might marry her himself, but anyway her son inherited eventually. A law introduced by *Solon permitted adoption by will, taking effect only on the testator's death. Another possibility was posthumous *adoption, by which the relatives arranged for one of themselves to become legally the deceased man's son. But a will or adoption could not be used to disinherit legitimate children.

The only other Classical Greek city from which detailed inheritance laws survive is *Gortyn. There sons and daughters shared the property, but a son's share was double a daughter's. The rights of a daughter without brothers resembled those of the Athenian *epiklēros*. In *Sparta there are said to have been 9,000 lots of land which, until the late 5th cent. BC, were passed down from father to son and could not be divided.

Roman Among the propertied classes of Rome making a will was regarded as a duty. But where there was no will or it was invalid, the first claimants were the *suī hērēdēs* (roughly 'direct heirs', those free persons in the paternal power (*patria potestas) of the deceased who by his death became independent); in their absence, second came the nearest agnates (see FAMILY, ROMAN).

Roman law recognized wills by the time of the *Twelve Tables (c.450 BC). The essential feature of a Roman will was the appointment of an heir or heirs. The whole estate of the deceased including debts devolved on the heir, whose liability was unlimited. Strictly, *sui heredes* could not refuse even an insolvent estate, but in practice the praetor allowed them to abstain. In his will a typical testator might appoint tutors to his children (see GUARDIANSHIP, *Rome*), manumit slaves, and charge his heir to pay legacies. They were payable provided the estate was solvent.

By the end of the republic certain relatives of the testator were regarded as having a legitimate expectation of sharing in his estate: if without good reason they were left less than a quarter of their prospective intestate share, they could bring the complaint of an undutiful will to upset the will. Earlier law had insisted only that *sui heredes* be either appointed heirs or formally disinherited, so that it was clear that they had not been forgotten. The complaint was a modest but important first step in recognizing a fixed entitlement, and marked a refinement of the conception of the duty owed by the Roman testator in composing his will.

initiation includes the set of rituals which transforms girls and boys into adults. (See also ELEUSIS; MYSTERY CULTS.) In Greece, these rituals were the combined product of the *Indo-European heritage and indigenous traditions. In historical times full rituals can be found only in Sparta and Crete. The Greeks had no term for initiation, but various cities used the term *agoge, lit. 'the leading (of a horse)', and related words. This view reflects itself not only in Archaic poetry, where boys and girls are often addressed as foals and fillies, but also in mythological naming: youths connected with initiation regularly have names with the element *hippos* ('horse'). Youths were seen as wild animals, that had to be domesticated before entering adult society.

Regarding girls, our best information comes from Sparta, where their 'education' prepared them for *motherhood through physical exercises and dancing in choruses. Aristocratic girls had to pass through a lesbian relationship (see HOMOSEXUALITY) to mark the contrast with their final destination, *marriage; a similar custom existed on Lesbos, where *Sappho instructed aristocratic girls. Stress was laid on enhancing the girls' beauty: sometimes, a beauty contest concluded the girls' initiation. See BRAURON. See also RITES OF PASSAGE.

iniūria **and defamation** In the late republic the delict of *iniuria* was infringing another's personality. In each case the offender had acted (1) in disregard of another person's personality, (2) contrary to sound morals and (3), typically, with the intention to insult. The penalty was 'as much money as may appear equitable' and involved disgrace (*infamia*).

inns, restaurants In primitive times hospitality towards strangers was universal. It remained common throughout antiquity, and for men of social standing was provided by the networks of guest-friendship (see FRIENDSHIP, RITUALIZED). In the Hellenistic and Roman world, with much more *travel, these relations were widespread. But from the 5th cent. BC there is evidence of inns in cities and by the roadside. Standards varied enormously: in the cheapest, travellers had to provide their own food and bedding, and even physical safety could not be taken for granted. Though hotels for higher-status people existed—ambassadors might have to use them for purposes of state— inns in general had a reputation for bedbugs, discomfort, rough-houses, and prostitution (see PROSTITUTION, SECULAR). Famous shrines in due course provided public accommodation, run either by the host city or by other cities for their own citizens—not always to their satisfaction.

In the Roman world conditions were similar. Men of standing tried to avoid using inns and were never seen in taverns or restaurants. They had their own 'halts' along roads which they travelled often (e.g. to their country seats), or could use those of their friends. Anyone might have to stop at an inn on a long journey (e.g. *Horace's to *Brundisium); and though innkeeping was classed among disgraceful trades, good and even luxurious establishments existed. Taverns were popular among the poor, many of whom had no adequate cooking facilities at home (see COOKERY), and became centres of their social life, often noisy and dangerous to public order. Various emperors passed legislation restricting the sale of prepared food and wine and, by building baths, provided alternative attractions.

In *Pompeii taverns, restaurants, and inns (some with accommodation for animals) were common. The inns clustered near the gates and the town centre. In superior places conditions would be pleasant, with dining-areas perhaps set out in a garden and musical entertainment and good food provided. The best hotels in *Pompeii were converted upper-class mansions. In lesser places, a colourful inn-sign might go with two or three dingy rooms, and customers had to eat sitting on stools and sleep on hard and bug-infested beds. Female company—no doubt of varying kinds—was provided if required. So, innkeepers were classed with pimps.

inscriptions See EPIGRAPHY, GREEK and LATIN; POTTERY, GREEK, INSCRIPTIONS ON.

institutes This was one of the titles given to elementary textbooks of Roman law. The best-known work of this kind is the *Institutes* of *Gaius (2), which was taken by *Justinian as the basis of his own *Institutes*. Though intended, like its model, as a students' manual, this work was given legislative validity.

intercessiō, 'interposition', was the right of one Roman magistrate (see MAGISTRACY, ROMAN) to veto the activity of another magistrate of equal or lesser authority. The possibility arose because magistrates were conceived as exercising collegiate power; only a magistrate with no peer, as the *dictator was, could act free of this possible interference. The tribunes of the people (*tribuni plebis*) shared with the regular magistrates the normal right of interposition against each other's acts, but in addition, at some point in the republic, they obtained a veto over all other, superior, magistrates and enactments of bodies presided over by magistrates, such as the comitial assemblies and the senate. They were able to exercise this extraordinary power, more revolutionary than constitutional in tendency, by virtue of their personal inviolability, which was ultimately guaranteed by the people.

interpretātiō Rōmāna, lit. 'Latin translation'; a phrase used to describe the Roman habit of replacing the name of a foreign deity with that of a Roman deity considered somehow comparable. The earliest of these 'translations' were from Greek: thus 'Zeus' was translated by 'Iuppiter' (see ZEUS; JUPITER). The process continued as the Romans came into contact with other cultures, so that the German 'Wodan' was called '*Mercurius' by Roman writers. Rarely were foreign divine names adopted directly into Latin, e.g. '*Apollo' and '*Isis'.

interpreters See BILINGUALISM.

interrex Under the Roman republic, if both *consuls died or left office without successors appointed, the 'auspices reverted to the *patrician senators' (see AUSPICIUM), who selected one of their number as *interrex*. *Interrēgēs*, who were of patrician birth and usually ex-consuls, held office in succession, each for five days, with consular powers. Their principal duty was to supervise the election of one or both new consuls.

intolerance, intellectual and religious

Sir K. Popper famously praised 5th cent. BC Athens as an 'open society', but the tolerance of that society had limits. There is some evidence for literary censorship, though of a haphazard and perhaps ineffective sort. *Phrynichus got into trouble near the beginning of the century for putting on a *tragedy dealing with a sensitive political topic. Between 440 and 437 there were formal restrictions on ridicule in theatrical comedy (see COMEDY (GREEK), OLD, 4). On the other hand there were no 'witch-hunts' against intellectuals, though *Anaxagoras and other associates of *Pericles were prosecuted in the courts. Anaxagoras' ostensible offence was impiety, and the decree of Diopeithes, if historical, would provide hard evidence for public control of teaching with religious implications. (See also

ATHEISM; THEODICY.) *Alcibiades and others were punished severely for profaning the Eleusinian *mysteries (see ANDOCIDES), but the offending action was hardly the product of earnest intellectual inquiry. The reasons for *Socrates' execution in 399 are still disputed, but political considerations were surely as relevant as religious: Socrates was critical of the working of *democracy, and had taught, in his fashion, prominent oligarchs (see OLIGARCHY). *Aeschines (1) explicitly makes the latter point, with which Socrates could not be charged in 399 because of the *amnesty.

In Rome, *censors, despite their name, were not responsible for literary or artistic censorship in the modern sense. Book-burning, is however attested in authoritarian periods of Roman history (see CREMUTIUS CORDUS). Roman attitudes to foreign religions were generally cosmopolitan; see RELIGION, ROMAN. The suppression of the *Bacchanalia in 186 BC was exceptional. For Roman treatment of Jews see JEWS and GAIUS (1): *Gaius and the Jews*; for persecution of Christians see CHRISTIANITY. See also PHILOSOPHERS AND POLITICS; PROTAGORAS.

invective is literature which, having regard to the customs and convictions of a given society, sets out to denigrate a named individual. Such denigration or abuse follows well-articulated rhetorical guidelines. The target is attacked on the grounds of birth, upbringing, 'banausic' occupation (see ARTISANS AND CRAFTSMEN; LABOUR), moral defects such as avarice, *corruption, profligacy, pleasure-seeking, sexual perversion, gluttony, or drunkenness (see ALCOHOLISM), physical shortcomings (see DEFORMITY), eccentricities of dress, ill fortune, offensiveness to the gods, and so on. These same categories of abuse are found irrespective of the *genre in which the invective is couched. This might be a senatorial or forensic speech, iambic poem, political pamphlet, curse-poem (see CURSES), or *epigram. Outstanding examples of invectives delivered in the public arena are *Demosthenes' (2) speech *On the Crown* and *Cicero's *Against Piso* and second *Philippic*.

The primary object of invective was to *persuade* the audience that one's accusations were true. Plausibility was thus more important than veracity. At the same time, invective aimed to give pleasure to the listeners. Cicero and Demosthenes both attest the enjoyment which derived from seeing others abused. The same factor underlies the personal attacks of Old Comedy (see COMEDY (GREEK), OLD), political lampoons, and the very existence of *iambic poetry, which was grounded in vituperation poetry. Despite the existence of legislation against defamation in Greece and Rome, invective flourished in both cultures.

invulnerability was commonly ascribed to the legendary heroes in the 'cyclic' epic tradition (see EPIC CYCLE), but is rigorously excluded from the Homeric poems (see HOMER) as incompatible with the principle that the great warriors are genuinely fighting for their lives. However, most examples have an 'escape clause'; there is one vulnerable spot, or one weapon which can wound.

Īo, in mythology, priestess of *Hera at the Argive Heraion. *Zeus seduces her, but when Hera discovers, she is transformed into a white cow, and tethered to an olive-tree in the Heraion grove with the monster Argos as guard. *Hermes kills Argos, but Hera inflicts a gadfly upon the bovine Io, who now wanders distraught around the world (in Aeschylus' *Prometheus Bound* past the remote Caucasus to receive a lecture from the enchained *Prometheus) until finally she reaches Egypt, where with a touch of his hand Zeus restores her, and soon Epaphus is born to her, the ancestor of *Danaus who will return to *Argos with the Danaids, his daughters.

Iocasta See OEDIPUS.

Īon of Chios, a versatile poet and prose author, seems to have been born in the 480s BC and to have come to Athens c.466. He was dead by 421, when *Aristophanes paid him a graceful tribute in *Peace*.

Works included the following. (1) *Tragedies and satyr-plays; see SATYRIC DRAMA. He was defeated by *Euripides in 438, but on another occasion he is said to have won first prize in both tragedy and *dithyramb and to have made a present of Chian *wine to every Athenian citizen. He was admitted by later critics into a canon of five great tragedians. **Longinus' found his plays faultless and elegant but lacking the inspired boldness of *Sophocles. (2) *Visits*, a book of reminiscences, in prose. This recounted Ion's meetings with, and impressions of, great men of his day, and was perhaps his most original work, and the most interesting to us. Surviving fragments describe meetings with *Cimon, *Aeschylus, and Sophocles, all of whom Ion admired (the conversation of Sophocles at a

symposium on Chios is the subject of a long extract).

Ionian festivals Festivals constitutive of the *Ionians on several levels of identity.

Festivals which were specific to the Athenian and Ionian festival-calendars were already in antiquity used as an argument for a common origin; they date back to before the Ionian migration (10th cent. BC). They include *Anthesteria, *Apaturia, *Lenaea, Plynteria, Pyanopsia, and *Thargelia. The Anthesteria attest a cult of *Dionysus already before the emigration. Exceptionally, common rituals confirm the connection, such as the expulsion of the *pharmakos* at the Thargelia.

The Ionians themselves articulated their identity in two festivals. In the Archaic period, first the Cycladic (see CYCLADES), then later all Ionians met at the festival of Delian Apollo. See DELOS. The (mainly Anatolian) Ionian cities held their common festival, the Panionia, in the *Panionium, a sanctuary of Poseidon Heliconios in the territory of Priene.

Ionian Revolt The east Greeks, prosperous and compliant subjects of *Persia from c.546/5 BC, remained uniquely quiet at *Darius I's irregular accession. Further Persian expansion in *Egypt, and *Thrace, however, increased imperial tax-exactions and reduced Hellenic market-share and attractive mercenary opportunities. Resenting *barbarian overlords, autocratic regimes (see TYRANNY), and conscript service for Persia, most Ionian cities (see IONIANS) followed Milesian *Aristagoras in deposing local tyrants (499). Enough Athenian and Eretrian assistance arrived to raze *Sardis. Ethnic religious assembly (*Panionium), political organization, and intercity operations proved east Greek capacities for unified action. So *Hellespontines, *Carians, and many *Cypriots joined the rebels. Samian and Lesbian interests (see LESBOS; SAMOS), however, diverged from Milesian and Carian. Inadequate revenues and budgetary mechanisms and disputed military hierarchies further weakened resolve.

Persia mobilized and defeated Hellenes and allies at *Ephesus, *Cyprus, and Labraunda, then reconquered Anatolian territories by amphibious, triple-pronged, city-by-city advances. Both commands welcomed a decisive naval battle near *Miletus (at Lade, 494). Approximately 70,000 allied Greeks in 353 ships, capable Dionysius of *Phocaea commanding, faced 600 largely Phoenician vessels. Co-operation among the predominantly Chian, Samian, Milesian, and Lesbian contingents—rivals to begin with—collapsed when battle commenced. Persian 'politics' and bribery succeeded where sheer force had not. Many fought bravely, but most Samians had agreed to defect. Miletus was sacked, the inhabitants killed, enslaved, or deported. The coastal and island mop-up was easy and ruthless.

*Herodotus' account, based on surviving losers' biased reconstructions, replays and exasperatedly explains the defeat. Like the westerners' later edifying victory, the east Greeks' edifying defeat demanded heroes and villains. Short-sighted tyrants, Ionian disorganization, and military disinclination are blamed throughout. Ionian achievements are trivialized or negated, as each *polis castigated the others' motives. Herodotus condemned the liberation as doomed from birth, but his facts allow alternative reconstructions. Initial successes and co-ordination suggest that liberation was possible.

Revolt produced three positive results. *Mardonius replaced some unpopular Hellenic tyrants on Persia's western borders with more democratic regimes. Artaphernes renegotiated tribute collections. Persian westward expansion was delayed.

Ionians, a section of the Greek people mentioned only once by Homer, but important later, after the central part of the west coast of *Asia Minor (still non-Greek in Homer) had become known as Ionia. Ionia was colonized, acc. to early traditions, by refugees from the Greek mainland, flying before the *Dorians and other tribes from NW Greece. Herodotus speaks of the mixed blood of the colonists, and adds that some of them took the women of the conquered *Carians. All were, however, reckoned as Ionians 'who trace their descent from Athens and keep the *Apaturia'.

The claim of Athens to be the mother-city of all Ionians will not hold, as Herodotus says; and the eponymous ancestor could only artificially be worked into the Athenian *genealogies, themselves extremely artificial (see XUTHOS). But the Athenian claim to be the 'eldest land of Ionia' was as old as *Solon, and long preceded any Attic claims to political predominance; and it receives confirmation from the appearance of some of the four ancient 'tribes' (see PHYLAI) of Attica in inscriptions of half-a-dozen Ionian cities. There may be some truth in the Athenian claim to have organized expeditions to Ionia,

but this was inflated in the time of the *Delian League (see below).

The Ionians, from about 750 BC, developed precociously (see the brilliant picture in the *Hymn to Delian Apollo*; see HYMNS, GREEK). Throughout the east 'Yawani' became the generic term for 'Greek'. They were, however, exposed to attack from the Lydian and Persian monarchies, and the effort to throw off Persian rule, exercised through Greek 'tyrants', ended in ruin after a struggle of six years (494), see IONIAN REVOLT. Then came Athenian overlordship and the devaluing of Ionians as unmanly. The generalization that credited Dorians with more steadfastness, Ionians with more intelligence, is in each case open to numerous exceptions. The Dorian–Ionian polarity was exaggerated (though not invented) by 5th-cent. Athenian propaganda.

See also ALPHABET, GREEK; AUTOCHTHONS; CHIOS; DORIANS; EPHESUS; IONIAN FESTIVALS; MILETUS; PANIONIUM; PHOCAEA; SAMOS.

Ionian Sea, used as an alternative to 'Adriatic Sea' for the waters between the Balkan peninsula and Italy, and like 'Adriatic', sometimes extended to include the sea east of Sicily. The name would seem to originate from early Ionian seafaring to the west.

Īphigenīa, the daughter of *Agamemnon and *Clytemnestra. *Artemis demanded her sacrifice as the price for sending a fair wind to the Greeks waiting at *Aulis to sail for Troy. In some versions Artemis was angry because Agamemnon had killed a deer—and boasted that he was a better hunter than Artemis. In another version he had killed a sacred goat kept in Artemis' grove and made the same boast. Acc. to one version, Agamemnon sent for Iphigenia on the pretext of marriage to *Achilles. In Aeschylus' *Agamemnon* it is suggested that she died at the altar—or at least that the spectators thought she did. In most versions Artemis snatched her away and saved her; a hind replaced her and was sacrificed in her place. In Euripides' *Iphigenia in Tauris* she becomes a priestess of Artemis, first in the Taurid (Crimea) and then at *Brauron. In the Taurid she was forced to preside over human sacrifices; on recognizing her brother (*Orestes) in one of the prospective victims she fled with him and Artemis' statue, which Athena instructed them to take to Attica. At Brauron she was associated with the rite of the *arkteia*, had a shrine, and received *hero-cult; the clothes of women who died in *childbirth were dedicated to her.

Īris, goddess of the rainbow and messenger of the gods. She is usually employed by *Zeus in *Homer's *Iliad*, once by *Hera, whose officious minister she later becomes. In Archaic art she has winged boots and short *chiton* like *Hermes, but later is winged, with long or short dress, and carries a herald's *sceptre. She appears in many divine or heroic scenes as messenger, as servant of Hera (*Parthenon frieze), and sometimes as a lone traveller beset by *satyrs or *Centaurs.

iron The new technical processes which introduced the widespread use of iron to the Mediterranean seem to have originated between the 13th and the 9th cents. BC. Iron was used for Mycenaean jewellery, and is mentioned in Homer. An iron bowl-stand was one of the *votives dedicated by *Alyattes at *Delphi. Greece possesses small iron-deposits. The main sources in classical times were Elba and the country behind Trapezus. Elba was a major source of iron, and the slag-heaps from Populonia in Etruria seem to represent an annual iron output of 1,600 to 2,000 tons from that city alone. Other ancient sources include *Thrace and, under the Roman republic, *Spain. Iron has a very high melting-point, and ancient furnaces could not reach such temperatures; so wrought, not cast, iron was produced. Weapons were made of mild steel. Quenching to harden is known to *Homer. The Romans produced blades which would not snap. See MINES AND MINING.

irrigation Mesopotamia (*Babylonia) and *Egypt were the main areas of the ancient world where agriculture depended on irrigation from a river rather than rainfall. In Mesopotamia the *Euphrates and Tigris permitted irrigation of extensive plains through a radial network of descending *canals. The more gentle gradient of the Nile and its very narrow valley meant that local basin irrigation was predominant in Egypt. Both these 'natural' systems required heavy communal work to clear canals and repair dykes, and careful drainage to avoid salination, but only the former, being an integrated system, demanded a single centralized control. 'Artificial' irrigation was necessary for land which lay above the flood-level and for additional watering of other land outside the period of inundation. The pole-mounted scoop (Arabic *shaduf*) was always the cheapest and commonest mechanical aid. 'Artificial' irrigation

was so laborious or costly in the ancient world that it remained confined to small plots of horticultural cultivation for the market. See AGRICULTURE, GREEK and ROMAN; WATER.

Īsaeus, Athenian speech-writer (*c*.420–340s BC), who specialized in inheritance cases. Some 64 speech-titles were known in antiquity, 50 of which were reckoned genuine. Eleven survive complete, of which four can be internally dated. The subject-matter of his speeches is fundamental for Athenian social history, lying as it does where the study of Athenian legal practice converges with those of oratorical professionalism, property acquisition strategies (see INHERITANCE), and private familial behaviour.

Īsis, 'mistress of the house of life', whose creative and nurturing functions made her the most popular divinity of the Late period in the Egyptian *Fayūm and delta. As such she absorbed, or was equated with, many other divinities, acquiring a universal character. A connected narrative of her myth appears late, doubtless under Greek influence. In the Egyptian versions, the myth generally begins with Set's murder of her brother and husband, Osiris, whom she and her sister revive by mourning. Impregnated by Osiris after his resurrection, Isis gives birth to Horus, who, after 'redeeming his father', ascends his throne, and later attacks and rapes Isis. In return, Isis chops off his hands. In the theology of the New Kingdom she has several linked roles: as a goddess who protects the coffin, she is 'mother', 'wet-nurse', of the dead, and brings about rebirth; as midwife, she protects women in giving birth and suckling; equated with Sothis (Sirius), she brings the Nile flood and the new year; equated with the snake-goddess Renenutet, the goddess of harvest, she is 'mistress of life'; as magician and protector, as in the Graeco-Egyptian magical papyri, she is 'mistress of heaven'. See MAGIC.

In Egyptian popular religion of the Hellenistic and Roman periods, these roles are simplified to three: protector of women and marriage; goddess of maternity and the new-born; guarantor of the fertility of fields and the abundance of harvests. Herodotus' identification of Isis with *Demeter, and the later view of Isis and Osiris as inventors of arable farming, reproduce only the last of these motifs. The version of Isis that was attractive in the Graeco-Roman world universalized this popular representation: dispenser of life, protector (esp. of the family), healer, deliverer, and so mistress of the universe. See EGYPTIAN DEITIES.

islands were and are one of the most obvious features of Greek life. 'The islands', as a geographical collective, formed one of the tribute districts of the 5th-cent. BC Athenian empire (see DELIAN LEAGUE), and 'islanders' is almost a synonym for Athens' subjects; but more often island status implies separateness. Islands in *Homer can symbolize remoteness and even magical strangeness (e.g. in *Odyssey*. 6, Scheria). Although in the real world 'islanders' could be a synonym for people in an exposed and defenceless situation, nevertheless island status was also seen as desirable because it meant security. Poets celebrated particular islands. *Relegation to islands was a punishment for members of the Roman élite in the imperial period. See also EUHEMERUS; ISLANDS OF THE BLEST; SEA POWER.

Islands of the Blest were originally, like the 'Gardens of the *Hesperides', the mythical winterless home of the happy dead, far west. Comparable is *Homer's description of *Elysium; in both cases entry is reserved for a privileged few. The islands were later identified with Madeira or more commonly with the Canaries, after their discovery. The Canaries were properly explored by King *Juba II. From the meridian line of this group *Ptolemy (*Geography, passim*) established his longitudes eastwards.

Īsocratēs (436–338 BC), distinguished Athenian *rhetor and writer of rhetorical texts. Although he lacked the voice and the confidence ever to address a large audience and so played no direct part in affairs of state, his written speeches provide us with a valuable commentary on the political issues of the 4th cent. His system of education in rhetoric influenced both the written and the spoken word: his many pupils included the historians *Ephorus and *Theopompus, the atthidographer *Androtion, the general Timotheus, and the orators *Hyperides and *Isaeus. Judgements of his importance have variously treated him as the prophet of the Hellenistic world, and as the specious adulator of personal rulers.

Life As son of a rich man, he studied under *Prodicus, *Gorgias, and *Theramenes. He was also a follower of *Socrates. In the 390s he turned his theoretical training to account and wrote speeches for others to use in the courts. Soon discontented with the profession of speech-writer, he began to train others in rhet-

oric. In *Against the Sophists* he advertised his principles. *Panegyric*, published in 380, was his version of a conventional subject treated by Gorgias and *Lysias; its demand that the Greeks unite under the shared hegemony of Athens and Sparta was familiar (see PANHELLENISM). As a result of Timotheus' successes Athens could make the peace (375) which embodied the principle of the shared hegemony. Isocrates began to address pleas to eminent individuals begging them to assume the lead against Persia.

The failure of Athens to suppress rebellious allies and the perilous financial position of the state in 355 stirred Isocrates to denounce the war policy of the imperialists as the way to bankruptcy, and to demand, in place of the limited peace being made with the allies, a Common Peace and the solution of economic difficulties by the foundation of colonies in *Thrace. On the question of a panhellenic crusade he is silent; a Persian ultimatum had ruled it out for the moment. Shortly after, in *Areopagiticus*, Isocrates advocated return to a sober constitution under which the *Areopagus would exercise its ancient general supervision of all aspects of life. The treatise must have made a curious impression on his countrymen. Certainly by 353 Isocrates was on the defensive. By then he had made a fortune unprecedented for his profession, and he had become liable to frequent *trierarchies; challenged in 354/3 to an *antidosis, Isocrates had emerged from the court unsuccessful and, imagining himself as a second Socrates, felt moved to write his apologia in his *Antidosis* of 353, in which he criticized his rivals and gave some account of what he himself professed. This is the chief source of our knowledge of his system of education.

In 346 he published his most important treatise, *Philippus*. It called on Philip 'to lead both the concord (see HOMONOIA) of the Hellenes and the campaign against the *barbarians' and to relieve the misery of Greece by planting colonies in the western satrapies of the Persian empire. In the following year, when Philip instead of beginning the crusade had got himself wounded in war against northern barbarians, Isocrates sent a letter urging him to begin the campaign against Persia and so acquit himself of slanderous accusations about his real intentions. In 342 he began the last of his great treatises, *Panathenaicus*. It was in part personal apologia, in part a comprehensive comparison of Athens and Sparta, glorifying the former. Nowhere did he manifest any further interest in the great theme of his *Panegyric* and his *Philippus*.

Events had disappointed him. One last effort remained. After discussion with *Antipater, when after *Chaeronea he came to negotiate, Isocrates wrote an appeal to Philip to set about the programme of *Philippus*. The Peace of *Demades was the answer, and in autumn 338 the aged Isocrates starved himself to death.

Significance Isocrates' various writings addressed to Philip probably helped him to form a clearer idea of the nature and strength of the panhellenist movement, the support of which he needed. His ideas about the partnership of Philip and the Greeks appear from the treatises to have been very imprecise. His new colonies would merely remove the impoverished from Greece, and he had no vision of the prosperity that could and did flow from the creation of new trading areas. On the other hand, he did provide answers to the two great problems of his age, viz. the discord (*stasis*) within cities due to poverty, and the discord between cities due to petty ambitions and rivalries.

In the history of education Isocrates has an important place. See EDUCATION, GREEK, 3. Apparently his pupils received under his personal supervision a course of instruction which was neither purely speculative nor a mere training in rhetoric. He disdained the business of the law-courts as well as 'astrology, geometry, and the like', which at best, he held, did no harm but were of no use 'either in personal matters or in public affairs', and he eschewed the logic-chopping of *dialectic, 'the so-called eristic dialogues'. For him the true concern of higher education was 'discussion of general and practical matters', the training of men for discussion and action in the sphere of the practical. In all this he differed from *Plato, whose chief concern was (hardly attainable) knowledge, moral and metaphysical. There was, not surprisingly, tension between the two, and with delicate irony Plato at the end of *Phaedrus* sneered at Isocrates, who defended himself and his system in *Antidosis*.

Writings Of the 60 orations extant under his name in Roman times 21 survive; six are court speeches. The works of Isocrates represent Attic prose at its most elaborate. He seems to have paid more attention to mere expression than any other Greek writer. His vocabulary is almost as pure as that of *Lysias, but while the simplicity of Lysias appears natural, the smoothness of Isocrates is studied.

Ister was the name given by the Greeks to the lower Danube (see DANUVIUS). From a know-ledge of its estuary, where they established a colony before 600 BC, the Greeks drew conclusions as to the size of the Danube. *Hesiod mentioned it as one of the four great rivers of the world. *Herodotus regarded it as the largest river of Europe and a northern counterpart to the *Nile. He correctly stated that it had a constant volume of water, but mistakenly assumed that its last bend was to the south and knew nothing of its source.

Isthmian Games The Isthmian Games were held at Isthmia, 16 km. (10 mi.) east of *Corinth, in honour of *Poseidon. They were reorganized as a *panhellenic festival c.582 BC, held biennially, and administered by Corinth, whose position as a commercial centre made them popular. Chariot- and horse-races were prominent (see HORSE- AND CHARIOT-RACES).

Italy Italy's greatest length is c.1,100 km. (680 mi.); the greatest breadth of the peninsula proper is c.240 km. (150 mi.). Its long coastline possesses few, mostly indifferent ports, Genua, *Puteoli, *Tarentum, *Brundisium, Ancona, and Pola being exceptions. Italy could, however, exploit its central position to build a Mediterranean empire. Mountains, valleys, and plains in juxtaposition feature the Italian landscape. The Alps form a natural but not impassable northern frontier: The Brenner from time immemorial has been used by invaders attracted by Italy's pleasant climate, fertility, and beauty; the Alps are steeper on the Italian side. Between Alps and Apennines lies the indefensible north Italian plain watered by the Po (see PADUS). The Apennines traverse peninsular Italy, impeding but not actually preventing communications. Italy contained few precious metals (see MINES AND MINING, *Roman*).

Despite fertile upland valleys, the mountain districts usually permitted only a frugal existence. The plains, however, were amazingly productive, being enriched partly by volcanic activity, partly by silt carried down by numerous rivers which in winter contained enough water. Northern Italy also possessed important lakes, but not central or southern Italy apart from Trasimene, Fucinus, and water-filled craters like *Albanusmons and Avernus. So Italy's natural products were abundant and varied: *olives, various fruits, *cereals, *timber, etc. The variety is explained chiefly by the climate, which is temperate if not cold in the mountains and north Italy, and warm if not hot in south Italy. Italy contains excellent pasturage; in many districts ranching supplanted agriculture (see TRANSHU-MANCE). Its seas abound in fish (see FISHING).

During the 8th cent. BC contact was established between Etruria, *Latium, and the early Greek colonies in south Italy (see COLONIZATION, GREEK). This was a stimulus to, and a profound influence upon, the emergence of the *Etruscan cities. The cities of Latium, including Rome, likewise expanded. Elsewhere in Italy a diverse mosaic of peoples began to achieve cultural and political identities. The coastal fringes of SW and south Italy, together with *Sicily, comprised *Magna Graecia. In the north, Gauls settled from c.400 or before. Some 40 languages were spoken altogether, and the peoples varied greatly in culture and level of civilization.

Ultimately, the peoples of Italy were for the first time united under the hegemony of Rome. This took the half-millennium between the 5th cent. BC and the reign of Augustus. *Romanization was slow and uneven, but was aided by the gradual creation of a new road network; by the founding of citizen, Latin and, later, veteran, colonies; and by the diffusion of the Latin language, mass-produced Roman goods, new concepts of town planning, and the spread of Romanized villas and farms. It was also fuelled by the profits brought in through the wars of conquest, which encouraged public and private patronage, as a means of social and political advantage.

With Italy finally unified, Augustus divided it into eleven administrative districts (regiōnēs):

   I. Latium, Campania, Picentini district
  II. Apulia, Calabria, Hirpini district
 III. Lucania, *ager Bruttius*
 IV. Region inhabited by, among others, Samnites (see SAMNIUM) and *Sabines
  V. Picenum, Praetuttii district
 VI. Umbria, *ager Gallicus*
 VII. Etruria
VIII. Gallia Cispadana
 IX. Liguria
  X. Venetia, Istria, Cenomani district
 XI. Gallia Transpadana

From the late 1st cent. AD, Italy's political and commercial pre-eminence began to wane. The process accelerated under the African and Syrian Severan dynasty (193–235), and, under *Diocletian, the imperial court moved to Mediolanum, 300.

Italy, languages of After the introduction of the *alphabet by the Greeks in the 8th cent. BC

and its adoption by the native peoples, *literacy gradually spread throughout Italy. Epigraphic remains (see EPIGRAPHY) provide evidence for a variety of languages down to the 1st cent. BC, when the spread of Latin that accompanied the extension of Roman power throughout the peninsula led to the disappearance of all other tongues (except only Greek), at least in their written form, by the Augustan period.

See ETRUSCAN LANGUAGE; LATIN LANGUAGE.

Ithōmē a prominent and easily fortified mountain rising isolated in the *Messenian plain, was the natural rallying point of the Messenians in their struggles for independence against *Sparta and, in 369 BC, site of the new city of Messene. In the first Messenian War (late 8th cent. BC) they held it for 20 years; on its fall they lost their freedom. In the rising of the *helots against Sparta in the late 460s it was fortified and became a chief centre of resistance.

itineraries, lists of settlements, way-marks, or posting-stations, often with distances between them. The genre originated with the Roman practice of making an *iter*, the military route into or through hostile territory which underlay the Roman theory of road-building. Thus the area of operation of Roman power could be marked out as a series of measured routes.

iūdex In the Roman civil process, with its division into two stages, before the magistrate (*in iūre*) and before the judge (*apud iūdicem*), the iūdex was a private person taken from the higher social classes, who was appointed to conduct the hearing in the second stage. No special legal knowledge was required. The choice of the judge lay with the parties and was normally, but not necessarily, made from a panel of qualified persons. The parties' choice was approved by the magistrate before whom the proceedings *in iure* were conducted. The iudex could not refuse the commission conferred on him by the magistrate's order to hear the case, except on recognized grounds. For the proceedings at the trial see LAW AND PROCEDURE, ROMAN, 2.

Iūlia (1), daughter of *Caesar and Cornēlia, b. c.73 BC, was married in 59 to *Pompey; their mutual affection bound Pompey more strongly to her father Caesar. In 55 the sight of Pompey returning from the *comitia spattered with blood allegedly caused a miscarriage; and next year she died in childbirth, the child dying a few days later. On the people's insistence, she was buried in the *Campus Martius, and in 46 Caesar held magnificent shows near her tomb.

Iūlia (2), only daughter of *Augustus (by Scribonia, divorced by him in 38 BC after Iulia's birth). She was brought up strictly by her father and stepmother *Livia Drusilla. In 25 she married her cousin *Claudius Marcellus (2) and in 21 *Agrippa, to whom she bore Gaius *Iulius Caesar (2) and Lucius Iulius Caesar, Iulia, *Vipsania Agrippina (2), and Agrippa *Iulius Caesar (Agrippa Postumus). Her third marriage, to *Tiberius (in 11) is said to have been happy at first, but estrangement followed. In 2 BC Augustus learned of her alleged adulteries and banished her to Pandateria; in AD 4 she was allowed to move to Rhegium. Scribonia voluntarily shared her exile. Augustus forbade her burial in his mausoleum, and Tiberius kept her closely confined and stopped her allowance, so that she died of malnutrition before the end of 14. *Macrobius speaks of her gentle disposition and learning, and gives anecdotes attesting her wit.

Iūlia Agrippīna, 'Agrippina the Younger' (AD 15–59), eldest daughter of *Germanicus and *Vipsania Agrippina (2). In 28 she was betrothed to Domitius Ahenobarbus, to whom she bore one son, the later emperor *Nero, in 37. During the principate of her brother *Gaius (1) (37–41) her name, like her sisters', was coupled with the emperor's in vows and oaths; but when she was discovered late in 39 to be involved in the conspiracy of Cornelius Lentulus Gaetulicus, she was banished. She was recalled by her uncle *Claudius, who married her in 49. Aided by *Antonius Pallas, *Seneca the Younger, and *Afranius Burrus, she quickly achieved her ambitious purpose. Receiving for herself the title Augusta (see AUGUSTUS, AUGUSTA AS TITLES), she persuaded Claudius to adopt Nero as guardian of his own son Britannicus. She was generally believed to have poisoned Claudius, to make room for Nero (54). In the first years of Nero's rule she was almost co-regent with him, but, after Pallas had fallen in 55 and Burrus and Seneca turned against her, she lost her power. In 59 she was murdered at Baiae by Anicetus, acting on Nero's instructions.

Iūlia Domna, daughter of Iūlius Bassiānus, priest of *Elagabalus at Emesa on Orontes, married *Septimius Severus in AD 187; her sons Marcus *Aurelius Antoninus (Caracalla) and *Septimius Geta were born in 188 and 189. She became Augusta (see AUGUSTUS, AUGUSTA AS TITLES) in 193 and 'mother of the camp' in 195; out of favour with Severus during the predominance of Fulvius Plautianus, she devoted herself to patronage of literature, inspiring *Philostratus' *Life of Apollonius*. She was in *Britain during the expedition of 208–11. Although trying in vain to save Geta, she was given a prominent role under Caracalla, becoming 'mother of the senate and of the fatherland' and managing his correspondence; she took her own life in 217, after Caracalla's murder.

Iūlia Drūsilla, b. probably in AD 16, the second daughter of *Germanicus and *Vipsania Agrippina (2). Her name, like her sisters', was compulsorily included in vows and oaths after the accession of her brother *Gaius (1) (Caligula). She was his favourite sister, and it was rumoured that their relations were incestuous. She was named as Gaius' heir during his illness (late 37), but died in 38. Public mourning was enforced throughout the empire and, though there was no precedent in Roman history for the deification of a woman, she was deified as Panthea, probably on the anniversary of Augustus' birthday.

Iūlius Agricola, Gnaeus (AD 40–93), son of a senator from Forum Iulii, was brought up by his mother after his father's execution by *Gaius (1). After study at *Massalia, he was *tribunus militum in *Britain during the *Boudiccan revolt (60–61). He then married, was *quaestor of Asia (63–64), tribune of the *plebs* (66; see TRIBUNI PLEBIS), and *praetor (68). Appointed by *Galba to recover temple property, after joining the Flavian side he recruited troops in Italy. Commanding *legion XX in Britain, he saw action under *Petillius Cerialis (71–73). He was made a *patrician, served as *legate of Aquitania (73–76), became *consul (76?) and *pontifex, then legate of Britain for seven years (77–84), winning *ornamenta triumphalia.

Apart from mentions by *Cassius Dio, a lapidary inscription at Verulamium, and inscribed lead pipes from Deva, Agricola is known entirely from the biography by his son-in-law *Tacitus. See BIOGRAPHY, ROMAN. He was certainly exceptional: the only senator known to have served three times in one province; unusually young as governor of Britain; the longest known tenure there. Favour from *Vespasian and *Titus may be surmised. In his first season (77) he conquered Anglesey; in the second he was in northern England and southern Scotland. Measures to promote *Romanization in his second winter are stressed by Tacitus. In his third season (79) he advanced to the Tay, leading to Titus' fifteenth imperatorial *acclamation; in the fourth (80) he consolidated along the Forth–Clyde. His fifth season (81) was in west Scotland: he drew up his forces facing Ireland, which he told Tacitus could easily have been conquered. He then tackled the Caledonians, victory narrowly eluding him in the sixth season (82) but being won at a great battle late in the seventh, mons Graupius, probably September 83. He ordered the fleet to circumnavigate Britain, finally proving that it was an island. Recalled, presumably in spring 84, he was denied further appointments because of *Domitian's jealousy, acc. to Tacitus. See BRITAIN, ROMAN.

Iūlius Agrippa (1) **I, Marcus** (10 BC–AD 44), called 'Herod' in the *Acts of the Apostles but 'Agrippa' on his coins. A grandson of *Herod (1) the Great and eventually ruler of his former kingdom. He lived in Rome from childhood, under the patronage of the widowed *Antonia (2) the Younger, until the death of his friend Drusus *Iulius Caesar in AD 23. Josephus narrates Agrippa's attempts to raise funds in Palestine and Italy. He was imprisoned by *Tiberius in 36 for a treasonable remark, but, when his friend *Gaius (1) acceded, appointed *tetrarch of territories NE of the Sea of Galilee. In 39 the substantially Jewish areas of Galilee and Peraea, until then under *Herod (2) Antipas, were added. Agrippa's appearance, when he passed through *Alexandria, provoked anti-Jewish riots. Shortly before Gaius' assassination, he dissuaded the emperor from desecrating the Temple. In 41 *Claudius, in whose accession Agrippa had been involved, added Judaea and Samaria, to complete his kingdom. But the emperor was later displeased by Agrippa's extension of the city wall in north *Jerusalem and by his inviting client kings to Tiberias. Agrippa's dramatic death in the *Caesarea amphitheatre is embroidered in tradition. His respect for Judaism was remembered. Acts of the Apostles makes him responsible for the execution of James brother of John and for Peter's imprisonment.

Iūlius Agrippa (2) **II, Marcus** (b. AD 27/8), did not succeed his father *Agrippa I in 44, but lived in Rome. There he supported the Jews before *Claudius against the Samaritans and the procurator. In 53 Agrippa was appointed king of the area in the Lebanon and anti-Lebanon region once ruled by his father. Nero added parts of Galilee and of Peraea. Agrippa's

coins carry the imperial portrait. He lavished attention on the Temple and had his *Jerusalem palace close by. But in 66 he and his sister Berenice were expelled from the city by the Jewish leadership, having failed to persuade the Jews to tolerate Gessius Florus' conduct as procurator. Unable to prevent revolt, Agrippa supplied cavalry and archers to the Romans throughout the war, and accompanied *Titus during its latter stages. He was rewarded by an enlargement of his territory. In 75, when Berenice went to live with *Titus in Rome, Agrippa received praetorian status there. He supplied *Josephus with information for his *Jewish War* and commended the work on publication. St *Paul appeared before him.

Iūlius Caesar, Agrippa (Marcus Vipsā-nius Agrippa Postumus), youngest son of *Vipsanius Agrippa and *Iulia (2), b. in 12 BC after his father's death, was adopted by *Augustus with *Tiberius in AD 4, becoming Agrippa Iulius Caesar. He had a fine physique, but, perhaps because he fell foul of Augustus, reports of his personality were unfavourable: *ferōcia* ('bloody-mindedness') is alleged. In AD 6 Augustus removed him from the Julian family, took over his property, and relegated him to Surrentum; in 7 the senate exiled him to Planasia. See ISLANDS; RELEGATION; EXILE, *Roman*. Probably a defeat in the struggle for the succession caused his disgrace rather than simple personality defects: the settlement of AD 4 gave more power to Tiberius than Agrippa, his sister Iulia, and their associates could accept. Attempts to rescue him and put him at the head of a military insurrection are alleged. He was killed immediately after the death of Augustus in 14, it is not clear on whose instructions.

Iūlius Caesar, Drūsus (*c*.13 BC–AD 23), only surviving son of the later emperor *Tiberius, by Vipsānia. Originally Nero Claudius Drusus, he became a Caesar in AD 4, on Tiberius' adoption by *Augustus. He married *Germanicus' sister *Livia Iulia (Livilla). He suppressed the mutiny of the Pannonian legions after Augustus' death in 14, was consul in 15, and did well in Illyricum (see ILLYRIANS) 17–20, celebrating an *ovation. His relations with Germanicus were friendly, despite mischief-makers. Germanicus' death (19) made him Tiberius' sole prospective successor: after his second consulship (21) he received tribunician power (22); his death in the next year opened the succession question. His taste for the games made him popular, though he is reported dissolute and violent. He had quarrelled with *Sejanus, and when Sejanus fell (31) it was alleged that Livilla, who was Sejanus' mistress, had poisoned Drusus.

Iūlius Caesar (1), **Gāius**, b. 100 BC of a *patrician family without social equals, as descendents of *Venus and *Aeneas, but with little recent political success. His father's sister Iulia married *Marius, but Caesar's father never became consul. *Cornelius Cinna while in power, gave Caesar his daughter Cornelia in marriage and made him *flamen Dialis* (see FLAMINES)—a post of supreme honour but normally precluding a consulship (no doubt thought unattainable). *Sulla, after his victory, annulled his enemies' measures, including this appointment, but as a fellow patrician spared Caesar's life, even though he refused to divorce Cornelia and voluntarily resign his priesthood.

Most of the next decade Caesar spent in Asia, studying and winning military distinction, including a victory over an advance force of *Mithradates VI and a *corona civica* (see CROWNS AND WREATHS, *Roman*); but two prosecutions of ex-Sullans, although unsuccessful, established his fame as an orator. In 73 he was co-opted a *pontifex*, largely through family connections, and returned to Rome. Elected *tribunus militum*, he supported amnesty for the associates of *Aemilius Lepidus (2). As quaestor 69, before going to his province of Further Spain, he lost both his aunt Iulia and his wife. He conducted their funerals in the grand aristocratic manner (see NOBILES), stressing his aunt's (and thus partly his own) descent from kings and gods and, for the first time since Sulla, displaying Marius' *imago* (see IMAGINES) and distinctions in public. On his return from Spain he found the Latin colonies beyond the Po (*Padus) vigorously demanding Roman citizenship and supported their agitation, but did nothing to further their cause in Rome. He also supported the laws of *Gabinius and *Manilius, conferring extraordinary commands on *Pompey (a most useful patron), and he married Pompeia, a granddaughter of Sulla. With Pompey overseas, he courted another powerful ex-Sullan, *Licinius Crassus, Pompey's enemy, joining him in various political schemes in return for financial support, which enabled Caesar to spend large sums as *curator* of the *via Appia and as aedile (65). In 64, in charge of the murder court, he resumed his vendetta against Sulla by offering to receive prosecutions of men who had killed citizens in Sulla's proscription.

In 63 Caecilius Metellus Pius' death left vacant the post of *pontifex maximus*, a post normally held by eminent ex-consuls. Although two such sought the office, Caesar announced his candidacy and through lavish bribery won the election. This and his election to a *praetorship for 62 established him as a man of power and importance. He supported *Sergius Catilina, who advocated a welcome cancellation of debts, but covered his tracks when Catiline turned to conspiracy. The consul *Cicero, who to the end of his days was convinced of Caesar's involvement, had to proclaim his innocence. In his prosecution of *Rabirius Caesar left the legality of the so-called *senatus consultum ultimum* in doubt, and when Cicero wanted the death penalty under that decree for the conspirators betrayed by the Allobrogan envoys, Caesar persuaded most senators to vote against it, until a speech by *Porcius Cato (2) changed their minds.

As praetor he joined the tribune Caecilius Metellus Nepos in agitating for the recall of Pompey against Catiline's forces. Suspended from office, he demonstratively submitted, and the senate, eager to avoid alienating him, reinstated and thanked him. In December, when Pompeia was *ex officio* in charge of the rites of the *Bona Dea, from which men were strictly excluded, *Clodius Pulcher gained access disguised as a woman—it was said, in order to approach Pompeia in her husband's absence—and was ejected. Caesar, while asserting the innocence of Clodius (a man congenial to him and worth cultivating) and of Pompeia, divorced her, proclaiming that his household must be free even from suspicion. With his consulship approaching, he could now seek a more advantageous marriage.

But first he had to go to his province of Further Spain. His creditors applied for an injunction to stop him from leaving, and he was saved from this unprecedented indignity by Crassus' standing surety for part of his debts: his provincial spoils would cover the rest. Largely neglecting his routine duties, he concentrated on attacking independent tribes. The *booty enabled him to clear his debts and pay large sums into the treasury, all without incurring a risk of prosecution. About mid-60 he returned to Rome, was voted a *triumph by a co-operative senate, and prepared to claim his consulship. There was a technical obstacle: to announce his candidacy for the consulship he had to enter Rome long before the triumph could be arranged, but that would forfeit his *imperium and right to triumph. The senate was ready to give him a dispensation, but his enemy Cato, although only an ex-tribune, arranged to be asked to speak and talked the proposal out. Caesar decided to put power before glory and entered the city.

He now could not afford to lose; so he needed allies and a massive infusion of money. A brilliant stroke secured both. In his absence Pompey and Crassus had failed—partly because each had opposed the other—to obtain what they each wanted from the senate: ratification of Pompey's eastern settlement and land for his veterans, and a remission of part of the price offered for the tithe of Asia by the *publicani. Caesar, on good terms with both, persuaded them to support his candidacy: he promised to give each what he wanted without harm to the other, provided they refrained from mutual opposition. Pompey now persuaded his rich friend Lucceius to join Caesar in his canvass: in return for paying the expenses for bribery (no doubt with Crassus' help), he could expect to succeed through Caesar's popularity. But Caesar's enemies, led by the upright Cato, collected a huge bribery fund for Cato's son-in-law *Calpurnius Bibulus, who secured second place after Caesar.

As consul Caesar appealed to the senate for co-operation in formulating the laws to satisfy his allies. Frustrated by his enemies, he passed them in the assembly by open violence, aided by friendly tribunes (see VATINIUS). Bibulus withdrew to his house, announcing that he was stopping all future meetings of the assemblies by watching the sky for omens. This unprecedented step, of doubtful legality, was ignored by Caesar, who satisfied Pompey and Crassus and went on to pass further legislation, *i.a.* on *extortion and on the publication of senate debates. Pompey and Crassus, satisfied (esp.) with his assuming the onus for his methods, now joined him in an open alliance (sometimes inaccurately called the 'First Triumvirate'). Pompey married *Iulia(1) and Caesar married *Calpurnia(1), whose father, *Calpurnius Piso Caesoninus, was made consul 58, with Pompey's aide Gabinius as colleague. For further insurance, Clodius was allowed to become a plebeian and tribune 58. Caesar's reward was a law of Vatinius, giving him Illyricum (see ILLYRIANS) and Cisalpine Gaul for five years. The senate obligingly added Transalpine Gaul. Early in 58 attempts to prosecute Caesar were averted, and moderates in the senate attempted conciliation by offering to have his legislation re-enacted in proper form. But Caesar refused, since this would admit guilt and impair his *dignitās*. The breach between him and the senate majority thus became irreparable.

A movement by the Helvetii gave him an unforeseen chance of starting a major war, which after nearly a decade and many vicissitudes led to the conquest of the whole of Gaul (see GALLIC WARS). It was in Gaul that he acquired the taste and the resources for monarchy and trained the legions that could 'storm the heavens'. Young Roman aristocrats flocked to him to make their fortunes, vast sums (sometimes made palatable as loans) flowed into the pockets of upper-class Romans and, as gifts, to cities and princes, to support Caesar's ambitions. The depleted treasury received none of the profits and was forced to pay for his legions. In his triumphs of 46 (see below) he displayed 63,000 talents of silver and spent *c*.20,000 of his own money, much of it booty from Gaul. Plutarch, on the basis of Caesar's figures, reports that a million Gauls were killed and another million enslaved. Requisitions of food and punitive devastations completed a human and economic disaster.

In Rome Caesar's position remained secure until 56, when his bitter enemy Domitius Ahenobarbus, confident of becoming consul 55, promised to recall and prosecute him, and Cicero, back from exile, hoped to detach Pompey from him. Crassus informed him of what was going on, and they summoned Pompey to Luca, where he was persuaded to renew the compact. Pompey and Crassus became consuls 55, receiving Spain and Syria respectively for five years, while Caesar's command was renewed for five years in Gaul; Pompey was to stay near Rome to look after their interests, governing Spain through *legati. But the alliance soon disintegrated. Iulia died (54), and Crassus, attacking *Parthia, was killed at Carrhae (53). In 52 Pompey married a daughter of Caesar's enemy Caecilius Metellus Pius Scipio and made him his colleague as consul. Caesar now secured authorization to stand for a consulship in absence in 49; but the legality of this became doubtful, and his claim that it included the right to retain *imperium* (hence immunity from prosecution) was denied by his enemies. (The legal position is obscured by partisan distortion.) Pompey was gradually (perhaps reluctantly) forced to co-operate with them, to avoid a consulship by Caesar in 48, which would have left him irreversibly at Caesar's mercy. In 49 Caesar, crossing the Rubicon, invaded Italy and started a civil war, nominally to defend the rights of tribunes who had been forced to flee to him for protection, but in fact, as he later admitted, to escape conviction and exile.

He rapidly overran Italy, where there were no reliable veteran legions to oppose him. As he moved down the peninsula, he kept making specious peace offers, retailed with considerable distortion in book 1 of his *Civil War*. Ahenobarbus was forced to surrender at Corfinium, and Pompey, knowing that Italy was untenable, to the chagrin of his aristocratic supporters crossed to Greece, hoping to strangle Italy by encirclement. Caesar broke it by defeating Pompey's *legati* in a brilliant campaign in Spain and then taking *Massalia. In 48 he crossed to Greece, though Pompey controlled the seas, and besieged him at Dyrrhachium. A tactical defeat there turned into *de facto* strategic victory when Pompey withdrew to Thessaly, where both sides received reinforcements. Persuaded, against his better judgement, to offer battle at *Pharsalus, Pompey was decisively defeated, escaped to Egypt and was killed. Caesar, arriving there in pursuit, intervened in a domestic conflict over the kingship and was cut off for months in Alexandria, until extricated by troops from Asia Minor and a Jewish force under Antipater, father of Herod (1) the Great. He spent three more months in Egypt, chiefly with *Cleopatra VII, whom he established on the throne and who after his departure bore a son whom she named Ptolemy Caesar. Then, moving rapidly through Syria and Asia Minor, he reorganized the eastern provinces, easily defeated the Bosporan (see BOSPORUS (2), CIMMERIAN) king Pharnaces II ('vēnī, vīdī, vīcī', 'I came, I saw, I conquered') and in September 47 returned to Italy. There he had to settle an army mutiny and serious social unrest, fanned during his absence by Caelius Rufus and *Annius Milo.

Meanwhile the republican forces had had time to entrench themselves in Africa, where Metellus Scipio assumed command, aided by King Juba I of *Numidia. Caesar landed in December. By deliberately inviting blockade at Thapsus, he won a decisive victory that led to the death of most of the republican leaders (including Scipio and Cato). On his return he was voted unprecedented honours and celebrated four splendid triumphs (20 September–1 October 46), nominally over foreign enemies, to mark the end of the wars and the beginning of reconstruction. But Pompeius Magnus, elder son of Pompey, soon joined by his brother Sextus and Labienus, consul for the second time, raised thirteen legions in Spain and secured much native support. In November Caesar hurriedly left Rome to meet the threat. The Pompeians were forced to offer battle at Munda and were annihilated with the loss of 30,000 men in Caesar's hardest-fought battle. After reorganizing Spain with massive *colonization, he returned to Rome and celebrated a triumph over 'Spain'.

Caesar had been *dictator (briefly), nominally for holding elections, in 49, consul for the second time 48, and dictator for the second time after Pharsalus; he was consul for the third time and 'prefect of morals' in 46 and dictator for the third time after Thapsus; he held his fourth, sole, consulship for nine months and his fourth dictatorship in 45, and was consul for the fifth time and (from about February) *dictator perpetuo* in 44. The specification of his dictatorships after the first is lost in the *fasti, but at least the third and fourth were probably, like Sulla's, 'for putting the state in order'. In addition to introducing the Julian calendar (see CALENDAR, ROMAN), his most lasting achievement, he greatly increased the numbers of senators, priests, and magistrates, for the first time since *c.*500 created new patrician families, founded numerous colonies, esp. for veterans and the city *plebs*, and passed various administrative reforms. His great-nephew Octavian, adopted by Caesar in his will in 45, was made a *pontifex* aged *c.*16 and, although he had no military experience, was designated *magister equitum* in 44, aged 18. Caesar, although he adopted the dress and ornaments of the old Roman kings, refused the invidious title of *rex, but, thinking gods superior to kings, aimed at deification (see RULER-CULT), which after gradual approaches he finally achieved shortly before his death (Marcus *Antonius was designated his *flamen*; see FLAMINES). It was the culmination of increasingly unprecedented honours voted by the senate, perhaps in part to see how far he would go, and he accepted most of them.

He had no plans for basic social, economic, or constitutional reforms, except to graft his divine and hereditary rule onto the republic. The abyss this opened between him and his fellow *nobiles* made him uncomfortable, and he planned to escape from Rome to wage a major Parthian war. As all remembered the disruption caused by his temporary absences during the Civil Wars, the prospect of being ruled by an absent divine monarch for years ahead proved intolerable even to his friends. He was assassinated in Pompey's Hall (next to his theatre), in a widespread conspiracy hastily stitched together to anticipate his departure, on 15 March 44.

Caesar was a distinguished orator in the 'Attic' manner, believing in '*analogy' (on which he wrote a treatise) and in the use of ordinary words. His speeches, at least some of which were published, and his pamphlet attacking Cato's memory (*Anticato*), are lost. Seven books on the Gallic War (an eighth was added by *Hirtius) and three on the Civil War survive, written to provide raw material for history and ensure that his point of view would prevail with posterity. Distortion at various points in the *Civil War* is demonstrated by evidence surviving in Cicero's correspondence.

Iūlius Caesar (2), **Gāius,** eldest son of *Agrippa and *Iulia (2), b. 20 BC, was adopted by *Augustus in 17. Augustus evidently hoped that he or his brother Lucius Iulius Caesar would succeed him, and the favour he showed them probably caused *Tiberius' retirement in 6. In 5, when Gaius assumed the *toga virilis*, he was designated consul for AD 1, admitted to the senate, and acclaimed by the *equestrians as *princeps iuventutis*. He was now virtually heir apparent. In 1 BC he married *Livia Iulia and was sent with proconsular authority to the east. In AD 2 he conferred with the Parthian king on the Euphrates and appointed a Roman nominee king of Armenia. This led to a revolt, which Gaius suppressed. Seriously wounded during a siege, he died eighteen months later on his way back to Italy (AD 4) to Augustus' great sorrow and dismay.

Iūlius Caesar, Germānicus elder son of Nero *Claudius Drusus and *Antonia (2) the Younger, was born in 15 or 16 BC and adopted in AD 4 by his uncle *Tiberius. As Tiberius was immediately adopted by *Augustus, Germanicus became a member of the Julian *gens* in the direct line of succession; and his career was accelerated by special dispensations. He served under Tiberius in Pannonia, and Germany. In 12 he was consul, and in 13, as commander-in-chief in Gaul and Germany, he won his first *acclamation as *imperator* in a campaign against the Germans, clearing them out of Gaul and re-establishing order there. By now he was a popular figure, held like his father to entertain 'republican' sentiments, and his affability contrasted with Tiberius' dour reserve. But, though by no means incapable, his judgement was unsteady. When, on the death of Augustus, the lower Rhine legions mutinied, his loyalty was proof against the (perhaps malicious) suggestion that he should supplant Tiberius, but his handling of the situation lacked firmness: he resorted to theatrical appeals and committed the emperor to accepting the mutineers' demands. On

dynastic matters the two were at one, but their political styles were different, and there was soon a marked difference of view as to how Germany should be handled, Tiberius adhering to the precept of the dying Augustus that rejected immediate territorial advance.

In the autumn of 14 Germanicus led the repentant legions briefly against the Marsi. But he was eager to emulate his father (Nero *Claudius Drusus) and reconquer parts of Germany lost after the defeat of *Quinctilius Varus. He campaigned in the spring of 15 against three tribes. In the summer he reached the *Teutoburgian forest, paid the last honours to Varus, and recovered legionary standards. For the main campaign of 16 a great fleet was prepared and the troops were transported via his father's canal and the lakes of Holland to the Ems, whence they proceeded to the Weser and defeated Arminius in two battles; the fleet suffered heavy damage from a storm on its homeward journey.

Although Germanicus claimed that one more campaign would bring the Germans to their knees, Tiberius judged that results did not justify the drain on Roman resources, and recalled him to a *triumph and a command to reorder the 'overseas' provinces as proconsul with *maius imperium* (subordinate to that of Tiberius). Germanicus entered on his second consulship (18) at Nicopolis in Epirus, crowned Zeno, king of Armenia (so winning an *ovatio*), and reduced Cappadocia and Commagene to provincial status. In 19 he offended Tiberius by entering Egypt, which Augustus had barred to senators without permission, and by the informal dress he wore there; his reception was tumultuous. On his return to Syria the enmity between him and Gnaeus *Calpurnius Piso, whom Tiberius had appointed governor as a check on Germanicus, led to his ordering Piso to leave the province. He fell mysteriously ill, and died near Antioch, convinced that Piso had poisoned him. His death—compared by some with that of *Alexander (2) the Great—provoked widespread demonstrations of grief and in Rome suspicion and resentment; many honours were paid to his memory; his ashes were deposited in the mausoleum of Augustus at Rome. His reputation remained as an overwhelming political advantage to his brother Claudius and descendants.

Germanicus married *Agrippina the Elder, the daughter of *Agrippa and *Iulia (2). She bore him nine children, among whom were *Gaius (1), *Agrippina the Younger, Iulia Drūsilla, and Iūlia Livilla. Eloquent and studious, he wrote comedies in Greek (all lost) and Greek and Latin epigrams; he also translated into Latin the *Phaenomena* of *Aratus, bringing it up to date and adding further matter on the planets and the weather.

Iūlius Frontīnus, Sextus, served as urban *praetor in AD 70 and then assisted in suppressing the revolt of the Batavian prince Iulius Civilis, receiving the surrender of 70,000 Lingones. Consul in 72 or 73, he served as governor of Britain (73/4–77), where he crushed the Silures in south Wales, establishing a fortress for *legion II Augusta at Isca, and then attacked the Ordovices. He was proconsul of Asia in 86, and was later appointed by *Nerva in 97 a commissioner for *aqueducts. He held his second, *suffect, consulship in 98, and his third, ordinary, consulship in 100, both times with *Trajan. *Pliny the Younger described him as one of the two most distinguished men of his day. He died in 103/4.

Works Frontinus wrote clearly about several technical subjects: the history, administration, and maintenance of the aqueducts of Rome; he cites engineers' reports, official documents, plans, and senatorial decrees, with details of quantity, supply, and abuses of the system. The book is an invaluable source for the study of the working of the Roman *water supply, and the history and administration of the city of Rome in general. It combines pride in the Roman achievement in this field with a willingness to list technical statistics. In his *Stratagems* Frontinus discusses techniques of military command, using stratagems drawn mainly from past commanders, though including several recent examples, esp. from Domitian's campaigns in Germany; the work is divided into three books by categories: before battle, during and after battle, sieges; a fourth book contains maxims on the art of generalship. Frontinus claims to provide practical guidance for contemporary commanders, and *Stratagems* may have served as a textbook in a society with no formal means of training men for public office.

Iūlius Vindex, Gāius, descended from the kings of Aquitania and son of a Roman senator, was governor of Gallia Lugdunensis (see GAUL (TRANSALPINE)) when he revolted from *Nero (spring AD 68). Vindex had no Roman troops under his command, and although he received support from many Gauls and the native noblemen in his province, he probably intended the overthrow of Nero, not nationalist secession. His

appeal to other governors for assistance was answered only by *Galba in Spain, and although Vienna in Narbonensis supported him, *Lugdunum rejected his approaches. The army of Upper Germany under *Verginius Rufus defeated the rebels at Vesontio, though the circumstances remain obscure, since Rufus had apparently been intriguing with Vindex before the battle, and his troops may have forced him to fight.

Iūnius Brūtus, Marcus, son of another Marcus Iunius Brutus (put to death by *Pompey in 77 after a promise of safe conduct) and of *Servilia, b. (probably) 85 BC. Brought up by *Porcius Cato (2), he was educated in oratory and philosophy and long retained hatred for Pompey. In 58 he accompanied Cato to *Cyprus and in 56 lent a large sum to Salamis at 48 per cent interest p.a., contrary to the law of Gabinius, procuring a senate decree to validate the loan. As moneyer (?55) he issued coins showing *Libertas and portraits of his ancestors. As quaestor 53 he went to Cilicia with Claudius Pulcher, whose daughter he had married. When *Cicero succeeded Appius, he found that an agent of Brutus had been made prefect of cavalry to extort money from Salamis and that five Salaminian senators had been killed. He cancelled the appointment, but to avoid offence to Brutus gave a similar post to Brutus' agent in Cappadocia and recognized the validity of the loan to Salamis. In 52 Brutus defended *Annius Milo and in a pamphlet attacked Pompey's wish for a dictatorship, but in 49 he joined the republican cause and was formally reconciled with Pompey. After Pompey's defeat at Pharsalus (48) he successfully begged Caesar for pardon and, no doubt through Servilia's influence, became one of his protégés. He was made a *pontifex* and in 47 sent to govern Cisalpine Gaul, while Caesar went to Africa to fight Cato and the republicans. During this time he developed relations with Cicero, who dedicated various philosophical and rhetorical works to him and, at his request, wrote a eulogy of Cato after Cato's death. (Finding it unsatisfactory, Brutus wrote one himself.) Although he now divorced Claudia and married Cato's daughter *Porcia, widow of *Calpurnius Bibulus, he remained on good terms with Caesar, met him on his return from Munda, assured Cicero of Caesar's laudable *optimate intentions, and was made urban praetor for 44 and designated consul for 41. But when Caesar became *dictator perpetuo* (February 44), Brutus joined, and *ex officio* took the lead in, the widespread conspiracy that led to Caesar's assassination before his departure for his Parthian war. Outmanœuvred by Marcus *Antonius, whose life he had spared on the Ides of March, he and *Cassius Longinus had to leave Rome and, failing to win popular approval, left Italy for Greece (August 44). With Antony now openly hostile, Brutus collected nearly 400 million sesterces from the treasuries of Asia and Syria and confiscated the supplies Caesar had prepared for his campaign. He and Cassius gradually seized all the eastern provinces, building up large armies, partly of veterans. When Cicero, in his *Philippics*, swung the senate behind them, they received *imperium maius* in the east. Brutus captured, and later executed, Antony's brother Gaius Antonius; after Cornēlius Dolabella's death he acquired Asia and completed its conquest, and during 43 and 42 squeezed it dry for his armies. The money was turned into a large coinage, and Brutus, alone among the republicans, put his own head on one of the gold coins. He also won the title of *imperator* in Thrace. In 42 he and Cassius, with about 80,000 legionaries plus auxiliaries, twice met Antony and *Octavian at *Philippi. In the first battle Cassius, defeated by Antony, committed suicide, while Brutus impressively defeated Octavian. In a second battle, forced on Brutus, he was defeated, deserted by his soldiers, and also committed suicide. His body was honourably treated by Antony.

Arrogant, rapacious, calculatingly ambitious, Brutus yet professed a deep attachment to philosophy. Cicero admired but never liked him, and ignored his warnings not to trust Octavian. A renowned orator, with an austere and dignified style, he despised Cicero's as 'effeminate and spineless'. His literary works are lost, as are his letters, except for a few surviving among Cicero's. With Cassius, he was officially condemned under the empire, but revered by many as the last defender of Roman freedom.

iūs cīvīle is the law of a particular state and usually the law of Rome. Alternatively, it is that part of the law of Rome which is applicable only to Roman citizens.

iūs gentium, or law of nations, has two main senses. (1) In a 'practical' sense it denotes that part of Roman private law which was open to citizens and non-citizens alike. The institutions of the old *ius civile* were accessible only to Romans, but the growth of international trade made it necessary to recognize some institutions which could be applied by Roman courts

to relations between foreigners and between foreigners and citizens.

(2) In a more 'theoretical' sense *ius gentium* is equated with the philosophical *law of nature.

iūs Italicum was a privilege granted to certain communities in the Roman provinces whereby their land was treated in law as if it were in Italy.

iūs Latiī, the Latin right, refers primarily to the legal status of those *Latins who after 338 BC shared the right of marriage and commerce with Romans. Latins settling in Rome acquired Roman *citizenship and vice versa.

iūs līberōrum ('the rights of parentage'). *Augustus' marriage laws rewarded parents. For example, precedence in public office was offered to married men and fathers. Three children (in Rome), four (for freed slaves and residents in Italy), or five (in the provinces) qualified parents for full exemptions, including, for women, exemption from being in *guardianship and, for men, from acting as guardians. The fictitious status of parent, esp. of three children (conferred e.g. on *Livia Drusilla), came to be granted as a privilege and favour by the emperors. See MARRIAGE, LAW OF, ROMAN; PATRONAGE, NON-LITERARY.

iūstitium ('stopping legal business'), was the temporary suspension of jurisdiction and judicial operations by magistrates and judges in civil and criminal matters. It was proclaimed by a magistrate in an *edict, usually on the senate's authority. It was originally used in a military crisis, esp. a *tumultus, to enable the people to concentrate on raising an army. Its use as a mark of mourning survived into the Principate. In the late republic we find it employed as a form of political pressure.

iuvenēs (or **iuventūs**), 'youths', 'youth', of military age. When a Roman boy adopted the *toga virīlis, usually at 14, he became a *iuvenis*. At 17 those intending to follow an *equestrian or senatorial career started the military service which was a normal preliminary. *Iuvenes* of 14–17 years of age who were of equestrian rank (including the sons of senators) served at Rome their *tīrocinium*, a preparation for military service. This institution originated in the Roman republic but was reorganized by *Augustus, to invigorate the youth of the upper classes at Rome, an important part of the imperial ideology. Two factors interested Augustus in the youth: concern to educate future generations in traditional Roman ways and offer them a model, and esp. his desire to recall military aspects of the equestrian order. They practised physical exercises and riding, paraded at great festivals, and held their own games.

ivory, a material derived from the tusk of the Asiatic or African *elephant. Capable of being carved in the round, or in relief, used as inlay, as a veneer, turned on a lathe, or even moulded, ivory was a multi-purpose commodity that was imported into the Mediterranean from North Africa and the Levant. At all periods, *furniture was decorated with ivory plaques. Ivory was used for the flesh parts of cult statues (e.g. *Phidias' *Athena Parthenos and his *Zeus at *Olympia), and for temple doors.

Ixīon, mythical king of *Thessaly, was a primal offender against divine order. *Pindar records two crimes: not only was he the world's first *parricide, but after *Zeus had purified him (see PURIFICATION) he reoffended by trying to rape his benefactor's wife *Hera. For his intended victim Zeus substituted a cloud-image, which conceived Centaurus ('Pokewind', named as usual after the father), sire of the *Centaurs. His punishment was to be crucified on a fiery wheel which revolves throughout eternity—i.e. presumably the sun; Ixion is condemned to become part of the operating mechanism of Zeus' universe, as *Sisyphus heaves the sun-disc up to the zenith only to see it roll back down.

Jānus, god of door and gate (*iānua*) (the term also for the type of honorific gateway that we misleadingly call "triumphal arch'). Like a door, he looked both ways, and is therefore depicted as a double-headed and bearded man (the image chosen for many early Roman coins). More generally he controlled beginnings, esp. as the eponym of the month January, and was linked with the symbolism of the gate at the beginning and end of military campaigns. This was most famously expressed in the ritual of the closing of the shrine of Janus Geminus in the Forum in times of complete peace: under King Numa, in 235 BC, three times under *Augustus, and more often in the imperial period. *Domitian transferred the cult to a new shrine in the forum Transitorium (see FORUM NERVAE).

This shrine (as depicted on coins) was little more than a gateway itself. It was probably *geminus*—'twin'—in being a four-way arch, like the 'arch of Janus' which survives in the *forum Boarium.

Jason (1), in myth, son of Aeson, and leader of the *Argonauts in their quest for the Golden Fleece. He was brought up in the Thessalian countryside by the *Centaur Chiron after *Pelias took the throne of Iolcus in place of Aeson. When Jason returned to Iolcus to claim his inheritance, Pelias, forewarned by an oracle to beware of a man wearing only one sandal, recognized the danger and devised the expedition to recover the Golden Fleece from the kingdom of Aia in the extreme east. The expedition itself follows a familiar pattern of *rite-of-passage stories in which young men must undergo terrible ordeals before claiming their rightful inheritance; *Apollonius (1) Rhodius' Jason resembles the tragic *Orestes in the hesitation he feels in the face of what he must do. The expedition is successfully completed with the assistance of *Hera, who wishes to punish Pelias for neglecting to honour her, and Aphrodite, who makes the Colchian princess *Medea fall in love with Jason. Already

in the *Odyssey* Jason is 'dear to Hera', and Apollonius explains that he once carried her across a torrent when she was disguised as an old woman; later sources combine this incident with the fateful loss of a sandal. After Jason and Medea had taken revenge upon Pelias, they fled to *Corinth where they lived until Jason decided to marry Creon's daughter; in the version made famous by *Euripides' *Medea*, Medea then killed their two sons and his new bride. There are various accounts of Jason's death, of which the most colourful are that he killed himself in despair, that he was killed when a plank from the rotting *Argo* fell on him as he slept, and that the stern-piece which he had dedicated to Hera fell on him when he entered her temple. Along with many other Argonauts, he was said to have taken part in the Calydonian boar-hunt (see MELEAGER (1)).

Jason (2), 4th-cent. BC tyrant (see TYRANNY) of Pherae in *Thessaly.

Jerome (Eusebius Hieronymus) (*c*.AD 347–420), biblical translator, scholar, and ascetic. Born into a Christian family in Dalmatia, he was educated in Rome at the school of Aelius Donatus, and later studied rhetoric. During a stay at *Augusta Treverorum, where he had probably intended to enter imperial service, his *Christianity took on greater meaning, and around 372, fired with ascetic zeal (see ASCETICISM), he set out for the east. After two years or more at Antioch, he finally withdrew to the desert to undertake the penitential life of an anchoritic monk. He began to learn Hebrew, with huge consequences for biblical scholarship. But after a year he returned to Antioch, where he was ordained priest. Back in Rome in 382, he quickly won the confidence of Pope Damasus I, at whose request he began work on what was to become the core of the Vulgate (Latin) version of the Bible. There he also formed friendships with several aristocratic women who had dedicated themselves to Christianity and were living austere and simple lives. His association with the widow Paula combined with other factors to put him in a bad light with the generality of Roman Christians, and after Damasus' death he was driven from the city (385). Paula followed him to Palestine, where, at Bethlehem, they founded a monastery and a convent. Here Jerome remained for the rest of his life, devoting himself to the ascetic way and to Christian learning.

Jerome was a prolific writer. In addition to his translations of Scripture, he produced numerous commentaries on books of the Bible, for which he drew heavily on previous commentators such as *Origen. Polemical works on a variety of religious issues reveal a bitter side to his nature. His surviving correspondence discloses a network of connections across the whole Mediterranean world and in high places. Other works of importance include his translation and expansion of *Eusebius' *Chronicle* of world history, and *On Famous Men*, a catalogue of 135 mainly Christian writers.

The dream in which Jerome saw himself accused of being not a Christian but a 'Ciceronian' (see TULLIUS CICERO (1), MARCUS), and which seems to have resulted in his giving up reading pagan literature for many years, is a reflection of the tension felt by many Christians of the time between their religious beliefs and their classical heritage. In the end Jerome himself succeeded in resolving this conflict, and perhaps more than any other of the Latin Fathers he can be seen as a man of the classical world who happened to be Christian. His classicism is evident not only in his frequent quotations from classical literature, but often in his style. While his scriptural translations and exegetical works tend to be simple and unadorned, other texts display the full fruits of rhetorical training and the verve of a great natural talent steeped in the best writings of an earlier age. If his enduring importance lay most of all in the Vulgate, in his teaching on celibacy, and in his contribution to western monasticism, he also ranks among the finest writers of Latin prose.

Jerusalem was repopulated and the Temple modestly restored with the blessing of *Cyrus (1), some 50 years after the destruction of 587 BC, by *Jews returning from the *Babylonian exile. In the 440s, the walls were rebuilt and their completion marked by a great celebration of the Tabernacles festival. Palestine as a whole came into *Alexander (2) the Great's empire after the battle of Issus (333). Under the Hasmoneans, the city became a major centre, expanding to the west and north. During *Pompey's siege of 63, to settle the war between two Hasmonean brothers, Aristobulus held out in the Temple, and in the aftermath Pompey personally inspected the shrine and removed Temple treasures; but little physical damage was inflicted. The capture and pillaging of Jerusalem by the *Parthians in 40 led to Sosius' siege and recapture in 37 and the installation of *Herod (1).

Herod transformed Jerusalem: the city acquired a theatre, hippodrome, and amphitheatre, all now vanished; a palace defended by three massive towers; the Antonia fortress, of which the paved courtyard and other installations remain. Above all, starting in 20/19 BC, the Temple was rebuilt, in white stone, with copious gold covering. The biblical prescriptions were still followed, but the height was doubled and the surrounding courts expanded. The Temple mount was erected on a vast retaining platform, of which the 'Western wall' ('Wailing wall') is a remnant. The valley between this and the élite residential quarter in the upper city was bridged. There the excavated houses, with their copious ablution cisterns, bear witness to the sophisticated but religiously correct lifestyle of the high priestly and lay élite of Second-Temple Jerusalem. The monumental tombs standing in the Kedron valley confirm the impression. Diaspora benefactors (see JEWS) had contributed to the Temple, and Jewish pilgrims converged from far afield during the three 'foot festivals'. For *Pliny (1) the Elder, Jerusalem was 'by far the most famous city of the east'.

In the revolt of AD 66, after the reduction of other parts of the country, Jerusalem became the centre first of fighting between the Zealots and two other factions, and then of unified resistance. The destruction of the city and the Temple by *Titus in 70, after a five-month siege, was a turning-point in its history. The walls were razed, leaving only the three towers. The priestly class all but disappeared. After the revolt, the camp of *legion X Fretensis was located at Jerusalem. After the Bar Kokhba revolt (132–135), *Hadrian refounded the city as a military colony, Aelia Capitolina, but there is little sign of large-scale reconstruction. Christian sources claim that Jews were barred. In any event, Jewish religious life perforce ceased to be focused on Jerusalem. The Christian holy places were not developed until Constantine I. The church of the Holy Sepulchre was dedicated in 335, and a second great basilica was built on the Mount of Olives, to mark the supposed site of the Ascension. Again, a pilgrim trade benefited the city. See PILGRIM-AGE (CHRISTIAN).

jewellery See DRESS; GEMS; PORTRAITURE, ROMAN.

Jews (in Greek and Roman times). The Jews at the beginning of the period were an ethnic group with distinctive religious practices. During the period, the religious definition acquired new emphasis, and many Jews were Jews by conversion rather than birth.

Palestine A racially mixed region, understood to be the homeland of the Jews throughout the period, though in fact housing a minority of them. More precisely, the Jews belonged to the small area around *Jerusalem known in Greek as Ioudaia, Lat. Iūdaea. However, the two revolts against Roman rule brought about the physical exclusion of the Jews from their centre.

From 538 to 332 BC the Jews of Palestine were a part of the *Persian empire. The high priest seems to have been the highest Jewish official. A century of Ptolemaic rule (see EGYPT, Ptolemaic) followed *Alexander (2) the Great's death.

In 200 Palestine passed into *Seleucid hands, and the pressure of Hellenism was manifested in Antiochus IV's installation of a pagan cult in the Temple (168/7), which was resisted by the Maccabees. Only in 142 was the Seleucid garrison expelled from Jerusalem. For the next 80 years, the Jews were ruled by the hereditary Hasmonean high priests. The expansion of Jewish territory involved a phenomenon new to Judaism, the conversion of neighbouring peoples at least partly by force.

*Pompey's intervention in 63, occasioned by a quarrel between the two sons of a defunct queen, led to the installation of one of them, Hyrcanus, and to the reduction of the kingdom, with the freeing of the conquered Greek cities. In 57 *Gabinius organized the ethnarchy into five self-governing communities, with Hyrcanus remaining as ethnarch until his removal by the *Parthians and the appointment of the Idumaean convert *Herod (1) as ruler.

In AD 6 Judaea was annexed, together with Samaria and Idumaea, to form the Roman province of Judaea, administered by *equestrian officials (prefects, later procurators). A census in that year crystallized opposition and generated an ideology of resistance. This tendency was evidently the source of the later, more famous rebel groupings, sīcāriī (daggermen) and zealots.

A pattern of procuratorial misgovernment turned the sympathies of the Jewish crowd in Jerusalem and of the poor in Galilee to the anti-Roman cause. The high-priestly and landowning élites criticized Rome only under extreme provocation, as when *Gaius (1) attempted to have his statue placed in the Temple (39/40). The installation of M. *Iulius Agrippa I (41–44) by Claudius was to prove merely a brief interlude in the regime of the procurators. Famines, banditry, and the breakdown of the working relationship between the Jewish ruling class and Rome marked the years before the outbreak of the First Jewish Revolt in 66. The Temple sacrifices for the emperor's welfare were ended, and a provisional government in Jerusalem appointed regional leaders (including *Josephus), chose a popular high priest by lot, abolished debt, and issued its own freedom coinage. But the Jews were deeply divided politically. In Galilee the conflict between pro- and anti-war elements made resistance ineffectual. In besieged Jerusalem, three rebel factions conducted a civil war until the last stages of the siege.

In 70 the Judaean victory of *Vespasian and *Titus, confirmed by the burning of Jerusalem and the (perhaps accidental) destruction of the Temple, was crucial in consolidating the Flavian seizure of power. Much was made of 'Iudaea capta' in Flavian propaganda, culminating in the *triumph over the Jews. Jewish-owned land in Judaea was expropriated. *Masada fell in 73 or 74. From 70 the province of Judaea was governed by *legates, and *legion X Fretensis was stationed in Jerusalem. Jewish religious and cultural life centred for a generation on Jamnia, an enclave on the Judaean coast, where a new definition of Judaism without a Temple was evolved by the first *rabbis.

The revolt in the Diaspora (see below) under Trajan, in 115–117, produced disturbances in Palestine, suppressed by the governor. More important was the Second Jewish Revolt in Palestine (132–135), led by Bar Kokhba. The immediate triggers were *Hadrian's prohibition of circumcision, and his plan to turn Jerusalem into the Roman colony of Aelia Capitolina. After the costly suppression of this revolt, the name of the province became *Syria Palaestina, another legion was stationed in Galilee, and, acc. to Christian sources, Jews were altogether excluded from Jerusalem. A further revolt occurred under *Antoninus Pius, in spite of his exemption of the Jews from Hadrian's ban on circumcision.

During the 3rd cent. Jewish life flourished in Galilee: synagogues began to proliferate, in villages as well as towns; rabbinic influence on daily life grew; and Jews played their part in some of the newly refurbished cities, esp. *Caesarea. The patriarch, located successively in several Galilean towns, operated as the representative of the Jews of Palestine and was closely associated with the rabbis. Greek was widely used by the educated élite, though the first great rabbinic compilation, the Mishnah, was written in Hebrew, c.200.

The Diaspora The dispersal of the Jews began in 586 BC, when Nebuchadnezzar took the inhabitants of Jerusalem into captivity. Many of them did not return when permitted by *Cyrus (1) of *Persia in 538, but remained voluntarily in *Babylonia, where flourishing communities existed for centuries, producing in late antiquity the greatest monument of rabbinic learning, the Babylonian Talmud. During the Hellenistic period, many Jews migrated from Palestine and also from Babylonia, settling around the eastern Mediterranean, esp. in Syria, Asia Minor, and Egypt. Jewish military colonists had lived at *Elephantine for centuries, and now they were joined by new military and civilian settlers in both countryside and town. The community at *Alexandria became the most important in the Diaspora, the splendour of its synagogue a byword, its mixed Jewish–Greek culture highly creative. Numbers alone made the Jews prominent inhabitants of the city. But by the 1st cent. AD there were sizeable communities in most of the cities of the eastern Mediterranean. The *Acts of the Apostles testifies to the local prominence of synagogues.

Expansion to Italy and the west began later, but the community in Rome was established by the mid-2nd cent. BC. Jews taken as slaves after the various wars in Palestine swelled the numbers of the Diaspora, as in due course did the voluntary attachment of pagans to the Jewish synagogues of Rome. Inscriptions from the Jewish *catacombs of Rome reveal the existence of eleven synagogues in the 2nd to 4th cents. AD, whose names suggest an earlier foundation.

Diaspora Jews retained their identity and the basic religious practices of Judaism—male circumcision, observance of the sabbath, and other festivals (esp. Tabernacles) and the avoidance of non-kosher meat. Until AD 70, their allegiance to the Temple and to Jerusalem as their mother city was signalled by the payment of the Temple tax and by the practice of pilgrimage at the major agricultural festivals.

Periodic expulsions of the Jews from the city of Rome were short-lived and did not undermine their standing elsewhere. Three expulsions are recorded: in 139 BC; by *Tiberius in AD 19; and by *Claudius. The authorities' fear of disturbance and of un-Roman practices, rather than overt proselytizing, was the immediate cause of anti-Jewish measures, as of those against other alien cults and practices.

In spite of—or because of—Jewish acculturation, friction between Jews and their neighbours was not uncommon. In Alexandria, anti-Semitic literature was produced in the Hellenistic period; but it was the Roman annexation of Egypt which shook a centuries-long political equilibrium by redefining the privileges accorded to Alexandrian citizens, and excluding the Jews from them. In 38, a visit of *Iulius Agrippa I to Alexandria provoked the first pogrom in Jewish history, when synagogues were burnt, shops looted, and the Jews herded into a ghetto.

In 115 the Jews of Cyrenaica rose against their pagan neighbours and against the Roman authorities, inflicting much damage and targeting pagan temples. The uprising spread to Alexandria and other parts of Egypt; and to *Cyprus. The rebellion in 116 in *Trajan's new Mesopotamian province (see MESOPOTAMIA), coinciding with these events, brought in the Jews of Babylonia. The revolts were suppressed by Marcius Turbo with much effort.

Jōsēphus (b. AD 37/8), was a Greek historian but also a Jewish priest of aristocratic descent, and a political leader in pre-70 *Jerusalem. Though a zealous defender of Jewish religion and culture, his writing is largely hostile to the various revolutionary groups, which he regarded as responsible for the fall of the Temple: his theology centres on the idea that God was currently on the Romans' side. Participation in a delegation to Rome (c.64) impressed on him the impracticality of resistance. When the Jerusalem leaders put him in charge of *Galilee, he played an ambiguous role. He was besieged at Jotapata, but when captured, evaded a suicide pact and, he claims, was freed when his prophecy of *Vespasian's accession came true. He remained close to *Titus until the fall of Jerusalem, making several attempts to persuade the besieged city to surrender. He was given Roman citizenship, and, after the war, an imperial house in Rome, a pension, and land in Judaea.

He first wrote an account of the war, now lost, in *Aramaic for the Jews of Mesopotamia. Most, if not all, of the seven books of the Greek *Jewish War* appeared between 75 and 79. The first book and a half sketch Jewish history from the revolt of 168/7 BC to AD 66. Much of the rest is based on Josephus' own experience, together with eye-witness reports from others and, probably, the diaries (*commentarii*) of Vespasian and Titus. The triumph at Rome over *Iudaea capta* is described in detail. The *Jewish Antiquities* is a history of the Jews from the Creation to just before the outbreak of revolt, ostensibly for Greek readers. In the later part, there is heavy dependence on the histories of *Nicolaus of Damascus. The famous *testimōnium* to Jesus is partly or even wholly an interpolation. Appended to the *Antiquities* was the *Life*—not a full autobiography, but a defence of Josephus' conduct in Galilee, responding to his critics. *Against Apion* was an apologia for Judaism in two books, showing its antiquity in comparison with Greek culture, and attacking anti-Semitic writers, from the 3rd cent. BC to Apion, a Greek teacher and lecturer, fl. AD 39/40. Josephus' writings were preserved by the early Church.

Juba II, king of Mauretania and son of Juba I, king of *Numidia, was led in *Caesar's triumph in 46 BC when still an infant, and brought up in Italy; he received the Roman *citizenship, apparently from *Octavian, and accompanied him on campaigns. In 25 he received from Augustus the kingdom of Mauretania. Deeply learned, Juba sought to introduce Greek and Roman culture into his kingdom. He organized an exploratory mission to the Canary Islands (See ISLANDS OF THE BLEST).

Jugurtha, grandson of *Masinissa outside the line of succession, served at *Numantia under *Cornelius Scipio Aemilianus, hereditary patron of the Numidian dynasty, and on his recommendation was adopted by King Micipsa and given pre-eminent rank over his brothers. After Micipsa's death (118 BC) the 'legitimate' brothers Hiempsal and Adherbal objected to his primacy, but he had Hiempsal assassinated and attacked Adherbal, who fled to Rome to appeal for assistance. A commission under *Opimius divided *Numidia, giving the more primitive western part to Jugurtha and the more developed eastern part to Adherbal. In 112 Jugurtha attacked Adherbal, besieged him in Cirta, and despite two Roman embassies captured Cirta and killed him. Some Italian businessmen who had helped in the defence were also killed, and this caused outrage in Rome and led to agitation for war. In

11 the consul Calpurnius Bestia invaded Numidia, but soon gave Jugurtha a tolerable peace, perhaps persuaded by his Roman friends, but certainly through hesitation over starting a long colonial war. Summoned to Rome under safe-conduct to reveal his protectors, Jugurtha was forbidden to speak by a tribune and left hurriedly. In Numidia the war was incompetently waged by Postumius Albinus (consul 110), and his brother and legate Aulus was forced to capitulate in his absence. An outcry over aristocratic 'corruption' in Rome led to the institution of a commission of enquiry and the election of *Caecilius Metellus Numidicus as consul for 109. Metellus in two campaigns achieved much success, but came no nearer to ending the war. His legate *Marius, profiting by this, intrigued to gain the consulship (107), promising quick victory, but he too was unable to deliver it, despite army reforms including the first enrolment of *proletarii in the legions. The war was finally won when *Sulla persuaded King Bocchus I of Maretania to surrender Jugurtha to Marius. He was executed after Marius' triumph (104).

As Sallust saw, the Jugurthine War marks an important stage in the decline of the oligarchy and the organization of attacks on it. Above all, Marius' army reform unwittingly prepared the way for the use of armies loyal to their commander in politics and civil war.

Julia, Julius, etc. For Roman personal names in 'J' (not a letter of the Latin alphabet) see under 'I', except for JULIAN, JUSTIN, JUSTINIAN, and JUVENAL.

Julian 'the Apostate', emperor AD 361–363, was born at *Constantinople in 331, the son of a half-brother of *Constantine I. After his father's murder in 337, Julian was placed by Constantius II in the care of an *Arian bishop and from 342 was confined for six years on an imperial estate in Cappadocia. He impressed his Christian tutors there as a gifted and pious pupil (see CHRISTIANITY), but his reading of the Greek classics was inclining him in private to other gods. In 351, as a student of philosophy, he encountered pagan Neoplatonists (see NEOPLATONISM) and was initiated as a theurgist (see THEURGY). For the next ten years Julian's *pagan 'conversion' remained a prudently kept secret. He continued his studies until summoned to Mediolanum by Constantius to be married to the emperor's sister Helena and proclaimed Caesar with charge over Gaul and Britain (355).

Successful Rhineland campaigns against the Alamanni and Franks between 356 and 359 proved Julian a talented general and won him great popularity with his army. When Constantius ordered the transfer of choice detachments to the east, the army mutinied and in February 361 proclaimed Julian Augustus (see AUGUSTUS, AUGUSTA, AS TITLES). Constantius' death late that year averted civil war, and Julian, now publicly declaring his paganism, entered Constantinople unopposed in December. A purge of the imperial court quickly followed, drastically reducing its officials and staff. In his brief reign Julian pursued ambitious aims with energy. An immediate declaration of general religious toleration foreshadowed a vigorous programme of pagan activism in the interest of '*Hellenism': the temples and finances of the ancestral cults were to be restored and a hierarchy of pagan priests appointed, while the Christian churches and clergy lost the financial subsidies and privileges gained under Constantine and his successors. Though expressly opposed to violent persecution of Christians, Julian overtly discriminated in favour of pagan individuals and communities in his appointments and judgements: measures such as his ban on the teaching of classical literature and philosophy by Christian professors and his encouragement of charitable expenditure by pagan priests mark a determination to marginalize Christianity as a social force. His attempts to revive the role of the cities in local administration by restoring their revenues and councils and his remarkable plan to rebuild the Jewish Temple at *Jerusalem are best appraised in the light of this fundamental aim.

Julian's military ambitions centred on an invasion of *Persia. To prepare his expedition he moved in June 362 to Antioch, where his relations with the mainly Christian population deteriorated markedly during his stay. The expedition set out in March 363, but despite some early successes it was already in serious difficulties when Julian was fatally wounded in a mêlée in June 363. He left no heir (Helena had died childless in 360, and Julian did not remarry), and after his death the reforms he had initiated came to nothing.

Julian's personal piety and intellectual and cultural interests are reflected in his surviving writings, which show considerable learning and some literary talent. They include panegyrics, polemics, theological and satirical works, and a collection of letters, public and private. Of his anti-Christian critique, *Against the Galileans*, only fragments remain. His own philosophic ideology was rooted in Iamblichan Neoplatonism (see IAMBLICHUS) and theurgy. How forcefully it impinged on his public religious reforms is controversial.

Julio-Claudian emperors and period See ROME, HISTORY, 2.2.

Jūnō, an old Italian goddess and one of the chief deities of Rome. Her roles as a goddess of women and as a civic deity were both ancient and widespread. Juno was widely worshipped under a number of epithets throughout central Italy. Some of her important civic cults in Rome were in fact imported from this region. Thus in the 5th cent. BC Juno Rēgīna ('Queen') was brought from *Veii and received a temple on the *Aventine. Also apparently Etruscan in origin was the Capitoline Triad of *Jupiter, Juno, and *Minerva; the Capitoline Juno was by the late republic also identified as Regina, and regularly carried that epithet in the imperial period. The cult of Juno Lūcīna, the goddess of childbirth, appears both in Rome and in other parts of *Latium. The foundation-day of her temple on the *Esquiline, March 1, was traditionally celebrated as the Matronalia, when husbands gave presents to their wives. Peculiar to Rome is Juno Monēta, whose cult dates to the 4th cent. BC. The ancient association of her epithet with *monērē* (to warn) is usually accepted. The first mint in Rome was later located in or near her temple on the Arx (see CAPITOL), hence the derivation of 'money' from Moneta. The Roman conception of Juno's character was deeply affected by her identification with similar goddesses of other cultures. The most important was the Greek *Hera: her mythology and characteristics were largely adopted for Juno, who was thus firmly established by the time of *Plautus as the wife of Jupiter and the goddess of marriage.

Jupiter (*Iuppiter*), sovereign god of the Romans, bears a name referring to the 'luminous sky'. He was known to all Italic peoples. Although associated with the sky, storms, and lightning, Jupiter was not just a god of natural phenomena. They expressed and articulated, in fact, his function as sovereign divinity. Jupiter was sovereign by virtue of his supreme rank and by the patronage derived from his exercise of supreme power. His supreme rank was signified by the fact that the god or his priest was always mentioned at the head of lists of gods or priests, and that the climactic point of the month, the Ides, was sacred to him. In addition, the Roman symbol of power, the *sceptre, belonged to him and functioned as his symbol. His supremacy was described by the traditional epithets of *optimus maximus*, 'the best and the greatest'. His patronage of human exercise of sovereign power expressed itself in the fact that no political action could be taken without his favourable and prior judgement, expressed through the auspices (see AUSPICIUM), and in the celebration of the *triumph, representing the fullest exercise of Roman supremacy.

In rituals as well as in mythical narratives, the exercise of sovereignty by Jupiter, which made him into a deity with a political function, is presented under two aspects. On the one hand Jupiter was patron of the violent aspect of supremacy. As well as falling lightning, the Roman triumph, ending at his temple, represented the inexorable side of this power. But Jupiter was also a political god, who agreed to exercise power within the limits imposed by law and good faith. By means of the auspices, he conferred legitimacy on the choices and decisions of the Roman people. Finally, he was the patron of *oaths and treaties, and punished perjurers in the terrible manner appropriate.

From the end of the regal period, the most brilliant of Jupiter's seats was his temple on the *Capitol, which he shared with *Juno Regina (in the cella or chamber to the left) and *Minerva (in the right-hand cella). This triad constituted the group of patron deities of the city of Rome, whose well-being was the subject of an annual vow; under the empire, vows for the health of the ruler and his family were celebrated on 3 January. The first political action of the new consuls was the discharge of these vows, formulated the previous year, and their utterance afresh. The anniversary of the Capitoline temple was celebrated during the *Ludi Romani on the Ides (13th) of September. On the Ides of November, during the Ludi Plebeii or Plebeian Games (see PLEBS), a great banquet was celebrated on the Capitol (*Iovis epulum*: see SEPTEMVIRI EPULONES), reuniting the Roman élite around the supreme god, along with Juno and Minerva.

Jupiter was often associated with other deities. From an early period he was associated with *Mars and Quirinus. On the Capitol he shared his temple with Juno and Minerva. Near this temple lay the temple of Fides (see above). The special priests of Jupiter were the *flāmen Dialis* and his wife (see FLAMINES) and, where the auspices were concerned, the *augurs, 'interpreters of Jupiter Best and Greatest'.

juries, jurors See LAW AND PROCEDURE, ATHENIAN (2) and ROMAN (2 and 3).

jurists See LAW, ROMAN, SOCIOLOGY OF; LAWYERS, ROMAN.

Justin Martyr (c. AD 100–165), a Christian apologist, flourished under *Antoninus Pius and died a martyr in Rome after his condemnation as a Christian (see CHRISTIANITY) by the city *prefect. At the beginning of his *First Apology* he tells us that he was born at Flavia Neapolis (the ancient Shechem in Samaria) of *pagan parents. He seems never to have been attracted to Judaism. His account of his early disappointments in philosophy is conventional, but he was certainly a Platonist (see PLATO) when converted to Christianity. The Stoics (see STOICISM) he knew and admired, but more for their lives than for their teachings, and his conversion owed much to the constancy of Christian confessors.

After leaving Samaria, he set up a small school in Rome, and wrote two *Apologies*, nominally directed to Antoninus Pius. One (c.155) defends Christianity in general against popular calumny and intellectual contempt; the second (c.162) is inspired by acts of persecution following denunciations of Christians to the authorities. It reveals that Christians served in the army and that Christian wives sometimes divorced their pagan spouses. Justin's pupil Tatian attributes his death to information given by a Cynic rival.

Justin's work is not so much a synthesis of Christianity, paganism, and Judaism as an attempt to discover an underlying homogeneity. This he effects by his doctrine of the Logos, which, as Christ, was present in many OT *epiphanies, and guarantees the unity of scriptural inspiration. In the *Apologies* he argues that a 'spermatic *logos*', identical with or related to Christ, instructs every man in wisdom, so that even pagan philosophers foreshadowed Christian truth. Like the other apologists, he accepts the civil authorities.

Justinian, eastern Roman emperor AD 527–565. He was born c.482 in *Thrace. His father Sabbatius had married a sister of the future emperor Justin, who adopted his nephew. He joined the guards, and became a personal imperial bodyguard. During the succession dispute in 518 Justinian was offered the throne but supported his more senior uncle, whose position he helped secure by eliminating potential rivals. He was now the dominant influence on imperial decisions. Promotion reflected his power: count in 519, general in attendance in 520, consul in 521, patrician and 'most noble' before 527. After 523 he married the former mime actress Theodora, but only after the empress, who strongly opposed the match, had died and Justinian had persuaded Justin to repeal the law prohibiting marriages between senators and actresses.

Justinian was crowned Augustus (see AUGUSTUS, AUGUSTA, AS TITLES) on 1 April 527, succeeded as sole emperor on Justin's death on 1 August, and soon began a campaign to enforce legislation against heretics, pagans, and male homosexuals, while in 530/1 permitting Monophysites exiled by Justin to return. (Monophysites believed that Christ had but one composite nature.) Imperial success depended on God's favour, a recurrent concern throughout Justinian's reign, so that deviants must be corrected or eliminated, but Justinian's conception of orthodoxy was sufficiently flexible to encourage him repeatedly to attempt religious reunification.

After religion Justinian's second great passion was law and administration. In 528 he established a commission to codify all valid imperial *constitutions from Hadrian to his own time: the *Codex Iustinianus* was first promulgated in 529, with a revised edition in 534. A second commission, appointed to excerpt and codify the works of classical jurists (see LAW, ROMAN, SOCIOLOGY OF; LAWYERS, ROMAN) published the *Digest* in 533 (see JUSTINIAN'S CODIFICATION). Thereafter Justinian continued to legislate energetically, with about 150 *Novellae* ('new constitutions') promulgated on a wide variety of administrative, legal, ecclesiastical, and criminal matters in a confident assertion of the efficacy of imperial action. Justinian also imposed his image on Constantinople after the Nika Riot (532) had necessitated extensive reconstruction, with the architecturally innovative St Sophia as centrepiece.

Warfare occupied much of Justinian's attention: he inherited conflict with *Sasanid Persia which dragged on until 561/2. His greatest ambition was to reconquer the provinces of the western empire: Africa was quickly recovered from the Vandals, but Ostrogothic Italy proved much harder, and the peninsula was not secured until 561/2; part of Spain was fortuitously recovered in 551. While intending to concentrate aggressive warfare in the west Justinian devoted much money and energy to improving the defences of the Balkans and eastern frontier: Armenia, Mesopotamia, and Syria required protection from the Persians; Thrace and Illyricum

from raids by Bulgars, Gepids, and Slavs, which on occasion even threatened the suburbs of Constantinople. Human and natural destruction had to be restored. *Procopius' *Buildings* provides a panegyrical survey of Justinian's efforts: fortifications were indeed improved. Beyond the frontiers diplomacy and money were exploited to maintain peace and dilute threats, with mixed success and adverse reaction from advocates of 'traditional' Roman aggression.

Justinian led an austere life, working hard for long hours and expecting the same of subordinates. He identified and exploited talent: John the Cappadocian and Peter Barsymas as administrators, *Tribonianus the lawyer, the generals Belisarius and Narses, the architect Anthemius, and the writers *Procopius and Paulus the Silentiary. Their various efforts ensured that the long reign presented, in general, a successful façade. Justinian's most trusted assistant, Theodora, died in 548; thereafter the childless Justinian failed to attend to the most pressing concern for every prudent emperor from *Augustus onwards, namely the identification and grooming of a successor.

Justinian's codification is a term loosely used to describe the three volumes (*Codex, Dīgesta* or *Pandectae, Institutes*) in which *Justinian tried to restate the whole of Roman law in a manageable and consistent form, though this restatement, which runs to over a million words, is too bulky and ill-arranged to count as a codification in the modern sense.

Within a few months of becoming emperor, Justinian ordered a commission of ten, mostly present or recent holders of public office, to prepare a comprehensive collection of imperial laws including those in the three existing codices, so far as they were still in force, together with more recent laws. The laws were to be edited in a short and clear form, with no repetition or conflict, but attributed to the emperors and dates at which they had originally been issued. The commission's head was the politically powerful layman John the Cappadocian. Within fourteen months the *Codex Iustinianus* in twelve books was finished and on 7 April 529 was promulgated as the exclusive source of imperial laws, the earlier codes being repealed. Its practical aim was to shorten lawsuits; and its compilation was widely regarded as a major achievement. It fitted a vision in which Justinian saw himself as rapidly restoring and extending the empire, in which process military and legal achievements would reinforce one another.

This 529 *Codex* does not survive, but the second edition of 534 does.

The writings of old legal authorities could still be cited in court, but they often conflicted; so Justinian first arranged for the 50 most prominent conflicts between the old writers to be settled, then in December 530 ordered that these old works, which ran to over 1,500 books, be condensed in 50 books and given the title *Dīgesta* ('Ordered Abstracts') or *Pandectae* ('Encyclopaedia'). For that purpose he set up a second commission consisting of élite lawyers under the quaestor *Tribonianus, who had shown his mettle as a member of the earlier commission, along with another official, four law professors, and eleven advocates. They were to read the works of authority, none of them written later than about AD 300, and excerpt what was currently valid. As with the *Codex*, the commissioners were to edit the texts in a clear form with no repetition or contradiction. 39 writers were used for the compilation. The commission was not to count heads but to choose the best view, no matter who held it. In the upshot *Ulpian, who provided two-fifths of the *Digest*, was their main source; Paulus provided one-sixth. The commission worked rapidly, and the *Digest* was promulgated in December 533. Justinian, in whose palace the commission was working, could be relied on to see that the timetable was kept to, as he did with the construction of St Sophia.

The compilers were authorized to alter the texts they kept. If the new version of a text differed from the old, the new prevailed, on the theory that Justinian was entitled to amend the previous law as he wished. But the amended texts were 'out of respect for antiquity' attributed to the original authors and books. This was a compromise, unsatisfactory from a scholarly point of view, which enabled Justinian to claim that everything in the *Digesta* was his, while in fact often reverting to the law as it was before 300.

The practical aims of the *Digest* were to shorten lawsuits and provide a revised law syllabus to be used in the schools of Berytus and *Constantinople. To complete the reform of law-teaching Justinian ordered Tribonianus and two of the professors to prepare an up-to-date edition of *Gaius' (2) lectures, the *Institutes*, making use also of other elementary teaching books by writers of authority. The professors perhaps each drafted two books, while Tribonianus brought the whole up to date by adding an account of recent legislation, esp. Justinian's. The *Institutes* like the *Digest* was promulgated in

December 533. It has survived and was for many centuries a successful students' first-year book. Then in 534 a second edition of the *Codex* of 529 was produced, which included the reforming laws of the intervening five years. This also has survived. The codification was now at an end. To avoid conflicting interpretations, commentaries on it were forbidden.

His codification had a practical and a political aim. Its practical impact, though considerable, was limited by its being wholly in Latin. Hence in the Greek-speaking Byzantine empire few could make proper use of it until the coming of a Greek collection of laws, the *Basilica*, which in the 9th and 10th cents. at last fused the two main sources of law, *Codex* and *Digest*.

The political aim of the codification was to renew, reform, and extend the Roman empire in its civil aspect. In this Justinian was in the long run successful, but not as he foresaw. He thought that the spread of Roman law depended on military conquest. In the west that proved short-lived; and when from the 11th cent. onwards his codification came to be taken as the basis of legal education and administration throughout Europe, it was not by force of arms but through its prestige and inherent rationality that his version of Roman law was adopted.

Juvenal (Decimus Iūnius Iuvenālis), Roman satirist. Known primarily for the angry tone of his early *Satires*, although in later poems he assumed an ironical and detached superiority. The highly rhetorical nature of his *Satires* has long been recognized, but only recently has the allied concept of the 'mask' been deployed to facilitate assessment of the *Satires* as self-conscious poetic constructs, rather than the reflections of the realities of Roman social life for which they have often been read. This approach is reinforced by rejection of the biographical interpretation, in which Juvenal's 'life' was reconstructed from details in his *Satires*. In fact, virtually nothing is known of his life: he is the addressee of three epigrams of *Martial (themselves highly sophisticated literary constructions) which indicate his skill in oratory. The absence of *dedication to a patron in Juvenal's *Satires* may suggest that he was a member of the élite. The few datable references suggest that the five books were written during the second and third decades of the 2nd cent. AD (or later), at about the same time as *Tacitus was writing his *Annals*. The *Satires* were written and published in books. Bk. 1 comprises *Satires* 1–5, bk. 2 *Satire* 6 alone, bk. 3 *Satires* 7–9, bk. 4 *Satires*

10–12, and bk. 5 *Satires* 13–16 (the last poem is unfinished).

In bk. 1 Juvenal introduces the indignant speaker who condemns Rome (satire is an urban genre), esp. the corruption of the patron–client relationship (see AMICITIA; CLIENS; PATRONAGE) (in *Satires* 1, 3, 4, and 5) and the decadence of the élite (in 1, 2, and 4). *Satire* 1 provides a justification for satire. The victims of satirical attack include the 'out-groups' that transgress sexual and social boundaries, such as the passive homosexuals of *Satire* 2 (see HOMOSEXUALITY) and the social upstarts, criminals, and foreigners attacked by Umbricius in *Satire* 3 (Umbricius figures himself as the last true Roman, driven from an un-Roman Rome). The Roman élite are portrayed as paradigms of moral corruption: the selfish rich are attacked in *Satires* 1 and 3, and *Domitian is portrayed as sexual hypocrite and autocrat in 2 and 4. Those dependent on these powerful men are not absolved from blame: the courtiers humiliated by Domitian by being asked to advise on what to do with an enormous fish in *Satire* 4, like the client humiliated by his wealthy patron at a dinner party in 5, are condemned for craven compliance.

The focus upon Roman men in bk. 1 is complemented by the focus upon Roman women in bk. 2, which consists of the massive *Satire* 6, comparable in length to a book of *epic. The speaker fiercely (but unsuccessfully) attempts to dissuade his addressee from marriage by cataloguing the (alleged) faults of Roman wives. Here Juvenal develops his angry speaker in the ultimate rant which seems to exhaust the possibilities of angry satire; thereafter he adopts a new approach of irony and cynicism. Initially (in bk. 3) Juvenal's new, calmer persona takes up the topics treated in bk. 1: clients and patrons (*Satires* 7 and 9) and the corruption and worthlessness of the élite (8). He then marks his change of direction explicitly at the start of bk. 4, where the speaker states his preference for detached laughter over tears as a reaction to the follies of the world; in *Satire* 10 he accordingly demolishes first the objects of human prayer, then the act of prayer itself. His programmatic declaration is borne out by the 'Horatian' tone and topics (see HORACE) of *Satire* 11 (where an invitation to dinner conveys a condemnation of decadence and a recommendation of self-sufficiency) and 12 (where true friendship is contrasted with the false friendship of legacy-hunters). The speaker of bk. 5 becomes still more detached and cynical as he turns his attention to the themes of crime and punishment, money and greed. The opening poem, *Satire* 13, offers a programmatic condemnation of anger in the form of a mock *consolation, which indicates clearly the development from bk. 1, where anger was apparently approved.

Juvenal claims that his satire replaces epic and *tragedy: his chief contribution to the genre is his appropriation of the 'grand style' from other more elevated forms of *hexameter verse, notably epic. This contrasts markedly with the sometimes coarse language of *Lucilius (1) and the tone of refined 'conversation' adopted by Horace in his satirical writings. Juvenal's satiric 'grand style' mingles different lexical levels, ranging from epic and tragedy (e.g. the epic parody in *Satires* 4 and 12) to mundanities, Greek words, and occasional obscenities. His penchant for oxymora, pithy paradoxes, and trenchant questions makes Juvenal a favourite mine for quotations, e.g. *mens sāna in corpore sānō* and *quis custōdiet ipsōs custōdēs?*: 'a healthy mind in a healthy body' and 'who guards the guards?'.

Juvenal's *Satires* apparently present reassuring entertainment for the Roman male élite audience. However, inconsistencies written into the texts allow alternative views of Juvenal's speakers as riddled with bigotry (chauvinism, misogyny, homophobia) or as cynically superior. In literary history, Juvenal's significance is in bringing to fullest development the indignant speaker: his 'savage indignation' had a lasting influence on Renaissance and later satire and remains central to modern definitions of 'satire'. See SATIRE.

Kairos, Opportunity personified.

kanēphoroi were usually young women who bore baskets or vessels in religious processions. In the Panathenaic procession (see PANATHE-NAEA) the young women were required to be of good family, unmarried, and of unsullied reputation; hence 'to be fit to carry the basket' is to live chastely, and to reject a candidate was a grave insult. Serving as a *kanephoros* was thus a mark of prominence. They were splendidly dressed; hair and garments were decked with gold and jewels; they were powdered with white barley-flour and wore a chain of figs. They carried vessels of gold and silver, which contained all things needed in the sacrificial ceremony: *first-fruits, the sacrificial knife, barleycorns, and garlands. The sacred utensils were kept in the Pompeion, the 'procession house'. The institution was very old, and its object was doubtless to secure the efficacy of the sacrificial materials by letting them touch nothing that was not virginal and therefore lucky and potent.

kingship The Mycenaean political system (see MYCENAEAN AGE CIVILIZATION) was monarchic, with the king at the head of a palace-centred economy. *Homer borrows elements from Mycenae and the near east, but seems essentially to be describing an aristocratic world, in which the word *basileus* is often used in the plural of an office-holding nobility. The earliest true monarchies were the 7th–6th-cent. BC *tyrannies, which were regarded as aberrations; the Spartan dual 'kingship' (see SPARTA) is a form of hereditary but non-monarchic military leadership. The Classical period knew kingship only from myth and as a *barbarian form of rule, found in tribal areas and in the near east. *Sophists established a theoretical table of constitutions, with kingship and tyranny as the good and bad forms of monarchy, opposed to the rule of the few and the rule of the many (see OLIGARCHY; DEMOCRACY; POLITICAL THEORY). In

the 4th cent., developments in *Thessaly, *Syracuse, *Caria, and *Cyprus, and esp. the rise of Macedon under *Philip II, demonstrated the practical importance of monarchy; and *Plato, *Xenophon, and *Isocrates elaborated theories justifying kingship.

After *Alexander (2) the Great, monarchy became a dominant form of government in the Greek world. The Hellenistic monarchies (see GREECE, HISTORY; HELLENISM) controlled vast territories by conquest ('land won by the spear'), and often made use of existing local administrative practices, presenting themselves as successors to earlier kings; they encouraged and adapted indigenous forms of king-worship (see RULER-CULT). In practice monarchies were hereditary, and claims were made to divine descent. In Greek cities the forms of king-worship were based on the idea of the king as saviour and benefactor (see EUERGETISM; SOTER), or new *founder of the city: the king and sometimes his family were living gods to be worshipped with temples, cult statues, and festivals. In the free cities such honours were often diplomatic, and reflected the needs of alliances. Roman proconsuls also found themselves honoured; and the emperors accepted and systematized emperor-worship in the Greek provinces of the empire.

A philosophical theory of monarchy developed in the early Hellenistic period: philosophers were often welcomed as advisers at court, and representatives from all major philosophical schools except the *Cynic are known to have written treatises *On Kingship* (all lost). They seem to have rested on a common theoretical basis: kingship was 'rule without accountability'; it was justified by the perfect virtue of the king, which should be exemplified in a series of actions towards his subjects. The main virtue was love of his subjects (*philanthrō-pia*); others were beneficence (*euergesia*), justice, self-control, wisdom, foresight, courage. Though the king need not himself be a philosopher, he should listen to their advice. The king's actions would ensure the love of his subjects. The doctrine of the king as 'living law' was not part of the theory, which was weak in legal justification.

This theory hardly affected Roman attitudes to the emperor until the mid-1st cent. AD. But thereafter a series of writers describe the duties of the emperor in language derived from Hellenistic kingship theory.

King's Peace, of 386 BC, epoch-making arrangement, imposed by king *Artaxerxes (2) II of Persia, whereby the *Corinthian War was ended. The peace guaranteed the *autonomy of the Greeks, in exchange for recognition that the cities in Asia, also the 'islands' Clazomenae (not actually an island) and *Cyprus, should belong to Persia. The Spartan *Antalcidas was prominent in the negotiations, hence the alternative name Peace of Antalcidas.

kinship Greek interest in *genealogy is securely attested. And Greeks of the Classical and Hellenistic periods were much interested in the idea of kinship between peoples or cities, and they based political claims and requests on such real, exaggerated, or imagined kinship-ties. The Romans also defined themselves in such terms; see AENEAS. All this might seem to encourage generalization about kinship in the ancient world, but it may be safer to pursue particular aspects.

See ADOPTION; FAMILY, ROMAN; FOUNDERS OF CITIES; GENEALOGY; GENOS; GENS; HOUSEHOLD; INCEST; INHERITANCE; MARRIAGE CEREMONIES and MARRIAGE LAW; PHRATRIES; PHYLAI; PROSOPOGRAPHY; TRIBUS; WOMEN.

koinē (standard Greek) See GREEK LANGUAGE.

korai See SCULPTURE, GREEK.

Korē See PERSEPHONE/KORE.

kouroi See SCULPTURE, GREEK.

Kourotrophos, 'child-nurturer', appears to be known both as a divine epithet and as an independent goddess over much of the Greek world. She is evidently an important figure of cult, appearing often in sacrifice groups connected with fertility and child care.

Kronos See CRONUS.

krypteia Part of the Classical Spartan upbringing (see AGOGE), during which (probably, selected) youths traversed the countryside, concealing themselves by day. Some sources present it as a lengthy test of individual endurance without equipment or prepared rations, others as a brief exercise by a group provided with supplies and daggers for killing prominent *helots; these may be sequential stages of the institution. Different modern interpretations of the *krypteia*—military preparation or a transitional period of 'opposition' to adult *hoplite life—are not necessarily incompatible.

labour, as a factor in the production of wealth, has no equivalent in Greek or Latin. Association of the terms *ponos* and *labor* with drudgery reflects the negative attitudes of ancient élites, for whom 'labour' was the antithesis of *scholē* and *ōtium* (leisure, for politics, education, and culture). So, the labour of theoretically free wage-earners and craftsmen tended to be assimilated to slavery. *Wages were seen as purchasing the person as opposed to labour-power; the supposedly degrading nature of craft-work (*banausia*) led to the downgrading of the individual worker (see ART, ANCIENT ATTITUDES TO; ARTISANS AND CRAFTSMEN). Our sources reveal nothing like modern unions or trade-guilds (see CLUBS), strikes, or common programmes of action; nor, aside from occasional epitaphs, is there any awareness of the 'dignity of labour'. There is no sign of sustained competition or resentment between types of labour. Instead we find shifting, complementary relationships between different forms of exploitation. Already in *Hesiod's Works and Days* (less clearly in the *Odyssey*) there exist crude equivalents of 'free', 'wage', and 'slave' labourer, combined on the *peasant farm. The dominant form of labour on the land throughout the ancient world may broadly be described as 'compulsory labour', whereby the politically weak performed obligatory labour dues for the powerful. From the Greek world, the *helots are the best known of these unfree agricultural workforces 'between freedom and slavery'. There was a similar pattern in the Roman empire, with Romans in the provinces retaining pre-existing systems of compulsory labour. In cities, the labour of independent artisans and their families would be supplemented by slaves (a permanent workforce) or wage labourers (for casual labour). Large public projects would require extensive hired labour. Exceptional were Classical Athens and Roman Italy and Sicily during the late republic, where chattel *slavery was widespread in the countryside (though supplemented by wage labour at harvest). In both cases, the citizen status of peasants made problematic their direct exploitation by landowning élites. Italian peasants, however, always remained vulnerable. As the number of chattel slaves gradually diminished, the later centuries of the empire saw a lowering of peasant status and their progressive re-exploitation.

labyrinth, a complex building constructed by *Daedalus for *Minos king of Crete and commonly identified with the Minoan palace of Cnossus (see MINOAN CIVILIZATION). The labyrinth's confusing system of passages, from which no one could escape, concealed the Minotaur, which fed on human victims until destroyed by *Theseus. The hero imitated its twists and turns in a ritual dance on *Delos. A plausible derivation of the non-Greek word from (Lydian) 'double axe' connects the labyrinth with a potent Minoan religious symbol *labrys*.

Lacedaemon See LACONIA; SPARTA (for which 'Lacedaemon' was the official name).

Laconia, the SE district of *Peloponnese, bordering Arcadia to the north and *Messenia to the west. Until the 190s BC, Laconia was controlled by *Sparta and was the 'nuclear territory' of the Spartans. A mountainous region, Laconia comprises the Parnon range in the east running south to the Malea peninsula, and the Taygetus range in the west, which towers over the plain of Sparta and extends south to the Mani peninsula. In between is the valley of the Eurotas, the main area of cultivable land.

By *c.*700 BC Sparta controlled most of Laconia and had begun its expansion into Messenia, reducing much of the conquered population to *helotry. Spartiate territory comprised the plain of Sparta and its surrounds, the rest of Laconia being divided among nominally independent perioecic towns (see PERIOIKOI). The northern frontiers were established *c.*540 after long disputes with *Argos and Tegea. Communications with the outside world were through Tegea to the north and Gytheum, Sparta's port and naval station, to the south. Spartan control of Laconia was uninterrupted until 338 BC.

Laelius, Gaius (c.190–after 129 BC), closest friend of *Cornelius Scipio Aemilianus. He became involved with the embassy of Athenian philosophers (155), esp. the Stoic Diogenēs, and with *Panaetius, whose work he was influential in publicizing at Rome. These connections earned him the nickname *Sapiens* ('wise'). In 147/6 he served with Scipio Aemilianus in Africa, and went on to be *praetor in 145 and *consul in 140. He was *augur from before 140 until his death. His reputation as an orator was considerable. He is the central figure in Cicero's *On Friendship* and appears also in his *Republic*.

Laius See OEDIPUS.

Lamachus (d. 414 BC), Athenian general, one of the *strategoi* as early as c.435 and well known for his military leadership by 425, when he was caricatured as a blustering soldier in *Aristophanes' *Acharnians*. In 424 he led an unsuccessful expedition into the Black (*Euxine) Sea. In 415 he was appointed with *Alcibiades and *Nicias to command the expedition to Sicily. He urged an immediate attack on *Syracuse, but failed to convince his colleagues. The rapid progress of the Athenian blockade in 414 seems to have been largely due to his energetic leadership; it ended abruptly when he was killed in a skirmish. In later plays Aristophanes pays tributes to his heroism.

Lamian War (323–322 BC), fought, after the death of *Alexander (2) the Great, by Macedon under *Antipater against a Greek coalition led by *Athens and Aetolia. It took its name from Lamia in *Thessaly, where Antipater was besieged (see LEOSTHENES). The war ended with the Greek defeat at Crannon.

lamps were made of *gold, *silver, *iron, *lead, *bronze, and ceramic. Only the last two kinds survive in any quantity. Lamps were used for *lighting, served as *votives in sanctuaries and as tomb-furniture. *Olive oil was the usual fuel.

land ownership See DOMAINS; LATIFUNDIA.

landscapes (ancient Greek) Greece has a rich flora and fauna, with many species peculiar to the country, or to one mountain or island (esp. *Crete).

The land comprises six ecological zones: (1) plains; (2) cultivable hillsides on softer rocks; (3) uncultivable hillsides on harder rocks; (4) high mountains; (5) fens; (6) coasts and sea. By classical times Greece looked not very different from Greece today, leaving aside urbanization, road-making, and bulldozing. One important difference is the disappearance of fens, which provided summer pasture for cattle. There have been changes in the coastline, famously at *Thermopylae. In land-use, the Classical Greeks had much more grain and legume cultivation than today (see CEREALS; FOOD AND DRINK), and much less *olive-growing; they kept cattle and pigs, as well as the sheep and goats which are the remaining livestock. At least half the land was natural vegetation, consisting as today of dwarf, *maquis* (shrubs), savannah (scattered trees), or woodland. The first three were valuable pasture-land. Woodland of oak, pine, fir, beech (in the north), and cypress (in Crete) was mainly in the uncultivable mountains. See TIMBER.

Ancient city-states varied hugely in territory and resources. Athens and Sparta, the two giants, had access to all six ecological zones. But even Athens was not self-sufficient in timber and not always in corn. It depended on buying imports with silver from *Laurium (smelted, presumably, with fuel from the *maquis* of uncultivable hills). Some tiny 'cities' (see POLIS) had only one or two zones. See AGRICULTURE, GREEK; GREECE (GEOGRAPHY).

land surveyors See GROMATICI.

languages See ARAMAIC; ETRUSCAN; GREEK; ITALY, LANGUAGES OF; LATIN; MYCENAEAN; PERSIAN, OLD.

Laocoön, a Trojan prince, brother of *Anchises and priest of *Apollo or *Poseidon. In the standard version of his story, he protested against drawing the Wooden Horse within the walls of *Troy, and two great serpents coming over the sea from the island of Tenedos killed him and his two sons. Acc. to *Virgil, the serpents were sent by *Athena because of his hostility to the Horse.

In art, Laocoön is the subject of the famous marble group in the Vatican (found in 1506) showing father and sons in their death-agony. It was made by three Rhodian sculptors. The group was exhibited in the palace of *Titus, and was said by *Pliny the Elder to have surpassed all other works of painting and sculpture.

The death of Laocoön is shown in two wall-paintings from *Pompeii.

Lāomedon, a legendary king of *Troy, son of Ilus (see DARDANUS), and father of several children, including *Priam and Hēsionē. He was renowned for his treachery: he had the walls of Troy built for him by *Apollo and *Poseidon, but then refused to pay them the agreed wage. As punishment, Apollo sent a plague and Poseidon a sea-monster which could be appeased only by the sacrifice of Hesione. But *Heracles saved her and killed the sea-monster, at which once again Laomedon refused to pay an agreed reward, this time the divine horses which *Zeus had once given him in exchange for kidnapping Ganymedes. In due course Heracles returned to Troy with an army, captured the city with the help of *Telamon, and killed Laomedon and all his sons except *Priam, giving Hesione to Telamon as a concubine and leaving Priam to rule Troy.

Lărēs Whatever their origins, the Lares, turned into (a) guardians of any crossway, including one in a city; (b) guardians of roads and wayfarers, including travellers by sea. The cult of the *Lar familiāris* ('of the *household') ultimately became universal, and so lar or lares is used like *penates, by metonymy, for 'home'.

lātifundia (large estates) 'have ruined Italy and are now ruining the provinces'. *Pliny the Elder put *latifundia* at the centre of debate about the development of the Roman rural economy. But what were *latifundia*? Divergent modern definitions abound and confuse: large pastoral ranches beginning in the 3rd cent. BC; slave-staffed oil- and wine-producing villas (either single properties or the scattered estates of one owner) first described by *Porcius Cato (1) *c.*160 BC (see VILLA; SLAVERY); any property above 500 *iugera* (125 ha.: 309 acres) of whatever period: all of which 'ruined' Italy by forcing *peasants from the land. Others dismiss Pliny's remark as generalized nostalgia and refer to archaeological surveys that not only emphasize the diversity of rural settlement but also show that villas and peasant farms often existed side by side. Yet if Pliny is to be believed, the term *latifundia* applies strictly to extensive unitary estates, resulting from an aggregation of properties, too large to farm according to the labour-intensive methods of cultivation of the slave-staffed villas recommended by the *agricultural writers. *Latifundia* are thus to be defined not so much by crop or measurement as by management principles.

Pliny refers to the reaping-machine and long-handled scythe typical of Gallic *latifundia*, which saved time and labour but wasted grain and hay. On such large estates tenants were probably increasingly employed alongside or in preference to poorly supervised (and thus uneconomical) slaves. In this interpretation *latifundia* 'ruined' an agriculture previously dominated by the slave-staffed villa. Some such process occurred in the 1st cent. AD both in Etruria, where field-survey and excavation indicate that medium-sized villas gave way to larger estates, and in the *ager Falernus* in *Campania, another heartland of the slave-staffed villa. Analysis of all literary references now suggests that *latifundia* developed in Italy in the Julio-Claudian period. But how widespread did they become? Only a generation later *Pliny the Younger readily contemplated just such an aggregation of two large estates on the upper *Tiber. As for the provinces specifically associated with *latifundia*, fieldwork in *Sicily suggests a similar trend of amalgamation in the late 1st and early 2nd cents. AD; evidence from northern Tunisia (see AFRICA, ROMAN) points to the formation of large estates consisting of a central villa and scattered, probably tenant, farms; while sculptural reliefs of the Gallic reaping-machine have been found at Reims and near *Augusta Treverorum. See AGRICULTURE, ROMAN; DOMAINS.

Latin language Latin belongs to the Italic group of *Indo-European languages, which includes Faliscan, Umbrian, and Oscan. It was originally spoken in Latium from 800 BC or earlier, and with the spread of Roman power it became the common language first of Italy, then of the western Mediterranean and Balkan regions of the Roman empire. The language of the illiterate majority of Latin-speakers, Vulgar Latin (VL), evolved through its regional dialects into the Romance languages. It is known from casual remarks by ancient grammarians, comparative Romance reconstruction, and deviations from classical norms in manuscript and epigraphic texts.

Refined versions of the language were developed early on for specific purposes—legal and ritual texts, public oratory, senatorial and priestly records, and *Saturnian verse. The earliest of these survive in corrupt and fragmentary forms, e.g. the *Twelve Tables and the 'Hymn of the Arval Brethren'. Later examples are the senate's decree on the cult of Bacchus (see BACCHANALIA) and the Cornelius Scipio Epitaphs (c.250–150 BC). The combination of these native written genres and the influence of Greek models from *c*.240 BC onwards led eventually to the written form of the Roman dialect, *sermō urbānus* 'urban(e) speech', that we know as Classical Latin (CL).

CL is defined by the characteristics common to literary authors in the period *c*.90 BC–*c*. AD 120. It is a highly artificial construct, which must be regarded linguistically as a deviation from the mainstream of the language, namely VL. Nevertheless for centuries a spectrum of usage linked the highest literary compositions through the informal idiom of the letters and conversation of their authors and the plain registers of legal, administrative, and technical writings to the Latin of the masses. The spectrum was ruptured long before the 9th century AD.

Latin right See IUS LATII.

Latins inhabited *Latium Vetus. They formed a unified ethnic group with a common name a common sentiment, and a common language; they worshipped the same gods and had similar political and social institutions. Archaeological evidence shows that a distinctive form of material culture spread throughout Latium Vetus from *c*.1000 BC. The Latins' sense of kinship was expressed in a common myth of origin: they traced their descent back to Latīnus (the father-in-law of *Aeneas), who after his death was transformed into *Jupiter Latiaris and worshipped on the Alban mount (see ALBANUS MONS). His annual festival was ancient. The main ritual event was a banquet, at which representatives of the Latin communities each received a share of the meat of a slaughtered bull (see SACRIFICE, ROMAN). Participation in the cult was a badge of membership; it was regularly attended by all the Latin peoples, including the Romans, well into the imperial period.

It is probable that the Latins formed a community long before the emergence of organized city-states in the 6th cent. BC. It is probable also that the rights that the Latin peoples shared in historical times were a relic of this pre-urban period. These shared rights, unparalleled elsewhere, include *conubium*, the right to contract a legal marriage with a partner from another Latin state; *commercium*, the right to deal with persons from other Latin communities and to make legally binding contracts; and the so-called right of migration, the capacity to acquire the citizenship of another Latin state simply by living there.

Acc. to tradition, Rome became dominant under the later kings (see REX), who established some kind of hegemony over much of *Latium. After the fall of the monarchy, however, the Latins rebelled from Rome, and formed an alliance centred at Aricia (25 km. (16 mi.) SE of Rome) The struggle between Rome and the Latin alliance culminated in the battle of Lake Regillus, and was finally resolved by the treaty of Cassius Vecellinus (493), which established peace and a defensive military alliance on equal terms between Rome and the so-called Latin League.

The alliance persisted into the 4th cent., and probably saved Latium from being overwhelmed by the encroachments of the Aequi and *Volsci. Successful campaigns that resulted in conquest of territory allowed the allies to found colonies, in which Romans and Latins both took part. The newly founded colonies became independent communities, with the same rights and obligations as the existing Latin states; they were therefore known as Latin colonies.

During the 4th cent. Roman territorial ambitions began to be seen as a threat by the Latins, who in 341 finally took up arms together with their southern neighbours. The ensuing 'Latin War' ended in disaster for the Latins and their allies, and in 338 the Romans imposed a settlement whereby some Latin and Volscian cities were incorporated in the Roman state with full *citizenship (e.g. Aricia and Antium). The other Latins remained allies and continued to share mutual privileges with Rome, but were forbidden to have any dealings with each other. The Latin League was thus finally dissolved. From now on Latin status meant that the city in question had a distinctive relationship with Rome, rather than being part of a wider community. The Romans also embarked on a new programme of colonization after the Latin War, and conferred Latin status on the newly founded colonies, even though they were outside Latium. By 200 the few remaining independent communities in Latium were only a small minority of the Latin name; most Latins lived in the colonies, which were spread throughout Italy. After the *Social War, when the Latins received full Roman citizenship, 'Latin' ceased to be an ethno-linguistic term and became a purely juridical category (see IUS LATII). See COLONIZATION, ROMAN.

Latium Ancient sources make a useful distinction between Old Latium (*Latium Vetus*), the land of the ancient *Latins, bounded to the NW by the rivers *Tiber and Anio and to the east by the Apennines and Lepinus mons, and Greater Latium (*Latium Adiectum*), which extended SE as far as the borders of *Campania. Under *Augustus Latium (Adiectum) was combined with Campania to form the first of the fourteen regions of *Italy. Physically Latium Vetus consists of a coastal plain (the name is connected etymologically with *lātus*, 'broad') with mountainous spurs extending towards the sea from the Apennines. It is dominated by the volcanic complex of the Alban hills, whose summit, the *Albanus mons, rises to nearly 1,000 m. (3,280 ft.).

laudātiō fūnebris, the funeral speech praising the accomplishments and virtues of the deceased. Because of the public nature of funerals, the speech offered an opportunity to display the family's status, to connect the deceased's merits with his or her illustrious ancestors, and to reinforce collective values. Important *gentes* (see GENS) preserved and displayed speeches over the years, thus creating a self-flattering if often fictional historical record. Funeral speeches devoted to women (see next entry) show the same combination of private and public concerns. See CONSOLATION; EPITAPHIOS.

'Laudātiō Turiae', the longest known private Roman inscription; originally in two long columns, the first of which is lost, but most of the second survives in four fragments. It is in the form of a *laudatio funebris, addressed by an aristocratic husband to a deceased wife, who had not only been an ideal Roman matron, but who had saved him and secured his rehabilitation during the triumviral *proscriptions. The inscription was set up in various places in Rome. The names of the couple are lost: 'Turia' is only a conjecture.

Laurium, a hilly district in southern *Attica near Cape *Sunium, was one of the largest mining districts of Greece, producing *silver from argentiferous lead ores. Early operations involved opencast and gallery mining, and later included the sinking of deep shafts. Athens' issue of silver *coinage stimulated production, enhanced by the finding of rich lodes at Maroneia before 483 BC; this financed Themistocles' fleet programme. The *mines flourished throughout the 5th cent. till the Decelean War, then declined, but revived greatly in the second half of the 4th cent. Copious industrial remains throughout the area include shafts, galleries, reservoirs, washing-tables, buildings, and smelteries. Excavations have revealed notable examples of surface workshops with cisterns, grinderies, cemented ore-washeries, workrooms and slave-quarters, some arranged in regular compounds. Mines, considered state property, were leased for fixed terms to private citizens by the *poletai, and surface installations were built by individuals for use or lease. Fragments of *poletai*-leases have been found in the Athenian Agora. See MINES AND MINING, Greek.

law, international 'Law' here includes customary, religious, and moral law. Some approach to statutory law can be seen in the amphictionic laws (see AMPHICTIONY), the covenant after the battle of *Plataea of 479 BC, and the *King's Peace; and the relations of states to each other were regulated by treaties. Nevertheless, international law remained essentially customary and, in contrast to the laws of individual states, which also had once been customary, was never officially recorded or codified.

By Homeric times *heralds and ambassadors were considered inviolable, and the sanctity of sworn agreements was recognized. Similar evidence is supplied for early Italy by the fetial code with its demand that every war be a just war (see FETIALES). Greek practice was soon expanded by the amphictionic oath and the truces for the panhellenic games (see PANHELLENISM).

Greek treaties were descended directly from the agreements of Homeric times, while the Roman organization of Italy indicates early use of treaties. Omitting armistices, the chief classes were treaties of peace, of alliance, and of friendship. The lack of treaties need not mean hostility. Thus, though Rome had treaties of friendship (*amicitia) with several states, friendly relations often existed without such a treaty. The oldest Greek treaties preserved in detail were made for a limited period, and treaties 'for all time' did not become the rule before the 4th cent. Many Greek treaties contained clauses providing for the arbitration of disputes, and even in their absence arbitration was frequently offered.

Regard for what was customary or morally right applied to the rules of war. Such a basis for law meant that standards varied over time and from place to place. Acc. to *Thucydides (2), a lowering of standards resulted from the *Peloponnesian War, while the accusation of *piracy constantly made against the people of Aetolia implies that their standard was lower than those of other states. Nor were all foreigners treated alike, but *barbarians were shown less consideration than closely related states.

Roman expansion, at first glance, seems to leave less scope for development of international law in the Roman empire than in Greece (see IMPERIALISM, ROMAN), but Rome's early organization of Italy was based on international law, and the existence of free and allied cities outside Italy and the control of states not formally annexed caused the Roman empire to be governed for long largely by a modified form of international law.

See also ALLIANCE; FETIALES; FOEDUS; HERALDS; LAW IN GREECE; PROXENOS; WAR, RULES OF.

law, Roman, sociology of During the later republic and early empire, Roman *jurists developed law, esp. private law, on the basis of what they called the 'art' of law-finding: they subjected existing legal rules and institutions to intense and sustained scrutiny, with the aim of isolating the basic principles that controlled the rules, and then applying these principles in the creation of new law. The activity of the Roman jurists opens a new chapter in the history of law. The sociological task is to evaluate how this new form of thinking contributed to Rome's broader social development.

The jurists' legal authority rested primarily on their accumulated knowledge of law and experience in manipulating it. They were independent legal experts who monopolized the study of law, but were available for consultation esp. by litigants and lay judges. However, during the empire the small corps of jurists (probably never more than ten to 20 at any time) was gradually transformed into a legal élite presiding over a much larger legal profession. This is esp. true after AD 150, when most jurists were absorbed into the emperor's central bureaucracy.

At first the jurists transmitted their methods and results from generation to generation internally, through writing and informal teaching. Formal elementary legal education is not attested before the mid-2nd cent. AD, as law became a more established and accessible profession.

The jurists' extensive writings were central to the continuity of their law-finding. Their writings were mainly problem-oriented; the jurists did not decide actual cases, but instead developed law through exploring hypothetical situations. Thus the jurists preserved a distance between themselves and the Roman judicial system; questions of law were solved abstractly, as general propositions not closely tied to the disputed facts of particular cases. The jurists resembled modern appellate judges.

Socially, the jurists belonged to the empire's élite, usually by birth, though some jurists seem to have risen by their legal talent. Their work is closely associated with the capital city, and esp. with the operation of its judicial system, which was, to be sure, widely imitated throughout the empire. Although the jurists differed somewhat in outlook, their social homogeneity is obvious: rich and powerful men drawn increasingly from across the empire, but not usually from the topmost ranks of the senatorial aristocracy.

Their social homogeneity doubtless contributes to a tendency to concentrate on legal problems affecting mainly the upper strata of Roman society; such problems also arose more often at trials in Rome than in the provinces. Although the jurists evaluate these problems even-handedly, both the framework of their analysis and their understanding of social reality are constricted. For example, they say almost nothing about ordinary wage labour, tenement housing, or peasant agriculture, but much about the management of large estates, succession to the rich, and commerce in staples and luxury items.

The narrowness of the jurists' vision raises difficult issues about the social reach of Roman private law: is it yet another manifestation of a highly stratified society, in which a few men control not only all common social goods, but also the apparatus of justice? None the less, the jurists display considerable sensitivity to the conflicting interests and demands of diverse social groups. Where juristic knowledge of social activity can be closely examined, it is accurate and deep, though casually acquired. The jurists develop Roman law incrementally, decision by decision, often after fierce debate among themselves. This process lent itself to the tacit accommodation of social interests. As the jurists became more confident in their methods, they increasingly justified decisions through reference to external social values such as fairness and practicality.

This incremental legal growth gradually raised the salience of law as a distinct institution within Roman society. Although lay criticism of the jurists and their law was common, it was also internalized as part of the process whereby new legal rules arise through reaction to existing law. The jurists, furthermore, could create new law without resort to cumbersome legislation; and the emperors left them largely free to do so. As a result law achieved, in the Roman world, substantial independence and social responsiveness.

The differentiation of law is a major Roman accomplishment, but its immediate consequence for Roman society is equivocal. The social and economic institutions of the empire do not appear to have altered significantly despite the encouragement of juristic liberalism. Juristic concepts of legality and due process probably did influence the growth of the imperial bureaucracy and judiciary; but except in private law, Roman progress was less than impressive.

The one obvious exception to this pattern is Roman law's contribution to integrating the empire's upper strata. As Roman *citizenship gradually spread, its élite became both larger and more disparate, no longer united by the traditional social values of earlier city-states; Roman aristocrats were forced to rub shoulders with rich *freedmen and provincial magnates. Law provided Romans with a predictable structure of expectations within their most vital social relationships: marriage, the family, contracts, and succession. It thus served to hold society together. The advantage was esp. marked for those members of the upper strata, such as the municipal nobilities, whose social position was not always well protected against their superiors (see DECURIONES). Most jurists were themselves members of these social groups, at least by birth. See HONESTIORES.

Insulated by their professionalism from directly contending social pressures, the jurists correctly defined justice, as *Ulpian did, primarily in formal terms: 'according each person his right'.

law and procedure, Athenian

1. **Legislation** Greeks used the same word (*nomos*) for both custom and law, and the beginning of law is hard to define. An unwritten rule can be regarded as a law if the community or the ruler approves it and imposes or authorizes punishment for infringement of it. In this sense laws forbidding some offences (e.g. murder, theft, bigamy) must have existed since primitive times. An alternative view is that only rules stated in writing are really laws. The transition from oral to written law began in the 7th cent. BC, but was not completed until the end of the 5th cent. in Athens (and later in other cities). See LITERACY; ORALITY.

The first written laws in Athens are attributed to *Draco. His laws, except that on homicide, were superseded in 594/3 by those of *Solon.

These laws were inscribed on wooden blocks for everyone to read. Later these inscriptions were transferred to stone and many additions and alterations were made, but the Athenians continued to refer to their code as the laws of Solon.

After democracy was established, new laws were made by majority vote in the *ekklesia. For most of the 5th cent. there was no distinction between a law (*nomos*) laying down a permanent rule and a decree (*psēphisma*) for a particular occasion. Legislation was not systematic, and confusions and contradictions arose. From 410 onwards efforts were made to rectify this situation. Existing laws were revised to remove obscurities or inconsistencies, and were all inscribed on stone; henceforth no uninscribed law was to be enforced, and no decree could override a law. New decrees were still made by the *ekklesia*, but the making of new laws was handed over to groups of citizens known as *nomothetai.

2. **Judicature** Until the early 6th cent. BC all verdicts were given by the archons (see ARCHONTES) or the *Areopagus or the *ephetai. Solon instituted a system of trial by the *eliaia, probably for appeals against the archons' verdicts or for imposition of penalties above certain limits. The next stages of development are obscure, but presumably appeals became so usual that the archons practically ceased to give verdicts, and the *eliaia* (if it was a single body) did not have time to hear all the cases referred to it. A system of juries was therefore set up, in which each jury consisted of a number of citizens who tried a case on behalf of all the citizens.

From *c.*450 we have fuller information. Volunteers for jury service (who had to be citizens aged over 30) were called for at the beginning of each year, and a list of 6,000 jurors for the year was drawn up. To encourage volunteers, each juror received a small fee for each day on which he sat to try a case. This payment was introduced by *Pericles, who probably fixed it at two obols; it was raised to three obols, probably on the proposal of *Cleon, not later than 425. Since the payment was less than an able-bodied man would earn by an ordinary day's work, one of its effects was that many of the volunteers were men who were too old for work. This state of affairs is satirized in Aristophanes' *Wasps*.

The size of a jury varied according to the type of case, but was normally several hundred. In the 4th cent. odd numbers (e.g. 501) were used, to avoid a tie in the voting. It is not known what method was used in the 5th cent. for allocating jurors to courts (*dikastēria*, sing. *dikastērion*). By the early 4th cent. a system of lot was used for this purpose, and later in the century a more complicated system of lot was introduced. The aim was to prevent *bribery by making it impossible to know beforehand which jurors would try which case.

Each trial was arranged and presided over by a magistrate or group of magistrates. Different magistrates had responsibility for different types of case. The archon had charge of cases concerning family and inheritance rights. The *basileus* had charge of homicide cases and most cases connected with religion. The *polemarch had charge of cases concerning non-Athenians. The *thesmothetai* had charge of a wide variety of cases; in general any type of public case which did not clearly fall within the province of another magistrate came to them. The *Eleven had charge of cases of theft and similar offences. The *strategoi* had charge of cases concerning military and naval service, and there were several lesser boards of magistrates with responsibility for particular types of case, such as the *apodektai* ('receivers' of the state's revenues). In the 4th cent. most types of private case were handled by four judges selected by lot for each of the ten tribes (see PHYLAI).

In the 5th cent. and the first half of the 4th each magistrate sat regularly in the same court. The *eliaia* was the court of the *thesmothetai*. Other courts, perhaps not all in use at the same time, included the *Odeum and the Painted *Stoa. In the later 4th cent. magistrates no longer sat regularly in the same courts, but were allocated to courts by lot each day. Distinct from all these courts were the Areopagus and the other special homicide courts, manned by the *ephetai*, in which a different procedure was followed. A few cases were tried by the *boule* or the *ekklesia*.

3. Actions The law on any particular subject generally specified the action to be raised against a transgressor; for some offences the prosecutor had a choice of actions. The principal distinction was between public actions and private actions. The following were the main differences. (*a*) A private action concerned a wrong done to an individual. A public action concerned an offence which was regarded as affecting the community as a whole. (*b*) A private action could be raised only by the person who claimed that he had suffered wrong. A public action might be raised by a magistrate or official acting on behalf of the state. But the scope of public pros-

ecution was widened by Solon to allow prosecution by 'anyone who wishes'; this meant any free adult male, except that some actions could not be brought by a non-citizen and none could be brought by a disfranchised citizen (see ATIMIA). (*c*) In a private action damages or compensation might be awarded to the prosecutor. In a public action any fine or penalty was paid to the state. However, to encourage public-spirited citizens to prosecute offenders on behalf of the state, financial rewards were given to successful prosecutors in certain public actions. This had the unintended effect of encouraging the rise of *sycophants (ill-motivated prosecutors). (*d*) To deter sycophants penalties were imposed, in most public actions, on a prosecutor who dropped a case after starting it or who failed to obtain at least one-fifth of the jury's votes; he had to pay a fine of 1,000 drachmas and forfeited the right to bring a similar action in future. These penalties did not apply in private actions.

The various public actions were named after their method of initiation. Five examples follow. (*a*) *Graphē* was the most ordinary public action, so named presumably because it had originally been the only one in which the charge had to be put in writing, though by the 4th cent. written charges had become the rule in other actions too. (*b*) *Apagōgē*. The prosecutor began proceedings by arresting the accused and handing him over to the appropriate magistrates, usually the *Eleven. (*c*) *Phasis*. The prosecutor pointed out goods or property involved in an offence, such as goods smuggled into Athens from abroad without payment of customs duties. If he won the case, he was rewarded with half of the fine exacted or property confiscated. This action is satirized in Aristophanes' *Acharnians*. (*d*) *Eisangelia* of the most serious type was initiated by a denunciation to the council or the assembly, which might either decide to try the case itself or refer it to a jury. (*e*) *Probolē* The prosecutor made a denunciation to the assembly. The ensuing procedure was used against men accused of sycophancy on of deceiving the people.

Homicide cases were treated differently from others. If a person was killed, his relatives were expected to prosecute the killer. The prosecution followed a special procedure, including a proclamation to the killer to keep away from sacred and public places. The trial, at which the prosecutor and the defendant each made two speeches, was held not in an ordinary court, but at one of several special open-air courts, with the *Areopagus or the *ephetai* as the jury.

4. Procedure   When anyone wished to raise either a private or a public action, he gave his charge to the appropriate magistrate. It was the responsibility of the prosecutor to deliver the summons to the defendant. The magistrate held an inquiry, at which he heard statements and evidence from both parties. Some minor cases could be decided by the magistrate forthwith, but generally the purpose of the inquiry was simply to satisfy him that the case should be taken to court.

At the trial the magistrate presided, but he did not give directions or advice to the jury, and did not perform the functions of a modern judge. The prosecutor spoke first and the defendant afterwards. If either litigant was a woman or child, the speech was made by the nearest adult male relative; but otherwise each litigant had to speak for himself, unless clearly incapable, though he might deliver a speech written for him by a speech-writer, and he might call on friends to speak too in his support. In the course of his speech he could request to have laws or other documents read out to the court. He could also call witnesses. See EVIDENCE, ATTITUDES TO. Until some date in the first half of the 4th cent., witnesses gave their evidence orally, and might be questioned by the speaker who called them (but not cross-examined by his opponent). Later in the 4th cent. witnesses gave evidence beforehand in writing, and at the trial merely signified assent when their statements were read out. Disfranchised citizens, women, children, and slaves could not speak as witnesses, although they could be present in court without speaking. A certain length of time, varying according to the type of case, was allowed for each litigant to make his speech, the time being measured by a water-clock (see CLOCKS).

When the speeches were over, the jury heard no impartial summing-up and had no opportunity for discussion, but voted at once. In the 5th cent. each juror voted by placing a pebble or shell in an urn; there was one urn for conviction and one for acquittal. In the 4th cent. each juror was given two bronze votes, one with a hole through the middle signifying conviction and one unpierced signifying acquittal, and he placed one in a 'valid' (bronze) urn and the other in an 'invalid' (wooden) urn; this method helped to ensure that the voting was secret and that each juror cast only one valid vote. When all had voted, the votes were counted, and the majority decided the verdict. A tie was treated as acquittal. There was no appeal from the jury's verdict. However, a losing litigant who proved

that a witness for his opponent had given false evidence could claim compensation from the witness.

For some offences the penalty was laid down by law, but in other cases the penalty or the amount of damages had to be decided by the jury. In such cases, when the verdict had been given against the defendant, the prosecutor proposed a penalty and the defendant proposed another (naturally more lenient). Each spoke in support of his proposal, and the jury voted again to decide between them. Payment of money was the most usual penalty, but other penalties regularly imposed were partial or total disfranchisement, confiscation of property, *exile, or death. See PUNISHMENT (GREEK AND ROMAN PRACTICE). Long terms of imprisonment were not normally imposed. See PRISON.

The chief fault of the Athenian courts was that a jury could too easily be swayed by a skilful speaker. Most jurors were men of no special intelligence; yet, without impartial advice or guidance, they had to distinguish true from false statements and valid from invalid arguments, and they had to interpret the law as well as decide the facts. It says much for the Athenians' alertness and critical sense that the system worked as well as it did. The advantages were that the large juries were hard to bribe or browbeat, and that the courts and the people were as nearly as possible identical; so an accused man felt that he was being judged by the Athenian people, not merely by some government official or according to an obscure written rule. Thus the institution of popular juries was one of the Athenians' greatest democratic achievements. See also DEMOCRACY, ATHENIAN.

law and procedure, Roman   The subject is here dealt with in three sections: civil law; civil procedure; criminal law and procedure.

1. Civil Law   (*ius civile*) in its broadest sense was the law of the city of Rome. In a narrower sense it refers to the secular law of Rome, private and public, to the exclusion of sacred law. This section deals, so far as the sources of law are concerned, with civil law in the first sense, but as regards substantive law is confined to the second.

From the standpoint of sources the beginning and end of Roman civil law are conveniently marked by the *Twelve Tables and *Justinian's codification. Dating from about 450 BC the law of the Twelve Tables was treated by the Romans as the starting-point of their legal history. Though much of it became obsolete, it was never technically superseded until Justinian's legislation of AD 529–534. These two documents, neither of which is systematic enough to be called a code in the modern sense, were of very different bulk, the first consisting of a few score laconic sentences, the second running to well over a million words.

Four periods of legal history are commonly distinguished in the interval between the Twelve Tables and Justinian's codification: (a) the early republic, a period of relatively primitive law ending in the 3rd cent.; (b) the late republic, a formative period in which an independent legal profession (see LAWYERS, ROMAN) took shape (c.200–31BC); (c) the classical period, spanning the first three cents. AD. Most of the important legal treatises were produced in the period down to 235, esp. 180–235. After the ensuing 60 years of disorder *Diocletian strove to revive classical law in its essential features. In (d) the post-classical period of the later empire, *Constantine I and his successors introduced important reforms in public and procedural law. In the east this period ends with Justinian's codification, which introduced some important reforms and simplifications, but often reverted to the law of the classical period. In the west the period ends with the disintegration of the empire in the 5th cent.

A striking mark of the law of the early Roman republic was its formalism. Both in legal transactions and litigation solemn oral forms were necessary and sufficient. The will of the parties was denied effect unless clothed in these forms. In this respect Roman law resembled primitive systems elsewhere; but it differed from them in the simplicity and economy of the forms used. Roman private law was confined to citizens. The community excluded foreigners from the use of the formulae it had devised. Within the Roman *family, only the male head (see PATRIA POTESTAS) could conduct legal transactions.

In the last two to three cents. BC, however, the expansion of Rome's commerce and empire over the Mediterranean world (see IMPERIALISM, ROMAN) made it impossible to maintain the exclusiveness of the old civil law. New, informal institutions appeared, which depended on the intention of the parties rather than the observance of external forms. An important example is the class of agreements binding by consent alone, which provided a way of enforcing the principal commercial transactions. These new institutions were open to foreigners and citizens alike (see IUS GENTIUM). A special magistrate for matters involving foreigners (praetor peregrīnus; see PRAETOR, Republic) was created c.242 with jurisdiction over these cases. In the same period the old rigid procedure for the trial of suits between citizens, called lēgis actiōnēs (actions in law) gave way to the less formal and more flexible 'formulary procedure' (see 2. 4 below).

Legislation (see COMITIA) played only a minor part in these changes. Apart from the Twelve Tables, legislation did little to develop private law during the republic. The chief factor in releasing the old civil law from its early rigidity was the development of magisterial law (see EDICT). The key magistrate in its development was the urban praetor in Rome (see PRAETOR, Republic). He like other magistrates published an annual edict setting out how he proposed to exercise his jurisdiction. In the last century of the republic this became an instrument by which, with the help of lawyers whom he consulted, significant innovations were introduced. A concurrent aspect of the development was the gradual introduction of the formulary procedure, by which the issue to be litigated no longer had to be expressed in one of the small number of ritual modes admitted by the old system of legis actiones. Instead it was embodied in a formula drawn up before the magistrate and adapted to the alleged facts of the case, though the actual trial was normally conducted by someone else. Thus the magistrate, who controlled the granting of formulae, the most important of which were incorporated in his edict, in effect acquired the power to amend and develop the law. Formally, his function was to administer the law and not to change it. But with the introduction of the new procedure he was able to grant new remedies by way both of right of action and defence, and thereby to 'support, supplement, and correct the civil law'. In some areas this power to supplement and correct produced a dualism between the old civil and newer magisterial law. Their integration in Justinian's codification is the outcome of the efforts of the law schools and lawyers of the later empire.

Augustus endeavoured to adhere to republican forms of legislation (*lex, *plebiscitum), but under his successors *senatus consulta took their place. Emperors influenced, and even dictated, the content of such of these decrees as were of general importance, and the emperor's speech proposing the decree came often to be cited in place of the decree itself. Thus the codification of the praetor's edict (131) was effected by a decree of the senate drafted by Iulianus on *Hadrian's behalf. See EDICT; PRAETOR (Caesar and imperial period).

The emperor's powers were at first conceived as modelled on those of republican magistrates. Thus the emperor might issue edicts, give instructions to officials, towns or provincial assemblies, grant charters or citizenship, decide cases as a judge, and reply to petitions from private individuals. By the time of Hadrian these various pronouncements came to be grouped together as *constitutions of the emperor. In the mid-2nd cent. AD *Gaius (2) treats them as having the force of law. Some constitutions, like edicts, could openly innovate, something which with the codification of the praetor's edict other magistrates could no longer do. Thus *Caracalla in 212 employed an edict to grant citizenship to the free inhabitants of the empire (see CONSTITUTION, ANTONINE). But the emperor along with *lawyers of authority continued in the Principate to make law indirectly, through rulings made in particular cases. Decisions made by the emperor acting as a judge (dēcrēta) and replies, or rescripts, on his behalf to petitions on points of law possessed a force which went beyond the case in point and served to fill gaps in the law and resolve ambiguities. Their force was greater than that of the opinions (responsa) of lawyers of authority. By the end of the classical period (69–235) this imperial case law, mainly embodied in rescripts, had supplanted the case law embodied in practitioners' opinions as an instrument for developing the law without legislating. In the reign of *Constantine I independent legal writing came to an end, and the imperial government, now firmly bureaucratized, monopolized legal development. The law schools of Rome and Berytus flourished, teaching classical law.

A factor disruptive of the earlier law was the development of institutions, which were imperial innovations and so cut across the old lines between civil and magisterial law. To enforce these new institutions, 'extraordinary' procedures and jurisdictions were created outside (Lat. extrā) the formulary system. These procedures of extraordinary inquiry (see 2.11, 12 below) gradually spread to jurisdiction over ordinary civil law cases and by the early 4th cent. entirely supplanted the formulary procedure.

2. Civil Procedure 1. The Roman civil trial was governed in the course of history by three systems of procedure: that of the lēgis actiōnēs (actions in law), the formulary system, and the cognitiō extrā ordinem or cognitio extrāordināria (extraordinary inquiry). The legis actiones prevailed until, probably in the second half of the 2nd cent. BC, they were largely replaced by the formulary system; the cognitio extraordinaria gradually encroached on the formulary system and finally superseded it after AD 284.

2. The first two systems shared a central feature: the division into two stages. The first took place before a magistrate, in iūre, and its purpose was to define and formulate the issue (i.e. the limits of the dispute between the parties). This stage culminated in joinder (joining) of issue, an acceptance by the parties, under the magistrate's supervision, of the issue thus formulated and the nomination of the iūdex authorized by the magistrate. It was the *iudex who presided in the second stage (apud iūdicem) when the case was heard and argued. He was a private person empowered by the magistrate's order to give judgement, but he was more than a mere private arbitrator, because that judgement was recognized by the state and enabled the successful plaintiff to put it into effect. For the first stage, in iure, certain formalities were observed; the stage apud iudicem was entirely informal. The differences between the legis actio system and the formulary system lay in the proceedings in iure.

3. The procedure by legis actio required the plaintiff and the defendant ritually to assert their rights in one or other of five sets of exactly prescribed formal words. Three of these sets served to open a lawsuit and the other two to enforce the execution (the responsibility of the plaintiff). Only the prescribed phraseology was allowed, and there was no appeal from the decision of the iudex.

4. The legis actio system had the disadvantage that it was inflexible. Apparently the praetor could neither create new forms of action nor extend the existing legis actiones to claims not recognized by the law. These defects were removed by the formulary system. Under it for each cause of action there was an appropriate form of action, expressed in a set of words or formula; and the praetor had the power to create new formulae to meet new needs. The formula constituted the pleadings. But while the formula varied from action to action, its structure was based on some permanent essential parts: the intentiō (concise formulation of the plaintiff's claim) and the condemnātiō, by which the judge was directed to condemn the defendant if he found after hearing the evidence and the arguments that the plaintiff's case was good, otherwise to acquit him. To suit the complexities of each case the formula might be extended by additional clauses. The whole formula was framed as a succession of conditional clauses governing an

order by the magistrate to the judge to condemn or acquit the defendant. Model *formulae* for all recognized actions, defences, etc. were published with the edict. The principle that each cause of action had its appropriate *formula*, coupled with the power of the praetor to create new *formulae* (or new parts of *formulae*) either generally in the edict or on the facts of a particular case, lay at the root of the law deriving from praetors and other magistrates.

5. All actions, except those intended only to settle a preliminary question, necessarily led to a *condemnatio* for a money sum to be paid by the defendant. The assessment of the sum was made by the *iudex*.

6. The formulary system was derived from the praetor's function of *iūrisdictiē*, administering justice. He could also, in virtue of his *imperium, take steps to enforce justice: e.g. he could issue an interdict protecting the plaintiff's interests; he could order seizure of property in order to secure compliance with some requirement; he could even set aside a general rule of law which appeared in the circumstances to produce an inequitable result.

7. The bringing of an action began with the plaintiff personally summoning the defendant to follow him before the magistrate. The Twelve Tables contained detailed provisions governing this summons.

8. Normally, the stage *in iure* was devoted to defining the issue. The proceedings ended with joinder of issue (agreement of the parties on the issue). This required the co-operation of the parties, but neither of them could prevent the achievement of this act by repeated refusal. After it there could not be another trial of the same issue; and it was with reference to this moment that the judge had to decide disputed matters.

9. The trial usually took place before a single *iudex*. He was bound to consider the issues as they were presented in the *formula* and in so doing to apply the law, but otherwise he was uncontrolled and could take what advice he chose. At the end of the hearing he was bound to announce his verdict to the parties in accordance with the *condemnatio*, unless he was willing to swear an oath that the matter was not clear to him. In that event the case would be remitted to another *iudex* for a retrial.

10. If the unsuccessful defendant did not carry out the terms of the judgement, the plaintiff could not proceed immediately to execution. He must first bring an action on the judgement. In this action the defendant could not dispute the merits of the judgement, but he might plead that it was invalid, e.g. for want of jurisdiction or defect of form, or that he had already satisfied it. In such a case there would be joinder of issue and a trial in the usual way. There were, however, two deterrents to frivolous defences: the defendant had to give security; and, if he lost, he would be condemned in double the amount of the original judgement. If the defendant neither satisfied the judgement nor defended the case, the magistrate would authorize the plaintiff to proceed either to personal or to real execution. In the latter case the magistrate made a decree putting the creditor in possession of all the debtor's property, and there followed what was in effect a bankruptcy.

11. The formulary system was the ordinary procedure from *c.*150 BC, but from the time of Augustus there developed beside it other forms of procedure in particular contexts, which are commonly referred to collectively as *cognitio extraordinaria* or *cognitio extra ordinem* (investigation outside the ordinary procedure of the formulary system). The *princeps* (rarely) or a magistrate or (most commonly) a delegated official conducted the entire trial; there was no division into two stages and no private *iudex*. The process was still, however, a judicial one and the development of a system of appeals served to secure uniformity. The trial was more like an investigation than of a hearing of a dispute between adversaries.

12. In the republic there was virtually no possibility of appeal. In the early Principate, however, some appeal to the emperor seems to have been allowed, and in cases dealt with by *cognitio extraordinaria* or *cognitio extra ordinem* where the trial would normally be before a delegated judge, it would be natural to allow an appeal to the person who had made the delegation. Certainly it soon became a regular institution, with the higher court not only quashing the original decision, but substituting its own. There were penalties for frivolous appeals.

3. **Criminal Law and Procedure 1.** When Roman law came to distinguish criminal wrongs from civil ones, it did not draw the line where we do. Theft for example was originally treated as a private wrong (delict) pursuable by civil action; only much later did it become usual to bring a criminal prosecution. *Adultery was not originally a matter for a civil suit (in Roman society no ground was needed for a divorce), but later became a crime. One can see a progression from private revenge towards a system

where public authority and those acting for the public undertake the pursuit of crimes, but this progression was never complete. We can distinguish phases in this development. In the oldest phase of criminal law we find, side by side with private revenge, the practice of settlements between offended and offender, at first voluntary and sporadic, later obligatory. By the end of this phase the beginnings of a new system can be seen: intervention of the community in punishing some crimes, esp. those directed against its own structure or existence. Next, the community undertakes the repression of offences, not only those which menace the public order or interest directly, but also those affecting private property or interest. The Twelve Tables represent a combination of the first two phases, while in the middle and late republic the intervention of public authority, hitherto exceptional, becomes increasingly common. Under the Principate it gains dominance, and under the late empire and Justinian it becomes exclusive, having absorbed nearly the whole field of private criminal law.

2. The Romans did not create a systematic body of statutes relating to criminal law. The Twelve Tables are primarily concerned with civil actions, and in the fragmentary provisions of tables 8 and 9 we find a mosaic of varied penal provisions rather than a code. The copious legislation of the republic dealt only with single crimes or groups of crimes. In the late republic some offences were treated by several laws voted within a short period of time. Under *Sulla there was some creation or revision of criminal procedures by the setting up of standing courts (*quaestiones) for particular types of offence. Imperial legislation was mainly concerned with adapting existing provisions to fit new circumstances, or with modifications of penalties.

3. The *jurists of the 2nd cent. AD—the best period of classical jurisprudence—contributed far less to the development of criminal law than to that of civil law, though they did contribute much to doctrines of private delicts, with which the praetor's edict dealt. Private delicts form a group apart: the wrongdoer is exposed to an action under the ordinary civil procedure by the person wronged, the effect of which is that he must pay a pecuniary penalty to the plaintiff. The state as such did not show any interest in the prosecution of these offences, except where the offender was a magistrate or other official (extortion, *repetundae), but the proceedings had a punitive character. The principal forms of private delict were theft; robbery (theft combined with violence); damage to property; assault, and in general all affronts to the plaintiff's dignity and personality (*iniuria). Praetorian law also introduced a category of actions for misdemeanours which affected public interest, e.g. violation of graves, and pouring liquids or throwing things out into the streets. In such cases anyone could be plaintiff and claim the penalty.

4. The special domain of criminal law is, however, the group of crimes prosecuted by public officials in public suits. The oldest law knew the intervention of the state, as avenger of offences against its security or against public order, only in exceptional cases such as treason (*perduellio), desertion to the enemy, or special forms of murder (*parricide). For the evolution of this group the series of criminal laws of the last two centuries of the republic (esp. those of Sulla and Caesar) were of the greatest importance. They instituted special criminal courts for particular crimes, extending in large measure the competence of the state to the prosecution and punishment of criminal acts. A survey of the various kinds of crimes allotted to the *quaestiones perpetuae shows that they included not only offences against the state, its security, and organization, or public order in the widest sense of the word, but also the more serious offences against life, personal integrity, private interests (falsification of wills and documents, serious injuries), and morality (adultery).

5. However, even with the help of the senate, imperial constitutions, and the jurists, this legislation covered only part of the offences needing repression. Furthermore, the quaestiones operated only in Rome and tried Roman citizens only (but not women or slaves or foreigners). Criminal jurisdiction in the provinces would normally have been a matter for the provincial governor or his legate. A solution was found for these and other problems with the development of cognitio extra ordinem or extraordinaria (see 2.11 above). The trials in these 'extraordinary' public suits were always conducted by public officials. Jurisdiction was exercised—apart from political offences and senatorial matters reserved for the senate—chiefly by the emperor and the *prefects and in particular provinces by *procurators as the emperor's delegates. The sphere of cognitio extra ordinem became, thanks to imperial policy, more and more extensive and superseded the quaestiones. Whilst in quaestiones only the penalty laid down by the statute could be pronounced, the imperial judges had discretion in

grading the penalty according to their appreciation of all the facts of the case. Moreover, penalties might vary according to the status (free/slave, man/woman) or rank of the convicted person: in particular, by the early 2nd cent. AD poorer citizens and others of low rank came to be punished more severely than those of higher rank. See HONESTIORES.

6. From the earliest times the intention of the wrongdoer was taken into consideration. Under the Principate the judge considered the intensity and persistence of the offending will, the question whether the act had been committed with premeditation or on sudden impulse, whether it had been provoked by a moral offence (e.g. murder of an adulterous wife when caught in the act) or was due to drunkenness.

7. The magistrates invested with *imperium, acting personally or by delegates, dispensed criminal justice. From early times their power of punishment was restricted by *provocatio ad populum (appeal to the people). There were two fundamentally different forms of procedure under the republic, trial before the assembly and quaestio (tribunal of inquiry). Both were originally based on the inquisitorial principle: before an assembly the magistrate acted both as prosecutor and president of the assembly simultaneously; in the early quaestiones he, aided by advisers, decided whether an accusation laid before him required investigation, controlled the investigation and production of evidence, and ultimately delivered a verdict and sentence. However, the latter procedure was modified when quaestiones perpetuae were set up by statute in the 2nd and 1st cents. BC. In these the investigation of crimes and production of evidence was a matter for the plaintiff or prosecutor; the selection of a jury was regulated by the relevant statute and both plaintiff and defendant had rights of rejection. At the trial itself, although the presiding magistrate might ask questions, procedure was adversarial, the verdict was determined by the jury, and the sentence was either fixed by the statute or a limited discretion was allowed to the jury, esp. with financial penalties. This accusatory system was, however, abolished in trials extra ordinem, where, once information had been laid about a crime, the magistrate had once more full initiative in prosecution and conducted the trial from beginning to end. The statutes establishing the quaestiones had specifically ruled out any appeal to another authority against verdict or sentence. Augustus' tribunician power (see TRIBUNI PLEBIS) was associated with the right to hear appeals and a prerogative of mercy.

8. The Roman penal system distinguished between public and private penalties, reflecting the division into public and private offences. The private penalty seems originally a substitute for private vengeance and retaliation (tāliō = infliction on the delinquent of the same injury as that done by him), but pecuniary compromise between the parties was already an option at the time of the Twelve Tables and later became compulsory. A private penalty consisted in payment of a sum of money to the person wronged, and differs from multa, a fine inflicted by a magistrate and paid to the state. Public penalties originated in the idea of public revenge, or religious expiation for crimes against the community, and, for serious offences, entailed the elimination of the guilty person from the community. The death penalty was inflicted in different ways. The Twelve Tables refer to burning for arson, and suspension (perhaps a form of *crucifixion) for using magic on crops. We later hear of decapitation, precipitation from the Tarpeian Rock, and drowning in a sack (for parricide). The more grotesque penalties were not all primitive. In republican times the execution (and even the sentence) could be avoided by voluntary *exile of the wrongdoer. Banishment was later applied as an independent penalty in various forms, including *relegation. Under the empire we find condemnation to heavy work in mines or public works or to the gladiatorial training-schools. These penalties were normally combined with loss of citizenship, while 'condemnation to the mines', considered as the penalty closest to death, normally also involved loss of liberty and flagellation; an accessory penalty was the total or partial confiscation of property. Execution might take the form of exposure to wild beasts in the arena (see VENATIONES). The Romans applied imprisonment only as a coercive or preventive measure, not as a penalty (see PRISON); the Roman conception of penalty laid more stress upon its vindictive and deterrent nature than on correction of the delinquent (see PUNISHMENT, GREEK AND ROMAN PRACTICE). The coming of Christianity led to some changes in the modalities of punishments but did not mitigate their severity.

law in Greece Classical Athenian law (see LAW AND PROCEDURE, ATHENIAN) is well documented from the *Attic Orators (c.420–320 BC): over 100 lawcourt speeches survive, though we rarely hear the result or even the opponent's case, and our manuscripts do not usually preserve the texts of witnesses' statements or legal statutes. Further information, esp. about judicial procedure, can be gleaned from Athenian comedy (esp. Aristophanes' *Wasps*) and from the Aristotelian **Athenaion Politeia*; and the Athenian habit of recording public decisions on stone has left large numbers of texts, though few of these are strictly legislative.

The other significant body of evidence comprises private documents written on papyrus (see PAPYROLOGY, GREEK). Papyrus was widely used throughout classical antiquity, but for climatic reasons virtually none survives except in Egypt, where Greek was the dominant language of administration under Ptolemaic and Roman rule (*c.*320 BC–*c.* AD 630). The range of these texts is vast (wills, letters, agreements, etc.), and though often fragmentary, they give us an unparalleled picture of law operating at ground level. See also GORTYN.

law of nature (*iūs nātūrālĕ*) embodies the belief that there are certain principles or institutions which are so rooted in 'nature' that they are of universal validity. *Aristotle divided law into that which was natural and that which was manmade, the former being the same everywhere and equally valid everywhere. This idea became a commonplace, esp. among the Stoics (see STOICISM), and is often echoed by *Cicero. For him, as for Aristotle, the fact that a principle is found everywhere is a proof of its naturalness and therefore of its validity. This leads to the identification, both by Cicero and by *Gaius (2), of natural law with *ius gentium. This is strictly a confusion of thought, since natural law is law which ought to be universally applied and *ius gentium* is law which is in fact so applied. Only in the case of *slavery did Gaius remark that according to natural law all men were born free, but by *ius gentium* they might be slaves.

lawyers, Roman or jurists were a specialized professional group in Roman society (see LAW, ROMAN, SOCIOLOGY OF) distinct from the humble clerks and notaries who copied documents and recorded proceedings. In the later republic and empire there emerged for the first time in history a class of secular legal experts who, whether they made a living from their profession or not, were regarded as the repositories of a special type of learning useful to the state and private citizens. Until the 3rd cent. BC knowledge of the law and its procedure was a monopoly of the patrician priesthood, the college of *pontifices, whose ad-

vice was sought not only on the law of the state cult but also on secular forms. From then on (see CORUNCANIUS) some who were not members of the priestly college began to give advice on law; but until the end of the republic the same people were often expert in sacred, public, and private law. Their functions resembled those of modern lawyers. They gave opinions (*responsa*) to people who consulted them, helped them to draft documents or take other measures to avoid legal pitfalls, and advised on litigation and its proper forms. They were consulted by magistrates such as the urban *praetor on the formulation of his *edict and by lay judges on the law they should apply in the cases before them (see IUDEX). They taught mainly by allowing others to listen to them as they practised, but sometimes actively undertook to instruct pupils. Some lawyers wrote books. In principle their services were free, but they were not forbidden to accept gifts from those who consulted or were taught by them, though unlike other professionals such as surveyors and doctors there was even in the empire no procedure by which they could sue for a fee.

In the republic and early empire lawyers were few. Membership of this élite group of intellectuals depended on being taught by another member and enjoying a sufficient regard from the group as a whole for one's independence of judgement and depth of learning. It continued, even in the empire, to depend on professional opinion and not on official recognition or employment. Legal learning often ran in families. The existence of such a small, intimate body of specialists explains why in their writings lawyers so often cite one another's opinions. They aim to convince other lawyers. *Advocacy was not in the republic and early empire a normal part of a lawyer's career, rhetoric being a separate discipline, but was not ruled out. In the republic and early empire lawyers often came from senatorial families, but legal learning could also be the avenue by which 'new men' (see NOVUS HOMO) rose in the world. Lawyers often held public office.

As a prestigious non-political group the legal profession presented Augustus with a problem since it comprised, for example, not only his supporter Trebatius Testa but the latter's republican pupil *Antistius Labeo. He declined to bring the profession directly under his own control (*Res Gestae* 6) but devised a system by which certain lawyers were granted the privilege of giving opinions publicly on his authority. *Tiberius gave the first such grant to a non-senator.

See also LAW, ROMAN, SOCIOLOGY OF.

lead is mined in part for the extraction of *silver from its ores. Some of the major sources in the Greek world were located at *Laurium, on Siphnos, and in *Macedonia. In the western Mediterranean, lead was mined on Sardinia and in Etruria (see ETRUSCANS). Roman extraction took place in *Spain, *Gaul, and *Britain. Stamped lead 'pigs' show that lead was being extracted from the Mendips soon after the Roman invasion of Britain. Buildings associated with the extraction of silver from the argentiferous lead ore have been excavated at Laurium. In the Greek world lead was used to fix *stelai to their bases. In the Roman period it was used for water pipes. See MINES AND MINING.

lectisternium, a Roman version of Greek *theoxenia, a banquet for gods whose images were placed on a cushioned couch or couches. The ceremony was meant to propitiate gods and repel pestilence or enemy. See MEALS, SACRED.

Lēda, mother of the *Dioscuri (Castor and Pollux/Polydeuces) and *Helen (as well as *Clytemnestra), wife of *Tyndareos. Most striking is the myth that *Zeus in the form of a swan copulated with Leda, who later produced an egg containing Helen and Polydeuces. Castor, thus the mortal twin, was born to Tyndareos on the same night. The story is rather out of place in Greek myth and might seem specially incredible.

Lefkandi, a coastal site in *Euboea between *Chalcis and *Eretria, inhabited from the early bronze age until its desertion *c.*700 BC, perhaps following the Lelantine War (see GREECE (HISTORY), *Archaic period*). During the Dark Age Lefkandi was an important centre. Cemeteries spanning the 11th to 9th cents. have revealed significant wealth and, from *c.*950 BC, abundant evidence for contact with *Cyprus and the Levant. A unique, massive apsidal building, with external and internal colonnades supporting a steep raking roof, prefigures Greek temple design. Inside the central hall were buried a man and woman, and four horses: woman and horses had apparently been killed in a chieftain's funeral ceremony. After a short life the building was demolished and covered with a mound. Whether it served as a chieftain's house, destroyed following his burial inside, or as a cult-place erected over a heroic warrior's tomb (see HERO-CULT), is debated.

legal literature is the works of *lawyers which went beyond mere collections of laws and formulae. Legal literature was the most spe-cifically Roman branch of Latin literature, and until the Byzantine age nearly all works on law were in Latin. They were for the most part written in plain but technically accurate language. For individual authors see the entries under their names.

legates/lēgāti in the late republic were senators serving on the staff of a military commander or governor, on whose recommendation they were appointed by the senate. *Pompey and *Caesar appointed their own *legati,* who had propraetorian power (see PRO CONSULE, PRO PRAETORE) and often exercised semi-independent command. 'The role of *legati* is distinct from that of commanders; the former must do everything according to orders, the latter must without restriction decide the overall strategy' (Caesar, *Civil War*). *Augustus developed this idea, appointing a *legatus,* a senator of consular rank who later held the title *legatus Augusti propraetore,* to govern each province for which he was responsible, except Egypt, which had *equestrian officers. Each legion in a province was commanded by a senator of praetorian rank, subordinate to the governor. In one-legion provinces, the governor also commanded the legion, except in Africa where *Gaius (1) appointed a separate legate, leaving the proconsul responsible for civil administration. *Legati Augusti* rarely held more than two senior commands, generally of about three years' duration.

legion

1. Early Republic By the end of the 5th cent. BC the legion numbered *c.*6,000 men, but *Polybius, writing *c.*150 BC, provides the earliest detailed account of its structure, and he probably refers to the army after the war against *Hannibal (see PUNIC WARS). The legion varied in size between 4,200 and 5,000 men subdivided into 30 maniples (see MANIPULUS) arranged in three lines; while light-armed troops (*vēlitēs*) formed a screen, the *hastātī* (spearmen) and *principēs* (chief men), chosen on the basis of age and experience, made up two ranks, followed by the most experienced soldiers (*triāriī* or 'third rank men'). The legion was supported by 300 cavalry.

2. Marius to Actium *Marius is credited with a change in the tactical structure of the legion from maniple to cohort (see COHORS); there were ten cohorts, each containing six centuries of 80 men, making the strength of a legion 4,800, although the first cohort may have been larger. Around this time an eagle (*aquila*) was adopted as the symbol of each legion, personifying its permanent existence. The *velites* and legionary cavalry were replaced by specialist auxiliary troops (see AUXILIA) from foreign or conquered peoples.

3. The Principate *Augustus created from the surviving legions of the *triumviral period a standing, professional army with which he aimed to meet all military needs. In AD 14 there were 25 legions in service, increasing by the Severan era (see ROME, HISTORY) to 33. Each legion, organized in cohorts, with 120 legionary cavalry, comprised *c.*5,400 men, had its own number and honorific title (e.g. Legio XX Valeria Victrix), and was commanded by a senatorial *legatus legiōnis* (see LEGATES), except in *Egypt and later in Mesopotamia (annexed in 198) where the legions were under *equestrian *prefects.

Legionaries were recruited from Roman citizens and increasingly from the provinces, so that by the time of *Hadrian, few Italians served in the legions. In addition, soldiers tended to be recruited locally as legions acquired permanent provincial bases. From the late 1st cent. legionaries served 25 years and were paid a salary of 1,200 sesterces (see STIPENDIUM). Pay was supplemented by *donatives, and legionaries enjoyed superannuation and various legal privileges (see CONTUBERNIUM).

4. Later Empire *Diocletian increased the legions to at least 67, though perhaps not retaining their traditional complement.

Lelantine War See GREECE (HISTORY), *Archaic period*; LEFKANDI.

Lēnaea, a Dionysiac festival (see DIONYSUS) celebrated in Athens on 12 Gamelion (January–February), which in other Ionian calendars is called Lenaion. The name is derived from *lēnē*, '*maenad*'. The official Athenian name, 'Dionysia at the Lenaion', proves that it took place in this *sanctuary, which was probably in the Agora. Officials of the Eleusinian mysteries (see ELEUSIS; MYSTERY CULTS) joined the *basileus* (see ARCHONTES) in the conduct of the festival. We hear of a procession. The rituals depicted on the so-called 'Lenaea vases' may have occurred at this festival. Dramatic contests at the Lenaea were formally organized only from *c.* 440 BC. In the 5th cent. it seems that the contests in comedy were arranged much as at the City *Dionysia, but that the tragic contests at the Lenaea were less prestigious, with only two tragedians

competing, each with two tragedies. See TRAGEDY, GREEK.

Leōnidas, Agiad king of *Sparta (reigned *c.*490–480 BC), succeeded on the mysterious death of his half-brother *Cleomenes I, whose daughter Gorgo he married. In 480, while the rest of the Spartans were prevented by the obligation to celebrate the *Carnea, he marched to Thermopylae (see THERMOPYLAE, BATTLE OF) with a hand-picked Spartiate advance guard of 300 (all 'men who had sons living'), some Greek volunteers picked up *en route*, and others brought under compulsion. The pass was apparently secured with some 7,000 hoplites, in time to enable the concurrent and linked naval operations off *Artemisium. But though Leonidas repelled Persian assaults for two days, he failed to prevent his flank being turned via the Anopaea path. Dismissing the main body, Leonidas remained with 1,100 Boeotians, some *helots and *perioikoi, and his own guard. The Spartiates died to a man, counter-attacking fiercely. Leonidas' corpse was mutilated.

Leonnatus (*c.*358–322 BC), Macedonian nobleman, related to the royal house through Eurydīcē, mother of *Philip II. As bodyguard of Philip, Leonnatus helped kill his murderer; under *Alexander (2) the Great, whom he accompanied to Asia, he fulfilled diplomatic missions, rose to Bodyguard in 332, and participated in all further political and military events of Alexander's expedition. At *Babylon (323) he was foreseen as protector for Roxanē's unborn child, but then received Hellespontine Phrygia as satrapy (see SATRAP). Both *Antipater and *Olympias offered him marriage alliances, but before either could be realized he was killed while moving to relieve Antipater in Lamia (322).

Leosthenēs, Athenian *strategos* (general) for home defence in 324/3. When Alexander died (323) Leosthenes and *Hyperides persuaded Athens to fight the Macedonians. He was chiefly responsible for early allied successes which shut up *Antipater in Lamia. His death that winter (323/2) devastated the Greek cause. In Athens Hyperides delivered the funeral speech (see EPITAPHIOS).

Leotychidas II, Eurypontid king of *Sparta (reigned 491–469 BC), succeeded his cousin and former marriage-rival, the deposed Dēmarātus. In 479, as commander-in-chief of the 'Hellenic League' fleet, he fomented the revolt of *Chios and *Samos, and decisively defeated the Persians on Cape Mycalē. He had some success against the medizing aristocracies of *Thessaly, but, on being recalled to face a charge of bribary, he fled to Tegea.

Lepcis (or **Leptis**) **Magna**, on the coast of Tripolitania, owed its prosperity to the fertility of its hinterland, where many farms with olive-presses are known: already by 46 BC *oil production was of a scale for *Caesar to levy an annual tribute on Lepcis of three million pounds of oil after Thapsus. Lepcis expanded rapidly under the early empire, becoming a *municipium under the Flavians (AD 69–96), and a colony under *Trajan. *Septimius Severus, a native of the city, adorned it with splendid buildings, including a new forum (Lepcis' third), a basilica, a four-way arch richly decorated with sculpture, and a colonnaded street with *nymphaeum leading to a newly built harbour. The esp. well-preserved ruins of Lepcis include—apart from the Severan buildings—the Augustan forum, theatre, and market, the amphitheatre and adjacent circus, and the Hadrianic baths. The small but virtually intact 'Hunting Baths' are so named from a *venatio* fresco (see VENATIONES).

Lesbos, the third largest Aegean island after *Crete and *Euboea, 10 km. (6 mi.) from NW *Anatolia. Lesbos was usually divided between five competing *poleis: Mytilene (the most powerful), Methymna, Pyrrha, Antissa, and Eresus. Some of the towns had land in Anatolia. Proximity to Anatolia and the *Hellespont partly explains the distinctive early culture. The earliest Greek settlers (10th cent. BC ?) may have brought to the island its Aeolic dialect (see GREEK LANGUAGE, 3).

The importance of seafaring is shown by the harbour moles at several of the towns. Lesbian transport *amphorae are found throughout the Greek world; amphora kilns have been located on the island. As élite wealth increased, a distinctive aristocratic culture grew up: Lesbos was the home of the poets *Sappho, *Alcaeus, Terpander, and *Arion; the historian *Hellanicus; and the philosopher *Theophrastus. Lesbians founded colonies in the Hellespont and challenged Athens for control of *Sigeum c.600 BC. The island came under *Persian domination during the *Persian Wars. The cities joined the Athenian alliance (see DELIAN LEAGUE), but their rivalries persisted: Methymna did not back Mytilene's revolt in 428, and was alone in not having an Athenian *cleruchy imposed afterwards. Lesbos revolted again in 412.

Lēto, a Titaness (see TITAN), daughter of Coeus and Phoebe. In myth, her only role is to be mother of *Apollo and *Artemis. Local legends locate the birth in various places. The main version is the one given in the Delian part of the Homeric *Hymn to Apollo, where the island of *Delos allows Leto to give birth to her twins on condition that it would became Apollo's main cult place (or that the island, hitherto floating, would become stable); grasping the palm-tree, Leto is delivered of Apollo (and, in later authors, of Artemis as well).

letters (i.e. correspondence), Greek Letters could be written on metal, wax-coated wood, *ostraka, animal skin, and (above all) papyrus (see BOOKS, GREEK AND ROMAN). At least until the late 5th cent. BC, and perhaps into the 4th, letter-writing was not a widespread habit.

Surviving letters are of many kinds. Roughly, one may distinguish:

1. Letters of otherwise unknown private individuals and officials, preserved either by mere chance, or because kept for personal or administrative *archives. Nearly all of these are known from papyrus finds in Graeco-Roman Egypt, and date from the middle of the 3rd cent. BC onwards. Ranging from business reports to soldiers' and students' letters home, they shed light on the social and economic life of both the Ptolemaic kingdom (see EGYPT, Ptolemaic) and the Roman province. See APOLLONIUS (3).

2. Official letters to and from the cities, senior officials, kings, and emperors of the Hellenistic and Roman periods, preserved and often 'published' because of their public importance to sender or recipient. They survive mainly as inscriptions.

3. Private correspondence of famous persons, collected and published because of the interest of contents, style, or author. The earliest extant set of such letters is that of *Julian; those of *Libanius enjoyed the greatest subsequent renown.

4. Exploitation of the letter form for various more public kinds of communication. This very broad category includes: (a) 'open' letters with apologetic or propagandistic aims. (b) Letters of personal advice and instruction, as written by *Epicurus and his disciples. Letters of *consolation belong in this category, as do the epistles of St *Paul.

5. Fictitious letters. This last category (again a broad one) covers both (a) pseudonymous letters of kinds (3) and (4) above, attributed to great names but in reality the products of

a later era, and (b) wholly 'literary' sets of letters attributed to entirely fictitious individuals or groups. Examples of (a) include some of the letters attributed to Isocrates and Demosthenes, and perhaps all of those attributed to Plato.

letters (i.e. correspondence), Latin Letters of all kinds played an even more important role in the vast Roman empire than in Greece, but we have fewer examples from the archaeological record because Latin was little used in Egypt, where most of the Greek examples have been found. Vindolanda in northern England has much increased the corpus, however (see VINDOLANDA TABLETS), and some public letters, esp. from emperors, have been preserved in inscriptions.

As in Greece, letters were normally written with a reed pen and ink on papyrus, which was then rolled up and sealed with a thread. *Cicero usually wrote to *Pomponius Atticus, his most intimate friend, in his own hand unless for some special reason, but an amanuensis was often used. Cicero's secretary *Tullius Tiro appears to have kept copies of letters dictated to him, and to have pasted together in rolls those which Cicero thought worth keeping. It is no doubt to this practice that we owe the preservation of Cicero's letters *To Friends*, though his intention, expressed in 44 BC, of revising and publishing a selection remained unfulfilled. His letters to Atticus and to his brother Quintus *Tullius Cicero were preserved by their recipients, and the former probably remained unpublished for a century after his death. There was never a public *postal service for private correspondence, although *Augustus instituted a system of post-couriers for official correspondence along the main routes of the empire: private individuals might have their own slave couriers, who could cover 50 Roman miles (c. 76 km.) a day, and the companies of tax-farmers (see PUBLICANI) had their own postal service.

Cicero's correspondence offers a broad cross-section of the different forms and registers of letter: bk. 13 of *To Friends*, is entirely devoted to letters of recommendation; see PATRONAGE, NON-LITERARY. *To Friends* offers in addition nearly 100 letters from other correspondents, including *Sulpicius Rufus' famous letter of *consolation to Cicero on the death of Tullia. The letters to Atticus, in contrast, tend to be less formal, and show a marked difference in linguistic register. The Ciceronian collections formed the model for *Pliny the Younger's epistolary self-presentation, and for other collections such as those of *Fronto.

A second model was that of the Greek philosophical letter, as represented by those of *Epicurus and the collection ascribed to *Plato. This tradition is best represented by Seneca's *Ethical Epistles* (see Seneca the younger).

The two traditions both influenced the poetic epistle, represented above all by *Horace's *Epistles* and *Ovid's collections of exile poetry, *Sorrows* and *Epistles from Pontus*. Horace constantly plays on the conventions of the everyday letter. Ovid's *Heroines' Epistles* represents a different tradition again. *Martial and *Statius have epistolary prose prefaces to their verse collections. Letter-writing of all kinds was esp. popular amongst Christian writers (see CHRISTIANITY), in part because of the use of the letter form in the NT.

Leuctra, place in SW *Boeotia where the Boeotians defeated the Spartans in 371 BC. *Epaminondas of Thebes massed his Thebans, 50 deep, on his left, opposite the Spartans themselves, with the élite Sacred Band perhaps forming the front ranks, and the remaining Boeotians, opposite Sparta's allies, echeloned back to the right. The battle opened with a clash between the cavalry, unusually placed in front of the phalanxes (see PHALANX), and the defeated Spartans reeled back into their advancing infantry. The latter's confusion was compounded by an attempt either to increase depth or to extend to the right, or both, and at this point the Sacred Band charged. The Spartan king, Cleombrotus, was mortally wounded, and although his men managed to recover his body, they eventually gave way, with heavy losses, esp. among the Spartiates. The battle ended two centuries of Spartan domination on the battlefield.

lex (pl. *lēgēs*), primarily, a statute, passed by one of the assemblies of the Roman people; the *lex Hortensia* of 287 BC conferred the force of statute on measures passed by a meeting of the *plebs*, and these came in time to be referred to loosely as *leges*. See PLEBISCITUM. The passage of a *lex* involved a magistrate presenting a proposal in the form of a question: 'Would you wish, would you order, Quirītes, that...? This then, as I have spoken, so I ask (*rogō*) you, Quirites.' (Quirites = assembled citizens of Rome.) The measure had normally to be promulgated at least three market-days, *nundinae*, beforehand (see TRINUNDINUM); and there could then be debate in a series of informal gatherings, *contiones* (see

CONTIO); but in the assembly the people could only answer yes or no. See ELECTIONS AND VOTING (*Roman*). Once the measure had been passed, the subjunctives of the dependent clauses of the *rogātiō* were converted into the future imperatives which are characteristic of Roman legislative style. The text was then both published and placed in the *archives. In the late republic and for the period of the early empire for which legislation survived, there was a tendency not to bother to carry out this process of conversion: only the enforcement clauses at the end appeared in the future imperative.

In the same period, there was increasing discussion of the sources of law, of which statutes formed only one kind; under the empire, decrees of the senate, which had been marginal under the republic, increased in importance (see SENATUS CONSULTUM); and imperial pronouncements became the principal source of law (see CONSTITUTIONS).

Major groups of *leges* were: *agrarian; laws regulating minimum ages for and intervals between different magistracies (see CAREERS, ROMAN); laws confirming *citizenship or Latinity on Latin or Italian communities; laws providing for the subsidized or free distribution of corn to (some of) the Roman people; laws dealing with the establishment and organization of the criminal courts; laws dealing with *extortion; laws regulating consumption and display; laws introducing and regulating the secret ballot for assembly votes.

Libanius, b. at Antioch (AD 314), died there (c.393), was a Greek *rhetor and man of letters who embodied in his work many of the ideals and aspirations of the pagan Greek urban upper classes of late antiquity. He belonged to a rich Antiochene family (see DECURIONES), and after a careful education at home was sent to study in Athens. Thereafter he taught *rhetoric in *Constantinople and then in *Nicomedia. Recalled to Constantinople by Constantius II, he was offered but declined a chair of rhetoric in Athens; in 354 he accepted a chair of rhetoric in Antioch, where he passed the rest of his life. His pupils numbered many distinguished men, pagan and Christian alike.

In his later years Libanius became a literary figure of renown throughout the Greek world, and was in correspondence with many of its leading figures, e.g. *Julian, for whom he had an unbounded admiration, and whose death was a bitter blow. In spite of his adherence to *paganism, he enjoyed great influence under

*Theodosius I, who granted him the honorary title of praetorian *prefect. Mostly, however, he avoided involvement in the politics of the empire.

Works His 64 surviving speeches deal with public or municipal affairs, educational and cultural questions. Many are addressed to emperors or high government officials, with whom he intervenes on behalf of the citizens or the curials of Antioch. Some of them were never actually delivered, but were sent to their addressees and published. Other speeches include his funeral oration on *Julian, his encomium of Antioch, and the autobiography which he composed in 374. There also survive some 1,600 letters. The speeches and letters are a mine of information on social, political, and cultural life in the eastern half of the empire in the 4th cent.

libations, *ritual pouring of *water, *wine, *oil, milk, or *honey in honour of gods, heroes, or the dead. Libations are an act of surrender, preceding human participation in meals and other acts. They mark beginnings and endings, such as mornings and evenings; at the *symposium, the group pours threefold libations to *Zeus and the Olympians (see OLYMPIAN GODS), to the heroes, and to Zeus Teleios, 'the Fulfiller'. *Dionysus 'himself' (i.e. wine) is poured to gain divine favour. Libations express blanket propitiation when associated with the unknown and new: having arrived in Colchis, the *Argonauts pour a libation of 'honey and pure wine to Earth (*Gaia) and the gods of the land and to the souls of dead heroes', asking for aid and a welcome (Apollonius Rhodius' *Argonautica*). The term *spondē*, usually associated with wine, refers also to the cry of invocation and to the solemn act it accompanies, such as the signing of truces. In iconography sacrificial acts may end with a libation over the fire on the altar (see SACRIFICE). Common is the 'departure of the *hoplite', where a woman is seen to the right, holding a libation vessel; the scene affirms the link between the group, the gods, the house, and the act. *Sponde* is controlled: libation is poured from a wine-jug into a shallow bowl, then onto an altar or the ground. *Choai*, 'total libations', often wineless, are characterized by greater quantities, esp. for the dead, and for gods of the Underworld.

libel and slander See INIURIA AND DEFAMATION.

Liber Pater, Italian god of fertility and esp. of *wine, later commonly identified with *Dionysus. He formed part of the *Aventine triad, *Ceres, Liber, and Libera, whose joint temple was founded in 493 BC, and became a centre for the plebeians (see PLEBS) in the 5th and 4th cents. Liber and Libera were concerned with seeds and therefore with the promotion of fertility both agricultural and human. At Liber's festival (the Liberalia), a *phallus was paraded through the fields and into town, accompanied by the singing of crude rustic songs, acc. to *Augustine. *Virgil also mentions the crude songs, together with *masks of Dionysus, hung on trees. At the Liberalia, too, Roman boys commonly put on the *toga of manhood: Liber was probably seen as the patron of the boy's transition (see RITES OF PASSAGE) into fertility.

Lībertās, 'freedom', Roman goddess, linked with *Jupiter in the cult of Jupiter Libertas and in the *censors' headquarters, the Atrium Libertatis; worshipped alone on the *Aventine in a temple built by Tiberius *Sempronius Gracchus. Her ideological connection with the freedoms of the ordinary citizen is apparent: freedom opposed both to the state of *slavery and to domination by the powerful. The term was often used in the late republic and early empire to designate the liberty of the politician to develop his career without interference, and so came to focus various types of resistance to the more autocratic aspects of the early Principate. But *Augustus had made a point of restoring the temples of both Libertas and Jupiter Libertas (*Res Gestae* 19). See FREEDOM IN THE ANCIENT WORLD.

Libitīna, Roman goddess of burials, which were registered at her grove on the *Esquiline.

libraries By the end of the 5th cent. BC, books were no rarity, even if some regarded them as a fad of intellectuals like *Euripides; Athens had booksellers, and exports reached the Black (*Euxine) Sea. Individuals collected the best-known poets and philosophers. Of famous collectors, *Aristotle took first place; but his library, like that of the other philosophic schools, remained private property.

Institutional libraries begin with the Hellenistic monarchies. The model was apparently the Peripatos (see PERIPATETIC SCHOOL), rather than the temple and palace libraries of the near east. The first Ptolemies (see PTOLEMY (1); EGYPT, *Ptolemaic*) collected ambitiously and systematically;

the Alexandrian Library (see ALEXANDRIA) became legend, and *Callimachus' *Pinakes* made its content accessible. There were rivals at Pella, Antioch, and esp. *Pergamum. Holdings were substantial: if the figures can be trusted, Pergamum held at least 200,000 rolls, the main library at Alexandria nearly 500,000—the equivalent, perhaps, of 100,000 modern books. Smaller towns had their own libraries, some at least attached to the *gymnasium.

The Romans inherited some libraries direct (*Aemilius Paullus (2) brought home the Macedonian royal library, *Sulla obtained Aristotle's books after the sack of Athens), together with the traditions of private collection and public endowment. *Cicero accumulated several libraries (and visited those of *Varro, Faustus *Cornelius Sulla, and Marcus Licinius Lucullus, son of Lucius *Licinius Lucullus); *Persius left 700 rolls of *Chrysippus. The private library became fashionable: Trimalchio boasted both Greek and Latin libraries; *Seneca the Younger and *Lucian satirize those whose books serve only for show. Successful Greeks and Romans founded libraries in their native cities. On the monarchic scale, *Caesar planned a public library in Rome, under Varro's direction; *Asinius Pollio actually founded one in the Atrium Libertatis (see LIBERTAS). There followed (among the grandest) *Augustus' library on the *Palatine, *Vespasian's near the *templum Pacis, *Trajan's in his *forum Traiani; libraries were included in the *baths of Trajan, *Caracalla, and *Diocletian. The new capital Constantinople was speedily provided with a library, which eventually reached 120,000 books. *Origen's library at *Caesarea provided the Christian exemplar.

Hellenistic libraries apparently consisted of simple storage-rooms attached to a *stoa or the like; such is the only ancient library to survive *in situ*, that of the Villa of the Papyri at *Herculaneum. The great Roman libraries provided reading-rooms, one for Greek and one for Latin, with books in niches round the walls. *Vitruvius advises that libraries should face east, to provide for good light and against damp. Books would be stored in cupboards, which might be numbered for reference. A statue of a divine (or imperial) patron occupied a central niche; busts of authors adorned the building. Catalogues listed authors under broad subject-headings; attendants fetched the books (borrowing was for a privileged few). The library of Pantaenus at Athens had its rules inscribed on stone: 'No book shall be taken out, for we have sworn.... Open from dawn to midday.' The staff would comprise a librarian; attendants, often slaves; copyists and restorers. New acquisitions might be provided by gift, or by purchase; *Pliny the Younger's library at Comum had an endowment of 100,000 sesterces.

Libraries came to rank among the grandest civic monuments. In the Bibliotheca Ulpia (forum Traiani), each reading-room covered 460 sq. m. (5,000 sq. ft.). Costs were substantial: 1,000,000 sesterces at Comum. Such libraries celebrated the ruling culture, and its representatives. They also preserved its texts. Ancient books were always vulnerable: material fragile, editions small, circulation desultory. The library offered a safe haven. Acceptance into a great library marked a work as authentic, or politically acceptable; emperors promoted favourite authors. But favour could do nothing against fire (the Palatine Library burnt down under *Nero or *Titus, again in AD 191, finally in 363); mould and 'the worst enemy of the Muses', worm, put paid to many immortalities. See also BOOKS, GREEK AND ROMAN.

Licinius Crassus, Lūcius, outstanding orator and master and model of *Cicero, who idealizes him, esp. in his *On the Orator*, where he is the chief speaker. Born 140 BC, he studied law under Publius Mucius Scaevola and Quintus *Mucius Scaevola (1). *Quaestor in Asia (see ASIA, ROMAN PROVINCE), he studied philosophy and rhetoric there and in Athens, and on his return became a leading orator in the courts. In 106 he supported the jury law of Servilius Caepio in a great speech attracting popular support for the senate. He became consul 95. In 92, as censor, he quarrelled with his colleague, but they jointly issued an *edict prohibiting the teaching of rhetoric in Latin, in part probably in order to restrict access to the powerful weapon of oratory.

Crassus taught a generation of ambitious young aristocrats, including *Livius Drusus, imbuing them with his ideas of aristocratic reform. He supported Drusus, who aimed at putting them into practice, in his tribunate (91), rallying the senate behind him against the consul in what Cicero called his 'swan song'. His death soon after led to Drusus' failure.

Licinius Crassus, Marcus, escaped from *Cornelius Cinna to Spain, joined *Sulla after Cinna's death, played a prominent part in regaining Italy for him, and made a fortune in Sulla's *proscriptions. After his praetorship he defeated *Spartacus (72–71 BC), but *Pompey, after crucifying many fugitives, claimed credit

for the victory, deeply offending Crassus. Formally reconciled, they were made *consuls 70 and presided over the abolition of Sulla's political settlement, though his administrative reforms were retained. During the next few years Crassus further increased his fortune and, relying on his connections, financial power, and astuteness, gained great influence. After 67, overshadowed by Pompey's commands (which he had opposed), he sought to expand his power and perhaps gain a military command. As *censor 65, he tried to enrol the Transpadanes (living north of the Po) as citizens and to have Egypt annexed; he was foiled by his colleague, and their quarrel forced both to abdicate. Always ready to help eminent or promising men in difficulty, he supported *Catiline until the latter turned to revolution and a programme of cancelling debts. A patron of *Caesar (without, however, detaching him from Pompey), he enabled him to leave for his province in 62 by standing surety for part of his debts. On Caesar's return, he was persuaded by him to give up his opposition to Pompey, which during 62–60 had prevented both of them from gaining their political objectives, and to join Pompey in supporting Caesar's candidacy for the consulship. As consul (59), Caesar satisfied him by passing legislation to secure remission of one-third of the sum owed by the *publicani of Asia for their contract (Crassus presumably had an interest in their companies), and he now joined Pompey and Caesar in an open political alliance. After Caesar's departure for Gaul he supported *Clodius Pulcher, who soon proved to be too ambitious to make a reliable ally. He welcomed Cicero on his return from exile, but in 56 alerted Caesar to the attempts by Cicero and others to recall him and attach Pompey to the *optimates. Caesar and Crassus met at Ravenna, and Pompey was persuaded to meet them at Luca and renew their alliance. The dynasts' plans were kept secret, but it soon became clear that Pompey and Crassus were to become consuls for a second time and to have special commands in Spain and Syria respectively assigned to them for five years (see TREBONIUS), while they renewed Caesar's command for five years.

Late in 55, ignoring the solemn curses of the tribune Ateius Capito, Crassus left for Syria, determined on a war of conquest against *Parthia. He won some early successes in 54 and completed financial preparations by extorting huge sums in his province. In 53 he crossed the Euphrates, relying on his long-neglected military skills and the recent ones of his son. Although deserted by two kings, he continued his advance into unfamiliar territory. After Publius died in a rash action, he himself was caught in a trap near Carrhae and, trying to extricate himself, died fighting.

After playing the game of politics according to the old rules, in which he was a master, he in the end found that unarmed power no longer counted for much in the changed conditions of the late republic, and he died while trying to apply the lesson. His death helped to bring Caesar and Pompey into the confrontation that led to the Civil War.

Licinius Lucullus, Lūcius, served in the *Social War under *Sulla and, as quaestor (88 BC), was the only officer who supported his march on Rome. As proquaestor in the east, he was Sulla's most reliable officer, charged with diplomatic missions, collecting ships and money, and letting *Mithradates VI escape from Flavius Fimbria in accordance with Sulla's policy. Aedile (79) with his brother, he gave splendid games. Praetor in 78, he became Sulla's literary executor and guardian of Faustus *Cornelius Sulla, and then governed Africa. As consul in 74, he opposed tribunician agitation and, worried by the threats of *Pompey, sent him generous supplies to Spain; after complicated intrigues, he secured an *imperium* against the pirates for Antonius (Creticus) and the command against Mithradates for himself.

He raised the siege of Cyzicus, then occupied much of Pontus, forcing Mithradates to flee to Armenia. In the province of Asia he tried to save the cities from financial ruin by drawing up a moderate and ultimately successful plan for payment of their debts and interest at moderate rates. After capturing Sinōpē, which he saved from plundering by his army, and Amaseia, he asked for a senate commission to organize the annexation of Pontus. When King Tigranes II of Armenia allied himself with Mithradates, Lucullus invaded Armenia, and in a battle against Tigranes won 'the greatest victory the sun had ever seen'. He captured the new capital Tigranocerta, allowed his troops to plunder it and celebrated victory games there. Tigranes had to evacuate his earlier conquests. But the enemy collected fresh forces, and the king of *Parthia threatened intervention. An invasion of the Armenian highlands had to be abandoned when the army mutinied. His brother-in-law *Clodius Pulcher had incited rebellion, and in Rome public opinion was turned against him, chiefly by those who had incurred losses in his organiza-

tion of Asia. His command was removed by stages (68–67); the army, hearing this, deserted him; and in the end he was superseded by Pompey under the law of Manilius.

Back in Rome, he had to divorce his wife (a sister of *Clodia) for adultery, and a second marriage, to a stepsister of *Porcius Cato (2), turned out no better. After long delays caused by his enemies, he finally triumphed in 63. But he took no leading part in politics, except for an attempt to oppose *Caesar and stop the ratification of Pompey's eastern arrangements (59), which ended in humiliation. He now concentrated on living in refined luxury, but lapsed into insanity before his death (57/6).

He was an able soldier and administrator, an Epicurean, a lover of literature and the arts, and a generous patron. But he lacked the easy demagogy that was needed for success in both war and politics in his day.

Licinius Mūciānus, Gāius, was three times *suffect consul. He served under *Domitius Corbulo in 58 and was governor of Lycia-Pamphylia. *Nero appointed Mucianus governor of *Syria roughly when he sent *Vespasian to Judaea (66). Reconciled with Vespasian after earlier disagreements, Mucianus encouraged his designs and secured the allegiance of Syria. Leading the Flavian army through Asia Minor and the Balkans, he was anticipated by Antonius Primus in the invasion of Italy and defeat of the Vitellians, but was able on the way to repel a Dacian incursion (see DACIA) into Moesia. He arrived in Rome a few days after its capture, repressed the ambitions of Primus, and controlled the government for Vespasian, whose chief adviser he remained. He is said to have urged him to banish philosophers from Rome.

lictors were attendants (*apparitores*), originally those, *Etruscan in origin, who carried the *fasces for magistrates with *imperium*. They accompanied the latter at all times inside and outside Rome, proceeding before them in single file, each carrying his bundle of *fasces* on his left shoulder. Their function was to announce the approach of the magistrate, clearing everyone except Vestals (see VESTA) and married women from his path, and to implement his rights of arrest, summons, and, in early times, execution. At Rome the ancient rule was that a consul's lictors preceded him only in the months when he was senior consul. Their number varied according to the nature of a magistrate's *imperium*. Among the *apparitores* lictors ranked higher than *viatores and lower than scri-bae (clerks and accountants). Their traditional dress was a toga in Rome, a red cloak outside Rome and in the triumphal procession, and a black mourning-dress at funerals. Although probably of undistinguished birth, they might derive status from their post.

lighthouses Tall monuments which might function as navigational marks were an early feature of ancient harbour-architecture. The idea became celebrated with the building of the 100-m. (328-ft.) tower on the Pharus island at *Alexandria, which gave its name to the architectural genre (c.300–280 BC, by Sostratus of *Cnidus), and the colossus of *Helios at *Rhodes (280 BC, by Chares of Lindus), both reckoned among the *Seven Wonders of the ancient world. Beacon-fires made such monuments visible by night as well as by day: but their function as signs of conquest and power was as important. Claudius' lighthouse tower at *Portus, intended to rival the Pharus, became a symbol of Rome's port and its activities.

lighting The ancients knew two methods: the burning of oil in a *lamp and the combustion of a solid substance. In classical times lamps were preferred for indoor illumination. The torch was more often used out of doors. Lanterns were also freely used, candles or lamps enclosed within horn or (in imperial times) *glass. Antioch was one of the few cities in antiquity to provide street lighting.

Ligurians The indigenous neighbours of the Greeks at *Massalia. Their territory is first defined clearly in the 3rd cent. BC. They were then allies of the *Celts and occupied lands adjacent to them: along the coast from the Rhône to the Arno and inland as far as the Durance and the mountains south of the Po (*Padus).

līmĕs (pl. līmitēs) originated as a surveyor's term for the path that simultaneously marked the boundaries of plots of land and gave access between them. It came to be used in a military sense, first of the roads that penetrated into enemy territory, and thence, as further conquest ceased, of the land boundaries that divided Roman territory from non-Roman. At this stage a whole paraphernalia of border control grew up— frontier roads with intermittent watch-towers and forts and fortlets to house the provincial garrisons which moved up to the frontier line. The term limes comes to embrace the whole border area and its control system. In Europe, where the frontiers faced onto habitable lands, and where they did not coincide with a river or other clear natural obstacle, the frontier line came to be marked off (rarely earlier than *Hadrian) by an artificial running barrier. In Britain this took the form of a stone wall (*wall of Hadrian) or one of turf (*wall of Antoninus); in Upper Germany (*Germania) and in Raetia timber palisades were originally built under Hadrian and *Antoninus Pius; they were strengthened in Upper Germany by a rampart and ditch, and replaced in Raetia by a narrow stone wall. In Europe beyond Raetia, the frontier ran along the Danube (*Danuvius) except where *Dacia projected northwards. Here earthwork barriers were used in discontinuous sectors where there were gaps in the encircling mountain ranges. The Upper German and Raetian frontiers were abandoned under Gallienus and the whole of Dacia under *Aurelian, leading to an intensification of military control on the rivers Rhine (*Rhenus) and Danube. In the eastern and southern parts of the empire the limites lay at the limits of cultivable land capable of supporting a sedentary population and were concerned with the supervision of trade routes and the control of cross-frontier migration by nomadic peoples (see NOMADS) whose traditional *transhumance routes took them into provincial territory. In the east, military bases were positioned along the major north–south communication line along the edge of the desert (the via nova Traiana, from the Red Sea past the Dead Sea), and concentrated on guarding watering-places and points where natural route-ways crossed the frontier line. The problems were similar in *Africa, where the use of intermittent linear barriers such as the Fossatum Africae was designed to channel and control rather than to halt nomadic movements.

Linear B See MYCENAEAN LANGUAGE.

linguistics is the scientific study of all aspects of language. More narrowly (as in the phrase core linguistics) it is the study of the components and their combinations in the grammar at its several levels of analysis, namely: phonology (the sound system), morphology (word-structure), syntax (clause- and sentence-structure, word order), semantics (meanings encoded in language), and the lexicon.

If modern western linguistics owes its birth to a single event, it is to the rediscovery of Sanskrit, by European scholars in the late 18th cent., and the consequent realization that many languages of Europe, Persia, and India must be related and descended from a common ancestor (*Indo-European). So 19th-cent. linguistics was predominantly historical (*diachronic*) and comparative. Research was devoted above all to writing the histories of languages, to understanding the principles of language-change, to establishing 'family trees' of related languages, and to reconstructing prehistoric ancestral languages by the comparative method of *comparative philology*.

At the beginning of the 20th cent., this emphasis on diachronic questions gave way to the *synchronic* approach that dominates linguistics today. The focus of interest was no longer, How does a language change over time? but rather, How is a language structured at a given point in time? and, How does it function as a system?

linguistics, ancient 1. Linguistics arose in western antiquity from two rather different sources: philosophical debate on the origin and nature of language, and the practical requirements of textual criticism and the teaching of Greek. It generally went under the name of 'grammar' (*grammatikē*), which had at first referred simply to the teaching of literacy, and came later to include what would now be called orthographical phonetics, phonology, morphology, and syntax. Linguistics developed along with other disciplines concerned with language, esp. *rhetoric and *literary criticism. Several well-known *grammatici engaged in one or both of these other subjects as well.

Linguistics began in Greece and was then taken up in the Latin world after the Greek-speaking countries had fallen under Roman control. There was some independent thought on language in Roman work, esp. with *Varro, but in general the Greeks set the pace and the Romans willingly and explicitly followed them. But Latin linguistics did not chronologically just follow Greek linguistics; from around 150 BC and up to the end of the classical era, c. AD 500, when Greek and Latin contacts began to weaken, Greek and Latin scholars were working contemporaneously and often in direct contact with each other.

2. Linguistic speculations of a sort are known to have occupied philosophers from the *Presocratic period, on such matters as the real-world correspondences of grammatical tenses and genders. *Aristophanes made fun of *Socrates engaging in such studies (in *Clouds*).

Two general questions arose: (*a*), To what extent was language an innate capacity of human beings, and how far was it the result of a tacit convention or social contract? and (*b*), How far

could general statements be made covering large numbers of word-forms and meanings, and how much individual irregularity must be accepted as inherent in language use? This latter went under the name of *analogy and anomaly.

*Plato's *Cratylus* deals with the nature of language, and in other dialogues he attributes to Socrates certain linguistic notions such as a nominal-subject element and a verbal predicate as the basic components of sentences. *Aristotle followed Plato's outlines and made reference to linguistic topics in several works.

3. It was the Stoics (see STOICISM) who recognized linguistics as a separate and essential part of philosophy or dialectic. Breaking away from the Platonic–Aristotelian school, the Stoics favoured the naturalist origin of language, laying stress on the irregularities necessarily found in it. Following their devotion to propositional logic as against the predominantly class-membership logic of Aristotle, they paid particular attention to syntax.

4. Though some details are lacking, we can follow the successive stages in the recognition of different word-classes (parts of speech) and of the grammatical categories which characterized them. Plato's distinction of nominal subject and verbal predicate was enriched by Aristotle's identification of a complex class of 'form words', lacking ostensive meaning and serving to ensure the unity of whole sentences. He also introduced the word *ptōsis*, 'falling', as a technical term for all grammatically relevant word-form variations. The Stoics later confined the term to its subsequent and current sense of nominal inflexion (Latin *cāsus* 'case'). This made possible a further subdivision of the Aristotelian class of form words. Their semantic analysis of Greek verbal tenses into their temporal and aspectual meanings was exploited by Varro in his analysis of Latin tenses.

Resulting from the conjoint work of Stoic philosophers and *Alexandrian teachers and critics, a system of eight word-classes—noun, verb, participle, (definite) article, pronoun, preposition, adverb, and conjunction—was established and preserved throughout the Greek grammatical tradition.

5. Alexandrian linguistics became the standard model in the Greek and Roman world and very largely formed the basis of both classical and modern grammars of European languages in the Renaissance. Alexandrian grammar, despite its general Aristotelian orientation, was driven less by philosophical considerations than by the needs of teachers of the Greek

language and of Greek, esp. Homeric, literature. The Macedonian successor states made themselves responsible for promoting Greek studies in their hitherto non-Greek territories. This Hellenizing process (see HELLENISM AND HELLENIZATION) was taken over and continued by the Romans, and during the four centuries of Roman rule the Greek orientation of education and culture was left intact.

*Alexandria became a centre of literary and linguistic studies, the latter comprising orthographical phonetics, morphology, syntax, lexical semantics, and dialect studies. *Aristarchus (2) was both a grammarian and a Homeric scholar, and his pupil Dionysius Thrax wrote what was probably the first authoritative grammar-book of the Greek language. It soon became known as 'The Manual'. A brief textbook entitled *Science of Grammar* has been attributed to him, but what we have is probably a Byzantine version. In it the sentence and the word were formally defined as the expression of a complete thought and as the minimal unit of syntax, respectively. Next came the eight word-classes.

6. Some Greek grammarians turned their attention to Latin after contacts with the Roman world, and they declared that, with just a few exceptions, the framework of Greek grammar would fit the Latin language. In their recognition of Greek superiority in intellectual matters this was what the Romans wanted to hear, and as far as possible the Alexandrian classes and categories were handed on to the later Latin grammarians.

However, Varro was the principal link between Greek and Latin linguistics, a learned man, knowing both languages well, and acquainted with the grammar-book of Dionysius in its original state. He understood both the Stoic and the Alexandrian views on language and applied them to Latin in his book *On the Latin Language*. This is not a grammar of Latin, but a lengthy discussion of the language, its structure, vocabulary, and, so far as he could trace it, its history.

Varro was the most original thinker about language that we know of in the Latin world. In addition to his application of Stoic semantics to the Latin verb he made an extensive study of word formation and inflexion, drawing on the principle of regularity ('analogy'), but recognizing existing irregularities as well. In his books he began the process of grouping Latin case forms together, leading to the later establishment of the traditional five declensions. These five were set out by the late Latin grammarians such as *Priscian (*c.* AD 500) several centuries before a comparable simplified account was applied to Greek.

Three main differences between Latin and Greek had to be noticed by Varro and others: (*a*) The Latin ablative case, not found in Greek and recognized by Varro as the 'sixth' or 'Latin' case. The term *ablative* was created later by reference to one of its major functions, 'taking away from'. (*b*) The absence of a definite article in Latin. (*c*) The conflation in Latin of the present completive ('have done') with the plain past ('did'), having differential verb forms in Greek but a single form in Latin. This was duly noted by Priscian.

7. The first grammarian dealing exclusively with syntax, whose work is, in part, extant, is Apollonius Dyscolus, writing in Alexandria *c.* AD 200. He was regarded by Priscian as his principal authority, and later Byzantine grammarians in the main wrote summaries and commentaries on the basis of Apollonius' books. The work of these Byzantine Greek grammarians between 500 and 1500 was the main vehicle for the reintroduction of Greek studies in the western Renaissance.

literacy The number of people who could read and write in the ancient world is hard to determine. We depend mostly on chance information and inference: e.g. the institution of *ostracism implies that most Athenian citizens could be expected to write a name. Our evidence (written) indicates the literate, not the illiterate, and esp. the highly educated élite. The ancient habit of reading aloud meant that written texts could often be shared the more easily by others; the existence of inscriptions (see EPIGRAPHY, GREEK) does not imply that they were read by everyone, since their symbolic value added another dimension to their written contents. There are also different levels of literacy, from the basic ability to figure out a short message, to functional literacy or 'craft literacy', to the skill required for reading a literary papyrus (reading and writing skills may also have been separate). However, certain broad generalizations are possible. The 'mass literacy' of modern industrial countries was never achieved in the ancient world. Women, slaves, and the lower social levels would be less literate. Archaic Greece and esp. Archaic Rome have left few instances of writing (graffiti, inscriptions), implying sparse literacy, and Archaic Greek cities sometimes try to ensure an official's power over the written word was not abused. However, there were pockets and periods where a higher rate of basic literacy among the adult citizen-body is probable: e.g. under the Athenian *democracy, when there was an unusually high level of reading-matter and incentives to read (in Aristophanes' *Knights*, even the sausage-seller can read a little); Hellenistic cities which made provision for elementary *education, esp. *Rhodes; the Roman empire, which probably had widespread craft literacy in the cities (see POMPEII) with increasingly elaborate use of writing; Roman Egypt, where the society was permeated by the need for written documentation. Literacy levels may to some extent be related to the functions of, or needs for, writing: *Sparta used written records very little until the Roman period, hence Classical Spartans were thought illiterate. The contexts in which writing was or could be used are essential in assessing the role or importance of literacy. It was often supplemented by oral communication and performance (see ARCHIVES; ORALITY; RECORDS AND RECORD-KEEPING). Literacy by itself was not a key to social advancement: one had to be able to sing and converse agreeably. Much reading and writing was done by slaves, esp. in Rome, ensuring that it was by itself of low status. However, it was not confined at any point in the Graeco-Roman world to scribes: writing is used from very early on in Greece for widely different purposes, informal graffiti and poetry, then inscriptions, suggesting it was not limited to a narrow social group, or to the public sphere. This spread may be partly linked to the comparative ease with which the alphabet can be learned, but the open nature of Archaic Greek society, and the early use of writing for memorials, should also be taken into account.

literary criticism in antiquity 1. The arts of formal speech played a big part in ancient life; so it was natural that vocabularies and conceptual frameworks should be developed for the purposes of evaluation, speculation about the nature and role of poetry, and practical advice for successful composition, esp. in oratory. In the resulting body of doctrine, this last element—which is the contribution of *rhetoric—is dominant, and it is this which seems the most striking difference between Graeco-Roman 'criticism' and most modern analogues.

2. *Homer and *Hesiod speak of their art as a gift of the *Muses, who inspire the poet, know all things, and can tell false tales as well as true. *Pindar too called himself the 'prophet'—i.e. 'spokesman'—of the Muses, and was proud to think of his 'wisdom' as the product of natural endowment, not teachable technique, which was for lesser mortals. The poets did not however escape criticism; they were the transmitters of a mythical tradition which had many offensive features—tales of the gods' immorality and the viciousness of heroic figures—and the early philosophers found these an easy target (see XENOPHANES). Allegory—e.g. the interpretation of the Battle of the Gods in Homer, *Iliad* 21, as a battle of the elements—began as a mode of defence against such attacks, and eventually (esp. with the Stoics (see STOICISM) in Hellenistic times and the Neoplatonists (see NEOPLATONISM) later) became the most significant and influential critical approach in all antiquity. The idea of inspiration and the demand for a moral and social commitment are not the only achievements of 'pre-Platonic' poetics. More sophisticated reflection is suggested by the paradox of *Gorgias, that tragedy 'offers a deception such that the deceiver is more just than the non-deceiver, and the deceived wiser than the undeceived'; and delicate connoisseurship is displayed by the comparison of 'high' and 'low' styles, as represented by *Aeschylus and *Euripides, in the great debate in Aristophanes' *Frogs*.

3. *Plato pulled the threads together but in a very radical and paradoxical way, in which irony may lurk. Inspiration, as claimed by the poets, was for him no road to knowledge, indeed a thing of no great worth; and in so far as poets failed to promote the right moral and social values, they were to be banished from the ideal state altogether. In rationalizing this attitude Plato developed for the first time a concept of 'imitation' (*mimēsis*) which, in various guises, was to be a central theme of later theory. He held strongly that the spectacle of degrading emotion nourished the same emotion in the hearer. Parallel to his attack on the poets was his criticism of contemporary rhetoric; here too he saw fraud, pretence, and contempt for truth. As a critic of style, he was superb, as is shown by his marvellous parodies, rivalled only by Aristophanes himself.

4. *Aristotle's *Poetics*, the fountain-head of most later criticism, is in part an answer to Plato; this is the context of the improved and very important analysis of *mimēsis* and of the much-debated doctrine that tragedy effects a *katharsis* of pity and fear. This crabbed and difficult book has many themes: a general theory of poetry as a 'mimetic' art, and a speculative account of its origins; a detailed analysis of

tragedy, stressing the primary importance of plot (*mȳthos*) over *character and ideas; an account of poetic diction, including much that we should call grammatical theory; and finally some discussion of *epic and its inferiority (as Aristotle held) to *tragedy as a *genre. A treatment of comedy is lost, but can to some extent be reconstructed from later writings. The *Poetics* is a seminal work for the Renaissance and for modern criticism.

5. Whereas Aristotle held poetry and rhetoric to be fundamentally distinct—the one was an 'imitative' art, the other a practical skill of persuasion—his successors tended more and more to blur the difference. *Theophrastus is credited with the observation that, while philosophers are concerned solely with facts and the validity of deductions, poets and orators alike are concerned with their relation with their audience, and this is why they have to use dignified words, put them together harmoniously, and in general produce pleasure and astonishment in order to cajole or bully their hearers into conviction. For criticism, the consequence of this kind of approach is that form may be judged apart from content. The main achievement of post-Aristotelian criticism is in the analysis of style, rather than in literary theory. The basic distinction between 'high' and 'low' writing (we might contrast *Homer and his followers with *Archilochus and his), the 'high' being associated with strong emotion and the 'low' with everyday life and character, goes back to Aristophanes; in terms of effect on the audience, it corresponds to the distinction between pleasure and astonishment, of which Theophrastus speaks. It was refined and modified in various ways.

6. Though this rhetorical and stylistic doctrine is the main achievement of critics after Aristotle, there were other developments as well. (*a*) The Stoics (see STOICISM) viewed poetry primarily as an educational instrument, and so in a sense continued Plato's moralizing approach. *Plutarch's essay on *How the Young should Study Poetry* is a later example of this tradition: though a Platonist, he tries to overcome Plato's objections to poetry by scholarly attention to context and historical circumstances. (*b*) The Epicurean *Philodemus is an important witness to Hellenistic theory: in his *On Poems*, parts of which are preserved, he discussed and refuted previous theorists, including Aristotle. He seems also to have had a positive view of his own, namely that form and content are inseparable, and cannot be judged separately. If this is right, Philodemus makes a sharp contrast with the prevailing 'rhet-

orical tradition'. (*c*) The *Alexandrian scholars who collected and edited classical poets and orators, and discussed the authenticity of the pieces they found, were also 'critics'. They needed historical, aesthetic, and grammatical insights. Much of *Dionysius (3) of Halicarnassus' work on orators is in their tradition.

7. In the classical period of Latin literature (as in the days of the Attic Old Comedy) criticism appears in topical writing in quite unacademic contexts; in *Lucilius (1) and *Horace, and later in *Persius and *Petronius Arbiter, it is an ingredient of satire. Horace not only defended his own literary position and expounded literary history in his *Satires* and *Epistles*, but wrote a humorous didactic poem (*Ars poëtica*) in which he combined traditional precepts on the drama and views on the poet's place in society with witty and urbane reflections on his own literary experience.

8. Cicero's achievement as a judge of oratory is unequalled—naturally, for he was himself a great orator. Political oratory died with him, and the age of the declaimers which followed produced critics of a different cast. *Seneca the Elder makes many shrewd points in commenting on his favourite declaimers. The dominant theme in the early empire seems to have been a consciousness of decline. In itself this was nothing new, since Greek critics of music and art as well as of oratory had long been drawing contrasts between admired works of the past and the degenerate efforts of the present. *Seneca the Younger and *Tacitus (*Dialogue*) reflect interestingly on the causes of 'decline'—moral and political, as well as intellectual. With *Quintilian, there is some renewed optimism and a return to Cicero's ideals. The chapter in which he catalogues the authors to be read by the budding orator summarizes traditional teaching on 'imitation' (his account of the Greek authors is based on Dionysius) but shows a capacity for independent judgement.

liturgy The liturgy (*leitourgia*, 'work for the people') is an institution known esp. from Athens, but attested elsewhere, by which rich men were required to undertake work for the state at their own expense. It channelled their expenditure and competitiveness into public-spirited directions, and was perhaps felt to be less confiscatory than an equivalent level of taxation.

In Athens liturgies were of two kinds: the *trierarchy, which involved responsibility for a warship for a year; and various liturgies in connection with festivals. The latter included the *choregia ('chorus-leading': the production of a chorus at the musical and dramatic festivals), the gymnasiarchy (responsibility for a team competing in an athletic festival), hestiāsis ('feasting': the provision of a banquet), and architheōria (the leadership of a public delegation to a foreign festival). At state level there were at least 97 in a normal year, at least 118 in a year of the Great *Panathenaea, and there were also some *deme liturgies.

Liability seems to have begun at a property level of c.3–4 talents; in some cases *metics as well as citizens could be called on. Appointment was made sometimes by one of the *archontes, sometimes by the tribes (*phylai). A man who thought that another was richer than himself but had been passed over could challenge the other to perform the liturgy in his place or else accept an exchange of property (*antidosis). The most that could legally be required of a man was to perform one festival liturgy in two years or one trierarchy in three, but in the atmosphere of competition surrounding the liturgies many men performed more liturgies and spent more money on them than the minimum possible.

In the 4th cent. BC it became hard to find enough men able to bear the cost of liturgies. Various measures were adopted to spread the cost of the trierarchy more fairly. Between 317 and 307 *Demetrius of Phaleron abolished all liturgies, and new magistrates were provided with funds for festivals by the state; but in the Hellenistic world there was a tendency to appoint rich men to offices of this kind and to expect them to add from their own pockets to what the state provided. See EUERGETISM.

Līvia Drūsilla, b. 58 BC, in 43 or 42 married Tiberius *Claudius Nero. She bore him *Tiberius, the future emperor, and Nero *Claudius Drusus. In 39, in order for her to marry Octavian (*Augustus), she was divorced though pregnant with her second son. Although she had no further children, she retained Augustus' respect and confidence throughout his life. As consort of the princeps, she became a model of old-fashioned propriety, her beauty, dignity, intelligence, and tact fitting her for her high position. She played a role in the Augustan system which was unusually formal and conspicuous for a woman, and on Augustus' death became a principal figure in his cult and (by his will) a member of his family, as Iulia Augusta. She was believed to have interceded successfully on behalf of conspirators, but

some took her influence on Augustus to be malign, and saw her as a ruthless intriguer (her grandson *Gaius (1) called her 'Ulixes stolatus', 'Odysseus dressed as a married woman'), while the tradition grew up that she had manipulated the affairs of Augustus' household on behalf of her sons, esp. Tiberius, to the extent of involvement in the deaths of *Claudius Marcellus (2), Gaius *Iulius Caesar (2), Lucius Iulius Caesar, Agrippa *Iulius Caesar (Agrippa Postumus), and *Germanicus, and even of Augustus himself. But after AD 14 her continuing influence caused discord between her and Tiberius, who was even supposed to have retired from Rome in 26 chiefly to avoid her. She died in 29, but Tiberius' hostility ensured that her will was not executed until Gaius' reign, and that she was not deified until that of *Claudius.

Līvius Andronīcus, Lūcius, a *freedman of the Livii, commonly held to be the first to compose poems of the Greek type in Latin. He produced a comedy and a tragedy at the *Ludi Romani of 240 BC and wrote the text of a hymn to *Juno sung by 27 young women at a moment of crisis in 207. Ancient biographers presented him as a half-Greek from *Tarentum who provided grammatical instruction in both Greek and Latin for the children of Livius Salinator (consul 207) and other aristocrats, and who played roles in the stage plays he composed. His prestige persuaded the Roman authorities to permit actors and stage-poets to assemble for religious purposes in the *Aventine temple of *Minerva.

Twenty-one fragments of his translation of *Homer's Odyssey in *Saturnian verses are unambiguously transmitted. Livius ignored the 24-book division introduced at *Alexandria. He seems to have kept fairly close to the general wording of the Homeric text but gave both the gods and the heroes (e.g. *Odysseus = Ulixes) local names and took account of the differences between Roman and Greek notions of story-telling. Conceptions shocking to Roman ears were toned down (e.g. Patroclus, 'counsellor equal to the gods', became 'first-rate leading man'). Undignified reactions to external events were replaced (e.g. 'Odysseus' knees were loosened' became 'Ulysses' heart froze').

*Cicero thought little of either the Odyssey translation or the plays. An eminent schoolmaster of the middle of the 1st cent. BC, *Orbilius, nevertheless beat the former into the heads of his charges.

Līvius Drūsus, Marcus, eldest of a circle of ambitious young nobles around *Licinius Crassus, to whom he owed his oratorical training and some of his ideas. A brilliant, hard-working, and arrogant man, he became tribune 91 BC. With the encouragement of *Aemilius Scaurus, who was himself in danger, and of Crassus, he proposed a solution for all of Rome's major problems: 300 *equestrians were to be raised to the senate (where their influence would be minimal: see NOVUS HOMO) and criminal juries were to be chosen from the enlarged senate. Thus the equestrians would be eliminated as a political force, with the most ambitious creamed off and the rest deprived of power. He also proposed colonies and land distributions to provide for the poor, and the enfranchisement of all Italians. The ruling oligarchy was to reap the political benefit and hold unchallenged leadership. But those who thought themselves adversely affected combined against him. After Crassus' death in September the consul Philippus gained the upper hand and had the laws already passed invalidated by the senate. Shortly after, Drusus was assassinated. The *Social War ensued. Drusus was the grandfather of *Livia Drusilla.

Livy (Titus Līvius), Roman historian, 59 BC–AD 17. He was born and died at Patavium, the most prosperous city of north Italy.

Livy entitled his work *Ab urbā conditē lībrā* ('Books from the Foundation of the City'): it covered Roman history from the origins of Rome to 9 BC in 142 books. Of these only 1–10 and 21–45 survive. Apart from a few references to topography and monuments, indicating *autopsy, Livy relied on literary sources; he did not regard it as his duty to consult documents. In books 31–45 it is clear that for events in the east Livy followed *Polybius closely, adapting his narrative for his Roman audience and making additions—sometimes tacitly. No Roman writer was so obviously superior on western events as was Polybius on eastern ones, and it may be that Livy sometimes produces an amalgam of the various works he had read. Livy's errors—anachronisms, geographical mistakes, misunderstandings of Polybius, and chronological confusions are not very many or striking in relation to the size of his work or in comparison with other writers.

Livy fulfilled Cicero's desire that history should be written by an orator. Cicero wanted a style that 'flowed with a certain even gentleness', and *Quintilian was to write of Livy's 'milky richness'. Livy, reacting against the contorted Thucydideanism of *Sallust (see THUCYDIDES (2)), first introduced fully developed periodic structure into Latin historiography. He had the ability to use language to embellish his material (comparison of Livy with Polybius in individual passages often shows the extent of Livy's originality) to convey an atmosphere and portray emotions. He gives special attention to major episodes, which are esp. numerous in the first decade (= ten books)—e.g. the rape of Lucretia, the stories of *Coriolanus. The mixture of direct and indirect speech is one of the features of his technique. Elsewhere the speed of action in a battle can be conveyed by short vivid sentences, while a dry style is adopted for lists of prodigies, elections, and assignments of provinces and armies.

Part of Livy's style is achieved by the use of poetical or archaic words avoided by Cicero and *Caesar. In this he is following in a tradition of historiography to which Sallust also belonged. These usages are most common in bks. 1–10. Livy makes particular use of vocabulary of this sort in those episodes which esp. attracted him, and these became progressively less common as his work proceeded—the diplomatic and military details of the early 2nd cent. did not compare in excitement with the great (and largely fictional) stories of the first decade. But some such episodes do occur in the later books, and it is just there that we find the greatest concentration of non-Ciceronian usages, e.g. in the story of the *Bacchanalia in book 39 or the account of the death of Cicero preserved by *Seneca the Younger.

Livy was a patriotic writer, though in narrative he never refers to Roman troops as 'our men', 'our army', and often, writing from their opponents' point of view, talks of the Romans as 'enemy'. His aim was to chronicle the rise of Rome to mastery first of Italy, then of the rest of the Mediterranean world, and to highlight the virtues which produced this result and enabled Rome to defeat *Hannibal. Livy intended his work to be morally improving, but though there are many passages where he writes with this aim in mind, a moral purpose is not all-pervasive. He believed that a serious moral decline had taken place by his own time, and appears to have doubted whether Augustus could reverse it.

If Livy shared Augustus' ideals, he was by no means a spokesman for the regime. *Tacitus makes *Cremutius Cordus, defending himself on a *maiestas charge, claim that Livy felt free to praise *Brutus and *Cassius; Cordus also claims that Livy was so lavish in his praise of *Pompey that Augustus called him a Pompeian, and adds that this did not harm their friendship. There are signs that Livy regarded the rule of Augustus as necessary, but only as a short-term measure.

loans See CREDIT; DEBT; HEKTEMOROI; MARITIME LOANS.

locus amoenus, 'pleasant spot', a phrase used by modern scholars to refer to the set description of an idyllic landscape, typically containing trees and shade, a grassy meadow, running water, song-birds, and cool breezes. The tradition goes back to *Homer's descriptions of the grotto of Calypso and the garden of Alcinous; the rural setting for the dialogue in Plato's *Phaedrus* was much imitated. In *Theocritus' and *Virgil's *Eclogues* such landscapes form the backdrop for the songs and loves of shepherds. *Horace criticizes the fashion for such descriptions. This perfect nature is also the setting for the innocence of the *golden age and the blessedness of the Elysian Fields (see ELYSIUM); among real places the vale of Tempē was idealized as a *locus amoenus*. There was an analogous fashion for ideal landscapes in Roman wall-*painting. See GARDENS.

logistics (Greek, military) In the ancient world, moving and supplying troops was most easily done by sea, and the Greeks believed their 'history' began with an overseas expedition—the Trojan War (see TROY). Certainly, by the 6th cent. BC the *Spartans were capable of attacking *Samos, and in the 5th the Athenians launched seaborne expeditions as far as *Egypt and *Sicily. In the latter case, *Thucydides (2) provides us with details of some of the preparations, including conscripting bakers from mills in Athens.

On land, unless they were cavalry, troops went on foot—*Xenophon and his comrades marched anything from 29 to 47 km. a day (18–29 mi.) on the way to *Cunaxa until they were near the enemy—and were housed either in skin tents or in the open. Foraging was common, but in friendly or neutral territory food was bought; see MARKETS). Where there was a likelihood that no provisions would be available, arrangements would be made to carry them, and there are examples of supply-lines being organized where an army remained in one place for any length of time, e.g. during the *Plataea campaign.

On land ox-carts, pack-animals, and human bearers were used to carry supplies, and Xenophon gives a vivid idea of what these might include. Wagons are often mentioned (see TRANSPORT), and could carry more than pack-animals—Xenophon reckons the average load 'per yoke' as 25 talents (*c.*920 kg. or 2,030 lb.). But they could not go everywhere, and Xenophon and his comrades burned their wagons before their long march home. The term most often used for the animals employed—*hypozugia* (lit. 'beasts under the yoke')—obviously included oxen, but also mules and *horses. *Philip II and *Alexander (2) the Great tended to restrict the size of baggage-trains, and to rely on the soldiers themselves, and their servants, for carrying equipment and supplies; for pack-animals, mules, horses, and *camels were used in preference to oxen or donkeys.

Food consumed varied with circumstances (see FOOD AND DRINK). Xenophon mentions wheat, barley, and chestnut bread, meat, including boiled beef and ass meat, olives, dates, raisins, vegetables, pickled dolphin, and dolphin fat used instead of olive oil. The daily rations allowed to the Spartans trapped on Sphacteria, under armistice terms, were two *choinikes* (2.16 kg. or $4^3/_4$ lb.) of ready-mixed barley meal, two *kotylai* (0.54 lt., almost 1 pint) of *wine, and some 'meat'. This would have provided something like 5,000 calories and 130 g. ($4^1/_2$ oz.) of protein, more than enough for a normal, active man, as the Spartan commander showed by hoarding some of it. Food brought in by *helots in boats, after the armistice, included wheat flour, wine, and cheese, and others swam over with poppy-seed mixed with honey and pounded linseed in skin bags.

logographers (Gk. *logographos*), as used by the contemporaries of *Demosthenes (2), commonly means a speech-writer for litigants in the courts, or else a writer of prose, as distinct from a poet. Modern practice, however, has followed *Thucydides (2) in applying the term to the predecessors and contemporaries of *Herodotus who were the pioneers of history-writing. Early writers of narrative prose are called *logopoioi*, 'tellers of tales', by Herodotus. But like the early philosophers and natural scientists, those who claimed to offer a faithful account of human activities considered their task as an investigation (*historia*), as scientific rather than poetic. If we grudge the title of 'historian' to the predecessors of Herodotus, it is largely because they wrote of gods and heroes as well as of men, and some of them professed to offer a true version of mythology as well as of history.

No manuscripts of these authors have survived, but there are numerous references to them and occasional direct quotations in later Greek writers. Some later writers have a low opinion of their accuracy and accuse them of fabricating names and incidents; others stress their lack of critical judgement; all agree that they wrote in simple style and language. Many of them came from Ionian cities. *Hecataeus of Miletus is a well-attested historical figure, mentioned several times by Herodotus; he was active politically in Miletus as early as 500 BC, and much can be learnt from surviving fragments about the range and character of his literary work.

The work of the logographers may be classified under various heads:

1. *Mythographic treatises, which involved attempts to rationalize and systematize Greek *mythology, and to trace the *genealogies of families who claimed descent from a god or hero.

2. Geographical works, describing the peoples and areas met with on a coasting voyage (see PERIPLOI) and the neighbouring peoples inland.

3. Accounts of the customs and history of non-Greek peoples. See BARBARIAN.

4. Local histories, esp. accounts of the Founding of Cities. See FOUNDERS OF CITIES.

5. Chronological works, which might include tables based on lists (real or apocryphal) of kings, magistrates, priests, or priestesses. See TIME-RECKONING.

Herodotus combines the various strains of the logographers' work, and was the first to provide a coherent history.

logos is one of the central terms of classical Greek culture, whose main range is covered by two different sets of terms in English: (*a*) 'speech', i.e. either the activity of speaking or the thing said (but not 'word'), and (*b*) 'reason', either in a wide sense or in the sense of 'argument'. In role (*a*) the term comes to be used esp. of prose speeches (as opposed to poetry), and of non-fictional accounts in general; but at this point it is already merging into role (*b*), for which compare e.g. *Protagoras' claim to be able 'to make the weaker *logos* the stronger' (see SOPHISTS), in those areas of ordinary life—esp. the lawcourts—where argument mattered.

Those ancient Greek philosophers who think of the world as having an ordered structure may express the idea by saying that it runs 'according to *logos*', i.e. is rational or intelligible. But they may also go on to suggest that the world is 'rational' in the sense of *possessing* reason; so, perhaps first, *Plato (whose *Timaeus* makes the world a living, rational creature with a soul which moves itself through the heavens), and after him the Stoics, who see everything as interpenetrated, activated, and ordered by *logos*—also identified with creative *fire, and with god/*Zeus (see STOICISM). Acc. to some (including the Stoics themselves), a view like the last is already to be found in *Heraclitus, and some Heraclitean fragments are more or less consistent with such an interpretation; but Heraclitus is more likely to have had in mind the less extravagant idea of the world as accessible to (speaking to?) human reason.

Lollia Paulīna was granddaughter of Marcus Lollius and very rich: *Pliny the Elder had seen her adorned in her fabulous pearls at an ordinary *betrothal dinner. She was forced to abandon her marriage to Memmius Regulus in order that she might marry the emperor *Gaius (1) in AD 38. Divorced by him in the following year, she was an unsuccessful candidate for the hand of *Claudius after the death of *Valeria Messallina in 48. *Iulia Agrippina secured her banishment (on the charge of consulting astrologers) in the following year, and she was driven to suicide.

Londinium. The Roman settlement was not established until *c.* AD 50, earlier routes crossing the Thames up river at Westminster. The settlement stood on Cornhill and Ludgate Hill north of the river, with a suburb across the bridge in Southwark. The original settlement was laid out around the northern bridgehead, beside modern London Bridge; it grew to *c.*25 ha. (62 acres) by the time of its destruction in the *Boudiccan revolt of 60/1, when *Tacitus says that it was an important trading centre. It was most likely a community of traders from other provinces.

After 61 there was a major public building programme including the construction of two successive fora (Flavian and early 2nd cent.), the latter huge, covering *c.*3.6 ha. (9 acres). There is strong evidence for vibrant economic activity. Substantial timber quays, stretching up to 300 m. (330 yds.) along the river, were constructed from the Flavian period. Epigraphic evidence shows the procurator was based here after 61, whilst a substantial Flavian building overlooking the river is interpreted as the provincial governor's palace, implying that London had become the provincial capital. The governor's guard and a staff seconded from other units were based here, probably in the Cripplegate fort, built *c.*90. Next to this was an early 2nd-cent. amphitheatre. The settlement suffered an economic decline during the later 2nd cent., and although there is good evidence for later Roman occupation, there was no resurgence of the productive economy. The later Roman city was instead dominated by town houses.

In the late 2nd cent. London was surrounded by a landward wall enclosing 133.5 ha. (330 acres), making it the largest town in Britain. The wall was extended along the riverside in the middle of the 3rd cent., whilst external towers were added in the mid-4th. Excavations show the city to have been cosmopolitan. A mid-3rd-cent. Mithraeum (see MITHRAS) has been excavated, and fine sculpture has also been found, including material from a monumental arch reused in the riverside wall.

'Longīnus' The literary treatise commonly called *On the Sublime*, of which two-thirds survives, is ascribed in the manuscript tradition both to 'Dionysius Longinus' and to 'Dionysius or Longinus'. Internal evidence, esp. the chapter on the decline of oratory, points to a date in the 1st cent. AD. The writer sets out to answer the *rhetor Caecilius of Caleacte, who had allegedly given an inadequate account of 'sublimity', failing in particular to give due weight to the emotional element (*pathos*).

On the Sublime is an important book. In discussing the quality of thought and style which marks writing as 'sublime', the author breaks free of the rhetorical tradition within which he works, and makes a connection between 'great writing' and greatness of mind. He is a sophisticated, original, and serious critic. Both his detailed analyses of passages of poetry and prose, and his general reflections on genius and the limitations of 'correct' writing, are distinguished work, and have deservedly been influential. See SUBLIME.

Long Walls, the, were built between 461 and 456 BC to connect Athens to her ports, Phaleron and *Piraeus. *Thucydides (2) records an attempt by enemies of the democracy to stop the building of the Long Walls, i.e. the walls were identified with *democracy. The Phaleric wall was replaced by a third, parallel to the northern or Piraeus wall, *c.* 445. They were destroyed by the Spartans to *aulos*-music in 404, rebuilt by *Conon (1) in 393, but allowed to fall into a

half-ruined state by 200. The walls to Piraeus were about 6.5 km. (4 mi.) long and *c.*180 m. (200 yds.) apart. The course of the Phaleric wall is uncertain. The main road from Piraeus to Athens lay outside, the road inside being primarily military. The Long Walls were used in the *Peloponnesian War to make Athens into an isolated fortress, in which most of the population of Attica could live on seaborne provisions. The example of Long Walls was followed elsewhere, notably at *Megara, and even Corinth.

lot See SORTITION.

love and friendship Greek philosophers place love and friendship within a structure of eudaimonism: an agent's own happiness (*eudaimonia*) is the final goal of all his deliberate actions.

*Plato discusses friendship (*philia*) most fully as an aspect of erotic desire (*erōs*). In his *Symposium*, Plato extends the Socratic psychology by making the ultimate goal of all desire not just being happy, but being happy for ever. Within this world, this may be achieved in a manner through passing on one's physical life to a child, or one's mental life to a beloved; the happiness counts as one's own in that it is a continuation of the life one has led. The ladder of love then advances the lover's attention from persons, through practices, laws, and sciences, to the Form of Beauty, until his goal becomes to beautify his (and arguably also a beloved's) *soul by the light of the Form. In *Phaedrus*, the lover is reminded by a beloved, congenial as well as beautiful, of the Forms he knew before birth, and of the kind of companionship that determined the manner in which he knew them; he then wishes them to re-create that companionship in a shared life, ideally of philosophy, that will restore to them after death the happiness they lost at birth. In *Republic*, the pederastic ideal (see HOMOSEXUALITY, *Pederasty*) applies between the sexes (viewed as naturally equal, and equally fit for public life), and yet erotic love is marginalized; the goal of a philosophical polity is a friendship that unites all the citizens, despite their differences of role, so that they identify with one another, applying the term 'mine' ('Mine has fared well' or 'badly') to each other's successes and sufferings.

*Aristotle defines friendship and classifies friendships, applying the term *philos* (in extension even of Greek idiom) far more widely than our 'friend'. Friends wish well to one another according to the manner in which they are friends: friends in utility (such as business partners) wish each other to be useful; in pleasure (such as lovers), to be pleasant; in goodness or virtue, to be good. Since, of these, only being good is intrinsic, and inherently beneficial, to the friend himself, only virtue-friendship can embody that goodwill (loving another for himself, and wishing him well for his own sake) which is definitive of *philia* in its strict sense. Happiness consists in activity, and is not a state of mind; through beneficence and co-operation, A acts upon and within B's life, making possible actions by B that are owed to A and count as A's also, so that their lives come to overlap. Friends pursue together the activities that they most value; even philosophy can be practised more continuously in company. Each may be improved by the other, taking from him the impression of the characteristics that please them. Aristotle lacks Plato's enthusiasm for pederasty, but concedes that, if the familiarity between a man and a boy produces a similarity of character, it may engender an enduring friendship. Though he views men and *women as naturally unequal, he allows a kind of virtue-friendship to link man and wife, each delighting in the proper virtue of the other. Cities are founded for living, but come to serve living well (see POLIS); through civic co-operation, the motive of self-interest is enriched by goodwill, as each citizen comes to wish every other to be good for his own sake. Women are to contribute to civic friendship not directly (as in Plato's utopias), but indirectly through the influence of the *household on its menfolk.

*Epicurus faces extra difficulties in that his ethic is not only eudaimonist but hedonist. Friendship inspires in him noble sentiments (e.g. the woozy 'Friendship dances round the world announcing to us all that we should wake up and felicitate one another') doubtfully consistent with the exclusive pursuit of one's own pleasure. The foundation of friendship is utility: it offers us not so much our friends' help, as confidence in their help. Yet it is not only a protector but a creator of pleasures: we rejoice in our friend's joy as in our own, and are equally pained by his distress; it is more blessed, because more pleasant, to give than to receive. Whether as a pleasure or as an insurance, one may run risks for a friend, take on the greatest pains on his behalf, and even die for him. Later Epicureans tried to explain *how* one can come to take joy in another's joy: perhaps we first form associations for utility, but then

affection 'blossoms' out of familiarity, so that we love our friends for their own sake; or else, knowing the advantages of altruism, we contract to love them no less than ourselves. Whether they arise or are adopted, altruistic attitudes make new pleasures possible. Epicurus' hedonism is discriminating, and disparages the pleasures of love: falling in love is not god-sent, and does not befall the wise; making love never did anyone any good. Characteristic of the Epicureans were calm collegiate friendships.

The Stoic goal was 'living in agreement with (human) nature' by acting virtuously (see STOICISM). A good friend is an external and instrumental good. Having friends is neither valuable in itself, nor necessary for happiness; but it gives virtue new scope. Only good men can be friends, for they do not compete for scarce commodities that are not really good, but co-operate in maintaining wisdom and exercising virtue. Benefiting another benefits oneself, for aiding another's virtue confirms one's own; in this manner, it is social to serve oneself. Ultimately, all good men are friends. This is the culmination of the process of 'appropriation' (*oikeiōsis*): animals have a natural tendency towards self-preservation; as the human animal grows up, it recognizes more and more things as belonging to it, so that its circle of concern extends. Personal familiarity nourishes common values that then create a solidarity uniting all the wise. The early Stoics were more tolerant of erotic relations than the Epicureans. In his Cynic vein, *Zeno (2) took making love to be evaluatively indifferent, whether with boy or girl, whether with boy-beloved or non-beloved. Being in love has real value for the wise: its stimulus is the 'apparent beauty', at once moral and visible, of the immature but potentially virtuous; its goal is a friendship that will foster that virtue. Consistently with that stimulus and goal, the young remain proper objects of love up to the age of 28. Outdoing Plato, Zeno politicizes love: Love is a god who, producing friendship, freedom, and unanimity, furthers the safety of the city.

See also FRIENDSHIP, GREECE; FRIENDSHIP, RITUALIZED; HOMOSEXUALITY.

Lucan (Marcus Annaeus Lucanus), Roman poet (AD 39–65), b. Corduba. His father, Annaeus Mela, was an *equestrian and brother of *Seneca the Younger. Mela came to Rome when his son was about eight months old. There Lucan received the typical élite education, ending with the school of rhetoric, where he was a great success (see EDUCATION, ROMAN); he probably also studied Stoic philosophy under Annaeus Cornutus, a connection of Seneca. He continued his studies at Athens, but was recalled by *Nero, who admitted him to his inner circle and honoured him with the offices of *quaestor and *augur. In 60, at the first celebration of the games called Neronia, he won a prize for a poem in praise of Nero. In 62 or 63 he published three books of his epic on the Civil War. Growing hostility between him and Nero finally led the emperor to ban him from public recitation of his poetry and from speaking in the lawcourts. Early in AD 65 Lucan joined the conspiracy of Gaius *Calpurnius Piso, and on its discovery was forced to open his veins in April 65; as he died, he recited some of his own lines on the similar death of a soldier.

Works Lucan was a prolific writer. The surviving epic 'The Civil War' contains ten books covering events in the years 49–48 BC beginning with *Caesar's crossing of the Rubicon; the poem breaks off, almost certainly unfinished, with Caesar in *Alexandria. Lucan freely manipulates historical truth where it suits his purpose, e.g. in introducing Cicero in *Pompey's camp on the eve of the battle of Pharsalus. The epic has no single hero; the three main characters are Caesar, an amoral embodiment of Achillean (see ACHILLES) and elemental energy; Pompey, figure of the moribund republic and shadow of his own former greatness; and *Cato (of Utica), an impossibly virtuous specimen of the Stoic saint (see STOICISM).

The Civil War is narrated as a tale of unspeakable horror and criminality leading to the destruction of the Roman republic and the loss of liberty; this message sits uneasily with the fulsome panegyric of Nero in the poem. From the moment when Caesar is confronted at the Rubicon by a vision of the distraught goddess Roma, in a scene that reworks Aeneas' vision of the ghost of Hector on the night of the sack of Troy, Lucan engages in continuous and detailed allusion to *Virgil's Aeneid, the epic of the birth and growth of Rome, in order to construct 'The Civil War' as an 'anti-Aeneid', a lament for the death of the Roman body politic as Roman military might is turned in against itself. Lucan's rhetorical virtuosity is exploited to the full to involve the audience (defined in the proem as Roman citizens, i.e. those most nearly concerned by the subject of civil war) in his grim tale. In an extension of tendencies present already in Virgil, an extreme of emotion is achieved through the use of lengthy speeches, apostrophe of characters in the narrative, and indignant epigrammatic utterances (*sententiae); in contravention of the objectivity associated with Homeric *epic, Lucan as narrator repeatedly intrudes his own reactions, as in the shocked meditation on the death of Pompey. Related to the goal of emotion are the features of hyperbole and paradox. Hyperbole is expressive both of the vast forces involved in the conflict, presented as a 'world war', and of the greatness of the crimes perpetrated. Lucan's use of paradox is rooted in the conceptual and thematic anti-structures of civil war, in which legality is conferred on crime, and the greatest exemplars of Roman military virtue, such as the centurion Scaeva, are at the same time the greatest criminals; but in this topsy-turvy world paradox also extends to the physical, as in the sea-battle at the end of bk. 3 which turns into a 'land-battle' because the ships are so tightly packed. Realism is not a goal; Lucan's notorious abolition of the traditional epic divine machinery is not determined by the desire for a historiographical plausibility; rather, Lucan replaces the intelligibility of the anthropomorphic gods of Homer and Virgil with a darker sense of the supernatural, in a world governed by a negative version of Stoic Providence or Fate. *Dreams, *portents, and *prophecies abound. Death fascinates Lucan, in both its destructive and its heroic aspects; a recurrent image is *suicide, viewed both as the symbol of Rome's self-destruction and as the Stoic's praiseworthy exit from an intolerable life. The Roman spectacle of ritualized killing in the *amphitheatre is reflected in the frequent gladiatorial imagery (see GLADIATORS) of the epic. In all of these features Lucan shows a close affinity with the tragedies of his uncle Seneca the Younger.

Lucan's style lacks the richness and colour of Virgil's, but his limited and repetitive vocabulary, often prosaic in tone, is deliberately geared to the bleak, remorseless, and unromantic nature of the subject-matter; a similar response may be made to the criticism of the monotony of Lucan's metre. Stylistic and metrical narrowness as a purposeful inversion of Virgilian norms finds an analogy in the device of 'negative enumeration', the listing of things that do not happen, but which might in normal circumstances be expected to happen.

Lucan's epic was avidly read and imitated for centuries after his death; his admirers include *Statius (whose mythological epic on civil war, the Thebaid, is permeated with echoes of Lucan),

Dante, Goethe, and Shelley. After a period of critical condemnation and neglect, the sombre baroque brilliance of the work is once more coming to be appreciated.

Lucian, of Samosata (b. *c.* AD 120), accomplished belletrist and wit in the context of the *Second Sophistic. His native language was probably *Aramaic; but he practised in the courts, then as an itinerant lecturer on literary-philosophical themes as far afield as Gaul. He presents a '"conversion' to philosophy aged *c.*40, and his natural milieu is Athens. He was known to *Galen for a successful literary fraud.

Works Lucian's work is difficult both to categorize and to assign to any sort of literary 'development'. Throughout he is a master of sensibly flexible Atticism (see ASIANISM AND ATTICISM). His *œuvre* runs to some 80 pieces, most of which are genuine. While some can be classified under traditional rhetorical headings such as 'exercises' and 'preambles', the most characteristic products of his repertoire are literary *dialogues which fuse Old Comic (see COMEDY (GREEK), OLD) and popular and/or 'literary' philosophy to produce an apparently novel blend of comic prose dialogue. But he is also an accomplished miniaturist, essayist, and raconteur: the 'Dialogues of the Sea-Gods' are esp. successful in exploiting the art of prose paraphrase of verse classics from *Homer to *Theocritus; 'How to Write History' gives a wittily commonsensical rather than commonplace treatment of a topical subject; while the 'Lovers of Lies' successfully combines satire of superstition with racy novella. He can be a lively and revealing commentator on his cultural and religious environment as when he attacks successful sophists, or figures such as Peregrinus or the oraclemonger Alexander, whom he sees as charlatans. In 'True Histories' he produced a masterpiece of Munchausenesque parody. His literary personality is engaging but elusive: he is cultivated but cynical, perhaps with a chip on his shoulder, but difficult to excel in his chosen field of versatile prose entertainment. His weakest moments to contemporary taste are perhaps as a repetitive and superficial moralist, his most successful when he plays with the full range of Classical Greek literature.

Lūcīlius (1), **Gāius,** Roman satirist, b. *c.*180 BC at Suessa Aurunca on the north edge of *Campania, d. in Neapolis 102/1. His family was of senatorial status, but Lucilius remained an *equestrian, a landowner with large estates

who never sought political power. He saw service under *Cornelius Scipio Aemilianus at the siege of *Numantia in 134/3, continued to enjoy the close friendship of Scipio and his companion *Laelius until the end of their lives, and attacked their enemies.

Works The extant fragments of Lucilius' 30 books consist of *c.*1,300 lines, either isolated lines or small groups. In spite of the severe difficulties in the interpretation of poems in a problematical transmission, Lucilius appears as a powerful personality and a major writer.

As a personal poet following *Archilochus, Lucilius attacked enemies by name and described without inhibition his own amatory exploits. In an epistolary poem he reproached a friend for having failed to visit him when he was ill. By recounting such mundane personal experiences he resembles *Catullus, but sometimes he used a persona. His account of a journey to Sicily suggests a genuine travelogue. Lucilius vilified reprobate consulars such as *Opimius and *Papirius Carbo, also undisciplined tribes and dishonest political lobbying. In denouncing gluttony and extravagance he shows an aptitude for popular moralizing. His definition of *virtūs* ('manly excellence') proposes a Roman aristocratic ideal with Stoic undertones (see STOICISM). Praised by *Pliny the Elder for his critical faculty, he wrote on principles of literary criticism and linguistic usage. Esp. noteworthy are Lucilius' own literary intentions, a polemic against *tragedy, and his defence of personal attacks, the 'Council of the Gods' on the chequered career of Cornelius Lentulus Lupus, *princeps senatus* (d. *c.*125), and the parody of the trial of the Stoic *Mucius Scaevola (1) accused of *extortion by the Epicurean Albucius, in which conflicting styles of rhetoric were ridiculed. Lucilius' style is conversational with some obscenity. He uses many Greek words including technical terms, and sometimes shows calculated elaboration and striking imagery.

At the end of the republic Lucilius was judged to be a writer of cultivated urbanity with characteristic Roman humour but formidable in his vituperation. *Horace discusses him in relation to his own writings: his predecessor's attack on named individuals and his improvisatory manner, his crude use of Greek words and unrefined style, and his autobiographical reflections and political *invective. Towards the end of the 1st cent. AD there was a short-lived enthusiasm for Lucilius, in which many preferred him to Horace. Viewed by the satirists *Persius and *Juvenal as the archetypal master of the genre, Lucilius had put a stamp on verse satire which it has retained. See SATIRE.

Lūcīlius (2), **Gāius,** friend of *Seneca (2) the Younger and the recipient of his *On Providence, Natural Questions,* and *Ethical Epistles;* b. in *Campania, without wealth or prospects. Talent, literary style, and distinguished connections brought him into prominence. His own energy made him an *equestrian. He was loyal to victims of *Valeria Messallina or *Narcissus under *Claudius. Under Claudius and *Nero he held four procuratorships (see PROCURATOR). The date of his death is unknown.

Seneca uses Lucilius as a sounding-board for the philosophical progression of the *Epistles.* Many of them start from some question Lucilius has supposedly put—generally philosophical, but sometimes literary, linguistic, or social. In spite of business, travel, ill health, and a tendency to grumble, he is depicted as a philosopher, perhaps an ex-Epicurean Stoic (see EPICURUS; STOICISM). On one occasion Seneca says to him 'meum opus es', 'you are my work', which may be read as testimony to Seneca's (re-)construction of his friend into the ideal philosophical novice and addressee. Seneca also warmly praises Lucilius' own philosophical work.

Lucrētius (Titus Lucrētius Cārus), Epicurean poet (see EPICURUS), author of the *Dē rērum nātūrā* (*DRN* hereafter), 'On the Nature of Things' (*c.*94–55 or 51 BC ?). Nothing is known of his place of birth or social status. *Cicero, in a letter to his brother written in 54, praises Lucretius' *poēmata* as possessing both flashes of genius and great artistry, i.e. as combining the qualities of an inspired and a craftsmanlike poet. This must refer to *DRN.*

The poem is in six books of *hexameter verse (*c.*7,400 lines, about three-quarters the length of the *Aeneid*) and is substantially complete: it opens with an elaborate prologue, and the prologue to bk. 6 states explicitly that this is the final book.

As well as the great initial prologue to bk. 1 (the first day of spring and the appeal to *Venus for help), each of the other books also has a prologue, and the concluding section of each book in some way stands apart from the rest of the book (see esp. the attack on love in bk. 4, and the final plague). In both structure and subject-matter each book is a unity. Bk. 1 deals with the basic metaphysical and physical premises of Epicureanism, beginning with the proposition that nothing comes to be out of nothing, and concluding with a description of the collapse of our world, which anticipates the Epicurean accounts of the death of our world at the end of bk. 2 and in bk. 5. Bk. 2 deals with the motion and shape of the atoms, and how they are relevant to the relationship between primary and secondary qualities: it concludes with the Epicurean doctrine of the infinite number of worlds in the universe, and the connected proposition that our world has both a birth and a death (recalling the end of bk. 1). Bk. 3 gives an account of the nature of the human soul, and argues both that it is mortal and that, because of this, death is not to be feared. Bk. 4 discusses a variety of psychological phenomena, esp. perception, and argues against scepticism: as remarked above, it concludes with an attack on love, seen as a delusion. Bk. 5 argues for the mortality of our world, and then gives a rationalist and anti-providentialist account of its creation and early history, concluding with the section on the development of human civilization, which is perhaps the most famous part of the poem. Bk. 6 then proceeds to account for those phenomena of our world which are most likely to lead to false belief in the gods—thunder and lightning, earthquakes, volcanoes, etc.—and ends with the aetiology of disease and the plague at Athens.

This clearly defined book-structure is more typical of prose philosophical treatises than of hexameter poetry, and it is replicated at levels both above and below that of the individual book. The books form three pairs, in which 1 and 2 deal with atomic phenomena up to the level of the compound (see ATOMISM), 3 and 4 deal with human beings, and 5 and 6 deal with the world: there is thus a clear sense of expanding horizons, as we move from the atomic to the macroscopic level. The twin targets of the work as a whole are fear of the gods and of death: the first and last pairs deal more with the former fear, by explaining phenomena that would otherwise be felt to require divine intervention in the world, while the central books, and esp. 3, tackle the fear of death head on. But the two motives are intermingled throughout the work. The six books may also be organized into two halves, with 1–3 dealing with basic premises, 4–6 with what follows from those basic premisses: the problematic prologue to 4 (repeated almost verbatim from 1. 921–950), with its stress on Lucretius' role as a poet and philosopher, thus functions as a 'proem in the middle' for the second half.

Below the level of the book, the subject-matter is carefully delineated and individual propositions within sections signposted with markers like 'First', 'Next', and 'Finally': the verse tends to group itself into blocks of two or more lines, with careful arrangement of words within the block. This division of the text corresponds to the Epicurean stress on the intelligibility of phenomena: everything has a systematic explanation, the world can be analysed and understood.

Every major proposition in *DRN* can be paralleled in other Epicurean sources, and it is likely that most at least of the arguments for these propositions also existed in the Epicurean tradition. There is a close correspondence with Epicurus' extant *Letter to Herodotus*, passages of which are closely translated. The *Letter to Herodotus* may have provided the core of the poem, which was expanded from a variety of other sources.

But *DRN* also draws on a wide range of literary texts in both Greek (esp. *Thucydides' (2) account of the *plague at Athens) and Latin. The main model is the lost poem of *Empedocles, 'On Nature': Empedocles' doctrine is criticized, but he is praised as a poet esp. for his stance as a 'master of truth' offering an important secret to his audience. Lucretius too writes to save humanity: although the work concentrates on physics and natural philosophy, this ethical purpose is clear throughout. Epicurus was opposed to poetry as a serious medium of enlightenment, and the Epicurean stress on clarity and simplicity of language and 'sober reasoning' in thought creates problems for an Epicurean didactic poem: by returning to the archaic models of Empedocles and *Parmenides, Lucretius was able to place himself in a tradition which made the alliance of philosophy and poetry more natural. Many of the resources of poetry, esp. the recall to the phenomenal world implicit in the use of metaphor and simile, can easily meet the needs of Epicureanism: poet and philosopher alike must make the reader *see*. The complexity and precision of Lucretius' imagery, always a central part of his claim to poetic excellence, is thus also an aspect of his role as philosopher and scientist.

Nevertheless, the old conception of a conflict between Lucretius the poet and Lucretius the philosopher was not perhaps wholly wrong. *DRN* became a most important text in the Renaissance and modern periods because of its rationalism. Similarly, the account of the development of civilization in bk. 5, and esp. the notion of the 'social contract', enabled historians and philosophers to free themselves from theistic models of the foundations of human society. But that stress on scientific rationalism as providing a single sure and certain answer to the troubles of life still fails to convince many thoughtful people. Lucretius the poet offers perhaps more ways of looking at the world than can be accommodated with comfort within the plain and simple truth of Epicureanism. Of necessity, his rationalism has its own sustaining myths, from the clear light of reason which pierces and disperses the clouds of ignorance to the secure citadel of the wise, from the nurturing female powers of Venus, Mother Earth, and Nature to the dread of the house of Hades that drives men to avarice and ambition, with their attendant crimes. Nevertheless, those myths in themselves continue to offer a powerful vision of a world by no means providentially ordered for humanity, but in which all humans can find happiness.

lūdī (including **ludi scaenicī**) (games) The chief uses of this word relate to diverse fields of Roman culture.

(1) Religious *festivals came to include formalized competitions and displays as a regular component, counting as religious rites just as much as *sacrifices and *processions. The numbers of days devoted to *ludi* in Rome increased over time: 57 in the late republic; 77 in the early 1st cent. AD; 177 in the mid-4th cent. There were three types of *ludi*. First, *ludi circensēs*, which consisted of chariot-racing, held in the circus in the *Campus Martius and eventually in the Circus Maximus (which could seat 150,000 people), see CIRCUS. Secondly, *ludi scaenici*, originating in 364 BC as *pantomime dances to the pipes, later including plays, first at the Ludi Romani of 240 (see LIVIUS ANDRONICUS); in 200 *Plautus' *Stichus* was produced at the Ludi Plebeii; in 191 the theatrical Ludi Megalenses were instituted; in 169 *Ennius' *Thyestēs* was performed at the Ludi Apollinares, instituted in 208; in 160 *Terence's *Adelphoe* was performed at the funeral games of *Aemilius Paullus (2). Under the empire performances chiefly consisted of *mime and pantomime. The cost was usually shared between state and presiding magistrate. Admission was free, with special seats designated for senators and others; women and slaves were admitted, but sat separately, at least from *Augustus onwards. Plays were staged initially in temporary settings associated with particular sanctuaries, and from the mid-1st cent BC onwards in permanent theatres (which became increasingly common

throughout the empire). Augustus' *Secular Games included both the 'archaic' games 'on a stage without a theatre and without seats', and more 'modern' games (in a purpose-built wooden theatre and in *Pompey's theatre). Thirdly, fights involving *gladiators and *venationes, which under the republic were given under private auspices. Originally they were staged in the Forum and elsewhere, but from 29 BC in the amphitheatre of *Statilius Taurus and from AD 80 in the *Colosseum (which could seat 50,000, with standing-room for another 5,000). Outside Rome, specialist amphitheatres were built and, in the Greek world, existing theatres adapted for the safety of the spectators. See AMPHITHEATRES; COLOSSEUM.

(2) Formal and informal games, of which the Romans had at least as many varieties as we do, retaining the practice of some of them even in mature years; the Campus Martius contained a 'multitude of those exercising themselves with ball and hoop and wrestling' (*Strabo). *Ludi*, part sport, part pre-military drill, entered into the routine of the formal associations of young men (see IUVENES), an allegedly ancient institution revived by Augustus.

(3) Schools of instruction, also training-schools for gladiators. There were four training-schools in Rome (including *Ludus Magnus* and *Ludus Mātūtīnus*) for the gladiators who were to perform in the Colosseum. Grammatical and literary instruction, originally in the hands of Greeks, was domesticated by the time of the empire (*see* GRAMMATICUS); training for public life (law, politics) was acquired through apprenticeship until the schools of *rhetoric replaced the old tradition. See EDUCATION, ROMAN.

Lugdūnum, colony founded in 43 BC by *Munatius Plancus, and to the mid-3rd cent. the *metropolis* of the NW of the Roman empire. Its position led to its becoming: the nodal point of *Vipsanius Agrippa's Gallic road system; the capital of the province of Lugdunensis (see GAUL (TRANSALPINE)); the religious, administrative, financial, and commercial centre of the Three Gauls and the Germanies; and the residence and birthplace of emperors. It even accommodated a branch of the imperial mint. The city's large and cosmopolitan population worshipped many deities, including those brought from the east. A Christian community (see CHRISTIANITY) developed early, and in 177 suffered savage and esp. well-documented persecution. Lugdunum declined from c.250, as imperial attention was directed increasingly to the Rhine frontier, and its primacy was usurped by *Augusta Treverorum.

Early Lugdunum occupied the heights west of the confluence of the Rhône and Saône. At the confluence itself (Gallic *Condate*), Drusus (see CLAUDIUS DRUSUS, NERO) established in 12 BC the altar of Rome and Augustus, to which aristocratic representatives of all the Gallic peoples came annually to show allegiance to Rome. On an island off Condate developed the city's main shipping and commercial quarter. On the heights, the main monuments are the theatre and odeum. The four aqueducts make extensive use of syphons. The museum contains the bronze tablets of *Claudius' speech on the admission of Gauls to the senate.

Lupercālia, a Roman *festival (15 February), conducted by the association (see SODALES) of Luperci. It included odd rites: goats and a dog were sacrificed at the Lupercal (a cave at the foot of the *Palatine where a she-wolf (*lupa*) reared *Romulus and Remus); the blood was smeared with a knife on the foreheads of two youths, and wiped with wool dipped in milk; then the Luperci, naked except for girdles from the skin of sacrificial goats, ran (probably) round the Palatine striking bystanders, esp. women, with goat-skin thongs. The rite combined purificatory *lustration and fertility magic. It was at the Lupercalia that Antony (Marcus *Antonius), consul and Lupercus, offered a royal diadem to Caesar (44 BC).

lustration is the performance of *lustrum*, a ceremony of *purification and of averting evil. The main ritual ingredient was a circular procession. The instruments of purification, such as torches and sacrificial animals (esp. the *suovetaurilia*; see MARS), were carried or led round the person(s) or the place to be purified, often to the accompaniment of music, chant, and dance. See SACRIFICE, ROMAN. The victims were sacrificed at the end of the ceremony, and their entrails inspected. Most important was *lustrātiō* of the Roman people as the concluding part of the *census, performed on the *Campus Martius by one of the *censors. The deity primarily invoked was Mars. The ceremony excluded evil, and kept the pure within the circle, but it also denoted a new beginning, esp. for the Roman people at the census or for an army when a new commander arrived or when two armies were joined together.

Lyceum See ARISTOTLE, 5; ATHENS, TOPOGRAPHY; PERIPATETIC SCHOOL.

Lycurgus (*c*.390–*c*.325/4 BC), Athenian statesman, active after the battle of *Chaeronea (338). He played the major part in the control of the city's finances for twelve years, raising the revenue to perhaps 1,200 talents a year, and financing projects by raising capital from individuals; scattered epigraphic evidence attests the wide range of his activities. The powers by which he did it all are obscure. Probably he occupied different offices including the position of steward of the military fund and controlled the whole by personal influence, which manifests itself to us in the varied decrees which he proposed. He carried through a diverse building programme including the completion of the arsenal begun by *Eubulus, the rebuilding of the theatre of Dionysus, the construction of docks, and the improvement of the harbours. The substantial increase in the navy in this period is ascribed to him. He concerned himself also with the arrangements for processions and festivals, and had statues of the three great tragic poets erected and an official copy made of their works (later borrowed by Ptolemy II Philadelphus for the library of *Alexandria and never returned). In politics he was bitterly suspicious of Macedon and was one of those at first demanded by *Alexander (2) the Great in 335. He prosecuted Lysicles who had been a general at Chaeronea and any who after the battle seemed to show signs of defeatism. The fragments of his speeches attest the wide range of his prosecution of corrupt practices.

Lydia was a territory in western Asia Minor, centred in the lower Hermus and Cayster valleys. Lydia contained much natural wealth, and lying on two main routes from the coast to the interior of Anatolia it was an entrepôt, exposed to Greek and Anatolian influences, which are reflected in its civilization, art, and cults. Under the Mermnad dynasty (*c*.700–546 BC) Lydia was a powerful kingdom, which by the time of its last king *Croesus had incorporated all the plateau of Anatolia up to the river Halys. After his defeat, Lydia became the chief Persian satrapy in the west, with its headquarters at *Sardis; this satrapy was in close political contact with the Greek city-states throughout the Persian period. The conquest by *Alexander (2) the Great opened Lydia to Graeco-Macedonian colonization. Lydian civilization, architecture, and art were influenced by Anatolian, Iranian, and Greek culture. Lydia was reputedly the first realm to mint gold–silver coinage (see COINAGE, GREEK) and invented the melodic form known as the Lydian mode. The Lydian language is *Indo-European.

lyric poetry

Greek The term 'lyric' is derived from *lyra* 'lyre'. As a designation of a category of poetry it is not found before the Hellenistic period (earlier writers term such a poem *melos*, 'song'. Though the term was extended to poetry sung to other stringed instruments or to the pipes, it is always used of sung poetry as distinct from poems which were recited or spoken.

The 'lyric' age begins in the 7th cent. BC, though the finished metres of the earliest exponents indicate that they are the heirs to a long tradition of popular song. So does the evidence of *Homer, whose narrative mentions sung paeans, *dirges, wedding songs (see EPITHALAMIUM), and more generally choral song and dance. However, the fact that no composer's name survives from this period suggests a context of anonymous folk-song. In the 7th cent. a change occurs, as named poets of distinction emerge.

Dividing lyric into choral and monodic (solo) corresponds to broad differences in form and content. Choral poetry was performed by a choir which sang and danced. The element of spectacle was enhanced further by the impressive costume of the chorus. The collective voice was ideally suited to represent the voice of the community, and so choral song in general has a pronounced 'public' quality. In origin choral performance was sacral, and even in the Classical period 'dance' may be synonymous with 'worship' (Sophocles, *OT* 896). Most of the attested types of choral song are religious or ritual in character: paean, usually addressed to *Apollo, *dithyramb, addressed to *Dionysus, processional song, maiden-song, dirge, wedding song. However, already in Homer we find choral song and dance as festive entertainment. During the late Archaic period there is a further secularization of choral music, as choral songs are composed in praise of rulers and aristocrats, as in the erotic and laudatory songs of Ibycus and the *encōmia* (originally 'party/revel songs', then 'songs of praise') and *epinīcia* (victory songs) of *Simonides, *Pindar, and *Bacchylides. Choral lyric is esp. associated with 'Dorian' states, though not exclusively (since Simonides and Bacchylides were from Ionic Ceos). The dialect is an artificial amalgam of western Greek,

Aeolic, and Homeric, though there are differences between authors. Choral compositions are either strophic (composed of stanzas which correspond metrically, strophē and antistrophē, which later writers associate with the movements of the chorus, 'turn' and 'counterturn') or triadic (each triad being composed of matching strophe and antistrophe, with a third stanza, epode, with a different metrical pattern). Metrical correspondence of stanzas is called 'responsion'. The metres are usually elaborate, and the metrical schema of each poem is almost always unique. The songs are almost always tied to a particular occasion. But celebration of the human or divine addressee is usually accompanied by succinct generalizations (*gnōmai*, see GNOME) which place the present celebration or its occasion in the broader context of human experience, and regularly a myth is narrated, usually occupying the centre of the ode; this pattern is already established for *Alcman in 7th-cent. Sparta. The choral lyric tradition reached its peak in the late Archaic and early Classical period in the work of Simonides, Bacchylides, and Pindar, the first 'freelance' professional panhellenic poets. The same period saw the beginning of the decline of choral lyric as a major literary genre. *Aristophanes and *Eupolis testify to a change in musical tastes at this period. The nature of choral lyric changed, with choral and monody mixed, the abandonment of strophic responsion in the interests of emotional realism, and an increasing dominance of music over words.

Monodic lyric is esp. associated with eastern Greece. *Sappho and *Alcaeus were natives of *Lesbos and *Anacreon of Teos. The metrical structures of monody are simpler, and unlike choral lyric are repeated from song to song. The dialect tends to be based on the vernacular of the poet. The subject-matter usually derives from the life and circumstances of the poet. The range of solo lyric is very wide. Love, politics, war, wine, abuse of enemies all figure, though to different degrees and with different emphases and approaches from poet to poet. To the modern reader, this personal poetry often seems remarkably impersonal, since there is a marked tendency to generalize personal experience through the medium of myth.

The major lyric poets were edited by the scholars of the *Library at *Alexandria. It is to them that we owe the list of nine lyric poets: Alcman, Alcaeus, Anacreon, Bacchylides, Ibycus, Pindar, Sappho, Simonides, Stesichorus. The list covers the period 650–450.

Latin The Roman poets knew the Alexandrian *canon of nine greek lyricists, and *Horace, who considers himself to be the first Latin lyric poet, memorably asks to be added to the list. Horace first combines Hellenistic technical refinement with the spirit of the lyric of *Alcaeus and *Pindar, and his *Odes* represent the crowning achievement of Latin lyric poetry. Before them the *cantica* of *Plautus provide genuine examples of lyric verse. After Horace, the tragedies of *Seneca the Younger include choral lyric, and *Statius' *Silvae* contain two lyric poems.

Lȳsander (d. 395 BC). Spartan general. His family, though of *Heraclid origin, was poor. He became the *erastēs* ('lover') of *Agesilaus, younger son of King *Archidamus II. Appointed admiral in 408 or 407, he gained the friendship and support of *Cyrus (2) the Younger, began to create a personal following, and won a victory at Notion which led to the dismissal of *Alcibiades. Resuming command in 405, he transferred his fleet to the *Hellespont and destroyed the Athenian fleet at Aegospotami. His personal success was celebrated through several monuments and dedications; at *Samos he was worshipped as a god, perhaps the first living Greek to receive divine worship. See RULER-CULT, GREEK.

Lysander established '*decarchies' of his oligarchical partisans in many cities. Obtaining Athens' surrender through blockade (spring 404), he secured the installation of the *Thirty Tyrants, but his policy was overturned by King *Pausanias' (2) restoration of democracy in 403. At some date before 396 the ephors withdrew support from the faltering decarchies. His continuing influence, however, led Sparta to support Cyrus' attempt on the Persian throne (401) and to make his protégé Agesilaus king.

Lysias, Attic orator, d. *c*.380 BC. His work is discussed in *Plato's *Phaedrus*; in Plato's *Republic*, his father Cephalus is an elderly *Syracusan, resident as a *metic in Athens, and friend of assorted Athenian aristocrats. Lysias and his brother Polemarchus left Athens after Cephalus' death to join the panhellenic colony (see PANHELLENISM) of *Thurii in south Italy, where he is said to have studied *rhetoric. They were expelled as Athenian sympathizers after the *Sicilian Expedition, and returned to Athens as metics in 412/11. In 403 the *Thirty Tyrants arrested both brothers, alleging disaffection but really (acc. to Lys. 12. 6) in order to confiscate their substantial property. Polemarchus was put to death; Lysias escaped, and gave financial and physical support to the democratic counter-revolutionaries. He was rewarded by *Thrasybulus' decree granting citizenship to all those who had assisted in the restoration, but this grant was promptly annulled as unconstitutional.

Works Modern editions contain 34 numbered speeches, although the titles of about 130 others are known. After 403, like his fellow metics *Isaeus and *Dinarchus, Lysias composed speeches for litigants to deliver in court; but his versatility was great. Like *Demosthenes (2) and *Hyperides, he wrote for both public and private cases. The two categories, however, are not formally distinguished in the collection, where few private speeches remain: most striking is 1, in which a cuckolded husband pleads justifiable homicide after killing his wife's lover, and the attack in 32 on an allegedly dishonest guardian. Underlying the public speeches are a variety of legal procedures, esp. the *dokimasia* or vetting of prospective officials, many of them compromised by their record under the *oligarchies of the *Four Hundred or the *Thirty Tyrants; other cases concern official malpractice (most notably 12, in which Lysias personally charged Eratosthenes, ex-member of the Thirty, with having killed Polemarchus). The shadow of the Thirty, indeed, hangs over much of Lysias' work.

Lysias' reputation attracted speeches. It is very hard to be sure which of those that survive are really the work of Lysias, but, with one or two exceptions, all the forensic pieces seem to be genuine speeches, written to be delivered on the occasion they purport to be.

Characteristics Lysias was noted in antiquity as a master of the language of everyday life: this 'purity' of style led to his being regarded by later rhetoricians as the pre-eminent representative of 'Atticism', as opposed to the florid 'Asiatic' school (see ASIANISM AND ATTICISM). By the time Lysias has finished telling a story, the audience has been beguiled by his apparent artlessness into accepting as true the most tendentious assertions.

Lȳsimachus (*c*.355–281 BC), Macedonian from Pella, was prominent in the entourage of *Alexander (2) the Great, achieving the rank of Bodyguard by 328. At *Babylon (323) he received *Thrace as his province, establishing himself with some difficulty against the dynast, Seuthes (322). He consolidated his power in the eastern coastal districts, but he made no mark in the wars of the Successors (see DIADOCHI) until in 302 he invaded Asia Minor and fought the delaying campaign against *Antigonus I which enabled *Seleucus I to bring up his army for the decisive battle of Ipsus (301). His reward was Asia Minor north of the *Taurus, the source of immense wealth, which he husbanded with legendary tight-fistedness and a degree of fiscal rapacity. These new reserves (*Pergamum alone held 9,000 talents) supported his impressive coinage and allowed him to consolidate in Europe, where he extended his boundaries north until he was captured by the Getic king, and forced to surrender his Transdanubian acquisitions (292). In 287 he joined *Pyrrhus in expelling Demetrius, son of Antigonus, from Macedon and two years later occupied the entire kingdom. His writ now ran from the Epirote border to the Taurus, but dynastic intrigue proved his nemesis, when he killed his heir at the instigation of his second wife, and alienated his nobility (283). Seleucus was invited to intervene and again invaded Asia Minor. The decisive battle at Corupedium (281) cost Lysimachus his life. Asia passed to the Seleucids while Macedonia dissolved into anarchy.

Macedonia links the Balkans and the Greek peninsula. Four important routes converge on the Macedonian plain. *Hesiod considered the 'Macedones' to be an outlying branch of the Greek-speaking tribes, with a distinctive dialect of their own. He gave their habitat as 'Pieria and Olympus'. A new dynasty, the Temenids, ruling the Macedonians, founded their early capital at *Aegae *c.*650 BC, and thereafter gained control of the coastal plain as far as the Axius. The Persian occupation of Macedonia 512–479 BC brought benefits. *Xerxes gave *Alexander (1) I control over western Upper Macedonia; and after Xerxes' flight Alexander gained territory west of the Strymon. His claim to be a Temenid, descended from *Heracles and related to the royal house of *Argos, was recognized at *Olympia; he issued a fine royal coinage and profited from the export of ship-timber.

The potential of the Macedonian kingdom was realized by *Philip II. By defeating the northern barbarians and incorporating the Greek-speaking Upper Macedonians he created a superb army (see ARMIES, GREEK), which was supported economically by other peoples who were brought by conquest into the enlarged kingdom: *Illyrians, Paeonians, and *Thracians—with their own non-Greek languages—and Chalcidians (see CHALCIDICE) and Bottiaeans, both predominantly Greek-speaking. 'He created a united kingdom from many tribes and nations' by a policy of tolerance and assimilation. His son *Alexander (2) the Great, inheriting the strongest state in eastern Europe, carried his conquests to the borders of Afghanistan and Pakistan. Later the conquered territories split up into kingdoms ruled mainly by Macedonian royal families, which fought against one another and contended for the original Macedonian kingdom. In 167 BC Rome defeated Macedonia and split it into four republics; and in 146 BC it was constituted a Roman province. Thereafter its history merged with that of the Roman empire.

From Philip II onwards the Macedonian court was a leading centre of Greek culture, and the policies of Alexander and his Successors (*Diadochi) spread the Greek-based 'Hellenistic' culture in the east, which continued to flourish for centuries after the collapse of Macedonian power. See COLONIZATION, HELLENISTIC; HELLENISM AND HELLENIZATION.

Macro See SUTORIUS MACRO.

Macrobius, Ambrosius Theodosius, *praetorian *prefect of Italy in AD 430. He wrote a comparison of the Greek verb with the Latin, and a *Neoplatonist commentary on *Cicero's *Dream of Scipio* (the end of his *Republic*). His *Saturnalia* is cast in the form of dialogues on the evening before the Saturnalia (see SATURNUS, SATURNALIA) of 383(?) and during the holiday proper. The guests include the greatest pagan luminaries of the time, and the grammarian Servius, still a shy youth but praised in accordance with his later eminence as a commentator on Virgil. Macrobius himself plays no part. After a few legal and grammatical discussions the night before, the three days are devoted to serious topics in the morning, lighter ones in the afternoon and evening. Having ranged over the Saturnalia, the calendar, and famous persons' jokes, the speakers devote the second and third mornings to *Virgil, represented as a master of philosophical and religious lore and praised almost without reserve in matters of rhetoric and grammar, including his use of earlier poets, Greek and Roman. The guests then turn to physiology, with special reference to eating and drinking. Sources include *Gellius (constantly used and never named), *Seneca the Younger's *Epistles*, and *Plutarch's *Sympotic Questions*. The work expresses the nostalgia of the Christianized élite in a diminished Rome for the city's great and pagan past; the new religion is ignored. Macrobius' style is elegant without extravagance.

Maecēnas, Gāius (year of birth unknown). Among Octavian's earliest supporters—he fought at *Philippi—he was his intimate and trusted friend and agent. (See AUGUSTUS.) His high position rested entirely on this: he never held a magistracy or entered the senate, remaining an *equestrian. He arranged Octavian's marriage with Scribonia, and represented him at the negotiations of the pact of Brundisium (40 BC) and that of Tarentum (37), when he took along his poets (Horace, *Satires* 1. 5). He went as envoy to Marcus *Antonius (Mark Antony) in 38, and in 36–33 and 31–29 he was in control of Rome and Italy in Octavian's absence, an unprecedented position: 'no title, only armed power'. In 30, claiming to uncover a conspiracy, he executed the son of the triumvir *Aemilius Lepidus (2). His enormous wealth must derive partly from the confiscations. He bequeathed the emperor everything, including his magnificent house and grounds on the *Esquiline. Many inscriptions survive of his slaves and *freedmen. Maecenas was famous, or notorious, for his luxury: wines, gourmet dishes, gems, fabrics, and love affairs (that with the dancer Bathyllus became scandalous). Astute and vigorous at need, he cultivated an image of softness. His name became proverbial as the greatest patron of poets (see PATRONAGE, LITERARY). He is the dedicatee of *Virgil's *Georgics*. Virgil introduced *Horace, who dedicated to Maecenas *Satires* 1, *Epodes*, *Odes* 1–3, and *Epistles* 1. Maecenas gave Horace his Sabine estate. Horace gives the fullest picture of Maecenas and his circle. Maecenas wrote poems which recall the metres and to some extent the manner of Catullus: extant fragments of two are addressed to Horace, intimate in tone. He also wrote in prose. His style was criticized for affectation. The fragments contain no trace of politics, but Maecenas must have been influential in inducing Virgil, Horace, and even Propertius to express support for the regime and the values it fostered. He was an important intermediary between *princeps* and poets, who lost contact after his death. His wife Terentia, eventually divorced, was Terentius Varro Murena's sister; apparently Maecenas, departing from his usual discretion, warned her of the detection of her brother's conspiracy (22). Thereafter his relations with Augustus, never openly impaired, seem to have been less close. He died in 8 BC.

maenads, women inspired to ritual frenzy (*mania*) by *Dionysus. Maenadic rituals took place in the mountains of Greece in mid-winter every other year. Having ceremonially left the city, maenads (probably upper-class women) would walk into the mountains crying 'to the mountains'. Here they removed their shoes, let their hair down, and pulled up their fawn-skins. After a sacrifice of cakes, they started their nightly dances (see DANCING) accompanied by *aulos* and *tympanon* (see MUSIC, 2 and 3). Stimulated by the high-pitched music, the flickering torches, the whirling dances, the shouting of *euhoi*, the headshaking, jumping, and running, the maenads eventually fell to the ground—the euphoric climax of their *ecstasy.

Maenadic ritual strongly stimulated the mythical imagination: the *Bacchae* of *Euripides shows us women who tear animals apart, handle *snakes, eat raw meat, and are invulnerable to iron and fire. Most likely, in Euripides' time maenads did not handle snakes or eat raw meat; however, their ecstasy may well have made them insensible to pain. Myth often exaggerates ritual, but the absence of contemporary non-literary sources makes it difficult to separate these two categories in *Bacchae*, where they are so tightly interwoven.

Maenadism was integrated into the city and should not be seen as a rebellion. It enabled women to leave their houses, to mingle with their 'sisters', and to have a good time. This social aspect, though, could be expressed only through the worship of Dionysus. To separate the social and religious aspect is not Greek. See WOMEN IN CULT.

Most likely, maenadism occurs in *Homer. In Athenian art it became popular on pots towards the end of the 6th cent. and again in the 4th cent. BC, with a selective interest expressed in the intervening period by painters of larger pots. Among the tragedians *Aeschylus pictured maenads in various lost plays, e.g. *Bassarids*, as did Euripides, esp. in *Bacchae*. Given these changing periods of interest in maenadism in literature and art, we should be wary of privileging *Bacchae* by ascribing to it a special influence on later maenadic ritual or by tying it too closely to contemporary new cults. The demise of maenadism started in the Hellenistic period and was complete by the 2nd cent. AD.

magi see MAGUS.

magic

1. **The concept** Antiquity does not provide clear-cut definitions of what was understood by magic, and there is a variety of terms referring to its different aspects. The Greek terms that lie at the root of the modern term 'magic',

magos, mageia, were ambivalent. Originally they referred to the rites of the Persian magi (see MAGUS) and their overtones were not necessarily negative. Soon, however, *magos* was associated with the doubtful practices of the Greek sorcerer and hence attracted the negative connotations of quack, fraud, and mercenary. Through *Aristotle, *Theophrastus, and Hellenistic authors this negative sense also affected the Latin terms *magus* etc. However, in late antiquity, esp. in *Greek Magical Papyri*, the term *magos* regained an authoritative meaning, somewhat like 'wizard', and was also embraced by philosophers and theurgists (see THEURGY). Since in these late texts prayer, magical formulae, and magical ritual freely intermingle, they challenge modern distinctions between magic and religion. However, definitions being indispensable, we here employ a broad description of the 'family resemblance' of magic: a manipulative strategy to influence the course of nature by supernatural ('occult') means. 'Supernatural means' involves an overlap with religion, 'manipulative (coercive or performative) strategy', as combined with the pursuit of concrete goals, refers rather to a difference from religion.

2. Sources Greek and Roman literature provides abundant examples of magical practice in both narrative and discursive texts. Myth affords many instances. Besides gods connected with magic (*Hermes and *Hecate), we hear of the Telchinēs, skilful but malignant smiths well versed in magic. Thracian *Orpheus was a famous magician, and so were *Musaeus, *Melampus, and others. But, as elsewhere, the female sex predominates. The most notorious witch was *Medea. *Thessaly boasted an old tradition of witchcraft, the Thessalian witches being notorious for their specialism of 'drawing down the moon'.

The earliest literary examples come from *Homer. Circe uses potions, salves, and a wand to perform magical tricks and teaches *Odysseus how to summon the ghosts from the Underworld. Folk magic glimmers through in a scene where an incantation stops the flow of blood from a wound. *Hesiod offers an aretalogy (see MIRACLES) of Hecate. Tragedy contributes magical scenes (e.g. the calling up of the ghost of *Darius I in Aeschylus' *Persians*) as well as whole plays (Euripides' *Medea*), while comedy ridicules magicians. *Theocritus' *Idyll* 2 ('Sorceress') became a model for many later witch scenes. Similarly, magical motifs in Greek epic tradition (e.g. Apollonius Rhodius' *Argonautica*

passim) were continued by Roman epic (e.g. Lucan's *Civil War*). Esp. informative is *Apuleius' *Metamorphoses*, which contains many a picturesque magical scene.

Another illuminating work by Apuleius belongs to the sphere of critical reflection. His *Apology* is a defence against the charge of magic and discusses various aspects of magic. Other discussions can be found in the satirical works of *Theophrastus (e.g. the 16th Character (*Deisidaimōn*)) and *Lucian. Although early philosophers were often associated with magical experiments, Greek philosophy generally rejected magic. *Plato wants the abuse of magic to be punished, and *Sceptics, Epicureans (see EPICURUS), and *Cynics never tired of contesting magic.

3. Objectives As to the intended effects, a rough distinction can be made between harmful 'black' magic and innocent or beneficial 'white' magic, although the boundaries cannot be sharply drawn. For the category of black magic curse-tablets are the most conspicuous evidence (see CURSES). Numerous other forms of black magic were widely applied and feared: incantations; the use of drugs and poison (Gk. *pharmakon* may refer to magic, poison, or medicine); the practice of 'sympathetic magic', e.g. the use of 'voodoo dolls' melted in fire or pierced with needles; and 'contagious magic', the destruction of the victim's hair, nails, part of his cloak, or other possessions as 'part for all', with the aim of harming the victim himself.

Some of these practices can function in 'white' magic as well. Its main objectives are protection against any kind of mishap, the attraction of material or non-material benefits, and the healing of illness. The first two are above all pursued by the use of *amulets, the last by the application of all sorts of medical material, often activated by charms and ritual (see 4 below); also by means of *purifications, exorcism, or divine healing.

Mixtures occur: love magic is generally pursued for the benefit of the lover, not for that of the beloved, who is sometimes bewitched in a very aggressive manner and by gruesome means. Other types of magic (e.g. prophecy) are more or less neutral, although uncanny aspects may render them suspect (e.g. the consultation of spirits of the dead).

4. Techniques Magic is based on secret knowledge of sources of power. The most important are (*a*) utterances, (*b*) material objects, and (*c*) performance.

(a) Utterances may consist of inarticulate sounds, cries, various types of noise (e.g. the use of bells), hissing, or whistling. More common are powerful words and formulae. One important category consists of strange, uncanny words not belonging to the Greek or Latin languages, whose (alleged) foreign origin and lack of normal communicable meaning were believed to enhance their magical power. Another category of effective words consists of Greek or Latin expressions in which the illness or the cure is compared with a model taken from myth or legend (esp. Homer, Virgil, the Bible) or nature. Stylistic and prosodic devices reinforce the formulae, as do other magical devices such as writing normal words from right to left or with foreign letters. A copious stock of magical formulae is provided by the *Greek Magical Papyri*, a collection of papyrus texts from Egypt that contain extended formulae with magical words and names of great gods and demons.

(b) Any object or material may have a magical force—iron, (precious) stones, pieces of wood, parts of animals, nails, hair, the blood of criminals. Most important are herbs and plants, where magic and folk medicine often coalesce in the wisdom of the root-cutter and herbalist (see PHARMACOLOGY).

(c) In the application of these objects and as independent magical acts, various performative actions play a part. The magical objects must be manipulated in a special way, various gestures are prescribed, etc.

These three technical aspects are often combined, strikingly so in the famous cure of a fracture in *Porcius Cato (1), On Agriculture*: a knife is brandished and two pieces of reed are brought together over the fracture while an untranslatable charm is sung.

5. Social setting The social and legal standing of magic is ambivalent. (Secret) wisdom and expertise in the application of supernatural means was indispensable and widely resorted to, hence highly valued. Many official 'religious' rites, esp. in Rome, contained 'magical' elements, which were accepted as long as they were publicly executed on behalf of the state. In the private sphere, however, magic's very secretiveness and association with asocial or even antisocial goals fostered suspicion and condemnation. Already in the 5th cent. BC, the author of *The Sacred Disease* made a clear distinction between religious and magical strategies and censured the latter. Plato (see 2 above) wanted the

abuse of magic to be penalized in his ideal state; the Romans, as early as 450 BC, actually did so in the *Twelve Tables. Under the first emperors many laws were issued to repress the growth of magical practices, and the 4th cent. AD saw a renaissance of anti-magical legislation. In this period, however, magic was practically identified with *prāva religiō* ('bad religion') and *superstitio* ('superstition'), which, together, served as conveniently comprehensive (and vague) classificatory terms to discredit social, political, and/ or religious opponents.

magister equitum, 'master of the horse', an emergency magistrate nominated by the *dictator. Apart from commanding the cavalry, he was the dictator's lieutenant and deputy, whether at Rome or on military service. He held *imperium* derived from the dictator and ranked with the praetors. His magistracy ended when his dictator laid down office.

magister libellorum ('master of petitions'), originally a *libellis* ('secretary for petitions'), an officer on the Roman emperor's staff whose duty was to deal with written petitions from private persons to the emperor and draft replies to them, known as rescripts. From *Hadrian onwards the office was entrusted to an *equestrian, and, since many petitions concerned points of law, the holder was often a lawyer, such as *Papinian or *Ulpian.

magistracy, Greek Magistracies (*archai*) in Greek states were the successors of the *kingships, which rarely survived into the Classical period. The powers of a hereditary king came to be divided between a plurality of magistrates, normally appointed for one year and often not eligible for reappointment. In addition to general offices of state, more specialized offices were sometimes created, e.g. to control a treasury or to supervise public works or the market. A small state could manage with few magistrates, but in a large one there might be many, and many duties might be given to boards rather than single individuals: Athens in the 5th cent. BC developed an esp. extensive range of offices— 700 internal and 700 external, acc. to the text of *Athenaion politeia*, though the second 700 is probably corrupt.

Magistrates tended to be more powerful, and to be appointed from a more restricted circle, in *oligarchies than in *democracies. Appointment by lot (see SORTITION) rather than by *election, to civilian posts which were not thought to require special ability, was esp. associated with democracy, but both that and a ban on reappointment to the same office can be found in oligarchies too. Athens and some other democratic states provided small salaries for magistrates (see DEMOCRACY, ATHENIAN, 2). One office might be regarded as the principal office in a state, but in general there was no hierarchy of offices and no *cursus honorum* (see CAREERS, GREEK). The citizens might control their magistrates through such procedures as *dokimasia* (vetting their qualifications before they entered office) and *euthynai* (examining their conduct after they left office), as well as by making them liable to prosecution for misconduct.

For an important further group of offices in the Greek city see LITURGY.

magistracy, Roman Magistrates at Rome may be divided between (*a*) the *ordināriī* (regularly elected), namely *consuls, *praetors, *censors, curule *aediles (these four offices were distinguished by privileges as 'curule', so called because they were entitled to use the official curule chair or *sella curūlis*), *quaestors, the *vigintisexvirate (vigintivirate under the empire), and (not formally magistrates of the whole people but only of the *plebs*) the *tribuni plebis* and aediles of the *plebs*, and (*b*) the *extraordinarii*, namely *interrex, city *prefect (altered by *Augustus), *dictator, *magister equitum, and a number of unique commissions (*tresviri rei publicae constituendae* (see TRIUMVIRI), etc.). More important is the distinction between those who possessed *imperium* (consuls, praetors, dictators, *magistri equitum*, and the *tresviri r. p. c.*) and those who did not (the rest). The competences and histories of the individual magistracies varied greatly and are treated separately. Most of them did, however, share certain features. They were elected (apart from the *interrex*, dictator, *magister equitum*, and city prefect). They were temporary: all the regular magistracies were annual, apart from the censorship. They were organized in colleges (usually of two, three, or ten members), and thereby subject to the *intercessio* (veto) of their colleagues; the dictatorship is the most significant exception, for which reason tenure of it was restricted to six months, until *Sulla and, *Caesar, whose dictatorship for life effectively re-created the *imperium* of the kings. They were unpaid: magistracy was regarded as an honour (*honōs* can be a synonym for *magistrātus*). The powers of magistrates with *imperium* were restricted over time, by the creation of the tribunate of the *plebs* and by the development

of *provocatio. But Roman magistrates, unlike Athenian, were never formally accountable to the people who elected them. Around the middle of the 2nd cent. BC it came to be felt that they ought to be. Magistrates and promagistrates (see PRO CONSULE, PRO PRAETORE) could be called to account, but this required special prosecutions which could be (and were) initiated by tribunes. Attempts formally to regulate the conduct, to enforce public scrutiny, and to facilitate public accountability of magistrates and promagistrates were made (chiefly by Gaius *Sempronius Gracchus and *Appuleius Saturninus), but this initiative foundered as the holders of high office dominant in (and, collectively, as) the senate defended their power and privilege, and as political principle gave way to internecine politics in the late republic.

Magna Graecia, the coastal region of *Italy colonized by the Greeks. Ancient sources use the term to refer to southern Italy—usually from *Cumae and *Tarentum southwards, and sometimes including Sicily. The colonies, founded between *c.*740 (Cumae) and 433 BC (Heraclea), prospered on the strength of fertile land and trade. In the 4th cent., pressure from the rapidly expanding Oscan peoples of Apennine Italy brought the Greeks into conflict with the Lucani and Bruttii. By the end of the Pyrrhic War (see PYRRHUS), the entire region was under Roman domination, and by 89 all surviving cities were Roman colonies or *municipia. The wars of the 4th–3rd cent. had undermined the prosperity of many cities, and some ceased to exist, but many were still viable. Neapolis, Cumae, Paestum, and Velia flourished, and Rhegium, Locri Epizephyrii, *Thurii, Croton, Heraclea, and Tarentum all maintained municipal status.

Magna Mater See CYBELE.

Magnesia, battle of The decisive battle of the war between Rome and the *Seleucid Antiochus III was fought near Magnesia by Mt. Sipylus in Lydia, in 189 BC. The nominal Roman commander was Cornelius Scipio Asiagenes, consul 190 (see also CORNELIUS SCIPIO AFRICANUS, PUBLIUS). After the scythe-chariots on Antiochus' left had been dispersed by *archers and *slingers, Rome's ally, *Eumenes II of Pergamum, led a massed cavalry charge which routed Antiochus' mailed cavalry, also on his left, and drove them into their centre. Meanwhile Antiochus had driven back the Roman left with his Iranian cavalry, but carried the pursuit too far.

His *phalanx, drawn up with gaps to accommodate his *elephants, resisted stubbornly until the elephants began to get out of hand, and Eumenes fell on its flank, whereupon it was annihilated.

magus/magi Only *Herodotus calls the Magi a Median tribe. In the pre-Hellenistic Greek tradition they are reciters of *theogonies, explainers of *dreams, royal educators and advisers. Magi are experts in the oral tradition rather than a class of priests, although they partake in sacrifices. In the *Persepolis administrative texts and in other *cuneiform documents magi often occur without a religious context. In the later Greek tradition the term often refers to specialists in exotic wisdom, astrology, and sorcery. See MAGIC; RELIGION, PERSIAN.

māiestās, (lit. 'greaterness'), used as an abbreviation for the crime *maiestas minūta populī Rōmānī*, 'the diminution of the majesty of the Roman people'. This charge was first introduced by *Appuleius Saturninus' *lex Appuleia*. He seems to have been provoked both by the incompetence and corruption of Roman generals in the wars against the Cimbri and Teutones and by the frustration of the will of popular assemblies through obstruction. However, the vagueness of the phrase made this a portmanteau charge, which could be deployed against any form of treason, revolt, or failure in public duty. Within a short time it virtually replaced charges of *perduellio ('treason') brought before an assembly. *Sulla's *lex Cornelia maiestatis* of 81 BC was an important part of his reorganization of the criminal law. It incorporated provisions restricting the conduct and movements of provincial governors. However, the law could still be applied to misbehaviour in a popular assembly. The *lex Iulia maiestatis* of *Caesar revised Sulla's law, incorporating *exile as the chief penalty. The scope of the existing law changed in the light of the existence of an emperor. Conspiracies against the emperor came naturally under the law, but its application was also gradually extended to cover *adultery with his daughter and then libel and slander (*Tiberius was initially reluctant to countenance such charges, but eventually they succeeded). The law was never redrafted to take precise account of these offences and, where conspiracy was concerned, *Domitian would say that an emperor's claim to have detected a conspiracy was not believed until he had been murdered. By Tiberius' reign prosecutions for *maiestas* might be brought before not only the *quaestio maiestatis* (see QUAESTIONES) but either the senate, sitting under the presidency of the emperor or consuls, or the emperor himself. Convicted persons were increasingly liable to the death penalty with no opportunity given to retire into exile; their property was confiscated for the imperial *fiscus* and their names were obliterated from public record (see DAMNATIO MEMORIAE). Since even the dead could be prosecuted, one could not be sure of escaping the last two consequences by killing oneself.

Information was laid and prosecutions brought by individuals (senators, where the senate was the court used). Certain men came to make a profession of this, being rewarded with at least a quarter of the accused man's property, if they secured conviction, and were labelled *dēlātōrēs*. Charges of *maiestas* were increasingly frequent under Tiberius and after AD 23 disfigured his reign. Many were made on apparently trivial grounds or as a complement to other charges, esp. *extortion and *adultery. One reason for this was that a charge of *maiestas* was held to warrant the hearing of a case in the senate, when it would otherwise have been heard in a *quaestio* under more rigid rules and with fewer opportunities for self-display by the accuser. Their political background from AD 23 to 31 was the growing power of *Sejanus at the expense of *Vipsania Agrippina (2), her sons, and friends; from 31 to 37 the determination of Sejanus' enemies to be avenged on his surviving friends. The hatred of one group for another was in the tradition of the late republic and the Civil War. Many of those convicted were guilty of something, but it usually fell short of an attempt to subvert the state.

There were convictions for *maiestas* under *Gaius (1) and *Claudius and in the latter half of *Nero's reign in contexts where an insecure emperor was being confronted with genuine conspiracies or threats to his position, even if not everyone convicted had acted treasonably. The condemnations under Domitian fall into the same pattern, but have a special importance for their impact on contemporaries, including *Tacitus, in whose work *maiestas* trials are a leitmotiv, and the later emperors *Nerva and *Trajan. They had the courage to follow the example of Titus and guarantee that they would not execute senators, so virtually suspending *maiestas* charges throughout their reigns. *Hadrian took a similar oath after executing some consulars for conspiracy but went back on it at the end of his reign. The *maiestas* law then remained dormant until it was revived by Marcus Aurelius after the conspiracy of Avidius Cassius, and later emperors found it indispensable.

malaria See DISEASE.

Mamertines ('sons of Mamers', the Oscan form of *Mars), a band of *Campanian *mercenaries who in 288 BC seized *Messana, whence they dominated and plundered NE Sicily. Their power was checked temporarily by *Pyrrhus and more seriously by *Hieron (2) II of Syracuse. Against the threat of Hieron they appealed in rapid succession to the Carthaginians, who installed a garrison, and to Rome. Roman acceptance of their appeal led to the ejection by the Mamertines of the Carthaginian garrison, to the dispatch to Messana of Appius Claudius Caudex, and ultimately to the First *Punic War.

mānēs See DEATH, ATTITUDES TO, ROMAN

Manetho (fl. 280 BC), Egyptian high priest at Heliopolis in the early Ptolemaic period, wrote a history of Egypt in three books from mythical times to 342. The human history was divided into 30 human dynasties (a 31st was added by a later hand) which still form the framework for ancient Egyptian chronology.

Mānīlius, Marcus, Stoic author (see STOICISM) of *Astronomica*, a *didactic astrological poem whose composition spans *Augustus' final years and *Tiberius' succession. *Astronomica* is no more a practical treatise than is Virgil's *Georgics*. Religious philosophy and political ideology are the driving forces. A blistering attack on *Lucretius' republican Epicurean poem underlies the poet's passionate Stoic hymns to the mystical order governing the multiplicity and diversity of creation. *Astrology allows Manilius to link heavenly macrocosm with earthly and human microcosm, and he claims the authority of a divinely inspired ascent to justify his vision. His *hexameters are fine and his poetic range unusual. Exploiting didactic's formal elements—prologue, 'digression', and epilogue—he reworks Lucretius' and Virgil's greatest excursuses and *Cicero's *Dream of Scipio*, but can also frame telling cameos of human foibles in comic and satiric vein, whilst his verbal point marks him as *Ovid's younger contemporary. Scaliger's view of Manilius, that he was as sweet as Ovid and more majestic, is returning to favour. See ASTROLOGY; CONSTELLATIONS.

manipulus (maniple), a tactical unit of a *legion; its adoption in the 4th century BC was associated with the introduction of the throwing spear (*pīlum*) which required a more open and manœuvrable formation. Legionaries were drawn up in three ranks, the first two each containing ten maniples of normally 120 men, the last, ten maniples of 60; light-armed troops were assigned in proportion. A maniple consisted of two centuries, each commanded by a centurion (see CENTURIO), the senior having overall responsibility. Intervals between maniples in battle formation were covered by the ranks behind, but were perhaps closed during advance. In the late 2nd cent. BC a larger tactical unit, the cohort (see COHORS), replaced the maniple.

Mantinēa, battles of The three battles of Mantinea (in eastern Arcadia), fought in 418, 362, and 207 BC, exemplify the main stages of Greek warfare. The first, fought between the *Spartans and a coalition mainly of Argives, Athenians (see ARGOS; ATHENS), and Mantineans, is the 'classic' *hoplite battle, with both sides edging to the right, as each man sought the protection of his right-hand neighbour's shield, with the result that each side won on its right, and only the discipline of the Spartans in not pursuing led to the rout of the allied right as it returned across the battlefield. The second battle, between the *Boeotians and their remaining allies, and a combination of Spartans, Mantineans, Elians (see ELIS), and Athenians, marks the transition between hoplite warfare and the more sophisticated warfare of integration of 'heavy' infantry with other troop types. Here the attack of the Theban *phalanx on the left was preceded by a charge of cavalry mingled with 'light' infantry trained to co-operate with cavalry. Finally, with the third battle, between Sparta and the *Achaean Confederacy, we are fully in the Hellenistic age, with both sides using all types of troops and weapons, including catapults (see ARTILLERY).

manubiae Roman military term, meaning that part of the *booty legitimately appropriated by an army commander as holder of *imperium*, and of which he was free to dispose as he wished without any legal restrictions. Custom rather than legal rule dictated the amount and type of booty defined as *manubiae*. The commander traditionally expended much of the proceeds of booty in distributions to his troops. Payments were also made to officers—legates, tribunes, quaestors, and even to relatives and friends of the commander, though usually to those who had taken part in the war. Commanders often used *manubiae* to celebrate their own name through the construction of public buildings and the provision of games and largess for the people. *Augustus suggested that distinguished commanders who had held a triumph could use their *manubiae* to help finance public road-projects. After 19 BC full *triumphs were no longer awarded to senators, and the custom of *manubiae* probably fell into disuse, all booty coming under the control of the emperor as commander-in-chief.

manumission of slaves See FREEDMEN, FREEDWOMEN; SLAVERY.

manus (lit. 'hand') was the power (akin to *patria potestas*) which a Roman husband might have over his wife. In early times it perhaps covered not only (as later) control of property, but the right, after due process, to execute. By entry into *manus* a woman was freed from any previous *paterfamilias* and entered the husband's family, coming under his control or that of his *paterfamilias*, merging her property in his, and gaining succession rights on intestacy equivalent to those of his children (see INHERITANCE, ROMAN). By the end of the republic, *manus* was evidently uncommon. See MARRIAGE LAW, ROMAN.

manuscripts See BOOKS, GREEK AND ROMAN; PALAEOGRAPHY; SCHOLARSHIP, ORIGINS OF MODERN CLASSICAL.

maps The *Ionian Greeks produced the first maps in the classical tradition (*Eratosthenes attributed the first map to *Anaximander); the one shown to *Cleomenes I of Sparta by *Aristagoras of Miletus is one such map: they fit into the context of new world-views that are also found in *Hecataeus and *Herodotus. These early maps were attempts to depict the wider order of the world. Distances on some land routes (such as the *Royal Road) and on *periploi were calculated. The place of maps in the geographical knowledge of *Alexander (2) the Great and his commanders is controversial.

The governmental purposes of the Ptolemies gave a new status to mapping in Alexandrian geography (see PTOLEMY (1); ALEXANDRIA). The greatest development of mapping in antiquity was associated with Roman imperial policy. The most complex known example of ancient surveying is the *Forma Urbis Romae, a plan of Rome on marble slabs which decorated a hall in the *templum Pacis complex at Rome and dates from the Severan period (the numerous fragments are a valuable source for the nature of the ancient city). A recently discovered fragment of perhaps Flavian date proves that there was an earlier version of neater draftsmanship and greater detail, with records of title to property as well as the names of public buildings.

It is likely that the ambitious plan of world surveying attributed to *Caesar was an attempt, and perhaps the first, to use geographical description as a sign of power. *Vipsanius Agrippa's world map, succeeding to Caesar's vision, in the Porticus Vipsania in Rome symbolized the control of space by the Augustan regime. It calibrated distances as well as representing the whole inhabited world.

Marathon, a large Attic *deme (see ATTICA) on the NE coast. Classical remains within the large fertile plain are extensive, and suggest that the Classical deme may have had several centres of habitation. Marathon and three neighbouring demes formed a religious confederacy known as the Tetrapolis, part of whose calendar is preserved in a 4th-cent. inscription. An early 5th-cent. inscription found here relates to the celebration of a festival of *Heracles. The plain was the scene of *Pisistratus' landing in c.545 as well as of the Persian landing in 490; see next article. The most famous demesman is *Claudius Atticus Herodes, traces of whose extensive estate can still be identified on the ground.

Marathon, battle of, fought at *Marathon in 490 BC, probably near the surviving mound covering the cremated remains of the Athenian dead. The Athenians and their allies from *Plataea had c.10,000 men, the Persians perhaps twice as many. After some delay, probably while the Greeks waited for the Spartans, the battle eventually took place before their arrival, probably because the Persians began to move on Athens. After lengthening their line by thinning their centre, the Greeks advanced, probably breaking into a run when within bowshot. Their stronger wings won easily and then perhaps turned inwards to envelop the victorious Persian centre as it returned from pursuing the broken Greek centre. The Greeks then pursued the Persian remnants to their ships, capturing seven. In all, 6,400 Persians were allegedly killed for only 192 Athenians. See PERSIAN WARS, various entries.

marble included granites, porphyries, and all stones capable of taking a high polish. The fine white marbles of Greece and the Greek islands were widely used for architecture and sculpture from the 7th cent. BC onwards. Grey Naxian and white Parian, the best of the island marbles, were used for both sculpture and architecture. The Pentelic quarries to the NE of Athens, still visible, supplied a fine-grained marble for the *Parthenon and other 5th-cent. buildings in the city and its territory. In Asia Minor, the white marble quarries at *Ephesus were exploited from the 6th cent.; other white marble quarries were opened in the Hellenistic period, e.g. at *Aphrodisias and Heraclea by Mt. Latmus. It was not until the 2nd cent. BC that quarries of coloured marble were exploited. In Italy the famous quarries at Luna (*Carrara) were not exploited on a large scale by the Romans until the mid-1st cent. BC. *Augustus employed marble extensively, esp. Luna and coloured marbles from the Aegean and North Africa, in his building programmes at Rome. From the time of *Hadrian marble was transported in large quantities to the cities of the empire, spreading architectural and decorative styles. A wide variety of coloured marbles was employed. Columns were often monolithic to exploit the veining in the stones. Apart from architectural decoration marble was also used for veneer and paving. For statuary the Romans used Luna marble, most of the Greek marbles, and some coloured marbles for specific subjects. Many of the major sources of supply were administered directly by the emperor through imperial representatives, or by contractors. The emperor apparently exercised a tight control over the quarrying, use, and distribution of certain stones, e.g. the granite and porphyry quarries in Egypt.

Marcellus, Claudius See CLAUDIUS MARCELLUS.

Marcius Coriolānus, Gnaeus, a Roman aristocrat who supposedly received his *cognōmen* from his part in the Roman capture of Corioli from the *Volsci (493 BC). Acc. to the story, he went into exile when charged with tyrannical conduct and opposing the distribution of corn to the starving *plebs*. Welcomed by the Volscians of Antium he became their leader in a war against Rome. In two devastating campaigns he captured a series of Latin towns and led his forces to the gates of Rome, where he was persuaded to turn back by his mother Veturia and his wife Volumnia. He was then killed by the

Volscians. It is uncertain how much, if any, of this story is based on fact.

Marcius Turbo, Quintus, from Dalmatia, is first recorded as *centurion in *legion II Adiutrix and rose through the primipilate, becoming tribune in the *vigiles* and urban cohorts at Rome, and commander of the imperial horse guard, then procurator of Ludus Magnus (see LUDI) and prefect of the fleet based at Misenum under *Trajan, the latter post taking him to the Parthian War, by which time he was already one of *Hadrian's friends. In AD 116 he was given the first of several special missions, to suppress the Jewish revolts in Egypt and Cyrenaica (see JEWS); soon after Hadrian's accession the next year he was sent to deal with an uprising in Mauretania. Next he had a special command in Pannonia (Lower) and *Dacia, with a rank equivalent to prefect of Egypt. In 119 he became praetorian *prefect and held this post for many years, although ultimately incurring Hadrian's dislike.

Marcus Aurēlius See AURELIUS, MARCUS.

Mardonius, nephew and son-in-law of *Darius I of Persia, took over command in Ionia *c.*492 BC, immediately after the *Ionian Revolt, and removed one major cause of discontent by abolishing government through tyrants (see TYRANNY) and permitting *democracies. He then restored Persian authority in southern Thrace, despite storm damage to his fleet off Mt. Athos. Herodotus makes him the moving spirit of Xerxes' invasion. Left in command in Greece after the battle of *Salamis, he vainly attempted to detach Athens from the Hellenic League by offers of favourable terms. Withdrawing from Attica in 479 in face of the Greek land-forces, he gave battle (perhaps reluctantly) near Plataea and was defeated and killed (see PERSIAN WARS).

maritime loans were a distinct category of *credit throughout antiquity. To pay for a cargo, a merchant or shipowner borrowed money for the duration of the voyage. Loan and interest were repaid out of proceeds of sale of the cargo only on condition that the ship returned safely; loss was otherwise borne by the lender. High risks justified high interest. As a guarantee against fraud, cargo and even the ship itself would be offered as security. Lenders tended to be those with experience of sea-trading. The importance of maritime loans in Athens' trade is indicated by their forming the substance of forensic speeches.

Marius, Gāius, b. *c*.157 BC near Arpinum, of a family probably of recent *equestrian standing, but with good Roman connections, including *Cornelius Scipio Aemilianus. He served with distinction under Scipio at *Numantia and, with his commendation, won a military tribunate by election. Quaestor *c*.123, he was helped to a tribunate by the Metelli (119), but fiercely attacked the consul Caecilius Metellus Delmaticus when he opposed Marius' law ensuring secrecy of individual votes in the *comitia*. Because of this breach of *fidēs* (loyalty) he failed to gain an aedileship, but became urban *praetor 115, barely securing acquittal on a charge of *ambitus*. Sent to Further Spain as proconsul, he showed aptitude at guerrilla warfare and added to his fortune. On his return he married a patrician Iulia, a distinguished match. In 109 Caecilius Metellus Numidicus, sent to fight a guerrilla war against *Jugurtha, chose Marius as his senior *legate. But when Marius requested leave to seek a consulship, Metellus haughtily rebuffed him. Marius now intrigued against Metellus among his equestrian and Italian friends in Africa and Rome and won election for 107 by playing on suspicions of the aristocracy. He superseded Metellus in *Numidia by special legislation. He ended the manpower shortage by the radical step of abolishing the property qualification for service and enrolled a volunteer army. After fighting for two years without decisive success, he captured Jugurtha through the diplomatic skill of his quaestor *Sulla, was elected consul for the second time for 104 by special dispensation, to deal with a threatened German invasion, and triumphed on 1 January.

He found an army reorganized and trained by *Rutilius Rufus (his fellow legate under Metellus and his enemy) as consul 105; and, re-elected consul year after year, with friendly colleagues, Marius improved the army's equipment and organization (see ARMIES, ROMAN) and defeated the Teutones at Aquae Sextiae and, with Lutatius Catulus, the *Cimbri at Vercellae, in 102 and 101 respectively, consenting to celebrate a joint triumph with Catulus. His immense prestige attracted nobles like Catulus into his following and confirmed the loyalty of *equestrians and *plebs*. He was elected to a sixth consulship (100), defeating Metellus' quixotic candidacy.

The tribune *Appuleius Saturninus had provided land for his African veterans in 103, and in 100 undertook to do so for the veterans of the German war. Marius gladly accepted his cooperation and was pleased when Metellus' intransigence in opposition led to his exile. But when Saturninus, with the help of Servilius Glaucia, threatened to achieve independent power, Marius turned against them, rejected Glaucia's consular candidacy, and, when they tried to force through a law overruling him, 'saved the republic' by forcibly suppressing them. But his stubborn opposition to Metellus' return alienated his optimate (see OPTIMATES) supporters. When the vote for Metellus' recall passed, he left for the east, 'to fulfil a vow', abandoning hope of a censorship. His firm words to *Mithradates VI earned him election to an augurate in absence and, with his *dignitās* restored, he returned. But he had frittered away his overwhelming stature. Some of his friends and clients were now attacked, and although he successfully defended them, his noble friends deserted him. When the senate openly expressed support for Sulla by allowing Bocchus I to dedicate on the Capitol a group showing Jugurtha's surrender, Marius was prevented from violent opposition only by the outbreak of the *Social War. In the war he was successful on the northern front, but when not offered supreme command, chose to retire.

With war against Mithradates imminent, Marius hoped for the command. He found an ally in *Sulpicius Rufus, tribune 88, in return for supporting his policies. When the optimates chose Sulla for the consulship and command (he married Caecilia Metella, widow of *Aemilius Scaurus), Sulpicius had the *plebs* transfer the command to Marius. Sulla responded by seizing Rome with his army. Marius, unprepared for this, had to flee. Having made arrangements that he hoped would last, Sulla left for the east. After the expulsion of *Cornelius Cinna from Rome, Marius returned and joined him with an army collected from his veterans. He sacked Ostia and organized Cinna's capture of Rome. Both were proclaimed consuls for 86 and Marius was to supersede Sulla in the east. He now took terrible vengeance on his enemies, esp. on faithless former friends; but his health gave out and he died before taking up his command.

A typical *novus homo*, Marius wanted to beat the nobles at their own game and win acceptance as a leader of their state. Unlike some aristocrats, from Gaius *Sempronius Gracchus to *Caesar, he had no plans for reform. Although favouring rewards for soldiers without distinction between citizens and Italians, he opposed *Livius Drusus' attempt to enfranchise the Italians and left it to Saturninus to look after his veterans' interests. His reform of enlistment accidentally created the client army: it was

Sulla who taught him the consequences. However, his early career first demonstrated the power inhering in an alliance of a successful commander with a demagogue and a noble following; and his opponents, in their attitude to him and to Sulla, revealed the lack of cohesion and of political principle besetting the *nobiles*.

Mark Antony See ANTONIUS, MARCUS.

markets

Greece The arrival of the market as an institution in the 8th cent. BC (see EMPORION; TRADE, GREEK), gradually replacing archaic mechanisms of exchange (see GIFT, GREECE), along with the concomitant beginnings of urbanization, prompted the *polis* to develop marketing arrangements. The installation of permanent retail-markets in urban centres, signalled in the shift in the meaning of *agora* from 'assembly (place of)' to 'market', is best followed at *Athens, where built shops are attested by c.500 BC and the first public edifice for commercial purposes by 391, although temporary booths and tables still typified the bazaar-area in the 4th cent.; colonnaded markets are a 3rd-cent. development. Elsewhere, as in the 'new town' at *Olynthus, private houses could act as retail outlets. The *polis* controlled the urban market through *agoranomoi* and drew revenues from taxing retailers; but it had no larger interest in intervention beyond seeking to assure (for essentially political reasons) an adequate *corn supply.

Although urban markets chiefly served an urban populace, additional periodic market-days, attested monthly at Classical Athens, point to their use by peasant farmers; in the 3rd cent. BC one Attic village (*Sunium, perhaps exceptional) had its own built market.

Rome The Forum was originally a market-site, the word surviving in this sense in the specialized markets of Rome (e.g. *forum Boarium), although by the 1st cent. BC *macellum* was the usual term for an alimentary market. A daily retail market existed in Rome by 210 and later was joined by others; wholesaling took place at the riverine Emporium, built in 193. The state supervised Rome's markets through *aediles.

marriage ceremonies

Greek Ceremonies were not identical all over Greece. For example, at Sparta they included a mock abduction. But they were shaped by largely similar perceptions about the ceremony and the deities concerned with it. Thus, *Artemis was concerned with the girl's transition to womanhood, *Hera, especially as Hera Teleia ('the Fulfiller'), with the institution of marriage, *Aphrodite with its erotic aspect. The evidence is more plentiful for Athens, where it includes images on vases, some of which (e.g. the *loutrophoroi*) were actually used in the wedding ceremony. What follows is centred on Athens. But the main elements were common to all; thus, the form of the preliminary *sacrifices and offerings may have varied from place to place, but such sacrifices and offerings were made everywhere. After a ritual bath, in water carried in *loutrophoroi* from a particular spring or river, in Athens Callirhoë, the bride and groom were dressed and (esp. the bride) adorned. Then the feast took place at the house of the bride's father, during which (almost certainly) there took place also the rite of the bride's unveiling in front of the groom, followed by gifts to the bride by the groom. Probably also during the feast, a boy with mother and father still living, carried a winnowing-basket full of bread and said, 'I escaped the bad, I found the better.' After the feast, in the evening, there was a procession from the bride's house to that of the groom, an important part of the ceremony, and a favourite image on black-figure vases. The couple went on foot or in a carriage or cart, accompanied by the groom's best friend. The bride's mother carried torches; the procession included the bride's attendants, musicians, and others who shouted congratulations to the couple. The bride was incorporated in her husband's house through the same rite as that by which newly acquired slaves were received into the house: when she first entered the house, she was led to the hearth (see HESTIA) where nuts, figs, and other dried fruit and sweetmeats were showered over her and the bridegroom. They then went to the bridal chamber where the marriage was consummated while their friends sang *epithalamia* outside. On the day after they were sent gifts. See also MARRIAGE LAW, GREEK.

Roman The favourite season was June. Usually on the previous day the bride put away her *toga praetexta*—she had come of age. Her dress and appearance were ritually prescribed: her hair was arranged in six locks, with woollen fillets, her dress was a straight white woven tunic fastened at the waist with a 'knot of Hercules', her veil was a great flame-coloured headscarf and her shoes were of the same colour. Friends and clients of both families gathered in the bride's father's house: the bridegroom arrived, words of consent were spoken, and the matron of honour performed the ceremony of linking bride's and bridegroom's right hands. This was followed by a *sacrifice (generally of a pig), and (in imperial times) the marriage contract (involving dowry) was signed. Then the guests raised the cry of *Felīciter!* ('Good Luck!'). There followed the wedding feast, usually at the expense of the bridegroom. The most important part of the ceremony then took place: the bride was escorted in procession to the bridegroom's house, closely accompanied by three young boys, whither the bridegroom had already gone to welcome her. The bridegroom carried her over the threshold to avert an ill-omened stumble; in the house she touched fire and water, was taken to the bedchamber and undressed by women who had known only one husband, and the bridegroom was admitted. Meanwhile an *epithalamium* might be sung. This is a generalized account of an upper-class wedding as it appears in literature. There could be many variations of detail, and there could be different forms of marriage (see MARRIAGE LAW, *Roman*).

marriage law

Greek Marriage in Greece was a process of transfer, by which the *kȳrios* ('controller') of a woman (normally her father; if he had died, her nearest adult male relative) gave her away to another man for the procreation of children. Originally this was merely a private arrangement between the two men; but, because the procreation of children affected inheritance of property and membership of the community, cities made laws regulating marriage in order to define legitimacy for those purposes.

In Athens a marriage was legal only if it began with *engyē* (see BETROTHAL, *Greek*), a formal statement by the *kyrios* granting the woman to a husband. (A woman with no father or brother living could be awarded to a husband by the archon, see ARCHONTES.) The woman's own consent was not legally required. She could not be married to a direct ascendant or descendant, nor to her brother or half-brother by the same mother, but marriage to a half-brother by the same father or to an uncle or cousin was permitted. From 451/0 BC marriage between an Athenian and a foreigner was forbidden (see CITIZENSHIP, GREEK). Bigamy was not allowed; a man could have a concubine as well as a wife, but the concubine's children were not legitim-

ate. A man could divorce his wife by sending her back to her father, who could then give her in marriage to a second husband.

Marriage was often accompanied by gifts of property or money: in Homeric times usually by gifts from the husband to the father, in Classical Athens by a dowry given by the father to support the wife and her future children. But these were customary, not legal requirements.

See also BETROTHAL; ENDOGAMY; INCEST; INHERITANCE, GREEK.

Roman Traditional expressions enshrine the view that a man took a wife for the procreation of children. No formalities were legally necessary for the inception of a marriage: the usual ceremonies had social and sometimes religious significance. All that was legally necessary was for a man and woman to live together with the intention of forming a lasting union (*affectiō maritālis*, the reciprocal attitude of regarding each other as husband or wife). The initial consent was given by both partners; if one (or both) was in (i.e. under) paternal power (see PATRIA POTESTAS), that of the respective fathers was needed. The social consequences of marriage followed. Wedding ceremonies, esp. the transfer of the bride to the husband's house (for the upper classes a procession) normally attested this intention (see MARRIAGE CEREMONIES, *Roman*). Moreover, the intention was necessary not merely at the beginning of a marriage, but throughout: hence if the intention ceased, the marriage was in principle at an end (see below). Roman marriage was essentially monogamous, for a man could have only one wife at a time for the purpose of breeding legitimate children, and intended to be lasting (provided that *affectio maritalis* persisted). But although the virtue and good fortune of a woman who in her lifetime had only one husband was valued, remarriage was acceptable and sometimes necessary.

Marriage in the ancient world was a matter of personal law, and therefore a full Roman marriage could exist only if both parties were Roman citizens or had *conubium* (right to contract marriage), either by grant to a group (e.g. Latins) or individually. Only such a marriage could place the children in the father's power and create rights of succession. Further, parties might have this general *conubium* but still lack *conubium* with each other. Impediments varied: (1) Age. Although consent, not consummation, made a marriage, the partners had to be physically capable. The minimum age became fixed at 12 for women and (apparently) 14, puberty, or both for men. (2) Relationship, by blood, adoption, or marriage, within certain degrees. (3) Disparate rank. The Augustan marriage laws of 18 BC and AD 9 prohibited marriage between senators (and their immediate descendants) and freed slaves. (4) Considerations of morals or public policy. *Augustus similarly prohibited marriage between free-born citizens and members of disreputable professions (see INFAMIA), or with a convicted adulteress. Serving soldiers (below a certain rank) were forbidden to marry until *Septimius Severus); later, to avoid undue influence, provincial officials were forbidden to marry women of the province during their term, and guardians (see GUARDIANSHIP, Rome) to marry their wards. Marriage was usually preceded by a formal *betrothal. Later, it became informal (though marked by celebration) and could be broken without legal penalty. But betrothal created relationships and moral obligations similar to those of marriage.

Except when accompanied by *manus (when all the wife's property became the husband's and she was under his control), marriage made no difference to the status or property rights of the wife. She remained either in the paternal power of her father or legally independent, with ownership of her property. Ideally, the separation of property of husband and wife was maintained. Dowry, on the other hand, was property transferred to the husband for the duration of the marriage, for the maintenance of the wife. Dowry was not legally necessary, but it was a moral duty to endow a woman so that she might make an eligible marriage. In early law, whoever gave the dowry could stipulate for its return at the end of the marriage; later, there developed a suit for return of dowry after divorce.

Marriage was ended by the withdrawal of *affectio maritalis* by one or both partners. No public authority had to give permission; even receipt of formal notice was not legally necessary, although in practice a husband or wife would usually inform the partner orally or in writing or by messenger and one would leave the marital home and recover personal property, and arrangements would be made about return of dowry. Augustus introduced documented notification, probably only when the husband needed evidence that he had divorced an adulteress. The husband normally kept any children. If the wife was in *manus*, formalities were necessary to free her. Divorce was by the husband or his *paterfamilias* in early times, but by the last century BC could also be decided by the wife (or her *paterfamilias*: the father's powers were gradually

curbed). The upper class of the late republic and early Principate exploited the possibility with relative freedom (despite inconvenient economic consequences, possible emotional suffering, e.g. because young children would stay under the father's control, and some public disapproval unless the motives were acceptable, e.g. for *adultery).

Mars (Māvors, Oscan **Māmers),** next to *Jupiter the chief Italian god. Months were named after him at Rome (*Martius*) and elsewhere. At Rome his festivals fell in March and October. Before starting a war the general shook the sacred spears of Mars in the *Regia, saying 'Mars vigila' (Wake up, Mars!); it is probable that they were the original embodiments of the god. His priest is the *flamen Martialis* (see FLAMINES) and his sacred animals the wolf and woodpecker (see BIRDS, SACRED). He is a war-god, equated with *Ares. Mars is a war- and warrior-god, who exercised his wild function in various contexts, e.g. by his presence on the border of a city, a territory, a field, or a group of citizens. This border-line was materialized, before an action or a period of time, by a *lustration, i.e. a circumambulation of three victims—a boar, a ram, a bull (*suovetaurilia*)—which were then sacrificed. His mythology is almost entirely borrowed from Ares. Under *Augustus he obtained an important new title, Ultor, 'Avenger', in recognition of the victory over *Caesar's assassins.

Marsyas, a silenus or *satyr. He invented the *aulos* ('double-oboe') or found it, cast aside by *Athena because playing it distorted her face, and challenged *Apollo on his *kithara* ('lyre') to a competition. He lost and, suspended from a tree, was flayed alive by Apollo. The moment when Marsyas spots the abandoned *aulos* was captured in a much-copied bronze statue-group by *Myron, and *Zeuxis painted a 'Marsyas Bound'. Vases from the later 5th cent. on depict the contest and the punishment.

Martial (Marcus Valerius Martiālis), Roman poet, (*c*. AD 40–*c*. 102), b. in Spain, came to Rome *c*.64. In Rome he was supported by *Seneca the Younger, then the most celebrated Spaniard in the city. He must have been well known to have been able in 80 to celebrate with a book of epigrams an important public event, the opening games for the new Flavian amphitheatre (see COLOSSEUM). This was probably when *Titus gave him the *ius trium liberorum*, an honour later confirmed by *Domitian, whose favour he assiduously courted. After another two collections with particular purposes, in 86 he began publishing the series of twelve books of varied epigrams which are his main claim to fame. They reveal a network of patronage and friendship involving a large cross-section of Roman upper-class society. He was also in contact with many distinguished writers: *Quintilian, *Pliny the Younger, *Silius Italicus, *Frontinus, *Juvenal. Martial became popular. His success gave him a central role in the literary scene and made it increasingly natural that his epigrams should be used to celebrate official events connected with imperial propaganda. Martial complains that this success did not bring him financial reward: without any copyright in his works, he depended on patrons (*see* PATRONAGE, LITERARY, *Roman*). He represents himself, doubtless with much exaggeration, as just another *cliens* forced to wander about the streets of Rome in search of tiny recompense for the humiliating attentions that had to be paid to his patrons. For a long time he rented a house like others of moderate means (see HOUSES, ITALIAN), but he had a property at Nomentum, and from 94 at least he also had a house in Rome: he had a number of slaves, and an honorary tribunate gave him *equestrian rank. After the death of Domitian he repudiated his earlier adulation and turned to Nerva and later Trajan. Both his personal position and his poetry had, however, been too closely involved with the court of Domitian, and in the new regime Martial must have felt less at home. Tired of city life and, as ever, nostalgic for the idealized 'natural' life in Spain that he had always set against the falsity and conventionality of Rome, he decided to return there in 98. Pliny helped him with the expenses of the journey, and even in Spain he depended on the generosity of friends, esp. a widow, Marcella, who gave him a house and farm, which finally enabled him to realize his dream of rural peace. Metropolitan life was, however, the source of his poetry, and in bk. 12, composed in Spain, he expresses with a new bitterness his sense of emptiness at the loss of the cultural and social stimuli that had made him a poet in the first place.

Works A Book of Epigrams described the games for the opening of the Colosseum: we have an incomplete selection of c.30 poems from the original volume.

Xenia and Apophoreta (now books 13 and 14), published between 83 and 85. They claim to be collections of mottos, each of a single elegiac couplet (see ELEGIAC POETRY, LATIN), and designed to accompany gifts at the Saturnalia (see SATURNUS).

Twelve Books of Epigrams (c.1,175 poems).

Martial's work does sometimes include *epigrams of the usual Greek type: epitaphs for friends and patrons, dedications celebrating both private and public events, and poems on contemporary or historical events, unusual happenings, or recoveries from illness. In these cases the traditional conventions are easily recognized, though the treatment may be original. In general, however, Martial's epigrams are very different. His main model was *Catullus, not as a love-poet but as a writer who had brought full literary dignity to the minor poetry of autobiography and comic realism. He takes from Catullus many formal elements, esp. his metres. Catullus had created a *genre of minor poetry which joined the influence of Greek *epigram, *iambic, and *lyric traditions to the Roman tradition of satirical verse full of personal and political polemic. Martial also had important models in late Hellenistic Greek epigram, which had already developed the tendency towards a clever final 'point', which marks much of his work.

Martial's growing success with his readers encouraged the conviction that this type of minor poetry (which he always termed 'epigram'), corresponded to a real need which the grander and more official genres could not satisfy. It was not a question of formal elegance or emotional intensity—the characteristics that had led *Callimachus (2) and Catullus to affirm the greater dignity of the shorter forms—but of a need for realism, for a closer link between the pages of the text and everyday life. The epigram, able to treat incisively every aspect of life, could better satisfy this need than the more distant and conventional genres, which continued to produce variations on the same old mythological themes. Most typical of Martial, and the reason for his success, is the humorous realistic epigram on contemporary characters and behaviour which moves from witty entertainment to a sharp picture of Roman society, revealing its multiple absurdities through the mirror of the gestures and behaviour of the various social classes. Both as a Spaniard born in a province which still retained a sense of rural life unspoilt, and as an intellectual in a world where poets were valued less highly than he thought their due, Martial observes Rome from the outside. His belief that his chosen poetic form, considered the lowest of all genres, might have more validity than the great works promoted by official culture, and his picture of Roman society together give Martial's work a strongly anti-establishment tone, which was well received by the general public, and eventually even by the higher classes and the court, albeit with a certain nervousness. The epigrams which Martial as a 'professional' poet offered to his patrons as a noble and cultured ornament of their lives give us an esp. concrete and direct representation of Roman high society, with its houses, parks, possessions, and rituals. The many epigrams devoted to Titus and esp. to Domitian are a fundamental document for the history of the imperial cult under the Flavians (see RULER-CULT). The first-person of the comic or satirical poems is a device to enliven the many social observations so that they seem to have been born from one man's experience, but there is also a more autobiographical 'I', the personality of a restless and unsatisfied poet who is proud of his accomplishments but disappointed in society and convinced that he could have achieved more in other circumstances.

Martial's work is extremely varied, and offers both realism and fantasy, subtlety and extravagance. One rarely feels that a poem has been written solely for piquant entertainment. His poetic language is influenced not only by Catullus but also by *Horace, and above all by *Ovid; it has a mastery of expression which knows how to preserve the appearance of nature even when artifice is most obvious. His realistic epigrams, while maintaining a high literary quality, open themselves to a lower and cruder language, including obscenity: in this area Martial is one of the boldest Roman poets, and, in general, many everyday objects and acts, and the words that describe them, enter Latin poetry for the first time with Martial. See also EPIGRAM, LATIN; DEDICATIONS, LITERARY, LATIN.

Masada is a small isolated plateau on the western shore of the Dead Sea, and accessible from there only by the tortuous 'snake path'. *Herod (1), having secured his family in its Hasmonean fortress during the Parthian invasion of 40 BC, later made it the most spectacular of his own fortress residences, with two ornate palaces, one built onto the northern rock terraces. Archaeology supplements *Josephus' detailed description of the architecture, revealing also a garrison-block, baths, storage rooms for quantities of food and weapons, cisterns, a surrounding casemate wall, and (probably) a synagogue. After the murder of their leader in Jerusalem early in the First Jewish Revolt, Jewish rebels occupied Masada; and it was the last fortress to hold out after the fall of *Jerusalem, succumbing in AD 73 or 74 to a six-month siege by Flavius Silva (see JEWS). The eight Roman *camps and circumvallation are visible, as well as the earth ramp which supported a platform for artillery. Josephus' graphic account of the mass suicide of the 960 defenders, with their leader, Eleazar ben Yair, after the breaching of the wall, supposedly based on the testimony of two women survivors, has aroused scepticism. But the remains of the revolutionaries' years of occupation of the site are at any rate extensive. These include domestic and personal objects, as well as Greek papyri and biblical texts of the Qumran type.

Masinissa, king of *Numidia (238–148 BC). After many adventures, he joined *Cornelius Scipio Africanus, when he landed in Africa in 204, and commanded the Numidian cavalry on Scipio's right at *Zama (202). His recognition as king by Scipio was confirmed by the senate; and the terms of the subsequent peace gave him virtual *carte blanche* in his dealings with Carthage. By loyally supporting Rome in her wars in Spain, Macedonia, and Greece, he usually enjoyed her support. His continuous aggression eventually led to Carthage's resorting to war against him, contrary to her treaty with Rome, and though Masinissa was victorious—or perhaps because he was—war with Rome became inevitable, Masinissa living to see its outbreak, though not its end.

Tough, brave, and ruthless, Masinissa was a skilled commander, esp. of cavalry, and a wily statesman. He was one of the very few Mediterranean potentates to grasp the overwhelming power of Rome and, caught up in a struggle between two great powers, he managed to emerge with his own territory enlarged. Although there are signs that even the Romans were becoming exasperated by, if not wary of, his ambitions, he managed to die in his bed, at the age of 90, and to bequeath his kingdom to his sons.

masks were used in Greece and Rome in cult and in dramatic representations. Masks were often worn in the cult of *Dionysus, and some ritual action centred on masks of Dionysus himself. The frightening gaze of the *Gorgon is mask-like. In Roman religion *imagines, ancestral masks, were displayed in the atrium of a noble family and worn by the living at funerals (along with the mask of the newly deceased).

Greek drama probably inherited the mask from Dionysiac ritual, but there are obvious dramaturgical advantages in the use of masks, esp. where the audience is (as often in ancient theatres) at some distance from the action. We have depictions of theatrical masks from the 5th cent. BC onwards, and a classification of them by Iulius Pollux, written in the 2nd cent. AD but based on earlier Alexandrian scholarship. Many terracotta representations of theatrical masks have been found on the island of Lipari. Masks were used in all the major dramatic genres. A common material was linen, and they generally covered the whole head. The masks of tragedy (naturalistic in the Classical period) and New Comedy mostly represented types rather than individuals (see TRAGEDY, GREEK; COMEDY (GREEK), NEW).

Massalia (**Massilia** in Roman writers) was founded *c*.600 BC by settlers from *Phocaea. Though preceded in the area by Rhodian and other traders, the Massaliotes eventually dominated the coast from Nicaea in the east to Emporiae in Spain. Massaliote venturing beyond the straits of Gibraltar is reflected in an anonymous 6th-cent. *periplous* (see PERIPLOI) and in the works of *Pytheas and Euthymenes, who explored the west African coast. In Gaul and eastern Spain the Greek presence had profound effects. Trade up the Rhône (Rhodanus), esp. in the 6th cent., contributed to the evolution of the culture of the *Celts, while among the *Ligurian and Iberian tribes of the coast all excavated hill-forts have yielded quantities of imported pottery and many show Greek influence in their fortifications, architecture, and art. The introduction of the vine (see WINE) and the *olive completed the picture of 'Gaul transformed into Greece'. Massalia's relations with Greece were maintained with a treasury at *Delphi. Renowned for the stability of its own aristocratic constitution, it was not involved in wars with other Greek cities, but victories over the Carthaginians are recorded in the 6th and 5th cents. Massalia early enjoyed Rome's *amicitia, which later developed into formal alliance; Massaliote ships helped Rome in the Second *Punic War. In 125 constant aggression by the Salluvii prompted an appeal to Rome, which led ultimately to the formation of the 'Province' (later Narbonensis; see GAUL (TRANSALPINE)). Having supported Pompey, the city was taken by *Caesar in 49, and lost most of its territory to Arelate. Massalia thereafter declined commercially, but retained a high reputation for Greek culture and learning (*Iulius Agricola was educated there).

Massilia See MASSALIA.

mathematics We know little about the origins and early development of mathematics among the Greeks. In *Babylon(ia) an advanced mathematics had existed since at least the time of Hammurabi (d. 1750 BC). Characteristic of this were problems in arithmetic and algebra, but many facts of elementary geometry were known, e.g. 'Pythagoras' theorem' and the mensuration formulae for a variety of plane and solid figures. It is probable that much of this knowledge reached the Greek world at some time, but it is difficult to say what came when, esp. as independent discovery can rarely be excluded. Greek tradition ascribed the invention of geometry to the Egyptians, whence it was made known to the Greeks in the 6th cent. BC by *Thales in Ionia or *Pythagoras in *Magna Graecia. However, there was little to learn from Egypt beyond elementary mensuration formulae, and since neither Thales nor Pythagoras left writings, there could be no foundation for the tradition. The most that can be said is that it is probable that 5th-cent. 'Pythagoreans' such as *Philolaus discussed the properties of numbers in the semi-mystical way imitated by *Speusippus in the 4th cent.

The first hard evidence we have concerns the mathematical activity of Hippocrates of Chios at Athens in the late 5th cent. While investigating the problem of squaring the circle (already considered a typical mathematical problem), he produced some ingenious theorems on the quadrature of lunes. The *content* of these is reasonably certain, but not our knowledge of the *form*. However, these theorems exhibit the concept of proof, the greatest single contribution and the most characteristic feature of Greek mathematics. There must have been a geometrical tradition before Hippocrates; but how old, and of what kind, we cannot say. It is possible that the arguments of *Zeno (1) of Elea in the mid-5th cent., showing that infinite division involved self-contradiction, were in part directed against contemporary mathematical procedures. It is certain that the logical difficulties he raised influenced the later course of Greek mathematics in its care to avoid infinitesimals. That this was a difficulty in the early stages is shown by *Democritus asking whether the two contiguous faces of a cone cut by a plane parallel to the base are equal or unequal.

Another difficulty was the existence of irrationals, specifically the incommensurability of the diagonal of a square with its side. Both arise only when one deals with continuous magnitudes (geometry), not with discrete (arithmetic in the Greek sense). Perhaps this explains the statement of *Archytas in the early 4th cent. that arithmetic can provide proofs where geometry fails. But these logical difficulties did not inhibit the practice of geometry, as is shown by Archytas' own ingenious solution to the problem of finding two mean proportionals (which Hippocrates had already shown to be equivalent to the problem of doubling the cube), and by the work of his contemporary Theaetetus, who made significant discoveries about irrationals and the five regular solids.

The difficulties were solved, or at least circumvented, by *Eudoxus, *c.*360. He formulated a general theory of proportion including both commensurable and incommensurable magnitudes, and also invented the method of approach to the limit which became the standard Greek way of dealing with problems involving infinitesimals. *Euclid's formulation of this is found in bk. 10, prop. 1: 'If from the greater of (any) two unequal magnitudes more than its half is subtracted, and from the remainder more than its half, and so on, there will (eventually) be left a magnitude less than the smaller of the original two.' *Archimedes quotes another formulation: 'The amount by which the greater of two unequal areas exceeds the smaller can, by being added continuously to itself, be made to exceed any given finite area.' He says that 'the earlier geometers' used this to prove among other things that pyramid and cone are one-third of prism and cylinder respectively with equal base and height. Since he tells us elsewhere that Eudoxus was the first to prove these theorems (although Democritus had stated them), the second formulation is probably that of Eudoxus. We may guess that Eudoxus, with his interest in logical rigour, was also chiefly responsible for the thorough axiomatization of geometry as we find it in Euclid. The great interest and progress in strict deductive logic during the 4th cent. is best seen in the logical works of *Aristotle, who also provides valuable evidence for the form of contemporary geometry.

We know many names of mathematicians active in the 4th cent., but few details of what they did. With the *Elements* of Euclid we come to the first extant mathematical treatise. This, though an introductory textbook, reflects the sophistication of contemporary geometry in both form

and content, but the axiomatic method of exposition necessarily obscures the historical development. A particular problem is raised by the propositions concerning the 'application of areas'—6. 28 gives a general solution, of which a particular case can be derived from 2. 5: 'To a given straight line (*b*) to apply a rectangle which shall be equal to a given area (*A*), and fall short of the rectangle formed by the straight line and one of its own sides by a square figure.' In algebraic terms this is $xy = A$, $x + y = b$ (in other words the quadratic equation $bx - x^2 = A$ is to be solved). This is exactly what one would arrive at if one were to transform the 'normal forms' of Babylonian numerical problems involving a quadratic equation into geometrical terms, and it is likely that this 'algebraic geometry' is just such a transformation. If so, some knowledge of advanced Babylonian mathematics had reached Greece by the 4th cent. (the same is true of Babylonian astronomy). As well as plane and solid geometry, the *Elements* included number theory, which (like other contemporary branches of mathematics) had not attained the same level of systematization as pure geometry. However, some remarkable results were reached, such as the proof that there is no limit to the number of primes.

In the case of conics this deficiency was supplied by *Apollonius (2), who transformed the approach to the field by extending the 'application of areas' to include it in a *tour de force* of generalization. A generation before him Archimedes had created new branches of mathematics by applying the axiomatic approach to statics and hydrostatics, but systematization was not his main interest. Most of his surviving work is in higher geometry, where he proves by traditional methods many theorems which are now proved by integral calculus. But his *Method* shows that he arrived at many of these results by using infinitesimals. This is only one of the ways in which his thought was so far ahead of its time that it had no effect in antiquity: thus the profound concept of a numerical system implicit in the *Sand-reckoner* has no echo in surviving literature. However, many of his results, such as the formula for the volume of a sphere and his approximation to π, became mathematical commonplaces.

The 3rd cent. was the great period of pure geometry, represented not only in the work of Apollonius and Archimedes, but also in that of a number of other mathematicians whose achievements can be judged from references by Pappus and others, although their works are lost. After this, most creative mathematics was done in other fields. Several of these were connected with *astronomy.

It is in later Greek mathematics that we find the non-axiomatic, numerical and algebraic techniques which are typical of Babylonian mathematics. But it is accidental that the first extant examples occur as late as the work of Heron, c. AD 60, for we cannot doubt that they are directly descended from Babylonian sources in a continuous tradition. A different branch of the same tradition is found in *Diophantus' Arithmetica. This is the Greek work which comes nearest to the modern conception of algebra, although it is not a textbook on the solution of equations, but rather groups of problems, mostly of indeterminate equations. Though the roots of this lie in Babylon, much of the content is probably original, and the form of exposition owes much to the Greek tradition.

In late antiquity, although there were still mathematicians competent to edit, excerpt, and comment on the classical works, mathematics had become sterile, so that the value of these authors lies in what they preserve from earlier periods. It was only after transmission to the Islamic world (translations into Arabic began in the 9th cent.) that the ancient mathematical tradition was revived and enlarged. This happened again, even more fruitfully, in 16th-cent. Europe, after the recovery of the Greek texts.

Mausoleum at Halicarnassus One of the *Seven Wonders of the ancient world, it was the tomb of the satrap *Mausolus of Caria. Begun shortly after 367, when Mausolus refounded *Halicarnassus, it was finished after his wife Artemisia died in 351, and is perhaps best interpreted as his hero-shrine (see HERO-CULT) as city-*founder. Its architect was Pythius of Priene; *Vitruvius records that he and Mausolus' court sculptor wrote a book on the building, and he and *Pliny the Elder note that four other sculptors, including Scopas, joined them. Pliny also outlines the building's form, reports that Scopas and his colleagues each took one side of it, and adds that Pythius made the chariot-group that crowned it. It stood until the 15th cent., when the Knights of Rhodes quarried it for their castle.

Excavation has supplemented and corrected the ancient accounts. The building consisted of a high podium, a colonnade of 36 Ionic columns, and a truncated pyramid of 24 steps. With the crowning chariot-group, it reached a total height of 42.7 m. (140 ft.). The tomb-chamber was encased in the podium, and sacrificial remains suggest the existence of a hero-cult. The podium's steps carried quantities of freestanding sculpture (hunts, battles, audience scenes, sacrifices, and portraits), and was crowned by an *Amazon frieze; portraits stood between the columns; coffer-reliefs embellished the peristyle's ceiling; lions ringed the cornice; and the base for the chariot carried a *Centaur frieze.

Mausōlus, son of Hecatomnus. Ruler of *Caria 377–353 BC, in conjunction with his sister and wife Artemisia, and a diffuser of *Hellenism in 4th-cent. Asia Minor, who nevertheless promoted or retained the local Carian element. (He made dedications in Greek, but only at culturally mixed sanctuaries.) Greek artists worked on his *Mausoleum, but it has some non-Greek features.

He ruled under Persian auspices (see PERSIA), and used the title *satrap in inscriptions. He moved his capital from Mylasa to *Halicarnassus in the 370s, perhaps announcing thereby an interest in Aegean politics. His area of direct control was large and his sphere of influence larger. He annexed *Rhodes, *Chios, and *Cos in the 350s.

Maxentius, Marcus Aurēlius Valerius (b. c. AD 283), son of *Maximian, was passed over when Diocletian and Maximian abdicated and *Galerius and *Constantius I succeeded as Augusti (305). On Constantius's death Flavius Valerius Severus became Augustus, but the *praetorian guard proclaimed Maxentius as princeps (306). In 307 he took the title Augustus and reconferred this on his father, calling him from retirement to assist him. Severus failed to suppress Maxentius, who had him executed; Galerius invaded Italy but failed against Maxentius, who now controlled all Italy and Africa. Maximian secured an alliance with Constantine in Gaul by giving him the title Augustus and his daughter Fausta in marriage. In 308 Maximian quarrelled with his son, failed to depose him, and fled to Constantine; at Carnuntum Galerius declared Maxentius a public enemy. A revolt in Africa was defeated by Maxentius's praetorian *prefect; famine at Rome was averted. Maximian's renewed attempt to become Augustus (310) caused Constantine to sever his alliance with the family and (312) invade Italy. He marched on Rome and defeated Maxentius' forces (said to have been four times as numerous) at Saxa Rubra; Maxentius was drowned near the Mulvian bridge.

Maximian Born *c.* AD 250, the son of shop-keepers, he rose through the ranks of the army. An excellent general, he was called by his old comrade-in-arms *Diocletian to assist him as his Caesar (285), with responsibility for Italy, Africa, Spain, Gaul, and Britain. Victorious in Gaul, he was promoted Augustus (286; see AUGUSTUS, AUGUSTA, AS TITLES). Against Carausius he was less successful: an expedition by sea failed, and the usurper was able to hold Britain and part of Gaul for some years, while Maximian was heavily engaged on the Rhine. He acted in close accord with Diocletian, to whom he remained utterly loyal.

In 293, under Diocletian's tetrarchic system (see TETRARCHY), he received Constantius I, as his Caesar. In 296 he came to guard the Rhine while Constantius recovered Britain from Allectus, who had killed Carausius. After fighting in Spain in autumn 296, Maximian crossed to Africa to deal with Mauretanian tribes; *c.*299 he entered Rome in triumph, and there he began the building of the baths of Diocletian. Late in 303 Diocletian joined him in Rome to celebrate a joint triumph and the twentieth anniversary of his reign.

When Diocletian abdicated on 1 May 305, Maximian, at Milan, reluctantly did likewise, but his son Maxentius, proclaimed emperor at Rome (306), named his father Augustus for the second time and called him from retirement. In spring 307, assisting his son, Maximian forced Flavius Valerius Severus to abdicate at Ravenna; then, to secure for Maxentius an alliance with *Constantine I against *Galerius, he went to Gaul and gave Constantine the title Augustus and his daughter Fausta in marriage. In April 308 Maximian failed to depose his son, with whom he had quarrelled, and fled to Constantine who sheltered him. Forced to abdicate again at the conference of Carnuntum, Maximian could not settle down to honourable inactivity. In revolt against Constantine he assumed the purple for the third time, but was quickly captured at Massilia (see MASSALIA) and killed himself (310). Proclaimed *Divus* by Maxentius and the senate, his memory was damned (see DAMNATIO MEMORIAE) by Constantine; after the Mulvian bridge (312) his widow swore that Maxentius had not been his son, and he was rehabilitated.

meals Among the Greeks the times and names of meals varied over time. In early times breakfast was taken shortly after sunrise, followed by a main meal (*deipnon*) at midday and supper in the evening. In Classical Athens two meals—a light lunch and dinner (*deipnon*) in the evening—appear to have been usual. From the 4th cent. BC onwards an earlier breakfast was again added, or substituted for lunch. For what was eaten, see FOOD AND DRINK.

Among the Romans dinner (*cēna*) was eaten in the middle of the day in early times, with a light supper in the evening. Eventually an evening *cena*, often beginning in the late afternoon, became usual. Lunch, consisting of fish or eggs and vegetables together with wine, was eaten towards midday. The day began with a very light breakfast, which might consist of only bread and salt. Cheese and fruit were sometimes added.

The *cena*, the biggest meal of the day, was eaten after the day's work was finished. It consisted of three parts. The hors d'œuvre, of eggs, shellfish, dormice, and *olives, with honeyed wine, was followed by the *cena* proper, comprising up to seven courses, with one chief item. This might be a whole roasted pig, accompanied by smaller, but substantial courses (e.g. lampreys, turbot, roast veal). The meal ended with dessert, consisting of snails, nuts, shellfish, and fruit. [Apicius] *On Cookery* (4th cent. AD) describes the meals of the rich, to whom most of our information relates. The appearance of ostriches, peacocks, cranes, etc. on the tables of the rich was largely due to the search for novelty. For peasant fare see e.g. Horace *Satires*. 2.6.63 f.

See COOKERY.

meals, sacred, either as part of a religious festival or functioning as religious festivals. The notion that a divinity is a participant in the meal with mortals distinguishes these meals from those in which acts of devotion are part of the standard ritual of dining.

The notion that a divinity could share in a meal with mortals was common to many cultures in the ancient Mediterranean and near east. In some cases, invitations would be issued in the name of the divinity, e.g. 'Sarapis invites you to dine at his temple'; in other cases the invitation would be issued by a priest. *Homer may illustrate the ideology of these events when he says that the gods could be seen eating with the Phaeacians. In all such cases, a god would participate with humans at a sacrificial banquet. The underlying principle was that the divinity shared the sacrificial food with those who had offered the sacrifice. Under such circumstances a specific portion of the sacrificial meal that was thought to be appropriate to the divinity in question was set aside, burned, or otherwise disposed of. A place might be set at the table for the divinity, and the divinity was the titular master of the banquet: thus numerous references in the sources to such items as 'the table of *Zeus', the 'couch of Sarapis', or 'the meal of the gods'.

The concept of the 'sacred meal' was important in classical polytheism since it represented the direct involvement of the divinities in the life of a community and generated numerous associations of worshippers who celebrated their own meals with divinities for their own benefit, in addition to those meals held in conjunction with state cults. It is also symbolic of the essential connection between group dining and the concept of community in the ancient world. See DINING-ROOMS; LECTISTERNIUM; SACRIFICE, GREEK and ROMAN; SANCTUARIES; THEOXENIA.

measures

1. Measures of Length Greek measures of length were based on parts of the human body, with the foot as unit both for fractions like finger and palm and for multiples like pace and arm-span. In Classical Greece many standard feet are found, the absolute values for which are derived from surviving stadia (preserved with starting and finishing lines). The later Greek unit, the *stadion* (see STADIUM), originally the distance covered by a single draught by the plough, contained 600 of such 'standard' feet.

The Roman foot of 296 mm. ($11^2/_3$ in.) was generally divided into 12 inches. For longer distances:

5 feet = 1 (double) pace
1,000 paces = 1 Roman mile
($1,480$ m.: $1,618^1/_2$ yds.).

2. Measures of Area Measures of area in both Greece and Rome were based on the amount ploughed in a day by a yoke of oxen. The Greek unit is the *plethron*, measuring $100 \times 100 = 10,000$ square 'Greek' feet. The Romans employed the a square of 120 feet, two of which formed the *iūgerum* of 28,800 square Roman feet.

3. Measures of Capacity Greek measures of capacity fall into two divisions, dry and wet, corresponding to the primary products, corn and wine, of ancient agriculture. In historic Greece the *kotylē* is basic to both dry and wet. Its absolute value in various local systems ranges from 210 ml. to more than 330 ml. ($7^2/_5$–$11^3/_5$ fl.

oz.). The basic unit in the Roman system is the *sextarius* (546 ml.: $19^1/_5$ fl. oz.), which is equivalent to two Greek *kotylai*.

See also WEIGHTS.

mechanics, specifically the description and explanation of the operations of machines (*mēchanai*); the ancient discipline embraces physical, geometric, and practical aspects. The earliest systematic effort to account for mechanical phenomena, the *Peripatetic Mechanica, adopts as its paradigm the lever, turning on the principle that weights are moved more easily as the distance of the moving force from the fulcrum increases. In his mechanical writings *Archimedes takes an alternative approach based on the principle of static equilibrium, as exemplified by the balance: that equilibrium holds when the weights are inversely proportional to their distances from the point of suspension. So in his efforts in statics and hydrostatics Archimedes introduces the conception of the centre of gravity, the point at which one can locate a body's entire contribution to a configuration of weights. In a more practical genre, treatises on machines were compiled by *Ctesibius, Philon, *Vitruvius, Heron, and others. Such of these works as survive include accounts of a wide range of machines, including water- and steam-powered devices, automata, ballistic engines and their deployment in sieges, and so on. The art of the ancient *mēchanikos* apparently combined enquiries into the theory and design of devices with meticulous concern over details of their manufacture and operation.

Mēdēa, in mythology, granddaughter of *Helios, and daughter of Aeētēs, king of Aia. She became the archetypal example of the scheming, *barbarian woman. In *Hesiod's *Theogony*, she is associated with the completion of *Jason (1)'s challenges in Aia in his quest for the Golden Fleece, and leaves Aia with him to live in Iolcus, but her mastery of salves and potions, a skill she shares with her aunt Circe, is not mentioned. This passage appears in a catalogue of goddesses who slept with mortal men, and Medea was clearly conceived as immortal. In one Archaic legend she married *Achilles in the Elysian Fields (see ELYSIUM) after the hero's death. In the best known account, that of *Pindar, and *Apollonius (1) Rhodius, *Argonautica*, Jason gains the Golden Fleece because Medea is made to fall in love with him and supplies him with a salve to protect him in the tasks Aeetes sets him; she then charms the dragon which guarded the fleece so that Jason can steal it. Acc. to some, Medea protected the *Argonauts from the pursuing Colchians by killing her baby brother, Apsyrtus, and scattering his limbs. Apollonius, however, makes Apsyrtus a young man, and Medea plots his murder by Jason on an Adriatic island. On their return to Iolcus, Medea rejuvenated Jason's aged father, Aeson; she then punished *Pelias by persuading his daughters to cut him up and boil him so that he too could be rejuvenated. After this, Jason and Medea fled to *Corinth, the setting of *Euripides' *Medea*, which, more than any other text, influenced later traditions about and iconographic representations of Medea. If Euripides did not actually invent Medea's deliberate killing of Jason's new bride and her own sons to punish Jason for abandoning her, he certainly gave it fixed form; in earlier tradition Medea had sought to make her children immortal, and in the historical period they were the object of cult in Corinth. Her association with that city, attested in a complex variety of stories, goes back at least to the early Archaic period.

Medea fled from Corinth to Athens in a chariot of the Sun; there she took shelter with King *Aegeus. When Aegeus' son, *Theseus, came to Athens from Troezen, Medea recognized him and sought to remove a threat to her position by attempting to poison him or having him sent to fight the bull of *Marathon, or both.

Medea in art Medea first appears on an *Etruscan vase of *c.*630 BC showing the cauldron of rejuvenation, with which she tricks the daughters of Pelias on Attic vases from a century later. The slaughter of the children appears mainly on southern Italian vases. From the later 5th cent., Medea usually wears eastern garb and carries potions.

medicine

1. Introductory Survey (a) Western literature begins with a *disease; in Homer's *Iliad* bk. 1 *Apollo sends a plague on the Greeks camped before Troy to avenge Chryses' treatment at the hands of *Agamemnon (see CHRYSEIS). No attempt is made to treat the plague; the activity of doctors in the Homeric epics is mostly limited to the treatment of wounds and injuries sustained in combat.

Greek opinion of those who treated diseases was divided. In Middle and New *Comedy mad doctors speak with strange, Doric accents (the accents of *Cos and *Cnidus). The first Greek doctor supposedly to arrive in Rome was nicknamed *carnifex* or 'butcher'. On the other hand, Homer had allowed that 'a doctor is worth many other men'. Medicine was never a profession in our sense. The pluralism of ancient medicine is striking. An increasing amount of archaeological evidence from Roman sites—medical instruments, *votives from temples, prescription stamps, wall-paintings, and so on—goes some way towards closing the gap between the archaeological and literary study of ancient medicine.

(b) Most of the literary evidence for early medical practice and theory is preserved either in the *Hippocratic writings or by *Galen, but there is much besides in early literary texts, esp. the Homeric epics. From earliest times, therapies might involve incantation (see MAGIC, 2), or the use of analgesic drugs, or the magical herb *mōly* to defend *Odysseus against *Circe's witchcraft, down to the use of *amulets and charms by the so-called 'purifiers' (see PURIFICATION) and 'mages' (see MAGUS). Medical treatment and advice was also supplied by drug-sellers, 'root-cutters', *midwives, athletic trainers, and surgeons. Anyone could offer medical services, and the early literary evidence for medical practice shows doctors working hard to distinguish their own ideas and treatments from those of their competitors.

(c) Various authorities, both ancient and modern (starting with *Herodotus) have sought links with Egypt to explain the origins of certain medical practices, esp. surgery, in the Greek world. Others have sought links with the near east, and esp. with Babylonian medicine although these have proved hard to establish. Some argue that the Hellenistic doctors working in *Alexandria were influenced by Egyptian traditional medicine. In the 5th cent. BC, when *Herodotus told the story of Darius' Greek physician, *Democedes, the really surprising feature of his career—apart from its conspicuous success—was Democedes' technical superiority over the Egyptian doctors.

(d) Medical practitioners often took their skills from town to town. *Thucydides (2)'s account of the *plague at Athens provides one of our few non-medical accounts of reaction to a great public crisis; he has little to say, however, about the doctors who treated the plague beyond the important observation that they were often the first to succumb. Herodotus is aware of the practice followed by various Greek states of hiring public physicians—he notes that Democedes held such a position at *Aegina. Just how public these public physicians were is unknown.

(e) The Hippocratic Oath is probably aimed at a specific, and perhaps rather small, group of doctors—in it, the doctor swears by Apollo, by Health (Hygieia), and Panacea to revere his teacher and his teacher's family, and never to administer poison, use the knife, abuse his patients, or breach their confidences. The Oath could be as much a sign of medical anarchy, as of a coherent acceptance of general standards. Anyone could practise; some were ex-slaves but many were free-born. In Rome, where traditional Italian medicine competed with foreign imports, many doctors were Greek. Sometimes training might take the form of an apprenticeship to another doctor, attendance at medical lectures, or even at public anatomical demonstrations.

(f) In the 1st cent. AD, *Cornelius Celsus reiterated the traditional division of medical therapy into *dietetics, *pharmacology, and surgery. The use of exercise and the regulation of one's way of life was traditionally associated with the training of athletes. Some dietetic lore is preserved in *cookery books. Surgery too, was employed from earliest times. The drug lore contained in bk. 9 of *Theophrastus' *Inquiry into Plants* gives a good idea of the persistence of certain beliefs about the magical powers of drugs and herbs, but Theophrastus also preserves much information new and old about the real powers of medicinal plants. This is equally true of the much later *Materials of Medicine* of *Dioscorides. See BOTANY; PHARMACOLOGY.

2. Temple Medicine Shrines and temples to *Asclepius formed one important focus for religious medicine. Most of the detailed evidence we have for temple medicine comes from later writers and inscriptions; and it is uncertain when Asclepius, rather than his father Apollo, began to become the object of veneration. That the practice of temple medicine was widespread in the 5th and 4th cents., however, seems clear from the extended parody in Ar. *Plut.* The most important temple was at *Epidaurus. Many inscriptions from here detail the advice that the faithful received from the god as they slept in the temple precincts—the practice of incubation. All manner of problems were solved here—monuments erected by grateful patients record cures for lameness, baldness, infestations with worms, blindness, aphasia, and snakebite.

Throughout antiquity the medical, magical, and religious seem to have coexisted. In Greek and Roman *sanctuaries, many stone and *terracotta votives survive—models of affected parts of the body which the god was able to cure. Important later accounts of experiences of temple medicine are preserved in the *Sacred Teachings* of Aelius *Aristides, and the importance of *dreams is shown by the *Oniro-critica* of *Artemidorus. In many cases, it seems, diagnoses of physicians could be rejected in favour of those acquired through dreams.

3. Early Medical Theory Certain Presocratic philosophers had well-attested interests in medical theory; most important was *Empedocles, a version of whose four-element theory was applied to the basic fluid constituents in the body. It is mirrored in a dominant strain of Hippocratic humoral pathology, as well as in the physiological theories of *Plato (see HUMOURS). An early statement of the idea that health can be ascribed to some kind of balance in the body (the political undertone is significant) is attributed to *Alcmaeon (2), who is also credited (controversially) with some of the first anatomical work based on dissection. Nearly all ancient doctors ascribed disease to an imbalance of some kind or other, and Plato's pathological theory in *Timaeus* similarly ascribes certain conditions to 'surfeit' or 'lack'.

4. Hippocratic Medicine (a) The large and heterogeneous corpus of writings which bears the name of *Hippocrates forms the core of our literary evidence for early Greek medicine. It was always agreed, even in antiquity, that the writings were not all by one person.

(b) The contents of the Hippocratic corpus had apparently stabilized by the time of *Hadrian, when Artemidorus Capito put together a canon of Hippocratic works. (Galen still felt the need to write a treatise (now lost) entitled *The Genuine Hippocratic Treatises*.) Several ancient authorities divided the writings into five categories.

(i) Semiotic works
'A doctor should pay much attention to prognosis.' The ability to interpret the signs (sēmata) presented by the patient and the patient's circumstances is regarded as an essential skill throughout the corpus. Hippocratic *diagnosis had to be based on careful study of a wide range of phenomena, from the general—age, climate, sex, way of life—to the very specific. There is much relevant material, esp. on charting the likely course of incurable diseases, in the case histories of the *Epidemics*.

(ii) Physiology
Hippocratic doctors were committed to the idea that the phenomena of health and disease are

explicable in the same way as other natural phenomena. Many treatises, notably *On the Nature of Man*, *Regimen*, *On Fleshes*, *On the Sacred Disease*, and *On Breaths* offer answers to the basic questions that most divided ancient doctors—how is the body constructed? how is it generated? what makes it prey to disease? what is disease? and so on. Whilst concepts of balance and morbid imbalance underly many pathological theories, the nature of the balance and the elements implicated in it could be explained in many ways. For the author of *On the Nature of Man*, the balance was one of fluids or 'juices' in the body (see HUMOURS). In this treatise, the humours are blood, yellow bile, black bile, and phlegm, and they are linked to the four *elements, earth, air, fire, and water, the four qualities associated with the elements (hot, cold, dry, moist), and the four seasons. This is not the only humoral pathological system in the Hippocratic corpus—but its later adoption and adaptation by Galen ensured its subsequent association with 'true' Hippocratic doctrine. The debate about the extent to which the search for causes can be narrowed down continued throughout antiquity. Theoretical disagreements apart, the names and symptoms of the major diseases were broadly accepted by Hippocratic doctors. Diseases tended to be named after the affected part, or the seat of the most significant symptoms; so pneumonia (lung), pleurisy (sides), hepatitis (liver), arthritis (joint), and so on; this was the case even for those doctors who either took a whole-body view of all disease, or denied altogether that diseases exist as specific entities.

(iii) Therapeutic works

Hippocratic therapy took many forms: treatises like *On Ancient Medicine* and *Airs, Waters, Places* stress the historical and practical debt of medicine to dietetics. The applications of dietetics were not confined to the sick; 'precepts of health' showed the way to the prevention of disease. Yet the drug-based treatment of disease is also an important strand in Hippocratic therapy. Pharmaceutical therapies and tests (e.g. for pregnancy or fertility) are esp. characteristic of the gynaecological treatises. Much ingenuity was expended in devising drugs to promote and test for conception—*On Barren Women* provides many examples. Explanations of why these treatments work tell us much about ancient speculative views on the internal structure of the female body (see GYNAECOLOGY). Surgery and invasive physical manipulation were also widely used, although the status of surgery was problematic because of the dangers involved. Several treatises deal with methods of reducing dislocations, bandaging, excision of haemorrhoids, treatment of cranial trauma, surgical removal of the dead foetus, and so on.

(iv) 'Mixed' works

'Mixed' works include practical compendia of material dealt with under the other headings. The seven books of *Epidemics* fell into this category, as did the highly influential and pithy summaries of Hippocratic practice contained in the *Aphorisms*.

(v) The art of medicine

Authors of many of the theoretical works in the corpus take care to describe their own methods. They often distinguish their enterprises from those of philosophers on one side, and alternative healers on the other. The constant concern with establishing the status of medicine as a *technē*, an art, gives us some idea how tenuous this status could be. In addition to these studies, a number of works deal with the problem of how the doctor should behave with his patients and in his dealings with society generally.

5. From the Hippocratics to Galen (a) The dominating figure of Galen eclipsed many of his predecessors, and very little Hellenistic medical writing survives intact. None the less, recent work on Hellenistic and Graeco-Roman medicine has brought to light much new material and goes some way towards recovering c.500 years of lost medical research. After the conquests of *Alexander (2) the Great, medicine like so much else spread east to the great new centres of learning and research in the Aegean, Egypt, and Asia Minor. Aristotle's pioneering work on scientific method, psychology, and zoology proved central to much post-Hippocratic medical research. Aristotle's famous exhortations to anatomical research found particular resonances in Alexandria, where Herophilus and Erasistratus made extraordinary progress in anatomy and physiology. It seems likely that they practised human *vivisection, using condemned criminals as subjects. Herophilus found the Greek language unequal to the task of describing his discoveries, and he is credited with a series of anatomical coinages, several of which remain in use today.

(b) The literary evidence for later Hellenistic medicine documents the rise of sectarian groups of doctors who espoused different approaches to medicine. The debate over how medicine should be studied, which can be discerned in much

Hippocratic writing, became far more vigorous. The so-called 'Empiricists', who espoused a medicine in which theory and speculation about diseases had no place, determined treatments on the basis of earlier experience of similar conditions, research into other doctors' experience, and, in special cases, a kind of analogical inference which justified thinking that what works for a complaint afflicting one part of the body may well work on a similar affection in another part. These doctors saw themselves as quite apart from so-called rationalist or dogmatic physicians who were committed to the value of theory. This latter group was never strictly a sect—adherents of medical theories hardly make up a coherent group—and often the term 'dogmatic' is used disparagingly.

One sect which named itself after its method became esp. successful in Rome. 'Methodism' was based on the idea that the whole of the diseased body (and not just the affected part) presents one of two morbid, phenomenally evident states, one called 'stricture', the other 'flux'. The appropriate treatment followed directly on the correct identification of the general state of the whole body. The most famous Methodist physician was *Soranus of Ephesus.

(c) Sectarian orthodoxy was rare, and much theoretical and practical variation can be found in all the groupings. Moreover, not all doctors were sectarian; evidence from inscriptions points to the existence of many independent medical practitioners who are likely to have been largely innocent of the theoretical debates going on elsewhere.

6. Galen dominates later Greek medicine. He is our main source for post-Hippocratic medicine, and the modern appreciation of Hippocratic medicine owes much to his version of Hippocratic doctrine. A daunting amount of his work survives—nearly three million words in Greek alone—and much remains to be edited and translated to modern standards. He wrote several guides to his own works. Surprisingly perhaps, he stresses before anything else the importance of what he calls 'demonstrative knowledge' in all medical work. He advises those embarking on medical studies to examine the methodological weakness of the medical sectarians, who lack, he claims, the logical equipment necessary to tell truth from fiction. (Galen's claim to possess the means to real knowledge needs to be treated with caution, but his logical skill is indeed considerable.) He then recommends an introductory study of anat-

omy and basic physiology. Of his own works which survive, he recommends that anatomy should begin with *On Pulses for Beginners*, and *On Bones for Beginners*, culminating in the great teleological analysis of the human body, *On the Usefulness of the Parts*. Important evidence for the nature of Galen's debt to the Hippocratics, Plato, Aristotle, and the Stoics is presented in *On the Doctrines of Hippocrates and Plato*, in which Galen investigates in very general terms the 'physical and psychical faculties of the body'. *On the Natural Faculties* presents Galen's reaction to the physiology of his Hellenistic predecessors.

Galen's physiological theory is based on a four-humour system which closely resembles the theory of the Hippocratic treatise *On the Nature of Man*. The application of the theory to the behaviour of drugs is dealt with in a series of extensive pharmacological treatises which draw together drug lore and theory from a variety of earlier sources. See also separate entry GALEN.

See also DIAGNOSIS; DIETETICS; DISEASE; GYNAECOLOGY; HUMOURS; PHARMACOLOGY; VIVISECTION.

Medism/Medizing (the 'med-' root is a linguistic fossil from the time of *Cyrus (1)'s conquest of Lydia: Ionian Greeks apparently perceived him as king of the Medes, perhaps because his mother was a Mede) was, usually, the offence of states or individuals (most famously, *Pausanias (1) and *Themistocles) that voluntarily collaborated with Persia in connection with invasions of mainland Greece; see PERSIAN WARS. The motive was commonly fear of attack or hatred of Greek rivals. See also HELLENISM; ORIENTALISM.

Mediterranean The Mediterranean sea united the classical world. From the Archaic period it was regarded as a unity (and distinct from the encircling ocean). *Caesar called it *marĕ nostrum* ('our sea').

Medusa See GORGON.

Megaclēs, son of Alcmaeon, of the family of the *Alcmaeonids at Athens. He was the successful suitor of Agaristē, daughter of *Cleisthenes (1), tyrant of Sicyon (perhaps 575 BC). Later he appears as factional leader of the *Paralioi* ('Shoremen'), in opposition to the *Pedieis* ('Plainsmen') led by Lycurgus, and the *Hyperakrioi* ('Uplanders') led by *Pisistratus. *Paralioi* perhaps refers to the SE promontory of *Attica where Alcmaeonid estates may have lain. When Pisistratus first seized power (*c*.560), Megacles joined with Lycurgus to expel him, but then helped him to a second period of tyranny on condition that Pisistratus married his daughter. This led to a further quarrel, and Pisistratus again retired before a combination of the other two factions (*c*.556). Nothing further is recorded of Megacles. He was father of *Cleisthenes (2) and of Hippocrates, father-in-law of *Xanthippus, and grandfather of *Pericles.

Megara, city between *Athens and *Corinth. It had only difficult access through mountains to the Corinthian Gulf, at Aegosthena and Pagae; its best territory, the plain near the city, was close to Nisaea, the Saronic Gulf port. Two important routes led through Megarian territory from *Peloponnese to central Greece: the Saronic Gulf coast road to *Eleusis, and the western route to *Boeotia. Megara suffered throughout her history from her more powerful neighbours but an independent Megara founded colonies after the mid-8th cent. BC, in *Sicily at Megara Hyblaea but esp. in the east, on the *Bosporus (1) (Chalcedon, *Byzantium) and the Black (*Euxine) Sea. The tyrant Theagenes (after 650?) assisted his son-in-law *Cylon in an unsuccessful attempt on the tyranny at Athens; we know little more except that he 'slaughtered the flocks of the rich'. *Salamis was disputed with Athens until *Pisistratus established Athenian control. Megara joined the Spartan alliance (see PELOPON- NESIAN LEAGUE) towards 500 and fought in the *Persian Wars, but Corinthian aggression *c*.460 caused her to join the Athenians, who helped to erect the first known *Long Walls, between the city and Nisaea; the First *Peloponnesian War soon followed. Another change in Megarian allegiance enabled Sparta to invade Attica in 446, and the *Thirty Years Peace was agreed, under which Athens agreed to give up Pagae and Nisaea. Athens' Megarian Decree restricted Megarian access to the Athenian Agora and harbours in the Athenian empire; it was a response to Megarian cultivation of sacred land on the border. Spartan diplomacy (and popular opinion) made it a significant factor in the outbreak of the Peloponnesian War; but *Thucydides (2) was right to judge that other issues were more important. Megara suffered two destructive invasions each year until 424. In that year democrats, having recently exiled oligarchic opponents, attempted to betray the city; Nisaea was taken, but *Brasidas saved Megara itself, and an extreme oligarchy was established. Megara rejected the terms of the Peace of *Nicias, since

they did not include the return of Nisaea; it was not recovered until 410/9.

Megasthenēs (*c*.350–290 BC), diplomat and historian. Megasthenes served on several embassies, 302–291. *Seleucus I sent him (perhaps more than once) to Chandragupta (*Sandracottus), founding king of the Maurya empire in northern India. He embodied his firsthand experience in an Indian history which covered geography, including peoples and cities, system of government, classification of the citizens and religious customs, and archaeology, history, and legends. Like *Herodotus, Megasthenes received much of his information first hand, through interpreters. But also like Herodotus on Egypt, he idealized Indian civilization by imposing Greek philosophical notions, and he accepted uncritically native fables. But appearing at a time when western interest in India had been stimulated by the campaigns of Alexander and his Successors (*Diadochi), his *Indīka* provided the Greeks with the fullest account yet of India. Together with the lesser works of the historians of Alexander's expedition, it was the source for many centuries of the western world's knowledge of the country.

Mela See POMPONIUS MELA.

Melampus, mythical seer and ancestor of the Melampodids, Greece's most renowned family of seers. The young, unmarried seer Melampus won a bride for his brother Bias, and for himself a part of a kingdom with its kingship. The kernel of this myth belongs to the older strata of Greek mythology, as Melampus' knowledge of the language of birds and woodworms demonstrates. Melampus is also connected with girls' *initiation. He is the king's son who with a band of youths catches the daughters of Proetus and cures them of madness.

Meleager (1), in myth son of Oeneus, king of the Aetolians of Calydon, and Althaea. He was the hero of the Calydonian boar-hunt, the story of which is first found in Homer's *Iliad*, told by Phoenix during the Embassy to *Achilles. Oeneus forgot to sacrifice to Artemis, and she, in anger, sent a wild boar to ravage the country. Meleager gathered huntsmen and hounds from many cities and killed the boar. The goddess then stirred up strife between Aetolians and Curetes over the head and hide of the boar, and a violent battle ensued. From this point on, Homer seems to develop the traditional story in order to create an example paralleling Achilles' situation, the better for Phoenix to persuade him back to battle. While Meleager fought, all went well for the Aetolians, but when he withdrew from battle (out of anger with his mother, who had cursed him for the 'slaying of a brother') the Curetes attacked their city more and more violently. Meleager was offered gifts and was entreated to return to battle by priests, his father, mother, and sisters; but he refused. Only when his wife entreated him did he go and fight, but then too late to receive the offered gifts.

Acc. to later legend, shortly after his birth the Moirai (see FATE) had said that he would live until a brand then on the fire burned away. His mother extinguished the brand and kept it safe for many years until, after the boar-hunt, Meleager killed her two brothers, either accidentally, or in anger when, after he had given the hide of the boar to *Atalanta with whom he was in love, they took it away from her. At this Althaea threw the brand into the fire and Meleager died, whereupon she killed herself.

Meleager (2) (fl. 100 BC), Greek poet and philosopher from Gadara in *Syria; lived in *Tyre and retired to *Cos in old age. His autobiographical poems claim that he spoke Greek, Syrian, and Phoenician. His chief claim to fame is his *Garland*, a substantial collection of *epigrams by poets of the preceding two centuries, artistically arranged. His preface names all his contributors, assigning each the name of a flower. His own poems are almost entirely erotic, addressed indifferently to boys and girls. His themes are taken from predecessors, but developed with extraordinary versatility and felicity of expression. His language is sometimes simple but often flamboyant, with all the traditional imagery of Cupids, bows, torches, thunderbolts, and honey, but his metre follows precise rules.

See too ANTHOLOGY; CYNICS; EPIGRAM, GREEK.

Mēlos, a volcanic island in the SW *Cyclades, exceptionally fertile and rich in minerals. It was settled c.900 BC from Laconia during the *Dorian colonization of the south Aegean. The ancient city occupied an acropolis overlooking the Great Bay, its early wealth apparent in its cemeteries. Melos contributed two pentekontors (see SHIPS) to the Greek fleet in 480 BC (see SALAMIS, BATTLE OF) and remained independent until the *Peloponnesian War, when Athens could no longer tolerate its neutrality. Following a failed expedition in 426, a more determined campaign in 416–415 ended in execution of the men,

enslavement of the women and children, and establishment of an Athenian *cleruchy. This was expelled by *Lysander in 405, and Melos was resettled with its former inhabitants. Prosperity returned and increased under the Roman empire.

Memmius, Gāius, married *Sulla's daughter Fausta. In 66 BC, apparently as tribune, he succeeded in delaying the *triumph of *Licinius Lucullus. As praetor 58 he was hostile to *Caesar. In 57 he went as governor to Bithynia. In 55 he divorced Fausta, who now married *Annius Milo, in 54 stood for consul with Caesar's support; but his chances were ruined by an electoral scandal which he himself revealed; eventually condemned for *ambitus*, he went into exile in Athens (52). Memmius was a literary patron; *Catullus and *Helvius Cinna accompanied him to Bithynia, and *Lucretius dedicated his *De rerum natura* to him.

Memmius Rēgulus, Publius, a *novus homo*, served as quaestor to *Tiberius and was promoted by him. He was *suffect consul in AD 31 and handled the overthrow of *Sejanus for Tiberius in the senate. He governed Moesia, Macedonia, and Achaia 35–44, but was forced to come to Rome in 38, to give his wife *Lollia Paulina in marriage to *Gaius (1), pretending to be her father. He was proconsul of Asia (probably) 48–49 and remained influential under Claudius and Nero until his death (61). Tacitus praises him.

Memnon, a mythical king of *Ethiopia, was the son of *Eos and Tithonus. He went with a large force to Troy to help *Priam, his uncle; and there, wearing armour made by *Hephaestus, he killed many Greeks including *Antilochus, son of *Nestor, who died saving his father's life. Finally he fought with *Achilles while the two mothers, Eos and *Thetis, pleaded with *Zeus for their sons' lives. Memnon was killed, and Eos asked Zeus to show him some special honour. Memnon's final combat with Achilles and his body being carried away by Eos were favourite themes in Archaic and Classical vase-painting. He is given regular heroic features, but often has black African attendants.

Memphis, though replaced as capital under *Ptolemy (1) I, remained an important city of both Ptolemaic and Roman Egypt. At least from the reign of Ptolemy V Epiphanes the Ptolemies were crowned according to Egyptian rites in the city's temple of Ptah. Important priestly edicts, including that of the Rosetta Stone (196 BC), derive from the city. Connected with the Ptah temple was the cult of Apis, which, together with other necropolis animal-cults, made the city a centre for tourists and pilgrims. Caches of Greek and demotic papyri from the necropolis illuminate the Hellenistic city.

Menander (? 344/3–292/1 BC), the leading writer of New Comedy (see COMEDY (GREEK), NEW), although in his own time less successful (with only eight victories) than *Philemon. An Athenian of good family, he is said to have studied under *Theophrastus, and to have been a friend of *Demetrius of Phaleron. He wrote over 100 plays, many of which must have been intended for performance outside Athens. Nearly 100 titles are known, but some may be alternatives attached to plays restaged (as happened often) after Menander's death.

Menander's plays were lost in the 7th and 8th cents. AD as a result of Arab incursions and Byzantine neglect, but in modern times many papyri have been discovered, attesting great popularity in Ptolemaic and Roman Egypt. These include one virtually complete play, *Dyskolos* ('Old Cantankerous': victorious at the *Lenaea in 316), and large enough portions of six others to permit some literary judgement. They include *Epitrepontes* ('Arbitration', a mature work half-preserved intact and named after a brilliant scene), *Perikeiromenē* ('Rape of the Locks', nearly half of its clear plot surviving), *Samia* ('Girl from Samos', four-fifths preserved), and *Aspis* ('Shield', first half).

Menander's plays are always set in contemporary Greece, often Athens or *Attica, but although the characters are aware of events in the wider world, the plots focus on private domestic problems. They often include situations less common probably in real life than on the stage (e.g. foundling babies, raped or kidnapped daughters). There is always a love-interest, but the range of situations is wide—a young man in love with a country girl or an experienced courtesan, an older man believing his mistress has been unfaithful, a husband doubting the paternity of his wife's new baby. Yet love is often only one ingredient in the drama; thus in *Dyskolos*, Sostratos' infatuation shares the limelight with his developing friendship with Gorgias, and Knemon's misanthropy.

Menander was a skilful constructor of plots, an imaginative deviser of situations, and a master of variety and suspense. He wrote for the theatre, highlighting the memorably emotive detail both in scenes of psychologically convincing dialogue and in long, vivid narrative speeches which sometimes recall the messengers of 5th-cent. tragedy. Tragedy may also have influenced the use of divine prologues, either beginning the play or following an appetite-whetting initial scene; they provided the audience with facts still unknown to the characters and enabled them to appreciate the irony of characters' ignorance.

Menander's plays were written in non-realistic verse, yet his lines give an illusion of colloquial speech, while variations of rhythm subtly modulate tone, emotion and presentation of character.

The characters are firmly rooted in a comic tradition of two-generation families, with important roles for slaves, courtesans, soldiers, parasites, and cooks. They are presented as credible individuals, and here two aspects of technique are significant. Menander often takes a type figure and either adds to it some unexpected touches or develops the expected traits in a new direction. Secondly, although almost every character speaks the same late Attic dialect, many of them are given individual turns of phrase that set them apart (e.g. in *Dyskolos* the cook Sikon's flamboyant metaphors and Knemon's simplistic exaggerations).

Menander attempts no profound psychological insights and leaves to his audiences the pleasure of inferring emotions and motives. Dialogue often moves so quickly that only the alert grasp all the implications. A single sentence may simultaneously advance the action, describe another person, and illuminate the speaker. Characters are portrayed typically with mingled irony and sympathy, and although the dramatist is primarily an entertainer, he quietly teaches that understanding, tolerance, and generosity are the keys to happiness in human relationships.

Menelaion, the *Laconian shrine of *Menelaus and *Helen at Therapne; from *c*.700 BC occupied a commanding position on a spur high above the Eurotas, 2.5 km. (1½ mi.) SE of *Sparta. A high rectangular terrace reached by a ramp, and retained by massive rectangular conglomerate ashlars, surrounded a small temple built on a conspicuous knoll.

Menelāus, younger brother of *Agamemnon and husband of *Helen; king of *Sparta. The abduction of his wife by *Paris caused the Trojan War. In *Homer's *Iliad* he is sometimes effective in battle, and he defeats Paris in a duel. He is consistently portrayed, however, as a (relatively) 'gentle spearman', inferior to the best fighters but honourable and courageous. In bk. 4 of Homer's *Odyssey*, he is seen at Sparta as a rich and hospitable king and recounts his adventures on his way home from Troy. They include his visit to Egypt and his encounter with Prōteus the mutable herdsman of seals, who prophesied that instead of dying he would finally be translated to *Elysium.

In tragedy his character deteriorates, like that of Helen. In *Euripides' *Trojan Women* he is a weak man, who clearly lacks the resolve to kill his guilty wife, while in *Sophocles' *Ajax* and Euripides' *Andromache* and *Orestes* he shows varying degrees of unpleasantness. He is a sympathetic character, however, in Euripides' more light-hearted *Helen*. He shared a tomb and cult with Helen at Therapne near Sparta (see MENELAION).

Menippean satire in the sense of a mixture of prose and many verse forms was, acc. to *Quintilian, introduced by *Varro, who in early compositions freely adapted works of Menippus of Gadara, combining jocularity with social comment and popular, esp. *Cynic philosophy. Some of the titles suggest inventive fantasy; many have a second explanatory title in Greek. The state of the extant fragments makes exegesis and reconstruction esp. daunting.

In AD 54 *Seneca the Younger wrote *Apocolocyntōsis* ('Pumpkinification'), a compact and savage *satire on the recent apotheosis of *Claudius, which is the only near-complete classical Menippean to have survived. The prose narrative is studded with quotations placed in incongruous situations; the verses include parody of a tragic speech and a mock funeral lament. The *Satyrica* of *Petronius Arbiter is a unique fusion of two genres, Menippean satire and the comic novel. Menippean elements are found in the mockery of a tasteless dinner party, the *Cena Trimalchionis*. Literary criticism and the long verse excerpts are spoken by a disreputable vagabond.

mercenaries

Greek and Hellenistic For there to be mercenaries, three conditions are necessary—*warfare, people willing to pay, and others to serve. Warfare persisted throughout Greek history, and there were probably always those whom love of adventure, trouble at home, or *poverty made willing to serve. In Archaic times Greek mercenaries usually found employment with tyrants or with near eastern potentates. Psammetichus I of Egypt, for example, used *Carians and *Ionians to seize power around 660 BC, and Pabis of Colophon and Elesibius of Teos were among those who carved their names on the statue of Ramesses II at Abu Simbel, while serving Psammetichus II (see SAÏTES).

There was probably always also a market for specialist troops like Cretan *archers and Rhodian *slingers, esp. when warfare became more complex. Cleon took *Thracian *peltasts to *Pylos, and Cretan archers and Rhodian slingers joined the *Sicilian Expedition in 415. By the end of the *Peloponnesian War there were enough Greeks eager for mercenary service for the Persian prince, *Cyrus (2), to raise more than 10,000 for his attempt on his brother's throne, including Athenians, Spartans, Arcadians, Achaeans, Boeotians, and Thessalians, as well as the usual Cretan and Rhodian specialists.

Poverty had probably always been the main factor in driving Greeks to become mercenaries—notably many were Arcadians—and the increasing number in the 4th cent. was probably partly due to the worsening economic situation. Greek mercenaries were now in great demand in Persia, and it is said that the Persian king promoted the *Common Peace of 375 in order to be able to hire Greeks for the reconquest of Egypt. But Greek states also increasingly employed mercenaries. *Jason (2) of Pherae is said to have had up to 6,000, and the 4th cent. saw many other 'tyrants' who relied on mercenaries to keep them in power, the most conspicuous being *Dionysius (1) I of Syracuse.

*Philip II and *Alexander (2) the Great certainly employed mercenaries, esp. as specialists and for detached duties such as garrisons, and the *Diadochi increasingly employed mercenaries in their *phalanxes as the supply of real Macedonians declined. However, as the Hellenistic world settled down after the battle of Ipsus (301), the great powers developed supplies of phalanx-troops from their own national resources—often the descendants of Greek mercenary settlers.

Roman Contact with foreign powers such as *Carthage and Macedon exposed Rome's weakness in cavalry and light-armed troops. This deficiency she remedied principally by obtaining contingents outside Italy. Some came from independent allies like *Masinissa, others were raised by forced levies or paid as mercenaries. Gauls served in the First *Punic War, 600 Cretan archers fought at Trasimene, Numidian cavalry (see NUMIDIA) turned the scale at *Zama. During the next two centuries the number and variety of contingents increased. Spain was a favourite recruiting-ground for cavalry and light infantry, while Caesar obtained his cavalry from Numidia, Gaul, and Germany, and his archers and slingers from Numidia, Crete, and the Balearic Islands. Under the Principate such troops became formalized within the *auxilia, but supplementary irregular troops were always employed on campaign.

Mercurius (Mercury), Roman god of circulation (see below), known as well in *Campania and Etruria. Acc. to ancient tradition, in 495 BC Mercury received an official temple on the SW slope of the *Aventine. His cult had close links with shopkeepers and transporters of goods, esp. corn. But his function was not simply the protection of businessmen (see NEGOTIATORES). If all the evidence for his cult is taken together, he emerges, like the Greek *Hermes, as the patron god of circulation, the movement of goods, people, and words and their roles. Mediator between gods and mortals, between the dead and the living, and always in motion, Mercury is also a deceiver, since he moves on the boundaries he is patron of the shopkeeper as much as the trader, the traveller as well as the brigand (see BRIGANDAGE).

Messallina See VALERIA MESSALLINA (third wife of emperor Claudius).

Messāna, an 8th-cent. BC colony, originally called Zanclē, founded by Cumaean and Euboean settlers on the straits of Messina (see CUMAE; EUBOEA). It prospered, founding colonies at Mylae and *Himera, but was overshadowed by Rhegium, whose tyrant seized it in 490/89. Samian and Messenian settlers arrived in 486, with Rhegine assistance, and changed the name of the city to Messana. It remained under Rhegine domination for most of the 5th cent., but by 427 was independent again. It was destroyed by Carthaginians in 396 and rebuilt by *Dionysius (1) I. In 288 it was seized by the *Mamertines, who ruled it until 264, when *Hieron (2) II attempted to oust them. Their appeal to Rome for help, and Roman agreement, was the occasion of the First *Punic War.

Messēnia, the SW region of *Peloponnese, bounded on the north by *Elis and Arcadia, and on the east by *Laconia. The Spartans had conquered central Messenia by (?) 700 BC, reducing the old population to the status of *helots or

*perioîkoi. The Third Messenian War, after the great earthquake of 464 BC, ended, like the first war, in the surrender of *Ithome after a long siege. Granted a safe conduct, many of the survivors were settled by the Athenians at Naupactus (455), a town in western Locris, with a small protected harbour commanding the entrance to the Corinthian Gulf. During the Peloponnesian War the Messenian helots were encouraged to sporadic revolts by the Athenian garrison established at Pylos after the victory at Sphacteria (425), in which Messenians from Naupactus played a decisive part. In 369 Messenia was liberated with the help of *Epaminondas.

metallurgy See MINES AND MINING, and BRONZE; GOLD; IRON; LEAD; SILVER.

metamorphosis, a type of tale focusing on a miraculous transformation. Tales of transformations of a divine or human being into an animal, plant, or inanimate object were very popular throughout antiquity. Attested in Homer, they were given a literary form later. Collections of these tales are known to have existed from the Hellenistic period onwards. They provided the model and material for *Ovid's *Metamorphoses*, recording some 250 transformations from the creation of the world to the reign of Augustus. After Ovid the most famous literary metamorphosis is that in *Apuleius' *Metamorphoses*, relating the transformation of Lucius into an ass and his final, miraculous, restoration to human shape by *Isis. Outside the realm of fiction, magicians (and gods) were generally believed to be able to change their own shapes and those of others.

metaphor and simile are features of literary language that have been extensively discussed by theorists and critics since antiquity. The first purposeful investigations are *Aristotle's. By the time of *Quintilian metaphor (implicit comparison) and simile (explicit comparison) have a place in an elaborate apparatus of 'tropes' and 'figures', with metaphor classed among the tropes, and simile generally associated with the figures. Figures comprise a variety of supposedly special 'conformations', from homoeoteleuton (see ASSONANCE, LATIN) to rhetorical question. Tropes comprise all deliberate deviations from established usage, including in particular (a) deviations based on contiguity or association, in modern analysis generally grouped together as 'metonymy' ('arma virumque cano', 'arms and the man I sing', Virgil, Aeneid 1. 1, where *arms* implies *war*) and (*b*) metaphor, a deviation based on similarity or analogy (a swarm of bees '*swims* through the summer air', Virgil, *Georgics*. 4. 59).

Metaphor proper differs from dead metaphor or cliché. Homer's 'shepherd of the people' may 'sound metaphorical' in translation, but in Homeric Greek is an established usage. Acc. to Quintilian, metaphor is the most important of the tropes, but not detached from them. Modern analysts of metaphor distinguish the vehicle (deviant element) from the tenor (non-deviant element) and both from the image as a whole, and likewise with the corresponding elements of similes.

In much Greek and Latin literature metaphor and allied figures occur sporadically. Representative are the short explanatory comparisons that crop up in technical prose ('in tetanus the jaws set hard like wood') and the orator's isolated and often half-familiar metaphors, commended by generations of rhetoricians ('the insurrection *awoke* Italy'). The intensive or intense use of imagery is in poetry and poetic prose. With the antiphonal epic simile, use is restricted: 'And *as when* a man *packs* the wall of a high house tight with stones . . . , *even so packed* were their helmets and bossed shields.' This is nevertheless much the most important mode of imagery in Homer, from whom it is transmitted as part of the epic repertoire to Apollonius Rhodius, Virgil, and beyond.

The main functions of metaphor and simile in ancient poetry are:

1. To make clearer, as through a diagram, usually by appeal to familiar experience. The function is chiefly associated with epic simile (as in the *Iliad* example just cited), or simile or analogy in scientific or philosophical contexts.

2. To make immediate, as if to the senses. This is a matter of making alien and thereby making listener or reader experience anew (the 'swimming' bees, cited above). The mechanism is usually short metaphor.

3. To exploit the associations, including the contrary associations, of the vehicle, beyond any limited point or ground of comparison. In *Iliad* 8 Gorgythion is killed and 'his head dropped like a poppy, weighed down with its fruit and the spring rain': poignant contrast of death with life and growth. In Aeschylus' *Agamemnon* Menelaus is 'Priam's great adversary *at law*': the implication that the Trojan War is somehow a legal event prefigures the way the whole cycle of conflict is eventually resolved in *Eumenides*. At the end of the *Aeneid* (*Aeneas killing Turnus): 'Pallās te hoc vulnere, Pallas immo-

lat' ('this wound is for you from Pallas; you are Pallas' *sacrificial offering*': the vehicle evokes the nexus of religious duty and destiny to which Aeneas is committed, even as he avenges himself on Turnus for killing young Pallas. Different functions readily coexist in a complex whole. Complexity is often intensified by clusters of imagery. The richest examples are in Aeschylus.

In some of the best ancient literature, however, metaphor and simile are not predominant. The most characteristic tropical movements in much Latin poetry and literary prose involve not metaphor but metonymy. *Juvenal writes of 'crimes worthy of the Venusian lamp', i.e. crimes that the satirist Horace, born at Venusia, might have got up early, or stayed up late, to write about. And in the *Aeneid*, which begins with a simple metonym ('arms'), the representative trope of the closing lines is not the metaphor in 'immolat' discussed above, but the agonized metonymic cluster that precedes it, 'Pallas te hoc vulnere, Pallas . . .'. Here 'wound' (i.e. weapon that deals the wound) and the repeated 'Pallas' (i.e. 'I, Aeneas, on behalf of Pallas') combine to create a harsh and powerful image: the absent Pallas is 'there' in the weapon's stroke to avenge his own 'wound' and Aeneas' too.

Metelli See CAECILIUS.

meteorology strictly means 'the study of things aloft', but the term was widely used in antiquity to cover both the study of what might now be called meteorological phenomena and the investigation of (supposedly) related phenomena on and within the earth itself, such as tides, earthquakes, volcanoes, and the formation of minerals and metals. Presocratic interest in meteorology is well attested, but the difficulty of providing explanations of such intractable phenomena sometimes made students of the subject figures of fun. *Aristophanes (1) in *Clouds* parodies 'meteorosophists' for their arcane and silly speculations about atmospheric and subterranean marvels. The author of *On Ancient Medicine* (see HIPPOCRATES; MEDICINE, 4) attacks those who are forced by the very nature of the subject to base their speculations on indemonstrable premisses. Even the Platonic *Socrates offers *Anaxagoras a backhanded compliment, claiming that he filled people with 'lofty' (i.e. meteorological) thoughts.

The earliest surviving work on the subject is *Aristotle's *Meteorology*. Aristotle describes his own work as an account of the*physics of the sublunary sphere—that is, the sphere closest to the earth; he includes accounts of comets and shooting stars (which were thought to originate in the upper atmosphere), and moves on to discuss weather, earthquakes, the origins of rivers, and the seas. Bk. 3 ends with an account of the formation of minerals. Bk. 4 (of disputed authenticity) deals with the physical properties of materials found in and around the earth and their behaviour.

metics As the Greek *polis* evolved, it sought to differentiate, amongst its inhabitants, between insiders and outsiders. Insiders *par excellence* were its own members, the citizens; palpable outsiders were its slaves, native or imported (see SLAVERY); but this simple dichotomy would have sufficed only for communities like *Sparta which discouraged immigration. Elsewhere it was necessary to recognize free persons who lived, temporarily or permanently, in the *polis* without becoming its citizens. Such a person was a *metoikos* ('home-changer', metic, immigrant). The precise nature and complexity of metic-status doubtless varied from place to place; evidence approaches adequacy only for Athens, atypical in its allure and so in the numbers of those who succumbed thereto (half the size of the (reduced) citizen body of *c*.313 BC; perhaps proportionately larger in the 5th cent.) With *Solon having created only indirect incentives to immigration, Athenian metic-status probably owes its formal origins to *Cleisthenes (2), after whom the presence of metics was recognized in law and could develop in its details at both city and local (*deme) level. The dividing line between visitors and residents seems to have been drawn on a common-sense basis in the 5th cent. BC but became more mechanical in the 4th. Definition as a metic brought some privileges but many burdens, largely fiscal (including the *metoikion*, 'poll-tax') and military. Socio-economically, Athens' metics were highly diverse, and contemporary attitudes to their presence deeply ambivalent.

Metōn, Athenian astronomer, is dated by his observation of the summer solstice, together with Euctemon, in 432 BC. He introduced the luni-solar calendaric cycle named after him, with nineteen solar years and 235 months, of which 110 were 'hollow' (containing 29 days) and 125 full (containing 30 days), making a total of 6,940 days. The basis of the cycle (though not the year-length of $365^5/_{19}$ days) was undoubtedly derived from Babylonian practice.

We may presume that Meton intercalated a thirteenth month in the same years as the Babylonians, and prescribed a fixed sequence of full and hollow months. He used the month-names of the Athenian calendar, but his cycle was intended not as a reform of that, but to provide a fixed basis for dating astronomical observations and for Meton's own astronomical calendar. Meton erected an instrument for observing solstices on the Pnyx, and appears as a character in Aristophanes' *Birds*. See ASTRONOMY.

metre, Greek (Some types of metre are described in 4.) Greek verse is quantitative: syllabic length is its patterning agent. (The patterning agent of English verse is stress.)

1. Prosody A syllable is long (—) either 'by nature', when its vowel-sound is long (long vowel—Eta, Omega (see ALPHABET, GREEK) and sometimes Alpha, Iota, Upsilon—or diphthong) or 'by position', when its vowel-sound is short but followed by two or more consonants, whether or not they belong to the same word. In this case, the consonants are said to 'make position'. (Zeta, Xi, Psi are double consonants.) However, plosive (mute) followed by nasal (Mu, Nu) or liquid (Lambda, Rho) does not always make position, depending on whether the plosive closes the syllable: *pāt-ros* but *pă-tros*. (The poet could usually choose whichever his metre required.) The plosives are: Pi, Beta, Phi (labials), Tau, Delta, Theta (dentals), Kappa, Gamma, Khi (velars). The voiced plosives, (Beta, Delta, Gamma) are the strongest: Gamma Mu, Gamma Nu, Delta Mu, Delta Nu always make position. The meeting of vowels at the junction between words gives rise to various modifications.

2. Basic Concepts While actual verse is composed of syllables (components of words), verses ('lines') in the abstract can be thought of as patterns of three types of 'position': long (–), short (∪) and *anceps* (×). This last admits either a long or a short syllable. So, × – ∪ – can be realized as either ∪ – ∪ – or – – ∪ –. One long counts as equivalent to two shorts. In some metres double short and long may be interchangeable. If double short does replace long, that is *resolution*. Much Greek verse is composed in sequences of uniform *metra*: short rhythmic phrases with their own rules for internal variation (e.g × – ∪ – iamb, – ∪∪ dactyl, etc.) So, × – ∪ – × – ∪ – is an *iambic dimeter*, and – ∪∪ – ∪∪ – ∪∪ – ∪∪ a *dactylic tetrameter* (four dactylic metra). The end of a verse (verse-end) may be marked by *catalexis*:

a verse is catalectic if its final or penultimate position is suppressed.

3. Verse and Stanza Stichic verse is composed in sequences of verses (*stichoi*, lines) of from three to six metra, uniform in metrical type and length. This kind of composition is associated with spoken delivery. Stichic verses must have word-end at or near mid-verse. Such word-end is called *caesura* if it falls within a metron. Distichs are couplets of unequal verses. Commonest is the *elegiac* distich or couplet: dactylic hexameter (4(b)) + –∪∪– ∪∪–|–∪∪–∪∪–. For the stanzas of choral lyric see LYRIC POETRY, *Greek*.

4. Types of Metre Types of poetic rhythm are associated in origin with different regions and poetic genres.

(*a*) Iambic and trochaic
These two metres can be seen as different segments of the sequence ×–∪–×. The iambic metron is, as above, ×–∪–, the trochaic –∪–×. Longs may be resolved. In the early iambic trimeter, caesura falls in the second metron, after anceps or after short: ×–∪–×|–∪|–×–∪–.

In the 5th cent. the iambic trimeter became the standard spoken verse of drama.

(*b*) Dactylic
Metron: –∪∪ or –– ('spondee'). The dactylic hexameter (six-metron line) is the metre of Homeric epic. *Aristotle describes it as the 'most solid and massive of metres', but he may have been swayed by the subject matter. The hexameter usually has caesura in the third metron, either after the long or between the two shorts: – ∪∪ – ∪∪ –|∪|∪– ∪∪ – ∪∪ – –. The fifth metron is usually a dactyl. In the elegiac distich or couplet (see 3), hexameters alternate with a verse made up of – ∪∪– ∪∪ –|∪∪ twice over (so-called 'pentameter'), with intervening word-end and long for double short permitted only in the first half.

(*c*) Anapaestic
In the earliest surviving anapaestic verse, Spartan marching songs, the metron seems to be ∪∪ – ∪∪ –, and ∪∪– remains the dominant movement. The catalectic (last or last-but-one position suppressed) tetrameter is much used in comedy, esp. in the *parabasis*, which is sometimes referred to as 'the anapaests'.

metre, Latin A tradition of writing Latin verses on the quantitative model of those of Classical Greek literature maintained itself from 240 BC down to the end of the western empire. The relation of the so-called *Saturnian verse to the classical tradition is disputed.

In the 3rd cent. BC some poets offered advice or information, others told stories in the Saturnian verse. Early in the 2nd cent. *Ennius proclaimed himself a Latin *Homer and composed an account of Roman history in a verse (the 'dactylic hexameter'; see METRE, GREEK, 4(*b*)) modelled on that of the *Iliad*. Where Ennius had led in Epic, later poets writing in different genres followed, devising appropriate Latin equivalents to their Greek metrical models.

mētropolis ('mother-city'). (*a*) The 'mother-city' of a Greek colony (*apoikia*) usually nominated the *founder, conducted rituals of *divination and departure, organized a body of settlers, and formulated the charter of their individual rights. Major mother-cities, such as *Chalcis or *Miletus, sometimes led mixed groups of settlers but would insist on their own founder and customs. The latter, *nomima*, would identify a colony either ethnically ('Dorian') or more specifically, as originating from a particular *polis. Nomima* could include cults, *calendar, script, *dialect, names and number of tribes (see PHYLAI) and other social divisions, titles of office-holders, and so on, and can aid modern research to determine colonial connections. Our sources in general are meagre, esp. for early mother-cities (8th–7th cents. BC), but three salient facts of the civic identity of colonies seem to emerge, stressing the importance attached to the *metropolis*: the identity of the mother-city, the date of foundation, and the name of the founder. The annual founder's cult in the colony probably commemorated, simultaneously, both the independence of the colony and its metropolitan, dependent origins. Taking sacred fire from the common hearth at the *prytaneion* of the mother-city to light a new fire in the colony similarly stressed both continuity and new sovereignty. Most colonies were independent *poleis* (see POLIS); the Locrian foundation decree of Naupactus repeats the formula 'when he becomes a Naupactian'. On the other hand, the articulation 'as parents to children', is also found in such decrees. The kinship-links were both real and metaphorical: descendants could point out graves of ancestors in the mother-city, and citizens from colonies could participate in cults and sacrifices in the *metropolis*, a right usually denied to strangers. Religion was often the only, albeit meaningful, expression of continuing relations. Whether or not a mother-city controlled its colonies depended on distance or on ambition combined with maritime capacity. *Corinth is known for its 'imperial' colonization in the Adriatic; its colony *Corcyra fought wars against it from the 7th cent. on, sometimes fell under its domination, and argued before the *Peloponnesian War that it was founded not to be a slave but an equal to its *metropolis*. (Corinthian art continued to dominate in Corcyra regardless of politics.) Primacy was naturally accorded to mother-cities, expressing a common and consistent opinion in Greece. War between a mother-city and colony was considered shameful, and alliance or military aid would rather be expected. Spartan generals kept appearing in Taras (see TARENTUM) centuries after its foundation in 706, and Sparta twice set out with esp. large contingents to help its motherland Doris in 457 and 426. Colonies often eclipsed the mother-cities (e.g. *Cyrene and Thera), reached more advanced forms of urban and country planning and political development (Achaean colonies were *poleis* before the *polis*-form had reached *Achaea), articulated law codes (see LAW IN GREECE), and significantly contributed to the emergence and formation of the Greek *polis* in general.

See also APOIKIA; COLONIZATION, GREEK; FOUNDERS OF CITIES; KINSHIP.

(*b*) In Roman times an honorary title granted to important cities.

Mīcōn, painter and sculptor, of Athens. His painting was closely connected with that of his contemporary *Polygnotus. He painted in the Theseum (soon after 475 BC) *Theseus and *Minos; probably also an Amazonomachy and Centauromachy (see AMAZONS; CENTAURS). In the *Stoa Poecile he is variously credited with Marathon and the Amazonomachy. The Amazonomachy and Centauromachy are reflected on vases: one Amazon is named Peisianassa, perhaps after Peisianax, who built the stoa. In the Anakeion (temple of *Dioscuri; see ATHENS, TOPOGRAPHY) were his *Argonauts. He painted the Peliads the daughters of *Pelias; he also painted Boutēs, brother of *Erechtheus, so that only head and eye appeared above a hill; analogies can be found on contemporary vases. He made a statue in *Olympia of Callias, victor in 472. See PAINTING, GREEK.

Midas (1), legendary king of Phrygia, a comical figure famous in Greek tradition for his interview with Silenus (see SATYRS AND SILENS), his golden touch, and his ass's ears (Ovid, *Met.* 11). Eager to learn the secret of life, he captured Silenus by spiking with wine the pool at which he drank; the *daimon* was brought before him bound (a scene attested in Greek art from *c*.560 BC) and revealed either the existence of a world beyond our own divided between the two races of the Blest and the Warriors, or the melancholy insight, which became proverbial, that the best thing for mankind was never to be born, otherwise to leave this world as soon as possible.

*Dionysus, grateful for Silenus' safe return to the wild, offered to grant the king any wish; Midas asked that everything he touched should turn to gold, but regretted his request when he saw that this made it impossible for him to eat or drink. The unwanted gift was washed off into the source of the river Pactolus, which thereafter carried gold dust down in its streams. A second divine encounter confirmed Midas' lack of judgement: invited to judge a musical contest between *Apollo and *Pan (or *Marsyas), he preferred Pan, and was rewarded by the god with the ironical gift of donkey's ears. A turban hid his shame from all except his barber, who, unable to contain the secret, told it to a hole in the ground; but reeds grew over the spot, and their wind-blown whispering propagates the unhappy truth for all time: 'Midas has ass's ears.'

Behind the character of legend there probably lies the historical king whom the Assyrians knew as Mita (see MIDAS (2)). Excavation of the largest of the tomb-mounds outside the Phrygian capital *Gordium recovered a skeleton which may be his; it shows no sign of auricular abnormality.

Midas (2), historical king of Phrygia, 738–696/5 BC. He was the first *barbarian king to make dedications at *Delphi, and is said to have married the daughter of the king of *Cyme, and to have killed himself by drinking bull's blood when the *Cimmerians overthrew his kingdom. In Assyrian records he appears as Mita: he joined a confederacy against King Sargon II (717), but became his vassal (707).

midwives and normal labour are rarely mentioned in the Hippocratic treatises (see HIPPOCRATES), perhaps because Hippocratic doctors concerned themselves with abnormal labour only. Occasional references to female 'helpers' and 'cord-cutters' survive. However, it is also possible that midwives are not discussed because any woman was thought able to take on the role if necessary. In *Soranus, in contrast, the midwife appears as a literate and highly knowledgeable professional, the ideal midwife being trained in all areas of therapy—diet, surgery, and drugs—and able to decide how each case should best be treated. Soranus' midwife does not have to have given birth herself, and can be old or young so long as she is sufficiently strong for the job. She must be free from superstition; labour, as a dangerous time for both mother and baby, was hedged around with taboos, and Soranus ridicules midwives who refuse to use iron when cutting the cord because they believe it is unlucky.

migration See COLONIZATION (various entries); EXILE; LIMES; METICS; NEGOTIATORES; NOMADS; POPULATION, GREEK and ROMAN; SYNOECISM; TRANSHUMANCE.

Milesian Tales See NOVEL, GREEK and LATIN.

milestones, a typical feature of Roman road-building. The earliest surviving Roman milestone dates from c.250 BC. Under the republic they are inscribed with the names of consuls or other magistrates concerned with the building or repair of roads. In the Principate the full names and titles of the emperor usually appear; in the Roman east the inscriptions are often bilingual. They may attest the date of new roads, or methods of funding construction. On trunk roads in Italy the distance given is often that from Rome, in the provinces from the administrative capital; but usually the distance is from the city on whose territory the milestone stood—often useful for the delimitation of those territories. Milestones were usually cylindrical, about 1.8 m. (6 ft.) high. See ROADS.

Milētus, southernmost of the great *Ionian cities of *Asia Minor. In *Homer the people of Miletus were Carians (see CARIA) who fought against the Achaeans (i.e. Greeks) at *Troy; and in later Greek prose tradition the Ionian settlers, seized Miletus from Carians (whose women they married). During the 7th and 6th cents. BC Miletus founded many colonies on the Black (*Euxine) Sea and its approaches (including Abydos, *Cyzicus, Sinōpē), led the way in Greek penetration of Egypt (Milesians' Fort and *Naucratis; Necho's offering to the nearby temple at *Didyma after Megiddo, 608; see SAÏTES). Miletus' sea power and colonies were partly cause, partly result of her long struggle with the Lydians (see LYDIA). *Alyattes made terms with Miletus (then under a tyrant Thrasybulus, friend of *Periander), which apparently kept a privileged

position when *Croesus subdued Ionia and when *Persia conquered Croesus' dominions c.546. In 499 Miletus, instigated by its ex-tyrant *Histiaeus and *Aristagoras, started the *Ionian Revolt. After the naval disaster at Lade the city was captured, the temple at Didyma was burnt, and Miletus was destroyed (494).

Lade ended a long period of prosperity, interrupted by intervals of internal political strife; to this period belong the philosophers *Thales, *Anaximander, and *Anaximenes and the chronicler *Hecataeus. Finds from recent excavations of local pottery of the 7th–6th cents., richly decorated with animal friezes, seem to indicate that Miletus was the main production centre of these types.

After the Persian defeat at Mycale (479) Miletus joined the *Delian League, but in the mid-5th cent. (probably after a revolt) the Athenians imposed a garrison and imperial controls on the city. In 412, during the *Peloponnesian War, Miletus revolted from Athens, and became the main Spartan naval base in the region. It became a Persian possession after the *King's Peace, until captured and liberated by *Alexander (2) the Great.

military training (Greek) There is little evidence that any troops, other than Spartans, were trained before the 4th cent. BC, and the sources imply that the Spartans were unique. Thus *Thucydides (2) has *Pericles contrast the courage instilled in the Spartans by 'laborious training' with the natural courage of the Athenians, and implies that the only trained troops opposed to the Spartans at the battle of *Mantinea in 418 were the 1,000 picked Argives trained at the state's expense. *Xenophon implies that it was only *after *Leuctra that the Boeotians began to train, and in his treatise on the Spartan constitution claims that manœuvres practised by the Spartans were beyond other Greeks. In the normal Greek state the main element in the armed forces, the *hoplites, consisted of men of a comparatively high social standing, and any kind of training might have been resented: it was much easier to train rowers for the fleet, since they came from a humble background, whether free or slave.

In his treatise on their constitution Xenophon implies that Spartan soldiers were trained to carry out manœuvres such as deploying from column-of-march into line-of-battle in various ways, depending on the direction of the enemy's approach, and without training they could not have carried out such drills as the one whereby files from the left or right wings of the *phalanx were withdrawn behind the centre to double its depth, or the counter-march for about-facing a phalanx. Nevertheless, much of this would have been at the level of 'square-bashing', and there is no evidence for any tactical training whether of officers or men.

In the 4th cent. there is increasing evidence for training. Xenophon's *Education of Cyrus* is fictional, but presumably he would not have had *Cyrus (1) train his troops, if such training was still unthinkable outside Sparta, and it seems unlikely that he would have written his *Cavalry Commander* unless there had also been works on infantry tactics. After Leuctra, the Thebans began to train, and there is some reason to believe that the two years' 'national service' of Athenian *epheboi began in the first half of the 4th cent. There was also an increasing use of specialized troops such as *peltasts, some of whom were highly trained, and of *mercenaries, who were at least experienced.

It seems likely that *Philip II instituted regular training in all branches of his Macedonian army, and when *Alexander (2) the Great succeeded, he was able to put on an impressive display for the *Illyrians. The army with which he conquered the Persian empire was highly trained, and with this and Hellenistic armies we enter the period of 'professional' soldiering at all levels.

military tribune(s) See TRIBUNI MILITUM.

Milo See ANNIUS.

Miltiadēs, Athenian aristocrat and general, a member of the rich and powerful family of the Philaïds. Archon (see ARCHONTES) in 524/3 BC, he was sent to recover control of *Chersonese by *Hippias (1) in succession to his brother, and his namesake and uncle, the elder Miltiades. There he married the daughter of the Thracian king, Olorus. Later he submitted to *Persia, and served *Darius I in the latter's Scythian expedition, allegedly supporting the Scythian suggestion that he and his fellow Greek tyrants should destroy the bridge over the Danube that Darius had left them to guard, though *Histiaeus persuaded the majority not to agree. Shortly afterwards he was driven out of Chersonese by a Scythian invasion, but returned when the nomads withdrew. He then appears to have joined in the *Ionian Revolt, and it was possibly then that he won control of Lemnos. But he was forced to flee to Athens when the revolt was crushed, and was

prosecuted for having held tyrannical power in Chersonese. Acquitted, he was shortly afterwards elected one of the ten generals (see STRATEGOI) for the year 490/89, and, acc. to tradition, it was he who was responsible for the Athenian decision to confront the Persians at *Marathon (see MARATHON, BATTLE OF), for persuading the *polemarchos *Callimachus (1) to give his casting-vote for fighting, and for choosing the moment. It is, however, impossible to be sure of his contribution to victory. He had never commanded a hoplite army of any size—and even *Herodotus does not make him responsible for the Athenian deployment. Since Callimachus was killed, and Miltiades' son *Cimon became the most influential man in Athens in the 470s and 460s, Miltiades' image as the victor of Marathon may owe much to family tradition.

After the victory, he commanded an Athenian fleet in an attack on *Paros, but having failed to take the town, and been severely wounded, he was brought to trial and condemned to pay a fine of 50 talents. He died of gangrene before he could pay, but his son dutifully discharged the debt.

mime The *mīmus* (Gk. *mīmos*) was an imitative performance or performer.

Greek In Greece, as elsewhere, the instinct for imitation found its expression in mimetic dance. From early times solo performers, by play of gesture, voice, and feature, gave imitations of neighing horses, etc., and small companies presented short scenes from daily life (e.g. 'The Quack Doctor') or mythology, probably on a hastily erected stage in the market-place or in a private house; such performers belonged to the social class of acrobats, etc. *Xenophon in his *Symposium* tells of a mime of '*Dionysus and *Ariadne', danced at a private banquet by a boy and girl; we note the connection with *Syracuse, the musical accompaniment, the use of dialogue, and the fact that the girl is also a sword-dancer and the concubine of the Syracusan dancing-master. In the 5th cent. BC Sophron of Syracuse wrote 'men's' and 'women's' mimes in Dorian rhythmic prose; the language was popular and included frequent proverbs; the surviving titles (e.g. 'The Old Fishermen', 'The Women Quacks', 'The Women Visitors to the Isthmia') indicate stock mime themes. In the 3rd cent. the taste for realism brought the mime to the fore; *Theocritus dressed some traditional themes in his courtly *hexameters; these pieces, like those of the more realistic *Herodas, were probably intended for semi-dramatic recitation. The emphasis of mime fell always on character and situation rather than on action.

Roman Barefoot clowns playing without masks improvised sketches in the streets of Rome and Italy before the popularity of mime won it regular official presentation at the Floralia (see FLORA). Early performers bear Greek names; no doubt many were Greek. Leading mimes trained their own companies, devising or modifying scenarios for their use. After Sulla associated with mime artists, mime became smart. Both men and women took part, exploiting sexual innuendo and display. Mime actresses won wealth and notoriety, and Cytheris, an ex-slave, was mistress of both Antony (Marcus *Antonius) and *Cornelius Gallus.

The scripts of literary mime composed by gentlemen like Decimus Laberius probably used the same plots based on change of fortune ('from rags to riches'), the pursuit and escape of tricksters, and disguise or concealment of adulterous lovers, but would be more carefully constructed. Non-dramatic literary texts could be performed as mime: *Ovid reports that his elegies were staged, as were *Virgil's *Eclogues* in his lifetime. *Augustus and his successors delighted in mime and presented it to win favour from the city crowd; audiences were entertained with 'real' fires, and the *crucifixion or rape on stage of condemned criminals and slaves. Star performers exploited their popularity to insert innuendos against emperors into their performance, or became imperial lovers or informers. The glamour of mime defeated the denunciations of *Tertullian and later of the official Christian Church: *Justinian made a mime actress his empress, and the mongrel genre survived to be reborn as *commedia dell'arte*.

mimēsis See IMITATIO; LITERARY CRITICISM IN ANTIQUITY; MUSIC, 3; PLAGIARISM.

Mimnermus, Greek *elegiac poet from Smyrna, later claimed by Colophon, whose foundation he described. His name may commemorate the Smyrnaeans' famous resistance to *Gyges at the river Hermus sometime before 660 BC, which would imply his birth at that time. He commented on a total solar *eclipse, probably that of 6 April 648. He was apparently still alive when *Solon criticized a line of his, but there is no sign that he survived *Alyattes' destruction of Smyrna c.600. His poetry was divided into two books, probably corresponding to the titles *Smyrneis* and *Nanno*. The *Smyrneis* was a quasi-epic on the battle against Gyges, with elaborate proemium and ample narrative with speeches. The shorter elegies stood under the collective title *Nanno*, said to be the name of a girl *aulos-player whom Mimnermus loved, though she is not mentioned in fragments, and he also celebrated the charms of boys. He was esp. famous for poems on the pleasures of love, youth, and sunlight. But one fragment seems to come from a call to arms, contrasting the citizens' present spirit with that of a hero of the Hermus battle.

Minerva, an Italian goddess of handicrafts, widely worshipped and regularly identified with *Athena. There is no trace of her cult in Rome before the introduction of the Capitoline Triad, where she appears with *Jupiter and *Juno in an Etruscan grouping. Apart from this she was worshipped in an ancient shrine on mons Caelius (see CAELIUS MONS) A much more important cult lay outside the *pomerium on the *Aventine; it was supposedly vowed in 263 or 262 BC. The Aventine Minerva was of Greek origin and was the headquarters of a guild of writers and actors during the Second Punic War and seems to have been the centre of organizations of skilled craftsmen.

mines and mining

Greek Greeks obtained *gold and *silver and 'utility' metals, copper, *tin (for bronze), *iron and *lead, by mining and by trade; *colonization extended their scope for both. Literary evidence for mining is mainly historical not technical. Epigraphical, archaeological, and scientific evidence has extended knowledge of industrial organization and techniques, and proved the early exploitation of certain ore-fields. Climate, geography, and geology dictated methods: panning for gold (as in Asia Minor and Black Sea regions) was rarely practicable in Greece and its islands, while low rainfall reduced mine-drainage problems and accounted for the elaborate catchment channels, cisterns and ore-washeries designed to recycle water in the *Laurium area. There the Athenian lead-silver mines were extensive (copper and iron ores were also exploited). In the same area, Thoricus has revealed sherd evidence for mining in late Mycenaean (see MYCENAEAN AGE CIVILIZATION) times. Sporadic mining continued in Laurium till the boom period of the 5th and 4th cents. BC. Opencast pits, oblique and vertical shafts (with cuttings for ladders, stagings, and windlasses), and underground galleries (some only 1 m. (39 in.) high) and chambers mark hillsides and valleys, along with extensive surface-works (cisterns, washeries). In Macedonia and Thrace (Mt. Pangaeus) and on Thasos, gold and silver were mined. Control of the mainland mines yielded *Philip II of Macedon an income of 1,000 talents annually. See SLAVERY.

Roman Imperial expansion gave Rome control over a wide variety of mineral resources. The Iberian peninsula (see SPAIN), *Gaul (Transalpine), *Britain, the Danubian provinces (Dalmatia, Noricum, and *Dacia), and *Asia Minor became the major mining regions of the empire, and *gold, *silver, copper, *lead, and *tin the main metals extracted. *Iron was found in many parts of the empire and, despite the presence of large-scale iron-mining districts in Noricum and the Kentish Weald, was usually exploited in smaller local units of production. Italy contained few precious metals, and Rome initially had to rely on imports from mines controlled by Hellenistic kings in the east and the Carthaginians in the west. After the defeat of *Hannibal in 202 BC, Romans and Italians were soon exploiting the *silver mines in SE Spain around *Carthago Nova. After the conquest of the Macedonian kingdom in 167, Rome regulated the operation of the Macedonian goldmines to suit its needs. The zenith of production at the major mines took place in the first two centuries AD. After the disruption of the 3rd cent., some mines were operating again in the 4th cent.

The Romans rarely opened up new areas of mining, but often expanded the scale of production and the variety of metals mined in regions already known for their mineral potential. Techniques of prospection relied heavily on observation of visible veins of mineralization in rock deposits and changes in soil colour. Of the precious metals only gold (and to a lesser degree copper) existed in a natural state. Silver, copper, lead, and tin occurred in compound metal deposits (ores) and required metallurgical processing to convert them into usable metals. Three main types of mining were practised: the exploitation of alluvial deposits; opencast mining of rock-deposits found near the surface; and underground mining of deeper-lying rock-deposits. The Romans exploited alluvial deposits of gold and tin by panning or, if they were larger in scale, by flushing the alluvium with large quantities of water released at high speed in sluices to separate the metal-bearing sands from the dross. In underground mines vertical shafts were sunk often in pairs occasionally to an impressive depth: 340 m. (1,115 ft.) at one mine near New Carthage. Horizontal galleries, often strengthened with wooden props, connected the shafts, increased ventilation, and allowed ore once mined to be removed from the ore-face. Terracotta oil-lamps were placed in niches to provide lighting. Drainage was a problem in deeper mines. Manual bailing was practised, but if possible, drainage adits were cut through sterile rock. In some mines chain-pumps, Archimedean screw-pumps, or a series of water-lifting wheels were used. Mining tools, including picks, hammers, and gads, were mainly of iron, while ore was collected in buckets made of esparto grass before being hauled, in some cases by pulleys, to the surface.

Many mines (especially gold and silver mines) over time became the property of the Roman state, but cities and private individuals continued to own and operate mines. In state-owned mines the state either organized production directly, as probably occurred in the gold-mining region of NW Spain, or it leased out contracts to work the mines to individuals, small associations or the larger *societates publicanorum* (see PUBLICANI). Mineworkers were often slaves, but prisoners of war, convicts, and free-born wage labourers also formed part of the workforce. Tombstones from mining settlements show that people often migrated long distances to work at mines. Soldiers were stationed at the larger mines, not just to supervise the labour force, but also to provide technological expertise. Any mining site needed a large number of ancillary workers to keep the labour force fed, clothed, and equipped, and to assist in processing ore into usable metals.

Minoan civilization, the bronze age civilization of *Crete (c.3500–1100 BC). The term 'Minoan' (after *Minos) was coined by Sir Arthur Evans to distinguish the prehistoric culture of Crete revealed in his excavations beginning in 1900 at Cnossus from the *Mycenaean civilization revealed by Schliemann on the Greek mainland.

Mīnos, mythical king of *Crete, who lived three generations before the Trojan War. The island's bronze age civilization has been named 'Minoan' after him (see preceding entry). He was a son of *Zeus and *Europa, whom Zeus in bull-form had carried to Crete from *Tyre or Sidon. In a contest for the kingship Minos prayed to *Poseidon to send him a bull from the sea for sacrifice. The god complied, but the bull was so handsome that Minos kept it for himself. Poseidon therefore caused Minos' wife Pāsiphaē to fall in love with the bull, and from their unnatural union the *Minotaur was born and kept in the *labyrinth built by *Daedalus. 'Labyrinth' occurs in Linear B (see MYCENAEAN LANGUAGE) and has been connected with the double axe (*labrys*), a Minoan religious symbol, and with the palace of Cnossus. The myth probably conceals bronze age cult involving Zeus, the bull, and Minos, although the king was not divine.

Minos was the most royal of mortal kings, the favourite of Zeus, who granted him kingship and renewed it every nine years. With his brother Rhadamanthys he gave the first laws to mankind, and acted as judge of the living and the dead. Minos' reputation as first thalassocrat see SEA POWER) recalls Minoan influence in the bronze age. Attic legend called him cruel. He made war on *Megara and Athens to avenge his son Androgeos, and he forced the Athenians to send an annual tribute of seven young men and women to be sacrificed to the Minotaur until *Theseus slew the monster: Minos died violently in Sicily. He had followed the fugitive Daedalus to the court of King Cocalus, whose daughters scalded him to death in his bath.

Minotaur See DAEDALUS; LABYRINTH; MINOS; THESEUS.

mint (for coins) see COINAGE, GREEK and ROMAN.

miracles Stories of the power of the gods were common throughout antiquity, many of them rooted in personal devotion, as appears e.g. from *votive inscriptions expressing gratitude for a miraculous recovery. A large group is linked with particular cults and cult places allegedly founded following miraculous deeds by the deity involved, who thus showed his/her divine power. Early instances can be found in the *Homeric *Hymns*, e.g. those to *Dionysus, *Demeter, and *Apollo. From the 4th cent. BC onwards there is a rapid increase in miracle-stories, and the connection with *epiphany receives ever more emphasis. Among the epigraphic evidence the miracles performed by *Asclepius in Epidaurus (4th cent. BC) are esp. significant. Slightly earlier, literature reveals a new impetus in *Euripides' *Bacchae*. Miracles (healing, punitive, and other) are now explicitly pictured as divine instruments to exact worship and submission. In the same period the term *aretē*—lit. the 'virtue' of a god—develops the meaning 'miracle',

which entails the rise of so-called aretalogies: quasi-liturgical enumerations of the qualities, achievements, and power of a specific god. All these features abound in and after the Hellenistic period in the cults of great foreign gods, e.g. Sarapis and *Isis, and no less in Christian texts. The fierce competition between, and radical demand of devout submission to, these new gods fostered a propagandistic tendency to publicize the gods' miraculous deeds. 'Miracle proved deity', and as such it was often welcomed with the exclamation ('God is one'), thus contributing to the shaping of 'henotheistic' religiosity.

mirrors See COSMETICS.

Mithradates Persian name borne most famously by six of the eight Hellenistic kings of Pontus in Asia Minor.

Mithradates VI Eupator Dionysus (120–63 BC) was the greatest king of Pontus, and Rome's most dangerous enemy in the 1st cent. BC. After murdering his mother and brother, his next exploit was conquering the Crimea and northern *Euxine. Ultimate control of most of the circuit of the Black Sea gave him almost inexhaustible supplies of men and materials for his military campaigns. In Cappadocia he continued to try to exert indirect control through agents. For the more aggressive annexation of Paphlagonia he took as ally his most powerful neighbour, Nicomedes III of *Bithynia, but later fell out with him. A famous meeting with *Marius in 99/8, and the armed intervention of *Sulla in Cappadocia c.95, made it clear that war with Rome was inevitable, and he prepared carefully. While Italy was preoccupied by the *Social War, he annexed Bithynia and Cappadocia. Skilful diplomacy, masterly propaganda and Roman overreaction enabled him to cast Rome in the role of aggressor and cause of the First Mithradatic War which followed (89–85). His armies swept all before them in Asia, where he ordered a massacre of resident Romans and Italians (the 'Asian Vespers'). He failed to capture Rhodes, but was welcomed in Athens and won over most of Greece. The Roman response came in 87, when Sulla arrived in Greece with five legions. He defeated the Pontic armies, besieged and captured Athens, and took the war to Asia. Mithradates surrendered at the Peace of Dardanus, and was allowed to retire to Pontus. The Second Mithradatic War (c.83–81) was no more than a series of skirmishes with Sulla's lieutenant, but when Nicomedes IV of Bithynia died and bequeathed his kingdom to

Rome, Mithradates again prepared for war. Having allied himself with *Sertorius, the Roman rebel in Spain, he invaded Bithynia, thus precipitating the Third Mithradatic War. The advance faltered immediately with a failure to capture *Cyzicus, and the Roman forces, ably led by *Licinius Lucullus, pushed Eupator out of Pontus into Armenia, where he took refuge with King Tigranes II, his son-in-law. He failed to win *Parthian support, but was able to return to Pontus in 68. *Pompey, newly appointed to the Mithradatic command, easily defeated him, and forced him to retreat to his Crimean kingdom. He was said to be planning to invade Italy by land, when his son led a revolt against him. Inured to poison by years of practice, he had to ask an obliging Gallic bodyguard to run him through with a sword. Mithradates presented himself both as a civilized philhellene—he consciously copied the portraiture and actions of Alexander the Great—and as an oriental monarch, and although in many ways he achieved a remarkably successful fusion of east and west, he failed either to understand or to match the power of Rome.

Mithras, an ancient Indo-Iranian god adopted in the Roman empire as the principal deity of a mystery cult which flourished in the 2nd and 3rd cents. AD. Iranian Mithra was a god of compact (the lit. meaning of his name), cattle-herding, and the dawn light, aspects of which survive (or were re-created) in his western manifestation, since Roman Mithras was a sun-god ('invincible sun god Mithras'), a 'bull-killer', and 'cattle-thief', and the saviour of the sworn brothers of his cult.

The cult is known primarily from its archaeological remains. Over 400 find-spots are recorded, many of them excavated meeting-places. These and the c.1,000 dedicatory inscriptions give a good idea of cult life and membership. Some 1,150 pieces of sculpture (and a few frescos) carry a rich sacred art, although the iconography remains elusive in default of the explanatory sacred texts. Literary references to Mithras and Mithraism are as scarce as the material remains are abundant.

Mithraism was an organization of cells. Small autonomous groups of initiates, exclusively male, met for fellowship and worship in chambers of modest size and distinctive design which they called 'caves'. A cave is an 'image of the universe', and acc. to *Porphyry the archetypal Mithraeum was designed and furnished as a kind of microcosmic model. Mithraea were sometimes sited in real *caves or set against rock-faces or were made to imitate caves by vaulting or decoration or by secluding them in dim interior or underground rooms. The Mithraeum's most distinctive (and unvarying) feature is the pair of platforms flanking a central aisle. It was on these that the initiates reclined for a communal meal. Visual representations show that this meal was the human counterpart of a divine banquet shared by Mithras and the sun-god (the latter appearing on the monuments as a separate being) on the hide of the bull killed by the former in his greatest exploit.

Initiates were ranked in a hierarchy of seven grades, each under the protection of one of the planets: Raven (Mercury), 'Nymphus' (Venus), Soldier (Mars), Lion (Jupiter), Persian (Moon), 'Heliodromus' (Sun), Father (Saturn). This was apparently a lay hierarchy, not a professional priesthood. Mithraists, as their monuments attest, remained in and of the secular world. It is unlikely that the full hierarchy was represented in each Mithraeum, although probable that most were presided over by one or more Fathers. The disparate connotations of the various ranks, the two idiosyncratic coinages ('Heliodromus' and 'Nymphus'—the latter would mean, if anything, 'male bride'), and the unique planetary order all signify an unusually inventive construct.

Actual Mithraea or traces of the cult have been found in almost every quarter of the Roman empire, though with two notable areas of concentration. The first was Rome itself and *Ostia. In Ostia, some fifteen Mithraea have been discovered in the excavated area that comprises about half of the town's total. Extrapolation to Rome, where some 35 locations are known, would yield a total of perhaps as many as 700 Mithraea. The number is impressive (if speculative), but individual Mithraea were small, and even if all were in service contemporaneously, they would accommodate no more than 2 per cent of the population. The other area of concentration was the empire's European frontier from Britain to the mouth of the Danube. As inscriptions confirm, Mithraism's typical recruits were soldiers and minor functionaries. Many were *freedmen or slaves. Mithraism did not attract the upper classes (except as occasional patrons) until its final days as the rather artificial creature of the pagan aristocracy of 4th-cent. Rome. It was always better represented in the Latin west than the Greek east.

Did the cult develop from and perpetuate a stream of Zoroastrianism, or was it essentially a western creation with 'Persian' trimmings? (See

RELIGION, PERSIAN; ZOROASTER.) Almost the only firm datum is *Plutarch's remark that the Cilician pirates suppressed by *Pompey had secret initiatory rites of Mithras, which had endured to his own day. These may have been a prototype of the developed *mysteries.

The cult's theology and its sacred myth must be recovered, if at all, from the monuments. Principal among these is the icon of Mithras killing a bull, which was always set as a focal point at one end of the Mithraeum. Mithras is shown astride the bull, plunging a dagger into its flank. The victim's tail is metamorphosed into an ear of wheat. Mithras is accompanied by dog, snake, scorpion, and raven; also by two minor deities, dressed like him in 'Persian' attire and each carrying a torch (one raised, the other inverted), whose names are known from dedications. Above the scene, which is enacted in front of a cave, are images of *Sol and Luna. This strange assemblage challenges interpretation. Clearly, the killing is an act of sacrifice, but to what end? It has been seen variously as an action which creates or ends the world or which in some sense 'saves' the world or at least the initiates within it.

The bull-killing is but one episode, albeit the most important, in a cycle of Mithraic myth represented (in no set order) on the monuments. Other episodes are Mithras' birth from a rock, the hunt and capture of the bull, and the feast celebrated with Sol. The banquet scene is sometimes shown on the reverse of bull-killing reliefs, as salvific effect from salvific cause. See MYSTERY CULTS.

Mithridates See MITHRADATES.

Mitylēnē See MYTILENE.

monarchy See KINGSHIP.

money may be regarded as a conventional means of representing a claim or a right to goods or services. Its existence may result from anything between a tacit understanding within a society and state legislation. And a wide variety of objects may function as money in its different uses—for payments, for storing wealth, for measuring value, and as a means of exchange. It is likely that at an early stage valuable and imperishable objects, such as metal, served to convert surplus produce into a means for the acquisition of other produce in the future; at the same time, any commodity, such as cattle, may have served for measuring value. A decisive step was taken when an organized community designated an official monetary unit, normally of precious metal, for collective purposes, whether for measuring value or for payments, for fines, or for taxes. This step had been taken in most near eastern kingdoms by the beginning of the iron age, in many Greek communities by 800 BC, in Rome by 500. The production of money in the form of coinage began in western Asia Minor about 600 and spread rapidly in the Greek world, more slowly in the Phoenician world, in the Roman world from the late 4th cent. In the Greek world, the use of spits, *oboloi*, as objects of value is reflected in the use of *oboloi* as monetary units and denominations of most Greek coinage systems. See COINAGE, GREEK and ROMAN.

Despite the spread of coinage, not only in the Greek, Phoenician, and Roman worlds, but also to communities on their fringes—from Parthia to Spain—even in the high Roman empire, there were large areas of the Mediterranean world in which coinage played a minimal role.

The ratio between the principal metals—*gold, *silver, *bronze—varied over time, with such factors as the increasing transfer to the Greek world of gold from Persia or the exploitation of silver-mines in Spain. these shifts naturally affected the relationships between different monetary units and different coin denominations.

See also BANKS; CREDIT.

monopolies In classical antiquity monopolistic control aimed above all at increasing revenues and was the prerogative of the state: 'cornering the market' by individuals was an almost mythical occurrence. State control and leasing of silver deposits in Attica (see LAURIUM) marks a long-term revenue-raising monopoly. In Ptolemaic *Egypt, monopoly control of goods and services, usually by sale and lease of rights, was a way of life (from oil and textiles to beer and goose-breeding). In the Roman empire, sale of monopolies by cities was a regular revenue-raising device. See ECONOMY, GREEK, HELLENISTIC, and ROMAN.

monotheism Apart from the influence of developed Judaism (see RELIGION, JEWISH) and *Christianity, no such thing as monotheism in the strict sense, i.e. the refusal to use the predicate 'god' of any but one being, existed in classical antiquity; even theistic philosophers, such as *Plato, *Aristotle, or the Stoics (see STOICISM), acknowledged the existence of subordinate deities (even if no more than planetary gods) beside the supreme one. Locally, it was usual enough to refer to one particular deity as 'the god' or 'the goddess', e.g. *Athena at Athens, *Apollo at *Delphi. But a further tendency towards monotheism may be detected, at any rate in Greek popular religion as interpreted by non-philosophical authors. The supremacy of *Zeus increases. Even in *Homer's (*Iliad* 8) he is much stronger than all the other gods put together; later authors tend to use 'Zeus', 'the gods', 'God' indiscriminately. To *Aeschylus Zeus is the supreme moral governor of the universe, though even there the existence of other gods is clearly recognized. Hellenistic writers favour vague phrases like 'the divine'. In the philosophical tradition, esp. that of Platonism, virtual monotheism is espoused, though there the single organizing principle of the universe is very much an impersonal force. See ANGELS.

months See CALENDAR, GREEK and ROMAN; TIME-RECKONING.

moon See ASTROLOGY; ASTRONOMY; CALENDAR, GREEK and ROMAN; SELENE; TIME-RECKONING.

mosaic Floors paved with natural pebbles arranged in simple geometric designs were used in the near east in the 8th cent. BC. In the Greek world, unpatterned pebble floors were known in Minoan and Mycenaean times; decorated pebble mosaics are first attested at the end of the 5th cent., at *Corinth and *Olynthus. The earliest examples had simple two-dimensional designs, both geometric and figured, usually light on a dark ground. Their use, mainly in private houses, spread throughout Greece during the 4th cent.; by its end a wider range of colours was used, and attempts were made to achieve more three-dimensional effects. Outstanding examples of this phase come from the palatial houses at Pella in Macedonia, late 4th cent. See HOUSES, GREEK.

The technique of tessellated mosaic, in which pieces of stone or marble were cut in cubes and fitted together in a bed of mortar, was invented during the 3rd cent. Tesserae were cut irregularly at first, then with greater precision; by the 2nd cent. a technique had appeared, in which tiny pieces, sometimes less than 1 mm. square, in a wide range of colours, were fitted so closely together as to imitate the effects of painting. Mosaics in this last technique often took the form of *emblēmata*: panels produced in the artists' studio, and then inserted into the floor at the centre of a coarser surround of tessellated

mosaic. Outstanding examples have been found near *Alexandria, and in *Pergamum; *Pliny the Elder records the mosaicist Sosus of Pergamum, famous for his representation of an 'unswept floor' littered with the debris of a meal, and for a scene of Drinking Doves, reflected in several Roman copies. The largest number of mosaics of the Hellenistic period is found in *Delos; they range from pavements of unshaped chips to very fine *emblēmata*.

In Italy mosaics of Hellenistic style are found in Rome, *Pompeii, and elsewhere from the late 2nd cent. onwards; outstanding examples are the Alexander mosaic (see ALEXANDER (2) THE GREAT) from the House of the Faun in *Pompeii and the Nile mosaic from *Praeneste. Tessellated mosaics with geometric patterns, coloured or black-and-white, became increasingly common in the 1st cent. BC.

Under the empire mosaics became mass-produced; they were widespread in private houses and superior apartments, and in large public buildings such as *baths. Geometric designs were much more common than figured work, and fine *emblēmata*, always objects of luxury, became rare. In Italy throughout the first three centuries AD, most mosaics were black-and-white, with all-over geometric or floral designs, or with figures in black silhouette. The figures might be set in panels, or as abstract all-over designs covering the greater part of the floor.

Much of the western empire adopted the use of mosaic under Italian influence during the 1st and 2nd cents. AD; a taste for polychromy prevailed over the black-and-white style. Each province tended to develop its own character, with a repertory of favourite designs and methods of composition. Among the most distinctive are those of North Africa; elaborate polychrome geometric and floral designs were favoured, and figure scenes often formed all-over compositions covering large areas of floor with minimal indication of depth or recession. Subject-matter here was often directly related to the interests and activities of the patrons, with scenes from the amphitheatre, the hunting-field, or the country estate. Closely related are the pavements of the 4th-cent. villa at *Piazza Armerina. In Spain the most striking mosaics come from villas of the late empire: they have much in common with the African floors, but include more mythological or literary subjects. In Britain some individual workshops have been distinguished, esp. from the 4th cent.

The development in the eastern empire is less well known, but a fine series has been excavated at Antioch. The Hellenistic tradition of the pictorial figure scene persisted. Fine pictorial mosaics of the 4th cent. have been found at several sites in *Syria. At the end of the 4th cent. they gave way to all-over two-dimensional designs, both geometric and figured, best exemplified by the 5th-cent. 'hunting-carpets' of Antioch.

The use of mosaic on walls and vaults was a Roman invention. In the late republic grottoes and fountains (see NYMPHAEUM) were decorated with shells, pumice-stone, and pieces of *glass, from which the use of regular glass tesserae developed. Numerous small fountains in Pompeii were decorated in this way, and more extensive mosaic decoration on walls is found there and in Rome in the 1st cent. AD; patterns and designs were more closely related to wall-painting than to floor mosaic. The technique was used on a large scale for vaults and walls in buildings such as baths and tombs in the 2nd and 3rd cents. The use of mosaic in Christian *churches from the 4th cent. onwards is an extension of this development.

Moschus, of *Syracuse, elegant *hexameter poet of the mid-2nd cent. BC; counted as second in the canonical list of three Bucolic poets, between *Theocritus and Bion. Like most Hellenistic poets, he combined creative writing with scholarship. His masterpiece is *Europa*, a 166-line pocket epic narrating the abduction of the Phoenician princess by Zeus in bull-form. It exhibits all the marks of the classic '*epyllion': neat exposition of the situation in time and space, brief but rhetorical speeches, dreams and prophecies, a summary conclusion, and esp. the elaborate, 25-line *ekphrasis of the golden basket which *Europa takes to the seaside meadow, inlaid by *Hephaestus with scenes which (unbeknown to her) prefigure her own imminent fate. The language is highly polished; indeed, polished can become precious.

mother-city See MĒTROPOLIS.

motherhood

Greek Women were deemed to have a right to *marriage and *children. Physicians maintained that intercourse and *childbirth were necessary to female health and prescribed pregnancy to cure pathological conditions; records of miraculous cures at the sanctuary of *Asclepius in *Epidaurus reflect a high level of sterility anxiety. Views of the maternal contribution to genetic inheritance differ: *Apollo's denial of female parentage in Aeschylus' *Eumenides* and *Aristotle's restriction of procreative agency to male spermatic fluid are countered by the Hippocratic belief (see HIPPOCRATES) that the embryo results from the union of male and female seed, its sex determined by the stronger of the two. From a judicial standpoint, *Pericles' law of 451/0 BC restricting citizenship to children of two Athenian parents made the mother's civic status fundamental to *inheritance questions.

Contrary to the Spartan practice of delaying marriage, Athenian girls married and bore children soon after puberty. Early pregnancy and inadequate hygiene made labour hazardous, as the comparison of childbirth and battle attests (Euripides, *Medea* 248–251). The male foetus was considered to be more active, healthier for the mother to bear, and easier to deliver. *Artemis was the chief divinity presiding over childbirth, although numerous lesser powers were also invoked. Women gave birth at home, attended by *midwives and friends; all participants incurred ritual *pollution, the mother's possibly lasting until post-partum bleeding stopped. Brides were not fully assimilated into conjugal families until after the birth of the first child.

Maternal love was idealized as unconditional, selfless, and stronger than that of a father. Though often assisted by wet-nurses or dry-nurses, the mother was accordingly viewed as the infant's primary care-giver. Boys were raised in the women's quarters until they began formal education at about age 6; girls remained with their mothers until marriage. Physical separation of mother and child was a regular consequence of divorce, as fathers retained custody. *Widows, however, might go on caring for their offspring, residing either in the dead husband's house or with other kin. Mothers continued to play an active part in the lives of adult children. Although the bond between mother and son was felt to be esp. close, hints of strain occur. *Aristophanes' comic representation of a spoiled only son in *Clouds*, *Plato's family history of the timocratic man in *Republic*, and *Herodas' vignette of a mother exasperated by a truant boy all depend upon the recognizable stereotype of a domineering mother. The legendary 'Spartan mother' may be a fictive projection of similar tensions. Real sons and mothers were nevertheless expected to assume mutual responsibilities to one another throughout their lives, the grown son becoming his mother's protector in her widowhood and old age. See LOVE AND FRIENDSHIP; WIDOWS.

Roman The Roman word for mother (*māter*) is reflected in such words as *māterfamiliās* and *mātrōna*, a respectable wife. The legendary 'first' Roman divorce was of a virtuous wife unable to bear children and thus fulfil the formal purpose of *marriage. The promotion of citizen marriage and procreation (see CHILDBIRTH) by the legislation of *Augustus included some honorific awards for mothers (see IUS LIBERORUM).

Roman ideal mothers tended to be praised for instilling the foundations of traditional morality and rhetorical skills, with the emphasis on the mother's influence on the education of her adolescent or young adult son. Roman authors praise the moral severity and hardheadedness of the ideal mother's guidance, as in the case of *Cornelia, mother of the *Gracchi, or Caesar's mother Aurelia. Being widows by the time their sons reached adolescence, these two mothers might have taken on socializing roles otherwise performed by fathers, but Roman marriage and mortality patterns meant that a fatherless adolescence was not abnormal. Roman literary historical sources stress the role played by such mothers in forming the character of famous sons of the political élite or imperial family. References to mothers and young children or mothers and daughters are rare and incidental. Mother–daughter combinations tend to figure in the context of *betrothal, where mothers played a greater role than might be expected from the legal concentration on the powers of the *paterfamilias. Iconographic, inscriptional, and legal sources flesh out our knowledge, but, like the literary sources, concentrate on ideal (or, in the case of law, problematic) aspects of family relations. Imaginative literature, such as satire, provides larger-than-life model mothers, monster mothers, and wicked stepmothers. Roman *children from an early age were likely to enjoy relations with a variety of care-givers rather than exclusively with the biological mother. Maternal breast-feeding, advocated by male moralists, would have depended in practice on social and economic considerations.

mountain cults Mountains were places of special cult, to the point that Mt. Maenalus in Arcadia (central *Peloponnese) was considered sacred to *Pan in its entirety. The location of a *sanctuary was rarely the exact summit of the mountain, but more often in the passes or on the slopes. The sanctuary could include a temple, as at *Bassae, or might be more rustic and simple (see CAVES). Worshippers were mainly shepherds, depicted on their *votives. The deities most often worshipped were *Zeus, the weather-god, *Artemis, goddess of the animal world and of boundaries, *Hermes, a country god and patron of shepherds, *Apollo, another pastoral god, and Pan, the divine herdsman and hunter of small game. Certain types of myth have a connection with mountains, such as myths of the birth of gods. The mountain solitude and the presence of divinities of nature in the form of *kourotrophos nymphs would give the young gods a secluded and suitable upbringing before their integration into divine society.

Mucius Scaevola (1), **Quintus,** called **'Augur',** Stoic (see STOICISM), eminent *lawyer. Praetor *c.*120 BC, he was accused of *extortion after governing Asia, but acquitted. (The trial was satirized by *Lucilius (1).) He was consul in 117, and in 100 opposed *Appuleius Saturninus. He taught (among others) his son-in-law *Licinius Crassus and, in his old age, *Cicero, who venerated his memory and introduced him into several dialogues. Alone among the *principēs* present in the city, he opposed *Sulla after his march on Rome (88) and aided *Marius, who had married his granddaughter. He died soon after.

Mucius Scaevola (2), **Quintus,** called **'Pontifex',** son of Publius Mucius Scaevola, whom he surpassed both as an orator and a *lawyer. In his most famous case, the *causa Curiana*, he defended the strict wording of a will, against the defence of equity and intention by *Licinius Crassus. As consuls (95 BC), he and Crassus passed the *lex Licinia Mucia* instituting a *quaestio* (see QUAESTIONES) against foreigners who had been illegally enrolled as citizens. He was sent as proconsul to govern Asia. He reorganized the troubled province with the aid of his *legate *Rutilius Rufus and, departing after nine months, left Rutilius in charge. When Rutilius was prosecuted in 92, he escaped prosecution, probably through his remote connection with *Marius and because of his high prestige, and in 89 he became *pontifex maximus*, the last civil lawyer known to have held this office. After Marius' death he was threatened but escaped harm and remained in Rome under the government of *Cornelius Cinna and *Papirius Carbo, loyal to the government and advising compromise with *Sulla. He was killed in 82.

Scaevola was perhaps the leading lawyer of the later Roman republic. His eighteen books on the civil law was the most famous legal treatise of the period. He was the first lawyer to give serious attention to classification; thus, he distinguished five types of *guardianship. But, despite his grounding in Greek culture, he did not succeed in reducing the civil law to a system, though he helped to make it morally more acceptable. Thus he fixed on the conscientious head of a family as the pattern of correct behaviour in avoiding harm to others. His large legal practice was attended by many pupils.

Mummius, Lūcius, as praetor and proconsul (153/2 BC) defeated the Iberian Lusitani, triumphing 152. As consul 146 he succeeded Caecilius Metellus Macedonicus in Macedonia and in the command against the revolt of the *Achaean Confederacy, which he defeated. He destroyed Corinth, making the land *ager publicus*, then, with a senatorial commission, organized the province of Macedonia and dealt with the Greek cities, calling on *Polybius for advice. He punished those involved in the revolt, dissolved the confederacy as a political unit, and arranged for Greece to be supervised by future commanders in Macedonia. The works of art taken, on an unprecedented scale, from Corinth and other cities (see BOOTY) were largely given to his friends or to Italian and provincial communities in his *clientela* (see CLIENS), or set up for display in Rome. He celebrated a triumph and became *censor (142) with *Cornelius Scipio Aemilianus, moderating his severity. He died soon after.

Munātius Plancus, Lūcius, of senatorial family, served under *Caesar in the Gallic and Civil Wars, and in 45 BC was one of Caesar's six prefects of the city. Proconsul of Gallia Comata (see GAUL (TRANSALPINE)) after Caesar's death, he founded *Lugdunum. In letters to Cicero he asserted his loyalty to the republic, while advising peace with Marcus *Antonius (Mark Antony). Probably after Octavian's march on Rome, he joined Antony and *Aemilius Lepidus (3). In the triumviral *proscriptions he was said to have put his own brother's name on the list. In December 43 he triumphed, became consul 42 with Lepidus, and then or later restored the temple of Saturn (see SATURNUS) out of his triumphal spoils. In the Perusine War he failed to assist *Antonius (Pietas), then escaped with *Fulvia to Antony in Greece. After governing Asia (40) and, during Antony's Parthian campaign, Syria as Antony's deputy (35), he joined Antony in *Alexandria and outdid himself in flattery of *Cleopatra VII. Before *Actium he joined Octavian, later claiming that he had refused to fight for Cleopatra. In 27 he moved that Octavian be called 'Augustus'. In 22 he was censor. He was buried at Caieta, where his tomb inscription was found. His daughter Munatia Plancina married Gnaeus *Calpurnius Piso.

mūnicipium, the institution through which the Roman state became incorporative, and thus developed from a city-state to accommodate much greater numbers of enfranchised citizens than had any *polis.

The term means 'the undertaking of duty'. Originally the duty in question no doubt varied. As the institution evolved, the duty to provide military assistance, and the reward of incorporation in the Roman body politic on settling in Rome, became paramount. In actuality, an asymmetry between Rome and any of its municipal partners grew steadily. Municipal status originally often went with citizenship without the vote at Rome, though the right of voting might be added, or acquired through movement to Rome. Roman supervision became more systematic. The line between second-class citizenship and subjugation was fine, and in the 3rd cent., e.g. in the case of *Capua, it can be hard to tell who in a municipal relationship with Rome thought the deal a privilege and who a disgrace. After the war against *Hannibal choices became more limited.

Municipia that had been given the vote retained the title *municipium*, and it was on this model that after the enfranchisement of Italy in 89 BC, all communities that were not *coloniae* became *municipia*. Some regularity in the charters and institutions of these communities was achieved, and a process of formation of civic nuclei in areas where there had been only villages was encouraged: this continued under *Augustus. Most of the cities of Italy from this point on were thus *municipia*, usually governed by magistrates called *quattuorviri*. But the institution was still mutating.

On the analogy of practice in Italy before the *Social War, some loyal communities in the provinces were made *municipia*: rewarded for military service, i.e. by a sort of citizen right, usually the *ius Latii*. Marius seems to have done this in Africa; *Caesar did it in Cisalpine Gaul (see GAUL (CISALPINE)), and then on a very grand scale in *Baetica. Augustus regularized the process in a law which also established a model charter. This is known through the versions of it which were used in the Flavian continuation of the process of municipalization in southern Spain. Under this charter the *quattuorviri* are replaced by two pairs of magistrates, and every five years there are to be censor-like special magistrates.

In its imperial form, the old theory of military service and reward is still present. As a way of spreading the citizenship and rewarding loyalty of a political kind, while encouraging responsible and governmentally helpful behaviour on the part of local élites, it became a standard benefaction from the centre to the provinces of the west; though the higher status of *colonia* replaced this function in the 2nd cent. AD. There remained in Gaul and Britain, and in the Rhine and Danube provinces, many *civitates* (see CIVITAS), communities with a legal status which had not been incorporated in this way. The dissemination of the citizenship, complete by 212, rendered the partial citizen rights of the *ius Latii* obsolete. See CITIZENSHIP, ROMAN; COLONIZATION, ROMAN.

mūnus, a gift or service, given or rendered freely (a lover's gift, or the gifts of gods to men) or, more commonly, out of a sense of duty (burial of the dead, sacrifices, or funeral games). The latter sense leads to its use in Roman public life, for what a person owes to the state or community of which he is a citizen or in which he lives. There are personal *munera*, esp. military service or service as a magistrate—for the latter, the word becomes common, as such service, under the empire, turns into an onerous obligation—and financial *munera*: taxes and contributions corresponding to Greek *liturgies. At least by the middle republic, men could be exempted by law from *munera* for various kinds of services, and such *immunitas* spread under the empire to whole classes of citizens deemed essential to the state, with increasing pressure on those not exempt. *Immunitas* could similarly be conferred on communities that would normally have owed taxes to Rome (see TRIBUTUM).

murder See LAW AND PROCEDURE, ATHENIAN and ROMAN (3); PARRICIDE.

Mūsaeus, a mythical singer with a descriptive name ('He of the Muses'). He belongs esp. to *Eleusis, where he is either autochthonous (see AUTOCHTHONS) or an immigrant from *Thrace, the land of mythical singers. He is father of *Eumolpus, the eponymous hero of the chief priestly family of Eleusis, and his wife has her grave beneath the Telesterion; the couple and their son Eumolpus are shown on a red-figure vase of the Meidias Painter.

Muses, goddesses upon whom poets—and later other artists, philosophers, and intellectuals generally—depended for the ability to create their works. They were goddesses, not only because they were the daughters of *Zeus and Mnēmosynē ('memory') and lived on *Olympus. They are called goddesses from the earliest sources on, and their attitude to mankind is identical to that of gods: they do not hesitate to destroy a mortal who dares to usurp their place (so Thamyris, in Homer's *Iliad* bk. 2, whom they paralysed), and they are divinely contemptuous of humankind (it does not matter to them whether the poetry they inspire is true or false. Muses appear both singly and in groups of varying sizes. Homer addresses a single goddess or Muse but knows there are more. The canonical nine and their names probably originated with *Hesiod. They were: Calliopē (epic poetry), Clīō (history), Euterpē (*aulos-playing), Terpsichorē (lyric poetry and dancing, esp. choral), Eratō (lyric poetry), Melpomenē (tragedy), Thalīa (comedy), Polyhymnia (hymns and pantomime), Ūrania (astronomy). But their names, functions, and number fluctuated.

The earliest sources locate the Muses at Pieria, just north of Olympus, and on Olympus itself; they are associated with so-called 'Thracian' bards, *Orpheus, Thamyris, and *Musaeus. That region appears to have been their first home. A southern group, the Muses of Mt. *Helicon, is identified by Hesiod with the Muses of Olympus and Pieria, perhaps because of an underlying connection between the two regions, but possibly because the young poet himself saw fit to make the association as a means to enhance his own reputation. NW of Helicon rises the sacred mountain Parnassus, with which also the Muses are associated.

Hesiod's influence led eventually to the establishment of a formal cult and sanctuary below Helicon in the Vale of the Muses. This may have been the first 'Mouseion' (*Museum: it housed, in the open air, statues of both legendary and historical notables). Philosophers, traditionally beginning with *Pythagoras, adopted the Muses as their special goddesses. From Hellenistic times they were a popular subject, individually or as a group, in sculpture and *mosaics.

Museum, originally a place connected with the *Muses or the arts inspired by them. When a religious meaning was attached, an altar or a temple was built to mark the spot. But the main meaning of the word was literary and educational. Thus Mt. *Helicon had a Museum containing the manuscripts of *Hesiod and statues of those who had upheld the arts. Almost any school could be called 'the place of the Muses'. There was a Museum in *Plato's *Academy and in *Aristotle's Lyceum.

By far the most famous Museum was that of *Alexandria, founded by *Ptolemy (1) I Soter. It was distinct from the *Library. Both were near the palace, but the exact site of neither is known. The Museum housed a band of scholars, who were supported by a generous salary granted by the Ptolemies and later by the Caesars, who appointed a president or priest as head of the institution. If lectures were given at all, they were secondary to research, but there were many discussions in which the kings joined. Dinners or symposia (see SYMPOSIUM), illuminated by witticisms, epigrams, and the solution of problems, were frequent. Acc. to one source, a record was kept of the solutions offered. The papyri suggest that the influence of the Museum stabilized the texts of authors, esp. *Homer, and ensured that a supply of *books could reach the smaller towns. The buildings, splendidly furnished by the Ptolemies, included a communal dining-hall, a recess with seats for discussions and lectures, a covered walk planted with trees.

Political upheavals *c*.146 BC caused learned men, including *Aristarchus (2), to flee from Alexandria, which was henceforth rivalled by *Pergamum as well as by Athens, *Rhodes, Antioch, Berytus, and Rome. The Museum suffered in reputation, but *Cleopatra VII, the last of the Ptolemies, still took part in its discussions. Acc. to a doubtful tradition, Mark Antony (Marcus *Antonius) gave the Pergamene library to Alexandria to make up for loss by fire during Caesar's siege, 47 BC. Prosperity returned under the *pax Augusta*. The early emperors visited the Museum and extended its buildings, and *Hadrian bestowed special care on it. The Museum was visited by famous literati like *Plutarch, Dio Cocceianus, *Lucian, and *Galen. In AD 216 it suffered under *Caracalla. It was destroyed, after the occupation of Alexandria by *Zenobia, in 272, but seems to have resumed its activities. It is unlikely to have survived long after *Theodosius I's edict of 391 requiring the destruction of pagan temples. The *Suda* gives the last member of the Museum as Theon, father of *Hypatia (*c*. AD 380). In the Ptolemaic period the Museum was famous for science and literary scholarship; in the 2nd cent. AD for the New Rhetoric; in the 3rd cent. for *Neoplatonism.

music

1. In Greek and Roman Life 'Let me not live without music', sings a chorus of greybeards in *Euripides. Expressions such as 'without music', 'chorusless', 'lyreless' evoked the dreary bitterness of war, the *Erinyes' curse, or death. Poetic pictures of unblemished happiness are correspondingly resonant with music; and in every sort of revel and celebration, Greeks of all social classes sang, *danced, and played instruments, besides listening to professional performances. Music was credited with divine origins and mysterious powers, and was a pivot of relations between mortals and gods. It was central to public religious observance (as in the north frieze of the Parthenon), and to such semi-religious occasions as weddings, funerals, and harvests. At the great *panhellenic *festivals and their many local counterparts, choruses and vocal and instrumental soloists competed no less than athletes for prizes and glory.

The best Greek soloists and composers were usually in some sense professionals, but choruses of singers and dancers remained citizen-amateurs until Hellenistic times (see DITHYRAMB; COMEDY (GREEK), OLD; TRAGEDY, GREEK), and often later. Well-bred Greek citizens could perform competently on an instrument (usually the lyre, sometimes the *aulos; see 2 below) as well as in singing and choral dance. When *Achilles, the toughest of the Greek warriors, is found playing the lyre and singing in his tent, no one is surprised. Humbler folk sang at their work, piped to their flocks, or kept time to music at their oars. Guests at the *symposium listened to girl *aulos*-players and other hired entertainers. Women made music in their domestic quarters. Music was essential to the pattern and texture of Greek life at all social levels, providing a widely available means for the expression of communal identity and values, and a focus for controversy, judgement, and partisanship, in which all citizens could enthusiastically engage.

Music seems to have been less important in Roman life than in Archaic or Classical Greece. It was nevertheless indispensable at Rome for all religious rituals and civic celebrations, prominent in public theatrical performance and private merrymaking, a fully institutionalized ingredient of military activities, and a common element in the education of well-bred citizens. Professional performers won great acclaim. All the same, Roman intellectuals seem to have thought of the musical elements in education either as a source of peripheral gentlemanly adornment, or as part of an ungentlemanly professional training. To most reflective Roman minds, music in their own milieu was no more than entertainment.

2. **Instruments** Through contact with their neighbours, esp. in the east, the Greeks knew of many kinds of instrument; yet they made substantial use of only two main sorts, lyres and *auloi* (pipes).

The *phorminx* of Homeric epic was a box-lyre, with a wooden soundbox and sides distinct from the back and face. Late in the 7th cent. BC, the great *kithara* (Lat. *cithara*) that became the main instrument of professional and public performance first appears in art. The pipe called *aulos* in Greece, *tibia* in Rome, was common around the Mediterranean. Despite the usual mistranslation, it was not a flute, but was sounded with a reed. Pipes were normally played in pairs, one fingered by each hand. Pipe music was emotionally stirring, capable of a wide range of effects. It was used in many religious contexts, in drama and other forms of choral performance, at weddings, symposia and revels. It was the main instrument of Dionysiac cult and the mystery religions (see DIONYSUS; MYSTERIES).

3. **History** In Homer the one specialized, professional musician is the minstrel who sings epic lays to his *phorminx*. The development of *kitharōdia* (the art of singing to one's own stringed accompaniment) in the context of the competitive festivals was associated with Terpander, who came from *Lesbos to Sparta (then a major cultural and artistic centre) perhaps as early as 680 BC: Terpander won victories at the *Carnea, and four times at the *Pythian Games. Many innovations were later attributed to him, esp. the establishment of a canon of set pieces known as citharodic *nomoi*. Nomoi, at least in 5th-cent. and later Greek usage, were solo pieces whose formal and stylistic outlines were regulated and distinguished by fixed rules, not unnaturally in a competitive setting. Aulodic *nomoi* were sung to a piper's accompaniment. Auletic *nomoi*, for pipes without the voice, were performed at *Delphi from the early 6th cent.

Choral lyric (see LYRIC POETRY, *Greek*), a blend of poetry, melody, accompaniment, and dance, was already an admired art in the 7th cent., esp. in Sparta and at the Delian (see DELOS) festivals; competition was essential in this genre too. *Dithyramb and *tragedy originated in the singing and dancing of choruses to the *aulos*, which always remained the accompanying

instrument; the dialogue of drama perhaps grew out of interchanges between the chorus and its leader. Other choral genres, such as paeans, maiden-songs, and victory-songs, were often accompanied by a *kithara*, sometimes by *aulos* and *kithara* together. Poet-composers of the late 6th and early 5th cents.—Lasus, *Pindar, *Simonides, and others—were often self-consciously reflective about their art: traces of musical controversies survive, and Lasus is said to have written the first treatise on music. Pindar repeatedly proclaims himself a musical innovator. But to moralists from *Aristophanes onwards, their period marks the pinnacle of the ancient, simple, educative, and edifying style: afterwards there is nothing but decline into theatricality and populism. During the 5th cent., melodies came to be embroidered with ornaments and turns, both in the vocal line and independently in its accompaniment. Modulations between scale-systems, facilitated by developments in instruments (more finger-holes on *auloi*, added strings on the *kithara*) became common, undermining old links between genre and musical structure. Traditionally distinct genres, such as *kitharodia* and choral dithyramb, began to merge into new and indeterminate forms. Technical expertise and startling dramatic effect were untiringly pursued: star instrumentalists and singers were idolized by the public, and enhanced their musical acts with striking costumes and histrionic bodily movements. Whereas previously the sense, rhythm, and cadence of the words had dictated their musical interpretation, now they were progressively subordinated to musical ideas worked out in their own terms and for their own sake. These developments spelled the downfall of an integrated art closely allied to religion and civic tradition; but it also meant the emancipation of pure music from ritual and, crucially, from poetry, which came gradually to be seen as a separate art. Chiefly associated with this musical revolution are Melanippides, Cinesias, Philoxenus, and esp. *Timotheus: Cinesias and other purveyors of the 'new music', including *Agathon and *Euripides, are regularly pilloried by Aristophanes.

Despite much condemnation of music and musicians, upper-class Romans usually arranged musical instruction for their children: their teachers were normally slaves. Well-born girls and boys, trained by *Horace, sang at the *Secular Games of 17 BC. Professional brass-players were essential to the military machine, their signals used for innumerable purposes.

Pipe-players always attended the rituals of sacrifice and libation, drowning any noises of ill omen. Ancient indigenous rites included the strange 'song' of the *fratrēs arvālēs* and the ferocious war-dances of the *Saliī, who swarmed twice a year through the streets singing and leaping to the sound of pipes, lyres, and percussion. Pipes and brass instruments were regularly played in funeral processions. The many foreign cults adopted in Rome brought their music with them. *Isis was worshipped in daily hymns with pipes and sistra (metal rattles). Pipes, cymbals, hand-drums, and ecstatic dancing were characteristic of Bacchic ritual, as in Greece; see BACCHANALIA; DIONYSUS; MAENADS. Musicians were most conspicuous in public entertainment (*see* LUDI (SCAENICI). In *Plautine comedy, an overture was played on the pipes, and there were interval performances of piping and dancing. Both comedies and tragedies included set-piece songs, often excerpted for the concert platform. *Pantomime was essentially dramatic solo dance, with a chorus and piper. In *mime, the actors sang and danced accompanied by pipes, brass, and percussion. Trumpets and later the water-organ (see CTESIBIUS) sounded an accompaniment to *gladiatorial combat. Solo recitals by pipe-players and citharodes were common: *Nero and *Domitian organized competitive festivals. Small groups of musicians entertained guests in rich households: streets and taverns were alive with buskers. Most musicians were of modest background, but the best, whatever their origins, attained extraordinary wealth and prestige: the spectacular case of the piper and singer Tigellius is esp. well documented.

4. Music and Morals Many 5th-cent. Greeks believed that music affects moral *character; that music of different styles and structures affects it differently; that appropriate musical training is essential to a citizen's education; and that music of the 'wrong' sort is morally and socially pernicious. Such ideas are taken for granted in Aristophanes. They were first articulated by *Damon. *Plato draws explicitly on his work when he bans from his ideal city ethically unsuitable rhythmic and melodic forms, on the grounds that they represent inappropriate or excessive emotions, and that the tendency of all music is to mould the structure of the listener's *soul in its own image. Only those melodic forms that represent and engender courage (Dorian) and moderation (Phrygian) are permitted. Also outlawed are instruments, including *auloi* and many-stringed harps, de-

signed to modulate readily between 'ethically' distinct musical structures. Plato applauds Damon's view that changes in musical styles invariably lead to change in fundamental political laws and social customs. Detailed plans for the ethical and social training of citizens through music, and critiques of contemporary musical practice, are elaborated in *Laws*. Perhaps the most thoughtful discussion of the subject is Aristotle's. He considers carefully the grounds for claims about music's powers and functions, the reasons why citizens should not only listen to music but learn to perform it (though not to professional levels), the emotional and ethical characteristics of instruments, melodic and rhythmic structures, and much else. While more pragmatic in approach than Plato, and more ready to value music for nonmoral reasons too, he nevertheless agrees that different rhythms and melodies are representations of different ethical characters, and have corresponding effects on the listener's soul.

5. Melodic Structure Greek music was primarily melodic, and the science of harmonics was concerned with the structures underlying melodies, not with 'harmony' in our sense. A lyre, for instance, cannot play an acceptable melody with its strings tuned at random. Harmonics seeks to analyse patterns of attunement and the features distinguishing them from uncoordinated jumbles of pitches, and to identify relations between patterns of different kinds.

Mȳcēnae is a rocky hill, situated on the NE edge of the Argive plain between larger hills. The increasingly rich and elaborate burials in the shaft-graves of Circle B, on a knoll to the west, and Circle A, in the middle of the SW slope, reflect its rise to power and wealth during the 16th cent. BC, and the number (probably seven) and quality of *tholos-tombs constructed during the 15th cent. similarly reflect the maintenance of this position.

The finest *tholos*-tombs (the 'Treasury of Atreus' and 'Tomb of Clytaemnestra') were most probably constructed during the 14th cent., to which the oldest parts of the surviving palace and fortifications belong; in the 13th cent. these were expanded and many other buildings were constructed. By this time there was an extensive settlement around the citadel and a wide spread of chamber-tomb cemeteries, probably used by satellite settlements, over the surrounding slopes. Mycenae was now at the height of its wealth and power, probably controlling a considerable territory and able to exert influence widely in the Aegean.

In the mid-13th cent. BC there was widespread damage by fire, followed by repairs and further building, mostly within the citadel. The cutting of a stepped passage through the rock to a water supply below the north wall, fed by an aqueduct from the nearby spring, may be a precaution against siege. There was considerable further destruction c.1200, esp. within the citadel. Mycenae was evidently in decline, and by about 1100 was no more than a village. It remained inhabited throughout the Dark Age, and had become reasonably prosperous by c.600. Politically it was subordinate to *Argos. It sent forces to the *Persian War in 480–479, but was destroyed by Argos c.468.

Mycenaean age civilization takes its name from the spectacular finds made by Schliemann at *Mycenae. The term 'Mycenaean' is now applied to the culture which developed on the mainland in the late bronze age.

Theories of Mycenaean responsibility for the collapse of *Minoan civilization c.1450 BC remain questionable, but the following period certainly saw a great expansion of Mycenaean culture and the establishment of a state in *Crete, centred on Cnossus, whose ruling class had strong Mycenaean connections in its burial customs and use of Greek, written in the Linear B script (see MYCENAEAN LANGUAGE), as the administrative language. The administrative skills of Crete were probably transmitted to the mainland at this time, when the first well-preserved antecedents of the later Mycenaean palaces were built (Tiryns, *Menelaion); but tombs continued to be richly provided with grave-goods at both mainland and Cretan sites. The final destruction of Cnossus during the 14th cent. removed the last major competitor to the mainland centres, and Mycenaean civilization now reached its zenith, dominating the southern Aegean and extending along the *Anatolian coast from *Miletus to *Cnidus.

The centres of this civilization were the palaces best preserved at Mycenae, Tiryns, *Pylos, and *Thebes. While much smaller than the Minoan palaces and differently laid out, they evidently functioned similarly, as centres of administration, ceremonial, storage, and craftwork. They presided over small societies: most settlements ranged in size from a few households to some hundreds, and even the largest do not look like towns. But there were more settlements on the mainland than ever before;

more of the land was being exploited, probably to provide commodities for trade as well as to support an increasing population. The highly specialized economies of the palaces concentrated on large-scale cultivation of a few crops and the production of perfumed olive oil, fine textiles, and other craftwork. The palace directly maintained a workforce of many hundreds, and controlled most of the distribution and working of bronze. Resources were now expended mainly on building and engineering projects rather than tombs, though the finest *tholoi* belong to the period.

The Linear B texts do not make the palaces' administrative system wholly clear, but ruling Pylos was the *wanax*; below him were various administrators. People of very varied status could hold land, generally by some form of lease, including priests, craftsmen, herdsmen.

Mycenaean language is the form of the Greek language written in the Linear B script and found in the Mycenaean palaces. There appears to be considerable uniformity between all the sites so far known. It is clear that the dialect forms part of the Greek language because of the presence of characteristic sound-changes, inflexions, and vocabulary. A dialect 500 years earlier than Homer can be expected to show archaic forms later abandoned. It appears to be most closely related to Classical Arcadian and Cypriot.

Myron, sculptor from Eleutherae (on the Boeotian–Attic border), active c.470–440 BC. He was the greatest representative of the post-Archaic period of experimentation in bronze sculpture, and was much interested in proportion; his œuvre encompassed gods, heroes, athletes, and animals. A detailed description by *Lucian has enabled the identification of copies of his Discobolus. Poised between the back- and foreswings, it is a brilliant study in arrested movement. His group of *Athena and *Marsyas has also been recognized in copy. It represented a moment of high drama: Athena has just thrown down the pipes, and Marsyas tentatively advances to pick them up.

mystery cults Graeco-Roman mystery cults were forms of personal religious choice that may be assigned to one of three groups: 'mystery' proper, an entire initiatory structure of some duration and complexity, of which the exemplar is Eleusis; 'mystic' cult, involving not initiation but rather a relation of intense communion, typically ecstatic or enthusiastic, with the divinity (e.g. Bacchic frenzy (see DIONYSUS)); and 'mysteriosophic' cult, offering an *eschatology, and a practical means of individual reunion with divinity—the primitive or original form is *Orphism.

myth and mythology is the field of scholarship dealing with myth but also a particular body of myths. 'Myth' derives from Gk. *mýthos*, which originally meant 'word, speech, message' but in the 5th cent. BC started to acquire the meaning 'entertaining, if not necessarily trustworthy, tale'. The Romans used the word *fābula*. Burkert's statement that 'myth is a traditional tale with secondary, partial reference to something of collective importance' gives a good idea of the main characteristics of myth.

*Homer mentions the *Argonauts, the *Theban Cycle, and the deeds of *Heracles. The myths of *Achilles, *Helen, and the cattle-raiding Heracles all seem to go back to *Indo-European times. It is typical of Greek myth that Homer and other Archaic poets tended to suppress strange and scandalous details which survived only in locally fixed traditions. The trend of Greek mythology was firmly anthropomorphic and away from the fantastic.

A more recent complex of myths came from the east. The Indo-Europeans had at the most only rudimentary *theogonical and cosmogonical myths. No wonder, then, that in this area Greece became greatly indebted to the rich mythologies of *Anatolia and *Mesopotamia. *Cronus' castration of his father *Uranus ultimately derives from the Hurrians, having passed through Hittite and *Phoenician intermediaries; the division of the world between Zeus, Poseidon, and *Hades through the casting of lots, as described in the *Iliad*, has a Babylonian origin; and when *Hera, in a speech to deceive Zeus, says that she will go to *Oceanus, 'origin of the gods', and Tēthys, the 'mother', she mentions a couple derived from the parental pair Apsu and Tiamat in the Babylonian creation epic *Enuma Eliš*.

The fertile contacts with the east probably took place in the early iron age. Somewhat later, the foundation of colonies (see COLONIZATION, GREEK) in the Mediterranean and the Black Sea (*c.*750–600 BC) led to the last great wave of mythical invention. The myths about the return of the heroes after the Trojan War, and also the expedition of the Argonauts, enabled many colonies to link themselves to the panhellenic past as created through these great myths. Traditional story-patterns quickly transformed historical events.

Whereas Archaic myth concentrated more on dynasties and heroic feats, in a later, more regulated society, myth tended to concentrate on relations within the family and, esp. in Athenian tragedy (see TRAGEDY, GREEK), on the relation between individual and *polis* or the value of democratic institutions (see DEMOCRACY, ATHENIAN).

Rome, on the other hand, was situated at the margin of the 'civilized' world and was late to assimilate Greek myth. However, the earliest extant literary account of the mythical origins of Rome, that of *Ennius, uses both the story of *Aeneas' arrival in Italy after the fall of Troy and also the purely Roman story of *Romulus and Remus (now presented as his descendants) and the foundation of Rome by the former. This becomes the canonical version of the early history of Rome in writers of the late republic and early empire, esp. *Livy and *Virgil. Greek versions of the pre-Romulan history of the site, and of the foundation of other towns, in Italy, largely supplant any native stories which may have existed. Likewise, the gods are assimilated to those of the Greek Pantheon. A few names of minor figures survive such as *Janus and Pīcus, but the lack of evidence for an originally rich mythology has led some scholars to suppose that the Romans had none. The foundation myths show that the temporal horizon was not the creation of gods or men but the birth of the native city; the foundation of the city was also the most important mythical theme in public declamations in imperial times (see FOUNDERS OF CITIES).

Greek poets were the main producers of myth. Poets performed at courts or local festivals in various genres, which successively became popular: epic in the 8th cent., choral lyric in the 6th and, finally, tragedy, the last public performance of myth, in the 5th. Yet myths were also related in other contexts. Temple friezes, sculptures, and vases (see IMAGERY; PAINTING; SCULPTURE) made myth as a subject visible almost everywhere. Mothers and nurses told myths to children, a significant factor in the continuing popularity of myth throughout antiquity.

The uses of myth varied over time, but the entertainment value was always important. Other uses included the explanation of the social and political order. Myth explained how in Athens males had arrived at their dominant position through the chaos caused by women; how cities originated, as *Thebes through a struggle against a dragon (see CADMUS), or how tribal groupings arose, as the *Ionians from Ion. It explained why Athens could claim *Aegina.

Myth also helped the Greeks to define the world around them and their own place in relation to the gods. By situating murderous women on mountains, by letting girls play on flowery meadows, these features of the landscape were assigned negative or positive values. By relating the unhappy endings of love affairs between gods and humans, e.g. *Semele being burnt to ashes through the appearance of Zeus in full glory, myth stressed the unbridgeable gap between mortals and immortals.

Finally, the aetiological function of myth was substantial. Many myths explained the birth or function of rituals; *Euripides often recounted the origins of Attic cults. Other myths highlighted or 'explained' unusual features of ritual. There is an important difference between myth and *ritual: myth can depict as real (murder and other horrors) what in ritual has to remain symbolic.

Myth was the product of an *oral society, but the arrival of writing brought important changes. Poets had now to share their leading intellectual role with philosophers and historians. The new intellectuals soon started to criticize mythical traditions. On the other hand, the force of tradition weighed heavily, which is why the two most popular ways of dealing with myth were rationalization, which starts with *Hecataeus (c.550–480 BC), and allegorization, decoding esp. the poems of Homer and Hesiod as accounts of the physical world or the truths of morality, which probably started in the late 6th cent.

These developments strongly diminished the public influence of poets as prime producers of myth. In Hellenistic times, the myths recorded and adapted by *Callimachus (2) and his contemporaries were directed at a small circle of connoisseurs, not the general public. However, these poets exercised an enormous influence in Rome, where in the last two centuries of the republic and during the early Principate mythical themes proliferate.

In the Hellenistic and early imperial period scholars started to collect myths in order to elucidate allusions in the Classical authors; most important in this respect was the collection of mythological *scholia on Homer which circulated as a separate book at least from the 1st to the 5th cent. AD. Other collections concentrated on one theme, such as *Eratosthenes' book of star-myths (see CONSTELLATIONS, 3) or the famous Library ascribed to *Apollodorus (2), which organized the mythical material by families. It is esp. these collections which have ensured modern knowledge of the less familiar myths of Greece. See MYTHOGRAPHERS.

mythographers make collections of heroic myths (see preceding entry), comprehensive or specialized and with various motives, including extracting history from certain myths (see HECATAEUS; HELLANICUS), and elucidating poetic texts. The greatest general account, arranged by family *genealogy, is the library, falsely ascribed to *Apollodorus (2).

Mytilēnē, the most important *polis in *Lesbos, situated on an islet (now a promontory) adjoining the east coast. Its walls, extending on to the mainland, enclosed an area similar to that of Athens; it possessed land in Asia Minor. Archaeology has revealed harbour moles, cemeteries, aqueducts, a theatre (possibly Pompey's prototype for Rome's first theatre), and a major sanctuary of *Demeter and Kore (see PERSEPHONE).

As the city grew powerful, its élite helped found the Hellenion at *Naucratis, and fought Athens over *Sigeum. *Alcaeus led one side in a civil war; his arch-enemy *Pittacus became sole ruler, but was reputedly a just man. Following a lengthy Persian domination, interrupted by the *Ionian Revolt, Mytilene became a steadfast ally of Athens; after its revolt in 428 a *cleruchy was installed. Mytilene remained mostly pro-Athenian until the Persians returned in 357.

Naevius, Gnaeus, stage poet of Campanian birth (see CAMPANIA). He saw military service in the last years of the First *Punic War. His theatrical career began in 235 and was over by 204. Many stories were told of the insulting remarks he made about men of the nobility from the stage or in other contexts.

Titles of 32 plays on themes of the Attic 'New' Comedy (see COMEDY (GREEK), NEW) are transmitted. Acc. to *Terence, Naevius was one of those who set a precedent for treating an Attic model with some liberty. He put both dialogues and monologues into musically accompanied metres of the type used by his contemporary *Plautus. On occasion he made his Greek characters allude to features of Italian life. Six titles suggest tragedies of the Attic type. Naevius also composed original tragedies.

Only one of the plays survived into the 1st-cent. BC stage repertoire. A narrative poem in *Saturnian verses concerning the First Punic War lasted longer. Naevius claimed inspiration by the Camenae and used a metrical and verbal style hard now to distinguish from that of *Livius Andronicus' translation of *Homer's *Odyssey*. Despite strong criticism by *Ennius, Naevius' poem continued to find readers in the 1st cent. BC.

names, personal, Greek In *Homer, one name only was the norm for men and women. Secondary names given in the Classical and Hellenistic periods to public figures such as politicians, *hetairai, and kings did not break this rule, since they were nicknames and were not handed down in the family.

In public contexts, such as decrees, dedications, and tombstones, the single name was normally followed by the name of the father in the genitive, the patronymic, or by the name of the husband (for women). The name and patronymic could be further qualified by an indication of location (*deme, tribe (see PHYLAI), or *phratry). In cities with a deme structure the demotic was regularly given after the patronymic when at home; city or regional *ethnics (e.g. *Athēnaios*) would not be used except when abroad.

Name-giving took place at the ceremony of the Amphidromia (see CHILDREN). It was common practice to name the first son after his paternal grandfather, the second after his maternal grandfather, paternal uncle, etc. Naming a son after his father was much less common. Daughters also were often named after family members.

Greek names could be simple or compound. In the first case a name could be identical to any noun or adjective, but it could also be a derivative of any word, formed by means of various suffixes including diminutive suffixes. Compound names such as *Xanthippos*, which were probably felt to have higher status, were often replaced by shortened forms.

An enormous range of concepts was drawn on to form names. Among the substantives forming simple names (and combining in compound names) were the names of animals, weapons, parts of the body, plants, rivers. Abstract nouns, including neuter nouns, were used esp. for women's names. They commonly carried notions of leadership and military prowess, civic organization, saving or defending, strength, beauty or nobility, liking, honouring, reputation. These and many other words combined to create thousands of different name-forms.

Theophoric names were a recognized category in antiquity. They were based not only on gods' names, but also on their cult titles, and on months named after them. Adjectival derivatives of a deity's name, *Apollonios/a, Dionysios/a, Demetrios/a* were among the commonest Greek names. Compound forms were likely to carry notions of giving/given (-*dōros*, -*dotos*), birth (-*genēs*, -*geneia*), repute or favour (-*klēs* /-*kleia*; -*phanēs* /-*phaneia*; -*charēs* /-*charis*, etc.). Thus, based on the name of *Zeus, with the root Dio-: *Diodōros, Diodotos, Diogenēs, Dioclēs, Diophanēs, Diocharēs*, etc.

Certain types of name were common among slaves, notably those derived from ethnics, esp. of those countries which were a regular source of slaves (e.g. *Aigyptios*). Many slaves had 'good' names indistinguishable from those of free people. The naming and renaming of slaves (see SLAVERY), on enslavement or at birth into slavery in the household, or at manumission, and the passing of manumitted slaves into the local population, are all factors tending to loosen the concept of a 'slave-name'. Servile status can never be inferred from the name alone.

names, personal, Roman 1. In the Classical period, the official designation of a free-born male Roman citizen embraced five components. Thus *M. Tullius M. f. Cor. Cicero* consists of the *praenōmen*, *M(arcus)*; the *nōmen* or *gentilicium*, the family-name, *Tullius*; the indication of the father's name, *M(arci) f(ilius)*; the indication of the Roman voting tribe (see TRIBUS) to which the citizen belonged, *Cor(nelia tribu)*; and the *cognōmen*, *Cicero* (optional in the republican age). The *tria nōmina* or 'three names' were thus: *praenōmen*, *nōmen*, and *cognōmen*.

2. It is probable, that the Italic peoples originally used one name only. This pattern was swept away by a revolution in Italic nomenclature: the creation of the hereditary family-name (*gentilicium* or *nomen*) from what had originally been patronymics, normally derived with a suffix *-ius* from the name of the father (so *Quintius* = 'son of *Quintus*'). At some point, these patronymics, having formerly changed from generation to generation, became invariable, a development reflecting the need to indicate membership of a large **gens*. The gentile name system seems to have become established in Rome *c.*600 BC.

3. Most gentile names of the early republic are in origin patronymics (another patronymic suffix beside *-ius* was *-ilius*, whence e.g. *Lucilius* from *Lucius*). Most Roman gentile names are probably derived from Latin individual names that vanished as a result of the *praenomen* reduction (see 4). Ethnics were another source for the formation of gentile names: the oldest Roman example is *Tarquinius*, derived from the name of the home town of two kings of Rome (see REX).

4. After the establishment of the gentile name system, the numerous old single names became the *praenomina*, identifying the individual within the family. For this purpose a limited selection sufficed, and the number of *praenomina* was gradually reduced. In the late republic some eighteen *praenomina* only were in general use: *Aulus, Decimus, Gaius, Gnaeus, Lucius, Manius, Mar-*

cus, *Numerius, Publius, Quintus, Servius, Sextus, Spurius, Tiberius, Titus*. The popularity of these *praenomina* varied greatly, the most frequent always being *Gaius, Lucius, Marcus, Publius, Quintus*. In inscriptions from the imperial period, *Tiberius* and *Titus* are also very frequent, but the popularity of *Tiberius* is entirely due to the Claudian emperors and to the numerous descendants of their freedmen. *Titus* mainly owes its wide diffusion to the Flavian emperors, *Vespasian, *Titus, *Domitian, who were all given that *praenomen*. As the number of *praenomina* was limited, in extra-familial use they were almost always abbreviated: *A.* = *Aulus, M.* = *Manius, P.* = *Publius, Q.* = *Quintus, S(p).* = *Spurius, Ser.* = *Servius, Sex.* = *Sextus, T.* = *Titus, Ti.* = *Tiberius*, etc.

5. The last component in the name of a Roman citizen was the *cognomen*. Originally unofficial surnames for individuals, thus complementing the function of the *praenomina*, the early *cognomina* of the Roman nobility (see NOBILES) became for the most part hereditary, designating a branch of a larger *gens*. Thus the Cornelii were split into several branches, the most famous being the *Cornēliī Scīpiōnēs*. Such a family could split still further, with an additional *cognomen*, e.g. the *Cornelii Scipiones Nāsīcae*. In the republican period noble *plebeian families also normally bore a *cognomen* (e.g. the *Semprōniī Gracchi*). see CORNELIUS and SEMPRONIUS. Ordinary people began to bear individual *cognomina* regularly only as late as the transition from the republic to the empire, but the usage established itself very quickly, and from the beginning of the empire the *cognomen* gradually superseded the *praenomen* as the individual name of a Roman.

There was a great variety of *cognomina*. They could be Latin, Greek, or '*barbarian'. They denote physical peculiarities, moral qualities, circumstances, esp. the so-called wish-names, circumstances of birth or sex, occupations, fauna and flora. *Cognomina* derived from other names, directly or with suffixes, are very popular: from *praenomina* (*Marcus, Marcellus*), gentile names (*Iulianus*), other *cognomina*, names of historical figures, divine and mythical names, and place-names; derivatives from adjectives are also common (*Cato* from *catus*, 'shrewd'). A person could bear more than one *cognomen*, esp. in old aristocratic families, where the first (and eventually the second) cognomen had become hereditary: *Publius Cornelius Scipio Nasica Corculum*. There were also *cognomina* given to victorious generals and derived from the name of the town or people conquered; some of these names became hereditary, as with *Messalla*, obtained by Manius *Valerius Maximus Messalla in 263 BC after the relief of *Messana and retained by the family into the imperial period. Comparable are the emperors' honorific titles, such as *Germānicus, Dācicus,* or *Arabicus.*

6. The indication of the father's name and the *tribus* was optional, because these two parts of the name do not designate a person directly. The indication of the father, in the form of his *praenomen* in the genitive and the word *filius* (normally abbreviated to *f.*) was placed after the gentile name.

7. *Women's names. The nomenclature of free-born women was similar to that of free-born men except that, normally, women did not have a *praenomen* in the Classical period. A woman inherited her gentile name from her father and did not usually change it on marriage. Thus the normal form of a woman's name in the republican period was—to take *Cicero's daughter as an example—*Tullia M. f.* (a woman was not inscribed in a *tribus*).

8. An adopted son took his adoptive father's full name, but could add an extra cognomen formed with the suffix *-ianus* from his original gentile name (*Scipio Aemilianus,* natural son of *Lucius Aemilius Paullus*). See CORNELIUS SCIPIO AEMILIANUS, LUCIUS.

9. Names of foreigners, *slaves, and *freedmen. Slaves and provincials without Roman (or Latin) *citizenship were known by an individual name, and thus lacked a *praenomen* and *nomen*; foreigners used their individual name followed by the father's name in the genitive and (optionally) by *f(ilius -ia)*, e.g. *Tritano Acali* and *Tritano Lani f.*, from Dalmatia. When enfranchised, new citizens normally retained their individual name as their *cognomen*. They were free to choose their *praenomen* and *nomen*; during the empire, it became common for new citizens to adopt those of the reigning emperor.

The usual form of a slave's name in the 1st cent. BC was *Pamphilus Servili M. s(ervus)*; from the Augustan age, the order of elements in the indication of the owner's name usually follows the pattern *Dama L. Titi ser(vus)*. When manumitted, slaves took the *nomen* of their master and, from the end of the republic, usually his *praenomen* too, retaining their slave name as a *cognomen*. The gentile name was followed by the indication of freed status, achieved by adding the master's *praenomen* in the genitive and the abbreviation *l.* or *lib.* for *libertus -a* (the official name of Cicero's freedman Tiro would thus have been *M. Tullius M. l. Tiro*). An imperial freedman was usually designated as *Aug. l.* or *lib. = Augusti libertus -a.*

Naqš-i Rustam, 7 km. (4½ mi.) north of *Persepolis, impressive rock-cut tombs of *Darius I, *Xerxes, *Artaxerxes (1) I, and *Darius II. Kings standing on thrones supported by subject peoples are carved in relief above palatial porticoes. Trilingual inscriptions proclaim the royal virtues of Darius I.

Narcissus, *freedman secretary for correspondence to *Claudius, acquiring 400 million sesterces and great political influence. He went to Gaul in AD 43 to embark the invasion force for Britain and received *quaestoria *ornamenta* in 48 for exposing *Valeria Messallina, with whom he had collaborated in removing threats to Claudius. The limits of his power appeared when he was given command of the *praetorians for one day only. It was weakened by the Messallina affair, involving the deaths of leading men, and eclipsed by that of *Antonius Pallas, whose ally *Iulia Agrippina married Claudius (Narcissus favoured another bride), and who obtained *praetoria ornamenta*. On Claudius' death in 54 he was immediately forced to kill himself.

narrative, narration Interest in narrative is developing fast. Two branches of this 'narratology' may be distinguished. The one is oriented towards the 'story' as signified ('what happened'); the other is oriented rather towards the narrative as signifier ('the way it is told'). Both approaches have been widely applied in classical studies, but the first has perhaps been more successful in the anthropological study of myth (see MYTH AND MYTHOLOGY), the second in literary studies, in that it focuses on the rhetorical construction of the work.

*Aristotle's *Poetics* may be considered the first treatise of narratology. He assigns a central place to *mỹthos* or 'plot', which is the criterion (rather than metre) that he uses to distinguish poetry from other forms of discourse. *Mythos,* analysed both in terms of content and of its representation, is required to have an organic unity which calls to mind the concept of *closure. The Aristotelian theory of narrative includes drama. Recently, the distinctive nature of the dramatic text, which is realized fully only in performance, has been stressed. One may certainly study narrative elements in non-narrative genres (e.g. *Pindar or the messenger speeches of tragedy; see TRAGEDY, GREEK), but these genres have different contexts of *reception and different purposes. For this reason, a narrower conception of *fictional* narrative, above all *epic and the *novel, may be preferable. The applicability of narratological approaches to *historiography has been esp. controversial.

The basic forms of western narrative occur in Homer. One may distinguish: the *order* in which events are narrated, their *duration* at the level of narrative in comparison to that of the underlying story, the mode or *mood* in which the information is conveyed ('focalization', point of view), and the *voice* which delivers it. Homeric narrative knows various ways of manipulating the linearity of story-time, such as the flashbacks of *Nestor in the *Iliad* and the *Odyssey*'s beginning *in mediis rebus*. At the level of duration, 'scenes' with dialogue predominate over more rapid 'summaries': the opposition is a version of the Platonic one (see PLATO) between *mimēsis* 'representation' and *diēgēsis* 'narration'. At the level of mood and voice, we are presented with a narrator who is (on the surface at least) impersonal, objective, and with a point of view superior to that of his characters. In comparison with this model, *Apollonius (1) Rhodius and *Virgil, under the influence of Hellenistic *epyllion, show a desire for a denser and more 'subjective' mode more oriented towards the present moment of narration: hence the greater use of anticipation of later events, of summary narration, and of focalization from the point of view of the characters (e.g. *Medea, *Dido).

The equivalence between poetry and fiction established by Aristotle had a long history in antiquity, and prose fiction developed late. The love novel or romance at first used a linear narrative technique (Chariton, Xenophon of Ephesus) but later turned to more complex forms in the phase influenced by the *Second Sophistic (Achilles Tatius, Longus, Heliodorus). In them, we find frequent use of a restricted point of view and the device of 'stories within stories'. This last technique is esp. prevalent in Heliodorus: the ultimate model is the *Odyssey*.

nationalism

Greece, Archaic and Classical City-state particularism (see POLIS), and the consciousness of the religious and linguistic differences between *Dorians and *Ionians, are not the same as nationalism. Such feelings are best considered under the heading of *ethnicity. The idea that Greece was a 'nation', in a way that transcended local differences, does occur in our sources, but only at exceptional times like the *Persian Wars (Herodotus 8. 144). The Persian Wars did affect Greek thinking (see PERSIAN-WARS TRADITION);

but the effect was negative rather than positive: in the 5th cent. BC '*barbarians' were viewed more disparagingly as a result of the Persian Wars, just as the opposition between Dorians and Ionians became sharper as tensions between Athens and Sparta increased in the same period. But no correspondingly increased sense of Greek national identity is traceable. It is, however, pointless to castigate the Greeks for their 'failure to achieve unity' when there is so little evidence that this was an aim they had or even understood.

Hellenistic and Roman Early Rome did not evolve into a nation because initial expansion was based, not on incorporation, but treaty-relationships (see SOCII); even when she extended her citizenship to all Italy, a Roman citizen belonged to a city, not a country.

Subject-resistance to the Hellenistic and Roman empires is sometimes scanned for 'national feeling'. But there was rarely a tradition of political unity even among ethnic groups sharing a common culture (e.g. the Gauls), so that nationalism in the modern sense could not exist. Important exceptions are the indigenous Egyptians under the Ptolemies, and the Jews of Judaea, who rebelled under both the *Seleucids and Rome; both groups could look back to a tradition of political independence. Otherwise, revolts against imperial Rome, when not occurring shortly after incorporation and constituting a continuation of the initial armed struggle, were chiefly occasioned by Roman misgovernment (e.g. the revolt of *Boudicca), the political ambitions of individuals, or other factors. Generally, Rome's political integration of subject élites (much more successful, and indeed purposeful, than in the Ptolemaic and Seleucid empires) kept local nationalisms underdeveloped.

nauarchos, 'admiral', the commander of a navy, of a squadron however small, and even of a single ship. As an official title it was slow to appear, since full-time *navies were hugely expensive and the geographical conditions of Greek warfare, which demanded amphibious operations, discouraged the separation of naval from military commands. Thus at Athens, Athenian and allied fleets were always commanded by *strategoi. But with the greater specialization of warfare, esp. in states lacking an established naval tradition, the title began to appear, in *Sparta (c.430–360 BC), Syracuse under *Dionysius (1) I and (2) II, Ptolemaic *Egypt, and *Rhodes. The *nauarchos* was everywhere admiral of the fleet, with no colleague; in republics such as Sparta his tenure was normally a single year (a rule that had to be circumvented to accommodate *Lysander), but admirals who served monarchs (e.g. in Syracuse and Egypt) might enjoy long commands.

Naucratis, a Greek city on the east bank of the Canopic branch of the *Nile 83 km. (52 mi.) SE of *Alexandria. It was founded as a trading station in the reign of Psammetichus I (664–610 BC). Under Amasis the Hellenion was erected by the Ionians from *Chios, Teos, *Phocaea, Clazomenae, the *Dorians of *Rhodes, *Cnidus, *Halicarnassus, Phaselis, and Aeolian *Mytilene. *Aegina, *Samos, and *Miletus had their own temples in honour of *Zeus, *Hera, and *Apollo.

naumachia This Gk. word was used for a naval battle, shown as a great spectacle, or for an artificial lake constructed for the purpose, the best known being that excavated by *Augustus in 2 BC on the right bank of the Tiber, with an island in the middle. *Caesar had been the first to give such an exhibition in 46 BC, on the left bank of the *Tiber. Prisoners of war and condemned criminals did the fighting; and some famous sea-fight of history (e.g. *Salamis, the Athenians at *Syracuse (413 BC), *Actium) was re-enacted. *Claudius exhibited a great *naumachia*, with 19,000 combatants, on the Fucine Lake in AD 52. Similar displays were sometimes given on private estates and by flooding *amphitheatres.

navies The Persian navy was created under *Cambyses (530–522 BC). It used *triremes and was crewed by the king's maritime subjects, arranged in territorial or ethnic squadrons (e.g. Egyptians, *Phoenicians, *Ionians). During much of the 5th cent. this navy fought in the eastern Mediterranean against the Greek city-states, led by Athens, whose ships were crewed by her citizens and subject allies. From the battle of *Salamis (480) to Aegospotami (405) the Athenians were the dominant naval power in the region. They developed considerable expertise in trireme warfare, which was put to good use in the *Peloponnesian War. During the 4th cent. the Athenian navy remained a powerful force, although lack of money and manpower prevented a return to its former dominance. Defeat by the Macedonians at Amorgos in 322 marked the end of the Athenian navy.

The Hellenistic period saw the development of larger warships, as the Hellenistic monarchs ap-

parently tried to outbuild each other in order to achieve supremacy and assert prestige. The Ptolemaic kings (see PTOLEMY (1); EGYPT, *ptolemaic*) used their navies extensively in the effort to secure their overseas possessions, but no single state gained lasting naval dominance until the Romans were forced to create a series of large fleets from the resources of Italy, initially in order to defeat the Carthaginians, and then to fight a series of wars in the Greek east.

Roman naval forces in the 2nd and 1st cents. BC were mainly drawn from allies in Italy and the Greek east. The value of a strong navy had been demonstrated to Octavian in his struggle with Sextus *Pompeius. He established permanent naval forces soon after the battle of *Actium. They consisted of a fleet to guard the NW coast of Italy and the Gallic coast, based at Forum Iulii, two praetorian fleets to secure the Italian coasts, based at Ravenna and Mīsēnum, commanded in AD 79 by *Pliny the Elder, and a small fleet based at *Alexandria.

The duties of the Roman navy included transporting Roman troops, supporting land campaigns, protecting coastal settlements, suppressing *piracy, and dealing with hostile incursions by barbarians into Roman waters. The fleets of the Roman imperial navy contained mainly triremes and smaller vessels, with only a few *quinqueremes or larger ships in the two praetorian fleets.

Naval craft were expensive to build and maintain. Most warships could not be used for *trade, and their crews were normally free men who required payment as well as provisioning. The creation of a navy was, therefore, a momentous step for any ancient state. *Samos acquired its navy during the prosperous period of *Polycrates (1)'s tyranny. The Athenian navy of the 5th cent. BC was founded on the proceeds of a rich silver strike in the *Laurium mines, and maintained through tribute payments and the wealth of private citizens (see TRIERARCHY). During the Peloponnesian War the Spartans were able to sustain their naval presence in the Aegean only with the support of the Persian king, who provided money for the wages of the crews. The achievement of the Rhodians (see RHODES), who maintained a substantial navy from the 4th to the 1st cent. BC, was exceptional and surpassed only by the Roman empire. See SEA POWER; SHIPS.

navigation is the art of guiding a ship at sea. The relatively calm, tideless waters of the Mediterranean encouraged travel by sea. Seagoing *ships were not normally used in the winter months, because storms and poor visibility made navigation hazardous, but *Hesiod's suggestion that sailing be limited to July and August is overcautious, the period between the vernal and autumnal equinoxes being the best season, with some leeway at either end. Ancient vessels were either paddled, rowed, or sailed. Their speed depended upon size, type of propulsion, and the weather. Sailing speeds of between four and six knots seem to have been the norm with favourable winds. Light or unfavourable winds might reduce speed to less than one knot, making it preferable to lie up and wait for a change in the weather.

Ancient seafarers guided their vessels without the benefit of instruments or charts. Wherever possible they coasted or sailed between fixed points on land. On clear nights the stars could be used to plot a course, as could the moon. Experienced ancient mariners would have had practical understanding of the phases of the moon and the movement of the stars, which they would have passed on orally. They would also have needed detailed knowledge of local conditions such as prevailing winds and currents, the presence of reefs, rocks, and shallows, and how to follow a course according to local landmarks.

Basic navigational equipment included oars and sails, steering oars, anchors, usually made of stone or wood, or both, and a variety of lines and cables. Leaded lines for checking the depth of the water were common. Flags and pennants were used to identify warships, or sometimes deliberately to misidentify them, and lanterns were used at night or in fog to enable flotillas to follow a flagship. Although detailed *maps were available from the early Hellenistic period onwards, there is no evidence of charts for use at sea. A few descriptions of sea routes and coastlines (*periploi) have survived from antiquity, but it is unlikely that they circulated among the mariners themselves.

Navigable rivers were also heavily used, especially the *Nile, the Rhine (*Rhenus), and the Rhône. In late republican and imperial times the Tiber would have been crowded with vessels carrying people and goods up to Rome from *Ostia. River-craft were mostly paddled, rowed, or sailed, but towing, either by teams of men or animals, or by use of a line fixed on shore and a capstan was also common. See LIGHTHOUSES; NAVIES.

Naxos, the largest of the *Cyclades, noted for its *marble. Its fertile western side contrasts with its rugged east. Ionian settlers arrived from Athens *c.*1025 BC. Naxos colonized Amorgos *c.*900 and joined in founding Sicilian Naxos in 735. Its Archaic prominence is revealed in dedications and monuments on *Delos (a colossal statue of *Apollo, the House of the Naxians, a Naxian stoa) and the Sphinx column at *Delphi, as well as in the marble temples and sculpture found on Naxos itself. Its craftsmen were pioneers in the development of monumental marble sculpture and architecture. At the peak of its power, following the overthrow of the tyrant Lygdamis (see TYRANNY) *c.*525, Naxos dominated the Cyclades, including its enemy *Paros, allegedly with 8,000 soldiers and a *navy at its command. In 500 it withstood a Persian siege, but in 490 city and temples were burnt and those captured enslaved. In 480 Naxian *triremes defected to the Greek fleet at *Salamis. Naxos was the first to revolt from the *Delian League *c.*467, later being reduced to tributary status. *c.*450, an Athenian *cleruchy was imposed.

Nearchus, of *Crete, boyhood friend of *Alexander (2) the Great and *satrap of Lycia/Pamphylia (334–329 BC); he commanded the fleet on the *Hydaspes and sailed along the coast from southern India to the Tigris. Prominent at Babylon in 323 (see GREECE (HISTORY), *Hellenistic period*), he served on the staff of *Antigonus I between 317 and 312. His memoirs of Alexander's campaign were popular, much used by *Strabo and *Arrian. The extant citations refer to events in India and to Nearchus' own voyage. Valuable detail is preserved, and there are traces of a critical attitude to Alexander (his account of the transit of Gedrosia is a catalogue of horrors); but there is much fantasy, and his own importance is systematically exaggerated.

nectar See AMBROSIA.

negōtiātōrēs, the businessmen of the Roman world. In literary sources of the republican period, esp. *Cicero, *negotiatores*, or people who *negōtia gerunt* ('do business deals'), are found as members of resident communities of Italian and Roman citizens in all the provinces of the empire, esp. in the major urban centres and ports. The term is used very broadly. Many who are described by Cicero as *negotiatores* were clearly of high *equestrian status. There were close links and involvement with the work of the *publicani* (tax companies), bankers, landowners, and with shipping. Indeed, one rhetorical remark of Cicero's about 'all the publicans, farmers, cattle-breeders, and the rest of the *negotiatores'* suggests that the term *negotia* could cover all those activities. The considerable expansion of trade in the Mediterranean in the Roman period depended upon organization of markets, investment in shipping, and, in a world where the money-supply was uncertain, *credit to facilitate deals (see also BANKS; MARITIME LOANS). This is what *negotiatores* provided. Such money-men always also had investments in land, which provided security. The scale and importance of the activities of the *negotiatores* was emphasized by Cicero in his speech on the command of *Pompey (66 BC) at the time of *Mithradates VI's disruption of Asia. The term *negotiator* was rarely defined precisely, because most such money-men had investments in a whole range of property and activities. The term had an air of respectability, which *mercātor* ('trader') did not.

Negotiatores, their families and their freed slaves, as Roman residents in the provinces, brought *Romanization, although, at least in the Greek east, the process of acculturation was importantly two-way. Their overall impact on the provinces is debated: that many—if well-connected enough—exploited Roman status to enrich themselves (esp. in the late republic) at provincials' expense is clear; but some at least also used their wealth to support the cities in which they resided (e.g. *Atticus, a 'super-negotiator', at Athens) and—in the east—local (Greek) culture. The scale of the eventual fortunes of a few settler-families is shown by the return of descendants to Italy as provincial senators from the 1st cent. AD on. See also TRADE, ROMAN.

Nēleus, son of *Poseidon and Tyro, and twin of *Pelias. Tyro exposed the twins, but animals suckled them. Years later, after a quarrel, Neleus leaves Pelias as king of Iolcus and either conquers or founds *Messenian *Pylos. Here he fathers twelve sons, with *Nestor the youngest. He reigns without playing a major role in the wars of Nestor's youth. But when he refuses to cleanse *Heracles from the murder of Iphitus (see POLLUTION; PURIFICATION), Heracles conquers Pylos and kills all the sons, except Nestor. Exposure and miraculous survival are typical for founders of dynasties and empires (*Romulus, *Darius (1), Moses), while the geographical dislocation hides the combination of different local traditions. The later events, as they appear in the *Iliad*, are determined by Pylian story-telling about the youth of Nestor.

Nemausus, a town in Gallia Narbonensis (see GAUL, TRANSALPINE). It was probably a *colōnia Latīna* (see IUS LATII) by 28 BC. In 16 BC it was laid out with walls enclosing *c*.220 ha. (543 acres). Remains include: amphitheatre, and a temple erected *c*. AD 2, and eventually dedicated to Gaius *Iulius Caesar (2) and Lucius Iulius Caesar (the 'Maison Carrée'). The Pont-du-Gard forms part of its *aqueduct.

Nemea Fertile upland valley in the NW Argolid sandwiched between the territories of ancient Phlius and Cleonae; legendary scene of *Heracles' encounter with the lion; site of the panhellenic sanctuary of *Zeus, where the Nemean games were held, every second and fourth year of each *Olympiad.

Nemesis 'Retribution'. Acc. to Hesiod, she was daughter of Night, and born as 'an affliction to mortal men'. Homer did not know the goddess. Nemesis' oldest cults were Ionian: in the Attic *deme of Rhamnus, and in Smyrna. Her first Rhamnusian temple was destroyed by the Persians and replaced in the late 5th cent. Agoracritus' image of Nemesis held an apple branch in her left hand and a bowl, decorated with *Ethiopians, in her right. A crown on her head showed figures of *Nike and deer. In, untypically Greek, myth Zeus pursued her in the shape of a fish and various animals; he finally changed into a swan and she into a goose. She laid an egg, which a shepherd found and took to *Leda, who nurtured *Helen after she was hatched. Nemesis' cultic past is obscured by her nature as indignant avenger. She is merciless, envies good fortune, and punishes *hubris. There is a Nemesis of gods, men, and even of the dead. She guards against excess; hence her attribute of a measuring-rod.

Neoplatonism, a modern term for *Plotinus' renewal of Platonic philosophy (see PLATO) in the 3rd cent. AD. It became the dominant philosophy of the ancient world down to the 6th cent. The following phases in its history may be distinguished. (*a*) After the Sceptical period of Plato's *Academy, philosophers in the 1st cent. BC, esp. Antiochus of Ascalon, initiated a revival of dogmatic Platonism. This revival (called today 'Middle Platonism') became widespread in the 2nd cent. AD when such writers as Albinus and Numenius, having recourse sometimes to Aristotelian and Stoic ideas, drew from Plato's dialogues a systematic philosophy. (*b*) Working in this intellectual context, Plotinus developed an unorthodox, compelling interpretation of Plato, a philosophy containing profound metaphysical and psychological ideas, which provided his successors with a fruitful basis of reflection. Plotinus' *Enneads* (published posthumously, *c.*300–305) are Neoplatonism's most important philosophical product. (*c*) Plotinus' school in Rome did not survive his death in 270. However, his closest pupils (esp. *Porphyry) did much to promote his philosophy. Porphyry published Plotinus' biography and works, on which he commented. He also innovated, esp. in metaphysics and in integrating Aristotle's logic into Neoplatonism, contributing also to the influence of Neoplatonism among Latin writers, pagan and Christian. Plotinus and Porphyry were also read in the east. (*d*) *Iamblichus, who founded an influential school in Syria, introduced a new phase. His systematic harmonization of Neoplatonic metaphysics with supposedly ancient pagan theologies made Neoplatonism suitable to the needs of the pagan reaction led by *Julian. *Sallustius' *On the Gods and the World* summarized the Neoplatonic interpretation of pagan religion. (*e*) Iamblichean philosophers contributed to the emergence of a Neoplatonic school in Athens, which produced works of learning and philosophical sophistication and had close relations with a Neoplatonist school in *Alexandria, from which came important commentaries on *Aristotle. *Justinian closed the Athenian school in 529. Its members took temporary refuge in Persia, whereas the Alexandrian school, perhaps through an understanding with the Church, survived for another century. Neoplatonism strongly influenced Byzantine thought, Islamic philosophy, medieval Latin thinkers and the Renaissance.

Neoptolemus, son of *Achilles and Dēidamīa; also known (but not to *Homer) as Pyrrhus.

The *Odyssey* relates how, after the death of Achilles, *Odysseus fetched Neoptolemus from Scyros to Troy, where he distinguished himself in counsel and battle and was one of the warriors in the Wooden Horse. After his return to Greece he married Hermione, daughter of *Menelaus and *Helen. Cyclic epics (see EPIC CYCLE) told how, in the sack of Troy, he killed *Priam and (acc. to the *Little Iliad*) the infant Astyanax (but the *Sack of Troy* attributed this to Odysseus), and chose *Andromache as his prize. Various writers made him responsible for the sacrifice of Polyxena. *Sophocles in *Philoctetes* makes Neoptolemus a companion of Odysseus on the expedition to fetch *Philoctetes from Lemnos. Here he is an essentially honourable youth, persuaded at first to assist in the plots of Odysseus but then finding his true nature through pity for Philoctetes.

Nēpos, Cornēlius (*c.* 110–24 BC), the earliest extant biographer in Latin. From Cisalpine *Gaul, by 65 he was living in Rome and moving in literary circles. He counted *Pomponius Atticus a friend.

Works 'On Famous Men', at least sixteen books containing perhaps 400 lives, grouped according to categories (those of generals and historians are firmly attested), and including non-Romans. It was first published before the death of Atticus; a second, expanded, edition appeared before 27. Of this we have 'On Eminent Foreign Generals' and the lives of *Porcius Cato (1) and Atticus from his 'Roman Historians'.

His defects are hasty and careless composition and lack of control of his material. He is mainly eulogistic, with an ethical aim, but also gives information about his hero's environment. As historian his value is slight; he names many sources, but rarely used them at first hand. His style is plain. His intended Roman readership was middlebrow. See BIOGRAPHY, ROMAN.

Nēreus, an old sea god, father of the Nereids; see NYMPHS. He lives with the Nereids in the depths of the sea, esp. in the *Aegean Sea. *Hesiod and *Pindar extol his righteousness. Like other 'Old Men of the Sea' he has wisdom and even the gift of prophecy. These abilities brought him into a strenuous contest with *Heracles. Heracles had to catch Nereus unawares in order to learn the whereabouts of the golden apples (see HESPERIDES). In his contest with Heracles Nereus transformed himself into fire, water, and many other shapes.

The earliest representations of him are of the early 6th cent. BC, as a fishtailed old man fighting Heracles and mutating. Vases from the mid-6th cent. to the early Classical show him fully human and holding a fish rather than mutating. Nereus attends the wedding of *Peleus and *Thetis (François vase), and watches them wrestle.

Nero (Nero Claudius Caesar), Roman emperor (AD 54–68), b. 37 to Gnaeus Domitius Ahenobarbus (consul 32) and *Iulia Agrippina.

To strengthen his doubtful claim to the throne, stories had been spread of his miraculous childhood and stress laid on his descent from the divine *Augustus. In 49 his mother, as *Claudius' new wife, had *Seneca the Younger recalled from exile in order to teach her son rhetoric and to secure his betrothal to Claudius' daughter *Claudia Octavia; in 50 Lucius Domitius Ahenobarbus was adopted by Claudius, thus becoming Tiberius Claudius Nero Caesar or Nero Claudius Caesar Drusus Germanicus. He assumed the *toga virilis at the early age of 13 and was clearly marked out for the accession. When Claudius died in 54, Nero was escorted into the *praetorian camp by the prefect *Afranius Burrus. The senate then conferred the necessary powers on Nero and declared his adoptive father a god and Agrippina his priestess.

The ancient tradition agrees that Nero's initial years of rule were excellent, a period hailed as a *golden age by contemporary poets. Of our three major authorities, *Suetonius and *Cassius Dio suggest that the young emperor at first left government to his mother, and Dio adds that Seneca and Burrus soon took over control, leaving the emperor to his pleasures. *Tacitus, however, regards the influence of Agrippina (visible on coins of 54 showing her head facing Nero's on the obverse) as more apparent than real and the role of his advisers as one of guiding his activities, as in Seneca's On Clemency, and managing court intrigue and public relations. Nero's first speech to the senate, written by Seneca, is described by Suetonius as a promise to rule according to Augustan precedent. Tacitus adds a renunciation of the abuses of the Claudian regime—and a pledge to share the responsibilities of government with the senate. The historian vouches for the fulfilment of these promises. Symbolic of the new attitude was the legend 'ex s c' ('in accordance with a senatorial decree') appearing regularly on the gold and silver coinage for the first ten years.

Nero at first heeded his advisers because they protected him from his domineering mother and indulged him. She had always used the menace of rivals to threaten him, and the presence of a considerable number of dynastic claimants was inevitable under the Augustan principate, which, not being an avowed monarchy, had no law of succession. When Agrippina decided to show sympathy for Claudius' natural son Britannicus in 55, she sealed his doom, though the poisoning was not overt and could be dissembled, as by Seneca, who wrote praising Nero's clemency in the next year. In 59 Agrippina's resistance to his affair with *Poppaea Sabina led Nero to enlist Anicetus, formerly his tutor and now perfect of the fleet at Mīsēnum, to drown her in a collapsible boat. When that failed, she was stabbed at her villa. This spectacular crime marked the end of the good part of Nero's reign, acc. to a contemporary view. But for Tacitus, the political deterioration did not set in until 62, when a treason charge of the unrepublican sort, based on irreverence towards the emperor, was admitted for the first time in the reign (see MAIESTAS), and Burrus died, thereby ending Seneca's influence as well. Nero now divorced his barren wife Octavia and married Poppaea.

The death of his mother already made him feel freer to indulge his artistic passions. His enthusiasm for art, chariot-racing, and Greek *athletics seems to have been genuine; he wanted to lead Rome from gladiatorial shows (see GLADIATORS) to nobler entertainments. At the Iuvenalia, private games held in 59 to celebrate the first shaving of his beard, he sang and performed on the lyre but also encouraged members of the upper classes to take lessons in singing and dancing. A year later he introduced for the first time at Rome public games in the Greek fashion (see AGONES) to be celebrated every five years (Nerōnia). In 61 he opened a *gymnasium and distributed free *oil to competitors. His interest in re-educating Rome was genuine: it was not until the second celebration of these games in 65 that the princeps himself performed, though he had already made his début in Neapolis a year earlier. His voice, described as 'slight and husky', may have been passable; his poetry was probably his own, for Suetonius had seen his notebooks with their erasures.

The emperor's popularity with the propertied classes had been further undermined by a fire in 64 which devastated the city. The emperor provided emergency shelter and helped with reconstruction, but he soon revealed that he would take the opportunity, not only to introduce a new code of safety for buildings, but also to use land previously in private occupation for a grand palace and spacious parks (the Golden House or *Domus Aurea) in the centre of Rome. The precious metal coinage shows the financial strain, to which the expense of the revolt of *Boudicca in *Britain in 60 and the wars with *Parthia over Armenia contributed: both the gold and silver were reduced in weight and the silver content of the dēnārius lowered by more than 10 per cent. With rumours circulating that Nero had instigated the fire and recited his own poems over the burning city, Nero made the Christians scapegoats, burning them alive to make the punishment fit the alleged crime (see CHRISTIANITY).

Nero never lost his popularity with the ordinary people of Rome, who loved his generosity and his games. The threat came from the upper classes and esp. from senators governing provinces where the propertied élite had become discontented as a result of confiscations after the Rome fire. Meanwhile his paranoiac prosecutions in Rome led to an unsuccessful conspiracy in 65 to assassinate him and make Gnaeus *Calpurnius Piso emperor. Piso and his accomplices, senators including *Lucan, *equestrians, officers of the praetorian guard, and one of the prefects, Faenius Rufus, were executed. Nero now suspected everyone, and more deaths followed, including Seneca, *Petronius, and the Stoics *Clodius Thrasea Paetus and Barea Soranus (see STOICISM). In the year after Poppaea's death, Nero married the talented and beautiful Statilia Messallīna, and, also in 66, Tiridates, a member of the ruling Parthian dynasty, came to Rome to receive the diadem of Armenia from Nero's hand. In September 66, despite another conspiracy, Nero himself left for Greece, to perform in all the Greek Games. The highpoint of his tour was his liberation of Greece from Roman administration and taxation.

While in Greece *Vespasian was selected from the emperor's entourage to deal with a revolt in Judaea (see JEWS). But Nero deposed and executed three senatorial commanders, *Domitius Corbulo, who had served him well in the east, and the Scribonii brothers, who governed the two Germanies. Disaffection was rumbling in the west. At last Nero returned to Italy. Soon after, March 68, *Iulius Vindex, governor of Gallia Lugdunensis (see GAUL (TRANSALPINE)), rose in arms. Although he was soon defeated by the governor of Upper Germany, Nero's failure to respond decisively had encouraged others to defect. In Spain *Galba declared himself 'Legate of the Senate and Roman People', and in Africa Clodius Macer revolted. The *praetorians were told that Nero had already fled abroad and were bribed by Nymphidius Sabinus, one of their prefects, to declare for Galba. The senate followed suit, decreeing Nero a public enemy. Nero took refuge in the villa of his freedman Phaon, and there he killed himself, reputedly lamenting, 'What an artist dies with me!'.

Nero's *philhellenism earned him the devotion of many in the Greek-speaking provinces. But the Christians naturally hated him for their persecution of 64 and the Jews for the mistreatment that led to the revolt which ultimately lost them the Temple in Jerusalem.

Nerva, Marcus Cocceius, Roman emperor AD 96–98, b. *c.* AD 35. His family, which came from Narnia and acquired distinction during the Civil Wars, had a remote connection with the Julio-Claudian dynasty. Nerva it seems did not serve as a provincial governor or hold any senior administrative post, but was influential as a confidant of *Nero, who admired his poetry and presented him with triumphal ornaments and other honours after the suppression of the conspiracy of Gaius *Calpurnius Piso. Even so, he was high in the Flavians' favour, being ordinary *consul with *Vespasian in 71 and again in 90 with *Domitian.

Nerva was seemingly not party to the plot to murder Domitian and was approached by the conspirators only after several others had rebuffed them. But he had qualities of good birth, a pleasant disposition, and long experience in imperial politics, and immediately set out to be a contrast to Domitian, who had been detested by the upper classes and whose memory was damned by the senate (see DAMNATIO MEMORIAE). The slogans on Nerva's coinage reflect his wish to create a new atmosphere. He released those on trial for treason, banned future treason charges, restored exiles, returned property confiscated by Domitian, displayed moderation in the public honours he accepted, and took advice from leading men. He built *granaries in Rome, dedicated the forum Transitorium (see FORUM NERVAE) begun by Domitian, distributed a largess to the people and the soldiers, removed the burden of the imperial post (see POSTAL SERVICE) from communities in Italy, and initiated moves to buy up land for distribution to the poorest citizens. Acc. to Tacitus, Nerva combined two incompatible elements— liberty and imperial rule.

However, Nerva was elderly, infirm and childless. Naturally there was speculation about the succession, and further problems appeared. The desire for vengeance against supposed agents of Domitian came close to anarchy. The appointment of a senatorial committee in 97 to effect economies suggests that there were financial difficulties, which perhaps resulted from extravagance in Nerva's regime. The most serious signs of disquiet occurred among the soldiers, with whom Domitian had been popular. One army was close to mutiny on the news of his death, and later there were rumours about the intentions of a governor of one of the eastern provinces in command of a substantial army. Coins celebrating 'Concord of the armies' probably express hope rather than confidence. There was also a plot against the emperor in Rome. Most ominously, rebellion broke out among the *praetorians, who had been stirred up by their prefect to demand the execution of the murderers of Domitian. Nerva had to accede, and was forced to give public thanks for the executions, thereby losing much of his authority and prestige. In October 97 amid gathering political crisis, he adopted *Trajan, whom he had previously appointed governor of Upper Germany, as his son, co-emperor, and successor. His own title *Germanicus*, granted for a minor victory over the Germans in Bohemia, was conferred on Trajan. It is impossible to discover the exact circumstances of Trajan's adoption. Pliny suggests that the empire was tottering above the head of an emperor who now regretted his elevation to imperial power, but this may have been exaggerated in order to please Trajan. However, if Nerva's regime faced increasing discontent, his advisers would doubtless take into consideration Trajan's distinguished background and career, popularity with the troops, and proximity to Rome. Nerva's death in January 98 marks a stage in the development of the empire, since he was the last strictly Italian emperor.

Nestor, in myth, the youngest son of *Neleus. He was king of Pylos, and went with *Menelaus around Greece to assemble the heroes ready for the expedition against *Troy, then himself accompanied them with 90 ships and his sons Antilochus and Thrasymedes, even though he was at that time a very old man. Homer portrays him as a highly respected elder statesman, the archetypal wise old man, but one still strong and valiant. He is always ready with advice: he tries to make peace between *Achilles and *Agamemnon, and later suggests the Embassy to Achilles, giving the ambassadors many instructions; he also suggests the spying raid on *Hector's camp in which Dolon is killed; he even offers Antilochus advice on chariot-racing which he himself admits is superfluous. He is much given also to long, rambling stories of the distant past, rich in reminiscences of his own achievements. But he is always listened to by his comrades with patience, and indeed with respect.

In the *Odyssey*, at Achilles' funeral, Nestor stopped the panic of the Greeks at the wailing of *Thetis and her attendants. After the fall of Troy he realized that disaster impended and sailed safely home to Pylos, where he entertained *Telemachus, who was seeking news of *Odysseus.

Nicander, of Colophon, (*c*.130 BC) was probably a priest of *Apollo at *Claros as well as a poet.

Works Surviving intact are two didactic poems in *hexameters, the *Thēriaca* ('Antidotes against Poisonous Bites') and *Alexipharmaca* ('Antidotes'). Forming the subject-matter of the *Theriaca* are snakes, spiders, scorpions, presumably poisonous insects, and related creatures, accompanied by remedies for their bites and stings; the *Alexipharmaca* retails botanical, animal, and mineral poisons and antidotes. Nicander is neither zoologist nor toxicologist: the lost tracts *Poisonous Animals* and *Poisonous Drugs* by Apollodorus of Alexandria (early 3rd cent. BC) were plagiarized for specifics. Noteworthy are descriptions of several cobras, the black widow spider, a number of scorpions, the blister beetle (from which came the aphrodisiac *kantharis*), the velvet ant (a wingless wasp), the wind scorpion or solifuge. Important are the accounts of opium, aconite, hemlock, and the thorn apple, showing careful study of widely known poisons.

Nicander has little poetic talent. His borrowing from Apollodorus indicates near-slavish dependence. Yet as a grammarian and commentator, Nicander is among the most diligent of the Alexandrians in searching for puns, double meanings, and allusions in the Homeric epics.

Nicander's two poems became standard for later students of toxicology, and these obscure hexameters owe their survival to their ease on the memory: one recalled Nicander's metrical lines far more easily than (e.g.) the lengthy treatises of Apollodorus. Nicander's poems were authoritative until the Renaissance. The delicious replication of superstitions about snakes, spiders, toads, frogs, salamanders, wasps, and so on are lodes for the folklorist and the historian of medicine, who note the meld of *magic and therapeutics. See PHARMACOLOGY.

Nīcias (*c*.470–413 BC), Athenian politician and general. After the death of *Pericles he became the main rival of *Cleon in the struggle for political leadership. He was a moderate and opposed the aggressive *imperialism of the extreme democrats, his aim being the conclusion of peace with Sparta as soon as it could be attained on terms favourable to Athens. Often elected *strategos, he led several expeditions in which, thanks to his cautious competence, he suffered no serious defeat and won no important victory. He was largely responsible for the armistice concluded in 423, and the Peace of 421 rightly bears his name.

He now favoured a policy of retrenchment and objected to the ambitious schemes of *Alcibiades, who advocated Athenian intervention in Peloponnese and later an expedition to Sicily. Despite his disapproval Nicias was appointed with Alcibiades and *Lamachus to command this enterprise. Alcibiades was soon recalled, and little was accomplished in 415, but in 414 Syracuse was besieged and almost reduced to capitulation. The death of Lamachus, the arrival of the Spartan Gylippus, and the inactivity of Nicias, now seriously ill, transformed the situation, and in spite of the efforts of *Demosthenes (1), who brought reinforcements in 413, the Athenians were themselves blockaded. Nicias, who refused to withdraw by sea until too late, led the vanguard in a desperate attempt to escape by land. His troops were overwhelmed at the river Assinarus, and he was later put to death. The narrative of *Thucydides (2), though giving due credit to Nicias for his selfless devotion, shows clearly that the Athenian disaster was largely due to his inadequate leadership. He was very rich (Xenophon. says he had 1,000 slaves working in the silver *mines; see SLAVERY) and spent lavishly. *Plutarch mentions the splendid procession he led to *Delos, where Athens has recently re-established the festival of the Delia. See PELOPONNESIAN WAR.

Nicolāus of Damascus, versatile author; friend and historian of *Herod (1) the Great; b. c.64 BC of distinguished family, very well-educated. He became a *Peripatetic and met leading figures of his day: he was tutor to the children of Antony (Marcus *Antonius) and *Cleopatra VII and from 14 BC close adviser of Herod, who employed him on diplomatic missions. Herod also studied philosophy, rhetoric, and history with Nicolaus and encouraged him to write. When Herod incurred *Augustus' displeasure on account of his Nabataean campaign (9?), Nicolaus succeeded in placating the *princeps* in Rome.

Works (1) *Histories*, universal history in 144 books from the earliest times to the death of Herod the Great, the most comprehensive work of universal history since *Ephorus. Bks. 1–7 dealt with the ancient east (Assyrians, Medes, Lydians, Persians) and early Greece. Only meagre fragments of bks. 8–144 are extant. Bks. 123–4, drawn on by *Josephus, contained the history of Herod the Great, for which Nicolaus, despite his tendentious and extenuating presentation, was an excellent primary source: he drew on his own experiences and on the king's memoirs. (2) *Life of Augustus*, apologetic

and panegyric account based on Augustus' autobiography, which reached down to c.25 BC. (3) *On My Own Life and Education*, autobiography. Education is seen from the viewpoint of Aristotelian ethics (see ARISTOTLE) and compared to 'a journey to one's own hearth'; an important source for the contemporary system of education.

Nicopolis, 'victory city', *Alexander (2) the Great's foundation to commemorate the battle of *Issus (333 BC), and, more importantly, its imitations in the eastern Mediterranean (with a Greek-speaking population), built to commemorate the victories of Roman commanders and emperors.

Nicopolis in Epirus was the most successful of these cities, on the isthmus of the peninsula opposite *Actium at the entrance to the Ambracian Gulf. Founded by Octavian (see AUGUSTUS) on the site of his army encampment, Nicopolis was not only a 'victory city' honouring his defeat of Antony (Marcus *Antonius) and *Cleopatra VII in this region, but was also a *synoecism of older cities. It was settled soon after 31 BC, and dedicated, perhaps, in 29. A *free city minting its own coinage, Nicopolis served as a regional administrative, economic, and religious centre. Augustus chose the city as the new site for the Actian Games, an ancient festival now celebrated every four years under Spartan stewardship and ranked equal to the major panhellenic *agones*. Surviving structures include impressive city walls, a theatre, stadium, bath structure, odeum, Actian victory monument, aqueduct, and four early Christian basilicas. It was home to *Epictetus.

Nīkē, the goddess of Victory, is first mentioned by *Hesiod as daughter of a *Titan and *Styx, and sister of Zēlos, Kratos, and Bia ('Rivalry', 'Strength', and 'Force'). With these she was honoured by *Zeus because she fought with the gods against the Titans. *Bacchylides depicts her standing next to *Zeus on *Olympus and judging the award for 'areta' (valour) to gods and men. In Pindar the victorious athlete sinks into the arms of Nike. Here Nike is victory in an athletic, not only a military, contest.

In cult Nike may be assimilated with other gods, like Zeus at *Olympia or *Athena at Athens, where from c.566 BC, she had an altar on the Acropolis, and later a Classical temple. *Pausanias (3) calls this Nike wingless, adding that the Athenians and Spartans had a wingless Nike so that she would stay with them always. In art, her winged appearance is readily confused with orientalizing figures, and later with Iris, esp. when she holds a herald's *sceptre. She appears from the early 6th cent., on vases. She may have two or four wings.

In the Classical period, her iconography is fully developed, attributes including garland, jug, shallow bowl, and censer. She is esp. popular on vases after the battle of *Marathon, often alone, or pouring a libation over an altar, for both gods and men; also in athletic and military contexts, sometimes holding weapons, or decorating a *trophy. She strides, runs, or flies. Sculptural representations attempt to evoke flight, such as the Nike of Paros (c.470) where she hovers or alights; so too the Nike of *Paeonius at Olympia of c.420. She was shown alighting on the hand of the Athena Parthenos and the Zeus at Olympia. The sculpted parapet of her temple on the Acropolis (c.410) shows her as messenger of Victory, setting a trophy, administering libations, leading bulls to sacrifice, and binding her sandal. In the Hellenistic period, Nike is used for political ends by *Alexander (2) the Great and the *Diadochi on coins and gems. The striding type is represented by the Nike of Samothrace (c.306–250).

Nile, Egypt's river was known to *Homer as 'Aegyptos river', to *Hesiod as 'Neilos'. *Cambyses (c.525 BC) reached the desert south of Korosko, but *Herodotus knew little beyond Meroë. *Anaxagoras made a good guess that the Nile flood was caused by melting snows, but the true cause was unknown. *Alexander (2) the Great's explorations disproved that the Nile joined the Indus. Under the Ptolemies (see PTOLEMY (1); EGYPT, *Ptolemaic*) the White Nile, the Blue Nile, and sources of the Astaboras became known. It was confirmed that the annual flood came from rains in *Ethiopia, as *Aristotle had guessed.

Nineveh Assyrian city on the east bank of the Tigris, also called 'Old Babylon' in astronomical tradition. It was the capital city of Assyria in the 7th cent. BC. The patron deity was Ishtar. Intermittent excavations have uncovered monumental palaces with sculptures and libraries of Sennacherib (704–681) and of Ashurbanipal (668–627) as well as religious buildings and city gates. Texts and sculptures attest fine gardens designed by Sennacherib. Although sacked in 612, its revival was encouraged by *Cyrus (1) the Great.

nōbilēs, nōbilitās When the *plebs* attained legal equality with the *patricians, the magistracies were in theory open to all citizens. In fact, the ruling class gradually co-opted powerful plebeian families into association, until (by the 3rd cent. BC) a new, increasingly plebeian, oligarchy emerges. In lists of consuls and priests, the same names tend to recur, with a slow trickle of newcomers. These new rulers are the *nobiles*, 'known' men—known (presumably) because they had the right to *imagines*, and actors representing their ancestors in full ceremonial dress were a common sight in the streets of Rome. These 'known' men naturally had an advantage in elections, and it was increased by a network of family and client relationships (see CLIENS) built up over generations. We do not know how and when the word '*nobilis*' acquired a more exclusive meaning: 'descended from a consul'. This is its quasi-technical meaning in the 1st cent. BC (although the general meaning 'known' always coexists with it outside the political sphere). Perhaps praetorships (six by 197/6, eight by 81) had become too common, and aedileships too humble.

As *Sallust says, with pardonable exaggeration, the *nobiles* tended to regard the accession of an outsider to the consulship as 'polluting' it. By the late republic, the defeat of a *nobilis* by an outsider sufficed to raise a presumption of *corruption. *Nobilitas* was never a necessary or a sufficient qualification for the consulship. There was fierce competition among *nobiles* for only two posts, and some outsiders of senatorial background gained admission. But very few men not born to senatorial families became consuls, and those few normally through the support of eminent families. They tended to be perfectly absorbed into the ethos of the oligarchy and became its defenders. (See NOVUS HOMO.) The proportion of *nobiles* in the consulship is never, over any lengthy period, less than 70 per cent (and this is a minimum); by the time of *Cicero, when many old families long unrepresented revive, it is close to 90 per cent. These proportions are remarkably untouched by the most violent political crises.

Under the empire the word was a social label, still chiefly applied to descendants (on either side) of republican, or at latest triumviral, consuls. *Nobiles* were raised to (usually harmless) dignity by 'good' emperors (the success of a patrician *Galba showed how dangerous they could be) and persecuted by 'bad' emperors. Most noble families were extinguished by the Antonine period.

nomads Greek (followed by Roman) writers lumped together as nomads all pastoral groups for whom wandering was a way of life, without distinguishing between semi-nomads—including those practising *transhumance—and fully nomadic societies of no fixed abode, such as the ancients met on the desert fringes of *Libya and Arabia and in *Scythia. *Homer's portrayal of the pastoral *Cyclopes as uncivilized and savage inaugurates a persistent hostility in Greek literature to nomads, whose lifestyle as cultivators of livestock, and esp. their different diet and desert habitat, set them apart from the sedentary communities of Greek farmers and encouraged a stereotyping taken to extremes in *Herodotus' account of the nomadic Scythian 'man-eaters'. Thus to turn nomads into settled agriculturalists ranked among the self-evident achievements of the Macedonian kings, *Philip II and *Alexander (2) the Great. see BARBARIAN; PASTORALISM.

nōmen See NAMES, PERSONAL, ROMAN.

nomos (1), 'nome', the Greek term for the administrative districts of ancient *Egypt. Though numbers varied, traditionally there were 42 nomes—22 in Upper and 20 in Lower Egypt.

nomos (2), Greek for 'law'. See LAW IN GREECE. For *nomos* as opp. *physis* (nature) see POLITICAL THEORY.

nomothetai, 'law-makers', were usually men like *Draco and *Solon, but in Athens in the late 5th and the 4th cent. BC large groups with this title were appointed. The earliest known was appointed in 411 in connection with the Five Thousand and must have lapsed when that regime fell. In 403, when democracy was restored, one group of *nomothetai* was appointed by the *boule to draft and display proposed additions to the laws, and another body of 500 *nomothetai* was elected by the demes to consider these proposals in conjunction with the *boule*.

Thereafter *nomothetai* were appointed regularly to consider proposed changes in the laws, on which they, not the *ekklesia*, now took the final decisions. In some cases (or in all, acc. to one view) they were drawn by lot from the list of 6,000 jurors; thus they were ordinary citizens, without special expertise, but their function was to examine proposals more closely than the *ekklesia* would do. The intention seems to have been to make legislating more difficult and less casual, and to prevent inconsistencies and contradictions arising within the legal code.

novel, Greek Extended prose narrative fiction is a latecomer to Greek literature (see NARRATIVE). Of the five novels to survive complete, Chariton probably belongs to the later 1st cent. AD; Xenophon to the first half of the 2nd cent., and Achilles Tatius to the 2nd; Longus is perhaps late 2nd or early 3rd cent. AD, while both early 3rd and late 4th cent. AD are claimed for Hēliodōrus.

These narratives vary a shared pattern. Boy and girl fall in love: Xenophon's heroine is 14, his hero 16, Longus' 13 and 15. Either before marriage (Achilles Tatius, Heliodorus) or soon after (Chariton, Xenophon) they are separated and survive storms, shipwreck, imprisonment, attempted seduction or rape, torture, and even what readers and characters believe to be death, before reunion at the book's end. Their ordeals usually traverse Egypt or other near eastern lands; but Heliodorus' couple have Meroë as their goal, Xenophon's reach south Italy, and Longus compresses the adventures of Daphnis and Chloē into a corner of *Lesbos, substituting sexual naïvety for external forces as obstacles to their union. The heroine typically preserves her virginity/fidelity to her husband, although Chariton's accepts a cultivated Greek as her second husband (to protect the hero's child she is carrying). Achilles' hero, however, succumbs to a married Ephesian, and Longus' receives sexual instruction, crucial to the plot's advancement, from a married city woman.

Love stories are found in earlier Greek literature, both verse (esp. of the Hellenistic period) and prose (esp. the other *Xenophon's *Cyropaedia*); the centrality of a young couple's love, their city origins and some speeches recall New Comedy (see COMEDY (GREEK), NEW); analogous story-patterns can be found in Mesopotamian or Egyptian literature. But the novel evolves from none of these. Rather it is a late Hellenistic or early imperial creation, whose literary effects include evocation of these Greek predecessors and of *Homer's *Odyssey* and Attic tragedy too (see TRAGEDY, GREEK). Elaborate 'documentation' of the story's 'origin' and apparently exact geographical detail entice readers to accept the 'events' as having once happened, albeit in the distant past: only Xenophon's world seems to be that of the empire, though Achilles' might be taken as such, and the élites from which the novels' characters are drawn (even the foundlings Daphnis and Chloe) resemble those of Greek cities of the Roman empire. But all authors exclude Rome and Romans. *Piracy is commoner than in the *pax Romana*, coincidences are far-fetched, but the impossible is avoided and only such miraculous events admitted (e.g. prophetic *dreams) as contemporary belief credited.

Characters are less convincing. The main ones, though morally admirable, are rarely interesting, but the often stronger heroines engage readers more effectively, and some minor characters (e.g. Heliodorus' Calasiris and even Cnemon) are more interesting because less predictable. Descriptions of actions and thoughts (usually conveyed by dialogue or monologue) are deployed rather to delineate emotion and raise suspense or excitement.

novel, Latin The Latin novel is mainly represented for us by two extant texts, the *Satyrica* of *Petronius Arbiter (1st cent. AD) and the *Metamorphoses* or *Golden Ass* of *Apuleius (2nd cent. AD); no previous long fictions are known in Latin. An influence on both were the lubricious *Milesian Tales*, short stories translated from the Greek of Aristīdēs in the first cent. BC. The adaptations by *Varro of the prose-and-verse Greek satires of Menippus (see MENIPPEAN SATIRE) also contributed something to the form and content of Petronius.

Petronius' *Satyrica* survives only in parts, but it ran to at least sixteen books. Its plot concerns the comic adventures of a homosexual couple as narrated by one of them, Encolpius; as its title implies, it has connections with Roman *satire, in its form and in its content, e.g. the comic meal (Trimalchio's Feast). Two of its inserted tales clearly reflect the tradition of *Milesian Tales*—the Widow of Ephesus and the Pergamene Boy; it also contains literary and social criticism and some complex narrative technique. Apuleius' *Metamorphoses* in eleven books, concerning the metamorphosis of a young man into an ass and his comic adventures before retransformation by *Isis, contains like the *Satyrica* a number of inserted tales, the most famous being that of Cupid and Psyche in two books. Some of them are clearly *Milesian Tales*, which Apuleius explicitly claims to use; the inserted tales make up a large proportion of the plot but also lend it unity and coherence by their close thematic relation to the main narrative. The *Metamorphoses* has marked Isiac and Platonic elements; in the final book, the conversion of Lucius to Isiac cult and the resulting reassessment of his adventures, coupled with the apparent revelation that the narrator is no longer Lucius but Apuleius himself, provide a problematic conclusion.

Both Petronius and Apuleius use the existing genre of the Greek ideal novel, but both alter its flavour in a characteristically Roman way, parodying its stress on virtuous young love, adding low-life realism, bawdy humour, and elements from other established literary genres, and using narrators, narrative levels, and inserted tales in a complex way.

nŏvus hŏmō ('new man'), term used in the late republic in various related senses: for the first man of a family to reach the senate, where he normally remained a 'small senator'; in a special sense, for such a man actually to rise to the consulship; and for the first man of a senatorial family to reach the consulship. The first of these achievements was not very difficult, provided a man had at least *equestrian standing, some military or oratorical ability, and good connections. The last also was far from rare: it was thus that the *nōbilēs* were constantly reinvigorated. But few men rose from outside the senate to a consulship, and the commonest use of the term characterizes this rare achievement. It took unusual merit and effort and either noble patronage (e.g. that of the Flacci for *Porcius Cato (1)) or a public emergency, as in the cases of *Marius and *Cicero.

The *novus homo* become consul contrasts with the *nobiles* (the 'known' men) as *per sē cognitus* ('known (only) through himself'). He has to win his own connections and *clientēlae* (see CLIENS) to balance those inherited by the *nobiles*. Hence a typical pattern of career and outlook develops, best seen in Marius and Cicero, about whom we know most. During his rise the *novus homo* prides himself on his ability and achievements and tends to compare them with those of the founders of noble families, as contrasted with their degenerate descendants. But Cicero is not a reformer of the system. After rising to the top, he aims at defending the order in which he has risen and gaining recognition as an equal from his social superiors. Some (e.g. Cato, in part through longevity) more or less succeed in this; others (e.g. Marius and Cicero) are never quite accepted. But they never favour the advancement of other new men.

Under the empire, men of this sort, of equestrian background, at first from Italy and gradually from the provinces, can rise high on their own merits, promoted by the emperor, to whom they give less cause for jealousy and suspicion.

Numa See REX.

Numantia, a strategic site on the upper Durius in Spain. It played a pivotal role in the Celtiberian resistance to Rome, repelling attacks by successive commanders, starting with *Porcius Cato (195). The capitulation of Hostilius

Mancinus (137) crowned a series of Roman failures and defeats. Finally, after an eight-month blockade, Numantia's 4,000 inhabitants capitulated to the overwhelming forces of *Cornelius Scipio Aemilianus in 133, a date which marks the end of concerted resistance to Rome in Iberia. *Marius, *Jugurtha, and *Rutilius Rufus witnessed Numantia's destruction.

nūmen, the 'expressed will of a divinity'. It was indicated esp. by the *nūtus*, an inclination of the head. The *numen* of a divinity shows the actual and particular will of this deity. In general the *numen* concerns the gods and, under the empire, the ruling emperor. The *numen* of Augustus received a cult from the beginning of our era, its function being to represent the exceptional power of the ruler, and it enabled the attribution of divine honours to him in his lifetime. See RULER-CULT.

numerals, Greek There were two main numeral systems:

(1) The 'alphabetic', probably originating in Ionia and the older of the two. It consisted of the ordinary letters of the Ionian *alphabet with three additions for 6, 90, and 900. Thus Alpha to Theta represent 1 to 9.

(2) The 'acrophonic'. Apart from |, the unit, the signs were the initial letters of the numeral words: $\Gamma = pente$ (5) (NB Gamma is Pī in Attic financial inscriptions); $\Delta = deka$ (10); H = *hekaton* (100); X = *Khīlioi* (1,000); M = *mȳrioi* (10,000).

(2) was the system used in all public inscriptions in *Attica down to *c*.100 BC. A zero sign is found in astronomical papyri.

numerals, Roman The numerals are represented by seven signs: I = 1, V = 5, X = 10, L = 50, C = 100, Ð = 500, ∞ = 1,000 (M was not used as a numeral, only as an abbreviation of the words *mille*, *milia*).

A notation could be constructed on this basis both by the additive method (IIII = 4; XXXX = 40) and by the subtractive (IV = 4; XL = 40) and both methods were employed, sometimes even in the same document. Inscriptions seem to show a preference for the additive method, esp. in official contexts, and this preference is occasionally carried to the extent of ignoring the signs V and L. The rule is that when two figures stand side by side, the smaller, if to the right, is to be added to its neighbour, if to the left, to be subtracted from it (VI = 6; IV = 4).

Numidia, originally the land of the Numidae or African *nomads, lying west and south of Carthaginian territory (see CARTHAGE). The original Berber inhabitants were nomad herdsmen, who sometimes practised a simple agriculture. Those on the coast came under the influence of *Utica, Carthage, and other Phoenician settlements. By the time of the Second Punic War their small clans had coalesced into tribal confederacies of the Masaesyli under Syphax (the more westerly of the two, occupying western Algeria above the Sahara), and the Massyli under *Masinissa. Their cavalry was formidable, but disunion made them difficult allies politically. Under Masinissa nomadism was abandoned for agriculture, and town life developed; Punic was adopted as the language of the élite, and worship of Baal-Hammon became popular alongside native cults. Masinissa was followed by Micipsa (148–118 BC), Adherbal (118–112), *Jugurtha (118–106), Hiempsal (106–60), and Juba I (60–46).

nymphaeum In Classical Greece a *nymphaeum* was a shrine to the *Nymphs, often a rural cave or grove with no architectural adornment. Several sculptured reliefs dedicated to *Pan and the Nymphs are known from Classical *Attica (see CAVES, SACRED).

The Nymphs were with river-gods the guardian spirits of sources of pure *water. When Theagenes of *Megara diverted fresh water for his city, he sacrificed to the *river-god at the point where the waters had been captured. By the Roman imperial period such sentiment was more publicly expressed at the urban terminus of *aqueducts, where the waters were filtered into a fountain, often richly decorated with statues and inscriptions recording the generosity, piety, and social status of the donor, and often referring to the river or spring from which the waters originated. The most intelligible surviving example was built by *Claudius Atticus Herodes in the sanctuary at *Olympia *c*. AD 150. The modern term *nymphaeum* applied to such buildings derives from late antique usage; in the early empire urban fountains were called *munera*, onerous burdens to those who held public office (see MUNUS). Ornate fountains built in many rich cities of the Roman empire, e.g. *Miletus, *Lepcis Magna, and *Carthage.

nymphs A varied category of female divinities anthropomorphically perceived as young women (Gk. *nymphē* means also 'bride'). They inhabit and animately express differentiated nature: *water, *mountains, *trees. Their ubiquitous presence in popular imagination, folklore, art, myth, and cult, provides a vivid illustration of ancient pantheism.

Cult of Nymphs, esp. associated with caves, is mentioned in *Homer and corroborated by archaeology. In the Polis cave at Ithaca, there was a cult to *Odysseus and also to the Nymphs. The grotto on Mt. Hymettus (SE of Athens) was sacred to Pan, *Apollo, and the Nymphs. See CAVES, SACRED. Nymphs were closely associated (mythically perceived as daughters or lovers) in worship with *river-gods, such as the archetypical *Achelous. They received both animal and cereal *sacrifices; *wine was usually forbidden in their worship. Nymphs are intimately, if vaguely, linked with productive and life-enhancing powers. Although mostly belonging to the countryside or to particular spots (streams, groves (see TREES, SACRED), hills), nymphs appear also in official state cult.

The association with other gods, such as Pan (esp.), *Hermes, and *Artemis appears both in cult and myth. Apollo and Dionysus are addressed as 'Nymph-leaders'. Often regarded as daughters of Zeus, nymphs were also perceived as belonging to an earlier stratum: the Meliads, nymphs of ash-trees, emerged from the drops of blood of *Uranus' castrated genitals. Nymphs are either lovers or mothers of gods, heroes, or satyrs; as virgins they roam the woods and mountains with Artemis. Eponymous nymphs, such as Aegina, filled up the landscape.

Nymphs may have other nymphs attending them (Calypso). They are either immortal or endowed with super-human longevity. They are often named after their respective elements: Hamadryads die with the particular trees with which they are identified; Oreads are mountain-nymphs; Naiads, water-nymphs, often daughters of the river-god; the Nereids are nymphs of the calm sea (daughters of the Old Man of the Sea, *Nereus); Oceanids are daughters of *Oceanus and Tethys.

Most nymphs are benevolent, although they may abduct handsome boys (*Hylas). They bring flowers, watch with Apollo and Hermes over the flocks, and, as patronesses of healing springs, aid the sick. See SPRINGS, SACRED. As divinities of woods and mountains they may help hunters. Folk-tales, similar to those about fairies and mermaids, are told about nymphs. A man who sees them becomes 'possessed by nymphs'. See POSSESSION, RELIGIOUS. They punish unresponsive lovers, as did the nymphs who blinded *Daphnis. See also NYMPHAEUM.

oaths An oath was a statement (assertory) or promise (promissory) strengthened by the invocation of a god as a witness and often with the addition of a *curse in case of perjury. A defendant in a lawsuit might swear by a god that his testimony was truthful and might specify the punishment for perjury. If the oath was false, the god, by effecting the provisions of the curse, would punish the individual, not for lying in court but for committing perjury. (See EVIDENCE, ATTITUDES TO.) Throughout antiquity oaths were required of signatories to treaties, of parties to legal disputes, commercial and private contracts, conspiracies, and marriages, of governmental officials, judges, and jurors, and, esp. by the Romans, of soldiers (*sacramentum), and, under the empire, of citizens to affirm their allegiance to the emperor.

Almost any deity could be invoked as a witness, but in formal oaths the Greeks often called upon a triad of gods representing the sky, earth, and sea (*Helios or *Zeus, Ge (see GAIA) or *Demeter, and *Poseidon); the Romans upon *Jupiter and 'all the gods'. Everyday language was apparently sprinkled with casual oaths, and Greek women often invoked *Artemis, the men Zeus or *Heracles; Roman women named Castor and the men Hercules or Pollux (see DIOSCURI). The gods themselves swore by the *Styx. The punishment for perjury, when specified, might suit the particular circumstances of the oath-taker, but often called for 'the complete destruction of the perjuror and his family'. An oath itself could be strengthened by being taken in a *sanctuary. In *Homer's *Iliad* the combatants, as they prayed to Zeus and poured a *libation to accompany their oath, said, 'whichever side first does harm contrary to this oath, may their brains flow to the ground like this wine.' Animal *sacrifice was performed for the same purpose.

The maintenance of oaths was an essential element of public and personal piety. The Spartans imagined that their defeats at *Pylos and elsewhere were caused by their disregard of an oath, and *Plato saw in the growing disregard of oaths signs of a breakdown of belief in the gods (see ATHEISM). See also MEDICINE, 1(e) (Hippocratic Oath).

Ōcĕanus (geographical) A circumambient ocean-river, the final destination of all streams, predates Greek and Roman culture, appears in *Homer and *Hesiod, and was confirmed by geographical theory: the accessible land-mass could cover only a small portion of the earth's surface. *Phoenician contacts with the metalliferous and fertile Guadalquivir valley (Tartessus) took them into Atlantic waters early, and that Greeks followed quite soon is reflected in *Herodotus' story of the voyage of Colaeus. Such pioneer navigators were a feature of the literary tradition about the Ocean from at least the 6th cent., and commercial exchanges certainly reached the Atlantic coasts of Gaul and southern Britain from the Classical period. Southward exploration to verify the circumnavigability of Africa, and northward to explore the seas around Europe were inconclusive, and the idea that the Caspian Sea was an inlet like the Red Sea, the Persian Gulf, and the *Mediterranean itself, persisted. The Indian Ocean, despite its size and the tides that in the Atlantic were regarded as a distinctive and worrying feature of Ocean, was regarded as analogous to these other inlets rather than being a part of Ocean proper; but the crossing to Britain, conversely, was, for political purposes, represented as going beyond Ocean in its most awesome sense.

Ōcĕanus (mythical), son of *Uranus (Sky) and Gē (*Gaia, Earth), husband of Tēthys (a combination probably derived from the Babylonian creation epic *Enuma Eliš*), and father of the Oceanids and river-gods. The Homeric Oceanus is the river encircling the whole world, from which through subterranean connections issue all other rivers; its sources are in the west where the sun sets. Such monsters as Gorgons (see

GORGON/MEDUSA) and Geryon (see HERACLES), and such outlandish tribes as Cimmerians, Ethiopians (see ETHIOPIA), and pygmies, live by the waters of Oceanus.

In Greek theories of the world Oceanus is conceived as the great cosmic power, water, through which all life grows, and in Greek mythology as a benign old god. Sometimes the elemental, sometimes the personal, aspect is more emphasized. The belief that sun and stars rise and set in the ocean is expressed mythologically by saying that stars bathe in Oceanus, and the Sun traverses it in a golden bowl by night to return to the east. See HELIOS. The rise of rational geographical investigation in *Herodotus and others reduced Oceanus to the geographical term 'Ocean'.

Octāvia, sister of *Augustus, married Claudius Marcellus. In 40 Marcellus died and, to seal the Pact of Brundisium, she was immediately married to Antony (Marcus *Antonius). She spent the winters of 39/8 and 38/7 with him in Athens, and in 37 helped with the negotiations which led to the Pact of Tarentum. When he returned to the east, Antony left her behind. In 35 Octavian (the future Augustus) sent her to Antony with token reinforcements for his army; Antony forbade her to proceed beyond Athens. She rejected Octavian's advice to leave Antony's house, and though divorced by him in 32 brought up all his surviving children by *Fulvia and *Cleopatra VII along with their two daughters and her three children by Marcellus. Her nobility, humanity, and loyalty won her wide esteem and sympathy. She died in 11 BC. The Porticus Octaviae in Rome was named after her.

Octāvia, the one extant *fabula praetexta*, dramatizes the fate of *Nero's neglected empress (see CLAUDIA OCTAVIA). *Seneca the Younger, who is brought in as a character trying to restrain Nero's cruelty with Stoic advice, can hardly be its author. Style and metrics differ in several respects from Senecan practice. Moreover, *Iulia Agrippina's ghost foretells Nero's doom in words so accurate that they were probably written after Nero's death in 68.

Octavian See AUGUSTUS.

Octāvius, Gnaeus became consul 87 BC with *Cornelius Cinna, whose attempt to reverse *Sulla's legislation he opposed, finally driving Cinna and his supporters out of Rome after a massacre in the Forum. He had Cinna deposed and the *flamen Dialis* (see FLAMINES) elected in his place, thus assuring himself of sole power. Cinna collected an army, and was joined by *Marius, *Papirius Carbo and *Sertorius. Besieged in Rome, Octavius summoned Pompeius Strabo and Caecilius Metellus Pius to aid him, but after Pompeius' death Metellus withdrew and his army disintegrated. The senate finally surrendered Rome to Cinna, and Octavius, refusing to flee, was killed wearing his consular robes, and his head was displayed in the Forum.

ōdēum (Gk. *ōdeion*), a small theatre or roofed hall for musical competitions.

The Odeum of *Pericles at Athens, an exceptional structure, placed near the then undeveloped theatre, was a square hall having a pyramidal roof supported on rows of internal columns supposedly utilizing the masts taken from the Persian fleet after the battle of *Salamis. It was used for the choral elements in the competitions of the *Dionysia festival (see PROAGŌN). There are no traces of the provision for the audience, but *Plutarch says it contained seats.

Developed odea are generally smaller and, when roofed, avoid the need for supports intruding into the auditorium. They usually take the form of miniature theatres, with seats arranged in a semicircle, contained within a rectangular outer structure. Since this form may also be used for theatres, the distinction depends on size, the larger theatres not being roofed. The developed type occurs at *Pompeii, where inscriptions refer to it as a covered theatre. A large example, the Odeum of Agrippa (see VIPSANIUS AGRIPPA), filled the centre of the Athenian agora. This had a free span of 25 m (82 ft.), roofed only as a result of Roman technological advance (and even this collapsed, so that the span had to be reduced).

Odysseus (Lat. Ulixes, from one of several Greek variants; hence English Ulysses), king of Ithaca; son of Laertes and Anticlea; husband of *Penelope; hero of *Homer's *Odyssey*.

In Homer's *Iliad*, despite his out-of-the-way kingdom, Odysseus is already one of the most prominent of the Greek heroes. He displays martial prowess, courage and resourcefulness, and above all wisdom and diplomacy. He shows little of the skill in deceit which is characteristic of him in the *Odyssey*, but such epithets as 'much enduring' and 'cunning', which occur in both epics, must refer to his exploits after the Trojan War (see TROY), and show that these were always his principal claim to fame.

In the *Odyssey* he is in some ways the typical 'trickster' of folktales, who uses guile and deception to defeat stronger opponents. Besides spear and sword he uses the bow, which was often considered a less manly weapon, and he even procures arrow-poison. He not only resorts to trickery by necessity but sometimes revels in it, as when he boasts of his triumph over the Cyclops (see CYCLOPES); and his lying tales on Ithaca are elaborated with relish, as *Athena observes. But Homer was concerned to make him a worthy hero, not just for a folktale, but for an epic. Bks. 1–4, where his son *Telemachus takes centre-stage, are largely devoted to building up our sense of his greatness: he is the ideal king, whose return is necessary to re-establish order on Ithaca, and a friend deeply honoured by *Nestor and *Menelaus. When we first see him in bk. 5—longing for home after his seven-year detention by Calypso, then no sooner released than shipwrecked—the emphasis is on his noble endurance. At his lowest point, naked and destitute on the shore of Scheria in bk. 6, he is still resourceful, and can be seen by the princess Nausicaa as an ideal husband. Even in the fantastic and magical episodes which he relates as bard-like storyteller to the Phaeacians in bks. 9–12 (see HOMER) there is pathos as well as adventure. When he finally reaches Ithaca, he spends much of the rest of the poem (bks. 17–21) in the most humiliating condition, disguised as a beggar in his own house; but in his final revenge over Penelope's suitors, although he takes the crafty and necessary precaution of removing their weapons, the main emphasis is on his strength in stringing the great bow and the skill with which he wields it (bks. 21–22).

(For the later works mentioned in the following paragraph see EPIC CYCLE.) The *Telegony* continued the story with further travels and martial adventures for Odysseus, who was finally killed unwittingly by Telegonus, his son by Circe. Other early poetry seems to have presented him less favourably. In the *Cypria* he feigned madness to evade his obligation to join the Trojan expedition, but the trick was exposed by *Palamedes. In revenge he and *Diomedes later brought about Palamedes' death. In the *Little Iliad* Odysseus and Diomedes stole the *Palladium, a Trojan talisman; and by some accounts Odysseus tried to kill Diomedes on the way back. The dispute with *Aias over the arms of Achilles, first mentioned in *Odyssey* 11, was related in the *Aethiopis* and *Little Iliad*, and *Pindar claims that Odysseus won the arms by dishonest

trickery. The killing of the infant Astyanax was attributed to *Neoptolemus by the *Little Iliad* but to Odysseus by the *Sack of Troy*.

The tragedians tended to be similarly unfavourable. *Sophocles, while presenting a noble and magnanimous Odysseus in *Aias*, makes him an unprincipled cynic in *Philoctetes*. *Euripides depicts the Homeric Odysseus straightforwardly in *Cyclops*, but evidently made him a villain in his lost *Palamedes* (as does *Gorgias in his *Defence of Palamedes*), and his character in other plays (on stage in *Hecuba*) is in keeping with this. His detractors now often call him the son, not of Laertes, but of the sinner *Sisyphus, who had allegedly seduced Anticlea before her marriage.

*Virgil's references to Ulixes in *Aeneid* 2 follow the Euripidean conception as does *Seneca the Younger in *Trojan Women*.

In art he is always a popular figure. The more spectacular adventures are illustrated esp. often in the Archaic period (the blinding of Polyphemus (see CYCLOPES) and the escape under the ram are found as early as the 7th cent.). Later these are joined by quieter subjects, such as the embassy to Achilles and the dispute over the arms.

Oedipus, son of Laius, the king of *Thebes, who killed his father and married his mother. His name appears to mean 'with swollen foot'.

*Homer's *Iliad* mentions him only in the context of the funeral games held after his death, implying that he died at Thebes and probably in battle. The *Odyssey*, however, tells how he unwittingly killed his father and married his mother Epicaste (the later Iocasta), but the gods soon made this known (this version allows no time for the couple to have children) and Epicaste hanged herself. Oedipus continued to reign at Thebes, suffering all the woes that a mother's *Erinyes can inflict.

Of the epic *Oedipodia* (see EPIC CYCLE) we know little except that it mentioned the *Sphinx, who killed Haemon son of *Creon (1) and must have been killed by Oedipus, and that Oedipus had children, not by his mother, but by a second wife. The children must have included *Eteocles and Polynices, and probably also *Antigone and Ismene.

Another epic, the *Thebais*, told how Oedipus, now probably blind, twice cursed his sons, first when Polynices disobeyed him by serving him wine in a gold cup on a silver table, and again when his sons served him the wrong joint of meat. He prayed that they would quarrel over their patrimony and die at each other's hands, and the epic went on to describe the Theban War that ensued. See SEVEN AGAINST THEBES.

It is uncertain when Oedipus was first said to have had children by his mother (see INCEST), and when the motif of his *exile arose.

In 467 *Aeschylus produced a tetralogy consisting of *Laius, Oedipus*, the extant *Seven against Thebes*, and the satyr-play *Sphinx*. Though much is debatable, the outlines of the Oedipus story can be gathered from fragments and from allusions in the *Seven*. Laius learned from the *Delphic oracle that to save the city he must die childless. Overcome by lust, however, he begot Oedipus, and sought to have the baby exposed. Oedipus somehow survived to kill his father at a fork in the road near Potniae. He came to Thebes and rid the city of the man-eating Sphinx, probably by answering her riddle. He married Iocasta, became an honoured king, and begot Eteocles and Polynices. The patricide and incest came to light (we do not know how, but *Tiresias may have played a role), and Oedipus in his anguish blinded himself and cursed the sons born of the incest: they were to divide their patrimony with the sword. In the *Seven* Oedipus is dead, having probably died at Thebes.

*Sophocles' *Antigone* mentions how Oedipus blinded himself and died and Iocasta hanged herself. But Sophocles' *Oedipus Tyrannus* (*King Oedipus*) became the definitive account. Here Laius received an oracle from Apollo that his son would kill him; so he ordered a shepherd to expose the infant Oedipus on Mt. Cithaeron. The shepherd, however, took pity on the baby, and Oedipus survived to be brought up as the son of Polybus, king of *Corinth, and his wife. An oracle warned him that he would kill his father and marry his mother; so he fled from Corinth. At a junction of three roads near Daulis he killed Laius in a rage, not knowing who he was. Coming to Thebes he answered the riddle of the Sphinx, married Iocasta, and became king. When the play opens, the city is being ravaged by a *plague, caused, so Apollo's oracle reveals, by the polluting presence of the killer of Laius (see POLLUTION). Oedipus, an intelligent and benevolent king, pronounces a *curse on the unknown killer and begins an investigation, which ends in the discovery of the whole truth. Iocasta hangs herself and Oedipus blinds himself with pins from her dress. The ending is problematic, as Oedipus does not go into the immediate exile foreshadowed earlier but remains, for the moment, in the palace.

*Euripides too wrote an *Oedipus*, in which the king was blinded by the servants of Laius, not by his own hand. In Euripides' *Phoenician Women* he is self-blinded and is still living in the palace at the time of his sons' death.

At the end of his life Sophocles returned to Oedipus with his *Oedipus at Colonus*. Here the blind man, led by Antigone, comes to the grove of the Eumenides (see ERINYES) at *Colonos near Athens, where he knows that he must die. Protected by *Theseus, he resists the attempts of Polynices and Iocasta's brother Creon, who banished him from Thebes, to bring him back there for their selfish purposes. He curses his sons for their neglect, and finally, called by the gods, he dies mysteriously at a spot known only to Theseus, where his angry corpse will protect Athens against Theban attack. The *Oedipus* of *Seneca the Younger is based on Sophocles' *Oedipus Tyrannus*. The confrontation with the Sphinx is often portrayed in art.

Oenoanda, a city in northern Lycia, whose Hellenistic walls enclose ruins largely of the Roman period. It has produced four remarkable inscriptions: an enormous genealogical inscription carved on a funerary monument (see GENEALOGY); the most complete epigraphic dossier from the Roman world concerning the creation of an artistic festival by a local citizen in AD 125 (see AGONES); the literary works of the local Epicurean philosopher *Diogenes (3), which were engraved for public display in the centre of the Roman city; and a theological *oracle of the 3rd cent. AD, which is a key text for the understanding of pagan religious mentality in the later Roman empire (see ANGELS).

Oenomaus See PELOPS.

Ogulnius Gallus, Quintus, as tribune of the plebs (see TRIBUNI PLEBIS) together with his brother Gnaeus, in 300 carried a law, despite the opposition of Appius *Claudius Caecus, by which the two major *priestly colleges were to be shared between *patricians and plebeians (see PLEBS). From then on five of the nine *augurs, and four of the eight *pontifices, were always plebeians. As curule aediles in 296, the Ogulnii used fines from usurers to set up a statue-group of the infants *Romulus and Remus beneath the teats of the she-wolf; in 269, when Quintus Ogulnius was consul, this group appeared on the reverse of Rome's earliest silver *coinage.

oil See OLIVE.

Old Oligarch is a modern name for a pamphlet about 5th-cent. BC Athens, preserved among the works of *Xenophon, but better referred to as *The Constitution of the Athenians*.

The pamphlet aims to show that the *demos* (common people) at Athens run affairs in their own interests, and it takes the curious form of a salute from an anti-democratic viewpoint. See OLIGARCHY. The author stresses the importance of the link between *sea power and *democracy: 'it is right that the the poor and the *demos* have more power there than the noble and rich because it is the *demos* which mans the fleet'. The date lies somewhere between 431 BC and 413.

It is hard to know what to make of the pamphlet. There are passages which would be valuable evidence for Classical Athens if they were straightforwardly usable (and they are often so used), e.g. on the licence allowed to slaves (see SLAVERY), on the use of the law-courts for the maintenance of the democracy (see LAW AND PROCEDURE, ATHENIAN), on sea power generally, on the refusal of the people to let comic poets mock the *demos* (something less than outright censorship may be meant; but see INTOLERANCE, INTELLECTUAL AND RELIGIOUS). The usual view sees the pamphlet as good evidence for facts and attitudes about Athenian democracy and the Athenian empire.

Old Persian See PERSIAN, OLD.

oligarchy ('the rule of the few'), with monarchy (see KINGSHIP) and democracy one of the three basic categories of constitution commonly used by the Greeks from the 5th cent. BC onwards. Whereas a democratic regime gave basic political rights to all adult males in the free native population, and had slight or non-existent limitations on eligibility for office, an oligarchic regime excluded some of the free population from even basic political rights, and might exclude even more of them from office-holding and reduce the amount of business which came the way of the full citizen body. In practice those who were admitted to political activity by democracies but not by oligarchies were the poor, and *Aristotle, after listing the three categories of constitution and distinguishing correct and deviant versions of each, went on to say that really oligarchy is the rule of the rich and democracy is the rule of the poor. (Most of the citizenry is 'poor', but not destitute.)

Before the 5th cent. the constitutions of most states were in fact oligarchic, though the term did not yet exist. In the 5th cent. Athens developed a self-conscious democracy (see DEMOCRACY, ATHENIAN) and posed as a champion of democracy elsewhere in Greece, while those who disliked democracy labelled themselves oligarchic, and Sparta, though not itself a typical oligarchy, posed as the champion of oligarchies. At the end of the 5th cent. there were oligarchic revolutions in Athens, resulting in the regimes of the *Four Hundred and of the (moderate but still not fully democratic) Five Thousand in 411–410, and of the *Thirty Tyrants in 404–403. In the Hellenistic period the distinction between oligarchy and democracy mattered less than in the Classical period as even states which were democratic in form tended in practice to be run by the rich; and government by the rich was preferred by the Romans. See also DEMOCRACY, NON-ATHENIAN AND POST-CLASSICAL; PATRIOS POLITEIA; POLITICS.

olive The olive is probably native to the Mediterranean region. It is long-lived and drought-resistant, though sensitive to frost, and thrives at low altitudes. Olives generally crop only every other year. Olives are easily propagated by cuttings, ovules (trunk growths), or by grafting, a technique well known in the classical world. Domesticated scions were often grafted onto wild stocks.

Olives were usually part of mixed farming regimes, including arable and other tree crops, since cropping and yields can be erratic. Sometimes olive cultivation was combined with pastoralism. Olives are harvested in autumn and winter. Greeks and Romans felt that the finest oil came from 'white' ('green') olives, picked early, a belief at variance with modern practice. Ripe, 'black' olives contain more oil than green ones—the scarcity of oil in the latter may partially explain why it was more highly valued.

Olives can be processed for either table-olives or oil: they are not edible raw. Olive oil was used for food, medicine, *lighting, perfume, bathing, and *athletics. Producing oil entails crushing, pressing, and separating. Oil, once separated, was stored in large jars or sold in *amphorae. Though most ordinary oil was probably consumed locally, fine oil was a luxury product traded over long distances, like vintage wine. Certain regions, e.g. *Attica, *Samos, and *Baetica, became famous for oil. In the case of Attica, the olive was a symbol of Athena and Athens, and oil from the sacred trees was given as prizes at the Panathenaic Games (see PANATHENAEA). However, it was probably never the most important Attic crop. See AGRICULTURE.

Olympia, *panhellenic *sanctuary of *Zeus located in hill country beside the river Alphēus in *Elis.

1. **Before 500** *Votives (tripods and figurines) in an ash layer in the innermost sacred area, the Altis, indicate cult activity from at least the late 10th cent. (perhaps with an early ash altar). The first *Olympiad was traditionally dated 776 BC (see TIME-RECKONING). Acc. to *Pindar, *Heracles founded the *Olympic Games; an alternative tradition attributed the foundation to *Pelops after his victory over Oenomaus. A sequence of wells on the eastern side of the sanctuary served visitors.

The first temple (ascribed to *Hera) was built c.590. A row of eleven treasuries (primarily of western Greek i.e. Italian and Sicilian cities) lay under Cronus Hill. The first phase of the *stadium (c. mid-6th cent.) consisted of a simple track west of the later stadium, extending into the Altis. The first building for the *boule* was built in c.520. From at least the 6th cent., sanctuary and festival were managed by Elis.

2. **Classical** The western Greeks always had close connections with Olympia. But Olympia, the paramount athletic sanctuary, was properly panhellenic. Thus the *Persian Wars were commemorated at Olympia, though less spectacularly than at *Delphi; for instance, the Athenians dedicated at Olympia a helmet 'taken from the Medes'; another splendid helmet-dedication by *Miltiades might be from Marathon (see MARATHON, BATTLE OF) but is probably earlier. The battle of *Plataea prompted a colossal bronze Zeus, inscribed with a roll of honour of the participating states, including Ionian Athens in second place after Sparta. But the *Dorian character of Olympia is marked, even if we deny political symbolism to the labours of *Heracles depicted on the temple metopes of the mid-5th cent Zeus temple, the second to be built within the Altis. Thus the Olympic Games of 428 were turned by Sparta into an overtly anti-Athenian meeting. But Athens was never, even in the *Peloponnesian War, formally denied access to Olympia, any more than to Delphi. We do hear from Thucydides of a Classical exclusion from the Olympic Games, but of Sparta not Athens.

3. **Hellenistic and Roman** Hellenistic kings affirmed by their dedications Olympia's panhellenic standing. New buildings included a *palaestra, *gymnasium, and (c.100 BC) the earliest Roman-style *baths found in Greece. Roman domination, signalled by the dedications of *Mummius (146 BC), at first saw Olympia decline in prestige: by 30 BC the games had dwindled into an essentially local festival. Imperial patronage prompted a marked revival: *Vipsanius Agrippa repaired the temple of Zeus, and both *Tiberius and *Germanicus won chariot-races, to be outdone by *Nero, who performed in person at irregularly convened games (67) including (uniquely) musical contests. In the 2nd cent., with the popularity of the games never greater, Olympia once more attracted orators (see SECOND SOPHISTIC), as well as cultural *tourism (*Phidias' statue of Zeus was among the *Seven Wonders of the ancient world).

Olympiad, four-year period between occurrences of the *Olympic Games; see HIPPIAS (2); TIMAEUS; TIME-RECKONING.

Olympian gods, Olympians See APHRODITE; APOLLO; ARES; ARTEMIS; ATHENA; DEMETER; DIONYSUS; HEPHAESTUS; HERA; HERMES; POSEIDON; ZEUS (these are the twelve on the *Parthenon frieze; but see RELIGION, GREEK, *Gods and Other Cult Figures*).

Olympias, daughter of Neoptolemus of Molossia, married *Philip II of Macedon (c.357 BC) and bore him two children, *Alexander (2) the Great and Cleopatra. Her husband's last marriage (to Cleopatra, niece of Attalus) led to a serious quarrel in which she retired to her native Epirus. Returning after Philip's assassination, she murdered her erst-while rival along with her infant daughter. After Alexander's departure (334) her relations with his viceroy, *Antipater, were turbulent, and by late 331 she had resumed residence in Epirus, which she treated as her fief. There she remained until 317, when the regent Polyperchon enlisted her aid against the nominal queen Eurydice, who had disowned him and sided with *Cassander. She invoked the memory of her husband and son, and the royal couple fell into her hands without a blow. That good will disappeared after she forced Eurydice and her wretched consort to their deaths and conducted a bloody purge in Macedon. Her armies in turn melted away before Cassander, and she was forced to surrender (spring 316). She was condemned by the Macedonian assembly and killed by relatives of her victims. Passionate in her political hatreds, she was devoted to ecstatic Dionysiac cults (see DIONYSUS; ECSTASY; MAENADS; WOMEN IN CULT), and her influence may have helped engender his son's belief in his divinity. See RULER-CULT.

Olympic Games They were held in the *sanctuary of *Zeus at *Olympia, once every four years in August or September. They honoured Zeus, and were said to commemorate the victory of *Pelops over Oenomaus, but also to have been founded by *Heracles. Lists of victors begin in 776 BC (see HIPPIAS (2); TIME-RECKONING), and a catalogue of the winners down to AD 217 is preserved by *Eusebius. They were abolished in 393 by *Theodosius I.

The original contest was the *stadion*, a sprint of about 200 m. (656 ft.) (see STADIUM). Other contests were added between the late 8th and 5th cents. BC, including races for chariots and single horses. Many early victors came from Sparta, but by the 6th cent. competitors were coming from all over the Greek world. *Hellānodikai* ('Greek judges'), prominent citizens of *Elis, presided over the games and exercised disciplinary authority over the athletes. In the 5th cent. the festival lasted five days. The main religious ceremony was the *sacrifice of a hecatomb on the great altar of Zeus. The contests were preceded by a procession from Elis to Olympia, and a ceremony at which athletes and officials swore an oath to observe the rules of the games, and they were followed by victory celebrations, with processions and banquets. From 472 the main sacrifice was preceded by the *pentathlon and horse-races, and on subsequent days there were the boys' contests, men's foot-races, *wrestling, *boxing, *pankration, and finally the race in armour. The prizes were crowns of wild *olive.

Olympiēum, the temple of *Zeus Olympios at Athens; begun by *Pisistratus, but abandoned after the latter's death, and the expulsion of his son, *Hippias (1), and not resumed until the *Seleucid Antiochus IV Epiphanes employed the Roman architect Cossutius to continue the work. It was completed for *Hadrian. The Pisistratean building was planned as a Doric temple. Cossutius changed the order to Corinthian, but in general seems to have adhered to the original plan. The Corinthian columns were 16.89 m. (53$\frac{1}{3}$ ft.) in height. The capitals are carved from two blocks of marble. *Vitruvius says the temple was open-roofed, which may have been true in its unfinished state at that time. It would have been roofed when completed by Hadrian to contain a gold and ivory cult-statue. Hadrian is certainly responsible for the impressive buttressed boundary wall, decorated with Corinthian columns on its interior, and with a gateway of Hymettan *marble on its northern side.

Olympus, the highest mountain in the Greek peninsula, dominating the Aegean to the east and the Macedonian and Thessalian plains. It rises at one point to 2,918 m. (9,573 ft.). Thought to be the throne of *Zeus and home of the gods, it held an important place in religion, mythology, and literature. Olympus proper was Macedonian; for the ancients the rest of the massif, shared between *Macedonia and *Thessaly, marked the northernmost limit of Greece. It was not, however, an obstacle to communication.

Olynthus, a city north of *Potidaea on the mainland of the Chalcidic peninsula (see CHALCIDICE). Originally Bottiaean, it became a Greek city after its capture by *Persia (479 BC) and repopulation from Chalcidice; its position and mixed population made it the natural centre of Greek Chalcidice against attacks from Athens, Macedon, and Sparta. In 433 the city was strengthened by further migration and received territory from Macedon, and it soon became the capital of a Chalcidian Confederacy issuing federal coinage (see FEDERAL STATES). In the end Olynthus fell to *Philip II of Macedon by treachery and was destroyed (348). Excavations have revealed the layout of the city (see URBANISM).

omens See PORTENTS.

Omphalē, queen of *Lydia. Acc. to Sophocles, *Heracles killed Iphitus, son of Eurytus of Oechalia, by treachery, and *Zeus decreed that he should expiate this crime by being sold in slavery to Omphale. Having endured this humiliation for a year, Heracles sacked Oechalia in revenge. Others say that after the murder of Iphitus *Apollo refused to give Heracles an oracle; so Heracles carried off the *Delphic tripod. The quarrel was halted by Zeus, and Apollo then decreed that Heracles should be sold to Omphale for three years and the price paid to Eurytus. Acc. to Ovid, Heracles as Omphale's slave had to dress as a woman and perform women's work (a paradox popular with Hellenistic and Roman authors).

omphalos, the navel. Metaphorically, the centre of a geographical area, e.g. the sea, a city (= the agora), the world. Title to the last was claimed by *Delphi, at least by early in the Classical period, and reinforced by identification with a solid object, namely an egg- (or navel-)

shaped stone. *Strabo gives the fullest description of the Delphic *omphalos*: it was covered by wreaths and had two images on it representing the two birds sent by *Zeus, one from the west, one from the east, meeting at Delphi. This stone was in the temple. The marble stone seen by *Pausanias (3)—and preserved to this day—is a man-made object, the wreaths depicted in relief. It stood on the esplanade outside the temple.

Opīmius, Lūcius, praetor 125 BC, was defeated in his bid for the consulship of 122, but he became consul 121 and, with his colleague fighting in Gaul, was in charge of Rome. When Gracchus and Fulvius Flaccus took to violence, he obtained the first *senatus consultum ultimum* from the senate, interpreted it to give him unlimited powers, and crushed the rebellion with considerable loss of life. He then (we are told) condemned a large number to death in a special *quaestio*. To commemorate this episode, he restored and dedicated the temple of *Concordia and built a *basilica in the Forum. Prosecuted by Decius Subulo, he was defended by Papirius Carbo and acquitted (120). This secured constitutional recognition of the *senatus consultum ultimum*. He headed a commission that divided Numidia between *Jugurtha and his brother, was later convicted by the 'Gracchan jurors' of the tribunal set up by Mamilius Limetanus and went into exile. The *wine produced in his consulship became proverbial for excellence.

optimātēs, populārēs Romans seem from an early time to have used words for 'good' (*bonus*, sup. *optimus*) to denote high birth and social standing, as well as moral excellence, qualities the upper class regarded as inherently combined. The social meaning is already found in *Plautus and *Ennius, though '*optimates*' (anglicized hereafter as 'optimate(s)') in a political sense does not appear in our sources until the 1st cent. BC. These 'best' men naturally assumed the right to rule the state. A 4th-cent. law ordered the censors to enrol in the senate *optimum quemque* ('all the best men'), *patricians and plebeians (see PLEBS). In due course this was understood to mean all men elected to high office (*de facto* limited to a small upper class). The senate was in charge of making policy, guided by the *nobiles. Its successful leadership in the Second *Punic War and the great wars in the east that followed led to unquestioning acceptance of its authority, though the assemblies' rights were respected, poverty was alleviated by

colonization and distribution (at times reluctant) of conquered land, and candidates for election conspicuously courted the favour of individual voters. The second half of the 2nd cent. BC saw a marked decline both in the success of senate leadership and in its care for the less fortunate. In foreign affairs the unpopular levies for the protracted wars in Spain (see NUMANTIA) led to resentment and actual resistance, organized by tribunes (see TRIBUNI PLEBIS). By the end of the century, the inglorious war against *Jugurtha and the disasters against the Gauls and Germans demolished the prestige of those born to command, and they came under increasing attack from men (usually tribunes) later described as '*populārēs*' ('supporters of the people'). Successive tribunician laws provided for ballot in assemblies (a tribunician law of *Marius made it secret ballot), and such laws were supported by aristocrats (e.g. *Cornelius Scipio Aemilianus) who believed in a 'mixed constitution'. At home the decline and proletarianization of the peasantry caused serious military, as well as social, problems, yet the senate majority resisted any attempt at distributing *ager publicus. Finally, a group of eminent senators supported Tiberius *Sempronius Gracchus (2) in putting a moderate law for the distribution of some *ager publicus* directly to the *plebs* (133). Stubborn resistance to this caused increasing tensions, which led to Tiberius' violent death. His younger brother Gaius *Sempronius Gracchus (tribune 123–122) then embarked on an ambitious programme of reform. While recognizing the senate's right to supervise administration, he sought to balance its power by replacing senators with *equites in the juries of *extortion trials. (Senatorial ex-governors were not to be judged by fellow senators.) When Gaius also was killed in a riot, the Gracchi became martyrs to later *populares*. Ambitious tribunes continued to provide leadership, and the tribunal set up by Mamilius in the Jugurthine War made it clear that the *equites*, although of the same eighteen *centuries as senators, resented the death of the Gracchi and despised senatorial incompetence. The election of the *novus homo Marius to the consulship and continued command seemed to threaten the birthright of the *nobiles*, and his admission of the *proletarii to the legions created a potential armed pressure group of the poor, which *Appuleius Saturninus and Servilius Glaucia tried to combine with the *equestrians.

The optimates never recovered the qualities of leadership and readiness to compromise that had made them successful and dominant. Attempts at reform met with resistance, which led to violence on both sides. *Livius Drusus, an aristocratic tribune in the mould of Gaius Gracchus, tried, again with the support of some aristocrats, to rally some of those who had usually supported *populares* (esp. poor citizens and the Italians seeking the Roman citizenship) behind the senate, but again the senate majority defeated the reforms on which the plan was based, resisting Italian enfranchisement (and thus causing the *Social War), land distribution (see AGRARIAN LAWS AND POLICY), and colonization. While refusing to assume the duty of providing for the veterans of proletarian armies, leaving them to become clients of their commanders, the senate merely opposed the commanders' attempts to secure benefits for their veterans. In the end, after prolonged civil war, *Sulla established personal power with the support of his client army, which he amply rewarded with land expropriated from his enemies. His legislation tried to eliminate the *populares*, establishing the senate securely in power against threats from equestrians, tribunes and ambitious commanders.

But the inefficiency and corruption of his senate led to the disintegration of his system within a decade. The consulship of *Pompey and *Licinius Crassus in 70 saw the abolition of all restrictions on tribunes, compromise with the equestrians and the integration of the Italians into the citizen body, which, by greatly enlarging that body, made it less amenable to senate control. Since the senate persisted in doing nothing for veterans and opposing their commanders' attempts to secure benefits for them, commanders were driven into opposition to the senate, alliance with tribunes, and the use of *populares* methods, esp. the passing of legislation by the people and *plebs* despite senate opposition. Pompey and *Caesar thus secured the distribution of corn to the city *plebs* and of land to veterans—and powerful commands for themselves. The Gracchi and Marius were so successfully cited as precedents, as heroes and martyrs, that even Cicero, at heart a convinced optimate, had to act as a *populares* and claim the heritage of those men when addressing people or *plebs*.

The *populares* of Cicero's age were generally devoid of serious principle. Whether new men like *Vatinius or patrician nobles like *Catiline, *Clodius Pulcher, and Caesar, they traded on the old traditions for personal advancement. Violence came to be used of set policy, with the poor and veterans hoping for benefits providing ready armies of the Forum. Men like Caesar and Catiline incurred huge debts to engage in unprecedented corruption. Characteristically, no *popularis* attempted to introduce elements of democracy into the system of Roman *comitia*, for real democracy might have counteracted optimate resistance and superseded the tactics on which they themselves relied for their own advancement (see DEMOCRACY, NON-ATHENIAN AND POST-CLASSICAL). The senate, on the other hand, while powerless against those tactics, continued in its failure to formulate any policy to set against them, but shielded continuing refusal to admit reforms by appeal to its traditional prestige. Many optimates now regarded their right to rule as divorced from any obligation for service, and most as limited to service in traditional offices, for their own political benefit. The decline that had begun after *c.*150 thus led to polarization and disintegration, without any organized movement for reform, which appeared to be in nobody's interest but that of the governed, who had no initiative.

Cicero saw a senate reawakened to its traditions as the only source of leadership. He tried to rally the equestrians behind it in a *concordia ordinum* (concord of the highest two orders in society) and all right-thinking citizens, concerned for the welfare of their country, in a consensus of all *bonī* (lit. 'good men'), a term that he used in this wide extension. In a programmatic passage in a speech before a jury of senators and equestrians he claimed the term 'optimates' for all (even *freedmen) who, under the leadership of the senate, resisted the attacks of unscrupulous and dangerous self-professed *populares*. However, he never went so far as to give positive programmatic content to his appeal.

Augustus, after disintegration had led to nearly two decades of bloody civil war, found the heirs to the optimates willing to give up the struggle for real power in return for peace and recognition of their social eminence and economic security. Like the old *populares*, he saw that the people did not want real power either (for they had no experience of it), but would be satisfied with modest, but secure, economic benefits. He also used the one point in which the optimates, *populares*, and the actual people had agreed, glory and the expansion of the empire, to cement unity behind a policy aiming at, and for a long time actually achieving, those objectives. As in a way the heir to both optimates and *populares*, he secured power for himself without permitting the revival of political conflict.

oracles Among the many forms of *divination known to the Greeks, the responses given by a god or hero when consulted at a fixed oracular site were the most prestigious. Such oracles were numerous. *Herodotus lists five in mainland Greece and one in Asia Minor which *Croesus supposedly consulted in the 6th cent. BC, and at least another five (including one 'oracle of the dead') appear in his pages; *Pausanias (3) mentions four lesser local oracles, and at least five more can be added from epigraphical evidence.

Healing oracles, esp. those of *Asclepius, are a specialized group, though even they never confined themselves to medical questions. The business of a general purpose oracle is best revealed by the lead question-tablets found at *Zeus' oracle at *Dodona. Most enquiries are from individuals; of those from states, most ask whether a particular alteration to cult practice is acceptable, or more generally by what sacrifices divine favour is to be maintained; one or two concern political issues. Individuals enquire whether their wife will conceive (or conceive a son), whether a proposed marriage or journey or change of career is wise, whether a child is legitimate; they also ask about health problems, and more generally about ways of gaining or retaining divine favour. The kind of answer envisaged is either 'yes' or 'no' or 'by sacrificing to X'.

Acc. to *Plutarch, similar everyday questions about 'whether to marry or to sail or to lend', or, from cities, about 'crops and herds and health' ('and cults', he might have added) formed the staple of Delphi's business in his day (see DELPHIC ORACLE). Before c.400, states had certainly also consulted Delphi about political issues, but even then a decision, e.g. to go to war or dispatch a colony (see COLONIZATION, GREEK), had normally been made by the state before approaching the oracle. What was sought was a divine sanction. And since no mortals were endowed with religious authority in the Greek system, all oracles always had an esp. important role in sanctioning adjustments to cult practice.

Techniques by which responses (another sense of 'oracle') were given were very various. The most prestigious was 'inspired' prophecy, the utterances of a human recipient (male or, more often, female) who spoke, probably in a trance. This was the method of several oracles of *Apollo in Asia Minor and the main, if not sole, method of Delphi too. The prophetic dream was characteristic of healing oracles, though not confined to them: the consultant slept a night or nights in the temple (*incubation), during which the god in theory appeared in a dream and issued instructions (or even, in pious legend, performed a cure direct). The oracle of Zeus at *Olympia worked by 'empyromancy', signs drawn from the flames on Zeus' *altar. To consult the hero *Trophonius at Lebadea, the client made a simulated descent to the Underworld: how the revelation then occurred is not recorded. Nor do we know anything certain about the practice at Dodona.

Apart from the Egyptian–Libyan oracle of *Ammon at the oasis of Siwa, which many Greeks consulted as an oracle of Zeus from the 5th cent. BC onwards, the great oracular shrines were Greek. In Italy, the oracle of the *Sibyl at *Cumae is well known from *Virgil, who (in *Aeneid* bk. 6) describes an ecstatic form of prophecy (see ECSTASY). Also prominent was the lot-oracle of Fortuna Primigenia at *Praeneste. On extraordinary occasions the Roman government or ruler consulted the Sibylline books (see SIBYL), which were kept by the *quindecimviri sacris faciundis*.

orality is reliance on oral communication rather than the written word. In the ancient world writing was used less than modern readers might expect. Orality can be sub-divided into (1) oral composition, (2) oral communication, (3) oral tradition.

Oral composition, entirely without the help of writing, is best known in relation to the tradition of oral poetry that persisted through the Greek Dark Age (see HOMER, 8). Parry and Lord sought to show how an oral poet could compose in performance. The importance of oral communication can be seen e.g. in the political activity of democratic Athens (see DEMOCRACY, ATHENIAN); in the use of contracts or wills relying on witnesses, not writing, in Athens and Rome (see EVIDENCE, ATTITUDES TO); in the habit of hearing literature. Silent reading was a rare accomplishment.

Most Greeks knew, or thought they knew, about their past from oral tradition. Over generations oral tradition tends to distortion. Its character and reliability depend heavily on who is transmitting the tradition and why (e.g. notions of honour, patriotism; see GENEALOGY). Although from the 7th cent. onwards poetry, and from the 6th cent. prose works and laws, were written down, verbal communication in Archaic Greece remained largely oral.

As written documents and the centrality of written literature increase in the 5th and 4th cents., elements of orality still remain fundamental, esp. the performance of poetry and prose (e.g. *sophists), and political and forensic oratory; the value of the written word was not uniformly accepted (see *Plato's criticisms in *Phaedrus*). Roman society was more book and library oriented, but even at the level of high culture one finds literary readings, the accomplishments of oratory, memory, and improvisation; the skill and advantages of shorthand were despised. The balance between oral communication and writing varied widely over time and between areas.

Orbilius Pupillus, Lūcius, *grammaticus* who migrated from Beneventum to Rome aged 50 (63 BC). A cross-grained character and severe critic of the capital's scholastic milieu, in which he did not prosper, he is recalled by his pupil *Horace for the beatings administered during lessons on *Livius Andronicus' *Odyssey*; yet he was honoured at Beneventum with a statue on the town's *capitolium*.

Orchomenus, city in NW *Boeotia located by the NW bay of Lake Copais, whose western basin it dominated. Rich in the Classical period, Orchomenus was famed as the city of the Graces (see CHARITES), to whom a venerable sanctuary was dedicated. Notable also was the grave of Hesiod.

Rivalry between Orchomenus and *Thebes for the hegemony of Boeotia became a constant factor throughout the Classical period. That tension notwithstanding, Orchomenus had joined the *Boeotian Confederacy by the time of *Xerxes' invasion (see PERSIAN WARS), when it Medized (see MEDISM). Upon the re-establishment of the Boeotian Confederacy, Orchomenus possessed two units within it. During the *Pentekontaetia Athens overran Boeotia after the battle of Oenophyta in 457, after which Orchomenus formed the principal base for the liberation of the region. Joining with other Boeotians, Orchomenus defeated Tolmides at Coronea in 447. In the new confederacy that was created in the wake of victory, Orchomenus maintained its position. At the battle of *Delion in 424 Orchomenians held a position on the left wing, but about this time the city lost control of *Chaeronea, which weakened its position within the confederacy.

orders (of architecture) The main Greek orders of architecture are Doric, Ionic, and Corinthian. The definitive form of Doric is established by the beginning of the 6th cent. BC, representing the translation into stone of forms which originated in wooden structures of the 7th cent. Ionic evolved at the same time, but took longer to reach definitive form; there are important local variations at least until the early Hellenistic period.

The Ionic order is inspired by near eastern architecture, copied even more closely in the variant Aeolic form of the NE Aegean. Both have volute capitals. Aeolic has two separate spirals springing from a central triangle, Ionic links the volutes across an abacus. In the entablature (the horizontal members, usually architrave, frieze, and cornice, which rest on the columns and support the roof) the architrave is normally surmounted by a row of dentils (projecting square blocks). Attic Ionic replaces this with a continuous carved frieze. In the Hellenistic period the Attic base is standard, while the entablature includes both continuous and dentil friezes.

Corinthian evolves in the 4th cent., using more ornate capitals decorated with acanthus leaves under volutes springing from the centre to all four corners. The earliest example of Corinthian (now lost) was in the temple of Apollo at *Bassae. Corinthian columns were used internally in temples and other buildings at Epidaurus and Delphi in the 4th cent. It gained favour as an external system in the Hellenistic period, culminating in the *Olympieum donated to Athens by the *Seleucid Antiochus IV.

All three orders are taken over by Roman architects: Doric in a primitive, variant form dating back to Archaic times, Ionic and Corinthian in the standardized Hellenistic models.

ordinary consuls (consulēs ordināriī) See CONSUL; SUFFECT.

Orestēs, in myth son of *Agamemnon and *Clytemnestra, and avenger of his father's murder by his mother and her lover *Aegisthus. Homer says that Orestes killed Aegisthus, having returned home from Athens in the eighth year after Agamemnon's death, and implies that he also killed Clytemnestra. This vengeance was an entirely praiseworthy deed, for which he won high renown; no regrets are expressed by anyone at his having to kill his mother, and there is no hint of any pursuit by the *Erinyes, who later play so large a part in the legend. Clytemnestra was simply 'hateful', and Orestes, as head of the family, would necessarily have been her judge and executioner.

5th-cent. tragedy provides the fullest details of Orestes' legend. At the time of Agamemnon's murder Orestes was taken to Strophius, king of *Phocis and brother-in-law of Agamemnon, and brought up by him together with his own son Pylades, who later accompanies Orestes when he secretly returns home, on the instruction of Apollo, to avenge his father's death. Here he encounters his sister Electra, and they recognize each other with mutual joy. In *Aeschylus' *Libation-bearers*, brother and sister join together in an invocation to Agamemnon's ghost, but the focus of this play is still mainly on Orestes, and Electra is not actively involved in the killings. Orestes gets access to the palace as a stranger, bringing news of his own death, and can scarcely bring himself to kill Clytemnestra. After her murder he is at once pursued by her Erinyes, who form the Chorus of the following play (*Eumenides*) where Orestes is put on trial and finally absolved by the homicide court on the *Areopagus, once Athena has given the casting vote in his favour. She also calms the Erinyes, who are to be settled in a shrine with the beneficent title of the Eumenides, 'the Kindly Ones'.

Electra's role in helping her brother is developed by *Sophocles and Euripides: in Sophocles' *Electra* she urges Orestes on from outside the door while he is inside killing their mother, and in Euripides' *Electra* she is the dominant figure, driving the weak and indecisive Orestes to kill Clytemnestra and even grasping the sword with him when his own hand fails. Here in Euripides, quite unlike Sophocles' play, brother and sister are entirely overcome with guilt and remorse once the deed is done; here too, again unlike Sophocles' version, the Erinyes will pursue Orestes. Elsewhere in Euripides we are aware of these Furies as the imagined phantoms of Orestes' guilty conscience (*Orestes*); and his release from their pursuit is a long process involving a journey to the land of the Taurians (*Iphigenia at Tauris*). In his *Andromache*, Orestes murders *Neoptolemus and carries off Hermione, whom he later marries.

Orientalism The central thesis of Edward Said's *Orientalism* (1978) is that the concepts 'Europe' and 'Orient', as polar opposites, have been created by Europeans, esp. in the context of European imperialism, to provide a positive, strong image of Europe, with which eastern civilizations (especially the Muslim world) can be negatively contrasted. The 'Orient' is thus presented as lacking all desirable, active characteristics. This pervasive perception of 'the east'

underlies most studies of near eastern history and culture and has profoundly shaped scholarly analysis. Said argues that Oriental stereotypes derive much of their imagery from early Greek literary works (e.g. *Herodotus; *Aeschylus' *Persians*). This has led several classicists and ancient historians to refocus their work and explore consciously the assumptions made in some traditional areas of study. Standard approaches to several subjects are now being scrutinized and reassessed. Most prominent among these are: the development of Greek art, esp. the '*orientalizing' phase, Attic tragedy, and *Achaemenid and Hellenistic history. An interesting, if partly maverick, study of Greek civilization, which adopts some of Said's political agenda, is M. Bernal's *Black Athena*; he argues that Greece was colonized by black Africans and *Phoenicians and owed its culture to them.

See also HELLENISM, HELLENIZATION.

orientalizing, an expression applied to certain phases of *Etruscan, Greek, Hellenistic, and Roman art when they appear to adopt stylistic traits characteristic of the near east. Examples include the influence of Phoenician and Cypriot silverware on Etruscan metalwork and pottery, or that of eastern textiles on the decoration of Greek *Geometric and Archaic vessels; the 'Achaemenidizing' character of some of the architectural details of Hadrian's Villa at *Tibur, which are probably dependent on Persian *booty won by *Alexander (2) the Great.

Origen (probably AD 184 or 185–254 or 255), b. at *Alexandria of Christian parents. Educated by his father (who perished in the persecution of 202) and later in the Catechetical School of Alexandria under Pantaenus and *Clement (of Alexandria), he became a teacher himself, with such success that he was recognized, first informally, then in 203 officially, as head of the school. He learned pagan philosophy from a *Peripatetic. The story of his self-castration in accordance with Matthew 19: 12 is supported by *Eusebius. His career as a teacher was interrupted in 215 by *Caracalla's massacre of Alexandrian Christians. He withdrew to Palestine, but after a time was recalled by his bishop, Demetrius. Through his extensive literary work he now acquired such influence in the eastern Church as to become its unofficial arbiter, and, on a journey to Greece in this capacity, allowed himself to be ordained priest by the bishops of *Caesarea and *Jerusalem. Demetrius, who had not given his consent, took offence at this and perhaps also at parts of Origen's teaching. On obscure grounds, Origen was banished from Alexandria and deposed from the presbyterate, but the decision was ignored in Palestine, and Origen settled at Caesarea in 231. He continued his labours until, after repeated torture in the Decian persecution (250–1), his health gave way and he died at Tyre at the age of 69. Origen's works were voluminous and of wide scope, but only a fraction has survived. He was a pioneer in textual criticism of the Bible, exegesis, and systematic theology.

ornamenta Ornaments were the decorations, costume, and status of a specific senatorial rank, quaestorian, praetorian, or consular, and in the republic were granted only in exceptional cases. In the imperial period these honours were granted more often, both to senators, who received precedence in voting associated with a higher rank without actual promotion (contrast *adlectio*; see ADLECTION), and to non-senators, for whom conferment of *ornamenta* was a mark of imperial favour, bestowing the appropriate senatorial status on public occasions, but not involving admission to the senate. Grants to non-senators were made most commonly to *praetorian prefects, who, from the Flavians onwards, probably received consular ornaments, but also under *Claudius to freedmen officials (*Narcissus receiving quaestorian, *Antonius Pallas praetorian ornaments). These developments indicate increasing imperial control of senatorial magistracies.

After 19 BC no senator outside the imperial family was permitted to celebrate a *triumph. Instead deserving commanders were on imperial initiative awarded *triumphālia ornamenta*—the insignia normally carried by a general in his triumphal procession.

Orpheus, the quintessential mythical singer, son of *Apollo and a *Muse, whose song has more than human power. He appears among the *Argonauts, whom he saves from the *Sirens by overcoming their song with his own. In the 5th cent. BC Orpheus enlarges his scope: his powerful song encompasses epic poetry, healing songs, oracles, and initiatory rites.

His main myth is his tragic love for Eurydĭcē, narrated by *Virgil and *Ovid but known already in some form in the 5th cent. In Virgil's version Eurydice, newly wed to Orpheus, died of a snakebite, and the singer descended to Hades to bring her back. His song enchanted *Hades; Eurydice was allowed to return, provided

Orpheus did not look back when leading her up; he failed, losing Eurydice for ever. He retired into wild nature where his lamenting song moved animals, trees, and rocks; finally a band of *Thracian women or *maenads (see DIONYSUS) killed him. The first representation of Eurydice, Orpheus, and *Hermes is the relief from the Athenian Altar of the Twelve Gods; earlier is the allusion in Euripides' *Alcestis* (438). Orpheus' death at the hands of maenads was presented in *Aeschylus' lost drama *Bassarids*, as the result of Dionysus' wrath (470/460 BC). Vases depicting Thracian women murdering him are somewhat earlier, without giving a reason for the killing; later, it is the aloofness of the widowed (and turned homosexual) singer which provokes the women. But even after his death, Orpheus' voice was not silenced: his head was carried by the sea to *Lesbos, where for a while it gave prophecies.

Generally, Orpheus is called a Thracian. A grave and a cult belong to Pieria in *Macedonia, NE of Mt. *Olympus, a region which formerly had been inhabited by Thracians and with which the Muses were associated. It may have been a recent invention, or point to the original home of Orpheus who has no certain place in the web of Greek mythological *genealogy.

One consequence of his miraculous song was his authorship of the so-called Orphic poetry: by the late 6th cent. the singer who had been down to Hades was thought esp. competent to sing about *eschatology and *theogony. *Pythagoreans and adherents of Bacchic mystery cults adopted him as their figurehead, and the *Neoplatonist philosophers esp. discerned deep theosophical knowledge in these poems and promoted Orpheus to the role of prime theological thinker.

In art the myth of Orpheus is treated from c.550 BC to late antiquity (main themes: as Argonaut; murder; in Hades; with the animals).

See MUSAEUS; ORPHIC LITERATURE; ORPHISM.

Orphic literature, the *pseudepigraphic literature ascribed to *Orpheus. *Neoplatonist authors esp. cite *hexameters from different poems attributed to Orpheus 'the theologian', and an entire corpus of hymns is preserved. The remains of a 4th-cent. BC papyrus commentary on a *theogony of Orpheus, found in 1962 in the remains of a funeral pyre in Derveni (Macedonia), considerably enlarged the corpus of texts.

The main texts attributed to Orpheus are theogonies. They follow the Oriental succession scheme established by *Hesiod, but extend it in both directions: *Uranus and *Gaia, Hesiod's first ruling couple, are preceded by Night and Protogonos or Phanes, and *Zeus' reign was succeeded by that of *Dionysus. The decisive invention is a double birth myth of Dionysus. Dionysus is the incestuous offspring of Zeus and his daughter *Persephone; *Hera, in anger, ordered the *Titans to kill the young god, which they did; they cooked and ate the boy. Zeus in turn killed the Titans with his thunderbolt. From the ashes of the burning Titans sprang mankind; from the heart of Dionysus which had been saved, Zeus reproduced with *Semele the second Dionysus. This myth is told only in Neoplatonist sources, and the consequence that man has a double nature, from the Titans and from the divine child they had eaten, is not drawn by the Orphic poet. Still the story explains why man's nature is wicked (he is an offspring of the wicked Titans), and why Dionysus could intercede on man's behalf with Persephone after death (Dionysus alone, if anyone, can assuage his mother's wrath against the offspring of the Titans). These elements are present already in classical times—in a much-discussed fragment of a *Pindaric *dirge, the overcoming of Persephone's 'ancient grief' is vital for the human *soul to attain the supreme stage in *transmigration. *Plato knows man's Titanic nature, and in a recently discovered gold tablet from *Thessaly (Pelinna, *c.*320 BC), the dead person has to appeal to Dionysus' help before the tribunal in the Underworld.

Orphism is basically *Orphic literature; it comprised, besides the dominant *theogonical and *eschatological poems, ritualistic texts, *hymns sung in ritual, and prescriptions about specific *initiation and other rites. They were used by two sets of people, followers of Bacchic *mystery groups, and individual ritual specialists, the itinerant Orpheotelests. The specialists used rituals to heal demonic possession, to harm by *magic, and to realize eschatological hopes.

Ostia, city at the mouth of the *Tiber, colony by the late 4th cent. BC, heavily involved with Rome's naval history, commerce, and communications, and one of the best preserved Roman cities. Abandoned in the 5th cent. AD, Ostia was covered with drifting sand from coastal dunes, and the area was sparsely populated until the 20th cent. because of malaria.

The Tiber was the route to the dockyard of Rome, the Nāvālia, and needed protection throughout the *Punic Wars, and on into the

age of *piracy, which destroyed a Roman fleet at Ostia in 67 BC. Since the 6th cent. it had also provided access for travellers and traders to the wharves of Rome (greatly improved and embellished during the 2nd cent.). The imperial power won by Rome at that time gave its sea access new importance, and, as the corn supply (see FOOD SUPPLY, *Roman*) of the city came under increased governmental supervision from the time of Gaius *Sempronius Gracchus, a resource of huge political sensitivity began regularly to pass through the difficult and insecure waters of Ostia. A circuit of walls enclosed 69 ha. (170 acres); *Marius captured Ostia by treachery in 87 and sacked it. In the Civil War the loyalty to Octavian's cause of members of the local élite benefited the city under the victorious regime. But Strabo describes Ostia in the Augustan period as 'a city without a harbour', and also says that the huge merchant-ships of southern Spain 'make for *Puteoli, and Ostia, the shipyard of Rome'; the city was still only a way-station on the route up the river, and the ports of *Campania (which long received much of the corn trade) were unrivalled until the construction of the basins of *Claudius and *Trajan at *Portus.

The good communications of the coastal area attracted the villas of the Roman élite even before the discomfiture of the pirates in the 60s, and there were spacious houses of the Pompeian type within Ostia's walls as well as large estates in the territory. These multiplied at the end of the republic, and from Ostia a resort coast stretched to Antium, where *Pliny the Younger owned a maritime *villa. Ostia itself became a 'very comfortable and convenient city'.

These comforts are very apparent. Most of the houses are well-built *insulae*, which, when first studied, gave a flattering impression of Roman urban conditions (some of the apartments have seven rooms), the streets were often colonnaded or arcaded, and there are areas of spacious houses. An aqueduct supplied at least seventeen bath-houses. Ostia was well equipped with taverns (see INNS, RESTAURANTS). A lavish theatre was originally probably a benefaction from *Vipsanius Agrippa. The buildings of the *forum (first given monumental form under Augustus and his successors; the large Capitoline temple is Hadrianic) occupied most of the area of the former colony, and are on a grand scale.

The principal testimony to Ostia's economic life are the great storehouses (see GRANARIES, *Roman*), including many used for the corn supply. There are a number of headquarters of *collēgia*, associations connected with commerce, the river, the harbour (Portus), or warehousing (see CLUBS, ROMAN); the elaborately decorated premises were intended to provide a place of visible, semi-public social interaction for the bosses rather than the rank and file. Our understanding of the relationship of the city to the river is hampered by changes in the Tiber's course and erosion of the site, but the main extent of the town was a long development beside the via Ostiensis, stretching towards Rome.

Most of what is visible at Ostia is a development of the Flavian, Antonine, and Severan periods. The uniformity of the kiln-fired brick construction and the regularity of the plan suggest wholesale redevelopment, and large-scale investment in urban property. Much of what we know of Ostia relates to the 2nd and 3rd cents., when the city appears to have been home to people who had made their money in harbour-activities; their descendants and successors moved further away from economic activity in the direction of comfort.

Ostia is quite small (there is no sign that the built-up area was ever larger than c.50 ha., and much of this was not primarily dwelling-places). It was a service-town, for the countryside, for the spread-out activities of the Tiber-bank, and the harbours of Portus, and for the numerous passers-by on their way to and from Rome (wide horizons are apparent in the diversity of its religious cults). Such service functions supported an economically fortunate population and a considerable number of their slaves, who are archaeologically largely invisible. Ostia was a focal point in a port-region rather than a harbour-town in the strict sense.

The serious study of the site was made possible by the eradication of malaria. About three-quarters of the inner part of the city is visible today. See HOUSES, ITALIAN.

Ostōrius Scapula, Publius (suffect consul before AD 46), of *equestrian background, succeeded Aulus *Plautius as governor of *Britain in 47. He consolidated Roman control by disarming some of the previously conquered peoples, and invaded north Wales, but was forced to turn back by a revolt of some western groups of the Brigantes of northern England (see CARTIMAN-DUA). *Legion XX was moved c.49 from *Camulodunum, which was then secured by a colony, for campaigns against the Silures and Ordovices in south and central Wales, which ended in the defeat of *Caratacus, although the war dragged on. Ostorius received *ornamenta triumphalia but died in 52, worn out by his responsibilities.

ostraca/*ostraka,* fragments of pottery used for writing on. See also OSTRACISM.

ostracism in Athens in the 5th cent. BC was a way to exile a citizen for ten years. Each year in the sixth prytany (see PRYTANEIS) the question whether an ostracism should be held that year was put to the *ekklēsia. If the people voted in favour of holding an ostracism, it was held on a day in the eighth prytany in the *Agora under the supervision of the *archontes and the *boule. Each citizen who wished to vote wrote on (more exactly, incised) a fragment of pottery (ostrakon) the name of the citizen whom he wished to be banished. The voters were marshalled by *phylai in an enclosure erected for the occasion, to ensure that no one put in more than one ostrakon. When all had voted, the ostraka were counted, and, provided that there was a total of at least 6,000, the man whose name appeared on the largest number was ostracized. He had to leave the country within ten days and remain in exile for ten years, but he did not forfeit his citizenship or property, and at the end of the ten years he could return to live in Athens without any disgrace or disability.

The date of the institution of ostracism is disputed. Acc. to *Athenaion Politeia, the law about it was introduced by *Cleisthenes (2) in 508/7, but the first ostracism was not held until 487. So long an interval is at least surprising.

The man ostracized in 487 was Hipparchus, a relative of the ex-tyrant *Hippias (1). He was followed in 486 by Megaclēs, an *Alcmaeonid, and in 485 by some other adherent of Hippias' family. No doubt these three had all become unpopular because it was thought that they favoured the Persian invaders and the restoration of the tyranny. *Xanthippus was ostracized in 484 and *Aristides in 482, but both of them returned from exile in 480 when an amnesty was declared in an attempt to muster the full strength of Athens to resist the invasion of Xerxes. Other prominent men known to have been ostracized are *Themistocles c.470, *Cimon in 461, *Thucydides (1) in 443, and *Damon. *Hyperbolus was the last victim of the system in c. 416. Ostracism then fell out of use, although the law authorizing it remained in force in the 4th cent. The *graphe paranomon was found to be a more convenient method of attacking politicians.

It is often hard to tell why a particular man was ostracized. Sometimes, as in the cases of Cimon and Thucydides, the Athenians seem to have ostracized a man to express their rejection of a policy for which he stood and their support for an opposing leader; thus an ostracism might serve a purpose similar to that of a modern general election. But no doubt individual citizens were often actuated by personal malice or other non-political motives, as is illustrated by the story of the yokel who wished to vote against Aristides because he was tired of hearing him called 'the Just'.

Over 10,000 *ostraka*, dumped in the Agora or *Ceramicus after use, have now been found. The names include not only men whom we know to have been actually ostracized but also a considerable number of others. Some are men quite unknown to us, and it may well be that they were not prominent politicians but merely had an odd vote cast against them by some malicious personal acquaintance. 190 *ostraka* found in a well on the northern slope of the Acropolis (see ATHENS, TOPOGRAPHY), are all inscribed with the name of Themistocles by only a few different hands. Presumably they were prepared for distribution by his opponents. This suggests that he was the victim of an organized campaign, and it illustrates the importance of ostracism as a political weapon in 5th-cent. Athens. See also LITERACY.

Othō (Marcus Salvius Otho) (AD 32–69), whose father received *patrician rank from *Claudius, was husband of *Poppaea Sabina and friend of *Nero. As Nero fell in love with his wife (afterwards divorced), he was sent to Lusitania as governor in 58 and remained there until Nero's death (68). He supported *Galba and hoped to be his heir. Disappointed, he organized a conspiracy among the *praetorians and was proclaimed emperor (Jan. 69). He posed as the legitimate successor of Nero. Egypt, Africa, and the legions of the Danube and the Euphrates declared for him. But the legions of the Rhine had already chosen *Vitellius. By early March their advanced guard had crossed the Alps, and an Othonian expedition to southern Gaul achieved little. His generals held the line of the Po, but his armies from the Danube arrived only gradually. Though defeated in a minor engagement, the Vitellians were soon heavily reinforced: yet Otho insisted on a decisive battle before he could oppose equal strength. His troops advanced from Bedriacum, and were irretrievably defeated. He killed himself on 16 April. Otho's profligacy seems not to have impaired his energy or his interest in government. But he was a slave to the praetorians who had elevated him.

Ouranos See URANUS.

ovātiō/ovation was a form of victory celebration less lavish and impressive than a *triumph. It could be granted to a general who was unable to claim a full triumph, e.g. because his victory had not involved the destruction of a large number of the enemy or because he had handed over his army to a successor. He entered Rome on foot or horseback instead of in a chariot, dressed in a *toga praetexta (not picta) and without a sceptre, wearing a wreath of myrtle instead of laurel, and the procession was much less spectacular.

Ovid (Publius Ovidius Nāsō, 43 BC–AD 17), Roman poet, b. at Sulmo. As the son of an old *equestrian family, Ovid was sent to Rome for his education. It was rounded off by the usual Grand Tour through Greek lands. After holding some minor judicial posts, he apparently abandoned public life for poetry—thus enacting one of the commonplaces of Roman elegiac (see below) autobiography. With early backing from *Valerius Messalla Corvinus, Ovid quickly gained prominence as a writer, and by AD 8 he was the leading poet of Rome. In that year he was suddenly relegated by *Augustus to *Tomis. In his *exile poetry Ovid refers to two causes of offence: *carmen, a poem, the Ars Amatoria; and error, an indiscretion. All that can be reconstructed from Ovid's own hints about the error is a vague picture of involuntary complicity in some scandal affecting the imperial house. Tomis, a superficially Hellenized town with a wretched climate on the extreme edge of the empire, was a cruel place in which to abandon Rome's most urbane poet. Public and private pleading failed to appease Augustus or (later) *Tiberius: Ovid languished in Tomis until his death. Several of the elegies from exile are addressed to his third wife, who remained behind in Rome.

Works (all extant poems except the Metamorphoses written in elegiac couplets; see ELEGIAC POETRY, LATIN).

Amōrēs, 'Loves'. Three books of elegies presenting the ostensibly autobiographical misadventures of a poet in love. Erotic elegy before Ovid had featured a disjunction in the first-person voice between a very knowing poet and a very unknowing lover. Ovid closes this gap, and achieves a closer fit between literary and erotic conventions, by featuring a protagonist who loves as knowingly as he writes. Ovid's lover is familiar with the rules of the *genre, understands the necessity for them, and manipulates them to his advantage. The result is a newly rigorous and zestful exploration of erotic elegy's possibilities.

Hērōidĕs, 'Heroines'. Of the 'single *Heroides*' 1–14 are letters from mythological female figures to absent husbands or lovers. In their argumentative ingenuity these poems show us the Ovid who was a star declaimer in the schools. The heroines tend to be well known. The epistolary form is sometimes archly appropriate ('what harm will a letter do?', Phaedra asks *Hippolytus), sometimes blithely inappropriate (where on her deserted shore will *Ariadne find a postman?); above all, perhaps, it effects a characteristically Alexandrian modernization by Ovid (see HELLENISTIC POETRY AT ROME) of the dramatic monologue by presenting the heroine as a writer, her impassioned speech as a written text, and the process of poetic composition as itself part of the action. In the paired letters, 16–21 the potential of the epistolary form is perhaps most fully realized.

Medicāmina Faciĕī Fēmineae, 'Cosmetics for the Female Face', a *didactic poem. Only the first 100 lines survive. See COSMETICS.

Ars Amātōria, 'Art of Love'. A didactic poem in three books on the arts of courtship and erotic intrigue; the mechanics of sexual technique receive but limited attention. The situations addressed owe much to previous elegy. The actors themselves are firmly located in contemporary Rome. Conventionally, didactic was a subset of *epic and written in hexameters; Ovid's choice of elegiac couplets, as it signals a continuity with his own *Amores*, signals a felt discontinuity with mainstream didactic. As successor to the *Amores*, the *Ars* achieves much of its novelty through a reversal of the implied roles of poet and reader: in the *Amores* the reader oversees the poet's love affair; in the *Ars* the poet oversees the reader's love affair. It may be that this newly direct implication of the Roman reader in the erotic text made the *Ars* the poem most likely to be picked on when the climate turned unfavourable to Ovid's work.

Remedia Amōris, 'Remedies for Love'. A kind of recantation of the *Ars Amatoria*; the poet now instructs his readers how to extricate themselves from a love affair.

Metamorphōsēs, 'Transformations'. An unorthodox epic in fifteen books, Ovid's only surviving work in hexameters, composed in the years immediately preceding his exile. The poem is a large collection of tales from classical and near eastern myth and legend, each of which describes or somehow alludes to a supernatural change of shape (see METAMORPHOSIS). Throughout the poem the theme calls attention to the boundaries between divine and human, animal and inanimate, raising fundamental questions about definition and hierarchy in the universe. Structurally the *Metamorphoses* is a paradox. The preface promises an unbroken narrative, epic in its scope, from the creation to the poet's own day; but throughout much of the poem chronological linearity takes second place to patterns of thematic association and contrast, book divisions promote asymmetry over symmetry, and the ingenious transitions do as much to emphasize the autonomy of individual episodes as to weld them into a continuum. Ovid engages with an unprecedented range of Greek and Roman writing; every genre, not just epic, leaves its mark in the poem's idiom. As narrative *Metamorphoses* brilliantly captures the infinite variety and patterning of the mythological tradition on which it draws (and which, for many later communities of readers, it supersedes). Ovid's poetic imagination, intensely verbal and intensely visual, finds here its finest expression. *Metamorphoses* tells utterly memorable stories about the aspirations and sufferings which define the human condition; from the poem's characteristic aestheticization of those sufferings comes both its surface brightness and its power to disturb.

Fastī, 'Calendar'. A poetical calendar of the Roman year with one book devoted to each month (see CALENDAR, ROMAN). At the time of Ovid's exile it was incomplete, and only the first six books (January–June) survive. The figure without whom the poem is ultimately inconceivable is Augustus, whose reclamation and appropriation of Roman religious discourse constitutes the basis of Ovid's own poetic appropriation. Long mined for its detailed information about the perceived roots of Roman religion and ritual, the *Fasti* has begun to attract new attention both as a complex work of art and as an exploration of religious thinking at a time of ideological realignment.

Tristia, 'Sorrows'. A series of books dispatched from exile between AD 9 and 12, containing poems addressed by Ovid to his wife and to various unnamed persons in Rome. The 'sorrows' of the title are the past, present, and anticipated sufferings associated with the relegation to the Black Sea: *Tristia*, and the later 'Epistles from Pontus', function as open letters in which the poet campaigns from afar for a reconsideration of his sentence. The second book, addressed to Augustus, differs from the other four. A single poem of over 500 lines, it uses an ostensibly submissive appeal for imperial clemency as the point of departure for a sustained defence of the poet's career and artistic integrity. The mood of *Tristia* is deeply introspective, with all the rich opportunities for geography and ethnography subsumed within the narrative of an inner journey: the ships on which Ovid voyages into exile merge with his metaphorical 'ship of fortune'; the icy torpor and infertility of the Pontic landscape become indices of the poet's own (allegedly) frozen creativity.

Epistulae ex Ponto, 'Epistles from Pontus'. Four books of poems from exile, differing from the *Tristia* only in that the addressees are named, and characterized with greater individuality.

Ibis. An elaborate curse-poem directed at an enemy whose identity is hidden under the name of a bird of unclean habits; both title and treatment derive from a lost work of Callimachus.

Lost works. Our principal loss is Ovid's tragedy *Medea*.

Ovid is not only one of the finest writers of antiquity; he is also one of the finest readers. Not since Callimachus, perhaps, had a poet shown such understanding in depth and in detail of the literary traditions of which he was the inheritor; never was such understanding carried so lightly. The same revisionary energy which he brings to alien texts is applied no less to his own. Ovid constantly reworks himself, at the level of the poem (the *Ars* reframes the *Amores*, the *Remedia* the *Ars*), of the episode (cross-referential Persephones in *Metamorphoses* and *Fasti*), and even of the individual line and phrase. This paradigm of self-imitation, together with the deceptively easy smoothness and symmetry which he bequeaths to the dactylic metres, make his manner (once achieved) endlessly imitable to later generations. What remains inimitable, however, is the wealth of the poet's invention. Ovid devoted most of his career to a single genre, elegy, so that by the time of the *Remedia* he was already able to claim that 'elegy owes as much to me as epic does to Virgil'. (The *Metamorphoses* still lay ahead, an epic which— although it is much else besides—can justly be said to be the epic of an elegist.) But within elegy he achieved an unparalleled variety of output by exploiting and extending the range of the genre as no poet had before. No Roman poet can equal Ovid's impact upon western art and culture. Esp. remarkable in its appropriations has been the *Metamorphoses*.

Oxyrhynchus, a nome capital (see NOMOS (1)) beyond the river Tomis west of the Nile, was the richest source of papyri ever found in Egypt. The finds came from rubbish mounds outside the town; they are now worked out. Most are Roman or Byzantine; the Ptolemaic levels lay beneath the water table. Over 70 per cent of surviving literary papyri come from Oxyrhynchus. Two sets of fragments belong to the same historical work (the 'Oxyrhynchus Historian'). It was a scholarly continuation of Thucydides from 411 to 395 BC.

Pācuvius, Marcus (220–c.130 BC), tragic poet of south Italian birth, nephew and pupil of *Ennius. Titles of thirteen tragedies of the Attic (see TRAGEDY, GREEK) type are transmitted. The themes of eight relate to the Trojan War. Several plots seem to have come from post-Euripidean pieces (see EURIPIDES). Pacuvius' borrowings of Greek poetic vocabulary, neologisms and deviant syntax incurred criticism from the grammatical purists of his own time. In the 1st cent. he was regarded as the greatest of the Latin tragic poets, surpassing *Accius in his use of the high tragic style.

Paeonius, Greek sculptor from Mende, active c.420 BC. Known from an original work found at *Olympia—a marble statue of a flying *Nike, mounted on a high triangular base, and displayed before the eastern face of the temple of *Zeus. The inscription on the base states that the monument was erected by the Messenians and Naupactians (see MESSENIA, *History*), and that Paeonius both made it and won the competition for the *acroteria for the temple.

The statue's style is certainly later than the *Parthenon, which confirms a Messenian tradition that it celebrated Sparta's defeat at Sphacteria in 425 (see PYLOS), and that they omitted to say so for fear of the Spartans. A virtuoso essay in marble-carving, the Nike represents the 'birthday' of the flamboyant or 'Rich' style in Greek sculpture, as the Tyrannicides had announced the birth of the Severe style (see CRITIUS). Her wet and windswept drapery clearly alludes to a battle at sea; she is also the first partially nude divinity in Classical Greek art.

pagan, paganism The Latin word *pāgānus* means literally one who inhabits a *pāgus* ('country district'). By imperial times, the term was applied to one who stayed at home or lived a civilian life. Christian reference implied one who was not a soldier of Christ. *Paganismus* was first used in the 4th cent.

painting, Greek (see also POTTERY, GREEK). When the Mycenaean palaces fell, c.1200 BC (see MYCENAEAN CIVILIZATION), the art of painting was lost. It is next practised in the early Archaic period. Sources for Archaic to Hellenistic are: literary references; artefacts echoing painting (primarily vases); surviving examples, mostly recent discoveries.

Writers of the Roman period tell us most. *Pliny the Elder gives a history of painting, detailing many works and careers, dividing artists into regional schools, notably (as in sculpture) a 4th-cent. Sicyonian school; see SICYON. *Pausanias (3)'s *autopsy and interest in art *per se* distinguish him from other writers. Philosophers like *Plato and *Aristotle made moral and aesthetic judgements on art (see ART, ANCIENT ATTITUDES TO); the *ekphrasis* employed by rhetoricians involved describing art for effect, not accuracy. Classical painters enjoyed high social standing (hence perhaps their prominence in the sources): esp. *Polygnotus' association with *Cimon, and *Apelles' with *Alexander (2) the Great. Painting was introduced into the school curriculum by Pamphilus (below).

Pliny places early painting's beginnings at Corinth or Sicyon. The temples at Corinth and neighbouring Isthmia, c.690–650, have painted walls: the former has blocks of colour, the latter figures c.30 cm. (12 in.) high and border patterns on stucco, using several colours. Contemporary is the rare use of a brown wash for flesh on vases from several regions. Tomb paintings preserved in Etruria appear to have been undertaken for Greek patrons (see ETRUSCANS); at Paestum in southern Italy, the Tomb of the Diver, c.480, closely resembles in pose and (in the *symposium) subject-matter contemporary Athenian vases.

Cimon of Cleonae (between *Argos and Corinth) is credited with inventing three-quarter views and a new disposition of figures. Substantial advances occur c.475–450, the age of Polygnotus and *Micon. Their work, often on historical and heroic themes in prominent public buildings, was characterized by variable groundlines, grouping, and disposition of figures, reflected in some contemporary vases. Panaenus is said to have painted portraits (among the earliest) in the Marathon painting of the *Stoa Poecile. The use of perspective was greatly developed by *Agatharchus, and *Sophocles is said to have introduced skēnē-painting (see THEATRE-STAGING, GREEK).

Apollodorus of Athens (fl. 407–404) opened 'the door of the art of painting' developing skiagraphia, balancing light and shade. Through the 'door', says Pliny, walked *Zeuxis. He is often contrasted with *Parrhasius, who worked mainly in Athens. Zeuxis was the painter of shade and mass, Parrhasius of contour lines. Euphranor (fl. 364) contrasted himself with Parrhasius, saying that the latter's Theseus was fed on roses, his own on meat. A debate on painting styles is reflected in *Xenophon, where Parrhasius talks with *Socrates. The most highly regarded of all painters was Apelles (fl. 332), pupil of Pamphilus of Sicyon, and court painter to Alexander.

Classical paintings were mainly painted on whitened wooden panels. Pliny and *Cicero give (differing) lists of four-colour painters, implying that the Classical range was limited to red, yellow, black, and white. Pliny divides colours into sombre and brilliant. The absence of green is incompatible with Vergina (see AEGAE), although the Alexander *mosaic (if it accurately reflects a late Classical painting) argues for the four-colour scheme.

Most paintings were done with brushes, but encaustic, applying pigments mixed with heated wax, is regularly used from the 4th cent. Pausias of Sicyon first became well known for encaustic, learning it from Pamphilus. Pausias is best known for introducing many kinds of flowers. 'Pausian' florals occur regularly on contemporary southern Italian vases, and on mosaics and paintings from *Macedonia (below), and elsewhere. Pausias painted *Eros and Drunkenness at *Epidaurus.

Recent finds include tomb paintings from Macedonia, notably Vergina, from 1976. See AEGAE. The smaller tomb (c.340?) contains a *Hades and *Persephone which eschews outline, painted impressionistically, with subtle shades of colour, hatching giving shading and depth. The 'tomb of *Philip II' (if so, soon after 336) features a hunt where human figures dominate, as in later Hellenistic and early Roman wall-painting. The treatment of landscape is paralleled in the Alexander mosaic. Hades and Perse-

phone are also painted on the back of a throne found at Vergina.

See IMAGERY; PAINTING, ROMAN; POTTERY, GREEK.

painting, Roman In late republican times Roman collectors avidly acquired Greek 'old master' pictures (see ART, ANCIENT ATTITUDES TO), and contemporary painters provided new works for the market; Greek artists were brought to, or migrated to, Rome to meet the demand. Pictures commemorating military campaigns were carried in triumphs (see TRIUMPH). But the advent of the empire saw a gradual shift of interest from portable panels to wall-paintings, a trend lamented by *Pliny the Elder.

Wall-painting on plaster is attested in tombs at Rome from an early date and became increasingly normal in private houses. At *Pompeii and *Herculaneum most residences eventually contained extensive paintings, ranging from simple schemes in minor rooms to rich, polychrome schemes in important rooms. The evidence from the Vesuvius region, together with contemporary material from Rome (including remains in *Augustus' properties on the *Palatine and Nero's *Domus Aurea), enable us to follow changing fashions up to the late 1st cent. AD. The evidence from later cents. is more fragmentary and difficult to date, but includes important decorations from the provinces. See IMAGERY; PORTRAITURE, ROMAN; SCULPTURE, ROMAN.

palaces In bronze age Crete and Greece palaces serve as complex administrative centres, as well as the residence of presumed monarchs (see MINOAN and MYCENAEAN AGE CIVILIZATION). With the rise of Macedon, monarchy is once more a significant political institution. The palace at Pella (late 4th cent.?), and the palace (late 4th or 3rd cent.) of *Aegae (Vergina), consist of rooms around substantial colonnaded courtyards. The ground-floor rooms at Aegeae are arranged almost entirely for formal feasting, one, with an antechamber, and marble and mosaic embellishment, being presumably that of the king and his closest 'friends' (see DINING-ROOMS).

Only written descriptions survive of the palace of the Ptolemies (see PTOLEMY (1); EGYPT, Ptolemaic) in *Alexandria. Here there was a mixture of separate administrative and related structures, together with special feasting buildings, one, built for Ptolemy II in the form of a Macedonian dining tent, having sufficient space for 130 feasting couches.

In Rome the favoured area was the Palatine hill (which gives its name to palaces as a type). The definitive construction is that of *Domitian. This comprises two large brick and concrete structures arranged around courtyards, one with large rooms designed for public receptions, the other with smaller rooms and dining-rooms, presumably the residential area. Before this Nero had built his *Domus Aurea (Golden House), sprawling over a large part of the city in imitation of the palace at Alexandria. Left unfinished at his suicide it was then demolished, or later incorporated into the baths of *Trajan. The rambling rural 'Villa' of *Hadrian at *Tibur probably reflects the type.

palaeography is the study of the history of writing upon papyrus (see PAPYROLOGY), wax, parchment, and paper, while *epigraphy deals with inscriptions carved in hard materials; from it we learn how to read old scripts and to observe their development, which may provide us with criteria for establishing the date and place of origin of a piece of writing. It is also concerned with the layout of the written page and the form of the book. In both Greek and Latin the written letters change under the influence of three forces: the first, the desire to form the letters with less effort, and the second, the need to be legible, oppose each other; the third, a concern for beauty, in the individual letter, the line as a whole or the page, makes the scribe careful, but sometimes, in his search for regularity and uniformity, he makes the letters hard to distinguish from each other.

palaestra was a wrestling-ground, a place for athletic exercise, whether public or private, which eventually took the standard form of an enclosed courtyard surrounded by rooms for changing, washing, etc. The application of the term to actual buildings is often uncertain; conventionally it is used for structures smaller than the developed gymnasia (see GYMNASIUM) which are similar in arrangement. See ATHLETICS; WRESTLING.

Palamēdēs ('the handy or contriving one'), a proverbially clever hero. Tradition from the *Cypria* on (see EPIC CYCLE) makes *Odysseus his enemy because he was forced by Palamedes to serve in the Trojan War (see TROY): Odysseus pretended to be mad to avoid going to Troy, but Palamedes exposed him, either by putting the infant *Telemachus in front of his ploughshare or by threatening the baby with a sword.

Odysseus saved his son, and thus gave himself away. In revenge he later forged a letter from *Priam to Palamedes, promising him a sum of gold if he would betray the Greeks, then buried this same amount of gold in Palamedes' quarters. *Agamemnon read the letter, found the gold, and handed over Palamedes to the army to be stoned. His father Nauplius avenged his death by causing some of the Greek leaders' wives to be unfaithful, and later by lighting false beacons at Cape Caphereus in *Euboea, with the result that the Greek fleet was wrecked. Palamedes was credited, alongside *Cadmus, with having invented certain letters of the *alphabet and the *games of draughts and dice to help while away the Trojan War.

Palatine, the chief of the *seven hills of Rome, traditionally the site of the oldest settlement there. Tradition assigns fortifications to the hill, and this seems to be confirmed by archaeology. Early settlement is represented by two archaic cisterns and rock-cut post-holes for iron age huts; one example, above the Lupercal (see LUPERCALIA) and *forum Boarium, is identified as the 'hut of *Romulus' which was preserved in historic times. Temples on the hill included those dedicated to *Victoria (294 BC), Victoria Virgo (193), and the Magna Mater (191; see CYBELE). Many aristocratic houses occupied the hill and the slopes which led down to the Forum, from the late 6th cent. BC onwards; famous owners including *Cicero, *Crassus, *Annius Milo, Marcus *Antonius (Mark Antony), *Livius Drusus, *Aemilius Scaurus (whose house has recently been excavated), and *Hortensius Hortalus. The house of Hortensius was acquired by *Augustus and became the nucleus of a group of palace-buildings which included a portico and libraries as well as the new temple of *Apollo. (see PALACES.) In the early Julio-Claudian period, the palace continued to be composed of individual houses, but *Gaius (1) extended it to the Forum and 'made the temple of Castor and Pollux his vestibule' (see CASTOR AND POLLUX), as recent excavations confirm. *Nero made important additions to the palace-buildings both before and after the great fire of 64. *Domitian was responsible for the Flavian palace-buildings, conventionally known as Domus Flavia and Domus Augustana, which included a monumental garden (*hippodromus*). Further construction was undertaken by *Hadrian, *Commodus, and *Septimius Severus, who built out towards the SE, where the Septizodium provided a monumental façade. The palace remained in use even after *Constantinople became the new imperial capital (see PALACES).

Palladium Miraculous guardian statues were common in ancient cities, but none was more famous than the Trojan Palladium, a small wooden image of armed *Athena. It fell from the sky, and the safety of *Troy depended on its possession. *Odysseus and *Diomedes carried it away, thus enabling the sack of Troy. But in the canonical Roman tradition it was *Aeneas who rescued the Palladium and brought it to Lavinium, whence it ultimately reached Rome. In Rome it was kept as a pledge of Rome's fate in the innermost part of *Vesta's temple, where only the chief Vestal could enter; when in 241 BC the temple burnt, the *pontifex maximus* saved the Palladium, but (so say some authorities) lost his sight.

Pallas, Marcus Antōnius See ANTONIUS PALLAS.

palliāta (sc. *fabula*, 'drama in a Greek cloak (*pallium*)'), the type of comedy written at Rome by *Plautus and *Terence, either known or mostly assumed to be adaptations of (Greek) New Comedy (see COMEDY (GREEK), NEW); since the plays of Plautus and Terence are our only complete Latin comedies, this term has come to mean Latin *comedy. Almost certainly a masked drama from the start, it shows Greek characters in a Greek setting, and in general the authors are believed to have preserved many of the essential elements of plot from their Greek originals. But Roman details sometimes intrude, esp. in Plautus, who adapted the Greek plays with considerable freedom and whose portrayal of stereotyped stock characters may well have been influenced by the *Atellana. Plautus was the first Latin playwright to devote himself exclusively to comedy: *Livius Andronicus, *Naevius, and *Ennius all wrote tragedies as well.

The Latin authors abandoned the five-act structure and choral interludes of Greek New Comedy, writing almost throughout for continuous performance; the act- and scene-divisions found in modern editions of Plautus and Terence do not go back to the authors. Like the Greek authors, they wrote in verse, but they increased the proportion of text with musical accompaniment. They were not restricted to the use of three speaking actors and wrote many scenes requiring more.

It was through Plautus and Terence that Greek New Comedy became the dominant type of comedy in the European dramatic tradition, with plots portraying love affairs, confusion of identity, and misunderstandings, and with casts including boastful soldiers, rediscovered foundlings, and scheming servants.

Pan, a god from Arcadia in central *Peloponnese. His name means 'guardian of flocks'. His appearance is mixed, half man and half goat, not surprising in a region where divine theriomorphism is well attested. His usual attributes of syrinx (Pan-pipes) and *lagobolon* (a device for catching hares) mark him out as a shepherd. Pan became a kind of national god of Arcadia. Starting at the beginning of the 5th cent., Pan spreads into Boeotia and *Attica, continuing in the 4th cent. to reach the rest of the Greek world.

The main myths concern his birth, and there are fourteen different versions of his parentage. Usually his father is *Hermes, another Arcadian god, but the name of his mother varies, though usually she is a *nymph, in harmony with the god's rustic nature. In Hellenistic times he loves the nymphs Echo and Syrinx, and *Selene, the moon.

Pan's activities and functions are tied to the pastoral world (see PASTORAL POETRY, GREEK). He is a shepherd god and protector of shepherds, who sacrifice in his honour kids, goats or sheep, and who dedicate to him statuettes showing herdsmen, with or without offerings. He is also a hunting god, concerned with small animals such as hares, partridges, and small birds, while *Artemis presides over larger game. This function is illustrated by an Arcadian ritual, whereby after an unsuccessful hunt, young men would beat Pan's statue with squills. In this way they would stimulate Pan's powers of fertility and direct it towards the animal domain. Pan is also linked to the world of the soldiers patrolling the rocky, lonely places where he lives. During the *Persian Wars, he intervened among the Athenian ranks at Marathon (see MARATHON, BATTLE OF). *Herodotus has the story of his appearance to *Phidippides, who was near Mount Parthenion in Arcadia on his way to *Laconia to get help from the Spartans; he offered to help the Athenians, in return for which the cult of Pan was established in Athens. From the Hellenistic period onwards, Pan is the god responsible for sowing panic in the enemy, a sudden, unforeseeable fear. Soldiers therefore pay cult to him.

The Greeks liked to worship Pan, together with Hermes and the nymphs, in sacred *caves, recalling the figure of the Arcadian goatherd. But in Arcadia, though he is fond of mountains, well away from human habitation, Pan does not live in caves, and he is not absent from cities. In Athens, his public cult involved the sacrifice of a castrated goat and a torch-race. Individual piety is typified by such *votives as vases, golden grasshoppers, oil-lamps (in the cave at Vari in *Attica), and reliefs which show the God in his cave in front of his worshippers, playing the syrinx and accompanied by Hermes, three nymphs, and sometimes *Achelous (see RIVER-GODS). In *Menander's *Dyskolos*, the mother of Sostratos arranges a religious celebration in honour of Pan at Phyle, in Attica, after the god appears to her in a dream. The sacrifice of a sheep is followed by a meal, and the happy and rowdy celebration continues all night at the cave, with drinking and dancing in the presence of the god.

The ancients quite early associated Pan with Gk. *pān*, 'all'. From this, word-play leads to the association which made Pan in the Roman period into a universal god, the All. This is the context of the story in *Plutarch, which has sometimes been linked with the rise of Christianity, of a mysterious voice announcing the death of 'great Pan'. Despite these developments, as *Pausanias (3) bears witness, in cult the god remained the god of shepherds.

Panaetius (*c*.185–109 BC), Stoic philosopher (see STOICISM) from *Rhodes. He studied with Crates of Mallus at *Pergamum and with the leaders of the Stoic school at Athens. He moved to Rome in the 140s and became, like *Polybius, part of the entourage of *Cornelius Scipio Aemilianus. He accompanied Scipio on a long journey in the Mediterranean (140/139). It is said that he lived alternately in Rome and Athens. In 129 he became head of the school. He died in Athens in 109.

Panaetius seems to have been more open to the views of *Plato and *Aristotle than were many Stoics, and to have questioned the earlier belief in a periodic world-conflagration. Unlike earlier Stoics, he doubted the efficacy of *astrology and *divination, though he retained a belief in divine providence. In ethics, he is associated with a more practical emphasis on the moral situation of ordinary men and a reduced emphasis on the morally perfect sage. Bks. 1–2 of *Cicero's *On Duty* were heavily influenced by Panaetius.

Panathēnaea, the great civic festival of Athens in honour of *Athena, celebrated in Hekatombaion (roughly August). Its core was the procession, evoked in the *Parthenon frieze, in which representatives of different sections of Athenian society and even *metics marched or rode from the *Ceramicus through the Agora to the Acropolis (see ATHENS, TOPOGRAPHY). There followed large sacrifices, the meat from which was publicly distributed. The night before, choirs of boys and maidens had celebrated a 'night festival' (*pannychis*). Every four years, the Panathenaea was extended to become the 'greater Panathenaea'. Only then, probably, did the procession bring to Athena the famous Panathenaic robe, embroidered with scenes from the battle of Gods and *Giants. Her ancient wooden statue was housed in the *Erechtheum. The greater Panathenaea also included major athletic and musical competitions (see AGONES), open to all Greece and lasting several days, winners in which received money prizes or *olive oil contained in the distinctive Panathenaic prize *amphoras. The games were added to the Panathenaea in the 6th cent. (in or near 566), doubtless to set it on a par with other recently founded panhellenic athletic festivals (see PANHELLENISM; PYTHIAN and ISTHMIAN GAMES). In the 5th cent. Athens' allies were required to participate in the procession, which thus became a symbol of imperial power; see DELIAN LEAGUE.

Pandōra, whose name combines 'all' and 'gifts', was a goddess connected with the earth, but she is better known as the first human female, the cause of all man's woes. If the name has any relevance here, it sounds ironic; but the two Pandoras may in fact be connected through the idea of the earth as first ancestor. Acc. to *Hesiod's poems, *Zeus caused Pandora to be created in order to punish *Prometheus and the human race. She was fashioned out of clay by *Hephaestus, given 'gifts' by 'all' the *Olympian gods, and sent as a gift herself to Prometheus' brother Epimetheus. Here she opened a large jar and released all manner of evils into the world; only Hope was left to counterbalance them.

panegyric, Latin, originates in the *laudatio funebris* or 'funeral eulogy'. Later came fertilization from Greek *rhetoric. The Latin tradition was much influenced by *Cicero's speeches in praise of *Pompey (66) and of *Caesar (46), and later by *Pliny the Younger's *Panegyric*, in which he gave thanks to *Trajan when Pliny took up his consulship in AD 100. By that time praise was ordinarily reserved for the emperor.

panhellenism, the idea that what the Greeks have in common, and what distinguishes them from *barbarians, is more important than what divides them. The word is not ancient, though *Panhellēnĕs* is used of the Greeks once in the *Iliad* (see HELLENES). The idea originates in the Greeks' resistance to the Persian invasions of 490 and 480–479 BC (see PERSIAN WARS), and in the *Delian League as a Greek alliance formed to continue the war against Persia. In the 4th cent., after the *Peloponnesian War, the argument that the heyday of the Greeks was when they (31 states) were united against Persia rather than fighting among themselves, and that to recover their greatness they should again unite against Persia, was advanced by *Gorgias and *Lysias and became a recurrent theme in the works of *Isocrates. The invasion of the Persian empire planned by *Philip II of Macedon and accomplished by *Alexander (2) the Great was partly inspired by this idea. Others might represent Macedon itself as a barbarian enemy. Panhellenic Games were games open to all Greeks; see AGONES, (2). The four great panhellenic *sanctuaries were *Delphi, *Olympia, Isthmia, and *Nemea, though there were panhellenic aspects to the *Panathenaea at Athens.

Panionium, meeting-place of the Ionian League (see IONIANS), from early 7th cent. BC?, where the common festival of the twelve member-cities took place and their *probouloi* met to discuss common policy in time of need. *Herodotus places it by Mt. Mycale; for security it was later moved near *Ephesus, before returning to Mycale, where it was still celebrated under the Principate. Sacrifice was offered to Heliconian *Poseidon; the priesthood was reserved for men from Priene. The site has been excavated: there was no temple, it seems, but an altar, 18 m. (59 ft.) long. The twelve members were: *Miletus, Myus, Priene, Ephesus, Colophon, Lebedus, Teos, Clazomenae, Erythrae, *Phocaea, *Chios, *Samos.

pankration In this event *boxing and *wrestling were combined with kicking, strangling, and twisting. It was a dangerous sport, but strict rules were enforced by the judges. Biting and gouging were forbidden (except at Sparta), but nearly every manœuvre of hands, feet, and body was permissible. You might kick your opponent in the stomach, twist his foot out of its socket, or break his fingers. All neck holds were allowed, a favourite method being the 'ladder-grip', in which you mounted your opponent's back, and

wound your legs round his stomach, your arms round his neck. See ATHLETICS.

Pantheon, a temple in the *Campus Martius dedicated to all the gods. The first Pantheon, built by *Vipsanius Agrippa in 27–25 BC, was completely rebuilt early in the reign of *Hadrian but retained Agrippa's name in the dedicatory inscription; it was later repaired by *Septimius Severus and *Caracalla. The building was entered from a long rectangular forecourt through a traditional octastyle Corinthian portico of red and grey granite columns, 48 Roman feet (11.8 m.) high. A rectangular block links this to the circular cella, 43.3 m. (142 ft.) in both diameter and height, lit from a single central oculus, 9 m. (30 ft.) in diameter. The cylindrical wall of the brick-faced concrete rotunda (6.2 m. (20 ft.) thick) supporting the dome is divided into eight piers by the doorway and alternating semicircular and rectangular recesses at the lower level. Richly coloured marble veneer, substantially preserved in the lower zone, decorated the interior; a small section of the attic decoration has been restored to its original form. The great bronze doors are ancient. The play of light from the oculus across the vast surface of the richly coffered dome is largely responsible for the building's enduring fascination.

pantomime, popular art-form under the Roman empire in which a solo dancer (*pantomīmus*) represented mythological themes without voice, supported by instrumental music and a chorus. The distinctive quality of pantomime is that the artist did everything by imitation, as in modern mime. The art was introduced at Rome in 22 BC by Pylades and Bathyllus (see MAECENAS). Pylades' innovation, acc. to himself, was to add the orchestra and the chorus. Bathyllus seems to have specialized in light themes related to comedy or satyric drama, such as Pan playing with a satyr; Pylades' style is said to have been 'high-flown, passionate' and related to tragedy. Tragic subjects were in fact a favourite. A highly sophisticated art, demanding much from both performers and spectators, pantomime was essentially serious, and enjoyed a higher status than *mime.

Performance took place in the theatre or privately. The artist, usually a handsome, athletic figure, wore a graceful silk costume permitting free movement and a beautiful mask with closed lips. Behind him stood the chorus and the musicians. Beside the artist there sometimes stood an assistant—perhaps an actor with a speaking part. The dancer might in one piece have to appear in five different roles, each with its own mask. The dancer's power to convey his meaning by steps, postures, and above all *gestures was aided by certain conventions, e.g. there was a traditional dance for 'Thyestes devouring his sons' (*see* ATREUS). The songs of the chorus were of secondary importance. *Lucan and *Statius wrote libretti for the pantomime. Pantomime-artists were popular in both halves of the empire.

Papiniānus/Papinian, lawyer: see AEMILIUS PAPINIANUS.

Papīrius Carbō, Gnaeus, a seditious tribune (see TRIBUNI PLEBIS) in 92 BC. He fought in the *Social War and supported *Cornelius Cinna in 87. He became Cinna's colleague as consul 85 and 84 and, as sole consul after Cinna's death, continued his moderate policy, giving citizenship to the last of the Italians and supporting a senate vote for disarmament. At the end of 84 he gave up the consulship, but with *Sulla advancing in Italy, became consul 82 with Marius, son of *Marius, and, with newly raised levies, fought unsuccessfully against Sulla, Caecilius Metellus Pius, and *Pompey. After failing to relieve Marius at *Praeneste he fled to Africa, was proscribed, captured by Pompey (whom he had once defended on a criminal charge) and executed.

papyrology, Greek Papyrus, manufactured in Egypt from a marsh plant, *Cyperus papyrus* (see BOOKS, GREEK AND ROMAN), was the most widely used writing material in the Graeco-Roman world. The object of papyrology is to study texts written on papyrus in Egyptian (hieroglyphs, demotic, Coptic), Hebrew, *Aramaic, Greek, Latin, Pahlavi, and Arabic. Greek papyrology also deals with Greek texts written on parchment (see PALAEOGRAPHY). Nearly all Greek papyri have been found in Egypt, preserved in the dry sand (see OXYRHYNCHUS). Outside Egypt, Greek papyri have been found at *Herculaneum, at Dura-Europus, in Palestine, and one text has come from Greece: the carbonized Orphic commentary found in a burial at Derveni near Salonica; see ORPHIC LITERATURE; ORPHISM. Today the sites which produced most of this material have been more or less exhausted; the most promising source of papyrus texts is now mummy cases made of papyrus cartonnage, i.e. layers of discarded papyri,

sometimes reinforced with linen cloth, covered with plaster and painted; they often contain Egyptian (demotic) and/or Greek texts of the Ptolemaic or Augustan periods. To date, an estimated 30,000 papyrus texts have been edited, while substantial quantities of unpublished texts, mostly documents, remain in collections in Europe, Egypt, and North America. They cover the period from the mid-4th cent. BC to the early 8th cent. AD, during most of which (332 BC to AD 641) Greek was the official language in Egypt.

papyrus See BOOKS, GREEK AND ROMAN; PALAEOGRAPHY; PAPYROLOGY, GREEK.

parasite, a stock character of Greek and Roman comedy. At first called *kolax* ('toady', 'flatterer', as in *Eupolis' *Kolakes* of 421 BC, named after its chorus), the type acquired as a joke in the 4th cent. the alternative label *parasitos* or 'sponger' (in origin a 'fellow diner', esp. denoting certain religious functionaries). Thereafter the two terms were largely interchangeable. Parasites attach themselves to their social superiors for their own advantage, esp. for free meals; in return they flatter or entertain their patron, run errands, and suffer much ill-treatment. Sometimes the patron is a vainglorious soldier, and soldier and parasite made a stock pair.

Paris, also called Alexandros (his usual name in *Homer), son of *Priam and *Hecuba. Homer refers several times to his abduction of *Helen, which was the cause of the Trojan War (see TROY). At an earlier stage in the development of the legend he was perhaps the principal warrior on the Trojan side. Even in the *Iliad* he is sometimes effective in battle, and he will be responsible, with *Apollo's help, for the death of *Achilles. In general, however, he is seen as greatly inferior to *Hector, who taunts him as handsome but unwarlike. He uses the bow, which tends (see ARCHERS) to be regarded as an unmanly weapon. He is defeated in a duel by *Menelaus, has to be rescued by *Aphrodite, and then consoles himself by making love to Helen.

The *Cypria* (see EPIC CYCLE) told the story of the Judgement of Paris, often mentioned in later literature. Incited to rivalry by *Eris ('strife'), *Hera, *Athena, and Aphrodite appointed Paris to decide between them. They were brought to him by *Hermes, and, bribed by the promise of Helen, he chose Aphrodite as the most beautiful. Acc. to the *Little Iliad* Paris was killed by

*Philoctetes. *Sophocles and *Euripides each wrote an *Alexandros*, and *Ennius an *Alexander*. In Euripides' play, Hecuba, before the birth of Paris, dreamt that she had given birth to a firebrand. So the child was exposed, and Hecuba initiated athletic games (*agones*) in his memory. But he survived and was raised among herdsmen. Grown to manhood, he was brought to Troy, where he competed in the games himself, winning several events. His brother *Deiphobus, furious at being defeated by a mere herdsman, urged Hecuba to kill him, and *Cassandra, recognizing him, prophesied disaster for Troy; but his identity was revealed and his life was spared. The nymph Oenōnē, who loved Paris when he lived as a herdsman on Mt. Ida, was abandoned by him for Helen, and later refused to cure him of the wound that killed him. In art his Judgement is esp. popular, and is identifiable from the 7th cent.

Parmenidēs of Elea is said to have legislated for his native city and (*c*.450 BC) to have visited Athens in his sixty-fifth year (Plato *Parmenides*). His philosophical poem, in hexameters (see METRE, GREEK, 4(b)), survives in large fragments. It opens with the narration of a journey taken by the initiate poet-speaker, apparently from the world of daily life and light to a mysterious place where night and day cross paths and opposites are undivided. Here he is greeted by a goddess whose instruction forms the remainder of the work. She urges him to cease relying on ordinary beliefs and to 'judge by reason the very contentious refutation' of those beliefs that she offers. Her address attends closely to logical rigour and connection. The proem is suffused with religious language, and one might conjecture that an initiation in reason is being substituted for the perception-suffused initiations of religious cult.

Central to the goddess's teaching is the idea that thought and speech must have an object that is there to be talked or thought about. So, if something is sayable or thinkable, it must *be*: 'You cannot say or think that it is not.' On this basis, she concludes not only that nothingness or the non-existent cannot figure in our speech, but also that temporal change, internal qualitative variation, and even plurality are all unsayable and unthinkable—on the grounds that talk about all these will commit the speaker to making contrasts and entail the use of negative language. Thus, whatever can be talked or thought about must be 'without birth or death, whole, single-natured, unaltering, and complete'.

A subsidiary argument invokes an idea of sufficient reason to rule out cosmogony: if what is had a beginning in time, there must have been some reason for that beginning. But what reason could there be, if (by hypothesis) there was nothing there previously?

Having described the 'Way of Truth', the goddess then acquaints her pupil with the deceptive contents of mortal beliefs. The cosmogony that follows is not intended to have any degree of truth or reliability. It is presumably selected because it shows the fundamental error of mortals in its simplest form. The decision to 'name' two forms, light and night, commits mortals to contrastive negative characterizations.

Parmenides was a great philosophical pioneer, who turned away from the tradition of Ionian cosmogony to attempt something fundamentally different: a deduction of the character of what is from the requirements of thought and language. His views were developed by his followers Melissus and *Zeno (1). *Empedocles, *Anaxagoras, and *Democritus all felt the need to respond to his arguments in defending plurality and change, though they did so without addressing his fundamental concern about language and thought. The core of his argument thus remained untouched until *Plato's *Sophist*, in which the Eleatic Stranger proposes a new understanding of the relation between language and the world in order to break the strong grip of the argument of 'father Parmenides'.

Parmenion (*c*.400–330 BC), Macedonian noble, the most respected general of *Philip II. Active in senior command as early as 356, he headed the expeditionary force in Asia Minor (336) and eased *Alexander (2) the Great's accession by helping to remove his colleague Attalus, the new king's bitterest enemy. So he was the automatic choice as Alexander's second-in-command in Asia, and two of his sons had command of the Companion (see HETAIROI) cavalry and the hypaspists (*see* ALEXANDER (2) THE GREAT, 2). At the major battles (the *Granicus, Issus, and *Gaugamela) he controlled the Macedonian left and had an indispensable defensive role. There is a tradition of disagreement between Parmenion and his king which is in part fabrication, but there appears to have been a genuine divergence of views on the terminus for conquest in Asia. As a result Parmenion was detached with increasing frequency on independent missions, and in the summer of 330 he was deputed to escort the treasures of *Persepolis to Ecbatana, where he remained, gradually isolated as his

Macedonian troops rejoined Alexander in the east. When his son *Philotas was executed for alleged treason, he was murdered at the king's command (autumn 330). He had been a long-standing curb on the king's ambitions and was too dangerous to be left alive.

parody, Greek Parody entails imitation, but an imitation which is intended to be recognized as such and to amuse. By exaggerating distinctive features, it may simply invite ridicule and criticism of the original; or it may exploit the humour of incongruity, coupled with exaggeration for ease of recognition, by combining the language and style of the original with completely alien subject-matter. In both cases, but esp. where incongruity is intended to achieve its effect, the targeted original may be a whole genre of literature rather than an individual author. The parodies of Aeschylean and Euripidean lyrics (see AESCHYLUS; EURIPIDES; TRAGEDY, GREEK) in *Aristophanes' Frogs are outstanding examples of the parody of individuals, while there are very many passages of Aristophanes in which high tragic style, identifiable by vocabulary and metre, is combined with matter which is down-to-earth.

Parody of tragedy in Aristophanes is not confined to language; characteristic constituents of tragedy, such as the messenger-speech, are also parodied, and so are whole scenes from particular tragedies. Nor is tragedy the only target. *Plato's parodies are often on a much larger scale than those of the comic poets, and he shows great subtlety and judgement in sustaining the character of the originals without lapsing into absurdity. *Agathon's speech in his Symposium is a notable example; it is described as being in the style of *Gorgias, and we can compare it with what survives of Gorgias' work. The display speech of *Protagoras in Protagoras 320c–8d is obviously parody, but our limited acquaintance with Protagoras' own work makes assessment of its success difficult. Eryximachus' speech in Symposium parodies the grandiloquent generalizations of a type of quasi-scientific literature current in the age of the *sophists. The first part of the funeral speech in the Menexenus is certainly parody, but the point (and purpose) of transition from the humorous to the serious in that speech remains an enigma. See ASPASIA; EPITAPHIOS.

Paros, a large island in the central *Cyclades, its fine white marble prized by sculptors and masons from Archaic times. It was settled by

*Ionians in the 10th cent. BC. Parian prosperity and power are exemplified in the 7th cent. by the poetry of *Archilochus and the colonization of Thasos, and in the 6th by marble temples, massive fortifications, and its sculpture workshops. A notable 6th-cent. monument is the hero-shrine of Archilochus, where later the Parian Chronicle (a marble record, of which two sizeable fragments survive, of a medley of events in years from mythical times to 264/3 BC) and Life of Archilochus were inscribed. Successfully resisting *Miltiades' attempt to punish collaboration in 490, but subject to an indemnity after the battle of *Salamis, its high tribute of 16–18 talents under the Athenian empire (see DELIAN LEAGUE) shows continuing prosperity.

Parrhasius, famous painter, son and pupil of Euenor of Ephesus, later Athenian. He made designs for reliefs on the shield of *Phidias' Athena Promachus (before 450). He was arrogant and wore a purple cloak and a gold wreath. He painted a 'rose-fed' *Theseus, *Demos, 'Healing of Telephus', *Philoctetes, 'Feigned madness of *Odysseus'. Such pictures displayed the details of expression which he discusses with *Socrates in the Socratic memoirs of *Xenophon. He wrote on painting. He was famed for subtlety of outline. His gods and heroes became types for later artists; his drawings on parchment and wood were used by craftsmen (probably metal workers) in Pliny's time.

parricide (Lat. parricīdium) was the killing of a par, a close relative. Under the republic the convicted murderer of a close relative was drowned in the sea, tied up in a sack with a dog, cock, ape, and viper. In later legislation the penalty was differentiated according to the gravity of the act, but the death-penalty remained the normal sanction.

Parthenon The Parthenon was the temple of *Athena built on the highest part of the Acropolis at Athens south of the Archaic temple. The name is properly that of the west room, but is generally extended to the entire building. Athena's title Parthenos (virgin) is descriptive; her status is Polias, protector of the city. It was begun in 447 BC in the time of *Pericles, the temple and cult statue were dedicated in 438, but work continued, esp. on the pedimental sculptures, until 432. A temple had been begun on the site after Marathon (490) (see MARATHON, BATTLE OF), but work was abandoned on the approach of *Xerxes' invasion (480–479). What had been built was destroyed by the Persians when they captured the city.

The Periclean building adapts the foundations and platform of this earlier structure. It was built to house the gold and ivory statue by *Phidias, who must have been responsible for at least the design of its sculptural decoration; it is unlikely that he also directed the architectural design, which was determined more by the existing foundations than the statue it was to house.

The architect was *Ictinus together with *Callicrates. In the Parthenon the Doric *order is seen at its most perfect in proportions and in refined details, though there are some unusual features. The material is fine marble readily available from the quarries of Pentelicon a few miles NE of Athens and generally used in the important Athenian buildings of the Periclean period. The temple measures about 69.5 × 30.8 m. (228 × 101 ft.) on the top step. It has eight columns at the ends, and seventeen on the sides. The inner structure has a porch of six columns at each end. The larger east room had a two-tiered inner colonnade running not only along the sides but round the west end, behind the great cult statue; there were windows high to the sides of the east door. The smaller west room opened off the back porch, and had its roof supported by four Ionic columns; it served as a 'treasury'.

The sculpture was more elaborate, more unified in theme, and more relevant to the cult than in most temples. It was also more extensive: every metope is carved, while the porch colonnades have a continuous frieze, extended abnormally the entire length of the cella's outer walls. The metopes must have been made first, and then the frieze. The pediments were the latest addition. They showed, in the east, Athena newly sprung from the head of *Zeus, and in the west, the contest of *Poseidon and Athena for the land of Attica. The metopes, in high relief, showed mythical combats, on the south side, best preserved, Lapiths and *Centaurs, on the east, Gods and *Giants, on the west, Greeks and *Amazons, on the north—less certainly, since this side is poorly preserved—Trojan scenes (see HOMER; TROY). Some of these themes were echoed in the minor decoration of the cult statue. The frieze, in low relief, shows a procession evocative of a *Panathenaic procession. It may depict or honour the young Athenian citizens who died at Marathon. A general allusion on these lines is certain. The whole temple, like its predecessor, is best interpreted as a thank-offering (after a false start) for the final, successful outcome of the *Persian Wars, and it is clear that the reliefs allude to this, to the glorification of the Greek, and specifically Athenian, contribution to the victory.

The temple was later converted into a church, dedicated to the Virgin, and then a mosque. It remained almost intact, though reroofed, until 1687, when a Turkish powder-magazine in it was exploded by the besieging Venetians. Earlier reconstruction work has been dismantled, and a thorough programme of conservation is being carried out, which has led to the identification of many of the fallen fragments. See also NATIONALISM.

Parthia, Parthians The people whom Greeks and Romans called Parthians were originally members of a semi-nomadic confederacy east of the Caspian. Their Greek name is derived from the *Achaemenid and then *Seleucid *satrapy called Parthia, which they occupied, traditionally in 247 BC, the year with which the Parthian ('Arsacid') era begins; later the *Arsacids ruled from the *Euphrates to the Indus, with Ctesiphon as their main residence. The territorial gains under Mithradates I and II not only changed their former eastern Iranian empire into an ethnically, politically, socially, and culturally diverse one needing new forms of administration, but also deeply influenced the relationship between the Parthian aristocracy and the rulers. It was the conflict between kings and nobles which shaped later history and often allowed Rome to intervene in Parthian affairs. Although we hear of large estates of Parthian aristocrats in the conquered parts of the empire, we do not know much about how their rights of possession and use were transferred to, and retained by them. Ambitious members of the great Parthian families (Suren, Karin, Gev and others), governors, petty and 'vassal' kings temporarily gained total or limited independence. Parthian rule was finally (AD 224) brought to an end by local dynasts from Istakhr (see SASANIDS).

The structure of Parthian society and the titulature of their élite are best known from the administrative documents from Nisa, the Sasanid inscriptions of the 3rd cent. AD, and the classical reports of Parthian warfare. They distinguish between a higher and a lower nobility and their dependants. Apart from these groups we find a middle stratum of artists, traders, doctors, bards, and other specialists and the non-Iranian native population of the conquered territories. In warfare the Parthians were famous for their mailed cavalry (cataphracts) and their horse archers, and they bred the Nisaean horses which were known even in China. They seem to have adopted the Zoroastrian cult of fire and its calendar (see ZOROASTER), but tolerated every other religion. The Parthians played an important role as middlemen in the trade between China, India, and Syria. Their art—a revived Iranian art, which absorbed both Mesopotamian and Greek elements—spread far.

Pasion (d. 370/69 BC) was the richest banker and manufacturer of his time in Athens (see BANKS). He began his career as a slave with a banking firm in *Piraeus, was made a freedman and later acquired ownership of the bank. He had two sons, *Apollodorus (1) and Pasicles. He later became an Athenian citizen, having spent lavishly on donations to the city. Information about his business activities derives from a speech written in the 390s for a disgruntled client (see Isocrates 17), and from the later speeches of Apollodorus (see esp. Demosthenes 36, 45, 46). He left real estate of 20 talents and outstanding loans of almost 40.

pastoral poetry, Greek For as long as peasants have tended their flocks and herds on grazing lands away from the village, song and music (esp. that of the pipe (*syrinx*), which is easily cut, fashioned and carried) have served as an anodyne against rustic tedium and brutality. This is esp. true of the goatherd, who ranges furthest into the wilderness of *Pan in search of shrubs on which only his omnivorous charges will browse; and in these lonely wastes it is natural that two herdsmen whose paths cross should not only perform in each other's company but that their songs should be competitive. This real-world situation provided the foundation upon which a literary *genre was established by *Theocritus in the 3rd cent. BC and developed by his followers in Hellenistic Greece, Rome, and the post-Renaissance world.

Two piping herdsmen are among the figures depicted on the Shield of Achilles (in bk. 18 of *Homer's *Iliad*), and Eumaeus the swineherd in the *Odyssey* reflects early literary interest in peasant characterization; even the *Cyclops Polyphemus, communing with his ram, arouses a moment of sympathy which will later stimulate his re-creation as a youthful lover. *Stesichorus is credited by *Aelian with having been the first to sing of the local bucolic hero *Daphnis, back in the 6th cent. But the conditions needed for pastoral themes to generate a genre were not met until literary life became concentrated in Hellenistic cities, alienated from the villages in which so many Greek cultural traditions had developed. One thread in the cultural amalgam of the 3rd cent. is an understandable nostalgia for the simpler world once dominated by Daphnis, Pan, *Priapus, and the *nymphs; a world now largely vanished but whose continued existence could at least be fantasized in the mountains of *Magna Graecia and Arcadia.

The basic form elaborated by Theocritus seems to have been essentially agonistic (see above). Theocritus 5 provides the clearest example. Two peasants meet; one proposes a contest; stakes are wagered, and a judge is sought; jockeying for the most favourable ground takes place; and after some preliminary boasting and badinage, each attempting to unsettle the other, the competition begins. This takes the form of an alternating sequence of couplets or quatrains in which the first singer, as proposer of each subject, has an inbuilt advantage, while the respondent must follow suit and if possible cap each theme. This goes some way to offset the fact that the initiator of the challenge—in this case, Lacon—has chosen the time and place. In poem 5, victory is suddenly and confidently claimed by Comatas, and immediately confirmed by the judge. Apparently, the first singer to contradict a previous statement is the loser. There is thus a limiting factor to the bucolic agon, for the longer it goes on the harder it gets.

Theocritus realized the possibilities offered by this half-crude, half-sophisticated model to the new style of self-conscious urban literature. His chosen form is artificial from the start; the Doric *dialect may impart a rustic flavour, but the metre is the Homeric *hexameter. Each poem works its own elegant variation on the fundamental pattern. The coarse duels of the grubby, garlic-chewing rustics are transmuted into allusive mandarin elegance, without ever quite pulling free of their roots in the vigorous Sicilian soil. The literary conventions which lead on to *Virgil, Milton, and Marie-Antoinette are all there.

pastoral poetry, Latin Among Latin pastoralists *Virgil stands supreme. He extended the boundaries of the genre which he had inherited from *Theocritus, whose inspiration he acknowledges, and upon whom he draws in all his *Eclogues, except 4 and 6, in which the poet strives to lift pastoral to a higher plane (see 4. 1, 'Sicilian Muses, let us sing a somewhat grander strain'). Virgil's originality is proclaimed at the start of the *Eclogue*-book. Whereas Theocritus had kept pastoral and court poems distinct, contemporary politics and pastoral are blended in the first *Eclogue*, which describes, in the persons of Meliboeus and Tityrus, the effects on the Italian countryside of the triumviral dispossessions of the late 40s BC (see TRIUMVIRI; PROSCRIPTION). So, the pastoral world may be said to exist no longer in isolation, but to suffer encroachments which disrupt the shepherds' *ōtium* ('tranquil existence').

Virgil also created the Arcadian setting, which was to prove so influential in European pastoral. But references to Arcadia in the *Eclogues* are actually few, and are combined with features of Italian topography. The precise import of Arcadia is disputed. It seems best to regard it as a lonely setting for lovers' plaints and for song (at which the Arcadians excelled). Both topics are central to pastoral. It is probably to the former of these that *Horace's description of the *Eclogues*, *molle atque facētum* ('*tender* and charming') refers, though both adjectives have a stylistic connotation as well. The *Eclogues* are self-reflexive, experimental, and challenging, but none of the authors who follow Virgil can rival him in complexity or suggestiveness.

paterfamiliās See PATRIA POTESTAS.

Pater Patriae ('Father of the Fatherland'), the title conferred on *Cicero for his action against the Catilinarian conspirators (see SERGIUS CATILINA), on *Caesar after the battle of Munda, and on Augustus in 2 BC (when he had reached the age of 60; see VALERIUS MESSALLA CORVINUS, MARCUS), in a gesture of unanimity by the Roman community, coinciding with the dedication of the *forum Augustum. *Tiberius never accepted the title, but after a show of refusal the later emperors took it if they lived long enough. The title suggested the protecting but coercive authority of the *paterfamiliās*.

pathology As defined in medical handbooks from at least AD 150 onwards, pathology was that part of medicine concerned with the causes of *disease. It went beyond the observation and classification implicit in *diagnosis to an identification of what might be invisible to the senses. From seeing, smelling, hearing, and touching the patient, and occasionally even tasting sweat or urine, the true physician could identify the cause of the illness, and work to eliminate or alleviate it. While this skill was used primarily in treatment, doctors might be called upon to testify in a lawcourt.

The investigation of the causes of illness was difficult in a pre-technological age. Although Herophilus is said to have invented a clock to time the pulse, and *Galen mentions urine being heated for examination, these are rare exceptions to what were otherwise impressionistic and qualitative judgements. In such circumstances establishing a cause of illness might be the mark of the truly distinguished medical expert or, as the Empiricist physicians argued, a waste of time. There was little agreement as to what these causes might be, as well as overlapping schemes of explanation.

For some conditions, esp. *plague, stroke, epilepsy, and some skin disfigurements like leprosy, divine punishment was suspected. An insult to a god or goddess, or, acc. to some Jewish and Christian authors, an individual's generally sinful behaviour, had called down physical retribution. A religious cause thus demanded, at least in part, a religious remedy.

Below the gods lay the heavens. For some, illness was determined by one's stars—hence the frequent mention of medical horoscopes. More sceptical writers like Galen preferred to think of *climate and seasons, each with their own particular air and mirroring in their ordered progression the cycle of remissions and relapses of febrile diseases like malaria, with their mathematically predictable 'critical days'. The importance of good air had been argued in the Hippocratic *Airs, Waters, and Places* (see HIPPOCRATES), which asserted a paramount role for environment in disease and assigned physical and moral peculiarities of the Scythians or Libyans to the effects of climate and geography. Many writers thought that the air itself became polluted, or miasmatic, and hence brought about epidemic diseases or plagues, but there was little agreement over what this *pollution was.

That those who had most to do with the sick were most likely to fall ill themselves was recognized by *Thucydides (2) in his account of the plague of Athens—he also noticed that those, like himself, who had recovered from one attack were less likely to fall ill of it again.

Hippocrates had reputedly considered disease the result of an imbalance of *humours. The idea of imbalance was shared by many physicians, even though there was little agreement on precisely what was out of balance. For some, it was the body's elements; for others its humours.

patria potestās was the power of a Roman male ascendant, normally father or grandfather (*paterfamiliās*), over descendants through males, provided that his marriage was valid in Roman law (see MARRIAGE LAW, *Roman*), and over adopted children. This power was seen by lawyers as practically unique to Roman citizens. Any male who became legally independent by being freed from *patria potestas* became a *paterfamilias*, even if he were a child too young to be a father. There was no comparable power held by women. It was not terminated on a child's arrival at any age of majority, but usually by the death or voluntary decision of the *paterfamilias*. Thus a woman might leave *patria potestas* if her *paterfamilias* transferred her into the control of a husband, *manus. *Adoption or becoming the *priest of *Jupiter (*flamen Dialis* (see FLAMINES)) or a *Vestal or the *exile of either party ended *patria potestas*; becoming a prisoner of war or the father's insanity suspended it. If a son in (i.e. under) his father's power married and his wife entered his marital power, the daughter-in-law was in his father's power, as were their subsequent children. Sons and daughters in power owned no property, though they might be allowed to administer property held by permission of the *paterfamilias*: this was called *peculium*. Anything they acquired (as earnings, by gift or bequest, etc.) belonged in law to the father. Action for delict by a child in power had to be brought against the father. Father's consent was necessary for the marriage of sons and daughters in power, and he might bring about a divorce. The *paterfamilias* also had power of life and death over children. This was exercised soon after birth, when a father chose to acknowledge and rear a child or not to do so. Legends and some accounts from the historic period show *patrēsfamilias* executing, banishing, or disowning adult children. Private judicial action, normally on the advice of a council, shows the exercise of *patria potestas*; execution of traitorous or insubordinate sons by public officials exemplifies paternal severity in a public role. Sons are portrayed as liable to punishment chiefly for offences against the state, daughters for unchastity. The Augustan adultery law (see AUGUSTUS) gave *patresfamilias* specific rights (with strict provisos) to kill on the spot adulterous daughters taken in the act. In historic times, paternal monopoly of control of property will have been more relevant to most sons in power than the father's theoretical capital jurisdiction. But the *peculium* might in practice be left in a child's control. Relatively low expectation of life will have meant that many fathers died before their children reached full adulthood. Those who gained independence by emerging from *patria potestas* or *manus* on the death of the *paterfamilias*, on his intestacy divided his property equally. If he made a will, he could make his own decisions, but children had a strong moral claim, and anyone who would become independent of *patria potestas* on the father's death had to be formally disinherited if not named heir and executor. *Patria potestas* remained a living institution throughout the classical period and was still important under Justinian (see JUSTINIAN'S CODIFICATION), while the comparable *manus* atrophied. Its continued relevance in changing times was probably more prominent in the minds of legal theorists than in those of ordinary fathers and children (Marcus *Tullius Cicero (1) and his brother Quintus *Tullius Cicero fail to invoke it when their teenage sons pose problems).

patricians formed a privileged class of Roman citizens. The word is probably connected with *patrēs* ('Fathers'), a formal collective term for patrician senators (see SENATE). In the republican period patrician status could be obtained only by birth.

One striking patrician prerogative was their control of affairs during an interregnum. Only a patrician could hold the office of *interrex* ('between-king'), evidently a relic of the regal period (see REX). The patricians may have chosen the king, whereas the king could not himself be a patrician. This would explain both the origin of patrician power and the fact that most of the kings were in some sense outsiders (many of them, indeed, foreigners).

The patricians monopolized all the important priesthoods, and they were probably a group defined by religious prerogatives. The nature of their political power is, by contrast, much less certain. Membership of the senate was not confined to patricians, since the senators were formally known as 'Fathers and Conscripts' of whom only the former were patricians (the *patrum auctoritas* was confined to them). The *Fasti suggest that in the earliest decades of the republic not all *consuls were patricians. The patrician monopoly of political office developed gradually during the 5th cent., and was successfully challenged in the 4th by the increasingly powerful *plebs*.

Although by 300 BC the patricians had lost their monopoly of office and of the major priestly colleges, they continued to exercise power out of all proportion to their numbers. Until 172 one of the two consuls was always a patrician, and they continued to hold half the places in the major priestly colleges as of right. Other priesthoods, such as the *flamines maiores* and the *Salii, remained exclusively patrician.

As an aristocracy of birth, the patriciate was unable to reproduce itself, and patrician numbers gradually declined. Of around 50 patrician clans that are known in the 5th cent., only fourteen survived at the end of the republic. *Caesar and *Octavian were given the right to create new patricians. Later emperors used their censorial powers to confer patrician status on favoured individuals, who then passed it on to their descendants.

patrios politeia, 'ancestral constitution (or way of life)', slogan apparently used in the late 5th cent. BC at Athens by proponents of *oligarchy, as a reassuring but fraudulent way of justifying constitutional change. The fraud lay in the implied claim that earlier reformers like *Solon and *Cleisthenes (2) had denied full citizen rights (see CITIZENSHIP, GREEK) to *thetes, confining them to *hoplites (*zeugitai) and above. Such general nostalgia for the imagined world of Solon and Cleisthenes is found in the 4th cent., and some of the tradition about the 5th cent. may reflect 4th-cent. arguments.

patronage, literary

Greek Literary patronage in Greece is associated chiefly with autocratic rulers (though in Classical Athens the *choregia was a kind of democratization of the patronage principle). The tyrants of Corinth, Pisistratid Athens, Samos, and the Greek cities of Sicily were notable examples, patronizing such writers as *Arion, *Alcman, *Anacreon, *Pindar, *Simonides, and *Bacchylides. See TYRANNY and the tyrants there listed. Later *Archelaus of Macedon collected at his court a coterie which included *Agathon, *Timotheus, and *Euripides. Later still the Hellenistic monarchs were often literary patrons, esp. the Ptolemies (see PTOLEMY (1)), who established and maintained at *Alexandria the *Museum and *Library.

Roman In Rome, it was not until the 1st cent. BC that literary texts began to circulate through the book trade, and this was never the only means of publication. Normally, an author received no money from booksellers. Much of the circulation of contemporary texts took place through the private dispatch of copies or the organization of *recitations, through the network of social relations which connected the élite of Rome, of Italy, and eventually of the provinces: an élite which was almost the sole public for literary production. So, writers needed the support of leading members of this élite, both materially if they were not themselves rich and more generally to enable them to become well known and appreciated. Writers might include the name of their patron in a work as a dedicatee (see DEDICATIONS, LITERARY), or they could celebrate the achievements of the patron or his family in epic poems or tragedies (*praetextae*; see FABULA) or compose occasional poems on various aspects of the patron's public or private life. To an extent patronage did lead to courtly literature, esp. in the imperial period, but as a system which brought writers into relation with the social and political élite, it may also be seen as forcing writers to confront important political and civic themes, without necessarily cramping their inspiration. Before the 1st cent. BC., writing, excepting historiography and oratory, was considered the activity of artisans. Theatrical pieces were commissioned by the city, and their authors received payment for them from the *aediles in charge of the performances: writers for the theatre continued in later periods also to be the only authors to get paid for their work. But writers also often entered into private relationships with one or more leading families interested in their work, sometimes as teachers. Through the support of these families they might obtain their freedom (*Livius Andronicus, *Terence; see FREEDMEN) or Roman *citizenship (*Ennius) and also probably help with getting their plays performed. *Naevius, Ennius, *Pacuvius, and *Accius wrote *praetextae* celebrating the families of their patrons, and Ennius did the same with his patrons in his *Annals*. Ennius also presents for the first time, as *Cicero noted with distaste, the figure of the poet who accompanies his patron on a military expedition in order to create a cultured environment and to be better able to celebrate his exploits. Literary patronage was already becoming an ostentatious tool that leading Roman politicians could use for their own ends, rather than a means of support for public benefactors. The great Roman families from the 2nd cent. on welcomed Greek intellectuals more and more warmly as clients to help them with their studies (now a sign of prestige), look after their rich *libraries, and commemorate them in learned works or celebrate them in verse. But as time went on, Latin literary production became separated from its craftsman associations: most of what we have from the 2nd cent. on is the work of senators, or more often of equestrians and members of well-off provincial families who through talent or family connections came to participate in the life of the Roman élite but were not involved in the normal military and political careers of that élite. Patronage by the great Roman families, which by the 1st cent. BC had made Rome a centre of attraction for Greek as well as Roman intellectuals, reached a peak in the triumviral period and the first years of Augustus' principate, when figures like *Asinius Pollio (patron of *Horace and *Virgil, founder of the first public *library in Rome, *Valerius Messalla Corvinus (patron of *Tibullus, *Ovid, and others), and *Maecenas gathered round them the greatest intellectual figures of the period and gave them both economic support and cultural stimulus. Maecenas esp., in his role as both close ally of Augustus and amateur of new poetry, gave to Virgil, Horace, *Propertius, and others personal friendship and generous financial support. The concentration of power in a single person made the patronage of the *princeps* himself a sort of state patronage: this was a novelty in Rome, but Augustus used it more and more directly as time went on, esp. after Maecenas faded from power *c*.20 BC and the regime became more rigid. In the imperial period, the ostentatious patronage of those figures who had competed for power at the end of the republic no longer had any point. The ultimate source of all patronage was the emperor, and this was true also of literary patronage. Some emperors were not interested in letters, but others employed patronage widely to make poetry an instrument of propaganda and courtly celebration, as in the case of *Nero and *Domitian, both of whom gave a powerful impetus to literature in their reigns. Nero introduced into Rome the Greek custom of literary contests (see AGONES), taken up again later by Domitian, and this gave Rome for the first time an official occasion for the publication of literary works and a means of public support for writers. *Pliny the Younger offers in his letters an optimistic portrait of imperial literary patronage, but *Juvenal presents a Rome inhabited by a host of starving writers in search of support from greedy and cruel patrons. *Martial also in part offers a more pessimistic picture, but while he laments that Rome no longer contains a Maecenas willing to give a poor poet the leisure to pursue his art, he also shows throughout his verse how the emperor and private patrons alike provided gifts and favours, sometimes considerable, even to a poet like himself writing within the minor genre of epigram. In fact, it would have been impossible to obtain regular financial support solely from the free exercise of literature—in this sense Juvenal's picture is correct. But literary talent could provide access to the social élite, and thus to the benefits that the friendship of the great could provide, from minor gifts to lucrative positions in private or public service. This sort of direct or indirect support could still enable a man like Martial to devote himself full time to literature. *See also* CLIENS; PATRONUS.

patronage, non-literary Greek and Roman society were both heavily stratified, and many forms of dependence tied people to their superiors in *wealth, power and *status. (Classical Athens was perhaps untypical, though see PATRONAGE, LITERARY, *Greek* for the *choregia.)

The letters of *Cicero and *Pliny the Younger combine with the legal evidence and epigraphy to give a more complete picture of patronage in the Roman world. In addition, the relationship between *patronus* and *cliens* among Roman citizens was recognized as being distinctive.

Two further forms of patronage complicate the picture. The first is the relationship of the master to a slave or former slave, which had precise definition in Roman law, and which entailed duties for *freedmen. The second is the relationship of Roman leaders to whole communities either in Italy or the provinces, and their protection of influential foreigners, for whom they might even obtain the Roman *citizenship. This relationship derived from the circumstances of Rome's growth as an imperial power, and drew on the behaviour of Hellenistic kings and their families. Augustus and his successors combined enormous households and very numerous dependants with an unsurpassed range of opportunities for bestowing favours of this second sort on communities and individuals all over the inhabited world.

Cicero's patronage is our most systematic guide to the late republican practice. He acquired relations with communities in southern Italy on his way to Sicily as quaestor; in the troubles of 63, retainers from three Italian towns gave him their physical support; around his villa at *Pompeii most of the towns were in his *clientela*; and his governorship in Cilicia gave him a special relationship with the whole of *Cyprus. All these places could count on Cicero for 'recommendation': a way into the personal politics of Rome, and in particular legal guidance and support. *Civitates* (see CIVITAS) were a natural object of this kind of patronage, but *collēgia* acquired patrons in this way too (see CLUBS, ROMAN).

Cicero provides us with an insight into the importance of patronage. Chains of this sort of relationship offered a way of dealing with the scale of ancient society: with the mechanics of representing, and making decisions concerning the rival interests of, either very numerous individuals in a large community, or thousands of communities in a world-empire. It thus offered a sort of brokerage, and promoted both active communication and reciprocal exchanges of information and esteem, and served to retain a real political role for patrons under a system in which their constitutional political position had been greatly weakened by the advent of the imperial system. Recommendation, moreover, could work only if there were agreed principles of comparison and standards of assessment, the maintenance of which fostered cultural cohesion. Finally, the system reflected and maintained change in hierarchic order, since the effectiveness of chains of influence varied, and the fortunes of the client with them. All of these effects ultimately worked in favour of social stability.

patrōnus, at Rome, was a man who gave assistance and protection to another person, Roman or non-Roman, who thereby became his client. In return clients gave their patrons respect, deference and services, which included personal attendance and political support. The social prestige and political influence of a Roman noble (see NOBILES) was made evident by the size and standing of his clientele, and competition for political office among the republican élite was partly a matter of obtaining the support of other powerful individuals and their personal followings. Under the empire patronage was the means by which imperial appointments were dispensed, and was fundamental to the working of the administration (see further CLIENS).

A special type of patronage (which was clearly defined by law) was exercised by a slave-owner over his *freedmen. He retained a certain amount of domestic jurisdiction over them and inherited their property if they died childless or intestate. Patrons and freedmen were often buried together, and inscriptions (esp. from the 2nd cent. AD onwards) suggest that genuine feelings of friendship often existed between them.

Under the later republic patrons also helped litigants by appearing in court to speak on their behalf (*advocāti*; see ADVOCACY). This practice became increasingly professionalized, as skilled orators (such as Cicero) were rewarded for their support in ways that circumvented a law of 204 BC that forbade the payment of fees to patrons for such services.

Roman generals assumed a diffused patronage over peoples conquered by them, and this patronage was transmitted to their descendants. The Claudii Marcelli undertook to look after the interests of Sicily (conquered in 210 BC by *Claudius Marcellus (1)). The patronage of *Pompey extended widely over the empire; in 83 he raised three legions of clients in his home region of Picenum, and his son Sextus *Pompeius could get help in Spain and Asia from his family's clients. It is probable that the emperors too exercised a patronage of this type over the provinces.

A similar form of patronage, which became common under the empire, originated in the action of Roman municipalities, which appointed one or more influential Romans to defend their interests in Rome and to provide them with personal access to the emperor. During the same period many *collēgia* (see CLUBS, ROMAN) appointed leading men as their patrons in the same way as the municipalities.

See PATRONAGE, NON-LITERARY.

patronymics See NAMES, PERSONAL, GREEK and ROMAN.

Paul, St St Paul, a Roman citizen from Tarsus, was a convert (see CONVERSION) from Pharisaic to Messianic Judaism as a result of a mystical experience (Galatians 1: 12 and 16) when he believed himself called to be the divine agent by whom the biblical promises about the *eschatological ingathering of the Gentiles would be fulfilled. That transference of allegiance led him to renounce his previous religious affiliations, even though the form of his religion remains in continuity with apocalyptic Judaism; see RELIGION, JEWISH. We know him as the result of letters which he wrote over a period of about ten years to maintain communities of Jews and Gentiles in Rome and several other urban centres in a pattern of religion which enjoined faithfulness to Jesus Christ as the determining factor in the understanding of the Mosaic Law. This subordination of the Law inevitably led to conflict with Jewish and Christian opponents who suspected him of antinomianism and apostasy. His doctrine of justification by faith was hammered out as a way of explaining his position in relation to the Jewish Law. He commended Christianity as a religion which was both the fulfilment of the Jewish tradition and also the negation of central precepts like food laws and circumcision, though he was emphatic in his rejection of idolatry. In his letters we have clear evidence of the emergence of identifiable Christian communities separate from Judaism with a loose adherence to the Jewish tradition as interpreted by Paul. At the end of his life he organized a financial offering for the poor in Jerusalem from the Gentile churches he had founded. Acc. to *Acts, his journey to Jerusalem with this collection preceded his journey to Rome, where later Christian tradition suggests that he died in the Neronian persecution (64). The letters in the NT which are widely assumed to be authentic are Romans, 1 and 2 Corinthians, Galatians, Philippians, 1 Thessalonians, and Philemon, and possibly Colossians and 2 Thessalonians. Ephesians, and 1 and 2 Timothy and Titus are probably pseudonymous. This last group of documents indicates the direction of the Pauline tradition after the apostle's death, when accredited teachers began to be ordained to ensure the preservation of the apostolic traditions and institutions in the face of emerging *gnosticism and antinomianism. See also CHRISTIANITY.

Paulus, lawyer. See IŪLIUS PAULUS.

Pausanias (1), son of the Agiad regent Cleombrotus (d. 480 BC), and nephew of *Leonidas. As regent for Pleistarchus, he commanded the combined Greek land forces at *Plataea in 479, while his Eurypontid co-king *Leotychidas assumed the overall command at sea. He immodestly ascribed the Greek victory to his leadership, thereby earning a reminder of his mortality from *Simonides and a rebuke from the Spartan authorities. Nevertheless in 478 he was placed in command of an allied 'Hellenic League' fleet and captured *Byzantium, but his arrogant behaviour and possibly treasonable negotiations with the Persian enemy provoked a mutiny that redounded to the benefit of Athens. Recalled to Sparta for trial on this charge, he escaped conviction and returned to Byzantium, apparently still on official business. Expelled in c.475 by *Cimon, leader of the new Athenian sea-league (see DELIAN LEAGUE), he removed to *Troas where he was believed to be continuing to negotiate with Persia on his own behalf. He

was again recalled to Sparta and tried c.470, but again acquitted. His enemies had more success with accusations of complicity with a *helot uprising and an alleged promise of citizenship to helot rebels. To escape arrest by the *ephors, he took refuge in a room in the temple of Athena on the Spartan acropolis, where he was left to starve; but shortly before he died, he was removed from the temple to avoid *pollution. Later, the Spartans made reparations with the erection of two statues and the founding of a hero-shrine in his (and Leonidas') honour; see HERO-CULT.

Pausanias (2), grandson of *Pausanias (1), Agiad king of Sparta 445–426 and 409–395 BC: his first reign was as a minor during the temporary deposition of his father Pleistoanax. In 403 he undermined *Lysander's dominance in Athens by obtaining command of a *Peloponnesian League expedition against the democratic resistance at *Piraeus, promoting reconciliation between them and the Three Thousand in Athens, and securing a treaty which restored democracy and brought Athens into Sparta's alliance. Back in Sparta he was prosecuted but acquitted. In 395 his army arrived at Haliartus after Lysander's defeat and retired without battle, partly due to Athenian military opposition. Sentenced to death, he fled to Tegea. In exile he continued to oppose his enemies in Sparta. He wrote a pamphlet which seemingly accused his enemies of violating traditional Lycurgan laws and advocated abolition of the ephorate. The pamphlet probably disseminated much basic documentation about Sparta, such as the 'Great Rhetra', but also contributed significantly to the distorted idealization of her society, the 'Spartan mirage'.

Pausanias (3), from Magnesia by Mt. Sipylus (?) (fl. c. AD 150), wrote an extant *Description of Greece* claiming to describe 'all things Greek'; in fact limited essentially to the province of *Achaia with the omission of Aetolia and the islands. Contents: 1. Attica, Megara; 2. Argolis etc.; 3. Laconia; 4. Messenia; 5–6. Elis, Olympia; 7. Achaea; 8. Arcadia; 9. Boeotia; 10. Phocis, Delphi.

His chief concern was with the monuments (esp. sculpture and painting) of the Archaic and Classical periods, along with their historical contexts, and the sacred (cults, rituals, beliefs), of which he had a profound sense. His work is organized as a tour of the *poleis* and extra-urban sanctuaries of Achaia, with some interest in topography, but little in the intervening countryside. His concern for objects after 150 BC is slight, although contemporary monuments attracted his attention, esp. the benefactions of *Hadrian. He wrote from *autopsy, and his accuracy (in spite of demonstrable muddles) has been confirmed by excavation. Although his approach was personal, his admiration for old Greece (Athens, Sparta, Delphi, and Olympia figure prominently) and its great patriots belongs to the archaizing enthusiasm for the Greek motherland fanned by the *Second Sophistic and Hadrian's Panhellenion, which attracted many overseas (esp. Asian) Greeks to Antonine Achaia; presumably Pausanias wrote partly with them in mind.

Pax, the personification of (political) peace. Scarcely heard of before Augustus, she comes (as Pax Augusta) to represent one of the main factors which made the imperial government both strong and popular, the maintenance of quiet at home and abroad (acc. to Tacitus, Augustus 'seduced everyone with the sweetness of peace'). The most famous monuments of the cult were the *Ara Pacis Augustae and the Flavian *templum Pacis, dedicated AD 75.

pay, political See DEMOCRACY, ATHENIAN, 2; EKKLESIA; LAW AND PROCEDURE, ATHENIAN, 2; PERICLES.

peace See JANUS; LIBATIONS; PAX; WARFARE, ATTITUDES TO (GREEK AND HELLENISTIC).

peasants are like postholes: it is easier to see where they ought to have been in the classical world than where they actually were. By 'peasants' most scholars have meant small-scale, low-status cultivators, whether free, tenant, or otherwise dependent, farming at subsistence level. Such people left little trace on the historical or archaeological record. Finds of modest farmsteads in archaeological survey or excavation (see ARCHAEOLOGY, CLASSICAL) can rarely be placed on the socio-economic scale with any certainty. Our suppositions are based largely on indirect evidence.

Much of the literary evidence is anecdotal, depicting the peasant as a 'type', e.g. Dicaeopolis in Aristophanes' *Acharnians*. Characters sometimes identified as 'peasants' (e.g. *Hesiod) are difficult to place in socio-economic terms, but are highly unlikely to be peasants. The peasant eventually becomes an 'ideal type' in classical literature, redolent of wholesome, simple, 'old-time' ideals. The peasant ethos of self-sufficiency appealed to élite classical writers as a moral ideal, surfacing often in treatises on farming. Peasants and similar types were romanticized, notably in the *pastoral poetry of the Hellenistic period.

It is generally assumed that in Athens peasants composed the bulk of the citizen population, but though many Athenians owned small amounts of land, the bulk of the acreage was held by the rich. To what extent the peasantry co-operated or could be mobilized as a political force is much debated.

Our view of the peasantry of republican and imperial Rome is equally blurred. Though ancient writers bemoaned the demise of small-scale cultivators in the countryside, recent studies have treated these complaints more as a rhetorical position than reality. The status of Roman 'peasants' is unclear and probably varied regionally. Many may have been tenants of or similarly dependent on the wealthy élite. The place of veterans' allotments and small-town market-centres in the social demography of the Italian countryside has also been much debated. Only in Egypt, where there are tax-collection documents surviving from the Ptolemaic and Roman periods, are very small-scale cultivators, often tenants, recorded. Though 'peasant values' were an important ideal in Roman thought, we can only guess at the political impact of 'real' peasants.

pecūlium Persons under *patria potestās could not own property, but, while technically having ownership, a father could allow his son, and a master his slave, to administer certain assets. These assets were known as *peculium* and might be extensive, including money, goods, land and slaves. In practice the assets were regarded as belonging to the son or slave, and a slave given his liberty on condition that he paid a sum of money could use his *peculium* to fulfil the condition. Much commercial and financial activity was conducted by slaves with their *peculium*.

pederasty See HOMOSEXUALITY.

Pedius, Quintus, son of an *equestrian and of Iulia, *Caesar's elder sister, served as Caesar's *legate in Gaul (58–56 BC?) and supported him in 49. Praetor 48, he suppressed the rising of *Annius Milo. In 46 he and Fabius Maximus commanded Caesar's forces in Spain; in 45 they took part in the campaign of Munda and were allowed to triumph. In 44 Pedius inherited one-eighth of Caesar's estate but was induced by

*Octavian to place it at his disposal. In 43 he became consul with him, carried a law providing for the trial of Caesar's murderers, and was left in charge of the city during Octavian's negotiations with Marcus *Antonius (Mark Antony) and *Aemilius Lepidus (2) at Bononia. Ordered to initiate the *proscriptions, he obeyed but died of anxiety over his task and the future.

Pēleus, in myth, son of *Aeacus, king of *Aegina. He and *Telamon killed their half-brother, at which their father *exiled them both, and Peleus went to Phthia where he was purified (see PURIFICATION, GREEK) by Eurytion, and married his daughter Antigone. But at the Calydonian boar-hunt (see ATALANTA; MELEAGER (1)) he accidentally killed Eurytion and was again exiled. This time he reached Iolcus, where Acastus son of *Pelias purified him, and he took part in Pelias' funeral games, in which he wrestled unsuccessfully with Atalanta. But Astydamia, Acastus' wife, fell in love with him; and when he refused her advances, she sent a lying message to Antigone that Peleus was about to marry Acastus' daughter. Antigone hanged herself. Astydamia then lied to Acastus that Peleus had tried to rape her. Acastus, unwilling to kill the man whom he had purified, instead took him hunting on Mt. *Pelion and hid his sword while he slept, thus leaving him defenceless against the *Centaurs. Either the gods sent Peleus a knife or Chiron gave him back his own sword. So he escaped, and took vengeance on Astydamia by capturing Iolcus and cutting her to pieces. He was given the extraordinary privilege of marriage to the goddess *Thetis, though he had to win her by wrestling with her while she changed into many different shapes. The gods came to their wedding-feast and brought gifts. But Thetis left Peleus because he interfered when she tried to make their son *Achilles immortal by burning away his mortality. In old age Peleus was alone and afflicted, but finally in death was reunited with Thetis and made immortal.

His wrestling at the funeral games for Pelias, his wrestling with Thetis, their wedding, and his bringing the infant Achilles to be brought up by Chiron, are favourite subjects in 6th- and 5th-cent. art.

Pĕlias, in myth, son of Tyro and *Poseidon and father of *Alcestis. *Hesiod portrays him as an evil man; when king of Iolcus he devised the expedition for the Golden Fleece to rid himself of *Jason (1)'s rightful claims to his throne.

After the expedition Jason and *Medea persuaded his daughters to cut him up so that Medea could rejuvenate him by boiling; thus did *Hera punish him for neglecting to honour her. The funeral games in his honour were a famous subject for Archaic epic and vase-painting.

Peloponnese/Peloponnesus, the large penninsula of south mainland Greece, joined to *Attice and *Boeotia by the Isthmus of *Corinth. It is a mountainous area with a complex topography. For many years the hegemony of Sparta promoted a regional solidarity, though it was never complete.

Peloponnesian League, the earliest known and longest-lasting Greek offensive and defensive *alliance. The name is modern and inaccurate, since the alliance was neither all and only Peloponnesian nor a league (the members were not all allied to each other, and when no League war was in progress, members were free to carry on separate wars even with other members); the usual ancient name was 'the Lacedaemonians (Spartans) and their allies'. In the 6th cent. Sparta used personal ties of *xenia* (see FRIENDSHIP, RITUALIZED) to negotiate treaties of alliance with Peloponnesian cities, the first being with either Tegea or *Elis. Allies swore to have the same friends and enemies as Sparta, and to follow the Spartans wherever they might lead; Sparta did not reciprocate these oaths, but did bind itself to go to the aid of an ally attacked by a third party with all strength and to the utmost of its ability. Sparta thus summoned and presided over the assembly of its allies, each of whom had one vote. Sparta could not be committed by the allies to a policy which it did not approve, but did require the approval of a majority vote of an allied congress to implement any joint policy it advocated. In war Sparta always held the command, appointed Spartan officers to levy and command allied contingents, and decided how many troops each ally must commit and the terms of engagement. In peace the League's main function from Sparta's standpoint was to act as a shield around its vulnerable domestic economic base (see HELOTS); for the allies the benefits were less clear-cut, except for aristocrats and oligarchs whom Sparta tended to champion, not always successfully, against incipient democratic movements. After victory over Athens in 404 a tendency to transform the League into an empire became more apparent (tribute was never directly levied on

League members) and the violations of allied political autonomy more flagrant. The sharp decline in Spartiate manpower was one of the main reasons behind a reform of the organization in the early 370s, but this did not halt the disaffection which culminated in allied satisfaction at Sparta's humiliation at *Leuctra in 371. Five years later, on the initiative of *Corinth, always the most important single ally, the League quietly dissolved.

Peloponnesian War, of 431–404, fought between *Athens and its allies (see DELIAN LEAGUE) on the one hand and *Sparta and its allies (see PELOPONNESIAN LEAGUE) on the other; most of it (down to 411) was recorded by *Thucydides (2), and that is the most interesting thing about it. The first ten years were the Archidamian War, a title first used by *Lysias, as far as we know, for what Thucydides called the 'ten-years war'. This phase was ended by the inconclusive Peace of *Nicias. The second main phase of the whole war, which Thucydides insisted on regarding as a unit, began with Athens' disastrous expedition to *Sicily (415–413) and continued with the 'Ionian' or 'Decelean' War until the Athenian surrender in 404. That is the Second or Main Peloponnesian War. The *First* Peloponnesian War is the modern name for the struggle between Athens and Corinth (with Sparta occasionally exerting itself) in *c.*461–446; it was ended by the *Thirty Years' Peace. See further ATHENS, HISTORY; CORINTH; GREECE (HISTORY); SPARTA.

Pĕlops, father of *Atreus, a hero worshipped at *Olympia and believed to be the eponym of *Peloponnese. As a child, he was killed and served up by his father *Tantalus, in order to test his guests, the gods. Only *Demeter, mourning the loss of her daughter, failed to notice, and ate part of his shoulder; the other gods restored him to life and replaced his shoulder with ivory. Later, he wooed Hippodāmīa, daughter of Oenomaus king of Pisa, the area round Olympia. Oenomaus had promised his daughter to any man who could carry her off in a chariot and escape his pursuit; unsuccessful contenders would be killed. Though skilled in horsemanship thanks to his former lover *Poseidon, Pelops won (in the usual version) by bribing Oenomaus' charioteer Myrtilus to loosen the linchpins on his master's chariot. Oenomaus was thus killed, but in dying cursed (see CURSES) Pelops; or he was cursed by Myrtilus, whom he killed on the homeward journey. The curse took

effect only in the next generation; Pelops himself prospered greatly, and had six sons by Hippodamia.

Just as Pelops' myth suggests a connection with the *Olympic Games, so his cult was most prominent at Olympia, where he had a precinct inside the Altis; many Archaic dedications were found here. There was a ritual opposition between this cult and that of Olympian *Zeus, whereby those who had eaten meat sacrificed to Pelops were refused entry to the precinct of Zeus (presumably for a specified time, or until purified; see PURIFICATION, GREEK).

In art, Pelops appears at Olympia itself, where the preparations for the chariot-race are the subject of the east pediment of the temple of Zeus.

peltasts Term originally used of *Thracians equipped with a small, light shield (*peltē*), but later probably of any light infantry similarly armed, their main offensive weapon being the javelin. Their first certain appearance was at *Pylos (425 BC). They were later used by *Brasidas in *Chalcidice, and in 409 Thrasyllus had 5,000 sailors equipped as peltasts. They were esp. useful in a skirmishing role, or as an advanced guard, e.g. for seizing passes and other strategic points. They could not hope to defeat *hoplites in pitched battle, but if they managed to keep their distance, they could wear them down by missile fire.

penalties See PUNISHMENT.

Penātēs, di, See WORSHIP, HOUSEHOLD.

Penelopē, wife of *Odysseus, and mother of *Telemachus. In *Homer's *Odyssey* she faithfully awaits Odysseus' return, although pressed to marry one of the many local nobles. She pretends that she must first finish weaving a shroud for Laertes, Odysseus' father, which she unravels every night for three years, until detected by a maid and forced to complete it. Finally, twenty years after Odysseus' departure, in despair she resolves to marry the suitor who can string Odysseus' bow and perform a special feat of archery. Odysseus, who has returned disguised as a beggar, achieves this and kills the suitors with the bow. She tests his identity by another trick concerning their marriage-bed and they are reunited. Homer portrays her as a model of fidelity, prudence, and ingenuity.

In art she is shown mourning Odysseus' absence (seated at her loom with head on hand, elbow on knee), at the departure of Telemachus, receiving gifts from the suitors, conversing with

Odysseus, at the foot-washing scene, and at the suitors' death.

pentathlon, a contest held at the *Olympic Games and elsewhere consisting of five events (long-jump, running, discus, javelin, *wrestling), precursor of the modern decathlon. Victory in three events was sufficient, but not necessary, for overall victory; if no competitor won three events, it is not known how it was decided who was the overall winner. Pentathletes would train and compete, esp. when long-jumping, to the sound of the *aulos. See ATHLETICS.

Pentēkontaĕtia the 'period of (almost) fifty years' between the end of the *Persian Wars in Greece in 479 and the beginning of the *Peloponnesian War in 431. The term is often applied to the account given by *Thucydides (2) at 1. 89–118 of the period from 478 to the early 430s, offered to justify his claim that the truest cause of the Peloponnesian War was Athens' growing power and Sparta's fear of it. The account is brief, selective, and lacking in precise dates.

Pentheus, in myth, son of Agavē, daughter of *Cadmus and Harmonia, and Echion. Euripides' *Bacchae* gives the most familiar version of his legend. The disguised *Dionysus returns from his conquests in the east to *Thebes, where the young king Pentheus is refusing to recognize his deity or to allow his worship. Pentheus imprisons Dionysus, in ignorance of his true identity and seeing him simply as a corrupting influence on the women of Thebes; but Dionysus escapes, and, by making Pentheus mad, inveigles him up on to Mt. Cithaeron to spy on the *maenads there. Pentheus, deranged and himself dressed as a maenad, is torn to pieces by the women led by his mother Agave. She carries his head home in triumph, believing it to be that of a lion killed in the hunt, where she is gently brought to sanity and grief by Cadmus.

Perdiccas (d. 321 BC), *Macedonian noble of the princely house of Orestis, commanded his native battalion in the phalanx of *Alexander (2) the Great. His military distinction, somewhat obscured by the hostile account of *Ptolemy (1) I, won him elevation to the rank of Bodyguard by 330. Later he ranked second only to *Craterus (1) in his effectiveness as marshal and succeeded *Hephaestion in his cavalry command and his position as chiliarch (Grand Vizier). The settlement at Babylon (323) confirmed him in the chiliarchy with command of the central army and gave him custody both of the new king,

Philip Arrhidaeus, and the unborn child of Alexander. In 322 his position strengthened after his successful invasion of Cappadocia, but his dynastic intrigues alarmed the commanders in Europe, *Antipater and Craterus, who declared war. Perdiccas was killed in Egypt.

perduelliō was the crime of activity hostile to the Roman state. It was probably not clearly defined. By the 3rd cent. BC prosecutions were mounted by *tribunes in an assembly. In the late republic such prosecutions became obsolete when crimes of this kind were actionable in the *quaestiō de maiestāte* (see MAIESTAS; QUAESTIONES).

peregrīnī, foreigners—the term used by Romans for the free citizens of any other community than the Roman people. This was the status of the peoples of non-Roman Italy, except the *Latins, until 90 BC and of allied and subject communities outside Italy until *Caracalla's reign (see CONSTITUTION, ANTONINE). The Latins were considered separate from the *peregrini* under the republic, though this distinction disappeared under the Principate. The rule that no Roman could be a citizen of two communities held until the end of the republic, but it seems to have been modified before the death of *Caesar. From the triumviral period onwards *peregrini* could receive Roman citizenship but remain effective members of their own communities.

Pergamum, in Mysia c.24 km. (15 mi.) from the Aegean, a natural fortress commanding the rich plain of the river Caïcus; important historically as the capital of the Attalid kings and, later, as one of the three leading cities of provincial *Asia, and archaeologically as the only excavated Hellenistic royal capital outside *Macedonia. Pergamum had adopted Greek civic organization (see POLIS) by c.300, and this was upheld by the Attalids, who maintained control in practice through their assumption of the right to appoint the chief magistrates. As a royal capital as well as a *polis*, the city was the chief showcase of Attalid patronage. From Attalus I on the kings promoted *Athena, the city's presiding deity, as dynastic protectress, esp. of military success; she acquired the title Nīkēphoros, 'victory-bearer', and her sanctuary in the upper city was adorned with famous statues of defeated Galatians. *Strabo credits above all *Eumenes II with the enlargement and beautification of the city. To his reign dates the 'Great Altar', masterpiece of the Pergamene 'school' of

Greek *sculpture, as well as the royal *libraries and the terraced, fan-shaped plan of the upper city, its focus the royal palace—a remarkable statement of royal absolutism (see URBANISM); an inscription preserves a royal law on municipal administration showing the efforts made to keep the city clean and in good repair. This royal programme aimed at transforming Pergamum into a Hellenistic cultural capital, for which the model was *Athens, recipient of generous Attalid patronage in the 2nd cent. BC. Declared exempt from tribute in his will by Attalus III, Pergamum lost its Roman status of allied city for its support of *Mithradates VI (88–85 BC).

Periander, tyrant of *Corinth c.627–587 BC, after his father *Cypselus; he was for many the typical oppressive tyrant; see TYRANNY. Advice that he should eliminate rivals is said by *Herodotus to have been given to Periander by Thrasybulus of *Miletus, who walked silently through a field of corn lopping off ears that were taller than the rest. Unlike his father, Periander recruited a bodyguard; he sent 300 Corcyraean boys to *Lydia for castration as punishment when Corcyraeans killed his son (see CORCYRA); he himself killed his wife Melissa, made love to her corpse and took the fine clothes off Corinthian women to burn for her spirit. There was also, however, a more favourable tradition: he was in many lists of the *seven sages. The burning of clothes probably reflects a more general attack on luxury, and restrictions on slave ownership may have been similar; his measures against idleness are a misinterpreted memory of the labour which his extensive building programme required: among other things, he constructed the *diolkos, and levied dues upon the use of it. If Cypselus had not brought Corcyra under control after the *Bacchiads fled there, Periander did, and installed his son as tyrant; this is the context of the joint Corinthian/Corcyraean foundations of Apollonia in Illyria and Epidamnus. He founded *Potidaea, the only Corinthian colony in the Aegean. He had a warlike reputation; probably his activity in particular lay behind *Thucydides (2)'s account of early naval affairs, which attributes more or less the naval practices of his own day, including suppression of *piracy, to Corinth. He attacked *Epidaurus and captured its tyrant, his own father-in-law. He arbitrated between Athens and *Mytilene in their dispute over *Sigeum. He advised *Thrasybulus (1) during his successful resistance to the Lydian siege of Miletus. On his death, the tyranny passed to his nephew Cypselus, who was soon killed.

Periclēs (c.495–429 BC), Athenian statesman, was the son of *Xanthippus and the *Alcmaeonid Agaristē, niece of *Cleisthenes (2) and granddaughter of Agariste of *Sicyon (see CLEISTHENES (1)) and Megaclēs. He was *choregos for *Aeschylus' Persians in 472, but first came to prominence as one of the elected prosecutors of *Cimon in 463/2. In 462/1 he joined with *Ephialtes (2) in the attack on the *Areopagus.

Acc. to *Plutarch, he became popular leader and one of the most influential men in Athens after Ephialtes' death and the *ostracism of Cimon. Little is recorded of him for some years, but it is reasonable to assume that he was in favour of the more ambitious foreign policy pursued by Athens in the 450s and of the further reforms of that decade. He is credited with a campaign in the Gulf of Corinth c.454 and with the sending out of *cleruchies to places in the *Delian League, and with the introduction of pay for jurors and the law limiting citizenship to those with an Athenian mother as well as an Athenian father. His proposal for a congress of all the Greeks, which came to nothing because of opposition from *Sparta (its authenticity has been challenged) perhaps belongs to the early 440s and was an attempt to convert the Delian League into a league of all the Greeks under Athens' leadership since the Delian League's war against Persia had ended. In 446 he commanded the expedition to put down the revolt of *Euboea; he returned to Athens when the Peloponnesians invaded, and was alleged to have bought off the Spartan king Pleistoanax; and he then went back to deal with Euboea. When *Samos revolted in 440, it took him eight months to subdue it.

Pericles was heavily involved in Athens' public building programme of the 440s and 430s. This was the issue on which opposition to him was focused by *Thucydides (1), a relative of Cimon, but Thucydides was ostracized (see OSTRACISM) c.443, and the building continued. Acc. to Plutarch, Pericles was elected general (see STRATEGOI) every year after that and was Athens' unchallenged leader; but it seems likely that attacks on Pericles and his friends, probably from the democratic end of the political spectrum, are to be dated to the early 430s. His partner *Aspasia and the philosopher *Anaxagoras were perhaps prosecuted, the sculptor *Phidias was prosecuted and left Athens, and

Pericles himself was charged with embezzlement but presumably acquitted.

In the 430s he led an expedition to the Black (*Euxine) Sea. The policies pursued by Athens in the late 430s, which led to the outbreak of the *Peloponnesian War, are presumably his: *Aristophanes represents him as being esp. obstinate over the decree imposing sanctions on *Megara, and *Thucydides (2) gives him a speech claiming that a policy of appeasement will not work. Acc. to Thucydides, his strategy for the Peloponnesian War was to stay inside the walls when the Peloponnesians invaded, and to rely on Athens' sea power and superior financial resources to outlast the Peloponnesians; but there are indications in the scale of Athens' expenditure and naval activity in the opening years of the war that Thucydides' picture may be distorted. In 430, when the hardship of the war was first felt, the Athenians deposed him from the generalship and attempted unsuccessfully to negotiate with Sparta; he was afterwards re-elected, but he was one of the many Athenians to suffer from the *plague, and he died in 429.

Pericles was an aristocrat who became a democratic leader. He won the admiration of Thucydides (*History* 2. 65), as a man who was incorruptible and far-sighted, and who led the people rather than currying favour with them. Plutarch reconciled this with the less favourable picture given by *Plato by supposing that Pericles was a *demagogue in the earlier part of his career and a statesman in the later. He was an impressive orator. His manner was aloof, and he is said to have been uninterested in his family's concerns. His marriage was unhappy, but after divorce he lived with Aspasia, and when his two sons by his Athenian wife had died of the plague, his son by Aspasia, Pericles, was made an Athenian citizen.

perioikoi, 'dwellers round about', were neighbouring people, often constituting groups of subjects or half-citizens, normally with local self-government. The best-known group of *perioikoi* are those of the Spartan state. The origins of their status and ethnic affiliation are unclear, though their *dialect was the Laconian Doric (see LACONIA) common to all the state's inhabitants.

Like the full citizen Spartiates, *perioikoi* were counted as Lacedaemonians in military contexts, serving not only in the Spartan army but even (after *c*.450) in the same regiments. But they had no say in the making of Spartan policy and seem to have been subject to special

taxation, and so can be considered at best second-class citizens of Sparta. Their status *vis-à-vis* Sparta was akin to that of an ally in the *Peloponnesian League. The perioikic *poleis* (see POLIS) possessed local *autonomy and their own religious *sanctuaries but were entirely subject to Sparta in foreign policy. Social stratification within the perioikic communities is on record; we read in *Xenophon both of 'gentlemen' *perioikoi* and of a named perioikic cavalryman; they were presumably substantial landowners. But humbler *perioikoi* profited from the Spartans' abstention from all economic activity, by providing them with raw materials (esp. iron) and objects of manufacture and trade; Gytheum, the most important community, served Sparta both as chief port and as naval dockyard and muster-station.

Peripatetic school of philosophers. *Aristotle was the first of them and by far the most significant. The school was located in a *sanctuary dedicated to *Apollo, called the Lyceum, a public space outside the city wall of Athens but within easy walking distance. A *gymnasium had been built there; by the end of the 5th cent. BC it was a favourite gathering place for Athenian young men. Visiting *sophists lectured there, *Socrates met his young interlocutors there. As in other such places, there were covered walks (*peripatoi*). The name 'Peripatos' stuck to the school begun there by Aristotle, formerly a member of the Academy, when he returned to Athens in 335.

The school was originally, perhaps always, a collection of people rather than a building: Aristotle, a *metic, could not own property. His successor *Theophrastus could and did, and he bequeathed real estate and a library to a group of his students, including Straton who was then elected Head. There is evidence of continuous philosophical activity until the 1st cent. BC, when Athens was captured by *Sulla and the Peripatetic library removed to Rome.

In the time of Aristotle and Theophrastus, the foundations were laid for systematic, co-operative research into nearly all the branches of contemporary learning. After Theophrastus' death in 287, however, Aristotle's 'school-treatises'—the works that have survived to this day—seem to have been mishandled: Theophrastus left the library to Neleus of Scepsis, and if the story in *Strabo is to be believed, it was removed from Athens. It is clear at least that Aristotle's fame then began to depend on his 'exoteric', more popular works. Straton continued the great tradition, esp. in *physics, but later members of the school devoted themselves to literary criticism, gossipy biography, and unimportant moralizing.

There was a revival in the 1st cent. BC, under the leadership of Andronicus of Rhodes. The school-treatises of Aristotle had been in some sense rediscovered, and Andronicus published an edition of them (probably after Cicero). In this period Peripatetic philosophy was not specifically located in Athens, and was not sharply distinguished doctrinally from the Academy and the Stoa; the Epicureans were opposed to them all.

In the 2nd cent. AD Marcus *Aurelius established teachers in the four main schools, including the Peripatos, in Athens. But the inheritance of Aristotle passed to the great commentators on his work, many of whom were themselves Neoplatonists; see NEOPLATONISM.

periploi, 'voyages around' (i.e. coasting) were the standard basis of ancient descriptive geography. Sequences of harbours, landings, watering-places, shelters from bad weather, landmarks, or hazards could be remembered in an oral tradition as a sometimes very long list, and in written culture offered much more room for detail than cartography (see MAPS). The *periplous* offered a peg on which to hang more information than the purely navigational. The first literary version was believed to have been prepared for *Darius I by Scylax of Caryanda, and the earliest Mediterranean *periplous* (actually late 4th cent.) goes by his name. *Alexander (2) the Great's captain Nearchus left a description of the coast between the Persian Gulf and the Indus. See also PYTHEAS.

perjury See CURSES; OATHS.

persecution, religious See CHRISTIANITY; INTOLERANCE, INTELLECTUAL AND RELIGIOUS.

Persephonē/Korē, goddess, *Demeter's daughter by *Zeus, *Hades' wife and queen of the Underworld. Her most important myth is that of her abduction by Hades, her father's brother, who carried her off when she was picking flowers in a meadow and took her to the Underworld, Demeter's unsuccessful search for her daughter (which took her to *Eleusis) and consequent withdrawal from her normal functions caused the complete failure of crops, and men would have starved if Zeus had not intervened. When Demeter did not respond to the persuasion of the divine messengers he sent to mediate, Zeus sent Hermes to persuade Hades to release Persephone, which he did; but Hades tricked Persephone and made her eat some pomegranate seeds, with the result that she could not leave Hades for ever, but had to spend part of the year with her husband in the Underworld and part of the year with her mother in the upper world. The story is told in the *Homeric *Hymn to Demeter*, a text which has a complex relationship with the most important cult involving Persephone and Demeter, that of the Eleusinian *mysteries, the celebration of which included a ritual search for Kore with torches.

In the images Kore/Persephone is represented as a young woman, often with the addition of attributes, among which torches, stalks of grain, and *sceptres are common.

The name Kore stresses her persona as Demeter's daughter, Persephone that as Hades' wife. The myth of her rape was perceived as, among many other things, an articulation of some perceptions pertaining to marriage from the viewpoint of the girl. Persephone's wedding and the flower-picking that preceded the abduction were celebrated in (amongst other places) Sicily.

She also had an awesome aspect as the queen of the Underworld. Everyone will eventually come under her authority. But she was not implacable, and she and Hades listened to reasonable requests, such as that to return to the upper world to perform proper burial or other rites—a trait abused and exploited by the dishonest *Sisyphus, who refused to return to Hades.

She was often worshipped in association with Demeter; a most important festival in honour of the two goddesses was the *Thesmophoria, which was celebrated by women all over the Greek world (Demeter bore the cult-title Thesmophoros, 'law-giving'). Not surprisingly, Persephone had an important place in the texts inscribed on the gold leaves that were buried with people who had been initiated into *Orphism.

Persepolis, in Persis, a residence of the *Achaemenid kings. *Alexander (2) the Great in 331 BC took and looted Persepolis and set fire to the palaces; this served to bake a number of clay sealings. The royal quarters, built on a hill-terrace, contained a treasury and symmetrically planned palaces with immense square columnar halls.

Excavations have revealed that *Darius I levelled the rock-terrace and began the great *apadana* (audience hall), the main palace-buildings, and the 'harem'. These were completed by *Xerxes; *Artaxerxes (1) I finished the Hall of a Hundred Pillars and built his own palace. Around the whole complex was a fortification wall, and a great gate and stairway led up to the terrace. The bas-reliefs of these palaces are among the finest extant examples of Achaemenid art. These include the Audience reliefs originally flanked by lions attacking bulls, and 23 delegations of tribute-bearers. The tombs of the Achaemenid kings are near by (see NAQŠ-I RUSTAM). In the palace and walls two collections of thousands of administrative texts written in Elamite have been found.

Perseus, a mythical hero. Acrisius, king of *Argos and brother of Proetus, being warned by an oracle that his daughter Danaë's son would kill him, shut her away in a bronze chamber. *Zeus visited her there in a shower of gold. Acrisius, learning that she had borne a son, whom she called Perseus, set mother and child adrift at sea in a chest. They drifted to the island of Serīphus, where a fisherman called Dictys rescued them and gave them shelter. When Perseus grew up, Polydectēs, the king of Seriphus and Dictys' brother, having fallen in love with Danae contrived to send him away to fetch the head of the *Gorgon Medusa. This Perseus achieved, with the help of *Athena and *Hermes, through whom he acquired the necessary implements of sickle, bag, cap of invisibility, and winged sandals. While returning home he came upon *Andromeda about to be devoured by a sea-monster, fell in love with her, rescued and married her. When they returned to Seriphus, he used the Gorgon's face to turn Polydectes and his followers into stone for persecuting Danae. He now gave the head to Athena, who put the face in the centre of her *aegis, and returned the bag, cap and sandals to Hermes. Leaving Dictys as king of Seriphus, he came with his wife and mother to Argos to see his grandfather. But Acrisius, learning of this and still fearing the oracle, hurried away to Pelasgiotis. Perseus followed, and, while competing in the funeral games for the late king of Larissa, he threw the discus and accidentally struck and killed Acrisius, thus fulfilling the oracle. Leaving Argos to the son of Proetus, he became king of Tiryns and founder of the Perseid dynasty. The adventures of Perseus, and esp. those relating to the beheading of Medusa, are favourite themes in art from the 7th cent.

Persia In the narrow sense, 'Persia' names the country lying in the folds of the southern Zagros mountains. From the start of the first millennium BC, an Iranian population lived in close contact with the Elamite inhabitants here. This led to the emergence of the Persian *ethnos* and the kingdom of Anshan, which appears fully on the historical scene beginning with the conquests of *Cyrus (1) the Great. Even with the extension and consolidation of the *Achaemenid empire under *Darius I, Persia proper retained a prominent place in the way in which the Great Kings visualized their territorial power. At the same time, members of the Persian aristocracy received the highest governorships and offices in the central and provincial government. In this respect, the empire created by Cyrus and his successors may be described as 'Persian'.

The Achaemenid period represents a turning-point in near eastern history: for the first time, countries from the Indus to the Balkans, from Central Asia to *Elephantinē in Upper Egypt were embraced by one, unifying, political structure. This political unification did not result in the disappearance of local ethno-cultural identities. In 334, despite the marked process of acculturation, *Asia Minor, *Egypt, *Babylonia, and *Bactria were still countries clearly distinguishable in language, culture, and religion. This was also true of Persia proper. In spite of partial and/or temporary set-backs (notably the secession of Egypt between 399 and 343), the empire held together for more than two centuries. Alexander himself often did little more than take over to his own advantage the Achaemenid ideological heritage and administrative techniques. *Mūtātīs mutandis*, the splintered geo-political pattern of the near east *c.*280 recalls the one which had prevailed before Cyrus the Great's conquests.

Persian, Old (abbr. OP), an *Indo-European language of western Iran (first millennium BC). Its writing is limited to royal inscriptions. The syllabic script has only 44 signs. The oldest extant and largest inscription is that of *Bisitun. It is debated whether the script was invented by *Darius I or had predecessors in western Iran. Most texts date from the reigns of Darius and *Xerxes. Thereafter texts are scarcer and contain more errors. OP was the first *cuneiform script to be deciphered.

Persian Wars, the two Persian expeditions against Greece in 490 and 480/79 BC. The origins of the conflict go back to mainland Greek involvement in the rebellion of the Asiatic Greeks against Persian rule, earlier in the 5th cent. (see IONIAN REVOLT), but although *Herodotus dramatizes their desire for revenge, the Persians already ruled many European Greeks in *Thrace and *Macedonia, and their primary reason for seeking to conquer the rest may well have been that their rule over existing Greek subjects would never be secure while others remained independent.

The first attack was by sea. After ravaging *Naxos and subduing other islands, forcing Carystus (see EUBOEA) to terms, and taking *Eretria by treachery, an invasion-force eventually reached *Marathon, where it was confronted by an army of Athenians and Plataeans (see PLATAEA). After several days' delay, the Persians perhaps provoked a battle by beginning to move on Athens, but were decisively defeated. See MARATHON, BATTLE OF.

The death of *Darius (1) and a revolt in Egypt delayed renewal of the attack, but when it came, it was on a grander scale and led by Darius' successor, *Xerxes, in person. How large his forces actually were is an intractable problem: the fleet may have contained the 1,207 triremes of tradition, but the army is unlikely to have had more than 100,000 men at most. Persian strategy clearly involved co-operation between the two, but the view that the army depended on sea-borne supplies is probably mistaken, since it continued to operate in 479 after the fleet had been defeated. More likely, naval forces were intended to prevent Greek ships from interfering with communications or in *Asia Minor, and also, possibly, to turn Greek defensive positions on land.

Once aware of the Persian preparations, the Greeks consulted the *Delphic oracle and received a series of gloomy prognostications. The Athenians, in particular, were advised to flee to the ends of the earth, and even a second approach elicited only the enigmatic response to rely on the 'wooden wall'. But interpreting this to refer to their newly built navy, they determined to resist, and probably late in 481, conferred with others of like mind. It was decided to patch up quarrels, to send spies to Asia Minor, and to appeal for help from uncommitted states. The appeals failed, and the spies were caught, be released on Xerxes' orders to spread alarming reports of his power. But, crucially, under Spartan leadership, an alliance (sometimes called 'the Hellenic League') was created.

At a second meeting, probably in spring, 480, a Thessalian appeal to defend the Tempē pass led, acc. to Herodotus, to the dispatch of 10,000 *hoplites by sea to the Gulf of Pagasae and thence on foot to the pass. They withdrew before Xerxes had even crossed the *Hellespont, allegedly because of a warning from the Macedonian king about Persian numbers, and the realization that the pass could be turned.

It was then decided to defend the *Thermopylae pass and to send the fleet to *Artemisium on the NE coast of *Euboea. But Thermopylae was turned through treachery, and what was probably a rear-guard under the king of Sparta, overwhelmed (see LEONIDAS; THERMOPYLAE, BATTLE OF), while, at sea, though the Persians suffered severely in storms, and the Greeks held the initiative for two days, they were so battered in the third day's fighting that they had almost decided to withdraw before the news from Thermopylae arrived. See ARTEMISIUM, BATTLE OF.

Falling back to *Salamis, the Greek fleet helped the Athenians to complete the evacuation of *Attica, which had probably been decided upon and largely carried out some months before, but there then followed a pause. Eventually, either because of a message from *Themistocles or because it was decided to try a surprise attack before the onset of winter, the Persian fleet entered the channel between Salamis and the mainland where its numbers and manoeuvrability were nullified. Decisively defeated, it withdrew to Asia. See SALAMIS, BATTLE OF.

Xerxes himself now also returned to Asia, but probably left most of his army in Greece under *Mardonius, who wintered in Thessaly and offered Athens generous terms to weaken her resolve. When this failed, he reoccupied the city (June 479), sending another envoy over to Salamis with a renewed offer. Despite stirring expressions of an undying will to resist, and the lynching of an unfortunate councillor who suggested the offer be considered, Athenian resolution was severely tested by Sparta's reluctance to take the offensive. But in the end, a combination of scarcely veiled Athenian threats and allied warnings broke the deadlock.

Mardonius withdrew from Attica, allegedly because it was not suitable for cavalry and a potential trap, but possibly, in reality, to avoid confrontation and thus continue to let diplomacy do his work. The Greeks followed him to *Boeotia, but clung to the foothills of Cithaeron (the mountain range which separates this part of Boeotia from Attica) until a success against the Persian cavalry, in which its commander was killed, led them to move nearer to the

Asopus, where Mardonius' main camp lay. There followed a delay during which they suffered increasingly from the harassment of Persian cavalry, and eventually, with their supply-lines severed and their water-supply at risk, they had to retreat.

Despite modern suggestions that the withdrawal was skilfully planned to lure Mardonius into attacking the apparently isolated right wing, whereupon the centre and left would converge to crush him, it is more likely that everything went wrong, as Herodotus suggests, with the centre's precipitate retirement to Plataea leaving the wings dangerously divided. However, in the ensuing battle, the Spartans and Tegeates on the right routed the Persians, while the Athenians on the left defeated their Greek allies. Mardonius himself was killed and most of his Asiatic troops with him, either on the field or in their palisaded camp. Only the Persian centre which had never become involved, managed to retreat in good order. See PLATAEA, BATTLE OF. Acc. to Greek legend, on the very same day, across the Aegean, a Greek fleet under *Leotychidas, king of Sparta, landed its men on the Mycale peninsula, defeated a Persian army and stormed the palisaded base where their ships had been beached. Thus the Greek triumph was complete.

There is no simple explanation for what happened, but in the two decisive battles the Greeks were better equipped. At Salamis, in confined waters, their possibly more stoutly constructed ships—Herodotus has Themistocles describe them as 'heavier'—stood up better to ramming head-on; at Plataea, as he emphasizes, their hoplites were certainly better equipped for hand-to-hand fighting. The Persians could have avoided both battles, and thus, as *Thucydides (2) has some speakers from *Corinth imply, it might be truer to say that they lost through their own mistakes.

Persian Wars: the Persian viewpoint A big problem for the historian is the absence of any direct reflection of the Persian angle on this celebrated conflict. In fact, apart from the *Bisitun inscription and relief, which recounts *Darius I's accession, the Persians have left us no narrative accounts of their history. The changes in the lists of provinces which appear regularly in the royal inscriptions cannot be used as a reliable criterion for tracing the growth or shrinkage of Persian territorial power. *Herodotus (1) is practically our only source. For him, the expeditions of 490 and 480 were the culmin-

ation of a long series of conflicts and misunderstandings. In his perspective, the *Ionian Revolt and decisions taken as a result played a key role. This is true of the burning of *Sardis (c.499) which, he says, gave the Persians the opportunity to declare a war of reprisals against the Greeks; similarly, the participation of an Athenian contingent alongside the Ionians 'was the beginning of disaster for Greeks and barbarians' (5. 97). Acc. to Herodotus' logic, Persian actions on their western frontier were part of a planned series of steps leading inevitably towards an expedition against the cities of mainland Greece: the conquest of *Samos by Syloson, the mission supposedly entrusted to *Democedes, the Saythian expedition of Darius in 513 and *Mardonius' campaign in *Thrace following the Ionian Revolt were all part of this plan. Herodotus' presentation is debatable, as it is not certain that Darius had determined on a plan for the conquest of mainland Greece from the moment of his accession. He did pursue a consistent Aegean policy, following that of *Cambyses, who is known to have been the founder of Achaemenid naval power. *Thucydides (2) understood this, when he placed Darius' conquest of the offshore islands in the long sequence of thalassocracies (see SEA POWER). The expedition of Datis and Artaphernes extended the Persian seizure of the eastern Aegean. Their expedition was different in aim from the campaign led by Xerxes in 480. The punishment meted out to Eretria and Athens in 490 was little more than a by-product of maritime expansion; in 480, the aim was to compel the mainland Greeks to acknowledge Xerxes' sovereignty. Although the so-called Persian Wars ended in 479, the Greek struggle against the Persians continued, with the Ionian cities asking Sparta, then Athens, to protect them in order to forestall a renewed Persian offensive. This request led to the birth in 478, under Athenian hegemony, of the tribute-paying *Delian League, 'a pretext for which was ravaging the lands of the King in revenge for the wrongs suffered'. The hostilities between Athens and Persia spanned the length and breadth of the Aegean front from Thrace to Egypt. In the first stage they were marked by a series of victorious Athenian offensives under the command of *Cimon (victor at Eurymedon in 466), until the Athenians suffered a serious defeat in Egypt. We have the first mention of direct intervention by the Persian court in Greek affairs on this occasion, i.e. when *Artaxerxes (1) I sent Megabazus to Sparta 'to bring about the retreat of the Athenian troops from

Egypt'. Acc. to *Diodorus (2) Siculus, a peace was concluded c.449/8 between the Great King and Athens, by whose terms Artaxerxes undertook not to intervene with military force on the Asia Minor coast. But, given Thucydides' silence on the matter, the historical veracity of this 'Peace of Callias' is a subject of continuing debate. See CALLIAS, PEACE OF. In the following years Persian *satraps intervened repeatedly in the cities of Asia Minor, e.g. Pissouthnes who, c.440, sent auxiliary troops to help the Samian exiles wishing to overthrow the island's democracy and Athenian hegemony. The Athenian disaster in Sicily spurred the satraps *Pharnabazus (Dascylium) and *Tissaphernes (Sardis) into making an alliance with Sparta (412). This led to the Ionian War (see PELOPONNESIAN WAR), when Spartans and Athenians fought each other under the watchful eye of the representatives of the Great King, who had ordered his satraps to collect the tribute due from the Greek cities of Asia. The Athenian defeat (404) did not put an end to hostilities, which resumed in Asia Minor and the islands in the early years of the 4th cent.; they continued down to 387/6, when *Artaxerxes (2) II imposed the *King's Peace, which gave control of the Greek cities of Asia Minor to Persia. This treaty was still determining relations between *Darius III and the Asiatic cities when *Alexander (2) the Great began his campaign in Asia Minor. See the next entry.

Persian-Wars tradition The glory-days of the Persian Wars loomed large in defining mainland Greek identities until well into the Roman age. In *Thucydides (2) 5th-cent. Athens justified its empire by them, in the tradition of the *epitaphios they are a cause for Athenian boasting (accompanied by distortion of the facts), and in *Aristophanes for nostalgia. In the 4th cent. *Macedon's rise prompted rhetorical appeals by Athenian politicians to ancestral resolve and self-sacrifice in the Persian Wars. *Philip II and *Alexander (2) the Great countered this (mainly) Athenian rhetoric by presenting Macedon's Persian adventure as a Greek war of revenge for Persian sacrilege in 480 BC. Roman emperors from *Augustus on equated Persia with *Parthia in presenting eastern policy and warfare, along the way fuelling subject-Greek memories of the Persian Wars, a favourite theme of the *Second Sophistic.

Persius Flaccus, Aulus (AD 34–62), Roman satirist. His ancient biography records that he was a rich *equestrian of *Etruscan stock who died young and who was connected with the Stoic opposition to *Nero (see STOICISM) through his links with *Clodius Thrasea Paetus and Annaeus Cornutus. However, Persius' satires are isolated and introverted works, more concerned with inner, philosophical freedom than with political liberty. The 'biting truth' he reveals is confined to moral crassness, literary bad taste, and his own failings.

Persius claims to take his lead from *Lucilius (1), but his language and ideas are similar to those of *Horace. He reduces Horace's 18 satires to 6 and a mere 650 *hexameters, offering 'something more concentrated', with 'the taste of bitten nails'. This formula provoked violent reactions in antiquity: *Lucan admired the satires as 'real poetry'; *Martial considered them a precious elixir worth more than bulky epics; but *Jerome is said to have burned them because of their obscurity. Persius certainly stretches satire to un-Horatian extremes: his characters are either aged or immature, tutors or students; his ideal is uncompromising Stoicism, not easy Epicureanism (see EPICURUS); Horace's mocking conversations become diatribes filled with bitter spleen.

Persius opens with a prologue in limping iambics, the metre of cynical sneering, exposing satire as a hybrid, semi-poetic genre, and the *patronage system as mutual back-scratching. (1) lifts the curtain on a disgusting orgy of modern poetry, in which specimens of literary decadence, possibly parodies of Nero's own works, corrupt Persius' avowedly straightforward style. His disgust with 'confused Rome' eventually explodes, and he mutters a cherished secret into a hole in the ground: all Romans have asses' ears. This echo of the Midas story (see MIDAS (1)) prompted an ancient legend that Cornutus, who edited Persius after his death, had been forced to change a specific attack on Nero to this vaguer generalization. (2) strips bare the hypocrisy of Roman citizens who sacrifice to the gods in the hope of material gain, not moral virtue. (3) is most often read as a dialogue between a lazy student in bed with a hangover and a Stoic tutor who urges him to pursue philosophy before it is too late (though both may be voices inside Persius' own head). (4) is a dialogue between a young politician (*Alcibiades) and a philosopher (*Socrates) where, again, self-knowledge is encouraged. In (5) Persius pays homage to his own tutor, Cornutus, who has taught him to use unadorned language. The two are united by their devotion to Stoicism in a topsy-turvy world where others are enslaved to material desires. In (6), a Horatian-style epistle to Caesius Bassus, Persius meditates on the contrast between his own tiny and worthless-seeming legacy to his profligate heirs and the infinite heaps of wealth coveted by others.

Persius is often regarded as a paragon of Stoic virtue, but he makes no secret of his own imperfections; in the confusion of different voices, he speaks as an erring student as well as a stern tutor. It is a mistake to try to extract clear messages from his disjointed outbursts. Although he claims to aspire to bluntness, his language is a tortuous mixture, full of jarring juxtapositions and strained links; he uses a dense tissue of images, often graphically anatomical, to revitalize dead metaphors and fuse disparate ideas. It was this black wit which struck a chord with the church fathers, and with later satirists, esp. John Donne. See SATIRE, ROMAN.

Pervigilium Veneris, a Latin poem of 93 trochaic tetrameters catalectic (see METRE, GREEK), has caught the romantic imagination perhaps more than any other poem in ancient literature. But while its beauty is unquestioned, interpretation is problematic; date and authorship are uncertain. The setting is *Sicily, on the eve of the spring festival of *Venus, and the poem celebrates the procreative power of the goddess in nature. The mood is mostly one of exhilaration, which is reflected in the metre and in numerous cases of verbal repetition, most notably the famous refrain (*Crās amet quī numqu(am) amāvit, quiqu(e) amavit cras amet* (the two bracketed syllables were not pronounced) 'Let who has never loved love tomorrow, and tomorrow let who has loved love'); but a serious, philosophical side is also evident, and the poem ends on a disquieting note as the poet asks anguishedly when *his* spring will come. A 4th cent. AD date is probable.

Pessimism, Greek See ĀTĒ; MIDAS (1); SIN, *Greece*.

Petillius Ceriālis, Quintus suffered a humiliating defeat while commanding *legion IX Hispana in Britain during *Boudicca's revolt (60). Entrusted with a cavalry force during the Flavian march on Rome, he was sent by Vespasian in 70 as governor of Lower Germany to put down the revolt of Iulius Civilis in the Rhineland. Despite some setbacks, which Tacitus attributes to rashness and carelessness, he had suppressed the rebellion by the end of 70. As governor of Britain (71–73/4) he crushed the Brigantes, Britain's largest tribe, penetrating to the northern Pennines.

Petrōnius (1), senator of consular rank and courtier of *Nero. Acc. to *Tacitus, he had been outstanding for his indolence, though this did not prevent him from being energetic as proconsul in *Bithynia and as consul. For a time he was influential enough to guide Nero in his choice of pleasures, and even when forced by Ofonius Tigellinus' intrigues to take his own life in 66, he showed himself not merely fearless but contemptuous of Stoic posturings. Instead of a will full of flattery of Nero or his current favourites, Petronius left a document denouncing him in embarrassing detail.

Petrōnius (2), author of the extant *Satyrica*, possibly identical with Petronius (1), the politician and *arbiter elegantiae* at the court of Nero. Given that the *Satyrica* belongs in style and factual detail to the Neronian period, and that *Tacitus' account of the courtier Petronius describes a hedonistic, witty, and amoral character which would well suit the author of the *Satyrica*, many find it economical to identify the two, but the matter is beyond proof.

Of the *Satyrica* itself we seem to have fragments of bks. 14, 15, and 16, with bk. 15 practically complete, containing *Trimalchio's Feast*. The whole work was evidently lengthy; one conjectural reconstruction has suggested twenty books and a length of 400,000 words. It is prosimetric in form, an inheritance from the similar satires of *Varro. The outline of the plot is naturally difficult to reconstruct; the main characters are the homosexual pair Encolpius (the narrator) and the younger Giton, who undergo various adventures in a southern Italian setting. They meet a number of characters, some of whom, e.g. the unscrupulous adventurer Ascyltus and the lecherous poet Eumolpus, try to divide the lovers; Giton is not esp. faithful, and this, like the sexual orientation of the lovers and many other elements in the novel, constitutes an evident *parody of the chaste fidelity of the boy–girl pairings of the ideal Greek *novel. Encolpius seems to be afflicted with impotence as the result of the wrath of *Priapus, and several episodes describe his sexual failures; the wrath of Priapus is evidently a parody of the wrath of *Poseidon in Homer's *Odyssey*, and other parallels between Encolpius and *Odysseus appear, esp. when he encounters a woman named Circe.

Many themes familiar from Roman satire appear, such as legacy-hunting and the comic meal (*Trimalchio's Feast*); in the latter Encolpius, Giton, and Ascyltus attend a dinner given by the rich *freedman Trimalchio, probably in *Puteoli, in the narrative of which both Trimalchio's vulgar and ignorant display of wealth and the snobbishness of the narrator emerge very forcibly, and which contains, in a parody of *Plato's *Symposium*, a collection of tales told by Trimalchio's freedman friends which gives some evidence for vulgar Latin (see LATIN LANGUAGE), though Petronius has naturally not reproduced colloquial speech exactly. Several other inserted tales are told in the novel, esp. those of the Pergamene Boy and the Widow of Ephesus, suitably lubricious stories for their narrator Eumolpus, but also clearly drawing on the Hellenistic tradition of Milesian tales (see NOVEL, LATIN). The inserted poems in various metres sometimes appear to comment on the novel's action; the two longest, presented as the work of Eumolpus, seem to relate to other Neronian writers: the 65-line *Capture of Troy* written in the iambic trimeters (see METRE, GREEK) of Senecan tragedy, and the *Civil War* in 295 *hexameters, closely recalling *Lucan's homonymous epic on the same subject (and restoring the divine machinery which Lucan had excluded). Literary and cultural criticism is certainly a concern of the novel; there are prominent attacks on contemporary oratory, painting, and poetry.

Petronius' novel seems not to have been widely known in antiquity, though a more extensive text than ours was available; it was rediscovered between the 15th and 17th cents., with great impact.

pets Animals were kept, inside and outside the house, as pets and for show, from early times. *Dogs that fed from their master's table are mentioned by *Homer, and *Penelope found pleasure in watching her flock of geese, though there is symbolism here (geese = suitors). For *Odysseus' dog Argos see *Odyssey* 17. The commonest pet was the small white long-coated Maltese terrier, represented on 5th-cent. BC Attic vases and gravestones. Epitaphs show the affection felt for pet dogs by their owners.

Tamed birds, esp. starlings, magpies, ravens, and crows, which could be taught to talk, were popular. Lesbia's 'sparrow' (Catullus 2; 3) was possibly a bullfinch. The more exotic parrot, introduced from India, was rarer. Nightingales and blackbirds were kept for their song. Monkeys amused the household with tricks they had been taught. The cat was a late introduction into the Roman house, probably because, being

a sacred animal in Egypt, its export from that country was forbidden. But *Seneca the Younger and *Pliny the Younger assume their readers' acquaintance with it as a household animal. In earlier times, its function in controlling vermin was performed by the ferret. Other animals were kept outside the house, more as a hobby and for showing off to visitors. The fishponds of the rich contained murenas and bearded mullet which might be trained to eat from their masters' hands. Aviaries and game-parks were fairly common from the late republic onwards. Here were kept singing birds, doves, pigeons, peacocks, flamingos, boars, hares, deer, and antelopes. See ANIMALS, ATTITUDES TO.

Peutinger Table conventional name for a manuscript made at Colmar *c*.1200 of a late Roman world-map, itself a 4th-cent. modification of a 2nd-cent. and perhaps even earlier design. The most valuable document of ancient cartography (see MAPS), it is also an important source for ancient topography. It represents the inhabited world from Spain and Britain (all but a fragment of which are missing) to India, though the *Mediterranean world occupies five-sixths of the whole (and Italy a third) of the scroll. The elongated form precludes constant scale or recognizable visual form for most land-masses and seas; but the dense and topologically correct network of roads (with posting-stations and distances) has a practical value. Major cities have pictorial images, middle-ranking ones conventional signs. Important rivers, mountains, and some other features of historical significance are included.

Phaedra See HIPPOLYTUS.

Phaedrus, Gāius Iūlius (*c*.15 BC–*c*. AD 50), a slave of Thracian birth, received a good schooling, became a freedman of Augustus, and composed five books of verse *fables. Under *Tiberius, he offended *Aelius Seianus through suspected allusions in his fables and suffered some unknown punishment. He is scarcely noticed by Roman writers. Prose paraphrases of his and of other fables were made in later centuries. The five books are clearly incomplete, and 30 further fables have been shown to belong to them; additional fables deriving from Phaedrus are contained in the prose paraphrases.

Phaedrus' achievement, on which he greatly prides himself, lies in his elevation of the fable, hitherto used in literature only as an adjunct, e.g. in satire, into an independent *genre. His fables consist of beast-tales based largely on '*Aesop', as well as jokes and instructive stories taken not only from Hellenistic collections but also from his own personal experience. His main source is likely to have been a collection of Aesopic fables compiled in prose by *Demetrius (1) of Phaleron. Philosophic weight is sought by borrowings from collections of maxims and from *diatribe; moral instruction is generally self-contained at the beginning or ending of the tale. Besides his professed purpose of providing amusement and counsel, Phaedrus sometimes satirizes contemporary conditions both social and political. His work evidently evoked considerable criticism, and retorts to his detractors are frequent. The presentation is animated and marked by a humorous and charming brevity of which Phaedrus is rightly proud, but which sometimes leads to obscurity. In language he stands in the tradition of *Terence.

phalanx In Homer the word is usually in the plural and means 'ranks', but in the singular it came to mean the close-packed formation characteristic of Archaic and Classical *hoplites. It usually formed eight deep, but as early as *Delion (424 BC) the *Thebans were 25 deep, and at *Leuctra (371) 50 deep. Though inflexible and unwieldy and thus vulnerable if caught on rough ground or attacked in flank or rear, the phalanx was formidable when driving forward, as the Persians found to their cost, and in the hands of the Spartans not even as cumbersome as it might seem. By articulating it down to units of 30–40 men, and by training, the Spartans were able to wheel wings forward at right angles to the main line of advance, or back behind the rest of the phalanx so as to double its depth, and even to countermarch it to face an attack from the rear; they also developed a technique for dealing with the threat of missile-armed troops—ordering the younger men in the front ranks to charge out and drive off the enemy.

The same term was applied to the infantry-of-the-line in Macedonian armies, though their task was primarily to pin the enemy while the cavalry exploited any opportunity so created. See ARMIES, GREEK AND HELLENISTIC. The Macedonian version was probably the creation of *Philip II, and it too achieved considerable flexibility through training and proper articulation into sub-units; its main offensive weapon was a formidable long pike (the *sarisa*). Philip and *Alexander (2) the Great's 'phalangites' were probably recruited from the peasantry of

Macedonia, rather than the rather better-off class from whom the hoplites had been drawn. This created problems after Alexander's conquest of the Persian empire, and for those of Alexander's successors who could not recruit in Macedonia. Alexander was already experimenting with a mixed force of Macedonians and Asiatics before his death. Though formidable enough to perturb even *Aemilius Paullus (2), the victor of *Pydna, Alexander's successors forgot that the secret of his and his father's success had been the integration of the phalanx with other arms: by itself it was no match for the legion. See MILITARY TRAINING (GREEK).

phallus, an image of the penis, often erect, to be found in various contexts, in particular (a) in certain rituals associated with fertility, esp. Dionysiac *processions (see DIONYSUS); (b) as a sacred object revealed in the Dionysiac *mysteries, as in the Villa of the Mysteries fresco at *Pompeii; (c) in the costume of comedy (see COMEDY (GREEK), OLD), *satyric drama and various low theatrical genres; *Aristotle says that comedy originated in phallic songs; (d) on permanent display, often as part of a statue such as those of *Priapus or the *herms identified with *Hermes; (e) as apotropaic: e.g. *Pliny the Elder says that it guards not only babies but also triumphal chariots (against envy). In general its appeal is as an expression of fertility and regeneration, but also of masculine strength (e.g. in the case of the herms marking boundaries).

pharmacology From earliest times, drugs formed an important part of *medicine, and *Homer has the first record of good drugs and bad drugs (poisons). Folklore incorporated many data on toxic substances, and Homer's *Circe and *Euripides' *Medea link *magic with poisons. Yet simultaneously there is another understanding of drugs and their actions: Pindar reflects *Asclepius' medicine as curative with drugs, surgery, and magical incantations. Drugs were contrasted with foods, but ancient thought overlapped the two, much as moderns fuse medical and culinary uses of spices. Until the *Enquiry into Plants* by *Theophrastus, Greek pharmacal *botany had not received clear organization, and folklore encompassed many famous drugs, e.g. the pennyroyal, used in a tea for female *contraception; the poisonous hemlock, infamous as the drug that killed *Socrates; the now-extinct silphium from *Cyrene, used as a cure-all distinguished by its fetid pungency; rose-oils of many varieties employed as essential in the manufacture of perfume. For female ailments, there are several hundred botanical substances recorded in the Hippocratic *Diseases of Women* and similar tracts (see GYNAECOLOGY).

Book 9 of Theophrastus' *Explanations of Plants* is mostly a collection of material derived from *rhizotomoi* ('root-cutters'), and incorporates their oral traditions and experiences with drugs, both beneficial and toxic; about 300 species appear, ranging from the detailed preparation of hemlock to the use of licorice. The *rhizotomoi* knew their pharmaceuticals as plant-parts, and Theophrastus reflects this ancient expertise as he classes his 'herbs' as seeds, roots, leaves, stems, and so on. His inclusion of *myrrh and frankincense shows long-term activity on trade routes from southern *Arabia. *Nicander summarized in *hexameters the toxicology of many plants, minerals, and animals; his *Theriaca* and *Alexipharmaca* became references for many later physicians and pharmacologists, but the *Materials of Medicine* by *Dioscorides gave the fullest and most accurate account of drugs and drug lore of Greek, Hellenistic, and early Roman imperial times. About 600 pharmaceuticals are described according to a drug affinity system, and this magnificent work became the textbook on the subject.

pharmakos, a human scapegoat. During the *Thargelia Athenians and Ionians expelled scapegoats, who were called 'offscourings', in order 'to purify' the cities. These *pharmakoi* were chosen from the poor and the ugly, received special treatment in the *prytaneion* ('town hall'), were led in a procession to the sound of unharmonious music around the city, beaten with wild or infertile plants like squill, and finally pelted with stones and chased over the border. See POLLUTION.

Pharnabazus, son of Pharnaces, hereditary *satrap of Dascylium (in Hellespontine Phrygia), distant cousin and son-in-law of *Artaxerxes (2) II. Instructed like *Tissaphernes to recover control of Asiatic Greek cities, he co-operated undeviously with Sparta, appearing personally at Abydos, Cyzicus (410), and Chalcedon (408) and providing relief after Cyzicus. *Cyrus (2)'s arrival (407) aborted Athenian negotiations with *Darius II via Pharnabazus, and he temporarily disappears. He had *Alcibiades murdered at *Lysander's request (404/3), but after Sparta's intervention in Anatolia his territory was invaded. *Agesilaus invited him to rebel but conceded his right to remain loyal to Artaxerxes

(395). The satrap's advice had already prompted *Conon (1)'s naval counter-offensive, and after Cnidus Pharnabazus took the fleet to mainland Greece (393)—unparalleled for a Persian after 479—attacked Spartan territory and supplied money to Athens and her allies. By 388/7 he had left to marry the King's daughter.

Pharus See ALEXANDRIA; LIGHTHOUSES; SEVEN WONDERS.

Phīdias, Athenian sculptor, active *c.*465–425 BC. His early works included the colossal bronze *Athena Promachos on the Acropolis; her spearpoint and helmet-crest were supposedly visible from *Sunium. His Athena Lemnia, perhaps preserved in Roman copy, and his Marathon group at *Delphi (see MARATHON, BATTLE OF) may also be early; some believe that the Riace bronzes (see 'RIACE WARRIORS') belong to the latter.

Phidias' reputation rested chiefly on his chryselephantine Athena (later called 'Parthenos') and his *Zeus at *Olympia. Both were of gold and ivory over a wooden core, with embellishments in jewels, silver, copper, enamel, glass, and paint; each incorporated numerous subsidiary themes to demonstrate the divinity's power. *Plutarch puts Phidias in charge not merely of the Athena but of *Pericles' entire building programme. He certainly belonged to Pericles' inner circle, and at the least probably directed the *Parthenon's exterior sculpture. The Athena recapitulated several of its themes. Almost 12 m. (40 ft.) high and draped in over a ton of gold, she was begun in 447 and installed in 438; descriptions by *Pliny the Elder and *Pausanias (3) have enabled the identification of many copies. Her right hand held out a *Nike, and her left held upright her grounded shield, embellished outside with the Amazonomachy and inside with the Gigantomachy (see AMAZONS; GIANTS); her spear leant against her shoulder. Lapiths and *Centaurs adorned her sandals, and her base carried the Birth of *Pandora in relief. A Gorgoneion (see GORGON) occupied the centre of her *aegis, and a sphinx and two Pegasi (see PEGASUS) supported the three crests of her helmet; griffins decorated its cheek-pieces.

Plutarch reports that Pericles' enemies prosecuted Phidias for embezzling some of the Parthenos' gold and for impiety, and that he died in prison; *Philochorus dated his trial to 438, but says that he fled to Olympia, where the Eleans killed him after he had made the Zeus. This seems more likely, for his workshop there belongs to the 430s and has yielded tools, terracotta moulds (for a colossal female statue), and even a cup bearing his name. As *Strabo and Pausanias describe it, the Zeus was even larger than the Parthenos. Enthroned, he held a Nike in his right hand and a *sceptre in his left; coins and vase-paintings reproduce the composition. The throne was richly embellished with Graces (see CHARITES), Seasons (see HORAE), Nikai, *sphinxes and Theban children, the slaughter of the children of Niobe (of which marble copies survive), and an Amazonomachy; paintings by Panaenus (Phidias' brother) on the screens between its legs included Hellas (Greece) and Salamis (see SALAMIS, BATTLE OF), some of the Labours of *Heracles, Hippodamia and her mother, and *Achilles and Penthesilea. Another Amazonomachy adorned Zeus' footstool, and the statue's base carried the Birth of *Aphrodite.

Ancient critics regarded Phidias as the greatest and most versatile of Greek sculptors. His pupils dominated Athenian sculpture for a generation (see PAEONIUS), and Hellenistic and Roman neo-classicism looked chiefly to him.

Phīdippidēs, a long-distance courier who *Herodotus says ran from Athens to Sparta in 490 BC to enlist help for the battle of Marathon (see MARATHON, BATTLE OF), reaching his destination 'next day'; a possible feat, since the winner of a race over the same ground in 1983 managed to cover the distance (c.240 km.; 149 mi.) in under 22 hours. On the way Phidippides encountered *Pan, who asked him why the Athenians did not yet honour him with a state cult; this was later put right.

Philēmon, 368/60–267/63 BC, New Comedy poet (see COMEDY (GREEK), NEW), granted Athenian *citizenship before 307/6. In a long life he wrote 97 comedies, of which over 60 titles are known; he won three times at the *Lenaea, coming immediately after *Menander in the victors' list, while his first victory at the *Dionysia is dated to 327.

Most of the titles seem typical of New Comedy; only two sound like mythological burlesques. Contemporary judgement awarded Philemon frequent victories over Menander—a judgement reversed by posterity. Nearly 200 fragments survive, emphasizing the moralizing aspect of Philemon's thought. There are many gnomic lines and couplets (see GNŌMĒ), often lacking Menander's terse precision. Acc. to *Apuleius, Philemon's plays contained wit, plots neatly turned, recognitions (or solutions) lucidly

arranged, realistic characters, maxims agreeing with life, and few seductions.

Philetas See PHILITAS.

philhellenism (in Roman republican history) is the nexus of two developments in the late 3rd and 2nd cent. BC. One of these is cultural, characterized by the actively favourable reception of Greek language, literature, and philosophy within the Roman ruling class. The other, political, is signalled by the adoption of policy and behaviour actively represented as beneficial to, and respectful of, Greece and Greeks. The phenomenon is associated esp. with *Quinctius Flamininus, *Aemilius Paullus (2), and *Cornelius Scipio Aemilianus and his circle.

Philip II (382–336 BC), king of Macedon and architect of Macedonian greatness. In his youth he witnessed the near dissolution of the kingdom through civil war and foreign intervention, and spent some time as hostage in *Epaminondas' *Thebes. The nadir came when his brother died in battle against *Illyrian invaders (360/59), who occupied the NW borderlands. On his accession his priority was to save Macedon from dismemberment by hostile powers; and from the outset he displayed a genius for compromise and intrigue. The Athenians, who backed a pretender, were defeated in a skirmish near *Aegae but wooed by the return of their prisoners (and by hints that he would recognize their claims to *Amphipolis). Other belligerents were bought off, and Philip used the time he acquired to train a new citizen army in mass infantry tactics, introducing the twelve-cubit pike (*sarisa*) as its basic weapon (see PHALANX). His efforts bore fruit in 358, when he decisively defeated the Illyrians and used his victory to integrate the previously independent principalities of upper Macedonia into his kingdom. Their nobility joined the companions of his court and the commons were recruited into the army. Philip's increased power was immediately deployed against Athens. He annexed Amphipolis and Pydna in 357, captured *Potidaea in 356, ceding it to the Olynthian federation (see CHALCIDICE; OLYNTHUS) in return for alliance, and acquired Methone (354)—at the cost of his right eye and permanent disfigurement. From the conquests came land which he distributed in part to a new aristocracy, recruited from all parts of the Greek world. Most important was Crenides, the Thracian settlement by Mt. Pangaeus, which Philip occupied and reinforced in 356, naming it

*Philippi after himself. The exploitation of the neighbouring gold mines allegedly yielded an annual income of 1,000 talents, which enabled him to maintain a large mercenary army and win the services of politicians in southern Greece.

*Thessaly rapidly became an annex of Macedon. An early marriage alliance brought an invitation to intervene in the internecine war between the Thessalian League and the tyrants of Pherae. In return for defeating the tyrants Philip was appointed archon of Thessaly with its revenues and superb cavalry at his disposal. In 349 he attacked Olynthus, and by September 348 had captured the city through internal treachery. The population was enslaved and Olynthus' land absorbed, but despite the shock of this exemplary treatment there was no response to the Athenian appeal for an international alliance against him, and in despondency the Athenians entered peace negotiations early in 346. Peace and alliance were concluded in April 346 (Peace of *Philocrates) at the same time that Philip accepted an appeal to lead an Amphictionic campaign against the Phocians (allies of Athens; see AMPHICTIONY; PHOCIS). With masterly prevarication he delayed ratifying the peace until he was near *Thermopylae, preventing the Athenians reinforcing their allies, and forced the Phocians to terms (July 346). The settlement which resulted left him master of Thermopylae with voting rights in the Amphictiony.

The years after 346 saw further expansion at the expense of the Illyrians and Thracians. Meanwhile Philip's influence had expanded in southern Greece. By 342 Athenian interpretations of his motives carried more conviction. The situation became graver in 340, when Philip laid siege to Perinthus and *Byzantium, and open war erupted in the late summer, when he commandeered the Athenian grain fleet.

The final act came when he assumed command of an Amphictionic expedition against the Locrians of Amphissa and used the campaign as a fulcrum to attack Thebes and Athens, now united in alliance against him. Its denouement was the battle of *Chaeronea (August 338), fought with a fraction of the forces at his disposal, which destroyed Thebes as a military power and made him undisputed master of the Greek world. Garrisons policed the settlement he imposed, and a conference at Corinth (summer 337) approved a common peace which guaranteed the stability of all governments party to it, prohibited constitutional change and entrenched Philip as executive head of the council

which directed its enforcement (see CORINTHIAN LEAGUE). It was intended to perpetuate Macedonian domination and did so. The meeting also witnessed Philip's proclamation of his war of revenge against Persia, a project doubtless long in gestation but only now publicized, and in 336 an expeditionary force under *Parmenion crossed the Hellespont to begin operations in Asia Minor.

Philip's last year was overshadowed by domestic conflict. His love match with Cleopatra provoked a rift in the royal house which saw his wife *Olympias in angry retirement and the heir-apparent, Alexander (see ALEXANDER (2) THE GREAT), in temporary exile in Illyria. There was a formal reconciliation; but tensions persisted, and Philip fell by an assassin's hand in autumn 336. The sources give personal motives, but there are also hints of a multiplicity of conspirators and the background to the murder is beyond speculation. He was interred at Aegae (many believe, in the splendid barrel-vaulted Tomb II in the Great Tumulus of Vergina), leaving his kingdom a military and economic giant but internally almost as distracted as it had been at his accession.

Philippi, a city in eastern *Macedonia on the *via Egnatia, overlooking a plain NE of Mt. Pangaeus. Its territory included rich gold mines, which were worked by *Thracians until in 360 BC Thasos annexed it and founded a city 'Crēnĭdēs'. The citizens of Crenides invoked the help of *Philip II against the Thracians. He enlarged the city, renamed it Philippi, and derived 1,000 talents a year from its mines. He treated it as a 'free' Greek city within his kingdom, drained its swamps and increased its territory. It became well known in 42 BC, when the forces of Marcus *Antonius (Mark Antony) and Octavian (see AUGUSTUS) defeated those of *Iunius Brutus and *Cassius Longinus; and the victors developed and enlarged Philippi as a Roman colony. The apostle *Paul founded the first Christian church at Philippi in AD 49. The site includes a fine theatre and four magnificent basilicas.

Philistus of *Syracuse, c.430–356 BC, friend, adviser, officer, and historian of *Dionysius (1) I and (2) II. He helped Dionysius I seize power in 406/5 and served for a long time as commander of the tyrant's stronghold on Ortygia. He was exiled for personal reasons in c.386 and on his return put in charge of the organization of colonies along the *Adriatic coast. He served as Dionysius II's political adviser and admiral.

A staunch opponent of *Plato's and Dion's re-forms, he died in 356 in the fight against the insurgent Syracusans.

Work His *History of Sicily* contained two parts, covering the time from the mythical beginnings until 363/2. The seven books of the first part brought the narrative down to the capture of *Acragas by the *Carthaginians in 406/5, the second part dealt in four books with the reign of Dionysius I from his accession in 406/5 until his death in 368/7. In addition there were two books on Dionysius II reaching down to 363/2. Philistus favoured the tyrants. Plutarch calls him 'the greatest lover of tyrants and more than any one else an admirer of the luxury, power, wealth, and marriage alliances of ty-rants'. He was nevertheless a very competent and important historian: ancient critics regarded him as an imitator of *Thucydides (2).

Philitas (or Philetas) of *Cos, poet and scholar, b. c.340 BC. Although little of his work has sur-vived, Philitas clearly influenced Hellenistic and Latin poetry. He came to represent the combin-ation of literary scholarship and poetic creativ-ity emulated by *Callimachus (2) and other 'learned poets'. His poetry was admired for its learning, small scale, and polish; his narra-tive elegy *Demeter* was esp. highly esteemed, and thought to be the object of many allusions by later poets. The character of Philetas in Longus' *Daphnis and Chloe* may be the vehicle for remin-iscences of P.'s poems. See NOVEL, GREEK.

Philo See PHILON (2).

Philochorus (c.340–260 BC) of Athens was a truly Hellenistic man. The mini-biography of him in the *Suda* reveals a man of religion, a patriot, and a scholar-historian, who wrote at least 27 works, of which the most famous was his *Atthis*. He was the last atthidographer and the most respected, to judge from the number of times his work was cited.

The *Atthis* was seventeen books long. We have over 170 fragments. It was arranged in the standard chronological form of the genre, by kings and archons (see ARCHONTES), and pre-sented its information in succinct factual no-tices in unadorned prose. Philochorus devoted only two books to the early period down to *Solon, and two more to the end of the 5th cent. The 4th cent., which had been treated in detail by *Androtion, was also reduced to two books. The remaining eleven books covered the 60 years from 320–260. So, Philochorus' main interest was the period of his mature years. Unfortunately nothing of significance has sur-vived from these books, because this period did not interest the later scholars who cited him. In his research Philochorus used documents and his own experience for his own time. For the earlier period he used Androtion. Philochorus was familiar with the works of *Herodotus, *Thucydides (2), *Ephorus, and *Theopompus.

Philocratēs, Athenian politician, mainly con-nected with the Atheno-Macedonian peace of 346. An attempt at negotiations in 348 was thwarted by a *graphē paranomōn, though *De-mosthenes (2) secured Philocrates' acquittal. In 346 he proposed crucial decrees authorizing dis-patch of the first embassy, acceptance of peace and alliance by Athens and her allies, and exten-sion of the treaty to *Philip II's descendants and political abandonment of Phocis, and he served on associated embassies. Athenian dissatisfac-tion with the outcome exposed him to prosecu-tion by *Hyperides for *bribery—alleged evidence included commercial ventures involv-ing wheat and *timber (a major Macedonian commodity), house-building, income from land provided by Philip, and ostentatious sexual and gastronomic self-indulgence—and he fled into exile (343). See INVECTIVE.

Philoctētēs, in myth leader of seven ships to *Troy, but left behind on *Lemnos suffering from a snakebite. The *Epic Cycle adds that while the Greeks were sailing to Troy they sac-rificed in Tenedos, and there Philoctetes was bitten and left behind on Lemnos because of the stench of his festering wound. Ten years later *Odysseus captured Priam's son Hele-nus, the Trojan seer, and learned from him that Troy could be taken only if Philoctetes was present; so *Diomedes fetched him from Lem-nos. He was healed by Machaon, then fought a duel with *Paris and killed him. *Aeschylus, *Sophocles, and *Euripides each wrote a *Philoc-tetes*, but only Sophocles' play survives. Sopho-cles adds that Philoctetes had the bow and inescapable arrows of *Heracles given to him for lighting the pyre on Mt. Oeta. Without the bow Troy would not fall; so *Neoptolemus is ordered by Odysseus to obtain it by trickery. But Neoptolemus' basic honesty causes compli-cations, and the play ends with Heracles *ex māchinā* ordering Philoctetes to Troy. Homer's *Odyssey* says that Philoctetes returned safely home after the war.

Philodēmus (c.110–c.40/35 BC), b. at Gadara in *Syria, d. probably at *Herculaneum; he came to Rome c.75 and eventually enjoyed the favour and powerful friendship of the Pīsōnēs. One of them, *Calpurnius Piso Caesoninus, was esp. attached to him and was perhaps the owner of the *Villa of the Papyri at Herculaneum. *Cicero's somewhat ironical praise of Philodemus shows that he was already well known to a Roman audience for his poetry in 55. His connections with Piso brought Philodemus the opportunity of influencing the brilliant young students of Greek literature and philosophy who gathered around him at Herculaneum and Neapolis, as is shown by Philodemus' addresses to and the responses of *Varius Rufus, *Virgil, Plotius Tucca, and *Horace (who names Philodemus in his *Satires*). Although his prose work, discovered in c.1,000 papyrus rolls in the philosophical library recovered at Herculaneum (see PAPYROLOGY, GREEK), is detailed in the strung-out, non-periodic style typical of Hellenistic Greek prose before the revival of the Attic style after Cicero (see ASIANISM AND ATTICISM), Philodemus like *Lucretius far surpassed the average literary standard to which most Epicureans aspired (see EPICURUS). In his elegant and often indecently frank erotic epigrams, some 35 of which are preserved in the *Palatine Anthology* (see ANTHOLOGY), he displays taste and ingenuity worthy of his fellow-citizen *Meleager (2). The success of these poems is proved by the allusions to, and imitations of, them in several passages of Horace, *Propertius, Virgil, and *Ovid. Although Cicero seems to imply that Philodemus' main activity was poetry, he makes clear that he also devoted himself, for Piso's benefit, to popularizing Greek philosophy, which he dealt with both systematically (Rhetoric, Poetics, Music, Ethics, Physics or, rather, Theology) and historically (in his comprehensive History of Philosophers, comprising an outline of the chronology of the Greek philosophical schools in ten books). His works covered a wide field, including in addition psychology, logic, aesthetics, and literary criticism. Esp. remarkable was his theory of art, which he conceived as an autonomous, non-philosophical activity, independent of moral and logical content, acc. to which artistic worth is determined not by its content or meaning, but by its form or aesthetic value. His particular originality is obscured by the fact that his works were not selected for preservation in the manner of other canonical authors. Philodemus succeeded in influencing the most learned and distinguished Romans of his age. No prose work of his was known until rolls of papyri, charred but largely legible, containing his writings, were discovered among the ruins of the villa at Herculaneum (now in Naples). See also PHILOSOPHERS ON POETRY.

Philolāus of Croton (c.470–390 BC) wrote one book, which was probably the first by a Pythagorean (see PYTHAGORAS). He was a contemporary of *Socrates and is mentioned in *Plato's *Phaedo* as arguing that *suicide is not permissible. Some fragments from his book survive. They show that it was the primary source for *Aristotle's account of Pythagoreanism. The book contained a cosmogony and presented astronomical, psychological, and medical theories. Philolaus argued that the cosmos and everything in it was made up not just of the unlimiteds (continua that are in themselves without limit, e.g. earth or void) used as *elements by other Presocratics, but also of limiters (things that set limits in a continuum, e.g. shapes). These elements are held together in a *harmonia* ('fitting together') which comes to be in accord with pleasing mathematical relationships. Secure knowledge is possible in so far as we grasp the number in accordance with which things are put together. Philolaus was the first to make the earth a planet. Along with the fixed stars, five planets, sun, moon, and a counter-earth (thus making the perfect number ten), the earth orbits the central fire.

Philon (1) of Larissa (159/8–84/3 BC), the last undisputed head of the *Academy. Philon studied in his native town under a pupil of *Carneades before he went to Athens, to study under Clitomachus, whom he succeeded as head of the Academy in 110/9. In 88, during the Mithradatic wars (see MITHRADATES), he left for Rome, where he numbered among his pupils *Cicero, who became his most devoted follower.

Under Philon, the sceptical Academy modified its attitude of strict suspension of judgement and adopted Carneades' account of the 'plausible impression' as a theory that would allow philosophers to accept the views they found most convincing, with the proviso that certain knowledge could not be achieved. Towards the end of his life Philon went a step further and claimed that knowledge was indeed possible, though not by the stringent standards of the *Stoic definition.

In accordance with the new fallibilism of his school, Philon also taught other philosophical subjects. Like the Stoics, he compared the philosopher to a doctor, and divided the teaching of ethics into five parts corresponding to the stages of a medical therapy, from persuading the pupil of the benefits of philosophy through the elimination of erroneous beliefs and the implanting of healthy views about goods and evils to teaching about the goal of life and advice for everyday living. Cicero tells us that Philon also taught rhetoric alongside philosophy; a combination that Cicero obviously found congenial.

Philon (2), **'Philo',** often known as **Philo Judaeus,** philosopher, writer and political leader, was the leading exponent of Alexandrian-Jewish culture (see ALEXANDRIA), and, together with *Josephus, the most significant figure in Jewish-Greek literature. Philo's voluminous works were a formative influence on *Neoplatonism and on Christian theology, from the NT on. His family was prominent in the Jewish diaspora and in the service of Rome in the east. The only fixed date in Philo's own life is AD 39/40, when, as an old man, he led the Jewish embassy to *Gaius (1); see *Gaius and the Jews*. Apart from those events, he himself seems to have confined his activities to the Alexandrian Jewish community. He made a pilgrimage to Jerusalem, but need not otherwise have had much contact with Palestine. Almost all his surviving works were apparently preserved in the library of *Caesarea built up by *Origen and then by *Eusebius. Some three-quarters of the corpus consists of exposition of the Pentateuch. Two tracts, *Against Flaccus* and *On the Embassy to Gaius* give a graphic account of the persecutions of the Jews under Gaius and of their political consequences. *Against Flaccus* dwells on the divine punishment inflicted on the persecutors of the Jews.

Philo operated within the Greek philosophical tradition and deployed an elaborate Greek literary language. At the same time, he was at home with the Greek Bible on which his commentaries were based. The sole authority of the Mosaic law was fundamental to him. The spuriousness of his Hebrew etymologies suggests, but does not prove, that he did not know Hebrew. His ontology was markedly Platonic: to provide a medium for the operation of a perfect God upon an imperfect world, he introduced a range of mediating powers. Philo's ethics are close to *Stoicism, but for him true morality is imitation of the Deity.

philosophers and politics *Plato in his *Republic* regarded good government as unattainable 'unless either philosophers become kings in our cities or those whom we now call kings and rulers take to the pursuit of philosophy'. He already recognized, however, that philosophers would either be reluctant to leave the contemplation of truth for the task of governing any but an ideal city, or would be ridiculed and rejected if they tried.

Philosopher-leaders were rare in the ancient world: *Cicero named only *Demetrius (1) of Phaleron. The Romans themselves sent philosophers to rule Tarsus, but it was in the 2nd cent. AD that admirers of Marcus *Aurelius could claim that Plato's ideal was finally fulfilled. Philosophers more commonly served their cities by educating and advising rulers or serving as ambassadors. In 155 BC when the Athenians wanted the senate to reduce a fine imposed on the city, they sent as envoys the *Stoic Diogenes, the *Peripatetic Critolaus, and the *Academic *Carneades. They succeeded in their missions, but also gave such attractive lectures that *Porcius Cato (1) objected that they were seducing Roman youth from traditional values.

The charge of corrupting the youth, already employed against *Socrates, was used at Rome as a reason for expelling philosophers from the city as early as 161 BC. As a preparation for public life, philosophy was suspect on several counts: (1) Philosophers, as Plato surmised, might reject practical politics. The Epicureans in fact advocated such abstention in normal circumstances. Stoics took the opposite line, so that their failure to participate was, or could be construed as, criticism of the existing regime. (2) Philosophers might insist on unrealistic moral standards in public life. The Romans were esp. prone to this view, so that whereas philosophers, except Epicureans, were regularly honoured at Athens and elsewhere in the Greek world for their contribution to educating the young, at Rome they were at first excluded from the privileges offered to doctors and teachers of rhetoric and literature for their services to the community.

The Hellenistic schools of philosophy were not interested in discussing ideal constitutions, but rather in prescribing moral conduct for rulers of any kind and in teaching their subjects how to preserve their integrity and exercise free speech. See KINGSHIP.

philosophers on poetry The engagement of philosophers with poetry was a recurrent and vital feature of the intellectual culture of

Graeco-Roman antiquity. By *c.*380 BC, *Plato in his *Republic* could already refer to 'a long-standing quarrel between philosophy and poetry'. Early Greek philosophy, while closely related to poetry (*Xenophanes, *Parmenides, and *Empedocles wrote in verse), set itself to contest and rival the claims of 'wisdom', *sophia*, made by and on behalf of poets. Xenophanes, repudiating anthropomorphic religion, cast ethical and theological aspersions on the myths of *Homer and *Hesiod; *Heraclitus expressed caustic doubts about the idea of poets as possessors and teachers of insight. Philosophy and poetry could be considered competing sources of knowledge and understanding. The stage was set for lasting debates about their relationship.

Plato, while emulating poetry in his myths and in features of his dramatic writing, produced a far-reaching critique of poetry's credentials as an educational force within Greek culture. Though sometimes scantily concerned with complexities of context, he responds to an existing tendency to regard poetic works as carrying normative significance: the putative 'truth' of poetry, which he so often (though not invariably) impugns, was in part a matter of taking poetry to provide models of human behaviour and morality. Plato's anxieties over poetry are based, besides, on an awareness of its immense psychological power, esp. in the theatre. Yet despite the *Republic*'s proposals for severe political censorship, Plato's dealings with poetry remain ambivalent and deeply felt: he quotes, echoes, and competes with it throughout his dialogues. But his critique rests, from first to last, on the premiss of philosophy's superior wisdom and judgement.

*Aristotle too is committed to the superior range of philosophical thought, but much readier than Plato to allow the independent cultural value of poetry. In *Poetics* 25 he asserts that poetic standards are not identical to those of *politikē* (ethics/politics), and the treatise as a whole, respecting generic traditions and recognizing the status of poetry as a distinct art, elaborates categories that focus upon the internal organization of poetic works. Yet Aristotle's stance is still markedly philosophical, not only in its method and many of its concepts, but also in discerning an affinity between poetry and philosophy. Poetry 'is more philosophical than history', because it 'speaks more of universals'. Aristotle's discussion of tragedy and epic ascribes to them the capacity to reveal deep features of human 'actions and life'; the pleasure of poetry arises from an experience that is simultaneously cognitive and strongly emotional.

By the later 4th cent., philosophical schools had established an institutional status which made their relationship to a traditional education in *mousikē* (poetry and music; see EDUCATION, GREEK, 1; MUSIC, 1) an urgent question. Both *Epicurus and *Zeno (2) are said to have rejected such conventional *paideia*. Yet the attitudes of their schools towards poetry were more complex and divergent than this suggests. Epicurus followed Xenophanes and Plato in attacking poetic myths as purveyors of false religious beliefs, to which the proffered antidote was his own natural philosophy. He asserted the need for philosophical judgement of poetry: 'only the wise man can discourse correctly about music and poetry'. Epicureans acquired a reputation for rejecting poetry; Metrodorus provocatively declared it unnecessary to know even the openings of Homer's epics. But the possibility of a more positive evaluation remained open, given the school's commitment to pleasure as the criterion of value: Epicurus himself allowed that philosophers could enjoy artistic performances. An Epicurean rapprochement with poetry was eventually effected both by *Lucretius' great work, and by the critical writings of *Philodemus, who regarded poetry as principally pleasurable, morally neutral in itself, yet capable of conveying ideas compatible with Epicurean philosophy. Lucretius and Philodemus demonstrate that Epicureanism had, by the 1st cent. BC, space for a subtle range of stances towards these issues.

Stoicism, by contrast, was solidly tied to a moralistic view of poetry—a view influenced by Plato, yet largely unplatonic in its inclination to 'save' poetry, wherever possible, either by allegorical interpretation or by exploiting the principle, propounded by Zeno himself, that not everything in poetry need be judged in terms of truth. Stoics as different as *Chrysippus and *Strabo, while acknowledging the scope (and sometimes the pleasures) of fiction, unequivocally sought ethical and didactic value in poetry; the habits of reading to which this led—habits immensely influential on later ages—can be seen in such figures as *Seneca the Younger, *Epictetus, and Marcus *Aurelius. At an extreme, Stoic subordination of poetry to philosophy amounted to redefinition: 'only the wise man can be a poet'.

Interpretive control, even to the point of appropriation, was perhaps the dominant tendency in ancient philosophy's dealings with poetry; Aristotle and Philodemus stand out as exceptionally liberal. Appropriation, but also reconciliation, reached a climax in the Neoplatonic reinterpretation of Homer as a fount of esoteric wisdom, symbolically expressed (see NEOPLATONISM). Thus, on the threshold of a new Christian synthesis of learning and culture, the 'ancient quarrel' was temporarily silenced.

philosophy, history of The *sophists of the later 5th cent. BC were probably the first to trace affiliations between the ideas of philosophers and their poetic predecessors (*Hippias (2)), and to classify views on the number and nature of the basic realities (*Gorgias). Both procedures are echoed in *Plato, but it is *Aristotle whose respect for the beliefs of the wise makes their employment a principled ingredient in philosophical enquiry, e.g. in the introduction to his *Metaphysics*, where he identifies and criticizes the first anticipations by previous thinkers of each of his four causes. Aristotle also composed monographs on the philosophies of individual thinkers or schools (e.g. *Democritus, the Pythagoreans; see PYTHAGORAS). It was left to his pupils to write systematic accounts of the growth of e.g. natural philosophy (*Theophrastus) and mathematics (*Eudemus), again focused on initial discoveries of key ideas. To the same period belong the first biographies of philosophers, as evidenced e.g. in surviving information about *Aristoxenus' account of Pythagoras.

The Hellenistic period saw the development of three further genres. (1) Successions. Following the model of institutions like the *Academy, where the headship of the school passed from one philosopher to his successor, scholars drew up lineages of teachers and pupils which included all the major and many of the minor figures known to us. *Philodemus' accounts of the Academy and the Stoa (see STOICISM) are early surviving examples. (2) Doxographies. For the dialectical purposes of dogmatists and *sceptics alike it was convenient to have to hand systematic accounts of the opinions (*doxai*) of philosophers on given topics, so arranged as to exhibit contradictions or at least differences between them. (3) 'On schools of thought'. Useful also were summary or introductory accounts of the main doctrines of different schools, such as those supplied in many of *Cicero's philosophical writings. These might include mention of variations or innovations introduced by later members of the schools. *Galen's little introduction on the medical 'sects' is a formal example of the genre. Much of the philosophical content

of *Diogenes (4) Laertius' *Lives of the Philosophers* will originally have belonged to it, although his work is principally biography organized according to the principles of succession literature.

If history of philosophy is taken to involve sympathetic reconstruction of an alien world of thought, no ancient writer practised history of philosophy. Mostly the past was appropriated for present use: whether to show the ingrained nature of another's error, or to invoke ancient authority, where the construction of an intellectual pedigree might be useful, or to illustrate the inevitability of contradiction between philosophers—or simply to provide materials for one or other of these purposes.

Philostratus, Lūcius Flāvius ('the Athenian'), enjoyed both a distinguished local career and a place in the circle of *Iulia Domna, wife of *Septimius Severus. She commissioned his 'Life' of *Apollonius (4) of Tyana, a philosophic holy man of the 1st cent. AD; later he produced 'Lives of the Sophists', and he is probably the author of most of a number of minor pieces, including '*Of Heroes*', a dialogue on the heroes of the Trojan War and their cults, and *Love Letters*.

The *Life of Apollonius* offers pagan hagiography under a sophistic veneer, and remains suspect both in sources and details; the *Lives of the Sophists* offer the foundation for our knowledge of the *Second Sophistic: they are sketches, sometimes affected and tendentious, of prestigious public speakers in action. *Of Heroes* offers an entertaining insight into how a sophistic writer might extend and 'correct' still vibrant Homeric materials.

In what we know of the work of Philostratus fluency and charm are often at odds with idiosyncrasy and rhetorical bravura, as well as a constantly equivocal attitude to facts and 'the real world'. Philostratus ranks as something of an arbiter of sophistic tastes and values; he is also an index of sophistic shortcomings.

Philōtas (d. 330 BC), Macedonian noble, son of *Parmenion and commander of the Companion cavalry during the early campaigns of *Alexander (2) the Great. After a career of distinction, in which he fought in all the major actions, he came to grief in 330, when he was accused of complicity in a court conspiracy, condemned by the Macedonian army, and executed after interrogation under torture. The details are mysterious, but nothing was proved against him other than failure to pass on information about the conspiracy. He was already under suspicion, victim of a covert investigation, and the conspiracy gave Alexander's younger marshals the opportunity to eradicate the influence of Parmenion.

philotīmia, lit. 'love of honour' (*tīmē*). The pursuit of honour(s), tangible or intangible, was a constant of élite behaviour throughout Graeco-Roman antiquity; all that changed was its context and the extent to which it was given unbridled expression or else harnessed to the needs of the community at large. Of the latter phenomenon Classical Athens (see DEMOCRACY, ATHENIAN) provides rich literary and epigraphic documentation, at city level and elsewhere; *philotimia* was good if its fruits brought communal benefit, and *tīmē* duly bestowed on the naturally competitive served as an object-lesson for all. See AGONES; EUERGETISM.

Phōcaea, northernmost of the *Ionian cities of Asia Minor (see PANIONIUM), occupying a site with twin harbours. Poorly endowed with land, the Archaic Phocaeans were renowned seafarers and traders, and *Herodotus stresses their close contacts with Tartessus in southern Spain; Greek *colonization of the French and Spanish coasts was largely their doing, above all *Massilia and Emporion. Besieged by a Persian army in 540, most citizens preferred emigration to submission, finally settling at Elea. Phocaea never recovered from their loss: Dionysius, the generalissimo of the Greek fleet in the *Ionian Revolt, was a Phocaean; but his city contributed only three ships.

Phōcion (402/1–318 BC), Athenian statesman and general, pupil of *Plato. No Athenian was *strategos* more often than Phocion's 45 times between 371 and 318. An incorruptible independent political thinker with conservative views, he opposed *Demosthenes (2)'s agitation against Macedon throughout, probably on grounds of practicability. This attitude did not prevent his pursuing Athenian interests as *strategos*. After *Chaeronea and again in 335 he negotiated milder treatment for Athens from the Macedonian kings.

Phōcis, a country of central Greece comprising the middle Cephissus valley and the valley of Crisa, which are linked loosely by passes over the southern spurs of Mt. Parnassus. Both areas were fertile. In the 6th cent. BC Phocis formed a strong federation (see FEDERAL STATES), issuing federal coinage and levying a federal army. Phocis' internal unity enabled it to resist the

aggression of its neighbours, who coveted the control of *Delphi and of the route to northern Greece via the Cephissus valley and the pass of Elatea to *Thermopylae, and the Phocians showed diplomatic skill.

Phoenicians, a people occupying the coast of the Levant; they are so named only in the classical sources; their own name for themselves is unknown, although the OT classes them as Canaanites. The royal Assyrian inscriptions (9th–7th cent. BC) refer to the cities of *Tyre, Sidon, Byblos, etc., as (in the form of *ethnics) do the Phoenician inscriptions. For the Classical Greeks, Phoenicia was the Phoenician homeland, without the precise boundaries later assigned by Rome. The Phoenicians were divided into several city-kingdoms.

The history of the Phoenicians is tied to the sea, as shown e.g. by their island-harbours at Tyre and Aradus and their harbour-settlements in the western Mediterranean; also by their expertise in ship-building (using wood from the Lebanon forests) and seafaring. This tie inspired two dominant trends in their history: their role in international trade—notably metals, textiles, *purple, foodstuffs, exotic materials, and craft-goods (see the trade of Tyre in Ezekiel, 27), and the spread of Phoenician settlements (trading posts and farming communities) from Spain via Africa to Egypt; of these *Carthage was the most famous. This movement began early in the 11th cent., reaching its climax in the 9th–8th cents., when Phoenician culture (arts, religion, and inscriptions) left traces over almost all of the Mediterranean.

The Phoenicians were also a vital element of the near east: the maritime strength of the region caused Assyrian and *Babylonian kings to conquer it several times, and the Phoenicians formed the backbone of the Persian navy in *Achaemenid times. They maintained close links with Palestine, Egypt (along with the Red Sea), Assyria and Arabia, and their arts were strongly influenced by the east.

From the beginning of their expansion, the Phoenicians came into contact with the Greeks, but it was only after the *Persian Wars that the Hellenization of Phoenicia began; see HELLENISM, HELLENIZATION. After their conquest (Tyre included) by Alexander, the Phoenician cities were gradually integrated into the Hellenistic *koinē* or shared culture, first under the Ptolemies (see PTOLEMY (1)), then the *Seleucids and finally Rome; but their political identity (based on their cities) and cultural character (notably their language) were partly preserved.

Phormion (1), Athenian admiral, first mentioned in 440 BC before *Samos. Thereafter he proved an excellent leader in Acarnania, at *Potidaea, and in *Chalcidice. In 430 he blockaded *Corinth from Naupactus; and next summer, by brilliant tactics, he defeated two larger Peloponnesian fleets, thus restoring Athenian influence in Acarnania. After his return (428), he is said to have been sentenced for peculation.

Phormion (2) (4th cent. BC) was the slave and later *freedman of the Athenian banker *Pasion (see BANKS), and himself worked in the bank. Shortly before Pasion's death he leased the bank from him, and later married his widow in accordance with his will. Persistent bad relations between him and his stepson *Apollodorus (2) led in c.349 to the latter unsuccessfully prosecuting him on a charge of embezzling money from the bank. Like Pasion, he was awarded Athenian *citizenship.

phratries, in Greek states, groups with hereditary membership and probably normally associated with specific locality(ies). The members were 'phrateres', related to words which in other *Indo-European languages mean 'brother'. Phratry names often, but not always, had the patronymic ending -idai.

Phratries are attested in a wide range of Greek states. Ionian Greeks, including Athenians, conceived of the institution as part of their Ionian heritage (see IONIANS). Celebration of the annual phratry festival *Apaturia was regarded as a criterion of Ionian identity.

We know most about phratries at Athens. In addition to numerous references in literary sources, esp. the orators, inscriptions attest them from the 7th to the 2nd cents. BC. Some nine phratries are now known by name. In total there were probably c.30. Before the reforms of *Cleisthenes (2) (508) every Athenian male belonged to a phratry, and phratries functioned as social groups concerned with matters of family and descent. Under *Draco's law on homicide, dating from the 620s, and re-enacted at the end of the 5th cent., members of the phratry of a victim of unintentional homicide are required to support the victim's family, and, if the victim has no family, to take on its role. This function as natural unit of community beyond the family was characteristic.

After Cleisthenes phratry membership continued to be necessary for a native-born Athenian citizen, along with membership of Cleisthenes' new institutional structure of *phylai, trittyes and *demes. The phratry apparently continued to play a major role in controlling matters relating to legitimacy of descent, including access to citizenship and inheritance of property. Phratry members appear as witnesses in 4th-cent. legal cases where matters of descent are in dispute. Down to the 2nd cent., naturalized citizens were normally enrolled in a phratry and a deme. The most substantial evidence for an individual Athenian phratry is three decrees, inscribed on stone in the early 4th cent., which regulate in detail admissions procedures.

Male children probably underwent a dual process of phratry introduction, in infancy at the meion and in adolescence at the koureion. There might also be a separate process of scrutiny, including a vote by the phratry on a candidate's eligibility. Under *Pericles' citizenship law, citizen descent was necessary in the female line as well as the male. The phratries seem to have taken greater account than the demes of women, who, while not normally regarded as phratry members, might sometimes be introduced to their fathers' phratries and were presented to their husbands' phratries at the gamēlia.

While phratries might pursue common activities throughout the year, phratry admissions normally took place at the Apaturia, at which there was also religious observance, esp. cult of *Zeus Phratrios and *Athena Phratria, feasting and competitions. Phratries could own property, which provided a source of income to support cultic and other activities and for loans to members; see CREDIT.

Phrynichus, an early Athenian tragic poet; see TRAGEDY, GREEK. The *Suda says that he won his first victory between 511 and 508 BC and was the first to introduce female characters in tragedy. *Themistocles was his chorēgos (see CHOREGIA) for a victorious production in 476, probably near the end of his career. At least two of his tragedies were on historical subjects. Soon after 494, when *Miletus, which had been aided by Athens, was sacked by the Persians (see IONIAN REVOLT), Phrynichus produced a Capture of Miletus, which, acc. to *Herodotus, so distressed the Athenians that they fined him 1,000 drachmas 'for reminding them of their own troubles'. He was remembered for the beauty of his lyrics and for inventive choreography.

He seemed to *Aristophanes to exemplify the 'good old days' of tragedy.

phȳlai The Greek word *phȳlē*, usually but mis-leadingly translated 'tribe', was widely used in the Greek world to denote the principal divisions of the citizen body. Two sets are well attested in the Archaic period: the *Dorian tribes Hylleis, Dymanes, and Pamphyloi, known as such in 7th-cent. Sparta and elsewhere, and the *Ionian–Attic tribes known in Archaic Athens, some Aegean islands, and Ionia. Archaic tribes appear to have functioned as military units (as *Tyrtaeus says) and as constituencies for the selection of magistrates or councillors.

The best-attested new system was that created by *Cleisthenes (2) for Attica in or just after 508/7 BC. The landscape was regarded as comprising three zones, Urban, Coastal, and Inland. Each zone was split into ten sections called *trittyes* ('thirdings'), to each of which were assigned between one and ten of the 139 existing settlements, villages, or town-quarters, which were henceforth termed *dēmoi* ('*demes'). Three sections, one each from Urban, Coastal, and Inland, were then put together to form a tribe. The 30 sections therefore yielded ten tribes, each named after a local hero and each with a geographically scattered membership roughly equal in size and hereditary in the male line thenceforward. They rapidly took on various functions. They became the brigading units for the army; constituencies for the election of magistrates, esp. the ten generals (see STRATEGOI), for the selection of members of the Council of 500 (see BOULE) and of the 6,000 jurors, and for the selection of boards of administrative officials of every kind; and bases for the selection of competing teams of runners, singers, or dancers at various festivals. They had their own corporate life, with officials and sanctuaries, and came to have an official order: Erechtheis, Aigeis, Pandionis, Leontis, Akamantis, Oineis, Kekropis, Hippothontis, Aiantis, and Antiochis.

physics today is distinguished from chemistry and biology. The same term, derived from the Greek word for 'nature', '*physis*', is used to describe a number of ancient inquiries where no such distinction is implied. 'Natural Philosophy' might be a reasonable definition of ancient physics. For some ancient authorities 'physics' explicitly excluded mathematics.

Before *Aristotle, physical inquiry ranged from the cosmological through to the observation and explanation of discrete natural phenomena. Early studies of the material origins of the world (see ELEMENTS), the position of the earth in space, along with speculation about what we now call magnetism, and the nature of sound and light, could all be thought of as parts of physical inquiry. In the first book of his *Metaphysics*, Aristotle reports in summary fashion that many of the earliest philosophers based their speculations about nature on the idea that the physical world is reducible to one or more basic starting-points or principles. *Thales is supposed to have given water a special status, *Anaximenes air, and so on. The *atomists Leucippus and *Democritus invented a theory of matter which, they hoped, would satisfy *both* strict logical demands for certain, immutable, knowledge about reality (laid down by *Parmenides) *and* account for the changing and unpredictable phenomena of the visible world. They posited a real world of first principles—atoms and void—and a secondary world of appearances, the result of the movement of the atoms in the void. (Aristotle praised Democritus for arguing 'physically' and not just 'logically', but criticized nearly all his predecessors for leaving important questions unanswered, notably about the origins of physical motion.)

2. *Plato's physical system is similarly based on a distinction between what is real and intelligible (the Forms) and the particulars we can see in the world around us, which share in different ways (though never completely) in the perfection of the Forms. Doubts about the extent to which the mathematical perfection of ultimate reality can ever be fully present in physical objects lie behind the reservations expressed by Plato about the reliability of the physical theory in his *Timaeus*. Matter, for Plato, is inherently chaotic, and the creator of Plato's universe had to struggle with the recalcitrant material substrate of physical being as he sought to model it in the image of the Forms.

Yet the desire to describe mathematically the behaviour of natural—physical—objects and phenomena did not always clash, even for Plato, and relations between mathematics and the physical world were studied throughout antiquity. Early evidence comes from the Pythagorean investigations into harmonics, but the idea that a mathematically describable order has left its imprint on at least some levels of creation was encouraged by Plato. In *Republic* 9, Plato prescribed a curriculum of physical subjects including *astronomy, stereometry, and harmonics for the education of the Guardians of his ideal state, because their study shows that the perfect order of the Forms is reflected to some extent at least in the world around us. See MUSIC, 5; PYTHAGORAS, 1; 9 below.

3. Aristotle is the author of the earliest surviving detailed work bearing the title *Physics*. For him, *physikē* is distinguished from the abstract study of number and shape in *mathēmatika* (see MATHEMATICS) and from divinity in *theologikē*. Physics involved going back to the first principles which underlie the phenomenal world of natural objects, and investigating their origins, number, behaviour, and interactions. The 'inquiry into nature' in Aristotle's view is the study of those things which do not exist independently of matter. It can thus be thought to include both the theoretical material contained in the *Physics* itself, the biological and zoological material in e.g. the *History of Animals*, what we might call the geophysical material in the *Meteorology*, along with the inherently more mathematical material of astronomy in *On the Heavens*.

In Aristotle's *Physics*, the first principles governing the behaviour of matter are investigated in detail. The nature of physical existence, of weight, qualitative variety, different types of motion and their origins, the nature of purpose-directed activity and its sources are all examined. It is here that the four types of causal question necessary for a full account of something's existence are formulated—the formal, final, material, and efficient. Aristotelian ideas about motion—notably his statements implying that the velocity of falling objects is inversely proportional to the resistance they meet and directly proportional to their weight, which made velocity in a void undefinable—were famously criticized and developed by much later commentators. Aristotle's successors as head of the Lyceum, *Theophrastus and *Straton, continued to stress the importance of the types of physical inquiry initiated by their master.

4. Many believe that Aristotle's criticisms of early atomic physics led *Epicurus and his followers to modify Democritean atomism. The extent of Epicurean innovation is hard to gauge, partly because of our lack of evidence for Democritus' own theory, and partly because Epicurus himself acknowledges few positive debts to any predecessors. Driven by the need to find arguments to dissolve fear, and esp. fear of death, Epicurean physics centres on proving the existence of ungenerated and permanent forms of matter—atoms—whose unpredictable and unpremeditated motion in the void can explain all natural phenomena. The Epicureans developed new arguments to prove the possibility of indivisible atoms, explain their motion and combination, and found new language to describe void. The phenomena of sensation and action at a distance (e.g. magnetic attraction) are all explained in terms of influxes or effluxes of atoms moving across the void. Purpose-directed activity in the domain of natural phenomena, and the active intervention of divine power in human life for good or ill, are denied. The study of the physical world is of value only insofar as it aids in the search for tranquillity.

5. With ethics and logic, physics was one of the cornerstones of Stoic philosophy. Although there is doctrinal variation within *Stoicism on the level of detail, *Diogenes (4) Laertius reports that the Stoics divided physics into the study of the world, of the elements, and the inquiry into causes. Stoic physics is an essential part of the broad Stoic inquiry into our place in the universe, and into the divine and guiding active principle which permeates everything, designing and steering it. Unlike the Epicureans, but following Plato and Aristotle, the Stoics denied the possibility of void within the cosmos, and many of the more sophisticated explanations of action at a distance in a continuum can be attributed to them.

6. Mathematical—geometrical—models of the behaviour of physical bodies developed rapidly in *mechanics, and also in what Aristotle calls the more 'physical' branches of *mathematics or the more 'mathematical' branches of physics, such as optics, acoustics and astronomy. Quite apart from the mathematical sophistication of these ancient inquiries, the level of methodological controversy, esp. between empiricist and rationalist positions, is striking. In the Aristotelian corpus there is a treatise on mechanics, almost certainly not by Aristotle himself, which deals with the theory and practical uses of balances, pulleys, and levers. *Archimedes' theoretical work on the behaviour of basic mechanical elements is characteristic of the subsequent application of strict geometry to the practical explanation of physical contrivances. Archimedes' *On the Equilibrium of Planes* deals with *i. a.* the problem of how to determine the centre of gravity in different types of figure. Other important ancient mechanical theoreticians include Heron of Alexandria and Pappus.

7. A group of ancient writers dealt with applied as well as theoretical mechanics. Heron and Philon of Byzantium wrote elaborate works on the subject, Philon dealing with the theory and practice of machines of war, Heron with mechanical automata.

8. The physics of sight, light, and colour occupied both physiologists and mathematicians. Natural philosophers and physiologists offered theories to explain the mechanisms of visual perception. Theoretical debate focused on the nature of light—was it a type of wave, or a tension in the continuum (a Stoic view), or the transport of something through the atomists' void? Geometrical optics was based on the assumption that light—or the visual ray—travels from the eye in straight lines. Systematic research into the behaviour of these lines begins (for us) with *Euclid's *Optics.

9. 'Pythagoras had no faith in the human ear', reports *Boethius. He sought instead fixed, mathematical ways of measuring consonances; the Pythagoreans were credited even in antiquity, with the discovery of the connection between the length of a vibrating body and its pitch. Further work on the subject was done by *Philolaus. Ancient harmonics was profoundly influenced by more general debates over how far the senses—the ear in this case—should be trusted over reason. There was also a long-running dispute over the nature of sound itself, which mirrors disagreements about the nature of light—is sound continuous, or discrete, to be analysed geometrically or arithmetically? The greatest ancient authority on harmonics is *Aristoxenus, whose *Elements of Harmonics* provided the basis for most subsequent treatments of both mathematical and practical harmonics.

physis (nature) as opp. *nomos (2) (law, convention). See POLITICAL THEORY.

Piazza Armerina, a hill-town of central south *Sicily famous for the remains of the most sumptuously appointed *villa so far discovered in the Roman empire. The complex, covering 1.5 ha. ($3^3/_4$ acres), consists of four parts: a triple-arched entrance with court beyond; the heart of the residential villa grouped around a peristyled garden, with a large reception hall and the private living quarters opening off a 70-m. (230-ft.)-long corridor; a banqueting suite to the south, set around another court; and an elaborate bath-suite. There are some 45 rooms in all; service quarters await identification. The reception hall was paved in marble, the remaining rooms and corridors with *mosaic floors of varying quality, some geometric but most figured. All are likely to have been laid by mosaicists from North Africa, probably based in *Carthage. The columns were of polychrome marble, the walls mostly frescoed. The villa was built within the first

three decades of the 4th cent. AD. The owner must have been a rich member of the senatorial order who had held magistracies at Rome—the assembling of animals for the games, and a chariot-race in the *Circus Maximus, are among the subjects depicted in the mosaics—but his identity has proved elusive.

pietās is the typical Roman attitude of dutiful respect towards gods, fatherland, and parents and other kinsmen. Pietās, personified, received a temple in Rome (vowed 191 BC, dedicated 181). She is often represented in human form, sometimes attended by a stork, symbol of filial piety; during the empire, Pietās Augusta appears on coins and in inscriptions. Some Romans adopted as *cognōmen* the term Pius; *Virgil's 'Pius *Aeneas' expresses the Roman ideal in his religious attitude, in his patriotic mission, and in his relations with father, son, and comrades. See RELIGION, ROMAN, TERMS RELATING TO.

piety See INTOLERANCE, INTELLECTUAL AND RELIGIOUS (for action against impiety); PRAYER; RELIGION (various entries); RITUAL; SACRIFICE.

pilgrimage (Christian) Despite the NT's disavowal of the localized cults of Judaism and the surrounding pagan world—the need was for holy lives rather than holy places—early Christians still clung to their sacred sites. Jesus' followers preserved some memory of the location of his tomb in *Jerusalem and (at least by the mid-2nd cent.) of his birthplace in Bethlehem; while further afield the burial places of martyrs on the outskirts of their cities attracted local gatherings. In maintaining these recollections of their sacred past, the first Christian pilgrims tried to assert some communal identity in a world indifferent or hostile to their faith.

Pindar, Greek lyric poet, native of Cynoscephalae in *Boeotia, b. probably in 518 BC. His last datable composition belongs in or shortly after 446. He achieved panhellenic recognition early; at the age of 20 he was commissioned by the ruling family of *Thessaly to celebrate the athletic victory of a favourite youth. His commissions covered most of the Greek world, from *Macedonia and Abdera in the north to *Cyrene in the south, from *Italy and *Sicily in the west to the seaboard of *Asia Minor in the east. He probably travelled widely. He is already a classic for *Herodotus, and was regarded by many in antiquity as the greatest of the nine poets of the lyric *canon.

The *Alexandrian editors divided Pindar's works into seventeen books: *hymns, paeans, *dithyrambs (2 books), processional songs (2), maiden-songs (3), dance songs (2), encomia, *dirges, and victory songs (4). Of these, the only books to survive intact are the choral victory songs composed for the formal celebration of victories in the four panhellenic athletic festivals (see AGONES). His patrons were the great aristocratic houses of the day, and the ruling families of Cyrene, *Syracuse and *Acragas. The scale of this section of the corpus indicates the value which Pindar, like other Greeks, placed on *athletics as a testing ground for the highest human qualities. The victory song was normally performed either at the athletic festival shortly after the victory or after the victor's return to his native city. Since time for composition and choir training was limited, the former type tends to be brief. Odes composed for performance after the victor's return are usually longer and more elaborate. The longer odes usually have three sections, with the opening and closing sections devoted to the victor and his success and the central section usually containing a mythic narrative. The opening is always striking, often elaborate, consisting either of an abrupt announcement of victory or a focusing process which sets the victory against a general background, usually through a hymnal invocation or a preparatory list of objects, experiences, or achievements (*priamel*). In the sections devoted to the victor conventional elements recur. The god of the games is honoured. Place of victory and event are announced, with details often surrendered slowly in order to maintain a forward tension (description of victory is rare, however). Earlier victories by the patron or other members of his family are listed; such lists are carefully crafted to avoid monotony. The city is praised, and in the case of boy victors the father and usually the trainer. Self-praise by the poet is also common. More sombre notes are struck. The poet often reminds the victor of his mortality or offers prayers to avert misfortune; these elements reflect the Archaic fear of divine envy and awareness of the psychological dangers of success; they function both to warn and to emphasize the extent of the achievement. Maxims (see GNŌMĒ) are frequent. Recurrent themes are the impossibility of achievement without toil, the need for divine aid for success, the duty to praise victory, the vulnerability of achievement without praise in song, the importance of inborn excellence and the inadequacy of mere learning. The effect of this moralizing is to give the ode a pronounced didactic as well as celebratory quality.

Pindar usually chooses myths dealing with the heroes of the victor's city. As with most Greek *lyric, the myth is not narrated in full. Usually a single incident is selected for narration, with other details dealt with briskly. Even the lengthy quasi-epic myth of *Pythian* 4 proceeds by a series of scenes, not an even narrative. Audience familiarity with the myth is assumed. Pindar regularly adopts an explicit moral stance with reference to the events narrated. The role of myth varies. Sometimes the myth has only a broad relevance to the victor, in that the deeds of the city's heroes highlight the tradition which has produced the victor's qualities. Sometimes myth presents a negative contrast to the victor. Often it appears to reflect an aspect of the victory or the victor's situation as developed in the direct praise.

His poems are written in regular stanzas, either strophic or triadic (see LYRIC POETRY (GREEK)). His manner of writing is both dense and elaborate. Words are used sparingly. Compound adjectives abound. The style is rich in *metaphor, and rapid shifts of metaphor are common. Transition between themes is rapid. He adhered throughout his life to a conservative set of standards. His thought impresses not for its originality but the consistency and conviction with which he presents the world view of the aristocrat of the late Archaic period. His religion is the traditional Olympian religion (see RELIGION, GREEK), combined in *Olympian* 2 and the dirges with elements of mystery cult and Orphico-Pythagorean belief (see ORPHISM; PYTHAGORAS, PYTHAGOREANISM).

piracy is armed robbery involving the use of ships. It is often hard to distinguish piracy from warfare in the ancient sources.

The earliest references to pirates are in the *Homeric poems, esp. the *Odyssey*, where piracy is an activity which brings no shame upon its practitioners, although it may be disapproved of for the misery it brings to the victims. None of the Homeric heroes is ever called a pirate, but they carry out seaborne raids which closely resemble the actions of those referred to as pirates.

Piracy begins to be differentiated from war in the Classical period, when the political aims of the Greek city-states began to take precedence over the economic goals of raiding and plundering. Nevertheless, pirates are often mentioned by *Thucydides (2) and *Xenophon in their accounts of the wars of the 5th and 4th cents. BC, and the speeches of the Attic orators show that accusations of piracy were made by both sides in the rivalries between Athens and *Macedon in the second half of the 4th cent.

In the Hellenistic period the main difference between piracy and warfare was the scale of activity. Many pirates operated on the fringes of wars in this period. Although attacks on ships at sea are mentioned occasionally in the ancient sources, the main threat from piracy seems to have been to coastal settlements. Numerous inscriptions from this period record sudden attacks by unidentified pirates on the islands and coastal cities of the Aegean, in search of both plunder and prisoners to be ransomed or sold. The abduction of a well-born young man or woman by pirates who sell their captive as a slave (see SLAVERY) became a common theme in literature.

The custom of plundering enemies in reprisal for injuries or insults suffered could be used by some groups to justify acts which others might have called piracy. Much of the piracy found in sources from the 5th to the 2nd cents. BC involves reprisals. The rules governing reprisals were vague. *Polybius criticized the Aetolians esp. for their abuse of this custom.

Thucydides credited *Minos with clearing the seas of pirates, but, until the 1st cent. BC, no ancient state possessed the resources to suppress piracy on anything more than a local scale, although even small successes might win fulsome praise and help to legitimize political power. Suppression of piracy required depriving pirates of bases on land, which entailed the conquest and control of territory. Without cooperation between states, or the imposition of a policy by a single imperial power, piracy could easily flourish in many parts of the Mediterranean. The Athenians took some action to limit piracy in their own interests in the 5th and 4th cents., as did the Rhodians (see RHODES) in the Hellenistic period. Both were warmly applauded by later writers. The rise of Roman power in the Mediterranean was accompanied by a gradual realization that the Romans should take a stand against those perceived as pirates, but little action had been taken by the 2nd cent., when pirates based in Cilicia began to cause serious problems in the eastern Mediterranean.

The attitude of the Romans towards piracy in the Mediterranean changed towards the end of the 2nd cent. The campaign of Marcus Antonius in Cilicia in 102 was specifically directed against pirates, and a law of 100 concerning the eastern provinces enjoins all Rome's allies and friends to assist in the suppression of piracy. Further campaigns by Roman magistrates in the 70s and 60s, most famously that of *Pompey in 67, reduced the areas from which pirates were able to operate, but piracy remained a problem at the start of Augustus' reign. It was only after the Roman emperors had secured control of the entire coastline of the Mediterranean that they could minimize piracy.

See NAVIES; SEA POWER.

Piraeus, the great harbour complex of Athens, is a rocky limestone peninsula some 7 km. (4–5 mi.) SW of Athens, which *Themistocles began to fortify in 493/2 as a base for Athens' rapidly expanding fleet in preference to the open roadstead of Phaleron. It has three harbours, Zea and Munichia on the east, used exclusively by naval shipping. Zea possessed 196 shipsheds and Philon's Arsenal. The biggest harbour, Kantharos (Goblet) or Megas Limēn (Great Harbour), lies to the west and accommodated, in addition to warships, a thriving emporium (see EMPORION) on its north and east shoreline comprising 'five stoas round about the harbour', of which some traces remain. Its urban development dates to *c.*450 BC when *Hippodamus of Miletus 'cut up Piraeus' by laying it out on an orthogonal plan. The presence of numerous *metics led to the establishment of many foreign cults here, including the *Thracian Great Goddess Bendis, *Isis, and Mother of the Gods (see CYBELE). In 458/7 Piraeus was joined to Athens by *Long Walls, and in *c.*446 the building of the Middle Wall eliminated Phaleron from the fortified area. In 429 moles were constructed on either side of each harbour's mouth which could be closed by chains in time of war. The fortifications were destroyed by the Spartans in 404 but rebuilt by *Conon (1) in 393. Though the port revived in the mid-4th cent. BC, it never became more than the ghost of its former *Periclean self. During the Macedonian occupation (322–229) it rapidly lost its pre-eminence as the trading capital of the eastern Mediterranean and its population dwindled. To this period, however, dates the well-preserved theatre in Zea. *Sulla's destruction of the town in 86 was so ruthless that little was visible to *Pausanias (3). Several important bronze statues, including those of *Apollo, *Artemis, and *Athena, which were buried at the time to escape destruction, came to light in 1959. As headquarters of the fleet, Piraeus constituted the heartland of Athenian *democracy and was the focus of the resistance to the *Thirty Tyrants, thereby justifying *Aristotle's claim that its population was 'more democratic' than that of Athens'.

Pīrithoŭs, in myth, a Lapith (see CENTAURS), son by *Zeus of *Ixion's wife. *Homer knows of him as fighting the Centaurs, presumably in the quarrel mentioned in *Odyssey* 21. Marrying Hippodamīa, he forgot to invite *Ares to his wedding-feast. For that or some other reason (the simplest is that they were very drunk) the Centaurs abused his hospitality by offering violence to Hippodamia, and a fierce fight began, ending in the victory of the Lapiths.

Pirithous was a close friend and comrade of *Theseus, and he took his share in the carrying off of *Helen, the war against the *Amazons, and finally Theseus' descent to *Hades, which, indeed, in one account was undertaken to get *Persephone as wife for Pirithous, in return for his services in the matter of Helen. Theseus in most accounts escapes; Pirithous generally does not.

The fight of Lapiths and Centaurs appears in early Archaic art as a pitched battle in armour. The brawl at the feast first appears in the early Classical period, in Attic vase-painting, and the west pediment of the temple of *Zeus at Olympia. Pirithous is also shown helping Theseus to abduct Helen, pictured from the mid-6th cent. Theseus and Pirithous were shown in the Underworld by *Polygnotus.

Pisander, Athenian politician, often attacked in comedy for corruption and cowardice, and ridiculed for being fat (see COMEDY (GREEK), OLD). As an apparent democrat he took a principal part in the investigation into the mutilation of the *herms (415 BC), but in 412 he showed still more energy in organizing the oligarchic revolution (see OLIGARCHY): he travelled between *Samos and Athens, and seems to have been the author of the motion which brought the régime of the *Four Hundred into being. On the fall of that régime he fled to Sparta and was convicted of treason in his absence.

Pīsistratus, tyrant of Athens (see TYRANNY). He first came to prominence through his success in the war against *Megara (c.565 BC). In a period of aristocratic faction between Lycurgus and the *Pedieis* ('Plainsmen') and the *Alcmaeonid Megaclēs and the *Paralioi* ('Shoremen'), he created a third faction, the *Hyperakrioi* or *Diakrioi* ('Hillsmen', probably of NE *Attica: the factions probably reflect regional bases of support). He

first seized power with the bodyguard granted him by the Athenians (c.560). Ousted by the other two factions, he returned with Megacles' support. However, the Alcmaeonid alliance disintegrated, and he went into exile in *Macedonia. He mustered support from *Eretria and other cities (e.g. *Thebes), and he exploited the mines of Mt. Pangaeus. Armed with money and Argive *mercenaries (see ARGOS), he landed near *Marathon, c.546, defeated opposition at the battle of Pallene, and established a tyranny that lasted for 36 years. He died in 527.

Sources agree that Pisistratus' rule, financed by a 5 per cent tax and perhaps family resources from the Strymon area (see THRACE), was benevolent and law-abiding. Despite the mention of exiles, he seems to have achieved a *modus vivendi* with other aristocratic families (who are later found holding archonships: see HIPPIAS (1)). Strained relations with the Philaïds may have been eased by *Miltiades' colonization of the *Chersonese, whose strategic importance suggests it had Pisistratus' blessing. Athenian interests were strengthened by Pisistratus' control of *Naxos, and recapture of *Sigeum, foreshadowing Athens' later maritime expansion. He lent money to poor farmers and instituted travelling judges.

From the 560s, Athens begins to acquire a monumental appearance and become a *panhellenic artistic centre. The archaeological record indicates rapidly increasing prosperity, as Attic black-figure becomes (from the 560s) the dominant exported pottery. How much can be attributed to Pisistratus, rather than to the indirect effects of internal peace and external expansion, is uncertain, and archaeological evidence is inconclusive. The *Panathenaea, reorganized in 566/5, and City *Dionysia prospered, but Pisistratus cannot securely be credited with establishing the former, or with erecting the (so-called 'old') temple of Athena on the Acropolis built about then. The beginning of Athenian *coinage, attested archaeologically by 550, might imply the ruler's support. Like other Archaic aristocrats, he probably used religious cult to consolidate his position or enhance *polis* cohesion. He purified *Delos and instituted a festival there. Other cults to Apollo were probably fostered by him in Athens, that of Pythian *Apollo and (perhaps) Apollo Patrōōs (first temple built in the Agora, c.550). Of secular buildings, as well as the Enneakrounos fountain-house, he can probably be associated with other building in the Agora, including the Stoa Basileios: in short with the further clearing of the Agora and its

development as civic centre. (See ATHENS, TOP-
OGRAPHY; HIPPIAS (1); HIPPARCHUS (1).

Pithēcūsae, the largest island in the Bay of
Naples and the site of the first and most northerly Greek base in the west. See COLONIZATION,
GREEK. The acropolis was in continuous use between the mid-8th and the 1st cents. BC. An
emporion rather than an *apoíkia*, Pithecusae
was settled by Chalcidians and Eretrians (see
CHALCIS; ERETRIA). Throughout the second half
of the 8th cent. it served as a large and vital 'pre-
colonial' staging-post—with a stable population
numbered in thousands—at the western end of
the route from the Aegean and the Levant. The
suburban industrial complex has yielded abundant evidence for early metallurgical production; competent local versions of Euboean Late
Geometric pottery (see POTTERY, GREEK) were
produced en masse, and expatriate Protocor-
inthian potters were also active.

Pittacus of *Mytilene (c.650–570 BC), statesman, lawgiver, and sage. He commanded in
the war against Athens for *Sigeum, on which
*Periander of Corinth later arbitrated; helped to
overthrow the tyrant Melanchros, then after
further complex factional struggles, was elected
'dictator' for ten years. After ten years he duly
laid down office and died ten years after that.
One of his sayings was that 'painted wood', i.e.
law, was the best protector of the city. His best-
remembered law doubled the penalty for all
offences committed when drunk. A moderate
reformer, like *Solon, he was violently attacked
by his fellow citizen and former ally *Alcaeus,
whose family had helped overthrow tyranny but
wished to perpetuate the old aristocratic rule.

plagiarism The more sophisticated ancient
critics distinguished 'imitation' of earlier
writers from 'theft'. 'Theft' involves derivative
copying and is condemned: this, and only this,
is plagiarism. 'Imitation' is an acceptable, even
normal, re-use, such that the 'borrowed' material is recreated as the borrower's 'own property'
and (perhaps because the original is well
known) the relationship between new and
old is acknowledged rather than concealed.
When *Seneca the Elder suggests that *Ovid
imitates *Virgil 'not as pilferer but as open ap-
propriator', the distinction is clear; so too when
'Longinus' praises a whole tradition of writers,
from *Archilochus to *Plato, for their re-use of
*Homer.

More often, however, the damaging label,
'plagiarism', was applied routinely to imitation
in general. *Aristophanes claimed that *Eupolis'
Maricas was his own *Knights* 'worn inside out',
and that other comic writers were copying his
comparisons. In Rome, *Terence was accused of
'theft' for reworking Greek material already
translated or adapted by his predecessors. Philosophers as eminent as *Anaxagoras, Plato, and
*Epicurus were all accused of stealing other
thinkers' ideas.

The preoccupation with plagiarism over
many centuries serves as a reminder that ancient literature, esp. poetry, was expected to be
'new'. Certainly, many writers, Greek and
Roman, are anxious to assert the necessity of
originality or their own claim to it.

plague, a term confusingly employed by ancient historians to designate epidemics of infec-
tious *diseases. Epidemics in antiquity were not
necessarily caused by the disease now called
plague. The major epidemic diseases are dens-
ity-dependent. The 'plague of Athens' (see
below) was an isolated event in Greek history,
but there is more evidence for great epidemics
during the Roman empire. Their frequency increased because of *population growth. Most of
the epidemics described by Roman historians,
e.g. *Livy who relied on the annalistic tradition,
are described so briefly that there is no hope of
identifying the diseases in question. Epidemics
are neglected in the major theoretical works of
ancient medicine (the Hippocratic corpus (see
HIPPOCRATES and GALEN)) because doctors had
no knowledge of the existence of micro-organ-
isms and had difficulty applying the types of
explanation they favoured (in terms of the diet
and lifestyle of individuals; also, later, the theory of the four *humours) to mass outbreaks of
disease.

*Thucydides (2) described the so-called
'plague of Athens' (430–426 BC), the most famous epidemic in antiquity. Unfortunately there
is no agreement regarding the identification of
the disease. Epidemic typhus and smallpox are
the strongest candidates, but true plague has
many advocates, along with the hypothesis
that the disease organism is now extinct. Thucydides recognized the role of contagion in
transmitting the infection.

The second famous plague in antiquity was
the 'Antonine plague', which attacked the
Roman empire in the 2nd cent. AD. Galen, the
main source, does not provide a comprehensive
description, but gives details which suggest

smallpox. Typhus and smallpox were probably the most important causes of epidemics in antiquity.

planets See ASTROLOGY; ASTRONOMY; PTOLEMY (2), 2.

plants, knowledge of See BOTANY.

plants, sacred Plants are associated with particular gods by virtue of their special properties of *purification and healing (see PHARMACOLOGY), or because of their symbolic value usually connected with fertility and growth. Thus corn is sacred to *Demeter who taught its cultivation to man. Similarly the vine belongs to *Dionysus as the god of *wine. The sexual symbolism of the pomegranate as the attribute of *Persephone and *Hera, goddess of women and marriage, is well known. In ritual, plants symbolized the annual death and rebirth of vegetation, as in the pre-Greek cult of Hyacinthus.

Corn also symbolized the recurring cycle of vegetation in the Eleusinian *mysteries (see ELEUSIS) but acquired moral and political overtones after 600 BC under Orphic influence (see ORPHISM) and after the annexation of Eleusis by Athens. Plants had *magical and medicinal properties: the withy (Gk. *lygos*; Lat., *agnus castus*) bound the image of Artemis Orthia in *Sparta. The use of the *lygos* in Demeter's *Thesmophoria was intended to reduce the sexual drive of the women worshippers. But it is doubtful if such plants were intrinsically sacred, any more than the wild olive awarded to the Olympic victor (see OLYMPIC GAMES), the bay leaves of the *Pythian Games or the wild celery of the *Nemean Games.

Roman interest in herbal medicine produced some specialist, also much superstitious and unscientific, literature in the early empire. *Pliny the Elder wrote extensively on healing and magic plants.

Plataea, a city in south *Boeotia situated between Mt. Cithaeron and the Asopus river, commanding a small plain. In the last quarter of the 6th cent. BC *Thebes tried to force it into the Boeotian Confederacy (see FEDERAL STATES). An appeal to *Sparta for support having failed, Plataea entered into an alliance with *Athens. The border between Plataea and Thebes became the Asopus river. The Plataeans turned out in force to support Athens at the battle of *Marathon, despite the denials of Athenian orators. A site on the battlefield has been claimed as the mass grave of the Plataeans. The greatest fame of Plataea comes from the final battle there between the Greeks and the Persians in 479 BC, when some 600 Plataeans fought alongside the other Greeks; in celebration of the victory the Greeks erected the altar of *Zeus Eleutherius. See next entry.

Plataea faded into temporary obscurity in the early 5th cent.. After the defeat of the Athenian Tolmides at the battle of Coronea in 447, however, it joined the new *Boeotian Confederacy. The Theban attack on it in 431 was the real start of the *Peloponnesian War. Most inhabitants having fled to Athens, the survivors, after a spirited defence, surrendered in 427 and were put to death. Rebuilt after the war, Plataea was independent under the terms of the *King's Peace until 373, when Thebes again seized it. Again survivors found refuge in Athens. After the battle of *Chaeronea in 338, *Philip II restored it. *Alexander (2) the Great gave Plataea its opportunity for revenge when he destroyed Thebes in 335.

Plataea, battle of (479 BC). The battle, which finished *Xerxes' attempt to conquer Greece (see PERSIAN WARS), falls into three stages. In the first, the Greeks, commanded by *Pausanias (1) clung to the lower slopes of Cithaeron (the mountain range which separates this part of *Boeotia from *Attica), and fought off the Persian cavalry, killing its commander. This encouraged them to move down towards the river Asopus, where water-supplies were better, but exposed them to continuous harassment by Persian cavalry, eventually leading to their being denied access to the Asopus, and the choking up of the Gargaphia spring. A planned night withdrawal then went disastrously wrong, leaving the Athenians isolated on the left, the Spartans and Tegeates on the right, and the centre just outside Plataea itself. This perhaps tempted the Persian commander, *Mardonius, to order a general attack, but his Asiatic troops were decisively beaten by the Spartans and their comrades, and his Boeotian allies by the Athenians.

plate, precious (Greek and Roman) Vessels of *gold and *silver are often mentioned in literary texts. *Pindar described a shallow gold bowl as 'the peak of all possessions'. Greek temple inventories list large quantities of plate and they often tell us the weights of items. Herodotus also records the gold and silver dedications made by various Lydian kings such as *Gyges, *Alyattes, and *Croesus. As silver and gold can be reworked, few items of ancient plate have survived in their original form. Likewise *sanctuaries as depositories of such wealth were often looted. The study of Roman plate is helped by the discovery of plate lost in the eruption of *Vesuvius in AD 79. Two major hoards have been recovered: one at Boscoreale and the other in the House of Menander at *Pompeii.

Plato of Athens (*c*.429–347 BC), descended from rich and influential Athenian families on both sides. His own family, like many, was divided by the disastrous political consequences of the *Peloponnesian War. His stepfather Pyrilampes was a democrat and friend of *Pericles, but two of his uncles, *Critias and *Charmides, became leading oligarchs. At some point Plato renounced ambition for a public career, devoting his life to philosophy. The major philosophical influence on his life was *Socrates, but in three important respects Plato turned away from the example of Socrates. He rejected marriage and the duty of producing citizen sons; he founded a philosophical school, the *Academy; and he produced large quantities of written philosophical works (as well as the shadowy 'unwritten doctrines' produced at some point in the Academy, for which we have only secondary evidence).

Apart from the *Apology*, his version of Socrates' speech in his own defence at his trial in 399, Plato's works are all *dialogues in which he does not himself appear. The philosophical point of this is to detach him from the arguments which are presented. Plato is unique among philosophers in this constant refusal to present ideas as his own, forcing the reader to make up his or her own mind about adopting them—a strategy which works best in the shorter dialogues where arguments are presented in a more lively way. For Plato this detachment and use of dialogue is not a point of style, but an issue of epistemology: despite various changes of position on knowledge, he remains convinced throughout that nothing taken on trust, second-hand, either from others or from books, can ever amount to a worthwhile cognitive state; knowledge requires effort from the person concerned. Plato tries to stimulate thought rather than to hand over doctrines.

This detachment also makes Plato himself elusive, in two ways. First, we know very little about him personally. Later biographies are patently constructed to 'explain' aspects of the dialogues. The seventh of a series of 'letters by Plato' has been accepted as genuine by some, and has been used to create a historical background to the dialogues. But such 'letters' are a

recognized fictional genre (see PSEUDEPIGRAPH-ICAL LITERATURE); it is misguided to use such material to create a basis for the arguments in the dialogues, which are deliberately presented in a detached way.

Second, the dialogues themselves are extremely varied and interpretatively often quite open. Since antiquity it has been debated whether Plato's philosophical legacy should be taken to be one of a set of doctrines, or of continuing debate and argument. The 'new', sceptical *Academy read Plato for the arguments, and Plato's heritage was taken to be a continuation of the practice of argument against contemporary targets. The dialogue most favourable to this kind of interpretation is *Theaetetus*, in which Socrates presents himself as a barren midwife, drawing ideas out of others but putting forward none himself. However, even in antiquity we find the competing dogmatic reading of Plato, in which the dialogues are read as presenting pieces of doctrine which the reader is encouraged to put together to produce 'Platonism', a distinctive system of beliefs. The dogmatic reading has to cope with the diverse nature of the dialogues and the unsystematic treatment of many topics, with apparent conflicts between dialogues and with the changing and finally disappearing role of Socrates as the chief figure. These problems are often solved by appeal to some development of Plato's thought.

Since the 19th cent. much energy has been expended on the chronology of the dialogues, but, in spite of computer-based work, no stylistic tests establish a precise order. In any case a chronology of the dialogues is interesting only if it tracks some independently established development of Plato's thought, and attempts to establish this easily fall into circularity. Stylistically, however, the dialogues fall into three comparatively uncontroversial groups. (1) The 'Socratic' dialogues, in which Socrates is the main figure, questioning others about their own positions but arguing for none himself, though characteristic views of his own emerge. This group includes *Ion*, *Laches*, *Lysis*, *Apology*, *Euthyphro*, *Charmides*, *Menexenus*, *Hippias Major*, *Hippias Minor*, *Protagoras*, *Crito*, *Cleitophon*, *Alcibiades*, *Lovers*, *Hipparchus* (the last three are often doubted as Plato's work). Two dialogues generally regarded as transitional between the Socratic and middle dialogues are *Gorgias* and *Meno*. Two dialogues which use the Socratic form but have much in common with the later works are *Euthydemus* and *Theaetetus*. (2) The 'middle' dialogues, in which Socrates remains the chief figure, but, no longer undermining others' views, sets out, at length, many positive ideas: this group includes *Phaedo*, *Republic*, *Symposium*, and *Phaedrus*. (3) The 'later' dialogues, in which Socrates retreats as the main interlocutor, and Plato deals at length, sometimes critically, with his own ideas and those of other philosophers, in a newly detailed and increasingly technical and 'professional' way: this group includes *Cratylus*, *Parmenides*, *Sophist*, *Statesman*, *Philebus*, and *Laws*. *Timaeus* and *Critias* are usually put in this group.

There is no uncontroversial way of presenting Plato's thought. Many aspects of his work invite the reader to open-ended pursuit of the philosophical issues; others present more developed positions, substantial enough to be characterized as 'Platonic' even for those who reject the more rigid forms of the dogmatic reading. While no brief survey of Plato's varied and fertile thought can be adequate, some major themes recur and can be traced through several works.

Ethical and Political Thought Plato insists on the objectivity of values, and on the importance of morality in personal life. The 'protreptic', exhorting (to philosophy), passage in *Euthydemus* anticipates the Stoics in its claim that what are called 'goods' (health, wealth, and so on) are not really so; the only good thing is the virtuous person's knowledge of how to use these things in a way consonant with morality. The assumption is explicitly brought out that everyone pursues happiness, though we have, before philosophical reflection, little idea of what it is, and most confuse it with worldly success; the choice of virtue (Gk. *aretē*) is embodied in the worldly failure Socrates. Many of the Socratic dialogues show Socrates trying to get people to rethink their priorities, and to live more morally; he is sure that there is such a thing as virtue, though he never claims to have it. He further identifies virtue with the wisdom or understanding that is at its basis, the unified grasp of principles which enables the virtuous to act rightly in a variety of situations, and to explain and justify their decisions and actions.

In *Protagoras*, we find the claim that this wisdom will be instrumental in achieving pleasure; this view is examined respectfully, and although we find attacks on the idea that pleasure could be our end in *Phaedo* and *Gorgias*, Plato reverts to some very hedonistic-seeming thoughts in *Philebus* and *Laws*. He is clearly tempted at times by the idea that some form of pleasure is inescap-

ably our aim, although after *Protagoras* he never thinks that our reason might be merely instrumental to achieving it. Apart from cryptic and difficult hints in *Philebus*, he never achieves a substantive characterization of the virtuous person's understanding.

In some of the early and middle dialogues Plato conflates the wisdom of the virtuous individual with that of the virtuous *ruler*; the skill of running one's own life is fused with that of achieving the happiness of others. The culmination of this is *Republic*, where individual and state are similar in structure, and the virtuous individual is produced only in the virtuous state. Later Plato divides these concerns again, so that *Philebus* is concerned with individual, and *Laws* with social morality.

Plato's treatment of social and political matters is marked by a shift of emphasis between two strands in his thought. One is his conviction that the best solution to political problems is the exercise of expert judgement: in an individual life what is needed is overall grasp based on correct understanding of priorities, and similarly in a state what is needed is expert overall understanding of the common good. This conviction is triumphant in *Republic*, where the rulers, the Guardians, have power to run the lives of all citizens in the state in a very broadly defined way: laws serve the purpose of applying the Guardians' expert knowledge, but do not stand in its way. Expert knowledge gives its possessor the right to enforce on others what the expert sees to be in their true interests, just as the patient must defer to the doctor and the crew to the ship's captain.

Plato is also, however, aware of the importance of law in ensuring stability and other advantages. In *Crito* the Laws of Athens claim obedience from Socrates (though on a variety of unharmonized grounds). In *Statesman* Plato admits that, although laws are in the real world a clog on expertise, they embody the past results of expertise and are therefore to be respected, indeed obeyed absolutely in the absence of an expert. In *Laws*, where Plato has given up the hope that an actual expert could exist and rule uncorrupted by power, he insists that problems of political division and strife are to be met by complete obedience to laws, which are regarded as the product of rational reflection and expertise, rather than the haphazard product of party strife.

Plato's best-known contribution to political thought is his idea, developed in *Republic*, that individual (more strictly the individual's *soul) and state are analogous in structure. Justice in the state is the condition in which its three functionally defined parts—the rulers, the rulers' auxiliaries, and the rest of the citizens (the producers)—work in harmony, guided by the expert understanding of the rulers, who, unlike the others, grasp what is in the common interest. Analogously, justice in the individual is the condition where the three parts of the individual's soul work in harmony. What this condition will be will differ for members of the three classes. All the citizens have souls whose parts are: reason, which discerns the interest of the whole or at least can be guided by grasp of someone else's reason which does; self-assertion; and appetite, the collection of desires aimed at their own satisfaction regardless of the interests of the whole. For all, justice consists in the rule of reason, and the subordination of self-assertion and appetite; but what this demands is different for the rulers, who understand and can articulate the requirements of reason, and for the producers, who do not. Plato identifies this condition of soul, which he calls psychic harmony, with justice, quite contrary to Greek intuitions about political justice. In *Republic*, the citizen's justice consists in identifying his or her overall interest, to the extent that that is possible, with the common interest, and this idea is taken to notorious lengths in the central books, where the rulers are to live a life in which individuality is given minimum scope. It has always been debated whether *Republic* is a contribution to political theory, or a rejection of the very basis of political theory, one which refuses to solve political conflicts, but unrealistically eliminates their sources. *Republic* has always been most inspiring as a 'pattern laid up in heaven' for individuals to use in the pursuit of individual justice.

Knowledge and its Objects In the early dialogues, Socrates is constantly in search of knowledge; this is provoked, not by sceptical worries about knowledge of matters of fact, but by the desire to acquire, on a larger and deeper scale, the kind of expert knowledge displayed by craftsmen. Socrates does not doubt that such globally expert knowledge, which he calls wisdom, exists, or that it would be most useful in the understanding and running of one's life, but he never claims to have it, and in the Socratic dialogues differences show up between it and everyday kinds of expert knowledge. Sophists, esp. *Hippias (2), are ridiculed as people who uncontroversially have everyday skills, but are

shown up as devoid of the global understanding which Socrates is seeking.

Socrates' conception of wisdom is an ambitious one; the person with this expert knowledge has a unified overall grasp of the principles which define his field and (as is stressed in *Gorgias*) he can give a *logos* or account of what it is that he knows, enabling him to explain and justify the judgements that he makes. In several dialogues this demand for giving a *logos* becomes more stringent, and prior conditions are set on an adequate answer. The person who putatively has knowledge of X is required to give an answer to 'What is X?' which is in some way explanatory of how particular things and kinds of thing are X. The answer is said to provide a 'form' which is itself in some way X, indeed X in a way which (unlike the Xness of other things) precludes ever being the opposite of X in any way. A number of complex problems arise over these 'forms', to which the text gives suggestive but incomplete solutions.

In the Socratic dialogues there is a mismatch between the goal of wisdom and the method that Socrates employs; for the latter is the procedure of *elenchus*, the testing of the opponent's views by Socrates' tenacious arguments. But the *elenchus* is a method that shows only inconsistency between beliefs; it has no resources for proving truth. Its result is negative; we have demonstrations of what friendship, courage, piety, and the like are not, but none of what they are. In *Meno* a different approach emerges; the theory of 'recollection' stresses that a person can get knowledge by thinking in a way not dependent on experience, and therefore entirely through his own intellectual resources. Although *Meno* is careful not to restrict knowledge entirely to such *a priori* knowledge, Plato goes on to develop an account of knowledge in which the model of skill is replaced by that of non-empirical, esp. mathematical reasoning. In *Phaedo* and *Republic* Plato stresses both the non-empirical nature of the objects of knowledge, the forms, and the structured and hierarchical nature of knowledge. Understanding now requires grasp of an entire connected system of thought, and insight into the difference between the basic and the derived elements, and the ways in which the latter are dependent on the former. As the conditions for having knowledge rise, knowledge becomes an ever more ideal state; in *Republic* it is to be achieved only by an intellectually gifted élite, who have spent many years in unremittingly abstract intellectual activities, and have lived a life strenuously devoted to the common good. In *Republic* Plato's account of knowledge, theoretically demanding yet practically applicable, is his most extensive and ambitious.

In later dialogues this synthesis, though never repudiated, lapses. In *Statesman* we find that theoretical and practical knowledge are now carefully separated; in *Laws* a continued stress on the importance of mathematics does little work, and contrasts with the work's extensive and explicit reliance on experience. *Theaetetus* examines knowledge with a fresh and lively concern, attacking various forms of relativism and subjectivism, but without reference to the *Republic* account.

Plato continues to talk about forms, but in elusive and often puzzling ways. The one sustained passage which appears to discuss forms as they appear in *Phaedo* and *Republic* is wholly negative—the first part of the *Parmenides*, where various powerful arguments are brought against this conception of forms, and no answers are supplied. Whatever Plato's own opinion of these arguments, forms in later dialogues revert to a role more like their earlier one. They are the objective natures of things, the objects of knowledge, and are to be grasped only by the exercise of thought and enquiry, not by reliance on experience. *Statesman* 262b–263d discusses the way that language can be misleading: there is no form of foreigner, since 'foreigner' simply means 'not Greek', and things are not put into a unified kind by not being Greek (see BARBARIAN). There is no single method, other than the continued use of enquiry, to determine which of our words do in fact pick out kinds that are natural, rather than merely contrived. However, Plato, though never renouncing forms as a demand of objectivity in intellectual enquiry, ceases to attach to them the mystical and exalted attitudes of the middle dialogues.

Soul and the Cosmos Throughout the dialogues Plato expresses many versions of the idea that a person's soul is an entity distinct from the living embodied person, attached to it by a relation which is inevitable but unfortunate. In *Phaedo* several arguments for the soul's immortality show that Plato is dealing indiscriminately with a number of different views of what the soul is: the principle of life, the intellect, the personality. The latter two are the ideas most developed. Soul as the intellect is the basis of Plato's tendency to treat knowledge as what transcends our embodied state; in *Meno* learning a geometrical proof is identified

with the person's soul recollecting what it knew before birth. Soul as the personality is the basis of Plato's use of myths of *transmigration of souls and afterlife rewards and punishments. In the middle dialogues these two ideas are united: *Phaedrus* gives a vivid picture of souls caught on a wheel of ongoing rebirth, a cycle from which only philosophical understanding promises release.

Plato's use of the idea that souls are immortal and are endlessly reborn into different bodies is a metaphorical expression of a deep body–soul dualism. He tends to draw sharp oppositions between active thinking and passive reliance on sense-experience, and to think of the senses as giving us merely unreflected and unreliable reports; the middle dialogues contain highly coloured disparagements of the world as revealed to us through the senses. However, there is also a strain in Plato which sets against this a more unified view of the person. In *Symposium* he develops the idea that erotic love can be sublimated and refined in a way that draws the person to aspire to philosophical truth; in *Phaedrus* he holds that this need not lead to repudiation of the starting-point. In *Republic* the soul has three parts, two of which are closely connected with the body; but in the final book only the thinking part achieves immortality.

Timaeus, an account of the natural world cast in the form of a description of how it was made by a creator god, treats the world itself as a living thing, with body and soul, and a fanciful cosmic account is developed. Other later dialogues, esp. *Philebus*, also introduce the idea that our souls are fragments of a cosmic soul in the world as a whole. Many aspects of the *Timaeus* cosmology depend on the assumption that the world itself is a living thing.

Later Problems and Methods The later dialogues do not display the same literary concerns as the Socratic and middle ones, nor do they contain the same themes. Rather, Plato moves to engaging with the ideas of other philosophers, and his own earlier ones, in a way strikingly unlike his earlier way of doing philosophy by the use of dialogue. In the later works the dialogue form is often strained by the need for exposition, and they are sometimes heavy and pedagogical. However, dialogue is often used brilliantly for long stretches of argument, as in *Parmenides* and *Sophist*.

Sophist presents, in a passage of challenging argument, Plato's solution to *Parmenides' challenge about the coherence of talking about not-being. *Timaeus* takes up the challenge of cosmology, replying to earlier thinkers with different cosmological assumptions. More fanciful treatment of cosmology is found in *Statesman*. *Cratylus* discusses questions of language and etymology in a semi-playful but systematic way. *Critias* (unfinished) and *Statesman* take up questions of political theory, discussing them by means previously rejected, like fiction and accounts which take folk memory and myth seriously. *Philebus*, discussing the place of pleasure in the good life, does so in a context of *Pythagorean metaphysics. *Laws* sketches an ideal state with considerable help from the lessons of history and of actual politics. These works show a larger variety of interests than hitherto, and an increased flexibility of methodology. Plato in these works shows both a greater respect for the views of others and an enlarged willingness to learn from experience, tradition and history. *Laws* 3 is a precursor of Aristotle's detailed research into political history. It is not surprising that we find many ideas which remind us of his pupil Aristotle, and the latter's methods and concerns, from the 'receptacle' of *Timaeus*, suggestive of matter, to the treatment of the 'mean' in *Statesman*.

Plato is original, radical, and daring, but also elusive. His ideas are locally clear and uncompromising, and globally fragmented, perennially challenging the reader to join in the dialogue and follow the argument where it leads. See DIALECTIC.

Plautius, Aulus (*suffect consul AD 29), of a family that became consular under *Augustus. He was governor of Pannonia in AD 42. In 43, commanding the British expedition, he defeated Cunobelinus' sons in battle, probably at the Medway and at the Thames, and staged Claudius' entry into *Camulodunum. Most of lowland Britain had been overrun before his departure (47) for the last *ovation awarded to a subject, a measure of Claudius' favour and of the family's ascendancy. In 57 (during a senatorial revival) Plautius tried his wife 'according to ancient custom' on charges of foreign religious practices—and acquitted her.

Plautus (Titus Maccius Plautus), comic playwright, author of *fabulae palliatae* (see FABULA) between *c.*205 and 184 BC; plays by Plautus are the earliest Latin works to have survived complete. *Varro drew up a list of 21 plays which were generally agreed to be by Plautus,

and doubtless they are the 21 transmitted in our manuscripts.

The plays are nearly all either known or assumed to be adaptations of (Greek) New Comedy, with plots portraying love affairs, confusion of identity and misunderstandings. Plautus adapted his models with considerable freedom and wrote plays that are in several respects different from anything we know of New Comedy. The musical element is much increased. The roles of stock characters such as the *parasite seem to have been much expanded. Consistency of characterization and plot development are sacrificed for the sake of an immediate effect. The humour resides less in the irony of the situation than in jokes and puns. There are 'metatheatrical' references to the audience and to the progress of the play, or explicit reminders that the play is set in Greece. Above all, there is a constant display of verbal fireworks, with alliteration, wordplays, unexpected personifications, and riddling expressions (e.g. *Mercator* ('The Businessman') 361, 'My father's a fly: you can't keep anything secret from him, he's always buzzing around'). Both the style of humour and the presentation of stock characters may well have been influenced by the *Atellana, but the verbal brilliance is Plautus' own.

The Greek originals have not survived, but a tattered papyrus contains the lines on which *Bacchides* ('The Bacchis Sisters') 494–561 are based (from Menander's 'Double Deceiver'), for the first time enabling us to study Plautus' techniques of adaptation at first hand, and confirming the freedom of his approach. Plautus has preserved the basic plot and sequence of scenes, but he has cut two scenes altogether and has contrived to avoid a pause in the action where there was an act-break in the original. The tormented monologue of a young man in love has had some jokes added to it. Passages spoken without musical accompaniment in the original Greek are turned into accompanied passages in longer lines. The play is still set in Athens, and the characters have Greek-sounding names; but Plautus has changed most of them, esp. that of the scheming slave who dominates the action, called Syrus (The Syrian) in Menander's play; Plautus calls him Chrysalus (Goldfinger) and adds some colour elsewhere in the play by punning on this name. Chrysalus even boasts of his superiority to slaves called Syrus.

The plots show considerable variety, ranging from the character study of *Aulularia* ('The Pot of Gold') (the source of Molière's *L'Avare*) to the transvestite romp of *Casina*, from the comedy of mistaken identity in *Amphitruo* and *Menaechmi* (both used by Shakespeare in *The Comedy of Errors*) to the more movingly ironic recognition comedy of *Captīvī* ('The Prisoners', unusual in having no love interest). *Trinummus* ('The Three-Pound Coin') is full of high-minded moralizing; *Truculentus* shows the triumph of an utterly amoral and manipulative prostitute. In several plays it is the authority-figure, the male head of the household, who comes off worst. Some plays glorify the roguish slave, generally for outwitting the father. These plays have been seen as providing a holiday release from the tensions of daily life, and their Greek setting must have helped: a world in which young men compete with mercenary soldiers for a long-term relationship with a prostitute was probably quite alien to Plautus' first audiences, a fantasy world in which such aberrations as the domination of citizens by slaves could safely be contemplated as part of the entertainment.

Plautus is at his most exuberant in the *cantica*, operatic arias and duets written in a variety of metres, with much technical virtuosity, and displaying many features of high-flown style. They often do little to advance the action, and we know of nothing like them in Greek New Comedy. Chrysalus has two strikingly boastful *cantica* in *Bacchides*. Some of his boasting is embroidered with triumph-imagery and other peculiarly Roman references; it is part of the fantasy of Plautus' Greek world that it can include Italian elements.

plēbiscītum, as opposed to *lex*, was in theory a resolution carried by any Roman assembly in which no *patrician cast his vote. In practice, it was a resolution of a plebeian tribal assembly (*concilium plēbis*: see COMITIA) presided over by a plebeian magistrate. At first the plebiscite was no more than a recommendation, and it attained the force of law only if re-enacted at the instance of a consul in the full assembly of the *populus*; but from an early date all plebiscites which had received the prior sanction of the patrician senators (*patrum auctōritās*) were recognized as universally binding). By the *lex Hortensia* of 287 BC (see HORTENSIUS) they were granted unconditional validity, and, with plebeian tribunes being drawn increasingly from within the governing class in the years which followed, they embodied much of the official routine legislation of the middle republic. In the post-Gracchan period they again became instruments of challenge to senatorial authority. Sulla therefore required in 88, and again in 81,

that all tribunician proposals should be approved by the senate before being put to the vote. This restriction was removed in 70.

plebs, the name given to the mass of Roman citizens, as distinct from the privileged *patricians. Our sources maintain that in the early republic the plebeians were excluded from religious colleges, magistracies, and the *senate; a law of the *Twelve Tables confirmed an existing ban on their intermarriage with patricians, only to be repealed within a few years by the *lex Canuleia*. However, they were enrolled in *curiae (see CURIA (1)) and *tribus, they served at all times in the army and could hold the office of *tribunus militum*. The 'Struggle of the Orders', by which the *plebs* (or, more precisely, its richer members) achieved political equality with the patricians, is an essential part of the story of the development of Rome. The *plebs* won because it turned itself into an association which held its own assemblies (*concilia plēbis*; see COMITIA), appointed its own officers, the *tribuni plebis and *aediles (usually selected from the richer members of the order), and deposited its own records in the temples of *Ceres and *Diana on the *Aventine. Its major tactic in crises was *sēcessio, secession *en masse* from Rome. During the first secession it secured inviolability for the persons of its officers by a collective undertaking to protect them. In fact the tribunes and aediles became in due course magistrates of the Roman people. The final secession in 287 BC led to the *lex Hortensia*, which made *plebiscita binding on the whole community. This is normally regarded as the end of the struggle of the Orders, since the plebeians were no longer significantly disadvantaged *qua* plebeians. However, there continued to be clashes between the interests of the aristocrats and the rich and those of the humbler citizens over issues such as public land (see AGER PUBLICUS), which had first emerged in the early republic. Under the later republic the name 'plebeian' acquired in ordinary parlance its modern sense of a member of the lower social orders. Hence from at least *Augustus' reign onwards those who did not belong to the senatorial or *equestrian orders or to the order of the local senate (see DECURIONES) in colonies or *municipia were often called the *plebs*.

Pliny the Elder (AD 23/4–79), Gaius Plīnius Secundus, prominent Roman *equestrian, from Cōmum in Gallia Cisalpina (see GAUL (CISALPINE)), and uncle of *Pliny the Younger, best known as the author of the 37-book *Natural History*, an encyclopaedia of all contemporary knowledge—animal, vegetable, and mineral—but with much that is human included too: 'Nature, which is to say Life, is my subject'.

Characteristic of his age and background in his range of interests and diverse career, Pliny obtained a cavalry command through the patronage of Pomponius Secundus (consul 41), and served in Germany, alongside the future emperor *Titus. Active in legal practice in the reign of *Nero, he was then promoted by the favour of the Flavians through a series of high procuratorships (including that of Hispania *Tarraconensis), in which he won a reputation for integrity. He became a member of the council of *Vespasian and Titus, and was given the command of the Misēnum fleet (see NAVIES). When *Vesuvius erupted in 79, duty and curiosity combined, fatally; he led a detachment to the disaster-area, landed at Stabiae, and died from inhaling fumes. For his career and death two letters of his nephew are the primary source.

Throughout this career Pliny was a most prolific author. His cavalry command produced a monograph on the use of the throwing-spear by cavalrymen, piety towards his patron demanded a biography in two books. *German Wars* in 20 books recounted Roman campaigns against the Germans, and was used by *Tacitus. The years of his procuratorships produced a 31-book history covering the later Julio-Claudian period; and, dedicated to Titus, the *Natural History*.

Pliny was impressed by scale, number, comprehensiveness, and detail. Characteristically he claims that there are 20,000 important facts derived from 2,000 books in his work, but this is a severe underestimate. The value of what he preserves of the information available to him far outweighs the fact that when he can be checked against the original, he often garbles his information through haste or insufficient thought. Our study of ancient *agriculture, *medicine, metallurgy, and the canon of great artists in antiquity, would all be impoverished if the work had perished (see ART, ANCIENT ATTITUDES TO). He can scarcely be blamed for not applying the standards of empirical enquiry to ancient medical lore, or for sharing widespread misconceptions about the world. Indeed, one of the interesting aspects of the work is the eloquent witness that he provides for precisely these pre-scientific ways of thinking.

Pliny was no philosopher, and the sections where Pliny's thought is least accessible are often those where subject matter such as the Cosmos or the Divine take him away from the

relatively concrete. Even here, though, there is an engaging personality at work, and there are enough asides and reflections on the world to give an impression of the author which is highly individual: as is the style and the imagery. The standard ethical *diatribe against luxury and aristocratic excess of the man from the municipality is given vivid historical and geographical colour, and if the Roman past is idealized, it is partly through the evocation of an image of the Roman people which is among the least hostile treatments of the many in any ancient author. The themes of the excellence of the natural endowment of Italy, and the moral threat posed by the exotic, form a laconic and memorable conclusion to bk. 37 (described in bk. 1, end, as 'nature compared in different lands; products compared in value').

Vita vigilia est: Life is being awake. The *Natural History* is a monument to keeping alert, and to the useful employment of time. Pliny's energy and diligence astonished his nephew, were intended to impress his contemporaries, and still amaze today; they were, moreover, intended as an ethical statement. For all his defects of accuracy, selection, and arrangement, Pliny achieved a summation of knowledge, deeply imbued with the mood of the time, and the greatness of his work was speedily recognized.

Pliny the Younger (c. AD 61–c.112), Gaius Plīnius Caecilius Secundus, is known from his writings and from inscriptions. Son of a landowner of Comum, he was brought up by his uncle, *Pliny the Elder, of *equestrian rank, who adopted him. He studied rhetoric at the feet of *Quintilian in Rome. After the usual year's service on the staff of a Syrian legion (c.81), he entered the senate in the later 80s through the patronage of such distinguished family friends as *Verginius Rufus and *Iulius Frontinus. He practised with distinction in the civil courts all his life, specializing in cases relating to inheritance, and conducted several prosecutions in the senate of provincial governors charged with *extortion. He climbed the senatorial ladder, becoming praetor in 93 (or 95) and consul in 100, and he also held a series of imperial administrative appointments, as *prefect of the military treasury (c.94–96), prefect of the treasury of Saturn (c.98–100) (see AERARIUM for both posts), and commissioner for the banks and channel of the *Tiber (c.104–106). He was thrice a member of the judicial council of *Trajan (c.104–107), who sent him as *legatus Augusti to govern *Bithynia-Pontus (c.110), where he apparently died in office (*c.*112). His career, very similar to that of his friend *Tacitus, is the best-documented example from the Principate of municipal origins and continuing ties, of the role of *patronage, of the nature of senatorial employment under emperors tyrannical and liberal, and of the landed wealth that underpinned the system.

Pliny published nine books of literary letters between 99 and 109 at irregular intervals, singly or in groups of three. Some letters comment elegantly on social, domestic, judicial, and political events, others offer friends advice, others again are references for jobs or requests for support for his own candidates in senatorial elections, while the tone is varied by the inclusion of short courtesy notes and set-piece topographical descriptions. Each letter is carefully composed, with great attention to formal style; Pliny uses the devices of contemporary rhetoric, with intricate arrangement and balance of words and clauses in sentences and paragraphs. Letters are limited either to a single subject treated at appropriate length, or to a single theme illustrated by three examples. Great care was also taken with the sequence of letters within each book. Pliny and his friends regularly exchanged such letters, which Pliny distinguished from boring business letters, from mere trivialities, and from the philosophical abstractions of the letters of *Seneca the Younger. The letters have their origins in day-to-day events, but Pliny aimed to create a new type of literature. He set out to write not an annalistic history, but a picture of his times with a strong moral element. He censures the cruelty of slave masters, the dodges of legacy hunters, and the meanness of the rich, but the targets of his criticisms are normally anonymous. He dwells for preference on positive aspects of the present, the benign role of Trajan, the merits of friends and acquaintances, the importance of education, and the literary life of Rome. Other letters describe the public life of senatorial debates, elections and trials, without concealing the weaknesses of senators, and recount, in a manner anticipating Tacitus, heroic episodes of the political opposition to *Domitian, with which Pliny liked to claim some connection. See LETTERS, LATIN.

Pliny was also active in other fields of literature. He wrote verses enthusiastically, publishing two volumes in the manner of his protégé *Martial, of which he quotes a few indifferent specimens. His surviving speech, the *Panegyric*, the only extant Latin speech between *Cicero and the late imperial panegyrics, is an expanded version of the original he delivered in the senate in thanks for his election to the consulship. Rhetorically a success (its popularity in the late-Roman rhetorical schools is responsible for its survival), it contrasts Trajan with the tyrannical Domitian. It is a major statement of the Roman political ideal of the good emperor condescending to play the role of an ordinary senator. See PANEGYRIC, LATIN.

The tenth bk. of letters contains all of Pliny's correspondence with Trajan: the first fourteen letters date between 98 and *c.*110, the remainder to Pliny's governorship of Bithynia-Pontus. The letters are much simpler in style than those in bks. 1–9 and were not worked up for publication, which probably occurred after Pliny's death. The provincial letters are the only such dossier surviving entire, and are a major source for understanding Roman provincial government. Each letter concerns a particular problem, such as the status of foundlings or the condition of civic finances, on which Pliny sought a ruling from Trajan. In *Epistle* 10. 96 Pliny gives the earliest external account of Christian worship, and the fullest statement of the reasons for the execution of Christians; see CHRISTIANITY.

Plōtīnus (AD 205–269/70), Neoplatonist philosopher. The main facts of his life are known from *Porphyry's memoir. His name is Roman, while his native language was almost certainly Greek. He turned to philosophy in his 28th year and worked for the next eleven years in *Alexandria under Ammonius Saccas, who had evoked from him the cry, 'The man I was looking for!' In 242–243 he joined Gordian III's unsuccessful expedition against Persia, hoping for an opportunity to learn something of eastern thought. The attempt was abortive, and at the age of 40 he settled in Rome as a teacher of philosophy, and remained there until his last illness, when he retired to *Campania to die. In Rome he became the centre of an influential circle of intellectuals, which included men of the world and men of letters, besides professional philosophers like Porphyry. He interested himself also in social problems.

Writings Plotinus wrote nothing until he was 50. He then began to produce a series of philosophical essays arising directly out of discussions in his seminars, and intended primarily for circulation among his pupils. These were collected by Porphyry, who classified them roughly according to subject, arranged them rather artificially in six *Enneads* or groups of nine, and eventually published them *c.*300–5. From this edition our manuscripts are descended. Save for the omission of politics, Plotinus' essays range over the whole field of ancient philosophy: ethics and aesthetics are dealt with mainly in *Enn.* 1; physics and cosmology in *Enns.* 2 and 3; psychology in *Enn.* 4; metaphysics, logic, and epistemology in *Enns.* 5 and 6. Though not systematic in intention, the *Enneads* form in fact a more complete body of philosophical teaching than any other which has come down to us from antiquity outside the Aristotelian corpus. Plotinus' favourite method is to raise and solve a series of 'difficulties': many of the essays give the impression of a man thinking aloud or discussing difficulties with a pupil. Owing to bad eyesight, Plotinus never revised what he wrote, and his highly individual style often reflects the irregular structure of oral statement. Its allusiveness, rapid transitions, and extreme condensation render him one of the most difficult of Greek authors; but when deeply moved he can write magnificently.

Philosophical Doctrine Recent writers see in him the most powerful philosophical mind between *Aristotle and Aquinas or Descartes; and in his work a logical development from earlier Greek thought, whose elements he arranged in a new synthesis designed to meet the needs of a new age. These needs influenced the direction rather than the methods of his thinking: its direction is determined by the same forces as resulted in the triumph of the eastern religions of salvation, but its methods are those of traditional Greek rationalism. Plotinus attached small value to ritual, and the religious ideas of the near east seem to have had little direct influence on the *Enneads*. To *Christianity Plotinus makes no explicit reference; but *Enn.* 2. 9 is an eloquent defence of Hellenism against *Gnostic superstition.

Plotinus holds that all modes of being, whether material or mental, temporal or eternal, are constituted by the expansion or 'overflow' of a single immaterial and impersonal force, which he identifies with the 'One' of the *Parmenides* and the 'Good' of the *Republic* (see PLATO), though it is strictly insusceptible of any predicate or description. As 'the One', it is the ground of all existence; as 'the Good', it is the source of all value. There is exact correspondence between degrees of reality and degrees of value, both being determined by the degree of unity, or approximation to the One, which any existence achieves. Reality, though at its higher levels it is non-spatial and non-temporal, may

thus be pictured figuratively as a series of concentric circles resulting from the expansion of the One. Each of these circles stands in a relation of timeless dependence to that immediately within it, which is in this sense its 'cause'; the term describes a logical relationship, not an historical event. Bare Matter is represented by the circumference of the outermost circle: it is the limiting case of reality, the last consequence of the expansion of the One, and so possesses only the ideal existence of a boundary.

Between the One and Matter lie three descending grades of reality—the World-mind *nous*, the World-soul *psŷchē*, and Nature *physis*. The descent is marked by increasing individuation and diminishing unity. The World-mind resembles Aristotle's Unmoved Mover: it is thought-thinking-itself, an eternal lucidity in which the knower and the known are distinguishable only logically; within it lie the Platonic Forms, which are conceived not as inert types or models but as a system of interrelated forces, differentiations of the one Mind which holds them together in a single timeless apprehension. The dualism of subject and object, implicit in the self-intuition of Mind, is carried a stage further in the discursive thinking characteristic of *Soul: because of its weaker unity, Soul must apprehend its objects successively and severally. In doing so it creates time and space; but the World-soul is itself eternal and transcends the spatio-temporal world which arises from its activity. The lowest creative principle is Nature, which corresponds to the immanent World-soul of the *Stoics: its consciousness is faint and dreamlike, and the physical world is its projected dream.

Man is a microcosm, containing all these principles actually or potentially within himself. His consciousness is normally occupied with the discursive thinking proper to Soul: but he has at all times a subconscious activity on the dreamlike level of Nature and a superconscious activity on the intuitive level of Mind; and his conscious life may lapse by habituation to the former level or be lifted by an intellectual discipline to the latter. Beyond the life of Mind lies the possibility of unification, an experience in which the Self by achieving complete inward unity is momentarily identified with the supreme unity of the One. This is the Plotinian doctrine of *ecstasy. The essays in which he expounds it, on the basis of personal experience, show extraordinary introspective power and are among the classics of mysticism. For Plotinus unification is independent of divine grace; is attainable very rarely, as the result of a prolonged effort of the will and understanding; and is not properly a mode of cognition, so that no inference can be based on it.

Plotinus also made important contributions to psychology, esp. in his discussion of problems of perception, consciousness, and memory; and to aesthetics, where for Plato's doctrine that Art 'imitates' natural objects he substitutes the view that Art and Nature alike impose a structure on Matter in accordance with an inward vision of archetypal Forms (see ART, ANCIENT ATTITUDES TO). His most original work in ethics is concerned with the nature and origin of evil, which in some passages he attempts to solve by treating evil as the limiting case of good, and correlating it with Matter, the limiting case of reality.

Plouton See HADES.

Ploutos See PLUTUS.

Plutarch (Lucius(?) Mestrius Plutarchus) of *Chaeronea; b. before AD 50, d. after AD 120; philosopher and biographer. The family had long been established in Chaeronea, and most of Plutarch's life was spent in that historic town, to which he was devoted. He knew Athens well, and visited both Egypt and Italy. He lectured and taught at Rome. Members of his family figure often in his dialogues; his wide circle of influential friends include the consulars Mestrius Florus (whose gentile name he bore) and Sosius Senecio (to whom the *Parallel Lives* and other works are dedicated), as well as magnates like the exiled Syrian prince Iulius Antiochus Philopappus. For the last 30 years of his life, Plutarch was a priest at *Delphi. A devout believer in the ancient pieties and a profound student of its antiquities, he played a notable part in the revival of the *sanctuary in the time of Trajan and Hadrian; and the people of Delphi joined with Chaeronea in dedicating a portrait bust of him 'in obedience to the decision of the *Amphictions'. He was a man of some influence in governing circles. In his writing he promoted the concept of a partnership between Greece, the educator, and Rome, the great power, and of the compatibility of the two loyalties.

A list of his works (4th cent.?), contains 227 items. Extant are 78 miscellaneous works and 50 Lives. We have lost the Lives of the Caesars (except *Galba* and *Otho*) and some others (notably *Epaminondas* and *Pindar*), and probably two-thirds of the miscellaneous works. Nevertheless, what remains is a formidable mass; Plutarch was a very prolific writer.

1. The group of *rhetorical* works includes 'The Glory of Athens', 'The Fortune of Rome', 'Against Borrowing Money'. Plutarch's richly allusive and metaphorical style is ill adapted to rhetorical performance, and these—with the exception of 'Against Borrowing', which is a powerful, satirical piece—are not very successful.

2. The many treatises on themes of popular moral philosophy are derivative in content, but homogeneous and characteristic in style. Among the best are 'Friends and Flatterers', 'Progress in Virtue', 'Superstition', 'The Control of Anger', 'Talkativeness', 'Curiosity', and 'Bashfulness'. In 'Rules for Politicians', Plutarch draws both on his historical reading and on his own experience, to give advice to a young man entering politics. The warm and sympathetic personality never far beneath the surface appears esp. in 'Consolation to my Wife' and 'Advice on Marriage'. Plutarch's teaching is less individualistic than that of many ancient moralists: family affections and friendly loyalties play a large part in it.

3. Many of Plutarch's works are *dialogues*, written not so much in the Platonic tradition as in that of *Aristotle (and *Cicero), with long speeches, enough characterization, and the frequent appearance of the author himself as a participant. The nine books of 'Sympotic Questions' are full of erudite urbanity and curious speculation. 'Socrates' Daimonion' combines exciting narrative (liberation of *Thebes from Spartan occupation in 379/8) with philosophical conversation about prophecy (a favourite theme) and an elaborate *Platonic myth of the fate of the soul after death (Plutarch attempted such myths elsewhere also, esp. in 'God's Slowness to Punish'). 'Eroticus' also combines narrative with argument, this time in a near contemporary setting: the 'kidnapping' of a young man by a widow who wishes to marry him forms the background to a discussion of heterosexual and homosexual love in general. Delphi is the scene of four dialogues, all concerned with prophecy, *daimones, and divine providence; and it is in these (together with *Isis and Osiris*) that the greater part of Plutarch's philosophical and religious speculation is to be sought.

4. He was a Platonist, and a teacher of philosophy; and the more technical side of this activity is to be seen in his interpretation of *Timaeus* and a series of polemical treatises against the Stoics and Epicureans.

5. We possess also important antiquarian works—'Roman Questions' and 'Greek Questions', mainly concerned with religious antiquities—and some on literary themes ('On Reading the Poets' is the most significant).

Plutarch's fame led to the inclusion in the corpus of a number of spurious works, some of which have been important: 'The Education of Children' was influential in the Renaissance; 'Doctrines of the Philosophers' is a version of a compilation to which we owe much of our knowledge of Greek philosophy, while 'Lives of the Ten Orators' and 'Music' are also important sources of information.

The 'Parallel Lives' remains his greatest achievement. We have 23 pairs, 19 of them with 'comparisons' attached. Plutarch's aims are set out e.g. in *Alexander*: his object was not to write continuous political history, but to exemplify individual virtue (or vice) in the careers of great men. Hence he gives attention esp. to his heroes' education, to significant anecdotes, and to what he sees as the development or revelation of character. Much depends on the sources available to him (*Alcibiades* is full of attested personal detail, *Antony* full of glorious narrative, esp. about *Cleopatra VII, *Phocion* and *Cato Maior* full of sententious anecdotes), but the general pattern is maintained wherever possible: family, education, début in public life, climaxes, changes of fortune or attitude, latter years and death. The *Lives*, despite the pitfalls for the historian, which have sometimes led to despair about their value as source-material, have been the main source of understanding of the ancient world for many readers from the Renaissance to the present day. Montaigne, Shakespeare, Dryden, Rousseau, and Emerson are among Plutarch's principal debtors. See also BIOGRAPHY, GREEK.

Pluto, Pluton See HADES.

Plūtus, Wealth, originally abundance of crops, hence associated with *Demeter at *Eleusis. He is son of Demeter and Iasion acc. to Hesiod, but at Athens, where he had an important role in the *mysteries, he is attested simply as son of Demeter. Demeter and Kore (see PERSEPHONE/ KORE) send him to those whom they favour, esp. Eleusinian initiates. Unlike the fertility god Plouton (see HADES), he is only a personification, never the object of worship. In Eleusinian art he is represented in the company of Demeter and Kore usually as a boy a few years old, naked, holding a cornucopia or bunch of grain stalks,

and wearing (in the Classical period) a loosely draped *himation* (see DRESS), as in the Great Eleusinian Relief. At a climactic moment in the mysteries he evidently made a dramatic appearance.

Po See PADUS.

polemarchos/polemarch, one of the nine *archontes appointed annually in Athens. The name indicates that the polemarch's original function was to command the army; presumably the office was created to take over this function from the king. Eventually military command was transferred to the *strategoi. At *Marathon in 490 BC the *strategoi* debated and voted on strategy, but *Callimachus (1) the polemarch had a casting vote, and he was the 'leader', it is disputed whether that means he was the real or merely the titular commander-in-chief. Certainly the polemarch no longer had military authority after 487/6, when *archontes* were appointed by lot (see SORTITION) and it could not be expected that every polemarch would make a competent commander. Thereafter the polemarch's main functions were legal. In the 4th cent. he had charge of trials of *metics' family, inheritance, and status cases. He also arranged the funeral ceremony for the war-dead.

Polemon of Athens, head of the *Academy 314/313–270/269 BC. Primarily a moralist, he dismissed the purely theoretical side of philosophy as sterile. He formulated the ideal of 'living according to nature'—later the official goal of *Stoicism, founded by his pupil *Zeno (2)—and maintained that virtue is both necessary and sufficient for happiness while accepting (unlike the Stoics) that there are bodily and external goods.

pōlētai 'sellers', were Athenian officials. They existed in the time of *Solon. In *Aristotle's time there were ten, appointed annually by lot from the ten *phylai. They conducted the selling or leasing of property belonging to the state, esp. property confiscated from convicted offenders. They sold as slaves *metics who failed to pay the metics' tax, and they let rights to work *mines, to collect taxes, and to carry out public works. The method generally used was an auction held in the presence of the *boule. The *poletai* then made out lists of the payments due from purchasers and tenants; sales of confiscated property and mining leases were inscribed on stone, and numerous fragments of these inscriptions have been found.

police Police forces did not exist in the ancient world. Ancient city-states did, however, recognize the need for publicly appointed officials to carry out functions of social regulation. For example, in Classical Athens annual boards of magistrates were charged with keeping the streets clean, supervising market transactions, and controlling corn prices. Officials of this kind are attested in Greek cities throughout the Hellenistic and Roman periods, and the same functions were performed in Rome and cities of the Latin west by the *aediles and their equivalents.

There were also magistrates appointed to deal with certain aspects of criminal activity. At Athens the *Eleven, appointed by lot, had the task of guarding prisoners in the city gaol, carrying out executions and occasionally arresting criminals. In Rome these functions were carried out by minor magistrates called *trēsvirī capitālēs*, who may also have exercised summary jurisdiction over slaves and humble citizens. But these magistrates, who were assisted by only a small number of public slaves, had neither the authority nor the resources to act as a police force. At Athens after the *Persian Wars a force of 300 Scythian slaves, armed with bows, was used to keep order in the assembly and the law courts, but the Scythian archers acted as policemen only in the most rudimentary sense; they were of low status, enjoyed little public respect and had no authority to investigate, arrest or prosecute. At Rome the *lictors who attended the senior magistrates were only symbols of the state's authority to discipline and punish; they had no power to coerce. The authority of magistrates depended absolutely on the acceptance by the citizens of their political institutions and the men who operated them.

In ancient societies the authorities were little involved in the suppression, investigation, and prosecution of criminal activity. These matters were left to the private initiative of citizens who relied on networks of kin, friends, and dependants in a system of self-help. Small-scale disturbances were resolved locally by neighbours and passers-by, who were expected to take sides and usually did so. The state became involved only when violence had a political dimension or when it became a threat to the community as a whole. In such circumstances the authorities mobilized ordinary citizens who took up arms on behalf of the state. This happened in Athens in the crisis of 415 BC, and in Rome in 186 BC at the time of the Bacchanalian affair (see BACCHANALIA). In the political crises of 121 and 100 the senators and *equestrians armed themselves and their dependants in order to crush Gaius *Sempronius Gracchus and *Appuleius Saturninus. The need to call upon the armed support of the citizens in a crisis was widely recognized, and is laid down in Roman colonial charters.

After the breakdown of public order in the late republic the Roman emperors instituted more permanent forces to police the city of Rome. These were the urban cohorts (see COHORTES URBANAE), commanded by the city *prefect, and the *vigiles, a corps of 7,000 freed slaves under an equestrian prefect, whose main task was to act as a fire brigade, but who could be used to enforce order if necessary. The *praetorian guard was also on hand to suppress major public disturbances. Urban cohorts similar to those at Rome existed in certain large cities, including *Lugdunum and *Carthage, and several cities apparently had fire brigades; but they were treated with suspicion by the central government, which saw them as potentially subversive. *Trajan advised *Pliny the Younger to provide fire-fighting equipment for the citizens of *Nicomedia to use when needed, rather than to set up a permanent fire brigade. But these paramilitary forces of the Roman empire, although closer to a police force than anything else in antiquity, were not involved in day-to-day law enforcement, which remained the responsibility of private citizens acting on their own behalf.

polis (pl. *poleis*), the Greek city-state. The *polis* is the characteristic form of Greek urban life; its main features are small size, local self-determination, sense of community and respect for law. It can be contrasted with the Mycenaean palace economy (see MYCENAEAN CIVILIZATION), and with the continuing existence of tribal types of organization in many areas of northern Greece. (See ETHNICITY. For a different sense of 'tribe' see below.) The *polis* is present in *Homer; the archaeological signs of city development (public space, temples, walls, public works, town planning) appear in an increasing number of sites in the 8th–7th cents. (Old Smyrna, *Eretria); the peaceful abandonment of smaller sites and the general decline of archaeological evidence from the countryside in the 7th cent. suggest early *synoecism or concentration of population in specific *polis* sites. The foundation of organized settlements in new areas (see COLONIZATION, GREEK) is part of the same process.

Each *polis* controlled a territory delimited geographically by mountains or sea, or by proximity to another *polis*; border wars were common, as were inter-city agreements and attempts to establish religious rights over disputed areas; *Athens and *Sparta possessed exceptionally large territories. *Autonomy was jealously guarded, but the necessities of collaboration made for a proliferation of foreign alliances, leagues, and hegemonies; and a constant struggle for domination or independence developed (see IMPERIALISM, *Greek and Hellenistic*). There was also constant interchange and competition between cities, so that despite their separate identities a common culture was maintained.

Economically the *polis* served an agrarian economy as a centre for local exchange, processing and manufacture; many cities were located by the sea, and had important overseas trading interests (see ECONOMY, GREEK). Socially the citizens (see CITIZENSHIP, GREEK) comprised an ethnically homogeneous group, composed of 'tribes' (*phylai*) and smaller *kinship groups, such as *phratries, *demes, and families (see HOUSEHOLD); new cities would replicate them. Each city had a patron deity and a religious calendar (see CALENDAR, GREEK) with other lesser cults and festivals; the older priesthoods belonged to specific aristocratic families, later ones were often appointed by the people (see PRIESTS). Animal sacrifice (see SACRIFICE, GREEK) was accompanied by equal distribution of the meat at civic festivals, which from the 6th cent. became the focus for city-organized competitions in athletics, music and dancing, and theatre (see AGONES). New cities required religious authorization, traditionally from *Apollo's oracle at Delphi (see COLONIZATION, GREEK; DELPHIC ORACLE); sacred fire was brought from the mother city, and established in the *prytaneion, which in all cities acted as the common hearth, where magistrates and others took meals provided at public expense; the *founder of a new city was given heroic honours after death, with a tomb within the walls and public rites. See HERO-CULT.

Economy, kinship groups, and religion were subordinate to the main focus of the *polis*, which was broadly political; and its development may be seen as the adaptation of these forces to a political end. Originating as an aristocratic system, the *polis* became a 'guild of warriors'. Women were never admitted to political rights. In origin all cities seem to have possessed similar institutions: magistrates (see MAGISTRACY, GREEK) elected annually, a council of elders (*gerousia*), and a warrior assembly; the common later contrast between *oligarchy and *democracy relates to differences in the distribution of

powers and eligibility for office. The first stage in the development of the *polis* (7th–6th cents.) was usually the establishment of a written or customary lawcode (often attributed to a named law-giver (Lycurgus (at Sparta), *Solon (at Athens)), which limited the arbitrary powers of the aristocratic magistrates and regulated social conflict; the ideal was often referred to as *eunomia* (see SPARTA, 2; TYRTAEUS). The second stage (late 6th cent.) was the evolution of the concept of the citizen (see CITIZENSHIP, GREEK) with defined privileges and duties; this often involved the establishment of equality of political rights (*isonomia*, or democracy), but also the establishment of clear membership rules excluding non-citizens, and creating subordinate statuses (see CLEISTHENES (2); METICS). The *polis* was always defined as its members, rather than geographically: the *polis* of Athens is always called 'the Athenians', and citizenship generally implied participation in all political, judicial, and governmental activities. In the 5th and 4th cents. a fully political society developed, centred on the making of complex decisions in the citizen assembly (see POLITICS).

This elaboration of a political culture affected all aspects of the *polis*. Religious and social institutions were not autonomous, but were continually being adapted to conform to the needs of *polis* organization. Sparta is a striking example: an initially normal Greek city substituted universal military commensality (the *syssitia*) in place of family structures, and adapted all religious *rituals to the needs of a hoplite *polis*. Other cities underwent less extreme forms of adaptation, but the constant subordination of family and religious structures and large parts of the legal system (such as inheritance) to the needs of the *polis* creates an impression of rationality in the development of social forms. Equally the dominance of the political led to an early recognition of the difference between the various spheres of social activity, and of the possibility of conflict between them, which is esp. exemplified in the public art of tragedy (see TRAGEDY, GREEK).

In the late 4th cent. the gradual loss of sovereignty eroded the power of the armed citizens, and increased that of rich notables. The Hellenistic *polis* was marked by a conflict between rich and poor citizens, moderated by the willingness of the rich to spend their *wealth on the duties of office and to engage in *euergetism, or subsidizing the expenses of office and of public festivals and culture, and providing buildings and other public works; this is expressed in the ideal of *homonoia. The extension of the polis as a civic form across the areas conquered by *Alexander (2) the Great under his successors created a colonial-style system, in which a Greek urbanized élite lived off the labour of a non-Greek countryside (see COLONIZATION, HELLENISTIC). The criterion of citizenship became education at the *gymnasium in Greek letters and athletics, and the concept of the polis became as much cultural as political.

The polis of the Roman age inherited a tradition of independence and competition within an imperial system, of civic pride expressed in public building programmes, and of cultural superiority over Romans and native peasantry; this was exemplified in the Greek renaissance of the '*Second Sophistic'. The Greek cities of the eastern empire were thus able to develop and continue a rich economic, cultural and social life into the early Byzantine period.

The origins of the rationalization and idealization of the polis lie deep in the reforming tendencies of the Archaic period. Greek political philosophy (see next entry) emerged in the fifth century with various attempts to imagine utopian cities whose institutions were directed towards specific ends; *Plato's Republic and Laws stand in this tradition. *Aristotle's Politics begins from the claim that 'man is by nature an animal of the polis', and seeks to draw conclusions from the whole experience of the polis, but fails to create an ideal philosophical state. Later thinkers (the *Cynics, *Zeno (2), *Epicurus) rebelled against the conception of man as subordinate to the polis, either by claiming his freedom from it, or by redefining the institution as a cosmopolis, in which all wise men were free. It is this mystical universalization of the polis which enabled first the Roman imperial panegyrists (see PANEGYRIC) and then *Augustine to conceive of the polis as a transcendental city embracing all the members of a community, whether empire or church.

See also ETHNICITY; FEDERAL STATES; FREEDOM IN THE ANCIENT WORLD; GREECE (HISTORY); LAW IN GREECE; POLITICAL THEORY; POLITICS; STASIS; URBANISM.

political theory Greek and Roman authors reflected constantly on justice, good government, the nature of law. Epic, tragedy, comedy, history, and oratory are rich in political thought, often intensely interacting with the thought of the philosophers.

Greek and Roman political theory is distinctive in its focus on the *soul. All the major thinkers hold that one cannot reflect well on political institutions without reflecting, first, on human flourishing, and on the psychological structures that facilitate or impede it. Their thought about virtue, education, and the passions is integral to their political theory, since they hold, for the most part, that a just city (*polis) can be achieved only by the formation of virtuous individuals—although they also hold that institutions shape the passions of individuals and their possibilities for flourishing.

The 5th cent. BC in Athens saw a flowering of political theory and a turning of philosophy from cosmology to human concerns. The *sophists and those influenced by them exchanged arguments about the status of ethical and political norms—whether these norms exist by nature (physis) or by convention or law (*nomos (2)), and whether they are absolute, or relative to the species and/or the individual. *Protagoras' famous saying that 'The human being is the measure of all things' probably means that the human species is the standard. But even such anthropocentrism constituted a challenge to the primacy of religious sources of value. Other thinkers championed more thoroughgoing forms of relativism. While Protagoras strongly defended conventions of justice as essential to well-being, others offered an immoralist teaching, urging individuals to pursue their own pleasure or power in so far as they could escape the tyranny of constraining law and custom.

*Socrates portrayed his relation to the Athenian democracy (see DEMOCRACY, ATHENIAN) as that of a gadfly on the back of a 'noble but sluggish horse': democracy was on the whole admirable but in need of critical self-examination. It is likely that he preferred democracy to other regimes, while advocating a larger role for expert judgement. In *Plato's Crito, he justifies his refusal to escape his penalty by insisting on the obligation of obedience to law imposed by a citizen's acceptance of the benefit and education of those same laws.

Plato's search for a just city, in his Republic, begins with the attempt to defend the life of the just person against *Thrasymachus' immoralist challenge, showing that this life is more eudaimōn (see DAIMON) than the unjust life. In order to understand justice in the individual, the interlocutors imagine an ideal city, in whose class relations justice may be seen. The relation between city and *soul turns out to be more complex than analogy, however, since the institutions of the ideal city prove necessary for the production of full justice in individuals; and the rule of just individuals is necessary for the maintenance of ideal institutions. The just individual is characterized by psychic harmony in which each part of the soul does its proper work, reason ruling and appetite and self-assertion being ruled; so too, in the just city, the reasoners are to rule and people dominated by appetite are to be ruled. On this basis Plato's Socrates develops his institutional proposals, which include: an education for the ruling class in which all traditional poetry is banished as bad for the soul; the abolition of the nuclear family and a communal scheme of marriage and child-rearing; the equal consideration of women for all functions, including that of ruler; a selective cultivation of the best souls to produce a ruling class of philosophers with knowledge of the good. Plato seems unconcerned about the limits he imposes on free choice, since he views most citizens as psychically immature and in need of permanent supervision.

Plato's later political works, *Statesman* and *Laws*, re-examine these psychic and institutional questions. *Statesman* develops the idea of practical wisdom as a flexible ability to grapple with the changing circumstances of human life, thus anticipating a prominent theme in the thought of *Aristotle. In *Laws* the emphasis on the guiding political role of wisdom is maintained, but, apparently, with a new emphasis on the importance of consent by and rational persuasion of the ruled, who now seem to be judged capable of some sort of fully-fledged virtue. The dialogue reflects at length on the justification and nature of punishment (see PUNISHMENT, GREEK THEORIES ABOUT).

Aristotle's political thought includes an account of the nature of human flourishing or *eudaimonia*, since, as he argues, the good things that politics distributes (property, possessions, offices, honours) are good not in themselves but as means to flourishing; an account of flourishing thus gives a 'limit' to the legislator, whose task will be to make an arrangement such that, barring catastrophic accidents, 'anyone whatsoever may do well and live a flourishing life'. Aristotle justifies the *polis* as essential to the complete realization of human ends, and details its development from the household and the village. While critical of 'artificial slavery', he defends a 'natural slavery' whose subjects are beings who 'altogether lack the deliberative faculty'. A more co-operative type of subordination is justified for women, apparently on the grounds that they deliberate ineffectually. Because he holds that virtue requires leisure, he denies citizenship to farmers, craftsmen, and

resident aliens. These exclusions aside, Aristotle's preferred constitution is that of free and equal citizens, ruling and being ruled by turns. His ideal city subsidizes the participation of poor citizens in common meals and other institutions out of the revenue from publicly held land; on the other hand, Platonic communism of property is thoroughly repudiated, as is Plato's attack on the family. Education is central, and Aristotle seems almost as insensitive as Plato to the issue of state control. In the central books of *Politics*, Aristotle describes various types of actual constitution and their mutations.

For *Epicurus, justice is a necessary condition for *eudaimonia*, not an end in itself. Political involvement is to be avoided as a source of disturbance. The moderation of bad desires, such as the fear of death and aggressive wishes, will ameliorate many social ills. *Lucretius either preserves or innovates a fuller account of politics, which includes the idea that justice arose out of an implicit contract for the sake of protecting the weak.

The Stoics (see STOICISM) also focus on the therapy of the soul, holding that anger, fear, and the other 'passions' should be extirpated by removing excessive attachments to external goods such as money and reputation. This will change politics by removing various bad forms of contention and self-assertion. *Zeno (2) and *Chrysippus propose an ideal city in which virtuous citizens will live in concord, inspired by bonds of love. Women are given full equality; the institution of marriage is replaced by free consensual sexual relations. To all Stoics, local and national affiliations are less morally salient than our membership in the worldwide community of reason; this theme of the *kosmou politēs* ('world citizen') is developed vividly in Roman Stoicism, esp. in Marcus *Aurelius. Roman Stoics debated the question of the best constitution: some preferred monarchy and conceived of the emperor as (ideally) a Stoic sage; others, such as *Clodius Thrasea Paetus, understanding the Stoic ideal of self-command to entail republican government, invoked Stoicism in their anti-imperial politics.

Other major contributors to Hellenistic political theory include *Cicero, with his account of the mixed constitution, and *Plutarch, with his wide-ranging reflections on virtue and rulership. See DEMOCRACY; FREEDOM IN THE ANCIENT WORLD; KINGSHIP; OLIGARCHY; POLIS; POLITICS.

politics

In Greece 1. Politics as power struggle. In the Archaic period there is some evidence for the existence of aristocratic groups supported by retainers, esp. in the poetry of *Alcaeus and at Athens before *Cleisthenes (2); in the Classical period organized aristocratic *hetaireiai occasionally emerged as politically important, but usually as a consequence of lack of success in normal political life. Organized political parties never existed, and political programmes were confined to groups trying to change the constitution.

2. Politics as ritualized *decision-making. Specific political institutions and methods for decision-making were first found in the Archaic period, and were highly developed by the Classical period; the best-known examples are *Sparta and *Athens (see LYCURGUS; SPARTA; DEMOCRACY, ATHENIAN). They involved a specific location for taking decisions, religious rituals for demarcating space and time, and a fixed procedure. In principle all citizens with full rights could participate in the assembly. The aim was to achieve consensus through structured discussion; arguments usually took the form of opposed speeches, and speakers were expected to maintain certain conventions of dignified behaviour: scandal was caused when these were infringed by Athenian *demagogues in the late 5th cent. At Athens political leaders were initially of aristocratic birth, but after the death of *Pericles they were simply those who spoke most often; they were regarded as responsible for decisions, and prided themselves on consistency of advice. There were four main issues on which they were expected to possess knowledge: city revenues, war and peace, defence, corn supply. Seventeen assembly speeches survive from the period 403–322 BC, by *Lysias, *Andocides, and (esp.) *Demosthenes (2); they are brief and well organized; their arguments are based on rational calculation of advantage and consequence, rather than appeals to sentiment, religion, or historical rights. The controls on assembly procedure in the 5th cent. were customary; but in the 4th cent. the formal distinction between laws and decrees, and the limitation of the assembly to the making of decrees, led to the constitutional check of the *graphe paranomon, whereby decrees could be challenged in the courts as being contrary to the laws. A decision once taken was accepted as the will of the community expressed in such phrases as 'the Athenians decided', and was binding on all: there was no mechanism for continued dissent.

This absence of a means for structuring permanent political oppositions was a basic weakness of Greek political life: *stasis, armed revolution, had as its aim the overthrow of the existing consensus, in order to return to a different political unity through the extermination of the opposition; it was common in many cities, and focused on the conflict between democracy and *oligarchy, or the question of equal or unequal distribution of political privileges in relation to social class; it caused much instability of political life. Stasis was regarded as a disease of the body politic, capable of destroying the community. Philosophers were unable to offer any solution to the problem.

At Rome Throughout the republic the kinship group and the clientēla (see CLIENS) played a large part in politics; the late republic saw also the growth of military clientship among the dynasts. Much of Roman political life was concerned with the struggle for election to those offices which gave access to legal power, military command, and the possibility of conquest (see IMPERIUM; MAGISTRACY, ROMAN; PRO CONSULE, PRO PRAETORE; PROVINCIA); it therefore involved a measure of participation by the people. Individuals might espouse conservative or radical attitudes and be designated by the political labels *optimates or populares; but there was much inconsistency, and these claims seldom involved clear differences in policy. Decision-making was divided between the aristocratic *senate and a number of different assemblies (see COMITIA), and was therefore complex and open to challenge. Roman political life seems closer to modern practices than does Greek, for it distanced the people from the process of decision-making and possessed a complex constitutional law based on precedent; but it still lacked the concept of institutionalized party politics. The political leadership was always aristocratic, and much concerned with its own dignity, privileges and 'equality'. The emperors continued to respect the claims of the senate to play a major role in the political system at least in principle during the 1st cent. AD, but the power of the people was not preserved under the principate; lībertās (see FREEDOM) became an aristocratic ideal.

See DEMOCRACY, ATHENIAN; DEMOCRACY, NON-ATHENIAN AND POST-CLASSICAL; FREEDOM IN THE ANCIENT WORLD; POLIS; TYRANNY.

pollution, Greek concept of Societies create order by stigmatizing certain disorderly conditions and events and persons as 'polluting', that is, by treating them as metaphorically unclean and dangerous. The pollutions generally recognized by the Greeks were birth, death, to a limited degree sexual activity, homicide except in war, and sacrilege; certain diseases, esp. madness, were also sometimes viewed in this way, while mythology abounds in instances of extreme pollutions such as *incest, *parricide, and cannibalism.

Pollution has a complicated relation to the sacred. In one sense they are polar opposites: the main practical result of the pollutions of birth and death was that the persons affected were excluded from temples for some days, and *priests and priestesses had to observe special rules of purity. But offenders against the gods became 'consecrated' to them in the sense of being made over to them for punishment; and such negative consecration (which could also be imposed by a human *curse) was comparable to a pollution.

Since some pollutions are natural and inescapable, rules of purity are not simply rules of morality in disguise. But the very dangerous pollutions were those caused by avoidable (if sometimes unintentional) actions such as bloodshed and sacrilege. In theory, one man's crime could through such pollution bring disaster to a whole state. There is a common mythological schema (best seen at the start of *Sophocles' OT), whereby pollution causes plague, crop-failure, infertility of women and of animals. Such pollution is fertility reversed, which is why such powers as the Eumenides (*Erinyes) are double-sided, agents of pollution and also givers of fertility (see esp. Aeschylus, *Eumenides*). Orators often attempted to brand political opponents as polluting demons, the source of the city's misfortunes (see INVECTIVE); and a question actually put to the *oracle of *Zeus at *Dodona shows that this conception of the polluting individual was not a mere anachronism in the historical period: 'is it because of a mortal's pollution that we are suffering the storm?'

But pollution is also often envisaged as working more selectively. Acc. to *Antiphon's *Tetralogies*, murder pollution threatens the victim's kin until they seek vengeance or prosecute, the jurors until they convict. Thus the threat of pollution encourages action to put right the disorder.

See also PURIFICATION, GREEK.

Polyaenus, a Macedonian *rhetor, dedicated his *stratagems* to Marcus *Aurelius and Lucius *Verus. It is wide-ranging, including exploits by gods, heroes, and famous women. Some entries are historically valuable. The underlying theme is didactic, to expound the methods of protecting an army and overcoming the enemy, and along with traditional clichés of military life, he recounts stratagems employed by historical Greek commanders, with some examples from Roman history, notably *Hannibal, *Caesar, and *Augustus. Polyaenus even claims a practical purpose, to assist the emperors in the *Parthian war (AD 162–166): 'You consider it part of the art of winning victories to study the ways by which commanders in the past triumphed.'

Polybius (*c.*200–*c.*118 BC), Greek historian. After Rome's victory over Perseus of Macedon at *Pydna (168), Polybius was denounced as insufficiently friendly to the Romans and became one of the 1,000 prominent Achaeans (see ACHAEA; ACHAEAN CONFEDERACY) deported to Rome and later detained without trial in various towns of Italy. He became friend and mentor to *Cornelius Scipio Aemilianus, and was allowed to remain in Rome during his captivity. He probably accompanied Scipio to Spain (151) and to Africa (where he met *Masinissa), returning to Italy over the Alps in *Hannibal's footsteps. After the release of the surviving detainees in 150 Polybius witnessed the destruction of *Carthage (146) in Scipio's company and undertook an exploratory voyage in the Atlantic. He helped to usher in the Roman settlement of Greece after the sack of Corinth (146), and visited *Alexandria and *Sardis.

His minor works are all lost. Of his *Histories* a substantial amount survives; he is the one Hellenistic historian of whom this is true. Only bks. 1–5 of the original forty survive intact. After that we are dependent upon excerpts and occasional quotations by other writers.

Polybius' original purpose was to describe and explain Rome's rise to world dominion, to answer the question 'how and under what sort of constitution' almost the whole of the known world was conquered and fell under Roman rule in a space of not quite 53 years, from 220 to the end of the Macedonian monarchy in 167: bks. 3–30). He was profoundly impressed by this process, both by the simple fact of the end of the monarchy that had dominated the affairs of Greece for almost two centuries and by the way in which the course of events seemed almost calculated to produce the final result. He later extended his purpose to show how the Romans exercised their dominion, how the world under them reacted to it, and how both were affected (bks. 30–39; bk. 40 contained a recapitulation and chronological survey). For his task Polybius developed both a structure and a kind of history. Given his theme and his belief that the process at issue was fundamentally unitary, the structure must allow for both universality and focus. This was made possible by combining chronological and geographical organization in an original way. Vertically, the arrangement is by Olympiads, each Olympiad containing four numbered years; these years were not rigidly fixed but were adapted to the flow of events. Horizontally, the framework is geographical. Within each year there is a fixed progression from west to east: first, events in Italy (with Sicily, Spain, and Africa), then Greece and Macedonia, then Asia, then Egypt. Bks. 1 and 2 focused primarily on Rome from the first Punic War to 220, providing a background for those little acquainted with the Romans and an explanation of how the Romans could with reason come to develop the aim of universal dominion that informed their actions after the Hannibalic war.

For the kind of history he wrote Polybius invented the term 'pragmatic history'. This kind of inquiry involves study of documents and written memoirs, geographical study (esp. *autopsy), first-hand knowledge of some events, and the most careful examination of eye-witnesses about the rest. The focus is upon political actions, but the scope of 'political' was for Polybius very wide, as may be inferred from the breadth of his account of the Roman *polīteia* in bk. 6: this embraced military, economic, religious, social, and political institutions and practice. (It also included the formulation of the theory of a tripartite constitution, incorporating elements of monarchy, aristocracy, and democracy, that influenced political thinking for the next 2,000 years.) Apprehension of all these was needed in order to describe things properly and, above all, to explain them. For Polybius the historian's primary task was explanation. 'The mere statement of a fact may interest us, but it is when the reason is added that the study of history becomes fruitful: it is the mental transference of similar circumstances to our own that gives us the means of forming presentiments about what is going to happen...'. This resembles *Thucydides (2) (1. 22), as does Polybius' insistence upon true and accurate narration of historical action (both deed and speech), but Polybius goes beyond his predecessor in his insistence upon the element of explanation and beyond everybody in his explicit formulation (3. 6–7) about beginnings and reasons. Beginnings are actions; actions are preceded by decisions to act; decisions to act are processes involving various elements: a proper explanation, for Polybius, must delineate these processes and identify these various elements. In dealing with the wars that led to Rome's dominion Polybius adheres rigorously to his principles: he aims to explain in a properly multifaceted way rather than to assign responsibility.

Having brought the writing of history to a methodological acme (and having access to Rome and Romans in a way that his Greek predecessors and contemporaries did not), Polybius was regularly critical of past and contemporary historians, often polemically and sometimes excessively, whether for their method or their bias (bk. 12 is the most concentrated statement about method and what survives of it contains much hostile criticism of *Timaeus). From bias he was himself manifestly not free, whether positive or negative. But he was honest, and he was, above all, concerned about the effect of undisputed dominion upon the society that wielded it and upon those who inhabited the world in which it was wielded.

Polyclītus, Argive sculptor, active *c.*460–410 BC. He worked only in metal; all his works were in bronze except the *Hera of *Argos, which was in gold and ivory. He made gods, heroes, and athletes, and his statues of mortals were unsurpassed. His reputation rested largely on a single work, the Doryphorus or Spearbearer; he also wrote a book called the *Canon, or Rule, that explained the principles of his art, apparently basing it on this statue. In it, he stated that 'perfection comes about little by little through many numbers', and described a system of proportion whereby, starting with the fingers and toes, every part of the body was related mathematically to every other and to the whole.

The Doryphorus (perhaps an *Achilles) is nowhere described in detail; we know only that it was a nude, 'virile boy', 'suitable for both war and athletics', and 'aimed at the mean'. He is now identified with a youth known in over 50 copies. He stands on his right leg with his left relaxed; his right arm hangs limp and his left is flexed to hold the spear; his head turns and inclines somewhat to his right. This compositional scheme, which unifies the body by setting up cross-relationships between weight-bearing and relaxed limbs, is called chiastic after the Greek letter *chi* (χ), see ALPHABET,

GREEK and thereafter becomes standard practice in Greek and Roman sculpture. His proportional scheme was equally influential, as was his system of modelling, which divided the musculature into grand (static) and minor (mobile) forms, alternating in ordered sequence throughout the body. Though sculptors such as Euphranor and Lysippus introduced their own variations upon this ideal, the Polyclitan ideal remained widely influential, and was esp. popular in Roman imperial sculpture. This and the longevity of Polyclitus' own school accounts for *Pliny the Elder's observation that later artists followed his work 'like a law'. *Varro criticized Polyclitus' work as being 'virtually stereotyped', and a series of copies that apparently reproduce his other statues bear this out. His *Amazon was placed first in a contest at Ephesus.

Polycratēs (1), tyrant (see TYRANNY) of *Samos, seized power c.535 BC, with his brothers, but soon made himself tyrant. Almost unrivalled in magnificence, he made Samos a great naval power (see NAVIES; SEA POWER), and subjected neighbouring islands, including Rheneia near *Delos, which he dedicated to *Apollo. He formed a defensive alliance with Amasis (see SAÏTES), but seems to have broken it off deliberately (contrast the moralizing tale of Polycrates' ring) when *Cambyses tried to acquire Egypt, and supplied him with 40 Samian ships. The Samians mutinied and went over to Sparta; *Sparta and *Corinth, apparently to prevent Polycrates Medizing, tried to overthrow him, unsuccessfully (525). He was lured to the mainland, c.522, by the *satrap Oroetes, who pretended to be plotting against *Darius I, and was crucified. He pursued a piratical and opportunist thalassocracy, upset by the gradual advance of Persian power, which he tried to court. He attracted poets, artists, and craftsmen (*Anacreon, Ibycus, *Theodorus). The three famous building achievements praised by *Herodotus, the temple of *Hera, the harbour mole, and the tunnelled *aqueduct bringing water to the city, may all be attributable to Polycrates.

Polycratēs (2) (c.440–370 BC) was an Athenian *sophist best known for his (lost) fictitious 'Accusation of *Socrates', written after 393/2 BC, and put in the mouth of *Anytus. It may have stimulated *Plato and *Xenophon to write in Socrates' defence. The speech was known to *Libanius, who composed an elaborate 'defence' partly at least in reply to it.

Polygnōtus, painter, of Thasos. *Pliny the Elder dates him before 420 BC. Three post-Persian-Wars buildings in Athens—the first two having links with *Cimon—housed panel paintings: the Theseum (hero-shrine of *Theseus), the *Stoa Poecile, and the Anakeion (the temple of the *Dioscuri). See ATHENS, TOPOGRAPHY. It is not certain that Polygnotus' work adorned the Theseum. He was represented in the Stoa Poecile by his earlier version of the 'Sack of Troy'. To the Anakeion he contributed his 'Rape of the daughters of Leucippus'. One of these two works earned him Athenian citizenship. Later, for the club-house for citizens of *Cnidus visiting Delphi, he painted a grander 'Sack of Troy' and also an 'Underworld'.

*Pausanias (3)'s description of the Cnidian club-house reveals Polygnotus' innovative variable groundline and distribution of figures, reflected in the Niobid Painter krātēr. He was praised by *Aristotle and *Lucian for livelier and more expressive faces than before. Pliny credits him with originating transparent drapery, and depicting open mouths. Many of the elements of his art had appeared sporadically before, but he combined them to represent men of high moral purpose (ēthos) and 'better than ourselves', often either taking a decision or in the reaction after the event. For *Theophrastus and others he was a primitive (he did not use shading), but still the first great painter. See PAINTING, GREEK.

Polynīcēs See ANTIGONE; ETEOCLES; OEDIPUS; SEVEN AGAINST THEBES.

Polyphēmus See CYCLOPES.

pōmērium was the line demarcating an *augurally constituted city. It was a religious boundary, and was distinct both from the city-wall and the limit of actual habitation, although it might coincide with the former and was often understood as the strip inside or outside the wall. Almost every aspect of the history of the *pomerium* of Rome is debatable.

Pompeii The best-preserved Roman city, this port and regional centre in the Sarnus plain of southern *Campania, destroyed by the eruption of AD 79, is central to the study of Roman art and domestic life.

The basics of Pompeii as we know it are 2nd cent. BC. Campanians were prominent participants in late Hellenistic prosperity. The formation of the distinctive 'Pompeian house' belongs in this setting. Benefactors who could afford dwellings like the palatial House of the Faun equipped the city with the larger theatre, the earlier *palaestra*, and the temple of *Isis, the first baths, the gymnasium around the Doric temple, the first systematization of the forum, and the paving of the main streets.

On this flourishing community, *Sulla imposed a colony of Roman veterans, led by his nephew, as a penalty for siding with the enemy in the *Social War (during which he had himself laid siege to Pompeii). See COLONIZATION, ROMAN. Latin replaced Oscan in the town's inscriptions. The new community continued the tradition of architectural benefaction with important monuments: the *amphitheatre, the covered theatre, the temple of Jupiter, which formed the main feature of the forum. Further important houses date from this period, as do the first monumental tombs of the inner suburbs and the first villas of the territory (Cicero was one proprietor).

Yet another phase of public building marked the city's response to the Augustan regime. Monumental complexes like the Macellum (see MARKETS, *Rome*) or the Porticus of Eumachia were added to the forum; the Great Palaestra was built alongside the amphitheatre, and the larger theatre remodelled.

The sudden destruction of 79 crystallized a problematic moment: the damage of the *earthquake of 62 was still being patchily repaired, and the opulence of some projects of the last phase (the temple of the town's patron Venus and the 'central' baths were both ambitious in scale) contrast with chaos and squalor. The centre of gravity of Campania was shifting towards *Puteoli. The inscriptions painted on the walls attest vigorous political life, but most surviving evidence relates to private life.

Local contacts included rivalry over spectacles (vividly illuminated by the slogans and notices on the walls), like that with Nuceria which caused a major riot in AD 59, untypically attracting attention from Rome. The city was the centre of a vigorous and varied cash-crop agriculture; excavation has revealed the intensiveness of cultivation on small garden-lots even within the walls. See GARDENS. The processing of agricultural produce is visible in many small commercial premises. Any assessment of Roman Pompeii must take into account the wealth of Campania, its dense network of overseas contacts (which are reflected in many aspects of the life of the city, esp. its religion), and the investment in the area that derived from its popularity as a resort.

The site (only haphazardly reoccupied in antiquity) was first rediscovered in 1748, rapidly acquiring a sensational fame. Systematic recording began in 1861; the excavations of the 1950s set a new standard; work today concentrates more on recording, conservation, and analysis, since the discoveries of the first excavators have often decayed irreparably. Some four-fifths of the walled area have been disinterred.

Pompeius Magnus, Gnaeus (Pompey), b. 106 BC (the official *cognomen* meaning 'the Great', in imitation of *Alexander (2), was assumed after 81 BC). He brought a private army of three legions from his father's veterans and clients in Picenum to win victories for *Sulla in 83. He was then sent *pro praetore* to Sicily, where he defeated and killed *Papirius Carbo, and from there to Africa, where he destroyed Domitius Ahenobarbus and King Iarbas. Though Pompey was still an *equestrian, Sulla grudgingly allowed him to triumph (March 81); and in 80, after the death of his wife Aemilia, Sulla's stepdaughter, he married Mucia Tertia, a close connection of the Metelli. He supported *Aemilius Lepidus (1) for the consulship of 78, for which Sulla cut him out of his will, but helped Lutatius Catulus to overcome Lepidus next year. Later in 77 he was sent *pro consule* to reinforce Caecilius Metellus Pius against *Sertorius in Spain. Thence he returned in 71 and attempted to steal from *Licinius Crassus the credit for finishing off the slave war (see SPARTACUS). He was rewarded with a second triumph and as his first magistracy, despite his youth, the consulship of 70, with Crassus as his colleague. They restored the legislative powers which Sulla had removed from the tribunes; and Aurelius Cotta reversed another of Sulla's arrangements by ending the senate's monopoly of representation on the courts: judges were now to be drawn equally from senators, *equestrians, and *tribuni aerarii* (a group similar to the equestrians).

Pompey took no consular province. But in 67 the *lex Gabinia* (see GABINIUS); authorized him to deal with *piracy. The command, for three years, covered the whole Mediterranean, and gave him unprecedented powers; but Pompey's campaign required only three months. In 66 a law of the tribune Manilius gave him the Asiatic provinces of Cilicia, *Bithynia, and Pontus, earlier held by *Licinius Lucullus, and the conduct of the war against *Mithradates VI. Pompey's eastern campaigns were his greatest achievement. Mithradates was defeated immediately, and though attempts to pursue him over the

Caucasus failed, he had himself killed in the Crimea in 63. Pompey founded colonies, annexed *Syria, settled Judaea, and laid the foundation of later Roman organization of the east (though he reached no agreement with *Parthia).

In 62 he returned, disbanded his army, and triumphed, no longer a *populāris* as hitherto (for *populārēs* see OPTIMATES). He made two requests: land for his veterans, and ratification of his eastern arrangements. But he had divorced Mucia for adultery, allegedly with *Caesar; and the Metelli, aided by Lucullus and *Porcius Cato (2), frustrated him until in 60 Caesar succeeded in reconciling him with Crassus. In 59 the three men formed a coalition and Pompey married Caesar's daughter *Iulia (1). His demands were satisfied by Caesar as consul; but his popularity waned, and in 58/7 *Clodius Pulcher flouted and attacked him. In 57, after securing *Cicero's return from exile, he received control of the corn-supply for five years with proconsular *imperium* and fifteen *legates. But no army was attached, nor could he secure the commission to restore *Ptolemy (1) XII Aulētēs ('*Aulos-player') in Egypt. In April 56 the coalition with Caesar and Crassus was renewed at Luca. Pompey became consul with Crassus for 55, and received both Spanish provinces for five years; he governed them through legates, staying in the suburbs of Rome. After Iulia's death in 54 he declined a further marriage alliance with Caesar, and the death of Crassus in 53 increased the tension between Caesar and Pompey. In 52 after Clodius' murder Pompey was appointed sole consul, with backing even from Cato. Pompey's immediate actions—the trial of *Annius Milo and his legislation on violence, on bribery, and on the tenure of *magistracies—were not necessarily intended specifically to injure Caesar, but the prolongation of his *imperium* for five years from this date destroyed the balance of power, and he took as his colleague Caecilius Metellus Pius Scipio, whose daughter Cornelia he married about the time that he became consul. At first he resisted attempts to recall Caesar, but his desire to pose as the arbiter of Caesar's fate was challenged in 50 by *Scribonius Curio, who insisted that both or neither should lay down their commands. Unable to accept the implications of parity, Pompey conditionally accepted from the consul Claudius Marcellus the command of the republic's forces in Italy. In 49 he transported his army from *Brundisium to Greece and spent the year mobilizing in *Macedonia. He met Caesar on the latter's arrival in 48 with a force powerful in

every arm, and inflicted a serious reverse when Caesar attempted to blockade him in Dyrrachium. But later (9 August), perhaps under pressure from his senatorial friends, he joined in a pitched battle at Pharsalus, and was heavily defeated. He fled to Egypt, but was stabbed to death as he landed (28 September 48).

The violence and unconstitutional character of Pompey's early career invite comparison with *Augustus, whose constitutional position his powers often prefigured: in 67 he had fifteen (or even 24) legates; from 55 he governed Spain through legates, and while doing so was made consul in 52. But still more significant were his wealth and his unofficial power: by 62 in Spain, Gaul, Africa and the east, and parts of Italy, there were colonists and clients (see CLIENS) bound to him by the relationship of *fidēs* (loyalty) and surrounding him with a magnificence unsurpassed by a Roman senator hitherto; the climax was reached with the dedication of his theatre in the *Campus Martius in 55. His military talents are hard to evaluate. Other commanders—Metellus, Crassus, Lucullus—often paved the way to his successes, and at Pharsalus he clearly panicked. Logistics seem to have been his strong point, as in the campaign against the pirates. But in politics he showed a mastery which it was easy for clever men to underrate (e.g., the epigram of *Caelius Rufus: 'he is apt to say one thing and think another, but is not clever enough to keep his real aims from showing'). 'Moderate in everything but in seeking domination' (*Sallust), by superb skill and timing he rose from his lawless beginnings to a constitutional pre-eminence in which he could discard the use of naked force. His aim was predominance, but not at the expense of at least the appearance of popularity. He did not wish to overthrow the republican constitution, but was content if its rules were bent almost to breaking-point to accommodate his extraordinary eminence. His private life was virtually blameless, and two women, Iulia and Cornelia, married to him for dynastic ends, became deeply attached to him, and his love for Iulia was noted by contemporaries. Cicero, though he never understood Pompey's subtleties, remained a devoted admirer; and despite the disappointments of the war years Pompey's death brought from him a muted but moving tribute: 'I knew him to be a man of good character, clean life, and serious principle.'

Pompeius Magnus (Pius), Sextus, younger son of Pompey (Gnaeus *Pompeius Magnus) and Mucia Tertia, b. *c*.67 BC. Left on Lesbos with *Cornelia during the campaign of Pharsalus (48), he accompanied his father to Egypt and after his murder went to Africa; after Thapsus (46) he joined his brother Gnaeus Pompeius Magnus in Spain, and during the campaign of Munda (45) commanded the garrison of Corduba. Later he contrived to raise an army, partly of fugitive Pompeians, and won successes against *Caesar's governors in Further Spain. In summer 44 *Aemilius Lepidus (2) arranged a settlement between him and the senate, under the terms of which he left Spain; but instead of returning to Rome, he waited on events in *Massalia with his army and fleet. In April 43 the senate made him its naval commander; but in August he was outlawed under the *lex Pedia* (see PEDIUS) and then used his fleet to rescue fugitives from the *proscriptions and to occupy *Sicily, at first sharing authority with the governor, but later putting him to death; and using the island as a base for raiding and blockading Italy. He repelled an attack by *Octavian's general in 42, supported Antony against Octavian in 40 and in 39 concluded the Pact of Misēnum with the triumvirs (see TRIUMVIRI), who conceded to him the governorship of Sicily, Sardinia and Corsica, and *Achaia, an *augurate and a future consulship in return for the suspension of his blockade. In 38 Octavian accused him of breaking the pact and again attacked him, but was defeated in sea fights off *Cumae and *Messana. In 36 the attack was renewed, and after *Vipsanius Agrippa's victory off Mylae, the war was decided by the battle of Naulochus. Sextus escaped with a few ships to Asia, where he was put to death.

Sextus was, like his father, an able and energetic commander. His brief career was spent entirely in the continuation—symbolized by his adoption of the surname Pius—of an inherited struggle. Despite his long absence from and blockade of Italy, he seems to have been popular in Rome.

Pompey See POMPEIUS MAGNUS, GNAEUS.

Pompilius, Numa See REX.

Pompōnius Atticus, Titus, b. 110 BC, the son of a cultured *equestrian of a family claiming descent from Pompilius Numa (see REX), was later adopted by a rich uncle, whose wealth he inherited. He was a friend of *Cicero from boyhood (Cicero's brother Quintus married Atticus' sister), and Cicero's *Letters to Atticus*, probably published in the reign of *Nero, are the best

source for his character, supplemented by an encomiastic biographical sketch by his friend *Nepos. In 85 Atticus left Italy after selling his assets there, in order to escape the civil disturbances he foresaw. He lived in Athens until the mid-60s (hence his *cognomen*), among other things studying Epicurean philosophy (see EPICURUS), to which however he never wholly subscribed. Henceforth he combined a life of cultured ease (*otium*; see LABOUR) with immense success in various business activities and an infallible instinct for survival. He privately urged Cicero to determined action on behalf of the *optimates, with whom he sympathized, but himself refused to take sides in politics and personally assisted many prominent politicians from *Marius to Octavian (see AUGUSTUS), without regard for their differences and conflicts. He was Cicero's literary adviser and had his works copied and distributed. He himself wrote a chronological table of world, and, esp. Roman, history, which became a standard work, eulogistic histories of some noble families, and minor works. (All are lost.) He lived to become a friend of *Vipsanius Agrippa, who married his daughter. In 32 he killed himself when incurably ill.

pontifex, pl. **pontificēs** The *pontifices* formed one of the four major colleges of the Roman priesthood. Their college was a more complicated structure than the other three, containing as full members the *rex sacrōrum* (the republican priest who took over the king's religious functions) and the three major *flamines* as well as the *pontifices* proper; the *Vestals and the minor *flamines* together with the pontifical scribe were also a subordinate part of the college. The *pontifices* themselves were originally three in number, all *patricians; new members were co-opted by the old ones.

The college's duties were wide-ranging: they had general oversight of the state cult—sacrifices (see SACRIFICE, ROMAN), games (see LUDI), festivals and other rituals; they advised magistrates and private persons on the sacred law and kept books which recorded their rules and decisions; they had special areas of concern in relation to families and clans (*gentes*; see GENS)—the control of adoptions, burial law, the inheritance of religious duties. They had no authority over priests outside the college; and their relationship with the state remained an advisory one—their rulings could be put into effect only by magistrates or by the assemblies.

The *pontifices*' position evolved gradually during the republic: the *lex Ogulnia* of 300 BC abolished the monopoly of the patricians and added extra places for the plebeians (see PLEBS). From then till the end of the republic the college, together with the *augurs, had as its members the dominant figures in the ruling élite, including *Iulius Caesar (1), *Aemilius Lepidus (2), and *Augustus himself.

The leading member of the college—the *pontifex maximus*—who had originally been selected by the college, was from the mid-3rd cent. BC onwards elected by a special procedure (only seventeen of the 35 tribes voted), which was later extended to the rest of the college—and the other colleges—by the *lex Domitia* of 104. He acted as spokesman for the college, esp. in the senate; but could be overruled by his colleagues. Perhaps as a result of the election by popular vote, the *pontifex maximus* came to be seen as the most prominent and influential of the priests; but it was not until Augustus united the position with other priesthoods and with the power of the *princeps*, that the *pontifex maximus* came to resemble a 'High Priest'. From then on the position was always held by the reigning emperor until Gratian refused to accept it.

Pontius Pīlātus, *prefect of Judaea AD 26–36. Offences against religious sentiment, perhaps not deliberate, created several serious disturbances which Pilatus handled badly. He yielded to determined protests against image-bearing standards being brought into *Jerusalem by troops. Shields set up in the palace, treated also as iconic, were removed at *Tiberius' behest. Control of a crowd objecting to the use of Temple funds for the building of an aqueduct was achieved with heavy violence. A military attack on Samaritans gathering at Mt. Gerizim finally led to accusations before *Vitellius, *legate of *Syria, and then to Pilatus' recall. A reliable account of his conduct of the trial of Jesus cannot be extracted from the conflicting Gospel accounts. John's portrayal of him giving judgement in front of his *praetorium* is plausible. Later Christian tradition and an apocryphal literature proliferated around him and his wife.

Poppaea Sabina, named after her maternal grandfather Gaius Poppaeus Sabinus (consul AD 9, governor of Moesia 12–35), was married first to Rufrius Crispinus, praetorian *prefect under Claudius, by whom she had a son, later killed by *Nero. By 58, during her second marriage, to the future emperor *Otho, she became mistress of Nero. Allegedly at her instigation, Nero murdered *Iulia Agrippina in 59 and in 62

divorced, banished, and executed *Claudia Octavia. Nero now married Poppaea, who bore a daughter Claudia in 63; both mother and child received the surname Augusta, but the child died at four months. Through Poppaea's influence, her native *Pompeii became a colony. In 65, pregnant again, she is supposed to have died from a kick which Nero gave her in a fit of temper, and was accorded a public funeral and divine honours.

populārēs See OPTIMATES.

population, Greek The demography of Greece is hard to investigate because of the shortage of statistical data. Owing to the stress on war in historiography most estimates of population size relate to the size of campaigning armies or to the manpower available for military purposes, i.e. free adult males only. Extrapolations must be attempted from such information to total population sizes because women, children, and slaves were not usually enumerated at all. The Greeks had a poor grasp of numbers and were prone to exaggeration, e.g. in relation to the size of Persian armies. *Thucydides (2) was a notable exception to this rule. (Unfortunately, he does not concern himself with Athenian naval manpower or recruiting.) Even in Classical Athens it seems unlikely that there was a central register of *hoplites, in addition to the deme registers. Greek states did not have taxes payable by all inhabitants that would have required the maintenance of records for financial purposes. Censuses of citizens were rare in the ancient Greek world.

Estimates of ancient population sizes inevitably involve much guesswork. It is often necessary to use estimates of carrying capacity based on land areas, soil fertility, etc. The assumptions underlying such estimates are usually controversial. Intensive archaeological field surveys are yielding information about changes in settlement patterns in ancient Greece, which are probably connected with population fluctuations. The general pattern is of a thinly populated landscape in the 11th–10th cents. BC, followed by substantial population growth in most areas from the 9th cent., suggesting that *colonization from the 8th cent. BC onwards was at least partly a product of population growth. A peak was reached in the 5th to the 3rd cents. The period of colonization after *Alexander (2) the Great (see COLONIZATION, HELLENISTIC) was at least partly a result of population increase. There was a substantial decline in the last two centuries BC, which continued into the early

Roman empire. There were always local variations on this broad pattern. However, the inference drawn from the field surveys, namely that Greece was more densely populated in the Classical period than at any time before or since until the late 19th cent. AD, correlates with the fact that even the lowest estimates of the size of the population of Classical Greece made by modern scholars, on the basis of the fragmentary literary sources, are substantially higher than figures derived from census data for parts of late medieval and early modern Greece. The total population in the 4th cent. BC may have been about two million people.

Demography is not just a matter of population size. It is also concerned with the age-structure of populations, which is mainly determined by fertility rates and also by mortality rates. Fertility and mortality rates are determined by many factors, esp. average age of marriage for fertility, and *disease patterns for mortality. There is as little information for vital rates in ancient Greece as for population size.

Excavations of *cemeteries suggest a high level of infant and early child mortality in Classical Greece (c.30 per cent at *Olynthus). Physical anthropologists attempt to determine the age of death of ancient skeletons. However, their methods suffer from various sources of uncertainty, esp. in relation to the age of death of adults. Individuals who survived infancy and early childhood may have had a reasonable chance of reaching old age. Moreover, conclusions drawn from cemeteries about populations, rather than individuals, are often controversial because it is not certain whether the individuals buried there were a representative sample of the whole population. Scholars are suspicious of ages given in literary sources because there were no birth or death certificates. (Greek men reported to have lived to a great age include *Gorgias, *Isocrates, *Sophocles.) The Greeks in the Classical period seldom recorded ages or causes of death on tombstones.

There is even less evidence for fertility rates than for mortality rates. However, fertility levels were almost certainly much higher than in modern advanced countries. In the context of high infant mortality (see CHILDBIRTH) parents needed several children to ensure that some reached adulthood, to provide an heir to the estate, support for the parents in old age, and additional farm labour. Each adult woman would have had to give birth four or five times to reproduce the population. There is little evidence for average age of marriage, esp. for

women, which is the most important factor influencing fertility levels. There were no marriage certificates. A few passages in literary sources suggest a pattern of late marriage for men (around the age of 30) and early marriage for women (mid- to late teens). Early marriage for women made very high fertility rates possible. So family limitation measures such as *infanticide or *abortion may have been practised in some social classes, regions, or periods.

Apart from calculations based on land areas, and scattered references to army strengths, the main body of information comes from *Athens, esp. for the 4th cent. BC. Such promising contemporary epigraphic sources as lists of *epheboi (two *age classes of young men undergoing military training), bouleutai (councillors, see BOULE) are usually fragmentary. It is unclear whether these groups were recruited from the entire adult male citizen body or only from the hoplite and upper classes (see PENTAKOSIOMEDIMNOI; HIPPEIS; ZEUGITAI). At Athens every boy at 18 was registered in his father's deme. The total of *deme registers formed the list of those entitled to attend the assembly. Unfortunately deme registers were not inscribed on stone. Other methods for calculating population size are hardly any more promising: *cereal production (the one extant figure may well refer to a year of drought); cereal imports (one estimate made in a year of drought, which may in any case total the imports for several years). Boys and girls were enrolled in their *phratries; but there were no other records of citizen women. *Metics were required to pay a tax and were registered in their deme of residence. The biggest area of uncertainty is the number of slaves (see SLAVERY).

For Classical Athens only one census is recorded, namely that carried out by *Demetrius (1) of Phaleron in the late 4th cent. BC. Acc. to information preserved by *Athenaeus, this census enumerated 21,000 citizens, 10,000 metics and 400,000 slaves. The number of citizens seems plausible, but it is uncertain whether it includes all citizens or merely those liable and fit for hoplite service. The number of metics is the only preserved figure for this status-group, whose numbers probably varied in accordance with the prosperity of Athens. The number of slaves is incredible. Attempts have been made to emend the text, but it is more likely that these figures for slaves were simply invented. Nevertheless there were probably many more slaves in the 5th cent. BC, at the time of the Athenian empire (see DELIAN LEAGUE), than there had been earlier. *Herodotus suggests that there were c.30,000 Athenian citizens in the early 5th cent. BC. This stock figure for the number of citizens was often repeated: the citizen body probably did not significantly exceed it during the 4th cent. BC. Multiplication by four to account for women and children indicates a total (citizen) population of around 120,000 then. There is no evidence that the sex-ratio diverged significantly from parity. Evidence for the size of Athenian military forces during the 5th-cent. empire suggests that by c.450 BC there were at least 50,000 citizens, revealing a substantial increase since the early 5th cent. BC. This level was maintained until the beginning of the *Peloponnesian War. Acc. to Thucydides, most Athenians still lived in the countryside then, rather than in Athens. During the war the citizen population gradually declined, first because of the '*plague', and second because of heavy casualties in battle, esp. during the *Sicilian Expedition.

*Sparta suffered from a serious manpower shortage, which *Aristotle identified as the reason for her downfall. Herodotus says that Sparta had 8,000 potential soldiers in 480 BC, and 5,000 actually took part in the battle of Plataea (see PLATAEA, BATTLE OF) in 479. By *Aristotle's time Sparta probably had fewer than 1,000 citizens. The causes of this decline are much debated. Such diverse factors as the structure of Spartan society, casualties in war, inheritance patterns, and the *earthquake of c.464 have been invoked to explain it. In any case, it is clear that the Spartan citizen body was only a small fraction of the total population of *Laconia and, before 371, *Messenia. Field-survey data suggest that these parts of the *Peloponnese were as densely populated in the 4th cent. as the rest of Greece.

There is even less evidence for other parts of Greece. Judging by evidence for military strengths, *Argos and *Boeotia had citizen bodies similar in size to that of Athens in the 4th cent., but probably had fewer resident aliens and slaves. Corinth's population was at most half the size of the Athenian population. Mountainous Arcadia produced many emigrants. However, migration occurred on a substantial scale from most regions of Greece from the Dark Age until well into the Hellenistic period, resulting in the foundation of many colonies abroad. The Greek colonies in *Sicily and Italy were esp. prosperous. The population of *Syracuse may have exceeded in size all the states of mainland Greece, including Athens. Several other colonies in these areas, such as *Acragas and *Tarentum, probably also surpassed virtu-

ally all states in mainland Greece in population size.

population, Roman There are two different kinds of question which historians might wish to ask about the population of the Roman world: how large was it or any of its constituent parts? and what were the patterns and tendencies of birth rates and death rates? Four kinds of information are available to offer imperfect answers to the first question: *census figures, mostly for the Roman republic and early empire, where they served for the levy and, originally, taxation; figures relating to the feeding of (part of) the population of the city of Rome; occasional references to the population of particular cities or areas, usually without any possibility of knowing on what they were based; and figures for the carrying capacity of different areas of the Roman world in the earliest periods for which reasonably reliable figures exist. Almost no information is available for the second question; and one has to try to find the best fit of such scraps as there are with the model life tables compiled in the modern period for a variety of populations at different stages of economic development.

The Roman census figures purport to give the adult male population from the early republic to the early empire. Leaving aside the problem of the reliability of the early figures, some scholars have argued that they give for the republic only the adult male population above the property qualification for military service, excluding *proletarii. If the figures really were only of those eligible, however, it would be hard to see why the Romans ever had problems of recruitment to the legions. On the other hand, it has also been argued that the rise in the total under Augustus is so large that it can be explained only on the assumption that the figures now included women and children:

| 70/69 BC | 910,000 |
| 28 BC | 4,063,000 |

This view is by no means universally accepted; and the alternative view argues that the difference is to be explained by the enfranchisement of Transpadane Gaul in 49 BC and by the greater efficiency of registration. In any case, the figure of 4,063,000 will have included large numbers of Romans living overseas, and comparisons with guesses as to the total (male) population of Italy in any earlier period are hazardous. Similarly, we cannot know how far rises in numbers after *Augustus are due to manumissions of slaves (see SLAVERY) and enfranchisements of provincials (see CITIZENSHIP, ROMAN).

There will always have been some under-registration in the census, probably substantial after *tributum ceased to be collected after 167. The rise in numbers between 131 and 125 is probably to be related to the agrarian law of Tiberius *Sempronius Gracchus (2); but it is not clear whether it is due to recipients of plots of land bothering to register for the first time or to men registering in order to prove their eligibility. The relatively low rise in 86, after the enfranchisement of peninsular Italy in 90 is probably to be explained by the difficulty of conditions in the aftermath of the *Social War.

All arguments about trends are made difficult by uncertainty over the scale of losses due to war casualties and the removal of Roman citizens to Latin colonies (see COLONIZATION, ROMAN), and of additions to citizen numbers through the manumission of slaves and the incorporation of new citizens from other communities.

The conventional view of Rome is that in the imperial period it had a total population of *c*.1 million; but it seems not to have been widely noticed that a fragment of *Livy implies that this figure had already been reached when *Pompey was controller of the corn supply (see CURA(TIO)) in 57.

Figures exist for a number of other cities, plausibly attesting that *Alexandria, *Carthage, Antioch, *Pergamum, *Ephesus, Apamea on the Orontes, and *Lugdunum had free populations in the range 300,000 to 100,000, probably including the free inhabitants of their territory. The numbers of slaves to be added to these figures are obviously uncertain, though *Galen implies that there were as many slaves in Pergamum as free male inhabitants.

For the total population of the Roman empire, *c*.54 million at the death of Augustus is a plausible guess and compatible with the figure of 7.5 million reported for Egypt, excluding Alexandria. The total may have risen slightly thereafter, declining with the series of *plagues which begin in the 160s AD and culminate in that under *Justinian.

When we turn to patterns and tendencies in the population as a whole, the best guess is that the population of the Roman world was relatively stable, both in size and in structure, with a high birth-rate and a high death-rate, esp. in infancy. Some confirmation for the use of model life tables as parallels comes from the few declarations of death which survive from Egypt. Ages of death recorded on tombstones

are worthless as demographic evidence: the surviving evidence is hopelessly skewed by underlying differences in who was commemorated and who was not.

The existence of the *ius (trium) liberorum shows that three surviving children was regarded as an attainable goal.

populus, a collective term for the Roman citizen body. The Roman People (*populus Rōmānus*) comprised the entire community of adult male citizens, but excluded women and children, as well as slaves and foreigners. In the later republic and during the early centuries of the empire *populus Romanus* was the technical designation of the Roman state: the Romans had no concept of 'the State' as an impersonal entity independent of the individuals who composed it. By means of its formal procedures in the *comitia, the *populus Romanus* elected magistrates, passed laws, declared war and ratified treaties; and it was the *populus Romanus* that had dealings with the gods in public religious ceremonies. The *rēs pūblica* was the affair (or property) of the people, as *Cicero observed, noting the formal equivalence '*res publica res populī*'.

Porcia was daughter of *Porcius Cato (2) and wife first of *Calpurnius Bibulus and from 45 BC of *Iunius Brutus. She shared the political ideals of her father and her husbands, insisted on being let into the secret of the plot to murder *Caesar, and took part with her mother-in-law *Servilia in the conference of republicans at Antium on 8 June 44. When Brutus sailed for the east, she returned to Rome, where she fell ill and in the early summer of 43 took her own life.

Porcius Cato (1), Marcus, 'Cato the Censor' (234–149 BC) was a dominant figure in both the political and the cultural life of Rome in the first half of the 2nd cent. BC. A *novus homo, b. in *Tusculum, he spent much of his childhood in the *Sabine country, where his family owned land. He served in the *Hannibalic War, winning particular praise for his contribution at the battle of the Metaurus in 207. He embarked on a political career under the patronage of the patrician Valerius Flaccus, who was his colleague in both consulship and censorship. As quaestor 204 he served under *Cornelius Scipio Africanus in Sicily and Africa; a constant champion of traditional Roman virtues, he looked with disfavour on Scipio's adoption of Greek customs and relaxed military discipline in Sicily. He is said to have returned from Africa via Sardinia, bringing

thence the poet *Ennius to Rome. He was plebeian aedile 199 and praetor 198. He governed
Sardinia, expelling usurers and restricting the
demands made on the Sardinians for the upkeep
of himself and his staff. He reached the consulship in 195: after unsuccessfully opposing the
repeal of the sumptuary lex *Oppia*, he went to
Spain, where he suppressed a major rebellion,
extended the area under Roman control, and
arranged for the exploitation of the gold and
silver mines; he returned to Rome to celebrate
a triumph. In 191, as military tribune, he played
an important part in the defeat of the *Seleucid
Antiochus III at *Thermopylae, and was sent to
Rome by Acilius Glabrio to report the victory.

Cato was constantly engaged in court cases,
both as prosecutor or prosecution witness and
as defendant. He was an instigator of the attacks
on the Scipios (Africanus and his brother), and
two of his other targets, Minucius Thermus and
Glabrio, can be seen as allies of the Scipios. The
attack on Glabrio was connected with the censorial elections of 189, when Cato and Flaccus
stood unsuccessfully. See CENSOR. Five years
later they were elected, having stood on a joint
programme of reversing the decline of traditional morality. They were severe in their review of the rolls of the senate and the
*equestrians. High levels of taxation were im-
posed on what the censors regarded as luxuries,
and the public contracts were let on terms most
advantageous for the state and least so for the
contractors. They undertook extensive public
works, including major repairs and extensions
to the sewage system. The controversies caused
by his censorship affected Cato for the rest of
his life. But he courted conflict and spoke his
mind to the point of rudeness. He rigidly applied to himself the standards he demanded of
others and made a parade of his own parsi-
mony: when in Spain he had shared the rigours
of his soldiers.

Though he held no further public offices, Cato
continued to play an active role in politics. In
171 he was one of the patrons chosen by the
peoples of Spain to present their complaints
against Roman governors. In 167 he opposed
the attempt by Sulpicius Galba to block the *triumph of *Aemilius Paullus (2); Cato's son later
married a daughter of Paullus, and apparently
the old enmity between Cato and the family of
the Scipios was at an end. In the last years of his
life, after serving on an embassy to *Carthage in
153, Cato convinced himself that the existence
of Carthage constituted a serious danger to
Rome; he ended each speech in the senate by
saying that Carthage must be destroyed. War
was eventually declared in 149. Shortly afterwards came the last speech of Cato's life, against
Galba (above).

Cato was the 'virtual founder of Latin prose
literature'. Among works that were known to
later generations—though not necessarily intended for publication by Cato himself—but of
which we know little, are 'To his Son', perhaps
no more than a brief collection of exhortations,
a letter to his son 'On Military Matters', a
work dealing with civil law, and a collection of
sayings.

The foremost orator of his age, Cato made
many speeches. Over 150 were known to *Cicero, and we possess fragments of 80. Doubtless
he intended his speeches to survive, though it is
a question whether he revised them for publication and conceived of himself as creating Latin
oratory as a literary genre.

Previous Roman historians, starting with *Fabius Pictor, had written in Greek; Cato's *Origines*,
begun in 168 and still in progress at the time of
his death, was the first historical work in Latin.
The first of its seven books dealt with the foundation of Rome and the regal period; Cato had
little or nothing to say about the early republic.
The second and third covered the origins and
customs of the towns of Italy (the title of the
work is appropriate for only these three books).
The remaining books described Rome's wars
from the First Punic War onwards. Cato is said
to have written in a summary fashion, though
some episodes were given detailed treatment,
and he devoted more space to the events of the
period during which he was writing; the last
two books cover less than 20 years. He chose to
omit the names of generals and included at least
two of his own speeches.

The only extant work of Cato is 'On Agriculture'. It is mainly concerned with giving advice
to the owner of a middle-sized estate, based on
slave labour, in Latium or Campania, whose
primary aim was the production of wine and
olive oil for sale. It also includes recipes, religious formulae, prescriptions, and sample contracts. The work is disordered, and some have
wondered whether Cato himself is responsible
for the shape of the text as we have it.

Cato sometimes expressed great hostility to
all things Greek: in 'To his Son' he called the
Greeks a vile and unteachable race; in 155, worried by the effect their lectures were having on
Roman youth, he was anxious that an embassy
of Athenian philosophers should leave Rome
rapidly. But he knew Greek and Greek literature

well. His objections were to an excessive *phil-hellenism.

Cato married twice, and had a son by each wife; the first died as praetor-designate in 152; the second, born when his father was 80, was the grandfather of Cato of Utica; see next entry.

Porcius Cato (2), **Marcus,** 'of Utica' (95–46 BC), great-grandson of Cato the Censor (see preceding entry), nephew of *Livius Drusus, and brought up in the Livian household with the children of his mother's earlier marriage to Servilius Caepio. In 63 he became tribune-designate, and intervened powerfully in the senate to secure the execution of the Catilinarians (see SERGIUS CATILINA). As tribune he conciliated the mob by increasing the numbers eligible to receive cheap corn, but in all else remained uncompromising; *Cicero deplores his lack of realism which prevented revision of the Asian tax-contracts (61)—thus alienating the *equestrians—and which frustrated every overture of *Pompey until the coalition between Pompey, *Caesar, and *Crassus was formed. In 59 he opposed Caesar obstinately and was temporarily imprisoned, but next year *Clodius Pulcher removed him by appointing him to undertake the annexation of *Cyprus. Though King Ptolemy of Cyprus killed himself and Cato's accounts were lost on the voyage home, his reputation for fairness remained unimpaired. After the conference of Caesar and Pompey at Luca he persuaded his brother-in-law Domitius Ahenobarbus not to give up hope of being elected consul for 55, but Domitius' candidature collapsed because of intimidation by the supporters of Pompey and Crassus. *Vatinius defeated Cato for the praetorship by bribery, but Cato was eventually praetor in 54. In 52, abandoning his constitutional principles, he supported Pompey's election as sole consul; he himself stood for 51 but failed. In the war he tried to avoid citizen bloodshed but resolutely followed Pompey: he served in Sicily, but was expelled from there. Then he served in Asia, and held Dyrrachium during the campaign of Pharsalus. After Pompey's defeat, Cato joined the quarrelling Pompeians in Africa and reconciled them; he had Caecilius Metellus Pius Scipio made general. During the war he governed *Utica with great moderation, and was honoured by the city's inhabitants when after Thapsus in April 46 he killed himself rather than accept pardon from Caesar, an act which earned him the undying glory of a martyr.

Cato's constitutionalism, a mixture of *Stoicism and old Roman principles, was genuine. After death he was more dangerous than ever to Caesar, who in his *Anticato*, a reply to Cicero's pamphlet *Cato*, pitched the hostile case too high, and allowed the fame of Cato's life and death to give respectability to the losing side, and to inspire later political martyrs: 'The victor had the gods on his side, but the vanquished had Cato' (*Lucan).

pornography presents people—esp. women —as mute, available, and subordinate sexual objects, often shown in a context of violence. Attic red-figure ware contains scenes of abuse and degradation of women, including some sado-masochism, in which women are typically threatened with a sandal. It is possible to read homosexual images on Attic vases as more 'romantic' in tone than the heterosexual images.

Erotic wall-paintings from such cities as *Pompeii were once used to define buildings as brothels, but it is now clear that erotic paintings as exemplars were found on the walls of private houses as well. Roman literary references to such images refer to small painted pictures on the bedroom walls of the Julio-Claudian emperors.

See HETEROSEXUALITY; HOMOSEXUALITY; PAINTING; SEXUALITY.

Porphyry (AD 234–c.305), scholar, philosopher, and student of religions. He was b. probably at Tyre; studied at Athens; became a devoted disciple of *Plotinus, with whom he studied in Rome (263–268). His varied writings may be classified as follows.

1. Commentaries and introductions to *Aristotle.

2. Commentaries on *Plato.

3. Our edition of Plotinus' *Enneads* arranged into sets of nine treatises; also a lost commentary on the *Enneads*.

4. Historical work includes scholarly research on chronology and a history of philosophy down to Plato, from which the extant *Life of Pythagoras* (see PYTHAGORAS) is an excerpt.

5. His metaphysical works are almost entirely lost but included the extant *Sententiae*, a succinct, but probably incomplete, introduction to Plotinian metaphysics which displays divergences from Plotinus.

6. His publications on religion show a consistent interest in and respect for most traditions allied to a searching but constructive critique of

the workings and significance of many pagan rituals. Despite his rejection of blood sacrifice in *On Abstinence* (see ANIMALS, ATTITUDES TO), he was in other respects a religious traditionalist. Porphyry raised but did not solve the problem of the relationship of philosophy to religion. In *Against the Christians* he used historical criticism to establish the lateness of the Book of Daniel.

7. Philological works include *Homeric Enquiries*, a landmark in the history of Homeric scholarship (see HOMER).

8. Extant works on technical subjects are a commentary (incomplete) on *Ptolemy (2)'s Harmonics*, and an introduction to his *Tetrabiblos*.

portents are phenomena seen as indicating the future, which are generally believed to be of divine origin. Such signs often occur spontaneously, although they may be sought. Roman theory thus distinguished between the unsolicited and the solicited (see AUGURS). Some sort of belief in portents was general in antiquity, but scepticism on particulars was widespread; there was much room for disagreement on what counted as a portent and on what it portended, as well as on its importance in relation to other factors.

In *Homer we can observe much that is characteristic of portents in the Greek world. Signs from the behaviour of birds (see BIRDS, SACRED) are frequent, and are sometimes explicitly said to come from *Zeus; they may simply confirm something that has been said or they may use symbolism to convey a more complex message. Typical of the latter kind is the portent in bk. 12 of the *Iliad*, where an eagle is bitten by a snake it is carrying and forced to drop it. This is interpreted by Polydamas to mean that the Trojans will eventually fail in their attack on the Achaean ships. Scepticism is shown by *Hector, who regards such signs as trivial ('one omen is best, to fight for your country')—but events will prove him wrong. Other portentous events in Homer include thunder and sneezing. Most of the portents recorded from later periods, Greek and Roman, conform to similar types. They are drawn from meteorological or astronomical phenomena (strange types of rainfall, *eclipses—also *earthquakes), from the behaviour of animals (birds, swarms of bees), and from the involuntary actions or unknowing words of humans. Other sources include the entrails of sacrificial victims, the unusual appearance of statues, and (esp. in Rome) deformed births, human or animal (See DEFORMITY). Wishing to interpret such an event, Greeks

might consult a professional diviner (see DIVINATION) or even send to an oracle, or they might, like Polydamas, draw their own conclusions. As with other forms of prophecy, much latitude was possible here. *Xenophon relates that when a Spartan expedition was demoralized by an earth tremor their leader and king Agesipolis interpreted it to indicate *Poseidon's approval, since the expedition was already under way. Once he had achieved part of his aim, however, he was prepared to accept a thunderbolt and a lobeless sacrificial liver as signs that the expedition should be disbanded.

Similar phenomena were regarded as portentous in the Roman world, but were conceived in a different way. Whereas certain signs, as among the Greeks, were simple indicators of the future, in particular of the success or otherwise of an undertaking, the more unusual or sinister-seeming—rains of blood, monstrous births—were classified as *prōdigia* and seen as signs of divine anger. Rather than exact interpretation, what was needed therefore was expiation, and the matter was likely to be the concern of the state. Prodigies were reported to the consuls, who prepared a list for the senate; the senate then decided which were authentic and of public concern. It might then take immediate action or more usually refer the matter to the *pontifices* or *haruspices*, or arrange a consultation of the *Sibylline Books. With this elaborate state mechanism, it is not surprising that more than in Greece portents were closely connected with politics and could be the subject of manipulation, conscious or unconscious. *Publica prodigia* decline in frequency during the 1st cent. BC, but omens and portents of other types continue to be reported throughout antiquity and beyond.

See also PROPHECIES.

portico, an extended colonnade and thus a possible translation of the Greek *stoa. The Latin term *porticus* can refer similarly to extended free-standing colonnades which are simply stoas erected in a Roman context. On the other hand, the Porticus Aemilia beside the Tiber, dating originally to 193 BC, was an extended, enclosed, market-hall with at least six rows of internal columns. The Latin term is often used to designate enclosed courtyards with colonnades surrounding all four sides, such as the Porticus Octaviae at Rome, shown on the Severan Forma Urbis; some fragments still stand. This was a temple precinct, enclosing the temples of *Juno Regina and *Jupiter Stator.

portōria were in origin duties on goods entering or leaving harbours, the upkeep of which was a charge on public funds. Such levies were made in Italian harbours under the republic. In the late republic and Principate internal customs-duties (raised for revenue) were extended to the provinces and levied on the major traffic-routes; for this purpose several provinces might form a single unit (e.g. the Gallic or the Danubian provinces) in the sense that duty was raised at a uniform rate (often, as in Gaul, $2\frac{1}{2}$ per cent) within the area. On the eastern frontiers, at least, customs duties, apparently fixed at 25 per cent, were levied on goods crossing the empire's borders. The collection of *portoria* was let out to *publicani. See FINANCE, ROMAN.

portraiture, Greek Greek portraiture proper begins after the Persian invasion of 480. The Tyrannicides (see CRITIUS) were generic representations of men long dead, but the *Themistocles from Ostia (a copy) modifies a pre-existing *Heracles type to make him into a heroic figure. Such 'role' portraiture, whereby standard types were personalized to a greater or lesser degree, was normative during the Classical period and into the Hellenistic. Early examples (all copies) include *Pericles (c.425: see CRESILAS), *Herodotus, *Thucydides (2), and *Socrates 'A' (c.380). Most if not all are Attic. Coiffure, attributes, posture, and gesture helped to locate the subject as belonging to a particular citizen and/or character type within the *polis.

Alexander's conquests both revolutionized the genre of ruler-portraiture and stimulated a massive demand for portraits at all levels. Lysippus idealized his features and blended them with a version of the nude spear-bearing Doryphorus (see POLYCLITUS) in order to show him as a latter-day *Achilles, while *Apelles represented him as a *Zeus on earth, complete with thunderbolt. They and others also first portrayed the ruler in narrative situations (hunts, battles, processions), and with gods and personifications. Alexander's successors eagerly followed suit, choosing the diadem (a white cloth headband, knotted behind with the ends dangling, which he had assumed in 330) as their royal symbol. Whether equestrian, armoured, cloaked, or nude; striding, standing, or seated; spear-bearing or with trident, *sceptre, or cornucopia, their statues, pictures, coins, and gems represented them as charismatic and often semi-divine rulers in their own right. While most are idealized, this seldom obscures their individuality, for easy recognition is one of their prime aims.

After Alexander, portraiture became the central Hellenistic art form. While the old categories continue, and bourgeois portraits are mostly conventional, others are markedly original, such as the sharp-featured *Menander, and the aged *Chrysippus. Portraits of Romans conformed both to traditional Greek attitudes about barbarians and the sitters' own tastes: examples range from the aquiline, impetuous *Quinctius Flamininus to the hard-boiled Italian merchants who settled on *Delos between 166 and 88 (see NEGOTIATORES). Athletes represent the opposite pole: surviving examples rarely suggest much individualization. See PORTRAITURE, ROMAN.

portraiture, Roman Roman portraiture is esp. noted for its verism, the meticulous recording of facial characteristics including such unflattering features as wrinkles, warts, and moles. The origins of the veristic style remain obscure, but republican customs suggest that portraits were used by the Romans to exemplify noble behaviour. *Polybius records the practice at the funeral processions of great men of dressing young men of the family in the clothes and death masks (see IMAGINES) of those distinguished ancestors whom they most resembled; he and *Pliny the Elder describe the ancestral portraits kept in genealogical order in noble houses together with a written record of the achievements of the dead. The right to keep and display such portraits was restricted to the nobility (see NOBILES) and to the families of serving magistrates.

Most surviving republican Roman portraits date to the 1st cent. BC, when the ancestral portrait was used in the struggle for political leadership in the late republic. Some aspiring political and military leaders adopted the fashions of Hellenistic court portraiture, but *Caesar favoured the veristic style, discrediting its republican origins by becoming the first Roman to have his own portrait on coins minted during his lifetime, and permitting his images to be carried on litters and set up on sacred platforms. *Augustus developed an idealized image drawn from the repertoire of Classical Greece, but recognizably Roman in its often modest presentation. From the beginning of the empire, men and women copied court portraiture from images of the emperor and his family on coins and statues intended for wide use and public view at Rome and in the provinces. The veristic style continued to be used by some nobles, but was also adopted by *freedmen who wished to celebrate the right of their families to Roman citizenship following legislation passed under Augustus; in the conventionalized portraits of freedmen and their families it is hard to trace the recording of individual features that was so marked a feature of republican portraiture of the aristocracy. Verism is also marked in the portraiture of emperors of modest origin such as *Vespasian.

The Julio-Claudian emperors and their successors were mostly clean-shaven, though *Nero and *Domitian were occasionally portrayed bearded (see COSMETICS). It is likely that his beard, comparable to that of *Pericles, expressed *Hadrian's commitment to Greek culture. During his reign women adopted the simple bun worn high on the crown, a revival of Hellenistic Greek fashion and a striking contrast to the elaborate tiered coiffures fashionable from the time of Nero to that of Trajan. Hadrian's adoption of the beard and the contemporary innovation of engraving the pupil and iris of the eye influenced subsequent imperial and private portraiture. Among beards there were idiosyncratic variations: Marcus *Aurelius wore the long beard of the philosopher, and *Septimius Severus a forked beard marking his interest in the cult of Sarapis. The soldier-emperors and tetrarchs (see TETRARCHY) of the later 3rd cent. were ill-shaven rather than bearded, with close-cropped hair. The clean-shaven portrait was revived by *Constantine I and his successors. Portraits, whether of imperial or private subjects, were made in a wide variety of media including silver, bronze, stone, terracotta, glass, mosaic, ivory, bone, and painted wood. Of the last the most striking examples are the mummy portraits made in the *Fayūm, the only naturalistically coloured portraits to survive from antiquity (see PAINTING, ROMAN). Many of these seem to represent individuals as they appeared in life; some present a type still current in NE Africa. These and the limestone funerary reliefs of Palmyra offer the best surviving evidence for the wearing of *dress and jewellery.

Roman portrait busts may be dated not only by their relationship to the fashions of the imperial court, but by changes in the shape and size of the bust, which by Flavian times had enlarged from head and neck to incorporate the shoulders. See ART, FUNERARY, ROMAN.

Portus *Claudius undertook the construction, which *Caesar had planned, of an enclosed harbour two miles north of *Ostia, linked to the Tiber by a *canal: to remedy the very difficult conditions of trans-shipment at Ostia; to provide Rome with a worthy gateway for seaborne visitors; and to help mitigate floods at Rome by improving the flow of the *Tiber. A deep basin was excavated and protected from the sea by two moles, with a *lighthouse rivalling that of *Alexandria.

The new harbour was not safe, as its wide-open expanse was prone to squalls; disaster struck in 62. *Trajan undertook the construction of an inner basin at Portus, hexagonal in plan, covering 32 ha. (79 acres), which rendered the harbour usable (despite some problem with silting) throughout antiquity.

Poseidon 'All men call Poseidon god of the sea, of *earthquakes, and of *horses', wrote *Pausanias (3), describing the three principal aspects of one of the most widely, and anciently, worshipped of the Greek gods. Pausanias' epithets for the earthquake god, Asphaleios, 'He who keeps things steady', and god of horses, Hippios, were common cult titles. Poseidon's importance at *Pylos is reflected in *Homer's *Odyssey* (*Nestor and nine groups of 500 Pylians sacrifice nine black bulls to the god on the seashore). Homer makes him a powerful figure, resistant to pressure from his brother Zeus while acknowledging the latter's seniority; this conflicts with the story in Hesiod's *Theogony* of Zeus being the last child of *Cronus and Rhea. In Homer he is largely the god of the sea, aside from the implications of earthquake in epithets meaning 'earth-shaker'. He causes storms and calms the waters; his wife is Amphitrītē, a sea-creature. Poseidon supports the Greeks in the *Trojan War, but is hostile to *Odysseus, the supreme seafarer. Eventually Odysseus will establish the god's cult far from the sea where an oar is mistaken for a winnowing fan.

Poseidon begets various monsters such as Odysseus' enemies the *Cyclopes. He is not associated, in myth or cult, with civic institutions. The violence of natural phenomena, sea and earthquake, are central to the Greek conception of him. In art he is always a grave, mature male, indistinguishable from Zeus when not accompanied by attributes.

Numerous sanctuaries of the god on coastal sites, such as the 5th-cent. BC marble temple on the promontory of *Sunium in Attica, where quadrennial boat races were held in his honour, and the oracular shrine at Taenarum in Laconia, which boasted a passage to the Underworld, show that his ties to the sea were prominent in cult, as do the dedications of sailors and fishermen. Many coastal settlements were named after him.

Mating with an *Erinys, he in the form of a stallion begets the marvellous horse Arion. With the *Gorgon Medusa he begets *Pegasus, whose name was connected with the springs (*pēgai*) of Ocean. His close association with the horse has led to the theory that he was introduced to Greece along with the horse by the speakers of an ancestral form of Greek early in the second millennium BC. Whatever the reasons for the original connection, the aristocratic and non-utilitarian associations of the horse were appropriate for a god often named as the ancestor of aristocratic families.

He was widely worshipped in Arcadia and Boeotia, and he had important cults around the Saronic Gulf. In the Archaic period, on the island of Calauria off Troezen, his *sanctuary was the centre of an *amphictiony of originally five small *poleis* on the Argolic and Saronic gulfs, together with Athens and Boeotian Orchomenus (Poseidon's son *Theseus moves in myth, as his cult may have moved historically, from Troezen to Athens). *Corinth, not a member of the amphictiony, developed the open-air shrine of the god on the Isthmus, dating from the Dark Age, into a major regional and then panhellenic sanctuary with one of the earliest ashlar-built temples (mid-7th cent. BC) and, in the early 6th cent., a biennial festival with games (see ISTHMIAN GAMES). It was the seat of the Hellenic League formed at the time of *Xerxes' invasion (see PERSIAN WARS).

In Athens Poseidon was shown contending with *Athena for the patronage of the city in the west pediment of the *Parthenon. He bore the epithet *Erechtheus. The same Attic *genos* provided the priest of Poseidon Erechtheus and the priestess of Athena Polias (the goddess of the Acropolis). Even so, no major Athenian festival was celebrated in his honour.

Posīdōnius (*c*.135–*c*.51 BC), *Stoic philosopher, scientist, and historian. A Syrian Greek from Apamea on the Orontes, he was educated at Athens under *Panaetius, but settled in *Rhodes, a prosperous free city with a reputation for philosophy and science. Granted citizenship, he took a significant part in public life. Probably in the 90s he embarked on long tours of research to the west, visiting Spain, southern Gaul, and Rome and Italy. Thereafter his school in Rhodes became the leading centre of Stoicism, and a mecca not only for intellectuals, but for the great and powerful of the Roman world such as *Pompey and *Cicero.

The range of his writing is astonishing. In addition to the conventional departments of philosophy (natural philosophy (*physics), ethics, logic), he wrote penetratingly on *astronomy, *meteorology, *mathematics, *geography, seismology (see EARTHQUAKES), zoology (see ANIMALS, KNOWLEDGE OF), *botany, *anthropology, and history. Some 30 titles survive over this field, but no complete work.

Posidonius believed in the development of philosophy by continued interpretation in the light of later criticism of the basic ideas of the founders and 'the old authorities'. At that level there had always been divergence of interpretation in the Stoa. So Posidonius had strikingly original things to say within the context of Stoic natural philosophy in defence of the ultimate principles as material without quality or form; on problems of destruction, generation, continuity and change related to the individual; on the problem of 'now' in time viewed as a continuum; on a finite cosmos surrounded by infinite void; and in logic, on the criterion of truth, *dialectic, and on the relational syllogism.

On the other hand, he was convinced that in ethics *Chrysippus had seriously distorted Stoicism with his monolithic rational psychology which defined emotion as mistaken judgement, and so failed to explain the cause and operation of emotions and hence the major questions in moral behaviour. Posidonius argued for a return to non-rational faculties of mind with affinities towards pleasure and power. These were natural, but not good. Only our rational affinity for moral virtue did he recognize as good and absolute. Hence the uncompromising Stoic end of virtue alone is preserved. Posidonius claimed that he could now explain the mechanics of moral choice, moral responsibility (since the root of evil lies within us), and moral education which required behavioural therapeutics as well as rational argument. His attack on Chrysippus in his book *On Emotions* rests on three grounds: respect for the facts, consistency derived from deductive proof, and understanding sprung from explanation of the causes of phenomena. Posidonius was himself famed for all three in antiquity. They are the key for the coherence of his own work.

In the first place, he promoted logic from being the organon or tool of philosophy to that organic part of it which as bones and sinews supplied the articulation and dynamic of its structure. From the model of Euclidean mathematics, in whose foundations he was much interested, he regarded axiomatic deductive proof as the top-down causal explanation of the cosmic nexus. The tools of philosophy, and this is explicitly stated, now become the special sciences, a completely original concept peculiarly apposite for the material continuum of the Stoic universe. The sciences were thus necessary for natural philosophy, and the two complementary, but not equal. For while science supplied the descriptive factual pattern of phenomena, only philosophy could provide final and complete explanation of causes or aetiology by its incontrovertible method of deductive proof from assured axiomatic premisses established by the natural philosophers. These procedures demanded precise distinction between different kinds of cause. Some of Posidonius' own research in the sciences is remarkable, such as a lunar theory of the periodicity of tides which held sway until Newton; or his ingenious method of measuring the circumference of the earth leading to the establishment of latitudinal bands. *On Ocean* was an extraordinary work ranging from the astronomical establishment of geographical zones and so physical and climatic conditions, to human geography and anthropology. It is one of the lost books of antiquity one would most like to recover.

The same relationship holds for history and ethics, for history with its descriptive framework of actual social behaviour was his necessary tool for moral philosophy. The *History* was a major work of 52 books covering the period from 146 BC probably to the mid-80s and possibly unfinished. Its scope was all-embracing of the Mediterranean-centred world, from the histories of *Asia Minor to *Spain, *Egypt and *Africa to Gaul and the northern peoples, Rome and Greece. It was packed with formidable detail of facts and events, both major and minor, global and local, and of social and environmental phenomena. But the unifying factor of the huge canvas, factually drawn and sharply critical of credulous legend, was a moralist's view of historical explanation, where events are caused by mind and character in the relationship between ruler and ruled, and by tribal or racial character in social movement and motives. Hence his detailed interest in ethnology (Italian, Roman, Gallic, Germanic). Again, such studies offer immediate historical explanation; final aetiology and principal causes come from the philosophical study of psychology and ethics.

His style, vivid, forceful and highly coloured, still gleams fitfully through the fragments. It so impressed Cicero that he begged Posidonius to write up his cherished consulship. The manner of declining showed a diplomat of enviable tact.

Posidonius' position in intellectual history is remarkable not for the scattered riches of a polymath and savant, but for an audacious aetiological attempt to survey and explain the complete field of the human intellect and the universe in which it finds itself as an organic part, through analysis of detail and the synthesis of the whole, in the conviction that all knowledge is interrelated.

In mainstream Stoicism he did not supplant Chrysippus, and it was often outside the School, and not least in the sciences and history that he was consulted. The riches of the details tended to obscure the grand design.

possession, religious That a human being might become possessed by a supernatural power was a fairly common ancient belief. The effect might be a prophetic trance as in the case of the Pythia (see DELPHIC ORACLE). Plato in *Phaedrus* further distinguishes between telestic (inspired by *Dionysus), poetic (inspired by the *Muses), and erotic (inspired by *Aphrodite and *Eros) possession. Words expressing the notion 'possessed by (a) god' carried an ambivalent meaning. On the one hand, they referred to terrifying pathological experiences, e.g. epileptic strokes or various types of insanity. On the other, possession involved direct contact with a god and thus could effect a kind of sacralization. Belief in the pathological connotations of possession, esp. possession by demons, grew stronger in the post-Classical period (cf. the stories about demoniacs in the NT) and reports of magical cures and exorcisms, pagan and Christian, abound. See ASCETICISM.

postal service The Greek *poleis* communicated by professional messengers like *Phidippides on land; there were also messenger-ships. The efficient Persian arrangements (see ROYAL ROAD) were maintained at the expense of local communities. From the first, the carrying of messages, the movement of goods due to the state, and the journeys of the ruler and his representatives were closely linked, and this is the system bequeathed by the *Achaemenid kingdom to the (*Diadochi) Successors of *Alexander (2) the Great, in *Syria and in Egypt.

For Rome in the republic, see TABELLARII. *Augustus' bold introduction of a public postal system for the whole empire was modelled on the Hellenistic kingdoms, and designed specifically for governmental purposes. In its developed form (the *cursus pūblicus*) it was one of the biggest administrative initiatives in antiquity. It could work only through a system of local requisitioning of animals, vehicles, and provisions.

Potīdaea, a Corinthian colony (see CORINTH; COLONIZATION, GREEK), founded *c.*600 BC for trade with *Macedonia and along the line of the later *via Egnatia. It struck coins from *c.*550. A strongly fortified port, it withstood a siege by Artabazus (480–479). It joined the *Delian League; but its connection with Corinth, which supplied its annual chief magistrate, rendered it suspect to Athens. After an increase of its tribute to fifteen talents (434 BC) it revolted (432), but although it received help from *Peloponnese it was reduced in 430, at a cost of 2,000. Athenian cleruchs (see CLERUCHY) occupied the site until 404, when it passed to the Chalcidians (see OLYNTHUS).

pottery, Greek

1. General Pottery is a primary source of evidence for Greek history. Pervasive and almost indestructible, its generally predictable development means that it provides a framework to which other arts can be related. The presence of clay in every region fostered local styles, whence trade patterns can be detected. Factors determining origin are clay, shape, and decoration, the last varying from none (most cookpots, coarsewares, storage *amphorae) to the elaborate mythological scenes exemplified by Archaic and Classical Athenian vases (see IMAGERY). Regular inscriptions give names of potters and painters and clues to workshop organization (see POTTERY, GREEK, INSCRIPTIONS ON) as do excavations like those in the Athenian Agora, the area of the *Academy, or the Potters' Quarter at Corinth. Sir John Beazley adopted Renaissance attribution methods to reconstruct the careers of many Archaic and Classical Athenian vase-painters, and to gauge master-pupil relations and workshop patterns. Recent trends have moved from attributions towards the social significance of pottery, with renewed interest in factors influencing shapes, imagery and composition, esp. wall-painting (see PAINTING, GREEK). Thus metalwork has been seen as a model for Classical vase shapes and decoration.

2. History The Protogeometric and Geometric periods (1050–700 BC) saw new shapes and

motifs (notably the meander). From restricted beginnings, decoration came to cover the whole vase in horizontal bands. This period is characterized by local schools, notably Argive and Attic; here the 8th cent. saw the development of figure scenes, including funerary subjects (*prothesis* and *ekphora*), chariot processions and battles. From the 8th cent. onwards, it is possible to identify 'hands' such as the Dipylon Master.

From the late-8th cent. the Geometric style developed into *Orientalizing, with the addition of motifs including florals and animals (real and fantastic) which replaced Geometric patterns. Although silhouette continued, the black-figure technique (invented in Corinth *c.*720) was most innovative; here lines are incised into a silhouette, with the addition of purple and white. The human figure was drawn with increasing naturalism, and mythological representations become complex. The chief 7th-cent. fabrics are Proto-Corinthian and Proto-Attic; contemporary is the peak of the island and eastern Greek schools. A mid-7th-cent. series of vases of various schools may reflect contemporary free painting, using such elements as a brown paint for flesh and mass battle scenes (e.g. works of the Corinthian Chigi (MacMillan) Painter).

By 600, black-figure was fully established in Attica, and by soon after 550 Corinth, Athens' main rival, had ceased producing figured wares, continuing with the patterned 'conventionalizing' style. Athenian potters produced a wider range of vases, introducing such shapes as the volute- and kalyx-*krātēr* (wine-mixing bowl), and a range of cups which are among the finest of Attic potting. The practice of inscribing vases helps us: the words *epoiēsen* and *egrapsen* probably mean 'potted' and 'painted', although the former may indicate ownership of the workshop.

Around 525, the red-figure technique was invented at Athens. In red-figure the decoration is left in the clay colour, and the background painted black; inner details are painted with lines of varying thickness. The use of the brush rather than the engraver allowed greater fluidity of drawing. Accessory colours are used sparingly in the 6th cent., white becoming common towards its end. The first generation trained in red-figure (*c.*520–500) Beazley called the Pioneers; they are characterized by adventurous anatomical depictions. Late Archaic vase-painting saw further advances by, e.g. the Berlin and Cleophrades Painters (who preferred large vases), and the cup specialists Duris and the Brygus Painter. Black-figure continued in quantity until the end of the Archaic period and, for Panathenaic prize amphorae (see PANATHE-NAEA), until the 2nd cent. BC.

In the early Classical period, vases of the Niobid Painter and others reflect the free painting recorded in literary sources as current in Athens and elsewhere in the works of *Polygnotus and *Micon (c.475–450). The later 5th cent. saw the ornate miniaturism of the Meidias Painter and others, often featuring boudoir scenes. White ground, at first mainly on cups, is used in the later 5th cent. for funerary lēkythoi (oil-flasks), often painted with delicate colours.

4th-cent. vases are characterized by greater use of accessory colours and gilding; red-figure ceased by c.320, but although much late work is poor, artists such as the Marsyas and Eleusinian Painters (c.350–330) gave unprecedented depth to their figures.

In Italy, painted wares imitating the contemporary Greek styles appeared from the 8th cent. BC, and by 525 native pottery was largely displaced by Greek (mainly Attic) imports and local copies. Independent schools of pottery in Apulia borrowed painted techniques from Greece, but remained local in style. Red-figure production began in southern Italy c.440, perhaps introduced by immigrant Athenian potters. A considerable output of vases, often large and elaborately decorated, continued into the early 3rd cent. Their inspiration was initially Athenian, but they increasingly diverged; their iconography owes much to the theatre.

pottery, Greek, inscriptions on Inscriptions can be painted on pots (dipinti), before or after firing, or incised (graffiti), normally after firing. Post-firing dipinti consist mainly of notations of a broadly commercial character on plain *amphorae. The bulk of written material from many parts of the Greek world earlier than c.400 BC, and esp. in the first generations of writing, before c.650, consists of texts on pots. Most are informally inscribed, though pre-firing dipinti can be used to aesthetic effect on decorated ware, and some graffito dedications (notably on Panathenaic amphorae; see PANATHENAEA) are in full 'lapidary' style. Vase inscriptions are a prime source of evidence for e.g. the identification of painted figures, names of potters and painters, distributors of pottery and its cost, aspects of local scripts, variations of *dialect and spelling, identity of cults (see OSTRAKA). Painted inscriptions are usually labels for figures, starting as near the head as possible; sometimes words uttered by the figures appear. Signatures

of potters and painters are first attested soon after 700, become common on Attic vases of c.525–475, but thin out over the following century. We also find the names of favoured youths (rarely girls) with the epithet kalos, 'beautiful'; these are of chronological, historical and social interest. Graffiti cover an enormous range; owner's marks and dedications, often abbreviated, are frequent; alphabets, shopping-lists and messages are much rarer. See also EPIGRAPHY, GREEK; POTTERY, GREEK.

pottery, Roman Roman potters provided a comprehensive range of vessels for table and kitchen use, and for storage and transport. At the top of the quality scale were vessels with a smooth glossy surface designed for the table, notably the bright red terra sigillāta, or Samian ware, mass-produced in Italy (Arretine ware) and elsewhere from the 1st cent. BC. Elaborately decorated cups and beakers with coloured surface coatings were used alongside this dinner service, while ornate pottery oil *lamps provided light. Most Roman pots were plain earthenware vessels designed for everyday household cooking and storage. The only really specialized forms were *amphorae, used for transporting wine and oil, globular dōlia, employed on farms for storage and fermentation, and mortāria, large bowls suitable for grinding and mixing. Many Roman buildings were constructed (wholly or partly) from bricks and roofed with ceramic tiles, while specialized clay elements aided the construction of bath-buildings and vaulted ceilings (see BUILDING MATERIALS).

The study of pottery reveals details of technology and methods of manufacture, and the analysis of patterns of production and distribution illuminates aspects of society and the economy. Pottery production ranged from a part-time activity that supplemented farming to full-time employment for specialized craft workers. Most vessels were formed on a potter's wheel and fired in carefully constructed kilns. Some industries made ranges of forms, others concentrated on particular categories. Distribution patterns of wares varied enormously; Italian terra sigillata could be found throughout the empire, whereas unspecialized kitchen wares might supply only a single town and its environs.

Rome conquered areas of Italy that already possessed well-established ceramic traditions—Celtic, Etruscan, and Greek. The kitchen and storage vessels made in most conquered areas resembled those of Italy, and they were normally adopted by the invaders once permanent garrison forts had been established. Name-stamps on *terra sigillata*, lamps and *mortaria* all confirm that some manufacturers either migrated to new provinces or set up branch workshops, presumably to avoid high transport costs involved in supplying distant markets. We are well informed about the diffusion of *terra sigillata* production from Italy to the provinces.

Roman military units included skilled artisans who often established facilities for the manufacture of bricks and roof tiles, commonly stamped with the name of their unit or legion. If local pottery supplies were inadequate, they also turned their hands to potting. Since many soldiers had been recruited in Italy or heavily Romanized provinces, most vessel forms made by military potters are closely comparable to those found in Italy itself. Military production tended to be short-lived, for when frontier areas were stabilized, supplies could be brought safely from non-military sources in the hinterland. Alternatively, civilian potters might set up production in a military region in order to take advantage of new markets created by forts and the civilian settlements (*canabae*) which grew up around them.

poverty See DIOGENES (2); WEALTH, ATTITUDES TO.

praefectus means 'put in charge' and describes a great variety of men set in authority—officers in the army and navy, major imperial officials, judicial officers delegated by the praetor and deputies for local magistrates.

Before the *Social War each wing (*āla*) of allied cavalry had six *praefectī*, three of whom were Roman officers. In *Caesar's time cavalry continued to be commanded by *praefecti*. Under the Principate units of allied troops (*auxilia*), both wings of cavalry and cohorts of infantry, were commanded by *equestrian *praefecti*. The administrative post of legionary camp commandant, *praefectus castrōrum*, was from *Claudius' reign onwards regularly held by an ex-centurion who had reached the rank of *primus pilus* (see PRIMIPILUS) but was unlikely to gain further promotion. *Praefecti* also held extraordinary appointments.

Some of the major appointments were also military: *praefecti* commanded the praetorian guard (see PRAEFECTUS PRAETORIO), the *vigiles* and the imperial fleets of *Ravenna and Misenum (see NAVIES), while the urban cohorts were under the *praefectus urbī* ('city prefect'). In the early Principate some governors of (mainly

minor) imperial provinces were called *praefecti* (this was the correct title of Pontius Pilate (*Pontius Pilatus*) in Judaea and this remained the title of the equestrian governor of Egypt. The legions in Egypt were commanded by equestrian *praefecti* instead of the normal senatorial *legati*.

praefectus praetōriō *Augustus first appointed praetorian prefects (see PRAEFECTUS) to command the *praetorians in 2 BC; there were usually two, of *equestrian rank. He recognized the importance of the prefecture, since it controlled the only significant military force in Rome. Prefects were selected personally by the emperor more for reliability than any specialist expertise, and their status and power increased because they had the ear of the emperor, who tended to confide in them and delegate some of his increasing administrative burden. The prefect was the only official permitted to bear a sword in the emperor's presence. The personal influence gained by several prefects enhanced the role of the prefecture itself, e.g. *Aelius Seianus, who also persuaded *Tiberius to concentrate the guard in one camp in Rome and became sole prefect (there were further instances of this, e.g. *Afranius Burrus, Ofonius Tigellinus). By AD 70, prefects were usually granted consular ornaments (see ORNAMENTA), and the prefecture had become the most important equestrian post, the climax of a career which had often begun with the equestrian military offices or even a chief centurionate. Prefects were often to become involved in political intrigues, and many met violent deaths.

As regular members of the emperor's advisory council (*consilium principis*), they helped to formulate imperial policy; they also had significant military responsibilities, since one prefect usually travelled with the emperor on campaign, sometimes even commanding an army in the field. Gradually they also acquired judicial functions (perhaps arising from their police powers in Rome), and by the late 2nd cent. exercised independent jurisdiction in Italy; *Septimius Severus confirmed their jurisdiction in Italy beyond the hundredth milestone from Rome (within was the responsibility of the city prefect; see PRAEFECTUS URBI).

praefectus urbī ('city prefect') A magistrate instituted by *Augustus to be the emperor's deputy at Rome. After a false start with *Valerius Messalla Corvinus *c.*25 BC, the regular series seems to have begun with Lucius Calpurnius

Piso in AD 13. The prefect was always a senator (see SENATE), usually a senior ex-consul, and served for a number of years. He was nominally an independent magistrate, with the duty of keeping order in the city, and for this purpose had *imperium* and the command of the urban cohorts (see COHORTES URBANAE). He also presided over his own court of justice, which by the 3rd cent. had practically superseded those of the regular magistrates; it heard cases both from Rome and outside, within a radius (from *c*.200) of 100 (Roman) miles (148 km.).

Praenestĕ occupied a cool, lofty spur of the Apennines 37 km. (23 mi.) ESE of Rome. It first appears in history in the 5th cent. BC as a powerful *Latin city, whose strategic site facing the Alban Hills was inevitably attacked by the neighbouring Aequi. In the 4th cent. it often fought Rome and, after participating in the Latin War, was deprived of territory and became a *civitās foederāta* (see FOEDUS). After 90 Praeneste became a Roman *municipium* devoted to *Marius' cause, which *Sulla sacked (82), transferred to lower ground, and colonized with veterans. It remained a colony in imperial times, famed chiefly as a fashionable *villa resort and seat of an ancient oracle, which Roman emperors, foreign potentates, and others consulted in the huge temple of Fortuna Primigenia, perhaps the largest in Italy. Its impressive remains probably belong to the second half of the 2nd cent. BC. Praeneste is known also for its spectacular Nile *mosaic, and Verrius Flaccus' calendar.

praenomen See NAMES, PERSONAL, ROMAN.

praetexta See FABULA.

praetor

Republic 'Praetor' (from *prae-īrĕ*, 'to precede', i.e. in battle) was originally the title borne by the two magistrates who were chosen annually to serve as heads of the republican state. In 367 BC the Romans decided to add a patrician 'praetor' as third colleague to these two chief magistrates, who were now (or were soon to be) called '*consuls'. The new praetor held *imperium, which was defined as being of the same nature as the consuls' but *minus, 'lesser', in relation to theirs. As a magistrate with this type of *imperium*, the praetor could perform almost all the activities of the consul, both in Rome and in the field, unless a consul stopped him; however, a praetor could not interfere with the consuls. The administration of law was merely one of the

praetor's areas of competence, which came with the grant of *imperium*. The praetor was, in the (quite common) absence of the consuls from the city, the chief magistrate in Rome and, as such, in charge of the legal system, as well as acting president of the senate and legislative *comitia*; but he also had the right to lead an army. Plebeians (see PLEBS) were first admitted to the office in 337.

The acceptance of extension of *imperium* beyond the year of the magistracy ('prorogation'), allowed the Romans, despite ever-increasing military commitments, to retain the system of two consuls and a sole praetor down to almost the end of the First *Punic War. Around 244 there was an increase from one to two praetors, now designated as *urbānus* ('urban') and *inter peregrīnōs* ('peregrine', i.e. 'over foreigners'). The Romans doubled the number of praetors to four *c*.228 to provide regular commanders for *Sicily and Sardinia, and in 198 created another two (with enhanced, i.e. consular, *imperium*) to serve in the Spanish provinces (see SPAIN). These additions made possible the transformation of the peregrine praetorship into a (mainly) city jurisdiction; they also led to an eventual insistence on the praetorship as a prerequisite for the consulship (*c*.197).

In 146, when *Macedonia and Africa (see AFRICA, ROMAN) were organized as praetorian provinces, the senate decided to keep the number of praetors at six, probably to control competition for the consulship. This decision made it impossible for all the provinces to be governed by regular magistrates in their year of office; routine prorogation of overseas commanders had to become actual policy. The Romans soon exploited what was, in effect, a new system of provincial government. In 126 came the annexation of Asia as a praetorian province, and in 123, Gaius *Sempronius Gracchus introduced a praetor's court at Rome to try cases of provincial extortion. Additional standing courts on the Gracchan model were established between 123 and 91 (see QUAESTIONES), while more territorial provinces were instituted—with no increase in praetors. By the 90s, even the city praetors (i.e. urban, peregrine and those in charge of a permanent court) had to be regularly prorogued, so that they could proceed to overseas provinces.

In 81 as dictator *Sulla raised the number of praetors to eight. He also institutionalized some earlier developments in a scheme aimed at ensuring regular annual succession, in which all praetors were restricted to Rome to attend to the city jurisdictions and the various courts, and were sent (with consular *imperium*) to govern an overseas province only after their year of office. However, the introduction of new standing courts (in 65 and then again in 55) coupled with increased bribery and violence at the consular elections (a praetor now had only a one-in-four chance of reaching the consulship) contributed to the collapse of this system by the late 50s BC.

Caesar and Imperial Period The number of praetors was increased by *Caesar to sixteen, as much to provide offices for partisans as to fulfil functions, although there were more posts in civil and criminal jurisdiction than could be filled by the praetors available in the late republic. Some praetors are found in military commands during their year of office in the Civil War period, but there is no clear evidence that this continued under *Augustus, who restricted the number of praetors at first to ten and then to twelve. Under the Principate the praetors retained their traditional republican functions at Rome—performing civil jurisdiction (for the consolidation of the edict of the urban praetor under Hadrian see EDICT), presiding over criminal courts, overseeing the games and occasionally presiding over the senate. In general they retained a high profile through presiding over and financing major games and also because the office was still a necessary step in the *cursus honorum*, the first occasion when a man received *imperium* as a magistrate. This enabled a holder to go on to be governor of a public province or to be a legate of a legion in an imperial province.

praetorian guard/praetorians The praetorian cohort was a small escort which accompanied an army commander in the republic, taking its name from his tent (see PRAETORIUM). During the Civil Wars the military dynasts had kept large personal bodyguards, and in 27 BC *Augustus established a permanent force consisting of nine cohorts, each containing 500 (or possibly 1,000) men, recruited mainly from Italy and Romanized provinces. The praetorians had superior service conditions, receiving more than three times legionary pay and serving for sixteen years, which marked them out as élite troops. Three cohorts, armed but in undress uniform, were stationed in Rome; the rest were dispersed among neighbouring towns, perhaps to ameliorate the politically sensitive idea of troops in the capital. In 2 BC Augustus appointed two prefects (see PRAEFECTUS PRAETORIO) to take overall charge, although he retained personal command.

In AD 23 *Aelius Seianus, now sole prefect, persuaded *Tiberius to base the praetorians in one permanent camp in the eastern suburbs of Rome. This made the guard a more coherent corps, which could be directly and speedily deployed in a crisis. Also in Tiberius' reign, the guard was probably increased to twelve cohorts. Its role was to protect the emperor and members of the imperial family, suppress disturbances, and discourage plots. A detachment of the guard accompanied the emperor on campaign.

*Vitellius increased the guard to sixteen cohorts of 1,000 men by adding legionaries from his army of the Rhine. In *Domitian's reign the number of cohorts was set at ten, each comprising 1,000 men and commanded by a tribune, who had usually served as a legionary chief centurion and as tribune in the other city forces, the *vigiles* and urban cohorts (see COHORTES URBANAE). The praetorians were still largely Italian and were supported by a cavalry arm—the *equitēs singulārēs Augustī*.

Inevitably the praetorians were drawn into political intrigue as it became obvious that their support could be crucial for a new emperor. In 41 after the murder of *Gaius (1), *Claudius won them over with a huge *donative, and thereafter every emperor at his accession granted a donative and, if in Rome, addressed the guard. *Commodus' indulgence subverted the praetorians' discipline, and in 193 his successor, Pertinax, was murdered by the guardsmen, who then proceeded to offer their support to the highest bidder for the purple. When later in 193 *Septimius Severus seized power, he disbanded the disgraced praetorians and replaced them with legionaries from the Danubian armies which had first supported him. But the guard retained its role until 312 when *Constantine I disbanded it after his defeat of *Maxentius.

Despite their special relationship with the emperor, the praetorians had no formal position of power, and lacked the political awareness to retain the influence that circumstances sometimes gave them.

praetōrium, the tent of a Roman commander, and also his council of senior officers. From this, *praetorium* came to mean the headquarters of a provincial governor, and in permanent forts of the imperial period indicates the private dwelling of the commanding officer, located close to the headquarters building or *principia*.

Praxitelēs, Athenian sculptor, active c.375–330 BC. He worked in both bronze and marble, though was more successful at the latter; he paid great attention to surface finish, by preference employing the painter Nicias for the final touches. A prolific artist, he specialized in statues of the younger gods, esp. *Aphrodite, *Dionysus, and their respective circles, and in portraits.

His masterpiece was the Cnidia, his Aphrodite of *Cnidus, supposedly modelled after his mistress Phrȳnē; reproductions on local coins have led to the identification of numerous copies. Displayed amid gardens in a colonnaded, circular shrine, remains of which have been discovered, the goddess was completely nude. Sculptors of the previous generation had occasionally represented her in transparent drapery or baring a breast, and Praxiteles himself may already have shown her topless. In the Cnidia, he took the final step: the essence of the love-goddess was her body; so it must be revealed. He showed her at the bath, with a water-pot beside her, holding her cloak in her left hand. No certain originals by Praxiteles exist. The *Hermes and Dionysus at *Olympia is almost certainly post-Praxitelean. His Apollo Sauroctonos ('lizard-killer') survives in copy.

Praxiteles' vision of a dreamy *Elysium inhabited by divine beings remote from the cares of mortals anticipates the philosophy of *Epicurus, and was widely influential. His fastidious manner was often imitated, esp. in *Alexandria, where it tended to degenerate into a facile slurring of surfaces enlivened by a luminous polish. His canon for the female nude (wide hips, small breasts, oval face, centrally parted hair, etc.) remained authoritative for the rest of antiquity (see BODY).

prayer Prayer was the commonest form of expression in ancient religion. It could be formal or informal and was often accompanied by other acts of worship, e.g. *sacrifice or vow. The earliest instance of an independent formal prayer, namely the prayer of Chrȳsēs (see CHRYSEIS) to *Apollo in bk. 1 of Homer's *Iliad*, presents a complete set of the fixed elements of ancient prayer. These are: (1) *invocation*. The god is addressed with his (cult) name(s), patronymic, habitual residence, functions, and qualities. This part serves both to identify and to glorify the god. (2) The *argument*, consisting of considerations that might persuade a god to help, e.g. a reminder of the praying person's acts of piety, or a reference to the god's earlier benefactions

or his natural inclination to help people. This part often expanded into a eulogy with narrative aspects, esp. in *hymns. (3) The *prayer* proper, the petition. Nearly all prayers, both private and public, contain a wish. There is a wide variation in 'egoistic' motifs. Drought, epidemics, or hail, for instance, can be prayed away, but also passed on to enemies or neighbours. This comes close to the *curse, which, too, may contain elements of prayer. Although gratitude was felt, the prayer of gratitude was rare. Instead of terms for gratitude, expressions of honour were generally employed, glorification being the most common expression of gratitude, as in human communication. Private prayer often lacked these formal aspects.

Although Greek influence is noticeable, esp. with respect to the formal aspects, Roman prayers distinguished themselves by their elaborate accuracy. Prayers for individual use were often equally formulaic, but both officially and privately less elaborate prayers occurred as well, e.g. *Mars vigilā* ('Mars, wake up').

Ancient prayer was spoken aloud. Silent or whispered prayer was reserved for offensive, indecent, erotic, or magical uses, but was later adopted as the normal rule in Christian practice. Kneeling down, though not unknown, was unusual, the gesture of entreaty being outstretched arms, with the hands directed to the god invoked (or his cult-statue).

prefect See PRAEFECTUS; PRAEFECTUS PRAETORIO ('praetorian prefect'); PRAEFECTUS URBI ('city prefect').

Presocratic philosophers, thinkers who lived not later than *Socrates. See ANAXAGORAS; ANAXIMANDER; ANAXIMENES; ATOMISM; DEMOCRITUS; EMPEDOCLES; HERACLITUS; HIPPIAS (2); LEUCIPPUS; PROTAGORAS; PYTHAGORAS; SOPHISTS; THALES; XENOPHANES; ZENO (1).

Priam, in myth, son of *Laomedon; king of *Troy at the time of its destruction by *Agamemnon. When Laomedon refused to pay *Heracles the promised reward for saving Hesione from the sea-monster, Heracles killed Laomedon and all of his sons except Priam, whom he spared and made king of Troy. Priam's principal wife was *Hecuba, though he had other wives and concubines. He was father of 50 sons including *Hector, *Paris, *Deiphobus, Helenus, and *Troilus, and daughters including *Cassandra and Polyxena (though the latter is not mentioned by *Homer). When the Greeks came to Troy with Agamemnon, Priam was already an old man. Homer depicts him as an amiable character, tender to *Helen, although he disapproves of the war and its cause, respected even by his enemies for his integrity and esteemed by most of the gods (though *Hera and *Athena are hostile) for his piety. He takes part in the truce and has returned to the city before it is broken. He tries to persuade Hector to come to safety within the walls after the rout of the Trojans and after his death goes to the Greek camp to ransom his body, moving *Achilles to pity (*Iliad* 24). The lost 'Sack of Troy' (see EPIC CYCLE) told of his death at the fall of Troy, killed by *Neoptolemus while taking refuge at the altar of *Zeus Herkeios in his own palace. The most powerful description in surviving literature is bk. 2 of *Virgil's *Aeneid*. Priam's name became almost proverbial for a man who had known the extremes of contrasting fortunes.

Neoptolemus killing Priam at the altar is a popular scene in art from the early 6th cent. on, as a separate scene or as the centre of a Sack of Troy, and is often associated with the death of Hector's young son, Astyanax. Priam is also shown coming to ransom Hector's body from Achilles.

Priāpus, an ithyphallic god most familiar from the sportively obscene short poems (Greek and Latin) called *Priape(i)a*: in these he typically threatens to punish by penetration any male or female intruder into the garden of which he is guardian. He was said to be a son of *Dionysus (the god he is most closely linked with in cult) by a *nymph or *Aphrodite. He is first mentioned in the 4th cent. BC, and allusions become common in the 3rd, when his cult seems to have spread rapidly out from the Lampsacus region in northern *Troas; he was later to be well known almost throughout the Roman empire. He is associated with sexuality, human fertility, gardens, and herds. His image was typically sited in a garden or house. His preferred victim in Lampsacus was the lustful ass, but elsewhere he received animal sacrifice of more normal type or, very commonly, offerings of fruit, flowers, and vegetables.

In the *Priape(i)a* he presents himself as a minor and disreputable god, and in texts of all kinds he is humorously handled. The prurience, embarrassment, disparagement, and humour associated with him are appropriate responses to that image of sexuality which, as much as of fertility, he presents. The association between ithyphallic display and protection of territory is found also among primates; how to fit this analogy into a broader account of the god is uncertain. See PHALLUS.

priests (Greek and Roman) Cities in the Graeco-Roman world always had men and women, often of high rank, specially chosen for the service of the gods and goddesses. They might be serving for life or for a fixed term; they might be holding a hereditary position, or be publicly elected or selected by some other method. The offices always carried honour, but often too, esp. in later periods, the expectation of high expenditure by the holders. (See EUERGETISM.) The duties varied widely, from quite humble service to high authority and power.

Greek and Latin have several terms referring to these positions—*hiereis* and *sacerdōtēs* are only the commonest in English, 'priest' is used as a generic term for all of them, but implies a potentially misleading unity of conception and an analogy with the roles of priesthood in later religions. Pagan priests did not form a separate group or caste and seldom devoted their whole lives to religious activity; characteristically, they performed their religious duties on special occasions or when required and otherwise continued with the same range of social or political activities as other members of their social groups. Above all, there was no religious community, separate from the civic community, with its own personnel or power-structure. Nor did priests monopolize religious action or communication with the gods and goddesses: fathers of families, leaders of social groups, officials of the city, all had the power of religious action, with priests as advisers or helpers. So far as the city itself was concerned, it might well be the city authorities who took the religious decisions and the magistrates (elected officials), not the priests, who took religious actions on the city's behalf.

To this extent, there was not much difference between the pagan practice of Greece and of Rome; but differences there are. Greek cities have female as well as male priests, female for goddesses, male for gods. They do not form priestly groups or colleges, but are attached to particular cults and even to particular temples, sanctuaries, or festivals; there is an alternative pattern where priesthood is carried in families. Priests seldom act as advisers to individuals, who consult ritual experts (*exēgētai*) or *diviners. They seem not to have been consulted on religious issues by the state, except the priests of an *oracle speaking on behalf of a god or when special *purifications or remedies were needed and a religious expert might be brought in.

In Rome on the other hand priests are (with the exception of the *Vestals) males, formed into colleges or brotherhoods (see SODALES). They are not attached to particular deities or temples, but rather to particular festivals (as the Luperci to the *Lupercalia) or areas of religion (the *augurs to the taking of auspices). The *flamines* are a spectacular exception, perhaps preserving a more archaic and far closer relationship between priest and deity; they therefore provide the model for the priesthood of the emperors after death (the Divi; see RULER-CULT). The most senior colleges were above all expert advisers, consulted by the senate when religious problems arose. The *pontifices* were also available to private individuals, in need of advice on the religious law.

In both Greece and Rome, the powers associated with priesthood were narrowly defined. They superintended particular cultic activities, but the financing of these activities was often carefully controlled by state officials, and the priests controlled no great temple incomes or resources, as equivalent officers did in other parts of the ancient world. The city would often vote funds for religious expenditure and might regard the treasures stored in temples as state reserves to be used in case of emergency and repaid later. There might also be city officials taking overall responsibility for state religious expenditure.

In the imperial period, both in the east and west, priesthood became closer than ever to the expression of public power. The flaminate in its new guise of an imperial priesthood became widespread in the provinces and cities, held by the leading members of the local élites as a mark of their authority and an opportunity for public generosity. Meanwhile, the emperor's image in priestly garb became one of the empire-wide expressions of his rule.

Apart from these official civic priesthoods, there was a wide range of religious expertise available for private consultation—diviners of all sorts, magicians, and astrologers; these had no official recognition and often attracted criticism. The mystery-cults also had their priests, who might attain great authority within a less controlled cultic environment than that of the civic priests; religious groups devoted to a particular cult might appoint priests of their own; the Bacchist movement of 186 BC (see BACCHANALIA) had priests and priestesses; but the clearest example of this development is the figure of the *Isis priest in *Apuleius' *Golden Ass*, who acts as mentor and spiritual adviser to the hero after his rescue from the spell that turned him into the ass. New currents within pagan religious life corresponded to, if they were not imitating, the new religious types evolving at the same time amongst Jews and Christians. Nothing, however, in pagan religious life corresponded to the Christian hierarchic structure of deacons, priests and bishops. See QUINDECIMVIRI SACRIS FACIUNDIS.

prīmipīlus In the army of the imperial period the *primipilus* was chief centurion (see CENTURIO) of a legion, commanding the leading century of the five in the first cohort. He probably held office for one year and usually gained *equestrian status immediately afterwards, with the opportunity of promotion to the camp prefecture and possibly the tribunates of the urban forces—*vigiles, urban cohorts (see COHORTES URBANAE), and *praetorian guard; favoured men could then be appointed to more senior equestrian posts. See PROCURATOR.

princeps When *Augustus selected '*princeps*' as the word which best indicated his own constitutional position, he chose a word which had good republican associations. It was not an abbreviation of *princeps senatus, though that, also, was a republican title and one which Augustus held. The *princeps senatus*, or First Senator, was before the time of *Sulla the man who had been placed by censors at the head of the list of members of the senate, and ranked as the senior member of that body. Augustus in the census of 28 BC enrolled himself as *princeps senatus*, and succeeding emperors held the same position.

Principēs in the plural, meaning the 'chief men of the state', was a phrase commonly employed by late republican writers, as *Cicero, and it continued to be used in the empire. It was the singular *princeps*, however, applied to *one* prominent statesman, esp. *Pompey, in republican times, which supplied *Augustus with something of a precedent. Early in 49 BC *Cornelius Balbus (1) wrote to Cicero: 'Caesar wants nothing more than to live without fear while Pompey is *princeps*.' Cicero used this designation of other statesmen besides Pompey. In 46 BC he used it of *Caesar. He used it also of himself in connection with the renown that he won by his action against the Catilinarian conspirators (see SERGIUS CATILINA) and by his rallying of the senate against Mark Antony (Marcus *Antonius) at the end of 44. Augustus' choice of *princeps* to designate his position was astute; it contrasted strongly with the dictatorship and the suspected monarchical intentions of Caesar and, in indicating an unquestioned but not a narrowly defined or clearly determined primacy, the word suited perfectly Augustus' definition of his own authority (*Res Gestae* 34.3): 'I excelled all in influence, although I possessed no more official power than others who were my colleagues in the various magistracies.' *Principātus* was in sharp opposition to *dominātiō*, *princeps* to *dominus*, and both Augustus and *Tiberius took pains to suppress the use of the title *dominus*, though it remained a conventional form of polite address within Roman society. The importance of this choice of title was appreciated by Roman historians; cp. Tacitus *Annals* 1. 1: 'He took control of a state exhausted by civil discord under the title of *princeps*'; 1. 9: 'He had put the state in order, not to make himself king or dictator, but under the title of *princeps*.'

Princeps was not an *official* title: it was assumed by Roman emperors at their accession and not conferred upon them by definite grant of the senate; nor does it appear in the list of official titles in documents and inscriptions. The nuance of the word, chosen by Augustus for its inoffensive character, was soon lost (though the use of the word itself persisted) as the government of the Roman emperors became more autocratic.

princeps iuventūtis or **princeps iuvenum** The phrase first appears with constitutional significance after the reorganization of the *iuventūs* by *Augustus (*see* IUVENES). Probably in 5 and 2 BC respectively the *equestrian order gave silver shields and spears to Augustus' grandsons Gaius *Iulius Caesar (2) and Lucius *Iulius Caesar, and hailed them as *principēs iuventutis*.

princeps senātūs The senator whose name was entered first on the *senate list compiled by the *censors. Once selected, he held his position for life (subject to confirmation by each new pair of censors), and longevity conferred increased influence. The *princeps senatus* had to be a *patrician. Apart from great dignity, the rank conferred the privilege of speaking first on any motion in the senate. Since there was usually not much debate, the *princeps senatus* moved all routine *senatus consulta*, and he influenced many debated ones. *Aemilius Lepidus (1), appointed six times, was the most powerful man of his generation. *Aemilius Scaurus was

appointed five or six times, and 'his nod all but ruled the world': it was he who moved the *senatus consultum ultimum* against *Appuleius Saturnnus and ceremonially handed *Marius a sword, and he pressed the legislation of *Livius Drusus. *Sulla abolished the office, since he did not want any one senator to have such power. Augustus revived it, appointing himself when he revised the senate list in 28 BC, even though Iulii were probably not eligible under the republic, and he held the office until his death. His successors took it as a matter of course.

Principate, the regime established by *Augustus (see PRINCEPS); also, the period of Roman history between Augustus and the late 3rd cent. AD. See ROME (HISTORY), 2, 3.

Priscian (5th–6th cent. AD) was the most prolific and important member of the late Latin grammarians. He spent most of his life as a teacher of Latin in *Constantinople. His surviving works include 'The Principles of Grammar' (974 printed pages). It comprises eighteen books, the first sixteen setting out the eight Latin word-classes (parts of speech) in great detail. Books 17 and 18 provide an account of the syntax of Latin, the first systematic treatment of Latin syntax known to us. The work represents a summation in Latin of the whole of grammatical theory and practice as it had developed in the Graeco-Latin world hitherto. It was of great importance in the western Middle Ages for the teaching of Latin and for philosophical grammar, some of whose concerns, e.g. universal grammar, are with us still.

prison Roman criminal law, like that of Athens, did not in general use public imprisonment of free persons as a form of punishment, although under the republic some criminals suffered private imprisonment at the hands of those they had wronged. The public prison (*carcer*) served normally only for a short incarceration, whether used as a coercive measure by magistrates against disobedience to their orders (see COERCITIO) or for convicted criminals awaiting execution. During inquiry in a criminal trial the accused person could be detained so as to be at the disposal of the authorities, but this was not necessarily in a public prison. Larger households had arrangements for imprisoning slaves, esp. in workhouses in the countryside. These were also used for convicted debtors and (under the republic) thieves, as well as other free men improperly seized.

proăgōn The *proagon* in Classical Athens was an official theatrical presentation which took place a few days before the City *Dionysia began. It was held in the *Odeum, a building east of the theatre reconstructed by *Pericles *c.*445 BC, where the poets appeared before the public with their choruses, actors, and presumably *chorēgoi* (see CHOREGIA), to give an exposition of the dramas with which they were to compete, perhaps little more than an indication of their general plot or subject-matter. Those involved in the forthcoming competitions were thereby identified before their civic peers: for, though garlanded, actors and choruses appeared without costumes or masks. We hear only of tragedy being presented in this way, but the procedure may have included comedy. The evidence for the *proagon* is meagre. An anecdote tells how at the *proagon* following Euripides' death, *Sophocles appeared in mourning, his troupe ungarlanded.

processions are a very common feature of Greek and Roman religious practice. It is above all in the procession that a group may ritually display its cohesion and power. And the route taken may express the control of space. The group may embody the whole community, as in the splendid festivals of the Greek *polis*— e.g. the *Panathenaic procession evoked in the *Parthenon frieze, with its various subgroups of virgins, youths, old men, musicians, chariots, and so on. Smaller groups form processions at funerals, weddings, and the like. Or a great procession may be centred around a single individual, as in the Roman *triumph. The procession almost always leads up to some action at its destination, often animal *sacrifice in a precinct (with the victims led in the procession); but also mystic *initiation (see MYSTERY CULTS), as in the mass of initiands proceeding on the sacred way from Athens to *Eleusis; theatrical performances, as at the Athenian City *Dionysia; the offering of a robe to the deity, as at the Panathenaea; games, as in the Roman procession to the *Circus Maximus; and so on. Special types of procession include those which escorted a deity (usually *Dionysus) into the city, and those conducted by children collecting contributions. Among the objects carried in processions were phalloi (see PHALLUS), baskets, the sacred objects of the mysteries, and branches hung with wool and fruit. Detailed accounts survive of magnificent processions at *Alexandria and at Rome (preceding the *Ludi Romani).

Proclus, Neoplatonist philosopher (AD 410 or 412–485; see NEOPLATONISM). Born in Lycia, he came to Athens in search of philosophical enlightenment, and there he spent the rest of his life. He studied with Syrianus, whom he succeeded as head of the Platonic school in 437. He is the last great systematizer of the Greek philosophical inheritance, and as such exerted a powerful influence on medieval and Renaissance thought. His learning was encyclopaedic and his output vast. Extant works include the following:

1. Philosophical treatises: *Elements of Theology*, a concise summary of Neoplatonic metaphysics; *Platonic Theology*, a more elaborate account of the same.

2. Commentaries on *Plato.

3. Scientific works: *Outline of Astronomical Theories*; *Commentary on the First Book of *Euclid's Elements*.

prō consulĕ, prō praetōrĕ, a magistrate (see MAGISTRACY, ROMAN) in place of a *consul or *praetor respectively, operating outside Rome and outside the regular annual magistracy.

The first instance is Publilius Philo, who was about to take Neapolis in 326 BC, when his consulship ran out. The people voted that he should retain his *imperium* in place of a consul (*pro consule*). He later triumphed as such. In the following centuries Rome's imperial expansion produced an endemic shortage of magistrates with *imperium*. Extensions were henceforth voted (*prōrogātiō imperiī*) for both consuls and praetors whenever necessary for military purposes or to enable the holder of *imperium* to *triumph. This became a routine measure requiring only a decree of the senate, not a popular vote. Similarly the magistracies of *quaestors could be prorogued *pro quaestore*.

In 295 four private citizens were given commands *pro praetore*; at least two of them had been delegated by a consul on his own authority. Such delegation of a promagistracy occurred later, when a magistrate or promagistrate was leaving his post abroad without receiving a successor sent from Rome (whatever his former status, the recipient would be given *imperium pro praetore*). However, the multiplication of Roman commanders or officials in a particular *provincia was normally achieved by the appointment of *legati, usually with more limited powers. Their nomination had to be approved by the senate, though it usually acceded to the wishes of the magistrate whose *legati* they were to be.

A promagistracy was exercised within a *provincia*, normally defined by the senate, in order to avoid collisions of rival authorities, and the holder was not permitted to go beyond it except in an emergency or for essential travel. During the Hannibalic War (see HANNIBAL) prorogation for long periods became common, and several private citizens were given *imperium pro magistrātū* by the people (but not, in this period, allowed to triumph). After the war long promagistracies became rare and the grant of *imperium* to private citizens was abandoned, but these practices revived (and a private citizen like *Pompey even triumphed) amid the troubles and shortage of commanders in the last century of the republic. Quaestors and *legati* could be given *imperium pro praetore* if necessary. Meanwhile, the multiplication of provinces and the development of *quaestiones perpetuae* entailed the integration of prorogation into the administrative system. By the late second century praetors normally went to their provinces abroad after their year of office, and the allocation of such provinces did not occur until then. Before Sulla consuls still undertook major wars in their year of magistracy. This practice became rare in the late republic and in any case they tended to continue as proconsuls after their consular year. The increase of the number of provinces in the 60s and the poor health or unwillingness of some magistrates to serve abroad led to a great increase in long tenures, and this trend was accelerated by the series of emergencies characterizing that period.

Consuls were always prorogued *pro consule*, praetors at first usually *pro praetore*; but both during and after their office their *imperium* might be raised to *pro consule* (with twelve *lictors), when the size of their armies or the importance of their tasks required it. After Sulla all governors seem to have ranked *pro consule*. Legates of proconsuls assigned extraordinary major commands by the people (e.g. of Pompey and Caesar) were now granted *imperium pro praetore* on appointment. The number of their lictors is uncertain. Pompey in 52 fixed a compulsory interval between magistracy and provincial government and seems to have tried to limit tenure of a promagistracy in principle to a year, in order to break the nexus of electoral bribery and corruption abroad and to prevent the dangerous accumulation of power. This meant that in the short term promagistracies had to be conferred on private citizens chosen by the senate (such as Cicero, who had declined a promagistracy after his consulship). This move Caesar

denounced as unconstitutional and he rescinded Pompey's law. However, *Augustus seems to have returned to Pompey's ideas in his organization of the 'public' provinces, though not with regard to his own. The emperor himself was consul from 27 to 23 and thereafter had proconsular *imperium*. So the governors on the spot of the provinces assigned to him ranked as *legati pro praetore* (with five lictors)—they would be either ex-praetors or ex-consuls, depending on the importance of their command. From 23 the emperor's proconsular *imperium* was also defined as greater (*maius*) with respect to that of proconsuls in the public provinces.

Procōpius Greek historian, b. in *Caesarea *c.*AD 500. After a thorough rhetorical and legal education, he obtained a post on the staff of *Justinian's general Belisarius, and carried out many difficult and sometimes dangerous missions for his commander. After accompanying Belisarius on his Persian, African, and Italian campaigns, he returned to *Constantinople. His fortunes no doubt fluctuated with those of his great patron, who incurred the enmity of Justinian's wife Theodora.

His principal work is his *History of the Wars of Justinian* in eight books. Bks. 1–2 deal with the first Persian war, 3–4 with the war against the Vandals in Africa, 5–7 with that against the Goths in Italy; these were probably published in 551. Bk. 8 contains supplementary material and a short history of the years 551–553. The *History* deals primarily with Justinian's campaigns, but there are many digressions on the political scene in Constantinople and on events elsewhere in the empire. Procopius, as Belisarius' confidant, had direct and comprehensive acquaintance with military affairs and was favourably placed to interrogate eyewitnesses of what he himself had not seen. These are the main sources upon which his *History* relies. But he also made use of documents and other written sources. His strength lies in clear narrative rather than in analysis. Procopius was a careful and intelligent man, generally of balanced judgement, though he favoured Belisarius. His attitude is somewhat old-fashioned and backward-looking. His claim to a sincere desire to establish the truth is somewhat vitiated by the very different picture which he paints of Justinian's regime in his *Secret History*, written at the same time as bks. 1–7 of his *History of the Wars*. It is a virulent, uncritical, and often scurrilous attack on the whole policy of Justinian and on the characters of the emperor and his consort, which can only have been circulated clandestinely so long as Justinian was alive. It provides a kind of sub-text to the *History of the Wars*, and reveals Procopius as a diehard adherent of the aristocratic opposition, which had briefly shown its hand at the time of the Nika riot of 532. The general reliability of his account of military events is unlikely to have been seriously affected by his reservations concerning Justinian's regime. His work *On Justinian's Buildings*, was composed (*c.*553–555) at the emperor's behest, and is panegyrical in tone. Whether this betokens a change in the author's views or merely proves his ability to ride two different horses at once, we cannot tell. The work is a first-class source for the geography, topography, and art of the period, and Procopius displays an unexpected talent for lucid architectural description.

All the works are written in a classicizing but generally clear Greek, with many echoes and reminiscences of earlier historians, esp. *Thucydides (2). Procopius is a historian of the first rank, helped rather than hindered by the literary tradition within which he wrote.

prōcūrātor signified an agent, and under the Principate came to be the distinctive term for the employees of the emperor in civil administration. They might be freedmen from the imperial household, but most, esp. the holders of the more important posts, were *equestrians. The principal types of procuratorial post were:

1. So-called 'presidial' procurators governed minor provinces such as Corsica, Judaea, Noricum, *Thrace, and the Mauretanias. These governors had originally been called *praefecti*; thus Pontius Pilate (*Pontius Pilatus) was officially entitled *Praefectus Iudaeae*. However, this term came to be reserved for the *equestrian governors of Egypt and, from 198, *Mesopotamia, where legionary troops were stationed. Presidial procurators commanded the auxiliary units in their provinces, exercised full civil and criminal jurisdiction, and supervised all fiscal matters. If at any time legionary forces were permanently stationed in such a province, the role of governor was transferred to a senatorial *legātus prō praetōre* (e.g. Judaea from the time of the revolt of AD 66; see LEGATES).

2. Procurators of imperial provinces, governed by *legati*, supervised the collection of direct taxes, indirect taxes (when special officials were not appointed, see below (5)), and of the revenues accruing from imperial properties. They were also responsible for the commissariat and pay of the troops. They had small detachments of troops at their disposal and official entitlement to requisitioned transport.

3. Procurators of the public provinces, governed by annual proconsuls, were originally in charge of only the properties of the emperor. They came to acquire responsibilities analogous to those of the procurators of the imperial provinces and, thus, to exercise joint supervision, with the proconsuls, of public taxation.

4. Procurators of imperial estates (see DOMAINS) were responsible for their general supervision. They possessed wide policing powers.

5. Procurators responsible for the supervision of specific indirect taxes appear in the 1st cent. and more widely in the 2nd (see PORTORIA and VECTIGAL). Their responsibility normally encompassed a set of adjacent provinces.

6. Throughout the first two centuries there was a steady accretion of procuratorial posts connected with the organization of such matters as the aqueducts, and the *annona* (see FOOD SUPPLY).

Entry to procuratorial posts followed normally on military service, either (for men who were already equestrians), the 'tres militiae' (see ALAE), or from the rank of *primipilus for men who had risen from the ranks. The 1st cent. saw the formation of the 'praetorian *cursus*' by which a *primipilus* went as tribune of a cohort successively in the three urban forces (*vigiles, urban cohorts (see COHORTES URBANI), *praetorian guard), went to another legion as *primipilus bis* (for the second time), and then moved to important procuratorships. A few of the most successful procurators could hope to gain promotion to the major prefectures, Egypt, the *annona*, and the praetorian guard and from the late 1st cent. to the secretarial posts with the emperor, previously the preserve of imperial freedmen. Procurators were the direct appointees of the emperor.

Prodicus of Ceos, a *sophist and contemporary of *Socrates. Little is known about his life. Acc. to *Plato, he served on diplomatic missions and took advantage of the opportunities these afforded to build up his clientele and to demand high fees. He was chiefly a teacher of *rhetoric, with a special interest in the correct use of words and the distinction of near-synonyms. Plato represents Socrates as being on friendly terms with him and paying tribute to the value of his teaching, though usually with a touch of irony. Of his writings all that survives is *Xenophon's paraphrase of his myth of the Choice of *Heracles between Virtue and Vice. He gave naturalistic accounts of the origin of religion, in some respects anticipating *Euhemerus, and is counted as an atheist by some sources. See also CULTURE-BRINGERS.

prodigies See PORTENTS.

progress See ANTHROPOLOGY.

progymnasmata were the 'preliminary exercises' which made up the elementary stage of instruction in schools of rhetoric. Some collections from the time of the empire survive. The principal exercises were *fable, *narrative, anecdotal apophthegm, maxim (see GNŌMĒ), refutation and confirmation, commonplace (see COMMUNES LOCI; TOPOS), speech written in character, description (see EKPHRASIS), general question, introduction of a law. While some of these exercises might prove useful for forensic or deliberative oratory, others (esp. 'narrative' and 'description') were closer to the needs of display oratory or history. The influence of these exercises on literature was very great and very long-lasting. See RHETORIC, GREEK.

prōlētāriī were the citizens of Rome too poor to contribute anything to the state except their children (*prōlēs*). They seem to have been equated with the *capite censī* ('counted by head; see CENSUS) as persons who paid no tribute and were exempt from military service except in an emergency (*tumultus*), when they were issued with armour and weapons.

In the mid-2nd cent. BC direct taxation for Romans was suspended (see TRIBUTUM) and the property qualification for military service was lowered. Nevertheless, the distinction between those who were rich enough to be regarded as both sound citizens and reliable defenders of their country and those who were not, remained important in Roman political ideology. *Marius in 107 BC set a precedent by enrolling *capite censi* volunteers when there was no emergency, but conscription from those financially qualified remained the main source of the legions throughout the republic. Although in Ciceronian times the *proletarii* must have constituted a large part of the total population, they had virtually no strength in the *comitia centuriata*, being collected in a single century, which voted only if the decision was still open after the decision of the five propertied classes had been declared.

Promētheus, son of Iapetus, associated with the origin of *fire and with *Hephaestus, developed by *Hesiod into a figure of greater weight. The name was given the sense 'Forethought' by Hesiod, who added a contrasting figure Epimetheus ('Thinking after the event').

In Hesiod's *Theogony* Prometheus is bound to a pillar, his liver eaten daily by an eagle and nightly renewed until finally he is freed by *Heracles. This is traced back to a meal shared by men and gods where Prometheus tricks the gods into feasting on bones and fat, explaining the division of victims after *sacrifice and also the distance which now separates men and gods. *Zeus in anger removes fire from men, but Prometheus steals it and gives it back to man, who is then further punished by Hephaestus' creation of woman, foolishly accepted by Epimetheus (see PANDORA). The portrait of Prometheus was developed by later authors: (Pseudo-?) *Aeschylus' *Prometheus Bound* makes him yet more of a *culture-bringer, responsible for man's skills and sciences. There is also a persistent tradition that Prometheus created man from clay, as commonly in mythologies, and this might lie behind Hephaestus' creation of woman in Hesiod.

Prometheus' defiance of the gods captured the romantic imagination and has profoundly influenced most modern artistic and literary genres, notably because of the nobility in the *Prometheus Bound* of Prometheus chained to the rock, hurling defiance at Zeus, and despising mere thunderbolts. The trickery with which Hesiod characterizes this culture-bringer has attracted interest in the light of trickster heroes in other mythologies, esp. North American. In any case, myths of the origin of fire and of man bring Greek myth closer than usual to world mythologies and folk-tale.

pronunciation, Greek The main features of the pronunciation of ancient Greek may be established through the study of contemporary documents, literary texts, spelling mistakes, puns, grammarians' statements, etc. (see next entry). In many points we may claim only approximate accuracy, but it is certain that the pronunciation of ancient Greek was different from that of Modern Greek. The early Greek accent was one of pitch, i.e. the prominence given within the word to the accented syllable was obtained through a rise of the pitch. The date at which the 'musical' or pitch accent was replaced by an accent like that of Modern Greek where stress is a primary component is uncertain. The change may have developed for a long time, but probably was completed by the end of the 4th cent. AD.

pronunciation, Latin Our knowledge of the pronunciation of classical Latin is derived from a variety of sources. Most direct are the specific statements of Latin grammarians and other authors (though allowance must be made for the fact that the former tend to be of later date). Other sources are: puns, word-play, contemporary etymologies, and onomatopoeia; the representation of Latin words in other ancient languages; later developments in the Romance languages; the spelling conventions of Latin, and esp. any deviations from these; the internal structure of Latin itself and of its metrical patterns (see ETYMOLOGY).

It is impossible to reconstruct the vocal totality of a dead language; but at least for the individual sounds it is feasible to reach an approximation which is probably as close as the average classical scholar comes to the sounds of a living foreign language.

prooemium

1. Verse. See HYMNS, GREEK; LYRIC POETRY, GREEK.

2. Prose. Applied originally to poetry Gk. *prooimion* was taken over by rhetorical theory to designate the first of the four (sometimes more) sections into which classical rhetoricians divided the prose speech. It is, together with the peroration, the part of the speech which contains the greatest accumulation of recognizable commonplaces, and the typical themes are already discernible in the 5th cent. Toward the end of the 5th cent. the custom arose of compiling collections of stock openings (and also perorations) to forensic and political speeches.

Propertius, Sextus, Roman *elegiac poet, between 54 and 47 BC, at Asisium, where his family were local notables. His father died early, and the family property was diminished by Octavian's confiscations of 41–40 BC (see AUGUSTUS; PROSCRIPTION)—not so diminished, however, that Propertius needed to earn a living. In the two last poems of bk. 1 the poet notably identifies with the side vanquished by Octavian at Perusia in 41; for the losing side see ANTONIUS (PIETAS). It is the first sign of a political independence that continues throughout his life, despite involvement in *Maecenas' circle. As the Augustan regime toughened, Propertius' modes of irreverence become more oblique, but irrever-

ence towards the government is maintained none the less. Propertius was dead by 2 BC. He is best known as a love poet. He celebrated his devotion to a mistress whom he called Cynthia (a name with Apollonian and Callimachean associations; see APOLLO; CALLIMACHUS (2)). *Apuleius says her real name was Hostia (*Apology* 10). Many of the incidents suggested in the poems seem conventional, but there is no reason to doubt Cynthia's basic reality. Her social status is uncertain.

Characteristic of Propertian love poetry is the claim to be the slave of his mistress, and the claim that love is his life's occupation; it replaces the normal career move of a young *equestrian (service in the cohort (see COHORS)) of a provincial governor—barely military service. Propertius distils this last point by referring to love as his military service. Typical too of his love poetry is his use of mythology: he cites figures and events from myth as 'romantic standards', as examples of how things in a romantic world might be.

Bk. 1, consisting almost entirely of love poems, is addressed to a variety of friends. Bk. 2, still largely devoted to love poems, evidences his entry to the circle of Maecenas, but there is no suggestion that he was ever economically dependent on him in the way that *Virgil and *Horace were (see PATRONAGE, LITERARY). Bk. 3 also contains a prominent poem to Maecenas, but bk. 4 omits all mention of him. Maecenas fades from Propertius' poetry as he fades from Horace's: probably because of the great patron's loss of favour with Augustus in the wake of the conspiracy led by Fannius Caepio in 23 BC.

Bk. 3 shows a greater diversity of subject-matter, and Propertius here first makes an ostentatious claim to be a Roman Callimachus. Some scholars think the claim is not well justified: Horace had claimed to be the Roman *Alcaeus; with some humour Propertius responds by making his claim to be the first Roman to adopt the mantle of another Greek poet. Notable among the many non-Cynthia poems in bk. 3 is 3. 18 on the death of Augustus' nephew *Claudius Marcellus (2). It is hard to imagine Propertius writing this a few years earlier. The toughening of the Augustan regime and the fading influence of the mediating Maecenas were having their effect. But Propertius can still be irreverent. The concluding poems of the book recall bk. 1 in various ways, and mark the end both of the affair with Cynthia and of his career as a love-poet (or so it seems).

Bk. 4 is more successful than bk. 3, and in it Propertius has a stronger claim to be called a Roman Callimachus. It consists partly of poems descended from Callimachus' *Aetia*; but these are Roman *Aetia*, one indeed explaining the temple of Apollo as a thank-offering for the victory at *Actium. 4. 6 is an example of Propertius' later subtle irreverence. It is largely devoted to an account of the battle of Actium, but tells it all in the manner of Callimachus, a style wholly unsuited to the subject-matter. The result is amusing to those with literary taste. To these aetiological poems are added poems on various subjects. The two in which he returns to the theme of Cynthia (7 and 8) are among Propertius' most original.

Some Romans, though not *Quintilian, thought Propertius the most 'refined and elegant' of the Roman elegists. Such epithets apply to many of his poems, but others seem to the modern reader obscure and jagged. Part of this is the reader's fault. The poet's wit is a demanding one. Other and real obscurities are due to a very corrupt manuscript tradition. The fact remains that Propertius often seems to cultivate complexity and convolution.

His vivid re-creation of his affair with Cynthia, his literary range, and his political independence make Propertius one of the most captivating of Latin poets.

prophecies, texts purporting to be the work of inspired sages, had an important role in Graeco-Roman thought. Collections of prophecies, which are attested from the 6th cent. BC, might be attributed to a divine or semi-divine character such as *Orpheus, Bacis, or a *Sibyl; they could be presented as accounts of moments where an individual was seized by a prophetic fit, or collections of significant oracles that either emanated, or were claimed to have emanated, from major oracular shrines.

The purveyors of such texts, usually called *chrēsmologoi* in Greek and by a number of titles in Latin, did not ordinarily claim inspiration for themselves, and it is impossible to know what role they played in the actual composition of such works. Evidence from Egyptian sources and from the manuscript traditions of the Sibylline Oracles does, however, suggest that there was considerable fluidity in their texts.

Recitation of these prophecies is often noted at times of public unrest. *Thucydides (2), *Aristophanes, and *Plutarch provide a sample of such prophecies (and parodies of the same) during the *Peloponnesian War. Other authors (e.g. *Plutarch and *Pausanias (3)) show that such writings were always in circulation.

See also DIVINATION.

prophētēs, the title of the mortal who speaks in the name of a god or interprets his will. It is properly used only of seers and functionaries attached to an established oracular shrine; the unattached seer is called *mantis* or *chrēsmologos*. And it is more often used of the officials who presided over oracular shrines than of the actual receivers of mantic inspiration: *Pindar can distinguish the two functions, inviting the *Muse to 'prophesy, and I will be your mouthpiece' (*prophetes*). At Delphi (see DELPHIC ORACLE) and *Didyma the immediate receiver of the divine revelation was a woman, while the 'prophets' were males who oversaw the oracular session: at Didyma, an annually elected magistrate, at Delphi (where the title was not official) two priests who served for life. The distinction is not absolute, however.

Propylaea A propylon is a monumental roofed gateway: the derivative term, 'propylaea', is applied to more complex structures, specifically the Periclean gateway (see PERICLES) to the acropolis of *Athens designed by Mnēsiclēs and built between 436 and 432 BC. It is approached by an inclined ramp continuing the natural slope of the rock. Started before the Persian Wars, it was burnt by *Xerxes' forces, but afterwards repaired; part survives behind the SW wing of Mnesicles' building. Mnesicles' plan was elaborated by lower flanking wings to north and south. On the west front are structures with porches each with three columns. That to the north was once decorated inside with paintings. Since it is approached by an off-centre door, it was probably a formal feasting room, holding seventeen couches (see DINING-ROOMS). A similar façade on the south cleverly embellishes an approach passage to the *Nike bastion. These were the last sections to be built, work being hastened (when all other building activity was stopped) at the approach of the *Peloponnesian War. The east rooms of the wings, clearly intended, were abandoned unbuilt. The central gateway building comprises two rooms with Doric hexastyle porticos facing outwards and inwards, the inner hall at a higher level. The dividing cross wall is pierced by five doors; the largest, centre, door is for a continuous inclined passage, used only for ceremonial *processions and animals. The others are at the top of a flight of five steps from the lower hall.

The Propylaea is built of Pentelic *marble, with the innovatory use of dark grey ('black') Eleusinian limestone for contrasting orthostats and string-courses. The front-gate hall has its roof supported on two rows of Ionic columns, the central passage having a span of nearly 4.26 m. (14 ft.). The architraves of the Ionic colonnades were reinforced with iron beams because of the weight imposed on them by the ceilings which were formed of marble beams and of slabs with deeply hollowed square coffers, richly decorated in blue and gold.

prorogation The extension of a Roman magistrate's *imperium* beyond his original year of office.

proscription, the publication of a notice, esp. a list of Roman citizens who were declared outlaws and whose goods were confiscated. This procedure was used by *Sulla in 82–81 BC, and by Marcus *Antonius (Mark Antony), *Aemilius Lepidus (2), and *Octavian in 43–42 as a means of getting rid of personal and political opponents and obtaining funds and land in virtue, or anticipation, of special powers of inappellable jurisdiction conferred on them as *dictator and *triumviri respectively. The proscribed were hunted down and executed in Rome and throughout Italy by squads of soldiers, and the co-operation of the victims' families and slaves and of the general public was sought by means of rewards and punishments.

Despite some wild exaggeration in ancient sources and modern calculations, Sulla's proscription, in part an act of revenge for massacres in 87 and 82 by *Marius and his son, targeted no more than perhaps 520 persons. The lists were closed on 1 June 81. The sons and grandsons of the proscribed were debarred from public life until restored by *Caesar in 49. The impression left was profound, and similar conduct was feared from Caesar or *Pompey, whichever should win the Civil War: as it was, Caesar's clemency was made an excuse for the proscriptions of the triumvirs: 'If traitors who had begged for mercy had not obtained it, and then conspired against their benefactors, Caesar would not have been killed by those he had saved by his clemency.' Their lists included about 300 senators and *equestrians; but many escaped, and some of them, including a fair proportion of senators, were afterwards restored.

proskynēsis See ALEXANDER (2) THE GREAT, 10; CALLISTHENES; RULER-CULT, *Greek*.

prosopography is the study of individuals, and is derived from Gk. *prosōpon*, one meaning of which is 'person'. Prosopography, as practised in ancient history, is a method which uses onomastic evidence (see NAMES, PERSONAL, GREEK and ROMAN) to establish (i) regional origins of individuals and (ii) family connections, esp. via marriage-ties but also via *adoption (which leaves traces on nomenclature), between individual and individual, and between group and group. (See GENOS and GENS for the basic large *kinship units.) Conclusions about the origins and family connections of individuals lead to inferences about their likely political sympathies and allegiances.

Traditional prosopography can be criticized for undue attention to the doings of élites and exceptional individuals; but the paucity of evidence for low-status groups and individuals is not a problem peculiar to prosopography but one which faces most attempts to investigate the ancient world. Roman republican history in its human and political complexity cannot be understood without proper attention to prosopographical detail. As for imperial Rome, prosopography, allied with *epigraphy, has transformed understanding of the Roman governing class under the Principate. Prosopography has made less impact on Greek history, but it has shown e.g. that in Classical Athens there is little overlap between politics at *deme level and at city level.

prostitution, sacred is a modern term and misleading in that it transfers to the institution an adjective which in ancient sources denotes only the status of the personnel involved (sometimes also their earnings, which likewise became sacred on dedication). In the cult of *Aphrodite at *Corinth, *Strabo, admittedly writing long after the city's destruction in 146 BC, gives a total of over 1,000 *hetairai dedicated by both men and women. Dedication is also emphasized in the cult of Aphrodite at Eryx in west Sicily.

prostitution, secular The exchange of sexual service for the economic benefits conferred by marriage is remarked upon by *Hesiod (*WD* 373–5). In both Greece and Rome, prostitution was considered to be as necessary as the institutions of *marriage, concubinage (see CONTUBERNIUM), or *slavery. Social attitudes and legislation generally stigmatized the prostitute, who—whether female or male—was usually of low status. In the Greek world there is a constant emphasis on the economic perils of the transaction for men and its concomitant provision of sexual release. The very terms *porneion* (brothel) and *pornē* (whore) are related to *pernēmi* (I sell). See HETAIRAI; HOMOSEXUALITY (for male prostitutes); PORNOGRAPHY; PROSTITUTION, SACRED.

Prōtagoras of Abdera (*c*.490–420 BC), the most celebrated of the *sophists. He travelled widely throughout the Greek world, including several visits to Athens, where he was associated with *Pericles. He was invited to write the constitution for the Athenian colony of *Thurii. The ancient tradition of his condemnation for impiety and flight from Athens is refuted by *Plato's evidence (*Meno* 91e) that he enjoyed a universally high reputation till his death and afterwards. See INTOLERANCE, INTELLECTUAL AND RELIGIOUS. He was famous in antiquity for agnosticism concerning the existence and nature of the gods, and for the doctrine that 'The human being is the measure of all things', i.e. the thesis that all sensory appearances and all beliefs are true for the person whose appearance or belief they are; on the most plausible construal that doctrine attempts to eliminate objectivity and truth altogether. It was attacked by *Democritus and Plato (in *Theaetetus*) on the ground that it is self-refuting; if all beliefs are true, then the belief that it is not the case that all beliefs are true is itself true. Protagoras also held that on every subject, there were two opposed arguments, and he wrote two books of 'Opposed Arguments'. In *Protagoras* Plato represents him as maintaining a fairly conservative form of social morality, based on a version of social contract theory; humans need to develop social institutions to survive in a hostile world, and the basic social virtues, justice and self-control, must be generally observed if those institutions are to flourish.

proverbs The proverb, or concise saying in common use, often summarizing experience or embodying practical wisdom, is a constant feature in Greek literature, both prose and verse, from *Homer onwards. It not only provided an ingredient calculated to please the ordinary hearer, but contributed to the formulation of moral philosophy. Many quotations from literature, and esp. from poetry, enjoyed an independent life as proverbs. See GNOME; SENTENTIA.

Prōvidentia, learned term for *prūdentia*, 'foresight', the capacity to distinguish good from bad, which became, under the influence of the *pronoia* ('forethought') of *Stoicism, a virtue of statesmen. *Providentia Augusti* became the object of cult at the beginning of the Principate. It expressed the wise forethought of *Augustus in regulating the succession in AD 4, before being extended to other fields of imperial forethought. The *Providentia Augusti* was invoked on the discovery of conspiracies and was a frequent theme in imperial coinage.

prōvincia/province 1. The basic meaning of *provincia* is the sphere in which a magistrate (perhaps originally a magistrate with *imperium*) is to function. See MAGISTRACY, ROMAN. By the 3rd cent. BC, the two consuls normally had their *provinciae* assigned by the *senate or by mutual agreement; later allotment was normal. A law of Gaius *Sempronius Gracchus (123) provided that the senate was to decide, before the consular elections, in a vote protected against tribunician *intercessio, which *provinciae* were to be consular: this was to prevent personal or political influences on that decision. At the beginning of the year the senate would decide which *provinciae* were to be praetorian (and, before 123, consular): for these, the magistrates would then draw lots. Any others would be filled by designated promagistrates (see PRO CONSULE, PRO PRAETORE). By the late 3rd cent., a magistrate or promagistrate was expected to confine his activities to his *provincia*, except in emergencies or by special permission. By 171 this had become a formal rule, enforced by the senate. It was at various times reaffirmed in legislation on provincial administration.

Originally the two consuls normally divided all duties between them. Since they had to campaign nearly every year, a *praetor with *imperium* was appointed and given the *provincia urbana* (affairs in the city, esp. legal business and the presidency of the senate and legislative assemblies when necessary). Until *c*.100, when consuls began to stay in Rome usually, this remained his task, but he came to specialize in civil law and in the end to confine himself to this. A second praetor was created at the end of the First *Punic War, probably to supervise the newly won territory of Punic *Sicily and perhaps later Sardinia. In 227 two new praetors were created for these overseas *provinciae* and the second praetor, though freely used in fighting in the Second Punic War, was normally assigned to judicial duties in the city, in due course those affecting foreigners (hence the popular title *praetor peregrīnus*, 'peregrine'). Two more praetors were created in 198/7, to command in the two newly won territories in *Spain, hitherto in the charge of private citizens with special *imperium*. Henceforth the word *provincia*, although it never lost its original meaning, was mainly used for overseas territories under permanent Roman administration, i.e. it came mainly to mean 'province'; but the two city *provinciae* were higher in prestige. By the second century provincial commanders were attended by *quaestors. The praetor of Sicily, where the territory of *Syracuse, annexed in the Second Punic War, remained under its traditional administration, was given two quaestors. Characteristically of Roman conservatism, he retained the two quaestors to the end of the republic, even after the administration of Sicily was unified on the more profitable model of the old kingdom of Syracuse.

After 197 the senate was unwilling to create more praetors (see PRAETOR) and, so on the whole to annex more territory. *Macedonia was 'freed' after the battle of *Pydna; *Numidia was not annexed after *Jugurtha's defeat; Transalpine Gaul (see GAUL (TRANSALPINE)), which provided the land connection with Spain, was not organized as a province until after the wars with the Cimbri and their allies (see MARIUS) had shown the danger this presented; *Cyrene was not properly organized until the 60s; and the bequest of Egypt by Ptolemy X (87) was refused by *Sulla. But some annexation became necessary, or was regarded as such: Macedonia and Africa (the territory of *Carthage; see AFRICA, ROMAN) in 146, Asia (129), Transalpine Gaul after 100. Unwillingness to create more praetors meant that the traditional city-state system of (in principle) annual magistracies was abandoned and promagistrates became an integral part of imperial administration. New quaestors were probably created, since quaestors, at that time not even guaranteed membership of the senate, did not endanger the political system. In 123-2, Gaius Gracchus, reforming the *extortion court, put a praetor in charge of it. Over the next generation, other *quaestiones were established on this model, so that by *c.*90 most, perhaps all, praetors were occupied in Rome during their year of office. Since consuls were not involved in routine provincial government, provinces were almost entirely left to promagistrates. As early as 114, the urban praetor Marius was sent as proconsul to Spain after his year of office—a major innovation as far as our records go. By the nineties praetors serving in the city might expect to be sent overseas the following year. Major foreign wars, the *Social War and civil wars added to the strain on the system, and tenures of promagistrates increased until they could reach six years. This, combined with the growth of the client army (see MARIUS), posed a serious danger to the republic, as Sulla soon showed.

Sulla, after his victory, aimed at stabilizing the state under senate control. He added at least two *quaestiones*, but also added two praetorships (and raised the number of quaestors to 20). Consuls (it seems) were encouraged to go to prestigious provinces (like Cisalpina) at the end of their year. It was apparently Sulla's idea that ten magistrates with *imperium, normally governing provinces after their year of office, would suffice to keep provincial tenures down to a year or at most two. But after 70 various factors—esp. the rise of *populārēs* (see OPTIMATES) with their programmes and ambitions, and increasing, hence increasingly expensive, competition for the consulship—led to accelerated annexation. *Crete was annexed by Caecilius Metellus (Creticus) to end Cretan *piracy—and to prevent its annexation by *Pompey. *Cyprus was annexed to pay for *Clodius Pulcher's corn distributions; Pompey annexed Syria and added Pontus to *Bithynia, as well as first organizing several territories (e.g. Judaea) as dependencies of provinces. He claimed to have added 85 million *dēnāriī* to Rome's previous revenue of 50 million. *Caesar, for reasons of personal ambition, extended Transalpine Gaul to the Rhine and the English Channel. Yet men not seeking glory or fortunes were often unwilling to serve in provinces, and Sulla had omitted to make acceptance of a promagistracy compulsory, as a magistrate's *provincia* always had been. Thus exploitation of provincials for private gain became a necessary incentive, tending to select those eager for it as provincial governors, while major wars and increasingly competitive ambitions for glory led to the granting of large *provinciae* with long tenure to *Licinius Lucullus, Pompey, Caesar and *Licinius Crassus. To stop the dangers inherent in this, Pompey, on the senate's advice, fixed an interval (perhaps of five years) between magistracy and promagistracy and made acceptance of provinces compulsory (52): thus *Cicero and *Calpurnius Bibulus belatedly had to accept provincial service. But the plan was nullified when civil wars supervened. It was later essentially restored by *Augustus.

2. A province was not an area under uniform administration. In Sicily, cities that joined the Romans had been declared 'free' (see FREE CITIES) when the territory was taken over from Carthage, and 'free' cities, granted various degrees of independence, remained characteristic

of eastern and some western provinces. Inevitably their rights tended to be whittled down: by the early 1st cent. BC, the free city of *Utica was the seat of the governor of Africa. Many governors were less than scrupulous in respecting the rights of free cities. Tribes could also be granted various degrees of self-government, and from the late 2nd cent. colonies of citizens were founded overseas (see COLONIZATION, ROMAN). A province was therefore a mosaic of territories with different statuses, from complete subjection to nominal independence, and provincial maps were kept in Rome to show this. Most provinces were annexed after wars, and in such cases the victorious commander would organize the peace settlement (including, if appropriate, annexation) with a commission of *legati according to a *senatus consultum. (Pompey, characteristically, refused to accept a commission, thereby causing serious anxiety regarding his political intentions.) This settlement, later confirmed by senate or people, the *lex provinciae* settled boundaries, local constitutions, taxation, and the administration of justice, in ways and degrees that differed considerably from one province to another. The *lex* might later be amended in detail, but remained the basis for the organization of the particular province.

Within the general framework, each governor issued his *edict, normally based on his predecessor's and relevant parts of those of urban praetors. But this was never compulsory. *Mucius Scaevola (2) in the 90s in Asia, and Cicero, modelling himself on him in 51 in Cilicia, introduced major judicial innovations. Scaevola's reforms were made mandatory for Asia by the senate, but any extension to other provinces was haphazard. The edict was not binding on the governor, at least until 67. Within the limits set by the general framework, he held absolute *imperium* over non-citizens. In fact, he was a commander and not, in the modern sense, a governor or administrator. On his departure from Rome, no matter how peaceful his province, he and his *lictors changed to military uniform, and his friends would escort him with prayers for his safety and success; and his return was accompanied by corresponding ceremonial. He could delegate his power to his quaestor and legates, and within limits to others. He was accompanied to his province by a large *cohors (a military term) of military and civilian attendants and friends of his and of his officers, many of them young men thus gaining their first experience of public service and rule. From them and provincial Romans, he would

choose his *consilium* (panel of advisers), to advise on, and vouch for, his judicial and other activities. Having *imperium*, he could not be challenged during his tenure, no matter how he behaved, and he could protect the actions of his officers and *cohors*, and also those of businessmen (see NEGOTIATORES) and *publicani, by armed force and sheer terror, for immense mutual profit. The chances of having him convicted in the *extortion court were slim, since he was rich and well connected: nearly all cases in the late republic ended in acquittal. Even conviction might not profit the provincials (see VERRES). The sum voted by the senate for the province offered further opportunities for profit: it was not expected that he would return the surplus, which was normally shared by him with his officers and *cohors*. As we have seen, these opportunities became an integral part of the system and were thus not subject to reform.

3. All indirect taxes were farmed by *publicani*. Direct taxes were originally collected by the quaestor, at greatly varying rates, though farmed at the local level. Gaius Gracchus arranged for the taxation of Asia, the richest province, to be sold to *publicani* under five-year contracts. This system was apparently extended by Pompey to the provinces he organized. Asia remained a centre of exploitation and consequent resentment, due more to warfare and the actions of governors than to the *publicani*, though the latter offered easier targets for complaint. Lucullus tried to save it by restructuring its huge debts, and after further civil war and oppression Caesar greatly reduced its tax and restored its collection to the quaestor. There was no change in other provinces before Augustus.

4. In 27 BC, Augustus was given a large consular *provincia*, originally (it seems) Gaul, Spain, and Syria, which he governed (after 23 as proconsul) through *legati pro praetore*, and which contained nearly all the legions. Its finances were administered by *procurators. The command was regularly renewed and the area changed over time. By the end of the reign the emperor's provinces were an accepted institution. The public (in fact, senatorial) provinces were governed by proconsuls, most (and within a generation all) of them without legions, but still with *imperium* and assisted by quaestors and legates. But the emperor had *imperium maius*, which we find Augustus exercising as early as the *Cyrene edicts. He also had to approve of all proconsular appointments, esp. the most prestigious ones to Asia (see ASIA, ROMAN PROVINCE)

and Africa. Egypt, though 'subject to the Roman people' was forbidden to senators and governed for the emperor by an *equestrian prefect with legionary forces (see PRAEFECTUS). Various minor provinces (e.g. Judaea and Noricum) were governed by prefects (later by procurators) without legions. Direct taxes were directly collected in all provinces; indirect taxes continued to be collected by *publicani*, now subject to strict regulation, but by the 3rd cent. AD were taken over by the central government.

The system established by Augustus was essentially maintained until well into the 3rd cent., although there were many changes in detail, some of them significant. *Britain was annexed by *Claudius and later extended, *Dacia and Arabia (i.e. Nabataea) by *Trajan. As expansion ceased, esp. after Trajan, frontiers were gradually marked out and defended by garrisons (see LIMES). Various *client kings were succeeded by governors and the subdivision of large provinces, begun by Augustus, was continued, esp. since a constant supply of senior men was soon available. Supervision of municipal government, made necessary by AD 100 because of financial incompetence, was gradually extended and stifled civic tradition. The whole system was finally reorganized, after the strains of civil wars and invasions, by *Diocletian.

In some provinces a *concilium* (provinicial council) of local notables had developed under the republic: it could serve as a vehicle for distributing the governor's messages and would propose honours for him; it might even occasionally complain about him to the senate. These *concilia*, extended to all provinces, became the organizations in charge of the imperial cult (see RULER-CULT, ROMAN), which grew out of the cult of the goddess Roma under the republic. The councils were headed by native high priests, who in due course could expect to gain citizenship; many of their descendants became equestrians or even senators. As more provincial notables gained the citizenship, the equestrian service and the senate were gradually opened up to provincials, although over a long time-span and at very varying rates for different provinces. Among the lower classes, Romanization was spread by army service (see AUXILIA), while the grant of *ius Latii* was extended among provincial communities; though the Latin language never spread to the east. By the time of *Caracalla's edict (see CONSTITUTION, ANTONINE), a unitary Roman state was *de facto* already in existence. See FINANCE, ROMAN.

prōvocātiō was an appeal made to the Roman people against the action of a magistrate (see MAGISTRACY, ROMAN), whether the latter was employing summary coercion (*coercitio) on the appellant or presiding over a judicial process. The *lex Valeria* of 300 BC made the disregard of *provocatio* by a magistrate a criminal offence. By 450 BC *provocatio* seems to have been recognized as a fact of Roman life. The least confrontational way for a magistrate opposed by *provocatio* to proceed further was to take the matter to an assembly, and from 300 BC the *lex Valeria* was an additional inducement so to do. During the 2nd cent. the protection of citizens against summary justice was enhanced by further laws, one of which abolished the flogging of Roman citizens and another extended *provocatio* to citizens in the military sphere (i.e. outside the city of Rome). A law of Gaius *Sempronius Gracchus not only reformulated one of the principles of *provocatio* by forbidding capital trials unsanctioned by the people (so helping to stimulate the growth of *quaestiones perpetuae* established by statute), but provided for assembly-trials of offenders against the law. Ultimately the grant of tribunician powers to *Augustus led to the substitution for *provocatio* of appeal to the emperor.

proxenos/proxeny Since Greek states did not send permanent diplomatic representatives abroad, local citizens served as *proxenoi* to look after the interests of other states in their community. By the beginning of the 5th cent. this 'proxeny' system had developed from earlier practices of hospitality under which some relied on hereditary ties with foreign families (see FRIENDSHIP, RITUALIZED) and others on the more general respect for strangers and suppliants. States selected their own *proxenoi* in other states and, in return for services already rendered and expected in the future, bestowed honours and privileges upon them. Such appointments were much coveted, and many voluntarily assumed the burdens in the hope of gaining the title. The position was often hereditary.

prytaneion, symbolic centre of the *polis, housing its communal hearth, eternal flame, and public dining-room where civic hospitality was offered; usually in or off the *agora. The privilege of permanent maintenance in the *prytaneion* was highly honorific and, in classical times, sparingly conceded; less honorific was the once-only invitation to a meal. Excavated *prytaneia* tend to be architecturally modest, as might have been the fare, at least in democratic Athens. See HESTIA.

prytaneis means 'presidents', sing. *prytanis*. In Athens the *boule*, after it was reorganized in 508/7 BC by *Cleisthenes (2), consisted of 50 men chosen by lot from each of the ten *phylai, and each group of 50 served as *prytaneis* for one-tenth of the year (see CALENDAR, GREEK). This period was called a prytany; owing to the vagaries of Athenian methods of reckoning a year, a prytany might be anything from 35 to 39 days. To decide which *phylē*'s group was to be *prytaneis* next, lots were drawn shortly before the beginning of each prytany except the last by all the groups which had not been *prytaneis* so far that year.

The *prytaneis* were on duty every day. They made arrangements for meetings of the *boule* and *ekklesia, received envoys and letters addressed to the state, and conducted other day-to-day business. Between 470 and 460 an office, called the *tholos* because of its circular shape, was built for them next to the *bouleuterion* on the west side of the Agora. There they dined every day at public expense.

Each day one of the *prytaneis* was picked by lot to be their chairman (*epistatēs*). He remained on duty in the *tholos* for one night and day, with one-third of the *prytaneis*. He had charge of the state seal and of the keys of the treasuries and *archives. In the 5th cent. he was the chairman at any meeting of the *boule* or *ekklesia* held on his day (see SOCRATES—the most famous *epistates*, and on a famous occasion), but in the 4th cent. this duty was taken over by the *proedroi*. No one could be chairman more than once, and so a considerable proportion (perhaps half) of the citizens held this position at some time in their lives. The whole system of the *prytaneis* and their chairman, based on lot and rotation, was a means of involving ordinary citizens in public administration, and thus a fundamental part of Athenian democracy and education.

pseudepigraphical literature Antiquity has left us a number of writings which evidence, internal or external, proves not to be the work of the authors whose names are traditionally attached to them. The causes of this include: (*a*) a tendency to ascribe anonymous pieces to a well-known author of like genre. Thus, the whole *Epic Cycle and other hexameter poems were at one time or another ascribed to *Homer. (*b*) Works by the followers of a philosopher

tended to be credited to their master; e.g. several short dialogues by members of the *Academy bear the name of *Plato. (*c*) Rhetorical exercises in the form of speeches, letters, etc., supposed to be by well-known persons, now and then were taken for their real works. The Epistles of Phalaris are the most notorious work of this kind, thanks to Bentley's exposure of them. (*d*) But the most frequent cases are of late date and connected with the craze for producing evidence of the doctrine one favoured being of great age. The numerous *Neopythagorean treatises are regularly attached to the names of prominent early Pythagoreans, including *Pythagoras himself, despite the tradition that he wrote nothing. The Sibylline oracles (see SIBYL) are an outstanding instance of this.

psȳchē is the Greek term for '*soul'. In Homer, we find a widespread soul system, in which *psyche* was the 'free-soul', which represented the individual personality only when the body was inactive: during swoons or at the moment of death. On the other hand, psychological functions were performed by 'body-souls', such as *thȳmos* and *menos*. It is also the *psyche* that leaves for the Underworld, and the dead are indeed often called *psychai*; on black-figure vases of *c*.500 BC we can see a homunculus, sometimes armed, hovering above the dead warrior. Towards the end of the Archaic age two important developments took place. First, *Pythagoras and other philosophers introduced the notion of *transmigration. The development is still unexplained, but it certainly meant an upgrading of the soul, which we find in *Pindar called 'immortal'. However, only in post-classical times did this notion become popular. Second, *psyche* started to incorporate the *thymos* and thus became the centre of consciousness. This development culminated in the Socratic notion that man had to take care of his *psychē* (see SOCRATES). In Greek philosophy, except *Aristotle, care for and cure of the soul now became an important topic of reflection. From the Hellenistic period onwards *Eros is often pictured with a girl, and it is attractive to see here a model for *Apuleius' fairy-tale-like story *Amor and Psyche*. Unfortunately, Psyche's ancestry remains obscure.

Ptolemy (Ptolemaeus) (1). The name of all the Macedonian kings of Egypt.

Ptolemy I Soter ('Saviour') (367/6–282 BC), childhood friend and general of *Alexander (2) the Great. At Susa in 324 he married a daughter of the satrap Artabazus. After divorcing her, he married the Macedonian Eurydice (6 children) and later Berenēcē I, mother of the dynastic line. On Alexander's death (323) he hijacked the conqueror's corpse and, taking it to *Memphis, established himself as satrap. In the following year he took *Cyrene. In the complex struggles of Alexander's successors he was not at first very successful. In 295 however he recovered Cyprus, and from 291 he increasingly controlled the Aegean League of Islanders. Ptolemy took the title of King in 305; this served as the first year of his reign. Responsible for initiating a Greek-speaking administration in Egypt, he consulted Egyptians (*Manetho and others), exploiting their local expertise. The cult of Sarapis, in origin the Egyptian *Osiris-Apis, was probably developed under Soter as a unifying force. There are few papyri from his reign, but hieroglyphic inscriptions from the Delta (esp. the 'Satrap Stele') present him as a traditional pharaoh. Moving the capital from *Memphis to *Alexandria, he brought Egypt into the mainstream of the Hellenistic world.

Ptolemy I as historian Ptolemy I wrote a history of the reign of Alexander. Its title, length and its date of composition are unknown. Apart from a single citation in *Strabo, our knowledge of it is wholly due to *Arrian who selected it, along with *Aristobulus, as his principal source. The work was evidently comprehensive, covering the period from at least 335 BC to the death of Alexander, and it provided much 'factual' detail, including most of our information about the terminology and organization of the Macedonian army. Ptolemy emphasized his personal contribution to the campaign and tended to suppress or denigrate the achievements of his rivals, both important in an age when service under Alexander was a big political asset. There is also a tendency to eulogize Alexander (whose body he kept interred in state) and gloss over darker episodes like the 'conspiracy' of *Philotas. So the king appears as a paradigm of generalship, his conquests achieved at minimum cost and maximum profit, and Ptolemy continuously figures in the action. His account is contemporary and valuable; but it needs to be controlled by other evidence.

Ptolemy (2) (Claudius Ptolemaeus) wrote at *Alexandria, between AD 146 and c.170, definitive works in many of the mathematical sciences (see MATHEMATICS), including *astronomy and geography. Ptolemy's earliest work, the *Canobic Inscription*, is a list of astronomical

constants dedicated by him in 146/7. Most of these are identical with those of the *Almagest*, but a few were corrected in the latter, which must have been published c.150. This, entitled *Mathematical Systematic Treatise* (the name 'Almagest' derives from the Arabic form of 'the greatest in Greek'), is a complete textbook of astronomy in thirteen books. Starting from first principles and using carefully selected observations, Ptolemy develops the theories and tables necessary for describing and computing the positions of sun, moon, the five planets and the fixed stars. The mathematical basis is the traditional epicyclic/eccentric model. In logical order, Ptolemy treats: the features of the geocentric universe and trigonometric theory and practice (bk. 1); spherical astronomy as related to the observer's location on earth (2); solar theory (3); lunar theory, including parallax (4 and 5); eclipses (6); the fixed stars, including a catalogue of all important stars visible from Alexandria (7 and 8); the theory of the planets in longitude (9–11); planetary stations and retrogradations (12) and planetary latitudes (13). The *Almagest* is a masterpiece of clear and orderly exposition, which became canonical, dominating astronomical theory for 1,300 years, in Byzantium, the Islamic world, and later medieval Europe. Its dominance caused the disappearance of all earlier works on similar topics, notably those of *Hipparchus (2) (to which Ptolemy often refers). Hence Ptolemy has been erroneously considered a mere compiler of the work of his predecessors. He should rather be regarded as a reformer, who established Greek astronomy on a valid (i.e. geometrically rigorous) basis, replacing in one sweep the confusion of models and methods which characterized practical astronomy after Hipparchus. He was an innovator in other ways, notably in introducing the 'equant' for the planets to produce remarkable agreement of theory with observation.

2. Other astronomical works are (a) *Planetary Hypotheses*, in two books, a résumé of the results of the *Almagest* and a description of the 'physical' models for use in constructing a planetarium. At the end of bk. 1 he proposes the system of 'nested spheres', in which each body's 'sphere' is contiguous with the next: he is thus able to compute the absolute distances of all heavenly bodies out to the fixed stars (in the *Almagest* this is done only for sun and moon). This feature was generally accepted throughout the Middle Ages, and determined the usual view of the (small) size of the universe to Dante and beyond. (b) *Planispherium*, describing the stereographic

projection of the celestial sphere on to the plane of the equator (the theoretical basis of the astrolabe). (c) *Analemma*, an application of nomographic techniques to problems of spherical geometry encountered in the theory of sundials (see CLOCKS). (d) *Handy Tables*, a revised and enlarged version of the *Almagest* tables; Ptolemy's own rules for their use survive. (e) *Phases of Fixed Stars*, on the heliacal risings and settings of bright stars, and weather predictions therefrom. This was part of traditional Greek astronomy, but Ptolemy introduced rigorous trigonometrical methods.

3. The *Geography*, in eight books, is an attempt to map the known world (see MAPS). The bulk (bks. 2–7) consists of lists of places with longitude and latitude, with brief descriptions of important topographical features. Ptolemy was probably the first to employ systematically latitude and longitude as terrestrial co-ordinates. Bk. 1 includes instructions for drawing a world map, with two different projections (Ptolemy's chief contribution to scientific map-making). Bk. 8 describes the breakdown of the world map into 26 individual maps of smaller areas. The maps accompanying the existing manuscripts are descended from a Byzantine archetype; whether Ptolemy himself 'published' maps to accompany the text is disputed. The work is certainly intended to enable the reader to draw his own maps. Given the nature of its sources (mainly travellers' *itineraries), the factual content of the *Geography* is inevitably inaccurate. The main systematic error, the excessive elongation of the *Mediterranean in the east–west direction, was due to one of the few astronomical data used, the lunar eclipse of 20 September 331 BC observed simultaneously at *Carthage and Arbela: the faulty report from Arbela led Ptolemy to assume a time difference of three (instead of two) hours between the two places, leading to a 50 per cent error in longitude. Although the general outlines of areas within the Roman empire and immediately adjacent are moderately accurate, there are numerous individual distortions, and beyond those areas the map becomes almost unrecognizable. A notorious error is a southern land-mass connecting Africa to China (making the Indian Ocean into a lake). Nevertheless, the *Geography* was a remarkable achievement for its time, and became the standard work on the subject (revised innumerable times) until the 16th cent. See GEOGRAPHY.

4. Other surviving works. (a) *Astrological Influences* or *Tetrabiblos* (from its four books) was the astrological complement to the *Almagest*, and

although not as dominant, was influential as an attempt to provide a 'scientific' basis for astrological practice (see ASTROLOGY). (b) *Optics*, in five books. Bk. 1 dealt with the theory of vision (using the doctrine of 'visual rays'); bk. 2 deals with the role of light and colour in vision, bks. 3 and 4 with the theory of reflection in plane and spherical mirrors, bk. 5 with refraction. This contains remarkable experiments, including some to determine the angles of refraction between various media (see PHYSICS). In comparison with the earlier optical work of *Euclid, Ptolemy's treatise is greatly advanced in mathematical refinement and the representation of physical and physiological reality, but it is difficult to estimate its originality. (c) *Harmonics*. Ptolemy criticizes the Pythagoreans for neglecting perceptual evidence: the credentials of rational theories of attunement must ultimately be assessed by ear. He pursues this approach with meticulous attention to mathematical detail, to the minutiae of experimental procedures, and to the design and use of the special instruments they demand.

pūblicānī Since the Roman republic had only a rudimentary 'civil service' (see *apparitores) and primitive budgeting methods, the collection of public revenue, except for the *tributum, was sold as a public contract to the highest bidder, who reimbursed himself with what profit he could, at the tax rate set by the state. In addition, there were contracts for public works, supplies and services (*ultrō tribūta*, 'outward payments'). The purchasers of these contracts provided the logistic background to the Roman victories in the *Punic Wars and in the eastern wars of the 2nd cent. BC, and managed the building of the Roman *roads. Roman expansion also expanded their activities; thus the traditional contracts for the exploitation of *mines were extended to the vastly profitable Spanish mines, and the profits of victory also financed a boom in public construction. Tax collection expanded correspondingly, as more harbours and toll stations came under Roman control and much conquered land became *ager publicus. In Italy there seems to have been a basic shift in sources of revenue between 179 and 167, with indirect taxes (esp. *portōria*, 'harbour dues') collected by *publicani* taking the place of *tributum*. The increase in their opportunities led to some conflicts with the senate and the *censors, in which the latter always prevailed. See *Porcius Cato (1).

In *Sicily the main tax was collected according to the law of *Hieron (2) II, which protected the population against serious abuse. In Spain, a *stipendium*, originally to pay for the Roman troops, was collected by the quaestors. We do not know how the taxes were collected in the provinces acquired in 146 and originally in Asia, but in 123 Gaius *Sempronius Gracchus changed history by providing that the tithe of Asia was to be sold in Rome by the censors every five years. The sums involved were spectacular: the companies had to become much larger and more complex in organization. Henceforth taxes far surpassed *ultro tributa* as sources of profit, esp. when *Pompey extended the Asian system to the provinces he organized. The richest of the *publicani* gained a dominant role in the *extortion court and other *quaestiones and in the *equestrian order. They became the most powerful pressure group in Rome, and they dominated finance in the provinces and allied states.

The companies, by special legislation, possessed privileges unknown in normal Roman company law. They consisted of *socii* (partners), who put up the capital and were governed by one or more *magistri*. Provincial offices were run by a *prō magistrō* (who might be an equestrian) and might have large staffs, including hundreds of slaves and freedmen. By the late republic they acted as bankers to the state (avoiding the shipment of large sums in coin) and their messengers (*tabellarii*) would transport mail for officials and important private persons.

Complaints about their abuses were frequent. Proconsuls found it more profitable to co-operate with them in exploitation than to protect the provincials. The fate of *Rutilius Rufus and *Licinius Lucullus shows the risks of opposing them; but these cases were exceptional and partly due to personal character. Cicero showed that tactful and honest governors could gain their co-operation in relieving provincials of unbearable burdens in return for secure profits. Extortion by senatorial commanders and their staffs seems to have far surpassed any extortion by *publicani*. In the late republic there was a market for unregistered shares in the companies in Rome, enabling senators (e.g. *Caesar and *Licinius Crassus), who were not allowed to be *socii*, to share in the profits of the companies and no doubt to be influential in running them. The largest companies now tended to form a cartel: thus the main company for *Bithynia consisted of all the other companies.

The Civil Wars brought the companies huge losses, as their provincial treasuries were appropriated by opposing commanders. They never recovered their wealth and power. Caesar somewhat restricted their activities by depriving them of the Asian title. Under the empire, tribute came to be collected by quaestors and *procurators, though *publicani* might be used at the local level. See FINANCE, ROMAN.

Publilius Syrus was brought to Rome as a slave in the 1st cent. BC. Acc. to *Macrobius, he was freed for his wit and educated by his master. He composed and performed his own *mimes throughout Italy. Invited by *Caesar to perform at the games of 46 (see LUDI) he challenged other mime-writers to improvise on a given scenario and was declared victor by Caesar over his chief rival. It became a commonplace that his aphorisms expressed moral teaching better than serious dramatists, and fourteen of them are quoted by *Gellius.

In the 1st cent. AD maxims uttered by various characters in the mimes were selected and alphabetically arranged as proverbial wisdom for schoolboys to copy or memorize. These formed a fixed syllabus with e.g. the distichs of *Porcius Cato (1), so that in the 4th cent. *Jerome learned in class a line which he quotes twice. It is hard to distinguish original Publilian *sententiae* (see SENTENTIA) from accretions.

One would not expect a common ethical standard among maxims spoken by different characters in a mime. Some contradict others, as proverbs often do. Although many advocate selfish pragmatism, their prevailing terseness of expression gives them an undeniable attraction.

Punic Wars (264–146 BC) or wars between Rome and *Carthage ('Carthaginians'=Lat. 'Poeni' = 'Phoenicians'). Down to 264, Carthage's relations with Rome and the Italian maritime peoples had been friendly. However, when Rome became the ruler of *Magna Graecia, and esp. of Rhegium, closely associated with *Messana, it was virtually inevitable that she would be drawn into the centuries-old conflict between the Greeks and Carthage for the control of Sicily.

The First Punic War (264–241) The war arose from an 'incident' that was allowed to escalate. Rome offered her protection to the *Mamertines, in order to prevent Messana from falling into the hands of either Carthage or *Hieron (2) II of Syracuse. Hieron and Carthage joined forces against Messana, probably expecting that the Carthaginian navy could prevent the Romans from landing in Sicily, and that a serious collision could be avoided. The consul Claudius Caudex, sent to relieve Messana, attempted to negotiate and then got his army across the straits on allied ships and raised the siege. His successor, Valerius Maximus Messalla, besieged Syracuse, forcing Hieron to accept generous terms, which left him, as the ally of Rome, in possession of much of his kingdom. This alliance, and the secession of some of her allies, alarmed Carthage for the security of her province, and in 262 she sent strong forces into Sicily. The Romans besieged *Acragas, Carthage's ally, defeated the Carthaginians in the field and sacked Acragas with a brutality that alienated many Sicilian communities. Inconclusive land-fighting and Carthaginian naval activity in 261 convinced the Romans that they must gain the command of the sea; and in the spring of 260 they built a fleet of 100 quinqueremes (larger and heavier than triremes) and fitted them with the *corvus*, a rotatable boarding-bridge; and with these *Duilius won the battle of Mylae. Neither side made much progress during the next three years; but in 256 the Romans, after defeating the enemy in a huge sea-battle off Ecnomus, put the consul Regulus Atilius ashore with his army at Clupea. Regulus defeated the Carthaginians and occupied Tunis, but the unreasonableness of his demands led to the breakdown of peace negotiations, and in 255 his army was almost annihilated by a mercenary force under a Spartan mercenary, Xanthippus, and he himself was captured. Indecisive naval operations ensued. Storms all but destroyed two Roman fleets. The Carthaginians' main effort was directed to the restoration of their dominion over the Libyans and Numidians (shaken by Regulus' invasion); but in 251 they reinforced their army in Sicily; however, the Romans enjoyed some military success, capturing Eryx. Neither side had the resources to mount a major offensive in Sicily; but in 247 the Carthaginians replaced a successful admiral by *Hamilcar Barca, who, after raiding the Italian coast, established himself near Panormus and waged guerrilla war, diversified with raids on Italy, until 244, when he recaptured Eryx and continued his guerrilla operations from there. In 243, the Romans, having been given a breathing-space from costly naval operations, raised another fleet (by contributions from the rich), with which Lutatius Catulus besieged Drepanum in 242, and in 241 defeated a Carthaginian relief fleet near the Aegātēs Isles. Carthage, financially exhausted, instructed Hamilcar to make peace. The Carthaginians evacuated Sicily—which (except for Hieron's kingdom) became Rome's first overseas province (see PROVINCIA)—and the adjacent

islands and undertook to pay an indemnity of 3,200 talents over a period of ten years. From 241 to 237 Carthage was involved in the Truceless (or Libyan) War, against its mutinous (because unpaid) mercenaries, supported by most of the Libyans and even by some cities, including Tunis and *Utica. The war was successfully concluded by the uneasy co-operation of Hamilcar and Hanno, the recent conqueror of Libya. Rome, alarmed by Carthage's recovery, exploited a revolt of the Sardinians to seize the island, so depriving Carthage of its principal granary and inducing a deep distrust of Rome in the minds of the rulers of Carthage. To compensate for the loss of Sardinia, to secure its supply of silver, and to provide a standing army for the defence of its empire, Carthage now decided to extend its control in Spain (where she had long had a foothold), entrusting this to Hamilcar, and after his death (229) to his son-in-law Hasdrubal. Mainly by diplomacy Hasdrubal advanced Carthage's suzerainty towards the river Ebro, which, in 226, he gave the Romans a formal undertaking not to cross, so alleviating their fears on the eve of the Celtic invasion of Italy. In 221 *Hannibal succeeded to his family's *satrapal position, and made conquests in cis-Ebro Spain on the eastern coast and inland. Seeing Saguntum, a Roman ally 'for many years', as a threat to Carthage's hold on Spain, Hannibal took the city (219), with the approval of Carthage, thus, from personal as well as imperial motives, provoking the Second Punic War.

The Second Punic War (218–201) For details of Hannibal's Italian campaign, see HANNIBAL. His crushing victory at *Cannae (216) led to the defection of most of southern Italy, apart from the Latin colonies; but this meant that Hannibal, obliged to protect his new allies (*Capua was to be the leader of a new Italian Confederation), was himself put on the defensive; and with Rome's adoption of the Fabian policy 'always to fight him where he is not', the initiative passed to her: see FABIUS MAXIMUS VERRUCOSUS, Hannibal remained invincible in the field, but he was unable either to widen effectively the area of revolt (despite the destruction of a Roman army in Gaul (216), the defections of *Syracuse (214) and *Tarentum (212), and unrest in Etruria) or to prevent the reconquest of rebel areas: a process which resulted in Hannibal's being confined, by the end of 211, to Lucania and Bruttium, and in 207, to Bruttium. Roman control of the sea, a crucial factor in the war (see SEA POWER), meant that few supplies or reinforcements could reach Hannibal from Carthage. In 215, the Carthaginians had diverted 13,500 men, with *elephants and ships, intended for Hannibal to Spain, and sent almost as many to Sardinia, in a disastrous attempt to recover the island. In 213 they sent 28,000 men, with elephants, to Sicily, but they failed to prevent *Claudius Marcellus (1) from taking Syracuse in 211, and Sicily was pacified in 210. In Spain, where Hannibal's brother Hasdrubal had been left in command, the brothers Publius Cornelius Scipio and Gnaeus Cornelius Scipio Calvus won a crushing victory just south of the Ebro in 216. They recovered Saguntum in 212; but in 211 they were both killed, with more than half their men, in the Tader valley. However, Publius *Cornelius Scipio Africanus (his *cognōmen*, 'Africanus' (see NAMES, PERSONAL, ROMAN), was actually acquired later), son of Publius Cornelius Scipio, above, was sent to Spain in 210 as proconsul. He captured *Carthago Nova in 209, after a forced march from the Ebro, and won over many Spanish tribes. In 208 he defeated Hasdrubal at Baecula. Hasdrubal escaped with a part of his forces to Italy, was joined by some Gauls, but in 207, while attempting to join forces with Hannibal, was defeated and killed at the Metaurus in Umbria. This disaster ended any hopes that Hannibal might still have entertained of winning the war. Scipio completed the defeat of the Carthaginians in Spain 206 and won over the Numidian princes Syphax (who later returned to his Carthaginian allegiance) and *Masinissa. In 204 Scipio (consul 205) crossed from Sicily to Africa but failed to take Utica. In 203 he defeated the Carthaginians and Syphax in two major battles and occupied Tunis; he recognized Masinissa as king of the Numidians and concluded a short-lived treaty with Carthage. Hannibal—by now confined to an area about Croton—was recalled to defend Carthage; but in the autumn of 202 he was completely defeated by Scipio near *Zama, and advised the Carthaginians to sue for peace. Carthage was allowed to retain all the cities and territory in Africa that it had held before the war, surrendered its fleet and elephants and all prisoners of war and deserters, undertook not to rearm or to make war without Rome's permission, to restore to Masinissa everything that had belonged to him or his ancestors, and to pay 10,000 talents in indemnity over a period of 50 years.

Hannibal and Carthage provoked the war in order to reverse the decision of the first war and, by permanently weakening Rome, to make

Carthage's western Mediterranean empire safe. They lost because the Romans, with huge reserves of fine manpower, refused to admit defeat; central Italy and the colonies did not revolt; the Gauls, as a nation, did not join Hannibal (or Hasdrubal); Carthage failed to gain command of the sea and dissipated its war-effort (as it had done in the first war), and to no effect; the Scipios confined Hasdrubal to Spain until 208, and produced, in Scipio Africanus, a soldier whose genius was at least the equal of Hannibal's. The war had profound effects on Italian life, and for centuries thereafter no foreign power could endanger Rome's existence. Carthage's rapid recovery after the war made the Romans apprehensive, and reawoke their hatred and desire for vengeance; and although Carthage offered, and gave, them assistance in their wars, they regularly countenanced Masinissa's endless encroachments upon Carthage's possessions. A more truculent nationalism emerged in Carthage, which led to the reiterated demand of *Porcius Cato (1), 'that Carthage should be wiped out'.

The Third Punic War (149–146) In 150, having paid off the war indemnity, Carthage supplied Rome with a pretext for war by rearming, crossing its borders and fighting Masinissa with over 31,000 men; and although this army was largely destroyed, and Carthage humbled itself, the Romans declared the war on which the senate had already secretly decided, and sent a large expeditionary force to Libya, where Utica had already defected. After agreeing surrender unconditionally and to hand over hostages and all their war-material, the Carthaginians were ordered to abandon their city and resettle at least ten (Roman) miles from the sea. They decided to fight, and successfully repulsed all the attempts of incompetent Roman generals either to take Carthage or to starve it into surrender. Finally, in 147 *Cornelius Scipio Aemilianus walled off both the city and its harbour and in 146 took Carthage by storm. The population was sold and the city utterly destroyed; its territory became the Roman province of Africa (see AFRICA, ROMAN).

punishment, Greek and Roman practice
Acc. to *Cicero *Solon said that a community was held together by rewards and penalties, and the ascription seems plausible, in so far as Archaic Greek law-codes already show the city asserting its authority in laying down penalties both for universally recognized crimes and for

failure to perform the duties imposed by its statutes. Cicero himself argued that the instinct to take vengeance is nature's gift to man to ensure his own and his family's survival. Both in Greece and Rome criminal law emerged as an attempt to circumscribe and gradually replace private revenge. Just as prosecution often fell to injured persons or their relatives, so the treatment of the convicted man was often a matter for his victims, e.g. in early homicide law and in cases of physical injury and *theft. The religious aspects of punishment extend beyond offences against the gods themselves—e.g. at Athens and Rome in relation to blood-guilt (see POLLUTION).

In fixing penalties legislators were guided to some extent both by the severity of the offence and the intention of the wrongdoer. Another consideration was the *status of the convicted person. Punishment of slaves was harsher and more humiliating than that of free men (see SLAVERY). Two other factors are relevant: first, limited financial resources made heavy expenditure on punishment impossible in practice in most communities, even if it was thinkable; secondly, the high value attached to *citizenship made the removal (or diminution) of this status, i.e. *exile or loss of political rights, an effective form of punishment.

The supreme penalty, execution, had a two-way relationship to exile. One might escape execution by voluntary exile, whereupon the self-imposed penalty was aggravated by a ban on return (on pain of death) and confiscation of property. Alternatively one might be condemned to exile with loss of property with the threat of a full capital penalty for illegal return. A form of inflicting dishonour less severe than exile was the removal of some citizen-privileges (*atimia at Athens, *infamia at Rome), e.g. loss of the right to speak or vote in an assembly or of membership of the senate at Rome or in a Roman municipality.

Long-term imprisonment by the community is not usually found in Greek cities or under the Roman republic (see PRISON), but a similar effect might be achieved by selling delinquents into chattel-slavery or turning them into virtual slaves to the person they had offended (the fate of condemned thieves under the Roman republic). Under the Principate we find condemnation to the *mines, *quarries, public works, or gladiatorial schools (see GLADIATORS and below) in Italy and the provinces.

Flogging was normally thought appropriate only for the punishment of slaves under Athenian democracy. Whips were associated with tyrants; thus the *Thirty Tyrants had 300 whip-carriers. However, whips were used on free men elsewhere in the Greek world, notably at the games (*agones). At Rome, apart from being an element in the traditional form of execution (symbolized in the *fasces, where the rods surrounded the axe), flogging was apparently inflicted on citizens at Rome as reprisal for disobedience to magistrates until the lex Porcia; even after this it remained a feature of military discipline and was employed on non-Romans anywhere.

Financial penalties were both employed to recompense injured parties, as in the Roman law on *extortion, and as fines paid to the community, in some instances being deliberately made so large as to entail the financial ruin of the convicted person—an early example is the ruinous fine imposed on *Miltiades.

Punishments which seem to us barbarous and grotesque may not be primitive. The Roman penalty for *parricide—drowning in a sack with a dog, cock, ape, and viper—must have been devised after a distinction had been drawn between the killing of parents and grandparents and that of other relatives. Under the Principate criminals provided entertainment when they were condemned to fight as gladiators or beast-fighters in the arena, often being forced to act mythological characters in dramas of blood which culminated in real death.

Reprisal, recompense, and the assertion of civic authority are the main themes in the Greek and Roman practice of punishment. The last involved rewarding the good and punishing the bad, hence encouraging citizens to virtue and deterring them from vice. To this extent only was punishment related to moral reform. See next entry.

punishment, Greek theories about Punishment may be defined as 'suffering inflicted on an offender in return for the suffering he inflicted'. On this definition the first holder of a theory of punishment is the Homeric hero (see HOMER); for when he retaliates against an offender he can articulate his purposes: (1) to restore or enhance his own tīmē (wealth, status) by exacting recompense, preferably large, from the offender; (2) satisfaction of his affronted feelings, in the shape of pleasure at the sight of the offender's discomfiture occasioned by (1); (3) publicity for his own superior strength; (4) deterrence of the offender (and of others) for the future. In achieving these aims he causes the offender to suffer reciprocally, as the definition requires.

Implicitly or explicitly, these four purposes dominated in penal contexts in all Greek life and literature. The strongly vindictive demand from injured parties for recompense in *some* form, even if only satisfaction of feelings, generated among other things: (*a*) severe penalties (confiscation of property, heavy fines, exile, and death were commonplace); (*b*) surrogate punishees, i.e. third parties who were themselves innocent, but somehow linked to the offender; (*c*) a belief in supernatural surrogate punishers, gods and *Erinyes etc., to deal with offenders who escaped human justice; (*d*) a certain fascination, chiefly in imaginative literature, with crime-specific punishments, i.e. those that neatly fit the offence.

Penology became a topic of public debate in Athens only to the extent that prosecutors and defendants adduced a wide variety of excuses, palliations, and aggravations, calculated to persuade juries to waive, mitigate, or increase penalties. Juries had therefore to consider the validity of general arguments in particular circumstances. But they could decide exactly as they pleased; there was no professional judiciary to ensure principled uniformity in sentencing.

The only challenges to the orthodoxy of (1)–(4) came from certain intellectuals. Diodotus, an Athenian speaker in *Thucydides (2), deprecated extreme punishments; so did *Isocrates, who also discussed the social causes of crime and advocated prevention in preference to cure; and *Protagoras recommended ignoring the past and using the reform/deterrence of the offender as the sole determinant of penalty. *Plato argued similarly, but even more radically: crime is a *mistake*; recompense must invariably be paid, but it is not a penal matter; the punishment proper, which may take *any* form (even 'gifts' for the offender) likely to be effective, must be precisely calibrated to 'cure' his mental and moral 'disease'. Plato seems to take the medical terminology literally: the *soul is something curable physically. This uncompromisingly utilitarian policy he attempts to build into the elaborate penal code of his *Laws*.

*Aristotle discusses punishment in many passages, esp. in his *Art of Rhetoric* and *Nicomachean Ethics*, in connection with such topics as justice, equity, and the emotions. Post-Aristotelian sources are scattered, but note *Seneca the Younger, *On Anger*; and *Plutarch, *On God's Slowness to Punish*. See PUNISHMENT, GREEK AND ROMAN PRACTICE; RECIPROCITY (GREECE); SIN; THEODICY.

purification, Greek The concept of 'purification', like that of *pollution, was applied in very diverse ways in Greek *ritual. Many purifications were performed not in response to specific pollutions, but as preparation for particular events or actions or as required by the calendar. The Athenian assembly (see EKKLESIA) was purified at the start of meetings (by carrying the body of a sacrificed piglet around it), and temples could be treated similarly; individuals purified themselves by washing before approaching the gods. Most drastically, some whole cities of ancient Ionia, not excluding Athens, were purified annually by the expulsion of human scapegoats (see PHARMAKOS) at the *Thargelia.

There were many different techniques of purification: by washing or sprinkling, by fumigation (esp. with sulphur), by 'rubbing off' with mud or bran; all admitted various degrees of symbolic elaboration (the use of sea-water, or water from a special *spring). *Sacrifice too, or modified forms of it, often functioned as a purification: the dead victim might be carried around the place to be purified (see above), while the blood supposedly sticking to a killer was 'washed off with blood' by pouring that of the animal victim over his hands. Where actual pollutions are concerned, however, these issues of technique and symbolism are less important than the question of the circumstances in which purification was permitted and deemed effective. Even minor and inescapable pollutions such as contact with a death could not be removed immediately: the major pollution of blood-guilt required a period of exile before the killer could (if at all) be readmitted to the community after purification. Thus the most powerful of all purifying agents was in a sense time.

Purification was given heightened significance by the other-worldly movements in Greek thought, *Orphism and Pythagoreanism (see PYTHAGORAS). For them, purification signified an escape not just from particular pollutions but from man's fallen condition, his imprisonment in the body. This was a new metaphorical extension of the traditional idea; but adherents of these movements also underwent purifications and observed abstinences of a more conventional type (see FASTING), so that the new 'purification' had a considerable psychological continuity with the old.

The god who presided over purification from blood-guilt was *Zeus Katharsios, 'Of purification'; this role derived from his general concern for the reintegration into society of displaced persons (cp. Zeus 'Of suppliants' and 'Of

strangers'). *Apollo too could be seen as a 'puri-
fier of men's houses' because his oracle at Delphi (see DELPHIC ORACLE) regularly gave advice
on such matters.

purification, Roman See LUSTRATION.

purple Of the two main kinds of purple-yield-
ing shellfish described by *Pliny the Elder, *purpura* and *pelagia* correspond to the Linnaean
murex, and *mūrex* and *būcinum* to the smaller
and less precious *purpura haemostoma*. In antiquity the purple of *Tyre always retained its
primacy, but purple dyeing was practised also in
the Greek cities of Asia, the Greek mainland and
islands, southern Italy, and North Africa. After
being gathered or caught in baskets and killed
suddenly to preserve the secretion, the molluscs
were either opened (esp. the larger) or crushed.
The mass was then left in salt for three days,
extracted with water, and slowly inspissated to
one-sixteenth of its original volume. Impurities
were removed during this process, and the liquid was then tested with flocks of wool until
the colour was right. Many shades within the
violet–scarlet range, and even a bluish green,
could be obtained by mixing the dyes from different species and by intercepting the photo-
chemical reaction which gives the secretion its
colour. In Rome the use of purple garments was
always a mark of rank (see REX; TOGA). See DYE-
ING; TEXTILE PRODUCTION.

Puteolī, 12 km. (7$\frac{1}{2}$ mi.) north of Neapolis.
The earliest settlement was a Greek foundation,
Dicaearchia (c.521 BC). Its early relations with
Rome are uncertain. It was an important harbour in the war against *Hannibal, and became a
Roman colony in 194 (see COLONIZATION,
ROMAN). In the 2nd cent., Puteoli's commercial
importance grew, thanks to the development of
trade between Italy and the east. It handled a
large proportion of trade with the eastern empire and corn imports for Rome. It was also a
fashionable resort, and many of the Roman élite
owned *villas there. Greek and Latin *epigraphy
attests a flourishing civic life. See OSTIA; PORTUS.

Pydna The battle of Pydna takes its name from
the town on the NE coast of Greece, where the
Romans under *Aemilius Paullus (2) ended the
Macedonian monarchy by defeating Perseus
(168 BC). The main Macedonian army deployed
faster than the Roman, and at first the *phalanx
carried all before it. But it became disrupted,
and the Romans were able to infiltrate its formation by dividing into *maniples. At the same

time, Roman cavalry and *elephants defeated
the Macedonian left wing, thus enveloping the
phalanx's left flank, and the same thing probably happened on the Macedonian right. Some
20,000 Macedonians were killed, and about
11,000 taken prisoner, only the cavalry escaping
in any numbers.

Pylos was the classical name of sites in *Elis,
Triphylia (south of Elis), and *Messenia, all of
which claimed to be the Pylos which is *Nestor's
capital in the Homeric poems; but many textual
references to 'sandy Pylos' better suit a region,
probably that around Navarino Bay. Messenian
Pylos was the rocky peninsula north of Navarino Bay and joined by a sand spit to the mainland. Its most famous moment occurred during
the *Peloponnesian War, in 425, when it was
occupied by an Athenian force. This occupation
led in turn to the capture of a force of Spartans
on the adjacent island of Sphacteria. This episode was fully described by *Thucydides (2). See
DEMOSTHENES (1); also CLEON; BRASIDAS. Anxiety
about the return of the prisoners taken 'on the
island', i.e. Sphacteria, was one main Spartan
motive for accepting peace in 421, the so-called
Peace of *Nicias. The Athenians held Pylos with
a garrison of Messenians until 409.

Pyrrhon of Elis (c.365–275 BC), the founder of
Greek Scepticism (see SCEPTICS). He wrote nothing, and what we know of him goes back to the
writings of his main pupil, Timon. Later accounts of Pyrrhon's philosophy tend to be heavily influenced by the philosophers of the
Pyrrhonist revival after *Aenesidemus. Acc. to a
passage attributed to Timon, Pyrrhon claimed
that nothing can be found out about the nature
of things because neither our sense-impressions
nor our opinions are true or false. Hence we
should be without opinions or inclinations, saying about all things that they no more are than
they are not. This attitude will result first in
non-assertion, then in tranquillity (*ataraxia*).
The claim that things cannot be known is stated
without reservations, and the emphasis lies on
the alleged result of suspending judgement—
tranquillity. This accords well with the rest of
our evidence from Timon, who satirized all
other philosophers by contrasting their empty
talk and fruitless worries with the supreme
calm and serenity of Pyrrhon.

Pyrrhus (1) See NEOPTOLEMUS.

Pyrrhus (2) of Epirus (319–272 BC), most famous of the Molossian kings, chief architect of a

large, powerful, and Hellenized Epirote state (see HELLENISM), and builder of the great theatre at *Dodona. Early in his reign he annexed southern *Illyria. He tried to emancipate Epirus from Macedon.

Appealed to by the people of *Tarentum, Pyrrhus went to assist them in their Hellenic struggle against Rome. With a force of 25,000 infantry, 3,000 horse, and 20 elephants he defeated the Romans at Heraclea (280), though not without loss, and won the support of the *Samnites, Lucanians, Bruttians, and Greek cities of the south. He marched towards Rome, but prolonged negotiations failed to secure peace. In 279 he defeated the Romans again, at Ausculum, but again with heavy losses. Late in the same year he received an appeal from *Syracuse and in 278 sailed to Sicily, where he fought the Carthaginians, then allies of Rome, and *Mamertines. In 276 he abandoned the campaign and returned to Italy, whither he was urgently summoned by his allies in the south. After more losses (including eight elephants and his camp) in battle with the Romans at Malventum (renamed thereafter Beneventum) in 275, he returned to Epirus with less than a third of his original force. A garrison was left behind at Tarentum, perhaps signifying future intent, but the Italian manpower at Rome's disposal had triumphed decisively.

Pythagoras, Pythagoreanism

1. Pythagoras Pythagoras, one of the most mysterious and influential figures in Greek intellectual history, born in *Samos in the mid-6th cent. BC, migrated to Croton in Sicily c.530. There he founded the sect or society that bore his name, and that seems to have played an important role in the political life of *Magna Graecia for several generations. Pythagoras himself is said to have died as a refugee in Metapontum. Pythagorean political influence is attested well into the 4th cent., with *Archytas of Tarentum.

The name of Pythagoras is connected with two parallel traditions, one religious and one scientific. He is said to have introduced the doctrine of *transmigration of souls into Greece, and his religious influence is reflected in the cult organization of the Pythagorean society, with periods of initiation, secret doctrines and passwords, special dietary restrictions (see ANIMALS, ATTITUDES TO), and burial rites. Pythagoras seems to have become a legendary figure in his own lifetime. His supernatural status was confirmed by a golden thigh, the gift of bilocation, and the capacity to recall his previous incarnations. Classical authors imagine him studying in Egypt; in the later tradition he gains universal wisdom by travels in the east. Pythagoras becomes the pattern of the 'divine man': at once a sage, a seer, a teacher, and a benefactor of the human race.

The scientific tradition ascribes to Pythagoras a number of important discoveries, including the famous geometric theorem that bears his name. Even more significant for Pythagorean thought is the discovery of the musical consonances: the ratios 2 : 1, 3 : 2, and 4 : 3 representing the length of strings corresponding to the octave and the basic harmonies (the fifth and the fourth). These ratios are displayed in the *tetractys*, an equilateral triangle composed of 10 dots; the Pythagoreans swear an oath by Pythagoras as author of the *tetractys*. The same ratios are presumably reflected in the music of the spheres, which Pythagoras alone was said to hear.

In the absence of written records before *Philolaus in the late 5th cent., it is impossible to tell how much of the Pythagorean tradition in *mathematics, *music, and *astronomy can be traced back to the founder and his early followers. The conception of Pythagorean philosophy preserved in later antiquity was, it seems, the creation of *Plato and his school, and the only reliable pre-Platonic account of Pythagorean thought is the system of Philolaus. *Aristotle reports that for the Pythagoreans all things are numbers or imitate numbers. In Philolaus we read that it is by number and proportion that the world becomes organized and knowable. The basic principles are the Unlimited and the Limiting. The generation of the numbers, beginning with One in the centre, seems to coincide with the structuring of the cosmos. There must be enough cosmic bodies to correspond to the perfect number 10; the earth is a kind of heavenly body, revolving around an invisible central fire. This fact permitted Copernicus to name 'Philolaus the Pythagorean' as one of his predecessors.

Plato was deeply influenced by the Pythagorean tradition in his judgement myths, in his conception of the soul as transcending the body, and in the mathematical interpretation of nature. *Phaedo* and *Timaeus*, respectively, became the classical formulations for the religious and cosmological aspects of the Pythagorean world view. In *Philebus* begins the transformation of Pythagoras into the archetype of philosophy. This view is developed by *Speusippus, who replaces Plato's Forms by Pythagorean numbers. Hence *Theophrastus can assign to Pythagoras the late Platonic 'unwritten doctrines' of the One and the Infinite Dyad, and these two principles appear in all later versions of Pythagorean philosophy.

In the 1st cent. BC, Nigidius Figulus revived the Pythagorean tradition in Rome, while in *Alexandria the Platonist Eudorus attributed to the Pythagoreans a supreme One, above the two older principles of One and Dyad. This monistic Platonism was developed by the Neopythagoreans. Their innovations were absorbed into the great Neoplatonic synthesis of *Plotinus (see NEOPLATONISM), and thereafter no distinction can be drawn between Pythagoreans and Neoplatonists. *Porphyry and *Iamblichus both wrote lives of Pythagoras in which he is represented as the source of Platonic philosophy.

2. Pythagoreanism (Religious Aspects) Pythagoreanism is the philosophical and religious movement allegedly derived from the teachings of Pythagoras. Reliable tradition on the early form of Pythagoreanism, coming chiefly from *Aristotle and his school, presents Pythagoras and his followers as a religious and political association in southern Italy (chiefly Croton), where they gained considerable influence, until their power was broken in a catastrophe c. 450. From then on, Pythagoreanism survived in two distinct forms, a scientific, philosophical form (the so-called *mathēmaticī*), which in the 4th cent. manifested itself in the thinking of *Philolaus and *Archytas of Tarentum and the Pythagoreans whom Plato knew and followed, and a religious, sectarian form (*acūsmaticī*), those following certain oral teachings (*akousmata*), which manifested itself in the migrant Pythagoristai of Middle Comedy (see COMEDY (GREEK), MIDDLE). Scientific Pythagoreanism is a reform of its earlier, religious way ascribed to Hippasus of Metapontum c.450.

The doctrines of the *acusmatici* laid down rules for a distinctive lifestyle, the 'Pythagorean life'. The originally oral *akousmata* contained unrelated and often strange answers to the questions 'What exists?', 'What is the best thing?', 'What should one do?'. Prominent among the rules of life is a complicated (and in our sources not consistent) vegetarianism, based on the doctrine of transmigration and already ascribed to Pythagoras himself during his lifetime; total

vegetarianism excludes participation in sacrifice and marginalizes those who profess it, at the same time binding them all the more tightly together in their own sect. Transmigration and, more generally, an interest in the afterlife connects Pythagoreanism with *Orphism; Plato associates vegetarianism with the Orphic lifestyle, and authors from c.400 BC onwards name Pythagoreans as authors of certain Orphic texts.

See ANIMALS, ATTITUDES TO; ORPHIC LITERATURE.

Pythĕas, Greek navigator of *Massalia, author of a lost work 'About the Ocean', object of ancient distrust. From *Strabo, *Diodorus (2), and *Pliny the Elder mostly, we learn that, sailing (c.310–306 BC) from Gades past Cape Ortegal, the Loire, NW France, and Uxisame (Ushant), he visited Belerium (Land's End) and the tin-depot at Ictis, circumnavigated *Britain, described its inhabitants and climate, reported an island Thūlē (Norway or Iceland), sailed perhaps to the Vistula, and reported an estuary (Frisian Bight?) and an island (Heligoland?) abounding in *amber. Pytheas calculated closely the latitude of Massalia and laid bases for cartographic parallels through northern France and Britain.

Pythia See DELPHIC ORACLE; WOMEN IN CULT.

Pythian Games Originally the Pythian festival at *Delphi took place every eight years, and there was a single contest, the singing of a hymn to *Apollo accompanied by the cithara (see MUSIC. After the First *Sacred War the festival was reorganized under the control of the *amphictiony, and further musical and athletic contests (see AGONES) were added. These games were next in importance to the *Olympic Games, and were held quadrennially in late August of the third year in each *Olympiad. The Pythiads were reckoned from 582 BC. The musical contests consisted in singing to the cithara, cithara-playing, and *aulos-playing, and the athletic contests resembled those at Olympia. The horse races were always held below Delphi in the plain of Crisa. The stadium lies above the sanctuary under Mt. Parnassus, and the *gymnasium and *palaestra are near the temple of *Athena Pronaia. The prize was a crown of bay leaves cut in the vale of Tempēe.

Python (mythical) See APOLLO; SNAKES.

Quadrivium See EDUCATION, GREEK, 3.

quaestiōnēs Roman tribunals of inquiry into crimes, later standing courts. By the 2nd cent. BC some political crimes and instances of mass law-breaking with serious public implications came to be handed over to a *quaestio*, at this point an ad hoc commission under a magistrate, appointed by the senate or the people or both, which investigated cases laid before it without the need for formal prosecution. See e.g. the *Bacchanalia. Trials of stabbers (*sīcāriī*) and poisoners (*venēficī*) were sometimes subject to a *quaestio* under a praetor or his deputy before permanent courts were set up (*c.*100).

Meanwhile, a new form of *quaestio*, a standing court (*q. perpetua*), was introduced by Calpurnius Piso Frugi, tribune of the *plebs* (see TRIBUNI PLEBIS) 149, to deal with *extortion cases. Like ad hoc *quaestiones* it was under the presidency and control of a praetor, and the jurors or assessors were drawn from senators, but prosecutions were conducted by a civil procedure. This court was completely overhauled by Gaius *Sempronius Gracchus, who substituted a form of denunciation for the civil procedure, introduced a large non-senatorial jury with full responsibility for verdict and damages, made these damages penal by doubling the amount originally taken, rewarded successful prosecutors, and formulated elaborate regulations for the conduct of the court.

In the next 40 years, while ad hoc *quaestiones* continued to be set up for special offences, several *quaestiones perpetuae*, modelled on the extortion court, were created—apart from those dealing with stabbers and poisoners; they concerned *maiestas and *ambitus. The composition of the juries in the *quaestiones* was changed several times. In 70 Aurelius Cotta created three jury *albums, assigning one to senators, one to *equestrians, and one to *tribūnī aerāriī* (akin to). From these albums juries were chosen by lot (one-third from each) for individual trials, with prosecution and defence having a limited right of rejection. The size of juries varied from court to court.

There was no public prosecutor at Rome, nor were prosecutions initiated by the magistrates in charge of *quaestiones perpetuae* (as opposed to ad hoc *quaestiones*). Originally in extortion cases charges were brought by the wronged individual, a member of his close family, or his chosen representative. Later, as in other *quaestiones*, any private citizen could request authority from a presiding magistrate to prosecute before his court. If several men wished to bring the same accusation against a person, then the relevant magistrate held a special pre-trial hearing, in which a panel of jurors, apparently not on oath, decided who should be the accuser. The authorized prosecutor then formally denounced the defendant to the magistrate, who accepted the charge, interrogated the defendant and, unless the latter pleaded guilty, formally recorded the indictment and fixed the date of the hearing. At the end of the trial the jury gave its decision by majority vote (a tie acquitted). The presiding magistrate did not vote but pronounced judgement and sentence, against which under the republic there was no appeal. Under most late republican statutes the maximum penalty seems to have been exile. Senior magistrates and men absent on public business could not be prosecuted in a *quaestio*.

After 70, although numerous laws were passed about individual courts (especially the *quaestio de ambitu*, since electoral bribery proved uncontrollable), the system remained basically unchanged, although it gradually lost importance during the Principate. Augustus reorganized some of the courts and added one for *adultery. He clearly intended the system of *quaestiones* to continue, and in fact it remained in use during the early Principate and became completely obsolete only in the 3rd cent. However, thanks to the development of senatorial and imperial jurisdiction in major cases (which also made our sources lose interest in the *quaestiones*) and the jurisdiction of the city *prefect and, later, the praetorian *prefect over the lower classes, the *quaestiones* became unimportant.

quaestors Financial quaestors were at first appointed by the consuls, one by each; after 447 BC they were elected by the tribal assembly. Two were added when plebeians were admitted (421), to administer the *aerarium* in Rome (hence *urbānī*) under the senate's direction. Four more were instituted in 267, and stationed in various Italian towns, notably *Ostia (see FOOD SUPPLY). More were added as various provinces were organized, until *Sulla, finding nineteen needed for all these duties, added one for the *water supply and raised the total to 20.

The quaestorship was commonly held at the age of 27 to 30 (often—in the late republic normally—after a military tribunate and/or a minor civil magistracy). It was the lowest of the regular magistracies. By the late 2nd cent. BC, most ex-quaestors were enrolled in the Senate, but the size of the Senate did not permit the enrolment of all. Sulla, who doubled the size of the Senate, made quaestors' entry automatic. *Provinciae* of quaestors were normally allotted, but magistrates could choose a quaestor for personal reasons. Quaestors attached to magistrates or promagistrates abroad did not normally serve more than two years. In addition to managing the provincial treasury, they had judicial and military duties. When their superior left or was disabled, they were expected to assume command *pro praetore* (see PRO CONSULE, PRO PRAETORE). Quaestors were supposed to remain bound to their commanders in loyalty for life. But their accounts were prime evidence in *extortion trials, and some were tempted to apply to prosecute their own commanders, to advance their own careers. Their charges seem normally to have been rejected.

*Augustus and *Nero removed the quaestors from the *aerarium*; but under the empire the *princeps*, as well as each consul, had two quaestors; the *quaestōrēs Caesaris*, chosen by the emperor himself, were often patricians and always young men of distinction. The duties of the quaestors in Italy were gradually taken over by imperial officials, but in the public provinces quaestors retained some financial functions throughout the Principate.

quarries Stone was an important material in both the Greek and Roman periods, not only for building, but also for decoration, sculpture, and vases. The Greeks started to extract stone by quarrying from the 7th cent. BC. Blocks were isolated by trenches using a quarry hammer. Metal wedges were then used to split them from the parent rock. The natural cleaving planes of the stone were at all times exploited. Open quarrying was preferred on grounds of ease and expense. However, if fine material ran out above ground, underground workings were often opened, e.g. in the marble quarries of *Paros. The Romans continued to use the same quarrying methods, also adopting some Egyptian techniques—e.g. the use of wooden wedges. However, the major difference between Greek and Roman quarrying was the scale of exploitation. The building records from Athens and *Epidaurus show the piecemeal nature of Greek quarrying. Roman quarrying was carried out on a more modular basis. This can be seen esp. clearly with the exploitation of decorative stones. A system of accountancy was developed in some quarries from the middle of the 1st cent. AD. Inscriptions were carved on blocks indicating the area of extraction and the personnel involved. Often objects were roughed out in the quarry before their export. In the Classical Greek period quarries probably belonged to and were administered by the nearest town. In the Roman period there was much more diversity in ownership. Some marble and granite quarries were owned by the emperor and administered by his representatives. The Egyptian quarries came under the jurisdiction of the military. Quarrying was a skilled activity, but convicts and slaves could perform unskilled tasks. See CARRARA; MARBLE.

Quinctilius Vārus, Publius, of a patrician family that had been unimportant for centuries. He owed his career to the favour of *Augustus. He was consul 13 BC with the future emperor *Tiberius; like him, Varus was at the time the husband of a daughter of *Vipsanius Agrippa. Later he married Claudia Pulchra, the grand-niece of Augustus, and was able to acquire political influence. Varus became proconsul of Africa (see AFRICA, ROMAN), and then *legate of *Syria. When *Judaea revolted after the death of *Herod (1) the Great, he marched rapidly southwards and dealt firmly with the insurgents. Varus is next heard of as legate of the Rhine army in AD 9. When marching back with three legions from the summer-camp near the Weser, he was treacherously attacked in difficult country by Arminius, war-chief of the Cherusci, whom he had trusted. The Roman army was destroyed in the *Teutoburgian Forest, and Varus took his own life. The defeat had a profound effect on Augustus (the regime noticeably deteriorates in the last few years). Varus was made the scapegoat for the signal failure of Augustus' whole German policy. He is alleged to have been grossly extortionate in Syria, torpid and incompetent in his German command.

Quinctius Flāminīnus, Titus, b. *c.*229 BC, military tribune 208 under *Claudius Marcellus (1), then quaestor, probably at *Tarentum, where he held praetorian *imperium* for some years from 205. He was Decemvir for distributing land to *Cornelius Scipio Africanus' veterans 201. In 198, against some opposition but with the support of the veterans he had settled, he was elected consul and sent to take over the war against Philip V of Macedon with a new army and a new political approach. Meeting Philip late in 198, he demanded the evacuation of all of Greece, but apparently hinted to Philip that the senate might modify the terms. He told his friends in Rome to work for peace if he could not be continued in command and for war if he could complete it; he was prorogued (see PROROGATION), and the senate insisted on his terms. In spring 197, after gaining the alliance of most of Greece, he decisively defeated Philip by superior tactical skill at Cynoscephalae, in eastern Thessaly. He now granted Philip an armistice on the same terms, which the senate confirmed as peace terms. In a spectacular ceremony he announced the unrestricted freedom of the Greeks in Europe at the *Isthmia Games of 196 and persuaded a reluctant senate commission that this pledge had to be carried out if Greek confidence was to be retained against the *Seleucid Antiochus III, who was about to cross into Europe. He now initiated a diplomatic effort to keep Antiochus out of Europe and deprive him of the Greek cities in Asia Minor. The final settlement of Greece involved a difficult war against Nabis of Sparta. In 194 all Roman troops were withdrawn. Henceforth Flamininus was showered with honours (including divine honours) in Greece. He issued a commemorative gold coin with his portrait and left for Rome to celebrate an unparalleled three-day triumph. A bronze statue with a Greek inscription was erected to him in Rome by his Greek clients.

In 193 he was entrusted with secret negotiations with Antiochus' envoys; when they refused his offer of undisturbed possession of Asia in return for withdrawal from Europe, he proclaimed to the Greek world that Rome would liberate the Greeks of Asia from Antiochus. Sent to Greece to secure the loyalty of the Greeks and of Philip, he was partly successful. In 189 he was censor. In 183, sent to Asia on an embassy, he took it upon himself to demand the extradition of *Hannibal from Prusias I of *Bithynia. (Hannibal killed himself.) Flamininus died in 174.

A typical patrician noble, his was a world of personal ambition, Roman patriotism, family loyalty, and patron–client relationships. He was the first to develop a policy of turning the Greek world—cities, leagues, and kings—into clients of Rome and of himself, nominally free or allied, but subject to interference for Rome's advantage. The Greeks, whom he had liberated, he expected to follow his instructions even without a public mandate. Aware of Greek history and traditions, he attracted many Greeks by charm and tact, but aroused antagonism by unscrupulous trickery. Midway between arrogant imperialists and the genuine philhellenes of a later period, he laid the foundations of the uneasy acceptance of Roman hegemony by the Greek world. See also PHILHELLENISM.

quindecimvirī sacrīs faciundīs ('the Priesthood of Fifteen'), one of the four major colleges (see COLLEGIUM) of the Roman priesthood (see PRIESTS). The size of the college increased gradually, starting at two, reaching ten, fifteen, and finally sixteen (though the name remained *quindecimviri*) in the late republic. Like the other colleges, they lost the right to select their own members, but continued to be recruited by popular election from the noblest families. Their main functions throughout their history were to guard the Sibylline books (Greek oracles, consisting mostly of ritual texts, not prophetic utterances; see SIBYL); to consult the books when asked to do so by the senate, esp. in response to prodigies (see PORTENTS) or other disasters; and to provide the appropriate religious remedies derived from them. Their recommendations led to the importation, from the 5th cent. BC onwards and esp. in the 3rd, of Greek cults and rituals, over which they maintained some oversight. They reached particular prominence in the early empire as the authorities responsible for the *Secular Games, radically reconstructed from the republican series to suit the new regime's ideas.

Quintilian (Marcus Fabius Quintiliānus), Roman *advocate and famous *rhetor b. *c.* AD 35 in Spain. In Rome the young Quintilian attached himself to the orator Domitius

Afer. *Jerome says that he was the first rhetor to receive a salary from the imperial treasury, a practice instituted by *Vespasian. His school brought him unusual wealth for one of his profession. He taught for 20 years, numbering *Pliny the Younger among his pupils, and retired with unimpaired powers, perhaps in 88, to write his masterpiece. *Domitian made him tutor to his two great-nephews and heirs, the sons of *Flavius Clemens, through whom he gained the *ornamenta consularia. His wife died while not yet 19, leaving two little sons; the younger child died aged 5, the elder aged 9, and his overwhelming grief at these losses is touchingly expressed in the preface to bk. 6 of his Institutio. He himself probably died in the 90s.

His one extant work is Institūtiō Ōrātōria, 'Education of the Orator', written and probably published before Domitian's death in 96. It covers the education of an orator from babyhood to the peak of his career. Bk. 1 discusses the education of the child, a practical and humane section, and goes on to the technicalities of grammar. In Bk. 2 the boy enters the school of *rhetoric; there is a memorable chapter on the Good Schoolmaster, and Quintilian gives a balanced account of the virtues and vices of *declamation, before going on to a discussion of rhētorikē, drawing on the prolegomena to Greek rhetorical handbooks. Bk. 3 goes into much detail on status-lore (classification of types of issue), besides giving most of what Quintilian has to say on deliberative and display oratory. Bks. 4–6 take us through the parts of a speech, with appendices on various topics, including the arousal of emotions and of laughter. Invention thus dealt with, Quintilian proceeds to arrangement in Bk. 7, with much on the different kinds of issue, and to style in bks. 8 and 9, full of examples from prose and poetry. Bk. 10, the most accessible, shows how the student is to acquire a 'firm facility' by reading, writing, and imitating good exemplars. The first chapter ends with a famous critique of Greek and Latin writers; Quintilian's concern is to direct his readers towards predecessors who will be useful in the acquisition of oratorical techniques; hence what might otherwise seem strange judgements, brevities ('some prefer Propertius'), and omissions: despite this limitation, many of his dicta have become classics of ancient criticism. The Greek section is derivative; the Latin, in which Quintilian is often at pains to show how Roman writers can stand up to Greek counterparts, is more original. In Bk. 11 the traditional five parts of rhetoric are rounded off with discussion of memory and delivery; fascinating details of dress and *gesture are here preserved. There is also an important chapter on propriety. The final book shows the Complete Orator, vir bonus dīcendī perītus ('the good man skilled in speaking') in action, a man of the highest character and ideals, the consummation of all that is best in morals, education, and stylistic discernment; Quintilian's insistence on eloquence as a moral force is here at its most impressive.

Quintilian's style, never less than workmanlike, is not without its variety and power. But it was content that most concerned him. Deeply imbued in Ciceronian ideas, and reacting sharply against the trends of his own century, his book is a storehouse of humane scholarship and good sense.

See also EDUCATION, ROMAN; LITERARY CRITICISM IN ANTIQUITY; RHETORIC, LATIN.

Rabirius, Gāius, an *equestrian, later a back-bench senator, prominent in the action against *Appuleius Saturninus in 100 BC. After some earlier attacks on him by *populārēs* (see OPTI-MATES), he was accused of *perduellio in 63 and condemned by *duoviri* (one of them *Caesar) in a revival of an archaic process. The aim was no doubt, as Cicero says, to impugn the senate's emergency decree (see SENATUS CONSULTUM ULTIMUM), which Cicero foresaw using against *Catiline.

race Greeks and Romans were avid observers in art and text of departures among foreigners from their own somatic norms. But general in-feriority was not ascribed to any ethnic group in antiquity solely on the basis of body-type. Al-though *Aristotle realized that pigmentation was biologically transmitted, popular *anthro-pology understood cultural variation among hu-mankind in terms, not of nature (i.e. heredity), but nurture, and specifically environment (thus the Hippocratic *Air, Waters, Places*; see HIPPOCRA-TES), which shaped 'customs, appearance and colour', the sunny south generating blackness, the north 'glacial whiteness'; thus, as *Strabo implies, it was only their poor soil which de-barred the Arians of eastern Iran from the pleas-ures of civilization as did the fact that both Greeks and Romans defined themselves in op-position to a *cultural* construct, the *barbarian, which embraced mainly peoples of similarly pale skin-tone.

rape See GORTYN; HETEROSEXUALITY; HUBRIS; SABINES; SEXUALITY.

readers, reading See LITERACY; RECEPTION; and entries listed under WRITING.

reception Studies of reception-history are studies of the reading, interpretation, appropri-ation, use, and abuse of past texts over the centuries, reception-theory the theory under-pinning such studies. All interpretation is held to take place *within history*, and to be subject to the contingencies of its historical moment; there is no permanently 'correct' reading of a text. Reception-theory stresses the importance of the reader, within the triangle writer–text–reader, for the construction of meaning. So Hor-ace, as a man, as a body of texts, as an authority for different ways of living, has been diversely read in the west over the last 500 years, by scholars, poets, and 'men of letters', and our current images are shaped in response to that reception-history.

reciprocity (Greece) The idea that giving goods or rendering services imposed upon the recipient a moral obligation to respond per-vaded Greek thought from its earliest documen-ted history. Reciprocity was one of the central issues around which the moral existence of the Homeric hero revolved; see HOMER. In the poems, it is consistently implied and sometimes plainly stated that a *gift or service should be repaid with a counter-gift or a counter-service. This need not be forthcoming immediately, and may not be in the same category as the original gift or service. In the long run, however, allow-ing for slight temporary imbalances, the gifts and services exchanged must be equal in value and bestow equal benefits upon both parties. Gain, profit, and loss belonged in Homer to the world of traders, or to that of aristocrats en-gaged in plunder and spoliation. Reciprocity aimed at the forging of binding relationships (see FRIENDSHIP, GREEK; FRIENDSHIP, RITUAL-IZED; MARRIAGE LAW) between status equals, from which a long series of unspecified mutual acts of assistance could be expected to flow.

The assumption of equivalence did not extend into the realm of hostile encounters. Here there was no taking of an eye for an eye. Instead, the 'head for an eye' principle prevailed: upon being provoked, offended, or injured, the hero was expected to give almost free rein to his desire for revenge. Although the more peaceful alternative of material compensation for an insult or an injury was also available, over-retaliation was the norm.

A system of thought striving at equivalence of give and take faces a practical difficulty: how to assess the values of exchangeable items with any precision. It is presumably this difficulty that precipitated the invention, at some time after Homer's day, of *coinage.

The *polis* brought about a threefold change in the operation of reciprocity. First, it turned communal interest into a new standard of individual morality, reinterpreting the norms inherited from the past accordingly. When *Themistocles tells *Artaxerxes (1) I, 'I deserve to be repaid for the help I gave you', *Thucydides (2) makes it clear that the first half of this reciprocal action gave rise to the suspicion that its other half was to be Themistocles' recruitment to the Persian court. This, in turn, posed a threat to the community to which no Athenian could be indifferent. In Homer no moral norms which compete with the unhindered exercise of reciprocity are visible. Secondly, the *polis* promoted the ideal of communal altruism: the performance of actions beneficial to the community but potentially detrimental to the individual performing them (e.g. nursing the sick during a *plague or donating money as liturgies; see LITURGY, GREEK). The pre-*polis* equation dictating equivalence of give and take here breaks down in favour of individual sacrifices for the benefit of the community. Thirdly, the *polis* in general, and Athens in particular, endorsed the ideal of self-control as a means of checking hostile encounters. When provoked, offended, or injured, the citizen was expected to refrain from retaliating, relinquishing the right to inflict punishment to the civic authorities.

recitātiō, the public reading of a literary work by the author himself. The practice originated in Greece. At Rome we are told that *Asinius Pollio 'was the first of all Romans to recite what he had written before an invited audience'. *Horace's allusion to reading his poems to select groups of friends probably refers to something less formal.

Recitation became common under the empire. We hear of readings of tragedy, comedy, lyric, elegy and history; and *Pliny the Younger employed recitation as a stage between delivery of a speech and its publication. A well-to-do author would hire a hall and send out invitations; a poorer poet might make do with a public place. Hadrian's Athenaeum eventually provided a formal venue in Rome. The satirists make fun of the affectation of some performances. Recitation was a good way of publicizing one's work; but it could be a trial to the listeners, and an audience might show its contempt openly.

Pliny regarded recitation as a convenient way of soliciting criticism from educated friends. But there was a risk of insincere flattery; certainly applause and extravagant compliment were habitual. And recitation, like *declamation, could encourage showy and superficial writing.

records and record-keeping Greeks and Romans kept records on stone or bronze, lead, wooden tablets (waxed or whitened), papyrus (see BOOKS, GREEK AND ROMAN), *ostraka*, even precious metals. The different materials often bear certain associations and reflect ancient attitudes to records: e.g. bronze documents in Athens have religious associations, as do the bronze tablets of Roman laws. Stone inscriptions promised permanence and importance, publicly visible reminders of the decree (etc.) they record: in *Athens, matters of particular concern to the gods went up on stone (e.g. the *tribute lists). Athenian inscriptions (see EPIGRAPHY, GREEK) are read and referred to, but they may also serve as memorials of the decision they record, so that their destruction signifies the end of that transaction. Inscribed laws and decrees are often dedicated to gods unspecified. The relation of the inscribed records to those in the *archives is complex.

Rēgia, traditionally the home of King Numa (see REX), was situated at the east end of the *forum Romanum, between the *via Sacra and the precinct of *Vesta. Under the republic it was the seat of authority of the *pontifex maximus and contained his *archives; also shrines dedicated to *Mars (which held the sacred shields carried in procession by the *Salii). Archaic huts on the site were in the late 7th cent. replaced by a stone building around a courtyard, recalling the palaces of Etruria. Rebuilt several times, the structure took on its definitive plan at the end of the 6th cent.; this was then preserved throughout antiquity.

regiō (pl. *regiōnēs*), ancient term for the four major subdivisions of the extensive area covered by the republican city of Rome. *Augustus (probably in 7 BC) divided Rome into fourteen *regiōnēs* (as he divided *Italy into eleven) as a basis for allotting some administrative competences, such as the watch (*vigíles*). The building-blocks of the new *regiones* were the *vīcī* or local units of the city population.

Reg(i)nī/Regnensēs, a *civitas* of Roman *Britain created from the kingdom of *Cogidubnus. Impressive Romanization was achieved under Cogidubnus, as indicated by early villas (Fishbourne, Angmering) and the monuments of the capital, Noviomagus, but thereafter slowed down. Apart from the iron industry of the Weald, agriculture was the basis of the economy; in the 4th cent. the Bignor villa, well-known for its mosaics, grew large.

reincarnation See TRANSMIGRATION.

relativism See POLITICAL THEORY; PROTA-GORAS; SOPHISTS; XENOPHANES.

relegation was a Roman form of *exile. It might be either decreed by a magistrate (from the late republic) as a coercive measure or imposed as a penalty in a criminal trial. The criminal penalty had gradations ranging from temporary expulsion to *dēportātiō* (introduced by Tiberius). The latter was a perpetual banishment to a particular place (see ISLANDS), combined with confiscation of property and loss of citizenship. Banishment in all its forms was esp. a punishment for the higher classes. The lower classes were punished for similar crimes with forced labour or even death. See PUNISHMENT, GREEK AND ROMAN PRACTICE.

relics, the remains (complete or partial) or property of a dead person (real or legendary) which were imbued with the power to benefit their possessor. The veneration of relics in ancient Greece occurs within the context of *hero-cult. Relics fall into three main categories: first, those put into a certain place on purpose and later worshipped there; second, those brought from one place to another for worship at the latter; third, those found by chance, given an identity, and venerated.

Examples of the first group are (*a*) the tombs of *founders of cities, (*b*) the tombs of fallen warriors (e.g. the fallen at Plataea; see PLATAEA, BATTLE OF); in the second group belong (*a*) the bones of *Orestes brought to Sparta from Tegea, (*b*) those of *Theseus from Scyros to Athens.

religion, Athenian See ATTIC CULTS AND MYTHS.

religion, Celtic The three main sources for Celtic religion are Romano-Celtic epigraphy and iconography, the comments of classical authors, and insular Celtic tradition as represented by recorded Irish and Welsh literature. The iconography is largely derived from Graeco-Roman models and reflects the religious and cultural *syncretism which obtained throughout the Romano-Celtic areas. Highly organized Celtic oral learning was maintained by three orders of practitioners headed by the priestly fraternity of the Druids and apparently replicated throughout the Celtic world. While the Druids were eliminated by the Romans in Britain (see SUETO-NIUS PAULINUS) and displaced by Christianity in Ireland, the other two orders—the Gallic *vates* ('prophet', 'seer') and bards—survived in Ireland and Wales as privileged praise-poets.

*Caesar names five principal gods of the Gauls—not a complete catalogue—together with their functions; unfortunately, he follows the *interpretatio Romana* in referring to them by the names of their nearest Roman equivalents. There certainly were gods whose cults were either panCeltic or enjoyed wide currency among the Celtic peoples. Caesar's Mercurius is the god Lugus, personification of kingship and patron of the arts, whose name is commemorated in place-names throughout Europe and survives in medieval Irish and Welsh literature as Lugh and Lleu respectively, and whose festival of Lughnasa is still widely celebrated. His Minerva corresponds to the multifunctional goddess best known as the Irish Brigit and British Brigantia, patron deity of the Brigantes. The divine triad of Father, Mother, and Son is attested throughout the Celtic realm, with matching names. Most of the Celtic gods and many of their myths are recognizably *Indo-European. The functions of the Celtic gods are less clearly differentiated in the literary sources than in Caesar's succinct, schematic version. The goddesses are closely linked to land and locality: in general they promote fertility, and as a personification of a given territory, e.g. Ireland or one of its constituent kingdoms, the goddess participates in the sacred marriage which legitimizes each new king, a sacred union which may form part of the symbolism of the many divine couples of Romano-Celtic iconography. Some of the more popular and widespread elements of Celtic belief and ritual, such as pilgrimage, healing wells, and the rich mythology of the otherworld, were easily assimilated to the Christian repertoire. See CELTS.

religion, Egyptian See EGYPTIAN DEITIES.

religion, Etruscan Our information comes from archaeological evidence (reliefs, tomb paintings, statues, mirrors, altars, temples, funerary urns) and Etruscan inscriptions, esp. the 'liturgical' texts. Roman scholars produced at the end of the republic antiquarian treatises containing translations from Etruscan ritual books. The surviving fragments often show a curious mixture of Etruscan, Egyptian, and Chaldaean tenets. Of extant authors esp. important is *Cicero.

Etruscan religion, unlike Greek and Roman, was a revealed religion. The revelation was ascribed to the semi-divine seer Tages, and to the *nymph Vegoia. Their teaching, with later accretions, formed a code of religious practices, *Etrusca disciplīna*, i.e. *divination. It included books of three kinds, interpreted by diviners called 'haruspices'.

The haruspical books dealt with inspecting the entrails of victims, esp. the liver. A bronze model of a sheep's liver found near Placentia has its convex side divided into 40 sections (16 border, 24 inner), inscribed with the names of some 28 deities. The liver reflected the heavens. Its sections corresponded to the abodes of the gods in the sky, and thus the *haruspex* distinguishing the favourable and inimical part of the liver and paying attention to the slightest irregularities was able to establish which gods were angry, which favourable or neutral, and what the future held.

The fulgural books concerned the interpretation of thunder (bolt) and lightning (*fulgur*); the portentous meaning depended on the part of the sky from which they were coming. Nine gods threw thunderbolts, Jupiter (*Tin*) three kinds: foretelling and warning, frightening, and destroying. The first he sent alone, the second on the advice of his counsellors, and the third with the approval of 'the higher and veiled gods' = the Fates.

The ritual books contained 'prescriptions concerning the founding of cities, the consecration of altars and temples, the inviolability of ramparts, the laws relative to city gates, also how tribes, *curiae* (see CURIA (1)), and centuries are distributed, the army constituted and ordered, and other things of this nature concerning war and peace'.

We know many Etruscan deities, but their functions and relations often remain obscure. They mostly bear Etruscan names, but were early subjected to Greek influences. The highest was the thundergod *Tin/Tinia* (*Zeus/*Jupiter). *Voltumna* presided over the league of twelve

Etruscan cities. *Neth/Nethuns* (*Neptunus) was a water god. *Apollo, *Artemis, and *Heracles kept their Greek names.

Etruscan religious expertise made a lasting impression upon the Romans. Livy called the Etruscans 'a nation more than any other devoted to religious rites, all the more as it excelled in the art of practising them'.

religion, Greek The cult practices and pantheons of different Greek communities have enough in common to be seen as one system, and were generally understood as such by the Greeks. Boundaries between Greek and non-Greek religion were not sharp. *Herodotus characterizes 'Greekness' as having common temples and rituals (as well as common descent, language, and customs).

Origins We can trace some Greek deities to *Indo-European origins: *Zeus, like *Jupiter, has evolved from an original Sky Father, while the relation between the *Dioscuri and the Aśvins, the twin horsemen of the Vedas, is too close for coincidence. The indigenous religious forms of the land will have influenced Greek-speaking invaders. Many of the names of the major Greek gods are found already in Linear B (see MYCENAEAN LANGUAGE).

At various periods the religion of Greece came under substantial influence from the near east See MYTHOLOGY AND MYTH. Cult practice, however, does not seem to have been open to influence from the east much before the Geometric period (see POTTERY, GREEK, 2), when we begin to find large temples containing cult images. A final 'source' for later Greek religion is the poems of *Homer and *Hesiod, who, though they did not, as Herodotus claims, give the gods their cult titles and forms, certainly fixed in Greek consciousness a highly anthropomorphic and more or less consistent picture of divine society, a pattern extremely influential throughout antiquity despite its frequent incompatibility with ritual practices and local beliefs.

General Characteristics In Archaic Greece we find a strong link between religion and society. Greek religion is community-based, and since the *polis forms the most conspicuous of communities, it is *polis*-based. To the end of antiquity Greek religion was more of a public religion than a religion of the individual. Reciprocally, religious observances contributed to the structuring of society, as kinship groups (real or fictitious), local communities, or less obviously related groups of friends constructed their corporate identity around shared cults. In the Greek world priesthood was not a special status indicating membership of a special group or caste, but resembled a magistracy, even where, as often, a particular priesthood was hereditary. See PRIESTS.

Cult   The central *ritual in Greek cult is animal *sacrifice, featured in nearly all religious gatherings. Sacrifice relates both to human–divine relations (the celebration of and offering to a deity) and to a bonding of the human community (the shared sacrificial meal). The rite might be celebrated at most times, but on certain dates it was celebrated regularly at a particular sanctuary, usually in combination with a distinctive ritual complex; the word '*festival' is loosely but conveniently applied to such rites, whether *panhellenic like the *Olympic Games or intimate and secret like the *Arrephoria in Athens. Festivals, at least those of the more public type, articulated the calendar year and provided an opportunity for communal recreation. A more exclusive gathering was provided by *mystery cults, participation in which was felt to confer special benefits, often a better fate after death. Secrecy was a prominent characteristic of these rites. More basic methods of communicating with the divine included above all *prayer. *Votive offerings were very common private religious acts throughout the Greek world. Individuals would greet deities whose shrines they happened to be passing, and might also show piety by garlanding an image (see CROWNS AND WREATHS) or making a personal, unscheduled sacrifice—often bloodless, consisting of cakes or other vegetarian foods, or a pinch of incense. Sometimes they might experience a divine *epiphany in the form of a dream or a waking vision. Both individuals and *poleis* might make use of *prophecies of various kinds.

Gods and Other Cult Figures   The pantheon showed local variation, but presented a recognizable picture throughout the Greek world. Zeus, *Demeter, *Hermes, for instance, were names to which any Greek could respond. Again, the fundamental qualities or 'personality' of a deity remained to some extent consistent across different areas of Greece, *Hera of *Samos is the same goddess as Hera of *Argos, differently imagined in the two cities. The boundaries of divine individuality could be drawn in different ways depending on context and circumstance.

An anthropomorphic view of the gods encouraged the concept of a divine society, probably influenced by west Asian models. Prayer formulae locate deities in their sanctuaries or favourite place on earth, but myth creates a picture of a group of gods living more or less together in (albeit rather eccentric) family relationships. Since their home was traditionally *Olympus, the gods most prone to this presentation were the 'Olympians', by and large those who were most widely known and worshipped. Sometimes these deities were schematized into the 'Twelve Gods', a group whose composition varied slightly. (The twelve on the *Parthenon frieze are *Aphrodite, *Apollo, *Ares, *Artemis, *Athena, Demeter, *Dionysus, *Hephaestus, Hera, Hermes, *Poseidon, Zeus.) However, any local pantheon would also exhibit deities who were not so universally known or who, though the object of widespread cult, were scarcely perceived as personal mythical figures. There were also 'new', 'foreign' gods such as *Adonis or Sabazius who were difficult to place in the pre-existing framework of divine personalities; and there were deities like the Cabiri of Samothrace who had a panhellenic reputation; although their cult remained confined to a very few locations. More localized still were the 'minor' figures of cult such as *nymphs and heroes (see HERO-CULT), for here there was much less tendency to assimilate figures with others more universally known. Nymphs and heroes were generally thought of as residing in one specific place, and though in that place their powers were often considerable, they were usually perceived as ranking lower than gods.

Later Developments   The above summary is mainly based on evidence from before the 3rd cent. BC. Much of the above is applicable also to Greece in the Hellenistic and Roman periods; religious thought and practice were constantly evolving rather than undergoing sudden transformation. During the period of *Alexander (2) the Great and his successors, many distinctive local practices were losing their hold. *Pausanias (3), writing in the 2nd cent. AD, still found a vast diversity of cult in mainland Greece. On the other hand, the worship of certain 'new' deities was steadily gaining in popularity over the whole Greek world. A striking example is the cult of *Tyche (Chance, Fortune), while also conspicuous in the later period were Egyptian deities such as *Isis and Sarapis, whose cults showed a large admixture of Greek elements. The payment of divine honours to rulers (see RULER-CULT), originating with Alexander, soon became standard.

religion, Jewish The main sources of knowledge of Judaism in Graeco-Roman antiquity are the OT and NT and other religious texts preserved in Greek within the Christian Church: the apocrypha and pseudepigrapha, and the writings of *Philon (2) and *Josephus. The works composed in Hebrew and *Aramaic produced by the rabbis (see below) after AD 70 stress rather different aspects. A fresh light has been shone on Judaism by the chance discovery of Jewish papyri in *Elephantine and esp. by the *Dead Sea Scrolls, which revealed the incompleteness of the later Jewish and Christian traditions. Pagan Greek and Latin writers emphasized the aspects of Judaism most surprising to outsiders, but many of their comments were ignorant and prejudiced.

The prime form of worship was by sacrifices and other offerings in the *Jerusalem Temple. In this respect the Jewish cult differed from most in the Greek and Roman world only in the exceptional scrupulousness of its observance; in the assumption of most Jews that sacrifices were valid only if performed in *Jerusalem in the role of the priestly caste, who inherited the prerogative to serve in the sanctuary under the authority of an autocratic high priest who at certain periods also operated as political leader of the nation; and in their strong sense of the special sanctity of the land of Israel and the city of Jerusalem and its shrine.

Of the special elements of Judaism noted in antiquity, most striking to pagans was the exclusive monotheism of Jews: most Jews worshipped only their own deity and either asserted that other gods did not exist or chose to ignore them. Equally strange was the lack of any cult image.

Jews were in general believed by outsiders to be esp. devoted to their religion, a trait interpreted sometimes negatively as superstition, sometimes positively as philosophy. The foundation of this devotion lay in the Torah, the law governing all aspects of Jewish life which Jews considered had been handed down to them through Moses on Mt. Sinai as part of the covenant between God and Israel. The Torah is enshrined in the Hebrew bible, pre-eminently in the Pentateuch (the first five books). Jews treated the scrolls on which the Torah was recorded with exceptional reverence; if written in the correct fashion, such scrolls were holy objects in themselves. The covenant, marked by circumcision for males, involved the observance of moral laws as well as taboos about food and sacred time (esp. the sabbath).

These main elements of Judaism were established by the 3rd and 2nd cents. BC, when the final books of the Hebrew bible were composed. But, among new developments, was the gradual emergence of the notion of a canon of scripture treated as more authoritative than other writings.

Agreement about the authority of particular books did not lead to uniformity, or even the notion of orthodoxy. From the 2nd cent. BC self-conscious philosophies began to proclaim themselves within Judaism: Pharisees, Sadducees, and Essenes, and perhaps others. These groups differed on correct practice in the Jerusalem cult as well as on quite fundamental issues of theology, such as the role of fate and the existence of an afterlife. However, apart perhaps from the Dead Sea sectarians, who saw themselves as the True Israel, all these Jews believed that they belonged within a united religion: Josephus, who described the three main Jewish philosophies in detail, boasted that Jews are remarkable for their unanimity on religious issues. The earliest followers of Jesus are best considered in the context of such variety within Judaism.

In the Hellenistic and early Roman periods some aspects of the biblical tradition were esp. emphasized by Jews. Ritual purity as a metaphor for holiness was stressed by Jews of all persuasions. Some Jews indulged in speculation about the end of days, which was variously envisaged as a victory of Israel over the nations under God's suzerainty or the total cessation of mundane life. In some texts a leading role was accorded to a messianic figure, but ideas about the personality and function of a messiah or messiahs varied greatly, and the extent to which messianic expectations dominated Judaism in any period is debated. Much of the extant *eschatological literature is composed in the form of apocalyptic, in which a vision is said to have been vouchsafed to a holy seer. All the apocalyptic texts from the post-biblical period are either anonymous or *pseudepigraphical, reflecting a general belief that the reliability of prophetic inspiration had declined since biblical times.

Acc. to Josephus in his defence and summary of Judaism, Jews were uniquely concerned to learn their own law. The primary locus of teaching was the synagogue, where the Pentateuch was read and explained at least once a week, on sabbaths. The increased ascription of sanctity to synagogues was in part a reaction to the destruction of the Jerusalem Temple by Roman forces under *Titus in AD 70 (see JEWS). The destruction, at the end of the First Jewish Revolt, had important consequences for the development of Judaism, although new theologies were slow to emerge: Josephus in the nineties AD still assumed that God is best worshipped by sacrifices in Jerusalem. In the diaspora (see JEWS, *The Diaspora*) the Temple had in any case always dominated more as an idea than as an element in religious practice, since only occasional pilgrimage was possible.

The Judaism of the rabbis differed from other forms of Judaism mainly in its emphasis on learning as a form of worship. Rabbinic academies, first in Jamnia immediately after AD 70, but from the mid-2nd cent. mainly in Galilee and (from the 3rd cent.) in *Babylonia, specialized in the elucidation of Jewish law, producing a huge literature by the end of antiquity. Their most important products, were the Mishnah and the two Talmuds, redacted (mainly in Aramaic) in Palestine in *c.* AD 400 and in Babylonia in *c.* AD 500. See CHRISTIANITY.

religion, Persian Two religious complexes are discernible in the first millennium BC in Iran.

1. The eastern Iranian tradition of Zarathuštra (see ZOROASTER), with the Avesta as its sacred writings. The texts were written down in *Sasanid times when Zoroastrianism became the state religion. This tradition cannot be provided with a historical or archaeological context.

2. The western Iranian religion of the *Achaemenids is attested in iconography, epigraphy, and in administrative texts; no sacred texts were preserved. *Ahuramazda is the only god invoked by name in the OP inscriptions (until *Artaxerxes II) and is portrayed as winged on reliefs and seals. Sanctuaries have not yet been identified in the Achaemenid residences, although *Darius I claims to have restored the sanctuaries destroyed by Gaumata. Two altar-plinths at Pasargadae remain the only cult structures. Evidence for cult-practices consists of tomb-reliefs where the king worships the sacred *fire. Around the residences, the picture is more diversified. *Persepolis administrative tablets (*PFT*) mention several Iranian gods, as well as Elamite Humban and *Babylonian Adad, who receive rations for sacrifices from the royal treasuries. Mithra (see MITHRAS) occurs often in names such as Mithradates, but is otherwise unattested until Artaxerxes II.

*Herodotus' description of Persian cult is substantially correct, although he confuses Mithra with Anahita. Sacrifices to fire, earth, and water are partly confirmed by the *PFT*. Fire-worship was known from personal observation in Asia Minor. Herodotus and *Plato emphasize the importance of 'truth' (OP *arta*) to the Persians.

religion, Roman The history of Roman religion might be said to begin with *Varro's *Human and Divine Antiquities* (47 BC), of which the second half, sixteen books on Divine Antiquities, codified for the first time Roman religious institutions: priests, temples, festivals, rites, and gods.

Defining 'Roman religion' is harder than it might seem. Scholarly emphasis has generally fallen on the public festivals and institutions, since they provided the framework for private rituals; only those committed to a protestant view of personal piety will argue that public rituals lack real religious feeling or significance. The geographical scope of the phrase changes radically over time, from the regal period when Rome was just one city-state through to Rome's acquisition of an empire stretching from Scotland to Syria. Two related themes run through that expansion: the role of specifically Roman cults outside Rome, and the religious impact of empire on Rome itself.

Our knowledge of the early phase of Roman religion is patchy, and subject, like all early Roman history, to later myth-making. For the republic, archaeological evidence, e.g. of temples, is important, and the literary tradition becomes increasingly reliable, esp. from the mid-4th or 3rd down to the 1st cent. BC. It becomes possible to produce a diachronic history of the changes to the public cults of the city of Rome, such as the introduction of the cult of Magna Mater (204; see CYBELE; PHILHELLENISM), the suppression of the *Bacchanalia (186), the creation in Italy and the provinces of colonies (see COLONIZATION, ROMAN) whose religious institutions were modelled on those of Rome, and the increasingly divine aura assumed by dynasts of the late republic.

The *Augustan 'restoration' of religion was in reality more a restructuring, with the figure of the emperor incorporated at many points. Some 'ancient' cults were given a fresh impetus, while Augustus also built major new temples in the city (*Apollo; *Mars Ultor), which expressed his relationship to the divine. This Augustan system remained fundamental to the public religious life of Rome to the end of antiquity. Roman religious life became increasingly cosmopolitan under the empire, with a flourishing of associations focused on gods both Roman and foreign, some within individual households, others drawing their membership from a wider circle. In the high empire the civic cults of Rome operated alongside associations devoted to *Isis, *Mithras, Yahweh, or Christ (see CHRISTIANITY). Outside Rome, civic cults in the west took on a strongly Roman cast. Pre-Roman gods were reinterpreted and local pantheons modelled on the Roman (see INTERPRETATIO ROMANA). In the 3rd and 4th cents., there was an increasing conceptual opposition between Roman religion and *Christianity, but elements of the Roman system proved to be very enduring: in Rome the *Lupercalia were still celebrated in the late 5th cent. AD.

religion, Roman, terms relating to

Lat. *rēligiō* was likened by the ancients to *relegere*, 'to go over again in thought' or to *religāre*, 'to bind', and designates religious scrupulosity as well as the sense of bonds between gods and humans. Knowledge of these bonds incites men and women to be scrupulous in their relations with gods, notably by respecting their dignity: the term *religio* is thus defined as 'justice rendered to the gods', and is parallel to *pietas, the justice rendered to parents. But *pius, pietas* apply equally to the religious domain: Virgil's Aeneas is *pius* because he observes right relations to all things human and divine. Usually *religio* is laudatory, but *religiōsus* often designates an exaggerated scrupulosity towards the gods and approaches *superstitiōsus* in sense (see SUPERSTITIO). There exists no idea of 'the sacred' in Rome. In Roman sacred law, *sacer* signifies 'consecrated to, property of' the gods, in contrast to what belongs to humans and the *di *manes*. A temple is *sacer*, likewise a duly consecrated object, a sacrificial victim after *immolatio* (see SACRIFICE, ROMAN), or a man consecrated to a deity after a crime. *Sanctus* is that which is guaranteed by an oath—thus what is inviolable, e.g. the walls of a city, certain laws, the tribunes of the *plebs*, deities.

repetundae

repetundae (*pecūniae*), (money) to be recovered. The *quaestiō dē repetundīs* (see QUAESTIONES) was an extortion court established to secure compensation for the illegal acquisition of money or property by Romans in authority abroad. Gaius *Sempronius Gracchus, finding the original standing court of 149 BC corrupt and its senatorial jurors unwilling to convict fellow-senators, had a law passed, of which major fragments survive on bronze. It was a radical reform: those liable were now all senators, ex-magistrates, or their close relatives (but not *equestrians, who did not fall into either of the last two categories); prosecution took place through denunciation to the *praetor; wronged parties or their delegates, even non-Romans, were themselves expected to prosecute; a 50-strong trial jury was drawn from an *album* of equestrians with no connections with the senate; the penalty was double repayment; rewards, including Roman citizenship, were offered to successful prosecutors; the whole trial procedure was set out in minute detail with emphasis on openness and accountability. Extortion was now clearly a criminal matter, and magistrates and senators might be convicted by their inferiors after being prosecuted by foreigners. The law caused understandable disquiet among the Roman aristocracy.

There was a reaction which led to variations in the composition of the juries (for which see QUAESTIONES), and also reforms which in some ways strengthened the court, but also made it less accessible to non-citizen victims of Roman misgovernment. *Caesar's *lex Iūlia de repetundis* of 59 included a number of provisions regulating the behaviour of magistrates in provinces, some of which had earlier formed part of other laws. This law, comprehensive and elaborate, remained the basis of controlling misbehaviour of men in authority in the provinces under the emperors.

The emphasis in the law was now on punishing improper behaviour and the interests of the Roman state. The losses and sufferings of the victims were not so important in their own right as they had been in the law of Gaius Gracchus. In 4 BC *Augustus procured a decree of the senate by which provincials who wished only simple restitution for their losses could with the senate's permission have their case investigated by five senatorial jurors. This return in effect to civil procedure, by reducing the defendant's liability, would be more likely to secure a conviction and compensation, and with less expense and inconvenience, thanks to the swift and simpler procedure. Cases involving criminal penalties continued alongside the new procedure and many were tried in the senate, after it came to be used as a court in the latter part of Augustus' reign. But senators were reluctant to condemn their peers, and men who enjoyed the emperor's favour were hard to convict. As a result, under *Trajan, his clemency was invoked to prevent the punishment even of known offenders.

representation, representative government See DEMES; FEDERAL STATES.

Res Gestae (of *Augustus). Augustus left four documents with the *Vestals to be read, after his death, in the senate. One of these was a record of his achievements, in the style of the claims of the *triumphātōrēs* (see TRIUMPH) of the Roman past, which was to be erected on bronze pillars at the entrance to his mausoleum in the *Campus Martius. This is known to us from a copy, updated after Augustus' death, which was piously affixed (with a Greek translation) in front of the temple of Rome and Augustus at Ancyra, capital of Galatia and therefore centre of the imperial cult of the province. Small fragments of other copies have been found at Apollonia and Antioch near Pisidia (also in Galatia); it is likely that copies were widely set up in the provinces.

As it stands, the document seems to have been composed immediately before Augustus' death, but it certainly existed in some form in AD 13. It makes remarkable claims for the legality and constitutional propriety of Augustus' position, and plays down a number of considerations, relating esp. to the period before *Actium, which might be seen less favourably.

It emphasizes, first, the honours bestowed on Augustus by the community; second, the expenses incurred by Augustus, as a great benefactor; third, the military achievements of the age and esp. the *imperium* and personal glory of Augustus. A final summary of the position justifies the resulting *auctōritās* and dwells on the conferment by all of the title *Pater Patriae. This is a record in the tradition of self-advertisement used by great men under the republic, and not a royal manifesto; it omits anything which might suggest an unconstitutional overall guidance of Roman decision-making, and is not a complete record of either his legislation or his administrative innovations. The document illustrates very well the speciously libertarian traditionalism which *Tacitus so deftly punctures in the opening chapters of his *Annals*; but it is also a very important source for much detail not provided elsewhere.

revenge See CURSES; ERINYES; LAW AND PROCEDURE, ROMAN, 3. 1; LAW IN GREECE; NEMESIS; PUNISHMENT (GREEK AND ROMAN PRACTICE); RECIPROCITY (GREECE).

rex, the Latin word for king. Traditionally Rome itself was ruled by kings during its earliest history, but the literary sources are reticent about kingship among other Italic peoples, including the *Latins.

That early Rome was ruled by kings is virtually certain, even if none of the traditional kings has yet been authenticated by direct testimony such as a contemporary inscription. There were supposedly seven kings, whose reigns spanned nearly 250 years, from the founding of the city to the expulsion of Tarquinius Superbus. This is far too long, and there are other reasons too for doubting the chronology of the regal period and for treating the traditional list of kings as artificial. Alternative traditions preserved the names of kings who were not included among the famous seven, and of these latter the first, *Romulus, is clearly no more than a legendary eponym. Of the others, who may be authentic, one (Tullus Hostilius) was Latin, two (Numa Pompilius, Ancus Marcius) were *Sabine, and two (the Tarquins) were *Etruscans. The origin of Servius *Tullius was disputed.

Acc. to tradition, the Roman monarchy was elective. Under the regular procedure the *patricians nominated the king through tenure of the office of *interrex*, but their choice had to be ratified by a vote of the *comitia curiata* and by favourable signs from the gods at an inauguration ceremony. None of the traditional kings was a patrician; most of them were in some sense outsiders, some indeed foreigners. This feature should not be dismissed as fictitious, nor should it be assumed that the accession of an Etruscan (Tarquinius Priscus) occurred because Rome had been the victim of an Etruscan conquest. The last two kings, Servius Tullius and Tarquinius Superbus, are presented in the sources as usurpers who adopted a tyrannical style of rule. This is quite possibly historical, given the close contacts between Rome and the Greek world in the 6th cent. BC: see TYRANNY.

The powers of the king cannot be reconstructed in detail. The accounts of the sources presuppose that the king's power was enshrined in the concept of *imperium*, which was taken over by the magistrates of the republic. It is probable enough that the trappings of power, which symbolized the absolute authority of the holder of *imperium*, go back to the time of the kings; they include the *fasces, purple robes, and the *sella curulis*, which were supposedly borrowed from the Etruscans. The ceremony of the *triumph, in which the victorious general bore all the regal insignia, was probably also a relic of the monarchy (it too was of Etruscan origin). It seems likely that the king commanded in war and exercised supreme jurisdiction; on the other hand, he probably had to work with an advisory council (the senate) and a popular assembly (the *comitia curiata*), both of which seem to have existed in the regal period.

The religious authority of the kings is more problematic. Even if the king, and his republican surrogate, the *rex sacrorum, held the highest priestly position, tradition also traces other major priesthoods, such as the *pontifices and the *augurs (see PRIESTS), back to the regal period. This must imply that the king did not have a monopoly of priestly authority.

During the republic the Romans are supposed to have been profoundly hostile to the very idea of kingship. It is doubtful, however, if this was ever a deeply held popular view; it seems rather to have been part of the aristocratic ideology of the Republic's ruling class, which viewed the rise of charismatic individuals with alarm, esp. if they were backed by popular support. It is no accident that all serious charges of monarchism (*regnum*) were levelled against mavericks from the ruling élite—the *Gracchi and their predecessors—who attempted to help the poor. When the Caesars revived the monarchy at Rome (see IULIUS CAESAR (1), GAIUS; AUGUSTUS), they avoided the title *rex* not because it was unpopular, but because it was unacceptable to the nobility.

rex nemorensis, the 'king of the grove', i.e. *Diana's grove near Aricia, at the foot of the Alban hills (see ALBANUS MONS). This priest was unique among religious officials of the Roman world, in being an escaped slave who acquired office by killing his predecessor, after issuing a challenge by plucking a branch from a particular tree in the grove. The 'mystery' of the priest of Nemi is the starting-point of J. G. Frazer's *The Golden Bough*.

rex sacrōrum On the expulsion of the kings from Rome (see REX) their sacral functions were partially assumed by a priest called *rex sacrorum* 'the king for sacred rites' (and his wife, the *rēgīna*, 'queen'). He sacrificed on the Kalends, and on the Nones he announced the days of festivals (see CALENDAR, ROMAN). He ranked first among priests, but was subordinate to the *pontifex maximus. He served for life, and might hold no other post.

rhapsodes were professional reciters of poetry, esp. of *Homer. The name, which means 'song-stitcher', is first attested in the 5th cent., but implies the formulaic compositional technique of earlier minstrels. Originally reciters of *epic accompanied themselves on the lyre, but later they carried a staff instead. Both are shown on vases; in his *Ion* *Plato distinguishes rhapsodes from *citharodes. In the 5th and 4th cents. rhapsodes were a familiar sight, esp. at public festivals and games, where they competed for prizes. They declaimed from a dais, and hoped to attract a crowd by their conspicuous attire and loud melodious voice. They would be likely to own texts of Homer, but recited from memory. They were carefully trained, and preserved a traditional pronunciation of Homer down to Alexandrian times. A good rhapsode might be filled with emotion while reciting, and communicate it to his audience, and there was felt to be a kinship between him and the actor. Rhapsodes were despised as stupid by the educated and a byword for unreliability. They looked up to the guild of *Homeridae, who claimed descent from Homer, and who recited his poems and told stories about his life, as authorities and arbiters.

Rhea See CRONUS; ROMULUS.

Rhēnus, the Rhine. The Rhine became the Roman frontier in *Caesar's time and, despite *Augustus' attempt (12 BC–AD 9) to move beyond it and a somewhat longer (Flavians to c. AD 260) projection of the Upper German frontier to the *limes, it remained so until the collapse of the western empire. A strong military presence on the Rhine gave Roman Gaul its shape and its *raison d'être* (the shielding of Italy); once the legions had gone, the NW provinces were just a burden.

As a means of communication the river, with its tributaries and outlets to the North Sea, was of vital military importance, as between units, between the armies of Germany and Britain, and during campaigns. From 12 BC the Romans maintained a fleet on it, with its headquarters at *Colonia Agrippinensis. It was also a great channel of commerce.

rhētor Teacher of *rhetoric. See EDUCATION, ROMAN, 2,3.

rhetoric, Greek The art of public speaking was vitally important in ancient city-states, and it was generally supposed to be teachable, at least to some extent. The concepts and terminology of rhetoric are almost entirely Greek: the Romans provided a wider field of activity for the teachers, rhetors. See entry above.

The teaching of rhetoric probably began (as *Aristotle thought) under the pressure of social and political needs in the 5th-cent. democracies of Syracuse and Athens (see GORGIAS). Even if the first mode of teaching was primarily by example (as in the display pieces of Gorgias, *Thrasymachus, and *Antiphon), this presupposes some theory of the parts of a speech (prologue, narrative, argument, counter-argument, epilogue) and some discussion of probable arguments and the value of different kinds of evidence. The early teachers cannot be responsible for the brilliant achievements of *Attic orators from *Antiphon to *Hyperides; they are due to individual genius and political stimulus. Behind the great orators, however, stood the mass of average Athenians, dependent for their success in life, and often for their personal safety, on the exertions of speechwriters (*Lysias and *Demosthenes (2) both wrote speeches for others). The large jury-courts made forensic oratory almost as much a matter of mass appeal as deliberative speeches in the assembly, but there were naturally big differences between these two genres. Ceremonial speeches (like the public funeral speeches, see EPITAPHIOS) again made different demands—less argument, more emotion, more ornamentation. The type of teaching available in the late 4th cent. was systematic, but arid, and with no attention to basic principles. But questions about the status and value of rhetoric were being asked; and both *Isocrates and the philosophers made important contributions. Isocrates' importance is as an educator, whose 'philosophy' was distinct from the *sophists' logic and rhetoric and also from the dialectic and mathematics of *Plato. He wished to give his pupils the right moral and political attitudes, and his method was to make them write about such matters and criticize and discuss his own work. This was to make a claim for instruction in writing and speaking, under the name of 'philosophy', as a complete education in itself. For Plato, Isocrates' approach was hardly more valid than that of the sophists and rhetors of the previous age. He attacks them all as deceivers and perverters of the truth. A 'philosophical' rhetoric, he says, would be based on an adequate psychology; this at least would have some value. Plato's hint was taken up by his pupil Aristotle, who gave instruction in rhetoric as well as in philosophy, and wrote the most influential of all treatises on the subject.

This work, *Rhetoric*, deals with three main topics: (*a*) the theory of rhetorical argument—argument from (merely) probable premises; (*b*) the state of mind of the audience and the ways of appealing to their prejudices and emotions; (*c*) style, its basic virtues (clarity, appropriateness), and the use of *metaphor.

When forensic and political oratory became less important, under the Hellenistic monarchies and later, rhetoric continued; outliving its original function, it became the principal educational instrument in the spread of Greek culture. Isocrates' attitudes triumphed. The *Rhetoric* of *Philodemus that gives us our best Greek evidence for the discussion of wider questions, e.g. whether rhetoric is an art. The stimulus of Rome, where significant political activity was in the hands of an aristocracy eager to learn, led to a revival of rhetoric in the 1st cent. BC (see RHETORIC, LATIN). With the revival of a more independent Greek literature in imperial times, Greek rhetoric took on a new lease of life; success in the schools might lead to a brilliant career as a sophist; see SECOND SOPHISTIC. Most of the extant works on rhetoric come from this period, or later.

Instruction remained the same. The basic divisions of a speech (prologue, etc.) and the basic classification of oratory (forensic, deliberative, display) go back, as we have seen, to the 4th cent. BC. They continue to fulfil a useful function in all later writers; but the method of organizing the whole subject which prevailed later derives ultimately from Aristotle's *Rhetoric*, and comprises five divisions:

1. 'Invention' is the most important. It teaches how to 'find' things to say to meet the question at issue.

2. 'Disposition' comprises prescriptions for the division of subject-matter within the 'parts' of a speech, and some common-sense advice about arrangement—e.g. 'put your weakest points in the middle'.

3. Diction was the area where rhetoric comes closest to literary criticism as it was practised in ancient times. Not only types of style, but figures and tropes (Gk. *tropoi*; see METAPHOR AND SIMILE), word-order, rhythm, and euphony were discussed.

4. Delivery was crucial, and ancient taste approved of much artifice in pronunciation and *gesture, so long as the orator's dignity was preserved.

5. 'Memory' was also a subject of instruction, and various forms of 'arts of memory' were taught, involving memorization of visual

features (e.g. columns in a colonnade) and the trick of associating these with the points to be made. It was bad form to read from a text, and speeches in court could be very long. See also DECLAMATION; PROGYMNASMATA.

rhetoric, Latin Oratory at Rome was born early. Rhetoric—speaking reduced to a method —came later, an import from Greece that aroused suspicion. *Porcius Cato (1), himself a distinguished speaker, pronounced *rem tenē, verba sequentur*, 'get a grip on the content; the words will follow'; and *rhetors professing to supply the words risked expulsion (as in 161 BC). But Greek teachers trained the Gracchi; and *Cicero marks out Aemilius Lepidus Porcina (consul 137) as the first master of a smoothness and periodic structure that rivalled the Greeks. In 92 Latin rhetors came under the castigation of the *censors; Cicero for one wanted to be taught by them, but was kept by his elders to the normal path of instruction in Greek exercises, doubtless *declamation.

In Cicero's major rhetorical work, *Dē ōrātōrē* ('On Oratory', 55), dialogue form militates against technical exposition; moreover, Cicero was concerned to inculcate his idea of the philosophic orator, with the widest possible education, able to speak 'ornately and copiously' on any topic, and this naturally went with criticism of those who thought that one could become an orator by reading a textbook. Nevertheless, *De oratore* contained much traditional material; as did the later *Orator* (46), in which Cicero contrasted the 'perfect orator', well educated and commanding every kind of style, modelled on Demosthenes and, implicitly, on Cicero himself, with the so-called Atticists, contemporaries who had a narrower and more austere ideal of oratory (see ASIANISM AND ATTICISM).

The *Philippics* of Cicero were the last examples of great oratory used to influence political action at Rome. Oratory went on under the Principate, but its practical effect was felt mainly in the lawcourts. Declamation continued to dominate the schools, fascinating even grown men; and it increasingly imparted a crisper style not only to public oratory but also to literature in general.

The massive *Institūtiō* ('Education of the Orator') of *Quintilian looks back to Cicero, and amidst all its detail retains Cicero's enthusiasm for a wide training and his dislike of trivial technicality. There was much in the *Institutio* that reflected contemporary conditions, esp. its concern with declamation; but it maintained, in defiance of history, the ideal of the 'good man

skilled in speaking' (*vir bonus dīcendī perītus*: Cato's phrase), whose eloquence should guide the senate and people of Rome. For a more realistic assessment of oratory under the early empire we have to look to *Tacitus' *Dialogue*.

For a summary of ancient rhetorical doctrine, which was usually Greek in origin but found some of its best surviving expositors in Latin, see RHETORIC, GREEK. See also COMMUNES LOCI; IMITATIO; INVECTIVE; TOPOS.

Rhodes, large island (*c*.1,400 sq. km./540 sq. mi.), lying close to the mainland of *Caria.

Dark Age Rhodes was settled by *Dorian Greeks who formed three city-states, Lindus, Ialysus, and Camirus. Their development in the Archaic period was typical for the time and place: they sent out colonies (Gela and Phaselis were Lindian foundations), they were ruled by local tyrants, they submitted to Persia in 490. In the 5th cent., they were members of the Athenian Alliance (see DELIAN LEAGUE), and all appear in the Athenian tribute-lists. The cities revolted from Athens in 412/11. In 408/7 the three cities renounced their independent political status, synoecized (see SYNOECISM), and founded a *federal state, Rhodes. The reason for this decision was probably commercial rather than military. Existing alongside the new federal capital (also called Rhodes) built on the northern tip of the island in Ialysian territory, the cities retained autonomy in local civic and religious matters and continued to be inhabited.

Rhodes suffered political turbulence for most of the 4th cent., but flourished in the age of the *Diadochi. The foundation of new cities in the east meant the transfer of trade to the eastern Mediterranean, and Rhodes with its five harbours was ideally placed for this commercial traffic. The year-long siege of Rhodes by Demetrius Poliorcetes in 305/4 arose when Demetrius tried to win the Rhodian fleet and dockyards for himself, thereby threatening a favourable Rhodian alliance with the Ptolemies (see PTOLEMY (1)). The Rhodians resisted heroically. Demetrius was forced to withdraw after wasting a year, and from the sale of his siege equipment the Rhodians financed the Colossus, a 33-m. (108-ft.) tall statue of their patron god *Helios standing on a hill overlooking the city (see SEVEN WONDERS OF THE ANCIENT WORLD). Rhodes' survival on this occasion increased its prestige and self-confidence, so that throughout the 3rd cent. it successfully avoided subservience to any of the larger powers, although close political and commercial ties with Egypt were maintained. By the second half of the century the Rhodian fleet replaced the Ptolemaic navy as the enemy of *piracy on the high seas and as protector of the island communities.

'Riace warriors', two masterpieces of Greek bronze-casting, from (it seems) an ancient *shipwreck; found off the toe of Italy in 1972. Standing nudes, 1.97–8 m. (6$\frac{1}{2}$-26 ft.) high, they originally held weapons; on technical grounds they are thought to come from the same workshop. A dating round the mid-5th cent. BC is gaining ground; later dates have advocates. Attempts to see in them famous lost works are speculative. See PHIDIAS; SCULPTURE, GREEK.

rings were used as signets from the early 6th cent. BC. The practice of wearing rings as ornaments is rare before the 4th cent. and reaches its height under the Roman empire. Rings had special uses at Rome: the gold ring as a military decoration and as a mark of rank, originally limited to *nobiles* and *equestrians, extended under the empire to denote free birth; and the betrothal ring, first of iron, later of gold.

rites of passage The main passages in the ancient life-cycle, between birth and death, were *initiation and *marriage, although in Rome initiation must have been abolished early because only traces of the institution have survived. It is sometimes possible to see which parts of the transitions received attention in which periods. Whereas on Attic black-figure vases of the late Archaic period the public procession of the couple to the bridegroom's home received all attention, the red-figure vases focused on the relationship of bride and groom: an illustration of a shift in attention from public to private.

Major symbols in the transitions were bathing or washing, change of clothes and hairstyle, and the use of *crowns. It is important to look at the timing and the shape of the symbol: the occurrence of a particular haircut, black or white clothes, crowns of fertile or fruitless plants. It is only the combination of symbols which gives meaning, not the individual symbols: both the dead and grooms wear white clothes, but they have different crowns. And when the Greek dead wear crowns but the mourners do not, it is the contrast which supplies meaning, not the crown itself.

ritual The study of ritual in Greek and Roman religion is hampered by lack of data. Ancient sources, local historians and antiquarians, as well as sacred laws, recorded only the exceptional and aberrant rituals, not the familiar and ordinary ones which were part of daily life; and because they recorded only the salient features, entire scenarios are very rare. Further, instruction in the correct performance of ritual was part of an oral tradition, from generation to generation or from *priest to priest, esp. in the Greek sacerdotal families like the Eumolpidae in *Eleusis (see EUMOLPUS), or in the *collegia* (see COLLEGIUM) in Rome. Elaborate ritual texts such as those known from near eastern sources, are therefore absent in Greece and Rome.

The central rite of Greek and Roman religion is animal *sacrifice. Greek and Roman analysis understood it as a gift to the gods; the myth of its institution by the trickster *Prometheus explained less its function as communication between man and god than an apparent deficiency in the gift from man to god. Beyond this indigenous interpretation, ordinary animal sacrifice with its ensuing meal repeated and reinforced the structure of society and was used to express societal values; changes of ritual reflected changes in values. Specific significations went together with specific forms of the ritual: the change from ordinary ovicaprine (sheep or goat) sacrifice to extraordinary sacrifice of bovines expressed a heightening of expense, festivity, and social status (religious reformers exposed the fundamental lack of moral values in such a differentiation); more specific animals were used for specific deities, chiefly as a function of their relationship to central *polis values (dog sacrifice to Enyalius (see ARES) or *Hecate). Holocaust sacrifice, which destroyed the entire animal, was offered in marginal contexts. See ANIMALS IN CULT.

Besides animal sacrifice, there were different kinds of bloodless sacrifice. A common gift was the cake, in specific forms which again were determined by the character of the divinity and its position in society. Other sacrifices comprised fruits or grains, often mixed and even cooked as a specific ritual dish (*kykeōn* in Eleusis, 'hot-pot' of Pyanopsia or *Thargelia, *puls* in Rome), as a function of the specific value of the festival. *Libation was used combined with animal sacrifice, but also as a ritual of its own. Again, the use of different liquids was determined by the function of the ritual; the main opposition was between mixed wine, the ordinary libation liquid, as it was the ordinary drink, and unmixed *wine, milk, *water, oil (see OLIVE), or *honey. Already *Peripatetic cultural theory explained many of the substances as survivals from an earlier period without wine libations and animal sacrifice (see *Porphyry, *On Abstinence*).

Another important group are purificatory rituals; see PURIFICATION; LUSTRATION. Their aim is to remove *pollution, either regularly, as in the ritual of the *pharmakos* of the Greek Thargelia or in the festivals of the Roman month Februarius, which derived its name from *februa*, a twig bundle used in purificatory rites, or in specific cases, to heal misfortune caused by pollution, as in the rites to cure epilepsy, or in the many rites instituted by oracles to avert a *plague. Cathartic rituals precede any new beginning; therefore, they belong to New Year cycles (Februarius precedes the new beginning of the Kalends of March) or initiatory rites. The forms of apotropaic rituals vary from ritual washing to holocaust sacrifices, and many forms used are not specific to cathartic rituals. A common idea, though, is to identify the pollution with an object and then to destroy it, by either burning it entirely (holocaust sacrifice of pigs) or expelling it (*pharmakos*; cure of epilepsy, where the *katharmata*, the unclean substances, are carried beyond the borders of the *polis*).

Some rituals retain the function of introducing (see INITIATION) the young generation into the community; beside the rituals in the archaic Spartan and Cretan societies, the institution of the *ephēbeia* (see EPHEBOI) belongs to this group. Other rituals concentrate upon a few selected members, like the Arrephori in the cult of the Athenian Athena (see ARREPHORIA), or the Roman *Salii where some rites preserve traces of their respective practical functions, namely to initiate women into weaving as the main female technology, or to initiate young men into armed dancing as training for *hoplite combat.

The social function of ritual was used by Hellenistic kings and Roman emperors alike to legitimate and base their rule on a religious foundation; in *ruler-cult, traditional forms like sacrifice were taken up to express these new concerns; modern negative judgements of such cults misunderstand the fundamental social and political meaning of much of ancient religion, where refusal of such rites by Christians was rightly understood as refusal to recognize the political supremacy of the ruler. See CHRISTIANITY.

river-gods Rivers and seas are ultimately derived from *Oceanus, the mythical father of all rivers. As personifications of seemingly animate powers river-gods such as Scamander in the Trojan plain may assume human form (conversation with *Achilles) but attack as gushing waters. River-gods also assemble in the council of *Zeus. Rivers are ancestors of 'older' heroes, articulating a differentiation of the landscape and humanity's link with it. Rivers can function as guardians. One-tenth of the property of the traitors of *Amphipolis (the city 'surrounded by river') was dedicated to the river.

River-gods, such as the *Nile or the *Tiber, are quintessentially male, and are often represented as bulls (also as horses and snakes) and appear thus—or as humans with bull-attributes, sometimes swimming—on coins (esp. from Sicily). Live bulls, a natural metaphor for the roaring waters, were occasionally sacrificed by throwing them into the river (horses too, sometimes). *Ritual acts and cult seem to have been ubiquitous. Before crossing a river one must, says *Hesiod, pray and wash one's hands. A vision of rivers is a sign of offspring, says *Artemidorus. River shrines were located at river-banks. Oaths are sworn by invoking rivers. During a battle diviners would offer sacrifices to the river.

*Acheloüs was perceived as the archetypal river. A son of Oceanus and *Tethys, it wrestled with *Heracles for Deianira; when it metamorphosed into a bull, Heracles won by breaking one of its horns. Acheloüs was a father of several nymphs associated with water, such as Castalia (the spring at *Delphi), and the *Sirens.

rivers See NAVIGATION; RIVER-GODS; names of particular rivers, e.g. NILE; TIBER.

roads Ramps, cuttings, stone pavements, zigzags, and lay-bys are found on local roads from Archaic Greek times, and were clearly designed to facilitate wheeled traction. Improved routes for specialized purposes such as the haulage-route to Athens from the *quarries of Pentelicon, or the *diolkos* across the isthmus of Corinth, are found, and fine paved processional ways like the Athenian Sacred Way or the approaches to great *sanctuaries like *Delphi. The technological repertoire was much increased by the use of arched construction on a large scale (see ARCHES), which made *bridges and viaducts feasible; and where labour was cheap, and petrology favourable, major cuttings and tunnels could be contemplated. Such things, like the use of the older road technologies on any grand scale, required large-scale organization, intercommunity co-operation, voluntary or enforced, and very large resources, all of which escaped the Archaic and Classical periods.

The *Royal Road (so Herodotus) of the Achaemenid empire probably did not comprise a continuous line of built structure; but what Persian power made possible along this 2,575-km. (1,600-mi.) stretch was the vision of a line joining distinct regions.

The road-building of the Roman republic was strikingly original. Between 312 (the date of the first stretch of the via Appia) and 147 BC (when the via Postumia joined *Adriatic to Tyrrhenian and spanned Cisalpine Gaul) Roman planners had perfected a way of turning the military journey-routes of commanders with *imperium (itinera) into a network which linked Roman communities to Rome, and spectacularly expressed Rome's power over the landscape. The system involved using the available skills to make showily straight connections across natural obstacles, and that was a precedent taken up with enthusiasm in the road plans of Gaius *Sempronius Gracchus. About then the first large-scale application of *milestones, docketing and measuring the domains of Rome, and the first really ambitious roads of the provincial empire are found, notably the *via Egnatia linking the Adriatic with the Aegean and eventually the *Bosporus (1), and the via Domitia running from the Alps across the Rhône and Pyrenees into *Spain.

Locally the layout of Roman roads resembles *Etruscan practice, e.g. in preferring to follow the summits of long ridges, but in geographical vision, already apparent in the *via Appia, even the Royal Road does not really provide a precedent.

The early emperors made road-building their own. *Augustus rebuilt the *via Flaminia as the highway to his *province in the settlement of 27; *Claudius commemorated his triumphal journey back to Rome from *Britain by piously completing the road which his father Nero *Claudius Drusus had begun on his own military expeditions across the Alps. The imitation of their practice by governors, and of both by municipal benefactors, spread a dense net of roads across the whole empire. While the routes of Augustus and Claudius were single highways, there is a growing sense of the application of a blueprint (developed long before in Italy), of boxing in territories with crisscross roads on a huge scale. These are the limites which were eventually to give their name to the frontier works of the empire (see LIMES). Strategic road-building on a scale large enough to cross provincial boundaries reaches its peak under the Flavians, Trajan and Hadrian, with the systematic reshaping of the networks of Anatolia and the whole eastern frontier, eventually down to Aqaba.

Romanization

1. In the West. This term refers to the processes by which indigenous peoples incorporated into the empire acquired cultural attributes which made them appear as Romans. Since the Romans had no single unitary culture but rather absorbed traits from others, including the conquered, the process was not a one-way passing of ideas and styles from Roman to indigene but rather an exchange which led to the metropolitan mixture of styles which characterized the Roman world. Styles of art and architecture, town-planning and villa-living, as well as the adoption of Latin and the worship of the Roman pantheon, are all amongst its expressions. The result of Romanization was not homogeneity, since indigenous characteristics blended to create hybrids like Romano-Celtic religion or Gallo-Roman sculpture.

Its manifestations were not uniform, and there is debate over the relative importance of directed policy and local initiative. Rome promoted aspects of her culture to integrate the provinces and facilitate government with least effort. Provincial centres like Tarraco and *Lugdunum were created to promote loyalty to the state through the worship of Roman gods, and their priesthoods became a focus for the ambitions of provincials. *Tacitus says that *Iulius Agricola in *Britain promoted public building and education for these purposes. Roman culture was also spread less deliberately by Roman actions. Mass movements of soldiers brought goods and ideas to newly conquered areas, whilst the construction of new *roads in their wake speeded communication and facilitated further cultural exchange. *Trade both within and beyond the frontiers brought Roman culture to new peoples. Equally, conquered people themselves sought to acquire Roman goods and values to curry favour with their conquerors and confer or maintain status within their own societies. In Gaul local aristocrats were obtaining Roman *citizenship in the Julio-Claudian period, establishing for themselves a new status in relation to Rome and their own peoples. Emulation of Roman customs and styles accompanied their rise. Thus in Claudian Britain, *Claudius Cogidubnus almost certainly constructed the highly sophisticated Roman villa at Fishbourne, and presided over a client kingdom where a temple of Neptune and

Minerva was built. This copying of things Roman by indigenes was probably the most important motive for these cultural changes.

2. In the East. No ancient writer provides any general account of the impact of Roman culture and institutions on the eastern provinces of the empire. The term 'Romanization' is best applied to specific developments which can be traced to the patterns of Roman rule.

Military The language used by the legions and most auxiliary regiments, both officially and privately, was Latin. Building inscriptions, gravestones, dedications, and casual graffiti provide evidence for a Latin-speaking culture in and around fortresses and also in towns which were accustomed to heavy military traffic on the roads to the eastern frontiers.

Citizenship and Law Roman *citizenship spread rapidly in the Greek east, and became almost universal with the Antonine constitution of AD 212 (see CONSTITUTION, ANTONINE). Roman citizens were notionally entitled to be tried or to conduct cases within the framework of Roman law. This will have swiftly led the Greek cities and other eastern communities to bring their own legal practices into conformity with Roman law.

Urbanization and Architecture The most characteristic form of Roman town, the colony, was introduced on a large scale to the Greek east. *Caesar and *Augustus settled veterans in colonies in Macedonia, Asia Minor, and Syria. The practice of introducing new settlers became rare under their successors, but existing communities were often raised to the status of colonies, esp. from the Severan period through the 3rd cent. More important than the practice of founding colonies (see COLONIZATION, ROMAN) was the fact that Roman provincial administration could function only in regions where an infrastructure of self-governing cities existed. Since much of the area between the Aegean and the Euphrates, esp. the interior of Asia Minor, was only thinly urbanized in the Hellenistic age, Roman rule led to the creation of hundreds of new cities. Although these had the constitution and institutions of Greek *poleis, they owed their existence directly to Roman control (see URBANISM). Civic culture, both in colonies and cities, also underwent radical changes. Since civic independence was now a thing of the past, much more emphasis was laid on the externals of city life, esp. splendid public buildings, which were the hallmark of a Roman city, esp. in the 1st and 2nd

cents. AD. Certain building types reflected specific Roman influence: temples and other structures associated with the imperial cult often dominated both old and newly founded cities; not only *amphitheatres (which were rare in the Greek east) but theatres were built to accommodate gladiatorial shows and other forms of public entertainment; above all, the *baths, *aqueducts, and spectacular fountain houses (see NYMPHAEUM), which were present everywhere and served almost as a defining characteristic of city life, were specifically Roman supplements to the existing character of a city.

Language Although no attempt was made to introduce or impose Latin as the spoken language of the population of the eastern provinces, it was the language of the army, of administration, and of the lawyers. During the 3rd and 4th cents. the attractions of a local career in a city were far outweighed by the prospect and possibilities of imperial service, as a soldier, an officer, or as a member of the imperial administrative cadre. Knowledge of Latin was a precondition for anyone wishing to enter this world. The law school at Berytus, whose students needed to master the language as well as the niceties of Roman law, provided a focal point where members of the Hellenized upper classes of the later empire acquired these two essential elements of the new, Romanized culture.

Religion and Cult The Roman *ruler-cult, whose origins lay in a collaboration between the Roman authorities, esp. provincial governors, and the upper classes of the eastern provinces, and which evolved a new form of politico-religious expression within the framework of imperial rule, had an enormous impact. Imperial temples and other buildings often dominated the cities; priesthoods and other offices concerned with the cult became the peak of a local political career; games and festivals in honour of the emperors dominated civic calendars. Much of the 'Romanness' of a city of the eastern provinces during the imperial period could therefore be traced directly to the institution of emperor-worship.

Rome (history)

1. From the Origins to 31 BC

1. The origins of Rome

Although the legends surrounding the beginnings of Rome (see AENEAS and ROMULUS; MYTHOLOGY) are ancient, they are broadly unhistorical, but certain details, like the location of early settlements, are consistent with the physical remains. The archaeology reveals hilltop settlements on the site of Rome from the end of the bronze age (c.1000 BC), such as those found throughout *Latium Vetus. By 700 the Palatine settlement included the Forum valley, and towards the end of the 7th cent. the Forum (see FORUM ROMANUM) was laid out as a public meeting-place with monumental buildings marking the transformation into an organized city-state. Although heavily influenced by the outside world, Rome remained fundamentally a Latin city. Acc. to the literary sources, the city was originally ruled by kings, which is likely enough, but no confidence can be placed in the complex dynastic history or the dating of the canonical seven (see REX).

2. The early republic and the 'Struggle of the Orders'
The received narrative of the last king, Tarquinius Superbus, says that he was expelled in an aristocratic coup, and replaced by a republic under two annually elected *consuls. Given that the *Fasti record consuls from c.500, a late 6th-cent. date for the beginning of the republic is probable. During the early republic an aristocratic clique (see PATRICIANS) retained power. During military and economic difficulties, the poorer citizens suffered most, esp. without the protection of the kings, who had relied on their support. In protest the aggrieved are said to have withdrawn from the city (see SECESSIO) in 494. The *plebs formed an assembly, elected their own officers (*tribuni plebis and *aediles), and set up their own cult (see LIBER PATER and CERES). In the 4th cent. (if not earlier) richer plebeians began to use these organizations to break down the privileges of the patricians. Through legislation between 367 and c.287, plebeians gained access to the higher magistracies, entrance into the major priestly colleges, and finally their *plebiscites became equivalent to laws (see HORTENSIUS). Other gains included the abolition of debt-bondage in 326, access to *ager publicus, and allotments of conquered territory for the poorer citizens. The alleviation of the burdens of the poor ended the plebeian struggle as a radical movement. The main result was the emergence of the nobility (see NOBILES), consisting of both patricians and plebeians, a new ruling class based on wealth, tenure of offices (see CURSUS HONORUM), and descent from former office-holders. After the lex Ovinia in the later 4th cent. the *senate took an increasingly important role in governmental administration and policy formation; this arose from the growing complexity of government and territorial expansion.

3. The Roman conquest of Italy
Despite the sack of the city by a Celtic war-band in 390 (or 386), the period from the beginning of the republic down to 275 saw Rome gain control of peninsular Italy. The Latins resisted Roman leadership in the early 5th cent. and again in the mid-4th cent. However, the overall strength of the Latin alliance allowed for successful forays in both the north and south. Notable adversaries and spheres of action included Sabines, Aequi, *Volsci, Etruscan Veii (captured in 396), *Samnium, *Campania, the territory of *Tarquinii and Caere. Rome completed the conquest of the peninsula by forcing all its peoples to become allies, either by defeating them in war or compelling them to surrender in advance, defeating an anti-Roman alliance of Samnites, Gauls, Etruscans, and Umbrians at Sentinum in 295. Final consolidation was marked by the defeat in 275 of *Pyrrhus of Epirus who had been summoned by *Tarentum to lead the war against Rome. This brought Rome to the attention of a wider world; the defeat of a powerful king by a hitherto unknown Italian republic astonished the Hellenistic east. Roman success relied on the foundation of strategic colonies on a network of well-built military roads, the loyalty of the local aristocracies within the allied states who saw the oligarchic republic as their natural advocate, and the cohesiveness of the system of alliances which resulted from continuous and successful warfare.

4. Roman *imperialism and its consequences
Rome's first overseas war, the First Punic War (264–241), despite initial heavy losses, led to the establishment of the first province, Sicily (see PROVINCIA). Twenty years later the Saguntum affair sparked the Second *Punic War, but *Hannibal's invasion of Italy (218) failed to win over Rome's Italian allies, in spite of spectacular victories, forcing his withdrawal from Italy in 204 and defeat at *Zama in 202.

Henceforth Rome's hegemony expanded throughout the Mediterranean. By c.175 Rome had overrun the Po valley, Liguria, and the Istrian peninsula, by 133 Lusitania and Celtiberia (see SPAIN), and finally Gallia Narbonensis (see GAUL, TRANSALPINE) by 121. The Romans ventured east of the *Adriatic into *Illyria in 229 and 219. Half-hearted engagements with the *Macedonian king, Philip V, began in 215 in response to his alliance with Hannibal, the so-called First Macedonian War (214–205). After Zama, Rome embarked in earnest on the Second Macedonian War (200), defeating Philip at Cynoscephalae (197). *Quinctius Flamininus pronounced 'the freedom of the Greeks' (194). However, Roman efforts to control events in the Greek world by diplomacy and threats were unsuccessful. In 191–188 the Romans invaded Asia Minor and defeated Antiochus III (see SELEU-CIDS), and in the Third Macedonian War (171–167) ended the Macedonian monarchy at the battle of *Pydna. The revolts of the 140s in Macedonia and Greece were crushed and provinces established (see ACHAIA). Dominance became equated with ruthlessness—Corinth and Carthage were razed in 146. Rome now took provinces in Africa (see AFRICA, ROMAN), Asia (133; see ASIA (ROMAN PROVINCE)), Cilicia (101), and *Cyrene (96).

This growth vastly increased the wealth of the elite, securing the dominance of the patrician-plebeian nobility. Through the influence of Greek culture rich Romans adopted the leisure style of the Hellenistic world (see HELLENISM). The *plebs* and the Italian allies acquiesced as long as they benefited from the proceeds of military conquest. But conquest had unforeseen effects on the economy and society of Italy. The peasant proprietors who formed the backbone of the Roman army could not maintain their farms due to prolonged military service and in the face of pressure from the land-hungry elite. The overseas conquests not only supplied the capital to purchase large estates, but also the slave labour needed to introduce new methods of farming, designed to provide absentee landlords with an income from cash crops. The new methods gave rise to further problems in the shape of a series of slave revolts, most notable in Sicily (132 and 103–101). Furthermore, the property qualification for army service made the impoverished peasants ineligible for recruitment. The result was a manpower crisis, as well as growing social tension, which increasingly threatened political consensus. See AGRICULTURE, ROMAN; LATIFUNDIA.

5. The Roman Revolution

In 133 a tribune (see TRIBUNI PLEBIS), Tiberius *Sempronius Gracchus (2), proposed to enforce the long-neglected limit of 500 *iugera* on holdings of *ager publicus*, and to redistribute the surplus to the poor (see AGRARIAN LAWS AND POLICY). Furious opposition led to his murder. Ten years later his brother, Gaius *Sempronius Gracchus

suffered the same fate, when he attempted to bring in a wide-ranging series of reforms, embracing provincial administration, the corn supply, judicial reform, and the status of the Italian allies. The outbreak of political violence set a destructive trend in republican politics.

In the following generation the oligarchy showed itself corrupt and incompetent in the face of military difficulties such as a war in Africa (see JUGURTHA) and an invasion of Italy by migrating German tribes. This allowed *Marius, a 'new man' (see NOVUS HOMO), to hold an unprecedented succession of consulships, and to recruit a professional army from the proletariat. These measures solved the military problems, but had fatal consequences. Ambitious nobles could now gain personal power through armed force by exploiting the desire of the poor to redress their grievances.

Matters were brought to a head by the enlargement of the citizen body resulting from the *Social War, and by an invasion of the eastern provinces by *Mithradates VI of Pontus (89). The senatorial appointment of *Cornelius Sulla to the command against Mithradates was overturned by the plebeian assembly in favour of Marius (88; see *SULPICIUS RUFUS). Over the next seven years Sulla's and Marius' supporters engaged in a series of bloody struggles for control of the city. As victor, Sulla assumed the *dictatorship in 81, purged his opponents by means of *proscriptions, and attempted to reform the constitution, strengthening the senate and abolishing most of the powers of the tribunes.

These efforts were ineffectual, however, and fresh military crises brought *Pompey and *Crassus to power (see AEMILIUS LEPIDUS (1); SERTORIUS; SPARTACUS). As consuls in 70 they repealed most of Sulla's laws. By tribunician plebiscite Pompey gained first unprecedented power to eradicate pirates (67), and then the command against Mithradates (66) to replace *Licinius Lucullus, the senate's commander. While Pompey completely reorganized the east, *Cicero ruthlessly put down the conspiracy of *Catiline (63). In 62 Pompey returned, a conquering hero, but the *optimates*, led by Lucullus and *Porcius Cato (2), blocked the land allotments promised to his veterans. This led to an irresistible alliance between Pompey, Crassus, and *Caesar, the so-called 'First Triumvirate', based on their respective popular support, unlimited funds, and unscrupulousness. As consul in 59 Caesar enacted his partners' desired measures, and rewarded himself with a special command in Gaul (conquered 58–50). (On the 50s, see also CLODIUS PULCHER and ANNIUS MILO.) After Crassus' death (53), fear of Caesar drove Pompey and the optimates closer together, as they attempted to frustrate Caesar's aim of passing directly from his Gallic command to a second consulship. Caesar refused to disarm, and in 49 he invaded Italy, sparking a civil war. Pompey was finally defeated at *Pharsalus (48).

As consul and dictator for life Caesar embarked on a series of visionary schemes, but his monarchical tendencies went against republican tradition of the nobles. On 15 March 44 a group of senators led by *Brutus and *Cassius stabbed him to death, but the conspirators failed to restore the republic. Mark Antony (see ANTONIUS, MARCUS) and Marcus *Aemilius Lepidus (2), supported by Caesar's armies, joined with Caesar's heir, the 19-year-old Caesar Octavian (see AUGUSTUS), to form a Triumvirate (see TRIUMVIRI), whereupon they divided the empire between them, and *proscribed their opponents (including Cicero). Octavian and Antony squeezed out Lepidus, and at the battle of *Actium in 31 Octavian gained full control.

2. From Augustus to the Antonines (31 BC–AD 192)

1. Augustus and the foundation of imperial rule

Shortly after Actium, the annexation of Egypt (30) brought Octavian full control of the Mediterranean world. The security of his position rested on his acceptance by most of the senatorial and *equestrian elite and the loyalty of the soldiery. Octavian and his political allies, like *Vipsanius Agrippa, proceeded cautiously towards an enduring political settlement. Grants of special powers by senate and people, most notably in 28/27, and 23, formalized Augustus' pre-eminent position. ('Augustus', meaning 'revered', was a title conferred on Octavian in 27.) Through such grants Augustus maintained his right to direct civic policy, the military, and the governance of the provinces. Such formally voted powers helped remove any hint of monarchy or dictatorship, and among his fellow aristocrats Augustus portrayed himself as 'first among equals' (*princeps).

The senate remained the principal political element in the state, even though its corporate powers were restricted through the transfer of major fiscal and military matters to Augustus and his advisers. Moreover, *equestrians were allotted important new positions of public authority (the *prefect of the corn supply, the prefects of the praetorian guard). Augustus had created Rome's first fully professional army with fixed terms and conditions of service; the state now maintained a force of c. 350,000 men. All senior commanders were appointed by the emperor from the senatorial and equestrian orders and the troops swore allegiance to the reigning emperor (see SACRAMENTUM). The loyalty of the troops was grounded in a system of material rewards (pay and *donatives), which privileged them in comparison to most free men and made the army the largest element in the state's budget. By the end of Augustus' reign the classic contours of the empire had been drawn: he secured Spain in 19, the Alpine regions by 14, and the Balkan peninsula up to the Danube in the same year. The line of the Rhine–Danube became *de facto* the empire's northern frontier. Augustus advised his successors to keep the empire within its current territorial limits.

2. The emperors and the empire

Under the emperors high politics came to centre on two interconnected issues, namely the relationship of individual emperors to the political élite, and the imperial succession. Extreme tension between sections of the political élite and the emperor, expressed most dramatically in treason-trials and executions, marked the reigns of Augustus' immediate successors, *Tiberius (AD 14–37), *Gaius (1) or Caligula (37–41), *Claudius (41–54), and *Nero (54–68), the Julio-Claudian dynasty. This tension derived from the façade of republicanism and the lack of any established law of succession. Thus, leading aristocrats, esp. if connected to the imperial family, might be regarded as threatening an emperor's rule. The personalities and backgrounds of these emperors sharpened the tension. Tiberius was designated successor only on the death of Augustus' two grandsons; Caligula and Nero gained power at a young age from the prestige of their parentage; Claudius was completely without experience of public life at his accession. Each turned to court-favourites to buttress his position. But the use of imperial slaves and freedmen as confidants antagonized the political élite.

The first imperial dynasty succumbed to insurrection and civil war in 68. After the brief reigns of *Galba (68–69), *Otho (69), and *Vitellius (69), stability were restored by *Vespasian (69–79). The new Flavian dynasty initiated by Vespasian was short-lived. His elder son *Titus ruled for two years (79–81) and was succeeded by Vespasian's younger son *Domitian (81–96). Under Domitian, who styled himself 'Lord and God', tension resurfaced. After his murder in

September 96, the senate nominated as his successor a leading, if elderly, senator, Cocceius *Nerva (96–98).

The ensuing 90 years represented a high-water mark of stability. The succession problem was resolved by the chance that a series of emperors had no surviving sons. Nerva adopted *Trajan (98–117). Trajan adopted *Hadrian (117–138), and Hadrian adopted *Antoninus Pius (138–161)—all previously leading senators. The transfer of key political offices at Rome (such as the handling of imperial correspondence or finances) from freedmen to senior equestrians further served to ameliorate relations between emperors and the élite. In 161 Marcus *Aurelius, adopted son of Pius, succeeded and immediately associated his adoptive brother Lucius *Verus (161–169) as co-emperor, but the problem of the succession resurfaced. Marcus had a surviving son, *Commodus. Commodus was made co-emperor in 177 and succeeded in March 180. He abandoned his father's senior advisers and placed his trust in confidants of servile status. On New Year's Eve 192 he was assassinated.

The empire of the 2nd cent. embraced a territory of c.5 million sq. km. (1,930,650 sq. mi.) with a population conventionally estimated at c. 55 million. Despite rudimentary technology and communication, the territorial integrity of the empire was not seriously threatened in this period. The principal aims of imperial rule were to maintain internal order and to extract resources via taxation (see FINANCE, ROMAN). Given these limited objectives, no large-scale bureaucracy was required. Although provincial governors had supreme authority for the maintenance of order and monopolized the legitimate use of violence within their territory, routine administrative activity was devolved on the local elites of the cities with each province operating as an agglomeration of civic units.

For nearly a century after Augustus consolidation, rather than conquest, epitomized Roman imperial policy. Some new territory was acquired through the assimilation of previously client territory as provinces. The only clear exception to this process of consolidation was *Claudius' invasion of *Britain in 43. Trajan led a temporary return to expansionism; expeditions on the Danube (101–102 and 105–106) saw the annexation of *Dacia and its goldmines, and there was an attempt to annex territory beyond the Euphrates from the *Parthians (113–117). Although successful at first, a serious Mesopotamian revolt (116–117) and the death of Trajan (117) led his successor Hadrian to abandon the attempt. The breach of the Danube frontier (166–167) and consequent Roman expeditions were perhaps followed by plans for annexation of land north of the Danube. Yet on Marcus' death at Vienna in 180 Commodus chose peace, and by his death the territorial extent of the empire was much, with the exception of Britain and Dacia, as it was in AD 14. The prime function of the Roman armed forces became the routine defence of the empire, with most legions and auxiliary units stationed on or near the frontiers in permanent fortified positions, served by an elaborate network of roads.

3. From Septimius Severus to Constantine (AD 193–337)

1. Political and dynastic history

The period from the Severans to Constantine the Great begins and ends with strong government, separated by a period of political and military turmoil. *Septimius Severus (193–211) rose to power in civil wars fought across the empire; his determined and ruthless reign did not endear him to senatorial opinion. His equally ruthless son *Caracalla succeeded him, but was killed in 217 during an eastern campaign by the supporters of his praetorian *prefect *Opellius Macrinus, the first candidate of equestrian rank to achieve the imperial dignity. Macrinus was quickly displaced by the religious innovator Elagabalus (see SOL INVICTUS), and then the ineffectual Severus Alexander. The following period down to the rise of *Diocletian in 284 has been called the 'third century crisis' and the age of the 'soldier-emperors'. In this half-century there were at least eighteen 'legitimate' emperors, and numerous usurpers; nearly all met violent deaths after short reigns. In response to this, Diocletian (284–305) promoted a conception of the imperial office as divisible, authority in different regions being devolved to separate, but collaborating, emperors. This conception is at the heart of the *Tetrarchy, in which Diocletian first (in 285) shared his power as Augustus with a single colleague, *Maximian, and (in 293) added to the Augusti two Caesars who would both share the burden of warfare and government and also ensure an orderly succession. The latter of these objectives was disrupted by the ambitions of rival contenders. From unrest following the joint retirements of Diocletian and Maximian in 305 emerged the figures of (the newly converted) Constantine in the west, and Licinius in the east, but Constantine's defeat of Licinius at Chrysopolis in 324 put him and his sons in sole control of the Roman empire.

2. Military policy and government

Despite internal difficulties and frequent military reverses, the territorial integrity of the Roman empire was maintained. Septimius Severus had converted his struggle for succession with Pescennius Niger into a war of conquest in which he annexed Mesopotamia, but half a century later the Persian campaign of Gordian III ended in defeat and the emperor's death (244). In the mid 250s Sapor I of the *Sasanid dynasty in Persia penetrated Roman territories, and in 260 the emperor Valerian was captured; but no territory was permanently lost, and the campaign of Galerius in the 290s was successful. On the lower Danube the 250s saw an invasion of Goths, who penetrated parts of Thrace and Asia Minor; the emperor Decius was killed in battle against this new enemy. In the 260s and 270s much was achieved in the name of Rome by the emergence of the Gallic 'empire' and Palmyrene 'empire' (see *ZENOBIA). Both these rebellions were suppressed by *Aurelian (270–275); but he was obliged to abandon Dacia to Gothic occupation. The only other territorial cession made in the period was the abandonment, also by Aurelian, of land between Rhine and Danube. The trend towards devolution of imperial power (see 3.1 above) is evident in these events. The rise of the Gallic and Palmyrene empires under Gallienus (sole ruler 260–268) secured frontiers which he could not have defended himself while also maintaining control in Italy and Illyricum. There was also progressive increase in the number, and reduction in the size, of provinces. After Diocletian there were more than 100 of these, compared with fewer than 50 in the time of Trajan, with greater numbers of equestrian governors.

3. Socio-Economic conditions

The economic history of the 3rd cent., like its political history, is one of distress and recovery. The radical debasement of the coinage is both a symptom and contributing factor to the rampant inflation of the later part of the period. But Diocletian and *Constantine I were able to restore a stable gold currency based on the *solidus* minted first at 60, then at 72 to the (Roman) pound; this coin was the foundation of the late Roman and Byzantine monetary economy. Over the longer term the prosperity of frontier regions benefited from the shift from the centre to the periphery of the resources necessary for defence. The *constitutio Antoniniana* of 212 (see CONSTITUTION, ANTONINE) extended the *citizenship to all free inhabitants of the Roman empire.

Fulfilling a long development, the *civitas Romana* was now without any ambiguity citizenship of the Roman empire and not of its capital. The army also underwent considerable changes: growing in size, reduced distinctions between legionaries and auxiliaries, and greater civil rights for soldiers, such as the right to contract legal marriages.

4. The Late Empire

1. Political and dynastic history

Upon the death of Constantine (337), competition between the three sons of Constantine—Constantine II (d. 340), Constans II (d. 350), Constantius II (d. 361)—and also the usurper Magnentius (d. 353), finally brought their cousin Julian to the throne. He had the support of his troops and attempted to restore the pagan cults of the Roman empire, but was cut short by his death in Persia (363; see 4.2 below). After the brief reign of Jovian (364), the firm military government of the brothers Valentinian I and Valens saw a division of the resources of eastern and western empires. The empire was briefly reunited by the accession of *Theodosius I (378), whose military successes have been overshadowed by his religious policies and by his confrontations with St Ambrose. At his death in 395 the empire was again divided: Theodosius' sons Arcadius (in the east) and Honorius (in the west) and their respective successors Theodosius II and Valentinian III were young, weak emperors, surrounded by competing courtiers and warlords. In the east, the competing successors to Theodosius II were effective commanders. Under Anastasius (491–518), Justin (518–527), and his formidable nephew and successor *Justinian (527–565) the Byzantine empire was able to hold its own and even, under Justinian, to attempt to make good its losses by reconquest.

2. Military policy

The real crisis of the Roman empire was generated on the Danube, as the Goths, under pressure from the Huns, negotiated or forced their way across the river, a process leading to their momentous victory at Adrianople (378). Despite the treaty concluded in 382 by Theodosius, the Romans were never able fully to recover, and the ensuing fragility of their command of the Balkans is the main strategic consideration in the division of the empire into eastern and western parts. In the 5th cent., the west was overrun by mainly Germanic invaders—Goths and then Franks in Gaul, Goths and Suebi in the Spanish peninsula, Vandals in North Africa—permitting greater or lesser degrees of Roman continuity. The Gallic upper classes and church preserved much of what was important to them—including the Latin language. Despite pressure from the Avars and other northern peoples, the eastern empire retained its territorial integrity until the expansion of Islam in the early 7th cent.

3. Government

The military and administrative achievements of later Roman government were based on structural reforms and changes that make it look very unlike the government of the early empire. It was a strongly bureaucratized state, with large and systematically organized departments of administration staffed by career officials (c.30,000). Since the military stresses of the late 2nd and 3rd cents., the 'consensual' mode of government of the early empire had been replaced by a more authoritarian system. The foundation of *Constantinople had much to do with this different system in the east. The later Roman empire enjoyed a stable currency in precious metals and limited inflation, regular taxation, good transport, stable borders, prosperous urban and rural life, and a flowering of literary and artistic culture. There was a price to pay—the late Roman penal code was one of unprecedented brutality, quite unmitigated by Christianity—but the success of the system is evident.

4. The impact of Christianity

Constantine's hopes that on his conversion the loyal bishops would deliver to him obedient tax-paying cities were disappointed by the levels of mutual disagreement within the Christian church. The emperors of the whole period were haunted by this problem, which they tended to exacerbate by taking sides themselves. *Paganism also proved recalcitrant, esp. in its associations with Classical culture and established patterns of life such as public games (see AGONES). But Christianity gave a model of imperial authority as deriving from divine. It gave to bishops an enhanced secular role, exemplified in their appointment as arbitrators in civil jurisdiction. The consequences, in an influx of Christian 'converts' using their religion to advance their personal and family interests, were apparent to such Christian writers as *Jerome, who held that the church had become richer and more powerful but poorer in virtue.

Rome (topography) The *Tiber valley at Rome is a deep trough, from 1 to 3 km. ($\frac{1}{2}$ - $1\frac{3}{4}$ mi.) wide, cut into the soft tufa floor of the river's lower basin. The edges of the trough are formed by steep weathered cliffs, seamed and even isolated by tributary streams. In this way the famous hills of Rome were formed: the Caelian (see CAELIUS MONS), Oppian, *Esquiline, Viminal, and Quirinal were flat-topped spurs, while the *Capitol, *Palatine and *Aventine were cut off from the main hinterland. (For the Oppian see ESQUILINE; it was not counted as one of the *seven hills of Rome.) On the valley floor itself the river meanders in an S-shaped curve, the northern twist containing the Campus Martius and skirting the Vatican plain, the southern curve skirting the Capitol, *forum Boarium, and Aventine, and enclosing Transtiberim, a smaller plain at the foot of the Janiculan ridge. Just below the middle of the S-curve the river runs shallow and divides at Tiber island. The ford here was the only feasible crossing-point between Rome and the sea, or for many miles upstream; so hills and spurs provided the natural strongholds suitable for defended settlement, and traffic across the heavily populated *Latium plain concentrated at the Tiber ford, which was to be the key to Rome's predominance.

Archaeology has revealed the presence of bronze-age settlement on the Capitol, and iron age settlements here and on many of the other hills, notably the Palatine, Esquiline, and Quirinal. Cemeteries crowded the edges of the marshy valley of the *forum Romanum; burials cease by the late 7th cent. BC, attesting the *synoecism of these different communities brought about as the area was drained by means of the *Cloaca Maxima and the Forum was created as a market-place. The fortification of Servius (see WALL OF SERVIUS) on the Viminal, and cliffs elsewhere, made this unified Rome a great promontory-fortress comparable with Veii; during the regal period, it grew to become one of the most substantial cities in the Mediterranean. Projects associated with the kings include the *Regia in the Forum, the temple of Jupiter Capitolinus, the temple of Diana on the Aventine, and the pons Sublicius which replaced the Tiber ford.

The Forum was the centre of civic life in republican Rome; political, religious, and commercial activities took place in a square which was also surrounded by housing and shops. As the city grew, however, ceremonial activities came to play an increasingly important role there; the Palatine became a centre of aristocratic housing, and the shops moved to the periphery of the Forum, as well as the Vēlābrum, a low-lying area between the capitol and Palatine, and the forum Boarium, close to the Tiber port.

Popular housing was concentrated in overcrowded and squalid areas such as the Subūra. As Rome's power in Italy and overseas grew, the *Campus Martius (where the *comitia centuriata met) was increasingly characterized by competitive building, as rival aristocrats sought to impress gods and voters with temples. Similarly, the construction of *basilicas around the Forum in the 2nd cent. BC provides an indication of aristocratic rivalry, while at the same time their architectural style demonstrates the Hellenization of the public spaces of the city. Meanwhile, *aqueducts were built to supply the city with enough water, together with bridges, quays, and newly paved roads. The rise of the dynasts in the 1st cent. BC was likewise reflected in the buildings of the city; *Sulla reconstructed the *Curia to reflect the increasing authority he granted to the senate; *Pompey built Rome's first permanent stone theatre, together with an impressive portico, on the Campus Martius, while of *Caesar's grandiose schemes, including a plan to divert the Tiber, only the *forum Caesaris, Basilica Iulia, and the Saepta lūlia (voting enclosure for the *comitia tributa) remain, finished by *Augustus.

Most of the surviving monuments of ancient Rome are, however, largely the work of the emperors, whose rebuildings or additions transformed or eclipsed the older monuments. Augustus built a *forum Augustum, decorated with statues of Roman heroes and members of the gens Iulia; his palace on the *Palatine was associated with the new temple of *Apollo, while many new monuments in the Campus, including the Mausoleum, were erected by him or *Vipsanius Agrippa, or by his *viri triumphales* (see TRIUMPH). The combination of Saepta, *Pantheon, and Agrippa's baths rivalled Pompey's theatre and portico for scale and grandeur. The east end of the forum Romanum was remodelled, with the temple of the Divine Iulius a new focal point, but ancient cult buildings were respected and in many cases restored; and the city was divided into fourteen new *regiones* (see REGIO). Tiberius' contributions to the urban landscape were limited, the Castra Praetoria on the outskirts of the Viminal reflecting the growing importance of the *praetorians. *Gaius (1) and *Nero, however, both sought to expand the imperial palace beyond Augustus' modest residence; Gaius linked it to the Forum by means of the temple of *Castor and Pollux. When Nero's first palace was destroyed in the fire of AD 64, he built another, the lavish *Domus Aurea, on a site which extended from the Palatine to the Esquiline. The effect of these building schemes was to drive the residential quarters off the Palatine to the villas and parks of the Quirinal, Pincian, and Aventine, and to make both emperors highly unpopular with the Roman élite; the Flavians spent much energy in returning the site of the Domus Aurea to the people of Rome, by replacing it with the *Colosseum and baths of Titus, and removing many of its treasures to the new temple of Peace (see TEMPLUM PACIS). Later, the baths of Trajan were built on the site. Domitian rebuilt the Palatine palace, further extending it to overlook the Circus Maximus; two new fora were built by *Nerva and Trajan. The centrepiece of the latter was *Trajan's Column; the complex also included the 'Markets of Trajan', which deliberately separated the commercial functions of the forum from the ceremonial. Hadrian sought to establish parallels between his rule and that of Augustus (and thereby legitimate his authority) by erecting a new Mausoleum, and rebuilding the Pantheon and baths of Agrippa in the Campus; his creation of a new temple to Venus and Rome (a deity worshipped in the provinces, but not previously in the city) showed that Rome had now become the capital of an empire, not Italy alone.

Then followed a pause in building activities: the Antonines could afford to live upon the prestige of their predecessors, adding only triumphal monuments and temples of the deified emperors. Later building schemes, apart from repairs, take the form of isolated monumental buildings, chiefly utilitarian in purpose; typical among these are the great *thermae* (see BATHS). These tended to be on the outskirts of the city, near residential areas, *Caracalla picking the low ground outside porta Capena, *Diocletian and *Constantine I choosing the Quirinal. Great fires offered the only chance of rebuilding in the older regions: thus, the fire of 283 created space for the basilica of *Maxentius, the noblest experiment in vaulting in the ancient world. The city had now reached the climax of its development; soon it was to give way to Constantinople as imperial capital.

Romulus and **Remus,** mythical founders of Rome. Their legend, though probably as old as the late 4th cent. BC in one form or another, cannot be very old or contain any popular element, unless it be the almost universal one of the exposed children who rise to a great position. 'Romulus' means simply 'Roman'.

In its normal form the story runs thus. Numitor, king of Alba Longa (see ASCANIUS), had a younger brother Amulius who deposed him. To prevent the rise of avengers, he made Numitor's daughter, R(h)ea Silvia, a *Vestal. But she was violated by *Mars himself, and bore twins. Amulius, who had imprisoned her, ordered the infants to be thrown into the Tiber. The river was in flood, and the receptacle in which they had been placed drifted ashore near the Ficus Rūminālis (a fig-tree at the foot of the *Palatine). There a she-wolf tended and suckled them, until they were found by *Faustulus the royal herdsman. He and his wife brought them up as their own; they increased mightily in strength and boldness, and became leaders of the young men in daring exploits. In one of these Remus was captured and brought before Numitor; Romulus came to the rescue, the relationship was made known, they rose together against Amulius, killed him, and made Numitor king again. The twins then founded a city of their own on the site of Rome, beginning with a settlement on the *Palatine; Romulus walled it, and he or his lieutenant killed Remus for leaping over the walls. He offered asylum on the *Capitol to all fugitives, and got wives for them by stealing women from the *Sabines, whom he had invited to a festival. After a successful reign of c.40 years he mysteriously vanished in a storm and became the god Quirinus.

Roscius Gallus, Quintus, the actor, was an *equestrian. Supreme in comedy, he also played tragic parts. His name became typical for a consummate actor, his popularity being prodigious. His earnings were enormous. He was on good terms with *Sulla and with *Cicero, to whom he gave one of his first important briefs, 81 BC, and who later defended him in a private suit.

rostra The earliest *rostra*, or speaker's platform, at Rome lay on the south side of the *comitium*; it existed in 338 BC when it was adorned with the prows (*rostra*) of ships captured from Antium. The long, straight platform is associated with the second level of the *comitium*. When rebuilt in the mid-3rd cent. it had a curved front. *Caesar replaced the republican *rostra* with a new curved structure at the west end of the forum in 44. *Augustus extended the Julian rostra, adding a rectangular platform faced with marble and decorated with bronze prows. The Augustan *rostra* were called the *rostra vetera* in contrast with the platform tribuna

in front of the podium of the temple of Divus Iulius (29), also treated as *rostra* with ships' prows from *Actium.

Royal Road *Herodotus describes what he calls the Royal Road, running from *Sardis to Susa, with its rest-houses and guard-posts. By comparing this with an *Aramaic letter of the satrap Arshama and tablets from *Persepolis (the so-called 'travel texts'), it is possible to refine and broaden analysis of the system. Although the most often cited journeys are those between Persepolis and Susa, the archive shows that all the imperial provinces were part of a network linking the royal residences from the Indus to Sardis. Authorized travellers carried a sealed document, which gave them the right to draw on the rations held in the official storehouses. This system also explains the existence of fast couriers, which so impressed the Greeks. See ROADS.

ruler-cult

Greek Greek ruler-worship is the rendering, as to a god or hero, of honours to individuals widely revered because of their achievements, position, or power.

In the aristocratic society of the Archaic period, as in the Classical *polis* of the 5th cent., no one could reach a position of such generally acknowledged pre-eminence as to justify the granting of divine honours: posthumous heroization (see HERO-CULT), rather than deification, was the honour for *founders of cities. The first case of divine honours occurred in the confused period at the end of the Peloponnesian War, when *Lysander, the most powerful man in the Aegean, received divine cult on *Samos.

Ruler-cult in a developed form first appears during the reign of *Alexander (2) the Great, and is directly inspired by his conquests, personality, and esp. his absolute and undisputed power. Alexander's attempt to force the Greeks and Macedonians in his entourage to adopt the Persian custom of prostration before the king (*proskynesis*), which for the Persians did not imply worship, was an isolated and ineffectual experiment. More important is his encounter with the priest of *Ammon at Siwa in 331 BC. The priest seemingly addressed Alexander as the son of Ammon, the traditional salutation due to any Pharaoh of Egypt, but the prestige which the oracle of Ammon then enjoyed throughout the Greek world had a decisive effect, not only on the Greeks, but also and esp. on the romantic imagination of the young king himself. It is probably the progressive development of these emotions which caused Alexander in 324, when he ordered the restoration of political *exiles, to press the Greek cities to offer him divine cult; some cities certainly responded, though contemporary evidence remains thin. Alexander also secured heroic honours for his dead intimate *Hephaestion, as official recognition of his achievements.

The cults of Alexander's successors are found in various different contexts. The principal context was that of the Greek cities dependent on particular kings, both ancient cities and those founded by the king himself. The cities acknowledged benefactions received from a king by the establishment of a cult, with temple or altar, priest, sacrifices, and games, modelled on that granted to the Olympian gods. Rulers were also honoured by having their statues placed in an already existing temple. The king was thought to share the temple with the god, and thus to partake in the honours rendered to the deity and, on occasion, in the deity's qualities.

The other main context was that of the court itself. The Greek monarchies of the east in time created their own official cults. The dynastic cult of the Ptolemies (see PTOLEMY (1)) at *Alexandria in its developed form by the end of the 3rd cent. BC consisted of priests: of Alexander, of each pair of deceased rulers, and of the reigning king and queen. In 280 Antiochus I deified his dead father *Seleucus I and dedicated to him a temple and precinct at Seleuceia Pieria; Antiochus III extended a court cult throughout his newly reconquered *Seleucid empire, with high priests of the living king and his divine ancestors in each province of the empire.

Cults are also found outside strictly Greek contexts. In Egyptian temples cult of the Ptolemies continued on the model of pharaonic practice. Incorporation of Greek practice might, however, be controversial: the erection of a statue of the Seleucid Antiochus IV in the Temple at Jerusalem stimulated the writing of the Book of Daniel, with its attack on Nebuchadnezzar's demand for worship.

Even within Greek contexts, at the outset there were debates about the propriety of divine honours for human beings, though the cults gradually became an accepted practice. That it became accepted does not prove it was essentially a political and not a religious phenomenon: to press the distinction is to deny significance to the creation of a symbolic system modelled on the cult of the gods. Those responsible for the cults, whether at court or in cities, were attempting to articulate an understanding of the power of the king.

Roman The offering of divine honours to humans was not indigenous to Italy. The Romans had long sacrificed to the ghosts of the dead (see MANES) and conceived of a semi-independent spirit (*genius*) attached to living people. But the myth of a deified founder, *Romulus, was invented only in or after the 4th cent. BC, under Greek influence, and developed in the new political circumstances of the late republic. From the time of *Claudius Marcellus (1)'s conquest of *Syracuse in 211 BC, Roman officials received divine honours in Greek cities; a notable instance is the 'liberator' of Greece, *Quinctius Flamininus (*c*.191), whose cult survived into the imperial period. At Rome such honours are met only from the late 2nd cent., and then exceptionally. Under Stoic influence (see STOICISM) the idea that worthy individuals might become divine after death appeared in *Cicero's *Dream of Scipio* and in the shrine he planned for Tullia. Though the evidence is controversial, *Caesar as dictator in 45–44 probably received divine honours, based on Roman models (cults of *Alexander (2) the Great and Hellenistic kings took different forms). After his assassination the *triumvirs, supported by popular agitation, secured from the senate his formal deification in 42 as Divus Iulius.

Worship of emperors and members of their families has two aspects, the worship of the living, including identification with the gods, and the deification of the dead. It took different forms in different contexts: Rome; provincial assemblies (see CONCILIUM); towns; and in private. At Rome *Augustus and later 'good' emperors avoided official deification in their lifetimes; *Gaius (1) Caligula and *Commodus were exceptional in seeking to emphasize their own divinity. Augustus was *divi filius* (son of the deified one), and enjoyed a mediating role with the divine, as implied by his name, and as a result of becoming *pontifex maximus* in 12. He also in 7 BC reorganized the cults of the 265 wards (*vici*) of the city: henceforth the officials of the wards, mainly *freedmen, worshipped the Augustan *Lares and the Genius of Augustus. The worship appropriate for a household was now performed throughout the city. Poets played with the association of Augustus with the gods, and assumed that he would be deified posthumously. In AD 14 Augustus' funeral managed both to evoke, on a grand scale, traditional aristocratic funerals and to permit his formal deification by the senate; it was the precedent for all subsequent emperors up to *Constantine. After *Livia Drusilla in 41, imperial relatives, male and female, could also be deified posthumously. After Constantine's avowal of *Christianity, it became harder and harder for traditional practices to continue: Christ alone had combined human and divine, and the prevalent doctrine, formulated by *Eusebius, was that the emperor ruled by divine favour.

In the Greek east provincial assemblies were permitted to establish cults of Roma and Augustus: the precedent was set in Asia (see ASIA, ROMAN PROVINCE) at *Pergamum and at Nicomedia in 29 BC. In 'civilized' western provinces provincial assemblies followed the Roman model, on the precedent of Hispania *Tarraconensis, which was granted permission to establish a temple and *flāmen* (see FLAMINES) to Divus Augustus at Tarraco in AD 15. Assemblies in more recently conquered western provinces had cults of the living Augustus and Roma (*Lugdunum; *Colonia Agrippinensis); they centred on *altars, not temples, and had *sacerdōtēs* not *flamines* (the title indicating that they were not Roman priesthoods).

Below the provincial level different forms of cult are found, depending in part on local traditions. In the (non-Greek) Egyptian temples Augustus and other emperors were accorded the position of high priest, like the Ptolemies and the pharaohs before them. In Greek contexts, in Egypt and the rest of the Greek east, emperors were generally accommodated within the context of the ordinary cult of the *Olympian gods. In cities throughout the east living emperors were granted temples and cult statues, priests and processions, sacrifices and games. At first the cult focused specifically on Augustus, and then often became a general cult of the emperors. Though some cults of Hellenistic kings did survive until Roman times, the imperial cult was more varied and more dynamic than Hellenistic cults had been. Towns in Italy and the west also established cults of the living Augustus and his successors; some, esp. colonies, chose to follow the Roman model.

Private households in Rome and elsewhere included associations of worshippers of Augustus, who will mainly have been the slaves and freedmen of the house. *Ovid in exile makes great play of his piety in praying at dawn each day before his household shrine with images of Augustus, Livia, *Tiberius, Germanicus *Iulius Caesar, and Drusus *Iulius Caesar. In Italy and the west there were also the *Augustales, a high-ranking status for Roman freedmen, whose officials are sometimes associated with the imperial cult.

To understand the imperial cult one must investigate the different ritual systems that honoured the emperor in their different social and cultural contexts. As the cult was in general not imposed from above, one must examine the contexts from which it sprang and which gave it meaning. There is a big difference between a Greek city with its stable Olympian pantheon within which the emperor was accommodated and a town in Gaul whose pre-Roman pantheon was restructured on Roman lines before the emperor found a place in it. Focus on actual divinization of the emperor is also too narrow. There was a range of religious honours, only some of which placed the emperor unambiguously among the gods. See CHRISTIANITY.

Rutilius Rūfus, Publius, b. c. 160 BC, studied philosophy under *Panaetius (becoming a firm Stoic), law under Mucius Scaevola (becoming an expert *jurist), and oratory under Sulpicius Galba (without becoming an effective speaker), then served as military tribune under *Cornelius Scipio Aemilianus at *Numantia. He was defeated for the consulship of 115 by *Aemilius Scaurus, prosecuted him, and was in turn prosecuted by him (both unsuccessfully) for *ambitus. In 109–108 he and *Marius served with distinction as *legates under *Caecilius Metellus Numidicus in Numidia, where they became bitter enemies. As consul 105 he restored Roman morale after the disaster of Arausio and introduced military reforms (among them arms drill), on which Marius later built his own army reforms and his German victories. As legate of *Mucius Scaevola (2) he was left in charge of Asia when Scaevola returned to Rome, and he offended the *publicani by strictly controlling their activities. In 92 he was prosecuted for *extortion (the prosecution was encouraged by Marius), took *Socrates as his model in his defence, and was convicted by the court manned by *equestrians. He went into exile at Smyrna and there wrote a largely autobiographical and highly personal history of his time, much used by later historians of the period. His conviction marked the bankruptcy of the equestrian courts first instituted by Gaius *Sempronius Gracchus and led to the attempted reform by his nephew *Livius Drusus.

Sabines, people of ancient Italy. The Sabines occupied an area to the NE of Rome along the east side of the *Tiber valley and extending to the *Apennine uplands. They play an important part in the legends of early Rome. The rape of the Sabine women, and the ensuing war and reconciliation, leading to the integration of the Sabines into the community under the joint rule of *Romulus and Titus Tatius are central elements in the story of how the city of Rome was formed.

sacrāmentum (military), the oath of allegiance, sworn by a Roman recruit; the most strictly observed of all Roman oaths, acc. to Dionysius of Halicarnassus' *Roman Antiquities*. Its content stressed obedience to the consuls or commanding officers and good discipline; in the mid-2nd cent. BC the military tribunes administered it. After the reforms of *Marius soldiers swore the oath to their general, and it took on a personal hue, thus encouraging the personal armies of the late republic. From *Augustus loyalty was sworn to the emperor, before the standards (see SIGNA MILITARIA); the oath was renewed annually on New Year's Day or the anniversary of the emperor's accession. In the Christian empire soldiers swore much the same oath but by God, Christ, and the Holy Ghost. See OATHS.

Sacred Wars Four wars declared by the Delphic *amphictiony (see DELPHI) against states allegedly guilty of sacrilege against *Apollo. The Third led to the destruction of *Phocis by *Philip II of Macedon (346 BC), and the Fourth to the battle of *Chaeronea (338).

sacrifice, Greek Sacrifice was the central rite in Greek religion (see RELIGION, GREEK), but there is no single Greek equivalent to the English word 'sacrifice'. The practices we bring together under this heading were described by a series of overlapping terms conveying ideas such as 'killing', 'destroying', 'burning', 'cut-ting', 'consecrating', 'performing sacred acts', 'giving', 'presenting'. As occasions for sacrifice *Theophrastus distinguished 'honour, gratitude, and need', but his categories do not correspond to fixed types, and in fact the rite could be performed on almost any occasion.

Vegetable products, esp. savoury *cakes, were occasionally 'sacrificed' (the same vocabulary is used as for animal sacrifice) in lieu of animals or, much more commonly, in addition to them. But animal sacrifice was the standard type. The main species used were sheep, goats, pigs, and cattle. In a few cults fish and fowl were offered, wild animals still more rarely; dogs and horses appear in a few sacrifices of special type that were not followed by a feast. Human sacrifice occurred only in myth and scandalous story. The choice between the main species was largely a matter of cost and scale, a piglet costing *c*.3 drachmae, a sheep or goat 12, a pig 20 or more, a cow up to 80. Within the species symbolic factors were sometimes also relevant: the virgins *Athena and *Artemis might require unbroken cattle, fertile Earth a pregnant sow. See ANIMALS IN CULT.

The most important step-by-step accounts of a standard sacrifice are a series of Homeric scenes, of which the fullest is in Homer's *Odyssey*, 3. 430–463. Attic practice differs or may have done from Homeric in details, but the basic articulations of the rite are the same in all sources. Vase-paintings and votive reliefs provide important supplementary evidence, though by their nature they rarely depict the full succession of actions. Three main stages can be distinguished:

1. Preparatory. An animal was led to the altar, usually in *procession. An *aulos played. The participants assembled in a circle, rinsed their hands in lustral water, and took a handful of barley grain from a basket. Water was sprinkled on the victim to force it to 'nod' agreement to its own sacrifice. The main sacrificer (not necessarily a priest) then cut hair from the victim, put it on the *altar fire, and uttered a *prayer which

defined the return that was desired (e.g. 'health and safety') for the offering. The other participants threw forwards their barley grains.

2. The kill. The victim's throat was cut with a knife; larger victims had been stunned with a blow from an axe first. Women participants raised the cry known as *ololygē*. In Attic practice it was important to 'bloody the altar'; small animals were held over it to be killed, the blood from larger ones was caught in a bowl and poured over it.

3. Treatment of the meat, which itself had three stages. First the god's portion, typically the thigh bones wrapped in fat with (in Homer) small portions of meat cut 'from all the limbs' set on top, was burnt on the altar fire. *Wine was poured on as it burnt. (Further portions for the gods were sometimes put on a table or even on the knees or in the hands of their statues; in practice, these became priests' perquisites.) Then the entrails were roasted on skewers and shared among all the participants. Finally the rest of the meat was boiled and distributed (normally in equal portions); in contrast to the entrails, this boiled meat was occasionally taken away for consumption at home, though a communal feast on the spot was the norm (see DINING-ROOMS). Omens (see PORTENTS) were often taken both from the burning of the god's portion and from the condition of the entrails.

Certain 'quasi-sacrifices' contained several of the actions listed above and could be described by some, though not all, of the group of words that denote sacrifice. The killing of animals to ratify an *oath, for instance, followed many of the stages mentioned under 1 and 2 above; stage 3, however, was omitted entirely, the carcass being carried away or thrown in the sea. And similar ritual killings occurred in certain *purifications and before battle.

Explicit early reflection on sacrifice is sparse. (But see ANIMALS, ATTITUDES TO.) The division whereby men received most of the meat was explained by a trick played on *Zeus by the man-loving *Titan *Prometheus at the time of the first sacrifice (Hesiod, *Theogony* 535–561). The rite of Bouphonia (part of the Attic festival Dipolieia; see ATTIC CULTS AND MYTHS) raised the issue of the institution's moral legitimacy: an ox sacrifice was followed by a 'trial' at which guilt for the killing was eventually fixed on the sacrificial axe or knife. *Plato's Euthyphro no doubt echoes popular usage in describing sacrifice as a form of 'gift' to the gods.

Recent interpretations are largely divided between those which see sacrifice (perhaps with reference to its hypothetical origins among prehistoric hunters) as a dramatization of killing, violence, and the associated guilt, and those for which by contrast it is a way of legitimizing meat-eating by treating the taking of life that necessarily precedes it as a ritual, i.e. a licensed act: the former approach stresses that rituals such as the Bouphonia raise the issue of sacrificial guilt, the latter that they resolve it. Sacrifice is normally killing followed by eating, but where does the emphasis lie? Almost always, clearly, on the eating; but all the uneaten sacrifices and quasi-sacrifices have to be set aside if the institution is to be understood by reference to the communal feast alone.

sacrifice, Roman Roman sacrificial practices were not functionally different from Greek, although the Roman rite was distinguishable from the Greek and Etruscan. As in the Greek world, sacrifice was the central ritual of religion. The expression *rem dīvīnam facerē*, 'to make a thing sacred', shows that sacrifice was an act of transfer of ownership. On its own or part of larger celebrations, the typical sacrifice embraced four phases: the *praefātio*, the *immolātiō*, the slaughtering, and the banquet.

1. After the purification (see LUSTRATION) of the participants and of the victims (always domestic animals) chosen in accordance with divinity's function and the context, a procession led them to the *altar of the divinity. There the presiding figure celebrated the *praefatio* ('preface') on a portable hearth set up beside the sacrificial altar. This rite consisted of offering *incense and *wine, and was the equivalent of a solemn salutation affirming the superiority of the gods. At the same time this rite opened a ritual space and announced what was to follow.

2. The second stage of the sacrifice was the *immolatio*. The presiding figure poured wine on the victim's brow, sprinkled its back with salted meal (*mola salsa*, whence *immolārē*), doubtless prepared by the *Vestals, and finally passed a sacrificial knife over the victim's spine. Acc. to the *prayer spoken during this rite, immolation transferred the victim from human possession to the divine.

3. Once this transfer was effected, the sacrificers felled the victim, butchered it, and opened the corpse, now on its back. The presiding figure then performed the inspection of the *exta* (vital organs: the peritoneum, liver, gall bladder, lungs, and, from the beginning of the 3rd cent. BC, the heart), to decide if they were in the good shape which would signal the god's acceptance

of the sacrifice. If the victim was unacceptable, the sacrifice had to begin again.

4. The banquet comprised two phases. Once acceptance was obtained, the sacrificers beheaded the victim, set aside the *exta*, and prepared them for offering: the *exta* of bovines were boiled in cooking-pots, those of ovines and porcines were grilled on spits. This cooking done, the *exta* were offered to the god, i.e. burnt, basted with *mola salsa* and wine. This was done on the altar if celestial gods were in question; offerings to aquatic gods were thrown into the water, those for *chthonian gods were placed on the ground or in ditches. Offerings for the *di *manes* were made on a pyre resting on the ground. When the offering to the god had been consumed, the rest of the victim was seized by the presiding figure, no doubt by imposition of the hand, and thus rendered fit for human consumption. In principle all sacrifices, except those addressed to gods of the Underworld, were followed by a sacrificial banquet. Sometimes the banquet was celebrated (doubtless on behalf of all) by just the immediate participants and their helpers, along with those possessing privileges in a particular *sanctuary (e.g. the pipe-players at the temple of Jupiter); sometimes the banquet united the chief sections of society (e.g. the Roman élite for the *epulum Iovis*; see SEPTEMVIRI EPULONES); sometimes the meat was sold in butchers' shops (i.e. it was accessible to all); sometimes, finally, it was eaten at great communal banquets, ultimately financed by benefactors. At the Ara Maxima of *Hercules, sacrificial meat had to be eaten or burnt before nightfall, a requirement giving rise to a very generous form of sacrificial banquet.

Communal sacrifices were celebrated by those who exercised power in the community in question: the *paterfamilias, magistrates and *priests, and the presidents of *clubs. Women could not normally sacrifice on behalf of the whole community. Many sacrifices were part of much larger celebrations, and in certain cases the sacrifices themselves were celebrated in more spectacular fashion (e.g. at the *lectisternium). Occasions for sacrifice were innumerable, from regular acts of homage shaped by sacred calendars and the ritual obligations of the city and its constituent associations to thank-offerings or contractual sacrifices. Faults and involuntary oversights committed in the celebration of the cult, or the involuntary deterioration of the patrimony of the gods, were expiated by *piācula*, sacrifices the purpose of which was to present excuses for past or imminent action (e.g. maintenance works in a sanctuary).

Traditional Roman sacrifice can be understood as establishing—with the help of a solemn sharing of food—a hierarchy between three partners: gods, humans, and animals (see ANIMALS IN CULT). To the gods was assured absolute priority in the course of a symbolic feast, during which they shared with humans an animal victim or a vegetable-offering. The different Roman myths which commented on sacrificial practices all insist on the fact that, by the privilege of priority, essential in Roman society, and the quality of the offerings (the *exta*, the incense and the pure wine, all reserved for the immortals), sacrifice fixed the superiority and immortality of the gods, along with the mortal condition and the pious submission of their human partners, at the expense of the animal victims. At the same time the sacrificial rite was capable of expressing, by the right to take part in the banquet and by the privilege of priority, the hierarchy among mortals.

Saïtes, the Egyptian 26th dynasty (664–525 BC), comprised six pharaohs: Psammetichus I (664–610), Necho II (610–595), Psammetichus II (595–589), Apries (589–570), Amasis (570–526), and Psammetichus III (526–525). Internally they faced the challenge of the native Egyptian warrior class and the Theban priesthood of *Ammon. The first was countered by basing Carian and Ionian mercenaries permanently in the Delta. An anti-Greek rebellion under Amasis, who defeated and expelled Apries in 570, brought only a brief reversal of this policy. Theban power, on the other hand, was neutralized by diplomatic means. Economically, close links were maintained with the Greeks, esp. through *Naucratis. Abroad, the Saites dealt effectively with Assyria, Nubia, and Chaldaea, but finally succumbed to the Persians in 525. Culturally, the period was a brilliant success with particular emphasis on the revival of past glories.

Salamis, an island in the Saronic Gulf between the west coast of *Attica and the east coast of the territory of *Megara, closes the bay of *Eleusis on the south. In the strait formed by the slopes of Mt. Aegaleus, the island of Psyttaleia, and the promontory of Cynosura on the south, and the small island of St. George on the west, the Persian fleet was crushingly defeated (September 480 BC). See PERSIAN WARS; SALAMIS, BATTLE OF. Though probably colonized by, and originally belonging to, *Aegina, and temporarily occupied by Megara (*c*.600), Salamis became an Athenian possession (thanks in part to propagandist use of the Ajax (see AIAS) connection) in the age of *Solon and *Pisistratus. It was declared a *cleruchy soon after *Cleisthenes (2)'s reforms.

Salamis, battle of (480 BC). The Persians, tempted, perhaps, by a message from *Themistocles, moved into the channel between the island and the mainland, almost certainly at night, to confront the Greek fleet, based on the island. Their intention was to surprise the Greeks at their anchorage, and prevent their escape by flanking their lines of retreat, but the Greeks were warned in time by a deserting ship from Tenos. When battle was joined in the morning, the two fleets were almost certainly aligned east–west, with the Persians along the shore of Attica, and in the initial stages the Phoenicians and other squadrons on the Persian right may have been isolated and outnumbered. But what actually happened is obscure. All we know is that the Persian fleet was defeated, and soon afterwards withdrew to Asia Minor.

Saliī (from *salīre*, 'to dance'), an ancient ritual *sodālitās* (see SODALES) found in many towns of central Italy, usually in association with the war-god. Their attachment at Rome was to *Mars. Salii had to be *patricians and to have both father and mother living. They wore the dress of an Archaic Italian foot-soldier. They also wore a sword and, on the left arm, carried one of the small figure-of-eight shields of which the original had fallen from heaven as a gift from *Jupiter to Numa Pompilius (see REX), but many copies were made to conceal which was the original; in the right hand they carried a spear or staff. When the Salii processed, they halted at certain spots and performed elaborate ritual dances, beating their shields with staves and singing the Carmen Saliare, of which fragments survive.

Sallust (Gāius Sallustius Crispus), Roman historian, probably 86–35 BC. A *Sabine from Amiternum, he probably derived from the municipal aristocracy. In 52 as tribune (see TRIBUNI PLEBIS) he acted against *Cicero and *Annius Milo. Perhaps for that reason, he was expelled from the senate in 50. He now joined *Caesar, commanding a legion in 49. As praetor in 46 he took part in the African campaign, and was appointed the first governor of New Africa. On his return to Rome he was charged with malpractice, allegedly escaping only on Caesar's intervention. With no immediate prospect of advancement, Sallust withdrew from public life—the proems of both *Cat.* and *Iug.* defend that decision—and turned to historiography.

In his first two works he avoided the usual annalistic presentation, preferring the monograph form. The first, the *Catilinarian War*, treats the conspiracy of Catiline (see SERGIUS CATILINA), 'esp. memorable for the unprecedented quality of the crime and the danger'. This is set against, and illustrates, the political and moral decline of Rome, begun after the fall of *Carthage, quickening after *Sulla's dictatorship, and spreading from the dissolute nobility to infect all Roman politics. There are no doubts about the guilt of the 'conspirators', and Sallust so far accepts the assessment of Cicero, who must have been one of his principal sources (supplemented by oral testimony). But Cicero himself is less prominent than might be expected; the heroes are Caesar and *Porcius Cato (2), the two examples of *virtūs* ('excellence') which stand out from the moral gloom of their day, and their speeches in the final debate are presented at a length which risks unbalancing the whole. Sallust's even-handedness between the two men would have struck contemporaries familiar with the fiercely polarized propaganda since Cato's death.

The second monograph, the more ambitious and assured *Jugurthan War* (see JUGURTHA), again emphasizes moral decline. This war is chosen 'both because it was great, bloody, and of shifting fortunes, and because it represented the first challenge to the arrogance of the nobility': a strange judgement, but one which reflects the work's interest in the interrelation of domestic strife and external warfare. The military narrative is patchy and selective. Politics is presented simply but vigorously, with decline again spreading from the venal nobility. This decline is presented more dynamically than in *Cat.*, as several individuals fail to live up to promising beginnings: Jugurtha himself, *Marius, *Sulla, and even Caecilius Metellus Numidicus, who comes closest to being a hero. Speeches and esp. digressions divide the work into distinct panels, and implied comparisons—Memmius and Marius, Metellus and Marius, Marius and Sulla—further plot the changes in political and military style. For sources Sallust perhaps used a general history and the autobiographies of *Aemilius Scaurus, *Rutilius Rufus, and Sulla.

Sallust's last work, the *Histories*, was annalistic. It covered events from 78, though it included a retrospect of earlier events. The last datable fragment, from book 5, concerns the year 67, hardly his chosen terminus. Speeches and letters survive entire, though the other fragments are scrappy. He again emphasized the decline of the state after Sulla, and was not generous to Pompey.

Sallust's leading theme is decline, but it is presented schematically and unsubtly; his characters have vigour, but seldom convince. The interpretation of Roman politics is often crude; but if the *nobiles* incur most criticism, this is because they set the pattern; their more popular opponents were no better. Still, the choice of the monograph form was enterprising, and he avoids the danger of drifting into biography; the use of particular episodes to illuminate a general theme is deft; he shows an increasing grasp of structure; the rhetoric, esp. in speeches and letters, has concentration and verve; and the man has style. The influence of *Thucydides (2) is pervasive, though he cannot match his model's intellectual depth. Many stylistic features are also owed to the Roman tradition, esp. *Porcius Cato (1). The characteristics are noted by ancient writers: archaisms, 'truncated epigrams, words coming before expected, obscure brevity', recherché vocabulary, rapidity. He won many admirers in later antiquity and was the greatest single influence on *Tacitus.

salūtātiō, a formal greeting; esp. at the *levée* of an eminent Roman. Etiquette required a *client to attend in formal dress (*togatus*) at his patron's house at dawn, to greet him and escort him to work, both for protection and for prestige. Friends of equal or nearly equal standing might also attend, out of special respect or flattery. A great man would admit his visitors in groups, according to class and his standing to some extent depended on the number and class of those attending him. Under the early empire lower-class clients degenerated into a parasitical claque, and the invitation to a meal or gift of money or food that they had traditionally received was generally converted to a standard payment of 25 asses, with special gifts at the *Saturnalia, and perhaps occasional invitations to dinner. Members of the upper classes continued to be assiduous in *salutatio*, and acc. to the satirists would also take their 25 asses. See PATRONAGE, NON-LITERARY; PATRONUS.

Samian Ware See POTTERY, ROMAN.

Samnium, an Oscan-speaking district in the central southern Apennines. A warlike people, the Samnites were divided into four tribal states, but were linked in a confederation. A generalissimo led the confederation in wartime. After their treaty with Rome (354 BC) the Liris evidently became their boundary with *Latium. Shortly thereafter their neighbours sought Roman protection. By granting it the Romans precipitated the three Samnite Wars. The First (343–341) resulted in Roman control of northern *Campania; the Second (327–321, 316–304), despite Samnite success at the Caudine Forks, prevented Samnite control of Apulia, *Lucania, and southern Campania; the Third (298–290) involved and at Sentinum decided the destiny of all peninsular Italy. Samnium, still unbowed, then supported *Pyrrhus, but the Romans defeated him and split Samnium apart with Latin colonies at Beneventum (268) and Aesernia (263). Samnium helped *Hannibal and lost both population and territory when the Second *Punic War was over. Samnites also fought implacably in the *Social War, and in the civil war against *Sulla. Romanization was slow. Under *Augustus, however, municipalization of the region (see MUNICIPIUM) greatly advanced, and from the late 1st cent. AD, men of Samnite stock were increasingly to be found in the *senate.

Samos, an important *polis on the large Aegean island of the same name (476 sq. km./184 sq. mi.), 1.8 km. (1 mi.) from Asia Minor. Though west and central Samos are each dominated by a mountain, Samos has arable slopes and coastal plains, and was considered fertile. Wheat was grown in its territory in Asia Minor. Exports included oil and Samian earth (a clay used in fulling); Samian transport *amphorae are distinctive.

The city lay in the SE lowlands; 8 km. (5 mi.) to the west along a sacred road lay the sanctuary of (*Hera *Heraion). Samos was reputedly *Carian before *Ionians arrived, perhaps in the 10th cent. The first Hera temple (early 8th cent.) was one of the earliest stone temples in Greece, receiving lavish dedications as an emerging élite developed overseas contacts. Samians colonized Cilicia, the Propontis, and the Black (*Euxine) Sea, helped found *Cyrene, and built a temple at *Naucratis (see COLONIZATION, GREEK).

Detailed history is lacking before the tyranny of *Polycrates (1) (*c*.550–522). His warships dominated nearby islands and towns, and his court was frequented by artists and poets (including Ibycus and *Anacreon). Refugees from the tyranny included *Pythagoras, who settled in Italy; others founded Dicaearchia (*Puteoli). Polycrates probably commissioned the three constructions mentioned by *Herodotus (3. 60), all of them extant. A new Hera temple begun earlier had proved unstable: its replacement, by *Theodorus, probably dates to Polycrates' reign. Though never finished, it was the largest Greek temple known to Herodotus.

The Persians killed Polycrates and installed tyrants friendly to themselves. Many Samian captains deserted the Ionians at Lade (see IONIAN REVOLT). Prominent in the *Delian League, Samos contributed ships until its revolt in 440, which took *Pericles eight months to suppress. Cleruchs (see CLERUCHY) were installed, and the ruling élite remained pro-Athenian in the *Peloponnesian War. For a time Samians shared Athens' radical democracy: in 405 they even received Athenian citizenship. After the war *Lysander installed a decarchy and received divine honours. After the fall of his regime Samos was generally pro-Athenian until *Mausolus renewed Persian domination. In 365 the Athenians again cleruchized the island, allegedly expelling the entire population. Liberated by *Alexander (2) the Great's Exiles' Decree (see EXILE, Greek), Samos was disputed between the Successors (see DIADOCHI); the historian Duris became tyrant of his own city. From 281 it was a Ptolemaic base; after being attacked by Philip V of Macedon it came under Rhodian hegemony (see RHODES), confirmed by Rome in 188.

sanctuaries in the Greek world were areas set aside for religious purposes and separate from the normal secular world. (Gk. temenos, originally used of a revenue-earning estate, came also to denote such an area.) The boundary might be an actual wall, but more often would be indicated by boundary markers. Traditional Greek and Roman worship was not restricted to initiates (except for the *mystery cults like *Eleusis) who had to be accommodated in closeable buildings suitable for private ritual: the open space of the sanctuary was where the worshippers congregated to observe and participate in the ritual which was enacted on their behalf; for this, the main requisite was sufficient space.

The *festivals which were the occasion for such worship were normally annual, though sanctuaries would be accessible for individual acts of worship and the performance of vows. Within the sanctuary space were the buildings and other structures for the use of the god, esp. the *altar at which the burnt *sacrifice, essential to the religious functioning of the sanctuary, was made. There is normally a *temple to house the image which was the god, which watched and so received the sacrifice. The temple was itself both an offering to the god, and a store room for *votives. The open area of the sanctuary round the *altar was the place where, at the god's festival, worshippers would witness the sacrifices. The meat from these was then divided amongst them, and normally consumed within the sanctuary. Most worshippers seem to have feasted al fresco, but certain sanctuaries contained special *dining-rooms for at least a privileged section of the worshippers. Other religious functions accommodated include contests of song and dance, as well as athletic ones (see AGONES). Specialized structures (see ODEUM; STADIUM; THEATRE) eventually developed for these.

In large sanctuaries it is often possible to distinguish between an innermost sacred area round the altar as place of sacrifice and the temple as the abode of the god, and an outer area given over to human activity, the feasting and contests. As a result theatres and stadia are often on the periphery. In healing sanctuaries, such as the Asclepieion at *Epidaurus, or the sanctuary of *Amphiaraus at Oropus in Boeotia, buildings where those seeking the god's cure might spend the night in the sanctuary (see INCUBATION) were normally next to the temple itself. In some sanctuaries the distinction between the two areas is clearly marked: at *Olympia a wall was eventually built round the innermost sanctuary (Altis), leaving outside gymnasia, stadium, and the course for the chariot-races. Here and at Epidaurus a vaulted passage leads from the inner area into the stadium. In other sanctuaries the distinction is not so clear. At the sanctuary of *Poseidon at *Isthmia the original running track has been found very close to the temple; later it was removed to a nearby valley, which perhaps afforded a better view for the spectators.

The sanctuaries of the Classical period had developed at the earliest in the 8th cent. BC. Reasons for the choice of a sanctuary site are unclear. Natural features such as *springs may be the attraction; *water is an important element in the performance of cult. A spring in the sanctuary, or its vicinity, was often embellished with a fountain house. Water may have to be provided artificially, as at the Corinthian sanctuary of Perachora, or by the construction of wells. It was needed for ritual *purification, but also, when dining-halls were provided, for more normal cleaning purposes. Sometimes the reason for the location of a sanctuary may be nothing more than an awareness of some unusual character of a place. Some sanctuaries are developed for particular communities, and each *polis* would possess one of major significance to it, dedicated to its protecting deity. Others belong to less important gods, or serve only limited sections of the community, classes in society, or villages outside the urban centre of the state. Within the *polis*-context, the location of major extra-urban sanctuaries could serve to demarcate a community's territory in the face of competing claims by neighbours. Other sanctuaries develop to serve more than one community, up to the 'international' sanctuary such as *Delphi or Olympia which attracts support and worshippers from all over Greece.

Control over the sanctuary, and responsibility for its development, rests with the community at large (see POLIS), through its political bodies, supervising finance, approving and supporting building programmes, and passing all necessary legislation for the conduct of its affairs. Immediate direction is often vested in groups of officials (who have a religious function but are not *priests): in democratic Athens, and elsewhere, the accounts were scrutinized and published as inscriptions. Many major sanctuaries were not limited to single cults. The acropolis of Athens within the surrounding walls and the *Propylaea was a sacred area, the pivot of which was the altar to *Athena. *Pausanias (3) lists a whole succession of cult-places within the sacred area, including e.g. a precinct of Brauronian Artemis (see ARTEMIS; BRAURON). See ATHENS, TOPOGRAPHY. Asclepius at Epidaurus shared his sanctuary with his father, Apollo (probably the original owner), as well as Hera.

The sanctuary would contain 'sacred property'. This might include the utensils and other paraphernalia of sacrifice and feasting, recorded on inscriptions. These both belonged to the god and were used by the god, or his worshippers. They include, at times, valuable *plate, in gold or silver, which in itself constitutes a special offering, but is still essentially a possession to be used. Other offerings are often described as *votives, strictly gifts made in response to the successful outcome of a vow, but even with these there may be a related purpose. A statue may well constitute an offering (see STATUES (CULT OF)), but is also a commemoration, of service by priests or priestesses (esp. those whose office was temporary), and of victory whether by the community in war or the individual in athletic contest. In 'international' sanctuaries, individual cities might dedicate '*thesauroi*'; the term means treasury, but this is a misleading translation, since they are not mere storehouses but offerings in their own right, often dedicated to the god to commemorate a victory in war. Some sanctuaries are oracular and thus need to provide for the consultation process; these might require modification of the temple plan (as at Delphi).

The sanctuaries of the Roman period embody the same concepts. An important right, confirmed by the Roman authorities in some cases, is that of asylum, though strictly all sanctuaries, being sacred places, offered potential refuge. In the early 5th cent. BC *Pausanias (1) sought refuge in a room of the temple of Athena Chalcioecus, where he could not be allowed to die (from starvation). In form, Roman sanctuaries are often more regularly planned, a characteristic inherited from Hellenistic architectural concepts. Such sanctuaries are normally rectangular, surrounded by porticos round the boundaries, and with formal gateway buildings which can be closed. The temple, with its altar directly in front, is placed within the resulting courtyard, and often situated to the back of it. The Severan marble plan of the city of Rome shows several such sanctuaries, but this form also characterizes the so-called imperial fora, such as those of Caesar, Augustus, and Trajan, which are essentially courtyard sanctuaries. See FORUM, various entries; ROME (TOPOGRAPHY). This concept, of the chief temple in its precinct, which continues over a road to form the civic forum, is typical of towns in the western Roman provinces.

See ALTARS; BOOTY; DINING-ROOMS; PRIESTS; SCULPTURE; THOLOS.

Sandracottus, the Greek form of the Sanskrit name Chandragupta. By 305 BC, before the encounter of *Seleucus I with Chandragupta, the latter appears to have controlled almost all the sub-continent north of the Vindhya mountains. Seleucus did not succeed in his designs, and he ceded to Chandragupta four eastern satrapies. Chandragupta made a present of 500 *elephants, and Seleucus sent a resident, *Megasthenes, to his court.

sanitation

Greek Developed arrangements in Greek towns for sanitation are a late phenomenon, coming in with the planned cities of the 4th cent. BC. Scenes of the *symposium on Greek vases depict the use of the chamber-pot, whose contents would be thrown out of the house, probably into open channels along the road surfaces. No systematic drainage scheme exists in Athens, other than the canalized stream which flows through the area of houses west of the Areopagus. The houses of *Olynthus provide evidence for bathrooms and tubs, with terracotta drainpipes leading the waste away from the house and along the streets.

Roman Despite Roman proficiency in hydraulic engineering, sanitation through supplying clean *water and the hygienic removal of human and other waste was a low priority. The role of impure water and ordure in causing *disease was little understood, and sewage was abhorred rather because it was noisome and might 'taint' other substances.

Private water-supplies were usually obtained from wells, and also from cisterns in dry climates. Only the rich could afford to tap the public *aqueducts. Domestic sanitation was provided by the cesspit (which might be near the well). Multi-storey buildings could be linked by gravity-fed pipes to a main cesspit. Night-soil was taken out to be spread on the fields. Chamber-pots, empty *amphorae, and the public gutters were also commonly used.

City aqueducts supplied drinkable water to street fountains. Covered sewers and drains were usually multi-purpose, combining sanitation with land- and rainfall-drainage, as in the *Cloaca Maxima (Great Drain) of Rome. Excess aqueduct water was used to flush these sewers. Open sewers and gutters ran down the centre or sides of streets. Bath-houses commonly contained latrines, using their water-supply. The latrines consisted of benches with holes over drains. Water for users' cleanliness was supplied in basins or channels. At Rome large urinal pots stood at street corners, the contents being used by the fullers (see TEXTILE PRODUCTION). When these were taxed by *Vespasian, the pots were nicknamed after him.

The army understood the value of hygiene in maintaining military effectiveness. Some temporary camps had cesspits, permanent forts had a clean water-supply and latrines which flushed outside the defences.

Sappho, Greek lyric poet. Born on *Lesbos in the second half of the 7th cent. BC, she was hailed in antiquity as 'the tenth Muse', and her poetry was collected into nine books (arranged according to metre) in the canonical Alexandrian edition. Only one complete poem and

some substantial fragments survive, culled from quotations in other writers or from papyrus finds. Most of her poems were for solo performance, and many refer to love between women or girls. Other subjects include *hymns to gods and apparently personal concerns such as her brother's safety. Wedding songs, and snatches from a lament for *Adonis are clearly for several singers.

Little about her life is certain. She was probably married, though only a brother and (probably) a daughter figure in the poems. Her sexual inclinations have occasioned much speculation. From Attic comedy onwards she was credited with an implausible selection of male lovers. She is described as a lover of women only in post-classical times. See HOMOSEXUALITY.

Her own poetry remains the main source for the question of how she related to the companions who formed her audience. An important parallel is *Alcman's maiden-songs. Sappho's term for her companions is *parthenos* (girl). This, and the frequent references to partings and absence in her poems, suggest that most of her circle shared their lives for only a limited period before marriage. Homoeroticism was probably institutionalized at this stage of life, as it was elsewhere for young men. The group's preoccupations—love, beauty, poetry—are indicated by the divinities most often invoked in Sappho: *Aphrodite, the Graces (see CHARITES), and the *Muses. Sappho in fr. 1, names herself in a prayer enlisting Aphrodite's help in winning the love of an unresponsive girl. In fr. 16 the singer links her own love for the absent Anactoria with that of *Helen for *Paris, and fr. 31 charts the singer's despair as she watches a beloved girl sitting next to a man. Sappho's love poetry differs from that of male writers in the almost complete absence of a sharp distinction between lover and beloved.

Poems such as these reveal an accomplished poet who can achieve effects of great subtlety beneath an apparently simple surface; other, less complex poems seem influenced by folksong. Her work was admired in antiquity for its euphony, and she was credited with musical invention; the Sapphic stanza was used by *Horace. Notable imitations include *Catullus 51, 61, and 62.

sarcophagi A sarcophagus is a coffin for inhumation, which in ancient times was often richly decorated. Sculptured stone sarcophagi appear first in the 5th cent. BC: the finest sarcophagi with sculptured reliefs were made by

Greek craftsmen for the kings of Sidon from the 5th cent. to *c.* 300 BC.

The *Etruscans used sculptured sarcophagi of clay and stone from the 6th cent.; the two commonest forms are the casket with gabled lid and the type with a reclining effigy of the dead. A few families of republican Rome buried their dead in sarcophagi. The prevailing rite of cremation in Rome gave way to inhumation in the early 2nd cent. AD, and the rich series of Roman sculptured marble sarcophagi begins about the time of *Trajan. These were made all over the Roman world.

See DEAD, DISPOSAL OF; ART, FUNERARY, ROMAN.

Sardis, the capital of *Lydia, lying under a fortified, precipitous hill in the Hermus valley, near the junction of roads from *Ephesus, Smyrna, *Pergamum, and inner *Anatolia. As the capital of the Lydian kingdom, esp. under *Croesus, and later as the headquarters of the principal Persian satrapy (see PERSIA; SATRAP), it was the political centre of the Lydian dynasty and of *Achaemenid Anatolia. Thus Sardis was captured and burned by Ionians in 498 BC (see IONIAN REVOLT), and *Xerxes mustered his troops there before he crossed the Hellespont. After *Alexander (2) the Great, it was controlled first by *Antigonus I, and then, from 282, by the *Seleucid kingdom. Its geopolitical importance and the Achaemenid heritage led the Seleucids to make Sardis one of the 'royal capitals' of their realm.

Sarmatians, nomadic tribe of Iranian origin, closely related to the Scythians (see SCYTHIA). Their women enjoyed more freedom, and, in the days of *Herodotus at least, hunted and fought alongside the men. Their fighters were all mounted, but while the rank and file were archers, the chieftains and their retainers wore armour and used heavy lances. By the time of *Augustus, the Sarmatians, who had moved slowly westward, displacing the Scythians, began to impinge on the Roman empire. Their two main branches were the Roxolani (on the Danube (*Danuvius) estuary) and the Iazyges (on the middle Danube).

Sarpēdon, in *Homer's *Iliad* the son of *Zeus and the daughter of *Bellerophon; he was joint commander of the Lycian contingent of *Priam's allies. He is one of the strongest warriors on the Trojan side and takes a prominent part in the fighting. The story of his death at the hands of *Patroclus is narrated in detail: Zeus,

knowing that he is fated to die, wishes to save his beloved son, but, rebuked by *Hera, allows his death and marks it by causing bloody rain to fall. There is a fierce fight over Sarpedon's corpse, until *Apollo rescues it on Zeus' instructions; it is then carried back home to Lycia by Sleep and Death (Hypnos and Thanatos; subject of a famous late-Archaic Attic vase by Euphronius) and given honourable burial.

Sasanids, kings of Iran AD 224–651. The dynasty, very often labelled heirs to the *Achaemenids, actually owed much more to the Parthians (see PARTHIA). Their empire at its greatest extent stretched from Syria to India and from Caucasian Iberia to the *Persian Gulf. The Sasanids constantly sought to alter the military *status quo* in the Mesopotamian, Armenian, and Syrian areas; and the forts of the *Euphrates *limes* were strengthened against attacks from them. Major campaigns were undertaken against them by various Roman emperors. Valerian was defeated and captured by Sapor I, *Diocletian and *Galerius defeated Narsēs in 297, Jovian had to make large concessions to Sapor II after the death of *Julian in Mesopotamia (363).

Though Zoroastrianism (see ZOROASTER) was the most important cult in Sasanid Iran, and although most kings tried to present themselves as devout Mazda-worshippers and a priestly hierarchy developed in the course of time, religious minorities like the Christians, the Manichaeans, and the *Jews were allowed to practise their faith.

satire (*satura*) was first classified as a literary form in Rome. 'Satire, at any rate, is all our own,' boasted *Quintilian of the genre that presented Rome in the least flattering light. Originally simply a hotch-potch (in verse, or in prose and verse mixed), satire soon acquired its specific character as a humorous or malicious exposé of hypocrisy and pretension; however, it continued to be a hold-all for mismatched subjects, written in an uneven style and overlapping with other genres. The author himself figured prominently in a variety of shifting roles: civic watchdog, sneering cynic, mocking or indignant observer, and social outcast. See also MENIPPEAN SATIRE; ENNIUS; HORACE, *Satires*; JUVENAL; LUCIAN; LUCILIUS (1); PERSIUS; PETRONIUS (2); SENECA THE YOUNGER; VARRO.

satrap, etymological meaning 'protector of power [kingdom]'. The Persian title (see PERSIA) appears first in the *Bisitun inscription to describe two of *Darius I's representatives charged with maintaining order in Bactria and Arachosia. It is found, in transliterated form, in all the languages of the Achaemenid empire.

Saturnian verse, a form of verse employed in the 3rd and 2nd cents. BC for epitaphs and triumphal commemorations. Acc. to *Ennius, the utterances of prophetic mediums had once been cast in it. A politician of the late 3rd cent. underlined a threat with its rhythm: *malum dabunt Metellī Naeviō poētae*, 'the Metelli will give the poet Naevius a thrashing'. *Livius Andronicus set in it a translation of *Homer's *Odyssey*, and *Naevius a narrative account of the First *Punic War. The poets of the Augustan period talked of its shaggy and unclean rhythm.

Sāturnus, Sāturnālia Saturnus is one of the most puzzling gods in Roman cult. The god, whose temple lay by the NW corner of the *forum Romanum, is now considered an Italo-Roman deity who underwent *Hellenization from the end of the 3rd cent. BC. His cult was celebrated according to the Greek rite, i.e. with head uncovered. To account for this, along with the other rites of the Saturnalia of 17 December, esp. the fact that the statue of Saturnus, bound for the rest of the year, was freed for this day, as well as other inversion-rituals, the god's function has been defined as that of liberation.

In *Cicero's day the Saturnalia lasted for seven days. *Augustus reduced it to three, but from the reigns of *Gaius (1) and *Claudius it attained five days, even though everyone continued to celebrate for seven days. The Saturnalia were celebrated down to the Christian age and beyond, and were the merriest festival of the year, 'the best of days' (Catullus). Slaves were allowed temporary liberty to do as they liked, and presents were exchanged. There was also a sort of mock king, 'leader of the Saturnalia', who presided over the feasts and amusements. Normal Roman behaviour was inverted at this time. Slaves dined before their masters and could allow themselves a certain insolence, leisure-wear was worn instead of the *toga, as well as the felt bonnet proper to slaves, and the time was spent eating, drinking, and playing. See also MACROBIUS.

satyric drama In the Classical period it was normal for a satyr-play to be written by each tragedian for performance after his set of three tragedies at the Athenian City *Dionysia. The chorus consists of satyrs (see next entry), closely associated with their father Silenus. One complete satyr-play 709 lines long (*Euripides' *Cyclops*), survives, together with numerous fragments, notably about half of *Sophocles' *Ichneutae* ('Trackers') preserved on papyrus, and numerous vase-paintings inspired by satyr-plays, notably the Pronomos vase, which displays the entire cast of a victorious play. The themes were taken from myth (sometimes connected with the theme of the trilogy), and the earthy preoccupations of the satyrs may have had the effect of reducing the dignity of various heroes, as happens to *Odysseus in *Cyclops*. Odysseus' speech is, metrically and stylistically, virtually indistinguishable from tragic speech, and even that of the satyrs and Silenus, though lower in tone, remains much closer to tragedy than to comedy. Horace describes tragedy as like a matron who does not descend to uttering trivial verses as she consorts modestly with the impudent satyrs at a festival.

There is a set of typical motifs, notably the captivity (explaining their presence in various myths) and eventual liberation of the satyrs, marvellous inventions and creations (of wine, the lyre, fire, etc.), riddles, emergence from the Underworld, the care of divine or heroic infants, and athletics. *Aristotle says that tragedy passed out of its satyric stage; and it seems that satyric drama was formally instituted in the festival to preserve what was being lost from tragedy as it turned to non-Dionysiac stories. Certainly it is too simple to see the function of satyric drama as merely to alleviate the effect of the seriousness of tragedy with comic relief, which could after all have been provided by comedy. Less universal in its appeal than tragedy and comedy, satyric drama had by the mid-4th cent. become detached from the tragic contest.

sătyrs and **sīlens** are imaginary male inhabitants of the wild, comparable to the 'wild men' of the European folk tradition, with some animal features, unrestrained in their desire for sex and wine, and generally represented naked. The first mention in literature of 'silens' is as making love to *nymphs in caves; of 'satyrs' it is as 'worthless and mischievous'. On the Attic François vase (c.570 BC) the horse–human hybrids accompanying *Hephaestus (with *Dionysus) back to *Olympus are labelled as silens. It seems that during the 6th cent. the (Attic-Ionic) silens were amalgamated with the (Peloponnesian) satyrs (so that the names were used interchangeably) to form, along with nymphs or *maenads, the sacred band (*thiasos*) of Dionysus. It is a *thiasos* of young satyrs that, in the 5th cent., forms the chorus of *satyric drama, with Silenus (in keeping with the ancient belief in individual silens) as father of the satyrs. In vase-painting satyrs are at first present in a few myths (the Return of Hephaestus, the Gigantomachy (see GIANTS), etc.), but in the 5th cent. this number grows considerably, at least partly under the influence of satyric drama.

Men dressed up as satyrs, e.g. at the Athenian *Anthesteria, where their frolics are depicted on the 'Choes' vases. Another part of the Anthesteria was the procession in which Dionysus arrived in a ship-cart accompanied by satyrs, who are prominent also in great *processions at *Alexandria and Rome. In contrast to this public presence, satyrs also conducted mystic *initiation (e.g. the paintings at the Villa of the *Mysteries at *Pompeii). To be initiated might be to join a satyric *thiasos*, a community of this world and the next. Hence the occurrence of satyrs in funerary art throughout most of antiquity.

Analogous to this contrast is the ambiguity of the satyrs as grotesque hedonists and yet the immortal companions of a god, cruder than men and yet somehow wiser, combining mischief with wisdom, lewdness with skill in music, animality with divinity. In satyric drama they are the first to sample the creation of culture out of nature in the invention of *wine, of the lyre, of the pipe, and so on. Silenus is the educator of Dionysus. King *Midas (1) extracted from a silen, whom he had trapped in his garden, the wisdom that for men it is best never to have been born, second best to die as soon as possible. And Virgil's shepherds extract from Silenus a song of great beauty and wisdom. This ambiguity is exploited in *Alcibiades' famous comparison of *Socrates to *Marsyas in Plato's *Symposium*.

At first somewhat equine, the satyrs become progressively more human in appearance (though from the Hellenistic period more caprine than equine, perhaps through association with *Pan), and may decorate a pastoral landscape or embody, for the visual artist, the charm of a not quite human body, as in the sculpted sleeping satyr known as the 'Barberini Faun'.

Sauromatians See SARMATIANS.

scapegoat See PHARMAKOS.

Sceptics, philosophers who hold no doctrine and suspend judgement on everything. The label *skeptikos* ('inquirer', but used with the implicit understanding that the inquiry does not end) was introduced in the 1st cent. BC, probably by the younger Pyrrhonists; before then, these philosophers would have been known as Pyrrhonists or Academics, respectively.

Early Pyrrhonism Acc. to the ancient tradition, the founder of scepticism was *Pyrrhon of Elis (c.365–275 BC). He held that it was not possible to determine whether things are one way rather than another, and that one should therefore refrain from asserting anything. Arguments to the effect that conflicts of appearances and opinions cannot be decided had been around since the time of *Protagoras and *Democritus, but Pyrrhon was probably the first to adopt the attitude of non-assertion and promote it as the foundation of peace of mind or tranquillity. Pyrrhon's school does not seem to have had any immediate followers after the time of his main pupil, Timon of Phlius.

Scepticism in the *Academy The second version of scepticism was developed in the Academy from *Arcesilaus in the 3rd cent. BC to *Philon (2) of Larissa in the first. The Academic sceptics saw themselves as followers of *Socrates. They practised his dialectical method by arguing for and against any given thesis and refuting the doctrines of other philosophers. Arcesilaus' criticism of the *Stoic theory of knowledge started a lively debate between the two schools that went on for two centuries and covered all parts of philosophy, including theology and ethics. Both sides were forced to revise and refine their arguments in the process. While the Academics would argue that, given Stoic assumptions, knowledge was impossible, the Stoics would defend their conception of knowledge and force the Academics to elaborate a sophisticated defence of the claim that it is possible to lead a normal life while suspending judgement on everything. The most detailed reply to the 'inactivity' argument, *Carneades' theory of the 'plausible impression'.

The Pyrrhonist Revival In the 1st cent. BC, when Academic scepticism had lost its vigour, Pyrrhonism was revived by Aenesidemus as a more radical form of scepticism. This new version of Pyrrhonism was clearly influenced by the preceding debate between Academics and Stoics. But Aenesidemus also picked up the older arguments from conflicting appearances, systematizing them in his list of ten 'Modes' for inducing suspension of judgement, and he revived the claim that scepticism can serve as a way to tranquillity. Unlike Pyrrhon, the later Pyrrhonists would avoid any dogmatic assertions about the impossibility of knowledge, presenting their views instead as an expression of what appeared to them to be the case. They also worked out a reply to the charge that scepticism makes life impossible, by saying that they would be guided in their everyday activities by simple appearances without strong assent.

Aenesidemus' main source of information about Pyrrhon was probably Timon, but it is likely that he was also influenced by the debates that had been going on between the different schools of medicine (see MEDICINE, 5.3). The list of Aenesidemus' followers contains the names of several prominent doctors, and the final and most sophisticated version of Pyrrhonism is preserved for us in the writings of the Empiricist physician *Sextus Empiricus (fl. *c.* AD 200). After Sextus, we do not hear of any important representatives of the school, and scepticism as a philosophical movement seems to have come to an end.

sceptre A stick carried in the hand, symbolic of kingly or priestly power, or of heraldic office; symbolic also of the right to speak in assembly.

scholarship, ancient

Greek In one sense of the term, scholarship began when literature became a central element of education and the prescribed texts had to be explained and interpreted to pupils in a class. An early reflex of this activity is the reported invention by Theagenes of Rhegium (late 6th cent. BC) of the allegorical method of interpretation, which could be used to deny the literal meaning of supposedly objectionable passages of *Homer. But scholarship, like literary criticism, was slow to develop in the Classical period. In the *Peripatetic school *Aristotle and his disciples were not primarily concerned with literature or history, but their discussions of Homer and concern with the chronology of Athenian dramatic festivals was a step forward. Recognizably scholarly work, including the composition of books or pamphlets about literary texts, began early in the 3rd cent. BC in *Alexandria under the patronage of the Ptolemies (see PTOLEMY (1)). The *Museum became a centre where literary topics were discussed regularly; acc. to one report, a record was kept of the discussions. The *Library acquired a virtually complete col-

lection of books written in Greek, to which *Callimachus (2) wrote an enormous bibliographical guide, and it looks as if copies of the classics, such as Homer, which reflected the results of work done in the Museum, came to be regarded as standard. Between *c.*285 and 145 a series of Alexandrian scholars, who variously combined one or more of the professions of poet, tutor to the children of the royal family, and librarian of the Museum, brought scholarship to a high level. They edited texts by comparing different exemplars, commented on them by writing either notes on difficult passages or extended running commentaries, and composed innumerable treatises on individual problems, some of them historical and antiquarian rather than literary. Questions of authenticity also had to be addressed. The leading figures in this process were *Zenodotus, Callimachus, *Eratosthenes, Aristophanes of Byzantium, and *Aristarchus (2). Not all their decisions about puzzles in Homer win the approval of a modern reader, and they seem to have been too prone to reject lines as being unworthy of Homer or inconsistent with the context; but luckily they did not remove such lines from the texts in circulation.

Latin During the 2nd cent. BC a 'great flock' of learned men came to Rome from Greece. By the end of the 2nd cent. and the start of the 1st not only was there substantial learning displayed in the *Didascalica* of *Accius and the satires of *Luclius (1), but Aelius had developed what would be the three main foci of Roman scholarship: 'antiquities', treating the institutions and beliefs of Rome and her neighbours; literary studies, including questions of authenticity and literary history (but little that we would recognize as 'literary criticism'); and the more or less systematic study of language, esp. (in this early period) *etymology and semantics. Aelius, Rome's first true scholar, in turn influenced *Varro, Rome's greatest scholar, whose antiquarian research ('Antiquities Human and Divine'), study of Latinity ('On the Latin Language'), and investigations of literary history ('On Poets') provided a model and a resource for all other scholars (e.g. Cornelius *Nepos, Verrius Flaccus) and some authors of imaginative literature (e.g. *Ovid).

scholarship, origins of modern classical

Classical texts formed the core of the arts curriculum in medieval schools and universities and were central to two of the three higher faculties, law and medicine, as well. But modern classical scholarship—the systematic effort to collect and study the written and material remains of the ancient world as a whole—came into being in 14th-cent. north Italy. Here teachers of rhetoric began to teach from *Cicero rather than the 'modern'—i.e. medieval—texts they had previously used. Formal imitation of the classics became systematic. Scholars began to see classical Latin texts as distinctively better than later ones: they copied, read, and studied a wide range of literary and historical texts that had not generally been read in the Middle Ages. Access to new material created new questions: problems of attribution and dating that had not interested medieval scholars arose and new techniques were devised to solve them. Before 1320 Giovanni de Matociis of Verona had established in a formal essay that the Pliny who wrote the *Natural History* could not have written the *Letters* as well (see PLINY THE ELDER and THE YOUNGER). He also wrote a history of the Roman emperors in which he drew on the evidence of coins as well as that of the ancient historians.

The poet and philosopher Petrarch (Francesco Petrarca, 1304–74) knitted these technical threads together into the programme for a new scholarship. Convinced that 'all history was but the praise of Rome' and that he himself lived in an inferior, 'dark' age, he dedicated his life to the study and imitation of the ancients—by which, as a list of his favourite books that he drew up reveals, he meant Romans like *Livy and *Virgil and St. *Augustine. Thanks to his connections with the papal curia, which spent much of the 14th cent. in Avignon, and with influential Italian clerics and statesmen, he gained access to the treasures of both Italian and northern libraries. Petrarch assembled a remarkable library of his own: his copy of Livy, brought together from diverse sources three decades, the bulk of the text that survives today, and though he never learned Greek, he had manuscripts of *Plato and *Homer. He studied and annotated his books with care and intelligence, hunted for other texts that they mentioned, and explored the ruins of Rome as well as its literary canon. His own works—which included an epic, bucolics, philosophical dialogues, historical compilations, and lively letters modelled on those of Cicero—represented a dramatic effort to revive the main genres of Latin literature. He insisted that the literature, history, and moral philosophy of the classical world could form a more solid and satisfactory basis for education and a better model for modern writers than the technical philosophy of Aristotle and his medieval commentators, which dominated the universities of northern Europe and were also becoming fashionable in Italian universities. He thus provided both a model for classical studies and a new justification for them: both proved vastly influential.

scholia are notes on a text, normally substantial sets of explanatory and critical notes written in the margin or between the lines of manuscripts. Many of them go back to ancient commentaries (which might fill volumes of their own). Scholia result from excerption, abbreviation, and conflation, brought about partly by readers' needs and partly by lack of space.

Like their modern successors, ancient commentators sometimes guessed or talked nonsense, but at their best scholia are a mine of information, though less in Latin than in Greek. *Aristophanes benefits most, because explanation of topical or literary references and allusions began at *Alexandria in the heyday of the Library.

science See particular sciences e.g. ASTRONOMY; BOTANY etc.; and see also EXPERIMENT.

Sciōnē, city near the tip of the western (Pallene) peninsula of *Chalcidice. It normally paid 6 talents tribute to Athens in the time of the *Delian League. Its most famous hour was its enthusiastic but unwise reception of *Brasidas in 423 BC; this led to harsh Athenian reprisals instigated by *Cleon (the men were put to death, the site given to exiles from *Plataea). Athenian treatment of Scione was a standard 4th-cent. reproach. In truth, Sparta's betrayal of Scione was no less of a disgrace.

Scipiō Aemiliānus See CORNELIUS SCIPIO AEMILIANUS AFRICANUS (NUMANTINUS).

Scipiō Africānus See CORNELIUS SCIPIO AFRICANUS.

scolia, drinking-songs, esp. *Attic. *Athenaeus and others identify various ways in which *scolia* were sung at *symposia, one of which obliged a drinker to sing when he was passed the lyre and/or myrtle branch.

Scrībōnius Cūriō, Gāius, was a friend of *Clodius Pulcher whose widow *Fulvia he later married. In the 50s he joined his father (who disapproved of his personal life) in supporting the *optimates. Elected tribune 50 as an enemy of *Caesar, he was bribed by him with a vast sum, perhaps when his own ambitious legislation was rejected by the senate. He tried to halt the drift towards civil war, proposing to disarm both Caesar and *Pompey. This was finally carried in the senate by 370 votes to 22, but the consul Claudius Marcellus refused to accept the vote. In 49 Curio served under Caesar in Italy, then was sent *prō praetōrĕ* to Sicily, which he occupied, and to Africa. There, after initial successes, he was trapped and killed by Juba I.

sculpture, Greek

Origins (*c.*1000–*c.*600 BC) Of Dark Age sculpture, only small bronzes and terracottas survive; unpretentious at first, by the 8th cent. they tend to imitate the geometrical forms of contemporary vase-painting. Some wooden cult images certainly existed, though most were perhaps aniconic or semi-iconic. Yet *Homer describes an *Athena at *Troy that was probably lifesize and fully human in form.

The Cretan *poleis* (see POLIS) were socially and politically precocious, and their eastern trade, in which *Corinth soon joined, set off a new cycle of experimentation *c.*700. In sculpture, the most popular of these *orientalizing styles is usually called 'Daedalic' after the mythical founder of Greek sculpture (see DAEDALUS). Daedalic is characterized by a strict frontality and an equally strict adherence to stylized, angular forms; coiffures are elaborately layered in the Syrian manner.

Meanwhile, *Cycladic sculptors were looking to Egypt, receptive to foreigners from 664 (see SAÏTES). After *c.*650 the walking, kilted Egyptian males were adapted to form the *kouros* type, nude and free-standing enter. *Marble was the preferred medium. The type soon spread to eastern Greece and the mainland. By *c.*600 rigid stylization was breaking down, as sculptors sought new ways of communicating male and female beauty, to delight the gods or to commemorate the dead.

Archaic sculpture (*c.*600–*c.*480) Archaic sculpture seeks exemplary patterns for reality, somewhat akin to the formulae of Homeric and archaic poetry. The aim was still to make sense of the phenomenal world, to generalize from experience, but in a more flexible and direct way. Though *kouroi* and *korai* (their draped female counter-parts) retained much in common, including the 'Archaic smile', wherever they were sculpted, each local school developed its own preferences in ideal beauty. Only in Athens did a thoroughgoing naturalism evolve. By *c.*500

Athenian *kouroi* were fully developed human beings, their anatomy closely observed, clearly articulated, and skilfully integrated with the underlying physical and geometric structure of the body.

Korai offered fewer opportunities for detailed physical observation, but just as many for displays of beauty appropriate to their subjects' station in life and value to a male-dominated world. Their sculptors concentrated upon refining the facial features, creating a truly feminine proportional canon, and indicating the curves of the body beneath the drapery. The mainland tunic or *peplos* offered little here, but from *c.*560 the possibilities of the more complex Ionian *chiton* and *himation* began to fascinate the eastern Greeks. See DRESS. Soon, refugees fleeing from the Persians helped the fashion to catch on elsewhere, esp. in Attica. Yet by *c.*500, serious interest in the behaviour of cloth had given way to a passion for novelty: sculptors now pursued a decorative brilliance enhanced by a lavish application of colour.

Both types could be adapted for cult statues, and the sources recount much work in this genre (see THEODORUS), often associated with the new stone *temples that now served as focal points of *polis* religion. Gold and ivory (chryselephantine) statues also begin to appear; several have been found at *Delphi. From *c.*600, temple exteriors were often embellished with architectural sculpture, first in limestone, then in marble; treasuries (see SANCTUARIES) were soon enhanced in the same way. Mythical narratives first supplemented, then supplanted primitive power-symbols like *gorgons and lions. Sculptors soon learnt to adapt their subjects to their frames, whether triangular (pediments or gables), rectangular (Ionic friezes), or square (metopes of the Sicyonian treasury at Delphi and temples at Paestum and Selinus); to carve pediments in higher relief and even in the round and to dramatize the story by judicious timing, lively postures and *gestures, and compelling rendering of detail.

By *c.*500 the drive to narrate convincingly had permeated almost all sculptural genres, from gravestones to statue-bases. Hollow-cast *bronze also began to replace marble (see ANTENOR), at least in free-standing sculpture. Its greater tensile strength now removed any technical restraint in the handling of narrative action poses. Only the *kouroi* and *korai* remained aloof—and so look increasingly old-fashioned.

Classical sculpture (*c.*480–*c.*330) Around 480 the automaton-like *kouros* gave way to more subtly mobile, narrative-oriented figures, monumental in physique and grave of countenance, pausing as if to think, like the 'Critius' boy, or resolute in action, like the Tyrannicides (see CRITIUS). This more flexible, holistic, and contextual view of man was abetted by a simultaneous repudiation of late Archaic 'excess' in decorative patterning in favour of a rigorously applied doctrine of formal restraint. The new style strongly recalls the *sōphrosynē* or 'self-control' urged by poets. This was an ethic much in vogue after the replacement of aristocracies at Athens and elsewhere by limited democracies, and esp. after the spectacular defeat of the hubristic and excessive Persians in 490 and 480/79. This early Classical phase is often (appropriately) called 'Severe'.

Sophrosyne is best exemplified in the sculptures of the temple of *Zeus at *Olympia, carved between 470 and 457. Their themes bespeak *hubris overcome by divinely inspired wisdom, and the participants act out their characters like participants in a tragedy. The expansive rendering brings power to the narrative, while a self-imposed economy of means allows bold distinctions in characterization, unhampered by distracting clutter. The same is true of bronzes like the Zeus from Artemisium and *Riace Warrior A, whose carefully calculated postures are eloquent, respectively, of divine might and heroic potency; and of works known only in copy like the Discobolus of *Myron, whose swinging curves capture the essence of athletic endeavour.

Throughout, the aim is to find forms or modes that express the general or typical, yet are open to some variation for individuality's sake: witness the differences between the two Riace warriors. Further progress was the work of two geniuses, *Polyclitus of Argos and *Phidias of Athens (active *c.*470–420). In his bronze *Doryphorus* or 'Spearbearer', Polyclitus created a new standard or *canon (also written up as a treatise) for the youthful nude male. Powerfully muscled, proportioned with meticulous exactitude, composed around carefully calibrated cross-relationships among the limbs, and finished with painstaking precision, it was a paradigm of measured humanity. The Mean personified, it was restrained yet limber, self-controlled yet ever-ready for action. Polyclitus produced many variations on this theme, and future generations were to follow it 'like a law'.

Polyclitus was remembered as supreme in the rendering of mortals, Phidias as the unsurpassed interpreter of the divine, master of chryselephantine, and propagandist for *Periclean Athens. In his Athena Parthenos and Zeus at Olympia he sought to convey the majesty of the gods by subtle manipulation of the rendering, and by surrounding them with mythical scenes to demonstrate their power. On the exterior sculptures of the *Parthenon Athena's power and reach are proclaimed by a closely co-ordinated programme of narratives, and her chosen people, the Athenians, are exalted by a rendering unsurpassed in Greek sculpture for its fluency, grace, harmony of body and clothing, and perfection of formal design. In this way the typical became the citizen ideal.

Phidias' followers, active during the *Peloponnesian War, both pressed his style to its limits and turned it to other ends (see PAEONIUS). Paeonius' *Nike and the parapet of the Nike temple on the Athenian Acropolis manipulate drapery to create a surface brilliance that seduces the spectator into believing that what he sees is truth: victory scintillates before his eyes. Hitherto a more-or-less objective analysis of reality, here sculpture becomes a vehicle for the subjective and rhetorical, initiating yet another phase of restless experiment. Henceforth, as the ancient critics realized, it is the phenomena that tend to coerce the sculptor, not vice versa.

Whereas in Peloponnese the war only benefited the conservative pupils of Polyclitus, in postwar Athens, demand for sculpture was virtually restricted to gravestones, revived *c.* 430 (see ART, FUNERARY, GREEK). Not until *c.*370 could the Athenians celebrate recovery by commissioning a bronze Eirēnē and Plutus (Peace and Wealth) from Cephisodotus, a work exuding Phidian majesty and harmony. Also seeking new ways to the divine, Cephisodotus' son *Praxiteles created his revolutionary Aphrodite of *Cnidus, proclaiming the power of the love goddess through total nudity and a beguiling radiance of feature and surface. Meanwhile, his contemporary Scopas sought to perfect an acceptable formula for conveying the passions of gods and men.

Scopas was a leading sculptor in the team engaged by *Mausolus of Caria for his gigantic tomb, the *Mausoleum. Its unparalleled magnificence announced the advent of the Hellenistic world; a pointer, too, was the hiring away of the best artistic talent by a *'barbarian' patron. The real revolutionary, though, was Lysippus of Sicyon (active *c.*370–310), who radically transformed Greek sculpture's central genre, the male nude. His Apoxyomenos or 'Body-scraper' not only rocks back and forth before our eyes and extends an arm into our space (see ATHLETICS for the role of the scraper), but was planned according to a new canon which sought slimness, elegance, and the appearance of greater height. This and his minute attention to details made him popular as a portraitist, esp. with *Alexander (2) the Great, from whose features he created a new ideal that was firmly rooted in reality. Greek *portraiture, which had hitherto veered between slight modifications to standard types and a sometimes trenchant realism, was transformed at a stroke.

Hellenistic Sculpture (c.330–c.30) The vast expansion of the Greek world under Alexander created a bonanza of opportunity for sculptors. Lysippus' pupils and others were hired to create commemorative, votive, and cult statues for the new kingdoms. Portraitists were esp. in demand to render and where necessary improve the features of Successor kings (see DIADOCHI), generals, and dignitaries.

Yet the political chaos after Alexander's death, together with the transformation of the independent *polis in mainland Greece, sculpture's homeland, undermined the art's social and religious foundations. Furthermore, Lysippus' commitment to the subjective had severely compromised whatever shared artistic values still existed; together with a feeling that little now remained to be discovered, this often tended to promote either eclectic blends of Scopaic, Praxitelean, and Lysippic (in portraiture) or a cautious neo-classicism.

Lysippus' school dominated Peloponnese and was popular with the Successors, while more conservative patrons could choose the Athenians. As Athens declined, her sculptors increasingly sought permanent employment abroad: *Alexandria, *Rhodes, and the Asian cities were the main beneficiaries. In Alexandria, Attic-style gravestones were popular for a while, and the affluent soon became avid consumers of grotesques; meanwhile, Ptolemaic royal portraits (see PTOLEMY (1)) exude an aura of superhuman calm. In *Pergamum, a liking for the vigorous realism of a local sculptor, in monuments celebrating the defeats of the *Celts and *Seleucids, did not preclude the hiring of the Athenian Phyromachus to create cult-images, portraits, and battle-groups in a turbulent 'baroque' style derived from late 4th-cent. art. Style was now a matter of choice.

The devastating wars c.200 mark a watershed in Hellenistic sculpture. The victorious Romans looted hundreds of statues and began to entice Greek sculptors west to work directly for them; realistic portraiture and Athenian neo-classical cult-images were most in demand. As the Roman market grew, Greek workshops began to respond with decorative copies and reworkings of classical masterpieces for direct shipment to Italy.

Meanwhile the main beneficiary of Rome's intervention, Pergamum, celebrated in style. *Eumenes II built the Great Altar, embellishing it with a 'baroque' Gigantomachy (see GIANTS) and a quasi-pictorial inner frieze narrating the life of the city's mythical founder, *Telephus. He also installed a copy of the Athena Parthenos in the Pergamene library to advertise his claim to rule the 'Athens of the east'.

Attalus III of Pergamum willed his domains to Rome in 133, bringing its sculptural tradition to a close, but the most crushing blow was dealt by the Mithradatic Wars (89–66; see MITHRADATES), which left Greece and Asia devastated and impoverished. Though some striking work was still produced, largely in portraiture, sculptors now moved to Italy in large numbers, creating the last of the great Hellenistic schools, but now on foreign soil and pledged to foreign masters. When the *Carrara quarries opened c.50 and *Augustus officially endorsed imperial classicism after *Cleopatra VII's defeat in 31, the west at last reigned supreme.

See IMAGERY; SCULPTURE, ROMAN.

sculpture, Roman Roman sculpture was produced in a variety of materials but *marble is seen as typically Roman because so much that survives is of marble. Sculpture was used for commemorative purposes (for display in public and in private contexts, esp. the tomb), for state propaganda, in religious settings, and for decorative purposes, and various forms were developed: statues and busts, relief friezes and panels, and architectural embellishments.

Early sculpture in Rome (e.g. the bronze she-wolf of c.500 BC) was heavily influenced by *Etruscan work, and Etruscan sculptors appear to have worked in Rome in the regal period and the early republic. Rome's contacts with the Greek world, at first with the colonies of southern Italy and later through wars of conquest in Greece and Asia Minor, resulted in a knowledge of and growing taste for Greek sculpture: at first statues arrived as war *booty, but growing demand created a flourishing trade in new work. The taste for sculpture in the Classical Greek style was fostered by the *Augustan regime, and had periodic revivals, esp. in the reign of *Hadrian, but from the late republic onwards there were developments in subject matter and style that are distinctly Roman, though owing much to Greek precursors. This is seen for example in the development of portraiture in late republican Rome (see PORTRAITURE, ROMAN).

Perhaps the most original Roman developments occurred in the series of historical reliefs used to decorate major state monuments and to express current ideologies. The taste for the representation of contemporary events first appears in the late republic: such a documentary approach continues under the empire, and can be seen at its most developed on the columns of *Trajan and Marcus *Aurelius, where the stories of Rome's wars with the barbarians are represented on a long relief spiralling round the column. These use 'continuous narrative': the episodes run into one another without obvious breaks between scenes, and esp. those on *Trajan's column show close attention to the factual recording of details. However, a more allegorical approach also developed alongside this realism, and some reliefs show a love of drama derived from the art of Hellenistic Greece (e.g. the so-called Great Trajanic Frieze). Realism and allegory appear side by side on one of the most complex and subtle Roman propaganda monuments, the *Ara Pacis Augustae, where 'realistic' procession scenes are placed next to mythological, allegorical, and decorative panels to express the ideals of the Augustan regime. Later state reliefs might combine the two approaches, as in the panels inside the arch of *Titus representing the Judaean *triumph (see JEWS): the carrying of the spoils of *Jerusalem is represented in a realistic (if dramatic) way, whereas the emperor in his triumphal chariot is accompanied by deities and allegorical figures. The deep, many-layered relief of these scenes was further developed in the 2nd cent. AD, with experiments in the representation of perspective, overlapping crowds, and the pictorial effects of light and shade. Towards the end of the century (Severan period) repetition and frontality of poses began to be used as a means of clarifying the narrative and isolating and emphasizing the emperor. This tendency is more marked by the time of the *tetrarchs and *Constantine I, and is a hallmark of late antique sculpture.

Sculptured relief was also produced for private patrons, esp. for the tomb: relief panels decorated the exterior walls, and ash-chests, grave *altars and *sarcophagi were placed inside. A rich repertoire of motifs was used, including mythological (and later, Christian) themes, battles, hunts, genre scenes, and portraits, drawing on Classical and Hellenistic Greek art and contemporary state reliefs as sources of inspiration. Sculpture was also widely used to decorate public buildings, temples, and private homes and *gardens.

In the provinces local styles and schools of sculpture developed. The sculptors of the eastern provinces, esp. Greece and Asia Minor, continued and developed the Classical and Hellenistic styles: they travelled widely around the empire, working on major monuments such as the forum of *Septimius Severus at *Lepcis Magna: they also created the large series of eastern sarcophagi exported to Rome and elsewhere. In the northern and western provinces Celtic traditions fused with Roman to produce interesting hybrids, such as the pediment of the temple of Sulis Minerva at *Aquae Sulis. See ART, ANCIENT ATTITUDES TO; ART, FUNERARY, ROMAN; IMAGERY; PAINTING, ROMAN.

Scythia The broad term used by Greeks and Romans to characterize the lands to their north and east, roughly from the Danube to the Don, Caucasus, and Volga. Typically, classical writers present Scythia as a chill wilderness, an 'otherness' of savages and uncivilized practices (from blinding, scalping, and flaying through tattooing to the drinking of *wine unmixed with water). Scythians and Scythian customs were a favourite literary theme from *Herodotus onwards. The historicity of such accounts is uncertain, but their ideological function has been established beyond doubt. Classical writers were esp. interested in Scythian *nomadism, uncivilized but attractive in its primitive simplicity (see BARBARIAN). So, Scythia might be imagined as a source of ignorance: e.g. the uncivilized Scythian archer-police-slaves of 5th-cent. Athens as mocked by *Aristophanes. But it can also be a source of wisdom, as personified by the legendary figure of the wise Scythian prince Anacharsis.

In the early 7th cent., acc. to Herodotus, Scythians forced the Cimmerians southwards across the Black (*Euxine) Sea and themselves campaigned deep through the near east. From c.600 the arrival of Greek settlers and traders on the north coast of the Black Sea brought Scythians into close contact with a new cultural influence. In 513 *Darius I launched an unsuccessful

Scythian expedition (see MILTIADES). The first fortified city appeared in Scythia on the steppes of the lower Dnieper *c*.400. Through the 4th cent. Scythia was at the height of its prosperity, esp. under King Atheas, who established his authority as far as the Danube, only to be killed by *Philip II. In 331 the Scythians were still strong enough to defeat the large army of Alexander (2) the Great's general Zopyrion. But, disunited, they were conquered in turn by a new force from the east, the Sauromatians (see SARMATIANS).

seals took the place of the modern signature on documents and, to some extent, of keys and locks. The materials for sealings were *lead and wax for documents; in commerce a lump of clay was commonly pressed down over the cordage. The seals themselves were generally of stone or metal and were often worn as signet *rings. The principal device on ancient seals was usually pictorial—a favourite deity, a mythical hero, animals, and later, portraits. *Augustus first used a *sphinx and later a portrait of *Alexander (2) the Great. Greek cities possessed civic seals, for public documents or public property; the Romans used a magistrate's personal seal. See ARCHIVES.

sea power Greeks started thinking seriously about command of the sea ('thalassocracy') in the 5th cent. BC, when Athens maintained its empire by naval power. The idea of Athens the great sea-power was balanced by that of Sparta the great land-power. *Thucydides (2) can, however, make *Pericles speak boldly of Athens' potential control of both elements. This combination, 'land and sea', was emotive for Greeks and Romans, a way of describing indefinite empire. It is found in the *Old Oligarch, like Thucydides' *History*, a product of the *Peloponnesian War (the writer stresses the advantages of being an *island). Fifth-cent. Greeks regarded *Minos as the first great 'thalassocrat'. Part of Thucydides' purpose in his *Archaeology* is to stress and trace the importance of sea power, hence his stress on *Delos, the actual and symbolic centre of the Aegean. Thus from Minos he passes to *Agamemnon and to historical wielders of sea power like *Polycrates (1); *Herodotus calls Polycrates the first *historical* thalassocrat.

After the end of the Athenian empire, when Sparta displaced Athens as leader of Greece, Sparta displaced Athens symbolically and emphatically at Delos too. But a combination of Athenian leadership and Persian money produced a fleet which defeated Sparta at *Cnidus in 394: Persian sea power tended to be exercised vicariously through *Phoenicians, Egyptians, and other subject peoples; this usually meant building a fleet from scratch over periods of up to three years. The *Second Athenian Confederacy gave Athens Delos again, and a further spell of sea power. *Alexander (2) the Great famously 'conquered the Persian fleet by land' i.e. by capturing Persian naval bases. No great naval victories mark his reign, or that of his father *Philip II before him.

It was not until the *Punic Wars that Rome became a real sea power. The contribution of the naval arm to Rome's success in the Hannibalic Wars was largely negative and defensive (preventing Carthaginian supplies and reinforcements from reaching Hannibal), but nevertheless crucial. Rome had trouble with *pirates until surprisingly late dates: this was due less to feebleness than lack of will (elimination of pirates would remove a source of slaves); but otherwise Rome controlled the Mediterranean from the 2nd cent. BC onwards. See also NAVIES; SHIPS; TRIREME.

sēcessio ('secession') is the Latin term for the withdrawal of the Roman *plebs* to a hill outside the sacred boundary (*pomerium*) of the city. It implies detachment from public life as well as emigration from Rome, and was an extreme form of civil disobedience, esp. as it entailed refusal of military service. The fact that the state was not immediately brought to its knees suggests that the *plebs* did not form a majority of the population, still less of the army. The first secession is said to have occurred in 494 BC, when the plebeians, oppressed by debt and arbitrary treatment, seceded to the Sacred Mount (Mons Sacer), a hill NE of Rome. The crisis, which was resolved by Agrippa Menenius Lanatus, produced the plebeian organization. See ROME (HISTORY), 1.2. The second secession was to the *Aventine, the last, to the Janiculum. The act of secession had an important place in the historical tradition of the *plebs*.

Second Athenian Confederacy A maritime defensive alliance-system open to Greek cities and dynasts outside *Anatolia, whose original motive was to ensure that Sparta respected the *freedom and *autonomy guaranteed by the *King's Peace. Its foundation (379/8) involved converting several existing bilateral alliances into a system which eventually (early 377) offered special rights, viz. a deliberative assembly; no internal political interference, tribute, governors, or garrisons; and no *cleruchy or private Athenian property-ownership within allied states. Starting with six members, the confederacy burgeoned in 378–373. Spartan naval challenges were crushed. In 375/4 Sparta conceded that the confederacy did not infringe autonomy. However, Athens failed to subdue a revolt led by *Rhodes, *Cos, and *Chios (Social War, 357–355). The Confederacy was dismantled after the creation of the *Corinthian League.

Second Sophistic is a term applied to the period *c.* AD 60–230 when *declamation became the most prestigious literary activity in the Greek world. *Philostratus coined the term in his *Lives of the Sophists*, claiming a link between the classical *sophists and the movement whose first member he identified as Nicetes of Smyrna in the reign of *Nero. The term 'sophist' seems restricted to *rhetors who entered upon a career of public displays.

On the evidence of Philostratus, whose 40 lives of imperial sophists include several Severan contemporaries, and of other literary and epigraphic texts, it is clear that for these 170 years declamation was not simply an exercise for rhetors and their pupils but a major art form in its own right. It flourished esp. in Athens and the great cities of western Asia Minor, esp. *Pergamum, *Smyrna, and *Ephesus. Rhetors, whether resident teachers of rhetoric or touring eminences, would draw aficionados in large numbers to private or imperial mansions, lecture halls in libraries, council-houses (see BOULE), concert halls (see ODEUM), and even theatres. After a less formal discourse which acted as a prelude, their formal speech was more often deliberative (Latin *suāsōria*; see RHETORIC, LATIN) recreating a historical situation, always from before 323 BC (e.g. Artabanus urges *Xerxes not to invade Greece), than forensic (*contrōversia*—e.g. should a man who both started and then halted civil war be rewarded or punished?), often involving tyrants, pirates, or rape. Rhetors also had opportunities to deliver diverse display speeches: e.g. *Polemon's speech commemorating the dedication of the Athenian *Olympieum in AD 131/2, or Aelius *Aristides' praise of Rome and lament for Smyrna devastated by an earthquake.

Many sophists, esp. many of those written up by Philostratus, were influential in their cities and even provinces, intervening to check civic disorder or inter-city rivalry, or dispatched as envoys to congratulate emperors on their accession or to win or secure privileges for their cities (and often themselves). We know of some omitted by Philostratus who, like his sophists, held city offices or were honoured with statues.

But for most teaching must have taken more time and energy than declamation, and it was to encourage education that *Vespasian gave rhetors, like *grammatici* (see EDUCATION, ROMAN) and doctors, immunities from city offices, judicial service, and priesthoods whether city or provincial, immunities confirmed by his successors and extended to philosophers by *Nerva or *Trajan (see IMMUNITAS; LITURGY). *Antoninus Pius limited holders to between three and five according to the city's size (and excluded philosophers), though those deemed of special excellence were supernumerary and, unlike the others, immune even when teaching outside their city. Emperors also established salaried chairs of rhetoric: Vespasian of both Greek and Latin at Rome, Pius allegedly throughout the empire. To the civic chair of Greek rhetoric then founded at Athens with a salary of a talent, Marcus *Aurelius added *c.*170 an imperial chair salaried at 10,000 drachmae. From no later than *Hadrian the *equestrian post of secretary for Greek correspondence was, appropriately, often held by a distinguished rhetor, and this led to a procuratorial career (see PROCURATOR) and further rewards. Some posts, however, and the elevation of sophists to the senate, like their authority within city or province, may be as much attributable to their birth into their cities' governing élites as to their skill in manipulating enthusiastic audiences.

Competition for such distinctions encouraged professional quarrels in a breed already competitive. Such rivalry added spice to performances and tempted fans to trap their hero's rival, as when *Herodes Atticus' pupils spoiled a supposedly extempore performance of Philagrus by reading out the speech, which had already been published.

The cultural change that occurred about the time of Nero may not have been so much one of the rhetors' role as of the theatre in which they played. The Greek world was recovering from Roman expansion and civil wars, Nero's short-lived gift of 'freedom' to *Achaia stirred consciousness, and Philostratus' period saw an economic, cultural, and even (to a degree) political recovery in the Greek world. What was uttered and done by rhetors in this period breathed more confidence and had a wider impact than what went before, and they themselves were prominent among the many elements of Greek culture that found a high place in Roman esteem and society.

Secular Games, theatrical games (see LUDI) and sacrifices (see SACRIFICE, ROMAN) performed by the Roman state to commemorate the end of one *saeculum* and the beginning of a new one. The *saeculum*, defined as the longest span of human life, was fixed in the republic as an era of 100 years. The ceremony took place in the *Campus Martius, near the Tiber, at a spot known as Tarentum.

*Augustus' plans to celebrate the *saeculum* were known in the 20s BC, and were referred to by Virgil in the *Aeneid*. At Augustus' request, the *quindecimviri consulted the Sibylline Books and discovered a prophecy sanctioning Secular Games with many novel features. The *ludi* of 17 BC are fully recorded in an inscription, set up at the Tarentum. The *saeculum* was now fixed at 110 years. The *ludi* retained three nights of sacrifices and games, but Dis pater and *Persephone were replaced by the Fates, the Goddesses of Childbirth, and Mother Earth, and three daytime celebrations were added, to *Jupiter, *Juno, and *Apollo and *Diana. The Augustan games marked not the passing of an era, but the birth of a new age. Other novelties include the addition of seven supplementary days of more modern entertainment in theatre and circus. After the offerings on the third day, 27 boys and 27 girls sang *Horace's *Secular Hymn*, first at the temple of Apollo and then on the *Capitol. In the hymn Horace brings into great prominence Augustus' patron god Apollo in his new *Palatine temple.

The antiquarian *Claudius next celebrated games, in AD 47, on a new cycle, the eight-hundredth birthday of Rome. Taking their lead from Claudius, games were also held the following two centuries, in 148 and 248, but these were not counted in the official numbered sequence of games. The next games on (or nearly on) the Augustan cycle were celebrated by *Domitian in 88 (six years early) and *Septimius Severus in 204 (back on the Augustan cycle). Another inscription from the Tarentum records this celebration (which included a new secular hymn). It was to be the last celebration, as games were not held in AD 314 by *Constantine I, newly converted to *Christianity.

seers See AUGURS; DIVINATION; MELAMPUS; PROPHECIES; PROPHETES; TIRESIAS.

Sejanus See AELIUS SEIANUS.

Selēnē, Greek moon-goddess, was acc. to *Hesiod, daughter of the sibling *Titans Hyperion and Theia, sister of *Helios and *Eos; she later became Helios' daughter, in recognition apparently of the idea that the moon shines by borrowed light. Selene drives the moon chariot, drawn by a pair of horses or oxen. In myth, she is best known for her love for *Endymion, which caused Zeus to cast him into an eternal sleep in a cave on Mt. Latmus in Caria, where Selene visits him; similar stories attach to Eos. Actual worship of Selene, as of Helios, is treated by *Aristophanes as characteristic of *barbarians in opposition to Greeks. A more important way in which the moon had a place in religious life was through the identification with it (but not necessarily with the mythological Selene) of major goddesses such as *Artemis or *Hecate.

Seleucids, rulers of the empire founded by *Seleucus I, governing a vast realm, stretching from *Anatolia, via Syria and Babylonia to Iran and thence to central Asia. The Seleucids from the start continued (and adapted) *Achaemenid institutions in the army (use of local peoples), in administration (e.g. taxation and satrapal organization; see SATRAP), colonizing policies, the use of plural 'royal capitals' (Seleucia on Tigris, Antioch, *Sardis), the use of local languages (and people) in local bureaucracy; also, from the beginning, *Babylon, *Babylonia, and the Babylonian kingship were central, in Seleucid planning, to an empire, the pivotal point of which, joining east and west, was the Fertile Crescent.

By the peace of Apamea (188), negotiated between Antiochus III and Rome, the Seleucids gave up possessions north of the Taurus mountains in Anatolia, retaining Pamphylia, Cilicia in southern Turkey, plus their large empire in the east. It was the complex interaction of dynastic strife, from the later 2nd cent., the advance of the Parthians, under Mithradates II of *Parthia, who had conquered Babylonia by the 120s, and the interference of Rome, that gradually destroyed the Seleucid empire. Pompey annexed Syria in 64 BC, ending just over two and a half centuries of Seleucid rule.

Seleucus I (Nicator: Conqueror) (c.358–281 BC), fought with *Alexander (2) the Great in the latter's campaigns from *Asia Minor to *Persia, Bactria, Sogdiana, and India, as a general. Later he was to replay this 'conquest' as he, and his son, Antiochus I, brought the eastern 'Upper Satrapies' (see SATRAP) of the former *Achaemenid empire gradually under Seleucid control and colonization, wisely negotiating after invasion (*c*.306) of the Indus region a settlement with Sandracottus. Seleucus ceded the Indus valley, and four adjacent satrapies.

After Alexander's death, Seleucus gained the satrapy of *Babylonia (321), which was to form the core of his later kingdom. There he initially supported *Antigonus I, but was ousted by him (316) and fled to Egypt. He regained Babylonia (312) with a small task force in a spectacular exploit and thence took *Media, Susiana, and perhaps Persis too; as a Babylonian chronicle shows, fighting against Antigonus continued until a battle (308) left Seleucus in control of Babylonia. Seleucus then embarked on further campaigns to the Upper Satrapies, to Bactria-Sogdiana, and the Indus region (above). He founded Seleucia on Tigris (*c*.305) as a royal capital, returning westwards to join the coalition of 'separatist' generals against Antigonus.

The victory of Ipsus (301) gave Seleucus northern Syria and access to the Mediterranean through Syria and Cilicia. He built Antioch (300) as another of his royal capitals to serve the then limits of his kingdom. Campaigns and colonization by Seleucus, Antiochus, and their officers, continued in the Upper Satrapies (e.g. Media, Sogdiana-Bactria, the Persian Gulf). See COLONIZATION, HELLENISTIC. Seleucus finally won Asia Minor with the victory of Corupedium over Lysimachus (281). A new Babylonian chronicle fragment reveals Seleucus' military objectives after Corupedium as 'Macedon, his land,' apparently aiming at the reconstitution of Alexander's unified empire of Macedon and Asia. He launched a campaign, but was assassinated by Ptolemy Ceraunus, who wanted Macedonia for himself.

Seleucus was married to the Bactrian princess Apame, mother of his successor and eldest son, the half-Iranian Antiochus, a prototype of the dynastic marriage alliances with non-Greek dynasties that the Seleucids pursued as a continuing policy in their relations with non-Greek peoples in and beyond their realms. Seleucus had prepared Antiochus for the throne since he acted as crown prince in Babylonia before he was appointed co-regent (292/1–281/0), a mechanism that facilitated the Seleucid succession and continued to be used. Seleucus' second marriage to Stratonice, daughter of Demetrius Poliorcetes (290s), seems mainly to have been directed by politics, i.e. a (temporary) pact with Demetrius. However, Stratonice was passed to Antiochus as queen and wife, and Antiochus was dispatched to the eastern satrapies as king with full royal authority (and armies). This looks like a recognition of the need to consolidate in the Upper Satrapies and for royal authority to do it, leaving Seleucus free to deal with problems in Syria and Anatolia.

Seleucus was one of the ablest of the Successors ('the greatest king of those who succeeded Alexander': *Arrian). Apart from his military victories, he took great care to 'respect' and utilize local traditions (e.g. the Babylonian kingship and Babylonian traditions) and to proffer patronage to non-Greek communities and their sanctuaries as well as Greek ones.

self-sufficiency See AUTARKY.

sella curūlis ('curule chair') was an ivory folding seat, without back or arms, used by the higher Roman magistrates (hence the title 'curule' magistrates; see MAGISTRACY, ROMAN). The name was derived from the chariot (Latin *currus*) in which the magistrate was conveyed to the place of judgement, and originally the *sella curūlis* served as the seat of justice.

Sĕmĕlē, a daughter of *Cadmus of *Thebes and Harmonia, seduced by *Zeus, who visited her unseen, and by whom she conceived a child. At the urging of *Hera, she persuaded Zeus to show himself to her: he appeared in the form of a thunderbolt, which killed her. Zeus removed the embryo from the corpse, sewed it into his own thigh, and eventually gave birth to *Dionysus, whom *Hermes handed over to Semele's sister *Ino, to rear. *Homer's version, although brief, implies that the birth was normal; so does Hesiod's. As a cult figure, Semele possessed an open-air enclosure, formerly her bridal chamber, on the acropolis at Thebes.

Sēmōnidēs of Amorgos in the SE *Cyclades, Greek iambic poet (see IAMBIC POETRY, GREEK), said to be one of those who led the Samian colonists to Amorgos (see SAMOS; COLONIZATION, GREEK), which would make him contemporary with *Archilochus. The longest fragment (118 lines, almost a complete poem) expounds the thesis that different types of women were created from different animals and have their qualities. Some fragments contain pessimistic moralizing, others suggest entertaining and obscene narratives. See also ANIMALS, KNOWLEDGE OF.

Semprōnius Gracchus, Gāius, younger brother of Tiberius *Sempronius Gracchus (2), served under his cousin and brother-in-law

*Cornelius Scipio Aemilianus at *Numantia. A member of his brother's land commission, he supported the plans (concerning Italian ownership of public land) of Fulvius Flaccus in 126 BC, then went to Sardinia as *quaestor. Returning before his commander in 124, he was accused before the censors but acquitted, and elected tribune for 123 and again for 122, when he was joined by Flaccus. After laws meant to avenge his brother and secure himself against a similar fate, he embarked on a programme of reform, aided by friendly colleagues. The most important measures were: (1) a law assuring citizens of corn, normally at a subsidized price; (2) laws providing for the resumption of land distribution and the foundation of colonies, including one on the ritually cursed site of *Carthage, which Gracchus himself, as commissioner, helped to establish; (3) laws regulating army service and providing for public works—all these to gain the support of the *plebs* and relieve poverty and exploitation; (4) a law to have the right to collect a tithe on the harvest of the new province of Asia sold by the censors in Rome; (5) laws regulating *extortion trials, the second (passed by Acilius Glabrio) introducing elements of criminal procedure and drawing on the *equestrian order for juries—these to protect provincials from magistrates' rapacity, to secure the treasury's major revenue against peculation, and to set up members of the non-political class to control politicians; (6) a law to make the senate's designation of consular provinces immune to tribunician veto and to have it before the elections—this to remove the most important administrative decision of the year from personal prejudice. This law shows how far he was from being a 'democrat'.

Finally, in 122, he proposed to offer citizenship to Latins and Latin status (see IUS LATII) to Italian allies, both to protect them from the excesses of Roman magistrates and to make them subject to his brother's agrarian law. The law was opposed by Fannius, whom he had supported for the consulship, and by the tribune Līvius Drūsus, who outbid him with an unrealistic colonial programme. It was defeated, and Gracchus was not re-elected. In 121, with his legislation under attack, Gracchus, supported by Flaccus, resorted to armed insurrection. It was suppressed after the first use of the so-called *senatus consultum ultimum*; they and many of their supporters were killed, others executed after arrest.

Gaius Gracchus had more ambitious plans than his brother, whose memory he revered. He saw the need for major administrative reforms. A proud aristocrat, he wanted to leave the senate in charge of directing policy and the magistrates in charge of its execution, subject to constitutional checks and removed from financial temptation, with the people sharing in the profits of empire without excessive exploitation of the subjects. The ultimate result of his legislation was to set up the *publicani* as a new exploiting class, not restrained by a tradition of service or by accountability at law. But this did not become clear for a generation.

Semprōnius Gracchus (1), **Tiberius,** was aedile 182 and demanded such heavy contributions from provincial clients that the senate limited future aediles' expenditure. As praetor and proconsul in Spain (180–178) he subdued the Celtiberians, imposed a settlement they regarded as bearable and founded a city for them. He was rewarded with a *triumph and the consulship of 177. He took *Sardinia from its commanders and in two ruthless campaigns subdued the Sardi, celebrating another triumph and recording his deeds in a temple on the *forum Boarium. As censor 169, he and his colleague supported the levies for the Macedonian War and dealt harshly with *equestrians and *publicani. Prosecuted by a tribune, they were acquitted. Gracchus restricted freedmen's votes and built the *basilica Sempronia. As consul for the second time (163) he again went to Sardinia, from where he remembered, as *augur, that the new consuls had been elected illegally, forcing them to resign. He headed two embassies to the east, establishing useful personal connections. He married *Cornelia, daughter of *Cornelius Scipio Africanus, who bore him twelve children, only three of whom (Tiberius *Sempronius Gracchus (2), Gaius *Sempronius Gracchus, and a daughter) survived.

Semprōnius Gracchus (2), **Tiberius,** son of (1) and of *Cornelia, served at Carthage under his cousin *Cornelius Scipio Aemilianus, who married his sister. As quaestor in Spain (137 BC), he used his father's connections to save the army of Hostilius Mancinus by a treaty later disowned by the senate on Scipio's motion. His good faith thus discredited, he joined a group hostile to Scipio: his father-in-law *Claudius Pulcher, *princeps senatus* and *augur; the consul for 133 Mucius Scaevola and his brother Licinius Crassus Dives Mucianus, both eminent lawyers and *pontifices* (see PONTIFEX). As tribune 133, in Scipio's absence, he proposed, with their aid and advice, a law designed to solve Rome's interlocking problems: departure or expulsion of small landowners from their properties, leading to insuperable difficulties in recruiting armies; danger from increasing numbers of slaves; and lack of an assured food supply for the capital. The law reaffirmed the long-ignored limit of 500 *iugera* of arable public land per person (see AGER PUBLICUS) and instituted a commission (to which he, his brother Gaius (see above) and his father-in-law were ultimately elected) to find and confiscate surplus land and distribute it in small lots to poor citizens. A compromise offering 250 additional *iugera* for each child was withdrawn when it failed to secure his opponents' acceptance of the law. Following good precedent and with his eminent supporters' approval, he submitted the law to the *plebs* without previous discussion in the senate. It was vetoed by Octavius, taken to the senate for adjudication, and rejected. Gracchus none the less resubmitted it, and Octavius persisted in his veto, both contrary to custom. To end the unprecedented impasse Gracchus had Octavius removed from office—again an unprecedented step, but without objection by the other tribunes, who did not veto it. When Pergamene envoys brought news of Attalus III's death and will, leaving his estate to Rome, Gracchus (with whom they probably stayed owing to his father's guest-friendship with the dynasty) proposed to prejudge the issue of acceptance, ignoring the senate's traditional right to guide foreign affairs, and to distribute Attalus' property to Roman citizens, perhaps as equipment grants for his new allotment-holders.

He next sought re-election, to escape certain conviction on *perduellio* charges. This last unprecedented step alienated earlier supporters and increased fear of tyranny among opponents. When the consul Scaevola refused to stop him by force, the *pontifex maximus* Cornelius Scipio Nasica Serapio led a mob of senators and their clients 'to save the republic'. Gracchus and many of his supporters were killed on the Capitol, others were later punished by a commission under Popillius Laenas, consul 132. The land commission, however, continued unimpeded until 129 (see CORNELIUS SCIPIO AEMILIANUS AFRICANUS).

His tribunate marks the beginning of 'the Roman Revolution': the introduction of murder into politics and the breakdown of *concordia* (the tradition of not pushing legal powers to extremes) on which the republic was based. See also AGRARIAN LAWS AND POLICY.

senate
Republican Age

Composition
In the time of the *Gracchi (c.133–121 BC) the senate was a body of c. 300 rich men of aristocratic birth, most of them ex-magistrates. Although the sources tend to assume that this state of affairs had always existed, it was in fact the product of historical development and change. Since in the early republic there were very few magistrates, and iteration of office was common, it follows that there was a time when either most senators had never held a magistracy, or their number was considerably less than 300. Probably both conclusions are true for the 5th cent.

A law passed before 318 BC (the *lex Ovinia*) laid down that the censors were to choose the senate according to fixed criteria; only men guilty of serious misconduct could be omitted from the list. As a result membership became effectively lifelong, and expulsion from the senate meant disgrace. The criteria of selection are not recorded, but it was probably as a consequence of this reform that ex-magistrates were chosen automatically. By the later 3rd cent. ex-magistrates were permitted to take part in sessions before being formally enrolled at the *census. The *censors nevertheless retained the right to make up numbers by choosing additional senators, and to exclude persons considered guilty of immoral behaviour or following disreputable professions. *Freedmen and sons of freedmen were not usually admitted. It is also evident that senators had to be qualified for membership of the *equestrian order, which meant ownership of landed property worth 400,000 sesterces. *Sulla increased the size of the senate by adding 300 new members and making entry dependent on tenure of the quaestorship; the number of *quaestors was raised to 20 to maintain numbers thenceforth. *Caesar rewarded his supporters by admitting them to the senate, which in 45 had 900 members; under the triumvirate the figure rose to over 1,000, but was reduced to c.600 by *Augustus.

Senators wore the *latus *clavus on their tunics and special shoes. They had reserved seats at religious ceremonies and games. They were not allowed to leave Italy without the senate's permission. Being excluded from state contracts and ownership of large ships, they were predominantly a landowning class. Although heredity was a strong recommendation for magisterial office, the senate was not an exclusively hereditary body; it seems always to have contained numbers of 'new men' (i.e. first-generation senators; see NOVUS HOMO), esp. among the lower ranks (though for a new man to rise to high office was naturally unusual).

Procedure

The senate was summoned by the presiding magistrates, either holders of *imperium or, later, tribunes of the plebs (see TRIBUNI PLEBIS), according to an order of precedence. Sessions were held between dawn and sunset, but were forbidden during the *comitia. Meetings had to take place in Rome (see CURIA (2)) or within a mile of the city boundary, in a place both public and consecrated. The first sitting of the year was in the temple of Jupiter Capitolinus.

Sittings were held in private, but with open doors, the tribunes sitting in the vestibule in the period before their admission to sessions (4th cent. BC?). A session opened with a statement by the chairman or another magistrate, outlining the matter for discussion. Each senator then gave his opinion (*sententia) in order of rank—beginning with ex-censors (censōriī), followed by consulārēs, praetōriī, and so on. The senior patrician ex-censor, who gave his opinion first, was known as the *princeps senatus. After Sulla the magistrate gave precedence to the consuls designate or, in their absence, to a senator of consular rank, and princeps senatus became a purely social title open to plebeians. Each senator spoke from his seat. Freedom of speech was unlimited in the republic, but Augustus imposed a time-limit. After the debate a vote was taken; the decree resulting from a positive vote was known as a *senatus consultum. Sometimes a vote was taken directly after the opening statement with no intervening debate; and on some issues a quorum was required. A senatus consultum could be vetoed by the tribunes. Records of proceedings were kept by the urban quaestors in the *aerarium, and in 59 BC Caesar ordered them to be published.

Functions

The senate's formal role was to advise the magistrates. Its advice covered all matters of domestic and foreign policy, finance, and religion. In the 3rd and 2nd cents. it was customary for magistrates (and tribunes) to submit legislative proposals to the senate for discussion, and to obtain a senatus consultum before presenting a bill to the comitia. The senate could also invalidate laws already passed by pointing out technical flaws in procedure.

Since the senate included ex-magistrates who were effectively (after the lex Ovinia) members

for life, its decisions inevitably came to bind those of its members who happened to be holding senior magistracies at any given time. And by the start of the 3rd cent. the growth of the Roman state and the increasing complexity of its affairs gave the senate an ever greater control of government business. It was the only permanent body with the necessary knowledge and experience to supervise policy in a wide range of fields. It controlled the state's finances, the levying and disposal of military forces, the allocation of magisterial tasks ('provinces'; see PROVINCIA), relations with foreign powers, and the maintenance of law and order in Rome and Italy. It was the senate that decided whether to extend the period of a magistrate's command (see PRO CONSULE, PRO PRAETORE), and although the people in the *comitia centuriata had the final say on declarations of war and the ratification of treaties, it is clear that, by the end of the 3rd cent. at least, they merely gave formal assent to decisions taken in advance by the senate. The senate supervised the religious life of the community, and the major priestly colleges consisted largely of senators. The senate received reports of prodigies and decided on the appropriate action; and it was the senate that ordered the performance of special religious ceremonies and decided on the introduction of new cults.

In the late republic the senate claimed the right to wield absolute power in certain circumstances. It could order dispensation from the observance of law, and during the Gracchan period it asserted the right to declare a state of emergency by passing its 'ultimate decree' (*senatus consultum ultimum), which gave the magistrates unfettered power to act as they saw fit. But these developments occurred at a time when the senate's authority was being challenged by the populares (see OPTIMATES), and in the succeeding decades it was completely undermined by armed force. The collapse of the senate's authority marked the end of the republic.

Imperial Age

Under *Augustus and his successors far-reaching modifications of the social origins and the corporate and individual functions of senators occurred. Despite those changes the senatorial order remained the most important political and social body in the empire, its first estate.

The order and its recruitment

By the end of the Civil Wars the ranks of senators had increased to about 1,000. Augustus initiated a series of revisions of the senate of which the most important occurred in 28 and

18 BC. After the latter the size of the senate was fixed at 600, which remained its normal figure through the first two and a half centuries of the Principate. A new property qualification of one million sesterces was introduced, which served to differentiate more clearly the senatorial from the *equestrian order. Sons of senators gained the automatic right to assume the *latus *clavus* at 17 years of age and to stand, later, for membership of the senate. Sons of senators normally served for one year as a military tribune, then held a post in the vigintivirate (see VIGINTISEX-VIRI) before standing for election to the senate (through the quaestorship; see QUAESTOR) at 25. Twenty quaestors were elected each year; from the beginning of *Tiberius' reign the election of junior magistrates (most notably the quaestors and praetors) was transferred to the senate.

The main thrust of Augustus' reforms was to introduce *dē iūre* a strong hereditary element into the senate. However, throughout the Principate some senatorial families were impoverished by over-expenditure, others fell into political disfavour or were eliminated; still other senatorial families had no surviving sons. In addition some sons of senators probably chose not to try to follow in their fathers' footsteps. So in each generation opportunities arose for new families, through the patronage of the emperors, to enter the senate. Emperors promoted new men into the senate either through the grant of the *latus clavus*, which gave individuals the right to stand for the quaestorship, or through direct *adlection. By these means imperial *patronage continuously transformed the social origins of senators.

The influx of new families recruited from the élites of the provinces transformed the geographic composition of the order. Under Augustus the senate remained primarily Italian in origin. Under the Julio-Claudian emperors provincial senators, esp. from *Baetica and Gallia Narbonensis (see GAUL (TRANSALPINE)), emerged. In the course of the later 1st and 2nd cents. new families emerged from the North African and eastern provinces, though very few senators ever came from the north or Danubian provinces. Under the Severi Italian senators were outnumbered. In the long term the social and geographic transformation of the senate allowed the socio-political élite of the conquered to be gradually fused with the élite of the conquerors. See next entry.

Functions and roles
Although financial policy, diplomacy, and military policy became the preserve of the em-

perors, the senate still exercised certain important corporate functions. It acted as a source of binding rule-making, as *senatus consulta* acquired the full force of law (see SENATUS CONSULTUM); surviving legislation predominantly concerns the rules of status and of inheritance and the maintenance of public order. As a court it tried its own members, chiefly on charges of *extortion. Most importantly it formally conferred powers on new emperors (and members of their families), and the acknowledgement of the senate was, therefore, the condition of legitimacy of any emperor. It also claimed the right to declare them public enemies, condemn their memory (*damnatio memoriae) and rescind their acts.

Senatorial membership, as in the republic, continued to be a precondition for exercising key individual political and administrative roles. For example, the civil and military administration of most provinces lay in the hands of individual senators in their role as provincial governors (proconsuls—see PRO CONSULE, PRO PRAETORE, and *legati Augusti*—see LEGATI). Even in AD 200 29 out of 33 legions were still commanded by senators. The civil and military posts, in Rome and the provinces, allocated to senators were ranked in a clear hierarchy; some were reserved for ex-praetors, others for ex-consuls. The most successful senators politically were those who governed the senior provinces reserved for ex-consuls. Senators also exercised direct influence on the administration, jurisdiction, and military policy of the emperors through their membership of the *consilium principis*. In short imperial rule required the active participation of the empire's political élite formed by the senate. Indeed in the 1st and 2nd cents. emperors, when they had no male heir, adopted a senator as their successor (so *Nerva adopted *Trajan who, in turn, adopted *Hadrian). When political legitimacy at Rome broke down and civil war occurred (as in 68–69 and 193–197), it was senior senators who vied for the purple.

senātūs consultum was the advice of the *senate to the magistrates, and was expressed in the form of a resolution or decree. In republican times it had no legal force, but in practice it was always obeyed and, except when vetoed, it acquired the force of law when implemented. During the empire *senatus consulta* were at first implemented by a clause in the *praetor's *edict; after Hadrian certain *senatus consulta* had immediate legal force. The *senatus consultum* was drafted after the session of the senate in the presence of the presiding magistrate and some witnesses, usually including the proposer. If necessary, it was translated into Greek. Many *senatus consulta* are preserved in Greek translations.

A *senatus consultum* usually contained: (1) the name of the presiding magistrate; (2) a statement by the proposing magistrate, ending with the formula *d(ē) e(ā) r(ē) i(ta) c(ensuērunt)* ('concerning the matter in hand they [i.e. the senators present] decreed as follows'); (3) the decree itself, often expressed in the form of advice to the magistrates: *s(ī) e(īs) v(idēbitur)* ('if it shall seem right to them'); (4) the mark of approval, indicated by the letter *C* (*censuerunt*, 'they decreed').

The texts of *senatus consulta* were deposited in the *aerarium*, and from an early date the plebeian *aediles were allowed to keep copies in the temple of Ceres (see AVENTINE). The documents were classified, but not sufficiently to prevent losses and falsifications.

senātūs consultum ultimum, 'the ultimate decree of the *senate', a modern term for a declaration of emergency (see TUMULTUS).

This decree urged magistrates, usually the consul or consuls, to take measures to defend the state and see that it came to no harm. It was interpreted as authorizing the magistrates to employ physical repression against (unspecified) public enemies without being bound by strict legality. Inevitably it was a matter of political controversy, since questions arose whether the circumstances merited this decree and what level of force and illegality was appropriate after it.

The decree was first both passed and accepted by the consul *Opimius in 121 BC, against Gaius *Sempronius Gracchus and Fulvius Flaccus. It was used nine times more in the years 100 to 40. It was originally passed after disturbances in Rome itself, but it came to be used when the primary threat came from outside Rome, as with the Catilinarians (63; see SERGIUS CATILINA), and later was employed against an alleged external enemy, when there was no threat of violence in Rome at all (so Caesar complained in 49, and this was certainly true in 43 and 40).

When this decree had led to deaths, esp. those of eminent men, there was bitter reaction after the event against magistrates responsible—Opimius, *Cicero—and, in the long-deferred case of *Rabirius (prosecuted in 63 for what he had done in 100), a man under *Marius' command. The usual ground of complaint was that citizens had been killed without proper trial—which

was true: the question was whether this illegality could be justified.

Seneca the Elder (Lucius Annaeus Seneca), writer on declamation, was born of an equestrian family at Corduba in Spain *c.*50 BC. Of his life we know little; he was certainly in Rome both as a young man and after his marriage, and his knowledge of the contemporary schools of *rhetoric implies that he spent much time in the capital. His family wealth was increased by his marriage to Helvia, a fellow countrywoman, by whom he had three sons, *Annaeus Novatus (Gallio), *Seneca the Younger, and Annaeus Mela, the father of *Lucan. He died *c.* AD 40.

His history of Rome 'from the start of the civil wars almost up to the day of his death' is lost. The partly preserved *Aphorisms, Distinctions, and Colours of Orators and Rhetors,* written for his sons in his old age, originally comprised ten books devoted to *contrōversiae*, each with a preface, and at least two devoted to *suāsōriae* (see DECLAMATION). As the cumbersome title suggests, the material is grouped under three rubrics. For each theme, striking and epigrammatic extracts from various speakers are followed by the author's analysis of the heads of their arguments and by remarks on their colours or lines of approach to the case. Extracts from Greek declaimers are often placed at the end, and the whole is spiced with comments and anecdotes of Seneca's own.

Seneca's sons were primarily interested in *epigram, and his book is biased towards smart sayings. The accumulated *sententiae*, vividly illustrative of an important aspect of *Silver Age Latin, tend to cloy. Relief is provided by the excellent prefaces, which sketch with graphic detail the characters of the major declaimers on whom Seneca, relying (it seems) only on a phenomenal memory, primarily drew. Elsewhere Seneca's own stories and digressions give priceless information on declamatory practice and on the literary scene of the early empire. His literary criticism is conservative and somewhat mechanical, and he is out of sympathy with a good deal of what he preserves for us (see LITERARY CRITICISM IN ANTIQUITY, 8).

Seneca the Younger (Lūcius Annaeus Seneca), Roman philosopher and tragic poet (b. at the turn of the eras; d. AD 65). He was born at Corduba in southern Spain, into a rich *equestrian family of Italian stock, being the second son of *Seneca the Elder and Helvia. He was happily married to Pompeia Paulina, but their only son died (41).

Brought to Rome by his aunt he studied grammar and rhetoric, and was attracted at an early age to philosophy. In 41 under *Claudius he was banished to Corsica for alleged adultery with a sister of Gaius (1) (Caligula), and remained in exile until 49, when he was recalled through the influence of *Iulia Agrippina and made praetor. He was appointed tutor to her son *Nero, then 12 years old and ready to embark on the study of rhetoric. In 51 *Burrus, who was to become Seneca's congenial ally and colleague during his years of political influence, was made *praetorian *prefect; and with Nero's accession in 54, Seneca exchanged the role of tutor for that of political adviser and minister.

During the next eight years, Seneca and Burrus managed to guide and cajole Nero sufficiently to ensure a period of good government, in which the influence of his mother was reduced and the worst abuses of the Claudian regime were corrected. As a friend (see AMICITIA) of the *princeps*, writing the emperor's speeches, exercising patronage, and managing intrigue, Seneca's power was ill-defined but real. On Clemency suggests the way in which Nero was encouraged to behave himself, but Seneca's reputation was tarnished by Nero's suspected murder of *Britannicus in 55 and certain murder of his mother in 59. As Nero fell under the influence of people more willing to flatter him and to encourage his inclination to seek popularity through exhibitionism and security through crime, Seneca's authority declined and his position became intolerable. In 62 the death of Burrus snapped his power, and Seneca asked to retire and offered to relinquish his vast wealth to Nero. The retirement was formally refused and the wealth not accepted until later; in practice he withdrew from public life and spent much time away from Rome. In 64, after Nero's sacrilegious thefts following the Great Fire in July, Seneca virtually retired to his chamber and handed over much of his wealth. He turned to philosophy, writing, and the company of friends. In 65 he was forced to kill himself for alleged participation in the unsuccessful Pisonian conspiracy (see CALPURNIUS PISO); his death, explicitly modelled on that of *Socrates, is vividly described by Tacitus.

Seneca's extant works comprise, first, ten ethical treatises: On Providence; On the Constancy of the Wise Man; On Anger (in three books); To Marcia, on Consolation; On the Happy Life; On Leisure. On Tranquillity of Mind; On the Brevity of Life; To Polybius, on Consolation; To Helvia, on Consolation (addressed to his mother, who is consoled for his exile).

We have four other prose works. On Clemency; On Kindness; Natural Questions, dedicated to *Lucilius (2) and written during Seneca's retirement. Moral Essays, the longest of the prose works, consists of 124 letters divided into 20 books. Their advertised recipient is again Lucilius, but the fiction of a genuine correspondence is only sporadically maintained. Despite the artificiality of the letter-form, the variety and informality of these essays have made them always the most popular of Seneca's prose works.

The obscurely entitled Apocolocyntosis, a *Menippean satire written in a medley of prose and verse, is an original and amusing skit on the deification of Claudius, containing serious political criticism and clever literary parody (even of Seneca himself).

The bulk of Seneca's prose work is philosophical and an important source for the history of *Stoicism. His moralizing is given all the force which an accomplished *rhetor can provide and is enlivened by anecdote, hyperbole, and vigorous denunciation. The style is brilliant, exploiting to the full the literary fashions of the day while remaining individual, and has an important place in the history of European prose. Nonperiodic and highly rhythmical, antithetical, and abrupt, it relies for its effect on rhetorical device, vivid metaphor, striking vocabulary, paradox, and point.

His most important poetical works are his tragedies. He drew inspiration from the whole tragic corpus, esp. from *Euripides. There is unmistakable influence from *Ovid's Heroides (Medea, Phaedra) and from episodes of violence and passion in the Aeneid and Metamorphoses: thus Trojan Women makes full use of Aeneid 2.

Seneca largely observes a post-classical pattern of five acts, opening with an expository monologue or prologue scene. Acts are divided by choral odes. Though the plays could be staged, discontinuity of action, with unanswered speeches and unexplained exits, suggests rather that they were primarily intended to be recited or read.

The plays have been called 'rhetorical': certainly their most conspicuous feature is the passionate rhetoric of the leading characters, displayed both in terse *stichomythia and extended harangues. They have been claimed as Stoic, since the dominant theme is the triumph of evil released by uncontrolled passion and the spread of destruction from man to the world of nature around him. Certainly Seneca both praises the beneficial persuasive effect of poetry and exonerates drama from the charge of fostering harmful emotions. However, although the plays reflect Stoic psychology, ethics, and physical theories, their predominantly negative tone and representation of life makes it unlikely that they were composed as Stoic lessons.

The tragedies exercised a powerful influence over the Renaissance theatres of Italy, France, and Elizabethan England, where the 'Tenne Tragedies' adapted from Seneca by various translators coloured the diction and psychology of Marlowe, Shakespeare, and Ben Jonson. 20th-century horrors make it easier to accept the violence and extravagance of Senecan and Elizabethan tragedy.

Seneca was a talented orator, statesman, diplomat, financier, and viticulturist, a prolific and versatile writer, a learned yet eloquent philosopher. Yet his style can weary us, as it did the generation of *Quintilian and *Tacitus, and as a man, he has continued to be criticized as a hypocrite: he preached the unimportance of wealth but did not surrender his until the end; he compromised the principles he preached by flattering those in power and by condoning many of Nero's crimes. Yet, as he says himself, effective exhortation can include preaching higher standards than can be realistically expected, and most moral teachers have urged attention to their words rather than to their example. Moreover, his teaching is more subtle and complex than is sometimes appreciated: he does not require the sacrifice of wealth, only the achievement of detachment from worldly goods; he advocates giving honest advice to rulers, while avoiding offence and provocation. Moreover, he confesses to having abandoned his youthful asceticism, to giving in on occasion to grief and anger, to being on only the first rung of moral progress. Above all, he conveys, as few moralists have, a sympathy with human weakness and an awareness of how hard it is to be good. For his disciples, then and later, Seneca's power as a healer of souls has more than made up for his shortcomings as a model of virtue.

sententia, whose basic meaning is 'way of thinking', came to have specialized senses, such as an opinion expressed in the *senate, the judgement of a judge, and the spirit (as opposed to the letter) of the law. In literary criticism, it came to mean a brief saying embodying a striking thought. Such sayings could be gnomic (see GNOME) and moralizing; a collection attributed to *Publilius Syrus survives. But they

were often specially coined for a particular context. They probably played a part in 'Asianic' rhetoric and *declamation (see ASIANISM AND ATTICISM); but Latin, with its terseness and love of antithesis and word play, took to them with especial enthusiasm. Even the florid *Cicero was thought not to lack them, and the declamation school gave them a natural home; in his book on rhetoric *Seneca the Elder makes *sententiae* a main rubric. At their worst, they descend to puerile punning; at their best they are pointed, allusive, witty. They are typical of *Silver Latin. Where declaimers might use them merely for pleasurable effect, orators and philosophers found they could be persuasive too, because they stuck in the mind; and they were perfectly designed to give emphatic *closure to speech or section. Tacitus used them masterfully (*sōlitūdinem faciunt, pācem appellant,* 'they make a desert and call it peace'). So too in verse of different kinds: *Seneca the Younger's drama, *Lucan's epic (*victrix causa deīs placuit, sed victa Catōnī,* 'the victor had the gods on his side, but the vanquished had Cato', typically hard to translate), *Juvenal's satire (*probitās laudātur et alget,* 'integrity is praised—and left in the cold'), and *Martial's epigrams rely heavily on them.

septemvirī epulōnēs, 'the Priesthood of Seven Diners', the last addition to the major colleges of Roman *priests. They were instituted by law in 196 BC and were then three in number, all apparently plebeians. Their first responsibility, from which they take their name, was the organization of the *epulum Iovis,* a great feast at the *Ludi Romani, attended by the senate and people and presided over by the images of the Capitoline deities (see CAPITOL). The number of priests increased from three to seven and later ten, though the seven remained their title.

Septimius Sevērus, Lūcius, emperor AD 193–211. The Septimii were of Punic origin, his mother's family of Italian descent. His *equestrian grandfather was the leading figure at *Lepcis Magna under *Trajan; his father held no office, but two Septimii were already senators when Severus was born (145). One of them secured senatorial rank for him from Marcus *Aurelius; he and his brother had normal careers under Marcus and *Commodus. Consul in 190, by now with a second wife, *Iulia Domna, and two young sons, he became governor of Upper Pannonia in 191. Twelve days after Pertinax's murder (March 193) he was proclaimed emperor at Carnuntum as avenger of Pertinax. Backed by all sixteen Rhine and Danube legions he marched on Rome, securing the support of Clodius Septimius Albinus, governor of Britain, by granting him the title 'Caesar'. By 1 June, 60 miles north of Rome, Severus was recognized by the senate; Pertinax's successor was murdered, and Severus entered Rome without opposition on 9 June. The *praetorians were dismissed and a new guard, twice as large, was formed from the Danubian legions; three new legions (I–III Parthicae) were raised, one of which (II Parthica) was to be based at Alba Longa. This, together with increases in the *vigiles*, urban cohorts (see COHORTES URBANAE), and other units, radically enlarged the capital's garrison. Army pay was raised (for the first time since AD 84) and the men gained new privileges, e.g. the right to marry (see CONTUBERNIUM). Then Severus moved against Pescennius Niger, proclaimed emperor in Syria in April. In spring 194 Niger was decisively defeated near Issus, and then captured and killed. Severus now launched a successful campaign against the Parthian vassals who had backed Niger. In 195 he proclaimed himself son of the deified Marcus and brother of the newly deified Commodus, renamed his elder son (Caracalla) Marcus *Aurelius Antoninus and made him Caesar, and gave his wife Iulia Domna the title 'mother of the camp'. This clearly dynastic move led his ally Albinus Caesar to rebel and cross to Gaul with the British army. Severus hurried back west for this final civil war, won at *Lugdunum (197).

In a purge of Albinus' supporters 29 senators, and numerous others in Gaul, Spain, and Africa were executed. Severus left in summer 197 for his Second Parthian War, invading in winter and capturing Ctesiphon, on 28 January 198. On this day, the centenary of Trajan's accession, he became *Parthicus Maximus*, raised Caracalla to the rank of Augustus, and made his younger son, Septimius Geta, Caesar. The new province of Mesopotamia was garrisoned by two of the new legions (I and III Parthicae), with an equestrian prefect as governor. After a lengthy stay in Syria, the imperial party entered Egypt before the end of 199, remaining for about a year. The province was reorganized, notably by the grant of a city council to *Alexandria and the other major cities. At the end of 200 Severus returned to Syria for another year; he was consul for the 3rd time at Antioch, with Caracalla as colleague, on 1 January 202.

Back at Rome in early summer he celebrated a tenth anniversary festival with lavish victory games (declining a triumph, although the *triumphal arch in the Forum had already been voted by the senate), followed by Caracalla's marriage to Fulvia Plautilla, daughter of the seemingly all-powerful praetorian *prefect Fulvius Plautianus. In the autumn the imperial family sailed for Africa: their native Lepcis, *Carthage and *Utica received *ius Italicum, while Severus crushed the desert tribes beyond Tripolitana. From 203 to 208 he remained in Italy, holding *Secular Games in 204. Early in 205 Caracalla had Plautianus killed, and he was replaced by Papinian (*Aemilius Papinianus), who, with his fellow-jurists Ulpian and Paulus (*Domitius Ulpianus, Iulius Paulus), made the Severan era a golden age of Roman jurisprudence. In 208 minor hostilities in Britain gave an excuse for another war, which Severus supposedly thought would benefit his quarrelling sons. The entire family, with Papinian, elements of the guard and other troops, crossed to Britain that year and took up residence at *Eburacum. Severus and Caracalla led two campaigns in north Scotland, with the professed intention of conquering the whole of Britain; a new advance base was built on the Tay, and victory was claimed in 210 with the title *Britannicus* for Severus and his sons, the younger becoming Augustus at last to ensure a joint succession. Long a victim of gout, Severus died at Eburacum in 211, leaving his sons the advice 'not to disagree, give money to the soldiers, and ignore the rest'. See BRITAIN, ROMAN.

Sergius Catilīna, Lūcius, of *patrician, but not recently distinguished, family, served with *Pompey and *Cicero under Pompeius Strabo in the *Social War. He next appears as a lieutenant of *Sulla both in the fighting after Sulla's invasion of Italy and in the *proscriptions. After his praetorship (68 BC), he governed Africa for two years. Prosecuted for *extortion on his return, he was prevented from standing for the consulship for 65 and 64, but was finally acquitted with the help of his prosecutor *Clodius Pulcher. Frustrated ambition now became his driving force. In the elections for 63 he made a compact with Antonius 'Hybrida' and gained the support of *Caesar and *Licinius Crassus, but was defeated by *Cicero. He then began to champion the cause of the poor and dispossessed. Again defeated for 62, he organized a widespread conspiracy with ramifications throughout Italy. Cicero, kept informed by his spies but lacking support, could not take decisive action, for Catiline—an old Sullan, a patrician, and now a demagogue—was both popular and well connected. In November Cicero succeeded in frightening Catiline into leaving Rome to join a force of destitute veterans in Etruria. Soon afterwards, some Allobrogan envoys, carelessly given letters by conspirators in Rome, provided Cicero with the written evidence he needed. The leaders of the conspiracy in Rome were arrested and, after a long debate and a vote in the senate, executed. The consul Antonius marched out against Catiline, who was caught between two armies and was defeated by Petreius and killed. Cicero was hailed as saviour of Rome, but was open to the charge of having executed citizens without trial.

Sertōrius, Quintus (c.126–73 BC), an *equestrian from Sabine Nursia, distinguished himself in the Cimbrian Wars under *Marius, and in Spain. Quaestor in 91, then a senior officer in the *Social War, he was thwarted by *Sulla in his candidacy for a tribunate and joined *Cornelius Cinna. He shared responsibility for the capture of Rome (87) and subsequent executions, but ended the indiscriminate terror of Marius' slave-bands. He became praetor (probably) in 85; kept in Italy by Sulla's impending return, he criticized, unsuccessfully, the Cinno-Marian leaders for their conduct of the civil war and finally took command of Spain (winter 83/2). Proscribed and driven out (81), he went to *Mauretania as a *condottiere*. Invited by the Lusitanians and anti-Sullan Roman exiles, he returned to Spain (80) and soon gained widespread support among the natives, owing to his bravery, justice, and skill in exploiting their religious beliefs. (His white doe was regarded as a sign of divine inspiration.) Through crafty employment of guerrilla methods (and, for naval support, 'Cilician' pirates) he was successful against many Roman commanders, and by 77 he held most of Roman Spain. He tried to Romanize Hispanic leaders and acted throughout as a Roman proconsul, relying heavily on Roman and Italian exiles in the province; creating a 'counter-senate' from among them, he made Spain the focal point of resistance against the post-Sullan regime in Rome. When approached by *Mithradates VI he concluded an alliance, yet refused to surrender Asia to him (76/5). The arrival of Perperna Veiento with substantial remnants of the army of *Aemilius Lepidus (1) enabled him to take the offensive against *Pompey—now commanding in Nearer Spain— whom he defeated at Lauro (77). But costly failures, of his own and his lieutenants, in several pitched battles (76) soon forced him to revert to

guerrilla warfare, with waning success after 75. Losing the confidence of his Roman and Hispanic followers alike and embittered by failure, he became increasingly despotic and was murdered by Perperna.

Servilia, b. c.100 BC, daughter of Servilius Caepio and Livia, who was by her second marriage the mother of *Porcius Cato (2). Servilia married first Iunius Brutus, to whom she bore Marcus *Iunius Brutus the tyrannicide, and then Iunius Silanus; one of her daughters by Silanus married *Cassius Longinus, the tyrannicide. *Caesar was her lover for many years and remained on good terms with her: it was rumoured (implausibly) that Brutus, for whom he showed particular favour, was his son, and she profited from his sale of the Pompeians' confiscated estates. She may have been discreetly involved in high politics before the Civil War, and after Caesar's death Cicero's letters show her playing a leading part in the tyrannicides' deliberations, always protecting her son's interests. After his death at *Philippi we hear no more about her, but for a short time, she was the most powerful woman of her generation.

Servius (Roman king). See REX.

sesterce See AES.

Seven against Thebes, myth, and play by *Aeschylus. *Oedipus' curse upon his sons *Eteocles ('True Glory') and Polynices ('Much Strife') results in their dispute over the throne of Thebes and in Polynices calling upon his father-in-law Adrastus, king of *Argos, and five other heroes. These seven heroes fight at, and match, the mythical seven gates of *Thebes. In particular, Zeus strikes Capaneus with a lightning-bolt, the two brothers slaughter each other, *Amphiaraus (who joins the expedition through the treachery of his wife Eriphyle) is swallowed up by the earth, and *Tydeus is denied immortality when *Athena finds him devouring the brains of Melanippus.

Aeschylus' *Seven against Thebes* was the last play of his Theban trilogy (467 BC), following *Laius* and *Oedipus*. It focuses on Eteocles' acceptance of the task of fighting his own brother and the impact of their deaths on the family—a catastrophic end to the House of Laius. It was an esteemed play, whose text appears to have been rehandled, esp. to allow a final view of *Antigone in the light of Sophocles' *Antigone*. See also EPIGONI.

Seven hills of Rome *Capitol; *Palatine; *Aventine; Quirinal; Viminal; *Esquiline; *Caelius Mons. See also ROME (TOPOGRAPHY).

Seven Liberal Arts See EDUCATION, GREEK, 4.

Seven Sages *Sophia*, which embraces wisdom, cleverness, and poetic skill, had always been admired in Greek society, as the character of *Odysseus shows; and with the rise of the agonistic spirit, fostered by the panhellenic games (see AGONES; PANHELLENISM) and displayed in such stories as that of Agaristē's suitors (see CLEISTHENES 1 and 2), there developed the idea that in wisdom too the Greek *poleis* should put up competing rivals. The original *sophoi* belong to the early decades of the 6th cent., and the usual list comprises four members from eastern cities (*Thales of Miletus, Bias of Priene, Cleobulus of Lindus on Rhodes, and *Pittacus of Mytilene) and three from the homeland (*Solon of Athens, *Chilon of Sparta, and *Periander the Corinthian tyrant). The way *Simonides sets out vigorously to refute the maxims of both Pittacus and Cleobulus—and claim a place for himself?—suggests that the *canon was forming, if not formed, by the beginning of the 5th cent.; though the first explicit attestation of a Group of Seven is in *Plato's *Protagoras*. Their wisdom was often expressed in pithy or 'Delphic' mottoes; but they were men involved with the problems of contemporary statecraft, not hermits. Herodotus gives many examples of their political and practical acuity.

Later generations felt it inappropriate that a tyrant with a brutal reputation like Periander should be included, and substitutes were proposed. Traditions about other 6th-cent. figures like *Heraclitus, *Cyrus (1), or the Saïte pharaoh Amasis show that their images, too, were brought into conformity with the developing standard profile.

Seven Wonders of the ancient world, *canon of seven 'sights' of art and architecture. First attested in the 2nd cent. BC, the canon comprises the pyramids of Egypt, the city walls of *Babylon, the hanging gardens of Semiramis there, the temple of Artemis at *Ephesus, the statue of Zeus at *Olympia, the *Mausoleum of *Halicarnassus, and the colossus of *Rhodes. The concept was developed in individual references to a single wonder and esp. in complete lists of seven, sometimes drawn up to celebrate an 'eighth' wonder (like the *Colosseum in Rome in Martial).

Later lists keep the number, but not always the identity of the wonders. While a late antique rhetorical treatise purporting to be a guidebook to the seven wonders for the armchair traveller and attributed to the engineer Philon of Byzantium still refers to the seven of the old canon, other wonders like the Pharus of *Alexandria, the *labyrinth, Egyptian Thebes, and the temple of Zeus at Cyzicus first feature in *Pliny the Elder's list.

Severan emperors and period See ROME (HISTORY), 3.1.

Severus (Roman emperor) See SEPTIMIUS SEVERUS.

Sextus Empiricus, Pyrrhonist Sceptic (see PYRRHON; SCEPTICS) and medical doctor. Nothing is known about his life, but the name 'Empiricus' shows that he was a member of the Empiricist school of medicine (see MEDICINE, 5(b)). He probably wrote towards the end of the 2nd cent. AD. His extant works are traditionally cited under two titles.

1. *Outlines of Pyrrhonism*, abbrev. *PH*, in three books; the first offers a general outline of Pyrrhonist scepticism, and a discussion of the differences between Pyrrhonism and other schools or philosophers alleged to have held similar views; the second and third books contain refutations of dogmatic philosophies, divided by subject-matter: theory of knowledge and logic, *physics, ethics.

2. *Against the professors*, abbrev. *M*, in eleven books, originally no doubt two different works. *M* 7–11, also entitled *Against the dogmatists*, is a critique of dogmatic philosophies parallel to but more detailed than *PH* 2–3; *M* 1–6 (*Against the professors*) criticizes other disciplines, as follows: grammar (1), rhetoric (2), geometry (3), arithmetic (4), astrology (5), music (6).

Sextus is the only Pyrrhonist philosopher whose work has survived. The first book of *PH* offers a detailed and subtle defence of scepticism, its aims, and methods. Though Sextus obviously draws upon his predecessors, he is an intelligent compiler who writes clearly and concentrates on argument rather than on anecdotes. His discussions of the doctrines of other schools have preserved valuable information, esp. about Stoic logic (see STOICISM) and Hellenistic theory of knowledge.

Sextus Pompeius See POMPEIUS MAGNUS (PIUS), SEXTUS.

sexuality Both Greeks and Romans divided sexual behaviour into active/passive as well as (some say, 'but not') homosexual/heterosexual. The normative role for adult males was penetrative ('active'); penetrated ('passive') partners were normally women, and boys aged 12 to 17. Texts generally convey the experience of penetrators, and evaluate passivity negatively, at worst (oral) as contaminating.

Philosophers debated the merits of intercourse—different for men and women—and regulated sexual desire along with other bodily appetites. Medical writers catalogued the human body, comprehending *gynaecology, embryology, and obstetrics, as well as male physiology. Greek scientists, notably Aristotle, defined the female body as physiologically inferior to the male, even repellent, and sometimes justified sexual hierarchy thereby. *Childbirth, and to some extent intercourse, conveyed *pollution; Roman menstrual revulsion is likely to have had Greek parallels. Sexual categories in *astrology, physiognomy, and dream-interpretation tally with their social valences (see DREAMS).

Sex with men for free women was defined in terms of marriage; girls married, often soon after puberty, and commonly remarried after divorce or widowhood. Virtue for women meant fidelity, though texts stereotype women as promiscuous. Their access to extramarital sex was always more or less controlled, *adultery being defined as sex with a married woman. Yet *Sulpicia voices her desire. Free men married later, and extramarital sex between male and (subordinate) female is again widely attested. Rape of woman or boy dishonoured the victim and was punished by law. Questions of sexuality within marriage include contraception, affection between husband and wife, fertility, pregnancy, and childbirth.

Class greatly affected sexual realities: slaves were by definition penetrable, and at Rome freed slaves bore a concomitant stigma. Non-marital alliances were available to non-élite classes. *Prostitution flourished, and many prostitutes were slaves; free Roman prostitutes were *infāmēs* (see INFAMIA), along with pimps and theatrical performers. Slaves' access to procreation was closely controlled. Graffiti suggest that slaves' own sexual norms matched those of free people; inscriptions commemorate freed slave marriages and families. *Race figures in hegemonic sexual discourse. Asia Minor was often associated in ancient texts with sexual luxury and effeminacy, and Roman texts express a preference for boys from Asia. Although some early and many late sources are available for Egypt and the near east, the sexual experience of indigenous peoples, esp. in northern Europe and Africa, is largely lost to us.

See ASCETICISM; HETEROSEXUALITY; HOMOSEXUALITY; LOVE AND FRIENDSHIP; PORNOGRAPHY; WOMEN.

shamans See; EMPEDOCLES; EPIMENIDES; PYTHAGORAS.

shame See HUBRIS; NEMESIS; SUICIDE.

ships From the Archaic period onwards the peoples of the eastern Mediterranean developed specialized types of ships which gradually came to be used throughout the ancient world. For war they used long ships, rowed by 50 or more oarsmen, on up to three levels, with masts and sails for long journeys. (The *pentecontor* or fifty-oared ship was largely superseded from perhaps the 6th cent. BC by the *trireme.) For *trade they commonly used ships of a more rounded appearance and deeper draft, which often required ballast to keep them afloat. They usually relied on sails for propulsion, which allowed more space for the storage of cargo, but also meant that they were at the mercy of the weather.

The typical sailing rig of ancient ships consisted of one square sail, hung from a yard attached to a mast, which was fixed in the centre of the ship. Sails were normally trimmed using brails, which gave great flexibility. In addition to the square sail, triangular or lateen sails might be used, as well as spritsails and lugsails. Large ships often had more than one mast and carried triangular topsails. Mediterranean ships generally used sails made of linen, which could be dyed and decorated. The sailcloth was often strengthened using leather patches in the corners and light lines stitched horizontally and vertically. Leather sails were used in NW Europe, as were sails strengthened with battens.

Wooden ships in the Mediterranean were mostly built by the 'shell first' method, with planking being attached directly to the keel, and inner frames added afterwards for strength. Ships were steered using one or two steering oars in the stern, usually fitted with transverse handles to make their handling easier. Steering was a skilled job, and the helmsman (Gk. *kybernētēs*, Lat. *gubernātor*) was the most important member of the crew.

Ancient ships varied greatly in size. Among the largest ancient *shipwrecks yet discovered were vessels that could carry cargoes weighing

250 tons or more. These ships mostly date to the period 100 BC to AD 200, when the conditions of the Roman empire encouraged maritime trade on a large scale.

See NAVIES; PUNIC WARS, *First*; SEA POWER; TIMBER; TRIREME.

shipwrecks, ancient Over 1,000 ancient shipwreck sites are known from the Mediterranean. Archaic wrecks tend to produce rare items, but more mundane, 'commercial' cargoes come to dominate the Aegean and then the rest of the Mediterranean from the 4th cent. BC onwards. Wrecks from the 1st cent. BC and 1st cent. AD are commonest, and reported sites are densest in the western Mediterranean, esp. along the French coast, where they reflect above all the export of Italian *wine to Gaul during the late republic.

See SHIPS; TRADE; WINE.

Sibyl Originally the Sibyl seems to have been a single prophetic woman, but by the time of Heraclides of Pontus, a number of places claimed to be the birthplace of Sibylla, traditions concerning a number of different Sibyls began to circulate, and the word came to be a generic term rather than a name. There are a number of Sibylline catalogues, of which the most important is that compiled by *Varro for his *On Religion*. It lists ten: (1) Persian; (2) Libyan; (3) Delphic; (4) Cimmerian (in Italy); (5) Erythraean; (6) Samian; (7) Cumaean; (8) Hellespontine; (9) Phrygian; (10) Tiburtine. The most important discussion of different traditions, which emphasizes the local connections of Sibyls, is given by *Pausanias (3). Inscriptions from Erythrae (see PANIONIUM) record sacrifices to the Sibyl.

The nature of Sibylline inspiration is diversely reported. *Virgil offers a famous description of the Cumaean Sibyl uttering ecstatic prophecy under the inspiration of *Apollo, but texts from Erythrae, or recorded by *Plutarch and Pausanias clearly state that the Sibyl spoke under her own inspiration. The evidence for Sibylline inspiration provided by the extant corpus of Sibylline oracles is inconsistent. All but one of the extant texts are in Greek *hexameter verse.

Widespread interest in Sibyls throughout the Mediterranean world probably stems from the connection between the Sibyl and Rome that dates to, at the very latest, the early 5th cent. BC. Legend has it that the collection first came to Rome in the reign of Tarquinius Priscus (see REX), who is said to have bought three books from the Cumaean Sibyl and placed them in the care of a priestly college (see QUINDECIMVIRI SACRIS FACIUNDIS), to be consulted only at the command of the senate; the senate could also vote to add new books to the state's collection after inspection by the college. This collection was housed in the temple of Capitoline Jupiter (see CAPITOL), where it was destroyed in the burning of the Capitol in 83 BC. After this the senate commissioned a board of three to make a collection from various places. Augustus moved this collection to the temple of *Palatine Apollo. The last known consultation of these books (to which additions had been made from time to time) was in AD 363. The books were consulted in times of crisis, and the one extant example suggests that the oracles contained a statement of the problem, followed by various remedies.

The Sibyl's intimate connection with Rome made her a natural choice for Christians who sought evidence from pagan sources for the truth of their beliefs. Belief that Virgil's *Fourth Eclogue* (modelled on sibylline prophecy) was in fact inspired by the Cumaean Sibyl combined with this interest to elevate the Sibyl to an important place in Christian literature and art.

Sicilian Expedition See PELOPONNESIAN WAR; SICILY, 4; SYRACUSE; THUCYDIDES (2).

Sicily

1. Prehistory Ancient writers distinguished three indigenous peoples—Sicans in central, Sicels in eastern, and Elymians in western Sicily. *Thucydides (2) attributes an Iberian origin to the Sicans, an Italic to the Sicels, and a Trojan to the Elymians. Archaeologically there is no differentiation of culture matching the Sicel–Sican distinction.

2. The Greek Settlement Despite Thucydides' account, the *Phoenicians did not apparently settle in Sicily before the Greeks, and their colonization was limited to Motya, Panormus, and Soloeis. The Elymians, whose principal centres were Segesta, Eryx, and Entella, became firm allies of the Carthaginians. From *c.*735 BC there followed a prolonged period of Greek *colonization. The indigenes were sometimes ejected from the colonized sites or reduced to dependent status; occasionally there was peaceful coexistence. Once established, the Greeks and their civilization gradually penetrated and transformed the indigenous area; sometimes the process was rapid. By the Hellenistic period the island was a Siculo-Greek amalgam. The Greeks exploited the island's economic potential, and

Corinthian, east Greek, and (later) Laconian and esp. Attic imported pottery (see POTTERY, GREEK) illustrates the considerable trade with Greece. Markets in Africa, southern Italy, and (after c.500) Rome were also available. Temple-building and rapid urbanization attest the wealth and culture of the Archaic period, and the first Sicilian coinage (see COINAGE, GREEK) belongs to the second half of the 6th cent. The Phoenicians acquiesced in the Greek settlement, but defended their enclave.

3. Early Tyrannies As in Greece, *tyranny emerged, but the aristocracies were tenacious, while the threat, potential or actual, of *Carthage and the Sicels affected internal politics; this in turn produced greater social instability. Early tyrannies in *Acragas and elsewhere foreshadowed the despotism of Hippocrates of Gela, who was the first of the great tyrants in Sicily. His successor *Gelon transferred his capital to *Syracuse. A Carthaginian attempt to check Gelon and his ally *Theron of Acragas, met with disaster at *Himera (480). Under Gelon and *Hieron (1) I Siceliot culture reached its zenith. It penetrated the Phoenician colonies, and the cities of the interior became increasingly Hellenized. After the deaths of Theron and Hieron I the tyrannies soon came to an end.

4. The Age of Dionysius In the latter part of the 5th cent. the cities maintained their mutual independence and were democratically governed. But *democracy did not strike such deep roots in Sicily as in Greece, and external dangers demanded a more authoritarian organization. The Athenians twice intervened in the island (427–424 and 415–413) on the basis of alliances with Leontini and Segesta, with hopes of ultimately controlling it; the first intervention did not succeed, and the second expedition ended in utter failure. Carthage now profited by the exhaustion of Syracuse to attempt the complete conquest of Sicily (409). Selinus and Himera fell in 409, Acragas and Gela in 406/5. In the days of crisis *Dionysius (1) I succeeded in establishing himself as tyrant of Syracuse; the Carthaginians were repulsed, and Syracuse, which came to control all Sicily outside Carthage's 'dominion' in the far west, prospered; but the cost was tyranny and the loss of liberty. Dionysius' death (367) was followed, after a decade, by civil war; petty tyrants established themselves in the various cities, and the Carthaginians again intervened.

5. The Hellenistic Period At this low ebb in their fortunes the Syracusans sent for the Cor-

inthian Timoleon, who defeated the Carthaginians and re-established settled government. His arrangements did not long survive his retirement (c.336), and oligarchy prevailed. In 317 Agathocles of Thermae seized the Syracusan tyranny and subjugated most of the island. When he died (289) fresh anarchy ensued; there were more local tyrants, Carthage again threatened, and the tyrant's ex-mercenaries (*Mamertines) carved out a dominion for themselves in *Messana. City-state Sicily was in dissolution. *Pyrrhus of Epirus was called in, but despite quick successes produced no lasting effect. *Hieron (2) II of Syracuse to some extent halted the decline, but his defeat of the Mamertines brought on a Carthaginian occupation of Messana and was the occasion for Roman interference and the First *Punic War (264–41), after which most of the island became a Roman province (see PRŌVINCIA). Hieron's kingdom remained autonomous and prosperous until his death in 215, when Syracuse went over to Carthage. After the Roman capture of Syracuse (211), all Sicily was unified as a Roman province.

6. The Roman Republican Period The province was under the control of a governor (praetor) with a quaestor in Syracuse and another in Lilybaeum, but the cities continued to enjoy a large measure of independence with their own self-government. Messana and Tauromenium, which had voluntarily accepted Rome's alliance, were distinguished as civitates foederatae (see FOEDUS); and five other communities, including Panormus and Segesta, were *free cities. Of the remainder some paid a tithe on a system established by Hieron II; the land of others became *ager publicus, for which they paid rent in addition to the tithe. Local autonomy was infringed by *Verres (73–71) but generally respected. Under the republic wheat-growing, vital to Rome's *food supply, was fostered; large *latifundia grew up, as a result of big Roman (and Sicilian) purchases of landed estates. These were worked by slaves whose conditions provoked the serious revolts of 137–133 and 104–101 BC. Some of the urban centres were attacked and damaged, but despite these setbacks most Sicilian towns flourished in the 2nd and 1st cents. BC. The NE of the island also suffered in 36 when Octavian (see AUGUSTUS) expelled Sextus *Pompeius, in whose occupation of Sicily (from 42) he and Antony had acquiesced in 39.

7. The Imperial Period The island continued to prosper under the empire, governed by a proconsul, and Latin and Greek culture long

co-existed. Augustus founded veteran colonies at Catana, Panormus, Syracuse, Tauromenium, Thermae, and Tyndaris (see COLONIZATION, ROMAN), and he gave Latin rights to a handful of others. A fixed levy replaced the tithe. *Latifundia*, among them large imperial estates (see DOMAINS), remained an important feature of the agricultural pattern. Yet village life and small-holdings evidently flourished also, and the population in general was more dispersed in the countryside than hitherto, esp. with the decline and abandonment of many of the old hill-towns of the interior. The coastal cities by contrast flourished, and the prosperity of the countryside in the 4th cent. is witnessed by such luxury villas such as that of *Piazza Armerina. Grain continued to be the most significant export, although Sicily was now less important to Rome's food supply than Africa and Egypt.

Sicyon, city west of *Corinth: they shared a rich coastal plain. The original site remains unknown. The *tyrant dynasty of the Orthagorids began c.650 BC and lasted for a century; it was the longest known to *Aristotle. *Cleisthenes (1) gave insulting names to the Dorian tribes (see DORIANS) as much for enmity to *Argos as to enhance the standing of his own non-Dorian tribe. He destroyed Crisa (or Cirrha) in the First *Sacred War. He held a magnificent contest for the hand of his daughter Agaristē, and through her became grandfather of *Cleisthenes (2) of Athens. Sparta ejected the last tyrant, and Sicyon became an ally. It played some part in the First Peloponnesian War; Athenians twice landed and won battles in its territory. Sparta intervened in 417 to make an already existing oligarchy narrower.

siegecraft, Greek The Greek national epics focused on the siege of a city, but it took ten years to capture *Troy, even if, in the end, the 'wooden horse' was some kind of siege device. The inability to take walled towns other than by treachery or blockade persisted into the historical period, despite a growing awareness of such techniques as the Persian siege-mound and undermining. *Pericles is said to have been the first to use 'siege-engines' (*mēchanai*) at *Samos in 440/39 BC—they included 'rams' and 'tortoises' (i.e. sheds to protect undermining parties). But despite the Athenian reputation for siegecraft, they took three years to capture *Potidaea (432–429), and mainly relied on blockade, though in 430 they made some use of 'siege-engines', perhaps towers. Similarly, though the Spartans and

their allies used a mound, battering-rams and even fire against *Plataea, this little town, too, stood a two-year siege (429–427), and only surrendered through lack of food. *Nicias also used ship-borne 'siege-engines' to capture two towers on Minoa near *Megara in 427, but against *Syracuse seems never to have tried anything but circumvallation (414–413).

Part of the reason for the poor showing of Classical Greeks in siege techniques may have been that their strength lay in hoplites, who were ill-suited to siege operations, and that there were too few archers and slingers to provide proper covering fire. When the *Boeotians attacked the *sanctuary at *Delion, which the Athenians had fortified, in 424, they sent for javelineers and slingers from Malis, though they eventually took the place by means of a primitive flame-thrower.

The first Greeks reliably attested to have used siege-towers were the Sicilians under *Dionysius (1) I, at the siege of Motya (397). Dionysius also used arrow-firing catapults. Such weapons were known in Greece by about 375 and are mentioned once by *Aeneas Tacticus, as are towers on wheels, 'masts'—perhaps pivoting beams holding leather or wicker cradles capable of carrying men—rams and 'drills', tortoises, scaling-ladders, and tunnelling.

Under *Philip II siegecraft began to develop in mainland Greece, though he still had only arrow-firing catapults—the 75 mm. (3-inch), three-barbed, bronze arrow-heads, inscribed with the king's name, found at *Olynthus, possibly came from these. But even Olynthus fell in the end through treachery, and Philip's 80-cubit towers and catapults failed to take Perinthus in 340. By this time, too, catapults were also being used in the defence of towns, and it was probably a bolt from one of these which put out Philip's eye at the siege of Methone.

Nevertheless, Philip clearly bequeathed both siege expertise and siege experts to his son, *Alexander (2) the Great, and it was under the latter that Greek siegecraft finally came into its own, playing a vital part in the conquest of Persia, esp. in the early years. With more powerful, torsion catapults, capable of throwing stones, it was now possible to smash battlements and even help to batter down walls. Alexander's sieges of *Miletus, *Halicarnassus, *Tyre, and Gaza display fully developed siege-techniques.

Some of the 'Successors', too, were notable besiegers, esp. *Demetrius, son of *Antigonus I, who was nicknamed 'Poliorcētēs' ('The Besieger'). *Diodorus (2) Siculus' accounts of Demetrius' sieges of Cyprian Salamis and, above all, *Rhodes, are a rich source of evidence for Hellenistic siegecraft. By the end of the 3rd cent. besiegers generally held the whip hand, though a rich city, such as Syracuse, was still capable of withstanding a lengthy siege. See ARTILLERY; FORTIFICATIONS.

siegecraft, Roman Early Roman besiegers employed blockade with methodical circumvallation, exploited surprise, and sometimes, esp. after weakening the besiegers by blockade, clinched matters by assault, using ladders and possibly ramps and rams. Veii, blockaded 405–396 BC, apparently fell to assault by mine.

From the 3rd cent., the Romans assimilated and improved the machinery and techniques of Hellenistic siegecraft, and continued to use elaborate fieldworks. Accounts of the sieges of *Syracuse by *Claudius Marcellus (1), of *Piraeus by *Sulla, and those of the Gallic, Jewish, Sasanid, and Gothic wars are instructive, as are the surviving technical treatises. Equipment included bolt-shooting and stone-throwing *artillery, mobile towers, mechanical ladders, movable siege-sheds, and rams, protective galleries, mobile screens, wall-borers, and hooks and crowbars for dislodging masonry (see VITRUVIUS, VEGETIUS). The design of equipment for going under, through, or over *fortifications was ingenious, but its quantity depended on the initiative of individual commanders.

During the Principate, Roman siege technology developed mainly in the eastern theatre; wars with Parthians and Sasanids were dominated by heavily fortified cities. In Roman literature the Sasanids are distinguished from their predecessors by their ability in siege-warfare, which they had learned from the Romans. Thus, Roman eastern fortresses were also on the defensive, using artillery and other equipment accordingly.

Republican sieges in the west are reflected archaeologically by camps, circumvallations, and missile artefacts (*Numantia, *Pompeii, Perusia, Gergovia, Alesia). Jewish War sites have fieldworks and projectiles.

Sīgēum, important site in *Troas, acquired by Athens—her first overseas possession—in the late 7th cent. BC, after arbitration by *Periander between Athens and *Mytilene (see also AL-CAEUS), but then lost by Athens to Mytilene, until reconquered by *Pisistratus. *Hippias (1) retired there after his eviction from Athens. In the *Delian League Sigeum was notably loyal.

signa mīlitāria, Roman military standards. The earliest standard (Lat. *signum*) of the Roman army was that of the *maniple. When the *cohort superseded the maniple as the tactical unit, the standard of the leading maniple became the chief standard of the cohort. The century had no separate standard. The basic form of a Roman standard was a hand on the top of a pole decorated with metal discs, crescents, laurel wreaths, mural crowns, and other emblems representing the battle honours won by the unit.

In the pre-Marian army (see MARIUS) there were also five legionary standards (see LEGION), which were placed for safety in battle between the first two lines. Marius replaced these by giving each legion an eagle (*aquila*) of silver or gold, with wreaths as its sole decoration. The eagle embodied the spirit of the legion and was the object of religious veneration. Its loss was the worst form of disgrace, and sometimes entailed the disbandment of the legion. Under the Principate the legion retained its eagle and standards, and to these were added standards bearing the portraits of the reigning and deified emperors. The cavalry standard was a *vexillum*, a square piece of cloth attached to a crossbar, borne on a pole.

sīlens, Sīlēnus See SATYRS AND SILENS.

Sīlius Italicus (c. AD 26–102), Roman politician and poet, author of *Punica*, an *epic of seventeen books on the Second *Punic War, at over 12,000 lines the longest poem in Latin. Before turning to the writing of poetry in retirement Silius had an outstanding public career. Zealous in prosecution under *Nero, he was the last consul appointed by the emperor in AD 68, at an early age for a *novus homo*. In the turmoil of the next year he was engaged in tense high-level negotiations between Aulus *Vitellius and *Vespasian's brother; his support for Vitellius did not harm him, for he reached the peak of a senator's career under Vespasian, as proconsul of Asia (c.77). One of his sons followed him to the consulship. He retired to *Campania, where he owned many *villas, and spent his last years as an artistic connoisseur, attracting adverse comment for conspicuous consumption. He owned one of *Cicero's villas and the tomb of *Virgil, whose memory he revered. Afflicted by an incurable ailment, Silius starved himself to death at the age of 76.

With *Livy's third decade as the principal historical source, and Virgil's *Aeneid* as the principal poetic model, the *Punica* traverses the entire

Second Punic War, presented as the fulfilment of the curse with which *Dido conjures eternal enmity between her people and *Aeneas'. A mythological dimension is immediately present, therefore: Hannibal is not just a formidable human antagonist but the hellish tool of Juno's unassuaged hate, and the gods participate throughout. Silius' decision not to follow *Lucan's removal of the gods as characters has attracted the censure of modern critics, but it is symptomatic of his forswearing of Lucan's nihilism in favour of a more traditional view of divine sanction for imperial destiny (debts to Lucan are ubiquitous, however, esp. in the Caesarian portrayal of Hannibal). The poem celebrates Roman fortitude by displaying such heroes as Atilius Regulus, *Fabius Maximus Verrucosus, *Claudius Marcellus (1), and *Cornelius Scipio Africanus, and by organizing the mass of fifteen years' history to centre on the catastrophic defeat at *Cannae (bks. 8–10, with seven books before and after): nostalgia for a simpler and nobler past is shot through with the apprehension that Rome's victory over Carthage held the seeds of contemporary decline.

silver While *gold could be easily obtained from alluvial deposits by washing, silver had to be extracted by regular mining processes. The *Phoenicians are said to have been the first to bring silver into general use; several of the silver objects mentioned in *Homer have Sidonian associations. The main sources for Classical Greece were Mt. Pangaeus in *Thrace, *Lydia, Colchis, Bactria, Siphnos, and *Laurium which provided abundant supplies for *Athens. In the western Mediterranean *Spain was the most prolific source of supply. The conquests of Spain and Asia made silver plentiful at Rome, where it had previously been rare.

Silver was worked with a hammer into plates which were soldered or riveted together and then decorated with repoussé work, stamping, chasing, or engraving. Vases might be hammered or cast from a mould and were often adorned with reliefs let into the body of the vessel or *crustae* soldered upon the surface. For coins molten dumps were struck between dies (see COINAGE, GREEK). To provide colour contrast silver objects were often gilded with gold leaf.

Silver was extensively used for statuettes, for temple offerings, and for the domestic *plate of rich Greeks and Romans. A few Greek vessels have survived in Thracian and Scythian tombs; many more Roman services have been preserved, examples being the *Esquiline and Mildenhall Treasures in London, of the late empire. See MINES.

Silver Age Latin Latin as distinctively written by Roman authors between, roughly, the death of Augustus (AD 14) and the death of Trajan (117). See JUVENAL; LUCAN; MARTIAL; SENECA THE ELDER and THE YOUNGER; STATIUS; TACITUS.

Simōnidēs, Greek poet, from Iulis on *Ceos. If he worked at the court of *Hipparchus (1), his career began before 514 BC; his *Battle of Plataea*, (see PLATAEA, BATTLE OF) was written in or after 479; he finished at the court of *Hieron (1) I, and his tomb was shown at *Acragas. Tradition made him live to be 90.

No poem of Simonides survives intact, except the epigrams attributed to him. But the fragments make it clear that Simonides commanded a wide variety of genres. In choral lyric, he composed victory odes, of which he and perhaps Ibycus are the first known practitioners; *dithyrambs, with which acc. to a (Hellenistic) epigram he won at least 57 competitions; *thrēnoi* (laments: see DIRGE); *paeans; encomia; maiden-songs and the like. His elegies included some sympotic pieces (see SYMPOSIUM LITERATURE), and some historical (on the battles of Artemisium (see ARTEMISIUM, BATTLE OF) and Plataea). Many *epigrams, esp. epigrams relating to the *Persian Wars, were collected under Simonides' name; the epitaph for the seer Megistias may be genuine. Simonides' clients included cities, individual athletes, tyrants, and various Thessalian dynasts.

For the next generation, Simonides belonged to the classic (old-fashioned) poets. He had the reputation of a money-grubber. He acquired also the reputation of a sage, like Bias and *Pittacus (see SEVEN SAGES); various pithy sayings were ascribed to him, mostly cynical. He was credited further with discovering the art of memory.

What little remains of Simonides shows a professional poet of great scope, much in demand over his long life, spanning the tyrants and the new democracy (see DEMOCRACY, ATHENIAN). Ancient critics admired him for simple pathos, and that appears in noble verses for the dead of Thermopylae (see THERMOPYLAE, BATTLE OF). In the elegies, lush eroticism contrasts with the pocket epic *Plataea*, whose form (a hymn to *Achilles introducing a narrative of the campaign) enforces the parallel between the Trojan and *Persian Wars, and between *Homer and Simonides.

Simplicius, 6th-cent. AD Neoplatonist (see NEOPLATONISM) and one of seven philosophers who left Athens for Ctesiphon on the Tigris after *Justinian had closed the Athenian Neoplatonist school in 529. He probably wrote all his commentaries after 532, when it was safe for the philosophers to leave Ctesiphon. He wrote commentaries, all extant, on *Aristotle's *On the Heavens*, *Physics*, and *Categories*, and on Epictetus' *Manual*. His are the fullest of all Aristotle commentaries, recording debates on Aristotle from the preceding 850 years, and embedding many fragments from the entire millennium. At the same time, Simplicius gave his own views on many topics. His commentaries express the revulsion of a devout Neoplatonist for Christianity.

sin The modern term has no equivalent in either Greek or Latin. Various aspects are denoted by such terms as Gk. *adikia* (wrongdoing, injustice), *anomia* (lawless conduct), *hamartia, hamartēma* (failure, fault, error), or Lat. *vitium* (fault, blemish), *scelus* (evil deed, crime), *peccātum* (fault, error), etc. The Greek term *hamartia* approximates most closely to (but cannot be identified with) our concept 'sin' and was adopted in the Septuagint (the collection of Jewish writings which became the Old Testament of Greek-speaking Christians) and early Christian scriptures for rendering and developing the biblical concept of sin.

Three of the most remarkable ancient characteristics as opposed to modern ones, are:

1. In the earlier period voluntary and involuntary offences against moral or divine laws were both equally reprehensible and hence liable to divine vengeance. Evil intention is not necessarily implied in the ancient definition of wrongdoing. The Greek concept of *ātē* (delusion, infatuation, through which 'evil appears good', Sophocles *Antigone* 622), which in the early period was often held responsible for human error, was either understood as divinely inspired—thus providing an escape from the problem of human responsibility, though *not* from divine punishment—or as rooted in personal (and condemnable) rashness, being a corollary of *hubris.

2. Closely related is the ancient belief that no clear distinction can be drawn between offences against ethical, legal, and social prescriptions on the one hand and violation of ritual rules on the other.

3. So, it is often impossible to draw a sharp line between the state of impurity (see PURIFI-

CATION) as result of a ritual fault and the state of moral blemish. Murder is a case in point. The earliest phases of Greek and Roman civilization did emphasize the ritual aspects, but even in *Homer there are unmistakable traces of moral codes warranted by the gods, and over time a gradual development towards a more personally felt experience of guilt can be perceived.

Greece In Homer it was esp. *Zeus who guarded the laws of hospitality in the house and the court and protected strangers and suppliants. Other transgressions did not affect him, except in cases of either ritual offence or personal acts of *hubris* defying his honour. *Dike* (man's duty to his fellows) is not synonymous with *themis* (man's duty according to divine institution). But the two may coincide, e.g. in the sin of *hubris* or disregard of the right of others (both mortals and gods). However, Hesiod pictures *dike* as Zeus' central responsibility, making Dike the daughter of Zeus. In his view, divine vengeance will equally follow both transgression of a certain branch of the moral code, such as ill-treatment of orphans or one's own parents, and ritual offences such as omitting to wash one's hands before pouring *libations. In fact the core of his poem is an appeal to the justice of Zeus: whoever offends human or divine laws will encounter divine anger.

Divine punishment
Early Greece made impressive attempts to bracket together two eternal problems: that of the cause of illness and disaster and that of *theodicy, the question of the justice of the gods. In the expression 'By day and by night diseases of themselves come upon man, and do him harm silently, for cunning Zeus removed their voice' (Hesiod, *Works and Days* 102–104), Zeus can be identified with blind fate or fortune, making man a plaything of an arbitrary and unfathomable divine power. Alternatively, illness is a penalty for evil acts, sent by Zeus in his role of divine judge. Both options were eagerly exploited, the former being a typical expression of 'Archaic pessimism', characteristic of much *lyric poetry, the latter providing an explanation that permits control, in cases of sudden unaccountable illness, esp. of epidemics (see DISEASE). These disasters were often seen as caused by the sin of one person, even by a sin unwittingly committed: 'Not willingly am I detained, but I must have sinned against the deathless gods', says *Odysseus. An oracle might then be consulted as to the nature of the unknown sin and the manner of its expiation.

The interpretation of illness as the punishment of sin must raise another question of theodicy: what if patent sinners do *not* fall ill? 'How, son of Cronus, does your mind manage to award the same portion to evil-doers and just men?' (Hesiod *Theogony* 377 f.). By way of solution, Archaic literature offers variations on the theme of temporary postponement. Evildoers will be punished but not always immediately, or the penalty will strike a later generation. Various options concerning sin and retribution coexisted, sometimes in the mind of one person. This is esp. marked in the idea of retribution in the afterlife and the Underworld.

Punishment in the hereafter

In Homer three conceptions are faintly discernible: (1) the Underworld as a cheerless and gloomy place where all souls assemble, without any suggestion of retribution or reward; (2) the *Islands of the Blessed, reserved for the (heroic) happy few; and (3) a place where the divine judges *Aeacus, *Minos, and Rhadamanthys judge the dead. The three great sinners mentioned, Tityus, *Tantalus, and *Sisyphus (Homer *Odyssey* 11. 576–600), are sentenced not for moral offences, but for an act of *hubris* against the honour of the gods.

The early doctrine of the *Eleusinian mysteries, as represented in the *Homeric Hymn to Demeter* (*c*.700 BC), though promising the initiated a blissful stay in the Underworld, did not require any proof of good behaviour; from a later period we learn that there was only one such requirement: not to have impure hands tainted with blood. On the other hand, we hear that the Samothracian mysteries required a confession of sins as a preliminary to the initiation: nothing more was apparently needed, the confession being an expiation of the state of sinfulness and impurity.

Most probably it was the Orphic movement (see ORPHISM) that helped two different solutions to develop: the first was the construction of something that can be called 'hell', with penalties of eternal suffering in mud, etc. Basically different, and no doubt inspired by influences from Pythagoreanism (see PYTHAGORAS), was the idea that evil was a corollary of bodily existence, the body being the prison of the *soul, which is thus punished for sins in previous lives. If these sins are not expiated during one incarnation, the soul *transmigrates to another body. Thus, this doctrine of reincarnation provided an elegant solution to the dilemma of divine justice and human suffering. Moreover, it opened an avenue to personal responsibility and an escape from the ritualist group solidarity which involved vicarious suffering for another's fault.

Classical developments

Attic *tragedy questioned all existing ideas on sin, retribution, and theodicy. *Aeschylus (esp. in his *Oresteia*), fascinated by the idea of hereditary curses, tested ways in which a descendant from a doomed house could escape his fate. *Sophocles explored both the question of guiltless guilt (*OT*) and the tensions between human and divine law (*Antigone*). *Euripides added a theological critique: gods who make unfair demands cannot be gods. Like other thinkers influenced by the *sophists, he showed that gods and ethics are often very difficult to reconcile. In the late 5th cent. this could (but in only a few instances actually did) lead to *atheistic expressions (Diagoras). In this same period the debate about the distinction between the laws of man and those of the gods begins. It is argued that the unwritten laws are in the hands of the gods and carry their own unavoidable punishment, whereas penalties resulting from violation of human law are avoidable. Others argued that the gods were the invention of a clever politician in order to bind people to laws which could not otherwise be enforced (most emphatically in the *satyr play *Sisyphus* by Euripides or *Critias.

From the 4th cent. onwards the major philosophical schools inherited from *Plato's *Socrates the basic conviction that 'no one sins willingly', wrongdoing being regarded as an error of judgement. *Stoicism esp. emphasizes individual autonomy within a human community whose cement is the divine principle of Reason (*logos*) which permeates the whole. Here universal laws are identical with divine laws, human life being a divine service. Sin is error, the violation of cosmic laws.

Sirens, enchantresses who live on an island near Scylla and Charybdis in *Homer's *Odyssey*. Sailors charmed by their song land and perish; their meadow is full of mouldering corpses. They attempt to lure *Odysseus by claiming omniscience, but on *Circe's advice he has himself bound to the mast and stops his comrades' ears with wax. Likewise *Orpheus saves the *Argonauts by overpowering their song with his lyre. In some versions they die or commit suicide if a mortal can resist them. The escape of Odysseus or of Orpheus leads to their death, as does their defeat in a singing contest with the *Muses.

In Homer there are two Sirens, later often three. They are often associated with death in both literature and art. They were located or received cults in various parts of Sicily or southern Italy.

In art they are usually represented as birds with women's heads. They are often shown crowning tombs, and also with musical instruments or in musical contexts. They are common on vases from 600 BC, esp. in scenes with Odysseus, and their suicide is already implied on some 6th-cent. examples. Early Sirens have claws like vultures or eagles, but in Classical and Hellenistic art they become beautiful, melancholy creatures, representative of music almost as much as the Muses. The Sirens were allegorized by both classical and Christian writers as representing the lusts of the flesh, the insatiable desire for knowledge, the dangers of flattery, or as celestial music drawing souls upwards to heaven.

Sīsyphus, son of *Aeolus, founder and king of *Corinth, of legendary cunning, a trickster who cheated death, and one of the sinners (see SIN) punished in *Hades in Homer's *Odyssey*: he is pushing a large boulder up a hill, and it keeps rolling back, and he has to start again. One way he cheated death was by persuading the Underworld deities to let him return to the upper world for some reason and then not returning below.

slavery

Greek From *Homer's claim that a man loses half his selfhood when 'the day of slavery' comes upon him (*Iliad* 6. 463) to *Aristotle's doctrine of the *barbarian as a 'natural' slave, and his flawed justification thereof (*Politics* bk. 1), Greek life and thought were inextricably bound up with the ideology and practice of human servitude.

In Athens there were gradations of *status and degrees of exploitation despite uniformity of legal status. At the top of the heap were the few hundreds of publicly owned slaves, who served as a token *police force or as other sorts of public functionary such as official coin-tester in the Agora or clerk to a jury-court. Below them were the privately owned, skilled slaves who 'lived apart' in craft workshops established with start-up capital by their owners to whom they remitted a share of their profits, or who were hired out for specific tasks such as harvesting. Then there were household slaves (*oiketai*), male and female, of whom the males of a smaller household might also work in the fields. Harder was the lot of the agricultural slaves of

a rich citizen householder. But worst of all was that of the mine-slaves who were either directly employed by or hired out to work the state-owned silver mines of *Laurium: for them an early death might be considered a happy release. Reliable numbers are lacking, but a reasonable guess would be that between 450 and 320 BC about 80,000–100,000 slaves of all kinds were active in Attica at any one time (out of a total population of perhaps a quarter of a million). See POPULATION, GREEK.

The Athenian model of chattel slavery became widely diffused in the Greek world, although the size and complexity of the original were never emulated or even approached. The prevalence of inter-Greek warfare ensured that Greek slave-dealers had plenty of custom, even if it was rare for a Greek to be removed from his or her native community into permanent servitude elsewhere in the Greek or non-Greek world. On the other hand, the flow of non-Greek slaves into the Greek world continued unabated.

By no means all those broadly labelled *douloi* ('unfree') in Greece were chattel-slave *douloi*. The two largest classes of these other unfree persons were those enslaved for *debt and the communally enslaved *helot-type populations. Debt-bondsmen technically forfeited their liberty only temporarily, pending repayment of their debt; in practice, the condition might be permanent and hereditary, and on occasion prompted violent political upheaval, as at Athens *c*.600. *Solon's response to that crisis was remarkable in several ways, not least in that he outlawed debt-bondage for citizens altogether. (This may help to explain the growth of chattel slavery.)

There were apparently some chattel slaves in Sparta, but nearly all its servile labour force was constituted by the native *helot class. The fact that they were Greek and enjoyed some privileges, above all a family life, suggested to one ancient commentator that they ought to be classified as somewhere between outright chattel slaves and completely free people. But this picture of relative privilege is darkened by the knowledge that at any time their masters might legally kill them with impunity. The helots were enslaved collectively as a community, a feature they shared with several other Greek and native servile populations. There may still be room for argument whether Greek civilization as a whole was 'based' on 'slavery', but the ubiquitousness and centrality of servitude in the Greek imagination as in Greek everyday reality are beyond question.

Roman Slavery in the strict sense of chattel slavery, whereby the slave-owner enjoyed complete mastery (*dominium*) over the slave's physical being, the power of life and death included, was evident throughout the central era of Roman history, and in Roman no less than Greek thought was regarded as both the necessary antithesis of civic freedom and the guarantee of their civic superiority to those who enjoyed it. Roman society, like Greek, was a genuine slave-society.

Although for no period of antiquity is it possible to determine accurately the size of the slave population, modern estimates of 2,000,000 slaves in Italy at the close of the republic conform to a slave : free ratio of roughly 1 : 3 in evidence from the major slave-societies of the New World. Slave-ownership was always a prerogative of the rich, although the scale of ownership was larger in the Roman world than the Greek, and the élite could possess hundreds of slaves. *Pompey's son Gnaeus Pompeius Magnus recruited 800 of his personal slaves and shepherds for the war against *Caesar, and the city prefect Pedanius Secundus maintained under *Nero *c*.400 slaves in his urban residence alone. Slave-owning, however, was not confined to the very rich. There is evidence to suggest that artisans in Roman Egypt regularly kept two or three slaves. Slave-owning was a mark of status to be sought for its own sake, and even slaves and ex-slaves became slave-owners, esp. those at Rome who belonged to the *familia Caesaris* and prospered from their favoured status.

Slaves were procured chiefly as prisoners of war (see BOOTY), as the victims of organized *piracy and *brigandage, through natural reproduction, and through *trade. The growth of the Roman empire in the 2nd and 1st cents. BC produced vast numbers of prisoners who were transported as slaves to the Italian heartland. Romans, like Greeks, tended to shun enslavement of co-nationals, assimilating slavery to the 'barbarian' character of other peoples; so Syrians and Jews were peoples born for enslavement (although classical slavery was never in itself racially grounded). Piracy is best illustrated from the activities of the Cilician bandits of the late republic, notorious for discharging great quantities of enslaved victims in *Delos, where traders swiftly redistributed them, esp. to the west. Children born to a slave mother were themselves slaves (the status of the father was immaterial); so natural reproduction constantly contributed to the slave supply.

Slaves can be observed in almost every area of human activity, the holding of public office apart. It was conventional in certain contexts (e.g. manufacturing) for slave and free to work side by side. In late republican Italy the extensive development of slave-run *latifundia* meant that the rural slave presence was very high; and it was still high, in some regions of Italy at least, under the Principate (see AGRICULTURE, ROMAN). Domestic labour and the dangerous and heavily exploitative work in the *mines were something of a slave preserve; the gold and silver mines in Roman Spain consumed human labour at a prodigious rate.

The slave-owner's prerogative of setting the slave free was frequently exercised in classical antiquity, and at Rome, contrary to Greek practice, the slave could even be admitted to citizenship (see FREEDMEN); but a high frequency of manumission does not entail that a high proportion of slaves were manumitted. Most slaves were probably not set free; many who were, paid their owners a price for their freedom from savings (see PECULIUM). Manumitted slaves could easily be replaced.

Almost all knowledge of classical slavery derives from sources representing the attitudes and ideology of slave-owners. So it is impossible to understand the life of slaves in Graeco-Roman society. Many slaves must have responded with obedience to the rewards for good behaviour—time off from work, superior rations of food and clothing, freedom—that owners offered them as incentives, knowing that physical coercion was always predictable if acquiescence were not forthcoming. As for resistance, it is most easily recognized in the occasional episodes of open revolt, notably the movement led by *Spartacus in Italy in the late 70s BC. Their object was not to eradicate slavery but to extricate the disaffected from its rigours. Slaves displayed resistance more commonly by running away, playing truant, working inefficiently, pilfering or sabotaging property—annoying and frustrating tactics for owners, but less personally threatening for the perpetrators.

At no time was there any serious questioning of the structural role of slavery in Graeco-Roman society. At Rome *Stoicism is said to have mitigated attitudes towards slaves and to have inspired humane legislation rendering slavery more tolerable, esp. under the Principate. In reality Stoic moralists were more concerned with the effects of slave-holding on the moral health of the slave-owners than with the conditions under which slaves lived, while Roman legislation, although showing an increasing interest in the public regulation of slavery, was primarily driven by the aim of perpetuating the slavery system as it was. *Christianity likewise displayed no interest in social change from which slaves might benefit, and the result of the Christian attitude symbolized by the repeated injunction that slaves should obey their masters 'with fear and trembling' (Ephesians 6: 5)—a vigorous reaffirmation that slavery was an institution based essentially on violence—was to make slavery even harsher in late antiquity than in earlier eras.

sleep See DREAMS; MEDICINE, 2; STATIUS.

slingers Thucydides mentions the Acarnanians from NW Greece as expert slingers in 429 BC, and in 424 the Boeotians (see BOEOTIA) sent for slingers from Malis before their assault on the Athenian fort at *Delion. By 415, at latest, the Rhodians (see RHODES) were known as expert slingers, and the Athenians took 700 of them to *Sicily; even Rhodians who had not originally enlisted as slingers proved expert with the weapon during the retreat of the 10,000. *Philip II of Macedon certainly used slingers at *Olynthus in 348, for many of their sling-bullets have been found. In the western Mediterranean Balearic slingers took the place of Rhodians.

Xenophon tells us that the Rhodian slingers among the 10,000 were able to improvise slings and lead bullets, and were even able to outrange most enemy archers; the maximum range of the sling was possibly as much as 350 m. (380 yards). Bullets could be either stone, clay, or lead. The lead bullets used by the Macedonians at Olynthus averaged about 30 grams, those of the defenders about 20. Bullets from Olynthus are often inscribed, some with the names of Philip or his officers, but some with slogans like 'take that' or 'a nasty present'.

snakes were regarded in Greek and Roman religion mostly as guardians, e.g. of houses, graves, *springs, and *altars. Probably evoking their hidden, secretive natural habitat of crevices and the world of 'under' in general, snakes were associated with gods linked with the Underworld. They were associated either with what emerges from the earth, such as trees or springs, or what is placed inside it, such as foundations of houses and altars, or graves.

Snakes guard sacred places (the garden of the Golden Apples of the *Hesperides) or objects (the Golden Fleece; see JASON (1)). *Apollo killed the Python which guarded *Delphi for its patron goddess, Earth (Ge, *Gaia); the sacred snake of Athena is said to have abandoned the Acropolis when the Athenians left for *Salamis. In art and ritual snakes often appear coiled around sacred trees, at the foot of altars, on gravestones, and as guardians of caves facing dedicants who present them with sacred *cakes (the *oracle of *Trophonius). In fantastic compositions we find men-snakes (*Cecrops, *Erichthonius), or metamorphoses: *Thetis took on the form of a snake to escape *Peleus. As an attribute of gods, snakes were close to *Demeter with her serpent-chariot, used also by *Athena (and *Medea). As healing powers, they were associated with *Asclepius, esp. in Hellenistic and Roman religion.

Feared for their deadly venom, the frightening aspect of snakes finds expression more in myth and art than in cult. Snakes (or 'dragons') were born of the earth or of the drops of Titans' blood (see TITAN); they are entwined in the *Gorgon's hair, coiled around the body of *Cerberus, accompany the Furies (see ERINYES), and sent by *Hera to kill baby *Heracles and his twin. To strike terror they were depicted on hoplites' shields or, as an expression of victory, on commemorative monuments (the Serpent Monument, dedicated at *Delphi as a thank-offering after the *Persian Wars).

Social Wars are conflicts collectively involving allies (Lat. *socii). The Social, Marsic, or Italic War (91–87 BC; the main fighting being in 90–89) was waged by Rome's Italian allies (among whom the Marsi were prominent) against her predominance. Rome gained the victory largely through the political concession of granting her citizenship to the enemy. Thereafter Italy, south of the Po (see PADUS), was united by the common bond of *citizenship.

socii were allies of Rome. The Roman conquest of Italy resulted in a system of military alliances by which native communities remained theoretically independent but were in practice reduced to subjects. This relationship was enshrined in treaties of alliance (see FOEDUS) which the Italian peoples made with Rome, on terms that were more or less favourable, depending on whether they joined Rome voluntarily or were defeated in war. By the time of the *Punic Wars more than 150 separate treaties had been concluded, and all the peoples of non-Roman Italy had become *socii*. Although the more equal treaties stipulated military partnership, in practice all the allies were obliged to assist the Romans by sending contingents of troops to fight alongside the legions. These obligations were set out in a document which seems to have defined the number of troops each allied community could be called upon to contribute. During the 3rd and 2nd cents. BC Roman *armies always contained a large proportion, varying between half and two-thirds, of allied troops. In exchange for their contribution the allies received security and a share of the profits of conquest, esp. the right to take part in land assignations and colonies. This doubtless explains the remarkable loyalty of the allies, even when tested to the limit in the *Hannibalic War. During the 2nd cent., however, the relationship changed, as *colonization ceased and the profits of empire, in the form of regular provincial taxation, were monopolized by Rome. By the time of *Marius the system had become exploitative, and in 91 allied discontent gave rise to the *Social War (i.e. the war against the *socii*). This bloody conflict ended when the allies were given Roman *citizenship and incorporated in the Roman state.

From early times Rome also had allies outside Italy, notably *Carthage and *Massilia, and their number increased rapidly after 200 as kings, city-states, and confederations made treaties with Rome on nominally equal terms. Unlike the Italian allies, they did not regularly contribute troops, although they were expected to undertake military action on Rome's behalf when local circumstances demanded it. With the growth of the empire these allied states gradually lost their independence and became merely the most privileged class of provincial communities; their number also declined during the Civil Wars, when many revolted or joined the wrong side, and so lost their privileged status. The few that survived into the Principate were known as *cīvitātēs foederātae*, while the term *socii* came increasingly to be used indiscriminately for all Rome's free provincial subjects.

Socratēs (469–399 BC), Athenian public figure and central participant in the intellectual debates so common in the city in the middle and late 5th cent. His influence has been enormous, although he himself wrote nothing.

Socrates' philosophy and personality reached a broad ancient audience mainly through the dialogues that a number of his associates wrote with him as protagonist. These were numerous and popular enough for *Aristotle to classify them in his *Poetics* as a species of fiction in their own right. But apart from the works of *Plato, only a few fragments survive of the dialogues of *Antisthenes, and *Aeschines of Sphettus, and nothing of the dialogues of Aristippus, and many others. In addition to Plato, most of our information about Socrates comes from *Aristophanes and *Xenophon, both of whom also knew him personally, and from Aristotle, who did not.

Socrates was the son of Sophroniscus, of the *deme of Alōpecē. Though Plato and Xenophon depict him as a poor man, he must at some time have owned sufficient property to qualify for service as a *hoplite in the battles of *Potidaea, *Amphipolis, and *Delium, through which he acquired a reputation for courage. He was married to Xanthippē and was the father of three sons.

Socrates avoided active participation in politics. He was, however, one of the presidents (see PRYTANEIS) of the assembly (*ekklesia*) when the generals at the sea-battle at *Arginusae were put on trial for abandoning the bodies of the Athenian dead there. Socrates (who was chairman of the *prytaneis* on the crucial day) alone voted against the illegal motion to try the generals as a single group, and they were executed. After the defeat of Athens in the *Peloponnesian War, he openly ignored an order by the *Thirty Tyrants to arrest an innocent citizen. For his likely political views, see POLITICAL THEORY.

Socrates' circle included a number of men who turned against democracy in Athens, including *Critias, Charmides, and *Alcibiades. (See OLIGARCHY; FOUR HUNDRED, THE; DEMOCRACY, ATHENIAN.) This may well have been the underlying reason why he himself was tried and put to death by drinking hemlock in 399. He was charged with impiety, specifically with introducing new gods and corrupting young men (see ATHEISM). This charge may have masked the political motives of his accusers, since the *amnesty of 403 BC prohibited prosecution for most offences committed before that date.

Socrates' execution prompted Plato and Xenophon to create portraits intended to refute the formal charge under which he was tried and to counter his popular image, which may have been inspired by Aristophanes' *Clouds*. Aristophanes had depicted Socrates engaged in natural philosophy and willing to teach his students how 'to make the weaker argument the stronger'—a commonplace charge against the *sophists. Both Plato and Xenophon were intent on distinguishing Socrates as radically as possible from other members of the sophistic movement, with whom he may actually have had some affinities. But their strategies differ. In both authors, Socrates devotes himself, like the sophists, to dialectical argument and the drawing of distinctions. In both, he refuses, unlike the sophists, to receive payment. In Xenophon, however, he uses argument to support, in contrast to the sophists, a traditional and conventional understanding of the virtues. In Plato, on the other hand, he disavows moral knowledge, and his main difference from the sophists is that, unlike them, he never presents himself as a teacher of any subject.

Plato's and Xenophon's portraits, inconsistent as they are with Aristophanes', are also inconsistent with each other. This is the root of 'the Socratic problem', the question whether we can ever capture the personality and philosophy of the historical Socrates or whether we must limit ourselves to the interpretation of one or another of his literary representations. Most contemporary scholars turn to Plato for information on Socrates' ideas and character.

That character is cool, distant, reticent and ironic, in contrast to Xenophon's more conventional, straightforward, almost avuncular figure. Plato's Socrates refrains from expounding positive views of his own, preferring instead to question those who do have such views. In Plato's early or 'Socratic' dialogues his questions mainly concern the nature and teachability of *aretē* ('virtue', 'excellence', or perhaps 'success') and what produces it, both in one's person and in one's activities, and its species—courage, wisdom, piety, self-control, and justice. By means of the procedure of question and answer which came to be known as the *elenchus* (see DIALECTIC), Socrates refutes all those who claim to know what *aretē* is by showing their views to be internally inconsistent.

The Platonic Socrates is utterly serious about *aretē* and the nature of the good and happy life. His commitment to do what is, by his best lights, the right thing to do in all cases is unwavering. This commitment ultimately cost him his life: acc. to Plato's *Apology*, he antagonized his jury by insisting that his life had been as good as any human being's and that far from having committed any wrongs he had brought the greatest benefits to Athens.

Socrates seems to have been convinced that wisdom and virtue were ultimately the same—that if one knows what the good is, one will always do it. His argument was that the good, or *aretē*, either leads to or is itself part of the happy life. Since everyone wants to be happy above everything else, no one who knows what the good is will not choose to do it. This 'intellectualist' approach to ethics implies that there is no such thing as 'weakness of will'. It is impossible to know the better and choose the worse: the only reason people choose a worse course of action is that they are ignorant of what is better. This is one of the 'Socratic paradoxes', which contradict everyday experience but have proved surprisingly resistant to analysis and refutation.

Plato's Socrates consistently denied that he had the knowledge of *arete* that he considered necessary for the good and happy life. He sometimes referred to this knowledge as 'divine', in opposition to the 'human' knowledge he himself possessed and which consisted in his awareness of his own ignorance. This, he claimed, made him wiser than others, who were both ignorant of *arete* and ignorant of their very ignorance. In the *Apology*, he claimed that this was the meaning of the Delphic oracle saying that no one in Athens was wiser that he was (see CHAEREPHON).

Socrates often, in both Plato and Xenophon, referred to a 'divine sign', a *daimonion*, which prevented him from taking certain courses of action—he attributes his reluctance to participate in active politics to this sign's intervention. His religious views, even though they sometimes overlapped with those of tradition (he acknowledged the authority of *Apollo, for example, when he received the *Delphic oracle), must have been quite novel, since he appears to have thought that the gods could never harm each other or human beings. He also seems, as we see in Plato's *Euthyphro*, to claim that the gods' approval or disapproval does not render actions right or wrong. On the contrary, rightness and wrongness are established independently, and the gods, knowing what they are, both engage in the former and shun the latter and approve of human beings for acting likewise.

Socrates' moral seriousness is counterbalanced by a worldly personality that enjoys good food and company—goods which he is also willing to forgo without complaint if they are not available or if they conflict with the much more important pursuit of *arete*. He had an uncanny ability, as we see in both Plato and Xenophon, not to do anything wrong, and his relation to positive philosophical views was fundamentally ambiguous. These features, along with the vividness with which Plato portrays his complex personality, are doubtless responsible for the fact that so many ancient philosophical schools, from the Academic *Sceptics and the *Cyrenaics to the Stoics (see STOICISM) and the *Cynics, considered him as the person most closely approximating their ideal.

Socrates provides the first model of a philosopher primarily devoted to the pursuit of ethical issues. His pursuit is systematic, and his emphasis on the necessity of knowing the definitions of the virtues if we are to decide securely what does and what does not fall under them provided an impetus for the development of logic. In addition, he still constitutes the paradigmatic figure in whom philosophy, even in its most abstract manifestations, is never severed from the concerns of life. He lived and—most importantly—he died in accordance with his philosophical principles. Plato's lively portrait makes it believable that such a life is possible. But since his principles are not always clear and we cannot be certain whether he himself knew exactly what they were, Socrates continues to constitute a mystery with which anyone interested in philosophy or in the writings of the Greeks must contend.

sodālēs are either 'companions, mates', or else 'members of a single college or fraternity'. Examples of the latter sense are the secondary religious groups of Rome: these include the *fētiālēs, who made treaties and declared war; and three sodalities that were concerned with performing specific annual rites—the *Salii; the Luperci, whose festival was the *Lupercalia; and best recorded of them all, the *fratrēs arvālēs*, whose cult of Dea Dia was originally agrarian and concerned with boundaries, later with the celebration of the imperial house.

Sōl Invictus ('the invincible Sun'), a Syrian god. The first attempt to make the Sun the chief object of Roman worship was that of the emperor Elagabalus (AD 218–222), who introduced the god of Emesa on the Orontes, whose priest and, apparently, incarnation he was, El Gabal. Elagabalus' excesses and consequent unpopularity and assassination checked the cult, but *Aurelian reintroduced a similar worship, also oriental; he was himself the son of a priestess of the Sun. This remained the chief imperial and official worship till *Christianity displaced it, although the cult of the older gods, esp. *Jupiter, did not cease, but rather the new one was somehow parallel to it, the Sun's clergy being called *pontifices Solis* (see PONTIFEX),

a significant name which was part of a policy of Romanizing the oriental god. Sol had a magnificent temple on the campus Agrippae. Its dedication day was 25 December.

Solon, Athenian politician and poet, was of noble descent but came to sympathize with the poor. He was prominent in the war against *Megara for the possession of the Island of *Salamis, urging the Athenians to renewed effort when they despaired of success (c.600 BC). In 594/3 he was archon (see ARCHONTES), and the link between his archonship and his reforms is probably to be accepted. He is said to have spent the ten years after his reforms in overseas *travel (see TOURISM), during which his measures were not to be altered: if he continued to travel after that, he may have met Amasis of Egypt, but if he died c.560/59, he is unlikely to have met *Croesus of Lydia (though that tradition is as old as *Herodotus). It may be true that he was in Athens at the time of the troubles in which *Pisistratus first seized power, and tried to warn the Athenians against Pisistratus.

For Herodotus Solon was a sage, a lawgiver, and a poet; *Thucydides (2) does not mention him. It was at the end of the 5th cent. that the democrats began to think of him as their founding hero: if 4th-cent. writers had access not only to his poems but also to the *axonēs* (revolving pillars) on which the laws were inscribed, they will have had a firm basis for their accounts of him, even though they were capable of anachronistic misinterpretation, and though the orators tended to ascribe to him all the laws current in the 4th cent.

Solon's *seisachtheia* ('shaking-off of burdens') is represented as a cancellation of all *debts, but should probably be seen as the liberation of the *hektēmoroi* ('sixth-parters'), men in a state of servitude who had to give a sixth of their produce to an overlord: their obligation was abolished and they became the absolute owners of their land; men who had been enslaved for debt (many of them, perhaps, *hektemoroi* who had defaulted on their obligation) were freed, and for the future enslavement for debt was banned. Grants of *citizenship to immigrant craftsmen, and a ban on the export of agricultural products other than olive oil, encouraging the growth of *olives, will have helped to move Athens from a largely self-contained towards a trading economy (see TRADE). Behind an alleged series of changes in Athens' measures, weights, and *coinage we should perhaps see legislation for the use of standard measures and weights (not necessarily different from those already in use in Attica); but even the earliest coins are almost certainly later than the time of Solon.

Solon divided the Athenian citizens into four property classes (*pentakosiomedimnoi*, *hippeis*, *zeugītai*, *thētĕs*). The property in question was agricultural produce: cereals, olive oil, wine. He made these classes the basis of all political rights, to break the monopoly of the noble families: the major offices were reserved for the two highest classes; the *zeugitai* were eligible for the minor offices; the *thetes* could not hold office but could attend the assembly (*ekklesia*) and *eliaia*. He probably created a council of 400 to prepare business for the assembly, and provided for regular meetings of the assembly. He compiled a new code of laws, superseding the more severe laws of *Draco except in the area of homicide, and probably extending written laws into areas not touched by Draco. He created a category of public lawsuits, in which any citizen might prosecute, in contrast to the private lawsuits in which only the injured party or his family could prosecute; and he provided for appeals against the verdicts of magistrates to the *eliaia* (possibly a judicial meeting of the assembly).

Solon shows in his poems that he was trying to achieve a compromise between the demands of the rich and privileged and of the poor and un-privileged, and that he satisfied neither: the *hektemoroi* were not given the total redistribution of land which some had wanted, but their liberation angered the deprived overlords; the nobles were reluctant to share political power with the many, and there was trouble over appointments to the archonship in the years that followed; tension continued until the three seizures of power by Pisistratus, between *c*.561/0 and *c*.546/5. Nevertheless, in the creation of a free peasantry, the weakening of the *aristocracy and the strengthening of the assembly and the judicial system, Solon laid the foundations for the successful and stable society of Classical Athens.

See also DEMOCRACY, ATHENIAN; PATRIOS POLITEIA.

sophists Itinerant professors of higher education. From its original senses of 'sage' and 'expert' the word came to be applied in the 5th. cent. BC in the technical sense given above to a number of men who travelled through the Greek world, giving popular lectures and specialized instruction in a wide range of topics. They were not a school, or even a single move-ment, having neither a common set of doctrines nor any shared organization.

Their activities included the popularization of Ionian natural philosophy, *mathematics and the 'human sciences' of history, *geography, and speculative *anthropology; *Hippias (2) was active in all and *Protagoras in at least some of these fields. They, and *Gorgias, pioneered the systematic study of techniques of persuasion and argument, which embraced various forms of the study of language, including grammar, *literary criticism, and semantics. Protagoras wrote a treatise on techniques of argument, and was notorious for his claim to 'make the weaker argument the stronger'.

The sophists aroused strong reactions, both positive and negative. On the positive side, the highly successful careers of the most celebrated testify to a considerable demand for their services, esp. in providing rhetorical training for aspiring politicians. On the negative, they were regarded, esp. by those of conservative views, as subversive of morality and tradition, in view both of their naturalistic outlook on morality and religion, and of their teaching (esp. to the young) of techniques of argument.

Various sophists did indeed subject morality to critical scrutiny. Protagoras maintained (apparently inconsistently with his universal subjectivism) a form of moral relativism, in which moral beliefs are true for the communities in which they are entertained. *Plato represents more radical critics of morality in the persons of Thrasymachus ('justice is the interest of the stronger.') and of Calliclës, a pupil of Gorgias. It is, however, oversimplified to regard the sophists as a group as having shared a generally sceptical or radical outlook on morality. *Xenophon reports Hippias as maintaining the traditional doctrine that there exist certain natural laws common to all societies, while Plato reports Protagoras as holding that the sophist complements, rather than subverts, the traditional educational institutions of the community in their task of imparting the basic social virtues.

As the writings of the sophists are lost, we depend for our information on others, mainly Plato, who is a hostile witness. He believed, very probably truly, that the suspicion which certain sophists had attracted had contributed to the unpopularity and ultimately to the condemnation of *Socrates, and therefore depicts the sophists predominantly as charlatans, in contrast to Socrates, the true philosopher. See EDUCATION, GREEK, 3.

Sophoclēs, Athenian tragic poet.

Career Sophocles, b. in the 490s BC, had a long career in the theatre, competing, almost always at the City Dionysia, from 468 to 406, when he died. He wrote more than 120 plays, of which only seven survive, and won at least 20 victories, eighteen at the City Dionysia: he was thus much the most successful of the three great 5th-cent. playwrights. He also figured in the public life of Athens: he was one of the Treasurers of the Greeks (see HELLENOTAMIAE) in 443–442 and a general (see STRATEGOI), with *Pericles, probably in 441/0, during the revolt of *Samos. In the political crisis that followed the defeat of the *Sicilian Expedition he is said to have been one of the ten 'advisers' appointed to deal with the state of emergency.

Plays of the seven only two can be dated: *Philoctētēs*, 409, and *Oedipus at Colōnus* (*OC*) 401 (a posthumous victory). The other five are: *Ajax, Antigonē, Electra, Oedipus Tyrannus* (*OT*), *Trachiniae* ('Women of Trāchis').

Theatricality Readings of Sophocles in the earlier part of the last century tended to be determined by the influence of *Aristophanes' passing remark about him, only months after his death, as 'easy-going' or 'relaxed' (*Frogs* 82) and by the judgement of later ancient critics of style which identified Sophocles' with the 'middle, well-blended' style, neither grand and austere (like Aeschylus and *Thucydides (2)) nor smooth and pedestrian (like *Isocrates and *Euripides). Sophocles thus emerged as 'middling'— stable, harmonious, and at ease with life. Such readings ignored the often discomforting nature of much Sophoclean theatre (esp. in *Antigone, OT*, and *Trāchīniae*) and largely denied his insistent theatricality. Sophocles is the master of the enacted metaphor—metaphors of e.g. blindness in the two *Oedipus plays and *Antigone*. The theatricality of such pervasive dramatic metaphors emerges in such moments as the messenger speech of *OT*, and the immediately following scene with the entry of the now blinded but 'seeing' Oedipus. Such moments are moments of theatrical power, and 'middling' is not a word to apply to them. Sophocles can produce equally powerful effects of the eerie and uncanny: e.g. in the opening scene of *Ajax*, where the unseen *Athena manipulates a puppet-like Ajax (see AIAS (1)) and is resisted by the matching subtlety of *Odysseus (the scene becomes even eerier in retrospect when his wife Tecmessa reports it as if Ajax had been speaking to a vacancy).

Much of Sophoclean theatricality resides in his dramatic use of significant objects and significant actions, esp. exits and entrances. *Electra* is a play of thwarted recognition (see below), and its centrepiece enacts a sinister game of illusion, of disguises and deceptions. The game involves not only a brilliantly theatrical messenger speech evoking and narrating, in the bravura style of such speeches, distant events which culminate in the violent death of *Orestes and which we know have not occurred, but also the bringing of Orestes' 'ashes', carried in an urn by the unrecognized Orestes himself. The urn is taken by Electra, whose grief for her dead brother and lament for the irreparable loss of her own hoped-for future are directed to it, focused on the 'little weight' which is his tomb and which she now holds in her hands. She begs to be allowed to join him in it, 'nothing with nothing', and even when Orestes struggles to disclose himself and to be recognized, she will not let go of it. The urn is 'what is closest' to her. The fusing of game-playing, irony, and intensity of tragic emotion is mediated through the simple 'prop'. Other such significant props are the sword in *Ajax* and the bow in *Philoctetes*.

Entrances and exits were always, given the layout of the theatre space, of more importance in Attic tragedy than in later forms of built theatre. Sophocles' use of them is, however, his own. The entrance of the self-blinded Oedipus in *OT*, immediately after one of Sophocles' most powerful messenger speeches, has already been mentioned. The final entrance of *Creon (1), carrying the body of his son, in *Antigone* is another *coup-de-théâtre*: it follows almost without pause on the exit of his wife, turning away in silence from the messenger's narrative of her son's death. As Creon enters, he is instantly met by the same messenger emerging from the palace to announce his wife's death and by the 'rolling out' of the *ekkyklēma* (see THEATRE STAGING, GREEK), carrying a tableau of his wife's body and the sword with which she has just killed herself (see SUICIDE). Entering and carrying one body, he confronts another.

Sophocles' last two plays offer a unique sense of space and 'place where', in relation to which alone the action has meaning. Lemnos in *Philoctetes* and the grove of the Semnai (see ERINYES) at Colonos in *OC* are heavily loaded with meaning as places to be left or reached. In both plays entrances and exits are thus equally full of significance. In *OC* the act of entering unknowingly upon sacred ground and esp. that of leaving it are given dramatic weight by the slow measured extension of the blind Oedipus' movements. Later in the play the entry of Ismene is similarly extended, this time from the moment the figures on stage first catch sight of her (in the approach to the acting area) until she is within range of speech and touch. These are adagio movements; in *Philoctetes*, it is the suddenness of Odysseus' entries at 974 (in mid-line) and 1293 that gives them their theatrical quality. But in *Philoctetes* it is above all the thwarted exit that defines the theatricality of the play. The play's action requires that Philoctetes leave Lemnos for Troy. That exit is four times launched, delayed, and then thwarted. Each thwarted exit is different in its implications from each of the others and the last, completed exit is itself ambiguous in its meaning.

Language, Form and Structure The language that Sophocles deploys in his plays has, arguably, a greater range than that of either Aeschylus or Euripides, from the baroque sonorities of Ajax' great 'deception speech' or the messenger's opening proclamation of his news in *OT* to the rambling, self-defensive preambles of the guard in *Antigone*. It is a language which is often difficult, even inscrutable (esp. in its syntax and particularly in the songs of the chorus); it is never less than formal, and it does not yield its sense easily. But it has a flexibility that is very much Sophocles'. It is a mark of Sophoclean writing that it operates within highly formalized structures but uses those structures with masterly tact and subtlety. Sophocles uses the iambic trimeter of tragic dialogue (see METRE, GREEK, 4(a)) mostly in its strict form, but he treats such formal boundaries as line-end, for example, with a relaxed ease; clauses, even prepositional phrases, may run over into the next line; occasionally a final vowel at the end of one line may be elided (i.e. run into) the opening vowel of the next. The pulse of the verse is kept steady but the rhythmical structure of the whole speech is given a new fluidity by Sophocles' informal treatment of metrical pause. So too with dialogue: like the other tragedians, Sophocles divides a line between speakers only as a sign of greatly heightened emotional tension, but the length of the speeches that are exchanged is left much more fluid than those of Euripides.

The fusion of formal symmetries with a more 'naturalistic' use of speech is well illustrated by the pivotal scene of *OT* which embraces the quarrel between Oedipus and Creon, the entry and intervention of Jocasta, and the following dialogue between Oedipus and Jocasta. With the entry first of Creon and then of Oedipus the quarrel develops from Oedipus' opening speech of denunciation into a rapid, heated exchange of short speeches which keeps drifting into and out of the formal severities of *stichomythia*; it culminates in Creon's long speech of reasoned self-defence and Oedipus' curt proclamation of death, not exile, as Creon's punishment. This in turn leads at once into a vicious exchange of tense, broken lines, a choral intervention in spoken iambics and Jocasta's entry. The three characters now on stage (most of our sources attribute to Sophocles the innovation of using three actors) engage in dialogue with a marked tendency towards symmetry. The formal severity of the scene is suddenly tightened still more when the chorus break in again, this time in song, and confront, first Oedipus, then Jocasta in a mixture of sung and spoken dialogue; the two confrontations, which respond with precise symmetry, are separated by the final, spoken exchanges between Oedipus and Creon, ending in another broken verse and Creon's exit. The chorus in song briefly assure Oedipus of their absolute loyalty, and Jocasta then begins a new scene of spoken, loosely structured dialogue in which it gradually emerges, with a high degree of psychological persuasive 'naturalness', that it may be Oedipus himself who killed his own predecessor as king, Jocasta's first husband, Laius.

The idea of flexibility in the deployment of a tightly controlled formal structure applies also to resonances and agreements between plays. Sophocles turned three times to the cycle of traditional stories associated with *Thebes, not to produce a continuous 'trilogy' in the manner of Aeschylus but to explore certain recurring themes. *Antigone* is often taken to be a broken-backed and structureless play (who is its 'hero'— Antigone, who disappears barely two-thirds of the way through the play, and never re-appears, or Creon, who is alienated from us almost from the first by the brutal autocracy of his language? *OT*, ever since *Aristotle's *Poetics*, has been read as the model of a well-constructed play. But in important ways Sophocles uses these two differently structured theatrical experiences to explore closely related themes. *OT* has a smoothly pivotal structure in which, with no appearance of discontinuity, we turn from one issue (the salvation of Thebes from plague brought on by *pollution) to another (is Oedipus guilty both of patricide and incest?). *Antigone* seems very different: it is more like a revolving stage on which, from Antigone's exit under sentence of death, one character is replaced by another until in the closing scene of the play all but Tiresias and the dead Antigone are assembled together in final confrontation with death and, for Creon, tragic recognition. But the two plays are tightly bound together by common themes (pollution through violent death; human blindness to truth; the impenetrability of the divine and the opaqueness of the riddling language of divinity); in both plays humans are left for carrion to devour, and boundaries between the two worlds of gods and men are thereby crossed with deadly results; in both the bonds of kinship have been distorted into horrific travesties of family. *Antigone* ends in inescapable bleakness; *OT*, more positively, with Oedipus re-confronting the world in his blindness.

Tragedy and 'Recognition' Aristotle in his *Poetics* makes much use of the idea of 'recognition' (*anagnōrisis*) in his analysis of the tragic effect. The idea is not of much help in reading Aeschylus and of intermittent usefulness in Euripides. But in Sophocles it is an illuminating critical tool. In play after play, one or more characters is brought to a realization that he or she has misperceived reality, and the realization is almost always associated with pain, suffering, and death. The idea of recognition is usually also associated with relationships between man and divinity. Between the two worlds of gods and men there is communication, in the imagined world of Sophoclean theatre: it comes in the form of dreams, oracles, and the reading of signs by seers like Tiresias. Men and women try to guide their decisions by their understanding of such communications. But such understanding is almost always false: the language and the signs used by divinity are everywhere ambiguous, however simple in appearance, and they are systematically and readily misunderstandable, even if they are to hand. In *Ajax*, at a crucial moment, men learn too late of the seer's reading of Athena's intentions and Ajax dies; in *Trachiniae* both Deiānīra and Heracles perceive the true meaning of a series of oracles and non-human communications only when it is too late and the recognition cannot save them from the consequences of catastrophically mistaken action. In *Antigone*, both Antigone and Creon believe that they are acting as the gods require of them: Antigone dies with that belief shaken and perhaps foundering, and Creon confronts his misreading of the requirements of divinity only when not just Antigone but his son

and wife also are already dead. In *Philoctetes* the oracle is never brought sharply into focus but none the less haunts the play; in *OT* the simplicities of the oracle's language become utterly opaque when read through the lens of Oedipus' 'knowledge' of the truth about himself. The recurring pattern of Sophoclean tragedy is that all falls into place and coheres only in retrospect: recognition comes after the event.

Soranus of Ephesus, physician under *Trajan and *Hadrian (AD 98–138), studied at *Alexandria and practised at Rome. He wrote *c*.20 books, their subjects including a wide range of medical topics, medical biography, commentaries, and discussions of grammar and etymology. Those surviving in Greek are sections and fragments of *On Signs of Fractures* and *On Bandages* and *Gynaecology*. The last gives valuable information on *gynaecology and obstetrics in the Roman empire, and is divided into (1) the midwife, female anatomy and conception; (2) *childbirth and the care of the newborn; (3) *pathology and *diet; (4) surgery and drugs (see PHARMACOLOGY). In the Greek east, Soranus' gynaecology survived in the work of the encyclopaedists. Esp. influential was his image of the ideal midwife: literate, sober, discreet, free from superstition, and equally well acquainted with both theory and practice (see MIDWIVES).

sortition, selection by lot, a method of appointing officials in Greek city-states, esp. in democracies (see DEMOCRACY, both entries). It was based on the idea of equality and reduced outside influence. Little is known of its use except at Athens. It was introduced there perhaps as early as *Solon. From 487/6 BC the archons (see ARCHONTES) were appointed by lot out of nominated candidates; later, this became a double sortition. From the time when the archons began to be selected by lot, they lost political leadership. But all ordinary magistrates, a few excepted, were thus appointed; also the *boulē (a prytany of 50 from each *phȳlē*; see PHYLAI; PRYTANEIS) and the juries (by a complicated procedure; see LAW AND PROCEDURE, ATHENIAN, 2). Lot decided many questions in political and social life. Politically, sortition, combined with the prohibition or at least severe restriction of a second term, enabled rotation in office, and electoral contests were avoided by its use; moreover, the power of magistrates was reduced, and thus the sovereignty of the assembly (see EKKLESIA) guaranteed. Sortition was practicable, as almost every citizen had a minimum of political experience, and nobody could be selected without having presented himself. Certain precautions were always taken (see DOKIMASIA), and military and some technical (esp. financial) officials were elected. Sortition was a necessary and fundamental element of the democratic *polis. See ELECTIONS AND VOTING, *Greek*.

soul The Gk. term nearest to English 'soul', *psȳchē* has a long history and a wide variety of senses in both philosophical and non-philosophical contexts. In *Homer, the psyche is what leaves the *body on death (i.e. life, or breath?), but also an insubstantial image (*eidōlon*) of the dead person, existing in *Hades and not something alive. But some vague idea of psyche as the essence of the individual, capable of surviving the body (and perhaps entering another) is well established by the 5th cent., though without necessarily displacing the older idea and even being combined with it. Simultaneously, in medical contexts and elsewhere, psyche begins to be found regularly in contrast with *sōma*, suggesting something like the modern contrast between mind and body.

All of these ideas are found, separately or in combination, in the philosophers. *Democritus stresses the interconnectedness of psyche ('mind') and body, while *Socrates regards the psyche primarily as our essence *qua* moral beings. Socrates was probably agnostic about whether it was something capable of surviving death; *Plato, by contrast, offers repeated arguments for the immortality of the psyche, which he combines with the (originally Pythagorean) idea that it *transmigrates, after the death of the person, into another body, human or animal. See PYTHAGORAS. Sometimes he represents the psyche as something purely (or ultimately) rational, sometimes as including irrational elements. At the same time his myths include many aspects of Homeric *eschatology, which may have retained an important place in popular belief. *Aristotle is remotest from popular belief, adopting a largely biological approach which says that the psyche is the 'form' of the living creature, i.e. the combination of powers or capacities to do the things which are characteristic of its species.

In philosophical contexts, the primary connotations of psyche are probably life, consciousness, and 'self-caused' movement. Psyche, or an aspect of it, is typically made the ultimate cause of all or most movement, whether in the shape of a world soul, as in Platonism, or of god, as in Aristotle and *Stoicism. The chief exception is *Epicureanism, which makes the movements of atoms primary.

sovereignty See AUTONOMY; DEMOCRACY; KINGSHIP; OLIGARCHY; PLEBISCITUM; POLIS; POLITICAL THEORY; SENATE.

Spain

Phoenicians, Greeks, Carthaginians Traditionally Phoenicians from *Tyre founded Gades *c.*1100 BC, although archaeologists have lowered the date to the 8th cent. Nine further colonies were later established along the coast of southern Spain. They traded with Tartessus until the 6th cent., when waning Phoenician power was replaced by that of *Carthage. In the mid-6th cent. Greeks from *Phocaea founded colonies in Iberia. Carthaginian power in Iberia was enhanced with the conquests in the south by *Hamilcar Barca and *Hannibal from 237. These culminated in the foundation of *Carthago Nova, as Carthage mobilized Iberian manpower and metal resources for the attack on Rome. The Second *Punic War, starting from Hannibal's siege of Saguntum and his approach to the Ebro, continued in the Iberian theatre until Carthage was driven out by *Cornelius Scipio Africanus in 206.

The Roman Provinces Roman territory was formally constituted as two separate provinces, Nearer Spain (the eastern coastal strip) and Further Spain (the SE coast and the Guadalquivir valley) in 197. Both provinces were gradually extended inland in rapacious and reactive campaigns against native peoples and tribes bordering the provinces, culminating in the Lusitanian (155–139) and Celtiberian (155–133) wars. This left the greater part of Iberia in Roman hands. Further conquest was halted, and further operations—sorties by triumph-hunting generals, and *Caesar's civil war (49–45; see POMPEIUS MAGNUS, SEXTUS)—were not attempts at expansion. Systematic exploitation of the provinces appears not to have begun before the 170s. Tribute eventually comprised a fixed money payment and one-twentieth of the grain crop. Cases of misgovernment led in 171 to the institution of trials for *extortion. *Mines (those of Carthago Nova yielded 2,500 *drachmae* daily) were rented out, for a fixed payment related to production, to Italian businessmen (see NEGOTIATORES), who settled in moderate numbers in centres like Carthago Nova, Corduba, and Tarraco.

The conquest of Iberia was completed by *Augustus in the Cantabrian Wars (26–19). This resulted in a largely new province of Lusitania and a great extension of Nearer Spain (renamed *Tarraconensis) to the north and west ocean. These provinces were assigned to the emperor; most of Further Spain (renamed *Baetica) was returned to the senate in 27. The new Augustan conquest required three *legions in NW Tarraconensis; by the time of *Vespasian they had been reduced to VII Gemina only. Twenty-two colonies were founded (see COLONIZATION, ROMAN), and a large number of *municipia created, under Caesar and Augustus, forming the basis for a Roman urban network within juridical *conventus (2) in each province. Following the development of a municipal imperial cult at Tarraco (AD 15), there soon followed the establishment of a conventual (Tarraconensis), and provincial imperial cult (under the Flavians). See RULER-CULT.

The density and sophistication of Hispano-Roman towns varied greatly from region to region. However, a substantial number of the 1st-cent. provincial senators at Rome came from Roman colonies in Spain. In literature they produced the Elder and Younger *Senecas and *Lucan; *Columella, *Quintilian, and *Martial were of native stock. The emperors *Trajan, *Hadrian, and Marcus *Aurelius had Spanish ancestry. However, despite *Vespasian's grant of Latin rights (see IUS LATII) to all Spanish communities, many retained native cultural traits. The systematic and large-scale exploitation of gold in NW Tarraconensis, as well as silver and other metals, provided important revenue for Rome and was supported by an extensive road network. Wine (from Tarraconensis) and fish-pickle (garum) were widely distributed, while the state monitored the production of Baetican olive oil for Rome and the frontiers (see AMPHORAE, ROMAN).

Sparta lies at the heart of the fertile alluvial valley of the Eurotas. See LACONIA. The initial relationship between Sparta and Amyclae, which by 700 had been incorporated on equal terms with the other four villages comprising Sparta town, is obscure. See SPARTA, SITE.

In a long war, much of neighbouring *Messenia was annexed and its population helotized (see HELOTS). The conquest transformed Sparta into a leading Greek state, culturally as well as militarily, as attested by numerous dedications at the sanctuary of *Artemis Orthia and numerous visits by foreign poets. But it also prompted the dispute surrounding the Partheniai, who departed to found Taras (*Tarentum) c.700; and

it saddled Sparta with lasting problems of security, both internal and external. During the 7th cent. Sparta was confronted with a major Messenian revolt (the 'Second Messenian War'), internal discontent from poor citizens, and probably military defeat by *Argos at Hysiae in 669. During the 6th cent. the external problem was solved by several successful wars—esp. against Argos c.545 and, after a serious defeat, against Tegea—followed by a new policy that created a system of unequal alliances which developed into the **Peloponnesian League'. The League, which underpinned Sparta's dominance until the mid-4th cent., provided external co-operation against the helots in return for support for broadly based oligarchies. An alliance with *Croesus and an expedition against *Polycrates (1) c.525 are signs of Sparta's prominence among Greek states.

Sparta's internal problems were tackled by extending her control over the whole of Messenia and by a thoroughgoing reorganization of Spartan institutions and way of life, which embodied a social compromise between rich and poor citizens. Later Spartans attributed the reorganization to a single, early lawgiver, Lycurgus. Most current opinion, while agreeing that the fundamental changes were consciously planned, views them as being implemented in a continuing process of adaptation between the 7th and 5th cents. There were three essential elements of the remodelled Spartan society. First, an economic system, according to which *citizenship was extended to a body of several thousand men who, as full-time hoplites supported by produce delivered by helots who worked their private estates, were debarred from agricultural labour, business activity, and a range of expenditures for consumption and display. These were the Spartiates or 'Peers' (see below). Secondly, a political system initiated by the 7th-cent. 'Great Rhetra', which combined a limited right of veto for the citizen assembly (see APELLAI) with the strong executive powers of the *ephors, the extra-constitutional influence of the two kings, and the formidable, conservative authority of the gerousia (council of 28 elders, plus the two kings; aged over 60, drawn from leading families, life-members; vacancies filled by shouts in the assembly). Thirdly, a social and ritual system, as part of which every Spartiate (except the two kings and their immediate heirs) underwent an austere public upbringing (the *agoge) followed by a common lifestyle of participation in the messes (*syssitia) and in military training and service in the army.

Thus was created *eunomia* ('good order'), admired by both contemporaries and later generations for its long-term stability. Few of its specific institutions were in themselves unique; many were transformations of earlier institutions or were paralleled elsewhere in Greece. What was distinctive was their combination into a coherent structure which attempted to produce a unified citizen body of *homoioi* ('Peers') whose subservience to collective interests and military training would ensure effective policing of the helots. The reorganization had its limits. The cultural impact was gradual: *Olympic athletic victories continued until *c.*550, and Laconian painted pottery and bronze vessel production until a generation later. Several spheres of Spartiate society were only partially affected, esp. the strength of family allegiances and more independent role of citizen women. Land tenure probably remained essentially private and its distribution unequal.

During the reign of *Cleomenes I (*c.*520–490) Sparta ousted the tyrants from Athens (see HIPPIAS (1)), but failed to control the subsequent democracy and declined various external appeals for assistance, esp. against Persia. Sparta commanded the Greek resistance to *Xerxes' invasion (480/79; see PERSIAN WARS); but afterwards its leadership of the Greek alliance and campaigns against *Medizing states in northern Greece foundered amidst the disgrace of the regent *Pausanias (1) and King *Leotychidas II. The 470s and 460s were decades of crisis marked both with her Arcadian allies and a long helot revolt following losses in the severe earthquake of *c.*465. The remainder of the 5th cent. was dominated by wars with Athens (the 'First' *Peloponnesian War *c.*460–446 as distinguished from that of 431–404). Their controversial origins were, on Sparta's side, connected with her fear that Athenian imperialism would destabilize the Peloponnesian League. Sparta's traditional strategy of invading Attic territory failed; but Athens was ultimately

starved into surrender after *Lysander, with Persian financial help, destroyed her fleet at Aegospotami (405). Sparta's ensuing imperialist activities in Asia Minor, central and northern Greece, and even in *Sicily, led to the *Corinthian War (394–387) against a hostile Graeco-Persian coalition. In the *King's Peace (387/6) Sparta traded her overseas empire for domination in mainland Greece, which was pursued vigorously against *Thebes by King *Agesilaus II; but her supremacy was destroyed at *Leuctra (371). Ensuing Theban invasions brought the liberation of Messenia (370/69), the foundation of Megalopolis (368) in SW Arcadia, and the demise of the Peloponnesian League (366), thereby reducing her to a second-rate power.

The roots of Sparta's international decline lay in internal difficulties. Inequalities in landholding developed during the 5th cent. as the employment of wealth for élite activities such as chariot-racing became increasingly significant as a determinant of status. Many poorer Spartiates became unable to provide their contributions to the common messes which were a necessary condition of citizenship. The Peers, 8,000 strong in 480, had dwindled to *c.*1 500 by 371. The sources' claim that Sparta was ruined by the influx of imperial wealth may be merely moralizing commonplace; but the development of independent foreign commands and of competing internal factions during the period of empire did mean enlarged opportunities for economic patronage. Unwilling to address the problems of poor Spartiates, the authorities' increasing reliance on non-Spartiate troops left Sparta unable to resist her enemies' dismantling of her power.

King-List. Until 491/90, the Spartans claimed, son had succeeded father, which is hard to believe. Thereafter relationship is indicated in brackets, the reference being to the preceding king.

AGIADS	EURYPONTIDS
Eurycratidas, *c.*615–590	Hippocratidas, *c.*600–575
Leon, *c.*590–560	Agasicles, *c.*575–550
Anaxandridas, *c.*560–520	Ariston, *c.*550–515
*Cleomenes (1) I, *c.*520–490	*Demaratus, *c.*515–491
*Leonidas (1) I (brother), 490–480	*Leotychidas II (cousin) 491–469
Pleistarchus (son), 480–459	
Pleistoanax (son), 459–409	*Archidamus II (grandson), 469–427
*Pausanias (2) (son), 409–395	
Agesipolis I (son), 395–380	
Cleombrotus I (brother), 380–371	*Agis II (son), 427–400
Agesipolis II (son), 371–370	*Agesilaus II (brother), 400–360

Sparta, site The only major public buildings of the classical 'city' identified to date are the *sanctuaries of *Artemis Orthia on the west bank of the Eurotas, and of *Athena Chalcioecus ('of the Bronze House') on the acropolis, both by their modesty (e.g. small *temples) supporting the claim of *Thucydides (2) that Sparta in its heyday lacked architecture to match its power (although the Persian Stoa, begun with *Persian Wars *booty, impressed later generations). The classical city was also notable because (1) Spartan military self-confidence allowed it to remain without *fortifications; and (2) its inhabitants lived in four villages, an old-fashioned pattern persisting into Augustan times. See also MENE-LAION.

Spartacus, a Thracian *gladiator (see THRACE) and former Roman auxiliary soldier (see AUX-ILIA), who led a revolt which began in the gladiatorial schools (see GLADIATORS) at *Capua in 73 BC. He was first supported by fighters of Thracian and Celtic extraction (see CELTS), but later acquired adherents from slaves and even the free proletariat in the countryside of southern Italy (many of these would have been working the large estates or *latifundia devoted to stock-raising in that area). Ultimately his army was estimated at figures ranging from 70,000 to 120,000. In 73 he defeated two Roman commanders and ranged over southern Italy. In 72, although his Celtic lieutenant Crixus was defeated, he himself overcame both consuls and reached Cisalpine *Gaul, whence, it is said, he hoped his followers would disperse to their homes. They, however, preferred to continue to ravage Italy. So Spartacus returned south and after at least one major victory, devastated Lucania and would have invaded Sicily, if he had succeeded in obtaining transport from the pirates. In 71 *Crassus, after trying to cut off Spartacus in Bruttium, caught and destroyed his army in Lucania, later crucifying any survivors he captured. Spartacus himself was killed, though his body was never found. *Pompey on his return from Spain annihilated others who had escaped. This revolt was outstanding for its scale and temporary success. It resembled the major slave-revolts in Sicily of 137–133 and 104–101, inasmuch as it drew in a depressed rural population. Spartacus quickly became a legend: he was competent, brave, physically powerful, and humane, with those he led. See SLAVERY.

Spartan cults The three greatest Spartan festivals, the ones that attracted visitors, all hon-oured *Apollo: the *Carnea, the Gymnopaedia (at which choirs competed for long hours in baking heat), and the Hyacinthia. This last comprised choral performances (again), spectacle, and feasting, spread over several days, only some of which were tinged with melancholy; it honoured Apollo of Amyclae and his dead lover Hyacinthus. The importance of Artemis Orthia is clear from the 100,000 or so small dedications found at her shrine; hers was a festival at which youths undergoing the Spartan military training (see AGOGE) sought to steal cheese from the altar and were whipped if caught. Other prominent cults honoured *Menelaus and *Helen, who were revered 'like gods' at the *Menelaion a couple of miles SE of the city; the *Dioscuri, glamorous local heroes, many dedications to whom have been found; Athena of the Bronze House, whose bronze-plated temple occupied the lowly Spartan acropolis; and *Poseidon of Taenarum, who in wrath at a violation of sanctuary supposedly caused the great earthquake of the 460s.

Speusippus (c.407–339 BC), Athenian philosopher, son of *Plato's sister. He accompanied Plato on his last visit to Sicily (361) and succeeded him as head of the *Academy from 347 to 339. Of his voluminous writings only fragments and later reports remain, but Aristotle treats him with respect, and it is clear that he continued and helped to shape some major philosophical interests which the Academy had acquired under Plato.

(a) Definition Speusippus argued that, since a definition is designed to identify its subject and differentiate it from everything else, it can be established only by knowing everything there is. This can hardly have been intended, as some ancient critics thought, to refute all attempts at defining. More probably it was this view of definition which prompted Speusippus in his ten books of *Homoia* ('Similar Things') to set about collecting the observable resemblances between different sorts of plant and animal, for he may have thought (as *Aristotle sometimes did), that a species can be defined by discovering a set of characteristics which it shares with various other species, taken collectively, but not with any one other species.

The Academy's interest in definition had led to the recognition that some expressions have more than one meaning. Speusippus marked this by drawing distinctions comparable to, but fuller than, those familiar from Aristotle's logic.

This gives Speusippus his place at the birth of logic in the Academy.

(b) Philosophy and Exact Science Speusippus wrote on *Pythagorean mathematics, endorsing the search for the *elements of numbers which Plato had taken over from the Pythagoreans. But he refused to equate numbers with Platonic Ideas, which like others in the Academy he rejected; and he further denied the claim, which Aristotle ascribes to the Pythagoreans and Plato, that the elements of number are the elements of everything else. Other sorts and levels of reality, he argued, need other sorts of element.

(c) Ethics In the Academic debate which can be heard behind Plato's *Philebus* and the ethical writings of Aristotle Speusippus makes two appearances. He holds, first, that pleasure is neither good nor evil in itself, and second, that goodness is to be found only in the final stages of development and not in the origins.

Under all these heads it is likely that the best of his work has been digested in that of Aristotle and his successors, and that his biological observations in *Homoia* were largely absorbed in the treatises of the Lyceum.

Sphactēria See PYLOS.

sphinx, a hybrid creature, like the Chimaera. Illustrations can be traced back to Egypt and Mesopotamia. The sphinx possessed the body of an animal (usually a lion) and a human head (male or female). The sphinx became a popular figure in Greek art—monumental and funerary—of the Archaic and later periods. This is an extension of her role as guardian spirit. The only literary references, whence the name, are to a monster of Theban legend (see THEBES), (S)phix, that inhabited a mountain at the western edge of Theban territory, waylaid passers-by, and wrought havoc on the Cadmeans (see CADMUS).

Her hostility to the Thebans may be connected with the traditional war between Minyan *Orchomenus and Cadmean Thebes. She would have been performing her accustomed role as guardian, this time of Minyan territory. Eventually she met her match in *Oedipus, who either answered her *riddle, causing her to kill herself, or actually killed her. The attachment of the sphinx to the Oedipus legend may have been grafted on to it from its original place in the story of the war.

spolia opīma were spoils offered by a Roman general who had slain an enemy leader in single combat.

springs, sacred Not every *sanctuary had access to running *water, nor, in all likelihood, was *every* spring sacred. A thing, place, or person became 'sacred' by being placed under the tutelage and control of a deity. It was a matter of function or utility. Thus, Castalia at *Delphi was a sacred spring because it was held to convey divinatory power from the god. Examples abound of springs performing similar functions, some *oracular, others merely inspirational (such as Hippocrene and Aganippe on Mt. *Helicon), artists being held to be human vessels transmitting divine messages.

At sanctuaries where cleanliness (e.g. *Asclepius and other medical gods) and purity (*mystery sanctuaries, as at *Eleusis) were important, water—from springs and elsewhere—was an essential element, and in this sense the springs concerned would have been regarded as sacred.

The waters of springs served as means of *purification at the critical points in life (see RITES OF PASSAGE): birth, *initiation, marriage, and death, but this function was shared by rivers, i.e. by any source of fresh, running water. In the Mediterranean world, this resource is as precious as it is scarce. It does not follow that the source itself is sacred for its own sake in the sense given above. On the other hand, the strategic location of a spring, as at a settlement site or a caravanserai, might be sufficient to imbue it with divine power (the sacred spring at *Corinth and the Boeotian spring Tilphossa *en route* to Delphi are examples of each). Sacred springs were usually presided over by female spirits—*nymphs—but it is not certain that every such spring had its nymph.

stadium (Gk. *stadion*), running track, about 200 m. long (the term also signifies a comparable unit of linear measurement (i.e. a 'stade'; see MEASURES). *Athletic activity often antedates the surviving stadia (e.g. at *Nemea); presumably any area of flat ground was used. One of the earliest definable stadia, that in the sanctuary of *Poseidon at *Isthmia, consists simply of a starting-gate on the relatively level ground of the sanctuary, with a bank raised artificially to one side for spectators. The architectural development of stadia can be seen by the 4th cent. BC with the running track and seats to one or, preferably, either side. Early examples may have both ends straight or near straight (*Olympia,

*Epidaurus). Later, for the convenience of spectators, one end is semicircular. Double races (the *diaulos*) and other long-distance races started at a straight starting-line at this closed end. This definitive form is still used in structures of the Roman period. One of the first examples is that at Nemea (*c*.325). A vaulted passage under the seating area gives access to the running tracks.

See ATHLETICS; SANCTUARIES.

standards, cult of Every permanent station of a Roman military unit, esp. legionary, and every camp regularly constructed contained a chapel, which, at least in imperial times, was in the charge of the first *cohort. This cohort kept both the statues of gods worshipped by the troops and of the emperors and also the standards (*signa militaria*) of the unit and its component parts; all received divine or quasi-divine honours. They were anointed and otherwise tended on feast-days. A suppliant might take refuge at them; an altar was sometimes dedicated at least partly to them or at all events to the most important, the eagle of the legion; sacrifice was made to them esp. after a victory. *Tertullian even says, rhetorically exaggerating, that the soldiers venerated them beyond all gods.

stars See ASTROLOGY; ASTRONOMY; CONSTELLATIONS AND NAMED STARS.

stasis (lit. 'standing'), a Greek word commonly used for a group of men who take a stand in a political dispute, i.e. a party or faction, and by extension for the dispute itself, esp. when the prosecution of the dispute goes beyond normal political activity to plotting and violence. The grounds for political dispute were various, in the Greek world as in the modern, but from the 5th cent. BC onwards there was a tendency for disputants to represent themselves, and for the sources to represent them, as champions of the rich or the poor, or of the oligarchs or the democrats, or of one outside power or another. *Herodotus writes of the rise of *Pisistratus in 6th-cent. *Athens in terms of three *staseis* with regional bases; later sources retain the regional bases for the *staseis* but give them ideological stances also. Despite the value placed on independence in Greek states, political leaders would often prefer to be on the winning side with the support of one of the greater states to being on the losing side in an independent state, and the leading states were glad to extend their influence in this way. Thus disputes which had a local origin often acquired an inter-state dimension; but in the 5th and 4th cents. *Sparta and Athens were able to give the states under their influence a measure of enforced stability by keeping their own supporters in power. The violence and the outside involvement to which *stasis* could lead had a damaging effect on the states: the worsening of this as attitudes were polarized in the *Peloponnesian War is analysed in Thucydides 3. 82–84.

state, states See BUREAUCRACY; DECISION-MAKING; DEMOCRACY (both entries); FEDERAL STATES; GOVERNMENT; POLIS; POLITICAL THEORY.

Statilius Taurus, Titus (suffect consul 37 BC, 2nd consulship 26), the greatest Augustan marshal after *Agrippa. By military talent and loyalty he attained wealth and honours; he was thrice acclaimed (see ACCLAMATION) *imperator* by the legions and held several priesthoods. His earliest recorded service was as admiral in the Sicilian campaign of 36. He then crossed to Africa and secured it, holding a triumph in 34 (the *amphitheatre erected in commemoration on the *Campus Martius was completed in 30). He also fought in Illyricum (34–33), commanded the land army in the campaign of *Actium (31). He was made city *prefect in 16 when Augustus left for the western provinces.

Statius, Publius Papinius, Roman poet. Born between AD 45 and the early 50s in Neapolis, Statius was the son of a man who had a glittering career first as a professional poet on the Greek festival circuit (see AGONES), and then as a *grammaticus* in Neapolis and in Rome, where the family moved when Statius was in his teens. Although Statius did not follow either of these careers, his debt to his father is manifest. Popular from a young age as a poet in Rome, he may have composed a *pantomime libretto for Paris, *Domitian's favourite (executed 83). He was victorious in the poetry competition at Domitian's annual Alban Games, but suffered a mortifying failure in the much more prestigious Capitoline Games, almost certainly later in the same year. By now he had married Claudia, widow of another poet, who brought him a step-daughter (he had no children of his own). The poem to Claudia, persuading her to leave Rome and follow him to Neapolis, speaks of her devoted support, and her nursing of Statius in illness. His epic, the *Thebaid*, was published in 91/2, after many partial recitations and many years of work (one for each of the twelve books he says, with suspicious symmetry. There followed the occasional poems of his *Silvae*. Bks. 1–3 were published together in 93 or 94; Bk. 4 was published in 95, by which time he had left Rome for Neapolis; and Bk. 5 (together with his unfinished second epic, the *Achilleid*) was published after his death, which is conventionally dated before the assassination of Domitian (Sept. 96).

Works

Thebaid. The only surviving Roman *epic which can safely be said to have been published as a completed work by its author, the *Thebaid* recounts the war between the sons of *Oedipus over the kingship of *Thebes (see SEVEN AGAINST THEBES). It is an acutely self-conscious masterpiece. The poem extravagantly explores human violence and madness. Its cosmic framework draws upon *Ovid's *Metamorphoses* to chart the problematic boundaries of human possibilities, and its political framework draws upon *Virgil and *Lucan to probe the imperial themes of absolutism and civil war. Seneca's tragedies (see SENECA THE YOUNGER) are the principal source for the atmosphere of doomed familial insanity. The diverse problems of succession and authority which face the brothers, the audience, and the poet reflect upon one another throughout, and this self-awareness disposes of the traditional criticism of Statius as derivative. Esp. in the divine action Statius shows himself to be a bold critic and innovator, undermining his inherited epic apparatus and experimenting with allegorical modes in ways which were to be profoundly influential in the Middle Ages. The verse is superbly accomplished, the style too aestheticized for many.

Silvae. Thirty-two poems, of which 26 are in *hexameters, the standard metre for post-classical Greek encomiastic poetry. Only the exceptional poem to Sleep has proved popular. The poems evince a not very intimate acquaintance with a not very large or eminent group, marking noteworthy moments such as marriage, official advancement, or bereavement, and celebrating the taste shown in artistic acquisition or architectural construction. In the service of these quasi-professional relationships Statius marshals the panoply of Greek praise-poetry inherited from his father, boasting self-depreciatingly of the impromptu production of the requisite verses. Generally knowing and light in touch, rather than ponderous, the poems none the less usually avoid banter and tease. Domitian, an intimidat-

ing and distant personality, receives six poems which modern taste has found repellent for sycophancy, though a more charitable reading might focus on the anxiety behind them.

statues, cult of

Greece The veneration of images of deities was well established by the 7th cent. BC, when monumental temples to house a cult's principal statue became common; in the manufacture of colossal cult-statues in precious metals from the 5th cent. sculptors like *Phidias may have sought to visualize the divine attributes of brightness and abnormal height. *Prayer was offered to statues of deities, including cult-statues, which probably were more accessible to worshippers than once thought.

Rome Acc. to *Varro the earliest Romans lacked cult-images. While archaeological evidence such as figurines of the *Di *penates contradicts this, the amorphous quality of *numen, a spiritual force common at all periods in Roman religion, lends the claim some support. Later, the gods were usually represented by cult-images.

Judaeo-Christian Worship of graven images was forbidden in Judaism (see RELIGION, JEWISH). This bemused pagans. Christianity appropriated the Jewish view. Worship of statues became part of anti-pagan polemic.

status, legal and social

Greek Greek social and legal status terminology was rich, if confused. There were hundreds of Greek communities (*poleis*; see POLIS), diverse in character, which although typically small were complex in organization. In all Greek societies the fundamental status division was between the free and the unfree. But whereas the former could be divided fairly simply into citizen and non-citizen, men and women, adults and children, the Greeks had a dozen words for various types and degrees of unfree people.

In all Greek societies the person of highest status was the full citizen (*politēs*), who was free, adult and male, qualifications for *citizenship varied, but birth—membership of a corporate descent-group—was primary. (Only in *Sparta was this coupled with a test of achievement, successful passage through the compulsory state educational curriculum and consequent election to a common mess.) Further distinctions were based on age, on sex (in Athens a female citizen was a *politis*) and, even to some extent in democratic Athens, on wealth. After

451 BC Athens insisted on double descent—from citizen mother as well as citizen father.

No Greek city gave women the political rights of citizenship, but Athens may have been unusual in the rigour with which married women were treated virtually as minors at law throughout their lives. Yet, paradoxically, the priestess of Athens' chief deity (*Athena Polias) was one of the city's most prominent public figures (see WOMEN IN CULT). She was always drawn from a particular noble lineage (see GENOS). Even in democratic Athens distinctions of birth continued to count for something, as they did more obviously in Sparta, another ideologically egalitarian peer-group society. Indeed, in Sparta there were not only noble families but also two hereditary royal houses.

Between the citizen and the free but non-resident foreigner came the free resident alien or *metic (*metoikos). This status is attested in c.70 communities but most extensively at Athens, where it was not esp. privileged. Metics were required to pay a poll tax and to be represented at law by a citizen patron; metic status, moreover, was that assigned to privately manumitted slaves (see SLAVERY, Greek), most of whom were non-Greek. It was very rare for an ex-slave such as *Pasion to crash the barrier of full citizen status.

Of the dozen Greek words for the unfree, doulos was the most general and the most common. Yet the term could be applied both to the chattel slaves of Athens, and to the *helot bondsmen of Sparta. The chattel slave was a socially dead being, categorizable as 'an animate tool'; but even chattel slaves were granted some legal protection, if only in virtue of their master's rights of property. Besides the helots, there were some other local collective groups of unfree persons each defined by a distinctive name. The classification of all such groups as 'between free people and douloi' illustrates both the complexity of Greek societies and the inadequacy of Greek social terminology.

Roman In Roman law, status describes the 'legal position' of an individual with respect to both that person's household (familia) and the civic community of Rome. The concept of status is linked to caput or persōna, an individual's legal 'personality'. Personality roughly defines the limits of what an individual is legally able to do: marry, make contracts, bring lawsuits, commit crimes or delicts, and so on.

The most systematic exposition of status comes in Roman sources discussing change of status, what *Cicero and the *jurists call capitis dēminūtiō. Three issues are paramount, and they are arranged hierarchically: freedom, citizenship, and membership of a household. The most fundamental division is between free persons and slaves (see SLAVERY, Roman); then, among free persons, between Roman citizens and others; and finally, esp. among Roman citizens, between those who head households and those subject to the power of a head.

The complex rules of capitis deminutio determine what happens when an individual's legal status changes; the consequences may concern not only the individual but others as well. For example, under the *senatus consultum Claudianum of AD 52, a woman who despite warning cohabits with another's slave can herself become that person's slave, thereby simultaneously losing her freedom, citizenship, and position as a household member.

Legal status is central to Roman private law. Other areas of Roman law, such as property, contracts, and testamentary succession, often appear remarkably liberal by modern standards; but all are subject to limitations that status imposes on legal capacity to act. For instance, although in principle Roman jurists permit owners to deal in virtually unrestricted fashion with their property, only sane heads of households have complete legal ownership of property. When resolution of a lawsuit hinges in part on a question of status, esp. whether an individual is free or a slave, this issue is always tried first.

Despite the importance of status, the Romans were casual in providing means to prove it. Beginning with *Augustus, children of a legitimate marriage were registered soon after birth; from Marcus *Aurelius, illegitimate children were also registered. But these evidently incomplete or inaccurate records did not have conclusive legal force. Marriages, upon the legitimacy of which the civil status of children depended, were not registered at all.

Proving one's freedom or citizenship could be challenging. The jurist Iulius Paulus drily observes that 'distinguishing a free person from a slave can be difficult'; just how difficult is demonstrated by many legal sources dealing with a free person 'serving in good faith', held as a slave by an 'owner' unaware of the person's true status. Free persons held as slaves could not assert their own freedom and had to find an outsider willing to take up the burden of proof.

As a result, civil status, though a cornerstone of Roman law, was always potentially at risk; at any moment it might be challenged, and it could disappear overnight. None the less, Roman citizens clung tenaciously to the belief that their civil status protected them from harm; as Cicero puts it, the cry 'I am a Roman citizen' brought safety the world over.

In modern social science, 'status' has a more than purely legal meaning: it refers to social position, esp. as determined by birth, wealth, and external markers like honour, place of residence, or badges of distinction. The Roman empire's small social élite was highly stratified by status: the 'orders' of *senators, *equestrians, and municipal councillors (*decuriones*). All three orders had minimum wealth requirements, but were also to a large extent hereditary. The rest of the free population was less formally stratified, though quasi-status groups often formed around a common occupation, residence, or civil status; of special note is the order of *freedmen, attested from the late republic on.

Such status groups played a significant social, political, and economic role, but were at first not clearly recognized by law; in theory, Roman citizens were equal before the law. However, during the early empire civic equality began to erode, esp. in criminal law; criminal procedure and punishment distinguished the 'more respected' (*honestiores*) from the 'less respected' (*humiliōrēs*). By the early 2nd cent. AD, this distinction was hardening into law; the *honestiores*, generally defined as the three uppermost social orders, received better legal treatment and milder penalties.

stēlē, (pl. *stēlai*) stone slab, esp. one bearing figured decoration or an inscribed text. In early Archaic Greece such *stelai* are rare, but in Athens *c*. 600 BC there begins a distinguished series with relief decoration on the shaft, topped first by a *sphinx, then by a palmette finial. The latter type originated in eastern Greece, and it persisted after 500 in the islands, after the Athenian series had already ended. A new type of *stele* in Athens appears after the mid-5th cent. It is broader, with pilasters at the side and a pediment above, and carries relief representations of the dead or scenes of parting. This ever more monumental series was stopped by a decree of *Demetrius (1) of Phaleron *c*.317–316, and later Attic grave markers are simple short cylindrical blocks. See ART, FUNERARY, GREEK; EPIGRAPHY, GREEK.

Stēsichorus, Greek lyric poet, active *c*.600–550 BC. Tradition made him contemporary with *Sappho and *Alcaeus; *Simonides referred to him and to *Homer.

Stesichorus' works were collected in 26 books; nothing survives but quotations and some fragmentary papyri. The poems are cited by title. The titles cover a range of major myths. These poems represent a kind of lyric epic. Their metre, 'Doric' dialect, and triadic form seem to attach them to the 'choral lyric' tradition represented by *Alcman and *Pindar. But their large scale and narrative sweep recall the traditional epic.

stichomȳthia is a form of dramatic dialogue in which each utterance by each speaker consists of a single line of verse. Under the same general heading come forms in which each utterance consists of two lines or half a line. *Stichomythia* is the form usually employed for rapid exchanges in Attic tragedy. Thus it is the usual alternative, in dialogue scenes, to extended speeches. It can extend for long stretches, esp. in *Euripides, despite the danger of monotony (to modern taste) and the occasional need for padding. *Stichomythia* may be used where one party questions and the other answers; where one persuades and the other resists; and where the two exchange insults.

stīpendium meant the regular cash payment received by soldiers at the end of the campaigning season, and so came to mean a period of military service, originally a season, but later a year. In the imperial period *stipendium* designated military pay, specifically one of the three annual instalments by which the troops were paid, or one year of service.

Pay During the war with Veii (*c*.400 BC) a payment was first made to Roman soldiers while on long campaigns to assist with their living expenses. In the 2nd cent. the legionary was probably receiving 180 *dēnarii* in a year of 360 days. After the revaluation of the coinage in the time of the *Gracchi this will have amounted to 112$\frac{1}{2}$ *denarii*, which accords with Suetonius' statement that *Caesar doubled legionary pay, since legionaries received 225 *denarii* under *Augustus, and there is no indication that he increased the sum. There were fixed deductions to meet the cost of food, clothing, and the repair or replacement of weapons. Deductions seem to have continued throughout the imperial period. *Domitian was the first emperor to increase military pay, by adding another instalment of 75 *denarii*, then *Septimius Severus increased it, probably to 600, and *Caracalla to 900 *denarii*.

*Praetorians received higher rates, more than three times legionary pay by AD 14 (750 *denarii*), and this differential was maintained. The salary of the soldiers of the urban cohorts (see COHORTES URBANAE) was 375 *denarii*. An *auxiliary infantryman probably received five-sixths of a legionary's pay, with higher rates for cavalrymen.

Junior officers below the rank of centurion were paid at one and a half times or twice the normal legionary rate, while centurions and *primipili* received substantial salaries (perhaps 13,500 *denarii* for a chief centurion in the early first century). By the end of the 3rd cent. inflation had so reduced the value of military salaries that a system of payment in kind was adopted.

Length of Service In the republic a man between the age of 17 and 46 was expected to be available for up to sixteen years service as an infantryman (ten years as a cavalryman), although in the 2nd cent. he would not normally serve more than six years continuously on active service. In 13 BC Augustus established or confirmed conditions of service for his troops— sixteen years for the legionaries (plus a further four years as a reservist), twelve years for the praetorians. However, it proved impossible to maintain this system, through shortage of recruits and the expense of discharge payments, and in AD 5 service was increased to 20 years (with probably five as a reservist) for legionaries, and sixteen for praetorians. But the mutineers in Pannonia and Lower Germany (AD 14) claimed that men were kept on long after their time, for 30 or 40 years. Sailors in the fleets served for 26 years, auxiliary soldiers for 25, and by the mid-1st cent. the service time had been set at 25 years for legionaries.

Pay scales from Domitian to Septimius Severus (in *denarii*):

praetorians	1,000	auxiliary *alae*	350
urban cohorts	500	part-mounted cohorts	300
legionaries	300	infantry cohorts	250

See ARMIES, ROMAN.

stoa The name 'stoa' is applied to various types of building, comprising essentially an open colonnade, generally in the Doric *order, and a roof over the space to a rear wall. There are many possible elaborations of this simplest type. An interior colonnade may be added, often of Ionic columns, supporting the ridge of the roof. This gives more usable space (the Ionic columns being at double the exterior interval to minimize obstruction). Rooms may be added, behind the wall.

In plan, they may be elaborated by construction of wings, to give Gamma or Pi (see ALPHABET) shaped structures, or completely surround a courtyard. Most are single-storey. In their simplest form they provide shade and shelter, whether for people watching religious activities in a *sanctuary (the stoa in the Samian temple of Hera (Heraion), of the 7th cent. BC; see SAMOS) or engaged in the various activities of the *agora; these can be political, judicial, or social, whether philosophical discussions (see STOA POECILE) or feasting (the south stoa of the Athenian agora has a series of rooms behind its double-aisled façade clearly arranged to accommodate dining couches).

In a sanctuary, stoas are inevitably ancillary to the main religious structures. As architecture, their main impact is on the agora, which they help to define by being placed on the boundary. In the agoras of planned cities this can lead to their being nothing more than linked lines of columns defining a regular shape. In the irregular agoras of unplanned cities, more variety is possible. Thus the agora at Athens, by the end of the 5th cent., had acquired several stoas of differing forms and functions.

Most stoas are less well built than temples. Stone work is limestone, not marble, columns are more spaced; the cheaper Doric is preferred to Ionic even in eastern Greece. Floors are often of beaten earth, walls may be mudbrick. Quality improves in the Hellenistic period.

See BASILICA; PORTICO.

Stoa Poecilē ('painted'). Known from over 50 literary testimonia, and excavated from 1981, it lies in the NW part of the Athenian agora; see ATHENS, TOPOGRAPHY. It measures 12.5 by c.36 m. (41 x 118 ft.), made of various limestones, with Doric exterior columns, and Ionic interior columns with marble capitals (see ORDERS), and is finely jointed. It dates from c.475–450, part of the *Cimonian improvement of the area. The name 'Poecile' derived from the panel paintings it housed. *Pausanias (3) gives the fullest account, mentioning scenes of the Athenians arrayed against the Spartans at Oenoë near *Argos (perhaps an error for the *Attic *deme Oenoe and preparations for Marathon; see MARATHON, BATTLE OF), the Amazonomachy, the sack of Troy, and, most famous, the battle of *Marathon. Sources name the painters as *Micon, *Polygnotus, and Panaenus.

The Poecile had no single function, being used for proclaiming the *Eleusinian *mysteries (see ELEUSIS), and occasional legal matters; shields from Sphacteria were displayed (see PYLOS). *Zeno (2) frequented it so much that his followers became known as 'Stoics'; see STOICISM.

Stoicism, philosophical movement, founded by *Zeno (2) of Citium, who came to Athens in 313 BC, and, after studying with various philosophers, taught in his own right in the *Stoa Poecile. Zeno developed a distinctive philosophical position divided into three parts, logic, *physics, and ethics. We know little of the institutional organization of the school, except that at Zeno's death one of his pupils, *Cleanthes, took over the headship of the school. He was not, however, the most famous of Zeno's pupils, and the original position was developed in different directions. Ariston of Chios stressed ethics to the exclusion of physics and logic; Cleanthes stressed a religious view of the world. Stoicism was in danger of dissolving into a number of different positions, but was rescued by Cleanthes' pupil *Chrysippus of Soli. He restated and recast Zeno's position in his voluminous writings, defending it with powerful arguments. It was correctly thought later that 'if there had been no Chrysippus, there would have been no Stoa'; the work of Zeno's earlier pupils came to be seen as unorthodox, and Chrysippus' works became the standard formulation of Stoicism. Chrysippus' own innovations were mainly in logic.

Stoicism is holistic: there is no foundational part which supports the others. Different Stoics disagreed radically both over the correct structure of their position and the correct order of teaching it. Thus the theory can be fully understood only as a whole, one of the respects in which it is markedly 'ideal' and makes high demands on the student. However, logic, physics, and ethics are distinguishable at a preliminary stage, and in fact the Stoics developed them with great sophistication. Logic includes logic in the technical sense, in which the Stoics made great advances in what is now called the logic of propositions. It also includes philosophy of language, including grammar and rhetoric, and theory of knowledge. The Stoics are radically empiricist; they give an account of knowledge which traces it from the impact made on the human mind by 'appearances' from the outside world. Some of these appearances, they claim, are such that they could not mislead; this gave rise to a debate with the Academic *Sceptics.

Knowledge proper, however, requires understanding of the principles which define the area in question.

Stoic physics gives an account of the world which is strongly materialist. It is also determinist; the world as a whole is made up of material objects and their interactions, which occur according to exceptionless laws, which are called 'fate'. However, their account is also strongly teleological; everything happens according to providence, which is identified with fate. Further, they are compatibilists; human action is free and morally responsible despite fate. The Stoics defended this problematic set of ideas with sophistication and power. The details of their physical account are more naïve: they take *fire to be the basic substrate from which things are produced, though Chrysippus, possibly influenced by contemporary medicine, used the mechanism of differing degrees of tension of *pneuma* or 'breath'.

Stoic ethics is marked by a set of uncompromising theses: virtue is sufficient for happiness; only virtue is good; emotions are always bad. Easily ridiculed in isolation, these theses can be defended when seen as contributing to an overall theory in which what is most important is the difference in kind between the value of virtue and other, 'non-moral' value, virtue being conceived of as the skill of putting other things to correct use. The Stoics give the most demanding account of virtue in ancient ethics, and put the most strain on their account of the happiness which is the virtuous person's aim.

In all areas of philosophy there is appeal to the notions of nature and of reason, which have two roles, in the world as a whole and in us humans. Humans should live in accordance with human nature, which is, for them, to live in accordance with human reason, humans being rational animals. Properly used, human reason will enable us to understand the role of reason in the world, and thus of the world's nature. Nature and reason are in Stoicism objective notions: for us to think rationally is for us to think in ways which converge with other rational thinkers and reach the truth. Those who use their reason form a kind of community of reason, which is sometimes characterized as the only true community, transcending mere earthly bonds.

Early Stoicism remained essentially unmodified in form until Diogenes of Babylon, who, as is increasingly clear from the *Herculaneum papyri, began changes of detail and presentation. The so-called 'Middle Stoa' attempted to make the position more accessible to educated

Romans (successfully in the case of *Panaetius) and was more hospitable to ideas from other philosophers, esp. *Plato and *Aristotle.

In the later period Stoicism survived in its standard form, and continued to be an object of philosophical discussion; some of the Church Fathers, such as *Tertullian, were influenced by it. We also find writers less interested in philosophical argument than in presenting Stoicism as an attitude or way of life. The letters and essays of *Seneca the Younger, the reported lectures of *Epictetus and the meditations of Marcus *Aurelius are examples of this. They tend to edifying and moralizing discussion and give little indication of the philosophical structure of their positions.

Strabo of Amaseia, author of a *Geography* in seventeen books, the most important source for ancient *geography, a priceless document of the Augustan age, and a compendium of important material derived from lost authors.

Born c.64 BC, he studied in Rome. He knew *Posidonius, whose work he used, and from whom he may have drawn his idea of a conjoint interest in history (with its ethical implications) and geography. The empires of Romans and Parthians allowed him to do for the Augustan empire what *Eratosthenes had been able to do in the aftermath of *Alexander (2) the Great.

In the debate over how to do geography, however, he is very critical of Eratosthenes (and many other experts); but, compared with them, he is inclined to be amateurish about mathematics and cosmology, preferring the practical to the theoretical and the particular to the general, which leads him to call his work 'chorography'. He therefore lays little stress on geographical wonders, and in searching for detailed information retails long passages of by then out-of-date description, which can make the interpretation of his evidence hazardous. He travelled extensively, but makes few boasts about *autopsy (he does mention a long stay in Egypt in the 20s, when his patron (see PATRONUS) Aelius Gallus was *prefect).

This experience of the patronage of Roman leaders and education among the foremost intellectuals (many Greeks of Asia like himself) made Strabo (almost certainly a Roman citizen, with a Latin *cognōmen*) an eloquent witness of the ways in which the Augustan settlement transformed the Mediterranean world of the late republic. Accommodation to Rome was part of the training of all his contemporaries, and he inherited the tradition of *Panaetius,

*Polybius and *Posidonius. He made his job the interpretation of Greek and Roman to each other, and at the same time uses the geographical necessities of Roman power to explain and the patriarchal hegemony of Augustus. No wonder this turning-point in Roman imperial power produced the masterpiece of ancient geography.

Strabo emphasizes the usefulness of geography for statesmen and generals, those 'who bring together cities and peoples into a single empire and political management'. He speaks from knowledge of the central concerns of Roman government and is a precious witness to them (as on the lack of profit to be had from lands on the fringes of the inhabited world such as *Britain). He is speaking from and about the centre of imperial power. The work is an extraordinary achievement—he likens it himself, apologetically, to a colossal statue whose detailing is less significant than the overall effect—and justifies his more ambitious claim to have fused the disciplines to produce out of a historical and chorographical framework a philosophy of geography. See also GEOGRAPHY.

stratēgoi was the ordinary term for military commanders in Greece, but in Athens in the 5th cent. BC *strategoi* had political as well as military importance. Little is known of the number and method of appointment of Athenian *strategoi* in the 6th cent., but in 501/0 a new arrangement was introduced by which ten *strategoi* were elected annually, one from each *phȳlē* (see PHYLAI). The ten were of equal status: at Marathon in 490 (acc. to Herodotus; see MARATHON, BATTLE OF) they decided strategy by majority vote, and each held the presidency in daily rotation. At this date the *polemarchos* had a casting vote, and one view is that he was the commander-in-chief; but from 487/6 onwards the polemarch, like the other *archontes*, was appointed by lot. Good leaders, whether military or political, obviously could not be regularly selected by lot; so now, if not before, the polemarch ceased to command the army, and the *strategoi*, who continued to be elected, not only were the chief military commanders, but in some cases became political leaders too.

*Themistocles, *Aristides (1), and *Cimon were early examples of *strategoi* who were politicians as well as generals. *Pericles was a *strategos* very often throughout his career; from 443 he held the office almost continuously until his death in 429. *Cleon, *Nicias, and *Alcibiades were all *strategoi*. But at the end of the 5th cent., with the collapse of the military and naval power of

Athens, and later because of an increasing tendency to specialization, military office ceased to be a means of acquiring political influence.

The annual election of *strategoi* was held in the spring, and their term of office coincided with the ordinary Athenian year, from midsummer to midsummer. If a *strategos* died or was dismissed from office, a by-election might be held to replace him for the remainder of the year. The original rule that one *strategos* was elected from each *phyle* underwent some modification after 450: in several years one *phyle* is known to have supplied two *strategoi* simultaneously. Representation of *phylai* was certainly abandoned in the 4th cent., when ten *strategoi* were elected annually from all Athenians.

Strategoi commanded both by land and by sea. A particular military or naval expedition might have one *strategos* or several in command; rarely did all ten go together. A *strategos* might be given special powers to take decisions in the field without reference back to Athens. At home the *strategoi* were responsible for calling up citizens and metics for military service, and for organizing the maintenance and command of ships by the system of *trierarchies. When a legal case arose from any of these matters, such as a prosecution for desertion or evasion of military service, or a dispute over the duty to perform a trierarchy, the *strategoi* were the magistrates responsible for bringing the case to court and presiding over the trial. Probably in the 4th cent. a systematic division of duties was made: one *strategos* led the *hoplites, one was in charge of the defence of *Attica, two were in charge of the defence of *Piraeus, and one supervised the trierarchies, leaving five available for other duties.

The Athenian people kept a close watch on their *strategoi*. Like other magistrates, at the end of their term of office they were subject to *euthyna, and in addition there was a vote in the *ekklesia* every prytany (see PRYTANEIS) on the question whether they were performing their duties well; if the vote went against anyone, he was deposed from office and as a rule tried by a jury. Pericles himself in 430 was removed from office as *strategos* and fined, and in 406 the eight *strategoi* who commanded the fleet at *Arginusae were all removed from office and condemned to death. These arrangements illustrate one of the most striking features of Athenian *democracy: reluctance to give power to individuals and fear that it might be abused.

Styx, eldest daughter of Ocean (see OCEANUS (MYTHICAL)) and Tēthys (see MYTHOLOGY, para.

3). Having helped *Zeus against the *Titans, she became the 'great oath of the gods'. (*Hesiod, *Theogony*). In later writers, the Styx is the river of the Underworld (see HADES). *Herodotus places the Styx in Arcadia, as do *Strabo, *Pliny the Elder, and *Pausanias (3).

sublime, that quality of genius in great literary works which irresistibly delights, inspires, and overwhelms the reader. Although ancient *rhetoric distinguished a grandiloquent style, for arousing the listeners' passions, from a dry one, for demonstrating by arguments, and a moderate or ornate one, for providing pleasure, the isolation and glorification of the sublime as a central aesthetic category is largely the achievement of the anonymous author of the treatise 'On the sublime' (1st cent. AD), long attributed to Cassius Longinus (see 'LONGINUS'). Applying Platonic views on poetic inspiration to the needs of the rhetorical schools, ps.-Longinus emphasizes the imaginative power of the canonical poets and prose authors of earlier periods (*Homer, *Demosthenes (2), but also Genesis and *Cicero), which enthrals, enhances, yet also annihilates the reader. The quality of the sublime usually attaches to works of literature rather than to natural phenomena and (much like Matthew Arnold's 'touchstones') less to whole works than to individual passages. It results from a superhuman natural capacity, not just study; yet specifiable rules and techniques produced it once and can produce it even today—or, if violated, can obstruct it, resulting in such faults as pomposity or frigidity. Hence, though the present age is mediocre in comparison with the greatness of the past, the sublime provides a channel whereby the ancients' *enthousiasmos* can lift us above our quotidian banalities and put us in touch with finer minds and, above all, with less obstructed emotions.

Suda is a lexicon, not an author. It is a historical encyclopaedia rather than a mere word-list, compiled about the end of the 10th cent. AD. It is a compilation of compilations, and like most works of its kind has suffered from interpolation. Nevertheless, in spite of its contradictions and other ineptitudes, it preserves (however imperfectly) much that is ultimately derived from the earliest or best authorities in ancient scholarship, and includes material from many departments of Greek learning and civilization.

Suētōnius (Gaius Suetonius Tranquillus) (b. *c*. AD 70), Roman biographer. Suetonius was the son of the *equestrian Suetonius Laetus, tribune (see TRIBUNI MILITUM) of *legion XIII at Bedriacum in 69. From the correspondence of *Pliny the Younger, he appears already to have attracted attention in Rome as an author and scholar by *c.*97, and also to have gained experience in *advocacy. He secured through Pliny's patronage a military tribunate in Britain *c.*102, which in the event he declined; *c.*110, however, he probably travelled with Pliny to *Bithynia as a member of the governor's retinue, gaining soon after, again through Pliny's intercession, the *ius trium liberorum*. In the later years of *Trajan's reign and under *Hadrian, Suetonius held three important posts in the imperial administration: literary adviser, librarian, correspondence secretary. As correspondence secretary, he is likely to have accompanied Hadrian to Germany and Britain in 121–122, but then for unknown reasons was dismissed from office when Hadrian simultaneously deposed as praetorian *prefect Septicius Clarus, the dedicatee of Suetonius' collection of imperial biographies, *Lives of the Caesars*.

Works 1. *On Famous Men*, a now incomplete set of biographies of Roman men of letters arranged in categories—*grammatici* and *rhetors (see EDUCATION, ROMAN, 2), poets, orators, historians, philosophers. The segment 'On *grammatici* and rhetors' is preserved independently, and a few other lives, variously abbreviated or corrupted, are known from manuscripts of other authors' works. The full collection may have contained as many as 100 lives. A particular interest in the age of Cicero and *Augustus and, to a lesser extent, in the Julio-Claudian era has been discerned in the work, while the relationship between authors and the public world in which they lived may have been its main theme.

  2. *Lives of the Caesars*, a series of twelve imperial biographies from *Caesar to *Domitian, composed in the early 2nd cent. and complete except for the first few chapters on Caesar.

  Suetonius was a scholar of wide-ranging antiquarian interests. But it is as an imperial biographer that he must be mainly judged. Apart from Cornelius *Nepos, he is the first Roman biographer whose work has survived. So his *Lives* have to be evaluated largely in their own context, with Suetonius' experience of imperial government during his years of administrative service very much in mind.

  A striking feature of the biographies is their thematic, rather than strictly chronological, arrangement: after an introductory section on ancestry and a second on the subject's early life and pre-accession career, a sequence of recurring rubrics follows, in which Suetonius details the emperor's accomplishments and his personal characteristics, often providing anecdotes to illustrate general statements. The lives conclude with an account of the subject's death, sometimes accompanied by a description of his physical appearance and idiosyncrasies. Though the manner of presentation varies from life to life, the principle of arrangement is consistent.

  The repetition from life to life of common topics, esp. the building operations or the public entertainments for which a particular emperor was responsible, suggests that the topics themselves had special significance for Suetonius and his contemporaries; and through comparison with other sources such as the *Res Gestae* of Augustus and the *Panegyric* of Pliny the Younger, where an ideal standard of imperial behaviour is clearly perceptible, it emerges that Suetonius used the topics to judge his subjects against a set of popular expectations of imperial behaviour that had taken shape by the time the *Lives* were composed. *Tiberius, for example, is repeatedly criticized for having failed to live up to expectation, whereas even *Nero and Domitian, rulers on whom Suetonius' final judgement is damning, can nevertheless be commended for having successfully met some of their imperial responsibilities. Suetonius' concern with such aspects of private behaviour as the subject's sexual and religious tastes has been taken also to reflect the increasing *Hellenization of upper-class Roman society.

  In modern times, simplicity has been seen as the main characteristic of Suetonius' writing, in the absence of any obvious literary artistry. He is notable for citing earlier writers verbatim and quotes liberally from various documents—the letters of Augustus for instance—in Greek as well as Latin. (Suetonius may have exploited his period of service under Trajan and Hadrian to seek out archival material for his biographies.) The Flavian lives are much shorter than those of the Julio-Claudians, and they in turn are less substantial than those of Caesar and Augustus. This again suggests that Suetonius' main historical interest was the period from which the Principate ultimately emerged.

  Suetonius was not, however, primarily a historian, and he should not therefore be compared with Sallust, Livy, or Tacitus. His main concern was to collect and present material pertinent to the biographical goal of realistically illustrating imperial performance and personality, and in this he stands apart from the historians; for while capable of detailed analysis and sustained narrative composition, he lacked their interest in the moralistic or didactic. As one author later expressed it, while the historians wrote 'eloquently', Suetonius wrote 'truthfully'. See BIOGRAPHY, ROMAN.

Suētōnius Paulīnus, Gāius, as ex-praetor in AD 41, commanded against the Mauretanians and was the first Roman to cross the Atlas mountains. In 58 he was appointed governor of *Britain and at once began a forward movement reaching the Irish Sea and subduing Mona, a stronghold of druidism (see RELIGION, CELTIC). During the campaign he learnt of *Boudicca's revolt (60) and swiftly returned with his advance-guard, but, unable to concentrate an adequate force, was compelled to abandon *Londinium and Verulamium to be sacked. Retreating (along Watling Street) to his main force, he routed Boudicca's attack. His severity towards the rebels led to discords with the *procurator Iulius Classicianus and his own recall (61).

suffect, suffectio *Suffectio* was the procedure by which a substitute or suffect (*suffectus*) was appointed whenever a Roman magistrate (see MAGISTRACY, ROMAN) resigned or died in office. It was employed to fill vacancies even of very short duration. Under the empire consuls ceased to hold office for a full year; those appointed after the original ('ordinary') pair were *suffecti*. They did not give their names to the year, unlike 'ordinary' ones, although they had the appropriate rank and title of *consulāris*.

suicide The Latin word *suicidium*, from which the English derives, is not Classical Latin: the word could only have meant 'the killing of a pig'.

The limited and unsystematic nature of our evidence for Greek and Roman suicide rules out quantitative studies. Reliant as we are for the most part on literary accounts (some fictional, even mythical, all artistically shaped), we can only draw conclusions about attitudes and values. If a sociological approach is difficult, so is a psychiatric one, for in antiquity suicide was described on the assumption that it was a conscious intentional act: mental imbalance was not the central case it has now become. The ancients, including hard-headed Roman *jurists who needed to distinguish suicides motivated by fear of condemnation from others that brought

exemption from confiscation, felt confident that they could distinguish individual motives. They were not troubled by notions of unconscious motivation. The suicide attempts reported in the ancient sources are relatively few when compared with the modern ratio of attempted to accomplished suicides.

Some of the chief motives mentioned are shame (typically, for men, because of defeat; for women, loss of chastity); severe pain, incurable illness, or old age; self-sacrifice for country or friend. Suicide was neither wholly approved nor wholly condemned: everything depended on the motive, the manner, and the method. When arising from shame and dishonour, suicide was regarded as appropriate; self-sacrifice was admired; impulsive suicide was less esteemed than a calculated, rational act; death by jumping from a height (including drowning) or by hanging was despised and regarded as fit only for women, slaves, or the lower classes, apparently because it was disfiguring; death by weapons was regarded as more respectable, even heroic.

The concern of philosophers with minimizing the fear of death by the application of reason led them to discuss suicide, and to consider, alongside obvious cases, compulsory suicide at one extreme and martyrdom at the other. The *locus classicus* for philosophical discussions of suicide was the death of *Socrates (which exemplifies both extremes), as described by *Plato in *Phaedo*. Although suicide, except under necessity, is there condemned, Socrates was adopted as a model, not only by *Seneca the Younger, who was ordered to kill himself, but by *Porcius Cato (2), who chose to refuse *Caesar's pardon. These were *Stoics, who advocated the rational exit from life, provided certain conditions were fulfilled. Plato and *Aristotle had been more negative, though Plato in his *Laws* admitted inevitable misfortune and intolerable shame as justifications and Aristotle allowed self-sacrifice for country or friends, while otherwise rejecting suicide as an injustice to society. The *Epicureans reluctantly permitted suicide when the balance of pleasure over pain could not be maintained. A calm demeanour and the giving of reasons to friends and relatives were the hallmark of the philosophically justified suicide: it could be histrionic, not only in literature but in life, for the jurists recognized 'showing off', as a motive for suicide characteristic of philosophers.

There seems to have been no blanket approval or condemnation of suicide, even though it was occasionally compared to murder. It was left to 4th-cent. *Christianity, confronting the incentive to suicide presented by the heavenly rewards of martyrdom, to throw its authority behind the Platonic belief that man must not pre-empt God's decision.

Sulla See CORNELIUS SULLA FELIX.

Sulpicia, daughter of Servius *Sulpicius Rufus, niece and ward of *Valerius Messalla Corvinus. Her six short elegies in the *Tibullan collection are the only extant poems by a woman in the Classical era. They record her love affair with a young man of her own class whom she calls, in accordance with the elegiac tradition, by the Greek pseudonym Cerinthus. Whether or not the affair was a prelude to marriage, the public display of sexual independence on the part of an unmarried female aristocrat runs counter to conventional morality. Syntactical idiosyncrasies have caused the poems to be branded as amateurish, but behind the apparent spontaneity and sincerity lies a self-conscious artistry and originality of thought and expression.

Sulpicius Rūfus, Publius, was a member (with *Livius Drusus) of a circle of brilliant and ambitious young nobles taught by *Licinius Crassus. As tribune in 88 BC he tried to carry on Drusus' ideas by securing the fair distribution of the enfranchised Italians in the tribes. Opposed by the *optimates, he began to stress the populāris (see OPTIMATES) aspects of his programme and turned for support to *Marius. In return for transferring the command against *Mithradates VI from *Sulla to Marius, he was able to pass his laws (with some violence), but, when Sulla reacted by marching on Rome, had to flee. He was captured and put to death and his laws were annulled.

Sulpicius Rūfus, Servius, Roman lawyer. He prosecuted Licinius Mūrēna when defeated by him in the consular elections for 62 BC; in his speech Pro Murena *Cicero makes fun of Sulpicius' legal expertise. He was eventually consul in 51. After hesitation he half-heartedly joined *Pompey in 49; Caesar pardoned him, and in 46 he governed *Achaia. He died on an embassy to Antony (Marcus *Antonius) in January 43, and was honoured with a public funeral. Known to lawyers as Servius, he was, next to *Mucius Scaevola (2), the leading lawyer of the Roman republic and the first after Mucius to attain the consulship. A student of philosophy, he extended Scaevola's efforts at classification, e.g.

by distinguishing four types of *theft. He wrote Cicero two celebrated letters (see CONSOLATION; LETTERS, LATIN). He was the father of *Sulpicia.

sumptuary legislation See DEMETRIUS (1) OF PHALERON; LEX; PERIANDER.

sun See ASTROLOGY; ASTRONOMY; HELIOS; HYPERION; MEDEA; SOL INVICTUS.

sundials See CLOCKS.

Sūnium, the name of the southernmost part of *Attica including the promontory with its temples to *Poseidon and *Athena and its fort. The *sanctuary seems to date from the 7th cent., at the end of which several kouroi (see SCULPTURE, GREEK) were dedicated, one of them colossal. The early 5th-cent. Ionic temple to Athena was of unusual asymmetrical design; the well-preserved Doric temple to Poseidon was architecturally closely related to the temple of *Nemesis at Rhamnus. See ORDERS. In 413 the Athenians fortified the promontory, and this fort was rebuilt in the 3rd cent. incorporating ship-sheds. The *deme of Sunium seems to have been centred to the north, in the Agrilesa valley (see LAURIUM), which is rich in marble quarries and silver-mining remains (see MINES AND MINING), where a deme decree concerning a new *agora was found.

superstitiō became for Romans a pejorative term from the end of the 1st cent. BC. Superstition was a free citizen's forgetting his dignity by throwing himself into the servitude of deities conceived as tyrants. The civic ideal of piety (see PIETAS) envisaged above all honouring the gods while preserving one's freedom—that is, with restraint and measure. Thus the superstitious were supposed to submit themselves to exaggerated *rituals, to adhere in credulous fashion to *prophecies, and to allow themselves to be abused by charlatans. The reproach was addressed to women as well as to the members of the social and intellectual élite portrayed by *Cicero in his On the Nature of the Gods and On Divination. This conception corresponded to that conveyed by the Greek *deisidaimonia, as it is discussed by *Plutarch in his On Deisidaimonia. As a rule the Romans considered strangers, and esp. *barbarians, as superstitious, either because they celebrated monstrous cults, like the Gauls (the severed head), or because they were terrified by each exceptional happening and attributed it to divine wrath. But one could equally be considered superstitious, like the Jews, in submitting without flinching to the prophecies of sacred books (see JEWS; RELIGION, JEWISH). With the coming of *Christianity, two new forms of superstition appeared, which could both be described as 'the cult of the wrong gods'. One was the retention, despite the strong disapproval of the doctors of the Church, of purely pagan beliefs. The other was the use of Christian names, holy books, etc. in *magic. See RELIGION, ROMAN, TERMS RELATING TO.

supplications, Roman (*supplicātiōnēs*). When calamity struck (pestilence, defeat) or danger threatened, the senate, advised by *priests, often decreed adoration by all the people, or some of them, esp. women, of all or certain gods to expiate transgressions or to ensure future support. *Supplicationes* were also decreed to render thanks for a signal victory. Originally lasting one day, they reached twelve days for *Pompey, 50 for *Caesar, and 55 supplications totalling 890 days for *Augustus (*Res Gestae* 4. 2).

Sūtōrius Macro, Quintus, of Alba Fucens. *Prefect of the *vigiles in AD 31, he was *Tiberius' agent in the overthrow of *Aelius Seianus, whom he succeeded as praetorian prefect; he may have been an instigator of the move against him. Macro predominated in politics while Tiberius lived and was influential in securing *Gaius (1)'s succession, but, appointed prefect of Egypt in 38, he was forced to *suicide with his wife before taking up office. His will, leaving his native city money for an amphitheatre, remained valid.

sycophants, habitual prosecutors. In Athens there were, for most offences, no public prosecutors, but any free man (for some offences, any citizen) who wished was allowed to prosecute in a public action. Some men made a habit of bringing prosecutions, either to gain the financial rewards given to successful prosecutors in certain actions (e.g. *phasis*; see LAW AND PROCEDURE, ATHENIAN), or to gain money by blackmailing a man who was willing to pay to avoid prosecution, or to earn payment from someone who had reasons for wanting a man to be prosecuted, or to make a political or oratorical reputation. Such persons came to be called sycophants (lit. 'fig-revealers'; the origin of the usage is obscure). The word is often used as a term of disparagement or abuse in the Attic orators and in *Aristophanes, who shows sycophants in action in *Acharnians*.

The Athenians wished to check sycophants, who prosecuted without good reason, but not to discourage public-spirited prosecutors. Therefore the rewards for successful prosecution were not abolished, but penalties were introduced in most public actions for a prosecutor who dropped a case after starting it, or whose case was so weak that he failed to obtain one-fifth of the jury's votes. In addition sycophancy was an offence for which a man could be prosecuted. It is not known how the offence was defined; perhaps there was no legal definition. It remains uncertain how the word got its modern sense of 'flatterers'.

symposium The warrior feast was central to the *Homeric image of society; under the influence of the near east in the period 750–650 BC more complex rituals of pleasure arose. The time of 'drinking together' (*symposion*) was separated from the preceding meal (*deipnon*; see MEALS) and became the focus of attention. The male participants wore garlands (see CROWNS AND WREATHS), and *libations and *prayers began and ended the proceedings. The Greeks adopted the practice of reclining on the left elbow (one or two to a couch); from this evolved a characteristic shape of room, and a standard size for the drinking group of between fourteen and 30: the *andrōn* or men's room was square, arranged with a door off centre to fit usually seven or fifteen couches; larger sizes tended to destroy the unity of sympotic space. Many such rooms have been recognized archaeologically, but the best representation is the painted Tomb of the Diver at Paestum (60km./37 mi. SE of Neapolis). They were supplied with low tables, cushions, decorated couches, and wall-hangings (see DINING-ROOMS). By the late 6th cent. a repertoire of vessels had been elaborated, including different cup shapes, jugs, wine-coolers, and wine-mixing bowls (Gk. *krātēr*): the decoration of these vases offers a set of self-conscious images related to the activities of the drinking group (see POTTERY, GREEK). Water was mixed with the *wine in a central *krater* to a strength determined by the president (usually three or four to one, or about the strength of modern beer); it was served by slave boys. Equality and order in distribution were maintained: each *krātēr* measured a stage in the progress towards drunkenness. At the end of the session a merry procession (*kōmos*) in the streets would demonstrate the cohesion and power of the group.

The symposium was a male and aristocratic activity, originally based on the warrior group;

its earliest poetry was the *elegiac poetry of war, and the Spartan reclining *syssition remained the basis of its military organization. Citizen women were excluded. It was a centre for the transmission of traditional values (*Theognis) and for the exploration of homoerotic relationships; it could provide the organization for political action in the aristocratic *hetaireia. But it was also a place of pleasure; drinking-songs (*scolia) were sung according to various rules, one of which required a drinker to sing when he was passed the lyre and/or myrtle branch; kottabos (see GAMES) was a favourite pastime; professional entertainers were hired. *Dionysus was accompanied by *Aphrodite and the *Muses, in the form of female companions (*hetairai) and solo *lyric poetry. In the Archaic period the symposium was the focus for an artistic patronage (see PATRONAGE, LITERARY, Greek) which reached its heights under the *tyrants; together with wine, 'drinking in the Greek style' was exported throughout the Mediterranean in a process of acculturation that profoundly affected Etruscans, Romans, and many other peoples.

The artistic and cultural importance of the symposium declined during the Classical period, but it remained important in social life well into the Hellenistic period. Later it fused with Roman customs. See also CONVIVIUM; SYMPOSIUM LITERATURE.

symposium literature Three overlapping types may be distinguished: 1. Poetry produced for the *symposium: this includes most or all Archaic solo *lyric poetry and at least some choral lyric, and much of *elegiac and *iambic poetry. There is a strong tendency in this poetry to relate content to context of performance; there is also a strong element of the normative: many elegiac and other poems offer rules for the conduct of symposia. Certain themes and forms like the *epigram and the *scolion (see previous entry) are characteristic. From the real context of the symposium a literary context developed: much Hellenistic and Roman poetry purports to be composed for the symposium, e.g. the lyric poetry of *Horace.

2. *Plato established the prose genre of the *Symposium*, an imagined dialogue of set speeches or discussions usually on themes appropriate to the occasion. Plato wrote on ideal love; *Xenophon's *Symposium* is more realistic and less serious; *Aristotle wrote on drunkenness, *Epicurus on the physical effects of wine and sex. *Maecenas wrote a literary *Symposium* which contained a discussion of wine and in which

*Virgil and *Horace appeared. The *Symposia* of *Menippus and *Lucian parodied the serious philosophic symposium. Banquets and symposia are a common setting in Roman satire.

3. Antiquarian works. These literary or learned discussions were probably originally modelled on the reality of Ptolemaic court symposia. They could serve to display collections of philosophical wisdom (*Plutarch's *Symposium of the Seven Wise Men*) or literary questions, or to structure information appropriate to the form, as in Plutarch's *Sympotic Questions*. The most systematic example is *Athenaeus' *Deipnosophistae* ('Doctors at Dinner'), an encyclopaedia of information on all aspects of the symposium, in which the topics are arranged for ease of reference as a discussion which takes place in the course of a meal and subsequent symposium. *Macrobius' *Saturnalia* purports to follow Plato, but uses the similar device of a succession of feast days to organize information centred on Virgil.

synoecism (*synoikismos*), in the Greek world, the combination of several smaller communities to form a single larger community. Sometimes the union was purely political and did not affect the pattern of settlement or the physical existence of the separate communities: this is what the Athenians supposed to have happened when they attributed a synoecism to *Theseus, commemorated by a festival in classical times (the Synoecia). On other occasions it involved the migration of citizens to the new city, as in the case of *Rhodes c. 408/7 BC.

Syracuse, on the east coast of *Sicily, was founded by the *Corinthians, c.734 BC. See COLONIZATION, GREEK. The original foundation lay on the island of Ortygia, with an abundant spring (Arethusa) and flanked by two fine natural harbours, but almost immediately, as shown by the distribution of 8th-cent. pottery, the settlement spread up to 1 km. (over $\frac{1}{2}$ mi.) inland on the adjacent mainland (Achradina); the two were joined by an artificial causeway. Its early government was aristocratic, the gamoroi forming an élite whose lands were worked by unfortunate native. Prosperity in the Archaic period is attested by colonies (see COLONIZATION, GREEK) at Camarina and elsewhere, as well as by architectural remains: temples of *Apollo, Olympian *Zeus, and *Athena, and an Ionic temple (see ORDERS) of unknown dedication, all belong to the 6th cent. Defeated by Hippocrates tyrant of Gela, the gamoroi were expelled in a democratic revolution. *Gelon espoused their cause, making himself tyrant of the city, of whose empire he thus became the founder. After Gelon's death (478/7), his brother *Hieron (1) I confirmed Syracusan primacy and added cultural splendour: *Aeschylus, *Simonides, and *Pindar all spent time at his court. After the battle of *Himera (480) he rebuilt the temple of Athena, the shell of which still stands, within the cathedral of Syracuse. The city expanded northwards and westwards from Achradina.

Soon after Hieron's death (466) Syracuse regained democratic freedom but lost her empire. The democracy operated through an assembly and council (*boule); annual *strategoi ('generals'), whose number varied, formed the chief executive. For a short time a device resembling *ostracism, called *petalismos*, sought to check abuses of power. In 412, after Athens' defeat, the democracy became more complete, but *Dionysius (1) I soon established his tyranny, preserving nevertheless the accepted organs of the constitution.

The post-466 democracy had difficulties with the tyrants' ex-soldiers and new citizens, and faced wars with *Acragas and with the Sicels. But these were surmounted, as later were the wars with Athens (427–424 and 415–413), in which the statesmanship of *Hermocrates was influential, as was the military leadership of the Spartan Gylippus, 414–413. After 406 *Carthage was the chief enemy. Dionysius I fought four Carthaginian wars, and more than once the Syracusans were hard pressed. But the early 4th cent. was a period of great prosperity, and it was now that the enormous girdle of *fortifications, 27 km. (17 mi.) long, were built to include the plateau of Epipolae (to the north of the city) within the defended area. Rigorously but astutely guided by its tyrant, Syracuse now controlled most of Sicily and much of southern Italy. *Dionysius (2) II enjoyed ten peaceful years before Dion challenged his rule (356); thereafter Syracusan affairs became increasingly anarchic, and the city's power and population declined. Timoleon of Corinth restored the situation, introducing a moderately oligarchic government, but after 20 years it was overthrown by Agathocles, who made himself first tyrant (317) and later king (305/4).

At Agathocles' death (289) a further period of instability ensued. Conflict with the *Mamertines in Messana produced a new leader, who as *Hieron (2) II led Syracuse into a prosperous Indian summer, when the city became a significant intellectual and artistic centre. The econ-omy prospered, with commercial contacts in both the eastern and western Mediterranean as well as with Carthage; and ambitious building projects included the great theatre, one of the largest in the Greek world, a grandiose Π-shaped stoa above the theatre, and a gigantic altar to Zeus Eleutherius. By now, however, Syracusan independence existed by courtesy of the Romans, and when in 215 Hieron's successor preferred Carthage to Rome, its end was at hand. After a long siege (213–211), in which *Archimedes played a substantial part, *Claudius Marcellus (1) plundered the city.

Under the Roman republic Syracuse became a city liable to pay a tithe and the centre of provincial government, retaining both its beauty and a certain importance. It suffered at *Verres' hands, and in 21 BC received an Augustan colony: a new public square near Hieron's altar, a monumental arch, and the amphitheatre belong to this period.

Syria This region was a satrapy ('Beyond the River', i.e. the *Euphrates) of the *Persian empire until it was conquered by *Alexander (2) the Great in 332 BC. On his death (323) it was assigned to the Macedonian Laomedon, who was ejected by *Ptolemy (1) I. Thereafter it was disputed between Ptolemy and *Antigonus I. After the battle of *Ipsus (301), *Seleucus I gained northern Syria. The whole region suffered from repeated wars between the Ptolemies and the *Seleucids in the 3rd cent. until Antiochus III won the strategically and economically important sectors of Coelē Syria and the *Phoenician cities, along with Judaea and Transjordania, bringing the southern borders of Seleucid rule in this area for the first time to the Sinai desert. *Pompey annexed Seleucid Syria in 64, and it became a Roman province, with Antioch on Orontes as its capital.

The Seleucids, esp. Seleucus I, as part of the physical occupation of the region and a policy of gaining control over major strategic routes, founded many colonies and cities in northern Syria, including Antioch (one of the Seleucid royal capitals).

Roman The Roman province comprised besides the cities, a few of which were free, the client kingdoms of Commagene and Arabia, and the ethnarchy of the Jews (Judaea). Syria was under the Principate an important military command; its *legate, a consular, had down to AD 70 normally four *legions at his disposal. Client kingdoms were gradually annexed.

Syrian deities Almost all the deities worshipped in Greek and Roman *Syria were Semitic. In spite of regional differences, a few main types of cult can be distinguished. The largest group consists of deities in human form. These are often divinities of agriculture and fertility, of the sky and thunder; they may be protectors, or bringers of military and commercial success; they may represent the sun, moon, or stars. Annual death and resurrection occur in some cults. Most characteristic of Syrian religion were the 'Lord' and 'Lady', the Ba'al and his consort the Ba'alat, pairs of deities who could take many of the above-mentioned forms. Each pair originally protected a Semitic tribe; when the tribe settled, the divine pair were regarded as owning the tribal territory, and sometimes their influence spread beyond it. Babylonian astrologers, the 'Chaldaeans' remained influential. In the Roman period, the Syrian deities were welded into one eternal and omnipotent power, manifest in the Sun.

Worship included ritual banquets, *processions in which symbols or statues of the deity were carried, dancing, *libations, and *sacrifices, *divination, sacred *prostitution, and *mysteries. Imposing temples in the traditions of Syrian Hellenistic architecture still stand at Palmyra and Baalbek; others have disappeared. Many Semitic deities received approximate Greek or Roman identifications. The local Ba'al was often romanized as *Jupiter. Syrian cults were carried west esp. during the Severan period, usually by soldiers, slaves, and merchants. See SŌL INVICTUS.

syssītia, the generic name for mess-companies of citizens, in various Greek cities, but esp. in *Sparta and *Crete. In Classical Sparta the messes, each some fifteen strong, were located in separate structures by the Hyacinthian Way. Membership of a mess, obtainable only by unanimous vote of its members, was a requirement of citizenship. Each member had to supply a fixed monthly amount of produce on pain of disfranchisement; from the later 5th cent. many poor citizens defaulted, thus becoming Inferiors. Prestigious additional donations came from hunting or from richer messmates; but the prohibition of excessive drinking and eating, and the range of ages within each mess, inhibited the violent behaviour attendant upon symposia elsewhere. Different messes probably combined into the basic army unit. Spartan boys had separate messes, but sometimes attended the adults' messes. A public mess housed both kings, who received double rations for sharing with honoured guests.

See RHETORIC, LATIN.

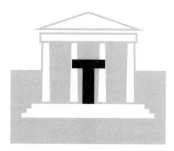

tabellāriī, *freedmen or slaves employed as couriers by the Roman state and by companies and private citizens of importance. To reduce costs, friends might share their services; and under the republic the couriers of the state and of the *publicani* would carry private mail for important men. An eminent Roman, when abroad, would put someone in Rome in charge of forwarding (as *Caesar did when in Gaul). But for reasons of security—esp. in times of trouble—it was essential to have one's own trusted letter-carriers for confidential messages. A good messenger, in the best conditions, could apparently cover 60 Roman miles or more in a day. For the Principate, see POSTAL SERVICE.

tabulārium The record-office in Rome (see ARCHIVES, *Roman*). It is traditionally associated with the trapezoidal building lying between the two summits of the *Capitol with its main front towards the Campus Martius. On the opposite side, closing the west end of the *forum Romanum, the elevation consisted of a massive substructure of ashlar masonry with an arcade of eleven arches flanked by Doric half-columns above it. A stairway from the Forum climbed through the ground floor of the substructure to the front hall of the building. Other *tabularia* in Rome included the *Aventine temple of *Ceres, for *plebiscites and decrees of the senate, and the *Atrium Lībertātis*, the *censors' registry of punishments and citizen-rolls.

Tacitus, Roman historian.
1. Publius(?) Cornelius Tacitus (b. *c.* AD 56, d. after 117), was perhaps a native of Narbonese Gaul. He had reached Rome by 75, where an uninterrupted career under *Vespasian, *Titus, and *Domitian brought him to the praetorship in 88. In 97 he was *suffect consul and pronounced the funeral oration upon *Verginius Rufus. Seniority brought him the proconsulship of Asia (See ASIA, ROMAN PROVINCE; PRO CONSULE) for 112–113.

2. Early in 98 Tacitus published his first work, *Agricola*, a biography of his father-in-law *Iulius Agricola, governor of *Britain for seven years. That governorship, culminating in the decisive victory of mons Graupius, forms the work's core. The work ends with a moving *consolation on the death of Agricola addressed to his widow and daughter; and the final words affirm that Agricola will live on through Tacitus' biography.

Later in the same year came *Germānia*. In its first half, after arguing briefly that the *Germans are indigenous and racially pure, Tacitus describes their public and private life. Its second half, devoted entirely to describing individual tribes, confirms that it is an ethnographical monograph, in which (naturally enough) a foreign people is viewed through Roman eyes.

The third of Tacitus' minor works, his *Dialogue on Oratory*, was perhaps written *c.*101/2. It is an urbane and good-natured discussion about the causes of the contemporary decline in oratory.

3. By *c.*105–106 Tacitus was collecting material for a historical work, almost certainly his *Histories*. When complete, it comprised twelve or fourteen books, covering the years 69–96; only the first four and a quarter books survive, bringing the narrative to 70.

The subject-matter of bks. 1–3, dealing with the civil wars between *Galba, *Otho, *Vitellius, and Vespasian, is predominantly military, and it is for his handling of this material that Mommsen called Tacitus 'most unmilitary of writers'. It is true that the reader is repeatedly puzzled or irritated by the absence of information on chronology, topography, strategy, and logistics. But Tacitus did not write according to the canons of modern historiography. His aim is to provide a narrative that will hold the reader's attention. By that standard chs. 12–49 of bk. 1 present a sustained narrative of unsurpassed pace and brilliance. From the moment when a handful of soldiers proclaim Otho emperor till Tacitus delivers his obituary over the murdered Galba ('omnium consensū capax imperiī, nisi imperasset': 'by universal consent fitted to rule—had he not ruled') the ebb and flow of fortune and emotion are portrayed with masterly skill. The loss of the later books is esp. frustrating, since they deal with a time when Tacitus was himself close to the centre of political activity.

4. At the beginning of his *Histories* Tacitus had spoken of going on to write of *Nerva and *Trajan. In the event he chose to go back to the Julio-Claudian dynasty from the accession of *Tiberius. The *Annals* (more exactly 'From the death of the deified Augustus') originally consisted of eighteen (or sixteen) books—six for Tiberius, six for Gaius and Claudius, six (or four) for Nero. Of these there are lost most of 5, all of 7–10, the first half of 11, and everything after the middle of 16. Whether Tacitus completed the *Annals* is not known.

The six books of Tiberius' reign are structured as two triads. The dichotomy, marked by the striking opening of bk. 4, emphasizes that the reign took a decisive turn for the worse in AD 23 with the rise to power of *Aelius Seianus. But even the excellence of the earlier years is attributed to Tiberius' concealment (*dissimulātiō*) of his true character. Whether that explanation, which does not originate with Tacitus, is consistent with Tacitus' claim to write impartially is open to question; but it is skilfully used to probe the ambiguities of Tiberius' behaviour, as the emperor sought to combine a *de facto* autocracy with a show of constitutional republicanism.

For *Claudius, Tacitus accepted the traditional picture of an emperor dominated by his wives and freedmen, and dwelt on the sexual scandals of *Valeria Messallina and the dynastic scheming of *Iulia Agrippina. But in much of his dealings with the senate Claudius emerges as a pedantically thoughtful personality, e.g. bk. 11. 13 and 24 (in the latter case uniquely we can compare Tacitus' version with the speech that Claudius actually delivered, on admitting Gauls to the senate).

*Nero's portrait also is simple: an initial quinquennium of mostly good government ends with the murder of Agrippina in 59, which frees Nero to follow his own desires. His extravagance, sexual depravity, and un-Roman innovations are depicted with verve and disapproval. Tacitus also pillories the servility of a senate that congratulates Nero when his mother is murdered, while *Clodius Thrasea Paetus' attempts to uphold senatorial independence lead only to his condemnation.

If political debate is less sharp in the Neronian books, foreign affairs and Nero's flamboyant behaviour fully extend Tacitus' descriptive powers. Their impact is strengthened by the organization of incidents into larger continuous units, a structural feature first observable in the Claudian books (so Messallina's final excesses and an account of British affairs covering several years; similarly, in the Neronian books: British affairs and the annual accounts of *Domitius Corbulo's eastern campaigns, and (at home) Agrippina's murder, the Great Fire of Rome and its aftermath, and the Pisonian conspiracy; see CALPURNIUS PISO, GAIUS.

5. None of the sources used by Tacitus has survived. For the *Annals*, esp. from bk. 6, similarities between Tacitus, *Suetonius, and *Cassius Dio suggest frequent use of a common source. But convention also allowed the ancient historian licence to elaborate or invent incidents to make his narrative more colourful and exciting. Yet, whatever the source, the resulting narrative is, by selection, arrangement, and interpretation, wholly Tacitean.

6. Though regret for the lost freedoms of the republic is evident throughout Tacitus, he accepted the necessity of the rule of one man and praised those few who served the state honourably but without servility. Yet pessimism and hints of a darker underlying reality are ever-present: motives are rarely simple; innuendo often suggests that the less creditable explanation is the more probable; and an awareness of the gulf in political life between what was professed and what was practised informs all his writing and finds fitting expression in a unique prose style.

7. That style is marked by a continuous avoidance of the trite. Elevation is lent to his language by archaic and poetic words and an admixture of neologisms, while his extensive use of *metaphor more closely resembles poetic than prose usage. In much of this he follows *Sallust. But to Sallust's renowned brevity Tacitus adds a greater compression of thought. The sinewy strength of his language is reinforced by a deliberate rejection of balance (*concinnitās*) in favour of syntactical disruption (*variātiō*), a device he uses with special effectiveness to underline alternative motives. The same aim is served by an esp. Tacitean type of sentence construction in which the main statement stands at or near the beginning, and then has appended to it (by various syntactical means, not least often the ablative absolute) comments that suggest motives or record men's reactions.

This type of sentence allows Tacitus to concentrate, often with sardonic comment, on the underlying psychology of men's actions and is tellingly employed in his portrait of Tiberius.

talents See WEIGHTS.

tamiai means 'treasurers'. In Athens the most important officials with this title were the treasurers of Athena. They were ten in number, appointed annually by lot, one from each of the ten *phylai*. They had charge of the money and treasures of Athena on the Acropolis. They kept the money in a building called *opisthodomos* (the location of which is doubtful), and they received and made payments in accordance with the decisions of the people. They paid out money not only for religious purposes but also for military use, esp. during the *Peloponnesian War, and to defray other secular expenses. Many of their records are preserved on stone and are an important source of information about Athenian finance.

Tantalus, legendary king of the area round Mt. Sipylus in Phrygia, son of *Zeus and father of *Pelops and *Niobe; like other Asian rulers (*Midas (1), *Croesus) he was proverbially rich. Along with *Tityus, *Ixion, and *Sisyphus, he belongs to the group of archetypal offenders against the honour of the gods, sinners (see SIN) whose exemplary punishment stands as a landmark for posterity. His offence was to abuse the great privilege he enjoyed, as one of the first generation of mortals, in being allowed to dine with the gods. Either he blabbed about the divine policy discussions he had overheard; or he stole and distributed to mortals the nectar and *ambrosia served at the feast; or, most commonly, he tested the gods by killing and cooking his son Pelops to see whether they would detect the forbidden food. Only *Demeter, distracted by sorrow for her missing daughter, ate a piece of shoulder from the stew; so when the child was reconstituted and brought back to life an ivory prosthesis was necessary. Tantalus suffers eternal and condign punishment, 'tantalized' by having to stand in a pool which drains away when he tries to drink, with fruit dangling before his eyes which is whisked away as soon as he reaches for it; other authors describe a rock teetering overhead, adding terror to the pains of hunger.

Tarentum (Gk. Taras), in southern Italy, an 8th-cent. Spartan colony (see COLONIZATION, GREEK; SPARTA) dominating the best harbour on the gulf of Tarentum. The colonists were said to be the offspring of *helots and Spartan women. Tarentum rose to prominence towards the end of the 5th cent. The early 4th cent. was marked by the ascendancy of *Archytas, who dominated Tarentine politics and successfully expanded Tarentine influence. After his death *c.*350, Tarentum adopted a policy of employing mercenary generals to control increasing pressure from the Lucanians and Messapians, but with limited success. The last of the *condottieri, *Pyrrhus, was involved in a full-scale war with Rome. After several inconclusive battles, he was forced to withdraw, and Tarentum fell to Rome, becoming an ally in 270. In 213 a faction of Tarentine aristocrats seized power and revolted from Rome. After a period of stalemate, during which *Hannibal held the town and Rome held the acropolis, Tarentum was recaptured, with heavy losses (209). For a time, it was directly governed by a Roman praetor. The foundation of *Brundisium and extension of the *via Appia undercut Tarentine trade.

Tarquinii, the chief of the twelve cities of Etruria, stood on a high plateau about 90 km. (56 mi.) from Rome. Its greatest glory is the series of painted chamber-tombs dating from the mid-6th cent. onwards. The wealth of material found in Tarquinii's vast cemeteries has made them basic to the study of *Etruscan arts and crafts. At Graviscae, the port of Tarquinii, a prosperous sanctuary was founded *c.*600 by Greek residents within the Etruscan community.

Tarquinius Priscus, Lūcius See REX.

Tarquinius Superbus, Lūcius See REX.

Tarracōnensis was the largest of Rome's Spanish provinces under the early empire. Its initial nucleus had been formed by the province originally (197 BC) called Nearer Spain, which had important *silver *mines at *Carthago Nova. It grew in size as Rome advanced westwards in the 2nd cent. and reached its full extent at the end of the Cantabrian wars (19). Under *Augustus (27) it came to be administered as an imperial province which comprised all of Iberia except for *Baetica and Lusitania. The province was subdivided into seven *conventus centred at Tarraco (the capital), Carthago Nova, Caesaraugusta, Clunia, Asturica, Bracara, and Lucus. By the reign of *Vespasian the military garrison comprised one legion, which helped administer the major gold mines in the territory of the Astures. This was the most culturally varied of the Spanish provinces. Its urban development was uneven, despite the creation of colonies (see COLONIZATION, ROMAN) and *municipia* by *Caesar and Augustus and the extension of the *ius Latii* by Vespasian. Tarraconensis was known for its fish-pickle, wine, and fish.

taxation See CENSORS; EISPHORA; FINANCE, GREEK AND HELLENISTIC, and ROMAN; GOVERNMENT; LITURGY; POLETAI; PORTORIA; PROCURATOR; PROVINCIA; PUBLICANI; VECTIGAL.

technology Most elements of Graeco-Roman technology were either inherited from prehistoric times, or adopted from '*barbarian' peoples. Some significant inventions were made, such as hydraulic concrete, the geared 'Vitruvian' water-mill, blown *glass, the screw-press, and a remarkable reaping-machine. Inventions that were applied included items for use in such essential activities as draining mines, and esp. processing the products of the single most important industry—*agriculture. The study of their date and application is complicated by the survival of a mere handful of detailed works by technical writers such as Heron or *Vitruvius, and the limited attention paid to technical matters by others, such as *Pliny the Elder. Archaeological evidence plays a growing role in establishing the date and diffusion of applied technology, and it also provides examples of devices that do not appear in the written sources, which (for example) give an incomplete view of the range of pumps. Interpretation is complicated by a tendency amongst classical scholars to approach Roman technology in the light of its Greek background, without adjusting the context from city-state to empire. A persistent stereotype contrasts Greek theory and invention with Roman practical application.

Technology remained stable (not stagnant) in most areas of metallurgy, stoneworking, *pottery, engineering, *architecture, agriculture, and *transport. Extraction and processing of silver at the Athenian mines at *Laurium varied in scale, not technique, from Classical Greek to Byzantine times. Finds from Egypt, Spain, and Wales show that the same techniques were applied across the entire empire in the Roman period. The Roman army evidently acted as an important agent of technology-transfer by spreading *literacy and skills to frontier regions. Thus, intensification rather than innovation characterized Roman technology, assisted by the geographical expansion of Rome and the reliance of its administration on secure and effective transport of men, foodstuffs, and both raw materials and finished goods. Roman engineers are remembered primarily because of the number of *roads, *bridges, and harbours that survive; archaeological evidence shows that these facilities were used by a wide range of vehicles and *ships whose size and technical complexity was matched to varying requirements. A similar flexibility—and availability—of *building materials and construction skills was able to create farms, workshops, and accommodation in rural and urban environments to house producers and consumers alike.

Greece and Rome constructed *marble buildings on an unprecedented scale, and minted millions of gold, silver, and bronze coins (see COINAGE). Thousands of ordinary farmers and urban craft-workers possessed more iron tools, architectural stonework, and fine tableware than ever before, to an extent that would not be matched until the post-medieval period. A combination of effective transport and appropriate coin denominations helped to sustain trade in these materials, far beyond the requirements of the state and the army alone. None of this caused, or resulted from, an Industrial Revolution; the significant growth factor was proliferation and intensification as a result of expanding conquest and trade. Evidence for extensive industries and widespread application of technology in the ancient world can be accepted without having to explain why they did not cause economic 'take-off'. See ECONOMY; INDUSTRY; MECHANICS; TRADE.

Teiresias See TIRESIAS.

Telamon, in mythology son of *Aeacus, and brother of *Peleus. He and Peleus were banished for killing their bastard half-brother; and Telamon settled in *Salamis, where he became king. He was one of the *Argonauts, and a participant in the Calydonian boarhunt (see MELEAGER (1)). By his wife, he fathered *Aias (1). By his slave-concubine Hēsionē, daughter of King *Laomedon of *Troy and given him by *Heracles for his help in taking Troy, he fathered Teucer. When Teucer came home from the Trojan War without Aias, Telamon banished him and he later founded Salamis in Cyprus.

Tēlemachus, the son of *Odysseus and *Penelope in *Homer's *Odyssey*, where he plays a prominent part, developing from a timid youth, unable to restrain the suitors, to a resourceful young man, who helps his father to kill them. In bks. 1–4, inspired by *Athena, he sails from *Ithaca to the mainland to inquire after his father at the courts of *Nestor at Pylos and *Menelaus and *Helen at Sparta. He sails home by a different route, thus avoiding an ambush laid for him by the suitors. After reaching Ithaca once more, he is reunited with his father in the hut of Eumaeus, and father and son together plot the suitors' destruction. Telemachus fights valiantly beside Odysseus in the final battle, in which all the suitors are killed.

temple The Greek temple was the house of the god whose image it contained, usually placed so that at the annual festival it could watch through the open door the burning of the sacrifice at the altar which stood outside (see STATUES, CULT OF). The worshippers gathered round the altar, where they would be given the meat of the victims to consume (see SACRIFICE, GREEK). *Orientation was generally towards the east, and often towards that point on the skyline where (allowing for the vagaries of ancient Greek calendars) the sun rose on the day of the festival. The temple also served as a repository for the property of the god, esp. the more valuable possessions of gold and silver *plate (see VOTIVES).

The core of the temple is the cella, a rectangular room whose side walls are prolonged beyond one end to form a porch, either with columns between them (*in antis*) or in a row across the front (prostyle). More prestigious temples surround this with an external colonnade (and are described as 'peripteral'). They generally duplicate the porch with a corresponding prolongation of the walls at the rear of the cella, *without*, however, making another doorway into the cella (the *opisthodomus*, or false porch). Some temples, such as the *Parthenon, have a double cella with a western as well as an eastern room, in which case the porch has a door in it.

The origins of this are uncertain. No provable temples exist before the 8th cent. BC.

By the end of the 7th cent. the rectangular form is normal. Cut stone replaces the earlier mudbrick structures, and important temples are peripteral 'hundred footers'; the 6th cent. sees a few huge 85-m. (300-ft.) examples, such as *Artemis at *Ephesus and *Hera at *Samos. From the 6th cent. stone-built temples are normal; *marble begins to be used where readily available. Doric temples (see ORDERS) generally stand on a base (*crēpis*) with three steps, though

the enlarged dimensions of the building make these excessively high for human use; they have to be doubled at the east-end approach, or replaced there by a ramp; Ionic temples often have more steps. Roofs are generally now of terracotta tiles; gutters occur rarely in Doric temples, regularly in Ionic. Marble tiles (introduced first in Ionic) are used in the Parthenon. The roof is supported on beams and rafters. Wider buildings require internal supports within the cella. Some of the very large Ionic temples do not seem to have had internal supports in their cellas, which must therefore have been unroofed, though the surrounding colonnades were roofed up to the cella wall. Each end of the roof enclosed a pediment or gable.

There are recognizable regional variations, even within the broad distinctions of Doric and Ionic. Approach ramps at the east end are regular in Peloponnesian temples, which often restrict carved decoration in the Doric metopes (square slabs) to those of the inner entablature (the part resting on the capitals above the columns) over the porch. Sicilian Doric temples may have four rather than three steps, and often have narrower cellas, without any internal supports.

Only exceptional buildings, such as the Parthenon, have full pedimental sculpture, let alone carved figures on every metope of the external entablature, while the frieze which replaces the metope frieze over the prostyle porches, and is continued along both sides of the cella, is a unique additional embellishment.

Roman temples derive from Etruscan prototypes, themselves possibly influenced by the simple Greek temples of the 8th and 7th cents. BC. They stand on high *podia*, with stepped approaches only at the front (temples of the Roman period in the Greek part of the empire often continue the tradition of the lower Greek stepped *crepis*). Roofs are steeper (reflecting perhaps the wetter climate of Etruria); more lavish carved decoration may derive from western Greek taste. The Corinthian order, used for some Hellenistic temples, became the preferred form. Marble is common in the Augustan period, white, with fluted columns; later polished smooth shafts of variegated marbles, granites, etc. are preferred. Regional variations continue to be important. The western provinces generally follow the example of Rome. See PAINTING; SANCTUARIES, GREEK; SCULPTURE GREEK.

temple officials Greek and Roman temples served as the houses of gods and goddesses, but also as centres of religious activity, meeting-places, storehouses for dedications, and secure locations for the keeping of valuables. They must have required regular control, care, and funding in fulfilling their tasks and maintaining their fabric.

We have a picture of how the temples operated in Greece. There were normally *priests or priestesses in charge of each one; in any large temple they would be assisted by minor officials of three types: first, there were cult officials who assisted in the sacrifices and rituals, who would have received their share of the sacrificial meat; secondly, there were caretakers who controlled access to the temple, carried out purifications of those entering, and cleaned the temple; thirdly, there were treasurers, who assisted with financial administration, took care of treasures and *votives, and oversaw the raising of revenue.

templum Pācis, later called forum Pacis or Vespasiani, was the precinct of the temple of Peace at Rome, dedicated by *Vespasian in AD 75. The area was surrounded by marble porticoes within an enclosure wall and laid out as a garden. The temple, a rectangular hall in the centre of the east side set flush with the portico, housed the spoils from *Jerusalem. It was flanked by a library, and various other halls. One of these carried the *Forma Urbis and may have housed the office of the city *prefect.

Terence (Publius Terentius Afer), Roman playwright, author of *fābulae *palliātae* in the 160s BC. Acc. to the *Life* by *Suetonius, he was born in Carthage, came to Rome as a slave in the household of a senator called Terentius Lucanus, was soon freed, but died still young in 159. We cannot check this information. He was patronized by prominent Romans, and his last play, *Adelphoe*, was commissioned by *Cornelius Scipio Aemilianus and his brother for performance at the funeral games for their father *Aemilius Paullus (1) in 160. The previous year, his *Eunuchus* had been an outstanding success, marked by a repeat performance and an unprecedentedly large financial reward. His one known failure was *Hecyra*, which twice had to be abandoned in the face of competition from rival attractions; Terence's account of these misfortunes in his prologue for the third production is exceptional evidence for conditions of performance at the time.

All his six plays survive: *Andria* ('The Girl from Andros', Megalesian Games 166; see LUDI); *Hecyra* ('The Mother-in-Law', MG 165, revived in 160 at Aemilius Paullus' funeral games);

H(e)autontīmōrūmenos ('The Self-Tormentor', MG 163); *Eunūchus* ('The Eunuch', MG 161); *Phormio* (Roman Games 161); and *Adelphoe* ('The Brothers', 160). *Hecyra* and *Phormio* were based on originals by Apollodorus of Carystus, the other four on plays by *Menander; Terence preserved the Greek titles of all but *Phormio* (named after the main character).

Terence used his prologues to conduct feuds with his critics; he never used one to tell the spectators about the background to the plot. Apparently he dispensed with expository prologues because he regarded them as unrealistic. Consistent with this is his avoidance of direct audience address in his plays.

Terence seems to have preserved the ethos of his originals more faithfully than *Plautus, with well-constructed plots, consistent characterization, and very few overtly Roman intrusions into the Greek setting. Like Plautus, he increased the proportion of lines with musical accompaniment. His plays repay thoughtful study and give a sympathetic portrayal of human relationships (*Haut.* and *Ad.* both deal with questions of openness and tolerance between fathers and adolescent sons). On the other hand, he added stock characters and boisterous scenes to *Eun.* and *Ad.*, and he was not faithful enough to the Greek originals for some of his contemporaries. He deserves his reputation for *hūmānitās*, sympathy for the predicaments of human beings, but his plays are also lively and entertaining situation comedies.

Terence's greatest contribution to the development of literary Latin was the creation of a naturalistic style far closer to the language of everyday conversation than that of Plautus or the other authors of *palliātae*, with much exclamation, aposiopesis, and ellipse; many of its features are paralleled in *Cicero's letters and *Catullus' shorter poems. But he did also sometimes use a more ornate and repetitive style, both in the plays themselves and above all in the prologues, which are highly elaborate rhetorical pieces with much antithesis, alliteration, etc. Terence was widely read for many centuries after his death, above all for his style and moral sentiments (*sententiae).

terracottas The term includes all objects made of fired clay; commonly, pots and household vessels are treated separately. Modellers were originally potters; later they were specialists who occasionally inscribed workshop or personal names. Earlier terracottas were modelled free-hand; after the 6th cent. BC they were usually made in moulds. Decoration at first resembled that of pots; from the 6th cent. figurative work was covered with a white slip and details painted. The status of terracotta was low. *Apollonius (4) of Tyana preferred 'to find an image of gold and ivory in a small shrine, than a big shrine with nothing but a rubbishy terracotta thing in it'.

Architectural Terracotta was used for: *sarcophagi, ash-urns, *altars, incense-burners, and roofing. Revetment that protected woodwork adorned all buildings in Archaic times; metal and stone have usually been robbed, but clay being intrinsically valueless has often survived. Roof tiles were commonly of terracotta. Ornamental elements were decorated with geometric and floral designs. In Italy and Sicily esp., architectural sculpture was made in terracotta. Large tiles were employed in Roman *heating systems (see BATHS) to support the floor and to permit hot air to circulate through walls.

Figurative Large representational terracottas were sometimes made in Greece as *votives (*Olympia); in Etruria (see ETRUSCANS) they were common. The Etruscan repertory was largely religious, but also included sarcophagi with life-size figures reclining on the lid. In Sicily large busts of the *Eleusinian deities were favoured. Small-scale representational terracottas—*masks, reliefs, and figurines—were made as votives for *sanctuaries, graves, and house-shrines. Female figures, numerous horses and riders characterize the terracottas of the late iron age. In the 7th cent. *orientalizing types, masks, and horses were made in *Cyprus, *Rhodes, and *Crete, and later all over the classical world. Local production centres developed, esp. in *Asia Minor, *Boeotia, *Corinth, *Laconia, *Argos, *Magna Graecia, and Etruria. In the 4th cent. the craft flourished, esp. in Athens and Boeotia (Tanagra). The repertory contained few religious types (Aphrodite and Eros), and many of theatrical genre (actors and comic figures). Cemeteries near Tanagra supplied so many charming figures in the 1870s that Greek figurines became a craze in Europe under the name 'Tanagras'. During the 3rd cent. these types spread everywhere.

Tertullian (AD c.160–c.240), b. in or near *Carthage, the son of a *centurion. He uses brilliant rhetorical gifts in favour of the rigorist party among the Carthaginian Christians. From the first he was steeped in the spirit of the martyrs. In works written c.197 he defended Christianity against pagan charges of atheism, black magic, and sedition, while maintaining that only in martyrdom could the Christian be assured of his salvation. Next (198–205) he devoted himself largely to Christian ethical problems, making high demands of Christians.

Tertullian's sole authority, apart from his verbal and intellectual acumen, was the Bible. Where he cites Stoics with approval, it is as the confirmation, not the source, of his beliefs. He maintains that all men have innate knowledge of God; yet heresy is found to result from the illegitimate substitution of philosophy for the 'rule of faith'. Against Marcion's belittlement of the OT and violent emendation of the NT, he argues for the integrity of scripture and a unity of purpose between the 'just' Father and the 'good' Son.

At some time he joined the Montanists, disciples of a new era of the Spirit, from whom they claimed to be receiving immediate direction. Believing that it was time for man to regain his unfallen image, he wrote (212) to a local pagan governor in defence of religious freedom. He wrote also against Christians who complied with the authorities; and he enjoined a rigour in discipline that went beyond scriptural teaching. See ASCETICISM; FASTING.

In his doctrinal writings of this period he fought against dualistic thought. Body and soul are one, God himself is a body (though its matter is Spirit), and the body of Christ that died on the cross is identical with the risen one. His last surviving work, *On Chastity*, was probably directed against measures by Callistus, bishop of Rome (217–222), to relax the Christian penitential system. The work is fundamental for the study of the western doctrine of the Holy Spirit.

Tertullian seems finally to have broken with the Montanists to found his own sect of Tertullianists, more rigorous than they. As a favourite of *Augustine, he exercised a great and abiding influence upon Christian theology in the west. He is unparalleled in both the originality and the difficulty of his Latin style.

tetrarchy The fourth part of an *archē* ('dominion'). In Roman times many Hellenized *client kings in Syria and Palestine were styled 'tetrarch', but the number of tetrarchies in any political organization ceased to be necessarily four, denoting merely the realm of a subordinate dynast. See also DIOCLETIAN.

Teutoburgian forest, the district where, in AD 9, the army of *Quinctilius Varus was destroyed on the march from summer to winter quarters. Its location was until very recently the subject of much speculation. However, striking archaeological discoveries (esp. of coins, legionary weaponry, and the usual impedimenta of a full Roman army on the march—including artillery and surgical equipment) now appear to confirm Mommsen's suggestion that the battle took place north of Osnabrück. Study of the remains of barricades reveals the skill of the German commanders in harassing, frustrating, and exhausting the Roman troops as they marched through a depression between a hillside and a moor.

textile production *Social Significance* Spinning and weaving held considerable symbolic and economic importance for women. In the *Gortyn law code a woman who was widowed or divorced could keep half of what she had woven in the marriage. Women took pride in men's praise of their skills and to 'keep the house and work in wool' was also a typical way of praising a woman after her death. Weaving also carries the suggestion of deception; in Athenian tragedy, *Heracles' wife *Deianira and *Medea trap men with fatal robes. The association with women is so strong that to accuse a man of weaving is to suggest that he is effeminate. In the empire, the strong gender connotations of spinning and weaving weakened; most weaving was done by men, although women were still clothes-makers and menders.

Thalēs of Miletus, the most scientific member of the *Seven Sages, was credited in antiquity with the prediction of a solar *eclipse that modern scholars have dated to 585 BC. He was reported to have advised the *Ionians to form a political union. Thales acquired legendary status as engineer, geometer, and astronomer; in *Aristotle's view he was the first natural philosopher and cosmologist. Since Thales left no written work, it is impossible to know how much historical basis there is for the achievements attributed to him in the ancient tradition. They include various geometrical discoveries and feats of mensuration (e.g. calculating the height of the pyramids by the length of their shadow), the study of solstices and measurement of the astronomical seasons, and several physical theses: that the earth floats on water, that a magnetic stone has a *psyche since it makes things move, that all things are full of gods, and that *water is the *archē*, the beginning or first principle of all things. The primeval import-

ance of water can be paralleled in Egyptian and Babylonian myths, and in the first verses of Genesis. Thales remains a marker of the moment when oriental science and myth were being transformed into the beginnings of Greek geometry, *astronomy, and cosmology.

Thamyris or **Thamyras** See MUSES.

Thargēlia, a festival of *Apollo held in Athens (7th of Thargelion, late May), some *Ionian cities, and their colonies; it belongs to the pre-colonial calendar (see CALENDAR, GREEK; COLONIZATION, GREEK). Scholars in antiquity explained its name from a *first-fruits sacrifice, a pot with the first cereals which was offered in Athens; the festival marks the beginning of the harvest season. At the same time, it had a cathartic character (see PURIFICATION), which explains the presence of Apollo: on the previous day in Athens, in the course of the festival in the Ionian towns, the citizens expelled the *pharmakos, the 'scapegoat'. At a crucial junction of the year, the expulsion of a member of society cleanses the town and prepares for the new harvest.

theatre staging, Greek Theatres in antiquity were constantly modified and rebuilt, and the surviving remains give few clear clues to the nature of the theatrical space available to the Classical dramatists of the 5th cent. There is, for example, no physical evidence for a circular orchēstra (dancing-place for chorus) earlier than that of the great theatre at *Epidaurus c.330. For 5th-cent. Athens, one might think of a metropolitan version of the *deme-theatre at Thoricus, where the audience was seated much closer to the stage in a rectilinear arrangement. The stage and probably the stage building (skēnē) were wooden at this period. Vases with scenes from Attic comedy from the late 5th and early 4th cents. suggest that by this time the stage was c.1 m. ($3^1/_4$ ft.) high with a flight of steps in the centre communicating with the *orchestra*. The stage was entered from either side, and from a central door in the stage building, representing palace, temple (and sometimes pavilion, tomb, or cave) in tragedy; for comedy, three doors are certain for the 4th cent., and were probably available in the 5th. The central door also housed the *ekkyklēma*, a wheeled platform large enough to display set-pieces of events that had taken place inside, like Ajax's torture and slaughtering of the animals in his tent in *Sophocles' *Ajax*. Towards the right (western) end of the stage area a crane (mēchanē, māchina) could be manipulated from behind the stage building to bring gods or heroes through the air onto the stage, or to have them fly up from it. The roof of the stage building was also accessible: it was used for the watchman on the roof in *Aeschylus' *Agamemnon*, but in later tragedy mostly for the appearance of gods. The contrast between the hidden interior of the stage building and the daylight outside, between the gods on high and the actors on stage, and between these and the chorus, half-way to the audience and virtually within its territory, are all factors which the playwrights exploited. In the 4th cent. the most important development was the so-called *Lycurgan theatre with its stone stage building faced with semi-columns.

It is hard to say much of the appearance of tragedy in the Classical period. *Masks probably had conventionalized, but not exaggerated features, with costumes rich and formal, as is suggested by the actors' costumes on the Pronomos vase of the end of the 5th cent.: that is presumably why Aristophanes could make jokes against Euripides when he abandoned some of its magnificence for his royal heroes in distress, like Telephus king of Mysia as an exile and a beggar. Comedy is better represented in the material remains. From the mid-6th cent. onwards comic choruses are shown in careful and colourful detail, and to identify a comedy by its chorus remained an artistic convention until the middle of the 4th cent. From the time of Aristophanes onwards we also find representations of actors, both in *terracotta figurines and in vase-paintings, where they are often shown in stage action.

The basic costume of Old and Middle *Comedy consisted of tights which terminated at ankle and wrist and which held heavy padding on the rump and belly. The costume appropriate to the role (male or female) was placed over this. Male characters wore a prominent leather *phallus. Certainly from the later part of the 5th cent. the masks were developed as standard types, recognizable once the characters came on stage, and the clothing was normally standardized to the part also, as the short tunic fastened at one shoulder for the slave, the cloak and conical hat for the traveller, and so on.

The award of prizes to actors from the middle of the 5th cent. is symptomatic of the growing importance given them as interpreters of roles. Actors became professional in the 4th cent. and gained increased *status. The growing popularity of theatre across the Greek world prompted the construction of huge theatres like that at

Epidaurus, with their audiences arranged round a circular *orchestra* and the stage raised higher to make the actors more visible. These conditions may have prompted the development of the crown of hair raised above the brow of tragic masks, a feature which appeared first in the later part of the 4th cent.; so too the platform soles for their boots.

The New *Comedy of *Menander and his contemporaries in the later 4th cent., however, was perceived as naturalistic not only in style and handling of plot but in presentation on stage. The grotesque padding and the artificial phallus worn by actors of Old and Middle Comedy were abandoned, and clothing was given a more naturalistic length and appearance. The range of mask-types was multiplied, esp. for the younger men and women, so as to allow a greater subtlety in their differentiation, paralleling the finer delineations of character in the text.

During the Hellenistic period theatre continued as the major form of public entertainment, and Menander's comedies became if anything more popular. But in later years, as his plays steadily came to be regarded as classics remote from the realities of the contemporary world, so the costume and performance style became more conventionalized. Many of the depictions of masks and comic scenes from *Pompeii are copies of the cultural heritage of the 2nd cent. BC.

theatre staging, Roman The staging of the plays of *Plautus and *Terence has to be worked out almost entirely from the texts themselves; the theatres in which they were performed have not survived. (The first Roman theatre to last for any length of time was built by *Pompey in 55 BC, with a seating capacity estimated at 10,000. Later theatres in the Roman world were increasingly elaborate. Plays put on at the Megalesian Games (see LUDI) were performed outside the temple of *Cybele on the *Palatine, others probably outside other temples or in the *forum Romanum, normally on wooden stages erected for the occasion. As in Greece, plays were performed in daytime in the open air, and the action was supposed to take place out of doors.

The stage generally represents a street, fronted by at most three houses, and with side-exits/-entrances to left and right. On the stage stood an altar. Further details of the setting may well have been left to the audience's imagination, and there was perhaps no painted scenery. The structure representing the houses had to be strong enough to withstand repeated opening and shutting of the doors (and knocking on them, if this was performed realistically), and in *Amphitruo* Mercury appears on the roof. There was no drop-curtain between the stage and the audience.

It is generally assumed that the actors in these comedies were male and wore *masks. They performed in Greek dress. Many of the conventions (such as asides and overheard monologues) were inherited from (Greek) New *Comedy, but many scenes differ from the surviving Greek remains in requiring four or more speaking actors.

Thebes was the birthplace of *Heracles, who, as its champion, threw off the tribute imposed upon it by the king of *Orchomenus. The legend of Heracles reflects the essence of Boeotian politics, which were moulded by rivalry between Thebes and Orchomenus. *Herodotus erroneously attributes to Thebes the introduction of the alphabet to Greece (though he is right to speak in this connection of *Phoenicians; see ALPHABET, GREEK; and for the allegedly Phoenician origins of the Thebans, see CADMUS). By the late 6th cent. BC Thebes had organized an alliance or rudimentary confederacy consisting of its neighbours, with Orchomenus conspicuously absent. Thereafter, it vied for the hegemony of all Boeotia. It maintained friendly relations with the Pisistratids (see ATHENS, HISTORY; HIPPIAS (1); HIPPARCHUS (1); PISISTRATUS), but hostility to Athens arose over *Plataea, which joined Athens in either 519 or 509. One group of Thebans stood with the other Greeks at Thermopylae, while other Thebans Medized (see MEDISM; PERSIAN WARS; THERMOPYLAE, BATTLE OF). The Greek victory at Plataea in 479 led to the temporary eclipse of Theban power. Thebes allied itself with Sparta in 457, but was overwhelmed by Athenian counter-attack at Oenophyta later that year. After a period of Athenian domination, the Boeotians rose against Athens, and defeated Tolmides at the battle of *Coronea in 447. Thebes and other major Boeotian cities thereupon formed the Boeotian Confederacy described in the *Oxyrhynchus historian (see FEDERAL STATES). Thebes at the outset possessed two of the eleven units of the federal government. It was instrumental in igniting the *Peloponnesian War by attacking Plataea in time of peace. Upon its surrender Thebes occupied its territory and took over its two units within the confederacy. Using the war to further its ambitions, Thebes destroyed the walls of Thespiae after the battle of *Delion in 424, and sometime later reduced

the power of Orchomenus. It had thereby gained a position of ascendancy within the confederacy. After the defeat of Athens, Thebes became estranged from Sparta, and offered sanctuary to Athenian exiles hostile to the *Thirty Tyrants. Thebes and the confederacy joined Athens, Corinth, and *Argos to oppose Sparta in the *Corinthian War, but defeat entailed the dissolution of the confederacy and the loss of Theban power. In 382 Sparta seized it in time of peace, only to lose it to a popular uprising in 379. Thebes thereupon re-established the confederacy, brought it fully under Theban control, and used its resources to defeat Sparta at *Leuctra in 371. The victory led to an ephemeral Theban hegemony of Greece under *Epaminondas and Pelopidas, which ended with the former's death at the battle of Mantinea in 362 (see MANTINEA, BATTLES OF). The fortunes of Thebes declined owing to losses during the Third *Sacred War, and its opposition to *Philip II at the battle of Chaeronea led to its downfall (see CHAERONEA, BATTLES OF). Although Philip spared the city, its revolt against *Alexander (2) the Great resulted in its destruction.

Thĕmis, daughter of *Gaia and *Ouranos. She is associated with Gaia in the myth of previous owners of the *Delphic oracle. She is a primordial goddess, but closely associated with Zeus' order, and with justice, with right, law, ordinances. In Hesiod's *Theogony* she is Zeus' second wife and she bore him the Seasons (*Horae)—Good Order (*Eunomia), Justice (*Dike) and Peace (Eirene)—and the Fates (see FATE). In the Homeric *Hymn to Apollo* Themis fed the new-born Apollo nectar and *ambrosia.

Themistoclēs (*c.*524–459 BC), Athenian politician, was a member of an ancient family but by a non-Athenian mother. *Herodotus' informants accused him of corruption and said that in 480 he had 'recently come to the fore', though he was archon (see ARCHONTES) in 493/2; but *Thucydides (2) admired him for his far-sightedness and considered him one of the greatest men of his generation.

As archon, Themistocles began the development of *Piraeus as Athens' harbour. In the *ostracisms of the 480s he regularly attracted votes but was not himself ostracized (altogether, 2,264 *ostraka* against him are known, including a set of 190 prepared by fourteen hands): the expulsion of *Xanthippus in 484 and *Aristides in 482 may represent a three-cornered battle in which Themistocles was the winner. He was behind the decision in 483/2 to spend a surplus from the silver mines (see LAURIUM) on enlarging Athens' navy from 70 to 200 ships—allegedly for use against *Aegina, but these ships played a crucial part in the defeat of the Persian navy in 480 (see PERSIAN WARS).

In 480 he was the general who commanded Athens' contingents in the Greek forces against the invading Persians: on land in *Thessaly, and then on sea at Artemisium and at Salamis (see ARTEMISIUM, BATTLE OF; SALAMIS, BATTLE OF); he interpreted an oracle to predict victory at Salamis, argued for staying at Salamis rather than retiring beyond the isthmus of Corinth, and tricked the Persians into throwing away their advantage by entering the straits. The Decree of Themistocles inscribed at Troezen in the 3rd cent. probably contains authentic material but has at least undergone substantial editing. In the winter of 480/79 he received unprecedented honours at Sparta, but in 479 we hear nothing of him, and Athens' forces were commanded by Aristides and Xanthippus.

After the Persian War there are various stories of his coming into conflict with Sparta (in the best attested he took delaying action at Sparta while the Athenians rebuilt their city walls). At the same time the pro-Spartan *Cimon was building up the *Delian League. In the main tradition the cunning, democratic Themistocles is opposed to the upright, aristocratic Aristides, but there are signs that Aristides was now a supporter rather than an opponent of Themistocles. Themistocles was ostracized *c.*470, went to live at *Argos, and 'visited other places in the Peloponnese', where an anti-Spartan alliance was growing. When Sparta became alarmed, and claimed to have evidence that he was involved with *Pausanias (1) in intrigues with Persia, he fled, first westwards but then via *Macedonia to *Asia Minor. The Athenians condemned him to death in his absence; after 465 the new Persian king, *Artaxerxes I, made him governor of Magnesia on Maeander, where coins bearing his name and portrait were issued. He probably died a natural death, though there was a legend that he killed himself; after his death, his family returned to Athens. Democracy did not become an issue while he was in Athens (see DEMOCRACY, ATHENIAN), but there are links between him and the democratic, anti-Spartan politicians who came to the fore at the end of the 460s.

Theocritus, Greek poet from *Syracuse, early 3rd cent. BC; creator of the bucolic genre, but a writer who drew inspiration from many earlier literary forms, cleverly blending them into a new amalgam, which nevertheless displays constant invention and seeks variety rather than homogeneity. Thirty poems and a few fragments, together with 24 epigrams, are ascribed to him, several clearly spurious and others of doubtful authenticity.

A near-contemporary of *Callimachus (2), Theocritus too was a remaker of the Greek poetic tradition, though his own method of propagating the gospel of tightly organized, perfectly finished writing on a miniature scale was to demonstrate by implicit example rather than engage in neurotic combat against real or imaginary enemies. The closest he comes to a manifesto, and a text that is central for understanding his art, is poem 7 in the collection, which bears the title *Thalýsia*, 'The Harvest Home'. Cast in elusively autobiographical form, it describes a journey undertaken by a conveniently assumed persona, 'Simichidas', during his younger days on *Cos. On the road he meets a Cretan called Lycidas, 'a goatherd—nor could anyone have mistaken him for anything else, since he looked so very like a goatherd'. The two engage in a song contest, preceded by a discussion of the current state of poetry; *Philitas and 'Sicelidas of Samos' (a near-anagram for Asclepiades, inventor of the erotic *epigram) are mentioned, and Lycidas praises his young companion for his refusal to write Homeric pastiche. The result of the 'competition' is a foregone conclusion, for Simichidas is promised his prize in advance; just as well, since his clumsy party-piece is no match for the smiling Lycidas' sophisticated song. And no wonder: for Lycidas is *Apollo, the god of poetry himself, and his *epiphany in the poem marks it out as an account of the 'poet's consecration' of the kind *Hesiod and *Archilochus had received from the Muses.

Other poems in the bucolic main sequence (1–7) also contain passages with programmatic implications—esp. the meticulous description of the wonderfully carved cup in poem 1, whose scenes seem intended as a visual correlative of Theocritus' poetic agenda. There are also pieces which refer more directly to the problems of the writer in the Hellenistic world. Poem 16 imaginatively reworks themes from *Simonides in appealing for *patronage to *Hieron (2) II of Syracuse, and 17 is a similar request to Ptolemy II Philadelphus, less inspired overall but with a splendidly impish portrayal of the afterlife which the king's father is fancied to be enjoying on *Olympus with *Alexander (2) the Great and *Heracles as his heavenly drinking-companions. Life in contemporary *Alexandria, and praise of its enlightened ruler, is again the theme of 14, an exploratory transposition of a scene of New *Comedy into *hexameter form; while 15, one of the two 'urban *mimes' in the collection, gives us a glimpse of the annual *Adonis festival in Ptolemy's palace. We watch the celebration, and hear the hymn through the eyes and ears of a pair of suburban housewives who have spent the first part of the poem stunning the reader by the banality of their conversation.

The other mime, 2, is cast as a monologue. A young Alexandrian woman, Simaetha, instructs her servant in the performance of a *magic ritual designed to charm back a wandering lover—or else destroy him; then, after the slave's departure with the drug, she recalls the occasion of her first sight of the youth, and her seduction. The poem is an excellent example of Theocritus' originality in expanding the range of material to be considered 'fit for poetry'; the effect was permanent. Though (like all of Theocritus' work) the piece is primarily designed for an audience of sophisticated readers, there is an emotional power here that makes it performable.

But Theocritus was also interested in staking a claim on more 'mainstream' territory, as his choice of the *hexameter as his regular vehicle suggests. *Epic remained the ultimate challenge. Two poems take up *Argonautic subjects, and must relate somehow to the contemporary long poem by *Apollonius (1) of Rhodes—perhaps Theocritus is showing his less radical rival how to do it properly. *Pindar is recast into epic and updated in the treatment of Heracles' cradle-confrontation with the snakes in 24; only as babies or lovers can the traditional heroes retain their tenuous grasp on the Hellenistic imagination. The rhetorical sequence at 16. 48–57 makes all clear: two lines for Homer's *Iliad* (and even here the emphasis is given to the losers, and to the *handsomest* Greek fighter at Troy, Cycnus, never even mentioned in Homer's poem) are followed by six for the *Odyssey*, with the peasants given pride of place over *Odysseus.

New, yet in some ways older, characters are brought forward to supplant the epic warrior Daphnis (1), Hylas (13), and Adonis (15), each of whom swoons in erotic death, and Polyphemus (see CYCLOPES), who joins Simaetha and the goatherd in 3 as a failed lover, and displaces Odysseus from centre-stage. Instead of the bloody duels of epic, the new model of compe-

tition is the agonistic singing of the goatherds (for which see PASTORAL POETRY, GREEK). Old false ideals and fantasies are pared away, and the new ones that Theocritus puts in their place are justified, paradoxically, by their very self-conscious artificiality. In an age of uncertainty and unbelief, Theocritus offers three beacons by which life may be orientated: love (which must ultimately fail, through rejection or death), personal determination, and art. Each of these is symbolically figured in turn on the cup, the 'marvel for goatherds', at 1. 27–56.

At some point in the ancient tradition Theocritus' poems acquired the generic title *Eidyllia*, 'vignettes'; in so far as the transliteration 'idylls' may conjure up a misleading image of rustic languor and passivity it is perhaps best avoided as a label for the poems of this energetic, engaged, and acutely intelligent writer.

theodicy seeks to explain (*a*) phenomena appearing to show a divinity's hostility to virtuous people, or (*b*), more generally, divine anger with humanity. Such explanations are well attested in Egyptian and Mesopotamian literature, and they form the basis for significant portions of the Hebrew bible. Theodicy is esp. important in societies that view divinity as upholding good.

*Hesiod is the most important early source for Greek theodicies. The story of *Pandora, which explains the existence of evil in the world as a response to *Prometheus' deceit, is one such, another the story that *Zeus decided to destroy the human race as a result of its *hubris. Early Greek elegy contains other examples in e.g. *Solon's poem on the subject of *Dike. The notion that a good person can be punished for the evil of an ancestor or ancestors is brought out perhaps most clearly in the *Delphic explanation of the fall of *Croesus, who is told that his misfortune is the consequence of the crime of *Gyges. *Aeschylus' *Oresteia* and *Sophocles *OT* are powerful explorations of the theme.

The fundamental concern with divine punishment in Greek religion is most obvious in the preoccupation with ritual purity and impurity (see POLLUTION; PURIFICATION, GREEK). A society that does not ensure the punishment or purification of individuals who have incurred *miasma* (pollution) invites divine punishment for the society as a whole. The prosecution of individuals for impiety is another illustration of this problem, raising the question of a society's responsibility for opinions that the gods might consider offensive as well as for actions. See INTOLERANCE, INTELLECTUAL AND RELIGIOUS.

In republican Rome, theodicy is intimately connected with conceptions of impiety or *impietās* (see PIETAS) and *vitium* (ritual fault). Both concepts provided powerful explanations for disasters affecting society as a whole. If *vitium* went undetected in the taking of the *auspices or at a sacrifice, it might be taken to explain military disaster, and the senate would take charge of the examination of ritual actions during a magistrate's term in office to determine the point at which *vitium* had occurred. Favourable signs observed after *vitium* had occurred would be taken as a sign of a divinity's determination to punish the previous error by leading a magistrate into a fatal situation. In such cases blame for disaster might be diffused quite widely through Roman society. Cases of open *impietas*, the wilful flouting of divine authority (the story that Claudius Pulcher threw sacred chickens into the sea before the battle of Drepanum) are less common.

Theodicean explanations for social disorder are common in the literature of the late republic and early empire. The preface to *Lucan's Civil War* suggests that the civil wars were the result of the general immorality of the Roman people, and Jupiter's explanation of the war against *Hannibal as an event necessary for the regeneration of the Roman people in *Silius Italicus' *Punica* is overtly theodicean. *Tacitus describes various disasters connected with the civil war of AD 69 as manifestations of the anger of the gods against the human race.

Theodicean ideas were not restricted to the realm of magistrates and intellectuals. There appears to have been much unrest in the reign of *Nero, resulting from his matricide, which might be taken to explain the Great Fire of 64. Various natural disasters resulted in the persecution of Christians, whose presence in a community might be thought to attract divine anger, and the sack of Rome in 410 was widely interpreted (by polytheists) as a manifestation of divine anger at a society that had fallen away from its proper religious customs.

In Christian society, concern with divine judgement is widely attested. In the first three centuries, its most important direct application was probably as an explanation of persecution. After the conversion of *Constantine I, the most important and wide-ranging exposition of a theodicean explanation for good and evil in the world appears in *Augustine's *City of God*. See SIN.

Theodora See JUSTINIAN.

Theodōrus, Samian architect (see SAMOS), sculptor, and metalworker, active *c.*550–520 BC. He made a massive silver mixing-bowl dedicated by *Croesus at *Delphi, *Polycrates' (1) famous ring, and a golden vine eventually owned by *Darius I. He also built the 'Scias' at Sparta (apparently an assembly-hall), and assisted in the construction of the temples of *Hera at Samos (upon which he wrote a book) and of Artemis at *Ephesus. He reportedly invented the line, rule, lathe, and lever, and made advances in bronze-casting. His bronze self-portrait was renowned for its realism, and showed him holding a file and a tiny chariot-and-four; the latter was exhibited at *Praeneste in *Pliny the Elder's time.

Theodosius I, 'the Great', the son of count Theodosius, b. *c.* AD 346. He was promoted early, serving as commander of Upper Moesia in 374. On his father's sudden disgrace and execution in 376 he retired to the family properties in NW Spain, but in 378, after the defeat and death of Valens at Adrianople, Gratian appointed him *magister mīlitum* to fight the Goths, and shortly afterwards proclaimed him Augustus of the eastern parts. For the next few years Theodosius conducted campaigns against the Goths. Failing to eject the Goths from the empire, he signed a treaty with them, recognizing them as federates and assigning them lands in *Thrace and Lower Moesia. In 386 he signed a treaty with Persia, whereby Armenia was partitioned between the two empires. Both these treaties are shown on the base of the obelisk of Theodosius, erected in the hippodrome at *Constantinople in 390, as triumphs of Roman arms. When the usurper Magnus Maximus killed Gratian in 383 and occupied the Gauls (see GAUL (TRANSALPINE)), Theodosius for a time recognized him, but when in 387 Maximus expelled Valentinian II from Italy, he marched west, defeated Maximus and put him to death. Theodosius stayed in the west for three years, and paid a state visit to Rome in 389. He returned to Constantinople in 391, but again had to march west in 394 to subdue the usurper Eugenius. He defeated him but died at Milan in January 395, to be succeeded by his sons Arcadius and Honorius in east and west respectively.

Theodosius was a pious Christian and an adherent of the Nicene creed, an allegiance which he owed to his origin and upbringing in the west. He was also surrounded by westerners, relatives and others, to whom he gave advancement, many of them individuals of intense personal piety. He was baptized early in his reign, during a serious illness. In February 380 (before he had come to Constantinople) he issued a constitution declaring that the faith professed by Pope Damasus was the true Catholic faith. In January 381 he ordered that all churches be surrendered to the Catholic bishops as defined by himself.

Theodosius was severe against heretics; he even ordained the death penalty for some extremist sects. Towards the pagans his policy was at first ambivalent. He did not forbid sacrifice, but was so severe against *divination as to prevent it. He did not close the temples, but allowed fanatical Christians to destroy them, or granted them to petitioners. In a law issued at Milan in 391 he abruptly closed all temples and banned all forms of pagan cult. This step was probably taken under the influence of Ambrose, bishop of Milan, who had obtained great ascendancy over him since his arrival in the west.

Theodosius' death was followed by what is often seen as the formal division of the Roman empire into eastern and western parts. His settlement with the Goths had long-term effects, as the Goths installed themselves ever more intimately into the political structure and society of the Roman empire. His religious policies mark a significant step in the developing alliance between Church and State, and were greeted with delight by *Augustine. He was brought to the throne at a time of major crisis, overcame it to the benefit of the empire, and imposed his personality on Roman history.

Theognis, elegiac poet, of *Megara. Chronographers dated him c.550–540 BC; historical allusions have been held to point to a much higher dating (c.640–600). A corpus of some 1,400 lines survives in manuscript tradition, labelled as Theognis' work, but it seems to be a composite from two or three ancient (Hellenistic) anthologies of elegiac excerpts, Theognis being only one of many poets represented. The corpus divides into five clear sections. 1–18: addresses to gods, gathered at the beginning. 19–254: nearly all addressed to his friend Cyrnus, serious in tone, with the first and last excerpts chosen to serve as prologue and epilogue. 255–1022: a much more diverse and disorderly collection, with a few Cyrnus-blocks here and there. 1023–1220: similar in character, but with a high proportion of couplets duplicated elsewhere. (1221–1230: added by editors from

other sources.) 1231–1389: amatory poems, mostly addressed to boys.

The addresses to Cyrnus, plus a few pre-Hellenistic citations naming the author, allow us to identify some 308 lines as Theognis'. Some of the rest may be his, but it is prudent to treat the greater part as anonymous and to call the corpus 'the Theognidea', not 'Theognis'. Theognis addresses Cyrnus in three roles: adviser, lover, and confederate. He makes many allusions to political turbulence. He appears as a man of standing in Megara, but subject to criticism and hostility, eventually betrayed by those he trusted, dispossessed of his estates in a civic upheaval, and forced into exile, where he dreams of revenge. He expects his poems to circulate at banquets everywhere, far into the future. Many of the anonymous Theognidea too were clearly composed for convivial gatherings (see SYMPOSIUM; SYMPOSIUM LITERATURE). Drinking and merry-making are frequent themes. Other pieces are reflective or philosophic. The amatory poems at the end are often banal, but sometimes touching. The collection as a whole contains many delightful things. It may be taken as a representative cross-section of the elegiac poetry circulating in social settings between the late 7th and early 5th cent., and it is our best source for the cultured man's ideas about life, friendship, fate, death, and other matters. See ELEGIAC POETRY, GREEK.

Theogony is the birth and genealogy of the gods.

Theophrastus (c.371 BC–c.287) of Eresus in Lesbos, associate and successor of *Aristotle. It is probable that he first joined Aristotle when the latter was at Assos in *Troas. He became head of the Lyceum (see ARISTOTLE, 5) when Aristotle withdrew from Athens on the death of *Alexander (2) the Great. His most famous pupil was *Demetrius of Phaleron, through whose influence he, though a *metic, was allowed to own property.

Theophrastus shared in, continued, and extended Aristotle's activity in every subject. His surviving works cover only a small part of the range of interests indicated by the lists of book-titles preserved by *Diogenes (4) Laertius and by numerous reports in later authors. It is likely that he saw himself as continuing and developing Aristotle's work of discussion and observation. Much of his writing seems, like the extant *Metaphysics*, to have raised questions rather than asserting a position.

Theophrastus made important modifications to Aristotle's modal logic. His research in propositional logic anticipated and probably influenced *Chrysippus; but it was Chrysippus rather than Theophrastus who made this the foundation of a new logical system. Theophrastus certainly rejected Aristotle's Unmoved Mover, and argued—though not necessarily against Aristotle—that teleological explanation could not be applied to every aspect of the natural world. He retained a belief in the divinity of the heavens and the eternity of the universe. He differed from Aristotle in involving material effluences in his explanation of the sense of smell. His collection of information about earlier philosophers (of which the extant treatise *On the Senses* formed part), undertaken in the context of his own philosophical concerns, was fundamental for later doxographers (see PHILOSOPHY, HISTORY OF). His work on *meteorology was exploited by *Epicurus and thence by *Lucretius.

In *botany, the only area in which most of Theophrastus' work survives intact, he so far surpassed his predecessors that the history of the subject in the west can be said to begin with him. In zoology (see ANIMALS, KNOWLEDGE OF) he was apparently more concerned with the behaviour and habitat of living creatures, and with physiological processes, than with anatomical description. His interest in human behaviour is shown by his best-known surviving work, the *Characters*—a series of sketches of 30 more or less undesirable types of personality. His work on friendship was used by *Cicero, who elsewhere portrays him as laying more emphasis on the importance of fortune and external goods for happiness than did Aristotle. He was best known in the Middle Ages for an attack on marriage preserved by *Jerome (included in the compilation which angered Chaucer's Wife of Bath); this may have been one side of a debate rather than a statement of Theophrastus' own views. The same may also apply to arguments for vegetarianism based on the affinity between men and animals, asserting that justice is relevant to relations between men and animals, whereas Aristotle had denied this (see ANIMALS, ATTITUDES TO). Theophrastus developed Aristotle's theory of the virtues of rhetorical style, wrote on rhetorical delivery, which Aristotle had neglected, and supplemented his political studies by the collection of laws and customs and the analysis of action in times of crisis.

Theopompus of *Chios, Greek historian of the 4th cent. BC, an exponent of rhetorical *his-

toriography, c.378/7, and still young when he and his father were exiled from Chios for sympathizing with Sparta. At the instigation of *Alexander (2) the Great he was allowed to return in 333/2, aged c.45. After Alexander's death he was again exiled; 'driven out from everywhere' he eventually reached the court of *Ptolemy I, who wished to have the 'trouble-maker' done away with. Theopompus was saved by the intervention of friends and died probably soon after 320. Acc. to ancient tradition, he was a pupil of *Isocrates and worked for a long time as an orator; in addition he wrote political pamphlets.

Historical works (1) *Epitome of Herodotus* (see HERODOTUS) the first known *epitome of an earlier work in antiquity; (2) *Hellenica* in twelve books: a continuation of *Thucydides (2) from 411 to 394, namely the sea battle of *Cnidus, which marked the end of Sparta's short-lived hegemony. With this work Th. entered into competition with *Xenophon's *Hellenica*, but he wrote in far greater detail than Xenophon. Only nineteen fragments are extant. (3) 'The History of Philip' in 58 books, Theopompus' main work, from which extensive quotations survive. It was not merely a history of Philip of Macedon, but a universal history including 'the deeds of Greeks and barbarians' centring on Philip II.

Characteristics (1) Theopompus had a universal conception of history; he focused not only on political and military events but showed an interest in ethnography, geography, cultural history, history of religion, day-to-day life, memorabilia, marvels, even myth. (2) He was fond of extensive digressions of all kinds: esp. noteworthy are the digressions on marvels; 'On the Athenian *demagogues'; and the three books on Sicilian history, covering the tyranny of *Dionysius (1) I and (2) II, 406/5–344/3. (3) Theopompus' historical writing was markedly rhetorical. He goes in for meticulous and skilful stylization, including numerous Gorgianic (see GORGIAS) figures of speech. (4) There is much moralizing in Theopompus. He incessantly denounced the depravity of leading politicians. (5) Political tendencies: Theopompus' attitude was that of a conservative aristocrat with Spartan sympathies. Philip II's patriarchal monarchy came closest to a realization of his ideal political and social system. Theopompus venerated him: 'Europe had never before produced such a man as Philip son of Amyntas.' (Th. had outlived his son Alexander.)

Sources The accounts of contemporary history are often based on *autopsy, personal research and experiences: Theopompus spent much time at Philip's court and travelled throughout Greece; for the earlier periods he used historical and literary material such as speeches, comedies, and pamphlets. He was one of the most widely read and influential Greek historians in Graeco-Roman times. *Dionysius (3) of Halicarnassus praises him for veracity, erudition, meticulous research, versatility, and his personal enthusiasm as well as for the purity, magnificence, and grandeur of his style. He does, however, find fault with Theopompus' *invectives and excessive digressions.

theōrika, 'spectacle' grants, paid by the state to the citizens of Athens to enable them to attend the competitions in drama. Attributions of these grants to *Pericles (who introduced payment for jurors) and to Agyrrhius (who introduced payment for attending the assembly) are both undermined by the silence of *Aristophanes on the subject, and the likeliest attribution is to *Eubulus in the 350s BC. In peace time the fund received not only a regular allocation but also any surplus revenue, and became rich enough to pay for a variety of projects; this, together with the fact that the treasurer of the fund was elected and could be re-elected, and shared with the council the oversight of the old financial committees, made the fund and its treasurer very powerful. A law of the 330s weakened the treasurer, but a similarly powerful position in Athenian finance was occupied in the 330s and 320s by *Lycurgus.

theos is the common Gk. word denoting a god, esp. one of the great gods (see OLYMPIAN GODS). Although often referring to an individual deity in his anthropomorphic representation, the term is rarely used to address a god: no vocative exists. The term is often used instead of the proper name of a god, e.g. when the god's name is under certain restrictions or reserved for direct dealings with the deity, as in the mysteries at *Eleusis: 'the two goddesses' is the normal expression there for *Demeter and Korē (*Persephone), 'the god' and 'the goddess' are Pluto (*Hades) and Persephone. It is also used when identification of an individual god is precarious, e.g. in the case of an *epiphany or vision, or as a comprehensive reference to any inarticulate, anonymous divine operator ('some god', 'the gods'); it alternates in Homer with *daimon to denote some unidentifiable divine operator. Later 'the divine power', 'divinity' becomes an equivalent, which, from Herodotus onwards, refers to occurrences that cannot be explained by natural causes. So, the term is often used in a predicative way to denote events or behaviour which are beyond human understanding: 'recognition of your own kin is *theos*.'

theoxenia ('theoxeny'), in myth and cult the entertaining of a god or gods by humans, usually at a meal. In Homer, the gods are said to 'meet' or be present at a sacrifice; more specifically, at *Odyssey* 17. 485–8 they roam the earth in disguise, testing the moral qualities of mortals. This is the germ of the typical theoxeny myth, in which a deity is given—or refused—hospitality, and after an *epiphany effects a reward or punishment. 'Failed' theoxenies are exemplified by the story of *Pentheus, while successful ones form an aetiology for very many cults, esp. of *Demeter and *Dionysus. In this pattern the host is often worshipped as a hero (see HERO-CULT), having been instructed by the deity and thus become the cult's first priest or the introducer of a new technique such as viticulture (see CULTURE-BRINGERS). The reception of Demeter at *Eleusis, narrated in the Homeric *Hymn to Demeter*, has elements of both success and failure. But perhaps the best-known literary version, probably deriving ultimately from local sources, is the story of *Baucis and Philemon.

In ancient usage, the term *theoxenia* is confined to cult, while as a festival name it indicates a specific type of worship in which a table is spread and a banqueting couch laid out for the divine guest or guests. The meal is commonly shared by the worshippers, thus contrasting with normal sacrifice, which distinguishes human from divine portions. One of the best-known examples was the Theoxenia of Delphi, which attracted delegates from all over Greece as well as numerous gods, among whom Apollo was predominant. A parallel ritual, partly influenced by Greek custom, is the Roman *lectisternium.

Thēramenēs (d. 404/3 BC), Athenian politician, son of Hagnon (see AMPHIPOLIS). He played an active part in establishing the *Four Hundred in 411, but four months later he was active in overthrowing them and establishing the Five Thousand, a more moderate but still not fully democratic regime, which succeeded the Four Hundred briefly. When full democracy was restored in 410 he was in the *Hellespont, assisting in the recovery of Athens' naval supremacy. At *Arginusae (406) he commanded only a single ship, but was one of those instructed to rescue survivors and corpses after the battle. Failure to achieve that was probably due only to bad weather, but later the blame was disputed between Theramenes and the generals (*strategoi), and after a largely illegal trial six generals were put to death. *Xenophon blames Theramenes for orchestrating this miscarriage of justice; but in *Diodorus (2) Siculus' account his role is less sinister, and *Aristophanes in *Frogs* next spring treated him lightly, as an adroit politician. In 404 he was sent to negotiate with *Lysander, and afterwards brought back the final terms of peace from Sparta. He was involved in setting up the *oligarchy of the *Thirty Tyrants, and was one of them, but he soon quarrelled with the extremists, esp. *Critias, who had him put to death.

His frequent changes of side were criticized both by democrats like *Lysias and by oligarchs like Critias, but in the 4th cent. he could be defended as a moderate seeking a genuine political mean. If he was sincere, he was at least guilty of misjudgement, and must bear a share of the blame for the internal troubles which weakened Athens in the last years of the *Peloponnesian War.

See also PATRIOS POLITEIA.

Therapne See MENELAION.

Thermopylae ('Hot Gates', from its hot sulphur springs) or just the 'Gates', strategic pass between Mt. Callidromus and the Euripus channel carrying the main land-route in antiquity from north to central and south Greece (since when the coast-line has receded); also site of the sanctuary of *Demeter, one of the twin cult-centres of the Delphic–Pylaean Amphictiony (see DELPHI; AMPHICTIONY), of which traces survive. As a defence position, where the road defiled between fierce cliffs and the sea, its weakness was that there is easy ground above, 'along the spine of the mountain', could an invader but find his way to it; and thus the pass was outflanked repeatedly. See PERSIAN WARS.

Thermopylae, battle of In the pass between the mountains and the sea (see preceding entry) 6,000–7,000 Greeks, led by *Leonidas king of Sparta, attempted to hold the invading Persians, probably in August 480 BC. See PERSIAN WARS. The small size of the army may have been due to religious scruples, or to Peloponnesian reluctance to send troops so far north. The Greeks held their position for two days, but then a local Greek betrayed the existence of an alter-

native route. The Phocians guarding this route withdrew to the nearest hill, leaving the way open, and when the rest of the Greeks learned of the enemy's approach, most retreated, either in panic, or because Leonidas told them to go. He, with the remnants of the Spartans, Thespians, *Thebans, and, possibly, *Mycenaeans, fought to the last, except possibly the Thebans, who are said to have surrendered.

Thēron, tyrant of *Acragas, c.489–473 BC; see TYRANNY. His seizure of *Himera (483), led to Hamilcar's invasion of Sicily (480), and to his defeat at Himera by Gelon and Theron. He beautified and enriched Acragas (public buildings and an enlightened agricultural policy), using Carthaginian spoils. A just and undespotic ruler and a patron of literature and the arts, he was honoured by the Acragantines as a hero after his death.

Thersītēs, acc. to Homer the ugliest man at Troy, lame, bow-legged, round-shouldered, almost bald, who abuses *Agamemnon until beaten into silence by *Odysseus. Here, he is of middling status; but in post-Homeric tradition he is related to *Diomedes. So, when he is killed by *Achilles for jeering at him because of his supposed love for the dead Penthesilea (*Aethiopis*—see EPIC CYCLE), a dispute arises, and Achilles sails to *Lesbos to be *purified.

Thēseus, a mythical king of Athens, who came to embody many of the qualities Athenians thought important about their city. Apparently originating without special Attic connections, he may have merged with a local hero of north *Attica, where several of his myths are located, and his prominence in Athenian tradition seems not to pre-date the 6th cent. BC, deriving at least in part from an epic or epics; the developed tradition of his life indicates a very different figure from older Athenian heroes such as *Cecrops or *Erechtheus.

Theseus' claim to membership of the Athenian royal line is shaky, since his father King *Aegeus was probably a late addition to the stemma, made precisely to accommodate Theseus. The alternative version, that his real father was *Poseidon, scarcely helps. In either case, his mother was Aethra, daughter of Pittheus of *Troezen. With her, Aegeus left instructions that if on reaching manhood their son was able to lift a certain rock under which Aegeus had placed sandals and a sword, he was to take the tokens and travel to Athens. This Theseus did, choosing the dangerous land-route, on which he encountered and defeated many brigands and monsters, such as Procrustes (the Stretcher) and the wild sow of Crommyon. On arrival in Athens, Theseus faced more dangers from *Medea, his father's new wife, and from his cousins the Pallantidae, but escaped their respective attempts at poisoning and ambush. He next defeated the *Marathonian bull. But the major exploit of this part of his life was the journey to Crete and killing of the *Minotaur. In revenge for the death of his son, Minos had laid upon Athens an annual tribute of seven youths and seven maidens to be given to the Minotaur; Theseus now travelled to Crete as one of the youths and killed the beast, escaping from the *labyrinth in which it was kept, with the help of a thread given him by Minos' daughter *Ariadne. He then fled Crete with Ariadne, but for reasons variously given abandoned her on *Naxos. On his return to Athens with his companions, he was unwittingly responsible for his father's death, by forgetting to hoist the white sails indicating his survival; Aegeus, thinking his son was dead, hurled himself off the Acropolis or into the sea.

Theseus thus became king. His greatest achievement as such was the *synoecism of Attica—the conversion of numerous small towns into one political unit centred on Athens. This was accomplished by persuasion, but other exploits, not all respectable, relied on force. Like (sometimes with) *Heracles, he undertook an expedition against the *Amazons, winning Antiope or Hippolyte for himself, but provoking an Amazon invasion of *Attica, which was finally defeated. His friendship with the Lapith *Pirithous led him to join the fight against the *Centaurs, and later to attempt to carry off *Persephone from the Underworld. In the usual version, after their failure and imprisonment, Theseus was rescued by Heracles, but Pirithous remained below. Theseus also kidnapped the child *Helen and kept her in the care of his mother until she should mature. He was forced to hand her back to her brothers the *Dioscuri when they invaded Attica. This gave Theseus' enemies their chance, and in the ensuing political confusion Theseus sent his sons to Euboea and himself fled to Scyros, where he was treacherously killed by King Lycomedes.

The formation of this tradition has clearly been influenced at several points by the figure of Heracles, notably in the monster-killing episodes at the beginning of his career. Evidently the developed Theseus saga was built up from pre-existing snippets to satisfy Athenian desire for a home-grown and clearly non-*Dorian hero of Heraclean type, a process which should be dated to roughly the last quarter of the 6th cent., when there is a dramatic increase in the popularity of Theseus in the visual arts (see below). It seems likely that the political significance of the 'new' hero soon became linked with *Cleisthenes (2), whose regional reforms could be seen as similar in spirit to the synoecism. Later, we may trace a connection with the family of *Miltiades and *Cimon, culminating in the latter's transfer of the hero's bones from Scyros to Athens (see RELICS). But by the time of the tragedies of the last 30 or so years of the 5th cent., far from being the property of any one party Theseus is a universally respected figure, the heroic representative of his city's greatness. True, *Euripides' Hippolytus presents him as incautious and mistaken (and outside drama, the distinctly negative traditions of the rape of Helen and the attempt on Persephone survived), but the usual picture of him in tragedy is of a strong, fair-minded, and compassionate man presiding with confidence over a proto-democracy (see DEMOCRACY, ATHENIAN), the antithesis of the tragic tyrant.

A latecomer to prominence, Theseus had few major sanctuaries in Attica. This was explained by the suggestion that the living Theseus had handed over all, or almost all, of his lands to Heracles, whose cult in Attica is clearly older. On the other hand, Theseus became deeply embedded in the festival cycle. As well as having his own festival, the Theseia, on 8 Pyanopsion, he was honoured to a lesser extent on the eighth day of every month (the day also sacred to Poseidon). Moreover, his journey to and return from Crete came to be associated with several cult-complexes and *rituals. Among these were the Oschophoria, where ritual *transvestism was explained by the story that two of the 'girls' sent to Crete had been young men in disguise, and the juxtaposed cries of joy and grief by the coincidence of Theseus' return with Aegeus' death; and the Pyanopsia, a festival of *Apollo said to derive from Theseus' *sacrifice in payment of a vow. Here and elsewhere Theseus can be seen as the heroic prototype of the young men whose transition to adulthood seems to be no concern of the rites. Outside Athens, Theseus was said on his return from Crete to have established various sacrifices and the 'crane-dance' on *Delos, a tradition helpful to the Athenians in their claim to *Ionian primacy. See also HIPPOLYTUS.

Theseus in Art The fight with the Minotaur, the only Theseus story regularly shown in Archaic art, is among the most popular of all scenes, continuing to imperial times in many media. The Minotaur is shown with bull's head (early, with human head), being killed.

From the late 6th cent. a cycle of Theseus' adventures on the road from Troezen appears, perhaps derived from poetry, or the adoption of Theseus as hero of the new democracy, resulting in the creation of a complementary series of 'Labours' to those of the Pisistratid (see PISISTRA-TUS) hero, Heracles. Such cycles appear on the metopes of the late Archaic Athenian treasury at Delphi and the Hephaesteion in Athens c.450 (see ATHENS, TOPOGRAPHY). Several vases depict cycles, but the scenes generally appear in groups or individually, mostly c.520–420. Theseus may be naked or wear a short cloak, and his weapons vary; his opponent is bearded and naked. Often, rocks and trees suggest Theseus' travels.

Theseus in the Underworld was painted in the club-house for citizens of *Cnidus visiting Delphi (see POLYGNOTUS); in the Stoa of Zeus at Athens he was painted with Democracy and the *Demos; in the *Stoa Poecile fighting the Amazons, and rising from the plain of Marathon; and in the Theseum (see MICON).

Thesmophoria, a married women's festival in honour of *Demeter, widespread across Greece, celebrated in the autumn (11–13 Pyanopsion in Athens), before the time of sowing. Men were excluded and the women camped out, sometimes at a little distance from the town, for three days. At Athens the first day was the *anodos*, 'way up', the second *nēsteia*, '*fasting*', the third *kalligeneia*, referring to a goddess of 'Fair Birth'. Pigs had been thrown into pits or caves, such as have been found at some Demeter shrines. The putrefied remains, brought up by 'Balers', and placed on altars of Demeter and Kore (see PERSEPHONE), ensured a good harvest when mixed with the seed corn. (It is uncertain when the pigs were cast down.) The festival included obscenity and a sacrifice. Otherwise, the secrets of the Thesmophoria have been well kept.

thesmothetai in Athens were the six junior of the nine *archontes, appointed annually. They were instituted in the 7th cent. BC. *Thesmos* is an early word for 'law' or 'rule', but it is unlikely that the *thesmothetai* ever made laws; their original function must have been 'laying down the

law' in the sense of pronouncing verdicts on accusations and disputes.

After the establishment of juries, the main function of the *thesmothetai* was to receive charges in various legal actions and arrange for a trial by jury, over which one *thesmothetēs* presided. Their trials were held in the building known as the *Eliaia*. The public actions for which they were responsible included *eisangelia for treason, *probolē* (see LAW AND PROCEDURE, ATHENIAN), and *graphe for many offences, including *graphe paranomon. They took trials arising from *dokimasia, and they also took some private actions. They could authorize the execution without trial of persons exiled for homicide who were afterwards found in Attica. In the 4th cent., after magistrates ceased to sit regularly in the same courts, it was the *thesmothetai* who arranged the dates for trials and allotted courts to magistrates each day.

Thessalonīca, a city of *Macedonia, founded by *Cassander, who *synoecized the small towns at the head of the Thermaic Gulf. It stood at the junction of the Morava–Axius route from the Danube basin with the route from the Adriatic to Byzantium (the later *via Egnatia). An open roadstead sheltered by *Chalcidice, Thessalonica became the chief Macedonian port. Strongly fortified, it withstood a Roman siege but surrendered after the battle of *Pydna. It became the capital of the Roman *province of Macedonia, and it served as *Pompey's base in the Civil War. As a '*free city' and as the main station on the via Egnatia, it enjoyed great prosperity. The population included a large Roman element and many Jewish settlers, who were visited by the apostle *Paul.

Thessaly, region of north Greece, divided into the four *tetradēs* (districts) of Thessaliotis, Hestiaeotis, Pelasgiotis, and Phthiotis. Comprising two vast plains divided by hills, Thessaly is enclosed by mountains (notably *Olympus, Ossa, Pelion, Othrys, and Pindus) which are pierced by valleys and passes, by which, in all periods, travellers, merchants, and armies have reached the Thessalian plains. Thessaly has access to the sea only by the gulf of Pagasae. It has a continental climate, with extremely fertile soils; it was rich in grain, horses, and other livestock, although its relative coolness largely precluded cultivation of the vine and olive.

From c.1000 BC Thessalians, from the southern half of the eastern plain, progressively took over more and more land, eventually coming to dominate (over the passage of 1,000 years) the two plains and also the surrounding mountains. The Thessalian *ethnos* early on formed itself into an organized state, with cities led by aristocratic families and grouped into a federation under the authority of a chief.

Their military power first gave the Thessalians access to the Peneus basin and part of the eastern plain, as well as the southern regions of the Othrys range, the Spercheios valley, and the coasts of the Maliac Gulf; then central Greece. Winning control of the *amphictiony formed by the population of these districts and based first at Anthela, then at *Delphi, the Thessalians were for a while a dominant power in central Greece. But from *c.*600 they were forced to fall back on Thessaly proper. In the second half of the 6th cent. the Thessalian state was reorganized by Aleuas the Red, who created the four tetrads each of four cities. Aleuas adapted the territories of each city for military mobilization by creating land-allotments controlled by officials charged with organizing the state's military units, and thus created an effective army.

In the 5th cent. the Thessalians strengthened their hold on Thessaly as a whole; of the population of the two plains a part was now integrated into the cities (which increased in number), the rest expelled to the mountains. Federal ties weakened following the rise to political and economic dominance over their neighbours of the cities of Larissa, Pherae, and Pharsalus. Urbanization progressed and wealth accumulated; aristocratic families engaged in their rivalries, but also were forced to cede to political pressure from ordinary citizens seeking a say in local government, which became progressively more democratic.

thētĕs, hired labourers, the lowest class of free men in a Greek state. At Athens, after *Solon, the lowest of the four property classes, comprising men who did not own land yielding as much as 200 *medimnoi* of corn or the equivalent in other produce. Solon admitted them to the assembly (*ekklesia) and *eliaia (indeed, probably they had never been formally excluded from the assembly), but not to *magistracies or, presumably, the council (*boule). Because they could not afford the armour, *thētĕs* did not fight as *hoplites, but when Athens became a mainly naval power, they acquired an important role as oarsmen in the fleet.

Thĕtis, a sea-*nymph, daughter of *Nereus, wife of *Peleus, and mother of *Achilles. The *Cypria* (see EPIC CYCLE) accounted for her marriage to Peleus by saying that she refused the advances of *Zeus to avoid offending *Hera and that Zeus, in anger, swore that she must marry a mortal. Acc. to *Pindar, however, she was desired by both Zeus and *Poseidon, but *Themis revealed that Thetis was fated to bear a son stronger than his father, and for this reason she was married off to Peleus. This version was exploited in the *Prometheus* plays attributed to *Aeschylus, where *Prometheus knew of the prophecy about Thetis and used the knowledge as a bargaining counter.

Before marrying Thetis, Peleus had to capture her while she assumed different forms to escape him. The wedding was attended by the gods, who brought gifts. Both the capture and the wedding are very popular subjects in Greek art. Most sources say that Thetis abandoned Peleus after her unsuccessful attempt to make the infant Achilles immortal; but *Homer sometimes implies that she stayed with him. She plays a crucial role in the *Iliad* as intermediary between Achilles and the gods, interceding with Zeus on his behalf, commissioning new armour for him, and bringing him the gods' command to release *Hector's body.

theurgy was a form of pagan religious *magic taken up by the later *Neoplatonists. It covered a range of magical practices, from rain-making and cures to animating statues of the gods. Like other forms of magic, theurgy was based on a theory of cosmic sympathy, but in theurgy, as in Neoplatonist metaphysics, sympathy was thought to extend beyond the material world and to unite it with a higher, divine world. So theurgy was believed to promote the union of the human soul with the divine. Plotinus shows no interest in theurgy, but in the next generation it became the focus of a dispute between *Porphyry and *Iamblichus. Iamblichus' *On the Mysteries* argues, against Porphyry, that the human soul cannot attain union with the divine purely by its own efforts of philosophical contemplation; such union requires the assistance of the gods, which can be brought about by theurgy. Most of the later Neoplatonists accepted Iamblichus' position, although they varied in the emphasis they placed on the practice.

Thirty Tyrants Upon Athens' defeat in the *Peloponnesian War (April 404 BC) Spartan support gave Athenian *oligarchs the upper hand. Under the peace terms imposed by *Lysander 30 men were chosen to run the government and write new laws following the 'ancestral constitution' (*patrios politeia*). These Thirty, with *Critias leading the extremists and *Theramenes the moderates, appointed sympathetic members to the new *boulē*, created a board of Ten to rule *Piraeus, abolished the popular juries, and began to remove their democratic opponents and certain *sycophants (ill-motivated prosecutors). The purge soon included respectable citizens and *metics. When Theramenes tried to broaden the franchise beyond the 3,000 citizens initially approved, Critias had him condemned and put to death. 1,500 are said to have been executed in all; many others left Athens. In January 403 *Thrasybulus (2) and a few democrats outside the city took up arms against the Thirty, who responded by stationing a Spartan garrison on the Acropolis thereby further alienating the Athenian people. Thrasybulus and his band grew larger and moved to Piraeus, where they defeated the forces of the Thirty in a battle in which Critias was killed (May 403). The Thirty were now replaced by a more moderate board of Ten; the same policies remained in force, but the Ten began negotiations with Thrasybulus' forces. Reconciliation was facilitated by the new Spartan commander, *Pausanias (2), and democracy was restored in September 403. *Amnesty was extended to all but the Thirty and a few others, who had fled to *Eleusis; most of them were killed two or three years later. They were first called the Thirty Tyrants, as far as we know, by *Diodorus (2) Siculus.

Thirty Years Peace, agreement between Sparta and Athens in 446, which ended the First *Peloponnesian War after *c*.15 years. Its exact terms are unknown, but by it Athens (after a recent defeat at Coronea in *Boeotia abandoned its recent land acquisitions (Nisaea, Pegae, Troezen, *Achaea, and esp. Boeotia), effectively in return for a free hand with revolted *Euboea. Armed attacks were renounced if the other side was prepared to go to arbitration. There was possibly a general clause stipulating *autonomy; at least, the *Aeginetans were to complain that theirs had been infringed. *Argos and other cities not included in the treaty could join whichever side they liked. There was *no* general clause of 446 recognizing possessions as they then stood, i.e. acknowledging the existence of the Athenian empire. Much of our evidence for the Peace comes from the late 430s, in the run-up to the main Peloponnesian War,

when the question arose whether Athens had broken the Peace.

tholos In classical architecture a *tholos* is a circular building. Examples include that on the west side of the Athenian Agora (otherwise referred to as the *Skias*, or parasol, from the shape of its roof; see ATHENS, TOPOGRAPHY). Built *c*.470 BC, it consisted of a drum with a conical roof supported by internal wooden posts on an elliptical plan. It was used as a dining-hall for the *prytaneis*. The *tholos* in the sanctuary of Athena Pronaea at *Delphi, dating to *c*.375, had a peristyle of 20 Doric columns (see ORDERS). Its function is uncertain.

Thrace The boundaries of Thrace varied at different times; in the 5th cent. BC the kingdom of the Odrysae, the leading tribe, extended from the Danube on the north to the *Hellespont and the Greek fringe on the south, and from *Byzantium to the sources of the Strymon.

Ancient writers considered the Thracians (who were *Indo-Europeans) a primitive people, consisting of the warlike and ferocious tribes dwelling in the mountains of Haemus and Rhodope, and the peaceable dwellers in the plain, who came into contact with the Greek colonies on the Aegean and the Propontis. Until classical times the Thracians lived in open villages; only in Roman times was urban civilization developed. *Herodotus remarks that, if they could have been united under a single king, they would have been invincible, a view corroborated by *Thucydides (2); in fact, unlike the Macedonians, the Thracians never achieved a national history. From the 8th cent. the coast of Thrace was colonized by Greeks at Abdera, Perinthus, Byzantium, and elsewhere, but the Thracians resisted Greek influence.

Thrasea Paetus See CLODIUS THRASEA PAETUS.

Thrasybūlus (1), tyrant of Miletus. See MILETUS.

Thrasybūlus (2), (d. 388 BC), Athenian general and statesman. In 411 he was a leader of the democratic state formed by the navy at *Samos in opposition to the *Four Hundred. He was responsible for the recall of *Alcibiades and contributed largely to the naval success of the following years.

He was banished by the *Thirty Tyrants and fled to *Thebes, where he organized a band of 70 exiles and occupied the Attic deme of Phȳlē (late autumn, 404). When his followers had increased to 1,000, he seized *Piraeus and defeated the troops of the Thirty. Thanks to an *amnesty proclaimed at the instance of Sparta, he led his men to Athens, and the democracy was restored. During the *Corinthian War he played a prominent part in reviving Athenian imperialism, and in 389/8 he commanded a fleet which gained many allies but lacked financial support. At Aspendus his troops plundered the natives, who murdered him in his tent.

Thrasybulus was an able and gallant commander. He championed democracy but was wise enough to make concessions in order to restore Athenian unity. In his last years he failed to appreciate that the imperialistic policy which he supported was far beyond the material resources of Athens at that time.

Thrasymachus of Chalcedon (fl. *c.*430–400 BC), *sophist, is best known for his defence, in *Plato's *Republic*, of the thesis that justice is the interest of the stronger. He played an important part in the development of Greek *rhetoric, by his elaboration of the appeal to the emotions by means of expression and delivery, and in the development of prose style by his attention to rhythm and to the building up of periods.

Thucydides (1), son of Melēsias, Athenian politician (b. *c.*500 BC). He was an aristocrat, connected by marriage with *Cimon. After the death of Cimon he succeeded him as the leading conservative opponent of *Pericles: he is said to have objected esp. to the building programme, and to have organized his supporters in a block in the assembly. His clash with Pericles led to his *ostracism *c.*443; he presumably returned to Athens after the statutory ten years, and acc. to Aristophanes' *Acharnians* he was prosecuted in old age. *Thucydides (2) the historian was probably a member of the same family.

Thucydides (2), author of the (incomplete) History of the *Peloponnesian War between Athens and Sparta, 431–404 BC, in eight books.

1. **Life** He was born probably between 460 and 455: he was general (see STRATEGOI) in 424 and must then have been at least 30 years old; while his claim that he was of years of discretion from beginning to end of the war may suggest that he was not much more than grown-up in 431. He probably died *c.*400. He shows no knowledge of 4th-cent. events. The revival of Athenian sea power under *Conon (1) and *Thrasybulus (2), from 394 on, made the decision of Aegospotami

(405: see ATHENS, HISTORY) less decisive than it had seemed to Thucydides. Of the three writers who undertook to complete his History, only *Xenophon took his view that the story ended in 404 (or 401).

Thucydides caught the *plague, some time between 430 and 427, but recovered, and in 424 failed to save *Amphipolis from *Brasidas. Not to have been a match for Brasidas does not prove him a bad soldier. He was exiled for this (424 winter) and returned 20 years later, after the war was over, and died within a few years.

He had property and influence in the mining district of *Thrace. His father's name was Olorus, the name of *Cimon's Thracian grandfather; his tomb was in Cimon's family vault. It is almost certain he was related by blood to Cimon, and probably to *Thucydides (1); born in the anti-Periclean opposition, he followed Pericles with a convert's zeal.

2. **Parts of the History** The History falls into five parts: A, an introduction (bk. 1); B, the ten years war (2. 1–5. 24); C, the precarious peace (5. 25–end); D, the Sicilian War (6 and 7); E, fragment of the Decelean War (8). It is convenient to take first B and D, the two complete wars.

B is enclosed between two statements that 'the continuous war has herein been described'. It was therefore provisionally finished (if these are Thucydides' words). It contains one allusion to the fall of Athens (2. 65. 12) and several allusions to events late in the 27 years: these are no doubt additions made to an already existing narrative, since one passage certainly was written before the last decade of the century. The narrative becomes more summary after Thucydides' exile: e.g. after the futile embassy to *Artaxerxes (1) I of *Persia nothing is said of the important negotiations with *Darius II.

D is the most finished portion. As it stands, it is adapted to a history of the whole war, and twice at least refers to events of 404 or later. But these may be revisions, and it has been suggested that Thucydides published it separately. B and D are connected by C, sequel to B and introduction to D, and so provided with a second preface. For symptoms of incompleteness, see below. C covers five and a half years, very unequally. Its two outstanding features are the description of the Mantinea campaign, and the *Melian Dialogue (see MANTINEA, BATTLES OF). The former should perhaps be regarded, with B and D, as a third completed episode.

E has the same symptoms of incompleteness as C and, moreover, stops abruptly in the middle of a narrative. It is very full, covering barely two years in its 109 chapters.

A consists of (1) a long preface, illustrating the importance of Thucydides' subject by comparison with earlier history (the so-called 'Archaeology') and stating his historical principles; (2) the causes of the war—i.e. mostly an account of the political manœuvres of 433–432; he adds important digressions, esp. 1. 89–117, a history of the years 479/8–440/39 (see PENTEKONTAETIA), partly to illustrate his view that the war was an inevitable result of Athens' growing power, partly to make his history follow without interval on that of *Herodotus. The second motive perhaps explains the length of another digression on the fate of *Pausanias (1) and *Themistocles.

3. Incompleteness E stops in mid-narrative, in winter 411: Thucydides intended to go down to 404. It shares with (roughly) C two peculiarities, absence of speeches and presence of documents, which are thought to show incompleteness; for these see below. The plan to make of BCDE a continuous history of the 27 years is only superficially achieved, even to 411: e.g. there is nothing of Atheno–Persian relations between 424 and 412, vital though these were (2. 65. 12). We shall see below that Thucydides kept his work by him and revised continually; so he left double treatments of the same theme, one of which he meant no doubt to suppress—e.g. the *tyrannicides. It is unlikely Thucydides left his unfinished work in no need of editing. If one looks for an editor, one thinks of Xenophon, who wrote his continuation (it seems) immediately after Thucydides' death; the suggestion was made in antiquity. His soldierly (if not his intellectual) qualities might commend him to Thucydides, but if it was indeed he, he worked with extreme piety, and his hand is very little apparent.

4. Speeches and Documents Ancient *craftsmen, and Thucydides notably, aimed at exactness; but in his speeches, Thucydides admits that exactness was beyond his powers of memory. Here, then, as in reconstructing the far past, he had to trust to his historical imagination, whose use generally he planned to avoid ('what I think they would have said'; and even here, he promises he will control its use as rigorously as he can by the tenor of the actual words. It is much debated whether he made this profession early or late; and it has been much explained

away. But it is unreasonable to doubt that from the start Thucydides took notes himself, or sought for hearers' notes, of the speeches he considered important. But since he used speeches dramatically, to reveal the workings of men's minds and the impact of circumstance, it is clear that verbatim reports would not have served even if he could have obtained them, and he was bound to compromise (unconsciously) between dramatic and literal truth. It is likely that, as his technique developed, dramatic truth would tend to prevail; it is tempting to put his profession of method early, a young man's intention. Even so, it is dangerous to treat the speeches as free fiction: their dramatic truth was combined with the greatest degree of literal truth of which Thucydides was capable. He tried to recreate real occasions.

There are no speeches in E, and (except the Melian Dialogue) none in C: Cratippus (a younger contemporary) says Thucydides had decided to drop their use. Modern critics treat their absence as a symptom of incompleteness; they would have been added had he lived. But these parts without speeches may be experiments in new techniques. Thucydides may have felt, as many readers do, that the narrative of the ten years is a compromise between the methods of tragedy and of a laboratory notebook, so that between the profoundest issues and the particular detail, the middle ranges (e.g. an intelligible account of strategy) are neglected. In the later narrative the methods are more separated. The Sicilian War was capable of almost purely dramatic treatment; C and E evidently not. And so in E at least a new technique is developed, less like either drama or chronicle, more of an organized narrative, with more of the writer's own judgements of values and interpretations of events. It is questionable if E would be improved by speeches.

Some of the speeches in books 1–4 may have been composed (or revised) very late. The new experiment would not entail eliminating the dramatic from those books; Thucydides experimented to the end and never solved his problem. Many believe that the Funeral Speech (see EPITAPHIOS) was written or rewritten after Athens' fall; and 2. 64. 3 surely was. The *Corcyra debate, on the contrary, may well be an actual report, written up soon after delivery. Though some speeches aim at dramatic characterization (e.g. Gorgianic (see GORGIAS) or Laconic), all are in Thucydides' idiom.

Those portions which lack speeches have (instead?) transcriptions of documents: that is,

E and (roughly speaking) C. If, then, we take C and E as experiments in a new method, the experiment begins in the latter part of B. These documents are usually thought (like the absence of speeches) a sign of incompleteness, since they offend against a 'law of style' which forbids the verbatim use of foreign matter in serious prose. With so inventive a writer as Thucydides, his laws of style are to be inferred from his practice, and 5. 24. 2 suggests that the end of B is provisionally finished. Are they part of the experiment? One may be surprised (though grateful) that Thucydides thought the full text of the Armistice worth its room. One of the documents survives in stone fragments and confirms the substantial accuracy of the copies. Another document conflicts with the narrative: apparently the narrative was written in ignorance of the exact terms, and has not been revised.

'Early' and 'Late' Thucydides says (1. 1. 1) he began to write his history as soon as war started; and it is arguable that much of the existing narrative, in all five parts of the work, was written, substantially as we have it, very soon after the events. But he worked slowly, and laboriously; correcting in the light of better information (we detect this process only where it is incomplete) or of later events. If his point of view, or his method, changed materially during this process, it becomes highly desirable to know from which point of view this or that portion is written. The attempt to recreate Thucydides' experience should (and will) never be dropped.

Truthfulness No historian is impartial; Thucydides certainly not, though unusually candid. His tastes are clear: he liked Pericles and disliked *Cleon. He had for Pericles a regard comparable to Plato's for *Socrates and an equal regard for Pericles' Athens. These things were personal: but in principle, concentrations of energy (like Athens or *Alcibiades) were to his taste. Their impact on a less dynamic world was likely to be disastrous—but whose fault was that? The world's, he says, consistently. Such judgements are rare, since Thucydides conceives his task as like medical research, where blame is irrelevant; the disconcerting simplicity of 2. 64. 3 (power and energy are absolute goods) is the more striking.

One version of the relationship between Thucydides, Pericles and the design of the History is this. Pericles (having planned an offensive war) lost his striking power, first because *Potidaea revolted, next because of the *plague. Forced to the defensive, he left the case for a defensive strategy as his testament. Thucydides was reluctant to face the fact of this failure, and accepted the testament, siding with the defeatist officer class against the revived offensive of Cleon. This is why Pericles' huge effort against *Epidaurus is recorded as a minor futility; why we hear nothing of the purpose of the Megarian decree; why, when that nearly bore fruit at last, Thucydides suggests that the capture of *Megara was of no great moment.

Such criticisms hardly detract much from his unusual truthfulness. Most readers will agree that he saw more truly, inquired more responsibly, and reported more faithfully than any other ancient historian. That is a symptom of his greatness, but not its core. Another symptom is his style: in its 'old-fashioned wilful beauty' (*Dionysius (3)) every word tells. It uses a language largely moulded by poets: its precision is a poet's precision, a union of passion and candour. Thucydides' concern for accuracy survived in the antiquarians, of whom he is the pioneer. To combine his predecessors' candour of vision with his successors' apparatus of scholarship was a necessity laid on him by his sense of the greatness of his subject.

Thucydides was not modest, but in his statement of his principles he seems strangely unaware of his unique equipment, and claims rather that he has spared no pains. The proper context for this statement is, first, his very similar statement about his own account of the plague, and then *Hippocrates' maxim, 'ars longa vita brevis'. The 'art' which outlasts individual lives is the study of man: the physician studied his clinical, Thucydides his political, behaviour. To know either so well that you can control it (and civilization is largely made up of such controls) is a task for many generations: a piece of that task well done is something gained for ever (1. 22. 4).

Style In one sentence *Dionysius (3) gives as the four 'tools' in Thucydides' workshop, 'poetical vocabulary, great variety of figures, harshness of word-order, swiftness in saying what he has to say'. The first, third, and fourth of these criticisms are undoubtedly true. Thucydides' style has a poetical and archaistic flavour (it is often difficult to distinguish between the two). 'Roughness' is to be seen in his bold changes of construction and his violent hyperbata, in which he wrests an emphatic word from its natural place in the sentence to give it more prominence. 'Speed' is perhaps the most striking of all his characteristics. He achieves an extreme concision, hardly to be paralleled in Greek prose except in the gnomic utterances of *Democritus (see GNOME). 'Great variety of figures' is more open to question. He is, for example, too austere to use metaphor at all freely, or asyndeton (more suited to the spoken word).

Some Recent Approaches The most noticeable feature of Thucydidean scholarship since 1970 has been the move away from preoccupation with the 'composition question' (the identification of layers of the History, with attempts to date them) to study of Thucydides' text as a literary whole.

The truthfulness of Thucydides came under scrutiny. Herodotus had for centuries found himself periodically in the pillory for alleged distortion and invention, but Thucydides' authoritative and apparently scholarly manner had usually been respected. Now it was suggested that Thucydides might simply have made things up, esp. his imputations of motive. More recently narratology has been tried on Thucydides. Narratology is the study of the principles underlying *narrative texts. Some narratological terms and insights are familiar to Thucydideans under other names; e.g. 'restricted access' means the difficulty encountered by a non-omniscient narrator interested in an agent's motives. The usual response, e.g. in messenger speeches in tragedy (and in Thucydides?) is for the narrator silently to assume an omniscient pose. But the main narratological weapon has been focalization, i.e. the point of view or perspective from which an event is described. Choice of Homeric (and Thucydidean?) vocabulary can sometimes be explained by the wish to present events or express emotions from a certain standpoint, which may or may not be that of the author rather than that of the imagined or historical agent. Provided it is recognized that there was a relation between what Thucydides says and the real world of the 5th cent. BC, only good can come of the recognition that his text is susceptible to literary 'close reading'. See HISTORIOGRAPHY, GREEK.

Thūriī, a Greek colony in southern Italy, founded in 444/3 BC on the site of Sybaris. It was a panhellenic foundation (see PANHELLENISM), but the main impetus was Athenian. *Herodotus and *Lysias were reputedly colonists, and it was planned by *Hippodamus of Miletus. There was initial *stasis* between the surviving Sybarites and the other colonists, but the city flourished.

Thyestēs See ATREUS.

Tiber rises in the *Apennines near Arretium, develops into central Italy's greatest river, meanders south to Narnia (confluence with the Nar), then SW past Rome (where it divides about Tiber Island), and enters the Tyrrhenian sea at *Ostia. The silt that it carries down with it on its 402-km. (250-mi.) journey accounts for its tawny colour, and constantly advances the coastline at Ostia. Tiber's tributaries include the Nar, Anio, and Allia. *Navigation, although possible as far as Narnia, was hazardous owing to the swift current. Inundations are first recorded in 241 BC, but were frequent in all periods, even after Augustus instituted officials responsible for the banks and channel of the Tiber (see CURA(TIO), CURATOR). The Tiber formed the eastern border of Etruria and the northern border of *Latium. In imperial times opulent *villas studded the banks of its lower course.

See also RIVER-GODS.

Tiberius, the emperor (Tiberius Iulius Caesar Augustus), was the son of *Claudius Nero and *Livia Drusilla, b. 42 BC. Livia was divorced and married *Octavian in 38 shortly before the birth of Tiberius' brother Nero *Claudius Drusus. After public service in Spain with *Augustus, Tiberius was quaestor in 23, five years earlier than normal. From 20 BC, when he crowned the Roman nominee Tigranes in *Armenia, until AD 12, when he returned to Rome after retrieving the situation on the Rhine after the Varian disaster (see QUINCTILIUS VARUS), Tiberius' military career was uniformly successful. In 15 and 14 BC he completed with Drusus the conquest of the Alps; from *Vipsanius Agrippa's death in 12 until 9 BC he was reducing Pannonia; from Drusus' death to 7 BC and again from AD 4 to 6 he campaigned in Germany. Between AD 6 and 9 he was engaged in suppressing the revolts of Pannonia and *Illyricum.

After Agrippa's death Tiberius divorced *Vipsania Agrippina (1) to marry Augustus' daughter *Iulia (2); their son died in infancy. After his second consulship (7 BC), Tiberius was granted tribunician power and *imperium* in the east for five years for a diplomatic mission, the restoration of Roman authority in Armenia, but the attempt to advance Augustus' grandson and adopted son Gaius *Iulius Caesar (2) to a premature consulship, made with or without the emperor's approval, helped provoke Tiberius' withdrawal to *Rhodes. He returned to Rome, still out of favour, in AD 2. By spring AD 4 both Augustus' adopted sons were dead, and he adopted Tiberius, together with Agrippa *Iulius Caesar (Agrippa Postumus), while Tiberius adopted his nephew Germanicus *Iulius Caesar. Tiberius received tribunician power (see TRIBUNI PLEBIS) for ten years, renewed in 13 for a further ten; concurrently he held proconsular *imperium* (see PRO CONSULE), in 13 made equal to that of Augustus.

When Augustus died in 14, Tiberius was thus in full power. The nature of the embarrassing 'accession debate' of 17 September remains unclear: a fresh conferment of power, or a political discussion of the (less autocratic) form to be taken by the new principate. Certainly, he abolished Augustus' advisory council (see CONSILIUM PRINCIPIS), which in his last months had made authoritative decisions; matters came directly to the senate. Abroad, Tiberius' dislike of extravagant honours was tempered by precedent and a need to conciliate his subjects which could prevent him making his wishes clear.

Tiberius respected Augustus and exploited his memory when taking unpopular steps. In dealing with the *Germans he followed the policy of containing the empire that Augustus had laid down in his political testament (Tiberius may have helped to draft it). This conflicted with the views of Germanicus, who was recalled in 16. Augustus' methods of coping with *Britain and Armenia were also followed: on his mission to the east (17–19) Germanicus established another Roman nominee in Armenia, who survived until 35. Tiberius did not shrink from annexing dependent monarchies: Germanicus took over Commagene and Cappadocia, which made it possible to halve the Roman sales tax.

Two innovations in provincial administration are credited to Tiberius: *prorogations of governors, and governorships in absence. Both were due to a shortage of satisfactory candidates, deplored by Tiberius. The second was clearly deleterious, and the first kept some poor governors in office (e.g. *Pontius Pilatus (Pilate) in *Judaea).

The most notorious feature of Tiberius' principate was the incidence of 'extraordinary' trials before the senate (introduced by Augustus). Most were for diminishing the majesty (*maiestas) of the Roman people, the emperor, his family, or other notables, by whatever means, however trivial; at first some were discouraged by the emperor. That of Gnaeus *Calpurnius Piso, also accused of extortion and of poisoning

Germanicus, is documented not only in the third book of Tacitus' *Annals* 3, but in the decree embodying the senate's decisions and approved by the emperor, which affords an unappetizing insight into the atmosphere of the reign.

Tiberius' reign opened with army mutinies, soon suppressed. Two factors undermined his principate. He inherited a poor military and economic situation: the German war was unprofitable; politicians were short of cash and were resorting to prosecutions to obtain it, there was unrest in Rome due to corn shortages, and provincials were chafing under tax burdens. Tiberius' answers (gifts to individuals, treasury disbursements when senators could no longer pay their debts in 33, and public economy), were inadequate, and his marked frugality (though personally generous, he built little, and gave donations and games sparingly) increased his unpopularity.

Second, there had been family jealousy since 7 BC, and the people and many senators favoured his stepsons. Rivalry after AD 4 led to the downfall of Agrippa Postumus and his adherents. Feared by former opponents, Tiberius could not make politicians trust his moderation and clemency. They looked forward to the succession of Germanicus (Tiberius was 55 in AD 14). On his death in 19 and that of Tiberius' son Drusus *Iulius Caesar in 23 the succession question opened up again, with the sons of Germanicus pitted against Sejanus, who seems to have supported Drusus' surviving son Tiberius Iulius Caesar Nero Gemellus. Instead of confronting the problem, Tiberius, encouraged by Sejanus, retired to *Campania and then to Capreae (mod. Capri, 27), never to enter Rome again. While he was under the influence of Sejanus and his freedmen, the struggle went on in Rome, until *Vipsania Agrippina (2) and her sons Nero Iulius Caesar and Drusus Iulius Caesar were disgraced (29–30), and Tiberius was given evidence that Sejanus was attempting the downfall of Germanicus' youngest son *Gaius (1) (31), who had become the only likely successor. Sejanus was arrested, tried before the senate, and executed. A purge of Sejanus' followers (and of supporters of Gemellus and rivals of Gaius' chief aide *Sutorius Macro) continued until Tiberius' death in 37, which was greeted with rejoicing.

Tiberius was a forceful orator, a poet, a connoisseur, and perhaps a *Sceptic (he was careless of religious ritual). Stories of vice on Capreae (and Rhodes) may be discounted; there remained real defects, a cultivated sense of superiority, relentlessness and lack of affability, meditated ambiguity of language, and concealment of intention and feeling (*dissimulātiō*). See TACITUS.

Tibullus, Albius, Roman *elegiac poet, b. between 55 and 48 BC. An anonymous and corrupt Life, tells us that he was good-looking and a dandy; also that he was of *equestrian rank and won military awards. He died in 19 BC.

Tibullus implies that his patrimony was diminished, presumably by Octavian's confiscations of 41–40 BC (see AUGUSTUS; PROSCRIPTION). But his claims to poverty should not be taken too seriously. He seems, no more than *Propertius, to have been reduced to economic dependence. *Horace indeed suggests that he was well-off, and possessed a *villa between *Tibur and *Praeneste. Tibullus refused, or did not attract, the patronage of *Maecenas, and instead addresses himself to *Valerius Messalla Corvinus. He set out to the east in Messalla's entourage, but fell ill at *Corcyra and returned to Italy.

Tibullus' manuscripts contain three books; these are commonly called the *Corpus Tibulliānum*, but only the first two belong to Tibullus himself. Tibullus' first book deals with his love for a mistress, Delia; surprisingly and provocatively it professes comparable devotion to a boy, Marathus. *Apuleius tells us that Delia existed and that her name was Plania. We need not doubt this, though her attributes (like those of Marathus) seem conventional. Bk. 2 celebrates a different mistress, whom the poet calls Nemesis. Nothing certain can be said about the social status of any of these lovers.

Tibullus, like Propertius, expresses the belief that love must be his life's occupation, and, like Propertius, he claims love to be his *mīlitia*, in spite of his actual forays into the world of action; like Propertius too he presents himself as the slave of his lovers. In his use both of military and servile figures Tibullus is more specific than Propertius. For example, his servile declarations express willingness to undergo servile punishments.

Unlike Propertius, Tibullus makes almost no use of mythology. Propertius' romantic, impossible dream had been that Cynthia would be like heroines of myth. Tibullus' impossible dream is that Delia will join him in his country estate to enjoy a rural idyll. Tibullus' aspirations to live the country life, expressed in more than one poem, separate him from the urban *Catullus and Propertius.

Apart from the love poems, bks. 1 and 2 contain poems in honour of Messalla, an elegy on the blessings of peace, and a charming representation of a rustic festival and the poet's song at it. Bk. 2 is *c*.400 lines long, and may be either defective or posthumous.

The third book is a collection of poems from the circle of Messalla. It includes five poems on the love of *Sulpicia for Cerinthus (known as the Garland of Sulpicia), and six short poems by Sulpicia herself.

In *Quintilian's view, Tibullus was the most 'refined and elegant' of the Roman elegists. The judgement is justified by the smooth finish of his poems; no other Roman poet writes with such refined plainness. Yet his simplicity is sometimes deceptive: the transitions by which he glides from one scene or subject to another often baffle analysis.

Tībur occupies a commanding site controlling the route up the Anio valley east into the central Apennines. It was a major settlement by the end of the 7th cent. BC. An important member of the Latin League, in the 4th cent. it often fought Rome until deprived of its territory in 338. Tibur, however, remained independent, acquiring Roman *citizenship only in 90. The monuments of the Roman town are conspicuous, and include the forum; a sanctuary to Hercules Victor and other temples; an amphitheatre and a rotunda. The airy foothills of the Apennines around Tibur were fashionable locations for villas (e.g. those of *Catullus and *Augustus). The most extraordinary was that of *Hadrian, begun *c*. AD 118 on the site of a republican–Augustan villa. The largest ever built, it incorporates many exotic buildings which reflect those that Hadrian had seen in the eastern Mediterranean. Among other important and luxurious buildings were the Poecilē, the island villa, the 'Piazza d'Oro', the baths, and a temple of *Venus resembling that of *Aphrodite at *Cnidus.

Tīmaeus of Tauromenium in *Sicily, *c*.350–260 BC, the most important western Greek historian. Timaeus was exiled in *c*.315 and spent at least 50 years of his exile in Athens, where he wrote his great historical work.

Works 1. *Olympionīkai*: a synchronic list of *Olympic victors, Spartan kings and *ephors, the Athenian *archontes, and the priestesses of *Hera in *Argos (2). Thereafter it became standard practice to date historical events by the years of the Olympic Games; see OLYMPIADS; TIME-RECKONING. 2. *Sicilian History* in 38 books from mythical times to the death of *Agathocles 289/8. The arrangement is known only in outline: the five books of the introduction dealt with the *geography and ethnography of the west and accounts of 'colonies, the foundation of cities, and their relations'. Bks. 6–15 contained the earlier history of Sicily until *Dionysius (1) I's accession to power in 406/5; bks. 16–33 treated the tyranny of Dionysius I and II (406/5–344/3) and events down to Agathocles. The last five (bks. 34–38) were devoted to the history of Agathocles. The work is known through 164 fragments, the extensive use made of it by *Diodorus (2), and *Polybius' criticism.

Characteristics 1. *Subject-matter*: Timaeus did not restrict his treatment to Sicily but dealt with the whole west including Carthage. He was the first Greek historian to give a comprehensive if summary account of Roman history until 264. 2. *Conception of history*: Timaeus took a broad view of history, including myth, geography, ethnography, political and military events, culture, religion, and marvels. 3. *Sicilian patriotism*: Timaeus frequently distorted events in favour of the Siceliots (Greeks who had settled in Sicily), and conversely wrote less favourably about the Athenians and Carthaginians; he always emphasized the contribution of the western Greeks to Greek intellectual life (e.g. *Pythagoras, *Empedocles, *Gorgias). 4. *Hatred of tyrants*: Timaeus, a conservative aristocrat, distorted not only the historical picture of Agathocles, who had exiled him, but also of other tyrants, e.g. *Hieron (1) I and *Dionysius I. 5. *Historical classification of his work*: Timaeus' work displays rhetorical, tragic, and 'pragmatic' (see POLYBIUS) features in equal proportion; hence it is an excellent example of the early blend of different kinds of historiography. 6. *Historical criticism*: Timaeus was the first Greek historian critically to appraise almost all of his predecessors, historians and other writers alike. He often went too far, which earned him the nickname *Epitimaeus* ('slanderer'). Timaeus in turn was criticized by Polybius for factual errors, his harsh criticism, and his historical methods (mere book-learning, want of *autopsy, lack of political and military experience).

timber was a valuable product in Greece and Rome. Many Mediterranean lands were forested in ancient times, but these timber stands were drastically reduced by human exploitation and by the grazing of animals, esp. goats. The Mediterranean climate is capable of sustaining forests so long as they are intact, but once the trees are cut, the combination of marginal

rainfall and grazing animals makes forest regeneration difficult, if not impossible. The history of timber supplies is one of gradual depletion, with little effort in antiquity to replant harvested lands. Only in those areas of continental rainfall conditions which lie at some distance from dense human settlement (e.g. the mountains of *Macedonia) have forests survived into modern times. Thus lacking much apparent physical correlation between modern scrubland and ancient forests we are dependent upon references in the ancient authors (e.g. *Theophrastus and *Pliny the Elder) for a description of the location and abundance of ancient timberland. Moreover, recent advances in palaeobotany have assisted in locating and describing some ancient forests not otherwise known to us. For example, *Cyprus was quite heavily forested from the central mountains down to its shorelines. Cypriot cedars of Lebanon and tall pines were much in demand for heavy construction and shipbuilding. The clearing of forest land for a variety of common uses (see below) was compounded in Cyprus by the extensive use of wood as fuel for the island's renowned smelting of copper. The result was the virtually complete stripping of the island of its famous forest cover.

With the growth and spread of the human population throughout the Mediterranean in antiquity, there were matching pressures on forest lands. They were cleared for conversion to agriculture, wood was harvested for fuel—either to be burned directly or to be converted into charcoal—and used for *furniture, tools, and other domestic needs. Coniferous tall timbers—which were light and strong—were used for the construction of private and public buildings and *ships. With the disappearance of nearby forests by late prehistoric times, the timber-starved cities of the Mediterranean turned further afield for their supplies. Beginning in the Classical period, the main sources were Macedonia and *Thrace (esp. for the pines and oaks necessary for shipbuilding, oars, and pitch), *Achaea, parts of *Crete and Cyprus, the south coast of the Black (*Euxine) Sea, Cilicia, the mountains of the Levant, southern *Italy, and *Sicily.

As tall timbers became scarcer, the competition among Greek city-states for remaining supplies increased. For example, when the forest products of Achaea were denied to Athens because of depletion and politics, the Athenians turned increasingly to Macedonia. *Brasidas' prolonged campaigns in Macedonia during the *Peloponnesian War can be seen in part as a

Spartan attempt to prevent Athenian access to the timberlands necessary to maintain the Athenian fleet (see NAVIES; SEA POWER).

The timber shortgage was never so acute for the Roman republic as for the Greek cities, due to the ample forest resources of lowland Italy, Sicily, and the accessible lower slopes of the Apennine and Alpine ranges. As wealth increased and tastes became more exotic, the Roman timber trade (like the trade in decorative building stone) went further afield to satisfy the demand for rarer and more exquisite woods. See LANDSCAPES (ANCIENT GREEK).

tīmē (honour) See PHILOTIMIA.

time-reckoning Ancient culture knew various expedients for dividing the day, for marking the succession of days in the month or year, and for dating important historical events. *Hesiod used the rising of particular *constellations to mark the changing seasons, and ascribed propitious and unpropitious qualities to the days of the month that corresponded to the phases of the moon. By the 5th cent. BC, Athenian astronomers—like their Babylonian colleagues—knew that the lunar month is approximately $29\frac{1}{2}$ and the tropical year approximately $365\frac{1}{4}$ days long, and could divide the day and night up into twelve 'seasonal' hours that varied with the length of daylight. *Astronomers from *Meton to *Hipparchus (2) and *Ptolemy (2) developed increasingly accurate luni-solar cycles and learned to explain and predict solar and lunar *eclipses. They also created public calendars, which traced the risings and settings of stars and predicted weather throughout the year. Civil practices, however, were never guided solely by astronomical expertise. Most people continued to divide the day and night into rough sections rather than precise hours. The Athenian calendar's failure to correspond with the actual movements of the moon was notorious, while the Roman months, before *Caesar reformed the calendar, deviated by a quarter of a year and more from what should have been their place in the seasons. Intercalation was often practised for political rather than calendrical ends. Only in the 1st cent. BC and after, when the spread of *astrology made it urgent to know the year, day, and hour of someone's birth, did an interest in precise calendar dates become widespread outside scientific circles. The chief motive for interest in the calendar lay, normally, in its days of ritual or ominous import rather than in its technical basis.

Historical events were at first normally dated, by both Greeks and Romans, by the year of a given priest or magistrate into which they fell: rough lengths for a single generation were used to date past dynasties of rulers. *Thucydides (2) protested against the first of these methods, but he himself (esp. in his introductory *Archaeology*) seems to have used the second, generation-count, method; and the temptation, to compute dates by means of assumptions about the length of human life, was persistent. Thus even in the 2nd cent., *Apollodorus (2) used an '*acmē*' system to date famous but poorly attested individuals like philosophers and historians; i.e. he assumed that an individual reached his acme (conventionally put at age 40) at the date of some well-known external event which had occurred in that person's life. From the end of the 4th cent., however, when the *Seleucid era of 312/11 came into widespread use, more precise eras and methods gradually came into use. Scholars like *Eratosthenes and *Timaeus tried to co-ordinate historical dates from different societies by measuring their distance from some single, common era, like that of the first *Olympic Games in 776 BC (see OLYMPIADS) or the founding of Rome in 753/2 BC. See also CALENDAR, GREEK and ROMAN; CLOCKS.

Tīmoleon, Corinthian, who expelled *Dionysius (2) II from *Syracuse, put down other *tyrants in *Sicily, and defeated *Carthage: the truth about him is not easy to discern behind our adulatory sources.

Tīmotheus (c.450–360 BC), of Miletus, famous *citharode and *dithyrambic poet. The comic poet Pherecrates speaks of him raping Music with his twelve-stringed lyre. He defeated the citharode Phrynis c.420. In a papyrus of the 4th cent. there survive large parts of his *Persians*, a citharodic *nomos* (see MUSIC, 3), for which *Euripides wrote the prologue. It is an account of the battle of Salamis mainly from a Persian point of view (see SALAMIS, BATTLE OF). The passages in which a shipwrecked Persian struggles for his life or the Persians invoke their homeland or beseech the victors in broken Greek give an esp. lively picture of the events and are a sign of the mimetic character of the music. In the final lines Timotheus proclaims the newness of his art. *Persians* is astrophic (see DITHYRAMB) and polymetrical. His music and language are said to have influenced *Euripides.

tin combined with copper is used to make the alloy of *bronze. Its addition to copper gives a product stronger than copper. Tin was also used to make pewter; five parts with two parts of lead. The main sources available to the classical world were the Erzgebirge and western Europe. The *Phoenicians probably controlled Spanish tin through their settlements in the western Mediterranean. *Massalia gave the Greeks access to supplies in northern Europe and possibly Cornwall via the Rhône valley. The mythical source of tin was the Cassiterides (Tin Islands'). There is ample evidence for the Roman pursuit of tin.

See MINES AND MINING.

Tīrēsias, legendary seer (Gk. *mantis*), whose ghost was consulted by *Odysseus. He was the resident seer of the Cadmeans of *Thebes, surviving from the time of *Cadmus (when he was, acc. to *Euripides' *Bacchae*, already old) to that of the *Epigoni, i.e. seven full generations. He was a pivotal figure in the Theban plays of *Sophocles and Euripides, and is presented by *Pindar as an outstanding interpreter of the will of *Zeus.

A tradition links Tiresias closely to the Theban legendary aristocracy, making him a descendant of one of the Spartoi. He was blinded because he caught sight of *Athena bathing: his mother Chariclo was a favourite of the goddess, and he was with her at the time. At her entreaty, Athena granted Tiresias the gift of prophecy (see DIVINATION, *Greek*) in compensation.

Acc. to the pseudo-Hesiodic *Melampodia*, the blinding and the gift of prophecy came from *Hera and Zeus respectively: the goddess was displeased because Tiresias said that women enjoyed sexual intercourse more than men. The gods had asked his opinion, as he was in an excellent position to give an accurate assessment, having been both man and woman: Tiresias had wounded copulating snakes on Mt. Cyllene in Arcadia and been turned into a woman; later, he saw them in action again and was turned back into a man.

*Callimachus locates the blinding of Tiresias on Mt. *Helicon, and it is at the base of the Helicon massif, at the spring Tilphossa, that Tiresias met his death. He was leading the Cadmeans from Thebes after its capture by the Epigoni, and died from drinking the water of the spring. He was buried near by.

Tissaphernēs. Having suppressed Pissuthnes' revolt, he succeeded him as *satrap of *Sardis (*c*.413 BC), receiving overall authority in western Anatolia. Instructed to collect tribute from the Greek cities, he interfered in the *Peloponnesian War, but, despite treaty-negotiations, active co-operation with Sparta soon dwindled (some blamed *Alcibiades' influence). *Cyrus' (2) arrival in 407 sidelined Tissaphernes—and the war prospered. He took revenge by accusing Cyrus of plotting against *Artaxerxes (2) II (404), disputing control of Asiatic Greek cities after Cyrus had cleared himself and resumed office, and denouncing Cyrus' insurrectionary plans in 401. Prominent at *Cunaxa and in the ensuing weeks (he negotiated with Cyrus' Greek generals and then murdered them at a meeting summoned to clarify and resolve mutual suspicions), he became Cyrus' effective successor in Anatolia. A demand for tribute from Ionia prompted Spartan intervention (400/399). His evasive military response and habit of diverting the Spartans against *Pharnabazus finally undermined his previously considerable credit with the king, perhaps even before *Agesilaus defeated his forces at Sardis (395). Invited to Phrygia, he was arrested in his bath and executed. A controversial figure, his behaviour after 399 is probably that of a deceiver whose bluff has been called rather than of a would-be rebel.

Tītan, name inherited by *Hesiod for gods of the generation preceding the *Olympians. Only *Cronus had cult. Hesiod seems to have padded them out into a set of twelve including also: *Oceanus, Rheā, *Themis, Mnēmosynē, Tēthys.

Mythologically, it is no less important to have former gods (Titans) than to have former people (e.g. Pelasgians) so that the current order may be defined, hence the battle between the two sides, the 'Titanomachy'. Hittite mythology too had its 'former gods', and the imprisonment of the Titans in Tartarus by *Zeus has its parallel (at least) in Marduk's treatment of the children of Tiamat in the Babylonian creation-epic, *Enuma Eliš*.

In *Orphic literature, the Titans destroyed the child *Dionysus as he played with toys and were blasted by Zeus' thunderbolt. We are, however, partly made out of their soot and as a result have a compulsive tendency to crime, to destroying the Dionysus within us, re-enacting the crimes of the Titans. Our word 'titanic' derives from the monstrous power and size of the creatures preceding the rule of Zeus.

Titus (Titus Flāvius Vespāsiānus), Roman emperor, AD 79–81, b. 39. He was the elder son of *Vespasian and was brought up at court along with *Britannicus, *Claudius' son. He had considerable physical and intellectual gifts, esp. in music and singing, and at one stage some viewed him as a possible second *Nero. He married the daughter of the praetorian *prefect of *Gaius (1) (Caligula); and she bore him a daughter, Iulia. After her death he married Marcia Furnilla, whom he later divorced. He spent his early career as a military tribune (see TRIBUNI MILITUM) in Germany and Britain, and it was probably in Lower Germany that he established his friendship with *Pliny the Elder, who later dedicated the *Natural History* to him. Although of only quaestorian rank, he joined his father in 67 in his mission to suppress the Jewish revolt, taking command of *legion XV Apollinaris and displaying great personal bravery. He was dispatched to convey Vespasian's congratulations to Galba, but turned back on hearing of the turmoil in Rome, pausing to consult the *oracle of Aphrodite at Paphos, whose allegedly encouraging response he brought to his father. He was closely involved in preparations for the Flavian bid for power which culminated on 1 July 69 when Vespasian was first acclaimed emperor by the troops in Egypt. Titus, however, remained in Judaea to take charge of the military operations and after the Flavian victory was created consul in his absence and given proconsular *imperium*. In 70 he captured *Jerusalem and was acclaimed *imperator* by his troops. His exploits on campaign were recorded by *Josephus, who had been befriended by the Flavians.

Hostile observers thought that Titus might use the affection of his troops to seize power for himself, since the soldiers in the east were demanding that he take them all back with him, but there is no sign of disloyalty to his father. Once back in Rome he celebrated a *triumph with Vespasian and was elevated to share his position, receiving the tribunician power (dated from 1 July 71), holding seven consulships with him, and sharing the office of *censor; he also became leader of the young men (*princeps iuventutis*) along with his brother, *Domitian. He was appointed praetorian prefect, a post normally held by *equestrians, and incurred hostility because of his ruthless suppression of the alleged conspiracy of Caecina Alienus and Eprius Marcellus. He was also disliked for his liaison with Berenice, whom he had met in Judaea and who came to Rome in 75, where she probably remained until 79.

Titus succeeded smoothly after Vespasian's death in 79, and belied the fears of some by the quality of his administration. He ended,

however unwillingly, his affair with Berenice, banished informers, and refused to accept treason charges. He declined to put any senator to death or confiscate property, and had a courteous relationship with the senate. Titus once remarked, on observing that he had benefited no one all day, 'Friends, I have lost a day.' He dedicated the *Colosseum begun by Vespasian, built baths, and provided lavish public spectacles. He reacted energetically to alleviate the natural disasters which occurred during his reign, the eruption of *Vesuvius in 79 and a serious fire and plague in Rome in 80. There were rumours that Titus' relationship with his brother Domitian was sometimes strained and even that he was poisoned, but he probably died from natural causes (81). He was remembered with affection as the 'delight and darling of the human race', though *Cassius Dio shrewdly commented that had he lived longer his regime might not have been judged so successful.

toga The toga was the principal garment of the free-born Roman man. It was usually made of undyed light wool, but for mourning was of dark wool, and, for children of high birth and the holders of high office, it had a *purple *prae-texta* border along its upper edge. A decorated version worn by victorious commanders in triumphal processions, the *toga picta*, was made of purple wool and gold thread. In shape the toga was a very large semicircle, a single piece of cloth. It was worn without a fastening and the wearer had to keep his left arm crooked to support its voluminous drapery.

As a result of Roman conquests the toga spread to some extent into the western provinces, but in the east it never replaced the Greek rectangular mantle, the *hīmation* or *pallium*. Its increased size and cost caused it to decline among ordinary Romans. See DRESS.

tolerance See INTOLERANCE, INTELLECTUAL AND RELIGIOUS.

topos, a standard form of rhetorical argumentation or a variably expressible literary commonplace. In classical rhetoric, *inventio* helps the orator to find elements of persuasion: *topoi* or *locī* are both the places where such elements (esp. plausible argumentative patterns) lurk, and also those patterns themselves; if universally applicable they can be called *locī commūnēs* ('commonplaces'). They are the habitual tools of ordinary thought but can also be studied and technically applied. No two *rhetors provide the same catalogue, but some of the more familiar *topoi* include arguments *ad hominem* or *ā fortiōrī*, from *etymology, from antecedents or effects.

See COMMUNES LOCI; PROGYMNASMATA.

torch-race, a spectacular ritual race, normally a relay, in which fire was taken from one altar to another. Most of the evidence comes from Athens, where lexicographers say three torch-races were held, at the *Panathenaea, the Hēphaestēa, and the Promēthēa (see PROMETHEUS); three more are in fact attested before the end of the 4th cent., for *Pan, for *Bendis (on horseback—a great novelty), and for *Nemesis of Rhamnus. It was the form of ritual activity most distinctively associated with the *epheboi, a matchless competitive display of dexterity and speed.

torture at Athens and under the Roman republic was normally thought inappropriate for citizens. It might be used on slaves (see SLAVERY) and perhaps on foreigners, e.g. prisoners of war. Slaves might be tortured in order to extract confessions of their own guilt or evidence against other persons (the unreliability of this second kind of evidence seems to have been recognized in practice at Athens). At Rome the evidence of the tortured was not *testimōnium*. Evidence under torture by slaves was not accepted against their own masters, except in such matters as treason and sacrilege, as with the Catilinarian conspirators (see SERGIUS CATILINA). Augustus extended these exceptions to include *adultery in certain situations but preserved the letter of the principle by having the slaves sold to a representative of the public. A master might prefer to free slaves liable to torture, and perhaps that is why we first hear of the torture of free men of humble status under the Principate. But we also find occasionally the torture of men of status suspected of conspiracy—a practice with a long history (e.g. *Philotas in the reign of *Alexander (2) the Great).

tourism (see TRAVEL). Well-known Greek tourists include *Solon, said by *Herodotus to have visited Egypt and Lydia 'for the sake of seeing', and Herodotus himself. Sea-borne *trade and sightseeing were surely companions from an early date. A genre of Greek travel literature arose by the 3rd cent.; the only fully preserved work of this type is *Pausanias (3). Under Rome ancient sightseeing came into its own. A papyrus of 112 BC gives instructions to prepare for a Roman senator's visit to the *Fayūm,

including titbits for the crocodiles; the colossi of Memnon (actually Amenophis III) and other pharaonic monuments are encrusted with Greek and Latin graffiti. Greece too was a firm favourite. Roman tourists were rich, their numbers limited; they might combine sightseeing (artworks, monuments, natural phenomena) with overseas study (as with *Cicero), thermal cures, and visits to *sanctuaries. See PILGRIMAGE (CHRISTIAN).

trade, Greek Exchange in some form has probably existed since the emergence of the first properly human social groups. Trade, whether local, regional, or international, is a much later development. It is a certain inference from the extant records in Linear B script that the Mycenaean palace-economy knew all three main forms of commerce (see MYCENAEAN AGE CIVILIZATION; MYCENAEAN LANGUAGE), and a reasonable guess that a considerable portion of the long-distance carrying trade was in the hands of specialized professional *traders. But whether that trade was 'administered' or 'free-enterprise' is impossible to say. It is one sign of the economic recession experienced by the Greek world between c.1200 and 800 BC that in this Dark Age regional and international trade dwindled to vanishing-point; the few known professional traders were typically men of non-Greek, esp. *Phoenician, origin.

In *Homer's *Odyssey* (bk. 8) the sea-battered hero finds his way at last to *Scheria, a never-never land set somewhere in the golden west, only to be abused by a young Phaeacian aristocrat for looking like a sordidly mercenary merchant skipper rather than a gentleman amateur athlete. *Hesiod, composing perhaps about the same time (c.700) in inland, rural *Boeotia, was prepared to concede that a moderately prosperous peasant farmer might load the surplus of the corn-crop produced by himself and his small workforce into his own modest boat and dispose of it down the nearby coast during the dead season of the agricultural year immediately after the harvest. But to be a full-time trader was no more acceptable to Hesiod than to Homer's Phaeacian aristocrat. Each in his way was objecting to the development of professional trading and traders.

This prejudice issued from a world dominated by landed aristocrats. It was quite all right for a Greek aristocrat to visit his peers in other communities, then just acquiring the novel constitutional form of the *polis, bearing gifts of richly woven garments or finely wrought metalwork, and to come home laden with comparable or even more lavish counter-gifts. It was quite another matter to spend most of the recognized sailing season (late March to late September) plying the Mediterranean with a mixed cargo of, say, perfume flasks from *Corinth, hides from *Euboea, salt fish from the Black (*Euxine) Sea, and wine-amphorae from *Chios, making only a humble living and precluded from participating in the military and political activities that defined the *status of leader of his *polis*. Such trading was considered an occupation suitable only for the lower orders of Greek society, the dependants (possibly unfree) of a big landlord.

Yet the significance of traders in the early *polis* era of Homer and Hesiod must not be confused with the significance of trade, esp. long-distance sea-borne commerce. Without the latter there would have been no opening from the Aegean to both east (e.g. the multinational *emporion* at Al Mina on the Orontes) and west (notably *Pithecusae), beginning in the half-century from 825 to 775, no movement of *colonization to south Italy, Sicily, or the Black (*Euxine) Sea, no knowledge of other, non-Greek cultures and thus no *alphabet—and so, maybe, no Homer or Hesiod. By 600 the status of traders may have improved, with the development of purpose-built sail-driven, round-hulled merchantmen (see SHIPS), the creation of institutions and techniques designed to facilitate multinational commerce, and the establishment of permanent *emporia* in Egypt and Etruria.

*Naucratis in the Nile delta was founded c. 630 by Greek traders from western Asia Minor, the adjacent Greek islands, and *Aegina, under the auspices of the pharaoh Psammetichus. In return for Greek oil, wine, and luxury goods, the Greek traders of Naucratis received Egyptian corn, metals, and slaves, from which exchange the Egyptian treasury derived extra value in taxes. Permanent transnational market-centres and ports of trade were thus established under governmental direction, linking economies of dissimilar type. Soon Naucratis had an Italian counterpart at Graviscae (see TARQUINII) in Etruria, the happy hunting-ground of one Sostratus of Aegina.

This Sostratus specialized in the run between Etruria and the Aegean by way of the haulway (*diolkos*) built across the isthmus of Corinth c. 600. He was a citizen, literate (in addition to his dedication to *Apollo at Graviscae he used personalized merchant-marks on the pots he carried), and an independent entrepreneur who presumably owned his own merchant ship (or ships). Perhaps he knew some Etruscan, as the Phocaean and Samian merchants who traded further westwards to the south of France and Spain knew the local Celtic languages and, as surviving business letters on lead attest, employed locals in their import–export businesses.

By the middle of the 5th cent. the place of Al Mina, Naucratis, and Graviscae had been taken by Athens' newly developed port city of *Piraeus. It was the Athenians' victory at *Salamis that enabled the development of Piraeus into a commercial as well as military harbour. A century later, *Isocrates hailed its creation: 'for Athens established Piraeus as a market in the centre of Hellas—a market of such abundance that the articles which it is difficult to obtain, one here, one there, from the rest of the world, all these it is easy to obtain from Athens.' This testimony is corroborated by archaeology and echoed by writers as diverse as *Thucydides (2), the *Old Oligarch, and Athenian comic poets. As early as 421, we learn from *Eupolis' *Maricas*, the characteristic institution of the *maritime loan had been developed to finance long-distance trade, esp. in the staple necessity, corn, on the regular large-scale importation of which Athens had come to depend both economically and (since it was the poor majority of citizens who mainly benefited) politically.

During her 5th-cent. empire Athens, thanks to her permanently commissioned fleet of *triremes, was able to suppress *piracy. Loss of empire was bad for Aegean Greek trade generally, and bad for Athens' access to corn and her collecting of taxes and dues on shipping and goods. During the 4th cent. a series of measures was enacted by Athens to compensate for loss of military power. A combination of the stick (penalties for residents who contracted loans on cargoes of corn bound elsewhere than for Piraeus, or for not offloading a certain minimum percentage of a cargo there, and so on) and the carrot (establishment for the benefit of Athens-based traders of new specialized maritime courts; granting permission to foreign traders to set up on Attic soil *sanctuaries for their native gods—*Isis and Astarte) was employed to good effect.

See also MARKETS.

trade, Roman The central issue for historians, is how to characterize the scale and importance of trade and commerce in the overall economy of the Roman empire. Some emphasize how different, and essentially backward, the Roman *economy was in comparison to the modern. They point to the Roman élite's apparent contempt for commerce. The primacy of *agriculture cannot be denied, and the Roman *agricultural writers, with the large landowner in mind, betray both very little interest in *markets and an aversion to risk, which did not inspire entrepreneurial experiments. Factories in the modern sense did not exist in the ancient world (see INDUSTRY). Cities did not grow up as centres of manufacturing; they are better represented as centres of consumption (see URBANISM). The cost and difficulty of transport, esp. over land, are claimed to have made it uneconomic to trade over long distances anything other than luxury products. Basic goods, such as *wine, *olive oil, and corn, also *pottery of all kinds, can be shown to have been carried in large quantities over long distances. But, it is argued, something other than the free-market mechanism is at work here. First, there was the considerable circulation of goods within the extensive households of the rich, from their estates to their town houses, to their retinues and clients. Further, staples could be exchanged in large quantities as gifts between members of the élite. Examples can be identified at all periods. The circulation of goods within the household of the emperor is the same phenomenon writ large. Secondly, and more importantly, it is claimed that the movement of staples was primarily an act of redistribution, directed by the central government, and on a smaller scale by local communities, to ensure the supply of essentials to the large cities, and to maintain the Roman armies, precisely because the private sector was not up to meeting needs on such a scale (see FOOD SUPPLY).

A different model has been proposed. The Roman aristocracy did on the whole keep a distance from direct involvement in trade, but even they benefited from its profits through intermediaries. Besides, beyond Rome, it is much less clear that local élites shared the same distaste for trade, with investments, often managed by their *freedmen, in potteries, *mines, *textile production, and the like. The landowners needed markets for their products, but were able to affect a lack of interest in trade, because the whole process, often starting with a contract to gather the crop, lay in the hands of *negotiatores. The landowner was provided with a certain return, while the *negotiator* had to arrange the trade and to take the risks. The number of *shipwrecks in the Mediterranean

recorded for the period 100 BC to AD 300 is much larger than for either the preceding period or the Dark Age; this suggests a level of operation which was not to be reached again until the high Renaissance. The greatest spur to the development of this trade was the creation of a fully monetarized economy throughout the empire (see MONEY). Barter continued to exist; but it is clear from Egyptian papyri that the use of money in transactions was the norm. *Strabo went out of his way to note the lack of coin among the Dalmatians, as a characteristic of barbarian peoples. The availability of coin varied between areas and over time. So *bankers who could provide *credit to facilitate deals were essential. The empire did not see the growth of large international banks; but at the local level money-lenders were the key to exchanges both large and small. Some historians see in the spread of the use of money the creation of a Roman unified 'world economy'. This is an exaggeration. The empire consisted of many regional economies at different stages of development, which linked up with each other in ways which changed over time.

At the regional level regular *markets were vital. They are found throughout the empire and were at least as important to the peasant as to the large landowner. The existence of these markets was strictly regulated. The senate had to be petitioned for permission to hold markets; many such requests came from large landowners who wished to hold markets on their estates. The reason for the control was probably to limit competition with well-established markets in the local towns. This suggests that the volume of trade in the countryside was limited. There are signs that some products circulated largely within regions (the distribution of Roman *lamps, which were traded over surprising distances, nevertheless reveals several broad regional patterns of trade).

At the other end of the scale came the huge cities, above all Rome. These constituted enormous markets. Much is made of the state-sponsored system for supplying Rome with corn. However, state corn met no more than a portion of the city's annual needs. The rest had to be supplied by the free market. Furthermore, the importation of the state corn depended upon private traders, who in times of crisis had to be offered considerable incentives to involve themselves in the trade. Monte Testaccio, the dump of Spanish oil amphorae, behind the port on the Tiber in Rome, is testimony to the enormous trade in oil (estimated at some 23 million kg. per year). The annual consumption of wine in the city has been put at between 1 and 1.8 million hectolitres (22–39.6 gal.). For much of the empire all this was provided by the free market. The city of Rome was an enormous stimulus to trade.

The expansion of the empire itself could open up major new markets to be exploited. Best known is the large market among the Gauls for Italian wine, from the west coast of Italy. However, it is easy to exaggerate the effect of these new markets on the agrarian economy of Italy. There were transformations, but they were largely confined to coastal regions within easy reach of ports, and they were short-lived. By the 1st cent. AD these regions had to compete with expanding trade in wine from Spain and southern Gaul. See AMPHORAE, ROMAN.

Because pottery survives on archaeological sites, its importance in trade can be exaggerated. However, the industrial scale of production of *terra sigillata* (see POTTERY, ROMAN) in Gaul presupposes something more than a local market. Pottery was not often the primary cargo of ships, but it was often a part-cargo and might be an important commodity for the return leg of voyages, whose primary concern was the transport of more valuable goods.

Trade was carried on beyond the limits of the Roman empire. Most notable was the trade in luxuries, spices, *ivories (see ELEPHANTS), etc. beyond the Red Sea with the east coast of *Africa and India. A Greek papyrus records one such transaction, involving nard, ivory, and textiles to a value of over 130 talents. Some of the large ships on the eastern run could carry up to 150 such cargoes. However, the handbook from the 1st cent. AD ('The Voyage round the Red Sea'; see PERIPLOI) shows that although the primary interest was in these very valuable goods, shippers were also on the look-out for more mundane staples to fill their holds.

traders in the ancient Mediterranean relied heavily on sea transport, reflecting terrain and the location of communities. *Plato describes the Greeks as huddled round the sea 'like ants and frogs round a pond'; his likening of traders (*emporoi*) to migrating summer birds reminds us of the realities of the Mediterranean *climate and the limitations of contemporary shipping, closing the seas for between six and ten months. Although in the Roman west extensive use was made of river and eventually even road transport, the primacy of sea trade was never challenged. Traders were liable to be marginalized as 'not belonging'. No formal bond existed between a *polis and those carrying on its trade: traders transporting goods to and from Athens were not necessarily Athenian citizens. Evidence for rich traders is slight. The norm seems to have been 'tramp trading': independent shipowners sailing wherever cargoes were to be bought and sold. Though traders might be of low status, maritime trade was crucially important: not necessarily in crude quantitative terms (as an engine of economic growth) but by way of redistributing essential raw materials (metals), alleviating temporary shortages of corn, and disseminating luxury goods. In addition, Classical Athens exceptionally depended on annual corn imports, made possible by a combination of *sea power and imperial tribute (with corresponding problems in the 4th cent.). The city of Rome was similarly exceptional, drawing as of right on the resources of empire to feed a massive urban population. Although the status of those actually involved in trade was low (senators were forbidden by law from owning a ship that could carry more than 300 *amphorae), there was probable élite involvement through agents. As provision of corn became more of a political preoccupation, and emperors eventually shouldered the burden of feeding the urban *plebs*, so traders came increasingly under state control. The *prefect of the corn supply regulated associations of shipowners, via the award of civic privileges. See CLUBS, ROMAN; FOOD SUPPLY; SHIPS; TRADE.

tragedy, Greek Tragedy, one of the most influential literary forms that originated in Greece, is esp. associated with Athens in the 5th cent. BC. All but one of the surviving plays date from the 5th cent., but these represent only a tiny sample of the vast body of material produced from the late 6th cent. onwards: thirteen new tragedies in a normal year in the latter part of the 5th cent. The popularity of the dramatic festivals at Athens attracted interest in other cities, with the result that performances of tragedy rapidly became common elsewhere, and what began as a medium reflecting the life of a particular community acquired universal appeal in the Greek-speaking world. By the end of the 3rd cent., Roman translations and adaptations began to extend the range of its influence still further.

1(a). The Dramatic Festivals in the Fifth Century It was in Attica that tragedy acquired its definitive form, and it is from Attica that we have almost everything that we know about it.

From the end of the 6th cent., if not before, tragedies were performed in the Athenian spring festival of Dionysus Eleuthereus, the City Dionysia. This remained the main context for tragic performances, although they occurred also at the Rural Dionysia, and (probably in the 430s) a competition for two tragedians each with two tragedies was introduced into the *Lenaea. In all these festivals the tragic performances were one feature of a programme of events which, at the City Dionysia, included processions, sacrifice, libations, the parade of war orphans, performances of dithyramb and comedy, and a final assembly to review the conduct of the festival.

At the City Dionysia three tragedians generally competed each with three tragedies and a satyr-play. In charge of the festival was the archon (see ARCHONTES), who chose the three tragedians. He also appointed the three rich men who bore the expenses of training and costuming the choruses (see CHOREGIA). Originally the tragedian acted in his own play, but later we find tragedians employing actors, as well as the appointment of protagonists (see 1 (b)) by the state. In a preliminary ceremony called the *proagon it seems that each tragedian appeared with his actors on a platform to announce the themes of his plays. Ten judges were chosen, one from each of the tribes (see PHYLAI), in a complex process involving an element of chance. The victorious poet was crowned with ivy in the theatre.

1(b). Form and Performance Some features of the tragic performances are best understood if set in the context of Greek festival practice. The notion of performers in athletics and the arts competing in honour of the gods was familiar throughout the Greek world (see AGONES). Individuals entered for athletic events like running (see STADIUM) or *boxing or for musical contests as solo instrumentalists, and groups participated in many forms of song and dance or in team activities such as relay races. In the City Dionysia the emphasis was on competition by choruses, whether for dithyramb, tragedy and satyr-play, or comedy; thus despite the novelty of dramatic representation there was a strong element of continuity with established practice, and the competition for the best leading actor (*prōtagōnistēs*), introduced in the mid-5th cent., can be compared with competitions among solo musicians or *rhapsodes.

The importance of the choral element is shown by the fact that the main responsibility of each of the financial sponsors was the recruiting and maintenance, costuming and training of the chorus, while the city paid the leading actors and the poets. Given the competitive nature of the events, it was important to have rules governing (e.g.) the choice of poets, the allocation of leading actors, and the procedures for judging; the apparent limitation on the number of speaking actors (often called the 'three-actor rule') may have been less a matter of strict regulation than a practical consequence of using *masks. In masked drama it is natural to confine the speaking in any one scene to a limited number of parts so that the audience can tell where each voice is coming from, and since the masks (with wigs attached) completely covered the actors' heads, one performer could easily play several different roles. All the surviving plays were evidently composed to be performed (with minor, mainly musical, exceptions) by not more than three speakers at a time, and the doubling of roles was certainly standard. Dramatists may well have exploited the effects to be gained from giving two related leading parts to the same actor (e.g. Deianira and *Heracles in Sophocles' *Women of Trachis* or *Pentheus and Agave in Euripides' *Bacchae*). Non-speaking roles for attendants, bodyguards, trains of captives, etc. were a different matter—powerful visual effects could be achieved by bringing groups on stage—and occasional extra solo singers or supplementary choruses might also be used. See also THEATRE STAGING, GREEK.

The metrical patterns of the surviving plays show that the typical 5th-cent. tragedy was formally much more complex than most modern drama. There was a strong musical element which bears some comparison with modern opera, most noticeably the sequences of song (and dance) performed by a chorus on its own which mark a break of some kind in the action and cover any necessary (usually short) lapse of time. Audiences could expect to see about five such performances within a single day, with the chorus in the orchestra as the centre of attention. Then there were the sung exchanges, or exchanges of alternating speech and recitative or song, between the chorus and one or more of the actors: these belonged to the same time-frame as the spoken dialogue and were used to intensify emotion or give a scene a ritual dimension, as in a shared lament or song of celebration. Singing by individual actors became steadily more important; Euripides was famous for his monodies, but there were striking examples from earlier tragedy. The musical accompaniment was provided by a player on a double pipe (*aulos*), who often appears in vase-paintings of dramatic scenes.

Virtuoso performance was not only musical: the speeches and dialogues in iambic trimeters (see METRE, GREEK) intended for spoken delivery were carefully designed to have an emotional impact, whether in the narrating of shocking off-stage events, the presentation of sharply conflicting points of view in formal debate scenes, or the cut and thrust of alternating lines or pairs of lines (*stichomythia*). All the surviving plays are designed to give the leading actor a series of 'big speeches', in which to show off his talent as an interpreter of character and feeling.

The physical circumstances of Greek theatres —open-air auditoria with a more or less central dancing-space for the chorus—clearly influenced acting style and dramatic design. The sense of the watching community must have been strong in open-air daylight performances in front of large crowds, and the constant presence of a choral group as witnesses to the action contributed to the public character of the events portrayed. This was not drama on an intimate scale: it depended on large effects of gesture and movement that could be 'read' by very diverse audiences, and the evidence suggests that it had popular appeal. The comic poets would not have spent so much time parodying past tragedies if tragedy had not meant something important to their audiences.

1(c). Subject-Matter and Interpretation All but one of the plots of the extant tragedies are drawn from heroic myth, familiar to 5th-cent. audiences from epic poetry and past tragic performances. Aeschylus' *Persians* (472) deals with events of 480 (see PERSIAN WARS), but these are refracted through a Persian setting, and no Greeks are named. The normal choice of material was from the heroic past, handled with no sign of antiquarian interest. Epic story-telling by rhapsodes must have been a shared experience, and many of the heroes continued to be deeply implicated in Greek life through their worship in cult. It is no accident that Athenian tragedy often deals with heroes who were the object of cult in Attica: *Theseus, *Heracles, *Aias (1), *Erechtheus and his family, *Iphigenia, *Oedipus.

*Plato called *Homer 'first of the tragic poets', and it is true that his poetry, esp. the *Iliad*, offered tragic interpretations of events, but it was from the *Epic Cycle that tragedians took most of their plots. All the same, their plays were relevant to the problems of the Athenian *polis*. Stories of intra-familial conflict like that of Oedipus could be re-cast to lay stress on the tensions between family and city, or the tale of *Jason (1) and *Medea could be shaped in such a way as to make an Athenian audience look closely at the categories of citizen and foreigner, male and female, civilized and barbarian as defined in their society.

The study of ritual practice and of ritual patterns in drama has helped to redefine the questions that it is appropriate to ask about the gods in Attic tragedy. As in epic, the gods are everywhere, but the plays are not about theology, and critics are less ready than they used to be to identify the religious beliefs of the individual dramatists. Even a more than usually god-focused play like Euripides' *Heracles* asks questions rather than finding answers, combining sceptical challenges to divine morality with aetiological reminders of Attic *hero-cult. But it would be wrong to underestimate the religious intensity of plays like Aeschylus' *Agamemnon*, Sophocles' *Oedipus at Colonus*, or Euripides' *Bacchae*; as always, it is through the use of language that the plays achieve their deepest effects. Existential issues of time and mortality, and questions that apply to individuals as well as to communities are strongly represented in tragedy alongside questions relating to contemporary society. This must have been an important factor in the spread of the medium beyond Attica and even outside the Greek-speaking world.

2(a). The Formation of a Repertoire Interest in Attic drama outside Athens can be traced to an early stage in its history: Aeschylus was invited to Sicily to compose a drama celebrating the foundation of the city of Aetna in 476/5 and returned to Sicily late in his life. Euripides had links with *Macedon, and there he died. But the most extensive range of evidence comes from the end of the 5th cent. onwards and is seen in theatre-building in different parts of the Greek world and in the production in southern Italy and Sicily of large quantities of painted pottery showing tragic scenes. This evidence needs to be combined with what is known from Attica about revivals of plays at the Rural *Dionysia (beginning in the 5th cent.) and eventually in the city as well. (Revivals of Aeschylus' plays had exceptionally been allowed in the city since his death.) The fact that revivals became popular need not mean that tragedy was in decline: it is hard to imagine an acting profession developing without a repertoire, and the wider the demand from different communities, whether local audiences in the Attic *demes or cities outside Attica eager to build a theatrical tradition, the greater must have been the incentive to re-perform successful plays.

There seems to have been no shortage of new writing, however, and the competition for new plays continued for centuries. Many names are known of tragic poets from other cities who came to Athens to compete. The fact that only a very small proportion of the most celebrated tragedies has survived may have more to do with the constraints of the school curriculum in late antiquity and the early Byzantine period than with the intrinsic quality of some of the lost material.

None the less, as tragedy became an 'international' medium, changes were taking place. Developments noted by Aristotle were the increasing influence and prestige of actors at the expense of dramatists, the habit of some tragedians of writing plays for reading rather than performance, and the growing tendency to use choral songs unconnected with the action of a particular play.

2(b). Actors and Festivals Growing professionalism must have been an important factor as the influence of tragedy began to spread, and it may have been helped at an early stage by the fact that the crafts of play-writing and producing, and of acting, often ran in families. It was actors who had the best opportunities of becoming well known in the Greek cities; as star performers they could command large fees for performances, and it was evidently they who took the initiative in putting on revivals. The organization of actors from the 3rd cent. onwards into powerful regionally defined guilds (see DIONYSUS, ARTISTS OF) gave them protection, immunities, and privileges as well as better access to the patronage of rulers and cities. This is the decisive development for the history of performance in Hellenistic and Roman times, and it linked tragic performers with comic actors, rhapsodes, and musicians of all kinds. Along with the growth in the power and influence of performers went the development of *festivals.

2(c). Tragedy in Adaptation and Translation Greek tragedy first reached Roman audiences through the plays of *Ennius, *Accius, and *Pacuvius; in the 1st cent. AD the tragedies of *Seneca the Younger offered a new reading of the same models, and it was through Seneca that the playwrights of the Renaissance made their first contact with the Greeks. The surviving Greek plays have had a profound influence on later literature and culture.

tragedy, Latin *Varro and *Pomponius Atticus dated the first performance of a Latin tragedy to 240 BC at the *Ludi Romani. Performances continued at this and other public festivals down to the end of the 1st cent. BC. Celebrations of temple dedications and funerals of aristocrats also provided occasions of performance. In 240 new plays were still being staged at the Athenian festivals of *Dionysus (see DIONYSIA; LENAEA), but the practice had grown up of reviving each year a number of old ones. At Rome adaptations of the better-known Attic works were offered at first under the names of the original authors. The makers of the adaptations sometimes took part in the performance of their own works.

Roman theatres probably never had much space in front of the stage platform for elaborate choral dancing. The Greek choral odes did not disappear, but the volume of singing and dancing assigned to the chorus was sharply reduced. The speeches of the heroic personages on the other hand were given much more musical accompaniment.

Themes from Roman legend and history were taken up by the 3rd cent. and developed within the dramatic structure which had arisen from the fusion of Attic text and local theatrical tradition. *Accius presented Tarquinius Superbus (see REX) talking with his councillors, much as *Aeschylus had dramatized the dialogue between Darius I's Queen Atossa and the chorus in *Persians*.

The 3rd- and 2nd-cent. plays remained popular at public festivals. The *Thyestes* composed by *Varius Rufus for performance at the festival celebrating Octavian's victory at *Actium (see AUGUSTUS) pleased the young, and *Ovid won praise for his *Medea*.

Composing for public festivals continued in the 1st cent. AD. Some men preferred, however, to compose poems they called tragedies for recitation to small groups in private. The eight extant plays of *Seneca (2) the Younger are each divided into five units separated by choral odes. Argument rages as to what kind of audience he sought.

training, military See MILITARY TRAINING (GREEK); VEGETIUS.

Trajan (Marcus Ulpius Trāiānus), Roman emperor AD 98–117, was born probably in 53 at Italica in *Baetica the son of a distinguished consular under the Flavians. His long period of service as a military tribune included a spell in *Syria during the governorship of his father c.75 (see TRIBUNI MILITUM). While legionary *legate in Spain he marched against the governor of Upper Germany, who revolted against Domitian in 89. He was consul in 91, and then having been appointed by *Nerva in 97 as governor of Upper Germany, was adopted by that emperor, who faced growing discontent among the praetorians, as his son and co-ruler, and became *consul ordinarius* for the second time in 98. After Nerva's death Trajan first inspected the armies in Pannonia and Moesia, and on his arrival in Rome re-established strict discipline by disposing of the praetorian mutineers against Nerva.

As emperor his personal conduct was restrained and unassuming, qualities also exhibited by his wife Pompeia Plotina, who from *c.*105 had the title *Augusta* (see AUGUSTUS, AUGUSTA AS TITLES). He was courteous and friendly to individual senators, and treated the senate with respect, avoiding confiscations of property and executions. Pliny's speech (*Panegyric*) delivered in 100, the year of Trajan's third consulship, gives a senatorial appreciation of his excellent qualities. Trajan intervened to help children who had been maltreated by their fathers, and free-born children exposed at birth, and made further exemptions from the inheritance tax. He required that candidates for public office in Rome should have at least one-third of their capital invested in Italian land, and he perpetuated the alimentary scheme, probably instituted by Nerva, through which sustenance was provided for poor children in Italian communities. Trajan undertook many utilitarian and celebratory building projects, including baths, a canal to prevent the river *Tiber from flooding, a new harbour near *Ostia (*Portus), the via Traiana which extended the via Appia from Beneventum to *Brundisium, a forum and basilica in Rome dedicated in 112 (see FORUM TRAIANI), and a column depicting the *Dacian Wars. He was generous to the Roman people, extending the corn doles, paying out enormous largess partly financed by the *booty of the Dacian Wars and the treasure of *Decebalus, and providing lavish spectacles; to celebrate the Dacian victory he gave games on 123 days in which 10,000 gladiators fought.

The correspondence between Trajan and Pliny, who had been specially appointed to resolve administrative and financial problems in the communities in *Bithynia, shows the kind of attitude towards provincial administration that the emperor had inspired in his officials, even if the emperor's replies were not directly composed by Trajan himself. They exhibit justice, fairness, and personal probity: 'You know very well that it is my established rule not to obtain respect for my name either from people's fears and anxieties or from charges of treason.' The letters about the treatment of Christians (see CHRISTIANITY) illustrate the fair-minded attitude of the emperor and his governor.

Experienced in military command, Trajan took a personal interest in the troops, whom he described as 'my excellent and most loyal fellow soldiers', in instructions issued to governors about the soldiers' testatory privileges. Two new *legions were formed, both named after himself—II Trajanic Brave and XXX Ulpian Victorious, and on campaign the emperor took personal charge, marching at the head of his men. Trajan's reign was marked by two great wars of conquest, in Dacia and *Parthia. His invasion in 101 of Decebalus' Dacian kingdom beyond the Danube (see DANUVIUS) could be justified on the grounds that the accommodation with the Dacians reached by Domitian was unsatisfactory to long-term Roman interests, and that Decebalus' power was increasing. However, his principal motive may have been to win military glory. Trajan crossed the Danube at Lederata and marched NE. The Dacians resisted with great determination and courage and inflicted heavy losses on the Romans in a pitched battle. In 102 Trajan resumed campaigning and by threatening Decebalus' capital at Sarmizegethusa forced the king to accept a peace by which he surrendered some territory and became a vassal of the Romans. Leaving garrisons behind, Trajan returned to Rome where he celebrated a triumph, accepted the title *Dācicus*, and issued coins depicting the defeat of Dacia. In 105 the emperor renewed the war, ostensibly because Decebalus was contravening the treaty, and crossed the Danube on a bridge built by *Apollodorus (3) at Drobeta. After Sarmizegethusa had fallen to the Romans, Decebalus killed himself, and his treasure was captured. Coins now proclaimed 'the capture of Dacia', and the area was turned into a Roman province with a consular governor and two legions. On the site of a legionary fortress about 30 km. (18 mi.) west of Sarmizegethusa a new colony was established, which served as the capital of the province. At Adamklissi a community called *Municipium Tropaeum Traiani* was set up, and a trophy was dedicated to *Mars the Avenger by Trajan in 107/8. In Rome, Trajan's column celebrated the emperor's prowess and the glorious achievement of the Roman army; his ashes were to be deposited in its base.

Expansion continued with the annexation of Arabia in 106 by the governor of Syria. Elsewhere in the east, contacts between Rome and Parthia, the only sophisticated empire on the edge of Roman territory, had been characterized by diplomatic rapport and avoidance of serious warfare during the previous 150 years. The kingdom of Armenia, between the two empires on the upper *Euphrates, though sometimes prey to Parthian influence and intervention, was generally ruled by a Roman nominee. Trajan took exception to the attempts of King Osroes to establish control of Armenia, and refusing all diplomatic advances arrived in Antioch early in 114. Without major opposition he incorporated Armenia into the empire and then launched an attack on Parthia through Mesopotamia while the Parthian king was beset with civil strife. In the campaigns of 115–116, the Romans crossed the Tigris into Adiabene and then advanced down the Euphrates, capturing the Parthian capital, Ctesiphon. Trajan was acclaimed *imperator, and accepted the title *Parthicus*. At least one new province (Mesopotamia) was created; coins celebrated the 'capture of Parthia', and 'Armenia and Mesopotamia brought under the power of the Roman People'. The emperor advanced to the Persian Gulf, but his success proved transitory as serious uprisings occurred in the captured territory to the army's rear, and a major insurrection of the *Jews in the eastern provinces spread to Mesopotamia in 116. Trajan tried to contain the military situation, and a vassal king was imposed on the Parthians. However, as the situation remained precarious, Trajan decided to retreat. The vassal king proved short-lived, despite grandiloquent Roman coins proclaiming a 'king granted to the Parthians', and with his health declining Trajan decided to return to Italy; but in early August he died suddenly at Selinus. *Cassius Dio attributed Trajan's expansion in the east to a desire for glory, and this remains the most likely explanation for a man who had already achieved great military success. The policy was a disastrous failure, but criticism was muted because he was generally popular with senators. By 114 the appellation 'Best' (*Optimus*), which had appeared early in the reign, had become one of his official titles, and is recalled in the ritual acclamation of the senate—'May you be even luckier than Augustus and even better than Trajan'.

Trajan's Column (see TRAJAN). Honorific column dedicated in AD 113 as part of the *forum Traiani in Rome. It consists of a 28.9-m. (95-ft.)-tall column standing on a 6.2-m. (20-ft.)-high pedestal. An internal spiral staircase, illuminated by 40 slit-windows, connects a door in the SE side of the base with a balcony at the top. Trajanic coin motifs represented the monument topped by an imperial statue. The pedestal has sculptured reliefs of barbarian military equipment on its four sides, and an inscription. The shaft bears a helical band, 200 m. long and $c.0.85$–1.45 m. high ($656 \times 2^3/_4$–$4^3/_4$ ft.), carved into its outer face with reliefs depicting Trajan's Dacian Wars (101–102, 105–106; see DACIA).

Many details of the pedestal reliefs can be paralleled in the archaeological record. The helical frieze depicts the two Wars separated by a Victory and trophies, and divided up into campaigns consisting of linked scenes. Beyond this, planning of content and 'narrative' was minimal. Some historical events were depicted and Trajan's own *commentarii probably contributed, but most of the scenes follow the unspecific formulae of imperial propaganda-art. However, some key compositions are arranged on vertical axes which cut across the helix to aid the viewer's comprehension.

The sculptors worked up the spiral without laying out the composition ahead of them; they did not follow detailed cartoons and they had a wide degree of compositional freedom. Human figure-types were defined with artificial uniformity to indicate the status and ethnic identities of participants. Some expert advice on camp design was used in garbled form, but most military material was provided through empirical observation in Rome. Thus, the reliefs are important for their propaganda function and as a sculptural *tour de force*, but the spiral frieze cannot be employed as a historical document or as a primary source for military studies. The pedestal was employed as Trajan's mausoleum after 117.

Transalpine Gaul See GAUL (TRANSALPINE).

transhumance, a form of semi-nomadism in which pastoralists move their flocks over long distances between summer and winter pastures. In Roman Italy, where the Apennines favour transhumance, the practice is well attested from the late republic on, *Varro providing the best evidence, and was presumably facilitated by the peninsula's political unification, although its scale and the extent of the Roman state's involvement (beyond extracting pasture-dues from shepherds using the drove-roads) are problematic. See NOMADS.

translation Members of the Roman élite learned, read, and spoke Greek, competing with each other in their familiarity with Greek literature: *Porcius Cato (1) ostentatiously addressed a Greek audience in Latin, using a translator, but could easily have spoken in Greek. Latin literature may be said to begin with *Livius Andronicus' versions of Greek plays and of *Homer's *Odyssey* in native *Saturnian verse. The republican dramatists closely adapted Greek comedy and tragedy for the Roman people. Acc. to Aulus *Gellius, *Virgil 'translated' *Theocritus, *Hesiod, and Homer (the boundary between translation and imitation is, in practice, impossible to police). Knowledge of the Greek language aided the expansion of Roman power; e.g. *Cicero, himself an experienced translator (he produced a version of *Aratus' *Phaenomena*), sought a unified Graeco-Roman culture as the basis of an ordered polity, while standardization of Latin *grammar on the model of Greek helped to cement a language for empire. Public documents were translated into Greek, often with adjustment to the different conceptual worlds (so Augustus' *Res Gestae*). Some prominent Roman authors came from non-Latin-speaking municipalities, while *Ennius spoke three languages: Latin, Greek, and Oscan. Translation also encouraged Roman self-consciousness about Latin and its limitations, fuelling a sense of both inferiority and competition; so *Lucretius complains of the poverty of the language.

The Greeks of the Classical and Hellenistic periods, by contrast, seem to have been primarily monoglot (with exceptions like *Polybius or *Philodemus)—foreigners were barbaroi (see BARBARIAN), i.e. people who did not speak Greek (in this respect at least the Romans emerge as more urbane and civilized). Colonization (see COLONIZATION, GREEK and HELLENISTIC) and contact with the empires of Asia Minor must have created a need for translation, but *Herodotus used native interpreters for his knowledge of matters Persian (there were also Greek officials in high places), Egyptian, etc. Initially most Greeks showed scant interest in reading the great Roman authors. It was not until the 3rd cent. AD, apparently, that Greeks in the eastern empire, seeking employment in the Roman administration and needing Latin for competence in law, started to study Latin liter-

ary texts on any scale; a writer like Claudian of Alexandria would have studied the same syllabus in Egypt as someone educated in Italy (and there are practical bilingual textbooks from this period known as hermēneumata). See BILINGUALISM.

It was the Romans, not the Greeks, who conceptualized the process of translation, establishing the framework and norms of western translation practice until the end of the 18th cent. *Pliny the Younger recommends practice in translating between Latin and Greek for promoting verbal fluency and critical discernment. The canonical case against undue 'literalism' is put by *Horace and by *Cicero, who describes translating speeches by *Demosthenes (2) and *Aeschines (1) not word for word, but so as to retain style and impact; *Jerome gave the classic formulation: 'not word for word but sense for sense'.

Translation must be a matter of concern to all students of antiquity. It is often thought of as the substitution for a foreign word of a word of the same or similar meaning, on the model of a dictionary: *amor* 'means' love. Indeed translatability, the idea that alien cultural and linguistic systems can be made intelligible to us, lies at the root of humanistic inquiry (often in conflict with a counter-claim that certain terms, e.g. *pietās* or *aretē*, are untranslatable). However, the semantic field of a word in one language is never identical with that of a word in another (*amor*, it can be argued, has different connotations and affiliations from *love*); and words are constantly changing their significations according to shifting context and use. So it is better to think of semantic 'equivalence' rather than identity; translation involves simultaneous sameness *and* difference. Indeed, any theory of translation implies, is dependent upon, a theory of language.

transmigration The belief that on death, some aspect of us—usually identified with the '*soul' (see PSYCHE)—survives to enter another body, is connected with the idea of immortality, supplying one possible destination for the disembodied soul. It is esp. associated with Pythagoreans (see PYTHAGORAS); in the 5th cent. it is attested in *Pindar, *Empedocles, and *Herodotus, who claims, probably wrongly, that Greeks borrowed it from Egypt). For Pythagoreans, the transmigrating entity retains its individual identity, but *Plato, who inherited the general idea from the Pythagoreans, specifies that souls do not remember previous bodily existences.

*Caesar reports that the Gallic Druids (see RELI-GION, CELTIC) believe that 'souls do not perish, but after death pass from (their original owners) to others'.

transport, wheeled and other (see also NAVIGATION; SHIPS; TRAVEL). The wheel played a prominent role in traction in the ancient Mediterranean lands. The role of chariots in *Homer (an echo of the late 2nd-millennium fashion for this form of warfare) established an élite function for light-wheeled vehicles: this was reinforced by their use for a variety of ritual movements of cult-personnel or objects. Such vehicles were for use over short distances, whether in war or religion. The light cart for rapid movement of people was a luxury but quite widespread where the terrain was suitable. Roman practice adapted the *Celtic chariot for light rapid transit. Carts and wagons for the movement of heavy materials, esp. bulk foodstuffs, remained in constant use in the Greek and Roman countryside, as well as for transporting goods for state-purposes, e.g. waging war.

Three factors govern the history of wheeled traction: vehicle design, source of traction energy, and environmental modification. For the first two we are dependent on the often inadequate representations of ancient stone reliefs. Harnessing techniques were primarily orientated towards the ox (large ox-teams were the main traction for very heavy loads like *building materials), but they were better adapted towards horses and mules than was once thought. *Road-building was not primarily designed to aid long-distance wheeled transport.

Other sources of traction therefore remained important: human porterage (of persons in sedan-chair or litter; or of goods, esp. over short distances in cities); trains of beasts of burden, horses, donkeys, mules, and increasingly in the east, *camels (as a means of carrying humans *horses retained a certain cachet, and wheeled transport was sometimes considered unmasculine or soft). Both of these were relatively efficient, but for certain very heavy loads (such as ships on the Corinthian *diolkos) there was no alternative to dragging, which was not. River-transport and coastal trans-shipment were naturally preferred.

In moneyed circles vehicles became elaborate. They were a regular feature of urban existence, as may be inferred from the rutted pavements of urban streets: civic regulations governed the hours of access and regulated the type of user. But the élite came to disregard earlier disapproval of the litter (which also had been subject to attempted control by legislation from time to time), and *lectīcāriī* (of whom eight might be required for an ornate litter) were a normal part of very rich households. The emperors expressed their standing through the opulence of their travelling-equipment.

transvestism, ritual, the wearing of a dress of the other sex during *ritual. Ritual transvestism belongs to rituals of reversal, where the values of ordinary life are temporarily abandoned. It is a special case of ritual change of dress; a structural equivalent is the taking up of freedmen's dress by Roman citizens during the Saturnalia (see SATURNUS). Persons who perpetually live on the margins of society might perpetually wear transvestite attire, as did the eunuch priests of *Cybele (see EUNUCHS, *Religious*).

travel Levels of personal mobility varied greatly in the ancient Mediterranean. Certain categories of men were regarded as mobile throughout: the *trader was a recognizable figure in the Homeric poems, and normally rootless wanderers of the Archaic period include such technical experts (see DEMIOURGOI), as healers, seers, scribes, practitioners of the visual and performance arts, and workers in special materials, esp. metalworkers. Traders remain a standard figure of mobility, from the great wanderers in *Herodotus to *negotiatores attested on Roman tomb-inscriptions.

The demand for the general *labour of the slave and the fighting skills of the soldier led to increased mobility. The Archaic period saw the development of structures for recruiting *mercenaries, through which large numbers of fighting men moved from Greece and Anatolia to Egypt, the Levant, and the Fertile Crescent; and the distribution of significant numbers of people by the nascent slave trade (as attested in *Solon's poems).

These circumstances combined to make the Mediterranean sea-ways a sphere of opportunity and danger, in which legality was tenuous and violence normal: the prevalence of plunder and *piracy reflects this. Early community action exploited the opportunities too, and the movements of colonists interested in agricultural produce, exchange-opportunities, and exploitable labour add to the picture (see COLONIZATION, GREEK). Women were involved in slave-mobility (witness the regulations on Hellenistic Greek islands keeping women indoors to protect them from being snatched by pirates).

Many of these tendencies survived the regulation of international relations and the increasing orderliness of contacts and communications over the Classical period. Leaving home to be a soldier, and perhaps settling far away, remained a standard experience through the early decades of the Successor (see DIADOCHI) kingdoms, and rising standards of urban living created an ever-growing demand for slaves, and increasing economic interdependence involved more people in trade. The Roman dominion also required a high level of mobility, and to the other processes added the development of movements which could be regarded as administrative, managing supplies and exactions and serving in the entourages of officials. As all of these processes developed, the opportunities for battening on them did so too, and piracy and rapine (see BRIGANDAGE) increased until the Roman state in the age of *Pompey and *Augustus had to extirpate it. Mobility under the Roman empire was thus more secure (the risks from robbers and brigands remained real, even in Italy), if still vulnerable to the weather and the multiple discomforts of ancient transport technology. Soldiers, traders, officials, and slaves retained a particular role in promoting it.

The development of widespread background mobility and its infrastructure made voluntary travel and its culture possible. The result was that *inns and eating-places came to be common, though the élite preferred to rely on reciprocal hospitality (see FRIENDSHIP, RITUALIZED). Journeying to panhellenic *sanctuaries seems to have become popular at least by the 4th cent. Élite journeying might turn into *tourism, excited by the descriptive and geographical literature that increased alongside mobility in general. Certain destinations in the Aegean and in Egypt (*Athens, *Sparta, *Memphis and the *Fayūm, Thebes and the Valley of the Kings) were esp. favoured. Travelling to acquire an education became common for the rich with the multiplication of centres of intellectual prestige from the 4th cent. Touring became a pastime of emperors, never more than in the journeys of *Hadrian, whose monument was his eclectic villa near *Tibur.

See also NAVIGATION; ROADS; TRANSPORT, WHEELED.

treason See EISANGELIA; MAIESTAS; PERDUELLIO.

treasurers (of Athena etc.) See TAMIAI.

treasuries (in sanctuaries) See SANCTUARIES; (in Roman public finance) see AERARIUM.

treaties See ALLIANCE; FOEDUS; LAW, INTERNATIONAL; LIBATIONS; OATHS.

Trebōnius, Gāius, quaestor *c*.60 BC, tribune of the *plebs* (see TRIBUNI PLEBIS) 55, when he carried the *lex Trebonia* conferring five-year commands on *Pompey and *Crassus. Pompey received the two Spanish provinces and Crassus Syria. As *legate he served with distinction in Gaul (55–50) and in 49 took *Massalia. Praetor in 48, he was sent next year to Spain, but failed against the Pompeians. Though appointed *suffect consul by *Caesar in 45, he is said to have plotted against him in that year, and he took part in the actual assassination in 44, detaining Marcus *Antonius (Mark Antony) outside. Proconsul of *Asia 43, he was treacherously murdered at Smyrna. He published a collection of Cicero's witticisms.

trees See ARBORICULTURE; TIMBER; TREES, SACRED.

trees, sacred Some trees were associated by Greeks and Romans with particular divinities for special reasons, like the oracular oak of *Zeus at *Dodona, Athena's *olive, which symbolized the source of Athens' prosperity, or the laurel of Apollo with its apotropaic and purifying properties. The palm was sacred to *Leto on *Delos. In popular belief trees housed some kind of 'soul'; spirits of the woods and mountains lived in them. The *nymphs haunted sacred groves, which were the first natural sanctuaries of the gods.

tribes (subdivisions of citizen body) See PHYLAI; TRIBUS; ETHNOS.

Tribōniānus, the main architect of *Justinian's codification of Roman law in the 6th cent. AD, was a lawyer from Side in Pamphylia, who practised as an advocate and rose to be master of offices and in September 529 quaestor (minister of justice). He was a member of the commission to prepare Justinian's *Codex* of imperial laws (528–529), and in 530 Justinian put him in charge of the preparation of the *Digesta* of legal writings (530–533), which he supervised throughout. He seems also to have played a full part in the detailed work of excerpting and editing the texts of earlier lawyers, of which he had a large personal collection and a deep knowledge. In 533 he headed a commission of three to prepare an up-to-date version of *Gaius' (2) Institutes*, and in 534 produced a second edition of the *Codex*. Accused of corruption and innovation, he was removed from office in January 532 as a sop to the public at the time of the Nika riots, but continued to work on the codification and by 535 had resumed the office of quaestor, which he held until his death in 541 or 542, continuing to draft new laws. The changes he made in the classical legal texts, apart from shortening and eliminating what was obsolete, were limited; they consisted largely in developing ideas found in the earlier writers, with whom Tribonianus considered himself to be on a par. See JUSTINIAN'S CODIFICATION.

tribūnī mīlitum The six most senior officers within a *legion, of whom at least five years' military experience was expected. They were *equestrians, though some were the sons of senators, and occasionally senior men took the post. The tribunes of the first four legions recruited each year were elected by the people, while those for additional legions were chosen by the commander. Two tribunes acting in rotation commanded a legion for two months, but they had no tactical responsibilities and their duties encompassed the welfare and discipline of the troops and supervision of the camp. Under *Caesar, as *legates were used extensively, tribunes declined in importance.

In the imperial period one of the six legionary tribunes was normally of senatorial rank (*tribunus lāticlāvius*), a young man early in his career, probably holding the post for one year. The other five tribunes were equestrians (*tribuni angusticlāviī*), who were often more experienced in army life. By the mid-1st cent. AD a pattern had emerged in which many equestrians held at least three military posts—*prefect of an auxiliary cohort (see COHORS), *tribunus militum*, prefect of an auxiliary *ala (see ALAE). Tribunes also commanded individual cohorts in the urban troops. See CURSUS HONORUM.

tribūnī plēbis/tribunes (of the *plebs*), were the officers of the *plebs first created in 500–450 BC (traditionally in 494, the date of the first *secession of the *plebs and their corporate recognition). The original number of the tribunes is variously given; by 449 it had risen to ten. The tribunes were charged with the defence of the persons and property of the plebeians. Their power derived not from statute (initially, at least) but from the oath sworn by the plebeians to guarantee their *sacrosanctitās*, or inviolability. Elected by the plebeian assembly (*comitia plebis tributa*) and exercising their power within the precincts of the city, the tribunes could summon the *plebs* to assembly and elicit resolutions (*plebiscita*; see PLEBISCITUM). They asserted a right of enforcing the decrees of the *plebs* and their own rights (*coercitio); connected with *coercitio* was a measure of jurisdiction, including, probably, capital. They possessed, moreover, a right of veto (*intercessio) against any act performed by a magistrate (or by another tribune), against elections, laws, *senatus consulta*.

This revolutionary power was gradually recognized by the state. The tribunes became indistinguishable from magistrates of the state, although without *imperium or insignia. The full acknowledgement of their power came with the recognition of *plebiscita* as laws binding upon the whole *populus* and not just the *plebs* (by the *lex Hortensia* of 287). Tribunes were first admitted to listen to senatorial debates; at least from the 3rd cent. they had the right to summon the senate; in the 2nd cent. the tribunate became sufficient qualification for membership of the senate. From the 4th and 3rd cents. the tribunate became in part an instrument by which the senate could control magistrates through the veto and the right to summon the senate. But the revolutionary potential and popular origins of the office did not disappear. From *c*.150, *Polybius states that 'they are bound to do what the people resolve and chiefly to focus upon their wishes'. Succeeding years saw the tribunate active in the pursuit of the people's interest and the principles of popular sovereignty and public accountability, as evidenced by the beginning of the practice of addressing the people in the Forum directly (145), the introduction of the secret ballot in assemblies (139 and 137), concern with the corn supply (138), the agrarian legislation of Tiberius *Sempronius Gracchus (2) (133), and above all by the legislation and speeches of Gaius *Sempronius Gracchus (123–122). This movement continued sporadically into the tribunates of *Appuleius Saturninus at the end of the 2nd cent. but did not long survive the domestic chaos of 100 and the convulsion of the *Social War and consequent enfranchisement of peninsular Italy. Active tribunes came increasingly to be associated with the particular interests and grievances of the urban *plebs* (and often with those of one or another of the emergent dynasts); the effective popular instrument was now the army. From the 130s on attempts were made to limit the legislative potential of the tribunate as well as the use of the veto. *Sulla excluded tribunes from the magistracies of the Roman People and abolished, or severely curtailed, their power to legislate, their judicial powers, and their veto. In 75 the bar from magistracies was removed, and in 70 the full *tribunicia potestas* was restored to the tribunes. This tribunician power, divorced from the office but retaining its associations, was valued by the architects of the imperial state in the construction of their personal power. *Caesar assumed at least the tribunician *sacrosanctitās*, and *Augustus, probably in three steps, gained a permanent *tribunicia potestas*. Reft of its power and all independence, the tribunate itself remained as a step in the senatorial career for plebeians alternative to the aedileship.

tribunicia potestas, tribunician power

See TRIBUNI PLEBIS (final section).

tribus, division of the Roman people.

In early times the Roman people were supposedly divided into three tribes. The three tribes were subdivided into *curiae* (see CURIA (1)) and were supposedly the basis of the earliest military organization of the state.

In republican times the three original tribes had been replaced by a system of local tribes, to which Roman citizens belonged by virtue of residence. Tradition ascribes the local tribes to Servius Tullius (see REX), who divided the city into four tribes, and the countryside into a number of 'rustic' tribes. By 495 BC there were seventeen rustic tribes. As Rome expanded during the 4th and 3rd cents., further tribes were created to incorporate newly won territory in which Roman citizens were settled or citizenship was conferred on the native inhabitants. By 241 the number of tribes had reached 35 (four urban, 31 rustic). After that it was decided not to create any further tribes, but to include all additional territory in the existing 35. As a result the tribes ceased to be confined to single districts, and came to include separate territories in different parts of Italy.

This process became more marked when Roman citizenship was extended to all of peninsular Italy after the *Social War. An attempt to restrict the new citizens to a small number of tribes (in order to diminish their voting power in the *comitia*) was thwarted, and they were distributed among the existing 31 rustic tribes.

The distribution of citizens among the tribes was always a sensitive political issue. In 312 the censor *Claudius Caecus caused a storm when he registered lower-class citizens (probably including *freedmen) in the rustic tribes. This act was reversed in 304, and in general during the republic freedmen were confined to the urban tribes, which came to be regarded as socially inferior and politically disadvantaged. The punishment of 'removal from a tribe', which the censors could inflict, in effect meant relegation to an urban tribe.

Every citizen had to belong to a tribe, a rule which continued in imperial times even for provincials who attained the Roman citizenship. It is not known how or why particular tribes were chosen in such cases, and no consistent rule was followed, although certain tribes tended to be favoured in certain provinces. The tribes were used as constituent voting units in political assemblies, and as the basis of army recruitment, the census, and taxation.

tribute lists (Athenian),

records of the *aparchai* (first-fruits) of one-sixtieth given as an offering to *Athena from the tribute paid by the members of the *Delian League after the treasury was moved from *Delos to Athens, very probably in 454/3 BC. From 453 the offerings were calculated separately on each member's tribute, and numbered lists of these offerings were inscribed in Athens: for the first fifteen years (453–439) on a single large block of marble, for the next eight (438–431) on another large block, and thereafter on a separate *stele* for each year. It is possible that no tribute was collected in 448, when war against Persia had come to an end and the future of the League was uncertain. In 413 a 5 per cent duty on all goods transported by sea was substituted for the tribute, but the tribute was probably reintroduced in 410/9. From the beginning there was a tendency to list neighbouring states together; in 442 the practice began of arranging the lists in five regional panels (Ionian, Hellespontine, Thracian, Carian, Island); in 437 some inland Carian states were abandoned and what remained of the Carian panel was combined with the Ionian. Assessments of tribute (ranging from 300 drachmas to the 30 talents of *Aegina and *Thasos) were normally revised every four years: the general level remained constant before the *Peloponnesian War, and in 430, but serious increases were needed in 428 (probably) and 425. In addition to the lists of *aparchai*, we have substantial parts of the assessment list of

425. In so far as they are preserved or can be reconstructed, the lists give us a valuable indication of which states paid tribute, and how much they paid, from one year to another.

tribūtum was a direct tax paid by individuals to the Roman state. Until 167 BC citizens of Rome were liable to pay a *tributum* which was in principle an extraordinary (in contrast to the regular *vectigalia*) levy on their property and might be repaid. The total size of the levy was decided by the senate and varied from year to year. In some years no *tributum* was levied. After its suspension in 167 this form of *tributum* was only again levied in the exigencies of the civil wars after *Caesar's murder. Under the emperors Rome and Roman Italy were exempt from direct taxation. After 167 *tributum* came to denote the direct taxes raised in the provinces, either in the form of a land-tax (*tributum solī*) or poll-tax (*tributum capitis*).

trīclīnium See CONVIVIUM; DINING-ROOMS; HOUSES, ITALIAN.

trierarchy Gk. *trierarchos* means '*trireme-commander*', but at Athens in the 5th and 4th cents. BC the trierarchy was a *liturgy, which the richest citizens could be called on to perform for a year. The state provided the ship and its basic equipment, and normally paid for the crew, but the trierarch had not only to command the ship but also to bear the costs of maintenance and repair, which could amount to as much as one talent. After 411 it became common for two men to share responsibility for a ship, and contractors could be found who would relieve the trierarchs of their personal involvement; reforms in 357 and later involved the organization of those liable in *symmoriai* ('partnerships'). The liturgy was abolished by *Demetrius of Phaleron.

Trinovantēs, a British tribe in Essex (see BRITAIN). Mandubracius, their prince, fled to *Caesar from *Cassivellaunus' aggression; the tribe later surrendered (54 BC) and brought over other tribes, making a turning-point in Caesar's British campaigning. The Trinovantes were protected in Caesar's peace-terms; they maintained an independent monarchy down to Cunobelinus' accession, *c.* AD 5. In 43 they were freed from *Catuvellaunian rule, but in 49 suffered deprivation of territory on the foundation of the colony (see COLONIZATION, ROMAN) at *Camulodunum. Aggrieved by the subsequent behaviour of the colonists, in 60 they joined *Boudicca's rebellion, and the colony was destroyed. After its refoundation, the primacy of Camulodunum as an emporium and provincial capital became eclipsed by London, but the provincial centre of the imperial cult remained there (see RULER-CULT).

trinundinum was a period including three *nundinae* (*market days, held every eight days), required between moving and voting a resolution, or between candidates' declaration of their intention to stand for office and the polling, or between the promulgation and execution of a sentence, etc.

trireme The trireme was the standard warship of the classical world for much of the time from the 5th cent. BC to the 4th cent. AD. A long rowing-ship, its main weapon was a bronze ram, fixed on the prow at the water-line. It was rowed by oarsmen arranged in groups of three, sitting one above the other and each oarsman pulling a single oar of equal length. On an Athenian trireme of the Classical period there were 170 oarsmen, ten marines, four archers, and sixteen sailors, including the helmsman, making a total of 200. Trials of a modern reconstruction of an Athenian trireme have shown that speeds above 9 knots are possible. Triremes could be rowed with only some of the oars manned, but this reduced speed considerably. For long sailing passages sails were used, but masts were usually removed and left on the shore before battle.

The trireme may have been invented by the *Phoenicians in the second half of the 6th cent. Its heyday was the 5th cent., when the finest practitioners of trireme warfare were the Athenians, who perfected the art of manœuvring at speed to ram and disable enemy ships.

From the mid-4th cent. BC larger warships with oarsmen arranged in groups of four, five, six, or more were developed. These ships relied far less on ramming and high speed manœuvring, and more on boarding and missile weapons (see PUNIC WARS, *First*). Thus the trireme became less important in Mediterranean fleets until the creation of the Roman imperial navy, which used triremes extensively until the 4th cent. AD. See NAVIES; SHIPS.

triumph, the procession of a Roman general who had won a major victory to the temple of *Jupiter on the *Capitol. It entered Rome through the *porta triumphālis* ('triumphal gate'), through which no one else might enter. It made its way to the Capitol by a long route including open spaces where large numbers could see it. It comprised the *triumphātor* (wearing the *toga picta*, said to have been the kings' and close to Jupiter's) in a four-horse chariot, with any sons of suitable age as outriders; eminent captives (normally destined for execution in the Tullianum, the underground cell of the prison) and freed Roman prisoners of war dressed as the *triumphator*'s freedmen; the major spoils captured; his army; and animals for sacrifice. The whole senate and all the magistrates were supposed to escort it. Increasingly costly and elaborate details were added from *c*.200 BC, including banners, paintings of sieges and battles, musicians, and torch-bearers. The *triumphator* was preceded by his *lictors, and a slave rode with him, holding a bay wreath over his head and reminding him that he was mortal. The soldiers chanted insulting verses, no doubt to avert the gods' displeasure. The right to triumph depended on a special vote of the people allowing him to retain his military *imperium* in the city, and so in fact on the senate's decision to ask for this vote.

In historical times the prerequisites for expecting such a decision were a victory in a declared war over a foreign enemy, with at least 5,000 of them killed and the ending of the war; the *triumphator* must have fought under his own *auspicia in his own *provincia and as a magistrate (or, later, as a promagistrate (see PRO CONSULE, PRO PRAETORE)). In the late republic *acclamation as *imperator was the first step, holding out hope of a triumph. Interpretation of entitlement was elastic and subject to intrigue, and the senate might even be by-passed. If the entitlement was judged defective, the general might be awarded a 'lesser triumph' called *ovātiō. The Capitoline triumph was the summit of a Roman aristocrat's ambition.

In the late republic interpretation of the rules came to be dominated by power and influence. Thus *Pompey celebrated two triumphs without having been a magistrate, and Caesar allowed two of his *legates to triumph. Under the empire, triumphs soon became a monopoly of the emperor and (with his permission) his family, while the actual commander would be granted 'triumphal *ornaments'. But as early as the 1st cent. AD these were deliberately cheapened and gradually lost their connection with military exploits.

triumphal arch, term used to denote the honorific arch, one of the most characteristically Roman of classical buildings. Though regu-larly erected to commemorate military victories, such arches often had religious or topographical associations that reflect the complex origins of the type, e.g. the posthumous arch of *Titus on the *via Sacra, with its representations both of his Jewish triumph and of his apotheosis (see RULER-CULT, *Roman*); or the frequent use of such arches on *bridges or to mark provincial or city boundaries. The earliest recorded examples were built in the first years of the 2nd cent. BC in Rome itself, and the principal development took place in Rome and Italy (over 100 known arches, many of early imperial date), Gaul (36), and Africa (118); but examples are recorded from every province of the empire. The earliest surviving arches, of Augustan date, are generally simple rectangular masses of masonry, with a single archway framed within a pair of half-columns or pilasters and a trabeated entablature, surmounted by an attic serving as the base for the statuary (often a chariot group) which was an integral and essential feature of the monument. Later architectural development was towards a steadily greater elaboration of the decorative framework. Triple arches are known from the later 2nd cent. BC and become a common variant from the early empire; important examples include the arches of *Septimius Severus, AD 203, and of *Constantine I, 312, in Rome. A specialized form, the tetrapylon, with two carriageways intersecting at right angles, though represented in Rome (arch in the *forum Boarium), was esp. common in Africa (e.g. *Lepcis Magna). See ARCHES.

triumvirī (or **trēsvirī**) were a board of three in Roman public life, of many different kinds, usually elected by the people. For the annual *tresviri monetales* and *capitales/nocturni* see VIGINTISEXVIRI. Apart from these, under the republic the most common *triumvirī* were agrarian. The most famous triumvirate consisted of Mark Antony (Marcus *Antonius), *Aemilius Lepidus (2), and Octavian (see AUGUSTUS), created in 43 BC by the *lex Titia*. This was originally to last until 1 January 37, but the triumvirs did not resign then, and it was renewed the following summer for another five years. Their title ('triumvirs for putting the state in order') was appropriate to a political crisis, but of the three only Octavian was to take a significant interest in Rome and Italy and even he undertook no major reforms as triumvir. Although republican institutions continued to function and their *imperium* was only consular, the triumvirs assumed a supreme authority, appropriate to an emergency, both in

Rome and abroad, one that overarched consuls, provincial governors (it is not clear whether their *imperium* was actually defined as *maius*), and, where necessary, the law. In particular they suspended normal judicial process in decreeing the *proscriptions. Lepidus was forced into retirement in 36; Antony used the title until his death in 30; Octavian seems to have dropped the title at the end of 33 but formally abolished the triumviral emergency only in 28.

Troas, or **Troad,** the mountainous NW corner of Asia Minor forming a geographical unit dominated by the Ida massif and washed on three sides by the sea. Its name derives from the belief that all this area was once under Trojan rule (see TROY). The interior is inaccessible, and the more important cities were situated on the coast. The historical significance of Troas derives from its strategic position flanking the *Hellespont (a factor which may already have weighed with the Achaeans in their attack on Troy). From the 6th cent. Athens became increasingly interested in holding the straits (see CHERSONESE; SIGEUM), but after Aegospotami (see ATHENS, HISTORY) Persia nominally controlled the Troas. It became the first battlefield in the struggle between east and west when *Alexander (2) the Great routed the Persian first line of resistance at the *Granicus.

Troilus, in myth, son of *Priam and *Hecuba. In *Homer's *Iliad* he is mentioned only as being dead. Later accounts, however, starting with the *Cypria* (see EPIC CYCLE), specify that he was killed by *Achilles. This was a popular story, for Achilles' ambush of Troilus with his sister Polyxena) at the fountain, the pursuit, the slaughter of the boy on the altar of Apollo, and the battle over the mutilated body, are favourite subjects in Archaic art from the early 6th cent. 'Troilus and Cressida' (i.e. *Chryseis) is a medieval fiction.

Trojan War See EPIC CYCLE; HOMER; TROY.

trophies (derived from Gk. *tropē*, a turning i.e. rout of the enemy). The act of dedicating on the field of battle a suit of enemy armour set upon a stake is a Greek practice. Originally intended as a miraculous image of the god who had brought about the defeat of the enemy, a trophy marked the spot where the enemy had been routed. Trophies were also dedicated in the *sanctuary of the deity to whom victory was ascribed. They appear in art at the end of the 6th cent. BC and were certainly in use during the *Persian Wars.

The trophies of the 4th cent. became permanent monuments. The battle of *Leuctra was commemorated by a tower surmounted by a trophy of arms, and from this period onwards the name was applied to various kinds of towers and buildings commemorating military and naval victories. Trophies became a common motif of art; sculptured trophies accompanied by statues of captives and victors decorated the buildings of Hellenistic kings and took an important place in Roman triumphal art from the 1st cent. BC.

Trophōnius was with his brother Agamedes a renowned master-builder, whose work included the lower courses of *Apollo's first temple at Delphi, and the treasury of the Boeotian hero Hyrieus. The latter provides the connection with Trophonius as cult figure and son of Apollo. While building the treasury, the brothers left a stone loose, so that they could make off with the treasure bit by bit. Hyrieus set a trap, which caught Agamedes. Trophonius cut off his brother's head, and ran off with it, pursued by Hyrieus. At Lebadea in west Boeotia, the ground opened up and swallowed Trophonius. He lived on underground as an oracular god (a fate similar to that of *Amphiaraus: in both cases an underground oracular god is identified with a figure of heroic tradition; see ORACLES). The oracle was well known to Athenians by the second half of the 5th cent. What caught the imagination was the means of consultation: there was no medium; instead the consultant, after suitable and lengthy preliminaries, descended underground and confronted the god himself. The experience was spectacular, frightening, notorious, and expensive.

Troy (mod. Hisarlik) lies in NW *Asia Minor, about 6.5 km. (4 mi.) from the Aegean coast and rather less from the *Hellespont. The site consists of a small citadel mound with c.25 m. (82 ft.) of gradually accumulated debris from human habitation, and a lower town at least 1 km. (½ mi.) square. The site was occupied from c.3000 BC to c. AD 1200, perhaps with some intervals, and has revealed well over 46 building phases. These are conventionally grouped in nine bands, sometimes misleadingly called 'cities'.

Hisarlik's identification with the Troy of *Priam has never been proved, but a ruined castle would have been visible in *Homer's day and its situation agrees with that of Troy in most classical tradition, *Strabo excepted. It is generally assumed that some residue of historical truth persists in the legends concerning the Trojan War, although how much and where is uncertain. Mycenaean Greeks (see MYCENAEAN AGE CIVILIZATION) could plausibly have destroyed Troy VI, VIIa, or VIIb. Of these Troy VI would fit best as dating to the peak of power at both *Mycenae and Troy.

Tullius, Servius See REX.

Tullius Cicero (1), **Marcus,** the orator **Cicero.**

Life

The first of two sons of a rich and well-connected *equestrian of Arpinum, b. 106 BC. His father gave his two sons an excellent education in philosophy and rhetoric in Rome and later in Greece. Cicero did military service in 90/89 under Pompey's father, and attended legal consultations of the two great Scaevolae (*Mucius Scaevola (1) and (2)). He conducted his first case in 81 and made an immediate reputation through his successful defence of Roscius of Ameria on a charge of *parricide in 80, a case which reflected discreditably on the contemporary administration of *Sulla. Cicero was then from 79 to 77 a student of philosophy and rhetoric both in Athens and in *Rhodes, where he heard *Posidonius; he visited *Rutilius Rufus at Smyrna.

He returned to Rome to pursue a public career, and was elected quaestor for 75, when he served for a year in western Sicily, and praetor for 66, in each case at the earliest age at which he could legally become a candidate. By securing the condemnation of *Verres for *extortion in Sicily in 70 he scored a resounding success against *Hortensius Hortalus, eight years his senior, whom he was to replace as the leading figure at the Roman bar. In a cleverly disarming speech delivered during his praetorship he supported, against strong *optimate opposition, the *tribune Manilius' proposal to transfer the command in the war against *Mithradates to *Pompey; this was the first public expression of his admiration for Pompey, who was, with occasional short interruptions, henceforward to be the focus of his political allegiance. He was elected consul for 63—the first *novus homo with no political background whatever since 94—because, in a poor field (including Catiline (see SERGIUS CATILINA), who had tried for the office twice before), his reputation as an orator and his cultivation of aristocrats, equestrians, and prominent Italians paid off. Hampered by a weak and indeed suspect colleague, Cicero did very well to secure evidence which convinced

the senate of the seriousness of Catiline's conspiracy. After the 'last decree' (*senatus consultum ultimum) had been passed, and Catiline had left Rome for his army in Etruria, five conspirators prominent in Roman society and politics, including a praetor, were arrested and executed on 5 December. Although, after debate, the senate, influenced by *Porcius Cato (2), had recommended their execution, the act itself, a violation of the citizen's right to a trial, could be justified only by the passing of the last decree and was Cicero's personal responsibility. Though approved in the first moment of panic by all classes of society in Rome, its legality was strictly questionable, and Cicero was unwise to boast of it as loudly as he did. He published his speeches of 63, including those against Catiline. To the end of his life he never wavered in his belief that he had acted rightly and had saved Rome from catastrophe.

Though it was unlikely that he would escape prosecution, Cicero refused overtures from *Caesar, which might have saved him at the price of his political independence. In 58 *Clodius Pulcher, whom he had antagonized in 61 when Clodius was charged with sacrilege, moved a bill as tribune re-enacting the law that anyone who had executed a citizen without trial should be banished. Without awaiting prosecution Cicero fled the country, to Macedonia, and Clodius passed a second bill, which Cicero regarded as unconstitutional, declaring him an exile. His house on the Palatine was destroyed by Clodius' gang, part of its site to be made a shrine of Liberty, and his villa at *Tusculum was also badly damaged. With Pompey's belated support and with the support of the tribune *Annius Milo, who employed violence as irresponsibly as Clodius had done in the previous year, Cicero was recalled by a law of the people in August 57 and was warmly welcomed on his return both in Italy and in Rome.

He returned to a busy winter, fighting to secure adequate public compensation for the damage to his property and, in the senate and in the courts, supporting those chiefly responsible for his recall. Hopes of dissociating Pompey from his close political connection with Caesar, attempts which Clodius was employed by Caesar to interrupt, were at an end when Caesar, Pompey, and *Licinius Crassus revived their political union at Luca in April 56, and Cicero was sharply brought to heel. He at once spoke warmly in the senate and on the public platform in favour of Caesar, as of a long-standing political friend. He claimed that it was the act of a realist, to accept the indisputable predominance of the Three and only revealed in conversation and in letters to such close friends as *Pomponius Atticus the deep wound which his pride—his *dignitās*—had suffered. He took no more part in the collapsing world of republican politics, devoting himself to writing, which he never regarded as anything but a poor substitute for active political life. *On the Orator* was published in 55, and *Republic* finished in 51; and he was humiliated by briefs which, under pressure from Pompey and Caesar, he was forced to accept. He was humiliated too by his failure, in a court packed with troops, to defend Milo adequately when, with the case already prejudiced, Milo was impeached for the murder of Clodius early in 52. The period brought him one consolation, when he was elected *augur.

Cicero was out of Rome during the eighteen months preceding the outbreak of the Civil War, being selected under regulations following Pompey's law on provinces of 52 to govern Cilicia as proconsul from summer 51 to summer 50. He was a just, if not a strong, governor, but he regarded his appointment with horror as a second relegation from Rome. However, his dispatches recording the successful encounter of his troops with brigands on mons Amanus earned a *supplication at Rome and he returned, the *fasces* of his *lictors wreathed in fading laurels, hoping that he might celebrate a triumph. Instead he was swept into the vortex of the Civil War.

Appointed district commissioner at *Capua by the government, he did not at first follow Pompey and the consuls overseas. Caesar saw him at Formiae on 28 March 49, and invited him to join the rump of the senate in Rome on terms which with great resolution Cicero refused to accept. His long indecision up to this point was now at an end, and he joined the republicans in Greece, irritating their leaders by his caustic criticism, himself dismayed by the absence of any idealistic loyalty on their part to the cause of republicanism. After *Pharsalus, in which he took no part, he refused Cato's invitation to assume command of the surviving republican forces and, pardoned by Caesar, he returned to Italy. But political life was at an end, and he was utterly out of sympathy with Caesar's domination. All that he could do was to return to his writing, his only important speech being that delivered in the senate in 46 (the year in which *Brutus* was written) in praise of Caesar's pardon of Claudius Marcellus (consul 51), who had done so much to precipitate the outbreak of the Civil War.

Cicero was not invited to participate in the conspiracy to kill Caesar in 44, but hailed the news of the murder on 15 March with intemperate delight. Political life began again, and Cicero had the prestige (*auctōritās*) of a senior consular. Within three months he was saying openly that Mark Antony (Marcus *Antonius) should have been killed too. He accepted the overtures of the young Caesar (Octavian; see AUGUSTUS), uncritical of the lawlessness of many of his acts, misled by his youth into an underestimate of his political acumen, and he closed his eyes to the fact that Octavian could never be reconciled to *Brutus and *Cassius. He struggled in speech after speech (the *Philippics*, the first delivered in September 44, the last on 2 April 43) to induce the senate to declare Antony a public enemy. After Antony's defeat in Cisalpine Gaul in April 43, Octavian fooled Cicero for a time, perhaps with the suggestion that they might both be consuls together. But Octavian's intentions were different. After his march on Rome to secure the consulship for himself and his uncle Quintus *Pedius, and the formation of the Triumvirate (see TRIUMVIRI), he did not oppose Antony's nomination of Cicero as a victim of the proscriptions which were the inauguration of the new regime (see PROSCRIPTION). The soldiers caught Cicero in a not very resolute attempt to escape by sea. His slaves did not desert him, and he died with courage on 7 December 43.

In politics he hated Clodius, with good reason, and he hated Crassus and, at the end of his life, Antony. For the character of Cato, eleven years his junior, he had unqualified respect, and he published a panegyric of Cato in 45, after his death; but in politics, esp. in the years following Pompey's return from the east in 62, he thought Cato's inflexibility (his *constantia*) impolitic, and Cato never concealed his distaste for Cicero's policy of temporizing expediency, both at this period and when he capitulated to the Three in 56. With Pompey Cicero never established the intimacy to which, esp. after Pompey's return in 62, he aspired, suggesting that he might play a second *Laelius to Pompey's Scipio (see CORNELIUS SCIPIO AEMILIANUS). Few of his contemporaries, perhaps, held him in higher esteem than did his constant opponent Caesar, who, though often with an imperiousness which Cicero could not tolerate, was always friendly in his approach. Cicero was a poor judge of the political intentions of others, being far too susceptible to, and uncritical of, flattery; and he was inevitably condemned to a certain political isolation.

Uncritically devoted to the existing republican constitution, and fascinated by the mirage of a '*concordia ordinum*', he was never a liberal reformer (*populāris*); yet he was never completely acceptable to the established optimates, the worst of whom despised his social origin, while the rest mistrusted his personality as much as he mistrusted theirs. And, not having the *clientela* (see CLIENS) of the noble (see NOBILES) or of the successful general, he lacked their *auctōritās*. It was this political isolation which enhanced the importance for him of his close association with Atticus, a man of the highest culture in both languages, his banker, financial adviser, publisher, and most generous and tolerant friend.

His marriage to Terentia had issue: Tullia, to whom he was devoted, and whose death in 45 was the hardest of the blows which afflicted his private life, and a son, also named Marcus (see TULLIUS CICERO (2)). His marriage survived the storms and stress of 30 years, until he grew irritated with Terentia and divorced her in winter 47/6, to marry the young Publilia, from whom in turn he was almost immediately divorced. Cicero was a good master to his slaves and, with the rest of his family, was devoted to Tiro (*Tullius Tiro), to whom 21 of his letters are addressed. He gave him his freedom in 53, 'to be our friend instead of our slave', as Quintus *Tullius Cicero wrote.

Cicero, who was never a really rich man, had eight country residences, in Campania, at Arpinum, at Formiae, and, his suburban villa, at Tusculum; in Rome he was extremely proud of his house on the *Palatine, which he bought in 62 for $3\frac{1}{2}$ million sesterces.

Apart from the surviving histories of the late republic and esp. Plutarch's Lives of Cicero and of his outstanding contemporaries, the bulk of our knowledge of him derives from his own writings, esp. his letters, only a few of which were written with any thought of publication. His reputation has suffered because we have intimate knowledge of the most private part of his personal life; in this respect he has been his own worst enemy, and his critics have given undue prominence to his extremes of exaltation and depression and to the frequent expression of his vanity.

Works

Speeches

Fifty-eight speeches of Cicero survive in whole or part; numerous others were unpublished or lost. Cicero's normal practice, if he decided to publish a speech, was to 'write up' a version after the event. In one case we know that he delivered a speech from a script; otherwise it seems that only a few important passages, chiefly the exordium and peroration, were written out *in extenso* beforehand. The published versions of many court speeches certainly represent a shortened version of the actual proceedings; the examination of witnesses is largely omitted, and some sections of argumentation are represented only by headings.

In certain cases there is firm evidence that our text does not represent a speech that was actually delivered. The five speeches of the *Actio secunda* against *Verres were prepared for use in court but were never actually delivered, since Verres withdrew into exile after the single speech of the *Actio prima*. The second *Philippic* was not delivered as a speech, but circulated as a pamphlet, although it observes the conventions of a senatorial speech. But these are exceptions.

Cicero's reputation as an orator depended on consistent practical success, although his detractors in antiquity made as much capital out of his rare failures as their modern equivalents have done. In these successes a large part must have been played by his manner of delivery, of which virtually no impression can be given by a written speech; yet it is possible to see in the published versions something of the powers of advocacy that made Cicero the leading courtroom orator of his time. The political speeches are perhaps more difficult for a modern reader to appreciate: Cicero's self-glorifications and his unbridled *invectives tend to repel modern western readers, while adverse judgement of his political position can hinder appreciation of his oratory. It is easy to be cynical about what *Juvenal called the 'divine Philippic' (the Second) without recognizing the historical circumstances that produced this and other speeches, and the oratorical qualities that made them into objects of near-universal admiration.

The style of Cicero's speeches depended to some extent on the occasion; there are variations in manner between Cicero's addresses to senate and people, to a full jury, and to a single arbitrator, and Cicero himself talks of the different styles appropriate for the different sections of a speech (plain for narration, grand for the final appeal to the emotions, etc.).

Cicero made good use of the theories of rhetoric current in his time, and, still more, of the models of Athenian oratory. Most of the ancient structural conventions, figures of speech, and standard modes of argument can be exemplified from his writings, and some of the speeches were consistently taken as copy-book examples by later *rhetors (teachers of rhetoric) such as *Quintilian.

Works on Rhetoric

(a) *Invention* (see RHETORIC, GREEK), written in Cicero's youth, is a treatise on some techniques of rhetorical argument, which has a close resemblance to parts of the anonymous *Rhetorica ad Herennium*.

(b) *On the Orator* (55), *Brutus*, and *Orator* (46) represent Cicero's major contribution to the theory of (Latin) *rhetoric, and he himself grouped them with his philosophical works. They present an idealized picture of the orator as a liberally educated master of his art, a picture in which the technical aspects of Greek rhetorical theory still have their place, but are supplemented by knowledge of literature, philosophy, and general culture, and by the qualities of character required of the ideal Roman aristocrat. This was endorsed by later Roman authors such as *Quintilian, and it was one of the formative influences on Renaissance ideals of character and education. *On the Orator* was closely linked with the more ambitious *Republic* which followed it, and the ideal orator depicted in the former is little different from the ideal statesman in the latter. *Brutus* is devoted largely to a history of Roman oratory, while *Orator* deals with more technical points of style.

Poems

Cicero early acquired a reputation as a bad poet on the basis of two lines from his autobiographical compositions, 'o fortunatam natam me consule Romam' ('O happy Rome, born in my consulship') and 'cedant arma togae, concedat laurea laudi' ('yield, arms, to the toga, the bay to achievement'). All that survives of his poetry in a manuscript tradition is 469 lines from a verse translation of *Aratus' *Phaenomena*.

Letters

Cicero's surviving correspondence is a precious collection of evidence for his biography, for the history of the time, and for Roman social life. The sixteen books *To Friends* were published after Cicero's death by his freedman *Tullius Tiro. Cicero's letters to *Pomponius Atticus were preserved (without the replies) by the latter and seen by *Cornelius Nepos. Our present collection *To Atticus* consists of sixteen books. We also have the smaller collections *To Quintus* (including the *Commentariolum petitionis*) and *To Brutus*. *To*

Friends contains, in addition to Cicero's own, letters from a variety of correspondents to him.

The letters were not originally written for publication; as far as is known, it was not until 44 that Cicero thought of publishing a selection of them, and it is not clear that this idea was ever carried out. They vary greatly in their level of formality. At the one extreme they include official dispatches and letters of a semi-public nature on matters of political importance, whose style is similar to that of the public speeches; at the other may be found casual notes to members of the family and informal exchanges with Atticus, often highly allusive and colloquial. See LETTERS, LATIN.

Philosophical works

Apart from the works on rhetoric, an important part of the Hellenistic philosophical curriculum, these fall into two parts: (a) the works on political philosophy and statecraft of the years just before Cicero's governorship of Cilicia, and (b) the works on theory of knowledge, ethics, and theology (standing in the place of *physics) which were produced in the very short period between February 45 and November 44.

In *Republic*, a dialogue between *Cornelius Scipio Aemilianus, *Laelius, and others, of which we have only parts of the six books (including *The Dream of Scipio*, preserved as a whole by *Macrobius), Cicero discusses the ideal state, always with an eye on the history of the Roman republic, and favours a constitution combining elements of all three main forms, monarchy, oligarchy, and democracy. His discussion reflects the political conditions of the time and looks to a wise counsellor (for which part Cicero may at one time have cast *Pompey) as a remedy for Rome's political sickness. But its chief attraction for posterity lay in its assertion of human rights and of man's participation in humanity and the cosmos, a notion which eclectic developments in *Stoicism and Cicero's own predilections helped to foster. Cicero probably worked on *Laws* immediately after *Republic*, but did not publish it. In the three extant books Cicero expounds the Stoic conception of divinely sanctioned law, based on reason, and discusses legal enactments connected with religion and magistracies.

Politically inactive under Caesar's dictatorship, the death of his daughter Tullia (45) finally led Cicero to seek consolation in writing about philosophical subjects which had always interested him. What had formerly been for Cicero a useful exercise and a source of oratorical material now became a haven. Cicero needed to re-assure himself, and hoped as well to make a name for himself as a philosophical writer. He was well prepared for the task, having learnt Stoic *dialectic from Diodotus, rhetoric and argu-ing both sides of a question from the *Peripate-tics, while the *Academics had taught him to refute any argument. In addition Cicero had lis-tened carefully to the most charismatic philo-sophers of his time, the showmen of the day. He had a profound admiration and respect for *Plato and *Aristotle. He aimed above all at giving the Romans a philosophical literature and termin-ology, which would take the place of the Greek philosophers, on whom the Romans had hitherto been intellectually dependent. The surviving work of the Hellenistic philosophers suggests that Cicero would not be alone in following his Greek sources closely in order to engage with them polemically.

Several lost works probably came first: a eu-logy of *Porcius Cato (2); his *Consolation, an at-tempt to console himself for the loss of Tullia (and unique in being addressed to himself); and Hortensius, a plea for the study of philosophy, which profoundly affected St *Augustine (it turned him to God). Cicero swiftly proceeded with the construction of what is by his own description an encyclopaedia of Hellenistic phil-osophy: Hortensius is followed by Academica, on theory of knowledge (esp. concerned with the criterion of truth). It treats of the views of the New Academy after *Arcesilaus, and esp. of *Carneades on the impossibility of attaining cer-tain knowledge. Cicero rejects the possibility of certain knowledge, but asserts the right to adopt whatever position seemed most com-pelling on each occasion.

Thus in questions of ethics Cicero often in-clined toward Stoic doctrine as he recoiled from the Epicurean, as is evident in Bests and Worsts, where he compiles and answers in turn the theories on the 'highest good' pro-pounded by the Epicureans and Stoics, before giving the views of the so-called 'Old Academy'. From this encyclopaedic survey of the various schools' positions on ethics, Cicero turned in Tusculan Disputations to the problems of the psychology of the happy life: death, grief, pain, fear, passion, and other mental dis-orders, and of what is essential for happiness, including (acc. to the Stoics) virtue. Concerned largely to allay his own doubts, and impressed by Stoic teaching on these subjects, he writes here with passionate intensity and lyrical beauty.

For Cicero theological speculation stands in the place of a full account of natural philosophy and physical causes (such as is found, for example, in *Lucretius, Epicurus, or *Chrysip-pus. Thus Cicero next composes The Nature of the Gods in three books, each devoted to the view of a different school (Epicurean, Stoic, Aca-demic) on the nature of the gods and the exist-ence of the divine, its role in human culture and the state. Having allowed Cotta to present the sceptical Academic view in bk. 3, after Velleius' presentation of the Epicurean in bk. 1, and Bal-bus' of the Stoic in bk. 2, Cicero rounds off the debate with a typically Academic expression of his own opinion: that the Stoic's argument is more likely to be right. Stoic beliefs concerning Fate and the possibility of prediction are exam-ined, with more use of anecdote and quotation, in the two books of Divination, published just after Caesar's murder. In this case Cicero dis-plays no sympathy with the views of the Stoics, whose commitment to the validity of *divin-ation was based on complex principles of logic and cosmic sympathy. Cicero's pious reaffirm-ation of his belief in the existence of a divine being, maintaining that it is prudent to keep traditional rites and ceremonies, belies his con-cerns in matters of theology and religion for the state above all else. Finally, the fragmentary Fate discusses the more specialized problem of vol-ition and decides against Stoic determinism.

Equally specialized are the two genial and polished essays Old Age and Friendship, which show once again Cicero's anxiety to reassure or occupy himself in times of stress and danger, and his last work on moral philosophy Moral Obligation (finished November 44) aims at giving advice, based on Stoic precepts and esp. on the teachings of *Panaetius, on a variety of prob-lems of conduct (ostensibly to Cicero's son).

These three works, along with Tusc. and The Dream of Scipio, were the most popular among readers in the Middle Ages, when the work of Cicero the politician and orator was almost for-gotten, to be rediscovered in the Renaissance. Cicero's influence on European thought and lit-erature ensured that what he found interesting and important in Greek philosophy became the philosophical curriculum of the Renaissance and Enlightenment. His achievement stands out as the creator of philosophical vocabulary in Latin, and as a philosophical stylist.

Tullius Cicero (2), **Marcus,** b. 65 BC, son of Cicero and Terentia and thirteen years younger than Tullia. He was educated under his father's supervision and taken out to Cilicia by him in 51. He was an obedient boy and a good soldier. He was a successful cavalry officer in the republican army in 49/8. Pardoned after *Pharsalus, he held office in the family's home town of Arpinum. He would have liked to serve under *Caesar in Spain, but instead was sent to study in Athens in 45. Cicero's *Moral Obligation* was written in the form of a letter to his son in 44. Marcus was serving under *Brutus, who praised him highly, when his father was killed in the *proscriptions. After *Philippi he joined Sextus *Pompeius Magnus, but took advantage of the amnesty of 39. He was elected to a priesthood and was colleague to *Octavian (see AUGUSTUS) as consul in 30; afterwards he governed Syria and then Asia. Though he was, by his own admission, idle in his student days and drank too much, and though his distinguished public career may have been partly due to Octavian's repentance for his father's murder, he must have had considerable administrative ability.

Tullius Cicero, Quintus (c.102–43 BC), younger brother of Cicero and similarly educated, had none of his brother's genius. He was irascible and often tactlessly outspoken; yet he was a good soldier and an able administrator. Plebeian aedile in 65 and praetor in 62 (helped, no doubt, by the fact that his brother Marcus was praetor and consul respectively when he was elected), he governed Asia (see ASIA, ROMAN PROVINCE) from 61 to 58, receiving two long letters of advice and criticism from his brother in Rome. He spent winter 57/6 in Sardinia as a *legate of *Pompey, when Pompey received his corn commission, and was evidently a hostage for Marcus' good behaviour in politics after his recall from exile. He was legate on *Caesar's staff in Gaul from 54 to early 51, taking part in the invasion of *Britain in 54 and earning praise for his courage in holding out against the Nervii when the Gauls attacked the winter camps in 54; though unwell, he drove himself so hard that his troops forced him to take some sleep at night. He was a valuable legate on Marcus' staff in Cilicia in 51/50, supplying military experience which Marcus lacked. He joined Pompey in the Civil War, was pardoned after Pharsalus and then, with his son, behaved badly in maligning his brother to Caesar. He returned to Rome in 47 by Caesar's permission. Victims of the *proscriptions in 43, he and his son were betrayed by their slaves.

The 27 surviving letters of Marcus to Quintus were written between 60 and 54, mostly when Quintus was serving abroad. Of the four short surviving letters of Quintus, one congratulated Marcus on enfranchising *Tullius Tiro and three were to Tiro. Quintus was a literary dilettante, writing four tragedies in sixteen days when in Gaul.

Like his brother, Quintus owned property near Arpinum. His marriage to Pomponia, who was older than he and the sister of Marcus' friend *Pomponius Atticus, lasted from 69 to 44 and was never happy. It produced one son, a gifted boy whom his father indulged.

Tullius Tīrō, Marcus, *Cicero's confidential secretary and literary adviser, freed by him 53 BC. From 51 he suffered from malaria (see DISEASE), which caused Cicero great concern. After Cicero's death he published some of his speeches and letters and perhaps a collection of his jokes, and wrote a biography of him. He devised a system of shorthand.

tumultus was a state of emergency decreed by the Roman state when facing attack. *Cicero says the ancients had distinguished two types, a war in Italy (which to Cicero and his contemporaries meant a civil war), and a Gallic attack (Gaul being the only province bordering Italy). When a *tumultus* was pronounced, there was a suspension of normal state business (*iustitium*), military leave was cancelled, and all the citizens, wearing the *sagum* (see DRESS), were levied. An emergency levy was the only time that *proletarii (citizens who fell below the census qualification for military service) could be enrolled, and on a famous occasion they were for the first time armed at public expense.

Twelve Tables Acc. to Roman tradition, popular pressure led to the appointment for 451 BC of ten men with consular *imperium*, for writing down statutes, in order to put an end to the patrician and priestly monopoly of the law. They compiled ten tables, were reappointed for 450, and compiled two more, including the ban on intermarriage between patricians and plebeians, which was rapidly abrogated by the *lex Canuleia* of 445. An attempt to remain in office for 449 also failed. The fundamental consequence was that customary law was now enacted by statute and given legislative basis; and the Twelve Tables were seen as the starting-point of the development of Roman law.

Tychē, fate, fortune both good and bad. Like Moira (see FATE), Tyche gives everything to mortals from birth. The mightiest of the Moirai in

*Pindar, she is the child of *Zeus Eleutherius. A splendid lyric fragment praises noble Tyche who dispenses more good than evil from her scales: grace shines about her golden wing, and she lights up the darkness. Though ambivalent by nature, she tends to be favourable, comparable with the *agathos daimōn*.

The popular view of a capricious, malignant Tyche emerges from New *Comedy: she was dangerous, senseless, blind, wretched, etc. In romances she figures large as a convenient plot device. Negative in *Thucydides (2) as blows of Fate, or an inscrutable element that confuses human affairs, she plays a larger role in *Polybius. Cunning Tyche is sudden, changeable, jealous. Nevertheless the historian contrasts this popular image of all-powerful Chance with what can be expected as reasonable historical development, like Rome's rise to power.

See also FORTUNA/FORS.

Tȳdeus legendary warrior of the generation before the Trojan War. Leaving home in Calydon, he came to *Argos, whose king, *Adrastus, gave him his daughter Dēïpȳlē in marriage; she bore him *Diomedes, who is always conscious at Troy of the need to match his father's exploits. Enrolled as one of the *Seven against Thebes, Tydeus first—acc. to *Homer's *Iliad*, drawing and no doubt embroidering upon earlier *Thebaid* traditions, see EPIC CYCLE—took part in an embassy to the city, triumphed over the locals in a series of games, then killed all but one of a 50-strong band sent to ambush him on his return to base. In the war itself, he proved himself a fierce fighter in spite of his stocky build; his thirst for slaughter drove him to put the Theban princess Ismēnē ruthlessly to the sword, and even in his own death-throes to try to eat out the brains of the wounded Melanippus—an act that cost him the immortality which Athena had arranged.

Tyndareōs, in mythology husband of *Leda and father, real or putative, of *Helen, *Clytemnestra, and the *Dioscuri. He succeeded eventually to the Spartan throne. When suitors came, wishing to marry Helen, Tyndareos made them take an oath to protect the marriage-rights of the chosen bridegroom, which led in due course to the Trojan War (see HOMER; TROY) when the Greek leaders marshalled troops to fetch back Helen after she deserted *Menelaus for *Paris. *Hesiod says that when sacrificing to the gods Tyndareos forgot *Aphrodite, so the goddess in anger made his daughters unfaithful, Helen with Paris, and Clytemnestra with *Aegisthus.

Tyndareos in due course bequeathed his kingdom to Menelaus. *Euripides has him live long enough to bring the charge of matricide against *Orestes.

tyrannicides, killers of tyrants (see TYRANNY) generally but specially used of (a) the killers of *Hipparchus (1) of Athens (see ARISTOGITON; also CRITIUS for a famous statue group) and (b) the killers of *Caesar (see esp. CASSIUS LONGINUS; IUNIUS BRUTUS).

tyranny (*tyrannos*, 'tyrant', was perhaps a Lydian word) was the form of monarchy set up by usurpers in many Greek states in the 7th and 6th cents. BC. The term first occurs in *Archilochus. Tyranny was not a special form of constitution, or necessarily a reign of terror; the tyrant might either rule directly or retain the existing political institutions but exercise a preponderant influence over their working, and his rule might be benevolent or malevolent. Tyranny acquired a bad reputation esp. from *Plato and *Aristotle, for whom it was the worst possible form of constitution.

The best known early tyrants were Pheidon of Argos, *Cypselus and *Periander of Corinth, *Cleisthenes (1) of Sicyon, *Pisistratus and his sons *Hippias (1) and *Hipparchus (1) in Athens, and *Polycrates (1) of Samos. Archaic tyranny seems to have been a response to the development of the *polis: typically a fringe member of the ruling *aristocracy would seize power with the support of discontented members of the community; but after a time the rule of the tyrant in turn became a cause of discontent, and tyranny rarely lasted more than two generations. These tyrants ruled in a period of growing confidence and prosperity: by encouraging national cults, by sponsoring public works, and by acting as patrons to writers and artists, they glorified both their cities and themselves. See PATRONAGE, LITERARY. Later tyrants were military dictators, among them *Gelon and *Hieron (1) I of Syracuse and *Theron of Acragas at the beginning of the 5th cent. and *Dionysius I and of Syracuse in the late 5th and 4th cents.

Tyre, a major city in southern *Phoenicia with a large territory, built on an island but extending ashore, and equipped with two harbours. It was the main founder of Phoenician colonies to the west (*Cyprus, *Carthage, etc.), and its international trade from Spain to the Persian Gulf is evoked in Ezekiel. The Tyrian *navy is often mentioned as an ally of the *Persians. In 332 BC it resisted *Alexander (2) the Great and was captured only after a long siege. It recovered quickly and became a Ptolemaic possession (see EGYPT, *Ptolemaic*). Conquered by the *Seleucids in 200, it became free in 126. It early struck a *foedus* with Rome. It was made a colony (see COLONIZATION, ROMAN) by *Septimius Severus. It was a great commercial city, with offices at *Puteoli and at Rome during the Principate, and was the seat of famous *purple-dyeing and *glass industries; its wealth is shown by the beautiful *sarcophagi of its Roman necropolis.

Tyrtaeus, Spartan *elegiac poet of the mid-7th cent. BC. His works are said to have filled five books; some 250 lines or parts of lines survive in quotations and papyri. They throw light on two crises affecting Sparta at the time. One was civic unrest that threatened the authority of the kings and elders. In a poem that later came to be entitled *Eunomia* ('Good Order'), Tyrtaeus reminded the citizens of the divine right by which the kings ruled, and of the oracle which had laid down the constitutional roles of kings, council, and *dēmos*. The other crisis was the Second Messenian War (see SPARTA, 2). Here too Tyrtaeus functioned as a state poet, exhorting the Spartans to fight to the death for their city. He addresses the fighting men as if they were already on the battlefield, and perhaps they were. Certainly in the 4th cent. when Tyrtaeus was an established classic, Spartan armies on campaign were made to listen to recitations of his poetry.

Ulpian, lawyer. See DOMITIUS ULPIANUS.

Ulysses See ODYSSEUS.

unconstitutional proposals, law against (in Athens). See GRAPHE PARANOMON.

Underworld See HADES.

Ūrănus (Gk. **Ouranos**), the divine personification of the sky in Greece. Scarcely known in cult, his best-known appearance is in *Hesiod's Theogony*. He is produced by *Gaia (Earth), then becoming her consort, but hating their children, he causes them to remain confined within her. At the instigation of Gaia, he is castrated by their son *Cronus; the severed genitals are cast into the sea and engender *Aphrodite.

urban cohorts See COHORTES URBANAE.

urbanism

Greek and Hellenistic Urban units are to be distinguished not simply by the size of the settlement, but by its topographical organization, occupational pattern, and cultural sophistication.

No Dark Age settlement deserves to be called a town, and the growth of towns in the 8th and 7th cents. seems often to be the result of separate village communities coalescing for political and economic reasons (*synoecism). At *Corinth the creation of a single town, with a specific area devoted to burial of the dead, and the creation of a separate potters' quarter go closely together, and are followed within half a century by temple-building and by *tyranny. Corinthian pottery already follows an independent tradition before the grouping of potting activity into the potters' quarter. The impetus to urbanism in Corinth may have come in part from the sending out of colonizing expeditions, which probably formed communities recognizably urban in their organization of civic space from the beginning. The members of a new community, formed from scratch, must have given thought to the requirements and organization of communal life. This may in turn have led to changes at home. Many early towns seem to have lacked walls; but at this stage colonizing and urbanism are phenomena of agriculturally marginal southern Greece, as also is the *polis.

Greek political thought did not recognize the existence of urban communities which were not also politically independent. Urbanism and political independence went closely together. One mark of both is the focusing of the community's religious life upon particular *sanctuaries, both central sanctuaries and those at the margins of a city's territory which stake out claims to territorial control.

The assumption that urban units should also enjoy political independence affected urban development across a single political territory. The main settlement tends to be much the largest settlement in a political territory, and even when there are other populous centres, they tend not to develop the full range of characteristically urban services—theatres, palaestras, diverse sanctuaries, dedicated community meeting-places. This is esp. clear in Athens, where some of the *demes were very much larger than *poleis* elsewhere in Greece (*Acharnae may have had a population of 8,000–10,000), but where none of them seems to have developed the facilities of a town.

In classical towns further attention is devoted to the space within which non-religious civic activities take place, and there are buildings specifically designed for such activities. The development of the *stoa, from the mid-6th cent. onwards, played an important part in this. Flanking the *agora with stoas became a popular way of marking out the civic centre.

During the 5th, 4th, and 3rd cents. urban forms spread to mainland northern Greece, both to the seaboard under the direct influence of southern cities, and inland in Macedonia, Thessaly, and even Epirus, in association with the greater political unification of those territories. These new towns were all marked by regular land division such as had marked most new developments since the 6th cent. and which had by this time become one of the hallmarks of a Greek city (see HIPPODAMUS). It is such regular planning, as well as specific Greek building types, that is exported to the near east with *Alexander (2) the Great.

See ARCHITECTURE, *Greek*; COLONIZATION, GREEK; ECONOMY, GREEK and HELLENISTIC; HOUSES, GREEK; MARKETS; SANITATION; WATER SUPPLY.

Roman The Romans based their city-policy and urban ideology mainly on their own city. Already in the 6th cent. BC extensive in surface-area, imposing in its public buildings and private houses, and complex in its use of space, Rome functioned as a show-case and pioneer of urban form. In the 4th cent. Rome's urban functions were transformed, through the economic and prestige gains of military success, the organization of a huge territory with the expanding tribal system, and new types of relations with neighbouring cities which foreshadowed the incorporative and co-operative citizenship policies on which a large urban population ultimately depended: the future megalopolis was conceived.

It is only from the perspective of the super-city that the long-lasting tradition of Roman urban policy can be understood. Other ancient cities produced offshoot communities which were essentially new cities. Rome alone deployed its population resources, citizen or Latin, in planned locations, maintaining a superior status, and a continuing political and governmental relationship which went far beyond any Greek or Carthaginian *mētropois–*apoikia tie.

The successes of the Roman élite from the Latin War to the *Pyrrhic transformed Rome, under the influence of the developing urban tradition of Greek southern Italy and Sicily. The new foundations adopted from the centre a repertoire of institutional architecture—forum, *porticoes, *comitium, *temples, streets, sewers (see SANITATION, *Roman*), monuments—which expanded as the city grew in grandeur through the 2nd cent. In mainly military installations, such as the maritime colonies, we are reminded of the *fortifications which many Italic peoples were building in the 4th and 3rd cents. on the model of Hellenic military engineering (see COLONIZATION, ROMAN).

In these cities a citizen egalitarianism (also found in the division of the territory: see CENTURIATION) was derived from Roman constitutional theory and (therefore) linked to military needs. It was esp. apparent in the regularity and uniformity of the plan, which have become the most famous features of Roman cities, and which echo the ideas of *Hippodamus; but is also reflected in the legal and political institutions and their architecture (e.g. comitium and *basilica), and increasingly by the late republic, the provision of the latest in the people's perks, such as *baths and places for spectacles.

By the age of *Cicero, the local élites of many Italian towns, enriched by a century of imperial success, had embellished their communities with the latest in Hellenistic taste, in a way that was still intermittent at Rome. Swollen by centuries of opportunistic influx and impossible to plan, the metropolis was less beautiful than its old enemy *Capua. *Sulla, *Pompey, and *Caesar made strenuous efforts to remedy this, and *Augustus completed the process of making Rome a worthy model for the founding and embellishing of cities everywhere.

Roman urbanism and its apparent uniformity in the early imperial period are the product of the imitation in local communities of canons of monumentality made fashionable by people further up the chain of patronage. Cities in the provinces came to have an ideological role, as exemplars of the values of Hellenic/Roman culture and a symbol of conversion from barbarism. Fortified settlements were moved from impregnable heights to the plain, gaining the easy communications and plain-land investment agriculture which were also signs of what the *pax Romana* offered local élites. Roman institutional statuses (see CIVITAS; MUNICIPIUM) helped the process, and the bases of the army and the veteran colonies which resembled them in function and planning, provided further examples, as at Arelate, and *Emerita Augusta. Meanwhile Rome itself came to resemble the other cities more. Fires and expansion into the periphery made possible the development of large areas of the city on a more regular plan. The great baths and prestige projects like the *Colosseum or *Pantheon were imitated in favoured centres; in projects like the *forum Traiani, however, or the great temples of the reigns from Hadrian to Aurelian, it is the grandiose architecture of the provinces that was being recreated on a grander scale in the centre.

Cities in more civilized places had always been the organs of communication, and the respecting (or not) of privileges, age, beauty, and so on became an important part of Roman government. The destruction of cities (*Carthage, *Corinth, *Jerusalem) must be considered part of Roman urban policy, throwing into relief the more desirable role of the Roman leader as founder of cities. Posing as the first or new founder of a city was a potent image that came to be often used. New imitations of the centre were made on an ambitious scale, and certain cities were singled out to enjoy the full benefit of imperial favour (*Lepcis, *Augusta Treverorum). The whole question of the standing of cities and their claims to favour, based on the past and present attainments of their citizens, became a central feature of life under the empire. The rhetoric in which the cities competed, and which is so apparent in Antonine literature, is a part of Roman urbanism, and relevant to its extension even into remote provinces. The aspirations of communities for a higher place in the formal hierarchy of city status is a real feature of this state of affairs, and the spreading of municipal status (see MUNICIPIUM), the upgrading of villages to cities, *municipia* to *coloniae*, and the increase in city institutions in places like *Egypt and *Syria where they had been less widespread, owes more to this competition than it does to imperial vision.

We should not credit Rome with planning the flowering of cities or their cultural uniformity, let alone with a set of social and economic goals to be achieved through urbanization. The symbolic importance of the city often concealed small structural change in the organization of the productive environment. Many cities probably had quite small permanent populations.

Utica by tradition the oldest Phoenician settlement on the north African coast, 33 km. (21 mi.) NE of Tunis. Utica was a busy port at the mouth of the river Bagradas. It was always an important part of the empire of *Carthage. It was besieged by *Cornelius Scipio Africanus in 204. A supporter of *Masinissa against Carthage in 149, Utica was rewarded by Rome with lands of the fallen city, and was made a *civitas libera* (see FREE CITIES) and the capital of the new Roman province of *Africa in 146. Italian financiers and merchants soon settled in the city, and *Pompey made the port his base for the swift campaign which won Africa from the Marians (81). Later Utica remained loyal to the Pompeian cause, and was the scene of *Porcius Cato (2)'s suicide. Heavily fined for its senatorial sympathies, Utica lost influence as Roman Carthage grew, but it received Latin rights (see IUS LATII) under *Augustus and became a *colony* (see COLONIZATION, ROMAN)) under *Hadrian.

utopias See EUHEMERUS; ISLANDS; POLIS.

Valentinian I, Roman emperor (AD 364–375), b. 321 in Pannonia. In 364 when Jovian died, he was commanding a guards regiment, and at Nicaea the generals and civil dignitaries elected him emperor. At Constantinople in March he proclaimed his brother Valens emperor of the eastern empire, and took the west for himself. Here he concentrated on frontier defence. The Alamanni who invaded Gaul were destroyed, and their homeland was devastated; fortifications on the Rhine and Danube were reconstructed for the last time. In Britain and Africa order was brutally restored. In 375 Valentinian left Gaul because Pannonia had been invaded, and while berating a delegation of those responsible, he suffered a stroke and died.

The fit of rage was characteristic, but Valentinian was a conscientious administrator who tried to control abuses and over-taxation. He was unusual in being a Catholic tolerant of pagans and most heretics; he intervened in Church politics only to maintain public order. Relations with the senatorial aristocracy were strained: he promoted professional soldiers and bureaucrats, and senators at Rome were executed by his ministers for sexual misdemeanours or magic.

Valeria Messallīna, great-granddaughter of *Augustus' sister *Octavia on her father's and mother's sides; b. before AD 20. In 39 or 40 she married her second cousin *Claudius, then c.50 years old and bore him two children, *Claudia Octavia and *Britannicus. Claudius alone was blind to her sexual profligacy (which *Juvenal travestied in Satires 6 and 10), even to her eventual participation in the formalities of a marriage service with a consul-designate in 48. *Narcissus turned against her and, while Claudius was in a state of stunned incredulity, ensured that an executioner was sent. Since she was unable to do the deed herself, the tribune ran her through.

Valerius Flaccus, Gāius, Roman poet, author of the *Argonautica*, *Flavian epic poem on the voyage of *Jason (1) and the *Argonauts to Colchis in search of the Golden Fleece.

Valerius' poem follows the Argonauts' expedition through many famous adventures to the point where Jason absconds from Colchis with *Medea. It breaks off as Medea is persuading Jason not to hand her back to her brother Absyrtus.

The poem owes much to *Apollonius (1) Rhodius' *Argonautica* as a quest with a strong interest in the problems of epic heroism. Valerius, though, departs radically from Apollonius when he concentrates on *Argo* as the first ship, harbinger of civilization, placing his poem in a long Roman tradition of appropriation of the *golden age and iron age myths. A cosmic frame is provided by Jupiter's concern for the expedition, which will reproduce on earth the patterns of order and dominance guaranteed universally by his own recent victory over the *Giants. The cycles set in train by *Argo*'s voyage will carry on down to the contemporary world of the Roman empire, where the Flavian house likewise rules after the chaos of civil war. Valerius recounts the origin of warfare and imperial institutions, so that the poem is studded with overt references to contemporary Roman practices. Valerius exploits Virgil's *Georgics* and *Seneca the Younger's *Medea* to stress the ambivalence of iron age achievement, for navigation is a violation of natural boundaries, and hence either magnificent or impious in its audacity. In cunning and ironic counterpoint to these grand themes is the love story which overtakes the narrative in bk. 5. Valerius rises to the daunting challenge of going where Apollonius, Virgil, and Ovid had gone before, exploiting his great goddesses to present a sombre and frightening image of Medea's passion. Valerius has suffered from being viewed as an earnest imitator of mightier models; his self-awareness and wry humour have gone largely unnoticed, although he has been commended for the poise of his versification and the acuity of his observation.

Valerius Maximus wrote a handbook of 'memorable deeds and sayings'. It is dedicated to *Tiberius, to whom constant flattery is addressed; and the violent denunciation of a conspirator safely identified with *Aelius Seianus suggests that it was published soon after his downfall in 31. The subject-matter has no clearly defined plan, but is divided under headings mostly moral or philosophical in character (e.g. Omens, Moderation, Gratitude, Chastity, Cruelty), usually illustrated by Roman and foreign examples. The latter, chiefly Greek, are admittedly less important, and in keeping with the strongly national spirit of the compilation are outnumbered by former by two to one. Valerius' chief sources seem to have been *Livy and *Cicero, but there are indications of many others. His use of this material is almost entirely non-critical, and varies greatly in extent and accuracy. The work has been condemned as shallow, sententious, and bombastic, full of the boldest metaphor and rhetorical artifices of the *Silver Age, esp. forced antitheses and far-fetched epigrams, only occasionally relieved by touches of poetic fancy or neat passages of narrative or dialogue; but its sources and alignment have begun to attract attention. The variety and convenience of the compilation ensured some measure of success in antiquity, and considerably more in the Middle Ages.

Valerius Messalla Corvīnus, Marcus (64 BC–AD 8), Roman public figure. He first distinguished himself in the *Philippi campaign (43–42), following his hero *Cassius. Declining command of the republican army after this defeat, he transferred his allegiance first to Antony (Marcus *Antonius), then to Octavian (see AUGUSTUS). He fought against Sextus *Pompeius (36), wrote pamphlets against Antony, and as consul with Octavian (31) fought in the battle of *Actium. After a command in *Syria he governed Gaul, where he conquered the Aquitani, celebrating a *triumph in 27. In 26 or 25 he was made city *prefect but resigned after a few days, claiming that he was uncertain how to operate or, more bluntly, that the power was unsuitable for a citizen amongst citizens. Thereafter he enjoyed less prominence, but there was no public breach with *Augustus. Already an *augur and by 20 BC an arval brother (a priestly college, of which the reigning emperor was always a member; in a festival the brethren sang a fam-

ous 'song'), he became the first permanent commissioner for the water supply in 11, and it was he who proposed the title of *Pater Patriae (see CURA(TIO), CURATOR) for Augustus (2 BC). He reconstructed part of the via Latina; he gained fame as an orator; he wrote his memoirs, and was patron of an impressive literary circle—*Tibullus, the young *Ovid, and his own niece *Sulpicia.

Varius Rūfus, an Augustan poet, friend of *Virgil and member with him, *Quinctilius Varus, and Plotius Tucca of an Epicurean (see EPICURUS) group referred to by *Philodemus. He was also a friend of *Maecenas, to whom he and Virgil introduced *Horace. He wrote a *hexameter poem *On Death*, probably intended on Epicurean lines to free men from the fear of death. It was apparently written *c*.43 BC and contained uncomplimentary allusions to Marcus *Antonius (Mark Antony); these and other passages were imitated by Virgil. Horace speaks of him as pre-eminent in *epic and suggests him as a panegyrist of *Vipsanius Agrippa. His tragedy *Thyestēs*, which was greatly admired, was commissioned by Augustus for his games of 29 in celebration of Actium and lavishly rewarded by him. After Virgil's death he prepared the *Aeneid* for publication.

Varrō, Marcus Terentius (116–27 BC), b. at *Sabine Reate. After studying at Rome with *Aelius, the first true scholar of Latin literature and antiquities, and at Athens with the Academic philosopher Antiochus of Ascalon, Varro began a public career that brought him to the praetorship and, ultimately, to service on the Pompeian side (see POMPEIUS MAGNUS, GNAEUS) in the Civil War. Having received *Caesar's clemency after *Pharsalus, he was asked to plan and organize the first public library (see LIBRARIES) at Rome. But this project went unrealized, and after Caesar's assassination he was proscribed by Mark Antony (Marcus *Antonius): his library at Casinum was plundered, but he escaped to live the rest of his life in scholarly retirement. He had completed 490 books by the start of his 78th year: 55 titles are known in all, and his *œuvre* has been estimated to include nearly 75 different works totalling *c*.620 books.

Works Varro's combination of methodical analysis, vast range, and original learning made him Rome's greatest scholar. His writings covered nearly every branch of inquiry: history, geography, rhetoric, law, philosophy, music, medicine, architecture, literary history, religion, agriculture, and language (at least ten works on this last alone). The achievements of the Augustans and of later authors, in both poetry and prose, are scarcely conceivable without the groundwork that he had laid. See also SCHOLARSHIP, ANCIENT, *Latin*.

Only two of his works survive substantially:

1. *On the Latin Language*, in 25 books, of which bks. 5–10 are partly extant (5 and 6 entirely). Bk. 1 provided an introduction; 2–7 dealt with *etymology, and the connection between words and the entities they represent; 8–13, with inflectional morphology and the conflict between 'anomalists' and 'analogists' (see ANALOGY AND ANOMALY); 14–25, with syntax and the proper formation of 'propositions'. Varro dedicated bks. 2–4 to his quaestor, the subsequent books to *Cicero; the work was published before Cicero's death, probably in 43.

2. *On Farming* (3 books), a treatise on farming in dialogue form, intended as an agreeable entertainment for men of Varro's own class. It deals with agriculture in general (bk. 1), cattle- and sheep-breeding (bk. 2), and smaller farm-animals (birds, bees, etc.: bk. 3). The work, which survives entirely and shows some amusing strokes of characterization, reveals very strikingly Varro's fondness for analysing his subjects into their parts, and those parts into their sub-parts: though this analysis is sometimes carried to unhelpful lengths, it also represents a new stage in the logical organization of prose at Rome. See AGRICULTURE, ROMAN; AGRICULTURAL WRITERS.

Varro's lost works include:

1. *Menippean Satires* (150 books), humorous essays on topics of contemporary vice and folly, mingling verse with prose; Varro professed to imitate Menippus of Gadara. See MENIPPEAN SATIRE.

2. *Antiquities Human and Divine*. Of the first 25 books, on human (i.e. Roman) antiquities, little is known: the introductory book was followed by four segments of (probably) six books each, on persons (the inhabitants of Italy), places, times, and things. The remaining sixteen books, dedicated to *Caesar as *pontifex maximus*, might be entitled *On Religion*: another book of general introduction, then five triads, on priesthoods, holy places, holy times, rites, and kinds of god. Among the lost works of republican prose, *Antiquities* is perhaps the one we miss most sorely.

3. *On Portraits*, a collection of 700 portraits of celebrated Greeks and Romans, in which each portrait was accompanied by an epigram.

4. *Disciplines*, a late work surveying the essential terms and principles of the learned 'disciplines' that a free man should command: these 'liberal arts' included 'grammar', rhetoric, dialectic, arithmetic, geometry, astronomy, music, medicine, and architecture (see EDUCATION, GREEK, 4).

vase-painting See PAINTING, GREEK; POTTERY, GREEK.

Vatican, an area outside the walls of Rome, on the right bank of the *Tiber around the mons Vaticanus. In the early empire the Vatican was the site of an imperial park (the gardens of Agrippina); and of entertainment structures, the *Naumachiae*, where mock sea-battles were exhibited, and the Vatican *circus, where *Gaius (1) set up a great obelisk from Heliopolis and which was traditionally the site of the martyrdom of St Peter; and along the two roads that crossed the area, the via Cornelia and the via Triumphalis, were cemeteries. A group of mausolea on the foot-slopes of the mons Vaticanus were excavated under St Peter's in the 1940s, and within this cemetery (directly under the high altar of St Peter's) was found a small 2nd-cent. shrine, marking the probable burial-site of the apostle Peter.

Vatīnius, Publius, tribune 59 BC (see TRIBUNI PLEBIS), sponsored the bills granting *Caesar Cisalpine Gaul (see GAUL (CISALPINE)) and Illyricum (see ILLYRIANS), and confirming the eastern settlement of *Pompey. He also features prominently in attacks on *Calpurnius Bibulus. In 56 he was a witness against Sestius, and *Cicero, defending Sestius, inveighed against Vatinius. But the forensic relationship was soon reversed: Vatinius was praetor 55, and in 54, obedient to Caesar, Pompey, and *Crassus, Cicero successfully defended Vatinius on a bribery charge arising from his election to the praetorship. After serving with Caesar in Gaul, Vatinius won a victory in the Adriatic in 47, and in December received the consulship, an office he had always boasted he would hold. As proconsul in Illyricum (45) he won a *supplicatio and, although he had surrendered to *Brutus in 43, was allowed an Illyrian triumph (42). Vatinius was an easy butt because of his personal disabilities; but he took raillery well, and in later life was genuinely reconciled with Cicero.

vectīgal meant primarily revenue derived from public land, mines, saltworks, etc., and in general, rents derived from state property. Such sources provided the basic revenues of the early republic, and remained the most important form of income for the *municipia and *civitates of the empire. The term was extended to cover indirect taxes of which only the *portoria and a tax of 5 per cent on the value of manumitted slaves, existed in the republic. In the Principate the number of *vectigalia* was increased, and they provided a considerable part of the state revenues. The inhabitants of Italy, who were exempt from *tributum, paid only *vectigalia*. The most important of the *vectigalia* were the *portoria*.

*Augustus, in order to raise revenues for the provision of discharge-donations to veterans, founded the *aerarium militare* into which was paid the yield of two new taxes. A tax of 1 per cent on sales by auction was halved by *Tiberius and abolished, in Italy, by *Gaius (1). The *vīcēsima hērēditātum* was a tax of 5 per cent, paid only by citizens, on significant sums bequeathed to persons other than near relatives. The spread of citizenship increased its yield. Augustus also established a 4 per cent tax on sale of slaves, to provide the pay of the *vigiles. The collection of *vectigalia* in the republic and early Principate was let out to companies of *publicani. See also FINANCE, ROMAN.

vegetarianism See ANIMALS, ATTITUDES TO.

Vegetius, wrote a *Short Account of Military Practice* in four books, which is the only such account to have survived intact. The work was written after AD 383 but before 450, and is addressed to an emperor.

Book 1 discusses the recruit, bk. 2 army organization, bk. 3 tactics and strategy, bk. 4 fortifications and naval warfare. Vegetius examines important matters—the maintenance of discipline and morale, vigilant preparations in enemy territory, establishing a camp, campaign planning, tactical adaptability in battle, conducting a retreat, and the use of stratagems. He also quotes some maxims which 'tested by different ages and proved by constant experience, have been passed down by distinguished writers'. Vegetius is convinced of the relevance of this approach. The emperor had instructed him to abridge ancient authors, and sought instruction from past exploits despite his own achievements.

Vegetius was not himself a soldier or historian, but served in the imperial administration. He took an antiquarian interest in the army, ignoring the detailed changes accomplished by

*Diocletian and *Constantine I, and for his manual collected material from many sources and chronological periods without adequate differentiation and classification. This impairs his value as a source for the organization and practices of the Roman army. He mentions some of his sources: *Porcius Cato (1), *Iulius Frontinus, and the ordinances of *Augustus, *Trajan, and *Hadrian. But there is no reason to assume that he always consulted these at first hand or that they were his only sources. The 'old legion' to which Vegetius refers, and which is clearly not from his own day, should probably be dated to the late 3rd cent.

See also ARMIES.

Velleius Paterculus, Roman historical writer, b. in (probably) 20 or 19 BC. He spent AD 4–12 serving under the future emperor Tiberius in Germany twice, Pannonia, and Dalmatia. In 6, having completed his service as an *equestrian officer, he returned to Rome and was elected quaestor for 7; in 12 he and his brother took part in Tiberius' *Illyrian *triumph; and, when *Augustus died in 14, both brothers were already designated 'candidates of Caesar' for the praetorship of 15.

Velleius' work begins with Greek mythology and ends in AD 29, a span of time which he encompassed in only two volumes. Like Cornelius *Nepos he is thus a writer of summary history, something to which he draws frequent attention. Almost all of bk. 1 is lost. It is separated from bk. 2 by two excursuses, which would be notable even in a full-length history (on Roman *colonization; on Greek and Latin literature); and bk. 2 begins, as the narrative part of bk. 1 had ended, with the destruction of *Carthage in 146 BC, which Velleius, like *Sallust, saw as a turning-point in Roman history. Although the following years to 59 BC are dispatched in a mere 40 chapters, which include three further excursuses of varying length (on Roman authors, and on Roman provincialization), Velleius devotes increasing amounts of space to *Caesar, Augustus, and esp. Tiberius, whose career forms the climax of his work.

Though Velleius constantly imitates the phraseology of both Sallust and *Cicero, it is the fullness and balance of the latter's style that he aimed generally to reproduce. His sentences, replete with antithesis and point, are often long and involved; and he has a gift for pithy characterization. Yet readers have been dismayed by the successive rhetorical questions and exclamations in his account of Tiberius, which in general, like his treatment of *Aelius Seianus, has been regarded as mere panegyric.

Yet in imperial times the traditional patriotism of Roman historians was inevitably focused on the emperor of the day, who in Velleius' case was also his former commander; and his account of Tiberius is valuable in presenting the establishment view of events for which Tacitus, from the safer perspective of the 2nd cent., supplies an opposition view. Even so the prayer, which forms the unconventional conclusion to his work, is arguably a recognition of the political crisis of 29, while the treatment of Sejanus, which is not a panegyric of the man but a defence of his elevation by Tiberius, betrays some of the very unease which it seems designed to dispel.

Velleius travelled widely; he was a senator, like Sallust and *Tacitus, and held magisterial office; like *Thucydides (2) he witnessed and took part in a significant number of the events he describes. He thus enjoyed many of the advantages conventionally associated with the ideal historian. He regularly provides information on topics about which we would otherwise be ignorant; and he is the only Latin historian of Roman affairs to have survived from the period between *Livy and Tacitus.

vēnātiōnēs 'Hunts', involving the slaughter of *animals, esp. fierce ones, by other animals or human fighters of wild beasts—and sometimes of criminals by animals, see below— were a major spectacle at Rome from 186 BC. They displayed the ingenuity and generosity of the sponsoring politician, and the reach of Rome, and its power over nature, in procuring exotic species (lions, panthers, bears, crocodiles, hippopotamuses, rhinoceroses, elephants): they admitted a privileged city-audience to the glories of traditional aristocratic hunting. Along with gladiatorial fights, they were a main reason for building *amphitheatres. The emperors gave esp. sumptuous displays: 5,000 wild and 4,000 tame animals died at the inauguration of *Titus' *Colosseum in 80, and 11,000 at *Trajan's *Dacian *triumph. Esp. in the later 1st cent. AD, criminals might be forced to re-enact gruesome myths (e.g. the killing of *Orpheus by a bear). See GLADIATORS; HUNTING.

vengeance See CURSES; ERINYES; LAW AND PROCEDURE, ROMAN, 3.1; LAW IN GREECE; NEMESIS; PUNISHMENT, GREEK AND ROMAN PRACTICE; RECIPROCITY.

Venus, an Italian goddess, the patron of all persuasive seductions, between gods and mortals, and between men and women (Venus Verticordia, 'changer of hearts'). Because of her links with the power of *wine, Venus is presented in the rites and myth of the festivals of wine-production (Vinalia) as a mediatrix between *Jupiter and the Romans. The first known temple is that of Venus Obsequens ('Propitious'), vowed in 295 BC and built some years later. During the *Punic Wars, the tutelary and diplomatic role of Venus grew continually, in proportion to the process of her assimilation to Greek *Aphrodite. In the 1st cent. BC she even acquired a political value. She was claimed by *Sulla as his protectress (his *agnomen* Epaphroditus means 'favoured by Venus'), as by *Pompey (Venus Victrix) and *Caesar (Venus Genetrix). Under the empire Venus became one of the major divinities of the official pantheon.

Vercingetorix, son of a powerful and ambitious Arvernian nobleman, raised the revolt against *Caesar in 52 BC and was acclaimed king of his people and general of the confederates. Defeated at Noviodunum Biturigum, he turned to depriving Caesar of supplies while tempting him either to attack or ingloriously decline to attack an impregnable foe. The policy succeeded admirably near Avaricum, where Caesar did not attack, and at Gergovia, where he did. Vercingetorix then risked another attack on Caesar in the field, which was badly defeated, so that he retreated to another prepared fortress, Alesia. Caesar had an unexpected weapon, the circumvallation, with which he beat off not only Vercingetorix but also additional Gallic forces summoned to relieve Alesia. Vercingetorix surrendered and was put to death after Caesar's *triumph (46). Vercingetorix's career shows how dangerous the developed Gallic nations were to Rome, yet how profoundly, once defeated, they succumbed to foreign rule: he was never apparently venerated as a national hero. See GALLIC WARS.

Vergil See VIRGIL.

Vergīnius Rūfus, Lūcius, from Mediolanum, consul AD 63, became governor of Upper Germany in 67. He apparently held discussions with the rebel *Iulius Vindex and may have been forced into battle at Vesontio by the precipitate action of his troops. Rejecting his army's attempts to proclaim him emperor, he was nevertheless slow to support *Galba, remitting the choice to the senate. Removed from office by the suspicious Galba, Verginius became *suffect consul for the second time under *Otho, and after his murder again refused the purple. Thereafter he lived quietly, becoming consul for the third time with *Nerva in 97. When he died soon after, his funeral oration was delivered by *Tacitus. He was *Pliny the Younger's guardian. His self-chosen epitaph reads (ambiguously): 'Here lies Rufus, who, after the defeat of Vindex, set free the imperial power, not for himself, but for his country'.

Verrēs, Gāius Quaestor in 84 BC. As *legate of Cornēlius Dolabella in Cilicia, he helped him plunder his province and Asia, but on their return helped to secure his conviction. As urban *praetor (74), he is charged by *Cicero with having flagrantly sold justice. Assigned Sicily as proconsul (73–71), he exploited and oppressed the province (except for *Messana, in league with him) and even Roman citizens living or trading there. Unwisely offending some senators and ill-treating clients of *Pompey, he yet evaded the effect of a senate decree censuring him, passed on the motion of the consuls of 72, and was again *prorogued. On his return, he used his great wealth (much of it acquired in Sicily) and his connections, and exploited the hostility of leading nobles (esp. most of the Metelli) to Pompey, to gain strong and eminent support. *Hortensius Hortalus, consul designate for 69 with a friendly Metellus, defended him against a prosecution launched in the extortion court (see QUAESTIONES; REPETUNDAE) by Cicero (70) and tried to drag the case on into his year of office. Outwitted by Cicero's speed and forensic tactics, and despite the efforts of a Metellus as Verres' successor in Sicily, Hortensius found the case caught up in the popular agitation for jury reform and succumbed to Pompey's influence exerted against Verres. On his advice, Verres fled into exile at *Massalia. Cicero nevertheless published the the five speeches of the second *actio* that he had prepared, to drive home Verres' guilt and demonstrate his own skill and efforts. The evidence seems overwhelming. But after his victory Cicero conciliated Verres' many noble supporters by agreeing to a low assessment of damages.

His *Verrines* give us our best insight into provincial administration and its abuses in the late republic. Verres died at Massalia, allegedly *proscribed for his stolen art treasures by Marcus *Antonius (Mark Antony).

Vērus, Lūcius, Roman emperor AD 161–169, was born in 130 and named Lucius Ceionius Commodus, son of Lucius Aelius Caesar. On Aelius' death, *Hadrian required his second choice as heir, *Antoninus Pius, to adopt Lucius along with his own nephew Marcus *Aurelius; he now had the names Lucius (Aelius) Aurelius Commodus, but unlike Marcus did not become Caesar. He became consul in 154 and was consul again in 161 with Marcus, who, following the death of Antoninus, at once made him co-emperor. He dropped the name Commodus, taking his adoptive brother's name Verus instead. He was thus the first joint Augustus, equal in all respects except for the position of *pontifex maximus*. When the *Parthians invaded the empire, he took nominal command of the ensuing Parthian War (162–166), in fact waged by his generals. In 164 he went to Ephesus to marry Marcus' daughter Annia Aurelia Galeria Lucilla, by whom he had several children. For his victories he assumed the titles *Armeniacus, Parthicus,* and *Mēdicus,* and held a *triumph jointly with Marcus in October 166. He reluctantly accompanied Marcus to the Danubian provinces in 168, to prepare for an offensive against the threatening German tribes, but, alarmed by the spread of *plague in winter-quarters at Aquileia, persuaded Marcus to set out for Rome in January 169; on the journey he suffered a stroke and died a few days later. He was deified as *divus Verus.*

Vespasian (Titus Flāvius Vespāsiānus), emperor AD 69–79, b. AD 9 at *Sabine Reātĕ. His father, Flavius Sabīnus, was a tax-collector (see PUBLICANI); his mother was of *equestrian family, but her brother entered the senate, reaching the praetorship. Vespasian was military tribune (see TRIBUNI MILITUM) in 27, serving in Thrace, quaestor in Crete in the mid-30s, aedile (at the second attempt) in 38, and praetor in 40. Claudius' freedman *Narcissus now advanced his undistinguished career, and he became *legate of *legion II Augusta, commanding it in the invasion of *Britain in 43 and subduing the SW as far as Exeter (43–47); for this he won triumphal *ornaments and two priesthoods (see PRIESTS). He was *suffect consul in 51 and is next heard of as an unpopular proconsul of *Africa c.62; any unemployment may be due to the deaths of Narcissus and Lucius *Vitellius and the eclipse of other supporters during the ascendancy of *Iulia Agrippina. In 66 he accompanied Nero to Greece and allegedly offended him by falling asleep at one of his recitals, but at the end of the year he was entrusted with suppressing the rebellion in Judaea. By mid-68 he had largely subdued Judaea apart from Jerusalem itself but conducted no further large-scale campaigns.

Vespasian now settled his differences with the governor of *Syria, *Licinius Mucianus. They successively recognized *Galba, *Otho, and Aulus *Vitellius, but the idea of using the eastern legions to attain power became a plan in the spring of 69. On 1 July the two Egyptian legions proclaimed Vespasian; those in Judaea did so on 3 July, and the Syrian legions a little later. Mucianus set out with a task-force against Italy while Vespasian was to hold up the grain ships at *Alexandria. However, the Danubian legions also declared for Vespasian, and the legionary *legate Antonius Primus invaded Italy. After his crushing victory at Cremona the city was sacked. (Primus fell from favour in 70 and took the blame. It was alleged that Primus' invasion was against orders (certainly Mucianus would have opposed his action), but victory could never have been bloodless.) Primus pressed on, entering Rome on 21 December, the day after Vitellius' death. The senate immediately conferred all the usual powers on Vespasian, though he dated his tribunician years from 1 July, negating the acts of senate and people and treating his legions as an electoral college.

There survives a fragment of an enabling law, conferring powers, privileges, and exemptions, most with Julio-Claudian precedents. It sanctioned all Vespasian had done up to the passing of the law and empowered him to act in whatever way he deemed advantageous to the Roman people. His *status was lower than that of any of his predecessors, and the law took the place of the *auctōritās* (prestige) he lacked. Vespasian was careful to publicize a number of omens which portended his accession; he often took the consulship, however briefly, and accumulated imperatorial *acclamations. Vespasian insisted that the succession would devolve on his son. Controversy over the dynastic principle, part of a wider controversy over the role of the senate in government, may have caused his quarrel with doctrinaire senators like *Helvidius Priscus, who was exiled and later put to death.

Vespasian returned to Italy in the late summer of 70. While at Alexandria he had been concerned with raising money, and his sales of imperial estates and new taxes caused discontent there. He claimed that 40,000 million sesterces were needed to stabilize the state. He increased, sometimes doubled, provincial taxation and revoked imperial immunities (see IMMUNITAS). Such measures were essential after the costs incurred by Nero and the devastation of the civil wars; contemporaries inevitably charged Vespasian with 'avarice'. He was able to restore the *Capitol, burnt in December 69, to build his forum and temple of Peace (see TEMPLUM PACIS), and to begin the *Colosseum. An attempt by senators in 70 to diminish expenditure by the state treasury (*aerarium), so promoting senatorial independence, was promptly vetoed.

It may have been partly for financial reasons that in 73–74 he held the censorship (see CENSOR) with *Titus. But both as censor and previously, he recruited many new members, Italian and provincial, to the senate, and conferred rights on communities abroad, notably a grant of Latin rights (see IUS LATII) to all native communities in Spain.

Vespasian restored discipline to the armies after the events of 68–69. Before his return Mucianus had reduced the *praetorian guard, enlarged by Vitellius, to approximately its old size, and they were entrusted to Titus on his return. The legions were regrouped so that Vitellian troops would not occupy dangerous positions. In the east Vespasian by the end of his reign had substituted three armies (six legions) in Syria, Cappadocia, and Judaea for the single army (until Nero's time only four legions) in Syria. After the Jewish rebellion and the Rhineland rebellion of Iulius Civilis had been suppressed, Vespasian continued imperial expansion with the annexation of northern England, the pacification of Wales, and an advance into Scotland (see IULIUS AGRICOLA), as well as in SW Germany between Rhine and Danube.

On his death in June 79 he was accorded deification. Unassuming behaviour had partially conciliated the aristocracy, although some of his friends were informers or otherwise disreputable; Tacitus claims that he was the first man to improve after becoming emperor, and the reign seems to have been tranquil after conflicts with the senate had been won. The years after 75 were marred (as far as is known) only by Titus' execution of Caecina Alienus and his forcing Eprius Marcellus to suicide.

Vespasian was industrious, and his simple life a model for contemporaries. Matching his rugged features he cultivated a bluff manner, parading humble origins and ridiculing a man who corrected his accent. His initial appointments (see PETILLIUS CERIALIS) show astuteness in building a powerful party of which the core was his own family. To have ended the wars was an achievement, and *Pax was a principal motif on his coinage. His proclaimed purposes were the restoration and enhancement of the state, and he made no great break with tradition.

Though Vespasian was no orator, he could quote *Homer, and his sons were cultivated. He attended to the needs of Rome and the empire by founding chairs of rhetoric and philosophy and by granting fiscal privileges to teachers and doctors.

Vespasian's wife Flavia Domitilla was alleged to be of only Latin status until her father proved her Roman citizenship. Besides his two sons she bore a daughter also named Flavia Domitilla; wife and daughter died before Vespasian's accession. He then lived with an earlier mistress, a freedwoman of *Antonia (2).

Vesta, Vestals Vesta was the Roman goddess of (the hearth-) fire, one of the twelve major deities. An ancient etymology linked Vesta to Greek *Hestia: her cult expressed and guaranteed Rome's permanence. Vesta's main public shrine was a circular building just SE of Augustus' arch in the *forum Romanum. In the late republic its form was taken to be that of a primitive house, intimating a connection between public and private cults of the hearth. In the historical period, the state cult effectively displaced private cults. There was no statue of Vesta within the shrine: it contained only the fire and, in the inner sanctum, the 'sacred things that may not be divulged'—esp. the *Palladium, and the *fascinum*, the erect *phallus that averted evil. On being elected *pontifex maximus* in 12 BC, Augustus created another shrine for Vesta on the *Palatine.

Vesta was thought of as virgin, by contrast with her sisters *Juno and *Ceres. She was 'the same as the earth', which also contains *fire, and was sacrificed to on low altars; she protected all altar-fires. Her character gains contour from a contrast with *Volcanus. The sacral status of the six Vestal Virgins (the sole female priesthood in Rome), was manifested in many ways. Though they were required to maintain strict sexual purity during their minimum of 30 years' service, their dress alluded to matrons' wear, their hair-style probably to a bride's. They were excised from their own family (freed from *patria potestas, ineligible to inherit) without acceding to another. It was a capital offence to pass beneath their litter (see TRANSPORT, WHEELED AND OTHER) in the street.

There were several restrictions upon eligibility; most known Vestals were of senatorial family. Though they had many ceremonial roles, their main ritual tasks were the preparation of the salted meal (*mola salsa*) for public *sacrifices and the tending of Vesta's 'undying fire'. The extinction of the fire provided the prima-facie evidence that a Vestal was impure: impurity spelled danger to Rome. The last known case of living entombment in the Campus Sceleratus (near Colline gate) occurred under *Domitian.

Vesuvius, volcano on the bay of Naples, rises out of the surrounding plain of *Campania. Its base is some 48 km. (30 mi.) in circumference, its central cone over 1,216 m. (4,000 ft.) high, and its appearance picturesque since the mountain-sides have been largely blown away. Vesuvius is mentioned only twice during the Roman republic: in the Latin War of 340, and in the revolt of *Spartacus, who used its crater as a stronghold in 73. It appeared extinct, and its fertile slopes were extensively cultivated, with vineyards mostly. In AD 63 a damaging earthquake presaged the first recorded eruption, the severe one of 24 August 79 that buried *Pompeii in sand, stones, and mud, *Herculaneum in liquid tufa, and *Stabiae in ashes, asphyxiated *Pliny the Elder, and is described by *Pliny the Younger, an eyewitness, in letters to *Tacitus.

veterans Legionaries in the late republic, though often serving for long periods, had no recognized right to discharge bounties. Such rewards, often plots of land since most soldiers came from a rural background, were organized through the initiative of individual commanders, and this fostered a close personal loyalty among their troops, which could then be exploited in politics. *Augustus, wishing to be sole benefactor of his army, but needing to avoid the land confiscations and disruption which often accompanied veteran settlements, between 30 and 2 BC spent 1,260 million sesterces in buying land and providing cash payments for veterans. In AD 5 he finally established a discharge bounty of 20,000 sesterces for praetorian veterans and 12,000 for legionary veterans; auxiliaries were apparently excluded, at least in the early empire, but received benefits of citizenship. Augustus funded superannuation from his own pocket, but in AD 6 he at last made the state responsible by establishing the military treasury (*aerarium militare) with a personal grant of 170 million sesterces, to be supported in perpetuity by taxes on inheritance and auctions (see VECTIGAL).

Land allocations to some veterans, either individually or in colonies, continued in the provinces until the 2nd cent. (in Italy until Flavian times), and in some areas colonies became an important source of recruits, although the practice of colonial settlement was neither systematic nor coherent. Veteran colonies often brought benefits to the vicinity: increased security, urban development, an influx of Roman citizens, and imperial benevolence (see URBANISM, *Roman*). Many prospered, e.g. Thamugadi, established (AD 100) in *Numidia for veterans of *legion III Augusta, on a plan reminiscent of a military camp, which became a highly developed community with extensive civic amenities. However, the founding of veteran colonies ended in the reign of Hadrian, because land was becoming more difficult and expensive to obtain, and, as local recruitment became more common, veterans increasingly preferred to settle close to the permanent camp where they had served rather than to be moved to a colony elsewhere. Veterans enjoyed exemption from certain taxes, compulsory public services, municipal duties, and degrading punishments.

veto See INTERCESSIO; TRIBUNI PLEBIS.

via Appia, the Romans' principal route to south Italy and beyond. Appius *Claudius Caecus, *censor 312 BC, built and named the 211-km. (132-mi.) section from Rome to *Capua. It had probably been extended by 244 through Beneventum, Venusia, and *Tarentum to *Brundisium (374 km., 234 mi.). Paving of the Appia began in 295 and apparently was complete by *Gracchan times. In imperial times a praetorian *curator kept the road in order. Its exact line can be traced most of the way to Beneventum. Between Rome and Beneventum one can still see roadside tombs (e.g. the Scipios', Caecilia Metella's), the ancient pavement, a rock-cutting (at Tarracina), embankments (e.g. at Aricia), *bridges (three between Caudium and Beneventum), and milestones. One of these proves that, even though travellers preferred the 30-km. (19-mi.)-long ship canal, the Appia from its earliest days crossed the Pomptine Marshes.

via Egnātia, Roman road built *c.*130 BC from the *Adriatic coast to *Byzantium; named after the proconsul in Macedonia Gnaeus *Egnatius, the via Egnatia was the main route from Rome to the east. Two branches of the road, starting respectively from Dyrrhachium and *Apollonia, united in the Skumbi valley, crossed the Balkan range by Lake Lychnidus, and descended to *Thessalonica by way of Pella, whence it followed the Thracian coast to Byzantium.

via Flāminia, the great northern highway of Italy, built 220 BC by *Flaminius, when censor. It was 334 km. (209 mi.) long from Rome by way of Narnia, to Fanum Fortunae, where it turned NW and followed the Adriatic coastline to Ariminum. From its earliest days the Flaminia was much frequented; its importance was, if anything, enhanced in late imperial times when the imperial court was at Mediolanum or *Ravenna. Large towns grew up along its tomb-lined course. The road was often repaired: by Gaius *Sempronius Gracchus, *Augustus (parts of whose bridge at Narnia and whose honorific arch at Ariminum survive), Vespasian (whose tunnel through the Intercisa Pass still exists), *Trajan, *Hadrian.

via Sacra, the 'sacred way', street connecting the *forum Romanum with the Velia, a ridge between the *Palatine and Oppian hills. In AD 64, *Nero planned the street anew as a noble colonnaded avenue, leading from the Forum to the entrance to the *Domus Aurea, which was flanked by shops for jewellers, and other luxury-traders.

viātōrēs were attendants on *magistrates, one of whose main functions was to summon persons to the magistrate's presence. Thus they might be used to call senators to a meeting from their country seats. However, they also had a function more akin to that of a bailiff, acting in the presence of a magistrate to seize a criminal or his property or indeed a recalcitrant political opponent. So *Caesar as consul had *Porcius (2) Cato dragged from the senate. This latter function was esp. useful to a tribune (see TRIBUNI PLEBIS), who, unlike a consul or praetor, lacked the help of *lictors. So Tiberius *Sempronius Gracchus (2) removed his fellow-tribune *Octavius from the platform. By the late republic *viatores* formed a corporation divided into several groups according to the rank of the magistrates. They are also found on the staffs of local magistrates and of Roman magistrates in the provinces. Although many were in origin freedmen or of low birth, the posts seem to have conferred prestige on those who held them.

vīcomagistrī, officials of a *vīcus*, which was a miniature body politic, and was entitled to possess property, administer common funds, and appoint officials. These officials, who were allowed to wear the *toga praetexta*, represented their community. In the late republic the *vici* offered a chance of finding a sense of community in the chaotic life of the city, and so they and their leaders, like the leaders of the *collegia* (see COLLEGIUM), played an important part in the organization of mass politics.

Augustus reorganized the *vici* at the same time as the *regiones. Their centre was a *compitum* or cross-roads, at which a cult of the *Lares or guardian deities of that locality was maintained. The cult now came to include Augustan Lares and the *genius* of the emperor.

Victoria, the Roman equivalent of *Nike. She is associated in cult with *Jupiter (Victor), oftener with Mars. She was worshipped by the army, as was natural. Her temple on the Clivus Victoriae leading up to the *Palatine dates from 294 BC; from 204 it housed temporarily the sacred stone of her future neighbour, the Magna Mater (see CYBELE). In 193 *Porcius Cato (1) added a shrine to her temple; in the early Principate both sanctuaries celebrated their anniversary on 1 August, no doubt because of Octavian's victory in *Alexandria in 30 BC; see AUGUSTUS.

vīcus (pl. *vīcī*), 'village', one of a series of Roman terms for settlements of lower status than towns. The term was also used of local subdivisions of the city, named after a street, local cult, or other landmark, and are found notably at Rome. *Pliny the Elder gives the number of *vici* at Rome as 265; they appointed officials known as *vicomagistri.

vigilēs ('the watch'). Ancient cities made various arrangements for maintaining security at night; bands of night-watchmen were more often aimed at the prevention of sedition than the protection of property from theft, but fire, accidental or deliberate, was always the main preoccupation. Order in republican Rome was the responsibility of junior magistrates called *tresviri capitales* (see VIGINTISEXVIRI), who were replaced at night by a team of five men with duties 'this side of *Tiber', because future senators could not be expected to be on duty at unsocial hours.

The political importance of fire-protection at Rome had been recognized by *Licinius Crassus and was exploited by Egnatius Rufus. Augustus gave the *aediles a force of 600 slaves to deal with the problem after a fire in 23 BC; in 7 BC the city was reorganized into *regiones and *vici, whose officials (see VICOMAGISTRI) were made

responsible for fire-prevention; in AD 6 he created a very substantial force from the freedman population. By the 3rd cent. some 7,000 *vigiles* were distributed in one cohort of 1,000 men for each pair of *regiones*, housed in purpose-built barracks. The earlier strength may have been little more than half this figure, but was still designed to cope with fires by the rapid deployment of manpower to demolish buildings rather than by extinguishing the flames directly (which was beyond the available technology).

Their commander was an *equestrian prefect, who became also a judge in petty criminal cases; the post was one of the more senior in the equestrian career path (see CURSUS HONORUM). See also POLICE.

vīgintīsexvirī, vīgintīvirī Six boards of minor magistrates at Rome were known by the collective designation *vigintisexviri* (the Twenty-Six) in the late republic: membership was a precursor to the quaestorship and the beginning of a senatorial career; see CURSUS HONORUM. The duties of two boards were as follows. The *trēsvirī capitālēs* or *nocturnī* had a police-function in Rome (see POLICE; TRIUMVIRI); the *trēsvirī monētālēs* were in charge of minting coin (for the *monetales* or moneyers see COINAGE, ROMAN). *Augustus reduced the 26 to 20.

villa was the Latin word for a rural dwelling associated with an estate, and ranging in character from functional farm to luxurious country seats. Most of the literary evidence relates to Italy and primarily describes farms run for the benefit of urban-based proprietors, though the most opulent seaside villas of the Roman aristocracy were sometimes built solely for pleasure. Aristocratic enjoyment of rural retreats and pride in creating architectural splendours there are well attested. However, the classic Italian villa, comprising a luxurious dwelling for the use of the owner on visits to the estate, the working farm buildings, and the storage buildings and barns, is perfectly illustrated by the excavations at Tuscan Settefinestre, with its aristocratic mansion, baths, slave quarters, wine- and oil-presses, piggery, substantial granary, and formal gardens. The development of villas in different regions of Italy from the 2nd cent. BC is generally equated with the rise of large slave-run estates (see LATIFUNDIA), though these regions commonly exhibit divergent patterns of rural settlement and varied types of villa (from simple farmhouses to 'palaces'). Similarly the relative success and longevity of villas differed from one part of Italy to another: certain coastal areas famous for viticulture in the late republic had declined markedly by the 2nd cent. AD, whereas villas in some inland areas survived into late antiquity.

Far more sites in NW Europe have been excavated and published than in the Mediterranean countries. In peripheral territories such as *Britain, where it may be hard to decide whether a particular structure would have been considered a villa by the Romans themselves, different criteria have commonly been used to define villas, encompassing aspects of Romanized construction or lifestyle (characterized by mosaics, painted plaster, hypocausts, baths, use of dressed stone and tile, etc.). Mediterranean-style peristyle houses are uncommon in Britain and Belgica (see GAUL (TRANSALPINE)), where winged corridor and aisled buildings tend to predominate.

Villius (Annālis), Lūcius, tribune of the *plebs* in 180 BC (see TRIBUNI PLEBIS), passed the first law to stipulate minimum ages for tenure of each (curule) magistracy (42 for the consulship); see MAGISTRACY, ROMAN. This law may have required an interval of two years between curule magistracies. Villius' measure probably aimed to regulate the number of men campaigning for higher office in any one year. The provisions of the *lex Villia annalis* remained largely unchanged until the Principate, when the minimum ages were lowered.

Vindolanda tablets During the 1970s and 1980s several hundred wooden writing-tablets were discovered at the Roman fort of Vindolanda behind Hadrian's Wall (see WALL OF HADRIAN); a further 400 turned up in 1993. Of the earlier finds, some were of the well-known stylus type, but most were made of thin, wooden leaves, written in ink with a pen. Very few such tablets were previously known, and the concentration of such numbers at one site is unique. They date between c. AD 90 and 120, when the fort was occupied first by *Cohors I of Tungrians and later by Cohors IX of Batavians.

The Vindolanda material includes the largest group of Latin letters ever discovered (see LETTERS, LATIN). There are also literary fragments, shorthand texts, military reports, applications for leave, and accounts. The letters often bear on the official and private concerns of the officers, their families, and slaves, while the military documents tell us much about the way the Romans organized a newly acquired frontier area. The tablets also provide valuable information on *palaeography and the *Latin language.

violence For Greece see HUBRIS; RECIPROCITY (GREECE). For Rome see VIS.

Vipsānia Agrippīna (1) (d. AD 20) was daughter of *Vipsanius Agrippa and granddaughter of *Pomponius Atticus. Married to *Tiberius, she bore him a son, Nero Claudius Drusus (see IULIUS CAESAR, DRUSUS), but he was forced by Augustus, against his will, to divorce her and marry *Iulia (2) in 11 BC. Vipsania then married Asinius Gallus and bore him at least five sons.

Vipsānia Agrippīna (2), 'Agrippina the Elder' (c.14 BC–AD 33), the daughter of *Vipsanius Agrippa and of *Iulia (2), daughter of *Augustus. She married *Germanicus (probably in AD 5), to whom she bore nine children. She was with Germanicus on the Rhine from 14 to 16 and in the east from 18 until his death in the following year. From 19 to 29 she lived in Rome, the rallying-point of a party of senators who opposed the growing power of Sejanus (see AELIUS SEIANUS). With *Tiberius, whom she suspected (without evidence) of causing her husband's death, her relations were consistently bad, and he refused her request in 26 for leave to marry again. She was arrested in 29 on the instruction of Tiberius and banished by the senate to Pandateria, where she starved to death in 33. She was survived by one son, the future emperor *Gaius (1), and three daughters, *Iulia Agrippina, *Iulia Drusilla, and Iulia Livilla.

Vipsānius Agrippa, Marcus, lifelong friend and supporter of *Augustus, b. c.63 BC of obscure but probably well-to-do family (he neglected his undistinguished family name). He accompanied Octavius (the future Octavian and Augustus) to Rome from Apollonia after *Caesar's murder, helped him to raise a private army, prosecuted *Cassius in the court set up by *Pedius in 43, and was prominent in the war against *Antonius (Pietas) (41/0). After holding the tribunate of the *plebs* (see TRIBUNI PLEBIS) c. 43, and so entering the *senate, he was urban *praetor in 40. As governor of Gaul in 38 he suppressed a rebellion in Aquitania, led a punitive expedition across the Rhine, and either now or in 20 settled the Ubii on the left bank. As consul (37) he fitted out and trained a new fleet for Octavian's war against Sextus *Pompeius, converting the lacus Avernus near *Cumae into a harbour for the purpose, and in 36 won two decisive naval engagements at Mylae and Naulochus, where his improved grapnel was highly effective. Although an ex-consul, he held the aedileship in 33, contributing greatly to Octavian's popularity. In 31 his vigorous naval operations were the primary cause of Mark Antony's defeat (see ANTONIUS, MARCUS); at *Actium he commanded the left wing. He next (31–29), with *Maecenas, managed affairs in Italy in Octavian's absence. On Octavian's return he helped carry out a purge of the senate and a *census (29–28), and he held second and third consulships in the crucial years 28 and 27. In 23 Augustus, ill and embroiled in political controversy, handed him his signet-ring, conferring an unofficial status (most importantly in the eyes of the armies) that would have meant his supremacy if Augustus had died. He was entrusted with a mission in the eastern empire, probably with proconsular power (see PRO CONSULE), which he carried out from *Mytilene. Agrippa had been put in easy reach of the armies of the Balkans and Syria if Augustus' position were undermined or his life threatened. He was recalled in 21 to represent Augustus in Rome; in 20 he proceeded to Gaul and in 19 to Spain, where he quelled the Cantabri. In 18 he was given tribunician power (see TRIBUNI PLEBIS, end of entry) for five years, a power held otherwise only by Augustus, and his *imperium was renewed for the same period. In 13 his tribunician power was renewed for five more years, and his *imperium* apparently made superior to that of all other holders, like that of Augustus. As a *quindecimvir sacris faciundis* he assisted in the celebration of the *Secular Games in 17. His second mission to the east (17/16–13) is notable for the establishment of Polemon in the Bosporan (see BOSPORUS (2)) kingdom, the settlement of veterans at Berytus and Heliopolis, and his friendship with *Herod (1) the Great and benevolent treatment of the *Jews. Early in 12 he went to Pannonia where there was a danger of revolt, but fell ill on his return and died. After a public funeral he was buried in the mausoleum of Augustus.

Agrippa's wealth was spent freely in the service of the Roman people and the empire, winning him lasting popularity. He restored the sewers of Rome (see CLOACA MAXIMA) and reorganized the water supply, constructing two new *aqueducts (Iulia, 33, and Virgo, 19), and a network of distribution installations. Virgo fed Rome's first public *baths, close to his *Pantheon, and the expanded Saepta Iulia (voting enclosure for the *comitia tributa*, 26), all in a huge recreational area. He also built a new bridge over the *Tiber. Constructions in the provinces included buildings at Nemausus and a road system radiating from *Lugdunum. By his will Augustus received the greater part of his property, including the Thracian *Chersonese; he also made large bequests to the people of Rome.

He wrote an autobiography (now lost) and a geographical commentary (also lost, but used by *Strabo and *Pliny the Elder) from which a map of the empire was constructed, to be displayed after his death on the porticus Vipsania (see MAPS).

Agrippa was married three times: in 37 to Caecilia Attica, in 28 to Augustus' niece the elder Marcella, whom he divorced in 21 to marry Augustus' daughter *Iulia (2). The first two wives produced daughters: Attica's including *Vipsania Agrippina (1), the first wife of the later emperor *Tiberius; Marcella's the Vipsania who married *Quinctilius Varus. Iulia had three sons, Gaius *Iulius Caesar (2) and Lucius Iulius Caesar, who were adopted by Augustus in 17, and Agrippa *Iulius Caesar (Agrippa Postumus); and two daughters, Iulia and *Agrippina (2); through her he was grandfather and great-grandfather respectively of the emperors *Gaius (1) and *Nero.

Agrippa, portrayed as upright, simple, and modest, a man who subordinated his ambitions to those of Augustus, was by 12 BC a partner nearly equal in power. Refusing three *triumphs (19 BC onwards) and failing even to report his Spanish successes inhibited private men from applying and contributed to the end of such triumphs. Like his advocacy of public display of works of art (he was a noted collector), it went against the interests of the ruling class, who boycotted his funeral games.

Virgil (Publius Vergilius Marō) (70–19 BC),
Roman poet. 'Virgil' is traditional in English. Most of the information in the extent lives derives from interpretation of the poems, and few details can be regarded as certain.

Virgil is said to have been born in 70 BC in a village near Mantua, and to have been educated in Cremona and Mediolanum before coming to Rome. At some stage Virgil was associated with the *Epicurean community in Neapolis: his name appears in a papyrus from *Herculaneum with Plotius Tucca, *Varius Rufus, and *Quinctilius Varus.

After the defeat of the *tyrannicides in 42, Octavian (see AUGUSTUS) attempted to settle members of his army on confiscated land (see PROSCRIPTION), a controversial move: war between Antony (Marcus *Antonius) and Octavian was narrowly (and temporarily) avoided by the Pact of *Brundisium in 40. Virgil's first collection of poems, his *Eclogues*, probably appeared *c.* 39–38 in the midst of the turmoil: the confiscations are a central topic in *Eclogues* 1 and 9. In the first poem, a slave Tityrus says that he has to thank a young man for freedom and security: this can only be Octavian. Virgil's father may have lost his land, and some personal experience of loss is suggested by 'Mantua, all too near unhappy Cremona' and 'the land unfortunate Mantua lost'. Some time after the publication of the *Eclogues*, Virgil entered the circle of *Maecenas, and thus of the future Augustus.

Virgil published the *Georgics*, 29; the battle of *Actium (31) is referred to in *Georgics* 3, and Virgil is said to have read the poem to Octavian 'after his return from the victory at Actium': Octavian reached Italy in the summer of 29.

Like the *Eclogues*, the *Georgics* are a constant presence in the poetry of the 20s, but by the time that the final poem of *Propertius' second book of elegies is published 'something greater than the *Iliad* is being brought to birth', that is, the *Aeneid*. The tradition claims that books 2, 4, and 6 were recited to Augustus, the reference to the young *Claudius Marcellus (2) in 6 causing *Octavia to faint; this episode, whether true or not, must be set after the death of Marcellus in 23. (What is certainly true is that one needs to hear Virgil's *hexameters as well as read them.) Virgil himself died in 19, with the poem apparently felt to be unfinished: 'in the 42nd year of his life, intending to finish the *Aeneid*, he decided to go off to Greece and Asia Minor, and to spend three straight years in simply correcting the poem, to leave the rest of his life free for philosophy. But when he had set out on his trip, he met Augustus in Athens returning to Rome from the east, and decided not to go off, and even to return with Augustus. He visited a small town near *Megara in very hot sun and caught a fever; this was made worse by his continued journey, to the extent that he was somewhat sicker when he put into Brundisium, where he died.' He was buried at Neapolis, and is said to have composed his own epitaph on his death-bed:

> Mantua me genuit, Calabri rapuere, tenetnunc
> Parthenope; cecini pascua rura duces.
> Mantua bore me, Calabria carried me off, now
> Neapolis holds me; I sang of pastures, fields, and kings.

Propertius' prophecy did not really come true (see below under *Aeneid* for status of Homer), but Virgil did become the Roman *Homer, the *Aeneid* in particular serving as the great Roman classic against which later epic poets and all Latin poets had to place themselves. Schoolboys studied it, even in Roman Egypt, and its opening words became a common graffito on the walls of *Pompeii. Already in his lifetime Virgil is said to have been famous, and his friendship with the great made him rich. As with Homer, all human learning came to be seen as condensed in the *Aeneid*, a view which finds full expression in *Macrobius' *Saturnalia*. The text of the *Aeneid* was consulted as an *oracle in the *sortēs Vergilianae*.

The Literary Works

The Eclogues

Virgil's first collection, the *Eclogues*, is made up of ten short poems in the *pastoral genre. The original title was *Būcolica*, 'cowherd songs'; *eclogae* means 'selections (from a larger corpus)' and it is unfortunate that a version of this later title has become usual in English. *Bucolica* as a title alludes clearly to *Theocritus, and the collection makes constant reference to his *Idylls*: commentators note four separate echoes in the first line. But the intertextuality with earlier Roman poetry is as dense. This combination of the Greek and the Roman, the ancient and the contemporary, and the rustic and the sophisticated is typical of the collection as a whole.

The *Eclogues* are highly 'artificial', and the relation of the world of song to the world outside is a central concern. Interwoven with and inseparable from the literary texture are the celebrated descriptive passages that so appealed to Romantic enthusiasts, the buzzing bees and cool springs of the pastoral world. The union of the two was an inheritance from Theocritus which Virgil passed on to the west, although 'Arcadia' is mentioned only rarely in the poems, the *Eclogues* came to signify Arcady as a place where poetry and love meet or avoid politics, cities, and empires.

One of the *Eclogues* came to have particular significance for later readers: *Eclogue* 4, with its description of the birth of a child whose lifetime will see a return of the world to the *golden age. There were several possible candidates for the identification of the child even for contemporary readers: the modern favourite is an anticipated son of Marcus *Antonius (Mark Antony) and Octavia, a hope already dashed by the time of the *Eclogues'* publication), but the poem can equally be read as a broader allegory of renewal;

Christian readers naturally saw reference to the birth of Jesus. See PASTORAL POETRY, GREEK and LATIN.

The Georgics

Virgil's call to himself to 'rise' at the end of the *Eclogues* was answered by a rise in *genre with his next work, the *Georgics*, a *didactic poem in four books on farming. Again there are Hellenistic Greek models. But there was also an important Archaic model in *Hesiod's *Works and Days*, and the relationship to *Lucretius' *De rerum natura* ('On the Nature of Things') is so central that the *Georgics* may be seen as an *anti-Lucretius*. Lucretius' confident exposition of the power of reason is 'remythologized' into a sceptical and yet more accepting attitude towards the natural world and its traditional divinities.

In the established manner of didactic poetry, passages of direct instruction are interspersed with 'digressions', descriptive or reflective passages with a less obvious relationship to the main theme, such as *Jupiter's paternal disruption of the golden age or the 'praises of Italy'. The concluding section of each book stands out: the troubles of Italy in 1, the virtues of country life in 2, the Cattle Plague in Noricum in 3, and esp. the '*epyllion' of Aristaeus and *Orpheus that ends bk. 4. This last section dramatizes the opposition between the successful conquest of nature through hard work (Aristaeus) and the pathos of loss and failure (Orpheus) which can be traced throughout the *Georgics* and which has led to a debate over the 'optimism' or 'pessimism' of the work. The contemporary relevance of this is reinforced by a constant comparison between the bee society of bk. 4 and Rome.

The poem concludes with an epilogue in which Virgil contrasts Augustus' 'thundering' on the *Euphrates with his own easeful retirement in Neapolis and looks back to the *Eclogues*, depicted as the playful work of his youth. At the opening of *Georgics* 3 he had promised to write a political *epic, and at the end of the *Georgics* we are left feeling that for Virgil the next move will be 'up' in the hierarchy of genres.

Aeneid

Virgil's final work was the *Aenēid* (Lat. *Aenēis*), an account in twelve books of the flight of *Aenēas from *Troy and his battles in Italy against *Turnus to found a new home, the origin of Rome. Epic was the sustained narration of great events ('kings and heroes' acc. to *Callimachus) by an inspired, omniscient, but distanced narrator; it was also the genre in which the fear of being thought too derivative was great-

est, since any epic was inevitably read against Homer's *Iliad* and *Odyssey*, by common consent the greatest poems of antiquity. Intertextuality with both poems is intense. The basic framework of the *Aeneid* is that of the *Odyssey* (note also the focus on the hero in the title): the first half of each epic describes the wanderings of the hero, the second his fight for victory in his home, and Aeneas is harried by *Juno as *Odysseus is by *Poseidon, but the anger of Juno also corresponds to the anger of *Achilles in the *Iliad*, and the end of the poem is more like the battle between Achilles and *Hector in *Iliad* 22 than the killing of the suitors in *Odyssey* 22. One may also contrast the first six books as 'Odyssean' with the second half as 'Iliadic'. But the correspondences with both epics go much further and much deeper. The relationship is signalled in the opening words of the poem, *arma virumque canō*, 'arms and the man I sing', where 'arms' points to the *Iliad*, 'man' to the *Odyssey*.

Two other epics are important: the *Argonautica* of *Apollonius Rhodius and *Ennius' *Annals*. But the range of material whose traces may be interpreted in the *Aeneid* is vast. The *Aeneid* both preserves the narrower norms of epic and expands the genre towards the variety that critics have reserved for the modern novel, a process taken further by *Ovid in his *Metamorphoses*.

Although the particular version of the Aeneas legend presented in the *Aeneid* has become canonical, these were many versions of the myth in the preceding tradition. Many of the details offered by Virgil were by no means standard in his day. His 'sources' were multiple, and there was no scruple against free invention. The *Aeneid* is not therefore a 'safe' text to use for the investigation of early Roman history and cult. The story as told by Virgil takes the reader, as in the *Odyssey*, *in medias res*. Aeneas on his way to Italy is blown off course to North Africa by a storm instigated by Juno (bk. 1). There he meets *Dido, and tells her the story of the fall of Troy (2) and his subsequent wanderings (3). He and Dido become lovers, and he forgets his mission; Mercury is sent to remind him, and his departure leads to Dido's suicide (4). In 5, the threat of another storm forces Aeneas to put into Sicily, where funeral games are celebrated for his dead father Anchises; after Juno incites the Trojan women to burn the ships, part of the group are left behind in Sicily, and Anchises appears in a dream to urge Aeneas to visit the *Sibyl of *Cumae. The first half of the epic concludes with the consultation of the Sibyl and their visit to the Underworld, where Aeneas meets his father and receives a vision of the future of Rome (6).

The events of the second half are described by Virgil as a 'greater work'. Landing at Lavinium in Latium, Aeneas sends a successful embassy of peace to the Latin king *Latinus; but Juno uses the Fury Allecto (see ERINYES) to stir up the young Rutulian king Turnus and Latinus' wife Amata to encourage war. Aeneas' son Iulus (see ASCANIUS) kills a pet stag while hunting, and from that small spark a war develops. Before battle commences we are given a catalogue of Italian forces (7). In 8 Aeneas, advised by the god of the river *Tiber in a dream, visits the Arcadian king Evander, who is living on the future site of Rome; Evander's young son Pallas joins the Trojan forces, and Aeneas receives a gift of armour from his mother Venus, including a shield which again depicts future events in the history of Rome, most notably the battle of Actium (8). In the succeeding books of fighting, emphasis falls on the terrible cost of the war, as the young lovers Nisus and Euryalus die in a night expedition (9), Turnus kills Pallas, and Aeneas kills both the equally tragic youth Lausus and his father the evil Mezentius (10), and Turnus' ally the female warrior Camilla is killed by an arrow to her breast (11). Finally in 12 Aeneas and Turnus meet in single combat, despite Juno's attempts to delay the duel; Aeneas is victorious, and hesitates over sparing Turnus until he sees the sword-belt that Turnus had taken from the dead Pallas. In a paroxysm of love and anger, he slaughters Turnus.

Throughout the *Aeneid* there is a strong narrative teleology, reaching beyond the events of the story to the future Rome. 'Fate' is a central concept; it coincides with the will of Jupiter, though the exact relationship is kept vague. Juno, pained and angry at past events, attempts always to retard the progress of the story, as a sort of 'counter-fate'. She is doomed to failure; at the end of the epic she is reconciled to the fate of Aeneas, but we know that this is only temporary. Onto the opposition between the king and queen of heaven may be projected many other oppositions in the poem: heaven and hell, order and disorder, reason and emotion, success and failure, future and past, epic and tragedy. The treatment of these oppositions has been the central issue in the criticism of the *Aeneid*. Although many of them coincide, the contrast is never absolute: if Juno naturally turns to Allecto and the Underworld, Jupiter god of the bright sky also uses the infernal Dirae (see ERINYES) as the instruments of his wrath; if Aeneas repre-

sents reason and self-control, he also concludes the epic with an act of passion.

Three particular aspects of these oppositions may be mentioned. First, the opposition between Jupiter and Juno is gendered, and many of the other contrasts drawn relate to ancient (and modern) conceptions of typically male or female characteristics, such as reason and emotion. Women in the *Aeneid* feature predominantly as suffering victims opposed to the progress of history (Juno, Dido, Amata, Camilla), and this may be read either as a reproach to the values of martial epic or as reinforcing them.

Second, the political aspects of the oppositions are more than implicit. The hero of the epic is *pius Aenēās* (see PIETAS; RELIGION, ROMAN, TERMS RELATING TO), a man marked out by attachment to communal values, who at the fall of Troy turns away from individual heroism to save his father and in *Carthage rejects personal happiness for the sake of his son's future and the destiny of Rome. This subordination of the individual to the collective is often seen as a prime component of Roman ideology, and its embodiment in Aeneas a central feature of the epic. At the same time, as in Virgil's earlier work, the pain and loss suffered by individuals are at least equally prominent in the poem. The question of the relationship between individual and community is raised in a different form by the question of the poem's relationship to the new autocratic rule of Augustus. The purpose of the *Aeneid* was commonly seen in antiquity as to praise Augustus, who receives explicit eulogy from Jupiter, Anchises, and the primary narrator in the description of Aeneas' divine shield. On the other hand, many have seen the poem's tragic elements as incompatible with a celebration of power. It is impossible to separate the question of the *Aeneid*'s political tendency—in its crudest form, whether we make it pro- or anti-Augustan—from the wider ideological issues mentioned above.

Finally, these same issues have also surfaced in relation to the philosophical aspects of the *Aeneid*. Just as the *Georgics* may be read as a reply to the *De rerum natura*, so the *Aeneid* may be seen as again 'remythologizing' Lucretian rationalism; as Aeneas rejects retirement in Carthage or Sicily for his fate in Italy, so the *Aeneid* turns from 'inglorious ease' to harsh commitment. The debates over the philosophy of the *Aeneid* have concentrated on ethics and the theory of the passions, esp. anger. Is the *Aeneid* essentially a Stoic text, which deprecates emotion? Or is it rather *Peripatetic, and thereby endorsing a right measure of anger? A similar ambivalence attends the depiction of the gods: although they may at times function as metaphors for psychological activity on the human plane, they cannot simply be reduced to allegory.

The classic status of the *Aeneid* is at once apparent from the *parody of its opening line as the epitome of epic openings in the first of Ovid's *Amores*. Intertextuality with the *Aeneid* is the central way in which Ovid's *Metamorphoses* and *Lucan's *Civil War* generate meaning: the *Aeneid* is taken as the official voice of the empire, to be subverted or reaffirmed. But just as all Greek literature must situate itself against Homer, so traces of the *Aeneid* can be seen in every genre of Latin verse and prose, Christian as well as pagan.

virginity See CHASTITY; VESTA, VESTALS.

vīs Latin word, means neutrally 'force' and pejoratively 'violence'. It is the latter sense that is treated here. For Greece see under VIOLENCE.

(*a*) Political Violence. Apart from the major non-violent *secessions, 'the Struggle of the Orders' in the early republic (see ROME (HISTORY), 1.2) seems to have involved small-scale violence between the *plebeians, defending each other and their tribunes, and the *patricians supported by their *clients (see TRIBUNI PLEBIS). However, in the last century of the republic violence became an ever-increasing factor, as a political weapon largely exploited by magistrates for limited ends. The notion of a police authority was alien to republican thought, and, if violence became serious, often the only counter was a state of emergency (see SENATUS CONSULTUM ULTIMUM). From 78 BC *vīs* was an offence. Laws passed by violence were sometimes annulled by the senate. Comprehensive legislation against all political violence was provided by a lex Iūlia dē vī pūblicā of *Augustus; practical security was provided for by Augustus' creation of the urban cohorts (see COHORTES URBANAE) and the *vigiles. See also POLICE.

(*b*) Private Violence. For the ordinary citizen both Rome and the Italian countryside were often violent places where it was necessary to defend oneself with the assistance of family, friends, patrons, or clients. Self-help was also originally recognized in the procedures of private law from the time of the *Twelve Tables onwards, most obviously as a means of bringing a reluctant opponent to court. In the later republic we find a particular interest in the restriction of violence in property disputes. After *Sulla an interdict was instituted specifically against the use of armed gangs, also actions for the recovery of property taken by armed gangs and extorted by force or menaces. In addition to these measures providing restitution and compensation, a lex Iūlia dē vī prīvātā established penalties. It is uncertain whether violence actually declined under the emperors.

Vitellius, Aulus (AD 15–69), Roman emperor in 69, son of Lucius *Vitellius, was friendly with *Gaius (1), *Claudius, and *Nero. Consul in 48, he became proconsul of Africa (see PRO CONSULE; AFRICA, ROMAN), then served as *legate to his brother in the same post. *Galba appointed him governor of Lower Germany in November 68. Vitellius won over the disaffected soldiers in the province by display of generosity. On 2 January 69 Vitellius was proclaimed emperor by his troops, and quickly won the support of the legions of Upper Germany, which had refused allegiance to Galba on 1 January. His main supporters were the legionary legates Fabius Valens and Caecina Alienus, and soon most of the western provinces and Africa were on his side. Galba had been replaced by *Otho, who killed himself on 16 April after his army had been defeated at Bedriacum by the Vitellian forces. After an undisciplined march Vitellius entered Rome in July; he made offerings to Nero, and had himself created consul in perpetuity. Hostile sources emphasize Vitellius' gluttony, indolence, and incompetence, though he displayed restraint in dealing with Otho's supporters. He replaced the existing *praetorian guard with sixteen *cohorts recruited from his German legions. But he did nothing to placate troops who had been defeated or betrayed at Bedriacum, and detachments of the three Moesian legions summoned by Otho returned to their bases.

At the beginning of July *Vespasian was proclaimed emperor, and soon all the troops in the east supported him. The legions in Pannonia, Dalmatia, and Moesia rapidly deserted Vitellius, and under the leadership of Antonius Primus, invaded Italy. Vitellius failed to block the Alpine passes, leaving the defence of Italy to Valens, who was ill, and Caecina, who occupied Cremona and Hostilia with an army including four legions; he had aimed to defend the line of the river Po, but collaborated with the Flavians. Caecina's army refused to follow his lead and arrested him. Junior officers led the army back to Cremona, between which and Bedriacum in a hard-fought battle (October 69) the Vitellian forces were defeated. As the Flavians advanced on Rome, there were steady desertions from Vitellius' cause, though his praetorians remained loyal. Vespasian's brother, Flavius Sabinus, city *prefect, persuaded Vitellius to abdicate, but the agreement was frustrated by the mob in Rome, and some of the emperor's soldiers, who forced Sabinus and his supporters to take refuge on the *Capitol, where the temple of *Jupiter was burnt down. The Flavian army now attacked the city and overcame Vitellian resistance in fierce street fighting. Vitellius was dragged through the streets, humiliated, tortured, and killed.

Vitellius, Lūcius, three times consul, father of the emperor *Vitellius, was a friend of the emperor *Claudius and the most successful politician of the age: he received a public funeral and a statue in the Forum commemorating 'unswerving devotion to the *princeps': it was indeed to the source of patronage and power that he attached himself, linking the history of three reigns. He was a vigorous *legate of *Syria (AD 35–37), inducing the Parthian king to pay homage and conciliating the Jews: acc. to *Tacitus, 'he acted with the integrity of ancient times'. At Rome, however, he earned a different reputation—'he is held by later generations to be an example of the ignominy that goes with sycophancy'. Claudius left him in charge of Rome during the invasion of Britain in 43 and chose him for colleague in the censorship (47). Adopting the cause of *Iulia Agrippina, Vitellius acted as a mouthpiece of a loyal senate in advocating her marriage to Claudius.

Vitrūvius, a Roman *architect and military engineer, in which capacity he served *Caesar. He built a basilica at Fanum Fortunae; but his fame rests chiefly on a treatise, *On Architecture*, on architecture and engineering, compiled partly from his own experience, partly from work by Hermogenes of Alabanda (to whom he is heavily indebted) and other Greek authors to which his own experiences have been added, sometimes in a disjointed fashion. It is a book for people who need to understand architecture. Perhaps its main function was place-seeking from Octavian (see AUGUSTUS), to whom it is addressed. His outlook is essentially Hellenistic, and there is a marked absence of reference to important buildings of Augustus' reign, though he knows of Roman technical developments, such as concrete construction (which he mistrusts). *On Architecture*, the only work of its kind which has survived, is divided into ten books. Bk. 1 treats of town-planning, architecture in general, and of the qualifications proper in an architect; 2 of building-materials; 3 and 4 of temples and of the 'orders' (see ORDERS); 5 of other civic buildings; 6 of domestic buildings; 7 of pavements and decorative plaster-work; 8 of *water supplies; 9 of geometry, mensuration, *astronomy, etc.; 10 of machines, civil and military. The information on materials and methods of construction in 2 and 7, and on rules of proportion in 3 and 4, is of great value.

Vitruvius' importance as an architect is very nearly matched by his significance as a historian of many different departments of ancient science and philosophy, ranging from mathematics to astronomy, meteorology, and medicine. Just as the Hippocratic doctors appreciated the importance of environment to good health, Vitruvius appreciated that in its general and most humane form, architecture included everything which touches on the physical and intellectual life of man and his surroundings.

Often, his encyclopaedic concern with covering a subject thoroughly seems odd to us. In 9, the highly abstract geometry of Plato is put to the use of the surveyor—something of which Plato himself might not have approved. Vitruvius is an important source for our knowledge of many early Greek scientists. (He preserved the story of Archimedes' discovery in his bathtub of a way of detecting the adulteration of *Hieron (2) II of Syracuse's golden crown.) And so Vitruvius goes on, often employing the theories of the most abstract Greek thinkers to elucidate his very practical subject. Astronomy is necessary for an understanding of the use of *sundials, and surveying instruments; astrology for the insights it offers into the organization of human life; machines and their principles (10) because of their utility in the manipulation of materials. As he remarks at 10. 1. 4, all machines are created by nature, and the revolutions of the universe ultimately set them in motion. For a man with interests practical and theoretical in equal measure, understanding the nature of nature was central to all.

vivisection Squeamishness about the dissection (let alone vivisection) of animals is a mark of much ancient medicine and zoology, and there is no firm evidence for vivisection in those Hippocratic works (see HIPPOCRATES) which are generally dated to the 5th or 4th cent. BC. Physicians and zoologists from *Aristotle onwards do, however, seem to have vivisected animals and in some cases humans. Practitioners themselves rarely show signs of concern with the morality of causing animals suffering in the name of knowledge, although such concern was voiced in other quarters (see ANIMALS, ATTITUDES TO and KNOWLEDGE OF).

Two ancient physicians are connected with the practice of human vivisection. *Cornelius Celsus reports that the Alexandrian anatomists Herophilus and Erasistratus vivisected criminals provided for them by the king. Erasistratus at least seems to have been motivated by the belief that the bodies of the living and the dead differ in important physical respects, and that conclusions drawn from the study of a cadaver will not necessarily hold for a living man. Celsus remarks that the practice had its supporters, who argued that agony for a few is justified by the widespread benefits that accrue from increased understanding of the body's vital functions, but Celsus himself regards it with distaste. The other major ancient witness, *Tertullian, manifests his Christian horror at the practice. The truth of these reports has been disputed in modern times. Some feel that it is difficult to *prove* that human subjects were ever used. Moreover, Galen himself based much of his own human anatomy on his dissections and vivisections of the Barbary ape and the Rhesus monkey, creatures which he thought most closely resembled humans. The implication is that, for Galen at least, humans were not possible subjects. The balance of modern opinion, however, seems to be in favour of accepting the veracity of Celsus' and Tertullian's reports.

Volcānus, an ancient Roman god of destructive, devouring *fire, in both the human environment and in nature: e.g. in volcanoes, which explains why his temple should always stand outside a city, on the authority of the Etruscan *haruspices* (see RELIGION, ETRUSCAN). He was worshipped at Rome from the earliest-known times, having a *flamen* (see FLAMINES) and a festival, the Volcanalia. His shrine, the Volcanal, stood in the *forum Romanum at the foot of the *Capitol. On the Volcanalia, he was given a curious and (at least for Rome) unexampled sacrifice: live fish from the *Tiber were flung into a fire. He had a considerable cult at *Ostia, where he seems to have been the chief god. In classical times he is fully identified with *Hephaestus.

Volscī, people of ancient Italy. It seems that in the early 5th cent. BC they overran *Latium and occupied the Monti Lepini, most of the Pom-

ptine plain, and the coastal region from Antium to Tarracina. During the 5th cent. they often attacked the territory of Rome and its Latin allies, often in concert with the Aequi. Both peoples were heavily defeated in 431, however, after which their raids virtually ceased. At the end of the 5th cent. and the first decades of the 4th the Romans took the initiative, and gradually conquered the Volsci, founding Latin colonies (see COLONIZATION, ROMAN), and annexing the Pomptine plain in 358. The Volsci opposed Rome in the Latin War, but were defeated in 338. The Volsci of the Liris valley were conquered during the Second Samnite War (see ROME, HISTORY; SAMNIUM). After that they were rapidly and thoroughly Romanized. *Marius and *Cicero (both from Arpinum) seem Roman enough.

voting See ELECTIONS AND VOTING, *Greek and Roman*; also (for *suffragium*) CITIZENSHIP, ROMAN; MUNICIPIUM.

votive offerings, votives are (durable) dedications to gods made by individuals or communities in circumstances usually of anxiety, transition, or achievement. Votives display many constant features in both Greek and Roman religion. Dedications consisted in renunciation and long-term symbolic investment in the divine, in expectation of good things to come. Whereas in *sacrifice one 'destroys', by depositing a solid object in a *sanctuary one both loses it and makes it permanent. One of the primary functions of *temples was to house expensive dedications; the temple itself was a communal dedication, *anathēma*, to the god.

On a personal level, just like *prayers, votives emphasize the individual's 'if-then' relationship with the gods. 'If my ship arrives safely, if I recover from illness, if my crop succeeds, etc. . . . I shall dedicate a statue, a tithe, a temple', and so on.

At transitional points in their lives (e.g. marriage, retirement) individuals dedicate objects that they are leaving behind. Boys and girls dedicate toys or locks of their hair (girls: also girdles to *Artemis). Retiring craftsmen may 'give up' tools of their trade: what sustained one's former life is renounced to become 'sacred' and permanent at a sanctuary. Personal victory at competitions could be followed by an offering of the prize: *Hesiod dedicated the tripod he won at the competition in *Chalcis to the *Muses at *Helicon, where they first taught him 'the way of clear song'. War served as occasion for both individual and collective offerings. In *Homer's *Iliad* *Hector swears to hang the arms of his foe in the temple of Apollo. After simultaneous victories over the Persians (see PERSIAN WARS) and *Carthage in 480 BC, *Themistocles and *Gelon dedicated temples. Collective dedications in the form of a tithe or the 'top' of the piles of *booty, a percentage from the sales of prisoners, and so on, became common from the Archaic period. Treasuries in the panhellenic sanctuaries contained dedicated memorials of victories won over centuries, serving as reminders of fluctuating fortunes and animosities.

The vow as well as the act of giving was made publicly. The dedicated object, such as a mask or a figurine, would be deposited at the shrine. The perpetuation of the gift might be enhanced by an inscription. The variety of dedicated objects might be enormous, depending on occasion and function of the deity. Representations of limbs (e.g. hands, legs, penises) were deposited at healing sanctuaries; cakes, garments, masks, arms, and esp. figurines were common (e.g. *c.*100,000 excavated at the sanctuary of *Artemis Orthia at Sparta). Most prominent and well known for their artistic value were the statues (not cult-images) 'set up' (*anathēmata*) in sanctuaries, advertising the donors and evoking the god. See next entry.

vōtum, Lat. for a vow. Both Greeks and Romans habitually made promises to gods, in order to persuade them to grant a favour stipulated in advance. If the gods fulfilled their part, the vow-maker was obliged to do as he had promised. Although the practice was no less popular in Greece, the vow developed an institutional form in Rome, due to the practical and juridical nature of Roman religion. In the private sphere *prayers for recovery and good health, crops, childbirth, safe return from an expedition, etc. were, in case of fulfilment, answered by a great variety of *votives. In public votive religion it was the magistrate who in the name of the state undertook to offer to a god or gods sacrifices, games, the building of a temple or an altar, etc., if the god on his side would give his assistance in such basic collective crises as war, epidemics (see PLAGUE), and drought. Formulas had to be pronounced in public and were very strict: mistakes required the repetition of the whole ceremony. In addition to these extraordinary vows there were also regular *vota*, pronounced for a definite period: e.g. the annually renewed *vota* of the magistrates for the welfare of the state on 1 January before the first regular sitting of the senate. Such vows found their direct continuation under the empire in the *vota* for the health or safety of the emperor and his family, and became periodical.

vows See PRAYER; VOTIVE OFFERINGS; VOTUM.

Vulcan See VOLCANUS.

wages, payment in cash or kind in return for labour services, are attested as early as the *thetes (landless labourers) of the *Iliad* and *Odyssey*. Homeric references point to the depressed status of the *thēs*: uncertain of receiving promised pay and, lacking the protection of the household, they ranked even lower than slaves. With significant exceptions, precariousness remained the characteristic of the wage-labourer through antiquity, dependent on availability of casual employment (e.g. at harvest time, on public building projects, in service as a *mercenary). The divisions between different types of *labour were fluid, with *peasants, *artisans, and *slaves potentially doubling up as wage-labourers. In late 5th-cent. Athens, the *metic Simias hired himself out along with his four slaves to work on the *Erechtheum. Roman law made special provision for the hiring out of slaves. In Athens, those looking for work gathered each day on a hill overlooking the *agora. From the mid-5th cent., Athens was exceptional among Greek states in offering an increasing range of payment for public service (jurors, council members, minor officials, and, eventually, those attending the assembly). The relationship between Athens as 'a *polis taking pay' and exploitation of the 5th-cent. empire is disputed, but public pay did buttress democracy (see DEMOCRACY, ATHENIAN) by enhancing participation and reducing dependence of the poor on the rich. Throughout the ancient world, wage rates were fixed more by custom than by demand and supply, and were slow to change. Figures have little meaning without detailed knowledge of circumstances and overall cost of living. The skilled workers on the Erechtheum earning one drachma per day would not always have found employment; likewise the jurors, receiving two obols (three after *c.*425) for each day in court. For the city of Rome, a combination of dependence on patrons and receipt of the corn dole (see FOOD SUPPLY) affects any overall assessment of rates of pay. *Diocletian's 'Price Edict' of

AD 296, has as its lowest maximum wage that of the farm labourer at 25 *denarii* per day, with an unspecified payment in kind. Comparisons of annual pay of legionaries (1,200 sesterces in 2nd cent.; 1,800 under Diocletian) are similarly complicated by payments in kind, *donatives, and deductions for equipment.

wall of Antōnīnus, a Roman frontier-wall 59 km. (37 mi.) long, running from Bridgeness on the Forth to Old Kilpatrick on the Clyde, built for *Antoninus Pius in AD 139–142 by Lollius Urbicus. The wall was of turf, standing upon a cobbled foundation. Some seventeen forts were built from one end to the other. The Antonine wall is structurally an advance upon Hadrian's turf wall (see WALL OF HADRIAN) in its economy of material and rubble foundation, allowing better drainage, while its garrison was distributed in small close-spaced forts instead of large forts and milecastles.

wall of Aurelian, the city wall of Rome, by *Aurelian in AD 271–275 in anticipation of a sudden barbarian inroad. The original wall, about 6.5 m. (21 ft.) high to the battlements, extended for 18.8 km. (11½ mi.) with 381 projecting rectangular towers at intervals of 100 Roman ft. (29.6 m.; 32⅓ yds.), except along the river. The wall was usually solid, but in places had an internal gallery or was treated as a revetment. It incorporated many earlier structures, such as the camp of the *Praetorian Guard, and the tomb of *Cestius. It enclosed most of the fourteen regions (see REGIO) but only a small part of Trastevere. The seventeen gates, mostly named from the principal roads, were flanked by simple semicircular towers. There were also at least six postern gates. The wall was thus designed to repel a raid rather than stand siege.

wall of Hadrian, a frontier-wall (see LIMES) of Roman *Britain, running for 80 Roman miles (see MEASURES) (118 km.; 73 mi.) from

Wallsend-on-Tyne to Bowness-on-Solway. Erected under the governor Platorius Nepos *c.* AD 122–126, it was first designed to start at Pons Aelius, the eastern 67 km. (42 mi.) being in stone 3 m. (10 ft.) thick and perhaps 4.2 m. (13$\frac{1}{2}$ ft.) high, and the western 46 km. (31 mi.) in turf, 6 m. (19$\frac{1}{2}$ ft.) broad at the base and some 4.2 m. (13$\frac{1}{2}$ ft.) high. In front of the wall ran a V-shaped ditch. Fortified gateways (milecastles), with towered gates to the north, occurred every Roman mile, and there were intermediate turrets (observation towers) every third of a mile. Milecastles and turrets continued to the west down the Cumbrian coast to St Bees Head. As construction progressed, changes came. The stone wall was reduced to 2.5 m. (7$\frac{1}{2}$ ft.) in width, and extended 6 km. (4 mi.) eastwards to Wallsend, and 6 km. westward (replacing some of the turf wall).

As planned, garrison forts (e.g. Vindolanda) remained behind the barrier on the Stanegate, the Trajanic road from Corbridge to Carlisle. At an early stage in construction the decision was taken to build a series of twelve forts astride the wall. After the decision to move forts onto the line of the frontier, the so-called *vallum* was added to the south of the wall. The vallum was a flat-bottomed ditch 6 m. (19$\frac{1}{2}$ ft.) wide and 3 m. (10 ft.) deep with the upcast disposed in two turf-curbed mounds, one on either side, set back 9 m. (29$\frac{1}{2}$ ft.) from the lip of the ditch. This provided a continuous cleared area behind the forts along the full length of the frontier. Crossings were limited to causeways at the forts. Lateral communication was first supplied by branches from the Stanegate; only later did the Military Way, between *vallum* and wall, connect forts and milecastles. Before the end of the reign of *Hadrian further forts were added to the system, bringing the garrison to *c.*9,090 men in auxiliary units.

After the accession of *Antoninus Pius the frontier was advanced to the *wall of Antoninus on the Forth–Clyde line. Hadrian's wall was rendered open to traffic by removing the gates from milecastles and filling in the *vallum*. In the 160s the wall was brought back into full use with the abandonment of the Antonine wall. There was extensive rebuilding and repair, but forts were reoccupied by units of similar size and type to those there before. Decreasing emphasis was placed on turrets and milecastles. The pattern so established endured for almost two centuries with only gradual modification, piecemeal rebuilding, and a slow decline in the size of the garrisons.

wall of Servius, the city-wall of republican Rome, traditionally assigned to Servius Tullius (see REX), actually belongs to 378 BC. It is of tufa, 4.5 m. (15 ft.) thick and at least 8.5 m. (28 ft.) high. The masons' marks, with Hellenistic affinities, suggest Greek contractors. The wall was some 11 km. (7 mi.) long, and its course, dictated by contours, enclosed an irregular area, estimated at 426 ha. (1,052 acres), and embracing the Quirinal, Viminal, Oppian, Caelian (see CAELIUS MONS), *Aventine, and fortified Capitoline hills (see CAPITOL). The names of the gates are well known, but the location of some is debated and their structure is uncertain. In the 2nd cent. the wall was heightened to some 16 m. (52 ft.), and was also supplied with casemates for *ballistae* (see ARTILLERY), covering approaches to the gates. During the 1st cent. BC neglect and encroachment made the course hard to find in places even by *Augustus' time, though elsewhere it remained visible, and one or two substantial sections are still standing.

war, art of, Greek Before the second half of the 5th cent. BC, the Greeks seem to have made no attempt to systematize military theory. The only such works to have survived are *Xenophon's *Cavalry Commander*, his fictional account of Cyrus' organization of his army in the *Cyropaedia*, and the treatise on siege-craft by *Aeneas Tacticus. We are thus largely left to infer the Greek art of war from the warfare itself.

Early wars, *Thucydides (2) says, were fought between neighbours, and even the exception he mentions—the 8th-cent. Lelantine War—seems just to have been a series of such conflicts; see GREECE (HISTORY), *Archaic Period*. They were also clearly fought for territory, involving a simple strategy, and this remained true even when the object was no longer territorial aggrandizement but hegemony, for ravaging could usually compel confrontation, and, if the invaders won, the acceptance of a more or less subordinate relationship.

As for tactics, it is hard to discern what, if any, were employed. The *Iliad* (see HOMER) is the earliest surviving account of warfare, but it is uncertain how far it reflects reality in giving prominence to a few heroes and their exploits. If it does, there was really no place for tactics, and even when *Tyrtaeus begins to emphasize the need to maintain cohesion, and missile-armed troops like Homer's spear-throwing heroes have become quite unimportant, we still learn nothing about how a battle was won, other than by an exemplary display of courage.

The first time the Greeks had to think in more complex strategic terms was probably during the *Persian Wars, but even then the Athenians probably never thought of anything else but of confronting the invader at Marathon (see MARATHON, BATTLE OF), and in 480, though confrontation in the open was evidently to be avoided, the Greeks initially seem to have decided just to try to hold the invader as far north as possible; in 479, when they took the offensive, they also simply moved to confront the enemy at Plataea (see PLATAEA, BATTLE OF). Tactics, too, seem still to have been primitive, with the possible exception of those employed at Marathon. At Thermopylae, acc. to Herodotus, the Spartans made use of feigned retreats (see THERMOPYLAE, BATTLE OF), but Plataea was again a matter of head-on collision.

The development of Athenian sea power added a new dimension to warfare, and during the *Peloponnesian War, the Spartans were initially baffled by the Athenian strategy of taking refuge in the fortified Athens–*Piraeus complex and relying on sea-borne supplies. But this was a recipe for survival rather than victory, and raids on the Peloponnese and even the establishment of permanent bases on and off its coast, could not defeat Sparta. The nearest Athens came to victory was when, as *Alcibiades is said to have claimed, the Spartans had to fight for their all at Mantinea (see MANTINEA, BATTLES OF), and it was the Spartans who eventually turned the tables by using *sea power to cut off Athens' sea-borne supplies.

The first battle of Mantinea was also the first battle won by tactics. The Spartan victory on the right may have been normal in a *hoplite battle, but the way in which they then took their opponents' right in its shieldless flank as it attempted to retreat across the battlefield, was not.

The drawback was that they involved sacrificing the left, and it was the Theban, *Epaminondas, who both perfected hoplite tactics at *Leuctra and ushered in a new era at the second battle of Mantinea. At the former he attacked with his best troops on the left, while holding back his right, at the latter with a combination of cavalry, hoplites, and infantry specially trained to co-operate with cavalry, which foreshadows the tactics of *Alexander (2) the Great.

We cannot be certain of *Philip II's place in the development of the art of war. In his first battle—against the *Illyrians—he seems to have used his newly created 'foot companions' (see HETAIROI) to pin the enemy, while his cavalry

(see HIPPEIS) attacked their flanks and rear, and at Chaeronea (see CHAERONEA, BATTLES OF) he may have feigned retreat with his right to stretch the enemy line and provide a gap for his cavalry to exploit. But strategically, Philip was a master of diplomacy, including the use of bribery, and of avoidance of confrontation wherever possible. The way in which he bypassed *Thermopylae in 339 and the manœuvres which led to Chaeronea show that he was also a master of campaign strategy.

Alexander, too, made the best possible use of the various elements in his forces, usually relying on cavalry to make the crucial breakthrough, but adding—at *Gaugamela—the holding back of part of his army as a reserve, and the pressing of pursuit to prevent any recovery. As a strategist, however, he seems to have lacked his father's ability to look ahead and to know when to stop. After him, warfare became even more complex, with *elephants and heavy-armed cavalry being added to the arms available, but there were few innovations in tactics, and when Hellenistic armies were confronted by a new kind of war-machine, the Roman army, they were decisively defeated. See ARMIES, GREEK AND HELLENISTIC.

war, art of, Roman The earliest Roman battle-order was probably the spear-armed *hoplite *phalanx, a single, close-order infantry formation. In the 4th cent. BC this was replaced by the more flexible *manipular organization whereby the *legion was drawn up in three lines of maniples behind a screen of light infantry and with cavalry on the wings. Each line was supported by, and could fall back upon, the line behind. All were spear-armed initially, but by the 2nd cent. the first two (*hastātī, principēs*) had javelins (*pīla*).

From the late 3rd cent. three maniples were grouped into a *cohort by taking one maniple from each line. First a tactical expedient, by the 1st cent. BC this became a permanent organization, coinciding with the equipping of all legionaries with *pīla*. Roman close-order infantrymen evolved from being primarily spearmen to swordsmen with javelins. The manipular organization proved flexible and resilient enough to defeat Celtic, Carthaginian, and Hellenistic infantry (see ROME (HISTORY), 1.3–4). The cohorts were sizeable tactical units with uniform equipment, reflecting the move away from socio-economic differentiation within the ranks. Shortages of light infantry and cavalry (esp. against Hannibal; see PUNIC WARS) were serious weaknesses only partially remedied during the republic.

Throughout the Principate legionaries remained armoured swordsmen, although fencing styles evolved from short- to long-sword. The *pilum* alone gave way to javelins and spears. Imperial commanders now had at their disposal the regular support troops (*auxilia*). The legions continued as the main-line troops, drawn up in the centre between wings and behind screens of auxiliaries. The tactical problems posed by mounted enemies in the Danubian and eastern theatres necessitated deepened legionary formations and increased effectiveness of missiles. Specialists were also transferred around the empire to best tactical advantage, e.g. oriental archers used against Germans, infantry bowmen and Moorish cavalry against *Sarmatians, western cavalry against eastern horse-archers. An increasing emphasis was placed on cavalry of all types.

Military treatises and accounts of campaigns demonstrate the care with which the imperial army's orders-of-march were formulated. Scouts, interpreters, and guides were institutionalized to ease passage and avoid ambushes of an advancing army. *Itineraries were used on known routes. Emphasis was placed on fortified camp-sites for protection overnight and as fallback positions.

The adoption and development of Hellenistic military technology gave Roman armies the option of 'scientific' siege operations. During the Principate military installations were lightly defended, and Roman armies hoped to operate offensively beyond the frontiers. However, Roman units tended to be strung out along frontier lines, and already in the 2nd cent. AD troops were becoming attached to their bases (see LIMES). To form campaigning armies increased recourse was had to drawing away detachments for service in other theatres. Many never returned to parent units.

Technical expertise for battle order, command/control, siegework, and camp-designing resided within the legions, esp. at centurial level, where a continuous tradition of skills was developed and passed on (see CENTURIONS). A militarized aristocracy exercised higher command during the republic and the Principate (see CAREERS, *Roman*), but from the later 2nd cent. a military élite developed within the army, providing professional commanders and emperors who preserved the empire. See AR-MIES, ROMAN; ARTILLERY; BOOTY; FORTIFICA-TIONS; MERCENARIES; SIEGECRAFT, ROMAN.

war, rules of   These, like much other international law (see LAW, INTERNATIONAL), depended on custom and showed a constant conflict between the higher standards of optimistic theory and the harsher measures permitted by actual usage, while passion and expediency often caused the most fundamental rules to be violated. Thus, the temptation to profit from a surprise at times led to the opening of hostilities without a declaration of war. Probably the law most generally observed was that of the sanctity of *heralds, for heralds were essential to communications between belligerents. Nor did Greeks often refuse a defeated army a truce for burying its dead, for the request of such a truce meant an admission of defeat and was usually followed by retreat. Beyond this there were few restraints except humanitarian considerations and the universal condemnation of excessive harshness. Plundering and the destruction of crops and property were legitimate, and were carried on both by regular armies and fleets, and by informal raiding-parties and privateers, and even the sanctity of temples was not always respected. Prisoners, if not protected by special terms of surrender, were at the mercy of their captors, who could execute them or sell them into *slavery or exact ransoms for them (see BOOTY). The warfare of the Hellenistic age was somewhat more humane. Roman warfare at its worst was extremely cruel and sometimes went to the length of killing all living things, even animals, in cities taken by storm, but it was often tempered by mercy. Though surrender gave full power to the captors, it was unusual to take extreme measures against a city that had surrendered and entrusted themselves to Rome. The protection of the rules of war was not extended to pirates (see PIRACY) and not always to *barbarians.

warfare, attitudes to (Greek and Hellenistic)   *Homer's *Iliad*, a poem about war, does not glorify war: it celebrates valour but also portrays the sufferings caused by war, and *Ares, god of war, is rebuked by Zeus as the most hateful of all the gods, to whom strife, wars, and slaughter are forever dear. The same ambivalence pervades Greek attitudes to warfare. War in Greece was a recurrent phenomenon, and conflicts grew in number and scale as larger power blocks emerged. Major wars provide the subject-matter of much of Greek historical writing. There were also countless local wars, less prominent in the record. 'War is the father of all things' (Heraclitus). It shaped Greek society and institutions. Military function and social and political *status were closely related; hence the predominance in the Classical period of the male citizen-warrior, the exclusion of *women from the political sphere, and literature's constant celebration of valour. Success in war was ascribed to divine favour and ostentatiously commemorated in *sanctuaries through dedications from enemy spoils, including captured weapons. In Classical Athens the war-dead received burial every year in a public ceremony, and the funeral speech (see EPITAPHIOS) linked the fallen warriors with the collective achievements of the *polis. On the other hand, literature constantly emphasized the destructive aspects of war. In the words of Herodotus: 'No one is so foolish as to prefer war to peace: in peace sons bury their fathers, while in war fathers bury their sons.' Tragedy and comedy exploited the theme in many ways. For *Thucydides (2), war was 'a teacher of violence'. Later historians often used the sacking of cities and the fate of the defeated for pathos and sensational effect. But attempts to limit war were few and ineffective, and it is doubtful whether there was any successful move towards humanizing warfare, even between Greeks. With the Persian Wars and the emergence of the antithesis between Greek and *barbarian, the view gained ground that Greeks should not fight wars against other Greeks or enslave Greek prisoners of war. After the failure of Athens in 355 in the Social War (see SECOND ATHENIAN CONFEDERACY) voices were raised in condemnation of Athenian imperialism and in favour of peace (*Xenophon, *Isocrates). But the legitimacy of war itself was not challenged: the same writers preached a profitable war of aggression against the Persian empire as an alternative to wars among Greeks. In short, throughout Greek history war was as much a part of life as earthquakes, droughts, destructive storms, and slavery. See also BOOTY; HOMONOIA; IMPERIALISM, *Greek and Hellenistic*; PANHELLENISM; PERSIAN-WARS TRADITION; TROPHIES; WAR, ART OF, GREEK; WAR, RULES OF.

water In a Mediterranean climate the availability of water shaped patterns of settlement. Erratic rainfall determined harvest-fluctuations and food-shortages (see FAMINE; FOOD SUPPLY). In *agriculture, although dry-farming was the norm in ancient Greece and Italy, *irrigation was not unknown. The use of hydraulic technology to increase the *water supply was an early concern of the *polis; some of the most spectacular installations were the work of the Archaic

tyrants (see POLYCRATES; TYRANNY); Rome pioneered raised *aqueducts. Communal fountains were a social focus; in Roman times they were civic status-symbols liable to lavish architectural embellishment (see NYMPHAEUM). Apart from drinking and *sanitation, ancient cities needed water for reasons of personal health (baths) as well as hygiene. In Greece domestic baths were increasingly common by the 4th cent. BC (terracotta bath-tubs or special bathrooms were found in one-third of the houses at *Olynthus). Public (including hot) *baths were common from at least the 4th cent.; baths were among the standard amenities of the Greek *gymnasium; in Roman cities they were a central social and cultural institution and, when based on therapeutic springs, the *raison d'être* of spa-towns. The play of water was an integral part of ancient, esp. Roman, gardens and of the Roman idea of the *locus amoenus*. In mythology spring-water had sacred power; in real life springs often prompted cult (see NYMPHS; SPRINGS, SACRED). Together with *fire, water was widely used in cult for *purification (including bathing), in *libations, and in *sacrifice; extra-urban *sanctuaries were as concerned as cities to secure a good supply. Purificatory water was also used in rites of birth, marriage, and death, the dead being considered 'thirsty'. Water was a primal *element in cosmogonic thought; this applies equally to philosophy (see THALES) and to the early mythical cosmogonies.

water supply

1. **Greece** The preferred source of water in Classical Greece is a natural perennial spring. Failing this, rainwater has to be conserved in cisterns, or raised from wells. Improvement of natural water supplies leads to the construction of fountain-houses, where water is fed through spouts (normally decorated in the form of a lion's head) into drawbasins; such constructions are usually placed behind architectural façades with a roof to shade (and keep cool) the drawbasins. These already existed in the 6th cent. BC (Enneakrounos at Athens, built by *Pisistratus). Pirene at Corinth was successively improved from Archaic to Roman times. The use of terracotta pipes and built or rock-cut conduits to lead water from a spring to a locality where it was needed develops from the Archaic period (see AQUEDUCT).

Cisterns may be rock-cut, but generally have to be lined with cement to retain water. They may be fed from rainwater trapped on roofs, or on the ground surface, led into settling tanks for cleaning before storage.

See NYMPHAEUM.

2. Rome See AQUEDUCTS and NYMPHAEUM.

wealth, attitudes to Classical societies developed a range of responses to the general ambition of people to amass property and possessions. One extreme response, characteristic of societies where the rich had retained or regained preponderant influence in public affairs, was to impose little or no restriction on accumulation: early Hellenistic Sparta and late republican Rome were examples. Conversely, Greek colonies were often founded on an 'equal and like' basis, and Roman colonial foundations regularly assigned the same land-area to each colonist. However, few colonies remained egalitarian for long. See COLONIZATION, GREEK and ROMAN.

More normally, attitudes oscillated unsystematically within such extremes. Amassing wealth, possessing it, and spending it aroused different responses, and varied also with the nature and the status of the gainful activity. Greeks saw the rich as potentially hubristic, extravagant, profiteering, and soft, probably dishonest if newly rich, and lucky rather than worthy if of longer standing, but also as prudent and as potentially generous benefactors. Romans likewise might profess contempt for usury while legally requiring *guardians to use their wards' spare capital profitably; might be represented as flaunting their wealth, as *Petronius' Trimalchio did or as the shippers of *Augusta Treverorum did on their grave-monuments, or as hoarding it; or might combine positive and negative attitudes in the same treatise, as *Seneca the Younger did repeatedly. Behind some such inconsistencies lay the influence of Greek philosophies. *Cynics preferred poverty and refused possessions, a pattern later followed by some rich Christians (see ASCETICISM; CHRISTIANITY), while some exponents of Stoicism associated joy with the use of wealth. Mainstream *Stoicism counted wealth among the 'useful indifferents', and *Aristotelian tradition (see PERIPATETIC SCHOOL) saw at least a comfortable independence as essential to the virtuous life. Other attitudes were less coherent. The idea that poverty had made Rome great, while wealth and luxury would ruin her, was a cliché of late republican ideology, explicit in *Sallust, *Horace, and *Livy, just when the rich of Rome and Italy were energetically exploiting every opportunity for investment and accumulation.

Some public policies, expressed in law or custom, attempted to restrain such behaviour. Partible inheritance (see INHERITANCE, *Greek*) ensured that an eldest son had no economic advantage, and the revocability of dowries checked some accumulation strategies, though the later freedoms of bequest and adoption largely eroded such restraints. The military need for citizen soldiers had long kept the number of free smallholders high, but was overtaken by army professionalization. Sumptuary laws (see LEX) attempted to restrict extravagant display, esp. at funerals or festivals. Most effective of all was the expectation that the rich would use at least some of their wealth for public benefit. The idea came closest to enforceable obligation in the institution of *liturgies at Athens and elsewhere, but normally emphasized the voluntariness of such benefaction and the goodwill thereby accruing to the benefactor (see EUERGETISM). In Greek contexts the objectives might be contributions to corn-buying or building funds, educational or cult foundations, help in manumission costs, or the ransoming of captives. In Roman contexts, expenditure on games, public spectacles, and food hand-outs tended to predominate, along with expenditure on *alimenta*-schemes (see CHILDREN), temple-building, and the patronage of *collegia* (see COLLEGIUM).

weaving See TEXTILE PRODUCTION.

weights, Athenian *Solon is said to have introduced into Athens-cum-Attica the system of weights prevailing in *Euboea. If the material in question is *silver, the table below gives the relationship between the units of Athenian money. Obols and drachmae are coined. 6,000 drachmae are equivalent to one talent of silver. See COINAGE, GREEK; WAGES.

The obol, or metal spit	0.72 g.
The drachma, bundle of 6 spits	4.31 g.
The *mna* or *mina*, 100 drachmae	431.00 g.
The talent, 60 minae	25.86 kg.

widows in Classical Athens were expected to live under the control (*kȳrieia*) of a male relative and to remarry if possible. There was usually an age-gap between husband and wife, and young widows were thought to be at risk of ill-health and sexual temptation. Older widows caused less anxiety and had more freedom of movement. The widow's dowry went to the man who took control of her, but in practice some widows kept control. Some men made provision by will for their widow's remarriage to a trusted friend. The archon (see ARCHONTES) had special responsibility for widows who might give birth to a posthumous heir.

Romans admired the *ūnivira*, the woman who married only once. But remarriage was not discouraged, except during the period of mourning, which traditionally lasted ten months. Both Greeks and Romans acknowledged that a second marriage could disadvantage the children of the first. Roman widows were sometimes given a life interest in their husband's property, provided they did not remarry. They could also be rich and influential on their own account. Some (including *Cornelia) were famous examples of motherhood. *Augustus restricted the inheritance rights (except from near relatives) of childless widows under 50 who did not remarry.

Many Christians opposed the remarriage of widows, on the grounds that death does not end a marriage and that celibacy is better anyway. A distinction was made between young widows who should remarry to avoid scandal and temptation, and 'real' widows, preferably aged 60 or above, devoted to prayer and good works.

wine (Greek and Roman) The grape vine grows naturally in the hills between the 10° C and 20° C annual isotherms (roughly between 30° and 50° N). By the earliest historical period wine had already become a fundamental part of classical culture. This is not simply the result of ecological determinism; viticulture represented an important cultural and social choice. Contemporaries were aware that the considerable geographical expansion of vine-growing which happened throughout classical history (in the Black (*Euxine) Sea region in the Hellenistic period, and esp. in southern Spain and Gaul (see MASSALIA) after the Roman conquest) was closely associated with the dissemination of classical culture.

The evidence, esp. the literary sources, for viticulture in Classical Greece is inadequate; not even *Theophrastus offers much detail. On the other hand, the techniques of wine-production figure prominently in the Roman *agricultural writers and *Pliny the Elder, whose information is derived not just from personal experience, but also the numerous handbooks produced in the Hellenistic period. Yet, even in Classical Greece it was already acknowledged that the particular character of a wine depended primarily on a combination of the type of vine, the soil, and the climate. Most of the modern methods of training and pruning vines were

already known, from the free-standing bush, propped vines, to trellising, and most notably the growing of vines up trees. This last was such a distinctive feature of some of the most prized vineyards of Roman Italy that Pliny could claim that 'classic wines can be produced only from vines grown on trees'. Cited yields varied enormously; but they depended on grape type and the density of planting. The choices here depended on which market the producer was aiming at: young wines for mass consumption or fine wines for the élite.

The descriptive lists of wines which can be found in such authors as Pliny and *Athenaeus, must be used with caution, because many of them are not the judgements of connoisseurs, but are derived from the accounts of medical writers, who assessed wines for their effects as remedies. Athenaeus has the most useful account of Greek wines with a wide selection of citations from ancient authors. Among the most noted Greek wines were those of five islands: *Cos, *Chios, Thasos, *Lesbos, and *Rhodes. A distinctive feature of several of these wines, esp. Coan, was the practice of cutting the must with quantities of sea water 'to enliven a wine's smoothness' (presumably to increase its acidity). So many of Greece's most prominent wines and the ones which were exported on a large scale down to the Roman imperial period came from the islands. Viticulture probably played a greater role in their economy than that of mainland areas such as *Attica. Two fragmentary inscriptions from 5th-cent. Thasos, an important producer and exporter, contain elaborate regulations about the sale of wine. Sometimes interpreted as trade protection, they are more likely a cumbersome attempt to assure the consumer of the genuineness and quality of their purchase.

In Roman Italy there was a close link between prestige vineyards and the favoured locations of the Roman élite's country estates, esp. the Alban hills; *Albanus mons (Alban, Setian wine), further south in Latium (Caecuban), the northern borders of Campania (Massic, Falernian), and round the bay of Naples. In the reign of *Augustus there was great interest in the wines of NE Italy. Most of the prized wines were sweet whites. Characteristically they were aged for a considerable number of years, with a resultant darkening of colour. This process of ageing was often accelerated by exposing the wine to heat by storing it in lofts above hearths. While it was accepted that ideally wine should be unadulterated, the long lists of additives in Pliny and

*Columella suggest that producers were often forced to disguise a deteriorating product.

The widespread finds of Italian *amphorae are testimony to the success of Italian wines in the growing markets of the city of Rome itself, in Spain and Gaul, and even in the Greek east. But Italian dominance of this trade lasted only from the late 2nd cent. BC to the mid-1st cent. AD. By then the wines of southern Spain and southern Gaul were competing successfully in these markets, so much so that Columella was forced to produce a detailed argument for the continued profitability of viticulture to counter growing scepticism in Italy.

Wine was the everyday drink of all classes in Greece and Rome. It was also a key part of one of the central social institutions of the élite, the dinner and drinking party (see CONVIVIUM; SYMPOSIUM). On such occasions large quantities of wine were drunk, but it was always heavily diluted with water. It was considered a mark of uncivilized peoples, untouched by classical culture, that they drank wine neat with supposed disastrous effects on their mental and physical health. See AGRICULTURE; ALCOHOLISM; DIONYSUS.

wisdom See SEVEN SAGES.

witchcraft, witches See AMULETS; CURSES; MAGIC.

witnesses See EVIDENCE, ATTITUDES TO.

wolf, wolves See APOLLO; LUPERCALIA; OGULNIUS, GALLUS; ROMULUS.

women Almost all information about women in antiquity comes to us from male sources. Athens alone produced every type of source material, but every type has its limitations, and relevant source material of every type must be used if significant progress is to be made; so, even in the case of Athens, solving the 'woman question' is much harder than once supposed. Many attributions to women are problematic.

One problem with the sources is how to weight different types of material. For example, in Sophocles' *Antigone* *Creon (1) orders *Antigone and Ismene to 'be women' and stay 'inside'. Is this evidence that women's domain was normally the home? Other types of source (philosophy, lawcourt speeches) suggest that Athenian women left the home to visit relatives, work in the fields, fetch water, and attend weddings and religious festivals. So is this ideal lived up to by only a few rich households?

In certain areas of life the similarities between the position and the experience of Greek and Roman women in all historical periods outweigh the differences; so some generalizations may be made. For all women, their main role was as bearers of legitimate children; even when Spartan women, seen as radically 'different' by the Athenian and Roman men who wrote about them, engaged in physical training, it was to strengthen their bodies for *childbirth. Concern with ensuring legitimacy of heirs led both to tight control of women's sexuality—including early marriage, at or before puberty—and fear of the power of that sexuality. Women must be tamed, instructed, and watched.

Ancient women lacked political rights; they could not attend political assemblies, nor could they hold office. However, some Athenian girls and women played prominent parts in public religion, as did *Delphi's Pythia. See next entry. In the Roman empire it has been argued that their political exclusion meant less after the decline in the roles of senate and assemblies, while the importance of the imperial family gave increased influence to its women. By the 2nd cent. AD the status of imperial women declined in a reaction against the roles of *Livia Drusilla and *Iulia Agrippina. When women are represented in Roman sources as taking a public role, this tends to be accompanied by allusions to female spite, treachery, or lack of self-control. References to women's political action are intended to discredit the men associated with them, as with *Aspasia and *Pericles.

To act for them in economic transactions, Athenian women needed a *kȳrios* or controller, normally father or husband; Roman women without father or husband needed a *tutor* (see GUARDIANSHIP, *Rome*). In the Roman world the exceptions were the *Vestals and, after Augustus, free-born women who had given birth to three children (see IUS LIBERORUM). However, the system could be used to give the appearance of male control over property; on the death of their husbands, *widows would take over their businesses, while in the eastern provinces women made contracts and used their wealth as benefactors of their communities from the Hellenistic period onwards (see EUERGETISM). By imperial times, male tutelage of Roman women had become a formality.

Although lower-class women in the ancient world often worked outside the home, in agriculture, as market-traders, and as craftswomen (see ARTISANS AND CRAFTSMEN), as well as in more obviously 'female' roles such as *midwives and wet-nurses, women were traditionally praised for silence and invisibility. Their appearances in lawcourts were restricted to displays of grief in support of male relatives; in Athens, their evidence was used only when a free woman swore an oath on the heads of her children. In Classical Greece a woman's name was not given in public unless she was dead, or of ill repute, and glory for a widow was defined in *Thucydides' (2) Funeral Speech of Pericles as 'not to be spoken of among the males, either in praise or blame' (see EPITAPHIOS). In Roman society, naming reflected this invisibility; women took the gentile name of their father, but in time they acquired a *cognomen*, so that sisters were differentiated as (e.g.) Iulia Agrippina and Iulia Drusilla. See NAMES, PERSONAL, ROMAN, 7; and entries under the names.

See next entry and also GYNAECOLOGY; HETEROSEXUALITY; HOMOSEXUALITY; MARRIAGE CEREMONIES; MARRIAGE LAW; MOTHERHOOD; PROSTITUTION; SEXUALITY.

women in cult Women played a prominent part in the public religious life of Greek cities. Most cults of a goddess were served by a priestess rather than a priest, each local *sanctuary following its own tradition here. A few cults of gods, as often those of *Dionysus, were also served by priestesses. Some cults stipulated that the priestess must be virgin (thus a little girl), a few that she have 'finished association with men', but most made no such stipulation: Lysimachē was priestess of *Athena Polias in Athens for 64 years in the 5th cent. BC. The role of a priestess was parallel to that of a *priest. Both sexes mediated between worshippers and worshipped, mainly by presiding over *sacrifices. Women other than the priestess also had a role in the sacrifice: the basket containing the sacrificial knife was carried in the procession by an unmarried girl (see KANEPHOROI), while the moment of the victim's death was marked by ululation from all women present.

Some women who were not strictly priestesses had special religious roles to play, most conspicuously the Pythia at *Delphi, a woman who, probably in a trance, appeared as the medium for *Apollo's prophecy; see DELPHIC ORACLE. In Athens the wife of the *basileus* (see ARCHONTES) performed various sacred functions, including becoming in some way the bride of Dionysus at the *Anthesteria. Quite different were the 'women's festivals', annual celebrations from which men were rigorously excluded. Some of them, like the *Arrephoria and the *Brauronian bear-ritual in Attica, involved unmarried girls and probably developed from *initiation ceremonies in which the girls in ritual seclusion were symbolically prepared for marriage and motherhood. Others, of which the widespread *Thesmophoria may be seen as typical, were largely the concern of married women and seem to have been esp. concerned with fertility—vegetable, animal, and human. Other types of celebration, such as some of the wilder forms of Dionysiac ritual (see MAENADS), or the 'unofficial' Adonia (see ADONIS), which became popular in Athens at the end of the 5th cent., seem to have involved women in a more overtly emotional, perhaps sometimes ecstatic, form of religious experience. Cults open to both sexes are amply attested by *votives and literary references.

The religious organization of the Roman state was radically different, and the place of women was correspondingly different. Most of the major priesthoods, even of female deities, were held by men. In contrast to normal Greek custom the wives of some of these priests held a quasi-sacerdotal office by virtue of their marriage; notable is the wife of the *flamen dialis*, known as *flaminica*, whose assistance was necessary at certain public rituals and whose death compelled her husband to relinquish office (see FLAMINES). An even more clearly priestly role was taken by the Vestals, unmarried women who served the cult of *Vesta for 30 years before puberty, whose peculiar status gave them elements akin to both married women and to men. Their presence was required at many public religious rites, at some of which they undertook parts of the sacrificial process which normally seem to have been barred to women. Like the Greek cities, however, Rome had its women's festivals, although such celebrations were perhaps marginal to the city's religious life. One was the festival of the *Bona Dea, celebrated with great secrecy in the house of the highest magistrate present in Rome, which attained notoriety when *Clodius Pulcher gained entry to *Caesar's house on this occasion. Women were often more conspicuous in cults with a 'foreign' tinge, ranging from the *Aventine cult of *Ceres (originating from southern Italy) which was served by a priestess, to the prominence of female devotees of *Isis. *Mithraic initiation was confined to men, but there is ample testimony of the interest many Graeco-Roman women took in Judaism (see RELIGION, JEWISH) and *Christianity. The epistles of *Paul show the difficulties faced by the new religion in assigning an agreed role to women.

women in philosophy are recorded in antiquity, though extant writings are few, and there is controversy over dating and authorship of texts. Most of the women whom ancient sources identify as philosophers are associated with schools or societies that admitted women, or are related to philosophers who made education available to them. Women are reported as writing philosophical and mathematical works, and teaching in positions of authority in established schools.

Pythagoreanism seems to have been hospitable to women from the start. *Pythagoras taught women as well as men, and many are associated with the society. In other schools, Axiothea (who dressed like a man) and Lastheneia are cited as students of *Plato and *Speusippus; *Epicurus admitted women to the Garden; Hipparchia, who married *Crates, is noted for her cynic way of life. Arētē, daughter of Aristippus, is cited among the *Cyrenaics. The Roman empress *Iulia Domna attracted a lively circle of philosophers and sophists (see SECOND SOPHISTIC). *Philostratus calls her 'the philosopher Iulia'.

The best-known woman in ancient philosophy lived in late antiquity. *Hypatia became head of the *Neoplatonic school in *Alexandria. A contemporary account of her hideous death at the hands of Christians in AD 415 is given by the ecclesiastical historian Socrates Scholasticus.

wool, the principal textile fibre of the Mediterranean region, was taken from the coat of the European domestic sheep. The structure of wool makes it warm, water-resistant and easy to spin; throughout antiquity fleece character was enhanced by selective breeding. Sheep were a core component of Greek upland agriculture. The finest wool came from *Miletus. The Greek colonies in Italy, esp. *Tarentum, set high standards for Roman wool-producers to emulate. Wool from farms in the Po valley (see PADUS) and several regions of *Spain was esp. prized. Some raw wool was converted directly into felt, but most was spun for the manufacture of all manner of clothing and furnishings; since wool takes dyes easily, they were often brightly coloured. See DYEING; TEXTILE PRODUCTION.

worship, household The domestic cult of a Greek family concerned the protection and prosperity of the house and its occupants, with daily small offerings and prayers to *Zeus Ktēsios (protector of the stores), Zeus Herkeios (protector of the wall or fence surrounding the house), and *Apollo Agyieus (of the streets) whose image stood at the house's street entrance. The hearth, as *Hestia, was sacred, and at mealtimes a bit of food was placed there as a *first-fruits offering. Similarly, before drinking wine, *libations were poured on the floor to Hestia or at formal banquets to Zeus and the heroes, to the Agathos Daimon, or to other deities. In these family cults the rituals seem of primary importance and hence were widespread, while the deities honoured varied from place to place. The father served as priest for the family, however, and that may partially explain the regular appearance of Zeus, father of the gods. The admission of new members to the family (brides, babies, and slaves) was marked by initiation rites, often involving the hearth and featuring fertility symbols. Death brought to the household a *pollution which was effaced only by the passage of a set period of time.

The Roman domestic cult was similar, centred on the hearth (*Vesta), with somewhat more elaborate table ritual, and with *Janus watching the door, the Di Penates guarding the stores, and the Lar Familiaris (see LARES) offering more general protection. Like their Greek counterparts these deities remained numinous, without distinct personality or mythology. The functions of the Lares and Di Penates were regularly confused. They were housed in the *larārium*, many examples of which are known from Pompeii.

wreaths See CROWNS AND WREATHS.

wrestling was a popular exercise among the Greeks. They used a wide variety of holds and throws, many of which are illustrated in vase-paintings and statuettes of wrestlers. The object was to throw an opponent to the ground, and usually three throws were required for victory. In the major *agones* wrestling was both a separate event and the last of the events of the *pentathlon; though weight was an advantage, general athletic ability was required too. Wrestling was also practised extensively to acquire physical fitness, and was considered esp. valuable, together with boxing, as a part of military training. See ATHLETICS.

writing See ALPHABET, GREEK; ARCHIVES; BELLEROPHON; BOOKS, GREEK AND ROMAN; BUREAUCRACY (GREEK); EPIGRAPHY, GREEK and LATIN; LETTERS, GREEK and LATIN; LIBRARIES; LITERACY; OSTRAKA; PALAEOGRAPHY; PAPYROLOGY, GREEK; POTTERY (GREEK), INSCRIPTIONS ON; RECORDS AND RECORD-KEEPING; VINDOLANDA TABLETS.

Xanthippus, husband of *Cleisthenes' (2) niece Agaristē and father of *Pericles. He prosecuted *Miltiades after his unsuccessful attack on Paros in 490–489 BC; he was ostracized in 484, but was recalled with the other victims of *ostracism before *Xerxes' invasion. As a general (see STRATEGOI) in 479 (see PERSIAN WARS) he commanded the Athenian contingent at Mycale (see LEOTYCHIDAS); after the Spartans had returned home, he led some of the Greeks in an attack on Sestus, which was captured from the Persians after a winter siege.

Xenophanēs of Colophon, poet, theologian, and natural philosopher, left *Ionia at the age of 25, probably after the Persian conquest in 545 BC, and led a wandering life for 67 years, as he tells us himself. He lived in several cities in Sicily, and is reported to have composed an epic on the colonization of Elea (see COLONIZATION, GREEK). The extant fragments, in various metres and genres, include two long elegiac (see METRE, GREEK) passages on how to conduct a civilized *symposium and on the civic importance of his own work and wisdom (see SEVEN SAGES).

A skilful poet in the tradition of *Tyrtaeus and *Solon, Xenophanes carried the Ionian intellectual enlightenment to *Magna Graecia. His natural philosophy is a somewhat simplified version of the new Milesian cosmology, supplemented by interesting inferences from observed fossils. Things originate from earth and water; meteorological and celestial phenomena (including sun, moon, and stars) are explained by clouds formed from the sea. In theology and theory of knowledge he was an original and influential thinker. He attacks *Homer and *Hesiod for portraying the gods as behaving in ways that are blameworthy for mortals. He mocks anthropomorphic conceptions of deity, and undermines the supernatural interpretation of natural phenomena. In place of the Homeric pantheon he offers the vision of a supreme god, 'greatest among gods and men, like unto mortals neither in body nor in mind', who without effort sways the universe with his thought. Moderns have imagined him a monotheist, but he seems rather to have preached a harmonious polytheism, without conflict among the gods. In our ignorance of Milesian speculation about the gods, Xenophanes appears as the first thinker systematically to formulate the conception of a cosmic god, and thus to found the tradition of natural theology followed by *Plato, *Aristotle, and the *Stoics. Pursuing a theme of Archaic poetry, Xenophanes is the first to reflect systematically on the distinction between human opinion or guesswork and certain knowledge.

Xenophon

Life Xenophon (c.428–c.354 BC), son of Gryllus, from the Athenian *deme of Erchia, came from a rich but politically inactive family. He presumably served in the cavalry (see HIPPEIS (2) and (3)) and certainly (like other rich young men) associated with *Socrates. This background did not encourage enthusiasm for democracy (see DEMOCRACY, ATHENIAN). He apparently stayed in Athens under the *Thirty Tyrants and fought the democratic insurgents in the civil war (404–403). The *amnesty of 403/2 theoretically protected him, and material in *Hellenica* and *Socratic Recollections* shows that (like *Plato) he was critical of the Thirty, but insecurity was surely one reason why he accepted the suggestion of a friend to enrol as a *mercenary with *Cyrus (2). He was thus among the 10,000 Greeks involved in Cyrus' rebellion and defeat at *Cunaxa (401). When *Tissaphernes murdered the Greek generals, Xenophon emerged as a replacement and led the survivors through Mesopotamia, Armenia, and northern Anatolia to *Byzantium and then into service with the Thracian Seuthes. He alleges a wish to go home at this stage but for various reasons neither did so nor availed himself of Seuthes' offers of land and marriage-alliance. So, when the Spartans under Thibron arrived in Anatolia for a war of 'liberation' (399) and took over Cyrus' veterans, he became a Spartan mercenary. Nothing is known of his role in ensuing campaigns except that he self-defensively endorsed criticisms which led to Thibron's dismissal. Subsequent Spartan commanders, Dercylidas and *Agesilaus, were more to his taste and he forged close associations with them. In 394 Agesilaus returned home to confront rebellion amongst Sparta's allies, and Xenophon fought for the Spartan cause at Coronea against, among others, his fellow Athenians. Exiled as a result of this (if not, as some think, earlier, as part of an Athenian attempt to win Persian goodwill) he was settled by the Spartans at Scillus, near *Olympia. As a Spartan protégé (he was their *proxenos at Olympia and his children were allegedly educated in Sparta) he became vulnerable during the disturbances which followed *Leuctra, was expelled, and spent the rest of his life in *Corinth. There was, however, a reconciliation with Athens. Works such as *Cavalry Commander* and *Revenues* disclose a sympathetic interest in the city; and in 362 his son Gryllus was killed fighting in the Athenian cavalry at *Mantinea. The posthumous eulogies this earned were in part a tribute to his father.

Works Most famous in antiquity as a 'philosopher' or mercenary-leader, Xenophon produced a large output, all known parts of which survive. Most works fall into three categories: long (quasi-) historical narratives, Socratic texts, and technical treatises. There are also four monographs, not unrelated to the major categories. Many are the earliest (or earliest surviving) examples of particular *genres. The clearest common features are (1) intimate relationship with Xenophon's personal experiences and (2) taste for didactic discourse. Xenophon's moral system is conventional, underpinned by belief in the gods and the importance of omen and ritual: divine power (often anonymous and often singular) is everywhere in Xenophon's writings, though not absolutely stultifyingly—when consulting the *Delphic oracle about going to Asia, he framed the question so as to get the 'right' answer; and at the climactic moment in *Anabasis* where the Greeks reach the sea they are too excited to think of sacrificing to the gods. But it is not these things in their own right so much as issues of leadership (by states as well as individuals) or military skill which engage his didactic muse. That even purely practical pursuits

have a moral component because they have social implications is a characteristic Xenophontic perception; and the would-be leader must earn his right to lead by superior wisdom and a capacity to match or outdo his subordinates in all the tasks which he demands of them.

In antiquity his style was judged to be simple, sweet, persuasive, graceful, poetic, and a model of *Attic purity. This is understandable, though there are deviations from standard Attic and some would call the style jejune; both rhetoric and narrative are sometimes awkward. The range of figures employed is modest (simile is common, with a penchant for animal comparisons). The overall effect (style *and* content) can seem naïve.

Hellenica. A seven-book history of Greek affairs, in two linguistically distinguishable parts, perhaps written at widely differing times. (*a*) The first part covers the *Peloponnesian War from 411 to the destruction of Athens' walls, the overthrow of democracy and the surrender of *Samos (404). The opening narrative links imperfectly with Thuc. 8. 109, but the intention must be to 'complete' the Thucydidean account, though this is achieved with little reproduction of Thucydides' *historiographical characteristics. (*b*) The second part continues the story, covering the *Thirty Tyrants (404–403), Sparta's Asiatic campaigns (399–394), the *Corinthian War and *King's Peace (395–387/6), Spartan imperialism in Greece (386–379), the rise of Thebes (379–371) and the Peloponnesian consequences of *Leuctra (371–362). The text ends at Mantinea (362; see MANTINEA, BATTLES OF), with Greece in an unabated state of uncertainty and confusion. The account is centred on Sparta and characterized by surprising omissions (e.g. the name of *Epaminondas the architect of Leuctra does not occur in bk. 6 where the battle is described), a tendency to expose the shortcomings of all states, including Sparta, and recurrent hostility to imperial aspirations. A curious amalgam of straight history and political pamphlet, it remains an indispensable source.

Anabasis ('March Inland'). An account of Cyrus' rebellion and the fate of his Greek mercenaries, dominated in bks. 3–7 by Xenophon's personal role in rescuing the army.

Cyropaedia ('Education of Cyrus'). A pseudo-historical account of the life of *Cyrus (1) I the Great, often invoked in accounts of the background of the Greek *novel. The chief concern is with techniques of military and political leadership. There is also a suggestion that even Cyrus can be corrupted by the acquisition of empire, and a final chapter (post-362) excoriates contemporary Persian vices.

Apology. A brief (perhaps early) work with a purported extract from the court-room defence of Socrates against charges of religious deviance and corruption of the young sandwiched between a preliminary dialogue with Hermogenes and various carefree observations made after the trial was over. The stated purpose is to explain the 'big-talking' which previous writers agreed was a feature of Socrates' reaction to prosecution and show why he did not fear death. (Opportunity is also found to note the prosecutor *Anytus' son's history of *alcohol abuse).

Symposium. 'In writing of great men it is proper to record not only their serious activities but their diversions', and entertainment at *Callias' (2) party is a mixture of cabaret (music, song, and dance, a sexually titillating tableau of *Dionysus and *Ariadne) and more-or-less serious conversation about the guests' account of their most prized assets (e.g. beauty, wealth, poverty, making people better, recitation, joke-telling, skill at procuring). There is much explicit or implicit reference to personal relationships (doubtless a feature of real sympotic conversation); so Socrates' eventual discourse on common and celestial love is an unsurprising development, though the Platonic model is probably relevant. See SYMPOSIUM LITERATURE.

Socratic Recollections. A collection of conversations, probably not planned as a coherent whole. The beginning of bk. 1 explicitly addresses charges advanced at Socrates' trial, but the whole work presents him as respecting the gods and helping (not corrupting) his fellowmen. Broad thematic patterns are visible—bk. 1 dwells on religion and moderate life-style, 2 on friendship and family, and 3 on Socrates' help to 'those ambitious of good things', while 4 is more disparate (education; the existence of god; temperance; justice) and pretentious—but the pleasure of the work is in its individual vignettes and convincing (not necessarily authentic) picture of a down-to-earth Socrates equally happy debating with sophists, courtesans, and victims of the collapse of Athenian imperialism, and concerned with practicalities as well as philosophy. (As with Plato, drawing the line between genuine Socratic conversational subjects and Xenophontic ones is not easy.)

Oeconomicus. A conversation with Critobūlus establishes the importance of *agriculture. Socrates then reports a conversation with Ischomachus—itself containing a conversation between Ischomachus and his wife—covering household organization, the daily pursuits of a rich Athenian, the role of bailiffs, and technical details of cereal and fruit cultivation. Much of it is effectively about leadership—a harder skill than agriculture, as Ischomachus remarks. The work is an important (though, given Socratic—and Xenophontic—unconventionality, slippery) source for social history. Ischomachus' wife, married young so she will be a *tabula rasa* on which her husband can write what he will, is accorded a significant—if sex-stereotyped—role in the running of the household (see HOUSEWORK; WOMEN).

Cavalry Commander deals with the management and improvement of the Athenian cavalry force (which ought to include foreign mercenaries); see HIPPEIS. Characteristically Xenophon begins and ends with the gods, asserts that no art should be practised more than warfare—boxing does not compare—and stresses the importance of leadership qualities. See WAR, ART OF, GREEK.

On Horsemanship. 'Instruction and exercises' for the private and apparently rather ignorant individual (the specific addressees are 'younger friends'). It is the earliest surviving such work. Its precepts are well regarded by modern experts. See HORSES.

*On *Hunting.* A technical treatise dealing with nets, *dogs and their training, and the timing and conduct of the hunt. The hunter is on foot, the normal prey a hare (an animal of notably good organic design), though Xenophon also mentions deer, boar, and the wild cats of *Macedonia, Mysia, and *Syria. (He disapproves of the hunting of foxes). The activity is non-utilitarian (quick capture shows perseverance, but is not real hunting), intensely pleasurable—the sight of a hare running is so charming that to see one tracked, found, pursued, and caught is enough to make a man forget all other passions—and a divine invention which promotes military, intellectual, and moral excellence. A contrast is drawn with the corrupt verbal wisdom of '*sophists' (a group not treated elsewhere in Xenophon as a coherent evil), and the hunter beats the politician in point of ethical standing and social value.

Agesilaus. Posthumous encomium of 'a perfectly good man'. An uneven chronological account is followed by a survey of principal virtues. Little solid information is offered which is not in *Hellenica*, but a new gloss (sometimes *panhellenic, occasionally critical) is put on already familiar facts. The work is an important contribution to the development of biography. See AGESILAUS; BIOGRAPHY, GREEK.

Hieron. A dialogue version of the 'wise man meets autocrat' scenario (cp. *Herodotus on *Solon and *Croesus) in which, contrary to expectation, *Hieron (1) I refutes *Simonides' claim that it is pleasant to be a *tyrant, while Simonides supplies suggestions for improving the situation, not least by manipulation of public opinion.

Revenues. Politicians claim that poverty compels Athens to treat other cities unjustly. So Xenophon advises alleviation of that poverty through innocent means, esp. (*a*) attracting revenue-creating foreign residents and (*b*) using state-owned slaves in the *Laurium silver *mines to increase income and generate a dole for citizens. The economic plan (a curious mixture of the apparently familiar and completely alien) has been much criticized; but the primary imperative is political—to devise a new imperialism based on peace and consensual hegemony.

Constitution of the Spartans. An account of the Spartan system (attributed to a single lawgiver, Lycurgus) intended to show the rationality of its constant contradiction of normal Greek practices. The tone is laudatory except in a final chapter (misplaced in the manuscripts) which notes the decline from Lycurgan values associated with 4th-cent. imperialism.

Xerxēs, son of *Darius (1) and Atossa, king of *Persia 486–465 BC, chosen by his father as successor. At the beginning of his reign he crushed a revolt in Egypt and later two rebellions in *Babylon. Plans for an expedition against Greece were inherited from Darius: for the course of events see PERSIAN WARS. No Persian document mentions the expedition.

The more important palaces on the terrace of *Persepolis were built in Xerxes' reign, including the *apadana with its impressive reliefs, illustrating the structure and the extent of the empire: king, court, and subject populations with their ethnographic characteristics. In the *daiva* inscription rebellion is equated with the neglect of Ahuramazda (see ZOROASTER) and the worship of *daivas* ('bad gods'). Xerxes' destruction of the *daiva*-sanctuary marks no breach with his ancestors' presumed religious tolerance, as is often thought, since the *Bisitun inscription already contains similar phraseology. Xerxes' reputation as weakling and womanizer depends on certain recognizably novelistic passages in Herodotus and on the reading of royal inscriptions as personal messages by the kings, rather than as formulaic royal statements. Seen from the heartland, his reign was a period of consolidation, not of incipient decay. Xerxes was murdered in 465.

Xūthus, a mythical figure connected with the perceived racial divisions among the Greeks. Acc. to *Hesiod, he was son of Hellen and brother of Dorus and Aeolus, the eponyms of the *Dorians and Aeolians (see AEOLIS); his sons by the Athenian Creusa, daughter of *Erechtheus, are Ion and Achaeus, who are also eponymous. This version reflects Athenian claims to *Ionian primacy.

year of the four emperors i.e. AD 69. See ROME (HISTORY), 2.2; VESPASIAN.

youth See AGE; CHILDREN; EDUCATION, *Greek* and *Roman*; EPHEBOI; HEBE; IUVENES.

Zama, battle of Zama is the name given to the final battle of the Second *Punic War, though it was not actually fought near any of the places so called. *Hannibal had perhaps 36,000 infantry, 4,000 cavalry and 80 *elephants, *Cornelius Scipio Africanus perhaps 29,000 infantry and 6,000 cavalry. The elephants, opening the battle, were either ushered down corridors Scipio had left in his formation or driven out to the flanks where they collided with Hannibal's cavalry, which was then routed by the Roman cavalry. When the infantry lines closed, the Roman first line may have defeated both Hannibal's first and second lines, though the remnants perhaps reformed on the wings of his third line, composed of his veterans from Italy. Scipio, too, reformed his lines at this point, and a titanic struggle developed until the Roman cavalry, returning from the pursuit, charged into Hannibal's rear, whereupon his army disintegrated.

Zēnō (1) of Elea is portrayed by *Plato as the pupil and friend of *Parmenides, and junior to him by 25 years. Their fictional meeting with a 'very young' *Socrates gives little basis for firm chronology. We may conclude only that Zeno was active in the early part of the 5th cent. BC.

The most famous of Zeno's arguments are the four paradoxes about motion paraphrased by *Aristotle, which have fascinated thinkers down to Bertrand Russell. The Achilles paradox proposes that a quicker can never overtake a slower runner who starts ahead of him, since he must always first reach the place the slower has already occupied. His task is in truth an infinite sequence of tasks, and can therefore never be completed. The Arrow paradox argues that in the present a body in motion occupies a place just its own size, and is therefore at rest. But since it is in the present throughout its movement, it is always at rest. The Dichotomy raises the same issues about infinite divisibility as the Achilles; the Arrow and the Stadium (an

obscure puzzle about the relative motion of bodies) are perhaps directed against the implicit assumption of indivisible minima.

Acc. to Plato, Zeno's method was to attack an assumption by deriving contradictory consequences from it. *Simplicius quotes fragments in which Zeno adopts precisely this strategy against the hypothesis of plurality. Thus fr. 3 proves that if there are many things, their number is both limited and unlimited. Frs. 1 and 2 evidently formed parts of a more elaborate argument from the same hypothesis. Each member of a plurality must be self-identical and one, and therefore (grounds for this inference are not preserved) so small as to be without magnitude. Anything with magnitude, by contrast, has an infinite number of parts, each possessing magnitude, and must accordingly itself be so large as to be infinite. No other examples survive, although it is conceivable that the paradoxes of motion originally took the form of antinomies about plurality.

Plato reads the antinomies as assaults on common sense; more specifically as an indirect defence of Parmenidean monism against outraged common sense. But perhaps Zeno intended not so much to shake belief in the existence of plurality and motion as to question the coherence of our understanding of these phenomena. On either interpretation Aristotle was right to see in Zeno the founder of *dialectic.

Zēnō (2) of Citium in *Cyprus, 335–263 BC, founder of *Stoicism. He came to Athens in 313 and is said to have studied with or been influenced by various philosophers, notably *Crates the Cynic, *Antisthenes the Socratic, and the Academics Xenocrates and esp. *Polemon. Zeno taught in the *Stoa Poecilē, which gave its name to Stoicism. He was well respected at Athens.

Zeno's writings established Stoicism as a set of ideas articulated into three parts: logic (and theory of knowledge), *physics (and metaphysics), and ethics. Later Stoics developed some of his ideas in differing ways until an orthodoxy on fundamentals was established by the writings of *Chrysippus. Stoicism is holistic in method: logic, say, or ethics can be developed in relative independence, but are ultimately to be seen to fit into the set of Stoic ideas as a whole, while no part serves as foundation for the others. Stoicism is materialist, regarding everything as part of a universal natural system subject to deterministic laws; however, it is also teleological and compatibilist. In method and theory of knowledge it is uncompromisingly empiricist, but again shows no reductive tendencies, laying great stress on reason and its capacities; Stoic propositional logic is one of its most distinctive and original contributions. Stoic ethics lays great stress on the difference of kind in value between virtue and other kinds of advantage such as health and wealth, although these are natural for us to pursue. This difference is such that virtue even without these is sufficient for happiness; thus stress on the importance of virtue leads to radical redefinition of happiness, our final end. The Stoics stressed the role of rules and principles in moral reasoning; early writings of Zeno stressed that even basic moral rules could have justified exceptions, but later Stoics downplayed this, and distanced themselves from Zeno's *Republic*, in which an ideal community, radically rejecting convention, was developed.

Zēnobia, the second wife of Septimius Odaenathus king of Palmyra. On his death in AD 267, in suspicious circumstances, she secured power for herself in the name of her young son, Septimius Vaballathus. As long as Zenobia kept the east secure, the emperors Gallienus and Claudius Gothicus were prepared to accept her regime, including its bestowal upon Vaballathus of his father's Roman titles, and hence of the claim to be more than just king of Palmyra. However, in 270 Zenobia exploited the political instability that followed the death of Claudius to expand beyond Syria by taking over Egypt and much of Asia Minor, and further to enhance Vaballathus' Roman titles, while continuing to recognize *Aurelian as emperor. When Aurelian finally moved against her in 272, her forces failed to stop him at Antioch and Emesa, and—now calling her son *Augustus* and herself *Augusta*—she was besieged in Palmyra. She was captured while attempting to escape, shortly before the fall of the city. She was spared. Many tales were told of her later life; little is certain, though it is likely that she was paraded in Aurelian's triumph.

Zēnodotus of Ephesus (b. *c.*325 BC), pupil of *Philitas, became the first head of the Library at *Alexandria (*c.*284) and undertook the classification of the Greek epic and lyric poets, some of whom he edited. His recension of *Homer's *Iliad* and *Odyssey*, in which the poems may have been divided into 24 books for the first time, represented the first scholarly attempt to get back to the original Homeric text by the collation of several manuscripts. He marked lines of the genuineness of which he felt doubt with a newly invented sign, the *obelus*.

zeugītai (from *zeugos*, 'yoke'), at Athens, *Solon's third property class, comprising men whose land yielded between 200 and 300 *medimnoi* of corn or the equivalent in other produce. The name identifies them as those who served in the army in close ranks, i.e. as *hoplites. Many of the farmers and craftsmen of *Attica fell into this class, and it provided the bulk of the city's hoplite army. Under Solon's constitution the *zeugitai* enjoyed full citizen rights except that they were not admitted to the highest *magistracies. The archonships (see ARCHONTES) were opened to them from 457/6.

Zeus, the main divinity of the Greek pantheon (see OLYMPIAN GODS; RELIGION, GREEK) and the only major Greek god whose *Indo-European origin is undisputed. His role as father, i.e. having the power of a father in a patriarchal system, is Indo-European. Thus in *Homer, Zeus is both *patēr* 'father', and *anax* 'king' or 'lord'.

Zeus, the Indo-European god of the bright sky, is transformed in Greece into Zeus the weather god, whose paramount and specific place of worship is a mountain top. Among his mountains, the most important is *Olympus, a real mountain, which was already a mythical place before Homer. Many mountain cults are reflected only in an epithet, which does not necessarily imply the existence of a peak *sanctuary. Few such sanctuaries have been excavated (e.g. on Mt. Hymettus); those attested in literature are mostly connected with rain rituals. As 'the gatherer of clouds' (a common Homeric epithet), he was generally believed to cause rain. With the god of clouds comes the god of thunder and of lightning; a spot struck by lightning is inviolable and often sacred to Zeus Kataibatēs, 'He who comes down'. As the master of tempest, he is supposed to give signs through thunder and lightning and to strike evildoers.

But already for the early Archaic Greeks, Zeus had much more fundamental functions. Acc. to the succession myth in Hesiod's *Theogony* (whose main elements are also known to Homer), Zeus deposed his father *Cronus, who had deposed and castrated his father *Uranus; after his accession to power, Zeus fought the *Giants and Typhon, who challenged his reign, and drew up the present world-order by assigning to each divinity his or her sphere: to his brothers *Poseidon and *Hades-Pluton, he allotted two-thirds of the cosmos, to the one the sea, to the other the Underworld, to his sisters Hera (also his wife) and *Demeter, and to his many divine children their domains in the human world. (His many matings with goddesses and mortal women are one manifestation of his prepotency.) Thus, Zeus became the ruler over both the other gods and the human world, which had existed before his reign; the current order of things is Zeus' work.

Closely related succession myths are attested from Hittite Anatolia and from Mesopotamia. In Hittite mythology, the succession passes through Anu, 'Sky', who is deposed and castrated by Kumarbi, finally to Teshub, the Storm God, who would correspond to Zeus. Myths from Mesopotamia present a similar, though more varied structure; the Babylonian *Enuma Eliš* moves from a primeval pair, Apsu and Tiamat, to the reign of Marduk, the city god of *Babylon and in many respects comparable to Ba'al and Zeus. The conception of Zeus as the kingly ruler of this world is unthinkable without oriental influence. In a similar way, the shift from Indo-European god of the bright sky to the Greek master of sky and storms is inconceivable without the influence of the weather gods of *Anatolia and Syria-Palestine with whom he was later identified.

Zeus is a king, not a tyrant. One of his main domains is right and justice: any transgression of his cosmic order is injustice; if necessary, Zeus punishes transgressors. Human kings are under his special protection, but they have to endorse his justice. Zeus himself protects those outside ordinary social bonds—strangers, suppliants and beggars. To preserve his order, he is himself subject to it: he is committed to *Fate.

In many instances (e.g. the Trojan War), human affairs follow the plan of Zeus despite apparent setbacks. He might hasten completion, if asked in prayer to do so, and he might signal his will, either asked for or unasked, in dreams, augural signs, thunder and lightning, but also by provoking ominous human utterances. In these cases, the prophetic power of Zeus is occasional and accessory. It becomes central in the only Greek *oracle of Zeus, *Dodona in Epirus, reputed to be the oldest Greek oracle, already known to Homer. It was active until late-Hellenistic times; though consulted by cities too, its main clients were private persons from NW Greece. Zeus is here paired with Diōnē, mother of *Aphrodite in ordinary Greek myth. Zeus manifested himself in the sounds of the holy oak-tree and in doves, whose call from the tree or whose flight were used as divine signs.

Zeus has only a few major *polis *festivals; and though he is often called Polieus, he has no major temple on an acropolis, unlike the Roman *Jupiter Capitolinus. Two festivals of his observed at Athens were the Dipolieia (see ATTIC CULTS AND MYTHS) and Diasia. The Dipolieia featured the guilt-ridden sacrifice of an ox on the altar of Zeus Polieus on the Acropolis, the Bouphonia. The ritual killing of the ox, the myth which makes all participants guilty, with the ensuing prosecution of the killer with the formal condemnation of axe and knife, enacts a crisis, not a bright festival.

The Diasia, 'the greatest Athenian festival of Zeus', had an even less auspicious character. The festival honoured Zeus Meilichios ('propitiable'), who appears in reliefs in the shape of a huge *snake. His cult took place just outside the city, with animal sacrifice or cakes; the victims were burnt whole. This meant no common meal to release the tension of the sacrifice; instead, there were feasts in small family circles and gifts to the children: the community passes through a phase of disintegration, characteristic of the entire month, Anthesterion, whose festival, the *Anthesteria, had an even more marked character of uncanny disintegration.

This paucity of *polis* festivals fits the general image of Zeus. The *polis* has to be under the protection of a specific patron deity, e.g. *Athena or *Apollo, while Zeus is the overall protector and cannot confine himself to one *polis*; his protection adds itself to that of the specific *polis* deities. From early on, he is prominent as a panhellenic deity. The founding hero of Dodona, *Deucalion, father of Hellēn, discloses the oracle's panhellenic aspirations. But Zeus' main Greek festival is the four-yearly *Olympic Games with the splendid sacrifice to Zeus Olympios and the ensuing panhellenic *agon. Their introduction in 776 BC, acc. to tradition, marked the end of the isolation of the Dark Age communities; the common festival took place at a spot outside an individual *polis* and under the protection of the supreme god.

In the *polis* at large, Zeus' own province is the *agora, where he presides, as Zeus Agoraios, over both the political and the commercial life of the community; thus, he can be counted among the main divinities of a city, like Athena Polias. Among the smaller social units, he is one of the patrons of *phratries and clans (see GENOS). He also protects individual households: as Zeus Herkeios, he receives sacrifices on an altar in the courtyard. See WORSHIP, HOUSEHOLD.

There are functions of Zeus at the level of the family which are easily extended both to individuals and to the *polis*. Since property is indispensable for the constitution of a household, Zeus is also protector of property (Ktēsios); as such, he receives cult from families, from cities and from individuals. In many places Zeus Ktesios has the appearance of a snake: property is bound to the ground, at least in the still agrarian mentality of ancient Greece, and its protectors belong to the earth.

As the most powerful god, Zeus has a very general function which cuts across all groups and gains in importance in the course of time: he is the Saviour (*Sōtēr*) par excellence. As such, he receives prayers and dedications from individuals, groups, and entire towns. These dedications reflect different possible situations of crisis, from very private ones to political troubles, natural catastrophes or military attacks.

The Zeus cults of *Crete fit only partially into this picture. Myth places both his birth and his grave in Crete: acc. to *Hesiod, in order to save him from Cronus, Rhea gave birth to Zeus and entrusted the baby to *Gaia, who hid it in a cave. Later authors replace Gaia by the Cūrētēs, young, semi-divine, Cretan warriors.

Already in Homer, Zeus had reached a very dominant position. During the Classical and Hellenistic periods, religious thinkers developed this into a sort of 'Zeus monotheism'. To *Aeschylus, Zeus had begun to move away from the object of simple human knowledge ('Zeus, whoever you are ...') to a nearly universal function ('Zeus is *aithēr* (upper air), Zeus is earth, Zeus is sky, Zeus is everything and more than that'); *Sophocles sees Zeus' hand in all human affairs ('Nothing of this is not Zeus'). The main document of this monotheism, however, is the hymn to Zeus by the Stoic *Cleanthes; Zeus, mythical image of the Stoic *logos* (see STOICISM;

LOGOS), becomes the commander of the entire cosmos and its 'universal law', and at the same time the guarantor of goodness and benign protector of man. This marks the high point of a development—other gods, though briefly mentioned, become insignificant besides this Zeus.

Zeus in art Zeus does not assume a type until early Archaic, when he strides with thunderbolt and, rarely, eagle. In the Classical period, Zeus is quieter, often seated and with a *sceptre: the prime example is *Phidias' cult statue at *Olympia, familiar from literature (esp. *Pausanias), coins, gems, and echoes on vases. The type continues in the Hellenistic period.

Zeus participates in many scenes. The east pediments of Olympia and the *Parthenon centred on him. He fights in the Gigantomachy (see GIANTS) from Attic and south Italian Archaic and Classical vases to the Hellenistic *Pergamum altar frieze. On Classical vases and sculpture, his pursuits include Aegina (the eponymous heroine of *Aegina, see EPONYMOI) and Ganymede. His transformations occur, esp. in depictions of his seduction of Europa from early Archaic, and *Leda from late Classical. He is common on coins. Zeus was favoured by *Alexander (2) the Great and some Roman emperors, esp. *Hadrian (see OLYMPIEUM).

Zeuxis, painter, of Heraclea in Lucania. His rose-wreathed *Eros is mentioned in Aristophanes' *Acharnians* (425). He painted *Archelaus' palace between 413 and 399. He 'entered the door opened by Apollodorus and stole his art' (see PAINTING, GREEK); he added the use of highlights to shading, and *Lucian in his *Zeuxis* praises in the *Centaur family (an instance of the unusual subjects which Zeuxis preferred) the subtle gradation of colour from the human to the animal body of the female Centaur; his paintings of grapes reputedly deceived birds; he said that if he had painted the boy carrying the grapes better, the birds would have been frightened off. His figures lacked the *ēthos* (character) of *Polygnotus, although his Penelope was morality itself, and his Helen an ideal picture compiled from several models. He was rich and arrogant, giving away his paintings since no price was sufficient for them.

Zodiac, twelve signs of the See CONSTELLATIONS AND NAMED STARS.

zoology See ANIMALS, KNOWLEDGE OF.

Zoroaster, is the Greek form of Iranian Zara-thuštra. It is not clear whether Zarathuštra was a reformer or the creator of a new religion, a prophet. In the oldest part of the Avesta, the seventeen Gāthās, ascribed to Zoroaster himself, he is called a *manthrān*, 'one who possesses the sacred formulas'. The Gāthās portray a dualistic system in which truth or rightness is opposed to lie or deceit, with Ahuramazda as the supreme deity. Some have doubted whether he was a his-torical figure. Of the various dates for Zoroaster, that of the 6th cent. BC is based on a late Zoroas-trian tradition, that of *c.*1000 BC is arrived at by linguistic arguments and therefore preferable. The Greeks had heard of Zoroaster by the 5th cent. By the time of Plato and Aristotle they had some notion of the content of his teaching. He is often called a **magus* and regarded as a sage. Legendary details of all sorts accumulated about him. See RELIGION, PERSIAN.

Money and its Value in the Classical World

1. The Monetary Systems

Greece

The Greek world was never unified by a single monetary system. In the Archaic and Classical periods, different city-states adopted different weight standards for their silver coinages. Moreover, different denominational structures were also used in different places. As in so many fields, we are best informed about the city of Athens. Thanks to the spread of Athenian influence in the 5th century BC, and the fact that the Athenian system was adopted and spread by *Alexander (2) the Great, Athenian coinage provides the clearest and most useful illustration of the structure of a Greek monetary system.

The basic unit was the drachma ('handful'), which was subdivided into 6 obols ('spits'). All other silver denominations were named by reference to these two basic units of account. The drachma and obol were not the most common denominations, however. In many states, Athens included, the main denomination was the tetradrachm (4 drachmas). Decadrachms (10 drachmas), didrachms (2 drachmas), drachms (1 drachma), and hemidrachms ($\frac{1}{2}$ drachmas) were also produced. In addition to the obol there were fractions down to $\frac{1}{8}$ obol. In this extensive array of denominations, Athens was exceptional. Most states confined themselves to one or two denominations. The principal denomination in some states was referred to as a 'statēr'.

For accounting purposes, units larger than the drachma were available. A 'mna' consisted of 100 drachmas, and a talent was equivalent to 60 mnas or 600 drachmas (mnas and talents were weights, not coins). The following table gives the equivalences in grams of silver of the basic Athenian units of account:

1 obol = 0.72g.
1 drachma = 6 obols = 4.3g.
1 mna = 100 drachmas = 430g.
1 talent = 60 mnas = 600 drachmas = 25.8 kg.

During the Hellenistic period bronze coinage became common in many states.

Rome

The Roman monetary system before the Second *Punic War (218–201 BC) was complex and unstable. The earliest silver coinage of the late 4th/early 3rd century was based on the Greek drachma system. From the start this coinage was accompanied by bronze money in various forms. The basic Roman bronze unit was the as, originally weighing one Roman pound (c.324 g. (12 oz.)). By the end of the 3rd century the weight of the as had dropped to 35 g. Around 212 the Roman state introduced a new silver denomination known as the *dēnārius* (10 as piece). This would remain the basic Roman silver coin until the 3rd century AD. In 141 BC the denarius was re-tariffed at 16 asses. The range of denominations issued in silver and bronze under the republic can be set out as follows:

Silver

1 dēnārius = 10 or 16 asses
1 quīnārius = $^1\!/_2$ denarius = 5 or 8 asses
1 sestertius = $^1\!/_4$ denarius = $2^1\!/_2$ or 4 asses

Bronze

1 as (= $^1\!/_{10}$ or $^1\!/_{16}$ denarius)
1 sēmis = half as
1 triens = quarter as
1 quadrans = third as
sextans = sixth as
uncia = twelfth as

Under Augustus the bronze coinage was reformed to produce the following denominations:

sestertius (4 asses or $^1\!/_4$ denarius)
dupondius (2 asses or $^1\!/_2$ sestertius)
as ($^1\!/_4$ sestertius) (hereafter, sesterce)
semis ($^1\!/_2$ as)
quadrans ($^1\!/_4$ as)

The gold aureus, which had started to be produced in serious quantities by Julius Caesar, was standardized at a value of 25 denarii.

2. The value of money

It is difficult to explain how much an ancient coin was worth, since there is no easy way of expressing that worth in terms of today's prices for goods. While we may occasionally know how much a certain commodity cost in certain places and at certain times, often the relative values of commodities have changed over time and distance. Moreover, the ancient world was far less well protected than the modern against seasonal variations in supply or the effects of good and bad harvests. Isolated evidence for the prices of goods may well be misleading: prices will have varied widely over time and between areas, even in the supposedly well-ordered Roman empire.

Similarly, it is not always easy to interpret figures given by ancient sources for workers' *wages for a working day, not least because modernistic expectations concerning hierarchies of pay to match hierarchies of skill are not straightforwardly applicable to the ancient evidence.

Greece

For Greece, the best evidence for wages and payments comes from Athens. The Aristotelian *Constitution of the Athenians* gives our most complete set of figures for Athenian public pay at one time. In the second half of the 4th century BC those who attended the assembly received 1 drachma per day (or 9 obols for the principal meeting of the assembly). This had risen from just 1 obol per day when pay was introduced at the end of the 5th century. Jurors received 3 obols per day. See LAW AND PROCEDURE, ATHENIAN, 2. Again this had increased from a payment of 1 or 2 obols per day when the payment was introduced by Pericles in the 5th century. Those serving on the council (*boule) received 5 obols per day except for the *prytaneis, in which case they received an extra obol (making a total of 1 drachma per day) as a subsistence payment. The nine archons (see ARCHONTES) received just 4 obols per day. During the first half of the Peloponnesian War (431–412) standard pay for Athenian soldiers and sailors seems to have been 1 drachma per day. The accounts that survive from the building of the *Erechtheum also attest to the figure of 1 drachma per day as a common wage. It was paid to workers of varying skills—from manual labourers to carpenters and other wood-workers. The same rate may even have applied to sculptors and masons.

Prices for goods at this period are less easy to come by. From the late 5th century at Athens we have some evidence for the price of slaves in an inscription recording the disposal of confiscated property, of upper-class men. An adult might cost c.160 drachmas, a child 70. The same, fragmentary inscription provides prices for some livestock. Two oxen sold for 70 drachmas; 67 goats and their young fetched 710 drachmas. From the island of *Delos during the 3rd and 2nd centuries BC we have a series of prices for certain commodities over a number of years, surviving in the accounts of the overseers of the temple of Apollo. Olive oil varied in price from 1 to 2 drachmas per khous (6 pints). Pigs could be purchased for as little as $1\frac{1}{2}$ drachmas each or as much as 8 drachmas, but usually for 3 to 4 drachmas (a price that accords well with the 3 drachmas for a piglet attested in Aristophanes' Peace). Barley could be had for 2 to 4 drachmas per medimnos (52 lt.); wheat was more expensive at c.6 drachmas per medimnos. Since one medimnos could feed a man for c.48 days, 1 drachma could purchase 8 day's wheat rations for a adult male.

Rome

The rates of pay earned by the rank and file Roman soldier are relatively well recorded. They rose from 450 sesterces ($112\frac{1}{2}$ denarii) per annum in the late republic to 900 sesterces (225 denarii) per annum under Caesar and Augustus to 3,600 sesterces (900 denarii) per annum under *Caracalla in the early 3rd century AD. Daily rates thus climbed from around $\frac{1}{3}$ denarius to $2\frac{1}{2}$ denarii over a period of three centuries or so. Soldiers would never see all of their pay, however. As much as 40–50% was apparently withheld by the army towards food, equipment, and clothing.

From the Roman fort at *Vindolanda we have some evidence for the quantities of commodities that could be bought by a soldier in the 2nd century AD. 100 nails for repairing boots cost 2 asses ($\frac{1}{8}$ denarius); Celtic beer came in at a little under 1 as per gallon; one centurion paid 8 denarii and 2 asses for 60 Roman pounds of pork and lard (a little under half an as per pound); a luxury item like a towel could sell for 1 to 2 denarii (16–32 asses).

For grain, in the late republic and early empire, an average price of 1 denarius per modius is suggested by the literary sources. One modius would have fed an adult male for around 8 days.

From Rome and Italy there is a certain amount of evidence for the prices of slaves or the purchase prices of their freedom (manumission). These range from 700,000 sesterces (175,000 denarii) for a Greek intellectual and teacher at Rome, to 600–725 sesterces (150–181 denarii) for slave boys and girls at Pompeii and

Herculaneum. An adult slave to do the cooking might sell for around 2,500 sesterces (625 denarii). A legionary could only dream of such luxuries. To the average senator, whose fortune may have been in the order 10 million sesterces (2.5 million denarii) such expenditure was negligible.

3. Conclusion

Despite the fragmentary nature of the evidence it is apparent that coinage in the Graeco-Roman world was ill-suited to the everyday use to which we put it. With the exception of Athens in the 5th to 4th centuries BC, no Greek state produced a coinage that could be used easily for purchasing daily requirements of food. Similarly at Rome, although a low-value coinage was introduced by Augustus, there was no such coinage before him, and in fact the low-value coins that his new system provided for were never consistently minted. Given this mismatch between coined money and everyday commodities, it becomes less surprising that it is difficult to put values on such commodities in a systematic way. It is also clear that there was a vast monetary chasm separating the average soldier or labourer from the average member of the élite.

Postscript. The Relative Values of Wages and Goods in the Later Roman Empire.

During the 3rd century AD the Roman empire suffered a period of severe inflation. Prices rose, while the coinage became more debased. *Diocletian (284–305) attempted to halt this process by issuing an empire-wide edict controlling prices. Although substantially inflated from the prices known from earlier periods, and thus not directly comparable, this homogeneous body of wage and price information is the largest available from antiquity and presents the best opportunity to compare relative prices and the relative purchasing power of different professions. A sample is presented below (all figures are denarii).

Daily Wages (with meals)		Food	
Picture painter	160	1 egg	1
Wall painter	75	5 lettuces	4
Baker	50	4 lb. of grapes	4
Farm labourer	25	1 lemon	24
Camel or donkey driver	25	1 lb. of fattened goose	200
Sewer cleaner	25	1 lb. of chicken	60
Shepherd	20	1 lb. of sea fish	24
		1 lb. of pork, lamb,	
Piece work		or goat	12
Teacher of rhetoric		1 lb. of freshwater fish	12
(per student, per month)	250	1 lb. of beef	8
Elementary teacher		1 sectārius (about 1 pint) of	
(per student, per month)	50	good olive oil	40
Scribe, per 100 lines	20	1 sectarius of best honey	40
Tailor			
(for thick socks)	4	**Drink**	
Barber, per man	2	1 sectarius of beer	4
Bath attendant, per person	2	1 sectarius of ordinary wine	8

1 sectarius of Falernian wine	30	1 lb. pure white silk	12,000
		1 male slave	30,000
Clothes and luxuries		1 racehorse	100,000
Pair of women's boots	60	1 lb. genuine emperor's	
Pair of senator's shoes	100	purple silk	150,000
Pair of farm labourer's boots	120		

Two-way Gazetteer: Ancient Place Names and their Modern Descendents

For the origin of this Gazetteer see Preface. In the Gazetteer there are two sets of place names, Ancient and Modern, most of which can be found in the pages of *ODCW*. Each set has 74 members. First, 74 Modern members, arranged in alphabetical order, are matched with the corresponding 74 Ancient, and then the Ancient with the Modern likewise.

MODERN	ANCIENT	MODERN	ANCIENT
Agrigento	Acragas/Agrigentum	Lincoln	Lindum
Aix-en-Provence	Aquae Sextiae	London	Londinium
Anglesey	Mona	Lyons	Lugdunum
Anzio	Antium	Mainz	Mogontiacum
Arezzo	Arretium	Marsala	Lilybaeum
Arles-sur-Rhône	Arelate	Marseilles	Massalia/Massilia
Athens	Athenai	Mérida	Emerita Augusta
Baalbek	Heliopolis	Messina	Messana
Bath	Aquae Sulis	Milan	Mediolanum
Behistun	Bisitun	Modena	Mutina
Beirut	Berytus	Naples/Napoli	Neapolis
Bodrum	Halicarnassus	Narbonne	Narbo
Brindisi	Brundisium	Nîmes	Nemausus
Cádiz	Gades	Orange	Arausio
Caerleon on Usk	Isca	Padua	Patavium
Capri	Capreae	Palermo	Panormus
Cartagena	Carthago Nova	Palestrina	Praeneste
Castellamare	Elea/Velia	Perugia	Perusia
Chester	Deva	Piacensa	Placentia
Chichester	Noviomagus	Póros	Calauria
Cirencester	Corinium	Pozzuoli	Puteoli
Colchester	Camulodunum	Reggio di	Rhegium
Cologne	Colonia Agrippinensis	Calabria	
Como	Comum	Rimini	Ariminum
Córdoba	Corduba	Rome	Roma
Corfu	Kerkyra/Corcyra	Sagunto	Saguntum
Crotone	Croton	St Albans	Verulamium
Cuma	Cyme/Cumae	Shohat	Cyrene
Durazzo	Dyrrhachium	Silchester	Calleva Atrebatum
Fréjus	Forum Iulii	Siracusa/Syracuse	Syrakousai/Syracusae
Gloucester	Glevum	Taranto	Taras/Tarentum
Harran	Carrhae	Tivoli	Tibur
Hisarlik	Troia/Troy	Trier	Augusta Treverorum
Ischia	Pithekoussai/Pithecusae	Utique	Utica
Istanbul	Byzantium/	Vergina	Aigeai/Aegae
	Constantinopolis	Wroxeter	Viroconium
Izmir	Smyrna	Yassilhüyük	Gordium
Izmit	Nicomedia	York	Eburaeum

ANCIENT	MODERN	ANCIENT	MODERN
Acragas/ Agrigentum	Agrigento	Halicarnassus	Bodrum
		Heliopolis	Baalbek
Aigeai/Aegae	Vergina	Isca	Caerleon on Usk
Antium	Anzio	Kerkyra/Corcyra	Corfu
Aquae Sextiae	Aix-en-Provence	Lilybaeum	Marsala
Aquae Sulis	Bath	Lindum	Lincoln
Arelate	Arles-sur-Rhône	Londinium	London
Ariminum	Rimini	Lugdunum	Lyons
Arretium	Arezzo	Massalia/Massilia	Marseilles
Athenai	Athens	Mediolanum	Milan
Augusta Treverorum	Trier	Messana	Messina
		Mogontiacum	Mainz
Berytus	Beirut	Mona	Anglesey
Bisitun	Behistun	Mutina	Modena
Brundisium	Brindisi	Narbo	Narbonne
Byzantium/ Constantinopolis	Istanbul	Neapolis	Naples/Napoli
		Nemausus	Nîmes
Calauria	Póros	Nicomedia	Izmit
CallevaAtrebatum	Silchester	Noviomagus	Chichester
Camulodunum	Colchester	Orange	Arausio
Capreae	Capri	Panormus	Palermo
Carrhae	Harran	Patavium	Padua
Carthago Nova	Cartagena	Perusia	Perugia
Colonia Agrippinensis	Cologne	Pithekoussai/ Pithecusae	Ischia
Comum	Como	Placentia	Piacensa
Corduba	Córdoba	Praeneste	Palestrina
Corinium	Cirencester	Puteoli	Pozzuoli
Croton	Crotone	Rhegium	Reggio di Calabria
Cyme/Cumae	Cuma	Roma	Rome
Cyrene	Shohat	Saguntum	Sagunto
Deva	Chester	Smyrna	Izmir
Dyrrhachium	Durazzo	Syrakousai/ Syracusae	Siracusa/Syracuse
Eburacum	York		
Elea/Velia	Castellamare	Taras/Tarentum	Taranto
Emerita Augusta	Mérida	Tibur	Tivoli
Forum Iulii	Fréjus	Troia/Troy	Hisarlik
Gades	Cádiz	Utique	Utica
Glevum	Gloucester	Verulamium	St Albans
Gordium	Yassilhüyük	Viroconium	Wroxeter

Chronology

Greece and the East

BC

*c.*1575-1200 Mycenaean civilization in Greece

*c.*1575-1100 New Kingdom in Egypt

*c.*1450 Mycenaeans take over palace settlements of Minoan Crete

*c.*1270 Troy VI, perhaps the Troy of legend, destroyed

c.1100-776 DARK age of Greece

*c.*1050-950 Migration of Ionian Greeks to the eastern Aegean

*c.*825-730 Colonization of the West begins

776 First Olympic Games

776-480 ARCHAIC period

*c.*750-700 Homer and Hesiod active

*c.*744-612 Assyrian empire at its height

*c.*740 Greek alphabet created from a Phoenician (Semitic) source

*c.*700 Greeks begin to colonize Black Sea area

*c.*700-600 Society remodelled at Sparta (Lycurgus)

*c.*680-625 The first tyrannies: Pheidon at Argos and Cypselus at Corinth

621/20 Draco's laws at Athens

*c.*610-575 Alcaeus and Sappho active on Lesbos

594/3 Solon's reforms at Athens

587 Capture of Jerusalem by Nebuchadnezzar; beginning of Jewish Diaspora

585 Thales of Miletus predicts eclipse of the sun

*c.*560-510 Tyranny of Pisistratus and his sons at Athens

*c.*557-530 Cyrus founds Persian empire

*c.*546/5 Persians conquer Ionian Greeks

*c.*534 First tragedy performed at City Dionysia in Athens

*c.*530 Pythagoras emigrates to south Italy

508 Reforms of Cleisthenes at Athens

499 Ionian Revolt against Persian rule

*c.*499-458 Aeschylus active (d. 456/5)

498-446 Pindar active

490 First Persian invasion of Greece; Battle of Marathon

*c.*487 State provision of comedies at City Dionysia in Athens begins

Rome and the West

BC

*c.*1500-1200 Bronze-age 'Apennine' culture in western central Italy

*c.*1300 Earliest Celtic culture emerges on Upper Danube

*c.*1000 Hill-top settlements are established on the hills of Rome, including the Palatine

*c.*900-600 Iron-age 'Villanovan' culture in western central Italy

*c.*800-700 Celtic culture spreads to Spain and Britain

753 Traditional date for founding of Rome

*c.*700 Palatine settlement expands; the Forum is laid out as a public meeting place

700-500 Etruscan civilization in Italy; their alphabet stimulates the spread of writing in Italy

*c.*600 Latin city states begin to emerge in central Italy; organization of Roman calendar and major priesthoods

509 Expulsion of last king and founding of the Republic

494 First secession of the plebeians

493 Treaty between Rome and Latins establishes peace and military alliance

Greece and the East

BC

480–323 CLASSICAL period

480–479 Second Persian invasion of Greece; battles of Thermopylae, Salamis, Plataea, and Mycale

478/7 Athens founds Delian League against Persia

*c.***468–406** Sophocles active (d. 406)

467 Cimon defeats Persians at Eurymedon

*c.***465–425** Phidias active

462/1 Ephialtes and Pericles initiate political reform at Athens

*c.***461–446** First Peloponnesian War

*c.***460–410** Polyclitus active

*c.***455–408** Euripides active (d. 406)

454 Treasury of the Delian League moved to Athens; growth of Athenian empire

447 Building of the Parthenon begins

*c.***440–420/10** Herodotus writes his history

431 Second Peloponnesian War begins

*c.***431–400** Thucydides writes his history

*c.***430** Democritus, Hippocrates, Socrates, and Protagoras active

430–426 Plague at Athens; death of Pericles (429)

*c.***427–388** Aristophanes active

415–413 Athenian expedition to Sicily

405 Battle of Aegospotami

405–367 Dionysius I is tyrant of Syracuse

404 Athens surrenders to Sparta; the Thirty Tyrants

*c.***404–355** Xenophon active

403 Democracy restored at Athens

399 Trial and execution of Socrates

395–386 Corinthian War

387 Plato (*c.*429–347) founds the Academy

386 King's Peace allows Persia to rule in Asia Minor

378 Foundation of Second Athenian Confederacy

377–353 Mausolus rules Caria

*c.***375–330** Praxiteles active

371 Sparta defeated by Thebes at Battle of Leuctra

*c.***370–315** Lysippus active

*c.***360–324** Diogenes the Cynic active

359–336 Philip II is king of Macedon

338 Philip defeats Athens and Thebes at Chaeronea

336 Alexander ('the Great') becomes king of Macedon (d. 323)

335 Aristotle (384–322) founds the Lyceum

334 Alexander crosses into Asia

331 Foundation of Alexandria

326 Alexander crosses the Indus

*c.***324–292** Menander active

Rome and the West

BC

*c.***450** Codification of the Twelve Tables; Rome on the offensive against neighbouring tribes

*c.***400** Earliest genuine archival records in Rome

396 Romans destroy Veii, inaugurating conquest of Etruria

390/86 Sack of Rome by Celts brings only temporary setback to Roman expansion

341–338 Latin War; Latin League is dissolved

Greece and the East

BC

323–331 HELLENISTIC period
*c.*323–281 Alexander's 'Successors' divide his
   empire
323–331 Egypt ruled by the Ptolemies
322 Death of Demosthenes (b. 384)
321 Seleucus gains satrapy of Babylon;
   beginning of Seleucid empire

*c.*310 Zeno (335–263) founds Stoicism
*c.*307 Epicurus (341–270) founds his school at
   Athens
301 Antigonus I killed at Battle of Ipsus
*c.*300 Euclid active

*c.*287 Theophrastus dies (b. *c.*371)
281 Battle of Corupedium: Seleucus finally wins
   Asia Minor
281/80 Achaean Confederacy revived
*c.*277/6–239 Antigonus Gonatas is king of
   Macedon
274–217 Four Syrian Wars fought between
   Ptolemies and Seleucids
*c.*270–245 Apollonius of Rhodes writes
   Argonautica

*c.*247–AD 224 Arsacids rule Parthia
241–197 Attalus I rules Pergamum
229 Illyrian piracy attracts Roman intervention
   in the East
227/6 Cleomenes III reforms Spartan state

200 Palestine comes under Seleucid rule

194 Eratosthenes, natural philosopher, dies
   (b. *c.* 285)

after 184 Great Altar of Pergamum
171–167 Third Macedonian War
168/7 Judaean Revolt against Antiochus IV
   Epiphanes, led by the Maccabees
166–188 Delos flourishes as free port

146 Macedonia a Roman province; Achaean
   War; destruction of Corinth

Rome and the West

BC

326–304 Second Samnite War

300 All Latium under Roman control
298–290 Third Samnite War
295 Battle of Sentinum, decisive for supremacy
   in Italy

275 Pyrrhus driven back to Epirus by the
   Romans
272 Capture of Tarentum, the final act in the
   Roman conquest of Italy

264–241 First Punic War; first gladiatorial
   games (264) in Rome
260 Rome builds large navy

241 Sicily becomes first Roman province

218–201 Second Punic War; Hannibal invades
   Italy
216 Crushing victory over Romans at Cannae
206 Carthaginians defeated in Spain
*c.*205–184 Career of Plautus
204 Scipio invades Africa
*c.*204–169 Career of Ennius
202 Scipio defeats Hannibal at Zama
200–197 Second Macedonian War between
   Rome and Philip V

192–188 Syrian War between Rome and
   Antiochus III
191 Rome completes conquest of Cisalpine Gaul

167 Kingdom of Macedon destroyed at Battle of
   Pydna
166–160 Plays of Terence
155–133 Celtiberian War leaves most of Iberia
   in Roman hands
149–146 Third Punic War; Carthage destroyed

Greece and the East

BC

142 Jews expel Seleucids; ruled by Hasmonean high priests (to 63)

120–163 Mithradates VI King of Pontus

89–85 First Mithradatic War
88 Sack of Delos
86 Sack of Athens

64 Syria a Roman province

47 Library of Alexandria burnt

40 Parthians capture Jerusalem; Rome intervenes backing Herod the Great as King of Judaea
30 Egypt a Roman province

AD
6 Judaea a Roman province

c.**30** Philon ('Philo'), Jewish writer, active; traditional date for crucifixion of Jesus of Nazareth

37/8 Josephus, Jewish Greek historian, born
c.**48** Birth of Plutarch

Rome and the West

BC

133 The tribune Tiberius Gracchus proposes land reform; annexation of Asia
121 Murder of Gaius Gracchus
c.**118** Death of Polybius (b. c.200)
112–106 War against Jugurtha of Numidia
107–100 Marius consul six times
91–89 Social War
88–82 Civil war between Sulla and Marius (d. 86)

81 Sulla dictator; proscriptions
73–71 Revolt of Spartacus
70 Crassus and Pompey consuls
70 Cicero's Verrine Orations delivered
63 Consulate of Cicero; conspiracy of Catiline; Pompey's settlement of the East
60 First Triumvirate (Pompey, Caesar and Crassus)
58–50 Caesar campaigns in Gaul; writes his *commentarii*
55–54 Caesar's invasions of Britain
55 (or 51) Death of Lucretius
54 Catullus dies (b. c.84)
49 Caesar crosses the Rubicon; Civil War
48 Caesar defeats Pompey at Pharsalus
44 Caesar made perpetual dictator; murdered (15 March); Cicero attacks Antony in his Philippics
43 Octavian seizes the consulship; Second Triumvirate (Octavian, Antony, and Lepidus); murder of Cicero (b. 106)
42 Republicans defeated at Philippi
31 Octavian defeats Antony and Cleopatra at Actium
28–23 Vitruvius writes *de Architectura*
27 Octavian's first constitutional settlement; he is given the name Augustus
23 Augustus' second constitutional settlement
20 Diplomatic triumph in Parthia

19 Death of Virgil (b. 70)
13–9 Roman control established up to the Danube

8 Death of Horace (b. 65)
2 Forum of Augustus dedicated

AD
9 Loss of three legions in Germany; Rhine–Danube becomes empire's northern frontier

14–37 Tiberius emperor
17 Death of Livy (b. 59 BC); death of Ovid (b. 43 BC)

37–41 Gaius ('Caligula') emperor
41–54 Claudius emperor

Greece and the East	Rome and the West
AD	AD
	54–68 Nero emperor
	64 Fire in Rome
	65 Suicides of Seneca (b. 4 BC/AD I) and Lucan (b. 39)
66 First Jewish revolt begins against Roman rule	*c.***65** Death of St Paul in Rome
66–68 Nero's tour of Greece	**69** Civil war
70 Destruction of the Temple at Jerusalem	**69–79** Vespasian emperor
73/4 Fall of Masada ends first Jewish Revolt	**79** Pompeii and Herculaneum destroyed by the eruption of Vesuvius; death of Pliny the Elder (b. 23/4)
	81–96 Domitian emperor
106 Arabia a Roman province	**98–117** Trajan emperor
	*c.***110–120** Tacitus writes Histories and Annals
	*c.***112** Death of Pliny the Younger (b. *c.*61)
	113 Trajan's Column dedicated
	117–138 Hadrian emperor; Suetonius and Juvenal active; the Pantheon built; Hadrian's Wall built (Britain); Soranus (physician) active
135 Revolt of Bar Kokhba in Palestine suppressed	**138–161** Antoninus Pius emperor
146–*c.***170** Ptolemy's writings on astronomy and geography	
150 Pausanias the travel writer flourishes	
	161–180 Marcus Aurelius emperor; Galen is court physician
	180–192 Commodus emperor
	193–211 Septimius Severus emperor
c.200 Mishnah, the first great Rabbinic compilation, is written	**198–217** Aurelius Antoninus ('Caracalla') emperor
224/5 Origen (b. *c.*184/5) dies, Sasanid dynasty seizes power in Persia (224)	*c.***202** Cassius Dio begins his Roman History
267 Athens sacked by Herulian Goths	**222–235** Aurelius Severus Alexander emperor
	235–284 Period of anarchy
	284–305 Diocletian emperor
	293 Tetrarchy established
c.300 Eusebius of Caesarea, Christian apologist, active; Christianity takes hold in Asia Minor	**306–337** Constantine I emperor
324 Constantinople founded	**313** Edict of Milan: Christianity tolerated
	354 Augustine of Hippo born (d. 430)
393 Olympic games abolished	**395** Division of the empire between East and West
	410 Sack of Rome by Alaric the Goth
	476 Last Roman emperor in the West deposed
420 Jerome, biblical translator (b. 347), dies in Palestine	**527–565** Justinian eastern emperor; codification of Roman law

Maps

Map 1   Greece and Western Asia Minor

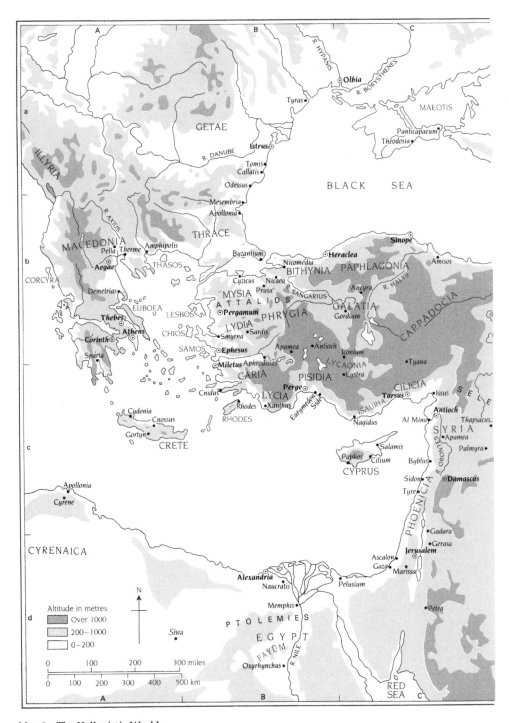

Map 2   The Hellenistic World

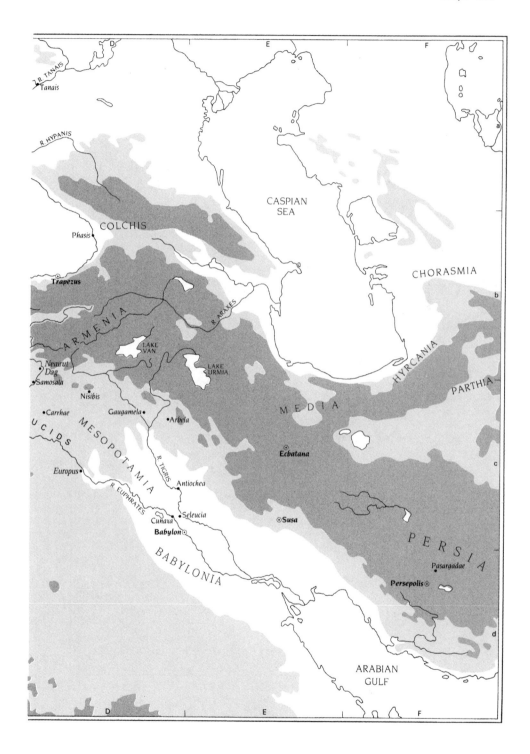

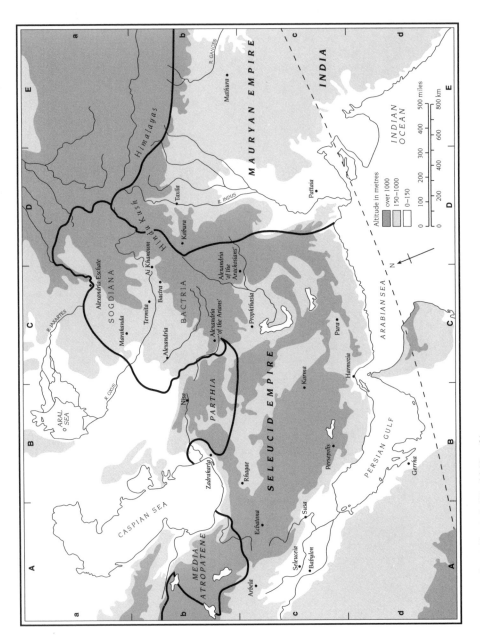

Map 2a   The Hellenistic World (*Contd.*)

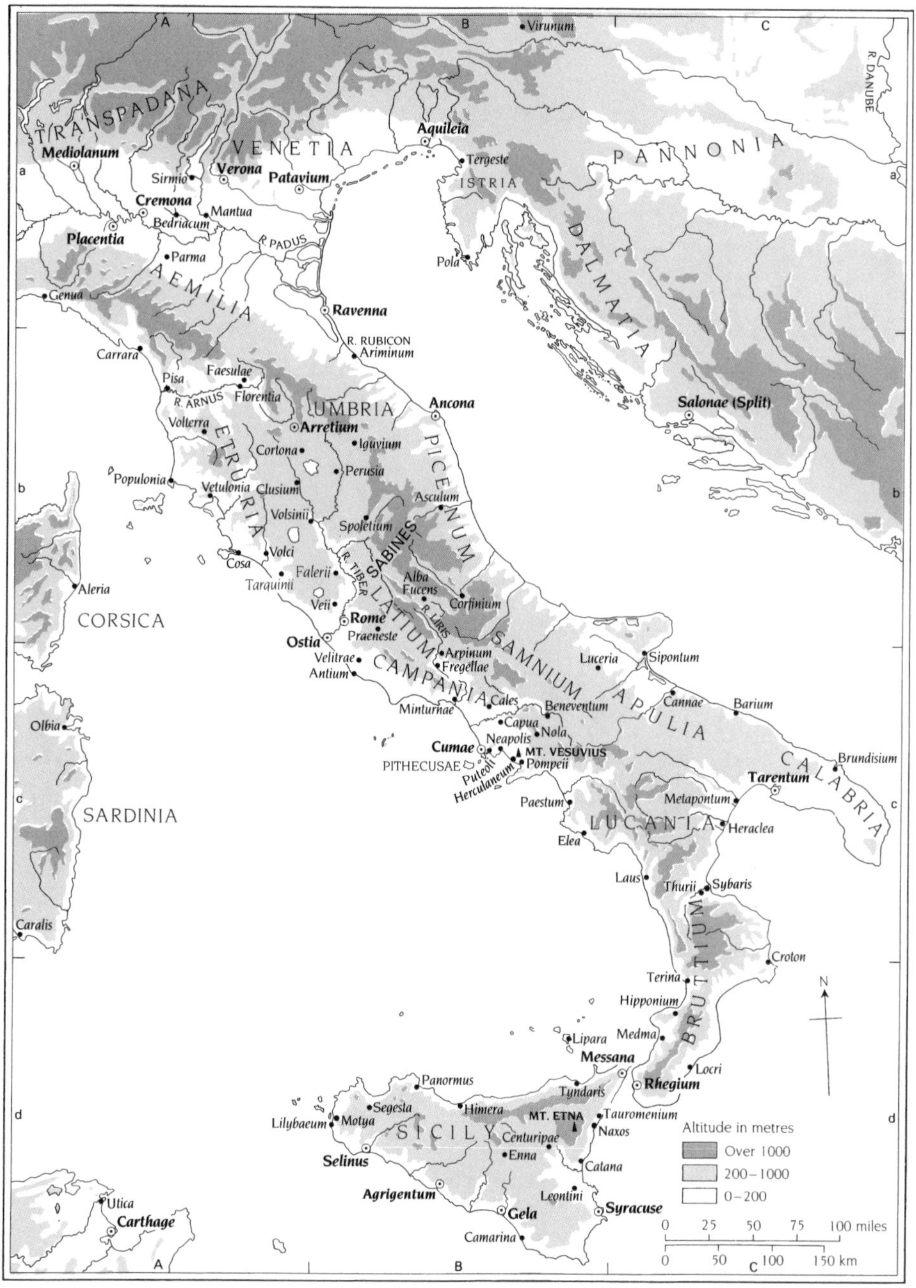
A
B
C
a
b
c
d
Virunum
R. DANUBE
TRANSPADANA
VENETIA
PANNONIA
Mediolanum
Aquileia
Tergeste
ISTRIA
Sirmio
Verona
Patavium
Cremona
Mantua
Bedriacum
Placentia
R. PADUS
Parma
Pola
DALMATIA
AEMILIA
Genua
Ravenna
R. RUBICON
Ariminum
Carrara
Faesulae
Pisa
R. ARNUS
Florentia
UMBRIA
Ancona
Salonae (Split)
Volterra
Arretium
Iguvium
ETRURIA
Cortona
Perusia
PICENUM
Populonia
Vetulonia
Clusium
Asculum
Volsinii
Spoletium
SABINES
Cosa
Volci
Aleria
Tarquinii
Falerii
R. TIBER
Alba Fucens
Corfinium
Veii
LATIUM
R. LIRIS
CORSICA
Rome
Praeneste
SAMNIUM
Ostia
Velitrae
Arpinum
Luceria
Sipontum
Antium
Fregellae
CAMPANIA
APULIA
Cales
Cannae
Barium
Minturnae
Beneventum
Olbia
Capua
Nola
Neapolis
Cumae
MT. VESUVIUS
CALABRIA
Brundisium
PITHECUSAE
Puteoli
Pompeii
Herculaneum
Tarentum
SARDINIA
Paestum
Metapontum
LUCANIA
Heraclea
Elea
Laus
Thurii
Sybaris
BRUTTIUM
Caralis
Croton
Terina
N
Hipponium
Medma
Lipara
Messana
Locri
Panormus
Tyndaris
Rhegium
Segesta
Himera
MT. ETNA
Tauromenium
Lilybaeum
Motya
SICILY
Naxos
Altitude in metres
Centuripae
Enna
Over 1000
Selinus
200–1000
Catana
0–200
Utica
Agrigentum
Leontini
Carthage
Gela
Syracuse
Camarina
0 25 50 75 100 miles
0 50 100 150 km

Map 3 Italy

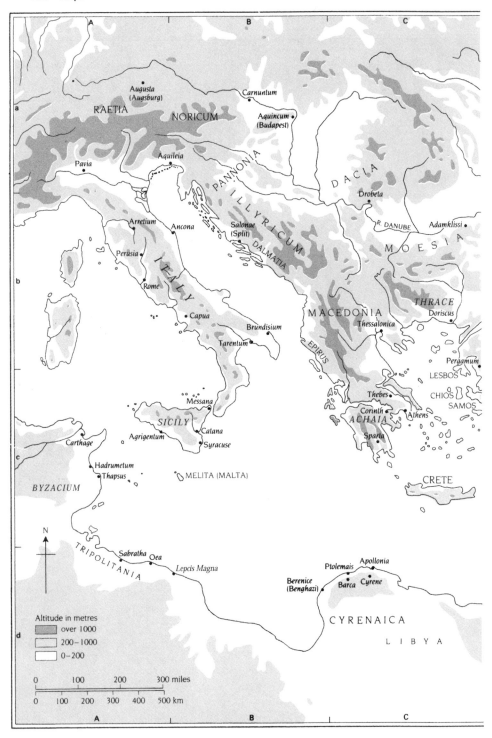

Map 4   The Roman Empire (Central and Eastern Provinces)

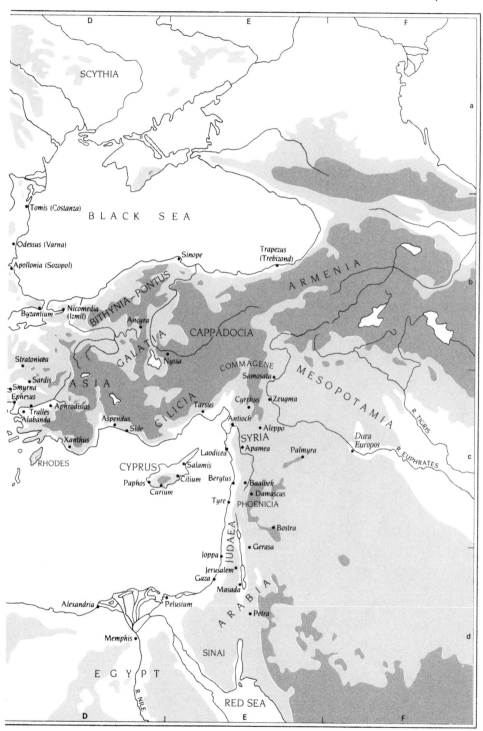

Map 5　The Roman Empire (Western Provinces)